$26.95

INTERNSHIPS
2004

D1358314

24th Edition

THOMSON

PETERSON'S

Australia • Canada • Mexico • Singapore • Spain • United Kingdom • United States

About The Thomson Corporation and Peterson's

The Thomson Corporation, with 2002 revenues of US$7.8 billion, is a global leader in providing integrated information solutions to business and professional customers. The Corporation's common shares are listed on the Toronto and New York stock exchanges (TSX: TOC; NYSE: TOC). Its learning businesses and brands serve the needs of individuals, learning institutions, corporations, and government agencies with products and services for both traditional and distributed learning. Peterson's (www.petersons.com) is a leading provider of education information and advice, with books and online resources focusing on education search, test preparation, and financial aid. Its Web site offers searchable databases and interactive tools for contacting educational institutions, online practice tests and instruction, and planning tools for securing financial aid. Peterson's serves 110 million education consumers annually.

For more information, contact Peterson's, 2000 Lenox Drive, Lawrenceville, NJ 08648; 800-338-3282; or find us on the World Wide Web at www.petersons.com/about.

CONTENTS

Manufacturing

Other Services

Professional, Scientific, and Technical Services

Public Administration

Real Estate and Rental and Leasing

Retail Trade

Transportation

Utilities

Indexes

Getting the Most Out of Your Internship Experience

by Joel F. Clark, Ph.D.

Joel F. Clark is Assistant Professor of Government and Co-Director of Internships at George Mason University and Director of Michigan State University's Washington Program. Professor Clark's book, *Intern to Success*, was published in 2002. For more advice on internships, visit www.internsuccess. com.

The Value of Internships Today

Each year thousands of interns work in a wide variety of places, including corporations, law firms, government agencies, media organizations, interest groups, clinics, labs, museums, and historical sites. How popular are internships? Consider the recent trends. In the early 1980s, only 1 in 36 students completed an internship or other experiential learning program. Compare this to 2000, where one study found that approximately 86 percent of college students had completed internships, with 69 percent reporting having had two or more.[1]

By definition, internships are a way to learn by doing, so you shouldn't be expected to know everything about them before you start. At the same time, intern success is not automatic. You must work to make it happen. An old saying applies here: "Success is a combination of preparation and luck." A stroke of luck gets you only so far if you are not prepared to maximize the opportunity. But preparation alone is insufficient for success. Good things must also happen to you. The trick is to increase the chances that good things will happen.

The Employer's Perspective

Students are obviously responding to the needs of employers in deciding to complete at least one internship. A survey by the National Association of Colleges and Employers, for example, reported that 70 percent of employers require new hires to have had internships or other on-the-job training, with 61 percent of respondents offering summer internships to provide that experience.[2]

Employers consider internships a good option in both healthy and ailing economies. In healthy economies, managers often struggle to fill their positions with eager workers who can adapt to changing technologies. Internships offer a low-cost way to get good workers into "the pipeline" without offering them a full-time position up front. In struggling economies, on the other hand, downsizing often requires employers to layoff workers without thinking about who will cover their responsibilities. Internships offer an inexpensive way to offset position losses resulting from these disruptive layoffs.

The Intern's Perspective

If you are looking to begin a career, change your career, or supplement your formal education with practical training, internships are a good bet for several reasons.

Internships offer a relatively quick way to gain work experience and develop job skills. Try this exercise: Scan the Sunday employment section of your newspaper. Choose a range of interesting advertisements for professional positions that you would consider taking. List the desired or required job skills and work experiences specified in the ads. How many of these skills and experiences do you have? Chances are, if you are still in school or a recent graduate, you don't have most of the skills and experience employers require of their new hires. What do you do?

You now face a dilemma confronted by numerous people before you. Although you are mentally prepared to start near the bottom of your chosen career, you don't even meet the prerequisites for the entry level! More than a few students have said in despair: "I know I must pay my dues to develop job skills and attain real work experience. But if no one will hire me with my current qualifications, how do I get those skills and experiences?" Good question.

The growing reality is that many entry-level positions require skills and experiences that schools and part-time jobs don't provide. Sure, you know your way around an office computer. You have some customer service experience. You may even have edited the college newspaper or organized a charity event for your sorority. But you still lack the relevant skills and on-the-job experiences that many hiring managers require.

A well-chosen internship can offer a way out of this common dilemma by providing you with job training and accumulated hours in an actual career field. Internships help you take your existing knowledge and skills and apply them in ways that will help you compete for good jobs. As Alan Goodman, Director of Career Services at Catholic University explains, "When you apply for a position and can explain during your interview what you did and what kinds of skills you gained, those are the things that employers really value."[3]

Internships offer a relatively risk-free way to explore a possible career path. Believe it or not, the best internship may tell you what you <u>don't</u> want to do for the next ten or twenty years. Think about it. If you put all your eggs in one basket, what happens if your

[1] Kristin Grimsley, "For Today's College Grads, It Isn't Just About Money," *Washington Post,* 5 May 2000, sec. H, p.1.

[2] Survey by the National Association of Colleges and Employers, reported in Steven Ginsberg, "Schools Out, Work's In," *Los Angeles Times,* 23 June 1997, sec. DD, p. 29.

[3] Quoted in Pat D'Angelo, "First Career Step: Good Internships Provide Students With Meaningful Work Experiences," *Washington Times,* 10 April 2000, sec. F, p. 8.

dream job turns out to be the exact opposite of what you want or who you are? This is what a student of mine who interned at a prestigious Washington, D.C., public relations firm told me recently. Unfortunately (or fortunately, depending on how you look at it), her story is quite common.

> I liked my coworkers and learned a lot about advertising and events management. But I learned that I don't have a passion for it. People work very long hours, and it always seems to be "crunch time." My last year's internship at a nonprofit women's advocacy group is looking a lot better in comparison. While the money may not be as good, they seem to be making a real difference in people's lives.

The point here is that internships offer a relatively low-cost opportunity to "try out" a career field to see if it's right for *you*. Of course, it's still important to complete one or more career assessments, which are readily available at your school's career center or through online educational resources. But a thorough career exploration should also include direct exposure to the fields you are considering. As Mary Wills, Career Center Director at Fresno Pacific University, puts it, internships provide a chance "to experience the good, the bad, and the ugly" of a career field.[4]

Internships offer real opportunities to do career networking and can significantly increase your chances of landing a good full-time position. Have you heard the saying: "It's not what you know, but who you know"? For good or ill, the reality is that who you know (or who knows you) can make a big difference in your job search. Studies show fewer than 20 percent of job placements occur through traditional application methods, including newspaper and trade journal advertisements, employment agencies, and career fairs. Instead, 60 to 90 percent of jobs are found through personal contacts and direct application.[5]

What's going on here? Put yourself in the place of a busy supervisor who must fill a vacant position. You can advertise the position, which requires a formal job announcement, review of resumes, and several interviews. Or you can rely on colleagues and subordinates to identify capable prospective applicants. Usually you will favor applicants who are referred to you by someone you know or those you personally know yourself. Even employers who must advertise a position don't always conduct a thorough review of all applicants. Instead, they employ "coping mechanisms" to streamline the process. One way to cope is to seriously consider only those applicants who have worked for you in the past or who are currently working as interns or part-time employees.

Career "networking" is a necessary strategy to break into this hidden hiring process. Simply put, networking is the exchange of information with others for mutual benefit. Your career network can tell you where the jobs are and help you compete for them. Isn't it better to develop your networking skills now, when the stakes aren't as high, than later when you are competing with everyone else for full-time jobs? The internship hiring process and the weeks you actually spend on the job provide excellent opportunities to talk with various people about careers, your skills, and ways to succeed.

---

[4] Quoted in Darina K. Lazo, "Learning By Doing. For Graduates Wanting to Work After Graduation, Internships Are Key," *The Fresno Bee*, 5 June 2000, sec. E, p. 1.

[5] Reported in *Moving On: A Guide for Career Planning and Job Search*, George Mason University Career Services, 1997, p. 43.

Choosing the Right Internship for You

Because internships today are so plentiful, chances are good that you will get hired somewhere. Finding an internship that is right for *you*, however, will take more effort. Unfortunately, too many people accept the first internship offer without seriously considering their goals, their personal values, and the broad range of available choices. Why leave to chance the choice of an internship where you will work part-time or full-time for several weeks, or months, or even longer? As you review numerous job listings, keep this thought in mind: *There is no "best" internship. There are only better and worse internships depending on my values, needs, and goals.*

An important step in developing your short list of internship choices is to learn about the range of jobs available to you. The internship universe is broad indeed, as you will soon see.

Workplace Size and Status

Workplaces vary greatly in their size, status, and overall mission. Obviously, your main consideration should be your basic interest in the job. But as you gather information to create a short list of possibilities, you might also consider the potential differences between high- and low-profile, and small and large workplaces.

What are high-profile workplaces? You should consider a workplace "high-profile" if most people have heard about it and, consequently, more interns want to work there. For example, high-profile government departments or agencies include the U.S. State Department, the White House, and the FBI. High-profile media organizations include ABC, NBC, CBS, and CNN.

As a general rule, high-profile workplaces tend to be more competitive. Typically, many more people apply for these internships than there are positions to fill. If you have personal contacts at a high-profile organization, talk to them about your application and the odds of getting hired. If you don't have contacts, expect your resume to land on a stack of dozens or even hundreds of others. Generally, applicants without personal contacts face more serious, although not insurmountable, hiring barriers.

High-profile internships often have more rigorous and lengthy application procedures, including letters of recommendation and writing samples. For example, the State Department's application process usually takes a minimum of nine months. So if you are interested in working at a high-profile internship, plan to spend more time and effort compiling your application materials.

You might now be thinking: "I know it's harder to land a high-profile internship. But shouldn't I strive for the best?" Of course you should. There is nothing inherently wrong with these places in that most offer excellent opportunities. But keep in mind that for every high-profile choice, there may be dozens of lesser-known workplaces that offer similar or better opportunities for some interns. For example, if your goal is to produce television documentaries, a smaller production company like Heintz Media Productions in Arlington, Virginia, could be a good alternative should the Discovery Channel not call you back. If you can't get hired at the United Nations or Amnesty International, the lesser-known Human Rights Watch is a great alternative. Usually these lower profile organizations are only lesser known to the general public. Employers in a particular field will likely know them because it's their job to know them.

Workplace size is also something to consider. Many large workplaces offer some obvious advantages. First, large workplaces tend to be more high profile. People are more likely to know about the larger workplace and be impressed that you worked there. Who cares if you spent your days answering phones, filing, and sorting mail? You DID work there. If your primary goal is to add impressive-sounding names to your resume, a large workplace could do the trick.

Second, internships at larger workplaces might be more integrated within the organization's personnel structure. This is good if you seek formal mentoring arrangements or training programs. Many larger workplaces provide more opportunities for getting hired in a paid position at your internship's completion, if that's what you seek. It's simple logic that the more employees and offices within an organization, the greater the chance of getting hired into a permanent position.

While larger workplaces can be good choices, they may have some downsides. For example, you could find the bureaucratic structure in a large workplace stifling. Or you may feel like a cog in a large wheel that has little or no connection to the organization's "end product." This might be tolerable if you can still develop your skills and make good contacts. But what if there is little real work because the office has too many interns? In this case your career portfolio will be quite thin at your internship's conclusion.

To thoroughly explore all your options, consider some possible merits of smaller (and lower profile) workplaces. Because smaller workplaces are generally less known, their internships are usually less competitive. Smaller workplaces often have streamlined application procedures, so you could get hired in a matter of days or weeks, not the months it often takes for larger organizations. Some smaller workplaces might even provide better opportunities to interact with supervisors and to be treated as a regular employee might. As Susan Binghamton, owner of a small political consulting firm explains, "I offer hands-on experience. I also refer my interns to other employers and go the extra mile for them in helping get them jobs."[1]

On the downside, a smaller workplace might offer fewer opportunities for structured interaction among interns and supervisory staff. There may be fewer mentoring opportunities simply because there are fewer employees. Also, the management may be less inclined to hold formal training sessions or provide enrichment activities, such as luncheon talks or in-service training.

These possible differences between workplaces are very rough guideposts. Obviously, organizations that fall within these categories will vary greatly. Make sure you investigate your internship choices thoroughly and prepare to ask specific questions about these issues during your job interviews.

Paid Versus Unpaid Internships

Given the choice, everyone would choose a paid over an unpaid internship, all else being equal. This is entirely understandable. After spending years in school and sacrificing your short-term monetary interests for long-term educational and career goals, why shouldn't you get paid for your labor? The problem is that rarely is all else equal in choosing between internships. In some cases a paid internship is a better choice for you, but in many cases it isn't. Internship compensation should be weighed among many factors.

The good news is that more internships are paid now than in the past. This trend reflects the increasing competition employers face in attracting good workers, especially in healthy economies. However, salary should not be your most important consideration if you can afford to temporarily work for free or very cheap. Remember you are interning to gain work experience and career-building opportunities, not to get rich.

The issue of compensation should also be considered alongside other recent changes in the career marketplace. Corporate recruiters report that college graduates rank salary lower on their list of job priorities than before. Less quantifiable "quality of life" factors, including the workplace mission, flex-time options, educational tuition support, and vacation time are increasingly important considerations for new recruits.[2] In choosing an internship, and ultimately a paid job, you should consider all these factors. And since this is your life we're talking about, the relative importance you assign to each should reflect your personal preferences, not those of your teachers, friends, or even relatives.

---

[1] Comments made at "Getting the Most Out of Your Internship," Career Panel II, George Mason University, 1997.

[2] Grimsley, "It Isn't Just About Money," 2000.

How to Apply for Internships

For many people, perfecting their application materials is a daunting process. Prospective interns are notorious for creating their resumes and cover letters at the last minute—and it shows. Since there are numerous resources available to help you do it right, there is no excuse for sending out flawed materials.

Your resume and cover letter won't get you hired. A job interview is usually necessary to secure the job. At the same time, well-crafted resumes and cover letters will help you get interviews, while flawed ones will certainly decrease your chances of advancing to the interview stage. When writing resumes and cover letters, aim for clarity and brevity. Your resume and cover letter should not exceed one page each.

Resumes

There are two basic types of resume: chronological and functional. *Chronological resumes* list your education, work, and extracurricular experiences separately in reverse chronological order (most recent first). *Functional resumes,* in contrast, group all your skills and experiences under broad functional categories. This format allows individuals who are changing careers to emphasize their most marketable attributes, while de-emphasizing problems such as long unemployment or specific jobs that didn't work out. Most individuals seeking internships don't fit the applicant profile for functional resumes and will therefore use the chronological resume.

Before you start crafting your resume, track down basic information, including the actual time periods you spent in schools and on jobs and the exact titles of clubs, organizations, and awards. You should also inventory your most important skills and experiences. The more you can place your skills in specific contexts, the more effective your resume will be.

As you complete the following steps, keep in mind the employers who will read your resume. They will quickly scan your resume, so make it easy to pick out your best qualifications and the contact information they need to arrange a job interview.

All resumes should contain certain categories of information. These are your personal contact information, your objective, your education, your work experience, any pertinent additional information that doesn't fit in these standard categories, and an offer to provide references upon request.

Your personal contact information. Write your name in capital letters, centered horizontally on the page, about one inch from the top. Use your formal name (not nickname) and include your middle initial to add some formality. You may choose to type your name in bold face or slightly increase the font. But don't get too carried away with this.

Enter your school address and phone number on the left-hand margin and your permanent home address and phone number (if different from your school address) on the right-hand margin, two or three lines below your name. If you only have one address, center it under your name or place it on the left-hand margin. If you will be traveling during the job search process, be sure to list the address and phone number of someone who always knows where to reach you. Employers who can't reach you right away might contact another applicant. Include the e-mail address that you check regularly.

Your objective statement. Your objective is important because it describes the type of internship you seek. Since you are applying for an internship, not a full-time job, your objective should balance your general employment goals with specific learning objectives. You should develop several objective statements for different internships. Here are some examples:

OBJECTIVE: A full-time internship in advertising to develop copywriting and administrative skills.

OBJECTIVE: A part-time internship at a nonprofit organization with opportunities to learn about grass-roots mobilization.

OBJECTIVE: An internship in federal legislative affairs that builds on my volunteer work for the Michigan State Senate.

Education. From most recent back, list your degrees completed (e.g., A.A., A.S., B.A., B.S.), major programs of study, institution(s) attended, minors or concentrations, and any noteworthy seminars, course work, projects, or study-abroad experiences. If your course work or projects don't add to your qualifications, don't include them. List your grade point average (GPA) if it's higher than 3.0 and any other relevant academic honors such as dean's list or honors program. If you are still pursuing a degree, use the phrase "Candidate for the degree of . . . ." If you have already graduated, use "Awarded the degree of . . . ."

If you have not graduated and are not currently pursuing a degree, simply list the dates you attended school and possibly several courses completed. If you transferred from one school to another, you may want to list the prior school depending on how long you attended and whether you achieved significant honors.

Work experience. In reverse chronological order, list the following: your position title, name of organization, location of work (city, state), and years of work. Then describe your work responsibilities and other relevant factors in succinct, active phrases. Unlike passive phrases ("assured attainment of balanced budgets in two consecutive years"), active phrases are crisp, action-oriented descriptions of the same tasks ("balanced the budget in two consecutive years"). List your most important responsibilities first and describe them more fully than less significant tasks. Emphasize your personal achievements rather than the activities themselves. For example, saying "security guard for clothing store" doesn't distinguish you from other security guards. Instead, emphasize what you accomplished as a security guard: "Supervised a team of 3 store security personnel, implemented new security training program, and achieved 30 percent drop in stolen merchandise as lead security guard." Note the use of action verbs: *supervised, implemented,* and *achieved.*

Additional activities. Optional categories such as "skills," "activities and interests," or "awards and honors" can group information that doesn't fit neatly in the above categories. A *skills* category lists any specialized skills you have, including computer skills (e.g., HTML, Lotus 123, PowerPoint, Excel), foreign language skills, or working knowledge of research programs (e.g., LexisNexis). Many employers value an applicant's specific office skills more than their major or academic achievements, so be sure to highlight your skills in ways that distinguish you from other applicants.

An ***activities and interests*** category is a good place for applicants to round out their personal profile. Activities that include community service, club involvement, or campus leadership can strengthen your resume, especially when they are linked to specific skills. Special interests that round out your "personality type" might include sports activities or hobbies.

An ***awards and honors*** category is useful for significant honors beyond those listed in other categories. For example, "Rotary Club Young Citizen Award" or "Eagle Scout Award" should be listed here, while things like "dean's list" or "employee achievement award" should be listed in the education or work experience sections.

References. It's best to just put "References available on request." Most career experts advise applicants not to list specific references on their resume because they should know when their references are called, and prospective employers won't hesitate to ask for them anyway. Make sure you have a list of at least 3 references (with updated contact information) should employers ask.

In describing your education, work experiences, and achievements, always strive for accurate and concise action-oriented phrases. Cut out nonessential words and transitions, and consistently use past tense for everything except what you are currently doing. Avoid overinflating your achievements and NEVER lie. It's okay to sell yourself but don't reinvent the truth. For example, if your job title was Office Receptionist, don't rename it Office Communications Facilitator. If you are not proficient in certain skills, don't say you are. Finally,

avoid using inflated terms like "expert," or "full knowledge." Few people in this world are true experts on anything. Claiming you are will raise doubts about your other claims and your general maturity. A White House official once complained to me that a student applicant described himself as an "expert" on Middle East politics. Instead, he should have simply indicated that his concentration was Middle East politics.

Cover Letters

Your cover letter is just as important as your resume. In fact, these two documents should always work together. A good cover letter will accomplish three things: (1) explain why you are interested in the job and organization; (2) give the recipient a reason to be interested in you; and (3) lay the groundwork for further contact. This is a lot to ask of a one-page letter but, with careful editing, it can be done.

The following is an outline of a standard cover letter:

Your mailing address
Your phone number/e-mail

Date

Mr./Ms./Dr. A. Recipient
Title
Company Name
Company Address

Dear Mr./Ms./Dr. A. Recipient. Avoid addressing your letter "To whom it may concern." Make the extra effort to find out the name and title of the person who will review your letter and resume and be sure to get the spelling right. This personal touch can make a big difference.

Introduce yourself. Your lead paragraph should clarify who you are, the intern position you seek, and, if possible, how the job will help promote your larger goals. For example: "Currently, I am a senior marketing major at Smith College who seeks an internship in Kent and Associates's advertising department. Since my ultimate goal is to be an account executive, an advertising internship can help me gain some necessary skills." If there isn't an identifiable internship position, describe what you seek in more general terms. Make sure you also mention how you learned of the position. Be as specific as you can. For example, if you spoke with someone over the phone, mention his or her name. Or if you learned about the internship through school or on a Web site, briefly describe the circumstances.

Highlight your most relevant skills and experiences. In your letter, refer specifically to the most relevant educational and work experiences listed on your resume and the useful skills you possess. For example: "As my resume states, last summer I gained advertising experience while working part-time at the San Francisco Symphony." In addition, describe briefly what you hope to gain from the internship. You might also mention your good personality traits or work ethic but keep it brief. The cover letter's purpose is to get your resume read, not list everything in it.

Set yourself up for the interview. Offer to come in for an interview or make yourself available for a phone interview if a personal visit is impractical. For example, you may want to say something like: "I am very interested in learning more about your internship position and DynaCorp's excellent work with defense contractors. You can reach me at [phone number and e-mail]. I will follow up with a phone call next week to arrange a meeting with you or another DynaCorp representative."

Sincerely,
Your signature
Type your formal name.

Use proper English and avoid slang and abbreviations. Keep your sentences short and use action verbs. Also, keep your total length to a single page. It's best if the actual text of the letter does not exceed a half page in length. This kind of brevity takes work, so keep drafting until you get it just right!

Students usually make the same simple mistakes on their resumes and cover letters. Employers often complain about typographical errors, passive voice, and inflated claims of knowledge or experience. Do you think your current drafts are perfect? Although you have scanned your materials numerous times for errors, you probably have missed one or more mistakes. To avoid sending out flawed application materials, be sure to have several trusted friends and family members read over your drafts. Also, have a professor or career guidance counselor review your work.

Interviews

You should take internship interviews seriously for several reasons. First, some intern positions are highly coveted and therefore highly competitive. Also, since most employers rely heavily on interns to help them accomplish their mission, they take the hiring process seriously. If they sense you are unprofessional or uncommitted, they will pass you over for someone else. Your job is to convince them that you are the best "fit" out of all applicants.

You should begin preparing for job interviews before you start scheduling them. Think carefully about what you bring to the internship and what you hope to gain from the experience. Before you contact your short list of employers, make sure you have the latest information on them and can use it to distinguish yourself from other applicants.

- What is the organization's mission?
- What are the principal products or services the organization provides?
- Who are the organization's principal clients, customers, and partners?
- What job positions are currently being offered?
- What are the organization's sales or other recent performance indicators?

Ideally, you will be able to speak to one or two current interns in the office. Tactfully try to find out about the workplace, the person who will interview you, and any special attributes they are looking for in an intern. During the interview, try to weave in comments that show you did your homework.

In addition to doing research, review the three basic job interview types: factual, situational, and conversational. In each instance your goal is to showcase your skills and experiences and to convey that you are a mature, personable, and trainable applicant.

Factual interviews focus on facts associated with grades, work, and experiences. A typical question might be: "So, you are a history major and economics minor. What does a minor in economics require?" In answering this type of question, aim to succinctly provide the information asked for and then steer your answer toward one of your major strengths. Your response might go something like this:

My economics minor required Micro- and Macroeconomics, Economic Theory and Practice, and three upper-level economics courses of my choosing. [*Note:* A weak answer might stop here.] For my electives I chose Political Economy, Monetary Policy, and International Markets because I am very interested in the economic and political dimensions of globalization. My economics minor also required me to do hands-on projects and analysis using economic forecasting methods. So I think it really complemented my history major, which was much more fact-based.

Just because your interviewer emphasizes facts in her questions doesn't mean you should take the interview lightly. Factual questions can be easily mishandled. A question like "Why do you want to intern at Sharpe Industries?" presents both traps and opportunities. Avoid answers that betray a poor understanding of what the company does or a haphazard way of choosing to apply for an internship there. For example, avoid saying things like "My friend Jim is also applying here, and we thought it would be cool to work in the same place this summer." Instead, be prepared to show that you have carefully researched the company and thought about your short- and long-term goals. For example:

In my career research, I kept coming across Sharpe Industries as a global leader in corporate management services, and I was impressed with the way Sharpe encourages its employees to constantly update their skills and training. I have already attained some experience with computer networks by working part-time at GlobeCom. While I learned a lot at GlobeCom, I also want to work at an industry leader to confirm my interest in management consulting as a career field.

Situational interviews often start with factual questions but move on to questions about how you would respond to certain (usually difficult) situations. For example: "Our interns at New Horizons interview youths locked up in county juvenile halls. How would you handle a situation where a male youth only wanted to talk about your dating life?" The point of this question is not to determine whether you read the training manual (you wouldn't be expected to), but instead how mature and tactful you are in responding to awkward situations. A good answer might go something like this:

I would remind the individual that we were talking for a specific purpose, and that his participation in the New Horizons program was a privilege that could be revoked if he didn't take the interview process seriously. If the youth persisted, I would terminate the interview and notify my supervisor immediately about what happened.

Like situational interviews, *conversational interviews* usually start out as factual ones. But instead of remaining a formal question-and-answer session, this interview quickly becomes an unstructured conversation between you and the interviewer about such things as the internship, the organization, your background, and any other topic that comes up. Often the style is relaxed—and even fun. While this interview is less stressful, don't take it any less seriously than the other two. Whether you realize it or not, your interviewer is still assessing your character, poise, articulation, and ability to relate to other people.

In a conversational interview you should adjust your style to better fit your interviewer's style. But don't get too chummy or informal, and avoid saying things that reflect badly on you as an applicant. For example, don't say things like the following, even in very light moments:

- I am really bored by school.
- Most of my professors are clueless.
- Nobody works because they like to, but because they have to.
- My main goals are to make money and retire early.
- I am a born leader.
- I'm not a morning person.

Even interview pros can be rattled by certain questions, so prepare as much as you can. You should avoid quick yes and no answers as well as rambling monologues. Instead, try to answer in succinct statements that put your record and personal attributes in the best light. For example: "Tell me about yourself" may seem easy. But for many applicants it's a minefield. If you are a "spontaneous" person, do you say so? Spontaneity may indicate flexibility in adapting to new situations, but it might also suggest you lack deliberation and the ability to follow through when things get tough. So be prepared to explain why your spontaneous personality is an asset.

At some point you will likely be asked if you have any questions. Make sure you always have some questions. In fact, you should interview them as much as they interview you. Now is the time to clarify what you will do, for whom you will work, and other benefits of the internship program.

Here are some possible questions to consider:

- Who would be my direct supervisor?
- What would be my primary tasks?
- How much interaction will I have with full-time staff?
- Will I have opportunities to take on more responsibilities?
- Is there a formal training program?
- Are there opportunities to do job shadowing?
- Will I be able to attend policy meetings or go to conferences?
- Is the internship paid? If not, are stipends available to offset my travel costs?
- How will I be evaluated?
- Is it possible to apply for a full-time job at the internship's conclusion?
- Have past interns been hired by the organization?

It is understandable that at this stage you are eager to please. But be careful not to promise your interviewers too much. As Michelle Rupp, a four-time intern, cautions: "Don't commit to something you can't do. Be realistic to yourself in terms of time. You don't want to have to stop your internship midway through."[1]

Punctuality and appearance are crucial to making good first impressions. So plan to arrive early. If you find you are very early, take a walk around the block. Review your resume. Clear your mind. If you are running late, make the best of a bad situation by calling ahead and informing your interviewer. Good personal grooming is just as important as finding the right outfit, so make sure your clothes fit and they, and you, are clean. Be sure to bring the right accessories. A briefcase

---

[1] "Getting the Most Out of Your Internship," Career Panel II, 1997.

or folder with extra copies of your resume, a pen, and writing paper are standard items.

Body language is also critical to interview success. Smile and offer a firm handshake. Maintain good posture and eye contact. Don't fidget or constantly shift your sitting position. Speak clearly and be a good listener. Instead of searching for complex words or phrases, stick to language you are comfortable with. Back up statements with brief personal anecdotes about real situations. Throughout the interview convey an attitude of interest in the job and an eagerness to work hard.

Telephone interviews. Many students intern away from home, which makes a phone interview necessary. Most tips for in-person interviews apply here, except visual cues. Since your job will likely include answer-ing the office phones, you are probably being evalu-ated on your phone demeanor. So make sure you listen carefully to each question and modulate your voice so that you can be heard clearly without speaking too loudly.

Scheduling is a major challenge for phone interviews, so make yourself as available as possible. Because employers are very busy, they will likely call another applicant if they can't complete your interview. Be will-ing to work around their schedule, and free up a suf-ficient block of time in case the interview is delayed or runs over.

For all interviews, be sure to send a typed or writ-ten thank-you letter within a day or two. Thank them for meeting with you and reaffirm your interest in working for the organization.

Making the Most of Your Internship Experience

Once you land your dream internship, how do you make the most of it? In my experience working with hundreds of interns, one point has proven true time and again: Intern success is not automatic; you must *work* at it. Remember, you—not your teachers, program administrators, or workplace supervisors—are primarily responsible for your internship success. Since all workplaces are different, you won't have the full picture until you actually start the job. Once you begin, it's up to you to evaluate your surroundings and adapt accordingly.

The Early Stage of Your Internship

Your internship program will usually require a written learning contract. This document covers the terms of your employment and identifies your learning objectives. It is best if you can sit down with your supervisor and complete the contract together. Think carefully about the skills and experiences you hope to gain, and encourage your supervisor to be specific about planned projects and activities.

If your workplace provides a formal orientation or training program for its interns, take it seriously. However, don't be surprised if your workplace doesn't provide any formal training. In their study of internship practices, for example, Cathy Ryan and Roberta Krapels found that most interns receive no formal training at all. Instead, they are expected to "learn the ropes" through informal means, such as reviewing workplace literature and anticipating the needs of their supervisors.[1] Obviously, this situation can be very disorienting if you are used to detailed directions provided by your teachers or work supervisors.

The vast majority of interns find their overall work experiences challenging and rewarding. But for many, the first week on the job is less than satisfying. Because you have built up high expectations about your internship, you may feel somewhat let down once you start work. Perhaps the workplace isn't as glamorous as you thought. Or maybe the office staffers are not outwardly enthusiastic about your arrival. As you experience feelings of doubt, keep in mind that most people feel uncomfortable starting a new job, whether it's their first job or fifth. Your challenge is to handle these early doubts with enthusiasm and grace. If you find yourself with little or nothing to do, don't panic. Keep yourself busy by studying your workplace training manual and other forms of literature, finding your way around and introducing yourself, and asking people if they need help.

Intern Dos and Don'ts

Here are general internship dos and don'ts that you should follow from day one. First, the "don'ts."

Don't be late or abuse your breaks. This seems obvious. But employers frequently complain about interns who show up late or not at all. Just because you are not paid doesn't mean you can set your own hours. No matter what else you do effectively on the job and how personable and otherwise competent you are, your consistent tardiness will become a serious mark against you, even if your supervisor doesn't seem to notice.

Don't make personal phone calls and don't play on the computer. Personal phone calls and personal computer use are pet peeves for many employers, even if they don't confront you on it right away. Workplaces are tightening their policies on these activities and monitoring their employees more closely. Don't find this out the hard way!

Don't dress inappropriately. Workplace dress codes vary widely. A general rule-of-thumb is to emulate existing office standards. Sloppy dress and grooming are never good practices; they convey the impression that you may also be sloppy in how you approach your job and life. Instead, aim for neat clothes that don't detract from who you are and what you do.

Don't disrespect other people's workspaces. Always leave the office workspaces cleaner than when you found them, even in very messy offices. If you use someone else's desk, clean up after yourself. This seems obvious, but you would be surprised at how often this simple rule is broken.

Don't be a complainer or a slacker. Bosses resent complainers because it's clear they are not team players. They are viewed as spoiled individuals who are not ready for the responsibilities of a real job. Interns who start out with an inflated belief in their worth as employees are bound to become resentful and disgruntled. Realistic expectations are the key to your whole experience. If you expect to make policy, supervise others, or land the big account, you are bound to be disappointed. Instead of complaining about mundane tasks from the very beginning, strive to complete them quickly and efficiently. When you demonstrate that you can cover the basics well, better projects should follow.

Don't be a "know-it-all." There is a fine line between being confident and assertive and knowing everything. At times you may know more than your coworkers or even your boss. However, no one likes to work with someone who thinks they have all the answers. It's okay to have opinions, even strong ones at times. But be sure to express them only when appropriate. Sometimes a better strategy is to hold back

---

[1] "Organizations and Internships," *Business Communications Quarterly* 60, no. 4. (1997): 126–131.

and quietly assess a situation before blurting out the most obvious answer. You may actually learn something. And you will avoid those simple yet costly gaffes that know-it-alls frequently make.

Don't be afraid to ask questions or speak up at the right time. If you have a legitimate question or need clarification, ask someone. Your bosses will appreciate your attempt to closely follow their instructions. A well-timed question can also help you avoid mistakes or costly delays in completing your tasks. Remember, as an intern you are not expected to fully understand everything you are asked to do on the first try.

The following "dos" are some best practices that can significantly improve your chances for intern success.

Do be an active and enthusiastic learner. Try to make a learning experience out of everything, even the most mundane tasks. Are you sorting and distributing mail? Try to learn who frequently contacts your organization and what they want. When you are photocopying, try to absorb the information contained in the originals. Elena Mayberry, an intern coordinator at the Smithsonian and a former intern herself, suggests that "intellectual sparkle" is what distinguishes a great intern from a mediocre one. This is "a desire to learn, a curiosity about a lot of things, and an enthusiasm for what you do."[2]

Do give your internship some time to develop before concluding there are problems. Interns often experience a lull in their jobs once the "honeymoon" period is over but before they gain more challenging tasks. How you handle this lull is crucial to your overall internship experience. If you become cynical, chances are you will sabotage your opportunities to gain better responsibilities. Instead, try to handle these challenges with patience. It is likely that your bosses are still assessing whether you can handle more.

After a few weeks, go back and review your learning contract and notes from your job interview and initial meetings with your supervisors or staff members. Did they promise that more substantial duties and projects would follow? Have they? If not, tactfully offer to take on more while still covering your basic responsibilities. As Bruce Craig, Communications Manager at the Smithsonian's Office of Museum Studies, explains, interns should "stand up for their rights and make sure they are not being taken advantage of." At the same time, they should also "make sure they work on the projects they were hired to."[3]

Do actively seek out opportunities to create your own projects. As you cover your basic tasks, look around the office to see where improvements can be made. Is the filing system a disaster? Are boxes of unrecorded data lying on the storage room floor? Is the company Web site horribly out of date? Instead of ignoring these problems, the savvy intern will try to fix them. Be sure to get permission before you start. This is also a good way to show that you are indispensable to the workplace. As Will Stone, Chief of Staff for U.S. Representative David Obey, says: "Look for the void, and ask about it. See if you can build a better mousetrap."[4]

There are other ways to expand your responsibilities. You can ask to "shadow" a regular employee on service calls or to meetings outside the office. Or you can seek feedback on your existing work. Ask how you could improve that summary report or letter to a client, or how you might have handled that rude caller differently. Asking for feedback shows that you want to improve yourself and do a good job for the benefit of the organization.

Do go the "extra mile" at times to demonstrate your willingness to pitch in and be a team player. Are there certain "crunch times" in your office? Instead of always dropping your work and leaving at 5 p.m., it's sometimes better to stay and finish the day's project or pitch in to help others finish theirs. Steve Selby, a Principal at Squier Knapp Dunn, looks for interns who can meet the challenges of working in a fast-paced political consulting firm. According to Selby: "The kind of people we like to hire are those who show some initiative and extra hustle. When it comes to hiring, those interns stand out in our mind."[5]

The more you look and act like a regular employee, the more likely you will be treated like one. Do you put in an honest day's work? Do you attend regular staff meetings (if allowed) and participate when you have something to contribute? Do you sit with other employees during lunch, even occasionally? Although you are still "just an intern," most supervisors and staff will treat you like a regular employee when you act like one. They may even decide they can't afford to let you go. That's what happened to Kristin Watkins. She is a former intern and now a full-time employee at Wider Opportunities, a national nonprofit association that creates employment opportunities for low-income women. According to Watkins, "Once you make yourself indispensable, it's very hard for the organization to let you go. They feel they have an investment in you."[6]

Do actively seek mentor relationships with supervisors and coworkers when appropriate. A frequent benefit of interning is the willingness of someone to mentor you. Mentors are more senior staff members and supervisors who take a special interest

---

[2] Comments made at "Getting the Most Out of Your Internship," Career Panel III, George Mason University, 1998.

[3] Comments made at "Getting the Most Out of Your Internship," Career Panel I, George Mason University, 1996.

[4] Comments made at Michigan State University's Washington Internship Seminar, 31 January 2001.

[5] Comments made at Michigan State University's Washington Internship Seminar, 10 April 2002.

[6] "Getting the Most Out of Your Internship," Career Panel III, 1998.

in your career aspirations and are willing to help you advance your career when they can. Often these mentors were interns themselves just a few short years ago and seek to help someone the way they were helped. Listen closely to successful people when they discuss their career histories; a mentor invariably shows up at critical points in their rise to the top.

Gaining a mentor may be one of the most important things you do at your internship. Once again, who you know is more important than what you know. While your immediate supervisors are good mentor candidates, don't neglect lower-level staff or contacts you make outside your office.

Do share your career aspirations with supervisors, coworkers, and those you encounter outside the workplace. This suggestion closely relates to the last one. Although you know what your immediate and long-term goals are, others don't unless you tell them. At appropriate times, you should make your goals known. This provides those who may want to help with the information they need to help you in the right way.

Try to take advantage of networking possibilities wherever they arise. When you network, you seek out and develop connections with others for mutual benefits. Networking is a socially acceptable practice, and all successful professionals do it. Begin with your friends and coworkers. Talk with them about their jobs and career paths. Ask them how they like their jobs, what their typical day is like, and what advice they have for someone who is considering a career in that field. You may be surprised at how helpful people can be.

Networking is not just talking about yourself but also being sincerely interested in others and what they do. A good networker is polite, personable, and genuine. To help you remember the names of contacts, be sure to exchange business cards. If your contact suggests you call or e-mail her later, do it. She may have a job lead or further contact in mind or genuinely want to help you in some other way.

Do build your own workplace portfolio. Employers are often impressed when job applicants can provide concrete examples of their work experiences and skill development. Providing them an actual copy of the newsletter you created at your internship, for example, will bolster your claim to "effective writing and organizational skills." What should go into your portfolio? The best strategy at this point is to save everything and decide later what you will actually keep. This includes letters and memos you wrote, research findings, reports you created, and newsletters you edited. Your academic assignments should also be included.

Do be open to learning from people whose backgrounds are different from yours. An underappreciated value of internships is that they can expose you to people with different backgrounds or life experiences. Try to meet and talk with as many people

as possible. Listen carefully to what they say and learn from them. Just because someone didn't go to college doesn't mean he or she doesn't have valuable wisdom to impart. In some instances, you may learn more from lower-placed staff than from your supervisors.

Ending Your Internship

How you end an internship is just as important as how you begin one. Your last days on the job are a time for personal satisfaction, honest evaluation, and looking forward.

Most academic internship programs require a written *work evaluation.* When possible, arrange personal meetings with your supervisors and possibly more senior staff to discuss the evaluation. While most interns receive good evaluations, some supervisors will indicate specific areas where you need improvement. Don't become defensive or resentful if you receive constructive criticism. Instead, take such advice for what it's worth and move on.

Final meetings with supervisors and regular staff members provide great opportunities to reemphasize your academic and career goals. If you are looking for a full-time job, now is a good time to reaffirm your interests. In some cases it's appropriate to directly ask for a job. In others, it isn't. If in doubt, just ask something like: "What can someone like me do to further prepare for a career in this field?"

Final meetings are also a good time to ask for a *letter of recommendation* for an existing job, for a future job, or for graduate school. Since you have worked for free or cheap for several weeks or months, it's not too much to ask of your employer. If you are not yet applying for jobs or graduate school, try to get a generic letter of recommendation. While a generic letter isn't great, it's better than nothing. Many employers are willing to revise a generic letter later when you do apply for jobs.

Your last days on the job are also a good time for *personal evaluation.* Take an inventory of what you accomplished and what remains to be done. Think about what you learned about the career field. Have your personal and work values been reinforced by your internship experience, or have they changed somewhat as a result of what you learned? Keep in mind that most people (even those who love their jobs) don't like something about their chosen career field. Try to realistically weigh the pros and cons of your internship experience.

An important part of intern success is *knowing when to leave.* Some interns become too comfortable with their position and decide to stay even though they have exhausted all the opportunities the internship offered. Your employer might even offer you a stipend to stay on. If so, be honest with yourself in deciding whether or not to take it. Often it's better to do two or three separate internships at different organizations than to remain at the same internship for a long period of time.

If you are disappointed with your internship experience, resist the temptation to burn your bridges. While that might make you feel good temporarily, it can hurt you in the long run. Also, interns who leave on a bad note may make it harder for future intern applicants who may be more suited to the organization.

Keep in touch with your former colleagues after you leave. A job position or other opportunity may open up later, or one of your network contacts may have a lead for you. A short e-mail to your contacts every couple of months can keep you on their radar screen.

Remember that it's primarily up to you to get the most out of your internship. Countless interns before you have achieved success, and you can too! Good luck.

International Applicants for U.S. Internships

by Elizabeth Chazottes

Elizabeth Chazottes is the Executive Director and CEO of the
Association for International Practical Training and has written
numerous articles on international training, overseas employment,
and international human resources issues.

International Applicants for U.S. Internships

Nothing is more exciting and rewarding than an international internship in the United States. International participants have been coming to the United States for years to learn American methods of business, to perfect their English skills, and to make international connections that last a lifetime. There are more opportunities today than ever before, but you must be well-informed. Take the time to learn about your options and which program will best meet your needs. The better prepared you are, the more successful your experience will be. All international students interested in coming to the U.S. for an internship or international program should make sure they are clear on what they can and cannot do in the workplace and on the type of visa they need to come to the U.S.

In an effort to provide guidance that is as accurate as possible for students from outside the United States, each employer listed in *Internships 2004* has been asked if applications will be accepted from international students. Peterson's has also asked if the employer is willing to undertake the necessary steps—either directly with the U.S. Immigration and Naturalization Service (INS) or through an educational exchange organization—to make it possible for the student to secure a proper U.S. visa that will allow them to complete the internship and legally receive a salary or stipend, if applicable, while in the United States.

There are significant penalties for employers who hire foreign nationals illegally. Foreign nationals can be deported and barred from returning to the United States for violating their visa status. If an employer in the United States offers you an internship, make certain that both you *and* the employer know and follow the requirements of U.S. law *before* you leave home.

Passports

In order to get a U.S. visa that permits employment in an internship, you must have a valid passport from your own country. Your passport must be valid for six months beyond the date on which you expect to leave the United States. A number of countries have special "passport validity" agreements with the United States under which a passport is considered to be valid for six months beyond the expiration date stated in the passport. In order to avoid last-minute problems, you should contact U.S. consular officials as early as possible to determine the exact requirement for your country.

Visas

Unlike many countries, the United States does not issue work permits or residence permits or require police registration. Instead, what an individual may or may not do while in the United States depends entirely on the specific type of visa granted. As a result, the United States has the world's most complex visa system—there are currently forty-six different kinds of nonimmigrant visas! Please note that although an individual may be a full-time student in his or her own country, a "student" visa for admission to the United States applies only to people attending an American school for full-time study. Therefore, the three kinds of student visas (F-1, J-1, and M) cannot be used by a student coming to the United States uniquely for an internship experience.

As a general rule, there are only two U.S. visas that are likely to be suitable for students coming to the United States for employment in an internship:

J-1 "Exchange Visitor" J-1 visa programs are managed by approved organizations or sponsors, such as U.S. government agencies, schools and universities, hospitals, companies, and private nonprofit educational exchange organizations. The Bureau of Educational and Cultural Affairs of the U.S. Department of State, formerly the U.S. Information Agency, has authority over these programs. There are fourteen different J-1 categories, each with its own specific rules and regulations. Among these categories are those that permit international high school students, university students, trainees, au pairs, and researchers to participate in programs in the U.S. Each sponsor is granted a "program description" that specifies the activities that are permitted for participants in the sponsor's program.

Of the fourteen J-1 categories, the "trainee" category is suitable for most international students coming to the U.S. for paid internships. J-1 trainees can come to the U.S. to receive training in their field for periods of up to eighteen months. A detailed training program must be prepared by the U.S. host employer, specifying the objectives and skills to be learned as well as the length of time required to complete the program. A trainee cannot replace a U.S. worker but comes to the U.S. to acquire skills and knowledge in U.S. methodology.

The number of trainee programs has grown over the years. Two of the long-standing trainee exchange organizations for students are the International Association of Students in Economics and Business Management (AIESEC)—for business and economics students—and the International Association for the Exchange of Students for Technical Experience (IAESTE)—for students in technical fields. The Council on International Educational Exchange (CIEE) is the largest of the student trainee programs, followed by the Association for International Practical Training (AIPT), which brings in students and professionals from some eighty countries annually. Other programs are also available that deal primarily with trainees from specific countries or regions of the world or specific industries. Some U.S. universities also run trainee programs.

There are three additional J-1 categories that may also be of interest to students who desire a work experience in the U.S.: Summer Travel/Work, Camp Counselor, and Au Pair.

Several organizations have been granted J-1 authorizations for "summer travel/work" programs. These permit university students to work in any job they may find during the summer months (November to February for students from the Southern Hemisphere). No extensions of visas are permitted, and changes to other J-1 visa categories are not allowed. Pre-placement is required for 50 percent of the participants, and students should check with the U.S. sponsoring organization about specific requirements. The Council on International Educational Exchange is the largest of these programs, but several other programs also operate summer travel/work programs.

The second type of J-1 visa is for placements in summer camps for camp counselor experience. Participants must be at least 18 years old. Placements are limited to a maximum of four months and must be for genuine camp counseling assignments in accredited U.S. camps. The YMCA, Camp America, and InterExchange operate several of the better-known camp counselor programs.

The third is the au pair category. Au pair programs allow participants to live with and participate in the home life of an American host family while providing child-care services and attending a U.S. postsecondary educational institution. The au pair participant cannot provide child-care services for more than 45 hours per week. All participants must register and attend classes offered by an accredited U.S. postsecondary institution. Au pairs must be between the ages of 18 and 26, be secondary school graduates or the equivalent, and be proficient in spoken English.

In some cases, an individual coming to the United States on the J-1 visa may be subject to something called the "two-year foreign residence requirement." Some countries have asked the U.S. government to establish a "skills list" for its citizens. If the person's field is included on the skills list for his or her country, that means that this particular skill is greatly needed in the home country, and it will generally be necessary for the individual to return to his or her country after completing their program in the U.S. Someone subject to this residence requirement must return to his or her home country for a minimum of two years before coming back to the United States on most of the nonimmigrant visas or as a "permanent resident." Most European countries do not have skills lists, but many other countries do. If the ability to return to the United States within a two-year period after training is of concern, you should get specific information regarding this from U.S. consular officials. Also, participants who receive funding from the sending foreign government or the U.S. government may also be subject to the two-year residency requirement.

J-1 Program Sponsors

Trainee Exchange Programs

Aiesec/US
127 West 26th Street, 10th Floor
New York, NY 10001
212-757-3774
Fax: 212-757-4062
E-mail: jimk@aiesecus.org
www.us.aiesec.org

American-Scandinavian Foundation
58 Park Avenue
New York, NY 10016
212-879-9779
Fax: 212-879-9779
E-mail: info@amscan.org
www.amscan.org

Association for International Practical Training (AIPT)
10400 Little Patuxent Parkway, Suite 250
Columbia, MD 21044-3519
410-997-2200
Fax: 410-992-3924
E-mail: aipt@aipt.org
www.aipt.org

CDS International
871 United Nations Plaza
New York, NY 10017-1814
212-497-3500
Fax: 212-497-3535
E-mail: info@cdsintl.org
www.cdsintl.org

Council on International Educational Exchange (CIEE)
633 Third Avenue, 20th Floor
New York, NY 10017-6706
800-40-STUDY
Fax: 212-822-2779
www.ciee.org

InterExchange, Inc.
161 Sixth Avenue
New York, NY 10013
212-924-0446
Fax: 212-924-0575
E-mail: info@interexchange.org
www.interexchange.org

YMCA International
5 West 63rd Street
New York, NY 10023
212-727-8800
888-477-9622 (toll-free)
Fax: 212-727-8814
www.ymcainternational.org

Agricultural and Agribusiness Trainee Programs

MAST International
395 VoTech Building
1954 Buford Avenue
St. Paul, MN 55108-6197
612-624-3740
Fax: 612-625-7031
E-mail: mast@tc.umn.edu
http://mast.coafes.umn.edu

Summer Travel / Work Programs

Council on International Educational Exchange, CIEE
(see address in previous list)

InterExchange, Inc.
(see address in previous list)

YMCA International
(see address in previous list)

Au Pair Programs

Au Pair in America
River Plaza
9 West Broad Street
Stamford, CT 06902-3788
800-727-2437
Fax: 203-863-6180
E-mail: aupair.info@aifs.com
www.aifs.org

EF Education Cambridge
One Education Street
Cambridge, MA 02141
617-619-1100
Fax: 617-619-1001
E-mail: aupair.ww@ef.com
www.ef.com/master

InterExchange Au Pair
(see address for InterExchange, Inc. in previous list)

Camp Counselor Programs

Camp America
River Plaza
9 West Broad Street
Stamford, CT 06902-3788
800-727-2437
Fax: 203-399-5590
E-mail: rhcow@aifs.com
www.aifs.com/camp

InterExchange—Camp USA Program
(see address in previous list)

International Camp Counselor Program—YMCA
(see address in previous list)

Q "International Cultural Exchange Visitor"

The "Q" visa allows the U.S. employer to apply to INS for permission to hire a person over 18 years of age from another country for a period of not more than fifteen months. The purpose of the program is for the international participant to work or train and to share or demonstrate his or her own culture with Americans.

A frequently cited example of a major Q employer is the EPCOT Center at Walt Disney World in Florida. Another example would be a museum or a department of a museum devoted to the art and culture of the student's home country.

The "cultural component" must be an integral part of the employment or training offered. The employer must demonstrate that the individual to be hired is fully able to communicate with Americans about his or her culture as well as being fully qualified for the work aspects of the position. Substantial documentation is required as part of the employer's application.

Visa Procedures

If an employer's applications for a Q visa are successful, the District Office of the Immigration and Naturalization Service will advise the U.S. Embassy in the student's country. The student can then obtain the visa and travel to the U.S. In the case of the J-1 visa, the sponsoring organization that is arranging the program issues a U.S. government document called an IAP-66 (a Certificate of Eligibility). The IAP-66, which is sent to the student, is used to apply for the J-1 visa in his or her own country.

When Q visa holders enter the United States, the admitting Immigration Inspector issues a Form I-94 (Arrival/Departure Record) that notes the specific visa granted and the date when the "Permit to Stay" expires. When J-1 visa holders enter, they are issued a Permit to Stay with the notation "D/S" (for duration of status). This means that J-1 trainees may remain in the U.S. as long as they are engaged in their training program or until the end date of their IAP-66, plus thirty days. The I-94 form (and IAP-66 for the J-1 trainee) is the only documentation needed for the student to proceed to the workplace and take up the assignment.

Employment Eligibility Verification

U.S. law requires employers to examine documentation proving that persons hired are either citizens of the United States or noncitizens legally authorized for employment during their stay in the United States.

Essentially, the law requires that within three business days after a person is hired, the employer must *physically examine* documentation that (a) establishes proof of the new employee's identity and (b) establishes that the person is either a U.S. citizen or is a noncitizen who has the legal right to be employed in the United States. The law requires that a record of the verification process be maintained in the employer's files for a period of three years after the date of hiring. For this purpose, the INS has developed the I-9 form.

Virtually all kinds of employment are covered, from a full-time job with a large employer such as IBM to selling hamburgers part-time at the local McDonald's. Certainly, all of the jobs listed in *Internships 2004* will require you and your employer to complete the I-9 form. The I-9 form is in two parts. The top half must be filled out by the employee—you. You then present the form, together with your documentation, to your employer, who will complete the bottom half of the form.

Social Security Number

In most cases, you will need to obtain a Social Security number. It is widely used in the United States as a basic identification number—and in most automated payroll systems, in university enrollment systems, and for transactions such as opening a bank account.

Individuals entering the U.S. on the F, J, M, and Q visas are usually exempt from the U.S. Social Security tax. But even if you are exempt from paying Social Security tax, you will still need to obtain a Social Security number. Social Security regulations require that you apply in person, and it is advised that you do this shortly after arrival. Normally, numbers are issued within a few weeks.

It will be important for you to provide full documentation that clearly shows you have a visa that permits employment. The Social Security official to whom you submit your application will want to see your passport, your I-94 form, visa documents (such as the triplicate copy of the IAP-66), and any documents related to your work placement. If you do not present the proper documentation, a Social Security card marked "Not Valid for Employment" will be issued. If this happens, you will not be able to receive a salary or stipend during your internship. If you have any problems getting your Social Security card, you should contact your sponsoring organization for assistance.

Income Tax

As a general rule, individuals coming to the United States on any of the visas discussed in this article will be subject to U.S. income tax (and possibly state and local income tax) on the money they earn while in the country, and they must file an income tax return. Between January 1 and April 15 of the year following your employment, you will have to submit an income tax return (Form 1040EZ or Form 1040) to the IRS. The 1040EZ is used if you have no dependents, earned less than $50,000 of income, and have no travel expense deductions. If you have remained in the country from one year to the next, you also must submit a Form 8843 to verify your non-resident status. Tax regulations and procedures are not simple, and you should seek help from your employer and/or your sponsoring organization if you are participating in a J-1 program. You may also wish to secure a copy of IRS Publication 519, *U.S. Tax Guide for Aliens*, which is available free of charge from the Internal Revenue Service. Forms are available online at www.irs.ustreas.gov/prod/forms_pubs/.

Full-Time Students at U.S. Schools

Individuals enrolled at U.S. colleges and universities for full-time academic study are usually admitted on the basis of the F-1 (student), M-1 (student), or student category of the J-1 visa. In each case, internship employment may be possible before graduation, after graduation, or both. When such employment may take place, the length of time allowed, and what the employment is called (practical training, curricular practical training, academic training) depend on the specific visa and circumstances of the individual student. A number of schools in the United States offer academic courses—usually known as cooperative education programs—that combine periods of study with periods of practical training employment. Under certain conditions, students from other countries who are enrolled as regular, full-time students in a cooperative education program are allowed to undertake the practical training assignments (usually paid) in the same manner as American students. For information on enrollment in cooperative education programs and the American colleges and universities that offer these opportunities, contact:

Cooperative Education & Internship Association
4190 S. Highland Dr., Suite 211
Salt Lake City, UT 84124
801-984-2026
800-824-0449 (toll-free)
Fax: 801-984-2027
E-mail: sher@ceiainc.org
www.ceiainc.org

Whether or not the student is enrolled in a cooperative education program, whether it is before or after graduation, and regardless of the type of visa (M-1, F-1, or J-1), the student remains under the legal sponsorship of his or her college, university, or in the case of some J-1 students, Exchange Visitor Program sponsor. Therefore, students should seek assistance from the international student adviser at their school.

Visa Violations or Overstays

In recent years, U.S. immigration laws have become more restrictive. All international visitors, trainees, and temporary work visa holders should make sure that they fully understand their responsibilities under the particular visa they use to enter the U.S. It is extremely important that you know exactly what you are permitted to do on the type of visa you have been granted and how long you are permitted to remain in the United States. If you have any questions about this, please check with your program sponsor, employer, or the INS. If your program ends early, you are not permitted to remain in the United States. You must either return home upon completion of your internship or work program or take the steps necessary to legally remain in the United States. There are severe penalties for foreign nationals who overstay their visas or who violate their status. You could be barred from returning to the U.S. for ten years or longer if you violate your visa status, even unintentionally.

In Conclusion

Most countries of the world have very strict regulations regarding employment for noncitizens in order to protect job opportunities for their own citizens. The United States is no different. What is different, however, is the U.S. system of visas and the rules and regulations that apply to each type (and subtype) of visa. The process of acquiring the proper visa takes a good deal of time (sometimes as long as four to six months) and can often be frustrating and confusing. Therefore, it is important to plan ahead and contact prospective employers as early as possible so that the employer has sufficient time to undertake the paperwork involved. If you have applied to or have been accepted by a "trainee" program, make sure that the employer knows the name of the organization, because each sponsoring organization has its own internal procedures that must be followed. Prepare well in advance, ask lots of questions, and make sure you understand what needs to be done. If you do your research and begin early, you will soon be on your way to a fulfilling internship experience in the United States.

What Sponsors Seek in an Intern

by Jay Heflin and Richard Thau

Jay Heflin and Richard Thau are freelance business writers from New York City.

What Sponsors Seek in an Intern

Graduating students usually discover that choosing a job is bewildering and aggravating. And to make matters worse, some students find themselves with jobs that they know very little about. But there is something that can teach a student the fundamentals of career life: an internship.

"College graduates who have served internships receive, on average, higher starting salaries and more job offers than those with no internship experience," says Maury Hanigan, president of New York–based Hanigan Consulting Group, a firm that studies the internship programs of Fortune 500 companies.

Indeed, internships can be the most impressive item

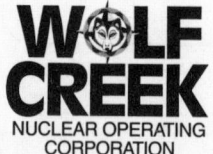

David Reynolds, Human Resource Specialist, Wolf Creek Nuclear Operating Corporation, Burlington, Kansas

"We look for candidates who have a unique interest in power generation," states David Reynolds, Human Resources Specialist with Wolf Creek Nuclear Operating Corporation, a commercial nuclear electric power generating station. His company employs, at about $10.50 an hour, junior and senior college students for one semester.

But interest is not the only requirement to secure an internship at Wolf Creek, as Mr. Reynolds explains. "Grades and the student's major are also important. We look for engineering students who have a GPA above a 2.5 or 2.7, something above average."

on a student's resume. It shows real experience and the ability to accomplish more than digesting college classroom theories. In some instances, participating in an internship will put a particular person ahead of the competition and can be the deciding factor in securing paid employment later.

Corporations know the advantages of hiring interns. In today's competitive economy, companies can no longer afford to spend valuable recruiting time on unknown entities. Internships allow a company to "test" a prospective employee nearly risk-free. A lot more can be learned about a person's work habits and attitudes within a semester internship than in a number of half-hour

Amy Leahy, Intern Coordinator, Omicon Cable, Hamtramck, Michigan

"Enthusiastic" is the way Amy Leahy describes the interns she hires. "Experience is something we give them [the interns] in return," she adds. Ms. Leahy works with Omicon Cable, a public-access cable company. Her company employs local programming interns of college or even high school level.

"We want to show the person interested in pursuing this career that it is not a 9 to 5 job and also that it could be for anyone," says Leahy. Interns who work at Omicon Cable are not paid for the first semester; if they decide to stay on, they receive a small monthly stipend.

interviews. It is common to find companies hiring 80 to 90 percent of their interns for full-time positions after graduation.

Companies also favor interns because they help to improve the bottom line. While most interns are paid a nominal stipend, their take-home pay is usually nowhere near what it would cost a company to employ someone full-time. "Some companies find investing in summer internships more cost effective than straight recruiting," stated Roger Muller, Placement Director at Northwestern University.

What do sponsors seek in an intern? The answer to this question is simple: It varies. Seemingly there are just as many different, specific qualifications needed

Catherine Councill, President, Maryland Film Office, Baltimore, Maryland

Catherine Councill at the Maryland Film Office believes in giving high school graduates a chance to learn a career. Her company markets the state of Maryland to film companies, enticing them to do their shooting there. "We like to bring the people on board who show the greatest amount of enthusiasm during the interview," she says.

But being a high school graduate isn't the only qualification required to interview with Ms. Councill's company. "Normally we like to have interns who are studying marketing or communication. That way they know the lingo that accompanies the marketing field."

Marya Warshaw, Director, Gowanus Arts Exchange, Brooklyn, New York

For Marya Warshaw at the Gowanus Arts Exchange, experience is needed to fill one of her internship slots. "For our arts administration intern," she explains, "we look for someone who has worked before. Especially on the technical side, it's hard to teach someone all that needs to be done and still get a show off the ground."

Gowanus' internships are as short as eight weeks or as long as a full year. The longer "experience required" positions are paid. "We try to be very accommodating [on both the time availability and salary] because having interns on our crew is very valuable, for us as well as for them."

to land an internship as there are companies within the broad scope of corporate America. No single criterion, such as grades, job experience, or major, can encapsulate what companies seek in their prospective interns. Each corporation has specific needs, and those needs must be filled by interns with specific skills.

Interest, Not Just Grades

"Good grades and related job experience are important. But we also look at what school activities they [prospective interns] participate in," said Kim Hendershot, personnel specialist at Burns and McDonnell in Kansas City, Missouri, an engineering consulting firm that hires about 30 paid interns each year.

Hendershot said the company considers school activities so important because they give insight about a student: "Belonging to the Greek system or being a member of an organization that is related to their discipline can often tell us more about a student than can be reflected in their grades or job experience."

Another company that considers school activities and personal interests in addition to grades and related job experience is *The Nation* magazine. "Grades and majors aren't as big a deal as interest in progressive causes and knowledge of such current events," said Sandy Wood, a staffer at *The Nation* in charge of recruiting interns.

The Nation employs 7 interns in New York and 1 in Washington, D.C. While at the magazine, interns must complete four "assignments" that require that they assist the publication's editors and columnists. "Their tasks on the assignments vary widely," said Mr. Wood. "There are some secretarial duties and research to be

done. But the biggest part they play is fact checking and assisting the publicity director with news releases."

Desire, Experience, and Grades

Still, there are companies that consider a candidate's grade point average as important as interpersonal skills and interests.

Jennifer Craig, the marketing director at Union Station, a mall in Indianapolis, said, "Careful attention to detail and a grade point average of at least 3.0" are required to intern with her company. Responsibilities for an intern include implementing special events, creating press releases, and assisting with programs that will enhance gross sales.

Craig went on to say that "qualified individuals for an internship program at Union Station should display a high drive, a willingness to be flexible, and related experience." Union Station employs 2 interns each year. Each intern is paid a weekly stipend of about $100.

Just as Craig said a related background in the field of marketing is important to becoming an intern in her company, so did Jeanine Triolo, marketing manager with *Vibe* magazine in New York City. "If they're majoring in marketing, I'd be more inclined to hire them," she said. "They are taught the fundamentals of marketing in school and are ready to apply what they've learned. I don't have to teach them anything; we can get right to work on projects that need to be accomplished for the magazine."

Triolo also sees availability of the intern's time as a crucial factor when considering who to hire. "I need someone for at least three or four days a week. We have

THE MEXICAN MUSEUM

Yalonda Perez, Intern Coordinator, Mexican Museum, San Francisco, California

At the Mexican Museum in San Francisco, California, possessing previous experience with the correct educational background can help secure an internship position. "Our interns are usually undergraduates majoring in art history or Latino history or graduate students with work experience," says Ms. Perez, an employee with the Museum.

Her museum accepts students into a wide range of internship programs. They range from curatorial to outreach programs. These positions are not paid, but the work completed does count toward college credit for the intern.

Council for Court Excellence

Priscilla Skillman, Program Analyst, Council for Court Excellence, Washington, D.C.

To be an intern at the Council for Court Excellence, the student has to be a triple threat: interested, experienced, and knowledgeable. "We require that our interns have an interest in public policy, a strong academic background, and be able to provide writing samples of past work," reports Priscilla Skillman, Program Analyst for the firm. Her group is a nonprofit, nonpartisan civic organization working to improve the administration of justice in local and federal courts.

Interns are not paid, but the experienced gained is immeasurable. "Our interns are usually with us for one semester," says Ms. Skillman, "but we would be delighted to have them stay longer." Skillman's firm accepts 1 to 3 interns per semester to assist in the development of selected projects.

projects lasting between fourteen and twenty days, and for [the interns] to get the best education possible about life in the marketing world, they have to see the project through all the way, from beginning to deadline."

The Universal Trait

Amid numerous company needs and intern qualifications, there was one universal trait that all internship sponsors hoped to see in internship candidates: a winning attitude. Possessing the desire to succeed is key to unlocking any door of opportunity.

How to Use This Book

Internships 2004 is a comprehensive directory of internship opportunities across the United States and abroad. The guide provides detailed, pertinent, annually updated information on tens of thousands of short-term positions available in numerous career areas.

Listings are categorized according to the type of company or organization that sponsors the internship. Most sponsors offer positions in career areas that extend beyond their specific field, so you should use the **Field of Interest Index** to find the types of programs that interest you. For example, this index will allow you to find a public relations position at an accounting firm or an accounting position at a public relations firm.

To help you make the most effective use of *Internships 2004*, entries contain the following groups of information:

What You'll Find in the Profiles

1. General Information
In this section you will find a brief description of the organization and its purpose and data on its size and the number of internship applications received each year.

2. Internships Available
Provides information about the type and number of positions available, basic job descriptions, duration of the internships, salaries, training, eligibility requirements, and whether international applicants are accepted.

3. Benefits
Provides information about the benefits available to interns, including training, housing, meal plans, health plans, whether an intern may arrange for college credit* through his or her own college or university, permanent employment opportunities, and placement services.

4. International Internships
Provides location of organization's internship placement opportunities outside the United States.

5. Contact
Includes the name, address, telephone number, and, when available, fax number, e-mail and World Wide Web addresses of the contact for the organization's internship program. Make special note of any application directions listed here to increase your chances for a positive response from the internship sponsor.

*College credit arrangements must be made prior to the student's participation in the internship.

GENERAL COMPANY
123 Main Street
Urban Center, NJ 08543

❶ **General Information** Entrepreneurial database publishing and communications company specializing in education and career reference books. Established 1966. Number of employees: 200. Division of Unified Corporation, Atlanta, Georgia. Number of internship applications received each year: 50.

❷ **Internships Available** ▶ *2 public relations interns:* responsibilities include drafting and disseminating press releases, establishing media contacts. Duration is 8 weeks. Paid. Candidates should have word processing skills. Open to college sophomores, college juniors, college seniors. ▶ *35 data editors:* responsibilities include reviewing survey data for internal consistency, resolving discrepant data with respondents over the phone, data entry. Duration is 6 months. $6 per hour. Open to college sophomores. International applications accepted.

❸ **Benefits** Formal training, opportunity to attend seminars/workshops, and free parking. Sponsor is willing to complete any necessary paperwork required for an intern to receive educational credit. Possibility of full-time employment. Placement assistance provided, including letters of recommendation, names of contacts. Housing provided at $95 per week. Meals provided at no cost.

❹ **International Internships** Available in Paris, France; Madrid, Spain.

❺ **Contact** Call or write to Internship Coordinator, P.O. Box 2123, Urban Center, New Jersey 08543. In-person interview required. Phone: 609-555-1212. Fax: 609-555-0923. E-mail: coord@gc.com. Application deadline: May 15 World Wide Web: http://www.gc.com.

A Note on International Internships

"Exciting Jobs Overseas," "Hundreds of Positions Worldwide: All Fields"—the ads sound great. Do your thing in another country. See the world. Maybe—but before you've gone too far, a closer look might be in order. What is an "international" career and what do *you* want from it? Are you interested in business, government, the United Nations, or nonprofit voluntary groups? Do you want to teach, undertake research, be a part of management, or assist in the needs of developing countries? And, perhaps most important of all, do you want to advance your career in the

United States, or do you want to pursue an international career in the fullest sense of the word by spending most of your working life in other countries? If you are honest with yourself in answering questions such as these, you will be a long way toward realizing your goal.

Far too many people seem to think that a strong interest in international work or some past foreign travel experience is sufficient to launch an international career. Unfortunately, this thinking can lead to a rude awakening.

First of all, you should think about the potential international applications of your chosen profession. Then, in addition to the training and preparation necessary to do your job, you should think about the additional preparation needed for an international career. What kind of language skills will you need? Do you have the ability to work with people of many different cultural backgrounds?

Use the listings in the **International Internships Index** and be a bit creative by making use of the **Employer Index.** While the opportunities listed in the **International Internships Index** are exclusively international in nature, many other employers listed in *Internships 2004* offer experiences with an international dimension. You can also find international opportunities in the **Field of Interest Index** under the International category.

The international dimension of every field of human endeavor expands as the world grows more interdependent, and challenging opportunities exist for the individual interested in an international career. Whether one's working life develops in a single country overseas, in a series of assignments in different countries, or in the United States with only occasional overseas travel, one or more international internship experiences will give you that all-important head start on an international career.

Some organizations accept interns of any age or academic level. Others limit their internships based on the academic level of the applicant. The **Academic Level Required Index** identifies organizations that have indicated the academic level(s) that are required for their internships. These may or may not be minimum requirements. An organization may indicate one or all of the options available, from high school student through college graduate.

If you are looking for an internship so that you have relevant experience to put on your resume, but whether you are going to be paid is still a concern, use the **Paid Internships Index** to find all of the organizations that are willing to pay for your talents and skills. Keep in mind that an unpaid internship will still give you valuable experience and will enhance your resume.

If you already have enough experience to know that you are on the right career path, check out the **Possibility of Permanent Employment Index** to find organizations that indicate they have an interest in keeping their best interns on the job on a full-time basis.

About the Data

The information in these listings was collected during the winter of 2002 and the spring of 2003 through questionnaire mailings and telephone interviews with representatives of each of the sponsoring organizations. For those few organizations that failed to respond to Peterson's survey in time to meet publication deadlines, information was drawn from Web sites. Although every entry has been completely updated, you should be aware that changes in the data may occur after the publication of the book; contact the sponsors directly for the most current information on their internship program.

Peterson's does not make any claim concerning the hiring policies or practices of sponsoring organizations in this book.

ACCOMMODATIONS AND FOOD SERVICES

GENERAL

AMELIA ISLAND PLANTATION
PO Box 3000
Amelia Island, Florida 32035-3000

General Information   1,350 acre internationally recognized, gated resort/residential community located in northeast Florida offering miles of sandy beach and many amenities. Established in 1974. Number of employees: 1,100. Number of internship applications received each year: 500.

Internships Available   ▶ *3–10 commercial recreation interns:* responsibilities include split duties in program design, implementation and evaluation of children's programs and group events, guest relations, major projects, pool maintenance, and minor facilities upkeep. Candidates should have ability to work with others, college courses in field, experience in the field, self-motivation, own transportation, fluency in conversational English (speaking, reading, writing, and comprehension), customer service skills, first aid, CPR, and life saving certificates (preferred). Duration is minimum of 16 weeks. $225 per week housing stipend. Open to college juniors, college seniors, graduate students. ▶ *3–6 culinary/ pastry interns:* responsibilities include gaining hands-on experience in a wide variety of culinary situations through a rotation that includes banquets, pastry, and restaurants. Candidates should have ability to work independently, ability to work with others, college courses in field, knowledge of field, plan to pursue career in field, own transportation, knife skills, customer service skills, fluency in conversational English (speaking, reading, writing, and comprehension). Duration is flexible. $7.50 per hour plus $1.00 per hour worked upon successful completion of internship. Open to college juniors, college seniors, graduate students. ▶ *1–2 environmental interpretation interns:* responsibilities include assisting nature science program manager in providing social and group guests, club members, property owners, employees and the community with nature programs; working closely with local animal sanctuaries in animal rescues on property; assisting with main nature displays and retail operations in-shop. Candidates should have college courses in field, knowledge of field, oral communication skills, personal interest in the field, self-motivation, own transportation, customer service skills, fluency in conversational English (speaking, reading, writing, and comprehension). Duration is minimum of 16 weeks. $225 per week housing stipend. Open to college juniors, college seniors, graduate students. ▶ *2 food and beverage interns:* responsibilities include assisting managers and staff in daily activities; learning scheduling practices, inventory control, tracking, and other administrative activities in addition to actual food service. Candidates should have ability to work independently, declared college major in field, experience in the field, plan to pursue career in field, strong interpersonal skills, customer service skills, must have own transportation. Duration is 14–16 weeks. $225 per week housing stipend. Open to college juniors, college seniors. ▶ *4–8 golf level I and turf management interns:* responsibilities include working as a golf level I intern (assisting guests, members, owners, and employees in golf experience) or as a turf management intern (mowing greens, collars, tees, fairways and roughs, raking sand bunkers, and changing cups). Candidates should have ability to work independently,

knowledge of field, plan to pursue career in field, strong interpersonal skills, own transportation, customer service skills, valid driver's license, a good driving record, basic knowledge of golf, fluency in conversational English (speaking, reading, writing, and comprehension). Duration is 16–32 weeks. $5.15 per hour plus tips. Open to college juniors, college seniors, graduate students. ▶ *12 lodging and housekeeping interns:* responsibilities include working as either a lodging intern (rotating through transportation, front desk/reservations departments) or housekeeping intern (assisting with daily activities including inspecting rooms and public areas, ordering supplies, and other duties). Candidates should have college courses in field, experience in the field, oral communication skills, strong interpersonal skills, must have own transportation, customer service skills, valid driver's license, good driving record, fluency in conversational English (speaking, reading, writing, and comprehension). Duration is minimum of 16 weeks. $225 per week housing stipend. Open to college juniors, college seniors, graduate students. ▶ *1 marketing intern:* responsibilities include working closely with the marketing, public relations, promotions, and graphics departments in implementation of new promotions, programs, events, by creating and distributing flyers, and preparing articles and press releases. Candidates should have ability to work independently, declared college major in field, knowledge of field, self-motivation, strong interpersonal skills, written communication skills, good time-management and problem-solving skills, valid driver's license, own transportation, proficiency in Microsoft Word and PowerPoint, fluency in conversational English (speaking, reading, writing, and comprehension). Duration is minimum of 16 weeks. $225 per week housing stipend. Open to college juniors, college seniors. ▶ *Real estate marketing interns:* responsibilities include creating and managing in-house collateral materials; assisting with a newsletter, reports, mailings, and a database; creating at least one press release; attending meetings and completing assigned projects. Candidates should have ability to work independently, computer skills, declared college major in field, editing skills, oral communication skills, customer service skills, own transportation, proficiency in Microsoft Word, PowerPoint, Excel, Publisher, and PhotoShop. Duration is 14–16 weeks. $225 per week housing stipend. Open to college juniors, college seniors. ▶ *2 retail interns:* responsibilities include total retail experience including rotation through 4-5 retail operations as well as the distribution center; assisting with displays, promotions and events, and purchasing. Candidates should have ability to work independently, declared college major in field, experience in the field, plan to pursue career in field, strong interpersonal skills, customer service skills, must have own transportation. Duration is 14–16 weeks. $225 per week housing stipend. Open to college juniors, college seniors. ▶ *1–2 tennis interns:* responsibilities include court maintenance, pro shop duties, tennis instruction, racquet stringing, organization, and implementation of tournaments. Candidates should have ability to work independently, college courses in field, knowledge of field, plan to pursue career in field, own transportation, customer service skills, 4.5 level of tennis playing ability, ability to string racquets, fluency in conversational English (speaking, reading, writing, and comprehension). Duration is 16–32 weeks. $5.15 per hour; additional pay for giving lessons. Open to college juniors, college seniors, graduate students.

Benefits   Formal training, free meals, job counseling, on-the-job training, opportunity to attend seminars/workshops, possible full-

Amelia Island Plantation (continued)

time employment, willing to act as a professional reference, willing to complete paperwork for educational credit, willing to provide letters of recommendation, assistance in locating housing and roommates, use of amenities/property at a discounted rate.
Contact Write, call, fax, e-mail, or through World Wide Web site Barbara Ross, Internship Coordinator. Phone: 904-277-5904. Fax: 904-491-4345. E-mail: intern@aipfl.com. Telephone interview required. Applicants must submit a formal organization application, letter of interest, resume, 2 academic and 2 professional references, 3 writing samples (for marketing positions). Applications are accepted continuously. World Wide Web: http://www.aipfl.com.

AMERICAN HOSPITALITY ACADEMY
PO Box 7832
Hilton Head, South Carolina 29938

General Information Company providing internships to college students in front office, food service, and resort activities. Established in 1986. Number of employees: 800. Number of internship applications received each year: 2,000.
Internships Available ▶ *500–750 interns:* responsibilities include working in one of the following areas: resort activities, front office, food service, or theme park. Candidates should have ability to work with others, knowledge of field, oral communication skills, personal interest in the field, self-motivation, ability to live and train with people from a diversity of cultures. Duration is 3–6 months. $300 per month. Open to college freshmen, college sophomores, college juniors, college seniors, recent college graduates, individuals 18-30 years old. International applications accepted.
Benefits Formal training, free housing, job counseling, on-the-job training, opportunity to attend seminars/workshops, possible full-time employment, willing to act as a professional reference, willing to complete paperwork for educational credit, willing to provide letters of recommendation, shuttled transportation to and from training site, local telephone, all utilities, cable television, weekly grocery trips, cultural nights, quarterly socials, rewards and recognition programs.
Contact Write, call, fax, e-mail, or through World Wide Web site Human Resources. Phone: 800-864-6762. Fax: 843-448-0621. E-mail: jgross@americanhospitalityacademy.com. Telephone interview required. Applicants must submit a formal organization application, letter of interest, resume, three personal references, letters of recommendation and college/university documentation of internship requirements may be requested; $300 program fee upon acceptance. Application deadline: at least 4 months in advance of desired start date. World Wide Web: http://www.americanhospitalityacademy.com.

BOLONGO BAY BEACH RESORT
7150 Bolongo
St. Thomas U.S. Virgin Islands

General Information Resort that includes hotel and restaurants. Established in 1974. Number of employees: 130. Number of internship applications received each year: 1,500.
Internships Available ▶ *1–2 culinary interns:* responsibilities include assisting executive chef throughout operation. Candidates should have ability to work independently, computer skills, knowledge of field, plan to pursue career in field, self-motivation. Duration is 3–4 months. Position available as unpaid or paid. Open to culinary academy students. ▶ *1 food and beverage intern:* responsibilities include assisting food and beverage director in carrying out daily operations in two restaurants, day sail, warehouses, and banquets. Candidates should have computer skills, declared college major in field, experience in the field, plan to pursue career in field, self-motivation, strong interpersonal skills. Duration is 3–4 months. Position available as unpaid or paid. Open to college seniors, recent college graduates.
Benefits Formal training, free housing, free meals, on-the-job training, possible full-time employment, willing to act as a profes-

sional reference, willing to complete paperwork for educational credit, willing to provide letters of recommendation.
Contact E-mail Douglas Porter, Food and Beverage Director. Fax: 340-693-2616. E-mail: dougporter506@yahoo.com. No phone calls. Telephone interview required. Applicants must submit a letter of interest, resume, 1-2 letters of recommendation. Applications are accepted continuously. World Wide Web: http://www.bolongobay.com.

BONAVENTURE HOTEL & SUITES
404 South Figueroa Street
Los Angeles, California 90071

General Information Hotel. Established in 1961. Number of employees: 750. Unit of Interstate Hotel Corporation, Pittsburgh, Pennsylvania. Number of internship applications received each year: 75.
Internships Available ▶ *Accounting interns:* responsibilities include assisting the department with general office work, compiling and researching information, and attending department meetings. Candidates should have ability to work with others, computer skills, knowledge of field, office skills, oral communication skills, organizational skills, personal interest in the field, self-motivation. Duration is year-round (at least 12 hours per week). Unpaid. Open to college freshmen, college sophomores, college juniors, college seniors, recent college graduates, graduate students, individuals re-entering work force and career changers only if enrolled in college program. ▶ *Food and beverage interns:* responsibilities include assisting outlet managers with organizing and implementing marketing concepts, developing new marketing and promotional strategies, and researching and tracking; sales promotion and follow-up to generate new business. Candidates should have office skills, oral communication skills, organizational skills, research skills, written communication skills, marketing skills and some knowledge of food and beverage (required), major in hotel restaurant management, business, or communications (preferred). Duration is year-round (at least 12 hours per week). Unpaid. Open to college freshmen, college sophomores, college juniors, college seniors, recent college graduates, graduate students, individuals re-entering the workforce and career changers only if enrolled in a college program. ▶ *Housekeeping interns:* responsibilities include communicating with customers, inspecting assigned guest rooms, reporting safety hazards, helping supervise staff, helping implement emergency training procedures, and special projects as needed. Candidates should have oral communication skills. Duration is year-round (at least 12 hours per week). Unpaid. Open to college freshmen, college sophomores, college juniors, college seniors, graduate students, individuals re-entering work force and career changers only if enrolled in college program. ▶ *Human resources interns:* responsibilities include helping plan and coordinate hotel-sponsored events, creating and implementing incentive programs for associates, screening applicants and checking references for recruitment, managing associate accounts, and coordinating associate benefits including discounts or worker's compensation. Candidates should have computer skills, office skills, oral communication skills, organizational skills, strong interpersonal skills, written communication skills, major in hotel management, business, or communications (preferred). Duration is year-round (at least 12 hours per week). Unpaid. Open to recent high school graduates, college freshmen, college sophomores, college juniors, college seniors, recent college graduates, graduate students, individuals re-entering the workforce and career changers only if enrolled in a college program. International applications accepted.
Benefits Formal training, free meals, on-the-job training, opportunity to attend seminars/workshops, possible full-time employment, travel reimbursement, willing to act as a professional reference, willing to complete paperwork for educational credit, one complimentary meal on days worked, complimentary parking pass.
International Internships Available.
Contact Write, call, fax, or e-mail Putri Sarnadi, Human Resources Manager, 404 South Figueroa Street, Los Angeles, California 90071. Phone: 213-612-4843. Fax: 213-612-4849. E-mail: putri.sarnadi@westin.com. Telephone interview required. Applicants must submit a letter of interest, resume, personal reference. Applications are accepted continuously.

CROWNE PLAZA RESORT
130 Shipyard Drive
Hilton Head Island, South Carolina 29928

General Information Resort hotel. Established in 1993. Number of employees: 300. Division of Six Continents Hotels & Resorts, Atlanta, Georgia. Number of internship applications received each year: 150.

Internships Available ▶ *10–12 rooms division/F&B/leisure activities/culinary interns:* responsibilities include hands-on operation training in resort hotel. Candidates should have ability to work independently, computer skills, declared college major in field, knowledge of field, oral communication skills, plan to pursue career in field, self-motivation, strong interpersonal skills, strong leadership ability, written communication skills. Duration is flexible. $7.25–$7.50 per hour. Open to college sophomores, college juniors, college seniors, recent college graduates. International applications accepted.

Benefits Formal training, housing at a cost, job counseling, meals at a cost, on-the-job training, opportunity to attend seminars/workshops, possible full-time employment.

Contact Write, fax, e-mail, or through World Wide Web site Tracy Sauer, Internship and Employment Coordinator. Phone: 843-842-2400. Fax: 843-785-4879. E-mail: tracy.sauer@6c.com. In-person interview recommended (telephone interview accepted). Applicants must submit a formal organization application, resume, two personal references. Applications are accepted continuously. World Wide Web: http://www.crowneplazaresort.com.

RADISSON SUITE BEACH RESORT
600 South Collier Boulevard
Marco Island, Florida 34145

General Information Hotel resort. Number of employees: 185. Affiliate of Interstate Hotels & Resorts, Washington, District of Columbia. Number of internship applications received each year: 350.

Internships Available ▶ *Food and beverage division interns:* responsibilities include learning all food and beverage positions including those of bartender, host, cashier and banquet server. Candidates should have ability to work with others, computer skills, oral communication skills, organizational skills, written communication skills. Duration is 12–18 months. $7 per hour. Open to recent high school graduates, college sophomores, college juniors, college seniors, recent college graduates, individuals reentering the workforce. ▶ *Rooms division interns:* responsibilities include front desk duties, including checking guests in and out; learning computer system; housekeeping duties, including supervising room attendants, working the desk in housekeeping, inspecting rooms. Candidates should have ability to work with others, computer skills, oral communication skills, organizational skills, self-motivation, written communication skills. Duration is 12–18 months. $7 per hour. Open to college freshmen, college sophomores, college juniors, college seniors, individuals reentering the workforce. International applications accepted.

Benefits Formal training, free meals, housing at a cost, on-the-job training, opportunity to attend seminars/workshops, willing to provide letters of recommendation.

Contact Write, fax, or e-mail June Drew, Human Resources Manager. Fax: 941-394-4312. E-mail: june.drew@ihrco.com. No phone calls. Telephone interview required. Applicants must submit a letter of interest, resume. Applications are accepted continuously.

SNOW MOUNTAIN RANCH
PO Box 169
Winter Park, Colorado 80482

General Information YMCA conference center and family resort. Established in 1907. Number of employees: 250. Branch of YMCA of the Rockies, Estes Park, Colorado. Number of internship applications received each year: 15.

Internships Available ▶ *2–10 adventure education instructors:* responsibilities include facilitating adventure/outdoor based programs, including low/high elements challenge course, environmental education, climbing wall, day hike interpretations, snowshoeing, and cross-country skiing. Candidates should have ability to work with others, knowledge of field, oral communication skills, organizational skills, plan to pursue career in field, self-motivation, strong leadership ability, current first aid and adult/child CPR certification required. Duration is 1–3 semesters. Position available as unpaid or at $155 per week. Open to college sophomores, college juniors, college seniors, recent college graduates, graduate students, individuals reentering the workforce. ▶ *1 chaplain's assistant:* responsibilities include supporting the office of the chaplain in providing leadership in the development of the religious and spiritual life and activities at Snow Mountain Ranch for guests and staff. Candidates should have ability to work independently, ability to work with others, computer skills, declared college major in field, knowledge of field, office skills, oral communication skills, organizational skills, personal interest in the field, self-motivation, strong leadership ability, writing skills, driver's license, previous experience leading and participating in church activities, musical background (preferred). Duration is 1–2 semesters. Position available as unpaid or at $155 per week. Open to college seniors, recent college graduates, graduate students. ▶ *1 craft shop supervisor:* responsibilities include providing supervision and guidance to staff and guests and teaching crafts to the guests and staff who visit the craft shop; will include training of new employees. Candidates should have ability to work independently, ability to work with others, experience in the field, oral communication skills, organizational skills, personal interest in the field, self-motivation, strong leadership ability. Duration is May to August/September. Position available as unpaid or at $170 per week. Open to college juniors, college seniors, recent college graduates, graduate students, career changers, individuals reentering the workforce. ▶ *2 family programs assistants:* responsibilities include developing, marketing, and implementing family programs for the guests of Snow Mountain Ranch. Candidates should have ability to work independently, ability to work with others, college courses in field, experience in the field, oral communication skills, organizational skills, plan to pursue career in field, self-motivation, strong leadership ability, written communication skills, guitar skills (helpful), first aid and CPR certification (required). Duration is summer (May to August). Position available as unpaid or at $155 per week. Open to college juniors, college seniors, recent college graduates. ▶ *1–5 food and beverage interns:* responsibilities include working on various assignments. Candidates should have ability to work independently, experience in the field, organizational skills, personal interest in the field, self-motivation, strong interpersonal skills, strong leadership ability. Duration is 1–3 semesters. Position available as unpaid or at $155 per week. Open to college sophomores, college juniors, college seniors, recent college graduates. ▶ *11 front-desk attendants:* responsibilities include ensuring the satisfaction of all potential and actual guests over the telephone and in person, accounting for all income during assigned shift, checking guests in and out, and operating computer and switchboard. Candidates should have college courses in field, computer skills, office skills, oral communication skills, organizational skills, plan to pursue career in field, strong interpersonal skills, strong leadership ability, fundamental math skills. Duration is 1–2 semesters. Position available as unpaid or at $155 per week. Open to college sophomores, college juniors, college seniors, recent college graduates, graduate students, career changers, individuals reentering the workforce. ▶ *1 human resources associate:* responsibilities include assisting with the daily operations of the human resources office by completing secretarial, receptionist, and driving duties. Candidates should have ability to work independently, computer skills, knowledge of field, office skills, oral communication skills, organizational skills, plan to pursue career in field, self-motivation, strong interpersonal skills, strong leadership ability, written communication skills, driver's license and acceptable driving record. Duration is 1 semester. Position available as unpaid or at $155 per week. Open to college juniors, college seniors, recent college graduates, graduate students. ▶ *1 recreation supervisor:* responsibilities include training, scheduling, and general supervision of recreation staff and facilities. Candidates should have ability to work independently, knowledge of field, oral communication skills, organizational skills, personal interest in the field, self-motivation, strong interpersonal skills, strong leadership ability, writing skills, current certifications in Lifeguard Training, First Aid, and CPR, minimum 3 years

Snow Mountain Ranch (continued)

lifeguarding and pool supervisory experience (preferred). Duration is 1–3 semesters. Position available as unpaid or at $170–$180 per week. Open to college sophomores, college juniors, college seniors, recent college graduates, graduate students. ▶ *1 staff activities coordinator:* responsibilities include developing, implementing, and evaluating activities for co-workers on their time off. Candidates should have ability to work independently, ability to work with others, knowledge of field, oral communication skills, organizational skills, personal interest in the field, self-motivation, strong leadership ability, written communication skills, driver's license and acceptable driving record. Duration is 1–2 semesters. Position available as unpaid or at $155 per week. Open to college juniors, college seniors, recent college graduates, graduate students, law students.

Benefits Formal training, free housing, free meals, job counseling, on-the-job training, opportunity to attend seminars/workshops, possible full-time employment, willing to act as a professional reference, willing to complete paperwork for educational credit, willing to provide letters of recommendation, free use of recreation facilities on-site and downhill ski benefits at nearby Winter Park Resort.

Contact Write, call, fax, e-mail, or through World Wide Web site Jeni Fuqua, Human Resources Director. Phone: 877-562-7962. Fax: 303-449-6781. E-mail: hrofficesmr@ymcarockies.org. Telephone interview required. Applicants must submit a formal organization application, letter of interest, resume, 3 reference forms (form provided by YMCA). Applications are accepted continuously. World Wide Web: http://www.ymcarockies.org.

SOUTH SEAS RESORT
PO Box 194
Captiva Island, Florida 33924

General Information Full-service destination resort property. Established in 1970. Number of employees: 750. Division of Interstate Hotels and Resorts, Washington, District of Columbia. Number of internship applications received each year: 300.

Internships Available ▶ *5–15 culinary interns:* responsibilities include working with chefs in three restaurants. Candidates should have ability to work independently, ability to work with others, experience in the field, oral communication skills, organizational skills, self-motivation. Duration is 6–18 months. $9 per hour. Open to recent high school graduates, college freshmen, college sophomores, college juniors, college seniors, recent college graduates, graduate students, law students, career changers, individuals reentering the workforce. ▶ *1 fitness intern:* responsibilities include assisting guests in proper use of equipment; coordinating and implementing fitness programs; registering and assisting guests at check-in; general customer service and fitness center support. Candidates should have college courses in field, oral communication skills, plan to pursue career in field, strong interpersonal skills, written communication skills, CPR certification, additional fitness certification (helpful). Duration is 7–15 weeks. $50 per week stipend. Open to college sophomores, college juniors, college seniors. ▶ *5–8 front desk/lodging interns.* Candidates should have ability to work independently, analytical skills, computer skills, editing skills, experience in the field, oral communication skills, organizational skills, research skills, self-motivation, strong interpersonal skills, writing skills. Duration is 12–18 months. $10 per hour plus commissions. Open to recent high school graduates, college freshmen, college sophomores, college juniors, college seniors, recent college graduates, graduate students, law students, career changers, individuals reentering the workforce. ▶ *15–20 housekeeping interns:* responsibilities include servicing and cleaning resort units. Candidates should have ability to work independently, ability to work with others, knowledge of field, oral communication skills, organizational skills, self-motivation. Duration is 9–18 months. $7 per hour. Open to recent high school graduates, college freshmen, college sophomores, college juniors, college seniors, recent college graduates, graduate students, law

students, career changers, individuals reentering the workforce. ▶ *5–10 landscaping interns:* responsibilities include manicuring and taking care of greenhouse, nursery stock, trees, and shrubs; maintaining interiorscapes; cleaning streets and grounds. Candidates should have ability to work independently, experience in the field, oral communication skills, personal interest in the field, self-motivation, strong interpersonal skills. Duration is 9–18 months. $7–$9 per hour. Open to recent high school graduates, college freshmen, college sophomores, college juniors, college seniors, recent college graduates, graduate students, career changers, individuals reentering the workforce. ▶ *1–6 recreation interns:* responsibilities include assisting in the planning and implementation of daily activities and special events, general office support, and completion of a major project. Candidates should have ability to work with others, college courses in field, personal interest in the field, self-motivation, strong leadership ability. Duration is 4 months or 1 semester. $750 per semester. Open to college juniors, college seniors, recent college graduates, graduate students. ▶ *20–50 server interns:* responsibilities include carrying trays and waiting on guests. Candidates should have ability to work independently, oral communication skills, organizational skills, self-motivation, strong interpersonal skills, strong leadership ability. Duration is 6–18 months. $7.75 per hour. Open to recent high school graduates, college freshmen, college sophomores, college juniors, college seniors, recent college graduates, graduate students, law students, career changers, individuals reentering the workforce. International applications accepted.

Benefits Health insurance, job counseling, names of contacts, on-the-job training, opportunity to attend seminars/workshops, possible full-time employment, willing to complete paperwork for educational credit, attendance at AHMA management classes, guest service and alcohol certification training, housing provided at $75–$150 biweekly, meals provided at a small cost.

Contact Write, call, fax, or e-mail Angie Cline, Recruiting Coordinator. Phone: 239-472-7588. Fax: 239-472-7548. E-mail: angie.cline@ihrco.com. In-person interview recommended (telephone interview accepted). Applicants must submit a formal organization application, letter of interest, resume. Applications are accepted continuously. World Wide Web: http://www.south-seas-resort.com.

STARWOOD HOTELS & RESORTS
1111 Westchester Avenue, 4th Floor
White Plains, New York 10604

General Information Largest hotel company in the world with more than 725 hotels in 80 countries. Established in 1997. Number of employees: 500. Subsidiary of Starwood Hotels & Resorts Worldwide, Inc., White Plains, New York.

Internships Available ▶ *1 public relations intern:* responsibilities include writing news releases, fact sheets, and executive biographies; handling media requests for information; organizing special events and programs; minor administrative duties. Candidates should have ability to work independently, ability to work with others, computer skills, editing skills, office skills, oral communication skills, organizational skills, plan to pursue career in field, self-motivation, writing skills, college courses in communications or public affairs (preferred). Duration is 1 semester. Position available as unpaid or at $5.50–$6.50 per hour. Open to college freshmen, college sophomores, college juniors, college seniors, recent college graduates. International applications accepted.

Benefits Possible full-time employment, willing to complete paperwork for educational credit, willing to provide letters of recommendation.

Contact Write or fax Mark Ricci, Public Relations Manager. Fax: 914-640-8458. No phone calls. In-person interview recommended (telephone interview accepted). Applicants must submit a resume, three writing samples, three personal references, cover letter. Application deadline: June 15. World Wide Web: http://www.starwood.com.

ADMINISTRATIVE AND SUPPORT SERVICES

EMPLOYMENT SERVICES

ASSOCIATION FOR INTERNATIONAL PRACTICAL TRAINING (AIPT), CAREER DEVELOPMENT PROGRAMS/IAESTE UNITED STATES
10400 Little Patuxent Parkway, Suite 250
Columbia, Maryland 21044-3519

General Information Organization that sponsors internships and arranges on-the-job training exchanges for students and young professionals in a variety of fields in more than 70 countries. Established in 1950. Number of employees: 50. Number of internship applications received each year: 4,000.
Internships Available ▶ *50–150 Career Development/IAESTE United States interns:* responsibilities include training in a field of choice ranging from technical fields to hospitality/tourism. Candidates should have ability to work independently, college courses in field, experience in the field, self-motivation, international interest. Duration is 1–18 months. Paid. Open to college freshmen, college sophomores, college juniors, college seniors, graduate students, law students. International applications accepted.
Benefits Formal training, health insurance, housing at a cost, meals at a cost, on-the-job training, opportunity to attend seminars/workshops, willing to complete paperwork for educational credit.
International Internships Available.
Contact Write, call, fax, e-mail, or through World Wide Web site Katie McDonough, Customer Service Representative. Phone: 410-997-2200. Fax: 410-992-3924. E-mail: aipt@aipt.org. Telephone interview required. Applicants must submit a formal organization application, letter of interest, resume, academic transcripts, portfolio, personal reference, essay. Application deadline: January 1. Fees: $25. World Wide Web: http://www.aipt.org.

COLLEGE WORKS PAINTING
1505 East 17th Street, Suite 210
Santa Ana, California 92705

General Information Organization providing training and financial support to organize and operate an independent house-painting business. Established in 1997. Number of employees: 4,000. Division of National Services Group, Santa Ana, California. Number of internship applications received each year: 8,000.
Internships Available ▶ *1,000 branch managers:* responsibilities include recruiting and training a 6-9 person team; marketing, pricing, and selling services; production, quality and cost control; collections; and promoting ethical business practices; positions available across U.S. Candidates should have ability to work independently, ability to work with others, analytical skills, oral communication skills, organizational skills, self-motivation, strong leadership ability. Duration is February-September (part-time in spring, full-time in summer). Average pay of $9200 per internship. Open to college freshmen, college sophomores, college juniors, college seniors, recent college graduates.
Benefits Formal training, job counseling, names of contacts, on-the-job training, opportunity to attend seminars/workshops, possible full-time employment, tuition assistance, willing to complete paperwork for educational credit, willing to provide let-

ters of recommendation, scholarships, trips to Cancun, special training workshops for top producers, multiple business contacts.
Contact Write, call, fax, e-mail, or through World Wide Web site Matthew Stewart, Vice President, 1505 East 17th Street, Suite 210, Santa Ana, California 92705. Phone: 714-564-7900. Fax: 714-564-8725. E-mail: nathan@collegeworks.com. Telephone interview required. Applicants must submit a formal organization application, resume, 3 in-person interviews. Application deadline: April 1. World Wide Web: http://www.nationalservicesgroup.com.

HANDS ON ATLANTA
1605 Peachtree Street, Suite 100
Atlanta, Georgia 30309

General Information Nonprofit, volunteer organization that organizes more than 250 flexible volunteer opportunities per month and matches 20,000 volunteer members to these opportunities. Established in 1989. Number of employees: 50. Affiliate of City Cares of America, New York, New York. Number of internship applications received each year: 50.
Internships Available ▶ *1–2 Martin Luther King Jr. service summit interns:* responsibilities include recruiting youth groups and AmeriCorps members from the Southeast to attend the service summit. Candidates should have ability to work independently, analytical skills, computer skills, oral communication skills, organizational skills, research skills, self-motivation, strong interpersonal skills, writing skills. Duration is 10 weeks. Unpaid. Open to college freshmen, college sophomores, college juniors, college seniors, recent college graduates, graduate students, law students, career changers, individuals reentering the workforce. ▶ *Service Entrepreneur Awards interns (SEA):* responsibilities include researching leadership training programs in the region as well as outstanding national models and developing an 8-month course curriculum and workbook for SEA winners. Candidates should have ability to work independently, analytical skills, computer skills, editing skills, oral communication skills, organizational skills, research skills, self-motivation, strong interpersonal skills, strong leadership ability, writing skills. Duration is 10 weeks. Unpaid. Open to college freshmen, college sophomores, college juniors, college seniors, recent college graduates, graduate students, law students, career changers, individuals reentering the workforce. ▶ *2–4 development interns:* responsibilities include assisting with grant writing, individual and corporate giving, and special events related to fund-raising. Candidates should have ability to work independently, ability to work with others, analytical skills, computer skills, editing skills, oral communication skills, organizational skills, personal interest in the field, research skills, self-motivation, writing skills. Duration is 10 weeks. Unpaid. Open to college freshmen, college sophomores, college juniors, college seniors, recent college graduates, graduate students, law students, career changers, individuals reentering the workforce. ▶ *Disability initiative interns:* responsibilities include helping make projects more accessible to Atlanta's disabled community, managing accessibility inspection visits to project sites, creating plans for improvement of project accessibility, and helping recruit teams of volunteers from the disabilities community. Candidates should have ability to work independently, computer skills, editing skills, oral communication skills, organizational skills, self-motivation, strong interpersonal skills, writing skills. Duration is 10 weeks. Unpaid.

Hands On Atlanta (continued)

Open to college freshmen, college sophomores, college juniors, college seniors, recent college graduates, graduate students, law students, career changers, individuals reentering the workforce. ▶ *1–2 issues in action interns:* responsibilities include recruiting participants; setting workshop dates, locations, and project dates at community organizations. Candidates should have ability to work independently, analytical skills, computer skills, editing skills, oral communication skills, organizational skills, self-motivation, strong interpersonal skills, writing skills. Duration is 10 weeks. Unpaid. Open to college freshmen, college sophomores, college juniors, college seniors, recent college graduates, graduate students, law students, career changers, individuals reentering the workforce. ▶ *7–12 program management interns:* responsibilities include working directly with volunteers to meet critical community needs; interns can choose among program areas including education, homelessness, or housing. Candidates should have ability to work independently, computer skills, editing skills, oral communication skills, organizational skills, personal interest in the field, self-motivation, strong interpersonal skills, writing skills. Duration is 10 weeks. Unpaid. Open to college freshmen, college sophomores, college juniors, college seniors, recent college graduates, graduate students, law students, career changers, individuals reentering the workforce. ▶ *1–2 reading and recruitment interns:* responsibilities include assisting the recruitment and marketing coordinator in preparing presentations, responding to inquiries, updating the Web site, and training. Candidates should have ability to work independently, computer skills, editing skills, oral communication skills, organizational skills, research skills, self-motivation, strong interpersonal skills, writing skills. Duration is 10 weeks. Unpaid. Open to college freshmen, college sophomores, college juniors, college seniors, recent college graduates, graduate students, law students, career changers, individuals reentering the workforce. ▶ *2–3 schools programs discovery interns:* responsibilities include assisting the discovery program manager with administrative tasks related to recruitment and tracking of volunteers, creating a newsletter and lesson plans, and assisting with school site visits. Candidates should have ability to work independently, computer skills, editing skills, oral communication skills, organizational skills, self-motivation, strong interpersonal skills, writing skills. Duration is 10 weeks. Unpaid. ▶ *Schools programs interns:* responsibilities include assisting the schools department with various activities from assisting AmeriCorps members in service project development to beginning Hands On Atlanta Day preparations. Candidates should have ability to work independently, analytical skills, computer skills, editing skills, office skills, oral communication skills, organizational skills, research skills, self-motivation, strong interpersonal skills, strong leadership ability, writing skills. Duration is 10 weeks. Unpaid. Open to college freshmen, college sophomores, college juniors, college seniors, recent college graduates, graduate students, law students, career changers, individuals reentering the workforce. ▶ *2 special events interns:* responsibilities include assisting in planning and implementing special events including event logistics, public relations, and advertising. Candidates should have computer skills, editing skills, oral communication skills, organizational skills, personal interest in the field, self-motivation, strong interpersonal skills, writing skills. Duration is 10 weeks. Unpaid. Open to college freshmen, college sophomores, college juniors, college seniors, recent college graduates, graduate students, law students, career changers, individuals reentering the workforce. ▶ *1 youth service program intern:* responsibilities include coordinating plan for a mass mailing of YSP information to metro area youth serving agencies and schools, and assisting youth service team on day of event in recruiting at the celebration of service for ongoing participation. Candidates should have ability to work independently, analytical skills, computer skills, editing skills, office skills, oral communication skills, organizational skills, research skills, self-motivation, strong interpersonal skills, strong leadership ability, writing skills. Duration is 10 weeks. Unpaid. Open to college freshmen, college sophomores, college juniors, college seniors, recent college graduates, graduate students, law students, career changers, individuals reentering the workforce. International applications accepted.

Benefits Formal training, on-the-job training, opportunity to attend seminars/workshops, possible full-time employment, willing to act as a professional reference, willing to complete paperwork for educational credit, willing to provide letters of recommendation.

Contact Write, call, fax, e-mail, or through World Wide Web site Tamala Fortson, Associate Director of Human Resources. Phone: 404-879-2753. Fax: 404-872-2251. E-mail: tfortson@handsonatlanta. com. In-person interview required. Applicants must submit a letter of interest, resume, two writing samples, two personal references. Applications are accepted continuously. World Wide Web: http://www.handsonatlanta.com.

JEWISH VOCATIONAL SERVICE
111 Prospect Street
East Orange, New Jersey 07017

General Information Service providing career/vocational counseling and job placement assistance, including college selection, to men and women in career transition, those returning to the workforce, or recent college graduates. Established in 1939. Number of employees: 100. Affiliate of Association of Jewish Vocational Service Professionals, Philadelphia, Pennsylvania. Number of internship applications received each year: 10.

Internships Available ▶ *Career/education counseling, rehabilitation, and emerge interns:* responsibilities include assisting with assessment, group counseling sessions, support groups, and interviews; helping keep library up to date; attending staff meetings and workshops; and dealing with placement and unemployed clients at all levels including rehabilitation, emigre, and middle income clientele. Candidates should have ability to work independently, analytical skills, college courses in field, computer skills, oral communication skills, organizational skills, personal interest in the field, research skills, self-motivation, strong interpersonal skills, written communication skills. Duration is 3–12 months. Unpaid. Open to recent college graduates, graduate students, career changes with master's degree or experience in career or job development. International applications accepted.

Benefits Formal training, job counseling, names of contacts, on-the-job training, opportunity to attend seminars/workshops, possible full-time employment, willing to complete paperwork for educational credit, willing to provide letters of recommendation.

Contact Write, fax, or e-mail Ms. Linda Zamer, Director of Career Counseling and Placement Services. Fax: 973-674-7773. E-mail: lzamer@jvsnj.org. No phone calls. In-person interview required. Applicants must submit a letter of interest, resume, two personal references. Applications are accepted continuously. World Wide Web: http://www.jvsnj.org.

JEWISH VOCATIONAL SERVICE/ KOHN SUMMER INTERN PROGRAM
77 Geary Street, Suite 401
San Francisco, California 94108

General Information Vocational, career, and employment specialists. Established in 1985. Number of employees: 65. Number of internship applications received each year: 100.

Internships Available ▶ *30 Kohn summer interns:* responsibilities include political advocacy, social service, journalism, Web site development, event coordination, curriculum development, marketing, or public relations. Candidates should have oral communication skills, strong interpersonal skills, strong leadership ability, written communication skills, demonstrated interest in Jewish community work. Duration is June 16 to August 8. $2000 per duration of internship. Open to college freshmen, college sophomores, college juniors, college seniors.

Benefits Job counseling, on-the-job training, opportunity to attend seminars/workshops, willing to act as a professional reference, willing to complete paperwork for educational credit, willing to provide letters of recommendation.

Contact Write, call, fax, e-mail, or through World Wide Web site Rebecca Bassin, Jewish Community Services Manager. Phone: 415-782-6223. Fax: 415-391-3617. E-mail: rbassin@jvs.org. In-person interview recommended (telephone interview accepted). Applicants must submit a formal organization application, two letters of recommendation. Application deadline: April 1 for summer. World Wide Web: http://www.jvs.org.

NATIONAL CONSORTIUM FOR GRADUATE DEGREES FOR MINORITIES IN ENGINEERING AND SCIENCE, INC.
PO Box 537
Notre Dame, Indiana 46556

General Information Organization that matches students who are interested in graduate degrees in engineering and science with employer sponsors; over 75 companies and over 80 universities participate. Established in 1976. Number of employees: 9. Number of internship applications received each year: 645.
Internships Available ▶ *40 PhD fellowships in engineering and science (20 each):* responsibilities include working on engineering and science projects. Duration is 1-3 summers. $14,000 living stipend per year towards graduate school tuition and fees. Open to students obtaining PhD in either engineering or science. ▶ *200 master's fellowships in engineering:* responsibilities include working on engineering projects. Candidates should have enrollment in engineering degree program (undergraduates must intend to pursue masters' degree in engineering). Duration is 1-3 summers. $10,000 living stipend per year towards graduate school tuition and fees. Open to college juniors, college seniors, graduate students.
Benefits Housing at a cost, on-the-job training, travel reimbursement.
Contact Write, call, fax, e-mail, or through World Wide Web site Valerie Washington, Coordinator of Information Services. Phone: 574-631-7771. Fax: 574-287-1486. E-mail: gem.l@nd.edu. Applicants must submit a formal organization application, resume, academic transcripts, two letters of recommendation. Application deadline: December 1. World Wide Web: http://www.gemfellowship.org.

UNITED STATES ARMY RECRUITING COMMAND
1307 Third Avenue
Fort Knox, Kentucky 40121-2726

General Information Unit that conducts recruiting of healthcare professionals for the Army Medical Department. Number of employees: 30. Unit of United States Department of the Army, Washington, District of Columbia. Number of internship applications received each year: 65.
Internships Available ▶ *60 advanced general dentistry interns.* Candidates should have ability to work with others, oral communication skills, research skills, strong leadership ability, written communication skills. Duration is October 1 to September 30. $3400 per month. Open to senior dental students, dental school graduates within 3 years after graduation. ▶ *5–10 clinical psychology interns.* Candidates should have analytical skills, college degree in related field, oral communication skills, strong interpersonal skills, strong leadership ability, written communication skills. Duration is 1 year. $35,000–$40,000 per year. Open to graduate students. ▶ *10 dietetics interns.* Candidates should have computer skills, oral communication skills, strong interpersonal skills, strong leadership ability, written communication skills. Duration is September to May. $2400 per month. Open to college seniors, recent college graduates, graduate students. ▶ *6 occupational therapy interns.* Candidates should have computer skills, oral communication skills, strong interpersonal skills, strong leadership ability, written communication skills. Duration is 7 months. $2400 per month. Open to college seniors, recent college graduates, graduate students.
Benefits Formal training, health insurance, meals at a cost, opportunity to attend seminars/workshops, possible full-time employment, travel reimbursement, tuition assistance, willing to complete paperwork for educational credit, on-post housing or housing allowance, subsistence allowance.
Contact Write, call, fax, e-mail, or through World Wide Web site Maj. Tanya Beecher, RA Operations Officer, 1307 Third Avenue, Fort Knox, Kentucky 40121. Phone: 502-626-0367. Fax: 502-626-0923. E-mail: tanya.beecher@usarec.army.mil. In-person interview required. Applicants must submit a formal organization application, letter of interest, resume, academic transcripts, three letters

of recommendation, other materials as specified by specific position; physical exam required (paid for by employer). Applications are accepted continuously. World Wide Web: http://www.healthcare.goarmy.army.com.

Y.E.S. TO JOBS
PO Box 3390
Los Angeles, California 90078

General Information Program designed to introduce minority high school students to career opportunities behind the scenes in the entertainment industry. Established in 1987. Number of employees: 3. Number of internship applications received each year: 800.
Internships Available ▶ *150–250 interns:* responsibilities include various duties as entry-level assistants working in the entertainment industry. Candidates should have computer skills, oral communication skills, personal interest in the field, self-motivation, strong interpersonal skills, written communication skills. Duration is 10 weeks. Paid. Open to high school students, individuals 16-18 years old.
Benefits Formal training, job counseling, names of contacts, on-the-job training, opportunity to attend seminars/workshops, willing to complete paperwork for educational credit, willing to provide letters of recommendation.
Contact Write, e-mail, or through World Wide Web site Marsha Cole, Program Coordinator. E-mail: yestojobs@aol.com. No phone calls. In-person interview recommended (telephone interview accepted). Applicants must submit a formal organization application, letter of interest, resume, academic transcripts, letter of recommendation. Application deadline: March 31 for summer. World Wide Web: http://www.yestojobs.org.

YMCA ALLIANCE
11 East Adams Street, Suite 300
Chicago, Illinois 60603

General Information Nonprofit organization that helps individuals achieve economic and career advancement by providing opportunities to enhance skills and self-esteem through job training and placement, literacy education, and referral services; also works with coalitions on issues relating to economic advancement and community development. Established in 1976. Number of employees: 35. Unit of YMCA of Metropolitan Chicago, Chicago, Illinois. Number of internship applications received each year: 8.
Internships Available ▶ *2 IT support interns:* responsibilities include assisting staff with desktop problems, providing technical support to instructors with new applications, developing program to provide legacy equipment for trainee graduates. Candidates should have ability to work independently, ability to work with others, experience in the field, office skills, oral communication skills, organizational skills, personal interest in the field, knowledge of common office applications and network software. Duration is flexible (minimum 8 weeks). Unpaid. Open to college juniors, college seniors, recent college graduates, technical school seniors. ▶ *1–2 employment interns:* responsibilities include assisting individuals in making career decisions and overcoming barriers to employment. Candidates should have computer skills, oral communication skills, organizational skills, self-motivation, strong interpersonal skills, strong leadership ability, written communication skills. Duration is flexible. Unpaid. Open to college sophomores, college juniors, college seniors, recent college graduates, graduate students, career changers. ▶ *1 fund-raising administration intern:* responsibilities include assisting in researching/writing grant proposals. Candidates should have ability to work independently, computer skills, editing skills, research skills, self-motivation, writing skills. Duration is flexible. Unpaid. Open to college juniors, college seniors, recent college graduates, graduate students, career changers. ▶ *1 literacy volunteer coordinator:* responsibilities include assisting with recruitment, referral to training and placement, and scheduling of students with literacy volunteers. Candidates should have ability to work with others, office skills, oral communication skills, organizational skills, self-motivation, written communication skills. Duration is flexible. Unpaid. Open to college seniors, recent college graduates, graduate students, career changers. ▶ *1*

YMCA Alliance (continued)

marketing associate: responsibilities include assisting in market research and development of marketing strategies and materials for the Alliance and its programs. Candidates should have editing skills, oral communication skills, plan to pursue career in field, research skills, self-motivation, written communication skills. Duration is flexible. Unpaid. Open to college seniors, recent college graduates, graduate students. ▶ *1 research and development intern:* responsibilities include gathering data and participating in preparing reports to study the effects of training and pre-employment activities on the economic self-sufficiency of low-income individuals. Candidates should have ability to work independently, ability to work with others, analytical skills, computer skills, editing skills, organizational skills, research skills, writing skills. Duration is flexible. Unpaid. Open to college juniors, college seniors, recent college graduates, graduate students, law students, career changers. ▶ *1 working knowledge intern:* responsibilities include tutoring, help-ing with curriculum development, and publishing a student-written journal. Candidates should have ability to work with others, computer skills, oral communication skills, personal interest in the field, self-motivation, written communication skills. Duration is flexible. Unpaid. Open to college juniors, college seniors, recent college graduates, career changers. International applications accepted.

Benefits Job counseling, on-the-job training, possible full-time employment, travel reimbursement, willing to complete paperwork for educational credit, willing to provide letters of recommendation.

Contact Write, call, fax, or e-mail Mr. Syd Lines, Technology and Volunteer Resources Manager. Phone: 312-913-2150 Ext. 25. Fax: 312-913-2157. E-mail: slines@ymcachgo.org. In-person interview recommended (telephone interview accepted). Applicants must submit a letter of interest, resume, two personal references. Applications are accepted continuously.

ARTS, ENTERTAINMENT, AND RECREATION

GENERAL

ABRAMS ARTIST AGENCY
9200 Sunset Boulevard, 11th Floor
Los Angeles, California 90069

General Information Talent agency. Established in 1986. Number of employees: 43. Number of internship applications received each year: 150.
Internships Available ▶ *Interns:* responsibilities include assisting agents and staff in all aspects of operations in order to learn how a talent agency works; screening calls; pulling submissions; script coverage; contact with all departments: MP/TV, Commercial, Voice Over, Hosting, and Business Affairs. Candidates should have ability to work independently, ability to work with others, oral communication skills, self-motivation, written communication skills. Duration is flexible. Unpaid. Open to high school seniors, recent high school graduates, college freshmen, college sophomores, college juniors, college seniors, recent college graduates, graduate students, law students, career changers, individuals reentering the workforce. International applications accepted.
Benefits Willing to complete paperwork for educational credit.
Contact Write or fax Internship Coordinator, 9200 Sunset Boulevard, Eleventh Floor, Los Angeles 90069. Fax: 310-276-6193. No phone calls. In-person interview required. Applicants must submit a letter of interest, resume. Applications are accepted continuously.

ABRAMS ARTIST AGENCY
275 7th Avenue, 26th Floor
New York, New York 10001

General Information Talent agency. Established in 1977. Number of employees: 39. Number of internship applications received each year: 20.
Internships Available ▶ *5 assistant agents.* Candidates should have ability to work with others, office skills, oral communication skills, organizational skills, personal interest in the field, writing skills. Duration is flexible. Unpaid. Open to college freshmen, college sophomores, college juniors, college seniors, graduate students, law students. International applications accepted.
Benefits Possible full-time employment, willing to complete paperwork for educational credit, willing to provide letters of recommendation, opportunity to attend NY theater, $10 per day travel reimbursement.
Contact Write, fax, or e-mail Mary Guzowski, Agent. Fax: 646-486-0100. E-mail: mary.guzowski@abramsart.com. No phone calls. In-person interview required. Applicants must submit a letter of interest, resume. Applications are accepted continuously.

ALL STARS PROJECT, INC./CASTILLO THEATRE
500 Greenwich Street, #201
New York, New York 10013

General Information Independent multicultural arts center housing off-off-Broadway Castillo Theatre, a laboratory for developmental theater and extensive inner-city youth programs. Established in 1983. Number of employees: 25. Number of internship applications received each year: 75.

Internships Available ▶ *4–6 All Stars Project/nonprofit management interns:* responsibilities include assisting in cultivation, research, volunteer program management, marketing, special events, and fund-raising. Candidates should have ability to work independently, ability to work with others, computer skills, office skills, oral communication skills, personal interest in the field, plan to pursue career in field, self-motivation. Duration is minimum 3 months (preferred); one weeknight or daytime weekend shift per week. Unpaid. Open to college freshmen, college sophomores, college juniors, college seniors, recent college graduates, graduate students, law students, career changers, individuals reentering the workforce. ▶ *2–4 All Stars Project/public relations interns:* responsibilities include working with skilled, public relations director promoting off-off-Broadway theater and nonprofit development programs for inner-city youth; hands-on experience dealing with major media outlets in the largest media market in the U.S. Candidates should have ability to work independently, computer skills, office skills, oral communication skills, personal interest in the field, strong interpersonal skills, English language skills required. Duration is minimum 3 months (preferred) including weekday hours. Unpaid. Open to college freshmen, college sophomores, college juniors, college seniors, recent college graduates, graduate students, career changers, individuals reentering the workforce. ▶ *3–6 theater costume design/construction and wardrobe interns:* responsibilities include working with resident designer at the Castillo Theatre; costume construction, makeup, wardrobe; qualified interns may participate in design; house staff shift part of internship requirement. Candidates should have ability to work independently, ability to work with others, oral communication skills, personal interest in the field, self-motivation. Duration is minimum 3 months; evenings and weekends preferred. Unpaid. Open to college freshmen, college sophomores, college juniors, college seniors, recent college graduates, graduate students, career changers, individuals reentering the workforce. ▶ *3–6 theater lighting design interns:* responsibilities include working with resident designer to produce lighting for Castillo Theatre; electrics; qualified interns may assist in design; weekly house staff shift part of internship requirement. Candidates should have ability to work independently, ability to work with others, knowledge of field, oral communication skills, personal interest in the field, self-motivation. Duration is minimum 3 months (preferred) evenings and weekends only. Unpaid. Open to recent high school graduates, college freshmen, college sophomores, college juniors, college seniors, recent college graduates, graduate students, career changers, individuals reentering the workforce. ▶ *3–6 theater management/theater assistant interns:* responsibilities include working with managing director of growing off-off-Broadway theater; hands-on experience in theatrical and event production, scheduling, budget management, staff development, and audience building. Candidates should have ability to work independently, ability to work with others, computer skills, office skills, organizational skills, personal interest in the field, self-motivation. Duration is minimum 3 months (preferred); flexible am/pm hours. Unpaid. Open to recent high school graduates, college freshmen, college sophomores, college juniors, college seniors, recent college graduates, graduate students, law students, career changers, individuals reentering the workforce. ▶ *4–8 theater production assistants/stage hands:* responsibilities include assisting producers and stage managers at the Castillo Theatre; attendance at rehearsals required. Candidates should have ability

All Stars Project, Inc./Castillo Theatre (continued)

to work independently, ability to work with others, oral communication skills, organizational skills, personal interest in the field. Duration is minimum 3 months (preferred); evenings and some weekends. Unpaid. Open to college freshmen, college sophomores, college juniors, college seniors, recent college graduates, graduate students, career changers, individuals reentering the workforce. ▶ *1–2 theater set construction and scenic painting interns:* responsibilities include working with resident designer to produce sets for Castillo Theatre productions: research, construction, scenic painting; qualified interns may assist in design; weekly house staff shift part of internship requirement. Candidates should have ability to work independently, ability to work with others, knowledge of field, oral communication skills, personal interest in the field, self-motivation, theater experience preferred. Duration is minimum 3 months (preferred); flexible hours including evenings. Unpaid. Open to recent high school graduates, college freshmen, college sophomores, college juniors, college seniors, recent college graduates, career changers, individuals reentering the workforce. ▶ *2–4 theater sound design interns:* responsibilities include working with resident designer at Castillo Theatre; research, sound engineering; weekly house staff shift part of internship requirement. Candidates should have ability to work independently, ability to work with others, oral communication skills, personal interest in the field, self-motivation. Duration is minimum 3 months (preferred); flexible hours evenings and weekends. Unpaid. Open to college freshmen, college sophomores, college juniors, college seniors, recent college graduates, graduate students, career changers, individuals reentering the workforce. ▶ *2–4 volunteer management assistants:* responsibilities include recruitment, placement, job development, recognition, training staff, and special volunteer event organizing. Candidates should have ability to work with others, oral communication skills, personal interest in the field. Duration is minimum 3 months (preferred); flexible hours (evenings possible). Unpaid. Open to recent high school graduates, college freshmen, college sophomores, college juniors, college seniors, recent college graduates, graduate students, career changers. International applications accepted.

Benefits Formal training, names of contacts, on-the-job training, opportunity to attend seminars/workshops, willing to act as a professional reference, willing to complete paperwork for educational credit, willing to provide letters of recommendation, credit available for most positions.

Contact Write, call, fax, e-mail, or through World Wide Web site Gail Elberg, Director, Volunteer and Intern Programs, 500 Greenwich Street, #201, New York, New York 10013. Phone: 212-941-9400. Fax: 212-941-8340. E-mail: gailelberg@aol.com. In-person interview recommended (telephone interview accepted). Applicants must submit a letter of interest, resume. Applications are accepted continuously. World Wide Web: http://www.allstars.org.

AMELIA WELLNESS CENTER
869 Sadler Road, Suite 5
Fernandina Beach, Florida 32034

General Information Health and fitness club. Established in 1987. Number of employees: 25. Subsidiary of Amelia Island Plantation, Amelia Island, Florida. Number of internship applications received each year: 30.

Internships Available ▶ *1–2 interns:* responsibilities include acting as manager-on-duty, group fitness leader, and customer service representative; fitness assessment, exercise prescription, promotion, advertising and selling fitness programs offered by club. Candidates should have computer skills, oral communication skills, organizational skills, plan to pursue career in field, self-motivation, strong interpersonal skills, strong leadership ability, writing skills. Duration is generally 3 to 4 months, but will accommodate to meet semester requirements. $300–$600 per month. Open to college seniors, recent college graduates, graduate students, career changers. International applications accepted.

Benefits Formal training, job counseling, names of contacts, on-the-job training, opportunity to attend seminars/workshops, possible full-time employment, tuition assistance, willing to act as a professional reference, willing to complete paperwork for educational credit, willing to provide letters of recommendation.

Contact Write, call, fax, e-mail, or through World Wide Web site Ms. Krissy Michaels, Intern Coordinator, 869 Sadler Road, Suite 5, Fernandina Beach, Florida 32034. Phone: 904-261-0557. Fax: 904-261-5671. E-mail: awc@net-magic.net. Telephone interview required. Applicants must submit a letter of interest, resume, writing sample, three personal references. Application deadline: April 1 for summer, December 1 for spring. World Wide Web: http://www.ameliawellnesscenter.com.

APERTURE FOUNDATION
20 East 23rd Street
New York, New York 10010-4463

General Information Not-for-profit organization devoted to the promotion of photography as a unique form of expression through publication, exhibition, and educational programs. Established in 1952. Number of employees: 30. Number of internship applications received each year: 500.

Internships Available ▶ *2 Paul Strand archive interns:* responsibilities include maintaining ongoing file of Strand material in print and other related material; organizing, cataloging, and preserving Aperture collection of artwork and photographs; inventorying and organizing book library; exhibition preparation work (Burden Gallery and Traveling Exhibitions); administration of copyright and permissions for use of photographs by Paul Strand; assembly, distribution, and recordkeeping of limited editions and portfolios; darkroom and on-camera copy work. Candidates should have ability to work independently, ability to work with others, office skills, organizational skills, personal interest in the field, research skills. Duration is minimum of 6 months. $250 per month. Open to college seniors, recent college graduates, graduate students. ▶ *2 design interns:* responsibilities include preparing files for color output, creating mechanicals, sizing art, scanning and placing photographs, conceptual design on selected projects, and general office support. Candidates should have ability to work independently, computer skills, experience in the field, office skills, personal interest in the field, strong interpersonal skills. Duration is minimum of 6 months. $250 per month. Open to college seniors, recent college graduates, graduate students. ▶ *2 development interns:* responsibilities include compilation of proposal packets (research, writing, and editing), updating donor listings, assisting with the annual appeal, assisting with board and donor relations, assisting with special events, maintaining the development database, and assisting with the coordination of Work-Scholar Program. Candidates should have oral communication skills, organizational skills, personal interest in the field, research skills, strong interpersonal skills, writing skills. Duration is minimum of 6 months. $250 per month. Open to college seniors, recent college graduates, graduate students. ▶ *2 director's office interns:* responsibilities include acting as liaison between Director's office and other departments; locating and requesting review copies of books, periodicals, and videos; maintaining the library; maintaining a database; and assisting with the preparation of important meetings. Candidates should have ability to work independently, office skills, oral communication skills, organizational skills, strong interpersonal skills, writing skills. Duration is minimum of 6 months. $250 per month. Open to college seniors, recent college graduates, graduate students. ▶ *4 editorial interns:* responsibilities include researching pictures and texts, reviewing manuscripts and portfolios, contacting outside sources to request artwork for reproduction, proofreading, compiling copy for catalogues and book jackets, some darkroom work, some development and publicity support, and registering copyrights. Candidates should have ability to work independently, editing skills, experience in the field, organizational skills, strong interpersonal skills, writing skills. Duration is minimum of 6 months. $250 per month. Open to college seniors, recent college graduates, graduate students. ▶ *2 foreign rights interns:* responsibilities include interfacing with foreign distributors and publishers, assisting with contracts and licensing agreements, arranging coeditions of Aperture books with publishers worldwide, identifying new publishing partners, preparing for the Frankfurt Book Fair, organizing pricing of books for potential foreign copublications. Candidates should have ability to work independently, computer skills, office skills, organizational skills, personal interest in the field, writing skills. Duration is minimum

of 6 months. $250 per month. Open to college seniors, recent college graduates, graduate students. ▶ *2 image resource interns:* responsibilities include gathering information for licensing program, maintaining research library, assisting in creation of photographer lists and mailing information packets, and general support as needed. Candidates should have computer skills, personal interest in the field, research skills, knowledge of contemporary photography, attention to details. Duration is minimum of 6 months. $250 per month. Open to college seniors, recent college graduates, graduate students. ▶ *2 information technology/systems interns:* responsibilities include assisting with client server and variety of other applications; assisting staff with daily computing functions as needed. Candidates should have interest in pursuing degree in information systems/technology, experience with Microsoft systems (preferred). Duration is minimum of 6 months. $250 per month. Open to college seniors, recent college graduates, graduate students. ▶ *2 marketing and circulation interns:* responsibilities include preparing sales materials, updating and mailing media kits, maintaining contact with distributors and sales representatives, creating and placing advertisements, selling ad space, maintaining the database, and producing direct mail. Candidates should have ability to work independently, computer skills, office skills, organizational skills, personal interest in the field, writing skills. Duration is minimum of 6 months. $250 per month. Open to college seniors, recent college graduates, graduate students. ▶ *2 production interns:* responsibilities include acting as liaison with outside companies, checking quotes and mechanicals, writing purchase orders, organizing and packaging original materials for transport, assisting with color corrections and some designing, and organizing information for invoicing, distribution, and billing. Candidates should have knowledge of field, office skills, organizational skills, plan to pursue career in field, strong interpersonal skills. Duration is minimum of 6 months. $250 per month. Open to college seniors, recent college graduates, graduate students. ▶ *2 publicity interns:* responsibilities include maintaining publicity books, assisting in the preparation of materials, creating first draft press releases, circulating reviews to sales representatives, updating files and mailing lists, research, assisting in promotion projects, and permissions. Candidates should have ability to work independently, office skills, organizational skills, personal interest in the field, strong interpersonal skills, writing skills. Duration is minimum of 6 months. $250 per month. Open to college seniors, recent college graduates, graduate students, law students. ▶ *2 traveling exhibition/gallery interns:* responsibilities include maintaining files on correspondence and venues contacted, researching potential venues, keeping the mailing list of potential venues up to date, assisting in the creation of exhibition kits, mailing the kits to potential venues, coordinating exhibitions, maintaining the museum/gallery database, and assisting with Burden Gallery openings and other gallery activities. Candidates should have ability to work independently, oral communication skills, organizational skills, personal interest in the field, research skills, strong interpersonal skills, writing skills. Duration is minimum of 6 months. $250 per month. Open to college seniors, recent college graduates, graduate students. International applications accepted.
Benefits On-the-job training, possible full-time employment, willing to act as a professional reference, willing to complete paperwork for educational credit, willing to provide letters of recommendation, limited edition print upon completion of internship.
Contact Write, call, fax, or e-mail Maria Decsey, Work-Scholar Coordinator. Phone: 212-505-5555 Ext. 336. Fax: 212-475-8790. E-mail: mdecsey@aperture.org. In-person interview recommended (telephone interview accepted). Applicants must submit a letter of interest, resume, two writing samples. Applications are accepted continuously. World Wide Web: http://www.aperture.org.

ARTISTS SPACE
38 Greene Street, 3rd Floor
New York, New York 10013

General Information Nonprofit organization that supports emerging artists in the visual arts, including video, performance,

architecture, and design. Established in 1972. Number of employees: 7. Number of internship applications received each year: 150.
Internships Available ▶ *1 artists file intern:* responsibilities include assisting artist file coordinator through updating database of artists, conducting appointments for the file, troubleshooting with the database, and possible Web site assistance if applicable. Candidates should have computer skills, personal interest in the field, self-motivation, strong interpersonal skills, strong art background and Macintosh skills. Duration is flexible. Unpaid. ▶ *1 curatorial intern:* responsibilities include working closely with curator and artists, reviewing artists' work, and assisting with events and exhibitions. Candidates should have ability to work independently, computer skills, personal interest in the field, self-motivation, strong art background. Duration is flexible. Unpaid. ▶ *Operations interns:* responsibilities include assisting with day-to-day operations of the gallery, working with intern coordinator, participating in special projects, and dealing with past and present exhibitions. Candidates should have ability to work independently, computer skills, organizational skills, personal interest in the field, self-motivation, strong interpersonal skills. Duration is flexible. Unpaid. Open to college freshmen, college sophomores, college juniors, college seniors, recent college graduates, graduate students. International applications accepted.
Benefits Job counseling, on-the-job training, willing to act as a professional reference, willing to complete paperwork for educational credit, willing to provide letters of recommendation, possibility of exhibiting samples of work, access to many NYC galleries and museums.
Contact Write, call, fax, e-mail, or through World Wide Web site Ms. Jennifer Chapek, Coordinator. Phone: 212-226-3970. Fax: 212-966-1434. E-mail: artspace@artissspace.org. In-person interview recommended (telephone interview accepted). Applicants must submit a formal organization application, letter of interest, resume, two personal references. Applications are accepted continuously. World Wide Web: http://www.artissspace.org.

ARTNET.COM
61 Broadway, 23rd Floor
New York, New York 10006-2701

General Information Company specializing in the buying, selling, and researching of fine art online; Online Gallery Network is largest of it's kind with over 1,300 galleries, 36,000 works, and 13,000 artists from around the globe.
Internships Available ▶ *Online Gallery Network interns (production):* responsibilities include involvement in creation and maintenance of individual gallery Web sites and artist information within online network and general administrative duties associated with network. Candidates should have familiarity with Adobe PhotoShop (recommended), attention to detail, dedication to accuracy (required), basic HTML knowledge (helpful, but not required). Unpaid. ▶ *Online Gallery Network sales interns:* responsibilities include coordinating art fairs, updating gallery/artist databases, preparing media kits, and general administrative duties. Candidates should have computer skills, oral communication skills, organizational skills, personal interest in the field, written communication skills, foreign language speaking ability (a plus). Unpaid.
Benefits $10 daily stipend to cover expenses.
Contact E-mail Internship Coordinator. Phone: 212-497-9700. Fax: 212-497-5007. E-mail: cruch@artnet.com. Applicants must submit Word-formatted resume and brief cover letter. Applications are accepted continuously. World Wide Web: http://www.artnet.com.

ASIAN AMERICAN ARTS CENTRE
26 Bowery, 3rd Floor
New York, New York 10013

General Information Multipurpose facility that offers ongoing visual arts exhibitions of contemporary Asian-Americans as well as one folk exhibit a year. Established in 1974. Number of employees: 4. Number of internship applications received each year: 5.
Internships Available ▶ *1 curatorial intern:* responsibilities include working closely with the director, researching and organizing

Asian American Arts Centre (continued)

exhibits. Candidates should have college courses in field, editing skills, knowledge of field, oral communication skills, personal interest in the field, strong interpersonal skills, written communication skills. Duration is 3 months. Unpaid. Open to college freshmen, college sophomores, college juniors, college seniors, recent college graduates, graduate students. ▶ *1 development assistant:* responsibilities include researching funding resources, writing grant proposals, and assisting in preparing grants. Candidates should have editing skills, research skills, strong interpersonal skills, strong leadership ability, writing skills. Duration is 3 months. Unpaid. Open to college freshmen, college sophomores, college juniors, college seniors, recent college graduates, graduate students. ▶ *1 gallery assistant:* responsibilities include various tasks depending on intern's abilities and interests. Candidates should have computer skills, knowledge of field, organizational skills, personal interest in the field, strong interpersonal skills, writing skills. Duration is 3 months. Unpaid. Open to college freshmen, college sophomores, college juniors, college seniors, recent college graduates, graduate students. ▶ *1–2 research assistants:* responsibilities include examining and archiving materials. Candidates should have computer skills, knowledge of field, oral communication skills, research skills, self-motivation, strong interpersonal skills, writing skills. Duration is 3 months. Unpaid. International applications accepted.
Benefits On-the-job training, willing to complete paperwork for educational credit, willing to provide letters of recommendation, general training, opportunity to learn working processes in all areas of exhibition and art administration and development.
Contact Write or e-mail Mr. Robert Lee, Director. E-mail: aaartsctr@aol.com. In-person interview required. Applicants must submit a resume, letter of interest specifying which position desired, one-page writing sample. Applications are accepted continuously. World Wide Web: http://www.artspiral.org.

BARBARA CAMPISI
400 Wythe Avenue
Brooklyn, New York 11211

General Information Art studio. Established in 1999. Number of employees: 1. Number of internship applications received each year: 2.
Internships Available ▶ *1 artist's assistant.* Candidates should have ability to work independently, oral communication skills, personal interest in the field, self-motivation, strong interpersonal skills. Duration is one semester or more, on a semester-to-semester basis. Unpaid. Open to high school seniors, recent high school graduates, college freshmen, college sophomores, college juniors, college seniors, recent college graduates. International applications accepted.
Benefits On-the-job training, willing to act as a professional reference, willing to complete paperwork for educational credit, willing to provide letters of recommendation.
Contact Write, call, fax, or e-mail Barbara Campisi, Sculptor. Phone: 718-782-8710. Fax: 212-620-7284. E-mail: campisib@msn.com. Telephone interview required. Applicants must submit a letter of interest, resume. Applications are accepted continuously.

BARBARA STRASEN
1724 South Pacific Avenue
San Pedro, California 90731

General Information Freelance visual artist who makes paintings (often combined with photography, mixed media, and installations) for exhibit and sale to galleries and museums nationally and internationally. Number of employees: 2. Number of internship applications received each year: 10.
Internships Available ▶ *1–3 studio assistants/interns:* responsibilities include painting under tutelage, canvas building, preparation imagery research, literary research, professional correspondence, framing and presenting artwork, and manufacturing 2-D and 3-D components of artwork. Candidates should have ability to work independently, ability to work with others, college courses in field, oral communication skills, personal interest in the field, research skills, self-motivation. Duration is flexible.

Unpaid. Open to college seniors, recent college graduates, graduate students, career changers. International applications accepted.
Benefits Formal training, job counseling, names of contacts, on-the-job training, willing to act as a professional reference, willing to complete paperwork for educational credit, willing to provide letters of recommendation, use of research facilities.
Contact Write or e-mail Ms. Barbara Strasen, Artist. E-mail: bstrasen@earthlink.net. No phone calls. In-person interview recommended (telephone interview accepted). Applicants must submit a letter of interest, resume, three letters of recommendation. Applications are accepted continuously.

BETSEY JOHNSON
498 Seventh Avenue, 21st Floor
New York, New York 10018

General Information Fashion designer showroom. Established in 1978. Number of employees: 50. Number of internship applications received each year: 100.
Internships Available ▶ *3–4 design interns:* responsibilities include assisting design team with fabric resourcing, arts and crafts, and running errands. Candidates should have ability to work independently, ability to work with others, knowledge of field, personal interest in the field. Duration is flexible. Unpaid. ▶ *4–5 sales interns:* responsibilities include assisting sales executives and customer relations, compiling sketch and swatch booklets, typing line sheets and letters, filing, and running errands. Candidates should have ability to work independently, ability to work with others, office skills, organizational skills, self-motivation, written communication skills. Duration is flexible. Unpaid. Open to recent high school graduates, college freshmen, college sophomores, college juniors, college seniors, recent college graduates, graduate students. International applications accepted.
Benefits Possible full-time employment, willing to complete paperwork for educational credit, willing to provide letters of recommendation.
Contact Write, call, or fax Jesika Homeijer, Sales. Phone: 212-244-0843. Fax: 212-244-0855. In-person interview required. Applicants must submit a letter of interest, resume. Applications are accepted continuously. World Wide Web: http://www.betseyjohnson.com.

BLAZING ADVENTURES
Box 5068, 48 Upper Village Mall
Snowmass Village, Colorado 81615

General Information Organization providing outdoor adventure tours. Established in 1969. Number of employees: 100. Number of internship applications received each year: 12.
Internships Available ▶ *1–2 group services interns:* responsibilities include working with conference coordinators to develop and manage active adventures and tour programs. Candidates should have ability to work independently, ability to work with others, computer skills, oral communication skills, organizational skills, personal interest in the field, self-motivation, strong leadership ability, written communication skills. Duration is May 15–August 31 (minimum 12 weeks). $150 per week plus 2% sales commission. ▶ *4–5 main office summer interns:* responsibilities include assisting guests with reservations in a knowledgeable and professional manner, resolving customer service issues and any operational problems, and utilizing the telephones and computers extensively to perform these responsibilities (all under the supervision of the office manager). Candidates should have ability to work independently, computer skills, office skills, oral communication skills, organizational skills, self-motivation. Duration is May 15–August 31. $150 per week plus 2% sales commission. ▶ *3–5 outdoor recreation guides:* responsibilities include training for a specific department and utilizing gained knowledge while providing professional service to guests. Candidates should have ability to work independently, ability to work with others, oral communication skills, personal interest in the field, self-motivation, strong leadership ability. Duration is May 5–August 31. Paid. Open to college freshmen, college sophomores, college juniors, college seniors, recent college graduates, graduate students, law students, career changers, individuals reentering the workforce.
Benefits Formal training, housing at a cost, job counseling, on-the-job training, possible full-time employment, willing to act as a

professional reference, willing to complete paperwork for educational credit, willing to provide letters of recommendation.
Contact Write, call, fax, e-mail, or through World Wide Web site Laurie Harris, Manager. Phone: 970-923-4544. Fax: 970-923-4994. E-mail: blazing@rof.net. Telephone interview required. Applicants must submit a formal organization application, resume, personal reference, letter of recommendation. Application deadline: May 1 for priority deadline; however, applications are accepted on a continuous basis. World Wide Web: http://www.blazingadventures.com.

BLOOMINGTON PARKS AND RECREATION
109 East Olive
Bloomington, Illinois 61704

General Information Parks and recreation program providing recreation for individuals of all ages, plus open space for passive involvement. Established in 1968. Number of employees: 250. Unit of City of Bloomington, Bloomington, Illinois. Number of internship applications received each year: 10.
Internships Available ▶ *1 marketing intern:* responsibilities include marketing recreation programs; working with local newspaper, radio, and cable TV. Candidates should have ability to work with others, oral communication skills, self-motivation, written communication skills. Duration is semester-basis; fitting requirements of school granting credit for internship. Position available as unpaid or paid. ▶ *2 recreation leaders:* responsibilities include planning, implementing, and evaluating recreation programs; learning about marketing, budgeting, and staffing. Candidates should have ability to work with others, experience in the field, oral communication skills, self-motivation, strong leadership ability. Duration is semester-basis; fitting requirements of school granting credit for internships. $80 per week. Open to college seniors, graduate students. International applications accepted.
Benefits On-the-job training, opportunity to attend seminars/workshops, possible full-time employment, willing to act as a professional reference, willing to complete paperwork for educational credit, willing to provide letters of recommendation.
Contact Write, call, or e-mail Barb Wells, Superintendent of Recreation. Phone: 309-434-2260. Fax: 309-434-2483. E-mail: bwells@cityblm.org. In-person interview recommended (telephone interview accepted). Applicants must submit a formal organization application, letter of interest, resume. Applications are accepted continuously. World Wide Web: http://www.cityblm.org/parks.

BONNI BENRUBI GALLERY
52 East 76th Street
New York, New York 10021

General Information Fine art gallery. Established in 1987. Number of employees: 5. Number of internship applications received each year: 75.
Internships Available ▶ *2–4 gallery interns:* responsibilities include office work, helping with shows and openings, and help in day-to-day functions of the gallery. Candidates should have ability to work independently, office skills, oral communication skills, personal interest in the field, self-motivation, strong interpersonal skills. Duration is one semester or summer. Unpaid. Open to college freshmen, college sophomores, college juniors, college seniors, recent college graduates. International applications accepted.
Benefits Job counseling, on-the-job training, willing to act as a professional reference, willing to complete paperwork for educational credit, willing to provide letters of recommendation.
Contact E-mail Jonathan Friedlander, Gallery Assistant. Fax: 212-288-7815. E-mail: jonathan@bonnibenrubi.com. No phone calls. In-person interview recommended (telephone interview accepted). Applicants must submit a resume. Applications are accepted continuously. World Wide Web: http://www.BonniBenrubi.com.

BOSTON PHOTO COLLABORATIVE
67 Brookside Avenue
Jamaica Plain, Massachusetts 02130

General Information Nonprofit community photography organization that brings photography to people traditionally without access to the medium. Established in 1991. Number of employees: 5. Number of internship applications received each year: 30.
Internships Available ▶ *5–20 interns:* responsibilities include positions available in fund-raising and special events, publicity, exhibits, program development, education, technology and Web design, and computer mentoring; most likely, interns will work in several areas at once, rather than one area exclusively. Candidates should have ability to work independently, ability to work with others, editing skills, office skills, oral communication skills, organizational skills, personal interest in the field, research skills, self-motivation, writing skills, creative thinking and problem-solving abilities, Mac-based computer skills (word-processing, design, database, and Internet). Duration is flexible; available throughout year, full- or part-time, days or evenings. Unpaid. Open to high school students, recent high school graduates, college freshmen, college sophomores, college juniors, college seniors, recent college graduates, graduate students, law students, career changers, individuals reentering the workforce. International applications accepted.
Benefits On-the-job training, opportunity to attend seminars/workshops, possible full-time employment, willing to act as a professional reference, willing to complete paperwork for educational credit, willing to provide letters of recommendation.
Contact Write, call, fax, or e-mail Heather Beard, Associate Director. Phone: 617-524-7729. Fax: 617-522-9891. E-mail: mail@bostonphoto.org. In-person interview recommended (telephone interview accepted). Applicants must submit a formal organization application, letter of interest, resume. Application deadline: February 29 for spring, May 31 for summer, July 1 for fall. World Wide Web: http://www.bostonphoto.org.

BRICK WALL MANAGEMENT
648 Amsterdam Avenue, Suite 4A
New York, New York 10025

General Information Music artist management company. Established in 1996. Number of employees: 3. Number of internship applications received each year: 100.
Internships Available ▶ *1–3 general interns:* responsibilities include general office administration. Candidates should have ability to work independently, computer skills, office skills, oral communication skills, organizational skills, personal interest in the field, plan to pursue career in field, research skills, strong interpersonal skills, writing skills. Duration is 3–5 months. Unpaid. Open to college freshmen, college sophomores, college juniors, college seniors, recent college graduates, career changers. International applications accepted.
Benefits On-the-job training, willing to act as a professional reference, willing to complete paperwork for educational credit, willing to provide letters of recommendation.
Contact Write, call, fax, or e-mail Abbie Johnson, Internship Coordinator. Phone: 212-501-0748. Fax: 212-724-0849. E-mail: jason@brickwallmgmt.com. In-person interview required. Applicants must submit a letter of interest, resume. Applications are accepted continuously. World Wide Web: http://www.brickwallmgmt.com.

BRISTOL-MYERS SQUIBB–CENTER FOR HEALTH AND FITNESS
1 Squibb Drive
New Brunswick, New Jersey 08903

General Information Corporate employee health and fitness center. Established in 1994. Number of employees: 1. Number of internship applications received each year: 6.
Internships Available ▶ *1–2 health and fitness interns:* responsibilities include working with participants to complete fitness assessments and exercise prescriptions, assisting in operation of facility and opening/closing routines. Candidates should have ability to work independently, college courses in field, computer skills, oral communication skills, personal interest in the field, self-motivation, strong interpersonal skills, CPR certification. Duration is 1 semester. Unpaid. Open to college freshmen, college sophomores, college juniors, college seniors, recent college graduates. International applications accepted.

Bristol-Myers Squibb–Center for Health and Fitness (continued)
Benefits Names of contacts, on-the-job training, possible full-time employment, willing to act as a professional reference, willing to complete paperwork for educational credit, willing to provide letters of recommendation.
Contact Write, call, or e-mail Sharon Combes-Kelemen, Supervisor of Health and Fitness, 1 Squibb Drive, New Brunswick, New Jersey 08903. Phone: 732-519-3900. Fax: 732-519-1727. E-mail: fitness.center@bms.com. In-person interview required. Applicants must submit a resume, academic transcripts. Applications are accepted continuously.

BRYNWOOD COUNTRY CLUB
6200 West Good Hope Road
Milwaukee, Wisconsin 53223

General Information Private country club with 18–hole golf course, tennis courts, swimming pool, banquet facility, fine dining room, and men's and lady's locker rooms. Established in 1928. Number of employees: 100. Number of internship applications received each year: 100.
Internships Available ▶ *1–3 interns:* responsibilities include working in facets of the club that need the most help for different time periods; primarily in food and beverage. Candidates should have ability to work independently, ability to work with others, oral communication skills, plan to pursue career in field, strong leadership ability, written communication skills. Duration is 3 to 6 months (one semester, one year, or 18 months). $7.50 per hour. Open to recent high school graduates, college freshmen, college sophomores, college juniors, college seniors, recent college graduates, graduate students, individuals at least 18 years old. ▶ *1 poolside cafe supervisor:* responsibilities include scheduling 10 employees for the summer supervising staff, maintaining consistent service in cafe, taking care of members' needs, working with assistant general manager. Candidates should have ability to work independently, ability to work with others, experience in the field, oral communication skills, strong leadership ability, written communication skills. Duration is June to September only. $7.50–$9 per hour. Open to college juniors, college seniors. International applications accepted.
Benefits Free housing, free meals, on-the-job training, possible full-time employment, willing to act as a professional reference, willing to complete paperwork for educational credit, willing to provide letters of recommendation, employee outings.
International Internships Available.
Contact Write, call, fax, or e-mail Gretchen Schlueter, Assistant General Manager. Phone: 414-353-8800 Ext. 19. Fax: 414-353-5905. E-mail: asstgmbrynwood@aol.com. Telephone interview required. Applicants must submit a letter of interest, resume. Applications are accepted continuously.

CAMPBELL SOUP COMPANY, HEALTH AND FITNESS CENTER
One Campbell Place
Camden, New Jersey 08103

General Information Health and fitness center for World Headquarters employees, spouses, and retirees. Established in 1984. Number of employees: 2. Unit of Campbell Soup Company, Camden, New Jersey. Number of internship applications received each year: 10.
Internships Available ▶ *1–2 interns:* responsibilities include working directly with exercise physiologists to assist in the administration, planning, and implementation of all health and fitness services programs by doing fitness evaluations, development of fitness programs, floor supervision, and class leadership. Candidates should have declared college major in field, knowledge of field, oral communication skills, personal interest in the field, self-motivation, strong interpersonal skills. Duration is 1 semester. $500 per duration of internship. Open to college juniors, college seniors. International applications accepted.
Benefits Names of contacts, on-the-job training, willing to act as a professional reference, willing to complete paperwork for educational credit, willing to provide letters of recommendation.

Contact Write, call, fax, or e-mail Bill Craig, Manager, Health and Fitness Center, One Campbell Place, Box 84, Camden, New Jersey 08103. Phone: 856-342-3940. Fax: 856-968-2984. E-mail: bill_craig@campbellsoup.com. In-person interview required. Applicants must submit a letter of interest, resume. Applications are accepted continuously.

CAMP SEALTH
14500 Southwest Camp Sealth Road
Vashon Island, Washington 98070

General Information Year-round camp providing summer resident camp programs to youth ages 6-17, school year environmental education programs to school age youth, and providing host services to rental groups throughout the year. Established in 1920. Number of employees: 180. Division of Camp Fire USA, Central Puget Sound Council, Seattle, Washington. Number of internship applications received each year: 10.
Internships Available ▶ *1–4 environmental education interns:* responsibilities include developing and teaching forest wetland and marine curriculum to students grade K-8; facilitating camp programs including challenge course and evening activities; assisting with other camp duties as assigned. Candidates should have ability to work independently, ability to work with others, personal interest in the field, self-motivation, strong leadership ability. Duration is April to June. Position available as unpaid or at $100–$180 per week. Open to college sophomores, college juniors, college seniors, recent college graduates, graduate students, career changers. ▶ *50 summer camp staff members:* responsibilities include various positions including cabin counselor, lifeguard, riding staff, program specialist, inclusion staff, plus many more; specific responsibilities vary. Candidates should have ability to work with others, knowledge of field, oral communication skills, organizational skills, personal interest in the field, self-motivation, strong leadership ability, written communication skills. Duration is June to September. $1350–$2200 per duration of internship. Open to high school seniors, recent high school graduates, college freshmen, college sophomores, college juniors, college seniors, recent college graduates, graduate students, career changers, individuals reentering the workforce.
Benefits Formal training, free housing, free meals, on-the-job training, willing to act as a professional reference, willing to complete paperwork for educational credit, willing to provide letters of recommendation.
Contact Write, call, fax, or e-mail Sarah Henderson, Program Coordinator, PO Box 13599, Burton, Washington 98013. Phone: 206-463-3174 Ext. 61. Fax: 206-463-6936. E-mail: campstaff@campfire-usa.org. In-person interview recommended (telephone interview accepted). Applicants must submit a formal organization application, 4-7 personal references. Application deadline: March 1 for environmental education interns, April 15 for summer. World Wide Web: http://www.campfire-usa.org.

CAROL BANCROFT AND FRIENDS
PO Box 266, 121 Dodgingtown Road
Bethel, Connecticut 06801

General Information Organization that specializes in art for children's and young adults' publications; represents over 50 artists and acts as an agent for illustrators. Established in 1973. Number of employees: 2. Number of internship applications received each year: 10.
Internships Available ▶ *1 promotional assistant:* responsibilities include assembling promotion packets, packaging and logging art on loan to clients, original art retrieving, caring for artist samples, and performing general clerical tasks. Candidates should have ability to work independently, ability to work with others, computer skills, knowledge of field, oral communication skills, organizational skills, personal interest in the field, plan to pursue career in field, self-motivation. Duration is flexible. Unpaid. Open to college freshmen, college sophomores, college juniors, college seniors, recent college graduates, individuals reentering the workforce. International applications accepted.
Benefits Job counseling, names of contacts, on-the-job training, opportunity to attend seminars/workshops, possible full-time employment, willing to act as a professional reference, willing to

complete paperwork for educational credit, willing to provide letters of recommendation, stipend upon completion of internship. **Contact** Write, call, fax, or e-mail Carol Bancroft, Artist Agent. Phone: 203-748-4823. Fax: 203-748-4581. E-mail: artists@carolbancroft.com. In-person interview recommended (telephone interview accepted). Applicants must submit a letter of interest, resume. Applications are accepted continuously. World Wide Web: http://www.carolbancroft.com.

CASA YBEL
2255 West Gulf Drive
Sanibel, Florida 33957

General Information Ocean-front resort with 114 one-or two-bedroom suites, tennis, restaurant, shuffleboard, and olympic-sized pool. Established in 1995. Number of employees: 79. Subsidiary of Coral Collections, Naples, Florida. Number of internship applications received each year: 100.
Internships Available ▶ *2–3 activity coordinators:* responsibilities include supervising groups of children, calculating daily/weekly/monthly financial totals, and maintaining supply inventory. Candidates should have college courses in field, knowledge of field, oral communication skills, organizational skills, personal interest in the field, self-motivation, strong interpersonal skills, strong leadership ability, CPR and first aid (recommended, but not required), knowledge of water safety a plus. Duration is 4–5 months. $300-$320 biweekly. Open to college juniors, college seniors.
Benefits Free housing, free meals, names of contacts, on-the-job training, willing to act as a professional reference, willing to complete paperwork for educational credit, willing to provide letters of recommendation, opportunity to meet staff from other area resorts.
Contact Write, call, fax, e-mail, or through World Wide Web site Recreation Director. Phone: 239-472-3145 Ext. 1319. Fax: 239-472-2109. E-mail: casaybelresort_rec@lycos.com. Telephone interview required. Applicants must submit a letter of interest, resume, two personal references. Application deadline: June 15 for fall, October 15 for spring, November 30 for summer. World Wide Web: http://www.casaybelresort.com.

CENTER FOR PHOTOGRAPHY AT WOODSTOCK
59 Tinker Street
Woodstock, New York 12498

General Information Nonprofit arts organization dedicated to promoting excellence in photography and the related arts through exhibition, publication, and education. Established in 1977. Number of employees: 5. Number of internship applications received each year: 30.
Internships Available ▶ *1–4 arts administration interns:* responsibilities include working in the Center's galleries as an administrative assistant, exploring programs and exhibitions, and assisting in the production of the *Center Quarterly* and other publications. Candidates should have ability to work with others, oral communication skills, personal interest in the field, self-motivation, written communication skills. Duration is 3 months. Unpaid. ▶ *3 photography workshop interns/assistants:* responsibilities include assisting in Woodstock Photography Workshops program, a summer and fall of workshops involving nationally recognized artists; handling publicity, hospitality, event facilitation, program documentation, and various administrative duties. Candidates should have ability to work independently, ability to work with others, oral communication skills, personal interest in the field, self-motivation. Duration is 4 months (June-October). $250 stipend. Open to college freshmen, college sophomores, college juniors, college seniors, graduate students.
Benefits Formal training, job counseling, names of contacts, on-the-job training, opportunity to attend seminars/workshops, possible full-time employment, travel reimbursement, willing to act as a professional reference, willing to complete paperwork for educational credit, willing to provide letters of recommendation, use of darkrooms, $5000 tuition remission for photography workshop internships.
Contact Write, call, fax, e-mail, or through World Wide Web site Kate Menconeri, Program Director. Phone: 845-679-9957. Fax: 845-679-6337. E-mail: info@cpw.org. In-person interview required. Applicants must submit three personal references, resume, portfolio, 2 personal references (for photography workshop internships). Application deadline: March/April for personal interviews (photography workshop); continuous for arts administration interns. World Wide Web: http://www.cpw.org.

CHICAGO ARTISTS COALITION
11 East Hubbard, 7th Floor
Chicago, Illinois 60611

General Information Service organization for visual artists providing information, a newspaper, workshops, and guidebooks to further artists' careers. Established in 1975. Number of employees: 4. Number of internship applications received each year: 5.
Internships Available ▶ *1–2 administrative assistants:* responsibilities include upgrading informational publications, helping with an art exhibition, helping to upgrade data, proofreading. Candidates should have ability to work with others, computer skills, office skills, oral communication skills, organizational skills, self-motivation. Duration is flexible. Unpaid. Open to college freshmen, college sophomores, college juniors, college seniors, recent college graduates, graduate students, career changers, individuals reentering the workforce. International applications accepted.
Benefits On-the-job training, opportunity to attend seminars/workshops, willing to act as a professional reference, willing to provide letters of recommendation, art-related job counseling.
Contact Write, call, or fax Arlene Rakoncay, Executive Director, 11 East Hubbard 7th Floor, Chicago 60611. Phone: 312-670-2060. Fax: 312-670-2521. In-person interview recommended (telephone interview accepted). Applicants must submit a letter of interest, resume. Applications are accepted continuously. World Wide Web: http://www.caconline.org.

CHILDREN'S MUSEUM OF RICHMOND (CMOR)
2626 West Broad Street
Richmond, Virginia 23220-1904

General Information Cultural art center. Established in 1981. Number of employees: 30. Number of internship applications received each year: 30.
Internships Available ▶ *1–2 Little CMOR specialists:* responsibilities include assisting in the planning/preparation, set-up, implementation and clean-up of the weekly early childhood programs; spending time in the Little CMOR exhibit area to interact with young children and their caregivers. Candidates should have experience in the field, personal interest in the field, plan to pursue career in field, patience. Duration is 1-2 semesters (Tuesday, Wednesday, and Friday mornings 9:00-noon). Unpaid. Open to college freshmen, college sophomores, college juniors, college seniors, recent college graduates. ▶ *1–2 accounting and finance interns:* responsibilities include assisting with accounting by supporting the payables and receivables staff in some of the following ways: data entry using Excel spreadsheets, accounting-related copying, filing, and distribution of materials to staff; assisting with bank reconciliations; assisting with other duties. Candidates should have ability to work independently, analytical skills, knowledge of field, office skills, oral communication skills, organizational skills, self-motivation, written communication skills. Duration is 1 semester. Unpaid. Open to college freshmen, college sophomores, college juniors, college seniors, recent college graduates, career changers. ▶ *2 art advocates:* responsibilities include preparing materials for group lessons and weekly projects; assisting in changing exhibitions by preparing signage, displays, and other visual aids; assisting in cleanup of the art studio; working with children, youth, and families to promote philosophy of children learning through art. Candidates should have organizational skills, personal interest in the field, self-motivation, strong interpersonal skills, written communication skills. Duration is 1 semester. Unpaid. Open to high school seniors, college freshmen, college sophomores, college juniors, college seniors, recent college graduates, career changers, individuals reentering the workforce. ▶ *1–2 development interns:* responsibilities include planning, execution, and documentation of a special project that will assist the development department while providing the intern with a learning

Children's Museum of Richmond (CMOR) (continued)

opportunity appropriate for his/her own skill level and career goals. Candidates should have ability to work independently, computer skills, oral communication skills, organizational skills, personal interest in the field, strong interpersonal skills, written communication skills. Duration is 1–2 semesters. Unpaid. Open to college sophomores, college juniors, college seniors, recent college graduates, career changers, individuals reentering the workforce. ▶ *1–2 marketing public relations interns:* responsibilities include assisting with marketing public relations needs related to the museum's special events, press releases, surveys, direct mail, earned income sales; providing support to these activities in the form of event operations, press kit compilation, collateral preparation, distribution, administrative support. Candidates should have knowledge of field, oral communication skills, organizational skills, strong interpersonal skills, written communication skills. Duration is 1–2 semesters. Unpaid. Open to college juniors, college seniors. ▶ *1–3 youth and family program assistant:* responsibilities include assisting with research and development of content and implementation and evaluation of diverse programs designed for audiences of children and their families; providing assistance with reservation process, customer service, and program supply inventory related to youth and family programs. Candidates should have ability to work independently, computer skills, office skills, oral communication skills, personal interest in the field, strong interpersonal skills. Duration is 1–2 semesters. Unpaid. Open to college freshmen, college sophomores, college juniors, college seniors, recent college graduates. International applications accepted.
Benefits On-the-job training, possible full-time employment, willing to act as a professional reference, willing to complete paperwork for educational credit, willing to provide letters of recommendation.
Contact Write, fax, or e-mail Irene Luu, Volunteer Resources Coordinator, 2626 West Broad Street, Richmond, Virginia 23220. Phone: 804-474-7029. Fax: 804-474-7099. E-mail: iluu@c-mor.org. In-person interview required. Applicants must submit a formal organization application, resume, three personal references. Application deadline: January 10 for spring, May 10 for summer, September 10 for fall. World Wide Web: http://www.c-mor.org.

CHRISTIE'S
20 Rockefeller Plaza
New York, New York 10020

General Information Auction sales company. Established in 1766. Number of employees: 600. Number of internship applications received each year: 100.
Internships Available ▶ *30 interns:* responsibilities include administrative assistance including telephones, faxing, and filing, in support of auction business processes. Candidates should have ability to work independently, ability to work with others, office skills, oral communication skills, personal interest in the field, written communication skills. Duration is flexible (usually 4 months or more). Position available as unpaid or paid. Open to college freshmen, college sophomores, college juniors, college seniors, graduate students. International applications accepted.
Benefits Job counseling, on-the-job training, possible full-time employment, willing to act as a professional reference, willing to provide letters of recommendation.
Contact Write, call, fax, e-mail, or through World Wide Web site Sara Fox, Recruiter, 20 Rockefeller Plaza. Phone: 212-636-2629. Fax: 212-636-4945. E-mail: sfox@christies.com. In-person interview recommended (telephone interview accepted). Applicants must submit a letter of interest, resume. Applications are accepted continuously. World Wide Web: http://www.christies.com.

CINEPARTNERS ENTERTAINMENT
3854 Beethoven Street, Unit #1
Los Angeles, California 90066

General Information Company that develops, packages, finances, and produces a variety of stories. Established in 1994. Number of employees: 4.

Internships Available ▶ *3 development and production interns:* responsibilities include reading screenplays, evaluating projects, and handling correspondence and phone calls. Candidates should have ability to work independently, ability to work with others, computer skills, oral communication skills, personal interest in the field, written communication skills. Duration is flexible. Unpaid. Open to recent high school graduates, college freshmen, college sophomores, college juniors, college seniors, recent college graduates, graduate students, career changers, individuals reentering the workforce. ▶ *2–3 film and TV production interns:* responsibilities include pre-production, script development, and production work. Candidates should have analytical skills, computer skills, oral communication skills, plan to pursue career in field, self-motivation. Duration is flexible. Unpaid. Open to recent high school graduates, college freshmen, college sophomores, college juniors, college seniors, recent college graduates, graduate students, career changers, individuals reentering the workforce. ▶ *3 graphic design/Web design interns:* responsibilities include designing posters and fliers and Web design. Candidates should have analytical skills, computer skills, knowledge of field, personal interest in the field, plan to pursue career in field. Duration is flexible. Unpaid. International applications accepted.
Benefits Job counseling, on-the-job training, possible full-time employment, willing to act as a professional reference, willing to complete paperwork for educational credit, willing to provide letters of recommendation.
Contact Write, call, fax, or e-mail Jeno Hodi, Chairman. Phone: 310-391-7229. Fax: 310-391-5950. E-mail: production@cinepartners. net. Applicants must submit a resume. Applications are accepted continuously. World Wide Web: http://www.cinepartners.net.

CITY OF CHULA VISTA RECREATION DEPARTMENT
270 F Street
Chula Vista, California 91910

General Information Recreation department that provides programs for individuals with developmental or physical disabilities. Established in 1979. Number of employees: 15. Division of City of Chula Vista, Chula Vista, California. Number of internship applications received each year: 2.
Internships Available ▶ *Recreation therapy interns:* responsibilities include assessments, program planning, evaluation, special events, case study, and the overall logistics of how city government works. Candidates should have ability to work independently, ability to work with others, college courses in field, computer skills, office skills, oral communication skills, organizational skills, plan to pursue career in field, self-motivation, strong leadership ability, written communication skills. Duration is 500 hours. $300 per duration of internship. Open to college seniors, graduate students, only those who have completed recreational therapy prerequisites. International applications accepted.
Benefits On-the-job training, opportunity to attend seminars/workshops, willing to act as a professional reference, willing to complete paperwork for educational credit, willing to provide letters of recommendation.
Contact Write, call, or e-mail Carmel Wilson, C.T.R.S., Recreation Supervisor. Phone: 619-409-5800. Fax: 619-476-8167. E-mail: cwilson@ci.chula-vista.ca.us. In-person interview recommended (telephone interview accepted). Applicants must submit a formal organization application, resume, city application; finger printing required. Applications are accepted continuously.

CITY OF GLEN COVE, DEPARTMENT OF PARKS AND RECREATION
9 Glen Street
Glen Cove, New York 11542

General Information Municipal parks and recreation department. Established in 1668. Number of employees: 160. Number of internship applications received each year: 5.
Internships Available ▶ *1–3 parks and recreation interns:* responsibilities include assisting in every aspect of operating a municipal parks and recreation program for a community of 25,000+ people; office work required as well as assisting with programs. Candidates

should have ability to work with others, computer skills, oral communication skills, plan to pursue career in field, self-motivation. Duration is flexible. Position available as unpaid or at hourly wage (varies, based on experience). Open to college juniors, college seniors, recent college graduates, graduate students.
Benefits On-the-job training, willing to act as a professional reference, willing to complete paperwork for educational credit, willing to provide letters of recommendation.
Contact Write, call, or e-mail Darcy Belyea, Director of Parks and Recreation. Phone: 516-676-3766. Fax: 516-676-0108. E-mail: glencoverec@aol.com. In-person interview required. Applicants must submit a formal organization application, letter of interest, resume, personal reference. Applications are accepted continuously. World Wide Web: http://glencove-li.com.

COCOA EXPO SPORTS CENTER
500 Friday Road
Cocoa, Florida 32926

General Information Multi-sports facility including baseball, soccer, football, lacrosse, volleyball, basketball, rugby, softball, and swimming. Established in 1986. Number of employees: 100. Number of internship applications received each year: 50.
Internships Available ▶ *2–3 athletic department assistants:* responsibilities include assisting in organization of baseball or soccer tournaments and events. Candidates should have ability to work independently, ability to work with others, computer skills, knowledge of field, oral communication skills. Duration is 4–6 months. Unpaid. Open to college juniors, college seniors, recent college graduates. International applications accepted.
Benefits Free housing, free meals, willing to act as a professional reference, willing to complete paperwork for educational credit, willing to provide letters of recommendation.
Contact Fax or e-mail Jeff Biddle, Athletic Director. Phone: 321-639-3976. Fax: 321-639-0598. E-mail: athleticdirector@cocoaexpo.com. In-person interview recommended (telephone interview accepted). Applicants must submit a letter of interest, resume, three personal references. Applications are accepted continuously. World Wide Web: http://www.cocoaexpo.com.

COLORADO COUNCIL ON THE ARTS
750 Pennsylvania Street
Denver, Colorado 80203-3699

General Information State arts agency that awards grants to arts organizations and artists and promotes the arts in Colorado. Established in 1967. Number of employees: 7. Unit of State of Colorado, Department of Higher Education, Denver, Colorado. Number of internship applications received each year: 12.
Internships Available ▶ *1 Arts in Public Places intern:* responsibilities include assisting director in administration of program. Duration is 3–12 months. Unpaid. ▶ *1 communications intern:* responsibilities include developing and monitoring agency communications, including press releases, newsletter, brochures, and Web site. Duration is 3–12 months. Unpaid. Candidates for all positions should have ability to work independently, college courses in field, computer skills, oral communication skills, personal interest in the field, written communication skills. Open to college freshmen, college sophomores, college juniors, college seniors, recent college graduates, graduate students, career changers.
Benefits Job counseling, names of contacts, on-the-job training, opportunity to attend seminars/workshops, willing to complete paperwork for educational credit, willing to provide letters of recommendation.
Contact Write, e-mail, or through World Wide Web site Renée Bovée, Deputy Director. E-mail: coloarts@state.co.us. No phone calls. In-person interview recommended (telephone interview accepted). Applicants must submit a letter of interest, resume. Applications are accepted continuously. World Wide Web: http://www.coloarts.state.co.us.

COMMUNITY ARTS ADMINISTRATION INTERNSHIP PROGRAM, NORTH CAROLINA ARTS COUNCIL
Department of Cultural Resources
Raleigh, North Carolina 27699-4653

General Information Council that works to enrich the cultural life of the state by nurturing and supporting excellence in the arts and providing opportunities for every North Carolinian to experience the arts. Established in 1974. Number of employees: 24. Division of North Carolina Arts Council/Department of Cultural Resources, Raleigh, North Carolina. Number of internship applications received each year: 35.
Internships Available ▶ *4 interns:* responsibilities include grant writing, fund-raising, financial management, interagency relationships, programming, planning, community arts administration and organizational structure. Candidates should have ability to work independently, college courses in field, oral communication skills, organizational skills, personal interest in the field, plan to pursue career in field, self-motivation, strong interpersonal skills, strong leadership ability. Duration is 3 months. $4000 per duration of internship. Open to recent college graduates, career changers, individuals reentering the workforce. International applications accepted.
Benefits Possible full-time employment, willing to provide letters of recommendation.
Contact Write, call, fax, or e-mail Viola Bullock. Phone: 919-733-7897. Fax: 919-715-8287. E-mail: viola.bullock@ncmail.net. Applicants must submit a formal organization application, letter of interest, resume, in-person interview (for persons accepted). Application deadline: May 1. World Wide Web: http://www.ncarts.org.

CONCRETE MARKETING
121 West 27th Street, Suite 1001
New York, New York 10001

General Information Music marketing company. Established in 1984. Number of employees: 16. Number of internship applications received each year: 100.
Internships Available ▶ *Web content assistants (music site):* responsibilities include Web research, light site updating, assisting in maintenance of site. Candidates should have ability to work independently, ability to work with others, editing skills, personal interest in the field, self-motivation, strong leadership ability, writing skills, graphic design skills (helpful but not necessary). Position available as unpaid or paid. Open to college freshmen, college sophomores, college juniors, college seniors, recent college graduates. ▶ *Marketing interns:* responsibilities include detailed phone tracking, computer work, and phone responsibility. Candidates should have ability to work independently, ability to work with others, oral communication skills, personal interest in the field, plan to pursue career in field, self-motivation, strong leadership ability. Position available as unpaid or paid. Open to college freshmen, college sophomores, college juniors, college seniors, recent college graduates, individuals reentering the workforce. International applications accepted.
Benefits Possible full-time employment, willing to complete paperwork for educational credit, willing to provide letters of recommendation.
Contact Fax or e-mail Dana Delbeke, Internship Coordinator. Fax: 212-645-2607. E-mail: info@concreteplanet.com. In-person interview required. Applicants must submit a letter of interest, resume. Applications are accepted continuously. World Wide Web: http://concreteplanet.com.

CONNIE ROGERS INC., CURATORIAL CONSULTANTS
152 East 94th Street
New York, New York 10128

General Information Art consulting firm that assembles large art collections, primarily contemporary, for major corporations and advises on acquisitions in impressionist and modern art for private collections. Established in 1979. Number of employees: 3.

Internships Available ▶ *3 interns:* responsibilities include performing administrative tasks and inventory, working with slide archives, photo documentation, cataloging art, and updating auction records. Candidates should have analytical skills, computer skills, office skills, organizational skills, personal interest in the field, research skills. Duration is flexible. Unpaid. Open to college sophomores, college juniors, college seniors, recent college graduates, graduate students, career changers, individuals reentering the workforce.
Benefits Job counseling, names of contacts, on-the-job training, possible full-time employment, willing to complete paperwork for educational credit, willing to provide letters of recommendation, invitations to art gallery openings.
Contact Write or call Ms. Connie Rogers. Phone: 212-410-3492. Applicants must submit a letter of interest, resume, call to follow up letter. Applications are accepted continuously.

CORNERSTONE HEALTH & FITNESS
Box 1308
Doylestown, Pennsylvania 18901

General Information Health and fitness center. Established in 1995. Number of employees: 60. Number of internship applications received each year: 30.
Internships Available ▶ *2–6 student interns:* responsibilities include fitness assessment, exercise prescription, nutrition counseling, exercise programming for special populations, project development, facility management, program administration, marketing, customer service, and attending lectures. Candidates should have declared college major in field, knowledge of field, oral communication skills, plan to pursue career in field, strong interpersonal skills, strong leadership ability, current CPR certification, personal liability insurance. Duration is variable as deemed appropriate through university requirements. Unpaid. Open to college sophomores, college juniors, college seniors, graduate students. International applications accepted.
Benefits Formal training, job counseling, names of contacts, on-the-job training, opportunity to attend seminars/workshops, possible full-time employment, willing to act as a professional reference, willing to complete paperwork for educational credit, willing to provide letters of recommendation.
Contact Write, call, or fax Tricia Kirkwood, Internship Coordinator, PO Box 1308, Doylestown, Pennsylvania 18901. Phone: 215-794-3700. Fax: 215-794-3922. In-person interview required. Applicants must submit a letter of interest, resume, three personal references. Applications are accepted continuously. World Wide Web: http://cornerstonehealthandfitness.com.

CORPORATE FITNESS WORKS
18558 Office Park Drive
Montgomery Village, Maryland 20886

General Information Health promotion and fitness management firm that customizes health promotion programs for businesses, government agencies, and office park developers; services range from providing on-site wellness/fitness management, health risk appraisals, health fairs, health screenings, facility design/layout, equipment purchase, and program consulting. Established in 1988. Number of employees: 9. Number of internship applications received each year: 100.
Internships Available ▶ *1–30 fitness specialists:* responsibilities include administering physical fitness assessments, developing individualized programs, supervising the exercise room, teaching classes or clinics, and assisting with the center newsletter. Duration is 12–16 weeks. Position available as unpaid or paid. ▶ *1–20 wellness/health promotion specialists:* responsibilities include coordinating and implementing health fairs, planning health screenings and lunch-n-learns, facilitating health seminars, and developing health information handouts and newsletter. Duration is 12–16 weeks. Position available as unpaid or paid. Candidates for all positions should have college courses in field, computer skills, oral communication skills, organizational skills, written communica-

tion skills, CPR and first aid certification. Open to college juniors, college seniors, recent college graduates, graduate students. International applications accepted.
Benefits Formal training, housing at a cost, job counseling, names of contacts, on-the-job training, opportunity to attend seminars/workshops, possible full-time employment, willing to act as a professional reference, willing to complete paperwork for educational credit, willing to provide letters of recommendation, opportunity for occasional part-time hours, possibility of stipend.
Contact Fax, e-mail, or through World Wide Web site Nicol Stephens, Internship Administrator, 18558 Office Park Drive, Montgomery Village, Maryland 20886. Fax: 301-417-0651. E-mail: info@corporatefitnessworks.com. No phone calls. In-person interview recommended (telephone interview accepted). Applicants must submit a formal organization application, letter of interest, resume, two letters of recommendation. Application deadline: April 15 for summer, July 15 for fall, November 15 for spring. World Wide Web: http://www.corporatefitnessworks.com.

THE CRAFTS CENTER
1001 Connecticut Avenue, NW, Suite 525
Washington, District of Columbia 20036

General Information Nonprofit organization assisting low-income artisans in the developing world. Established in 1986. Number of employees: 6. Number of internship applications received each year: 30.
Internships Available ▶ *2–3 interns:* responsibilities include researching projects related to crafts proposal research, fundraising activities, and content development for newsletter. Candidates should have ability to work independently, computer skills, editing skills, office skills, oral communication skills, personal interest in the field, research skills, self-motivation, writing skills, written and oral Spanish skills (a plus). Duration is 1–12 months. Position available as unpaid or at $500–$900 per month. Open to college seniors, recent college graduates, graduate students, career changers. International applications accepted.
Benefits Names of contacts, on-the-job training, opportunity to attend seminars/workshops, willing to act as a professional reference, willing to complete paperwork for educational credit, willing to provide letters of recommendation.
Contact Write, fax, or e-mail Program Manager. Fax: 202-296-2452. E-mail: info@craftscenter.org. No phone calls. In-person interview recommended (telephone interview accepted). Applicants must submit a letter of interest, resume. Applications are accepted continuously. World Wide Web: http://www.craftscenter.org.

CREATIVE TIME, INC.
307 Seventh Avenue, Suite 1904
New York, New York 10001

General Information Public arts organization presenting multidisciplinary artworks in the public setting in and around New York City. Established in 1973. Number of employees: 9. Number of internship applications received each year: 250.
Internships Available ▶ *1–2 curatorial assistants:* responsibilities include maintaining and updating artists files and researching prospective projects. Candidates should have ability to work independently, analytical skills, office skills, organizational skills, personal interest in the field, research skills, self-motivation, strong interpersonal skills, written communication skills. Duration is flexible. Unpaid. ▶ *2 development interns:* responsibilities include assisting in research, maintaining current files on foundations and corporate sponsors, drafting and mailing correspondences, maintaining development database, updating publicity packets on the organization, and maintaining artist files. Candidates should have ability to work independently, ability to work with others, computer skills, office skills, organizational skills, personal interest in the field, research skills, self-motivation, writing skills. Duration is flexible. Unpaid. ▶ *1 operations and research intern:* responsibilities include assisting in site management of the production sites and office, researching and cultivating interns and volunteers, researching venues and production resources for potential projects, researching potential purchases, vendor research, and involvements with long term planning including technology plan. Candidates should have ability to work independently, ability to

work with others, computer skills, office skills, oral communication skills, organizational skills, personal interest in the field, research skills, self-motivation, written communication skills. Duration is flexible. Unpaid. ▶ *Production interns:* responsibilities include working with visual and performing artists and other on-site personnel in the creation and de-installation of site specific projects, as well as planning and research in pre-production. Candidates should have ability to work independently, computer skills, office skills, organizational skills, personal interest in the field, research skills, self-motivation, strong interpersonal skills, writing skills. Duration is flexible. Unpaid. ▶ *1–2 public relations assistants:* responsibilities include assisting in organizing publicity for individual projects, research on media sources for projects, outreach, updating the press database with current masthead information, sending out press releases, assisting at box office for performance events, updating mailing lists, and surveying. Candidates should have ability to work independently, computer skills, editing skills, office skills, oral communication skills, organizational skills, personal interest in the field, research skills, self-motivation, strong interpersonal skills, writing skills. Duration is flexible. Unpaid. ▶ *1 technology and Web intern:* responsibilities include developing Web site to reflect current and upcoming programming and maintaining and expanding Web archives. Candidates should have ability to work independently, editing skills, organizational skills, personal interest in the field, research skills, self-motivation, solid HTML skills, knowledge of PhotoShop, Javascript (a plus). Duration is flexible. Unpaid. Open to college freshmen, college sophomores, college juniors, college seniors, recent college graduates, graduate students. International applications accepted.

Benefits Job counseling, names of contacts, possible full-time employment, willing to complete paperwork for educational credit, willing to provide letters of recommendation, hands-on art experience.

Contact Write, call, fax, e-mail, or through World Wide Web site Kelly Evans, Operations Manager. Phone: 212-206-6674 Ext. 200. Fax: 212-255-8467. E-mail: staff@creativetime.org. In-person interview recommended (telephone interview accepted). Applicants must submit a letter of interest, resume. Applications are accepted continuously. World Wide Web: http://www.creativetime.org.

CULTUREFINDER, LLC
850 Seventh Avenue, Suite 704
New York, New York 10019-5230

General Information Leading Web site for arts information covering Broadway, theater, classical music, opera, dance, jazz, and the visual arts. Established in 1995. Number of employees: 5. Number of internship applications received each year: 150.

Internships Available ▶ *2 editorial assistants:* responsibilities include assisting the producer with day-to-day publishing responsibilities on the Web including editing text and graphics. Candidates should have ability to work independently, computer skills, knowledge of field, oral communication skills, organizational skills, self-motivation, written communication skills, proactive approach, interest and/or experience in the arts (highly recommended). Duration is 3 months. stipend. Open to college freshmen, college sophomores, college juniors, college seniors, recent college graduates, graduate students, career changers, individuals reentering the workforce. International applications accepted.

Benefits Names of contacts, on-the-job training, willing to act as a professional reference, willing to complete paperwork for educational credit, willing to provide letters of recommendation.

Contact Fax, e-mail, or through World Wide Web site Eugene Carr, President, 850 Seventh Avenue, Suite 703, New York 10019-5230. Fax: 212-271-0207. E-mail: business@culturefinder.com. No phone calls. In-person interview recommended (telephone interview accepted). Applicants must submit a letter of interest, resume. Application deadline: April 30 for summer, July 15 for fall, December 15 for spring. World Wide Web: http://www.culturefinder.com.

DACTYL FOUNDATION FOR THE ARTS AND HUMANITIES
64 Grand Street
New York, New York 10013

General Information Not-for-profit organization that offers opportunities and awards in the fields of visual arts, film, theory, music, poetry, and lectures. Established in 1996. Number of employees: 5. Number of internship applications received each year: 100.

Internships Available ▶ *4–10 gallery attendants:* responsibilities include working as gallery attendant, updating database, event planning, telephone work, and assisting the managing director in public relations, fund-raising, membership, and general operating support. Candidates should have computer skills, knowledge of field, office skills, oral communication skills, personal interest in the field, plan to pursue career in field, self-motivation, writing skills. Duration is flexible (year-round). Unpaid. Open to recent high school graduates, college freshmen, college sophomores, college juniors, college seniors, recent college graduates, graduate students. International applications accepted.

Benefits On-the-job training, willing to act as a professional reference, willing to complete paperwork for educational credit, willing to provide letters of recommendation.

Contact Through World Wide Web site Carmen Cruz, Internship Coordinator. Phone: 212-219-2344. Fax: 212-226-7320. E-mail: email@dactyl.org. Applicants must submit a formal organization application, letter of interest, resume. Application deadline: November/December for winter/spring positions, May for summer positions. World Wide Web: http://www.dactyl.org.

DAVID FINDLAY JR FINE ART
41 East 57th Street, Suite 1115
New York, New York 10022-1908

General Information American late 19th- and 20th-century painting and sculpture gallery. Established in 1870. Number of employees: 5. Number of internship applications received each year: 30.

Internships Available ▶ *1 summer intern:* responsibilities include working on projects involving aspects of the gallery's operations including administrative tasks, inventories, photographing paintings, catalog layout and research, organizing artist's files, researching master paintings, developing marketing programs for particular works, exhibitions, and scheduling. Candidates should have computer skills, oral communication skills, personal interest in the field, research skills, self-motivation, writing skills. Duration is one summer. Unpaid. Open to college freshmen, college sophomores, college juniors, college seniors, recent college graduates, graduate students, career changers.

Benefits Job counseling, names of contacts, willing to complete paperwork for educational credit, willing to provide letters of recommendation, paid lunch.

Contact Write, call, fax, or e-mail Katie Leonard, Gallery Manager. Phone: 212-486-7660. Fax: 212-980-2650. E-mail: gallery@findlayart.com. In-person interview required. Applicants must submit a letter of interest, resume. Applications are accepted continuously. World Wide Web: http://www.artnet.com/dfindlay.html.

THE DIRECTOR'S COMPANY
311 West 43rd Street, Suite 307
New York, New York 10036

General Information Theater that specializes in the development of the director. Established in 1980. Number of employees: 4. Number of internship applications received each year: 40.

Internships Available ▶ *2–3 interns:* responsibilities include performing general office duties and working on projects during rehearsals. Candidates should have ability to work with others, computer skills, experience in the field, self-motivation, writing skills. Duration is 3 months minimum. Position available as unpaid or paid. Open to high school seniors, recent high school graduates, college freshmen, college sophomores, college juniors, college seniors, recent college graduates, graduate students. International applications accepted.

The Director's Company (continued)

Benefits On-the-job training, opportunity to attend seminars/workshops, possible full-time employment, willing to complete paperwork for educational credit, willing to provide letters of recommendation.

Contact Write or fax Veronica Bainbridge, Internship Coordinator. Fax: 212-246-5882. No phone calls. In-person interview recommended (telephone interview accepted). Applicants must submit a letter of interest, resume. Applications are accepted continuously. World Wide Web: http://www.thedirectorscompany.org.

DISABLED SPORTS USA–FAR WEST
PO Box 9780
Truckee, California 96162

General Information Organization that provides high challenge sports to people with physical, cognitive, or developmental disabilities. Established in 1967. Number of employees: 50. Unit of Disabled Sports USA- Far West, Citrus Heights, California. Number of internship applications received each year: 20.

Internships Available ▶ *2 Tahoe Adaptive Ski School winter interns:* responsibilities include involvement in all aspects of an adaptive ski program; attending clinics; assisting and teaching lessons; working on outreach, fund-raising, and other administrative projects. Candidates should have ability to work independently, computer skills, oral communication skills, strong interpersonal skills, written communication skills, strong intermediate alpine skiing abilities. Duration is December to April (4 days per week). Unpaid. Open to college sophomores, college juniors, college seniors, recent college graduates, graduate students, career changers, individuals reentering the workforce. ▶ *1–3 program assistants for executive offices:* responsibilities include recreation program design and implementation/administration, client registration and follow-up, volunteer and equipment coordination. Candidates should have ability to work independently, ability to work with others, office skills, oral communication skills, organizational skills, written communication skills. Duration is June to August (3 to 4 days per week). Unpaid. Open to college sophomores, college juniors, college seniors, recent college graduates, graduate students, law students, career changers. ▶ *Summer interns:* responsibilities include leading and assisting with white water rafting, waterskiing, and the Donner Lake camp-outs summer programs. Candidates should have oral communication skills, organizational skills, strong interpersonal skills, strong leadership ability, background in camping, water-skiing, or rafting helpful. Duration is May to August (3 days per week). Unpaid. Open to college sophomores, college juniors, college seniors, recent college graduates, graduate students, career changers, individuals reentering the workforce.

Benefits Formal training, names of contacts, on-the-job training, opportunity to attend seminars/workshops, possible full-time employment, willing to act as a professional reference, willing to complete paperwork for educational credit, willing to provide letters of recommendation, skiing privileges, $100 per month stipend.

Contact Write, call, fax, or e-mail Haakon Lang-Ree, Program Director, PO Box 9780, Truckee, California 96162. Phone: 530-581-4161. Fax: 530-581-3127. E-mail: haakon@dsusafw.org. In-person interview recommended (telephone interview accepted). Applicants must submit a formal organization application, letter of interest, resume, three personal references, written response to 6 questions. Application deadline: April 15 for summer, October 31 for winter/spring. World Wide Web: http://www.dsusafw.org.

DISTRICT OF COLUMBIA JEWISH COMMUNITY CENTER (DCJCC)
1529 16th Street, NW
Washington, District of Columbia 20036

General Information Nonprofit Jewish community center, educational, cultural and exercise center. Number of employees: 250. Unit of Jewish Community Center Association.

Internships Available ▶ *1–4 camp interns:* responsibilities include some administrative work, some substitute work in classrooms. Candidates should have ability to work independently, computer skills, knowledge of field, office skills, oral communication skills, organizational skills, personal interest in the field, self-motivation, strong interpersonal skills, strong leadership ability, written communication skills, experience with children between 4-18 years old, flexibility, energy. Duration is flexible (June to August). Position available as unpaid or at $7.50–$10 per hour. Open to recent high school graduates, college freshmen, college sophomores, college juniors, college seniors, recent college graduates, graduate students, law students, career changers, individuals 18 years old and over. International applications accepted.

Benefits Names of contacts, on-the-job training, opportunity to attend seminars/workshops, possible full-time employment, willing to act as a professional reference, willing to provide letters of recommendation, JCC membership, 2 free meals per week.

Contact Write, fax, e-mail, or through World Wide Web site Stephanie Nanwin, Director, Center for Youth and Family and Acting Preschool Director. Fax: 202-518-9420. E-mail: stephanie@dcjcc.org. No phone calls. In-person interview recommended (telephone interview accepted). Applicants must submit a letter of interest, resume, 2-4 personal references. Application deadline: June 1. World Wide Web: http://www.dcjcc.org.

DOLPHIN DREAMS IMAGES
PMB 529 75-5629 Kuakini Highway, Suite R
Kailua-Kona, Hawaii 96740

General Information Underwater video and still photography production facility, Hawaiian Marine Life Research Organization, and scuba diving training organization. Established in 1991. Number of employees: 18. Number of internship applications received each year: 150.

Internships Available ▶ *6 logistics assistants:* responsibilities include insuring that all scuba and camera gear is delivered to and from designated location and ready for use. Candidates should have ability to work independently, analytical skills, organizational skills, self-motivation, strong interpersonal skills. Duration is 4–12 weeks. Unpaid. Open to high school students, recent high school graduates, college freshmen, college sophomores, college juniors, college seniors, recent college graduates, graduate students, law students, career changers, individuals reentering the workforce. ▶ *6 research assistants:* responsibilities include assisting by monitoring resident dolphins, green sea turtle, and manta ray populations and keeping accurate records. Candidates should have ability to work independently, ability to work with others, analytical skills, computer skills, office skills, organizational skills, research skills, self-motivation, written communication skills, willingness and ability to keep accurate records. Duration is 4–12 weeks. Unpaid. Open to high school seniors, recent high school graduates, college freshmen, college sophomores, college juniors, college seniors, recent college graduates, graduate students, law students, career changers, individuals reentering the workforce. ▶ *6 scuba diving assistants:* responsibilities include assisting underwater cameramen by delivering and/or carrying camera and lighting equipment (on scuba) and operating underwater vehicles. Candidates should have ability to work independently, ability to work with others, self-motivation, diving certification (preferred but will train). Duration is 4–12 weeks. Unpaid. Open to high school seniors, recent high school graduates, college freshmen, college sophomores, college juniors, college seniors, recent college graduates, graduate students, law students, career changers, individuals reentering the workforce. ▶ *6 video/photo editors:* responsibilities include linear and nonlinear video editing on PC and Macintosh, DVD production, photo editing, and all image duplication. Candidates should have ability to work independently, ability to work with others, computer skills, editing skills, organizational skills, self-motivation, must be "coachable". Duration is 4–12 weeks. Unpaid. Open to high school seniors, recent high school graduates, college freshmen, college sophomores, college juniors, college seniors, recent college graduates, graduate students, law students, career changers, individuals reentering the workforce. International applications accepted.

Benefits Formal training, housing at a cost, meals at a cost, on-the-job training, possible full-time employment, willing to act as a professional reference, willing to complete paperwork for educational credit, willing to provide letters of recommendation, scuba diving opportunities.

Contact E-mail or through World Wide Web site Martina Wedig-Wing, Owner. E-mail: internship@dolphindreams.com. No phone calls. Telephone interview required. Applicants must submit three personal references, completion of online application. Applications are accepted continuously. Fees: $25. World Wide Web: http://www.dolphindreams.com.

THE DRAWING CENTER
35 Wooster Street
New York, New York 10013

General Information Not-for-profit art institution focusing on the exhibition of drawings, both contemporary and historical, with an emphasis on providing opportunities for emerging and under-recognized artists. Established in 1977. Number of employees: 14. Number of internship applications received each year: 400.
Internships Available ▶ *10 art museum rotational interns:* responsibilities include rotating through several departments based on the interns' interests and needs of the institution, working with staff members on various special and ongoing projects, assisting with exhibition installations and de-installations, and handling daily operating tasks. Candidates should have ability to work independently, college courses in field, college degree in related field, computer skills, office skills, oral communication skills, organizational skills, self-motivation. Duration is September–December, January–April, or May–July (fifteen hours per week minimum). Position available as unpaid or at $6 to $11 per hour if student has work-study award through school; salary varies according to school work-study rates. Open to college sophomores, college juniors, college seniors, recent college graduates, graduate students. International applications accepted.
Benefits Job counseling, willing to act as a professional reference, willing to complete paperwork for educational credit, willing to provide letters of recommendation, opportunity to attend a variety of public programming including lectures, readings, and artists' talks; various professional development activities and resources including weekly meetings with staff members; possibility of stipend for summer positions.
Contact Write, call, fax, or e-mail Ms. Meryl Zwanger, Education Coordinator. Phone: 212-219-2166 Ext. 119. Fax: 212-966-2976. E-mail: merylzwanger@drawingcenter.org. In-person interview recommended (telephone interview accepted). Applicants must submit a formal organization application, resume, two personal references. Application deadline: April 15 for summer, August 15 for fall, December 15 for winter/spring. World Wide Web: http://www.drawingcenter.org.

EASTCOAST ENTERTAINMENT
8910-E Lenox Pointe Drive
Charlotte, North Carolina 28273

General Information Booking agency for entertainment and events. Established in 1976. Number of employees: 15. Branch of EastCoast Entertainment, Richmond, Virginia. Number of internship applications received each year: 50.
Internships Available ▶ *1–3 interns:* responsibilities include accumulating information for updating records, communicating with customers, faxing and e-mailing information, and working with promotional materials. Candidates should have ability to work independently, computer skills, office skills, oral communication skills, organizational skills, strong interpersonal skills, written communication skills. Duration is one quarter or semester. Unpaid. Open to high school students, recent high school graduates, college freshmen, college sophomores, college juniors, college seniors.
Benefits On-the-job training, willing to complete paperwork for educational credit, willing to provide letters of recommendation.
Contact Write or e-mail Sherry Callahan, Business Administrator. Fax: 704-339-0762. E-mail: ssigmon@eastcoastentertainment.com. No phone calls. Telephone interview required. Applicants must submit a resume. Applications are accepted continuously. World Wide Web: http://eastcoastentertainment.com.

ELITE MODEL MANAGEMENT, LOS ANGELES
345 North Maple Drive, Suite 397
Beverly Hills, California 90210

General Information Modeling agency for men and women including runway/fashion print. Established in 1985. Number of employees: 10. Affiliate of Elite Model Management, New York, New York. Number of internship applications received each year: 50.
Internships Available ▶ *2–3 assistants to model agents.* Candidates should have ability to work independently, ability to work with others, computer skills, oral communication skills, personal interest in the field, self-motivation. Unpaid. Open to recent high school graduates, college freshmen, college sophomores, college juniors, college seniors. International applications accepted.
Benefits Possible full-time employment, willing to act as a professional reference, willing to complete paperwork for educational credit, willing to provide letters of recommendation.
Contact Write or fax Intern Coordinator. Fax: 310-278-7520. E-mail: elitemodels@elitelosangeles.com. No phone calls. In-person interview required. Applicants must submit a letter of interest, resume. Applications are accepted continuously. World Wide Web: http://www.elitelosangeles.com.

EVEN SPACE PRODUCTIONS/PYRAMAXIS RECORDS
3200 La Rotonda Drive, Suite 114
Rancho Palos Verdes, California 90275

General Information Music publishing, production, artist development, and record company. Established in 1982. Number of employees: 4.
Internships Available ▶ *1 office manager:* responsibilities include daily operations and learning the areas of the music, entertainment business, and dealing with industry people contacts. Candidates should have analytical skills, computer skills, office skills, oral communication skills, organizational skills, personal interest in the field, research skills, self-motivation, strong interpersonal skills, strong leadership ability, written communication skills. Duration is flexible. Unpaid. Open to high school students, recent high school graduates, college freshmen, college sophomores, college juniors, college seniors, recent college graduates, graduate students, law students, career changers, individuals reentering the workforce. International applications accepted.
Benefits Free meals, names of contacts, on-the-job training, opportunity to attend seminars/workshops, possible full-time employment, travel reimbursement, willing to act as a professional reference, willing to complete paperwork for educational credit, willing to provide letters of recommendation.
Contact Write, call, fax, or e-mail Evan Pace, President, Rancho Palos Verdes. Phone: 310-544-5003. Fax: 310-514-0178. E-mail: evanpace@hotmail.com. In-person interview recommended (telephone interview accepted). Applicants must submit a formal organization application, letter of interest. Applications are accepted continuously.

FILM ROMAN, INC.
12020 Chandler Boulevard, Suite 300
North Hollywood, California 91607

General Information Animation studio responsible for working on the Simpsons, King of the Hill, X-Men, and Free for All. Number of employees: 300. Number of internship applications received each year: 75.
Internships Available ▶ *4–5 production assistants:* responsibilities include cut and pasting, copying, databasing, post-production, and helping production staff get a show ready to ship. Candidates should have ability to work independently, ability to work with others, college courses in field, computer skills, personal interest in the field, plan to pursue career in field, self-motivation. Duration is flexible. Unpaid. Open to college sophomores, college juniors, college seniors.

Film Roman, Inc. (continued)

Benefits Job counseling, opportunity to attend seminars/workshops, possible full-time employment, willing to complete paperwork for educational credit, willing to provide letters of recommendation.
Contact Write or e-mail Shelley McCully, Intern Coordinator. E-mail: shelleyg@filmroman.com. In-person interview recommended (telephone interview accepted). Applicants must submit a letter of interest, resume. Applications are accepted continuously. World Wide Web: http://www.filmroman.com.

FISHERMEN'S BEND RECREATION SITE
PO Box 785
Mill City, Oregon 97360

General Information Multiple resource management agency involved in the operation and maintenance of one multiple-use recreation site and four small recreation sites. Established in 1964. Number of employees: 8. Unit of Bureau of Land Management, Salem District, Salem, Oregon. Number of internship applications received each year: 2.
Internships Available ▶ *2–4 park rangers:* responsibilities include park maintenance and public relations. Candidates should have ability to work independently, ability to work with others, oral communication skills, personal interest in the field, self-motivation, willingness to work outdoors under variable conditions. Duration is 3–4 months. Position available as unpaid or at weekly subsistence pay of $100 per week. Open to recent high school graduates, college freshmen, college sophomores, college juniors, college seniors, recent college graduates, individuals reentering the workforce. International applications accepted.
Benefits Free housing, on-the-job training, opportunity to attend seminars/workshops, willing to complete paperwork for educational credit, willing to provide letters of recommendation, field trips.
Contact Write, call, fax, or e-mail J. B. Grant, Park Manager. Phone: 503-897-2406. Fax: 503-897-3098. E-mail: jgrant@or.blm. gov. Telephone interview required. Applicants must submit a resume, personal reference, letter of recommendation. Application deadline: January 1 for spring, March 1 for summer, July 1 for fall.

FRANKLIN FURNACE ARCHIVE, INC.
45 John Street, Suite 611
New York, New York 10038-3706

General Information Presenters of live art on the Internet. Established in 1976. Number of employees: 4. Number of internship applications received each year: 100.
Internships Available ▶ *Volunteers:* responsibilities include working with artists, fund-raising and development, administration, technical assistance, Web site maintenance and development, production assistance, and archiving/cataloging of artists' information. Candidates should have love of contemporary art. Duration is flexible. Unpaid. Open to high school students, recent high school graduates, college freshmen, college sophomores, college juniors, college seniors, recent college graduates, graduate students, law students, career changers, individuals reentering the workforce. International applications accepted.
Benefits Job counseling, names of contacts, on-the-job training, opportunity to attend seminars/workshops, possible full-time employment, willing to act as a professional reference, willing to complete paperwork for educational credit, willing to provide letters of recommendation.
Contact Write, call, fax, e-mail, or through World Wide Web site Harley Spiller, Internship Coordinator. Phone: 212-766-2606. Fax: 212-766-2740. E-mail: harley@franklinfurnace.org. Applicants must submit a letter of interest, resume, in-person interview recommended (telephone or e-mail interview acceptable). Applications are accepted continuously. World Wide Web: http://www.franklinfurnace.org.

FREDERICK COUNTY DEPARTMENT OF PARKS AND RECREATION
118 North Market Street
Frederick, Maryland 21701

General Information Parks and recreation department. Number of employees: 90. Division of Frederick County Government, Frederick, Maryland. Number of internship applications received each year: 10.
Internships Available ▶ *1 public relations intern:* responsibilities include development of parks and recreation brochure, program promotion, calendar of events development, and additional promotional activities using TV, radio and newspapers. Candidates should have ability to work independently, computer skills, knowledge of field, oral communication skills, organizational skills, written communication skills. Duration is 1 semester. Stipend of $1000 for every 400 hours worked. Open to high school students, recent high school graduates, college sophomores, college juniors, college seniors, recent college graduates, career changers, individuals reentering the workforce. ▶ *1 recreation and parks intern:* responsibilities include assisting administration with a focus on recreation programming and administration; some exposure to volunteer management, park management, historic site interpretation, and nature programming. Candidates should have computer skills, knowledge of field, organizational skills, personal interest in the field, self-motivation, strong interpersonal skills. Duration is 1 semester. Stipend of $1000 for every 400 hours worked. Open to high school students, recent high school graduates, college freshmen, college sophomores, college juniors, college seniors, career changers, individuals reentering the workforce.
Benefits On-the-job training, possible full-time employment, willing to act as a professional reference, willing to complete paperwork for educational credit, willing to provide letters of recommendation.
Contact Write, call, fax, or e-mail Jeremy Kortright, Recreation Superintendent. Phone: 301-696-2936. Fax: 301-694-2595. E-mail: parksandrecreation@fredco-md.net. In-person interview required. Applicants must submit a formal organization application, letter of interest, resume. Applications are accepted continuously. World Wide Web: http://www.co.frederick.md.us/govt/parks.

HADLEY'S PARK
6234 Montrose Road
Rockville, Maryland 20852

General Information Nonprofit organization dedicated to designing and building universally accessible playgrounds for children with and without disabilities. Established in 1996. Number of employees: 3. Number of internship applications received each year: 20.
Internships Available ▶ *1–2 development interns:* responsibilities include researching potential funders, writing proposals and letters of inquiry, aiding in mailings, some event planning, and miscellaneous office administration. Candidates should have ability to work independently, ability to work with others, editing skills, research skills, written communication skills. Duration is year-round. $7 per hour. ▶ *1–2 event coordinator interns:* responsibilities include following up phone calls, newsletter, organizing meetings, logistics for event, and aiding in mailings. Candidates should have computer skills, oral communication skills, organizational skills, strong interpersonal skills, writing skills. Duration is year-round. $7 per hour. Open to college juniors, college seniors, graduate students.
Benefits On-the-job training, opportunity to attend seminars/workshops, willing to act as a professional reference, willing to complete paperwork for educational credit, willing to provide letters of recommendation.
Contact Write, fax, or e-mail Danielle Milo, Development Director. Fax: 301-770-2265. E-mail: danielle@hadleyspark.org. No phone calls. In-person interview required. Applicants must submit a letter of interest, resume, two writing samples, three personal references. Applications are accepted continuously. World Wide Web: http://www.hadleyspark.org.

HEADLANDS CENTER FOR THE ARTS
Building 944, Fort Barry
Sausalito, California 94965

General Information   Interdisciplinary art center providing residencies across the country and abroad for artists from the Bay Area, and programs for the public, including art talks and open houses. Established in 1982. Number of employees: 12. Number of internship applications received each year: 50.
Internships Available   ▶ *2–4 interns:* responsibilities include performing administrative duties including slide library documentation, publicity, membership management, and events coordination; building duties, including research and construction; periodically assisting national and international artists-in-residence; processing residency applications. Candidates should have ability to work independently, ability to work with others, computer skills, office skills, organizational skills, plan to pursue career in field. Duration is flexible (typically 6 weeks). Unpaid. Open to college seniors, recent college graduates, graduate students. International applications accepted.
Benefits   Free housing, willing to complete paperwork for educational credit, willing to provide letters of recommendation, free attendance at all activities, readings, and art talks; opportunity to do work in exchange for meals.
Contact   Write, call, fax, or e-mail Ms. Holly Blake, Residency Manager. Phone: 415-331-2787 Ext. 24. Fax: 415-331-3857. E-mail: hblake@headlands.org. In-person interview recommended (telephone interview accepted). Applicants must submit a letter of interest, resume. Application deadline: March 1. World Wide Web: http://www.headlands.org.

HENSEL ECKMAN YMCA
615 Oakhurst Avenue
Pulaski, Virginia 24301

General Information   Association that provides the best in fitness, child development, and aquatics. Established in 1947. Number of employees: 25. Affiliate of YMCA of the USA, Chicago, Illinois. Number of internship applications received each year: 10.
Internships Available   ▶ *3–8 aquatic assistants:* responsibilities include lifeguarding, cleaning pool, teaching swim lessons, and leading water aerobics. Candidates should have ability to work independently, ability to work with others, organizational skills, self-motivation, strong leadership ability. Duration is flexible. Unpaid. Open to high school students, recent high school graduates, college sophomores, college juniors, college seniors, recent college graduates, graduate students, career changers, individuals reentering the workforce. ▶ *3–8 child development assistant teachers:* responsibilities include teaching and supervising children. Candidates should have ability to work independently, ability to work with others, oral communication skills, organizational skills, self-motivation, strong leadership ability. Duration is flexible. Unpaid. Open to high school seniors, recent high school graduates, college freshmen, college sophomores, college juniors, college seniors, recent college graduates, graduate students, career changers, individuals reentering the workforce. ▶ *3–10 fitness assistants:* responsibilities include assisting with fitness evaluations, assessments, exercise classes; keeping equipment in good condition. Candidates should have ability to work independently, ability to work with others, organizational skills, self-motivation, strong leadership ability. Duration is flexible. Unpaid. Open to high school students, recent high school graduates, college freshmen, college sophomores, college juniors, college seniors, recent college graduates, graduate students, career changers, individuals reentering the workforce. International applications accepted.
Benefits   Formal training, job counseling, names of contacts, on-the-job training, opportunity to attend seminars/workshops, possible full-time employment, willing to act as a professional reference, willing to complete paperwork for educational credit, willing to provide letters of recommendation.
Contact   Write, call, fax, or e-mail Jerry Duncan, Program Director. Phone: 540-980-3671. Fax: 540-980-7422. E-mail: pulaski6@i-plus. net. In-person interview recommended (telephone interview accepted). Applicants must submit a letter of interest, resume, three personal references. Applications are accepted continuously. World Wide Web: http://www.i-plus.net/~pulaski6/.

HERSHEY PARK
100 West Hersheypark Drive
Hershey, Pennsylvania 17033

General Information   Amusement park. Number of employees: 3,760. Unit of Hershey Entertainment and Resorts Company, Hershey, Pennsylvania.
Internships Available   ▶ *Interns:* responsibilities include positions in various areas including: criminology, culinary/food service, business, recreation/sports medicine, hospitality management, human resources/training and development, marketing/public relations, information technology. Duration is 3 months. $7–$9 per hour. Open to college juniors, college seniors, graduate students.
Contact   Call or through World Wide Web site Internship Coordinator. Phone: 717-520-JOBS. Applicants must submit materials as specified on Web site. Applications are accepted continuously. World Wide Web: http://www.hersheypa.com.

HI FREQUENCY
103 Bayard Street, 3rd Floor
New Brunswick, New Jersey 08901

General Information   Entertainment, marketing, and promotions company that works with music, movies, and entertainment industries. Established in 1995. Number of internship applications received each year: 1,200.
Internships Available   ▶ *Entertainment marketing field representatives:* responsibilities include grassroots marketing to build an interest in new music, movies, and products in locations across the country. Candidates should have ability to work independently, computer skills, oral communication skills, personal interest in the field, self-motivation, written communication skills. Duration is minimum of 3 months (8-10 hours per week). Unpaid. Open to recent high school graduates, college freshmen, college sophomores, college juniors, college seniors, recent college graduates, graduate students, career changers, individuals reentering the workforce.
Benefits   Willing to act as a professional reference, willing to complete paperwork for educational credit, willing to provide letters of recommendation, free CDs, tickets for concerts and consumer goods.
Contact   Through World Wide Web site Internship Coordinator. No phone calls. Applicants must submit online application. Applications are accepted continuously. World Wide Web: http://www.findyourfrequency.com.

HIGHLANDER ELITE FITNESS AND RACQUET CLUB
13825 West Burleigh Road
Brookfield, Wisconsin 53005

General Information   Multi-purpose health club. Established in 1986. Number of employees: 125. Number of internship applications received each year: 20.
Internships Available   ▶ *2–3 fitness specialists:* responsibilities include fitness testing, exercise orientations, and assisting in group programming. Candidates should have ability to work independently, college degree in related field, oral communication skills, personal interest in the field, self-motivation, strong interpersonal skills. Duration is 2–3 months (40 hours per week). $400 per month. Open to college seniors. International applications accepted.
Benefits   On-the-job training, possible full-time employment, willing to complete paperwork for educational credit, willing to provide letters of recommendation.
Contact   Write, call, fax, or e-mail Tony Bieri, Fitness Director. Phone: 262-786-0880. Fax: 262-786-9619. E-mail: eliteclubs@voyager. net. In-person interview recommended (telephone interview accepted). Applicants must submit a resume, 1–2 letters of recommendation. Application deadline: March 1 for summer, November 1 for spring.

HORNBLOWER CRUISES AND EVENTS
Pier 3 on The Embarcadero
San Francisco, California 94111

General Information Dining cruise company. Established in 1981. Number of employees: 200. Number of internship applications received each year: 100.

Internships Available ▶ *1–2 marketing interns:* responsibilities include marketing communication between satellite offices and the corporate office, as well as day-to-day support functions. Candidates should have ability to work with others, computer skills, office skills, oral communication skills, organizational skills, personal interest in the field, self-motivation, writing skills. Duration is flexible. Unpaid. Open to high school seniors, recent high school graduates, college freshmen, college sophomores, college juniors, college seniors, recent college graduates. International applications accepted.

Benefits On-the-job training, possible full-time employment, willing to act as a professional reference, willing to complete paperwork for educational credit, willing to provide letters of recommendation.

Contact Fax or e-mail Mary Anne Kazemi, Human Resources Manager. Phone: 415-788-8866. Fax: 415-394-8444. E-mail: mkazemi@hornblower.com. In-person interview required. Applicants must submit a formal organization application, letter of interest, resume. Applications are accepted continuously. World Wide Web: http://www.hornblower.com.

HURRICANE ISLAND OUTWARD BOUND SCHOOL–SOUTHERN PROGRAMS
177 Salem Court
Tallahassee, Florida 32301

General Information Wilderness-based counseling. Established in 1964. Number of employees: 200. Unit of Hurricane Island Outward Bound School, Rockland, Maine. Number of internship applications received each year: 100.

Internships Available ▶ *40–60 adolescent instructor practicums:* responsibilities include working within team to facilitate wilderness expeditions and complete treatment plans with students. Candidates should have ability to work independently, oral communication skills, plan to pursue career in field, strong interpersonal skills, written communication skills, wilderness skills. Duration is approximately 3 months. $15–$35 per day depending on experience. Open to college seniors, recent college graduates, graduate students, law students, career changers, individuals reentering the workforce, must be over 21 years of age.

Benefits Formal training, free housing, free meals, job counseling, on-the-job training, opportunity to attend seminars/workshops, possible full-time employment, travel reimbursement, willing to act as a professional reference, willing to complete paperwork for educational credit, willing to provide letters of recommendation, propurchase program.

Contact Write, call, fax, e-mail, or through World Wide Web site Alyse Ostreicher, Staff Developer. Phone: 850-487-4365. Fax: 850-922-6721. E-mail: flrecruit@hurricaneisland.org. Telephone interview required. Applicants must submit a formal organization application, letter of interest, resume, wilderness resume (if applicable), total of 3 personal references/letters of recommendation. Applications are accepted continuously. World Wide Web: http://www.members.tripod.com/outward.bound.

INDEPENDENT CURATORS INTERNATIONAL (ICI)
799 Broadway, Suite 205
New York, New York 10003

General Information International, nonprofit traveling exhibit service specializing in contemporary art. Established in 1975. Number of employees: 10. Number of internship applications received each year: 50.

Internships Available ▶ *1 development intern:* responsibilities include assisting in planning benefit dinner and donor events; researching individual, foundation, and corporate prospects; and preparing grant applications and other proposals. Candidates should have ability to work independently, computer skills, office skills, organizational skills, strong interpersonal skills, written communication skills, interest in field of contemporary art. Duration is 8–12 weeks. Unpaid. Open to college sophomores, college juniors, college seniors, recent college graduates, graduate students, law students, career changers. ▶ *1–2 exhibitions interns:* responsibilities include assisting with maintenance of files and records; preparing checklists, condition reports, installation instructions, and catalog information; and collecting and maintaining visual materials. Candidates should have ability to work independently, computer skills, knowledge of field, office skills, oral communication skills, organizational skills, interest in field of contemporary art. Duration is minimum of 3 months (minimum of 15 hours per week). Unpaid. Open to college sophomores, college juniors, college seniors, recent college graduates, graduate students, career changers. ▶ *1 registration intern:* responsibilities include assisting with maintenance of files and records; preparation of registration forms and installation instructions. Candidates should have ability to work independently, ability to work with others, computer skills, knowledge of field, office skills, oral communication skills, organizational skills, written communication skills, interest in field of contemporary art. Duration is minimum of 3 months (minimum of 15 hours per week). Unpaid. Open to college sophomores, college juniors, college seniors, recent college graduates, graduate students, career changers. International applications accepted.

Benefits Willing to complete paperwork for educational credit, willing to provide letters of recommendation, possibility of stipend, reimbursement of local travel expenses.

Contact Write, fax, e-mail, or through World Wide Web site Sue Scott, Executive Assistant. Fax: 212-477-4781. E-mail: info@ici-exhibitions.org. No phone calls. In-person interview recommended (telephone interview accepted). Applicants must submit a letter of interest, resume, letter of recommendation. Applications are accepted continuously. World Wide Web: http://www.ici-exhibitions.org.

THE INSTITUTE FOR UNPOPULAR CULTURE
PMB 1523, 1850 Union Street
San Francisco, California 94123

General Information Nonprofit organization devoted to fostering and promoting obscure, subversive art and music. Established in 1989. Number of employees: 5. Number of internship applications received each year: 30.

Internships Available ▶ *5–10 interns:* responsibilities include various clerical duties, writing, graphic design and layout, fundraising, research, and use of numerous computer programs; internships designed to meet interests of individual intern. Candidates should have ability to work independently, office skills, personal interest in the field, research skills, self-motivation, writing skills. Duration is flexible. Unpaid. Open to college freshmen, college sophomores, college juniors, college seniors, recent college graduates, graduate students, law students, career changers, individuals reentering the workforce. International applications accepted.

Benefits Job counseling, names of contacts, on-the-job training, opportunity to attend seminars/workshops, possible full-time employment, willing to act as a professional reference, willing to complete paperwork for educational credit, willing to provide letters of recommendation.

Contact Write, call, fax, e-mail, or through World Wide Web site David Ferguson, Executive Director. Phone: 415-986-4382. Fax: 415-986-4354. E-mail: ifuc2002@hotmail.com. Telephone interview required. Applicants must submit a letter of interest, resume. Applications are accepted continuously. World Wide Web: http://www.ifuc.org.

INTERNATIONAL ARTS AND ARTISTS
3061 M Street, NW, 2nd Floor
Washington, District of Columbia 20007

General Information Nonprofit arts management services organization. Established in 1995. Number of employees: 14. Number of internship applications received each year: 250.

Internships Available ▶ *1–2 design department interns:* responsibilities include project work, maintenance of Web site, and assisting designer on catalogues/publications/brochures. Candidates should have ability to work with others, computer skills, declared college major in field, experience in the field, oral communication skills, written communication skills. Duration is 3–12 months. Unpaid. Open to college freshmen, college sophomores, college juniors, college seniors, recent college graduates, graduate students, career changers, individuals reentering the workforce. ▶ *1–2 education department interns.* Candidates should have ability to work independently, ability to work with others, computer skills, oral communication skills, personal interest in the field, written communication skills. Duration is 3–12 months. Unpaid. Open to recent high school graduates, college freshmen, college sophomores, college juniors, college seniors, recent college graduates, graduate students, career changers, individuals reentering the workforce. ▶ *1 fund-raising and arts management intern:* responsibilities include grant writing, fund-raising, assisting the President, and research. Candidates should have ability to work independently, experience in the field, office skills, oral communication skills, organizational skills, written communication skills. Duration is 3–12 months. Unpaid. Open to recent high school graduates, college freshmen, college sophomores, college juniors, college seniors, recent college graduates, graduate students, career changers, individuals reentering the workforce. ▶ *1–3 marketing and exhibition development interns:* responsibilities include marketing, research, press releases, creative writing, and project management. Candidates should have ability to work with others, editing skills, experience in the field, oral communication skills, writing skills. Duration is 3–12 months. Unpaid. Open to high school seniors, recent high school graduates, college sophomores, college juniors, college seniors, recent college graduates, graduate students, career changers, individuals reentering the workforce. International applications accepted.

Benefits Names of contacts, on-the-job training, opportunity to attend seminars/workshops, possible full-time employment, willing to act as a professional reference, willing to complete paperwork for educational credit, willing to provide letters of recommendation.

Contact Write, call, fax, e-mail, or through World Wide Web site Elaine Yan, Internship Program Manager. Phone: 202-338-0680. Fax: 202-333-0758. E-mail: elainey@artsandartists.org. In-person interview recommended (telephone interview accepted). Applicants must submit a formal organization application, letter of interest, resume, academic transcripts, portfolio, writing sample, personal reference, 1 or 2 letters of recommendation. Applications are accepted continuously. World Wide Web: http://www.artsandartists.org.

INTERNATIONAL SCULPTURE CENTER
14 Fairgrounds Road, Suite B
Hamilton, New Jersey 08619-3447

General Information Nonprofit arts service organization. Established in 1960. Number of employees: 7. Number of internship applications received each year: 5.

Internships Available ▶ *10 arts administrator assistants:* responsibilities include assisting in administrative management, marketing, and promotion of public programs; research on the Internet; assisting in clerical and grantwriting projects. Candidates should have ability to work independently, ability to work with others, office skills, oral communication skills, personal interest in the field, self-motivation, written communication skills. Duration is flexible. Unpaid. Open to recent high school graduates, college freshmen, college sophomores, college juniors, college seniors, recent college graduates, graduate students, career changers, individuals reentering the workforce. ▶ *5 researchers/writers for Web site:* responsibilities include assisting in identification and preparation of text and images for award-winning art Web site. Candidates should have ability to work independently, ability to work with others, college courses in field, computer skills, editing skills, organizational skills, research skills, self-motivation, writing skills, interest in art (preferred). Duration is flexible. Unpaid. Open to college freshmen, college sophomores, college juniors, college seniors, recent college graduates, graduate students, career changers, individuals reentering the workforce. International applications accepted.

Benefits Opportunity to attend seminars/workshops, willing to act as a professional reference, willing to complete paperwork for educational credit, willing to provide letters of recommendation, attendance at local art events.

Contact Write, fax, or e-mail Carol Sterling, Director of Education. Fax: 609-689-1061. E-mail: carol@sculpture.org. No phone calls. In-person interview recommended (telephone interview accepted). Applicants must submit a letter of interest, resume, writing sample, 1-2 personal references. Applications are accepted continuously. World Wide Web: http://www.sculpture.org.

J. E. JASEN STUDIO
36 East Tenth Street
New York, New York 10003-6219

General Information Studio that designs and produces enamel art objects. Established in 1979. Number of internship applications received each year: 20.

Internships Available ▶ *1 art studio intern:* responsibilities include working in studio. Candidates should have knowledge of field, oral communication skills, personal interest in the field, self-motivation. Unpaid. Open to recent high school graduates, college freshmen, college sophomores, college juniors, college seniors, recent college graduates, graduate students, career changers, individuals reentering the workforce. International applications accepted.

Benefits On-the-job training, opportunity to attend seminars/workshops, willing to act as a professional reference, willing to complete paperwork for educational credit, willing to provide letters of recommendation.

Contact Write, call, or fax Ms. June Jasen, Owner. Phone: 212-674-6113. Fax: 212-777-6375. In-person interview recommended (telephone interview accepted). Applicants must submit a letter of interest, resume, portfolio. Applications are accepted continuously.

JONATHAN SLAFF AND ASSOCIATES
55 Perry Street
New York, New York 10014

General Information Editorial press representative for cultural institutions, domestic and foreign government agencies, professional theater and dance companies, fund-raising events, and civic events in NYC and vicinity.

Internships Available ▶ *1 theatrical public relations intern:* responsibilities include working with up to twelve professional theater groups at high management level. Duration is 1–2 semesters. Unpaid. Open to college freshmen, college sophomores, college juniors, college seniors, graduate students.

Benefits On-the-job training, opportunity to attend seminars/workshops, willing to act as a professional reference, willing to complete paperwork for educational credit, willing to provide letters of recommendation.

Contact E-mail Internship Coordinator. E-mail: printernship@jsnyc.com. Applicants must submit a resume, writing sample. Applications are accepted continuously. World Wide Web: http://www.jsnyc.com.

JON SIMS CENTER FOR THE ARTS
1519 Mission Street
San Francisco, California 94103

General Information Arts organization. Established in 1978. Number of employees: 5. Number of internship applications received each year: 10.

Internships Available ▶ *1–4 administrative assistants:* responsibilities include database management, graphics and publicity, public relations, general office support, marketing outreach, publicity distribution, e-mail list management, box office reservations. Candidates should have ability to work independently, computer skills, self-motivation, strong interpersonal skills, written communication skills. Duration is 1 semester. Unpaid. ▶ *1–4 program assistants:* responsibilities include assisting with set-up, box office, house management, light board or sound operation, strike and post-performance discussion; opportunities to get experience in theatrical production and to work with individual artists in technical design and implementation. Candidates should have computer

Jon Sims Center for the Arts (continued)

skills, organizational skills, self-motivation, strong interpersonal skills, written communication skills. Duration is 1 semester. Unpaid. Open to college freshmen, college sophomores, college juniors, college seniors, recent college graduates, graduate students, career changers, individuals reentering the workforce. International applications accepted.

Benefits On-the-job training, opportunity to attend seminars/workshops, willing to act as a professional reference, willing to complete paperwork for educational credit, willing to provide letters of recommendation.

Contact Write, call, fax, or e-mail Charles Wilmoth, Executive Director. Phone: 415-554-0402. Fax: 415-621-4637. E-mail: director@jonsimsctr.org. Applicants must submit a formal organization application, letter of interest, resume. Applications are accepted continuously. World Wide Web: http://www.jonsimsctr.org.

KENTUCKY STATE PARKS, DIVISION OF RECREATION & INTERPRETATION
Capitol Plaza Tower, 11th Floor, 500 Mero Street
Frankfort, Kentucky 40601

General Information Provider of recreational and leisure opportunities for visitors to the commonwealth while protecting and promoting historical, cultural, and natural resources. Established in 1924. Number of employees: 200. Department of Tourism Development Cabinet, Frankfort, Kentucky. Number of internship applications received each year: 12.

Internships Available ▶ *8–12 naturalists:* responsibilities include planning, organizing, implementing, and evaluating interpretive programs; inspecting and maintaining hiking trails; researching new and various trends in the field of recreation and interpretation; other projects as assigned. Candidates should have ability to work independently, college courses in field, computer skills, knowledge of field, oral communication skills, organizational skills, personal interest in the field, plan to pursue career in field, research skills, self-motivation, strong interpersonal skills, strong leadership ability, writing skills, minimum 2.25 GPA at time of application, valid driver's license. Duration is minimum of 20 hours per week. Position available as unpaid or at $5.50 per hour. ▶ *15–24 recreation leaders:* responsibilities include planning, organizing, implementing, and evaluating recreational and interpretive programs for park visitors; researching new and various trends in the field of parks and recreation; inspection of various recreational facilities, and special projects as assigned. Candidates should have ability to work independently, college courses in field, computer skills, office skills, oral communication skills, organizational skills, personal interest in the field, plan to pursue career in field, research skills, self-motivation, strong interpersonal skills, strong leadership ability, writing skills, minimum 2.25 GPA at time of application, valid driver's license. Duration is minimum of 20 hours per week. Position available as unpaid or at $5.50 per hour. Open to college juniors, college seniors, graduate students, college sophomores who are registered for junior year.

Benefits Formal training, meals at a cost, names of contacts, on-the-job training, opportunity to attend seminars/workshops, possible full-time employment, willing to act as a professional reference, willing to complete paperwork for educational credit, willing to provide letters of recommendation.

Contact Write, call, fax, e-mail, or through World Wide Web site Cynthia Howard-Cottongim, Assistant Recreation Director, Capitol Plaza Tower, 11th Floor, 500 Mero Street. Phone: 502-564-2172 Ext. 223. Fax: 502-564-9015. E-mail: cynthia.howard-cottongim@mail.state.ky.us. In-person interview recommended (telephone interview accepted). Applicants must submit a formal organization application, letter of interest, resume, academic transcripts, two personal references, two letters of recommendation, division application and work agreement. Application deadline: March 1 for summer, July 1 for fall, November 1 for spring. World Wide Web: http://www.kystateparks.com.

LOCHEARN CAMP FOR GIRLS
Lake Fairlee
Post Mills, Vermont 05058

General Information Girls residential summer camp. Established in 1916. Number of employees: 80. Number of internship applications received each year: 10.

Internships Available ▶ *Interns:* responsibilities include serving as cabin counselors and activity instructors in land and water sports, fine and performing arts, English riding, and outdoor adventure; activity staff write and implement daily lesson plans combining skill acquisition and character development; senior staff positions as leadership trainers, division heads, and program coordinators. Candidates should have organizational skills, personal interest in the field, strong interpersonal skills, strong leadership ability, well versed in area(s) of instruction, prepared to follow lesson plans to promote active learning, strong activity skills, enthusiasm and compassion, prior teaching experience not required. Duration is June-August. $1700–$2800 per duration of internship. Open to college freshmen, college sophomores, college juniors, college seniors, recent college graduates, graduate students, students earning academic credit are welcome. International applications accepted.

Benefits Formal training, free housing, free meals, on-the-job training, willing to act as a professional reference, willing to complete paperwork for educational credit, willing to provide letters of recommendation, travel allowance.

Contact Write, call, fax, or e-mail Ginny Maxson, Co-Director, Post Mills, Vermont 05058. Phone: 802-333-4211. Fax: 802-333-4856. E-mail: lochearn@comcast.net. Telephone interview required. Applicants must submit a formal organization application, three personal references, three letters of recommendation. Applications are accepted continuously.

LOS ANGELES MUNICIPAL ART GALLERY
433 South Spring Street, 10th Floor
Los Angeles, California 90013-2012

General Information City-run gallery supporting the southern California art community and its artists. Established in 1971. Number of employees: 30. Division of Cultural Affairs Department, Los Angeles, California. Number of internship applications received each year: 30.

Internships Available ▶ *3–5 education interns:* responsibilities include working as gallery educators while evaluating and exploring the potential of art galleries and museums as educational sources. Candidates should have ability to work independently, college courses in field, computer skills, oral communication skills, personal interest in the field, research skills, self-motivation, strong interpersonal skills, writing skills. Duration is 3–4 months. Unpaid. Open to college freshmen, college sophomores, college juniors, college seniors, recent college graduates, graduate students, career changers, individuals reentering the workforce, college graduates who are interested in museum education. International applications accepted.

Benefits Names of contacts, opportunity to attend seminars/workshops, willing to act as a professional reference, willing to complete paperwork for educational credit, willing to provide letters of recommendation, formal training in museum education.

Contact Write, call, fax, or e-mail Laurel Granger, Education Coordinator, 433 South Spring Street, 10th Floor, Los Angeles, California 90013. Phone: 213-473-8436. Fax: 213-473-8527. E-mail: lgranger@cad.lacity.org. In-person interview recommended (telephone interview accepted). Applicants must submit a formal organization application, letter of interest, resume. Application deadline: May 1 for summer, August 1 for fall, December 1 for spring.

MAGNUM PHOTOS, INC.
151 West 25th Street, 5th Floor
New York, New York 10001

General Information Cooperative photo agency with active editorial, archive, corporate, and advertising departments; archive contains over 1 million pictures representing 55 photographers. Established in 1947. Number of employees: 30.

Internships Available ▶ *1–6 interns:* responsibilities include working in department on different projects, assisting in production, taking part in basic office duties, and performing some computer work, editing, and archive research. Candidates should have ability to work independently, ability to work with others, office skills, organizational skills, plan to pursue career in field, research skills, self-motivation, writing skills. Duration is 3–4 months. Unpaid. Open to recent high school graduates, college freshmen, college sophomores, college juniors, college seniors, recent college graduates, graduate students, career changers, individuals reentering the workforce. International applications accepted.
Benefits Possible full-time employment, willing to complete paperwork for educational credit, willing to provide letters of recommendation.
Contact Write, call, fax, or e-mail Vanessa Churchill, Intern Coordinator. Phone: 212-929-6000. Fax: 212-929-9325. E-mail: vanessa@magnumphotos.com. In-person interview recommended (telephone interview accepted). Applicants must submit a letter of interest, resume, letter of recommendation. Applications are accepted continuously. World Wide Web: http://www. magnumphotos.com.

MANUS & ASSOCIATES LITERARY AGENCY
375 Forest Avenue
Palo Alto, California 94301

General Information Literary agency representing authors to publishing houses, TV/movie producers, or studios/networks. Established in 1985. Number of employees: 10. Number of internship applications received each year: 100.
Internships Available ▶ *5–10 editorial interns:* responsibilities include reading and assessing manuscripts, correspondence with writers, and management of submissions database. Candidates should have editing skills, oral communication skills, self-motivation, writing skills, personal interest in field preferred. Duration is up to 1 year. Unpaid. Open to college sophomores, college juniors, college seniors, recent college graduates, graduate students, career changers.
Benefits Names of contacts, on-the-job training, willing to act as a professional reference, willing to complete paperwork for educational credit, willing to provide letters of recommendation.
Contact Write, fax, or e-mail Ms. Stephanie Lee, Internship Coordinator and Agent, 375 Forest Avenue, Palo Alto, California 94301. Fax: 650-470-5159. E-mail: manuslit@manuslit.com. No phone calls. In-person interview required. Applicants must submit a letter of interest, resume, evaluation of five 100-page manuscript excerpts (available from organization). Applications are accepted continuously. World Wide Web: http://www.manuslit.com.

MARCO ISLAND FILM FESTIVAL
601 Elkcam Circle, B-6
Marco Island, Florida 34145

General Information Film festival organizer. Established in 1997. Number of employees: 3. Number of internship applications received each year: 200.
Internships Available ▶ *1 assistant director/special events intern:* responsibilities include coordinating scheduling of all programs and parties; inviting panelists, interviewers, and celebrities for program; coordinating and posting daily program changes; assisting the director with all other necessary tasks. Candidates should have ability to work with others, computer skills, office skills, oral communication skills, written communication skills. Duration is negotiable. Unpaid. Open to college sophomores, college juniors, college seniors, recent college graduates, graduate students. ▶ *1 community relations/sponsorship intern:* responsibilities include assisting marketing/promotions director in special events, setting-up festival parties, stocking food and beverages for parties and hospitality, developing ongoing mailing campaign, and putting together sponsorship packages. Candidates should have ability to work with others, computer skills, editing skills, office skills, oral communication skills, organizational skills, research skills, self-motivation. Duration is negotiable. Unpaid. Open to college juniors, college seniors, recent college graduates. ▶ *1 graphic designer/marketing intern:* responsibilities include designing all festival print advertising, flyers, posters; layout of monthly newslet-

ters and festival programs; correspondence with Web site host to keep Web site current. Candidates should have ability to work independently, analytical skills, computer skills, office skills, oral communication skills, organizational skills, strong interpersonal skills, strong leadership ability, writing skills. Duration is negotiable. Unpaid. Open to college freshmen, college sophomores, college juniors, college seniors, recent college graduates, graduate students. International applications accepted.
Benefits Formal training, free housing, names of contacts, on-the-job training, willing to act as a professional reference, willing to complete paperwork for educational credit, willing to provide letters of recommendation.
Contact E-mail Patricia Berry, Executive Director. Phone: 239-642-3378. Fax: 239-394-1736. E-mail: info@marcoislandfilmfest.com. In-person interview recommended (telephone interview accepted). Applicants must submit a letter of interest, resume. Applications are accepted continuously. World Wide Web: http://www. marcosislandfilmfest.com.

MARYLAND ART PLACE
8 Market Place, Suite 100
Baltimore, Maryland 21202

General Information Nonprofit regional art center exhibiting the work of contemporary artists in all media. Established in 1981. Number of employees: 6. Number of internship applications received each year: 20.
Internships Available ▶ *6 programming/development interns:* responsibilities include assisting staff with programming, fundraising, installation of exhibitions; performing administrative duties and public relations work; archiving electronic database work; maintaining Web site and artist registry. Candidates should have ability to work independently, ability to work with others, computer skills, office skills, oral communication skills, organizational skills, personal interest in the field, research skills, self-motivation, writing skills. Duration is 1–3 semesters. Unpaid. Open to high school students, recent high school graduates, college freshmen, college sophomores, college juniors, college seniors, recent college graduates, graduate students, career changers, individuals reentering the workforce.
Benefits Formal training, on-the-job training, opportunity to attend seminars/workshops, possible full-time employment, willing to act as a professional reference, willing to complete paperwork for educational credit, willing to provide letters of recommendation, acquisition of marketable skills.
Contact Write, call, or e-mail Joy McClure, Registry Coordinator/ Program Coordinator. Phone: 410-962-8565. Fax: 410-244-8017. E-mail: jmcclure@mdartplace.org. In-person interview recommended (telephone interview accepted). Applicants must submit a letter of interest, resume, personal reference. Applications are accepted continuously. World Wide Web: http://www.mdartplace. org.

MICHAEL PEREZ GALLERY
49 Jobs Lane
Southampton, New York 11968

General Information Art gallery showing only the owner's work. Established in 1998. Number of employees: 2. Division of Apple Graphics and Advertising of Merrick, Inc., Merrick, New York. Number of internship applications received each year: 40.
Internships Available ▶ *3–5 gallery assistants:* responsibilities include interacting with clients, selling art, organizing, answering questions, answering the telephone, and credit card sales. Candidates should have ability to work independently, oral communication skills, personal interest in the field, self-motivation, strong interpersonal skills, strong leadership ability, reliability, timeliness, and honesty. Duration is flexible (April to November). Position available as unpaid or at 5% commission on each piece an intern sells. Open to high school students, recent high school graduates, college freshmen, college sophomores, college juniors, college seniors, recent college graduates, graduate students, law school graduates, career changers, individuals reentering the workforce.

Michael Perez Gallery (continued)

Benefits On-the-job training, possible full-time employment, willing to act as a professional reference, willing to complete paperwork for educational credit, willing to provide letters of recommendation.
Contact Write or e-mail Allison Schneider, Partner, 8 Merrick Avenue, Merrick, New York 11566. E-mail: mperezgallery@aol.com. No phone calls. In-person interview recommended (telephone interview accepted). Applicants must submit a letter of interest, resume, photograph. Applications are accepted continuously. World Wide Web: http://www.michaelperez-artist.com.

MOSAIC MEDIA GROUP
9200 Sunset Boulevard, Suite 1000
Los Angeles, California 90069

General Information Entertainment company specializing in talent management, music management, and film production. Established in 1999. Number of employees: 80. Number of internship applications received each year: 200.
Internships Available ▶ *6–10 interns:* responsibilities include assisting with script reading/coverage, promoting bands, setting up shows, and clerical duties. Candidates should have oral communication skills, personal interest in the field, plan to pursue career in field, self-motivation. Duration is 1 semester. Unpaid. Open to college freshmen, college sophomores, college juniors, college seniors, graduate students, law students, must be receiving academic credit.
Benefits Opportunity to attend seminars/workshops, possible full-time employment, willing to act as a professional reference, willing to complete paperwork for educational credit, willing to provide letters of recommendation.
Contact Fax or e-mail Erin Smith, Internship Coordinator. Fax: 310-777-2103. E-mail: erin@mosaicla.com. No phone calls. In-person interview recommended (telephone interview accepted). Applicants must submit a letter of interest, resume. Applications are accepted continuously.

NATIONAL SCULPTURE SOCIETY
237 Park Avenue
New York, New York 10017

General Information Not-for-profit arts organization. Established in 1893. Number of employees: 4. Number of internship applications received each year: 12.
Internships Available ▶ *1–3 Geffken Educational Intern:* responsibilities include working in the areas of history of American sculpture/archival restoration, publishing, and arts administration. Candidates should have ability to work with others, computer skills, office skills, plan to pursue career in field, self-motivation, interest in arts administration, art history, and/or American sculpture. Duration is 3 months to 1 year (at least 16 hours per week). Stipend varies with intern's time commitment. Open to recent college graduates, graduate students, career changers. International applications accepted.
Benefits On-the-job training, opportunity to attend seminars/workshops, travel reimbursement, willing to act as a professional reference, willing to complete paperwork for educational credit, willing to provide letters of recommendation.
Contact Write, fax, e-mail, or through World Wide Web site Gwen Pier, Executive Director. Fax: 212-764-5651. E-mail: nss1893@aol.com. No phone calls. In-person interview required. Applicants must submit a letter of interest, resume. Application deadline: January 15 for January to May, May 15 for summer, August 15 for fall. World Wide Web: http://www.nationalsculpture.com.

NAXOS OF AMERICA, INC.
416 Mary Lindsay Polk Drive, #509
Franklin, Tennessee 37067

General Information Record label and music distribution company. Established in 1987. Number of employees: 40. Subsidiary of HNH International, Hong Kong, China. Number of internship applications received each year: 30.
Internships Available ▶ *1 advertising/design assistants:* responsibilities include assisting marketing manager and design coordinator with daily activities including placement and creation of advertising, publicity, writing and inputting copy, coordination of promotional campaigns, image research, design layout, processing artwork requests, product development, creation of merchandising, and general office duties. Candidates should have ability to work independently, self-motivation, graphic design experience, familiarity with PhotoShop and Quark, good typing skills, creative thinking skills, attention to deadlines, knowledge of classical music (a strong plus). Duration is flexible. Unpaid. ▶ *1 assistant to the Label Manager:* responsibilities include assisting label manager daily with activities of running record label, including A & R submissions, research, correspondence, organization, supervising marketing teams/activities, filing creative press kits and bios. Candidates should have ability to work independently, organizational skills, research skills, self-motivation, strong interpersonal skills, writing skills, Internet experience, good phone manner, multitasking, and interest in other cultures, (love of world music, knowledge of other languages/cultures a plus). Duration is one or multiple semesters (flexible days/hours). Position available as unpaid or paid. ▶ *3 licensing administration assistants:* responsibilities include contacting song publishers, data entry, and calculating mechanical royalties; assisting in creating song licenses, research, and general clerical duties. Candidates should have knowledge of field, strong computer skills in Word and Excel, desire to learn and gain experience in field. Duration is flexible. Unpaid. ▶ *2 marketing/world assistants:* responsibilities include assisting marketing manager with daily activities including placement of advertising, implementation of marketing campaigns, and general office activities; marketing Naxos World label, tracking marketing trends and campaign results, and market research. Candidates should have computer skills, organizational skills, desire to work hard, detail-orientation, good follow-up skills, creative thinking skills (a plus). Duration is flexible. Unpaid. ▶ *1 publicity intern:* responsibilities include compiling reviews on a weekly and quarterly basis, working on press mailings; generally assisting manager of publicity and promotions. Candidates should have personal interest in the field. Duration is flexible. Unpaid. Open to college freshmen, college sophomores, college juniors, college seniors, recent college graduates, graduate students. International applications accepted.
Benefits On-the-job training, possible full-time employment, willing to act as a professional reference, willing to complete paperwork for educational credit, willing to provide letters of recommendation.
Contact Write, fax, or e-mail Dolores Canavan, Label Manager. Phone: 615-771-9393 Ext. 25. Fax: 615-771-6747. E-mail: dcanavan@naxosusa.com. In-person interview recommended (telephone interview accepted). Applicants must submit a letter of interest, resume, writing sample, two personal references. Applications are accepted continuously. World Wide Web: http://www.naxosusa.com.

NEW DRAMATISTS
424 West 44th Street
New York, New York 10036

General Information Nonprofit workshop for playwrights dedicated to finding gifted playwrights and giving them time, space, and tools to develop their craft to fulfill their potential and make lasting contributions to the theater. Established in 1949. Number of employees: 7. Number of internship applications received each year: 100.
Internships Available ▶ *1 development/administrative intern:* responsibilities include assisting in fund-raising projects, grant proposal writing, and bookkeeping. Candidates should have ability to work independently, oral communication skills, self-motivation, strong interpersonal skills, written communication skills. Duration is 3 months (minimum). $25 per week. ▶ *2 literary management interns:* responsibilities include communicating directly with member playwrights and getting involved with ScriptShare (a national script distribution service) and International Playwrights Exchange Program. Candidates should have ability to work independently, oral communication skills, personal interest in the field, self-motivation, strong interpersonal skills, written communication skills. Duration is 3 months (minimum).

$25 per week. ▶ *2 stage management/directing interns:* responsibilities include managing more than one stage, setting up and planning auditions, assisting member playwrights in the smooth running of rehearsals and readings, and regulating all maintenance and behind-the-scenes activities. Candidates should have ability to work independently, oral communication skills, organizational skills, self-motivation, strong interpersonal skills, written communication skills. Duration is 3 months (minimum). $25 per week. Open to recent high school graduates, college freshmen, college sophomores, college juniors, college seniors, recent college graduates, graduate students, law students, career changers, individuals reentering the workforce. International applications accepted.
Benefits Willing to complete paperwork for educational credit, complimentary tickets to Broadway and off-Broadway productions.
Contact Write, call, fax, e-mail, or through World Wide Web site Ms. Melissa Kievman, Internship Coordinator. Phone: 212-757-6960 Ext. 20. Fax: 212-265-4738. E-mail: newdramatists@newdramatists.org. In-person interview required. Applicants must submit a letter of interest, resume, online application. Applications are accepted continuously. World Wide Web: http://www.newdramatists.org.

NEW YORK CITY PERCENT FOR ART PROGRAM
330 West 42nd Street, 14th Floor
New York, New York 10036

General Information Government art organization that commissions artwork for city-owned property. Established in 1982. Number of employees: 3. Unit of New York City Department of Cultural Affairs, New York, New York. Number of internship applications received each year: 60.
Internships Available ▶ *2 program assistants:* responsibilities include answering requests, processing artists' applications, assisting with research, and preparing correspondence and minutes of meetings. Candidates should have computer skills, office skills, oral communication skills, personal interest in the field, self-motivation, written communication skills. Duration is flexible (year-round). Unpaid. Open to college freshmen, college sophomores, college juniors, college seniors, recent college graduates, graduate students, career changers, individuals reentering the workforce. International applications accepted.
Benefits Job counseling, names of contacts, opportunity to attend seminars/workshops, travel reimbursement, willing to complete paperwork for educational credit, willing to provide letters of recommendation.
Contact Write, call, fax, or through World Wide Web site Cathie Behrend, Deputy Director. Phone: 212-643-7791. Fax: 212-643-7780. E-mail: cbehrend@culture.nyc.gov. In-person interview recommended (telephone interview accepted). Applicants must submit a letter of interest, resume. Applications are accepted continuously. World Wide Web: http://www.nyc.gov.

THE ORCHARD
133 5th Avenue, 4th Floor
New York, New York 10003

General Information Music distribution company that provides independent music content to every major interest store and traditional retail stores. Established in 1998. Number of employees: 10. Number of internship applications received each year: 250.
Internships Available ▶ *1–5 operations/content acquisition interns:* responsibilities include all aspects of operation including account processing, artwork scanning, data processing for artist Web pages, artist and label relation support, distribution purchase processing, and A&R research for new artists. Candidates should have computer skills, oral communication skills, personal interest in the field, research skills, self-motivation, strong interpersonal skills. Duration is flexible. Unpaid. Open to college sophomores, college juniors, college seniors, recent college graduates. International applications accepted.
Benefits Possible full-time employment, willing to complete paperwork for educational credit, willing to provide letters of recommendation.
Contact E-mail Andy Dushey, Director of Operations. Fax: 212-253-7614. E-mail: andyd@theorchard.com. No phone calls. In-person interview recommended (telephone interview accepted). Applicants

must submit a letter of interest, resume. Applications are accepted continuously. World Wide Web: http://www.theorchard.com.

PERA CLUB
PER 200, PO Box 52025
Phoenix, Arizona 85072

General Information Recreation facility for public utility company that provides park facility for programming, large scale special events, fitness, sports programs, private parties, business functions, and rental groups. Established in 1952. Number of employees: 60. Unit of Salt River Project, Tempe, Arizona. Number of internship applications received each year: 15.
Internships Available ▶ *1–2 coordinator interns:* responsibilities include working as a full-time staff member with the same responsibilities as coordinators (store, maintenance, fitness, office, booking, pool, and other operations). Candidates should have major in recreation (preferred). Duration is flexible. Minimum wage. Open to college freshmen, college sophomores, college juniors, college seniors, recent college graduates, graduate students.
Benefits Names of contacts, opportunity to attend seminars/workshops, willing to complete paperwork for educational credit, willing to provide letters of recommendation, use of facility (store, fitness center, pool).
Contact Write, call, or fax John Madden, Activities Supervisor. Phone: 602-236-2088. Fax: 602-236-5920. E-mail: jlmadden@srpnet.com. In-person interview recommended (telephone interview accepted). Applicants must submit a formal organization application, resume. Applications are accepted continuously.

PHOTOGRAPHY WEST GALLERY
PO Box 5306
Carmel, California 93921

General Information Fine art photography gallery that sells photography, posters, books, and notecards; publisher of 5 major photography books. Established in 1980. Number of employees: 5. Number of internship applications received each year: 20.
Internships Available ▶ *2 gallery interns:* responsibilities include talking to customers about photography, inventorying artwork, answering phones, restocking gallery, clerical work. Candidates should have college courses in field, knowledge of field, oral communication skills, personal interest in the field, strong interpersonal skills, written communication skills. Duration is 3–6 months. $8–$10 per hour. Open to recent high school graduates, college freshmen, college sophomores, college juniors, college seniors, recent college graduates, graduate students.
Benefits Names of contacts, on-the-job training, possible full-time employment, willing to act as a professional reference, willing to complete paperwork for educational credit, willing to provide letters of recommendation.
Contact Write, fax, e-mail, or through World Wide Web site Carol Williams, Owner. Fax: 831-625-1288. No phone calls. In-person interview recommended (telephone interview accepted). Applicants must submit a resume, three personal references. Applications are accepted continuously. World Wide Web: http://www.photographywest.com.

THE POETRY PROJECT
131 East 10th Street
New York, New York 10003

General Information Literary center with an arts program featuring readings, performances, workshops, and publications. Established in 1966. Number of employees: 11. Number of internship applications received each year: 35.
Internships Available ▶ *1–5 interns:* responsibilities include filing, researching archives, updating archives and documentation, assisting with market research, preparing and distributing publications, organizing tape and video archives, updating and mailing membership lists, and documenting ongoing programs and events. Candidates should have ability to work independently, ability to work with others, editing skills, office skills, plan to pursue career in field, research skills, self-motivation, writing skills, strong interest in contemporary poetry. Duration is 1–2 semesters. Unpaid. Open to high school students, recent high school graduates, col-

The Poetry Project (continued)
lege freshmen, college sophomores, college juniors, college seniors, recent college graduates, graduate students. International applications accepted.

Benefits Opportunity to attend seminars/workshops, willing to act as a professional reference, willing to complete paperwork for educational credit, willing to provide letters of recommendation, opportunity to attend literary events, use of research facilities, work-study points.

Contact Write, call, e-mail, or through World Wide Web site Ms. Maureen Owen, Program Coordinator. Phone: 212-674-0910. Fax: 212-529-2318. E-mail: poproj@poetryproject.com. In-person interview recommended (telephone interview accepted). Applicants must submit a letter of interest, resume. Applications are accepted continuously. World Wide Web: http://www.poetryproject.com.

PRICE TOWER ARTS CENTER
510 Dewey Avenue
Bartlesville, Oklahoma 74005

General Information Fine arts complex dedicated to art, architecture, and design with a particular emphasis on Frank Lloyd Wright and his Price Tower. Established in 1985. Number of employees: 14. Number of internship applications received each year: 35.

Internships Available ▶ *1–3 curatorial interns:* responsibilities include assisting with collections, inventory, and exhibition work. Candidates should have ability to work independently, ability to work with others, organizational skills, personal interest in the field, plan to pursue career in field, self-motivation. Duration is 200–400 hours. Unpaid. Open to high school seniors, recent high school graduates, college freshmen, college sophomores, college juniors, college seniors, recent college graduates, graduate students, career changers, individuals reentering the workforce.

Benefits Willing to act as a professional reference, willing to complete paperwork for educational credit, willing to provide letters of recommendation, membership with the Price Tower Arts Center.

Contact Write, fax, or e-mail K. Hurst, Curator, PO Box 2464, Bartlesville, Oklahoma 74005. Phone: 918-336-4949. Fax: 918-336-7117. E-mail: khurst@pricetower.org. In-person interview recommended (telephone interview accepted). Applicants must submit a formal organization application, letter of interest, resume, three personal references. Applications are accepted continuously. World Wide Web: http://www.pricetower.org.

PRINCE GEORGES PARKS AND RECREATION DEPARTMENT
6600 Kenilworth Avenue
Riverdale, Maryland

General Information Local government parks, recreation, and leisure services. Established in 1927. Number of employees: 1,500. Division of Maryland National Capital Park and Planning Commission, Upper Marlboro, Maryland. Number of internship applications received each year: 10.

Internships Available ▶ *Interns:* responsibilities include positions in area operations, arts and cultural heritage, maintenance and development, natural and historical resources, park planning and development, public affairs, special programs, sports/athletics. Candidates should have ability to work independently, college courses in field, computer skills, knowledge of field, office skills, oral communication skills, research skills, self-motivation, strong interpersonal skills, strong leadership ability, writing skills. Duration is fall, winter/spring, or summer semesters. Unpaid. Open to college sophomores, college juniors, college seniors, recent college graduates. International applications accepted.

Benefits On-the-job training, opportunity to attend seminars/workshops, possible full-time employment, willing to act as a professional reference, willing to complete paperwork for educational credit, willing to provide letters of recommendation.

Contact Write, call, fax, or e-mail Laurence J. Zimmerman, Departmental Intern Coordinator. Phone: 301-699-2510. Fax: 301-864-6941. E-mail: larry.zimmerman@pgparks.com. In-person interview recommended (telephone interview accepted). Applicants must

submit a letter of interest, resume, academic transcripts, portfolio. Application deadline: April 1 for summer, July 1 for fall, December 1 for winter/spring.

PUBLIC ARTS FOR PUBLIC SCHOOLS, DIVISION OF SCHOOL FACILITIES
28-11 Queens Plaza North
Long Island City, New York 11101

General Information Curator of 1350 artworks in New York City public schools including murals, paintings, sculptures, stained glass, and graphics from 1850 to the present. Established in 1989. Number of employees: 3. Unit of New York City Board of Education, New York, New York. Number of internship applications received each year: 5.

Internships Available ▶ *1–2 assistant registrars:* responsibilities include inspection and evaluation of condition of artwork throughout New York City schools in cooperation with curator; creation of condition reports; data entry; incidental art handling. Candidates should have computer skills, office skills, organizational skills, research skills, self-motivation, background in art history and/or studio art. Duration is flexible (minimum 4 months, one day per week). Unpaid. Open to college freshmen, college sophomores, college juniors, college seniors, recent college graduates, graduate students. International applications accepted.

Benefits Formal training, on-the-job training, willing to act as a professional reference, willing to complete paperwork for educational credit, willing to provide letters of recommendation, opportunities to meet major public artists, introduction to conservation community.

Contact Write or e-mail Gregory W. Frux, Project Manager. Phone: 718-391-6517. Fax: 718-391-6564. E-mail: gfrux@nycboe. net. In-person interview required. Applicants must submit a letter of interest, resume. Applications are accepted continuously.

REAL ART WAYS, INC.
56 Arbor Street
Hartford, Connecticut 06106

General Information Nonprofit presenter of new and experimental art, performance, video, film, spoken word, and music; showcases a variety of emerging and nationally recognized artists in Hartford and is dedicated to serving the culturally diverse communities of the Hartford area. Established in 1975. Number of employees: 15. Number of internship applications received each year: 50.

Internships Available ▶ *2–4 arts management interns:* responsibilities include assisting the executive director and program coordinator in day-to-day operations including researching and compiling grants, assisting in audience development, coordinating events, scheduling, promoting, and corresponding with artists. Candidates should have computer skills, oral communication skills, research skills, self-motivation, writing skills. Duration is 1 semester. Unpaid. ▶ *2–4 development interns:* responsibilities include assisting development director with research for potential foundation funding, grant preparation, and grant writing. Candidates should have computer skills, office skills, oral communication skills, organizational skills, writing skills. Duration is 1 semester. Unpaid. ▶ *Gallery interns:* responsibilities include assisting the gallery curator with all aspects of the visual art gallery operations, including arrangements for transportation, installation, documentation, and promotion of art exhibitions. Candidates should have ability to work independently, ability to work with others, knowledge of field, oral communication skills, personal interest in the field, self-motivation. Duration is 1 semester. Unpaid. ▶ *Music interns:* responsibilities include assisting in artist research and contact, preconcert publicity and media relations, and concert production. Candidates should have computer skills, knowledge of field, oral communication skills, organizational skills, research skills, written communication skills. Duration is 1 semester. Unpaid. ▶ *Public relations interns:* responsibilities include assisting in writing and distributing press releases and other press materials, performing electronic and written media contact and follow-up, and assisting with community outreach, membership communication, and event promotion. Candidates should have computer skills, oral communication skills, research skills, self-motivation, strong interpersonal

skills, writing skills. Duration is 1 semester. Unpaid. ▶ *Technical interns:* responsibilities include assisting in the coordination of technical requirements for a diversified series of performances and artist residencies and working in the areas of audio and video, lighting, and sound systems. Candidates should have computer skills, knowledge of field, oral communication skills, organizational skills, written communication skills. Duration is 1 semester. Unpaid. Open to college sophomores, college juniors, college seniors, recent college graduates. International applications accepted.
Benefits Names of contacts, possible full-time employment, travel reimbursement, willing to complete paperwork for educational credit, willing to provide letters of recommendation.
Contact Write, call, fax, e-mail, or through World Wide Web site Jennifer Banach, Visual Arts Program Assistant. Phone: 860-232-1006 Ext. 113. Fax: 860-233-6691. E-mail: jbanach@realartways. org. In-person interview recommended (telephone interview accepted). Applicants must submit a letter of interest, resume. Applications are accepted continuously. World Wide Web: http:// www.realartways.com.

THE REGISTRY RESORT & CLUB
475 Seagate Drive
Naples, Florida 34103

General Information   23-acre resort located on the Gulf of Mexico's "platinum coast" with over 400 rooms, 5 pools, health club, recreation department, 15 tennis courts, and 3 miles of beaches. Established in 1986. Number of employees: 1,200. Subsidiary of Boca Resorts, Inc., Miami, Florida. Number of internship applications received each year: 100.
Internships Available   ▶ *4–8 recreation coordinators:* responsibilities include working as a recreation coordinator, pool attendant, or beach attendant. Candidates should have ability to work with others, knowledge of field, oral communication skills, self-motivation, strong leadership ability, own transportation, major in recreation, hospitality, tourism, or related field, certification in CPR, safety, and first aid, ability to lift 50 pounds (minimum), run, walk, climb, and swim. Duration is spring (January to May), summer (May to September), fall (September to January). $400 per month. Open to college juniors, college seniors, graduate students.
Benefits Formal training, free housing, free meals, job counseling, names of contacts, on-the-job training, opportunity to attend seminars/workshops, possible full-time employment, willing to act as a professional reference, willing to complete paperwork for educational credit, willing to provide letters of recommendation, discounted rates on golf, tennis, and merchandise.
Contact Write, call, fax, or e-mail Eric Carlson, Director of Recreation and Pool Operations. Phone: 239-597-3232 Ext. 5612. Fax: 239-597-7168. E-mail: ecarlson@naplesresort.com. Telephone interview required. Applicants must submit a formal organization application, letter of interest, resume, three personal references. Applications are accepted continuously. World Wide Web: http://registryresort.com.

ROTUNDA GALLERY
33 Clinton Street
Brooklyn, New York 11201

General Information   Contemporary visual art gallery. Established in 1981. Number of employees: 4. Unit of Brooklyn Information and Culture (BRIC), Brooklyn, New York. Number of internship applications received each year: 5.
Internships Available   ▶ *5 interns.* Candidates should have ability to work independently, office skills, oral communication skills, personal interest in the field, self-motivation, strong interpersonal skills. Duration is 1 semester. Position available as unpaid or paid. Open to college freshmen, college sophomores, college juniors, college seniors, recent college graduates, graduate students, individuals reentering the workforce, working artists. International applications accepted.
Benefits On-the-job training, willing to act as a professional reference, willing to complete paperwork for educational credit, willing to provide letters of recommendation, federal work-study participants accepted.

Contact Write, call, fax, or e-mail Meridith McNeal, Director of Education. Phone: 718-875-4047 Ext. 13. Fax: 718-488-0609. E-mail: rotunda@brooklynx.org. In-person interview recommended (telephone interview accepted). Applicants must submit a letter of interest, resume. Applications are accepted continuously. World Wide Web: http://www.brooklynx.org.

SALT RIVER PROJECT (SRP)–PROJECT EMPLOYEES RECREATION ASSOCIATION (PERA)
1 East Continental Drive
Tempe, Arizona 85281

General Information   Private club for Salt River Project employees and their immediate families. Established in 1952. Number of employees: 50. Division of Salt River Project (SRP), Tempe, Arizona. Number of internship applications received each year: 12.
Internships Available   ▶ *Recreation interns:* responsibilities include working in the fitness center; assisting with facility booking, snack bar operations, maintenance, bartending, and special events; assembling educational classes; working on promotional flyers and billings; overseeing the recreational aids; assisting with swimming pool. Candidates should have ability to work with others, computer skills, knowledge of field, organizational skills, plan to pursue career in field, self-motivation. Duration is flexible. $5.25 per hour. Open to high school seniors, college freshmen, college sophomores, college juniors, college seniors, graduate students. International applications accepted.
Benefits Formal training, job counseling, names of contacts, on-the-job training, opportunity to attend seminars/workshops, possible full-time employment, willing to act as a professional reference, willing to complete paperwork for educational credit, willing to provide letters of recommendation, use of facility (store, fitness, pool).
Contact Write, call, fax, or e-mail Nadia Cerini, Activities Coordinator. Phone: 602-236-5782. Fax: 602-236-5920. E-mail: nrcerini@srpnet. com. In-person interview recommended (telephone interview accepted). Applicants must submit a formal organization application, letter of interest, resume. Applications are accepted continuously.

SALZMAN INTERNATIONAL
824 Edwards Street, PO Box 41
Trinidad, California 95570-0041

General Information   Agency for freelance illustrators working in communicating arts including publishing and advertising. Established in 1982. Number of employees: 1. Number of internship applications received each year: 50.
Internships Available   ▶ *1 personal assistant:* responsibilities include general office, clerical, phone, and some household duties. Candidates should have ability to work independently, computer skills, oral communication skills, organizational skills, strong interpersonal skills, written communication skills. Duration is 3–4 months. Unpaid. Open to recent high school graduates, college freshmen, college sophomores, college juniors, college seniors, recent college graduates, graduate students, career changers, individuals reentering the workforce. International applications accepted.
Benefits Free housing, job counseling, names of contacts, on-the-job training, opportunity to attend seminars/workshops, possible full-time employment, willing to act as a professional reference, willing to complete paperwork for educational credit, willing to provide letters of recommendation.
Contact Write or e-mail Mr. Richard Salzman, Artist Representative, 524 Edwards Street, PO Box 41, Trinidad, California 95570-0041. Phone: 707-677-0241. Fax: 707-677-0242. E-mail: richard@ salzmaninternational.com. Telephone interview required. Applicants must submit a letter of interest. Applications are accepted continuously. World Wide Web: http://www.salzmaninternational. com.

SAN FRANCISCO ART COMMISSION GALLERY
401 Van Ness Avenue
San Francisco, California 94102

General Information Municipal art gallery exhibiting a broad range of Bay Area contemporary art. Established in 1970. Number of employees: 3. Unit of San Francisco Art Commission, San Francisco, California. Number of internship applications received each year: 35.

Internships Available ► *1–4 gallery assistants:* responsibilities include working with staff and assisting in all areas of gallery operations. Candidates should have ability to work independently, ability to work with others, computer skills, oral communication skills, organizational skills, self-motivation, written communication skills. Duration is 5–6 months. Unpaid. Open to college freshmen, college sophomores, college juniors, college seniors, recent college graduates, graduate students, career changers, individuals reentering the workforce. International applications accepted.

Benefits Willing to complete paperwork for educational credit, willing to provide letters of recommendation.

Contact Write, call, fax, e-mail, or through World Wide Web site Internship Coordinator. Phone: 415-554-6080. Fax: 415-252-2595. E-mail: gallery@thecity.sfsu.edu. In-person interview required. Applicants must submit a letter of interest, resume. Applications are accepted continuously. World Wide Web: http://www.sfacgallery.org.

SCRIPTAPALOOZA, INC.
7775 Sunset Boulevard, PMB 200
Hollywood, California 90046

General Information Company that presents annual screenwriting competition and film festival. Established in 1998. Number of employees: 3.

Internships Available ► *1–2 office assistants:* responsibilities include answering phones, scheduling meetings, database upkeep, typing, and filing. Candidates should have ability to work with others, college courses in field, office skills, oral communication skills, personal interest in the field, written communication skills. Duration is 1–6 months. Unpaid. ► *2–10 script readers:* responsibilities include reading scripts, database upkeep, and filing. Candidates should have ability to work independently, college courses in field, computer skills, organizational skills, personal interest in the field, self-motivation. Duration is 2–12 weeks. Unpaid. Open to college freshmen, college sophomores, college juniors, college seniors, recent college graduates.

Benefits On-the-job training, willing to act as a professional reference, willing to complete paperwork for educational credit, willing to provide letters of recommendation.

Contact Write or e-mail Genevieve Cibor, Vice President. E-mail: gen@scriptapalooza.com. No phone calls. In-person interview required. Applicants must submit a letter of interest, resume. Applications are accepted continuously. World Wide Web: http://www.scriptapalooza.com.

SIRI BERG STUDIO
9 Mercer Street, #6E
New York, New York 10012-4453

General Information Studio that exhibits in New York City, nationally, and globally; artist whose paintings, collages, and assemblages are in museums and galleries; sells to collectors and the general public. Established in 1980. Number of internship applications received each year: 6.

Internships Available ► *1–3 business intern:* responsibilities include mailing for national and global exhibitions, assisting in planning and installing art shows, consignment of art work, contacting collectors, and assisting with Japanese woodblock printing. Candidates should have computer skills, experience in the field, office skills, organizational skills, plan to pursue career in field. Duration is one day a week for up to 2 years. Unpaid. ► *1–3 studio interns:* responsibilities include assisting artist in Japanese woodblock printing, curating exhibitions, planning and installing a slide and catalog system, consignment, mailings and press releases, and exhibits research. Candidates should have college courses in field, computer skills, knowledge of field, personal interest in the field, plan to pursue career in field. Duration is 1 day a week for up to 2 years. Unpaid. Open to college freshmen, college sophomores, college juniors, college seniors, recent college graduates, graduate students, career changers, individuals reentering the workforce.

Benefits Job counseling, names of contacts, on-the-job training, willing to act as a professional reference, willing to complete paperwork for educational credit, willing to provide letters of recommendation, opportunity to learn Japanese woodblock printing and collaging.

Contact Write, call, fax, e-mail, or through World Wide Web site Siri Berg, Artist, New York. Phone: 212-966 Ext. 3063. Fax: 212-966 Ext. 3063. E-mail: siriberg@earthlink.net. In-person interview recommended (telephone interview accepted). Applicants must submit a letter of interest, resume, personal reference, letter of recommendation, portfolio (if possible). World Wide Web: http://www.siriberg.com.

SITE SANTA FE
1606 Paseo de Peralta
Santa Fe, New Mexico 87501

General Information Not-for-profit contemporary art space. Established in 1995. Number of employees: 20. Number of internship applications received each year: 35.

Internships Available ► *1 administrative intern:* responsibilities include organizing and updating the director's Rolodex, working with artists' files, assisting with travel arrangements for artists, faxing, and gathering information for visiting artists under the direction of the director's assistant. Candidates should have computer skills, oral communication skills, organizational skills, strong interpersonal skills, writing skills. Duration is 1–2 semesters. Unpaid. Open to college sophomores, college juniors, college seniors, recent college graduates, graduate students. ► *1 curatorial intern:* responsibilities include assisting with research, correspondence, curatorial worksheets, condition reports, and shipping; interns will identify educational goals and will construct a project that will meet specific requirements of their home institution. Candidates should have ability to work independently, computer skills, oral communication skills, plan to pursue career in field, writing skills. Duration is 3–5 months. Unpaid. Open to graduate students. ► *1–2 education and public programming assistants:* responsibilities include assisting with the implementation and design of outreach programs for school children and the elderly and working with the public in the capacity of a docent. Candidates should have ability to work independently, oral communication skills, organizational skills, personal interest in the field, research skills, strong interpersonal skills. Duration is 3–5 months. Unpaid. Open to college freshmen, college sophomores, college juniors, college seniors, graduate students. ► *1–2 public relations interns:* responsibilities include assembling and managing mailings, slide duplication and labeling, maintaining press clippings book, and working on the phone with local and national press. Candidates should have ability to work independently, computer skills, editing skills, knowledge of field, writing skills. Duration is 3–5 months. Unpaid. Open to college freshmen, college sophomores, college juniors, college seniors, recent college graduates, graduate students. ► *1–2 special events and membership assistants:* responsibilities include producing and sending out membership acknowledgements and packages weekly, helping update and maintain membership files, and researching new target markets and methods of reaching them; helping plan and organize private exhibition previews, private receptions, benefit events, and tours and gallery talks for members, donors, and trustees. Candidates should have ability to work independently, computer skills, oral communication skills, organizational skills, research skills, strong interpersonal skills. Duration is 3–5 months. Unpaid. Open to college freshmen, college sophomores, college juniors, college seniors, recent college graduates, graduate students, career changers, individuals reentering the workforce. International applications accepted.

Benefits On-the-job training, willing to act as a professional reference, willing to complete paperwork for educational credit, willing to provide letters of recommendation.

Contact Write, call, fax, e-mail, or through World Wide Web site Kirsten Mundt, Education Coordinator. Phone: 505-989-1199 Ext. 19. Fax: 505-989-1188. E-mail: education@sitesantafe.org. In-person interview recommended (telephone interview accepted). Applicants must submit a formal organization application, letter of interest, resume, two letters of recommendation. Applications are accepted continuously. World Wide Web: http://www.sitesantafe.org.

SONY MUSIC ENTERTAINMENT, INC.
550 Madison Avenue
New York, New York 10022

General Information Music entertainment corporation including CBS Records, Columbia and Epic Records, and Sony Classical. Established in 1988. Number of employees: 1,500. Division of Sony, Inc., Japan. Number of internship applications received each year: 1,500.
Internships Available ▶ *35–40 summer interns (NY/Santa Monica):* responsibilities include working in promotions, publicity, retail marketing, artists and repertoire (A&R), A&R administration, business, affairs, accounting, or MIS. Candidates should have ability to work with others, computer skills, office skills, oral communication skills, organizational skills, personal interest in the field, minimum 3.0 GPA in declared major, prior work experience a plus. Duration is 10 weeks. $8 per hour. Open to minority (African-American, Latino, Asian, American Indian) undergraduate college students, college seniors considered only if returning to school in fall. ▶ *7 summer interns (sales and distribution branches):* responsibilities include working with sales representatives, progressive music marketing representative, marketing manager, sales manager, and branch manager. Candidates should have ability to work with others, computer skills, oral communication skills, organizational skills, personal interest in the field, self-motivation, minimum 3.0 GPA in declared major, record industry experience desired, one year retail or other music industry experience a plus; car required. Duration is 10 weeks. $8 per hour. Open to minority (African-American, Latino, Asian, American Indian) undergraduate college students; college seniors considered only if returning to school in fall.
Benefits Job counseling, opportunity to attend seminars/workshops, possible full-time employment, willing to act as a professional reference, willing to provide letters of recommendation, travel reimbursement possible for second application interview invitees, access to on-site employee store, possible promotional freebies, housing provided for engineering interns who are relocated to manufacturing facilities outside of New York.
Contact Write or fax Internship Coordinator, 550 Madison Avenue, Room 203, New York, New York 10022. Fax: 212-833-5024. No phone calls. In-person interview required. Applicants must submit a letter of interest, resume. Application deadline: March 31 for undergraduates, December 31 for first-year law and first-year MBA students. World Wide Web: http://www.sony.com.

SOUTHERN EXPOSURE
401 Alabama Street
San Francisco, California 94110

General Information Nonprofit artists' organization providing opportunities for noncommercial activity and challenging artists to exhibit work in a supportive and open environment. Established in 1974. Number of employees: 4. Unit of Project Artaud, San Francisco, California. Number of internship applications received each year: 40.
Internships Available ▶ *2–4 artists in education interns:* responsibilities include facilitating and administering a hands-on education program for schools and youth organizations that consists of workshops on relevant aesthetic and social issues; serving as an artist's classroom assistant, program coordinator, artist's liaison, program developer, and fund-raiser. Candidates should have knowledge of field, oral communication skills, organizational skills, personal interest in the field, strong interpersonal skills, strong leadership ability. Duration is 1 summer or minimum of 6 months during academic year (minimum of 6 hours per week). Position available as unpaid or at stipend between $300-$600. Open to recent high school graduates, college freshmen, college sophomores, college juniors, college seniors, recent college graduates, graduate students, career changers. ▶ *2–3 arts administration interns:* responsibilities include working in the areas of membership development/coordination, publicity/public relations, graphic

design, Web site design/maintenance, and grants management. Candidates should have computer skills, office skills, oral communication skills, organizational skills, personal interest in the field, self-motivation, strong interpersonal skills, writing skills. Duration is 1 summer or minimum of 6 months during academic year (minimum of 6 hours per week). Unpaid. Open to college freshmen, college sophomores, college juniors, college seniors, recent college graduates, graduate students, career changers. ▶ *1–2 installation/exhibition coordinators:* responsibilities include assisting in the facilitation and installation of monthly visual arts exhibitions and acting as liaison between artists and staff; serving as volunteer coordinator and recruiter; assisting with presentation coordination; serving as technical assistant, event staffer, and fund-raiser. Candidates should have ability to work independently, computer skills, office skills, oral communication skills, organizational skills, personal interest in the field, self-motivation, strong interpersonal skills, written communication skills. Duration is 1 summer or minimum of 6 months during academic year (minimum of 6 hours per week). Unpaid. Open to college freshmen, college sophomores, college juniors, college seniors, recent college graduates, graduate students, career changers.
Benefits Job counseling, names of contacts, willing to act as a professional reference, willing to complete paperwork for educational credit, willing to provide letters of recommendation.
Contact Write, call, fax, e-mail, or through World Wide Web site Lisa Ricci, Associate Director. Phone: 415-863-2141. Fax: 415-863-1841. E-mail: soex@soex.org. In-person interview recommended (telephone interview accepted). Applicants must submit a letter of interest, resume. Applications are accepted continuously. World Wide Web: http://www.soex.org.

STEEN ART STUDY
961 East California Boulevard 329
Pasadena, California 91106-4057

General Information Independent art historian and educator who performs research; involved in publishing, curating, and lecturing; and conducts classes and study trips. Established in 1983. Number of employees: 1. Number of internship applications received each year: 5.
Internships Available ▶ *1 intern:* responsibilities include assisting in research, conducting classes, and curatorial and registrar work on a private collection. Candidates should have ability to work independently, ability to work with others, computer skills, office skills, oral communication skills, plan to pursue career in field, research skills, self-motivation, written communication skills. Duration is 1 year. Unpaid. Open to high school students, recent high school graduates, college freshmen, college sophomores, college juniors, college seniors, recent college graduates, graduate students, law students, career changers, individuals reentering the workforce. International applications accepted.
Benefits Formal training, job counseling, names of contacts, opportunity to attend seminars/workshops, possible full-time employment, willing to complete paperwork for educational credit, willing to provide letters of recommendation.
Contact Write, call, fax, or e-mail Mr. Ronald E. Steen, Art Historian and Art Educator. Phone: 323-681-6343. Fax: 626-577-7384. E-mail: ronaldsteen@att.net. In-person interview recommended (telephone interview accepted). Applicants must submit a resume. Applications are accepted continuously. World Wide Web: http://www.steenartstudy.com.

SUMMIT TALENT AND LITERARY AGENCY
9454 Wilshire Boulevard, Suite 203
Beverly Hills, California 90212

General Information Literary agency representing writers and directors in motion pictures and television. Established in 2000. Number of employees: 2. Number of internship applications received each year: 100.
Internships Available ▶ *1–3 interns:* responsibilities include administrative duties; phones, handling mail, script reading, preparation of submissions, contract administration. Candidates should have knowledge of field, office skills, oral communication skills, personal interest in the field, strong interpersonal skills, written communication skills. Duration is as needed. Position avail-

Summit Talent and Literary Agency (continued)

able as unpaid or paid. Open to college freshmen, college sophomores, college juniors, college seniors, graduate students, law students.
Benefits Names of contacts, willing to act as a professional reference, willing to complete paperwork for educational credit, willing to provide letters of recommendation, stipend.
Contact Fax Jeremy Ross, Assistant. Fax: 310-205-9734. No phone calls. Telephone interview required. Applicants must submit a letter of interest, resume. Application deadline: May 1.

TRAIL BLAZERS
45 East 20th,, 9th Floor
New York, New York 10003

General Information Summer educational opportunity for disadvantaged/underprivileged youth. Established in 1887. Number of employees: 7. Number of internship applications received each year: 200.
Internships Available ▶ *10–20 group leaders:* responsibilities include providing leadership in all areas of small camp-living for a group of 8 to 9 children in an informal, family-like setting. Candidates should have ability to work independently, ability to work with others, oral communication skills, self-motivation, strong leadership ability. Duration is June-August. $1600–$1700 per duration of internship. Open to college freshmen, college sophomores, college juniors, college seniors, recent college graduates, graduate students. ▶ *4 program support staff interns:* responsibilities include organizing, coordinating, and managing specified program areas and activities that support small camp group leaders. Candidates should have ability to work independently, ability to work with others, oral communication skills, self-motivation, strong leadership ability, written communication skills. Duration is June to August. $1700–$3000 per duration of internship. Open to college sophomores, college juniors, college seniors, recent college graduates, graduate students.
Benefits Free housing, free meals, names of contacts, on-the-job training, opportunity to attend seminars/workshops, travel reimbursement, tuition assistance, willing to act as a professional reference, willing to complete paperwork for educational credit, willing to provide letters of recommendation.
Contact Write, call, fax, e-mail, or through World Wide Web site Dennis Kramer-Wine, Staff Recruitment Coordinator. Phone: 212-529-5113. Fax: 212-529-2704. E-mail: dkramerwinetbcny@aol.com. In-person interview recommended (telephone interview accepted). Applicants must submit a formal organization application, three personal references, online application at www.trailblazers.org. Applications are accepted continuously. World Wide Web: http://www.trailblazers.org.

TRURO CENTER FOR THE ARTS AT CASTLE HILL
PO Box 756
Truro, Massachusetts 02666

General Information Summer art school offering a wide range of workshops in painting, printmaking, drawing, sculpture, writing, photography, book arts, metal, and clay taught by well-established artists and craftspeople. Established in 1971. Number of employees: 8. Number of internship applications received each year: 20.
Internships Available ▶ *1–3 art assistants:* responsibilities include assisting art teacher in working with students/children. Candidates should have ability to work with others, experience in the field, organizational skills, personal interest in the field, self-motivation. Duration is 1–2 months. Unpaid. Open to high school students, recent high school graduates, college freshmen, college sophomores, college juniors, college seniors, recent college graduates, graduate students, individuals reentering the workforce. ▶ *1 ceramic assistant:* responsibilities include working with the ceramic studio manager, assisting in ceramic studio, and assisting with firing kilns. Candidates should have ability to work with others, oral communication skills, personal interest in the field, self-motivation, knowledge of ceramics. Duration is 1–2 months. Unpaid. Open to high school seniors, college freshmen, college sophomores, college juniors, college seniors, recent college graduates, gradu-

ate students. ▶ *General interns:* responsibilities include assisting in daily maintenance of buildings and grounds, preparing studios for workshops, mixing clay and glazes, doing odd jobs connected with special public events, and assisting in office work. Candidates should have ability to work independently, analytical skills, office skills, oral communication skills, organizational skills, personal interest in the field, plan to pursue career in field, self-motivation, strong interpersonal skills, strong leadership ability, must be prepared to make significant time commitment. Duration is 1–2 months. Unpaid. Open to high school seniors, recent high school graduates, college freshmen, college sophomores, college juniors, college seniors, recent college graduates, graduate students, law students, career changers, individuals reentering the workforce. International applications accepted.
Benefits Willing to complete paperwork for educational credit, willing to provide letters of recommendation, opportunity to attend seminars/workshops with leading artists.
Contact Write, fax, e-mail, or through World Wide Web site Cherie Mittenthal, Director. Fax: 508-349-7513. E-mail: castlehilltruro@aol.com. No phone calls. In-person interview recommended (telephone interview accepted). Applicants must submit a letter of interest, resume. Application deadline: June 1 for summer. World Wide Web: http://www.castlehill.org.

UNIVERSAL STUDIOS, INC.
100 Universal City Plaza, Building 1220-1
Universal City, California 91608

General Information Entertainment (TV, film, music) company. Established in 1912. Number of employees: 6,000. Division of Vivendi Universal, New York, New York.
Internships Available ▶ *Interns.* Candidates should have ability to work with others, computer skills, oral communication skills, personal interest in the field, plan to pursue career in field, self-motivation, written communication skills. Duration is 12–15 weeks. Position available as unpaid or paid. Open to college freshmen, college sophomores, college juniors, college seniors, graduate students, 2-year students. International applications accepted.
Benefits Job counseling, names of contacts, on-the-job training, possible full-time employment, willing to act as a professional reference, willing to complete paperwork for educational credit, willing to provide letters of recommendation.
Contact Fax or through World Wide Web site College Intern Recruiter. Fax: 818-866-9459. No phone calls. In-person interview recommended (telephone interview accepted). Applicants must submit a resume. Applications are accepted continuously. World Wide Web: http://www.universalstudios.com.

UNIVERSITY OF FLORIDA–STEPHEN C. O'CONNELL CENTER
PO Box 115850, Suite 1232
Gainesville, Florida 32611-5850

General Information Center whose mission is to serve as an academic, athletic, recreational, and entertainment facility. Established in 1980. Number of employees: 300. Unit of University of Florida, Gainesville, Florida. Number of internship applications received each year: 150.
Internships Available ▶ *1–2 business interns:* responsibilities include working in various areas such as facility management, special event planning, marketing, accounting, advertising and public relations, financing, journalism, and management. Candidates should have computer skills, oral communication skills, self-motivation, strong interpersonal skills, written communication skills. Duration is fall, spring, and summer semesters. Position available as unpaid or paid. ▶ *1–2 facility interns/special events:* responsibilities include event management, guest services, personnel management, client/promoter relations, booking/scheduling; working closely with the associate director with a focus on the operational aspects of a multi-purpose facility and special events planning. Candidates should have computer skills, oral communication skills, self-motivation, strong interpersonal skills, written communication skills. Duration is fall, spring, and summer semesters. Position available as unpaid or paid. ▶ *1 human resources intern:* responsibilities include semester hire program, scheduling

of personnel, booking of services and equipment, employee training, coordination and execution of continuous hire, guest service, and client relations. Candidates should have office skills, oral communication skills, self-motivation, strong interpersonal skills, written communication skills. Duration is fall, spring, and summer semesters. Position available as unpaid or paid. Open to college freshmen, college sophomores, college juniors, college seniors, recent college graduates, graduate students, priority given to college juniors and above. International applications accepted.

Benefits Formal training, names of contacts, on-the-job training, opportunity to attend seminars/workshops, willing to act as a professional reference, willing to complete paperwork for educational credit, willing to provide letters of recommendation, compensation on contracted hourly basis after 24 hours in any given work week.

Contact E-mail or through World Wide Web site Renee Musson, Internship Coordinator. Phone: 352-392-5500. Fax: 352-392-7106. E-mail: musson@ufl.edu. In-person interview recommended (telephone interview accepted). Applicants must submit a formal organization application, letter of interest, resume, three personal references. Application deadline: March 1 for summer, July 1 for fall, October 1 for spring. World Wide Web: http://www.oconnellcenter.ufl.edu.

VISUAL STUDIES WORKSHOP
31 Prince Street
Rochester, New York 14607

General Information Center for the study of the visual image, especially the photographic image; projects include an exhibition program and a research center; educational programs including an MFA program; offices of the journal *AFTERIMAGE*; publishing program, print shop, bookstore, gallery, and media center. Established in 1969. Number of employees: 15. Number of internship applications received each year: 50.

Internships Available ▶ *1 AFTERIMAGE intern:* responsibilities include learning critical writing, news reporting, and production. Duration is 1 semester. Unpaid. ▶ *2 exhibitions program interns:* responsibilities include working in curating, exhibitions, gallery management, and a traveling exhibition service. Duration is 1 semester. Unpaid. ▶ *2 media center interns:* responsibilities include assisting with video equipment access and performing research and public relations tasks for lecture screening series. Duration is 1 semester. Unpaid. ▶ *2 research center interns:* responsibilities include assisting in print collection management, cataloging, and exhibition preparation and installation. Duration is 1 semester. Unpaid. ▶ *2 special graphics interns:* responsibilities include working on book design, production, distribution, and media projects. Duration is 1 semester. Unpaid. Open to college freshmen, college sophomores, college juniors, college seniors, recent college graduates, graduate students. International applications accepted.

Benefits Opportunity to attend seminars/workshops, willing to complete paperwork for educational credit, access to photo, film, video, and book collections.

Contact Write, call, fax, or e-mail Scot Gulbransen, Coordinator. Phone: 716-442-8676. Fax: 716-442-1992. E-mail: info@vsw.org. Applicants must submit a resume, letter of recommendation, letter of interest indicating program area preferred. Applications are accepted continuously. World Wide Web: http://www.vsw.org.

WALL STREET MUSIC
28545 Greenfield, Suite 200
Southfield, Michigan 48076

General Information Record company and distributor specializing in the marketing, promotion, and sales of various musical genres. Established in 1985. Number of employees: 10. Branch of Wall Street Productions, Atlanta, Georgia. Number of internship applications received each year: 100.

Internships Available ▶ *1–2 engineering/production interns:* responsibilities include learning the inner workings of the music production industry using Digidesign random-access multitrack recording software, digital soundfile editors, digital multitrack tape machines, video/audio machine control interfacing, and digital sequencing software during all stages of the audio production chain, and

exercising organizational skills. Candidates should have computer skills, declared college major in field, experience in the field, oral communication skills, organizational skills, plan to pursue career in field. Duration is 15–20 weeks. Unpaid. Open to college freshmen, college sophomores, college juniors, college seniors, recent college graduates, graduate students, law students. ▶ *1–2 marketing interns:* responsibilities include assisting in maintaining databases for each marketing area, contacting and negotiating with mailing list brokers, helping prepare international direct-mail campaigns, composing press releases for international newswires, and disseminating press kits for radio, television, and print. Candidates should have ability to work independently, computer skills, oral communication skills, organizational skills, plan to pursue career in field, written communication skills. Duration is 15–20 weeks. Unpaid. Open to college freshmen, college sophomores, college juniors, college seniors, recent college graduates, graduate students, law students. ▶ *1–2 promotions interns:* responsibilities include assisting in contacting radio, retail, press, and record pools to maintain status and contact reports on computer, providing advance notice of new releases, coordinating promotional mailings, determining need for promotional products, informing of artists' activities, mediating with venues regarding promotional events, exploring advertising opportunities, seeking out additional contacts, and troubleshooting problems. Candidates should have ability to work independently, computer skills, oral communication skills, organizational skills, plan to pursue career in field, written communication skills. Duration is 15–20 weeks. Unpaid. Open to college freshmen, college sophomores, college juniors, college seniors, recent college graduates, graduate students. ▶ *1–2 public relations interns:* responsibilities include writing news releases, biographies, and fact sheets; compiling and packaging press kits; acquiring performance information regarding artist tours and assisting in promotional mailings to magazines and press; arranging for interviews and promotional events and requesting and cataloging tearsheets from press; electronically pasting up press coverage for press kits, tracking inventory of artists' promotional materials, assisting in follow-up of targeted media personnel, exploring media advertising based upon media plan, helping coordinate record release parties, and interacting with Wall Street artists on all promotional issues. Candidates should have ability to work independently, computer skills, oral communication skills, organizational skills, plan to pursue career in field, written communication skills. Duration is 15–20 weeks. Unpaid. Open to college freshmen, college sophomores, college juniors, college seniors, recent college graduates, graduate students, law students. International applications accepted.

Benefits Job counseling, names of contacts, opportunity to attend seminars/workshops, possible full-time employment, willing to act as a professional reference, willing to complete paperwork for educational credit, willing to provide letters of recommendation, use of company computers for resumes and mass mailings.

Contact Write or e-mail Mr. Jeffrey Richardson, Internship Coordinator. Phone: 248-395-2772. Fax: 248-395-2773. E-mail: jr@wallstreetmusic.com. In-person interview recommended (telephone interview accepted). Applicants must submit a formal organization application, letter of interest, resume, two writing samples. Applications are accepted continuously. World Wide Web: http://www.wallstreetmusic.com.

WALT DISNEY WORLD COMPANY
Walt Disney World College Program, PO Box 10900
Lake Buena Vista, Florida 32830-0090

General Information Hospitality and entertainment industry comprising 14 resorts, 4 theme parks, 3 water parks, and numerous recreational venues; over 1,500 different types of jobs support the operation of the resort. Established in 1971. Number of employees: 55,000. Number of internship applications received each year: 1,000.

Internships Available ▶ *Culinary assistants:* responsibilities include assisting in food preparation for guest meals by mixing, peeling and dicing, grillwork, and sandwich and salad preparations. Candidates should have ability to work independently, ability to work with others, oral communication skills, organizational skills,

Walt Disney World Company *(continued)*

personal interest in the field, formal education required for some culinary positions. Duration is spring (January-May/August); fall (June/September-December). $6 per hour. Open to college freshmen, college sophomores, college juniors, college seniors, recent college graduates. ▶ *Custodial cast members:* responsibilities include answering guest questions, emptying trash cans, cleaning restrooms, sweeping park areas, and assisting with busing and cleaning restaurants. Candidates should have ability to work independently, oral communication skills, organizational skills, self-motivation, strong interpersonal skills. Duration is spring (January-May/August); fall (June/September-December). $6 per hour. Open to college freshmen, college sophomores, college juniors, college seniors, graduate students. ▶ *Full-service food and beverage cast members:* responsibilities include greeting, assigning, and seating guests; handling cash, preparing food, rolling silverware into linens, folding napkins, and some custodial duties. Candidates should have ability to work independently, oral communication skills, organizational skills, self-motivation, strong interpersonal skills, written communication skills. Duration is spring (January-May/August); fall (June/September-December). $6 per hour. Open to college freshmen, college sophomores, college juniors, college seniors, graduate students. ▶ *Hospitality cast members:* responsibilities include working in one of Disney's themed resorts or campgrounds, including guest services, bell services, or front desk operations. Candidates should have ability to work independently, knowledge of field, oral communication skills, organizational skills, personal interest in the field, self-motivation, strong interpersonal skills, strong leadership ability, written communication skills, major in the hospitality field (preferred). Duration is January to August; June to December. $6 per hour. Open to college freshmen, college sophomores, college juniors, college seniors, graduate students. ▶ *Housekeeping cast members:* responsibilities include making beds, dusting, cleaning bathrooms, and putting out fresh towels; lifting, bending, and pulling; attending regular informal meetings with hotel management. Candidates should have ability to work independently, organizational skills, personal interest in the field, self-motivation, strong interpersonal skills. Duration is spring (January-May/August); fall (June/September-December). $6 per hour. Open to college freshmen, college sophomores, college juniors, college seniors, graduate students. ▶ *Lifeguarding cast members:* responsibilities include monitoring guests' safety as they swim, keeping the pool areas clean, and answering questions in any of Disney's pools, marinas, or water parks; Disney conducts the certification process. Candidates should have ability to work independently, oral communication skills, organizational skills, personal interest in the field, self-motivation, strong interpersonal skills, strong leadership ability, previous certification (helpful, not required). Duration is spring (January-May/August); fall (June/September-December). $6 per hour. Open to college freshmen, college sophomores, college juniors, college seniors, graduate students. ▶ *Merchandise cast members:* responsibilities include working in any of Disney's theme parks, resorts, or downtown Disney area; answering guest questions, stocking shelves, ringing up merchandise, and cleaning work areas; may also work in wheelchair and stroller rental areas. Candidates should have ability to work independently, oral communication skills, organizational skills, self-motivation, strong interpersonal skills. Duration is spring (January-May/August); fall (June/September-December). $6 per hour. Open to college freshmen, college sophomores, college juniors, college seniors, graduate students. ▶ *Operations cast members interns:* responsibilities include greeting guests and collecting tickets, operating ride systems, giving long narrations, assisting guests on and off the rides, custodial duties, cash handling, and parking lot duties. Candidates should have ability to work independently, oral communication skills, organizational skills, self-motivation, strong interpersonal skills, script memorization ability. Duration is spring (January-May/August); fall (June/September-December). $6 per hour. Open to college freshmen, college sophomores, college juniors, college seniors, graduate students. ▶ *Quick-service food and beverage interns:* responsibilities include serving guests at over 240 restaurants, fast food counters, and snack bars; rotating different stations while filling orders, cashiering, cleaning, stocking, preparing, and assembling food items. Candidates should have ability

to work independently, oral communication skills, organizational skills, self-motivation, strong interpersonal skills. Duration is spring (January-May/August); fall (June/September-December). $6–$6.25 per hour. Open to college freshmen, college sophomores, college juniors, college seniors, graduate students. ▶ *Recreation cast members:* responsibilities include handling ticket sales and towel rentals, keeping marinas and water parks clean, and answering guest questions. Candidates should have ability to work independently, oral communication skills, organizational skills, self-motivation, strong interpersonal skills, interest in working outdoors. Duration is spring (January-May/August); fall (June/September-December). $6 per hour. Open to college freshmen, college sophomores, college juniors, college seniors, graduate students. ▶ *Transportation cast members:* responsibilities include assisting guests on and off boats and monorails; keeping transportation lines moving smoothly, as well as answering guest questions and giving information while guests are waiting. Candidates should have ability to work independently, oral communication skills, organizational skills, self-motivation, strong interpersonal skills, valid driver's license. Duration is spring (January-May/August); fall (June/September-December). $6 per hour. Open to college freshmen, college sophomores, college juniors, college seniors, graduate students. International applications accepted.

Benefits Formal training, housing at a cost, job counseling, meals at a cost, names of contacts, on-the-job training, opportunity to attend seminars/workshops, possible full-time employment, willing to act as a professional reference, willing to complete paperwork for educational credit, willing to provide letters of recommendation, transportation provided from on-site housing to work location.

Contact Call or through World Wide Web site College Recruiting, College Program, PO Box 10900, Lake Buena Vista, Florida 32830-0090. Fax: 407-934-6878. E-mail: wdw.college.recruiting@ disney.com. In-person interview required. Applicants must submit a formal organization application, attendance at recruitment presentation at one of over 400 colleges/universities nationwide (consult Web site for dates and locations). Application deadline: between September and November for spring positions; between February and April for fall positions; no summer only positions. World Wide Web: http://www.wdwcollegeprogram.com.

WARD-NASSE GALLERY
178 Prince Street
New York, New York 10012

General Information Nonprofit, artist-administered alternative space dedicated to the presentation of visual, spoken, and performing arts. Established in 1970. Number of employees: 2. Number of internship applications received each year: 10.

Internships Available ▶ *2–4 gallery assistants:* responsibilities include dealing with public, signing up new artists for membership and exhibitions, and helping with sales. Candidates should have ability to work independently, ability to work with others, office skills, oral communication skills, personal interest in the field, written communication skills, some computer skills. Duration is June to September. Position available as unpaid or at $15–$20 per day. Open to college freshmen, college sophomores, college juniors, college seniors. ▶ *2–5 interns:* responsibilities include organizing exhibits; installing art; assisting with press, advertisements, sales, and financial matters; opening and closing the gallery; general office duties; and working on a special project if desired. Candidates should have ability to work with others, organizational skills, personal interest in the field. Duration is 3 months to 1 year. $10 per day. Open to recent high school graduates, college freshmen, college sophomores, college juniors, college seniors, recent college graduates, graduate students, law students, career changers, individuals reentering the workforce. ▶ *Office assistants:* responsibilities include working on mailing list, filing, typing, helping with sales labeling, and packing artwork for shipping. Candidates should have ability to work with others, computer skills, office skills, personal interest in the field, self-motivation. Position available as unpaid or at $10 per day. Open to college freshmen, college sophomores, college juniors, college seniors, recent college graduates, graduate students. International applications accepted.

Benefits Job counseling, names of contacts, on-the-job training, possible full-time employment, travel reimbursement, willing to complete paperwork for educational credit, willing to provide letters of recommendation, possibility of sales commissions.
Contact Write, call, or e-mail Mr. Harry Nasse. Phone: 212-925-6951. E-mail: wardnasse@hotmail.com. In-person interview required. Applicants must submit a letter of interest. Applications are accepted continuously. World Wide Web: http://www.wardnasse.org.

WILDERNESS INQUIRY
808 14th Avenue SE
Minneapolis, Minnesota 55414-1516

General Information Nonprofit organization integrating people of all ages, backgrounds, and abilities through outdoor education and adventure programs (in wilderness); 3 areas: adventure trips, training, and accessibility assessment of trails/facilities. Established in 1978. Number of employees: 50. Number of internship applications received each year: 80.
Internships Available ▶ *1–3 development interns:* responsibilities include assisting with facilitation, administration, and enhancement of Wilderness Inquiry's development components; helping with special events, fund-raising, and organization and recruitment of volunteers. Candidates should have ability to work independently, ability to work with others, oral communication skills, organizational skills, research skills, written communication skills. Duration is 6–15 weeks. Unpaid. ▶ *4–20 outdoor leader interns:* responsibilities include working in trail leadership, trip logistics, and outdoor education; equipment maintenance, transportation, food systems; office/administration work. Candidates should have ability to work with others, oral communication skills, organizational skills, personal interest in the field, strong leadership ability. Unpaid. ▶ *2–5 outreach interns:* responsibilities include assisting the outreach staff with press relations, information services, publications, presentation development and administration; may also participate in integrated outdoor adventures. Candidates should have ability to work with others, computer skills, oral communication skills, research skills, written communication skills. Duration is 6–15 weeks. Unpaid. Open to college seniors, recent college graduates, career changers. International applications accepted.
Benefits Free housing, on-the-job training, opportunity to attend seminars/workshops, possible full-time employment, willing to act as a professional reference, willing to complete paperwork for educational credit, willing to provide letters of recommendation.
Contact Call, fax, e-mail, or through World Wide Web site Stephanie Schmit, Internship Coordinator. Phone: 612-676-9427. Fax: 612-676-9401. E-mail: stephschmit@wildernessinquiry.org. Telephone interview required. Applicants must submit a formal organization application, letter of interest, resume, three personal references. Applications are accepted continuously. World Wide Web: http://www.wildernessinquiry.org.

WINE COUNTRY FILM FESTIVAL
PO Box 303
Glen Ellen, California 95442

General Information Film festival that sponsors an annual showcase of 100+ films from around the world in which many filmmakers present their work. Established in 1987. Number of internship applications received each year: 43.
Internships Available ▶ *1–2 assistants to the director:* responsibilities include assisting festival director in securing films and filmmakers; organizing seminars; supervising other interns as needed. Candidates should have ability to work independently, ability to work with others, computer skills, editing skills, oral communication skills, organizational skills, self-motivation, written communication skills, personal interest in film and world culture. Duration is end of May to mid-August. Unpaid. Open to college juniors, college seniors, recent college graduates, graduate students. ▶ *1–2 graphic designers:* responsibilities include designing flyers, advertisements, brochures, and souvenir program. Candidates should have ability to work independently, computer skills, editing skills, experience in the field, oral communication skills, organizational skills, personal interest in the field, self-motivation, written communica-

tion skills. Duration is June to end of July/early August. Unpaid. Open to college juniors, college seniors, recent college graduates, graduate students. ▶ *1–2 marketing and promotions interns:* responsibilities include marketing festival, securing sponsors, press releases, and public relations events. Candidates should have ability to work independently, computer skills, editing skills, experience in the field, oral communication skills, organizational skills, personal interest in the field, plan to pursue career in field, self-motivation, writing skills. Duration is flexible. Unpaid. Open to college freshmen, college sophomores, college juniors, college seniors, recent college graduates, graduate students. ▶ *1–2 volunteer/host coordinators:* responsibilities include coordinating and enrolling hosts for filmmakers and interns; supervising and enrolling volunteers. Candidates should have ability to work independently, ability to work with others, organizational skills, self-motivation, writing skills. Duration is flexible. Unpaid. Open to college freshmen, college sophomores, college juniors, college seniors, recent college graduates, retirees (seniors welcome). International applications accepted.
Benefits Free housing, on-the-job training, opportunity to attend seminars/workshops, willing to act as a professional reference, willing to complete paperwork for educational credit, willing to provide letters of recommendation.
Contact Write, call, fax, or e-mail Justine Ashton, Executive Director. Phone: 707-996-2536. Fax: 707-996-6964. E-mail: wcfilmfest@aol.com. In-person interview recommended (telephone interview accepted). Applicants must submit a letter of interest, resume, two personal references, two letters of recommendation. Application deadline: February 1 for summer. World Wide Web: http://www.winecountryfilmfest.com.

WOMEN'S STUDIO WORKSHOP
PO Box 489
Rosendale, New York 12472

General Information Studio arts programs offering specialized studios in intaglio, papermaking, photography, screenprinting, offset, letterpress, book arts, and ceramics; offers residencies, grants and fellowships to professional artists, a studio-based art in education program, and intensive workshop. Established in 1974. Number of employees: 8. Number of internship applications received each year: 40.
Internships Available ▶ *3 studio interns:* responsibilities include maintaining studio facilities and assisting artists in residence and instructors. Candidates should have ability to work independently, ability to work with others, college degree in related field, knowledge of field, personal interest in the field, plan to pursue career in field, self-motivation. Duration is 6 months. Position available as unpaid or at $150 per month. Open to recent college graduates, graduate students. International applications accepted.
Benefits Formal training, free housing, on-the-job training, opportunity to attend seminars/workshops, willing to act as a professional reference, willing to complete paperwork for educational credit, willing to provide letters of recommendation.
Contact Write, call, e-mail, or through World Wide Web site Ellen Kucera, Internship Coordinator. Phone: 845-658-9133. Fax: 845-658-9031. E-mail: wsw@ulster.net. Telephone interview required. Applicants must submit a letter of interest, resume, portfolio, 3 personal references or letters of recommendation. Application deadline: April 1 for August-December, October 15 for January-July. World Wide Web: http://www.wsworkshop.org.

YMCA CAMP GRADY SPRUCE
3000 Park Road 36
Graford, Texas 76449

General Information 856-acre waterfront resident outdoor center for youth that provides a summer camp, outdoor education, conferences, and family programs with an emphasis on Christian values. Established in 1949. Number of employees: 100. Branch of YMCA Metro Dallas, Dallas, Texas. Number of internship applications received each year: 5.
Internships Available ▶ *1–4 naturalist interns:* responsibilities include being a member of the residential outdoor education staff team, developing and leading outdoor activities with 5th and

YMCA Camp Grady Spruce (continued)

6th graders; participating in teacher workshops, basic upkeep and maintenance, and other essential duties. Candidates should have ability to work with others, oral communication skills, personal interest in the field, strong leadership ability, written communication skills, desire to work with children in the outdoors. Duration is 4 months or more in fall or spring. $200–$250 per week. Open to individuals 19 and older. ▶ *1–3 summer camp interns:* responsibilities include being a member of the camp delivery team, developing and leading programs, scheduling, and other administrative duties. Candidates should have ability to work independently, oral communication skills, personal interest in the field, strong interpersonal skills, strong leadership ability, written communication skills. Duration is 2–12 months. Position available as unpaid or at $140–$200 per week. Open to college freshmen, college sophomores, college juniors, college seniors, recent college graduates, graduate students. ▶ *Up to 120 summer camp staff interns:* responsibilities include residing at camp whose activities include horseback riding, swimming, sailing, crafts, snorkeling, fishing, archery, canoeing, kayaking, water skiing, challenge course, and traditional camp activities; positions include counselors, unit leaders, waterfront directors, ski team sports directors, wranglers, and trip leaders. Candidates should have oral communication skills, personal interest in the field, strong interpersonal skills, strong leadership ability, written communication skills, interest in working with children ages 8–16. Duration is 10 weeks. $140–$210 per week. Open to individuals 19 and older. International applications accepted.

Benefits Formal training, free housing, free meals, on-the-job training, opportunity to attend seminars/workshops, possible full-time employment, willing to act as a professional reference, willing to complete paperwork for educational credit, willing to provide letters of recommendation, job listings provided when available.

Contact Write, call, fax, e-mail, or through World Wide Web site Kevin Spaeth, Outdoor Education Director. Phone: 940-779-3411. Fax: 940-779-2939. E-mail: kevincgs@hotmail.com. In-person interview recommended (telephone interview accepted). Applicants must submit a letter of interest, resume, three personal references, three letters of recommendation. Application deadline: February 1 for summer, June 30 for fall, October 30 for spring. World Wide Web: http://campgradyspruce.com.

YMCA CAMP POTAWOTAMI
PO Box 38
South Milford, Indiana 46786

General Information Outdoor education center, summer camp, adventure education, conference and retreat center. Established in 1920. Number of employees: 40. Branch of YMCA of Greater Fort Wayne, Fort Wayne, Indiana.

Internships Available ▶ *1 leadership/conference director assistant:* responsibilities include leading participants through challenge course and teambuilding course; working with weekend retreat groups; helping with outdoor education and summer staff; leading whitewater and rock climbing trips; running climbing tower. Candidates should have ability to work independently, knowledge of field, oral communication skills, personal interest in the field, self-motivation, strong interpersonal skills, strong leadership ability. Duration is April to November. Position available as unpaid or at $150–$180 per week. Open to recent high school graduates, college freshmen, college sophomores, college juniors, college seniors, recent college graduates. ▶ *2–4 outdoor education instructors:* responsibilities include developing and implementing programs, serving as liaisons to schools, and working with school groups. Candidates should have analytical skills, oral communication skills, personal interest in the field, self-motivation, strong interpersonal skills. Duration is 3–6 months. Position available as unpaid or at $150–$215 per week. Open to recent high school graduates, college freshmen, college sophomores, college juniors, college seniors, recent college graduates, graduate students, law students, career changers, individuals reentering the workforce. ▶ *3–10 summer camp counselors:* responsibilities include supervising children, organizing and implementing activities; other duties as needed. Candidates should have ability to work independently, ability to

work with others, oral communication skills, personal interest in the field, self-motivation, strong leadership ability. Duration is 10 weeks. Position available as unpaid or at $150–$200 per week. Open to recent high school graduates, college freshmen, college sophomores, college juniors, college seniors, recent college graduates, graduate students, law students, career changers, individuals reentering the workforce. International applications accepted.

Benefits Formal training, free housing, free meals, job counseling, names of contacts, on-the-job training, opportunity to attend seminars/workshops, possible full-time employment, travel reimbursement, willing to act as a professional reference, willing to complete paperwork for educational credit, willing to provide letters of recommendation.

Contact Write, call, fax, e-mail, or through World Wide Web site Ms. Angie Cole, Outdoor Education Director. Phone: 219-351-2525. Fax: 219-351-3915. E-mail: ymcacamp@camp-potawotami. org. In-person interview recommended (telephone interview accepted). Applicants must submit a formal organization application, letter of interest, resume, three personal references. Applications are accepted continuously. World Wide Web: http://www. camp-potawotami.org.

YMCA CAMP RALPH S. MASON
23 Birch Ridge Road
Hardwick, New Jersey 07825

General Information Camp for children, outdoor education facility, and retreat center. Established in 1900. Number of employees: 150. Number of internship applications received each year: 5.

Internships Available ▶ *3–7 naturalists:* responsibilities include leading children through adventures in outdoor education. Candidates should have ability to work independently, ability to work with others, oral communication skills, organizational skills, personal interest in the field, self-motivation, strong leadership ability, healthy attitude. Duration is 3–9 months. Position available as unpaid or at $215–$230 per week. Open to college freshmen, college sophomores, college juniors, college seniors, recent college graduates, graduate students, career changers. International applications accepted.

Benefits Free housing, free meals, possible seasonal employment.

Contact Write, call, fax, e-mail, or through World Wide Web site Marcus Forester, Senior Program Director. Phone: 908-362-8217. Fax: 908-362-5767. E-mail: marcus@campmason.org. In-person interview recommended (telephone interview accepted). Applicants must submit a formal organization application, letter of interest, resume, three personal references. Applications are accepted continuously. World Wide Web: http://www.campmason.org.

YMCA OF GREATER OKLAHOMA CITY/CAMP CLASSEN
Route 1, Box 47
Davis, Oklahoma 73030-9801

General Information 2400-acre resident camp offering a summer youth camp, school-year outdoor education programs, family programs on weekends, and seeking to help people grow in mind, body, and spirit. Established in 1940. Number of employees: 25. Unit of YMCA of Greater Oklahoma City, Oklahoma City, Oklahoma. Number of internship applications received each year: 10.

Internships Available ▶ *3 program assistants:* responsibilities include assisting in the operation of programs including nature education, cooperative courses and games, and helping in facility care and development. Candidates should have analytical skills, oral communication skills, personal interest in the field, self-motivation, strong interpersonal skills, love of children and willingness to learn. Duration is 2 semesters. Position available as unpaid or at $225 per week. Open to college freshmen, college sophomores, college juniors, college seniors, recent college graduates, graduate students, career changers, individuals reentering the workforce.

Benefits Formal training, free housing, free meals, job counseling, names of contacts, on-the-job training, opportunity to attend seminars/workshops, possible full-time employment, willing to act as a professional reference, willing to complete paperwork for educational credit, willing to provide letters of recommendation. **Contact** Write, call, fax, e-mail, or through World Wide Web site Bill Hinton, Outdoor School Director. Phone: 580-369-2272. Fax: 580-369-2284. E-mail: bhinton@ymcaokc.org. In-person interview recommended (telephone interview accepted). Applicants must submit a formal organization application, letter of interest, resume, three personal references. Applications are accepted continuously. World Wide Web: http://www.campclassenymca.org.

MUSEUMS, HISTORICAL SITES, ZOOS, AND NATURE PARKS

ACADIA NATIONAL PARK
PO Box 177
Bar Harbor, Maine 04609

General Information Resource protection and resource-based recreation/educational agency. Established in 1916. Number of employees: 150. Unit of United States National Park Service, Washington, District of Columbia. Number of internship applications received each year: 35.
Internships Available ▶ *2 environmental education interns:* responsibilities include working with park education staff in presenting natural and cultural history curriculum-based programs for grades 3 through 6, both in the classroom and at the park; custom programs and special projects related to environmental education possible. Candidates should have ability to work independently, ability to work with others, knowledge of field, oral communication skills, personal interest in the field, strong leadership ability. Duration is 10 weeks in spring or fall. Position available as unpaid or at $100 per week (32 hours). Open to college freshmen, college sophomores, college juniors, college seniors, recent college graduates, graduate students, career changers, individuals reentering the workforce. International applications accepted.
Benefits Formal training, free housing, job counseling, on-the-job training, opportunity to attend seminars/workshops, willing to act as a professional reference, willing to complete paperwork for educational credit, willing to provide letters of recommendation.
Contact Write, call, fax, or e-mail Cynthia Ocel, Education Coordinator, PO Box 177, Bar Harbor, Maine 04609. Phone: 207-288-3893. Fax: 207-288-5507. E-mail: cynthia_ocel@nps.gov. Telephone interview required. Applicants must submit a letter of interest, resume, three personal references. Application deadline: February 1 for spring, July 1 for fall. World Wide Web: http://www.nps.gov/acad.

AGATE FOSSIL BEDS NATIONAL MONUMENT
301 River Road
Harrison, Nebraska 69346-2734

General Information National monument set aside for mammalian paleontological resources and Captain James H. Cook's Oglala Lakota Sioux Native American artifacts collection; set in a mixed prairie high plains ecosystem with extensive wetlands. Established in 1965. Number of employees: 13. Unit of National Park Service, Washington, District of Columbia. Number of internship applications received each year: 5.
Internships Available ▶ *1–2 SCA interns:* responsibilities include various tasks depending upon specific research interpretation and/or management needs. Candidates should have ability to work independently, analytical skills, computer skills, oral communication skills, organizational skills, self-motivation, strong interpersonal skills, writing skills. Duration is 3 months (usually in summer). $50 per week. Open to recent high school graduates, college freshmen, college sophomores, college juniors, college seniors, recent college graduates, graduate students, law students, law school graduates, career changers, individuals reentering the workforce. ▶ *Volunteers-in-Parks interns:* responsibilities

include interpreting for public and/or performing curatorial duties, library research, resource management, and general clerical duties. Candidates should have ability to work independently, computer skills, oral communication skills, personal interest in the field, self-motivation, strong interpersonal skills, writing skills. Duration is flexible (at least 1 month). Unpaid. Open to individuals 18 or older. International applications accepted.
Benefits Formal training, free housing, job counseling, on-the-job training, opportunity to attend seminars/workshops, willing to act as a professional reference, willing to complete paperwork for educational credit, willing to provide letters of recommendation, 2 trailer pads with full hookups, reimbursement for mileage, small stipend for meals, 3-bedroom house available for occupancy, tuition assistance and health insurance supported (if funds available).
Contact Write, call, fax, e-mail, or through World Wide Web site Lil Morava, Superintendent. Phone: 308-668-2211. Fax: 308-668-2318. E-mail: agfo_superintendent@nps.gov. Telephone interview required. Applicants must submit a formal organization application, letter of interest, resume, three personal references. Applications are accepted continuously. World Wide Web: http://www.nps.gov/agfo/.

THE ANDY WARHOL MUSEUM
117 Sandusky Street
Pittsburgh, Pennsylvania 15212

General Information Museum that features extensive permanent collections of art and archives and presents the work of one of the most influential American artists of the second half of the 20th century. Established in 1994. Number of employees: 64. Unit of Carnegie Institute, Pittsburgh, Pennsylvania. Number of internship applications received each year: 300.
Internships Available ▶ *1–2 archives interns:* responsibilities include assisting with all aspects of archival collection including inventory, exhibits, research, and special projects as assigned by the archivist. Candidates should have computer skills, knowledge of field, office skills, organizational skills, personal interest in the field, self-motivation. Duration is flexible. Unpaid. Open to high school students, recent high school graduates, college freshmen, college sophomores, college juniors, college seniors, recent college graduates, graduate students, law students, career changers, individuals reentering the workforce. ▶ *Education department interns.* Candidates should have oral communication skills, personal interest in the field, self-motivation, strong interpersonal skills, strong leadership ability. Duration is flexible. Unpaid. Open to high school students, recent high school graduates, college freshmen, college sophomores, college juniors, college seniors, recent college graduates, graduate students, law students, career changers, individuals reentering the workforce. ▶ *1 film and video intern:* responsibilities include administrative and research duties. Candidates should have computer skills, knowledge of field, organizational skills, self-motivation. Duration is flexible. Unpaid. International applications accepted.
Benefits Job counseling, names of contacts, opportunity to attend seminars/workshops, possible full-time employment, willing to complete paperwork for educational credit, willing to provide letters of recommendation, lectures and special events.
Contact Write Rachel Baron, Administrative and Financial Coordinator. No phone calls. In-person interview recommended (telephone interview accepted). Applicants must submit a letter of interest, resume. Applications are accepted continuously. World Wide Web: http://www.warhol.org.

ANGELINA NATIONAL FOREST
111 Walnut Ridge Road
Zavalla, Texas 75980

General Information National forest offering multiple uses including recreation, wildlife, timber, soil, and water resources. Number of employees: 23. Unit of National Forests and Grasslands in Texas, Lufkin, Texas. Number of internship applications received each year: 5.
Internships Available ▶ *2–3 volunteer campground hosts:* responsibilities include greeting campers, informing visitors of campground rules, assisting in cleaning and maintaining the area. Candidates

Angelina National Forest (continued)

should have ability to work independently, oral communication skills, self-motivation, strong interpersonal skills. Duration is 3 months. Unpaid. Open to graduate students, career changers, individuals reentering the workforce. ▶ *1–20 volunteers:* responsibilities include assisting with recreation or wildlife habitat management, maintaining campgrounds and hiking trails, and assisting with various other duties. Candidates should have ability to work with others, oral communication skills, personal interest in the field, self-motivation, written communication skills. Duration is variable. Unpaid. Open to anyone willing to work outside.

Benefits Formal training, job counseling, names of contacts, opportunity to attend seminars/workshops, willing to complete paperwork for educational credit, willing to provide letters of recommendation, free campsite for volunteer campground hosts.

Contact Write, call, or fax Karen Tinkle, District Ranger. Phone: 936-897-1068. Fax: 936-897-3406. In-person interview recommended (telephone interview accepted). Applicants must submit a letter of interest, resume. Applications are accepted continuously. World Wide Web: http://www.southernregion.fs.fed.us/texas.

ANTIETAM NATIONAL BATTLEFIELD
PO Box 158
Sharpsburg, Maryland 21782

General Information Preserves and protects the site of the Battle of Antietam and provides information about the battle of Antietam or Sharpsburg. Established in 1890. Number of employees: 56. Branch of Department of Interior–National Park Service, Washington, District of Columbia. Number of internship applications received each year: 15.

Internships Available ▶ *Volunteers in the Park (VIP):* responsibilities include staffing the information desk, assisting librarian/historian as library aide, accessioning books, manuscripts, conducting research, and assisting researchers/visitors with research. Duration is flexible. Unpaid. Open to people of all ages. International applications accepted.

Benefits Formal training, willing to complete paperwork for educational credit, protection for on-the-job injury, limited reimbursement of travel and meal expenses.

Contact Write, call, fax, e-mail, or through World Wide Web site Mrs. Stephanie Gray, Volunteer-in the Parks (VIP) Coordinator. Phone: 301-432-5124. Fax: 301-432-4590. E-mail: stephanie_gray@nps.gov. In-person interview required. Applicants must submit a letter of interest, resume. Applications are accepted continuously. World Wide Web: http://www.nps.gov/anti.

ARCHIVE OF FOLK CULTURE, AMERICAN FOLKLIFE CENTER, LIBRARY OF CONGRESS
101 Independence Avenue, SE
Washington, District of Columbia 20540-4610

General Information National archive of folk music, ethnomusicology, and folklore. Established in 1928. Number of employees: 25. Division of Library of Congress, Washington, District of Columbia. Number of internship applications received each year: 40.

Internships Available ▶ *4–8 interns:* responsibilities include performing reference work, reader service, cataloging, processing, photocopying, accessioning, filing, and working on a special project that will benefit both the intern and the Archive. Candidates should have ability to work with others, computer skills, experience in the field, organizational skills, personal interest in the field, research skills. Duration is 200-1000 hours or more. Unpaid. Open to recent high school graduates, college freshmen, college sophomores, college juniors, college seniors, recent college graduates, graduate students, career changers, individuals reentering the workforce. International applications accepted.

Benefits Job counseling, names of contacts, on-the-job training, opportunity to attend seminars/workshops, willing to act as a professional reference, willing to complete paperwork for educational credit, willing to provide letters of recommendation.

Contact Write, call, fax, e-mail, or through World Wide Web site Ann Hoog, Folklife Specialist (Reference). Phone: 202-707-5510. Fax: 202-707-2076. E-mail: folklife@loc.gov. In-person interview

recommended (telephone interview accepted). Applicants must submit a letter of interest, resume. Applications are accepted continuously. World Wide Web: http://www.loc.gov/folklife.

BADLANDS NATIONAL PARK
PO Box 6
Interior, South Dakota 57750

General Information Organization that protects park resources, and provides enjoyment and education for park visitors. Established in 1939. Number of employees: 50. Number of internship applications received each year: 70.

Internships Available ▶ *2–3 Enos Mills Nature Education interns:* responsibilities include preparing and presenting guided walks and talks; staffing visitor center; coordinating special events. Candidates should have ability to work with others, computer skills, oral communication skills, plan to pursue career in field, self-motivation, writing skills. Duration is May 23 to August 20. $1000 reimbursement of expenses. Open to college sophomores, college juniors, college seniors, recent college graduates, graduate students, law students, career changers, individuals reentering the workforce. ▶ *1–3 John C. Clark Paleontological Educational interns:* responsibilities include preparing and presenting interpretive programs on paleontology and geology to park visitors. Candidates should have ability to work independently, college courses in field, computer skills, knowledge of field, office skills, oral communication skills, personal interest in the field, plan to pursue career in field, research skills, self-motivation, strong interpersonal skills, writing skills. Duration is 13 weeks. $1000 per duration of internship. Open to college sophomores, college juniors, college seniors, recent college graduates, graduate students, career changers. ▶ *2 curatorial interns:* responsibilities include assisting park curator in cataloging and organizing museum collections (fossils, rocks, plant and animal specimens, and photographs). Candidates should have ability to work independently, ability to work with others, analytical skills, computer skills, office skills, personal interest in the field, research skills, self-motivation. Reimbursement for $1000 in expenses. Open to college sophomores, college juniors, college seniors, recent college graduates, graduate students, career changers, individuals reentering the workforce, curators on sabbatical. ▶ *2–4 fall nature education interns:* responsibilities include preparing and presenting school programs on geology, ecology, or history; staffing visitor center; writing; and school activity preparation. Candidates should have ability to work independently, college courses in field, experience in the field, oral communication skills, self-motivation, strong interpersonal skills, written communication skills. Duration is September to early December. $1000 reimbursement of expenses plus uniforms. Open to college juniors, college seniors, recent college graduates, graduate students, law students, career changers, individuals reentering the workforce. ▶ *1 library intern:* responsibilities include cataloging library books, slides, and museum objects in database. Candidates should have ability to work independently, ability to work with others, computer skills, knowledge of field, office skills, self-motivation. Duration is September to November. $500 reimbursement of expenses. Open to college freshmen, college sophomores, college juniors, college seniors, recent college graduates, graduate students, law students, career changers, individuals reentering the workforce, librarians on sabbatical. ▶ *2–10 mini-internships:* responsibilities include submitting proposal for project relating to Badlands National Park at least 8 weeks prior to proposed start date. Candidates should have ability to work independently, computer skills, personal interest in the field, research skills, self-motivation, strong interpersonal skills, writing skills. Duration is 8 weeks (year-round). Unpaid. Open to college freshmen, college sophomores, college juniors, college seniors, recent college graduates, graduate students, law students, career changers, individuals reentering the workforce, teachers on sabbatical. ▶ *1–4 spring education interns:* responsibilities include preparing and presenting programs in schools on geology, ecology, or history; staffing visitor center; developing lesson plans; leading guided walks. Candidates should have ability to work independently, college courses in field, oral communication skills, plan to pursue career in field, strong interpersonal skills, written communication skills. Duration is March 1 to May 23 (approximate).

$1000 reimbursement of expenses plus uniforms. Open to college juniors, college seniors, recent college graduates, graduate students, law students, career changers, individuals reentering the workforce. ▶ *1–2 winter education interns:* responsibilities include developing lesson plans, children's materials, exhibits, and related curricula-based activities; staffing visitor center; creative writing. Candidates should have ability to work independently, ability to work with others, experience in the field, plan to pursue career in field, research skills, written communication skills. Duration is December to February. $1000 reimbursement of expenses. Open to college seniors, recent college graduates, graduate students, career changers, teachers on sabbatical. International applications accepted.

Benefits Formal training, free housing, free meals, job counseling, on-the-job training, opportunity to attend seminars/workshops, travel reimbursement, willing to act as a professional reference, willing to complete paperwork for educational credit, willing to provide letters of recommendation, worker's compensation.

Contact Write, call, fax, e-mail, or through World Wide Web site Marianne Mills, Chief, Resource Education. Phone: 605-433-5245. Fax: 605-433-5248. E-mail: badl_internships@nps.gov. Applicants must submit a formal organization application, letter of interest, writing sample, three personal references, letter of recommendation. Application deadline: March 15 for summer, July 15 for fall, October 15 for winter/spring. World Wide Web: http://www.nps.gov/badl/.

BALTIMORE MUSEUM OF INDUSTRY
1415 Key Highway
Baltimore, Maryland 21230

General Information History museum that preserves and interprets Baltimore's and Maryland's rich industrial heritage, focusing on education and archival holdings and collections that include a steam tug and working machinery. Established in 1981. Number of employees: 55. Affiliate of American Association of Museums, Washington, District of Columbia. Number of internship applications received each year: 15.

Internships Available ▶ *1–3 archives interns:* responsibilities include processing holdings and working on cleaning and documenting archives. Duration is flexible. Unpaid. Open to college freshmen, college sophomores, college juniors, college seniors, recent college graduates, graduate students, law students, career changers, individuals reentering the workforce. ▶ *1 curatorial intern:* responsibilities include performing historical research on artifacts and processing. Candidates should have organizational skills, research skills. Duration is flexible. Unpaid. Open to college freshmen, college sophomores, college juniors, college seniors, recent college graduates, graduate students, law students, career changers, individuals reentering the workforce. ▶ *1–5 education interns:* responsibilities include helping to research, plan, and implement Museum educational programs with emphasis on interactive activities for children. Candidates should have ability to work independently, ability to work with others, oral communication skills, organizational skills, personal interest in the field, self-motivation, some college courses in related fields of history and/or technology. Duration is flexible. Unpaid. Open to college freshmen, college sophomores, college juniors, college seniors, recent college graduates, graduate students, law students, career changers, individuals reentering the workforce. ▶ *1–2 exhibits interns/school programs:* responsibilities include helping design and build exhibits. Candidates should have ability to work independently, computer skills, self-motivation, art, design, or museum skills, history or education background. Duration is Flexible. Unpaid. Open to recent high school graduates, college juniors, college seniors, recent college graduates. ▶ *1–3 library interns:* responsibilities include duties as needed, including data entry, shelving, and materials preparation. Candidates should have ability to work independently, self-motivation, attention to detail. Duration is flexible. Unpaid. Open to college freshmen, college sophomores, college juniors, college seniors, recent college graduates, graduate students, law students, career changers, individuals reentering the workforce. ▶ *1 public relations intern:* responsibilities include helping with mailings and daily operation of public relations office. Candidates should have computer skills, knowledge of field,

office skills, oral communication skills, personal interest in the field, written communication skills. Duration is flexible. Unpaid. Open to college juniors, college seniors, recent college graduates, graduate students, law students, career changers, individuals reentering the workforce. ▶ *1–3 research interns:* responsibilities include performing historical research for Museum files. Duration is flexible. Unpaid. Open to college freshmen, college sophomores, college juniors, college seniors, recent college graduates, graduate students, law students, career changers, individuals reentering the workforce. International applications accepted.

Benefits On-the-job training, possible full-time employment, willing to act as a professional reference, willing to complete paperwork for educational credit, willing to provide letters of recommendation.

Contact Write, call, fax, or e-mail Eliner T. Elgin, Director of Education. Phone: 410-727-4808. Fax: 410-783-8541. E-mail: bmi@thebmi.org. In-person interview required. Applicants must submit a letter of interest, resume. Application deadline: March 15 for summer, July 15 for fall, November 15 for spring. World Wide Web: http://www.thebmi.org.

BALTIMORE ZOO
Druid Hill Park
Baltimore, Maryland 21217

General Information Zoo involved in education, conservation, research, and recreation. Established in 1876. Number of employees: 150. Number of internship applications received each year: 50.

Internships Available ▶ *Animal embassy interns:* responsibilities include assisting keepers with weighing food, preparing and distributing diets, cleaning animal habitats, assisting as needed with facilitating animal behavior, and enrichment activities. Candidates should have ability to work with others, self-motivation, written communication skills, ability to stand 3 to 6 hours and lift moderately heavy loads, must complete training to handle animals, must complete research report. Duration is year-round (8 hours per week minimum). Unpaid. Open to college freshmen, college sophomores, college juniors, college seniors. ▶ *Education department interns:* responsibilities include working on educational lesson plans, animal fact sheets, local educational trips, mobile teaching units, and presentations. Candidates should have ability to work with others, college courses in field, oral communication skills, plan to pursue career in field, written communication skills. Duration is 1 semester. Unpaid. Open to college juniors, college seniors, graduate students, individuals reentering the workforce. ▶ *Group sales interns:* responsibilities include assisting with coordinating, planning, and promoting two summer overnight events; booking reservations; answering calls regarding events; and coordinating volunteers with assigned duties. Candidates should have ability to work with others, college courses in field, computer skills, experience in the field, oral communication skills, self-motivation. Duration is year-round. Unpaid. Open to college freshmen, college sophomores, college juniors, college seniors, recent college graduates, graduate students, career changers, individuals reentering the workforce, must be at least 18 years old. ▶ *Horticulture interns:* responsibilities include weeding, watering, mulching, planting, pruning, bed preparation, plant propagation, flowerbed layout, installation of plants in exhibits, and IPM. Candidates should have ability to work with others, college courses in field, personal interest in the field, plan to pursue career in field, self-motivation, basic understanding of plant care. Duration is June to August or April to May. Unpaid. Open to college freshmen, college sophomores, college juniors, college seniors, graduate students, must be at least 18 years old. ▶ *Keeper aid interns:* responsibilities include assisting with cleaning animal habitats and exhibits; weighing, preparing, and distributing diets; assisting with collecting and recording data on animal behavior and eating habits; assisting with enrichment activities. Candidates should have ability to work with others, personal interest in the field, self-motivation, additional training to handle animals. Duration is 4 consecutive months. Unpaid. Open to recent high school graduates, college freshmen, college sophomores, college juniors, college seniors, must be at least 18 years old. ▶ *Marketing interns:* responsibilities include assisting with on-grounds and radio promo-

Baltimore Zoo (continued)

tions, coordinating with promotion partners, answering inquiries, and evaluating effectiveness of zoo's advertising efforts. Candidates should have ability to work with others, college courses in field, computer skills, oral communication skills, writing skills, excellent portfolio of writing samples, knowledge of Baltimore, ability to handle multiple tasks. Duration is year-round. Unpaid. Open to college freshmen, college sophomores, college juniors, college seniors, graduate students, individuals reentering the workforce, must be at least 18 years old. ▶ *Public relations interns:* responsibilities include writing media alerts and press releases, maintaining media list, tracking news coverage, hosting media events, providing zoo tours for media, setting up interviews, and coordinating story coverage. Candidates should have computer skills, experience in the field, oral communication skills, strong interpersonal skills, written communication skills, knowledge of Baltimore area, ability to handle multiple tasks. Duration is year-round. Unpaid. Open to college freshmen, college sophomores, college juniors, college seniors, recent college graduates, graduate students, career changers, individuals reentering the workforce, must be at least 18 years old. International applications accepted.

Benefits Names of contacts, on-the-job training, possible full-time employment, willing to act as a professional reference, willing to complete paperwork for educational credit, willing to provide letters of recommendation, discounts at all concessions, free parking, stipend for horticulture and education positions.

Contact Write, call, or fax Hannah Katz, Volunteer Manager. Phone: 410-396-7623. Fax: 410-396-6464. In-person interview required. Applicants must submit a formal organization application, letter of interest, resume, academic transcripts, TB test for animal embassy and keeper aid positions. Application deadline: April 1 for summer/fall, November 1 for winter/spring.

BEAVER LAKE NATURE CENTER
East Mud Lake Road
Baldwinsville, New York 13027

General Information A 580-acre park with a 200-acre lake and 10 miles of trails established to enhance visitors' understanding and appreciation of the natural world. Established in 1970. Number of employees: 12. Unit of Onondaga County Parks, Syracuse, New York. Number of internship applications received each year: 50.

Internships Available ▶ *4 naturalist interns:* responsibilities include presenting a wide range of on-site interpretive programs to students and youth or family groups and assisting with exhibit production and program development. Candidates should have knowledge of field, oral communication skills, personal interest in the field, self-motivation, strong interpersonal skills. Duration is 3 months minimum. $125–$165 per week. Open to college juniors, college seniors, recent college graduates.

Benefits Free housing, job counseling, names of contacts, on-the-job training, opportunity to attend seminars/workshops, possible full-time employment, willing to act as a professional reference, willing to provide letters of recommendation.

Contact Write, call, fax, or e-mail Mr. Greg Smith, Park Naturalist, East Mud Lake Road, Baldwinville, New York 13027. Phone: 315-638-2519. Fax: 315-638-7488. E-mail: prgsmit@nysnet.net. In-person interview recommended (telephone interview accepted). Applicants must submit a letter of interest, resume, three personal references. Applications are accepted continuously. World Wide Web: http://www.ongov.net/parks/blnc.html.

BOOKER T. WASHINGTON NATIONAL MONUMENT
12130 Booker T. Washington Highway
Hardy, Virginia 24101

General Information National park service site where Booker T. Washington was born in 1856; focuses on interpretive programs about the influence of slavery on Washington's life. Established in 1956. Number of employees: 13. Unit of United States National Park Service, Washington, District of Columbia. Number of internship applications received each year: 10.

Internships Available ▶ *1 costumed interpreter:* responsibilities include presenting interpretive programs to the general public. Candidates should have ability to work independently, oral communication skills, personal interest in the field, strong interpersonal skills, writing skills. Unpaid. Open to high school students, recent high school graduates, college freshmen, college sophomores, college juniors, college seniors, recent college graduates, graduate students, law students, career changers, individuals reentering the workforce. ▶ *1–10 information desk receptionists:* responsibilities include greeting visitors, explaining primary theme of park story, explaining available programs and facilities, and operating book sales area. Candidates should have ability to work independently, computer skills, oral communication skills, personal interest in the field, strong interpersonal skills. Unpaid.

Benefits Job counseling, willing to complete paperwork for educational credit.

Contact Write or e-mail Ms. Betsy Haynes. E-mail: betsy_haynes@ nps.gov. In-person interview required. Applications are accepted continuously. World Wide Web: http://www.nps.gov/bowa/.

BROOKFIELD ZOO
3300 South Golf Road
Brookfield, Illinois 60513

General Information Zoo that strives to enhance appreciation of the earth's biological heritage and to help visitors achieve a sustainable relationship with the natural world through conservation. Established in 1934. Number of employees: 470. Number of internship applications received each year: 200.

Internships Available ▶ *1 development intern:* responsibilities include development/fund-raising projects, activities, events, and hands-on learning in department operations. Candidates should have computer skills, knowledge of field, office skills, oral communication skills, organizational skills, personal interest in the field, self-motivation, strong interpersonal skills, writing skills. Duration is 6–12 weeks. Unpaid. Open to college juniors, college seniors. ▶ *6–9 education department interns:* responsibilities include involvement in school programs, casual visitor program, community outreach, public programs, and accessibility for the disabled. Candidates should have college courses in field, computer skills, office skills, oral communication skills, organizational skills, personal interest in the field, plan to pursue career in field, self-motivation, strong interpersonal skills, written communication skills. Duration is 6–12 weeks. Unpaid. Open to college juniors, college seniors, recent college graduates, graduate students. ▶ *1–2 human resources interns:* responsibilities include working on various human resource projects and learning human resource department operations. Candidates should have analytical skills, college courses in field, computer skills, editing skills, office skills, oral communication skills, organizational skills, personal interest in the field, plan to pursue career in field, research skills, self-motivation, strong interpersonal skills, writing skills. Duration is 6–12 weeks. Unpaid. Open to college juniors, college seniors. ▶ *18–20 interns:* responsibilities include working in areas of human resources, education, zookeeping, photographic services, animal nutrition, publications, and exhibit design. Candidates should have ability to work independently, college courses in field, computer skills, office skills, oral communication skills, organizational skills, personal interest in the field, plan to pursue career in field, self-motivation, strong interpersonal skills, written communication skills. Duration is 6–12 weeks. Unpaid. Open to college freshmen, college sophomores, college juniors, college seniors, recent college graduates, graduate students, career changers, individuals reentering the workforce. ▶ *1 water quality lab intern:* responsibilities include performing water quality analysis, analytical testing on various samples, project management, record keeping, database management, and maintaining water systems in exhibits throughout the zoo. Candidates should have ability to work independently, analytical skills, computer skills, knowledge of field, oral communication skills, organizational skills, personal interest in the field, research skills, self-motivation, strong interpersonal skills. Duration is 6–12 weeks. Unpaid. Open to college juniors, college seniors, recent college graduates, graduate students. ▶ *18–19 zookeeper interns:* responsibilities include working in all aspects of captive animal management, including exhibit/enclosure maintenance, animal husbandry, diet preparation, record keeping, and observations duties. Candidates should have ability to work independently, college courses in field, knowledge of field, oral communication skills, organizational skills, personal interest in the field, plan to pursue career in field, self-motivation, strong interpersonal skills. Duration is 6–12 weeks. Unpaid. Open to college juniors, college seniors, recent college graduates, graduate students. International applications accepted.

Benefits On-the-job training, opportunity to attend seminars/workshops, possible full-time employment, willing to act as a professional reference, willing to complete paperwork for educational credit, willing to provide letters of recommendation, hands-on experience with exotic, native, and domestic animals in all aspects of captive animal management.

Contact Write, call, fax, or e-mail Ms. Sandra Dornhecker, Human Resources Director. Phone: 708-485-0263 Ext. 334. Fax: 708-485-0986. E-mail: interns@brookfieldzoo.org. In-person interview required. Applicants must submit a formal organization application, letter of interest, resume, academic transcripts, two letters of recommendation. Application deadline: February 1 for summer (zookeeper), August 1 for fall (zookeeper), December 1 for winter (zookeeper); all non-zookeeper applications accepted continuously. Fees: $15. World Wide Web: http://www.brookfieldzoo.org.

BROOKLYN BOTANIC GARDEN
1000 Washington Avenue
Brooklyn, New York 11225

General Information Botanical garden. Established in 1910. Number of employees: 200. Number of internship applications received each year: 150.

Internships Available ▶ *7–9 horticultural education interns.* Candidates should have ability to work with others, knowledge of field, oral communication skills, personal interest in the field, strong leadership ability, written communication skills, experience working with children. Duration is June 1 through September 1. $7 per hour. Open to college sophomores, college juniors, college seniors. ▶ *7–9 horticulture/general interns:* responsibilities include performing gardening work. Candidates should have ability to work independently, ability to work with others, personal interest in the field, plan to pursue career in field, self-motivation, driver's license. Duration is April through December. $7 per hour. Open to recent college graduates, career changers, individuals reentering the workforce, individuals 18 years or older. ▶ *1–3 junior botanist summer interns:* responsibilities include teaching botany, horticulture, and environmental science to a class of 12 students in grades 4-6; hands-on experience in children's garden; a three-day trip away from the garden, supervising cooking, and environmental skills. Candidates should have ability to work independently, college courses in field, computer skills, knowledge of field, oral communication skills, organizational skills, research skills, self-motivation, strong interpersonal skills, strong leadership ability, written communication skills. Duration is 7–8 weeks. $7–$10 per hour. Open to college freshmen, college sophomores, college juniors, college seniors, recent college graduates. ▶ *6 science department interns:* responsibilities include developing and implementing individual plant science research projects, field work, herbarium management, and computer applications. Candidates should have ability to work independently, ability to work with others, oral communication skills, organizational skills, personal interest in the field, research skills, self-motivation, written communication skills. Duration is one semester or one summer. $5.15 per hour. Open to high school students. International applications accepted.

Benefits Names of contacts, on-the-job training, possible full-time employment, willing to complete paperwork for educational credit, continuing education courses.

Contact Write, call, fax, e-mail, or through World Wide Web site Rochelle Cabiness, Director of Human Resources. Phone: 718-623-7216. Fax: 718-622-7826. E-mail: rochellecabiness@bbg.org. In-person interview recommended (telephone interview accepted). Applicants must submit a letter of interest, resume, two letters of recommendation. Application deadline: January 15 for horticulture/general interns, March 15 for horticulture education interns, June

1 for junior botanist interns; one month prior to beginning of semester for science department interns. World Wide Web: http://www.bbg.org.

THE BROOKLYN MUSEUM OF ART
200 Eastern Parkway
Brooklyn, New York 11238

General Information Art museum with a collection of more than one million items and a program of exhibitions, educational activities, and community events; collection ranges from ancient to contemporary art. Established in 1823. Number of employees: 240. Number of internship applications received each year: 100.

Internships Available ▶ *1–2 adult programs intern educators:* responsibilities include assisting in the development and execution of permanent collection, special exhibition, and non-collection based programs for adult audiences; assisting with the museum's presentation of gallery talks, seminars, workshops, and lectures and with the production of film, video, music, dance, poetry, and performance art programs; research, logistical support, outreach, and production of writing materials. Candidates should have ability to work independently, ability to work with others, oral communication skills, organizational skills, plan to pursue career in field, strong leadership ability, written communication skills. Duration is September to June (full-time). $13,500 per duration of internship. ▶ *5–6 school, youth, and family programs intern educators:* responsibilities include researching, preparing, and teaching daily school group and family programs in a particular area of the museum's permanent collection; preparing teaching materials related to special exhibitions; assisting in researching, writing, and producing a wide variety of materials for children, teachers, and families. Candidates should have ability to work independently, ability to work with others, analytical skills, oral communication skills, organizational skills, plan to pursue career in field, self-motivation, strong leadership ability, written communication skills. Duration is September to June (full-time). $13,500 per duration of internship. Open to recent college graduates, career changers. International applications accepted.

Benefits Formal training, health insurance, on-the-job training, opportunity to attend seminars/workshops, willing to act as a professional reference, willing to provide letters of recommendation, transit check.

Contact Write, call, fax, or e-mail Internship Coordinator, Education Division. Phone: 718-501-6229 Ext. 229. Fax: 718-501-6129. E-mail: education.internships@brooklynmuseum.org. In-person interview recommended (telephone interview accepted). Applicants must submit a letter of interest, resume, two letters of recommendation, send letters of recommendation and other materials in the same envelope if possible. Application deadline: March 31. World Wide Web: http://www.brooklynart.org.

BRUKNER NATURE CENTER
5995 Horseshoe Bend Road
Troy, Ohio 45373

General Information Nature center whose mission is to provide environmental education and wildlife rehabilitation. Established in 1974. Number of employees: 9. Number of internship applications received each year: 75.

Internships Available ▶ *2–3 education/wildlife rehabilitation assistants:* responsibilities include learning and participating in all phases of operation, assisting in the care of native Ohio wildlife, and providing programs for schools using live animals. Candidates should have ability to work independently, oral communication skills, personal interest in the field, self-motivation, strong interpersonal skills. Duration is 3–9 months. $75 per week. Open to college juniors, college seniors, recent college graduates, graduate students. International applications accepted.

Benefits Free housing, job counseling, names of contacts, on-the-job training, opportunity to attend seminars/workshops, possible full-time employment, willing to act as a professional reference, willing to complete paperwork for educational credit, willing to provide letters of recommendation.

Contact Write or e-mail Ms. Debra K. Brill, Administrative Director. Phone: 937-698-6493. Fax: 937-698-4619. E-mail: brukner@juno.

Brukner Nature Center (continued)

com. Telephone interview required. Applicants must submit a letter of interest, resume. Applications are accepted continuously.

BUFFALO BILL HISTORICAL CENTER
720 Sheridan Avenue
Cody, Wyoming 82414

General Information Nonprofit organization with five museums that advances knowledge of the western United States. Established in 1917. Number of employees: 127. Number of internship applications received each year: 30.
Internships Available ▶ *3–4 Native American interns:* responsibilities include working in curatorial or education departments. Candidates should have ability to work independently, ability to work with others, college courses in field, computer skills, organizational skills, personal interest in the field, research skills, self-motivation, writing skills. Duration is 3 months. $1000 per month. Open to college sophomores, college juniors, college seniors, recent college graduates, graduate students. ▶ *6–8 general interns:* responsibilities include working in various departments at any of five BBHC museums according to museum's needs and intern's desire and ability. Candidates should have ability to work independently, ability to work with others, computer skills, organizational skills, personal interest in the field, self-motivation, written communication skills, research skills helpful. Duration is 3-months (average). Position available as unpaid or at $1000 per month. Open to college juniors, college seniors, recent college graduates, graduate students. International applications accepted.
Benefits On-the-job training, opportunity to attend seminars/workshops, willing to act as a professional reference, willing to complete paperwork for educational credit, willing to provide letters of recommendation, stipends for some internships.
Contact Write, call, fax, e-mail, or through World Wide Web site Trent Reed, Internship Coordinator. Phone: 307-578-4007. Fax: 307-578-4090. E-mail: trentr@bbhc.org. Telephone interview required. Applicants must submit a formal organization application, letter of interest, resume, academic transcripts, three letters of recommendation. Application deadline: February 1 for summer. World Wide Web: http://www.bbhc.org.

BUFFALO NATIONAL RIVER
402 North Walnut, Suite 136
Harrison, Arkansas 72601

General Information National river site that conserves and interprets an area containing unique scenic and scientific features, and preserves a free-flowing stream in an important segment of the Buffalo River for the benefit and enjoyment of present and future generations. Established in 1972. Number of employees: 78. Unit of United States National Park Service, Washington, District of Columbia. Number of internship applications received each year: 2.
Internships Available ▶ *1–2 archaeology/museum interns:* responsibilities include inputting archeological data, preparing artifacts for storage, and research/analysis of data. Candidates should have ability to work independently, computer skills, knowledge of field, research skills, writing skills. Duration is flexible. Unpaid. Open to college juniors, college seniors, recent college graduates, graduate students, individuals reentering the workforce. ▶ *1 cultural resources assistant:* responsibilities include creating and maintaining cultural resources files and documents, both graphic and written; preparing research information for use by park managers and public. Candidates should have ability to work independently, computer skills, editing skills, research skills, writing skills. Duration is flexible, (April to December preferred). Unpaid. Open to recent high school graduates, college freshmen, college sophomores, college juniors, college seniors, recent college graduates, graduate students. ▶ *1–5 interpretation interns:* responsibilities include performing visitor center program development and presentation, school outreach, and other resource-oriented duties. Candidates should have ability to work independently, ability to work with others, college courses in field, oral communication skills, personal interest in the field, writing skills. Duration is 8 weeks. Unpaid. Open to college sophomores, college juniors, college seniors,

recent college graduates, graduate students, career changers, individuals reentering the workforce. ▶ *1–3 visitor services interns:* responsibilities include assisting with visitor use monitoring in campgrounds, backcountry, and river; monitoring natural and cultural resources for impact; maintaining fire, EMS and search and rescue caches; participating in fire and search and rescue to a limited degree. Candidates should have ability to work independently, oral communication skills, organizational skills, personal interest in the field, self-motivation. Duration is flexible (April to October preferred). Unpaid. Open to college freshmen, college sophomores, college juniors, college seniors, recent college graduates, graduate students, law students, career changers, individuals reentering the workforce.
Benefits Formal training, free housing, job counseling, names of contacts, on-the-job training, willing to complete paperwork for educational credit, willing to provide letters of recommendation, possible reimbursement of in-park travel expenses.
Contact Write, call, or e-mail Volunteer/Intern Coordinator. Phone: 870-741-5443. E-mail: buff_information@nps.gov. Telephone interview required. Applicants must submit a letter of interest, resume, three personal references. Applications are accepted continuously. World Wide Web: http://www.nps.gov/buff.

BUTTERFLY HOUSE
15193 Olive Boulevard
Chesterfield, Missouri 63017

General Information Public educational facility specializing in the exhibit of tropical butterflies and insects. Established in 1995. Number of employees: 22. Division of Missouri Botanical Garden, St. Louis, Missouri. Number of internship applications received each year: 15.
Internships Available ▶ *2–3 education interns:* responsibilities include assisting in adapting existing and creating new curriculum to be used in-house and for Web site visitors; helping with classes and Outreach programs. Candidates should have ability to work independently, college courses in field, computer skills, editing skills, knowledge of field, office skills, oral communication skills, organizational skills, personal interest in the field, research skills, self-motivation, strong interpersonal skills, writing skills. Duration is 1 semester. Unpaid. Open to college freshmen, college sophomores, college juniors, college seniors, recent college graduates, graduate students. ▶ *2–3 entomology interns:* responsibilities include working with all non-venomous invertebrates and other animals, helping to maintain the collection, and processing butterfly shipments. Candidates should have ability to work with others, knowledge of field, personal interest in the field, self-motivation, college courses in biology. Duration is 1 semester. Unpaid. Open to college sophomores, college juniors, college seniors, recent college graduates, graduate students. ▶ *1–4 guest and volunteer services interns:* responsibilities include assisting in greeting and helping guests, meeting group sales and education classes, maintaining the facility, recruiting and training new volunteers, and volunteer scheduling. Candidates should have college courses in field, computer skills, office skills, oral communication skills, organizational skills, self-motivation, strong interpersonal skills, writing skills, interest in working with people. Duration is 1 semester. Unpaid. Open to college freshmen, college sophomores, college juniors, college seniors, recent college graduates, graduate students. ▶ *2–3 horticulture interns:* responsibilities include helping maintain the tropical conservatory garden, native habitat, prairie garden, annual garden, and grounds; planting, pruning, watering, pest management, weeding, and propagation. Candidates should have ability to work with others, college courses in field, knowledge of field, personal interest in the field, self-motivation. Duration is 1 semester. Unpaid. Open to college freshmen, college sophomores, college juniors, college seniors, recent college graduates, graduate students. ▶ *2–3 retail interns:* responsibilities include assisting with admissions, sales, inventory, and guest services. Candidates should have college courses in field, computer skills, knowledge of field, office skills, oral communication skills, organizational skills, self-motivation, strong interpersonal skills, writing skills. Duration is 1 semester. Unpaid. Open to college freshmen, college sophomores, college juniors, college seniors, recent college graduates, graduate students, individuals reenter-

ing the workforce. ▶ *2–3 special events marketing interns.* Candidates should have computer skills, editing skills, knowledge of field, office skills, oral communication skills, organizational skills, personal interest in the field, self-motivation, strong interpersonal skills, written communication skills. Duration is May to August. Unpaid. Open to college freshmen, college sophomores, college juniors, college seniors, recent college graduates, graduate students. International applications accepted.

Benefits Names of contacts, on-the-job training, willing to act as a professional reference, willing to complete paperwork for educational credit, willing to provide letters of recommendation. **Contact** Write, call, fax, or e-mail Laura Chisholm, Invertebrate Specialist. Phone: 636-530-0076. Fax: 636-530-1516. E-mail: chisholm@mobot.org. In-person interview recommended (telephone interview accepted). Applicants must submit a formal organization application, letter of interest, resume. Applications are accepted continuously. World Wide Web: http://www.butterflyhouse.org.

CABRILLO NATIONAL MONUMENT
1800 Cabrillo Memorial Drive
San Diego, California 92106-3601

General Information Agency that seeks to preserve park scenery, natural and historical objects, and wildlife. Established in 1913. Number of employees: 25. Unit of United States National Park Service, Washington, District of Columbia. Number of internship applications received each year: 15.

Internships Available ▶ *1 natural resource science intern:* responsibilities include working with numerous aspects of the natural resources in the National Park Service; , may include field work, office assistance, and computer work. Candidates should have ability to work independently, ability to work with others, computer skills, personal interest in the field, self-motivation. Duration is flexible. Unpaid. ▶ *1–2 park ranger interns:* responsibilities include developing and presenting interpretive programs; introducing film presentations; conducting nature walks; assisting with education programs and natural resource management projects; staffing visitor center information desk; assisting with exhibit design, brochure publications, museum collection management, desktop publishing, and Web page design. Candidates should have ability to work independently, oral communication skills, personal interest in the field, self-motivation, strong interpersonal skills, written communication skills. Duration is flexible, depending on availability. Unpaid. Open to recent high school graduates, college freshmen, college sophomores, college juniors, college seniors, recent college graduates, graduate students, career changers, individuals reentering the workforce. International applications accepted.

Benefits Formal training, job counseling, names of contacts, on-the-job training, opportunity to attend seminars/workshops, willing to act as a professional reference, willing to complete paperwork for educational credit, willing to provide letters of recommendation, aid on the application process provided. **Contact** Write, call, fax, or e-mail Marcy Marquez, Internship Coordinator. Phone: 619-523-4573. Fax: 619-557-5469. E-mail: marcy_marquez@nps.gov. In-person interview recommended (telephone interview accepted). Applicants must submit a formal organization application. Applications are accepted continuously. World Wide Web: http://www.nps.gov/cabr.

CALAVERAS BIG TREES STATE PARK
22708 Broadway Street
Columbia, California 95310

General Information State park established to protect two groves of Giant Sequoia (largest trees in the world); located in the central Sierra Nevada, California. Established in 1931. Number of employees: 26. Unit of California Department of Parks & Recreation, Sacramento, California. Number of internship applications received each year: 15.

Internships Available ▶ *2 interns:* responsibilities include conducting interpretive programs, operating and maintaining all equipment, conducting sales of merchandise, working with volunteers and paid staff, and working in visitor center. Candidates should have ability to work independently, analytical skills, college courses in field, computer skills, knowledge of field, oral communication

skills, personal interest in the field, plan to pursue career in field, research skills, self-motivation, strong interpersonal skills, written communication skills. Duration is 3 months (June-September). $195 per month. Open to college freshmen, college sophomores, college juniors, college seniors, recent college graduates, graduate students. International applications accepted.

Benefits Free housing, job counseling, names of contacts, on-the-job training, opportunity to attend seminars/workshops, willing to complete paperwork for educational credit, willing to provide letters of recommendation. **Contact** Write, call, fax, or e-mail Bruce Thomsen, District Interpretive Specialist. Phone: 209-532-0150. Fax: 209-532-5064. E-mail: bthom@parks.ca.gov. In-person interview recommended (telephone interview accepted). Applicants must submit a letter of interest, resume. Application deadline: February 15 for summer.

CALLAWAY GARDENS
PO Box 2000
Pine Mountain, Georgia 31822-2000

General Information Horticulture display garden and resort with conservatories, nature trails, lodging, golf, tennis, and manmade beach. Established in 1952. Number of employees: 1,200. Number of internship applications received each year: 50.

Internships Available ▶ *1 arboriculture intern:* responsibilities include tree climbing and pruning, use of hand tools, chain saws, chippers, bucket trucks; tree trimming and cabling, bracing, hedge pruning, and tree health evaluation. Candidates should have college courses in field, knowledge of field, personal interest in the field, self-motivation, strong interpersonal skills. Duration is late May to mid- August. $7.26 per hour. Open to college freshmen, college sophomores, college juniors, college seniors, recent college graduates, graduate students, career changers, (college juniors, seniors, graduate students, and technical students preferred). ▶ *3 education interns:* responsibilities include conducting and assisting with education programs in home horticulture and natural history. Candidates should have knowledge of field, oral communication skills, personal interest in the field, self-motivation, strong interpersonal skills, written communication skills. Duration is late May to mid- August. $7.26 per hour. Open to college freshmen, college sophomores, college juniors, college seniors, recent college graduates, graduate students, (college juniors, seniors, graduate students preferred). ▶ *1 entomology intern:* responsibilities include practical, physical, hands-on experience in butterfly rearing, exhibit design and maintenance, mechanical operations, animal husbandry, exhibit horticulture, and tropical plants and insects. Candidates should have college courses in field, knowledge of field, personal interest in the field, self-motivation, strong interpersonal skills. Duration is late May to mid- August. $7.26 per hour. Open to college freshmen, college sophomores, college juniors, college seniors, recent college graduates, graduate students, career changers, (college juniors, seniors, graduate students preferred). ▶ *1 floriculture intern:* responsibilities include growing, harvesting and post-harvest care of cut flowers, display and maintenance of interior foliage and blooming plants, floral design; and research. Candidates should have college courses in field, knowledge of field, personal interest in the field, self-motivation, strong interpersonal skills. Duration is late May to mid- August. $7.26 per hour. Open to college freshmen, college sophomores, college juniors, college seniors, recent college graduates, graduate students, career changers, (college juniors, seniors, graduate students preferred). ▶ *1 fruit and vegetable production and landscape maintenance intern:* responsibilities include wide variety of horticulture activities including tending small gardens, pruning, helping to design display beds; care for vegetables, herbs, small fruits, floral borders and home landscape demonstration garden. Candidates should have college courses in field, knowledge of field, personal interest in the field, self-motivation, strong interpersonal skills. Duration is late May to mid- August. $7.26 per hour. Open to college freshmen, college sophomores, college juniors, college seniors, recent college graduates, graduate students, career changers, (college juniors, seniors, graduate students preferred). ▶ *1 horticulture production intern:* responsibilities include practical, hands-on experience in greenhouse production; assisting growers in production of annuals, perennials, woody

Callaway Gardens (continued)

ornamentals, natives, tropicals, and floriculture crops. Candidates should have college courses in field, knowledge of field, personal interest in the field, self-motivation, strong interpersonal skills. Duration is late May to mid- August. $7.26 per hour. Open to college freshmen, college sophomores, college juniors, college seniors, recent college graduates, graduate students, career changers, (college juniors, seniors, graduate students preferred). ▶ *1 trails intern:* responsibilities include planting, watering, weeding, flora identification and inventory; woodland gardening and restoration; maintaining and enhancing collections of native and cultivated azaleas, hollies, and rhododendrons. Candidates should have college courses in field, knowledge of field, personal interest in the field, self-motivation, strong interpersonal skills. Duration is late May to mid- August. $7.26 per hour. Open to college freshmen, college sophomores, college juniors, college seniors, recent college graduates, graduate students, career changers, (college juniors, seniors, graduate students preferred). International applications accepted.

Benefits Formal training, housing at a cost, job counseling, meals at a cost, names of contacts, on-the-job training, possible full-time employment, willing to act as a professional reference, willing to complete paperwork for educational credit, willing to provide letters of recommendation, opportunity to attend classes and field trips.

Contact Write, call, fax, or e-mail Patricia L. Collins, Director of Education. Phone: 706-663-5155. Fax: 706-663-6720. E-mail: plcolli@ callawaygardens.com. Applicants must submit a formal organization application, letter of interest, resume, three letters of recommendation. Application deadline: February 1 for summer. World Wide Web: http://www.callawaygardens.com.

CAMBRIDGE HISTORICAL SOCIETY
159 Brattle Street
Cambridge, Massachusetts 02138-3300

General Information Museum that emphasizes the history of Cambridge, Massachusetts. Established in 1905. Number of employees: 3. Number of internship applications received each year: 12.

Internships Available ▶ *1 volunteer researcher:* responsibilities include corresponding with individuals seeking historical information and conducting research for the museum. Candidates should have ability to work independently, computer skills, editing skills, knowledge of field, oral communication skills, research skills, self-motivation, writing skills. Duration is flexible. Unpaid. Open to college sophomores, college juniors, college seniors, recent college graduates, graduate students, career changers.

Benefits Job counseling, names of contacts, on-the-job training, willing to act as a professional reference, willing to complete paperwork for educational credit, willing to provide letters of recommendation, informal training.

Contact Write, call, fax, or e-mail Sally Purrington Hild, Executive Director. Phone: 617-547-4252. Fax: 617-661-1623. E-mail: camhistory@aol.com. In-person interview recommended (telephone interview accepted). Applicants must submit a letter of interest, resume, personal reference. Applications are accepted continuously. World Wide Web: http://www.cambridgehistory.org.

CARLSBAD CAVERNS NATIONAL PARK
3225 National Parks Highway
Carlsbad, New Mexico 88220

General Information Park consisting of 47,000 acres of Chihuahuan desert and more than 92 caves; established to conserve resources and to provide for understanding, appreciation, and enjoyment of park resources. Established in 1923. Number of employees: 100. Unit of United States Department of Interior, Washington, District of Columbia. Number of internship applications received each year: 100.

Internships Available ▶ *1–3 education program assistants:* responsibilities include developing, presenting, and assisting others with curriculum-based programs in schools and at the park; assisting in organizing and implementing ParKids summer day camp for third to eighth graders; developing kids activities and displays for the park's visitor center. Candidates should have ability to work independently, ability to work with others, oral communication skills, organizational skills, written communication skills, outgoing personality and interest in working with children and the National Park Service. Duration is May to September; or any period therein (12 week minimum). Unpaid. Open to college juniors, college seniors, recent college graduates, graduate students, career changers, individuals reentering the workforce, educators on summer break. ▶ *1 park historian assistant:* responsibilities include assisting the park historian with oral history transcripts, research, and filing. Candidates should have ability to work independently, computer skills, organizational skills, research skills, writing skills. Duration is flexible. Unpaid. Open to individuals 18 years or older with interest in history. ▶ *1–2 visitor services assistants:* responsibilities include working with the public, answering questions, and providing visitor assistance while staffing the information desk; roving cave trails; and presenting cave orientations and short interpretive talks. Candidates should have ability to work with others, experience in the field, oral communication skills, personal interest in the field, self-motivation. Duration is flexible (10 week minimum). Unpaid. Open to individuals 18 years or older with interest in working with the public. ▶ *1 wildlife research assistant:* responsibilities include field research requiring hiking 4 to 8 miles per day in rocky, desert conditions; conducting surveys of plant species and animal sign; maintaining a database of natural resource information; and writing reports. Candidates should have computer skills, experience in the field, personal interest in the field, self-motivation, writing skills, good physical condition. Duration is March to June or September to November. Position available as unpaid or paid. International applications accepted.

Benefits Job counseling, on-the-job training, opportunity to attend seminars/workshops, willing to complete paperwork for educational credit, protection from tort claims, worker's compensation for on-the-job injuries.

Contact Write, call, fax, e-mail, or through World Wide Web site Volunteer Coordinator. Phone: 505-785-2232. Fax: 505-785-2302. E-mail: samuel_franco@nps.gov. Telephone interview required. Applicants must submit a letter of interest, resume. Applications are accepted continuously. World Wide Web: http://www.nps.gov/ cave.

CATOCTIN MOUNTAIN PARK
6602 Foxville Road
Thurmont, Maryland 21788-1598

General Information Park dedicated to the preservation and protection of historical objects and wildlife. Established in 1936. Number of employees: 40. Unit of United States National Park Service, Washington, District of Columbia. Number of internship applications received each year: 24.

Internships Available ▶ *1–7 cabin camp hosts:* responsibilities include providing people with assistance, performing office duties, receiving cabin reservations, and checking visitors into and out of cabins. Candidates should have ability to work independently, office skills, oral communication skills, personal interest in the field, strong interpersonal skills. Duration is 1 month. Unpaid. Open to college juniors, college seniors, recent college graduates, graduate students, law students, career changers, individuals reentering the workforce. ▶ *1–5 campground hosts:* responsibilities include answering questions for visitors, maintaining campground, and keeping track of how many campsites are open. Candidates should have ability to work independently, oral communication skills, personal interest in the field, self-motivation, strong interpersonal skills. Duration is 1 month. Unpaid. Open to college juniors, college seniors, recent college graduates, graduate students, law students, career changers, individuals reentering the workforce. ▶ *1–4 resource education interns:* responsibilities include providing visitor services and interpretive programs. Candidates should have ability to work independently, oral communication skills, personal interest in the field, self-motivation, strong interpersonal skills. Duration is 10–12 weeks. Unpaid. Open to high school seniors, recent high school graduates, college freshmen, college sophomores, college juniors, college seniors, recent college graduates, graduate students, law students, career changers, individuals reentering the workforce. ▶ *1–4 resource management interns:* responsibilities include performing education, vegetation, water quality, and wildlife studies. Candidates should have ability to work independently, ability to work with others, knowledge of field, oral communication skills, personal interest in the field, written communication skills. Duration is 10–12 weeks. Unpaid. Open to high school students, recent high school graduates, college freshmen, college sophomores, college juniors, college seniors, recent college graduates, graduate students, law students, career changers, individuals reentering the workforce. International applications accepted.

Benefits Free housing, willing to complete paperwork for educational credit, willing to provide letters of recommendation.

Contact Write Chief Ranger. Phone: 301-663-9388. Telephone interview required. Applicants must submit a resume. Application deadline: March 1 for summer, August 1 for fall; continuous for cabin camp hosts and campground hosts. World Wide Web: http://www.nps.gov/cato/.

CHESAPEAKE AND OHIO CANAL NATIONAL HISTORICAL PARK
1850 Dual Highway, Suite 100
Hagerstown, Maryland 21740

General Information National park that seeks to preserve the cultural and natural history of the Chesapeake and Ohio Canal. Established in 1971. Number of employees: 120. Unit of United States National Park Service, Washington, District of Columbia. Number of internship applications received each year: 25.

Internships Available ▶ *1–2 geographic information systems interns:* responsibilities include map production, data acquisition, and field data collection with Global Positioning Systems. Candidates should have ability to work independently, college courses in field, computer skills, knowledge of field, organizational skills, plan to pursue career in field, self-motivation. Duration is minimum 12 weeks, 16 hours per week. Position available as unpaid or at $100 weekly stipend. Open to college freshmen, college sophomores, college juniors, college seniors, graduate students. ▶ *1–3 living history interpreters:* responsibilities include working as part of a living history canal boat crew, presenting third-person living history programs, operating lock gates, handling mules, assisting in boat operation. Candidates should have ability to work with others, college courses in field, knowledge of field, oral communication skills, personal interest in the field, research skills, self-motivation. Duration is minimum 20 hours per week per semester. Position available as unpaid or at $100 weekly stipend. Open to college freshmen, college sophomores, college juniors, college seniors, graduate students. ▶ *1–3 natural resource assistants:* responsibilities include assisting natural resource management specialist with breeding bud count, wetland monitoring, tree planting, data entry, PC-based map making. Candidates should have ability to work independently, college courses in field, knowledge of field, oral communication skills, plan to pursue career in field, self-motivation, writing skills. Duration is minimum 20 hours per week up to 12 weeks. Position available as unpaid or at $100 weekly stipend. Open to college freshmen, college sophomores, college juniors, college seniors, graduate students. ▶ *1 public affairs assistant:* responsibilities include setting up communication with regional media, developing media kits and county specific information guides. Candidates should have college courses in field, computer skills, editing skills, knowledge of field, office skills, organizational skills, personal interest in the field, self-motivation, writing skills. Duration is minimum 20 hours per week per semester. Position available as unpaid or at $100 weekly stipend. Open to college freshmen, college sophomores, college juniors, college seniors, graduate students. ▶ *1–3 research interns:* responsibilities include conducting research on historic 185-mile towpath canal and on archaeological and natural history aspects of a canal park encompassing approximately 22,000 acres along the Potomac River. Candidates should have ability to work independently, college courses in field, knowledge of field, personal interest in the field, research skills, self-motivation, writing skills. Duration is minimum 20 hours per week per semester. Position available as unpaid or at $100 weekly stipend. Open to recent college graduates, graduate students. ▶ *1–5 visitor services interns:* responsibili-

ties include staffing visitor center desk, researching and presenting talk, slide program and/or information for brochure on history of some aspect of the C&O Canal. Candidates should have ability to work independently, ability to work with others, computer skills, oral communication skills, personal interest in the field, research skills, self-motivation, strong leadership ability, written communication skills. Duration is minimum 20 hours per week per semester. Position available as unpaid or at $100 weekly stipend. Open to college freshmen, college sophomores, college juniors, college seniors, recent college graduates, graduate students, career changers. International applications accepted.

Benefits Formal training, names of contacts, on-the-job training, possible full-time employment, willing to complete paperwork for educational credit, willing to provide letters of recommendation.

Contact Write, call, fax, or e-mail John Noel, Volunteer Outreach Coordinator. Phone: 301-714-2238. Fax: 301-739-6179. E-mail: john_noel@nps.gov. In-person interview recommended (telephone interview accepted). Applicants must submit a letter of interest, resume, academic transcripts, personal reference. Application deadline: April 15 for summer, July 15 for fall, November 15 for spring. World Wide Web: http://www.nps.gov/choh/.

CHICAGO CHILDREN'S MUSEUM
Navy Pier, 700 East Grand Avenue, Suite 127
Chicago, Illinois 60611-3428

General Information Interactive children's museum that inspires creative learning. Established in 1982. Number of employees: 80. Number of internship applications received each year: 250.

Internships Available ▶ *1 design intern:* responsibilities include assisting with 3-D and 2-D design projects and exhibit enhancements; helping with illustrations, production and execution of printed materials; other assignments as needed. Candidates should have ability to work independently, oral communication skills, organizational skills, strong art background, ability to work as team member, knowledge of MAC and graphic software, Quark, PhotoShop. Duration is 3–5 months (15–20 hours per week). Unpaid. ▶ *1 development intern:* responsibilities include researching potential donors and assisting in creating fund-raising proposals. Candidates should have computer skills, research skills, strong interpersonal skills, written communication skills. Duration is 2–3 months. Unpaid. Open to college sophomores, college juniors, college seniors, recent college graduates, graduate students, career changers, individuals reentering the workforce. ▶ *2–3 education interns:* responsibilities include planning workshops, developing educational programs, and facilitating activities. Candidates should have computer skills, organizational skills, self-motivation, strong interpersonal skills. Duration is 2–3 months. Unpaid. Open to college sophomores, college juniors, college seniors, recent college graduates, graduate students, career changers. ▶ *1 exhibits intern:* responsibilities include researching products and services, keylining exhibit labels, and creating temporary displays. Candidates should have editing skills, research skills, written communication skills. Duration is 2–3 months. Unpaid. Open to college sophomores, college juniors, college seniors, recent college graduates, graduate students, career changers, individuals reentering the workforce. ▶ *1 human resource intern:* responsibilities include performing duties relating to all aspects of the volunteer program including recruitment, training, retention, and recognition. Candidates should have analytical skills, computer skills, oral communication skills, organizational skills, strong interpersonal skills, written communication skills. Duration is 2–3 months. Unpaid. Open to college juniors, college seniors, recent college graduates, graduate students, career changers. ▶ *1 marketing intern:* responsibilities include soliciting membership and assisting in social events and public relations/marketing. Candidates should have analytical skills, computer skills, office skills, oral communication skills, strong interpersonal skills, written communication skills. Duration is 2–3 months. Unpaid. Open to college sophomores, college juniors, college seniors, recent college graduates, graduate students, career changers, individuals reentering the workforce. ▶ *1 public relations intern:* responsibilities include assisting in writing press materials, photo releases, Web site updates, and calendar of events; assisting with research, follow-up media calls, photo shoots, media tours, and

Chicago Children's Museum (continued)

other special events. Candidates should have ability to work independently, computer skills, oral communication skills, strong interpersonal skills, written communication skills, attention to detail, knowledge of photography (helpful). Duration is 3–5 months (15–20 hours per week). Unpaid. International applications accepted.

Benefits Job counseling, willing to complete paperwork for educational credit, willing to provide letters of recommendation, $100 travel stipend after 200 hours.

Contact Write, call, fax, or e-mail Catherine Patyk, Director of Human Resources. Phone: 312-464-7733. Fax: 312-464-8241. E-mail: cpatyk@chichildrensmuseum.org. In-person interview recommended (telephone interview accepted). Applicants must submit a resume, writing sample, two personal references. Application deadline: January 30 for winter/spring, June 1 for summer, September 30 for fall. World Wide Web: http://www.chichildrensmuseum.org.

THE CHILDREN'S MUSEUM
300 Congress Street
Boston, Massachusetts 02210

General Information Museum whose mission is to help children understand the world in which they live; believes that real objects, direct experiences, and enjoyment support learning. Established in 1913. Number of employees: 140. Number of internship applications received each year: 150.

Internships Available ▶ *15–20 exhibit floor staff:* responsibilities include staffing exhibits and providing a quality experience for visitors. Candidates should have ability to work independently, oral communication skills, self-motivation, strong interpersonal skills, strong leadership ability, ability to speak to large groups and work with diverse public, ability to work weekend and holiday hours (required). Duration is mid-June to end of August. $7.50 per hour. Open to high school seniors, recent high school graduates, college sophomores, college juniors, college seniors, recent college graduates, graduate students, law students, career changers, individuals reentering the workforce. ▶ *15–20 program interpreters:* responsibilities include teaching programs for preschool, kindergarten, elementary grades, and general public. Candidates should have ability to work independently, oral communication skills, self-motivation, strong interpersonal skills, strong leadership ability, ability to speak to large groups and work with diverse audience, ability to work weekend and holiday hours (required). Duration is end of August through beginning of June. $8.50 per hour. Open to high school seniors, recent high school graduates, college freshmen, college sophomores, college juniors, college seniors, recent college graduates, graduate students, law students, career changers, individuals reentering the workforce. International applications accepted.

Benefits On-the-job training, possible full-time employment.

Contact Write, fax, e-mail, or through World Wide Web site Kathryn Willis, Human Resources Associate. Fax: 617-423-3213. E-mail: willis@bostonkids.org. No phone calls. In-person interview required. Applicants must submit a letter of interest, resume, two personal references. Application deadline: March 1 for summer, June 1 for fall. World Wide Web: http://www.bostonkids.org.

THE CHILDREN'S MUSEUM OF INDIANAPOLIS
PO Box 3000
Indianapolis, Indiana 46206

General Information Museum that strives to enrich the lives of children by creating excellent exhibits, programs, and experiences that share knowledge, stimulate imagination, kindle curiosity, and affirm the joy of lifelong learning. Established in 1925. Number of employees: 400. Number of internship applications received each year: 400.

Internships Available ▶ *2–5 collections interns:* responsibilities include working with curators to record, handle, and preserve the collection. Candidates should have ability to work independently, ability to work with others, college courses in field, computer skills, knowledge of field, office skills, oral communication skills, organizational skills, personal interest in the field, plan to pursue

career in field, research skills, self-motivation, writing skills. Duration is flexible. Position available as unpaid or paid. Open to college freshmen, college sophomores, college juniors, college seniors, recent college graduates, graduate students. ▶ *2–5 communications/ marketing interns:* responsibilities include working in various areas including public relations, photography, and/or written communications as well as marketing projects. Candidates should have ability to work independently, ability to work with others, analytical skills, college courses in field, computer skills, editing skills, knowledge of field, office skills, oral communication skills, organizational skills, personal interest in the field, plan to pursue career in field, research skills, self-motivation, strong leadership ability, writing skills. Duration is 3 months (usually). Position available as unpaid or paid. Open to college freshmen, college sophomores, college juniors, college seniors, recent college graduates, graduate students, law students. ▶ *1–3 development interns:* responsibilities include working with development department on fund-raising projects. Candidates should have ability to work independently, ability to work with others, analytical skills, college courses in field, computer skills, editing skills, knowledge of field, office skills, oral communication skills, organizational skills, personal interest in the field, plan to pursue career in field, research skills, self-motivation, strong leadership ability, writing skills. Duration is flexible. Position available as unpaid or paid. Open to college freshmen, college sophomores, college juniors, college seniors, recent college graduates, graduate students, law students. ▶ *1–20 education/programs interns:* responsibilities include working with gallery educators to develop activities and working with visitors. Candidates should have ability to work independently, ability to work with others, analytical skills, college courses in field, computer skills, editing skills, knowledge of field, office skills, oral communication skills, organizational skills, personal interest in the field, research skills, self-motivation, strong leadership ability, writing skills. Duration is flexible. Position available as unpaid or paid. Open to college freshmen, college sophomores, college juniors, college seniors, recent college graduates, graduate students. ▶ *1–4 exhibits interns:* responsibilities include working with exhibit designers to create exhibits and do graphic arts work for exhibits. Candidates should have ability to work independently, ability to work with others, analytical skills, college courses in field, computer skills, editing skills, knowledge of field, office skills, oral communication skills, organizational skills, personal interest in the field, plan to pursue career in field, research skills, self-motivation, strong leadership ability, writing skills. Duration is flexible. Position available as unpaid or paid. Open to college freshmen, college sophomores, college juniors, college seniors, recent college graduates, graduate students. ▶ *1–3 facilities interns:* responsibilities include building operation maintenance and grounds keeping. Candidates should have ability to work independently, ability to work with others, analytical skills, college courses in field, computer skills, knowledge of field, oral communication skills, organizational skills, personal interest in the field, self-motivation, writing skills. Duration is flexible. Position available as unpaid or paid. Open to college freshmen, college sophomores, college juniors, college seniors, recent college graduates, graduate students. ▶ *1–3 human resources interns.* Candidates should have ability to work independently, ability to work with others, analytical skills, college courses in field, computer skills, editing skills, knowledge of field, office skills, oral communication skills, organizational skills, personal interest in the field, plan to pursue career in field, research skills, self-motivation, strong leadership ability, writing skills. Duration is flexible. Position available as unpaid or paid. Open to college freshmen, college sophomores, college juniors, college seniors, recent college graduates, graduate students, law students. ▶ *1–3 information systems interns:* responsibilities include Web design and computer programming. Candidates should have ability to work independently, ability to work with others, analytical skills, college courses in field, computer skills, editing skills, knowledge of field, office skills, oral communication skills, organizational skills, personal interest in the field, research skills, self-motivation, strong leadership ability, writing skills. Duration is flexible. Position available as unpaid or paid. Open to college freshmen, college sophomores, college juniors, college seniors, recent college graduates, graduate students. ▶ *2–4 public policy/ community initiatives interns:* responsibilities include taking leadership roles in the areas of visitor information, neighborhood initiatives, legislative updates, and strategic events. Candidates should have ability to work independently, ability to work with others, analytical skills, college courses in field, computer skills, editing skills, knowledge of field, office skills, oral communication skills, organizational skills, personal interest in the field, plan to pursue career in field, research skills, self-motivation, strong leadership ability, writing skills. Duration is flexible. Position available as unpaid or paid. Open to college freshmen, college sophomores, college juniors, college seniors, recent college graduates, graduate students, law students. ▶ *1–3 retail services interns:* responsibilities include working in all aspects of retail services including sales, management, and accounting. Candidates should have ability to work independently, ability to work with others, analytical skills, computer skills, knowledge of field, office skills, oral communication skills, organizational skills, personal interest in the field, research skills, self-motivation, strong leadership ability, writing skills. Duration is flexible. Position available as unpaid or paid. Open to college freshmen, college sophomores, college juniors, college seniors, recent college graduates, graduate students. ▶ *1–3 security interns:* responsibilities include safety and security projects. Candidates should have ability to work independently, ability to work with others, analytical skills, college courses in field, computer skills, editing skills, knowledge of field, office skills, oral communication skills, organizational skills, personal interest in the field, research skills, self-motivation, strong leadership ability, writing skills. Duration is flexible. Position available as unpaid or paid. Open to college freshmen, college sophomores, college juniors, college seniors, recent college graduates, graduate students, law students. ▶ *1–4 visitor relations interns:* responsibilities include research, working with visitors, and working in call center and box office. Candidates should have ability to work independently, ability to work with others, analytical skills, college courses in field, computer skills, editing skills, knowledge of field, office skills, oral communication skills, organizational skills, personal interest in the field, plan to pursue career in field, research skills, self-motivation, strong leadership ability, writing skills. Duration is flexible. Position available as unpaid or paid. Open to college freshmen, college sophomores, college juniors, college seniors, recent college graduates, graduate students. International applications accepted.

Benefits Formal training, job counseling, names of contacts, on-the-job training, opportunity to attend seminars/workshops, possible full-time employment, willing to act as a professional reference, willing to complete paperwork for educational credit, willing to provide letters of recommendation, field trips to other museums/arts organizations, discount at restaurant.

Contact Write, call, fax, e-mail, or through World Wide Web site Emily Clossin, Intern Program Manager. Phone: 317-334-3830. Fax: 317-920-2028. E-mail: emilyc@childrensmuseum.org. In-person interview recommended (telephone interview accepted). Applicants must submit a formal organization application, letter of interest, resume, 2-3 personal references, portfolio (or graphic design (exhibits) internship), writing sample (for public relations/grant-writing internships). Applications are accepted continuously. World Wide Web: http://www.childrensmuseum.org.

CLAUDE MOORE COLONIAL FARM
6310 Georgetown Pike
McLean, Virginia 22101

General Information Privately operated, nonprofit national park which has 18th century living history farm, environmental education, history, horticulture, and crafts programs. Established in 1973. Number of employees: 8. Number of internship applications received each year: 20.

Internships Available ▶ *1–2 historical interpreter interns:* responsibilities include serving as historical interpreter to visiting public and school groups; completing a research project; supervising youth volunteers; performing basic farm tasks. Candidates should have ability to work independently, oral communication skills, research skills, strong interpersonal skills, written communication skills. Duration is 12–16 weeks. $6.50–$7.50 per hour. Open to recent high school graduates, college sophomores, college juniors, college seniors, recent college graduates, graduate students, career

changers, individuals reentering the workforce. ▶ *1 history education intern:* responsibilities include presenting historical agriculture classes to school children, researching and developing educational materials, and working at special events. Candidates should have ability to work independently, ability to work with others, oral communication skills, research skills, writing skills, interest in history, education, or agriculture. Duration is March 15 to December 15 (in semesters or quarters). $6.50–$7.50 per hour. Open to recent high school graduates, college freshmen, college sophomores, college juniors, college seniors, recent college graduates, graduate students, career changers, individuals reentering the workforce. ▶ *1 horticulture production assistant:* responsibilities include operating small (1500 sq ft) greenhouse operation with 1-acre nursery for heirloom plants, using Horicopia software, conducting sales, and working with horticulture volunteers. Candidates should have ability to work independently, ability to work with others, college courses in field, computer skills, experience in the field, organizational skills. Duration is February 15 to October 31 (in semester or quarters). $6.50–$7.50 per hour. Open to college freshmen, college sophomores, college juniors, college seniors, recent college graduates, graduate students, career changers, individuals reentering the workforce. ▶ *1 marketing/public relations assistant:* responsibilities include maintaining a database of contacts, developing and maintaining relationships with various press organizations, preparing and issuing press releases, and assisting in development of marketing plan. Candidates should have computer skills, editing skills, oral communication skills, strong interpersonal skills, writing skills. Duration is January to December (in semesters/quarters). $6.50–$7.50 per hour. Open to recent high school graduates, college freshmen, college sophomores, college juniors, college seniors, recent college graduates, graduate students, career changers, individuals reentering the workforce. ▶ *1 retail sales assistant:* responsibilities include assisting with management and operation of a small museum gift shop, assisting with inventory control and management, and assisting in development of new sources of merchandise. Candidates should have ability to work independently, computer skills, oral communication skills, organizational skills, strong interpersonal skills. Duration is January to December (in semesters/quarters). $6.50–$7.50 per hour. Open to recent high school graduates, college freshmen, college sophomores, college juniors, college seniors, recent college graduates, graduate students, career changers, individuals reentering the workforce.

Benefits On-the-job training, possible full-time employment, willing to act as a professional reference, willing to complete paperwork for educational credit, willing to provide letters of recommendation.

Contact Write, e-mail, or through World Wide Web site Anna C. Eberly, Executive Director. Fax: 703-847-0726. E-mail: aeberly@1771.org. No phone calls. In-person interview recommended (telephone interview accepted). Applicants must submit a formal organization application, letter of interest, resume, personal reference, letter of recommendation. Applications are accepted continuously. World Wide Web: http://www.1771.org.

THE CLOISTERS
Fort Tryon Park
New York, New York 10040

General Information Museum devoted to the art of medieval Europe with a collection including architectural fragments, sculptures, frescoes, illuminated manuscripts, tapestries, stained glass, medieval metal works, and paintings. Established in 1938. Number of employees: 60. Branch of Metropolitan Museum of Art, New York, New York. Number of internship applications received each year: 300.

Internships Available ▶ *8 interns:* responsibilities include teaching day campers (ages 4-12) about medieval art and giving gallery talks on a specialized topic to the general public. Candidates should have ability to work independently, college courses in field, knowledge of field, oral communication skills, personal interest in the field, research skills, self-motivation, strong interpersonal skills, ability to work with children. Duration is 9 weeks. $2500

The Cloisters (continued)

per duration of internship. Open to college freshmen, college sophomores, college juniors, college seniors. International applications accepted.

Benefits Names of contacts, on-the-job training, opportunity to attend seminars/workshops, willing to complete paperwork for educational credit, willing to provide letters of recommendation.

Contact Write, call, or through World Wide Web site Terry McDonald, Internship Coordinator. Phone: 212-650-2280. In-person interview required. Applicants must submit a letter of interest, resume, academic transcripts, two letters of recommendation. Application deadline: February 7 for summer. World Wide Web: http://www.metmuseum.org.

COLONIAL NATIONAL HISTORICAL PARK
PO Box 210
Yorktown, Virginia 23690

General Information National historical park that preserves, protects, and interprets the site of the first permanent English settlement in the New World (Jamestown) and the site of the last major battle of the American Revolutionary War (Yorktown). Established in 1930. Number of employees: 80. Unit of United States National Park Service, Washington, District of Columbia. Number of internship applications received each year: 10.

Internships Available ▶ *1 cataloging intern:* responsibilities include cataloging artifacts. Candidates should have ability to work independently, ability to work with others, analytical skills, college courses in field, experience in the field, office skills, organizational skills. Duration is 4–6 weeks. Position available as unpaid or paid. Open to college juniors, college seniors, recent college graduates, graduate students. ▶ *4–6 division of historical interpretations interns:* responsibilities include historical research and preparing and presenting interpretive programs; internship can be tailored to meet the intern's interests and the park's needs. Candidates should have college courses in field, editing skills, knowledge of field, oral communication skills, personal interest in the field, research skills, strong interpersonal skills, writing skills. Duration is 9–12 weeks. Position available as unpaid or paid. Open to college freshmen, college sophomores, college juniors, college seniors, recent college graduates, graduate students. ▶ *1 landscape architect:* responsibilities include working closely with park landscape architect on a variety of projects mostly relating to historic landscape inventory, landscape maintenance plans, design projects, and historic documentation. Candidates should have ability to work independently, analytical skills, computer skills, declared college major in field, knowledge of field, oral communication skills, plan to pursue career in field, research skills, self-motivation, strong interpersonal skills, written communication skills. Duration is 3 months to 1 semester. Unpaid. Open to college juniors, college seniors, recent college graduates, graduate students. International applications accepted.

Benefits Formal training, free housing, names of contacts, on-the-job training, opportunity to attend seminars/workshops, willing to act as a professional reference, willing to complete paperwork for educational credit, willing to provide letters of recommendation, possibility of stipend.

Contact Write, call, fax, or e-mail Chris Bryce, Volunteer Coordinator, PO Box 210, Yorktown, Virginia 83690. Phone: 757-898-2414. Fax: 757-898-6346. E-mail: chris_bryce@nps.gov. In-person interview recommended (telephone interview accepted). Applicants must submit a letter of interest, resume, academic transcripts. Application deadline: March 25 for summer, July 1 for fall, October 1 for spring. World Wide Web: http://www.nps.gov/colo/.

THE COLONIAL WILLIAMSBURG FOUNDATION
PO Box 1776
Williamsburg, Virginia 23187-1776

General Information Living history museum that interprets the lives and times of 18th-century Williamsburg and colonial Virginia residents. Established in 1926. Number of employees: 3,400. Number of internship applications received each year: 75.

Internships Available ▶ *5–15 interns:* responsibilities include working in various areas including architecture, architectural research, archives and records, historic trades programs, decorative arts administration, historic research, interpretive education, program development, and personnel. Candidates should have ability to work independently, computer skills, organizational skills, personal interest in the field, written communication skills, experience and/or college courses in field. Duration is 2–12 months. Unpaid. Open to college juniors, college seniors, recent college graduates, graduate students, career changers.

Benefits Willing to complete paperwork for educational credit.

Contact Write, call, fax, or e-mail Ms. Peggy McDonald Howells, Manager, Museum Professional Services, PO Box 1776, Willilamsburg, Virginia 23187-1776. Phone: 757-220-7211. Fax: 757-565-8213. E-mail: phowells@cwf.org. In-person interview recommended (telephone interview accepted). Applicants must submit a letter of interest, resume, 1 to 2 personal references, 1 to 2 letters of recommendation. Applications are accepted continuously. World Wide Web: http://www.history.org.

COLORADO DIVISION OF PARKS AND RECREATION, TRINIDAD LAKE STATE PARK
32610 Highway 12
Trinidad, Colorado 81082

General Information Organization overseeing Trinidad Lake State Park, located in the Purgatoire River Valley among pinion/juniper forests, whose goals are to ensure safety, provide resource protection and enforce administrative regulations and laws. Established in 1980. Number of employees: 5. Unit of Colorado Division of Parks & Recreation, Denver, Colorado. Number of internship applications received each year: 15.

Internships Available ▶ *1 intern:* responsibilities include working in various areas of Colorado State Park operations including interpretation, research, programming, public safety, resource protection, revenue collection, visitor contact, conducting surveys, maintenance, and attending management meetings. Candidates should have ability to work independently, ability to work with others, oral communication skills, plan to pursue career in field, self-motivation, writing skills. Duration is 2–6 months. Position available as unpaid or paid. Open to college juniors, college seniors.

Benefits Formal training, job counseling, names of contacts, opportunity to attend seminars/workshops, possible full-time employment, willing to complete paperwork for educational credit, willing to provide letters of recommendation, housing available.

Contact Write or e-mail Lisa Minton, Park Ranger. E-mail: lisa.minton@state.co.us. No phone calls. In-person interview recommended (telephone interview accepted). Applicants must submit a resume. Application deadline: May 1 for summer, August 1 for winter. World Wide Web: http://www.parks.state.co.us.

COLORADO HISTORICAL SOCIETY
1300 Broadway
Denver, Colorado 80203

General Information Educational institution that collects, preserves, and interprets the history and prehistory of Colorado and the West. Established in 1879. Number of employees: 120. Division of State of Colorado, Department of Higher Education, Denver, Colorado. Number of internship applications received each year: 150.

Internships Available ▶ *Interns:* responsibilities include working in education, publications, public relations, books and manuscripts, decorative/fine arts, material culture, photography, design and production, or the historian's office. Candidates should have ability to work independently, ability to work with others, college courses in field, organizational skills, personal interest in the field, self-motivation. Duration is up to 1 year. Unpaid. Open to college freshmen, college sophomores, college juniors, college seniors, recent college graduates, graduate students. International applications accepted.

Benefits Job counseling, names of contacts, possible full-time employment, willing to complete paperwork for educational credit, willing to provide letters of recommendation.

Contact Write, fax, e-mail, or through World Wide Web site Jennifer Adams, Program Assistant. Fax: 303-866-4464. E-mail: jennifer. adams@chs.state.co.us. No phone calls. In-person interview recommended (telephone interview accepted). Applicants must submit a letter of interest, resume, two letters of recommendation. Applications are accepted continuously. World Wide Web: http://www.coloradohistory.org.

COLORADO STATE PARKS, STEAMBOAT LAKE STATE PARK
PO Box 750
Clark, Colorado 80428

General Information State park reservoir for camping, fishing, water sports, winter recreation, wildlife, and hunting. Established in 1967. Number of employees: 20. Division of Department of Natural Resources, Denver, Colorado. Number of internship applications received each year: 40.

Internships Available ▶ *1 environmental education/interpretation specialist:* responsibilities include developing, scheduling, promoting, and conducting environmental education and interpretive programs to be presented at Steamboat Lake and Pearl Lake State Parks and the local community. Candidates should have ability to work independently, computer skills, knowledge of field, office skills, oral communication skills, organizational skills, personal interest in the field, plan to pursue career in field, self-motivation, strong interpersonal skills, writing skills, valid driver's license, willingness to work weekends, holidays, and evening shifts. Duration is 6 months from May-September (40 hours per week). $8.41 per hour. Open to college freshmen, college sophomores, college juniors, college seniors, recent college graduates. ▶ *3-4 maintenance technicians:* responsibilities include daily maintenance of park facilities and special projects (fencing, construction, trails); special project assignments based on intern's interests and the needs of the park. Candidates should have ability to work independently, ability to work with others, oral communication skills, organizational skills, personal interest in the field, self-motivation, valid driver's license, willingness to work weekends and holidays. Duration is 5 months from May-September (40 hours per week). $7.26 per hour. Open to recent high school graduates, college freshmen, college sophomores, college juniors, college seniors, recent college graduates. ▶ *4-6 seasonal park rangers:* responsibilities include supervising the safety of park visitors; enforcing rules and regulations; patrolling park area; performing public relations, interpretive programs, maintenance, and office and administrative duties. Candidates should have ability to work independently, computer skills, oral communication skills, plan to pursue career in field, self-motivation, strong interpersonal skills, written communication skills, valid driver's license, willingness to work weekends, holidays, and evening shifts, successful completion of personal background investigation. Duration is 5 months from May-September (40 hours per week). $7.84 per hour. Open to college juniors, college seniors, recent college graduates, graduate students, individuals at least 21 years old. ▶ *4-5 visitor services technicians:* responsibilities include assisting visitors by providing information about park, local community, and surrounding public lands; operating visitor center; assisting with interpretive activities; maintenance duties as assigned. Candidates should have ability to work independently, computer skills, office skills, oral communication skills, organizational skills, personal interest in the field, self-motivation, strong interpersonal skills, valid driver's license, willingness to work weekends, holidays, and evening shifts. Duration is 5 months from May-September (40 hours per week). $7.26 per hour. Open to college freshmen, college sophomores, college juniors, college seniors, recent college graduates. ▶ *1 winter intern:* responsibilities include visitor center operation; public relations; interpretation/environmental education; snow removal; maintenance; administrative tasks; and assisting with patrol functions by foot, motor vehicle, and snowmobile. Candidates should have ability to work independently, declared college major in field, oral communication skills, plan to pursue career in field, self-motivation, strong interpersonal skills, valid driver's license, willingness to work weekends and holidays; current CPR and first aid certification. Duration is December to April

(flexible). Unpaid. Open to college juniors, college seniors, recent college graduates, individuals at least 21 years old.
Benefits Formal training, housing at a cost, names of contacts, on-the-job training, opportunity to attend seminars/workshops, possible full-time employment, willing to act as a professional reference, willing to complete paperwork for educational credit, willing to provide letters of recommendation.
Contact Write, call, fax, e-mail, or through World Wide Web site Joyce Wetterberg, Administrative Assistant. Phone: 970-879-3922. Fax: 970-879-8258. E-mail: steamboat.lake@state.co.us. In-person interview recommended (telephone interview accepted). Applicants must submit a formal organization application, three personal references. Application deadline: January 15 for summer (suggested deadline), October 1 for winter (suggested deadline). World Wide Web: http://www.parks.state.co.us.

CONTEMPORARY ART MUSEUM
PO Box 66
Raleigh, North Carolina 27602-0066

General Information Nonprofit art museum that presents new and innovative works by regional, national, and international artists and designers through a schedule of diverse exhibits that explore aesthetic cultural and ideological issues. Established in 1983. Number of employees: 3. Number of internship applications received each year: 5.
Internships Available ▶ *1 curatorial intern:* responsibilities include assisting the curator of exhibits with aspects of planning, research, and implementation of the exhibit schedule. Candidates should have ability to work independently, ability to work with others, computer skills, declared college major in field, knowledge of field, office skills, oral communication skills, research skills, self-motivation, writing skills. Duration is 1-2 semesters. Unpaid. Open to college juniors, college seniors, recent college graduates, graduate students, career changers, individuals reentering the workforce. ▶ *1-2 education interns:* responsibilities include assisting in the development of educational programs for exhibits, community outreach, and working on special educational projects with local high schools and middle schools. Candidates should have ability to work independently, college courses in field, computer skills, office skills, oral communication skills, organizational skills, personal interest in the field, written communication skills. Duration is 1-2 semesters. Unpaid. Open to college sophomores, college juniors, college seniors, recent college graduates, graduate students, career changers, individuals reentering the workforce. ▶ *1-2 marketing interns:* responsibilities include working with a membership committee, performing public relations work, assisting the development director, and assisting with all phases of marketing. Candidates should have ability to work independently, ability to work with others, computer skills, office skills, oral communication skills, personal interest in the field, self-motivation, written communication skills. Duration is 1 semester. Position available as unpaid or paid. Open to college sophomores, college juniors, college seniors, recent college graduates, graduate students, career changers, individuals reentering the workforce. International applications accepted.
Benefits Opportunity to attend seminars/workshops, possible full-time employment, willing to act as a professional reference, willing to complete paperwork for educational credit, willing to provide letters of recommendation.
Contact Write, call, or e-mail Nicole Welch, Curator of Education. Phone: 919-836-0088. Fax: 919-836-2239. E-mail: nw@camnc.org. In-person interview recommended (telephone interview accepted). Applicants must submit a letter of interest, resume, three personal references, three letters of recommendation, 2-3 writing samples. Applications are accepted continuously. World Wide Web: http://www.camnc.org.

COOPER-HEWITT NATIONAL DESIGN MUSEUM, SMITHSONIAN INSTITUTION
2 East 91st Street
New York, New York 10128

General Information Museum serving as a resource for architects, designers, studio artists, craftpeople, and scholars; the

Cooper-Hewitt National Design Museum, Smithsonian Institution (continued)

nearly quarter-million object collection includes decorative arts, drawings and prints, textiles and wallcoverings, and an extensive library. Established in 1897. Number of employees: 150. Unit of Smithsonian Institution, Washington, District of Columbia. Number of internship applications received each year: 300.
Internships Available ▶ *1 Kell-Munoz Education Fellow.* Candidates should have ability to work independently, analytical skills, oral communication skills, plan to pursue career in field, written communication skills. Duration is September 1 to June 1 (24 hours per week). $10,000 per duration of internship. Open to graduate students, individuals of Latino descent. ▶ *6–8 Peter Krueger interns:* responsibilities include assisting on special projects for a specific curatorial, educational, or administrative department and participating in daily museum activities. Candidates should have analytical skills, office skills, organizational skills, research skills, self-motivation, strong interpersonal skills, career consideration in art history, design, museum studies, or museum education. Duration is 10 weeks in summer. $2500 per duration of internship. Open to college freshmen, college sophomores, college juniors, college seniors, recent college graduates, graduate students. ▶ *Smithsonian Institution minority interns.* Candidates should have ability to work independently, ability to work with others, computer skills, office skills, oral communication skills, organizational skills, written communication skills. Duration is 10 weeks in summer. Position available as unpaid or at $3500 per duration of internship. Open to college freshmen, college sophomores, college juniors, college seniors, recent college graduates, graduate students. ▶ *10–25 volunteer interns:* responsibilities include learning about the programs, policies, procedures, and operations of the National Design Museum and of museums in general. Candidates should have office skills, organizational skills, personal interest in the field, self-motivation, strong interpersonal skills. Duration is 10 weeks. Unpaid. Open to college freshmen, college sophomores, college juniors, college seniors, recent college graduates, graduate students. International applications accepted.
Benefits On-the-job training, opportunity to attend seminars/workshops, willing to complete paperwork for educational credit, willing to provide letters of recommendation, stipend available for minority intern program.
Contact Write, fax, or through World Wide Web site Intern Coordinator. Phone: 212-849-8380. Fax: 212-849-8328. E-mail: edu@ch.si.edu. Telephone interview required. Applicants must submit a resume, academic transcripts, two letters of recommendation, 1-2 page essay describing career goals and specific areas of interest. Application deadline: February 1 for summer (postmarked), December 1 for spring. World Wide Web: http://www.si.edu/ndm/.

DANFORTH MUSEUM OF ART
123 Union Avenue
Framingham, Massachusetts 01702-8291

General Information Community museum that presents changing exhibits, many drawn from its permanent collection; operates an art school with 70 courses for adults and children; offers Junior Gallery experiences, workshops, and curriculum kits to teachers and students. Established in 1975. Number of employees: 16. Number of internship applications received each year: 50.
Internships Available ▶ *2 Danforth Museum School interns:* responsibilities include assisting in the management of an art school. Candidates should have background in studio arts/art history, knowledge of Microsoft Word (desirable). Duration is 4–6 weeks. Unpaid. Open to college freshmen, college sophomores, college juniors, college seniors. ▶ *1–3 curatorial assistants:* responsibilities include assisting director with research, formation of archives, packing/unpacking art work, and exhibition installation. Candidates should have college courses in field, knowledge of field, knowledge of Microsoft Word. Duration is 1 semester (8–10 hours per week). Unpaid. Open to college juniors, college seniors, recent college graduates, graduate students, career changers. ▶ *1–3 development and marketing interns:* responsibilities include donor information processing and research, benefit events, grant research and writing, and drafting public relations and marketing brochures. Candidates should have computer skills, knowledge of field,

personal interest in the field. Duration is 1 semester (8–10 hours per week). Unpaid. Open to college juniors, college seniors, recent college graduates, graduate students, career changers. ▶ *2–3 education interns:* responsibilities include assisting education coordinator in school outreach, scheduling guided tours, docent training, developing Art on the Move curriculum kits, and conducting student tours. Candidates should have knowledge of Microsoft Word. Duration is 1 semester (8–10 hours per week). Unpaid. Open to college juniors, college seniors, recent college graduates, graduate students, career changers. International applications accepted.
Benefits On-the-job training, willing to act as a professional reference, willing to complete paperwork for educational credit, willing to provide letters of recommendation, job lists provided when available.
Contact Write, call, or fax Internship Coordinator, 125 Union avenue, Framingham, Massachusetts 01702. Phone: 508-620-0050. Fax: 508-872-5542. In-person interview recommended (telephone interview accepted). Applicants must submit a letter of interest, resume, academic transcripts. Applications are accepted continuously. World Wide Web: http://www.danforthmuseum.org.

D. C. BOOTH HISTORIC NATIONAL FISH HATCHERY
423 Hatchery Circle
Spearfish, South Dakota 57783

General Information Historic federal fish hatchery with museum and archives of fish culture. Established in 1896. Number of employees: 8. Unit of U.S. Fish and Wildlife Service, Washington, District of Columbia. Number of internship applications received each year: 10.
Internships Available ▶ *1–2 archives aides:* responsibilities include assisting with archival processing, storage, and research. Candidates should have ability to work independently, knowledge of field, research skills, self-motivation, written communication skills. Duration is 2–6 months. Position available as unpaid or at $8–$10 per hour. Open to high school seniors, recent high school graduates, college freshmen, college sophomores, college juniors, college seniors, recent college graduates, graduate students, career changers, individuals reentering the workforce. ▶ *1–2 museum aides:* responsibilities include assisting with collection care, pest management, preservation maintenance, monitoring environmental conditions, cataloging, photographing, and aiding in conservation. Candidates should have ability to work independently, knowledge of field, research skills, self-motivation, written communication skills. Duration is 2–6 months. Position available as unpaid or at $8–$10 per hour. Open to high school seniors, recent high school graduates, college freshmen, college sophomores, college juniors, college seniors, recent college graduates, graduate students, career changers, individuals reentering the workforce. ▶ *1–2 youth volunteer coordinators:* responsibilities include coordinating Youth Volunteer Program of approximately 15 children aged 11-14, supervising work program, and planning educational opportunities and reward programs. Candidates should have oral communication skills, organizational skills, self-motivation, strong interpersonal skills, strong leadership ability, patience. Duration is flexible. Position available as unpaid or at up to $900 per internship. Open to college freshmen, college sophomores, college juniors, college seniors, recent college graduates, graduate students, law students, career changers, individuals reentering the workforce, retirees. International applications accepted.
Benefits Names of contacts, on-the-job training, possible full-time employment, willing to act as a professional reference, willing to complete paperwork for educational credit, willing to provide letters of recommendation.
Contact Write, call, fax, or e-mail Ms. Randi Sue Smith, Curator. Phone: 605-642-7730. Fax: 605-642-2336. E-mail: randi_smith@fws.gov. Applicants must submit a formal organization application, letter of interest, resume, three personal references. Application deadline: March 15 for summer (museum and archive interns); continuous for other positions. World Wide Web: http://dcbooth.fws.gov.

DECATUR HOUSE
1610 H Street , NW
Washington, District of Columbia 20006

General Information Historic house museum located near the White House that interprets its residents' history and Washington, DC history from 1819 to 1956. Established in 1956. Number of employees: 39. Unit of National Trust for Historic Preservation, Washington, District of Columbia. Number of internship applications received each year: 20.

Internships Available ▶ *1–2 curatorial assistants:* responsibilities include assisting curator of collections with cataloging, caring for and maintaining museum's collection, and aiding in exhibit preparation, installment, and coordination. Candidates should have ability to work independently, computer skills, personal interest in the field, research skills, self-motivation, strong interpersonal skills, writing skills. Duration is at least 6-8 weeks. Unpaid. Open to college sophomores, college juniors, college seniors, recent college graduates, graduate students, career changers. ▶ *1–3 education assistants:* responsibilities include assisting curator of education with school group tours, developing educational materials, and working with tour guides to learn about museum and collections. Candidates should have ability to work independently, computer skills, experience in the field, knowledge of field, oral communication skills, organizational skills, personal interest in the field, self-motivation, strong interpersonal skills, writing skills. Duration is 3-6 months (2-4 days per week). Unpaid. Open to college juniors, college seniors, recent college graduates, graduate students, career changers. ▶ *1–2 marketing assistants:* responsibilities include assisting the director of marketing with site and program promotion, advertisements, upkeep of contact information, and public relations. Candidates should have editing skills, experience in the field, oral communication skills, organizational skills, plan to pursue career in field, self-motivation, strong interpersonal skills, writing skills. Duration is 3-6 months (2-4 days per week). Unpaid. Open to college juniors, college seniors, recent college graduates, graduate students, career changers. ▶ *1–3 research interns:* responsibilities include researching certain areas pertaining to Decatur House collection and its occupants and utilizing on-site materials and local organizations to gather research information. Candidates should have ability to work independently, computer skills, editing skills, research skills, self-motivation, strong interpersonal skills, writing skills. Duration is at least 6-8 weeks. Unpaid. Open to college juniors, college seniors, recent college graduates, graduate students, career changers. International applications accepted.

Benefits Names of contacts, on-the-job training, opportunity to attend seminars/workshops, willing to complete paperwork for educational credit, willing to provide letters of recommendation, membership after 30 hours service, opportunity to become immersed in the workings of a medium historic house museum.

Contact Write, call, fax, or e-mail Ms. Sheri J. Levinsky, Director of Education and Programs. Phone: 202-842-0920. Fax: 202-842-0030. E-mail: sheri_levinsky@nthp.org. In-person interview recommended (telephone interview accepted). Applicants must submit a resume, portfolio, one-page letter of interest. Application deadline: April 15 for summer (suggested), July 15 for fall (suggested), September 15 for winter (suggested), November 15 for spring (suggested). World Wide Web: http://www.decaturhouse.org.

DELTA AREA STATE PARKS
PO Box 682
Delta Junction, Alaska 99737

General Information District that includes 5 recreation sites, 1 historical park, salmon and trout fishing, and numerous campgrounds and serves as a main access point for the Interior. Established in 1975. Number of employees: 3. Branch of Alaska Division of Parks and Outdoor Recreation, Anchorage, Alaska. Number of internship applications received each year: 10.

Internships Available ▶ *2–3 ranger assistants:* responsibilities include janitorial and park maintenance, camper registration, offering visitor information, conducting firewood sales and distribution, and visitor center staffing. Candidates should have ability to work independently, oral communication skills, organizational

skills, self-motivation, strong interpersonal skills. Duration is 6–12 weeks. Unpaid. Open to recent high school graduates, college juniors, college seniors, recent college graduates, graduate students, career changers. International applications accepted.

Benefits Free housing, on-the-job training, opportunity to attend seminars/workshops, possible full-time employment, willing to act as a professional reference, willing to complete paperwork for educational credit, willing to provide letters of recommendation, meal stipend.

Contact Write, fax, or e-mail Mr. Brooks Ludwig, Ranger. Fax: 907-895-5043. E-mail: brooks_ludwig@dnr.state.ak.us. Applicants must submit a formal organization application, letter of interest, resume, academic transcripts, three personal references. Application deadline: February 28 for summer. World Wide Web: http://www.dnr.state.ak.us.

DENALI NATIONAL PARK AND PRESERVE
PO Box 9
Denali Park, Alaska 99755

General Information National park serving to preserve, protect, and interpret the natural and cultural history of 6 million acres, recognized for its wildlife and North America's tallest peak, Mount McKinley. Established in 1917. Number of employees: 241. Unit of United States National Park Service, Washington, District of Columbia. Number of internship applications received each year: 300.

Internships Available ▶ *1–2 backcountry volunteers:* responsibilities include issuing bear-resistant food containers to backcountry users, advising visitors of safe hiking and minimum impact techniques, issuing permits at VAC, conducting backcountry patrols, and special projects. Candidates should have ability to work independently, computer skills, knowledge of field, oral communication skills, personal interest in the field, self-motivation, strong interpersonal skills. Duration is 1 summer (mid-May to early September). Unpaid. Open to college freshmen, college sophomores, college juniors, college seniors, recent college graduates, graduate students, career changers, individuals reentering the workforce. ▶ *1–2 interpretive naturalists:* responsibilities include preparing and presenting educational programs and providing information at the Visitor Center (VAC). Candidates should have ability to work independently, computer skills, knowledge of field, oral communication skills, organizational skills, personal interest in the field, self-motivation, strong interpersonal skills, strong leadership ability, writing skills. Duration is 1 summer (mid-May to early September). Unpaid. Open to recent college graduates, graduate students, career changers. ▶ *1–2 resource management volunteers:* responsibilities include assisting researchers and resource managers in a variety of field and office work. Candidates should have ability to work independently, knowledge of field, organizational skills, personal interest in the field, research skills, self-motivation, strong interpersonal skills, written communication skills. Duration is 1 summer (mid-May to early September). Unpaid. Open to recent college graduates, graduate students, career changers. International applications accepted.

Benefits Formal training, job counseling, on-the-job training, minimum stipend and/or housing may be provided depending on availability of housing and funding.

Contact Write, call, fax, or e-mail Mark Motsko, VIP Coordinator. Phone: 907-683-2294. Fax: 907-683-9617. E-mail: mark_motsko@nps.gov. Applicants must submit a formal organization application, resume or the official NPS/Land Management Agency volunteer applications. Application deadline: March 15. World Wide Web: http://www.nps.gov/dena.

DENVER ART MUSEUM
100 West 14th Avenue Parkway
Denver, Colorado 80204

General Information Art museum with world collection (Asian, pre-Columbian, Spanish Colonial, American Indian, American, European, and African) and special emphasis on museum education and outreach. Number of employees: 125. Number of internship applications received each year: 55.

Internships Available ▶ *5–8 museum education interns:* responsibilities include applying research to educational tasks including

Denver Art Museum (continued)

didactic exhibits; performing outreach to culturally diverse individuals; assisting with school, family, and adult programs; and teaching youth and adults in Museum galleries. Candidates should have ability to work independently, ability to work with others, computer skills, knowledge of field, oral communication skills, personal interest in the field, research skills, written communication skills. Duration is 1–12 months. Position available as unpaid or paid. Open to college sophomores, college juniors, college seniors, recent college graduates, graduate students, career changers, individuals reentering the workforce. International applications accepted.

Benefits Formal training, job counseling, opportunity to attend seminars/workshops, possible full-time employment, willing to act as a professional reference, willing to complete paperwork for educational credit, willing to provide letters of recommendation.

Contact Write, call, fax, or e-mail Jeannie Hendrick, Education Administrator. Phone: 720-913-0065. Fax: 720-913-0005. E-mail: jhendrick@denverartmuseum.org. In-person interview recommended (telephone interview accepted). Applicants must submit a formal organization application, letter of interest, resume, academic transcripts, three personal references, letter of recommendation. Application deadline: April 15 for summer; continuous for other positions. World Wide Web: http://www.denverartmuseum.org.

DENVER BOTANIC GARDENS
909 York Street
Denver, Colorado 80206

General Information Urban botanical gardens headquartered on 23 acres within 2 miles of downtown Denver with additional property located in the foothills (6,000-8,000 feet), montane (8,000-10,000 feet), and alpine (above timberline) zones. Established in 1951. Number of employees: 100. Number of internship applications received each year: 20.

Internships Available ▶ *Applied horticulture interns:* responsibilities include working with garden professionals. Candidates should have ability to work independently, ability to work with others, college courses in field, knowledge of field, oral communication skills, personal interest in the field, plan to pursue career in field, written communication skills. Duration is 10 weeks in summer. $8–$9 per hour. Open to college juniors, college seniors, graduate students, older students returning to school.

Benefits Names of contacts, on-the-job training, opportunity to attend seminars/workshops, willing to complete paperwork for educational credit.

Contact Write, call, or e-mail Gail Martinez, Recruiter/Training Coordinator. Phone: 720-865-3531. E-mail: martinezg@botanicgardens.org. In-person interview recommended (telephone interview accepted). Applicants must submit a formal organization application, resume, academic transcripts, three letters of recommendation. Application deadline: February 28. World Wide Web: http://www.botanicgardens.org.

DISCOVERY CREEK CHILDREN'S MUSEUM OF WASHINGTON
2233 Wisconsin Avenue, Suite 410
Washington, District of Columbia 20007

General Information Children's museum focusing on the environment and education, located on 12-acre site that includes the only remaining one-room schoolhouse in Washington, D.C. as well as a renovated historic stable at Glen Echo Park in Glen Echo, MD and a mobile exhibition "The Rolling Rainforest". Established in 1991. Number of employees: 25. Number of internship applications received each year: 50.

Internships Available ▶ *1–13 education interns:* responsibilities include assisting with development and teaching of Museum's school and weekend public programs utilizing live wildlife, art activities, and outdoor exploration; working with children ages 4-12 in an outdoor summer nature camp. Duration is 3 months to 1 year. Position available as unpaid or at $1200 per month. ▶ *1–13 spring/summer/fall interns:* responsibilities include assisting and leading various environmental programs with children ages

3-11 years old; programs include live animals, art activities, science experiments, outdoor exploration, and sports. Duration is 3–6 months. Position available as unpaid or at $1200 per month. Candidates for all positions should have ability to work independently, ability to work with others, experience in the field, oral communication skills, organizational skills, personal interest in the field, self-motivation, strong leadership ability. Open to high school seniors, recent high school graduates, college freshmen, college sophomores, college juniors, college seniors, recent college graduates, graduate students, career changers, individuals reentering the workforce. International applications accepted.

Benefits Names of contacts, on-the-job training, opportunity to attend seminars/workshops, possible full-time employment, willing to act as a professional reference, willing to complete paperwork for educational credit, willing to provide letters of recommendation.

Contact Write, call, fax, e-mail, or through World Wide Web site Ms. Anne Knight, Intern Program Manager. Phone: 202-337-5111. Fax: 202-337-5344. E-mail: aknight@discoverycreek.org. In-person interview recommended (telephone interview accepted). Applicants must submit a formal organization application, letter of interest, resume, three personal references, two letters of recommendation. Applications are accepted continuously. World Wide Web: http://www.discoverycreek.org.

FILOLI
86 Canada Road
Woodside, California 94062

General Information Early 20th-century country estate with a 16-acre formal garden. Established in 1975. Number of employees: 30. Number of internship applications received each year: 35.

Internships Available ▶ *2 garden apprentices:* responsibilities include performing public garden maintenance including mowing, blowing, edging, caring for displays, pruning, and greenhouse work. Candidates should have ability to work with others, oral communication skills, plan to pursue career in field, major in horticulture, public garden management, landscape maintenance, landscape preservation, landscape architecture, environmental studies, botany, or biology. Duration is 6 months (40 hours per week). $8 per hour. ▶ *5 garden interns:* responsibilities include performing public garden maintenance including mowing, blowing, edging, caring for displays, pruning, and greenhouse work. Candidates should have oral communication skills, plan to pursue career in field, strong interpersonal skills, major in horticulture, public garden management, landscape maintenance, landscape preservation, landscape architecture, environmental studies, botany, or biology. Duration is 10 weeks in spring, summer, or fall (40 hours per week). $8 per hour. Open to college freshmen, college sophomores, college juniors, college seniors, recent college graduates, graduate students. International applications accepted.

Benefits Formal training, on-the-job training, opportunity to attend seminars/workshops, willing to complete paperwork for educational credit.

Contact Write, call, fax, e-mail, or through World Wide Web site Ms. Lucy Tolmach, Director of Horticulture. Phone: 650-364-8300 Ext. 214. Fax: 650-366-7836. E-mail: filoli@earthlink.net. In-person interview recommended (telephone interview accepted). Applicants must submit a formal organization application, letter of interest, academic transcripts, three personal references, three letters of recommendation. Application deadline: January 14 for spring (March-May), March 31 for summer (June-August), July 16 for fall (September-November), August 14 for 6-month (January-June) apprenticeship. World Wide Web: http://www.filoli.org.

FLORIDA PARK SERVICE
3900 Commonwealth Boulevard, MS 535
Tallahassee, Florida 32399

General Information Organization that manages 151 state parks. Established in 1935. Number of employees: 1,080. Division of Department of Environmental Protection, Tallahassee, Florida. Number of internship applications received each year: 10.

Internships Available ▶ *10–20 interns:* responsibilities include providing general assistance in the state park system; specific interests and assignments can be accommodated. Candidates

should have ability to work with others, knowledge of field, oral communication skills, personal interest in the field, plan to pursue career in field. Duration is flexible. Unpaid. Open to high school students, recent high school graduates, college freshmen, college sophomores, college juniors, college seniors, recent college graduates, graduate students, career changers, individuals reentering the workforce. International applications accepted.
Benefits Formal training, job counseling, names of contacts, on-the-job training, possible full-time employment, travel reimbursement, willing to act as a professional reference, willing to complete paperwork for educational credit, willing to provide letters of recommendation, housing may be provided, camping may be available.
Contact Write, call, fax, e-mail, or through World Wide Web site Mr. Phillip A. Werndli, Coordinator of Volunteer Programs. Phone: 850-243-3098. Fax: 850-245-3091. E-mail: phillip.werndli@dep.state.fl.us. In-person interview required. Applicants must submit a formal organization application, letter of interest, resume. Applications are accepted continuously. World Wide Web: http://www.dep.state.fl.us/parks/.

FLORISSANT FOSSIL BEDS NATIONAL MONUMENT
PO Box 185
Florissant, Colorado 80816

General Information National park providing interpretive services to the public while managing 6000-acre site containing Ponderosa pine forests, grassy wildflower meadows, and 35-million-year-old plant and insect fossils. Established in 1969. Number of employees: 18. Unit of United States National Park Service, Washington, District of Columbia. Number of internship applications received each year: 25.
Internships Available ▶ *1–3 interpretive interns:* responsibilities include developing and presenting programs to groups of all ages; providing information to the public about fossil resources and natural and cultural history of the area. Candidates should have ability to work independently, oral communication skills, strong interpersonal skills, written communication skills, basic knowledge of natural sciences or geology. Duration is late May to mid-August (2½ months or 12 weeks). Stipend of $150 per week. Open to college freshmen, college sophomores, college juniors, college seniors, recent college graduates, graduate students, law students, career changers, individuals reentering the workforce. ▶ *1–2 paleontology interns:* responsibilities include fossil collection and curation; assisting with excavation, inventory, and monitoring of sites; database development; self-directed research. Candidates should have ability to work independently, analytical skills, computer skills, research skills, written communication skills, declared college major in geology or paleontology. Duration is late May to mid-August (usually 12 weeks). Stipend of $150 a week. Open to recent college graduates, graduate students, career changers, college seniors preparing thesis. ▶ *1–3 resource management interns:* responsibilities include weed and fire management; water quality monitoring; vegetation and wildfire monitoring. Candidates should have ability to work independently, analytical skills, computer skills, research skills, written communication skills. Duration is 12 weeks. Stipend of $150 per week. Open to college sophomores, college juniors, college seniors, recent college graduates, graduate students, career changers. International applications accepted.
Benefits Formal training, free housing, job counseling, names of contacts, on-the-job training, opportunity to attend seminars/workshops, willing to act as a professional reference, willing to complete paperwork for educational credit, willing to provide letters of recommendation, uniforms provided.
Contact Write, call, fax, or e-mail Jeff Wolin, Volunteer Coordinator. Phone: 719-748-3253. Fax: 719-748-3164. E-mail: flfd_information@nps.gov. Telephone interview required. Applicants must submit a letter of interest, resume, academic transcripts, two personal references. Application deadline: March 20 for summer. World Wide Web: http://www.nps.gov/flfo.

FORT LARAMIE NATIONAL HISTORIC SITE
HC72 Box 389
Fort Laramie, Wyoming 82212

General Information Restored military outpost in southeastern Wyoming, near the Laramie Mountains, about 100 miles north of Cheyenne. Established in 1938. Number of employees: 21. Unit of United States National Park Service, Washington, District of Columbia.
Internships Available ▶ *1–5 interpretation volunteers:* responsibilities include interacting with visitors and preparing and presenting information on surroundings. Candidates should have ability to work independently, knowledge of field, strong interpersonal skills, written communication skills, public speaking skills. Duration is 1 summer. Unpaid. Open to college freshmen, college sophomores, college juniors, college seniors, recent college graduates. ▶ *1–2 natural resource volunteers:* responsibilities include working with resource management branch in dealing with exotic plants. Candidates should have ability to work independently, ability to work with others, knowledge of field, oral communication skills, personal interest in the field, self-motivation. Duration is one summer/fall. Unpaid. Open to high school students, college freshmen, college sophomores, college juniors, college seniors, recent college graduates, graduate students, individuals reentering the workforce. International applications accepted.
Benefits Formal training, opportunity to attend seminars/workshops, willing to complete paperwork for educational credit.
Contact Write, call, fax, or e-mail Kathie Perry, Administrative Officer. Phone: 307-837-2221. Fax: 307-837-2120. E-mail: fola_superintendent@nps.gov. Applicants must submit a formal organization application, resume, academic transcripts. Applications are accepted continuously.

FORT NECESSITY NATIONAL BATTLEFIELD
1 Washington Parkway
Farmington, Pennsylvania 15437

General Information Site commemorating the start of the French and Indian War in 1754. Established in 1931. Number of employees: 22. Unit of United States National Park Service, Washington, District of Columbia. Number of internship applications received each year: 5.
Internships Available ▶ *1 interpretive aide:* responsibilities include working in the contact station, performing guided talks and walks, and preparing brochures. Candidates should have oral communication skills, personal interest in the field, strong interpersonal skills. Duration is flexible. Unpaid. Open to high school seniors, recent high school graduates, college freshmen, college sophomores, college juniors, college seniors, recent college graduates, graduate students. International applications accepted.
Benefits Formal training, free housing, job counseling, on-the-job training, willing to complete paperwork for educational credit, willing to provide letters of recommendation, limited reimbursement for meals and travel.
Contact Write, e-mail, or through World Wide Web site Carney Rigg, Volunteer Coordinator. E-mail: carney_rigg@nps.gov. Applicants must submit a formal organization application, three personal references. Applications are accepted continuously. World Wide Web: http://www.nps.gov/fone.

FOSSIL BUTTE NATIONAL MONUMENT
PO Box 592
Kemmerer, Wyoming 83101

General Information Preserves paleontological sites and related geological phenomena and provides for the display and interpretation of scientific specimens. Established in 1972. Number of employees: 7. Unit of United States National Park Service, Washington, District of Columbia. Number of internship applications received each year: 50.
Internships Available ▶ *2 interpretation/resource management interns:* responsibilities include staffing information desk and presenting interpretive programs; labor intensive conservation projects such as trail maintenance, stream erosion projects; cultural and natural resource management projects that may include preparation of specimens and organization of museum collections, wildlife and

Fossil Butte National Monument (continued)

plant surveys, and documentation of archaeological sites; preparation and presentation of programs to school groups including guided hikes. Candidates should have knowledge of field, oral communication skills, personal interest in the field, self-motivation, strong interpersonal skills. Duration is 12 weeks. Unpaid. Open to recent high school graduates, college freshmen, college sophomores, college juniors, college seniors, recent college graduates, graduate students, law students, career changers, individuals reentering the workforce. ▶ *1–2 paleontology interns:* responsibilities include fossil collection and preparation. Candidates should have ability to work independently, ability to work with others, declared college major in field, oral communication skills, personal interest in the field, self-motivation. Duration is 12 weeks. Unpaid. Open to college freshmen, college sophomores, college juniors, college seniors, recent college graduates, graduate students. International applications accepted.
Benefits Formal training, free housing, names of contacts, on-the-job training, travel reimbursement, willing to complete paperwork for educational credit, willing to provide letters of recommendation, $50 stipend.
Contact Write, call, or e-mail Marcia D. Fagnant, Park Ranger/Lead Interpreter. Phone: 307-877-4455. E-mail: marcia_fagnant@nps.gov. Telephone interview required. Applicants must submit a formal organization application, resume, academic transcripts, three personal references. Application deadline: March 15 for spring and summer, July 1 for fall. World Wide Web: http://www.nps.gov/fobu.

FRANKLIN D. ROOSEVELT PRESIDENTIAL LIBRARY AND MUSEUM
4079 Albany Post Road
Hyde Park, New York 12538

General Information Library and museum containing the papers, books, and personal memorabilia of President Franklin D. Roosevelt, the papers of his wife, Anna Eleanor Roosevelt, and those of many of his political associates and contemporaries. Established in 1941. Number of employees: 25. Unit of Office of Presidential Libraries, National Archives & Records Administration, Washington, District of Columbia. Number of internship applications received each year: 40.
Internships Available ▶ *5–6 William R. Emerson interns:* responsibilities include organizing and automating archival materials, making indices, finding aids and databases, digitizing documents and photographs, and assisting with other archival and museum projects. Candidates should have ability to work with others, college courses in field, computer skills, personal interest in the field, research skills, written communication skills. Duration is 6-8 weeks during summer. $250 per week. Open to college freshmen, college sophomores, college juniors, college seniors, recent college graduates. International applications accepted.
Benefits On-the-job training, willing to complete paperwork for educational credit, willing to provide letters of recommendation.
Contact Write, call, fax, e-mail, or through World Wide Web site Ms. Lynn Bassanese, Director of Public Programs. Phone: 845-486-7741. Fax: 845-486-1147. E-mail: lynn.bassanese@nara.gov. In-person interview recommended (telephone interview accepted). Applicants must submit a formal organization application, letter of interest, two letters of recommendation. Application deadline: April 15. World Wide Web: http://www.fdrlibrary.marist.edu.

FREDERICKSBURG AND SPOTSYLVANIA NATIONAL MILITARY PARK
120 Chatham Lane
Fredericksburg, Virginia 22405

General Information National historic park whose main objective is to preserve and interpret four major Civil War battles and related Civil War structures. Established in 1927. Number of employees: 50. Unit of United States National Park Service, Washington, District of Columbia. Number of internship applications received each year: 10.
Internships Available ▶ *2 curatorial assistants:* responsibilities include cataloging and recordkeeping associated with museum

objects and other projects, including exhibit guides. Candidates should have ability to work independently, knowledge of field, organizational skills, personal interest in the field, self-motivation. Duration is 2–4 months. Unpaid. Open to college juniors, college seniors, recent college graduates, graduate students. ▶ *4 historical interpreters:* responsibilities include assisting visitors at information desk and park library and and providing walking tours. Candidates should have knowledge of field, oral communication skills, personal interest in the field, self-motivation, strong interpersonal skills. Duration is 2–4 months. Position available as unpaid or at $10.35–$11.58 per hour. Open to college juniors, college seniors, recent college graduates, graduate students. ▶ *3 historical researchers:* responsibilities include indexing manuscripts, writing brochures, and assisting with various other historical and cultural resource management projects. Candidates should have ability to work independently, knowledge of field, personal interest in the field, research skills, self-motivation, writing skills. Duration is 2–4 months. Unpaid. Open to college juniors, college seniors, recent college graduates, graduate students. ▶ *1–2 natural resource assistants:* responsibilities include monitoring water quality, agricultural pests, fire, weather, and/or gypsy moths. Candidates should have ability to work independently, college courses in field, personal interest in the field, self-motivation. Duration is 2–4 months. Unpaid. Open to college juniors, college seniors, recent college graduates, graduate students. ▶ *2 restoration assistants:* responsibilities include working on various projects related to the preservation or restoration of historic structures. Candidates should have ability to work with others, experience in the field. Duration is 2–4 months. Unpaid. Open to recent high school graduates, college freshmen, college sophomores, college juniors, college seniors, recent college graduates, career changers, individuals reentering the workforce.
Benefits Formal training, free housing, job counseling, names of contacts, on-the-job training, travel reimbursement, tuition assistance, willing to complete paperwork for educational credit, willing to provide letters of recommendation, possibility of seasonal employment; summer housing generally limited to historical interpreter interns; meals stipend.
Contact Write, call, fax, or e-mail Mr. Gregory A. Mertz, Supervisory Historian. Phone: 540-373-6124. Fax: 540-654-5521. E-mail: greg_mertz@nps.gov. In-person interview recommended (telephone interview accepted). Applicants must submit a formal organization application. Applications are accepted continuously. World Wide Web: http://www.nps.gov/frsp.

FRIENDSHIP HILL NATIONAL HISTORIC SITE
223 New Geneva Road
Point Marion, Pennsylvania 15474

General Information Historic site located along the Monongahela River that contains the home of Albert Gallatin, Secretary of the Treasury under Presidents Jefferson and Madison. Established in 1978. Number of employees: 8. Unit of National Park Service, Washington, District of Columbia. Number of internship applications received each year: 2.
Internships Available ▶ *1 curatorial aide:* responsibilities include cataloging, photographing, preparing items for storage, general conservation, record keeping, and inventories. Candidates should have ability to work independently, ability to work with others, computer skills, experience in the field, organizational skills, personal interest in the field. Duration is flexible. Unpaid. Open to college freshmen, college sophomores, college juniors, college seniors, recent college graduates, graduate students, career changers, individuals reentering the workforce. ▶ *2–3 interpretive aides:* responsibilities include working in the contact station, performing guided talks and walks, and preparing brochures. Candidates should have ability to work independently, oral communication skills, research skills, strong interpersonal skills, written communication skills. Duration is flexible. Unpaid. Open to high school seniors, recent high school graduates, college freshmen, college sophomores, college juniors, college seniors, recent college graduates, graduate students, law students, career changers, individuals reentering the workforce. ▶ *1 resource management aide:* responsibilities include monitoring water, flora, and fauna and performing vegetation studies, reforestation, and other

projects. Candidates should have ability to work independently, college courses in field, experience in the field, oral communication skills, research skills, written communication skills. Duration is flexible. Unpaid. Open to college freshmen, college sophomores, college juniors, college seniors, recent college graduates, graduate students, career changers, individuals reentering the workforce. International applications accepted.

Benefits Formal training, job counseling, on-the-job training, opportunity to attend seminars/workshops, willing to act as a professional reference, willing to complete paperwork for educational credit, willing to provide letters of recommendation, limited reimbursement of travel and meal expenses.

Contact Write, call, fax, e-mail, or through World Wide Web site Kathryn Seifert, Volunteer Coordinator, 223 New Geneva Road. Phone: 724-725-9190. Fax: 724-725-1999. E-mail: kitty_seifert@nps. gov. Telephone interview required. Applicants must submit a formal organization application, letter of interest, resume, two personal references. Applications are accepted continuously. World Wide Web: http://www.nps.gov/frhi/.

FULLER MUSEUM OF ART
455 Oak Street
Brockton, Massachusetts 02301

General Information Art museum and museum school with permanent collection and rotating exhibits whose mission is to serve as an educational and cultural institution to the region. Established in 1969. Number of employees: 8. Number of internship applications received each year: 10.

Internships Available ▶ *Administrative interns:* responsibilities include assisting the director in researching available sources of foundation and grant income and obtaining corporate support; researching for present and upcoming exhibits; book reviewing; lobbying; and planning meeting sessions. Candidates should have ability to work independently, computer skills, oral communication skills, research skills, self-motivation. Duration is 1 semester. Unpaid. ▶ *Curatorial/registration interns:* responsibilities include surveying and researching the permanent collection for various purposes (education, condition, reports, preliminary cataloging, insurance, and restoration) and researching particular artists or works. Candidates should have ability to work independently, computer skills, office skills, personal interest in the field, plan to pursue career in field, research skills, self-motivation. Duration is 1 semester. Unpaid. ▶ *Education interns:* responsibilities include assisting in researching exhibits for creation of teacher materials and guides, cataloging museum slide collection. Candidates should have ability to work independently, personal interest in the field, plan to pursue career in field, research skills, self-motivation, writing skills. Duration is 1 semester. Unpaid. ▶ *Museum school interns:* responsibilities include assisting the coordinator in a variety of tasks. Candidates should have ability to work independently, office skills, oral communication skills, self-motivation. Duration is 1 semester. Unpaid. ▶ *Public relations interns:* responsibilities include assisting in writing news releases and public service announcements, promoting all Museum exhibits and events, writing and editing quarterly newsletters, and maintaining accurate and up-to-date art listings and calendar of events in all area newspapers. Candidates should have ability to work independently, computer skills, editing skills, research skills, self-motivation, writing skills. Duration is 1 semester. Unpaid. Open to college freshmen, college sophomores, college juniors, college seniors, recent college graduates, graduate students, law students, career changers, individuals reentering the workforce.

Benefits Willing to provide letters of recommendation, opportunity to research, study, and be part of an organization serving the community.

Contact Write, fax, or e-mail Jennifer Atkinson, Director. Fax: 508-587-6191. E-mail: jatkinson@fullermuseum.org. No phone calls. In-person interview recommended (telephone interview accepted). Applicants must submit a letter of interest, resume. Applications are accepted continuously. World Wide Web: http://www.fullermuseum.org.

GREENBURGH NATURE CENTER
99 Dromore Road
Scarsdale, New York 10583

General Information Nature center that provides exhibits and programs for all ages on natural history and the environment; 33-acre site includes woods, pond, field, orchard, vineyard, nature trails, and cultivated lawns and gardens; indoor exhibits include petting zoo with over 140 live animals, greenhouse with botanical exhibits on plant adaptation room, and changing natural history exhibits. Established in 1975. Number of employees: 12. Number of internship applications received each year: 80.

Internships Available ▶ *1–2 naturalist interns:* responsibilities include teaching programs for children 2-8 years, caring for and presenting live animals, and directing activities of high school and adult volunteers. Candidates should have ability to work independently, experience in the field, oral communication skills, personal interest in the field, self-motivation, drivers license. Duration is 3–4 months. $180–$200 per week. Open to college freshmen, college sophomores, college juniors, college seniors, recent college graduates, graduate students. International applications accepted.

Benefits Free housing, on-the-job training, opportunity to attend seminars/workshops, willing to complete paperwork for educational credit, willing to provide letters of recommendation, free local phone service and Internet in intern's room.

Contact Write, call, fax, or e-mail Rene Catano, Naturalist/Intern Coordinator. Phone: 914-723-3470. Fax: 914-725-6599. E-mail: gbhntr@aol.com. In-person interview recommended (telephone interview accepted). Applicants must submit a formal organization application, resume, academic transcripts, three personal references, letter of interest including which season preferred. Application deadline: April 15 for summer, July 15 for fall, December 1 for winter/spring. World Wide Web: http://www.townlink.com/community_web/gnc.

GREENWOOD FURNACE STATE PARK
RR 2, Box 118
Huntingdon, Pennsylvania 16652-9006

General Information State park that offers a full range of camping and activities, including a visitor center offering historical interpretation of the former iron furnace. Established in 1929. Number of employees: 30. Unit of Department of Conservation and Natural Resources, Bureau of State Parks, Harrisburg, Pennsylvania. Number of internship applications received each year: 3.

Internships Available ▶ *1–2 interpretation interns:* responsibilities include operating visitor center/gift shop; visitor contact; conducting programs on environmental, historical, and cultural topics (including hikes, talks, demonstrations, living history reenactments); historical and environmental research; all training provided. Candidates should have computer skills, oral communication skills, personal interest in the field, self-motivation, strong interpersonal skills, good relational skills with general public. Duration is flexible (dependent upon student's academic needs). Unpaid. Open to high school students, recent high school graduates, college freshmen, college sophomores, college juniors, college seniors, recent college graduates, graduate students, individuals reentering the workforce. International applications accepted.

Benefits Free housing, job counseling, names of contacts, on-the-job training, opportunity to attend seminars/workshops, willing to act as a professional reference, willing to complete paperwork for educational credit, willing to provide letters of recommendation, worker's compensation coverage, service effectiveness training.

Contact Write, call, fax, or e-mail Paul T. Fagley, Cultural Educator. Phone: 814-667-1805. Fax: 814-667-1802. E-mail: greenwoodfurnacesp@state.pa.us. In-person interview recommended (telephone interview accepted). Applicants must submit a formal organization application, letter of interest, resume. Applications are accepted continuously. World Wide Web: http://www.dcnr.state.pa.us.

HARPERS FERRY NATIONAL HISTORICAL PARK
PO Box 65
Harpers Ferry, West Virginia 25425

General Information Park whose mission is to preserve and protect the natural and cultural resources of the Harpers Ferry area including natural heritage, transportation, water-powered industry, John Brown's raid, the Civil War, and African-American history for the education of current and future generations. Established in 1944. Number of employees: 125. Unit of United States National Park Service, Washington, District of Columbia. Number of internship applications received each year: 10.

Internships Available ▶ *1 camp aide-history day camp:* responsibilities include assisting camp director in direct supervision of boys and girls ages 10-12 in a day camp setting held in a national historical park; campers will participate in daily outdoor activities related to the park. Candidates should have ability to work independently, ability to work with others, oral communication skills, personal interest in the field, self-motivation. Duration is 1 week. $60 per day. Open to high school seniors, recent high school graduates, college freshmen, college sophomores, college juniors, college seniors. ▶ *1 curatorial/collections management assistant:* responsibilities include documenting, cataloging, and inventory control of primary and secondary source materials; care and maintenance of artifact collections with proper curatorial methods; performing research duties and assisting outside researchers. Candidates should have ability to work independently, ability to work with others, computer skills, knowledge of field, oral communication skills, written communication skills. Duration is 10 weeks. $100 per week. Open to college freshmen, college sophomores, college juniors, college seniors, recent college graduates, graduate students. ▶ *1–6 park/ living history and period exhibits interns:* responsibilities include management and operation of the Historic Exhibits and Living History Program; duties and responsibilities assigned in interpretive exhibit/tour program development, volunteer staff assistance, black powder/living history activity, and special event support. Candidates should have ability to work with others, oral communication skills, research skills, written communication skills, knowledge of 19th-century history. Duration is 6–12 weeks. Position available as unpaid or at $100 per week. Open to high school seniors, college freshmen, college sophomores, college juniors, college seniors, recent college graduates, graduate students, individuals reentering the workforce. ▶ *1 visitor services assistant:* responsibilities include assisting in the operation of visitor information desks, museum tours, and special event organization; involves frequent public contact and/or special research projects. Candidates should have oral communication skills, organizational skills, personal interest in the field, self-motivation, strong interpersonal skills. Duration is 12 weeks. $100 per week. Open to high school seniors, college freshmen, college sophomores, college juniors, college seniors, recent college graduates, graduate students. International applications accepted.

Benefits Free housing, job counseling, names of contacts, on-the-job training, opportunity to attend seminars/workshops, travel reimbursement, willing to act as a professional reference, willing to complete paperwork for educational credit, willing to provide letters of recommendation.

Contact Write, call, fax, or e-mail David Fox, Volunteer Coordinator. Phone: 304-535-6282. Fax: 304-535-2912. E-mail: david_fox@nps.gov. In-person interview recommended (telephone interview accepted). Applicants must submit a formal organization application, letter of interest, resume, three personal references. Application deadline: March 15 for visitor services summer interns; living history summer interns; camp aide summer intern, December 1 for curatorial summer interns. World Wide Web: http://www.nps.gov/hafe/home.htm.

THE HERMITAGE
4580 Rachel's Lane
Hermitage, Tennessee 37076

General Information Organization that presents the home of Andrew Jackson to visitors, a public museum. Established in 1889. Number of employees: 80. Number of internship applications received each year: 100.

Internships Available ▶ *6–10 historical archaeology interns:* responsibilities include participating in all phases of field excavation and laboratory processing of finds. Candidates should have college courses in field, knowledge of field, oral communication skills, plan to pursue career in field, self-motivation, strong interpersonal skills. Duration is 5 weeks in summer; flexible from year to year. $1000 per duration of internship. Open to college juniors, college seniors, recent college graduates, graduate students, career changers.

Benefits Free housing, job counseling, names of contacts, on-the-job training, willing to act as a professional reference, willing to complete paperwork for educational credit, willing to provide letters of recommendation.

Contact Write, call, or e-mail Elizabeth J. Kellar, Director of Archaeology. Phone: 615-889-2941 Ext. 200. Fax: 615-889-9289. E-mail: ekellar@thehermitage.com. Applicants must submit a letter of interest, resume, two personal references. Application deadline: April 10. World Wide Web: http://www.thehermitage.com.

HIGH MUSEUM OF ART
1280 Peachtree Street, NE
Atlanta, Georgia 30309

General Information Art museum. Established in 1926. Number of employees: 142. Division of Woodruff Arts Center, Atlanta, Georgia. Number of internship applications received each year: 75.

Internships Available ▶ *10–15 interns:* responsibilities include duties in one of the following departments: community relations, curatorial, development, education, exhibitions, library, marketing, membership, public relations, and registration; duties will vary based on Museum's current needs. Candidates should have knowledge of field, personal interest in the field. Duration is at least 6 weeks. Unpaid. Open to college freshmen, college sophomores, college juniors, college seniors, recent college graduates, graduate students. International applications accepted.

Benefits Opportunity to attend seminars/workshops, possible full-time employment, willing to act as a professional reference, willing to complete paperwork for educational credit, willing to provide letters of recommendation, discounts at gift shop and cafe.

Contact Write, fax, or e-mail Laura Malek, Internship Coordinator. Fax: 404-733-4538. E-mail: laura.malek@woodruffcenter.org. No phone calls. In-person interview recommended (telephone interview accepted). Applicants must submit a resume, two letters of recommendation, 3-page writing sample, cover letter indicating up to 3 areas of interest. Application deadline: April 15 for summer interns; continuous for all other positions. World Wide Web: http://www.high.org.

HIRSHHORN MUSEUM & SCULPTURE GARDEN
Smithsonian Institution, Room 410, MRC 350
Washington, District of Columbia 20560

General Information Museum of 19th- and 20th-century paintings, sculptures, and graphics emphasizing 20th-century and contemporary art. Established in 1974. Number of employees: 60. Number of internship applications received each year: 80.

Internships Available ▶ *Conservation interns.* Candidates should have declared college major in field, knowledge of field, plan to pursue career in field. Duration is 10 weeks. Position available as unpaid or paid. Open to college juniors, college seniors, recent college graduates, graduate students. ▶ *Exhibit and design interns.* Candidates should have college courses in field, experience in the field, plan to pursue career in field. Duration is 10 weeks. Unpaid. Open to college juniors, college seniors, recent college graduates, graduate students. ▶ *Graduate interns.* Candidates should have declared college major in field. Duration is 1 semester. Unpaid. Open to graduate students. ▶ *Photography interns.* Candidates should have college courses in field, experience in the field, plan to pursue career in field. Duration is 10 weeks. Unpaid. Open to college sophomores, college juniors, college seniors, recent college graduates, graduate students. ▶ *Public programs interns:* responsibilities include assisting in curatorial, education, publications, or public affairs division. Candidates should have ability to work with others, college courses in field, computer skills, experience in the field, oral communication skills, research skills, written communication skills. Duration is 10 weeks. Unpaid. Open to college juniors, college seniors, recent college graduates, graduate students. ▶ *Undergraduate interns:* responsibilities include working in a specific department of the museum and participating in a series of seminars on the museum's collection and organization. Candidates should have college courses in field, computer skills, knowledge of field, organizational skills, research skills, writing skills. Duration is 10 weeks. Unpaid. Open to college juniors, college seniors, recent college graduates, graduate students. International applications accepted.

Benefits Opportunity to attend seminars/workshops, willing to act as a professional reference, willing to complete paperwork for educational credit, willing to provide letters of recommendation.

Contact Write or fax Teresia Bush, Intern Coordinator. Fax: 202-786-2682. No phone calls. Applicants must submit a letter of interest, resume, academic transcripts, three letters of recommendation. Application deadline: March 1 for summer, June 1 for fall, November 1 for spring. World Wide Web: http://hirshhorn.si.edu.

HISTORICAL SOCIETY OF DELAWARE
505 Market Street
Wilmington, Delaware 19801

General Information Historical society with research library, urban museums, historic house museum, publications, and outreach programs. Established in 1864. Number of employees: 49. Number of internship applications received each year: 10.

Internships Available ▶ *1–4 curatorial interns:* responsibilities include working with artifacts. Candidates should have ability to work with others, analytical skills, computer skills, organizational skills, research skills, self-motivation. Duration is 13 weeks. Position available as unpaid or at $5–$10 per hour. ▶ *1–3 library interns:* responsibilities include assisting with researching and processing. Candidates should have ability to work with others, computer skills, organizational skills, plan to pursue career in field, research skills, self-motivation. Duration is minimum of 10 weeks. Position available as unpaid or at $5–$10 per hour. ▶ *1–4 programs interns:* responsibilities include assisting with educational activities. Candidates should have computer skills, oral communication skills, organizational skills, self-motivation, strong interpersonal skills. Duration is minimum of 10 weeks. Position available as unpaid or at $5–$10 per hour. Open to high school students, college freshmen, college sophomores, college juniors, college seniors, graduate students.

Benefits Formal training, job counseling, names of contacts, on-the-job training, willing to act as a professional reference, willing to complete paperwork for educational credit, willing to provide letters of recommendation.

Contact Write, fax, e-mail, or through World Wide Web site Dr. Barbara E. Benson, Executive Director. Fax: 302-655-7844. E-mail: hsd@hsd.org. No phone calls. In-person interview required. Applicants must submit a resume. Application deadline: April 1 for summer, November 1 for spring. World Wide Web: http://www.hsd.org.

HISTORIC DEERFIELD
Box 321
Deerfield, Massachusetts 01342

General Information Nonprofit museum dedicated to promoting the understanding and appreciation of New England history, architecture, and decorative arts. Established in 1952. Number of employees: 162. Number of internship applications received each year: 60.

Internships Available ▶ *3–4 summer and fall interns:* responsibilities include working with staff in curatorial, collections management, development office, architectural conservation, research, and archives on a variety of projects tailored to needs of Historic Deerfield and talents and interests of students. Candidates should have ability to work independently, ability to work with others, organizational skills, research skills, self-motivation, written communication skills. $2000–$3500 per semester. Open to college sophomores, college juniors, college seniors, recent college gradu-

ates, graduate students. ▶ *6–10 summer fellows:* responsibilities include studying early American history and material culture, visiting other museums in New England and beyond, receiving training as guides and as interpreters of history to the general public, and researching and writing a paper. Candidates should have ability to work independently, oral communication skills, self-motivation, strong interpersonal skills, written communication skills. Duration is mid-June to mid-August. Unpaid. Open to college sophomores, college juniors, college seniors. International applications accepted.

Benefits Free housing, free meals, opportunity to attend seminars/workshops, willing to complete paperwork for educational credit, archaeological digs, tours of various historic sites; all program tuition costs covered.

Contact Write, call, fax, e-mail, or through World Wide Web site Joan Morel, Office Manager. Phone: 413-775-7201. Fax: 413-775-7224. E-mail: sfp@historic-deerfield.org. Applicants must submit a formal organization application, academic transcripts, two letters of recommendation, personal statement explaining interest in internship. Application deadline: February 21 for summer fellows; continuous for summer/fall interns. Fees: $15. World Wide Web: http://www.deerfield-fellowship.org.

THE HOLDEN ARBORETUM
9500 Sperry Road
Kirtland, Ohio 44094

General Information 3,500-acre museum of wood plants intended for educational and scientific purposes. Established in 1931. Number of employees: 90. Number of internship applications received each year: 70.

Internships Available ▶ *1 conservation intern:* responsibilities include maintaining conservation collections. Candidates should have ability to work independently, ability to work with others, college courses in field, knowledge of field, personal interest in the field, self-motivation. Duration is 3–5 months. $7–$7.50 per hour. ▶ *1 education intern:* responsibilities include teaching and producing educational materials. Candidates should have ability to work independently, college courses in field, computer skills, knowledge of field, office skills, oral communication skills, personal interest in the field, plan to pursue career in field, research skills, self-motivation, strong interpersonal skills, writing skills. Duration is 1 year. $8.25–$8.75 per hour. ▶ *7 horticultural maintenance/production interns:* responsibilities include caring for horticultural collections and gardens. Candidates should have ability to work independently, ability to work with others, college courses in field, personal interest in the field, plan to pursue career in field, self-motivation. Duration is 3 months. $7–$7.50 per hour. ▶ *1 horticultural therapy intern:* responsibilities include working with special populations and teaching. Candidates should have ability to work independently, ability to work with others, college courses in field, computer skills, oral communication skills, personal interest in the field, plan to pursue career in field, self-motivation, writing skills. Duration is 6 months. $7–$7.50 per hour. ▶ *1 horticulture intern:* responsibilities include keeping plant records and horticultural collections. Candidates should have ability to work independently, ability to work with others, college courses in field, computer skills, knowledge of field, office skills, plan to pursue career in field, self-motivation. Duration is 1 year. $8.25–$8.75 per hour. ▶ *1 landscape gardening intern:* responsibilities include maintaining intensive horticulture plantings on a 5-acre estate within the arboretum. Candidates should have ability to work independently, ability to work with others, college courses in field, personal interest in the field, plan to pursue career in field, self-motivation. Duration is 3–5 months. $7–$7.50 per hour. Open to college freshmen, college sophomores, college juniors, college seniors, recent college graduates, graduate students. International applications accepted.

Benefits Formal training, housing at a cost, job counseling, names of contacts, on-the-job training, possible full-time employment, willing to complete paperwork for educational credit, health insurance and paid vacation and holiday time for 12-month positions.

Contact Write, call, fax, e-mail, or through World Wide Web site Greg J. Wright, Horticulture Education Manager. Phone: 440-946-4400. Fax: 440-602-3857. E-mail: gwright@holdenarb.org. Applicants must submit a letter of interest, resume, three personal references. Application deadline: February 1. World Wide Web: http://www.holdenarb.org.

HOPEWELL FURNACE NATIONAL HISTORIC SITE
2 Mark Bird Lane
Elverson, Pennsylvania 19520

General Information   Historic site preserving a 19th-century ironmaking community and a 200,000-object museum collection on 848 acres. Established in 1938. Number of employees: 16. Unit of United States National Park Service, Washington, District of Columbia. Number of internship applications received each year: 45.

Internships Available ▶ *4 education coordinator assistants:* responsibilities include assisting the education coordinator in planning, developing, and implementing a variety of education programs for a wide range of ages and interests. Candidates should have ability to work independently, ability to work with others, computer skills, knowledge of field, self-motivation, writing skills. Duration is 90 days. Unpaid. Open to recent high school graduates, college freshmen, college sophomores, college juniors, college seniors, recent college graduates, graduate students, career changers, individuals reentering the workforce. ▶ *1–3 farm assistants/collier apprentices:* responsibilities include routine livestock care and/or historical charcoal-making, often in reproduction period clothing; qualified candidate will be trained. Candidates should have ability to work independently, ability to work with others, oral communication skills, organizational skills, self-motivation. Duration is 2 weeks to 4 months. Unpaid. Open to recent high school graduates, college freshmen, college sophomores, college juniors, college seniors, recent college graduates. ▶ *2–3 historical interpretation interns:* responsibilities include making living history presentations and cultural demonstrations, developing programs, and performing educational programming. Candidates should have knowledge of field, oral communication skills, personal interest in the field, self-motivation, strong interpersonal skills. Duration is 200 hours. Unpaid. Open to recent high school graduates, college freshmen, college sophomores, college juniors, college seniors, recent college graduates, graduate students, law students, career changers, individuals reentering the workforce. ▶ *2–3 museum/curatorial interns:* responsibilities include cataloging, archival preservation, photography preservation, and environmental monitoring. Candidates should have ability to work independently, computer skills, personal interest in the field, research skills, self-motivation, written communication skills. Duration is 200 hours. Unpaid. Open to recent high school graduates, college freshmen, college sophomores, college juniors, college seniors, recent college graduates, graduate students, law students, career changers, individuals reentering the workforce. ▶ *2–3 research assistants:* responsibilities include conducting program-specific research using on-site archives to provide biographical/occupational data on individuals represented in living history program. Candidates should have ability to work independently, computer skills, knowledge of field, personal interest in the field, research skills, written communication skills. Duration is 200 hours. Unpaid. Open to recent high school graduates, college freshmen, college sophomores, college juniors, college seniors, recent college graduates, graduate students, law students, career changers, individuals reentering the workforce. ▶ *1–4 visitor center assistants:* responsibilities include serving as front line contact for visitors, collecting and accounting for fees and bookstore sales, operating cash registers, running audio/visual programs, and other duties as assigned. Candidates should have ability to work independently, oral communication skills, personal interest in the field, strong interpersonal skills. Duration is 4–12 weeks. Unpaid. Open to high school seniors, recent high school graduates, college freshmen, college sophomores, college juniors, college seniors, recent college graduates, individuals reentering the workforce. International applications accepted.

Benefits Formal training, free housing, job counseling, on-the-job training, opportunity to attend seminars/workshops, willing to act as a professional reference, willing to complete paperwork for educational credit, willing to provide letters of recom-

mendation, guidance through federal government hiring practices, $5 per day meal reimbursement, mileage reimbursement.
Contact Write, call, fax, or e-mail Mr. Frank Hebblethwaite, Volunteer Coordinator. Phone: 610-582-8773 Ext. 229. Fax: 610-582-2768. E-mail: hofu_superintendent@nps.gov. Telephone interview required. Applicants must submit a formal organization application, letter of interest, resume, two personal references. Applications are accepted continuously. World Wide Web: http://www.nps.gov/hofu.

INDIANAPOLIS ZOO AND WHITE RIVER GARDENS
1200 West Washington Street
Indianapolis, Indiana 46222

General Information   Zoo and garden providing recreational learning experiences through exhibition and presentation of elements of natural environments. Established in 1944. Number of employees: 350. Unit of Indianapolis Zoological Society, Indianapolis, Indiana. Number of internship applications received each year: 200.

Internships Available ▶ *5–15 animal care interns:* responsibilities include daily cleaning duties, food preparation, animal observation, and/or study with participation in ongoing projects. Candidates should have ability to work independently, ability to work with others, college courses in field, personal interest in the field, plan to pursue career in field, self-motivation. Duration is 3-4 months (40 hours per week). Unpaid. Open to college freshmen, college sophomores, college juniors, college seniors, recent college graduates. ▶ *1–5 environmental education (programs) interns:* responsibilities include participating in informal educational setting with classes, summer camps, distance learning programs, or in the departmental interactive area. Candidates should have oral communication skills, organizational skills, personal interest in the field, strong interpersonal skills, written communication skills. Duration is 3-4 months (20-40 hours per week). Unpaid. Open to college freshmen, college sophomores, college juniors, college seniors, recent college graduates, graduate students. ▶ *2–4 environmental education-naturalist supervisors:* responsibilities include attending zoo naturalist training sessions and overseeing adult and teen naturalists; first-hand interpretation with the public using hands-on artifacts (bones, pelts, teeth); on-grounds education. Candidates should have ability to work independently, ability to work with others, oral communication skills, personal interest in the field, self-motivation, strong leadership ability. Duration is May-August; minimum of 12 weeks (20-40 hours per week). Unpaid. Open to college freshmen, college sophomores, college juniors, college seniors, recent college graduates, graduate students. ▶ *4–6 horticulture interns:* responsibilities include assisting in planting and horticulture maintenance; performing watering, pruning, weeding, mulching, fertilization, mowing, pest and disease control. Candidates should have ability to work independently, ability to work with others, knowledge of field, personal interest in the field, ability to exert 50-100 pounds of force regularly. Duration is minimum of 6 weeks (40 hours per week). Position available as unpaid or at $7.50 per hour. Open to college freshmen, college sophomores, college juniors, college seniors, recent college graduates, graduate students, career changers. ▶ *1–2 institutional advancement interns:* responsibilities include assisting with the coordination of regular fund-raising programs and special events: tracking income, preparing reports, data entry, managing development of planned giving newsletter, arranging seminars, and conducting research. Candidates should have computer skills, oral communication skills, organizational skills, research skills, self-motivation, written communication skills. Duration is minimum of 6 weeks (20 hours per week). Position available as unpaid or at $7–$9 per hour. Open to college freshmen, college sophomores, college juniors, college seniors, recent college graduates, graduate students. ▶ *1–3 marketing interns:* responsibilities include working with marketing department to design, implement, and manage market research program focusing on customer satisfaction; participating in radio and print campaigns and event planning. Candidates should have computer skills, office skills, oral communication skills, plan to pursue career in field, strong interpersonal skills. Duration is May to August (minimum of 20 hours per week). Unpaid. Open to college freshmen, college sophomores, college juniors, college seniors, recent college graduates. ▶ *1 veterinary externship/preceptorship:* responsibilities include assisting zoo veterinarians with clinical cases, treatments, immobilizations, surgeries, neuropsies, and medical record-keeping; completing and presenting a project. Candidates should have ability to work with others, analytical skills, declared college major in field, oral communication skills, plan to pursue career in field, written communication skills. Duration is minimum of 4 weeks (40 hours per week). Position available as unpaid or paid. Open to veterinary students only. ▶ *1 veterinary technician:* responsibilities include assisting veterinarian with animal procedures; performing in-house lab work; assisting in maintaining hospital, and maintaining patient logs. Candidates should have ability to work independently, ability to work with others, analytical skills, declared college major in field, research skills, self-motivation. Duration is minimum of 4 weeks (40 hours per week). Unpaid. Open to college sophomores, college juniors, college seniors, recent college graduates, graduate students, veterinary technician students. International applications accepted.

Benefits Formal training, job counseling, names of contacts, on-the-job training, possible full-time employment, willing to complete paperwork for educational credit, willing to provide letters of recommendation.

Contact Write, call, fax, e-mail, or through World Wide Web site Mr. Joel Vanderbush, Manager of Volunteer Services. Phone: 317-630-2041. Fax: 317-630-5119. E-mail: volunteer@indyzoo.com. In-person interview recommended (telephone interview accepted). Applicants must submit a formal organization application, letter of interest, resume, academic transcripts, two letters of recommendation. Application deadline: March 10 for summer, July 10 for fall, November 10 for winter/spring. World Wide Web: http://www.indianapoliszoo.com.

INTERNATIONAL CENTER OF PHOTOGRAPHY
1114 Avenue of the Americas, School and Administration Offices
New York, New York 10036

General Information Museum and school dedicated to the understanding and appreciation of photography. Established in 1974. Number of employees: 85. Number of internship applications received each year: 150.

Internships Available ▶ *1–2 community programs interns:* responsibilities include archive program documentation, assisting with tour program, off-site community program activities, research, program exhibitions, and learning about photographic education. Candidates should have ability to work independently, computer skills, oral communication skills, organizational skills, personal interest in the field, strong interpersonal skills. Duration is flexible; summer or semester(s). Unpaid. Open to college juniors, college seniors, recent college graduates. ▶ *1–2 digital media lab interns:* responsibilities include helping students in open labs and/or classrooms with using computers, printers, scanners, and various software (PhotoShop, Illustrator, Dreamweaver, and Final Cut Pro); helping in office, phone coverage, checking students in and out, and issuing equipment and supplies. Candidates should have computer skills, experience in the field, oral communication skills, strong interpersonal skills. Duration is June 22-August 29. Unpaid. Open to college freshmen, college sophomores, college juniors, college seniors, recent college graduates, graduate students. ▶ *5–8 exhibitions department interns:* responsibilities include research, general administrative duties, assisting staff members with projects, and general support. Candidates should have computer skills, office skills, organizational skills, personal interest in the field, research skills, knowledge of PhotoShop. Duration is 12–15 weeks. Unpaid. Open to college juniors, college seniors, recent college graduates, graduate students. ▶ *1–2 library interns:* responsibilities include library support such as filing, labeling, and bibliographic searching depending on skills and desired level of credit and experience; to be arranged in coordination with librarian. Candidates should have ability to work independently, ability to work with others, analytical skills, computer skills, knowledge of field, office skills, oral communication skills, organizational skills, self-motivation, written communication skills, interest in photography and ease with English language are both essential, experience,

college courses, major, or degree in related field preferred, but not required. Duration is 1 semester. Unpaid. Open to college freshmen, college sophomores, college juniors, college seniors, recent college graduates, graduate students. ▶ *1–2 membership/development interns:* responsibilities include mailings, events (openings, member days), general administrative duties, miscellaneous project work. Candidates should have ability to work independently, ability to work with others, office skills, personal interest in the field, written communication skills, knowledge of PhotoShop. Duration is flexible; summer or semester(s). Unpaid. Open to college juniors, college seniors, recent college graduates, graduate students. ▶ *1–4 photo lab interns:* responsibilities include general lab and/or TA duties, helping in office, student check-in, and equipment check-out. Candidates should have ability to work independently, organizational skills, personal interest in the field, self-motivation, strong interpersonal skills. Duration is 8-12 weeks in summer. Unpaid. Open to high school students, recent high school graduates, college freshmen, college sophomores, college juniors, college seniors. ▶ *1–2 public information interns:* responsibilities include assisting public information department with filing, archiving slides, negatives and photographs; updating contact database; mailings to press; answering telephones. Candidates should have ability to work with others, computer skills, office skills, oral communication skills, organizational skills, research skills, knowledge of PhotoShop. Duration is flexible; summer or semester(s). Unpaid. Open to college freshmen, college sophomores, college juniors, college seniors, recent college graduates, graduate students. ▶ *3 summer program interns.* Candidates should have ability to work independently, ability to work with others, college courses in field, computer skills, knowledge of field, office skills, oral communication skills, organizational skills, personal interest in the field, self-motivation, written communication skills. Duration is June to August 16 (20 hours per week). Unpaid. Open to high school students, recent high school graduates, college freshmen, college sophomores, college juniors, college seniors, recent college graduates, graduate students, law students, career changers, individuals reentering the workforce. International applications accepted.

Benefits Willing to act as a professional reference, willing to complete paperwork for educational credit, willing to provide letters of recommendation, discounts on classes and access to labs.

Contact Write, call, fax, or e-mail Greg Murphy, Internship Coordinator, 1114 Avenue of the Americas, New York, New York 10036. Phone: 212-857-0022. Fax: 212-857-0090. E-mail: info@icp. org. In-person interview recommended (telephone interview accepted). Applicants must submit a letter of interest, resume. Application deadline: April 7 for summer, July 28 for fall, November 24 for spring. World Wide Web: http://www.icp.org.

IRON MISSION STATE PARK
635 North Main Street
Cedar City, Utah 84720

General Information State park museum that preserves Southwestern pioneer memorabilia and transportation and farming equipment. Established in 1973. Number of employees: 3. Division of Utah Department of Parks and Recreation, Salt Lake City, Utah. Number of internship applications received each year: 5.

Internships Available ▶ *1–2 museum aides:* responsibilities include assisting curator in cataloging and preserving artifacts. Candidates should have computer skills, organizational skills, research skills, writing skills. Duration is 10–14 weeks. $250–$500 per duration of internship. Open to college sophomores, college juniors, college seniors, recent college graduates, graduate students. International applications accepted.

Benefits Names of contacts, on-the-job training, opportunity to attend seminars/workshops, willing to act as a professional reference, willing to complete paperwork for educational credit, willing to provide letters of recommendation.

Contact Write, call, fax, or e-mail Todd Prince, Park Manager. Phone: 435-586-9290. Fax: 435-865-6830. E-mail: ironmission@utah. gov. Applicants must submit a formal organization application, letter of interest, resume. Application deadline: January 15 for spring, March 15 for summer, July 1 for fall, October 1 for winter.

Iron Mission State Park (continued)

ISLE ROYALE NATIONAL PARK
800 East Lakeshore Drive
Houghton, Michigan 49931

General Information Wilderness park containing historic and cultural resources located on the largest island in Lake Superior; features 165 miles of hiking trails and is home to moose, wolves, foxes, and a variety of water fowl including loons, great blue herons, and ducks. Established in 1940. Number of employees: 100. Unit of United States National Park Service, Washington, District of Columbia. Number of internship applications received each year: 75.

Internships Available ► *1 assistant purser:* responsibilities include assisting the purser in NPS vessel RANGER III on voyages to and from Isle Royale, assisting with visitor information and interpretive programs, issuing backcountry permits and collecting fees. Candidates should have computer skills, oral communication skills, organizational skills, personal interest in the field, self-motivation, strong interpersonal skills. Duration is 3 months (June-August). Unpaid. ► *1–2 backcountry campground host/ranger assistants:* responsibilities include living and working in a remote backcountry campground; assisting Ranger division by checking camping permits, providing information to visitors, conducting interpretive programs, providing first aid and emergency assistance, and campground maintenance. Candidates should have ability to work independently, experience in the field, oral communication skills, plan to pursue career in field, self-motivation, strong interpersonal skills. Duration is 3 months (June-August). Unpaid. ► *1 interpretive resource center manager:* responsibilities include locating and providing information and materials for park staff in support of interpretive program, managing park library, maintaining audiovisual equipment and slide collection. Candidates should have ability to work with others, computer skills, office skills, personal interest in the field, self-motivation, written communication skills. Duration is 3 months (June-August). Unpaid. ► *1 photo/cultural resources volunteer:* responsibilities include maintaining park historic photo collection, documentary photographs and slides of park projects and operations, designing brochures, and historical research. Candidates should have ability to work independently, computer skills, experience in the field, organizational skills, self-motivation, written communication skills. Duration is 3 months (June-August). Unpaid. ► *1–2 resource management technicians:* responsibilities include assisting with air, water quality, and acid rain monitoring; field sampling; inventory and monitoring of bird populations; compiling backcountry camping permit data; location and removal of exotic plant species; assisting with field research. Candidates should have ability to work independently, college courses in field, experience in the field, personal interest in the field, research skills, written communication skills. Duration is 3 months (June-August). Unpaid. ► *1–4 trail crew interns:* responsibilities include maintaining trails and campgrounds; performing erosion control, trail tread and bridge work, brushing, sign maintenance, and tool sharpening; campsite rehabilitation. Candidates should have ability to work with others, knowledge of field, personal interest in the field, self-motivation, camping and back country skills, experience with hand tools (helpful). Duration is 1–6 weeks. Unpaid. ► *1–3 visitor center assistants:* responsibilities include general staffing of visitor center; collecting fees, issuing camping permits, trip planning, greeting and orienting visitors, meeting ferry boats, conducting interpretive programs, hikes, selling books. Candidates should have computer skills, office skills, oral communication skills, personal interest in the field, self-motivation, strong interpersonal skills. Duration is 3 months (June-August). Unpaid. Open to recent high school graduates, college freshmen, college sophomores, college juniors, college seniors, recent college graduates, graduate students, law students, career changers, individuals reentering the workforce. International applications accepted.

Benefits Formal training, free housing, job counseling, names of contacts, on-the-job training, possible full-time employment, willing to complete paperwork for educational credit, willing to provide letters of recommendation, uniform, meal reimbursement.

Contact Write, call, e-mail, or through World Wide Web site Ms. Elizabeth Valencia, Volunteer Coordinator. Phone: 906-487-7153.

Fax: 906-487-7170. E-mail: liz_valencia@nps.gov. Applicants must submit a formal organization application. Application deadline: March 15. World Wide Web: http://www.nps.gov/isro/.

ISLIP ART MUSEUM
50 Irish Lane
East Islip, New York 11730

General Information Art museum emphasizing contemporary and avant-garde works and mixed media installations. Established in 1971. Number of employees: 10. Number of internship applications received each year: 10.

Internships Available ► *1–2 assistants to curators:* responsibilities include assisting with all curatorial functions and gallery sittings. Candidates should have computer skills, plan to pursue career in field, research skills, strong interpersonal skills, writing skills. Duration is flexible. Unpaid. Open to college freshmen, college sophomores, college juniors, college seniors, recent college graduates, graduate students, must be resident of Long Island area. ► *1–2 director's assistants:* responsibilities include assisting in fund development, research, and special projects. Candidates should have ability to work independently, plan to pursue career in field, self-motivation, strong interpersonal skills, word processing skills, residence within commuting distance of the Museum. Duration is flexible. Unpaid. Open to recent high school graduates, college freshmen, college sophomores, college juniors, college seniors, recent college graduates, graduate students, career changers, must be resident of Long Island area. ► *1–2 museum school assistants:* responsibilities include helping with art classes at museum and other museum programs. Candidates should have ability to work independently, oral communication skills, self-motivation, strong interpersonal skills. Duration is flexible. Unpaid. Open to recent high school graduates, college freshmen, college sophomores, college juniors, college seniors, recent college graduates, graduate students, career changers, must be resident of Long Island area.

Benefits Job counseling, names of contacts, willing to complete paperwork for educational credit, willing to provide letters of recommendation.

Contact Write, fax, or e-mail Ms. Mary Lou Cohalan, Director. Fax: 631-224-5417. E-mail: info@islipartmuseum.org. No phone calls. In-person interview required. Applicants must submit a letter of interest, resume. Applications are accepted continuously. World Wide Web: http://www.islipartmuseum.org.

JAMESTOWN-YORKTOWN FOUNDATION
PO Box 1607
Williamsburg, Virginia 23187-1607

General Information Educational institution that operates Jamestown Settlement and the Yorktown Victory Center, museums that preserve and interpret the first English settlement in the New World and the story of the American Revolution. Established in 1956. Number of employees: 466. Number of internship applications received each year: 20.

Internships Available ► *1 Celebration 2007 intern.* Duration is 3 months. Unpaid. ► *1 curatorial intern:* responsibilities include assisting with various curatorial projects. Candidates should have ability to work with others, editing skills, research skills, self-motivation, writing skills. Duration is 3 months. Unpaid. ► *1 education intern:* responsibilities include assisting with educational programs. Candidates should have ability to work independently, ability to work with others, knowledge of field, oral communication skills, plan to pursue career in field, written communication skills. Duration is 3 months. Unpaid. ► *1 finance intern:* responsibilities include assisting with financial operations. Candidates should have ability to work independently, ability to work with others, knowledge of field, oral communication skills, plan to pursue career in field, written communication skills. Duration is 3 months. Unpaid. ► *1 marketing intern:* responsibilities include assisting with marketing programs. Candidates should have ability to work with others, knowledge of field, oral communication skills, plan to pursue career in field, self-motivation, written communication skills. Duration is 3 months. Unpaid. ► *1 research intern:* responsibilities include researching selected topics. Candidates should have ability to work with others, plan to pursue career in field, research skills, strong leadership ability, writing skills. Duration is 3 months.

Unpaid. Open to college juniors, college seniors, recent college graduates, graduate students. International applications accepted.
Benefits Formal training, on-the-job training, opportunity to attend seminars/workshops, possible full-time employment, willing to act as a professional reference, willing to complete paperwork for educational credit, willing to provide letters of recommendation, discounted meals in cafe and discount in gift shop.
Contact Write, call, fax, or e-mail Elaine Cannon, Volunteer Services Coordinator, Williamsburg, Virginia 23187-1607. Phone: 757-253-4034. Fax: 757-253-4997. E-mail: ecannon@jyf.state.va.us. In-person interview recommended (telephone interview accepted). Applicants must submit a formal organization application, letter of interest, resume, three personal references, three letters of recommendation. Applications are accepted continuously. World Wide Web: http://www.historyisfun.org.

JEWEL CAVE NATIONAL MONUMENT
RR 1, Box 60 AA
Custer, South Dakota 57730

General Information Organization that administers and manages the natural resources of Jewel Cave. Established in 1908. Number of employees: 42. Unit of United States National Park Service, Washington, District of Columbia. Number of internship applications received each year: 8.
Internships Available ▶ *2–3 interpreter interns:* responsibilities include researching, preparing, and presenting scenic cave tours and a variety of surface programs; working at the information desk, answering public information requests; and possibly other projects, which may include assisting with production of interpretive publications, resource management projects, photography, and library work. Candidates should have ability to work independently, oral communication skills, personal interest in the field, self-motivation, strong interpersonal skills, educational background in geology, environmental education, recreational resource management, natural history, or related area. Duration is 1 summer (generally, May 18 to August 31). Position available as unpaid or at $9.80–$12.32 per hour. Open to recent high school graduates, college freshmen, college sophomores, college juniors, college seniors, recent college graduates, graduate students, career changers. International applications accepted.
Benefits Formal training, job counseling, names of contacts, on-the-job training, willing to act as a professional reference, willing to complete paperwork for educational credit, willing to provide letters of recommendation, housing may be available at a cost for paid positions; free housing for unpaid positions.
Contact Write, call, or fax Ms. Karen Rosga, Chief of Interpretation, RR1, Box 60 AA, Custer, South Dakota 57730. Phone: 605-673-2288 Ext. 1237. Fax: 605-673-3294. Telephone interview required. Applicants must submit a formal organization application, letter of interest, resume, 2-3 personal references; academic transcripts may be required. Application deadline: March 15 for summer, July 25 for fall. World Wide Web: http://www.nps.gov/jeca.

THE JEWISH MUSEUM
1109 5th Avenue
New York, New York 10128

General Information Museum of Jewish interest and of art. Established in 1904. Number of employees: 130. Unit of Jewish Theological Seminary of America, New York, New York. Number of internship applications received each year: 50.
Internships Available ▶ *1–5 interns:* responsibilities include clerical support to Museum department heads, including phone, light research, and some computer work (data entry, word processing). Candidates should have ability to work independently, ability to work with others, analytical skills, computer skills, knowledge of field, office skills, oral communication skills, organizational skills, personal interest in the field, research skills, writing skills. Duration is 8–20 weeks. Unpaid. Open to college freshmen, college sophomores, college juniors, college seniors, recent college graduates, graduate students, law students, career changers, individuals reentering the workforce. International applications accepted.

Benefits On-the-job training, opportunity to attend seminars/workshops, possible full-time employment, willing to act as a professional reference, willing to complete paperwork for educational credit, willing to provide letters of recommendation.
Contact Write, call, fax, or e-mail Patricia Gurevich, Internship Coordinator. Phone: 212-423-3208. Fax: 212-423-3232. E-mail: pgurevich@thejm.org. In-person interview required. Applicants must submit a formal organization application, letter of interest, resume. Applications are accepted continuously. World Wide Web: http://thejewishmuseum.org.

JOHN F. KENNEDY PRESIDENTIAL LIBRARY AND MUSEUM
Columbia Point
Boston, Massachusetts 02125

General Information Presidential library. Established in 1964. Number of employees: 55. Unit of National Archives and Records Administration, College Park, Maryland. Number of internship applications received each year: 60.
Internships Available ▶ *3–5 audiovisual archives interns:* responsibilities include assisting staff in cataloging historic films/video/audio tapes, and still photos; duties include copying, data entry, researching answers to questions from the public, assisting researchers with operation of audio/video/film equipment, identifying scenes in films, and simple preservation practices involving film, photos, and magnetic media. Candidates should have ability to work independently, ability to work with others, analytical skills, oral communication skills, research skills, self-motivation, written communication skills. Duration is flexible (minimum of 8 weeks). $11 per hour. Open to college freshmen, college sophomores, college juniors, college seniors, graduate students. ▶ *1–3 museum collections and exhibits interns:* responsibilities include assisting in collections processing, inventory and care of objects, group and independent projects, contributing to the documentation, preservation, and exhibition of the collection. Candidates should have ability to work independently, ability to work with others, oral communication skills, organizational skills, personal interest in the field, college courses in museum studies, history, or American studies. Duration is flexible (minimum of 10 weeks). $11 per hour. Open to college juniors, college seniors, recent college graduates, graduate students, career changers, individuals reentering the workforce. ▶ *2–3 research room interns:* responsibilities include assisting research room archivist with handling reference queries from the public from phone, fax, e-mail, or in person; involves registering researchers, retrieving archival materials from stack areas, data entry, and answering telephones. Candidates should have ability to work independently, ability to work with others, office skills, oral communication skills, research skills, written communication skills. Duration is flexible (minimum of 8 weeks). $11 per hour. Open to college freshmen, college sophomores, college juniors, college seniors, graduate students. ▶ *3–5 textual archives interns:* responsibilities include assisting in the processing and cataloging of collections of historic papers; involves photocopying, data entry, some moderate lifting. Candidates should have ability to work independently, ability to work with others, analytical skills, research skills, self-motivation, written communication skills. Duration is flexible (minimum of 8 weeks). $11 per hour. Open to college freshmen, college sophomores, college juniors, college seniors, graduate students. International applications accepted.
Benefits Formal training, on-the-job training, opportunity to attend seminars/workshops, willing to complete paperwork for educational credit, willing to provide letters of recommendation.
Contact Write, call, fax, e-mail, or through World Wide Web site Intern Coordinator. Phone: 617-514-1624. Fax: 617-514-1625. E-mail: kennedy.library@nara.gov. In-person interview recommended (telephone interview accepted). Applicants must submit a formal organization application, letter of interest, resume, academic transcripts, letter of recommendation. Application deadline: February 28 for summer; continuous for other positions. World Wide Web: http://www.jfklibrary.org.

JOSHUA TREE NATIONAL PARK
74485 National Park Drive
Twentynine Palms, California 92277

General Information National park in southern California desert that provides protection of cultural and natural resources of the Mojave and Colorado deserts. Established in 1936. Number of employees: 65. Number of internship applications received each year: 10.

Internships Available ▶ *1–2 education interns:* responsibilities include working with school children off-site and in park for field trips; utilizing park curriculum to plan lessons and activities. Candidates should have ability to work independently, oral communication skills, personal interest in the field, self-motivation, strong interpersonal skills. Duration is 12–14 weeks. $50–$100 per week. Open to college sophomores, college juniors, college seniors, recent college graduates, graduate students, career changers. ▶ *Field studies interns.* Candidates should have background in ecology, wildlife biology, or natural science. $50–$100 per week. Open to college juniors, college seniors, recent college graduates, graduate students. ▶ *Interpreters/volunteers:* responsibilities include operating the visitor center, assisting in field studies, and conducting walking tours. Duration is 3 months. Unpaid. Open to U.S. citizens 18 or older. ▶ *Visitor center interns:* responsibilities include providing information to traveling public about park services and recreation opportunities and preparing guided activities. Candidates should have oral communication skills, strong interpersonal skills. Duration is 12 weeks. $50–$60 per week. Open to college juniors, college seniors, recent college graduates, graduate students.

Benefits Formal training, job counseling, willing to complete paperwork for educational credit, willing to provide letters of recommendation.

Contact Write, call, fax, or through World Wide Web site Internships. Phone: 760-367-5500. Fax: 760-367-6392. Applicants must submit a letter of interest, resume. Applications are accepted continuously. World Wide Web: http://www.nps.gov/jotr/.

THE J. PAUL GETTY TRUST
1200 Getty Center Drive
Los Angeles, California 90049-1687

General Information Art museum of European art; research institute for the history of art and humanities; conservation institute; grant program. Established in 1953. Number of employees: 1,200. Number of internship applications received each year: 200.

Internships Available ▶ *20 Getty graduate interns:* responsibilities include working in one of the Getty programs. Candidates should have ability to work with others, college degree in related field, knowledge of field, plan to pursue career in field, research skills, writing skills. Duration is 8–12 months. $17,296 for 8 months; $25,000 for 12 months. Open to graduate students. International applications accepted.

Benefits Health insurance, on-the-job training, opportunity to attend seminars/workshops, willing to provide letters of recommendation, educational travel stipend of $1200.

Contact Write, call, e-mail, or through World Wide Web site Josephine Ramirez, Administrator, Graduate Grant Program, Education Department, 1200 Getty Center Drive, Los Angeles, California 90049-1687. Phone: 310-440-7129. E-mail: interns@getty.edu. Applicants must submit a formal organization application, letter of interest, academic transcripts, two letters of recommendation. Application deadline: early January. World Wide Web: http://www.getty.edu/about/opportunities/intern.html.

KANSAS STATE HISTORICAL SOCIETY
6425 Southwest Sixth Avenue
Topeka, Kansas 66615-1099

General Information Society that collects, preserves, and interprets Kansas history. Established in 1875. Number of employees: 140. Number of internship applications received each year: 10.

Internships Available ▶ *1 Lela Barnes intern:* responsibilities include managing archives and manuscript records. Candidates should have ability to work independently, computer skills, organizational skills, plan to pursue career in field, research skills, written communication skills. Duration is 10 weeks. $1800 per duration of internship. ▶ *3–5 interns:* responsibilities include working in the archaeology, archives, or education department, the historical preservation office, or the Kansas Museum of History. Candidates should have ability to work independently, ability to work with others, computer skills, oral communication skills, research skills, written communication skills. Duration is 6–10 weeks. Unpaid. Open to college juniors, college seniors, graduate students. International applications accepted.

Benefits Job counseling, names of contacts, possible full-time employment, willing to complete paperwork for educational credit, willing to provide letters of recommendation.

Contact Write, call, fax, e-mail, or through World Wide Web site Dr. David A. Haury, Associate Director. Phone: 785-272-8681 Ext. 209. Fax: 785-272-8682. E-mail: dhaury@kshs.org. In-person interview recommended (telephone interview accepted). Applicants must submit a formal organization application, letter of interest, resume, academic transcripts, letter of recommendation. Application deadline: April 15 for summer, June 15 for fall, November 15 for spring. World Wide Web: http://www.kshs.org.

KRESGE ART MUSEUM
Michigan State University
East Lansing, Michigan 48824

General Information Art museum that collects, preserves, exhibits, and interprets works of art of all periods. Established in 1959. Number of employees: 7. Unit of Michigan State University, East Lansing, Michigan. Number of internship applications received each year: 30.

Internships Available ▶ *1 museum intern:* responsibilities include learning all facets of museum work including exhibit development, grant writing, registration, and publicity. Candidates should have ability to work independently, ability to work with others, college degree in related field, computer skills, oral communication skills, written communication skills. Duration is 10 months. $13,000 per duration of internship. International applications accepted.

Benefits Health insurance, job counseling, names of contacts, opportunity to attend seminars/workshops, travel reimbursement, willing to provide letters of recommendation, inexpensive faculty housing.

Contact Write Ms. Carol Fisher, Education Coordinator. Telephone interview required. Applicants must submit a letter of interest, three personal references. Application deadline: March 15. World Wide Web: http://www.msu.edu/unit/kamuseum.

LASSEN VOLCANIC NATIONAL PARK
PO Box 100, 38050 Highway 36 East
Mineral, California 96063-0100

General Information National park with the mission of preserving and protecting the park's natural resources and providing for the continued enjoyment of the land. Established in 1916. Number of employees: 130. Number of internship applications received each year: 40.

Internships Available ▶ *5–7 campground hosts:* responsibilities include representing National Park Service within campgrounds; answering visitor questions, distributing information, checking compliance with regulations, maintaining user statistics, and assisting with fee collection. Candidates should have ability to work independently, oral communication skills, self-motivation, strong interpersonal skills, good money handling and administrative skills, must provide own transportation, RV, or tent. Duration is 2–4 months. Unpaid. Open to recent high school graduates, college freshmen, college sophomores, college juniors, college seniors, recent college graduates, graduate students, career changers, individuals reentering the workforce, retirees. ▶ *1 cultural resources assistant:* responsibilities include assisting with museum cataloging and curatorial tasks of historical, archival, and botanical collections; assisting with cataloging and organizing photo, slide, and library collections. Candidates should have ability to work independently, ability to work with others, computer skills, knowledge of field, organizational skills, personal interest in the

field, research skills, written communication skills. Duration is flexible. Unpaid. Open to recent high school graduates, college freshmen, college sophomores, college juniors, college seniors, recent college graduates, graduate students, career changers, individuals reentering the workforce. ▶ *1–3 resource management aides:* responsibilities include working either independently of or in direct support of resource management staff on defined field project work, computer database entry, and other projects. Candidates should have ability to work independently, ability to work with others, knowledge of field, personal interest in the field, self-motivation. Duration is 3 months in summer (June through August). Unpaid. Open to college juniors, college seniors, recent college graduates, graduate students, career changers. ▶ *1 sign mapping technician:* responsibilities include updating park sign inventory, sign mapping, and photo editing. Candidates should have ability to work independently, computer skills, experience in the field, organizational skills, personal interest in the field, self-motivation. Duration is May 1 to October 1. Unpaid. Open to college juniors, college seniors, recent college graduates, graduate students, career changers. ▶ *1–4 spring and summer interpretive aides:* responsibilities include supporting junior ranger, living history, and field interpretive programs and helping in the visitor center. Candidates should have ability to work independently, oral communication skills, personal interest in the field, self-motivation, strong interpersonal skills, written communication skills. Duration is February or March through early June and June through August. Unpaid. Open to recent high school graduates, college freshmen, college sophomores, college juniors, college seniors, recent college graduates, graduate students, career changers, individuals reentering the workforce. ▶ *1–2 winter interpretive aides:* responsibilities include assisting with winter interpretive programs; working with slide, photo, and museum collections; and recording wildlife sightings. Candidates should have ability to work independently, oral communication skills, personal interest in the field, self-motivation, strong interpersonal skills, strong leadership ability, written communication skills. Duration is January through March. Unpaid. Open to recent high school graduates, college freshmen, college sophomores, college juniors, college seniors, recent college graduates, graduate students, career changers, individuals reentering the workforce. International applications accepted.
Benefits Formal training, free housing, names of contacts, on-the-job training, willing to complete paperwork for educational credit, willing to provide letters of recommendation, possible reimbursement for some expenses and/or park campsite.
Contact Write, call, fax, or e-mail Nancy Bailey, Volunteers in Parks Coordinator. Phone: 530-595-4444 Ext. 5133. Fax: 530-595-3408. E-mail: nancy_bailey@nps.gov. In-person interview recommended (telephone interview accepted). Applicants must submit a formal organization application, two personal references. Application deadline: March 1 for summer, October 1 for winter, December 1 for spring.

LIBRARY OF CONGRESS–CAROLINE AND ERWIN SWANN FOUNDATION FOR CARICATURE AND CARTOON
101 Independence Avenue, SE
Washington, District of Columbia 20540-4730

General Information Foundation that promotes caricature and cartoon through scholarship, publication, exhibition, cataloging, and preservation. Established in 1967. Number of employees: 4. Unit of Library of Congress, Washington, District of Columbia. Number of internship applications received each year: 18.
Internships Available ▶ *1 Swann Foundation fellowship:* responsibilities include making use of the collections of the Library of Congress during research for at least two weeks during fellowship, giving a public lecture on work in progress, and giving the Library of Congress a copy of any publication produced as a result of the fellowship support for the Swann Foundation Archives. Duration is September through June. $15,000 per duration of internship. Open to graduate students, those enrolled in an MA or PhD program or within 3 years of having completed an MA or PhD. International applications accepted.

Benefits Willing to complete paperwork for educational credit, access to collections of the Library of Congress, public lectures.
Contact Write, call, e-mail, or through World Wide Web site Martha Kennedy, Curatorial Assistant, Prints and Photographs Division, Washington 20540-4730. Phone: 202-707-9115. Fax: 202-707-6647. E-mail: swann@loc.gov. Applicants must submit a formal organization application, resume, academic transcripts, writing sample, three letters of recommendation, accompanying visual materials (slides or photocopies). Application deadline: February 13. World Wide Web: http://lcweb.loc.gov/rr/print/swann/swann_foundation.html/fellow.

LIBRARY OF CONGRESS JUNIOR FELLOWS PROGRAM
Library of Congress, LM-642
Washington, District of Columbia 20540-4600

General Information Library that collects and preserves material from a wide range of disciplines including history, area studies, film, fine arts, literature, and music. Established in 1800. Number of employees: 5,000. Unit of United States Federal Government, Washington, District of Columbia. Number of internship applications received each year: 600.
Internships Available ▶ *6 junior fellows:* responsibilities include assisting in selected divisions to reduce arrearage, producing finding aids and bibliographic records, preparing materials for preservation and service, and doing bibliographical research; working in areas such as music, rare book and special collections, American history and literature, cataloging, photography, sound recordings, American popular culture, librarianship, preservation, film, television, and radio. Duration is 2-3 months in summer (40 hours per week). $300 per week. Open to college juniors, college seniors, recent college graduates, graduate students. International applications accepted.
Contact Write, call, fax, or e-mail Angela Reid-Ampey, Junior Fellows Program Coordinator, Library Services. Phone: 202-707-3660. Fax: 202-707-6269. E-mail: jrfell@loc.gov. Applicants must submit academic transcripts, letter of recommendation, cover letter indicating area(s) of interest, resume or Application for Federal Employment (SF 171). Application deadline: April 4. World Wide Web: http://lcweb.loc.gov/rr/jrfell/.

LINCOLN PARK ZOO
2001 North Clark Street
Chicago, Illinois 60614

General Information Nonprofit zoological park whose missions include education, conservation of wild and captive populations, and research. Established in 1868. Number of internship applications received each year: 100.
Internships Available ▶ *4–6 research interns:* responsibilities include conducting independent research projects supervised by staff scientists; project design, background research, data collection and analysis, and write-up. Candidates should have ability to work independently, analytical skills, computer skills, knowledge of field, research skills, written communication skills. Duration is 3–12 months. $9–$10 per hour. Open to college sophomores, college juniors, college seniors, recent college graduates. International applications accepted.
Benefits Job counseling, on-the-job training, opportunity to attend seminars/workshops, possible full-time employment, willing to act as a professional reference, willing to complete paperwork for educational credit, willing to provide letters of recommendation.
Contact Write, call, fax, e-mail, or through World Wide Web site Lisa Faust, Research Biologist. Phone: 312-742-7227. Fax: 312-742-7220. E-mail: lisa@lpzoo.org. In-person interview recommended (telephone interview accepted). Applicants must submit a resume, academic transcripts, three letters of recommendation, statement of research interests. Application deadline: March 14. World Wide Web: http://www.lpzoo.org/conservation.

LONGWOOD GARDENS
PO Box 501
Kennett Square, Pennsylvania 19348

General Information Display garden promoting the art and enjoyment of horticulture for the public, while providing opportunities for research and learning. Established in 1954. Number of employees: 350. Number of internship applications received each year: 150.

Internships Available ▶ *2 arboriculture interns:* responsibilities include assisting the arborist crew in maintaining the tree collection; further responsibilities described on Web site. Candidates should have personal interest in the field, plan to pursue career in field, arboriculture/urban forestry experience (preferred). Duration is 3–12 months. $6.50 per hour. ▶ *1 continuing education intern:* responsibilities include assisting with continuing education program; refer to Web site. Candidates should have ability to work independently, computer skills, office skills, oral communication skills, strong interpersonal skills, writing skills. Duration is 1 year. $6.50 per hour. Open to college freshmen, college sophomores, college juniors, college seniors, recent college graduates. ▶ *1 curatorial intern:* responsibilities include assisting curator in daily activities; refer to Web site. Candidates should have ability to work with others, computer skills, oral communication skills, self-motivation, written communication skills, familiarity with plant nomenclature. Duration is 1 year. $6.50 per hour. Open to college freshmen, college sophomores, college juniors, college seniors, recent college graduates. ▶ *4 greenhouse production interns:* responsibilities include working with production crops and unusual crop; refer to Web site. Candidates should have ability to work independently, ability to work with others, knowledge of field, personal interest in the field, self-motivation. Duration is 3–12 months. $6.50 per hour. Open to college freshmen, college sophomores, college juniors, college seniors, recent college graduates. ▶ *2 integrated pest management interns:* responsibilities include assisting integrated pest manager; refer to Web site. Candidates should have ability to work independently, ability to work with others, oral communication skills, personal interest in the field, self-motivation, written communication skills. Duration is 3–12 months. $6.50 per hour. Open to college freshmen, college sophomores, college juniors, college seniors, recent college graduates. ▶ *1 landscape design intern:* responsibilities include various duties; refer to Web site. Candidates should have computer skills, declared college major in field, knowledge of field, oral communication skills, personal interest in the field, plan to pursue career in field, self-motivation, strong interpersonal skills, written communication skills, CAD experience. Duration is 6–12 months. $6.50 per hour. Open to college freshmen, college sophomores, college juniors, college seniors, recent college graduates. ▶ *1 library science intern:* responsibilities include helping maintain horticultural library collection; refer to Web site. Candidates should have ability to work with others, computer skills, office skills, organizational skills, personal interest in the field, self-motivation. Duration is 1 year. $6.50 per hour. Open to college freshmen, college sophomores, college juniors, college seniors, recent college graduates. ▶ *2 nursery interns:* responsibilities include general nursery work; refer to Web site. Candidates should have ability to work independently, ability to work with others, college courses in field, knowledge of field, personal interest in the field, plan to pursue career in field. Duration is 3–9 months. $6.50 per hour. Open to college freshmen, college sophomores, college juniors, college seniors, recent college graduates. ▶ *8 outdoor display or groundskeeping interns:* responsibilities include maintenance of annuals and perennials; working with herbs, ground covers, vegetables, fruits, and roses; or various groundskeeping duties; refer to Web site. Candidates should have ability to work independently, ability to work with others, knowledge of field, personal interest in the field, plan to pursue career in field, self-motivation. Duration is 3–12 months. $6.50 per hour. Open to college freshmen, college sophomores, college juniors, college seniors, recent college graduates. ▶ *2 performing arts interns (administrative or technical):* responsibilities include assisting with publicity/marketing for 350-event program; refer to Web site. Candidates should have ability to work independently, oral communication skills, personal interest in the field, self-motivation,

written communication skills. Duration is 1 year. $6.50 per hour. Open to college freshmen, college sophomores, college juniors, college seniors, recent college graduates. ▶ *1 research intern:* responsibilities include assisting in care and evaluation of plant materials; refer to Web site. Candidates should have ability to work independently, ability to work with others, knowledge of field, organizational skills, personal interest in the field, research skills, self-motivation. Duration is 3–12 months. $6.50 per hour. Open to college freshmen, college sophomores, college juniors, college seniors, recent college graduates. ▶ *5 special display/indoor display interns:* responsibilities include assisting in development of floral and special displays and maintaining display garden; refer to Web site. Candidates should have ability to work independently, ability to work with others, personal interest in the field, plan to pursue career in field, self-motivation. Duration is 3–12 months. $6.50 per hour. Open to college freshmen, college sophomores, college juniors, college seniors, recent college graduates. ▶ *1 student programs intern:* responsibilities include working with students; refer to Web site. Candidates should have ability to work independently, computer skills, office skills, oral communication skills, organizational skills, self-motivation, strong interpersonal skills, strong leadership ability, writing skills. Duration is 1 year. $6.50 per hour. Open to college freshmen, college sophomores, college juniors, college seniors, recent college graduates. ▶ *2 visitor education interns:* responsibilities include interpreting gardens; refer to Web site. Candidates should have computer skills, office skills, oral communication skills, organizational skills, strong interpersonal skills, writing skills. Duration is 9–12 months. $6.50 per hour. Open to college freshmen, college sophomores, college juniors, college seniors, recent college graduates. International applications accepted.

Benefits Formal training, free housing, job counseling, names of contacts, on-the-job training, opportunity to attend seminars/workshops, possible full-time employment, willing to act as a professional reference, willing to complete paperwork for educational credit, willing to provide letters of recommendation.

Contact Write, call, fax, e-mail, or through World Wide Web site Bill Simeral, Student Programs Coordinator. Phone: 610-388-1000 Ext. 508. Fax: 610-388-2908. E-mail: studentprograms@longwoodgardens.org. Applicants must submit a formal organization application, resume, academic transcripts, two letters of recommendation, statement of professional objectives. Application deadline: February 1 for summer, May 1 for fall, November 1 for winter and spring. World Wide Web: http://www.longwoodgardens.org.

LOS ANGELES COUNTY MUSEUM OF ART
5905 Wilshire Boulevard
Los Angeles, California 90036

General Information Museum with more than 110,000 works of art spanning ancient times to the present. Established in 1938. Number of employees: 322. Number of internship applications received each year: 500.

Internships Available ▶ *Interns:* responsibilities include working in various departments as determined by interests of intern and needs of department. Duration is 2–12 months. Position available as unpaid or paid. Open to college freshmen, college sophomores, college juniors, college seniors, graduate students. International applications accepted.

Benefits Job counseling, meals at a cost, on-the-job training, possible full-time employment, willing to complete paperwork for educational credit.

Contact Fax, e-mail, or through World Wide Web site Adam Kaplan, Recruiter. Fax: 323-857-4720. E-mail: jobs@lacma.org. No phone calls. In-person interview required. Applicants must submit a formal organization application, letter of interest, resume, academic transcripts, contact information for 2 professional references. Applications are accepted continuously. World Wide Web: http://www.lacma.org.

THE MARITIME AQUARIUM AT NORWALK
10 North Water Street
Norwalk, Connecticut 06854

General Information Aquarium, maritime museum, and educational center that encourages and excites appreciation of science and the interrelationship of global ecology and natural and cultural events as they relate to Long Island Sound. Established in 1988. Number of employees: 150. Number of internship applications received each year: 100.
Internships Available ▶ *5–8 college interns:* responsibilities include opportunities to work in Education, Animal Husbandry, Seal Census Study, Volunteer, Marketing or Exhibit departments; interns required to complete a project related to their internship. Candidates should have ability to work independently, ability to work with others, computer skills, oral communication skills, personal interest in the field, plan to pursue career in field, research skills, self-motivation, writing skills, ability to interact with public. Duration is 1 month (minimum). Unpaid. Open to college freshmen, college sophomores, college juniors, college seniors, recent college graduates, graduate students. ▶ *5–10 high school interns:* responsibilities include rotation through 3 different departments (Education, Aquarium, and Volunteers), participating in a variety of jobs from preparing seal food to helping teach educational programs. Candidates should have ability to work independently, ability to work with others, computer skills, oral communication skills, personal interest in the field, research skills, self-motivation, strong leadership ability, writing skills, ability to interact with public. Duration is minimum of 6 weeks. Unpaid. Open to high school students, recent high school graduates, individuals at least 16 years old. International applications accepted.
Benefits Names of contacts, on-the-job training, possible full-time employment, willing to act as a professional reference, willing to complete paperwork for educational credit, willing to provide letters of recommendation.
Contact Write, fax, e-mail, or through World Wide Web site Amy Ferland, Internship Coordinator. Fax: 203-838-5416. E-mail: internships@maritimeaquarium.org. No phone calls. In-person interview recommended (telephone interview accepted). Applicants must submit a formal organization application, letter of interest, resume, academic transcripts, two personal references, letter of recommendation. Application deadline: April 1 for summer, August 1 for fall, November 1 for spring. World Wide Web: http://maritimeaquarium.org.

MEADOWSIDE NATURE CENTER
5100 Meadowside Lane
Rockville, Maryland 20855

General Information Nature center located within a 2700-acre regional park outside of Washington, D.C. Established in 1927. Number of employees: 5. Unit of Maryland National Capital Park and Planning Commission, Department of Parks, Silver Spring, Maryland. Number of internship applications received each year: 20.
Internships Available ▶ *1–2 paid field experiences:* responsibilities include developing and presenting interpretive programs for diverse audiences including conservation clubs and special events; assisting with field studies and maintenance of wildlife and heritage gardens, rehabilitated animal display, and other exhibits. Candidates should have college courses in field, oral communication skills, personal interest in the field, self-motivation, strong interpersonal skills, ability to deal with the general public. Duration is 14–16 weeks. Position available as unpaid or at hourly minimum wage or a little higher, as funds are available. Open to college juniors, college seniors, recent college graduates, graduate students, career changers, individuals reentering the workforce.
Benefits Formal training, on-the-job training, opportunity to attend seminars/workshops, willing to act as a professional reference, willing to complete paperwork for educational credit, willing to provide letters of recommendation, outings to other park facilities, park housing available at cost.
Contact Write, call, or fax Sandy Staples, Intern Coordinator. Phone: 301-924-4141. Fax: 301-924-1034. In-person interview recommended. Applicants must submit a letter of interest, resume,

academic transcripts, evidence of academic coursework. Application deadline: March 1 for summer, June 1 for winter, November 1 for spring.

MEMPHIS BROOKS MUSEUM OF ART, INC.
1934 Poplar Avenue, Overton Park
Memphis, Tennessee 38104

General Information Fine arts museum whose collection spans from the ancient to the contemporary. Established in 1916. Number of employees: 65. Number of internship applications received each year: 20.
Internships Available ▶ *1–2 curatorial interns:* responsibilities include assisting curator with research of collections and exhibitions. Candidates should have ability to work independently, college courses in field, computer skills, knowledge of field, plan to pursue career in field, research skills, writing skills. Duration is 1 semester. Unpaid. Open to college juniors, college seniors, recent college graduates, graduate students. ▶ *1–2 media/public relations interns:* responsibilities include writing press releases, assisting in media outreach/contact, and supporting public relations staff. Candidates should have ability to work independently, computer skills, oral communication skills, self-motivation, strong interpersonal skills, written communication skills. Duration is June to August. Unpaid. Open to college juniors, college seniors, recent college graduates, graduate students. ▶ *Membership interns:* responsibilities include promotion of memberships, outreach, researching and identifying potential new members, and helping design membership information and recruitment plan. Candidates should have ability to work independently, oral communication skills, organizational skills, self-motivation, strong interpersonal skills, written communication skills. Duration is June to August. Unpaid. Open to college juniors, college seniors, recent college graduates. ▶ *1 registrar's office intern:* responsibilities include assisting in general office work, helping upkeep collections, and preparing exhibits. Candidates should have ability to work independently, computer skills, declared college major in field, plan to pursue career in field, research skills. Duration is 1 semester. Unpaid. Open to college seniors, recent college graduates, graduate students. International applications accepted.
Benefits On-the-job training, willing to complete paperwork for educational credit, willing to provide letters of recommendation.
Contact Write or e-mail Charlene A Mitchell, Human Resources Manager. Fax: 901-725-4071. E-mail: brooks@brooksmuseum.org. No phone calls. In-person interview required. Applicants must submit a letter of interest, resume, writing sample. Applications are accepted continuously. World Wide Web: http://www.brooksmuseum.org.

THE METROPOLITAN MUSEUM OF ART
1000 Fifth Avenue
New York, New York 10028-0198

General Information Art museum that emphasizes encyclopedic collection of master works of art. Established in 1870. Number of employees: 2,500. Number of internship applications received each year: 450.
Internships Available ▶ *Interns:* responsibilities include varied duties for college and graduate students interested in art museum and related careers; contact the Education Department for further information. Candidates should have ability to work with others, computer skills, oral communication skills, written communication skills, background in art history, knowledge of foreign languages. Duration is 10 weeks to 12 months (part-time or full-time). Position available as unpaid or paid. Open to college freshmen, college sophomores, college juniors, college seniors, recent college graduates, graduate students. International applications accepted.
Benefits Meals at a cost, on-the-job training, opportunity to attend seminars/workshops, willing to complete paperwork for educational credit, letters of recommendation provided (if appropriate).
Contact Write, call, e-mail, or through World Wide Web site Internship Program. Phone: 212-570-3710. E-mail: mmainterns@metmuseum.org. In-person interview required. Applicants must submit a letter of interest, resume, academic transcripts, two letters of recommendation, essay of not more than 500 words which

states reason for application and career goals and a list of art history and other relevant courses taken. Application deadline: contact Internship Programs for exact dates. World Wide Web: http://www.metmuseum.org/.

MILWAUKEE PUBLIC MUSEUM
800 West Wells Street
Milwaukee, Wisconsin 53233

General Information   Natural and human history museum. Established in 1882. Number of employees: 260. Number of internship applications received each year: 200.
Internships Available   ▶ *1–3 anthropology interns:* responsibilities include collections work in the following areas: American Indian, Africa, Pacific Islands, and Central and South America. Candidates should have ability to work independently, ability to work with others, analytical skills, college courses in field, computer skills, office skills, organizational skills, plan to pursue career in field, research skills, self-motivation, writing skills. Duration is 1–3 months. Unpaid. Open to college sophomores, college juniors, college seniors, recent college graduates, graduate students. ▶ *1–2 botany interns:* responsibilities include assisting with collections management, lab work, and local fieldwork. Candidates should have ability to work independently, analytical skills, college courses in field, computer skills, organizational skills, plan to pursue career in field. Duration is 1–3 months. Unpaid. Open to college juniors, college seniors, recent college graduates, graduate students. ▶ *1–2 development interns:* responsibilities include assisting in the coordination, development, and implementation of special events and programs at the museum. Candidates should have ability to work independently, office skills, organizational skills, self-motivation, strong interpersonal skills. Duration is 1–6 months. Unpaid. Open to college juniors, college seniors, recent college graduates, graduate students. ▶ *1–3 education interns:* responsibilities include presenting educational programs to groups and performing collection research and program development. Candidates should have ability to work independently, college courses in field, oral communication skills, organizational skills, personal interest in the field, self-motivation, strong interpersonal skills, written communication skills. Duration is 1–3 months. Unpaid. Open to college sophomores, college juniors, college seniors, recent college graduates, graduate students. ▶ *1–3 exhibit programs interns:* responsibilities include assisting in the production of various components of permanent and temporary exhibits, the installation of special exhibits, and upkeep of exhibits. Candidates should have ability to work independently, college courses in field, experience in the field, plan to pursue career in field. Duration is 1–2 semesters. Unpaid. Open to college juniors, college seniors, recent college graduates. ▶ *1–2 geology interns:* responsibilities include assisting with collections management, lab work, and local fieldwork. Candidates should have ability to work independently, analytical skills, college courses in field, organizational skills, plan to pursue career in field, research skills. Duration is 1–3 months. Unpaid. Open to college juniors, college seniors, recent college graduates, graduate students. ▶ *1–2 history interns:* responsibilities include working on collections from colonial America, European societies, North Africa, Middle East, classical civilizations, Asia, and specific areas in textiles and military weapons. Candidates should have ability to work independently, analytical skills, college courses in field, computer skills, editing skills, office skills, organizational skills, plan to pursue career in field, research skills, self-motivation, writing skills. Duration is 1–3 months. Unpaid. Open to college seniors, graduate students. ▶ *1–3 marketing interns:* responsibilities include working in public relations, communications, advertising, and journalism. Candidates should have ability to work independently, college courses in field, computer skills, editing skills, knowledge of field, office skills, oral communication skills, organizational skills, self-motivation, strong interpersonal skills, writing skills. Duration is 1–3 months. Unpaid. Open to college sophomores, college juniors, college seniors, recent college graduates. ▶ *1–2 zoology interns:* responsibilities include assisting with collections maintenance, lab work, and local fieldwork. Candidates should have ability to work independently, analytical skills, college courses in field, computer skills, knowledge

of field, plan to pursue career in field, research skills, self-motivation, written communication skills. Duration is 1–3 months. Unpaid. Open to college juniors, college seniors, recent college graduates, graduate students. International applications accepted.
Benefits Job counseling, names of contacts, on-the-job training, opportunity to attend seminars/workshops, willing to complete paperwork for educational credit, willing to provide letters of recommendation.
Contact Write, call, fax, or e-mail Ms. Dawn Scher Thomae, Museum Internship Coordinator. Phone: 414-278-6157. Fax: 414-278-6100. E-mail: thomae@mpm.edu. In-person interview recommended (telephone interview accepted). Applicants must submit a letter of interest, resume. Application deadline: March 1 for summer, November 1 for spring. World Wide Web: http://www.mpm.edu.

THE MINNEAPOLIS INSTITUTE OF ARTS
2400 Third Avenue, South
Minneapolis, Minnesota 55404

General Information   Art museum that emphasizes collection of master works of art in the areas of painting, sculpture, decorative arts, prints, drawings, photography, textiles, and Asian, African, Oceanic, and Native-American arts. Established in 1883. Number of employees: 200. Number of internship applications received each year: 75.
Internships Available   ▶ *1–2 curatorial interns:* responsibilities include assisting in preparation of object files and occasionally researching and writing gallery and catalog materials. Candidates should have ability to work with others, college courses in field, organizational skills, research skills, writing skills. Duration is dependent on project requirements. Unpaid. Open to college freshmen, college sophomores, college juniors, college seniors, recent college graduates, graduate students, career changers, individuals reentering the workforce. ▶ *2–3 development interns:* responsibilities include assisting department in various capacities relating to fund-raising. Candidates should have computer skills, knowledge of field, office skills, oral communication skills, research skills, written communication skills. Duration is dependent on project requirements. Unpaid. Open to college freshmen, college sophomores, college juniors, college seniors, recent college graduates, graduate students. ▶ *5–10 education interns:* responsibilities include assisting in preparation of teaching materials for use in schools and researching and writing gallery and catalog materials. Candidates should have ability to work independently, computer skills, editing skills, plan to pursue career in field, research skills, writing skills. Duration is dependent on project requirements. Unpaid. Open to college freshmen, college sophomores, college juniors, college seniors, recent college graduates, graduate students. ▶ *3–5 library interns:* responsibilities include working on various projects relating to library exhibits including museum object files. Candidates should have college courses in field, computer skills, experience in the field, organizational skills, strong interpersonal skills, written communication skills. Duration is dependent on project requirements. Unpaid. Open to college freshmen, college sophomores, college juniors, college seniors, recent college graduates, graduate students, career changers, individuals reentering the workforce. ▶ *1–2 marketing/ communications interns:* responsibilities include compiling press clippings and other various duties and opportunities. Candidates should have ability to work with others, college courses in field, computer skills, editing skills, experience in the field, written communication skills. Duration is dependent on project requirements. Unpaid. Open to college freshmen, college sophomores, college juniors, college seniors. ▶ *1 registration intern:* responsibilities include working on various projects including inventory of parts of a collection. Candidates should have ability to work with others, college courses in field, experience in the field, office skills, organizational skills, plan to pursue career in field. Duration is dependent on project requirements. Unpaid. Open to college freshmen, college sophomores, college juniors, college seniors, recent college graduates, graduate students. International applications accepted.

Benefits Names of contacts, opportunity to attend seminars/workshops, possible full-time employment, willing to complete paperwork for educational credit, willing to provide letters of recommendation.
Contact Write, call, fax, e-mail, or through World Wide Web site Treden P. Wagoner, Intern Coordinator. Phone: 888-642-2787 Ext. 3189. Fax: 612-870-3004. E-mail: twagoner@artsmia.org. Applicants must submit a formal organization application, letter of interest, resume, academic transcripts, two letters of recommendation, writing samples and interviews may be required. Application deadline: March 1 for summer, June 1 for fall/winter, October 1 for winter/spring. World Wide Web: http://www.artsMIA.org.

MINNESOTA MUSEUM OF AMERICAN ART
75 West Fifth Street, Landmark Center, Suite 505
St. Paul, Minnesota 55102

General Information Art museum that collects, preserves, enriches, and educates the community on 19th- and 20th-century American art. Established in 1927. Number of employees: 10. Number of internship applications received each year: 50.
Internships Available ▶ *1 curatorial assistant:* responsibilities include assisting curator with didactics, gallery installation, and research. Candidates should have computer skills, knowledge of field, oral communication skills, research skills, written communication skills. Duration is 3 months. Unpaid. Open to college seniors, recent college graduates, graduate students. ▶ *1 education assistant:* responsibilities include assisting director of education with educational materials for use by museum visitors, volunteers, and docents. Candidates should have computer skills, knowledge of field, office skills, research skills, self-motivation, writing skills. Duration is 3–12 months. Unpaid. Open to college seniors, recent college graduates, graduate students. ▶ *1 public relations/marketing assistant:* responsibilities include assisting PR coordinator with writing and distributing press releases and other publications. Candidates should have ability to work independently, computer skills, editing skills, knowledge of field, office skills, oral communication skills, organizational skills, written communication skills. Duration is 3 months. Unpaid. Open to college juniors, college seniors, recent college graduates, graduate students, career changers. International applications accepted.
Benefits Opportunity to attend seminars/workshops, willing to complete paperwork for educational credit, willing to provide letters of recommendation, complimentary museum membership.
Contact Write, call, fax, e-mail, or through World Wide Web site Tami Miller, Assistant Director of Education. Phone: 651-292-4395. Fax: 651-292-4340. E-mail: tmiller@mmaa.org. In-person interview recommended (telephone interview accepted). Applicants must submit a formal organization application, letter of interest, resume, academic transcripts. Applications are accepted continuously. World Wide Web: http://www.mmaa.org.

THE MINNESOTA ZOO
13000 Zoo Boulevard
Apple Valley, Minnesota 55124

General Information Conservation organization and facility whose goal is to help people realize the importance of animals and their impact on the world. Established in 1977. Number of employees: 250. Number of internship applications received each year: 80.
Internships Available ▶ *10–30 animal management interns:* responsibilities include caring for exotic and domestic animals, preparing diets, cleaning exhibits; learning techniques of zoo animal management, observing, reporting, and evaluating animal behavior; responding to animal emergencies, observing medical procedures; and effectively communicating with visitors on animal-related questions. Candidates should have college courses in field, oral communication skills, strong interpersonal skills. Duration is 10-14 weeks (30-40 hours per week). Unpaid. Open to college juniors, college seniors. ▶ *1 butterfly hoop house/garden entomologist/interpretive naturalist:* responsibilities include daily maintenance of insect collection and butterfly hoop house; interaction with zoo guests and volunteers while staffing butterfly garden; providing interpretive information to zoo volunteers and guests; monitoring hoop house area to prevent damage, butterfly/moth escapes, and pest

problems; accurate recordkeeping; assisting in developing and implementing a conservation message or project; replying to pertinent correspondence; assisting with reference work or additional tasks as needed. Candidates should have ability to work independently, college courses in field, plan to pursue career in field, self-motivation, strong interpersonal skills. Duration is May to September. Unpaid. Open to college juniors, college seniors. ▶ *2–4 education interns:* responsibilities include teaching in the informal setting of a zoo, handling animals for interpretive demonstrations, developing effective presentations, responding to questions from diverse audiences, structuring lesson plans, developing curriculum, working effectively with students and zoo education staff, and becoming environmental interpreters. Candidates should have college courses in field, oral communication skills, plan to pursue career in field, strong interpersonal skills, written communication skills. Duration is 10-14 weeks (30-40 hours per week). Unpaid. Open to college juniors, college seniors. ▶ *2 farmkeepers:* responsibilities include assisting with cleaning and maintenance of animal pens and exhibits; groundskeeping and horticulture maintenance; interpreting various farm animals to the public; assisting with demonstrations and domestic animal training. Candidates should have ability to work independently, college courses in field, plan to pursue career in field, self-motivation, strong interpersonal skills. Duration is 3-months (April to July or July to October). Unpaid. Open to college juniors, college seniors. ▶ *1–2 horticulture interns:* responsibilities include assisting with horticulture projects throughout the Zoo and assisting in maintenance of greenhouse plants. Candidates should have ability to work independently, college courses in field, plan to pursue career in field, self-motivation, strong interpersonal skills. Duration is 10-14 weeks (30-40 hours per week). Unpaid. Open to college juniors, college seniors, second-year technical college students.
Benefits Willing to act as a professional reference, willing to complete paperwork for educational credit, willing to provide letters of recommendation.
Contact Write, call, fax, e-mail, or through World Wide Web site Jill Wallin, Personnel Aide. Phone: 952-431-9219. Fax: 952-431-9211. E-mail: jill.wallin@state.mn.us. In-person interview recommended (telephone interview accepted). Applicants must submit a formal organization application, letter of interest, resume, academic transcripts, letter of recommendation. Application deadline: March 1 for summer, August 1 for fall, October 1 for winter, December 1 for spring. World Wide Web: http://www.mnzoo.com.

MISSOURI BOTANICAL GARDEN
PO Box 299
St. Louis, Missouri 63166-0299

General Information Botanical garden and research center that provides educational programs. Established in 1859. Number of employees: 350. Number of internship applications received each year: 50.
Internships Available ▶ *5–6 horticulture interns:* responsibilities include participating in day-to-day horticulture maintenance operations and working side-by-side with skilled staff. Candidates should have college courses in field, plan to pursue career in field, ability to work outside in heat and humidity. Duration is 12 weeks. $6.24 per hour. Open to college freshmen, college sophomores, college juniors, college seniors.
Benefits Housing at a cost, job counseling, names of contacts, on-the-job training, opportunity to attend seminars/workshops, possible full-time employment, willing to complete paperwork for educational credit, willing to provide letters of recommendation.
Contact Write, call, fax, or e-mail Dr. Shannon Smith, Director of Horticulture. Phone: 314-577-5190. Fax: 314-577-9465. E-mail: lisa.francis@mobot.org. Applicants must submit a formal organization application, letter of interest, resume, three letters of recommendation, additional materials available on Web site. Application deadline: February 1 for horticulture interns; visit Web site for information regarding other departmental internships. World Wide Web: http://www.mobot.org/hort/.

THE MONTCLAIR ART MUSEUM
3 South Mountain Avenue
Montclair, New Jersey 07042

General Information Art museum with a permanent collection spanning 3 centuries of American art with strengths in 19th-century American landscapes, Hudson River School, and American impressionist paintings, in addition to a Native American collection of almost 4000 objects which represent nearly every North American indigenous culture. Established in 1914. Number of employees: 30. Number of internship applications received each year: 30.
Internships Available ▶ *3–18 interns:* responsibilities include assisting staff in various areas including communications, curatorial, education, development, library, volunteer, exhibit design and installation, museum store, or Yard School of Art. Candidates should have ability to work independently, computer skills, oral communication skills, plan to pursue career in field, self-motivation, strong interpersonal skills, strong leadership ability, written communication skills, interest in art. Duration is 3 months. Unpaid. Open to high school seniors, recent high school graduates, college freshmen, college sophomores, college juniors, college seniors, recent college graduates, graduate students, career changers. International applications accepted.
Benefits Job counseling, names of contacts, on-the-job training, willing to complete paperwork for educational credit, willing to provide letters of recommendation.
Contact Write, fax, or e-mail Rachel Wynne, Associate Educator. Fax: 973-746-0536. E-mail: rachel@montclair-art.org. No phone calls. In-person interview required. Applicants must submit a letter of interest, resume, academic transcripts, two letters of recommendation. Application deadline: February 15 for spring, May 31 for summer, August 16 for fall.

MONTSHIRE MUSEUM OF SCIENCE
One Montshire Road
Norwich, Vermont 05055

General Information Science museum that uses materials and devices, natural objects, exhibits, live animals, and indoor/outdoor settings as catalysts in experiencing science and encouraging observation, curiosity, intuition, problem-solving, and imagination. Established in 1974. Number of employees: 26. Number of internship applications received each year: 16.
Internships Available ▶ *1 Internet and education intern:* responsibilities include developing bibliography of global Internet resources. Candidates should have ability to work independently, computer skills, experience in the field, oral communication skills, strong interpersonal skills. Duration is 15 weeks. $1000 stipend. Open to college juniors, college seniors, recent college graduates, graduate students, career changers. ▶ *4 environmental education interns:* responsibilities include planning, development, and teaching in environmental day camps. Candidates should have ability to work with others, personal interest in the field, ability to work with children. Duration is 10 weeks in summer. $1500 stipend. Open to college freshmen, college sophomores, college juniors, college seniors, recent college graduates, graduate students. ▶ *1–2 exhibit/design fabrication interns:* responsibilities include researching, designing, constructing, and refining exhibits. Candidates should have ability to work independently, oral communication skills, research skills, written communication skills. Duration is 15 weeks. $1000 stipend. Open to college juniors, college seniors, recent college graduates, graduate students, career changers. ▶ *1 land management intern:* responsibilities include following master plan and management objectives for 100-acre property, doing trail and grounds work. Candidates should have ability to work independently, personal interest in the field, self-motivation, ability to operate chain saw. Duration is 15 weeks. $1000 stipend. Open to college juniors, college seniors, recent college graduates, graduate students, career changers. ▶ *1 membership and development intern:* responsibilities include development and coordination of annual fund, major gifts, and planned giving programs; working with Montshire Associates, a local forum for business, education, and government; providing support for family and individual members. Candidates should have ability to work independently, oral communication skills, organizational skills,

strong interpersonal skills, written communication skills. Duration is 15 weeks. $1000 stipend. Open to college juniors, college seniors, recent college graduates, graduate students, career changers. ▶ *1 public relations intern:* responsibilities include working in the various avenues of communication. Candidates should have editing skills, oral communication skills, plan to pursue career in field, research skills, strong interpersonal skills, written communication skills. Duration is 15 weeks. $1000 stipend. Open to college juniors, college seniors, recent college graduates, graduate students, career changers. ▶ *1–4 science education interns:* responsibilities include teaching a variety of science and ecology classes to preschoolers, school children, teachers, and families; participating in environmental camps, overnights, and demonstrations; developing curricula; interpreting exhibits, outreach programs, teacher workshops, and courses. Candidates should have ability to work independently, personal interest in the field, strong interpersonal skills, interest in working with children and adults. Duration is 15 weeks. $1000 stipend. Open to college juniors, college seniors, recent college graduates, graduate students, career changers.
Benefits Free housing, on-the-job training, willing to act as a professional reference, willing to complete paperwork for educational credit, willing to provide letters of recommendation.
Contact Write, call, fax, e-mail, or through World Wide Web site Lou-Anne Conroy, Intern Coordinator, One Montshire Road. Phone: 802-649-2200. Fax: 802-649-3637. E-mail: montshire@montshire.net. In-person interview recommended (telephone interview accepted). Applicants must submit a formal organization application, letter of interest, resume, writing and art sample (for exhibit/design interns), writing sample (for public relations interns). Applications are accepted continuously. World Wide Web: http://www.montshire.net.

MOORES CREEK NATIONAL BATTLEFIELD
40 Patriots Hall Drive
Currie, North Carolina 28435

General Information Site that preserves the site of the Revolutionary War Battle of Moores Creek. Established in 1926. Number of employees: 6. Unit of United States National Park Service, Washington, District of Columbia. Number of internship applications received each year: 4.
Internships Available ▶ *1–4 visitor use assistants:* responsibilities include performing interpretation, managing resources, and conducting historical research. Candidates should have computer skills, knowledge of field, oral communication skills, personal interest in the field, strong interpersonal skills. Duration is year-round. Unpaid. Open to recent high school graduates, college freshmen, college sophomores, college juniors, college seniors, only those 18 years and older and accepted for college study. International applications accepted.
Benefits Names of contacts, travel reimbursement, willing to complete paperwork for educational credit, experience in a national park.
Contact Write, call, fax, or e-mail Linda L. Brown, Lead Park Ranger. Phone: 910-283-5591. Fax: 910-283-5351. E-mail: linda_brown@nps.gov. In-person interview recommended (telephone interview accepted). Applicants must submit a resume, two personal references. Applications are accepted continuously. World Wide Web: http://www.gov.nps.mocr.

MORRIS ARBORETUM OF THE UNIVERSITY OF PENNSYLVANIA
100 Northwestern Avenue
Philadelphia, Pennsylvania 19118

General Information University arboretum that emphasizes teaching, research, and outreach programs. Established in 1932. Number of employees: 55. Unit of University of Pennsylvania, Philadelphia, Pennsylvania. Number of internship applications received each year: 50.
Internships Available ▶ *1 arborist intern:* responsibilities include working in all phases of tree care. Candidates should have ability to work with others, personal interest in the field, climbing experience. Duration is 1 year. $8 per hour. Open to college

juniors, college seniors, recent college graduates. ▶ *1 education intern:* responsibilities include working closely with education staff and volunteer guides to develop workshops for experienced guides and training sessions to recruit new guides; supervising school tour program; running special programs for school children; developing specialized tours for the public; and helping coordinator prepare adult-education course brochures by selecting course topics and instructors and writing promotional copy. Candidates should have ability to work independently, college courses in field, computer skills, editing skills, experience in the field, oral communication skills, self-motivation, strong interpersonal skills, written communication skills. Duration is 1 year. $8 per hour. Open to college seniors, recent college graduates, graduate students, career changers, individuals reentering the workforce. ▶ *1 flora of Pennsylvania intern:* responsibilities include working in a major herbarium and creating a modern flora using computerized systems. Candidates should have ability to work independently, analytical skills, college courses in field, computer skills, knowledge of field, personal interest in the field, plan to pursue career in field, research skills, self-motivation, written communication skills. Duration is 1 year. $8 per hour. Open to college seniors, recent college graduates, graduate students, career changers, individuals reentering the workforce. ▶ *1 flower garden intern:* responsibilities include working with experienced horticulturist to plan, plant, and maintain Arboretum's rose garden display. Candidates should have ability to work independently, ability to work with others, college courses in field, knowledge of field, personal interest in the field, self-motivation. Duration is 1 year. $8 per hour. Open to college juniors, college seniors, recent college graduates, graduate students, career changers, individuals reentering the workforce. ▶ *1 horticultural intern:* responsibilities include assisting arboretum horticulturists in all phases of garden development and care and supervising gardening activities of volunteers and part-time staff. Candidates should have ability to work independently, college courses in field, knowledge of field, organizational skills, personal interest in the field, self-motivation, strong interpersonal skills. Duration is 1 year. $8 per hour. Open to college juniors, college seniors, recent college graduates, graduate students, career changers, individuals reentering the workforce. ▶ *1 plant protection intern:* responsibilities include assisting the arboretum's plant pathologist with the Integrated Pest Management (IPM) program. Candidates should have ability to work independently, analytical skills, college courses in field, personal interest in the field, research skills, self-motivation. Duration is 1 year. $8 per hour. Open to college seniors, recent college graduates, graduate students, career changers, individuals reentering the workforce. ▶ *1 propagation intern:* responsibilities include assisting propagator in the development of plant production and propagation schemes. Candidates should have ability to work independently, ability to work with others, college courses in field, knowledge of field, organizational skills, personal interest in the field, self-motivation. Duration is 1 year. $8 per hour. Open to college seniors, recent college graduates, graduate students, career changers, individuals reentering the workforce. ▶ *1 urban forestry intern:* responsibilities include working on community landscape consultation projects. Candidates should have college courses in field, computer skills, editing skills, oral communication skills, organizational skills, personal interest in the field, self-motivation, strong interpersonal skills, written communication skills. Duration is 1 year. $8 per hour. Open to college seniors, recent college graduates, graduate students, career changers, individuals reentering the workforce. International applications accepted.

Benefits Formal training, health insurance, on-the-job training, opportunity to attend seminars/workshops, tuition assistance, willing to act as a professional reference, willing to complete paperwork for educational credit, willing to provide letters of recommendation, vacation and dental benefits.

Contact Write, call, fax, e-mail, or through World Wide Web site Ms. Jan McFarlan, Education Coordinator. Phone: 215-247-5777 Ext. 156. Fax: 215-247-7862. E-mail: jlm@pobox.upenn.edu. Telephone interview required. Applicants must submit a letter of interest, resume, academic transcripts, three letters of recommendation. Application deadline: February 15 for June start date. World Wide Web: http://www.morrisarboretum.org.

MOUNT DESERT ISLAND HISTORICAL SOCIETY
373 Sound Drive, PO Box 653
Mount Desert, Maine 04660

General Information Society that manages a museum and archive, offers educational programs, acts as a voice for historic preservation on Mount Desert Island, and publishes an annual history journal. Established in 1931. Number of employees: 2. Number of internship applications received each year: 15.
Internships Available ▶ *1 museum assistant:* responsibilities include assisting with tours of museum, cataloging, collection care, research assistance, and program development assistance. Candidates should have ability to work independently, computer skills, oral communication skills, personal interest in the field, research skills, strong interpersonal skills, written communication skills. Duration is 3 months (June 1 to August 31). $1000 stipend. Open to college freshmen, college sophomores, college juniors, college seniors, recent college graduates, graduate students. International applications accepted.
Benefits Free housing, willing to act as a professional reference, willing to complete paperwork for educational credit, willing to provide letters of recommendation, opportunity to gain basic experience in small museum management.
Contact Write, call, or e-mail Jaylene Roths, Executive Director. Phone: 207-276-9323. Fax: 207-276-4204. E-mail: mdihistory@gwi.net. Telephone interview required. Applicants must submit a letter of interest, resume. Application deadline: March 1. World Wide Web: http://www.mdihistory.org.

MOUNT RUSHMORE NATIONAL MEMORIAL
PO Box 268
Keystone, South Dakota 57751-0268

General Information National Park Service site that commemorates the first 150 years of American democracy with a mountain carving of four important Presidents' faces. Established in 1925. Number of employees: 70. Unit of National Park Service, Washington, District of Columbia. Number of internship applications received each year: 10.
Internships Available ▶ *1–2 interpretation interns:* responsibilities include developing and presenting interpretive talks and guided walks, staffing information desk, performing informal roving interpretation, assisting speaker at evening program, and assisting with special events and museum curator research. Candidates should have ability to work independently, ability to work with others, oral communication skills, personal interest in the field, self-motivation, written communication skills. Duration is 12 to 16 weeks in fall, winter, and spring, (possibly in summer, if housing is available). Stipend of $75 per week (40 hours per week). Open to college sophomores, college juniors, college seniors, graduate students, career changers, individuals reentering the workforce, college students in a related field. ▶ *1 museum intern:* responsibilities include accessioning and cataloging, database management, preventive conservation, museum storage and security, exhibit planning, and possibly collections research. Candidates should have ability to work with others, college courses in field, organizational skills, plan to pursue career in field, research skills, self-motivation, written communication skills. Duration is 12 to 16 weeks in fall, winter, and spring. Stipend of $75 per week. Open to recent college graduates, graduate students, career changers, college students actively enrolled in museum studies for academic credit. ▶ *2–3 resource management and visitor protection interns:* responsibilities include assisting with visitor services and monitoring trails, climbing areas, and boundaries. Candidates should have ability to work independently, ability to work with others, oral communication skills, personal interest in the field, self-motivation. Duration is 12–16 weeks. Stipend of $75 per week (40 hours per week). Open to college freshmen, college sophomores, college juniors, college seniors. International applications accepted.
Benefits Formal training, job counseling, meals at a cost, on-the-job training, willing to act as a professional reference, willing to complete paperwork for educational credit, willing to provide letters of recommendation, potential seasonal job opportunities with the National Park Service, limited reimbursement for some expenses, free housing (if available), free uniform.

Mount Rushmore National Memorial (continued)
Contact Write, call, fax, or e-mail Blaine Kortemeyer, Volunteer Coordinator. Phone: 605-574-3170. Fax: 605-574-2307. E-mail: blaine_kortemeyer@nps.gov. Telephone interview required. Applicants must submit a letter of interest, resume, three personal references. Applications are accepted continuously. World Wide Web: http://www.nps.gov/moru.

MUSEUM OF ARTS AND SCIENCES
1040 Museum Boulevard
Daytona Beach, Florida 32114

General Information Museum of art, science, and history that emphasizes the conservation of and education about its permanent collections in the areas of American art, Cuban art, African art, French art, Chinese art, decorative arts, Indian and Persian miniatures, as well as the prehistory of Florida. Established in 1954. Number of employees: 23. Number of internship applications received each year: 20.
Internships Available ▶ *1–2 anthropology interns:* responsibilities include assisting in coordinating anthropological/archaeological programming and materials; artifact interpretation, identifying, and exhibition. Candidates should have college courses in field, computer skills, knowledge of field, organizational skills, research skills, writing skills. Duration is minimum 6 weeks; 2-month commitment preferred. Unpaid. Open to college freshmen, college sophomores, college juniors, college seniors, recent college graduates, graduate students. ▶ *1–3 collections department/registrar assistants:* responsibilities include research, cataloging, object handling; specialized projects may be developed based on personal interest. Candidates should have college courses in field, computer skills, organizational skills, personal interest in the field, research skills, self-motivation. Duration is year-round (minimum 6 weeks). Unpaid. Open to college sophomores, college juniors, college seniors, recent college graduates, graduate students. ▶ *1–2 decorative art curatorial interns:* responsibilities include researching decorative arts objects on display and preparing short summaries which will be entered into an interactive computer database in gallery. Candidates should have college courses in field, computer skills, organizational skills, personal interest in the field, research skills, writing skills, Macintosh knowledge (a plus). Duration is minimum 6 weeks; 2-month commitment preferred. Unpaid. Open to college juniors, college seniors, recent college graduates, graduate students. ▶ *1–4 environmentalist assistants:* responsibilities include coordination and development of environmental and educational programming and materials; guest services; special activities; and basic upkeep of environmental/historical sites. Candidates should have college courses in field, computer skills, knowledge of field, organizational skills, research skills, writing skills. Duration is minimum 6 weeks; 2-month commitment preferred. Unpaid. Open to college freshmen, college sophomores, college juniors, college seniors, recent college graduates, graduate students. ▶ *1–2 fine art curatorial interns:* responsibilities include research, cataloging, object handling; specialized projects may be developed based upon personal interests. Candidates should have college courses in field, computer skills, organizational skills, personal interest in the field, research skills, writing skills. Duration is minimum 6 weeks; 2-month commitment preferred. Unpaid. Open to college sophomores, college juniors, college seniors, recent college graduates, graduate students. ▶ *2–3 museum education interns:* responsibilities include curriculum development, research, and tours. Candidates should have ability to work with others, computer skills, oral communication skills, personal interest in the field, research skills, writing skills. Duration is minimum 6 weeks; 2-month commitment preferred. Unpaid. Open to college freshmen, college sophomores, college juniors, college seniors, recent college graduates, graduate students. ▶ *1–2 museum store assistants:* responsibilities include creating marketing plans and merchandising programs for store. Candidates should have knowledge of field, oral communication skills, organizational skills, self-motivation, written communication skills. Duration is flexible (2-month commitment preferred). Unpaid. Open to college juniors, college seniors, recent college graduates, graduate students. ▶ *1–3 paleontology interns:* responsibilities include assisting in coordinating archaeological programming and materials; artifact identification, interpretation, and exhibition; development of curriculum; and cataloging. Candidates should have college courses in field, computer skills, knowledge of field, organizational skills, research skills, writing skills. Duration is minimum 6 weeks; 2-month commitment preferred. Unpaid. Open to college freshmen, college sophomores, college juniors, college seniors, recent college graduates, graduate students. ▶ *1 public relations assistant:* responsibilities include writing, editing, and distributing news releases on a variety of museum events and programs; organizing and archiving museum photos and slides. Candidates should have declared college major in field, editing skills, organizational skills, writing skills. Duration is 1 semester. Unpaid. Open to college juniors, college seniors. International applications accepted.
Benefits Formal training, names of contacts, possible full-time employment, willing to complete paperwork for educational credit, willing to provide letters of recommendation.
Contact Write, call, or fax Monica Kelley, Volunteer Coordinator. Phone: 386-255-0285. Fax: 386-255-5040. In-person interview required. Applicants must submit a letter of interest, resume, three personal references. Application deadline: May 1 for summer, October 1 for spring. World Wide Web: http://www.moas.org.

MUSEUM OF CONTEMPORARY ART
220 East Chicago Avenue
Chicago, Illinois 60611

General Information Contemporary art museum focusing on international, multimedia work from 1945 to present; maintains permanent collection of over 2000 works and over 3000 artist books. Established in 1967. Number of employees: 190. Number of internship applications received each year: 200.
Internships Available ▶ *1–3 collections and exhibitions interns:* responsibilities include assisting director with daily operations of collections management, exhibition organization and tours, research, contracts, and budget management. Candidates should have ability to work independently, ability to work with others, computer skills, office skills, organizational skills, research skills, writing skills. Duration is 3 months (16 hours per week). Unpaid. Open to college freshmen, college sophomores, college juniors, college seniors, recent college graduates, graduate students, law students. ▶ *3–4 curatorial interns:* responsibilities include assisting curatorial staff with research, preparing artists' biographies, handling correspondence, general research inquiries, and daily departmental activities. Candidates should have ability to work independently, organizational skills, personal interest in the field, research skills, self-motivation, writing skills. Duration is 3 months (16 hours per week). Unpaid. Open to college freshmen, college sophomores, college juniors, college seniors, recent college graduates, graduate students. ▶ *1–2 development and membership interns:* responsibilities include conducting research, developing lists of prospects, sending proposals in the area of restricted fund-raising, and assisting with grant writing. Candidates should have office skills, organizational skills, personal interest in the field, research skills, self-motivation, written communication skills. Duration is 3 months (16 hours per week). Unpaid. Open to college freshmen, college sophomores, college juniors, college seniors, recent college graduates, graduate students. ▶ *1–2 editorial interns:* responsibilities include assisting museum editor and designer in all phases of production of museum gallery and working on invitations and calendar, including proofreading and basic editing. Candidates should have computer skills, editing skills, knowledge of field, organizational skills, writing skills. Duration is 3 months (16 hours per week). Unpaid. Open to college freshmen, college sophomores, college juniors, college seniors, recent college graduates, graduate students. ▶ *2–3 education interns:* responsibilities include assisting in art historical research and providing on-site support for outreach program, public lectures, and docent training sessions. Candidates should have computer skills, office skills, oral communication skills, organizational skills, research skills, strong interpersonal skills. Duration is 3 months (16 hours per week). Unpaid. Open to college freshmen, college sophomores, college juniors, college seniors, recent college graduates, graduate students. ▶ *1–3 graphic design interns:* responsibilities include developing and producing materials related to MCA's graphic needs, including exhibition catalogues, gallery signage, and

brochures. Candidates should have ability to work independently, ability to work with others, college courses in field, computer skills, knowledge of field, organizational skills. Duration is 3 months (16 hours per week). Unpaid. Open to college freshmen, college sophomores, college juniors, college seniors, recent college graduates, graduate students. ▶ *1–2 library interns:* responsibilities include organizing library resources by sorting and labeling books. Candidates should have ability to work independently, computer skills, office skills, organizational skills, personal interest in the field, written communication skills. Duration is 3 months (16 hours per week). Unpaid. Open to college freshmen, college sophomores, college juniors, college seniors, recent college graduates, graduate students. ▶ *3–4 marketing interns:* responsibilities include conducting research on prospective audience markets, assisting in analysis of demographic admissions, and working in database. Candidates should have oral communication skills, organizational skills, personal interest in the field, research skills, strong interpersonal skills, writing skills. Duration is 3 months (16 hours per week). Unpaid. Open to college freshmen, college sophomores, college juniors, college seniors, recent college graduates, graduate students. ▶ *3–4 media relations interns:* responsibilities include assisting in planning and implementing publicity; writing press releases, public service announcements, and media alerts; and conducting visitor surveys. Candidates should have ability to work independently, office skills, organizational skills, personal interest in the field, self-motivation, writing skills. Duration is 3 months (16 hours per week). Unpaid. Open to college freshmen, college sophomores, college juniors, college seniors, recent college graduates, graduate students. ▶ *2–4 performance programs interns:* responsibilities include participating in various aspects of developing and producing MCA programs in performance art, dance, music, literature, and video/film; maintaining resource files; completing marketing and administrative tasks; and assisting with artists and house management at performances. Candidates should have ability to work with others, knowledge of field, office skills, organizational skills, self-motivation, writing skills. Duration is 3 months (16 hours per week). Unpaid. Open to college freshmen, college sophomores, college juniors, college seniors, recent college graduates, graduate students. ▶ *1–3 photo archives interns:* responsibilities include assisting library staff in the slide library by sorting, relabeling, and organizing. Candidates should have computer skills, knowledge of field, office skills, organizational skills, personal interest in the field, self-motivation. Duration is 3 months (16 hours per week). Unpaid. Open to college freshmen, college sophomores, college juniors, college seniors, recent college graduates, graduate students. ▶ *1–3 special events/hospitality interns:* responsibilities include maintaining special events calendar, organizing on-site problem solving, offering creative input, and assisting with planning and coordinating events. Candidates should have ability to work with others, computer skills, knowledge of field, oral communication skills, organizational skills, self-motivation. Duration is 3 months (16 hours per week). Unpaid. Open to college freshmen, college sophomores, college juniors, college seniors, recent college graduates, graduate students. International applications accepted.

Benefits Formal training, on-the-job training, opportunity to attend seminars/workshops, willing to complete paperwork for educational credit, willing to provide letters of recommendation, opportunity to attend staff events, receptions, meetings, lecture series, access to MCA job boards.

Contact Write, call, fax, or through World Wide Web site Lauren Cumbia, Internship Coordinator. Phone: 312-280-2660. Fax: 312-397-4095. In-person interview recommended (telephone interview accepted). Applicants must submit a formal organization application, letter of interest, resume, two letters of recommendation. Application deadline: March 15 for summer, July 15 for fall, November 15 for winter/spring. World Wide Web: http://www.mcachicago.org.

MUSEUM OF FINE ARTS, DEPARTMENT OF MUSEUM LEARNING AND PUBLIC PROGRAMS
465 Huntington Avenue
Boston, Massachusetts 02115

General Information Nonprofit organization whose mission is to educate the public about the MFA. Established in 1876. Number of employees: 45. Division of Museum of Fine Arts, Boston, Boston, Massachusetts. Number of internship applications received each year: 60.

Internships Available ▶ *Interns:* responsibilities include assisting with teaching art classes for community groups; working on services for disabled visitors; promoting lectures, concerts, and programs; some clerical work. Candidates should have ability to work with others, computer skills, experience in the field, office skills, oral communication skills, organizational skills, personal interest in the field, plan to pursue career in field, self-motivation, written communication skills. Duration is flexible. Unpaid. Open to college juniors, college seniors, recent college graduates, graduate students. International applications accepted.

Benefits Opportunity to attend seminars/workshops, willing to act as a professional reference, willing to complete paperwork for educational credit, willing to provide letters of recommendation, discounts in museum store and free admission to the museum at all times.

Contact Write or through World Wide Web site Karen Strangfeld. Fax: 617-267-9328. No phone calls. In-person interview recommended (telephone interview accepted). Applicants must submit a formal organization application, letter of interest, two letters of recommendation. Applications are accepted continuously. World Wide Web: http://www.mfa.org.

THE MUSEUM OF FINE ARTS, HOUSTON
PO Box 6826
Houston, Texas 77265-6826

General Information Museum dedicated to serving all people by pursuing excellence in art through collection, exhibition, and education. Established in 1900. Number of employees: 500. Number of internship applications received each year: 100.

Internships Available ▶ *5 summer interns:* responsibilities include working in various curatorial and administrative departments. Candidates should have personal interest in the field, research skills, writing skills. Duration is 10 weeks. $2000–$2500 per duration of internship. Open to college sophomores, college juniors, college seniors. International applications accepted.

Benefits Health insurance, job counseling, names of contacts, on-the-job training, possible full-time employment, willing to act as a professional reference, willing to complete paperwork for educational credit, willing to provide letters of recommendation.

Contact Write, call, fax, or through World Wide Web site George Ramirez, Student and Faculty Programs Manager. Phone: 713-639-7727. Fax: 713-639-7707. In-person interview required. Applicants must submit a letter of interest, resume, academic transcripts, letter of recommendation, one-page essay describing applicant's interest in internship. Application deadline: January 18. World Wide Web: http://www.mfah.org.

MUSEUM OF SCIENCE
Science Park
Boston, Massachusetts 02114

General Information Museum designed to stimulate interest in science and technology and to further understanding of their importance to individuals and society. Established in 1830. Number of employees: 450. Number of internship applications received each year: 500.

Internships Available ▶ *Interns:* responsibilities include writing and editing print materials, working with the public and school groups, and serving in a variety of departments within the Museum. Candidates should have personal interest in the field, other requirements listed on Web site. Duration is 3-12 months in winter/spring and summer/fall periods. Position available as unpaid or at $6.75–$7 per hour. Open to recent high school graduates, college freshmen, college sophomores, college juniors,

college seniors, recent college graduates, graduate students, career changers, individuals reentering the workforce, high school seniors who have volunteered at the museum.
Benefits Names of contacts, on-the-job training, opportunity to attend seminars/workshops, possible full-time employment, willing to act as a professional reference, willing to complete paperwork for educational credit, meals at a discount, informal job counseling.
Contact Write, call, fax, e-mail, or through World Wide Web site Daniel Gomez-Palacio, Internship Program Coordinator. Phone: 617-589-0314. Fax: 617-589-0454. E-mail: interncoordinator@mos.org. In-person interview recommended (telephone interview accepted). Applicants must submit a letter of interest, resume. Application deadline: April 10 for summer; continuous for fall/spring positions. World Wide Web: http://www.mos.org.

THE MUSEUM OF TELEVISION & RADIO
25 West 52nd Street
New York, New York 10019

General Information Museum that collects, preserves, and exhibits radio and television programs. Established in 1975. Number of employees: 180. Number of internship applications received each year: 500.
Internships Available ▶ *2–4 curatorial department interns:* responsibilities include compiling information about programs and individuals significant in the history of the media, listening to and reviewing programs in the museum's collection, and drafting correspondence. Candidates should have ability to work independently, editing skills, office skills, organizational skills, research skills, self-motivation, written communication skills, knowledge of field (helpful). Duration is flexible (year-round). Unpaid. Open to high school seniors, college freshmen, college sophomores, college juniors, college seniors, recent college graduates, graduate students. ▶ *1 development department intern:* responsibilities include researching sources of corporate/individual underwriting, coordinating department activities, and preparing press kits. Candidates should have ability to work independently, computer skills, oral communication skills, organizational skills, research skills, strong interpersonal skills, written communication skills. Duration is according to need. Unpaid. Open to high school seniors, college freshmen, college sophomores, college juniors, college seniors, recent college graduates, graduate students, career changers, individuals reentering the workforce. ▶ *1–2 education department interns:* responsibilities include assisting in the research, preparation, and teaching of group presentations and scheduling groups for education programs. Candidates should have computer skills, oral communication skills, personal interest in the field, strong interpersonal skills, written communication skills. Duration is according to need. Unpaid. Open to college freshmen, college sophomores, college juniors, college seniors, recent college graduates, graduate students, career changers. ▶ *1–4 library services department interns:* responsibilities include watching videotapes, listening to audio tapes, using microfilm and reference sources to research facts, and indexing. Candidates should have ability to work independently, computer skills, editing skills, office skills, research skills, self-motivation, writing skills. Duration is flexible (year-round). Unpaid. Open to high school seniors, college freshmen, college sophomores, college juniors, college seniors, recent college graduates, graduate students, career changers, individuals reentering the workforce. ▶ *1–2 public relations department interns:* responsibilities include working closely with the staff on routine duties (typing, filing, photocopying) and long-term projects (press releases, telephone projects, organization of exhibition openings, and press conferences). Candidates should have ability to work independently, computer skills, office skills, oral communication skills, organizational skills, personal interest in the field, research skills, self-motivation, strong interpersonal skills, written communication skills. Duration is flexible (year-round). Unpaid. Open to college freshmen, college sophomores, college juniors, college seniors, recent college graduates, graduate students, career changers, individuals reentering the workforce. ▶ *2–4 research services interns:* responsibilities include assisting in organization of extensive print information received daily, assisting in all

aspects of television and communications, and working on special projects as needed. Candidates should have ability to work independently, computer skills, editing skills, office skills, organizational skills, research skills, written communication skills. Duration is flexible (year-round). Unpaid. Open to college freshmen, college sophomores, college juniors, college seniors, recent college graduates. ▶ *1–2 special events/membership interns.* Candidates should have ability to work independently, computer skills, office skills, organizational skills, research skills, strong interpersonal skills. Duration is according to need. Unpaid. Open to high school seniors, college freshmen, college sophomores, college juniors, college seniors, recent college graduates, graduate students, career changers, individuals reentering the workforce.
Benefits Formal training, opportunity to attend seminars/workshops, willing to complete paperwork for educational credit, willing to provide letters of recommendation.
Contact Call, fax, or e-mail Robert Eng, Director. Phone: 212-621-6620. Fax: 212-621-6700. E-mail: reng@mtr.org. In-person interview recommended (telephone interview accepted). Applicants must submit a formal organization application, letter of interest, resume, two letters of recommendation. Applications are accepted continuously. World Wide Web: http://www.mtr.org.

MUSKEGON MUSEUM OF ART
296 West Webster Avenue
Muskegon, Michigan 49440

General Information Art museum that collects and exhibits early through contemporary American and European artwork including paintings, prints, drawings, sculpture, glass, and photography. Established in 1911. Number of employees: 16. Unit of Muskegon Public Schools, Muskegon, Michigan. Number of internship applications received each year: 10.
Internships Available ▶ *2 collections management interns:* responsibilities include working with the registrar to learn aspects of collection data management, data entry, inventory, label production, condition reports, exhibit installation, loans, and art accessions. Candidates should have ability to work independently, ability to work with others, computer skills, editing skills, office skills, oral communication skills, organizational skills, research skills, self-motivation. Duration is flexible. Unpaid. Open to recent high school graduates, college freshmen, college sophomores, college juniors, college seniors, recent college graduates, graduate students, career changers, individuals reentering the workforce. ▶ *1–2 curatorial interns:* responsibilities include conducting in-depth research on selected areas of the permanent collection and exhibition training. Candidates should have ability to work independently, analytical skills, computer skills, editing skills, oral communication skills, organizational skills, research skills, self-motivation, strong interpersonal skills, writing skills. Duration is flexible. Unpaid. Open to college juniors, college seniors, recent college graduates, graduate students, career changers. ▶ *1–2 education interns:* responsibilities include interpretation of selected portions of the permanent collection; writing didactic labels, exhibit brochures, and family gallery guides; organizing programming and art education stations; working with the Museum Docent program in-museum tours and classroom outreach. Candidates should have computer skills, editing skills, oral communication skills, research skills, strong interpersonal skills, writing skills. Duration is flexible. Unpaid. Open to recent high school graduates, college freshmen, college sophomores, college juniors, college seniors, recent college graduates, career changers, individuals reentering the workforce. ▶ *1 gift shop intern:* responsibilities include working with manager, buying and selling museum merchandise, doing inventory and budget, creating design and layout, and working on some advertising. Candidates should have computer skills, oral communication skills, personal interest in the field, self-motivation, strong interpersonal skills. Duration is flexible. Unpaid. Open to college freshmen, college sophomores, college juniors, college seniors, recent college graduates, graduate students, career changers, individuals reentering the workforce. ▶ *1 public relations and development intern:* responsibilities include coordinating communications, media relations, general museum communications, visitor services, marketing, special projects, grant preparation, and campaign and membership development.

Candidates should have computer skills, editing skills, oral communication skills, organizational skills, personal interest in the field, research skills, strong interpersonal skills, writing skills. Duration is flexible. Unpaid. Open to college juniors, college seniors, recent college graduates, career changers. International applications accepted.
Benefits Job counseling, on-the-job training, willing to act as a professional reference, willing to complete paperwork for educational credit, willing to provide letters of recommendation, assistance with preparing job applications.
Contact Write, call, fax, or e-mail Art Martin, Registrar. Phone: 231-720-2575. Fax: 231-720-2585. E-mail: artjmartin@yahoo.com. In-person interview recommended (telephone interview accepted). Applicants must submit a formal organization application, letter of interest, resume, academic transcripts, letter of recommendation. Applications are accepted continuously. World Wide Web: http://www.muskegonartmuseum.org.

NANTUCKET MARIA MITCHELL ASSOCIATION
4 Vestal Street
Nantucket, Massachusetts 02554

General Information Association that celebrates the memory of Nantucket astronomer, librarian, and educator, Maria Mitchell, by continuing her work in education, social reform, and scientific research. Established in 1902. Number of employees: 13. Number of internship applications received each year: 75.
Internships Available ▶ *1 Historic House intern:* responsibilities include guiding tours of the museum, assisting with history classes for children, participation in conservation and cleaning projects, accessioning program for historical collection, and developing and facilitating research projects. Candidates should have ability to work with others, college courses in field, experience in the field, oral communication skills, self-motivation. Duration is 10 weeks. $2000 per duration of internship. Open to college sophomores, college juniors, college seniors, recent college graduates, graduate students. ▶ *1 Natural Science Museum intern:* responsibilities include daily operations of the Natural Science Museum, participating in bird and flower ecology field trips, participating in on-going biodiversity surveys, and developing a personal research project. Candidates should have ability to work independently, college courses in field, plan to pursue career in field, self-motivation, strong interpersonal skills. Duration is 11 weeks. $2100–$2280 per duration of internship. Open to college sophomores, college juniors, college seniors, recent college graduates, graduate students. ▶ *3 aquarium interns:* responsibilities include daily operations of the aquarium, assisting with marine ecology field trips, participating in on-going biodiversity surveys, and developing a personal research project. Candidates should have college courses in field, plan to pursue career in field, self-motivation, strong interpersonal skills. Duration is 11 weeks. $2100–$2280 per duration of internship. Open to college sophomores, college juniors, college seniors, recent college graduates, graduate students. ▶ *7 discovery class teaching interns:* responsibilities include planning and teaching discovery classes for children ages 4-15, assisting with management of Natural Science Museum, and involvement in special projects. Candidates should have college courses in field, personal interest in the field, self-motivation, strong interpersonal skills, ability to work well with children. Duration is 10 weeks. $1750–$1900 per duration of internship. Open to college freshmen, college sophomores, college juniors, college seniors, recent college graduates, graduate students.
Benefits Free housing, on-the-job training, willing to act as a professional reference, willing to provide letters of recommendation.
Contact Write, call, fax, e-mail, or through World Wide Web site Annalisa Helm, Education Coordinator. Phone: 508-367-7878. Fax: 508-228-1031. E-mail: ahelm@mmo.org. Telephone interview required. Applicants must submit a formal organization application, letter of interest, resume, three personal references. Application deadline: March 15 for Historic House intern; continuous for all other positions. World Wide Web: http://www.mmo.org.

NATIONAL BUILDING MUSEUM
401 F Street, NW
Washington, District of Columbia 20001

General Information Museum whose exhibits and educational programs interpret the worlds of engineering and architectural design, environmental and urban planning, building crafts and materials, and historic preservation. Established in 1980. Number of employees: 75. Number of internship applications received each year: 50.
Internships Available ▶ *8–15 student interns:* responsibilities include working in one of the following departments: exhibitions, collections, education, public affairs, or development. Candidates should have ability to work independently, ability to work with others, editing skills, oral communication skills, personal interest in the field, self-motivation, writing skills. Duration is flexible. Unpaid. Open to college freshmen, college sophomores, college juniors, college seniors, recent college graduates, graduate students. International applications accepted.
Benefits Names of contacts, opportunity to attend seminars/workshops, possible full-time employment, willing to act as a professional reference, willing to complete paperwork for educational credit, willing to provide letters of recommendation, weekly intern enrichment program for summer interns, complimentary member benefits, discount at Museum Shop.
Contact Write, call, fax, e-mail, or through World Wide Web site Emily Mudd-Hendricks, Director of Volunteers. Phone: 202-272-2448 Ext. 3300. Fax: 202-272-2564. E-mail: ehendricks@nbm.org. In-person interview recommended (telephone interview accepted). Applicants must submit a formal organization application, academic transcripts, writing sample, two letters of recommendation. Applications are accepted continuously. World Wide Web: http://www.nbm.org.

NATIONAL MUSEUM OF AMERICAN HISTORY
14th Street and Constitution Avenue, NW, Room 1040
MRC 0605
Washington, District of Columbia 20560-0605

General Information Museum that investigates, interprets, collects, preserves, exhibits, and honors the heritage of the American people. Established in 1964. Number of employees: 350. Unit of Smithsonian Institution, Washington, District of Columbia. Number of internship applications received each year: 500.
Internships Available ▶ *50–100 interns:* responsibilities include assisting in scholarly research, museum practices, and developing professional skills in a variety of career fields; contact office for list of current projects. Candidates should have ability to work independently, computer skills, research skills, self-motivation, strong interpersonal skills, various skills (depending on project). Duration is 8 weeks minimum, up to 1 year. Unpaid. Open to high school seniors, recent high school graduates, college freshmen, college sophomores, college juniors, college seniors, recent college graduates, graduate students, career changers, individuals reentering the workforce, minimum age of 16 years and at least a high school junior. International applications accepted.
Benefits On-the-job training, opportunity to attend seminars/workshops, willing to act as a professional reference, willing to complete paperwork for educational credit, willing to provide letters of recommendation.
Contact Write, call, fax, or e-mail Suzanne McLaughlin, Intern Manager, PO Box 37012 AHB 1040 MRC 605, Washington, District of Columbia 20013-7012. Phone: 202-357-1606. Fax: 202-786-2851. E-mail: intern@nmah.si.edu. Applicants must submit a formal organization application, resume, academic transcripts, two letters of recommendation, personal essay as outlined on the application. Application deadline: February 15 for summer, July 15 for fall, October 15 for spring. World Wide Web: http://www.americanhistory.si.edu/interns.

NATIONAL MUSEUM OF WOMEN IN THE ARTS
1250 New York Avenue, NW
Washington, District of Columbia 20005

General Information Art museum whose permanent collection (renaissance to present), temporary exhibits, and educa-

National Museum of Women in the Arts (continued)

tion programs recognize the achievements of women artists. Established in 1981. Number of employees: 96. Number of internship applications received each year: 100.
Internships Available ▶ *1 Coca-Cola intern:* responsibilities include working in any of the following departments: accounting, administration, development, curatorial, education, exhibit design and production, library and resource center research, national programs, publications, public relations, registrar, retail operations, special events, information technology, member services. Candidates should have college courses in field, knowledge of field, oral communication skills, organizational skills, personal interest in the field, research skills, strong interpersonal skills, written communication skills, plan to pursue museum career, prior experience (exhibit design and production), minimum GPA of 3.25. Duration is 1 summer (June to August); 1 fall; 1 winter (12 weeks). $1500 per duration of internship. Open to college sophomores, college juniors, college seniors, recent college graduates, graduate students. ▶ *1 Lebovitz intern:* responsibilities include working in any of the following departments: accounting, administration, development, curatorial, education, exhibit design and production, library and resource center research, national programs, publications, public relations, registrar, retail operations, special events, member services. Candidates should have ability to work with others, computer skills, editing skills, knowledge of field, oral communication skills, personal interest in the field, research skills, self-motivation, writing skills, plan to pursue career in art, prior experience (exhibition design and production), minimum GPA of 3.25. Duration is June-August (12 weeks, full-time). $1500 per duration of internship. Open to college sophomores, college juniors, college seniors, recent college graduates. ▶ *12–14 general interns:* responsibilities include working in any of the following departments: accounting, administration, development curatorial, education, exhibit design and production, library and resource center research, national programs, publications, public relations, registrar, retail operations, special events, information technology, member services. Candidates should have ability to work with others, computer skills, knowledge of field, oral communication skills, organizational skills, personal interest in the field, research skills, writing skills, prior experience (exhibit design and production), minimum GPA of 3.0. Duration is 12 weeks. Unpaid. Open to college sophomores, college juniors, college seniors, graduate students. International applications accepted.
Benefits Formal training, opportunity to attend seminars/workshops, possible full-time employment, willing to complete paperwork for educational credit, willing to provide letters of recommendation, art history course on women artists (fall and winter only), tours of exhibits at other museums in Washington, DC featuring women artists.
Contact Write, call, fax, e-mail, or through World Wide Web site Mieke Fay, Volunteer Coordinator. Phone: 202-783-7996. Fax: 202-393-3234. E-mail: mfay@nmwa.org. Applicants must submit a letter of interest, resume, academic transcripts, letters of recommendation including one personal letter and one academic letter; applicants for Coca-Cola, Lebovitz, and publications/PC internships must submit one writing sample (1-2 pages) in addition to other requirements. Application deadline: March 15 for summer, June 15 for fall, October 15 for winter. World Wide Web: http://www.nmwa.org.

NATIONAL PARK SERVICE OZARK NATIONAL SCENIC RIVERWAYS
PO Box 490
Van Buren, Missouri 63965

General Information Park that conserves outstanding examples of the natural and cultural resources of the United States for the benefit and enjoyment of present and future generations. Established in 1964. Number of employees: 100. Unit of United States National Park Service, Washington, District of Columbia. Number of internship applications received each year: 5.
Internships Available ▶ *1–2 archival assistants:* responsibilities include assisting in cataloging and organizing archival material. Duration is flexible. Unpaid. Open to college juniors, college

seniors, recent college graduates, graduate students. ▶ *1 landscape architect:* responsibilities include updating public land records; developing public sign proposals, plans, and drawings for public park facilities and trails; reviewing scenic easements, rights of way, and park boundaries. Duration is May-September. Unpaid. Open to college juniors, college seniors, recent college graduates, graduate students. ▶ *2 natural resources interns:* responsibilities include assisting in monitoring waterways, conducting bacteria sampling, lab work, and other natural resource duties. Duration is flexible. Position available as unpaid or paid. Open to college juniors, college seniors, recent college graduates, graduate students. ▶ *5 park ranger interns:* responsibilities include helping and dealing with visitors, leading trail walks, and evening talks. Candidates should have oral communication skills, strong interpersonal skills, strong leadership ability. Duration is 4 months. Unpaid. Open to high school students, recent high school graduates, college freshmen, college sophomores, college juniors, college seniors, recent college graduates, graduate students, law students, career changers, individuals reentering the workforce. International applications accepted.
Benefits Formal training, job counseling, willing to complete paperwork for educational credit, willing to provide letters of recommendation.
Contact Write, call, or fax Debbie Wisdom, Personnel Specialist. Phone: 573-323-4236. Fax: 573-323-4140. In-person interview recommended (telephone interview accepted). Applicants must submit a resume. Applications are accepted continuously. World Wide Web: http://www.nps.gov/ozar/.

THE NAVAL HISTORICAL CENTER
805 Kidder Breese Street, SE
Washington Navy Yard, District of Columbia 20374-5060

General Information Museum that undertakes historical research and writing, archival management, documentary editing, museum exhibits, educational and public programs, collections management, and library services for the Navy and the public. Established in 1801. Number of employees: 90. Unit of Department of the Navy, Washington, District of Columbia. Number of internship applications received each year: 100.
Internships Available ▶ *1–6 archival interns:* responsibilities include processing and cataloging documents, answering public inquiries, and assisting researchers. Candidates should have ability to work independently, analytical skills, organizational skills, personal interest in the field, research skills, self-motivation. Duration is 120–800 hours. Position available as unpaid or at $400 per duration of internship. Open to college freshmen, college sophomores, college juniors, college seniors, recent college graduates, graduate students, career changers, individuals reentering the workforce. ▶ *1–4 art curator interns:* responsibilities include supporting the organizing of the Navy's art collection as well as researching and writing for the collection's exhibit program. Candidates should have ability to work with others, college courses in field, computer skills, knowledge of field, research skills, written communication skills. Duration is 120–800 hours. Position available as unpaid or at $400 per duration of internship. Open to college freshmen, college sophomores, college juniors, college seniors, recent college graduates, graduate students, career changers, individuals reentering the workforce. ▶ *1–4 conservation interns:* responsibilities include assisting with conservation projects and independent artifact care. Candidates should have ability to work independently, ability to work with others, organizational skills, personal interest in the field, appreciation of artifacts. Duration is 120–800 hours. Position available as unpaid or at $400 per duration of internship. Open to individuals majoring in conservation. ▶ *1–4 copyediting interns:* responsibilities include editing publications for printed products of the branches, including books, booklets, brochures, and magazines. Candidates should have ability to work independently, computer skills, editing skills, organizational skills, self-motivation, written communication skills. Duration is 120–800 hours. Position available as unpaid or at $400 per duration of internship. Open to college juniors, college seniors, recent college graduates, graduate students, law students, career changers. ▶ *1–20 curator interns:* responsibilities include assisting the museum curator with research and developing an exhibition script or text for

publications. Candidates should have ability to work independently, research skills, self-motivation, strong interpersonal skills, writing skills. Duration is 120–800 hours. Position available as unpaid or at $400 per duration of internship. Open to high school seniors, recent high school graduates, college freshmen, college sophomores, college juniors, college seniors, recent college graduates, graduate students, career changers, individuals reentering the workforce. ▶ *1–5 design interns:* responsibilities include making models, preparing shop drawings, type design, graphic photography, photo silkscreening, mounting photographs, and assisting in matting, framing, and installation. Candidates should have ability to work independently, ability to work with others, computer skills, experience in the field, self-motivation. Duration is 120–800 hours. Position available as unpaid or at $400 per duration of internship. Open to high school seniors, recent high school graduates, college freshmen, college sophomores, college juniors, college seniors, recent college graduates, graduate students, career changers, individuals reentering the workforce. ▶ *1–4 education interns:* responsibilities include working independently and with the director of education to conceive, develop, and implement education programs directly relating to the museum's collection. Candidates should have ability to work independently, personal interest in the field, research skills, strong interpersonal skills, written communication skills. Duration is 120–800 hours. Position available as unpaid or at $400 per duration of internship. Open to college juniors, college seniors, recent college graduates, graduate students, career changers, individuals reentering the workforce. ▶ *3–20 historian interns:* responsibilities include historical research and writing for the branches dealing with post-1945 U.S. Naval history, U.S. commissioned ships, and aviation history of the U.S. Navy. Candidates should have ability to work independently, analytical skills, college courses in field, research skills, writing skills. Duration is 120–800 hours. Position available as unpaid or at $400 per duration of internship. Open to college freshmen, college sophomores, college juniors, college seniors, recent college graduates, graduate students, career changers, individuals reentering the workforce. ▶ *2 library interns:* responsibilities include all aspects of library work. Candidates should have ability to work independently, ability to work with others, computer skills, organizational skills, personal interest in the field, research skills. Duration is 120–800 hours. Position available as unpaid or at $400 per duration of internship. Open to college freshmen, college sophomores, college juniors, college seniors, recent college graduates, graduate students, career changers. ▶ *1–6 public relations interns:* responsibilities include writing press releases and public service announcements, developing mailing lists, and creating and implementing strategies to increase local and national awareness of The Navy Museum. Candidates should have ability to work independently, editing skills, oral communication skills, organizational skills, writing skills. Duration is 120–800 hours. Position available as unpaid or at $400 per duration of internship. Open to college freshmen, college sophomores, college juniors, college seniors, recent college graduates, graduate students, career changers, individuals reentering the workforce. ▶ *2–10 registrarial interns:* responsibilities include collections management of the Navy's artifact collection, including accessioning, cataloging, and identifying artifacts. Candidates should have ability to work independently, ability to work with others, computer skills, organizational skills, research skills, self-motivation. Duration is 3–10 weeks. Position available as unpaid or at $400 per duration of internship. Open to high school seniors, recent high school graduates, college freshmen, college sophomores, college juniors, college seniors, recent college graduates, graduate students, career changers, individuals reentering the workforce. International applications accepted.

Benefits On-the-job training, opportunity to attend seminars/workshops, willing to act as a professional reference, willing to complete paperwork for educational credit, willing to provide letters of recommendation, small stipend.

Contact Write, call, fax, or e-mail Dr. Edward M. Furgol, Curator. Phone: 202-433-6901. Fax: 202-433-8200. E-mail: edward.furgol@navy.mil. In-person interview recommended (telephone interview accepted). Applicants must submit a formal organization application, academic transcripts, writing sample, letter of recommendation, portfolio for design interns. Applications are accepted continuously. World Wide Web: http://www.history.navy.mil.

NEW YORK BOTANICAL GARDEN
200th Street and Kazimiroff Boulevard
Bronx, New York 10458-5126

General Information Internationally recognized center for botanical research, dedicated to environmental education and the conservation of plant diversity; operations at this facility include scientific research, horticulture, and education. Established in 1891. Number of employees: 552. Number of internship applications received each year: 90.

Internships Available ▶ *2–3 Bronx green-up interns:* responsibilities include implementing programs in community gardening and composting and supporting the development of school garden lessons and curriculum. Candidates should have ability to work independently, knowledge of field, oral communication skills, personal interest in the field, self-motivation, strong interpersonal skills. Duration is variable (according to funding). Salary depends on funding. Open to college freshmen, college sophomores, college juniors, college seniors, recent college graduates. ▶ *5–7 Everett Public Service Internship Program positions:* responsibilities include working on community outreach, research, education projects. Candidates should have college courses in field, computer skills, knowledge of field, oral communication skills, personal interest in the field, plan to pursue career in field, research skills, strong interpersonal skills, strong leadership ability, writing skills. Duration is 10 weeks. $230 per week. Open to college freshmen, college sophomores, college juniors, college seniors, recent college graduates, graduate students. ▶ *1–7 botanical science interns:* responsibilities include working side-by-side with prominent scientists in various areas including economic botany, systematic botany, molecular systematics, and the Harding Laboratory, Library, and Herbarium, (the largest in the Western Hemisphere, containing six million plant specimens). Candidates should have analytical skills, college courses in field, computer skills, knowledge of field, personal interest in the field, plan to pursue career in field, research skills, writing skills. Duration is variable (according to funding). Salary depends on funding. Open to college freshmen, college sophomores, college juniors, college seniors, recent college graduates, graduate students. ▶ *10 horticulture interns:* responsibilities include assisting gardeners, curators, and managers in the care of plants, gardens, collection, and records. Candidates should have ability to work independently, college courses in field, knowledge of field, plan to pursue career in field, self-motivation, strong interpersonal skills. Duration is 6–8 months. Position available as unpaid or at $7.50 per hour. Open to college freshmen, college sophomores, college juniors, college seniors, recent college graduates, career changers. ▶ *8–10 instructors:* responsibilities include assisting with children's gardening programs; interpreting hands-on exhibits at interactive Children's Garden; presenting science activities to children and adults. Candidates should have ability to work with others, oral communication skills, personal interest in the field, self-motivation, strong leadership ability. Duration is 4–8 months. $8.50–$10.50 per hour. Open to high school students, recent high school graduates, college freshmen, college sophomores, college juniors, college seniors, recent college graduates, graduate students. International applications accepted.

Benefits On-the-job training, opportunity to attend seminars/workshops, possible full-time employment, willing to act as a professional reference, willing to complete paperwork for educational credit, willing to provide letters of recommendation.

Contact Write, call, fax, or e-mail Claribel Irizarry, Human Resources Representative. Phone: 718-817-8872. Fax: 718-220-6504. E-mail: hr2@nybg.org. In-person interview recommended (telephone interview accepted). Applicants must submit a formal organization application, letter of interest, resume, academic transcripts, three personal references. Application deadline: March 31 for horticulture interns and Everett positions; continuous for other positions. World Wide Web: http://www.nybg.org.

NEW YORK HISTORICAL SOCIETY
2 West 77th Street
New York, New York 10024

General Information Collecting institution including a museum and library. Established in 1804. Number of employees: 200. Number of internship applications received each year: 100.

Internships Available ▶ *10–20 interns:* responsibilities include working in several different departments including public relations, development, special events, exhibitions, public programs, research, decorative arts, collection management, curatorial, and library (manuscripts and archives). Candidates should have ability to work independently, office skills, oral communication skills, organizational skills, personal interest in the field, research skills, self-motivation, strong interpersonal skills, writing skills. Duration is 8 to 12 weeks (usually a full semester). Position available as unpaid or paid. Open to college freshmen, college sophomores, college juniors, college seniors, graduate students.

Benefits Opportunity to attend seminars/workshops, willing to complete paperwork for educational credit, willing to provide letters of recommendation.

Contact Call, fax, or e-mail Internship Coordinator. Phone: 212-893-3400 Ext. 236. Fax: 212-921-6905. E-mail: internships@nyhistory. org. In-person interview recommended (telephone interview accepted). Applicants must submit a formal organization application, letter of interest, resume, two personal references. Application deadline: April 11. World Wide Web: http://www.nyhistory. org.

NORLANDS LIVING HISTORY CENTER
290 Norlands Road
Livermore, Maine 04253

General Information Museum that brings to life the daily activities of 19th-century rural New England through role playing, hands-on experience, and demonstrations performed in historic buildings. Established in 1974. Number of employees: 23. Unit of Washburn-Norlands Foundation, Livermore, Maine. Number of internship applications received each year: 12.

Internships Available ▶ *2 agricultural interns:* responsibilities include performing 19th-century farm activities, working with school groups, working with livestock, and maintaining site. Candidates should have ability to work independently, oral communication skills, personal interest in the field, self-motivation, strong interpersonal skills, flexibility and good sense of humor. Duration is 2 to 6 months (possibly longer depending on organization's needs). $50 per week; increases to $75 a week after 3 months, to $100 a week after 6 months. Open to recent high school graduates, college freshmen, college sophomores, college juniors, college seniors, recent college graduates, graduate students, law students, career changers, individuals reentering the workforce, individuals with farming backgrounds. ▶ *1 archival intern:* responsibilities include researching, organizing, and maintaining the archives; working with visiting scholars. Candidates should have ability to work independently, computer skills, organizational skills, personal interest in the field, research skills, self-motivation. Duration is dependent on the amount of time needed to complete projects. $50 per week; increases to $75 a week after 3 months, to $100 a week after 6 months. Open to college juniors, college seniors, recent college graduates, graduate students, law students, career changers, librarians and teachers. ▶ *1 curatorial intern:* responsibilities include working in an 1870s mansion that has recently undergone major restoration and maintaining collections. Candidates should have ability to work independently, ability to work with others, computer skills, organizational skills, research skills, self-motivation. Duration is 2–6 months. $50 per week; increases to $75 a week after 3 months, to $100 a week after 6 months. Open to college juniors, college seniors, recent college graduates, graduate students, career changers. ▶ *2–4 interpretation/ education interns:* responsibilities include guiding tours and groups, working as living-history interpreter for hands-on educational programs, possibility of working with livestock and site maintenance. Candidates should have oral communication skills, organizational skills, personal interest in the field, self-motivation, strong interpersonal skills, strong leadership ability. Duration is 2-6 months (may be extended longer than 6 months). $50 per week;

increases to $75 a week after 3 months, to $100 a week after 6 months. Open to college juniors, college seniors, recent college graduates, graduate students, law students, career changers, individuals reentering the workforce, retired teachers, history buffs, and individuals with farming backgrounds. International applications accepted.

Benefits Free housing, on-the-job training, possible full-time employment, willing to act as a professional reference, willing to complete paperwork for educational credit, willing to provide letters of recommendation.

Contact Write, call, fax, or e-mail Judith Bielecki, Executive Director. Phone: 207-897-4366. Fax: 207-897-4963. E-mail: norlands@ norlands.org. In-person interview recommended (telephone interview accepted). Applicants must submit a formal organization application, letter of interest, resume, 2-page essay, 3 letters of recommendation or personal references. Applications are accepted continuously. World Wide Web: http://www.norlands. org.

NORTH CAROLINA MUSEUM OF ART
2110 Blue Ridge Road, 4630 Mail Service Center
Raleigh, North Carolina 27699-4630

General Information Art museum with collections ranging from ancient through contemporary; strengths in American and Old Masters paintings, particularly Dutch, Flemish, and Italian. Established in 1956. Number of employees: 150. Branch of North Carolina State Department of Cultural Resources, Raleigh, North Carolina. Number of internship applications received each year: 25.

Internships Available ▶ *1 design department intern:* responsibilities include assisting the head exhibition designer. Candidates should have ability to work independently, college courses in field, computer skills, experience in the field, plan to pursue career in field, self-motivation. Duration is 2–3 months. Unpaid. Open to college juniors, college seniors, recent college graduates, graduate students. ▶ *1 development office intern:* responsibilities include devising and maintaining tracking system for travel program participation and correlation to giving history. Candidates should have ability to work independently, computer skills, knowledge of field, office skills, oral communication skills, organizational skills, personal interest in the field, self-motivation, strong interpersonal skills, strong leadership ability, written communication skills. Duration is 2–3 months. Unpaid. Open to college juniors, college seniors, recent college graduates, graduate students. ▶ *3 education department interns:* responsibilities include researching and writing on objects in collection; slide library work, including research, labeling, and filing; assisting with studio art classes; and assisting museum programmers in planning, coordinating, and implementing educational programs. Candidates should have ability to work independently, college courses in field, computer skills, knowledge of field, office skills, oral communication skills, organizational skills, personal interest in the field, research skills, self-motivation, strong interpersonal skills, strong leadership ability, written communication skills. Duration is 2-3 months minimum. Unpaid. Open to college juniors, college seniors, recent college graduates, graduate students. ▶ *3 educational outreach interns:* responsibilities include researching and writing on objects in the collection; slide library work, including research, labeling, and filing; assisting with studio art classes; assisting museum programmers in planning and implementing programs; making contact with special populations and minorities; calling outreach volunteers; and compiling outreach data. Candidates should have ability to work independently, college courses in field, computer skills, knowledge of field, oral communication skills, organizational skills, personal interest in the field, research skills, self-motivation, strong interpersonal skills, written communication skills. Duration is 2–3 months. Unpaid. Open to college juniors, college seniors, recent college graduates, graduate students. ▶ *3 graphic design interns:* responsibilities include assisting the head graphic designer in maintaining contact with museum staff "project managers" throughout the length of a project. Candidates should have ability to work independently, college courses in field, computer skills, editing skills, knowledge of field, office skills, organizational skills, writing skills. Duration is 2–3 months. Unpaid. Open to college juniors, college seniors, recent college graduates, graduate students. ▶ *1 public programs intern:* responsibilities include helping produce, promote, coordinate, and implement departmental events. Candidates should have ability to work independently, college courses in field, knowledge of field, office skills, oral communication skills, organizational skills, personal interest in the field, strong interpersonal skills. Duration is 2–3 months. Unpaid. Open to college seniors, recent college graduates, graduate students. ▶ *1 registration department intern:* responsibilities include recordkeeping in regard to the permanent collection. Candidates should have ability to work independently, college courses in field, computer skills, knowledge of field, office skills, organizational skills, personal interest in the field, research skills, self-motivation, written communication skills. Duration is 1 semester. Unpaid. Open to college juniors, college seniors, recent college graduates, graduate students. ▶ *3 volunteer services interns:* responsibilities include assisting in planning, coordinating, and implementing of special events. Candidates should have ability to work independently, computer skills, oral communication skills, organizational skills, personal interest in the field, strong interpersonal skills. Duration is 2–3 months. Unpaid. Open to college juniors, college seniors, recent college graduates, graduate students. International applications accepted.

Benefits Travel reimbursement, willing to complete paperwork for educational credit, free admission to museum events (lectures, films, concerts).

Contact Write, call, or fax Office Manager, Education Department. Phone: 919-839-6262 Ext. 2143. Fax: 919-733-8034. In-person interview recommended (telephone interview accepted). Applicants must submit a letter of interest, resume, academic transcripts. Application deadline: April 1 for summer, July 1 for fall, November 1 for winter/spring. World Wide Web: http://www.ncartmuseum.org.

NORTH CAROLINA STATE PARKS AND RECREATION, CLIFFS OF THE NEUSE STATE PARK
345-A Park Entrance Road
Seven Springs, North Carolina 28578-8971

General Information Park serving the people of North Carolina and protecting a unique area of scientific value and scenic beauty. Established in 1945. Number of employees: 8. Unit of North Carolina State Park System, Raleigh, North Carolina. Number of internship applications received each year: 6.

Internships Available ▶ *1 museum/librarian/researcher:* responsibilities include working in park museum cataloging slides, conducting research on cliff deposits, and writing papers on findings. Candidates should have ability to work independently, college courses in field, knowledge of field, oral communication skills, personal interest in the field, research skills. Duration is 4 months. Unpaid. Open to college juniors, college seniors, recent college graduates, graduate students. ▶ *Researchers:* responsibilities include collecting and cataloging a plant collection of flora found in the park to be stored in the park's herbarium. Candidates should have ability to work independently, college courses in field, knowledge of field, oral communication skills, personal interest in the field, research skills. Duration is 4 months. Unpaid. Open to college seniors, recent college graduates, graduate students. ▶ *1 trails specialist:* responsibilities include coordinating and initiating maintenance and repairs on trails. Candidates should have ability to work independently, ability to work with others, knowledge of field, oral communication skills, organizational skills, personal interest in the field, self-motivation, strong leadership ability, writing skills. Duration is 1 semester. Unpaid. Open to college freshmen, college sophomores, college juniors, college seniors. International applications accepted.

Benefits Free housing, names of contacts, possible full-time employment, willing to complete paperwork for educational credit, willing to provide letters of recommendation.

Contact Write or call Mr. Daniel G. Smith, Park Superintendent. Phone: 919-778-6234. In-person interview required. Applications are accepted continuously.

NORTH CAROLINA STATE PARKS AND RECREATION, HANGING ROCK STATE PARK
PO Box 278
Danbury, North Carolina 27016

General Information State park that strives to preserve and protect an area of scenic and natural beauty and provide a recreational area for the public. Established in 1936. Number of employees: 11. Unit of North Carolina Division of Parks and Recreation, Raleigh, North Carolina. Number of internship applications received each year: 5.

Internships Available ▶ *1 assistant ranger:* responsibilities include park operations and interpretation. Candidates should have college courses in field, knowledge of field, oral communication skills, self-motivation, strong interpersonal skills. Duration is 7 months. Position available as unpaid or at $7.25 per hour. Open to college freshmen, college sophomores, college juniors, college seniors, recent college graduates. ▶ *1 lifeguard:* responsibilities include lifeguarding lake. Candidates should have knowledge of field, oral communication skills, self-motivation, strong interpersonal skills, American Red Cross certification. Duration is 3 months. $7.15 per hour. Open to high school seniors, recent high school graduates, college freshmen, college sophomores, college juniors, college seniors, recent college graduates. ▶ *1 naturalist/interpreter:* responsibilities include presenting natural and cultural interpretive programs to park visitors. Candidates should have ability to work independently, college courses in field, knowledge of field, oral communication skills, strong interpersonal skills. Duration is 3-6 months (40 hours per week). Unpaid. Open to college juniors, college seniors, recent college graduates, graduate students. ▶ *1 park attendant:* responsibilities include maintaining and operating campgrounds and resource management. Candidates should have knowledge of field, oral communication skills, personal interest in the field, self-motivation, strong interpersonal skills. Duration is 6 months. Position available as unpaid or at $6 per hour. Open to college freshmen, college sophomores, college juniors, college seniors. ▶ *1 resource management specialist:* responsibilities include working on assigned resource management problems and issues; some research may be involved. Candidates should have ability to work independently, declared college major in field, experience in the field, research skills, strong interpersonal skills, written communication skills. Duration is 3-6 months (40 hours per week). Unpaid. Open to college juniors, college seniors, recent college graduates, graduate students. International applications accepted.

Benefits Housing at a cost, names of contacts, possible full-time employment, willing to complete paperwork for educational credit, willing to provide letters of recommendation.

Contact Write, call, fax, or e-mail Mr. Tommy R. Wagoner, Park Superintendent. Phone: 336-593-8480. Fax: 336-593-9166. E-mail: hangingrock@mindspring.com. In-person interview recommended (telephone interview accepted). Applicants must submit a formal organization application, resume. Application deadline: February 1 for summer, December 1 for spring.

NORTH CAROLINA STATE PARKS AND RECREATION, JOCKEY'S RIDGE STATE PARK
West Carolina Drive
Nags Head, North Carolina 27959

General Information Park providing high-quality management of scenic, ecological, and cultural values for public benefit. Established in 1975. Number of employees: 16. Unit of North Carolina State Park System, Raleigh, North Carolina. Number of internship applications received each year: 50.

Internships Available ▶ *2–3 assistant rangers:* responsibilities include planning and providing public education. Candidates should have ability to work independently, knowledge of field, oral communication skills, personal interest in the field, research skills, self-motivation, strong interpersonal skills. Duration is 3 months for 2 assistants and 9 months for other assistant. $7.25 per hour. ▶ *2 volunteer/ naturalist interns:* responsibilities include planning and providing public education. Candidates should have ability to work independently, college courses in field, knowledge of field, oral communication skills, personal interest in the field,

North Carolina State Parks and Recreation, Jockey's Ridge State Park (continued)
research skills, self-motivation, strong interpersonal skills. Duration is flexible. Unpaid. Open to high school students, recent high school graduates, college freshmen, college sophomores, college juniors, college seniors, recent college graduates, graduate students, law students, career changers, individuals reentering the workforce. International applications accepted.

Benefits Names of contacts, on-the-job training, possible full-time employment, willing to act as a professional reference, willing to complete paperwork for educational credit, willing to provide letters of recommendation, free housing for volunteers working over 16 hours per week.

Contact Write, call, or fax Mr. John Fullwood, Park Ranger II, PO Box 592, Nags Head, North Carolina 27959. Phone: 252-441-7132. Fax: 252-441-8416. In-person interview recommended (telephone interview accepted). Applicants must submit a formal organization application, letter of interest. Application deadline: March 1 for summer, July 1 for fall.

NORTH CAROLINA STATE PARKS AND RECREATION, NEW RIVER STATE PARK
1477 Wagoner Access Road, PO Box 48
Jefferson, North Carolina 28640

General Information Recreational park that seeks to preserve and protect an area of scenic beauty and environmental and ecological significance. Established in 1976. Number of employees: 22. Unit of North Carolina State Park System, Raleigh, North Carolina. Number of internship applications received each year: 15.

Internships Available ▶ *1–3 archaeological researchers:* responsibilities include researching and documenting archaeology of the river area. Candidates should have ability to work independently, ability to work with others, analytical skills, college courses in field, computer skills, editing skills, knowledge of field, personal interest in the field, research skills, self-motivation, writing skills. Duration is 4–10 months. Unpaid. Open to college juniors, college seniors, recent college graduates, graduate students. ▶ *1 bird surveyor:* responsibilities include developing accurate bird lists, conducting PIF and Birds in Forested Landscapes study, conducting Warbler Atlas Project. Candidates should have ability to work independently, analytical skills, computer skills, editing skills, knowledge of field, organizational skills, personal interest in the field, research skills, self-motivation, strong interpersonal skills, writing skills. Duration is 8–10 weeks. Position available as unpaid or at $6.75 per hour. Open to college juniors, college seniors, graduate students. ▶ *1 botanical surveyor of New River State Park:* responsibilities include organizing botanical information previously gathered; gathering new information on plants and plant communities within the park; mapping plant communities. Candidates should have ability to work independently, analytical skills, computer skills, knowledge of field, organizational skills, personal interest in the field, research skills, self-motivation, strong interpersonal skills. Duration is 8–10 weeks. Position available as unpaid or at $6.75 per hour. Open to college juniors, college seniors, graduate students. ▶ *1–2 butterfly study interns:* responsibilities include identifying different species of butterflies within park boundaries, preparing a list of different species and noting rare findings, and producing butterfly brochure for the use of the public. Candidates should have ability to work independently, ability to work with others, computer skills, knowledge of field, office skills, personal interest in the field, research skills, self-motivation, writing skills. Duration is 3–4 months. Position available as unpaid or at $6.75 per hour. Open to college juniors, college seniors, recent college graduates, graduate students. ▶ *1 canoe trail specialist:* responsibilities include conducting a natural and historical investigation of the New River in order to create a 26.5-mile self-guided canoe trail; information in the guide should include local history, ecology, and geology, as well as provide basic stewardship principles. Candidates should have ability to work independently, analytical skills, computer skills, editing skills, knowledge of field, organizational skills, personal interest in the field, research skills, self-motivation, strong interpersonal skills, writing skills. Duration is 3 months. Position available as unpaid or at $6.75 per hour. Open to college juniors, college seniors, graduate students.

▶ *2–4 exhibit and publications specialists:* responsibilities include design, layout, and construction of new exhibits and publications for park interpretive programs and materials. Candidates should have ability to work independently, analytical skills, college courses in field, computer skills, editing skills, knowledge of field, organizational skills, personal interest in the field, research skills, self-motivation, strong interpersonal skills, writing skills, desktop publishing skills (preferred). Duration is 3–10 months. Position available as unpaid or at $6.75 per hour. Open to college freshmen, college sophomores, college juniors, college seniors, recent college graduates, individuals reentering the workforce. ▶ *1–4 interpretive specialists:* responsibilities include developing school and evening group programs and identifying species in the field. Candidates should have ability to work independently, analytical skills, college courses in field, computer skills, editing skills, knowledge of field, office skills, oral communication skills, organizational skills, personal interest in the field, research skills, self-motivation, strong interpersonal skills, writing skills. Duration is 3–10 months. Position available as unpaid or at $6.75 per hour. Open to college sophomores, college juniors, college seniors, recent college graduates, graduate students, career changers. ▶ *1–4 mapping interns:* responsibilities include mapping the state park using GIS software and GPS devices. Candidates should have ability to work independently, analytical skills, college courses in field, computer skills, editing skills, knowledge of field, organizational skills, personal interest in the field, research skills, self-motivation, strong interpersonal skills, writing skills. Duration is 4–6 months. Position available as unpaid or at $6.75 per hour. Open to college juniors, college seniors, recent college graduates, graduate students, career changers. ▶ *1–2 natural heritage researchers:* responsibilities include identifying and documenting endangered species and performing floristics or faunal inventory. Candidates should have ability to work independently, analytical skills, college courses in field, computer skills, editing skills, knowledge of field, organizational skills, personal interest in the field, research skills, self-motivation, strong interpersonal skills, writing skills. Duration is 3–12 months. Position available as unpaid or at $6.75 per hour. Open to college juniors, college seniors, recent college graduates, graduate students, career changers. ▶ *1–2 park photographers:* responsibilities include photographing flora and fauna of the state park. Candidates should have ability to work independently, knowledge of field, personal interest in the field, self-motivation, strong interpersonal skills. Duration is 3 months. Unpaid. Open to recent high school graduates, college freshmen, college sophomores, college juniors, college seniors, recent college graduates, graduate students, career changers. ▶ *1–3 river user surveyors:* responsibilities include conducting survey of river water levels to ensure safe use by rafters and canoers. Candidates should have ability to work independently, analytical skills, college courses in field, computer skills, knowledge of field, office skills, personal interest in the field, research skills, self-motivation, strong interpersonal skills, writing skills. Duration is 3–6 months. Position available as unpaid or at $6.75 per hour. Open to college juniors, college seniors, recent college graduates, graduate students. ▶ *5–10 trails construction technicians:* responsibilities include design, layout, and construction of hiking trails using hand tools and natural materials; supervision of volunteer and court-assigned laborers. Candidates should have ability to work independently, personal interest in the field, self-motivation, strong interpersonal skills. Duration is 3–10 months. Position available as unpaid or at $6.75 per hour. Open to recent high school graduates, college freshmen, college sophomores, college juniors, college seniors, recent college graduates, graduate students, career changers, individuals reentering the workforce. International applications accepted.

Benefits Free housing, job counseling, names of contacts, possible full-time employment, willing to act as a professional reference, willing to complete paperwork for educational credit, willing to provide letters of recommendation, paid internships (for North Carolina residents only).

Contact Write, call, fax, or e-mail Mr. Jay Wild, Superintendent. Phone: 336-982-2587. Fax: 336-982-3943. E-mail: neri@skybest.com. In-person interview recommended (telephone interview accepted). Applicants must submit a resume, academic transcripts, three personal references, letter of recommendation. Application deadline: January 31 for paid interns; continuous for volunteer interns. World Wide Web: http://www.ncsparks.net.

NORTH CAROLINA STATE PARKS AND RECREATION, PETTIGREW STATE PARK
2252 Lakeshore Road
Creswell, North Carolina 27928

General Information State park whose goal is to preserve and protect unique state natural areas and provide public enjoyment. Established in 1939. Number of employees: 8. Unit of North Carolina Division of Parks and Recreation, Raleigh, North Carolina. Number of internship applications received each year: 5.

Internships Available ► *1 general utility worker:* responsibilities include working with the administrative staff, maintenance staff, and generally doing what needs to be done. Candidates should have ability to work independently, ability to work with others, personal interest in the field. Duration is March to September (40 hours per week). $6.75 per hour. Open to recent high school graduates, college freshmen, college sophomores, college juniors, college seniors, individuals reentering the workforce, must be 18 years or older. ► *1–2 naturalists:* responsibilities include conducting aquatic plant surveys, rare plant species surveys, and new plant experimentation. Candidates should have personal interest in the field, plan to pursue career in field. Duration is flexible. Unpaid. Open to college sophomores, college juniors, college seniors. ► *1 park attendant:* responsibilities include maintaining grounds and facilities. Candidates should have ability to work independently, ability to work with others, personal interest in the field, plan to pursue career in field, valid driver's license. Duration is 3 months in summer. $6 per hour. Open to recent high school graduates, must be 18 years or older. ► *1 volunteer:* responsibilities include performing various duties around the park. Candidates should have ability to work independently, ability to work with others, personal interest in the field, plan to pursue career in field, self-motivation. Duration is flexible. Unpaid. Open to college freshmen, college sophomores, college juniors, college seniors, recent college graduates, graduate students. International applications accepted.

Benefits Names of contacts, possible full-time employment, willing to act as a professional reference, willing to complete paperwork for educational credit, willing to provide letters of recommendation, free camping.

Contact Write, call, fax, or e-mail Internship Coordinator. Phone: 252-797-4475. Fax: 252-797-7405. E-mail: pettigrew@ncmail.net. In-person interview recommended (telephone interview accepted). Applications are accepted continuously. World Wide Web: http://ils.unc.edu/parkproject/ncparks.html.

NORTH CAROLINA STATE PARKS AND RECREATION, RAVEN ROCK STATE PARK
3009 Raven Rock Road
Lillington, North Carolina 27546

General Information State park that conserves and protects natural resources and provides opportunities for recreation and environmental education. Established in 1916. Number of employees: 5. Unit of North Carolina Department of Environment and Natural Resources, Raleigh, North Carolina. Number of internship applications received each year: 1.

Internships Available ► *1 facilities and grounds intern:* responsibilities include assisting in the routine maintenance of park facility and grounds. Candidates should have ability to work independently, ability to work with others, self-motivation. Duration is 3–4 months. Unpaid. ► *1 natural resource interpreter:* responsibilities include utilizing interpretive materials on a rotating basis to provide information on the park's natural resources. Candidates should have ability to work independently, oral communication skills, personal interest in the field, research skills, self-motivation, written communication skills. Duration is flexible. Unpaid. ► *1 trail maintenance intern:* responsibilities include assisting staff in maintenance of hiking and bridle trails, trimming overgrowth and fallen trees from trail path, and maintaining water bars, footbridges, trail blazes, signs, and markers. Candidates should have ability to work

independently, ability to work with others, self-motivation. Duration is 3–4 months. Unpaid. Open to recent high school graduates, college freshmen, college sophomores, college juniors, college seniors, recent college graduates, graduate students, law students, career changers, individuals reentering the workforce. International applications accepted.

Benefits Names of contacts, possible full-time employment, willing to complete paperwork for educational credit, willing to provide letters of recommendation.

Contact Write, call, fax, or e-mail Eric Folk, Park Ranger 1. Phone: 910-893-4888. Fax: 910-814-2200. E-mail: ravenroc@infi.net. In-person interview required. Applicants must submit a formal organization application. Applications are accepted continuously. World Wide Web: http://ils.unc.edu/parkproject/ncparks.htm.

OFFICE OF HISTORIC ALEXANDRIA
PO Box 178, City Hall
Alexandria, Virginia 22313

General Information Office involved with the preservation of historic sites, artifacts, records, and the enhancement and preservation of the cultural diversity of Alexandria; provides programs to bring people and business to the city. Established in 1983. Number of employees: 70. Unit of City of Alexandria, Alexandria, Virginia. Number of internship applications received each year: 40.

Internships Available ► *3–4 Alexandria archaeology interns:* responsibilities include assisting with archaeological field work, public programs, collections management, and research. Candidates should have ability to work independently, ability to work with others, computer skills, personal interest in the field, self-motivation. Duration is 4–12 weeks. Unpaid. Open to high school students, college freshmen, college sophomores, college juniors, college seniors, graduate students. ► *1 Archives and Records Center intern:* responsibilities include preparing and finding records and cataloging the collection of archival materials relating to history of the city. Candidates should have ability to work independently, ability to work with others, analytical skills, college courses in field, computer skills, knowledge of field, office skills, organizational skills, plan to pursue career in field, self-motivation, writing skills. Duration is 6–8 weeks. Position available as unpaid or at Paid at hourly rate (if funding available). Open to college juniors, college seniors, recent college graduates, graduate students. ► *1–2 Black History Center volunteers:* responsibilities include assisting with interpretation, public programs, and cataloging. Candidates should have computer skills, oral communication skills, plan to pursue career in field, strong interpersonal skills, written communication skills, graphics skills. Duration is 6 weeks. Unpaid. Open to high school students, college freshmen, college sophomores, college juniors, college seniors, graduate students, career changers. ► *1 Black History Resource Center intern:* responsibilities include assisting with interpretation, public programs, and cataloging. Candidates should have oral communication skills, plan to pursue career in field, strong interpersonal skills, written communication skills. Duration is 8-10 weeks in summer. Paid. Open to high school students, college freshmen, college sophomores, college juniors, college seniors, recent college graduates, graduate students, career changers. ► *1–2 Ft. Ward Museum interns:* responsibilities include cataloging. Candidates should have editing skills, knowledge of field, plan to pursue career in field, research skills, writing skills. Duration is 8 weeks (minimum). Unpaid. Open to college sophomores, college juniors, college seniors, recent college graduates, graduate students. ► *4 Gadsby's Tavern Museum interns:* responsibilities include assisting with interpretation and public programs. Candidates should have knowledge of field, oral communication skills, plan to pursue career in field, writing skills. Duration is 6–8 weeks. Unpaid. Open to high school seniors, college freshmen, college sophomores, college juniors, college seniors, recent college graduates, graduate students. ► *1–3 Lyceum interns:* responsibilities include assisting with exhibits and public programs. Candidates should have ability to work independently, oral communication skills, personal interest in the field, self-motivation, strong interpersonal skills, written communication skills. Duration is 6–8 weeks. Unpaid. Open to high school seniors, college freshmen, college sophomores, college juniors, college seniors,

recent college graduates, graduate students, individuals reentering the workforce. International applications accepted.
Benefits Formal training, job counseling, names of contacts, on-the-job training, opportunity to attend seminars/workshops, willing to act as a professional reference, willing to complete paperwork for educational credit, willing to provide letters of recommendation.
Contact Write, call, fax, e-mail, or through World Wide Web site Ms. Jean Taylor Federico, Director. Phone: 703-838-4554. Fax: 703-838-6451. E-mail: jean.federico@ci.alexandria.va.us. In-person interview recommended (telephone interview accepted). Applicants must submit a letter of interest, resume, three personal references, three letters of recommendation. Applications are accepted continuously. World Wide Web: http://ci.alexandria.va.us/oha.

OLYMPIC NATIONAL PARK
600 East Park Avenue
Port Angeles, Washington 98362

General Information National park managing 923,000 acres of coast, rainforest, and mountains. Established in 1938. Number of employees: 140. Unit of United States National Park Service, Washington, District of Columbia. Number of internship applications received each year: 75.
Internships Available ▶ *8–9 backcountry rangers:* responsibilities include assisting park rangers with various tasks including visitor contacts, providing information to the public, patrolling trails and roads, operating backcountry stations, minor trail maintenance, various resource management projects, light maintenance, and search-and-rescue operations. Candidates should have ability to work independently, ability to work with others, oral communication skills, personal interest in the field. Duration is 1–3 months. Position available as unpaid or at $50 per month. Open to college freshmen, college sophomores, college juniors, college seniors, recent college graduates, graduate students, law students, career changers, individuals reentering the workforce. ▶ *14 campground hosts:* responsibilities include assisting area park rangers with operations and light maintenance of campgrounds in a designated location within the park. Candidates should have ability to work independently, ability to work with others, oral communication skills, personal interest in the field, access to recreation vehicle or trailer. Duration is usually June to Labor Day. Position available as unpaid or at $50 per month. Open to college seniors, recent college graduates, graduate students, career changers, individuals reentering the workforce. ▶ *4–8 education rangers:* responsibilities include assisting with daily operations of a major visitor center, providing environmental education programs to local schools, conducting nature walks and talks, planning exhibits, and assisting with search-and-rescue. Candidates should have ability to work independently, computer skills, oral communication skills, strong interpersonal skills, strong leadership ability, written communication skills. Duration is 3–4 months. Position available as unpaid or at $100 per month. Open to college freshmen, college sophomores, college juniors, college seniors, recent college graduates, graduate students. ▶ *4–6 natural resource management interns:* responsibilities include aiding park scientists and resource managers in a variety of projects, including fish and other wildlife studies and wilderness revegetation; conducting plant ecology research; monitoring programs; and collecting and inputting resource data. Candidates should have ability to work independently, ability to work with others, college courses in field, oral communication skills, personal interest in the field, written communication skills. Duration is 2–5 months. Position available as unpaid or at $50–$100 per month. Open to college freshmen, college sophomores, college juniors, college seniors, recent college graduates, graduate students. ▶ *1–3 wilderness information center interns:* responsibilities include developing a working knowledge of park wilderness destinations, regulations, and "Leave No Trace" outdoor skills; issuing camping reservations and permits; answering phone and mail. Candidates should have ability to work independently, ability to work with others, computer skills, oral communication skills, strong leadership ability, written communication skills. Duration is April to September. Position available as unpaid or at $50 per month. Open to college freshmen, college

sophomores, college juniors, college seniors, recent college graduates, graduate students, law students, career changers, individuals reentering the workforce. International applications accepted.
Benefits Free housing, job counseling, names of contacts, opportunity to attend seminars/workshops, willing to complete paperwork for educational credit, willing to provide letters of recommendation.
Contact Write, call, fax, or e-mail Volunteer Coordinator. Phone: 360-565-3000. Fax: 360-565-3015. E-mail: olym_mail_room@nps.gov. Applicants must submit a formal organization application, resume. Application deadline: March 15 for natural resource management, campground host, and summer education rangers, October 1 for winter education rangers; continuous for all other positions. World Wide Web: http://www.nps.gov/olym.

ORLANDO MUSEUM OF ART
2416 North Mills Avenue
Orlando, Florida 32803

General Information Museum featuring public programs and activities that interpret its permanent collections and special exhibits. Established in 1924. Number of employees: 40. Number of internship applications received each year: 20.
Internships Available ▶ *3 education interns:* responsibilities include performing activities tailored to the needs of the department that plans museum programs. Candidates should have ability to work independently, computer skills, oral communication skills, organizational skills, strong interpersonal skills, knowledge of pre-Columbian, African, or contemporary American art (helpful). Duration is minimum of 2 months. Unpaid. Open to college sophomores, college juniors, college seniors, recent college graduates, graduate students, individuals reentering the workforce.
Benefits Formal training, names of contacts, on-the-job training, opportunity to attend seminars/workshops, willing to complete paperwork for educational credit, willing to provide letters of recommendation.
Contact Write or e-mail Ms. Susan Rosoff, Curator of Education. E-mail: srosoff@omart.org. No phone calls. In-person interview recommended (telephone interview accepted). Applicants must submit a letter of interest, resume, letter of recommendation. Applications are accepted continuously. World Wide Web: http://www.omart.org.

PASADENA MUSEUM OF HISTORY
470 West Walnut Street
Pasadena, California 91103

General Information Museum operating exhibition galleries, an historic 1906 mansion, a museum of Finnish folk art, and a library archive. Established in 1924. Number of employees: 13. Number of internship applications received each year: 5.
Internships Available ▶ *1 assistant educator:* responsibilities include assisting with ongoing educational programs, exhibition development, and updating docent training materials. Candidates should have ability to work independently, office skills, oral communication skills, organizational skills, personal interest in the field, strong interpersonal skills. Duration is flexible. Unpaid. Open to high school students, recent high school graduates, college freshmen, college sophomores, college juniors, college seniors, recent college graduates, graduate students, law students, career changers, individuals reentering the workforce. ▶ *1 assistant manager of membership:* responsibilities include data entry, mailings, scheduling of meetings and organizing events; some clerical work. Candidates should have ability to work independently, computer skills, office skills, organizational skills, self-motivation, written communication skills. Duration is flexible. Unpaid. Open to recent high school graduates, college freshmen, college sophomores, college juniors, college seniors, recent college graduates, graduate students, law students, career changers, individuals reentering the workforce. ▶ *1 collections intern:* responsibilities include assisting with research and care of extensive collection of circa 1900 art and antiques. Candidates should have ability to work independently, computer skills, knowledge of field, organizational skills, personal interest in the field, research skills. Duration is summer (two to three months). $3000 per duration of internship. Open to college freshmen, college sophomores, college juniors, college seniors, recent college graduates, graduate students, law students, career

changers, individuals reentering the workforce. ▶ *1 facilities/ operations assistant manager:* responsibilities include working with committees to schedule set-up of meetings and events; maintenance and organizing. Candidates should have ability to work independently, ability to work with others, organizational skills, self-motivation. Duration is flexible. Unpaid. Open to recent college graduates, graduate students, career changers, individuals reentering the workforce. ▶ *1 public relations intern:* responsibilities include developing/producing ads, flyers, promotional materials, database and news clippings; possible presentations. Candidates should have computer skills, editing skills, oral communication skills, personal interest in the field, strong interpersonal skills, writing skills. Duration is flexible. Unpaid. Open to recent high school graduates, college freshmen, college sophomores, college juniors, college seniors, individuals reentering the workforce. ▶ *1–3 research library interns:* responsibilities include assisting researchers in use of library; conservation of documents, books, and photographs; researching reference questions; and assisting in cataloging library and archival materials. Candidates should have ability to work with others, analytical skills, computer skills, office skills, research skills, self-motivation. Duration is 3–12 months. Unpaid. Open to high school seniors, recent high school graduates, college freshmen, college sophomores, college juniors, college seniors, recent college graduates, graduate students, law students, career changers, individuals reentering the workforce. International applications accepted.

Benefits Formal training, names of contacts, on-the-job training, willing to act as a professional reference, willing to complete paperwork for educational credit, willing to provide letters of recommendation.

Contact Write, fax, or e-mail Ardis Willwerth, Director of Exhibitions. Fax: 626-577-1662. E-mail: awillwerth@pasadenahistory.org. No phone calls. In-person interview required. Applicants must submit a letter of interest, resume, two personal references, two letters of recommendation. Application deadline: May 15 for summer. World Wide Web: http://www.pasadenahistory.org.

PENNSBURY MANOR
400 Pennsbury Memorial Road
Morrisville, Pennsylvania 19067

General Information Historic site of William Penn's reconstructed home. Established in 1939. Number of employees: 20. Unit of Pennsylvania Historical and Museum Commission, Harrisburg, Pennsylvania. Number of internship applications received each year: 10.

Internships Available ▶ *1 Alice Hemenway Memorial intern:* responsibilities include doing curatorial/research work, developing educational programs, or doing horticultural work. Candidates should have personal interest in the field, plan to pursue career in field. Duration is flexible. Paid. Open to college juniors, college seniors, recent college graduates, graduate students, career changers, individuals reentering the workforce. ▶ *1 PHMC intern:* responsibilities include doing research/curatorial work, developing educational programs, or doing horticultural work. Candidates should have college courses in field, knowledge of field, personal interest in the field, plan to pursue career in field. Duration is 12-15 weeks in summer. $6.50 per hour. Open to those who live in or attend school in Pennsylvania, must have student status for the semester before and after internship. ▶ *Interns (for credit or experience):* responsibilities include doing curatorial/research work, developing educational programs, or doing horticultural work. Candidates should have personal interest in the field. Duration is flexible. Unpaid. International applications accepted.

Benefits On-the-job training, willing to act as a professional reference, willing to complete paperwork for educational credit, willing to provide letters of recommendation.

Contact Write Mary Ellyn Kunz, Museum Educator. In-person interview recommended (telephone interview accepted). Applicants must submit a formal organization application, letter of interest, resume, academic transcripts. Application deadline: December 15 for summer positions; continuous for others. World Wide Web: http://www.Pennsburymanor.org.

PICTURED ROCKS NATIONAL LAKESHORE
PO Box 40
Munising, Michigan 49862-0040

General Information Recreation area that strives to protect natural and cultural resources. Established in 1966. Number of employees: 30. Unit of United States National Park Service, Washington, District of Columbia. Number of internship applications received each year: 20.

Internships Available ▶ *1 biological technician:* responsibilities include researching and documenting flora, fauna, and other natural resources. Candidates should have ability to work independently, computer skills, knowledge of field. Duration is 4–5 months. Unpaid. Open to college seniors, recent college graduates, graduate students.

Benefits Free housing, job counseling, names of contacts, on-the-job training, willing to complete paperwork for educational credit, willing to provide letters of recommendation.

Contact Write, call, or fax Administrative Manager. Phone: 906-387-2607. Fax: 906-387-4025. Applicants must submit a letter of interest, resume, academic transcripts, three personal references. Application deadline: February 1 for summer. World Wide Web: http://www.nps.gov/piro.

REYNOLDA HOUSE MUSEUM OF AMERICAN ART
2250 Reynolda Road, PO Box 11765
Winston-Salem, North Carolina 27116-1765

General Information Historic house/art museum emphasizing interdisciplinary learning in American art, music, and literature; collection includes American paintings, prints, and sculpture. Established in 1964. Number of employees: 49. Affiliate of Wake Forest University, Winston-Salem, North Carolina. Number of internship applications received each year: 75.

Internships Available ▶ *1 education assistant:* responsibilities include assisting coordinator of education in scheduling, leading tours, development and implementation of public programs, special research projects and planning trips. Candidates should have ability to work independently, college degree in related field, experience in the field, oral communication skills, plan to pursue career in field, strong interpersonal skills, written communication skills. Duration is September through August. Stipend of $15,000. Open to recent college graduates, graduate students. ▶ *3–4 education interns:* responsibilities include leading school tours, performing general research and an independent research project, assisting with operation of education department. Candidates should have ability to work independently, college courses in field, oral communication skills, personal interest in the field, research skills, written communication skills. Duration is 1 semester. Unpaid. Open to college juniors, college seniors, recent college graduates, graduate students. ▶ *1 public relations assistant:* responsibilities include assisting in writing, editing, and mailing press releases on museum events and exhibits; maintaining press kits; serving as liaison with local publications and organizations; and providing assistance to the public relations department. Candidates should have ability to work independently, computer skills, organizational skills, personal interest in the field, strong interpersonal skills, written communication skills. Duration is September to August. Stipend of $15,000. Open to recent college graduates, graduate students. ▶ *1 public relations intern (summer):* responsibilities include writing copy and conducting program outreach. Candidates should have computer skills, oral communication skills, organizational skills, personal interest in the field, self-motivation, written communication skills. Duration is one summer. Unpaid. Open to college juniors, college seniors, recent college graduates, graduate students, individuals reentering the workforce.

Benefits Job counseling, names of contacts, on-the-job training, opportunity to attend seminars/workshops, willing to act as a professional reference, willing to complete paperwork for educational credit, willing to provide letters of recommendation, health insurance (for year-long positions only).

Contact Write, call, fax, or e-mail Ms. Kathleen Hutton, Curator of Education. Phone: 336-725-5325 Ext. 115. Fax: 336-725-7475. E-mail: khutton@reynoldahouse.org. In-person interview recommended (telephone interview accepted). Applicants must submit a formal organization application, letter of interest, resume, two

Reynolda House Museum of American Art (continued)
letters of recommendation. Application deadline: May 1 for 1-year paid position, July 1 for fall, November 1 for January position, December 1 for spring. World Wide Web: http://www.reynoldahouse. org.

SAGAMORE INSTITUTE, INC.
PO Box 146, Sagamore Road
Raquette Lake, New York 13436

General Information Nonprofit National Landmark offering public tours and programs in regional culture and outdoor and environmental education. Established in 1972. Number of employees: 25. Number of internship applications received each year: 150.
Internships Available ▶ *3 acting/performance interpretation interns:* responsibilities include performing play (4 performances per week), interpreting camp's history, and leading public tours in character. Candidates should have ability to work with others, analytical skills, oral communication skills, acting skills, experience, and liberal arts education. Duration is June 15-September 5 and/or September 5-October 31. $150 per week. Open to college juniors, college seniors, recent college graduates, graduate students, career changers. ▶ *3 historic interpreters:* responsibilities include leading public tours of National Landmark; interpreting architectural, socio-economic, regional, and national land-use history. Candidates should have analytical skills, college courses in field, oral communication skills, strong interpersonal skills, strong leadership ability, writing skills. Duration is June 15-September 5 and/or September 5-October 31. $150 per week. Open to college juniors, college seniors, recent college graduates, graduate students, career changers, individuals reentering the workforce. ▶ *2 management interns:* responsibilities include assisting innkeeper, registrar, and bookshop/craft shop. Candidates should have ability to work independently, office skills, oral communication skills, organizational skills, strong interpersonal skills, retail experience desirable. Duration is June 15-September 5 and/or September 5-October 31. $150 per week. Open to college freshmen, college sophomores, college juniors, college seniors, recent college graduates, graduate students. ▶ *1 oral historian:* responsibilities include managing and developing archives of resident artisans and families and assisting with public interpretation. Candidates should have ability to work independently, declared college major in field, knowledge of field, oral communication skills, research skills, strong interpersonal skills. Duration is June 15-September 5 and/or September 5-October 31. $150 per week. Open to college juniors, college seniors, recent college graduates, graduate students. ▶ *2 outdoor environmental educators:* responsibilities include assisting guiding staff with environmental education program for wide variety of ages. Candidates should have college courses in field, experience in the field, oral communication skills, strong interpersonal skills, strong leadership ability, first aid/CPR certifications, water safety instruction/wilderness, first responder certification (desirable). Duration is June 15-September 5 and/or September 5-October 31. $150 per week. Open to college juniors, college seniors, recent college graduates, graduate students. ▶ *1 theater technician intern:* responsibilities include managing visitor's center performance space for multiple use, lighting/sound design and run, and some changeovers. Candidates should have ability to work independently, computer skills, oral communication skills, strong interpersonal skills, basic lighting and sound design/run skills, liberal arts education (preferred). Duration is June 15 to September 5 and/or September 5 to October 15. $150 per week. Open to college sophomores, college juniors, college seniors, recent college graduates, graduate students, career changers. ▶ *1 tour supervisor:* responsibilities include managing tours and training. Candidates should have analytical skills, college degree in related field, oral communication skills, strong interpersonal skills, strong leadership ability, writing skills, teaching/interpretive experience. Duration is June 15-September 5 and/or September 5-October 31. $150 per week. Open to recent college graduates, graduate students, career changers. International applications accepted.
Benefits Formal training, free housing, free meals, job counseling, on-the-job training, opportunity to attend seminars/workshops,

willing to act as a professional reference, willing to complete paperwork for educational credit, willing to provide letters of recommendation.
Contact Write, call, fax, e-mail, or through World Wide Web site Dr. Michael S. Wilson, Associate Director, 9 Kiwassa Road, Saranac Lake, New York 12983. Phone: 518-891-1718. Fax: 518-891-2561. E-mail: mwilson@northnet.org. In-person interview recommended (telephone interview accepted). Applicants must submit a letter of interest, resume, three personal references, one expository writing sample. Application deadline: May 1 for summer (mid-June to early September), July 31 for fall (September to October). World Wide Web: http://www.sagamore.org.

THE SAINT LOUIS ART MUSEUM
1 Fine Arts Drive, Forest Park
St. Louis, Missouri 63110-1380

General Information Comprehensive, free public art museum with diverse collection from cultures worldwide, strong educational programs, and a regular schedule of special exhibits. Established in 1879. Number of employees: 200. Number of internship applications received each year: 30.
Internships Available ▶ *1 museum Fellow:* responsibilities include working primarily with elementary students, as well as giving public lectures, researching and writing on collection and/or special exhibits, and other responsibilities contingent upon the Fellow's background and the Museum's current programs. Candidates should have ability to work with others, oral communication skills, plan to pursue career in field, research skills, major and/or at least 1 year graduate work in art education, art history, anthropology, museum studies, area studies, archaeology, or related field (no studio artists, except as an undergraduate field with graduate work in qualifying area). Duration is 1 year. $23,000 per year. Open to career changers, those with at least one year of graduate school by starting date. International applications accepted.
Benefits Names of contacts, opportunity to attend seminars/ workshops, willing to complete paperwork for educational credit, willing to provide letters of recommendation, health benefits, and travel reimbursement, assistance with resume preparation.
Contact Write, call, fax, e-mail, or through World Wide Web site Janet Hawkins, Human Resources. Phone: 314-655-5295. Fax: 314-721-4911. E-mail: jhawkins@slam.org. Applicants must submit a letter of interest, resume, academic transcripts, 1 writing sample in a humanities area (research positions), cover letter indicating exact dates and times of availability to work, names and phone numbers of 3 professional or academic references. Application deadline: March 1. World Wide Web: http://www.slam.org.

THE SMITHSONIAN ASSOCIATES
PO Box 23293
Washington, District of Columbia 20026-3293

General Information Educational and cultural outreach arm of the Smithsonian Institution that creates and administers special programs and educational activities as well as providing membership services. Number of employees: 100. Unit of Smithsonian Institution, Washington, District of Columbia. Number of internship applications received each year: 75.
Internships Available ▶ *Interns:* responsibilities include researching and planning educational programs for children and adults working in any of the other departments including public affairs, national outreach, marketing/membership, study tours, young associates, Discovery Theater, or administration. Candidates should have strong interest in TSA's mission and in educational programming. Duration is flexible. Unpaid. Open to college freshmen, college sophomores, college juniors, college seniors, graduate students. International applications accepted.
Benefits Opportunity to attend seminars/workshops, willing to complete paperwork for educational credit, hands-on learning experience.
Contact Write, call, e-mail, or through World Wide Web site Volunteer Coordinator. Phone: 202-786-3234. E-mail: volunof@tsa. si.edu. In-person interview recommended (telephone interview accepted). Applicants must submit a formal organization application, writing sample, cover letter explaining areas of interest and

proposed dates of availability, 2 letters of recommendation from professors. Applications are accepted continuously. World Wide Web: http://www.si.edu/tsa/rap.

SMITHSONIAN INSTITUTION, ANACOSTIA MUSEUM AND CENTER FOR AFRICAN AMERICAN HISTORY AND CULTURE
1901 Fort Place SE, MRC 520
Washington, District of Columbia 20020

General Information Museum and center devoted to increasing public understanding and awareness of the historical experiences and cultural expressions of people of African descent and heritage living in the Americas. Established in 1967. Number of employees: 25. Division of Smithsonian Institution, Washington, District of Columbia. Number of internship applications received each year: 60.
Internships Available ▶ *3–6 education, research, and public programs interns:* responsibilities include research, database acquisition, interacting with visitors, working Internet, online word processing, and occasional site visitation in Washington, D.C. area. Candidates should have ability to work independently, ability to work with others, analytical skills, computer skills, oral communication skills, organizational skills, research skills, self-motivation, written communication skills. Duration is 6 weeks to 2 months (possibility of extension). Unpaid. Open to college sophomores, college juniors, college seniors, graduate students. International applications accepted.
Benefits Names of contacts, on-the-job training, opportunity to attend seminars/workshops, willing to complete paperwork for educational credit, willing to provide letters of recommendation.
Contact Write, call, fax, or e-mail Toni Brady, Public Program Specialist, 1901 Fort Place, SE, Washington, District of Columbia 20020. Phone: 202-610-3370. Fax: 202-287-3183. E-mail: bradyt@am.si.edu. Applicants must submit a formal organization application, resume, academic transcripts, three letters of recommendation, statement of interest. Applications are accepted continuously. World Wide Web: http://www.si.edu.

SMITHSONIAN INSTITUTION, ARCHITECTURAL HISTORY AND HISTORIC PRESERVATION
Arts and Industries Building, Room 2263, MRC 417
Washington, District of Columbia 20560

General Information Office that integrates the architectural history of Smithsonian buildings with their preservation, conducts research on history of all Institution buildings, reviews proposed changes which affect historical integrity of buildings, and possesses holdings and records relating to the design and construction of Institution buildings. Established in 1986. Number of employees: 6. Division of Smithsonian Institution, Washington, District of Columbia. Number of internship applications received each year: 40.
Internships Available ▶ *1–2 architectural history interns:* responsibilities include integrating original documentation, such as correspondence and memoranda, architectural drawings, photographs, and other architectural materials to explore history of the Smithsonian buildings. Candidates should have ability to work independently, analytical skills, college courses in field, research skills, writing skills. Duration is 10 weeks. Position available as unpaid or at $2000 per duration of internship. Open to college freshmen, college sophomores, college juniors, college seniors, recent college graduates, graduate students. International applications accepted.
Benefits Job counseling, names of contacts, opportunity to attend seminars/workshops, willing to act as a professional reference, willing to complete paperwork for educational credit, willing to provide letters of recommendation.
Contact Write, call, or e-mail Sabina Wiedenhoeft, Intern Coordinator. Phone: 202-357-2571. Fax: 202-633-9324. E-mail: ahhpmx@sivm.si.edu. Applicants must submit a letter of interest, resume, academic transcripts, writing sample, two letters of recommendation. Application deadline: January 1 for spring, April 1 for summer. World Wide Web: http://www.si.edu.

SMITHSONIAN INSTITUTION ARCHIVES
Arts and Industries Building, 900 Jefferson Drive, SW, Room 2135
Washington, District of Columbia 20560-0414

General Information Repository for documents of historic value about the Smithsonian. Established in 1846. Number of employees: 25. Unit of Smithsonian Institution, Washington, District of Columbia.
Internships Available ▶ *Interns:* responsibilities include working as an apprentice to a staff specialist in the areas of archives, institutional history, oral history, or national collections. Candidates should have prior course work in American history, humanities, museum studies, collections management, or the sciences (desirable, but not a pre-requisite). Duration is negotiable. Position available as unpaid or paid. Open to college freshmen, college sophomores, college juniors, college seniors, graduate students. International applications accepted.
Benefits Formal training, on-the-job training, opportunity to attend seminars/workshops, willing to act as a professional reference, willing to complete paperwork for educational credit, willing to provide letters of recommendation, possible stipend.
Contact Write, call, fax, e-mail, or through World Wide Web site Tracy Elizabeth Robinson, Internship Coordinator, PO Box 37012, MRC 414, Washington, District of Columbia 20013-7012. Phone: 202-357-1420 Ext. 33. Fax: 202-357-2395. E-mail: osiaref@osia.si.edu. Applicants must submit a formal organization application, academic transcripts, two letters of recommendation, essay, application (which can be downloaded from Web site). Application deadline: March 15 for summer, July 1 for fall, November 1 for spring. World Wide Web: http://www.si.edu/archives.

SMITHSONIAN INSTITUTION, ARCHIVES OF AMERICAN ART
750 9th Street, NW, Suite 2200
Washington, District of Columbia 20560-0937

General Information Organization that collects the personal papers of American artists, art dealers, and critics and makes them available to historians and students. Established in 1954. Number of employees: 35. Unit of Smithsonian Institution, Washington, District of Columbia. Number of internship applications received each year: 80.
Internships Available ▶ *2 interns:* responsibilities include research on a variety of staff projects. Candidates should have ability to work independently, computer skills, organizational skills, research skills, self-motivation, written communication skills, background in American studies, art history, or library science. Duration is flexible. Unpaid. Open to college juniors, college seniors, recent college graduates, graduate students, career changers, individuals reentering the workforce. International applications accepted.
Benefits Formal training, job counseling, names of contacts, on-the-job training, opportunity to attend seminars/workshops, willing to act as a professional reference, willing to complete paperwork for educational credit, willing to provide letters of recommendation.
Contact Write or e-mail Dr. Liza Kirwin, Curator of Manuscripts. E-mail: kirwinl@aaa.si.edu. No phone calls. Applicants must submit a letter of interest, resume, academic transcripts, two letters of recommendation. Applications are accepted continuously. World Wide Web: http://www.aaa.si.edu.

SMITHSONIAN INSTITUTION, JOSEPH HENRY PAPERS
Arts and Industries Building 2188, 900 Jefferson Drive, SW
Washington, District of Columbia 20024

General Information Historical documentary editing project preparing a 11-volume selective letterpress edition of the papers of Joseph Henry (1797-1878), an eminent American physicist, professor at Princeton University, and the first Secretary of the Smithsonian Institution. Established in 1967. Number of employees:

Smithsonian Institution, Joseph Henry Papers (continued)

5. Division of Smithsonian Institution, Washington, District of Columbia. Number of internship applications received each year: 25.

Internships Available ▶ *1–3 research interns:* responsibilities include conducting historical research on selected or assigned topics relating to documents or themes to be treated in current or future volumes of *The Papers of Joseph Henry.* Candidates should have ability to work independently, ability to work with others, personal interest in the field, research skills, self-motivation, written communication skills. Duration is 2–3 months. Unpaid. Open to college sophomores, college juniors, college seniors, recent college graduates, graduate students, career changers. International applications accepted.

Benefits Health insurance, job counseling, opportunity to attend seminars/workshops, willing to act as a professional reference, willing to complete paperwork for educational credit, willing to provide letters of recommendation, use of research facilities, 20% discount at museum store; stipends may be available.

Contact Write, call, fax, e-mail, or through World Wide Web site Mr. Marc Rothenberg, Internship Coordinator/Editor, PO Box 37012, Washington, District of Columbia 20013-7012. Phone: 202-357-1421 Ext. 18. Fax: 202-786-2878. E-mail: rothenbergm@osia. si.edu. Applicants must submit a formal organization application, academic transcripts, writing sample, letter of recommendation. Application deadline: April 1 for summer. World Wide Web: http://www.si.edu/archives/ihd/jhp.

SMITHSONIAN INSTITUTION LIBRARIES
NHB 26A, MRC 154, 10th and Constitution Avenue, NW
Washington, District of Columbia 20560

General Information System of branch libraries that contains hard-bound volumes, rare books, current journals, and manuscripts. Unit of Smithsonian Institution, Washington, District of Columbia. Number of internship applications received each year: 50.

Internships Available ▶ *Collection management interns.* Duration is flexible. Unpaid. ▶ *Planning and administration interns.* Duration is flexible. Unpaid. ▶ *Research services interns.* Duration is flexible. Unpaid. ▶ *Systems and technical services interns.* Duration is flexible. Unpaid. Open to college freshmen, college sophomores, college juniors, college seniors, recent college graduates, graduate students. International applications accepted.

Benefits Job counseling, names of contacts, opportunity to attend seminars/workshops, willing to complete paperwork for educational credit, willing to provide letters of recommendation.

Contact Write, call, fax, e-mail, or through World Wide Web site Internship Coordinator, NHB 26A, MRC 154, 10th and Constitution Avenue, NW. Phone: 202-357-1851. Fax: 202-357-4532. E-mail: averav@si.edu. In-person interview recommended (telephone interview accepted). Applicants must submit a formal organization application, letter of interest, resume, academic transcripts. Applications are accepted continuously. World Wide Web: http://www.sil.si.edu.

SMITHSONIAN INSTITUTION, NATIONAL MUSEUM OF AFRICAN ART
950 Independence Avenue, SW
Washington, District of Columbia 20560-0708

General Information Major research and reference center and the only national museum in the United States dedicated to the collection, exhibition, conservation, and study of African art. Established in 1978. Number of employees: 55. Unit of Smithsonian Institution, Washington, District of Columbia. Number of internship applications received each year: 50.

Internships Available ▶ *Interns:* responsibilities include assisting museum staff in the following departments: administration, conservation, curatorial, education, exhibition and design, photo archives, public affairs, or registration. Candidates should have ability to work with others, plan to pursue career in field, research skills, self-motivation, writing skills, background in art history, museum studies, anthropology, or related disciplines. Duration is 10-week minimum (20 hours per week) in fall, spring or summer. Unpaid. Open to college juniors, college seniors, recent college graduates, graduate students, individuals interested in exploring museum professions. International applications accepted.

Benefits On-the-job training, willing to complete paperwork for educational credit, willing to provide letters of recommendation.

Contact Write, call, fax, or e-mail Dr. Veronika Jenke, Internship Coordinator, PO Box 37012, National Museum of African Art, 0708, Washington, District of Columbia 20013-7012. Phone: 202-357-4600 Ext. 225. Fax: 202-357-4879. E-mail: jenkev@nmafa.si. edu. Telephone interview required. Applicants must submit a formal organization application, letter of interest, resume, academic transcripts, personal reference, two letters of recommendation, essay. Application deadline: February 15 for summer, June 15 for fall, October 15 for spring. World Wide Web: http://www.si.edu/nmafa/.

SMITHSONIAN INSTITUTION, NATIONAL MUSEUM OF NATURAL HISTORY
10th Street and Constitution Avenue, NW
Washington, District of Columbia 20560-0166

General Information Museum that employs curatorial and scientific staff to collect specimens, conduct research, and study in the natural sciences. Established in 1910. Number of employees: 550. Unit of Smithsonian Institution, Washington, District of Columbia. Number of internship applications received each year: 200.

Internships Available ▶ *Natural science interns:* responsibilities include beginning and completing a project assigned and supervised by curator or museum specialist. Candidates should have ability to work independently, ability to work with others, oral communication skills, personal interest in the field, written communication skills. Duration is 1–12 months. Unpaid. Open to high school seniors, recent high school graduates, college freshmen, college sophomores, college juniors, college seniors, recent college graduates, individuals reentering the workforce. ▶ *20 research training program interns.* Candidates should have college courses in field, knowledge of field, personal interest in the field, plan to pursue career in field. Duration is 10 weeks. $3000 stipend plus housing and travel allowance. Open to college freshmen, college sophomores, college juniors. International applications accepted.

Benefits Names of contacts, on-the-job training, opportunity to attend seminars/workshops, willing to act as a professional reference, willing to complete paperwork for educational credit, willing to provide letters of recommendation.

Contact Write, fax, e-mail, or through World Wide Web site Mary Sangrey, Program Director, PO Box 37012, Washington, District of Columbia 20023-7012. Phone: 202-357-4548. Fax: 202-786-2563. E-mail: sangrey.mary@nmnh.si.edu. Applicants must submit a formal organization application, two letters of recommendation, cover letter, academic transcripts (desirable). Application deadline: February 1. World Wide Web: http://www.nmnh.si.edu/rtp/.

SMITHSONIAN INSTITUTION, NATIONAL PORTRAIT GALLERY
PO Box 37012, Victor Building, Suite 8300, MRC 973
Washington, District of Columbia 20013-7012

General Information Free public museum for the exhibition and study of portraiture and statuary depicting men and women who have made significant contributions to the history, development, and culture of the people of the United States and the artists who created such works. Established in 1962. Number of employees: 100. Unit of Smithsonian Institution, Washington, District of Columbia. Number of internship applications received each year: 100.

Internships Available ▶ *15–20 interns:* responsibilities include assistance with varied projects depending on needs of the departments as well as intern's skills and interests. Candidates should have computer skills, editing skills, knowledge of field, oral communication skills, research skills, writing skills. Duration is 2-3 months (20 hours per week). Unpaid. Open to college freshmen, college sophomores, college juniors, college seniors, recent college graduates, graduate students. International applications accepted.

Benefits Opportunity to attend seminars/workshops, willing to complete paperwork for educational credit, willing to provide letters of recommendation.

Contact Write, call, fax, or e-mail Shirlee Lampkin, Intern Coordinator, Education Department. Phone: 202-275-1811. Fax: 202-275-1904. E-mail: lampkins@npg.si.edu. Applicants must submit a formal organization application, resume, academic transcripts, two letters of recommendation, 500-1000 word essay. Application deadline: March 31 for summer; continuous for other times of year. World Wide Web: http://www.npg.si.edu/.

SMITHSONIAN INSTITUTION, NATIONAL POSTAL MUSEUM
2 Massachusetts Avenue, NE
Washington, District of Columbia 20560-0570

General Information One of the largest and most comprehensive collections of stamps and philatelic materials in the world, housing six major galleries. Established in 1993. Number of employees: 25. Unit of Smithsonian Institution, Washington, District of Columbia. Number of internship applications received each year: 24.

Internships Available ▶ *10 interns:* responsibilities include working with professional staff on current projects relating to exhibits, education, collections, curatorship, and membership/public affairs. Candidates should have ability to work with others, computer skills, office skills, oral communication skills, personal interest in the field, research skills. Duration is flexible. Unpaid. Open to college freshmen, college sophomores, college juniors, college seniors, recent college graduates, graduate students, some high school students. International applications accepted.

Benefits Job counseling, names of contacts, on-the-job training, opportunity to attend seminars/workshops, willing to act as a professional reference, willing to complete paperwork for educational credit, willing to provide letters of recommendation.

Contact Write, fax, or through World Wide Web site Intern Coordinator, Education Department, 2 Massachusetts Avenue, NE, Washington, District of Columbia 20560-0570. Fax: 202-633-9393. No phone calls. Applicants must submit a formal organization application, resume, academic transcripts, two letters of recommendation, essay. Applications are accepted continuously. World Wide Web: http://www.si.edu/postal/.

SMITHSONIAN INSTITUTION, OFFICE OF IMAGING, PRINTING, AND PHOTOGRAPHIC SERVICES
PO Box 37012, AHB1040, MRC 605
Washington, District of Columbia 20013-7012

General Information Central photographic unit in support of the Smithsonian's research and publications, for museum's collections, for documenting the Institution's history, and for the needs of the public. Established in 1846. Number of employees: 22. Division of Smithsonian Institution, Washington, District of Columbia. Number of internship applications received each year: 50.

Internships Available ▶ *Digital imaging interns:* responsibilities include digitizing photographs used in various departments throughout the museum. Candidates should have knowledge of scanners, digitizing, Adobe PhotoShop 6 or 7, and Web pages. Duration is 8–20 weeks. Unpaid. Open to college freshmen, college sophomores, college juniors, college seniors, recent college graduates, graduate students, law students, career changers. ▶ *Digital library archives interns:* responsibilities include editing, cataloging, and preparing photographic images for scanning, converting, and linking to image databases. Candidates should have knowledge of photography, Adobe PhotoShop 6 or 7, and archival procedures. Duration is minimum 30 hours per week. Unpaid. Open to college freshmen, college sophomores, college juniors, college seniors, recent college graduates, graduate students, law students, career changers. ▶ *Electronic imaging interns:* responsibilities include assisting staff in scanning photographic images and cataloging them into the master database, digital restoration, retouching, printing, and conversion of photo CD images. Candidates should have ability to work independently, analytical

skills, editing skills, office skills, oral communication skills, personal interest in the field, research skills, strong interpersonal skills, strong leadership ability, writing skills, knowledge of professional cameras and lighting equipment, knowledge of Adobe PhotoShop 6 or 7 and Macintosh computers. Duration is 8–20 weeks. Unpaid. Open to college freshmen, college sophomores, college juniors, college seniors, recent college graduates, graduate students, law students, career changers, individuals reentering the workforce. ▶ *Museum photography interns:* responsibilities include assisting staff photographers with photographing objects including studio, documentary, public relations, and use of professional digital equipment. Candidates should have experience with professional cameras, lighting equipment and Adobe PhotoShop 6 or 7. Duration is 4 to 20 weeks (minimum 30 hours per week). Unpaid. Open to college freshmen, college sophomores, college juniors, college seniors, recent college graduates, graduate students, law students, career changers. International applications accepted.

Benefits Job counseling, on-the-job training, opportunity to attend seminars/workshops, willing to act as a professional reference, willing to complete paperwork for educational credit, willing to provide letters of recommendation.

Contact Write, call, fax, or e-mail Suzanne McLaughlin, Intern Coordinator. Phone: 202-357-1606. Fax: 202-786-2851. E-mail: nmahintern@si.edu. Applicants must submit a formal organization application, academic transcripts, two personal references, portfolio on Web site or CD. Application deadline: February 15 for summer, July 15 for fall, October 15 for winter. World Wide Web: http://www.photo2.si.edu.

THE SOCIETY FOR THE PRESERVATION OF NEW ENGLAND ANTIQUITIES
141 Cambridge Street
Boston, Massachusetts 02114

General Information Museum of cultural history that preserves, interprets, and collects buildings, landscapes, and objects reflecting New England life from the 17th-century to the present. Established in 1910. Number of employees: 100. Number of internship applications received each year: 50.

Internships Available ▶ *2–6 interns:* responsibilities include working with collections, archaeology, archives, education, public relations, and research departments on current and special projects in museum interpretation, social history, architectural history, and landscape and agricultural history. Candidates should have ability to work independently, analytical skills, college courses in field, computer skills, knowledge of field, oral communication skills, organizational skills, personal interest in the field, plan to pursue career in field, research skills, self-motivation, strong interpersonal skills, writing skills. Duration is flexible. Unpaid. Open to college sophomores, college juniors, college seniors, recent college graduates, graduate students, career changers, individuals reentering the workforce. International applications accepted.

Benefits On-the-job training, opportunity to attend seminars/workshops, willing to act as a professional reference, willing to complete paperwork for educational credit, willing to provide letters of recommendation.

Contact Write, call, fax, e-mail, or through World Wide Web site Ms. Susan L. Porter, Research Manager. Phone: 617-227-3957 Ext. 251. Fax: 617-227-3956. E-mail: sporter@spnea.org. In-person interview recommended (telephone interview accepted). Applicants must submit a formal organization application, letter of interest, resume, three personal references, three letters of recommendation. Application deadline: May 1 for summer; continuous for other times of year. World Wide Web: http://www.spnea.org.

SOUTHERN OHIO MUSEUM AND CULTURAL CENTER
PO Box 990, 825 Gallia Street
Portsmouth, Ohio 45662

General Information Art museum that presents 11-month schedule of temporary exhibits, primarily in the visual arts in addition to performing arts and films; offers classes, workshops, and special programs. Established in 1979. Number of employees: 11. Number of internship applications received each year: 2.

Southern Ohio Museum and Cultural Center (continued)

Internships Available ▶ *1 exhibit curator:* responsibilities include assisting in organizing exhibits, making contacts, and following up with paperwork. Candidates should have computer skills, oral communication skills, organizational skills, research skills, strong interpersonal skills, written communication skills. Duration is 3 months minimum. Unpaid. Open to recent college graduates, graduate students. ▶ *1 history curatorial assistant (photography):* responsibilities include scanning and digitizing historical photographs and organizing into categories, working on documentation. Candidates should have ability to work independently, computer skills, organizational skills, research skills, self-motivation, strong interpersonal skills, written communication skills. Duration is 3 months. Unpaid. Open to college seniors, recent college graduates, graduate students. ▶ *1 public relations assistant:* responsibilities include assisting in publicizing museum programs, preparation of newsletters and news releases, and some graphic arts work. Candidates should have computer skills, editing skills, oral communication skills, strong interpersonal skills, writing skills. Duration is 3 months minimum. Unpaid. Open to college juniors, college seniors, recent college graduates, graduate students. International applications accepted.

Benefits Names of contacts, on-the-job training, opportunity to attend seminars/workshops, possible full-time employment, willing to complete paperwork for educational credit, willing to provide letters of recommendation.

Contact Write, fax, or e-mail Ms. Kay Bouyack, Administrative Director, Portsmouth, Ohio. Fax: 740-354-4090. E-mail: museum82@falcon1.net. No phone calls. In-person interview required. Applicants must submit a letter of interest, resume, two personal references, letter of recommendation. Applications are accepted continuously.

SOUTH STREET SEAPORT MUSEUM
207 Front Street
New York, New York 10038

General Information Maritime history museum, located in a 12-block historic district in downtown Manhattan, that interprets the role of the seaport in the development of the city, the state, and the nation through education programs, exhibitions, and the preservation of buildings and ships. Established in 1967. Number of employees: 100. Number of internship applications received each year: 150.

Internships Available ▶ *1–2 collections management interns:* responsibilities include artifact cataloging, re-housing and research, maintaining artifact files and home computer work. Candidates should have ability to work independently, ability to work with others, computer skills, organizational skills, personal interest in the field, research skills. Duration is flexible (one or more days per week). Unpaid. Open to college seniors, recent college graduates, graduate students, career changers. ▶ *2–4 curatorial assistants:* responsibilities include assisting curators with research; development and implementation of new exhibits. Candidates should have knowledge of field, personal interest in the field, research skills, strong interpersonal skills, written communication skills. Duration is flexible (weekdays). Unpaid. Open to recent high school graduates, college sophomores, college juniors, college seniors, recent college graduates, graduate students, law students, career changers, individuals reentering the workforce. ▶ *1–2 development interns:* responsibilities include providing research support to busy fund-raising office; assisting with grant applications and reports. Candidates should have ability to work independently, ability to work with others, office skills, personal interest in the field, research skills, written communication skills. Duration is flexible (2-3 half days per week). Unpaid. Open to college juniors, college seniors, recent college graduates, graduate students, career changers, individuals reentering the workforce. ▶ *5–10 docents/educators:* responsibilities include giving tours of ships/galleries and historic district; giving tours of new building to school groups; answering questions and providing information for visitors to new galleries. Candidates should have ability to work independently, oral communication skills, personal interest in the field, self-motivation, strong interpersonal skills. Duration is flexible. Unpaid. Open to college freshmen, college sophomores, college juniors, college seniors, recent college graduates, graduate students, law

students, career changers, individuals reentering the workforce, retirees, senior citizens. ▶ *Interns:* responsibilities include working in any of the following areas: archaeology, education, fundraising/development, maritime crafts, marketing/special events, printing and stationers shop, schooner *Lettie G. Howard*, ship restoration and maintenance, collections management, exhibit research, library, membership, publications, tour marketing, schooner *Pioneer*, boat building, volunteer department, and Elderhostel. Candidates should have ability to work independently, ability to work with others, computer skills, office skills, personal interest in the field, written communication skills. Duration is flexible. Unpaid. Open to high school students, recent high school graduates, college freshmen, college sophomores, college juniors, college seniors, recent college graduates, graduate students, career changers, individuals reentering the workforce, must be at least 16 years old. ▶ *1–4 schooner crew interns:* responsibilities include acting as deck hands on one or both of the vessels including deckwork underway duties, watch keeping, and ship maintenance. Candidates should have ability to work with others, oral communication skills, personal interest in the field, self-motivation, physical agility. Duration is flexible. Unpaid. Open to high school students, recent high school graduates, college freshmen, college sophomores, college juniors, college seniors, recent college graduates, graduate students, law students, career changers, individuals reentering the workforce, must be at least 16 years old. ▶ *2–4 wet lab interns:* responsibilities include guiding visitors through wet lab during open hours; feeding and care of animals; and maintenance of wet lab aquarium. Candidates should have ability to work independently, oral communication skills, personal interest in the field, knowledge of biology helpful. Duration is April 15 to October 15 (flexible). Unpaid. Open to high school students, recent high school graduates, college freshmen, college sophomores, college juniors, college seniors, recent college graduates, any individual willing to be trained (must be 16 years old or over). International applications accepted.

Benefits Formal training, on-the-job training, opportunity to attend seminars/workshops, possible full-time employment, willing to act as a professional reference, willing to complete paperwork for educational credit, willing to provide letters of recommendation.

Contact Write, call, fax, or e-mail Richard Dorfman, Director of Volunteers and Community Outreach. Phone: 212-748-8727. Fax: 212-748-8610. E-mail: rdorfman@southstseaport.org. In-person interview required. Applicants must submit a letter of interest, resume. Applications are accepted continuously. World Wide Web: http://www.southstseaport.org.

SPRINGFIELD ARMORY NATIONAL HISTORIC SITE
1 Armory Square
Springfield, Massachusetts 01105-1299

General Information Site commemorating the critical role Springfield Armory played in the nation's military history; preserves, researches, and interprets the firearms collection, archives, library, and structures; provides the story of technological developments of the Armory complex and their impacts on civilization. Established in 1974. Number of employees: 14. Unit of National Park Service, Washington, District of Columbia. Number of internship applications received each year: 10.

Internships Available ▶ *1–2 archives summer interns:* responsibilities include organizing, boxing, and cataloging archives; housekeeping and environmental monitoring. Candidates should have analytical skills, computer skills, oral communication skills, organizational skills, research skills, written communication skills. Duration is 12 weeks (minimum of 30 hours per week). Unpaid. Open to college freshmen, college sophomores, college juniors, college seniors. ▶ *1–2 collections management interns:* responsibilities include environmental monitoring; housekeeping, including cleaning exhibits; using the collection management database, Automated National Catalog System (ANCS). Candidates should have ability to work with others, computer skills, editing skills, self-motivation, writing skills. Duration is 2 semesters (minimum of 240 hours). Position available as unpaid or paid. Open to college juniors, college seniors, recent college graduates, graduate students, law students, career changers, individuals reentering the workforce.

► *1–2 conservation interns:* responsibilities include rehousing archaeological collection; cleaning and housing paper, metal, and wood materials. Candidates should have ability to work with others, computer skills, editing skills, self-motivation, writing skills. Duration is 1 semester. Position available as unpaid or paid. Open to college juniors, college seniors, recent college graduates, graduate students, law students, career changers, individuals reentering the workforce. ► *1–3 interpretive program assistants:* responsibilities include assisting with development of museum exhibits and public programs, testing curriculum-based education programs. Candidates should have ability to work independently, oral communication skills, self-motivation, strong interpersonal skills, writing skills. Duration is 120 hours. Position available as unpaid or paid. Open to college juniors, college seniors, recent college graduates, graduate students, law students, career changers, individuals reentering the workforce. ► *4–6 library/archives interns:* responsibilities include cataloging new books, rehousing archives, participating in housekeeping, and making phase boxes for historic books. Candidates should have analytical skills, computer skills, oral communication skills, organizational skills, research skills, written communication skills. Duration is 1 semester (minimum of 120 hours). Unpaid. Open to college juniors, college seniors, recent college graduates, graduate students, law students, career changers, individuals reentering the workforce. ► *1–2 maintenance resource evaluators:* responsibilities include gathering and entering data into the inventory assessment program, entering reports and evaluating the maintenance program. Candidates should have ability to work with others, computer skills, editing skills, self-motivation, writing skills. Duration is 8–10 weeks. Position available as unpaid or paid. Open to college juniors, college seniors, recent college graduates, graduate students, law students, career changers, individuals reentering the workforce. ► *1 market plan developer:* responsibilities include creating a plan to publicize the Historic Site and available services and programs. Candidates should have oral communication skills, organizational skills, strong interpersonal skills, strong leadership ability, writing skills. Duration is flexible (minimum of 10 hours per week). Position available as unpaid or paid. Open to college juniors, college seniors, recent college graduates, graduate students, law students, career changers, individuals reentering the workforce. ► *4–6 oral history interns:* responsibilities include transcribing, compiling, and cataloging information on the 100 oral histories into the parks database; intern will need to read *Transcribing and Editing Oral History* by Willa K. Baum. Candidates should have ability to work independently, computer skills, editing skills, knowledge of field, organizational skills, ability to understand elderly voices on audio tape. Duration is 1 semester (minimum of 120 hours). Unpaid. Open to college juniors, college seniors, recent college graduates, graduate students, law students, career changers, individuals reentering the workforce. ► *1 pre-program intern (art conservation):* responsibilities include practicing a group of completed conservation treatments, including all relevant documentation materials, organized for portfolio presentation. Candidates should have ability to work with others, analytical skills, computer skills, knowledge of field, plan to pursue career in field, research skills, written communication skills. Duration is 8–10 weeks. Unpaid. Open to applicants to graduate programs in art conservation. ► *1 promotional development intern:* responsibilities include creating brochures, flyers, and other non-personal materials for the public and schools; researching and developing concepts with park rangers. Candidates should have ability to work independently, computer skills, knowledge of field, personal interest in the field, strong leadership ability, writing skills. Duration is flexible (minimum of 10 hours per week). Unpaid. Open to college juniors, college seniors, recent college graduates, graduate students, law students, career changers, individuals reentering the workforce. ► *1–2 research assistants:* responsibilities include researching publications, archives, microfilm, or newspapers for park staff or outside researchers. Candidates should have ability to work independently, ability to work with others, analytical skills, computer skills, research skills, written communication skills. Duration is 1 semester (minimum of 120 hours). Unpaid. Open to college juniors, college seniors, recent college graduates, graduate students, law students, career changers, individuals reentering the workforce. ► *1 summer intern (art conservation):* responsibilities include full participation in the routine activities of a small objects conservation cab; emphasis will be on treatment, documentation, and preventive conservation; research opportunities also possible. Candidates should have ability to work independently, ability to work with others, computer skills, declared college major in field, plan to pursue career in field, written communication skills. Duration is 8–10 weeks. Unpaid. Open to graduate students in art conservation. International applications accepted.

Benefits Formal training, names of contacts, on-the-job training, opportunity to attend seminars/workshops, willing to act as a professional reference, willing to complete paperwork for educational credit, willing to provide letters of recommendation, worker's compensation, local travel expenses (mileage).

Contact Write, call, fax, e-mail, or through World Wide Web site Joanne Gangi, Chief of Visitor Services, Volunteer Parks Program Coordinator. Phone: 413-734-8551. Fax: 413-747-8062. E-mail: joanne_gangi@nps.gov. In-person interview recommended (telephone interview accepted). Applicants must submit a letter of interest, resume, writing sample, two personal references, security background check required. Application deadline: July 1 for fall and January winter break, November 1 for spring and summer. World Wide Web: http://www.nps.gov/spar.

SPRINGFIELD LIBRARY AND MUSEUMS
220 State Street
Springfield, Massachusetts 01103

General Information Administrative organization for the Springfield libraries and 4 separate museums. Established in 1857. Number of employees: 275. Number of internship applications received each year: 10.

Internships Available ► *Archives interns:* responsibilities include organizing and processing small collection and creating a finding aid to it, working under the supervision of the archives staff. Candidates should have ability to work independently, organizational skills, research skills, self-motivation, written communication skills. Duration is usually 120 hours per semester. Unpaid. Open to college juniors, college seniors, graduate students. ► *1 curatorial assistant (art):* responsibilities include assisting in various duties depending on intern's interest. Candidates should have ability to work independently, ability to work with others, computer skills, declared college major in field, knowledge of field, oral communication skills, plan to pursue career in field, research skills, written communication skills. Duration is one semester (flexible). Unpaid. Open to college seniors, graduate students. ► *1 curatorial assistant (science):* responsibilities include cataloguing natural history collections, exhibit preparation, possibly some animal care. Candidates should have ability to work independently, ability to work with others, computer skills, declared college major in field, knowledge of field, plan to pursue career in field. Duration is 1 semester. Unpaid. Open to college juniors, college seniors, graduate students. ► *1–2 development interns:* responsibilities include grant research and grant writing; corporate sponsor research and proposal drafting; assistance with mailings, membership solicitations, and special fund-raising event. Candidates should have ability to work independently, research skills, strong interpersonal skills, writing skills. Duration is January-May, possibly June-August. Unpaid. Open to college freshmen, college sophomores, college juniors, college seniors, recent college graduates, graduate students, career changers, individuals reentering the workforce. ► *1 drawings into DeltaCad intern (Science Museum):* responsibilities include transferring hand-drawn museum floor layouts into computer generated drawings using the DeltaCad program. Candidates should have ability to work independently, computer skills, oral communication skills, personal interest in the field, written communication skills. Duration is flexible. Unpaid. Open to college freshmen, college sophomores, college juniors, college seniors, recent college graduates, graduate students, career changers. ► *1–2 museum preparation interns (Science Museum):* responsibilities include assisting the exhibit preparator in museum work ranging from permanent exhibit maintenance to traveling exhibition installation. Candidates should have ability to work with others, oral communication skills, personal interest in the field, self-motivation. Duration is flexible. Unpaid. Open to college freshmen, college sophomores, college juniors, college seniors, recent

Springfield Library and Museums (continued)

college graduates, graduate students, career changers. ▶ *1 public relations intern:* responsibilities include writing press releases, writing for a variety of audiences, and performing various other publicity-related duties. Candidates should have ability to work independently, college courses in field, computer skills, editing skills, oral communication skills, organizational skills, plan to pursue career in field, research skills, strong interpersonal skills, writing skills. Duration is 1 semester. Unpaid. Open to college seniors, graduate students.

Benefits Job counseling, on-the-job training, willing to act as a professional reference, willing to complete paperwork for educational credit, willing to provide letters of recommendation.

Contact Write or e-mail Mary Morisi, Public Relations Secretary. Fax: 413-263-6807. E-mail: mmorisi@spfldlibmus.org. No phone calls. In-person interview required. Applicants must submit a letter of interest, resume, academic transcripts, writing sample may be required. Application deadline: March 1 for summer, June 1 for fall, November 1 for spring. World Wide Web: http://www. quadrangle.org.

STATEN ISLAND INSTITUTE OF ARTS AND SCIENCES
75 Stuyvesant Place
Staten Island, New York 10301-1998

General Information Organization that focuses on Staten Island and its people and has strong collections in these subjects. Established in 1881. Number of employees: 32. Number of internship applications received each year: 35.

Internships Available ▶ *2 archival assistants:* responsibilities include working on special research projects requiring direct involvement with original material (including artifacts and archival holdings such as oral and written personal histories, documents, photographs, leaflets, fliers, and memoirs); identifying and locating appropriate artifacts, archival holdings, and materials relating to the material culture and contributions of working-class people on Staten Island. Candidates should have ability to work independently, ability to work with others, personal interest in the field, research skills, self-motivation, writing skills. Duration is 15 weeks. Unpaid. Open to high school seniors, recent high school graduates, college freshmen, college sophomores, college juniors, college seniors, recent college graduates, individuals reentering the workforce. ▶ *1 art collections intern:* responsibilities include inventorying, cataloging, and storing art collection objects, entering art collection objects into database, marking museum objects with permanent identification numbers, tracking incoming donations to the permanent collection, completing condition reports for incoming loans, updating incoming loan files, assisting with installation and removal of exhibits, and other assigned collections-related duties. Candidates should have ability to work independently, ability to work with others, organizational skills, personal interest in the field, research skills, self-motivation. Duration is flexible, 2 days per week (4 hours per day preferred). Unpaid. Open to college freshmen, college sophomores, college juniors, college seniors. ▶ *1 marketing intern:* responsibilities include assisting in preparation of media and newsletter mailings, distribution of printed materials, and direct marketing of group programs and public events through contact with tourism professionals and community groups. Candidates should have ability to work with others, computer skills, editing skills, organizational skills, personal interest in the field, self-motivation, writing skills. Duration is flexible. Unpaid. Open to college freshmen, college sophomores, college juniors, college seniors, recent college graduates, graduate students, career changers, individuals reentering the workforce. ▶ *2 science assistants:* responsibilities include performing various duties within the science department; possible areas of work include archaeology collection, entomology, botany, zoology, data entry, geology, Staten Island paleontology, mounted bird collection, herbarium, and myxomycete collection. Candidates should have ability to work independently, college courses in field, computer skills, knowledge of field, personal interest in the field, research skills, self-motivation. Duration is flexible. Unpaid. Open

to college freshmen, college sophomores, college juniors, college seniors, recent college graduates. International applications accepted.

Benefits Formal training, job counseling, on-the-job training, opportunity to attend seminars/workshops, possible full-time employment, willing to act as a professional reference, willing to complete paperwork for educational credit, willing to provide letters of recommendation.

Contact Write, call, fax, or e-mail Bart Bland, Director of Exhibitions. Phone: 718-727-1135. Fax: 718-273-5683. E-mail: blandsiias@aol.com. In-person interview required. Applicants must submit a letter of interest, resume, academic transcripts. Applications are accepted continuously. World Wide Web: http://www. siiasmuseum.org.

STATEN ISLAND ZOO, EDUCATION DEPARTMENT
614 Broadway
Staten Island, New York 10310

General Information Zoological park focusing on the goals of conservation, education, and recreation in order to present exotic animals to the public. Established in 1936. Number of employees: 50. Unit of Staten Island Zoo, Staten Island, New York. Number of internship applications received each year: 50.

Internships Available ▶ *1 camp art teacher:* responsibilities include teaching art programs and creating curriculum. Candidates should have ability to work independently, experience in the field, plan to pursue career in field, strong interpersonal skills, college courses in education or art. Duration is 3 months. $250 per week. Open to college juniors, college seniors. ▶ *1 camp recreation teacher:* responsibilities include teaching recreation and creating curriculum. Candidates should have ability to work independently, experience in the field, personal interest in the field, strong interpersonal skills. Duration is 3 months. $250 per week. Open to college juniors, college seniors, recent college graduates. ▶ *1 camp science teacher:* responsibilities include teaching science programs and creating curriculum. Candidates should have ability to work with others, experience in the field, oral communication skills, plan to pursue career in field, ability to work with animals. Duration is 3 months. $250 per week. Open to college juniors, college seniors, recent college graduates. ▶ *1 zoomobile teacher:* responsibilities include teaching outreach programs with live animals and feeding and taking care of animals in education department. Candidates should have ability to work independently, college degree in related field, experience in the field, strong interpersonal skills, ability to work with animals. Duration is 9 months. $375 per week. Open to recent college graduates, graduate students. International applications accepted.

Benefits Formal training, job counseling, names of contacts, on-the-job training, opportunity to attend seminars/workshops, willing to act as a professional reference, willing to complete paperwork for educational credit, willing to provide letters of recommendation.

Contact Write, call, or fax Ella Viola, Assistant Director of Education. Phone: 718-442-3101 Ext. 37. Fax: 718-981-8711. In-person interview recommended (telephone interview accepted). Applicants must submit a letter of interest, resume. Application deadline: May 24 for summer, August 23 for fall. World Wide Web: http://www.statenislandzoo.org.

STEPHENSON COUNTY HISTORICAL SOCIETY
1440 South Carroll Avenue
Freeport, Illinois 61032

General Information Historical society and museum. Established in 1944. Number of employees: 1. Number of internship applications received each year: 5.

Internships Available ▶ *Accessioning assistants:* responsibilities include describing new items in the collection and rating their condition, entering information into database; additional research may be necessary to accurately describe some items. Candidates should have computer skills, personal interest in the field, research skills, self-motivation, written communication skills, attention to detail, knowledge of antiques and historical artifacts (helpful). Duration is flexible. Unpaid. Open to high school students, recent high school graduates, college freshmen, college sophomores, college juniors, college seniors, recent college graduates, graduate students, law students, career changers, individuals reentering the workforce. ► *Fall or spring school tour guides:* responsibilities include specializing in the Victorian Home, School House, Log Cabin, or Farm Museum (intern's choice); guide will be taught touring and educational techniques along with ways to gear history to children. Candidates should have oral communication skills, personal interest in the field, strong interpersonal skills, strong leadership ability. Duration is flexible. Unpaid. Open to high school students, recent high school graduates, college freshmen, college sophomores, college juniors, college seniors, recent college graduates, graduate students, law students, career changers, individuals reentering the workforce. ► *Museum gift shop assistant:* responsibilities include helping staff the gift shop, stocking shelves, ordering supplies, advertising, plus answering visitor's questions and showing them the Victorian home decorated for Christmas. Candidates should have oral communication skills, organizational skills, personal interest in the field, written communication skills. Duration is November-December (flexible). Unpaid. Open to high school students, recent high school graduates, college freshmen, college sophomores, college juniors, college seniors, recent college graduates, graduate students, law students, career changers, individuals reentering the workforce. ► *Special project or research interns:* responsibilities include intern's project or research ideas that would benefit society. Candidates should have organizational skills, personal interest in the field, research skills, self-motivation. Duration is flexible. Unpaid. Open to high school students, recent high school graduates, college freshmen, college sophomores, college juniors, college seniors, recent college graduates, graduate students, law students, career changers, individuals reentering the workforce. ► *Summer assistant to the director:* responsibilities include helping the director in planning special events, guiding tours, accessioning collection pieces, marketing and promoting the museum, and/or daily activities of operating a museum; may be assigned a special project, event, or exhibit or his/her own. Candidates should have ability to work with others, office skills, oral communication skills, personal interest in the field, research skills, written communication skills. Duration is May to October (flexible). Unpaid. Open to high school students, recent high school graduates, college freshmen, college sophomores, college juniors, college seniors, graduate students, law students, career changers, individuals reentering the workforce.

Benefits On-the-job training, willing to act as a professional reference, willing to complete paperwork for educational credit, willing to provide letters of recommendation, membership in Historical Society.

Contact Write, fax, or e-mail Suzy Beggin, Executive Director. Phone: 815-232-8419. Fax: 815-297-0313. E-mail: director@stephcohs. org. In-person interview recommended (telephone interview accepted). Applicants must submit a letter of interest, resume. Applications are accepted continuously. World Wide Web: http:// www.StephCoHS.org.

STEPPING STONES MUSEUM FOR CHILDREN
303 West Avenue
Norwalk, Connecticut 06850

General Information Children's museum. Established in 1992. Number of employees: 50.

Internships Available ► *1–2 elementary education interns:* responsibilities include program development, school and group programs, and gallery facilitation. Candidates should have ability to work independently, declared college major in field, oral communication skills, organizational skills, plan to pursue career in field, self-motivation, strong interpersonal skills. Duration is 1–2 semesters. Unpaid. ► *1 human resources intern:* responsibilities include general human resource responsibilities including recruiting, payroll, and insurance benefits. Candidates should have ability to work with others, computer skills, declared college major in field, office skills, organizational skills, personal interest in the field, research skills, self-motivation. Duration is 1–2 semesters. Unpaid. ► *1 marketing intern:* responsibilities include developing membership programs, handling facility rentals, and school groups services. Candidates should have computer skills, declared college major in field, editing skills, office skills, oral communication skills, organizational

skills, personal interest in the field, research skills, self-motivation, strong interpersonal skills, writing skills. Duration is 1–2 semesters. Unpaid. Open to college seniors, recent college graduates, graduate students.

Benefits Job counseling, meals at a cost, on-the-job training, willing to act as a professional reference, willing to complete paperwork for educational credit, willing to provide letters of recommendation.

Contact Write, call, fax, e-mail, or through World Wide Web site Debby Ury, Human Resources Coordinator. Phone: 203-899-0606. Fax: 203-899-0530. E-mail: jobs@steppingstonesmuseum.org. In-person interview required. Applicants must submit a letter of interest, resume, writing sample, two letters of recommendation. Applications are accepted continuously. World Wide Web: http:// steppingstonesmuseum.org.

STONES RIVER NATIONAL BATTLEFIELD
3501 Old Nashville Highway
Murfreesboro, Tennessee 37129-3094

General Information Organization dedicated to preserving the natural and cultural features of the national battlefield site and providing for the study and interpretation of the Battle of Stones River. Established in 1927. Number of employees: 19. Unit of United States National Park Service, Washington, District of Columbia. Number of internship applications received each year: 75.

Internships Available ► *1 clerical assistant:* responsibilities include performing office work including filing and data entry. Candidates should have computer skills, editing skills, knowledge of field, office skills, organizational skills. Duration is 8–10 weeks. Unpaid. Open to recent high school graduates, college freshmen, college sophomores, college juniors, college seniors, recent college graduates, graduate students, career changers, individuals reentering the workforce. ► *1 historian:* responsibilities include conducting historical research. Candidates should have college courses in field, computer skills, knowledge of field, oral communication skills, research skills, writing skills. Duration is flexible. Unpaid. Open to recent college graduates, graduate students, career changers, individuals reentering the workforce. ► *1 interpreter:* responsibilities include preparing and presenting interpretive programs and operating the visitor's center. Candidates should have ability to work with others, knowledge of field, oral communication skills, personal interest in the field, research skills, writing skills. Duration is flexible. Unpaid. Open to recent high school graduates, college freshmen, college sophomores, college juniors, college seniors, recent college graduates, graduate students, career changers, individuals reentering the workforce. ► *1 library assistant:* responsibilities include cataloging and classifying library. Candidates should have computer skills, knowledge of field, office skills, organizational skills. Duration is flexible. Unpaid. Open to college juniors, college seniors, recent college graduates, graduate students, career changers, individuals reentering the workforce. ► *1 maintenance worker:* responsibilities include maintaining trails, landscape management, and cleaning cemetery headstones. Candidates should have ability to work independently, knowledge of field, organizational skills, personal interest in the field, self-motivation. Duration is flexible. Unpaid. Open to recent high school graduates, college freshmen, college sophomores, college juniors, college seniors, recent college graduates, graduate students, career changers, individuals reentering the workforce. ► *1 museum technician:* responsibilities include caring for museum collection. Candidates should have analytical skills, computer skills, knowledge of field, organizational skills, research skills. Duration is flexible. Unpaid. Open to college juniors, college seniors, recent college graduates, graduate students, career changers, individuals reentering the workforce. ► *1 natural resource management technician:* responsibilities include vegetation management, eradicating exotic species, and biological monitoring. Candidates should have ability to work independently, analytical skills, college courses in field, research skills, self-motivation. Duration is flexible. Unpaid. Open to college juniors, college seniors, recent college graduates, graduate students, career changers, individuals reentering the workforce.

Stones River National Battlefield (continued)

Benefits Formal training, job counseling, on-the-job training, opportunity to attend seminars/workshops, willing to complete paperwork for educational credit, willing to provide letters of recommendation, worker's compensation.
Contact Write, call, fax, or e-mail Volunteer Coordinator. Phone: 615-893-9501. Fax: 615-893-9508. E-mail: stri_information@nps. gov. In-person interview recommended (telephone interview accepted). Applicants must submit a formal organization application, two personal references. Applications are accepted continuously. World Wide Web: http://www.nps.gov/stri.

STRONG MUSEUM
1 Manhattan Square
Rochester, New York 14607

General Information Public educational institution that collects, preserves, and interprets historic artifacts, manuscripts, and other materials that depict everyday life in America after 1820, emphasizing the Northeast during the era of industrialization. Established in 1982. Number of employees: 173. Number of internship applications received each year: 25.
Internships Available ▶ *1–20 volunteer interns:* responsibilities include working in one of the following: collections, research, conservation, or education. Candidates should have ability to work with others, oral communication skills, plan to pursue career in field, research skills, self-motivation, written communication skills. Duration is 10–12 weeks. Unpaid. Open to college juniors, college seniors, recent college graduates, graduate students. International applications accepted.
Benefits Job counseling, names of contacts, on-the-job training, opportunity to attend seminars/workshops, willing to act as a professional reference, willing to complete paperwork for educational credit, willing to provide letters of recommendation.
Contact Write, call, fax, or e-mail Kathleen S. Dengler, Vice President for Human Resources. Phone: 585-263-2701 Ext. 267. Fax: 585-263-3598. E-mail: kdengler@strongmuseum.org. In-person interview required. Applicants must submit a formal organization application, letter of interest, resume, three writing samples, two personal references, letter of recommendation. Applications are accepted continuously. World Wide Web: http://www.strongmuseum.org.

SUNSET CRATER VOLCANO, WALNUT CANYON, AND WUPATKI NATIONAL MONUMENTS
Route 3, Box 149
Flagstaff, Arizona 86004

General Information Three national monuments managed by the National Park Service including a volcano, cliff dwellings, and pueblo archaeological sites; provides for visitor enjoyment, education, and resource protection. Number of employees: 50. Unit of Flagstaff Area National Monuments, Flagstaff, Arizona. Number of internship applications received each year: 100.
Internships Available ▶ *2–3 environmental education/interpretation/ visitor services interns:* responsibilities include staffing visitor center; developing and conducting interpretive programs for park visitors; developing and conducting environmental education programs for school groups; creating educational displays and publications; roving trails and making visitor contacts to discourage theft and vandalism of natural and cultural resources; preparing equipment for wildfire management; assisting in first aid and emergency situations. Candidates should have oral communication skills, personal interest in the field, self-motivation, strong interpersonal skills, written communication skills. Duration is 3–6 months. Unpaid. Open to recent high school graduates, college freshmen, college sophomores, college juniors, college seniors, recent college graduates, graduate students, career changers, individuals reentering the workforce. ▶ *1–2 maintenance interns:* responsibilities include providing maintenance of park facilities including janitorial services, trail maintenance, trash collection, painting, minor repairs, and other physical labor duties as skills allow. Candidates should have ability to work independently, ability to work with others, experience in the field, personal interest in the field, self-motivation, ability to do physical labor. Duration is

3–6 months. Unpaid. Open to high school seniors, recent high school graduates, college freshmen, college sophomores, college juniors, college seniors, recent college graduates, graduate students, career changers, individuals reentering the workforce. ▶ *1–2 resource management interns:* responsibilities include assisting in studying and protecting cultural and natural resources; performing curatorial work, roving archaeological sites, conducting scientific studies, assisting in planning efforts, entering data in computer, and assisting interpretive staff in preparing educational material. Candidates should have analytical skills, knowledge of field, personal interest in the field, research skills, self-motivation. Duration is 3–6 months. Unpaid. Open to college freshmen, college sophomores, college juniors, college seniors, recent college graduates, graduate students, individuals reentering the workforce. International applications accepted.
Benefits Formal training, free housing, job counseling, names of contacts, on-the-job training, opportunity to attend seminars/ workshops, willing to act as a professional reference, willing to complete paperwork for educational credit, willing to provide letters of recommendation, coverage for on-the-job injury or tort claim, uniform provided.
Contact Write, call, fax, or e-mail Karen Carswell, Volunteer Coordinator. Phone: 928-526-0502. Fax: 928-714-0565. E-mail: karen_carswell@nps.gov. Telephone interview required. Applicants must submit a formal organization application, letter of interest, resume, three personal references. Applications are accepted continuously. World Wide Web: http://www.nps.gov/sucr.

SUPREME COURT OF THE UNITED STATES, OFFICE OF THE CURATOR
1 First Street, NE
Washington, District of Columbia 20543

General Information Office that preserves the history of the Supreme Court; creates the historical exhibits in the building; develops, catalogues, and preserves the collections of the Supreme Court; and offers private tours and lectures. Established in 1973. Number of employees: 7. Unit of Supreme Court of the United States, Washington, District of Columbia. Number of internship applications received each year: 150.
Internships Available ▶ *2–8 curatorial interns:* responsibilities include conducting lectures and tours for visitors and assisting with curatorial projects which may include cataloging photographs, papers, and memorabilia; assisting with the development and installation of exhibits; researching and responding to public information requests. Candidates should have computer skills, office skills, oral communication skills, personal interest in the field, strong interpersonal skills, written communication skills. Duration is minimum of 24 hours per week for 12 weeks; or 40 hours per week for 3 weeks, mid-December to first week in January. Position available as unpaid or at $10 per hour for summer positions; academic credit for other positions. Open to college freshmen, college sophomores, college juniors, college seniors, recent college graduates, graduate students. International applications accepted.
Benefits Willing to complete paperwork for educational credit, willing to provide letters of recommendation, training in curatorial work, museum procedures, and public speaking; reimbursement for some commuting expenses.
Contact Write, call, or fax Trisha Brooks, Visitor Programs Coordinator. Phone: 202-479-2940. Fax: 202-479-2926. In-person interview recommended (telephone interview accepted). Applicants must submit a formal organization application, letter of interest, resume, three personal references, three letters of recommendation. Application deadline: March 1 for summer (May-August), July 1 for fall (September-December), October 1 for winter (mid-December to 1st week of January), November 1 for winter (January-May). World Wide Web: http://www.supremecourtus.gov.

THEODORE ROOSEVELT NATIONAL PARK
315 Second Avenue, PO Box 7
Medora, North Dakota 58645

General Information National park preserving the Little Missouri Badlands and 70,000 acres that are home to a variety of plants, wildlife including bison, elk, wild horses, and almost 200 species of birds. Established in 1947. Number of employees: 80. Number of internship applications received each year: 20.

Internships Available ▶ *2–3 biological science technicians:* responsibilities include performing resource management duties including exotic pest control and wildlife surveys. Candidates should have ability to work independently, ability to work with others, oral communication skills, research skills, self-motivation, written communication skills. Duration is 2–3 months. Position available as unpaid or paid. Open to college freshmen, college sophomores, college juniors, college seniors, recent college graduates, graduate students, career changers, individuals reentering the workforce. ▶ *3–5 interpretive volunteers:* responsibilities include working at the information desk, presenting information to the public at talks and formal evening programs, leading guided nature hikes, and undertaking special projects that employ the skills of the volunteer. Candidates should have ability to work independently, ability to work with others, oral communication skills, organizational skills, self-motivation, written communication skills. Duration is 2–3 months. Unpaid. Open to college freshmen, college sophomores, college juniors, college seniors, recent college graduates, graduate students, individuals reentering the workforce. International applications accepted.

Benefits Formal training, free housing, job counseling, names of contacts, on-the-job training, willing to complete paperwork for educational credit, willing to provide letters of recommendation, subsistence pay.

Contact Write or call Bruce M. Kaye, Chief of Interpretation. Phone: 701-623-4466. E-mail: bruce_kaye@nps.gov. Telephone interview required. Applicants must submit a letter of interest, resume, two personal references. Application deadline: February 15 for spring/summer, June 15 for fall. World Wide Web: http://www.nps.gov/thro.

TONGASS NATIONAL FOREST, ADMIRALTY NATIONAL MONUMENT
8461 Old Dairy Road
Juneau, Alaska 99801

General Information National monument and wilderness dedicated to preserving natural, cultural, geological, historical, scientific, recreational, wildlife, and wilderness resources and monitoring and protecting a coastal, temperate rain forest. Established in 1978. Number of employees: 15. Unit of United States Forest Service, Washington, District of Columbia. Number of internship applications received each year: 10.

Internships Available ▶ *1–2 wilderness rangers:* responsibilities include backcountry monitoring of wilderness campsites, cabins, and recreation sites; conducting campsite cleanup; and assisting with visitor contact and wilderness education. Candidates should have ability to work with others, oral communication skills, personal interest in the field, self-motivation. Duration is April 23 to August 25. Unpaid. Open to college juniors, college seniors, recent college graduates, graduate students, law students, career changers. International applications accepted.

Benefits Free housing, free meals, job counseling, names of contacts, travel reimbursement, willing to complete paperwork for educational credit, willing to provide letters of recommendation.

Contact Write, call, fax, or e-mail Mr. John Neary, Wilderness Assistant. Phone: 907-790-7481. Fax: 907-586-8795. E-mail: jneary@fs.fed.us. In-person interview recommended (telephone interview accepted). Applicants must submit a formal organization application. Application deadline: March 31. World Wide Web: http://www.fs.fed.us/r10/chatham/anm.

TRAILSIDE MUSEUMS AND WILDLIFE CENTER
Palisades Interstate Park Commission
Bear Mountain, New York 10911

General Information Large park and recreational facility that promotes conservation of natural resources and provides space for outdoor recreation, home to non-releasable native New York wildlife; also performs wildlife rehabilitation. Established in 1927. Number of employees: 15. Number of internship applications received each year: 10.

Internships Available ▶ *1 environmental interpretation and wildlife care intern:* responsibilities include providing care for permanently injured or orphaned park wildlife in zoo setting under the supervision of zookeeper; preparing food and diets; maintaining enclosures and exhibits; practicing enrichment; interacting with the public answering questions, interpreting exhibits, and offering short interpretive talks. Candidates should have oral communication skills, enthusiasm, high comfort level handling animals, and motivation to learn. Duration is mid-May to mid-August or end of August to early November. Unpaid. Open to college freshmen, college sophomores, college juniors, college seniors, individuals 18 years or older. ▶ *4 zookeeper assistants:* responsibilities include providing care for permanently injured or orphaned park wildlife in zoo setting under the supervision of a park ranger/zookeeper. Candidates should have ability to work independently, ability to work with others, oral communication skills, plan to pursue career in field, self-motivation, animal-related experience helpful, but will train. Duration is mid-May to mid-August (2 positions) or end of August to mid- November (2 positions). Unpaid. Open to college freshmen, college sophomores, college juniors, college seniors. International applications accepted.

Benefits Formal training, names of contacts, on-the-job training, possible full-time employment, willing to act as a professional reference, willing to complete paperwork for educational credit, willing to provide letters of recommendation, payment for pre-exposure rabies shots ($300 value) at conclusion of internship.

Contact Write, call, fax, or e-mail Ms. Jennifer Verstraete, Park Ranger/Zookeeper. Phone: 845-786-2701 Ext. 278. Fax: 845-786-0496. E-mail: uncl@icu.com. In-person interview recommended (telephone interview accepted). Applicants must submit a resume. Application deadline: May 1 for summer, August 31 for fall. World Wide Web: http://www.bearmountainzoo.org.

UCR/CALIFORNIA MUSEUM OF PHOTOGRAPHY
University of California, Riverside
Riverside, California 92501

General Information Facility that promotes understanding of photography and related media through collections, research, exhibition, and instruction. Established in 1973. Number of employees: 10. Unit of University of California, Riverside, Riverside, California. Number of internship applications received each year: 75.

Internships Available ▶ *3–5 museum assistants:* responsibilities include assisting with educational programs and exhibitions installation and performing administrative, collections, curatorial, marketing, and publications duties. Candidates should have ability to work independently, computer skills, oral communication skills, personal interest in the field, written communication skills. Duration is minimum of 3 months. Unpaid.

Benefits Job counseling, willing to complete paperwork for educational credit, willing to provide letters of recommendation.

Contact Write, fax, e-mail, or through World Wide Web site Jennifer Stratton, Museum Store Assistant. Fax: 909-787-4797. E-mail: jenstrat@pop.ucr.edu. No phone calls. In-person interview recommended (telephone interview accepted). Applicants must submit a letter of interest, resume, portfolio. Applications are accepted continuously. World Wide Web: http://www.cmp.ucr.edu.

U.S. HOLOCAUST MEMORIAL MUSEUM
100 Raoul Wallenberg Place, SW
Washington, District of Columbia 20024-2126

General Information Leading institution for the documentation, study, and interpretation of Holocaust history. Established in 1993. Number of employees: 600. Branch of United States Holocaust Memorial Council, Washington, District of Columbia. Number of internship applications received each year: 200.

Internships Available ▶ *Academic publications interns:* responsibilities include reviewing submitted memoirs, articles, and books for possible publication and assisting in production of the museum's journal *Holocaust and Genocide Studies.* Candidates should have ability to work independently, college courses in field, computer skills, editing skills, knowledge of field, organizational skills, research skills, written communication skills, European language skills. Duration is 12 weeks. Position available as unpaid or at $1000

U.S. Holocaust Memorial Museum (continued)

monthly (full-time); $500 (part-time). Open to college sophomores, college juniors, college seniors, recent college graduates, graduate students, career changers, individuals reentering the workforce. ▶ *Archives interns:* responsibilities include translating and summarizing wartime trial records. Candidates should have college courses in field, computer skills, knowledge of field, research skills, writing skills, European language skills. Duration is 10–12 weeks. Position available as unpaid or at $1000 monthly (full-time); $500 (part-time). Open to college sophomores, college juniors, college seniors, recent college graduates, graduate students, career changers, individuals reentering the workforce. ▶ *Collections interns:* responsibilities include assisting with research projects and cataloging holdings of the Museum's collections. Candidates should have ability to work independently, ability to work with others, computer skills, research skills, writing skills. Duration is 10–12 weeks. Position available as unpaid or at $1000 monthly (full-time); $500 (part-time). Open to college sophomores, college juniors, college seniors, recent college graduates, graduate students, career changers. ▶ *Education interns:* responsibilities include assisting with the development of various educational projects including teacher resources. Candidates should have ability to work independently, ability to work with others, computer skills, knowledge of field, oral communication skills, research skills, writing skills. Duration is 10–12 weeks. Position available as unpaid or at $1000 monthly (full-time); $500 (part-time). Open to college sophomores, college juniors, college seniors, recent college graduates, graduate students, career changers. ▶ *International programs interns:* responsibilities include assisting with the development of programs sponsored by the Museum throughout the world. Candidates should have computer skills, knowledge of field, oral communication skills, research skills, strong interpersonal skills, writing skills, knowledge of eastern European language (helpful). Duration is 10–12 weeks. Position available as unpaid or at $1000 monthly (full-time); $500 (part-time). Open to college sophomores, college juniors, college seniors, recent college graduates, graduate students, career changers. ▶ *2–3 legal interns:* responsibilities include preparing briefs, researching, editing. Candidates should have analytical skills, college courses in field, knowledge of field, research skills, writing skills. Duration is 10–12 weeks. Position available as unpaid or at $1000 monthly (full-time); $500 (part-time). Open to recent college graduates, law students. ▶ *Membership interns:* responsibilities include assisting with the development and maintenance of the membership program. Candidates should have computer skills, office skills, oral communication skills, strong interpersonal skills, written communication skills. Duration is 10–12 $1000 monthly (full-time); $500 (part-time). Position available as unpaid or paid. Open to college sophomores, college juniors, college seniors, recent college graduates, graduate students, career changers. ▶ *Photo archive department interns:* responsibilities include maintaining archives of Holocaust photographs. Candidates should have ability to work independently, ability to work with others, analytical skills, computer skills, organizational skills, research skills. Duration is 10–12 weeks. Position available as unpaid or at $1000 monthly (full-time); $500 (part-time). Open to college sophomores, college juniors, college seniors, recent college graduates, graduate students, career changers. ▶ *Research interns:* responsibilities include assisting senior research scholars. Candidates should have ability to work independently, ability to work with others, computer skills, editing skills, research skills, writing skills. Duration is 10–12 weeks. Position available as unpaid or at $1000 monthly (full-time); $500 (part-time). Open to college sophomores, college juniors, college seniors, recent college graduates, graduate students, law students, career changers, individuals reentering the workforce. ▶ *Visitor services interns:* responsibilities include assisting with the development of a volunteer program for a diverse constituency. Candidates should have ability to work independently, computer skills, oral communication skills, strong interpersonal skills, writing skills. Duration is 10–12 weeks. Unpaid. Open to college sophomores, college juniors, college seniors, recent college graduates, graduate students, career changers. International applications accepted.

Benefits Formal training, job counseling, names of contacts, on-the-job training, opportunity to attend seminars/workshops,

willing to act as a professional reference, willing to complete paperwork for educational credit, willing to provide letters of recommendation.

Contact Write, call, fax, or through World Wide Web site Internship Coordinator. Phone: 202-479-9738. Fax: 202-488-6568. Telephone interview required. Applicants must submit a formal organization application, letter of interest, resume, academic transcripts, two letters of recommendation. Application deadline: March 15 for summer, June 15 for fall, October 15 for winter/spring. World Wide Web: http://www.ushmm.org.

WADSWORTH ATHENEUM MUSEUM OF ART
600 Main Street
Hartford, Connecticut 06103-2990

General Information Fine arts museum housing a collection with strengths in 19th-century American painting, Renaissance and Baroque European painting, European and American decorative arts, the Amistad Foundation Collection of African-American art and artifacts, and the Nutting Collection of Colonial American furniture. Established in 1842. Number of employees: 150. Number of internship applications received each year: 100.

Internships Available ▶ *1 Amistad Foundation intern:* responsibilities include providing general curatorial support, writing label copy, research, and cataloging. Candidates should have ability to work independently, analytical skills, computer skills, organizational skills, self-motivation, written communication skills. Unpaid. Open to college seniors, recent college graduates, graduate students. ▶ *1 business office intern:* responsibilities include performing office duties. Candidates should have ability to work with others, computer skills, office skills, organizational skills, self-motivation. Duration is flexible. Unpaid. Open to college freshmen, college sophomores, college juniors, college seniors, recent college graduates, graduate students, career changers, individuals reentering the workforce. ▶ *1 curatorial intern:* responsibilities include conducting research on permanent collection, labeling objects, and cataloging entries. Candidates should have ability to work independently, ability to work with others, computer skills, knowledge of field, research skills, self-motivation, written communication skills. Duration is flexible. Unpaid. Open to college freshmen, college sophomores, college juniors, college seniors, recent college graduates, graduate students, career changers, individuals reentering the workforce. ▶ *1 design and installation intern:* responsibilities include assisting with 2- and 3-dimensional designs within the organization. Candidates should have ability to work independently, ability to work with others, knowledge of field, personal interest in the field, self-motivation. Duration is flexible. Unpaid. Open to college freshmen, college sophomores, college juniors, college seniors, recent college graduates, graduate students, career changers, individuals reentering the workforce. ▶ *1 development intern:* responsibilities include fund-raising, writing grants, learning how to solicit corporate contributions/individual patrons, conducting market research, and building databases. Candidates should have ability to work independently, ability to work with others, computer skills, office skills, organizational skills, self-motivation. Duration is flexible. Unpaid. Open to college freshmen, college sophomores, college juniors, college seniors, recent college graduates, graduate students, career changers, individuals reentering the workforce. ▶ *1 education intern:* responsibilities include assisting in implementing public programs including lectures, concerts, films, symposia, teachers' workshops, and children's programs; writing educational material including gallery handouts and slide programs; grant writing; and surveying educational programs. Candidates should have ability to work independently, computer skills, office skills, organizational skills, research skills, written communication skills. Duration is flexible. Unpaid. Open to college freshmen, college sophomores, college juniors, college seniors, recent college graduates, graduate students, career changers, individuals reentering the workforce. ▶ *1 library intern:* responsibilities include serving museum staff and the public. Candidates should have ability to work independently, ability to work with others, computer skills, office skills, organizational skills, self-motivation. Duration is flexible. Unpaid. Open to college freshmen, college sophomores, college juniors, college seniors, recent college graduates, graduate students, career changers, individu-

als reentering the workforce. ▶ *1 membership intern:* responsibilities include assisting in membership drives, organizing membership activities and exhibit openings, and coordinating publication of membership materials. Candidates should have computer skills, office skills, oral communication skills, strong interpersonal skills, written communication skills. Duration is flexible. Unpaid. Open to college freshmen, college sophomores, college juniors, college seniors, recent college graduates, graduate students, career changers, individuals reentering the workforce. ▶ *1 museum shop intern:* responsibilities include assisting in retail facility within museum. Candidates should have ability to work with others, oral communication skills, organizational skills, self-motivation. Duration is flexible. Unpaid. Open to college freshmen, college sophomores, college juniors, college seniors, recent college graduates, graduate students, career changers, individuals reentering the workforce. ▶ *1 photographic services intern:* responsibilities include maintaining museum's extensive slide holdings, handling all slide loans to staff and public, processing all requests regarding rights and reproductions, planning photo shoots, and filing and maintaining photographic archives. Candidates should have ability to work independently, ability to work with others, office skills, organizational skills, research skills, self-motivation. Duration is flexible. Unpaid. Open to college freshmen, college sophomores, college juniors, college seniors, recent college graduates, graduate students, career changers, individuals reentering the workforce. ▶ *1 public information intern:* responsibilities include assisting public relations staff with writing press releases. Candidates should have ability to work with others, computer skills, editing skills, self-motivation, written communication skills. Duration is flexible. Unpaid. Open to college freshmen, college sophomores, college juniors, college seniors, recent college graduates, graduate students, career changers, individuals reentering the workforce. ▶ *1 registrar intern:* responsibilities include maintaining provenance files on permanent collections, making accession cards, and researching objects for inventory. Candidates should have ability to work with others, computer skills, office skills, oral communication skills, self-motivation, written communication skills. Duration is flexible. Unpaid. Open to college freshmen, college sophomores, college juniors, college seniors, recent college graduates, graduate students, career changers, individuals reentering the workforce. International applications accepted.
Benefits Job counseling, names of contacts, opportunity to attend seminars/workshops, possible full-time employment, willing to complete paperwork for educational credit, willing to provide letters of recommendation, opportunity to attend all museum education programs.
Contact Write, call, fax, or e-mail Dana Engstrom DeLoach, Assistant Curator of Public Programs. Phone: 860-278-2670 Ext. 3121. Fax: 860-249-7780. E-mail: dana.deloach@wadsworthatheneum.org. In-person interview recommended (telephone interview accepted). Applicants must submit a letter of interest, resume, academic transcripts, writing sample, two letters of recommendation. Application deadline: March 15 for summer, July 15 for fall/winter, November 1 for spring. World Wide Web: http://www.wadsworthatheneum.org.

WHITE SANDS NATIONAL MONUMENT
PO Box 1086
Holloman A.F.B., New Mexico 88330

General Information National monument that preserves the world's largest gypsum dunefield. Established in 1933. Number of employees: 24. Unit of United States National Park Service, Washington, District of Columbia. Number of internship applications received each year: 4.
Internships Available ▶ *1 environmental interpretation intern:* responsibilities include performing interpretive ranger duties, developing and presenting talks, conducting nature walks, staffing information desk, and performing roving interpretation on foot. Candidates should have college courses in field, oral communication skills, self-motivation, strong interpersonal skills, written communication skills. Duration is 12-14 weeks in spring, fall, or winter. Unpaid. Open to college juniors, college seniors, recent college graduates, graduate students, career changers. ▶ *1 geology interpretation intern:* responsibilities include performing interpre-

tive ranger duties, developing and presenting programs on geology and ecology of the dunes, staffing information desk, and developing exhibits/informational brochures. Candidates should have oral communication skills, self-motivation, strong interpersonal skills, written communication skills, major in geology or earth science education. Duration is 12-14 weeks in summer. Unpaid. Open to college juniors, college seniors, graduate students. International applications accepted.
Benefits Formal training, free housing, job counseling, names of contacts, on-the-job training, travel reimbursement, willing to act as a professional reference, willing to complete paperwork for educational credit, willing to provide letters of recommendation, $50 per week food reimbursement for environmental interpretation positions.
Contact Write, call, fax, e-mail, or through World Wide Web site Mr. John Mangimeli, Chief of Interpretation. Phone: 505-679-2599 Ext. 230. Fax: 505-479-4333. E-mail: john_mangimeli@nps.gov. Applicants must submit a formal organization application, resume, academic transcripts, two letters of recommendation, materials through Student Conservation Association application process (603)543-1700. Application deadline: January 1 for spring (March to late May), March 1 for summer (mid-May to mid-August), August 1 for fall (October to December), October 15 for winter (late December to mid-March). World Wide Web: http://www.nps.gov/whsa.

WHITNEY MUSEUM OF AMERICAN ART
945 Madison Avenue
New York, New York 10021

General Information Museum dedicated to collecting, preserving, and interpreting 20th and 21st century American art with an emphasis on contemporary art. Established in 1930. Number of employees: 200. Number of internship applications received each year: 250.
Internships Available ▶ *Interns:* responsibilities include working in a variety of areas including curatorial, branch museum, communications, education, film and video, library, registration, marketing, development, rights and reproductions, and traveling exhibitions. Candidates should have ability to work with others, college courses in field, computer skills, office skills, research skills, self-motivation, written communication skills. Duration is 2–4 months. Position available as unpaid or paid. Open to college sophomores, college juniors, college seniors, graduate students. International applications accepted.
Benefits On-the-job training, opportunity to attend seminars/workshops, possible full-time employment, willing to complete paperwork for educational credit, willing to provide letters of recommendation, stipend of $626 for summer program, free admission at museum.
Contact Write or e-mail Lisa Dowd, Human Resources Manager. Fax: 212-606-0210. E-mail: hr@whitney.org. No phone calls. In-person interview required. Applicants must submit a letter of interest, resume, academic transcripts, personal reference, letter of recommendation, one-page statement of purpose stating what the intern hopes to gain from the internship and what he/she hopes to contribute to the organization. Application deadline: March 1 for summer; no deadlines for academic-year placements. World Wide Web: http://www.whitney.org.

WILDLIFE PRAIRIE STATE PARK
3826 North Taylor Road, RR 2, Box 50
Peoria, Illinois 61615

General Information Zoological and botanical park that encompasses 2000 acres of grazing land, lakes, and woodlands, presenting the wild animals once native to Illinois. Established in 1978. Number of employees: 50. Number of internship applications received each year: 50.
Internships Available ▶ *3–4 education interns:* responsibilities include greeting school groups and assisting with various interpretive programs including day camps, guiding tours, presenting daily interpretive programs to the general public, assisting with special events, performing certain opening and closing procedures, trail monitoring, and completing a special project. Candidates should have ability to work independently, oral communication skills,

Wildlife Prairie State Park (continued)

strong interpersonal skills, biology and/or environmental interests. Duration is 12 weeks or longer. Position available as unpaid or paid. Open to college juniors, college seniors, recent college graduates, graduate students.

Benefits On-the-job training, possible full-time employment, willing to act as a professional reference, willing to complete paperwork for educational credit, willing to provide letters of recommendation, leadership skills, possibility of free housing.

Contact Write, call, fax, or e-mail Rebecca Rees, Internship Coordinator. Phone: 309-676-0998 Ext. 6758. Fax: 309-676-7783. E-mail: wppnat@aol.com. In-person interview recommended (telephone interview accepted). Applicants must submit a letter of interest, resume, three personal references. Application deadline: March 1 for summer; continuous for other positions. World Wide Web: http://www.wildlifeprairiestatepark.org.

WIND CAVE NATIONAL PARK
RR1 Box 190
Hot Springs, South Dakota 57747

General Information National park that preserves and protects an exceptional maze-cave with a rare cave formation called "boxwork", and maintains a beautiful mixed-grass prairie complete with representative wildlife. Established in 1903. Number of employees: 75. Unit of National Park Service, Washington, District of Columbia. Number of internship applications received each year: 25.

Internships Available ▶ *2–4 interpretive park guides:* responsibilities include preparing and presenting interpretive programs including cave tours, visitor center demonstrations, prairie hikes, and staffing visitor center desk. Candidates should have ability to work independently, oral communication skills, personal interest in the field, self-motivation, strong interpersonal skills. Duration is 3–5 months. $50–$75 per week. Open to college sophomores, college juniors, college seniors, recent college graduates, graduate students, law students, career changers.

Benefits Formal training, free housing, job counseling, names of contacts, on-the-job training, travel reimbursement, willing to complete paperwork for educational credit, willing to provide letters of recommendation, uniform allowance, meal stipend.

Contact Write, call, fax, or e-mail Phyllis Cremonini, Assistant Chief of Interpretation, RR1, Box 190, Hot Springs, South Dakota 57747. Phone: 605-745-4600. Fax: 605-745-4207. E-mail: phyllis_cremonini@nps.gov. Telephone interview required. Applicants must submit a letter of interest, resume, academic transcripts, two personal references. Application deadline: March 15 for summer, August 1 for fall/winter, November 1 for spring. World Wide Web: http://www.nps.gov/wica.

WINTERTHUR MUSEUM, GARDEN AND LIBRARY
Winterthur, Delaware 19735

General Information Complete community for the presentation, preservation, and exploration of American arts and historic structures; naturalistic garden; research library and academic center. Established in 1951. Number of employees: 613. Number of internship applications received each year: 30.

Internships Available ▶ *1 arborist intern:* responsibilities include assisting arborists in maintaining health and vigor of the trees throughout Winterthur garden; learning good arboricultural techniques and safety practices. Duration is 2 months (June to August). $9.50 per hour. ▶ *7 horticulture interns:* responsibilities include assisting the horticulturist of a particular garden and/or plant group; working with a horticulturist or production supervisor in maintaining the design of the garden or plant group by practicing good horticulture techniques. Duration is 2 months (June to August). $9.50 per hour. Candidates for all positions should have ability to work with others, knowledge of field, personal interest in the field. Open to college freshmen, college sophomores, college juniors, college seniors. International applications accepted.

Benefits Meals at a cost, opportunity to attend seminars/workshops, possible full-time employment, willing to complete paperwork for educational credit, willing to provide letters of recommendation, field trips, safety training.

Contact Write, call, fax, or e-mail Shonie Castle, Employment Manager. Phone: 302-888-4830. Fax: 302-888-4956. E-mail: acastle@winterthur.org. In-person interview required. Applicants must submit a formal organization application, letter of interest, resume. Application deadline: March 31.

WOMEN'S HISTORY AND RESOURCE CENTER
1734 N Street, NW
Washington, District of Columbia 20036

General Information Archives and library devoted to women's history with an emphasis on women in volunteerism. Established in 1984. Number of employees: 25. Unit of General Federation of Women's Clubs, Washington, District of Columbia. Number of internship applications received each year: 100.

Internships Available ▶ *Interns:* responsibilities include working with books and archival materials, researching answers to reference inquiries, assisting researchers, receiving training for archival computer project tasks, and archival processing and cataloging. Candidates should have ability to work independently, ability to work with others, college courses in field, computer skills, office skills, organizational skills, research skills, strong interest in archives, women's history, and volunteerism. Duration is fall, spring, or summer (flexible hours). Unpaid. Open to college freshmen, college sophomores, college juniors, college seniors, graduate students, individuals reentering the workforce. International applications accepted.

Benefits Willing to act as a professional reference, willing to complete paperwork for educational credit, willing to provide letters of recommendation, small stipend at completion of internship.

Contact Write, fax, or e-mail Suzanne Gould, Director, 1734 N Street, NW, Washington, District of Columbia 20036. Fax: 202-835-0246. E-mail: whrc@gfwc.org. In-person interview required. Applicants must submit a resume. Applications are accepted continuously. World Wide Web: http://www.gfwc.org/whrc.htm.

YESHIVA UNIVERSITY MUSEUM
15 West 16th Street
New York, New York 10011

General Information Museum that preserves, exhibits, and interprets Jewish life, art history, and culture through multidisciplinary exhibitions, contemporary shows, and scholarly catalogs. Established in 1973. Number of employees: 10. Affiliate of Yeshiva University, New York, New York. Number of internship applications received each year: 25.

Internships Available ▶ *Archives interns:* responsibilities include organizing and maintaining museum's press and exhibition archives and updating press archive database. Candidates should have ability to work independently, analytical skills, computer skills, office skills, organizational skills, written communication skills. Duration is minimum 3 months. Unpaid. Open to high school seniors, college freshmen, college sophomores, college juniors, college seniors. ▶ *1 curatorial intern:* responsibilities include research, cataloging, and exhibitions. Candidates should have ability to work independently, ability to work with others, computer skills, editing skills, office skills, research skills, writing skills. Duration is 3 months minimum. Unpaid. Open to high school students, recent high school graduates, college freshmen, college sophomores, college juniors, college seniors, recent college graduates, graduate students, individuals reentering the workforce. ▶ *2 education interns:* responsibilities include assisting in the preparation of youth programs and art workshops for visiting school groups. Candidates should have ability to work independently, ability to work with others, office skills, oral communication skills, written communication skills. Duration is 2–12 months. Unpaid. Open to high school students, college freshmen, college sophomores, college juniors, college seniors, graduate students, individuals reentering the workforce. ▶ *1 registration intern:* responsibilities include collections, research, and record keeping. Candidates should have ability to work independently, ability to work with others, computer skills, editing skills, office skills, research skills, writing skills. Duration is minimum of 3 months. Unpaid. Open to high school students, college freshmen, college sophomores, college juniors, college seniors, graduate students, individuals reentering the workforce. International applications accepted.

Benefits Job counseling, names of contacts, opportunity to attend seminars/workshops, willing to complete paperwork for educational credit, willing to provide letters of recommendation.

Contact Write, fax, or e-mail Mary Kiplok, Internship Coordinator. Fax: 212-294-8335. E-mail: mkiplok@yum.cjh.org. No phone calls. In-person interview required. Applicants must submit a letter of interest, resume, 2 personal references/letters of recommendation. Applications are accepted continuously. World Wide Web: http://www.yu.edu/museum/.

ZOO NEW ENGLAND
One Franklin Park Road
Boston, Massachusetts 02121

General Information Private, nonprofit organization that manages the Franklin Park Zoo and Stone Zoo. Established in 1911. Number of employees: 230. Number of internship applications received each year: 12.

Internships Available ▶ *1–6 animal care interns:* responsibilities include assisting the animal care staff at the Franklin Park Zoo (Boston) and/or Stone Zoo (Stoneham). Candidates should have ability to work independently, ability to work with others, oral communication skills, organizational skills, plan to pursue career in field, self-motivation. Duration is 12 weeks (full-time). Unpaid. Open to college juniors, college seniors, recent college graduates, graduate students, career changers. ▶ *1 animal records assistant:* responsibilities include assisting with animal and library records. Candidates should have ability to work independently, computer skills, office skills, organizational skills, research skills, written communication skills. Duration is 6 months or 1 semester. Unpaid. Open to recent high school graduates, college freshmen, college sophomores, college juniors, college seniors, recent college graduates, graduate students, career changers. ▶ *2–3 education assistants:* responsibilities include assisting with or leading programs for school-aged children; gathering program materials for classes; interpreting exhibits. Candidates should have ability to work independently, college courses in field, editing skills, knowledge of field, office skills, oral communication skills, organizational skills, personal interest in the field, self-motivation, strong interpersonal skills, strong leadership ability, writing skills. Duration is 3–4 months. Unpaid. Open to college juniors, college seniors, recent college graduates, graduate students. ▶ *1–3 horticulture interns:* responsibilities include assisting with the preparation, installation, and maintenance of extensive plant collection at Franklin Park Zoo (Boston) or Stone Zoo (Stoneham). Candidates should have ability to work independently, ability to work with others, knowledge of field, personal interest in the field, research skills, self-motivation. Duration is 1 semester. Unpaid. Open to college sophomores, college juniors, college seniors, recent college graduates, graduate students, career changers. ▶ *1 marketing intern:* responsibilities include assisting with special events, promotions, marketing, and administrative tasks. Candidates should have office skills, oral communication skills, organizational skills, personal interest in the field, strong interpersonal skills, writing skills. Duration is 1 semester. Unpaid. Open to college sophomores, college juniors, college seniors, recent college graduates, graduate students, career changers. ▶ *2 youth programs coordinators (ZooTeen program):* responsibilities include recruitment, orientation, development, training and supervision of the ZooTeen Program, including managing payroll, scheduling, and maintaining records and daily logs; evaluating teens, planning special events, assessing the program, creating and implementing curriculum and coordinating professional developmental workshops. Candidates should have ability to work independently, computer skills, declared college major in field, editing skills, experience in the field, office skills, oral communication skills, organizational skills, personal interest in the field, plan to pursue career in field, self-motivation, strong interpersonal skills, strong leadership ability, writing skills. Duration is 4 months (full-time). $2000 per duration of internship. Open to college sophomores, college juniors, college seniors, recent college graduates, graduate students. International applications accepted.

Benefits Formal training, job counseling, meals at a cost, on-the-job training, opportunity to attend seminars/workshops, possible full-time employment, willing to act as a professional reference, willing to complete paperwork for educational credit, willing to provide letters of recommendation, free entrance to zoos anywhere in U.S., reimbursement for project expenses.

Contact Write, call, fax, or e-mail James L. Brantley, III, Director of Community Relations and Volunteer Services. Phone: 617-989-2017. Fax: 617-541-0732. E-mail: jbrantley@zoonewengland.com. In-person interview recommended (telephone interview accepted). Applicants must submit a formal organization application, letter of interest, resume, academic transcripts, personal reference, two letters of recommendation, TB test required. Applications are accepted continuously. World Wide Web: http://www.zoonewengland.org.

PERFORMING ARTS COMPANIES

THE ACTING COMPANY–GROUP I ACTING COMPANY, INC.
630 9th Avenue, #214
New York, New York 10036

General Information Professional touring classical repertory theater. Established in 1972. Number of employees: 9. Number of internship applications received each year: 30.

Internships Available ▶ *1 education intern:* responsibilities include assisting director of education with educational programming and coordinating classroom residencies and workshops. Candidates should have ability to work independently, ability to work with others, computer skills, oral communication skills, organizational skills, self-motivation. Duration is 1–2 semesters. $50–$100 per week. ▶ *1 marketing/development intern:* responsibilities include assisting director of development in planning, research for, and execution of special events, fund-raising and grant writing; assisting in managing promotional materials. Candidates should have ability to work independently, ability to work with others, computer skills, oral communication skills, organizational skills, self-motivation. Duration is 1–2 semesters. $50–$100 per week. ▶ *1–2 stage management interns:* responsibilities include assisting with rehearsals. Candidates should have ability to work independently, computer skills, oral communication skills, organizational skills, personal interest in the field, plan to pursue career in field, written communication skills. Duration is 4 months (mid-September to mid-January). $100 per week. Open to college freshmen, college sophomores, college juniors, college seniors, recent college graduates, graduate students. International applications accepted.

Benefits Job counseling, names of contacts, on-the-job training, possible full-time employment, willing to act as a professional reference, willing to complete paperwork for educational credit, willing to provide letters of recommendation, free/reduced theater tickets.

Contact Write, fax, or e-mail Intern Coordinator, PO Box 898, Times Square Station, New York, New York 10108-0898. Fax: 212-258-3299. E-mail: mail@theactingcompany.org. No phone calls. In-person interview recommended (telephone interview accepted). Applicants must submit a letter of interest, resume, letter of recommendation, 1-2 personal references. Application deadline: April 15 for summer, July 15 for fall, November 15 for spring. World Wide Web: http://www.theactingcompany.org.

ACTORS THEATRE OF LOUISVILLE
316 West Main Street
Louisville, Kentucky 40202

General Information Professional regional repertory theater that produces 30 or more plays a season including one major festival. Established in 1964. Number of employees: 200. Number of internship applications received each year: 100.

Internships Available ▶ *1 apprentice/intern company intern:* responsibilities include curriculum development, recruiting, and updating and maintaining library and archives. Candidates should have ability to work independently, computer skills, organizational skills,

Actors Theatre of Louisville (continued)

self-motivation, strong interpersonal skills, attention to detail. Duration is late August to early June. Unpaid. Open to college freshmen, college sophomores, college juniors, college seniors, recent college graduates, graduate students, career changers, individuals reentering the workforce. ▶ *1 casting and company management intern:* responsibilities include weekly attendance at rehearsals; maintaining communication with artists, designers, and other regional theaters; research, scheduling general auditions, arranging local casting needs, maintaining resume files, and performing reference checks. Candidates should have experience in the field, office skills, strong interpersonal skills, sense of humor, computer skills (a plus). Duration is last August to early June. Unpaid. Open to college freshmen, college sophomores, college juniors, college seniors, recent college graduates, graduate students, career changers, individuals reentering the workforce. ▶ *1 company and volunteer management intern:* responsibilities include initiating contact with contracted artists, coordinating transportation and housing needs, and assisting Development Board with audience recruitment. Candidates should have oral communication skills, organizational skills, strong interpersonal skills, sense of humor, discretion, computer skills (a plus). Duration is late August to early June. Unpaid. Open to college freshmen, college sophomores, college juniors, college seniors, recent college graduates, graduate students, career changers, individuals reentering the workforce. ▶ *4–6 costume interns:* responsibilities include working with the staff in one of the following areas: assistant to the designer, technical costume/shop management, wardrobe, or wigs. Candidates should have oral communication skills, organizational skills, strong interpersonal skills, design skills (for some positions). Duration is late August to early June. Unpaid. Open to college freshmen, college sophomores, college juniors, college seniors, recent college graduates, graduate students, career changers, individuals reentering the workforce. ▶ *1 festival management intern:* responsibilities include events and project coordination, producing numerous publications and flyers, setting up exhibits and merchandise displays, coordinating travel and lodging arrangements for guests, coordinating volunteers. Candidates should have computer skills, oral communication skills, organizational skills, strong interpersonal skills, experience with word processing, database management, and desktop publishing (helpful). Duration is January to April. Unpaid. Open to college freshmen, college sophomores, college juniors, college seniors, recent college graduates, graduate students, career changers, individuals reentering the workforce. ▶ *1 lighting intern:* responsibilities include production work (hanging and focusing, etc.); drafting, paperwork, assisting professional lighting designers. Candidates should have computer skills, experience in the field. Duration is late August to early June. Unpaid. Open to college freshmen, college sophomores, college juniors, college seniors, recent college graduates, graduate students, career changers, individuals reentering the workforce. ▶ *2 literary management interns:* responsibilities include attending rehearsals, assisting with playwright residencies, library research, reading new plays, writing articles for ATL publications, administrative support for various literary projects, dramaturgy. Candidates should have ability to work with others, oral communication skills, organizational skills, research skills, self-motivation, written communication skills. Duration is late August to early June. Unpaid. Open to college freshmen, college sophomores, college juniors, college seniors, recent college graduates, graduate students, career changers, individuals reentering the workforce. ▶ *Properties interns:* responsibilities include working with full-time staff in props shop. Candidates should have ability to work with others, knowledge of field, personal interest in the field, self-motivation. Duration is late August to early June (40 hours per week). Unpaid. ▶ *2 public relations/marketing interns:* responsibilities include media relations, single ticket and subscription audience development, promotions, writing press releases. Candidates should have ability to work with others, analytical skills, oral communication skills, organizational skills, written communication skills. Duration is late August to early June. Unpaid. Open to college freshmen, college sophomores, college juniors, college seniors, recent college graduates, graduate students, career changers, individuals reentering the workforce. ▶ *1 scenic design intern:* responsibilities include working as a member of the theater's design staff. Candidates should have abil-

ity to work independently, experience in the field, personal interest in the field, self-motivation. Duration is late August to early June. Unpaid. Open to college freshmen, college sophomores, college juniors, college seniors, recent college graduates, graduate students, career changers, individuals reentering the workforce. ▶ *1 sound intern:* responsibilities include running sound board during performances and assisting sound engineer; assistant design opportunities. Candidates should have ability to work independently, personal interest in the field. Duration is 1/2 season or full season. Unpaid. Open to college freshmen, college sophomores, college juniors, college seniors, recent college graduates, graduate students, career changers, individuals reentering the workforce. ▶ *3 stage management interns:* responsibilities include assisting at rehearsals, running mainstage productions, keeping track of props, and pre-show and post-show duties for mainstage production. Candidates should have experience in the field, organizational skills, strong interpersonal skills. Duration is late August to early June. Unpaid. Open to college freshmen, college sophomores, college juniors, college seniors, recent college graduates, graduate students, career changers, individuals reentering the workforce. ▶ *1 volunteer and audience relations intern:* responsibilities include front-of-house activities, assisting with volunteer programs, and Audience (Accessible) Services. Candidates should have ability to work independently, oral communication skills, organizational skills, strong interpersonal skills. Duration is late August to early June (approximately 20 hours per week). Unpaid. Open to college freshmen, college sophomores, college juniors, college seniors, recent college graduates, graduate students, career changers, individuals reentering the workforce. International applications accepted.

Benefits Names of contacts, on-the-job training, opportunity to attend seminars/workshops, possible full-time employment, willing to act as a professional reference, willing to complete paperwork for educational credit, willing to provide letters of recommendation.

Contact Write, call, fax, e-mail, or through World Wide Web site Wendy McClellan, Director of the Apprentice/Intern Company. Phone: 502-584-1265. Fax: 502-561-3300. E-mail: wmcclellan@ actorstheatre.org. In-person interview required. Applicants must submit a formal organization application, letter of interest, resume, academic transcripts, portfolio, two letters of recommendation. Application deadline: April 15. World Wide Web: http://www. actorstheatre.org.

ALLEY THEATRE
615 Texas Avenue
Houston, Texas 77002

General Information Theater presenting plays of merit performed by a company of actors for a subscription audience. Established in 1947. Number of employees: 100. Number of internship applications received each year: 75.

Internships Available ▶ *1–3 company management interns:* responsibilities include assisting with management of actors, including travel and housing arrangements. Candidates should have office skills, oral communication skills, organizational skills, self-motivation, strong interpersonal skills, written communication skills. Duration is 10–16 weeks (full or part-time). Unpaid. Open to college freshmen, college sophomores, college juniors, college seniors, recent college graduates, graduate students, career changers. ▶ *1–3 costumes/wigs interns:* responsibilities include assisting shop manager and wigmaster. Candidates should have ability to work independently, knowledge of field, plan to pursue career in field, research skills, self-motivation, strong interpersonal skills. Duration is 10–16 weeks (full or part-time). Position available as unpaid or at $200 per week. Open to college freshmen, college sophomores, college juniors, college seniors, recent college graduates, graduate students, career changers. ▶ *1–3 development interns:* responsibilities include fund-raising, special events, development office support. Candidates should have computer skills, office skills, oral communication skills, organizational skills, personal interest in the field, self-motivation, strong interpersonal skills, writing skills. Duration is 10–16 weeks (full or part-time). Unpaid. Open to high school seniors, college freshmen, college sophomores, college juniors, college seniors, recent college graduates, graduate students, career changers. ▶ *1–3 dramaturgy interns:* responsibilities include reading new plays and performing literary research. Candidates should have ability to work independently, analytical skills, computer skills, editing skills, oral communication skills, personal interest in the field, research skills, self-motivation, strong interpersonal skills, writing skills. Duration is 10–16 weeks (full or part-time). Unpaid. Open to college freshmen, college sophomores, college juniors, college seniors, recent college graduates, graduate students, career changers. ▶ *1–3 education and community outreach interns:* responsibilities include assisting with outreach programming. Candidates should have computer skills, office skills, organizational skills, strong interpersonal skills, written communication skills. Duration is 10–16 weeks (full or part-time). Unpaid. Open to college freshmen, college sophomores, college juniors, college seniors, graduate students. ▶ *1–3 lighting and sound interns:* responsibilities include operating Prestige 3000 lighting system. Candidates should have ability to work independently, ability to work with others, college courses in field, computer skills, knowledge of field, self-motivation. Duration is 10–16 weeks (full or part-time). Position available as unpaid or at $200 per week. Open to college freshmen, college sophomores, college juniors, college seniors, recent college graduates, graduate students, career changers. ▶ *1–3 marketing interns:* responsibilities include devising advertising strategies. Candidates should have computer skills, knowledge of field, office skills, oral communication skills, organizational skills, personal interest in the field, research skills, self-motivation, strong interpersonal skills, writing skills. Duration is 10–16 weeks (full or part-time). Unpaid. Open to college freshmen, college sophomores, college juniors, college seniors, recent college graduates, graduate students, career changers. ▶ *1–3 production management interns:* responsibilities include production and theater management. Candidates should have ability to work independently, computer skills, office skills, oral communication skills, organizational skills, plan to pursue career in field, writing skills. Duration is 10–16 weeks (full or part-time). Unpaid. Open to high school seniors, recent high school graduates, college freshmen, college sophomores, college juniors, college seniors, recent college graduates, graduate students, career changers. ▶ *1–3 props interns.* Candidates should have ability to work independently, analytical skills, knowledge of field, personal interest in the field, research skills, self-motivation, strong interpersonal skills. Duration is 10–16 weeks (full or part-time). Position available as unpaid or at $200 per week. Open to college freshmen, college sophomores, college juniors, college seniors, recent college graduates, graduate students, career changers, individuals reentering the workforce. ▶ *1–3 scenery interns:* responsibilities include carpentry, painting scenery, and assisting technical director. Candidates should have ability to work with others, college courses in field, experience in the field, organizational skills, plan to pursue career in field, self-motivation. Duration is 10–15 weeks. Unpaid. Open to college freshmen, college sophomores, college juniors, college seniors, recent college graduates, graduate students. ▶ *1–3 stage management interns:* responsibilities include assisting stage managers with preparation for rehearsals and performances. Candidates should have computer skills, experience in the field, oral communication skills, organizational skills, plan to pursue career in field, strong interpersonal skills. Duration is 10–15 weeks. Unpaid. Open to college freshmen, college sophomores, college juniors, college seniors, recent college graduates, graduate students.

Benefits Names of contacts, on-the-job training, possible full-time employment, willing to act as a professional reference, willing to complete paperwork for educational credit, willing to provide letters of recommendation, flexible hours.

Contact Write, call, fax, e-mail, or through World Wide Web site Joe Angel Babb, Education and Community Outreach Coordinator. Phone: 713-228-9341 Ext. 425. Fax: 713-227-7116. E-mail: joeab@alleytheatre.org. In-person interview recommended (telephone interview accepted). Applicants must submit a formal organization application, letter of interest, resume, two letters of recommendation. Application deadline: April 15 for summer, July 15 for fall, October 30 for spring. World Wide Web: http://www.alleytheatre.org.

ALLIANCE THEATRE COMPANY
1280 Peachtree Street, NE
Atlanta, Georgia 30309

General Information Theater company offering a diverse 8-play season of contemporary plays, musical theater, world and regional premieres, and classics in its 784-seat mainstage and 200-seat studio theaters; also offers 2 children's theater productions. Established in 1966. Number of employees: 100. Division of Woodruff Arts Center, Atlanta, Georgia. Number of internship applications received each year: 30.

Internships Available ▶ *2 stage management apprentices:* responsibilities include performing clerical work, maintaining rehearsal halls during rehearsal, assisting with all rehearsals, preparation and distribution of rehearsal and performance notes, operating backstage positions. Candidates should have ability to work with others, computer skills, experience in the field, oral communication skills, organizational skills, plan to pursue career in field. Duration is 8–9 months. $275 per week plus overtime after 40 hours. ▶ *2 stage management production assistants:* responsibilities include performing clerical work, maintaining rehearsal halls during rehearsal, assisting with all rehearsals, preparation and distribution of rehearsal and performance notes, operating backstage positions. Candidates should have ability to work with others, computer skills, experience in the field, oral communication skills, organizational skills, personal interest in the field. Duration is 8–9 months. $350 per week plus overtime after 40 hours. Open to recent college graduates, graduate students.

Benefits Job counseling, names of contacts, on-the-job training, possible full-time employment, willing to act as a professional reference, willing to provide letters of recommendation.

Contact Write or fax Mr. Rixon Hammond, Production Manager, 1280 Peachtree Street, NE. Fax: 404-733-4773. No phone calls. In-person interview recommended (telephone interview accepted). Applicants must submit a formal organization application, letter of interest, resume, three personal references, two letters of recommendation. Application deadline: May 18. World Wide Web: http://www.alliancetheatre.org.

AMERICAN CONSERVATORY THEATER
30 Grant Avenue
San Francisco, California 94108

General Information One of the nation's largest and most active resident professional theaters. Established in 1967. Number of employees: 500. Number of internship applications received each year: 75.

Internships Available ▶ *1–3 artistic department interns:* responsibilities include working with the directors and artistic staff in the artistic, casting, and literary departments; projects include new play development, visiting artist support, artistic planning, and script evaluation. Candidates should have ability to work independently, analytical skills, computer skills, editing skills, experience in the field, office skills, oral communication skills, organizational skills, plan to pursue career in field, research skills, self-motivation, strong interpersonal skills, writing skills. Duration is 2–10 months. $6.75 per hour. Open to college freshmen, college sophomores, college juniors, college seniors, recent college graduates, graduate students, career changers. ▶ *1 arts management intern:* responsibilities include assisting managing director and front of house manager with budget projections, research, general administration, event coordination, and volunteer coordination. Candidates should have computer skills, experience in the field, office skills, oral communication skills, organizational skills, plan to pursue career in field, research skills, strong interpersonal skills, strong leadership ability. Duration is 2–10 months. $6.75 per hour. Open to college juniors, college seniors, recent college graduates, graduate students. ▶ *1 costume rental intern:* responsibilities include maintaining large stock of period costumes; organizing and creating a unified look for business, personal, and theatrical rentals; and furnishing rehearsal costumes for mainstage theater productions. Candidates should have ability to work independently, college courses in field, computer skills, experience in the field, office skills, oral communication skills, organizational skills, plan to pursue career in field, research skills, self-motivation, strong interpersonal skills,

American Conservatory Theater (continued)

written communication skills. Duration is 9–10 months. $6.75 per hour. Open to college freshmen, college sophomores, college juniors, college seniors, recent college graduates, graduate students, career changers, individuals reentering the workforce. ▶ *1 costume shop intern:* responsibilities include assisting in costume shop including shopping, stitching, and various costume building duties as determined by the shop manager. Candidates should have ability to work independently, ability to work with others, college courses in field, computer skills, editing skills, experience in the field, office skills, oral communication skills, organizational skills, plan to pursue career in field, research skills, self-motivation, strong leadership ability, writing skills. Duration is 9–10 months. $6.75 per hour. Open to college freshmen, college sophomores, college juniors, college seniors, recent college graduates, individuals reentering the workforce. ▶ *1 lighting design intern:* responsibilities include assisting the lighting design associate in maintaining all records necessary for upkeep of the repertory plot and inventory, drafting designs for special effects, assisting the designers in hanging and focusing lights, and supervising technical rehearsals. Candidates should have ability to work independently, ability to work with others, college courses in field, computer skills, experience in the field, office skills, oral communication skills, organizational skills, plan to pursue career in field, research skills, self-motivation, strong leadership ability, written communication skills. Duration is 9–10 months. $6.75 per hour. Open to college seniors, recent college graduates, graduate students. ▶ *1 makeup and wig construction intern:* responsibilities include working under the direction of the theater's wigmaster in the repertory shop and on special projects. Candidates should have ability to work independently, ability to work with others, analytical skills, knowledge of field, oral communication skills, organizational skills, plan to pursue career in field, research skills, self-motivation, practical experience in related field, college degree in related field (preferred). Duration is 9–10 months. $6.75 per hour. Open to college freshmen, college sophomores, college juniors, college seniors, recent college graduates, graduate students, career changers, individuals reentering the workforce. ▶ *1 marketing/public relations intern:* responsibilities include learning day-to-day operations: writing, proofreading, photo production, developing and executing signage and posters, and maintaining the database. Candidates should have ability to work independently, analytical skills, college courses in field, computer skills, editing skills, experience in the field, office skills, oral communication skills, organizational skills, plan to pursue career in field, research skills, self-motivation, strong interpersonal skills, strong leadership ability, written communication skills. Duration is 2 months (minimum). $6.75 per hour. Open to college sophomores, college juniors, college seniors, recent college graduates, graduate students. ▶ *1 production management intern:* responsibilities include assisting the production management team in operation of production departments; learning about season schedule, budget planning, contracts, design development, and day-to-day production operations. Candidates should have ability to work independently, analytical skills, college courses in field, computer skills, editing skills, experience in the field, office skills, oral communication skills, organizational skills, plan to pursue career in field, research skills, self-motivation, strong interpersonal skills, written communication skills. Duration is 8–10 months. $6.75 per hour. Open to college seniors, recent college graduates, graduate students, career changers. ▶ *1 properties intern:* responsibilities include creation and fabrication of hand props and set dressings for mainstage productions. Candidates should have ability to work independently, analytical skills, college courses in field, experience in the field, office skills, oral communication skills, organizational skills, plan to pursue career in field, research skills, self-motivation, strong interpersonal skills, written communication skills. Duration is 9–10 months. $6.75 per hour. Open to college freshmen, college sophomores, college juniors, college seniors, recent college graduates, graduate students, career changers. ▶ *1 sound design intern:* responsibilities include assisting the repertory designer in mounting each production. Candidates should have ability to work independently, college courses in field, experience in the field, office skills, oral communication skills, organizational skills, plan to pursue career in field, research skills,

self-motivation, strong interpersonal skills, writing skills. Duration is 9–10 months. $6.75 per hour. Open to college seniors, recent college graduates, graduate students. ▶ *2–3 stage management interns:* responsibilities include assisting by becoming an integral member of stage management team on specifically assigned mainstage shows. Candidates should have ability to work independently, analytical skills, college courses in field, computer skills, editing skills, experience in the field, office skills, oral communication skills, organizational skills, plan to pursue career in field, research skills, self-motivation, strong interpersonal skills, strong leadership ability, written communication skills. Duration is 8–10 months. $6.75 per hour. Open to college freshmen, college sophomores, college juniors, college seniors, recent college graduates, graduate students, career changers, individuals reentering the workforce. ▶ *1 technical design intern:* responsibilities include working under the direction of the design associate and the technical supervisor to learn the specific techniques and construction methods developed by the theater staff; emphasis on drafting and mold building. Candidates should have ability to work independently, ability to work with others, college courses in field, computer skills, knowledge of field, office skills, oral communication skills, organizational skills, plan to pursue career in field, research skills, written communication skills. Duration is 9–10 months. $6.75 per hour. Open to college juniors, college seniors, recent college graduates, graduate students.

Benefits Formal training, job counseling, names of contacts, on-the-job training, opportunity to attend seminars/workshops, possible full-time employment, willing to act as a professional reference, willing to provide letters of recommendation, assistance with resume preparation.

Contact Write or through World Wide Web site Jennifer Caleshu, Internship Coordinator, 30 Grant Avenue, San Francisco, California 94108-5800. No phone calls. In-person interview recommended (telephone interview accepted). Applicants must submit a formal organization application, letter of interest, resume, portfolio, writing sample, three letters of recommendation. Application deadline: April 15 for production positions; continuous for artistic and administrative positions. Fees: $15. World Wide Web: http://www.act-sfbay.org.

THE AMERICAN PLACE THEATRE
266 West 37th Street, 22nd Floor
New York, New York 10018

General Information Theater producing the work of American writers that strives for an uncompromising commitment to unconventional and daring plays. Established in 1963. Number of employees: 10. Number of internship applications received each year: 75.

Internships Available ▶ *1 assistant to artistic director:* responsibilities include assisting artistic director in script evaluations, fundraising, correspondence, and daily maintenance of activities schedule. Candidates should have ability to work independently, analytical skills, college courses in field, computer skills, editing skills, knowledge of field, office skills, oral communication skills, organizational skills, plan to pursue career in field, research skills, self-motivation, strong interpersonal skills, writing skills. Duration is one academic year. Position available as unpaid or paid. Open to college seniors, recent college graduates, graduate students, career changers, individuals reentering the workforce. ▶ *3 education interns:* responsibilities include assisting education directors in the coordination and creative planning of 3 education programs: Urban Writes, Literature to Life, and Teacher's Place. Candidates should have ability to work independently, analytical skills, college courses in field, computer skills, knowledge of field, office skills, oral communication skills, organizational skills, self-motivation, strong interpersonal skills, writing skills, interest in production/stage management. Duration is one academic year. Position available as unpaid or paid. Open to college seniors, recent college graduates, graduate students. ▶ *1–2 fund-raising interns:* responsibilities include assisting the director of development in tracking funders and writing grants. Candidates should have ability to work independently, ability to work with others, computer skills, editing skills, office skills, organizational skills, personal interest in the field, research skills, writing skills. Duration is 1 semester. Position available as unpaid or paid. Open to college seniors, recent college graduates, graduate students, individuals reentering the workforce. ▶ *2–4 literary interns:* responsibilities include assisting artistic director in reading and processing incoming submissions and with new play development programs. Candidates should have ability to work independently, ability to work with others, analytical skills, college courses in field, computer skills, office skills, oral communication skills, organizational skills, personal interest in the field, research skills, self-motivation, writing skills, interest in playwriting or dramaturgy. Duration is 1 semester. Position available as unpaid or paid. Open to college juniors, college seniors, recent college graduates, graduate students. ▶ *4 marketing assistants:* responsibilities include assisting staff with day-to-day functions of office. Candidates should have ability to work independently, computer skills, editing skills, office skills, oral communication skills, organizational skills, self-motivation, strong interpersonal skills, writing skills. Duration is flexible. Position available as unpaid or paid. Open to college juniors, college seniors, recent college graduates, graduate students. ▶ *2 production interns:* responsibilities include assisting production manager in rehearsal and running of productions. Candidates should have ability to work independently, ability to work with others, college courses in field, computer skills, experience in the field, office skills, oral communication skills, organizational skills, plan to pursue career in field, self-motivation, written communication skills. Position available as unpaid or paid. Open to college juniors, college seniors, recent college graduates, graduate students. International applications accepted.

Benefits Job counseling, names of contacts, on-the-job training, opportunity to attend seminars/workshops, possible full-time employment, travel reimbursement, willing to act as a professional reference, willing to complete paperwork for educational credit, willing to provide letters of recommendation.

Contact Write, call, fax, or e-mail Vanessa Sparling, Administrative Assistant/Internship Coordinator. Phone: 212-594-4482 Ext. 10. Fax: 212-594-4208. E-mail: edu@americanplacetheatre.org. In-person interview recommended (telephone interview accepted). Applicants must submit a letter of interest, resume, three letters of recommendation. Applications are accepted continuously. World Wide Web: http://www.americanplacetheatre.org.

APPEL FARM ARTS AND MUSIC CENTER
457 Shirley Road
Elmer, New Jersey 08318

General Information Fine and performing arts center concentrating on 3 areas: presenting arts (music, dance, theater) to the local community; providing affordable meeting and work space for artists and art organizations; and offering arts education for children through a summer camp. Established in 1960. Number of employees: 18. Number of internship applications received each year: 50.

Internships Available ▶ *1 assistant events coordinator:* responsibilities include house manager for Evening and Family Matinee Series in a 250-seat house, assisting with coordination of 2,000-seat Country Music events and 10,000-seat Arts and Music Festival, assisting with Community Arts Outreach program, and miscellaneous other office duties. Candidates should have ability to work independently, oral communication skills, organizational skills, self-motivation, strong interpersonal skills, strong leadership ability. Duration is 3–9 months. $300 per month. ▶ *1–2 marketing associates/box office coordinators:* responsibilities include box office management for 16 plus shows (250-seat house), 3 plus shows (2,000-seat house), 1 show (10,000-seat house); assisting with marketing to radio, press, and audience; tabulating audience surveys and selling ads for program book. Candidates should have ability to work independently, ability to work with others, oral communication skills, organizational skills, self-motivation, written communication skills. Duration is 3–9 months. $300 per month. ▶ *1 outreach coordinator:* responsibilities include coordinating and executing outreach programs with schools and artists, maintaining surveys and records of program, and miscellaneous office duties. Candidates should have ability to work independently, oral communication skills, organizational skills, strong interpersonal skills, written com-

munication skills. Duration is 3–9 months. $300 per month. Open to college seniors, recent college graduates, graduate students, individuals reentering the workforce.

Benefits Free housing, free meals, names of contacts, on-the-job training, possible full-time employment, willing to act as a professional reference, willing to complete paperwork for educational credit, willing to provide letters of recommendation.

Contact Write, call, fax, e-mail, or through World Wide Web site Ms. Heather A. Yelle, Internship Coordinator, PO Box 888, Elmer, New Jersey 08318. Phone: 856-358-2472. Fax: 856-358-6513. E-mail: appelarts@aol.com. Telephone interview required. Applicants must submit a formal organization application, letter of interest, resume, three letters of recommendation. Applications are accepted continuously. World Wide Web: http://www.appelfarm.org.

ARDEN THEATRE COMPANY
40 North Second Street
Philadelphia, Pennsylvania 19106

General Information Nonprofit, professional theater company whose mission is to tell the greatest stories by the greatest storytellers of all time, stories that arouse, provoke, illuminate, and inspire. Established in 1988. Number of employees: 35. Number of internship applications received each year: 300.

Internships Available ▶ *6 apprentices:* responsibilities include working in every aspect of operations including artistic direction, marketing, box office, development, production (load-in/strike, run crew, prop/set/costume building), stage management, finance, and general management. Candidates should have ability to work with others, oral communication skills, plan to pursue career in field, self-motivation. Duration is one season (August to June). $275 per week plus full health benefits. Open to college seniors, recent college graduates, graduate students, law students, career changers, individuals reentering the workforce. ▶ *1 artistic intern:* responsibilities include assisting artistic office staff. Candidates should have office skills, oral communication skills, organizational skills, strong interpersonal skills. Duration is flexible. Unpaid. Open to high school seniors, recent high school graduates, college freshmen, college sophomores, college juniors, college seniors, recent college graduates, law students, career changers, individuals reentering the workforce. ▶ *1–2 development assistants:* responsibilities include assisting development staff in all areas of fund-raising. Candidates should have computer skills, office skills, oral communication skills, strong interpersonal skills, written communication skills. Duration is flexible. Unpaid. Open to high school seniors, recent high school graduates, college freshmen, college sophomores, college juniors, college seniors, recent college graduates, graduate students, law students, career changers, individuals reentering the workforce. ▶ *1–3 front-of-house interns:* responsibilities include assisting in all front-of-house responsibilities including house management and box office. Candidates should have oral communication skills, strong interpersonal skills. Duration is flexible during September-June season. Unpaid. Open to recent high school graduates, college freshmen, college sophomores, college juniors, college seniors, recent college graduates. ▶ *1–2 marketing assistants:* responsibilities include assisting staff in all areas of marketing. Candidates should have computer skills, office skills, strong interpersonal skills. Duration is flexible. Unpaid. Open to high school seniors, recent high school graduates, college freshmen, college sophomores, college juniors, college seniors, recent college graduates, graduate students, law students, career changers, individuals reentering the workforce. ▶ *15–20 production assistants:* responsibilities include running crew and assistants, working in areas of lighting, sound, props, costumes, and sets. Candidates should have ability to work with others, personal interest in the field. Duration is show-by-show for season of 7 shows. Position available as unpaid or at $80–$175 per week. Open to high school seniors, recent high school graduates, college freshmen, college sophomores, college juniors, college seniors, recent college graduates, law students, career changers, individuals reentering the workforce. International applications accepted.

Benefits Job counseling, names of contacts, on-the-job training, opportunity to attend seminars/workshops, possible full-time

Arden Theatre Company (continued)

employment, willing to act as a professional reference, willing to complete paperwork for educational credit, willing to provide letters of recommendation.

Contact Write, fax, or through World Wide Web site Intern or Apprentice Coordinator. Fax: 215-922-7011. No phone calls. In-person interview recommended (telephone interview accepted). Applicants must submit a letter of interest, resume. Application deadline: May 1 for Arden Professional Apprentice Program; continuous for other positions. World Wide Web: http://www.ardentheatre.org.

ARENA STAGE
1101 Sixth Street, SW
Washington, District of Columbia 20024

General Information One of the country's leading resident theater companies consisting of a core of resident artists, craftspeople, theater technicians, and administrators who seek to illuminate the American spirit through the highest professional standard of theater art; 8-play season runs mid-August through mid-June. Established in 1950. Number of employees: 180. Number of internship applications received each year: 300.

Internships Available ▶ *8 Allen Lee Hughes Fellowships:* responsibilities include working with seasoned professionals in the areas of artistic and technical production, arts and administration, and community engagement. Candidates should have ability to work independently, college courses in field, knowledge of field, plan to pursue career in field, strong interpersonal skills. Duration is July/August to May/June. $265 per week. Open to recent college graduates, graduate students. ▶ *7–11 artistic interns:* responsibilities include assisting in directing, literary management, casting/production, or community engagement/education/audience enrichment. Candidates should have analytical skills, college courses in field, experience in the field, organizational skills, research skills, writing skills. Duration is flexible (full-time); may follow production cycle (6-8 weeks). $120 per week. Open to college freshmen, college sophomores, college juniors, college seniors, recent college graduates, graduate students, career changers. ▶ *14–20 arts administration interns:* responsibilities include assisting the executive director or finance/personnel office or working with communications/marketing/media relations/graphic design; development (fund-raising), information systems, casting/production office, access ability/house management, or sales office. Candidates should have knowledge of field, office skills, oral communication skills, organizational skills, strong interpersonal skills, writing skills. Duration is flexible (full-time). $120 per week. Open to college freshmen, college sophomores, college juniors, college seniors, recent college graduates, graduate students, career changers. ▶ *10–20 technical/production interns:* responsibilities include assisting with costumes, lighting, production management, properties, scene painting/set construction, sound, or stage management. Candidates should have ability to work independently, college courses in field, knowledge of field, plan to pursue career in field, strong interpersonal skills. Duration is flexible (full-time); not available in summer. $120 per week. Open to college freshmen, college sophomores, college juniors, college seniors, recent college graduates, graduate students, career changers. International applications accepted.

Benefits Job counseling, names of contacts, opportunity to attend seminars/workshops, possible full-time employment, willing to act as a professional reference, willing to complete paperwork for educational credit, willing to provide letters of recommendation, modest stipend, minority fellowships available.

Contact Write, call, fax, e-mail, or through World Wide Web site Maya Robinson, Intern Program Coordinator. Phone: 202-554-9066. Fax: 202-488-4056. E-mail: interns@arenastage.org. Applicants must submit a letter of interest, resume, academic transcripts, two personal references, statement of how internship matches career objective; 2 letters of recommendation (one academic, one professional); mandatory interview in person or by phone; a critical writing sample (directing and administrative applicants only); see Web site for details. Application deadline: March 1 for summer, April 1 for Allen Lee Hughes fellowship, May 1 for fall, October 1 for winter/spring. World Wide Web: http://www.arenastage.org.

ASH LAWN OPERA FESTIVAL
1941 James Monroe Parkway
Charlottesville, Virginia 22902-8722

General Information Summer festival producing 2 operas and 1 musical theater production for a total of 28 performances; hosts additional musical and theatrical productions for all ages. Established in 1978. Number of employees: 60. Unit of The College of William and Mary, Williamsburg, Virginia. Number of internship applications received each year: 20.

Internships Available ▶ *1 administrative intern:* responsibilities include maintaining databases, organizing fund-raising mailings, designing summer festival programs, providing general office support. Candidates should have computer skills, office skills, organizational skills, self-motivation, writing skills. Duration is flexible. Unpaid. Open to high school seniors, recent high school graduates, college freshmen, college sophomores, college juniors, college seniors, recent college graduates, graduate students. ▶ *1 arts management intern:* responsibilities include working in administrative office, with production staff, and in the costume shop and box office. Candidates should have ability to work with others, computer skills, office skills, organizational skills, self-motivation. Duration is flexible. Unpaid. Open to college freshmen, college sophomores, college juniors, college seniors, recent college graduates, graduate students. ▶ *1 development intern:* responsibilities include composing development materials and fund-raising strategies and expanding and maintaining databases. Candidates should have ability to work independently, ability to work with others, computer skills, organizational skills, research skills, self-motivation, writing skills. Duration is flexible. Unpaid. Open to college juniors, college seniors, recent college graduates, graduate students. ▶ *1 marketing intern:* responsibilities include developing marketing strategies and contacts; researching, organizing, and updating grant information; and assisting with grant writing. Candidates should have ability to work with others, computer skills, office skills, organizational skills, research skills, self-motivation, writing skills. Duration is flexible. Unpaid. Open to college freshmen, college sophomores, college juniors, college seniors, recent college graduates, graduate students. ▶ *1 press intern:* responsibilities include composing press releases and calendar listings; organizing press databases; and developing contacts with area newspapers, magazines, and radio and television stations. Candidates should have ability to work independently, ability to work with others, computer skills, organizational skills, self-motivation, writing skills. Duration is one summer. Unpaid. Open to college freshmen, college sophomores, college juniors, college seniors, recent college graduates, graduate students. ▶ *1 production intern:* responsibilities include scene painting, scene shifting, lighting design, theatrical sewing, and carpentry. Candidates should have ability to work independently, ability to work with others, knowledge of field, self-motivation. Duration is one summer. Unpaid. Open to high school seniors, recent high school graduates, college freshmen, college sophomores, college juniors, college seniors, recent college graduates, graduate students. International applications accepted.

Benefits Free housing, job counseling, names of contacts, willing to complete paperwork for educational credit, willing to provide letters of recommendation, hands-on experience in the operation and production of professional opera company.

Contact Write, call, fax, e-mail, or through World Wide Web site Assistant to the General Director. Phone: 434-293-4500. Fax: 434-293-0736. E-mail: opera@avenue.org. Applicants must submit a letter of interest, resume. Application deadline: February 1 for spring, April 1 for summer. World Wide Web: http://www.ashlawnopera.org.

ATLANTIC THEATER COMPANY
336 West 20th Street
New York, New York 10011

General Information Nonprofit off-Broadway acting ensemble dedicated to producing new theater and featuring a distinctive acting technique. Established in 1985. Number of employees: 19. Number of internship applications received each year: 25.

Internships Available ▶ *2–4 development/marketing interns:* responsibilities include marketing, fund-raising, and organizing development and benefits. Candidates should have ability to work independently, ability to work with others, computer skills, organizational skills, personal interest in the field, self-motivation, writing skills. Duration is flexible. Unpaid. Open to college freshmen, college sophomores, college juniors, college seniors, recent college graduates, graduate students. ▶ *3 office interns:* responsibilities include managing house and box office, and performing general office work. Candidates should have editing skills, office skills, oral communication skills, organizational skills, self-motivation, strong interpersonal skills, writing skills. Duration is September 1-May 31. Unpaid. Open to college freshmen, college sophomores, college juniors, college seniors, recent college graduates. ▶ *3 production interns:* responsibilities include working on lighting, sets, props, costumes, and running crew for all productions. Candidates should have knowledge of field. Duration is flexible. Unpaid. Open to college freshmen, college sophomores, college juniors, college seniors, recent college graduates. International applications accepted.

Benefits Names of contacts, on-the-job training, opportunity to attend seminars/workshops, willing to complete paperwork for educational credit, willing to provide letters of recommendation.

Contact Write or fax Internship Coordinator. Fax: 212-645-8755. No phone calls. In-person interview recommended (telephone interview accepted). Applicants must submit a letter of interest, resume. Applications are accepted continuously. World Wide Web: http://www.atlantictheater.org.

BALLET INTERNATIONALE
502 North Capital Avenue, Suite B
Indianapolis, Indiana 46204-1392

General Information Professional performing ballet company offering home, educational, and tour performances. Established in 1973. Number of employees: 47. Number of internship applications received each year: 10.

Internships Available ▶ *1 administrative intern:* responsibilities include performing a variety of functions or working on special projects in the Executive, Artistic Operations and/or Human Resources areas. Candidates should have ability to work independently, computer skills, office skills, oral communication skills, organizational skills, research skills, self-motivation, strong interpersonal skills. Duration is flexible. Unpaid. Open to high school seniors, recent high school graduates, college freshmen, college sophomores, college juniors, college seniors, recent college graduates, graduate students, career changers, individuals reentering the workforce. ▶ *1 artistic administrative intern:* responsibilities include working with the principal ballet mistress on administrative tasks associated with casting, training, and coordinating the annual holiday performance of "The Nutcracker". Candidates should have ability to work independently, computer skills, office skills, oral communication skills, organizational skills, self-motivation, strong interpersonal skills, written communication skills. Duration is flexible. Unpaid. Open to recent high school graduates, college freshmen, college sophomores, college juniors, college seniors, recent college graduates, graduate students, career changers, individuals reentering the workforce. ▶ *1 ballet school intern:* responsibilities include support in maintaining student records, helping with organizing student bulletin boards, and assisting in the day-to-day operations of the school. Candidates should have ability to work independently, computer skills, office skills, oral communication skills, organizational skills, personal interest in the field, self-motivation, written communication skills. Duration is flexible. Unpaid. Open to high school seniors, recent high school graduates, college freshmen, college sophomores, college juniors, college seniors, recent college graduates, graduate students, career changers, individuals reentering the workforce. ▶ *2 development/special events interns:* responsibilities include proposal development, prospect identification and research, mailing preparation, and general office duties. Candidates should have ability to work independently, computer skills, editing skills, office skills, organizational skills, research skills, self-motivation, strong

interpersonal skills, writing skills. Duration is flexible. Unpaid. Open to high school students, recent high school graduates, college freshmen, college sophomores, college juniors, college seniors, recent college graduates, graduate students, law students, career changers, individuals reentering the workforce. ▶ *1 education and outreach intern:* responsibilities include assisting with general office duties and research to support education/outreach efforts. Candidates should have ability to work independently, computer skills, office skills, oral communication skills, organizational skills, research skills, self-motivation, strong interpersonal skills, written communication skills. Duration is flexible. Unpaid. Open to college juniors, college seniors, recent college graduates, graduate students. ▶ *2 marketing/publicity interns:* responsibilities include writing, organizing, and coordinating various projects. Candidates should have ability to work independently, analytical skills, college courses in field, computer skills, editing skills, office skills, oral communication skills, organizational skills, plan to pursue career in field, research skills, self-motivation, strong interpersonal skills, writing skills. Duration is flexible. Unpaid. Open to recent high school graduates, college freshmen, college sophomores, college juniors, college seniors, recent college graduates, graduate students, career changers. ▶ *1 production/stage management intern:* responsibilities include assisting the technical staff with planning and mounting a production. Candidates should have ability to work with others, college courses in field, computer skills, knowledge of field, organizational skills, plan to pursue career in field, self-motivation. Position available as unpaid or at $200 per week (maximum). Open to college freshmen, college sophomores, college juniors, college seniors, recent college graduates, graduate students. ▶ *1 ticketing services intern:* responsibilities include working with ticketing services manager to provide group and VIP sales services to ballet subscribers and patrons; may also be involved in gathering research. Candidates should have ability to work independently, computer skills, office skills, oral communication skills, organizational skills, research skills, self-motivation, strong interpersonal skills. Duration is flexible. Unpaid. Open to college juniors, college seniors, recent college graduates, graduate students, career changers, individuals reentering the workforce. ▶ *1 wardrobe intern:* responsibilities include assisting with costume construction and professional shop operations. Candidates should have college courses in field, knowledge of field, strong stitching ability, costume experience (helpful). Duration is flexible (no summers). Unpaid. Open to college sophomores, college juniors, college seniors, recent college graduates, graduate students. International applications accepted.

Benefits Formal training, names of contacts, on-the-job training, opportunity to attend seminars/workshops, possible full-time employment, willing to act as a professional reference, willing to complete paperwork for educational credit, willing to provide letters of recommendation.

Contact Write, fax, e-mail, or through World Wide Web site Pat Hanford, Executive Director. Fax: 317-637-1637. E-mail: phanford@balletinternationale.org. No phone calls. In-person interview recommended (telephone interview accepted). Applicants must submit a letter of interest, resume, letter of recommendation. Applications are accepted continuously. World Wide Web: http://www.balletinternationale.org.

BARROW GROUP
312 West 36th Street
New York, New York 10018

General Information Theater performing full-length new works. Established in 1986. Number of employees: 5. Number of internship applications received each year: 20.

Internships Available ▶ *1–3 development interns:* responsibilities include grant writing, fund-raising, and publicity. Candidates should have ability to work independently, computer skills, editing skills, oral communication skills, organizational skills, research skills, self-motivation, writing skills. Duration is 3–6 months. Unpaid. Open to college juniors, college seniors, recent college graduates, graduate students, career changers. ▶ *1–4 general management interns:* responsibilities include assisting the managing director in all aspects of production, fund-raising, Web site management, and Board of Trustees relationship. Candidates should

Barrow Group (continued)

have computer skills, office skills, oral communication skills, organizational skills, self-motivation, written communication skills. Duration is flexible. Unpaid. Open to recent high school graduates, college freshmen, college sophomores, college juniors, college seniors, recent college graduates, graduate students, career changers. ▶ *1–3 literary management interns:* responsibilities include reading and responding to scripts, helping organize reading series, recommending projects for production. Candidates should have ability to work independently, computer skills, editing skills, knowledge of field, oral communication skills, organizational skills, personal interest in the field, self-motivation, writing skills. Duration is 3–6 months. Unpaid. Open to recent high school graduates, college freshmen, college sophomores, college juniors, college seniors, recent college graduates, graduate students. ▶ *1–3 production interns:* responsibilities include assisting director and/or stage manager; helping with box office, house/stage management, and running crew. Candidates should have ability to work with others, personal interest in the field, plan to pursue career in field, self-motivation. Duration is one fall or spring. Unpaid. Open to high school students, recent high school graduates, college freshmen, college sophomores, college juniors, college seniors, recent college graduates, individuals reentering the workforce.

Benefits On-the-job training, opportunity to attend seminars/workshops, possible full-time employment, travel reimbursement, willing to complete paperwork for educational credit, willing to provide letters of recommendation.

Contact Write, e-mail, or through World Wide Web site Eric Paeper, Managing Director. E-mail: barrowgroup@earthlink.net. In-person interview recommended (telephone interview accepted). Applicants must submit a letter of interest, resume. Applications are accepted continuously. World Wide Web: http://www. barrowgroup.org.

BATTERY DANCE COMPANY
380 Broadway, 5th Floor
New York, New York 10013-3518

General Information Dance company that tours internationally, works extensively in the public schools, and produces an annual free public dance festival in New York City's financial district; also organizes domestic tours by foreign dance troupes. Established in 1976. Number of employees: 15. Number of internship applications received each year: 25.

Internships Available ▶ *1 administrative assistant:* responsibilities include performing office management duties. Candidates should have ability to work independently, ability to work with others, computer skills, office skills, oral communication skills, personal interest in the field, self-motivation, writing skills. Duration is flexible. Unpaid. ▶ *1 intern:* responsibilities include coordinating contracts and publicity, acting as site liaison, assisting in ad campaign, and administration. Candidates should have ability to work independently, ability to work with others, oral communication skills, personal interest in the field, self-motivation, written communication skills. Duration is flexible. Unpaid. Open to high school students, recent high school graduates, college freshmen, college sophomores, college juniors, college seniors, recent college graduates, graduate students, law students, career changers, individuals reentering the workforce. International applications accepted.

Benefits Job counseling, names of contacts, on-the-job training, possible full-time employment, willing to act as a professional reference, willing to complete paperwork for educational credit, willing to provide letters of recommendation, opportunity to attend seminars/workshops and performances.

Contact Write, call, fax, e-mail, or through World Wide Web site Jonathan Hollander, Artistic/Executive Director. Phone: 212-219-3910. Fax: 212-219-3911. E-mail: jonathan@batterydanceco.com. In-person interview recommended (telephone interview accepted). Applicants must submit a letter of interest, resume, writing sample, applications by e-mail encouraged. Applications are accepted continuously. World Wide Web: http://www.batterydanceco.com.

BILINGUAL FOUNDATION OF THE ARTS
421 North Avenue 19
Los Angeles, California 90031

General Information Bilingual Spanish-English theater company that performs plays by Hispanic and Hispanic-American playwrights and also has a touring children's theater company and teen theater. Established in 1973. Number of employees: 14. Number of internship applications received each year: 10.

Internships Available ▶ *1–2 development/marketing interns:* responsibilities include fund-raising and development. Candidates should have college courses in field, computer skills, knowledge of field, personal interest in the field, research skills, self-motivation, strong interpersonal skills, strong leadership ability, writing skills. Duration is 3–12 months. Unpaid. ▶ *1–2 marketing interns/development grantwriters, researchers:* responsibilities include performing data entry, compiling statistical data, preparing audience surveys, reporting survey results, assisting in preparation of marketing plan, and writing grants to request supporting funds and researching new funding sources. Candidates should have college courses in field, computer skills, knowledge of field, office skills, organizational skills, personal interest in the field, research skills, self-motivation, strong interpersonal skills, writing skills. Duration is flexible. Unpaid. Open to college seniors, recent college graduates, graduate students, career changers, individuals reentering the workforce.

Benefits On-the-job training, possible full-time employment, willing to provide letters of recommendation.

Contact Write, fax, or e-mail Aracely Alvarez, Managing Director. Fax: 323-225-1250. E-mail: bfa99@earthlink.net. No phone calls. In-person interview required. Applicants must submit a letter of interest, resume, three personal references, two letters of recommendation. Applications are accepted continuously. World Wide Web: http://www.bfatheatre.org.

BOND STREET THEATRE
2 Bond Street
New York, New York 10012

General Information Theater focusing on original work having a physical style; tours internationally performing socially relevant material with minimal use of language. Established in 1976. Number of employees: 5. Number of internship applications received each year: 100.

Internships Available ▶ *1 acting intern:* responsibilities include acting as understudy for all roles, standing-in for actors as necessary in rehearsals, attending all rehearsals (as possible), learning all skills (musical, physical). Candidates should have experience in the field, plan to pursue career in field, self-motivation, strong interpersonal skills, strong physical training or capability of physical training (dance, gymnastics), musical skills (a plus). Duration is open. Position available as unpaid or paid. Open to college freshmen, college sophomores, college juniors, college seniors, recent college graduates, graduate students. ▶ *1 business intern:* responsibilities include helping to design, implement, and produce company projects with artistic director and managing director. Candidates should have ability to work independently, ability to work with others, computer skills, organizational skills, personal interest in the field, writing skills. Duration is open. Position available as unpaid or paid. Open to college freshmen, college sophomores, college juniors, college seniors, recent college graduates, graduate students, career changers, individuals reentering the workforce. ▶ *1 costume design intern.* Candidates should have ability to work independently, knowledge of field, personal interest in the field, research skills, self-motivation, strong interpersonal skills. Duration is open. Position available as unpaid or paid. Open to college freshmen, college sophomores, college juniors, college seniors, recent college graduates, graduate students, career changers, individuals reentering the workforce. ▶ *1 development intern:* responsibilities include identifying and drafting applications for grants, foundations, and awards. Candidates should have ability to work independently, computer skills, personal interest in the field, research skills, self-motivation, writing skills. Duration is open. Position available as unpaid or paid. Open to college freshmen, college sophomores, college juniors, college seniors, recent college graduates, graduate students, career changers, individuals reentering the workforce. ▶ *1 directing intern:* responsibilities include assisting the director and dramaturgical functions. Candidates should have oral communication skills, personal interest in the field, plan to pursue career in field, research skills, strong interpersonal skills, writing skills. Duration is open. Position available as unpaid or paid. Open to college freshmen, college sophomores, college juniors, college seniors, recent college graduates, graduate students. ▶ *1 general management intern:* responsibilities include general office management and management/coordination of company projects. Candidates should have ability to work independently, computer skills, office skills, organizational skills, self-motivation, written communication skills. Duration is open. Position available as unpaid or paid. Open to college freshmen, college sophomores, college juniors, college seniors, recent college graduates, graduate students, career changers, individuals reentering the workforce. ▶ *1 press/marketing intern:* responsibilities include primarily marketing productions to festivals and other venues, both in U.S. and globally; some press work also. Candidates should have computer skills, oral communication skills, personal interest in the field, self-motivation, strong interpersonal skills, writing skills. Duration is open. Position available as unpaid or paid. Open to college freshmen, college sophomores, college juniors, college seniors, recent college graduates, graduate students, career changers, individuals reentering the workforce. ▶ *1 production intern:* responsibilities include all around production assistance. Candidates should have ability to work independently, organizational skills, strong interpersonal skills, versatility, a wide range of interests and abilities in the field. Duration is open. Position available as unpaid or paid. Open to college freshmen, college sophomores, college juniors, college seniors, recent college graduates, graduate students, career changers, individuals reentering the workforce. ▶ *1 set design intern.* Candidates should have ability to work independently, knowledge of field, personal interest in the field, research skills, self-motivation, strong interpersonal skills. Duration is open. Position available as unpaid or paid. Open to college freshmen, college sophomores, college juniors, college seniors, recent college graduates, graduate students, career changers, individuals reentering the workforce. ▶ *1 stage management intern.* Candidates should have ability to work independently, ability to work with others, knowledge of field, organizational skills, personal interest in the field, self-motivation. Duration is open. Position available as unpaid or paid. Open to college freshmen, college sophomores, college juniors, college seniors, recent college graduates, graduate students, career changers. International applications accepted.

Benefits Formal training, on-the-job training, opportunity to attend seminars/workshops, willing to complete paperwork for educational credit, willing to provide letters of recommendation, possibility of international travel, possible stipend.

Contact Write, call, e-mail, or through World Wide Web site Joanna Sherman, Artistic Director. Phone: 212-254-4614. E-mail: info@bondst.org. In-person interview recommended (telephone interview accepted). Applicants must submit a letter of interest, resume, photo (recommended) for acting interns. Applications are accepted continuously. World Wide Web: http://www.bondst.org.

CENTER STAGE
700 North Calvert Street
Baltimore, Maryland 21202

General Information Professional, regional theater whose artistic goal is to explore a wide range of dramatic literature and production approaches, from fresh visions of the classics to active support for contemporary writing. Established in 1963. Number of employees: 110. Number of internship applications received each year: 120.

Internships Available ▶ *1 audience services intern:* responsibilities include assisting volunteer and events coordinator in all aspects of program and assisting audience services staff in administration of patron and front-of-house services. Candidates should have oral communication skills, good customer service skills and be detail oriented. Duration is August/September to May/June. $85 per week. Open to recent college graduates, students willing to take a year off from college. ▶ *1 company management intern:* responsibilities include assisting with all aspects of company and facilities management, including actor, director, and other theater consultants' contacts, travel arrangements, and accommodations; auditions; management of all theater-owned housing units; and attending to the needs and requirements of visiting artists. Candidates should have ability to work independently, computer skills, organizational skills, self-motivation, strong interpersonal skills. Duration is August/September to May/June. $85 per week. Open to recent college graduates, students willing to take a year off from school. ▶ *1 costumes/wardrobe intern:* responsibilities include assisting in costume shop with construction, shopping for shows, and maintenance of stock, as well as assisting with running crew and daily wardrobe maintenance as needed; opportunities to learn more about crafts or wig maintenance also available. Candidates should have knowledge of field, self-motivation, strong interpersonal skills, fast and accurate sewing skills. Duration is August/September to May/June. $85 per week. Open to recent college graduates, career changers, students willing to take a year off from school. ▶ *1 development/fund-raising intern:* responsibilities include active participation in all fund-raising activities, including the annual direct mail and telefunding campaigns, special events, funding research, special projects, and day-to-day booking and acknowledgement of gifts. Candidates should have computer skills, office skills, oral communication skills, organizational skills, self-motivation, strong interpersonal skills. Duration is August/September to May/June. $85 per week. Open to recent college graduates, career changers, students willing to take a year off from school. ▶ *1 education intern:* responsibilities include assisting in scheduling workshops and other programs for middle and high schools, universities, and colleges; facilitating theater artists' school visits; developing educational and outreach activities and materials; and other special projects. Candidates should have computer skills, oral communication skills, organizational skills, self-motivation, strong interpersonal skills, written communication skills. Duration is August/September to May/June. $85 per week. Open to recent college graduates, students willing to take a year off from school. ▶ *1 electrics intern:* responsibilities include assisting electricians with hanging and focusing, creation of special effects, maintenance of lighting equipment, and running of each show. Candidates should have ability to work with others, computer skills, knowledge of field, oral communication skills, self-motivation. Duration is August/September to May/June. $85 per week. Open to recent college graduates, career changers, students willing to take a year off from school. ▶ *1 marketing intern:* responsibilities include assisting with market research and ticket promotions, coordinating complimentary gift certificate program, distributing marketing materials, and working with the on-campus sales team. Candidates should have computer skills, knowledge of field, office skills, oral communication skills, self-motivation, strong interpersonal skills, written communication skills. Duration is August/September to May/June. $85 per week. Open to recent college graduates, students willing to take a year off from college. ▶ *1 media relations intern:* responsibilities include managing the student critics program, generating publicity for the theater's educational programs, producing the in-house newsletter, and assisting with publications, press relations, advertising, and promotions. Candidates should have computer skills, knowledge of field, office skills, oral communication skills, self-motivation, strong interpersonal skills, writing skills. Duration is August/September to May/June. $85 per week. Open to recent college graduates, students willing to take a year off from college. ▶ *1 properties intern:* responsibilities include assisting in all aspects of procuring and creating props for each production; this includes carpentry, sculpting, metalwork, sewing, upholstery, painting, drawing, and research. Candidates should have knowledge of field, research skills, self-motivation, strong interpersonal skills. Duration is August/September to May/June. $85 per week. Open to recent college graduates, career changers, students willing to take a year off from school. ▶ *1 scenic art intern:* responsibilities include assisting the charge painter in the painting and occasional sculpting of all scenic elements. Candidates should have experience in the field, personal interest in the field, self-motivation, strong interpersonal skills, painting and drawing skills. Duration is August/September to May/June. $85 per week. Open to recent college graduates, career changers, students willing to take a year off from school. ▶ *1 scenic carpentry intern:* responsibilities include working

Center Stage (continued)

in the scene shop on construction of scenery for six mainstage productions. Candidates should have ability to work independently, ability to work with others, knowledge of field, oral communication skills, self-motivation, experience with wood construction and standard shop tools. Duration is August/September to May/June. $85 per week. Open to recent college graduates, students willing to take a year off from college. ▶ *1 sound intern:* responsibilities include assisting audio engineers in maintaining and installing equipment and with the running of each show. Candidates should have ability to work with others, computer skills, knowledge of field, oral communication skills, self-motivation. Duration is August/September to May/June. $85 per week. Open to recent college graduates, career changers, students willing to take a year off from school. ▶ *2 stage management interns:* responsibilities include working in all aspects of stage management, with primary duties in the rehearsal hall and as part of the running crew. Candidates should have computer skills, experience in the field, oral communication skills, organizational skills, self-motivation, strong interpersonal skills. Duration is August/September to May/June. $105 per week. Open to recent college graduates, career changers, students willing to take a year off from school.

Benefits Free housing, job counseling, names of contacts, on-the-job training, opportunity to attend seminars/workshops, possible full-time employment, willing to act as a professional reference, willing to complete paperwork for educational credit, willing to provide letters of recommendation, assistance with resume and interview preparation, free e-mail, complimentary tickets, opportunities to supplement living allowance, laundry facilities, and common room (with cable TV) in intern housing.

Contact Write, call, fax, or through World Wide Web site Katharyn Davies, Internship Coordinator. Phone: 410-685-3200 Ext. 330. Fax: 410-539-3912. In-person interview recommended (telephone interview accepted). Applicants must submit a formal organization application, letter of interest, resume, two letters of recommendation, portfolio or writing sample may be required. Application deadline: April 15 for upcoming season. World Wide Web: http://www.centerstage.org.

CENTRAL PARK SUMMERSTAGE
830 Fifth Avenue
New York, New York 10021

General Information New York's premier free performing arts festival that presents productions of superior artistic caliber. Established in 1983. Number of employees: 15. Subsidiary of City Parks Foundation, New York, New York. Number of internship applications received each year: 200.

Internships Available ▶ *1 Swedish Cottage Marionette Theatre intern:* responsibilities include box office duties, ushering guests, answering phones, booking group ticket sales, confirming reservations, correspondence, and documenting theatre revenue. Candidates should have oral communication skills, ability to multi-task, personal interest in small theatre atmosphere. Unpaid. Open to high school students. ▶ *1 VIP/Guest List Coordinator:* responsibilities include compiling and managing guest lists; scheduling interns to work VIP table; coordinating with publicist; setting up staffing, supervising, and coordinating VIP table with publicist. Candidates should have oral communication skills, organizational skills, knowledge of MS Office, foreign language skills (a plus). Duration is May ot August (30 hours per week plus events as necessary). Unpaid. Open to college freshmen, college sophomores, college juniors, college seniors, recent college graduates, graduate students. ▶ *1 Web intern:* responsibilities include day-to-day upkeep of Web site; updating site, pictures, and e-mail list; assisting with online activities. Candidates should have oral communication skills, organizational skills, knowledge of MS Office and graphics programs, experience on PCs and Macintosh. Duration is May to August (25 hours, 3 days per week). Unpaid. Open to college freshmen, college sophomores, college juniors, college seniors, recent college graduates, graduate students. ▶ *2 community outreach interns:* responsibilities include assisting marketing and media relations departments in creating and distributing season information in NYC; coordination flyering events throughout NYC as necessary. Candidates should have ability to work independently,

oral communication skills, written communication skills, computer graphics skills and fluency in a foreign language (a plus). Duration is may to august (20 or 40 hours per week plus events as needed). Unpaid. Open to college freshmen, college sophomores, college juniors, college seniors, recent college graduates, graduate students. ▶ *2 design interns:* responsibilities include coordinating ads for print campaign; designing community outreach fliers, venue directional/informational signage, and contesting/survey signage; designing fall/spring direct mail campaigns; designing and layout of final report templates for fall/winter. Candidates should have organizational skills, experience with PC/Macintosh and computer graphics programs, design skills. Duration is May to August (25 hours per week). Unpaid. Open to college freshmen, college sophomores, college juniors, college seniors, recent college graduates, graduate students. ▶ *1 event marketing intern:* responsibilities include event management for VIP sections; placing signage; overseeing drink tickets, food, beverages, decorations, and logistics; and communication with production staff. Candidates should have ability to work independently, oral communication skills, organizational skills, strong interpersonal skills, written communication skills. Duration is May to August (20 hours per week plus events). Unpaid. Open to college freshmen, college sophomores, college juniors, college seniors, recent college graduates, graduate students. ▶ *1 media partnership marketing intern:* responsibilities include coordinating promotional/production needs for media partners, assigning vehicle permits, compiling guest list names, producing and implementing contests, and assisting media partners with on-site needs. Candidates should have ability to work independently, oral communication skills, organizational skills, written communication skills, knowledge of MS Office and graphics programs, fluency in a foreign language (a plus). Duration is May to August (40 hours per week). Unpaid. Open to college freshmen, college sophomores, college juniors, college seniors, recent college graduates, graduate students. ▶ *1 membership program intern:* responsibilities include processing all new memberships, upkeep of membership database, servicing members with materials, answering e-mail and phone inquiries, gathering and maintaining guest list spreadsheets, and checking in members at free events. Candidates should have oral communication skills, strong interpersonal skills, ability to multi-task and work under deadlines, knowledge of MS Office programs. Duration is May to August (40 hours per week). Unpaid. Open to college freshmen, college sophomores, college juniors, college seniors, recent college graduates, graduate students. ▶ *1 merchandise intern:* responsibilities include managing store, overseeing production of merchandise/status reports, handling all monetary issues, and keeping track of inventory and sales. Candidates should have oral communication skills, organizational skills, written communication skills, ability to use MS Office programs. Duration is May to August (10 hours per week plus events as necessary). Unpaid. Open to college freshmen, college sophomores, college juniors, college seniors, recent college graduates, graduate students. ▶ *1 music programming intern:* responsibilities include office duties; maintaining artist files and CDs; assisting with talent offer letters; organizing contact letters and press materials; assisting in supplying marketing with artist bios, photos, and contact information; and assisting in coordinating travel and accommodations. Candidates should have office skills, organizational skills, knowledge of Windows programs and database software, interest in all types of music. Duration is May to August (40 hours per week). Unpaid. Open to college freshmen, college sophomores, college juniors, college seniors, recent college graduates, graduate students. ▶ *2 partnership marketing interns:* responsibilities include phones/messages, RSVPs, VIP/guest list additions, scheduling meetings, maintaining media kits and sales material, creating sell sheets on marketing programs, taking minutes and follow-ups for meetings, assisting at select events, assisting in contests, tracking, and receiving promotional materials. Candidates should have oral communication skills, written communication skills, knowledge of MS Office programs and File Maker Pro, knowledge of NYC geography. Duration is May to August (20 or 40 hours plus events as needed). Unpaid. Open to college freshmen, college sophomores, college juniors, college seniors, recent college graduates, graduate students. ▶ *1 photo and archive intern:* responsibilities include photoghaphing promotional activities; providing event shots for

Web site; and archiving materials including CDs, videos, publicity, and artist information. Candidates should have written communication skills, excellent photography skills (must provide own camera, digital preferred), knowledge of MS Office programs, File Maker Pro, PhotoShop, Illustrator, and Quark. Duration is May to August (20 to 30 hours per week). Unpaid. Open to college freshmen, college sophomores, college juniors, college seniors, recent college graduates, graduate students. ▶ *2 publicity interns:* responsibilities include assisting with creation/distribution of promotional and marketing materials; coordinating projects between sponsors, media outlets, and the public; and creating Web site content. Candidates should have computer skills, oral communication skills, written communication skills, Internet experience, fluency in a foreign language a plus. Duration is May to August (20 or 40 hours per week plus events as needed). Unpaid. Open to college freshmen, college sophomores, college juniors, college seniors, recent college graduates, graduate students. ▶ *2 summer community outreach interns:* responsibilities include creating advance awareness of specific performances and series; audience development; and duties on-site and in office. Candidates should have ability to work independently, personal interest in the field, knowledge of NYC and previous experience (a plus), driver's license required. Duration is May to August. Unpaid. Open to college freshmen, college sophomores, college juniors, college seniors, recent college graduates, graduate students. ▶ *2 summer field coordinators:* responsibilities include implementing Reading in the Parks or Arts in the Parks programs in the field. Candidates should have ability to work independently, personal interest in the field, positive attitude and sense of adventure, knowledge of NYC and previous experience (a plus), driver's license required. Duration is May to August (part-time to full-time). $10–$12 per hour. Open to college freshmen, college sophomores, college juniors, college seniors, recent college graduates, graduate students. International applications accepted.
Benefits Names of contacts, possible full-time employment, travel reimbursement, willing to act as a professional reference, willing to complete paperwork for educational credit, willing to provide letters of recommendation.
Contact Write, fax, e-mail, or through World Wide Web site Carter Angus, Internship Coordinator. Fax: 212-360-2754. E-mail: info@summerstage.org. No phone calls. Telephone interview required. Applicants must submit a letter of interest, resume, two writing samples. Application deadline: February 25 for spring, April 25 for summer, September 20 for fall. World Wide Web: http://www.summerstage.org.

THE CHILDREN'S THEATRE COMPANY
2400 Third Avenue South
Minneapolis, Minnesota 55404

General Information North America's largest professional theater for young people and adults dedicated to producing excellence in theater for audiences in the Twin Cities and nationwide. Established in 1965. Number of employees: 270. Number of internship applications received each year: 100.
Internships Available ▶ *3–4 costume construction interns:* responsibilities include working as assistant draper, painter/dyer, milliner, design assistant, or general shop. Candidates should have ability to work independently, ability to work with others, declared college major in field, experience in the field, oral communication skills, organizational skills. Duration is 3 months minimum. Unpaid. Open to college juniors, college seniors, recent college graduates, graduate students. ▶ *1–2 development interns:* responsibilities include focusing on the process of networking, fund-raising, grant writing, building and maintaining databases, and research on funding sources. Candidates should have ability to work independently, computer skills, knowledge of field, organizational skills, research skills, writing skills. Duration is 3 months minimum (20 hours per week minimum). Unpaid. Open to college juniors, college seniors, recent college graduates, graduate students. ▶ *1–2 directing interns:* responsibilities include assisting during the rehearsal process as an in-house critic and dramaturg as well as being an active participant in the development and direction of the plays. Candidates should have ability to work with others, analytical skills, experience in the field, office skills, organizational skills, research

skills. Duration is 3 months. Unpaid. Open to college seniors, recent college graduates, graduate students. ▶ *1–2 education outreach interns:* responsibilities include working directly with students and teachers to coordinate and schedule summer programs; school partnership programs; teacher training workshops; assisting staff in creating curriculum. Candidates should have ability to work independently, ability to work with others, computer skills, declared college major in field, experience in the field, office skills, organizational skills, plan to pursue career in field, research skills, strong leadership ability. Duration is 3 months. Position available as unpaid or paid. Open to college seniors, recent college graduates, graduate students. ▶ *2–3 lighting and sound interns:* responsibilities include duties based on intern's abilities and department needs. Candidates should have ability to work independently, ability to work with others, experience in the field, oral communication skills, organizational skills, plan to pursue career in field. Duration is 3 months minimum. Unpaid. Open to college juniors, college seniors, recent college graduates, graduate students. ▶ *1–2 marketing interns:* responsibilities include helping create the institution's public persona; areas of focus include media relations, database maintenance, and departmental organization. Candidates should have computer skills, editing skills, knowledge of field, office skills, organizational skills. Duration is 3 months minimum. Unpaid. Open to college juniors, college seniors, recent college graduates, graduate students. ▶ *6–8 performing apprentices:* responsibilities include acting in productions, classes, and studio theater production. Candidates should have college courses in field, oral communication skills, plan to pursue career in field, self-motivation, strong interpersonal skills. Duration is 11 months. Stipend. Open to college juniors, college seniors, recent college graduates, graduate students. ▶ *1 properties apprentice.* Candidates should have ability to work independently, declared college major in field, experience in the field, oral communication skills, plan to pursue career in field. Duration is 3 months minimum. Stipend. Open to college seniors, recent college graduates, graduate students. ▶ *2–3 properties construction interns:* responsibilities include learning basic techniques for building both hard and soft props; hand and large props construction, furniture building, and welding techniques. Candidates should have ability to work independently, declared college major in field, experience in the field, oral communication skills, plan to pursue career in field, self-motivation. Duration is 3 months minimum. Unpaid. Open to college juniors, college seniors, recent college graduates, graduate students. ▶ *1 stage management apprentice:* responsibilities include assisting with preproduction and rehearsals, run of 3–4 mainstage and/or tour productions, and stage managing 1–3 studio theater projects. Candidates should have computer skills, declared college major in field, experience in the field, organizational skills, plan to pursue career in field, strong leadership ability. Duration is 8–10 weeks. Stipend. Open to college juniors, college seniors, recent college graduates, graduate students. ▶ *4–5 stage management interns:* responsibilities include learning Actor's Equity Association rules and regulations and becoming an integral part of the rehearsal and performance process. Candidates should have ability to work with others, experience in the field, office skills, organizational skills, plan to pursue career in field, strong leadership ability. Duration is 3 months minimum. Unpaid. Open to college juniors, college seniors, recent college graduates, graduate students. International applications accepted.
Benefits Formal training, names of contacts, possible full-time employment, willing to complete paperwork for educational credit, willing to provide letters of recommendation.
Contact Write, fax, or e-mail Dana Ward, Education Department Manager. Fax: 612-874-8119. E-mail: education@childrenstheatre.org. No phone calls. In-person interview recommended (telephone interview accepted). Applicants must submit a letter of interest, resume, portfolio, two letters of recommendation. Applications are accepted continuously. World Wide Web: http://www.childrenstheatre.org.

CHILD'S PLAY TOURING THEATRE
2518 West Armitage Avenue
Chicago, Illinois 60647

General Information Professional touring children's theater that performs stories and poems written by children and adapted by

Child's Play Touring Theatre (continued)

professional actors and musicians. Established in 1978. Number of employees: 19. Number of internship applications received each year: 50.

Internships Available ▶ *1–3 administrative/public relations interns:* responsibilities include producing newsletter and assisting general manager and office manager. Candidates should have ability to work with others, computer skills, office skills, oral communication skills, research skills, written communication skills. Duration is flexible. Position available as unpaid or paid. Open to high school seniors, recent high school graduates, college freshmen, college sophomores, college juniors, college seniors, recent college graduates, graduate students, law students, career changers, individuals reentering the workforce. ▶ *1–3 assistants to executive director/producer:* responsibilities include all aspects of running a theater, including board development, fund-raising, and marketing. Candidates should have computer skills, oral communication skills, organizational skills, personal interest in the field, strong interpersonal skills, written communication skills. Duration is flexible. Position available as unpaid or paid. Open to college seniors, recent college graduates, graduate students, law students, career changers, individuals reentering the workforce. ▶ *1–3 development interns:* responsibilities include researching funding sources and assisting with proposal preparation. Candidates should have analytical skills, computer skills, oral communication skills, research skills, self-motivation, strong interpersonal skills, written communication skills. Duration is flexible. Position available as unpaid or paid. Open to college freshmen, college sophomores, college juniors, college seniors, recent college graduates, graduate students, law students, career changers, individuals reentering the workforce. ▶ *1–3 special project interns:* responsibilities include overseeing various aspects of Writing Our World (WOW) project. Candidates should have ability to work independently, ability to work with others, analytical skills, research skills, written communication skills, computer skills (Internet and Web site updates). Duration is flexible. Position available as unpaid or paid. Open to recent college graduates, graduate students, law students, career changers, individuals reentering the workforce. ▶ *3 story readers/coordinators:* responsibilities include reading, categorizing, culling, filing young authors' works, contacting young authors, and helping to script stories. Candidates should have computer skills, office skills, oral communication skills, organizational skills, written communication skills, bilingual ability (Spanish desired). Duration is September to June. Position available as unpaid or paid. Open to college freshmen, college sophomores, college juniors, college seniors, recent college graduates, graduate students, law students, career changers, individuals reentering the workforce. ▶ *2–6 technical production interns:* responsibilities include assisting production manager with sets, props, and costumes. Candidates should have ability to work with others, knowledge of field, personal interest in the field, self-motivation. Duration is flexible. Position available as unpaid or paid. Open to college freshmen, college sophomores, college juniors, college seniors, recent college graduates, graduate students, law students, career changers, individuals reentering the workforce. International applications accepted.

Benefits Names of contacts, on-the-job training, opportunity to attend seminars/workshops, possible full-time employment, willing to act as a professional reference, willing to complete paperwork for educational credit, willing to provide letters of recommendation, reimbursement of work-related travel expenses, lunch allowance (for those who work 20 hours or more per week), occasional stipends.

Contact Write, call, fax, e-mail, or through World Wide Web site Ms. June Podagrosi, Executive Director and Producer. Phone: 773-235-8911. Fax: 773-235-5478. E-mail: interns@cptt.org. In-person interview recommended (telephone interview accepted). Applicants must submit a formal organization application, letter of interest, resume, portfolio, personal reference, letter of recommendation. Applications are accepted continuously. World Wide Web: http://www.cptt.org.

THE CHORAL ARTS SOCIETY OF WASHINGTON
5225 Wisconsin Avenue, NW, Suite 603
Washington, District of Columbia 20015-2016

General Information 200-member symphonic chorus that performs a season subscription series at the Kennedy Center in addition to concerts with the National Symphony Orchestra, international tours, and recordings. Established in 1965. Number of employees: 12. Number of internship applications received each year: 50.

Internships Available ▶ *1 development intern:* responsibilities include assisting with fund-raising activities including donor tracking and recognition, silent auction tracking, funder research, proposal coordination, and other duties as assigned. Candidates should have computer skills, editing skills, office skills, oral communication skills, organizational skills, research skills, self-motivation, strong interpersonal skills, written communication skills. Duration is flexible. Unpaid. Open to college sophomores, college juniors, college seniors, recent college graduates, graduate students. ▶ *1 education/outreach intern:* responsibilities include assisting director of education in coordinating a choral tribute to Dr. Martin Luther King, Jr.; arranging preconcert lectures for students; providing area students with complimentary tickets for concerts; coordinating elementary school music program; and strategic planning. Candidates should have ability to work independently, office skills, oral communication skills, organizational skills, self-motivation, strong interpersonal skills, written communication skills. Duration is flexible. Unpaid. Open to college sophomores, college juniors, college seniors, recent college graduates, graduate students. ▶ *1 production intern:* responsibilities include assisting production department in administrative tasks including arranging concert season, chorus management, cataloging scores and music library, and other tasks as assigned. Candidates should have ability to work independently, ability to work with others, computer skills, editing skills, office skills, oral communication skills, organizational skills, research skills, self-motivation, written communication skills. Duration is flexible. Unpaid. Open to college sophomores, college juniors, college seniors, recent college graduates. ▶ *1 public relations/marketing intern:* responsibilities include writing press releases, designing brochures, assisting with marketing research and group sales, designing and editing the quarterly newsletter, updating press lists, and photographing and assisting with special events. Candidates should have computer skills, oral communication skills, organizational skills, self-motivation, strong interpersonal skills, written communication skills. Duration is flexible. Unpaid. Open to college sophomores, college juniors, college seniors, recent college graduates, graduate students. International applications accepted.

Benefits Formal training, job counseling, names of contacts, on-the-job training, opportunity to attend seminars/workshops, possible full-time employment, willing to act as a professional reference, willing to complete paperwork for educational credit, willing to provide letters of recommendation.

Contact Write, call, fax, e-mail, or through World Wide Web site Alicia Mills, Director of Community and Education Programs, 5225 Wisconsin Avenue, NW, Suite 603, Washington, District of Columbia 20015. Phone: 202-244-3669. Fax: 202-244-4244. E-mail: aliciamills@choralarts.org. In-person interview required. Applicants must submit a letter of interest, resume, three personal references, writing sample upon request for certain positions. Applications are accepted continuously. World Wide Web: http://www.choralarts.org.

CINCINNATI PLAYHOUSE IN THE PARK
Box 6537
Cincinnati, Ohio 45206

General Information Live theater company that presents professional theater productions to the Cincinnati region; member of the League of Regional Theaters. Established in 1960. Number of employees: 75. Number of internship applications received each year: 20.

Internships Available ▶ *3–5 stage management interns:* responsibilities include helping union stage management staff run rehearsals and performances; possible opportunity to stage manage outreach touring show. Candidates should have ability to work with others, analytical skills, organizational skills, knowledge of stage management techniques. Duration is part or all of 2003-2004 season. $250 per week. Open to college freshmen, college sophomores, college juniors, college seniors, recent college graduates, graduate students. International applications accepted.

Benefits Possible full-time employment, willing to act as a professional reference, willing to complete paperwork for educational credit, willing to provide letters of recommendation.

Contact Write, call, fax, e-mail, or through World Wide Web site Bruce Coyle, Production Stage Manager. Phone: 513-345-2242 Ext. 233. Fax: 513-345-2254. E-mail: bruce.coyle@cincyplay.com. In-person interview recommended (telephone interview accepted). Applicants must submit a letter of interest, resume, two letters of recommendation. Application deadline: May 30. World Wide Web: http://www.cincyplay.com.

CIRCA '21 DINNER PLAYHOUSE
1828 Third Avenue
Rock Island, Illinois 61201

General Information Theater that produces a year-round season of musicals, modern comedies, a series of children's plays, and special guest artist concerts as well as national tours. Established in 1977. Number of employees: 65. Number of internship applications received each year: 10.

Internships Available ▶ *Marketing/sales interns:* responsibilities include participating in marketing campaigns and sales program. Candidates should have ability to work independently, ability to work with others, computer skills, oral communication skills, written communication skills. Duration is minimum of 6 weeks. Unpaid. Open to recent high school graduates, college juniors, college seniors, graduate students. ▶ *1–2 public relations interns:* responsibilities include writing copy for ads and press releases; creating flyers, promotional materials, and mailing lists; assisting with group sales. Candidates should have college courses in field, computer skills, personal interest in the field, self-motivation, strong interpersonal skills, written communication skills, artistic skills (helpful). Duration is flexible. Unpaid. Open to college juniors, college seniors, recent college graduates. ▶ *1 stage management intern:* responsibilities include assisting resident stage manager with rehearsal duties and functioning as a running crew member. Candidates should have declared college major in field, experience in the field, organizational skills, personal interest in the field, strong interpersonal skills, strong leadership ability. Duration is linked to the production schedule. Unpaid. Open to college juniors, college seniors, recent college graduates, graduate students. ▶ *1–2 technical interns:* responsibilities include assisting in building of scenery and/or painting, maintaining the show, and functioning as a running crew member. Candidates should have ability to work independently, ability to work with others, college courses in field, experience in the field, organizational skills, technical skills. Duration is linked to the production schedule. Unpaid. Open to college sophomores, college juniors, college seniors, recent college graduates.

Benefits Job counseling, names of contacts, on-the-job training, possible full-time employment, tuition assistance, willing to act as a professional reference, willing to complete paperwork for educational credit, willing to provide letters of recommendation, possible reimbursement for academic credit.

Contact Write, fax, e-mail, or through World Wide Web site Mr. Dennis Hitchcock, Producer. Fax: 309-786-4119. E-mail: dpjh@circa21.com. No phone calls. In-person interview recommended (telephone interview accepted). Applicants must submit a letter of interest, resume, two letters of recommendation. Application deadline: January 1 for spring, April 1 for summer, October 1 for winter. World Wide Web: http://www.circa21.com.

CLASSIC STAGE COMPANY
136 East 13th Street
New York, New York 10003

General Information Nonprofit 178-seat theater dedicated to the reimagination of classics for an American audience; produces a season of 4 plays committed to new directorial or authorial

perspectives on the classics. Established in 1967. Number of employees: 54. Number of internship applications received each year: 25.

Internships Available ▶ *1 marketing/development intern:* responsibilities include assisting in research, grant compilation, and related clerical work. Candidates should have ability to work independently, analytical skills, computer skills, knowledge of field, research skills, writing skills. Duration is flexible. Unpaid. Open to college seniors, recent college graduates, graduate students. ▶ *1 production/management intern:* responsibilities include assisting with budget research, acquisition of production needs, actual production work, company and facilities management. Candidates should have ability to work with others, computer skills, experience in the field, office skills, oral communication skills, organizational skills, self-motivation. Duration is flexible. Unpaid. Open to college freshmen, college sophomores, college juniors, college seniors, recent college graduates, graduate students.

Benefits Formal training, job counseling, names of contacts, opportunity to attend seminars/workshops, possible full-time employment, willing to act as a professional reference, willing to complete paperwork for educational credit, willing to provide letters of recommendation, complimentary tickets to off-Broadway productions.

Contact Write, fax, e-mail, or through World Wide Web site Reed Ridgley, General Manager. Fax: 212-477-7504. E-mail: reed.ridgley@classicstage.org. No phone calls. In-person interview recommended (telephone interview accepted). Applicants must submit a letter of interest, resume, two personal references. Applications are accepted continuously. World Wide Web: http://www.classicstage.org.

THE CLEVELAND PLAY HOUSE
8500 Euclid Avenue
Cleveland, Ohio 44106

General Information Theater dedicated to the presentation of new and classical plays. Established in 1915. Number of employees: 60. Number of internship applications received each year: 200.

Internships Available ▶ *1–8 assistant directors:* responsibilities include assisting directors during rehearsals. Duration is 6–8 weeks. Unpaid. ▶ *1 business intern:* responsibilities include helping in all areas of business office. Duration is 8–10 weeks. Unpaid. ▶ *2 development interns:* responsibilities include grant writing, telemarketing, and fund-raising. Duration is 2–12 months. Unpaid. ▶ *2 literary interns:* responsibilities include reading and evaluating scripts and assisting dramaturg. Duration is 6 weeks to 9 months. Unpaid. ▶ *4 marketing interns:* responsibilities include assisting in all aspects of marketing. Duration is 2–12 months. Unpaid. ▶ *1 playwriting intern:* responsibilities include assisting literary manager. Duration is 6 weeks to 9 months. Unpaid. ▶ *2 production assistants:* responsibilities include assisting stage managers in rehearsal and performance. Duration is 6 weeks to 9 months. Unpaid. ▶ *6 shop interns:* responsibilities include working with costumes, lights, sound, and props. Duration is 2–9 months. Unpaid. Open to recent college graduates, graduate students.

Benefits Job counseling, possible full-time employment, willing to act as a professional reference, willing to complete paperwork for educational credit, willing to provide letters of recommendation.

Contact Write, call, fax, or e-mail Mr. David Colacci, Director of Apprentice Program. Phone: 216-795-7000 Ext. 205. Fax: 216-795-7005. E-mail: dcolacci@clevelandplayhouse.com. Applicants must submit a letter of interest, resume, photo. Applications are accepted continuously. World Wide Web: http://www.clevelandplayhouse.com.

COLLEGE LIGHT OPERA COMPANY
Highfield Theatre, PO Drawer 906
Falmouth, Massachusetts 02541

General Information Summer stock music theater serving as training ground for all aspects of theater performance, production, and management. Established in 1969. Number of employees: 80. Number of internship applications received each year: 400.

Internships Available ▶ *1 assistant business manager:* responsibilities include assisting business manager in various tasks, maintain-

College Light Opera Company (continued)

ing mailing lists, and supervising snack bar operation. Candidates should have ability to work independently, computer skills, experience in the field, office skills, oral communication skills, writing skills. Duration is June to August. $1600 per duration of internship. Open to college freshmen, college sophomores, college juniors, college seniors, recent college graduates. ▶ *2 box office treasurers:* responsibilities include managing box office. Candidates should have ability to work independently, ability to work with others, experience in the field, office skills, oral communication skills, organizational skills, written communication skills. Duration is June to August. $1600 per duration of internship. Open to high school seniors, recent high school graduates, college freshmen, college sophomores, college juniors, college seniors, graduate students. ▶ *1 cook:* responsibilities include menu planning, food buying and cooking for 80 people in co-op setting. Candidates should have ability to work independently, ability to work with others, knowledge of field, organizational skills, personal interest in the field, self-motivation, strong leadership ability. Duration is June to August. $5000–$6500 per duration of internship. Open to college freshmen, college sophomores, college juniors, college seniors, recent college graduates, career changers, individuals reentering the workforce. ▶ *6 costume crew interns:* responsibilities include assisting with making costumes. Candidates should have ability to work independently, ability to work with others, sewing skills. Duration is June to August. $2000 per duration of internship. Open to high school seniors, recent high school graduates, college freshmen, college sophomores, college juniors, college seniors, recent college graduates, graduate students. ▶ *1 costume designer:* responsibilities include designing or pulling from stock costumes for 9 musicals. Candidates should have ability to work with others, college courses in field, experience in the field, organizational skills, strong leadership ability, costume design and building skills. Duration is June to August. $4000–$5000 per duration of internship. Open to college sophomores, college juniors, college seniors, recent college graduates, graduate students. ▶ *18 orchestra musicians:* responsibilities include performing in 9 musicals. Candidates should have ability to work with others, experience in orchestra work. Duration is June to August. $1000 per duration of internship. Open to high school seniors, recent high school graduates, college freshmen, college sophomores, college juniors, college seniors, recent college graduates, graduate students. ▶ *1 publicity director:* responsibilities include writing press releases, distributing literature and posters, preparing weekly programs, maintaining theater bulletin boards, house managing, and supervising ushers. Candidates should have ability to work independently, ability to work with others, computer skills, editing skills, experience in the field, oral communication skills, organizational skills, self-motivation, writing skills. Duration is June to August. $1600 per duration of internship. Open to college freshmen, college sophomores, college juniors, college seniors, recent college graduates. ▶ *32 singers/actors:* responsibilities include performing in 9 musicals. Candidates should have ability to work with others, personal interest in the field, self-motivation, strong singing/acting skills. Duration is June to August. Unpaid. Open to college freshmen, college sophomores, college juniors, college seniors, recent college graduates, graduate students. ▶ *6 stage crew interns:* responsibilities include assisting with building scenery. Candidates should have ability to work independently, ability to work with others, knowledge of field, experience in set construction, set painting, and lighting. Duration is June to August. $2000 per duration of internship. Open to high school seniors, recent high school graduates, college freshmen, college sophomores, college juniors, college seniors, recent college graduates. ▶ *1 stage set designer:* responsibilities include designing and building stage sets and lights for 9 musicals using a crew of 6 stage hands. Candidates should have ability to work independently, ability to work with others, college courses in field, experience in the field, organizational skills, strong leadership ability, skills in designing and building stage scenery. Duration is June to August. $4000–$5000 per duration of internship. Open to college juniors, college seniors, recent college graduates, graduate students. International applications accepted.

Benefits Formal training, free housing, free meals, job counseling, names of contacts, on-the-job training, willing to act as a professional reference, willing to complete paperwork for educational credit, willing to provide letters of recommendation.
Contact Write, call, fax, e-mail, or through World Wide Web site Mr. Robert A. Haslun, Producer, 162 South Cedar Street, Oberlin, Ohio 44074. Phone: 440-774-8485. Fax: 440-775-8642. E-mail: bob.haslun@oberlin.edu. Applicants must submit a formal organization application, resume, two letters of recommendation, audition tape or CD for orchestra and vocal company. Application deadline: March 15 for summer; continuous after March 15 if openings remain. World Wide Web: http://www.collegelightopera.com.

CORTLAND REPERTORY THEATRE, INC.
37 Franklin Street
Cortland, New York 13045

General Information Professional summer stock theater whose mission is to bring affordable cultural opportunities to a primarily rural area. Established in 1972. Number of employees: 2. Number of internship applications received each year: 250.
Internships Available ▶ *6 performing interns:* responsibilities include acting in productions and doing shop duties. Candidates should have ability to work with others, college courses in field, knowledge of field, personal interest in the field, self-motivation. Duration is up to 14 weeks in summer. $90 per week. Open to college freshmen, college sophomores, college juniors, college seniors, graduate students. ▶ *4 production interns:* responsibilities include performing, props, scenery, costume, light, sound duties, and running crews. Candidates should have ability to work with others, college courses in field, knowledge of field, oral communication skills, self-motivation. Duration is up to 14 weeks in summer. $90 per week. Open to college freshmen, college sophomores, college juniors, college seniors, recent college graduates, graduate students. International applications accepted.
Benefits Formal training, free housing, on-the-job training, opportunity to attend seminars/workshops, willing to provide letters of recommendation.
Contact Write, fax, or e-mail Kerby Thompson, Producing Director. Fax: 607-753-0047. E-mail: cortlandrep@hotmail.com. No phone calls. In-person interview required. Applicants must submit a letter of interest, resume, three personal references, 3 professional references, audition (for performing internships). Application deadline: April 1 for summer. World Wide Web: http://www.cortlandrep.org.

COURT THEATRE (THE PROFESSIONAL THEATRE AT THE UNIVERSITY OF CHICAGO)
5535 South Ellis Avenue
Chicago, Illinois 60637

General Information Professional residence Equity theater company located on the University of Chicago campus. Established in 1954. Number of employees: 20. Unit of University of Chicago, Chicago, Illinois. Number of internship applications received each year: 50.
Internships Available ▶ *1 casting intern:* responsibilities include developing schedules, assisting with organizational research, setting up auditions, and processing new actor pictures and resumes. Candidates should have knowledge of field, oral communication skills, organizational skills, personal interest in the field, plan to pursue career in field, self-motivation, written communication skills. Duration is flexible. Unpaid. Open to college juniors, college seniors, recent college graduates. ▶ *1 costume shop intern:* responsibilities include researching, shopping for, and coordinating costume and prop elements. Candidates should have experience in the field, knowledge of field. Duration is flexible. Unpaid. Open to college juniors, college seniors, graduate students. ▶ *1–3 dramaturgy interns:* responsibilities include researching and writing playnotes. Candidates should have computer skills, editing skills, research skills, writing skills. Duration is 6–14 weeks. Unpaid. Open to college juniors, college seniors, graduate students. ▶ *1–3 production assistants:* responsibilities include developing projects with various staff members. Candidates should have knowledge of field, personal interest in the field, plan to pursue career in field. Duration is flexible. Unpaid. Open to college juniors, col-

lege seniors, graduate students. ▶ *2 stage management interns:* responsibilities include working directly with stage manager and assistant stage manager in all areas of preparation and the rehearsal process, including the technical rehearsal; may lead to a paid position. Candidates should have computer skills, knowledge of field, office skills, organizational skills, personal interest in the field, self-motivation. Duration is 6–14 weeks. Unpaid. Open to college seniors, recent college graduates, graduate students.

Benefits On-the-job training, opportunity to attend seminars/ workshops, possible full-time employment, willing to act as a professional reference, willing to complete paperwork for educational credit, willing to provide letters of recommendation.

Contact Write Executive Assistant to Executive Director. Fax: 773-834-1897. E-mail: directors@courttheatre.org. No phone calls. In-person interview recommended (telephone interview accepted). Applicants must submit a letter of interest, resume, two personal references, two letters of recommendation. Applications are accepted continuously. World Wide Web: http://www.courttheatre. org.

DALLAS THEATER CENTER
3636 Turtle Creek Boulevard
Dallas, Texas 75219

General Information Theater committed to supporting the work of the most exciting, daring, and uncompromising artists as well as serving the community through the plays presented and special programs offered. Established in 1959. Number of employees: 75. Number of internship applications received each year: 100.

Internships Available ▶ *1–3 arts administrators:* responsibilities include working in the areas of fund-raising, marketing, development, and general management; assisting department heads in daily operations, special events and planning. Candidates should have ability to work independently, analytical skills, computer skills, editing skills, office skills, oral communication skills, organizational skills, personal interest in the field, self-motivation, strong interpersonal skills, writing skills. Duration is August to May. Minimum wage. Open to college freshmen, college sophomores, college juniors, college seniors, recent college graduates, graduate students. ▶ *1 company manager:* responsibilities include assisting in all areas required to maintain efficient company operations including booking travel, housing, and hospitality arrangements for visiting artists. Candidates should have ability to work independently, computer skills, office skills, oral communication skills, organizational skills, personal interest in the field, self-motivation, strong interpersonal skills, strong leadership ability, written communication skills. Duration is August to May. Minimum wage. Open to college freshmen, college sophomores, college juniors, college seniors, recent college graduates, graduate students. ▶ *2 director/literary managers:* responsibilities include assisting mainstage productions, directing workshop production, reading new scripts, gathering and organizing research for mainstage productions, attending local productions, maintaining correspondence with playwrights, and providing administrative assistance. Candidates should have ability to work independently, computer skills, knowledge of field, office skills, oral communication skills, organizational skills, plan to pursue career in field, research skills, self-motivation, strong interpersonal skills, strong leadership ability, written communication skills. Duration is August to May. Minimum wage. Open to college juniors, college seniors, recent college graduates, graduate students. ▶ *1 education and community programs intern:* responsibilities include assisting the director of education in overseeing all education and community programs; serving as teaching assistant for school outreach programs; communicating with other departments, including artistic, production and marketing, and DISD schools to gather information and facilitate scheduling. Candidates should have ability to work independently, computer skills, office skills, oral communication skills, organizational skills, personal interest in the field, self-motivation, strong interpersonal skills, written communication skills. Duration is August to May. Minimum wage. Open to college juniors, college seniors, recent college graduates, graduate students. ▶ *6–8 production interns:* responsibilities include working in various areas such as props, electrics, sound,

carpentry, scenic art, wardrobe, or stage operations. Candidates should have ability to work independently, ability to work with others, college courses in field, experience in the field, plan to pursue career in field, self-motivation. Duration is August to May. Minimum wage. Open to college freshmen, college sophomores, college juniors, college seniors, recent college graduates, graduate students, career changers. ▶ *1 production management intern:* responsibilities include assisting producing manager in overseeing all production-related concerns, including scheduling and the facilitation of communication between production departments and visiting artists. Candidates should have ability to work independently, ability to work with others, computer skills, office skills, oral communication skills, organizational skills, personal interest in the field, self-motivation. Duration is August to May. Minimum wage. Open to college juniors, college seniors, recent college graduates, graduate students. ▶ *2 stage managers:* responsibilities include working with Equity stage managers in all aspects of their work, including involvement in production from the beginning of the rehearsal process through the run of mainstage productions. Candidates should have ability to work independently, computer skills, editing skills, experience in the field, oral communication skills, organizational skills, self-motivation, strong interpersonal skills, strong leadership ability. Duration is August to May. Minimum wage. Open to college freshmen, college sophomores, college juniors, college seniors, recent college graduates, graduate students, career changers. International applications accepted.

Benefits On-the-job training, opportunity to attend seminars/ workshops, possible full-time employment, willing to act as a professional reference, willing to complete paperwork for educational credit, willing to provide letters of recommendation.

Contact Write, call, fax, or through World Wide Web site Lisa Lawrence Holland, Director of Education and Community Programs. Phone: 214-252-3916. Fax: 214-521-7666. E-mail: lisa. holland@dallastheatercenter.org. Applicants must submit a formal organization application, letter of interest, resume, three letters of recommendation. Application deadline: July 1. World Wide Web: http://www.dtcinfo.org.

DENVER CENTER THEATRE COMPANY
1050 13th Street
Denver, Colorado 80204

General Information Nonprofit regional theater producing 12 productions in four theaters and tour productions locally, nationally, and internationally. Established in 1978. Number of employees: 400. Division of Denver Center for the Performing Arts, Denver, Colorado. Number of internship applications received each year: 100.

Internships Available ▶ *1–2 administration interns:* responsibilities include assisting in various aspects of administration for nonprofit regional theater. Candidates should have ability to work independently, computer skills, office skills, oral communication skills, organizational skills, personal interest in the field, self-motivation, strong interpersonal skills, written communication skills. Position available as unpaid or paid. Open to recent college graduates, graduate students, law students. ▶ *1–2 costume/ wigs/wardrobe interns:* responsibilities include running crew assignment involving costume and accessories maintenance and quick change techniques. Candidates should have ability to work independently, oral communication skills, personal interest in the field, self-motivation, strong interpersonal skills, flexibility for long working hours. Duration is 6–8 weeks. Position available as unpaid or at $8–$10 per hour. Open to high school seniors, recent high school graduates, college freshmen, college sophomores, college juniors, college seniors, recent college graduates, graduate students, law students, career changers, individuals reentering the workforce. ▶ *1 lighting design intern:* responsibilities include working with resident and guest professional staff members during the season with a focus on drafting, equipment maintenance, electrics, special effects, and special projects. Candidates should have ability to work independently, ability to work with others, knowledge of field, personal interest in the field, plan to pursue career in field, self-motivation. Duration is September to May. Position available as unpaid or paid. Open to high school students, college

Denver Center Theatre Company (continued)

sophomores, college juniors, college seniors, recent college graduates. ▶ *Marketing interns:* responsibilities include assisting in various aspects of marketing and communication for nonprofit regional theater. Candidates should have ability to work independently, computer skills, office skills, personal interest in the field, self-motivation, written communication skills. Duration is 1–2 semesters. Position available as unpaid or paid. Open to college seniors, recent college graduates, graduate students. ▶ *1 properties intern:* responsibilities include using techniques in welding, vacuforming plastics, painting, carving, furniture construction and upholstery, and other crafts. Candidates should have ability to work with others, knowledge of field, personal interest in the field. Position available as unpaid or paid. Open to college juniors, college seniors, recent college graduates, graduate students. ▶ *1 scene design intern:* responsibilities include drafting, model building, design and technical research in scenic and prop areas, and scene painting. Candidates should have ability to work independently, computer skills, knowledge of field, oral communication skills, plan to pursue career in field, self-motivation, strong interpersonal skills. Duration is 8–40 weeks. Position available as unpaid or paid. Open to college juniors, college seniors, recent college graduates, graduate students. ▶ *1 scene painting intern:* responsibilities include using traditional methods and innovative techniques, assisting the DCTC scenic artists in painting and finishing scenery and technical effects for productions. Candidates should have ability to work with others, knowledge of field, personal interest in the field. Position available as unpaid or paid. Open to high school seniors, recent high school graduates, college juniors, college seniors, recent college graduates, graduate students, career changers, individuals reentering the workforce. ▶ *1 sound intern:* responsibilities include assisting sound designers in fabrication of show recordings, including recording and editing of music and sound effects; setting up sound recording, reproducing, amplification, and communication equipment for rehearsals and performances; maintaining sound department equipment, libraries, and facilities; and other related activities as may be required for the actualization of theater sound. Candidates should have ability to work independently, ability to work with others, computer skills, knowledge of field, oral communication skills, personal interest in the field, written communication skills. Position available as unpaid or paid. Open to high school seniors, recent high school graduates, college freshmen, college sophomores, college juniors, college seniors, recent college graduates, graduate students. ▶ *1–3 stage management/production interns:* responsibilities include organizing daily schedules, conducting rehearsals, attending design and production meetings, and focusing on the detail work surrounding productions. Candidates should have ability to work independently, knowledge of field, oral communication skills, plan to pursue career in field, self-motivation, strong interpersonal skills. Duration is 10–38 weeks. Unpaid. Open to college freshmen, college sophomores, college juniors, college seniors, recent college graduates, graduate students, law students, career changers. ▶ *1 technical production intern:* responsibilities include working in a master/apprentice relationship with the technical director, learning a variety of disciplines, ranging from fiscal management to high tech invention of scenic solutions. Candidates should have ability to work independently, ability to work with others, college courses in field, knowledge of field, organizational skills, personal interest in the field, plan to pursue career in field. Position available as unpaid or paid. Open to college seniors, recent college graduates, graduate students. International applications accepted.

Benefits Formal training, names of contacts, on-the-job training, possible full-time employment, willing to act as a professional reference, willing to complete paperwork for educational credit, willing to provide letters of recommendation, limited stipends and free housing may be available in some departments.

Contact Write, call, fax, or e-mail Lyle Raper, Production Stage Manager, 1101 13th Street. Phone: 303-572-4446. Fax: 303-825-2117. E-mail: lraper@dcpa.org. In-person interview recommended (telephone interview accepted). Applicants must submit a letter of interest, resume. Applications are accepted continuously. World Wide Web: http://www.denvercenter.org.

DORSET THEATRE FESTIVAL
Box 510
Dorset, Vermont 05251-0510

General Information Professional, nonprofit Equity theater company producing summer seasons of 5 mainstage plays and children's play. Established in 1976. Number of employees: 76. Program of American Theatre Works Inc., Dorset, Vermont.
Internships Available ▶ *4–5 arts management interns:* responsibilities include helping with fund-raising, publicity, box office duties, special events planning, and related managerial tasks. Candidates should have experience in the field, organizational skills, plan to pursue career in field, self-motivation, strong interpersonal skills, writing skills. Duration is 3-4 months in summer. $125 per week. Open to college freshmen, college sophomores, college juniors, college seniors, recent college graduates, graduate students, career changers, individuals reentering the workforce. ▶ *4–5 technical theater interns:* responsibilities include working closely with designers on costumes, props, sets, and lighting. Candidates should have ability to work independently, ability to work with others, college courses in field, knowledge of field, plan to pursue career in field. Duration is 3-4 months in summer. $125 per week. Open to college freshmen, college sophomores, college juniors, college seniors, recent college graduates, graduate students, individuals reentering the workforce. International applications accepted.
Benefits Free housing, names of contacts, on-the-job training, opportunity to attend seminars/workshops, willing to act as a professional reference, willing to complete paperwork for educational credit, willing to provide letters of recommendation.
Contact Write, call, fax, e-mail, or through World Wide Web site Barbara Ax, General Manager. Phone: 802-867-2223. Fax: 802-867-0144. E-mail: theatre@sover.net. In-person interview recommended (telephone interview accepted). Applicants must submit a letter of interest, resume, two personal references. Application deadline: April 15. World Wide Web: http://www.dorsettheatrefestival.org.

THE DRAMA LEAGUE
520 8th Avenue, Suite 320
New York, New York 10018

General Information Organization whose purpose is to develop and administer programs that foster the growth of artists and audiences. Established in 1916. Number of employees: 6. Number of internship applications received each year: 200.
Internships Available ▶ *1 administrative intern:* responsibilities include daily mail, receptionist work, special projects (including archival work), and sending out mailings. Candidates should have ability to work independently, office skills, oral communication skills, organizational skills, personal interest in the field, research skills, self-motivation, strong interpersonal skills, writing skills, knowledge of MS Word, Excel, QuarkXpress, and ACCESS. Duration is 12 weeks. $50 per 20-hour week. Open to college freshmen, college sophomores, college juniors, college seniors. ▶ *1 directors project intern:* responsibilities include liaison with casting directors, creating newsletter (with supervision), attending rehearsals as needed, helping box office for performances (if needed), and assisting with mailings. Candidates should have ability to work independently, computer skills, office skills, organizational skills, plan to pursue career in field, writing skills. Duration is 10–12 weeks. $50 per week. Open to college freshmen, college sophomores, college juniors, college seniors, recent college graduates. ▶ *1–3 member services assistants:* responsibilities include assisting in data entry, financial processing, member services, theatre and publicist relationships, special events, and vendor activity. Candidates should have ability to work independently, computer skills, knowledge of field, office skills, oral communication skills, plan to pursue career in field, self-motivation, strong interpersonal skills, written communication skills, passion for theatre and its audiences. Duration is September to May. $50 per week. Open to college juniors, college seniors, recent college graduates, graduate students, individuals reentering the workforce. ▶ *2–3 special events interns:* responsibilities include assisting with the preparation, production, and coordination of all fund-raising, memberships, and educational events; includes securing donations, coordinating mailings, and ticket sales. Candidates should have ability to work independently, computer skills, knowledge of field, oral com-

munication skills, strong interpersonal skills, written communication skills. Duration is 3–4 months. $50 per week. Open to college juniors, college seniors, recent college graduates, graduate students.

Benefits Job counseling, names of contacts, opportunity to attend seminars/workshops, travel reimbursement, willing to complete paperwork for educational credit, willing to provide letters of recommendation.

Contact Write, fax, or e-mail Jane Ann Crum, Executive Director, 520 Eighth Avenue, Suite 320, New York, New York 10018. Fax: 212-244-9191. E-mail: jacrum@dramaleague.org. No phone calls. In-person interview recommended (telephone interview accepted). Applicants must submit a letter of interest, resume. Application deadline: January 1 for spring, April 1 for summer, July 1 for fall, October 1 for winter. World Wide Web: http://www.dramaleague.org.

FAIRFAX SYMPHONY ORCHESTRA
PO Box 1300
Annandale, Virginia 22003

General Information Nonprofit, professional symphony orchestra that performs year-round in northern Virginia and greater metropolitan Washington, D.C. Established in 1956. Number of employees: 4. Number of internship applications received each year: 30.

Internships Available ► *1 administrative intern:* responsibilities include assisting executive director and acting as board liaison. Candidates should have ability to work independently, computer skills, office skills, oral communication skills, organizational skills, self-motivation, strong interpersonal skills, writing skills. Duration is 8–12 weeks. Unpaid. Open to high school students, recent high school graduates, college freshmen, college sophomores, college juniors, college seniors, recent college graduates, graduate students, individuals reentering the workforce. ► *1 marketing intern:* responsibilities include assisting with press relations and promotional projects. Candidates should have ability to work independently, ability to work with others, computer skills, editing skills, experience in the field, office skills, oral communication skills, organizational skills, self-motivation, writing skills. Duration is 8–24 weeks. Unpaid. Open to high school seniors, recent high school graduates, college freshmen, college sophomores, college juniors, college seniors, recent college graduates, graduate students, career changers, individuals reentering the workforce.

Benefits Job counseling, on-the-job training, opportunity to attend seminars/workshops, possible full-time employment, willing to complete paperwork for educational credit, willing to provide letters of recommendation, tickets to concerts.

Contact Write, fax, or e-mail Rachael M. Garrity, Executive Director, 4024 Hummer Road, Annandale, Virginia 22003. Fax: 703-642-7205. E-mail: rgarrity@fairfaxsymphony.org. In-person interview recommended (telephone interview accepted). Applicants must submit a letter of interest, resume, two personal references. Application deadline: May 1 for summer, November 1 for winter. World Wide Web: http://www.fairfaxsymphony.org.

THE 52ND STREET PROJECT
500 West 52nd Street, 2nd Floor
New York, New York 10019

General Information Nonprofit organization that serves inner-city children by putting them together with adult actors to create original theater. Established in 1981. Number of employees: 7. Number of internship applications received each year: 30.

Internships Available ► *1–3 education interns:* responsibilities include assisting the director of education in all aspects of homework help and the Smart Partner mentoring program. Candidates should have oral communication skills, self-motivation, strong interpersonal skills, writing skills, interest in and experience working with children ages 9-18. Duration is flexible. Unpaid. Open to recent high school graduates, college freshmen, college sophomores, college juniors, college seniors, recent college graduates, graduate students. ► *1–3 youth theater interns:* responsibilities include working with staff in the areas of marketing, development, business, production, and teaching. Candidates should have computer skills, office skills, oral communication skills, personal

interest in the field, self-motivation, strong interpersonal skills, strong desire to work with children. Duration is 1 semester. Unpaid. Open to high school seniors, recent high school graduates, college freshmen, college sophomores, college juniors, college seniors, recent college graduates, graduate students. International applications accepted.

Benefits Names of contacts, on-the-job training, opportunity to attend seminars/workshops, willing to act as a professional reference, willing to complete paperwork for educational credit, willing to provide letters of recommendation, weekend or week-long trips to the country with children.

Contact Write, call, fax, e-mail, or through World Wide Web site Megan Sandberg-Zakian, Associate Artistic Director. Phone: 212-333-5252. Fax: 212-333-5598. E-mail: intern@52project.org. In-person interview recommended (telephone interview accepted). Applicants must submit a letter of interest, resume, 3 personal references or 3 letters of recommendation. Applications are accepted continuously. World Wide Web: http://www.52project.org.

FIJI COMPANY/PING CHONG AND COMPANY
47 Great Jones Street
New York, New York 10012

General Information Center focusing on contemporary avant-garde theater and art. Established in 1975. Number of employees: 4. Number of internship applications received each year: 10.

Internships Available ► *1 general management intern:* responsibilities include duties tailored to intern's abilities and center's needs. Candidates should have office skills, oral communication skills, personal interest in the field, research skills, strong interpersonal skills, written communication skills. Duration is flexible (at least 3 months preferred). Unpaid. Open to college freshmen, college sophomores, college juniors, college seniors, recent college graduates, graduate students, individuals reentering the workforce. International applications accepted.

Benefits Job counseling, willing to complete paperwork for educational credit, willing to provide letters of recommendation, small stipend available.

Contact Write, fax, or e-mail Sachiko Willis, General Manager. Fax: 212-529-1703. E-mail: pingchong@earthlink.net. No phone calls. In-person interview recommended (telephone interview accepted). Applicants must submit a letter of interest, resume. Applications are accepted continuously. World Wide Web: http://www.pingchong.org.

FLAT ROCK PLAYHOUSE
PO Box 310
Flat Rock, North Carolina 28731

General Information Theater that produces ten shows annually from May through December. Established in 1952. Number of employees: 70. Number of internship applications received each year: 30.

Internships Available ► *15–18 apprentices/interns:* responsibilities include learning through practical experience and exposure to as many facets of theatre as possible, including acting, technical/design, improvisation, scene design, lighting, costumes, and resume preparation (apprentices). Candidates should have ability to work with others, experience in the field, plan to pursue career in field, self-motivation. Duration is 10–30 10 to 30 weeks; May 31 to August 17 (apprentices). Position available as unpaid or at $175 per week. Open to recent high school graduates, college freshmen, college sophomores, college juniors, college seniors, recent college graduates, graduate students, individuals reentering the workforce.

Benefits On-the-job training, opportunity to attend seminars/workshops, willing to act as a professional reference, willing to complete paperwork for educational credit, willing to provide letters of recommendation, Equity Membership Candidacy Program; free housing and meals for interns.

Contact Write, call, fax, e-mail, or through World Wide Web site Dennis C. Maulden, Director of Educational Programs. Phone: 828-693-0403 Ext. 18. Fax: 828-693-6795. E-mail: frp@flatrockplayhouse.org. Applicants must submit a formal organization application, resume, two personal references, in-person audi-

Flat Rock Playhouse (continued)

tion recommended (video tape acceptable), $400 fee for apprentices for room/board. Application deadline: April 1 for summer. World Wide Web: http://www.flatrockplayhouse.org.

FLORIDA GRAND OPERA
1200 Coral Way
Miami, Florida 33145

General Information   Grand opera producing company presenting 35 performances of 5 grand operas each session in addition to a small-scale touring production and various other performance programs. Established in 1942. Number of employees: 25. Number of internship applications received each year: 500.

Internships Available   ▶ *8–10 Young Artist Studio Singers:* responsibilities include performing and covering main-stage roles; in-school performances, community performances, and master classes and coaching. Duration is September to April. $200 weekly stipend plus additional compensation for chorus participation. Open to singers who have completed their training and are ready for career. ▶ *1 Young Artist Studio coach/accompanist:* responsibilities include working extensively with the resident and visiting musical staff; duties include coaching the Young Artists, taking part in school and community performances, accompanying chorus rehearsals, and preparing and calling titles (projected English, translations). Duration is September to April. $200 weekly stipend plus additional remuneration for calling titles. Open to coaches who have completed their training and are ready for career. Candidates for all positions should have ability to work independently, ability to work with others, oral communication skills, plan to pursue career in field, self-motivation.

Benefits   Free housing, health insurance, job counseling, opportunity to attend seminars/workshops, possible full-time employment, willing to complete paperwork for educational credit, willing to provide letters of recommendation, utilities (except phone), round-trip transportation to Miami.

Contact   Write, fax, e-mail, or through World Wide Web site Auditions Coordinator. Fax: 305-856-1042. E-mail: auditions@fgo.org. No phone calls. Applicants must submit a resume, application (available in summer 2002); to be placed on mailing list e-mail: auditions@fgo.org, CD or tape of 2 arias. Application deadline: October 27. Fees: $20. World Wide Web: http://www.fgo.org.

FLORIDA STUDIO THEATRE
1241 North Palm Avenue
Sarasota, Florida 34236

General Information   Professional, nonprofit theater that runs a mainstage season of contemporary plays October through August under Actor's Equity Contract, a cabaret club theater with a three-show mainstage program, November through May, and various new play festivals. Established in 1973. Number of employees: 75. Number of internship applications received each year: 500.

Internships Available   ▶ *3–4 children's education interns:* responsibilities include organizing and teaching children's acting programs and performing on children's tour. Candidates should have oral communication skills, personal interest in the field, strong interpersonal skills. Duration is October to May. $75–$100 per week. Open to recent college graduates. ▶ *2–3 development or marketing administration interns:* responsibilities include working box office or concessions, development, or marketing. Candidates should have ability to work independently, ability to work with others, computer skills, office skills, oral communication skills, organizational skills, written communication skills. Duration is summer (late May to late August); or year (September to May). $75–$100 per week. Open to recent high school graduates, college freshmen, college sophomores, college juniors, college seniors, recent college graduates. ▶ *2 literary management interns:* responsibilities include providing literary assistance to the new play program, script analysis and evaluation, and general clerical support. Candidates should have ability to work independently, computer skills, office skills, organizational skills, research skills, writing skills. Duration is May to August and September to June. $75–$100 per week. Open to recent high school graduates, college freshmen,

college sophomores, college juniors, college seniors, recent college graduates. ▶ *2–3 production interns:* responsibilities include building sets, working with props and costumes, and loading and running shows. Candidates should have ability to work independently, ability to work with others, experience in the field, organizational skills, personal interest in the field, self-motivation. Duration is 3–12 months. $75 per week. Open to recent high school graduates, college freshmen, college sophomores, college juniors, college seniors, recent college graduates. ▶ *3–4 stage management interns:* responsibilities include assisting Equity stage managers with rehearsals and running mainstage productions and cabarets. Candidates should have analytical skills, knowledge of field, organizational skills, strong interpersonal skills, strong leadership ability. Duration is October to May; summer position also available. $75–$100 per week. Open to recent high school graduates, college freshmen, college sophomores, college juniors, college seniors, recent college graduates. International applications accepted.

Benefits   Formal training, free housing, on-the-job training, possible full-time employment, willing to act as a professional reference, willing to complete paperwork for educational credit, willing to provide letters of recommendation.

Contact   Write, call, fax, e-mail, or through World Wide Web site James Ashford, Casting and Literary Coordinator. Phone: 941-366-9017. Fax: 941-955-4137. E-mail: james@fst2000.org. Telephone interview required. Applicants must submit a formal organization application, letter of interest, resume, 2-3 personal references, 2-3 letters of recommendation, audition required for children's education interns. Applications are accepted continuously. World Wide Web: http://www.fst2000.org.

FOOLS COMPANY, INC.
423 West 46th Street
New York, New York 10036-3510

General Information   Not-for-profit cultural and educational organization whose mission is to produce and present innovative and unconventional works and workshops in all areas of the performing arts. Established in 1970. Number of employees: 5. Number of internship applications received each year: 50.

Internships Available   ▶ *5 administration interns:* responsibilities include working in funding, publicity, and public relations for performing arts productions and workshops. Duration is 3 months. Unpaid. ▶ *2 production interns:* responsibilities include assisting with company productions and workshops. Duration is 3–6 months. Unpaid. Candidates for all positions should have ability to work independently, oral communication skills, self-motivation, strong interpersonal skills, written communication skills. Open to high school seniors, recent high school graduates, college freshmen, college sophomores, college juniors, college seniors, recent college graduates, graduate students, law students, career changers, individuals reentering the workforce. International applications accepted.

Benefits   Formal training, job counseling, names of contacts, on-the-job training, opportunity to attend seminars/workshops, possible full-time employment, willing to act as a professional reference, willing to complete paperwork for educational credit, willing to provide letters of recommendation.

Contact   Write, call, or e-mail Ms. Jill Russell, Executive Director. Phone: 212-307-6000. E-mail: foolsco@nyc.rr.com. In-person interview required. Applicants must submit a letter of interest, resume, telephone interview acceptable for international applicants only. Applications are accepted continuously.

GEVA THEATRE
75 Woodbury Boulevard
Rochester, New York 14607

General Information   Theater that strives to present and advance the art of theater so that its artists, audience, and the community can celebrate the human experience through an active participation in this art form. Established in 1972. Number of employees: 75. Number of internship applications received each year: 35.

Internships Available   ▶ *1 literary intern:* responsibilities include script analysis and heavy duty play development work. Candidates should have computer skills, knowledge of field, organizational skills, personal interest in the field, writing skills. Duration is 9 months. Unpaid. ▶ *2 stage management apprentices:* responsibilities include assisting in running shows. Candidates should have computer skills, experience in the field, oral communication skills, organizational skills, plan to pursue career in field, self-motivation. Duration is 10 months. $206–$250 per week. Open to recent college graduates, graduate students.

Benefits Job counseling, names of contacts, possible full-time employment, willing to complete paperwork for educational credit, willing to provide letters of recommendation.

Contact Write, e-mail, or through World Wide Web site Skip Greer, Director of Education. Fax: 585-232-4031. E-mail: sgreer@ gevatheatre.org. No phone calls. In-person interview recommended (telephone interview accepted). Applicants must submit a letter of interest, resume. Applications are accepted continuously. World Wide Web: http://www.gevatheatre.org.

GLIMMERGLASS OPERA
PO Box 191
Cooperstown, New York 13326

General Information Summer opera festival. Established in 1975. Number of employees: 300. Number of internship applications received each year: 300.

Internships Available ▶ *18 administrative interns:* responsibilities include duties in one of the following areas: accounting/finance, box office, development, house management, housing and transportation, marketing/public relations, and operations/special events, general administration. Candidates should have computer skills, oral communication skills, organizational skills, personal interest in the field, strong interpersonal skills. Duration is May to August. Weekly stipend. Open to college freshmen, college sophomores, college juniors, college seniors, recent college graduates, graduate students. ▶ *6 artistic interns:* responsibilities include duties in one of two areas: music (locating and copying music, transporting instruments, orchestra pit set-up), Young American Artist Program Administration (acting as liaison between young artists and Director of Artistic Administration). Candidates should have computer skills, knowledge of field, oral communication skills, organizational skills, strong interpersonal skills, driver's license. Duration is May to August. Weekly stipend. Open to college juniors, college seniors, recent college graduates, graduate students, career changers, individuals reentering the workforce. ▶ *32 production interns:* responsibilities include duties in the following areas: audio/video, costume construction or crafts, costume shop management, electrics, hair and make-up, projected titles, properties, scene painting, scenery construction, shop management, stage operations, or wardrobe, production shop management, stage management. Candidates should have ability to work with others, experience in the field, oral communication skills. Duration is May to August. Weekly stipend. Open to college freshmen, college sophomores, college juniors, college seniors, recent college graduates, graduate students. International applications accepted.

Benefits Free housing, on-the-job training, opportunity to attend seminars/workshops, possible full-time employment, willing to act as a professional reference, willing to complete paperwork for educational credit, willing to provide letters of recommendation.

Contact Write, call, fax, e-mail, or through World Wide Web site Internship Coordinator. Phone: 607-547-5704. Fax: 607-547-6030. E-mail: interns@glimmerglass.org. Telephone interview required. Applicants must submit a letter of interest, resume, two personal references. Application deadline: March 8. World Wide Web: http://www.glimmerglass.org.

GOODMAN THEATRE
170 North Dearborn
Chicago, Illinois 60601

General Information Oldest and largest nonprofit theater in Chicago producing classic, contemporary, and new works. Established in 1925. Number of employees: 100. Number of internship applications received each year: 200.

Internships Available ▶ *1 casting intern:* responsibilities include scheduling and monitoring auditions, corresponding with actors

and agents, and maintaining actor files. Candidates should have ability to work independently, computer skills, office skills, plan to pursue career in field, strong interpersonal skills, written communication skills. Duration is 3–5 months. Stipend (varies from season to season). Open to college juniors, college seniors, recent college graduates, graduate students. ▶ *1 costuming intern:* responsibilities include general costume construction and assisting with office clerical tasks. Candidates should have ability to work independently, ability to work with others, experience in the field, organizational skills, plan to pursue career in field. Duration is 2 to 3 months in fall/winter only (20 hours per week maximum). Stipend (varies from season to season). Open to college juniors, college seniors, recent college graduates, graduate students. ▶ *1 development intern:* responsibilities include researching prospective contributors and grants, writing for newsletters and the annual report, developing fund-raising campaigns, and writing solicitation letters. Candidates should have ability to work with others, computer skills, knowledge of field, oral communication skills, plan to pursue career in field, written communication skills. Duration is 3-5 months; special, short-term placements are an option. Stipend (varies from season to season). Open to college juniors, college seniors, recent college graduates, graduate students. ▶ *1 dramaturgy intern:* responsibilities include researching various subjects for newsletter articles and program notes, assisting with preparation of scripts for rehearsals, maintaining in-house library, working on script changes once play is in production, and assisting with new script reading and evaluation. Candidates should have ability to work independently, computer skills, editing skills, organizational skills, research skills, written communication skills. Duration is 3–5 months. Stipend (varies from season to season). Open to college juniors, college seniors, recent college graduates, graduate students. ▶ *1 education and community programs intern:* responsibilities include assisting with student matinee performances, writing articles or exercises for study guides, compiling information from student and teacher evaluations, helping to coordinate high school teacher seminars, corresponding with school groups or other community organizations, and assisting with organization of archival material. Candidates should have ability to work independently, computer skills, oral communication skills, organizational skills, personal interest in the field, written communication skills. Duration is 3–5 months. Stipend (varies from season to season). Open to college juniors, college seniors, recent college graduates, graduate students. ▶ *1 literary management intern:* responsibilities include assisting in solicitation and recording of new manuscripts; maintaining extensive script library; analyzing and evaluating solicited manuscripts; corresponding with playwrights, agents, theaters, and play development programs; and researching playwright production histories. Candidates should have ability to work independently, computer skills, editing skills, organizational skills, research skills, written communication skills. Duration is 3–5 months. Stipend (varies from season to season). Open to college juniors, college seniors, recent college graduates, graduate students. ▶ *1 marketing/public relations/press intern:* responsibilities include assisting in areas of marketing and advertising, proofreading newsletter and program copy, compiling audience survey results, distributing promotional materials, and facilitating special events. Candidates should have ability to work with others, computer skills, knowledge of field, office skills, plan to pursue career in field, written communication skills. Duration is 3–5 months. Stipend (varies from season to season). Open to college juniors, college seniors, recent college graduates, graduate students. ▶ *1 production management intern:* responsibilities include assisting with coordination and management of overall technical production, assisting with routine tasks and projects, conducting research for specific productions, and attending production meetings. Candidates should have ability to work with others, computer skills, knowledge of field, organizational skills, personal interest in the field, research skills. Duration is 3–5 months. Stipend (varies from season to season). Open to college juniors, college seniors, recent college graduates, graduate students. ▶ *Sound interns:* responsibilities include helping to create sound scores for mainstage and studio productions, and learning advanced procedures for installing, operating, and maintaining sound equipment. Candidates should have ability to work with others, experience in the field, plan to pursue career in field, self-motivation. Duration is 2 to 3 months in fall/

Goodman Theatre (continued)

winter only; 20 hours per week maximum. Stipend (varies from season to season). ▶ *1–2 stage management interns:* responsibilities include assisting stage managers with pre-production preparation and continuing through technical rehearsals, preview weeks, and opening nights. Candidates should have computer skills, experience in the field, organizational skills, plan to pursue career in field, strong interpersonal skills. Duration is 6-8 weeks or length of production. Stipend (varies from season to season). Open to college seniors, recent college graduates, graduate students. International applications accepted.

Benefits Job counseling, names of contacts, on-the-job training, opportunity to attend seminars/workshops, willing to act as a professional reference, willing to complete paperwork for educational credit, willing to provide letters of recommendation.

Contact Write, call, e-mail, or through World Wide Web site Ms. Julie Massey, Intern Coordinator. Phone: 312-443-3813. Fax: 312-443-7448. E-mail: juliemassey@goodman-theatre.org. In-person interview recommended (telephone interview accepted). Applicants must submit a formal organization application, letter of interest, resume, two letters of recommendation. Application deadline: March 5 for summer, June 6 for fall, October 3 for winter. World Wide Web: http://www.goodman-theatre.org.

GOODSPEED MUSICALS
Box A
East Haddam, Connecticut 06423

General Information Professional, award-winning theater with a 30-year history of producing musical theater. Established in 1963. Number of employees: 100. Number of internship applications received each year: 200.

Internships Available ▶ *2 carpentry interns:* responsibilities include running crew and building sets. Candidates should have ability to work independently, college courses in field, oral communication skills, personal interest in the field, strong interpersonal skills. Duration is 1–2 semesters. $6.90 per hour. Open to college freshmen, college sophomores, college juniors, college seniors, graduate students. ▶ *2 electrics interns:* responsibilities include running follow spots for production and helping shop build shows. Candidates should have ability to work independently, college courses in field, oral communication skills, personal interest in the field, strong interpersonal skills. Duration is 1–2 semesters. $6.90 per hour. Open to college freshmen, college sophomores, college juniors, college seniors, graduate students. ▶ *2 props interns:* responsibilities include running crew and building props. Candidates should have ability to work independently, college courses in field, oral communication skills, personal interest in the field, strong interpersonal skills. Duration is 1–2 semesters. $6.90 per hour. Open to college freshmen, college sophomores, college juniors, college seniors, graduate students. ▶ *1 scenic art intern:* responsibilities include helping the scenic artists paint scenery. Candidates should have ability to work independently, college courses in field, oral communication skills, personal interest in the field, strong interpersonal skills. Duration is 1–2 semesters. $6.90 per hour. Open to college freshmen, college sophomores, college juniors, college seniors, recent college graduates. ▶ *2–4 stage management interns:* responsibilities include assisting stage manager during rehearsals and performances. Candidates should have ability to work independently, college degree in related field, computer skills, editing skills, knowledge of field, office skills, oral communication skills, organizational skills, plan to pursue career in field, self-motivation, strong interpersonal skills, strong leadership ability, writing skills. Duration is 4–16 weeks. Stipend of $200 per week. Open to recent college graduates. ▶ *2 wardrobe interns:* responsibilities include working in the costume shop and running wardrobe. Candidates should have ability to work independently, college courses in field, oral communication skills, personal interest in the field, strong interpersonal skills. Duration is 1–2 semesters. $6.90 per hour. Open to college freshmen, college sophomores, college juniors, college seniors, graduate students. International applications accepted.

Benefits Housing at a cost, names of contacts, on-the-job training, opportunity to attend seminars/workshops, possible full-time employment, willing to act as a professional reference, willing to complete paperwork for educational credit, willing to provide letters of recommendation.

Contact Write, fax, e-mail, or through World Wide Web site Heather Auden, Assistant Production Manager, Box A, East Haddam, Connecticut 06243. Fax: 860-873-2480. E-mail: hauden@goodspeed.org. No phone calls. Telephone interview required. Applicants must submit a formal organization application, letter of interest, resume, three personal references. Applications are accepted continuously. World Wide Web: http://www.goodspeed.org.

HARTFORD STAGE
50 Church Street
Hartford, Connecticut 06103

General Information Regional theater company that produces top-quality professional theater for Connecticut's capital city and its surrounding communities; under the direction of Michael Wilson since April 1998, Hartford Stage has deepened its commitment to new works and reinterpretations of classic plays. Established in 1964. Number of employees: 50. Number of internship applications received each year: 50.

Internships Available ▶ *5–7 interns:* responsibilities include working in theatre/education teaching, literary/artistic management and new play development, and marketing and public relations. Candidates should have ability to work independently, computer skills, organizational skills, plan to pursue career in field, strong interpersonal skills, college courses or experience in field. Duration is flexible. Unpaid. Open to college freshmen, college sophomores, college juniors, college seniors, recent college graduates, graduate students, individuals planning to pursue a career in theatre. ▶ *1–3 production apprentices:* responsibilities include working with leading designers, actors, and craftspeople. Candidates should have ability to work independently, oral communication skills, organizational skills, plan to pursue career in field, strong interpersonal skills, BA in theatre production. Duration is 7–9 months. Paid. Open to recent college graduates.

Benefits On-the-job training, willing to act as a professional reference, willing to provide letters of recommendation.

Contact Write, fax, or e-mail Edward Duran, Internship Coordinator. Fax: 860-525-4420. E-mail: eddieduran@hartfordstage.org. No phone calls. In-person interview recommended (telephone interview accepted). Applicants must submit a formal organization application, letter of interest, resume, three letters of recommendation. Application deadline: April 1 for summer, November 1 for spring. World Wide Web: http://www.hartfordstage.org.

HERE ARTS CENTER
145 Avenue of the Americas, Ground Floor
New York, New York 10013

General Information Theater and gallery that develop new works. Established in 1993. Number of employees: 25. Unit of Home for Contemporary Theatre and Art, New York, New York. Number of internship applications received each year: 300.

Internships Available ▶ *1–2 arts administration interns:* responsibilities include assisting general manager, executive director, and finance director with programming, operations, and fiscal control in support of 5000 artists per year. Candidates should have ability to work independently, ability to work with others, analytical skills, knowledge of field, office skills, organizational skills, self-motivation. Duration is flexible. Unpaid. Open to recent high school graduates, college freshmen, college sophomores, college juniors, college seniors, recent college graduates, individuals reentering the workforce. ▶ *1–2 development interns:* responsibilities include assisting the development director in writing grant proposals and database management. Candidates should have ability to work independently, computer skills, editing skills, oral communication skills, organizational skills, research skills, self-motivation, written communication skills. Duration is flexible. Unpaid. Open to recent high school graduates, college freshmen, college sophomores, college juniors, college seniors, recent college graduates, individuals reentering the workforce. ▶ *1–2 gallery interns:* responsibilities include assisting the gallery director in organizing gallery shows and loading in. Candidates should have oral communication skills, personal interest in the field, strong interpersonal skills, written communication skills. Duration is flexible. Unpaid. Open to high school students, recent high school graduates, college freshmen, college sophomores, college juniors, college seniors, recent college graduates, individuals reentering the workforce. ▶ *1–4 production interns:* responsibilities include assisting the production manager with running and maintaining 3 theaters; possibility of running tech on shows. Candidates should have ability to work independently, organizational skills, personal interest in the field, self-motivation, strong interpersonal skills. Duration is flexible. Unpaid. Open to recent high school graduates, college freshmen, college sophomores, college juniors, college seniors, recent college graduates, career changers, individuals reentering the workforce. ▶ *1–2 programming interns:* responsibilities include assisting the programming director in reviewing artists and booking space. Candidates should have ability to work independently, oral communication skills, organizational skills, self-motivation, strong interpersonal skills. Duration is flexible. Unpaid. Open to high school seniors, recent high school graduates, college freshmen, college sophomores, college juniors, college seniors, recent college graduates, individuals reentering the workforce. ▶ *1–2 publicity/marketing interns:* responsibilities include database management, some graphic design and layout, print and Internet advertising. Candidates should have computer skills, editing skills, oral communication skills, personal interest in the field, self-motivation, strong interpersonal skills, written communication skills. Duration is flexible. Unpaid. Open to recent high school graduates, college freshmen, college sophomores, college juniors, college seniors, recent college graduates, individuals reentering the workforce. International applications accepted.

Benefits Possible full-time employment, willing to complete paperwork for educational credit, willing to provide letters of recommendation, exposure to a wide range of artistic activity, possibility of travel reimbursement.

Contact Write, fax, e-mail, or through World Wide Web site David Winitsky, Internship Coordinator, 145 Avenue of the Americas Ground Floor, New York, New York 10013. Fax: 212-647-0257. E-mail: david@here.org. No phone calls. In-person interview recommended (telephone interview accepted). Applicants must submit a letter of interest, resume. Applications are accepted continuously. World Wide Web: http://www.here.org.

HORSE CAVE THEATRE
Box 215
Horse Cave, Kentucky 42749

General Information Nonprofit repertory theater bringing professional theater to the area at an affordable price while promoting educational outreach programs and student theatre workshops. Established in 1976. Number of employees: 8. Number of internship applications received each year: 15.

Internships Available ▶ *6–9 apprentices:* responsibilities include assisting with lighting, scene shop, costumes, props, box office management, sound, administration, and possible roles in certain plays. Candidates should have ability to work independently, ability to work with others, knowledge of field, personal interest in the field, self-motivation, strong leadership ability. Duration is 3–6 months. $50–$75 per week. Open to high school seniors, recent high school graduates, college freshmen, college sophomores, college juniors, college seniors, recent college graduates, graduate students, career changers, individuals reentering the workforce. International applications accepted.

Benefits Free housing, on-the-job training, opportunity to attend seminars/workshops, willing to act as a professional reference, willing to complete paperwork for educational credit, willing to provide letters of recommendation.

Contact Write, call, fax, or e-mail Jacklyn Spangler, Administrative Assistant. Phone: 270-786-1200. Fax: 270-786-5298. E-mail: hctjacklyns@hotmail.com. In-person interview recommended (telephone interview accepted). Applicants must submit a formal organization application, letter of interest, resume, two letters of recommendation, three letters of recommendation. Application deadline: April 1. World Wide Web: http://www.horsecavetheatre.org.

INDIANA REPERTORY THEATRE
140 West Washington Street
Indianapolis, Indiana 46204

General Information Theater company that produces 6 mainstage and 3 upperstage productions in a season that operates from September to May. Established in 1972. Number of employees: 100. Number of internship applications received each year: 30.

Internships Available ▶ *3–4 administrative interns:* responsibilities include assisting professional staff in a variety of areas including marketing/sales, education, public relations, or development. Candidates should have computer skills, office skills, oral communication skills, organizational skills, plan to pursue career in field, research skills, written communication skills. Duration is minimum of 3 months. Unpaid. ▶ *5–6 production interns:* responsibilities include working in various areas including stage management, costume shop, properties, company management, production management, scene shop, scenic art, and electrics/sound; working side-by-side with professional staff. Candidates should have ability to work with others, oral communication skills, organizational skills, personal interest in the field, plan to pursue career in field, self-motivation. Duration is minimum of 3 months. Unpaid. Open to college freshmen, college sophomores, college juniors, college seniors.

Benefits Names of contacts, possible full-time employment, willing to complete paperwork for educational credit, willing to provide letters of recommendation.

Contact Write or e-mail Josh Friedman, Production Supervisor. E-mail: jfriedman@indianarep.com. No phone calls. In-person interview recommended (telephone interview accepted). Applicants must submit a formal organization application, letter of interest, resume, three letters of recommendation. Application deadline: July 1 for fall, December 1 for winter/spring; no summer positions. World Wide Web: http://www.indianarep.com.

JEAN COCTEAU REPERTORY THEATER
330 Bowery
New York, New York 10012

General Information Permanent residential acting company performing in repertory presenting classical plays. Established in 1971. Number of employees: 7. Number of internship applications received each year: 15.

Internships Available ▶ *10 production interns:* responsibilities include assisting in all areas of production, including scenery, properties, costumes, lighting, and sound; some administrative work. Candidates should have ability to work independently, ability to work with others, knowledge of field, self-motivation. Duration is flexible. Unpaid. Open to high school seniors, recent high school graduates, college freshmen, college sophomores, college juniors, college seniors, recent college graduates, individuals reentering the workforce. International applications accepted.

Benefits Willing to complete paperwork for educational credit, willing to provide letters of recommendation.

Contact Write, fax, or e-mail Ernest Johns, Production Director. Fax: 212-777-6151. E-mail: cocteau@jeancocteaurep.org. Applicants must submit a resume, letter of inquiry and statement of purpose. Applications are accepted continuously. World Wide Web: http://www.jeancocteaurep.org.

JENNIFER MULLER/THE WORKS
131 West 24th Street
New York, New York 10011

General Information New York City-based contemporary dance company that does national and international touring. Established in 1974. Number of employees: 15. Number of internship applications received each year: 15.

Internships Available ▶ *1 accounting intern:* responsibilities include working on general ledger and bookkeeping tasks. Candidates should have ability to work independently, computer skills. Duration is flexible. Unpaid. Open to college freshmen, college sophomores, college juniors, college seniors, recent college graduates, graduate students, dancers. ▶ *2 administration interns:* responsibilities include assisting managers in day-to-day operations, special events, and fund-raising. Candidates should have ability to work

Jennifer Muller/The Works (continued)

independently, ability to work with others, computer skills, oral communication skills, research skills, written communication skills. Duration is flexible. Unpaid. Open to college freshmen, college sophomores, college juniors, college seniors, recent college graduates, graduate students. ▶ *1 tour planning intern:* responsibilities include contacting sponsors; travel and hotel bookings. Candidates should have ability to work independently, oral communication skills, organizational skills, personal interest in the field, strong interpersonal skills. Duration is flexible. Unpaid. Open to college freshmen, college sophomores, college juniors, college seniors, recent college graduates, graduate students, dancers. International applications accepted.

Benefits Job counseling, on-the-job training, possible full-time employment, willing to complete paperwork for educational credit, willing to provide letters of recommendation.

Contact Write Ms. Lynette Muller, Office Manager. Phone: 212-691-3803. Fax: 212-206-6630. E-mail: theworksnyc@compuserve. com. Telephone interview required. Applicants must submit a letter of interest, resume. Applications are accepted continuously. World Wide Web: http://jennifermullertheworks.org.

JOHN DREW THEATER OF GUILD HALL
158 Main Street
East Hampton, New York 11937

General Information Performing arts presenter and Equity theater associated with art museum. Established in 1931. Number of employees: 14. Unit of Guild Hall of East Hampton, East Hampton, New York. Number of internship applications received each year: 50.

Internships Available ▶ *1 intern (Executive Director's Office):* responsibilities include computer trouble shooting, Web site update, and special projects. Candidates should have ability to work independently, computer skills, office skills, oral communication skills, strong interpersonal skills, writing skills. Duration is flexible. Position available as unpaid or at $8–$12 per hour. Open to high school seniors, recent high school graduates, college freshmen, college sophomores, college juniors, college seniors, recent college graduates, graduate students, individuals reentering the workforce. ▶ *1 marketing/PR intern:* responsibilities include researching/drafting press releases; media list maintenance; administrative duties; distribution and organization of materials. Candidates should have ability to work independently, computer skills, editing skills, organizational skills, personal interest in the field, self-motivation, writing skills. Duration is June to mid-August (10–15 hours per week). Position available as unpaid or at up to $200 per week. Open to recent high school graduates, college freshmen, college sophomores, college juniors, college seniors, recent college graduates, graduate students, career changers, individuals reentering the workforce. ▶ *1 production management intern:* responsibilities include assisting production manager. Candidates should have theater background. Duration is one summer. Position available as unpaid or at up to $200 per week. Open to high school seniors, recent high school graduates, college freshmen, college sophomores, college juniors, college seniors, recent college graduates, graduate students. ▶ *1–2 technical interns:* responsibilities include completing general backstage assignments. Candidates should have ability to work with others, college courses in field, personal interest in the field. Duration is one summer. Position available as unpaid or at up to $200 per week. Open to high school seniors, college freshmen, college sophomores, college juniors, college seniors, recent college graduates, graduate students. ▶ *1–2 theater administration interns:* responsibilities include assisting with daily operation of theater office; assisting with house management and company management; contract management; artist relations; patron relations. Candidates should have computer skills, oral communication skills, personal interest in the field, self-motivation, strong interpersonal skills. Duration is 1–3 months. Position available as unpaid or at up to $1000 per internship. Open to high school seniors, recent high school graduates, college freshmen, college sophomores, college juniors, college seniors, recent college graduates, graduate students. International applications accepted.

Benefits Job counseling, names of contacts, on-the-job training, willing to act as a professional reference, willing to complete paperwork for educational credit, willing to provide letters of recommendation, academic credit can be arranged.

Contact Write, fax, e-mail, or through World Wide Web site Josh Gladstone, Artistic Director. Fax: 631-324-2722. E-mail: joshgladstone@ guildhall.org. No phone calls. In-person interview required. Applicants must submit a letter of interest, resume, letter of recommendation. Applications are accepted continuously. World Wide Web: http://www.GuildHall.org.

LIMELIGHT PRODUCTIONS, INC.
471 Pleasant Street
Lee, Massachusetts 01238-9322

General Information Theatrical supply and rental shop with regional and national accounts; involved in sales, service, rental, fabrication, installation of theatrical equipment, supplies, and custom constructions. Established in 1972. Number of employees: 12. Number of internship applications received each year: 10.

Internships Available ▶ *1 assistant to curtain fabricator:* responsibilities include assisting curtain fabricator in production and installation of stage curtains; involves cutting and sewing large pieces of fabric. Candidates should have ability to work with others, analytical skills, oral communication skills, organizational skills, self-motivation, experience using sewing machines. Duration is 2–12 months. $270–$360 per week. Open to recent high school graduates, college freshmen, college sophomores, college juniors, college seniors, career changers, individuals reentering the workforce. ▶ *1 technical intern (rigging):* responsibilities include acting as part of 3-4 person rigging crew installing stage/studio counterweight, motorized or rope-type rigging systems; travel required. Candidates should have ability to work with others, analytical skills, oral communication skills, organizational skills, personal interest in the field, self-motivation. Duration is 3–12 months. $270–$400 per week. Open to college seniors, recent college graduates, graduate students, career changers, individuals reentering the workforce. ▶ *1–2 technical interns (lighting):* responsibilities include checking rentals on load-ins and load-outs, installations, and mounting and running lights for clients' productions under supervision of in-house staff. Candidates should have ability to work with others, declared college major in field, oral communication skills, organizational skills, personal interest in the field, self-motivation. Duration is 2–12 months. $270–$360 per week. Open to college juniors, college seniors, recent college graduates, graduate students. International applications accepted.

Benefits Job counseling, names of contacts, on-the-job training, possible full-time employment, willing to complete paperwork for educational credit, willing to provide letters of recommendation.

Contact Write or through World Wide Web site Mr. William Beautyman, President. Fax: 413-243-4993. E-mail: wbeautyman@ limelightproductions.com. No phone calls. In-person interview recommended (telephone interview accepted). Applicants must submit a letter of interest, resume, academic transcripts, three letters of recommendation. Applications are accepted continuously. World Wide Web: http://www.limelightproductions.com.

LINCOLN CENTER FOR THE PERFORMING ARTS
70 Lincoln Center Plaza
New York, New York 10023-6583

General Information Producer and presenter of 300 events annually and manager of the Lincoln Center complex. Established in 1956. Number of employees: 500.

Internships Available ▶ *Arts management interns:* responsibilities include providing assistance on projects to be chosen by the intern in consultation with senior staff members. Candidates should have ability to work independently, analytical skills, computer skills, oral communication skills, plan to pursue career in field, written communication skills. Paid. Open to graduate students, recent graduate-level graduates. International applications accepted.

Benefits Names of contacts, possible full-time employment, willing to complete paperwork for educational credit, willing to provide letters of recommendation, tickets to performances.

Contact Write, fax, or e-mail Human Resources. Fax: 212-875-5185. E-mail: humanresources@lincolncenter.org. No phone calls. In-person interview required. Applicants must submit a resume, cover letter. Application deadline: July 31. World Wide Web: http://www.lincolncenter.org.

MABOU MINES
150 First Avenue
New York, New York 10009

General Information Avant-garde theater company emphasizing the creation of new theater pieces from original texts and the theatrical use of existing texts staged from a specific point of view. Established in 1970. Number of employees: 4. Number of internship applications received each year: 75.

Internships Available ▶ *1–3 administrative interns:* responsibilities include assisting in maintaining archives, preparing promotional materials, running errands, handling telephone calls, general filing, computer input, and general office maintenance. Candidates should have ability to work with others, office skills, organizational skills, self-motivation, written communication skills. Duration is 1 semester. Unpaid. Open to college freshmen, college sophomores, college juniors, college seniors, recent college graduates, priority given to those familiar with company's work. International applications accepted.

Benefits Job counseling, opportunity to attend seminars/workshops, willing to complete paperwork for educational credit, willing to provide letters of recommendation, opportunity to accompany artistic directorate to art events.

Contact Write, call, fax, or e-mail Joe Stackell, Company Manager. Phone: 212-473-0559. Fax: 212-473-2410. E-mail: manager@maboumines.org. In-person interview required. Applicants must submit a letter of interest, resume. Applications are accepted continuously. World Wide Web: http://www.maboumines.org.

MAINE STATE MUSIC THEATRE
22 Elm Street
Brunswick, Maine 04011

General Information Theater dedicated to polishing, preserving, and producing musical plays and training young theater professionals. Established in 1959. Number of employees: 150. Number of internship applications received each year: 1,000.

Internships Available ▶ *4 administrative interns:* responsibilities include working with company management, marketing, box office, and house management. Candidates should have ability to work independently, computer skills, office skills, oral communication skills, organizational skills, strong interpersonal skills. Duration is May to August. $60 per week. Open to recent high school graduates, college freshmen, college sophomores, college juniors, college seniors, recent college graduates, graduate students, must be 18 years old. ▶ *8 performers.* Candidates should have ability to work with others, experience in the field, organizational skills, plan to pursue career in field, self-motivation. Duration is May to August. $60 per week. Open to recent high school graduates, college freshmen, college sophomores, college juniors, college seniors, recent college graduates, graduate students. ▶ *12 technicians:* responsibilities include working in stage management, painting, scenery, props, electrics, costumes, and wardrobe; building and installing sets. Candidates should have ability to work independently, ability to work with others, experience in the field, oral communication skills, plan to pursue career in field, self-motivation. Duration is May to August. $60 per week. Open to recent high school graduates, college freshmen, college sophomores, college juniors, college seniors, recent college graduates, graduate students, must be 18 years old.

Benefits Free housing, names of contacts, on-the-job training, opportunity to attend seminars/workshops, willing to complete paperwork for educational credit, willing to provide letters of recommendation, 13-14 Actors Equity membership candidate points (for performers and technical interns), one meal per day.

Contact Write, call, fax, or e-mail Kathi Kacinski, Company Manager. Phone: 207-725-8760 Ext. 11. Fax: 207-725-1199. E-mail: msmtjobs@blazenetme.net. In-person interview recommended (telephone interview accepted). Applicants must submit a formal organization application, resume, two letters of recommendation. Application deadline: March 1. World Wide Web: http://www.msmt.org.

MANHATTAN CLASS COMPANY
145 West 28th Street, 8thFloor
New York, New York 10001

General Information Off-Broadway theater. Established in 1983. Number of employees: 9. Number of internship applications received each year: 100.

Internships Available ▶ *1 arts in education intern:* responsibilities include assisting the Education Department with special projects, correspondence, Youth Theater Company meetings, general office help, errands, and filing. Candidates should have computer skills, office skills, oral communication skills, personal interest in the field, strong interpersonal skills, written communication skills. Duration is flexible. Unpaid. Open to high school seniors, recent high school graduates, college freshmen, college sophomores, college juniors, college seniors, recent college graduates, graduate students, career changers, individuals reentering the workforce. ▶ *1 development intern:* responsibilities include correspondence, working in database, working on special projects including the Annual Benefit, research, data entry, and running errands. Candidates should have ability to work with others, computer skills, office skills, oral communication skills, personal interest in the field, written communication skills. Duration is flexible. Unpaid. Open to college freshmen, college sophomores, college juniors, college seniors, recent college graduates, career changers, individuals reentering the workforce. ▶ *2–3 general management interns:* responsibilities include running errands, filing, copying, assisting with mailings and correspondence, and working on special projects. Candidates should have ability to work independently, computer skills, office skills, oral communication skills, strong interpersonal skills, writing skills. Duration is based on applicant's availability. Unpaid. Open to college freshmen, college sophomores, college juniors, college seniors, recent college graduates, graduate students, career changers, individuals reentering the workforce. ▶ *1 literary intern.* Duration is flexible. Unpaid. Open to graduate students. ▶ *1 marketing intern.* Duration is flexible. Unpaid. Open to college freshmen, college sophomores, college juniors, college seniors. International applications accepted.

Benefits Names of contacts, travel reimbursement, willing to complete paperwork for educational credit, willing to provide letters of recommendation.

Contact Write, fax, e-mail, or through World Wide Web site Eric Bornemann, Office Manager, 120 West 26t Street, 2nd Floor, New York, New York 10001. Phone: 212-727-7722. Fax: 212-727-7780. E-mail: ebornemann@mcctheater.org. In-person interview required. Applicants must submit a resume, cover letter. Applications are accepted continuously. World Wide Web: http://www.mcctheater.org.

MANHATTAN THEATRE CLUB
311 West 43rd Street, 8th Floor
New York, New York 10036

General Information Major on and off-Broadway theater with a commitment to developing and producing new works; sponsors a variety of special events including readings of plays-in-progress and Writers-in-Performance series. Established in 1970. Number of employees: 70. Number of internship applications received each year: 500.

Internships Available ▶ *15–18 theater/management interns:* responsibilities include working in the following departments: artistic, casting, development/fund-raising, executive producing, business, education, literary, marketing, production management, Writers-in-Performance, technical direction, and props. Candidates should have ability to work independently, ability to work with others, office skills, oral communication skills, personal interest in the field, written communication skills. Duration is 1–3 semesters. $200 per week. Open to college freshmen, college sophomores, college juniors, college seniors, recent college graduates, graduate students, career changers. International applications accepted.

Benefits Names of contacts, on-the-job training, opportunity to attend seminars/workshops, possible full-time employment, willing to act as a professional reference, willing to complete paperwork for educational credit, willing to provide letters of recommendation, free and discounted tickets to cultural events in New York City.

Contact Write, fax, e-mail, or through World Wide Web site Jamie Beth Cohen, Assistant Education Director and Coordinator, Paul A. Kaplan Theatre Management Program. Fax: 212-399-4329. E-mail: interns@mtc-nyc.org. No phone calls. In-person interview recommended (telephone interview accepted). Applicants must submit a formal organization application, letter of interest, resume, two letters of recommendation. Application deadline: March 15 for summer, July 15 for fall, November 15 for winter/spring. World Wide Web: http://www.ManhattanTheatreClub.com.

MCCARTER THEATRE–CENTER FOR THE PERFORMING ARTS
91 University Place
Princeton, New Jersey 08540

General Information Performing arts center producing and presenting world-class artists in drama, music, dance, and special events; received 1994 Tony Award for outstanding regional theater. Established in 1974. Number of employees: 150. Number of internship applications received each year: 150.

Internships Available ► *1 company/production management intern:* responsibilities include coordinating artists' travel and housing arrangements, scheduling use of company car, tracking company management expenses, and providing administrative support to the business office. Candidates should have ability to work independently, computer skills, office skills, oral communication skills, organizational skills, self-motivation, strong interpersonal skills, strong leadership ability. Duration is 9–10 months. $75 weekly stipend. Open to recent college graduates, career changers, individuals reentering the workforce, graduating college seniors. ► *1 costumes/wardrobe intern:* responsibilities include planning, building, and maintaining costumes. Candidates should have ability to work independently, ability to work with others, college courses in field, knowledge of field, organizational skills, personal interest in the field, research skills, self-motivation. Duration is 9–10 months. $75 weekly stipend. Open to recent college graduates, graduate students, career changers, individuals reentering the workforce, graduating college seniors. ► *1 development intern:* responsibilities include involvement with government, corporate, foundation, and individual solicitations for support; compiling statistics, donor record management, gift entry, and acknowledgement and special event operations. Candidates should have ability to work independently, ability to work with others, computer skills, editing skills, office skills, organizational skills, personal interest in the field, research skills, self-motivation, written communication skills. Duration is 9–10 months. $75 weekly stipend. Open to recent college graduates, graduate students, career changers, individuals reentering the workforce, graduating college seniors. ► *2 directing/producing interns:* responsibilities include administrative work for the office of the artistic director, assisting with in-house casting, NY/NJ production coverage, reading of new material for the artistic team, serving as assistant to the director on mainstage production (subject to the artistic director's discretion). Candidates should have ability to work independently, analytical skills, college courses in field, computer skills, knowledge of field, office skills, oral communication skills, organizational skills, personal interest in the field, plan to pursue career in field, research skills, self-motivation, strong interpersonal skills, strong leadership ability, written communication skills. Duration is 9–10 months. $75 weekly stipend. Open to recent college graduates, graduate students, career changers, individuals reentering the workforce, graduating college seniors. ► *1 education teaching artist intern:* responsibilities include assisting with school contacts, coordinating staffing of student performances, traveling with in-school tours, serving as assistant instructor, team teaching one or more Creative Drama and Youth Theater programs, and participating in educational touring shows and in-school residencies. Candidates should have ability to work independently, college courses in field, computer skills, experience in the field, office skills, oral communication skills, organizational skills,

personal interest in the field, plan to pursue career in field, self-motivation, strong interpersonal skills. Duration is 9–10 months. $75 weekly stipend. Open to college seniors, recent college graduates, graduate students, individuals reentering the workforce. ► *1 literary management intern:* responsibilities include participating in the administration of the Literary Office, script reading, organizing playreadings, dramaturgical research, play coverage, and report writing. Candidates should have ability to work independently, analytical skills, college courses in field, computer skills, editing skills, knowledge of field, office skills, oral communication skills, organizational skills, personal interest in the field, plan to pursue career in field, research skills, self-motivation, strong interpersonal skills, writing skills. Duration is 9–10 months. $75 weekly stipend. Open to college juniors, college seniors, recent college graduates, graduate students, career changers, individuals reentering the workforce, graduating college seniors. ► *1 marketing/special events intern:* responsibilities include working with Marketing and Sales Departments in all aspects including assignments in advertising/promotion, publicity, Web development, and special events planning related to group sales. Candidates should have ability to work independently, ability to work with others, college courses in field, computer skills, experience in the field, office skills, oral communication skills, organizational skills, personal interest in the field, plan to pursue career in field, research skills, self-motivation, writing skills. Duration is 9–10 months. $75 weekly stipend. Open to recent college graduates, graduate students, career changers, individuals reentering the workforce, graduating college seniors. ► *1 marketing/special events management:* responsibilities include work with Marketing and Group Sales Departments in all aspects of branding, publicity, promotion, and direct mail marketing; responsibilities will include assignments in advertising/promotion, publicity, Web development, and special events planning related to group sales. Candidates should have ability to work independently, college courses in field, computer skills, editing skills, office skills, oral communication skills, organizational skills, personal interest in the field, research skills, self-motivation, strong interpersonal skills, strong leadership ability, writing skills. Duration is 9–10 months. $75 weekly stipend. Open to recent college graduates, graduate students, career changers, individuals reentering the workforce. ► *1 properties intern:* responsibilities include participating in the procurement, construction, set-up, running, and maintenance of props, beginning with the design process and continuing through to strike. Candidates should have ability to work independently, ability to work with others, knowledge of field, organizational skills, personal interest in the field, research skills, self-motivation. Duration is 9–10 months. $75 weekly stipend. Open to recent college graduates, graduate students, career changers, individuals reentering the workforce, graduating college seniors. ► *1 stage management intern:* responsibilities include preparing for and attending rehearsal with shared responsibility for organizing and tracking production needs, communicating with various departments, and maintaining a work environment conducive to the best artistic efforts. Candidates should have college courses in field, knowledge of field, oral communication skills, organizational skills, plan to pursue career in field, self-motivation, strong interpersonal skills, strong leadership ability. Duration is 9–10 months. $75 weekly stipend. Open to recent college graduates, graduate students, individuals reentering the workforce, graduating college seniors. ► *1 technical direction/scene shop intern:* responsibilities include working in all aspects of scenery development for a large proscenium stage operating on a repertory schedule and participating on changeover and running crews. Candidates should have analytical skills, college courses in field, knowledge of field, organizational skills, self-motivation, strong interpersonal skills, strong leadership ability. Duration is 9–10 months. $75 weekly stipend. Open to recent college graduates, graduate students, career changers, individuals reentering the workforce, graduating college seniors. International applications accepted.

Benefits Free housing, names of contacts, opportunity to attend seminars/workshops, possible full-time employment, willing to act as a professional reference, willing to complete paperwork for educational credit, willing to provide letters of recommendation.

Contact Write, fax, e-mail, or through World Wide Web site Grace Shackney, Intern Coordinator. Fax: 609-497-0369. E-mail: gshackney@

mccarter.org. No phone calls. In-person interview recommended (telephone interview accepted). Applicants must submit a formal organization application, letter of interest, resume, two personal references, two letters of recommendation, writing samples (for literary and marketing internships). Application deadline: March 31 for fall. World Wide Web: http://www.mccarter.org.

MERRIMACK REPERTORY THEATRE
50 East Merrimack Street
Lowell, Massachusetts 01852

General Information Professional theater producing 7 quality productions from September through June. Established in 1979. Number of employees: 20. Number of internship applications received each year: 30.
Internships Available ▶ *2 administrative interns:* responsibilities include assisting administrative staff with special projects, data entry, answering phones, bulk mailings, and typing. Candidates should have ability to work independently, computer skills, organizational skills, personal interest in the field, self-motivation, strong interpersonal skills. Duration is flexible (at least 12 weeks). Unpaid. ▶ *4 production interns:* responsibilities include assisting production staff in areas of stage management, electrics, and scenery. Candidates should have ability to work independently, knowledge of field, personal interest in the field, self-motivation, strong interpersonal skills. Duration is 9 months. Position available as unpaid or paid. Open to high school students, recent high school graduates, college freshmen, college sophomores, college juniors, college seniors, recent college graduates, graduate students. International applications accepted.
Benefits Possible full-time employment, willing to act as a professional reference, willing to complete paperwork for educational credit, willing to provide letters of recommendation, 2 free tickets to each production.
Contact Write, call, fax, or e-mail Linda Trudel, Office Manager. Phone: 978-454-6324 Ext. 224. Fax: 978-934-0166. E-mail: info@merrimackrep.org. In-person interview recommended (telephone interview accepted). Applicants must submit a resume, three personal references. Applications are accepted continuously. World Wide Web: http://www.merrimackrep.org.

MILWAUKEE REPERTORY THEATER
108 East Wells Street
Milwaukee, Wisconsin 53202

General Information Major regional theater producing a broad range of classical and contemporary theater pieces. Established in 1953. Number of employees: 150. Number of internship applications received each year: 125.
Internships Available ▶ *12–16 actors:* responsibilities include understudying all mainstage roles, performing ensemble roles. Candidates should have college courses in field, knowledge of field, plan to pursue career in field, self-motivation, strong interpersonal skills. Duration is 1 full season (August to May). Position available as unpaid or at $50 per week. Open to college seniors, recent college graduates, graduate students, individuals reentering the workforce, semi-professional actors. ▶ *3 directing interns:* responsibilities include assisting directors with projects, running understudy rehearsals, and directing readings of new materials. Candidates should have ability to work independently, experience in the field, oral communication skills, organizational skills, personal interest in the field, plan to pursue career in field, research skills, strong interpersonal skills, strong leadership ability, writing skills. Duration is 1 full season (August to May). Position available as unpaid or at $50 per week. Open to college seniors, recent college graduates, graduate students, individuals reentering the workforce, early career directors. ▶ *1 literary intern:* responsibilities include reading new scripts, researching projects, and assisting with research for specific productions. Candidates should have ability to work independently, editing skills, knowledge of field, organizational skills, personal interest in the field, research skills, self-motivation, writing skills. Duration is 1 full season (August to May). Position available as unpaid or at $50 per week. Open to college seniors, recent college graduates, graduate students, individuals reentering the workforce, semi-professional playwrights or literary managers. ▶ *1 production apprentice (lights and sound):* responsibilities include assisting light and sound supervisor in the preparation of designs for shows at the Milwaukee Repertory; intern will also run "A Christmas Carol" crew. Candidates should have analytical skills, declared college major in field, experience in the field, organizational skills, plan to pursue career in field, self-motivation, strong interpersonal skills. Duration is August 1 to May 12. $7.50 per hour. Open to recent college graduates, graduate students. ▶ *2 production apprentices (A Christmas Carol):* responsibilities include assignments in specific areas of production including electrics, sound, paint, and running the production of "A Christmas Carol" at the Pabst Theater. Candidates should have declared college major in field, experience in the field, personal interest in the field, self-motivation, strong interpersonal skills. Duration is November 4 to December 27. $225 per week. Open to high school seniors, recent college graduates, graduate students. International applications accepted.
Benefits Free housing, job counseling, on-the-job training, opportunity to attend seminars/workshops, willing to act as a professional reference, willing to complete paperwork for educational credit, willing to provide letters of recommendation, earn points toward Actors Equity Association membership.
Contact Write, call, or e-mail Sandy Ernst, Company Intern Director. Phone: 414-224-1761 Ext. 374. Fax: 414-224-9097. E-mail: sernst@milwaukeerep.com. In-person interview recommended (telephone interview accepted). Applicants must submit a formal organization application, letter of interest, resume, writing sample, three personal references, three letters of recommendation, auditions required for acting internships. Application deadline: April 1 for acting interns. World Wide Web: http://www.milwaukeerep.com.

MONTE BROWN DANCE
1170 Broadway
New York, New York 10001

General Information International 9-member contemporary touring dance company. Established in 1981. Number of employees: 3.
Internships Available ▶ *1 administrative intern:* responsibilities include assisting with duties related to fund-raising, booking, financial management, programming, marketing, attending staff and board meetings, taking turns with the management staff in the general upkeep of the office/studio. Candidates should have strong interest in dance and arts administration. Duration is one summer or 1-2 semesters. Unpaid. Open to college juniors, college seniors, recent college graduates, graduate students.
Benefits Names of contacts, opportunity to attend seminars/workshops, willing to complete paperwork for educational credit, willing to provide letters of recommendation, 3 hours of credit if arranged by student in advance of internship.
Contact Write, call, fax, or e-mail Managing Director. Phone: 212-251-0789. Fax: 212-251-0743. E-mail: jcolandrea@elisamontedance.org. In-person interview required. Applicants must submit a letter of interest, resume. Applications are accepted continuously. World Wide Web: http://www.elisamontedance.org.

THE NEW CONSERVATORY THEATRE CENTER
25 Van Ness Avenue, Lower Lobby
San Francisco, California 94102

General Information Nonprofit theater school and performing arts company for children ages 7-18 emphasizing new and socially aware plays for family audiences; offers seven educational theater touring companies for youths in grades K-12; school provides theater and musical theater training as well as performance opportunities for youth ages 7-18. Established in 1981. Number of employees: 20. Number of internship applications received each year: 25.
Internships Available ▶ *3 Pride Season interns:* responsibilities include working in production (stage management, design, or with assistant directors); program is designed to feature work for and by gay and lesbian artists. Candidates should have ability to work independently, analytical skills, office skills, oral communication skills, personal interest in the field, self-motivation, strong interpersonal skills. Duration is flexible (evening hours). Position available as unpaid or at $5.75–$7 per hour. Open to col-

The New Conservatory Theatre Center (continued)

lege freshmen, college sophomores, college juniors, college seniors. ▶ *1 development intern.* Candidates should have ability to work independently, analytical skills, computer skills, editing skills, office skills, oral communication skills, organizational skills, plan to pursue career in field, research skills, self-motivation, strong interpersonal skills, strong leadership ability, writing skills. Duration is 3–6 months. Position available as unpaid or at $5.75–$9 per hour. Open to high school students, recent high school graduates, college freshmen, college sophomores, college juniors, college seniors, recent college graduates, graduate students. ▶ *2 general audience interns:* responsibilities include working in production or audience development and marketing. Candidates should have ability to work independently, office skills, oral communication skills, organizational skills, strong interpersonal skills, strong leadership ability. Duration is flexible (evening hours). Position available as unpaid or at $5.75–$7 per hour. Open to recent high school graduates, college freshmen, college sophomores, college juniors, college seniors, recent college graduates. ▶ *1 marketing and promotion intern.* Candidates should have ability to work independently, college courses in field, computer skills, knowledge of field, office skills, oral communication skills, personal interest in the field, research skills, self-motivation, strong interpersonal skills, strong leadership ability, writing skills. Duration is 3–9 months. Position available as unpaid or at $7–$9 per hour. Open to college freshmen, college sophomores, college juniors, college seniors, recent college graduates, graduate students. ▶ *3 teaching assistants.* Candidates should have oral communication skills, strong interpersonal skills, strong leadership ability. Duration is 1–9 months. Position available as unpaid or at $5.75–$6.75 per hour. Open to recent high school graduates, college freshmen, college sophomores, college juniors, college seniors, recent college graduates, graduate students, must be at least 18 years old. ▶ *1 touring program intern:* responsibilities include providing technical assistance for Youth Aware program, a 7-production touring program that travels to schools in northern California. Candidates should have ability to work with others, analytical skills, computer skills, office skills, oral communication skills, organizational skills, personal interest in the field, research skills, self-motivation, strong leadership ability, writing skills. Duration is 3–9 months. Position available as unpaid or at $5.75–$7 per hour. Open to recent high school graduates, college freshmen, college juniors, college seniors, career changers. International applications accepted.

Benefits On-the-job training, opportunity to attend seminars/workshops, possible full-time employment, travel reimbursement, willing to provide letters of recommendation.

Contact Write or through World Wide Web site Mr. Ed Decker, Executive Director. No phone calls. In-person interview recommended (telephone interview accepted). Applicants must submit a letter of interest, resume. Application deadline: April 1 for summer, July 1 for fall. World Wide Web: http://www.nctcsf.org.

NEW JERSEY SHAKESPEARE FESTIVAL
36 Madison Avenue
Madison, New Jersey 07940

General Information Actor's Equity theater devoted to producing the works of Shakespeare and other classic masterworks. Established in 1962. Number of employees: 250. Number of internship applications received each year: 200.

Internships Available ▶ *2–3 box office interns:* responsibilities include functioning as junior staff members, dealing with the public, and learning the important and intricate workings of ticketing procedures. Candidates should have ability to work independently, computer skills, knowledge of field, office skills, oral communication skills, organizational skills, strong interpersonal skills. Duration is flexible. Position available as unpaid or paid. Open to college freshmen, college sophomores, college juniors, college seniors, recent college graduates, graduate students, law students, career changers, individuals reentering the workforce. ▶ *3–5 costume design interns:* responsibilities include assisting costume shop supervisor and designers for the productions. Candidates should have ability to work independently, ability to work with others, analytical skills, college courses in field, knowledge of field, oral communication skills, organizational skills, personal interest in

the field, plan to pursue career in field, self-motivation. Duration is summer (late May through August) or fall (mid-August through December). Position available as unpaid or paid. Open to college freshmen, college sophomores, college juniors, college seniors, recent college graduates, graduate students, law students, career changers, individuals reentering the workforce. ▶ *5–6 directing interns:* responsibilities include assisting on mainstage productions, coaching apprentices on scenes and monologues, and directing projects with non-equity company members. Candidates should have ability to work independently, analytical skills, college courses in field, computer skills, knowledge of field, oral communication skills, organizational skills, personal interest in the field, plan to pursue career in field, research skills, self-motivation, strong interpersonal skills, strong leadership ability, written communication skills. Duration is flexible. Unpaid. Open to college freshmen, college sophomores, college juniors, college seniors, recent college graduates, graduate students, law students, career changers, individuals reentering the workforce. ▶ *1–2 house management interns:* responsibilities include functioning as house manager for the festival, reporting to the managing director, and dealing with the public. Candidates should have ability to work independently, analytical skills, experience in the field, office skills, oral communication skills, organizational skills, self-motivation, strong interpersonal skills, strong leadership ability, written communication skills. Duration is flexible. Unpaid. Open to college freshmen, college sophomores, college juniors, college seniors, recent college graduates, graduate students, law students, career changers, individuals reentering the workforce. ▶ *3 lighting design interns:* responsibilities include assisting with mainstage productions and working under the supervision of the master electrician. Candidates should have ability to work independently, college courses in field, computer skills, knowledge of field, personal interest in the field, strong interpersonal skills. Duration is flexible. Unpaid. Open to college freshmen, college sophomores, college juniors, college seniors, recent college graduates, graduate students, law students, career changers, individuals reentering the workforce. ▶ *2 production management interns:* responsibilities include assisting with logistical operations, including transporting actors, pricing and purchasing supplies, theater maintenance, and load-ins. Candidates should have ability to work independently, analytical skills, computer skills, office skills, oral communication skills, organizational skills, personal interest in the field, research skills, self-motivation, strong interpersonal skills, written communication skills. Duration is flexible. Unpaid. Open to college freshmen, college sophomores, college juniors, college seniors, recent college graduates, graduate students, law students, career changers, individuals reentering the workforce. ▶ *2–3 props interns:* responsibilities include coordinating and acquiring props for each show and acting as properties manager throughout the season. Candidates should have experience in the field, oral communication skills, personal interest in the field, research skills, strong interpersonal skills, painting and craftwork experience. Duration is flexible. Unpaid. Open to college freshmen, college sophomores, college juniors, college seniors, recent college graduates, graduate students, law students, career changers, individuals reentering the workforce. ▶ *2–4 set construction interns:* responsibilities include working as part of the team that builds and mounts productions for the festival. Candidates should have ability to work independently, analytical skills, knowledge of field, organizational skills, personal interest in the field, research skills, strong interpersonal skills, drafting skills (preferred). Duration is flexible. Unpaid. Open to college freshmen, college sophomores, college juniors, college seniors, recent college graduates, graduate students, law students, career changers, individuals reentering the workforce. ▶ *3–4 set design interns:* responsibilities include assisting with the construction and painting of sets and props for each show. Candidates should have ability to work independently, analytical skills, college courses in field, computer skills, knowledge of field, organizational skills, plan to pursue career in field, research skills, strong interpersonal skills, painting skills, carpentry skills. Duration is summer (May through August) or fall (August through December). Unpaid. Open to college freshmen, college sophomores, college juniors, college seniors, recent college graduates, graduate students, law students, career changers, individuals reentering the workforce. ▶ *1–2 sound design interns:* responsibilities include working directly with resident sound designer and taking responsibility for the operation of sound for each show. Candidates should have ability to work independently, ability to work with others, computer skills, editing skills, knowledge of field, oral communication skills, research skills. Duration is flexible. Unpaid. Open to college freshmen, college sophomores, college juniors, college seniors, recent college graduates, graduate students, law students, career changers, individuals reentering the workforce. ▶ *6 stage management interns:* responsibilities include assisting Equity stage managers for each show. Candidates should have analytical skills, computer skills, knowledge of field, office skills, oral communication skills, organizational skills, personal interest in the field, plan to pursue career in field, strong interpersonal skills, written communication skills. Duration is summer (May through August) or fall (August through December). Unpaid. Open to college freshmen, college sophomores, college juniors, college seniors, recent college graduates, graduate students, law students, career changers, individuals reentering the workforce. ▶ *6–12 theater administration interns:* responsibilities include working in publicity, development, general management, and/or casting divisions. Candidates should have ability to work independently, computer skills, editing skills, office skills, oral communication skills, organizational skills, personal interest in the field, research skills, strong interpersonal skills, writing skills, experience in specific area (preferred). Duration is summer (May through August) or fall (August through December). Unpaid. Open to recent high school graduates, college freshmen, college sophomores, college juniors, college seniors, recent college graduates, graduate students, law students, career changers, individuals reentering the workforce. International applications accepted.

Benefits Formal training, housing at a cost, job counseling, names of contacts, on-the-job training, opportunity to attend seminars/workshops, possible full-time employment, travel reimbursement, willing to act as a professional reference, willing to complete paperwork for educational credit, willing to provide letters of recommendation, limited stipend available.

Contact Write, call, fax, e-mail, or through World Wide Web site Jake Berger, Associate Director of Education. Phone: 973-408-3278. Fax: 973-408-3361. E-mail: jberger@njshakespeare.org. In-person interview recommended (telephone interview accepted). Applicants must submit a formal organization application, letter of interest, resume, portfolio, three personal references, work samples (if applicable to area of interest). Application deadline: May 2 for summer. Fees: $25. World Wide Web: http://www.njshakespeare.org.

NEW YORK STATE THEATRE INSTITUTE
Russell Sage Campus, 37 First Street
Troy, New York 12180

General Information Professional theater company and statewide arts-in-education program that develops one new musical theater production a season for family audiences, and performs a range of classical, modern, contemporary, and new works for school, family, and general audiences. Established in 1976. Number of employees: 32. Number of internship applications received each year: 100.

Internships Available ▶ *20–30 interns:* responsibilities include working in areas of technical theater, arts management, performance, and arts-in-education; participating in the operation of a professional theater. Candidates should have theater skills. Duration is 5 months. Unpaid. Open to high school seniors, recent high school graduates, college freshmen, college sophomores, college juniors, college seniors, recent college graduates, graduate students, career changers, individuals reentering the workforce. International applications accepted.

Benefits Formal training, job counseling, names of contacts, opportunity to attend seminars/workshops, travel reimbursement, tuition assistance, willing to complete paperwork for educational credit, willing to provide letters of recommendation, academic credit granted by State University of New York at Albany and Russell Sage College.

Contact Write, call, fax, e-mail, or through World Wide Web site Ms. Arlene Leff, Intern Program Administrator/Education Director. Phone: 518-274-3573. Fax: 518-274-3815. E-mail: nysti@capital.

net. In-person interview recommended (telephone interview accepted). Application deadline: June 1 for summer, December 1 for spring. World Wide Web: http://www.nysti.org.

NORTH SHORE MUSIC THEATRE
62 Dunham Road, PO Box 62
Beverly, Massachusetts 01915-0062

General Information Professional theater dedicated to the American musical and programs for young audiences, serving over 300,000 patrons from April through December. Established in 1955. Number of employees: 100. Unit of North Shore Community Arts Foundation, Beverly, Massachusetts. Number of internship applications received each year: 100.

Internships Available ▶ *2 company management interns:* responsibilities include assisting company manager with housing, transportation, and services for Equity companies and concert road groups. Candidates should have office skills, self-motivation, strong interpersonal skills. Duration is 4–8 months. $270 per week. Open to individuals 21 years of age and older. ▶ *2–4 electrics interns:* responsibilities include hanging and focusing instruments and running follow spots for musicals and concerts. Candidates should have strong interpersonal skills, no fear of heights. Duration is 4–8 months. $270 per week. Open to individuals 18 years of age and older. ▶ *6–8 production assistants:* responsibilities include working within various departments to gain basic understanding and assisting in various departments with show runs. Candidates should have strong interpersonal skills. Duration is 4–8 months. $270 per week. Open to individuals 18 years of age and older. ▶ *1 scenic art intern:* responsibilities include scenic painting for musicals and concerts; emphasis is on painting 3-dimensional units. Candidates should have ability to work independently, ability to work with others, experience in the field, personal interest in the field. Duration is 4–8 months. $270 per week. Open to individuals 18 years of age and older. ▶ *2 sound interns:* responsibilities include maintaining equipment, sound setup, and operating wireless microphones for musicals and concerts. Candidates should have knowledge of field, personal interest in the field, plan to pursue career in field, strong interpersonal skills. Duration is 4–8 months. $270 per week. Open to individuals 18 years of age and older. ▶ *1–2 stage management interns:* responsibilities include assisting Equity stage manager or running crew supervisor in rehearsing and running musicals and children's shows. Candidates should have knowledge of field, personal interest in the field, self-motivation, strong interpersonal skills, strong leadership ability. Duration is 4–8 months. $270 per week. Open to individuals 18 years of age and older. ▶ *1–2 wardrobe interns:* responsibilities include providing fitting, maintenance, and dressing needs for musicals and concerts. Candidates should have knowledge of field, strong interpersonal skills, sewing skills. Duration is 4–8 months. $270 per week. Open to individuals 18 years of age and older. International applications accepted.

Benefits Names of contacts, opportunity to attend seminars/workshops, possible full-time employment, willing to complete paperwork for educational credit, willing to provide letters of recommendation.

Contact Write, fax, or e-mail Associate Production Manager. Fax: 978-922-0768. E-mail: amignone@nsmt.org. No phone calls. In-person interview recommended (telephone interview accepted). Applicants must submit a formal organization application, letter of interest, resume, three personal references. Applications are accepted continuously. World Wide Web: http://www.nsmt.org.

OPERA COMPANY OF PHILADELPHIA
1420 Locust Street, Suite 210
Philadelphia, Pennsylvania 19102

General Information Company presenting performances of grand opera in the original language of composition with internationally acclaimed performers and rising young talent, staged at the Academy of Music. Established in 1975. Number of employees: 30. Number of internship applications received each year: 20.

Internships Available ▶ *1 box office intern:* responsibilities include taking subscription and single ticket orders, performing data entry, answering phones, and filing. Candidates should have ability to

Opera Company of Philadelphia (continued)

work with others, computer skills, office skills, oral communication skills. Duration is flexible. Unpaid. ▶ *1 business office intern:* responsibilities include data entry, accounting, filing, and typing. Candidates should have computer skills, experience in the field, office skills. Duration is flexible. Unpaid. ▶ *1 development intern:* responsibilities include typing and data entry, filing, recordkeeping, planning special events, scheduling, and acknowledging donors. Candidates should have computer skills, knowledge of field, office skills. Duration is flexible. Unpaid. ▶ *1–3 education office interns:* responsibilities include coordinating dress rehearsal attendance, corresponding, entering data, maintaining teacher contact, coordinating special events, assisting with general clerical and administrative tasks, researching opera background for educational materials, and some public relations duties. Candidates should have computer skills, editing skills, office skills, personal interest in the field, research skills, writing skills. Duration is flexible. Unpaid. ▶ *1 general administration intern:* responsibilities include answering phones, typing, and filing. Candidates should have ability to work with others, computer skills, office skills, organizational skills, personal interest in the field. Duration is flexible. Unpaid. ▶ *1 marketing intern:* responsibilities include creating target marketing mailings, researching possible audience members, and designing advertisements. Candidates should have computer skills, office skills, oral communication skills, personal interest in the field, written communication skills. Duration is flexible. Unpaid. ▶ *1 public relations intern:* responsibilities include assisting with mass mailings; editing and producing press releases, media packages, and newsletters; scheduling press and artists' interviews and conferences; and filing. Candidates should have computer skills, editing skills, office skills, organizational skills, personal interest in the field. Duration is flexible. Unpaid. International applications accepted.

Benefits Names of contacts, possible full-time employment, willing to complete paperwork for educational credit, willing to provide letters of recommendation, work-study granted to in-state residents (when possible).

Contact Write, call, fax, or e-mail Judy L. Williams, Director of Educational Operations. Phone: 215-893-3600 Ext. 216. Fax: 215-893-7801. E-mail: williams@operaphilly.com. In-person interview recommended (telephone interview accepted). Applicants must submit a letter of interest, resume. Applications are accepted continuously. World Wide Web: http://www.operaphilly.com.

THE PEARL THEATRE COMPANY
80 Saint Mark's Place
New York, New York 10003

General Information Nonprofit classical theater company. Established in 1982. Number of employees: 9. Number of internship applications received each year: 75.

Internships Available ▶ *1–3 administrative interns:* responsibilities include assisting in all administrative departments including marketing, development, finance, production, and artistic direction; position can be tailored to suit intern's interests. Candidates should have ability to work independently, computer skills, knowledge of field, office skills, oral communication skills, personal interest in the field, plan to pursue career in field, self-motivation, strong interpersonal skills, writing skills. Duration is part-time and flexible; minimum length of commitment required. Position available as unpaid or paid. Open to college juniors, college seniors, recent college graduates, graduate students, career changers. ▶ *1 costume intern:* responsibilities include assisting costume designer on 5 classical plays and wardrobe maintenance. Candidates should have ability to work independently, ability to work with others, plan to pursue career in field, self-motivation, positive attitude, reasonable background in theatrical costumes. Duration is 5-10 months (full-time), from August through June. $200 weekly stipend. Open to college juniors, college seniors, recent college graduates, graduate students. ▶ *2 stage management interns:* responsibilities include assisting stage manager with 3 to 5 productions, scheduling, prompting, blocking, production meetings, light board, sound, and floor managing. Candidates should have ability to work independently, analytical skills, knowledge of field, oral communication skills, organizational skills, plan to pursue career in

field, self-motivation, strong interpersonal skills. Duration is 5 to 10 months (full-time), from August through June. $200 weekly stipend. Open to college juniors, college seniors, recent college graduates. International applications accepted.

Benefits Job counseling, names of contacts, on-the-job training, opportunity to attend seminars/workshops, possible full-time employment, willing to act as a professional reference, willing to complete paperwork for educational credit, willing to provide letters of recommendation, Equity membership candidacy points for stage management interns.

Contact Write, fax, or e-mail Meghan Beals, Programs Manager. Phone: 212-505-3401. Fax: 212-505-3404. E-mail: mbeals@pearltheatre. org. In-person interview recommended (telephone interview accepted). Applicants must submit a letter of interest, resume, two writing samples, three personal references. Application deadline: March 31 for fall, October 31 for spring. World Wide Web: http://www.pearltheatre.org.

PENINSULA PLAYERS
W4351 Peninsula Players Road
Fish Creek, Wisconsin 54212-9799

General Information Professional resident summer theater. Established in 1935. Number of employees: 40. Number of internship applications received each year: 40.

Internships Available ▶ *2–4 administrative interns:* responsibilities include assisting with box office operation, promotion and publicity, accounting, and house management. Candidates should have office skills, oral communication skills, personal interest in the field, strong interpersonal skills, written communication skills. Duration is 1 summer, June 1 to Labor Day. $75 per week. ▶ *6 production interns:* responsibilities include working in areas of costume, carpentry, electrical, design, props, and stage management. Candidates should have ability to work with others, knowledge of field, personal interest in the field, self-motivation. Duration is 1 summer, June 1 to Labor Day. $75 per week. Open to high school seniors, recent high school graduates, college freshmen, college sophomores, college juniors, college seniors, recent college graduates, graduate students, career changers. International applications accepted.

Benefits Free housing, free meals, possible full-time employment, travel reimbursement, willing to act as a professional reference, willing to complete paperwork for educational credit, willing to provide letters of recommendation.

Contact Write or call Ms. Audra Baakari Boyle, Business Manager, W4351 Peninsula Players Road, Fish Creek, Wisconsin 54212. Phone: 920-868-3287. Telephone interview required. Applicants must submit a formal organization application, letter of interest, resume, two letters of recommendation. Application deadline: May 1. World Wide Web: http://www.peninsulaplayers.com.

PIONEER PLAYHOUSE
840 Stanford Road
Danville, Kentucky 40422

General Information Summer stock theater that produces plays. Established in 1950. Number of employees: 30. Number of internship applications received each year: 50.

Internships Available ▶ *5–10 acting and technical interns:* responsibilities include assisting in all aspects of play productions. Candidates should have ability to work with others, plan to pursue career in field, self-motivation, strong leadership ability. Duration is June to September. Unpaid. Open to high school students, recent high school graduates, college freshmen, college sophomores, college juniors, college seniors, recent college graduates, graduate students, law students, career changers, individuals reentering the workforce, must be between the ages of 14 and 60. International applications accepted.

Benefits Housing at a cost, meals at a cost, names of contacts, on-the-job training, opportunity to attend seminars/workshops, possible full-time employment, tuition assistance, willing to act as a professional reference, willing to complete paperwork for educational credit, willing to provide letters of recommendation.

International Internships Available.

Contact Write, call, fax, or e-mail Col. Eben Henson, Production Manager. Phone: 859-236-2747. Fax: 859-236-2341. E-mail: pioneer@

mis.net. In-person interview recommended. Applicants must submit a letter of interest, $900 tuition includes room and board (high school students); $50 per week for college students for room and board. Application deadline: May 1. World Wide Web: http://www. pioneerplayhouse.com.

PITTSBURGH CIVIC LIGHT OPERA
719 Liberty Avenue
Pittsburgh, Pennsylvania 15222

General Information Producer of Broadway-scale, professional musicals in a 2,837-seat theater during the summer. Established in 1946. Number of employees: 60. Number of internship applications received each year: 250.
Internships Available ▶ *1–2 Gene Kelly Awards interns:* responsibilities include coordinating award ceremony patterned after Tony Awards for Allegheny County High Schools; marketing to production. Candidates should have computer skills, oral communication skills, personal interest in the field, self-motivation, strong interpersonal skills, strong leadership ability, writing skills. Duration is January–May. $50 per week. ▶ *1 Web design intern.* Duration is 8–10 weeks. $100 per week. ▶ *1 lighting intern.* Duration is 8–10 weeks. $100 per week. ▶ *1 music director.* Duration is 8–10 weeks. $100 per week. ▶ *1 production manager.* Duration is 8–10 weeks. $100 per week. ▶ *2 property coordinators.* Duration is 8–10 weeks. $100 per week. ▶ *1 sound design intern.* Duration is 8–10 weeks. $100 per week. ▶ *2 stage directors.* Duration is 8–10 weeks. $100 per week. ▶ *2 stage management interns.* Duration is 8–10 weeks. $100 per week. ▶ *1 summer development intern.* Candidates should have ability to work independently, computer skills, office skills, oral communication skills, organizational skills, strong interpersonal skills, written communication skills. Duration is 8–10 weeks. $100 per week. ▶ *1 summer education and outreach intern:* responsibilities include performing general duties including data entry and assisting with a variety of outreach programs. Candidates should have computer skills, office skills, oral communication skills, organizational skills, strong interpersonal skills, written communication skills. Duration is 8–10 weeks. $100 per week. ▶ *1 summer general administration intern:* responsibilities include working for the executive director and handling a full range of administrative tasks in company office. Candidates should have ability to work independently, computer skills, office skills, oral communication skills, organizational skills, research skills, self-motivation, strong interpersonal skills, written communication skills. Duration is 8–10 weeks. $100 per week. ▶ *1 summer hair/wig intern:* responsibilities include assisting wig and hair designer with preparation, styling, and maintaining of performers' hair and wigs. Candidates should have ability to work independently, knowledge of field, personal interest in the field, self-motivation, strong interpersonal skills. Duration is 8–10 weeks. $100 per week. ▶ *1 summer promotion/marketing intern:* responsibilities include performing a broad range of tasks including writing press releases, distributing flyers and posters, and escorting stars on interviews. Candidates should have ability to work independently, college courses in field, computer skills, editing skills, office skills, oral communication skills, organizational skills, personal interest in the field, self-motivation, strong interpersonal skills, writing skills. Duration is 8–10 weeks. $100 per week. Open to recent high school graduates, college freshmen, college sophomores, college juniors, college seniors. International applications accepted.
Benefits Names of contacts, on-the-job training, willing to act as a professional reference, willing to complete paperwork for educational credit, willing to provide letters of recommendation.
Contact Write, call, fax, e-mail, or through World Wide Web site Buddy Thompson, Education Director, Penn Avenue Place, 130 CLO Academy Way, 8th Floor, Pittsburgh, Pennsylvania 15222. Phone: 412-281-2234 Ext. 2. Fax: 412-281-2232. E-mail: bthompson@ pittsburghclo.org. In-person interview recommended (telephone interview accepted). Applicants must submit a formal organization application, letter of interest, resume, two personal references, photo. Application deadline: February 28 for summer, November 15 for Gene Kelly interns. World Wide Web: http://www.pittsburghCLO.org.

PLAYHOUSE ON THE SQUARE
51 South Cooper
Memphis, Tennessee 38104

General Information Nonprofit, professional theater with a mission to create challenging, truthful, entertaining, and culturally diverse high-quality theater that reflects, improves, and reaches the present and future community. Established in 1969. Number of employees: 23. Number of internship applications received each year: 300.
Internships Available ▶ *7 acting interns:* responsibilities include acting and technical or administrative work. Candidates should have ability to work with others, knowledge of field, plan to pursue career in field, self-motivation. Duration is 1 year. $100 per week. Open to recent college graduates. ▶ *1 administrative intern:* responsibilities include assisting with clerical duties, box office, house management, and subscription drive. Candidates should have ability to work independently, computer skills, knowledge of field, oral communication skills, self-motivation, strong leadership ability. Duration is 1 year. $100 per week. Open to recent college graduates. ▶ *1 costumes intern:* responsibilities include assisting with costuming. Candidates should have college courses in field, knowledge of field, organizational skills, plan to pursue career in field, self-motivation. Duration is 1 year. $100 per week. Open to recent college graduates. ▶ *1 props intern:* responsibilities include gathering, building, renting, buying, running, and organizing properties. Candidates should have ability to work independently, ability to work with others, experience in the field, plan to pursue career in field, self-motivation. Duration is 1 year. $100 per week. Open to recent college graduates. ▶ *2 stage management interns:* responsibilities include assisting with management and technical tasks. Candidates should have ability to work independently, ability to work with others, knowledge of field, organizational skills, self-motivation, strong leadership ability. Duration is 1 year. $100 per week. Open to recent college graduates. ▶ *1 technical/set design intern:* responsibilities include assisting with set construction. Candidates should have ability to work with others, knowledge of field, organizational skills, personal interest in the field, self-motivation. Duration is 1 year. $100 per week.
Benefits Free housing, health insurance, job counseling, names of contacts, on-the-job training, possible full-time employment, willing to act as a professional reference, willing to complete paperwork for educational credit, willing to provide letters of recommendation, free utilities, local phone, laundry facilities.
Contact Write Jackie Nichols, Executive Producer. Phone: 901-725-0776. Fax: 901-272-7530. E-mail: info@playhouseonthesquare.org. In-person interview required. Applicants must submit a resume, two letters of recommendation. Applications are accepted continuously. World Wide Web: http://playhouseonthesquare.org.

PORTLAND STAGE COMPANY
PO Box 1458
Portland, Maine 04104

General Information Resident professional theater producing a 6-play mainstage season and providing numerous other educational and cultural services. Established in 1974. Number of employees: 30. Number of internship applications received each year: 100.
Internships Available ▶ *1–3 directing/dramaturgy interns:* responsibilities include assisting directors on mainstage productions, conducting dramaturgical research, and assisting artistic staff on day-to-day administrative activities. Candidates should have knowledge of field, plan to pursue career in field, research skills, self-motivation, strong interpersonal skills, writing skills. Duration is September to May. $65 per week. Open to recent high school graduates, college freshmen, college sophomores, college juniors, college seniors, recent college graduates, graduate students. ▶ *1 literary/education intern:* responsibilities include assisting literary staff with reading and evaluating scripts, playwright correspondence, researching and preparing educational resource guides, and assisting with student matinees, school workshops and discussions. Candidates should have ability to work independently, computer skills, oral communication skills, organizational skills, research skills, writing skills. Duration is September to May. $65 per week.

Portland Stage Company (continued)

Open to college freshmen, college sophomores, college juniors, college seniors, recent college graduates, graduate students. ▶ *2 marketing/development interns:* responsibilities include assisting with publicity, media relations, fund-raising, grant research, ticket promotions, press releases, and all aspects of promoting a regional theater. Candidates should have ability to work independently, computer skills, knowledge of field, personal interest in the field, self-motivation, writing skills. Duration is September to May. $65 per week. Open to college freshmen, college sophomores, college juniors, college seniors, recent college graduates, graduate students. ▶ *3–5 production interns:* responsibilities include working in all production departments with areas of specialization in carpentry/props, costumes/wardrobe, electrics/sound; assisting construction and maintenance; and serving on run crew. Candidates should have ability to work independently, ability to work with others, knowledge of field, plan to pursue career in field, self-motivation. Duration is September to May. $65 per week. Open to recent high school graduates, college freshmen, college sophomores, college juniors, college seniors, recent college graduates, graduate students. ▶ *2 stage management interns:* responsibilities include assisting Equity stage managers in all areas of production and preproduction. Candidates should have ability to work with others, knowledge of field, organizational skills, plan to pursue career in field, self-motivation. Duration is September to May. $65 per week. Open to recent high school graduates, college freshmen, college sophomores, college juniors, college seniors, recent college graduates, graduate students. International applications accepted.

Benefits Formal training, free housing, on-the-job training, opportunity to attend seminars/workshops, possible full-time employment, willing to act as a professional reference, willing to complete paperwork for educational credit, willing to provide letters of recommendation.

Contact Write, call, fax, e-mail, or through World Wide Web site Lindsay Cummings, Education Manager. Phone: 207-774-1043. Fax: 207-774-0576. E-mail: education@portlandstage.com. Telephone interview required. Applicants must submit a formal organization application, letter of interest, resume, writing sample, two letters of recommendation. Application deadline: April 30 for full-season positions; continuous for partial-season positions. World Wide Web: http://www.portlandstage.com.

PRIMARY STAGES
131 West 45th Street, 2nd Floor
New York, New York 10036

General Information Producer of new American plays. Established in 1985. Number of employees: 8. Number of internship applications received each year: 40.

Internships Available ▶ *1–4 assistant director/production assistants.* Candidates should have oral communication skills, organizational skills, plan to pursue career in field, self-motivation, strong interpersonal skills. Duration is 5–10 weeks. Unpaid. Open to college juniors, college seniors, recent college graduates, graduate students, career changers. ▶ *1–4 literary interns:* responsibilities include reading and analysis of play submissions, upkeep of database, correspondence with agents/playwrights, participation in attending workshops/readings in New York City. Candidates should have analytical skills, computer skills, office skills, personal interest in the field, self-motivation, written communication skills. Duration is 9 weeks or more. Unpaid. Open to college juniors, college seniors, recent college graduates, graduate students, career changers. ▶ *1–4 publicity and marketing interns:* responsibilities include assisting publicity/marketing staff in marketing production, special events, and subscription campaigns. Candidates should have oral communication skills, self-motivation, strong interpersonal skills, writing skills. Duration is flexible. Unpaid. Open to college freshmen, college sophomores, college juniors, college seniors, recent college graduates, graduate students, career changers, individuals reentering the workforce. ▶ *1–4 stage management interns:* responsibilities include assisting the manager in rehearsals and serving as running crew backstage. Candidates should have knowledge of field, oral communication skills, personal interest in the field, self-motivation, strong interpersonal skills.

Duration is 9 weeks or more. Unpaid. Open to college freshmen, college sophomores, college juniors, college seniors, recent college graduates, graduate students, career changers, individuals reentering the workforce.

Benefits Job counseling, names of contacts, on-the-job training, opportunity to attend seminars/workshops, willing to complete paperwork for educational credit, willing to provide letters of recommendation.

Contact Write, fax, or e-mail Tyler Marchant, Associate Artistic Director. Fax: 212-840-9725. E-mail: tyler@primarystages.com. No phone calls. In-person interview recommended (telephone interview accepted). Applicants must submit a letter of interest, resume, two personal references, letter of recommendation. Applications are accepted continuously. World Wide Web: http://www.primarystages.com.

PULSE ENSEMBLE THEATRE
432 West 42nd Street
New York, New York 10036

General Information Ensemble theater company that produces mainstage shows, Bare Bones Classic Season (a studio season), and readings of new plays. Established in 1989. Number of employees: 8. Number of internship applications received each year: 60.

Internships Available ▶ *12–20 acting interns:* responsibilities include playing small parts in shows and providing general assistance in the preparation of shows. Candidates should have acting experience or training. Duration is 6 months. Unpaid. Open to recent high school graduates, college freshmen, college sophomores, college juniors, college seniors, recent college graduates, graduate students, law students, career changers, individuals reentering the workforce. ▶ *2–4 business management interns.* Candidates should have college courses in field, computer skills, knowledge of field, personal interest in the field, plan to pursue career in field. Duration is flexible. Unpaid. Open to college juniors, college seniors, recent college graduates, graduate students, law students, career changers. ▶ *2–4 directing interns:* responsibilities include assisting the director in taking a play from casting through to performance. Candidates should have ability to work independently, ability to work with others, experience in the field, oral communication skills, research skills, strong leadership ability. Duration is 6–8 weeks. Unpaid. Open to recent high school graduates, college seniors, recent college graduates, graduate students, individuals reentering the workforce. ▶ *2–6 fund-raising interns:* responsibilities include finding funding sources, helping to complete grant applications, and helping at fund-raising events. Candidates should have ability to work independently, computer skills, knowledge of field, organizational skills, research skills, writing skills. Duration is 3–12 months. Unpaid. Open to recent college graduates, graduate students, law students, career changers. ▶ *2–4 management interns:* responsibilities include assisting the general manager, organizing volunteer groups, and assisting at the box office. Candidates should have ability to work independently, computer skills, organizational skills, personal interest in the field, research skills, writing skills. Duration is 6 months. Unpaid. Open to high school seniors, recent high school graduates, college freshmen, college sophomores, college juniors, college seniors, recent college graduates, graduate students, law students, career changers, individuals reentering the workforce. ▶ *2–4 marketing interns:* responsibilities include typing and distributing publicity and making promotional telephone calls. Candidates should have ability to work independently, computer skills, office skills, organizational skills, research skills, writing skills. Duration is 3 months minimum. Unpaid. Open to high school seniors, recent high school graduates, college freshmen, college sophomores, college juniors, college seniors, recent college graduates, graduate students, law students, career changers, individuals reentering the workforce. ▶ *2–3 production interns:* responsibilities include setting up scenery, working on sound tapes, and running lighting boards. Candidates should have ability to work independently, knowledge of field, organizational skills, personal interest in the field, research skills, written communication skills. Duration is 3 months minimum. Unpaid. Open to recent high school graduates, college freshmen, college sophomores, college juniors, college seniors, recent college graduates, graduate students, law students, career changers, individuals reentering the workforce. ▶ *1–3 stage management interns:* responsibilities include operating shows and sound and light equipment and setting props. Candidates should have computer skills, editing skills, experience in the field, oral communication skills, personal interest in the field, writing skills. Duration is 2 months minimum. Unpaid. Open to high school seniors, recent high school graduates, college freshmen, college sophomores, college juniors, college seniors, recent college graduates, graduate students, law students, career changers, individuals reentering the workforce. International applications accepted.

Benefits Formal training, job counseling, on-the-job training, opportunity to attend seminars/workshops, possible full-time employment, willing to act as a professional reference, willing to complete paperwork for educational credit, willing to provide letters of recommendation, reimbursement for job-related travel.

Contact Write, e-mail, or through World Wide Web site Alexa Kelly, Artistic Director. E-mail: intern@pulseensembletheatre.org. No phone calls. In-person interview required. Applicants must submit a letter of interest, resume, two letters of recommendation, headshot, audition (for acting interns). Application deadline: June 1 for fall, December 1 for spring. World Wide Web: http://www.pulseensembletheatre.org.

QUEENS THEATER IN THE PARK
PO Box 520069
Flushing, New York 11352

General Information Performing arts center. Established in 1989. Number of employees: 47. Number of internship applications received each year: 20.

Internships Available ▶ *1–3 office interns.* Candidates should have computer skills, office skills, oral communication skills, organizational skills, self-motivation, strong interpersonal skills. Duration is 1 semester. Unpaid. ▶ *1–3 stage production interns:* responsibilities include performing production work for theater, assisting stage manager, production manager, and other production personnel. Candidates should have computer skills, knowledge of field, organizational skills, personal interest in the field, self-motivation, strong interpersonal skills. Duration is 1 semester. Unpaid. Open to high school students, recent high school graduates, college freshmen, college sophomores, college juniors, college seniors, recent college graduates, graduate students, law students, career changers, individuals reentering the workforce. International applications accepted.

Benefits On-the-job training, possible full-time employment, willing to act as a professional reference, willing to complete paperwork for educational credit, willing to provide letters of recommendation.

Contact Write, call, fax, or e-mail Ms. Gail Koelln, Development Director. Phone: 718-760-0686. Fax: 718-760-5092. E-mail: qtipgail@aol.com. In-person interview required. Applicants must submit a letter of interest, resume. Applications are accepted continuously. World Wide Web: http://www.queenstheatre.org.

REPERTORIO ESPANOL
138 East 27th Street
New York, New York 10016

General Information Spanish language theater company that presents plays from Spain's Golden Age, contemporary Latin-American classics, and works by new playwrights. Established in 1968. Number of employees: 15. Number of internship applications received each year: 3.

Internships Available ▶ *Interns:* responsibilities include performing duties in the areas of community affairs, media relations, and fund development; preparing press packages for groups and responding to inquiries; arranging rehearsals, changing sets, helping with various production activities. Candidates should have ability to work independently, ability to work with others, computer skills, knowledge of field, office skills, oral communication skills, plan to pursue career in field, writing skills, Spanish ability (helpful). Duration is flexible. Unpaid. Open to recent high school graduates, college freshmen, college sophomores, college juniors, college seniors, recent college graduates. International applications accepted.

Benefits Names of contacts, possible full-time employment, willing to complete paperwork for educational credit, willing to provide letters of recommendation, free tickets to performances.

Contact Write, call, fax, or e-mail Allison Astor-Vargas, Special Projects Manager. Phone: 212-889-2850. Fax: 212-686-3732. E-mail: a.astorvargas@repertorio.org. In-person interview recommended (telephone interview accepted). Applicants must submit a letter of interest, resume. Applications are accepted continuously. World Wide Web: http://www.repertorio.org.

SAN FRANCISCO OPERA
301 Van Ness Avenue
San Francisco, California 94102

General Information Opera producing a season of international opera and regularly presenting premiers of new operas and commissioned works. Established in 1932. Number of employees: 1,120. Number of internship applications received each year: 100.

Internships Available ▶ *1–2 artistic interns:* responsibilities include acting as liaison with artists, managers, and other theaters; conducting research; entering computer data about auditions; organizing audition material; filing confidential artistic information. Candidates should have ability to work independently, computer skills, office skills, organizational skills, personal interest in the field, strong interpersonal skills. Duration is open. Unpaid. Open to recent high school graduates, college freshmen, college sophomores, college juniors, college seniors, recent college graduates, graduate students, individuals reentering the workforce. ▶ *1–2 costume shop interns:* responsibilities include running errands, shopping for fabrics and materials, maintaining notion inventory, sorting fabric samples, recording and arranging trimmings, pulling and replacing costumes from stock. Candidates should have ability to work with others, knowledge of field, oral communication skills, personal interest in the field, self-motivation, good physical stamina in order to move heavy boxes and costumes, as well as freedom from colorblindness and vertigo. Duration is open. Unpaid. Open to recent high school graduates, college freshmen, college sophomores, college juniors, college seniors, recent college graduates, graduate students, career changers, individuals reentering the workforce. ▶ *1–2 development interns:* responsibilities include individual and institutional gifts fund-raising, assisting with grant writing, prospect research, fund-raising systems, planned giving, telefunding, preparation of collateral materials design, and copy writing. Candidates should have office skills, oral communication skills, self-motivation, strong interpersonal skills, writing skills. Duration is open. Unpaid. Open to recent high school graduates, college freshmen, college sophomores, college juniors, college seniors, recent college graduates, graduate students, career changers. ▶ *1–2 finance/accounting interns:* responsibilities include filing and organizing financial documents, reconciling and analyzing accounts, and assisting with special projects. Candidates should have ability to work with others, analytical skills, computer skills, knowledge of field, organizational skills, self-motivation. Duration is open. Unpaid. Open to recent high school graduates, college freshmen, college sophomores, college juniors, college seniors, recent college graduates, graduate students, career changers, individuals reentering the workforce. ▶ *1–2 guild activities and events interns:* responsibilities include working with the board of directors; assisting with special events, education and outreach program, volunteer management, and fund-raising development. Candidates should have ability to work with others, computer skills, office skills, oral communication skills, organizational skills, self-motivation, written communication skills. Duration is open. Unpaid. Open to recent high school graduates, college freshmen, college sophomores, college juniors, college seniors, recent college graduates, graduate students, career changers, individuals reentering the workforce. ▶ *1–2 human resources:* responsibilities include assisting with recruiting/hiring, health and safety fair, employee training and development, managing personnel records, compensation and benefit coordination, and policies and procedures administration. Candidates should have ability to work independently, ability to work with others, computer skills, editing skills, office skills, oral communication skills, organizational skills, self-motivation, writing skills. Dura-

San Francisco Opera (continued)

tion is open. Unpaid. Open to recent high school graduates, college freshmen, college sophomores, college juniors, college seniors, recent college graduates, graduate students, career changers, individuals reentering the workforce. ▶ *1–2 information systems interns:* responsibilities include assisting with data backup and maintenance, equipment and software inventory management, conducting Internet research and file searches, routine network and hardware maintenance, and with Sybase, C++, PowerBuilder, Access, and RPG programming. Candidates should have ability to work independently, ability to work with others, computer skills, knowledge of field, office skills, personal interest in the field, research skills. Duration is open. Unpaid. Open to recent high school graduates, college freshmen, college sophomores, college juniors, college seniors, recent college graduates, graduate students, career changers, individuals reentering the workforce. ▶ *1–2 marketing interns:* responsibilities include composing collateral copy, collecting art/images for brochures, compiling information from a variety of sources, editing/proofreading documents and coordinating proofreading throughout organization; placing advertisements or event-related media; assisting with budgeting, sales reporting; and compiling statistics. Candidates should have ability to work with others, computer skills, editing skills, knowledge of field, office skills, oral communication skills, organizational skills, writing skills. Duration is open. Unpaid. Open to recent high school graduates, college freshmen, college sophomores, college juniors, college seniors, recent college graduates, graduate students, career changers, individuals reentering the workforce. ▶ *1–2 opera center interns:* responsibilities include assisting with events and performances, preparations for Western Opera Theater (national touring company), public relations and marketing, artist services, and with various aspects of the Merola Opera Program (11-week training for young artists). Candidates should have ability to work with others, computer skills, oral communication skills, personal interest in the field, written communication skills. Duration is open. Unpaid. Open to recent high school graduates, college freshmen, college sophomores, college juniors, college seniors, recent college graduates, graduate students, career changers, individuals reentering the workforce. ▶ *1–2 orchestra administration interns:* responsibilities include providing general assistance to the orchestra manager by assisting with musicians' employment records, assisting with engaging substitute and extra musicians, assisting with rehearsals and performances, tracking attendance and breaks, and assisting with financial reports. Candidates should have computer skills, oral communication skills, personal interest in the field, strong interpersonal skills, written communication skills. Duration is open. Unpaid. Open to recent high school graduates, college freshmen, college sophomores, college juniors, college seniors, recent college graduates, graduate students, individuals reentering the workforce. ▶ *1–2 public relations interns:* responsibilities include assisting members of public relations team with daily activities, assisting with mailings and photo distribution; maintaining photo and artist files; assisting during performances, events, and conferences when necessary; maintaining press database. Candidates should have ability to work with others, computer skills, editing skills, knowledge of field, office skills, oral communication skills, organizational skills, personal interest in the field, self-motivation, written communication skills. Duration is open. Unpaid. Open to recent high school graduates, college freshmen, college sophomores, college juniors, college seniors, recent college graduates, graduate students, career changers, individuals reentering the workforce. ▶ *1–2 special events interns:* responsibilities include producing and coordinating 75-125 donor recognition and cultivation events per year; development and management of event budgets and timelines; coordinating event logistics including catering, decor, seating, guest check-in; training and supervising volunteers; production of printed materials including programs and invitations; enlisting the support of and communicating with the opera's executive office, artistic and production staff; and development and marketing departments. Candidates should have computer skills, office skills, oral communication skills, organizational skills, strong interpersonal skills, written communication skills. Duration is open. Unpaid. Open to recent high school graduates, college freshmen, college sophomores, college juniors, college seniors, recent college gradu-

ates, graduate students, individuals reentering the workforce. ▶ *1–2 technical production interns:* responsibilities include participating in production meetings, assisting with the design and management of productions from scene shop to stage, creating and manipulating information on department network. Candidates should have ability to work with others, computer skills, personal interest in the field. Duration is open. Unpaid. Open to recent high school graduates, college freshmen, college sophomores, college juniors, college seniors, recent college graduates, graduate students, individuals reentering the workforce. International applications accepted.

Benefits Possible full-time employment, willing to act as a professional reference, willing to complete paperwork for educational credit, willing to provide letters of recommendation, opportunity to attend dress rehearsals and performances.

Contact Write, call, fax, e-mail, or through World Wide Web site Erin Johnson, Human Resources Assistant/Internship Coordinator. Phone: 415-861-4008. Fax: 415-551-6297. E-mail: ejohnson@sfopera. com. In-person interview recommended (telephone interview accepted). Applicants must submit a formal organization application, resume, 2-3 personal references. Applications are accepted continuously. World Wide Web: http://www.sfopera.com.

SEACOAST REPERTORY THEATRE
125 Bow Street
Portsmouth, New Hampshire 03801

General Information Year-round professional theater that presents 9 mainstage shows, 9 children's shows, and classes. Established in 1987. Number of employees: 15. Number of internship applications received each year: 10.

Internships Available ▶ *1–2 administrative interns.* Candidates should have knowledge of field, office skills, oral communication skills, organizational skills, strong interpersonal skills, computer literacy and knowledge of graphics a plus. Duration is June to September. Position available as unpaid or paid. Open to high school students, recent high school graduates, college freshmen, college sophomores, college juniors, college seniors, recent college graduates, graduate students, career changers, individuals reentering the workforce. ▶ *4–8 theatre production interns:* responsibilities include working in the areas of props, sets, electrics, sound, paint, costumes, and running of the shows. Candidates should have ability to work independently, ability to work with others, knowledge of field, oral communication skills, organizational skills, self-motivation, strong leadership ability. Duration is 6–52 weeks. Position available as unpaid or paid. Open to high school seniors, recent high school graduates, college freshmen, college sophomores, college juniors, college seniors, recent college graduates, graduate students, law students, career changers, individuals reentering the workforce. International applications accepted.

Benefits On-the-job training, possible full-time employment, willing to act as a professional reference, willing to provide letters of recommendation, possible housing.

Contact Write or fax Eileen Rogosin, Associate Producer. Fax: 603-431-7818. E-mail: info@seacoastrep.org. No phone calls. In-person interview recommended (telephone interview accepted). Applicants must submit a formal organization application, letter of interest, resume, two letters of recommendation. Application deadline: April 15 for summer interns; continuous for other positions. World Wide Web: http://www.seacoastrep.org.

SEATTLE OPERA
PO Box 9248
Seattle, Washington 98109

General Information Opera company producing 5 full-scale operas per season, plus one educational outreach show. Established in 1964. Number of employees: 65. Number of internship applications received each year: 30.

Internships Available ▶ *3 assistant direction interns:* responsibilities include observing rehearsals, keeping a "blocking book," walking roles for absent performers, and other duties as determined by the stage director. Candidates should have ability to work independently, knowledge of field, oral communication skills, personal interest in the field, plan to pursue career in field, strong interpersonal skills. Duration is 4 weeks. Unpaid. Open to college seniors, recent college graduates, graduate students, career changers, individuals reentering the workforce. ▶ *5 costume interns:* responsibilities include assisting the costume shop manager in shopping and other duties based on the ability of the intern. Candidates should have ability to work independently, knowledge of field, oral communication skills, personal interest in the field, strong interpersonal skills, ability to sew at an intermediate level. Duration is 6 weeks. Unpaid. Open to recent high school graduates, college freshmen, college sophomores, college juniors, college seniors, recent college graduates, graduate students, career changers, individuals reentering the workforce, individuals studying fashion design or college theater costume design/construction. ▶ *5 hair and make-up interns.* Candidates should have ability to work independently, knowledge of field, oral communication skills, personal interest in the field, strong interpersonal skills, previous experience in make-up application for stage. Duration is 3 weeks. Unpaid. Open to recent high school graduates, college freshmen, college sophomores, college juniors, college seniors, recent college graduates, graduate students, career changers, individuals reentering the workforce, those studying wig and make-up application for theater and opera or those studying at salon schools. ▶ *5 music library interns:* responsibilities include working directly with the music librarian, marking scores, and performing other duties as determined by the music librarian. Candidates should have ability to work independently, ability to work with others, knowledge of field, personal interest in the field, self-motivation, ability to read music well and in different clefs. Duration is 6–10 weeks. Unpaid. Open to recent high school graduates, college freshmen, college sophomores, college juniors, college seniors, recent college graduates, graduate students, career changers, individuals reentering the workforce, high school seniors over 18 years of age. ▶ *5 stage management interns:* responsibilities include working as part of the stage management team in rehearsals and performances and managing backstage elements. Candidates should have ability to work independently, ability to work with others, computer skills, oral communication skills, organizational skills, personal interest in the field. Duration is 6–8 weeks. Unpaid. Open to recent high school graduates, college freshmen, college sophomores, college juniors, college seniors, recent college graduates, graduate students, career changers, individuals reentering the workforce. International applications accepted.

Benefits On-the-job training, willing to act as a professional reference, willing to complete paperwork for educational credit, willing to provide letters of recommendation, opportunities to attend rehearsals and coachings and to meet with artists and staff.

Contact Write, call, fax, e-mail, or through World Wide Web site Paula Podemski, Production Supervisor, PO Box 9248, Seattle, Washington 98109. Phone: 206-676-5812. Fax: 206-389-7651. E-mail: paula.podemski@seattleopera.org. In-person interview recommended (telephone interview accepted). Applicants must submit a formal organization application, letter of interest, resume, three personal references. Applications are accepted continuously. World Wide Web: http://www.seattleopera.org.

SHADOW BOX THEATRE
325 West End Avenue, 12B
New York, New York 10023

General Information Theater focusing on children's theater and Arts-in-Education for inner-city children, home-based theater, in-school and after-school workshop program, and summer touring group. Established in 1967. Number of employees: 20. Number of internship applications received each year: 20.

Internships Available ▶ *1–2 administrative interns:* responsibilities include assisting with telephone bookings, marketing, publicity, general administrative duties. Candidates should have ability to work independently, ability to work with others, computer skills, office skills, oral communication skills, organizational skills, research skills, written communication skills. Duration is flexible. Unpaid. ▶ *2–4 theater interns:* responsibilities include assisting with technical aspects of theater, house management, box office, and assisting the director. Candidates should have college courses in field, knowledge of field, personal interest in the field, strong

interpersonal skills. Duration is flexible. Unpaid. Open to college freshmen, college sophomores, college juniors, college seniors. International applications accepted.

Benefits Willing to complete paperwork for educational credit, willing to provide letters of recommendation, small stipend, local travel/lunch.

Contact Write, call, fax, or e-mail Marlyn Baum, Managing Director. Phone: 212-724-0677. Fax: 212-724-0767. E-mail: sbt@ shadowboxtheatre.org. In-person interview required. Applicants must submit a letter of interest, resume, two letters of recommendation. Applications are accepted continuously. World Wide Web: http://www.shadowboxtheatre.org.

SOHO REPERTORY THEATRE
86 Franklin Street, 5th Floor
New York, New York 10013

General Information Theater specializing in new and avant-garde plays. Established in 1975. Number of employees: 5.

Internships Available ▶ *Interns.* Candidates should have computer skills, office skills, oral communication skills, organizational skills, personal interest in the field, self-motivation. Duration is flexible. Unpaid. ▶ *Literary interns.* Candidates should have ability to work independently, analytical skills, personal interest in the field, self-motivation, writing skills. Duration is flexible. Unpaid. Open to college freshmen, college sophomores, college juniors, college seniors, recent college graduates, graduate students, law students, career changers, individuals reentering the workforce.

Benefits Willing to complete paperwork for educational credit, willing to provide letters of recommendation.

Contact Write, call, fax, or e-mail Young Jean Lee, Administrative Manager, 86 Franklin Street, Fifth Floor, New York, New York 10013. Phone: 212-941-8632 Ext. 202. Fax: 212-941-7148. E-mail: yjlee@sohorep.org. Applicants must submit a letter of interest, resume. Applications are accepted continuously. World Wide Web: http://www.sohorep.org.

STEPPENWOLF THEATRE COMPANY
758 West North Avenue, 4th floor
Chicago, Illinois 60610

General Information Not-for-profit Tony Award winning theater company. Established in 1976. Number of employees: 70. Number of internship applications received each year: 300.

Internships Available ▶ *1–3 artistic interns:* responsibilities include various activities; see company Web site for complete description. Candidates should have computer skills, oral communication skills, research skills, self-motivation, strong interpersonal skills, written communication skills, strong varied background in theater. Duration is 3–4 months. Position available as unpaid or at $3.61 per hour. Open to college juniors, college seniors, recent college graduates, graduate students. ▶ *1–2 arts exchange interns:* responsibilities include various activities; see company Web site for complete description. Candidates should have ability to work with others, office skills, oral communication skills, organizational skills, research skills, writing skills, interest in education, strong background in dramatic literature. Duration is 3–4 months. Position available as unpaid or at $3.61 per hour. Open to college freshmen, college sophomores, college juniors, college seniors, recent college graduates, graduate students, career changers, individuals reentering the workforce. ▶ *1 company management intern:* responsibilities include various activities; see company Web site for complete description. Candidates should have computer skills, office skills, oral communication skills, organizational skills, personal interest in the field, strong interpersonal skills, written communication skills. Duration is 3–4 months. Position available as unpaid or at $3.61 per hour. Open to college freshmen, college sophomores, college juniors, college seniors, recent college graduates, graduate students, career changers, individuals reentering the workforce. ▶ *1–3 costuming interns:* responsibilities include various activities; see company Web site for complete description. Candidates should have ability to work with others, experience in the field, oral communication skills, plan to pursue career in field, self-motivation. Duration is 3–12 months. Position available as unpaid or at $3.61 per hour. Open to college sophomores, college juniors, college seniors, recent college graduates, graduate students. ▶ *1–2 develop-*

Steppenwolf Theatre Company (continued)

ment interns: responsibilities include various activities; see company Web site for complete description. Candidates should have ability to work independently, computer skills, oral communication skills, organizational skills, personal interest in the field, self-motivation, strong interpersonal skills, written communication skills. Duration is 3–4 months. Position available as unpaid or at $3.61 per hour. Open to college freshmen, college sophomores, college juniors, college seniors, recent college graduates, graduate students. ▶ *1–3 lighting interns:* responsibilities include various activities; see company Web site for complete description. Candidates should have ability to work with others, experience in the field, oral communication skills, plan to pursue career in field, self-motivation. Duration is 3–12 months. Position available as unpaid or at $3.61 per hour. Open to college sophomores, college juniors, college seniors, recent college graduates, graduate students. ▶ *1–2 marketing interns:* responsibilities include various activities; see company Web site for complete description. Candidates should have ability to work with others, office skills, oral communication skills, personal interest in the field, self-motivation, writing skills. Duration is 3–4 months. Position available as unpaid or at $3.61 per hour. Open to college freshmen, college sophomores, college juniors, college seniors, recent college graduates, graduate students, career changers, individuals reentering the workforce. ▶ *1–2 production management interns:* responsibilities include various activities; see company Web site for complete description. Candidates should have computer skills, knowledge of field, oral communication skills, organizational skills, personal interest in the field, written communication skills. Duration is 3–4 months. Position available as unpaid or at $3.61 per hour. Open to college sophomores, college juniors, college seniors, recent college graduates, graduate students. ▶ *1–3 properties interns:* responsibilities include various activities; see company Web site for complete description. Candidates should have ability to work with others, experience in the field, oral communication skills, plan to pursue career in field, self-motivation. Duration is 3–12 months. Position available as unpaid or at $3.61 per hour. Open to college sophomores, college juniors, college seniors, recent college graduates, graduate students. ▶ *1–2 publicity interns:* responsibilities include various activities; see company Web site for complete description. Candidates should have ability to work with others, office skills, oral communication skills, personal interest in the field, self-motivation, writing skills. Duration is 3–4 months. Position available as unpaid or at $3.61 per hour. Open to college freshmen, college sophomores, college juniors, college seniors, recent college graduates, graduate students, career changers, individuals reentering the workforce. ▶ *1–3 scenic art interns:* responsibilities include various activities; see company Web site for complete description. Candidates should have ability to work with others, experience in the field, oral communication skills, plan to pursue career in field, self-motivation. Duration is 3–12 months. Position available as unpaid or at $3.61 per hour. Open to college sophomores, college juniors, college seniors, recent college graduates, graduate students. ▶ *1–3 scenic carpentry:* responsibilities include various activities; see company Web site for complete description. Candidates should have ability to work with others, experience in the field, oral communication skills, plan to pursue career in field, self-motivation. Duration is 3–12 months. Position available as unpaid or at $3.61 per hour. Open to college sophomores, college juniors, college seniors, recent college graduates, graduate students. ▶ *1–3 sound interns:* responsibilities include various activities; see company Web site for complete description. Candidates should have ability to work with others, experience in the field, oral communication skills, personal interest in the field, self-motivation. Duration is 3–12 months. Position available as unpaid or at $3.61 per hour. Open to college sophomores, college juniors, college seniors, recent college graduates, graduate students. ▶ *1–2 special events interns:* responsibilities include various activities; see company Web site for complete description. Candidates should have ability to work with others, office skills, oral communication skills, organizational skills, personal interest in the field, self-motivation, written communication skills. Duration is 3–4 months. Position available as unpaid or at $3.61 per hour. Open to college freshmen, college sophomores, college juniors, college seniors, recent college gradu-

ates, graduate students. ▶ *1–5 stage management interns:* responsibilities include various activities; see company Web site for complete description. Candidates should have experience in the field, oral communication skills, organizational skills, plan to pursue career in field, self-motivation, strong interpersonal skills. Duration is several months to full season (1 year). Position available as unpaid or at $50–$300 per week. Open to college juniors, college seniors, recent college graduates, graduate students. International applications accepted.

Benefits Formal training, job counseling, names of contacts, opportunity to attend seminars/workshops, willing to act as a professional reference, willing to complete paperwork for educational credit, willing to provide letters of recommendation, opportunity to attend all productions and events.

Contact Write, call, fax, e-mail, or through World Wide Web site Internship Coordinator, 758 West North Avenue, 4th Floor, Chicago, Illinois 60610. Phone: 312-335-1888. Fax: 312-335-0808. E-mail: internships@steppenwolf.org. In-person interview recommended (telephone interview accepted). Applicants must submit a formal organization application, resume, portfolio, two letters of recommendation, personal statement. Application deadline: February 14 for summer, May 1 for fall, November 1 for winter. World Wide Web: http://www.steppenwolf.org.

TADA!
15 West 28th Street
New York, New York 10001

General Information Nonprofit children's theater ensemble producing high-quality productions performed by children for family audiences. Established in 1984. Number of employees: 10. Number of internship applications received each year: 15.

Internships Available ▶ *1 arts administrative assistant:* responsibilities include assisting in running the office. Candidates should have ability to work with others, experience in the field, office skills, research skills, writing skills. Duration is flexible (minimum 4 weeks). Unpaid. ▶ *1 arts education intern.* Candidates should have ability to work with others, computer skills, knowledge of field, office skills, oral communication skills, organizational skills, self-motivation. Duration is flexible (minimum of 4 weeks). Unpaid. ▶ *1 assistant stage manager:* responsibilities include assisting stage manager with rehearsals and performances. Candidates should have background in technical theater. Duration is 3 months. Paid. ▶ *1 box office intern.* Candidates should have ability to work independently, computer skills, office skills, oral communication skills, organizational skills, strong interpersonal skills. Duration is flexible. Paid. ▶ *1 house manager:* responsibilities include dealing with the audience. Candidates should have experience in the field, oral communication skills, strong interpersonal skills, strong leadership ability. Duration is flexible. Paid. ▶ *1 theater electrician/ board operator:* responsibilities include assisting with technical work and performances. Candidates should have background in technical theater. Duration is 2 months. Paid. ▶ *1 wardrobe supervisor:* responsibilities include maintaining costumes and working backstage with children. Candidates should have experience in the field. Duration is 2 months. Paid. Open to college freshmen, college sophomores, college juniors, college seniors.

Benefits Names of contacts, willing to complete paperwork for educational credit, willing to provide letters of recommendation.

Contact Write, fax, or e-mail Bonnie Butkas, Managing Director. Fax: 212-243-6736. E-mail: tada@tadatheater.com. No phone calls. In-person interview recommended (telephone interview accepted). Applicants must submit a letter of interest, resume, letter of recommendation. Application deadline: May 15 for summer; continuous for other positions. World Wide Web: http://www.tadatheater.com.

TEXAS NONPROFIT THEATRES, INC.
3505 West Lancaster Avenue
Fort Worth, Texas 76107-3002

General Information Service organization for nonprofit theatres. Established in 1972. Number of employees: 2. Number of internship applications received each year: 20.

Internships Available ▶ *1–4 multicultural initiatives summer theatre interns:* responsibilities include working in two theatres,

administratively, artistically, technically, or a combination. Candidates should have declared college major in field, self-motivation, strong interpersonal skills, ability to travel within Texas. Duration is May to August. $200–$250 per week. Open to college sophomores, college juniors, college seniors, recent college graduates, graduate students, career changers.
Benefits Free housing, on-the-job training.
Contact Write, call, fax, e-mail, or through World Wide Web site Linda M. Lee, Executive Director. Phone: 817-731-2238. Fax: 817-731-2239. E-mail: tnt@texastheatres.org. In-person interview required. Applicants must submit a formal organization application, resume, academic transcripts, letter of recommendation. Application deadline: December 10. World Wide Web: http://www.texastheatres.org.

THEATER FOR THE NEW CITY FOUNDATION, INC.
155 First Avenue
New York, New York 10003

General Information Nonprofit off-off-Broadway theater that presents 44 shows each season. Established in 1970. Number of employees: 10. Number of internship applications received each year: 50.
Internships Available ▶ *Administrative interns:* responsibilities include assisting executive and administrative director. Candidates should have ability to work independently, ability to work with others, analytical skills, office skills, oral communication skills, organizational skills, self-motivation, strong leadership ability, writing skills. Duration is flexible. Unpaid. ▶ *Financial development/fund-raising interns:* responsibilities include writing grants, typing, and performing foundation research and clerical duties. Duration is flexible. Unpaid. ▶ *Technical interns:* responsibilities include assisting technical director. Candidates should have ability to work independently, ability to work with others, analytical skills, office skills, oral communication skills, organizational skills, self-motivation, strong leadership ability, writing skills. Duration is flexible. Unpaid. Open to individuals 17 and older. International applications accepted.
Benefits Possible full-time employment, willing to act as a professional reference, willing to complete paperwork for educational credit, willing to provide letters of recommendation.
Contact Write, call, fax, or e-mail Crystal Field, Executive Director. Phone: 212-254-1109. Fax: 212-979-6570. E-mail: info@theaterforthenewcity.org. In-person interview recommended (telephone interview accepted). Applicants must submit a letter of interest, resume. Applications are accepted continuously. World Wide Web: http://www.theaterforthenewcity.org.

THEATRE DE LA JEUNE LUNE
105 First Street North
Minneapolis, Minnesota 55401

General Information Theater company with an interactive, highly physical style of performance. Established in 1978. Number of employees: 82. Number of internship applications received each year: 50.
Internships Available ▶ *3–12 assistant designers:* responsibilities include assisting set, costume, and lighting designers in research and construction. Duration is 6–8 weeks. Unpaid. ▶ *3–6 assistant directors:* responsibilities include keeping up scripts and assisting in blocking and scheduling. Duration is 6–12 weeks. Unpaid. ▶ *3–9 assistant stage managers:* responsibilities include assisting the stage manager in running rehearsals, doing fittings, and scheduling. Duration is 6–18 weeks. Unpaid. ▶ *1–3 business interns:* responsibilities include assisting the finance manager with accounting work reconciliations, balances, and budget. Duration is flexible. Unpaid. ▶ *1–4 development interns:* responsibilities include assisting with mailings, project research, and donor events. Duration is 8–10 weeks. Unpaid. ▶ *1–3 dramaturgical interns:* responsibilities include assisting in writing scripts, keeping updates, and performing research. Duration is flexible. Unpaid. ▶ *1–3 front-of-house interns:* responsibilities include assisting in usher recruitment and front-of-house duties, managing and conducting inventory on concessions, and working the box office. Duration is flexible. Unpaid. ▶ *1–2 music interns:* responsibilities include assisting the composer and music director, providing accompaniment at rehearsals, and

copying music. Duration is flexible. Unpaid. ▶ *1–3 properties interns:* responsibilities include locating, arranging, and constructing show props. Duration is 6 weeks. Unpaid. ▶ *3 technical interns:* responsibilities include assisting the technical director in building, drafting, shop organization, and building management. Duration is 3–12 weeks. Unpaid. Open to high school students, recent high school graduates, college freshmen, college sophomores, college juniors, college seniors, recent college graduates, graduate students, law students, career changers, individuals reentering the workforce. International applications accepted.
Benefits Job counseling, names of contacts, opportunity to attend seminars/workshops, possible full-time employment, willing to complete paperwork for educational credit, willing to provide letters of recommendation, tickets.
Contact Write, call, fax, or e-mail Operations Associate. Phone: 612-332-3968. Fax: 612-332-0048. E-mail: info@jeunelune.org. In-person interview recommended (telephone interview accepted). Applicants must submit a letter of interest, resume. Applications are accepted continuously. World Wide Web: http://www.jeunelune.org.

THEATRE OF YUGEN
2840 Mariposa Street
San Francisco, California 94110

General Information Experimental theater company informed by stylized Asian theatre traditions. Established in 1978. Number of employees: 5. Number of internship applications received each year: 6.
Internships Available ▶ *2–4 administrative assistants:* responsibilities include making final reports of grants received, maintaining board meeting minutes, handling membership mailings, scheduling, development, and fund-raising. Candidates should have ability to work with others, computer skills, office skills, oral communication skills, personal interest in the field, written communication skills. Duration is 3–6 months. Position available as unpaid or paid. Open to college juniors, college seniors, recent college graduates, graduate students, career changers, individuals reentering the workforce. ▶ *1 technical director's assistant:* responsibilities include scheduling rentals, maintaining space and equipment, and running light board and sound equipment. Candidates should have ability to work with others, computer skills, knowledge of field, organizational skills, personal interest in the field, some background in technical theater (preferred). Duration is 3–6 months. Position available as unpaid or at $10–$12 per hour. Open to college freshmen, college sophomores, college juniors, college seniors, recent college graduates, career changers, individuals reentering the workforce. ▶ *1 theater publicity relations assistant.* Candidates should have ability to work with others, computer skills, editing skills, knowledge of field, writing skills. Duration is 3–6 months. Position available as unpaid or paid. Open to college juniors, college seniors, recent college graduates, graduate students, career changers, individuals reentering the workforce. International applications accepted.
Benefits Willing to act as a professional reference, willing to complete paperwork for educational credit, willing to provide letters of recommendation, complimentary theater tickets, theater discounts, formal training in movement.
Contact Write, fax, e-mail, or through World Wide Web site Libby Zilber, Joint Artistic Director. Fax: 415-621-0223. E-mail: libby@theatreofyugen.org. No phone calls. In-person interview recommended (telephone interview accepted). Applicants must submit a letter of interest, resume. Applications are accepted continuously. World Wide Web: http://www.theatreofyugen.org.

THE THEATRE-STUDIO, INC.
750 Eighth Avenue, Suite 200
New York, New York 10036

General Information Studio theater that focuses on growth of theater arts for the community. Established in 1980. Number of employees: 10. Number of internship applications received each year: 50.
Internships Available ▶ *1–3 administrative assistant interns:* responsibilities include monitoring daily trafficking schedule and logging phone messages, telephone contact work, correspondence, fil-

The Theatre-Studio, Inc. (continued)

ing, and organizing and monitoring play scripts. Candidates should have ability to work independently, computer skills, oral communication skills, organizational skills, strong interpersonal skills, written communication skills. Duration is 3–6 months. Unpaid. ▶ *1–5 grant researchers:* responsibilities include researching types of grants available to theater production companies, organizing and presenting findings to artistic director, and selecting and writing grants. Candidates should have ability to work independently, editing skills, knowledge of field, research skills, written communication skills. Duration is flexible. Position available as unpaid or paid. ▶ *1–3 production assistant interns:* responsibilities include tech crew on two performances per week with various duties including operation of simple sound/light equipment, setting up house, working on set changes and strikes, prop/costume searches, updating fliers and programs, and running errands. Candidates should have ability to work independently, computer skills, knowledge of field, office skills, oral communication skills, organizational skills, personal interest in the field, research skills, self-motivation, strong interpersonal skills, written communication skills. Duration is 3–6 months. Unpaid. Open to high school students, recent high school graduates, college freshmen, college sophomores, college juniors, college seniors, recent college graduates, graduate students, law students, career changers, individuals reentering the workforce.

Benefits Formal training, opportunity to attend seminars/workshops, willing to complete paperwork for educational credit, willing to provide letters of recommendation, opportunity to work in a professional production, opportunity to attend and participate in Artistic Director's Actor/Director/Writer sessions.

Contact Write, call, fax, or e-mail A. M. Raychel, Producing/Artistic Director. Phone: 212-719-0500. Fax: 212-719-0537. E-mail: arayche@attglobal.net. Applicants must submit a letter of interest, resume, two writing samples, three personal references, three letters of recommendation, in-person interview within 2 weeks of receipt of application/letter of interest. Application deadline: February 1 for spring, April 1 for summer, October 1 for winter. World Wide Web: http://www.theatrestudio.org.

THEATREWORKS
1100 Hamilton Court
Menlo Park, California 94025

General Information Nationally recognized, professional, nonprofit theater company presenting high-quality live theater that reflects the diversity of its community. Established in 1970. Number of employees: 37. Number of internship applications received each year: 75.

Internships Available ▶ *5–15 artistic interns:* responsibilities include working in the areas of directing, literary, casting, or musical directing. Candidates should have ability to work with others, oral communication skills, personal interest in the field, research skills, directing experience required for assistant directors, music theory and piano skills required for assistant music directors. Duration is 3-9 months (30 hours per week). Unpaid. Open to college freshmen, college sophomores, college juniors, college seniors, recent college graduates, graduate students, law students, career changers, individuals reentering the workforce. ▶ *3–6 arts management interns:* responsibilities include working in the areas of development/events, outreach, ticket services, marketing, or operations. Candidates should have computer skills, office skills, oral communication skills, organizational skills, personal interest in the field, written communication skills. Duration is 3-9 months (10-30 hours per week). Unpaid. Open to college freshmen, college sophomores, college juniors, college seniors, recent college graduates, graduate students, law students, career changers, individuals reentering the workforce. ▶ *10–15 production interns:* responsibilities include working in the areas of scenic/props, costumes, lighting, sound, stage management, or production management. Candidates should have ability to work with others, experience in the field, oral communication skills, personal interest in the field, plan to pursue career in field, self-motivation. Duration is 3-9 months (35 hours per week). Unpaid. Open to recent high school graduates, college freshmen, college sophomores, college juniors, college

seniors, recent college graduates, graduate students, law students, career changers, individuals reentering the workforce.

Benefits Job counseling, names of contacts, on-the-job training, opportunity to attend seminars/workshops, travel reimbursement, willing to act as a professional reference, willing to complete paperwork for educational credit, willing to provide letters of recommendation, complimentary tickets to productions, first option on short-term paid contracts within theater operations.

Contact Write, fax, e-mail, or through World Wide Web site Jodi Corwin, Manager of Intern and Volunteer Programs. Fax: 650-463-1963. E-mail: interns@theatreworks.org. In-person interview recommended (telephone interview accepted). Applicants must submit a formal organization application, letter of interest, resume. Application deadline: March 1 for summer; continuous for all other positions. World Wide Web: http://www.theatreworks.org.

THIRTEENTH STREET REPERTORY COMPANY
50 West 13th Street
New York, New York 10011

General Information Nonprofit off-off-Broadway theater that operates 52 weeks per year and performs full-length plays every 3 months, children's plays every Saturday and Sunday, Sunday Reading Series, and other ongoing projects. Established in 1972. Number of internship applications received each year: 25.

Internships Available ▶ *1 Webmaster intern:* responsibilities include updating theater Web site; updating shows, archives, and actor's information; some Web design. Candidates should have ability to work independently, ability to work with others, computer skills, organizational skills, personal interest in the field, self-motivation, strong working knowledge of HTML and Web site design. Duration is flexible. Unpaid. Open to high school seniors, recent high school graduates, college freshmen, college sophomores, college juniors, college seniors, recent college graduates, graduate students, individuals reentering the workforce. ▶ *2 assistant literary managers:* responsibilities include organizing and cataloging incoming and outgoing plays, organizing play evaluations and entering results in computer, reading and evaluating plays from National Playwriting Contest. Candidates should have computer skills, knowledge of field, oral communication skills, organizational skills, personal interest in the field, college courses in drama criticism. Duration is ongoing. Unpaid. Open to college freshmen, college sophomores, college juniors, college seniors, recent college graduates, graduate students. ▶ *3 assistants to general manager:* responsibilities include handling scheduling of 60 volunteers, investigating marketing possibilities on Internet, evaluating plays, creating programs for new shows, entering accounting information into computer, running box office, and handling media listings. Candidates should have ability to work independently, computer skills, oral communication skills, organizational skills, written communication skills, Internet skills. Duration is ongoing. Unpaid. Open to high school seniors, recent high school graduates, college freshmen, college sophomores, college juniors, college seniors, recent college graduates, graduate students, career changers, individuals reentering the workforce. ▶ *2 marketing interns.* Candidates should have college courses in field, computer skills, oral communication skills, research skills, self-motivation, written communication skills. Duration is ongoing. Unpaid. Open to college freshmen, college sophomores, college juniors, college seniors, recent college graduates, graduate students, career changers. ▶ *3 publicity interns.* Candidates should have ability to work independently, college courses in field, computer skills, oral communication skills, self-motivation, written communication skills. Duration is ongoing. Unpaid. Open to college freshmen, college sophomores, college juniors, college seniors, recent college graduates, graduate students, career changers. ▶ *10–15 stage managers/technicians/assistant directors:* responsibilities include assisting with lights and sound, auditioning, understudying, acting, and assisting play director and artistic director. Candidates should have ability to work independently, ability to work with others, computer skills, knowledge of field, oral communication skills, self-motivation. Duration is several months. Unpaid. Open to high school seniors, recent high school graduates, college freshmen, college sophomores, college juniors, college seniors, recent college graduates, graduate students, career changers, individuals reentering the workforce. International applications accepted.

Benefits Names of contacts, on-the-job training, opportunity to attend seminars/workshops, willing to act as a professional reference, willing to complete paperwork for educational credit, willing to provide letters of recommendation.

Contact Write, call, or e-mail Sandra Nordgren, General Manager. Phone: 917-363-2369. E-mail: sandranord@aol.com. In-person interview recommended (telephone interview accepted). Applicants must submit a formal organization application, letter of interest, resume, two personal references, two letters of recommendation. Applications are accepted continuously. World Wide Web: http://www.13thStreetRep.org.

TRINITY REPERTORY COMPANY
201 Washington Street
Providence, Rhode Island 02903

General Information Professional regional theater engaging the audience as participants. Established in 1964. Number of employees: 120. Number of internship applications received each year: 75.

Internships Available ▶ *3–6 administration interns:* responsibilities include working in general management, literary management, communications/PR, marketing, and education. Candidates should have computer skills, experience in the field, office skills, oral communication skills, strong interpersonal skills, written communication skills, accounting skills. Duration is August 15 to June 1 (full-time) or one summer. Position available as unpaid or at $60–$75 per week. Open to high school seniors, recent high school graduates, college freshmen, college sophomores, college juniors, college seniors, recent college graduates. ▶ *4–6 production interns:* responsibilities include working in one of several positions including production management, stage management, electrical, scenic carpentry, sound, costume, and props. Candidates should have college courses in field, experience in the field, oral communication skills, plan to pursue career in field, strong interpersonal skills. Duration is August 15 to June1 (full-time) or one summer. $60–$75 per week. Open to recent college graduates. International applications accepted.

Benefits Formal training, job counseling, names of contacts, on-the-job training, opportunity to attend seminars/workshops, possible full-time employment, willing to act as a professional reference, willing to complete paperwork for educational credit, willing to provide letters of recommendation, 2 complementary tickets for each production, stipend, free housing for year-round interns.

Contact Write, call, fax, or e-mail Brian Ruggiero, Associate Education Director. Phone: 401-521-1100 Ext. 255. Fax: 401-751-5577. E-mail: bruggiero@trinityrep.com. In-person interview recommended (telephone interview accepted). Applicants must submit a letter of interest, resume, three letters of recommendation, writing sample (for education, literary, and public relations positions only). Application deadline: June 1 for full-time seasonal interns; continuous for all other positions. World Wide Web: http://www.trinityrep.com.

UNTITLED THEATER COMPANY #61
235 West 102nd Street, Suite 16-S
New York, New York 10025

General Information Nonprofit producer of experimental and philosophic plays off-Broadway. Established in 1992. Number of employees: 3. Number of internship applications received each year: 10.

Internships Available ▶ *1–3 artistic associates:* responsibilities include assisting in the directorial and playwriting aspects of theater, including the positions of assistant director and dramaturg. Candidates should have ability to work with others, knowledge of field, oral communication skills, organizational skills, personal interest in the field, research skills, writing skills. Duration is 2 months. Unpaid. Open to college freshmen, college sophomores, college juniors, college seniors, recent college graduates. ▶ *1–5 assistants to the artistic director:* responsibilities include assisting the artistic director in all areas, including publicity, grant writing, and scheduling. Candidates should have ability to work independently,

knowledge of field, office skills, oral communication skills, organizational skills, personal interest in the field, research skills, writing skills. Duration is flexible. Unpaid. Open to high school students, recent high school graduates, college freshmen, college sophomores, college juniors, college seniors, recent college graduates. ▶ *1–3 company managers:* responsibilities include organizing performances, readings, and rehearsals. Candidates should have ability to work independently, ability to work with others, knowledge of field, organizational skills. Duration is flexible. Unpaid. Open to college freshmen, college sophomores, college juniors, college seniors, recent college graduates. ▶ *Design assistants:* responsibilities include assisting in costume, set, lighting, and sound design. Candidates should have ability to work with others, personal interest in the field, aptitude in art/design areas. Duration is 2 months. Unpaid. Open to high school seniors, recent high school graduates, college freshmen, college sophomores, college juniors, college seniors, recent college graduates. ▶ *1–5 stage managers:* responsibilities include supervising all the technical aspects of a production including organizing props, light, and sound. Candidates should have knowledge of field, oral communication skills, organizational skills, personal interest in the field, strong interpersonal skills. Duration is 2 months. Unpaid. Open to high school students, recent high school graduates, college freshmen, college sophomores, college juniors, college seniors, recent college graduates. International applications accepted.

Benefits Names of contacts, on-the-job training, opportunity to attend seminars/workshops, willing to act as a professional reference, willing to complete paperwork for educational credit, willing to provide letters of recommendation.

Contact Write, call, or e-mail Edward Einhorn, Artistic Director. Phone: 212-866-1073. E-mail: utc61@hotmail.com. In-person interview recommended (telephone interview accepted). Applicants must submit a letter of interest, resume. Applications are accepted continuously. World Wide Web: http://www.untitledtheater.com.

VICTORY GARDENS THEATER
2257 North Lincoln Avenue
Chicago, Illinois 60614

General Information World premiere theater emphasizing the development of Chicago playwrights. Established in 1974. Number of employees: 24. Number of internship applications received each year: 30.

Internships Available ▶ *1 administrative intern:* responsibilities include assisting managing director, director of development, and marketing director in daily tasks and projects. Candidates should have ability to work independently, analytical skills, college courses in field, computer skills, editing skills, knowledge of field, office skills, oral communication skills, organizational skills, personal interest in the field, research skills, self-motivation, strong interpersonal skills, writing skills. Duration is 3-5 months (variable). Unpaid. Open to college seniors, recent college graduates, graduate students, individuals reentering the workforce. ▶ *2 artistic interns:* responsibilities include assisting literary manager. Candidates should have ability to work independently, college courses in field, computer skills, editing skills, knowledge of field, office skills, oral communication skills, organizational skills, personal interest in the field, research skills, self-motivation, strong interpersonal skills, writing skills. Duration is 3–6 months. Unpaid. Open to college seniors, recent college graduates, graduate students, career changers, individuals reentering the workforce. ▶ *3 production interns:* responsibilities include assisting production manager. Candidates should have ability to work independently, ability to work with others, knowledge of field, plan to pursue career in field, self-motivation, carpentry, electrical, technical theater skills. Duration is 8–12 weeks. Unpaid. Open to recent high school graduates, college freshmen, college sophomores, college juniors, college seniors, recent college graduates, graduate students, law students, career changers, individuals reentering the workforce. International applications accepted.

Benefits Names of contacts, on-the-job training, opportunity to attend seminars/workshops, possible full-time employment, willing to complete paperwork for educational credit, willing to provide letters of recommendation.

Victory Gardens Theater (continued)

Contact Write, fax, or e-mail Jonathan Heuring, Production Manager, 2257 North Lincoln Avenue, Chicago, Illinois 60614. Fax: 773-549-2779. E-mail: jheuring@victorygardens.org. No phone calls. In-person interview recommended (telephone interview accepted). Applicants must submit a letter of interest, resume, two personal references, two letters of recommendation. Applications are accepted continuously. World Wide Web: http://www.victorygardens.org.

VINEYARD THEATER
108 East 15th Street
New York, New York 10003-9689

General Information Theater that specializes in developing and producing new dramatic and musical theater. Established in 1981. Number of employees: 10. Number of internship applications received each year: 20.

Internships Available ► *1–6 interns:* responsibilities include working in production, development, marketing, or literary/artistic areas. Candidates should have ability to work independently, computer skills, office skills, personal interest in the field, self-motivation, strong interpersonal skills. Duration is flexible. Unpaid. Open to high school seniors, recent high school graduates, college freshmen, college sophomores, college juniors, college seniors, recent college graduates, graduate students, career changers, individuals reentering the workforce. International applications accepted.

Benefits Job counseling, names of contacts, travel reimbursement, willing to complete paperwork for educational credit, willing to provide letters of recommendation.

Contact Write, fax, or e-mail Rebecca Habel, Business Manager. Fax: 212-353-3803. E-mail: rhabel@vineyardtheatre.org. No phone calls. In-person interview recommended (telephone interview accepted). Applicants must submit a letter of interest, resume. Applications are accepted continuously. World Wide Web: http://www.vineyardtheatre.org.

VIRGINIA SYMPHONY ORCHESTRA
880 North Military Highway, Suite 1064
Norfolk, Virginia 23518

General Information Symphony orchestra offering 140 performances each season. Established in 1920. Number of employees: 19. Number of internship applications received each year: 12.

Internships Available ► *1–4 department assistants:* responsibilities include assisting director in development, marketing, production, or education departments and assisting administration. Candidates should have ability to work independently, ability to work with others, college courses in field, computer skills, personal interest in the field, self-motivation, dependability and reliability. Duration is flexible. Unpaid. Open to college sophomores, college juniors, college seniors, recent college graduates, graduate students. International applications accepted.

Benefits Possible full-time employment, willing to act as a professional reference, willing to complete paperwork for educational credit, willing to provide letters of recommendation, complimentary admission to all concerts/courses.

Contact Write, fax, or e-mail Ashley Clayton, Development and Special Events Coordinator. Fax: 757-466-3046. E-mail: aclayton@virginiasymphony.org. No phone calls. In-person interview required. Applicants must submit a letter of interest, resume, two personal references, letter of recommendation. Applications are accepted continuously. World Wide Web: http://www.virginiasymphony.org.

VPSTART CROW PRODUCTIONS
9005 Church Street, Suite 203
Manassas, Virginia 20110

General Information Professional nonprofit theater company. Established in 1994. Number of employees: 2. Number of internship applications received each year: 20.

Internships Available ► *1–3 arts administration interns:* responsibilities include working with communications director on publicity, media contacts, advertising; also trained in ticket sales, office duties and others as assigned. Candidates should have ability to work with others, office skills, oral communication skills, personal interest in the field, written communication skills. Duration is 1 semester. Unpaid. Open to high school seniors, recent high school graduates, college freshmen, college sophomores, college juniors, college seniors, recent college graduates, graduate students, career changers, individuals reentering the workforce. ► *1 assistant house manager:* responsibilities include assisting with preparation of theater for audience, training to operate ticket equipment, running box office, supervising ushers, concession workers, and other duties as assigned. Candidates should have ability to work with others, office skills, oral communication skills, personal interest in the field, strong leadership ability. Duration is 1 semester. Unpaid. Open to high school students, recent high school graduates, college freshmen, college sophomores, college juniors, college seniors, recent college graduates, graduate students, career changers, individuals reentering the workforce. ► *1–3 assistant stage manager/crew interns:* responsibilities include assisting with stage management duties, load-in, prep, strike of sets, and props; assisting stage manager with calling cues and other duties as assigned. Candidates should have oral communication skills, personal interest in the field, plan to pursue career in field, self-motivation, strong interpersonal skills, strong leadership ability. Duration is 1 semester. Unpaid. Open to high school students, recent high school graduates, college freshmen, college sophomores, college juniors, college seniors, recent college graduates, graduate students, career changers, individuals reentering the workforce. International applications accepted.

Benefits Names of contacts, on-the-job training, willing to act as a professional reference, willing to complete paperwork for educational credit, willing to provide letters of recommendation.

Contact Write, call, e-mail, or through World Wide Web site Lindsay Eagle, Managing Director. Phone: 703-365-0240. E-mail: information@vpstartcrow.org. In-person interview recommended (telephone interview accepted). Applicants must submit a formal organization application, letter of interest, resume, two letters of recommendation. Applications are accepted continuously. World Wide Web: http://www.vpstartcrow.org.

WALNUT STREET THEATRE
825 Walnut Street
Philadelphia, Pennsylvania 19107

General Information Major regional theater. Established in 1809. Number of employees: 50. Number of internship applications received each year: 250.

Internships Available ► *4 acting interns (including 2 reserved for African Americans):* responsibilities include performing, teaching youth acting classes, understudying mainstage shows, and acting as readers at auditions. $285 per week. ► *1–2 casting and literary management interns:* responsibilities include assisting casting director in all local and New York auditions; working in literary office reviewing scripts. $285 per week. ► *1–2 development interns:* responsibilities include assisting the development manager in grantmanship, responding to volunteers for theater, and fundraising. $285 per week. ► *1 directing intern:* responsibilities include assisting in all areas of the theater including mainstage, studio and education productions. $285 per week. ► *1–2 general management interns:* responsibilities include assisting the general manager with space management, housing, building maintenance, and agreed contracts. $285 per week. ► *1–2 house management interns:* responsibilities include assisting house manager on all mainstage plays, including lobby duty and tickets. $285 per week. ► *1–2 marketing interns:* responsibilities include assisting the marketing staff. $285 per week. ► *1–2 painting interns:* responsibilities include learning extensive scene-painting techniques in a large paint shop operation and working closely with the charge scenic artist in all phases of scene painting. $285 per week. ► *1–2 props interns:* responsibilities include assisting the properties manager in construction and acquisition of props for all productions and learning skills in sewing, upholstery, carpentry, sculpturing, painting, and/or calligraphy. $285 per week. ► *1–2 run crew interns:* responsibilities include moving sets, load-ins, and load-outs. $285 per week. ► *3–5 stage management interns:* responsibilities include assisting in all facets of rehearsals and productions. $285 per week. ▶ *1–2 subscriptions interns:* responsibilities include phone management, subscription, and ticket exchange. $285 per week. Open to recent college graduates. International applications accepted. **Benefits** Formal training, health insurance, opportunity to attend seminars/workshops, possible full-time employment, willing to act as a professional reference, willing to complete paperwork for educational credit, willing to provide letters of recommendation, job placement opportunities.

Contact Write, call, fax, or through World Wide Web site Susan Nicodemus Quinn, Director of Education, 9th and Walnut Streets, Philadelphia, Pennsylvania 19107. Phone: 215-574-3550 Ext. 510. Fax: 215-574-3598. In-person interview recommended (telephone interview accepted). Applicants must submit a formal organization application, letter of interest, resume, three personal references, download application and information at wstonline.org. Application deadline: March 31 for acting interns, June 1 for fall interns. World Wide Web: http://www.wstonline.org.

WESTPORT COUNTRY PLAYHOUSE
PO Box 629
Westport, Connecticut 06881

General Information Professional summer theater in a historic building. Established in 1931. Number of employees: 50. Unit of Connecticut Theatre Foundation, Westport, Connecticut. Number of internship applications received each year: 150.
Internships Available ▶ *12–15 interns:* responsibilities include working in various areas including scenic design and construction, properties, costume design/wardrobe, lighting, sound, press and marketing, or production/company management. Candidates should have ability to work independently, college courses in field, experience in the field, plan to pursue career in field, strong interpersonal skills. Duration is 3 months in summer. $100 per week. Open to college freshmen, college sophomores, college juniors, college seniors, recent college graduates, graduate students.
Benefits Free housing, names of contacts, on-the-job training, opportunity to attend seminars/workshops, possible full-time employment, willing to act as a professional reference, willing to complete paperwork for educational credit, willing to provide letters of recommendation.
Contact Write, call, fax, e-mail, or through World Wide Web site Hyla Crane, Education Coordinator. Phone: 203-227-5137. Fax: 203-221-7482. E-mail: hcrane@westportplayhouse.org. In-person interview recommended (telephone interview accepted). Applicants must submit a formal organization application, resume, two letters of recommendation, letter of interest stating which internships desired. Application deadline: March 3. World Wide Web: http://www.westportplayhouse.org.

WILLIAMSTOWN THEATER FESTIVAL
1000 Main Street, PO Box 517
Williamstown, Massachusetts 01267

General Information Summer theater presenting productions of revivals of classics and new works by new and established playwrights. Established in 1953. Number of employees: 330. Number of internship applications received each year: 600.
Internships Available ▶ *60–70 acting apprenticeships:* responsibilities include taking acting classes and alternate days of crew work. Candidates should have plan to pursue career in field, self-motivation, strong interpersonal skills, written communication skills. Duration is 1 summer (June-August). Unpaid. Open to high school students, recent high school graduates, college freshmen, college sophomores, college juniors, college seniors, recent college graduates, graduate students, career changers, individuals reentering the workforce, individuals 17 and over. ▶ *60 administrative and technical interns:* responsibilities include working in any of the following areas: scenic design/scenic art, costume design/construction, lighting design/electrics, sound design/production, scenic carpentry, directing, publications/graphic design, photography, general management, production management, company management, house management, box office, publicity, stage management, literary management/dramaturgy, cabaret management/production/development. Candidates should have knowledge of field, organizational skills, self-motivation, strong interpersonal

skills. Duration is 1 summer (June-August). Unpaid. Open to high school students, recent high school graduates, college freshmen, college sophomores, college juniors, college seniors, recent college graduates, graduate students, career changers, individuals reentering the workforce. International applications accepted.
Benefits Formal training, housing at a cost, meals at a cost, names of contacts, on-the-job training, opportunity to attend seminars/workshops, willing to act as a professional reference, willing to complete paperwork for educational credit, willing to provide letters of recommendation, opportunity to work with professionals in field.
Contact Write, call, fax, or e-mail Michael Coglan, Company Manager, 229 West 42nd Street #801, New York, New York 10036. Phone: 212-395-9090. Fax: 212-395-9099. E-mail: mcoglan@wtfestival. org. In-person interview recommended (telephone interview accepted). Applicants must submit a formal organization application, letter of interest, resume, portfolio, two personal references, two letters of recommendation, $30 application fee (for acting apprentice workshop only). Application deadline: April 1 for acting apprentices; continuous for other positions. World Wide Web: http://www.wtfestival.org.

THE WILMA THEATER
265 South Broad Street
Philadelphia, Pennsylvania 19107

General Information Nonprofit, professional, innovative theater under the artistic direction of Jiri Zizka and Blanka Zizka. Established in 1973. Number of employees: 35. Number of internship applications received each year: 150.
Internships Available ▶ *1 artistic fellow:* responsibilities include assisting artistic directors and literary manager/dramaturg, assistant directing, directing understudies and extras, note-taking for directors, and serving as the artistic directors' personal assistant. Candidates should have ability to work independently, college degree in related field, editing skills, experience in the field, knowledge of field, oral communication skills, organizational skills, personal interest in the field, plan to pursue career in field, research skills, self-motivation, strong interpersonal skills, strong leadership ability, written communication skills. Duration is full theater season (August to June). $250 per week. Open to recent college graduates, graduate students. ▶ *1–3 development interns:* responsibilities include working with development director on researching new prospects, helping to coordinate fund-raising events, assisting with correspondence, and maintaining development files. Candidates should have ability to work independently, computer skills, office skills, oral communication skills, organizational skills, research skills, strong interpersonal skills, written communication skills. Duration is flexible. Unpaid. Open to college sophomores, college juniors, college seniors, recent college graduates, graduate students, career changers, individuals reentering the workforce. ▶ *1 education intern:* responsibilities include assisting with administration, registration, and promotion of school; researching; symposium coordination; summer camp planning; assisting with outreach programming. Candidates should have ability to work independently, ability to work with others, office skills, oral communication skills, organizational skills, personal interest in the field, self-motivation, written communication skills. Duration is flexible. Unpaid. Open to college sophomores, college juniors, college seniors, recent college graduates, career changers. ▶ *1 graphic design intern:* responsibilities include working with director of communications and director of marketing on all aspects of theater design including the program book, Wilma2advertising, studio school brochure, advertisements, flyers, brochures, and show-specific pieces. Candidates should have ability to work independently, college courses in field, computer skills, editing skills, experience in the field, plan to pursue career in field, self-motivation, written communication skills, familiarity with Quark Xpress, PhotoShop, Word. Duration is 2–6 months (15–20 hours per week). Unpaid. Open to college sophomores, college juniors, college seniors, recent college graduates, graduate students. ▶ *1–2 literary interns:* responsibilities include assisting literary manager/dramaturg with script reading and evaluation, script solicitation, administration, correspondence, and performing dramaturgical research for quarterly newsletter. Candidates should have ability

The Wilma Theater (continued)

to work independently, analytical skills, editing skills, knowledge of field, oral communication skills, organizational skills, personal interest in the field, research skills, strong interpersonal skills, writing skills. Duration is flexible. Unpaid. Open to college sophomores, college juniors, college seniors, recent college graduates, graduate students, individuals reentering the workforce. ▶ *1–2 marketing interns:* responsibilities include assisting marketing director with various aspects of theater promotion; projects may include subscription, single ticket and group sales marketing, coordination of direct mail campaigns, assisting with graphic design, and promotion of printed materials. Candidates should have ability to work independently, computer skills, editing skills, oral communication skills, personal interest in the field, self-motivation, strong interpersonal skills, written communication skills. Duration is flexible. Unpaid. Open to college sophomores, college juniors, college seniors, recent college graduates, graduate students, career changers, individuals reentering the workforce. ▶ *1–2 marketing/publicity interns:* responsibilities include working with marketing/publicity associates, understudying all aspects of theater promotion, mass mailing, graphic design, editing playbill, photographic archiving, analysis of audience, and development of theater literature. Candidates should have ability to work with others, computer skills, oral communication skills, organizational skills, personal interest in the field, written communication skills. Duration is flexible. Unpaid. Open to college sophomores, college juniors, college seniors, recent college graduates, graduate students, career changers, individuals reentering the workforce. ▶ *1 production fellow:* responsibilities include working closely with the production manager and technical director; duties may include set construction, painting, load-in, strike, electrics, lighting, running crew and costume work. Candidates should have ability to work independently, experience in the field, oral communication skills, personal interest in the field, plan to pursue career in field, self-motivation, strong interpersonal skills. Duration is full theater season, August to June. $250 per week. Open to recent college graduates, graduate students. ▶ *1 public relations intern:* responsibilities include working with director of communications coordinating varying aspects of community and press relations; projects may include compiling, writing and editing program book, targeting marketing research, writing and editing press releases, and updating press contacts. Candidates should have ability to work independently, computer skills, editing skills, knowledge of field, office skills, oral communication skills, organizational skills, personal interest in the field, self-motivation, strong interpersonal skills, written communication skills. Duration is flexible. Unpaid. Open to college sophomores, college juniors, college seniors, recent college graduates, graduate students. ▶ *1 special events intern:* responsibilities include assisting with vital fundraising portion of annual gala; projects may include creating an ad book and event program, soliciting corporation sponsorships, and assisting during special events. Candidates should have ability to work independently, office skills, oral communication skills, organizational skills, personal interest in the field, self-motivation, strong interpersonal skills, written communication skills. Duration is flexible. Unpaid. Open to college sophomores, college juniors, college seniors, recent college graduates, graduate students. ▶ *1–2 stage management fellow:* responsibilities include serving as the assistant to the production stage manager, performing duties including note-taking, cleaning, prepping, serving as a liaison between the actors and PSM, and attending all rehearsals and performances. Candidates should have knowledge of field, oral communication skills, organizational skills, personal interest in the field, self-motivation, strong interpersonal skills, ability to thrive under pressure. $250 per week. Open to recent college graduates, graduate students. International applications accepted.

Benefits Job counseling, names of contacts, on-the-job training, possible full-time employment, willing to act as a professional reference, willing to complete paperwork for educational credit, willing to provide letters of recommendation, free tickets, discounts on studio school classes.

Contact Write, fax, e-mail, or through World Wide Web site Deborah Braak, Education Director. Fax: 215-893-0895. E-mail: dlb@wilmatheater.org. No phone calls. In-person interview recommended (telephone interview accepted). Applicants must submit a letter of interest, resume, writing sample. Applications are accepted continuously. World Wide Web: http://www.wilmatheater.org.

WOLF TRAP FOUNDATION FOR THE PERFORMING ARTS
1645 Trap Road
Vienna, Virginia 22182

General Information Performing arts organization that presents music, dance, theater, opera, and related educational programs. Established in 1971. Number of employees: 87. Number of internship applications received each year: 300.

Internships Available ▶ *1 Internet programs intern:* responsibilities include assisting with development and maintenance of content on Wolf Trap's Web site. Candidates should have ability to work independently, editing skills, knowledge of field, organizational skills, personal interest in the field, research skills, writing skills, experience with HTML, Adobe Photo Shop, and Web-related applications development. Duration is 12 weeks during summer. $210 per week. Open to college freshmen, college sophomores, college juniors, college seniors, recent college graduates, graduate students. ▶ *1 accounting intern:* responsibilities include assisting in the reporting of all foundation financial activities. Candidates should have ability to work independently, ability to work with others, analytical skills, computer skills, declared college major in field, office skills. Duration is 12 weeks during summer. $210 per week. Open to college freshmen, college sophomores, college juniors, college seniors, recent college graduates, graduate students, career changers. ▶ *1 associates intern:* responsibilities include assisting in coordinating special events, volunteers, and membership efforts. Candidates should have ability to work independently, computer skills, oral communication skills, organizational skills, strong interpersonal skills, written communication skills. Duration is 12 weeks during summer. $210 per week. Open to college freshmen, college sophomores, college juniors, college seniors, recent college graduates, graduate students. ▶ *6 communications and marketing interns:* responsibilities include working in media relations, advertising, publications, marketing, graphic design, or photography; performing such tasks as research, writing, and editing. Candidates should have ability to work independently, ability to work with others, college courses in field, computer skills, editing skills, knowledge of field, office skills, oral communication skills, organizational skills, personal interest in the field, research skills, self-motivation, strong leadership ability, written communication skills. Duration is dependent upon position. $210 per week. Open to college freshmen, college sophomores, college juniors, college seniors, recent college graduates, graduate students, career changers. ▶ *1–3 development interns:* responsibilities include researching, organizing, and preparing reports on individual, corporate, and foundation prospects. Candidates should have ability to work independently, computer skills, editing skills, office skills, oral communication skills, organizational skills, personal interest in the field, research skills, self-motivation, strong interpersonal skills, writing skills. Duration is 12 weeks during summer and spring. $5.25 per hour; $210 per week for summer interns. Open to college freshmen, college sophomores, college juniors, college seniors, recent college graduates, graduate students, career changers. ▶ *1 directing intern (Wolf Trap Opera Company):* responsibilities include participating in the rehearsal process alongside professional members of the artistic and production staffs. Candidates should have ability to work independently, knowledge of field, oral communication skills, self-motivation, strong interpersonal skills, strong leadership ability, written communication skills, interest in pursuing career in opera stage direction. Duration is 10 weeks during summer. $210 per week. Open to college freshmen, college sophomores, college juniors, college seniors, recent college graduates, graduate students. ▶ *1–2 education interns:* responsibilities include assisting with scheduling and coordination of education activities, including artist residencies, field trips, children's performances, and others. Candidates should have ability to work independently, computer skills, editing skills, office skills, oral communication skills, organizational skills, personal interest in the field, self-motivation, strong interpersonal skills, writing skills. Duration is 12 weeks during summer, fall, and spring. $5.25 per hour; $210 per week for summer interns. Open to college freshmen, college sophomores, college juniors, college seniors, recent college graduates, graduate students, career changers. ▶ *1 group sales/box office intern:* responsibilities include assisting director of group sales in interacting with groups, researching market expansion, and creating marketing materials to boost group sales. Candidates should have computer skills, office skills, oral communication skills, organizational skills, strong interpersonal skills, writing skills. Duration is 12 weeks during spring. $5.25 per hour. Open to college freshmen, college sophomores, college juniors, college seniors, recent college graduates, graduate students, career changers. ▶ *1 human resources intern:* responsibilities include assisting director with employee relations, benefits, policies, and recruiting. Candidates should have ability to work independently, analytical skills, computer skills, editing skills, office skills, oral communication skills, organizational skills, personal interest in the field, research skills, self-motivation, strong interpersonal skills, strong leadership ability, writing skills. Duration is 12 weeks during summer. $210 per week. Open to college freshmen, college sophomores, college juniors, college seniors, recent college graduates, graduate students, career changers. ▶ *1 information systems intern:* responsibilities include maintaining and repairing all the systems and networks, including network administration, system maintenance, system upgrade, and Internet connectivity. Candidates should have ability to work independently, college courses in field, computer skills, knowledge of field, personal interest in the field, self-motivation, strong interpersonal skills. Duration is 12 weeks during summer. $210 per week. Open to college freshmen, college sophomores, college juniors, college seniors, recent college graduates, graduate students. ▶ *1 opera administration intern (Wolf Trap Opera Company):* responsibilities include attending production meetings, rehearsals, and performances; updating company history, repertoire lists, contact sheets, and mailings lists; and assisting the administrative director and staff in daily office operations. Candidates should have ability to work independently, computer skills, editing skills, office skills, oral communication skills, organizational skills, personal interest in the field, self-motivation, strong interpersonal skills, strong leadership ability, writing skills. Duration is 12 weeks during summer. $210 per week. Open to college freshmen, college sophomores, college juniors, college seniors, recent college graduates, graduate students, career changers. ▶ *1 planning and initiatives intern:* responsibilities include coordinating with staff and outside partners on projects such as planning, government relations, long-term commissions, special productions, new series, and cooperative projects with other arts organizations and community partnerships. Candidates should have ability to work independently, computer skills, oral communication skills, organizational skills, research skills, strong interpersonal skills, written communication skills. Duration is 12 weeks during summer. $210 per week. Open to college freshmen, college sophomores, college juniors, college seniors, recent college graduates, graduate students, career changers. ▶ *1–3 special events interns:* responsibilities include assisting with preparations for special events, organizing volunteers, and assisting the staff with daily office operations. Candidates should have ability to work independently, computer skills, office skills, oral communication skills, organizational skills, personal interest in the field, research skills, self-motivation, strong interpersonal skills, writing skills. Duration is 12 weeks during summer, fall, and spring. $210. $5.25 per hour; $210 per week for summer interns. Open to college freshmen, college sophomores, college juniors, college seniors, recent college graduates, graduate students, career changers. ▶ *2 stage management interns (Wolf Trap Opera Company):* responsibilities include assisting stage management team in all aspects of the rehearsal process and running one side of stage during performance. Candidates should have ability to work independently, experience in the field, oral communication skills, organizational skills, plan to pursue career in field, self-motivation, strong interpersonal skills, ability to read music. Duration is 12 weeks during summer. $210 per week. Open to college freshmen, college sophomores, college juniors, college seniors, recent college graduates, graduate students. ▶ *1–4 technical theater interns (Wolf Trap Opera Company):* responsibilities include working in general technical theater, scenic/prop painting, and costuming; all work side by side with professional direc-

tors, designers, and technicians in mounting and running two operas. Candidates should have ability to work independently, ability to work with others, experience in the field, oral communication skills, organizational skills, self-motivation. Duration is 8-10 weeks during summer. $210 per week. Open to college freshmen, college sophomores, college juniors, college seniors, recent college graduates, graduate students, career changers. International applications accepted.

Benefits Job counseling, names of contacts, on-the-job training, opportunity to attend seminars/workshops, possible full-time employment, willing to act as a professional reference, willing to complete paperwork for educational credit, willing to provide letters of recommendation, complimentary performance tickets when possible, opportunity to join in 403(b) plan, field trips to local arts organizations, mentor program.

Contact Write, call, fax, e-mail, or through World Wide Web site Mia De Mezza, Assistant Director, Education Outreach. Phone: 703-255-1933. Fax: 703-255-1924. E-mail: internships@wolftrap.org. In-person interview recommended (telephone interview accepted). Applicants must submit a letter of interest, resume, two writing samples, two letters of recommendation. Application deadline: March 1 for summer, July 1 for fall, November 1 for spring. World Wide Web: http://www.wolftrap.org.

WOMEN'S PROJECT AND PRODUCTIONS
55 West End Avenue
New York, New York 10023

General Information Nonprofit theater organization that seeks to develop and produce original works written and directed by women in the off-Broadway theater and to promote women in the theater nationally. Established in 1978. Number of employees: 8. Number of internship applications received each year: 100.

Internships Available ▶ *1 administrative intern:* responsibilities include assisting office personnel with general administrative duties and working with the managing director on special projects. Candidates should have ability to work with others, computer skills, office skills, oral communication skills, organizational skills, self-motivation. Duration is flexible. Unpaid. Open to high school students, recent high school graduates, college freshmen, college sophomores, college juniors, college seniors, recent college graduates, graduate students, career changers, individuals reentering the workforce. ▶ *1–2 development assistants:* responsibilities include assisting development director in researching funding sources, drafting development-related correspondence, coordinating mail solicitation, and helping with the ongoing activities of development department. Candidates should have ability to work independently, computer skills, oral communication skills, personal interest in the field, research skills, written communication skills. Duration is 20 hours per week. Unpaid. Open to college freshmen, college sophomores, college juniors, college seniors, recent college graduates, graduate students, career changers, individuals reentering the workforce. ▶ *1–5 education interns:* responsibilities include teaching in New York public schools, creating lesson plans, and assisting with a final production in the Women's Project Theatre. Candidates should have college courses in field, experience in the field, organizational skills, personal interest in the field, strong interpersonal skills. Duration is flexible. Unpaid. Open to college juniors, college seniors, recent college graduates, graduate students, career changers, individuals reentering the workforce. ▶ *2 literary assistants:* responsibilities include reading and evaluating play scripts, assisting in processing scripts and updating artistic files, and assisting literary manager with the reading series and ongoing activities of the literary department. Candidates should have ability to work independently, analytical skills, computer skills, knowledge of field, research skills, written communication skills. Duration is 20 hours per week. Unpaid. Open to college freshmen, college sophomores, college juniors, college seniors, recent college graduates, graduate students, career changers, individuals reentering the workforce. ▶ *1–2 marketing interns:* responsibilities include copywriting for programs, helping to prepare mailings, telemarketing, and assisting in writing newsletter. Candidates should have ability to work independently, computer skills, knowledge of field, oral communication skills, organizational skills. Duration is 6 weeks (minimum). Unpaid.

Women's Project and Productions (continued)

Open to college freshmen, college sophomores, college juniors, college seniors, recent college graduates, graduate students, career changers, individuals reentering the workforce. ▶ *1–5 production interns:* responsibilities include assisting crew during rehearsals or performances of full productions and possibly serving as general production assistant or assisting the director. Candidates should have ability to work independently, experience in the field, self-motivation, strong interpersonal skills, maturity and ability to handle pressure. Duration is 25 to 35 hours per week. Unpaid. Open to college freshmen, college sophomores, college juniors, college seniors, recent college graduates, graduate students, career changers, individuals reentering the workforce. International applications accepted.

Benefits Names of contacts, possible full-time employment, willing to complete paperwork for educational credit, willing to provide letters of recommendation, complimentary tickets to all performances by WPP and to other New York theaters (when available).

Contact Write, call, fax, or e-mail Cory Hinkle, Assistant to Artistic Director/Intern Coordinator. Phone: 212-765-1706. Fax: 212-765-2024. E-mail: info@womensproject.org. In-person interview recommended (telephone interview accepted). Applicants must submit a letter of interest, resume. Applications are accepted continuously. World Wide Web: http://www.womensproject.org.

PERFORMING ARTS, SPECTATOR SPORTS, AND RELATED INDUSTRIES

AMERICAN DANCE FESTIVAL
Box 90772
Durham, North Carolina 27708

General Information Organization that supports modern dance artists through performance, education, and special programs and works to promote dance consciousness in the American public. Established in 1934. Number of employees: 17. Number of internship applications received each year: 60.

Internships Available ▶ *1 box office intern:* responsibilities include selling single tickets on a computerized box office system (Prologue). Candidates should have ability to work independently, ability to work with others, computer skills, oral communication skills, organizational skills, self-motivation, must have own transportation. Duration is late May through late July. $1100 per duration of internship. Open to college sophomores, college juniors, college seniors, recent college graduates. ▶ *1 executive intern:* responsibilities include working on a development project, working on activities for international participants and special guests, assisting with video dance film festival, and general office management duties. Candidates should have ability to work independently, computer skills, office skills, organizational skills, ability to work nights and weekends. Duration is late May to late July. $950 per duration of internship. Open to college freshmen, college sophomores, college juniors, college seniors, recent college graduates, graduate students, career changers, individuals at least 21 years old (or who own a car). ▶ *2 facility services interns:* responsibilities include facilitating the technical, studio, housing, food and transportation needs for the entire ADF community; assisting in virtually all aspects of setting up and running an international arts festival. Candidates should have ability to work independently, computer skills, oral communication skills, organizational skills, self-motivation, strong interpersonal skills, video experience (a plus). Duration is late May through late July. $1100 per duration of internship. Open to college freshmen, college sophomores, college juniors, college seniors, recent college graduates, graduate students, law students, career changers. ▶ *1*

food and housing intern: responsibilities include planning and implementing receptions/parties and arranging food/housing requests with Duke University for ADF students and professionals throughout the Festival. Candidates should have ability to work independently, ability to work with others, oral communication skills, organizational skills, self-motivation, evening and weekend work required. Duration is late May through late July. $1100 per duration of internship. Open to college sophomores, college juniors, college seniors, recent college graduates, graduate students. ▶ *1 merchandising intern:* responsibilities include displays, inventory control, ordering, daily cash reports, supervision of the scholarship students and volunteers who work in the store and at the theater. Candidates should have ability to work independently, ability to work with others, oral communication skills, self-motivation, accounting and business skills (helpful) and creative eye for visual display. Duration is late May through July. $1100 per duration of internship. Open to college sophomores, college juniors, college seniors, recent college graduates, graduate students. ▶ *2 performance interns:* responsibilities include administrative coordination of all activities connected with the professional performing companies. Candidates should have ability to work independently, oral communication skills, organizational skills, personal interest in the field, strong interpersonal skills, written communication skills, ability to handle multiple tasks, attention to detail, must have own transportation. Duration is late May through late July. $950 per duration of internship. Open to college juniors, college seniors, recent college graduates, graduate students, law students, career changers. ▶ *2 press interns:* responsibilities include contacting artists for program information; editing and proofing; design work in newspaper advertisements and invitations. Candidates should have computer skills, editing skills, organizational skills, self-motivation, writing skills, responsibility, attention to detail, ability to work under pressure, must have own transportation. Duration is 8 weeks. $950 per duration of internship. Open to college freshmen, college sophomores, college juniors, college seniors, recent college graduates, graduate students, career changers. ▶ *Production interns:* responsibilities include various assignments including: stage management, wardrobe, sound, electrics, and carpentry. Candidates should have ability to work with others, experience in dance production (preferred). Duration is late May through July. $1100 per duration of internship. Open to college sophomores, college juniors, college seniors, recent college graduates, graduate students. ▶ *2 school interns:* responsibilities include working with an international student body and faculty of over 500 people; maintaining the school's master schedule, as well as publishing the daily and weekly calendars; assisting in academic relationships with Duke University; assisting school VIP's; and assigning jobs to scholarship students. Candidates should have ability to work independently, analytical skills, computer skills, experience in the field, oral communication skills, personal interest in the field, self-motivation, strong interpersonal skills. Duration is 8–9 weeks. $950 per duration of internship. Open to college freshmen, college sophomores, college juniors, college seniors, recent college graduates, graduate students, law students, career changers. ▶ *1 technical production intern.* Candidates should have self-motivation, experience in dance production, ability to work nights and weekends, and be detail oriented. Duration is late May to late July. $1100 per duration of internship. Open to college freshmen, college sophomores, college juniors, college seniors, recent college graduates, graduate students, career changers. ▶ *1 video production intern:* responsibilities include working with the videographer at every video taped event and performance and working with the archive to manage season's videos. Candidates should have ability to work independently, experience with audio visual equipment required. Duration is late May through late July. $950 per duration of internship. Open to college sophomores, college juniors, college seniors, recent college graduates, graduate students, law students. International applications accepted.

Benefits Job counseling, names of contacts, on-the-job training, opportunity to attend seminars/workshops, possible full-time employment, willing to complete paperwork for educational credit, willing to provide letters of recommendation, free dance classes, free admission to dance concerts.

Contact Write, fax, e-mail, or through World Wide Web site Intern Coordinator. Fax: 919-684-5459. E-mail: adf@americandancefestival.org. Telephone interview required. Applicants must submit a formal organization application, letter of interest, resume, two letters of recommendation. Application deadline: February 15 for summer. World Wide Web: http://www.americandancefestival.org.

AMERICAN SYMPHONY ORCHESTRA LEAGUE
33 West 60th Street, 5th Floor
New York, New York 10023

General Information National service organization for symphony, chamber, youth, and university orchestras in America working to ensure the artistic, organizational, and financial strength of American orchestras. Established in 1942. Number of employees: 30. Number of internship applications received each year: 50.
Internships Available ▶ *5 orchestra management fellows:* responsibilities include duties and projects while on rotating 6 to 16-week assignments at American orchestras, including assisting in orchestra operations, marketing, public relations, development, volunteerism, governance, contract negotiations, financial management, long-range planning, artistic administration, education, and outreach. Candidates should have knowledge of field, personal interest in the field, plan to pursue career in field, strong interpersonal skills, strong leadership ability. Duration is 1 year. $25,000 stipend. Open to college seniors, recent college graduates, graduate students, law students, career changers, individuals reentering the workforce. International applications accepted.
Benefits Formal training, health insurance, job counseling, names of contacts, on-the-job training, opportunity to attend seminars/ workshops, travel reimbursement, willing to provide letters of recommendation, access to employment services offered by the League.
Contact Write, call, fax, e-mail, or through World Wide Web site Melanie Hausmann, Program Coordinator. Phone: 212-265-5161 Ext. 220. Fax: 212-262-5198. E-mail: mhausmann@symphony.org. In-person interview required. Applicants must submit a formal organization application, resume, academic transcripts, three writing samples, three letters of recommendation. Application deadline: January 1. Fees: $45. World Wide Web: http://www.symphony.org.

ARCADY MUSIC SOCIETY
PO Box 37
Bass Harbor, Maine 04653

General Information Organization that presents high-quality chamber music. Established in 1980. Number of employees: 2. Number of internship applications received each year: 10.
Internships Available ▶ *1–2 summer festival interns:* responsibilities include assisting executive director and regional committees in all logistics of festival presentation including selling ads, distributing posters, and handling publicity, ticket sales, and artists' housing arrangements. Candidates should have ability to work with others, computer skills, office skills, oral communication skills, organizational skills, personal interest in the field, self-motivation. Duration is 3–4 months. $1000–$1200 per duration of internship. Open to high school seniors, recent high school graduates, college freshmen, college sophomores, college juniors, college seniors, recent college graduates, graduate students, career changers, individuals reentering the workforce. International applications accepted.
Benefits Free housing, job counseling, names of contacts, on-the-job training, willing to act as a professional reference, willing to complete paperwork for educational credit, willing to provide letters of recommendation, some free meals on concert nights.
Contact Write, call, fax, e-mail, or through World Wide Web site Dean Stein, Executive Director. Phone: 207-288-2141. Fax: 207-288-2141. E-mail: arcady@arcady.org. In-person interview recommended (telephone interview accepted). Applicants must submit a letter of interest, resume, two personal references. Application deadline: March 15 for summer, August 1 for fall. World Wide Web: http://www.arcady.org.

ARCHIVE OF CONTEMPORARY MUSIC
54 White Street
New York, New York 10013

General Information Nonprofit music library and research center, with over one million recordings, dedicated to the collection and preservation of all types of popular music from around the world, 1950 to the present. Established in 1986. Number of employees: 3. Number of internship applications received each year: 100.
Internships Available ▶ *12 interns:* responsibilities include assisting in cataloging, filing press clippings, conducting research, and performing general office duties. Candidates should have ability to work with others, computer skills, knowledge of field, office skills, organizational skills, personal interest in the field, research skills, self-motivation. Duration is flexible. Unpaid. Open to high school students, college freshmen, college sophomores, college juniors, college seniors, graduate students. International applications accepted.
Benefits Job counseling, opportunity to attend seminars/ workshops, willing to complete paperwork for educational credit, willing to provide letters of recommendation, computer training, $10 per day for transportation and lunch (entire day); $5 per day (minimum of 4 hours).
Contact Write, call, fax, e-mail, or through World Wide Web site Mr. Bob George, Director. Phone: 212-226-6967. Fax: 212-226-6540. E-mail: arcmusic@inch.com. In-person interview recommended (telephone interview accepted). Applicants must submit a resume. Applications are accepted continuously. World Wide Web: http://www.arcmusic.org.

ATLANTA BALLET
1400 West Peachtree Street
Atlanta, Georgia 30309

General Information Professional ballet company and education facility. Established in 1929. Number of employees: 90. Number of internship applications received each year: 50.
Internships Available ▶ *1–3 marketing and public relations interns:* responsibilities include ad trafficking, writing correspondence and press releases, donation requests, researching, and other duties to be assigned. Candidates should have ability to work independently, oral communication skills, personal interest in the field, strong interpersonal skills, written communication skills. Duration is flexible. Unpaid. Open to high school seniors, college freshmen, college sophomores, college juniors, college seniors, recent college graduates. International applications accepted.
Benefits Formal training, job counseling, names of contacts, on-the-job training, opportunity to attend seminars/workshops, tuition assistance, willing to act as a professional reference, willing to complete paperwork for educational credit, willing to provide letters of recommendation.
Contact Call or e-mail Heather Berry, Associate Director of Marketing and Public Relations. Phone: 404-873-5811 Ext. 203. Fax: 404-874-7905. E-mail: hberry@atlantaballet.com. In-person interview recommended (telephone interview accepted). Applicants must submit a letter of interest, resume, 2-3 writing samples. Applications are accepted continuously. World Wide Web: http://www.atlantaballet.com.

BALLET MET
322 Mount Vernon Avenue
Columbus, Ohio 43215

General Information Professional dance company and academy. Established in 1978. Number of employees: 100. Number of internship applications received each year: 150.
Internships Available ▶ *1–4 marketing interns:* responsibilities include working on special events, press coordination, marketing, and some design. Candidates should have ability to work independently, computer skills, editing skills, oral communication skills, written communication skills, design experience helpful. Duration is 3 months. $200 stipend. Open to college sophomores, college juniors, college seniors. International applications accepted.
Benefits Names of contacts, willing to complete paperwork for educational credit, willing to provide letters of recommendation.

Ballet Met (continued)

Contact Write, call, fax, or e-mail Brandi Pennington, Marketing Manager. Phone: 614-229-4860 Ext. 163. Fax: 614-229-4858. E-mail: bpennington@balletmet.org. In-person interview recommended (telephone interview accepted). Applicants must submit a letter of interest, resume, writing sample. Applications are accepted continuously. World Wide Web: http://www.balletmet.org.

BASEBALL EXPOS L.P.
C.P. 500, Succursale M/PO Box 500, Station M
Montreal, Quebec H1V 3P2 Canada

General Information Major league baseball team. Established in 1969. Number of employees: 1,300. Number of internship applications received each year: 50.

Internships Available ▶ *1–3 interns.* Candidates should have computer skills, office skills, oral communication skills, research skills, writing skills. Duration is March 1 to September 30. Position available as unpaid or at $300 Canadian dollars per week. Open to college seniors, graduate students, career changers. International applications accepted.

Benefits Formal training, job counseling, names of contacts, on-the-job training, opportunity to attend seminars/workshops, possible full-time employment, willing to act as a professional reference, willing to complete paperwork for educational credit, willing to provide letters of recommendation.

International Internships Available.

Contact Write or fax Claude Delorme, Vice President, Stadium Operations. Fax: 514-251-4205. No phone calls. In-person interview recommended (telephone interview accepted). Applicants must submit a formal organization application, resume, academic transcripts, three personal references. Application deadline: January 30.

BOWIE BAYSOX
PO Box 1661
Bowie, Maryland 20717

General Information Minor league baseball team affiliated with Baltimore Orioles. Unit of Comcast, Philadelphia, Pennsylvania. Number of internship applications received each year: 300.

Internships Available ▶ *10th Player Program coordinators:* responsibilities include sales and marketing of new program to area businesses via telemarketing and mass direct marketing techniques; aggressive telephone selling. Candidates should have ability to work independently, computer skills, self-motivation, strong interpersonal skills, strong leadership ability, writing skills, ability to work in fast-paced environment. Duration is 1 semester. Unpaid. ▶ *Audio visual interns:* responsibilities include taping and production of pre-recorded AV pieces on Baysox players for broadcast on video board; coordination of all camera operators for in-stadium game broadcast; installation of digital pictures, graphics, and video into click effects program; game-day operation of click effects program in press box for fan entertainment. Candidates should have ability to work independently, computer skills, knowledge of field, oral communication skills, organizational skills, personal interest in the field, research skills, self-motivation, strong interpersonal skills, strong leadership ability, writing skills, ability to work in fast-paced environment. Duration is 1 semester. Unpaid. ▶ *Box office assistants:* responsibilities include assisting ticket manager with daily operations of the ticket box office; taking incoming phone orders for individual game ticket sales; processing ticket orders using select ticketing system; assisting in completing multiple mass-mail jobs for renewal of season tickets. Candidates should have ability to work independently, computer skills, oral communication skills, organizational skills, personal interest in the field, self-motivation, strong leadership ability, writing skills, ability to work in fast-paced environment. Duration is 1 semester. Unpaid. ▶ *Group event coordinators:* responsibilities include aggressive selling; helping event coordinator at all times; generating leads through cold calling; servicing clients during events. Candidates should have ability to work independently, ability to work with others, computer skills, knowledge of field, oral communication skills, organizational skills, personal interest in the field, self-motivation, writing skills, ability to work in fast-paced

environment. Duration is 1 semester. Unpaid. ▶ *Group events assistants:* responsibilities include assisting full-time group event manager with follow up phone calls; generating leads; coordinating events and servicing clients during events; processing group event orders and mailing group event packages to clients; group database management and maintenance. Candidates should have ability to work independently, computer skills, knowledge of field, oral communication skills, personal interest in the field, strong interpersonal skills, strong leadership ability, written communication skills, ability to work in fast-paced environment. Duration is 1 semester. Unpaid. ▶ *Marketing assistants:* responsibilities include assisting marketing staff with development and implementation of innovative and fun promotions designed to attract fans to the stadium; working with local media to promote the visibility of the Baysox; mass marketing via mailing and pocket schedule distribution. Candidates should have ability to work independently, oral communication skills, organizational skills, strong interpersonal skills, strong leadership ability, writing skills, ability to work in fast-paced environment. Duration is 1 semester. Unpaid. ▶ *Public relation assistants:* responsibilities include assistance with production of Baysox Playbill; dissemination of press releases; assisting director in coordinating media interviews with staff and players; distribution of media credentials; management of press box during games; providing updated scores to wire services; assisting local and national sports media; contacting media with scores. Candidates should have ability to work independently, computer skills, oral communication skills, organizational skills, personal interest in the field, self-motivation, strong interpersonal skills, strong leadership ability, writing skills, ability to work in fast-paced environment. Duration is 1 semester. Unpaid. ▶ *Sponsor sales assistants:* responsibilities include assisting full-time sponsorship sales account managers with follow-up-phone calls; generating leads; coordinating events and serving clients during events; telemarketing and mass direct marketing to area businesses. Candidates should have ability to work independently, computer skills, knowledge of field, oral communication skills, personal interest in the field, self-motivation, strong leadership ability, writing skills, ability to work in fast-paced environment. Duration is 1 semester. Unpaid. ▶ *Theme night assistants:* responsibilities include assisting theme night coordinator with setting up particular nights throughout the season by focusing on targeted audiences with the goals of driving revenues and turnstile attendance on those nights; setting up meetings in and out of office with community groups and organizations; selling pre- and post-game group events. Candidates should have ability to work independently, computer skills, knowledge of field, personal interest in the field, self-motivation, strong interpersonal skills, strong leadership ability, writing skills, ability to work in fast-paced environment. Duration is 1 semester. Unpaid. ▶ *Ticket sales assistants:* responsibilities include aggressive selling; lead generation through cold calling area businesses; use of mass direct marketing techniques to business and residences to sell partial and full-season ticket packages; servicing of clients during events; and box office assistance. Candidates should have ability to work independently, ability to work with others, computer skills, oral communication skills, organizational skills, personal interest in the field, self-motivation, strong leadership ability, writing skills, ability to work in fast-paced environment. Duration is 1 semester. Unpaid. Open to college juniors, college seniors, recent college graduates, graduate students, must be working for academic credits.

Benefits Formal training, on-the-job training, opportunity to attend seminars/workshops, possible full-time employment, willing to act as a professional reference, willing to complete paperwork for educational credit.

Contact Write, call, fax, e-mail, or through World Wide Web site Curt A. Wilson, Recruiter, Human Resources, 3601 South Broad Street, Philadelphia 19148-5290. Phone: 215-389-9502. Fax: 215-389-9413. E-mail: cwilson@comcast-spectacor.com. In-person interview required. Applicants must submit a formal organization application, letter of interest, resume, writing sample, personal reference, letter of recommendation. Applications are accepted continuously. World Wide Web: http://www.baysox.com.

BROOKLYN ACADEMY OF MUSIC
30 Lafayette Avenue
Brooklyn, New York 11217-1486

General Information Internationally recognized performing arts center. Established in 1861. Number of employees: 150. Number of internship applications received each year: 200.

Internships Available ▶ *1–2 fiscal interns.* Candidates should have college courses in field, computer skills, knowledge of field, office skills, organizational skills, personal interest in the field. Position available as unpaid or at stipend of $150 per week. Open to college sophomores, college juniors, college seniors, recent college graduates, graduate students, career changers, individuals reentering the workforce. ▶ *1–2 fund-raising interns:* responsibilities include writing reports and proposals for grants. Candidates should have ability to work independently, computer skills, office skills, organizational skills, personal interest in the field, writing skills. Duration is flexible. Position available as unpaid or at stipend of $150 per week. ▶ *1 general management intern:* responsibilities include administrative/clerical duties, answering phones, answering questions about renting the theaters, running errands, and proofreading contracts and schedules. Candidates should have ability to work independently, computer skills, knowledge of field, office skills, oral communication skills, self-motivation, strong interpersonal skills. Duration is flexible. Unpaid. Open to college freshmen, college sophomores, college juniors, college seniors, recent college graduates, graduate students, career changers. ▶ *1 human resources intern:* responsibilities include administrative/clerical duties; (answering phones, filing, possible data entry). Candidates should have ability to work with others, knowledge of field, office skills, organizational skills, personal interest in the field, research skills, ability to keep confidential information. Duration is flexible. Unpaid. Open to college freshmen, college sophomores, college juniors, college seniors, recent college graduates, graduate students, law students, career changers. ▶ *1–2 marketing and communications interns:* responsibilities include providing general administrative support services. Candidates should have ability to work independently, computer skills, office skills, oral communication skills, organizational skills, personal interest in the field, written communication skills. Duration is flexible. Position available as unpaid or at stipend of $150 per week. Open to high school seniors, recent high school graduates, college freshmen, college sophomores, college juniors, college seniors, recent college graduates, graduate students, career changers, individuals reentering the workforce. ▶ *1 production intern:* responsibilities include working with stagehands, technical, and wardrobe personnel to provide administrative support. Candidates should have ability to work independently, computer skills, office skills, oral communication skills, organizational skills, personal interest in the field, self-motivation, strong interpersonal skills. Duration is flexible. Unpaid. Open to college freshmen, college sophomores, college juniors, college seniors, recent college graduates, graduate students. ▶ *1–2 special events interns:* responsibilities include assisting in fund-raising, planning, and execution of events. Candidates should have computer skills, office skills, organizational skills, personal interest in the field, self-motivation, strong interpersonal skills. Duration is flexible. Position available as unpaid or at stipend of $150 per week. Open to high school students, recent high school graduates, college freshmen, college sophomores, college juniors, college seniors, recent college graduates, graduate students, career changers, individuals reentering the workforce. International applications accepted.

Benefits Names of contacts, possible full-time employment, willing to complete paperwork for educational credit.

Contact Write, fax, or e-mail Sarah Weinstein, Director of Human Resources, 30 Lafayette Avenue, Brooklyn, New York 11217-1485. Fax: 718-636-4179. E-mail: hrresumes@bam.org. No phone calls. In-person interview required. Applicants must submit a resume, letter of interest specifying which internship requested and dates of availability. Applications are accepted continuously. World Wide Web: http://www.bam.org.

BUFFALO BILLS
One Bills Drive
Orchard Park, New York 14127

General Information Professional football team. Established in 1960. Number of employees: 150. Number of internship applications received each year: 150.

Internships Available ▶ *3–5 marketing department interns:* responsibilities include assisting in all facets of marketing, including marketing partnerships, tickets and premium seats, merchandise, community relations, and marketing communications. Candidates should have ability to work independently, college courses in field, computer skills, editing skills, office skills, oral communication skills, organizational skills, plan to pursue career in field, strong interpersonal skills, written communication skills. Duration is spring, summer, or fall semesters. Unpaid. Open to college sophomores, college juniors, college seniors, recent college graduates, graduate students. International applications accepted.

Benefits Willing to act as a professional reference, willing to complete paperwork for educational credit, willing to provide letters of recommendation.

Contact Write Chris Voigt, Manager, Marketing Programs. Phone: 716-648-1800 Ext. 344. Fax: 716-648-3126. E-mail: chrisv@bill.nfl.com. In-person interview recommended (telephone interview accepted). Applicants must submit a letter of interest, resume, three personal references. Application deadline: January 1 for spring, April 1 for summer, August 1 for fall. World Wide Web: http://buffalobills.com.

BURNS SPORTS & CELEBRITIES, INC.
1007 Church Street, Suite 306
Evanston, Illinois 60201

General Information Sports and entertainment marketing company. Established in 1970. Number of employees: 9. Number of internship applications received each year: 400.

Internships Available ▶ *Up to 3 interns:* responsibilities include general office duties, database management, research marketing, travel arrangements, contracts. Candidates should have computer skills, office skills, oral communication skills, organizational skills, personal interest in the field, research skills, self-motivation, strong interpersonal skills, written communication skills. Duration is 1 semester. Position available as unpaid or paid. Open to college freshmen, college sophomores, college juniors, college seniors, preference given to students receiving credit. International applications accepted.

Benefits Possible full-time employment, willing to act as a professional reference, willing to complete paperwork for educational credit, willing to provide letters of recommendation, case-by-case stipend or travel reimbursement.

Contact Write or fax Tim Ketterman, Account Executive. Fax: 847-491-9778. E-mail: timk@burnssports.com. No phone calls. In-person interview recommended (telephone interview accepted). Applicants must submit a letter of interest, resume, three personal references. Applications are accepted continuously. World Wide Web: http://www.burnsports.com.

CARNEGIE HALL
881 Seventh Avenue
New York, New York 10019

General Information Concert hall providing concerts of classical, jazz, and other styles of music. Established in 1891. Number of employees: 270. Number of internship applications received each year: 250.

Internships Available ▶ *Interns:* responsibilities include various possibilities throughout Carnegie Hall (typically in marketing, public affairs, and development). Candidates should have ability to work independently, ability to work with others, oral communication skills, plan to pursue career in field, written communication skills, MS Office skills. Duration is typically 3 to 5 months (may be longer). Position available as unpaid or paid. Open to recent high school graduates, college freshmen, college sophomores, college juniors, college seniors, recent college graduates, graduate students. International applications accepted.

Carnegie Hall (continued)

Benefits On-the-job training, willing to complete paperwork for educational credit, willing to provide letters of recommendation, opportunity to attend concerts.

Contact Write, fax, or e-mail Human Resources. Fax: 212-581-6539. E-mail: humanresources@carnegiehall.org. No phone calls. In-person interview required. Applicants must submit a formal organization application, letter of interest, resume, 1-2 writing samples. Applications are accepted continuously. World Wide Web: http://www.carnegiehall.org.

CAVS/GUND ARENA COMPANY
1 Center Court
Cleveland, Ohio 44115-4001

General Information Company that sponsors 2 basketball teams and various entertainment activities.

Internships Available ▶ *1 CAVS public relations intern:* responsibilities include helping distribute newspaper clips on CAVS and archive stories, assisting in operations of public relations department, assisting in updating records, and working/editing international and marketing documents. Candidates should have computer skills, oral communication skills, written communication skills, experience in related activities at college level (preferred), study in sports management and/or communications. Duration is one summer or semester (full-time); must be receiving academic credit. Unpaid. Open to college juniors, seniors, and graduate students (preferred). ▶ *Corporate partnerships:* responsibilities include assisting with administrative and telephone support, providing various public relations/customer service functions, and assisting with season's game operations and promotions. Candidates should have computer skills, oral communication skills, written communication skills, study in sports management, marketing, or a related field. Duration is one summer or semester (full-time); must be receiving academic credit. Unpaid. Open to college juniors, seniors, and graduate students (preferred). ▶ *1 facility operations intern:* responsibilities include assisting with administrative functions including budgeting, cost control, equipment inventory, preventive maintenance, safety reports, event follow-up, and payroll functions. Candidates should have computer skills, organizational skills, study in facility management or related field, previous "hands-on" experience (helpful). Duration is one summer or semester; must be receivig academic credit. Unpaid. Open to college juniors, seniors, and graduate students (preferred). ▶ *3 marketing/community relations/public relations interns:* responsibilities include assisting in coordinating special events based on seasonal projects; assisting in planning, coordinating, and implementing community relations programs; writing media advisories; and editing and working for newsletter. Candidates should have computer skills, oral communication skills, organizational skills, self-motivation, written communication skills, study in marketing, public relations/journalism, sports administration, or related field. Duration is one summer or semester; must be receiving academic credit. Unpaid. Open to college juniors, seniors, or graduate students (preferred). ▶ *3 sales interns:* responsibilities include participating in all sales renewal activities, assisting with coordination/implementation of special events, assisting with pre-and/or post-game activities, compiling sales reports, and other projects as assigned. Candidates should have computer skills, oral communication skills, organizational skills, written communication skills, study in sports administration, marketing, or related field. Duration is one summer or semester; must be receiving academic credit. Unpaid. Open to college juniors, seniors, and graduate students (preferred). International applications accepted.

Benefits Tickets to games, free parking.

Contact Write, call, or fax Kevin R. Lednik, Internship Coordinator. Phone: 216-420-2214. Fax: 216-420-2235. Applicants must submit a formal organization application, resume, cover letter. Application deadline: 3-6 months prior to start of internship. World Wide Web: http://www.gundarena.com.

CHAMBER MUSIC AMERICA
305 Seventh Avenue, 5th Floor
New York, New York 10001-6008

General Information National service organization for professional chamber music ensembles and presenters. Established in 1977. Number of employees: 13. Number of internship applications received each year: 10.

Internships Available ▶ *2–3 Chamber Music Magazine interns:* responsibilities include assisting with editorial and production duties. Candidates should have computer skills, editing skills, oral communication skills, organizational skills, written communication skills. Duration is flexible. Position available as unpaid or paid. Open to college seniors, recent college graduates, graduate students. ▶ *1 arts administration intern:* responsibilities include assisting with general administration duties. Candidates should have computer skills, office skills, oral communication skills, organizational skills, personal interest in the field, written communication skills. Duration is flexible. Position available as unpaid or paid. Open to college seniors, recent college graduates, graduate students, career changers. ▶ *1 conferences intern:* responsibilities include assisting in administrative duties related to national conference. Candidates should have analytical skills, office skills, organizational skills, personal interest in the field, strong interpersonal skills. Duration is flexible. Position available as unpaid or paid. Open to college freshmen, college sophomores, college juniors, college seniors, graduate students. ▶ *4–6 development interns:* responsibilities include assisting in fund-raising efforts. Candidates should have ability to work independently, computer skills, office skills, research skills, written communication skills. Duration is flexible. Position available as unpaid or paid. Open to college seniors, recent college graduates, graduate students. International applications accepted.

Benefits Job counseling, names of contacts, opportunity to attend seminars/workshops, possible full-time employment, willing to act as a professional reference, willing to complete paperwork for educational credit, willing to provide letters of recommendation, possible stipends.

Contact Write, fax, e-mail, or through World Wide Web site Kevin-Sky Russell, Director of Administration. Fax: 212-242-7955. E-mail: info@chamber-music.org. No phone calls. In-person interview recommended (telephone interview accepted). Applicants must submit a letter of interest, resume. Applications are accepted continuously. World Wide Web: http://www.chamber-music.org.

CHARLOTTE WILCOX COMPANY
1560 Broadway, Suite 315
New York, New York 10036

General Information Organization managing Broadway, touring-shows, and undertaking various responsibilities including contracts, budgets, taxes, and union rulings. Established in 1976. Number of employees: 5. Number of internship applications received each year: 25.

Internships Available ▶ *1–2 office assistants:* responsibilities include assisting with general office duties including filing, phone work, running errands, computer input, typing, and working on special projects. Candidates should have ability to work independently, computer skills, office skills, oral communication skills, personal interest in the field, plan to pursue career in field, research skills, self-motivation, strong interpersonal skills, writing skills. Duration is flexible. Stipend of $200 per 40-hour week. Open to college freshmen, college sophomores, college juniors, college seniors, recent college graduates. International applications accepted.

Benefits Names of contacts, on-the-job training, possible full-time employment, willing to act as a professional reference, willing to complete paperwork for educational credit, willing to provide letters of recommendation.

Contact Write or fax Charlotte Wilcox, General Manager. Fax: 212-764-5766. No phone calls. In-person interview recommended (telephone interview accepted). Applicants must submit a letter of interest, resume. Applications are accepted continuously.

CITY LIGHTS YOUTH THEATRE
300 West 43rd Street, Suite 402
New York, New York 10036

General Information Nonprofit theater arts education program for students K-12, offering process-oriented classes, workshops, and residencies that engage New York youth from diverse backgrounds in the performance of theater. Established in 1991. Number of employees: 42. Number of internship applications received each year: 25.

Internships Available ▶ *2–3 assistant stage managers:* responsibilities include working closely with the professional stage manager during rehearsals and production of plays that are cast entirely with youth. Candidates should have ability to work independently, ability to work with others, computer skills, oral communication skills, organizational skills, personal interest in the field, self-motivation. Duration is 3–6 months. Unpaid. Open to high school students, recent high school graduates, college freshmen, college sophomores, college juniors, college seniors, recent college graduates, graduate students. ▶ *1 office assistant:* responsibilities include assisting the management team and the office manager; some light bookkeeping; interaction with children, teenagers, and parents necessary. Candidates should have ability to work independently, ability to work with others, computer skills, office skills, oral communication skills, organizational skills, personal interest in the field, self-motivation, word processing and telephone skills. Duration is flexible. Unpaid. Open to high school students, recent high school graduates, college freshmen, college sophomores, college juniors, college seniors, recent college graduates, graduate students. ▶ *6–10 teaching artist assistants:* responsibilities include being matched with a professional theater arts teaching artist for support in the classroom, working with children or teenagers in a theater arts educational setting. Candidates should have ability to work independently, ability to work with others, oral communication skills, personal interest in the field, self-motivation. Duration is 9–15 weeks. Unpaid. Open to recent high school graduates, college freshmen, college sophomores, college juniors, college seniors, recent college graduates, graduate students. International applications accepted.

Benefits On-the-job training, opportunity to attend seminars/workshops, willing to act as a professional reference, willing to complete paperwork for educational credit, willing to provide letters of recommendation.

Contact Write, e-mail, or through World Wide Web site Warren Baumgart, Jr., Artistic Director. Fax: 212-262-1888. E-mail: citylights@clyouththeatre.org. No phone calls. In-person interview required. Applicants must submit a letter of interest, resume, three personal references. Applications are accepted continuously. World Wide Web: http://www.clyouththeatre.org.

COMCAST
3601 South Broad Street
Philadelphia, Pennsylvania 19148-5290

General Information Sports and entertainment company that operates the First Union Spectrum/Center facilities, 3 professional sports franchises, and a cable broadcast sports network. Established in 1967. Number of employees: 3,150. Number of internship applications received each year: 300.

Internships Available ▶ *1 accounting intern:* responsibilities include maintaining data files, preparing bank reconciliations, assisting with payroll functions, analyzing G/L accounts, and entering accounts payable invoices in the accounting system. Candidates should have analytical skills, college courses in field, computer skills, knowledge of field, office skills, Lotus experience (helpful), ability to meet deadlines. Duration is 1 semester in fall, spring, or summer. Unpaid. Open to college juniors and seniors or graduate students working for academic credit. ▶ *1 advertising sales intern:* responsibilities include developing new concepts for advertising venues at the First Union Spectrum/Center, assisting staff with research and design for various projects, handling phone inquiries, coordinating promotions and special events, and assisting with client sponsorship agreements. Candidates should have knowledge of field, oral communication skills, organizational skills, self-motivation, strong interpersonal skills, written communication skills, ability to use Word, WordPerfect, PowerPoint, and Lotus 123 (preferred). Duration is spring or fall semester. Unpaid. Open to college juniors and seniors or graduate students working for academic credit. ▶ *1 building public relations intern:* responsibilities include assisting with generating and pitching story ideas to media; assisting with brainstorming, planning, and executing publicity events; assisting with media tours; handling correspondence and assisting with mailings; and keeping a comprehensive record of events. Candidates should have oral communication skills, organizational skills, research skills, writing skills, good phone skills, ability to use WordPerfect 5.1/6.0. Duration is 1 semester in fall, spring, or summer. Unpaid. Open to college juniors and seniors or graduate students working for academic credit. ▶ *1 electronic media engineering intern:* responsibilities include learning the various computer-controlled systems that operate video, audio, intercom, and electronic message systems throughout the First Union Center; assisting the engineer in event set-up and troubleshooting. Candidates should have analytical skills, college courses in field, computer skills, editing skills, basic understanding of electronic circuit theory including video and audio system signals, component-level understanding of DC electronic (helpful). Duration is 1 semester in fall, spring, or summer. Unpaid. Open to 2nd-year technical school students with audio and television major leading to an associate degree or equivalent. ▶ *1 event production intern:* responsibilities include participating in event-related duties, assisting with coordination of amenities for First Union Center tours, assisting event production staff on various projects, and assisting with coordination of vendor functions. Candidates should have office skills, oral communication skills, strong interpersonal skills, written communication skills, ability to use word processing and spreadsheet applications (Microsoft Word, WordPerfect, Lotus 123, and Excel), good phone skills, and the ability to meet deadlines. Duration is 1 semester in fall, spring, or summer. Unpaid. Open to college juniors and seniors or graduate students working for academic credit. ▶ *1 event public relations intern:* responsibilities include organizing photo files and show files, handling event-related correspondence, helping to plan and execute publicity events, assisting with mailings, and providing support during events. Candidates should have college courses in field, oral communication skills, organizational skills, writing skills, good phone skills, ability to use WordPerfect 5.1/6.0, experience with database management (preferred). Duration is 1 semester in fall, spring, or summer. Unpaid. Open to college juniors and seniors or graduate students working for academic credit. ▶ *2 event services interns:* responsibilities include assisting in promotion of shows and sporting events to group customers, helping to promote and implement the Public Tour program, processing orders, and customer service. Candidates should have ability to work with others, office skills, oral communication skills, organizational skills, written communication skills, ability to use WordPerfect and Lotus software. Duration is 1 semester in fall, spring, or summer. Unpaid. Open to college juniors and seniors or graduate students working for academic credit. ▶ *2 graphic services interns:* responsibilities include assisting in design, layout, and production of printed materials; maintaining computer files; assisting with production of game-day materials; and participating in brainstorming on proposed graphics projects. Candidates should have college courses in field, knowledge of field, plan to pursue career in field, strong Macintosh computer skills, working knowledge of QuarkXpress, Illustrator, and PhotoShop. Duration is 1 semester in fall, spring, or summer. Unpaid. Open to college juniors and seniors or graduate students working for academic credit. ▶ *1 human resources intern:* responsibilities include working with recruiter to promote and administer the internship program, assisting in orientation of interns, maintaining internship files, and screening incoming employment applications and mailing responses to applicants. Candidates should have oral communication skills, organizational skills, self-motivation, written communication skills, ability to use Microsoft Word (or WordPerfect), Excel, and cc:Mail. Duration is 1 semester in fall, spring, or summer. Unpaid. Open to college juniors and seniors or graduate students working for academic credit. ▶ *2 marketing interns:* responsibilities include promoting shows and sporting events; assisting the security, operations, and promotions departments on days of events, creating post-event marketing summaries, and performing demographic and psychographic market research.

Comcast (continued)

Candidates should have college courses in field, oral communication skills, research skills, self-motivation, written communication skills, basic knowledge of word processing and spreadsheet applications, computer graphics experience (helpful). Duration is 1 semester in fall, spring, or summer. Unpaid. Open to college juniors and seniors or graduate students working for academic credit. ▶ *2 operations interns:* responsibilities include assisting with event-related activities, assisting with changeover tasks, and helping to create a production book concerning events held at the First Union Spectrum/Center. Candidates should have analytical skills, knowledge of field, self-motivation, strong interpersonal skills, ability to use WordPerfect, Microsoft Word, and Excel, ability to adapt to a wide variety of projects, ability to meet deadlines. Duration is 1 semester in fall, spring, or summer. Unpaid. Open to college juniors and seniors or graduate students working for academic credit. ▶ *1 tour guide intern:* responsibilities include leading individuals and groups on informative tours of the First Union Center, providing office support, scheduling tours, telemarketing prospective clients, and assisting in marketing and promoting tours. Candidates should have ability to work independently, oral communication skills, self-motivation, strong interpersonal skills, willingness to work some weekends, ability to speak to large groups and to do extensive walking, ability to use WordPerfect and Lotus software. Duration is 1 semester in fall, spring, or summer. Unpaid. Open to college juniors and seniors or graduate students working for academic credit.

Benefits Formal training, names of contacts, on-the-job training, opportunity to attend seminars/workshops, possible full-time employment, willing to act as a professional reference, willing to complete paperwork for educational credit.

Contact Write, call, fax, e-mail, or through World Wide Web site Curt A. Wilson, Human Resources Recruiter, 3601 South Broad Street, Philadelphia, Pennsylvania 19148-5290. Phone: 215-389-9502. Fax: 215-389-9413. E-mail: cwilson@comcast-spectacor.com. In-person interview required. Applicants must submit a formal organization application, resume, letter of recommendation, cover letter indicating reasons for choosing internship and the qualities or attributes that will help make a contribution, faculty recommendation form (sent with application). Applications are accepted continuously. World Wide Web: http://www.comcast-spectacor.com.

COTUIT ATHLETIC ASSOCIATION
PO Box 411
Cotuit, Massachusetts 02635-0411

General Information Sponsor of Cotuit Kettleer Baseball team; manages and maintains Lowell Park facility; sponsors youth baseball clinics and teams; conducts nonprofit fund-raising. Established in 1950. Number of employees: 16. Unit of Cape Cod Baseball League, Barnstable Village, Massachusetts. Number of internship applications received each year: 40.

Internships Available ▶ *1 announcer intern:* responsibilities include announcing players and recorded information from announcers book and assisting in preparing announcers book. Candidates should have ability to work independently, ability to work with others, knowledge of field, oral communication skills, organizational skills, personal interest in the field. Duration is mid-June through August 15. Unpaid. Open to high school students, recent high school graduates, college freshmen, college sophomores, college juniors, college seniors, recent college graduates. ▶ *4 game day interns:* responsibilities include assisting with game day activities including statistical sheets, raffles, counting and recording money, and putting up and taking down sponsor banners; assisting with public relations. Candidates should have ability to work independently, ability to work with others, organizational skills, personal interest in the field. Duration is mid-June through August 15. Unpaid. Open to high school students, recent high school graduates, college freshmen, college sophomores, college juniors, college seniors, recent college graduates. ▶ *1 photographer intern:* responsibilities include taking game day and special event photos. Candidates should have ability to work independently, ability to work with others, knowledge of field, personal interest in the field. Duration is mid-June through August 15. Unpaid.

Open to high school students, recent high school graduates, college sophomores, college juniors, college seniors, recent college graduates, graduate students. ▶ *1 scoreboard operator.* Candidates should have ability to work independently, ability to work with others, knowledge of field, personal interest in the field. Duration is mid-June through August 15. Unpaid. Open to high school students, recent high school graduates, college freshmen, college sophomores, college juniors, college seniors, recent college graduates. International applications accepted.

Benefits Housing at a cost, on-the-job training, willing to act as a professional reference, willing to complete paperwork for educational credit, willing to provide letters of recommendation.

Contact Write or e-mail Clyde Takala, Game Day Coordinator, PO Box 1987, Cotuit 02635-1987. Phone: 508-420-3473. Fax: 508-420-3473. E-mail: ttak@gis.net. In-person interview required. Applicants must submit a letter of interest, resume, two personal references. Application deadline: April 1. World Wide Web: http://www.kettleers.org.

DANCETODAY
528 Hennepin Avenue, Suite 510
Minneapolis, Minnesota 55403

General Information Dance support organization that builds audiences and visibility for dance. Established in 2002. Number of employees: 4. Number of internship applications received each year: 10.

Internships Available ▶ *Assistant to the communications director:* responsibilities include assisting with publicity and press/artist/community relations; researching local media; helping with publications and Web site; working on other projects as needed. Candidates should have editing skills, organizational skills, personal interest in the field, self-motivation, strong interpersonal skills, written communication skills. Duration is flexible. Unpaid. Open to high school seniors, recent high school graduates, college freshmen, college sophomores, college juniors, college seniors, recent college graduates, graduate students, law students, law school graduates, career changers, individuals reentering the workforce. ▶ *Assistants to community development manager:* responsibilities include assisting with community and artist relations; helping coordinate residency activities; helping research communities; working on other projects as needed. Candidates should have organizational skills, personal interest in the field, research skills, self-motivation, strong interpersonal skills, written communication skills. Duration is flexible. Unpaid. Open to high school seniors, recent high school graduates, college freshmen, college sophomores, college juniors, college seniors, recent college graduates, graduate students, law students, career changers, individuals reentering the workforce. ▶ *Intern assistants to the executive director:* responsibilities include assisting with grant writing and research into funding opportunities, helping prepare final reports, assisting with board meetings and relations, and working on other projects as needed. Candidates should have organizational skills, personal interest in the field, research skills, self-motivation, strong interpersonal skills, written communication skills. Duration is flexible. Unpaid. Open to high school seniors, recent high school graduates, college freshmen, college sophomores, college juniors, college seniors, recent college graduates, graduate students, law students, law school graduates, career changers, individuals reentering the workforce. International applications accepted.

Benefits Names of contacts, on-the-job training, opportunity to attend seminars/workshops, possible full-time employment, willing to complete paperwork for educational credit, willing to provide letters of recommendation.

Contact Write, call, fax, or e-mail Sandra Sullivan, Director of Communications. Phone: 612-340-1900. Fax: 612-340-9919. E-mail: info@dancetoday.org. In-person interview recommended (telephone interview accepted). Applicants must submit a letter of interest, resume, two personal references. Applications are accepted continuously. World Wide Web: http://www.dancetoday.org.

DELMARVA SHOREBIRDS
6400 Hobbs Road
Salisbury, Maryland 21804

General Information Minor league baseball team affiliated with Baltimore Orioles. Established in 1995. Number of employees: 91. Unit of Comcast, Philadelphia, Pennsylvania. Number of internship applications received each year: 300.

Internships Available ▶ *Graphic design interns:* responsibilities include working with marketing director to create marketing and game-day pieces as needed, 4-color art, video board slides; assisting in production and finishing of game and event-related materials; performing other duties as assigned. Candidates should have ability to work independently, ability to work with others, oral communication skills, organizational skills, personal interest in the field, strong leadership ability, writing skills, knowledge of Quark Xpress, PhotoShop, and Illustrator (necessary), animation experience (a plus), ability to work night and weekend slides. Duration is 1 semester. Unpaid. ▶ *Marketing and events interns:* responsibilities include working with director of marketing on implementation of corporate marketing strategy; includes media campaigns, implementation of fan survey system, involvement with mascot and community performances, radio, print and television ads, coordination of special events and game-day events. Candidates should have ability to work independently, computer skills, oral communication skills, organizational skills, personal interest in the field, self-motivation, strong interpersonal skills, strong leadership ability, writing skills, customer service background, ability to work nights and weekends. Duration is 1 semester. Unpaid. ▶ *Public relations interns:* responsibilities include working with PR director and marketing director in all aspects of promoting game and events at the park; creating press releases, writing articles, working with media, and keeping game statistics. Candidates should have ability to work independently, computer skills, oral communication skills, organizational skills, personal interest in the field, self-motivation, strong interpersonal skills, strong leadership ability, writing skills, major in public relations, communications or journalism, ability to work nights and weekends. Duration is 1 semester. Unpaid. Open to college juniors, college seniors, recent college graduates, graduate students, must be working for academic credits.

Benefits Formal training, on-the-job training, opportunity to attend seminars/workshops, possible full-time employment, willing to act as a professional reference, willing to complete paperwork for educational credit.

Contact Write, call, fax, e-mail, or through World Wide Web site Curt A. Wilson, Recruiter, Human Resources, 3601 South Broad Street, Philadelphia 19148-5290. Phone: 215-389-9502. Fax: 215-389-9413. E-mail: cwilson@comcast-spectacor.com. Telephone interview required. Applicants must submit a formal organization application, letter of interest, resume, writing sample, letter of recommendation. Applications are accepted continuously. World Wide Web: http://www.dshorebirds.com.

DIXON PLACE
258 Bowery, 2nd Floor
New York, New York 10012

General Information Organization that nurtures theater, performance, dance, and literary artists by encouraging the development of new work and assists emerging and established artists in exploring the creative process by providing a safe, supportive environment. Established in 1986. Number of employees: 10. Number of internship applications received each year: 50.

Internships Available ▶ *1 administrative intern:* responsibilities include preparing monthly calendars, handling press listings and press releases, updating the mailing list, scheduling artists' rehearsal times, and box office management. Candidates should have ability to work independently, computer skills, office skills, personal interest in the field, self-motivation, strong interpersonal skills. Duration is minimum of 3 months. $75–$100 per week. ▶ *1 administrative/artistic intern:* responsibilities include preparing monthly calendars, press listings, and press releases; updating the mailing list; scheduling artists' rehearsal time; reviewing submissions; correspondence with artists; house management; and archiving past-performances. Candidates should have computer

skills, experience in the field, oral communication skills, self-motivation, strong interpersonal skills. Duration is minimum of 3 months. $75–$100 per week. ▶ *1 technical intern:* responsibilities include providing technical assistance for artists, setting up light, sound, and video; working the box office, opening and closing the theater, videotaping performances, and operating sound and light during performances. Candidates should have ability to work independently, experience in the field, oral communication skills, organizational skills, self-motivation, strong interpersonal skills. Duration is minimum of 3 months. $75–$100 per week. Open to college sophomores, college juniors, college seniors, recent college graduates, graduate students, career changers. International applications accepted.

Benefits On-the-job training, opportunity to attend seminars/workshops, willing to complete paperwork for educational credit, willing to provide letters of recommendation.

Contact Write, call, fax, e-mail, or through World Wide Web site Ms. Ellie Covan, Executive Director. Phone: 212-219-0736. Fax: 212-219-0761. E-mail: contact@dixonplace.org. In-person interview recommended (telephone interview accepted). Applicants must submit a letter of interest, resume. Application deadline: April 15 for summer, August 1 for fall, December 1 for winter/spring. World Wide Web: http://www.dixonplace.org.

ELITE MODEL MANAGEMENT, CHICAGO
58 West Huron
Chicago, Illinois 60610

General Information Model management. Established in 1982. Number of employees: 40. Unit of Elite Model Management, New York, New York. Number of internship applications received each year: 100.

Internships Available ▶ *3–5 management assistants:* responsibilities include office duties including filing, fax, phone coverage, and assisting model bookers. Candidates should have ability to work independently, computer skills, office skills, oral communication skills, organizational skills, personal interest in the field, self-motivation, strong interpersonal skills, writing skills. Duration is 2-4 months (flexible). Unpaid. Open to recent high school graduates, college freshmen, college sophomores, college juniors, college seniors, recent college graduates.

Benefits On-the-job training, willing to act as a professional reference, willing to complete paperwork for educational credit, willing to provide letters of recommendation.

Contact Write or fax Shannon E. Hill, New Faces Agent. Fax: 312-943-2590. E-mail: shill@elitechicago.com. No phone calls. Applicants must submit a letter of interest, resume, interview after review of resume. Applications are accepted continuously. World Wide Web: http://www.elitechicago.com.

FREDERICK KEYS
3201 Design Road
Frederick, Maryland 21703

General Information Minor league baseball team affiliated with Baltimore Orioles. Established in 1989. Number of employees: 22. Unit of Comcast, Philadelphia, Pennsylvania. Number of internship applications received each year: 300.

Internships Available ▶ *Box office management trainees:* responsibilities include assisting box office manager in all areas of ticket operations; data entry; processing payments; building accounts; conducting mailings and updating season ticket holders; creating literature; ticket sales promotions; and other special interest projects as needed. Candidates should have ability to work independently, computer skills, office skills, oral communication skills, organizational skills, personal interest in the field, self-motivation, strong interpersonal skills, writing skills, ability to work night and weekends, customer service background (preferred). Duration is 1 semester. Unpaid. ▶ *Group event interns:* responsibilities include customer service; game day and event preparation; assistance with game day reports and mailings; and performing other duties as assigned. Candidates should have ability to work independently, ability to work with others, computer skills, oral communication skills, organizational skills, personal interest in the field, self-motivation, strong leadership ability, writing skills, ability to work nights and weekends, enthusiasm with a desire to

work hard. Duration is 1 semester. Unpaid. ▶ *Public relations management trainees:* responsibilities include assisting the public relations department with the Keys for Reading Program, Junior Keys Program, and articles for Keys souvenir program; game day duties and special promotional projects as assigned; and assisting in advertising and printing. Candidates should have ability to work independently, computer skills, oral communication skills, organizational skills, personal interest in the field, self-motivation, strong interpersonal skills, strong leadership ability, writing skills, ability to work nights and weekends. Duration is 1 semester. Unpaid. Open to college juniors, college seniors, recent college graduates, graduate students, must be working for academic credits.
Benefits Formal training, on-the-job training, opportunity to attend seminars/workshops, possible full-time employment, willing to act as a professional reference, willing to complete paperwork for educational credit.
Contact Write, call, fax, e-mail, or through World Wide Web site Curt A. Wilson, Recruiter, Human Resources, 3601 South Broad Street, Philadelphia 19148-5290. Phone: 215-389-9502. Fax: 215-389-9413. E-mail: cwilson@comcast-spectacor.com. In-person interview required. Applicants must submit a formal organization application, letter of interest, resume, writing sample, personal reference, letter of recommendation. Applications are accepted continuously. World Wide Web: http://www.frederickkeys.com.

GREER LANGE TALENT AGENCY
40 Lloyd Avenue, Suite 104
Malvern, Pennsylvania 19355

General Information Full-service talent agency representing union and non-union actors, models, and extras. Established in 1986. Number of employees: 4. Number of internship applications received each year: 100.
Internships Available ▶ *1–3 talent agency interns:* responsibilities include photo scanning/digitizing, assisting in talent booking activities, updating Web site content, talent relations/service, and general office assistance. Candidates should have ability to work independently, ability to work with others, oral communication skills, organizational skills, personal interest in the field, strong computer skills in photo software (preferred), must have car. Duration is year-round. $10 per day for travel. Open to high school students, recent high school graduates, college freshmen, college sophomores, college juniors, college seniors, recent college graduates, graduate students, career changers. International applications accepted.
Benefits On-the-job training, possible full-time employment, willing to act as a professional reference, willing to complete paperwork for educational credit, willing to provide letters of recommendation, free lunches.
Contact E-mail Stacy Bell, Vice President, Sales and Marketing. Fax: 610-889-3097. E-mail: info@greerlange.com. No phone calls. In-person interview required. Applicants must submit a letter of interest, resume, two personal references. Applications are accepted continuously. World Wide Web: http://www.greerlange.com.

GUS GIORDANO JAZZ DANCE CHICAGO
614 Davis Street
Evanston, Illinois 60201

General Information Nonprofit American jazz dance company that tours internationally and nationally and offers local performances in the Chicago area. Established in 1962. Number of employees: 12. Number of internship applications received each year: 5.
Internships Available ▶ *1–2 office interns:* responsibilities include word processing, writing press releases, dancers' biographies and other marketing material; assisting with grant writing; providing research assistance; and performing general administration work. Candidates should have ability to work independently, ability to work with others, computer skills, office skills, oral communication skills, written communication skills. Duration is 2–12 months. Unpaid. Open to college freshmen, college sophomores, college

juniors, college seniors, recent college graduates, individuals reentering the workforce. International applications accepted.
Benefits On-the-job training, willing to act as a professional reference, willing to complete paperwork for educational credit, willing to provide letters of recommendation.
Contact Write, fax, or e-mail Ben Hodge, Executive Director. Fax: 847-866-9228. E-mail: ggjdc@giordanojazzdance.com. No phone calls. In-person interview recommended (telephone interview accepted). Applicants must submit a letter of interest, resume, two personal references. Applications are accepted continuously.

THE HOUSE FOUNDATION FOR THE ARTS
306 West 38th Street, #401
New York, New York 10018

General Information Foundation that works specifically to raise funds and manage the artistic career of Meredith Monk. Established in 1968. Number of employees: 4. Number of internship applications received each year: 10.
Internships Available ▶ *1–2 archivists:* responsibilities include organizing archive of theatrical, film, opera, dance, and music materials. Candidates should have ability to work independently, computer skills, office skills, organizational skills, personal interest in the field, writing skills. Duration is 3–6 months. Unpaid. ▶ *1–2 assistants to the company manager:* responsibilities include assisting in the production of tours and the New York season, booking, travel arrangements, pre-production, and maintenance of all elements. Candidates should have experience in the field, oral communication skills, organizational skills, personal interest in the field, self-motivation, strong interpersonal skills. Duration is 3–6 months. Unpaid. ▶ *1–3 assistants to the development director:* responsibilities include grant research and fund-raising. Candidates should have ability to work independently, editing skills, office skills, plan to pursue career in field, research skills, writing skills. Duration is 3–6 months. Unpaid. ▶ *1–3 general administrative interns:* responsibilities include answering phones and maintaining correspondence. Candidates should have ability to work independently, computer skills, office skills, organizational skills, personal interest in the field, strong interpersonal skills. Duration is 3–6 months. Unpaid. Open to college juniors, college seniors, recent college graduates, graduate students.
Benefits Possible full-time employment, willing to complete paperwork for educational credit, willing to provide letters of recommendation.
Contact Write or fax Ms. Barbara Dufty, Managing Director. Fax: 212-904-1305. E-mail: monk@meredithmonk.org. In-person interview required. Applicants must submit a letter of interest, resume. Applications are accepted continuously. World Wide Web: http://www.meredithmonk.org.

THE JOHN F. KENNEDY CENTER FOR THE PERFORMING ARTS
2700 F Street, NW
Washington, District of Columbia 20566

General Information National performing arts center. Established in 1971. Number of employees: 1,000. Number of internship applications received each year: 700.
Internships Available ▶ *1 Alliance for Arts Education intern:* responsibilities include assisting with national recognition programs for outstanding school administrators and local school boards, administering fellowships, and working with a national network of state organizations. Candidates should have computer skills, knowledge of field, oral communication skills, strong interpersonal skills, writing skills. Duration is 3–4 months. $800 per month. Open to college juniors, college seniors, recent college graduates, graduate students. ▶ *1 American College Theater Festival intern:* responsibilities include assisting with technical coordination of ACTF national festival, responding to telephone inquiries, updating mailing lists, and handling national festival ticket distribution. Candidates should have computer skills, oral communication skills, personal interest in the field, plan to pursue career in field, strong interpersonal skills, writing skills. Duration is 3–4 months. $800 per month. Open to college juniors, college seniors, recent college graduates, graduate students. ▶ *1 Arts Edge intern:* responsibili-

ties include assisting director and staff with research, collection, and organization of information to be disseminated through the Arts Edge Web site. Candidates should have computer skills, knowledge of field, oral communication skills, strong interpersonal skills, writing skills. Duration is 3–4 months. $800 per month. Open to college juniors, college seniors, recent college graduates, graduate students. ▶ *1 Friends of Kennedy Center intern:* responsibilities include working in special events production, volunteer management, retail management, visitor services, and community relations. Candidates should have computer skills, oral communication skills, personal interest in the field, strong interpersonal skills. Duration is 3–4 months. $800 per month. Open to college juniors, college seniors, recent college graduates, graduate students. ▶ *2–4 National Symphony Orchestra interns:* responsibilities include assisting with organization of special concerts for young people, administering training programs and competitions for high school musicians, fielding phone inquiries, researching programming issues, working with volunteers, and compiling material for NSO education programs. Candidates should have computer skills, knowledge of field, oral communication skills, plan to pursue career in field, strong interpersonal skills, writing skills. Duration is 3–4 months. $800 per month. Open to college juniors, college seniors, recent college graduates. ▶ *2 advertising interns:* responsibilities include providing administrative support and dealing with advertising trafficking and placements, broadcast production, editing, and promotional event planning. Candidates should have computer skills, knowledge of field, oral communication skills, plan to pursue career in field, writing skills. Duration is 3–4 months. $800 per month. Open to college juniors, college seniors, recent college graduates, graduate students. ▶ *3–4 development interns:* responsibilities include assisting in administration of fund-raising campaigns and working on project research, special projects, membership services, grants, sponsorship, corporate fund, and Circle Fund. Candidates should have computer skills, oral communication skills, organizational skills, strong interpersonal skills, writing skills. Duration is 3–4 months. $800 per month. Open to college juniors, college seniors, recent college graduates, graduate students. ▶ *6–8 education department interns:* responsibilities include assisting with the administration of arts education events and evaluating programs, workshops, discussions, master classes, and performances. Candidates should have computer skills, oral communication skills, personal interest in the field, plan to pursue career in field, strong interpersonal skills, writing skills. Duration is 3–4 months. $800 per month. Open to college juniors, college seniors, recent college graduates, graduate students. ▶ *1 production intern:* responsibilities include serving as a production or design assistant for shows and events in the Center's six theater and non-theater spaces. Candidates should have computer skills, knowledge of field, oral communication skills, personal interest in the field, strong interpersonal skills. Duration is 3–4 months. $800 per month. Open to college juniors, college seniors, recent college graduates, graduate students. ▶ *1–2 programming interns:* responsibilities include contract preparation, supernumerary coordination, artist hospitality, and special performance event management. Candidates should have ability to work independently, computer skills, organizational skills, plan to pursue career in field, strong interpersonal skills, writing skills. Duration is 3–4 months. $800 per month. Open to college juniors, college seniors, recent college graduates, graduate students. ▶ *1 special events intern:* responsibilities include assisting with the planning and implementation of all special events including the Kennedy Center Honors, Spring Gala, and cast parties. Candidates should have knowledge of field, organizational skills, personal interest in the field, strong interpersonal skills, writing skills. Duration is 3–4 months. $800 per month. Open to college juniors, college seniors, recent college graduates, graduate students. ▶ *1 youth and family programs intern:* responsibilities include assisting with theater training program, contributing to audience and program development projects, supporting the artistic and production staff, acting as production interns by assisting the stage managers or design assistants, or working with the artistic and production staff. Candidates should have computer skills, knowledge of field, oral communication skills, plan to pursue career in field, writing skills. Duration is 3–4 months. $800 per month. Open to

college juniors, college seniors, recent college graduates, graduate students. International applications accepted.
Benefits Formal training, names of contacts, opportunity to attend seminars/workshops, willing to act as a professional reference, willing to complete paperwork for educational credit, willing to provide letters of recommendation, opportunity to attend performances.
Contact Write, call, e-mail, or through World Wide Web site Caitlin Albers, Internship Program Coordinator. Phone: 202-416-8821. Fax: 202-416-8853. E-mail: rcalbers@kennedy-center.org. Applicants must submit a formal organization application, letter of interest, resume, academic transcripts, two letters of recommendation, 1–3 page writing sample. Application deadline: March 1 for summer, June 15 for fall, November 1 for winter/spring. World Wide Web: http://www.kennedy-center.org.

MELLON ARENA
66 Mario Lemieux Place
Pittsburgh, Pennsylvania 15219

General Information Public sports and entertainment facility. Established in 1961. Number of employees: 400. Unit of SMG, Philadelphia, Pennsylvania. Number of internship applications received each year: 50.
Internships Available ▶ *2–4 marketing/group services interns:* responsibilities include preparing and implementing marketing plans for Mellon Arena events; preparing recaps of event sponsorships; maintaining client database; assisting with Web site; field group/corporate sales phone work. Candidates should have ability to work independently, computer skills, oral communication skills, organizational skills, research skills, strong interpersonal skills. Duration is May to August, September to December, or January to April. Position available as unpaid or paid. Open to college sophomores, college juniors, college seniors, recent college graduates, graduate students. International applications accepted.
Benefits Names of contacts, opportunity to attend seminars/workshops, possible full-time employment, willing to act as a professional reference, willing to complete paperwork for educational credit, willing to provide letters of recommendation.
Contact Write or fax Marketing Manager. Fax: 412-391-8454. No phone calls. In-person interview recommended (telephone interview accepted). Applicants must submit a letter of interest, resume. Applications are accepted continuously. World Wide Web: http://www.mellonarena.com.

METROPOLITAN OPERA GUILD EDUCATION DEPARTMENT
70 Lincoln Center Plaza
New York, New York 10023-6593

General Information Program dedicated to furthering music education in schools and communities across the nation through a variety of activities including school residencies, lecture series, backstage tours, multimedia resources, and special performances for students at the Metropolitan Opera House. Established in 1935. Number of employees: 9. Unit of Metropolitan Opera Guild, New York, New York. Number of internship applications received each year: 15.
Internships Available ▶ *2–4 interns:* responsibilities include performing office tasks, managing the box office, editing and producing study materials, and coordinating students in the Opera House. Candidates should have ability to work independently, computer skills, experience in the field, office skills, oral communication skills, plan to pursue career in field. Duration is 3 months minimum (15 hours minimum per week). $500 per duration of internship. Open to college freshmen, college sophomores, college juniors, college seniors, recent college graduates. International applications accepted.
Benefits Job counseling, on-the-job training, opportunity to attend seminars/workshops, willing to act as a professional reference, willing to complete paperwork for educational credit, willing to provide letters of recommendation, $500 stipend.
Contact Write, call, fax, e-mail, or through World Wide Web site Ms. Nevena Arizanovic, Program Coordinator, Urban Voices.

Metropolitan Opera Guild Education Department (continued)
Phone: 212-769-7027. Fax: 212-769-8519. E-mail: narizanovic@
operaed.org. In-person interview required. Applicants must submit
a letter of interest, resume, three letters of recommendation.
Application deadline: May 1 for summer, July 1 for fall, December
1 for spring. World Wide Web: http://www.operaed.org.

MILWAUKEE BREWERS BASEBALL CLUB
1 Brewers Way
Milwaukee, Wisconsin 53214

General Information Professional sports franchise. Established
in 1970. Number of employees: 90. Number of internship
applications received each year: 75.
Internships Available ▶ *2–5 media relations interns:* responsibilities include correspondence with fans, research projects, day-to-
day operations in media, and writing projects. Candidates should
have ability to work independently, computer skills, editing skills,
knowledge of field, research skills, writing skills. Duration is 3–4
months (year-round). Unpaid. Open to college sophomores, college juniors, college seniors, graduate students, only those earning college credit. International applications accepted.
Benefits Names of contacts, willing to act as a professional reference, willing to complete paperwork for educational credit, willing to provide letters of recommendation.
Contact Write, fax, or e-mail Jason Parry, Assistant Director, Media
Relations, 1 Brewers Way, Milwaukee, Wisconsin 53201-3099.
Phone: 414-902-4500. Fax: 414-902-4053. E-mail: jparry@
milwaukeebrewers.com. Telephone interview required. Applicants
must submit a letter of interest, resume, writing sample, letter of
recommendation. Application deadline: February 1 for summer,
August 1 for fall, December 1 for spring. World Wide Web: http://
www.milwaukeebrewers.com.

MISSOURI SYMPHONY SOCIETY
203 South 9th Street
Columbia, Missouri 65201

General Information Private nonprofit corporation dedicated
to bringing fine music to central Missouri, educating central
Missouri youth about music, and preserving and restoring the
historic Missouri Theatre. Established in 1970. Number of
employees: 4. Number of internship applications received each
year: 10.
Internships Available ▶ *1 marketing intern:* responsibilities include
assisting with corporate development and marketing of programs
of the professional Missouri Chamber Orchestra and the Historic
Missouri Theatre. Candidates should have computer skills, office
skills, oral communication skills, organizational skills, writing skills.
Duration is 10 weeks (summer, fall, or winter) or 9 months
(September to May). Position available as unpaid or paid. Open
to college freshmen, college sophomores, college juniors, college seniors, recent college graduates, graduate students, career
changers.
Benefits Possible full-time employment, willing to complete
paperwork for educational credit, willing to provide letters of
recommendation.
Contact Write, fax, or e-mail David A. White, III, Executive
Director. Fax: 573-449-4214. E-mail: daw3moss@socket.net. No
phone calls. In-person interview recommended (telephone interview
accepted). Applicants must submit a letter of interest, resume.
Application deadline: March 1 for summer, August 1 for fall,
November 1 for winter.

MUSIC MOUNTAIN INC.
PO Box 1739
Sharon, Connecticut 06069

General Information Showcase for string quartets and summer chamber music festival; presents 33 concerts from June
through September and offers 8 seminars. Established in 1930.
Internships Available ▶ *1 intern:* responsibilities include working in box office, ticket sales, press, publicity, and artist/seminar
participant relations. Candidates should have ability to work
independently, ability to work with others, must have own vehicle.
Duration is 3 months. $250 per week. Open to college freshmen,

college sophomores, college juniors, college seniors, graduate
students, career changers, individuals reentering the workforce.
Benefits Free housing, job counseling, names of contacts, opportunity to attend seminars/workshops, willing to provide letters of
recommendation, concerts.
Contact Write, call, fax, or e-mail Mr. Nicholas Gordon, President,
Board of Managers. Phone: 860-364-2080. Fax: 860-364-2090.
E-mail: ngordon@snet.net. In-person interview recommended
(telephone interview accepted). Application deadline: April 30
for summer. World Wide Web: http://www.musicmountain.org.

NATIONAL BASKETBALL ASSOCIATION
645 Fifth Avenue
New York, New York 10022

General Information Fully-integrated global sports marketing
and entertainment organization. Established in 1946. Number
of employees: 1,200. Number of internship applications received
each year: 2,000.
Internships Available ▶ *20–30 summer interns:* responsibilities
include working in various areas including television production,
finance, NBA photos, global merchandising, international public
relations, human resources, and events and attractions. Candidates
should have ability to work with others, computer skills, oral communication skills, organizational skills, self-motivation. Duration
is June to August. Salary competitive with sports and entertainment industries. Open to college sophomores, college juniors.
International applications accepted.
Benefits Formal training, job counseling, names of contacts,
on-the-job training, opportunity to attend seminars/workshops,
possible full-time employment, willing to act as a professional reference, willing to complete paperwork for educational credit, willing to provide letters of recommendation.
Contact Through World Wide Web site Karel Rhoades, Manager,
Recruiting and Staffing. No phone calls. Telephone interview
required. Applicants must submit a letter of interest, resume.
Application deadline: September 9. World Wide Web: http://www.
nba.com/help/jobs.html.

NATIONAL COLLEGIATE ATHLETIC ASSOCIATION
PO Box 6222
Indianapolis, Indiana 46206-6222

General Information Voluntary association of 1200 colleges and
universities, athletic conferences, and sports organizations devoted
to the sound administration of intercollegiate athletics. Number
of internship applications received each year: 150.
Internships Available ▶ *11 Ethnic Minority and Women's Enhancement Intern Program participants:* responsibilities include duties in
areas of championships, enforcement, education services, finance,
men's and women's basketball governance, and broadcasting/
branding and promotions. Candidates should have ability to work
with others, computer skills, oral communication skills, personal
interest in the field, plan to pursue career in field, written communication skills. Duration is 1 year (June-June, full-time). Paid.
Open to college seniors, recent college graduates, graduate
students, law students, career changers.
Benefits Health insurance, opportunity to attend seminars/
workshops, travel reimbursement, willing to act as a professional
reference.
Contact Write, call, fax, e-mail, or through World Wide Web site
Arthur J. Hightower, II, Assistant Director of Professional
Development. Phone: 317-917-6263. Fax: 317-917-6336. E-mail:
ahightower@ncaa.org. Applicants must submit a formal organization application, letter of interest, resume, academic transcripts,
three letters of recommendation, in-person interview (if selected).
Application deadline: February 1. World Wide Web: http://www.
ncaa.org.

NATIONAL DANCE EDUCATION ORGANIZATION
4948 St. Elmo Avenue, Suite 301
Bethesda, Maryland 20814

General Information National organization serving dance educators teaching Pre-K–12, higher education, private studios, professional preparation programs, and outreach programs of perform-

ing arts organizations; offers national/regional conferences, Journal of Dance Education, resources (books, CDs, videos), and technical assistance to individuals, organizations, and departments of education seeking to develop standards/guidelines for dance (content, curriculum, assessments, professional development, certification); membership is individual (professional, student, retiree), institutional, affiliate, or business/corporation. Established in 1997. Number of employees: 5. Number of internship applications received each year: 50.

Internships Available ▶ *2 arts administration/business interns:* responsibilities include helping coordinate 6 divisions (membership, finance, conference, publications and periodicals, grants, and programs); assisting in budget development and running a nonprofit business; liaison with national organizations in dance, arts, and education communities; attending national partnership meetings. Candidates should have experience in the field, oral communication skills, personal interest in the field, strong interpersonal skills, strong leadership ability, writing skills. Duration is 1–2 semesters. Unpaid. Open to college seniors, graduate students, law students. ▶ *2 grant procurement and implementation interns:* responsibilities include researching funding sources using electronic databases for Foundation Center and government publications; assisting with implementing any grant NDEO is supporting at national, state, and local levels. Candidates should have analytical skills, computer skills, knowledge of field, research skills, self-motivation, writing skills. Duration is 1–2 semesters. Position available as unpaid or paid. Open to college seniors, recent college graduates, graduate students, career changers. ▶ *1 marketing intern:* responsibilities include helping develop new markets and sustain current markets; coordinating activities with press and media; developing innovative ways to promote NDEO and dance education to public, educators and administrators. Candidates should have computer skills, oral communication skills, organizational skills, research skills, self-motivation, written communication skills. Duration is 15–30 weeks. Unpaid. Open to college seniors, recent college graduates, graduate students, career changers. ▶ *1 membership development intern:* responsibilities include developing new programs in membership; coordinating and implementing membership campaigns; interacting with members (new, renewals, and prospective); facilitating all membership services (individual and institutional); maintaining membership database. Candidates should have computer skills, oral communication skills, organizational skills, strong interpersonal skills, strong leadership ability, written communication skills. Duration is 15–30 weeks. Unpaid. Open to college seniors, recent college graduates, graduate students, career changers. ▶ *1 programs intern:* responsibilities include participating in initiating, implementing, and maintaining national, state and NDEO programs in dance and arts education. Candidates should have analytical skills, computer skills, organizational skills, strong interpersonal skills, strong leadership ability, writing skills. Duration is 15–30 weeks. Unpaid. Open to college juniors, college seniors, recent college graduates, graduate students. ▶ *2 research interns:* responsibilities include working with key personnel on defining research topic, tools, review of literature, design, methodology, conclusions and recommendations; monitoring initialization, collection, and analysis of data; writing drafts about research in process; seeking funding and support research (commissioned or RFPs). Candidates should have ability to work independently, analytical skills, college courses in field, organizational skills, research skills, writing skills. Duration is 1–2 semesters. Unpaid. Open to college seniors, recent college graduates, graduate students. ▶ *1 standards and curriculum intern:* responsibilities include assisting in the development of national, state, and local school district standards, curricular frameworks, and assessments for teachers and students in dance arts education; assisting in state certification programs. Candidates should have ability to work with others, analytical skills, knowledge of field, organizational skills, writing skills. Duration is 1–2 semesters. Unpaid. Open to college seniors, recent college graduates, graduate students, career changers.

Benefits Formal training, job counseling, names of contacts, on-the-job training, opportunity to attend seminars/workshops, possible full-time employment, willing to act as a professional reference, willing to complete paperwork for educational credit, willing to provide letters of recommendation.

Contact Write, call, fax, e-mail, or through World Wide Web site Dr. Jane Bonbright, Executive Director, 4948 St. Elmo Avenue, Suite 301. Phone: 301-657-2880. Fax: 301-657-2882. E-mail: info@ndeo.org. In-person interview recommended (telephone interview accepted). Applicants must submit a formal organization application, letter of interest, resume, two writing samples, personal reference, two letters of recommendation. Applications are accepted continuously. World Wide Web: http://www.ndeo.org.

NEW YORK JETS, LLC
1000 Fulton Avenue
Hempstead, New York 11550

General Information Professional football team. Established in 1959. Number of employees: 85. Number of internship applications received each year: 150.

Internships Available ▶ *30–35 Jets Fest interns:* responsibilities include running Jets Fest, an interactive football theme park; includes corporate sponsorships and interactions with sponsors and VIP's. Candidates should have personal interest in the field, self-motivation, strong interpersonal skills, strong leadership ability, major in marketing, sports management, or sports marketing. Duration is June to August. $200 per week or school credit. Open to college freshmen, college sophomores, college juniors, college seniors, recent college graduates, graduate students, law students. International applications accepted.

Benefits Free meals, names of contacts, willing to act as a professional reference, willing to complete paperwork for educational credit, willing to provide letters of recommendation.

Contact Write, fax, or e-mail Ken Zore, Special Events Assistant. Fax: 516-560-8296. E-mail: kzore@jets.nfl.com. No phone calls. In-person interview recommended (telephone interview accepted). Applicants must submit a resume. Application deadline: March 7. World Wide Web: http://www.newyorkjets.com.

NORFOLK CHAMBER MUSIC FESTIVAL–YALE SUMMER SCHOOL OF MUSIC
PO Box 208246
New Haven, Connecticut 06520-8246

General Information Festival that presents high-quality performances of chamber music and other classical music repertoire by world-renowned artists, while providing training and performance opportunities for young professional musicians. Established in 1941. Number of employees: 10. Unit of Yale University, New Haven, Connecticut. Number of internship applications received each year: 150.

Internships Available ▶ *1–2 administrative interns:* responsibilities include general administration and concert hall work. Candidates should have knowledge of field, organizational skills, personal interest in the field, self-motivation, strong interpersonal skills. Duration is June to August. Unpaid. Open to college juniors, college seniors, recent college graduates, career changers. ▶ *1 artist liaison/facilities manager:* responsibilities include handling artist relations and managing housekeepers, concessions workers, and parkers. Candidates should have plan to pursue career in field, self-motivation. Duration is June to August. $2750 per season. Open to recent college graduates, graduate students, career changers, individuals reentering the workforce. ▶ *1 associate administrator:* responsibilities include acting as artist liaison, scheduling, and office work. Candidates should have computer skills, knowledge of field, office skills, organizational skills, self-motivation, strong interpersonal skills. Duration is June to August. $2750 per season. Open to recent college graduates, graduate students, career changers, individuals reentering the workforce. ▶ *1 box office manager:* responsibilities include performing general box office duties. Candidates should have computer skills, organizational skills, self-motivation, strong interpersonal skills. Duration is June to August. $2750 per season. Open to recent college graduates, graduate students, career changers, individuals reentering the workforce. ▶ *1 concert hall manager:* responsibilities include scheduling and performing concert hall management duties. Candidates should have organizational skills, self-motivation, stage management experience. Duration is June to August. $2750 per season. Open to recent college graduates, graduate students, career changers,

individuals reentering the workforce. ▶ *1 music librarian:* responsibilities include assisting in the music library. Candidates should have knowledge of field, organizational skills, research skills, strong interpersonal skills. Duration is June to August. $2750 per season. Open to recent college graduates, graduate students, career changers, individuals reentering the workforce. ▶ *1 production intern:* responsibilities include concert production, recording, and festival organization. Candidates should have ability to work with others, organizational skills, personal interest in the field, self-motivation. Duration is June to August. Unpaid. Open to college juniors, college seniors, recent college graduates, career changers. ▶ *1 recording engineer:* responsibilities include recording all festival concerts. Candidates should have computer skills, self-motivation, strong leadership ability, recording experience and knowledge of equipment. Duration is June to August. $2750 per season. Open to recent college graduates, graduate students, career changers, individuals reentering the workforce. International applications accepted.
Benefits Formal training, free housing, free meals, names of contacts, opportunity to attend seminars/workshops, willing to act as a professional reference, willing to complete paperwork for educational credit, willing to provide letters of recommendation, opportunity to attend music performances.
Contact Write, fax, e-mail, or through World Wide Web site Festival Manager. Fax: 203-432-2136. E-mail: norfolk@yale.edu. No phone calls. In-person interview recommended (telephone interview accepted). Applicants must submit a letter of interest, resume, three personal references. Applications are accepted continuously. World Wide Web: http://www.yale.edu/norfolk.

OAKLAND A'S
7000 Coliseum Way
Oakland, California 94621

General Information Professional baseball club. Established in 1901. Number of employees: 400. Number of internship applications received each year: 300.
Internships Available ▶ *Interns:* responsibilities include working in various areas of the organization. Candidates should have personal interest in the field. Duration is 3-6 months (beginning in February/March). Stipend. Open to college freshmen, college sophomores, college juniors, college seniors, graduate students. International applications accepted.
Benefits On-the-job training, possible full-time employment, willing to act as a professional reference, willing to complete paperwork for educational credit, willing to provide letters of recommendation.
Contact Write, fax, or e-mail Intern Coordinator. Fax: 510-563-2397. E-mail: hr@oaklandathletics.com. No phone calls. In-person interview required. Applicants must submit a resume. Applications are accepted continuously. World Wide Web: http://www.oaklandathletics.com.

ORLANDO MAGIC
8701 Maitland Summit Boulevard
Orlando, Florida 32810

General Information Professional basketball team in the NBA. Established in 1989. Number of employees: 500. Number of internship applications received each year: 650.
Internships Available ▶ *30–40 interns:* responsibilities include duties in areas of basketball operations/coaching, broadcast/production, broadcast/radio, corporate sales, community relations, creative services, human resources, team marketing, team media, ticket sales, or team charities. Candidates should have ability to work independently, computer skills, knowledge of field, organizational skills, self-motivation, writing skills. Duration is 1 season (9 months) or 1 semester (4 months). Stipend of $232 bi-weekly. Open to college juniors, college seniors, graduate students, recent college graduates (within 18 months following graduation).
Benefits Job counseling, names of contacts, on-the-job training, opportunity to attend seminars/workshops, possible full-time

employment, willing to complete paperwork for educational credit, tickets to games, job-shadowing, athletic club access, free meals at games while working.
Contact Fax, e-mail, or through World Wide Web site Cindy Anderson, Human Resources Generalist. Fax: 407-916-2884. E-mail: canderson@rdvsports.com. No phone calls. Telephone interview required. Applicants must submit a formal organization application, resume, three writing samples, drug screen, background check required; in-person interview required for finalists; demo tape required for some positions; driver's license check required for some positions. Application deadline: February 20 for summer, June 30 for fall, October 31 for spring. World Wide Web: http://www.orlandomagic.com.

THE PENNSYLVANIA STATE UNIVERSITY WILKES-BARRE CAMPUS OF THE COMMONWEALTH COLLEGE
PO PSU
Lehman, Pennsylvania 18627-0217

General Information Athletic, intramural, and recreational sport department of major university. Established in 1916. Number of employees: 250.
Internships Available ▶ *1–2 assistant directors/assistant managers:* responsibilities include recreational programming/sports instruction (lifeguard certification and water safety instructor certification), management of lifeguards and swimming areas, and related lifeguard duties. Candidates should have computer skills, organizational skills, personal interest in the field, self-motivation, strong interpersonal skills, written communication skills. Duration is 1 semester at PSU; April-September at Valley Club. Position available as unpaid or at $6–$6.50 per hour. Open to college freshmen, college sophomores, college juniors, college seniors, recent college graduates, graduate students, career changers. ▶ *1–2 athletic, intramural, recreational sports assistants:* responsibilities include organizing and managing all responsibilities of a trained professional in the recreation and athletic field. Candidates should have oral communication skills, organizational skills, plan to pursue career in field, self-motivation, strong leadership ability, written communication skills. Duration is fall to spring; spring to summer; or summer. Position available as unpaid or at $6–$6.25 per hour. Open to college seniors, recent college graduates, graduate students. International applications accepted.
Benefits Formal training, housing at a cost, job counseling, meals at a cost, names of contacts, on-the-job training, possible full-time employment, willing to act as a professional reference, willing to complete paperwork for educational credit, willing to provide letters of recommendation, opportunity for experience at other facilities.
Contact Write, call, fax, or e-mail Jack Monick, Athletic Director/Manager. Phone: 570-675-9262. Fax: 570-675-9177. E-mail: jxm15@psu.edu. In-person interview recommended (telephone interview accepted). Applicants must submit a formal organization application, letter of interest, resume, academic transcripts, two personal references, two letters of recommendation, first aid/CPR, Water Safety, Lifesaving certifications or recreation degree. Application deadline: March 1 for summer, July 1 for fall, November 15 for spring. World Wide Web: http://http://www.wb.psu.edu/.

PGA TOUR, INC.
100 PGA Tour Boulevard
Ponte Vedra Beach, Florida 32082

General Information Professional Golf Sports Association supporting pro golfers on three tours: PGA Tour, Champions Tour, Nationwide Tour; manages over 130 tournaments worldwide. Established in 1968. Number of employees: 550. Number of internship applications received each year: 175.
Internships Available ▶ *3–4 communications interns:* responsibilities include working with communications department staff; research; assisting in press releases; working with sports media; assisting in developing minority intern program yearbook and application. Candidates should have ability to work independently, analytical skills, computer skills, editing skills, office skills, oral communication skills, organizational skills, research skills, self-

motivation, strong interpersonal skills, writing skills. Duration is 9 weeks. $9 per hour. Open to college juniors, college seniors, graduate students, law students. ▶ *4–6 corporate marketing interns:* responsibilities include assisting in marketing proposals and promoting to corporate clients; tracking marketing results; attending client meetings; and working with tournaments and sponsors. Candidates should have ability to work independently, analytical skills, computer skills, oral communication skills, research skills, self-motivation, strong interpersonal skills, written communication skills. Duration is 9 weeks. $9 per hour. Open to college juniors, college seniors, graduate students, law students. ▶ *Up to 5 event promotions interns:* responsibilities include working for a sister company, MBNA and AJGA, and traveling to regional golf events. Candidates should have ability to work independently, computer skills, oral communication skills, self-motivation, strong interpersonal skills. Duration is 9–13 weeks. $9 per hour. Open to college juniors, college seniors, graduate students, law students. ▶ *1 human resources assistant:* responsibilities include administration of minority intern program, job descriptions, special HR projects, training, and recruitment. Candidates should have ability to work independently, analytical skills, computer skills, office skills, oral communication skills, organizational skills, personal interest in the field, research skills, self-motivation, strong interpersonal skills, strong leadership ability, writing skills. Duration is 9 weeks. $9 per hour. Open to college juniors, college seniors, graduate students, law students. ▶ *2 information systems interns:* responsibilities include help-desk duties, troubleshooting problems, answering phones, and on-site roll out of new computer software and hardware. Candidates should have ability to work independently, analytical skills, computer skills, knowledge of field, office skills, oral communication skills, organizational skills, personal interest in the field, self-motivation, strong interpersonal skills, written communication skills. Duration is 9 weeks. $9 per hour. Open to college juniors, college seniors, graduate students. ▶ *2 television production interns:* responsibilities include working with PGA Tour productions, editing, logging tapes, assisting production staff with post-event shows; may work with TV broadcast staff, analyzing program ratings domestically and internationally. Candidates should have ability to work independently, analytical skills, computer skills, editing skills, knowledge of field, office skills, oral communication skills, organizational skills, research skills, self-motivation, strong interpersonal skills, strong leadership ability, writing skills. Duration is 9 weeks. $9 per hour. Open to college juniors, college seniors, graduate students. ▶ *6–8 tournament operations interns:* responsibilities include working with sponsors, setting up golf operations, helping with managing the events, scoring, working with volunteers; based either at specific tournament or traveling on a weekly basis. Candidates should have ability to work independently, ability to work with others, office skills, oral communication skills, plan to pursue career in field, self-motivation, strong leadership ability, written communication skills, knowledge or experience in playing golf (preferred). Duration is 9–13 weeks. $9 per hour. Open to college juniors, college seniors, graduate students, law students.

Benefits Housing at a cost, job counseling, names of contacts, on-the-job training, opportunity to attend seminars/workshops, possible full-time employment, travel reimbursement, willing to act as a professional reference, willing to complete paperwork for educational credit, willing to provide letters of recommendation, temporary membership to golf course.

Contact Write or e-mail Mike Cooney, Director, Human Resources. Phone: 904-273-3520. Fax: 904-273-3588. E-mail: mip@mail.pgatour.com. In-person interview recommended (telephone interview accepted). Applicants must submit a formal organization application, letter of interest, resume, academic transcripts, writing sample, three personal references. Application deadline: March 15 for summer, May 25 for fall. World Wide Web: http://www.pgatour.com.

PHILADELPHIA 76ERS
3601 South Broad Street
Philadelphia, Pennsylvania 19148-5290

General Information Professional basketball team playing in the National Basketball Association. Unit of Comcast, Philadelphia, Pennsylvania. Number of internship applications received each year: 250.

Internships Available ▶ *2 box office interns:* responsibilities include processing contracts, processing and mailing season tickets and game-day tickets, and handling customer questions and complaints. Candidates should have office skills, oral communication skills, organizational skills, strong interpersonal skills, ability to use Windows 95 programs such as Microsoft Excel and WordPerfect. Duration is 1 semester in spring or fall. Unpaid. ▶ *1 community relations intern:* responsibilities include handling phone inquiries; maintaining database files; ordering merchandise for charitable donations; assisting staff with correspondence and special projects; and responding to requests for autographed items, financial donations, tickets, and speaking appearances. Candidates should have oral communication skills, organizational skills, strong interpersonal skills, strong leadership ability, ability to use Microsoft Word, Excel, and WordPerfect (preferred). Duration is 1 semester in fall, spring, or summer. Unpaid. ▶ *2 fan relations interns:* responsibilities include responding to requests for fan club information, selling fan club memberships at home games, and tracking inventory and mailing for fan club. Candidates should have oral communication skills, organizational skills, strong interpersonal skills, ability to work game days outside normal business hours, proficiency in use of the Internet and Microsoft applications (Word, Access, and Excel). Duration is 1 semester in fall or spring. Unpaid. ▶ *1 marketing intern:* responsibilities include following up on promotions/marketing events and advertising, updating the Web site, assisting the director of fan relations, and responding to customer phone inquiries. Candidates should have oral communication skills, strong interpersonal skills, written communication skills, ability to use Microsoft Office and the Internet, experience with PageMaker (desirable), ability to work some game nights and weekends. Duration is 1 semester in fall, spring, or summer. Unpaid. ▶ *1 operations intern:* responsibilities include handling phone inquiries and clerical tasks, assisting coaching and scouting staff, assisting with operation of scouting database, and helping with a variety of duties related to team practices and games. Candidates should have office skills, organizational skills, research skills, strong interpersonal skills, written communication skills, excellent phone skills, ability to use Microsoft Word and Excel. Duration is 1 semester in fall, spring, or summer. Unpaid. ▶ *1 promotions intern:* responsibilities include following up on event promotions and creating post-event marketing summaries, updating computer kiosks, assisting in game operations/promotional events, and scripting advertising that will appear on Arenavision and message boards. Candidates should have oral communication skills, organizational skills, strong interpersonal skills, written communication skills, ability to use Microsoft Office applications, WordPerfect, and Lotus 123, event production background (preferred). Duration is 1 semester in fall, spring, or summer. Unpaid. ▶ *1 public relations intern:* responsibilities include acting as liaison with media, attending home games (including weekends), assisting with publications, organizing team and individual photo files, organizing mass mailings, handling press clippings, and participating in a variety of public relations projects. Candidates should have editing skills, oral communication skills, organizational skills, strong interpersonal skills, writing skills, ability to use PageMaker, MS Word, WordPerfect, or Lotus 123 software. Duration is 1 semester in fall, spring, or summer. Unpaid. ▶ *1–2 sales interns:* responsibilities include assisting in mass marketing campaigns and in prospecting leads for corporate sales managers; coordinating trade shows, open houses, and off-site presentations; helping with clerical duties, customer service, and phone relations. Candidates should have oral communication skills, organizational skills, research skills, strong interpersonal skills, written communication skills, professional phone skills, attention to detail. Duration is 1 semester in fall, spring, or summer. Unpaid. ▶ *5 statistics interns:* responsibilities include recording, deciphering, and logging box scores; updating individual and team statistics as well

Philadelphia 76ers (continued)

as play-by-play records for 76ers and other NBA teams; and assisting staff on various projects. Candidates should have ability to work independently, computer skills, office skills, research skills, self-motivation, attention to detail and accuracy with numbers, interest in basketball statistics (preferred). Duration is 1 semester in fall, spring, or summer. Unpaid. Open to college juniors, college seniors, graduate students, must be working for academic credit. International applications accepted.

Benefits Names of contacts, on-the-job training, possible full-time employment, willing to complete paperwork for educational credit, excellent experience in the sports and entertainment industry.

Contact Write or through World Wide Web site Internship Program, Human Resources Department. In-person interview required. Applicants must submit a formal organization application, resume, cover letter indicating reasons for choosing a particular internship and the qualities/attributes that will help make a contribution, faculty recommendation form (sent with application). Application deadline: at least 2 months prior to intended start date. World Wide Web: http://www.comcast-spectacor.com.

PHILADELPHIA FLYERS
3601 South Broad Street
Philadelphia, Pennsylvania 19148-5290

General Information Professional hockey team in the National Hockey League. Unit of Comcast, Philadelphia, Pennsylvania.

Internships Available ▶ *1 community relations intern:* responsibilities include scheduling and arranging Flyers School program, corresponding with elementary schools, handling charitable donation requests, sorting and answering fan mail, scheduling birthday packages and get well cards, organizing and assisting in team/individual public appearances and promotional events, and data entry. Candidates should have oral communication skills, strong interpersonal skills, written communication skills, ability to use Microsoft Word, WordPerfect, Lotus 123, and Goldmine software (preferred). Duration is 1 semester in fall, spring, or summer. Unpaid. ▶ *1 fan development/youth hockey intern:* responsibilities include assisting fan development staff on research, design, and brainstorming for proposed projects; assisting in coordination of NHL BREAKOUT event, and performing minimal clerical duties. Candidates should have oral communication skills, written communication skills, interest in sports marketing and/or public relations, hockey background (preferred). Duration is June 1 through July 31. Unpaid. ▶ *2 public relations interns:* responsibilities include assisting with production and distribution of game notes for media, obtaining post-game quotes from participants, organizing publications database and photo files, assisting in coordination of NHL All-Star balloting, assisting with press releases and publicity events, and handling daily and weekly press clippings. Candidates should have oral communication skills, organizational skills, written communication skills, ability to use WordPerfect 5.1/6.0, ability with database management (preferred). Duration is 1 semester in fall, spring, or summer. Unpaid. ▶ *1 rink management and development intern:* responsibilities include assisting rink development staff with projects involving facility marketing, public relations, site analysis, and construction-related issues; helping with clerical duties as assigned. Candidates should have oral communication skills, written communication skills, interest in facility management, marketing, group sales and/or public relations, or construction management is preferred. Duration is May 1 through September 1. Unpaid. ▶ *1 sales/marketing intern:* responsibilities include assisting sales/marketing staff with projects and brainstorming sessions, responding to phone inquiries, helping with season ticket database mailings and game-day promotions, maintaining data files, and game-day customer relations. Candidates should have oral communication skills, organizational skills, written communication skills, ability to meet deadlines, friendly manner for customer service contacts, knowledge of WordPerfect (required) and Goldmine (helpful), ability to work game nights and game weekends. Duration is 1 semester in fall, spring, or summer. Unpaid. Open to college juniors, college seniors, graduate students, must be working for academic credit.

Benefits Names of contacts, possible full-time employment, willing to complete paperwork for educational credit, excellent experience in the sports and entertainment industry.

Contact Write or through World Wide Web site Internship Program, Human Resources Department. No phone calls. In-person interview required. Applicants must submit a formal organization application, resume, cover letter indicating reasons for choosing internship and qualities/attributes that will help make a contribution, faculty recommendation form (sent with application). Application deadline: at least 2 months prior to intended start date. World Wide Web: http://www.comcast-spectacor.com.

PHILADELPHIA PHANTOMS
3601 South Broad Street
Philadelphia, Pennsylvania 19148-5290

General Information The American Hockey League affiliate of the Philadelphia Flyers. Unit of Comcast, Philadelphia, Pennsylvania. Number of internship applications received each year: 200.

Internships Available ▶ *2 assistants to the ticketing manager:* responsibilities include assisting with phone sales, customer service inquiries, and internal data entry/accounting tasks; distributing Phantoms literature at selected events; and working on a variety of promotional projects. Candidates should have ability to work independently, oral communication skills, strong interpersonal skills, written communication skills, ability to use WordPerfect and Lotus 123 software. Duration is 1 semester in fall, spring, or summer. Unpaid. ▶ *1 marketing intern:* responsibilities include assisting staff with marketing projects, following up event promotions, and creating post-event marketing summaries; writing and handling press releases and statistics; assisting in day-of-event operations; and coordinating media publicity. Candidates should have oral communication skills, self-motivation, strong interpersonal skills, ability to use Word, WordPerfect, and Lotus 123. Duration is 1 semester in fall, spring, or summer. Unpaid. ▶ *1 public relations intern:* responsibilities include writing and handling press releases and statistics, corresponding with season ticket holders, assisting in advertising and printing, coordinating media publicity, and working on various projects with staff. Candidates should have editing skills, oral communication skills, writing skills, ability to use Word, WordPerfect, and Lotus 123. Duration is 1 semester in fall, spring, or summer. Unpaid. Open to college juniors, college seniors, graduate students, must be working for academic credit. International applications accepted.

Benefits Names of contacts, possible full-time employment, willing to complete paperwork for educational credit, excellent experience in the sports and entertainment industry.

Contact Write or through World Wide Web site Internship Program, Human Resources Department. In-person interview required. Applicants must submit a formal organization application, resume, cover letter indicating reasons for choosing a particular internship and the qualities or attributes that will help make a contribution, faculty recommendation form (sent with application). Application deadline: at least 2 months prior to intended start date. World Wide Web: http://www.comcast-spectacor.com.

POSEY SCHOOL OF DANCE, INC.
PO Box 254
Northport, New York 11768

General Information Community school of dance offering education and professional training. Established in 1953. Number of employees: 10. Number of internship applications received each year: 25.

Internships Available ▶ *1 studio manager.* Candidates should have oral communication skills, strong interpersonal skills, strong leadership ability, knowledge of dance techniques, ballet, and modern dance. Duration is 10–12 months. Position available as unpaid or at $100–$450 per month. Open to recent college graduates, graduate students, career changers. ▶ *1 summer studio manager.* Candidates should have oral communication skills, strong interpersonal skills, strong leadership ability, written communication skills, knowledge of dance techniques, ballet, and modern dance. Duration is 2–3 months. $250–$300 per duration of internship. Open to recent college graduates, graduate students, career changers, performers entering education field.

Benefits Formal training, job counseling, names of contacts, opportunity to attend seminars/workshops, possible full-time employment, willing to act as a professional reference, willing to complete paperwork for educational credit, willing to provide letters of recommendation, personal introductions.

Contact Write, call, or e-mail Ms. Elsa Posey, President. Phone: 631-757-2700. E-mail: eposey@optonline.net. Telephone interview required. Applicants must submit a letter of interest, resume. Applications are accepted continuously.

READING PHILLIES BASEBALL TEAM
1900 Centre Avenue
Reading, Pennsylvania 19605

General Information Minor league baseball team. Established in 1967. Number of employees: 400. Number of internship applications received each year: 200.

Internships Available ▶ *8–10 Reading Phillies junior associates:* responsibilities include sales, promotions, and customer service. Candidates should have ability to work with others, computer skills, oral communication skills, organizational skills, written communication skills, outgoing personality. Duration is 5–8 months. $600 per month with housing or $800 per month without housing. Open to college freshmen, college sophomores, college juniors, college seniors, recent college graduates, graduate students, law students, career changers. International applications accepted.

Benefits On-the-job training, opportunity to attend seminars/ workshops, possible full-time employment, willing to act as a professional reference, willing to provide letters of recommendation.

Contact Write, call, fax, e-mail, or through World Wide Web site Ashley Forlini, Director of Fan Development, PO Box 15050, Reading, Pennsylvania 19612-5050. Phone: 610-375-8469 Ext. 225. Fax: 610-373-5868. E-mail: ashley@readingphillies.com. In-person interview recommended (telephone interview accepted). Applicants must submit a resume. Application deadline: November 1. World Wide Web: http://www.readingphillies.com.

RICHARD FRANKEL PRODUCTIONS
729 7th Avenue, 12th Floor
New York, New York 10019

General Information Independent theatrical production and general management company that manages and produces plays and musicals and acts as general manager for other theatrical producers. Established in 1985. Number of employees: 60. Number of internship applications received each year: 1,000.

Internships Available ▶ *12–15 interns:* responsibilities include assignments under the supervision of the general manager of one show, compiling daily sales figures, assisting company managers at theater, providing production assistant services for shows in rehearsal and pre-production, and implementing grassroots marketing campaigns. Candidates should have ability to work independently, computer skills, oral communication skills, organizational skills, personal interest in the field, self-motivation, strong interpersonal skills, strong leadership ability, written communication skills. Duration is 3-5 months full-time (Monday through Friday 10 AM to 6 PM). Position available as unpaid or at $206 per week. Open to college freshmen, college sophomores, college juniors, college seniors, recent college graduates, graduate students, law students. International applications accepted.

Benefits Formal training, job counseling, names of contacts, on-the-job training, opportunity to attend seminars/workshops, possible full-time employment, willing to act as a professional reference, willing to complete paperwork for educational credit, willing to provide letters of recommendation.

Contact Write, fax, e-mail, or through World Wide Web site Lori Steiger-Perry, Internship Coordinator, 729 Seventh Avenue, 12th Floor, New York, New York 10019. Fax: 212-302-8094. E-mail: lori@rfpny.com. In-person interview required. Applicants must submit a letter of interest, resume, academic transcripts. Application deadline: April 15 for summer, July 15 for fall, November 15 for spring. World Wide Web: http://www.rfpny.com.

ROCKPORT CHAMBER MUSIC FESTIVAL
PO Box 312
Rockport, Massachusetts 01966

General Information Four-week festival in June-July presenting chamber music featuring nationally known groups. Established in 1982. Number of employees: 2. Number of internship applications received each year: 10.

Internships Available ▶ *1 summer intern/stage manager:* responsibilities include handling office, selling tickets, and assisting artistic director. Candidates should have ability to work with others, computer skills, knowledge of field, office skills, oral communication skills, personal interest in the field, self-motivation, ability to read music well. Duration is 5 weeks. $200 per week. Open to college freshmen, college sophomores, college juniors, college seniors, recent college graduates. International applications accepted.

Benefits Free housing, free meals, job counseling, names of contacts, willing to complete paperwork for educational credit, willing to provide letters of recommendation, opportunity to interact with musicians.

Contact Write, call, fax, e-mail, or through World Wide Web site Laura C. Tapley, General Manager. Phone: 978-548-7391. Fax: 978-546-7391. E-mail: rcmf.info@verizon.net. Telephone interview required. Applicants must submit a letter of interest, resume, two letters of recommendation. Application deadline: April 1. World Wide Web: http://www.rcmf.org.

SAN DIEGO PADRES BASEBALL CLUB
8880 Rio San Diego Drive, Suite 400
San Diego, California 92108

General Information Professional major league baseball club. Established in 1969. Number of employees: 160. Number of internship applications received each year: 250.

Internships Available ▶ *5–8 interns.* Candidates should have ability to work independently, analytical skills, computer skills, oral communication skills, plan to pursue career in field, self-motivation, strong interpersonal skills, writing skills. Duration is April to October. $7.25–$8.25 per hour. Open to college freshmen, college sophomores, college juniors, college seniors, recent college graduates, graduate students, law students. International applications accepted.

Benefits Names of contacts, on-the-job training, opportunity to attend seminars/workshops, possible full-time employment, willing to act as a professional reference, willing to complete paperwork for educational credit, willing to provide letters of recommendation, some free meals.

Contact Write, call, fax, or e-mail Tim Katzman, Corporate Communications. Phone: 619-881-6539. Fax: 619-497-5338. E-mail: tkatzman@padres.com. In-person interview required. Applicants must submit a letter of interest, resume, writing sample, two personal references. Application deadline: February 15.

SAN FRANCISCO 49ERS
4949 Centennial Boulevard
Santa Clara, California 95054

General Information Professional football team. Established in 1946. Number of employees: 90. Number of internship applications received each year: 100.

Internships Available ▶ *1–2 season interns:* responsibilities include assisting public relations department with interview requests, fan mail requests, and research for publications. Candidates should have ability to work with others, knowledge of field, office skills, oral communication skills, personal interest in the field, written communication skills. Duration is 7–8 months. $7 per hour. Open to college sophomores, college juniors, college seniors, recent college graduates, graduate students. ▶ *2 summer camp interns:* responsibilities include assisting public relations department staff at training camp, handling interview requests, writing features, and general office work. Candidates should have ability to work with others, knowledge of field, oral communication skills, personal interest in the field, written communication skills. Duration is 1 month. $7 per hour. Open to college freshmen, college sophomores,

San Francisco 49ers (continued)
college juniors, college seniors, recent college graduates, graduate students. International applications accepted.

Benefits Names of contacts, on-the-job training, possible full-time employment, willing to act as a professional reference, willing to complete paperwork for educational credit, willing to provide letters of recommendation.

Contact Write Internship Coordinator. Fax: 408-727-2760. No phone calls. Applicants must submit a letter of interest, resume. Application deadline: May 15. World Wide Web: http://www.sf49ers.com.

SEATTLE SONICS AND STORM
351 Elliot Avenue W, Suite 500
Seattle, Washington 98119

General Information Professional basketball team. Established in 1967. Number of employees: 300. Number of internship applications received each year: 500.

Internships Available ▶ *1 community relations intern:* responsibilities include assisting with organizational and administrative duties within the Community Relations Department. Candidates should have computer skills, oral communication skills, personal interest in the field, strong interpersonal skills, written communication skills. Duration is one quarter or semester. Unpaid. ▶ *1–4 guest relations interns:* responsibilities include learning the duties associated with the coordination and administration of all activities and correspondence within the Guest Relations department. Candidates should have personal interest in the field, oral, written, and interpersonal skills (preferred). Duration is one quarter or semester. Unpaid. ▶ *1 public relations intern:* responsibilities include assisting with organizational and administrative duties within the Public Relations Department. Candidates should have computer skills, editing skills, oral communication skills, personal interest in the field, strong interpersonal skills, written communication skills. Duration is one quarter or semester. Unpaid. ▶ *1–4 sales development interns:* responsibilities include learning the duties associated with the coordination and administration of all activities and correspondence within the Sales Development Department. Candidates should have computer skills, oral communication skills, personal interest in the field, self-motivation, strong interpersonal skills, written communication skills. Duration is one quarter or semester. Unpaid. Open to college juniors, college seniors.

Benefits On-the-job training, possible full-time employment, opportunity to attend Sonics and Storm games.

Contact Write, fax, or e-mail Internship Coordinator. Fax: 206-272-2795. E-mail: employment@sonics-storm.com. No phone calls. In-person interview required. Applicants must submit a resume. Applications are accepted continuously. World Wide Web: http://www.supersonics.com.

SOMERSET PATRIOTS
1 Patriots Park
Bridgewater, New Jersey 08807

General Information Member of the Atlantic League of Professional Baseball. Established in 1998. Number of employees: 50. Number of internship applications received each year: 100.

Internships Available ▶ *3 group sales/promotions interns:* responsibilities include assisting directors with data entry, tracking, and organizing day-to-day sales activities; mailings; printing and distribution of tickets. Candidates should have computer skills, oral communication skills, organizational skills, strong interpersonal skills, written communication skills, management and sales skills, video/scoreboard experience a plus. Duration is April to September. $750 per month or college credit. ▶ *2 operations interns:* responsibilities include assisting director of operations with daily operations of Commerce Bank Ballpark; planning/coordinating game-day staff and community use of the facility; and general office work. Candidates should have ability to work independently, computer skills, organizational skills, strong interpersonal skills, management skills. Duration is April to September. $750 per month or college credit. ▶ *2 ticketing interns:* responsibilities include assisting director of ticketing with all ticketing aspects at ballpark. Candidates should have computer skills, oral communication skills, organizational

skills, strong interpersonal skills, written communication skills, experience with ticketing is a plus, but not required. Duration is April to September. $750 per month or college credit. Open to college freshmen, college sophomores, college juniors, college seniors, recent college graduates, graduate students. International applications accepted.

Benefits Formal training, names of contacts, on-the-job training, possible full-time employment, willing to act as a professional reference, willing to complete paperwork for educational credit, willing to provide letters of recommendation.

Contact Write or fax Brendan P. Fairfield, Assistant General Manager. Fax: 908-252-0776. E-mail: bfairfield@somersetpatriots.com. No phone calls. In-person interview recommended (telephone interview accepted). Applicants must submit a resume. Applications are accepted continuously. World Wide Web: http://www.somersetpatriots.com.

SPOLETO FESTIVAL USA
PO Box 157
Charleston, South Carolina 29402-0157

General Information Arts festival that produces and presents world-class opera, dance, theater, chamber music, symphonic music, jazz, visual arts, and experimental multimedia works of all kinds. Established in 1977. Number of employees: 20. Number of internship applications received each year: 200.

Internships Available ▶ *2–3 artist services interns:* responsibilities include assisting with artist transportation, preparing mailings and artist welcome packets, scheduling and set-up of backstage hospitality, answering phones, correspondence, filing, and other administrative tasks. Candidates should have ability to work independently, ability to work with others, computer skills, office skills, organizational skills, self-motivation. Duration is 4–6 weeks. $250 per week. ▶ *15–20 box office interns:* responsibilities include assisting with box office window/telephone sales, program information, ticket collection, and processing mail orders. Candidates should have ability to work with others, computer skills, oral communication skills, strong customer service skills. Duration is 4–5 weeks. $250 per week. ▶ *1–2 business office intern:* responsibilities include assisting with recording cash receipts, preparing and recording disbursements, and personnel and payroll operations. Candidates should have computer skills, organizational skills. Duration is 4–5 weeks. $250 per week. ▶ *2 development interns:* responsibilities include assisting with development report, distribution of contributor benefits, and coordination of special events; extensive phone work; managing invitation mailings and RSVP's. Candidates should have ability to work independently, ability to work with others, organizational skills, self-motivation. Duration is 4–5 weeks. $250 per week. ▶ *4 merchandising interns:* responsibilities include assisting with sales of souvenir merchandise. Candidates should have ability to work with others, oral communication skills, organizational skills, self-motivation, strong customer service skills. Duration is 4 weeks. $250 per week. ▶ *6–7 orchestra management interns:* responsibilities include assisting in the transport and setup of equipment and large instruments for rehearsals and performances. Candidates should have ability to work independently, ability to work with others, self-motivation, knowledge of music helpful. Duration is 4–5 weeks. $250 per week. ▶ *30 production interns:* responsibilities include working in stage carpentry and electrics, wardrobe, properties, wigs and makeup, sound, and production administration. Candidates should have ability to work independently, ability to work with others, college courses in field, experience in the field, plan to pursue career in field, self-motivation. Duration is 4–5 weeks. $250 per week. ▶ *5 public relations interns:* responsibilities include staffing the press room and assisting the press in obtaining interviews, photos, and story information for print, radio, and television coverage. Candidates should have ability to work with others, computer skills, office skills, oral communication skills, written communication skills. Duration is 4–5 weeks. $250 per week. Open to college freshmen, college sophomores, college juniors, college seniors, recent college graduates, graduate students. International applications accepted.

Benefits Free housing, possible full-time employment, willing to complete paperwork for educational credit, willing to provide letters of recommendation, access to performances.

Contact Write, fax, e-mail, or through World Wide Web site Apprentice Coordinator. Fax: 843-723-6383. E-mail: apprentice@ spoletousa.org. No phone calls. Telephone interview required. Applicants must submit a formal organization application, letter of interest, resume, two letters of recommendation, 2 writing samples (public relations positions only). Application deadline: February 1. World Wide Web: http://www.spoletousa.org.

THE SUCHIN COMPANY
12747 Riverside Drive, Suite 208
Valley Village, California 91607-3333

General Information Production/management company that represents actors, writers, singers, comedians; advises and counsels with regard to career aspirations/TV product; makeup artists, and costumes. Established in 1979. Number of employees: 5. Number of internship applications received each year: 150.
Internships Available ▶ *4 assistants:* responsibilities include phones, marketing, computers, filing, script reading and analysis. Candidates should have ability to work independently, office skills, research skills, strong interest in entertainment business. Duration is 3–6 months. Unpaid. Open to college freshmen, college sophomores, college juniors, college seniors, career changers. International applications accepted.
Benefits Job counseling, names of contacts, on-the-job training, opportunity to attend seminars/workshops, possible full-time employment, willing to act as a professional reference, willing to complete paperwork for educational credit, willing to provide letters of recommendation, chance to be with entertainment industry members.
Contact Write, fax, or e-mail Milton B. Suchin, President. Phone: 818-505-0044. Fax: 818-505-0110. E-mail: starmgri@aol.com. In-person interview recommended (telephone interview accepted). Applicants must submit a letter of interest, resume. Applications are accepted continuously.

THEATRE BUILDING CHICAGO
1225 West Belmont Avenue
Chicago, Illinois 60657

General Information Live theater with three-space multiplex that emphasizes new musicals. Established in 1969. Number of employees: 10. Number of internship applications received each year: 20.
Internships Available ▶ *1–2 "Stages" summer interns:* responsibilities include acting as stage manager or production manager for intense weekend festival of musical; coordinating 12 plays; 36 authors, and 125 performing artists. Candidates should have ability to work with others, oral communication skills, organizational skills, self-motivation, strong leadership ability, written communication skills. Duration is June 17 to August 17. $500 per duration of internship. Open to high school students, recent high school graduates, college freshmen, college sophomores, college juniors, college seniors. ▶ *1–3 box office and marketing interns:* responsibilities include ticketing, phone work, customer service; correspondence and marketing tools including Web site, flyers, programs, and broadsides. Candidates should have ability to work with others, computer skills, office skills, oral communication skills, writing skills. Duration is 1 year (full-time). $500 monthly stipend. Open to recent college graduates, graduate students, career changers, individuals reentering the workforce. ▶ *1–3 marketing and fundraising interns:* responsibilities include assisting executive director in grant writing; individual donor campaigns, marketing and public relations planning for renting their space and for presenting musical productions. Candidates should have ability to work with others, computer skills, organizational skills, self-motivation, writing skills. Duration is 1 year (full-time). $500 monthly stipend. Open to recent college graduates, graduate students, career changers, individuals reentering the workforce. International applications accepted.
Benefits Health insurance, on-the-job training, opportunity to attend seminars/workshops, willing to act as a professional reference, willing to complete paperwork for educational credit, willing to provide letters of recommendation.
Contact Write, call, fax, or e-mail Joan Mazzonelli, Executive Director. Phone: 773-929-7367 Ext. 221. Fax: 773-327-1404. E-mail:

joan@theatrebuildingchicago.org. In-person interview recommended (telephone interview accepted). Applicants must submit a formal organization application, resume. Applications are accepted continuously. World Wide Web: http://www. theatrebuildingchicago.org.

TSE SPORTS & ENTERTAINMENT
14 Penn Plaza, Suite 1517
New York, New York 10122

General Information Sports and entertainment marketing firm. Established in 1997. Number of employees: 25. Number of internship applications received each year: 100.
Internships Available ▶ *2–4 general interns:* responsibilities include researching for client needs, coordinating ad/sales campaigns, organizing sports and entertainment packages. Candidates should have ability to work with others, computer skills, office skills, oral communication skills, personal interest in the field, research skills, self-motivation, creative enthusiasm. Duration is 1–3 semesters. Unpaid. Open to high school seniors, recent high school graduates, college freshmen, college sophomores, college juniors, college seniors.
Benefits Willing to act as a professional reference.
Contact Fax or e-mail Human Resources. Fax: 212-564-8098. E-mail: resume@tseworld.com. No phone calls. In-person interview recommended (telephone interview accepted). Applicants must submit a resume. Applications are accepted continuously. World Wide Web: http://www.tseworld.com.

WASHINGTON PERFORMING ARTS SOCIETY
2000 L Street, NW, Suite 510
Washington, District of Columbia 20036-4907

General Information Nonprofit organization focused on presenting classical music, traditional and contemporary dance, world music, jazz, Latino artforms, gospel, and performance art in concert halls, theaters, schools, senior citizen centers, and embassies throughout the Washington, DC area. Established in 1965. Number of employees: 40. Number of internship applications received each year: 25.
Internships Available ▶ *1 administrative assistant:* responsibilities include general assistance to the Finance and Administration Department, including general office work, maintenance of databases and spreadsheets, as well as organization and evaluation of new information. Candidates should have computer skills, office skills, organizational skills, research skills, self-motivation, writing skills. Duration is 1–2 semesters. Position available as unpaid or paid. Open to college juniors, college seniors, recent college graduates, graduate students, career changers. ▶ *1 development assistant:* responsibilities include researching corporate, foundation, and individual donors; processing mail; assisting with writing of grants and special events; general office work. Candidates should have ability to work with others, computer skills, plan to pursue career in field, research skills, writing skills, ability to work some evening hours. Duration is 1 semester. Position available as unpaid or paid. Open to college seniors, recent college graduates, graduate students, career changers. ▶ *1 graphic design assistant.* Candidates should have ability to work with others, computer skills, knowledge of field, personal interest in the field, self-motivation, fluency in Quark, knowledge of PhotoShop. Duration is 1–2 semesters. Position available as unpaid or paid. Open to college juniors, college seniors, recent college graduates, graduate students, career changers. ▶ *1 programming assistant:* responsibilities include transporting artists, coordinating/booking hotel accommodations, assisting with front-of-house and ticketing at performances, and general office work. Candidates should have computer skills, knowledge of field, organizational skills, personal interest in the field, research skills, strong interpersonal skills. Duration is 4–9 months. Position available as unpaid or paid. Open to college seniors, recent college graduates, graduate students, career changers. ▶ *1–2 public relations and marketing assistants:* responsibilities include writing and distributing press releases; writing copy for promotions, sales pieces, and newsletters; assisting with special promotions, direct mail campaigns, list management, and response tracking and analysis; proofing; preparing reviewer kits for concerts; maintaining press kits and department files; and general office

Washington Performing Arts Society *(continued)*

work. Candidates should have editing skills, knowledge of field, organizational skills, research skills, self-motivation, writing skills. Duration is 1–2 semesters. Position available as unpaid or paid. Open to college juniors, college seniors, recent college graduates, graduate students, career changers.

Benefits Names of contacts, willing to complete paperwork for educational credit, willing to provide letters of recommendation.

Contact Write, fax, e-mail, or through World Wide Web site Education Manager. Fax: 202-331-7678. E-mail: wpas@wpas.org. No phone calls. In-person interview recommended (telephone interview accepted). Applicants must submit a letter of interest, resume, writing sample, personal reference. Application deadline: April 15 for summer, July 15 for fall, November 15 for winter/spring. World Wide Web: http://www.wpas.org.

EDUCATIONAL SERVICES

GENERAL

ACADEMIC STUDY ASSOCIATES–ASA
10 New King Street
White Plains, New York 10604

General Information Summer pre-college programs for high school students. Established in 1984. Number of employees: 10. Number of internship applications received each year: 400.
Internships Available ▶ *80–100 resident advisors:* responsibilities include introducing high school students to academic, social, and recreational aspects of college life. Candidates should have ability to work with others, oral communication skills, self-motivation, creativity, flexibility, interest in working with high school students. Duration is 4–8 weeks. $300 per week. Open to college juniors, college seniors, recent college graduates, graduate students, must be 21 years of age.
Benefits Free housing, free meals.
International Internships Available in France; Spain; United Kingdom.
Contact Through World Wide Web site Lisa Siggia, Summer Staff Coordinator. Phone: 800-752-2250 Ext. 110. Fax: 914-686-7740. E-mail: summerstaff@asaprograms.com. In-person interview required. Applicants must submit a formal organization application, two letters of recommendation. Applications are accepted continuously. World Wide Web: http://www.asaprograms.com.

AIM FOR THE HANDICAPPED
945 Danbury Road
Dayton, Ohio 45420

General Information Educational facility that offers specialized movement education program to handicapped children and adults. Established in 1958. Number of employees: 7. Number of internship applications received each year: 15.
Internships Available ▶ *1–3 education department assistants:* responsibilities include teaching handicapped children and adults, setting up programs in schools, working on the newsletter, and performing general office duties. Candidates should have ability to work with others, office skills, oral communication skills, personal interest in the field, self-motivation, written communication skills. Duration is flexible. Unpaid. Open to high school students, recent high school graduates, college freshmen, college sophomores, college juniors, college seniors, recent college graduates, graduate students, career changers, individuals reentering the workforce. International applications accepted.
Benefits On-the-job training, possible full-time employment, willing to act as a professional reference, willing to complete paperwork for educational credit, willing to provide letters of recommendation, assistance in locating housing.
Contact Write, call, fax, or e-mail Lynn E. Switzer, Education Director. Phone: 937-294-4611. Fax: 937-294-3783. E-mail: aimeducation@hotmail.com. In-person interview recommended (telephone interview accepted). Applicants must submit a letter of interest, resume, three personal references, three letters of recommendation. Applications are accepted continuously.

ALICE PAUL CENTENNIAL FOUNDATION
128 Hooten Road
Mt. Laurel, New Jersey 08054

General Information Nonprofit corporation created to celebrate Alice Paul's birth in 1885; goals are to enhance public awareness of the life and work of Alice Paul and to educate women and girls to accept leadership challenges in their lives, communities, and work places. Established in 1984. Number of employees: 3. Number of internship applications received each year: 1.
Internships Available ▶ *1–3 administrative interns/research assistants:* responsibilities include research, assistance with specific programs or events, database management, and education research. Candidates should have ability to work independently, ability to work with others, analytical skills, college courses in field, computer skills, knowledge of field, oral communication skills, organizational skills, personal interest in the field, plan to pursue career in field, research skills, self-motivation, strong leadership ability, writing skills. Duration is flexible. Unpaid. Open to high school students, recent high school graduates, college freshmen, college sophomores, college juniors, college seniors, recent college graduates, graduate students, law students, career changers, individuals reentering the workforce. International applications accepted.
Benefits On-the-job training, opportunity to attend seminars/workshops, willing to act as a professional reference, willing to complete paperwork for educational credit, willing to provide letters of recommendation.
Contact Write, call, fax, e-mail, or through World Wide Web site Rhonda Carboni, President. Phone: 856-231-1885. Fax: 856-231-4223. E-mail: info@alicepaul.org. In-person interview recommended (telephone interview accepted). Applicants must submit a formal organization application, letter of interest, resume, personal reference. Applications are accepted continuously. World Wide Web: http://www.alicepaul.org.

AMERICAN ASSOCIATION OF OVERSEAS STUDIES
9933 65th Road
New York, New York 11374

General Information International placement service working with over 200 universities and 150 preparatory and high schools to place 100 students annually in business, law, theater, communications/media, sciences, journalism, politics, arts/museums, psychology, women's studies, music, fashion, and food and wine areas. Established in 1984. Number of employees: 2. Affiliate of Anglo International Education Consultants, London, United Kingdom. Number of internship applications received each year: 50.
Internships Available ▶ *60–100 interns:* responsibilities include various duties according to the internship; positions available in New York or London. Candidates should have ability to work independently, computer skills, office skills, oral communication skills, organizational skills, personal interest in the field, self-motivation, strong interpersonal skills, writing skills, enthusiasm, willingness to help. Duration is 1–3 months. Unpaid. Open to high school seniors, recent high school graduates, college freshmen, college sophomores, college juniors, college seniors, recent college graduates, graduate students, law students. International applications accepted.
Benefits Housing at a cost, job counseling, names of contacts, opportunity to attend seminars/workshops, willing to act as a professional reference, willing to complete paperwork for educational credit, willing to provide letters of recommendation.

American Association of Overseas Studies (continued)

International Internships Available in London, United Kingdom.
Contact Write, call, fax, e-mail, or through World Wide Web site
Ms. Janet Kollek Evans, Director, 51 Drayton Gardens, London
SW10 9EX United Kingdom. Phone: 44-20-7835-2143. Fax: 44-20-
7244-6061. E-mail: aaos2000@hotmail.com. Telephone interview
required. Applicants must submit a formal organization application, personal reference, letter of recommendation. Applications
are accepted continuously. Fees: $200. World Wide Web: http://
www.worldwide.edu/uk/aaos/.

AMERICAN COUNCILS FOR INTERNATIONAL EDUCATION
1776 Massachusetts Avenue, NW, Suite 700
Washington, District of Columbia 20036

General Information Nonprofit organization dealing with
educational development and exchange with the former Soviet
Union and Eastern Europe. Established in 1975. Number of
employees: 100. Number of internship applications received each
year: 800.
Internships Available ▶ *10–15 interns:* responsibilities include
communications, setting up conferences, clerical work, and general
office duties. Candidates should have computer skills, oral communication skills, personal interest in the field, strong interpersonal
skills, written communication skills. Duration is May to August.
$8–$10 per hour. Open to college sophomores, college juniors,
college seniors. International applications accepted.
Benefits Names of contacts, opportunity to attend seminars/
workshops, possible full-time employment, willing to act as a
professional reference, willing to complete paperwork for educational
credit, willing to provide letters of recommendation.
Contact Through World Wide Web site Internship Coordinator.
No phone calls. In-person interview recommended (telephone
interview accepted). Applicants must submit a letter of interest,
resume, academic transcripts. Applications are accepted continuously.
World Wide Web: http://www.americancouncils.org.

AMERICAN INSTITUTE FOR FOREIGN STUDY
River Plaza, 9 West Broad Street
Stamford, Connecticut 06902

General Information Institute providing educational/cultural
exchanges for high school and college students and interested
adults on 15 campuses in Europe, Asia, Australia, Africa, Russia
and South America. Established in 1964. Number of employees:
125. Number of internship applications received each year: 100.
Internships Available ▶ *Interns in Florence, Cannes, and Salzburg.*
Candidates should have oral communication skills, personal interest in the field, written communication skills, minimum 2.5 GPA,
language proficiency. Duration is 1 semester. Unpaid. ▶ *25–40
interns in London:* responsibilities include attending classes for 4
weeks and working for 11 weeks full-time in business (marketing,
finance, management), communications (media), fine arts (design
and lens media), politics, and theater. Candidates should have
minimum 2.5 GPA. Duration is 12–15 weeks. Unpaid. Open to
college sophomores, college juniors, college seniors. International
applications accepted.
Benefits Formal training, opportunity to attend seminars/
workshops, possible full-time employment, willing to complete
paperwork for educational credit, willing to provide letters of
recommendation, health insurance, housing, and some meals.
International Internships Available in Sydney, Australia; Salzburg, Austria; Cannes, France; Florence, Italy; Amsterdam,
Netherlands; London, United Kingdom.
Contact Write, call, fax, e-mail, or through World Wide Web site
Sharman Hedayati, College Division, Director of Admissions.
Phone: 800-727-AIFS Ext. 5057. Fax: 203-399-5597. E-mail: info@
aifs.org. Applicants must submit a formal organization application, academic transcripts, writing sample, two personal refer-
ences, tuition payment required upon acceptance. Application
deadline: May 15 for fall, November 1 for spring. Fees: $75. World
Wide Web: http://www.aifs.com.

THE AMERICAN-SCANDINAVIAN FOUNDATION
58 Park Avenue
New York, New York 10016

General Information Nonprofit organization that promotes
international understanding through educational and cultural
exchange between the United States and Denmark, Finland,
Iceland, Norway, and Sweden. Established in 1910. Number of
employees: 22. Number of internship applications received each
year: 60.
Internships Available ▶ *5–10 English teachers in Finland:* responsibilities include teaching English as a foreign language in Finnish
kindergartens, schools, colleges, private and public institutions
and universities. Candidates should have experience in education, pre-school education, English, or closely related fields. Duration is 1–2 semesters. $750–$900 per month. Open to college
juniors, college seniors, recent college graduates, graduate students.
▶ *5–10 TEFOL positions (Finland):* responsibilities include teaching English as a foreign language to Finns at a variety of age
levels in Finnish public schools, institutes, or private firms.
Candidates should have declared college major in field, experience in the field, plan to pursue career in field, English, education, ESL, or related major. Duration is 3–10 months. $750–$900
per month. Open to college juniors, college seniors, recent college graduates, graduate students. ▶ *20–30 engineering interns
(Scandinavia):* responsibilities include computer programming,
performing entry-level engineering fieldwork, and assisting with
projects. Candidates should have declared college major in field,
knowledge of field, self-motivation, openness to a cross-cultural
experience. Duration is 2–6 months. $775–$1110 per month.
Open to college juniors, college seniors, graduate students. ▶ *20–
30 interns in Scandinavia:* responsibilities include working in
Scandinavia by undertaking an internship; see Web site for further
detail. Candidates should have college courses in field, college
degree in related field, self-motivation. Duration is 2–6 months.
$775–$1110 per month. Open to college juniors, college seniors.
Benefits Health insurance, on-the-job training, temporary work
permit may be issued if intern arranges internship and housing.
International Internships Available in Finland; Sweden.
Contact Write, call, e-mail, or through World Wide Web site Training Program. Phone: 212-879-9779. Fax: 212-249-3444. E-mail:
trainscan@amscan.org. Applicants must submit a formal organization application, letter of interest, resume, academic transcripts,
letter of recommendation. Application deadline: January 1 for
interns in Scandinavia, March 1 for English teachers in Finland.
Fees: $50. World Wide Web: http://www.amscan.org.

AMERICAN UNIVERSITY IN MOSCOW
1800 Connecticut Avenue, NW
Washington, District of Columbia 20009

General Information Educational institute that conducts conferences, seminars, and educational programs for students and leaders in business, politics, and academia in the U.S. and the Commonwealth of Independent States. Established in 1991. Number
of employees: 5. Number of internship applications received each
year: 50.
Internships Available ▶ *5 assistants to program coordinators:*
responsibilities include assisting in all work related to the programs.
Candidates should have computer skills, editing skills, office skills,
oral communication skills, writing skills. Duration is 1–6 months.
Unpaid. Open to recent high school graduates, college freshmen, college sophomores, college juniors, college seniors, recent
college graduates. International applications accepted.
Benefits Names of contacts, opportunity to attend seminars/
workshops, possible full-time employment, travel reimbursement,
willing to complete paperwork for educational credit, willing to
provide letters of recommendation.
Contact Write, call, fax, e-mail, or through World Wide Web site
Dr. Edward Lozansky. Phone: 202-986-6010. Fax: 202-667-4244.
E-mail: lozansky@aol.com. Telephone interview required. Applicants
must submit a resume. Applications are accepted continuously.
World Wide Web: http://www.RussiaHouse.org.

AMERISPAN UNLIMITED
PO Box 58129
Philadelphia, Pennsylvania 19102-8129

General Information Company that specializes in internships, volunteer work, and language programs in Latin America and Europe. Established in 1993. Number of employees: 10. Number of internship applications received each year: 200.

Internships Available ▶ *1–4 ESL teachers:* responsibilities include planning and implementing ESL classes for small groups of people of various ages and levels. Candidates should have ability to speak high-intermediate level of Spanish, ESL certification and/or experience, college degree. Duration is 3–6 months. Unpaid. Open to recent college graduates, graduate students, career changers, individuals reentering the workforce. ▶ *10–30 environmental and/or zoological interns:* responsibilities include working in animal rescue and/or conservation, cloud forests, national parks, eco/adventure tourism, orchard gardens, botany, bird and butterfly sanctuaries, and environmental education. Candidates should have ability to work independently, experience in the field, self-motivation, ability to speak high-intermediate level of Spanish, experience living in remote areas, good physical condition. Duration is 4 weeks to 6 months. Unpaid. Open to recent high school graduates, college juniors, college seniors, recent college graduates, graduate students, law students, career changers, individuals reentering the workforce. ▶ *Professional interns:* responsibilities include working in a professional environment in one of the following fields: accounting, banking, economics, education, engineering, government, hotel, law, marketing, medicine, psychology, social work, or tourism. Candidates should have college degree in related field, knowledge of field, organizational skills, plan to pursue career in field, self-motivation, good Spanish skills (oral and written). Duration is 1–6 months. Unpaid. Open to recent college graduates, graduate students, law students, career changers, individuals reentering the workforce. ▶ *5–20 social work/education/health-care interns:* responsibilities include working with abused, poor and/or street children; addiction counseling; physically and/or mentally disabled children, adults, and elderly; teaching arts and crafts; teaching English; working in rural villages or health clinics/hospitals. Candidates should have ability to work independently, personal interest in the field, ability to speak high-intermediate level of Spanish, related experience and/or certification. Duration is 4 weeks to 6 months. Unpaid. Open to recent high school graduates, college freshmen, college sophomores, college juniors, college seniors, recent college graduates, graduate students, law students, career changers, individuals reentering the workforce. ▶ *1–4 student services coordinators:* responsibilities include administrative duties, computer work, correspondence, translations, organizing activities, and helping on special projects. Candidates should have ability to work independently, computer skills, self-motivation, strong interpersonal skills, ability to speak high-intermediate level of Spanish, administrative and customer service experience, college degree. Duration is 3–6 months. Unpaid. Open to recent college graduates, graduate students, law students, career changers, individuals reentering the workforce. International applications accepted.

Benefits Health insurance, meals at a cost, names of contacts, willing to act as a professional reference, willing to complete paperwork for educational credit, willing to provide letters of recommendation, travel insurance, free housing or housing at cost available depending on internship position.

International Internships Available in Argentina; Bolivia; Brazil; Chile; Costa Rica; Ecuador; Guatemala; Mexico; Peru; Spain.

Contact Write, call, fax, e-mail, or through World Wide Web site Liz Cleveland, Volunteer/Internship Program Director, 117 South 17th Street, Suite 1401, Philadelphia, Pennsylvania 19103. Phone: 800-879-6640. Fax: 215-751-1986. E-mail: info@amerispan.com. Telephone interview required. Applicants must submit a formal organization application, letter of interest, resume, two letters of recommendation, $300 placement fee. Application deadline: 2 months prior to start of internship. Fees: $50. World Wide Web: http://www.amerispan.com.

ARCADIA UNIVERSITY CENTER FOR EDUCATION ABROAD
450 South Easton Road
Glenside, Pennsylvania 19038-3295

General Information University-based study abroad provider that arranges junior and senior year abroad for transfer credit. Established in 1948. Unit of Arcadia University, Glenside, Pennsylvania.

Internships Available ▶ *Australia Parliamentary interns:* responsibilities include positions in government or government-related fields in Canberra, Australia's capital city. Candidates should have ability to work independently, oral communication skills, organizational skills, research skills, strong interpersonal skills, written communication skills. Duration is 1 semester. Unpaid. ▶ *Dublin Parliamentary interns:* responsibilities include acting as an aide to a member of the Irish Parliament in Dublin. Candidates should have ability to work independently, oral communication skills, organizational skills, research skills, strong interpersonal skills, written communication skills. Duration is 1 semester. Unpaid. ▶ *London interns:* responsibilities include holding positions in public policy, social science, communications, business, and health care. Candidates should have ability to work independently, college courses in field, oral communication skills, strong interpersonal skills, written communication skills. Duration is 1 semester or 1 summer. Unpaid. ▶ *Scottish Parliamentary interns:* responsibilities include research project under the direction of a member of the Scottish Parliament. Candidates should have ability to work independently, oral communication skills, organizational skills, research skills, strong interpersonal skills, written communication skills. Duration is 1 semester. Unpaid. ▶ *Sydney interns:* responsibilities include positions in the humanities, arts, business, and social science. Candidates should have ability to work independently, college courses in field, oral communication skills, strong interpersonal skills, written communication skills. Duration is one semester or summer. Unpaid. Open to college juniors, college seniors.

Benefits Health insurance, tuition assistance, willing to complete paperwork for educational credit, guaranteed housing, orientation, ongoing host country support, ISIC card, Arcadia University transcript.

International Internships Available in Canberra, Australia; Sydney, Australia; Dublin, Ireland; Edinburgh, United Kingdom; London, United Kingdom.

Contact Write, call, fax, e-mail, or through World Wide Web site Program Coordinators, Arcadia University, 450 South Easton Road, Glenside, Pennsylvania 19038-3295. Phone: 866-927-2234. Fax: 215-572-2174. E-mail: cea@arcadia.edu. In-person interview required. Applicants must submit a formal organization application, resume, academic transcripts, personal reference, letter of recommendation, personal essay. Application deadline: March 10 for summer (London); March 31 for summer (Sydney), April 20 for fall (Sydney, Dublin, London); April 2 for fall (Scotland), October 15 for spring (Sydney, Dublin, London, Scotland), November 15 for spring (Canberra); March 15 for fall (Canberra). Fees: $35. World Wide Web: http://www.arcadia.edu/cea.

ASHAY: EDUCATIONAL RESOURCES FOR A MULTICULTURAL WORLD
1800 South Robertson Boulevard, Suite 408
Los Angeles, California 90035

General Information Organization that develops educational curriculum designed to help people understand and appreciate human differences from race and ethnicity to sexuality, age, and ability. Established in 1995. Number of employees: 2. Number of internship applications received each year: 20.

Internships Available ▶ *1–3 event planning interns:* responsibilities include helping plan and implement programs to expose people to Ashay and cultivate further involvement, working on small receptions in people's homes and larger special events, overseeing logistics, including invitations and food. Candidates should have ability to work independently, organizational skills, self-motivation, strong interpersonal skills, strong leadership ability. Duration is 3–6 months. Position available as unpaid or paid.

Ashay: Educational Resources for a Multicultural World (continued)

Open to college seniors, recent college graduates, graduate students, career changers, individuals reentering the workforce. ▶ *1–2 fund-raising interns:* responsibilities include researching, writing for grants and corporate sponsorships, planning/implementing fund-raising events, and helping with direct mail campaign. Candidates should have ability to work independently, computer skills, organizational skills, research skills, self-motivation, written communication skills. Duration is 4–6 months. Position available as unpaid or paid. Open to college seniors, recent college graduates, graduate students, career changers, individuals reentering the workforce. ▶ *1–3 marketing and promotion interns:* responsibilities include helping to plan and implement teachers focus groups, researching leads for multicultural communication game distribution, identifying conferences at which game can be presented, working to have game included in educational resource catalogs. Candidates should have ability to work independently, organizational skills, research skills, self-motivation, strong interpersonal skills, written communication skills. Duration is 3–6 months. Position available as unpaid or paid. Open to college seniors, recent college graduates, graduate students, career changers, individuals reentering the workforce. ▶ *1–3 multicultural communication game interns:* responsibilities include promoting game with schools, camps, and other organizations; facilitating the game with various groups; researching new questions and additional resources. Candidates should have ability to work independently, computer skills, self-motivation, strong interpersonal skills, strong leadership ability. Duration is 4–6 months. Position available as unpaid or paid. Open to college juniors, college seniors, recent college graduates, graduate students, career changers, individuals reentering the workforce. ▶ *1–3 special projects interns:* responsibilities include varied duties depending on intern's skills/interests and project needs; possible areas include Web master, database design and maintenance, public speaking, outreach and networking, and graphic design. Candidates should have ability to work independently, ability to work with others, computer skills, organizational skills, research skills, self-motivation. Duration is 4–6 months. Position available as unpaid or paid. Open to college juniors, college seniors, recent college graduates, graduate students, career changers, individuals reentering the workforce. International applications accepted.

Benefits On-the-job training, willing to act as a professional reference, willing to complete paperwork for educational credit, willing to provide letters of recommendation, learning valuable transferable skills, possible stipends.

Contact Write, call, fax, e-mail, or through World Wide Web site Ms. Shifra Teitelbaum, Director, 1800 South Robertson Boulevard, Suite 408, Los Angeles, California 90035. Phone: 310-842-9125. Fax: 310-204-6221. E-mail: shifra@ashay.org. In-person interview recommended (telephone interview accepted). Applicants must submit a letter of interest, resume, two personal references. Applications are accepted continuously. World Wide Web: http://www.ashay.org.

ASSOCIATED WESTERN UNIVERSITIES, INC.
4190 South Highland Drive, Suite 211
Salt Lake City, Utah 84124

General Information Nonprofit educational consortium linking students, postgraduates, and faculty with fellowship, internship, and sabbatical research opportunities in science and engineering at federal and industrial laboratories. Established in 1959. Number of employees: 30. Number of internship applications received each year: 2,500.

Internships Available ▶ *200–300 graduate fellowships:* responsibilities include conducting research towards master's or doctoral thesis or exploring research and technology career options at a cooperating facility. Candidates should have computer skills, oral communication skills, research skills, continuous enrollment in a university thesis program (required during tenure). Duration is up to 12 months. Stipend of $1300 per month (minimum). Open to graduate students in science and engineering. ▶ *200–300 postgraduate research fellowships.* Candidates should have ability to work independently, ability to work with others, college degree in related field, oral communication skills, personal interest in

the field, research skills. Duration is 1–3 years. Stipend paid by the facility. Open to individuals with recent bachelor's degree, master's degree, or PhD graduates. ▶ *500–600 student research fellowships:* responsibilities include working in primarily research and applied technology positions under the guidance of experienced scientists and engineers; facilities range from federal to private industry. Candidates should have ability to work with others, college courses in field, computer skills, knowledge of field, oral communication skills, research skills. Duration is 8–16 weeks. $300 per week. Open to college sophomores, college juniors, college seniors, recent college graduates, graduate students. International applications accepted.

Benefits Health insurance, housing at a cost, names of contacts, opportunity to attend seminars/workshops, possible full-time employment, travel reimbursement, tuition assistance, willing to act as a professional reference, willing to complete paperwork for educational credit, willing to provide letters of recommendation.

Contact Write, call, fax, e-mail, or through World Wide Web site Mariann Bleazand, Program Coordinator. Phone: 888-841-5745. Fax: 801-277-5632. E-mail: info@awu.org. Applicants must submit a resume, academic transcripts, two letters of recommendation, formal organizational application (can be completed on-line). Applications are accepted continuously. World Wide Web: http://www.awu.org.

ASSOCIATION FOR EXPERIENTIAL EDUCATION (AEE)
2305 Canyon Boulevard, Suite 100
Boulder, Colorado 80302

General Information Not-for-profit international professional membership association with roots in adventure education, committed to the development, practice, and evaluation of experiential learning in all settings. Established in 1972. Number of employees: 5. Number of internship applications received each year: 100.

Internships Available ▶ *1–5 administrative interns:* responsibilities include duties that are dependent upon the applicant's experience and interests and the needs of AEE. Candidates should have computer skills, office skills, organizational skills, self-motivation, strong interpersonal skills. Duration is 1-6 months (3 months preferred). Unpaid. ▶ *1–3 publications and marketing interns:* responsibilities include various duties dependent on the applicant's interest and experience, as well as on the needs of AEE. Candidates should have editing skills, research skills, self-motivation, writing skills. Duration is 1 to 12 months (3 months preferred). Unpaid. Open to high school students, recent high school graduates, college freshmen, college sophomores, college juniors, college seniors, recent college graduates, graduate students, law students, career changers, individuals reentering the workforce. International applications accepted.

Benefits Formal training, job counseling, names of contacts, on-the-job training, opportunity to attend seminars/workshops, possible full-time employment, willing to act as a professional reference, willing to complete paperwork for educational credit, willing to provide letters of recommendation.

Contact Write, fax, or e-mail Bill Zimmerman, Director of Accreditation. Fax: 303-440-9581. E-mail: bill@aee.org. No phone calls. Applicants must submit a formal organization application, letter of interest, resume. Applications are accepted continuously. World Wide Web: http://www.aee.org.

AURORA UNIVERSITY–LAKE GENEVA CAMPUS
PO Box 210
Williams Bay, Wisconsin 53191

General Information Educational conference center providing outdoor and nontraditional learning experiences and sponsoring regional conferences. Established in 1886. Number of employees: 100. Affiliate of Aurora University, Aurora, Illinois. Number of internship applications received each year: 50.

Internships Available ▶ *6–8 adventure education interns:* responsibilities include facilitating team building and leadership development programs for adolescents, colleges, and adult groups by utilizing trust building, group initiatives, high and low ropes courses, team and individual climbing elements, and off-campus rock climbing. Candidates should have experience in the field, oral communication skills, organizational skills, strong interpersonal skills, strong leadership ability. Duration is March-November. $320–$350 per week. Open to college seniors, recent college graduates, graduate students, career changers. ▶ *1 outdoor recreation intern:* responsibilities include coordinating conference groups and leading activities, including sports, games, natural awareness, and orienteering. Candidates should have ability to work independently, ability to work with others, experience in the field, self-motivation, strong leadership ability, waterfront skills, qualified life guard, experience in sailing, canoeing, windsurfing, skiing (downhill or cross country). Duration is 1 summer or 1 winter (12 to 15 weeks each). $200–$250 per week. Open to college seniors, recent college graduates, graduate students. ▶ *7 outdoor/environmental education interns:* responsibilities include coordinating school groups and teaching classes in natural awareness, wetlands, lake study, astronomy, and weather. Candidates should have ability to work with others, organizational skills, personal interest in the field, plan to pursue career in field, self-motivation, strong leadership ability. Duration is September-May. $265–$300 per week. Open to recent college graduates, graduate students. International applications accepted.

Benefits Formal training, names of contacts, on-the-job training, willing to act as a professional reference, willing to complete paperwork for educational credit, willing to provide letters of recommendation, supplemental medical policy, use of recreational facilities (tennis, golf, waterfront), free room and board for outdoor/environmental education and outdoor recreation positions, room and board at a cost for adventure education positions.

Contact Write, fax, e-mail, or through World Wide Web site Cathy Coster, Associate Director of Adventure Education. Fax: 262-245-8549. E-mail: ccoster@aurora.edu. No phone calls. In-person interview recommended (telephone interview accepted). Applicants must submit a letter of interest, resume, three personal references. Application deadline: February 1 for adventure education interns (March), April 1 for summer, August 1 for outdoor/environmental education interns (September), November 1 for winter. World Wide Web: http://www.aurora.edu.

BOSTON UNIVERSITY SARGENT CENTER FOR OUTDOOR EDUCATION
36 Sargent Camp Road
Hancock, New Hampshire 03449

General Information Program offering environmental and outdoor education, including initiatives, trust activities, and ropes-course work, for 5th- through 8th-graders. Established in 1912. Number of employees: 20. Unit of Boston University, Boston, Massachusetts. Number of internship applications received each year: 50.

Internships Available ▶ *1 nature center coordinator:* responsibilities include assisting in teaching environmental lessons, providing interns with new ideas or facts for lessons, supervising students in the nature center during free time, creating new displays, working on the physical appearance of the nature center, and attending most meals. Candidates should have ability to work independently, knowledge of field, oral communication skills, organizational skills, personal interest in the field, research skills, self-motivation. Duration is 4 up to 9 months. $225 per week. ▶ *15–16 school program instructors:* responsibilities include teaching groups of 8-10 students environmental and outdoor education, supervising students, and attending weekly staff meetings. Candidates should have ability to work with others, oral communication skills, personal interest in the field, self-motivation, strong leadership ability, written communication skills. Duration is 3–9 months. $150–$200 per week. Open to recent high school graduates, college freshmen, college sophomores, college juniors, college seniors, recent college graduates, graduate students, law students, career changers, individuals reentering the workforce. International applications accepted.

Benefits Formal training, free housing, free meals, names of contacts, on-the-job training, opportunity to attend seminars/workshops, possible full-time employment, willing to complete paperwork for educational credit, willing to provide letters of recommendation, job lists provided when available, health insurance assistance.

Contact Write, call, fax, e-mail, or through World Wide Web site Kelly Meyer, School Program Coordinator. Phone: 603-525-3311. Fax: 603-525-4151. E-mail: school_program@busc.mv.com. In-person interview recommended (telephone interview accepted). Applicants must submit a formal organization application, three letters of recommendation. Application deadline: July 31 for fall, December 15 for winter/spring. World Wide Web: http://www.bu.edu/outdoor.

THE BREAKTHROUGH COLLABORATIVE
40 First Street, 5th Floor
San Francisco, California 94105

General Information Education program that provides free academic enrichment to middle school students and teaching, mentorship, and tutoring opportunities to high school and college students at 26 program sites nation wide and in Hong Kong. Established in 1991. Number of employees: 14. Number of internship applications received each year: 1,300.

Internships Available ▶ *500–800 school-year tutors:* responsibilities include providing one-to-one mentoring, teaching, and tutoring to children. Duration is September through May. Unpaid. Open to high school students, college freshmen, college sophomores, college juniors, college seniors, recent college graduates, graduate students. ▶ *800–900 summer teachers:* responsibilities include planning daily lessons, planning and overseeing special events, and acting as mentors. Duration is 2–3 months. Position available as unpaid or at $500-$2500 per internship; stipend enhancement may be possible upon request. Open to high school students, recent high school graduates, college freshmen, college sophomores, college juniors, college seniors, recent college graduates. Candidates for all positions should have ability to work with others, oral communication skills, organizational skills, self-motivation, strong leadership ability, writing skills. International applications accepted.

Benefits Formal training, on-the-job training, opportunity to attend seminars/workshops, possible full-time employment, tuition assistance, willing to act as a professional reference, willing to complete paperwork for educational credit, willing to provide letters of recommendation, room and board for out-of-town interns may be available.

International Internships Available in Hong Kong.

Contact Write, call, e-mail, or through World Wide Web site Rhea Wong, Admissions and Alumni Coordinator. Phone: 415-422-0600 Ext. 105. E-mail: admissions@breakthroughcollaborative.org. Telephone interview required. Applicants must submit a formal organization application, resume, academic transcripts, general application via Web site. Application deadline: early February (round 1); early April (round 2). World Wide Web: http://www.breakthroughcollaborative.org.

BRECKENRIDGE OUTDOOR EDUCATION CENTER
Box 697
Breckenridge, Colorado 80424

General Information Education center offering year-round wilderness and adventure programs for individuals of all abilities, as well as team building, leadership development, and adaptive skiing opportunities for individuals with disabilities and other special needs, and team building programs for professionals; accredited by Association of Experiential Education. Established in 1976. Number of employees: 25. Number of internship applications received each year: 100.

Internships Available ▶ *Business administration interns:* responsibilities include working with business manager learning about the general accounting, budget, and overall business side of the organization. Candidates should have ability to work independently, ability to work with others, computer skills, office skills, oral communication skills, self-motivation. Duration is flexible. Unpaid. ▶ *Development interns:* responsibilities include working with the grants and contributions manager; grant writing, research, and field work. Candidates should have ability to work with others, computer skills, editing skills, research skills, self-motivation, writing skills. Duration is flexible. Unpaid. ▶ *Events and marketing interns:* responsibilities include assisting in planning, implementation, and evaluation of special events and marketing plans. Candidates should have organizational skills, personal interest in

Breckenridge Outdoor Education Center (continued)

the field, self-motivation, strong interpersonal skills, writing skills. Duration is flexible. Unpaid. ▶ *1–2 program administration interns:* responsibilities include working with program directors 90% of the time and working in the field 10% of the time; outreach, database work, and special projects. Candidates should have ability to work independently, ability to work with others, computer skills, office skills, personal interest in the field, self-motivation. Duration is flexible. Unpaid. ▶ *10–12 summer wilderness interns:* responsibilities include planning, implementation/facilitation/evaluation of wilderness courses, administrative duties, and assisting with professional challenge courses. Candidates should have oral communication skills, personal interest in the field, self-motivation, strong interpersonal skills, CPR and first aid certifications. Duration is May 15 to September 30. $50 per month stipend. ▶ *10–12 winter adaptive ski interns:* responsibilities include serving as adaptive ski instructor, assisting on wilderness courses, assisting on professional challenge courses, and administrative duties. Candidates should have ability to work independently, ability to work with others, personal interest in the field, self-motivation, strong leadership ability, CPR and first aid certifications. Duration is November 1 to April 30. $50 per month stipend. Open to individuals at least 21 years old. International applications accepted.
Benefits Formal training, free housing, free meals, names of contacts, on-the-job training, possible full-time employment, willing to act as a professional reference, willing to complete paperwork for educational credit, willing to provide letters of recommendation, ski pass in winter, worker's compensation, athletics club pass.
Contact Write, call, fax, e-mail, or through World Wide Web site Robyn Graber, Internship Coordinator. Phone: 970-453-6422 Ext. 11. Fax: 970-453-4676. E-mail: internship@boec.org. In-person interview recommended (telephone interview accepted). Applicants must submit a letter of interest, resume, letter of recommendation, formal application (available on Web site). Application deadline: March 1 for summer, September 1 for winter. World Wide Web: http://www.boec.org.

BROOKINGS INSTITUTION–CENTER FOR PUBLIC POLICY EDUCATION (CPPE)
1775 Massachusetts Avenue, NW
Washington, District of Columbia 20036

General Information Nonprofit public policy research organization that designs and conducts executive education programs for corporate and government executives. Established in 1917. Number of employees: 20. Number of internship applications received each year: 50.
Internships Available ▶ *1–2 interns:* responsibilities include working with senior staff members to identify possible topics and speakers for public policy conferences, researching new companies to visit as part of conferences on understanding business policy, working with marketing staff to identify potential companies to attend programs, and performing clerical duties as assigned. Candidates should have computer skills, oral communication skills, organizational skills, research skills, self-motivation, strong interpersonal skills. Duration is one semester or summer. Unpaid. Open to college juniors, college seniors.
Benefits On-the-job training, opportunity to attend seminars/workshops, willing to complete paperwork for educational credit.
Contact Write, fax, or e-mail Rick Henry, Program Associate, 1775 Massachusetts Avenue, NW, Washington, District of Columbia 20036. Fax: 202-797-6319. E-mail: rhenry@brookings.edu. No phone calls. Telephone interview required. Applicants must submit a resume, writing sample, cover letter. Application deadline: March 1 for summer, July 1 for fall, November 1 for spring. World Wide Web: http://www.brookings.edu/execed.

CALIFORNIA ACADEMY OF SCIENCES, CAREERS IN SCIENCE
Golden Gate Park
San Francisco, California 94118

General Information Work-based youth-development program focusing on youth traditionally under-represented in the sciences.

Established in 1996. Number of employees: 32. Number of internship applications received each year: 100.
Internships Available ▶ *3–5 level one interns:* responsibilities include teaching science on museum floor and through outreach to community partners; providing administrative assistance to the Education Department; opportunities to assist research scientists or graduate assistants with original research. Candidates should have ability to work independently, oral communication skills, personal interest in the field, self-motivation, strong interpersonal skills. Duration is year-round; can stay in program until age 20. $7–$9.50 per hour. Open to high school students, recent high school graduates, college freshmen, must be between the ages of 15 and 17.
Benefits Formal training, names of contacts, on-the-job training, opportunity to attend seminars/workshops, tuition assistance, willing to act as a professional reference, willing to provide letters of recommendation, career and educational planning.
Contact Write, call, fax, or e-mail Ashley Conrad–Saydah, Careers in Science Manager. Phone: 415-750-7366. Fax: 415-750-7367. E-mail: cis@calacademy.org. In-person interview required. Applicants must submit a formal organization application. Application deadline: April 30. World Wide Web: http://www.calacademy.org/education/internships.

CASA XELAJU
3034 47th Avenue South
Minneapolis, Minnesota 55406

General Information Cultural institute. Established in 1987. Number of employees: 40. Number of internship applications received each year: 75.
Internships Available ▶ *2 business/computer interns:* responsibilities include working on Web site, assisting international coordinator in organizing field trips, translating lectures, and working with banks and local businesses. Candidates should have ability to work independently, college courses in field, self-motivation, written communication skills, ability to speak Spanish. Duration is 6 weeks. Unpaid. Open to college sophomores, college juniors, college seniors. ▶ *6 human rights/labor union interns.* Candidates should have ability to work independently, analytical skills, college courses in field, computer skills, knowledge of field, office skills, oral communication skills, organizational skills, research skills, self-motivation, strong interpersonal skills, strong leadership ability, writing skills, ability to read, write, and speak Spanish. Duration is 6 weeks. Unpaid. Open to college freshmen, college sophomores, college juniors, college seniors, recent college graduates, graduate students, law students. ▶ *6 journalism interns:* responsibilities include working on newspapers on different tasks including photojournalism, business office, layout, news, wire services, reporting. Candidates should have ability to work independently, ability to work with others, analytical skills, editing skills, writing skills, ability to write, read, and speak Spanish. Duration is 6 weeks. Unpaid. Open to college juniors, college seniors, recent college graduates, graduate students. ▶ *5 medical interns:* responsibilities include working with the grassroots organization Clinica Alemana and working in a national hospital as a resident. Candidates should have declared college major in field, oral communication skills, self-motivation, ability to write, read, and speak Spanish. Duration is 6 weeks. Unpaid. Open to college seniors, recent college graduates, graduate students. ▶ *2–4 research community development interns:* responsibilities include working with a rural community in Quetzaltenango, Guatemala; researching issues in the community and developing solutions. Candidates should have ability to work independently, ability to work with others, analytical skills, computer skills, editing skills, knowledge of field, office skills, oral communication skills, organizational skills, personal interest in the field, research skills, self-motivation, strong leadership ability, writing skills. Duration is 6–12 months. Unpaid. Open to college juniors, college seniors, recent college graduates, graduate students, law students, career changers. ▶ *2 senior advisors (Women's Sewing Association):* responsibilities include helping to develop broader markets for selling goods in USA and European countries. Candidates should have ability to work independently, ability to work with others, analytical skills, college courses in field, computer skills, editing skills, office skills, oral communication skills, organizational skills, personal interest in the field, plan to pursue

career in field, research skills, self-motivation, strong leadership ability, writing skills. Duration is 6–12 months. Unpaid. Open to college juniors, college seniors, recent college graduates, graduate students, law students. ▶ *4 social work interns:* responsibilities include helping a local women's shelter address domestic violence; helping children with homework; and working with local community. Candidates should have analytical skills, knowledge of field, office skills, oral communication skills, strong interpersonal skills, strong leadership ability, written communication skills, ability to read, write, and speak Spanish. Duration is 7 weeks. Unpaid. Open to college juniors, college seniors, recent college graduates, graduate students. International applications accepted.

Benefits Housing at a cost, opportunity to attend seminars/ workshops, possible full-time employment, willing to act as a professional reference, willing to complete paperwork for educational credit, willing to provide letters of recommendation.

International Internships Available in Guatemala.

Contact Write, call, fax, e-mail, or through World Wide Web site Julio E. Batres, Director, 3034 47th Avenue South, Minneapolis, Minnesota 55406. Phone: 888-796-CASA. Fax: 612-729-9264. E-mail: info@casaxelaju.com. Telephone interview required. Applicants must submit a formal organization application, letter of interest, resume, two letters of recommendation. Applications are accepted continuously. Fees: $50. World Wide Web: http://www.casaxelaju. com.

THE CENTER FOR CROSS-CULTURAL STUDY
446 Main Street
Amherst, Massachusetts 01002

General Information Educational institution/study abroad program combining academic coursework and internships in a variety of fields. Established in 1969. Number of employees: 40. Number of internship applications received each year: 10.

Internships Available ▶ *1–2 interns (Seville, Spain):* responsibilities include duties based on type of position and field of study. Candidates should have ability to work with others, knowledge of field, oral communication skills, self-motivation, written communication skills, one semester of advanced college-level Spanish or equivalent, participation in an Upper-Division, CC-CS Semester or Academic Program in Seville, Spain. Duration is one semester (10-15 hours per week). Unpaid. Open to college freshmen, college sophomores, college juniors, college seniors. International applications accepted.

Benefits On-the-job training, willing to act as a professional reference, willing to complete paperwork for educational credit, possibility of 3-6 credits per semester for equine science and educational positions.

International Internships Available in Seville, Spain.

Contact Write, call, fax, e-mail, or through World Wide Web site Dr. Judith Ortiz, Director, United States. Phone: 413-256-0011. Fax: 413-256-1968. E-mail: ortiz@cccs.com. In-person interview required. Applicants must submit a formal organization application, letter of interest, resume, academic transcripts, three letters of recommendation. Application deadline: May 15 for fall, November 15 for spring. Fees: $30. World Wide Web: http://www. StudyinSpain .org.

CENTER FOR CULTURAL INTERCHANGE
17 North Second Avenue
St. Charles, Illinois 60174

General Information Nonprofit student and adult exchange organization that sends American college-age students and recent graduates abroad for internship opportunities. Established in 1985. Number of employees: 21. Number of internship applications received each year: 20.

Internships Available ▶ *Up to 100 interns:* responsibilities include working in business, accounting/finance, travel/tourism, social service, or other fields depending on the intern's educational background and destination. Candidates should have college courses in field, office skills, personal interest in the field, language skills may be necessary. Duration is 1–3 months. Unpaid. Open to college juniors, college seniors, recent college graduates, graduate students. International applications accepted.

Benefits Health insurance, housing at a cost, meals at a cost, names of contacts, on-the-job training, opportunity to attend seminars/workshops, willing to act as a professional reference, willing to complete paperwork for educational credit, willing to provide letters of recommendation.

International Internships Available in France; Dublin, Ireland; Florence, Italy; London, United Kingdom.

Contact Write, call, fax, e-mail, or through World Wide Web site Jacqui Metcalf, Outbound Programs Director. Phone: 888-227-6231. Fax: 630-377-1944. E-mail: jacqui@cci-exchange.com. Applicants must submit a formal organization application, letter of interest, resume, letter of recommendation, language interview may be necessary, $250 deposit ($175 refunded if not accepted for program). Applications are accepted continuously. World Wide Web: http://www.cci-exchange.com.

CENTER FOR TALENTED YOUTH/JOHNS HOPKINS UNIVERSITY
2701 North Charles Street
Baltimore, Maryland 21218

General Information Organization that provides academically talented pre-college students with the opportunity to take rigorous courses in mathematics, science, computer science, humanities, and writing at college campuses in the United States. Established in 1980. Number of employees: 150. Unit of Johns Hopkins University, Baltimore, Maryland. Number of internship applications received each year: 3,000.

Internships Available ▶ *20–25 health assistants:* responsibilities include overseeing medication and medical appointments for live-in, pre-college students; contacting parents when necessary; and completing reports. Candidates should have oral communication skills, organizational skills, personal interest in the field, self-motivation, strong interpersonal skills, written communication skills. Duration is late June through early August. $2200 per 6-week internship. Open to college juniors, college seniors, recent college graduates, graduate students, medical or pre-med students. ▶ *20 office managers:* responsibilities include managing an office, overseeing petty cash account, and supervising office staff at a fast-paced, live-in camp for gifted pre-college students. Candidates should have computer skills, experience in the field, office skills, organizational skills, strong interpersonal skills, strong leadership ability. Duration is late June through early August. $3600 per 7-week internship. Open to college juniors, college seniors, recent college graduates, graduate students, business students. ▶ *400 resident assistants:* responsibilities include caring for the needs of live-in, pre-college students and sponsoring and leading daily activities. Candidates should have ability to work with others, oral communication skills, organizational skills, self-motivation, strong leadership ability. Duration is late June through early August. $2000 per 6-week internship. Open to college freshmen, college sophomores, college juniors, college seniors, recent college graduates. ▶ *40–45 residential program assistants:* responsibilities include answering phones, covering office, purchasing supplies, and conducting recreational activities at a residential camp for gifted pre-college students. Candidates should have computer skills, office skills, oral communication skills, self-motivation, strong interpersonal skills, written communication skills. Duration is late June through early August. $2200 per 6-week internship. Open to college juniors, college seniors, recent college graduates, age 21 and over preferred in order to drive rental vehicles. ▶ *400 teaching assistants/laboratory assistants:* responsibilities include supporting instructor with clerical work for the class, tutoring the students, proctoring study hall, and teaching some lessons. Candidates should have college courses in field, oral communication skills, personal interest in the field, strong interpersonal skills, strong leadership ability, written communication skills. Duration is late June through early August. $1800 per 6-week internship. Open to college freshmen, college sophomores, college juniors, college seniors, recent college graduates, graduate students, law students. International applications accepted.

Benefits Formal training, free housing, free meals, job counseling, names of contacts, on-the-job training, opportunity to attend seminars/workshops, possible full-time employment, willing to act

Center for Talented Youth/Johns Hopkins University (continued)
as a professional reference, willing to complete paperwork for educational credit, willing to provide letters of recommendation. **Contact** Write, call, fax, e-mail, or through World Wide Web site Summer Employment Opportunities, 3400 North Charles Street, Baltimore, Maryland 21218. Phone: 410-516-0053. Fax: 410-516-0093. E-mail: ctysummer@jhu.edu. Telephone interview required. Applicants must submit a formal organization application, letter of interest, resume, academic transcripts, letter of recommendation. Application deadline: January 27 for priority deadline. World Wide Web: http://www.cty.jhu.edu/summer/employment.

CENTRO DE DISENO ARQUITECTURA Y CONTRUCCION
Apartado Postal 3900
Tegucigalpa Honduras

General Information Private university specializing in architecture and design that is committed to investigation and community outreach. Established in 1996. Number of employees: 54. Number of internship applications received each year: 5.
Internships Available ▶ *1 computer services intern:* responsibilities include providing support to users of computer lab; offering training opportunities for students and staff; helping design operational programs; developing database for university operations. Candidates should have ability to work independently, computer skills, knowledge of field, self-motivation, strong interpersonal skills, minimum of intermediate-level Spanish. Duration is 1–3 semesters. Position available as unpaid or paid. Open to college juniors, college seniors, recent college graduates, graduate students, career changers. ▶ *1–2 construction technology interns:* responsibilities include giving workshops on specific construction skills, such as building types, the use of specific materials, and building models. Candidates should have ability to work with others, experience in the field, oral communication skills, personal interest in the field, minimum of intermediate-level Spanish. Duration is 1–15 weeks. Position available as unpaid or paid. Open to college seniors, recent college graduates, graduate students, career changers, individuals reentering the workforce, people with specific construction skills. ▶ *1 librarian:* responsibilities include activities to strengthen library services, managing Internet access and monitoring for topics of interest, soliciting additional library resources. Candidates should have ability to work independently, computer skills, knowledge of field, research skills, self-motivation, minimum of intermediate-level Spanish. Duration is 1–3 semesters. Position available as unpaid or paid. Open to college seniors, recent college graduates, graduate students, career changers, individuals reentering the workforce, professionals in the field desiring overseas experience. ▶ *1 marketing intern:* responsibilities include helping design and write public relations and promotional materials, designing ad campaigns, organizing promotional events, working with student admissions process, investigating need for new degree and extension courses. Candidates should have ability to work with others, computer skills, experience in the field, self-motivation, minimum of intermediate-level Spanish. Duration is 2–6 months. Position available as unpaid or paid. Open to college seniors, recent college graduates, graduate students, career changers, individuals reentering the workforce, professionals in the field desiring overseas experience. ▶ *1–2 municipal support interns:* responsibilities include helping develop materials to train municipal employees and elected officials on basic urban planning issues. Candidates should have ability to work independently, declared college major in field, knowledge of field, self-motivation, written communication skills, minimum of intermediate-level Spanish. Duration is 1–3 semesters. Position available as unpaid or paid. Open to college seniors, recent college graduates, graduate students, career changers, individuals reentering the workforce, professionals in the field desiring overseas experience or research opportunities. ▶ *1–3 research interns:* responsibilities include locating and translating background materials; participating in testing, experiments, and design; providing logistical support; helping design final reports, and drafting proposals for additional research projects. Candidates should have ability to work independently, ability to work with others, analytical skills, knowledge of field, research skills, minimum of

intermediate-level Spanish. Duration is 1–3 semesters. Position available as unpaid or paid. Open to college juniors, college seniors, recent college graduates, graduate students, career changers, individuals reentering the workforce, professionals in the fields of architecture, design, engineering, or construction desiring overseas experience. ▶ *1–3 teaching assistants:* responsibilities include providing support for teachers in workshop settings, helping prepare exercises and materials, evaluating and proposing teaching methods, proposing and developing new courses, and helping draft proposals for program needs. Candidates should have declared college major in field, knowledge of field, oral communication skills, self-motivation, strong interpersonal skills, minimum of intermediate-level Spanish. Duration is 1–3 semesters. Position available as unpaid or paid. Open to college seniors, recent college graduates, graduate students, career changers, individuals reentering the workforce, architecture or design professionals desiring overseas or teaching experience. ▶ *1–4 urban and regional planning interns:* responsibilities include working with municipal governments to develop plans and offering courses or training on the subject. Candidates should have ability to work with others, declared college major in field, oral communication skills, written communication skills, minimum of intermediate-level Spanish. Duration is 1–12 months. Position available as unpaid or paid. Open to college seniors, recent college graduates, graduate students, individuals reentering the workforce, professionals in the field desiring overseas experience. International applications accepted.
Benefits Housing at a cost, meals at a cost, on-the-job training, opportunity to attend seminars/workshops, possible full-time employment, willing to act as a professional reference, willing to complete paperwork for educational credit, willing to provide letters of recommendation, participation in CEDAC courses free of charge.
International Internships Available in Tegucigalpa, Honduras.
Contact Write, fax, or e-mail Lorette Pellettiere Calix, Internship Coordinator, TGU-00390, PO Box 025387, Miami, Florida 33102-5387. Phone: 011-504-232-4195. Fax: 011-504-231-0729. E-mail: administracion@cedac.edu.hn. Applicants must submit a letter of interest, resume, academic transcripts, three letters of recommendation, e-mail address if possible. Applications are accepted continuously. World Wide Web: http://www.cedac.edu.hn.

CHOATE ROSEMARY HALL
333 Christian Street
Wallingford, Connecticut 06492

General Information Secondary school with summer enrichment and credit programs for middle and high school students. Established in 1916. Number of employees: 125. Number of internship applications received each year: 100.
Internships Available ▶ *25–30 teaching interns:* responsibilities include teaching two classes, serving as residential house adviser, and coaching two afternoons per week. Candidates should have ability to work with others, organizational skills, personal interest in the field, plan to pursue career in field, self-motivation, strong leadership ability. Duration is 5 weeks. $2400–$2500 per duration of internship. Open to college juniors, college seniors, recent college graduates, graduate students, career changers. International applications accepted.
Benefits Free housing, free meals, job counseling, names of contacts, on-the-job training, willing to act as a professional reference, willing to provide letters of recommendation, training with two different senior teachers.
Contact Write, call, fax, e-mail, or through World Wide Web site Jim Irzyk, Director of Summer Programs. Phone: 203-697-2365. Fax: 203-697-2519. E-mail: jirzyk@choate.edu. In-person interview recommended (telephone interview accepted). Applicants must submit a formal organization application, letter of interest, resume, academic transcripts, two letters of recommendation. Application deadline: March 1 for teaching interns (submissions by January encouraged). World Wide Web: http://www.choate.edu/summer.

CITY OF DETROIT–WORKFORCE PLANNING AND COMMUNITY OUTREACH UNIT
2 Woodward Avenue, Suite 314, Coleman A. Young Municipal Center
Detroit, Michigan 48226

General Information Program that has over 40 departments and agencies that offer college students an internship program opportunity to receive paid work experience in their area of study. Established in 1701. Number of employees: 19,000. Unit of City of Detroit–Human Resources Department, Detroit, Michigan. Number of internship applications received each year: 100.
Internships Available ▶ *1–20 urban government interns (I and II):* responsibilities include performing varied tasks depending upon position and department requirements. Candidates should have ability to work independently, computer skills, declared college major in field, oral communication skills, plan to pursue career in field, research skills, strong interpersonal skills, writing skills. Duration is 10–12 weeks. Position available as unpaid or at $10–$14 per hour. Open to college juniors, college seniors, graduate students. International applications accepted.
Benefits Opportunity to attend seminars/workshops, possible full-time employment, willing to complete paperwork for educational credit, willing to provide letters of recommendation.
Contact Write, fax, or e-mail Mary K. Shanks-Allen, Internship Coordinator, 2 Woodward Avenue, Suite 314, Coleman A. Young Building, Detroit, Michigan 48226. Fax: 313-224-3410. E-mail: allenm.po1.ccb@href.ci.detroit.mi.us. No phone calls. In-person interview required. Applicants must submit a letter of interest, resume, academic transcripts. Application deadline: April 15 for summer. World Wide Web: http://www.ci.detroit.mi.us.

COLLEGE OF DUPAGE–MULTIMEDIA SERVICES
425 Fawell Boulevard
Glen Ellyn, Illinois 60137

General Information Images production of monthly news and public affairs program produced by College of DuPage. Established in 1970. Number of employees: 1,700. Number of internship applications received each year: 25.
Internships Available ▶ *1–2 assistant editors/videographers of images:* responsibilities include logging and capture of media, lighting and shooting interviews and b-roll segments both in studio and field locations, and assisting in editing segments. Candidates should have college courses in field, computer skills, organizational skills, personal interest in the field, plan to pursue career in field, research skills, background in lighting and videography, care and handling of DVCAM and Betacam video equipment. Duration is 1 semester at intern's college (20 hours per week). Unpaid. Open to college juniors, college seniors. ▶ *1–2 assistant producers of images:* responsibilities include arranging studio time, scheduling and assisting with interviews, writing segments, coordinating crew and equipment, and assisting in production, editing, and distribution of program. Candidates should have college courses in field, organizational skills, personal interest in the field, plan to pursue career in field, research skills, writing skills, background in scripting, production, interviewing techniques, and principles of editing. Duration is 1 semester at intern's college (20 hours per week). Unpaid. Open to college juniors, college seniors. ▶ *1 streaming media/electronic graphics intern:* responsibilities include logging, capture, and compression of media. Candidates should have analytical skills, college courses in field, computer skills, personal interest in the field, plan to pursue career in field, background in new media, Web design, video compression Flash, Shockwave, and other new media software. Duration is 1 semester at intern's college (20 hours per week). Unpaid. Open to college sophomores, college juniors, college seniors. International applications accepted.
Benefits On-the-job training, willing to act as a professional reference, willing to complete paperwork for educational credit, willing to provide letters of recommendation, entry into the Chicago area production market.
Contact Call or e-mail Kevin Willman, Producer. Phone: 630-942-3352. Fax: 630-942-2788. E-mail: willman@cdnet.cod.edu. In-person interview recommended (telephone interview accepted). Applicants

must submit a formal organization application, resume, two letters of recommendation. Application deadline: February 10 for spring, April 10 for summer, July 10 for fall, November 10 for winter. World Wide Web: http://www.cod.edu/multimedia.

THE COLLEGE SETTLEMENT OF PHILADELPHIA AND KUHN DAY CAMP
600 Witmer Road
Horsham, Pennsylvania 19044

General Information Resident and day camp that stresses environmental awareness in all activities including rock climbing, backpacking, outpost camping, and ""regular" camping; offers a residential outdoor school program for schools in the Philadelphia area during the fall and spring. Established in 1922. Number of employees: 63. Number of internship applications received each year: 200.
Internships Available ▶ *50–65 counselors:* responsibilities include living with children and directing activities. Candidates should have ability to work independently, experience in the field, oral communication skills, self-motivation, strong interpersonal skills, strong leadership ability. Duration is 9 weeks (summer only). $1800–$2000 per duration of internship. Open to college freshmen, college sophomores, college juniors, college seniors, recent college graduates, graduate students. ▶ *2 health providers:* responsibilities include living at Health Center; providing first day screenings, administering medications, and attending to sick or injured campers and staff. Candidates should have knowledge of field, organizational skills, personal interest in the field, plan to pursue career in field, strong interpersonal skills, RN or BSN required, Pennsylvania license required. Duration is 9 weeks (summer only). $4000 per duration of internship. Open to college juniors, college seniors, recent college graduates, graduate students, individuals reentering the workforce. ▶ *3 lifeguards:* responsibilities include instructing swimming and ensuring safety of recreational program participants. Candidates should have knowledge of field, oral communication skills, strong interpersonal skills, strong leadership ability, lifeguard training (required), water safety instruction (helpful). Duration is 9 weeks (summer only). $2000 per duration of internship. Open to college sophomores, college juniors, college seniors, recent college graduates, graduate students. ▶ *5 teachers/naturalists:* responsibilities include teaching small groups of children and leading large group and environmental activities. Candidates should have knowledge of field, oral communication skills, personal interest in the field, strong interpersonal skills, strong leadership ability. Duration is 3 months (spring and fall only). $225 per week. Open to college juniors, college seniors, recent college graduates, graduate students. ▶ *2 teen adventure leaders:* responsibilities include leading adventure trips with 13- and 14-year-olds. Candidates should have experience in the field, oral communication skills, personal interest in the field, self-motivation, strong interpersonal skills, strong leadership ability. Duration is 9 weeks (summer only). $3000 per duration of internship. Open to college seniors, recent college graduates, graduate students, individuals reentering the workforce. International applications accepted.
Benefits Formal training, free housing, free meals, names of contacts, opportunity to attend seminars/workshops, willing to act as a professional reference, willing to complete paperwork for educational credit, willing to provide letters of recommendation.
Contact Write, call, fax, or e-mail Andrew Fielding, Program Director. Phone: 215-542-7974. Fax: 215-542-7457. E-mail: camps@collegesettlement.org. In-person interview recommended (telephone interview accepted). Applicants must submit a formal organization application, resume, three personal references, background check required. Application deadline: January 1 for spring (recommended), May 1 for summer (recommended), August 1 for fall (recommended). World Wide Web: http://www.collegesettlement.org.

COOPERATIVE CENTER FOR STUDY ABROAD
Northern Kentucky University, BEP 301 Nunn Drive
Highland Heights, Kentucky 41099

General Information Organization that develops, plans, and coordinates study abroad programs to English speaking countries.

Established in 1984. Number of employees: 4. Number of internship applications received each year: 25.

Internships Available ▶ *Interns:* responsibilities include duties specific to intern's interests. Duration is 8–9 weeks. Unpaid. Open to college freshmen, college sophomores, college juniors, college seniors, graduate students, minimum age 18.

Benefits Housing at a cost, meals at a cost.

International Internships Available in Dublin, Ireland; London, United Kingdom.

Contact Write, call, fax, or e-mail Robin Byerly, Assistant to the Director. Phone: 800-319-6015. Fax: 859-572-6650. E-mail: ccsa@nku.edu. Applicants must submit a formal organization application, letter of interest, resume, two personal references, two letters of recommendation, 2 passport-size photos. Application deadline: February 14 for summer, April 11 for fall, October 3 for spring. Fees: $200. World Wide Web: http://www.ccsa.cc.

CORO
911 Washington Avenue, Suite 510
St. Louis, Missouri 63101

General Information Organization that conducts research, education, and training in public affairs; participants learn from their experiences in field assignments, interviews, and projects with diverse organizations. Established in 1942. Number of employees: 40. Number of internship applications received each year: 300.

Internships Available ▶ *64 Coro Fellows Program in Public Affairs:* responsibilities include working a minimum of 1600 hours over 9.5 months in 5 field assignments of public affairs (government, business, labor unions, nonprofit, and political campaigns); dozens of group interviews, 2 projects, 2-3 three-day retreats, and bi-weekly seminars. Candidates should have ability to work independently, analytical skills, oral communication skills, organizational skills, personal interest in the field, self-motivation, strong interpersonal skills, strong leadership ability, writing skills, commitment to public service. Duration is September to June. Position available as unpaid or paid. Open to college seniors, recent college graduates, graduate students, law students, career changers, individuals reentering the workforce. International applications accepted.

Benefits Formal training, names of contacts, on-the-job training, opportunity to attend seminars/workshops, willing to act as a professional reference, willing to complete paperwork for educational credit, willing to provide letters of recommendation, monthly stipends available based on financial need (ranging from $400–$800).

Contact Write, call, fax, e-mail, or through World Wide Web site Fellows Recruiter, 911 Washington Avenue, Suite 510, St. Louis, Missouri 63101. Phone: 314-621-3040 Ext. 28. Fax: 314-621-1874. E-mail: pzayas@coro.org. Applicants must submit a formal organization application, academic transcripts, three writing samples, three letters of recommendation, participation (for finalists) in a series of group "exercises" and interviews in March/April. Application deadline: February 1. Fees: $50. World Wide Web: http://www.coro.org.

CORO CENTER FOR LEADERSHIP
425 Sixth Avenue, Suite 1790
Pittsburgh, Pennsylvania 15219

General Information Leadership training center. Established in 1999. Number of employees: 12. Affiliate of Coro National, San Francisco, California. Number of internship applications received each year: 500.

Internships Available ▶ *3 Allegheny County Executive Fellows:* responsibilities include complying with specifications set by the county's requirements, attending training, meetings, sessions, and completing assigned projects. Candidates should have ability to work independently, ability to work with others, analytical skills, knowledge of field, oral communication skills, personal interest in the field, self-motivation, strong leadership ability, writing skills. Duration is July to June. $37,500 per year. Open to graduate students, law students, career changers, individuals reentering the workforce. ▶ *16 Coro Community Problem Solving Fellows:* responsibili-

ties include completing field assignments, attending weekly seminars and evening networking events, completing a group project, and conducting leadership interviews. Candidates should have ability to work independently, ability to work with others, oral communication skills, self-motivation, strong leadership ability, written communication skills. Duration is June to August. $2000 stipend. Open to college freshmen, college sophomores, college juniors, college seniors, recent college graduates. ▶ *64 Fellows in Public Affairs:* responsibilities include attending seminars, participating in five multi-sector placements, participating in group and individual projects. Candidates should have ability to work independently, ability to work with others, analytical skills, oral communication skills, personal interest in the field, self-motivation, strong leadership ability, written communication skills. Duration is September to May; full-time. Position available as unpaid or at $7000 to $12,000 stipend based on financial need. Open to recent college graduates, graduate students, law students, career changers, individuals reentering the workforce. ▶ *20–25 Information Technology Fellows:* responsibilities include meeting weekly, attending site visits and related events, and conducting interviews with professionals in this field of study. Candidates should have knowledge of field, personal interest in the field, plan to pursue career in field, self-motivation, strong leadership ability. Duration is June to August. Unpaid. Open to graduate students, career changers, individuals reentering the workforce. International applications accepted.

Benefits Formal training, names of contacts, on-the-job training, opportunity to attend seminars/workshops, tuition assistance, willing to act as a professional reference, willing to provide letters of recommendation, stipends; possible graduate school credit for Fellows in Public Affairs.

Contact Write, call, fax, e-mail, or through World Wide Web site Paul Leger, Associate Director. Phone: 412-258-2673. Fax: 412-201-0672. E-mail: pleger@coro.org. Applicants must submit a formal organization application, resume, academic transcripts, writing sample, personal reference, letter of recommendation, $50 fee for some applications. Application deadline: February for Fellows in Public Affairs, March for Community Problem Solving Fellows, March for Allegheny County Executive Fellows, April for Information Technology Fellows. World Wide Web: http://www.coro.org.

CORO NEW YORK LEADERSHIP CENTER
42 Broadway, 18th Floor
New York, New York 10004

General Information Organization that conducts research, education, and training in public affairs; participants' learning comes from their experiences in field assignments, interviews, and projects with diverse organizations. Established in 1942. Number of employees: 8. Affiliate of Coro Foundation National Organization, San Francisco, California. Number of internship applications received each year: 100.

Internships Available ▶ *12 Coro Fellows in Public Affairs:* responsibilities include working a minimum of 1600 hours over 9.5 months in 6 field assignments in public affairs (government, business, labor unions, nonprofit, media, and political campaigns); dozens of group interviews, individual and group consulting projects, 2-3 three-day retreats, and bi-weekly seminars. Candidates should have ability to work independently, oral communication skills, personal interest in the field, self-motivation, strong interpersonal skills, strong leadership ability. Duration is September-June. Position available as unpaid or paid. Open to college seniors, recent college graduates, graduate students, law students, career changers, individuals reentering the workforce. International applications accepted.

Benefits Formal training, housing at a cost, names of contacts, on-the-job training, opportunity to attend seminars/workshops, possible full-time employment, tuition assistance, willing to act as a professional reference, willing to complete paperwork for educational credit, willing to provide letters of recommendation, need-based financial aid including loan deferments, scholarships, stipends, subsidized housing; graduate credit.

Contact Write, call, fax, e-mail, or through World Wide Web site Rebecca Skaroff, Director of Outreach, 42 Broadway, 18th Floor,

New York, New York 10004. Phone: 212-248-2935 Ext. 230. Fax: 212-248-2970. E-mail: rskaroff@coro.org. In-person interview required. Applicants must submit a formal organization application, resume, academic transcripts, three writing samples, three letters of recommendation, participation (for finalists) in a series of group "exercises" and interviews in mid-March. Application deadline: January 3. Fees: $50. World Wide Web: http://www.coro. org.

CORO NORTHERN CALIFORNIA
580 California Street, 7th Floor
San Francisco, California 94104

General Information Private, nonprofit, nonpartisan, educational institution providing experiential and classroom training in public affairs through comprehensive training involving proprietary curriculum, internships, group participation, interviews, and seminars. Established in 1942. Number of employees: 8. Number of internship applications received each year: 100.
Internships Available ▶ *12 Coro Fellows in Public Affairs:* responsibilities include working a minimum of 1600 hours over 9.5 months in 6 field assignments of public affairs (government, business, labor unions, nonprofit, media, and political campaigns); dozens of group interviews, 2 projects, 2-3 three-day retreats, bi-weekly seminars, and Focus Weeks. Candidates should have ability to work independently, analytical skills, computer skills, editing skills, office skills, oral communication skills, organizational skills, personal interest in the field, research skills, self-motivation, strong interpersonal skills, strong leadership ability, writing skills. Duration is September to June. Paid at up to $15,000 stipend for duration of internship (need-based). Open to college seniors, recent college graduates, graduate students, law students, career changers, individuals reentering the workforce.
Benefits Formal training, names of contacts, on-the-job training, opportunity to attend seminars/workshops, possible full-time employment, willing to act as a professional reference, willing to complete paperwork for educational credit, willing to provide letters of recommendation.
Contact Write, call, fax, e-mail, or through World Wide Web site Mahvish Jafri, Program Associate. Phone: 415-986-0521. Fax: 415-986-5522. E-mail: recruitsf@coro.org. Applicants must submit a formal organization application, academic transcripts, three writing samples, three letters of recommendation, participation (for finalists) in a series of group "exercises" and interviews in late March/early April. Application deadline: first week of January. Fees: $50. World Wide Web: http://www.coro.org.

CORO SOUTHERN CALIFORNIA
811 Wilshire Boulevard, Suite 1025
Los Angeles, California 90017-2624

General Information Organization that conducts research, education, and training in public affairs; participants' learning comes from their experiences in field assignments, interviews, and projects with diverse organizations. Established in 1942. Number of employees: 12. Number of internship applications received each year: 100.
Internships Available ▶ *12 Coro Program in Public Affairs fellows:* responsibilities include working a minimum of 1600 hours in 6 field assignments of public affairs (government, business, labor unions, non-profit, media, and political campaigns); dozens of group interviews, 2 projects, 2-3 three-day retreats, and bi-weekly seminars. Candidates should have ability to work independently, analytical skills, computer skills, editing skills, office skills, oral communication skills, organizational skills, personal interest in the field, research skills, self-motivation, strong interpersonal skills, strong leadership ability, writing skills. Duration is September-June. Paid. Open to college seniors, recent college graduates, graduate students, law students, career changers, individuals reentering the workforce. International applications accepted.
Benefits Formal training, names of contacts, on-the-job training, opportunity to attend seminars/workshops, possible full-time employment, willing to act as a professional reference, willing to complete paperwork for educational credit, willing to provide letters of recommendation, monthly stipends available based on financial need (ranging from $800-$1200).

Contact Write, call, fax, e-mail, or through World Wide Web site Cynthia Rodriguez, Program Manager, 811 Wilshire Boulevard, Suite 1025, Los Angeles, California 90017-2624. Phone: 213-623-1234 Ext. 25. Fax: 213-680-0079. E-mail: crodriguez@coro.org. In-person interview required. Applicants must submit a formal organization application, resume, academic transcripts, three writing samples, personal reference, three letters of recommendation, all finalists must participate in a selection event in late March/early April. Application deadline: January 3. Fees: $50. World Wide Web: http://www.coro.org.

CUBAN STUDIES INSTITUTE
Tulane University, Caroline Richardson Building
New Orleans, Louisiana 70118-5698

General Information Organization that promotes academic and cultural collaboration and exchanges with Cuban institutions and scholars. Established in 1995. Number of employees: 3. Unit of Roger Thayer Stone Center for Latin American Studies. Number of internship applications received each year: 4.
Internships Available ▶ *6 development interns:* responsibilities include working side by side with community members on grassroots development projects. Candidates should have ability to work independently, oral communication skills, self-motivation, strong interpersonal skills, basic Spanish skills (highly recommended). Duration is 3 weeks to 1 semester. Unpaid. Open to college freshmen, college sophomores, college juniors, college seniors, recent college graduates, graduate students, law students, career changers, individuals reentering the workforce. International applications accepted.
Benefits Health insurance, housing at a cost, meals at a cost, names of contacts, on-the-job training, opportunity to attend seminars/workshops, willing to act as a professional reference, willing to complete paperwork for educational credit, willing to provide letters of recommendation.
International Internships Available in Ecuador.
Contact Write, call, fax, e-mail, or through World Wide Web site Deborah Ramil, Program Coordinator, Caroline Richardson Building, Tulane University, New Orleans 70118. Phone: 504-862-8629. Fax: 504-862-8678. E-mail: cuba@tulane.edu. In-person interview recommended (telephone interview accepted). Applicants must submit a formal organization application, letter of interest, academic transcripts, two letters of recommendation, medical clearance and housing forms, $500 deposit; passport copy. Application deadline: May 15 for summer interns; continuous for all other positions. World Wide Web: http://www.cuba.tulane.edu.

THE CUSHMAN SCHOOL
592 North East 60th Street
Miami, Florida 33137

General Information Non-denominational, non-discriminatory independent school designed for preschool through 8th grade boys and girls of average and above average development and learning ability. Established in 1924. Number of employees: 54. Number of internship applications received each year: 15.
Internships Available ▶ *2-4 educational interns:* responsibilities include helping with small reading groups, assisting in the writing process, and generating thematic projects. Candidates should have knowledge of field, oral communication skills, personal interest in the field, strong interpersonal skills. Duration is 1 semester. Paid. Open to recent college graduates, graduate students. International applications accepted.
Benefits Opportunity to attend seminars/workshops, possible full-time employment, willing to complete paperwork for educational credit, opportunity to teach, stipend of $2000 for U.S. residents, $3000 for foreign residents.
Contact Write, fax, or e-mail Ann Gorman, Internship Coordinator. Fax: 305-757-1632. E-mail: 1234567111@msn.com. No phone calls. Applicants must submit a letter of interest, resume, photo of applicant. Application deadline: May 1 for spring positions for following year, December 5 for fall positions for following year. World Wide Web: http://www.cushmanschool.org.

DUBLIN INTERNSHIPS
8 Orlagh Lawn, Scholarstown Road
Dublin 16 Ireland

General Information Organization that provides professional-level internships in Dublin, Ireland across the spectrum of majors and career options. Established in 1989. Number of employees: 4. Number of internship applications received each year: 120.
Internships Available ▶ *Interns:* responsibilities include professional level work under supervision in area of intern's interest. Candidates should have ability to work with others, college courses in field, computer skills, knowledge of field, flexibility. Duration is 10 weeks in summer; 15 weeks in fall and spring. Unpaid. Open to college juniors, college seniors, recent college graduates, graduate students, law students, career changers. International applications accepted.
Benefits Housing at a cost, meals at a cost, on-the-job training, opportunity to attend seminars/workshops, tuition assistance, willing to act as a professional reference, willing to complete paperwork for educational credit, willing to provide letters of recommendation, orientation, information and advice about cultural and historical visits.
International Internships Available.
Contact Write, call, fax, e-mail, or through World Wide Web site Mary H. Rieke, Director. Phone: 353-1-494-5277. Fax: 353-1-494-5277. E-mail: mhrieke@eircom.net. Applicants must submit a formal organization application, letter of interest, resume, academic transcripts, two letters of recommendation, photograph. Application deadline: March 1 for summer, May 1 for fall, October 1 for spring. World Wide Web: http://homepage.eircom.net/~dublinternships.

DYNAMY, INTERNSHIP YEAR
27 Sever Street
Worcester, Massachusetts 01609

General Information Nine-month internship program for students exploring their career interests; interns complete a three-week Outward Bound course and a series of three 9-week internships during the program. Established in 1969. Number of employees: 14. Number of internship applications received each year: 60.
Internships Available ▶ *40 interns:* responsibilities include completing 1 to 3 internships (areas include business, education, government, radio, TV, theater, social service, fine arts, medicine, restaurant/hotel management, retail, and environmental science), meeting weekly with a Dynamy Internship year adviser, and participating in community service activities and a 3-week outdoor education program. Candidates should have ability to work independently, oral communication skills, self-motivation, strong interpersonal skills, strong leadership ability. Duration is 4–9 months. Unpaid. Open to recent high school graduates, college freshmen, college sophomores, college juniors, college seniors, individuals ages 17-22. International applications accepted.
Benefits Formal training, housing at a cost, job counseling, on-the-job training, opportunity to attend seminars/workshops, tuition assistance, willing to act as a professional reference, willing to complete paperwork for educational credit, willing to provide letters of recommendation, up to 12 college credits available through Clark University.
Contact Write, call, fax, e-mail, or through World Wide Web site Mr. Keith Robichaud, Director of Admissions. Phone: 508-755-2571. Fax: 508-755-4692. E-mail: krobichaud@dynamy.org. In-person interview recommended (telephone interview accepted). Applicants must submit a formal organization application, academic transcripts, two writing samples, three letters of recommendation. Applications are accepted continuously. Fees: $50. World Wide Web: http://www.dynamy.org.

EDUCATE THE CHILDREN
PO Box 414
Ithaca, New York 14851

General Information International development organization. Established in 1991. Number of employees: 3. Number of internship applications received each year: 22.

Internships Available ▶ *1 program assistant:* responsibilities include research, secretarial tasks, newsletter production, and design and execution of promotional campaigns. Candidates should have ability to work independently, computer skills, office skills, oral communication skills, research skills, written communication skills. Duration is flexible. Unpaid. Open to college freshmen, college sophomores, college juniors, college seniors, recent college graduates, graduate students, career changers. International applications accepted.
Benefits On-the-job training, opportunity to attend seminars/workshops, willing to act as a professional reference, willing to complete paperwork for educational credit, willing to provide letters of recommendation, housing and/or meals for some placements in Nepal.
Contact Write or e-mail Susanna Pearce, Co-Director. E-mail: info@etc-nepal.org. In-person interview recommended (telephone interview accepted). Applicants must submit a formal organization application, resume, two personal references. Applications are accepted continuously. World Wide Web: http://www.etc-nepal.org.

EDUCATIONAL PROGRAMMES ABROAD (EPA)
350 East Michigan Avenue, Suite 225
Kalamazoo, Michigan 49007

General Information Educational organization that offers academic internships in London, Bonn, Berlin, Brussels, Madrid, Paris, Melbourne, and Edinburgh. Established in 1977. Number of employees: 3. Division of Educational Programmes Abroad, London, United Kingdom. Number of internship applications received each year: 600.
Internships Available ▶ *Interns:* responsibilities include working in national or regional government, various businesses, social services, health administration, medical research, media, or environmental organizations in London, Bonn, Berlin, Brussels, Madrid, Paris, Melbourne, or Edinburgh. Candidates should have ability to work independently, knowledge of field, personal interest in the field, self-motivation, strong interpersonal skills, written communication skills. Duration is 1 semester or summer. Unpaid. Open to college juniors, college seniors, recent college graduates, graduate students, law students. International applications accepted.
Benefits Housing at a cost, meals at a cost, willing to complete paperwork for educational credit.
International Internships Available in Melbourne, Australia; Brussels, Belgium; Paris, France; Bonn and Berlin, Germany; Madrid, Spain; London and Edinburgh, United Kingdom.
Contact Write, call, fax, e-mail, or through World Wide Web site Administrative Manager. Phone: 269-382-0139. Fax: 269-382-5222. E-mail: usoffice@epa-internships.org. Applicants must submit a formal organization application, resume, academic transcripts, writing sample, personal reference, letter of recommendation. Application deadline: March 1 for summer, May 1 for fall, November 15 for spring. World Wide Web: http://www.studyabroad.com/epa/.

EDUCATIONAL TESTING SERVICE
Rosedale Road
Princeton, New Jersey 08541

General Information Private not-for-profit educational measurement institution and leader in educational research that develops and administers achievement and admission tests. Established in 1948. Number of employees: 2,000. Number of internship applications received each year: 80.
Internships Available ▶ *3 ETS Postdoctoral Fellowship Award Program interns:* responsibilities include conducting original research at ETS in fields relevant to education, psychology, psychometrics, statistics, computer science, linguistics, testing, minority issues, or policy research. Candidates should have analytical skills, computer skills, knowledge of field, oral communication skills, organizational skills, research skills, written communication skills, academic scholarship with relevance to ETS research mission. Duration is 1 year. $38,000 per internship plus relocation expense reimbursement. Open to doctoral-level scholars. ▶ *1 Sylvia Taylor Johnson Minority Fellowship in Educational Measurement:* responsibilities include car-

rying out independent research outlined in 5-page research proposal under the mentorship of ETS senior scientist. Candidates should have ability to work independently, analytical skills, experience in the field, oral communication skills, research skills, written communication skills. Duration is 1 year. Paid. Open to minority scholars who hold a PhD or EdD, must be U.S. citizen. ► *8–12 summer program in research (graduate students):* responsibilities include independent research with access to a mentor in fields relevant to education, psychology, psychometrics, statistics, computer science, linguistics, testing, minority issues, or policy research; participation in seminars and workshops. Candidates should have ability to work with others, computer skills, knowledge of field, oral communication skills, research skills, written communication skills, scholarship with relevance to ETS mission. Duration is 8 weeks. $4000 per duration of internship. Open to doctoral students who have completed one year of full-time graduate study. International applications accepted.
Benefits Housing at a cost, meals at a cost, names of contacts, on-the-job training, opportunity to attend seminars/workshops, possible full-time employment, willing to act as a professional reference, willing to complete paperwork for educational credit, willing to provide letters of recommendation, reimbursement of roundtrip travel expenses (minimal compensation if accompanied by spouse or child).
Contact Write, call, fax, e-mail, or through World Wide Web site Ms. Linda J. DeLauro, Fellowship Program Administrator, Rosedale Road, Mail Stop 09R, Princeton, New Jersey 08541. Phone: 609-734-1806. Fax: 609-734-1755. E-mail: ldelauro@ets.org. Telephone interview required. Applicants must submit a formal organization application, letter of interest, resume, academic transcripts, writing sample, three letters of recommendation, 2-3 personal references; additional requirements vary by program (contact ETS for specifics). Application deadline: February 1 for summer program interns and postdoctoral positions. World Wide Web: http://www.ets.org.

EVERETT PUBLIC SERVICE INTERNSHIP PROGRAM
c/o Co-op America, 1612 K Street, NW, Suite 600
Washington, District of Columbia 20006

General Information Group of over 60 nonprofit organizations offering paid internships for 10 weeks in the summer. Established in 1989.
Internships Available ► *200 interns:* responsibilities include duties as assigned by organization selected. Duration is 10 weeks in summer. $230 per week. Open to college sophomores, college juniors, college seniors, graduate students, law students.
Benefits On-the-job training, opportunity to attend seminars/workshops, possible full-time employment, willing to act as a professional reference, willing to complete paperwork for educational credit, willing to provide letters of recommendation.
Contact Through World Wide Web site Internship Coordinator. E-mail: info@everettinternships.org. In-person interview recommended (telephone interview accepted). Applicants must submit a letter of interest, resume, some organizations require writing samples or references. Application deadline: March 1. World Wide Web: http://www.everettinternships.org.

EXCHANGE NETWORK INTERNATIONAL
1508 Birchwood Court
North Brunswick, New Jersey 08902

General Information Internship placement organization. Established in 2001. Number of employees: 1. Affiliate of Exchange Network International, Accra, Ghana. Number of internship applications received each year: 40.
Internships Available ► *2–4 customer service interns:* responsibilities include responding to, and dealing with clients on policy and claims issues, as well as making inquiries on behalf of clients. Candidates should have college courses in field, office skills, oral communication skills, organizational skills, strong interpersonal skills. Duration is 4–12 weeks. Paid. Open to college sophomores, college juniors, college seniors. ► *4–8 distant bankers:* responsibilities include formation of new groups, writing appraisal reports,

disbursing of loans to groups, monitoring clients performance, loan recovery, and preparing monthly reports. Candidates should have ability to work independently, analytical skills, oral communication skills, organizational skills, self-motivation, strong interpersonal skills, written communication skills. Duration is 4–12 weeks. Paid. Open to college juniors, college seniors, graduate students. ► *2–4 service support interns:* responsibilities include service support for software development, networking, and Internet access/services. Candidates should have ability to work with others, analytical skills, college courses in field, computer skills, organizational skills. Duration is 4–8 weeks. Paid. Open to college juniors, college seniors, recent college graduates. International applications accepted.
Benefits Free housing, free meals, health insurance, names of contacts, on-the-job training, opportunity to attend seminars/workshops, willing to act as a professional reference, willing to complete paperwork for educational credit, willing to provide letters of recommendation, communication facilities (personal mobile phone and Internet access).
International Internships Available in Ghana.
Contact Write, e-mail, or through World Wide Web site Internship Placement Department. E-mail: exchange@exchangenet.org. Telephone interview required. Applicants must submit a letter of interest, resume, completion of pre-internship form on line. Applications are accepted continuously. World Wide Web: http://www.exchangenet.org.

EXPLORATIONS IN TRAVEL, INC.
2458 River Road
Guilford, Vermont 05301

General Information Organization that provides travel opportunities and volunteer placements for students and adults. Established in 1990. Number of employees: 3. Number of internship applications received each year: 50.
Internships Available ► *1–5 agricultural/conservation volunteers (New Zealand):* responsibilities include working on small farms, teaching in schools, working with environmental and conservation organizations. Candidates should have ability to work independently, oral communication skills, self-motivation, strong interpersonal skills. Duration is flexible. Unpaid. Open to high school seniors, recent high school graduates, college freshmen, college sophomores, college juniors, college seniors, recent college graduates, graduate students, career changers, individuals reentering the workforce. ► *1–5 agroforestry and rainforest reserve volunteers (Costa Rica):* responsibilities include working with a small rainforest reserve in Costa Rica, including trail maintenance, tree planting, connection with local school and students. Candidates should have ability to work independently, ability to work with others, self-motivation, Spanish language skills. Duration is flexible. Unpaid. Open to recent high school graduates, college freshmen, college sophomores, college juniors, college seniors, recent college graduates, graduate students, career changers, individuals reentering the workforce, retired persons. ► *1–5 animal shelter volunteers (Puerto Rico):* responsibilities include working with an animal shelter/clinic in Puerto Rico caring for dogs, cats, and horses, and assisting veterinarian. Candidates should have ability to work independently, ability to work with others, personal interest in the field, self-motivation, Spanish language skills useful. Duration is flexible. Unpaid. Open to recent high school graduates, college freshmen, college sophomores, college juniors, college seniors, recent college graduates, graduate students, career changers, individuals reentering the workforce, retired persons. ► *1–5 conservation interns (Guatemala):* responsibilities include instruction in ecology, agriculture, animal husbandry, environmental education and history; volunteers assist with reforestation projects, trail maintenance, organic gardening, farm animals, and medicinal plants. Candidates should have ability to work independently, oral communication skills, self-motivation, strong interpersonal skills, strong leadership ability, written communication skills. Duration is flexible. Unpaid. Open to recent high school graduates, college freshmen, college sophomores, college juniors, college seniors, recent college graduates, graduate students, career changers, individuals reentering the workforce, retired persons. ► *1–5 environmental education/conservation volunteers (Mexico):* responsibili-

Explorations in Travel, Inc. (continued)

ties include teaching environmental education to student and community members in Mexico, assisting with field research on environmental changes to conservation areas. Candidates should have ability to work independently, ability to work with others, self-motivation, Spanish language skills useful. Duration is flexible. Unpaid. Open to recent high school graduates, college freshmen, college sophomores, college juniors, college seniors, recent college graduates, graduate students, career changers, individuals reentering the workforce, retired persons. ▶ *1–5 environmental/ conservation project volunteers (Ecuador):* responsibilities include working on environmental and conservation projects. Candidates should have ability to work independently, ability to work with others, self-motivation, Spanish language skills. Duration is flexible. Unpaid. Open to recent high school graduates, college freshmen, college sophomores, college juniors, college seniors, recent college graduates, graduate students, career changers, individuals reentering the workforce, retired persons. ▶ *1 individual and group projects intern (Nepal):* responsibilities include conservation and community group projects available in 2-week blocks; individual positions in schools and orphanages can also be arranged. Candidates should have ability to work independently, oral communication skills, self-motivation, strong interpersonal skills. Duration is 2 weeks to one year. Unpaid. Open to recent high school graduates, college freshmen, college sophomores, college juniors, college seniors, recent college graduates, graduate students, career changers, individuals reentering the workforce, retired persons. ▶ *1–5 rainforest conservation volunteers (Australia):* responsibilities include working in a tropical research center which focuses on the study, care, and rehabilitation of flying foxes in Australia; rainforest protection activism opportunity also available. Candidates should have ability to work independently, oral communication skills, personal interest in the field, self-motivation, strong interpersonal skills. Duration is flexible. Unpaid. Open to college freshmen, college sophomores, college juniors, college seniors, recent college graduates, graduate students, career changers, individuals reentering the workforce, retired persons. ▶ *1–5 rainforest reserve volunteers (Puerto Rico):* responsibilities include working with a small rainforest reserve in Puerto Rico on trail maintenance, reforestation projects, receiving visiting eco-tourist groups. Candidates should have ability to work independently, self-motivation, strong interpersonal skills. Duration is flexible. Unpaid. Open to high school seniors, recent high school graduates, college freshmen, college sophomores, college juniors, college seniors, recent college graduates, graduate students, career changers, individuals reentering the workforce, retired persons. ▶ *1–5 rainforest/conservation volunteers (Costa Rica):* responsibilities include working on a small rainforest reserve, including trail maintenance, tree planting, and connection with local school and students. Candidates should have ability to work independently, ability to work with others, personal interest in the field, self-motivation, Spanish language skills. Duration is flexible. Unpaid. Open to high school seniors, recent high school graduates, college freshmen, college sophomores, college juniors, college seniors, recent college graduates, graduate students, career changers, individuals reentering the workforce, retired persons. ▶ *1–5 sea turtle project volunteers (Costa Rica):* responsibilities include working with an environmental organization that focuses on protecting beaches and monitoring sea turtles, night patrols of beaches, and documenting turtle activity. Candidates should have ability to work independently, ability to work with others, personal interest in the field, self-motivation, Spanish language skills useful. Duration is flexible (April to August). Unpaid. Open to recent high school graduates, college freshmen, college sophomores, college juniors, college seniors, recent college graduates, graduate students, career changers, individuals reentering the workforce, retired persons. ▶ *1–5 teaching assistant volunteers (Costa Rica):* responsibilities include working with rural elementary and secondary schools in Costa Rica, including teaching English and other subjects and organizing recreational activities. Candidates should have ability to work independently, oral communication skills, self-motivation, strong interpersonal skills, strong leadership ability, written communication skills, Spanish language skills. Duration is flexible. Unpaid. Open to recent high school graduates, college freshmen, college sophomores, college juniors, college seniors,

recent college graduates, graduate students, career changers, individuals reentering the workforce, retired persons. ▶ *1–5 teaching assistant volunteers (Ecuador and Guatemala):* responsibilities include working with rural elementary and secondary schools in Ecuador, including teaching English and other subjects and organizing recreational activities. Candidates should have ability to work independently, oral communication skills, self-motivation, strong interpersonal skills, strong leadership ability, written communication skills, Spanish language skills. Duration is flexible. Unpaid. Open to recent high school graduates, college freshmen, college sophomores, college juniors, college seniors, recent college graduates, graduate students, career changers, individuals reentering the workforce, retired persons. ▶ *1–5 teaching assistant volunteers (Mexico):* responsibilities include working with secondary schools in the Yucatan including teaching English and other subjects and organizing recreational activities. Candidates should have ability to work independently, oral communication skills, self-motivation, strong interpersonal skills, strong leadership ability, written communication skills, Spanish language skills. Duration is flexible. Unpaid. Open to recent high school graduates, college freshmen, college sophomores, college juniors, college seniors, recent college graduates, graduate students, career changers, individuals reentering the workforce, retired persons. ▶ *1–5 wildlife rescue volunteers (Costa Rica):* responsibilities include working with an environmental education center and wildlife rehabilitation. Candidates should have ability to work independently, ability to work with others, self-motivation, Spanish language skills useful. Duration is flexible (one month minimum). Unpaid. Open to recent high school graduates, college freshmen, college sophomores, college juniors, college seniors, recent college graduates, graduate students, career changers, individuals reentering the workforce, retired persons. International applications accepted.
Benefits Housing at a cost, meals at a cost, names of contacts, willing to act as a professional reference, willing to complete paperwork for educational credit, willing to provide letters of recommendation, opportunity for language study.
International Internships Available in Costa Rica; Ecuador; Guatemala; Puerto Rico.
Contact Write, call, fax, e-mail, or through World Wide Web site Debbie Jacobs, Volunteer Coordinator. Phone: 802-257-0152. Fax: 802-257-2784. E-mail: explore@volunteertravel.com. Telephone interview required. Applicants must submit a formal organization application, letter of interest, resume, two letters of recommendation, placement fee of $975 upon acceptance. Applications are accepted continuously. Fees: $35. World Wide Web: http://www.volunteertravel.com.

FINANCIAL MARKETS CENTER
PO Box 334
Philomont, Virginia 20131

General Information Nonprofit research and education institute. Established in 1997. Number of employees: 5. Number of internship applications received each year: 75.
Internships Available ▶ *1–2 interns:* responsibilities include data collection and analysis; literature reviews; documents and survey research; preparing reports and summaries; Web site maintenance and promotion; and general office support. Candidates should have ability to work independently, analytical skills, computer skills, oral communication skills, research skills, writing skills. Duration is 1–3 semesters. $8–$17 per hour. Open to college freshmen, college sophomores, college juniors, college seniors, recent college graduates, graduate students, law students. International applications accepted.
Benefits On-the-job training, opportunity to attend seminars/ workshops, possible full-time employment, travel reimbursement, willing to act as a professional reference, willing to provide letters of recommendation, stipend.
Contact Write, e-mail, or through World Wide Web site Tom Schlesinger, Executive Director. Fax: 540-338-7757. E-mail: tom@ fmcenter.org. No phone calls. In-person interview recommended (telephone interview accepted). Applicants must submit a letter of interest, resume, writing sample, 3 personal references (for

top applicants). Application deadline: March 15 for summer, July 30 for fall, November 30 for spring. World Wide Web: http://www.fmcenter.org.

FLORIDA INTERNATIONAL UNIVERSITY
University Park
Miami, Florida 33199

General Information Large multicampus, multicultural university in Miami-Dade County, Florida. Established in 1965. Number of employees: 4,000. Number of internship applications received each year: 10.
Internships Available ▶ *1–2 exercise and sports science interns:* responsibilities include conducting exercise prescriptions, fitness testing, and fitness workshops. Candidates should have ability to work with others, computer skills, oral communication skills, plan to pursue career in field, research skills, self-motivation. Duration is preferably January to April, May to August, or August to December. Position available as unpaid or at stipend of $250–$500 (must work minimum of 200 hours). Open to college juniors, college seniors, recent college graduates. ▶ *1–2 health promotion/health education interns:* responsibilities include health promotion planning, implementation, and evaluation; development and dissemination of health communication materials; providing one-on-one health consultations; and teaching workshops on a variety of topics. Candidates should have ability to work independently, ability to work with others, computer skills, declared college major in field, knowledge of field, oral communication skills, self-motivation, ability to work with diverse population. Duration is preferably January to April, May to August, or August to December. Position available as unpaid or at stipend of $500–$1000 (must work minimum of 40 hours per week for 15 weeks). Open to college seniors, recent college graduates. ▶ *1–2 wellness interns:* responsibilities include coordinating special health promotion events; creating and disseminating health promotion materials; conducting one-on-one consultations; and teaching workshops on a variety of health-related topics. Candidates should have computer skills, knowledge of field, oral communication skills, self-motivation, strong interpersonal skills, written communication skills. Duration is flexible (ideally January-April, April-August, or August to December). Position available as unpaid or at $500–$1000 stipend (must work minimum of 40 hours per week for 15 weeks). Open to college freshmen, college sophomores, college juniors, college seniors, recent college graduates, graduate students. International applications accepted.
Benefits Formal training, job counseling, names of contacts, on-the-job training, opportunity to attend seminars/workshops, possible full-time employment, willing to act as a professional reference, willing to complete paperwork for educational credit, willing to provide letters of recommendation.
Contact Write, call, fax, e-mail, or through World Wide Web site Mariela Gabaroni, Wellness Coordinator, University Park, HWC 215, Miami, Florida 33199. Phone: 305-348-4020. Fax: 305-348-6655. E-mail: xgabaron@fiu.edu. Telephone interview required. Applicants must submit a formal organization application, letter of interest, resume, two personal references. Application deadline: March 1 for summer, May 1 for fall, October 1 for spring. World Wide Web: http://http://www.fiu.edu/.

FOOD SERVICE MANAGEMENT INTERNSHIP COMMITTEE
Lawyers Club Dining Service, 551 South State Street
Ann Arbor, Michigan 48109-1208

General Information Educational program whose purpose is to introduce aspiring professionals to the food service industry and to provide on-the-job experience that will better qualify them to assume responsibilities related to college and university food service. Established in 1961. Unit of Association of College and University Housing Officers–International/National Association of College and University Food Services. Number of internship applications received each year: 120.
Internships Available ▶ *55–65 food service management interns:* responsibilities include working with food service employees to develop understanding of personnel, production, service, sanita-

tion, and safety issues; working with professional staff to learn policies and issues affecting decisions in food service; gaining experience in supervision; and planning and coordinating food service functions. Candidates should have ability to work with others, college courses in field, knowledge of field, oral communication skills, organizational skills, personal interest in the field. Duration is 8 weeks. Stipend of $1600. Open to college sophomores, college juniors, college seniors, recent college graduates, graduate students. International applications accepted.
Benefits Free housing, free meals, job counseling, names of contacts, on-the-job training, opportunity to attend seminars/workshops, possible full-time employment, willing to act as a professional reference, willing to complete paperwork for educational credit, willing to provide letters of recommendation.
Contact Write, call, fax, e-mail, or through World Wide Web site Holly Downey, Assistant Manager, 551 South State Street, Ann Arbor, Michigan 48109-1208. Phone: 734-763-5161. Fax: 734-763-2313. E-mail: hkdowney@umich.edu. Telephone interview required. Applicants must submit a formal organization application, letter of interest, resume, academic transcripts, letter of recommendation. Application deadline: January 24 for summer. World Wide Web: http://www.nacufs.org.

THE FULBRIGHT COMMISSION
62 Doughty Street
London United Kingdom

General Information Educational exchange between the U.S. and the U.K. Established in 1948. Number of employees: 7. Number of internship applications received each year: 15.
Internships Available ▶ *1–2 information officers:* responsibilities include working in the U.S. Educational Advisory Service providing information and advice about studying in the U.S., project work on events, researching publications and handouts, and some general administrative work. Candidates should have office skills, personal interest in the field, research skills, self-motivation, strong interpersonal skills, written communication skills, marketing and/or IT skills (highly desirable). Duration is 6 months. $8 per hour. ▶ *4–8 student information officers:* responsibilities include answering inquiries about studying in the U.S., project work on events, information sheets, publications, newsletters, and some general administrative work. Candidates should have ability to work independently, ability to work with others, office skills, oral communication skills, organizational skills, written communication skills, marketing and/or IT skills (highly desirable). Duration is 3 months. Unpaid. Open to college juniors, college seniors, recent college graduates, graduate students. International applications accepted.
Benefits On-the-job training, willing to act as a professional reference, willing to complete paperwork for educational credit, willing to provide letters of recommendation, possible reimbursement of fee for work visa, free lunch, reimbursement for travel in London.
International Internships Available.
Contact Write, call, fax, or e-mail Anthony Nemecek, Director, U.S. Educational Advisory Service, London WC1N 2JS United Kingdom. Phone: 44-20-7404-6994. Fax: 44-20-7404-6874. E-mail: anemecek@fulbright.co.uk. In-person interview recommended (telephone interview accepted). Applicants must submit a letter of interest, resume, names and contact details of two referees. Applications are accepted continuously. World Wide Web: http://www.fulbright.co.uk.

THE FUND FOR AMERICAN STUDIES
1706 New Hampshire Avenue, NW
Washington, District of Columbia 20009

General Information Internship coordinating foundation. Number of employees: 20. Number of internship applications received each year: 1,500.
Internships Available ▶ *25–40 Capital Semester interns:* responsibilities include taking classes on corporate politics and economics at Georgetown University while working full-time with political, economic, and business agencies in DC. Candidates should have oral communication skills, plan to pursue career in field, self-motivation, written communication skills. Duration is 1 semester.

The Fund for American Studies (continued)

Unpaid. Open to college freshmen, college sophomores, college juniors, college seniors. ▶ *70–85 Institute on Political Journalism interns:* responsibilities include working with media organization and taking classes on ethics and journalism at Georgetown University. Candidates should have computer skills, oral communication skills, plan to pursue career in field, self-motivation, writing skills. Duration is 8 weeks (June-July). Unpaid. Open to college freshmen, college sophomores, college juniors, college seniors, sophomores and juniors preferred. ▶ *40–50 The Bryce Harlow Institute on Business and Government Affairs interns:* responsibilities include working with DC firm and taking classes in economics and business. Candidates should have computer skills, office skills, oral communication skills, plan to pursue career in field, self-motivation, written communication skills. Duration is 8 weeks (June-July). Unpaid. Open to college freshmen, college sophomores, college juniors, college seniors, graduate students, law students, sophomores and juniors preferred. ▶ *100–115 The Institute on Comparative Political and Economic Systems interns:* responsibilities include taking classes on corporate politics and economics at Georgetown University and working with political international organization in DC. Candidates should have oral communication skills, plan to pursue career in field, self-motivation, written communication skills. Duration is 8 weeks (June-July). Unpaid. Open to college freshmen, college sophomores, college juniors, college seniors, graduate students, law students, sophomores and juniors preferred. International applications accepted.

Benefits Housing at a cost, names of contacts, on-the-job training, opportunity to attend seminars/workshops, willing to act as a professional reference, willing to provide letters of recommendation, college credit through Georgetown University, tuition assistance (scholarship).

International Internships Available in Hong Kong, China; Prague, Czech Republic; Athens, Greece.

Contact Call, e-mail, or through World Wide Web site Tim Sprinkle, Director of Recruitment. Phone: 202-986-0384. Fax: 202-318-0441. E-mail: admissions@tfas.org. Applicants must submit a formal organization application, resume, academic transcripts, two letters of recommendation, essay (writing sample for journalism program). Application deadline: March 15 for summer, June 1 for fall, November 1 for spring. Fees: $30. World Wide Web: http://www.dcinternships.org.

GEORGIA GOVERNOR'S INTERN PROGRAM
245 State Capitol
Atlanta, Georgia 30334

General Information Internship program that offers hands-on experience working with state and nonprofit agencies. Established in 1971. Number of employees: 3. Unit of Governor's Office, Atlanta, Georgia. Number of internship applications received each year: 500.

Internships Available ▶ *200–300 Governor's interns:* responsibilities include working at entry level in field of intern's choice. Candidates should have analytical skills, college courses in field, computer skills, office skills, oral communication skills, organizational skills, personal interest in the field, research skills, self-motivation, strong interpersonal skills, strong leadership ability, writing skills. Duration is 10–13 weeks. Stipend consistent with hourly federal minimum wage. Open to college juniors, college seniors, graduate students, law students. ▶ *Law interns.* Duration is one summer. $7.50 per hour. Open to law students. International applications accepted.

Benefits Formal training, names of contacts, opportunity to attend seminars/workshops, tuition assistance, willing to act as a professional reference, willing to complete paperwork for educational credit, willing to provide letters of recommendation.

Contact Write, call, fax, e-mail, or through World Wide Web site Julie Smith, Director. Phone: 404-656-3804. Fax: 404-651-5110. E-mail: jsmith@gov.state.ga.us. In-person interview recommended (telephone interview accepted). Applicants must submit a formal organization application, resume, two personal references. Application deadline: February 1 for law interns, April 1 for summer, July 1 for fall, October 1 for spring. World Wide Web: http://www.ganet.org/governor/intern.

GLOBAL CAMPUS STUDY ABROAD, UNIVERSITY OF MINNESOTA
230 Heller Hall, 271 19th Avenue South
Minneapolis, Minnesota 55455

General Information Study abroad program designed to give students an opportunity to accent program curriculum by working as an intern in a variety of fields. Established in 1972. Number of employees: 40. Number of internship applications received each year: 100.

Internships Available ▶ *50 London interns:* responsibilities include working in one of a variety of fields. Candidates should have college courses in field, oral communication skills, personal interest in the field. Duration is 4 months. Unpaid. Open to college sophomores, college juniors, college seniors, recent college graduates. ▶ *Minnesota Studies in International Development interns:* responsibilities include working in a variety organizations, most often in rural areas of Ecuador, Ghana, India, Kenya, and Senegal. Candidates should have ability to work independently, analytical skills, knowledge of field, oral communication skills, personal interest in the field, research skills, self-motivation, strong interpersonal skills, strong leadership ability, written communication skills. Duration is 16–20 weeks. Unpaid. Open to college juniors, college seniors, recent college graduates, graduate students, law students, career changers. ▶ *Montpellier interns:* responsibilities include various activities depending upon internship placement; goal of internship is to introduce students to the organization and French working life and is one course in a full-time study program. Candidates should have ability to work with others, knowledge of field, oral communication skills, personal interest in the field, self-motivation, written communication skills, strong French language skills. Duration is 5–10 months. Unpaid. Open to college freshmen, college sophomores, college juniors, college seniors. ▶ *25 Toledo interns:* responsibilities include working in one of a variety of fields. Candidates should have college courses in field, personal interest in the field, strong Spanish language skills. Duration is 4 months. Unpaid. Open to college sophomores, college juniors, college seniors, recent college graduates. International applications accepted.

Benefits Health insurance, housing at a cost, meals at a cost, names of contacts, on-the-job training, opportunity to attend seminars/workshops, willing to act as a professional reference, willing to complete paperwork for educational credit, willing to provide letters of recommendation, participants earn 15 University of Minnesota semester credits while on the International Program (3 or 6 of those credits go towards the internship).

International Internships Available in Ecuador; Montpellier, France; Ghana; India; Kenya; Senegal; Toledo, Spain; London, United Kingdom.

Contact Write, call, fax, e-mail, or through World Wide Web site Internship Coordinator. Phone: 612-626-9000. Fax: 612-626-8009. E-mail: umabroad@umn.edu. In-person interview required. Applicants must submit a formal organization application, letter of interest, resume, academic transcripts, writing sample, 1-2 personal references, 1-2 letters of recommendation. Application deadline: April 15 for fall (England); May 15 fall or academic year (France), July 30 for fall or academic year (Spain), October 15 for spring (England), November 15 for spring (Spain and France); March 1 for summer (Spain). Fees: $50. World Wide Web: http://www.umabroad.umn.edu/.

GLOBAL SERVICE CORPS
300 Broadway, Suite 28
San Francisco, California 94133

General Information Nonprofit organization providing international cultural immersion and service learning programs in HIV/AIDS prevention, sustainable agriculture, environmental education, health care, and ESL (English as a second language). Established in 1993. Number of employees: 7. Unit of Earth Island Institute, San Francisco, California. Number of internship applications received each year: 125.

Internships Available ▶ *1–15 Buddhist cultural immersion/Thailand project interns:* responsibilities include learning about Buddhism through daily interface and conversation with monks at a local monastery while helping monks with conversational English. Candidates should have ability to work with others, oral communication skills, personal interest in the field, self-motivation, written communication skills. Duration is 3 weeks to 6 months (year-round). Unpaid. Open to recent high school graduates, college freshmen, college sophomores, college juniors, college seniors, recent college graduates, graduate students, law students, career changers, individuals reentering the workforce, retirees. ▶ *1–15 English instructors (Thailand):* responsibilities include assisting Thai teachers; leading classes in conversation, vocabulary, pronunciation, reading, writing, and games and songs; possibility of working with teachers in media presentation, environmental education, HIV/AIDS awareness, "Say No to Drugs," and classroom presentation skills. Candidates should have ability to work independently, ability to work with others, oral communication skills, plan to pursue career in field, self-motivation, written communication skills. Duration is 3 weeks to 6 months (year-round). Unpaid. Open to recent high school graduates, college freshmen, college sophomores, college juniors, college seniors, recent college graduates, graduate students, law students, career changers, individuals reentering the workforce, retirees. ▶ *1–15 HIV/ AIDS awareness and education interns (Tanzania):* responsibilities include teaching and spreading awareness of HIV/AIDS through talks and specific curricula in schools and at community meetings; reporting on this work and successes/failures. Candidates should have ability to work independently, oral communication skills, personal interest in the field, self-motivation, strong interpersonal skills, written communication skills. Duration is 4 weeks to 6 months (year-round). Unpaid. Open to college sophomores, college juniors, college seniors, recent college graduates, graduate students, law students, career changers, individuals reentering the workforce, individuals over 20 years of age. ▶ *1–4 Thailand program assistants (headquarters office):* responsibilities include recruiting, registering and corresponding with Thailand program participants, communicating with Thailand in-country program director, and preparing packets. Candidates should have computer skills, oral communication skills, organizational skills, personal interest in the field, written communication skills, travel and/or work experience (helpful). Duration is 3-6 months or longer. $200 per month. Open to college freshmen, college sophomores, college juniors, college seniors, recent college graduates, graduate students, law students, career changers, individuals reentering the workforce. ▶ *Web marketing assistants (headquarters office):* responsibilities include Web research, Web page linking, search engine positioning, communicating with colleges and universities, and database administration. Candidates should have ability to work independently, computer skills, experience in the field, personal interest in the field, research skills, written communication skills. Duration is 3–6 months. $200 per month plus local transportation costs. Open to college freshmen, college sophomores, college juniors, college seniors, recent college graduates, graduate students, law students, career changers, individuals reentering the workforce. ▶ *Environmental educators (Thailand):* responsibilities include teaching environmental education classes in English at local schools. Candidates should have ability to work independently, oral communication skills, personal interest in the field, self-motivation, written communication skills. Duration is 3 weeks to 6 months (year-round). Unpaid. Open to recent high school graduates, college freshmen, college sophomores, college juniors, college seniors, recent college graduates, graduate students, law students, career changers, individuals reentering the workforce. ▶ *4–8 headquarters office assistants (special projects):* responsibilities include responding to e-mail, overseeing mailings, assisting with international program administration, assisting with accounting, and special projects. Candidates should have ability to work independently, computer skills, office skills, oral communication skills, organizational skills, written communication skills. Duration is 3-6 months or longer. $200 per month plus local transportation costs. Open to college freshmen, college sophomores, college juniors, college seniors, recent college graduates, graduate students, law students, career changers, individuals reentering the workforce. ▶ *1–15 health-care interns (Thailand):* responsibilities include shadowing doctors at a hospital or nurses at a rural health clinic; presenting conversational English classes. Candidates should have knowledge of field, oral communication skills, plan to pursue

career in field, self-motivation, strong interpersonal skills, written communication skills. Duration is 3 weeks to 6 months (year-round). Unpaid. Open to recent high school graduates, college freshmen, college sophomores, college juniors, college seniors, recent college graduates, graduate students, law students, career changers, individuals reentering the workforce, retirees. ▶ *1–15 international health interns (Tanzania):* responsibilities include training teachers and students in HIV/AIDS prevention; community health service projects; visits to health-care facilities; shadowing health professionals and visiting AIDS patients in their homes. Candidates should have oral communication skills, personal interest in the field, self-motivation, strong interpersonal skills, written communication skills. Duration is 4 weeks to 6 months (year-round). Unpaid. Open to college sophomores, college juniors, college seniors, recent college graduates, graduate students, individuals reentering the workforce, individuals over 20 years of age, health professionals and pre-med, health, and medical students. ▶ *1–15 sustainable agriculture teachers (Tanzania):* responsibilities include learning the methods and mechanics of biointensive agriculture and organic gardening; teaching biointensive agriculture to others in Tanzania; reporting on work and successes/failures. Candidates should have ability to work independently, oral communication skills, organizational skills, personal interest in the field, self-motivation, strong interpersonal skills. Duration is 4 weeks to 6 months (year-round). Unpaid. Open to college freshmen, college sophomores, college juniors, college seniors, recent college graduates, graduate students, law students, career changers, individuals reentering the workforce, individuals over 20 years of age. International applications accepted.

Benefits Formal training, names of contacts, on-the-job training, possible full-time employment, willing to act as a professional reference, willing to complete paperwork for educational credit, willing to provide letters of recommendation, cost of program includes meals, homestay, travel in country, excursions (including safaris), and project administration; college credits and financial aid through SUNY-Albany.

International Internships Available in Thailand; United Republic of Tanzania.

Contact Write, call, fax, e-mail, or through World Wide Web site Stacy Readal, Manager of Operations. Phone: 415-788-3666 Ext. 128. Fax: 415-788-7324. E-mail: gscprograms@earthisland.org. Telephone interview required. Applicants must submit a formal organization application, letter of interest, resume. Application deadline: January 1 for spring, April 1 for summer, July 1 for fall, October 1 for winter. Fees: $150. World Wide Web: http://www.globalservicecorps.org.

GLOBAL VOLUNTEER NETWORK
PO Box 2231
Wellington New Zealand

General Information Volunteer placement organization. Established in 2000. Number of employees: 4. Number of internship applications received each year: 2,500.

Internships Available ▶ *20 Uganda community project interns:* responsibilities include aiding awareness programs, mothers and widows empowerment program, micro-credit scheme, and adult education. Candidates should have knowledge of field, oral communication skills, personal interest in the field, strong interpersonal skills. Duration is 2 weeks to 6 months. Unpaid. ▶ *40 airline interns:* responsibilities include working as a flight attendant. Candidates should have ability to work independently, oral communication skills, self-motivation, strong interpersonal skills, written communication skills. Duration is 13 months or longer. $800 per month. Open to recent high school graduates, college freshmen, college sophomores, college juniors, college seniors, recent college graduates, graduate students, law students, career changers, individuals reentering the workforce. ▶ *20 environmental program in Ecuador interns:* responsibilities include reforestation, trail care, and maintenance of reserves in Amazon rainforests; teaching English and environmental issues (optional); plant and nursery care. Candidates should have ability to work independently, knowledge of field, personal interest in the field, self-motivation, strong interpersonal skills. Duration is 1–6 months. Unpaid. Open to recent high school graduates, college freshmen, college

Global Volunteer Network (continued)

sophomores, college juniors, college seniors, recent college graduates, graduate students, career changers, individuals reentering the workforce. ▶ *50 teachers of English as a second language (China):* responsibilities include teaching English as a second language including conversational, grammar, listening, and speaking comprehension; aiding Chinese teachers. Candidates should have oral communication skills, self-motivation, strong interpersonal skills, written communication skills. Duration is 1–12 months. Unpaid. Open to college freshmen, college sophomores, college juniors, college seniors, recent college graduates, graduate students, law students, career changers, individuals reentering the workforce. ▶ *20–30 teaching in Ghana interns:* responsibilities include teaching a range of subjects at either pre-school, primary , or secondary schools. Candidates should have ability to work independently, oral communication skills, self-motivation, strong interpersonal skills, written communication skills, college degree in related field (for specific subjects). Duration is 1–6 months. Unpaid. Open to college freshmen, college sophomores, college juniors, college seniors, recent college graduates, graduate students, career changers, individuals reentering the workforce. ▶ *10 teaching in Nepal interns:* responsibilities include teaching English as a second language, teaching environmental awareness, and homestay cultural exchange. Candidates should have ability to work independently, experience in the field, oral communication skills, personal interest in the field, strong leadership ability, written communication skills. Duration is 2 weeks to 6 months. Unpaid. Open to recent high school graduates, college freshmen, college sophomores, college juniors, college seniors, recent college graduates, graduate students, law students, career changers, individuals reentering the workforce. ▶ *4 volunteers in Romania:* responsibilities include working in group home for disabled children between 8 months and 26 years; teaching, counseling, helping with feeding, cooking, and cleaning depending on skills and experience. Duration is minimum of 10 weeks (maximum of 6 months). Unpaid. Open to individuals 23 years of age or older. International applications accepted.
Benefits Formal training, names of contacts, on-the-job training, travel reimbursement, willing to complete paperwork for educational credit, willing to provide letters of recommendation, possibility of meals and housing at a cost or free.
International Internships Available in Yantai, China; Ecuador; Ghana; Kathmandu, Nepal; Tecuci, Romania.
Contact Write, call, fax, e-mail, or through World Wide Web site Colin Salisbury, Executive Director. Phone: 64-4-569 9080. Fax: 64-8326-7788. E-mail: info@volunteer.org.nz. Applicants must submit a formal organization application, telephone interview for Romanian program. Applications are accepted continuously. Fees: $250. World Wide Web: http://www.volunteer.org.nz.

GREAT SMOKY MOUNTAINS INSTITUTE AT TREMONT
9275 Tremont Road
Townsend, Tennessee 37882

General Information Residential environmental education center dedicated to creating environmentally literate students who want to help preserve and protect places such as the Smokies. Established in 1969. Number of employees: 21. Number of internship applications received each year: 25.
Internships Available ▶ *5–6 environmental education summer interns.* Candidates should have ability to work independently, oral communication skills, personal interest in the field, self-motivation, strong interpersonal skills. up to $100 per week. Open to college sophomores, college juniors, college seniors, recent college graduates, graduate students. International applications accepted.
Benefits Formal training, free housing, free meals, job counseling, names of contacts, on-the-job training, opportunity to attend seminars/workshops, possible full-time employment, willing to act as a professional reference, willing to complete paperwork for educational credit, willing to provide letters of recommendation.
Contact Write, e-mail, or through World Wide Web site Mr. Ken Voorhis, Director. E-mail: mail@gsmit.org. In-person interview recommended (telephone interview accepted). Applicants must submit a formal organization application, letter of interest, resume,

three personal references. Application deadline: February 7 for summer. World Wide Web: http://www.nps.gov/grsm/Tremont.htm.

HIDDEN VILLA ENVIRONMENTAL EDUCATION PROGRAM
26870 Moody Road
Los Altos Hills, California 94022

General Information School-year program introducing 4-12 year olds to the wonders and magic of an organic farm and garden and the natural world. Established in 1970. Number of employees: 10. Unit of The Trust for Hidden Villa, Los Altos Hills, California. Number of internship applications received each year: 40.
Internships Available ▶ *4 environmental education interns:* responsibilities include teaching on a farm, in the wilderness, and in a classroom for 25 hours per week; working on a farm for 10 hours per week; and spending 5 hours per week on special projects and in meetings. Candidates should have ability to work independently, oral communication skills, personal interest in the field, plan to pursue career in field, self-motivation, strong interpersonal skills, strong leadership ability, desire to work outdoors and with children. Duration is September through May. $500 per month. Open to recent high school graduates, college freshmen, college sophomores, college juniors, college seniors, recent college graduates, graduate students, law students, career changers, individuals reentering the workforce. International applications accepted.
Benefits Formal training, free housing, health insurance, job counseling, names of contacts, opportunity to attend seminars/workshops, willing to complete paperwork for educational credit, willing to provide letters of recommendation, reimbursement for mileage, seasonal farm-grown food.
Contact Write, call, fax, or e-mail Claire Elliott, Internship Coordinator. Phone: 650-949-8643. Fax: 650-948-1916. E-mail: hveep@hiddenvilla.org. Telephone interview required. Applicants must submit a formal organization application, letter of interest, resume. Application deadline: April 11. World Wide Web: http://www.hiddenvilla.org.

HIGHER EDUCATION CONSORTIUM FOR URBAN AFFAIRS, INC.
2233 University Avenue, Suite 210
St. Paul, Minnesota 55114-1629

General Information Nonprofit education consortium providing college-level study programs in U.S. and abroad, focusing on strategies to address social inequality; programs include internships, field projects, and independent research. Established in 1971. Number of employees: 15. Number of internship applications received each year: 100.
Internships Available ▶ *25 City Arts interns:* responsibilities include working in one of many Minneapolis-St. Paul arts-related projects combined with seminars that explore the connections between the arts, cultural expression, social change, and the impact of class, race, and gender. Candidates should have ability to work with others, analytical skills, oral communication skills, personal interest in the field, self-motivation, written communication skills. Duration is February to May. Position available as unpaid or paid. Open to college sophomores, college juniors, college seniors. ▶ *40–50 Metro Urban Studies Term (MUST) interns:* responsibilities include working in one of many Minneapolis-St.Paul public, nonprofit, or community agencies combined with seminars that examine issues of social inequality in the urban environment and strategies for change. Candidates should have ability to work with others, analytical skills, oral communication skills, personal interest in the field, self-motivation, written communication skills. Duration is September to December or February to May. Position available as unpaid or paid. Open to college sophomores, college juniors, college seniors. ▶ *20 Partners Internship Program participants:* responsibilities include working in a nonprofit organization in Minnesota, Wisconsin, and North Dakota. Candidates should have ability to work with others, analytical skills, oral communication skills, organizational skills, personal interest in the field, self-motivation, strong leadership ability, written communication skills.

Duration is June-August. $8.50 per hour. Open to college freshmen, college sophomores, college juniors. ▶ *15–20 community interns (Latin America):* responsibilities include working in one of many community agencies based in Quito, Ecuador, combined with seminar and independent project, all focussing on community participation for social change. Candidates should have ability to work independently, personal interest in the field, self-motivation, strong interpersonal skills, two years college-level Spanish. Duration is September to December. Unpaid. Open to college sophomores, college juniors, college seniors. ▶ *20 democracy and social change interns (Northern Ireland):* responsibilities include working in one of many organizations in Northern Ireland combined with seminar and independent project; focusing on democracy, peace and conflict resolution, and social change. Candidates should have ability to work with others, analytical skills, oral communication skills, personal interest in the field, self-motivation, strong leadership ability, written communication skills. Duration is February to May. Unpaid. Open to college sophomores, college juniors, college seniors. ▶ *20 environmental sustainability interns:* responsibilities include working in one of many Minneapolis-St. Paul public, nonprofit, or community agencies combined with seminars that examine issues of science, politics, and public policy; focuses on the upper Mississippi River Basin. Candidates should have ability to work with others, analytical skills, oral communication skills, organizational skills, personal interest in the field, self-motivation, written communication skills. Duration is September-December. Position available as unpaid or paid. Open to college sophomores, college juniors, college seniors. ▶ *3–6 fellowships in philanthropy:* responsibilities include working on a substantive project at philanthropic organization in human rights and social justice. Candidates should have oral communication skills, organizational skills, personal interest in the field, plan to pursue career in field, self-motivation, strong interpersonal skills, strong leadership ability, written communication skills. Duration is 6 months-1 year. $6000 per semester (stipend or scholarship). Open to graduate students. International applications accepted.

Benefits Opportunity to attend seminars/workshops, willing to complete paperwork for educational credit, willing to provide letters of recommendation, full semester of academic credit.

International Internships Available in Quito, Ecuador; United Kingdom.

Contact Write, call, fax, e-mail, or through World Wide Web site Michael Eaton, Director of Student Services. Phone: 800-554-1089. Fax: 651-659-9421. E-mail: info@hecua.org. Applicants must submit a formal organization application, resume, academic transcripts, two letters of recommendation. Application deadline: contact organization for deadlines. Fees: $75. World Wide Web: http://www.hecua.org.

HOPE CHAPEL
Church Office, 300 Ohukai Road, Building C-210
Kihei, Hawaii 96753

General Information Christ-centered interdenominational church with an emphasis on Bible teaching and inspirational worship serving a membership base of 1200 people. Number of employees: 32.

Internships Available ▶ *8 interns:* responsibilities include assignment to a ministry overseer whose gifts and talents compliment those of the intern; ministry areas include pastoral, children's, junior and senior high school, worship/special events, small groups, and administration; comprehensive exposure to all areas of ministry; all projects will be tailored to interest and gifts of intern. Duration is 1 year (August to August); 60 hours per week (40 hours in specialty area and the remainder in other areas). $400 monthly stipend. Open to college-age individuals who are seriously considering full-time vocational ministry. International applications accepted.

Benefits Free housing, paid utilities.

Contact Write, call, fax, e-mail, or through World Wide Web site Jason Spence, Associate Pastor. Phone: 808-879-3853 Ext. 232. Fax: 808-874-2886. E-mail: eydis@hopemaui.org. Application deadline: May 15. World Wide Web: http://www.hopemaui.org.

HORIZONS FOR YOUTH
121 Lakeview Street
Sharon, Massachusetts 02067

General Information Residential environmental education center that works with children. Established in 1938. Number of employees: 20. Number of internship applications received each year: 100.

Internships Available ▶ *1–3 field instructor/teachers:* responsibilities include developing and teaching outdoor activities related to ecology, environmental science, and group dynamics. Candidates should have ability to work with others, oral communication skills, personal interest in the field, self-motivation, previous work with children. Duration is 12–17 weeks. $250 per week. Open to college sophomores, college juniors, college seniors, recent college graduates, graduate students, law students, career changers. ▶ *1 kitchen assistant:* responsibilities include working to support a kitchen that serves up to 250 people. Candidates should have ability to work independently, ability to work with others, oral communication skills, organizational skills, personal interest in the field, self-motivation, cooking knowledge. Duration is 12–17 weeks. $250 per week. Open to college sophomores, college juniors, college seniors, recent college graduates, graduate students, career changers. International applications accepted.

Benefits Free housing, free meals, on-the-job training, opportunity to attend seminars/workshops, possible full-time employment, willing to act as a professional reference, willing to complete paperwork for educational credit, willing to provide letters of recommendation.

Contact Write, call, fax, e-mail, or through World Wide Web site Mr. James Barnett, School Program Director. Phone: 781-828-7550. Fax: 781-784-1287. E-mail: outdoors@hfy.org. In-person interview recommended (telephone interview accepted). Applicants must submit a formal organization application, letter of interest, resume, 3 references. Applications are accepted continuously. World Wide Web: http://www.hfy.org.

HOSPITALITY MANAGEMENT TRAINING INSTITUTE, INC.
760 Market Street, Suite 1009
San Francisco, California 94102

General Information Hotel/restaurant management college teaching certified management classes with diploma programs, internships, and job placement services worldwide. Established in 1991. Number of employees: 16. Affiliate of American Hotel and Lodging Association, Washington, District of Columbia. Number of internship applications received each year: 7.

Internships Available ▶ *1–10 hospitality administration interns:* responsibilities include front desk and concierge duties, event planning. Candidates should have ability to work with others, computer skills, oral communication skills, organizational skills, personal interest in the field. Duration is flexible. Position available as unpaid or at $10–$15 per hour. Open to recent high school graduates, college freshmen, college sophomores, college juniors, college seniors, recent college graduates, career changers, individuals reentering the workforce. ▶ *1–10 hospitality operations interns:* responsibilities include front desk duties, concierge positions in hotels, and events planning. Candidates should have ability to work with others, computer skills, oral communication skills, organizational skills, personal interest in the field, writing skills. Duration is flexible. Position available as unpaid or at $12–$15 per hour. Open to recent high school graduates, college freshmen, college sophomores, college juniors, college seniors, recent college graduates, career changers, individuals reentering the workforce. ▶ *2 marketing interns:* responsibilities include placing international phone calls, creating marketing reports, and assisting with update of business plan. Candidates should have ability to work with others, computer skills, oral communication skills, bilingual ability. Duration is flexible. Position available as unpaid or at $7–$10 per hour. Open to college seniors, recent college graduates, graduate students. ▶ *2 preschool teachers:* responsibilities include assisting head teacher with adult teacher certification students. Candidates should have ability to work with others, computer skills, oral communication skills. Duration is flexible.

Hospitality Management Training Institute, Inc. (continued)

Position available as unpaid or at $7–$10 per hour. Open to college seniors, recent college graduates, graduate students. International applications accepted.

Benefits Formal training, job counseling, names of contacts, on-the-job training, possible full-time employment, willing to act as a professional reference, willing to complete paperwork for educational credit, willing to provide letters of recommendation.

International Internships Available in Australia; Paris, France; Tokyo, Japan; Mexico; London, United Kingdom.

Contact Write, fax, e-mail, or through World Wide Web site Sherris Goodwin, Executive Director. Fax: 415-677-9810. E-mail: hotelscool@aol.com. No phone calls. In-person interview recommended (telephone interview accepted). Applicants must submit a formal organization application, letter of interest, resume, academic transcripts, three personal references, two letters of recommendation, three letters of recommendation. Applications are accepted continuously. World Wide Web: http://www.hotelcollege.com.

IACOCCA INSTITUTE, GLOBAL VILLAGE FOR FUTURE LEADERS OF BUSINESS & INDUSTRY
111 Research Drive
Bethlehem, Pennsylvania 18015

General Information Institution of higher learning. Established in 1988. Number of employees: 56. Division of Lehigh University, Bethlehem, Pennsylvania. Number of internship applications received each year: 350.

Internships Available ▶ *Global Village Iacocca interns:* responsibilities include attending all lectures/seminars and other scheduled learning activities, sharing information about home culture and history with other interns, hosting executive visitors, and producing results on assigned projects. Candidates should have oral communication skills, self-motivation, strong interpersonal skills, strong leadership ability, well-developed personal value system. Duration is 6 weeks (June 21 to August 2). Unpaid. Open to college juniors, college seniors, recent college graduates, graduate students, law students, career changers, young entrepreneurs, family-owned business members, corporate new-hires. International applications accepted.

Benefits Formal training, housing at a cost, job counseling, names of contacts, on-the-job training, opportunity to attend seminars/workshops, willing to act as a professional reference, willing to complete paperwork for educational credit, willing to provide letters of recommendation.

Contact Write, call, fax, e-mail, or through World Wide Web site M. Frances Schurtz-Leon, Candidate Manager, 111 Research Drive, Bethlehem, Pennsylvania 18015. Phone: 610-758-4440. Fax: 610-758-6550. E-mail: mfs2@lehigh.edu. Applicants must submit a formal organization application, letter of interest, resume, academic transcripts, personal reference, two letters of recommendation. Applications are accepted continuously. Fees: $50. World Wide Web: http://www.lehigh.edu/~village.

INNER QUEST, INC.
34752 Charles Town Pike
Purcellville, Virginia 20132

General Information Outdoor education organization teaching personal growth and skill development through outdoor adventure activities including rock climbing, caving, canoeing, kayaking, and challenge courses. Established in 1979. Number of employees: 20. Number of internship applications received each year: 100.

Internships Available ▶ *10 apprentice instructors:* responsibilities include teaching climbing, caving, canoeing, kayaking, and challenge courses. Candidates should have oral communication skills, personal interest in the field, self-motivation, strong interpersonal skills, strong leadership ability. Duration is March 16-June 7; May 18-August 9; August 17-November 8. $1800 per duration of internship. Open to individuals 18 or older.

Benefits Formal training, on-the-job training, possible full-time employment, willing to complete paperwork for educational credit, willing to provide letters of recommendation.

Contact Write, call, fax, or e-mail Sara Smith, Director. Phone: 540-668-6699. Fax: 540-668-6253. E-mail: innerquestinfo@cs.com. In-person interview recommended (telephone interview accepted). Applicants must submit a formal organization application, letter of interest, resume, three personal references. Application deadline: February 15 for spring, April 15 for summer, July 15 for fall. World Wide Web: http://www.InnerQuestOnline.com.

THE INSTITUTE FOR EARTH EDUCATION
Cedar Cove
Greenville, West Virginia 24945

General Information Designer of educational programs that will help people increase their understanding of, appreciation for, and harmony with the earth's natural systems and communities. Established in 1974. Number of employees: 3. Number of internship applications received each year: 10.

Internships Available ▶ *1–6 earth education interns:* responsibilities include development and maintenance of the center; helping with food production and preservation; and assisting in the international office. Candidates should have oral communication skills, plan to pursue career in field, self-motivation, strong interpersonal skills, written communication skills, willingness to work hard and follow instructions when needed. Duration is 2–12 months. Unpaid. ▶ *1 landcare coordinator:* responsibilities include assisting in master planning, housing rehabilitation, trail design, and establishing teepee and treehouse villages; developing wild cave tours; some basic maintenance. Candidates should have ability to work independently, knowledge of field, oral communication skills, personal interest in the field, self-motivation, strong interpersonal skills. Duration is 2–12 months. Unpaid. ▶ *2–4 organic gardeners:* responsibilities include planning, sowing, harvesting, and preserving organic produce. Candidates should have ability to work independently, ability to work with others, knowledge of field, oral communication skills, personal interest in the field, self-motivation. Duration is 2–12 months. Unpaid. Open to recent high school graduates, college freshmen, college sophomores, college juniors, college seniors, recent college graduates, graduate students, career changers, individuals reentering the workforce. International applications accepted.

Benefits Formal training, free housing, free meals, job counseling, names of contacts, on-the-job training, opportunity to attend seminars/workshops, willing to act as a professional reference, willing to complete paperwork for educational credit, willing to provide letters of recommendation.

Contact Write, call, fax, e-mail, or through World Wide Web site Internship Coordinator. Phone: 304-832-6404. Fax: 304-832-6077. E-mail: iee1@aol.com. Telephone interview required. Applicants must submit a formal organization application, resume, letter of recommendation. Applications are accepted continuously. World Wide Web: http://www.eartheducation.org.

THE INSTITUTE FOR EXPERIENTIAL LEARNING
1776 Massachusetts Avenue, NW, Suite 201
Washington, District of Columbia 20036

General Information Institute that works to advance the theory of experiential education through internship programs for graduate and undergraduate students in all majors. Established in 1990. Number of employees: 6. Number of internship applications received each year: 650.

Internships Available ▶ *80–100 interns:* responsibilities include participating fully in office life by attending meetings and special events, performing research, writing reports, and preparing briefings. Candidates should have ability to work independently, analytical skills, knowledge of field, office skills, oral communication skills, organizational skills, personal interest in the field, research skills, self-motivation, strong interpersonal skills, strong leadership ability, writing skills. Duration is 10-15 weeks, 4 days per week. Position available as unpaid or paid. Open to college sophomores, college juniors, college seniors, recent college graduates, graduate students, law students, career changers. International applications accepted.

Benefits Formal training, housing at a cost, job counseling, names of contacts, opportunity to attend seminars/workshops, possible full-time employment, willing to act as a professional reference, willing to complete paperwork for educational credit, willing to provide letters of recommendation, career counseling and professional development.

Contact Write, call, fax, e-mail, or through World Wide Web site Lauren Day, Program Coordinator, 1776 Massachusetts Avenue, NW Suite 201, Washington, District of Columbia 20036. Phone: 202-833-8580. Fax: 202-833-8581. E-mail: info@ielnet.org. Telephone interview required. Applicants must submit a formal organization application, academic transcripts, three letters of recommendation. Application deadline: April 1 for summer, June 1 for fall, November 15 for spring. Fees: $50. World Wide Web: http://www.ielnet.org.

INSTITUTE FOR INTERNATIONAL COOPERATION AND DEVELOPMENT
PO Box 520
Williamstown, Massachusetts 01267

General Information Nonprofit organization training volunteers for work in Africa and Latin America; involves people from local communities in fields of education, health, and small-scale construction. Established in 1987. Number of employees: 10. Number of internship applications received each year: 3,000.

Internships Available ▶ *15–20 volunteers in Angola:* responsibilities include preventive health care, teaching in schools, and community environmental projects. Candidates should have oral communication skills, personal interest in the field, self-motivation, strong interpersonal skills, strong leadership ability. Duration is 13 months. Unpaid. ▶ *15–20 volunteers in Brazil:* responsibilities include helping in community construction, collecting information from local people, and working with street children. Duration is 6 months. Unpaid. ▶ *15–20 volunteers in Mozambique:* responsibilities include teaching in schools for street kids and in vocational schools, teacher training, and village health campaigns. Candidates should have oral communication skills, personal interest in the field, self-motivation, strong interpersonal skills, strong leadership ability. Duration is 19 months. Unpaid. ▶ *10–15 volunteers in Nicaragua:* responsibilities include working with families in rural villages to provide health care, assisting small-scale farmers in improving food production, and HIV prevention. Candidates should have oral communication skills, personal interest in the field, self-motivation, strong interpersonal skills. Duration is 13 months. Unpaid. ▶ *15–20 volunteers in Zimbabwe:* responsibilities include working with families in rural villages to provide health care, assisting small-scale farmers in improving food production, and HIV prevention. Candidates should have oral communication skills, personal interest in the field, self-motivation, strong interpersonal skills, strong leadership ability. Duration is 13 months. Unpaid. Open to individuals over 18 years old. International applications accepted.

Benefits Formal training, health insurance, job counseling, names of contacts, on-the-job training, opportunity to attend seminars/workshops, possible full-time employment, tuition assistance, willing to act as a professional reference, willing to complete paperwork for educational credit, willing to provide letters of recommendation, housing, meals, and education are provided with tuition.

International Internships Available in Angola; Brazil; Mozambique; Nicaragua; Zimbabwe.

Contact Write, call, fax, e-mail, or through World Wide Web site Uli Stosch, Director. Phone: 413-458-9828. Fax: 413-458-3323. E-mail: info@iicd-volunteer.org. In-person interview recommended (telephone interview accepted). Applicants must submit a formal organization application, letter of interest, resume. Applications are accepted continuously. World Wide Web: http://www.iicd-volunteer.org.

INSTITUTE FOR LEADERSHIP DEVELOPMENT
1810-2 Assiniboine, York University
Toronto, Ontario M3J 1P3 Canada

General Information United Nations Global Partnership Institute that builds leadership skills in young professionals and entrepreneurs in Canada and around the world through skills enhancement programs, distance learning, and work placements. Established in 1995. Number of employees: 5. Affiliate of United Nations, New York, New York.

Internships Available ▶ *35–40 interns:* responsibilities include a variety of assignments with UN agencies, international institutions, and private sector organizations. Candidates should have ability to work with others, college degree in related field, computer skills, plan to pursue career in field, strong leadership ability, second language skills often required. Duration is 6 to 8 months on average. $700–$1400 Canadian dollars per month. Open to those with a graduate degree or equivalent, undergraduates considered for some positions.

Benefits Health insurance, opportunity to attend seminars/workshops, possible full-time employment, willing to act as a professional reference, willing to provide letters of recommendation, job search support, pre-placement training, housing at a cost/free housing (depending on placement).

International Internships Available in Ecuador; Ethiopia; Kenya; Philippines.

Contact E-mail Nadira Ramkissoon, Programmes Coordinator, 1810-2 Assiniboine, York University, 4700 Keele Street, Toronto, Ontario M3J 1P3 Canada. Phone: 416-736-2100 Ext. 88704. Fax: 416-736-5693. E-mail: nadira@wtuglobal.org. In-person interview recommended (telephone interview accepted). Applicants must submit a resume, two letters of recommendation, cover letter, formal application (must be submitted by mail or courier; faxes and e-mails are not acceptable). Applications are accepted continuously. World Wide Web: http://www.ildglobal.org.

INSTITUTE FOR THE INTERNATIONAL EDUCATION OF STUDENTS (IES)
33 North LaSalle Street, 15th Floor
Chicago, Illinois 60602-2602

General Information Study abroad program provider. Established in 1950. Number of employees: 52.

Internships Available ▶ *Arts/museum interns:* responsibilities include assignments in England, Ireland, Australia, Japan, Germany, Spain, Italy, Chile, and China. Candidates should have ability to work with others, knowledge of field, oral communication skills, personal interest in the field, self-motivation, strong grasp of country's native language (usually needed). Duration is one semester, year, or summer (London, Melbourne, and Madrid only). Unpaid. Open to college juniors, college seniors. ▶ *Business and marketing interns:* responsibilities include assignments in Australia, China, Germany, Argentina, Spain, France, Japan, Ireland, England, Austria, and Italy. Candidates should have ability to work with others, knowledge of field, oral communication skills, personal interest in the field, self-motivation, strong grasp of country's native language (usually needed). Duration is one semester, academic year, or summer (Melbourne, Dublin, London, Madrid). Unpaid. Open to college juniors, college seniors. ▶ *Education and teaching interns:* responsibilities include assignments in China, Germany, Argentina, France, Spain, Japan, Austria, England, Australia, Italy, and Chile. Candidates should have ability to work with others, knowledge of field, oral communication skills, personal interest in the field, self-motivation, strong grasp of country's native language (usually needed). Duration is one semester, year, or summer (London only). Unpaid. Open to college juniors, college seniors. ▶ *International relations and government interns:* responsibilities include assignments in Germany, England, Spain, France, Japan, Australia, Ireland, Chile, Italy, and Austria. Candidates should have ability to work with others, knowledge of field, oral communication skills, personal interest in the field, self-motivation, strong grasp of country's native language (usually needed). Duration is one semester, academic year, or summer (London, Madrid, and Dublin only). Unpaid. Open to college juniors, college seniors. ▶ *2–4 marketing interns (Chicago):* responsibilities include working with vice president of marketing, recruitment, and information systems to review ongoing research projects, developing processes and designs for approaching the marketing questions at hand, and implementing market research projects. Candidates should have ability to work independently, ability to work with others, analytical skills, computer skills, organizational skills, personal interest in the field, research skills,

Institute for the International Education of Students (IES) (continued)

strong critical thinking skills, study abroad experience (preferred). Duration is 2–3 months. $2000 stipend for full-time interns; prorated share for part-time interns. Open to college sophomores, college juniors, college seniors, recent college graduates. ► *Science interns:* responsibilities include assignments in Australia, Germany, and France. Candidates should have ability to work with others, knowledge of field, oral communication skills, personal interest in the field, self-motivation, strong grasp of country's native language (usually needed). Duration is one semester, academic year, or summer (London only). Unpaid. Open to college juniors, college seniors. ► *Social and political activism interns:* responsibilities include assignments in Australia, China, Germany, France, Ireland, Argentina, England, Spain, Italy, Japan, Austria, and Chile. Candidates should have ability to work with others, knowledge of field, oral communication skills, personal interest in the field, self-motivation, strong grasp of country's native language (usually needed). Duration is one semester, academic year, or summer (London, Madrid, and Dublin only). Unpaid. Open to college juniors, college seniors. ► *Theater interns:* responsibilities include assignments in England, Germany, and Ireland. Candidates should have ability to work with others, knowledge of field, oral communication skills, personal interest in the field, self-motivation, strong grasp of country's native language (usually needed). Duration is one year, semester, or summer (London and Dublin only). Unpaid. Open to college juniors, college seniors. International applications accepted.
Benefits Opportunity to attend seminars/workshops, willing to complete paperwork for educational credit, housing and meals included with some programs.
International Internships Available.
Contact Call, e-mail, or through World Wide Web site IES Representative. Phone: 800-995-2300. Fax: 312-944-1448. E-mail: info@iesabroad.org. In-person interview required. Applicants must submit a formal organization application, letter of interest, resume, academic transcripts, must be participant in IES study abroad program; program fees vary by placement. Application deadline: March 1 for summer (London), May 1 for spring and summer (except London summer), June 15 for fall. World Wide Web: http://www.IESabroad.org.

INSTITUTE OF CENTRAL AMERICAN STUDIES
PO Box 1524-2050
San Pedro Costa Rica

General Information Institute that provides education about the realities of Central America, specializing in acquisition, maintenance, and dissemination of information. Established in 1981. Number of employees: 15. Number of internship applications received each year: 25.
Internships Available ► *12–20 research assistants and/or journalism.* Candidates should have ability to work independently, ability to work with others, computer skills, editing skills, experience in the field, personal interest in the field, research skills, writing skills. Duration is usually 6 months. Unpaid. Open to college juniors, college seniors, recent college graduates, graduate students. International applications accepted.
Benefits Housing at a cost, meals at a cost, on-the-job training, opportunity to attend seminars/workshops, willing to act as a professional reference, willing to complete paperwork for educational credit, willing to provide letters of recommendation, journalistic experience.
International Internships Available in San Jose, Costa Rica.
Contact Write, call, e-mail, or through World Wide Web site Linda Holland, Executive Director, Apdo. 1524-2050, San Pedro 2050 Costa Rica. Phone: 011-506-253-3195. Fax: 011-506-234-7682. E-mail: mesoamer@sol.racsa.co.cr. Applicants must submit a letter of interest, resume, two writing samples, three letters of recommendation, $100 fee upon acceptance. Applications are accepted continuously. World Wide Web: http://www.mesoamericaonline.net.

INSTITUTE OF INTERNATIONAL EDUCATION–OFFICE FOR LATIN AMERICA
Londres 16, 2nd Floor, Col. Juarez
Mexico City, DF 06600 Mexico

General Information Nonprofit educational exchange organization. Established in 1974. Number of employees: 14. Division of Institute of International Education, New York, New York. Number of internship applications received each year: 15.
Internships Available ► *1–3 scholarship program interns:* responsibilities include supporting the administering of scholarship and training programs, including promotion, selection, and monitoring of grantees; managing databases; communicating on a formal level with clients and sponsors; and designing program brochures. Candidates should have ability to work independently, computer skills, organizational skills, strong interpersonal skills, writing skills, proficiency in Spanish. Duration is 3–4 months. $400 per month. ► *1–3 student advising interns:* responsibilities include advising the public on all aspects of U.S. education, including information about the admissions process and testing programs; working on assigned research projects; assisting with outreach activities; editing publications; developing presentations; and managing databases. Candidates should have ability to work independently, computer skills, organizational skills, research skills, strong interpersonal skills, proficiency in Spanish. Duration is 3–4 months. $400 per month. Open to college sophomores, college juniors, college seniors, recent college graduates, graduate students. International applications accepted.
Benefits Names of contacts, on-the-job training, opportunity to attend seminars/workshops, possible full-time employment, willing to act as a professional reference, willing to complete paperwork for educational credit, willing to provide letters of recommendation.
International Internships Available.
Contact Write, e-mail, or through World Wide Web site Internship Coordinator, PO Box 9000, IIE/PD/Educational Center, Brownsville, Texas 78520-0900. E-mail: iie@solar.sar.net. Applicants must submit a formal organization application, letter of interest, resume, academic transcripts, two letters of recommendation. Application deadline: March 15 for summer, June 15 for fall, October 15 for spring. World Wide Web: http://www.iie.org/latinamerica.

INTERLOCKEN
19 Interlocken Way
Hillsboro Upper Village, New Hampshire 03244

General Information Experiential learning center that offers educational summer adventures for young people ages 9-18, an international residential summer camp in New Hampshire, and travel programs in the U.S. and abroad. Established in 1961. Number of employees: 45. Number of internship applications received each year: 200.
Internships Available ► *25–30 camp counselors:* responsibilities include teaching specialty areas and being responsible for living units. Candidates should have self-motivation, strong interpersonal skills, skills for teaching in particular area and experience working with children. Duration is 9 weeks. $1400–$2500 per duration of internship. Open to college freshmen, college sophomores, college juniors, college seniors, recent college graduates, graduate students. ► *1 computer programmer:* responsibilities include helping with camp computer network and database. Candidates should have ability to work independently, declared college major in field, oral communication skills, organizational skills, personal interest in the field, self-motivation, strong interpersonal skills, written communication skills, knowledge of Microsoft, SQL, and HTML. Duration is 10–12 weeks. $200–$250 per week. Open to college juniors, college seniors, recent college graduates, graduate students. ► *25–30 travel interns:* responsibilities include leading a small group travel adventure in the U.S., Europe, Latin America, Africa or Asia. Candidates should have ability to work independently, knowledge of field, self-motivation, strong interpersonal skills, strong leadership ability, experience working with teenagers, willingness to work 24 hours a day 7 days a week. Duration is 4–6 weeks. $1550–$2250 per duration of internship. Open to gradu-

ate students, minimum age of 24. ▶ *1 video editing instructor:* responsibilities include working with students to make video documentaries of their summer experiences. Candidates should have ability to work independently, declared college major in field, editing skills, knowledge of field, oral communication skills, personal interest in the field, plan to pursue career in field, strong interpersonal skills, written communication skills, computer video editing skills. Duration is 10–12 weeks. $200–$300 per week. Open to college juniors, college seniors, recent college graduates, graduate students. International applications accepted.

Benefits Free housing, free meals, names of contacts, willing to act as a professional reference, willing to complete paperwork for educational credit, willing to provide letters of recommendation.
International Internships Available in Quebec, Canada; Cuba; Paris, France; Venice, Italy.
Contact Write, fax, e-mail, or through World Wide Web site Tom Herman, Marketing Director. Fax: 603-478-5260. E-mail: staff@ interlocken.org. In-person interview recommended (telephone interview accepted). Applicants must submit a formal organization application, letter of interest, resume, three letters of recommendation. Application deadline: March 30. World Wide Web: http://www.interlocken.org.

INTERNATIONAL FIELD STUDIES
PO Box 428, 30 Public Square
Nelsonville, Ohio 45764

General Information Nonprofit organization that provides logistical support to get students and educators into the marine biology field. Two programs are offered: marine biology field station in Andros Island, Bahamas, and sailing programs in the northern and central Bahamas. Established in 1970. Number of employees: 6. Number of internship applications received each year: 40.
Internships Available ▶ *1–3 co-directors:* responsibilities include overseeing staff and working with group leaders to coordinate trips. Candidates should have experience in the field, oral communication skills, organizational skills, self-motivation, strong interpersonal skills, strong leadership ability. Duration is 1–2 years. $200–$500 per month. Open to recent college graduates, graduate students. ▶ *2–6 field station interns:* responsibilities include supporting staff at field station. Candidates should have ability to work with others, experience in the field, oral communication skills, personal interest in the field, self-motivation, mechanical abilities desirable. Duration is 1–2 years. $200–$500 per month. Open to recent college graduates, must be 21 or over. ▶ *1–3 sailing first-mates:* responsibilities include supporting crew on sailing program. Candidates should have ability to work with others, oral communication skills, personal interest in the field, self-motivation, strong leadership ability, mechanical abilities. Duration is 1–2 years. $200–$500 per month. Open to recent college graduates, must be 21 or over. International applications accepted.
Benefits Free housing, free meals, on-the-job training, opportunity to attend seminars/workshops, possible full-time employment, willing to act as a professional reference, willing to complete paperwork for educational credit, willing to provide letters of recommendation, stipend, transportation to Bahamas (when available).
International Internships Available in Andros Island, Bahamas.
Contact Write, call, fax, e-mail, or through World Wide Web site Paula A. Inman, Intern Coordinator, 30 Public Square PO Box 428, Nelsonville, Ohio 45764. Phone: 800-962-3805. Fax: 740-753-5100. E-mail: employment@intlfieldstudies.com. In-person interview required. Applicants must submit a formal organization application, letter of interest, resume, two personal references, $595 for on-site interview (one week); reimbursed after 12 months of employment. Application deadline: May 1. World Wide Web: http://www.intlfieldstudies.com.

THE INTERNATIONAL PARTNERSHIP FOR SERVICE-LEARNING
815 Second Avenue, Suite 315
New York, New York 10017

General Information Organization that administers international graduate and undergraduate study-abroad programs, combining academic study with service-learning/hands-on community service. Established in 1982. Number of employees: 6. Number of internship applications received each year: 150.
Internships Available ▶ *100–200 student program interns:* responsibilities include providing service to communities in need, teaching/ tutoring at all levels (preschool-adult), providing rehabilitation for mentally or physically handicapped people, or assisting with health care, counseling, recreation, and community development. Candidates should have oral communication skills, personal interest in the field, strong interpersonal skills, written communication skills, minimum score of 550 (213 CBT) on the TOEFL (nonnative English speakers). Duration is variable. Unpaid. Open to recent high school graduates, college freshmen, college sophomores, college juniors, college seniors, recent college graduates, graduate students, career changers, individuals reentering the workforce, retirees. International applications accepted.
Benefits Housing at a cost, meals at a cost, on-the-job training, opportunity to attend seminars/workshops, willing to act as a professional reference, willing to complete paperwork for educational credit, willing to provide letters of recommendation, academic study and credit.
International Internships Available in Prague, Czech Republic; Guayaquil and Quito, Ecuador; Montpellier, France; Calcutta, India; Beer-Sheva, Israel; Kingston, Jamaica; Guadalajara, Mexico; Manila, Philippines; Moscow, Russian Federation; Chaing Mai, Thailand; London and Glasgow, United Kingdom.
Contact Write, call, fax, e-mail, or through World Wide Web site Director of Student Programs. Phone: 212-986-0989. Fax: 212-986-5039. E-mail: info@ipsl.org. Applicants must submit a formal organization application, academic transcripts, two personal references, two letters of recommendation, $250 deposit as part of program fees. Application deadline: April 15 for summer, July 15 for fall, November 15 for spring. Fees: $50. World Wide Web: http://www.ipsl.org.

INTERNATIONAL YMCA
Go Global, 5 West 63rd Street, 2nd Floor
New York, New York 10023

General Information Organization providing global awareness programs for children to promote understanding of international cultures and peoples. Branch of YMCA of Greater New York, New York, New York.
Internships Available ▶ *Diversity workshop leaders:* responsibilities include designing workshop to present to children (ages 5-12); workshop must be inspired by and directly related to intern's personal skills, area of expertise, or cultural background; workshop must be interactive, comparative, and highlight realities of multiculturalism and diversity in the world. Candidates should have ability to work independently, ability to work with others, computer skills, office skills, self-motivation, strong leadership ability, proficiency in an art from, subject, or talent from a country or region in the world, willingness and ability to work with children (prior experience desired but not necessary). Duration is minimum of 3 months; 5 month commitment preferable. Unpaid. Open to recent high school graduates, college freshmen, college sophomores, college juniors, college seniors, recent college graduates, graduate students, law students, career changers. ▶ *Educational research and program design interns:* responsibilities include designing lesson plans related to cultural identity awareness and global education for high school students ages 15-18; possibility of working off-site with weekly consultations. Candidates should have self-motivation, knowledge of Microsoft software, experience working with high school students (helpful). Duration is 3–5 months. Unpaid. ▶ *Graphic and web site designers:* responsibilities include print and HTML design of outgoing communication and press materials. Candidates should have ability to work independently, ability to work with others, computer skills, editing skills, self-motivation, written communication skills, proficiency in Publisher, Illustrator, PhotoShop, and other design programs, knowledge of HTML and Internet-related database. Duration is 3 months (up to 20 hours per week). Unpaid. Open to college sophomores, college juniors, college seniors, recent college graduates.

International YMCA (continued)

Benefits Opportunity to attend seminars/workshops, possible full-time employment, travel reimbursement, willing to act as a professional reference, willing to complete paperwork for educational credit, willing to provide letters of recommendation.
Contact Write, call, or e-mail Leeza Ahmady, Project Coordinator. Phone: 212-727-8800 Ext. 4303. E-mail: lahmady@ymcanyc.org. In-person interview recommended (telephone interview accepted). Applicants must submit a letter of interest, resume. Applications are accepted continuously. World Wide Web: http://www.ymcainternational.org.

INTERN EXCHANGE INTERNATIONAL LTD.
1858 Mallard Lane
Villanova, Pennsylvania 19085

General Information Organization offering travel to London and the opportunity to participate in career-based internships, arts activities, special interest activities, and cultural trips/tours. Established in 1987. Number of employees: 1. Branch of Intern Exchange International Ltd., Woodmere, New York. Number of internship applications received each year: 225.
Internships Available ▶ *15–20 resident/teaching assistants (London):* responsibilities include supervising interns studying in London. Candidates should have plan to pursue career in field, self-motivation, strong interpersonal skills, strong leadership ability, background in journalism, theater, film/video, photography, psychology, business, fashion and design, fine arts, or Web site design. Duration is 31 days in June-July. Stipend. Open to college seniors, recent college graduates, graduate students, must be at least 20 years of age. ▶ *150–240 student travel interns (London):* responsibilities include interning in any of the following academic areas: archaeology, architecture, art history/appreciation, business (banking/finance, marketing), communications, government and politics, health sciences, journalism, prelaw, premed, social services, video, photography, fashion and design, and community service. Candidates should have ability to work independently, oral communication skills, personal interest in the field, self-motivation, strong interpersonal skills, strong leadership ability. Duration is 30 days in June-July. Unpaid. Open to individuals ages 16-18. International applications accepted.
Benefits On-the-job training, willing to complete paperwork for educational credit, willing to provide letters of recommendation, cultural trips available, housing provided for resident assistants.
International Internships Available in London, United Kingdom.
Contact Write, call, fax, e-mail, or through World Wide Web site Nina Miller Glickman, Director, 130 Harold Road, Woodmere, New York 11598. Phone: 516-374-3939. Fax: 516-374-2104. E-mail: info@internexchange.com. Applicants must submit a formal organization application, letter of interest, academic transcripts, fee of approximately $5495 and deposit of $450 upon acceptance (for student-travel interns only), 1-2 letters of recommendation (depending on field). Applications are accepted continuously. Fees: $50. World Wide Web: http://www.internexchange.com.

INTERNSHIPS IN FRANCOPHONE EUROPE
26 Rue Cmdt. Mouchette J-108
75014 Paris France

General Information Semester-long academic program that includes 12 weeks full-time professional experience in French public life, preceded by 5 weeks of intensive preparation. Established in 1988. Number of employees: 4.
Internships Available ▶ *5–10 interns:* responsibilities include working in various institutions in the public sector and non-governmental organizations. Candidates should have ability to work independently, ability to work with others, analytical skills, self-motivation, adequate command of French. Duration is 12–17 weeks. Unpaid. Open to college sophomores, college juniors, college seniors, recent college graduates, graduate students. International applications accepted.
Benefits Formal training, job counseling, opportunity to attend seminars/workshops, tuition assistance, willing to complete paperwork for educational credit, willing to provide letters of recommendation, faculty advising throughout the internship.

International Internships Available.
Contact Write, call, fax, e-mail, or through World Wide Web site Timothy Carlson, Co-Director. Phone: 33-1-43-21-78-07. Fax: 33-1-42-79-94-13. E-mail: ifeparis@ifeparis.org. Applicants must submit a formal organization application, resume, academic transcripts, writing sample, two letters of recommendation, other materials as specified on Web site. Application deadline: June 1 for fall, November 1 for spring. Fees: $50. World Wide Web: http://www.ifeparis.org.

INTERNSHIPS INTERNATIONAL
1612 Oberlin Road, #5
Raleigh, North Carolina 27608

General Information Placement service for quality unpaid internships in locations worldwide. Established in 1994. Number of employees: 5. Number of internship applications received each year: 50.
Internships Available ▶ *Interns:* responsibilities include working in all fields as requested by interns. Duration is 8 weeks to 3 months. Unpaid. Open to college seniors, recent college graduates, graduate students, law students, career changers.
Benefits On-the-job training, willing to act as a professional reference, willing to provide letters of recommendation.
International Internships Available in Melbourne, Australia; Santiago, Chile; Shanghai and Beijing, China; Paris, France; Dresden, Germany; Budapest, Hungary; Dublin, Ireland; Capetown, South Africa; Bangkok, Thailand; Glasgow/Edinburgh, United Kingdom; London, United Kingdom.
Contact Write, call, e-mail, or through World Wide Web site Judy Tilson, Director. Phone: 919-832-1575. E-mail: intintl@aol.com. In-person interview recommended (telephone interview accepted). Applicants must submit a formal organization application, letter of interest, resume, academic transcripts, two letters of recommendation, 2 photos; program fees vary from $800-$1500. Applications are accepted continuously. World Wide Web: http://www.rtpnet.org/~intintl.

JAPAN–AMERICA STUDENT CONFERENCE, INC.
606 18th Street, NW, 2nd Floor
Washington, District of Columbia 20006-5202

General Information 30-day exchange program for 30-40 Japanese and 30-40 American university students; alternates annually between Japan and the United States; freshman to PhD levels. Established in 1934. Number of employees: 3. Number of internship applications received each year: 5.
Internships Available ▶ *1–3 interns:* responsibilities include fundraising, general administrative duties, coordinating alumni activities, acting as university liaison, working with database and other computer systems, and archival research. Candidates should have ability to work with others, computer skills, office skills, organizational skills, personal interest in the field, research skills, self-motivation. Duration is flexible. Unpaid. Open to college freshmen, college sophomores, college juniors, college seniors, recent college graduates, graduate students, law students, career changers, individuals reentering the workforce. International applications accepted.
Benefits On-the-job training, opportunity to attend seminars/workshops, willing to act as a professional reference, willing to complete paperwork for educational credit, willing to provide letters of recommendation.
Contact Write, call, fax, or e-mail Ms. Gretchen Hobbs Donaldson, Executive Director. Phone: 202-289-4231. Fax: 202-789-8265. E-mail: jascinc@jasc.org. In-person interview required. Applicants must submit a letter of interest, resume, two personal references. Applications are accepted continuously. World Wide Web: http://www.jasc.org.

JOHN C. CAMPBELL FOLK SCHOOL
One Folk School Road
Brasstown, North Carolina 28902

General Information School with weekend classes and one-week sessions throughout the year that teaches crafts, wood, metal, fiber, painting, song/dance, and musical instruments. Established in 1925. Number of employees: 38. Number of internship applications received each year: 30.

Internships Available ▶ *2 hosts:* responsibilities include supporting programming operations. Candidates should have ability to work independently, oral communication skills, organizational skills, self-motivation, strong interpersonal skills, strong leadership ability. Duration is 6 months. Unpaid. Open to recent high school graduates, college freshmen, college sophomores, college juniors, college seniors, recent college graduates, graduate students, law students, career changers, individuals reentering the workforce. ▶ *3–8 work/study interns:* responsibilities include general indoor and outdoor maintenance. Candidates should have ability to work independently, oral communication skills, self-motivation, strong interpersonal skills, interest in arts and crafts. Duration is 6–12 weeks. Unpaid. Open to recent high school graduates, college freshmen, college sophomores, college juniors, college seniors, recent college graduates, graduate students, law students, law school graduates, career changers, individuals reentering the workforce. International applications accepted.

Benefits Free housing, free meals, opportunity to attend seminars/workshops, tuition assistance, willing to provide letters of recommendation, free classes.

Contact Write, call, fax, or e-mail Hanne Dalsemer, Registrar, 1 Folk School Road, Brasstown, North Carolina 28902. Phone: 828-837-2775. Fax: 828-837-8637. E-mail: hanne@folkschool.org. Telephone interview required. Applicants must submit a formal organization application, two personal references, personal statement (1-2 pages). Applications are accepted continuously. Fees: $35. World Wide Web: http://www.folkschool.org.

JUILLIARD SCHOOL
60 Lincoln Center Plaza
New York, New York 10023-6588

General Information Specialized professional school for the performing arts. Established in 1905. Number of employees: 550. Number of internship applications received each year: 200.

Internships Available ▶ *1 concert office intern:* responsibilities include general assistance in box office management, preparation of recital programs/publicity, concert production, and scheduling in numerous venues. Candidates should have computer skills, organizational skills, self-motivation, strong interpersonal skills, music background (helpful). Duration is September to May. $246 per week. Open to college freshmen, college sophomores, college juniors, college seniors, recent college graduates, graduate students, career changers, individuals reentering the workforce. ▶ *5 costume shop interns:* responsibilities include constructing costumes, dyeing, painting, and performing alterations and repairs. Candidates should have ability to work with others, knowledge of field, plan to pursue career in field, self-motivation, sewing experience. Duration is September to May. $246 per week. Open to recent high school graduates, college freshmen, college sophomores, college juniors, college seniors, recent college graduates, graduate students, career changers. ▶ *1 dance division intern:* responsibilities include assisting the dance production coordinator who manages the daily and long-term planning of dance productions. Candidates should have ability to work independently, computer skills, experience in the field, oral communication skills, organizational skills, personal interest in the field, self-motivation, strong interpersonal skills. Duration is September to May. $246 per week. Open to college freshmen, college sophomores, college juniors, college seniors, recent college graduates, graduate students, career changers. ▶ *1 drama division intern:* responsibilities include assisting administrative director in daily administrative and production operations. Candidates should have ability to work independently, ability to work with others, computer skills, office skills, oral communication skills, organizational skills, self-motivation, written communication skills. Duration is September to May. $246 per week. Open to recent high school graduates, college freshmen, college sophomores, college juniors, college seniors, recent college graduates, graduate students, career changers. ▶ *3 electrics interns:* responsibilities include reading light plots and assisting master electricians with hanging, focusing, and maintaining equipment. Candidates should have ability to work

with others, experience in the field, plan to pursue career in field, self-motivation. Duration is September to May. $246 per week. Open to recent high school graduates, college freshmen, college sophomores, college juniors, college seniors, recent college graduates, graduate students, career changers. ▶ *1 facilities management intern:* responsibilities include assisting the associate vice president of facilities and engineering. Candidates should have ability to work independently, college courses in field, computer skills, oral communication skills, organizational skills, plan to pursue career in field, self-motivation, strong interpersonal skills, written communication skills. Duration is September to May. $246 per week. Open to college freshmen, college sophomores, college juniors, college seniors, recent college graduates, graduate students, career changers, individuals reentering the workforce. ▶ *1 orchestra library intern:* responsibilities include assisting orchestra librarian in securing and preparing all of the music for Juilliard's Performing Ensembles. Candidates should have ability to work independently, experience in the field, plan to pursue career in field, self-motivation, strong interpersonal skills, music background essential. Duration is September to May. $246 per week. Open to recent college graduates, graduate students, career changers. ▶ *2 production assistants:* responsibilities include working with resident production stage managers on various productions and special events. Candidates should have ability to work independently, ability to work with others, computer skills, oral communication skills, organizational skills, self-motivation. $246 per week. Open to college freshmen, college sophomores, college juniors, college seniors, recent college graduates, graduate students, career changers, individuals reentering the workforce. ▶ *2 props interns:* responsibilities include reviewing script for props breakdown; researching, designing, and constructing prop designs; and running crew assignments. Candidates should have ability to work with others, experience in the field, plan to pursue career in field, self-motivation. Duration is September to May. $246 per week. Open to recent high school graduates, college freshmen, college sophomores, college juniors, college seniors, recent college graduates, graduate students, career changers. ▶ *2 scene painting interns:* responsibilities include assisting design, layout, scene painting, texturing, sculpturing, and paint shop maintenance. Candidates should have ability to work independently, ability to work with others, experience in the field, plan to pursue career in field, self-motivation. Duration is September to May. $246 per week. Open to college seniors, recent college graduates, graduate students, career changers. ▶ *6 stage management interns:* responsibilities include assisting production stage managers on opera, drama, and dance productions. Candidates should have ability to work independently, ability to work with others, knowledge of field, oral communication skills, plan to pursue career in field, self-motivation, written communication skills. Duration is September to May. $246 per week. Open to college sophomores, college juniors, college seniors, recent college graduates, graduate students. ▶ *1 vocal arts intern:* responsibilities include assisting administrative staff with daily operations of vocal arts department. Candidates should have computer skills, oral communication skills, organizational skills, personal interest in the field, self-motivation, strong interpersonal skills, written communication skills. Duration is September to May. $246 per week. Open to college freshmen, college sophomores, college juniors, college seniors, recent college graduates, graduate students, career changers.

Benefits Health insurance, names of contacts, possible full-time employment, willing to complete paperwork for educational credit, willing to provide letters of recommendation.

Contact Write, call, fax, e-mail, or through World Wide Web site Helen Taynton, Intern Director. Phone: 212-799-5000 Ext. 621. Fax: 212-724-0263. E-mail: htaynton@juilliard.edu. In-person interview recommended (telephone interview accepted). Applicants must submit a formal organization application, resume, three letters of recommendation, 250-word statement of expectations of the internship program and how it relates to career goals. Application deadline: June 1. Fees: $15.

LANGLEY AEROSPACE RESEARCH SUMMER SCHOLARS (LARSS)
NASA, Mail Stop 400-LARSS
Hampton, Virginia 23681

General Information Education office that promotes opportunities related to university affairs for students, teachers, and faculty. Division of NASA Langley Research Center, Hampton, Virginia. Number of internship applications received each year: 400.
Internships Available ▶ *125–150 LARSS participants.* Candidates should have computer skills, declared college major in field, knowledge of field, plan to pursue career in field, research skills. Duration is early June to mid-August (40 hours per week). $4500 per duration of internship. Open to rising college juniors, seniors, and graduate students.
Benefits Housing at a cost, on-the-job training, opportunity to attend seminars/workshops, possible full-time employment, willing to act as a professional reference, willing to complete paperwork for educational credit, willing to provide letters of recommendation.
Contact Write, call, fax, e-mail, or through World Wide Web site Heidi Davis, Director, LARSS Program, NASA Mail Stop 400-LARSS, Hampton 23681. Phone: 757-864-5298. Fax: 757-864-9701. E-mail: h.b.davis@larc.nasa.gov. Applicants must submit a formal organization application, letter of interest, resume, academic transcripts, writing sample, two letters of recommendation. Application deadline: February 1. World Wide Web: http://edu.larc.nasa.gov/larss.

LANGUAGE STUDIES ABROAD, INC. (LSA)
1801 Highway 50 East, Suite I
Carson City, Nevada 89701

General Information Company that has established partners in countries outside the U.S.A. to provide opportunities for foreigners to develop an understanding of languages and cultures through education and work experiences. Established in 1985. Number of employees: 4. Number of internship applications received each year: 12.
Internships Available ▶ *Interns.* Candidates should have ability to work with others, oral communication skills, self-motivation, written communication skills. Duration is 8–24 weeks. Unpaid. Open to college freshmen, college sophomores, college juniors, college seniors, recent college graduates, graduate students. International applications accepted.
Benefits Health insurance, housing at a cost, meals at a cost, on-the-job training.
International Internships Available in Vienna, Austria; Paris, France; Berlin, Germany; Florence and Rome, Italy; Cuernavaca and Morelin, Mexico; Madrid, Sevilla, Salamanca, Grenada, and Barcelona, Spain.
Contact Write, call, fax, e-mail, or through World Wide Web site Internship Coordinator. Phone: 800-424-5522. Fax: 775-883-2266. E-mail: info@languagestudiesabroad.com. Applicants must submit a formal organization application. Application deadline: 2 months prior to departure. Fees: $100. World Wide Web: http://www.languagestudiesabroad.com.

LITTLE KESWICK SCHOOL, INC.
Keswick, Virginia 22947

General Information Special education residential school for 30 emotionally disturbed or learning disabled boys ages 10-15. Established in 1963. Number of employees: 35. Number of internship applications received each year: 5.
Internships Available ▶ *1–2 interns:* responsibilities include working as a classroom, recreation, or residential aide. Candidates should have ability to work with others, experience in the field, oral communication skills, personal interest in the field, self-motivation. Duration is 1–2 semesters. Unpaid. Open to college seniors, recent college graduates, graduate students. International applications accepted.
Benefits Formal training, free meals, names of contacts, opportunity to attend seminars/workshops, possible full-time employ-

ment, willing to act as a professional reference, willing to complete paperwork for educational credit, willing to provide letters of recommendation.
Contact Write, call, or fax Ms. Terry Columbus, Director, PO Box 24, Keswick, Virginia 22947. Phone: 434-295-0457. Fax: 434-977-1892. E-mail: lks@avenue.org. In-person interview required. Applicants must submit a formal organization application, resume. Applications are accepted continuously. World Wide Web: http://monticello.avenue.org/lks/.

MANHATTAN COUNTRY SCHOOL FARM
Roxbury, New York 12474

General Information Rural Catskill Mountains campus of a New York City independent elementary and junior high school; students take part in raising their own food and fibers and study nature. Established in 1968. Number of employees: 9. Unit of Manhattan Country School, New York, New York. Number of internship applications received each year: 5.
Internships Available ▶ *1 environmental education intern:* responsibilities include working as member of team of veteran farm educators teaching students from age 8 to 14 in one of main curriculum areas: farming, cooking, textiles, nature study, Catskills studies; intern will also be able to conduct research in area of his or her interest related to farm program; student supervision and residential duties. Candidates should have ability to work independently, ability to work with others, research skills, self-motivation, interest in teaching children about the environment, valid driver's license. Duration is 1–2 semesters. Monthly stipend of up to $750. Open to individuals who have completed one or more years of undergraduate study (preferred).
Benefits Free housing, some board provided.
Contact Write, call, or e-mail Virginia Scheer, Farm Director. Phone: 607-326-7049. E-mail: mcsfarm@catskill.net. In-person interview required. Applicants must submit a letter of interest, resume. Application deadline: April 1 for fall (suggested), October 1 for winter/spring. World Wide Web: http://www.manhattancountryschool.org.

MANICE EDUCATION CENTER
68 Savoy Road
Florida, Massachusetts 01247

General Information Residential environmental/wilderness education program serving economically disadvantaged New York City youth through challenging outdoor adventures. Established in 1897. Number of employees: 15. Unit of Christodora, Inc., New York, New York. Number of internship applications received each year: 25.
Internships Available ▶ *2 AmeriCorps Teaching Internships:* responsibilities include working five months in New York City teaching about the environment through hands-on experiences; remaining six months (April-October) will be spent in Massachusetts at the Manice Education Center leading wilderness trips and teaching environmental education to NYC students. Candidates should have ability to work with others, college courses in field, knowledge of field, oral communication skills, strong leadership ability, wilderness camping skills, first aid/CPRskills, street smarts. Duration is 11 months (January-November). $160 per week plus educational award. Open to college sophomores, college juniors, college seniors, recent college graduates, graduate students, career changers. ▶ *4 environmental education interns:* responsibilities include teaching ecology, wilderness, and group leadership skills; facilitating environmental debates; leading science labs and cooperative games; and being responsible for the overnight supervision of 6 students, 4 nights per week. Candidates should have knowledge of field, oral communication skills, personal interest in the field, self-motivation, strong interpersonal skills, strong leadership ability. Duration is spring (April 20-June 15) or fall (September to October). $170–$200 per week. Open to college sophomores, college juniors, college seniors, recent college graduates, graduate students, career changers. ▶ *4 wilderness leadership interns:* responsibilities include co-leading wilderness expeditions; teaching low-impact wilderness travel skills, general ecology, and interpretation; facilitating environmental debates; leading science labs and cooperative games; and supervising students overnight. Candidates should

have experience in the field, oral communication skills, personal interest in the field, self-motivation, strong interpersonal skills, strong leadership ability. Duration is June 15 to August 29. $170–$200 per week. Open to college sophomores, college juniors, college seniors, recent college graduates, graduate students. International applications accepted.

Benefits Formal training, free housing, free meals, health insurance, job counseling, names of contacts, on-the-job training, possible full-time employment, willing to act as a professional reference, willing to complete paperwork for educational credit, willing to provide letters of recommendation, job lists provided when available, equipment discounts, wilderness first aid training for summer interns.

Contact Write, fax, e-mail, or through World Wide Web site Ileana Farris, Administrative Assistant, One East 53rd Street, Suite 1401, New York, New York 10022. Phone: 212-371-5225. Fax: 212-371-2111. E-mail: info@christodora.org. In-person interview recommended (telephone interview accepted). Applicants must submit a formal organization application, letter of interest, resume, academic transcripts, two personal references, three letters of recommendation. Application deadline: March 1 for spring/summer, July 1 for fall. World Wide Web: http://www.christodora.org.

MARIST COLLEGE–MARIST INTERNATIONAL PROGRAMS
3399 North Road
Poughkeepsie, New York 12601-1387

General Information Study abroad programs designed to give undergraduate students enrolled at U.S. colleges/universities the opportunity to participate actively in another culture by combining an internship overseas with coursework at a host institution. Number of internship applications received each year: 60.

Internships Available ▶ *Student interns:* responsibilities include working for overseas organization or business as determined by intern's interest. Candidates should have college courses in field, plan to pursue career in field, self-motivation, strong interpersonal skills. Duration is 1 semester (part-time). Unpaid. Open to college sophomores, college juniors, college seniors.

Benefits On-the-job training, willing to complete paperwork for educational credit, undergraduate academic credit.

International Internships Available in Sydney, Australia; Dublin, Ireland; Madrid, Spain; Leeds, United Kingdom.

Contact Write, call, fax, e-mail, or through World Wide Web site Carol Toufali, Coordinator. Phone: 845-575-3330. Fax: 845-575-3294. E-mail: international@marist.edu. In-person interview required. Applicants must submit a formal organization application, letter of interest, resume, academic transcripts, writing sample, two letters of recommendation. Application deadline: March 15 for fall semester, October 1 for spring semester. Fees: $35. World Wide Web: http://www.marist.edu/international.

MARYMOUNT STUDY ABROAD PROGRAM
Marymount College
Tarrytown, New York 10591-3796

General Information Academic program providing opportunity for undergraduate study at universities in central London combined with internships and work experience placements according to individual interests. Established in 1924. Number of employees: 3. Department of Marymount College of Fordham University, Tarrytown, New York. Number of internship applications received each year: 20.

Internships Available ▶ *London interns:* responsibilities include working in a variety of fields including fashion design, merchandising, public relations, publishing, art gallery/museums, journalism, communications, British education, or international business. Candidates should have ability to work independently, college courses in field, oral communication skills, strong interpersonal skills, written communication skills. Duration is 1 semester. Unpaid. Open to college juniors, college seniors.

Benefits Job counseling, willing to complete paperwork for educational credit, academic study abroad opportunity.

International Internships Available in London, United Kingdom.

Contact Write, call, fax, e-mail, or through World Wide Web site Ekaterina Michailidis, Assistant Dean, Study Abroad Program. Phone: 914-332-8222. Fax: 914-631-3261. E-mail: studyab@mmc.marymt.edu. Applicants must submit a formal organization application, resume, academic transcripts, two personal references, two letters of recommendation, study abroad application. Application deadline: March 15 for London fall or full term, October 15 for spring term. Fees: $125. World Wide Web: http://www.marymt.edu/international/studyab/index.html.

MCKEEVER ENVIRONMENTAL LEARNING CENTER
55 McKeever Lane
Sandy Lake, Pennsylvania 16145

General Information Resident environmental education center for grades K-12 that specializes in preservice and in-service teacher education. Established in 1974. Number of employees: 10. Department of Slippery Rock University of Pennsylvania, Slippery Rock, Pennsylvania. Number of internship applications received each year: 15.

Internships Available ▶ *2 co-op interns:* responsibilities include assisting in implementing special programs, supervising student teachers, providing alternate evening coverage, overseeing props and program supplies, providing on-line status with rental group activities, and assisting with office support. Candidates should have ability to work independently, ability to work with others, oral communication skills, organizational skills, strong leadership ability. Duration is 12 months. $8 per hour. Open to recent college graduates. ▶ *1–3 teaching interns:* responsibilities include teaching in the Center's residential environmental education programs. Candidates should have ability to work with others, oral communication skills, organizational skills, desire to work with children in an outdoor setting. Duration is 2 months. $8 per hour. Open to college seniors, recent college graduates. International applications accepted.

Benefits Formal training, free housing, free meals, job counseling, names of contacts, on-the-job training, opportunity to attend seminars/workshops, travel reimbursement, willing to act as a professional reference, willing to provide letters of recommendation.

Contact Write, call, fax, e-mail, or through World Wide Web site Mr. Francis M. Bires, Director. Phone: 724-376-1000. Fax: 724-376-8235. E-mail: info@mckeever.org. In-person interview required. Applicants must submit a formal organization application, letter of interest, resume, academic transcripts, three letters of recommendation. Applications are accepted continuously. World Wide Web: http://www.mckeever.org.

MINIWANCA EDUCATION CENTER
8845 West Garfield Road
Shelby, Michigan 49455

General Information Multi-purpose youth center on the shores of Lake Michigan offering retreat, conference, leadership development, team building, and community building services for a variety of populations. Established in 1924. Number of employees: 16. Unit of American Youth Foundation, St. Louis, Missouri. Number of internship applications received each year: 20.

Internships Available ▶ *1–10 program interns:* responsibilities include assisting in program development and implementation for a variety of populations, facilitating ropes courses and other experience-based activities, providing hospitality for retreats and conferences, assisting in support services for all programs, assisting with administration, marketing, public relations, and evaluations of all programs. Candidates should have ability to work independently, ability to work with others, knowledge of field, self-motivation, strong leadership ability, experience working with children, CPR and first aid certification (required), lifeguard training (preferred). Duration is 1–2 semesters. $500 per month. Open to individuals at least 18 years of age. International applications accepted.

Benefits Formal training, free housing, health insurance, job counseling, names of contacts, on-the-job training, opportunity to attend seminars/workshops, willing to act as a professional reference, willing to complete paperwork for educational credit, willing to provide letters of recommendation, meals (when programs are running).

Miniwanca Education Center (continued)

Contact Write, call, fax, e-mail, or through World Wide Web site Jennifer Dudley Gilburg, Program Director. Phone: 231-861-2262 Ext. 1109. Fax: 231-861-5244. E-mail: jennifer.dudley@ayf.com. In-person interview recommended (telephone interview accepted). Applicants must submit a formal organization application, letter of interest, resume, three personal references, letter of recommendation. Application deadline: January 15 for winter. World Wide Web: http://www.ayf.com.

MINNETRISTA
1200 North Minnetrista Parkway
Muncie, Indiana 47303

General Information Organization that creates awareness, understanding, and appreciation of the natural and cultural heritage of east central Indiana. Established in 1988. Number of employees: 65. Number of internship applications received each year: 30.

Internships Available ▶ *1 Children's Garden assistant:* responsibilities include maintenance and upkeep of the Children's Garden, developing educational programs and materials, and leading small activities or programs. Candidates should have ability to work independently, ability to work with others, experience in the field, oral communication skills, self-motivation, written communication skills. Duration is minimum of one semester (20 hours per week). Unpaid. Open to college sophomores, college juniors, college seniors, recent college graduates, graduate students, career changers. ▶ *1 assistant archivist (general projects):* responsibilities include arranging and describing archival collections and assisting in reference service and other projects as assigned. Candidates should have ability to work independently, ability to work with others, computer skills, knowledge of field, organizational skills, interest in local history. Duration is minimum of one semester (10 to 20 hours per week). Unpaid. Open to college sophomores, college juniors, college seniors, recent college graduates, graduate students, career changers. ▶ *1–3 collection assistants (specific collections):* responsibilities include researching and cataloging objects; measuring and marking objects; providing a written record of objects prior to storage; overseeing photographing of objects; proper packing and assigning permanent storage location; other duties as assigned. Candidates should have ability to work independently, knowledge of field, self-motivation, ability to lift 30-40 pounds and climb a ladder. Duration is minimum of one semester (30 hours per week). Unpaid. Open to college sophomores, college juniors, college seniors, recent college graduates, graduate students, career changers. ▶ *1 educational resource developer/assistant:* responsibilities include inventorying cultural artifacts; implementing a system for record keeping and coding using computer resources available; developing educational kits with lesson plans using inventoried items, questionnaire to determine educational kit needs for teachers, and strategy for future kits. Candidates should have ability to work independently, ability to work with others, computer skills, knowledge of field, organizational skills, ability to lift 20-30 pounds. Duration is one semester (minimum of 20 hours per week). Unpaid. Open to college sophomores, college juniors, college seniors, recent college graduates, graduate students, career changers. ▶ *3–5 environmental education assistants:* responsibilities include surveying and research; planning, development, coordination, implementation and documentation of project; leading groups, interacting with visitors, training volunteers, and assisting staff. Candidates should have ability to work independently, oral communication skills, organizational skills, strong interpersonal skills, background in research pertaining to area of study. Duration is minimum one semester or college release time. Unpaid. Open to college sophomores, college juniors, college seniors, recent college graduates, graduate students, career changers. ▶ *2–3 events and promotion assistants (specific events):* responsibilities include development of programs; assisting with planning and promotion; coordination of promotional mailings; making contacts and arrangements; other duties as assigned. Candidates should have ability to work independently, organizational skills, personal interest in the field, strong interpersonal skills, creativity, good marketing background, some event planning experience (helpful), average knowledge of Microsoft Office. Duration is dependent upon event. Unpaid. Open to college sophomores, college juniors, college seniors, recent college graduates, graduate students, career changers. ▶ *1 exhibit design assistant:* responsibilities include assisting in the design of exhibits (working within limitations of space and material); assuring exhibits meet museum standards; and developing a driving tour depending upon subject matter. Candidates should have ability to work independently, ability to work with others, college courses in field, organizational skills, personal interest in the field. Duration is minimum of one semester (10 to 20 hours per week). Unpaid. Open to college sophomores, college juniors, college seniors, recent college graduates, graduate students, career changers. ▶ *Marketing assistants:* responsibilities include developing a marketing plan for a project; providing edited copy, as necessary, to graphics; developing and contacting targeted audience; overseeing and implementing distribution of pieces; developing measures of effectiveness; preparing and presenting evaluation and summary of project. Candidates should have ability to work independently, ability to work with others, computer skills, declared college major in field, knowledge of field, office skills, oral communication skills, organizational skills, self-motivation, written communication skills. Duration is minimum of one semester (15-40 hours per week). Unpaid. Open to college juniors, college seniors, recent college graduates, graduate students, career changers. ▶ *1 merchandising assistant:* responsibilities include assisting with inventory control, purchasing, displays, sales analysis, and sales during peak periods; analyzing merchandising trends, making projections for future needs; other duties as assigned. Candidates should have ability to work independently, ability to work with others, computer skills, oral communication skills, organizational skills, written communication skills, basic knowledge of retail concepts and merchandising. Duration is minimum one semester (15-20 hours per week). Unpaid. Open to college sophomores, college juniors, college seniors, recent college graduates, graduate students, career changers. ▶ *2 natural resource research assistants:* responsibilities include working with current grid system of plants and animals to update records, monitoring water quality and updating records, working with volunteers to teach data collection, taking photographs for documentation. Candidates should have ability to work independently, ability to work with others, knowledge of field, organizational skills, some experience with a GIS system, knowledge of digital and 35mm cameras (necessary). Duration is February to June or June to October (minimum of 10-15 hours per week). Unpaid. Open to college sophomores, college juniors, college seniors, recent college graduates, graduate students, career changers. ▶ *Oral/public historians:* responsibilities include conducting and transcribing tape recorded oral history interviews and providing recordings and written transcripts. Candidates should have ability to work independently, ability to work with others, computer skills, knowledge of field, oral communication skills. Duration is by project, 10-20 hours per interview. Unpaid. Open to college sophomores, college juniors, college seniors, recent college graduates, graduate students, career changers. ▶ *1 professional development program assistant:* responsibilities include schedule making and developing of time lines; event planning, contacting presenters by letter/phone, assisting with development and implementation of the publication of each event, implementation of events, developing and implementing evaluations of event. Candidates should have ability to work independently, ability to work with others, experience in the field, oral communication skills, organizational skills, self-motivation, written communication skills. Duration is minimum of one semester (average of 20 hours per week). Unpaid. Open to college sophomores, college juniors, college seniors, recent college graduates, graduate students, career changers. ▶ *1–3 research analysts/assistants:* responsibilities include marketing research and analysis of information on east central Indiana or a specific area, researching using the library and Internet as well as other appropriate sources, developing a profile of participants in cultural activities and a bench mark as it relates to other cultural institutions, putting all information into a usable format that includes the sources. Candidates should have ability to work independently, ability to work with others, computer skills, knowledge of field, research skills. Duration is one semester (minimum of 20 hours per week). Unpaid. Open to college sophomores, college juniors, college seniors, recent college graduates, graduate students, career changers. ▶ *2–3 research assistants:* responsibilities include assisting with primary documents research on a task-by-task or project-by-project basis; archival and census research; meeting with staff to receive individual assignments; participation in research plan development. Candidates should have ability to work independently, ability to work with others, analytical skills, written communication skills, some archival/library research experience, attention to detail, experience with primary document research (preferred but not necessary). Duration is dependent on project (minimum 8-10 hours per week). Unpaid. Open to college sophomores, college juniors, college seniors, recent college graduates, graduate students, career changers. International applications accepted.

Benefits Names of contacts, on-the-job training, willing to act as a professional reference, willing to complete paperwork for educational credit, willing to provide letters of recommendation.
Contact Write, call, fax, e-mail, or through World Wide Web site Sandy Dunn, Staff and Volunteer Manager. Phone: 765-213-3540 Ext. 130. Fax: 765-741-5110. E-mail: sdunn@mcc.mccoak.org. In-person interview recommended (telephone interview accepted). Applicants must submit a formal organization application, letter of interest, resume, portfolio. Applications are accepted continuously. World Wide Web: http://www.mccoak.org.

MISS PORTER'S SCHOOL
60 Main Street
Farmington, Connecticut 06032

General Information Independent boarding and day school for girls grades 9-12. Established in 1843. Number of employees: 120. Number of internship applications received each year: 50.
Internships Available ▶ *1–2 teaching interns:* responsibilities include teaching 1-2 sections within discipline, acting as Assistant House Director, and coaching or advising the equivalent of two seasons of activity. Candidates should have ability to work independently, ability to work with others, college courses in field, computer skills, oral communication skills, strong interest in working with adolescents. Duration is 2 semesters. $14,000 per internship. Open to recent college graduates, graduate students. International applications accepted.
Benefits Free housing, free meals, health insurance, job counseling, names of contacts, on-the-job training, opportunity to attend seminars/workshops, possible full-time employment, travel reimbursement, willing to act as a professional reference, willing to complete paperwork for educational credit, willing to provide letters of recommendation, mentorship by teacher.
Contact Write, call, fax, e-mail, or through World Wide Web site Alan P. Sherman, Director, New Teacher Program. Phone: 860-409-3664. Fax: 860-409-3515. E-mail: alan_sherman@missporters. org. In-person interview required. Applicants must submit a letter of interest, resume, academic transcripts, two letters of recommendation. Applications are accepted continuously. World Wide Web: http://www.missporters.org.

MOUNTAIN LAKE BIOLOGICAL STATION, UNIVERSITY OF VIRGINIA
238 Gilmer Hall, PO Box 400327
Charlottesville, Virginia 22904-4327

General Information Academic center for teaching and research in field biology. Established in 1929. Number of employees: 6. Academic Research Center/Institute of University of Virginia, Charlottesville, Virginia. Number of internship applications received each year: 150.
Internships Available ▶ *10 REU interns:* responsibilities include supervised independent research. Candidates should have ability to work independently, ability to work with others, analytical skills, college courses in field, computer skills, oral communication skills, personal interest in the field, plan to pursue career in field, self-motivation, writing skills. Duration is June 1 to August 15. $3250 scholarship. Open to college freshmen, college sophomores, college juniors, only U.S. citizens or permanent residents.
Benefits Free housing, free meals, names of contacts, opportunity to attend seminars/workshops, possible full-time employment, travel reimbursement, tuition assistance, willing to act as a

professional reference, willing to complete paperwork for educational credit, willing to provide letters of recommendation.
Contact Write, call, fax, e-mail, or through World Wide Web site Eric Nagy, REU Coordinator, Gilmer Hall Room 238, Charlottesville, Virginia 22904-4327. Phone: 434-982-5486. Fax: 434-982-5626. E-mail: enagy@virginia.edu. Applicants must submit a formal organization application, academic transcripts, letter of recommendation, essay. Application deadline: March 1. World Wide Web: http://www.mlbs.org.

MOUNTBATTEN INTERNSHIP PROGRAMME
50 East 42nd Street, Suite 2000
New York, New York 10017-5405

General Information Exchange visitor program providing one-year professional internships for British, New Zealand, and Australian citizens in New York and for U.S. citizens only in London, UK. Established in 1984. Number of employees: 14. Number of internship applications received each year: 1,250.
Internships Available ▶ *35–50 internships in London:* responsibilities include general entry-level work in various fields including finance, marketing, banking, commerce, legal, and information technology. Duration is 12 months beginning in September (some beginning in March). Approximately 1100 British pounds per month. Open to recent college graduates, graduate students, law students, career changers, only those who are U.S. citizens. ▶ *150–160 internships in New York:* responsibilities include general entry-level work in management, business, commerce, and finance with clerical, administrative, research, paralegal, analytical, and information technology duties. Duration is 1 year beginning in January, May, or September. $960 per month. Open to recent college graduates, graduate students, law students, career changers, only those who are citizens of Great Britain, Australia, or New Zealand (no U.S. citizens). Candidates for all positions should have computer skills, office skills, oral communication skills, self-motivation, strong interpersonal skills, written communication skills. International applications accepted.
Benefits Formal training, free housing, health insurance, job counseling, on-the-job training, opportunity to attend seminars/ workshops, willing to act as a professional reference, willing to complete paperwork for educational credit, willing to provide letters of recommendation.
International Internships Available in London, United Kingdom.
Contact Write, call, fax, e-mail, or through World Wide Web site Ellen S. Lautz, Administrative Director, 50 East 42nd Street, Suite 200, New York, New York 10017-5405. Phone: 212-557-5380. Fax: 212-557-5383. E-mail: info@mountbatten.org. In-person interview required. Applicants must submit a formal organization application, resume, academic transcripts, three personal references, three letters of recommendation, personal statement (essay form). Application deadline: May 31 for internships in London. Fees: $50. World Wide Web: http://www.mountbatten.org.

NAFSA
1307 New York Avenue, NW, 8th Floor
Washington, District of Columbia 20005

General Information Nonprofit membership association that provides training, information, and other educational services to professionals in the field of international educational exchange. Established in 1963. Number of employees: 50. Number of internship applications received each year: 50.
Internships Available ▶ *Interns:* responsibilities include working on a specific project in areas including publications, conference, membership, accounting, human resources, special programs, public policy and press relations. Duration is flexible. Position available as unpaid or paid. Open to college freshmen, college sophomores, college juniors, college seniors, recent college graduates, graduate students, law students, career changers, individuals reentering the workforce. International applications accepted.
Benefits On-the-job training, willing to act as a professional reference.
Contact Write, fax, or e-mail Jill Erbland, Executive Assistant. Fax: 202-737-3657. E-mail: internship@nafsa.org. Applicants must submit a letter of interest, resume. Applications are accepted continuously. World Wide Web: http://www.nafsa.org.

NATIONAL COALITION OF ALTERNATIVE COMMUNITY SCHOOLS TEACHER EDUCATION PROGRAM
Upattinas Resource Center, 429 Greenridge Road
Glenmoore, Pennsylvania 19343

General Information Coalition that offers internships in alternative education in grades K-12, public and private, with the possibility of international placement. Established in 1993. Number of employees: 1. Affiliate of National Coalition of Alternative Community Schools (NCACS), Ann Arbor, Michigan. Number of internship applications received each year: 12.
Internships Available ▶ *10 alternative/experiential teaching interns:* responsibilities include teaching at a member school. Candidates should have ability to work independently, oral communication skills, personal interest in the field, self-motivation, strong interpersonal skills. Duration is 1 year. Position available as unpaid or paid. Open to college seniors, recent college graduates, graduate students, career changers, individuals reentering the workforce. International applications accepted.
Benefits Formal training, job counseling, names of contacts, on-the-job training, opportunity to attend seminars/workshops, possible full-time employment, tuition assistance, willing to act as a professional reference, willing to complete paperwork for educational credit, willing to provide letters of recommendation, some housing (depending on placement).
International Internships Available in Yokohama, Japan.
Contact Write, call, fax, e-mail, or through World Wide Web site Ms. Sandra M. Hurst, Director of Teacher Education Program, Upattinas Resource Center, 429 Greenridge Road, Glenmore, Pennsylvania 19343. Phone: 610-458-5138. Fax: 610-458-8688. E-mail: sandy@upattinas.org. In-person interview recommended (telephone interview accepted). Applicants must submit a formal organization application, letter of interest, resume, academic transcripts, personal reference, $3000 fee for tuition upon acceptance. Applications are accepted continuously. Fees: $25. World Wide Web: http://www.ncacs.org.

NATIONAL 4-H CENTER
7100 Connecticut Avenue
Chevy Chase, Maryland 20815

General Information Conference center that teaches political awareness and the history of Washington, D.C. Established in 1951. Number of employees: 180. Number of internship applications received each year: 120.
Internships Available ▶ *2–6 fall program assistants for WOW:* responsibilities include participation in 3 to 4 week training period; leading workshops and assemblies; escorting groups; working with a wide range of youth; learning routes; field trip logistics; learning political awareness workshops. Candidates should have ability to work independently, ability to work with others, office skills, oral communication skills, organizational skills, research skills, self-motivation, strong leadership ability, writing skills. Duration is 11–20 weeks. $250–$300 per week. Open to high school seniors, recent high school graduates, college freshmen, college sophomores, college juniors, college seniors, recent college graduates, 18 through 26 year olds. ▶ *4–8 spring program assistants for WOW:* responsibilities include participation in 3 to 4 week training period; learning to teach workshops on political awareness; coordinating field trip logistics; learning routes; leading workshops and assemblies; office work. Candidates should have ability to work independently, ability to work with others, computer skills, office skills, oral communication skills, organizational skills, research skills, self-motivation, strong leadership ability, writing skills. Duration is 17–21 weeks. $250–$300 per week. Open to high school seniors, recent high school graduates, college freshmen, college sophomores, college juniors, college seniors, recent college graduates, 18 through 26 year olds. ▶ *9–15 summer program assistants for CWF:* responsibilities include participation in 3 to 4 week training period; leading workshops and assemblies; escorting groups; working with high school youth; learning routes; field trip logistics; learning political awareness workshops. Candidates should have ability to work independently, ability to work with others, office skills, oral communication skills, organizational skills, research

skills, self-motivation, strong leadership ability, writing skills. Duration is 13–17 weeks. $250–$300 per week. Open to high school seniors, recent high school graduates, college freshmen, college sophomores, college juniors, college seniors, recent college graduates, 18 through 26 year olds. ▶ *2–5 summer program assistants for WOW:* responsibilities include participation in 3 to 4 week training period; learning workshops and assemblies; escorting groups; working with a wide range of youth; learning routes; field trip logistics; learning political awareness workshops. Candidates should have ability to work independently, ability to work with others, office skills, oral communication skills, organizational skills, research skills, self-motivation, strong leadership ability, writing skills. Duration is 13–17 weeks. $250–$300 per week. Open to high school students, recent high school graduates, college freshmen, college sophomores, college juniors, college seniors, recent college graduates, 18 through 26 year olds. International applications accepted.
Benefits Free housing, free meals, opportunity to attend seminars/workshops, willing to provide letters of recommendation.
Contact Write, call, fax, e-mail, or through World Wide Web site Joel Ann Hawthorne, Sales Director. Phone: 301-961-2801. Fax: 301-961-2922. E-mail: jhawthorne@fourhcouncil.edu. Telephone interview required. Applicants must submit a resume, two writing samples, three letters of recommendation, application package available on line. Application deadline: January 15 for summer, June 1 for fall, November 1 for spring. World Wide Web: http://www.n4h.org.

NATIONAL SOCIETY FOR EXPERIENTIAL EDUCATION
9001 Braddock Road, Suite 380
Springfield, Virginia 22151

General Information Nonprofit education association and resource center that supports colleges and universities, high schools, community agencies, and businesses by helping students learn through meaningful work and service experiences. Established in 1971. Number of employees: 4.
Internships Available ▶ *1 conference workshop intern:* responsibilities include assisting in a wide variety of duties including logistics for meetings and training institute, fund-raising, and membership services. Candidates should have ability to work independently, ability to work with others, oral communication skills, organizational skills, self-motivation, written communication skills. Duration is flexible. Position available as unpaid or paid. ▶ *1 publications intern:* responsibilities include assisting with writing and editing publications and publications order fulfillment. Candidates should have ability to work independently, ability to work with others, computer skills, organizational skills, self-motivation, writing skills. Duration is flexible. Position available as unpaid or paid. Open to college freshmen, college sophomores, college juniors, college seniors, recent college graduates, graduate students. International applications accepted.
Benefits Job counseling, names of contacts, willing to complete paperwork for educational credit, willing to provide letters of recommendation, possible membership, publications, stipend.
Contact Write, fax, e-mail, or through World Wide Web site Charles Walker, Executive Director. Fax: 703-426-8400. E-mail: info@nsee.org. No phone calls. In-person interview recommended (telephone interview accepted). Applicants must submit a letter of interest, resume, writing sample. Applications are accepted continuously. World Wide Web: http://www.nsee.org.

NEW CANAAN COUNTRY SCHOOL
PO Box 997
New Canaan, Connecticut 06840

General Information Independent elementary school enrolling 575 students in grades pre-K through 9. Established in 1936. Number of employees: 120. Number of internship applications received each year: 200.
Internships Available ▶ *16–18 teaching fellowships:* responsibilities include assisting in all areas of program in a self-contained K-6 homeroom. Candidates should have oral communication skills, personal interest in the field, self-motivation, strong interpersonal

skills, written communication skills. Duration is September to June. $18,000 taxable stipend. Open to college seniors, recent college graduates, graduate students, career changers. International applications accepted.

Benefits Formal training, health insurance, housing at a cost, job counseling, names of contacts, opportunity to attend seminars/workshops, possible full-time employment, tuition assistance, willing to provide letters of recommendation.

Contact Write or call Ms. Dana Mallozzi, Fellowship Coordinator. Phone: 203-972-0771. Fax: 203-966-5924. E-mail: dmallozzi@countryschool.net. In-person interview required. Applicants must submit a letter of interest, resume, academic transcripts, three letters of recommendation. Application deadline: April 1. World Wide Web: http://www.nccs.pvt.k12.ct.us.

NEW CANAAN NATURE CENTER
144 Oenoke Ridge
New Canaan, Connecticut 06840

General Information Environmental education center and sanctuary dedicated to helping people of all ages understand, appreciate, and care for the natural world. Established in 1960. Number of employees: 30. Number of internship applications received each year: 150.

Internships Available ▶ *2–3 fall and school year teachers/naturalists:* responsibilities include planning and presenting natural science programs for pre-kindergarten through middle school students, teaching selected public programs, and assisting with animal care. Candidates should have ability to work independently, ability to work with others, knowledge of field, oral communication skills. Duration is 9 months (Labor Day to Memorial Day). $275 per week. Open to recent college graduates, graduate students, career changers, individuals reentering the workforce. ▶ *1–2 spring teachers/naturalists:* responsibilities include planning and presenting natural science programs for pre-kindergarten through middle school students, teaching selected public programs, and assisting with animal care. Candidates should have ability to work independently, ability to work with others, knowledge of field, oral communication skills. Duration is 5 months (January 1-Memorial Day). $275 per week. Open to recent college graduates, graduate students, career changers, individuals reentering the workforce. ▶ *1–15 summer teachers/naturalists:* responsibilities include planning and team-teaching diverse programs that include the study of natural science, nature crafts, sensory awareness, and general environmental education in day camp setting with groups of up to 14 children (pre-K through 4th grade). Candidates should have ability to work independently, ability to work with others, knowledge of field, oral communication skills, personal interest in the field. Duration is 11 weeks. $250 per week. Open to college freshmen, college sophomores, college juniors, college seniors, recent college graduates, graduate students, career changers, individuals reentering the workforce. International applications accepted.

Benefits Formal training, free housing, job counseling, on-the-job training, opportunity to attend seminars/workshops, possible full-time employment, willing to act as a professional reference, willing to complete paperwork for educational credit, willing to provide letters of recommendation.

Contact Write, fax, or e-mail Ms. Ann Kozlowicz, Director of School Programs. Phone: 203-966-9577 Ext. 38. Fax: 203-966-6536. E-mail: akozlowicz@newcanaannature.org. In-person interview recommended (telephone interview accepted). Applicants must submit a letter of interest, resume, three personal references. Application deadline: January 1 for spring, April 1 for summer, July 1 for fall and school year. World Wide Web: http://www.newcanaannature.org.

NEWFOUND HARBOR MARINE INSTITUTE
1300 Big Pine Avenue
Big Pine Key, Florida 33043

General Information Nonprofit residential education center offering programs in marine environmental education to groups seeking to increase their understanding of the ocean and natural ecosystems. Established in 1965. Number of employees: 80. Number of internship applications received each year: 70.

Internships Available ▶ *10–18 science interns:* responsibilities include teaching, dorm duty, dining hall management, housekeeping, and daily interaction with children. Candidates should have ability to work with others, declared college major in field, oral communication skills, plan to pursue career in field, strong leadership ability. Duration is 3–5 months. $50 per week. Open to college sophomores, college juniors, college seniors, recent college graduates, graduate students, career changers. International applications accepted.

Benefits Formal training, free housing, free meals, job counseling, names of contacts, opportunity to attend seminars/workshops, possible full-time employment, willing to act as a professional reference, willing to complete paperwork for educational credit, willing to provide letters of recommendation.

Contact Write, call, fax, or e-mail Assistant Science Program Director. Phone: 305-872-2331. Fax: 305-872-2555. E-mail: info@nhmi.org. Telephone interview required. Applicants must submit a formal organization application, letter of interest, resume, academic transcripts, three letters of recommendation. Application deadline: April 30 for summer, July 1 for fall, October 15 for spring. World Wide Web: http://www.nhmi.org.

NORTHFIELD MOUNT HERMON SCHOOL
206 Main Street
Northfield, Massachusetts 01360-1089

General Information Private co-educational boarding school with 1100 students in 9th grade through the post-graduate level. Established in 1879. Number of employees: 500. Number of internship applications received each year: 250.

Internships Available ▶ *6–8 First-Year Teacher Program interns:* responsibilities include working closely with master teacher during fall term; full responsibility for classes during winter and spring terms; coaching two seasons; living in dormitory apartments; serving as advisor to 6-8 students. Duration is September to June. $22,500 per year. ▶ *1–3 administrative interns:* responsibilities include working closely with administrator in a specific program; teaching courses where appropriate; living in dormitory apartments; advising group of 6-8 students; coaching athletic (if appropriate). Duration is September to June. $16,000 per year. Candidates for all positions should have college degree in related field, oral communication skills, strong interpersonal skills, written communication skills, competitive athletics experience. Open to college seniors, recent college graduates, graduate students. International applications accepted.

Benefits Formal training, free housing, free meals, health insurance, job counseling, names of contacts, on-the-job training, opportunity to attend seminars/workshops, possible full-time employment, willing to act as a professional reference, willing to provide letters of recommendation, life insurance.

Contact Write, call, fax, e-mail, or through World Wide Web site Office of Faculty Recruitment. Phone: 413-498-3410. Fax: 413-498-3054. E-mail: faculty_recruitment@nmhschool.org. In-person interview recommended (telephone interview accepted). Applicants must submit a letter of interest, resume, academic transcripts, two letters of recommendation, optional formal application (see Web site). Applications are accepted continuously. World Wide Web: http://www.nmhschool.org.

NORTHFIELD MOUNT HERMON SUMMER SESSION
206 Main Street
Northfield, Massachusetts 01360

General Information Summer coeducational boarding school with a curriculum focusing on credit and enrichment for junior and senior high school students; students come from all over the U.S. and the world. Established in 1961. Number of employees: 110. Number of internship applications received each year: 150.

Internships Available ▶ *35–40 teaching interns:* responsibilities include assistant teaching a major and minor course, leading a sport, and assisting with dorm supervision. Candidates should have ability to work independently, college courses in field, organizational skills, personal interest in the field, self-motivation, strong interpersonal skills. Duration is 6 weeks. $2000 per duration of internship. Open to college juniors, college seniors, recent college graduates, graduate students. International applications accepted.

Benefits Formal training, free housing, free meals, job counseling, names of contacts, possible full-time employment, willing to complete paperwork for educational credit, willing to provide letters of recommendation.

Contact Write, call, fax, e-mail, or through World Wide Web site Debra J. Frank, Associate Director. Phone: 413-498-3290. Fax: 413-498-3112. E-mail: summer_school@nmhschool.org. Applicants must submit a formal organization application, letter of interest, resume, academic transcripts, two letters of recommendation, either in-person or telephone interview. Application deadline: March 1. World Wide Web: http://www.nmhschool.org/summer.

OAK RIDGE INSTITUTE FOR SCIENCE AND EDUCATION
PO Box 53
Aberdeen Proving Ground, Maryland 21010-0053

General Information Department of Energy initiative focusing on scientific initiatives to educate the next generation of scientists. Established in 1946. Unit of Oak Ridge Associated Universities, Oak Ridge, Tennessee. Number of internship applications received each year: 400.

Internships Available ▶ *Interns:* responsibilities include performing practical research experiences closely related to intern's academic pursuits. Candidates should have ability to work independently, research skills, self-motivation, strong interpersonal skills, strong leadership ability. Duration is 1-12 months (up to 3 years). Monthly stipend. Open to college freshmen, college sophomores, college juniors, college seniors, recent college graduates, graduate students. International applications accepted.

Benefits On-the-job training, opportunity to attend seminars/workshops, possible full-time employment, travel reimbursement in some cases.

International Internships Available in Germany; Japan.

Contact Write, call, fax, e-mail, or through World Wide Web site Jody Osborne, Recruiter. Phone: 410-436-7258. Fax: 410-436-5811. E-mail: joanna.osborne@apg.amedd.army.mil. Applicants must submit a formal organization application, resume, academic transcripts, 3 professional references. Applications are accepted continuously. World Wide Web: http://www.orau.gov.

OAK RIDGE INSTITUTE FOR SCIENCE AND EDUCATION (ORISE)
MS36, PO Box 117
Oak Ridge, Tennessee 37831-0117

General Information Organization that conducts multidisciplinary science and engineering internships. Established in 1946. Number of employees: 300. Unit of United States Department of Energy, Washington, District of Columbia.

Internships Available ▶ *Project Education Research Experiences (HERE) interns:* responsibilities include participating in research in sciences and engineering technology. Candidates should have ability to work independently, ability to work with others, analytical skills, computer skills, research skills, writing skills, major in science, mathematics, engineering, or technology fields, minimum GPA of 3.0. Duration is 3–12 months. $350 per week (undergraduates); $400 per week (graduates). Open to college freshmen, college sophomores, college juniors, college seniors, recent college graduates, graduate students. ▶ *Professional interns:* responsibilities include participating in fossil energy-related research in the areas of chemistry, computer science, engineering, environmental sciences, geology, mathematics, physics, and statistics at any of the following sites: Savannah River, National Energy Laboratory Center at Pittsburgh (PA), or Morgantown (WV). Candidates should have a declared college major in field, minimum GPA 2.5. Duration is 3–18 months. $250–$871 per week. Open to college freshmen, college sophomores, college juniors, college seniors, graduate students, college graduates with BS received no longer than 2 years ago. ▶ *Technology interns:* responsibilities include

research in the areas of chemistry, physics, engineering, mathematics, computer science, safety, and health at National Energy Laboratory Center at Pittsburgh (PA). Duration is 3–18 months. $300 per week. Open to college sophomores at 2-year colleges.

Benefits Travel reimbursement, possible tuition assistance (for off-campus students only).

Contact Write, call, fax, e-mail, or through World Wide Web site Kathy Ball, Specialist. Phone: 865-576-8807. Fax: 865-241-5220. E-mail: ballk@orau.gov. Applicants must submit a formal organization application, academic transcripts, two letters of recommendation. Application deadline: February 15 for summer, February 1 for HERE positions, June 1 for fall, October 1 for spring. World Wide Web: http://www.orau.gov/orise.htm.

OFFICE OF INTERNSHIPS AND EXPERIENTIAL EDUCATION
Taft Hall, The University of Rhode Island
Kingston, Rhode Island 02881

General Information Internship office that administers full-time and part-time internships for academic credit; internship opportunities available nationwide as well as in Dublin, Ireland. Established in 1975. Number of employees: 2. Unit of University of Rhode Island, University College, Kingston, Rhode Island. Number of internship applications received each year: 300.

Internships Available ▶ *Interns.* Candidates should have ability to work independently, oral communication skills, plan to pursue career in field, self-motivation, strong interpersonal skills, written communication skills, 60 credits completed, with a 2.5 GPA. Duration is 1 semester or summer, full- or part-time. Unpaid. Open to college juniors, college seniors.

Benefits Job counseling, on-the-job training, opportunity to attend seminars/workshops, willing to act as a professional reference, willing to complete paperwork for educational credit, willing to provide letters of recommendation, interviewing assistance.

International Internships Available in Dublin, Ireland.

Contact Write, call, fax, e-mail, or through World Wide Web site Moira Keating, Ph.D., Intern Advisor. Phone: 401-874-2160. Fax: 401-874-4573. E-mail: intern@etal.uri.edu. In-person interview required. Applicants must submit a formal organization application, academic transcripts, telephone interview acceptable for non-URI students. Application deadline: April 20 for summer, August 20 for fall, November 20 for spring. World Wide Web: http://www.uri.edu/univco/internships.

THE OUTDOORS WISCONSIN LEADERSHIP SCHOOL (OWLS)
350 Constance Boulevard
Williams Bay, Wisconsin 53191-0210

General Information Leading provider of adventure education in the Midwest focusing on leadership, communication, creativity, risk-taking, trust-building, and problem solving. Unit of Aurora University, Lake Geneva Campus, Williams Bay, Wisconsin.

Internships Available ▶ *Interns.* Candidates should have some course work in related areas and experience working with people. Paid. Open to college seniors, recent college graduates.

Benefits Free housing, free meals, supplemental health insurance.

Contact Write or e-mail Cathy Coster. Phone: 262-245-5531 Ext. 8544. Fax: 262-245-8549. E-mail: owls@aurora.edu. Applicants must submit a letter of interest, resume, names of 3 references. Applications are accepted continuously. World Wide Web: http://www.augeowms.org/owls.html.

PACIFIC AND ASIAN AFFAIRS COUNCIL (PAAC)
1601 East-West Road, 4th Floor
Honolulu, Hawaii 96848

General Information Nonprofit organization that has been providing global education for over 47 years; member of the World Affairs Council of America and has organized forums featuring speakers including the Dalai Lama and Bob Dole. Established in 1954. Number of employees: 5. Number of internship applications received each year: 5.

Internships Available ▶ *1–2 assistant program coordinators:* responsibilities include helping to plan educational programs and doing basic office duties. Candidates should have computer skills, office skills, organizational skills, research skills, self-motivation, writing skills. Duration is flexible. Unpaid. Open to college freshmen, college sophomores, college juniors, college seniors, recent college graduates, graduate students, law students, career changers. International applications accepted.
Benefits Names of contacts, on-the-job training, opportunity to attend seminars/workshops, possible full-time employment, willing to act as a professional reference, willing to complete paperwork for educational credit, willing to provide letters of recommendation.
Contact Write, call, fax, or e-mail Lisa Maruyama, Executive Director, 1601 East-West Road, 4th Floor, Honolulu, Hawaii 96848. Phone: 808-944-7780. Fax: 808-944-7785. E-mail: ed@paachawaii. org. In-person interview recommended (telephone interview accepted). Applicants must submit a letter of interest, resume. Applications are accepted continuously. World Wide Web: http:// www.paachawaii.org.

PARK SCHOOL
171 Goddard Avenue
Brookline, Massachusetts 02445

General Information Independent day school of more than 500 students from nursery through 9th grade. Established in 1888. Number of employees: 100. Number of internship applications received each year: 150.
Internships Available ▶ *8–10 teaching interns:* responsibilities include teaching full-time with a mentor teacher in 2 different classroom placements during the year and learning to handle all aspects of teaching, coaching, and play directing. Candidates should have knowledge of field, oral communication skills, personal interest in the field, self-motivation, strong interpersonal skills, written communication skills. Duration is academic year (9 months). $15,000 per internship plus additional pay for coaching, drama, and after school program help. Open to recent college graduates, graduate students, career changers. International applications accepted.
Benefits Formal training, health insurance, job counseling, names of contacts, on-the-job training, opportunity to attend seminars/ workshops, tuition assistance, willing to act as a professional reference, willing to complete paperwork for educational credit, willing to provide letters of recommendation, free lunches.
Contact Write, fax, or e-mail Linda Knight. Fax: 617-277-2456. E-mail: linda_knight@parkschool.org. Applicants must submit a letter of interest, resume, academic transcripts, three letters of recommendation, in-person interview (held February to May). Applications are accepted continuously. World Wide Web: http:// www.parkschool.org.

PEAK PERFORMANCE
627 West Valley Boulevard
Big Bear City, California 92314

General Information Company that designs and delivers experiential adventure learning for businesses, schools, churches, and families. Established in 1994. Number of employees: 25. Number of internship applications received each year: 50.
Internships Available ▶ *1 marketing intern:* responsibilities include market research, writing copy and releases, maintaining database, conducting presentations, planning special events, and assisting with program delivery. Candidates should have computer skills, oral communication skills, personal interest in the field, research skills, self-motivation, writing skills. Duration is 2–6 months. $50–$100 per week. Open to recent college graduates, graduate students, law students, career changers, individuals reentering the workforce. ▶ *1–4 program specialists:* responsibilities include designing and delivering adventure education programs to varied audiences. Candidates should have ability to work with others, oral communication skills, personal interest in the field, self-motivation, strong leadership ability. Duration is 3–8 months. Position available as unpaid or at $50 per week. Open to college

juniors, college seniors, recent college graduates, graduate students, career changers, individuals reentering the workforce. International applications accepted.
Benefits Formal training, free housing, free meals, job counseling, on-the-job training, opportunity to attend seminars/workshops, possible full-time employment, travel reimbursement, willing to act as a professional reference, willing to complete paperwork for educational credit, willing to provide letters of recommendation, discounts on equipment.
Contact Write, fax, e-mail, or through World Wide Web site Mark H. Rowland, President. Fax: 909-584-9764. E-mail: info@peaktraining. com. No phone calls. Telephone interview required. Applicants must submit a letter of interest, resume, three personal references. Applications are accepted continuously. World Wide Web: http:// www.peaktraining.com.

THE PHILADELPHIA CENTER
121 South Broad Street, 7th Floor
Philadelphia, Pennsylvania 19107

General Information Off-campus experiential education program comprised of a full-time internship with opportunities in all disciplines, academic seminars, and independent living. Established in 1967. Number of employees: 10. Affiliate of Great Lakes College Association, Inc., Ann Arbor, Michigan. Number of internship applications received each year: 250.
Internships Available ▶ *180–200 interns:* responsibilities include working in numerous fields including communications, business, education, law, government, psychology, social service, science, and the arts. Duration is 1 semester. Unpaid. Open to college freshmen, college sophomores, college juniors, college seniors, recent college graduates, graduate students. International applications accepted.
Benefits Formal training, job counseling, names of contacts, on-the-job training, opportunity to attend seminars/workshops, willing to act as a professional reference, willing to complete paperwork for educational credit, willing to provide letters of recommendation, college credit, more than 700 placements from which to choose, program student advisors act as career and academic counselors, networking possibilities.
Contact Write, call, fax, e-mail, or through World Wide Web site Ilene Baker, Information Director. Phone: 215-735-7300. Fax: 215-735-7373. E-mail: admin@philactr.edu. Applicants must submit a formal organization application, resume, academic transcripts, two letters of recommendation, proof of eligibility for off-campus study (determined by applicant's school), $8000 tuition cost upon acceptance. Applications are accepted continuously. World Wide Web: http://www.philactr.edu.

PHILLIPS ACADEMY
180 Main Street
Andover, Massachusetts 01810-4161

General Information Private secondary boarding and day preparatory school. Established in 1778. Number of employees: 550. Number of internship applications received each year: 300.
Internships Available ▶ *10–12 fellowships:* responsibilities include teaching two sections of a departmental offering, acting as assistant house counselor in dormitory, and participating in athletics. Candidates should have ability to work independently, college courses in field, knowledge of field, oral communication skills, plan to pursue career in field, self-motivation, strong interpersonal skills, strong leadership ability, written communication skills. Duration is September to June. $18,000 per year. Open to college seniors, recent college graduates, graduate students. ▶ *20 teaching assistants:* responsibilities include assisting in the teaching of two courses, running a dormitory, coaching an afternoon activity, chaperoning, and facilitating nearly every facet of boarding school life. Candidates should have ability to work independently, oral communication skills, plan to pursue career in field, self-motivation, strong interpersonal skills, strong leadership ability, writing skills, interest in working with adolescents. Duration is June 26 to August 8. $2400 per duration of internship. Open to recent college graduates, graduate students. ▶ *12–14 teaching assistants (math and science for minority students):* responsibilities include assisting with teaching minority students two courses in

Phillips Academy (continued)

mathematics, biology, chemistry, physics, or English; college counseling; running help sessions or study halls; and occasional chaperoning of on- and off-campus activities. Candidates should have declared college major in field, oral communication skills, strong interpersonal skills, written communication skills, interest in working with minority adolescents. Duration is June 28 to August 8. $2400 per duration of internship. Open to college seniors, recent college graduates, graduate students. ▶ *1 teaching fellowship in community service:* responsibilities include serving as assistant director of the community service program, managing various aspects of the program, mentoring, student coordinators, meeting with agency contacts, transporting student volunteers, and participating on the faculty advisory board. Candidates should have ability to work independently, ability to work with others, knowledge of field, oral communication skills, personal interest in the field, plan to pursue career in field, self-motivation, strong leadership ability, written communication skills. Duration is September to June. $18,000 per year. Open to college seniors, recent college graduates, graduate students, career changers, those who have one-year work in service learning environment (preferred). International applications accepted.

Benefits Free housing, free meals, health insurance, job counseling, names of contacts, on-the-job training, opportunity to attend seminars/workshops, willing to act as a professional reference, willing to provide letters of recommendation, life insurance, dental insurance.

Contact Write, call, or e-mail Lynda Diamondis, Dean of Faculty. Phone: 978-749-4003. Fax: 978-749-4033. E-mail: ldiamondis@andover.edu. In-person interview required. Applicants must submit a formal organization application, letter of interest, resume, academic transcripts, writing sample, personal reference, two letters of recommendation. Application deadline: February 1 for fellowships (September start), February 15 for teaching assistants (June start). World Wide Web: http://www.andover.edu.

PRESIDENTIAL CLASSROOM
119 Oronoco Street
Alexandria, Virginia 22314-2015

General Information Nonprofit, nonpartisan educational organization that brings high school students to Washington, D.C. for 1-week experiential government programs. Established in 1968. Number of employees: 15. Number of internship applications received each year: 200.

Internships Available ▶ *12–14 program interns:* responsibilities include providing administrative, logistical, and academic support. Candidates should have ability to work independently, oral communication skills, organizational skills, strong interpersonal skills, strong leadership ability. Duration is 6 weeks in summer; 10 weeks in winter. Small stipend. Open to college sophomores, college juniors, college seniors, recent college graduates, graduate students, law students. International applications accepted.

Benefits Formal training, free housing, free meals, job counseling, names of contacts, opportunity to attend seminars/workshops, possible full-time employment, willing to act as a professional reference, willing to complete paperwork for educational credit, willing to provide letters of recommendation.

Contact Write, call, fax, e-mail, or through World Wide Web site Natanya Levioff, Director of Logistics and Special Projects. Phone: 800-441-6533. Fax: 703-548-5728. E-mail: intern@presidentialclassroom.org. Telephone interview required. Applicants must submit a formal organization application, two letters of recommendation. Application deadline: March 1 for spring, October 1 for winter. World Wide Web: http://www.presidentialclassroom.org.

PROJECT USE, URBAN SUBURBAN ENVIRONMENTS
PO Box 837, 76 East Front Street
Red Bank, New Jersey 07701-0837

General Information Year-round experiential educational organization for children and adults from all backgrounds; activities include initiative games, high ropes courses, backpacking,

canoeing, kayaking, rock climbing, and environmental education. Established in 1970. Number of employees: 15. Number of internship applications received each year: 3.

Internships Available ▶ *1 builder:* responsibilities include assisting with the design and building of challenge courses and training the client in facilitation techniques. Candidates should have oral communication skills, self-motivation, strong interpersonal skills, strong leadership ability, building skills. Duration is 3 months. $100–$150 per week. Open to high school seniors, recent high school graduates, college freshmen, college sophomores, college juniors, college seniors, recent college graduates, graduate students, career changers, individuals reentering the workforce. ▶ *1–3 field instructors:* responsibilities include preparing for, conducting, and concluding safe wilderness experiences for all courses. Candidates should have ability to work independently, oral communication skills, personal interest in the field, self-motivation, strong interpersonal skills, love of outdoors and related activities. Duration is 3 months. $100–$150 per week. Open to high school seniors, recent high school graduates, college freshmen, college sophomores, college juniors, college seniors, recent college graduates, graduate students, law students, career changers, individuals reentering the workforce, must be 18 years old. International applications accepted.

Benefits Formal training, free housing, free meals, names of contacts, on-the-job training, opportunity to attend seminars/workshops, possible full-time employment, willing to act as a professional reference, willing to complete paperwork for educational credit, willing to provide letters of recommendation.

Contact Write, call, fax, e-mail, or through World Wide Web site Nancy Medrow, Human Resources Coordinator, PO Box 837, 76 East Front Street, Redbank, New Jersey 07701. Phone: 732-219-7300. Fax: 732-219-7305. E-mail: projectuse@monmouth.com. In-person interview recommended (telephone interview accepted). Applicants must submit a formal organization application, two personal references. Applications are accepted continuously. World Wide Web: http://www.projectuse.com.

PUBLIC ALLIES DC
1120 Connecticut Avenue, NW, Suite 435
Washington, District of Columbia 20036

General Information Nonprofit organization aimed at developing strong community leadership by creating opportunities for diverse young leaders to strengthen communities through paid professional apprenticeships in community organizations. Established in 1992. Number of employees: 3. Unit of Public Allies, Inc., Milwaukee, Wisconsin.

Internships Available ▶ *1–2 hiring assistants:* responsibilities include assisting in all aspects of recruitment selection and placement of program participants, including, but not limited to, creating/editing recruitment materials, facilitating recruitment sessions, reviewing applications, and interviewing. Candidates should have computer skills, oral communication skills, self-motivation, strong interpersonal skills, written communication skills, knowledge of human resources (useful but not required). Duration is flexible. Unpaid. Open to college juniors, college seniors, recent college graduates, graduate students. ▶ *Up to 20 public allies apprentices:* responsibilities include serving four days a week at nonprofit organization; fifth day spent in leadership training and personal development workshops. Candidates should have ability to work with others, personal interest in the field, self-motivation, strong leadership ability, written communication skills. Duration is September to July. Paid at up to $15,000 plus health insurance and tuition assistance. Open to recent high school graduates, college sophomores, college juniors, college seniors, recent college graduates, graduate students, individuals reentering the workforce, U.S. citizens or legal permanent residents ages 18-30 (required). International applications accepted.

Benefits Names of contacts, on-the-job training, willing to act as a professional reference, willing to complete paperwork for educational credit, willing to provide letters of recommendation, health insurance, tuition assistance, formal training, and possibility of full-time employment (apprentice program only).

Contact Write, call, or e-mail Jay Kim, Executive Director. Phone: 202-293-3969. Fax: 202-822-1199. E-mail: jayk@publicallies.org.

In-person interview recommended (telephone interview accepted). Applicants must submit a resume, academic transcripts, writing sample, three personal references, 2 letters of recommendation and in-person interviews (for public allies apprenticeships) letter of interest (hiring assistant position). Application deadline: May 31 for hiring assistants, July 1 for public allies apprenticeships. World Wide Web: http://www.publicallies.org.

PUBLIC BROADCASTING SERVICE (PBS)
1320 Braddock Place
Alexandria, Virginia 22314

General Information Nonprofit media, television, and online education corporation. Established in 1969. Number of employees: 500. Number of internship applications received each year: 200.
Internships Available ▶ *10–15 interns:* responsibilities include working in various departments including accounting, broadcast operations, human resources, information technology, Web site development/editing, program operations, and communications. Duration is 6–12 weeks. Position available as unpaid or at $6 per hour. Open to college freshmen, college sophomores, college juniors, college seniors, recent college graduates, graduate students, law students. International applications accepted.
Benefits On-the-job training, possible full-time employment, willing to complete paperwork for educational credit, willing to provide letters of recommendation.
Contact Write, fax, or through World Wide Web site Internship Program. Fax: 703-739-8689. E-mail: jobs@pbs.org. No phone calls. In-person interview recommended (telephone interview accepted). Applicants must submit a letter of interest, resume. Applications are accepted continuously. World Wide Web: http://www.pbs.org.

PUBLIC LEADERSHIP EDUCATION NETWORK (PLEN)
1001 Connecticut Avenue, NW, Suite 900
Washington, District of Columbia 20036-5507

General Information National consortium of women's and other colleges that runs public policy programs and places students as interns in organizations working with public policy. Established in 1978. Number of employees: 3. Number of internship applications received each year: 30.
Internships Available ▶ *12–20 women and public policy interns:* responsibilities include performing various duties, including research, writing reports, and attending hearings. Candidates should have knowledge of field, office skills, oral communication skills, organizational skills, personal interest in the field, research skills, written communication skills. Duration is one summer or semestser. Position available as unpaid or paid. Open to college freshmen, college sophomores, college juniors, college seniors, recent college graduates, graduate students. International applications accepted.
Benefits Formal training, job counseling, names of contacts, on-the-job training, opportunity to attend seminars/workshops, willing to act as a professional reference, willing to complete paperwork for educational credit, willing to provide letters of recommendation, opportunity to attend classes focusing on women and public policy, information on locating housing.
International Internships Available in London, United Kingdom.
Contact Write, call, fax, or e-mail Liz Swanson, Executive Director, 1001 Connecticut Avenue, NW, Suite 900, Washington, District of Columbia 20036-5607. Phone: 202-872-1585. Fax: 202-457-0549. E-mail: plen@plen.org. In-person interview recommended (telephone interview accepted). Applicants must submit a formal organization application, letter of interest, resume, writing sample, letter of recommendation. Application deadline: February 12 for summer, July 14 for fall, November 4 for spring. Fees: $45. World Wide Web: http://www.plen.org.

PUBLIC SERVICE CORPS, NEW YORK CITY, DEPARTMENT OF CITYWIDE ADMINISTRATIVE SERVICES
1 Centre Street, Room 2435
New York, New York 10007

General Information Agency that provides internship opportunities throughout city agencies. Established in 1966. Number of employees: 8. Division of New York Department of Citywide Administrative Services, New York, New York. Number of internship applications received each year: 1,600.
Internships Available ▶ *1,000 Federal Work-Study Program interns:* responsibilities include working in a broad range of fields including government administration, creative arts, social work, health care, research, education, computer science, economic development, finance, accounting, labor relations, transportation, and management. Duration is to be determined by each school. $5.90–$12.48 per hour. Open to undergraduates, graduate students, and law students who are eligible for Federal Work-Study Program. ▶ *Academic credit interns:* responsibilities include working in a broad range of fields including government administration, creative arts, social work, health care, research, education, computer science, economic development, finance, accounting, labor relations, transportation, and management. Duration is flexible. Unpaid. Open to college freshmen, college sophomores, college juniors, college seniors, graduate students, law students. Candidates for all positions should have specific college courses and/or skills by internship.
Benefits On-the-job training, opportunity to attend seminars/workshops, willing to complete paperwork for educational credit, experience in public service; credit can be arranged with college approval.
Contact Write, call, fax, or e-mail Dr. Marjorie Jelin, Director. Phone: 212-669-3255. Fax: 212-669-3633. E-mail: mjelin@dcas.nyc.gov. In-person interview required. Applicants must submit a formal organization application. Applications are accepted continuously. World Wide Web: http://www.nyc.gov/html/dcas/html/psc.html.

THE PULLIAM FELLOWSHIPS
307 North Pennsylvania Street
Indianapolis, Indiana 46204

General Information Journalism work-study program for college students serious about pursuing a career in journalism. Established in 1974. Number of employees: 2. Unit of Gannett Co., Inc., McLean, Virginia. Number of internship applications received each year: 200.
Internships Available ▶ *20 Pulliam fellowships:* responsibilities include reporting and copy editing. Candidates should have ability to work independently, analytical skills, computer skills, editing skills, experience in the field, oral communication skills, organizational skills, personal interest in the field, plan to pursue career in field, research skills, self-motivation, strong interpersonal skills, strong leadership ability, written communication skills. Duration is 10 weeks. $6600 stipend. Open to college sophomores, college juniors, college seniors. International applications accepted.
Benefits Job counseling, names of contacts, on-the-job training, opportunity to attend seminars/workshops, possible full-time employment, travel reimbursement, willing to act as a professional reference, willing to provide letters of recommendation, 2 lunches and 1 dinner provided weekly.
Contact Write, call, fax, e-mail, or through World Wide Web site Russell B. Pulliam, Fellowship Director. Phone: 317-444-6001. Fax: 317-444-6750. E-mail: russell.pulliam@indystar.com. Applicants must submit a formal organization application, academic transcripts, three letters of recommendation, editorial (400-600 words) on any topic, photo of self suitable for reproduction, 5-10 writing samples. Application deadline: March 1 for final entries; other early admissions applicants will be considered with later entries, November 15 for early admissions applicants; up to five winners will be notified by December 15. World Wide Web: http://www.indystar.com/pjf.

QUEST–UNIVERSITY FRIENDS MEETING
4001 9th Avenue NE
Seattle, Washington 98105

General Information Social service/social justice internship program for young adults. Established in 1992. Number of employees: 6. Number of internship applications received each year: 30.
Internships Available ▶ *6 quest interns:* responsibilities include entry-level positions in social service, social justice, peace, and environmental organizations. Candidates should have ability to work independently, computer skills, oral communication skills, strong interpersonal skills, writing skills. Duration is September 1 to August 31. $100 per month living allowance; $525 exit stipend; $4700 AmeriCorps Education Award. Open to college seniors, recent college graduates, graduate students, young adults age 21-30. International applications accepted.
Benefits Free housing, free meals, health insurance, on-the-job training, opportunity to attend seminars/workshops, tuition assistance, willing to provide letters of recommendation.
Contact Write, call, e-mail, or through World Wide Web site Lynn Fitz Hugh, Program Coordinator. Phone: 206-417-0422. Fax: 206-368-0116. E-mail: questprogramufm@yahoo.com. Telephone interview required. Applicants must submit a formal organization application, resume, two letters of recommendation. Application deadline: March 1 for fall. World Wide Web: http://www.scn.org/spiritual/friends/quest.html.

REGIONAL INTERNSHIP CENTER OF SWPA
425 6th Avenue, Suite 1790
Pittsburgh, Pennsylvania 15219

General Information Clearinghouse for internships in southwest Pennsylvania. Established in 2001. Number of employees: 3.
Internships Available ▶ *Multi-industries and sectors interns.* Position available as unpaid or paid. Open to college freshmen, college sophomores, college juniors, college seniors, recent college graduates, graduate students.
Contact Call, fax, e-mail, or through World Wide Web site Becky Reitmeyer, Outreach Coordinator. Phone: 412-258-2686. Fax: 412-201-0672. E-mail: rreitmeyer@coro.org. Applicants must submit a resume. Applications are accepted continuously. World Wide Web: http://www.ric-swpa.org.

RHODE ISLAND STATE GOVERNMENT INTERN PROGRAM
Room 8AA, State House Building
Providence, Rhode Island 02903

General Information Program that places college, graduate, and law students in Rhode Island's government agencies for internships. Established in 1969. Number of employees: 5. Number of internship applications received each year: 450.
Internships Available ▶ *200 interns:* responsibilities include working in a state government agency such as the Department of Health, the Department of Education, or the Attorney General's office. Duration is 8–12 weeks. Position available as unpaid or at $20 per day for Rhode Island residents; work-study available for out-of-state residents. Open to high school seniors, college freshmen, college sophomores, college juniors, college seniors, law students, career changers. International applications accepted.
Benefits Job counseling, names of contacts, opportunity to attend seminars/workshops, possible full-time employment, willing to complete paperwork for educational credit, willing to provide letters of recommendation.
Contact Call, fax, or e-mail Mr. Robert W. Gemma, Executive Director. Phone: 401-222-6782. Fax: 401-222-6142. E-mail: rgemma@rilin.state.ri.us. In-person interview required. Applicants must submit a letter of interest, resume, writing sample (law students only). Application deadline: May 15 for summer. World Wide Web: http://www.rilin.state.ri.us.

RIVER BEND NATURE CENTER
PO Box 186
Faribault, Minnesota 55021

General Information Provider of environmental and natural education programs to schools and the community. Established in 1980. Number of employees: 8. Number of internship applications received each year: 50.
Internships Available ▶ *2–4 naturalist interns:* responsibilities include providing natural history programs to the public and children; writing press releases, curriculum, and newsletters; and assisting with land management and maintenance practices. Candidates should have ability to work independently, oral communication skills, plan to pursue career in field, self-motivation, strong interpersonal skills, written communication skills. Duration is seasonal. $150 per week. Open to college juniors, college seniors, recent college graduates, graduate students, career changers. ▶ *4 summer program naturalists:* responsibilities include developing and teaching programs for youth environmental day camps; designing and completing individual project; teaching weekend programs for all ages; assisting with facility management, displays, and publications. Candidates should have oral communication skills, plan to pursue career in field, self-motivation, strong interpersonal skills, strong leadership ability. Duration is 12 weeks. $170 per week. Open to college juniors, college seniors, recent college graduates, graduate students, career changers, individuals reentering the workforce.
Benefits Formal training, free housing, job counseling, names of contacts, on-the-job training, opportunity to attend seminars/workshops, willing to act as a professional reference, willing to complete paperwork for educational credit, willing to provide letters of recommendation, professional development fund.
Contact Write, e-mail, or through World Wide Web site John Blackmer, Chief Naturalist. E-mail: blackmer@rbnc.org. No phone calls. In-person interview recommended (telephone interview accepted). Applicants must submit a letter of interest, resume, three personal references, application packet (must be requested). Application deadline: February 15 for summer, May 8 for school-year positions. World Wide Web: http://www.rbnc.org.

ROGERS ENVIRONMENTAL EDUCATION CENTER
2721 State Highway 80
Sherburne, New York 13460

General Information Group of environmental education centers dedicated to teaching the public about natural resources, environmental issues, natural history, and ecological principles. Established in 1967. Number of employees: 6. Unit of New York State Department of Environmental Conservation, Albany, New York. Number of internship applications received each year: 50.
Internships Available ▶ *15–20 naturalist interns:* responsibilities include teaching groups, writing articles, and working on special projects. Candidates should have ability to work with others, college courses in field, oral communication skills, personal interest in the field, self-motivation, written communication skills. Duration is 10–12 weeks. $200 per week. Open to college sophomores, college juniors, college seniors, recent college graduates, graduate students, career changers, individuals reentering the workforce. International applications accepted.
Benefits Formal training, free housing, job counseling, names of contacts, on-the-job training, opportunity to attend seminars/workshops, willing to act as a professional reference, willing to complete paperwork for educational credit, willing to provide letters of recommendation.
Contact Write, call, fax, or e-mail Mr. Fred von Mechow, Environmental Educator II. Phone: 607-674-4017. Fax: 607-674-2655. E-mail: rogers@gw.dec.state.ny.us. In-person interview recommended (telephone interview accepted). Applicants must submit a formal organization application, resume, three personal references. Application deadline: February 15 for summer, May 1 for fall, August 1 for winter, December 1 for spring. World Wide Web: http://www.ascent.net/rogers/.

ST. JOHNSBURY ACADEMY
1000 Main Street
St. Johnsbury, Vermont 05819

General Information Academy that provides educational programs to 950 students. Established in 1842. Number of employees: 180. Number of internship applications received each year: 275.

Internships Available ▶ *1–4 teaching interns:* responsibilities include teaching 2 sections, increasing to 3 sections in the second semester, living in residence, working closely with a mentor teacher, and observing classes. Candidates should have college degree in related field, computer skills, oral communication skills, plan to pursue career in field, strong leadership ability, written communication skills. Duration is August 15 to June 15. $12,000 per duration of internship. Open to recent college graduates with a minimum 3.0 GPA.

Benefits Formal training, free housing, free meals, health insurance, job counseling, names of contacts, opportunity to attend seminars/workshops, possible full-time employment, tuition assistance, willing to provide letters of recommendation.

Contact Write, call, fax, or e-mail Carl Martin-Nelson, Director of New Faculty. Phone: 802-748-8171 Ext. 2257. Fax: 802-748-4703. E-mail: sinternships@stj.k12.vt.us. In-person interview required. Applicants must submit a letter of interest, resume, academic transcripts, three personal references, three letters of recommendation. Application deadline: April 1. World Wide Web: http://www.stjohnsburyacademy.org.

ST. PAUL'S SCHOOL
325 Pleasant Street
Concord, New Hampshire 03301-2591

General Information Coeducational boarding school offering year-round college preparatory programs. Established in 1856. Number of employees: 200. Number of internship applications received each year: 150.

Internships Available ▶ *30–35 Advanced Studies Program interns:* responsibilities include offering classroom assistance and dormitory supervision and supervising recreational activities. Candidates should have college courses in field, oral communication skills, personal interest in the field, self-motivation, strong interpersonal skills. Duration is 6 weeks in summer. $2000 per duration of internship plus up to $200 in qualifying travel expenses. Open to college juniors, college seniors, recent college graduates. ▶ *2–4 teaching fellows:* responsibilities include teaching, coaching, and supervising students in dormitories. Candidates should have college courses in field, knowledge of field, oral communication skills, self-motivation, strong interpersonal skills. Duration is 9 months. $15,000 per duration of internship. Open to college seniors, recent college graduates. International applications accepted.

Benefits Formal training, free housing, free meals, job counseling, names of contacts, on-the-job training, opportunity to attend seminars/workshops, possible full-time employment, willing to act as a professional reference, willing to provide letters of recommendation, health insurance for academic-year interns.

Contact Write, call, fax, e-mail, or through World Wide Web site Mr. Thomas P. Bazos, Director, Apprentice Teaching Programs. Phone: 603-229-4777. Fax: 603-229-4767. E-mail: asp@sps.edu. In-person interview required. Applicants must submit a formal organization application, resume, academic transcripts, three letters of recommendation, 2-page personal statement. Application deadline: January 20 for application, resume, personal statement, February 1 for academic transcripts, recommendations. World Wide Web: http://www.sps.edu.

SCHUYLKILL CENTER FOR ENVIRONMENTAL EDUCATION
8480 Hagy's Mill Road
Philadelphia, Pennsylvania 19128-1998

General Information Environmental education facility presenting programming for kindergarten through graduate school with a yearly audience of 80,000. Established in 1965. Number of employees: 5.

Internships Available ▶ *2 education interns:* responsibilities include teaching daily class, assisting education staff, and working on projects. Candidates should have ability to work independently, college courses in field, plan to pursue career in field, self-motivation, writing skills, previous experience working with children, natural history background (preferred). Duration is 4–16 weeks. Unpaid. Open to college sophomores, college juniors, college seniors, recent college graduates, graduate students, career changers, individuals reentering the workforce. ▶ *2–4 forest restoration ecologists:* responsibilities include accumulating baseline data for Piedmont Forest restoration; includes some physical labor. Candidates should have ability to work independently, ability to work with others, analytical skills, experience in the field, plan to pursue career in field, research skills. Duration is flexible. Unpaid. Open to college sophomores, college juniors, college seniors, graduate students.

Benefits Formal training, names of contacts, on-the-job training, opportunity to attend seminars/workshops, willing to complete paperwork for educational credit, willing to provide letters of recommendation.

Contact Write, call, fax, or e-mail Kathy Bright, Director of Education. Phone: 215-482-7300 Ext. 124. Fax: 215-482-8158. E-mail: kbright@schuylkillcenter.org. In-person interview recommended (telephone interview accepted). Applicants must submit a formal organization application, letter of interest, resume, personal reference, letter of recommendation. Applications are accepted continuously. World Wide Web: http://www.schuylkillcenter.org.

SMITHSONIAN CENTER FOR EDUCATION AND MUSEUM STUDIES
Arts and Industries Building, 900 Jefferson Drive, SW, Suite 2235
Washington, District of Columbia 20560-0427

General Information Office that provides professional development for teachers, publishes information and curriculum materials for schools, and encourages productive relationships between schools and museums; also supports educational efforts within the Smithsonian's various museums, offices, and institutes. Established in 1846. Number of employees: 6,000. Unit of Smithsonian Institution, Washington, District of Columbia. Number of internship applications received each year: 25.

Internships Available ▶ *600–700 interns:* responsibilities include working in education, public programs, diversity initiatives, school and teacher partnerships, heritage months, internship services, professional development, and Web and print publications. Candidates should have oral communication skills, organizational skills, written communication skills, familiarity with computers. Duration is 4–52 weeks. Position available as unpaid or paid. Open to individuals 16 or older having completed 2 years of high school. International applications accepted.

Benefits Opportunity to attend seminars/workshops, willing to act as a professional reference, willing to complete paperwork for educational credit, willing to provide letters of recommendation, discounts at Smithsonian shops and restaurants.

International Internships Available.

Contact Call, e-mail, or through World Wide Web site Tracie Spinale, Internship Coordinator, 900 Jefferson Drive, SW, Suite 2235, Washington, District of Columbia 20560-0427. Phone: 202-357-3102. E-mail: interninfo@scems.si.edu. Applicants must submit a formal organization application, academic transcripts, writing sample, two letters of recommendation, resume; see Web site (www.si.edu/cms/intern.htm) for more specifics. Application deadline: February 15 for summer, June 15 for fall, October 15 for winter/spring. World Wide Web: http://museumstudies.si.edu.

SMITHSONIAN INSTITUTION, OFFICE OF FELLOWSHIPS
750 9th Street NW, Suite 9300, MRC 902, PO Box 37012
Washington, District of Columbia 20013-7012

General Information Office that offers fellowships and internships for research and study in fields that are actively pursued by the museums and research organizations of the Institution.

Smithsonian Institution, Office of Fellowships (continued)

Internships Available ▶ *James E. Webb Minority Graduate interns:* responsibilities include interning in the areas of business and public administration. Duration is 10 weeks. $400 per week. ▶ *Minority Internship Program interns:* responsibilities include participating in research or museum-related activities in one of the many museums or departments of the Smithsonian Institution. Duration is 10 weeks. $350 per week. ▶ *Native American Internship Program interns:* responsibilities include participating in research or museum activities related to Native American studies. Duration is 10 weeks. $350 per week.

Benefits Opportunity to attend seminars/workshops, travel reimbursement, willing to complete paperwork for educational credit, willing to provide letters of recommendation.

Contact Write, call, e-mail, or through World Wide Web site Ms. Pamela Hudson, Program Manager, 750 9th Street, NW, Suite 9300, MRC 902 PO Box 37012, Washington, District of Columbia 20013-7012. Phone: 202-275-0655. Fax: 202-275-0489. E-mail: siofg@si.edu. Application deadline: February 1 for James E. Webb Minority Graduate, Minority Internship Program, and summer Native American Program, June 1 for fall Native American Program, October 1 for spring Native American Program. World Wide Web: http://www.si.edu/research+study.

SPANISH EDUCATION DEVELOPMENT CENTER
1840 Kalorama Road, NW
Washington, District of Columbia 20009

General Information Hispanic nonprofit organization that offers educational programs for children and adults. Established in 1971. Number of employees: 25.

Internships Available ▶ *20–40 English as a second language teachers:* responsibilities include leading a small group by implementing teacher's lesson plans, observing and learning selected ESL techniques from the teacher, and working with individual students who have been absent or who need extra assistance. Candidates should have ability to work independently, ability to work with others, oral communication skills, self-motivation. Duration is 10 weeks (7:00-9:00 pm Monday through Friday, or 11:00 m-2:00 pm, Saturday and Sunday. Unpaid. Open to college freshmen, college sophomores, college juniors, college seniors, recent college graduates, graduate students, law students. ▶ *8–10 after school teacher aides (Silver Spring, Maryland):* responsibilities include conducting small group activities with children. Candidates should have ability to work independently, ability to work with others, oral communication skills, self-motivation. Duration is flexible (3:00 pm-6:30 pm, Monday to Friday). Unpaid. Open to high school students, recent high school graduates, college freshmen, college sophomores, college juniors, college seniors, recent college graduates, graduate students, law students. ▶ *10–20 preschool teacher assistants:* responsibilities include helping classroom teacher supervise children; preparing educational materials; interacting with children through stories, games, teaching, and songs; working with children in small group activities designed either by the teacher or the assistant. Candidates should have ability to work independently, ability to work with others, oral communication skills, self-motivation. Duration is flexible (7:00 am-6:00 pm, Monday to Friday). Unpaid. Open to high school students, recent high school graduates, college freshmen, college sophomores, college juniors, college seniors, recent college graduates, graduate students. ▶ *2–5 proposal writing interns:* responsibilities include performing foundation research and proposal writing. Candidates should have computer skills, editing skills, research skills, writing skills. Duration is flexible. Unpaid. Open to college freshmen, college sophomores, college juniors, college seniors, recent college graduates, graduate students, individuals reentering the workforce. ▶ *6–10 special project assistants:* responsibilities include conducting foundation research, public relations, fund-raising, and material and curriculum development. Candidates should have computer skills, editing skills, research skills, writing skills. Duration is flexible. Unpaid. Open to college freshmen, college sophomores, college juniors, college seniors, recent college graduates, graduate students, individuals reentering the workforce. International applications accepted.

Benefits Formal training, willing to complete paperwork for educational credit, willing to provide letters of recommendation. **Contact** Write, call, fax, or e-mail Ms. Doris Ruano, Director, Volunteer Program. Phone: 202-462-8848. Fax: 202-462-6886. E-mail: dorisruano@sedcenter.com. In-person interview recommended (telephone interview accepted). Applicants must submit a resume. Applications are accepted continuously.

SPONSORS FOR EDUCATIONAL OPPORTUNITY (SEO) CAREER PROGRAM
30 West 21st Street
New York, New York 10010

General Information Nonprofit organization that provides training, orientation, and summer internships to undergraduate students of color in the areas of accounting, asset management, corporate law, investment banking, management consulting, information technology, media, and philanthropy. Established in 1963. Number of employees: 22. Unit of Sponsors for Educational Opportunity, New York, New York. Number of internship applications received each year: 2,000.

Internships Available ▶ *5–10 Chicago Investment Banking Program interns.* Candidates should have ability to work independently, ability to work with others, analytical skills, computer skills, knowledge of field, strong desire to pursue post-graduation career opportunities in Chicago. Duration is minimum 10 weeks in summer. Competitive salary. Open to college sophomores, college juniors. ▶ *4–8 Hong Kong Investment Banking interns.* Candidates should have analytical skills, computer skills, knowledge of field, strong interpersonal skills, strong desire to pursue post-graduation career opportunities in Hong Kong and/or Greater Asia. Duration is minimum 10 weeks in summer. Competitive salary. Open to college sophomores, college juniors. ▶ *4–6 San Francisco Investment Banking Program interns.* Candidates should have ability to work independently, ability to work with others, analytical skills, computer skills, knowledge of field, prior financial services experience (preferred). Duration is minimum 10 weeks in summer. Competitive salary. Open to college juniors. ▶ *10–15 accounting interns:* responsibilities include working as full member of auditing teams on client engagements; or working in either internal audit division, the comptroller's office, or on the staff of the chief financial officer at a major investment banking firm. Candidates should have ability to work independently, ability to work with others, analytical skills, college courses in field, computer skills, knowledge of field. Duration is minimum 10 weeks in summer. Competitive salary. Open to college juniors. ▶ *15–25 asset management interns:* responsibilities include working as research assistants to one or more portfolio managers, and in marketing to identify potential clients. Candidates should have ability to work independently, analytical skills, computer skills, knowledge of field, strong interpersonal skills, coursework in economics, finance, or accounting (desirable). Duration is minimum 10 weeks in summer. Competitive salary. Open to college juniors, exceptional sophomores (may be considered), seniors who will have one semester to complete at the time of the internship (may be considered). ▶ *25–30 corporate law interns:* responsibilities include document indexing, distributions, citation checking and document review, working side- by-side with established attorneys on significant assignments that range from closing of major corporate transactions to pro bono projects. Candidates should have ability to work independently, ability to work with others, analytical skills, oral communication skills, plan to pursue career in field, written communication skills. Duration is minimum 10 weeks in summer. Competitive salary. Open to graduating seniors who plan to attend law school in the fall, exceptional juniors (may be considered). ▶ *15–20 information technology interns:* responsibilities include developing, testing, maintaining, installing, and/or deploying third party proprietary technologies. Candidates should have analytical skills, knowledge of field, research skills, self-motivation, coursework in computer science, engineering, and other quantitative subjects. Duration is minimum 10 weeks in summer. Competitive salary. Open to college freshmen, college sophomores, college juniors. ▶ *125–150 investment banking interns:* responsibilities include working in finance, research, or sales and trading at major investment firm; performing tasks similar to those of full-time analysts. Candidates should have ability to work independently, analytical skills, computer skills, knowledge of field, strong interpersonal skills, coursework in economics, finance, or accounting (desirable). Duration is minimum 10 weeks in summer. Competitive salary. Open to college juniors, exceptional freshmen and sophomores (may be considered), seniors who will have one semester to complete at the time of the internship (may be considered). ▶ *5–15 management consulting interns:* responsibilities include research for presentations, data analysis, "number crunching" and preparation of presentation documents; interfacing with clients and travel to client offices to conduct on-site analyses. Candidates should have analytical skills, computer skills, knowledge of field, oral communication skills, self-motivation, written communication skills. Duration is minimum 10 weeks in summer. Competitive salary. Open to college juniors, college seniors who will have one semester to complete at the time of the internship (may be considered). ▶ *3–6 media interns:* responsibilities include meeting and analyzing data for strategic marketing plans, content, ratings, and financial analysis. Candidates should have ability to work with others, analytical skills, oral communication skills, self-motivation, written communication skills, comfort with financial/business modeling in Excel. Duration is minimum 10 weeks in summer. Competitive salary. Open to college sophomores, college juniors. ▶ *10–20 philanthropy interns:* responsibilities include site visits, budget preparation, program evaluation, research, and report writing. Candidates should have ability to work independently, ability to work with others, computer skills, knowledge of field, oral communication skills, research skills, self-motivation, written communication skills, demonstrated commitment to the nonprofit field. Duration is minimum 10 weeks in summer. Competitive salary. Open to college sophomores, college juniors, college seniors, students who will have graduated one semester before to start of internship may also be considered. International applications accepted.

Benefits Formal training, housing at a cost, job counseling, names of contacts, on-the-job training, opportunity to attend seminars/workshops, possible full-time employment, willing to complete paperwork for educational credit.

International Internships Available in Hong Kong, China; London, United Kingdom.

Contact Write, call, e-mail, or through World Wide Web site SEO Career Program. Phone: 212-979-2040. Fax: 212-647-7010. E-mail: careerprogram@seo-ny.org. In-person interview required. Applicants must submit a formal organization application, resume, academic transcripts, writing sample, two letters of recommendation. Application deadline: January 15 for early action deadline, February 15 for final deadline. World Wide Web: http://www.seo-ny.org.

SUMMER STUDY AT PENN STATE
University Park, Pennsylvania 16802

General Information Pre-collegiate academic summer program. Established in 1991. Number of employees: 83. Unit of Summer Study Programs, Melville, New York. Number of internship applications received each year: 250.

Internships Available ▶ *40–50 staff advisors/enrichment instructors:* responsibilities include teaching one or two enrichment classes per day; organizing and supervising afternoon activities; chaperoning nightly events; residing in dedicated residence halls and chaperoning weekend excursions. Candidates should have ability to work independently, college courses in field, knowledge of field, oral communication skills, organizational skills, personal interest in the field, self-motivation, strong interpersonal skills, strong leadership ability, interest in teaching high school students. Duration is June 29-August 3 or July 6-July 30. $700–$1200 per duration of internship. Open to college juniors, college seniors, recent college graduates, graduate students, law students. ▶ *3–5 staff advisors/office support staff members:* responsibilities include completing office rotations involving performing administrative tasks, scheduling and confirming activities, planning and coordinating special events and chaperoning afternoon, evening, and weekend events. Candidates should have ability to work independently, computer skills, office skills, oral communication skills, organizational skills, self-motivation, strong interpersonal skills, strong leadership ability, writing skills. Duration is June 29-August 9 or July

6-July 30. $700–$1200 per duration of internship. Open to college juniors, college seniors, recent college graduates, graduate students, law students, career changers. ▶ *10–12 staff advisors/sports clinic instructors:* responsibilities include instructing a sports clinic; organizing and supervising afternoon and evening activities; residing in dedicated residence hall, and chaperoning weekend excursions. Candidates should have ability to work independently, knowledge of field, oral communication skills, organizational skills, personal interest in the field, self-motivation, strong interpersonal skills, strong leadership ability, athletic ability. Duration is June 29-August 9 or July 6-July 30. $700–$1200 per duration of internship. Open to college juniors, college seniors, recent college graduates, graduate students, law students. ▶ *8–10 staff advisors/supervision staff interns:* responsibilities include organizing and supervising afternoon and evening activities; residing in dedicated residence hall; and chaperoning weekend excursions. Candidates should have ability to work independently, oral communication skills, self-motivation, strong interpersonal skills, strong leadership ability. Duration is June 29-Augsut 9 or July 6-July 30. $700–$1200 per duration of internship. Open to college juniors, college seniors, recent college graduates, graduate students, law students.

Benefits Formal training, free housing, free meals, willing to act as a professional reference, willing to complete paperwork for educational credit, willing to provide letters of recommendation, ability to develop and instruct courses.

Contact Call, e-mail, or through World Wide Web site Lina Yacovelli, Director of Personnel, 900 Walt Whitman Road, Melville, New York 11747. Phone: 800-666-2556. Fax: 631-424-0567. E-mail: lyacovelli@summerstudy.com. Applicants must submit a formal organization application, resume, academic transcripts, three personal references, letter of recommendation, in-person interview recommended video interview acceptable). Applications are accepted continuously. World Wide Web: http://www.summerstudy.com.

SUNY CORTLAND CAREER SERVICES/INTERNSHIP OFFICE
State University of New York
Cortland, New York 13045

General Information 4-year liberal arts college. Established in 1868. Number of employees: 1,000. Unit of State University of New York at Albany, Albany, New York. Number of internship applications received each year: 5.

Internships Available ▶ *1 career services intern:* responsibilities include learning all areas of career service, including: counseling; career exploration; event planning and implementation; information/library management; experiential education; recruitment and job search skills; interacting with all levels of administration and students. Candidates should have office skills, oral communication skills, organizational skills, personal interest in the field, strong interpersonal skills, writing skills. Duration is flexible. Unpaid. Open to graduate students, career changers. International applications accepted.

Benefits Formal training, job counseling, names of contacts, opportunity to attend seminars/workshops, willing to complete paperwork for educational credit, willing to provide letters of recommendation, possibility of housing at reduced rate in summer.

Contact Write, fax, or e-mail Mr. John Shirley, Assistant Director. Fax: 607-753-2937. E-mail: johns@em.cortland.edu. No phone calls. In-person interview recommended (telephone interview accepted). Applicants must submit a letter of interest, resume. Applications are accepted continuously. World Wide Web: http://www.cortland.edu/www/career/.

TANDEM, ESCUELA INTERNACIONAL MADRID
Calle Marques de Cubas, 8
Madrid, 28014 Spain

General Information Center that specializes in foreign language teaching and teacher preparation in Spanish, German, and English as a foreign language. Established in 1982. Number of employees: 80. Number of internship applications received each year: 40.

Tandem, Escuela Internacional Madrid (continued)
Internships Available ▶ *1 accounting assistant (consulting):* responsibilities include working with MS Access and statistics programs within the accounting department of an international consulting firm. Candidates should have ability to work independently, analytical skills, college courses in field, plan to pursue career in field, upper-intermediate level Spanish. Duration is 3–6 months. Unpaid. Open to college juniors, college seniors, recent college graduates, graduate students. ▶ *1 administrative assistant (German importing company):* responsibilities include translations (English, German, Spanish), pricing, telephone customer service, billing, and various other duties. Candidates should have ability to work with others, computer skills, office skills, oral communication skills, organizational skills, upper-intermediate knowledge of Spanish. Duration is 2–6 months. Unpaid. Open to recent high school graduates, college freshmen, college sophomores, college juniors, college seniors, recent college graduates, graduate students, career changers, individuals reentering the workforce. ▶ *1 administrative assistant (international commerce-software):* responsibilities include technical documentation projects, databases, commercial tasks, and translation of documents from Spanish into other languages. Candidates should have ability to work with others, computer skills, knowledge of field, oral communication skills, written communication skills, upper-intermediate level Spanish. Duration is 3–6 months. Unpaid. Open to college sophomores, college juniors, college seniors, recent college graduates, graduate students, career changers, individuals reentering the workforce. ▶ *1 assistant linguistic travel agency intern:* responsibilities include informing clients about different travel options to study abroad, updating databases, organizing travel packages, and researching travel opportunities. Candidates should have ability to work independently, oral communication skills, organizational skills, research skills, written communication skills, upper-intermediate level Spanish. Duration is 3 months. Unpaid. Open to college sophomores, college juniors, college seniors, recent college graduates, graduate students. ▶ *1 hotel management intern:* responsibilities include working possibilities in administration, reservations, catering, and various other tasks. Candidates should have knowledge of field, oral communication skills, self-motivation, strong interpersonal skills, upper-intermediate level Spanish. Duration is 3–6 months. Unpaid. Open to college freshmen, college sophomores, college juniors, college seniors, recent college graduates, graduate students, career changers, individuals reentering the workforce. ▶ *1 international relations intern (UN Information Centre):* responsibilities include revision of Spanish newspapers, summarizing and translating pertinent articles, and sending them to UN Headquarters in New York. Candidates should have ability to work independently, college courses in field, knowledge of field, personal interest in the field, written communication skills, upper-intermediate level Spanish. Duration is 6 months. Unpaid. Open to college juniors, college seniors, graduate students. ▶ *1 journalism (nonprofit Web site) intern:* responsibilities include maintaining databases, answering the telephone, visiting NGOs, and writing articles for the Web site. Candidates should have ability to work independently, computer skills, editing skills, knowledge of field, written communication skills, upper-intermediate level Spanish. Duration is 3–6 months. Unpaid. Open to college sophomores, college juniors, college seniors, recent college graduates, graduate students, career changers. ▶ *1 language school assistant (ESL):* responsibilities include helping with classes and test preparation for cadets at The Military School of Languages, translation of documents and internal information, computer and data processing, and public relations support. Candidates should have ability to work independently, office skills, oral communication skills, personal interest in the field, written communication skills, upper-intermediate level Spanish. Duration is 3–5 months. Unpaid. Open to college juniors, college seniors, recent college graduates, graduate students. ▶ *1 marketing assistant (international transportation company):* responsibilities include commercial tasks, databases, customer/client services, and marketing-related duties. Candidates should have ability to work independently, office skills, oral communication skills, personal interest in the field, written communication skills, upper-intermediate level Spanish. Duration is 3–6 months. Unpaid. Open to college sophomores, college juniors, college seniors, recent college graduates, graduate students, career changers, individuals reentering the workforce.

▶ *1 marketing assistant (language school):* responsibilities include marketing, advertising, and the cultural program; translation of advertising texts; working with computers and databases. Candidates should have ability to work with others, computer skills, office skills, oral communication skills, personal interest in the field, upper-intermediate level Spanish. Duration is 3–6 months. Unpaid. Open to recent high school graduates, college freshmen, college sophomores, college juniors, college seniors, recent college graduates, graduate students, career changers, individuals reentering the workforce. ▶ *1 public relations intern:* responsibilities include promoting the company including trips to cities in Spain, intercultural parties, and customer services. Candidates should have oral communication skills, organizational skills, strong interpersonal skills, strong leadership ability, upper-intermediate level Spanish. Duration is 3 months. Unpaid. Open to college sophomores, college juniors, college seniors, recent college graduates, graduate students. ▶ *1 video production company assistant:* responsibilities include video production, assisting during video shoots, and post-production; working in editing, and storing images. Candidates should have ability to work independently, ability to work with others, computer skills, plan to pursue career in field, written communication skills, upper-intermediate level Spanish. Duration is 3 months. Unpaid. Open to recent high school graduates, college freshmen, college sophomores, college juniors, college seniors, recent college graduates, graduate students. International applications accepted.
Benefits Formal training, housing at a cost, on-the-job training, willing to act as a professional reference, willing to complete paperwork for educational credit, willing to provide letters of recommendation, language course at a cost.
International Internships Available in Madrid, Spain.
Contact Write, call, fax, e-mail, or through World Wide Web site Almendra Staffa-Healey, Director of Internship Programs. Phone: 34-91-532-2715. Fax: 34-91-522-4539. E-mail: internships@tandem-madrid.com. In-person interview recommended (telephone interview accepted). Applicants must submit a formal organization application, letter of interest, resume, academic transcripts, personal reference, letter of recommendation, language-level test in Spanish. Application deadline: March 15 for fall and summer, November 1 for spring academic semester plus intern program; continuous for course plus intern program. Fees: $250. World Wide Web: http://www.tandem-madrid.com.

THOMAS JEFFERSON UNIVERSITY
Eleventh and Walnut Streets
Philadelphia, Pennsylvania 19107

General Information Internationally recognized academic health-care center whose mission is to promote state-of-the-art research, quality education, and quality health care. Established in 1824. Number of employees: 11,500. Number of internship applications received each year: 10.
Internships Available ▶ *2 voluntary human resources interns:* responsibilities include rotation of employee relations and employment divisions, data entry, report production and analyses, applicant tracking, reference checks, surveys. Candidates should have ability to work independently, computer skills, declared college major in field, office skills, oral communication skills, organizational skills, personal interest in the field, plan to pursue career in field, self-motivation, strong interpersonal skills. Duration is 1 summer or 1 semester. Unpaid. Open to college juniors, college seniors.
Benefits Job counseling, on-the-job training, opportunity to attend seminars/workshops, possible full-time employment, willing to act as a professional reference, willing to complete paperwork for educational credit, willing to provide letters of recommendation.
Contact Write, fax, or e-mail Kimberly Nichols, Coordinator, Recruitment Systems, 201 South 11th Street, 1st Floor, Martin Building, Philadelphia, Pennsylvania 19107. Phone: 215-503-8219. Fax: 215-503-2183. E-mail: kimberly.nichols@mail.tju.edu. In-person interview required. Applicants must submit a formal organization application, resume. Application deadline: April 1 for summer, October 1 for spring. World Wide Web: http://http://www.jefferson.edu/.

TOUCH OF NATURE ENVIRONMENTAL CENTER
Southern Illinois University, Mailcode 6888
Carbondale, Illinois 62901-6888

General Information Year-round educational, recreational, and service facility specializing in outdoor education, therapeutic recreation, environmental and experiential education, and conference services; supports academic and public service mission of the University. Established in 1949. Number of employees: 80. Unit of Southern Illinois University Carbondale, Carbondale, Illinois. Number of internship applications received each year: 20.

Internships Available ▶ *2–5 Environmental Ed-Ventures apprentices and interns:* responsibilities include lending logistical support to programs; program support to senior staff; co-facilitating environmental activities with groups of all ages in outdoor settings; co-leading travel expeditions with ecological and environmental focus; facilitating evening programs. Candidates should have knowledge of field, oral communication skills, personal interest in the field, strong interpersonal skills, strong leadership ability, flexibility, CPR, lifeguard, WFR (desirable). Duration is 1–6 months. $250–$1000 per month. Open to college juniors, college seniors, recent college graduates, graduate students, career changers. ▶ *1 Underway Outdoor Program intern:* responsibilities include assisting in field and in the office. Candidates should have ability to work independently, ability to work with others, knowledge of field, organizational skills, self-motivation, writing skills. Duration is May to August. Position available as unpaid or at $500–$800 per month. Open to college freshmen, college sophomores, college juniors, college seniors, recent college graduates, graduate students, individuals reentering the workforce. ▶ *6–12 spectrum interns:* responsibilities include assisting lead and assistant instructors in providing outdoor therapeutic programs for youth at risk. Candidates should have knowledge of field, oral communication skills, plan to pursue career in field, strong interpersonal skills, strong leadership ability, written communication skills. Duration is 3–6 months. $250–$1000 per month. Open to high school students, recent high school graduates, college freshmen, college sophomores, college juniors, college seniors, recent college graduates, graduate students, law students, career changers, individuals reentering the workforce. ▶ *1–5 therapeutic recreation/ fieldwork interns:* responsibilities include observing and participating in various facets of Camp operations including camper intake and placement, staff training, camper care and supervision, program planning and presentation, evaluations and reviews; meeting regularly with director to address specific educational requirements. Candidates should have ability to work independently, knowledge of field, personal interest in the field, strong interpersonal skills, strong leadership ability, some coursework and experience in the field desirable. Duration is year-round. $365–$600 per month. Open to college freshmen, college sophomores, college juniors, college seniors, recent college graduates, graduate students. International applications accepted.

Benefits Free housing, on-the-job training, possible full-time employment, willing to complete paperwork for educational credit, willing to provide letters of recommendation, meals during program operation.

Contact Write, call, fax, e-mail, or through World Wide Web site Internship Coordinator, Southern Illinois University, Mailcode 6888. Phone: 618-453-1121. Fax: 618-453-1188. E-mail: tonec@siu. edu. In-person interview recommended (telephone interview accepted). Applicants must submit a formal organization application, letter of interest, resume, three personal references. Applications are accepted continuously. World Wide Web: http://www. pso.siu.edu/tonec.

UNIVERSITY OF CINCINNATI COLLEGE OF MEDICINE
231 Albert Sabin Way, ML 0552
Cincinnati, Ohio 45267-0552

General Information College of medicine. Established in 1819. Number of employees: 3,000. Division of University of Cincinnati, Cincinnati, Ohio. Number of internship applications received each year: 150.

Internships Available ▶ *17 Summer Premedical Enrichment Program (SPEP) interns:* responsibilities include full-time participation in all program events, classes, and activities. Candidates should have college courses in field, self-motivation, demonstrated interest in career in medicine. Duration is 6 weeks. $1000 per duration of internship. ▶ *4 Summer Research Scholars (SRS):* responsibilities include functioning as full participating member of biomedical research team, preparation and presentation of research results at research symposium at end of program. Candidates should have ability to work independently, ability to work with others, analytical skills, college courses in field, personal interest in the field, research skills. Duration is 8 weeks. $2000 per duration of internship. Open to college sophomores, college juniors, college seniors, recent college graduates, graduate students.

Benefits Free housing, job counseling, on-the-job training, opportunity to attend seminars/workshops, travel reimbursement, willing to act as a professional reference, willing to complete paperwork for educational credit, willing to provide letters of recommendation, stipend, some free meals, other meals at cost.

Contact Write, call, fax, e-mail, or through World Wide Web site Roberta Handwerger, Director, Recruitment Programs. Phone: 513-558-7212. Fax: 513-558-1165. E-mail: roberta.handwerger@uc. edu. Applicants must submit a formal organization application, academic transcripts, two letters of recommendation, written personal statement regarding motivation for participating. Application deadline: March 1 for priority deadline, April 15 for final deadline. World Wide Web: http://www.med.uc.edu.

UNIVERSITY OF CONNECTICUT SCHOOLS OF MEDICINE, DENTAL MEDICINE, AND GRADUATE SCHOOL
263 Farmington Avenue
Farmington, Connecticut 06030-1905

General Information Medical, dental, and graduate schools. Established in 1968. Number of employees: 4,000. Branch of University of Connecticut, Storrs, Connecticut. Number of internship applications received each year: 150.

Internships Available ▶ *20–30 summer research fellows:* responsibilities include a research enrichment experience and some exposure to clinical medicine or dental medicine; faculty develop and make available suitable project descriptions from which interns may select a research opportunity; intern will meet with faculty sponsor and develop research protocol; 30+ hours per week working on project with faculty sponsor and/or designates; 8-10 hours per week for clinical experientials and enrichments. Candidates should have ability to work independently, ability to work with others, plan to pursue career in field, research skills, self-motivation, completion of some college biology and chemistry (preferably through organic chemistry), previous lab experience (desirable). Duration is June to August (10 weeks). $2500–$3000 per duration of internship. ▶ *6 summer research interns:* responsibilities include a research enrichment experience; a faculty sponsor will be identified for each intern; faculty develop and make available suitable project descriptions; interns will spend 30+ hours per week on project working with faculty sponsor and/or designates; lab positions available in: cell, developmental, molecular, and oral biology, immunology, biochemistry, neuroscience, and cellular and molecular pharmacology. Candidates should have ability to work independently, ability to work with others, plan to pursue career in field, research skills, self-motivation, completion of some college biology and chemistry, previous lab experience (desirable). Duration is June to August (10 weeks). $3000 per duration of internship. Open to college sophomores, college juniors.

Benefits Job counseling, on-the-job training, willing to complete paperwork for educational credit, willing to provide letters of recommendation.

Contact Write, call, e-mail, or through World Wide Web site Robin Walsh, Director of Student Activities. Phone: 860-679-3971. Fax: 860-679-1282. E-mail: rwalsh@nso1.uchc.edu. In-person interview recommended (telephone interview accepted). Applicants must submit a formal organization application, academic transcripts, writing sample, two letters of recommendation. Application deadline: March 15. Fees: $25.

UNIVERSITY OF GEORGIA, MARINE EDUCATION CENTER AND AQUARIUM
30 Ocean Science Circle
Savannah, Georgia 31411

General Information Marine education center and aquarium that emphasizes teaching about the coastal environment. Established in 1970. Number of employees: 19. Unit of University of Georgia, Athens, Georgia. Number of internship applications received each year: 60.

Internships Available ▶ *3–4 marine education interns:* responsibilities include teaching a wide variety of marine-related topics to K-12 students and adults at location on Skidaway Island, Georgia; completing an education project. Candidates should have oral communication skills, personal interest in the field, plan to pursue career in field, self-motivation, strong interpersonal skills, recent college degree in science or science education (completed before start of internship). Duration is 50 weeks. $287 per week. Open to recent college graduates, college seniors who will graduate before start of internship. International applications accepted.

Benefits Formal training, free housing, job counseling, names of contacts, on-the-job training, opportunity to attend seminars/workshops, willing to provide letters of recommendation, some meals provided.

Contact Write, call, fax, e-mail, or through World Wide Web site Dr. Willis B. Hayes, Associate Director for Education, Marine Extension Service. Phone: 912-598-2356. Fax: 912-598-2302. E-mail: hayes@uga.edu. Telephone interview required. Applicants must submit a letter of interest, resume, academic transcripts, three letters of recommendation. Application deadline: April 30 for fall. World Wide Web: http://www.uga.edu/aquarium.

UNIVERSITY OF MICHIGAN, SCHOOL OF PUBLIC HEALTH, POPULATION FELLOWS PROGRAMS
1214 South University, 2nd Floor
Ann Arbor, Michigan 48104-2548

General Information Programs offering internships and fellowships in population, family planning, reproductive health, and population-environment. Established in 1984. Number of employees: 20. Number of internship applications received each year: 180.

Internships Available ▶ *2–4 HBCU/HSI/TCU graduate interns:* responsibilities include applied internship in international population or population-environment and additional professional development as appropriate. Candidates should have analytical skills, knowledge of field, organizational skills, personal interest in the field, plan to pursue career in field. Duration is 3–6 months. Stipend. Open to individuals with graduate degrees from historically black colleges or universities, Hispanic-serving institutions, or tribal colleges and universities. ▶ *20 HBCU/HSI/TCU undergraduate interns:* responsibilities include entry-level, professional work in international population and population-environment. Candidates should have analytical skills, oral communication skills, organizational skills, personal interest in the field, strong interpersonal skills, written communication skills. Duration is 12 weeks. Stipend. Open to juniors and seniors from historically black colleges and universities, Hispanic-serving institutions, or Tribal Colleges and Universities. ▶ *10–15 Population Fellows:* responsibilities include population, family planning, and reproductive health programming, including program design, implementation, administration, and evaluation. Candidates should have experience in the field, personal interest in the field. Duration is 2 years. Yearly professional-level stipend and benefits. Open to U.S. citizens or permanent residents with graduate degree in population-related area. ▶ *5 Population-Environment Fellows:* responsibilities include design, implementation, and evaluation of programs that link population, family planning, and reproductive health service delivery with environmental programming. Candidates should have knowledge of field, personal interest in the field. Duration is 2 years. Yearly professional-level stipend and benefits. Open to U.S. citizens or permanent residents with graduate degree and expertise in population/environment fields. ▶ *20–30 population graduate internship funding opportunities:* responsibilities include positions in international population, family planning, and reproductive health or population-environment

which are unpaid or require significant additional support (candidate must have identified or secured full-time internship). Candidates should have personal interest in the field, plan to pursue career in field. Duration is 2–4 months. taxable stipend up to $5000 (overseas internship) or $3000 (U.S.-based internship). Open to U.S. citizens or permanent residents in the first year of graduate program in relevant area.

Benefits Health insurance, names of contacts, on-the-job training, opportunity to attend seminars/workshops, travel reimbursement, willing to act as a professional reference, willing to provide letters of recommendation, housing assistance.

International Internships Available.

Contact Write, call, fax, e-mail, or through World Wide Web site Population Fellows Programs. Phone: 734-763-9456. Fax: 734-647-0643. E-mail: michiganfellows@umich.edu. In-person interview recommended (telephone interview accepted). Applicants must submit a formal organization application, letter of interest, resume, academic transcripts, writing sample, three letters of recommendation. Application deadline: February 1 for HBW/HSI/TCU undergraduate interns, March 10 for population graduate internship funding positions, April 1 for fall fellows and HBCU/HSI/TCU graduate interns, November 1 for spring fellows and HBCU/HSI/TCU graduate interns. World Wide Web: http://www.sph.umich.edu/pfps.

U.S. ENVIRONMENTAL PROTECTION AGENCY, OFFICE OF ENVIRONMENTAL EDUCATION, NNEMS FELLOWSHIP PROGRAM
1200 Pennsylvania Avenue, NW (1704A)
Washington, District of Columbia 20460

General Information The NNEMS Fellowship Program offers undergraduate and graduate students research opportunities nationwide. Established in 1987. Division of Environmental Protection Agency, Washington, District of Columbia. Number of internship applications received each year: 350.

Internships Available ▶ *70–80 national network for environmental management studies fellowship positions:* responsibilities include research in the areas of environmental policy, regulation and law; environmental management and administration; environmental science; public relations and communications; computer programming and development. Candidates should have ability to work independently, ability to work with others, personal interest in the field, research skills, written communication skills, minimum GPA of 3.0 (undergraduates), enrollment in an academic program directly related to pollution abatement and control, one semester of graduate work (graduate students). Duration is full-time summer or part-time school year. $2100–$3500 per month. Open to college freshmen, college sophomores, college juniors, college seniors, graduate students.

Benefits On-the-job training, opportunity to attend seminars/workshops, willing to act as a professional reference, willing to complete paperwork for educational credit, willing to provide letters of recommendation, work-related travel reimbursement, stipend for fellowship period.

Contact Write, e-mail, or through World Wide Web site Sheri Jojokian, Environmental Education Specialist. E-mail: jojokian.sheri@epa.gov. Telephone interview required. Applicants must submit a formal organization application, resume, academic transcripts, letter of recommendation, 1-page work plan proposal, 1 letter of reference from a professor or advisor, NNEMS Liability Agreement (obtained from Web site or Career Service Center of participating universities). Application deadline: February 24 for summer. World Wide Web: http://www. epa.gov/enviroed/students.html.

U.S. SERVAS, INC.
11 John Street, Suite 505
New York, New York 10038

General Information Cultural exchange and peace organization created to give people the opportunity to have a short homestay with hosts in other cultures; strives for peace through education and the understanding of cultural differences both in the U.S. and abroad. Established in 1948. Number of employees: 4. Unit of Servas, International, New York, New York. Number of internship applications received each year: 20.

Internships Available ▶ *1 administrative intern:* responsibilities include educating potential members about the program; answering members' questions, e-mails, phone calls, and mail; small projects; helping with Web site; some filing and data entry. Candidates should have ability to work independently, ability to work with others, computer skills, office skills, oral communication skills, writing skills. Duration is 1–6 months. $4 per day lunch stipend; $3 per day transportation stipend. Open to high school students, recent high school graduates, college freshmen, college sophomores, college juniors, college seniors, recent college graduates, graduate students, law students, career changers, individuals reentering the workforce, senior citizens. ▶ *1–3 peace and social justice outreach interns:* responsibilities include assisting organization with outreach initiatives, especially to college students, but may include other target groups; tasks will include researching, establishing contacts, organizing publicity packets and mailings, and event planning. Candidates should have knowledge of field, oral communication skills, organizational skills, research skills, strong interpersonal skills, writing skills. Duration is 1–6 months. $4 per day lunch stipend; $3 per day transportation stipend. Open to college freshmen, college sophomores, college juniors, college seniors, recent college graduates, graduate students, law students, career changers. International applications accepted.

Benefits Names of contacts, on-the-job training, opportunity to attend seminars/workshops, possible full-time employment, willing to act as a professional reference, willing to complete paperwork for educational credit, willing to provide letters of recommendation.

Contact Write, call, fax, or e-mail Julie Schumacher Cohen, Intern Coordinator/Program Assistant. Phone: 212-267-0252. Fax: 212-267-0292. E-mail: info@usservas.org. In-person interview recommended (telephone interview accepted). Applicants must submit a resume, two personal references, cover letter. Applications are accepted continuously. World Wide Web: http://www.usservas.org.

VOYAGEUR OUTWARD BOUND SCHOOL
101 East Chapman Street
Ely, Minnesota 55731

General Information Adventure-based school using wilderness experiences to enhance students' self-reliance, compassion, physical fitness, and cooperation. Established in 1964. Number of employees: 135. Unit of Voyageur Outward Bound, Ely, Minnesota. Number of internship applications received each year: 200.

Internships Available ▶ *20–25 interns:* responsibilities include initial field training and support work assignments in all program areas. Candidates should have experience in the field, self-motivation, strong interpersonal skills, flexibility, sense of humor. Duration is 8 weeks. $300 per month. Open to college sophomores, college juniors, college seniors, recent college graduates, graduate students, law students, career changers, individuals reentering the workforce, individuals age 21 or older (preferred). International applications accepted.

Benefits Free housing, free meals, job counseling, names of contacts, on-the-job training, willing to act as a professional reference, willing to complete paperwork for educational credit, willing to provide letters of recommendation.

Contact Write, fax, e-mail, or through World Wide Web site Staffing Coordinator. Fax: 218-365-7079. E-mail: staffing@vobs.com. No phone calls. Telephone interview required. Applicants must submit a formal organization application, three letters of recommendation. Application deadline: March 1 for summer. World Wide Web: http://www.vobs.com.

WAHSEGA 4-H CENTER
77 Cloverleaf Trail
Dahlonega, Georgia 30533

General Information Outdoor and environmental education center for youth. Established in 1937. Number of employees: 15. Unit of University of Georgia, Athens, Georgia. Number of internship applications received each year: 50.

Internships Available ▶ *5–8 environmental education instructors:* responsibilities include teaching environmental education classes for students in third through eighth grade from public and private schools throughout Georgia. Candidates should have ability to work independently, oral communication skills, personal interest in the field, self-motivation, strong interpersonal skills, patience and ability to work with youth. Duration is 3–9 months. $240 per week before taxes. Open to college sophomores, college juniors, college seniors, recent college graduates, graduate students, law students. International applications accepted.

Benefits Free housing, free meals, health insurance, on-the-job training, willing to act as a professional reference, willing to complete paperwork for educational credit, willing to provide letters of recommendation, certification in American Red Cross Standard First Aid and CPR.

Contact Write, call, fax, or e-mail Program Coordinator. Phone: 706-864-2050. Fax: 706-867-2901. E-mail: wahsega@uga.edu. In-person interview recommended (telephone interview accepted). Applicants must submit a letter of interest, resume. Applications are accepted continuously. World Wide Web: http://www.wahsega4h.org.

THE WASHINGTON CENTER FOR INTERNSHIPS AND ACADEMIC SEMINARS
2301 M Street, NW, Fifth Floor
Washington, District of Columbia 20037-1427

General Information Center that provides off-campus full-time internships and 1–2 week academic seminars in all fields for students from more than 750 colleges and universities. Established in 1975. Number of employees: 55. Number of internship applications received each year: 1,500.

Internships Available ▶ *50 College Plus One interns:* responsibilities include varied duties depending on student's interests and expertise. Candidates should have analytical skills, office skills, oral communication skills, plan to pursue career in field, self-motivation, written communication skills. Duration is 10–12 weeks. Position available as unpaid or paid. Open to recent college graduates, graduate students, law students. ▶ *50 Law Plus One interns:* responsibilities include varied law-related duties depending upon student's interests. Candidates should have analytical skills, knowledge of field, office skills, oral communication skills, plan to pursue career in field, written communication skills. Duration is 10 weeks in the summer. Position available as unpaid or paid. Open to law students. ▶ *30 North American Free Trade Agreement (NAFTA) Program interns:* responsibilities include varied duties related to bi- or tri-lateral trade issues between U.S., Canada, and Mexico. Candidates should have analytical skills, knowledge of field, office skills, oral communication skills, personal interest in the field, written communication skills. Duration is 10–15 weeks. Minimum $2000 financial assistance guaranteed and applied toward housing. Open to college juniors, college seniors, graduate students. ▶ *50–75 diversity in Congress program interns:* responsibilities include being placed in congressional offices; general staff work. Candidates should have ability to work with others, analytical skills, office skills, oral communication skills, self-motivation, written communication skills. Duration is 10–15 weeks. $2000 minimum guaranteed financial assistance applied toward housing. Open to college juniors, college seniors, graduate students. ▶ *25–75 diversity leaders interns:* responsibilities include variety of tasks for students in any major field, with an emphasis on quantitative and analytical skills. Candidates should have analytical skills, office skills, oral communication skills, self-motivation, strong leadership ability, written communication skills. Duration is 10–15 weeks. Housing fees paid (minimum value of $2925). Open to college juniors, college seniors, graduate students. ▶ *50–75 environment interns:* responsibilities include varied duties related to environmental issues. Candidates should have analytical skills, knowledge of field, office skills, oral communication skills, self-motivation, written communication skills, major in any field related to environment. Duration is 10–15 weeks. Guaranteed minimum financial assistance of $1000 applied toward housing. Open to college juniors, college seniors, graduate students. ▶ *10–25 federal government interns:* responsibilities include working for federal government agencies, such as Commerce, Interior, and EPA on various projects and initiatives. Candidates should have computer skills, oral com-

The Washington Center for Internships and Academic Seminars (continued)

munication skills, organizational skills, research skills, written communication skills. Duration is 10–15 weeks. Position available as unpaid or at $4500–$8000 per duration of internship. Open to college juniors, college seniors. ▶ *500 main program interns:* responsibilities include working in American studies, arts management, business, communications, computer science, consumer advocacy, environment, government affairs, health and science, international relations/studies, labor relations/studies, law, politics/public policy, public administration, social work, urban studies, or women's studies. Candidates should have analytical skills, office skills, oral communication skills, organizational skills, self-motivation, written communication skills. Duration is 10–15 weeks. Position available as unpaid or at $1000–$8000 per semester depending on placement. Open to college juniors, college seniors, recent college graduates, graduate students, law students. ▶ *50–75 mass communications interns:* responsibilities include working in journalism, public relations, public affairs, or advertising. Candidates should have college courses in field, knowledge of field, oral communication skills, plan to pursue career in field, self-motivation, written communication skills. Duration is 10–15 weeks. Guaranteed financial assistance of $250 minimum applied toward housing. Open to college juniors, college seniors, graduate students. ▶ *50–75 nonprofit leaders interns:* responsibilities include working for a nonprofit organization, such as an advocacy group, or trade or professional associations. Candidates should have ability to work with others, analytical skills, office skills, oral communication skills, self-motivation, written communication skills. Duration is 10–15 weeks. Guaranteed financial assistance of $1000 minimum applied toward housing. Open to college juniors, college seniors, graduate students. ▶ *50 study abroad in DC interns:* responsibilities include varied duties with an international component possibly involving the use of foreign language and cultural skills. Candidates should have office skills, oral communication skills, organizational skills, self-motivation, written communication skills. Duration is 10–15 weeks. Position available as unpaid or paid. Open to college juniors, college seniors, graduate students. ▶ *50–75 women leaders interns:* responsibilities include varied duties related to public policy. Candidates should have ability to work independently, ability to work with others, analytical skills, office skills, oral communication skills, self-motivation, written communication skills. Duration is 10–15 weeks. Guaranteed financial assistance of $1000 (minimum) applied toward housing. Open to college juniors, college seniors, graduate students. International applications accepted. **Benefits** Formal training, housing at a cost, names of contacts, opportunity to attend seminars/workshops, possible full-time employment, willing to act as a professional reference, willing to complete paperwork for educational credit, willing to provide letters of recommendation, financial aid available in certain fields. **Contact** Write, call, fax, e-mail, or through World Wide Web site Dr. Eugene J. Alpert, Senior Vice President, 2301 M Street NW, Fifth Floor, Washington, District of Columbia 20037-1427. Phone: 800-486-8921. Fax: 202-336-7609. E-mail: info@twc.edu. Applicants must submit a formal organization application, resume, academic transcripts, two letters of recommendation, short essay on topic related to internship request area. Application deadline: March 15 for summer, June 15 for fall, November 15 for spring. Fees: $60. World Wide Web: http://www.twc.edu.

WOLF CREEK EDUCATION CENTER/REDWOOD NATIONAL AND STATE PARKS
1111 Second Street
Crescent City, California 95531

General Information   School for students in grades 4-6 offering programs in awareness and value clarification, campfire programs, and old growth, stream, and prairie studies. Established in 1972. Number of employees: 3. Division of Redwood National and State Parks, Crescent City, California. Number of internship applications received each year: 30.
Internships Available ▶ *6 environmental education interns:* responsibilities include instructing 4th, 5th, and 6th grade students; leading activities involving environmental education. Candidates should have ability to work independently, college courses in field, oral communication skills, strong interpersonal skills, written com-

munication skills, desire to work with children, camp experience (helpful). Duration is 12 weeks. $10 per day. Open to college freshmen, college sophomores, college juniors, college seniors, recent college graduates. International applications accepted.
Benefits Formal training, free housing, names of contacts, on-the-job training, travel reimbursement, willing to complete paperwork for educational credit, willing to provide letters of recommendation. **Contact** Write, call, fax, or e-mail Deborah Savage, Park Ranger/Director. Phone: 707-822-7611 Ext. 5266. Fax: 707-488-2861. E-mail: debbie_savage@nps.gov. Applicants must submit a formal organization application, letter of interest, resume. Applications are accepted continuously. World Wide Web: http://www.nps.gov/redw/index.html.

WOLVERINE CAMPS OUTDOOR EDUCATION CENTER
Wolverine Camps
Wolverine, Michigan 49799

General Information   Residential outdoor education program for grades 5-8. Established in 1968. Number of employees: 8. Number of internship applications received each year: 3.
Internships Available ▶ *1–3 instructors:* responsibilities include teaching classes in natural history, pioneer living, orienteering, survival, and ropes course; performing light maintenance duties; and program planning. Candidates should have ability to work with others, declared college major in field, oral communication skills, plan to pursue career in field, self-motivation, willingness to learn new skills. Duration is 6 months (January 2-June 10). $100–$125 per week. Open to college freshmen, college sophomores, college juniors, college seniors, recent college graduates.
Benefits Formal training, free housing, free meals, names of contacts, on-the-job training, opportunity to attend seminars/workshops, possible full-time employment, willing to complete paperwork for educational credit, willing to provide letters of recommendation.
Contact Write, call, fax, e-mail, or through World Wide Web site Mr. Eric Schupbach, Director. Phone: 231-525-8211. Fax: 231-525-6112. E-mail: camps@wolverinecamps.com. In-person interview recommended (telephone interview accepted). Applicants must submit a resume. Applications are accepted continuously. World Wide Web: http://www.wolverinecamps.com.

WOMEN'S SPORTS FOUNDATION
Eisenhower Park
East Meadow, New York 11554

General Information   Nonprofit national education organization that promotes sports and fitness opportunities for girls and women. Established in 1974. Number of employees: 35. Number of internship applications received each year: 150.
Internships Available ▶ *17–48 interns:* responsibilities include researching topics in women's sports, staffing the Information Referral Service and toll-free hot line, assisting staff with projects according to abilities and skills, writing for the newsletter, and planning fund-raising projects and events. Duration is 3–12 months. $450–$700 per month. ▶ *2–6 minority interns:* responsibilities include researching topics in women's sports, staffing the Information Referral Service and toll-free hot line, assisting staff with projects according to abilities and skills, writing for newsletter, and planning fund-raising projects and events. Duration is 3–12 months. $1000 per month. Candidates for all positions should have ability to work independently, computer skills, editing skills, knowledge of field, office skills, oral communication skills, organizational skills, personal interest in the field, research skills, self-motivation, strong interpersonal skills, writing skills. Open to recent high school graduates, college freshmen, college sophomores, college juniors, college seniors, recent college graduates, graduate students, law students, career changers, individuals reentering the workforce. International applications accepted.
Benefits Job counseling, names of contacts, on-the-job training, opportunity to attend seminars/workshops, willing to complete paperwork for educational credit, willing to provide letters of recommendation.

Contact Write, call, fax, e-mail, or through World Wide Web site Ramona Collins, Educational Services Coordinator. Phone: 516-542-4700. Fax: 516-542-4716. E-mail: wosportrc@aol.com. In-person interview recommended (telephone interview accepted). Applicants must submit a formal organization application, resume, two letters of recommendation. Applications are accepted continuously. World Wide Web: http://www.womenssportsfoundation.org.

WOMEN'S STUDIES PROGRAM/AFRICAN AND LATIN AMERICAN STUDIES PROGRAM
Colgate University, 13 Oak Drive
Hamilton, New York 13346-1398

General Information Educational services organization. Established in 1819. Department of Colgate University, Hamilton, New York. Number of internship applications received each year: 60.
Internships Available ▶ *1 African and Latin American Studies Program Assistant:* responsibilities include assisting the director and secretary in planning and execution of programming (lectures, film series, workshops, study groups); acting as liaison among student groups and faculty members. Candidates should have college courses in field, computer skills, knowledge of field, organizational skills, self-motivation, strong interpersonal skills, ability to speak and write Spanish well (optional). Duration is August 15 to June 1. $18,000 per duration of internship. ▶ *1 Women's Studies Program assistant:* responsibilities include assisting director in administration of the Center for Women's Studies; programming (film series, workshops, brown bag lunch series, lectures). Candidates should have ability to work independently, college courses in field, computer skills, knowledge of field, self-motivation, strong interpersonal skills. Duration is August 15 to June 1. $18,000 per duration of internship. Open to recent college graduates, graduate students. International applications accepted.
Benefits Health insurance, on-the-job training, opportunity to attend seminars/workshops, travel reimbursement, willing to act as a professional reference, willing to provide letters of recommendation, faculty/staff privileges.
Contact Write, call, or e-mail Mary Keys, Administrative Assistant, WMST/ALST Programs, Hamilton 13346-1398. Phone: 315-228-7546. Fax: 315-228-7098. E-mail: mkeys@mail.colgate.edu. Applicants must submit a letter of interest, resume, academic transcripts, portfolio, writing sample, telephone interview followed by in-person interview if appropriate. Application deadline: March 26. World Wide Web: http://www.colgate.edu.

WOODBERRY FOREST SUMMER SCHOOL
Woodberry Station
Woodberry Forest, Virginia 22989

General Information Summer school program that provides developmental, remedial, and advanced credit academic work and enrichment for high school-age students. Established in 1889. Number of employees: 21. Unit of Woodberry Forest School. Number of internship applications received each year: 200.
Internships Available ▶ *20–25 teaching interns:* responsibilities include assisting with classroom instruction, tutoring and reviewing with students, monitoring study hall, supervising dormitories, supervising athletics and fine arts programs, and chaperoning trips. Candidates should have knowledge of field, oral communication skills, self-motivation, strong interpersonal skills, strong leadership ability, written communication skills. Duration is 4–5 weeks. $1400 per duration of internship. Open to college juniors, college seniors, recent college graduates, graduate students, career changers, individuals reentering the workforce, must be at least 21 years old. International applications accepted.
Benefits Free housing, free meals, on-the-job training, willing to complete paperwork for educational credit, willing to provide letters of recommendation.
Contact Write, call, fax, or e-mail David McRae, Director. Phone: 540-672-6047. Fax: 540-672-9076. E-mail: wfs_summer@woodberry.org. In-person interview recommended (telephone interview accepted). Applicants must submit a letter of interest, resume,

academic transcripts, two personal references. Application deadline: March 15 for summer. World Wide Web: http://www.woodberry.org.

WORLDTEACH
CID–Harvard University, 79 John F. Kennedy Street
Cambridge, Massachusetts 02138

General Information Private, nonprofit organization that sends volunteers to teach in Africa, Asia, and Latin America. Established in 1986. Number of employees: 10. Unit of Center for International Development, Cambridge, Massachusetts. Number of internship applications received each year: 300.
Internships Available ▶ *250–300 teachers:* responsibilities include primarily teaching English and occasionally science and mathematics to students in developing countries. Candidates should have ability to work independently, oral communication skills, self-motivation, strong interpersonal skills, strong leadership ability, interest in other cultures, commitment to service. Duration is 6–12 months. Small monthly living allowance (varies from country to country). Open to recent college graduates, graduate students, law students, career changers. ▶ *20–300 volunteer summer teachers:* responsibilities include teaching English and taking part in cultural exchange with people of the host country (Ecuador, Costa Rica, China, or Namibia). Candidates should have computer skills, oral communication skills, personal interest in the field, strong interpersonal skills, English fluency, commitment to service. Duration is 8 weeks (June to August). Unpaid. Open to recent high school graduates, college freshmen, college sophomores, college juniors, college seniors, recent college graduates, graduate students, law students, career changers, individuals reentering the workforce. ▶ *30 volunteer teachers:* responsibilities include teaching English and other class subjects. Candidates should have ability to work independently, oral communication skills, self-motivation, strong interpersonal skills, strong leadership ability. Duration is July to June (11 months). Position available as unpaid or paid. Open to college seniors, recent college graduates, graduate students, law students, career changers. International applications accepted.
Benefits Formal training, health insurance, housing at a cost, meals at a cost, names of contacts, opportunity to attend seminars/workshops, possible full-time employment, willing to act as a professional reference, willing to provide letters of recommendation, student loans deferrable, possible scholarships to help cover the program fee.
International Internships Available in China; Costa Rica; Ecuador; Marshall Islands; Mexico; Namibia.
Contact Write, call, fax, e-mail, or through World Wide Web site Admissions Department, CID-Harvard University, 79 John F. Kennedy Street, Cambridge, Massachusetts 02138. Phone: 800-4-TEACH-0. Fax: 617-495-1599. E-mail: info@worldteach.org. In-person interview recommended (telephone interview accepted). Applicants must submit a formal organization application, resume, 3 essays, 2 personal references or letters of recommendation, academic transcripts for full-year programs. Application deadline: February 1 for April departures, April 1 for summer departures, July 1 for September departures, November 15 for January departures. World Wide Web: http://www.worldteach.org.

WYMAN CENTER
600 Kiwanis Drive
Eureka, Missouri 63025

General Information Youth development organization that focuses on educational readiness, citizenship, self-esteem, self-motivation, leadership, communication, intercultural understanding, environment, and community/relationship building. Established in 1898. Number of employees: 50. Number of internship applications received each year: 25.
Internships Available ▶ *5–7 Camp Coca-Cola St. Louis team leaders:* responsibilities include supervising, coaching, and supporting groupleaders; instilling positive camper outcomes. Candidates should have ability to work independently, experience in the field, oral communication skills, strong interpersonal skills, strong leadership ability. Duration is May/June to August. $2400–$2700 per duration of internship. Open to college freshmen, college sophomores, college juniors, college seniors, recent college gradu-

Wyman Center (continued)

ates, graduate students, law students, career changers, individuals reentering the workforce. ▶ *4–6 Camp Coca-Cola activity instructors:* responsibilities include teaching skills to campers and groupleaders in skill areas: waterfront, relief, camping and nature, and arts and crafts. Candidates should have ability to work independently, experience in the field, oral communication skills, strong interpersonal skills, strong leadership ability. Duration is May/June to August. $2000–$2400 per duration of internship. Open to college freshmen, college sophomores, college juniors, college seniors, recent college graduates, graduate students, law students, career changers, individuals reentering the workforce. ▶ *10–15 Camp Coca-Cola group leaders:* responsibilities include supervising campers and creating a cohesive community; developing personal relationships with campers; and teaching activities and skills through the CCC outcomes. Candidates should have ability to work independently, experience in the field, oral communication skills, strong interpersonal skills, strong leadership ability. Duration is May/June to August. $1800–$2200 per duration of internship. Open to college freshmen, college sophomores, college juniors, college seniors, recent college graduates, graduate students, law students, career changers, individuals reentering the workforce. ▶ *2–4 Camp Wyman activity instructors:* responsibilities include planning and implementing program in one area: archery, canoeing, swimming, arts and crafts, or adventure. Candidates should have ability to work independently, oral communication skills, self-motivation, strong interpersonal skills, strong leadership ability. Duration is June to mid-August. $1800–$2240 per duration of internship. Open to high school seniors, recent high school graduates, college freshmen, college sophomores, college juniors, college seniors, recent college graduates, graduate students, law students, career changers, individuals reentering the workforce. ▶ *1–20 Camp Wyman group leaders:* responsibilities include supervising campers in a residential camp setting (up to 8 campers per cabin; children 7 to 16 years old). Candidates should have oral communication skills, self-motivation, strong leadership ability, interest in mentoring children and working in a residential camp setting. Duration is June to mid-August. $1800–$2100 per duration of internship. Open to high school students, recent high school graduates, college freshmen, college sophomores, college juniors, college seniors, recent college graduates, graduate students, law students, career changers, individuals reentering the workforce. ▶ *4–8 Camp Wyman team leaders:* responsibilities include supervising group leaders; program design and implementation; and administrative work. Candidates should have ability to work independently, oral communication skills, self-motivation, strong interpersonal skills, strong leadership ability. Duration is June to mid-August. $2400–$2600 per duration of internship. Open to college freshmen, college sophomores, college juniors, college seniors, recent college graduates, graduate students, law students, career changers, individuals reentering the workforce. ▶ *1–3 activity instructors:* responsibilities include planning and implementing age-appropriate activities for youth enrolled in day camp located in St. Louis. Candidates should have analytical skills, oral communication skills, organizational skills, self-motivation, strong interpersonal skills, strong leadership ability, strong desire to work with youth in a community-based setting. Duration is May 28th to July 25th. Paid. Open to college freshmen, college sophomores, college juniors, college seniors, recent college graduates, graduate students, law students, career changers. ▶ *1–16 group leaders:* responsibilities include supervising youths aged 6-16 in a summer day-camp setting. Candidates should have ability to work independently, oral communication skills, self-motivation, strong interpersonal skills, strong leadership ability, strong desire to work with youths from various backgrounds. Paid. Open to high school seniors, recent high school graduates, college freshmen, college sophomores, college juniors, college seniors, recent college graduates, graduate students, law students, career changers. ▶ *1–8 program interns:* responsibilities include instructing and facilitating groups in environmental and adventure activities includingg caving, orienteering, high and low-challenge courses, evening activities; training and supervising counselors; participating in presentations and outreach programs; designing curriculum and teaching materials; community-based programs for youth; other positions available in community-based programs

for youth, teens, and families. Candidates should have experience in the field, oral communication skills, personal interest in the field, self-motivation, strong interpersonal skills. Duration is flexible. $400–$800 per month. Open to recent high school graduates, college freshmen, college sophomores, college juniors, college seniors, recent college graduates, graduate students, law students, career changers, individuals reentering the workforce. ▶ *1 social work practicum intern:* responsibilities include working with community-based groups in after-school programs, community leadership development, and large-scale community events. Candidates should have ability to work independently, oral communication skills, organizational skills, personal interest in the field, self-motivation, strong interpersonal skills, written communication skills, strong desire to work with children, youth and adults from an asset-based philosophy. Duration is 1–2 semesters. Paid. Open to college juniors, college seniors, graduate students. International applications accepted.

Benefits Formal training, free housing, free meals, names of contacts, on-the-job training, opportunity to attend seminars/workshops, possible full-time employment, willing to act as a professional reference, willing to complete paperwork for educational credit, willing to provide letters of recommendation.

Contact Write, fax, or through World Wide Web site Cheryl Estwanick, Executive Secretary. Fax: 636-938-5289. No phone calls. In-person interview recommended (telephone interview accepted). Applicants must submit a formal organization application, letter of interest, resume, three personal references, child abuse and criminal background checks required. Application deadline: February 1 for spring, April 15 for summer, August 1 for fall. World Wide Web: http://www.wymancenter.org.

YMCA CAMP CHINGACHGOOK
1872 Pilot Knob Road
Kattskill Bay, New York 12844

General Information Outdoor environmental and adventure education center in the Adirondacks that teaches school children, college students, families, and adult groups. Established in 1913. Number of employees: 100. Branch of Capital District YMCA, Albany, New York. Number of internship applications received each year: 10.

Internships Available ▶ *3–4 outdoor educators:* responsibilities include leading environmental, recreational, adventure, and outdoor classes for school children, families, college students, and adults. Candidates should have knowledge of field, personal interest in the field, strong interpersonal skills, strong leadership ability. Duration is 8–20 weeks. Position available as unpaid or at $125–$200 per week. Open to recent high school graduates, college freshmen, college sophomores, college juniors, college seniors, recent college graduates. International applications accepted.

Benefits Formal training, free housing, free meals, names of contacts, on-the-job training, opportunity to attend seminars/workshops, possible full-time employment, tuition assistance, willing to act as a professional reference, willing to complete paperwork for educational credit.

Contact Write, call, fax, or e-mail Kenis Sweet, Outdoor Education Director. Phone: 518-656-9462 Ext. 14. Fax: 518-656-9362. E-mail: ksweet@cdymca.org. In-person interview recommended (telephone interview accepted). Applicants must submit a letter of interest, resume, three personal references. Application deadline: February 1 for spring, June 1 for fall. World Wide Web: http://www.chingachgook.org.

YMCA OF GREATER NEW YORK–GREENKILL OUTDOOR ENVIRONMENTAL EDUCATION CENTER
300 Big Pond Road, PO Box B
Huguenot, New York 12746

General Information Center that provides outdoor education and other camping/conference-related services to elementary school-age students to help develop teamwork and an understanding of natural resources. Established in 1975. Number of employees: 40. Branch of YMCA of Greater New York, New York, New York. Number of internship applications received each year: 50.

Internships Available ▶ *2–6 naturalists interns:* responsibilities include teaching outdoor environmental education and assisting with operating the residential center. Candidates should have college courses in field, personal interest in the field, plan to pursue career in field, strong interpersonal skills, strong leadership ability. Duration is 8–16 weeks. $50–$100 per week. Open to college juniors, college seniors, recent college graduates, career changers. International applications accepted.

Benefits Formal training, free housing, free meals, names of contacts, on-the-job training, possible full-time employment, willing to complete paperwork for educational credit, willing to provide letters of recommendation, worker's compensation.

Contact Write, call, fax, or e-mail Heather Chadwick, Director. Phone: 845-858-2200. Fax: 845-858-7823. E-mail: camps@ymcanyc. org. In-person interview recommended (telephone interview accepted). Applicants must submit a formal organization application, letter of interest, resume, three personal references. Application deadline: January 15 for spring, March 15 for summer, April 15 for fall, October 15 for winter. World Wide Web: http://www. ymcanyc.org.

YOUTH FOR UNDERSTANDING USA INTERNATIONAL EXCHANGE
6400 Goldsboro Road, Suite 100
Bethesda, Maryland 20817

General Information Private, nonprofit educational student exchange organization dedicated to international understanding and world peace. Established in 1951. Number of employees: 40. Number of internship applications received each year: 100.

Internships Available ▶ *Accounting interns:* responsibilities include working with accounting system, using Excel documents, and assisting in payroll process. Candidates should have analytical skills, computer skills, declared college major in field, office skills, strong interpersonal skills, written communication skills. Duration is 1–4 months. Unpaid. ▶ *1 admissions and registration intern:* responsibilities include creating database record; processing and updating documentation; coordinating and processing transfer of documentation between U.S. and overseas partners; undertaking file processing projects; and analyzing the results. Candidates should have ability to work independently, analytical skills, computer skills, office skills, strong interpersonal skills, written communication skills. Duration is 3–6 months. Unpaid. Open to college freshmen, college sophomores, college juniors, college seniors. International applications accepted.

Benefits Formal training, possible full-time employment, willing to complete paperwork for educational credit, willing to provide letters of recommendation.

Contact Write or e-mail Monty Melchior, Internship Coordinator. E-mail: melchior@yfu.org. No phone calls. In-person interview recommended (telephone interview accepted). Applicants must submit a letter of interest, resume. Applications are accepted continuously. World Wide Web: http://yfu-usa.org.

FINANCE AND INSURANCE

GENERAL

ALTERNATIVES FEDERAL CREDIT UNION
125 North Fulton Street
Ithaca, New York 14850

General Information Community development credit union that focuses services toward low income residents of Tompkins County, New York. Established in 1979. Number of employees: 35. Number of internship applications received each year: 100.
Internships Available ▶ *1 Dollars for Dreams assistant:* responsibilities include assisting the adult adviser with goal projects, fundraising, and motivating youth for this branch credit union run for and by youth under age 19. Candidates should have ability to work independently, oral communication skills, organizational skills, plan to pursue career in field, strong interpersonal skills. Duration is flexible (approximately 10 hours per week). Unpaid. Open to recent high school graduates, college freshmen, college sophomores, college juniors, college seniors, recent college graduates, graduate students, law students, law school graduates, career changers, individuals reentering the workforce. ▶ *1 community partnership lending intern:* responsibilities include working with potential partner lists to promote program to community nonprofit organizations. Candidates should have ability to work independently, oral communication skills, organizational skills, strong interpersonal skills, written communication skills. Duration is one semester (5-10 hours per week). Unpaid. Open to college freshmen, college sophomores, college juniors, college seniors, recent college graduates, graduate students, law school graduates. ▶ *1 computer instruction intern:* responsibilities include providing one-to-one and small group instruction on basics of Lotus123, Excel, Wordperfect, or other computer programs to assist staff in becoming more proficient. Candidates should have computer skills, oral communication skills, personal interest in the field, strong interpersonal skills. Duration is 200–300 hours. Unpaid. Open to college freshmen, college sophomores, college juniors, college seniors, recent college graduates, graduate students, law school graduates. ▶ *1–3 loan operations clerks:* responsibilities include clerk-level duties allowing intern to gain experience in office procedures, work habits, and corporate structure and process. Candidates should have ability to work with others, organizational skills, self-motivation. Duration is flexible. Unpaid. Open to high school students, recent high school graduates, college freshmen, college sophomores, college juniors, college seniors, recent college graduates, graduate students, law students, law school graduates, career changers, individuals reentering the workforce. ▶ *1 loan procedures manual intern:* responsibilities include updating loan procedures manual, including interviewing staff and editing. Candidates should have ability to work independently, organizational skills, written communication skills, business background and loan knowledge (helpful). Duration is one semester (10 hours per week). Unpaid. Open to college freshmen, college sophomores, college juniors, college seniors, recent college graduates, graduate students, law school graduates. ▶ *1–2 micro enterprise development interns:* responsibilities include working on database, videotape classes, research, identifying share ware and other business resources online, collecting anecdotal information and success stories from participants. Candidates should have ability to work independently, college courses in field, computer skills, oral communication skills, organizational skills, personal interest in the field, research skills, self-motivation, strong interpersonal skills, writing skills. Duration is 200–300 hours. Unpaid. Open to college sophomores, college juniors, college seniors, recent college graduates, graduate students, law school graduates, small business owners. ▶ *Student loan products interns:* responsibilities include researching non-guaranteed and other student loan products offered by local lenders. Candidates should have ability to work independently, organizational skills, strong interpersonal skills. Duration is one semester (3-5 hours per week). Unpaid. Open to college freshmen, college sophomores, college juniors, college seniors, recent college graduates, graduate students, law school graduates. International applications accepted.
Benefits On-the-job training, possible full-time employment, willing to act as a professional reference, willing to complete paperwork for educational credit, willing to provide letters of recommendation.
Contact Write, call, fax, e-mail, or through World Wide Web site Sharon Kinnan, Human Resource Manager. Phone: 607-273-4611 Ext. 821. Fax: 607-277-6391. E-mail: skinnan@alternatives.org. In-person interview recommended (telephone interview accepted). Applicants must submit a formal organization application, resume, 3 professional references. Applications are accepted continuously. World Wide Web: http://www.alternatives.org.

APPLIED CARD SYSTEMS
50 Applied Cards Way
Glen Mills, Pennsylvania 19342

General Information Credit card service company with offices in Delaware, Kentucky, West Virginia, and Florida. Established in 1987.
Internships Available ▶ *Interns:* responsibilities include positions in various departments including collections, customer service, learning and development, information technology, payment processing, facilities, human resources, credit, audit, and accounting. Duration is 8 weeks. Paid. Open to college freshmen, college sophomores, college juniors, college seniors.
Contact Write, e-mail, or through World Wide Web site Human Resources. E-mail: acshr@appliedcard.com. Applicants must submit a resume. Applications are accepted continuously. World Wide Web: http://www.appliedcard.com.

CAREFIRST BLUECROSS BLUESHIELD
10455 Mill Run Circle
Owings Mills, Maryland 21117

General Information Managed care organization (insurance company). Established in 1937. Number of employees: 1,800. Number of internship applications received each year: 300.
Internships Available ▶ *1–5 interns.* Candidates should have office skills, oral communication skills, personal interest in the field, strong interpersonal skills, written communication skills, Microsoft computer software knowledge (desirable). Duration is full-time in summer, part-time during academic year. $8–$12 per hour depending on experience. Open to college freshmen, college sophomores, college juniors, college seniors, graduate students. International applications accepted.
Benefits On-the-job training, opportunity to attend seminars/workshops, possible full-time employment, willing to complete paperwork for educational credit.
Contact Write, call, fax, or e-mail Tony Davis, Employment Associate. Phone: 410-998-7880. Fax: 410-998-5313. E-mail: tony.davis@carefirst.com. In-person interview required. Applicants must

submit a letter of interest, resume. Applications are accepted continuously. World Wide Web: http://www.carefirst.com.

CIGNA CORPORATION
1601 Chestnut Street, 2 Liberty Place
Philadelphia, Pennsylvania 19192

General Information Premier global employee benefits provider. Established in 1792. Number of employees: 2,500. Number of internship applications received each year: 1,000.
Internships Available ▶ *100–150 associate leadership development program interns:* responsibilities include working in actuarial science, risk management, finance, human resources, computer science, computer engineering, or MIS; working on project-based, meaningful assignments; attending luncheons, informational panel discussions, and developmental workshops. Candidates should have analytical skills, oral communication skills, self-motivation, strong interpersonal skills, strong leadership ability, written communication skills. Duration is 10–12 weeks. $11–$16.50 per hour. Open to college sophomores, college juniors, college seniors, graduate students. International applications accepted.
Benefits Job counseling, names of contacts, on-the-job training, opportunity to attend seminars/workshops, possible full-time employment, willing to complete paperwork for educational credit, willing to provide letters of recommendation, housing stipend.
Contact Write, fax, e-mail, or through World Wide Web site Mary Ann Gaio, Summer Internship Program Manager, Building A-125, 900 Cottage Grove Road, Bloomfield, Connecticut 06002. Fax: 860-226-1537. E-mail: maryann.gaio@cigna.com. No phone calls. In-person interview recommended (telephone interview accepted). Applicants must submit a letter of interest, resume, writing sample. Application deadline: March 31 for winter, September 1 for fall, December 1 for summer. World Wide Web: http://www.cigna.com.

COMMUNITY FINANCIAL SERVICES, LLP
216 Haddon Avenue, Suite 327
Westmont, New Jersey 08108

General Information Firm specializing in debt reduction for corporations. Established in 1987. Number of employees: 6. Unit of Community Financial Management Services, Atlanta, Georgia. Number of internship applications received each year: 25.
Internships Available ▶ *1–4 accounting assistants:* responsibilities include organizing and entering client supplied data into accounting programs, completing routine sales and income tax returns. Candidates should have computer skills, knowledge of field, organizational skills, plan to pursue career in field. Duration is 10–13 weeks. $10–$12 per hour. Open to recent high school graduates, college freshmen, college sophomores, college juniors, graduate students, law students.
Benefits On-the-job training, travel reimbursement, willing to act as a professional reference, willing to complete paperwork for educational credit, willing to provide letters of recommendation.
Contact Write, fax, or e-mail Stephan L. Schneider, National Partner, PO Box 355, Collingswood 08108. Phone: 856-869-4236. Fax: 856-869-4239. E-mail: sschneider1@compuserve.com. In-person interview required. Applicants must submit a letter of interest, resume. Application deadline: April 15 for summer.

FANNIE MAE
3900 Wisconsin Avenue, NW
Washington, District of Columbia 20016

General Information Financial services company, whose mission is to tear down barriers, lower costs, and increase the opportunities for home ownership and affordable rental housing for all Americans. Established in 1938. Number of employees: 4,500. Number of internship applications received each year: 200.
Internships Available ▶ *Business interns:* responsibilities include handling professional-level assignments in business units across the company, including: financial analysis, market research, and systems testing and development. Candidates should have analytical skills, computer skills, oral communication skills, plan to pursue

career in field, written communication skills, 3-5 years of relevant work experience, fluency in English, minimum GPA of 3.3. Duration is 10 weeks. Paid. Open to first-year MBA students specializing in finance, MIS, and/or real estate; first-year MS students specializing in industrial or computer engineering. International applications accepted.
Benefits Formal training, job counseling, on-the-job training, opportunity to attend seminars/workshops, possible full-time employment, willing to complete paperwork for educational credit, assignment to a peer mentor, possible free housing.
Contact Write, fax, or e-mail Jane Marie Maselli, Campus Recruiting Manager, 3900 Wisconsin Avenue, NW, Washington, District of Columbia 20016. Fax: 202-752-4934. E-mail: janemarie_maselli@fanniemae.com. No phone calls. Applicants must submit a letter of interest, resume, writing sample. Application deadline: January 31. World Wide Web: http://www.fanniemae.com.

HORSMAN BROTHERS, INC.
139 Sunrise Avenue, Suite 308
Palm Beach, Florida 33480

General Information Financial advisory and marketing firm for hedge funds for wealthy private investors. Established in 1998. Number of employees: 3. Number of internship applications received each year: 40.
Internships Available ▶ *2–6 administrative assistant interns:* responsibilities include assisting in weekly and monthly strategic and tactical trading conferences; assisting in marketing activities, newsletter formatting and production; assisting in seminar presentations and in telephone follow-ups. Candidates should have ability to work independently, ability to work with others, computer skills, oral communication skills, written communication skills. Duration is 6–18 months. Unpaid. Open to college seniors, recent college graduates, graduate students, law students. International applications accepted.
Benefits Formal training, on-the-job training, opportunity to attend seminars/workshops, willing to act as a professional reference, willing to complete paperwork for educational credit, willing to provide letters of recommendation.
Contact Write or e-mail L. Horsman, Vice President. E-mail: horsmanbrothers@worldnet.att.net. No phone calls. In-person interview recommended (telephone interview accepted). Applicants must submit a formal organization application, letter of interest, personal references or letters of recommendation in some instances. Applications are accepted continuously.

INTERNATIONAL MONETARY FUND
700 19th Street, NW
Washington, District of Columbia 20431

General Information International financial institution responsible for monitoring the international monetary system. Established in 1946. Number of employees: 3,000. Number of internship applications received each year: 1,100.
Internships Available ▶ *37–40 summer interns:* responsibilities include undertaking a research project on a subject set by the employing department and preparing a paper. Candidates should have ability to work independently, analytical skills, college degree in related field, computer skills, knowledge of field, organizational skills, research skills, self-motivation, writing skills. Duration is 13 weeks. $3800 per month (paid on daily basis). Open to graduate students in international economics or a related field, preferably at end of third or fourth year in PhD program. International applications accepted.
Benefits Health insurance, opportunity to attend seminars/workshops, possible full-time employment, travel reimbursement.
Contact Fax, e-mail, or through World Wide Web site Summer Intern Program, Recruitment and Staffing Division, 700 19th Street, NW, Washington, District of Columbia 20431. Fax: 202-623-7333. E-mail: recruit@imf.org. Applicants must submit a resume, academic transcripts, college campus interview during IMF recruitment (desirable); formal applications should be made on line at www.imf.org/recruitment. Application deadline: January 31. World Wide Web: http://www.imf.org.

NATIONAL ACADEMY OF SOCIAL INSURANCE
1776 Massachusetts Avenue, NW, Suite 615
Washington, District of Columbia 20036

General Information Nonprofit, nonpartisan organization made up of the nation's leading experts on social insurance whose mission is to promote understanding and informed policy-making on social insurance and related programs. Established in 1986. Number of employees: 15. Number of internship applications received each year: 50.
Internships Available ▶ *1 Nathan J. Stark internship for nonprofit development positions:* responsibilities include learning about nonprofit boards and fund-raising. Candidates should have analytical skills, organizational skills, personal interest in the field, strong interpersonal skills, written communication skills. Duration is June to August (12 weeks). $2000 per duration of internship. Open to college freshmen, college sophomores, college juniors, college seniors, recent college graduates, graduate students. ▶ *5 Somers aging and long-term care research interns:* responsibilities include researching and focusing on long-term care issues. Candidates should have analytical skills, personal interest in the field, research skills, written communication skills. Duration is June to August (12 weeks). $2000 per duration of internship. Open to college freshmen, college sophomores, college juniors, college seniors, recent college graduates, graduate students, law students. ▶ *10–12 social insurance interns (Washington, DC):* responsibilities include working closely with experts on social policy issues. Candidates should have analytical skills, personal interest in the field, research skills, writing skills. Duration is June to August (12 weeks). $2000 per duration of internship. Open to college freshmen, college sophomores, college juniors, college seniors, recent college graduates, graduate students, law students. International applications accepted.
Benefits Opportunity to attend seminars/workshops, possible full-time employment, willing to act as a professional reference, willing to complete paperwork for educational credit, willing to provide letters of recommendation.
Contact E-mail or through World Wide Web site Kate Robie, Program Associate and Internship Coordinator. Phone: 202-452-8097. Fax: 202-452-8111. E-mail: krobie@nasi.org. Telephone interview required. Applicants must submit a formal organization application, resume, academic transcripts, three letters of recommendation, one-page essay on interest in the program, one 5-10 page writing sample. Application deadline: March 15. World Wide Web: http://www.nasi.org.

NATIONAL ASSOCIATION OF PROFESSIONAL SURPLUS LINES OFFICES, LTD.
6405 North Cosby Avenue, #201
Kansas City, Missouri 64151

General Information Trade association representing the surplus lines segment of the insurance industry. Established in 1975. Number of employees: 6. Number of internship applications received each year: 100.
Internships Available ▶ *6–8 summer interns:* responsibilities include placement with NAPSLO member firms across the U.S., 5 weeks working with a company member, 4 weeks working with a surplus lines broker agent member; 4 interns selected to attend the NAPSLO Annual Convention; one intern selected to receive an additional internship in London. Candidates should have ability to work with others, computer skills, oral communication skills, plan to pursue career in field, self-motivation, written communication skills, major in business, finance, insurance (insurance preferred). Duration is 9 weeks. Stipend paid by NAPSLO; up to $400 per week paid by host company. Open to college juniors, college seniors, recent college graduates, graduate students. International applications accepted.
Benefits Free housing, names of contacts, on-the-job training, possible full-time employment, travel reimbursement, willing to act as a professional reference, willing to complete paperwork for educational credit, willing to provide letters of recommendation.
International Internships Available in London, United Kingdom.
Contact Write, call, fax, e-mail, or through World Wide Web site Jessica Myers, Internship Coordinator. Phone: 816-741-3910. Fax: 816-741-5409. E-mail: internship@napslo.org. Applicants must submit a formal organization application, resume, academic transcripts, two letters of recommendation, selected applicants will be contacted for telephone and/or personal interview. Application deadline: January 15. World Wide Web: http://www.napslo.org.

NONPROFIT FINANCIAL CENTER
29 East Madison, Suite 1700
Chicago, Illinois 60602-4415

General Information Comprehensive financial services provider for nonprofit organizations; programming falls into five main areas of service: financing, training, consulting, informational resources, and member services. Established in 1980. Number of employees: 10. Number of internship applications received each year: 25.
Internships Available ▶ *1–2 marketing interns:* responsibilities include assisting marketing director with campaigns and design materials and overseeing publication production; working with Webmaster to update Web site; and creating new marketing campaigns. Candidates should have ability to work independently, college courses in field, computer skills, oral communication skills, personal interest in the field, written communication skills. Duration is flexible. Unpaid. Open to college freshmen, college sophomores, college juniors, college seniors, recent college graduates, graduate students, individuals reentering the workforce. ▶ *1–2 operations interns:* responsibilities include overseeing internal operations projects; verifying databox information; directing filing projects; creating new forms for databox; and other duties as assigned. Candidates should have office skills, oral communication skills, organizational skills, strong interpersonal skills, written communication skills. Duration is flexible. Unpaid. Open to college sophomores, college juniors, college seniors, recent college graduates, graduate students, individuals reentering the workforce. ▶ *2–4 program services interns:* responsibilities include assisting program services department; coordinating consulting and instructional projects; conducting related research and development duties; attending and coordinating related conferences; and some lending-related duties. Candidates should have ability to work with others, computer skills, oral communication skills, research skills, writing skills. Duration is flexible. Unpaid. Open to college juniors, college seniors, recent college graduates, graduate students, individuals reentering the workforce. International applications accepted.
Benefits Job counseling, opportunity to attend seminars/workshops, willing to act as a professional reference, willing to complete paperwork for educational credit, willing to provide letters of recommendation.
Contact Write, call, fax, e-mail, or through World Wide Web site Etta M. Davis, Assistant Director of Operations. Phone: 312-252-0420. Fax: 312-252-0099. E-mail: etta@nfconline.org. In-person interview recommended (telephone interview accepted). Applicants must submit a letter of interest, resume. Applications are accepted continuously. World Wide Web: http://www.NFConline.org.

PRINCIPAL FINANCIAL GROUP
711 High Street
Des Moines, Iowa 50392-0550

General Information Organization that provides financial services. Established in 1879. Number of employees: 8,500. Number of internship applications received each year: 500.
Internships Available ▶ *8–12 accounting interns:* responsibilities include assisting on accounting projects in a team environment. Candidates should have declared college major in field, plan to pursue career in field, self-motivation, strong interpersonal skills, strong leadership ability. Duration is 3 months. $12.25–$13.90 per hour. Open to college sophomores, college juniors, college seniors, graduate students. ▶ *5–6 actuarial interns:* responsibilities include assisting in the performance of the actuarial function. Candidates should have analytical skills, college courses in field, plan to pursue career in field, self-motivation, strong interpersonal skills, strong leadership ability. Duration is 3 months. Salary plus housing stipend. Open to college sophomores, college juniors. ▶ *2–4 capital management interns:* responsibilities include researching possible entities of investing and funding. Candidates should have

ability to work independently, analytical skills, declared college major in field, plan to pursue career in field, research skills, strong interpersonal skills, strong leadership ability. Duration is 3 months. $12–$13 per hour. Open to college juniors, college seniors, graduate students. ▶ *8–10 commercial real estate interns:* responsibilities include assisting in purchasing, underwriting, and liquidating corporate owned property. Candidates should have ability to work independently, analytical skills, college courses in field, plan to pursue career in field, strong interpersonal skills, experience in finance and/or real estate (preferred). Duration is 6–9 months. $12 to $13 per hour plus housing subsidy. Open to college juniors, college seniors. ▶ *1 corporate wellness intern:* responsibilities include fitness testing, personal training, conducting seminars, teaching fitness classes, research and administrative duties, and special interest projects. Candidates should have ability to work independently, declared college major in field, knowledge of field, oral communication skills, personal interest in the field, plan to pursue career in field, self-motivation, strong interpersonal skills. Duration is 6–8 months. Unpaid. Open to college juniors, college seniors. ▶ *30–40 information analyst interns:* responsibilities include application development, database administration, and networking. Candidates should have ability to work independently, declared college major in field, plan to pursue career in field, self-motivation, strong interpersonal skills, strong leadership ability, Cobol experience. Duration is 3–12 months. $14 per hour plus housing stipend. Open to college sophomores, college juniors, college seniors.

Benefits Job counseling, on-the-job training, opportunity to attend seminars/workshops, possible full-time employment, willing to act as a professional reference, willing to complete paperwork for educational credit, willing to provide letters of recommendation, access to on-site wellness centers.

Contact Through World Wide Web site Internship Coordinator. No phone calls. In-person interview recommended (telephone interview accepted). Applicants must submit a letter of interest, resume, academic transcripts. Applications are accepted continuously. World Wide Web: http://www.principal.com/careers.

STATE TEACHERS RETIREMENT SYSTEM OF OHIO (STRS OHIO)
275 East Broad Street
Columbus, Ohio 43215-3771

General Information One of the largest pension funds in the United States managing assets totaling over $48 billion at market value and providing benefits to more than 400,000 public educators. Established in 1920. Number of employees: 725. Number of internship applications received each year: 1,500.

Internships Available ▶ *Interns:* responsibilities include working in different departments including member benefits, information technology, investments, and finance/accounting. Candidates should have analytical skills, office skills, organizational skills, self-motivation, strong interpersonal skills. Duration is 3–4 months. $15–$20 per hour. Open to college junior and seniors (at least a 3.0 GPA). International applications accepted.

Benefits Formal training, free housing, job counseling, on-the-job training, opportunity to attend seminars/workshops, possible full-time employment, travel reimbursement, tuition assistance, willing to act as a professional reference, willing to complete paperwork for educational credit, willing to provide letters of recommendation, free fitness center membership.

Contact Write, call, fax, e-mail, or through World Wide Web site Michael Mancuso, Human Resources Generalist. Phone: 614-227-2881. Fax: 614-233-8795. E-mail: mancusom@strsoh.org. In-person interview recommended (telephone interview accepted). Applicants must submit a formal organization application, letter of interest, resume, 1 personal/2 business references; drug screen required.

Application deadline: April 30 for summer; continuous for other positions. World Wide Web: http://www.strsoh.org/jobs.htm.

THRIVENT FINANCIAL FOR LUTHERANS
625 Fourth Avenue, South, MS869
Minneapolis, Minnesota 56415

General Information Faith-based financial services organization. Established in 1917. Number of employees: 3,000. Unit of Lutheran Brotherhood Home Office, Minneapolis, Minnesota. Number of internship applications received each year: 1,000.

Internships Available ▶ *100–150 financial services interns:* responsibilities include strengthening regional markets, exploring high-touch selling techniques/strategies, volunteering at local congregations, and building relationships with professional networks. Candidates should have ability to work independently, college courses in field, computer skills, oral communication skills, organizational skills, personal interest in the field, research skills, self-motivation, strong interpersonal skills, strong leadership ability, written communication skills, minimum GPA of 3.0 (highly recommended), valid driver's license. Duration is May to September (40 hours per week). Position available as unpaid or at stipend of $150-$250 per week plus commissions. Open to college sophomores, college juniors, college seniors, graduate students, law students, must be 18 years or older. International applications accepted.

Benefits Formal training, on-the-job training, opportunity to attend seminars/workshops, possible full-time employment, willing to act as a professional reference, willing to complete paperwork for educational credit, willing to provide letters of recommendation, expense-paid trip to Minneapolis home office, assistance in earning insurance licenses.

Contact E-mail or through World Wide Web site Justin Pickar, Internship Specialist, 625 Fourth Avenue South, MS 869, Minneapolis, Minnesota 55415. Phone: 800-688-6027. Fax: 612-340-7142. E-mail: jobs@thrivent.com. In-person interview recommended (telephone interview accepted). Applicants must submit a letter of interest, resume, three personal references, application and contracting kit; background check required. Application deadline: March 31. World Wide Web: http://www.thrivent.com.

VENTUREPLEX
701 B Street, Suite 300
San Diego, California 92101

General Information Venture capital and private equity research firm. Established in 1999. Number of employees: 5. Number of internship applications received each year: 300.

Internships Available ▶ *5–15 interns:* responsibilities include working on many projects that entail research, financial presentation preparation, marketing and sales, and document preparation; each intern will work some part of the day researching venture capital activity. Candidates should have ability to work with others, computer skills, oral communication skills, organizational skills, research skills, written communication skills, minimum GPA of 3.0. Duration is 3–9 months. Unpaid. Open to college freshmen, college sophomores, college juniors, college seniors, graduate students. International applications accepted.

Benefits On-the-job training, possible full-time employment, willing to act as a professional reference, willing to complete paperwork for educational credit, willing to provide letters of recommendation.

Contact E-mail Dante Fichera, President. Phone: 619-544-7475. Fax: 619-544-7477. E-mail: dante@ventureplex.com. Applicants must submit a letter of interest, resume, some evidence of English ability. Applications are accepted continuously. World Wide Web: http://www.ventureplex.com.

HEALTH CARE AND SOCIAL ASSISTANCE

HEALTH-CARE SERVICES

ACCREDITED CARE, INC.
106 West Third Street, Suite 707
Jamestown, New York 14701

General Information Provider of home health-care services. Established in 1979. Number of employees: 50. Number of internship applications received each year: 10.
Internships Available ▶ *1 general intern:* responsibilities include assisting with all aspects of home health care. Duration is flexible (minimun of 2months). Position available as unpaid or at $5–$7 per hour. ▶ *1 general office assistant (part-time):* responsibilities include administrative duties. Duration is flexible (minimum of 2 months). Position available as unpaid or at $5–$7 per hour. Candidates for all positions should have oral communication skills, organizational skills, personal interest in the field, strong interpersonal skills, written communication skills. Open to high school students, recent high school graduates, college freshmen, college sophomores, college juniors, college seniors, recent college graduates, graduate students, law students, career changers, individuals reentering the workforce. International applications accepted.
Benefits Formal training, job counseling, on-the-job training, opportunity to attend seminars/workshops, possible full-time employment, willing to act as a professional reference, willing to complete paperwork for educational credit, willing to provide letters of recommendation.
Contact Write, call, or e-mail Mr. Fred Press, Director. Phone: 212-517-8110. E-mail: acihomehealth@aol.com. In-person interview recommended (telephone interview accepted). Applicants must submit a letter of interest, resume. Applications are accepted continuously.

ADVOCATE FITNESS
Northern Trust Fitness Center, 801 South Canal Street, C-P1
Chicago, Illinois 60607

General Information Health-care organization. Established in 1898. Number of employees: 22,000. Branch of Advocate Health Care, Oak Brook, Illinois. Number of internship applications received each year: 100.
Internships Available ▶ *7–8 site interns:* responsibilities include various duties, depending on intern's developmental needs and interests. Candidates should have ability to work independently, college courses in field, knowledge of field, organizational skills, self-motivation, strong interpersonal skills. Duration is 400 hours. Position available as unpaid or at $250–$500 per duration of internship. Open to college juniors, college seniors, recent college graduates, graduate students.
Benefits Names of contacts, on-the-job training, opportunity to attend seminars/workshops, possible full-time employment, willing to act as a professional reference, willing to complete paperwork for educational credit, willing to provide letters of recommendation.

Contact Write, call, fax, or e-mail Eric M. Nelson, Manager, Fitness Programs, Northern Trust Fitness Center, 801 South Canal Street, C-P1, Chicago, Illinois 60607. Phone: 312-557-2201. Fax: 312-557-5707. E-mail: en4@ntrs.com. In-person interview recommended (telephone interview accepted). Applicants must submit a resume. Applications are accepted continuously.

AIR FORCE HEALTH PROFESSIONS
500 East Boulevard, Suite 102
Montgomery, Alabama 36117

General Information Residency that provides broad-based clinical training. Established in 1978. Number of employees: 365,000. Number of internship applications received each year: 50.
Internships Available ▶ *10–28 clinical psychology residents:* responsibilities include intensive, in-depth experience and supervision in assessment and treatment of a diverse patient population with a broad range of emotional and behavioral disorders during required clinical rotations through the Outpatient Mental Health/Life Skills Support Center, Clinical Health Psychology/Primary Care Clinic, and Neuropsychology. Candidates should have college degree in related field, U.S. citizenship. Duration is 48 months. $45,000–$55,000 per year. Open to student in final year of doctorate program only, maximum age 39.
Benefits Formal training, free housing, health insurance, names of contacts, opportunity to attend seminars/workshops, possible full-time employment, travel reimbursement, tuition assistance, willing to act as a professional reference, willing to provide letters of recommendation.
Contact Write, call, fax, or e-mail T. Sgt. George Adams, Air Force Health Profession. Phone: 334-270-3129. Fax: 334-271-6315. E-mail: george.adams@rs.af.mil. In-person interview recommended. Applicants must submit a formal organization application, resume, academic transcripts, letter of recommendation, physical, (if applicant is qualified an application is completed). Application deadline: December 1. World Wide Web: http://airforce.com.

AMERICAN ACADEMY OF PEDIATRICS
Department of Federal Affairs, 601 13th Street, NW, Suite 400 North
Washington, District of Columbia 20005

General Information Organization of 55,000 primary care pediatricians, pediatric medical subspecialists, and pediatric surgical specialists dedicated to the health and well-being of infants, children, adolescents, and young adults. Established in 1930.
Internships Available ▶ *3 Washington Office interns:* responsibilities include attending and reporting on congressional hearings and Department of Health and Human Services meetings/hearings, research, coalitions, association work, and medical work. Duration is minimum of 4 weeks. Unpaid. Open to college freshmen, college sophomores, college juniors, college seniors, graduate students, medical students, residents, and AAP members and family.
Contact Write, call, or e-mail Mary McGowan, Internship Coordinator. Phone: 202-347-8600. E-mail: mmcgowan@aap.org. Applicants must submit letter of interest; see Web site for details. Applications are accepted continuously. World Wide Web: http://www.aap.org/advocacy/washing/intern.html.

AMERICAN CANCER SOCIETY NATIONAL HOME OFFICE
1599 Clifton Road, NE
Atlanta, Georgia 30329

General Information Nationwide, community-based voluntary health organization dedicated to eliminating cancer as a major health problem. Established in 1913. Number of employees: 600. Number of internship applications received each year: 200.
Internships Available ▶ *5–10 student interns:* responsibilities include assisting in challenging projects within research, education, advocacy, and patient support programs. Candidates should have computer skills, oral communication skills, organizational skills, personal interest in the field, strong interpersonal skills, written communication skills. Duration is 8 weeks or more. Position available as unpaid or at $2500 stipend per 8 weeks. Open to college sophomores, college juniors, college seniors. International applications accepted.
Benefits On-the-job training, opportunity to attend seminars/workshops, possible full-time employment, willing to act as a professional reference, willing to complete paperwork for educational credit, willing to provide letters of recommendation.
Contact Write, fax, or e-mail Kim Loccisano, Recruiter. Fax: 404-982-3677. E-mail: internships@cancer.org. No phone calls. In-person interview required. Applicants must submit a formal organization application, resume, academic transcripts, three letters of recommendation, essay. Application deadline: January 20 for spring, May 2 for summer, September 10 for fall. World Wide Web: http://www.cancer.org.

AMERICAN FOUNDATION FOR THE BLIND
11 Penn Plaza, Suite 300
New York, New York 10001

General Information Nonprofit organization with offices in Atlanta, Chicago, Dallas, San Francisco, Huntington, WV, and Washington, DC serving as the national resource for the public and for local services for blind and visually-impaired persons. Established in 1921. Number of employees: 150. Number of internship applications received each year: 5.
Internships Available ▶ *1 communications intern:* responsibilities include all facets of communications work including writing press releases, articles, letters, editing/proofreading, media follow-up, and reporting; assistance with special events and other projects as assigned. Candidates should have ability to work with others, computer skills, editing skills, organizational skills, plan to pursue career in field, writing skills. Duration is flexible. Unpaid. Open to college freshmen, college sophomores, college juniors, college seniors, recent college graduates, graduate students. ▶ *1–3 social science research assistants:* responsibilities include conducting policy research and program evaluation. Candidates should have ability to work independently, ability to work with others, computer skills, organizational skills, personal interest in the field, research skills. Duration is 1–2 semesters. Position available as unpaid or at $6-$16 per hour depending on experience (if funding permits). Open to college juniors, college seniors, recent college graduates, graduate students, law students, career changers, individuals reentering the workforce. International applications accepted.
Benefits Job counseling, names of contacts, on-the-job training, opportunity to attend seminars/workshops, possible full-time employment, willing to act as a professional reference, willing to complete paperwork for educational credit, willing to provide letters of recommendation.
Contact Write, call, fax, e-mail, or through World Wide Web site Corinne Kirchner, PhD, Director of Policy Research and Program Evaluation. Phone: 212-502-7640. Fax: 212-502-7773. E-mail: corinne@afb.net. In-person interview recommended (telephone interview accepted). Applicants must submit a resume, 2 personal references or letters of recommendation; one writing sample may be required. Applications are accepted continuously. World Wide Web: http://www.afb.org/afb.

AMERICAN LUNG ASSOCIATION OF CENTRAL FLORIDA
1333 West Colonial Drive
Orlando, Florida 32804

General Information Nonprofit health organization. Established in 1904. Number of employees: 10. Affiliate of American Lung Association, New York, New York. Number of internship applications received each year: 20.
Internships Available ▶ *1–2 health sciences interns:* responsibilities include coordinating various programs related to lung disease and assisting program director as needed. Candidates should have ability to work independently, computer skills, knowledge of field, personal interest in the field, self-motivation, strong interpersonal skills. Duration is flexible. Stipend of $500 upon completion of internship. Open to high school seniors, recent high school graduates, college freshmen, college sophomores, college juniors, college seniors, recent college graduates, graduate students, career changers, individuals reentering the workforce. ▶ *1–3 public relations/communications interns:* responsibilities include public relations, media relations, special events, fund-raising; assignments made based on intern's talents and interests. Candidates should have ability to work independently, computer skills, oral communication skills, self-motivation, strong interpersonal skills, written communication skills. Duration is flexible, typically semester-long. Stipend of $500 upon completion of internship. Open to college freshmen, college sophomores, college juniors, college seniors, recent college graduates.
Benefits Names of contacts, on-the-job training, opportunity to attend seminars/workshops, possible full-time employment, travel reimbursement, willing to act as a professional reference, willing to complete paperwork for educational credit, willing to provide letters of recommendation.
Contact Write, call, fax, or e-mail Heather Dowling, Program Manager, 1333 West Colonial Drive, Orlando, Florida 32804. Phone: 407-425-5864. Fax: 407-425-2876. E-mail: hdowling@alacf.org. In-person interview recommended (telephone interview accepted). Applicants must submit a letter of interest, resume. Applications are accepted continuously. World Wide Web: http://www.lungusa.org.

AMERICAN LUNG ASSOCIATION OF THE DISTRICT OF COLUMBIA (ALADC)
475 H Street, NW
Washington, District of Columbia 20001-2617

General Information Voluntary private health association working to prevent lung disease and promote lung health. Established in 1902. Number of employees: 10. Unit of American Lung Association, New York, New York. Number of internship applications received each year: 20.
Internships Available ▶ *1–2 communications interns:* responsibilities include assisting in researching information as requested; providing concept plans for promotion of a lung disease program or event; producing at least one news release for a program or event; maintaining program participant and contact records in database. Candidates should have computer skills, office skills, organizational skills, research skills, strong interpersonal skills, written communication skills. Duration is 2 to 3 months. Unpaid. ▶ *1 creative design/special events marketing intern:* responsibilities include assisting in production of ALADC's annual report and newsletter, designing graphics, updating Web site, and assisting with design and layout of brochures and other promotional and educational materials; assisting with development and implementation of marketing plans; conducting marketing research and analysis; maintaining marketing contacts database. Candidates should have computer skills, office skills, oral communication skills, strong interpersonal skills, written communication skills, knowledge of desktop publishing and familiarity with Internet and HTML. Duration is 4 weeks minimum. Unpaid. ▶ *1–2 program interns:* responsibilities include providing staff support to lung health, environmental health and tobacco, and asthma education programs; assisting with information research as well as production and distribution of program promotional materials; maintaining program contact records in database, and assisting

American Lung Association of the District of Columbia (ALADC) (continued)

in the coordination of health fairs; assisting with the development and implementation of marketing plans. Candidates should have computer skills, office skills, oral communication skills, organizational skills, strong interpersonal skills, written communication skills, knowledge of desktop publishing and familiarity with Internet and HTML. Duration is 2 to 3 months. Unpaid. Open to college sophomores, college juniors, college seniors, recent college graduates, graduate students, career changers. International applications accepted.

Benefits Names of contacts, on-the-job training, opportunity to attend seminars/workshops, willing to act as a professional reference, willing to complete paperwork for educational credit, willing to provide letters of recommendation, reimbursement of expenses while on official assignments.

Contact Write, fax, or e-mail Mr. Rolando Andrewn, Executive Director. Fax: 202-682-5874. E-mail: randrewn@aladc.org. No phone calls. In-person interview recommended (telephone interview accepted). Applicants must submit a letter of interest, resume, two personal references. Applications are accepted continuously. World Wide Web: http://www.aladc.org.

AMERICAN RED CROSS BLOOD SERVICES
1925 Monroe Drive, NE
Atlanta, Georgia 30324

General Information Organization responsible for collecting and distributing half of the nation's blood supply. Number of employees: 700. Branch of American Red Cross National Headquarters, Washington, District of Columbia.

Internships Available ▶ *2 interns:* responsibilities include working in various areas of the organization. Candidates should have computer skills. Duration is flexible. Unpaid. Open to college freshmen, college sophomores, college juniors, college seniors, recent college graduates, graduate students, law students, career changers.

Benefits Willing to act as a professional reference, willing to complete paperwork for educational credit, willing to provide letters of recommendation.

Contact Fax, e-mail, or through World Wide Web site Suzanne Waldron, Human Resources. Fax: 404-253-5336. E-mail: waldronsu@usa.redcross.org. Applications are accepted continuously. World Wide Web: http://www.redcross.org.

ANXIETY DISORDERS ASSOCIATION OF AMERICA
8730 Georgia Avenue, Suite 600
Silver Spring, Maryland 20910

General Information Nonprofit association dedicated to promoting the prevention, treatment, and cure of anxiety disorders. Established in 1980. Number of employees: 10. Number of internship applications received each year: 12.

Internships Available ▶ *2 administrative assistants:* responsibilities include assisting all departments with administrative duties such as typing, filing, copying, large mailings, word processing, and computer work. Candidates should have ability to work independently, computer skills, office skills, organizational skills, strong interpersonal skills, writing skills. Duration is 1 semester. Unpaid. Open to recent high school graduates, college freshmen, college sophomores, college juniors, college seniors, career changers. ▶ *Communications interns:* responsibilities include assisting in creation of a media database, production of the bimonthly newsletter (organizing article submissions, research for articles, advertiser correspondence), and development and maintenance of a photo archives and resources database. Candidates should have ability to work independently, computer skills, experience in the field, organizational skills, research skills, writing skills. Duration is flexible (15 hours per week). Unpaid. Open to college freshmen, college sophomores, college juniors, college seniors, recent college graduates. ▶ *1 government affairs intern:* responsibilities include monitoring news and legislation related to mental health issues; drafting issue briefs and legislative alerts and updates for association Web site and bimonthly newsletter; and developing online surveys to gauge constituent attitudes towards key issues. Candidates should have computer skills, knowledge of field, self-

motivation, writing skills. Duration is 1 semester. Unpaid. Open to college freshmen, college sophomores, college juniors, college seniors, recent college graduates. ▶ *2–4 marketing development interns:* responsibilities include assisting with all marketing tasks related to membership including drafting correspondence, developing new member benefits, working with membership committee, and overseeing member-related content on the Web site and in the newsletter. Candidates should have ability to work independently, ability to work with others, knowledge of field, oral communication skills, self-motivation, writing skills. Duration is flexible (16 hours per week). Unpaid. Open to college freshmen, college sophomores, college juniors, college seniors, recent college graduates, graduate students.

Benefits Names of contacts, possible full-time employment, willing to act as a professional reference, willing to complete paperwork for educational credit, willing to provide letters of recommendation.

Contact Write, call, fax, or e-mail Clare Dell'Olio, Intern Coordinator. Phone: 240-485-1001. Fax: 240-485-1035. E-mail: cdellolio@adaa.org. In-person interview recommended (telephone interview accepted). Applicants must submit a resume, writing sample. Applications are accepted continuously. World Wide Web: http://www.adaa.org.

ARIZONA HEART INSTITUTE MESA
6335 East Main Street, Suite 4
Mesa, Arizona 85205

General Information Outpatient clinic dedicated to prevention and treatment of heart and vascular diseases. Established in 1975. Number of employees: 30. Division of Arizona Heart Institute, Phoenix, Arizona. Number of internship applications received each year: 25.

Internships Available ▶ *6–8 exercise physiology interns (undergraduate):* responsibilities include completing flow chart of experiences and observations; participating in Phase II and III cardiovascular rehabilitation program; patient education, supervision, and follow-up. Candidates should have computer skills, knowledge of field, oral communication skills, strong interpersonal skills, current CPR certification. Duration is 350–700 hours. Unpaid. Open to college seniors, recent college graduates, graduate students. ▶ *2 graduate exercise physiology interns (cardiovascular conditioning):* responsibilities include completing flow chart of clinical observations and experiences, participating in operation of Phase II and III cardiovascular rehabilitation program, and supervising and instructing undergraduate interns. Candidates should have college degree in related field, computer skills, knowledge of field, oral communication skills, strong interpersonal skills, current CPR certification. Duration is September to December or January to April. Unpaid. Open to recent college graduates, graduate students. International applications accepted.

Benefits Formal training, on-the-job training, opportunity to attend seminars/workshops, possible full-time employment, willing to act as a professional reference, willing to complete paperwork for educational credit, willing to provide letters of recommendation, occasional free meals.

Contact Call, fax, or e-mail Denise Gonzales, Program Director, Cardiovascular Conditioning, 6335 East Main Street, Suite 4, Mesa, Arizona 85205. Phone: 480-641-5400. Fax: 480-218-4353. E-mail: dgonzales@azheart.com. In-person interview recommended. Applicants must submit a formal organization application, letter of interest, resume, academic transcripts, two letters of recommendation. Applications are accepted continuously. World Wide Web: http://www.azheart.com.

ARTHRITIS FOUNDATION, NORTHERN CALIFORNIA CHAPTER
657 Mission Street, Suite 603
San Francisco, California 94105

General Information Foundation that seeks to improve lives through leadership in the prevention, control, and cure of arthritis and related diseases. Established in 1948. Number of employees: 13. Unit of Arthritis Foundation, Atlanta, Georgia. Number of internship applications received each year: 40.

Internships Available ▶ *6–8 summer science fellowship interns:* responsibilities include working on arthritis research in laboratory. Candidates should have ability to work with others, knowledge of field, personal interest in the field, plan to pursue career in field. Duration is 8 weeks. $1500–$2000 per duration of internship. Open to high school seniors, recent high school graduates, college freshmen, college sophomores, college juniors, college seniors, high school juniors. International applications accepted.
Benefits Stipend, hands-on laboratory experience.
Contact Write, fax, or e-mail Molly Klarman, Community Programs Coordinator. Fax: 415-356-1240. E-mail: mklarman@arthritis.org. No phone calls. Applicants must submit a formal organization application, academic transcripts, three letters of recommendation. Application deadline: March 3. World Wide Web: http://www.arthritis.org.

BAXTER INTERNATIONAL
1 Baxter Parkway
Deerfield, Illinois 60015

General Information Worldwide leader in critical therapies for people with life-threatening conditions. Established in 1931. Number of employees: 1,300. Number of internship applications received each year: 1,000.
Internships Available ▶ *40–60 interns:* responsibilities include working in finance, engineering, human resources, research and development, marketing, and strategy. Candidates should have ability to work independently, analytical skills, computer skills, oral communication skills, organizational skills, self-motivation, strong interpersonal skills, strong leadership ability, writing skills. Duration is 3 months (May to August). Salary depends on year at school, field, or degree. Open to college sophomores, college juniors, recent college graduates, graduate students, individuals reentering the workforce.
Benefits Housing at a cost, meals at a cost, on-the-job training, opportunity to attend seminars/workshops, possible full-time employment, travel reimbursement, willing to complete paperwork for educational credit, willing to provide letters of recommendation.
Contact Write, fax, e-mail, or through World Wide Web site Ana M. Trbojevich, Manager, Global College Relations. Fax: 847-948-4494. E-mail: internships@baxter.com. No phone calls. In-person interview required. Applicants must submit a letter of interest, resume, academic transcripts. Application deadline: May 15. World Wide Web: http://www.baxter.com.

BEVERLY HEALTHCARE GREENVILLE
527 Moye Boulevard
Greenville, North Carolina 27834

General Information Long-term care facility also specializing in short-term rehabilitation for a primarily geriatric population. Established in 1964. Number of employees: 170. Division of Beverly Enterprises, Fort Smith, Arkansas. Number of internship applications received each year: 15.
Internships Available ▶ *1–2 social work interns:* responsibilities include associated duties related to social work in the health-care setting. Candidates should have declared college major in field, oral communication skills, self-motivation, strong interpersonal skills, written communication skills. Duration is flexible (as designated by program). Unpaid. Open to college juniors, college seniors. ▶ *1–2 therapeutic recreation interns:* responsibilities include associated duties related to therapeutic recreation in a health-care setting. Candidates should have ability to work independently, ability to work with others, declared college major in field, oral communication skills, self-motivation, written communication skills. Duration is 12 weeks (or as designated by program). Unpaid. Open to college juniors, college seniors, individuals seeking national certification. International applications accepted.
Benefits Formal training, job counseling, meals at a cost, names of contacts, on-the-job training, opportunity to attend seminars/workshops, willing to act as a professional reference, willing to complete paperwork for educational credit, willing to provide letters of recommendation.
Contact Write, call, fax, or e-mail Amy Smith, Recreation Services Director. Phone: 252-758-4121. Fax: 252-758-8037. E-mail: amy_smith@

beverlycorp.com. In-person interview recommended (telephone interview accepted). Applicants must submit a letter of interest, resume, two personal references, letter of recommendation, affiliation agreement with university. Applications are accepted continuously.

CAMP LA JOLLA
176 C Avenue
Coronado, California 92118

General Information Fitness and weight loss camp. Established in 1979. Number of employees: 86. Number of internship applications received each year: 75.
Internships Available ▶ *15–20 counselors:* responsibilities include working with campers, teaching three physical activity classes per day, and acting as counselor. Candidates should have ability to work with others, knowledge of field, organizational skills, personal interest in the field, strong leadership ability. Duration is 8–10 weeks. Position available as unpaid or paid. Open to college freshmen, college sophomores, college juniors, college seniors, recent college graduates, graduate students. International applications accepted.
Benefits Free housing, free meals, names of contacts, on-the-job training, willing to complete paperwork for educational credit, willing to provide letters of recommendation.
Contact Write, call, fax, e-mail, or through World Wide Web site Donna Volpe, Personnel Director, 176 C Avenue, Coronado, California 92118. Phone: 800-825-8746. Fax: 619-435-8188. E-mail: staff@camplajolla.com. In-person interview recommended (telephone interview accepted). Applicants must submit a formal organization application, personal reference, letter of recommendation. Application deadline: April 1 for priority deadline; however, applications are accepted on a continuous basis. World Wide Web: http://www.camplajolla.com.

CHILDREN'S HOSPICE INTERNATIONAL
901 North Pitt Street, Suite 230
Alexandria, Virginia 22314

General Information Organization that provides advocacy and outreach services for children with life-threatening conditions and their families. Established in 1983. Number of employees: 4. Number of internship applications received each year: 20.
Internships Available ▶ *1–2 interns:* responsibilities include performing office duties, coordinating resources, disseminating information, and working on special projects. Candidates should have computer skills, oral communication skills, organizational skills, strong interpersonal skills, written communication skills. Duration is flexible. Unpaid. Open to college freshmen, college sophomores, college juniors, college seniors, recent college graduates, graduate students, law students, career changers, individuals reentering the workforce. ▶ *1 receptionist/administrative assistant:* responsibilities include answering information requests, performing general office activities, and preparing mailings. Candidates should have computer skills, editing skills, oral communication skills, organizational skills, research skills, self-motivation. Unpaid. Open to high school students, recent high school graduates, college freshmen, college sophomores, college juniors, college seniors, recent college graduates, graduate students, law students, career changers, individuals reentering the workforce. International applications accepted.
Benefits On-the-job training, opportunity to attend seminars/workshops, possible full-time employment, willing to complete paperwork for educational credit, willing to provide letters of recommendation.
Contact Write, call, fax, or e-mail Ann Armstrong-Dailey, Founding Director. Phone: 703-684-0330. Fax: 703-684-0226. E-mail: chiorg@aol.com. In-person interview recommended (telephone interview accepted). Applicants must submit a letter of interest, resume. Application deadline: March 1 for summer, December 15 for spring. World Wide Web: http://www.chionline.org.

CLINICAL DIRECTORS NETWORK, INC.
54 West 39th Street, 11th Floor
New York, New York 10018

General Information Nonprofit network that arranges conferences, workshops, and training for clinicians research; emphasizes clinical trials, health-care services, research and development, and finding alternative treatments for AIDS through community programs. Established in 1985. Number of employees: 15. Number of internship applications received each year: 75.

Internships Available ▶ *1 AIDS program intern:* responsibilities include gathering and entering information into the database and assisting at a health center. Candidates should have ability to work independently, college courses in field, personal interest in the field, strong interpersonal skills, computer literacy in IBM-compatible programs, interest in public health and/or public administration. Duration is 1 summer to 1 year. Unpaid. Open to recent high school graduates, college freshmen, college sophomores, college juniors, college seniors, recent college graduates, graduate students. ▶ *1–2 administrative interns:* responsibilities include setting up conferences, preparing contacts, making hotel arrangements, data entry, and assisting in fund-raising events. Candidates should have ability to work independently, analytical skills, office skills, oral communication skills, organizational skills, self-motivation, strong interpersonal skills, written communication skills, computer literacy in IBM-related programs, interest in public health and/or public administration. Duration is year-round. Unpaid. Open to recent high school graduates, college freshmen, college sophomores, college juniors, college seniors, recent college graduates, individuals reentering the workforce. ▶ *1–2 asthma/SMART/cardiovascular interns:* responsibilities include assisting coordinator with health centers. Candidates should have ability to work independently, analytical skills, college courses in field, office skills, oral communication skills, personal interest in the field, research skills, self-motivation, strong interpersonal skills, written communication skills, computer literacy in IBM-related programs, interest in public health and/or public administration. Duration is year-round. Unpaid. Open to recent high school graduates, college freshmen, college sophomores, college juniors, college seniors, recent college graduates, graduate students. ▶ *1–2 marketing interns:* responsibilities include assisting in the marketing department, research for future conference sponsors, and developing marketing tools. Candidates should have ability to work independently, declared college major in field, office skills, oral communication skills, organizational skills, self-motivation, strong interpersonal skills, written communication skills, computer literacy in IBM-compatible programs, interest in public health and/or public administration. Duration is year-round. Unpaid. Open to college freshmen, college sophomores, college juniors, college seniors, recent college graduates. ▶ *4–6 research programs interns:* responsibilities include assisting research program coordinator with administrative and research tasks at office and health centers. Candidates should have ability to work independently, analytical skills, oral communication skills, organizational skills, plan to pursue career in field, research skills, self-motivation, strong interpersonal skills, written communication skills, computer literacy in IBM-compatible programs, interest in public health and/or public administration. Duration is year-round. Unpaid. Open to recent high school graduates, college freshmen, college sophomores, college juniors, college seniors, recent college graduates, graduate students. International applications accepted.

Benefits On-the-job training, opportunity to attend seminars/workshops, willing to act as a professional reference, willing to complete paperwork for educational credit, willing to provide letters of recommendation, networking opportunities.

Contact Write, fax, e-mail, or through World Wide Web site Internship Department, 54 West 39 Street, 11th Floor, New York, New York 10018. Fax: 212-382-0669. E-mail: info@cdnetwork.org. No phone calls. In-person interview required. Applicants must submit a formal organization application, letter of interest, resume. Applications are accepted continuously. World Wide Web: http://www.cdnetwork.org.

COUNCIL ON ALCOHOLISM AND DRUG ABUSE
232 East Canon Perdido
Santa Barbara, California 93101

General Information Organization that actively provides prevention, education, intervention, referral and treatment services throughout Santa Barbara County. Established in 1949. Number of employees: 125. Affiliate of National Council on Alcoholism (NCA). Number of internship applications received each year: 25.

Internships Available ▶ *Perinatal Program interns:* responsibilities include assisting in childcare, daycare, and parenting skills activities and other duties assigned by childcare specialist or perinatal manager. Candidates should have college courses in field, experience in the field, personal interest in the field, strong interpersonal skills, written communication skills. Unpaid. Open to college freshmen, college sophomores, college juniors, college seniors, recent college graduates, graduate students, law students, career changers, individuals reentering the workforce. ▶ *Teen Court Program interns.* Candidates should have ability to work with others, oral communication skills, plan to pursue career in field, self-motivation, written communication skills, ability to work well with at-risk youth. Duration is 6 months (8-10 hours per week). Unpaid. Open to college sophomores, college juniors, college seniors, recent college graduates, graduate students, law students, only those working toward bachelor's degree or have degree in related field. ▶ *1–3 coordinators for special events interns:* responsibilities include coordination of multiple special events for youth and families. Candidates should have ability to work independently, editing skills, office skills, oral communication skills, organizational skills, self-motivation, strong interpersonal skills, writing skills. Duration is flexible. Unpaid. Open to college freshmen, college sophomores, college juniors, college seniors, recent college graduates. ▶ *Information and referral counselors.* Candidates should have knowledge of field, oral communication skills, personal interest in the field, strong interpersonal skills, written communication skills, six months of sobriety required. Duration is 2 hours per week. Unpaid. Open to recent high school graduates, college freshmen, college sophomores, college juniors, college seniors, recent college graduates, graduate students, law students, career changers, individuals reentering the workforce. International applications accepted.

Benefits Job counseling, on-the-job training, opportunity to attend seminars/workshops, possible full-time employment, willing to act as a professional reference, willing to complete paperwork for educational credit, willing to provide letters of recommendation. **Contact** Write, call, fax, or e-mail Maria Long, Director of Special Events. Phone: 805-963-1433. Fax: 805-963-4099. E-mail: mlong@cadasb.org. In-person interview recommended (telephone interview accepted). Applicants must submit a letter of interest, resume. Applications are accepted continuously. World Wide Web: http://www.sbcada.org.

THE EVANGELICAL LUTHERAN GOOD SAMARITAN SOCIETY
PO Box 5038
Sioux Falls, South Dakota 57117-5038

General Information Society that provides shelter and services to the frail elderly and others in need and operates approximately 250 nursing centers and residential facilities throughout the country. Established in 1922. Number of employees: 270. Number of internship applications received each year: 250.
Internships Available ▶ *4–6 administrators in training:* responsibilities include operating and administering a long-term care facility. Candidates should have ability to work independently, analytical skills, college courses in field, computer skills, knowledge of field, oral communication skills, organizational skills, personal interest in the field, plan to pursue career in field, self-motivation, strong interpersonal skills, strong leadership ability, written communication skills. Duration is 6–12 months. Monthly stipend. Open to college seniors, recent college graduates, graduate students, law students, career changers, individuals reentering the workforce. International applications accepted.

Benefits Formal training, free meals, health insurance, on-the-job training, opportunity to attend seminars/workshops, possible full-time employment, travel reimbursement, willing to complete paperwork for educational credit.

Contact Write, call, fax, or e-mail Dean Mertz, Vice President for Human Resources, 4800 West 57th Street, Sioux Falls, South Dakota 57117-5038. Phone: 605-362-3100 Ext. 120. Fax: 605-362-3240. E-mail: dmertz@good-sam.com. In-person interview required. Applicants must submit a formal organization application, letter of interest, resume, academic transcripts, three personal references. Applications are accepted continuously. World Wide Web: http://www.good-sam.com.

EXTENDICARE HEALTH SERVICES, INC.
111 West Michigan Street
Milwaukee, Wisconsin 53203

General Information Nationwide operator of over 200 long-term care, subacute, and assisted living facilities. Established in 1968. Number of employees: 350. Subsidiary of Extendicare, Inc., Markham, Ontario, Canada. Number of internship applications received each year: 100.

Internships Available ▶ *5 accounting analysts:* responsibilities include working in accounts payable, tax accounts receivable, and general accounting. Candidates should have ability to work with others, office skills, organizational skills, research skills, self-motivation, knowledge of Microsoft Access and Excel (helpful). Duration is May to August. $10–$12 per hour. Open to college juniors, college seniors, recent college graduates. ▶ *5 administrators in training:* responsibilities include preparing to take the licensure exam to become a nursing home administrator. Candidates should have ability to work independently, analytical skills, oral communication skills, organizational skills, plan to pursue career in field, self-motivation, strong interpersonal skills, strong leadership ability, written communication skills, prior experience in the service or health-care industry (preferred). Duration is 6 months. Paid. Open to college seniors, recent college graduates, graduate students, law students, career changers.

Benefits Possible full-time employment.

Contact Write, call, fax, or e-mail Angela Komarek, Human Resources. Phone: 414-908-8418. Fax: 414-908-8143. E-mail: akomarek@extendicare.com. Telephone interview required. Applicants must submit a letter of interest, resume, in-person interview (travel expenses paid) for finalists. Application deadline: May 15 for summer. World Wide Web: http://www.extendicare.com.

FAMILY SERVICE BUREAU OF NEWARK
393 Central Avenue
Newark, New Jersey 07103

General Information Behavioral health organization providing counseling to all ages concerning most mental health issues; psychiatrist available; substance abuse programs. Established in 1882. Number of employees: 30. Affiliate of New Community Corporation, Newark, New York. Number of internship applications received each year: 20.

Internships Available ▶ *1–2 clerical interns:* responsibilities include answering phones, scheduling clients, setting up files, typing, copying, and collating. Candidates should have ability to work independently, knowledge of field, organizational skills, self-motivation, strong interpersonal skills. Unpaid. Open to high school students, recent high school graduates, college freshmen, college sophomores, college juniors, college seniors, recent college graduates, graduate students, law students, career changers, individuals reentering the workforce. ▶ *2–3 marriage and family therapy interns:* responsibilities include telephone intakes; face-to-face intakes; individual/couple/family/group counseling; working in agency committees; collaborating with other service providers. Candidates should have ability to work independently, ability to work with others, declared college major in field, oral communication skills, self-motivation, written communication skills. Duration is 1 year. Unpaid. Open to graduate students. ▶ *4–5 master social work interns:* responsibilities include telephone intakes; face-to-face intakes; individual/couple/family/group counseling; participating on agency committees; collaborating with

other service providers; administrative track student would work in policy; procedures; grant proposals; strengthening relationships with other service providers. Candidates should have ability to work independently, ability to work with others, declared college major in field, oral communication skills, self-motivation, written communication skills. Duration is 1-2 semesters; may be year-round. Unpaid. Open to graduate students. ▶ *1–2 substance abuse counselor interns:* responsibilities include assessment and treatment of suspected/known substance abusers of all ages; facilitating groups; working collaboratively with other community service providers; assisting in program development; working with other agency professionals to provide comprehensive services. Candidates should have ability to work independently, ability to work with others, oral communication skills, plan to pursue career in field, self-motivation, written communication skills. Duration is 1 year. Unpaid. Open to college freshmen, college sophomores, college juniors, college seniors, recent college graduates, graduate students, career changers, individuals reentering the workforce. International applications accepted.

Benefits On-the-job training, opportunity to attend seminars/workshops, possible full-time employment, willing to act as a professional reference, willing to complete paperwork for educational credit, willing to provide letters of recommendation, willing to work in collaboration with intern's academic program.

Contact Write, fax, or e-mail Linda Combs, Training Director, Newark, New Jersey 07103. Fax: 732-484-3452. E-mail: lcombs@newcommunity.org. No phone calls. In-person interview required. Applicants must submit a formal organization application, resume, two personal references. Applications are accepted continuously. World Wide Web: http://www.newcommunity.org.

FEMINIST HEALTH CENTER OF PORTSMOUTH, INC.
559 Portsmouth Avenue, PO Box 456
Greenland, New Hampshire 03840

General Information Free-standing, nonprofit clinic providing the following services: GYN care, primary care, abortions, STD/HIV counseling and testing, pregnancy testing, birth control, health education, and community outreach. Established in 1980. Number of employees: 20. Number of internship applications received each year: 5.

Internships Available ▶ *1–5 health-care counselors:* responsibilities include information sharing, client interviewing and assessing, communicating effectively, and utilizing strong interpersonal skills while working as part of a team in the delivery of care. Candidates should have college courses in field, oral communication skills, personal interest in the field, strong interpersonal skills, pro-choice views. Position available as unpaid or at $6.50–$9 per hour. Open to college freshmen, college sophomores, college juniors, college seniors, recent college graduates, graduate students, career changers, individuals reentering the workforce.

Benefits Formal training, job counseling, names of contacts, on-the-job training, possible full-time employment, willing to act as a professional reference, willing to complete paperwork for educational credit, willing to provide letters of recommendation.

Contact Write, call, or fax Diana Braun, Executive Director. Phone: 603-436-7588. Fax: 603-431-0451. In-person interview recommended (telephone interview accepted). Applicants must submit a letter of interest, resume, academic transcripts, three personal references, three letters of recommendation. Applications are accepted continuously.

FRONTIER NURSING SERVICE
132 FNS Drive
Wendover, Kentucky 41775

General Information Rural health-care provider; midwife and nurse practitioner educator. Established in 1925. Number of employees: 300. Number of internship applications received each year: 30.

Internships Available ▶ *4–5 "Courier" volunteers:* responsibilities include delivering supplies, hosting dinners, assisting with office work, participating in various community events, acting as teaching aide in local schools, and accompanying health care profes-

Frontier Nursing Service (continued)

sionals during daily routine. Candidates should have ability to work independently, self-motivation, strong interpersonal skills, valid driver's license, access to a car. Duration is 8–12 weeks. Unpaid. Open to recent high school graduates, college freshmen, college sophomores, college juniors, college seniors, recent college graduates, graduate students, law students, career changers, individuals reentering the workforce, individuals at least 18 years old. International applications accepted.

Benefits Housing at a cost, meals at a cost, willing to complete paperwork for educational credit, willing to provide letters of recommendation.

Contact Write, call, fax, e-mail, or through World Wide Web site Barb Gibson, Courier Coordinator. Phone: 606-672-2317. Fax: 606-672-3022. E-mail: courierprogram@yahoo.com. Telephone interview required. Applicants must submit a formal organization application, three letters of recommendation, $250 room and board fee to be paid by applicant or applicant's college/school (upon acceptance). Applications are accepted continuously. World Wide Web: http://www.frontiernursing.org.

GLOBAL HEALTH ACTION
PO Box 15086
Atlanta, Georgia 30333

General Information Organization that sponsors health leadership and management training programs around the globe; community development and empowerment. Established in 1972. Number of employees: 12. Number of internship applications received each year: 300.

Internships Available ▶ *1 fund-raising/development intern:* responsibilities include conducting prospect research; updating donor/prospect files; assisting with special events, production of collateral materials, and correspondence and mailings. Candidates should have computer skills, knowledge of field, organizational skills, plan to pursue career in field, research skills, strong interpersonal skills, written communication skills. Duration is January to May or August to December (15 weeks, 10 hours per week). $300–$500 per semester. Open to college sophomores, college juniors, college seniors, graduate students. ▶ *1 fund-raising/development/public relations intern:* responsibilities include participating in development plan; conducting prospect research; updating donor/prospect files; assisting with special events, the production of collateral materials, and correspondence and mailings. Candidates should have computer skills, knowledge of field, organizational skills, plan to pursue career in field, research skills, strong interpersonal skills, written communication skills. Duration is May/June to August/September (14 weeks, 20 hours per week). $1500 per duration of internship. Open to college sophomores, college juniors, college seniors, graduate students. ▶ *1 health programs spring or fall intern:* responsibilities include analyzing and reporting on participant evaluation data; preparing general correspondence to training program applicants; supporting course participants with identified needs; creating, updating, and sending course-related promotional material; participating in program-related meetings and events; supporting course trainers with materials, classrooms, and handouts; coordinating volunteers for GHA course events; conducting research on topics relevant to GHA course development and special events. Candidates should have computer skills, organizational skills, plan to pursue career in field, research skills, strong interpersonal skills, written communication skills. Duration is January to May or August to December, (15 weeks, 10 hours per week). $300–$500 per semester. Open to college sophomores, college juniors, college seniors, graduate students. ▶ *1 health programs summer intern:* responsibilities include preparing general correspondence to training program applicants; supporting course participants with identified needs; creating, updating, and sending course-related promotional materials; participating in program-related meetings and events; supporting course trainers with materials, classrooms, and handouts; coordinating volunteers for GHA course events; conducting research on topics relevant to GHA course development and special events. Candidates should have computer skills, organizational skills, plan to pursue career in field, research skills, strong interpersonal skills, written communication skills.

Duration is May/June to August/September, (14 weeks, 20 hours per week). $1500 per duration of internship. Open to college sophomores, college juniors, college seniors, graduate students. ▶ *1 high school summer intern:* responsibilities include administrative duties, some Web-based research, and assistance with course materials. Candidates should have computer skills, office skills, oral communication skills, organizational skills, self-motivation, written communication skills. Duration is May to August (10 hours per week). Unpaid. Open to high school students, recent high school graduates. ▶ *1 marketing/public relations intern:* responsibilities include writing press releases; developing media list; pitching stories; compiling/updating presentations, photo files, and media book; coordinating speakers bureau training and materials; participating in development of marketing plan and marketing audit; Web-based research and publicity opportunities; and updating Web site. Candidates should have editing skills, knowledge of field, organizational skills, plan to pursue career in field, research skills, written communication skills. Duration is January-May or August-December (15 weeks, 10 hours per week). $300–$500 per semester. Open to college sophomores, college juniors, college seniors, graduate students. ▶ *1 marketing/public relations summer intern:* responsibilities include writing press releases; developing media list; pitching stories; compiling/updating presentations, photo files, and media book; coordinating speakers bureau training and materials; participating in development of marketing plan and marketing audit; Web-based research and publicity opportunities; and updating Web site. Candidates should have editing skills, knowledge of field, organizational skills, plan to pursue career in field, research skills, written communication skills. Duration is May/June—August/September (14 weeks, 20 hours per week). $1500 per duration of internship. Open to college sophomores, college juniors, college seniors, graduate students. International applications accepted.

Benefits On-the-job training, opportunity to attend seminars/workshops, possible full-time employment, willing to act as a professional reference, willing to complete paperwork for educational credit, willing to provide letters of recommendation, work-related travel reimbursement.

Contact Write or fax Virginia M. Thompson, Director of Administration and Finance, PO Box 15086, Atlanta, Georgia 30333. Fax: 404-634-9685. E-mail: gha@globalhealthaction.org. No phone calls. In-person interview recommended (telephone interview accepted). Applicants must submit a letter of interest, resume, one short writing sample. Application deadline: March 31 for summer, June 30 for fall, November 29 for spring. World Wide Web: http://www.globalhealthaction.org.

GOULD FARM
Box 157, 100 Gould Road
Monterey, Massachusetts 01245-0157

General Information Rural residential center providing integrated, structured rehabilitation for adults with psychiatric disorders and a continuum of services through the Boston Area Program. Established in 1913. Number of employees: 45. Number of internship applications received each year: 100.

Internships Available ▶ *1 community resources workleader:* responsibilities include helping clients to improve personal, social, and work skills. Candidates should have ability to work independently, computer skills, office skills, oral communication skills, organizational skills, strong interpersonal skills, strong leadership ability, written communication skills, public relations skills. Duration is 12 months. $250 per month. Open to college juniors, college seniors, recent college graduates, graduate students, career changers. ▶ *1–2 farm workleaders:* responsibilities include making assignments for animal care, field work, haying, and fencing; working with clients; teaching work habits and skills. Candidates should have oral communication skills, personal interest in the field, strong interpersonal skills, strong leadership ability, knowledge in the field and ability to drive farm equipment a plus. Duration is 12 months. $250 per month. Open to college juniors, college seniors, recent college graduates, graduate students. ▶ *1–2 forestry and grounds work leaders:* responsibilities include providing leadership and direction to landscaping and forestry teams, clearing forest trails, mowing lawns, trimming yards and flower gardens. Candidates should have

knowledge of field, oral communication skills, organizational skills, self-motivation, strong interpersonal skills, strong leadership ability. Duration is 12 months. $250 per month. Open to college seniors, recent college graduates, graduate students, career changers. ▶ *1 gardens workleader:* responsibilities include making assignments for maintaining the grounds and gardens, teaching work habits and skills, helping clients develop social skills. Candidates should have ability to work with others, experience in the field, oral communication skills, personal interest in the field, self-motivation, strong leadership ability. Duration is 3 months in summer. $250 per month. Open to college juniors, college seniors, recent college graduates, graduate students. ▶ *1–4 kitchen and roadside store workleaders:* responsibilities include making assignment for meals and operating restaurant; helping clients to improve work habits, work, and social skills. Candidates should have ability to work independently, experience in the field, oral communication skills, personal interest in the field, strong interpersonal skills, strong leadership ability. Duration is 12 months. $250 per month. Open to college juniors, college seniors, recent college graduates, graduate students, career changers. ▶ *1 maintenance workleader:* responsibilities include leading maintenance work groups for the upkeep/repair of residential facilities. Candidates should have experience in the field, oral communication skills, self-motivation, strong interpersonal skills, strong leadership ability, general handy person skills. Duration is 12 months. $250 per month. Open to college seniors, recent college graduates, career changers, retirees. ▶ *2–3 residential advisors:* responsibilities include working as house advisors in one of three houses; assisting with social skills, medications, goal setting, recreation, and informal counseling. Candidates should have oral communication skills, organizational skills, personal interest in the field, self-motivation, strong interpersonal skills, driver's license, college residential work a plus. Duration is 12 months. $250 per month. Open to college juniors, college seniors, recent college graduates, graduate students, career changers. ▶ *1–2 volunteer case managers (Boston program):* responsibilities include providing support to clients who have moved on from Gould Farm to more independent living, facilitating meal preparation and providing rides, helping with job searches, assisting with medication, attending meetings and training, organizing and leading activities. Candidates should have oral communication skills, personal interest in the field, self-motivation, strong interpersonal skills, strong leadership ability, driver's license required. Duration is 12 months. $250 per month. Open to college juniors, college seniors, recent college graduates, graduate students, career changers.
Benefits Formal training, free housing, free meals, health insurance, on-the-job training, opportunity to attend seminars/workshops, possible full-time employment, willing to complete paperwork for educational credit, willing to provide letters of recommendation, AmeriCorps Education Awards.
Contact Write, call, fax, e-mail, or through World Wide Web site Ms. Cynthia Meyer, Director, Human Resources, Box 157 Gould Road, Monterey, Massachusetts 01245-0157. Phone: 413-528-1804 Ext. 17. Fax: 413-528-5051. E-mail: humanresources@gouldfarm.org. In-person interview recommended (telephone interview accepted). Applicants must submit a letter of interest, resume, total of 3 references or letters of recommendation. Application deadline: February 1 for spring, March 1 for summer, June 1 for fall. World Wide Web: http://www.gouldfarm.org.

GRACIE SQUARE HOSPITAL
420 East 76th Street
New York, New York 10021

General Information Psychiatric hospital with the following inpatient services: geriatric, drug/alcohol detoxification and rehabilitation, Asian, and general psychiatric patients. Established in 1958. Number of employees: 400. Unit of New York Presbyterian Hospital Network, New York, New York. Number of internship applications received each year: 100.
Internships Available ▶ *1–2 psychology externs:* responsibilities include performing psychodiagnostic testing, individual and group psychotherapy, and attending staff meetings and workshops. Duration is September through May. $2000 per duration of internship. Open to graduate students. ▶ *1–2 psychology interns:* responsibili-

ties include attending workshops and staff meetings; doing psychodiagnostic testing and psychotherapy commensurate with skills. Duration is 10 weeks minimum from May to August; start and end dates flexible. $2000 per duration of internship. Open to college juniors, college seniors, recent college graduates, graduate students. Candidates for all positions should have ability to work independently, analytical skills, editing skills, oral communication skills, research skills, self-motivation, strong interpersonal skills, written communication skills.
Benefits On-the-job training, opportunity to attend seminars/workshops, willing to complete paperwork for educational credit, willing to provide letters of recommendation.
Contact Write, call, fax, e-mail, or through World Wide Web site Dr. Fran Luckom-Nurnberg, Director, Department of Psychological Services. Phone: 212-434-5378. Fax: 212-434-5373. E-mail: frl9006@nyp.org. In-person interview required. Applicants must submit a formal organization application, resume, academic transcripts, writing sample, two letters of recommendation. Application deadline: February 28 for summer, February 15 for academic year. World Wide Web: http://www.nygsh.org.

HARRIS COUNTY PUBLIC HEALTH AND ENVIRONMENTAL SERVICES
2223 West Loop South, #718
Houston, Texas 77027

General Information Agency that provides health inspection, education, and health care for the county excluding the City of Houston. Established in 1950. Number of employees: 200. Number of internship applications received each year: 10.
Internships Available ▶ *2–4 environment interns:* responsibilities include monitoring water, air, mosquitoes, and animals; research and other tasks. Candidates should have ability to work independently, computer skills, office skills, plan to pursue career in field, research skills, writing skills, college courses in field including environmental engineering and chemistry. Duration is 1 semester. Unpaid. Open to college seniors, recent college graduates, graduate students. ▶ *3–6 public health interns:* responsibilities include research; surveys, data entry, according to the division; pollution, animal, mosquito control, community health services, health education, and administration. Candidates should have ability to work independently, ability to work with others, computer skills, oral communication skills, plan to pursue career in field, self-motivation, written communication skills. Duration is 200 hours. Unpaid. Open to recent college graduates, graduate students. International applications accepted.
Benefits Names of contacts, on-the-job training, opportunity to attend seminars/workshops, possible full-time employment, willing to act as a professional reference, willing to complete paperwork for educational credit, willing to provide letters of recommendation.
Contact Write, call, fax, e-mail, or through World Wide Web site Lyndall Maxwell, Volunteer and Student Services Coordinator, 2223 West Loop South #718, Houston, Texas 77027. Phone: 713-439-6000. Fax: 713-439-6080. E-mail: lmaxwell@hd.co.harris.tx.us. In-person interview recommended (telephone interview accepted). Applicants must submit a formal organization application, letter of interest, resume, three personal references. Applications are accepted continuously. World Wide Web: http://www.hd.co.harris.tx.us.

HEALTH AND MEDICINE POLICY RESEARCH GROUP
29 East Madison Street, Suite 602
Chicago, Illinois 60602

General Information Nonprofit organization that performs policy research work on health-care issues affecting the poor, women, children, and the general population. Established in 1980. Number of employees: 6. Number of internship applications received each year: 30.
Internships Available ▶ *1–4 policy interns:* responsibilities include policy research, policy writing, office administration, and conference development. Candidates should have ability to work independently, analytical skills, college courses in field, computer

Health and Medicine Policy Research Group (continued)

skills, editing skills, knowledge of field, office skills, oral communication skills, organizational skills, personal interest in the field, plan to pursue career in field, research skills, self-motivation, strong interpersonal skills, written communication skills. Duration is dependent on intern's availability. Unpaid. Open to college freshmen, college sophomores, college juniors, college seniors, recent college graduates, graduate students, law students. International applications accepted.

Benefits Names of contacts, on-the-job training, opportunity to attend seminars/workshops, willing to act as a professional reference, willing to provide letters of recommendation.

Contact Write, call, fax, or e-mail Margie Schaps, Executive Director, 29 East Madison Street, Suite 602, Chicago, Illinois 60602. Phone: 312-372-4292. Fax: 312-372-2753. E-mail: info@hmprg.org. In-person interview recommended (telephone interview accepted). Applicants must submit a letter of interest, resume, writing sample, personal reference. Application deadline: January 1 for spring, April 1 for summer, October 1 for winter. World Wide Web: http://www.hmprg.org.

HEALTH CAREER OPPORTUNITY PROGRAM, RUSK INSTITUTE OF REHABILITATION MEDICINE
New York University Medical Center, 560 First Avenue, Greenberg Hall, Room C-95
New York, New York 10016

General Information Full-service rehabilitation facility. Established in 1948. Number of employees: 1,000. Unit of New York University Medical Center, New York, New York. Number of internship applications received each year: 300.

Internships Available ▶ *50–150 interns/Reader's Digest Fellows:* responsibilities include performing tasks related to either a research area or a clinical area such as nursing, rehabilitation medicine, recreation therapy, occupational therapy, physical therapy, and horticultural therapy, and attending lectures, films, demonstrations, and presentations on the various careers in rehabilitation. Candidates should have ability to work independently, analytical skills, oral communication skills, personal interest in the field, plan to pursue career in field, self-motivation, strong interpersonal skills. Duration is 4 weeks. Unpaid. Open to high school seniors, college freshmen, college sophomores, college juniors, college seniors, career changers, individuals reentering the workforce. International applications accepted.

Benefits Formal training, meals at a cost, on-the-job training, opportunity to attend seminars/workshops, willing to provide letters of recommendation, housing provided at $575 for the months of June and July.

Contact Write, call, fax, or e-mail Mr. Glenn Goldfinger, Director, HCOP, New York University Medical Center, 560 First Avenue, Greenberg Hall, C-95, New York, New York 10016. Phone: 212-263-6496. Fax: 212-263-0750. E-mail: hcop@med.nyu.edu. Applicants must submit a formal organization application, letter of interest, resume, writing sample, personal reference, letter of recommendation. Application deadline: March 1 for summer fellows/interns.

HEALTH FITNESS CORPORATION AT GE CORPORATE HEADQUARTERS
3135 Easton Turnpike
Fairfield, Connecticut 06431

General Information Corporate health and fitness facility. Established in 1982. Number of employees: 2. Branch of Health Fitness Corporation, Minneapolis, Minnesota. Number of internship applications received each year: 12.

Internships Available ▶ *1–2 health and fitness interns:* responsibilities include assisting in the daily operation of the fitness facility, including fitness testing, program orientation, one-on-one training, group exercise classes, and development of motivational and health education programs. Candidates should have college courses in field, oral communication skills, personal interest in the field, self-motivation, strong interpersonal skills, CPR certification. Dura-

tion is 12–15 weeks. Position available as unpaid or paid. Open to college seniors, recent college graduates, graduate students. International applications accepted.

Benefits Possible full-time employment, willing to act as a professional reference, willing to complete paperwork for educational credit, willing to provide letters of recommendation.

Contact Write, call, fax, or e-mail Carrie Williams, Assistant Program Director/Intern Coordinator. Phone: 203-373-2183. Fax: 203-373-3131. E-mail: carrie.williams@corporate.ge.com. In-person interview recommended (telephone interview accepted). Applicants must submit a letter of interest, resume. Application deadline: April 1 for summer, July 1 for fall, October 31 for spring.

INDIAN HEALTH SERVICE
801 Thompson
Rockville, Maryland 20852

General Information Provider of health care to over 1.5 million American Indians and Alaska Natives; seeks to elevate health status to the highest level possible. Established in 1955. Number of employees: 375. Unit of Department of Health and Human Services, Washington, District of Columbia. Number of internship applications received each year: 180.

Internships Available ▶ *1–20 COSTEP externs (commissioned corps):* responsibilities include assisting an administrative or health professional in carrying out the program. Candidates should have ability to work independently, ability to work with others, declared college major in field, plan to pursue career in field, self-motivation, strong leadership ability. Duration is 120 days. Salary depends on experience and college credit. Open to college juniors, college seniors. ▶ *180 civil interns:* responsibilities include working in area in health profession related to intern's course of study. Candidates should have analytical skills, declared college major in field, knowledge of field, oral communication skills, self-motivation, written communication skills. Duration is 120 days. Paid. Open to college sophomores, college juniors, college seniors.

Benefits Job counseling, names of contacts, on-the-job training, possible full-time employment, travel reimbursement, willing to provide letters of recommendation, tuition assistance for students who receive an Indian Health Service scholarship.

Contact Write, call, fax, or e-mail Vickye M. Santiago, Intern Coordinator. Phone: 301-443-6197. Fax: 301-443-6048. E-mail: vsantiag@hqe.ihs.gov. Applicants must submit a letter of interest, resume, academic transcripts, proof of Indian eligibility (if needed). Application deadline: March 15 for summer, July 15 for winter. World Wide Web: http://www.ihs.gov.

INNISFREE VILLAGE
5505 Walnut Level Road
Crozet, Virginia 22932

General Information Lifesharing community with adults with disabilities. Established in 1971. Number of employees: 12. Number of internship applications received each year: 25.

Internships Available ▶ *5–10 residential counselors:* responsibilities include living in family-style homes with 3–8 coworkers (adults with mental disabilities); caring for personal needs and helping to run the house; assisting in therapeutic workstations of weavery, woodwork, cooking, baking, and gardening. Candidates should have ability to work independently, ability to work with others, oral communication skills, patience, flexibility. Duration is minimum of one year. $215 monthly stipend. Open to individuals 21 years old and over. International applications accepted.

Benefits Free housing, free meals, health insurance, on-the-job training, willing to provide letters of recommendation, 15 vacation days paid at $45 per day.

Contact Write, call, fax, e-mail, or through World Wide Web site Nancy Chappell, Community Coordinator. Phone: 434-823-5400. Fax: 434-823-5027. E-mail: innisfreevillage@prodigy.net. In-person interview recommended (telephone interview accepted). Applicants must submit a formal organization application, three personal references, police record and TB test required. Applications are accepted continuously. World Wide Web: http://www.avenue.org/innisfree.

INSTITUTE FOR MENTAL HEALTH INITIATIVES
2175 K Street, NW, Suite 700
Washington, District of Columbia 20037

General Information   Not-for-profit organization promoting mental health by making the latest research accessible and understandable to the general public and the media industry. Established in 1982. Number of employees: 10. Unit of The George Washington University, Washington, District of Columbia. Number of internship applications received each year: 35.

Internships Available ► *1 business intern:* responsibilities include supporting IMHI's staff in general office management as well as fiscal and personnel budgeting and management. Duration is flexible. Unpaid. ► *1 community intervention intern:* responsibilities include supporting programs directed toward community interventions including IMHI's RETHINK anger management program and resilience interventions. Duration is flexible. Unpaid. ► *1 development intern:* responsibilities include assisting staff in development phase of projects and support IMHI's fund-raising efforts. Duration is flexible. Unpaid. ► *1 media intern:* responsibilities include assisting media team in design and implementation of media projects including IMHI's publication, "Dialogue" as well as the development of relationships with media professionals. Duration is flexible. Unpaid. Candidates for all positions should have ability to work independently, ability to work with others, oral communication skills, organizational skills, self-motivation, written communication skills. Open to college freshmen, college sophomores, college juniors, college seniors, recent college graduates, graduate students. International applications accepted.

Benefits   Names of contacts, opportunity to attend seminars/workshops, possible full-time employment, willing to complete paperwork for educational credit, willing to provide letters of recommendation.

Contact   Write, call, fax, e-mail, or through World Wide Web site Intern Coordinator. Phone: 202-467-2285. Fax: 202-467-2289. E-mail: imhi-info@gwumc.edu. In-person interview recommended (telephone interview accepted). Applicants must submit a letter of interest, resume, two personal references, 1-2 page writing sample. Application deadline: April 1 for summer (priority deadline), August 1 for fall, December 1 for spring. World Wide Web: http://www.imhi.org.

INTERMOUNTAIN PLANNED PARENTHOOD
721 North 29th Street
Billings, Montana 59101

General Information   Organization that serves 25,000 patients per year for birth control, cancer screening, treatment for sexually transmitted diseases, counseling, and education; the organization believes in wanted children, loving and committed parents, decisions based on knowledge, and the right to make those decisions. Established in 1969. Number of employees: 118. Affiliate of Planned Parenthood Federation of America, New York, New York. Number of internship applications received each year: 5.

Internships Available ► *Interns:* responsibilities include working in education, development, administration, patient services, or other positions; each position has varying responsibilities, duties, and requirements. Candidates should have ability to work independently, ability to work with others, computer skills, oral communication skills, personal interest in the field, self-motivation. Duration is flexible. Unpaid. Open to high school students, recent high school graduates, college freshmen, college sophomores, college juniors, college seniors, recent college graduates, graduate students, law students, career changers, individuals reentering the workforce. International applications accepted.

Benefits   On-the-job training, willing to complete paperwork for educational credit, willing to provide letters of recommendation, basic reproductive healthcare and family planning services provided free after 50 hours of work.

Contact   Write, call, fax, e-mail, or through World Wide Web site Diana Baldwin, Human Resource Director. Phone: 406-248-3636 Ext. 120. Fax: 406-254-9330. E-mail: diana.baldwin@ppfa.org. Applicants must submit a formal organization application, letter of interest, resume. Applications are accepted continuously. World Wide Web: http://www.impp.org.

KAIROS DWELLING
2945 Gull Road
Kalamazoo, Michigan 49048

General Information   Home for the terminally ill. Established in 1998. Number of employees: 4. Number of internship applications received each year: 4.

Internships Available ► *2 personal caregivers.* Candidates should have ability to work independently, personal interest in the field, self-motivation, strong interpersonal skills, loving and compassionate presence, flexibility. Duration is 2 months-1 year (minimum of 40 hours per week). Unpaid. Open to recent high school graduates, college freshmen, college sophomores, college juniors, college seniors, recent college graduates, graduate students, law students, career changers, individuals reentering the workforce, persons out of high school who are looking for a volunteer experience. International applications accepted.

Benefits   Free housing, free meals, on-the-job training, opportunity to attend seminars/workshops.

Contact   Write, call, fax, or e-mail Sue Shaw, Director. Phone: 269-381-3688. Fax: 269-388-8016. E-mail: kairosdwelling@aol.com. In-person interview recommended (telephone interview accepted). Applicants must submit a formal organization application, letter of interest, resume, three personal references, three letters of recommendation. Applications are accepted continuously.

LANCASTER GENERAL CARDIAC AND VASCULAR REHABILITATION
2100 Harrisburg Pike
Lancaster, Pennsylvania 17604

General Information   Cardiac and vascular rehabilitation unit combining exercise training to increase strength and stamina, education to reduce risk, and help with lifestyle changes for those who have experienced a cardiac event. Established in 1986. Number of employees: 12. Division of Lancaster General Heart Center, Lancaster, Pennsylvania. Number of internship applications received each year: 30.

Internships Available ► *2 exercise physiology interns:* responsibilities include actively participating in roles and responsibilities of the exercise physiologists, observing in other health-care settings, and working in conjunction with the registered nurses to provide a safe, therapeutic environment for patients. Candidates should have ability to work independently, ability to work with others, declared college major in field, oral communication skills, self-motivation. Duration is 10–14 weeks. Unpaid. Open to college seniors, recent college graduates.

Benefits   Formal training, names of contacts, on-the-job training, opportunity to attend seminars/workshops, willing to act as a professional reference, willing to complete paperwork for educational credit, willing to provide letters of recommendation.

Contact   Write, call, fax, or e-mail D.C. Clark, Exercise Physiologist. Phone: 717-290-3126. Fax: 717-290-3124. E-mail: dfclark@lancastergeneral.org. In-person interview recommended (telephone interview accepted). Applicants must submit a letter of interest, resume, academic transcripts. Applications are accepted continuously. World Wide Web: http://www.lancastergeneral.org.

L & T HEALTH AND FITNESS
7309 Arlington Boulevard #202
Falls Church, Virginia 22042

General Information   Premier provider of innovative health and fitness management services including health fitness programming, facility management, facility design consultation, and health promotional services. Established in 1984. Number of employees: 300. Number of internship applications received each year: 75.

Internships Available ► *Fitness specialist interns:* responsibilities include learning all aspects of facility management and operations, assisting staff with creation and implementation of health promotion programs, and supervising group and one-on-one fitness activities. Candidates should have ability to work independently, oral communication skills, personal interest in the field, strong interpersonal skills, writing skills. Duration is flexible. $100 per week stipend based on full-time (40 hours); $50 per week stipend

L & T Health and Fitness (continued)

based on part-time (20 hours). Open to college sophomores, college juniors, college seniors, graduate students, only those enrolled in health/fitness-related degree program. International applications accepted.

Benefits On-the-job training, opportunity to attend seminars/workshops, possible full-time employment, willing to act as a professional reference, willing to provide letters of recommendation.

Contact Write, call, fax, e-mail, or through World Wide Web site Rose Cooper, Director of Recruiting, 7309 Arlington Boulevard, #202, Falls Church, Virginia 22042. Phone: 703-204-1355 Ext. 33. Fax: 703-204-2332. E-mail: r.cooper@ltwell.com. In-person interview recommended (telephone interview accepted). Applicants must submit a formal organization application, resume. Applications are accepted continuously. World Wide Web: http://www.ltwell.com.

LIFEWISE HEALTH AND FITNESS CENTER
200 West 12th Street
Kansas City, Missouri 64105

General Information Fitness and wellness club. Established in 1985. Number of employees: 12. Branch of Saint Luke's Hospital, Kansas City, Missouri. Number of internship applications received each year: 20.

Internships Available ▶ *2 fitness specialists:* responsibilities include conducting fitness assessments, body composition, exercise prescription, personal training, facility operation, and group exercise. Candidates should have ability to work with others, college courses in field, knowledge of field, oral communication skills, personal interest in the field, plan to pursue career in field. Duration is 8–10 weeks. Unpaid. Open to college juniors, college seniors, recent college graduates. International applications accepted.

Benefits Names of contacts, on-the-job training, opportunity to attend seminars/workshops, possible full-time employment, willing to act as a professional reference, willing to complete paperwork for educational credit, willing to provide letters of recommendation.

Contact Call or e-mail Gina Hofstetter, Internship Coordinator. Phone: 816-283-0794. Fax: 816-283-3384. E-mail: ghofstetter@saint-lukes.org. In-person interview recommended (telephone interview accepted). Applicants must submit a formal organization application, resume, academic transcripts. Applications are accepted continuously. World Wide Web: http://www.saint-lukes.org.

MACOMB-OAKLAND REGIONAL CENTER, INC.
16200 19 Mile Road, PO Box 380710
Macomb, Michigan 48038-0070

General Information Internationally renowned mental health agency providing case management and clinical support services to persons with developmental disabilities and mental illness. Established in 1972. Number of employees: 500. Number of internship applications received each year: 15.

Internships Available ▶ *1–3 occupational therapy interns:* responsibilities include training/in-service; care consultation; assessments and evaluations, program planning and review; providing and monitoring adaptive and functional equipment; resource/liaison with community. Candidates should have ability to work independently, ability to work with others, computer skills, declared college major in field, self-motivation. Duration is flexible. Position available as unpaid or at $13.58 per hour. Open to college seniors. ▶ *1–5 social work interns:* responsibilities include providing case management services to a community-based population of people with developmental disabilities. Candidates should have ability to work independently, ability to work with others, college courses in field, computer skills, self-motivation. Duration is flexible. Position available as unpaid or at $15.20 per hour. Open to college juniors, college seniors. ▶ *1–3 speech and language pathology interns:* responsibilities include assessment, program planning, training; case consultation, monitoring and review. Candidates should have ability to work independently, ability to work with others, college degree in related field, self-motivation, computer skills helpful. Duration is flexible. Position available as unpaid or at $13.58 per hour. Open to graduate students. ▶ *1–2 therapeutic recreation special-*

ists: responsibilities include performing therapeutic recreation assessments; in-service training to consumers and their families, home staff, and other professionals; adapting equipment for consumers independent use; and developing programs and clinical treatments designed to assist in consumer development and independence. Candidates should have ability to work independently, ability to work with others, computer skills, declared college major in field, self-motivation, background in aquatics helpful. Duration is flexible. Position available as unpaid or at $13.58 per hour. Open to college seniors. International applications accepted.

Benefits Formal training, names of contacts, on-the-job training, opportunity to attend seminars/workshops, possible full-time employment, travel reimbursement, willing to act as a professional reference, willing to complete paperwork for educational credit, willing to provide letters of recommendation.

Contact Write or fax Peter J. Lynch, Director of Human Resources, 16200 19 Mile Road, PO Box 380710, Clinton Township 48038-0070. Fax: 586-286-3832. No phone calls. In-person interview recommended (telephone interview accepted). Applicants must submit a formal organization application, letter of interest, resume, academic transcripts. Applications are accepted continuously. World Wide Web: http://morcndc.org.

THE MAY INSTITUTE
1 Commerce Way
Norwood, Massachusetts 02062

General Information Organization with over 170 behavioral, health-care, education, and rehabilitation work sites serving 8000 individuals and families each year. Established in 1955. Number of employees: 2,000. Number of internship applications received each year: 20.

Internships Available ▶ *Classroom teachers:* responsibilities include working in a classroom setting providing direct instruction to children, adolescents, and young adults with brain injury, autism, or other developmental disabilities. Candidates should have oral communication skills, personal interest in the field, strong interpersonal skills, written communication skills. Duration is 3–6 months. $10–$12 per hour. ▶ *Residential counselors:* responsibilities include working in a group home setting providing direct instruction to children, adolescents, and young adults with autism, brain injury, or other developmental disabilities. Candidates should have ability to work with others, oral communication skills, personal interest in the field, written communication skills. Duration is 3–6 months. $10–$12 per hour. Open to recent high school graduates, college freshmen, college sophomores, college juniors, college seniors, recent college graduates, graduate students, law students, career changers, individuals reentering the workforce.

Benefits Formal training, on-the-job training, possible full-time employment, willing to act as a professional reference, willing to complete paperwork for educational credit, willing to provide letters of recommendation.

Contact Write, call, fax, or e-mail Jennifer Jenkins, College Recruiter. Phone: 781-440-0400 Ext. 285. Fax: 781-440-0414. E-mail: jjenkins@mayinstitute.org. In-person interview required. Applicants must submit a formal organization application, letter of interest, resume, two professional references. Applications are accepted continuously. World Wide Web: http://www.mayinstitute.org.

MEMORIAL HEALTH AND LIFESTYLE CENTER
111 West Jefferson
South Bend, Indiana 46601

General Information Medically-based fitness center offering personalized exercise program, recreational programs, and group exercise programming. Established in 1985. Number of employees: 30. Subsidiary of Memorial Hospital, South Bend, Indiana. Number of internship applications received each year: 2.

Internships Available ▶ *1–4 fitness specialists:* responsibilities include assisting members with fitness assessments, orientations, open/close, and educational seminars. Candidates should have college courses in field, computer skills, knowledge of field, oral communication skills, self-motivation, strong interpersonal skills. Duration is 1–6 months. Unpaid. Open to college juniors, college seniors, recent college graduates, career changers, individuals reentering the workforce. ▶ *1–4 personal trainers/wellness special-*

ists: responsibilities include personal training a variety of clientele, developing specific exercise programs, and working on educational series. Candidates should have ability to work independently, ability to work with others, knowledge of field, oral communication skills, self-motivation. Duration is 1–6 months. Unpaid. Open to college juniors, college seniors, recent college graduates. International applications accepted.

Benefits Formal training, job counseling, on-the-job training, possible full-time employment, willing to act as a professional reference, willing to complete paperwork for educational credit, willing to provide letters of recommendation.

Contact Write, call, or e-mail Maria Rearick, Fitness Manager. Phone: 219-233-7178 Ext. 302. Fax: 219-239-6458. E-mail: mrearick@ memorialsb.org. In-person interview required. Applicants must submit a letter of interest, resume, academic transcripts. Applications are accepted continuously. World Wide Web: http://www. qualityoflife.org.

NATIONAL ASSOCIATION OF ANOREXIA NERVOSA AND ASSOCIATED DISORDERS (ANAD)
PO Box 7
Highland Park, Illinois 60035

General Information National, nonprofit, educational, and self-help association offering a variety of services to aid anorexics, bulimics, compulsive eaters, and their families. Established in 1976. Number of employees: 10. Number of internship applications received each year: 70.

Internships Available ▶ *6 interns:* responsibilities include research, national hot line, correspondence with eating disorders sufferers, organizing a national conference, and coordinating and administering special projects. Candidates should have ability to work independently, oral communication skills, self-motivation, strong interpersonal skills, writing skills. Duration is flexible. Unpaid. Open to college juniors, college seniors, recent college graduates, graduate students.

Benefits On-the-job training, willing to complete paperwork for educational credit, willing to provide letters of recommendation.

Contact Write, call, fax, e-mail, or through World Wide Web site Dawn Ries, Administrator. Phone: 847-831-3438. Fax: 847-433-4632. E-mail: anad20@aol.com. Applicants must submit a letter of interest, resume. Application deadline: March for summer. World Wide Web: http://www.anad.org.

NATIONAL BRAIN TUMOR FOUNDATION
414 13th Street, Suite 700
Oakland, California 94612-2603

General Information Nonprofit health organization. Established in 1981. Number of employees: 10. Number of internship applications received each year: 6.

Internships Available ▶ *1–2 patient services interns:* responsibilities include assistance in staffing patient information line, editing, writing and producing national newsletter, and coordinating resources for national network of support groups. Candidates should have ability to work independently, knowledge of field, office skills, oral communication skills, organizational skills, plan to pursue career in field, self-motivation, strong interpersonal skills, writing skills. Duration is 3–12 months. Position available as unpaid or at Small stipend for graduate social work interns. Open to college juniors, college seniors, recent college graduates, graduate students. International applications accepted.

Benefits On-the-job training, opportunity to attend seminars/ workshops, willing to act as a professional reference, willing to complete paperwork for educational credit, willing to provide letters of recommendation.

Contact Write, call, fax, or e-mail Patient Services, Oakland. Phone: 510-839-9777. Fax: 510-839-9779. E-mail: nbtf@braintumor. org. In-person interview recommended (telephone interview accepted). Applicants must submit a letter of interest, resume. Applications are accepted continuously. World Wide Web: http:// www.braintumor.org.

NATIONAL HEALTHY MOTHERS, HEALTHY BABIES
121 North Washington Street, Suite 300
Alexandria, Virginia 22314

General Information Public health education resource coalition promoting and enhancing culturally and linguistically appropriate services for mothers, babies, and families. Established in 1981. Number of employees: 9. Number of internship applications received each year: 100.

Internships Available ▶ *8 interns:* responsibilities include drafting articles for HMHB publications; assisting with Web site and list servers; gathering information from Internet, publications, and direct contacts with members and experts; working on special projects in a core program area; administrative duties as assigned. Candidates should have oral communication skills, organizational skills, strong interpersonal skills, written communication skills, commitment to maternal and child health, knowledge of nonprofit sector, experience working with underserved populations. Duration is 3 months (20-35 hours per week). Unpaid. Open to college freshmen, college sophomores, college juniors, college seniors, recent college graduates, graduate students.

Benefits Job counseling, names of contacts, opportunity to attend seminars/workshops, willing to act as a professional reference, willing to complete paperwork for educational credit, willing to provide letters of recommendation.

Contact Write, call, fax, e-mail, or through World Wide Web site Intern Coordinator. Phone: 703-836-6110 Ext. 234. Fax: 703-836-3470. E-mail: info@hmhb.org. In-person interview recommended (telephone interview accepted). Applicants must submit a resume, cover letter, three personal references (two must be non-academic). Applications are accepted continuously. World Wide Web: http://www.hmhb.org.

NATIONAL LYMPHEDEMA NETWORK
1611 Telegraph Avenue, Suite 1111
Oakland, California 94612

General Information Nonprofit support and mutual assistance organization for sufferers of lymphedema and their caregivers, providing treatment referrals, educational materials, individual guidance counseling, support groups, and conferences. Established in 1988. Number of employees: 5. Number of internship applications received each year: 4.

Internships Available ▶ *1–2 program assistants:* responsibilities include working on variety of projects including development of chapter manuals, assisting in setting-up of local NLN chapters, establishment of nationwide speakers bureau, researching possible grant makers/funders. Candidates should have office skills, oral communication skills, organizational skills, self-motivation, strong interpersonal skills, written communication skills. Duration is flexible. Unpaid. Open to recent high school graduates, college freshmen, college sophomores, college juniors, college seniors, recent college graduates, graduate students, law students, career changers, individuals reentering the workforce, senior citizens. ▶ *1–3 project development interns:* responsibilities include various projects; development of National Speakers Bureau, grant writing, fund-raising special events, statistical analysis, on-site resource library development. Candidates should have ability to work independently, analytical skills, oral communication skills, research skills, self-motivation, writing skills. Duration is flexible (minimum of 10 hours per week for 8 weeks). Unpaid. Open to high school seniors, recent high school graduates, college freshmen, college sophomores, college juniors, college seniors, recent college graduates, graduate students, law students, career changers, disabled volunteers. International applications accepted.

Benefits Names of contacts, on-the-job training, willing to act as a professional reference, willing to complete paperwork for educational credit, willing to provide letters of recommendation.

Contact Write, call, fax, e-mail, or through World Wide Web site Megan O'Brien, Outreach Coordinator. Phone: 510-208-3200. Fax: 510-208-3110. E-mail: nln@lymphnet.org. In-person interview required. Applicants must submit a formal organization application, letter of interest, resume, personal reference. Applications are accepted continuously. World Wide Web: http://www.lymphnet. org.

NATIONAL MULTIPLE SCLEROSIS SOCIETY
1867 Lackland Hill Parkway
St. Louis, Missouri 63146

General Information Nonprofit voluntary health agency dedicated to ending the devastating effects of multiple sclerosis. Established in 1955. Number of employees: 27. Branch of National Multiple Sclerosis Society, New York, New York. Number of internship applications received each year: 50.

Internships Available ▶ *1–2 client programs interns:* responsibilities include participating in development, implementation, and documentation of services to people with multiple sclerosis. Candidates should have ability to work independently, office skills, oral communication skills, strong interpersonal skills, written communication skills. Duration is 240 hours. $500 stipend toward tuition. Open to college juniors, college seniors, graduate students. ▶ *Donor development interns:* responsibilities include assisting with the development, marketing, and implementation of the volunteer-driven campaigns. Candidates should have ability to work independently, office skills, oral communication skills, organizational skills, strong interpersonal skills, written communication skills. Duration is 240 hours. $500 stipend toward tuition. Open to college juniors, college seniors, graduate students, career changers, individuals reentering the workforce. ▶ *1 policy intern:* responsibilities include supporting the advocacy efforts of the Chapter by monitoring proposed legislation, communicating with and organizing grassroots volunteers, and various other duties. Candidates should have ability to work independently, declared college major in field, oral communication skills, organizational skills, personal interest in the field, written communication skills. Duration is spring semester only. $500 stipend toward tuition. Open to graduate students. ▶ *1–2 program department interns:* responsibilities include participating in health services promotion to people with multiple sclerosis and their families; planning, organizing, and promoting family events and wellness programs. Candidates should have ability to work independently, computer skills, office skills, oral communication skills, organizational skills, written communication skills. Duration is 240 hours. $500 stipend toward tuition. Open to college sophomores, college juniors, college seniors, graduate students, career changers, individuals reentering the workforce. ▶ *2–4 public relations interns:* responsibilities include supporting overall communications efforts of the agency including media relations, news and feature-story development, and Web site updates. Candidates should have ability to work independently, editing skills, oral communication skills, strong interpersonal skills, writing skills. Duration is 240 hours. $500 stipend toward tuition. Open to college juniors, college seniors, recent college graduates, graduate students, individuals reentering the workforce. ▶ *2–4 special events interns:* responsibilities include assisting fundraising staff with the organization, marketing, and/or implementation of the events and campaigns that make our programs possible. Candidates should have ability to work independently, office skills, oral communication skills, organizational skills, strong interpersonal skills, written communication skills. Duration is 240 hours. $500 stipend toward tuition. Open to college sophomores, college juniors, college seniors, recent college graduates, graduate students, career changers, individuals reentering the workforce. International applications accepted.

Benefits Formal training, names of contacts, on-the-job training, opportunity to attend seminars/workshops, willing to act as a professional reference, willing to complete paperwork for educational credit, willing to provide letters of recommendation.

Contact Write, call, fax, e-mail, or through World Wide Web site Victoria Love, Volunteer Development Coordinator. Phone: 314-781-9020. Fax: 314-781-1440. E-mail: victoria.love@mos.nmss.org. In-person interview recommended (telephone interview accepted). Applicants must submit a letter of interest, resume, writing sample. Applications are accepted continuously. World Wide Web: http://www.mos.nmss.org.

NATIVE AMERICAN HEALTH EDUCATION RESOURCE CENTER
PO Box 572, 809 High Street
Lake Andes, South Dakota 57356-0572

General Information Nonprofit grassroots organization committed to providing education, empowerment skills for women and children, self-help skills, and other resources to the Native American community of the Yankston Sioux Reservation, the surrounding area, and nationwide. Established in 1985. Number of employees: 17. Affiliate of Native American Community Board, Lake Andes, South Dakota.

Internships Available ▶ *1 domestic violence advocate intern:* responsibilities include sheltering, rape advocacy, support groups, outreach projects, court advocacy, referrals to other service agencies, housing referrals, and assistance getting re-established in the community after leaving abusive partners. Candidates should have ability to work independently, knowledge of field, office skills, oral communication skills, self-motivation, strong interpersonal skills. Duration is 3–12 months. $500 per month. Open to college juniors, college seniors, recent college graduates, graduate students. ▶ *1–2 reproductive health educators:* responsibilities include planning and executing a community-wide reproductive health program designated to provide health education information and workshops on reproductive tract infections (RTI's); writing public service announcements for Native radio; and coordinating focus groups and round tables. Candidates should have ability to work independently, college courses in field, computer skills, personal interest in the field, research skills, self-motivation, strong leadership ability, writing skills. Duration is 6–12 months. $1000 per month for Native Americans; $500 per month for others. Open to college juniors, college seniors, recent college graduates, graduate students, law students, Native Americans (preferred). ▶ *2–4 reproductive health educators/interns:* responsibilities include working with staff to provide support services in the various programs of the Native American Women's Health Education Resource and the Women's Lodge (shelter for battered women); developing health education materials; contributing to the newsletter; and assisting on the 24-hour youth hot line. Candidates should have ability to work independently, college courses in field, computer skills, personal interest in the field, research skills, self-motivation, strong leadership ability, writing skills. Duration is 3–12 months. $500 per month. Open to college juniors, college seniors, recent college graduates, graduate students, law students. International applications accepted.

Benefits Formal training, free housing, on-the-job training, opportunity to attend seminars/workshops, willing to act as a professional reference, willing to provide letters of recommendation, some food provided.

Contact Write, call, fax, e-mail, or through World Wide Web site Altina Mace, Internship Coordinator. Phone: 605-487-7072. Fax: 605-487-7964. E-mail: altina@charles-mix.com. Telephone interview required. Applicants must submit a letter of interest, resume, personal references. Applications are accepted continuously. World Wide Web: http://www.nativeshop.org.

NEW YORK PRESBYTERIAN HOSPITAL, WEILL CORNELL WESTCHESTER
21 Bloomingdale Road
White Plains, New York 10605

General Information Nonprofit and voluntary comprehensive psychiatric facility with inpatient, partial hospitalization, day hospital programs, clinics, and outpatient departments. Established in 1894. Number of employees: 1,000. Division of New York Presbyterian Hospital, New York, New York. Number of internship applications received each year: 50.

Internships Available ▶ *1–2 administrative volunteers:* responsibilities include working in an administrative office assisting with daily operations. Candidates should have ability to work independently, computer skills, office skills, oral communication skills, organizational skills, strong interpersonal skills, writing skills. Duration is June to August (full-time). Unpaid. ▶ *10–20 clinical volunteers:* responsibilities include working in an inpatient unit, partial hospitalized program, or day hospital program. Candidates should have ability to work independently, knowledge of field, oral communication skills, personal interest in the field, strong interpersonal skills. Duration is June to August (full-time). Unpaid. ▶ *8–10 research volunteers:* responsibilities include working on a clinical or scientific research project, collecting data, interviewing subjects, and entering data into computer. Candidates should have analytical skills, computer skills, research skills, background in biology or chemistry. Duration is June to August (full-time). Unpaid. Open to college sophomores, college juniors, college seniors, recent college graduates. International applications accepted.

Benefits Opportunity to attend seminars/workshops, possible full-time employment, willing to complete paperwork for educational credit, willing to provide letters of recommendation, participation in orientation program.

Contact Write, call, or fax Diane A. Clark, Manager, Volunteer and Patient Services, 21 Bloomingdale Road. Phone: 914-997-5780. Fax: 914-682-6909. In-person interview recommended (telephone interview accepted). Applicants must submit a formal organization application, resume, one academic and one personal letter of recommendation. Application deadline: April 1 for summer, August 1 for fall. World Wide Web: http://nyp.org.

NORTHWESTERN MEMORIAL HOSPITAL
WELLNESS INSTITUTE
251 East Huron Street
Chicago, Illinois 60611

General Information Leading academic medical center serving the entire Chicago area; an organization of caregivers who consistently aspire to high standards of quality and cost effectiveness. Established in 1972. Number of employees: 4,000. Number of internship applications received each year: 75.

Internships Available ▶ *1 intern:* responsibilities include assisting in marketing services to physicians and the Chicago community; coordinating special events to promote awareness; developing of marketing materials including letters, flyers, and promotional posters; conducting and implementing direct mailings to target markets; managing and developing marketing databases; and initiating projects as appropriate. Candidates should have ability to work independently, computer skills, declared college major in field, knowledge of field, oral communication skills, self-motivation, written communication skills. Duration is 8–12 weeks. Unpaid. Open to college seniors, recent college graduates, graduate students. International applications accepted.

Benefits Housing at a cost, names of contacts, on-the-job training, opportunity to attend seminars/workshops, possible full-time employment, travel reimbursement, willing to act as a professional reference, willing to complete paperwork for educational credit, willing to provide letters of recommendation.

Contact Write, call, or fax Leigh Ginther, Marketing Coordinator, 150 East Huron Street, Suite 1100, Chicago, Illinois 60611. Phone: 312-926-8895. Fax: 312-926-5444. In-person interview required. Applicants must submit a letter of interest, resume. Applications are accepted continuously. World Wide Web: http://www.NMH.org.

PATHWAYS
2501 West University, M/S 8018
McKinney, Texas 75071

General Information Employee association providing health and wellness benefits as well as business assistance to employees of Raytheon. Established in 1990. Number of employees: 8. Subsidiary of Raytheon Corporation, McKinney, Texas. Number of internship applications received each year: 20.

Internships Available ▶ *1 corporate fitness intern:* responsibilities include learning and using skills used by the fitness specialist; gaining knowledge in the operations of the fitness program. Candidates should have ability to work independently, oral communication skills, personal interest in the field, strong interpersonal skills, written communication skills. Duration is 480–600 hours. Position available as unpaid or at $400 per month. Open to recent high school graduates, college freshmen, college sophomores, college juniors, college seniors, recent college graduates, graduate students, career changers. ▶ *1 health promotions intern:* responsibili-

ties include participating in planning of programming designed to target employees and their wellness needs. Candidates should have ability to work independently, oral communication skills, personal interest in the field, strong interpersonal skills, written communication skills. Duration is 480–600 hours. Position available as unpaid or at $400 per month. Open to college freshmen, college sophomores, college juniors, college seniors, recent college graduates. ▶ *1 marketing intern:* responsibilities include marketing the employee association to corporate employees. Candidates should have ability to work independently, oral communication skills, organizational skills, strong interpersonal skills, written communication skills. Duration is 480–600 hours. Unpaid. Open to college sophomores, college juniors, college seniors, recent college graduates, graduate students.

Benefits Formal training, names of contacts, on-the-job training, opportunity to attend seminars/workshops, willing to act as a professional reference, willing to provide letters of recommendation.

Contact Write, fax, or e-mail Chris Schappaugh, Strength and Conditioning Coordinator. Fax: 972-952-2138. E-mail: schappaugh@raytheon.com. No phone calls. In-person interview recommended (telephone interview accepted). Applicants must submit a formal organization application, letter of interest, resume. Applications are accepted continuously. World Wide Web: http://www.pathwayswellness.org.

PLANNED PARENTHOOD OF WESTERN
PENNSYLVANIA
209 9th Street, Suite 400
Pittsburgh, Pennsylvania 15222

General Information Nonprofit organization that offers services and programs to meet the community's reproductive health care, advocacy, and educational needs. Established in 1930. Number of employees: 28. Affiliate of Planned Parenthood Federation of America, New York, New York. Number of internship applications received each year: 20.

Internships Available ▶ *1–4 general internships.* Candidates should have ability to work independently, ability to work with others, analytical skills, computer skills, office skills, oral communication skills, organizational skills, personal interest in the field, research skills, self-motivation, strong leadership ability, written communication skills, knowledge of field (helpful). Duration is 1–3 semesters. Unpaid. Open to college freshmen, college sophomores, college juniors, college seniors, recent college graduates, graduate students, career changers, individuals reentering the workforce. International applications accepted.

Benefits Opportunity to attend seminars/workshops, willing to act as a professional reference, willing to complete paperwork for educational credit, willing to provide letters of recommendation.

Contact Write, call, fax, e-mail, or through World Wide Web site Volunteer and Intern Coordinator. Phone: 412-434-8969. Fax: 412-434-8974. E-mail: volunteer@ppwp.org. In-person interview required. Applicants must submit a formal organization application, letter of interest, resume, three personal references. Applications are accepted continuously. World Wide Web: http://www.ppwp.org.

PROJECT CONCERN INTERNATIONAL
3550 Afton Road
San Diego, California 92123

General Information International health development organization. Established in 1961. Number of employees: 30. Number of internship applications received each year: 350.

Internships Available ▶ *Student internships.* Candidates should have ability to work independently, college courses in field, personal interest in the field, plan to pursue career in field, self-motivation. Duration is one fall or summer. Unpaid. Open to college freshmen, college sophomores, college juniors, college seniors, recent college graduates, graduate students, individuals reentering the workforce. International applications accepted.

Benefits Willing to act as a professional reference, willing to complete paperwork for educational credit, willing to provide letters of recommendation.

International Internships Available in Bolivia; El Salvador; Guatemala; Honduras; Indonesia; Nicaragua.

Project Concern International (continued)
Contact E-mail Lorna Reese, Volunteer and Intern Coordinator. Fax: 858-694-0294. E-mail: lhirae-reese@projectconcern.org. No phone calls. In-person interview recommended (telephone interview accepted). Applicants must submit a formal organization application, letter of interest, resume, three personal references. Applications are accepted continuously. World Wide Web: http://www.projectconcern.org.

ROSWELL PARK CANCER INSTITUTE
Elm and Carlton Streets
Buffalo, New York 14263

General Information Comprehensive cancer center with faculty in research and clinical and education studies. Established in 1898. Number of employees: 2,200. Number of internship applications received each year: 250.
Internships Available ▶ *25 summer medical student fellows.* Candidates should have oral communication skills, plan to pursue career in field, research skills, self-motivation, strong interpersonal skills. Duration is 8 weeks. $250 per week. Open to first and second year medical and dental students. ▶ *20 summer research fellows (college).* Candidates should have ability to work with others, declared college major in field, oral communication skills, plan to pursue career in field, research skills, self-motivation, written communication skills. Duration is 10 weeks. $250 per week. Open to college students in summer between junior and senior year. ▶ *25–30 summer research fellows (high school).* Candidates should have ability to work independently, ability to work with others, oral communication skills, plan to pursue career in field, research skills, self-motivation, written communication skills. Duration is 7 weeks. Position available as unpaid or at $150 per week. Open to high school students between junior and senior years, and seniors. International applications accepted.
Benefits Opportunity to attend seminars/workshops, willing to act as a professional reference, willing to provide letters of recommendation, room and board for interns from out of town.
Contact Write, call, e-mail, or through World Wide Web site Mary Wisnicki, Program Secretary. Phone: 716-845-8134. E-mail: mary.wisnicki@roswellpark.org. Applicants must submit a formal organization application, resume, academic transcripts, letter of recommendation, essay. Application deadline: February 1 for summer research fellows (college juniors), February 15 for summer research fellows (high school juniors), February 15 for first or send year medical students. Fees: $5. World Wide Web: http://www.roswellpark.org.

RUTH SHEETS ADULT CARE CENTER
228 West Edenton Street
Raleigh, North Carolina 27603

General Information Care center specializing in the care of dementia patients, most of whom have been diagnosed with Alzheimer's disease. Established in 1991. Number of employees: 4. Number of internship applications received each year: 12.
Internships Available ▶ *1–2 social work interns:* responsibilities include performing intake work and keeping progress notes, service notes, and service plans. Candidates should have ability to work independently, oral communication skills, personal interest in the field, self-motivation, strong interpersonal skills, strong leadership ability. Duration is 1 semester. Position available as unpaid or at $220 per month. Open to college freshmen, college sophomores, college juniors, college seniors.
Benefits Job counseling, names of contacts, opportunity to attend seminars/workshops, possible full-time employment, willing to complete paperwork for educational credit, willing to provide letters of recommendation, free lunches.
Contact Write, call, or fax Judith A. Shotts, Director. Phone: 919-832-7227. Fax: 919-829-5780. In-person interview recommended (telephone interview accepted). Applicants must submit a resume, two personal references, letter of recommendation. Application deadline: November 15 for spring.

UCSF AIDS HEALTH PROJECT
Box 0884
San Francisco, California 94143-0884

General Information HIV education, prevention, and counseling organization. Established in 1984. Number of employees: 105. Unit of University of California, San Francisco, San Francisco, California. Number of internship applications received each year: 80.

Internships Available ▶ *1 AHP Services Center operations intern:* responsibilities include assisting with production and dissemination of forms, flyers, notices, and manuals; assisting with data compilation for monthly statistical reports. Candidates should have ability to work with others, computer skills, office skills. Duration is one year (July 1 to June 30). Unpaid. Open to recent college graduates, graduate students, law students, career changers, college graduates with interest in health professions, social services, or nonprofit management. ▶ *3 HIV counseling and testing program interns:* responsibilities include fielding calls from individuals needing appointments or basic information; meeting clients at AHP test sites throughout San Francisco; recording client data in database (training provided). Candidates should have computer skills, oral communication skills, strong interpersonal skills, ability to do accurate data entry. Duration is one year (July 1 to June 30). Unpaid. Open to recent college graduates, graduate students, law students, career changers, individuals reentering the workforce, college graduates with interest in health professions, social services, or nonprofit management. ▶ *1 Risk Evaluation and Counseling for Health (REACH) intern:* responsibilities include assisting in all daily activities of unit; assisting in design of publicity for specialized workshops, forums, and other community events; production of brochures, newsletters, and other public relations materials. Candidates should have computer skills, office skills, strong interpersonal skills, written communication skills. Duration is one year (July 1 to June 30). Unpaid. Open to recent college graduates, graduate students, law students, career changers, college graduates with interest in health professions, social services, or nonprofit management. ▶ *1 psychological support services intern:* responsibilities include assisting with daily administrative tasks and assuring clinical staff receive needed support (training provided). Candidates should have computer skills, office skills, strong interpersonal skills. Duration is one year (July 1 to June 30). Unpaid. Open to recent college graduates, graduate students, law students, career changers, college graduates with interest in health professions, social services, or nonprofit management. ▶ *2 research program interns:* responsibilities include assisting in the day-to-day implementation of a research study; assisting in recruiting research subjects; securing informed consent; attending monthly meetings with researchers; assisting with entering, cleaning, and coding research project data; generating reports. Candidates should have computer skills, office skills, oral communication skills, strong interpersonal skills. Duration is one year (July 1 to June 30). Unpaid. Open to recent college graduates, graduate students, law students, career changers, college graduates with interest in health professions, social services, or nonprofit management. ▶ *1 training program intern:* responsibilities include researching current information regarding HIV-related statistics, psychological and legal issues, and medication updates; assisting administrators in preparation for trainings; delivering training modules under guidance of program's trainees. Candidates should have computer skills, strong interpersonal skills. Duration is one year (July 1 to June 30). Unpaid. Open to recent college graduates, graduate students, law students, career changers, college graduates with interest in health professions, social services, or nonprofit management. International applications accepted.

Benefits On-the-job training, opportunity to attend seminars/workshops, willing to act as a professional reference, willing to complete paperwork for educational credit, willing to provide letters of recommendation, $800 monthly housing stipend.

Contact Write, call, fax, e-mail, or through World Wide Web site Carol Music, Staffing Coordinator. Phone: 415-476-3890. Fax: 415-476-3613. E-mail: cmusic@itsa.ucsf.edu. Telephone interview required. Applicants must submit a formal organization application, resume. Application deadline: March 31. World Wide Web: http://www.ucsf-ahp.org.

VILLA MARIA
2300 Dulaney Valley Road
Timonium, Maryland 21093

General Information Organization that provides mental health and special education programs to children, families, and adults. Number of employees: 600. Division of Catholic Charities, Baltimore, Maryland. Number of internship applications received each year: 100.

Internships Available ▶ *15–20 educational treatment assistant interns:* responsibilities include developing and maintaining a therapeutic environment in the classroom; intern is assigned to a class setting where he/she will assist with the preparation and implementation of lesson plans under the direction of the teacher. Candidates should have ability to work independently, declared college major in field, oral communication skills, self-motivation, strong interpersonal skills. Duration is 1 semester. Unpaid. Open to college juniors, college seniors, graduate students, law students, career changers. ▶ *10–15 graduate therapists:* responsibilities include providing individual and family therapy to clients on an assigned caseload under supervision of a licensed practitioner; will be responsible for all case management responsibilities. Candidates should have ability to work independently, oral communication skills, plan to pursue career in field, strong interpersonal skills, written communication skills. Duration is 1 to 2 semesters depending on graduate program requirements. Unpaid. Open to graduate students. ▶ *10–15 residential treatment interns:* responsibilities include helping develop and maintain a therapeutic environment for children; involves creating opportunities for corrective emotional experiences and socialization as well as fostering relationships that promote development and growth. Candidates should have ability to work independently, declared college major in field, oral communication skills, self-motivation, strong interpersonal skills. Duration is minimum of 100 hours. Unpaid. Open to college juniors, college seniors, recent college graduates, graduate students, law students, career changers. ▶ *2–4 therapeutic after school program assistants:* responsibilities include assisting in activity programming; transportation and general supervision of children ages 5-13. Candidates should have ability to work independently, college courses in field, oral communication skills, self-motivation, strong interpersonal skills. Duration is 1 semester. Unpaid. Open to college juniors, college seniors, recent college graduates, graduate students, law students, career changers. International applications accepted.

Benefits Formal training, free meals, job counseling, on-the-job training, opportunity to attend seminars/workshops, possible full-time employment, willing to act as a professional reference, willing to complete paperwork for educational credit, willing to provide letters of recommendation.

Contact Write, call, fax, or e-mail Carol Shear, Director of Volunteer Services, 2300 Dulaney Valley Road (Villa Maria), Timonium 21093. Phone: 410-252-4700. Fax: 410-252-3040. E-mail: cshear@catholiccharities-md.org. In-person interview recommended (telephone interview accepted). Applicants must submit a formal organization application, resume, academic transcripts, three personal references, letter of recommendation. Applications are accepted continuously.

VISITING NURSE SERVICE OF NEW YORK
107 East 70th Street
New York, New York 10021

General Information Full-service home health-care organization. Established in 1893. Number of employees: 8,000. Number of internship applications received each year: 15.

Internships Available ▶ *1 foundation research and communications intern:* responsibilities include researching and drafting/creating grant proposals and reports for current donors; researching donors (corporations and foundations) through a variety of sources; working internally and externally to increase funding revenue. Candidates should have ability to work independently, computer skills, oral communication skills, personal interest in the field, research skills, self-motivation, writing skills. Duration is year-round (minimum of 3 months). Position available as unpaid or paid. Open to college juniors, college seniors, recent college graduates, graduate students, career changers. ▶ *1 marketing and*

community relations intern: responsibilities include conducting research on corporate, foundation, and individual donors; preparing donor and prospect profiles; drafting fund-raising correspondence including solicitation materials, acknowledgement letters, and VNSNY fact sheets. Candidates should have computer skills, oral communication skills, personal interest in the field, research skills, self-motivation, written communication skills. Duration is year-round (minimum of 3 months). Position available as unpaid or paid.

Benefits On-the-job training, willing to act as a professional reference, willing to provide letters of recommendation, education grant/stipend.

Contact Write, call, fax, or e-mail Michael Ambrosini, Volunteer Coordinator. Phone: 212-794-6342. Fax: 212-794-6480. E-mail: kharrington@vnsny.org. Applicants must submit a resume, two personal references, two letters of recommendation. Applications are accepted continuously. World Wide Web: http://www.vnsny.org.

YMCA NEW HORIZONS
12831 Newport Avenue, Suite 250
Tustin, California 92780

General Information Organization serving the developmentally disabled in Orange County. Established in 1972. Number of employees: 300. Branch of YMCA of Orange County, Tustin, California. Number of internship applications received each year: 30.

Internships Available ▶ *2–4 counselors:* responsibilities include counseling new horizons participants, supervising clients, initiating program scheduled activities. Candidates should have ability to work with others, oral communication skills, self-motivation, strong leadership ability. Duration is 3–6 months. Unpaid. Open to high school students, recent high school graduates, college freshmen, college sophomores, college juniors, college seniors, recent college graduates, graduate students, law students, career changers, individuals reentering the workforce, court referral. International applications accepted.

Benefits Free meals, job counseling, possible full-time employment, willing to act as a professional reference, willing to complete paperwork for educational credit, willing to provide letters of recommendation, certification.

Contact Call or e-mail Catherine Doezie, Program Coordinator. Phone: 714-838-0181. Fax: 714-838-6478. E-mail: crupp@ymcaoc. net. In-person interview recommended (telephone interview accepted). Applicants must submit a formal organization application. Applications are accepted continuously. World Wide Web: http://www.ymcaoc.org.

SOCIAL ASSISTANCE

AFFILIATED SANTE GROUP AND THE ROCK CREEK FOUNDATION
700 Roeder Road, 4th Floor
Silver Spring, Maryland 20910

General Information Behavioral health-care company utilizing students and volunteers seeking to fulfill academic and personal community service roles. Established in 1973. Number of employees: 300. Number of internship applications received each year: 500.

Internships Available ▶ *5 business and nonprofit management interns:* responsibilities include working with director of marketing on development projects, marketing campaigns, and managing referral base. Candidates should have ability to work independently, analytical skills, computer skills, declared college major in field, editing skills, knowledge of field, office skills, oral communication skills, organizational skills, personal interest in the field, plan to pursue career in field, research skills, self-motivation, strong interpersonal skills, strong leadership ability, writing skills. Duration is 3 months minimum (2 days weekly). Unpaid. Open to college juniors, college seniors, recent college graduates, gradu-

Affiliated Sante Group and the Rock Creek Foundation (continued)
ate students, career changers, individuals reentering the workforce.
▶ *5 computer volunteers/interns:* responsibilities include assessment, management, research, database maintenance, or programming. Candidates should have ability to work independently, ability to work with others, analytical skills, computer skills, editing skills, knowledge of field, office skills, organizational skills, personal interest in the field, self-motivation, writing skills. Duration is 3 months minimum (2 days weekly). Unpaid. Open to high school students, recent high school graduates, college freshmen, college sophomores, college juniors, college seniors, recent college graduates, graduate students, career changers, individuals reentering the workforce.
▶ *5 employment consultants:* responsibilities include assisting adults with disabilities to integrate into the community and on the job. Candidates should have ability to work independently, computer skills, knowledge of field, oral communication skills, organizational skills, personal interest in the field, self-motivation, strong interpersonal skills, strong leadership ability, writing skills. Duration is 3 months minimum (2 days weekly). Unpaid. Open to college juniors, college seniors, recent college graduates, graduate students, individuals reentering the workforce. ▶ *10 leadership/ volunteerism/service learning interns:* responsibilities include working with individuals with disabilities. Candidates should have ability to work independently, analytical skills, computer skills, editing skills, experience in the field, organizational skills, personal interest in the field, self-motivation, strong interpersonal skills, strong leadership ability, writing skills. Duration is 3 months minimum (2 days weekly). Unpaid. Open to high school students, recent high school graduates, college freshmen, college sophomores, college juniors, college seniors, recent college graduates, graduate students, law students, career changers, individuals reentering the workforce, participants in community volunteer programs. ▶ *5 organizational development interns:* responsibilities include working with directors and staff to conduct surveys on policy, procedures, systems of companies, meetings, and infrastructure. Candidates should have ability to work independently, analytical skills, college courses in field, computer skills, editing skills, knowledge of field, office skills, oral communication skills, organizational skills, personal interest in the field, self-motivation, strong interpersonal skills, strong leadership ability, writing skills. Duration is 3 months minimum (2 days weekly). Unpaid. Open to college juniors, college seniors, recent college graduates, graduate students, career changers, individuals reentering the workforce. ▶ *5 psychology interns:* responsibilities include developing and teaching consumer life skills such as community adaptation. Candidates should have ability to work independently, oral communication skills, organizational skills, personal interest in the field, self-motivation, strong interpersonal skills, strong leadership ability, written communication skills. Duration is 3 months minimum (2 days weekly). Unpaid. Open to college sophomores, college juniors, college seniors, recent college graduates, graduate students, career changers, individuals reentering the workforce. ▶ *5 public relations/ marketing interns:* responsibilities include marketing duties, technical writing, media networking, and special event planning. Candidates should have ability to work independently, analytical skills, computer skills, editing skills, knowledge of field, oral communication skills, organizational skills, personal interest in the field, plan to pursue career in field, research skills, self-motivation, strong interpersonal skills, strong leadership ability, writing skills, declared major in nonprofit management, mental health management, special event planning, or fund-raising. Duration is 3 months minimum (2 days weekly). Unpaid. Open to college juniors, college seniors, graduate students. ▶ *5 recreation specialists:* responsibilities include facilitating groups and assisting with community integration and special events. Candidates should have ability to work independently, computer skills, knowledge of field, oral communication skills, organizational skills, personal interest in the field, self-motivation, strong interpersonal skills, strong leadership ability, writing skills. Duration is 3 months minimum (2 days weekly). Unpaid. Open to high school seniors, recent high school graduates, college freshmen, college sophomores, college juniors, college seniors, recent college graduates, graduate students, career changers, individuals reentering the workforce, therapeutic recreation majors. ▶ *5 rehabilitation counseling interns:* responsibilities include performing assessments; case management,

attending interdisciplinary team meetings; and assisting with vocational goal planning. Candidates should have ability to work independently, analytical skills, college degree in related field, computer skills, oral communication skills, organizational skills, personal interest in the field, plan to pursue career in field, self-motivation, strong interpersonal skills, strong leadership ability, writing skills. Duration is 3 months minimum (2 days weekly). Unpaid. Open to graduate students. ▶ *3 research interns:* responsibilities include performing special research projects in behavioral applications, neuropsychology, human relations, and recreation. Candidates should have ability to work independently, analytical skills, college courses in field, computer skills, editing skills, knowledge of field, office skills, organizational skills, personal interest in the field, plan to pursue career in field, research skills, self-motivation, strong interpersonal skills, strong leadership ability, writing skills, grant writing and/or fund-raising experience (encouraged). Duration is 3 months minimum (2 days weekly). Unpaid. Open to college seniors, recent college graduates, graduate students, career changers. ▶ *10 social work/counseling interns:* responsibilities include case management, facilitating groups and one-on-one, and performing assessments. Candidates should have ability to work independently, college courses in field, knowledge of field, oral communication skills, organizational skills, personal interest in the field, plan to pursue career in field, self-motivation, strong interpersonal skills, strong leadership ability, written communication skills. Duration is 3 months minimum (2 days weekly). Unpaid. Open to college juniors, college seniors, recent college graduates, graduate students, career changers, individuals reentering the workforce. ▶ *5 student/volunteer career counselors:* responsibilities include assisting staff with interviewing students, surveying satisfaction, updating database for community referrals, and attending seminars/community collaborations. Candidates should have ability to work independently, college courses in field, computer skills, editing skills, knowledge of field, office skills, oral communication skills, organizational skills, personal interest in the field, self-motivation, strong interpersonal skills, strong leadership ability, writing skills. Duration is 3 months minimum (2 days weekly). Unpaid. Open to college freshmen, college sophomores, college juniors, college seniors, recent college graduates, graduate students, career changers, individuals reentering the workforce. International applications accepted.
Benefits Formal training, job counseling, names of contacts, on-the-job training, opportunity to attend seminars/workshops, possible full-time employment, travel reimbursement, willing to act as a professional reference, willing to complete paperwork for educational credit, willing to provide letters of recommendation, possibility of partial parking reimbursement.
International Internships Available.
Contact Write, call, fax, e-mail, or through World Wide Web site Ms. Beth Albaneze, Director of Students and Volunteers. Phone: 301-589-8303 Ext. 417. Fax: 301-589-5861. E-mail: balbaneze@santegroup.org. In-person interview required. Applicants must submit a formal organization application, letter of interest, resume, personal reference, letter of recommendation, learning contract from school, TB/physical required if in direct service; application may be downloaded from Web site. Applications are accepted continuously. World Wide Web: http://www.thesantegroup.org.

ALLIANCE FOR CHILDREN AND FAMILIES POLICY OFFICE
1701 K Street, NW, Suite 200
Washington, District of Columbia 20006-1503

General Information Organization representing nationwide voluntary nonprofit agencies that provide a wide range of services to children and families. Established in 1911. Number of employees: 6. Division of Alliance for Children and Families, Milwaukee, Wisconsin. Number of internship applications received each year: 60.
Internships Available ▶ *2–3 public policy interns:* responsibilities include monitoring and analyzing proposed legislation on child and family issues; attending congressional hearings and national advocacy coalition meetings; writing issue briefs, policy updates, and articles for monthly newsletter; assisting with planning of annual Public Policy Conference; attending staff meetings and

updating office on specific policy issue areas; assisting with national and grassroots advocacy initiatives. Candidates should have ability to work independently, analytical skills, college courses in field, oral communication skills, personal interest in the field, research skills, self-motivation, writing skills, knowledge of legislative process, familiarity with MS Windows, MS Office and Outlook, or Outlook Express. Duration is flexible. Unpaid. Open to college juniors, college seniors, recent college graduates, graduate students, law students, career changers. International applications accepted.
Benefits Names of contacts, on-the-job training, opportunity to attend seminars/workshops, willing to complete paperwork for educational credit, willing to provide letters of recommendation.
Contact Write, call, fax, or e-mail Carmen Delgado Votaw, Senior Vice President. Phone: 202-223-3447. Fax: 202-331-7476. E-mail: cvotaw@alliance1.org. In-person interview required. Applicants must submit a letter of interest, resume, writing sample. Applications are accepted continuously. World Wide Web: http://www.alliance1.org.

ALTERNATIVE HOUSE
2136 Gallows Road, Suite E
Dunn Loring, Virginia 22027

General Information Shelter and outreach program that builds on the innate strengths and resiliency of children, youth, and families through individual, group, and family interaction. Established in 1972. Number of employees: 25. Unit of Alternative House, Inc., Dunn Loring, Virginia. Number of internship applications received each year: 30.
Internships Available ▶ *1–6 emergency teen shelter interns:* responsibilities include planning and initiating recreational, educational, and group activities for youths aged 13-17; supervising youths; maintaining documentation of activities; adhering to professional standards. Candidates should have oral communication skills, self-motivation, strong interpersonal skills, strong leadership ability, written communication skills. Duration is 3–12 months. Unpaid. Open to high school seniors, recent high school graduates, college freshmen, college sophomores, college juniors, college seniors, recent college graduates, graduate students, law students, career changers, individuals reentering the workforce. ▶ *1–3 outreach programs interns:* responsibilities include implementing new programs in outreach and teen center programs; planning and initiating recreational, educational, and group activities for youths aged 13-17; networking with people within the community and other agencies; adhering to professional standards. Candidates should have ability to work independently, oral communication skills, self-motivation, strong interpersonal skills, strong leadership ability. Duration is 3–12 months. Unpaid. Open to college sophomores, college juniors, college seniors, recent college graduates, graduate students, law students, career changers. International applications accepted.
Benefits Formal training, free meals, possible full-time employment, willing to complete paperwork for educational credit, willing to provide letters of recommendation.
Contact Write, call, or fax Volunteer Coordinator. Phone: 703-820-9039. Fax: 703-820-0788. In-person interview recommended (telephone interview accepted). Applicants must submit a formal organization application, letter of interest, resume, three personal references. Application deadline: April 15 for summer, August 1 for fall, December 15 for spring.

AMERICAN RED CROSS–GREATER HARTFORD CHAPTER
209 Farmington Avenue
Farmington, Connecticut 06032

General Information Human service organization helping individuals and communities to prevent, prepare for, and respond to emergencies; programs and services include health and safety, emergency services (education and response) and blood services. Established in 1969. Number of employees: 50. Unit of American Red Cross–National Capital Chapter, Washington, District of Columbia. Number of internship applications received each year: 10.

Internships Available ▶ *1–3 communication interns:* responsibilities include researching, writing, and editing articles for newsletter "Real Heroes" and News for chapter Web site; assisting with public relations on special events and/or at the scene of a disaster. Candidates should have ability to work independently, college courses in field, computer skills, strong interpersonal skills, writing skills. Duration is 10–15 weeks (minimum 8 hours a week). Unpaid. Open to college sophomores, college juniors, college seniors, recent college graduates, career changers, individuals reentering the workforce. ▶ *1–3 community outreach interns:* responsibilities include identifying opportunities to promote services and programs within the community; helping with general outreach and network community resources focusing on Hispanic and African-American organizations and groups, helping recruit volunteers. Candidates should have ability to work independently, oral communication skills, organizational skills, self-motivation, written communication skills, Spanish-speaking ability. Duration is 10–15 weeks, (minimum 8 hours per week). Unpaid. Open to college sophomores, college juniors, college seniors. ▶ *1–2 disaster services interns (planning and preparedness):* responsibilities include working with volunteers and paid staff to increase readiness and ability to respond to meet community disaster needs; assisting with implementation of disaster programs, planning of disaster drills and exercises; coordinating volunteer recruitment, retention, and recognition. Candidates should have ability to work with others, computer skills, organizational skills, personal interest in the field, self-motivation, public speaking skills. Duration is 10–15 or more weeks, (minimum 8 hours a week). Unpaid. Open to college juniors, college seniors, recent college graduates, career changers, individuals reentering the workforce. ▶ *1 emergency services caseworker:* responsibilities include working with disaster services staff to assess client needs for Red Cross Disaster services and coordinating emergency and long-term service delivery. Candidates should have office skills, oral communication skills, self-motivation, strong interpersonal skills, written communication skills, sensitivity to various cultures/backgrounds. Duration is 10 to 15 weeks (minimum 8 hours a week). Unpaid. Open to college sophomores, college juniors, college seniors, recent college graduates, career changers. ▶ *1–2 grant writing interns:* responsibilities include researching potential sources of grant funding, compiling new prospects in system; researching, developing, and completing grant proposals to be submitted with the support of chapter staff; tracking and follow-up with existing grants in the community. Candidates should have ability to work independently, oral communication skills, research skills, self-motivation, writing skills, creativity. Duration is 10–15 weeks, or more (minimum 8 hours a week). Unpaid. Open to college juniors, college seniors, recent college graduates, career changers, individuals reentering the workforce. ▶ *1–3 health and safety services community instructors:* responsibilities include teaching first aid and CPR to members of the community. Candidates should have ability to work independently, ability to work with others, oral communication skills, personal interest in the field, self-motivation, administrative skills. Duration is 10 to 15 weeks (minimum 8 hours a week). Unpaid. Open to recent high school graduates, college freshmen, college sophomores, college juniors, college seniors, recent college graduates, career changers, individuals reentering the workforce. ▶ *1 market research intern–AED Project:* responsibilities include assisting in development of sales and marketing plan for new programs and products, including AED (automated external defibrillator); analyzing program activity, patterns, and audience motivations; establishing communications and collaborations with other agencies. Candidates should have ability to work independently, analytical skills, college courses in field, oral communication skills, organizational skills, written communication skills. Duration is 10–15 weeks. Unpaid. Open to college seniors, career changers, individuals reentering the workforce. ▶ *1 market research intern–Babysitter's Training Program:* responsibilities include establishing Babysitter's Training Program; analyzing program activity, patterns, and audience motivations; identifying current customers and competitors in order to increase participation in ARC Health Services Courses; designing and developing a data collection system; analyzing data to provide recommendations for increasing course enrollment. Candidates should have ability to work independently, college courses in field, oral com-

American Red Cross–Greater Hartford Chapter (continued)

munication skills, organizational skills, written communication skills. Duration is 10–15 weeks. Unpaid. Open to college juniors, college seniors, career changers, individuals reentering the workforce. ▶ *1–2 multi-media presentation coordinators (communication):* responsibilities include working as part of a team to develop a multi-media presentation (slide show/video/PowerPoint) to be shown at the greater Hartford chapters annual volunteer recognition event. Candidates should have ability to work with others, editing skills, knowledge of field, writing skills, knowledge of Microsoft Office and the Internet, photography skills, interview skills, knowledge of PowerPoint. Duration is 10 to 15 weeks (minimum 8 hours a week, January to May). Unpaid. Open to college sophomores, college juniors, college seniors, recent college graduates, career changers, individuals reentering the workforce. International applications accepted.

Benefits Names of contacts, on-the-job training, opportunity to attend seminars/workshops, willing to act as a professional reference, willing to complete paperwork for educational credit, willing to provide letters of recommendation, formal training possibility for certain positions.

Contact Write, call, fax, e-mail, or through World Wide Web site Anouchka Bayard-Blanchard, Manager, Youth Services. Phone: 860-678-2799. Fax: 860-678-5461. E-mail: bayarda@usa.redcross.org. In-person interview required. Applicants must submit a formal organization application, resume, two writing samples, two personal references, telephone interview acceptable for international applicants. Applications are accepted continuously. World Wide Web: http://www.greaterhartfordredcross.org.

AMERICAN RED CROSS NATIONAL HEADQUARTERS
8111 Gatehouse Road, 6th Floor
Falls Church, Virginia 22042

General Information Humanitarian organization that provides relief to victims of disasters and helps people prevent, prepare for, and respond to emergencies. Established in 1881. Number of employees: 1,000. Number of internship applications received each year: 200.

Internships Available ▶ *10–30 Presidential interns:* responsibilities include working in positions throughout NHQ including finance, government relations, biomedical services, international services, communications, health and safety, disaster, and the Holland Laboratory. Candidates should have college courses in field, oral communication skills, personal interest in the field, self-motivation, strong interpersonal skills, written communication skills. Duration is 10 weeks. $9.40 per hour. Open to college freshmen, college sophomores, college juniors, college seniors, recent college graduates, graduate students, law students.

Benefits On-the-job training, opportunity to attend seminars/workshops, possible full-time employment, willing to complete paperwork for educational credit, willing to provide letters of recommendation.

Contact Write, call, fax, e-mail, or through World Wide Web site Jennifer Carino, Diversity Associate. Phone: 703-206-8368. Fax: 703-206-8572. E-mail: carinoj@usa.redcross.org. In-person interview recommended (telephone interview accepted). Applicants must submit a letter of interest, resume. Application deadline: March 1 for summer. World Wide Web: http://www.redcross.org.

THE ARCH, INC.
175-43 Hillside Avenue
Jamaica, New York 11432

General Information Organization that provides human services through diversity education and arts outreach programs; assists at-risk communities, families, and individuals with arts performance/classes/workshops, food distribution, advocacy, stress relief, and multimedia services (by-donation). Established in 1998. Number of employees: 10. Number of internship applications received each year: 2,500.

Internships Available ▶ *2 accounting interns:* responsibilities include undertaking pro bono or reduced fee work maintaining 'The Arch' accounts, as required of a 501 (C) (3) not-for-profit

corporation. Duration is flexible. CPAs are paid. Open to high school students, recent high school graduates, college freshmen, college sophomores, college juniors, college seniors, recent college graduates, graduate students, law students, career changers, individuals reentering the workforce, certified public accountants (encouraged). ▶ *Computer support/graphics designers:* responsibilities include maintaining Web page; designing, producing, and formatting newsletters, brochures, posters, letterheads, and official letters (written by others); maintaining computer files, address book, e-mail records, and correspondence records. Candidates should have ability to work with others, organizational skills. Duration is flexible. Position available as unpaid or at up to $10 per hour. Open to high school students, recent high school graduates, college freshmen, college sophomores, college juniors, college seniors, recent college graduates, graduate students, law students, career changers, individuals reentering the workforce. ▶ *5 customer services interns:* responsibilities include attending meetings, answering phones, customer accounts, front office, and administrative duties. Candidates should have ability to work with others. Duration is flexible. Position available as unpaid or at up to $9 per hour. Open to high school students, recent high school graduates, college freshmen, college sophomores, college juniors, college seniors, recent college graduates, graduate students, law students, career changers, individuals reentering the workforce. ▶ *Grant writers:* responsibilities include researching information about potential funding sources; taking part in the process of funding, regularly sharing reports with the directors of Arch; providing detailed accounts on requirements for sources, as well as liaison with sources and funders. Duration is flexible. Position available as unpaid or paid. Open to high school students, recent high school graduates, college freshmen, college sophomores, college juniors, college seniors, recent college graduates, graduate students, law students, career changers, individuals reentering the workforce. ▶ *1–2 legal expert/advisors:* responsibilities include advising on legal issues and taking necessary action for "The Arch" on a pro bono/reduced fee basis. Candidates should have personal interest in the field, self-motivation. Duration is flexible. Unpaid. Open to practicing attorneys or law professors only. ▶ *Marketing and sales interns:* responsibilities include assisting in media market research; calling newspaper and magazine editors, radio and T.V. producers to develop a database of media contacts for the organization. Duration is flexible. Position available as unpaid or paid. Open to high school students, recent high school graduates, college freshmen, college sophomores, college juniors, college seniors, recent college graduates, graduate students, law students, career changers, individuals reentering the workforce. ▶ *Media associates (videography):* responsibilities include assisting with development of 5-minute music capsules featuring undiscovered artists for broadcast by college radio stations; archiving/documenting in multimedia. Candidates should have ability to work independently, knowledge of field. Duration is flexible. Paid up to $10 per hour. Open to high school students, recent high school graduates, college freshmen, college sophomores, college juniors, college seniors, recent college graduates, graduate students, law students, career changers, individuals reentering the workforce. ▶ *1–5 office managers:* responsibilities include light bookkeeping; receiving/disbursing funds; maintaining records and files; filing, typing, and maintaining records of correspondence, addresses, and E-mail; making telephone calls; interacting with respondents; running errands connected with office work. Candidates should have office skills, organizational skills, strong interpersonal skills. Duration is flexible. Position available as unpaid or at up to $10 hour. Open to high school students, recent high school graduates, college freshmen, college sophomores, college juniors, college seniors, recent college graduates, graduate students, law students, career changers, individuals reentering the workforce. International applications accepted.

Benefits Formal training, free meals, health insurance, job counseling, names of contacts, on-the-job training, opportunity to attend seminars/workshops, possible full-time employment, willing to act as a professional reference, willing to complete paperwork for educational credit, willing to provide letters of recommendation, fruits, vegetables, variety of bread and baked goods provided, free housing or at a discounted cost, some health care and local travel expenses.

Contact Write, call, fax, e-mail, or through World Wide Web site Craig Kaufman, Director. Phone: 718-883-7770. Fax: 718-262-8234. E-mail: kaufman@thearch.org. Applicants must submit a letter of interest, resume. Applications are accepted continuously. World Wide Web: http://www.thearch.org.

AUDUBON YMCA
2460 Boulevard of the Generals
Norristown, Pennsylvania 19403

General Information Organization that provides the community with services that promote healthy spirits, minds, and bodies. Established in 1984. Number of employees: 70. Branch of Phoenixville Area YMCA, Phoenixville, Pennsylvania. Number of internship applications received each year: 4.

Internships Available ▶ *2–5 child-care interns:* responsibilities include assisting with staffing schedules, designing lesson plans for various age groups, assisting in provider care, learning state licensing requirements, developing promotional piece for services offered. Candidates should have oral communication skills, plan to pursue career in field, self-motivation, strong interpersonal skills, strong leadership ability, written communication skills. Duration is summer or 1-3 semesters. Position available as unpaid or paid. Open to high school seniors, college freshmen, college sophomores, college juniors, college seniors, recent college graduates, individuals pursuing child-care certificates. ▶ *1–3 community and family recreation interns:* responsibilities include designing lesson plan for outdoor education, designing youth and/or family special events, creating promotional strategy for youth and/or family programs, assisting in day camp program during summer internship. Candidates should have ability to work independently, oral communication skills, personal interest in the field, self-motivation, strong interpersonal skills, strong leadership ability. Duration is summer or 1-3 semesters. Position available as unpaid or paid. Open to college freshmen, college sophomores, college juniors, college seniors, recent college graduates, PHEAA work-study eligibles. ▶ *1 technology assistant:* responsibilities include assisting with implementing computer use in child-care programs; troubleshooting computer problems in departments and administration areas; assisting with computer upgrades; instructing staff in Word, Excel, and entry-level graphics programs. Candidates should have ability to work independently, computer skills, knowledge of field, oral communication skills, self-motivation, strong interpersonal skills. Duration is 1 summer or 1-3 semesters. Position available as unpaid or paid. Open to college sophomores, college juniors, college seniors, recent college graduates, individuals reentering the workforce. ▶ *5–10 volunteers:* responsibilities include performing office duties and assisting in childcare, administration, physical education, or marketing. Candidates should have ability to work independently, office skills, oral communication skills, personal interest in the field, self-motivation, strong interpersonal skills. Duration is flexible. Unpaid. Open to college freshmen, college sophomores, college juniors, college seniors, recent college graduates, graduate students, career changers.

Benefits Job counseling, names of contacts, on-the-job training, opportunity to attend seminars/workshops, possible full-time employment, willing to complete paperwork for educational credit, willing to provide letters of recommendation.

Contact Write, call, fax, or e-mail Janet Genuardi. Phone: 610-539-0900. Fax: 610-539-2975. E-mail: jlg@net-thing.net. In-person interview recommended (telephone interview accepted). Applicants must submit a letter of interest, resume, two personal references, two letters of recommendation. Applications are accepted continuously. World Wide Web: http://www.phoenixvilleareaymca.org.

BAILEY HOUSE, INC
275 7th Avenue, 12th Floor
New York, New York 10001

General Information Nonprofit agency that provides housing and supportive services for families living with HIV and AIDS. Established in 1983. Number of employees: 80. Number of internship applications received each year: 12.

Internships Available ▶ *INVEST interns:* responsibilities include working with the INVEST Team to create and maintain innovative services to residents on projects including "The Book Club" and "Back to Work Clothing Closet". Candidates should have ability to work independently, analytical skills, computer skills, editing skills, knowledge of field, office skills, oral communication skills, organizational skills, personal interest in the field, research skills, self-motivation, strong interpersonal skills, strong leadership ability, writing skills. Unpaid. Open to high school seniors, recent high school graduates, individuals reentering the workforce. ▶ *Administrative interns:* responsibilities include providing coverage when necessary to accomplish short-term administrative tasks for all departments including greeting visitors, answering phones, forwarding messages, faxing, and creating documents. Candidates should have ability to work with others, analytical skills, computer skills, editing skills, knowledge of field, office skills, oral communication skills, organizational skills, personal interest in the field, plan to pursue career in field, research skills, self-motivation, strong leadership ability, writing skills. Unpaid. Open to high school seniors, recent high school graduates, college freshmen, college sophomores, college juniors, college seniors, recent college graduates, graduate students, law students, career changers, individuals reentering the workforce. ▶ *Volunteer service interns:* responsibilities include assisting the coordinator of volunteer services with recruitment, interviewing, and retention of volunteers and interns; assisting with the production of the volunteer newsletter, creating flyers, and organizing mass mailings; helping staff volunteers for special events and agency needs. Candidates should have ability to work independently, analytical skills, computer skills, editing skills, knowledge of field, office skills, oral communication skills, organizational skills, personal interest in the field, plan to pursue career in field, research skills, self-motivation, strong interpersonal skills, strong leadership ability, writing skills. Unpaid. Open to high school seniors, recent high school graduates, college freshmen, college sophomores, college juniors, college seniors, recent college graduates, career changers, individuals reentering the workforce.

Benefits Names of contacts, on-the-job training, travel reimbursement, willing to act as a professional reference, willing to complete paperwork for educational credit, willing to provide letters of recommendation.

Contact Write, call, fax, e-mail, or through World Wide Web site Tamesha Harper, Placement Services Manager. Phone: 212-633-2500 Ext. 215. Fax: 212-633-2932. E-mail: tharper@baileyhouse.org. In-person interview required. Applicants must submit a formal organization application, resume, two personal references. Applications are accepted continuously. World Wide Web: http://www.baileyhouse.org.

BERKSHIRE FARM CENTER AND SERVICES FOR YOUTH
Route 22
Canaan, New York 12029

General Information Nonprofit social service agency serving at-risk adolescents of New York State and their families. Established in 1886. Number of employees: 350. Number of internship applications received each year: 15.

Internships Available ▶ *10–15 teaching assistants:* responsibilities include assisting teacher in diverse subjects in public junior and high schools. Candidates should have ability to work independently, ability to work with others, oral communication skills, plan to pursue career in field, self-motivation, strong leadership ability, written communication skills, interest in at-risk adolescents. Duration is flexible. Unpaid. ▶ *Youth counselors/advocates/mentors/tutors:* responsibilities include assisting in supervision of troubled adolescents. Candidates should have personal interest in the field, self-motivation, strong interpersonal skills, interest in at-risk adolescents, possible plan to pursue career in field. Duration is flexible. Unpaid. Open to recent high school graduates, college freshmen, college sophomores, college juniors, college seniors, recent college graduates, graduate students, law students, career changers, individuals reentering the workforce. International applications accepted.

Berkshire Farm Center and Services For Youth (continued)

Benefits Formal training, free meals, job counseling, names of contacts, on-the-job training, opportunity to attend seminars/workshops, possible full-time employment, willing to act as a professional reference, willing to complete paperwork for educational credit, willing to provide letters of recommendation, opportunity to clarify career interest in field by practical experience working with at-risk adolescents.

Contact Write, call, fax, e-mail, or through World Wide Web site Lawrence "Lari" Brandstein, Director of Volunteer Services. Phone: 518-781-4567 Ext. 322. Fax: 518-781-3710. E-mail: lbrandstein@berkshirefarm.org. In-person interview recommended (telephone interview accepted). Applicants must submit a formal organization application, letter of interest, resume, three personal references. Applications are accepted continuously. World Wide Web: http://www.berkshirefarm.org.

BETHESDA LUTHERAN HOMES AND SERVICES, INC.
600 Hoffmann Drive
Watertown, Wisconsin 53094-6204

General Information Facility that provides residential and training services to individuals with developmental disabilities. Established in 1904. Number of employees: 700. Number of internship applications received each year: 21.

Internships Available ▶ *1 Camp Matz intern:* responsibilities include supervising and coordinating all activities for the Servant Event Program at Camp Matz. Candidates should have ability to work independently, ability to work with others, oral communication skills, strong leadership ability, written communication skills, camp experience desirable, Lutheran background. Duration is 12 weeks in summer. $7.50 per hour. ▶ *1 chaplaincy representative:* responsibilities include providing spiritual nurture for people with developmental disabilities, leading Bible classes, and serving as a chapel aide. Candidates should have ability to work independently, oral communication skills, personal interest in the field, strong interpersonal skills, Lutheran background. Duration is 12 weeks in summer. $7.50 per hour. ▶ *1 nursing student intern:* responsibilities include performing nursing duties designed to enhance the student's knowledge of the role of a professional nurse in a facility that provides care and treatment for people who have physical and mental disabilities. Candidates should have ability to work with others, declared college major in field, experience in the field, personal interest in the field, plan to pursue career in field. Duration is 12 weeks in summer. $7.50 per hour. ▶ *1 psychology intern:* responsibilities include assisting in preparing resident annual summaries and psychological assessments, preparing and analyzing data collection materials, assisting in the development of behavior treatment programs. Candidates should have ability to work with others, analytical skills, college courses in field, organizational skills, personal interest in the field. Duration is 12 weeks in summer. $7.50 per hour. ▶ *1 public relations intern:* responsibilities include writing articles and stories, doing layouts and photographic assignments, constructing displays, giving tours of Bethesda, and assisting with special events as required. Candidates should have ability to work with others, computer skills, editing skills, oral communication skills, plan to pursue career in field, self-motivation, writing skills. Duration is 12 weeks in summer. $7.50 per hour. ▶ *1 student social worker intern:* responsibilities include working directly with residents individually or in groups in social skill development or behavior training; assisting with writing and monitoring Individual Program Plans (in conjunction with an assigned social worker/QMRP). Candidates should have ability to work with others, college courses in field, organizational skills, personal interest in the field, plan to pursue career in field. Duration is 12 weeks in summer. $7.50 per hour. ▶ *1 student teacher intern:* responsibilities include working as a team, assisting in organizing and planning classroom activities, seeking materials and preparing for activities outlines in lesson plans, and assisting with all record keeping as assigned by the supervising teacher. Candidates should have declared college major in field, knowledge of field, personal interest in the field, plan to pursue career in

field, strong interpersonal skills, strong leadership ability. Duration is 12 weeks in summer. $7.50 per hour. Open to college juniors, college seniors, graduate students.

Benefits Formal training, free housing, meals at a cost, on-the-job training, opportunity to attend seminars/workshops, possible full-time employment, willing to act as a professional reference, willing to complete paperwork for educational credit, willing to provide letters of recommendation.

Contact Write, call, fax, e-mail, or through World Wide Web site Thomas Heuer, Coordinator, Outreach Programs and Services, 600 Hoffmann Drive. Phone: 800-369-4636. Fax: 920-262-6513. E-mail: theuer@blhs.org. In-person interview recommended (telephone interview accepted). Applicants must submit a formal organization application, two personal references, letter of recommendation, cover letter, resume desirable; preference given to Lutheran students. Application deadline: March 1 for interns. World Wide Web: http://www.blhs.org.

BIG BROTHERS BIG SISTERS OF BEAVER COUNTY
426 Adams Street
Rochester, Pennsylvania 15074

General Information Youth development agency that recruits, screens, and supervises adult volunteers in one-to-one mentoring relationships with disadvantaged school-age youth. Established in 1976. Number of employees: 8. Affiliate of Big Brothers Big Sisters of America, Philadelphia, Pennsylvania. Number of internship applications received each year: 10.

Internships Available ▶ *1–3 caseworker interns:* responsibilities include assisting caseworkers with recruitment, screening, training, supervising volunteers, and fund-raising. Candidates should have ability to work with others, college courses in field, oral communication skills, plan to pursue career in field, self-motivation. Duration is 3 months. Unpaid. Open to college sophomores, college juniors, college seniors, graduate students. International applications accepted.

Benefits On-the-job training, opportunity to attend seminars/workshops, possible full-time employment, travel reimbursement, willing to act as a professional reference, willing to complete paperwork for educational credit.

Contact Write or fax Pam Webb, Executive Director, 426 Adams Street, Suite 2, Rochester, Pennsylvania 15074. Fax: 724-728-3674. No phone calls. In-person interview required. Applicants must submit a letter of interest, resume. Applications are accepted continuously.

BIG BROTHERS BIG SISTERS OF BERRIEN & CASS, INC.
1 South Fifth, PO Box 194
Niles, Michigan 49120-0194

General Information Organization that prepares children for the future by enhancing their strengths through new experiences and friendship with qualified mentors. Established in 1967. Number of employees: 4. Unit of Big Brothers Big Sisters of America, Philadelphia, Pennsylvania. Number of internship applications received each year: 4.

Internships Available ▶ *Case work assistants:* responsibilities include supervising unmatched clients, conducting volunteer and client trainings, contributing to the agency newsletter, and membership on the Activities Committee. Candidates should have oral communication skills, plan to pursue career in field, self-motivation, strong interpersonal skills, written communication skills. Duration is flexible. Unpaid. ▶ *General office assistants:* responsibilities include general office, typing, answering phones, telemarketing and fund-raising, and filing. Candidates should have ability to work with others. Duration is flexible. Unpaid. International applications accepted.

Benefits On-the-job training, possible full-time employment, willing to act as a professional reference, willing to complete paperwork for educational credit, willing to provide letters of recommendation, approved mileage reimbursement.

Contact Write, call, fax, or e-mail Carol Milburn, Executive Director. Phone: 616-684-1100. Fax: 616-684-1490. E-mail: cmilburn@

lycos.com. In-person interview required. Applicants must submit a formal organization application, resume, two personal references. Applications are accepted continuously.

BIG BROTHERS BIG SISTERS OF BUCKS COUNTY
2875 Old York Road
Jamison, Pennsylvania 18929

General Information Organization that provides mentoring services to youth. Established in 1963. Number of employees: 23. Affiliate of Big Brothers Big Sisters of America, Philadelphia, Pennsylvania. Number of internship applications received each year: 4.
Internships Available ▶ *1 administrative intern:* responsibilities include answering telephones, data entry, providing customer service to clients, and assisting in file organization. Candidates should have ability to work independently, ability to work with others, office skills, oral communication skills, self-motivation, written communication skills. Duration is year-round (5 days per week). Unpaid. Open to high school seniors, recent high school graduates, college freshmen, college sophomores, college juniors, college seniors, recent college graduates, individuals reentering the workforce. ▶ *Case manager interns:* responsibilities include recruitment, screening, matching, and supervision of volunteers, in addition to screening, matching, and supervision of youth. Candidates should have ability to work independently, ability to work with others, college courses in field, computer skills, oral communication skills, organizational skills. Duration is year-round. Unpaid. Open to college freshmen, college sophomores, college juniors, college seniors, recent college graduates, graduate students, career changers, individuals reentering the workforce. ▶ *1 recruitment intern:* responsibilities include community recruitment of Big Brothers and Little Sisters. Candidates should have ability to work independently, experience in the field, office skills, oral communication skills, self-motivation, writing skills. Duration is year-round. Unpaid. Open to recent high school graduates, college sophomores, college juniors, college seniors, recent college graduates, graduate students, career changers, individuals reentering the workforce. International applications accepted.
Benefits Formal training, names of contacts, on-the-job training, opportunity to attend seminars/workshops, possible full-time employment, travel reimbursement, willing to act as a professional reference, willing to complete paperwork for educational credit, willing to provide letters of recommendation.
Contact Write, call, fax, e-mail, or through World Wide Web site Susan Bartels, Director of Program Development. Phone: 215-343-8260 Ext. 15. Fax: 215-343-8265. E-mail: bartels@bbbsbc.org. In-person interview required. Applicants must submit a formal organization application, letter of interest, resume, three personal references. Applications are accepted continuously. World Wide Web: http://www.bbbsbc.org.

BIG BROTHERS BIG SISTERS OF CAMDEN AND GLOUCESTER COUNTIES
246 South White Horse Pike
Audubon, New Jersey 08106

General Information Organization with mission to provide positive role models and to enhance the development of youth in need. Established in 1959. Number of employees: 5. Affiliate of Big Brothers Big Sisters of America, Philadelphia, Pennsylvania. Number of internship applications received each year: 5.
Internships Available ▶ *1–3 fund development assistants:* responsibilities include assisting with planning and organizing special events and fund-raising campaigns. Candidates should have office skills, oral communication skills, organizational skills, personal interest in the field, self-motivation, written communication skills. Duration is flexible. Unpaid. Open to recent high school graduates, college freshmen, college sophomores, college juniors, college seniors, recent college graduates, graduate students. ▶ *1–3 grant and program development interns:* responsibilities include assisting in researching and writing grants; also assisting with strategic planning and other initiatives such as program development, public relations, and recruitment. Candidates should have ability to work independently, ability to work with others, editing skills, research

skills, writing skills. Duration is flexible. Unpaid. Open to college seniors, recent college graduates, graduate students. ▶ *1–3 program assistants:* responsibilities include assisting with follow-up co-worker activities with existing matches; may participate in screening of potential volunteers and clients; assisting with planning certain programs and campaigns. Candidates should have ability to work with others, college courses in field, oral communication skills, plan to pursue career in field, written communication skills. Duration is flexible. Unpaid. Open to college juniors, college seniors, recent college graduates, graduate students. ▶ *1–3 program coordinators:* responsibilities include assisting in coordinating an aspect of program; interviewing potential volunteers and clients; making and following-up with all mentor matches in the program and assisting in other aspects such as recruiting. Candidates should have ability to work independently, ability to work with others, oral communication skills, organizational skills, written communication skills. Duration is flexible. Unpaid. Open to graduate students. ▶ *1–2 public relations assistants:* responsibilities include planning and implementing public relations efforts; developing brochures; writing press releases; planning and scheduling speakers bureau. Candidates should have oral communication skills, personal interest in the field, self-motivation, strong interpersonal skills, writing skills. Duration is flexible. Unpaid. Open to college sophomores, college juniors, college seniors, recent college graduates, graduate students.
Benefits Names of contacts, on-the-job training, possible full-time employment, willing to act as a professional reference, willing to complete paperwork for educational credit, willing to provide letters of recommendation.
Contact Write, call, fax, or e-mail Robert Jakubowski, Executive Director. Phone: 856-546-1221. Fax: 856-546-6721. E-mail: bbbscg@snip.net. In-person interview recommended (telephone interview accepted). Applicants must submit a letter of interest, 2-3 personal references. Application deadline: April 15 for summer, August 1 for fall, December 1 for spring.

BIG BROTHERS BIG SISTERS OF CENTRAL SUSQUEHANNA VALLEY
335 Market Street, Suite 2B
Sunbury, Pennsylvania 1780

General Information Program that matches adult volunteers one-to-one with children needing additional adult companionship, support, guidance and understanding; provides group activities for children and youth. Established in 1982. Number of employees: 2. Affiliate of Big Brothers Big Sisters of America, Philadelphia, Pennsylvania.
Internships Available ▶ *1–2 adjunct caseworkers:* responsibilities include contacting clients to monitor progress of client matches; writing and recording case notes reports; maintaining records of clients, cases, volunteers, and parents' inquiries; performing routine clerical work; assisting with social and fund-raising functions; and attending group meetings, staff meetings, and board of director meetings. Candidates should have ability to work independently, oral communication skills, personal interest in the field, strong interpersonal skills, written communication skills. Duration is 1–2 semesters. Unpaid. Open to college freshmen, college sophomores, college juniors, college seniors. International applications accepted.
Benefits Opportunity to attend seminars/workshops, travel reimbursement, willing to act as a professional reference, willing to complete paperwork for educational credit, willing to provide letters of recommendation.
Contact Write, call, fax, or e-mail Peggy Reichenbach, Executive Director, 356 Market Street, Sunbury, Pennsylvania 17801-2338. Phone: 570-286-3127. Fax: 570-286-3150. E-mail: csv_bbbs@msn.com. In-person interview recommended (telephone interview accepted). Applicants must submit a formal organization application, resume, three personal references. Applications are accepted continuously.

BIG BROTHERS BIG SISTERS OF NEVADA
4045 South Spencer, Suite A-57
Las Vegas, Nevada 89119

General Information Youth-mentoring organization that matches children ages 6-17, with mature, responsible, caring adults and

Big Brothers Big Sisters of Nevada (continued)

older high school students. Established in 1973. Number of employees: 20. Affiliate of Big Brothers Big Sisters of America, Philadelphia, Pennsylvania. Number of internship applications received each year: 2.

Internships Available ▶ *1–3 case management and intake interns:* responsibilities include managing a designated case load, interviewing prospective clients and volunteers, and documenting results of interviews. Candidates should have ability to work independently, declared college major in field, oral communication skills, self-motivation, strong interpersonal skills, written communication skills. Duration is 3–12 months. Position available as unpaid or paid. Open to college sophomores, college juniors, college seniors, recent college graduates, graduate students, career changers, individuals reentering the workforce. ▶ *1 school program intern:* responsibilities include interviewing prospective clients, volunteers, and documentation case management. Candidates should have ability to work independently, declared college major in field, oral communication skills, self-motivation, strong interpersonal skills, written communication skills. Duration is flexible. Position available as unpaid or paid. Open to college freshmen, college sophomores, college juniors, college seniors. ▶ *1–2 youth intervention interns:* responsibilities include interviewing prospective clients and volunteers, documentation. Candidates should have ability to work independently, declared college major in field, oral communication skills, self-motivation, strong interpersonal skills, written communication skills, Spanish-speaking preferred. Duration is flexible. Position available as unpaid or paid. Open to college freshmen, college sophomores, college juniors, college seniors, recent college graduates. International applications accepted.

Benefits Names of contacts, on-the-job training, opportunity to attend seminars/workshops, possible full-time employment, willing to complete paperwork for educational credit, willing to provide letters of recommendation, mileage reimbursement.

Contact Write, fax, or through World Wide Web site Veronica Torres, Vice President of Program Services. Fax: 702-737-9209. No phone calls. In-person interview recommended (telephone interview accepted). Applicants must submit a letter of interest, resume, academic transcripts, 2-3 letters of recommendation. Applications are accepted continuously. World Wide Web: http://www.bbbssn.org.

BIG BROTHERS BIG SISTERS OF NORTH ALABAMA
3322 South Memorial Parkway, Suite 617
Huntsville, Alabama 35801

General Information Organization that provides friends and role models for children ages 5-15 and fosters one-to-one mentoring relationships with adult volunteers. Established in 1982. Number of employees: 4. Unit of Big Brothers Big Sisters of America, Philadelphia, Pennsylvania. Number of internship applications received each year: 4.

Internships Available ▶ *1–4 long-term interns:* responsibilities include observing interviews, home visits, and empowerment training of volunteers, children, and their parents; working with staff to process applications to programs; participating in matching children and volunteers; helping to recruit volunteers; and participating in agency fund-raisers. Candidates should have ability to work with others, office skills, oral communication skills, plan to pursue career in field, self-motivation, written communication skills, case management experience, background in social science or education. Duration is minimum of 500 hours. Unpaid. Open to college juniors, college seniors. ▶ *1–4 short-term interns:* responsibilities include observing interviews, home visits, and empowerment training of volunteers, children, and their parents; working with staff to process applications to programs, participating in matching children and volunteers, helping to recruit volunteers, and participating in agency fund-raisers. Candidates should have computer skills, oral communication skills, strong interpersonal skills, written communication skills. Duration is under 500 hours. Unpaid. Open to high school seniors, recent high school graduates, college freshmen, college sophomores, college juniors, college seniors, individuals reentering the workforce. International applications accepted.

Benefits Formal training, names of contacts, on-the-job training, possible full-time employment, willing to complete paperwork for educational credit, willing to provide letters of recommendation.

Contact Write, call, or fax Camille Solley, Executive Director, 3322 South Memorial Parkway Suite 617, Huntsville, Alabama 35801. Phone: 256-880-2123. Fax: 256-880-2177. E-mail: camilles@bbbsna.com. In-person interview required. Applicants must submit a resume, personal reference. Applications are accepted continuously.

BIG BROTHERS BIG SISTERS OF ORANGE COUNTY
253 South William Street
Newburgh, New York 12550

General Information Human service agency dedicated to youth development through mentoring and life skills programs. Established in 1977. Number of employees: 10. Affiliate of Big Brothers Big Sisters of America, Philadelphia, Pennsylvania. Number of internship applications received each year: 6.

Internships Available ▶ *2–4 mentoring manager assistants.* Candidates should have computer skills, declared college major in field, organizational skills, personal interest in the field, self-motivation, strong interpersonal skills. Duration is 4–12 months. Unpaid. ▶ *1 public relations intern.* Candidates should have computer skills, knowledge of field, oral communication skills, self-motivation, strong interpersonal skills, written communication skills. Duration is 4–12 months. Unpaid. Open to college juniors, college seniors, recent college graduates, graduate students.

Benefits On-the-job training, opportunity to attend seminars/workshops, possible full-time employment, willing to act as a professional reference, willing to complete paperwork for educational credit, willing to provide letters of recommendation.

Contact Write, e-mail, or through World Wide Web site Nancy A. Kosloski, Executive Director. Phone: 845-562-5900. Fax: 845-562-1408. E-mail: bbbsoc@warwick.net. In-person interview required. Applicants must submit a letter of interest, resume, two personal references. Applications are accepted continuously. World Wide Web: http://www.mentorachild.org.

BIG BROTHERS BIG SISTERS OF RACINE, INC.
824 Sixth Street
Racine, Wisconsin 53403

General Information Organization that seeks to achieve positive development of minors from single-parent homes by pairing them with carefully screened adult volunteers. Established in 1960. Number of employees: 6. Unit of Big Brothers Big Sisters of America, Philadelphia, Pennsylvania. Number of internship applications received each year: 4.

Internships Available ▶ *2–4 caseworkers/social workers:* responsibilities include performing intake and assessments of clients and volunteers and supervising matches. Candidates should have ability to work independently, college courses in field, oral communication skills, organizational skills, personal interest in the field, written communication skills. Duration is 1–2 months. Unpaid. Open to college freshmen, college sophomores, college juniors, college seniors, recent college graduates, graduate students, career changers, individuals reentering the workforce. International applications accepted.

Benefits Formal training, job counseling, on-the-job training, opportunity to attend seminars/workshops, travel reimbursement, willing to act as a professional reference, willing to complete paperwork for educational credit, willing to provide letters of recommendation.

Contact Write, call, fax, or e-mail Tom Weiss, Executive Director. Phone: 262-637-7625. Fax: 262-632-1156. E-mail: bbbsrk@rootcom.net. In-person interview required. Applicants must submit a letter of interest, resume, criminal background check required. Applications are accepted continuously.

BIG BROTHERS BIG SISTERS OF ROCK AND WALWORTH COUNTIES
2433 South Riverside Drive
Beloit, Wisconsin 53511

General Information Organization that matches children ages 6-14 from single-parent families with adult role models and provides opportunities for the emotional growth of children. Established in 1971. Number of employees: 7. Affiliate of Big Brothers Big Sisters of America, Philadelphia, Pennsylvania. Number of internship applications received each year: 2.
Internships Available ▶ *1–2 fund-raising coordinators:* responsibilities include planning annual bowling and golf events, writing grant proposals, and general fund-raising. Candidates should have ability to work independently, knowledge of field, oral communication skills, organizational skills, self-motivation, written communication skills. Duration is flexible. Position available as unpaid or at $5.50–$10.50 per hour. Open to college freshmen, college sophomores, college juniors, college seniors, recent college graduates, graduate students, law students, career changers, individuals reentering the workforce. ▶ *1–2 general office interns:* responsibilities include billing, data entry, telephoning, and computer input. Candidates should have ability to work with others, computer skills, knowledge of field, office skills, oral communication skills, writing skills. Duration is flexible. Position available as unpaid or at $5.50–$10.50 per hour. Open to recent high school graduates, college freshmen, college sophomores, college juniors, college seniors, recent college graduates, graduate students, career changers, individuals reentering the workforce. International applications accepted.
Benefits Formal training, names of contacts, opportunity to attend seminars/workshops, travel reimbursement, willing to act as a professional reference, willing to complete paperwork for educational credit, willing to provide letters of recommendation.
Contact Write, call, or e-mail Nancy Mignon, Executive Director. Phone: 608-362-8223. Fax: 608-362-5835. E-mail: bbbsnancy@aol.com. In-person interview required. Applicants must submit a letter of interest, resume, two personal references, two letters of recommendation. Applications are accepted continuously.

BIG BROTHERS BIG SISTERS OF SALEM COUNTY
29 South Main Street
Woodstown, New Jersey 08098

General Information Organization that provides positive opportunities for growth and development for children and at-risk youth through one-to-one matches with volunteers, educational programs, and recreational activities. Established in 1986. Number of employees: 2. Affiliate of Big Brothers Big Sisters of America, Philadelphia, Pennsylvania. Number of internship applications received each year: 1.
Internships Available ▶ *1 fund developer:* responsibilities include helping plan fund-raisers, distributing flyers, and soliciting door prizes and corporate sponsors. Candidates should have ability to work independently, computer skills, oral communication skills, organizational skills, personal interest in the field, self-motivation, strong interpersonal skills. Duration is 6–12 months. Unpaid. Open to recent high school graduates, college freshmen, college sophomores, college juniors, college seniors, recent college graduates, graduate students, law students, career changers, individuals reentering the workforce. ▶ *1 program intern:* responsibilities include providing casework services, interviewing children and families, and matching supervision and assistance with recreational and educational activities. Candidates should have ability to work independently, ability to work with others, computer skills, experience in the field, oral communication skills, self-motivation, written communication skills. Duration is 12 months. Unpaid. Open to college freshmen, college sophomores, college juniors, college seniors, recent college graduates, graduate students, law students, career changers, individuals reentering the workforce. ▶ *1 volunteer recruiter:* responsibilities include creating brochures of information to be distributed throughout the county; calling and writing to local businesses asking for volunteers. Candidates should have ability to work independently, ability to work with others, computer skills, oral communication skills, self-motivation, strong leadership ability. Duration is 3–6 months. Unpaid. Open to high school seniors, recent high school graduates, college freshmen, college sophomores, college juniors, college seniors, recent college graduates, graduate students, law students, career changers, individuals reentering the workforce. International applications accepted.
Benefits Formal training, job counseling, names of contacts, on-the-job training, opportunity to attend seminars/workshops, possible full-time employment, travel reimbursement, willing to act as a professional reference, willing to complete paperwork for educational credit, willing to provide letters of recommendation.
Contact Write, call, or fax Lori Tesauro, Executive Director. Phone: 856-769-3556. Fax: 856-769-3566. E-mail: salemcountybbbs@hotmail.com. In-person interview required. Applicants must submit a letter of interest, resume, personal reference, three letters of recommendation. Applications are accepted continuously.

BOULDER COUNTY AIDS PROJECT
2118 14th Street
Boulder, Colorado 80302

General Information AIDS service organization. Established in 1984. Number of employees: 15. Number of internship applications received each year: 10.
Internships Available ▶ *2 Latino outreach interns:* responsibilities include assisting coordinator with speaking engagements and other outreach activities. Candidates should have ability to work independently, oral communication skills, self-motivation, strong interpersonal skills, bilingual English/Spanish ability. Duration is flexible. Unpaid. Open to college juniors, college seniors, recent college graduates, graduate students. ▶ *1–3 special events associates:* responsibilities include coordinating special events for fund-raising. Candidates should have ability to work independently, oral communication skills, organizational skills, self-motivation, strong interpersonal skills. Duration is commitment of 1 academic year, but will accept 1 semester. Unpaid. Open to college juniors, college seniors, recent college graduates, career changers, individuals reentering the workforce.
Benefits On-the-job training, opportunity to attend seminars/workshops, willing to act as a professional reference, willing to complete paperwork for educational credit, willing to provide letters of recommendation.
Contact Write, fax, e-mail, or through World Wide Web site Jenny Schwartz, Intern Coordinator, 2118 14th Street, Boulder, Colorado 80302. Fax: 303-444-0260. E-mail: jaschwartz@worldnet.att.net. No phone calls. In-person interview required. Applicants must submit a letter of interest, resume, two writing samples, two personal references, letter of recommendation. Applications are accepted continuously. World Wide Web: http://www.bcap.org.

BOYS & GIRLS CLUB AND YMCA AT THE ALFOND YOUTH CENTER
126 North Street
Waterville, Maine 04901

General Information Nonprofit youth agency that provides social, educational, and recreational activities to persons ages 6–20. Established in 1924. Number of employees: 90. Number of internship applications received each year: 5.
Internships Available ▶ *1 aquatics director assistant:* responsibilities include teaching swimming, coaching swim team, and maintaining indoor pools. Candidates should have ability to work independently, college courses in field, computer skills, knowledge of field, oral communication skills, personal interest in the field, self-motivation, strong interpersonal skills, strong leadership ability, written communication skills. Duration is one semester with option to extend. Unpaid. Open to recent high school graduates, college freshmen, college sophomores, college juniors, college seniors, recent college graduates, career changers, individuals reentering the workforce. ▶ *1 arts and crafts instructor:* responsibilities include teaching an art curriculum. Candidates should have ability to work independently, analytical skills, knowledge of field, oral communication skills, organizational skills, personal interest in the field, plan to pursue career in field, self-motivation, strong interpersonal skills, strong leadership ability.

Boys & Girls Club and YMCA at the Alfond Youth Center (continued)

Duration is September 1 to June 30. Unpaid. Open to high school students, recent high school graduates, college freshmen, college sophomores, college juniors, college seniors, recent college graduates, graduate students, career changers, individuals reentering the workforce. ▶ *1 assistant athletic director:* responsibilities include organizing athletic games, activities, and teams. Candidates should have ability to work independently, college courses in field, computer skills, knowledge of field, oral communication skills, organizational skills, personal interest in the field, self-motivation, strong interpersonal skills, strong leadership ability, writing skills. Duration is one semester with option to extend. Unpaid. Open to recent high school graduates, college freshmen, college sophomores, college juniors, college seniors, recent college graduates, career changers, individuals reentering the workforce. ▶ *1 human resources intern:* responsibilities include assisting the human resources director in all aspects of human resources including assisting in volunteer coordinating. Candidates should have ability to work independently, analytical skills, college courses in field, computer skills, editing skills, knowledge of field, office skills, oral communication skills, organizational skills, personal interest in the field, plan to pursue career in field, self-motivation, strong interpersonal skills, strong leadership ability, written communication skills. Duration is one semester with option to extend. Unpaid. Open to college juniors, college seniors. ▶ *1 marketing intern:* responsibilities include assisting the development department in promoting programs and participating in fund raising events. Candidates should have ability to work independently, analytical skills, college courses in field, computer skills, knowledge of field, office skills, oral communication skills, organizational skills, personal interest in the field, plan to pursue career in field, research skills, self-motivation, strong interpersonal skills, strong leadership ability, written communication skills. Duration is one semester with option to extend. Unpaid. Open to college juniors, college seniors. ▶ *1–3 recreation management or physical education interns:* responsibilities include individual and group programming with at-risk teens. Candidates should have ability to work independently, college courses in field, computer skills, declared college major in field, knowledge of field, oral communication skills, organizational skills, personal interest in the field, plan to pursue career in field, self-motivation, strong interpersonal skills, strong leadership ability, written communication skills. Duration is one semester with option to extend. Unpaid. Open to recent high school graduates, college freshmen, college sophomores, college juniors, college seniors, recent college graduates, graduate students, career changers, individuals reentering the workforce. ▶ *1 sports management intern:* responsibilities include assisting the assistant executive director. Candidates should have ability to work independently, college courses in field, computer skills, knowledge of field, oral communication skills, organizational skills, personal interest in the field, self-motivation, strong interpersonal skills, strong leadership ability, written communication skills. Duration is one semester with option to extend. Unpaid. Open to recent high school graduates, college freshmen, college sophomores, college juniors, college seniors, recent college graduates, career changers, individuals reentering the workforce. International applications accepted.

Benefits Formal training, housing at a cost, job counseling, meals at a cost, names of contacts, on-the-job training, opportunity to attend seminars/workshops, possible full-time employment, willing to complete paperwork for educational credit, willing to provide letters of recommendation.

Contact Write, call, fax, or e-mail Christian Gajowski, Volunteer Coordinator. Phone: 207-873-0684. Fax: 207-861-8016. E-mail: cgajowski@alfondyouthcenter.org. In-person interview recommended (telephone interview accepted). Applicants must submit a letter of interest, resume, academic transcripts, three personal references. Application deadline: January 1 for spring, April 1 for summer, July 1 for fall, November 1 for winter. World Wide Web: http://www.aplaceforkidstogo.org.

BOYS & GIRLS CLUBS OF ALBANY
21 Delaware Avenue
Albany, New York 12210

General Information Organization that promotes the social, educational, and vocational development of at-risk boys and girls by building self-esteem, values, and skills during youth and adolescence. Established in 1891. Number of employees: 35. Affiliate of Boys & Girls Clubs of America, Atlanta, Georgia. Number of internship applications received each year: 10.

Internships Available ▶ *1–10 program assistants:* responsibilities include working with children, implementing activities, supervising children, and working with the site director and coordinator. Candidates should have oral communication skills, personal interest in the field, self-motivation, strong interpersonal skills, strong leadership ability. Duration is flexible. Unpaid. Open to high school students, recent high school graduates, college freshmen, college sophomores, college juniors, college seniors, recent college graduates, graduate students, law students, career changers, individuals reentering the workforce. ▶ *1–5 program counselors:* responsibilities include helping youth to achieve and maintain fitness to acquire a broad range of physical skills; to develop a sense of teamwork, cooperation, and fairness; and to lead healthy, active lifestyles. Candidates should have ability to work independently, ability to work with others, knowledge of field, organizational skills, self-motivation, strong leadership ability. Duration is flexible. Unpaid. Open to high school students, recent high school graduates, college freshmen, college sophomores, college juniors, college seniors, recent college graduates, graduate students, law students, career changers, individuals reentering the workforce, senior citizens. International applications accepted.

Benefits Formal training, names of contacts, on-the-job training, opportunity to attend seminars/workshops, possible full-time employment, willing to act as a professional reference, willing to complete paperwork for educational credit, willing to provide letters of recommendation.

Contact Write, call, or fax Doretha Holmes, Deputy Executive Director. Phone: 518-462-5528. Fax: 518-462-5540. In-person interview required. Applicants must submit a formal organization application, letter of interest, resume, two writing samples, three personal references, three letters of recommendation. Applications are accepted continuously.

BOYS & GIRLS CLUBS OF BROCKTON, INC.
233 Warren Avenue
Brockton, Massachusetts 02301-4321

General Information Youth development organization that provides guidance and offers programs to serve youth of disadvantaged circumstances. Established in 1988. Number of employees: 30. Unit of Boys & Girls Clubs of America, Atlanta, Georgia. Number of internship applications received each year: 5.

Internships Available ▶ *1 fund-raising intern:* responsibilities include assisting in implementing the annual financial development plan, grant writing, assisting with board and youth fund-raising events, and directing mail campaigns. Candidates should have ability to work independently, analytical skills, computer skills, editing skills, organizational skills, personal interest in the field, research skills, self-motivation, written communication skills. Duration is flexible. Unpaid. Open to college sophomores, college juniors, college seniors. ▶ *1–3 health promotion interns:* responsibilities include assisting in supervising teen leaders in planning and implementing prevention programs for peers and younger members. Candidates should have ability to work independently, ability to work with others, oral communication skills, organizational skills, personal interest in the field, self-motivation, strong leadership ability. Unpaid. Open to college juniors, college seniors. ▶ *1–5 learning center interns:* responsibilities include helping to coordinate and implement learning center programs in computer learning, homework assistance, tutoring, SAT preparation, and career awareness activities; and leading field trips, special activities, and programs. Candidates should have ability to work independently, ability to work with others, oral communication skills, self-motivation, strong leadership ability, written communication skills. Duration is flexible. Unpaid. Open to college fresh-

men, college sophomores, college juniors, college seniors, individuals reentering the workforce. ▶ *1–3 leisure studies interns:* responsibilities include working with the sports programs in basketball, soccer, volleyball, and baseball, working in the games room, and planning special events. Candidates should have ability to work independently, computer skills, knowledge of field, oral communication skills, organizational skills, personal interest in the field, self-motivation, strong interpersonal skills, strong leadership ability. Duration is flexible. Unpaid. Open to college freshmen, college sophomores, college juniors, college seniors, individuals reentering the workforce. ▶ *1 marketing intern:* responsibilities include promoting club programs, implementing annual marketing plan, maintaining media relations, organizing membership and volunteer recruitment campaigns, planning and implementing regional campaigns, updating brochures, and assisting with annual newsletter and annual report. Candidates should have ability to work independently, analytical skills, computer skills, organizational skills, research skills, self-motivation, writing skills. Duration is flexible. Unpaid. Open to college freshmen, college sophomores, college juniors, college seniors. International applications accepted.
Benefits Formal training, names of contacts, on-the-job training, possible full-time employment, willing to act as a professional reference, willing to complete paperwork for educational credit, willing to provide letters of recommendation.
Contact Write, call, or fax Jenn Aldworth, Assistant Executive Director. Phone: 508-586-3503. Fax: 508-588-2772. E-mail: jennaldworth@aol.com. In-person interview required. Applicants must submit a resume, personal reference, two letters of recommendation, criminal background check required. Application deadline: August 1 for fall; continuous for remainder of year.

BOYS & GIRLS CLUBS OF CENTRAL WYOMING
353 West 'A' Street
Casper, Wyoming 82601

General Information Youth-serving organization. Established in 1969. Number of employees: 11. Affiliate of Boys & Girls Clubs of America, Atlanta, Georgia.
Internships Available ▶ *1 program coordinator:* responsibilities include working on program sustainability, new programs, and volunteer recruitment. Candidates should have ability to work independently, analytical skills, computer skills, knowledge of field, office skills, oral communication skills, organizational skills, personal interest in the field, self-motivation, strong interpersonal skills, strong leadership ability, writing skills. Duration is 1 semester. Position available as unpaid or paid. Open to college freshmen, college sophomores, college juniors, college seniors, recent college graduates, graduate students.
Benefits Formal training, job counseling, on-the-job training, opportunity to attend seminars/workshops, willing to act as a professional reference, willing to complete paperwork for educational credit, willing to provide letters of recommendation.
Contact Write, call, fax, or e-mail Ashley Bright, Chief Professional Officer. Phone: 307-235-5694. Fax: 307-235-5697. E-mail: bgccw@coffey.com. In-person interview recommended (telephone interview accepted). Applicants must submit a formal organization application, letter of interest, resume, academic transcripts, four personal references, three letters of recommendation.

BOYS & GIRLS CLUBS OF CLIFTON
822 Clifton Avenue
Clifton, New Jersey 07013

General Information Youth serving organization for boys and girls ages 2½-17. Established in 1958. Number of employees: 72. Unit of Boys & Girls Clubs of America, Atlanta, Georgia. Number of internship applications received each year: 20.
Internships Available ▶ *9 "School's Out" program supervisors:* responsibilities include implementing care programs from 2:30-6:30 for 35 students ages 6-11. Candidates should have experience in the field, oral communication skills, personal interest in the field, self-motivation, strong interpersonal skills. Duration is 10 months. $8.50–$10 per hour. Open to individuals 18 years or older. ▶ *6–8 after-school program counselors:* responsibilities include acting as group leader for elementary school children and provid-

ing supervision and instruction in the after-school program 3-6:30 daily. Candidates should have experience in the field, oral communication skills, organizational skills, personal interest in the field, self-motivation, strong interpersonal skills. Duration is from September-June. $7–$10 per hour. Open to high school seniors, college freshmen, college sophomores, college juniors, college seniors. ▶ *4–6 lifeguards:* responsibilities include lifeguarding pool for all open swims, lessons, swim team, and adult swims. Candidates should have lifeguard training , first aid/CPR certification. Duration is 12 months. $7.50–$8.50 per hour. ▶ *1 summer assistant program director:* responsibilities include implementing and supervising summer day camp program; working with staff and children (Monday-Friday) to direct summer program activities. Candidates should have experience in the field, oral communication skills, personal interest in the field, self-motivation, strong interpersonal skills, written communication skills. Duration is June to August. $9–$10.50 per hour. Open to college juniors, college seniors, recent college graduates. ▶ *6–10 summer group counselors:* responsibilities include supervising and conducting activities for a group of 25 youngsters ages 6-12, overseeing specific age groups in a highly structured camp-at-home program, and performing administrative duties. Candidates should have experience in the field, oral communication skills, personal interest in the field, self-motivation, strong interpersonal skills, strong leadership ability. Duration is June 25-August 24. $7–$8.50 per hour. Open to high school seniors, college freshmen, college sophomores, college juniors, college seniors. ▶ *1 summer trip program coordinator:* responsibilities include implementing summer trip program for three age groups (6-8, 9-10, 11-16); one trip per week per age group; supervision, chaperoning, and administration of program. Candidates should have ability to work with others, office skills, oral communication skills, personal interest in the field, self-motivation, written communication skills, responsibility, maturity. Duration is June to September. $9–$10.50 per hour. Open to college juniors, college seniors. ▶ *4–6 water safety instructors:* responsibilities include teaching American Red Cross swim lessons levels I-VII plus safety and life saving classes. Candidates should have experience in the field, current WSI, first aid, and CPR certifications. Duration is 12 months. $10.50 per hour. Open to high school seniors, recent high school graduates, college freshmen, college sophomores, college juniors, college seniors, individuals reentering the workforce.
Benefits Formal training, names of contacts, possible full-time employment, willing to complete paperwork for educational credit, willing to provide letters of recommendation, access to Boys and Girls Club of America job listings and career services.
Contact Write, call, fax, e-mail, or through World Wide Web site Robert Foster, Director of Operations. Phone: 973-773-2697 Ext. 19. Fax: 973-773-3103. E-mail: rfoster@bgcclifton.org. In-person interview required. Applicants must submit a resume, two personal references, letter of recommendation. Application deadline: April 15 for summer, August 15 for fall, December 15 for winter/spring. World Wide Web: http://www.boysandgirlsclbclifton.org.

BOYS & GIRLS CLUBS OF EAST AURORA
24 Paine Street
East Aurora, New York 14052

General Information Youth service organization. Established in 1939. Number of employees: 18. Affiliate of Boys and Girls Club of America, Atlanta, Georgia. Number of internship applications received each year: 1.
Internships Available ▶ *1 fund development director:* responsibilities include applying for grants from local government and foundation resources; assisting with coordination of special events; marketing club through newsletters. Candidates should have computer skills, knowledge of field, oral communication skills, research skills, writing skills. Duration is 3–6 months. Position available as unpaid or at percentage of funds raised. Open to college seniors, recent college graduates, graduate students, career changers. ▶ *1–2 youth development professionals:* responsibilities include organizing, directing, and supervising youth in a variety of program settings including athletics, social recreation, social work, drug, alcohol, and sex prevention, mentoring, tutoring, homework help, and technology. Candidates should have organizational skills, personal interest in the field, self-motivation,

Boys & Girls Clubs of East Aurora (continued)

strong interpersonal skills, strong leadership ability. Duration is 3–6 months. Position available as unpaid or at $6–$8 per hour. Open to high school students, recent high school graduates, college freshmen, college sophomores, college juniors, college seniors, recent college graduates, graduate students, career changers. International applications accepted.
Benefits Formal training, job counseling, on-the-job training, opportunity to attend seminars/workshops, possible full-time employment, willing to act as a professional reference, willing to complete paperwork for educational credit, willing to provide letters of recommendation.
Contact Write, call, fax, or e-mail Mr. Gary D. Schutrum, Executive Director. Phone: 716-652-1060. Fax: 716-652-0212. E-mail: gschutrum@bgcea.org. In-person interview required. Applicants must submit a formal organization application, letter of interest, resume, academic transcripts, letter of recommendation. Applications are accepted continuously. World Wide Web: http://www.bgcea.org.

BOYS & GIRLS CLUBS OF LAKELAND, INC.
PO Box 763
Lakeland, Florida 33802

General Information Organization that helps local disadvantaged youth to become responsible citizens and leaders. Established in 1939. Number of employees: 27. Unit of Boys & Girls Clubs of America, Atlanta, Georgia. Number of internship applications received each year: 1.
Internships Available ▶ *1–4 interns:* responsibilities include working with youth ages 6-18 from disadvantaged urban backgrounds. Candidates should have ability to work independently, ability to work with others, oral communication skills, organizational skills, personal interest in the field, self-motivation. Duration is flexible. Unpaid. Open to high school students, recent high school graduates, college freshmen, college sophomores, college juniors, college seniors, recent college graduates, graduate students, career changers, individuals reentering the workforce. International applications accepted.
Benefits Formal training, job counseling, names of contacts, opportunity to attend seminars/workshops, possible full-time employment, willing to complete paperwork for educational credit, willing to provide letters of recommendation.
Contact Write or call Rex Perry, Executive Director. Phone: 863-686-1719. In-person interview recommended (telephone interview accepted). Applicants must submit a letter of interest, resume. Applications are accepted continuously.

BOYS & GIRLS CLUBS OF LARIMER COUNTY
103 Smokey Street
Fort Collins, Colorado 80525

General Information Organization that helps all youth to develop maximum potential by providing personal growth and educational and recreational programs in an environment of mutual trust and respect. Established in 1988. Number of employees: 21. Unit of Boys & Girls Clubs of America, Atlanta, Georgia.
Internships Available ▶ *Gameroom/recreation interns:* responsibilities include supervising and assisting full-time staff with playtime and recreational activities for children ages 6-18. Candidates should have ability to work independently, ability to work with others, organizational skills, personal interest in the field. Duration is flexible. Unpaid. ▶ *Learning-lab/computer technicians:* responsibilities include planning, implementing, and coordinating activities of the computer lab with full-time staff for youth ages 6-18. Candidates should have ability to work with others, computer skills, knowledge of field, organizational skills, self-motivation. Duration is flexible. Unpaid. ▶ *Program interns:* responsibilities include helping full-time staff with the planning and supervision of programs for children ages 6-18. Candidates should have ability to work with others, computer skills, knowledge of field, organizational skills, self-motivation. Duration is flexible.

Unpaid. Open to college freshmen, college sophomores, college juniors, college seniors, recent college graduates, graduate students. International applications accepted.
Benefits Names of contacts, opportunity to attend seminars/workshops, possible full-time employment, willing to complete paperwork for educational credit, willing to provide letters of recommendation.
Contact Write, call, fax, e-mail, or through World Wide Web site Tammy Chandler, Business Manager/Controller. Phone: 970-223-1709. Fax: 970-206-9531. E-mail: bgclc@frii.com. In-person interview recommended (telephone interview accepted). Applicants must submit a formal organization application, background check required. Applications are accepted continuously. World Wide Web: http://www.lcbgc.org.

BOYS & GIRLS CLUBS OF NASH/EDGECOMBE COUNTIES
405 Raleigh Road
Rocky Mount, North Carolina 27802

General Information Youth development center. Established in 1969. Number of employees: 33. Affiliate of Boys and Girls Club of America, Atlanta, Georgia. Number of internship applications received each year: 25.
Internships Available ▶ *5–15 human service interns:* responsibilities include developing and coordinating programs; participating in fund-raising and marketing; performing administrative duties as required. Candidates should have ability to work with others, computer skills, oral communication skills, personal interest in the field, self-motivation, strong leadership ability. Duration is 12 weeks. Position available as unpaid or paid. Open to college freshmen, college sophomores, college juniors, college seniors, recent college graduates, graduate students. International applications accepted.
Benefits Formal training, job counseling, on-the-job training, opportunity to attend seminars/workshops, possible full-time employment, willing to act as a professional reference, willing to complete paperwork for educational credit, willing to provide letters of recommendation.
Contact Write, call, or e-mail Misty L. Miller, Director of Operations, PO Box 1622, Rocky Mount 27802. Phone: 252-977-9924. Fax: 252-985-0277. E-mail: mmiller@bgcne.org. In-person interview recommended (telephone interview accepted). Applicants must submit a formal organization application, letter of interest, resume, three personal references. Applications are accepted continuously. World Wide Web: http://www.bgcne.org.

BOYS & GIRLS CLUBS OF NEWARK
155 Washington Street, Suite 202
Newark, New Jersey 07102-2001

General Information Youth development agency. Established in 1938. Number of employees: 42. Affiliate of Boys & Girls Clubs of America, Atlanta, Georgia. Number of internship applications received each year: 15.
Internships Available ▶ *1 accounting assistant.* Candidates should have analytical skills, declared college major in field, knowledge of field, office skills, self-motivation, strong interpersonal skills. Duration is flexible. Unpaid. Open to college sophomores, college juniors, college seniors, recent college graduates, graduate students. ▶ *2 office assistants:* responsibilities include general office help. Candidates should have ability to work with others, computer skills, office skills, self-motivation, writing skills. Duration is flexible. Unpaid. Open to high school students, recent high school graduates, college freshmen, college sophomores, college juniors, college seniors, recent college graduates, graduate students, law students, career changers, individuals reentering the workforce. ▶ *3 social workers.* Candidates should have ability to work independently, knowledge of field, oral communication skills, organizational skills, strong interpersonal skills, writing skills. Duration is flexible. Unpaid. Open to college freshmen, college sophomores, college juniors, college seniors, recent college graduates. ▶ *10–30 tutors:* responsibilities include assisting students with homework. Candidates should have oral communication skills, strong interpersonal skills, strong leadership ability. Dura-

tion is flexible. Unpaid. Open to high school students, recent high school graduates. International applications accepted.

Benefits Formal training, job counseling, on-the-job training, opportunity to attend seminars/workshops, possible full-time employment, willing to act as a professional reference, willing to complete paperwork for educational credit, willing to provide letters of recommendation.

Contact Write, call, fax, or e-mail John Mack, Executive Director. Phone: 973-242-1200. Fax: 973-242-8629. E-mail: jmack@bgcn. org. In-person interview required. Applicants must submit a formal organization application. Applications are accepted continuously. World Wide Web: http://www.bgcn.org.

BOYS & GIRLS CLUBS OF PLYMOUTH, INC.
PO Box 3479
Plymouth, Massachusetts 02361

General Information Organization that provides area youth with activities designed to build self-esteem, develop leadership skills, and promote positive life choices. Established in 1911. Number of employees: 12. Unit of Boys & Girls Clubs of America, Atlanta, Georgia. Number of internship applications received each year: 6.

Internships Available ▶ *1 junior staff intern:* responsibilities include interacting with children, handling small amounts of money. Candidates should have ability to work with others, oral communication skills, personal interest in the field, self-motivation, patience. Duration is 10 months. Position available as unpaid or at $6.75 per hour. Open to high school students. ▶ *1–2 youth counselors:* responsibilities include running programs, dealing with children and parents, answering phones, and overseeing recreational activities. Candidates should have ability to work independently, oral communication skills, personal interest in the field, self-motivation, strong interpersonal skills. Duration is 10–30 weeks. Position available as unpaid or at $7 per hour. Open to recent high school graduates, college freshmen, college sophomores, college juniors, college seniors, recent college graduates, graduate students, career changers, individuals reentering the workforce. International applications accepted.

Benefits Names of contacts, on-the-job training, willing to act as a professional reference, willing to complete paperwork for educational credit, willing to provide letters of recommendation.

Contact Write, call, fax, or e-mail Ms. Mary Leavenworth, Executive Director. Phone: 508-746-6070. Fax: 508-746-5953. E-mail: mleavenworth@aol.com. In-person interview required. Applicants must submit a formal organization application, resume, three letters of recommendation. Applications are accepted continuously.

BOYS & GIRLS CLUBS OF TAMPA BAY, INC.
3020 West Laurel Street
Tampa, Florida 33607

General Information Youth agency with 20 sites in Hillsborough County that serves school-age children after school, all day on school holidays, and during the summer by providing educational, athletic, cultural, enrichment, and prevention programs with a focus on the disadvantaged. Established in 1929. Number of employees: 150. Affiliate of Boys & Girls Clubs of America, Atlanta, Georgia. Number of internship applications received each year: 3.

Internships Available ▶ *1–3 career program directors:* responsibilities include working with youth on college and career program development: goal-setting classes, job readiness, and volunteer activities (community service). Candidates should have oral communication skills, personal interest in the field, self-motivation, strong interpersonal skills, strong leadership ability. Duration is 1–2 semesters. Unpaid. Open to recent high school graduates, college freshmen, college sophomores, college juniors, college seniors, individuals reentering the workforce, individuals 18 years or older with high school diploma or GED. ▶ *2–14 cultural arts specialists:* responsibilities include working with small groups of youths to develop singing, musical instrument, dance, or artistic talents; auditioning students and working on a show group; working with youths in developing skills in painting, sculpting, and related media. Candidates should have ability to work independently, oral communication skills, organizational skills, personal interest

in the field, strong interpersonal skills, strong leadership ability. Duration is 1 semester, school year, or summer. Unpaid. Open to recent high school graduates, college freshmen, college sophomores, college juniors, college seniors, recent college graduates, career changers, individuals reentering the workforce, individuals 18 years of age or older. ▶ *2–5 data collection specialists:* responsibilities include obtaining data on club membership, program participation, and attendance from clubs and schools; entering data into main system and relating it to grant reports. Candidates should have ability to work independently, computer skills, personal interest in the field, research skills, self-motivation, written communication skills. Duration is 1 semester. Unpaid. Open to college freshmen, college sophomores, college juniors, college seniors, recent college graduates, graduate students, law students, career changers, individuals reentering the workforce, individuals 18 years of age or older. ▶ *10–19 girls' sports coordinators:* responsibilities include planning and implementing athletic events for girls only. Candidates should have oral communication skills, organizational skills, personal interest in the field, strong interpersonal skills, strong leadership ability. Duration is 1–2 semesters. Unpaid. Open to recent high school graduates, college freshmen, college sophomores, college juniors, college seniors, recent college graduates, career changers, individuals reentering the workforce, individuals 18 years of age or older. ▶ *1–6 outreach program specialists:* responsibilities include delivering outreach and prevention programs to public and private schools and public housing sites; planning and implementing school outreach programs with educational and athletic activities; and conducting county-wide outreach events. Candidates should have ability to work independently, oral communication skills, organizational skills, personal interest in the field, self-motivation, strong interpersonal skills. Duration is 1 semester, school year, or summer. Unpaid. Open to recent high school graduates, college freshmen, college sophomores, college juniors, college seniors, recent college graduates, graduate students, career changers, individuals reentering the workforce, individuals 18 years of age or older. ▶ *10–19 prevention specialists:* responsibilities include conducting group sessions with school-age children in violence prevention, drug abuse prevention, AIDS education, peer pressure response, and similar programs. Candidates should have analytical skills, oral communication skills, personal interest in the field, strong interpersonal skills, written communication skills. Duration is 1–2 semesters. Unpaid. Open to recent high school graduates, college freshmen, college sophomores, college juniors, college seniors, recent college graduates, career changers, individuals 18 years of age or older. ▶ *1–3 research associates:* responsibilities include researching grant opportunities, collecting data, and assisting with grant writing and monitoring. Candidates should have ability to work independently, editing skills, plan to pursue career in field, research skills, self-motivation, written communication skills. Duration is 1 semester, school year, or summer. Unpaid. Open to college freshmen, college sophomores, college juniors, college seniors, recent college graduates, graduate students, career changers, individuals reentering the workforce, individuals 18 years of age or older. ▶ *1 special events coordinator:* responsibilities include working with management staff to develop and implement special events and fund-raisers. Candidates should have ability to work independently, organizational skills, personal interest in the field, self-motivation, strong interpersonal skills. Duration is 1 semester, school year, or summer. Unpaid. Open to college freshmen, college sophomores, college juniors, college seniors, recent college graduates, graduate students, career changers, individuals reentering the workforce, individuals 18 years of age or older. ▶ *2 teen services coordinators:* responsibilities include working directly with teens developing leadership skills and enhancing their educational pursuits. Candidates should have oral communication skills, personal interest in the field, strong interpersonal skills, strong leadership ability, written communication skills. Unpaid. Open to recent high school graduates, college freshmen, college sophomores, college juniors, college seniors, recent college graduates, graduate students, career changers, individuals reentering the workforce. ▶ *14–28 tutor/homework assistants:* responsibilities include working with children one-to-one and in small groups to improve their academic achievement. Candidates should have ability to work independently, oral communication skills, personal

Boys & Girls Clubs of Tampa Bay, Inc. (continued)
interest in the field, self-motivation, strong interpersonal skills, written communication skills. Duration is 1–2 semesters. Unpaid. Open to recent high school graduates, college freshmen, college sophomores, college juniors, college seniors, recent college graduates, graduate students, law students, career changers, individuals reentering the workforce, individuals 18 years of age or older.
▶ *14–56 youth development professionals:* responsibilities include coordinating and leading appropriate activities within a group while acting as program assistant to year-round staff. Candidates should have ability to work independently, oral communication skills, organizational skills, personal interest in the field, self-motivation, strong interpersonal skills. Duration is up to 2 years (10-30 hours per week). Unpaid. Open to recent high school graduates, college freshmen, college sophomores, college juniors, college seniors, recent college graduates, graduate students, career changers, individuals reentering the workforce, individuals 18 years of age or older. ▶ *1–3 youth development professionals/aquatics coordinators:* responsibilities include assisting in program areas designated by club director, working with small groups of children on specific programs, supervising aquatic activities, coaching and managing synchronized swimming team. Candidates should have ability to work independently, oral communication skills, organizational skills, personal interest in the field, self-motivation, strong interpersonal skills, lifeguard and WSI certification. Duration is 2 semesters. Unpaid. Open to recent high school graduates, college freshmen, college sophomores, college juniors, college seniors, recent college graduates, graduate students, career changers, individuals reentering the workforce, individuals 18 years of age or older. International applications accepted.
Benefits Formal training, job counseling, names of contacts, on-the-job training, opportunity to attend seminars/workshops, possible full-time employment, willing to act as a professional reference, willing to complete paperwork for educational credit, willing to provide letters of recommendation.
Contact Write, call, fax, or e-mail Lisbeth Moore, Director of Services to Clubs. Phone: 813-875-5771. Fax: 813-875-4428. E-mail: bmoore@bgctampa.org. In-person interview required. Applicants must submit a formal organization application, letter of interest, resume. Applications are accepted continuously. World Wide Web: http://www.bgctampa.org.

BOYS & GIRLS CLUBS OF TRACY
753 West Lowell Avenue
Tracy, California 95376

General Information Youth service organization providing a safe, supportive, and nurturing environment with programs that enrich the lives of the young people of the community. Established in 1989. Number of employees: 24. Affiliate of Boys & Girls Clubs of America, Atlanta, Georgia.
Internships Available ▶ *Program assistants:* responsibilities include supervising and interacting with children; helping implement and plan special events and programs; assisting with membership tracking; maintaining positive relationship with community. Duration is flexible. Unpaid. Open to college sophomores, college juniors, college seniors, recent college graduates, graduate students, law students, career changers, individuals reentering the workforce.
▶ *Programmers:* responsibilities include national character and leadership development, educational and career development, health and life skills programs. Duration is flexible. Unpaid. Open to college freshmen, college sophomores, college juniors, college seniors, recent college graduates, graduate students, law students, career changers, individuals reentering the workforce. Candidates for all positions should have ability to work independently, ability to work with others, analytical skills, computer skills, editing skills, knowledge of field, office skills, oral communication skills, organizational skills, personal interest in the field, research skills, self-motivation, strong leadership ability, writing skills. International applications accepted.
Benefits Job counseling, on-the-job training, opportunity to attend seminars/workshops, possible full-time employment, willing to act as a professional reference, willing to complete paperwork for educational credit, willing to provide letters of recommendation.

Contact Write, call, or fax Steven Gough, Director of Operations. Phone: 209-832-2582. Fax: 209-832-4687. In-person interview recommended (telephone interview accepted). Applicants must submit a formal organization application, personal reference. Applications are accepted continuously. World Wide Web: http://bgca.org.

BOYS & GIRLS CLUBS OF WESTERN BROOME, INC.
1 Clubhouse Road
Endicott, New York 13760

General Information Educational/recreational nonprofit organization that provides for the educational, psychological, and physical needs of infants to seniors, with an emphasis on youth development. Established in 1994. Number of employees: 60. Unit of Boys & Girls Clubs of America, Atlanta, Georgia. Number of internship applications received each year: 1.
Internships Available ▶ *1–2 child-care mentors:* responsibilities include working with children in an after-school program. Candidates should have ability to work independently, oral communication skills, organizational skills, plan to pursue career in field, self-motivation, strong interpersonal skills, strong leadership ability, written communication skills, interest in working with young children 6-12 years or adolescents 12-14 years (experience in field desirable). Duration is 10 months. Unpaid. Open to recent high school graduates, college freshmen, college sophomores, college juniors, college seniors, recent college graduates, graduate students, individuals reentering the workforce. ▶ *1–2 computer class assistant teachers:* responsibilities include assisting instructor in one-on-one direction and mentoring. Candidates should have analytical skills, college courses in field, computer skills, knowledge of field. Duration is January to June or September to December. Unpaid. Open to college freshmen, college sophomores, college juniors, college seniors, recent college graduates. ▶ *1 marketing/public relations intern:* responsibilities include building community relations and seeking additional publicity. Candidates should have computer skills, oral communication skills, plan to pursue career in field, research skills, self-motivation, strong interpersonal skills, written communication skills. Duration is 2–6 months. Position available as unpaid or paid. Open to college freshmen, college sophomores, college juniors, college seniors, recent college graduates, graduate students. ▶ *1–3 summer fun club unit leaders/assistants:* responsibilities include planning, organizing, and implementing programs and age-appropriate activities for children in a day camp unit; teaching cooking and crafts; and leading hikes. Candidates should have ability to work with others, personal interest in the field, self-motivation, strong leadership ability. Duration is 2 months. $5.55 per hour. Open to recent high school graduates, college freshmen, college sophomores, college juniors. International applications accepted.
Benefits Job counseling, names of contacts, on-the-job training, willing to act as a professional reference, willing to complete paperwork for educational credit, willing to provide letters of recommendation.
Contact Write, call, fax, or e-mail Darlene Cacialli, Executive Director. Phone: 607-754-0225. Fax: 607-754-2801. E-mail: bgclubwb@stny.rr.com. In-person interview required. Applicants must submit a letter of interest, resume, three personal references. Applications are accepted continuously. World Wide Web: http://www.boysandgirlsclubofwesternbroome.com.

BOYS & GIRLS CLUBS OF WORCESTER
2 Ionic Avenue
Worcester, Massachusetts 01608

General Information Youth development agency that provides daily programs in character and leadership development, educational and career development, the arts, health/life skills and sports, and fitness and recreation. Established in 1889. Number of employees: 33. Unit of Boys & Girls Clubs of America, Atlanta, Georgia. Number of internship applications received each year: 5.
Internships Available ▶ *Youth development interns:* responsibilities include assisting staff with delivery of programs. Candidates should

have ability to work independently, oral communication skills, organizational skills, plan to pursue career in field, self-motivation, strong interpersonal skills, strong leadership ability. Duration is flexible. Unpaid. Open to college freshmen, college sophomores, college juniors, college seniors, recent college graduates. International applications accepted.

Benefits Formal training, job counseling, names of contacts, on-the-job training, opportunity to attend seminars/workshops, possible full-time employment, willing to act as a professional reference, willing to complete paperwork for educational credit, willing to provide letters of recommendation, some free meals.

Contact Write, call, fax, e-mail, or through World Wide Web site Joe Hungler, Director of Operations. Phone: 508-754-2686. Fax: 508-754-7635. E-mail: jhungler@bgcworcester.org. In-person interview recommended (telephone interview accepted). Applicants must submit a letter of interest, resume, academic transcripts, two personal references. Application deadline: April 1 for summer, October 1 for spring. World Wide Web: http://www.bgcworcester.org.

BOYS HOPE GIRLS HOPE NATIONAL OFFICE
12120 Bridgeton Square Drive
Bridgeton, Missouri 63044-2607

General Information National organization that provides family-like homes and college preparatory educational opportunities for at-risk, yet academically capable, boys and girls ages 10 to 14. Established in 1977. Number of employees: 125. Number of internship applications received each year: 125.

Internships Available ▶ *1–2 administrative interns:* responsibilities include providing administrative support and office support for executive office resource development efforts. Candidates should have ability to work with others, computer skills, office skills, oral communication skills, organizational skills, personal interest in the field, plan to pursue career in field, written communication skills. Duration is flexible. Unpaid. Open to college juniors, college seniors, recent college graduates, graduate students, career changers. ▶ *50 tutors:* responsibilities include providing tutoring assistance to boys or girls at a local program. Candidates should have editing skills, oral communication skills, organizational skills, strong interpersonal skills, strong leadership ability. Duration is flexible. Unpaid. Open to recent college graduates, graduate students, career changers. ▶ *40–50 volunteer residential counselors:* responsibilities include living with children and other staff, maintaining a structured and stable home environment for up to 8 boys or girls, assuming a mentoring role, assisting students in academics, assisting houseparents in daily home operation, and exploring college and career opportunities with students. Candidates should have ability to work independently, oral communication skills, personal interest in the field, self-motivation, strong interpersonal skills, strong leadership ability, background in education and/or recreation (preferred). Duration is 12 months. $200 per month. Open to recent college graduates, graduate students, career changers.

Benefits Formal training, free housing, free meals, health insurance, on-the-job training, opportunity to attend seminars/workshops, possible full-time employment, travel reimbursement, willing to act as a professional reference, willing to complete paperwork for educational credit, willing to provide letters of recommendation.

Contact Write, call, fax, e-mail, or through World Wide Web site Laurie Keefe, Volunteer Coordinator. Phone: 877-878-HOPE. Fax: 314-298-1251. E-mail: lkeefe@bhgh.org. In-person interview recommended (telephone interview accepted). Applicants must submit a formal organization application, resume, academic transcripts, three personal references, criminal history background check required, physical exam, driver's license, 1 immediate family member reference. Application deadline: April 1 for fall; continuous for other positions. World Wide Web: http://www.boyshopegirlshope.org.

BOYS HOPE GIRLS HOPE OF ARIZONA
3443 North Central Avenue, Suite 713
Phoenix, Arizona 85012

General Information Private, nonprofit residential scholarship program working with bright and gifted at-risk youth; provides 100% support for youth in high school and assistance in college. Established in 1989. Number of employees: 11. Affiliate of Boys Hope Girls Hope, St. Louis, Missouri. Number of internship applications received each year: 3.

Internships Available ▶ *1–2 program assistants:* responsibilities include program development and enhancement; community networking and public speaking; recruitment and assessment of potential participants in the program; case management. Candidates should have ability to work independently, oral communication skills, personal interest in the field, plan to pursue career in field, self-motivation, strong interpersonal skills. Duration is flexible. Position available as unpaid or paid. Open to college juniors, college seniors, recent college graduates, graduate students, career changers. ▶ *2–3 residential counselors:* responsibilities include direct care and supervision of up to 8 youth; live-in position to support and empower youth to develop intellectually, emotionally, socially, physically, and spiritually. Candidates should have ability to work with others, knowledge of field, oral communication skills, organizational skills, personal interest in the field. Duration is one year (August to August). Position available as unpaid or at $200 per month; AmeriCorps stipend at end of service. Open to recent college graduates, graduate students.

Benefits Formal training, free housing, on-the-job training, opportunity to attend seminars/workshops, possible full-time employment, willing to act as a professional reference, willing to complete paperwork for educational credit, willing to provide letters of recommendation, stipend and other benefits negotiable.

Contact Write or call Melanie McClintlock, Executive Director. Phone: 602-266-4873. Fax: 602-200-8426. E-mail: mmcclintock@bhgh.org. In-person interview required. Applicants must submit a formal organization application, letter of interest, resume. Applications are accepted continuously. World Wide Web: http://www.boyshopegirlshope.org.

BREAK THE CYCLE
PO Box 64996
Los Angeles, California 90064

General Information Nonprofit organization whose mission is to end domestic violence by providing preventative education, free legal representation, advocacy, and support to young people ages 12-22. Established in 1995. Number of employees: 11. Number of internship applications received each year: 30.

Internships Available ▶ *1 development intern:* responsibilities include updating donor database; conducting grant research; assisting in planning fund-raising events. Candidates should have ability to work independently, computer skills, oral communication skills, personal interest in the field, research skills, self-motivation, strong interpersonal skills, written communication skills. Duration is 1 semester. Unpaid. Open to college sophomores, college juniors, college seniors, recent college graduates, graduate students. ▶ *2 interns:* responsibilities include providing wide range of administrative support to programs; performing research and writing on various domestic violence, youth, and women's issues; assisting in fund-raising; conducting outreach. Candidates should have computer skills, office skills, oral communication skills, self-motivation, strong interpersonal skills, written communication skills. Duration is June to August (with possibility of extension) or one semester. Unpaid. Open to recent high school graduates, college freshmen, college sophomores, college juniors, college seniors, recent college graduates. ▶ *1–2 law interns:* responsibilities include exposure to a wide range of legal work and experiences, including performing traditional legal research on public interest law issues that affect the lives and safety of the youth that Break-the-Cycle serves; co-teaching "Ending Violence: A Curriculum for Educating Teens on Domestic Violence and the Law"; and conducting various forms of outreach and client advocacy. Candidates should have computer skills, oral communication skills, personal interest in the field, self-motivation, strong interpersonal skills, written communication skills. Duration is 1 semester. Unpaid. Open to law

Break the Cycle (continued)

students. ▶ *1 nonprofit management intern:* responsibilities include assisting associate director with variety of tasks relating to nonprofit management, including but not limited to operations, program services, and fund-raising. Candidates should have computer skills, oral communication skills, personal interest in the field, self-motivation, written communication skills, strong attention to detail. Duration is 1–2 semesters. Unpaid. Open to college freshmen, college sophomores, college juniors, college seniors, recent college graduates, graduate students. International applications accepted.

Benefits On-the-job training, opportunity to attend seminars/workshops, possible full-time employment, willing to complete paperwork for educational credit.

Contact Write, call, fax, or e-mail Volunteer Coordinator. Phone: 310-286-3366. Fax: 310-286-3386. E-mail: volunteer@breakthecycle.org. In-person interview recommended (telephone interview accepted). Applicants must submit a letter of interest, resume. Application deadline: March 1 for summer; continuous for year-round positions. World Wide Web: http://www.break-the-cycle.org.

BRETHREN VOLUNTEER SERVICE
1451 Dundee Avenue
Elgin, Illinois 60120

General Information Volunteer organization with goals that include working for peace, advocating justice, serving basic human needs, and maintaining the integrity of creation. Established in 1948. Number of employees: 4. Unit of Church of the Brethren, Elgin, Illinois. Number of internship applications received each year: 100.

Internships Available ▶ *80–100 domestic volunteers:* responsibilities include performing duties that vary according to project and volunteer's skills, experience, and interest. Duration is 1 year. $60–$80 per month. Open to individuals 18 years or older. ▶ *20–30 overseas volunteers:* responsibilities include performing duties that vary according to project and volunteer's skills, experience, and interest; possibly working in Europe, Latin America, Japan, and Nigeria. Duration is minimum of 2 years. $60–$80 per month. Open to college graduates 21 years or older. International applications accepted.

Benefits Free housing, free meals, health insurance, cost of travel expenses to and from project for U.S. positions; some projects may qualify for educational award.

International Internships Available.

Contact Write, call, fax, e-mail, or through World Wide Web site Brethren Volunteer Service Recruitment. Phone: 800-323-8039 Ext. 454. Fax: 847-742-0278. E-mail: bvs_gb@brethren.org. Applicants must submit a formal organization application, letter of interest, resume, academic transcripts, current photo and essay, $400 for overseas travel. Applications are accepted continuously. World Wide Web: http://www.brethrenvolunteerservice.org.

BUTLER COUNTY RAPE CRISIS CENTER
110 South College Avenue
Oxford, Ohio 45056

General Information Social service agency providing information and support to adult and child survivors of sexual assault as well as community education and prevention services. Established in 1990. Number of employees: 9. Affiliate of Community Counseling and Crisis Center, Oxford, Ohio. Number of internship applications received each year: 20.

Internships Available ▶ *10–30 volunteer victim advocates:* responsibilities include providing crisis counseling and advocacy for a 24-hour service that responds to sexual assault victims by phone or face-to-face in Butler County hospitals and police stations. Candidates should have ability to work independently, oral communication skills, personal interest in the field, self-motivation, strong interpersonal skills. Duration is summer (May start) or fall (September start). Unpaid. Open to recent high school graduates, college freshmen, college sophomores, college juniors, college seniors, recent college graduates, graduate students, law

students, career changers, individuals reentering the workforce, must be over age of 18 and living in or near Butler County. International applications accepted.

Benefits Formal training, on-the-job training, opportunity to attend seminars/workshops, willing to act as a professional reference, willing to complete paperwork for educational credit, willing to provide letters of recommendation.

Contact Write, call, or e-mail Jennifer Weigel, Assistant Director. Phone: 513-523-4149. Fax: 513-523-4145. E-mail: rcp@one.net. In-person interview required. Applicants must submit a formal organization application. Application deadline: April 30 for summer, September 30 for fall. World Wide Web: http://www.helpandhealing.org.

CAMP FIRE BOYS AND GIRLS
PO Box 3275
San Diego, California 92163-1275

General Information Nonprofit organization providing clubs, camping, and self-reliance for youth to develop self-esteem and the skills to function as caring, self-directed individuals. Established in 1929. Number of employees: 6. Unit of Camp Fire USA, Kansas City, Missouri. Number of internship applications received each year: 6.

Internships Available ▶ *1 resident camp program coordinator:* responsibilities include coordinating program schedule for summer resident camp for 100 at-risk youth per week; supporting counseling staff and organizing all camp activities and programs. Candidates should have ability to work independently, knowledge of field, oral communication skills, organizational skills, personal interest in the field, self-motivation, strong interpersonal skills, strong leadership ability, desire to work with children in an outdoor setting. Duration is July 6-11. Position available as unpaid or paid. Open to college freshmen, college sophomores, college juniors, college seniors, recent college graduates, graduate students.

Benefits Formal training, names of contacts, possible full-time employment, willing to complete paperwork for educational credit, willing to provide letters of recommendation.

Contact Write, call, or fax Nancy Thompson, Administrative Assistant. Phone: 619-291-8985. Fax: 619-291-8988. E-mail: campfiresd@aol.com. In-person interview required. Applicants must submit a resume, three personal references. Applications are accepted continuously.

CAMP FIRE USA CENTRAL COAST COUNCIL
PO Box 1269
Arroyo Grande, California 93421

General Information Youth development organization for boys and girls through club and camp programs. Established in 1939. Number of employees: 4. Unit of Camp Fire USA, Kansas City, Missouri.

Internships Available ▶ *1–5 community club leaders:* responsibilities include planning and running club meetings with 10-12 boys and girls, coordinating parent helpers, recruiting members, and staying within approved budget. Duration is 9–12 months. $8–$8.50 per hour. Open to recent high school graduates, college sophomores, college juniors, college seniors, recent college graduates, graduate students, career changers, individuals reentering the workforce. ▶ *1 resident camp director:* responsibilities include planning and organizing camp season, hiring and managing staff, overseeing all programs and facilities at camp, and working with volunteer camp committee. Duration is March to August. $9 per hour for 10 hours per week (March-June 15); $2500 for 6-week season (June to August). Open to college seniors, recent college graduates, graduate students, career changers, individuals reentering the workforce, must be at least 25 years of age. Candidates for all positions should have ability to work independently, ability to work with others, experience in the field, oral communication skills, organizational skills, strong leadership ability. International applications accepted.

Benefits Job counseling, on-the-job training, possible full-time employment, willing to act as a professional reference, willing to complete paperwork for educational credit, willing to provide letters of recommendation.

Contact Write, call, fax, or e-mail Ms. Joey Hughes, Executive Director. Phone: 805-489-7345. Fax: 805-489-6556. E-mail: campfirejh@onemain.com. In-person interview recommended (telephone interview accepted). Applicants must submit a formal organization application, resume, three personal references. Application deadline: March 31 for summer, July 15 for fall. Fees: $10.

CAMP FIRE USA GEORGIA COUNCIL
100 Edgewood Avenue, NE, Suite 528
Atlanta, Georgia 30303

General Information Organization that provides fun, experiential programs which enable youth to develop into caring, confident future leaders. Established in 1910. Number of employees: 18. Unit of Camp Fire USA, Kansas City, Missouri. Number of internship applications received each year: 10.

Internships Available ▶ *1 clerical assistant:* responsibilities include entering data from outcome measurement surveys. Candidates should have ability to work independently, computer skills, office skills, organizational skills, written communication skills. Duration is 1 semester. Position available as unpaid or paid. Open to high school seniors, recent high school graduates, college freshmen, college sophomores, college juniors, college seniors. ▶ *1–2 program assistants:* responsibilities include assisting program staff in all areas of program delivery in underserved areas. Candidates should have ability to work independently, ability to work with others, oral communication skills, personal interest in the field, self-motivation, strong leadership ability, Spanish language skills helpful. Duration is 1–2 semesters. Unpaid. Open to recent high school graduates, college freshmen, college sophomores, college juniors, college seniors, recent college graduates, graduate students, individuals reentering the workforce. ▶ *1 public relations intern:* responsibilities include writing press releases, designing flyers, and taking photographs. Candidates should have ability to work independently, computer skills, editing skills, writing skills. Duration is 1 semester. Unpaid. Open to college juniors, college seniors, recent college graduates, graduate students, career changers, individuals reentering the workforce.

Benefits Formal training, names of contacts, on-the-job training, opportunity to attend seminars/workshops, willing to complete paperwork for educational credit, willing to provide letters of recommendation, housing and meals (summer only).

Contact Write, call, fax, or e-mail Karen Sullivan, CEO. Phone: 404-527-7125. Fax: 404-527-7139. E-mail: kasullivan@campfireusaga.org. In-person interview recommended (telephone interview accepted). Applicants must submit a letter of interest, resume, three writing samples, personal reference, background check required. Applications are accepted continuously. World Wide Web: http://www.campfireusaga.org.

CAMP FIRE USA, NORTH OAKLAND COUNCIL
4450 Walton Boulevard, Suite C
Waterford, Michigan 48329

General Information Organization that provides, through a program of informal education, opportunities for youth to realize their potential and to function as caring, self-directed individuals, responsible to themselves and to others. Established in 1910. Number of employees: 4. Unit of Camp Fire USA, Kansas City, Missouri.

Internships Available ▶ *Club leaders:* responsibilities include conducting a Camp Fire program for a group of 5-15 children. Candidates should have oral communication skills, organizational skills, self-motivation, strong interpersonal skills, strong leadership ability. Duration is 2 semesters. Unpaid. Open to recent high school graduates, college freshmen, college sophomores, college juniors, college seniors, recent college graduates, individuals reentering the workforce. ▶ *1–15 day camp counselors:* responsibilities include working with a group of 10 campers in a day camp setting on a pre-planned program. Candidates should have oral communication skills, organizational skills, self-motivation, strong interpersonal skills, strong leadership ability. Duration is 4 weeks in the summer. $125 per week. Open to recent high school graduates, college freshmen, college sophomores, college juniors, college seniors, recent college graduates, graduate students, law students, career changers, individuals reentering the workforce. ▶ *1–4 school club leaders:* responsibilities include conducting a bi-weekly pre-planned Camp Fire meeting for at-risk youth. Candidates should have oral communication skills, organizational skills, plan to pursue career in field, self-motivation, strong interpersonal skills. Duration is 2 semesters. Position available as unpaid or at $7 per hour. Open to high school seniors, recent high school graduates, college freshmen, college sophomores, college juniors, college seniors, recent college graduates, graduate students, law students, career changers, individuals reentering the workforce. International applications accepted.

Benefits Formal training, names of contacts, opportunity to attend seminars/workshops, willing to complete paperwork for educational credit, willing to provide letters of recommendation.

Contact Write, call, fax, e-mail, or through World Wide Web site Ms. Barb Zelinski, Program Director. Phone: 248-618-9050. Fax: 248-618-9052. E-mail: campfireusano@aol.com. In-person interview required. Application deadline: May 1 for summer camp. World Wide Web: http://www.comnet.org/campfirenoc.

CAMP FIRE USA WATHANA COUNCIL
16250 Northland Drive, #301
Southfield, Michigan

General Information Nonprofit youth development organization. Established in 1910. Number of employees: 7. Unit of Camp Fire USA, Kansas City, Missouri.

Internships Available ▶ *1 communications associate:* responsibilities include assisting director of communications with public/media relations, special events, grant writing, newsletter, and Web site development. Candidates should have ability to work independently, ability to work with others, computer skills, office skills, oral communication skills, written communication skills. Duration is 1 semester. Position available as unpaid or at $8.50–$10 per hour. Open to college seniors. ▶ *2–3 summer camp interns:* responsibilities include working with camp director to plan and implement youth programs at summer residential camp in Holly, Michigan. Candidates should have ability to work with others, oral communication skills, self-motivation, strong leadership ability, commitment to work with youth. Duration is June to August. $8.50–$10 per hour. Open to college juniors, college seniors. ▶ *1–2 youth program associates:* responsibilities include working directly with program staff to plan and implement a multi-faceted youth development program. Candidates should have ability to work with others, oral communication skills, plan to pursue career in field, self-motivation, commitment to work with youth. Duration is 1 semester. Position available as unpaid or at $8.50–$10 per hour. Open to college sophomores, college juniors, college seniors.

Benefits Formal training, job counseling, on-the-job training, opportunity to attend seminars/workshops, possible full-time employment, willing to act as a professional reference, willing to complete paperwork for educational credit, willing to provide letters of recommendation.

Contact Write, fax, or e-mail Linda Tarjeft, Executive Director. Fax: 248-599-4307. E-mail: campfirewc@msn.com. No phone calls. In-person interview required. Applicants must submit a letter of interest, resume, three personal references, two letters of recommendation. Applications are accepted continuously.

CAMPHILL SOLTANE
224 Nantmeal Road
Glenmoore, Pennsylvania 19343

General Information Life-sharing community that provides a bridge from youth to adulthood for people with developmental disabilities through community life, further education and training, the arts, and job placement in the surrounding area. Established in 1988. Number of employees: 36. Affiliate of Camphill Association of North America, Hudson, New York. Number of internship applications received each year: 50.

Internships Available ▶ *1 orchardist:* responsibilities include leading work crew in caring for 300-tree orchard and 1 acre of berries according to biodynamic gardening methods; householding and direct care activities. Candidates should have ability to work with others, knowledge of field, personal interest in the field,

Camphill Soltane (continued)

strong leadership ability. Duration is 1–5 years. Unpaid. Open to recent college graduates, career changers. ▶ *8–10 special education interns:* responsibilities include householding, direct care as needed, and helping with workshops and activities. Candidates should have ability to work independently, oral communication skills, self-motivation, strong interpersonal skills, personal interest in developmental disabilities, community living, and personal growth. Duration is ten to twelve months (late August to late July preferred), full-time. Unpaid. Open to recent high school graduates, college freshmen, college sophomores, college juniors, college seniors, recent college graduates, graduate students, career changers, individuals reentering the workforce, individuals 19 years of age or older (required). International applications accepted.

Benefits Formal training, free housing, free meals, names of contacts, on-the-job training, opportunity to attend seminars/workshops, willing to act as a professional reference, willing to complete paperwork for educational credit, willing to provide letters of recommendation, monthly stipend, health insurance (after initial 3 months), vacation funds in July, possibility of continuing involvement, student loan assistance available for AmeriCorps participants.

Contact Write, call, fax, e-mail, or through World Wide Web site Anne-Marie McMahon, Projects Administrator. Phone: 610-469-0933. Fax: 610-469-1054. E-mail: amcmahon@camphillsoltane. org. In-person interview recommended (telephone interview accepted). Applicants must submit a formal organization application, three personal references. Applications are accepted continuously. World Wide Web: http://www.camphillsoltane.org.

CAMP WOODSON
741 Old U.S. Highway 70
Swannanoa, North Carolina 28778

General Information Year-round therapeutic wilderness camping program for juvenile delinquents and/or at-risk youth. Established in 1976. Number of employees: 21. Division of Department of Juvenile Justice and Delinquency Prevention, State of North Carolina, Raleigh, North Carolina. Number of internship applications received each year: 15.

Internships Available ▶ *3–5 fieldwork interns:* responsibilities include hiking, camping, canoeing, horseback riding, and/or rock climbing with students and staff; assisting with office paperwork including documentation, treatment plans, and records; and daily counseling of individuals and groups. Candidates should have ability to work independently, oral communication skills, self-motivation, strong interpersonal skills, strong leadership ability, must have own transportation. Duration is 1–4 months. Unpaid. Open to college freshmen, college sophomores, college juniors, college seniors, recent college graduates, graduate students, law students, career changers, individuals reentering the workforce. International applications accepted.

Benefits Formal training, free meals, job counseling, names of contacts, opportunity to attend seminars/workshops, possible full-time employment, willing to complete paperwork for educational credit, willing to provide letters of recommendation, use of equipment.

Contact Write, call, fax, or e-mail Melanie Derry, Internship Coordinator. Phone: 828-686-9595 Ext. 237. Fax: 828-686-7671. E-mail: melanie.derry@ncmail.net. In-person interview recommended (telephone interview accepted). Applicants must submit a letter of interest, resume, three personal references. Application deadline: March 1 for spring.

CAPITAL CITY YOUTH SERVICES
2407 Roberts Avenue
Tallahassee, Florida 32310

General Information Nonprofit youth services agency that provides counseling, short-term residential, and community/school outreach to youth and families in crisis. Established in 1974. Number of employees: 43. Number of internship applications received each year: 18.

Internships Available ▶ *1 business intern:* responsibilities include computer data entry, accounts receivable, setting up and using spreadsheets, organizing file system, accounts payable, and some general ledger duties. Candidates should have ability to work with others, analytical skills, college courses in field, organizational skills, personal interest in the field, plan to pursue career in field. Duration is 1–2 semesters. Unpaid. Open to college sophomores, college juniors. ▶ *1 communications intern:* responsibilities include outreach, event planning, designing literature and other PR activities as needed. Candidates should have ability to work independently, oral communication skills, organizational skills, personal interest in the field, strong interpersonal skills, written communication skills. Duration is flexible. Unpaid. Open to college freshmen, college sophomores, college juniors, college seniors, recent college graduates, graduate students, career changers, individuals reentering the workforce. ▶ *1–3 residential program interns:* responsibilities include case management, youth development, follow-ups, direct supervision, crisis calls, program management, educational assistance, and group counseling. Candidates should have ability to work independently, oral communication skills, personal interest in the field, self-motivation, strong interpersonal skills, written communication skills. Duration is flexible. Unpaid. Open to college juniors, college seniors, recent college graduates, graduate students. International applications accepted.

Benefits On-the-job training, opportunity to attend seminars/workshops, possible full-time employment, willing to act as a professional reference, willing to complete paperwork for educational credit, willing to provide letters of recommendation.

Contact Write, call, fax, or e-mail Melanie Carty, Communications Director. Phone: 850-576-6000. Fax: 850-576-2580. E-mail: melanie@ccys.org. In-person interview required. Applicants must submit a formal organization application, letter of interest, resume, two personal references, in-depth background check required. Applications are accepted continuously. World Wide Web: http://www.ccys.org.

CATHOLIC BIG BROTHERS BIG SISTERS
3300 West Temple Street
Los Angeles, California 90026

General Information Social service organization that provides healthy role models for at-risk youth. Established in 1925. Number of employees: 50. Affiliate of Big Brothers Big Sisters of America, Inc, Philadelphia, Pennsylvania. Number of internship applications received each year: 3.

Internships Available ▶ *1 development assistant:* responsibilities include assisting director of development, locating foundations, researching criteria for grant applications, and writing letters to donors. Candidates should have computer skills, office skills, oral communication skills, organizational skills, research skills, strong interpersonal skills, written communication skills. Duration is flexible. Unpaid. Open to recent high school graduates, college freshmen, college sophomores, college juniors, college seniors, recent college graduates, graduate students, career changers, individuals reentering the workforce. ▶ *1–8 director's assistants:* responsibilities include assisting director of programs, keeping records, assuring quality, and planning and follow-up. Candidates should have office skills, oral communication skills, personal interest in the field, self-motivation, strong interpersonal skills, written communication skills. Duration is flexible. Unpaid. Open to college freshmen, college sophomores, college juniors, college seniors, recent college graduates, graduate students, career changers, individuals reentering the workforce. ▶ *1 marketing/public relations assistant:* responsibilities include assisting director of marketing/public relations, contacting media, coordinating events, and preparing press releases. Candidates should have oral communication skills, personal interest in the field, self-motivation, strong interpersonal skills, writing skills. Duration is flexible. Unpaid. ▶ *1–3 school-based mentoring programs assistants:* responsibilities include assisting director of programs, working with youth and volunteers, record keeping and reports, tutoring, and mentoring. Candidates should have oral communication skills, personal interest in the field, self-motivation, strong interpersonal skills, written communication skills. Duration is flexible. Unpaid. Open to recent high school graduates, college freshmen, college sophomores, college juniors, college seniors, recent college graduates, graduate students, career changers, individuals reentering the workforce.

▶ *1–8 social work interns:* responsibilities include assisting directors with programs, case management, working with youth, counseling, tutoring, mentoring youth. Candidates should have office skills, oral communication skills, personal interest in the field, plan to pursue career in field, self-motivation, strong interpersonal skills, written communication skills. Duration is flexible (6 months to 12 months). Unpaid. Open to recent high school graduates, college freshmen, college sophomores, college juniors, college seniors, recent college graduates, graduate students, career changers, individuals reentering the workforce. International applications accepted.

Benefits Formal training, on-the-job training, possible full-time employment, travel reimbursement, willing to act as a professional reference, willing to complete paperwork for educational credit, willing to provide letters of recommendation.

Contact Write, call, fax, e-mail, or through World Wide Web site Douglas Ferraro. Phone: 213-251-9800. Fax: 213-251-9855. E-mail: info@catholicbigbrothers.org. In-person interview required. Applicants must submit a letter of interest, resume. Applications are accepted continuously. World Wide Web: http://www. catholicbigbrothers.org.

CATHOLIC CHARITIES FLEMINGTON
6 Park Avenue
Flemington, New Jersey 08822

General Information Multi-service agency providing a wide range of quality mental health and substance abuse services to individuals, families, neighborhoods, and communities. Established in 1982. Number of employees: 25. Number of internship applications received each year: 8.

Internships Available ▶ *4–6 family service office interns:* responsibilities include conducting assessments and case management with an emphasis on family therapy; individual, couples, family, and group counseling. Candidates should have ability to work independently, college courses in field, plan to pursue career in field, strong interpersonal skills, written communication skills. Duration is 9–12 months. Unpaid. Open to graduate students, college students pursuing master's-level degree for social work or counseling psychology. International applications accepted.

Benefits Names of contacts, on-the-job training, opportunity to attend seminars/workshops, possible full-time employment, willing to complete paperwork for educational credit.

Contact Write, call, fax, or e-mail Jeanne Hahn, Program Director. Phone: 908-782-7905. Fax: 908-782-5934. E-mail: jhahn@ccdom. org. In-person interview required. Applicants must submit a resume, school referral. Applications are accepted continuously.

CENTRAL VERMONT COUNCIL ON AGING/ NEIGHBOR TO NEIGHBOR AMERICORPS
30 Washington Street, Suite 2
Barre, Vermont 05641-4279

General Information AmeriCorps program hosted by five area agencies on aging that works to connect volunteers to meet the needs of elders in their community; 25 members statewide develop and organize successful programs for the aged. Established in 1975. Number of employees: 30. Number of internship applications received each year: 40.

Internships Available ▶ *25 Neighbor to Neighbor AmeriCorps Members:* responsibilities include working independently or on teams of 6; balancing time between providing direct service to elders and adults with disabilities and recruiting volunteers to meet the needs of clients; positions available statewide. Candidates should have ability to work independently, organizational skills, personal interest in the field, self-motivation, strong interpersonal skills. Duration is September to August. Stipend of $10500 upon completion of internship. Open to college seniors, recent college graduates, graduate students, individuals reentering the workforce.

Benefits Formal training, health insurance, job counseling, names of contacts, on-the-job training, opportunity to attend seminars/workshops, possible full-time employment, travel reimbursement, tuition assistance, willing to act as a professional reference, willing to complete paperwork for educational credit, willing to provide letters of recommendation, child care.

Contact Call, e-mail, or through World Wide Web site Nancy Sherman, Program Director. Phone: 802-479-0531. Fax: 802-479-4235. E-mail: nsherman@cvcoa.org. In-person interview recommended (telephone interview accepted). Applicants must submit a formal organization application, letter of interest, resume, 3 personal references or 2 letters of recommendation. Application deadline: September 1. World Wide Web: http://www. N2Namericorps.org.

CHILD AND FAMILY SERVICES OF NEWPORT COUNTY
19 Valley Road
Middletown, Rhode Island 02842

General Information Nonprofit agency providing services for children, their families, and the communities in which they live. Established in 1867. Number of employees: 275. Number of internship applications received each year: 30.

Internships Available ▶ *1–5 child-care interns:* responsibilities include assisting teachers with classroom management, one-on-one parent contacts. Candidates should have ability to work independently, college courses in field, oral communication skills, personal interest in the field, self-motivation, strong interpersonal skills. Duration is 1 semester. Unpaid. Open to college sophomores, college juniors, college seniors, graduate students. ▶ *1–4 community-based interns:* responsibilities include assisting staff in the provision of wide range of home-based services to families in process of reunification or seeking to avoid separation. Candidates should have ability to work independently, declared college major in field, oral communication skills, self-motivation, strong interpersonal skills. Duration is 6 months. Unpaid. Open to college sophomores, college juniors, college seniors, graduate students. ▶ *5–15 residential program interns:* responsibilities include working with staff to provide safe, nurturing environment in which youth 6-18 can learn and grow; includes one-on-one and group activities. Candidates should have ability to work independently, ability to work with others, declared college major in field, oral communication skills, personal interest in the field, self-motivation. Duration is minimum of 6 months. Unpaid. Open to college sophomores, college juniors, college seniors, graduate students. ▶ *1–5 school-based interns:* responsibilities include assisting in classroom with special programs; developing group programs; working one-on-one with students needing special attention. Candidates should have ability to work independently, declared college major in field, oral communication skills, personal interest in the field, self-motivation, strong interpersonal skills. Duration is 1 semester. Unpaid. Open to college juniors, college seniors, graduate students. International applications accepted.

Benefits On-the-job training, opportunity to attend seminars/workshops, possible full-time employment, willing to act as a professional reference, willing to complete paperwork for educational credit, willing to provide letters of recommendation.

Contact Write, call, or e-mail Martha Parks, Volunteer/Intern Program Director. Phone: 401-848-4210. Fax: 401-848-2336. E-mail: mparks@cfsnewport.org. In-person interview required. Applicants must submit a formal organization application, resume, three personal references. Applications are accepted continuously.

CHILD CARE, INC.
275 7th Avenue
New York, New York 10001

General Information Nonprofit child-care and early education resource organization that offers programs on public policy work, training for child-care providers, and referrals for parents. Established in 1982. Number of employees: 35. Number of internship applications received each year: 40.

Internships Available ▶ *3–5 development interns:* responsibilities include assisting with coordination of memberships, researching prospective funders, writing articles for newsletter, writing and editing correspondence with funders and members, and planning for annual event. Candidates should have ability to work independently, ability to work with others, computer skills, office skills, personal interest in the field, research skills, self-motivation, writing skills, creative thinking skills, some awareness of child-

Child Care, Inc. (continued)

care issues (helpful). Duration is 2–3 months in summer; positions during school year negotiable. Position available as unpaid or paid. Open to college freshmen, college sophomores, college juniors, college seniors, recent college graduates, graduate students, career changers.

Benefits Names of contacts, on-the-job training, opportunity to attend seminars/workshops, willing to act as a professional reference, willing to complete paperwork for educational credit, willing to provide letters of recommendation, stipend, transportation reimbursement provided.

Contact Write, fax, or e-mail Brian Rausse, Development Associate. Fax: 212-929-5785. E-mail: brausse@childcareinc.org. No phone calls. In-person interview required. Applicants must submit a letter of interest, resume, writing samples for some positions. Applications are accepted continuously. World Wide Web: http://www. childcareinc.org.

CHRYSALIS: A CENTER FOR WOMEN
4432 Chicago Avenue, S
Minneapolis, Minnesota 55407-3522

General Information Multi-service organization serving women and their families; programs include mental health, chemical dependency, legal assistance, family education, resource referral, supportive counseling, and education and support groups. Established in 1974. Number of employees: 50. Number of internship applications received each year: 100.

Internships Available ▶ *2 chemical health interns:* responsibilities include developing a caseload of clients in a feminist-based, high quality chemical dependency outreach program. Candidates should have college courses in field, knowledge of field, personal interest in the field, plan to pursue career in field, strong interpersonal skills. Duration is flexible. Unpaid. Open to college seniors, graduate students, those enrolled in or graduates of chemical dependency certification program. ▶ *2–3 family education interns:* responsibilities include providing support in several capacities to children in various stages of development. Candidates should have knowledge of field, oral communication skills, personal interest in the field, self-motivation, strong interpersonal skills. Duration is 150 hours or more. Unpaid. Open to college freshmen, college sophomores, college juniors, college seniors, recent college graduates, career changers, individuals reentering the workforce. ▶ *2–3 legal and resource interns:* responsibilities include helping empower women through education and advocacy; hosting legal education sessions; facilitating legal advice clinics and offering peer support through the resource counseling program. Candidates should have ability to work independently, knowledge of field, oral communication skills, personal interest in the field, strong interpersonal skills. Duration is 150 hours or more. Unpaid. Open to college freshmen, college sophomores, college juniors, college seniors, recent college graduates, graduate students, law students, career changers, individuals reentering the workforce. ▶ *1–2 marketing and communications interns:* responsibilities include working with development, marketing, and communications team on a variety of projects, particularly outreach to the community and event coordination. Candidates should have knowledge of field, oral communication skills, personal interest in the field, strong interpersonal skills, written communication skills. Duration is 150 hours or more. Unpaid. Open to college sophomores, college juniors, college seniors, recent college graduates, graduate students, career changers, individuals reentering the workforce. ▶ *3 mental health clinic interns:* responsibilities include participating in all aspects of clinic operations, including intakes and individual, group, and family therapy. Candidates should have college courses in field, knowledge of field, oral communication skills, plan to pursue career in field, strong interpersonal skills. Duration is 9 month minimum, September through June. Unpaid. Open to graduate students. ▶ *10–15 resource counseling interns:* responsibilities include providing support, resources, and referrals to women who call or walk into the Center. Candidates should have oral communication skills, personal interest in the field, self-motivation, strong interpersonal skills. Duration is 150 hours or more. Unpaid. Open to college freshmen, college sophomores, college juniors,

college seniors, recent college graduates, graduate students, law students, career changers, individuals reentering the workforce. International applications accepted.

Benefits Formal training, names of contacts, on-the-job training, opportunity to attend seminars/workshops, possible full-time employment, willing to act as a professional reference, willing to complete paperwork for educational credit, willing to provide letters of recommendation.

Contact Call, e-mail, or through World Wide Web site Ms. Karen Smith, Volunteer Services Manager, 4432 Chicago Avenue S, Minneapolis, Minnesota 55407-3522. Phone: 612-870-2420. Fax: 612-870-2403. E-mail: ksmith@chrysaliswomen.org. In-person interview recommended (telephone interview accepted). Applicants must submit a letter of interest, resume, 2 professional references. Application deadline: January 1 for spring, May 21 for summer, September 1 for fall. World Wide Web: http://www.chrysaliswomen.org.

COLUMBUS YOUTH CAMP
12454 West Youth Camp Road
Columbus, Indiana 47201

General Information Nonprofit youth organization. Established in 1928. Number of employees: 3. Division of Foundation for Youth, Columbus, Indiana. Number of internship applications received each year: 10.

Internships Available ▶ *1–2 interpretation interns:* responsibilities include interpretive needs assessment; developing nature trail and signage; researching historical information of camp history. Candidates should have ability to work independently, oral communication skills, organizational skills, personal interest in the field, research skills, written communication skills. Duration is 3 months. $750 per duration of internship. ▶ *2–6 outdoor recreation resource management interns:* responsibilities include assisting in program planning and implementation; supervising seasonal staff; inspection and maintenance of challenge course elements; assisting in leading adventure trips; assisting with administrative responsibilities. Candidates should have ability to work independently, personal interest in the field, self-motivation, strong interpersonal skills, strong leadership ability. Duration is 3 months. $1000 per duration of internship. Open to college sophomores, college juniors, college seniors, recent college graduates, graduate students. International applications accepted.

Benefits Free housing, names of contacts, on-the-job training, opportunity to attend seminars/workshops, possible full-time employment, willing to act as a professional reference, willing to complete paperwork for educational credit, willing to provide letters of recommendation.

Contact Write, call, fax, or e-mail Laura Boggess, Director of Programs. Phone: 812-342-2698. Fax: 812-372-3226. E-mail: laura@ columbusyouthcamp.com. In-person interview recommended (telephone interview accepted). Applicants must submit a letter of interest, resume. Application deadline: February 15 for summer, May 15 for fall, December 1 for spring. World Wide Web: http://www.columbusyouthcamp.com.

COMMISSION FOR WOMEN–COUNSELING AND CAREER CENTER
401 North Washington Street, Suite 100
Rockville, Maryland 20850

General Information Commission that conducts research and advocacy activities for women's issues and operates a counseling and career center primarily for women. Established in 1976. Number of employees: 20. Department of Montgomery County Government, Rockville, Maryland. Number of internship applications received each year: 15.

Internships Available ▶ *1–3 Commission for Women interns:* responsibilities include researching and preparing reports. Candidates should have ability to work independently, analytical skills, computer skills, editing skills, knowledge of field, oral communication skills, organizational skills, personal interest in the field, research skills, self-motivation, strong interpersonal skills, strong leadership ability, writing skills. Duration is 1 year. Unpaid. Open to college seniors, recent college graduates, graduate students, law students, career changers, individuals reentering the workforce. ▶ *1–5 counseling interns:* responsibilities include providing psychosocial and career counseling to adults using short term, problem-solving approach; facilitating workshops/seminar. Candidates should have ability to work with others, analytical skills, college degree in related field, oral communication skills, plan to pursue career in field, counseling experience (preferred). Duration is 2 semesters (preferred). Unpaid. Open to second-year graduate students enrolled in a master's program for social work or counseling and are using this experience as part of a formal practicum or internship approved by their university for credit. ▶ *5 information and referral specialists:* responsibilities include assisting with information and referral services and providing intake for the counseling center. Candidates should have analytical skills, computer skills, knowledge of field, oral communication skills, organizational skills, personal interest in the field, research skills, strong interpersonal skills, written communication skills. Duration is 2 semesters (preferred). Unpaid. Open to college juniors, college seniors, recent college graduates, graduate students, career changers. International applications accepted.

Benefits Job counseling, on-the-job training, opportunity to attend seminars/workshops, willing to complete paperwork for educational credit, willing to provide letters of recommendation, supervision for counseling interns and those who need supervision in order to earn certification.

Contact Write, fax, e-mail, or through World Wide Web site Alyssa Philipp, Supervisor, Intake and Referral Services. Phone: 240-777-8307. Fax: 301-279-1318. E-mail: philia@co.mo.md.us. In-person interview recommended (telephone interview accepted). Applicants must submit a formal organization application, resume, letter of interest including time of availability. Applications are accepted continuously. World Wide Web: http://www.montgomerycountymd.gov/cfw.

COMMON GROUND SANCTUARY
1410 South Telegraph
Bloomfield Hills, Michigan 48302

General Information Comprehensive voluntary counseling and psychiatric assessment services for children, youth, and families; residential and non-residential care for people who are in crisis situations. Established in 1971. Number of employees: 198. Number of internship applications received each year: 60.

Internships Available ▶ *1 accountant:* responsibilities include tracking daily receipts and disbursements, performing general ledger, payroll, budgeting, and budget analysis duties. Candidates should have ability to work independently, analytical skills, computer skills, experience in the field, organizational skills, self-motivation, strong interpersonal skills, written communication skills. Duration is minimum of 1 semester. Unpaid. Open to recent high school graduates, college freshmen, college sophomores, college juniors, college seniors, career changers, individuals reentering the workforce. ▶ *1 business administrator:* responsibilities include assisting in developing business plans, strategic planning, internal information management, and personnel policies. Candidates should have ability to work independently, analytical skills, experience in the field, office skills, oral communication skills, organizational skills, self-motivation, strong interpersonal skills, strong leadership ability, written communication skills. Duration is minimum of 1 semester. Unpaid. Open to college freshmen, college sophomores, college juniors, college seniors, recent college graduates. ▶ *6 counselors:* responsibilities include directing case load of 2-10 youth and families and providing after-care and advocacy counseling. Candidates should have college courses in field, knowledge of field, oral communication skills, personal interest in the field, self-motivation, strong interpersonal skills, writing skills. Duration is 14–52 weeks. Unpaid. ▶ *4–20 direct care workers:* responsibilities include performing daily supervision, intakes, group counseling, recreational supervision, and teen consultation. Candidates should have personal interest in the field, strong interpersonal skills, written communication skills. Duration is minimum of 1 semester. Unpaid. Open to recent high school graduates, college freshmen, college sophomores, college juniors, college seniors, recent college graduates, law students, career changers, individuals reentering the workforce. ▶ *2 marketing and*

public relations interns: responsibilities include assisting in development and implementation of a corporate public relations strategic plan, including written, oral, and media relations, as well as marketing publications. Candidates should have ability to work with others, computer skills, knowledge of field, oral communication skills, personal interest in the field, self-motivation, written communication skills. Duration is 10–52 weeks. Unpaid. Open to high school seniors, recent high school graduates, college freshmen, college sophomores, college juniors, college seniors, recent college graduates, graduate students, individuals reentering the workforce. ▶ *2 victim assistance advocates:* responsibilities include providing advocacy, counseling, and support services to victims of crime; providing education and awareness classes/outreach, and supporting research and statistics. Candidates should have ability to work with others, college courses in field, computer skills, knowledge of field, oral communication skills, research skills, self-motivation, written communication skills. Duration is 12–52 weeks. Unpaid. Open to college freshmen, college sophomores, college juniors, college seniors, graduate students. International applications accepted.

Benefits Free meals, opportunity to attend seminars/workshops, possible full-time employment, travel reimbursement, willing to complete paperwork for educational credit, willing to provide letters of recommendation.

Contact Write, fax, or e-mail James A. Perlaki, Vice President of Community Intervention Services. Fax: 248-456-8147. E-mail: sanctuary6@aol.com. No phone calls. In-person interview required. Applicants must submit a formal organization application, resume, academic transcripts, three personal references. Application deadline: February 1 for spring/summer (recommended), November 1 for winter (recommended). World Wide Web: http://commongroundsanctuary.org.

COMMUNITY CRISIS CENTER
PO Box 1390
Elgin, Illinois 60121

General Information Center providing immediate, twenty-four hour, caring and professional services in response to requests from individuals and families affected by domestic violence, sexual assault, and other crisis situations. Established in 1975. Number of employees: 80. Number of internship applications received each year: 15.

Internships Available ▶ *4–6 case managers:* responsibilities include crisis intervention on the hot line, individual counseling with an assigned shelter resident client, providing information to walk-in clients. Duration is 400 hours. Unpaid. Open to college seniors. ▶ *1–2 children's workers:* responsibilities include assisting Children's Program staff with individual and group activities with the children in the shelter. Duration is 1 semester (20 hours per week). Unpaid. Open to college sophomores. ▶ *2–4 counselors:* responsibilities include crisis intervention via hot line, individual and group counseling with residents and walk-in clients, family counseling with resident adults and their minor children. Duration is September to May. Unpaid. Open to graduate students. ▶ *2–4 shelter workers:* responsibilities include assisting resident case managers in responding to the needs of the women and children in the shelter. Duration is 1 semester (20 hours per week). Unpaid. Open to college sophomores. Candidates for all positions should have college courses in field, oral communication skills, strong interpersonal skills, written communication skills. International applications accepted.

Benefits Formal training, names of contacts, on-the-job training, opportunity to attend seminars/workshops, possible full-time employment, willing to act as a professional reference, willing to complete paperwork for educational credit, willing to provide letters of recommendation.

Contact Call or fax Maureen Manning-Rosenfeld, Director of Client Services. Phone: 847-697-2380. Fax: 847-742-4182. In-person interview required. Applicants must submit a letter of interest, resume. Application deadline: March 1 for summer, April 1 for fall, October 1 for spring.

COMMUNITY MEDIATION CENTER
165 South Main Street, Suite A
Harrisonburg, Virginia 22801

General Information Mediation center providing services to individuals, families, organizations, and communities, as well as mediation and conflict resolution training. Established in 1982. Number of employees: 9. Number of internship applications received each year: 15.

Internships Available ▶ *5 case managers:* responsibilities include interviewing clients referred to mediation (by phone or in court) and scheduling cases for mediation. Candidates should have ability to work independently, college courses in field, oral communication skills, personal interest in the field, self-motivation, strong interpersonal skills, written communication skills. Duration is flexible. Unpaid. Open to college juniors, college seniors, recent college graduates, graduate students, law students, career changers. International applications accepted.

Benefits Formal training, names of contacts, on-the-job training, opportunity to attend seminars/workshops, willing to act as a professional reference, willing to complete paperwork for educational credit, willing to provide letters of recommendation.

Contact Write, call, fax, e-mail, or through World Wide Web site Timothy Ruebke, Director of Mediation Services. Phone: 540-434-0059. Fax: 540-574-0174. E-mail: cmcmediation@adelphia.net. In-person interview recommended (telephone interview accepted). Applicants must submit a letter of interest, resume. Application deadline: April 1 for summer, July 1 for fall, November 1 for spring. World Wide Web: http://www.cmcmediation.com.

CONNECTICUT JUVENILE TRAINING SCHOOL
1225 Silver Street
Middletown, Connecticut 06457

General Information Juvenile justice residential treatment facility for youths ages 12 to 16; provides custody and treatment of juvenile offenders. Established in 1971. Number of employees: 400. Unit of Department of Children and Families, State of Connecticut, Middletown, Connecticut. Number of internship applications received each year: 5.

Internships Available ▶ *2 clinical interns:* responsibilities include supervising counseling and group work. Candidates should have oral communication skills, personal interest in the field, strong interpersonal skills, writing skills. Duration is flexible. Unpaid. Open to graduate students. ▶ *4 residential interns:* responsibilities include assisting paraprofessional group leader. Candidates should have college courses in field, oral communication skills, personal interest in the field, self-motivation, strong interpersonal skills. Duration is flexible. Unpaid. Open to college freshmen, college sophomores, college juniors, college seniors, recent college graduates, graduate students.

Benefits Formal training, opportunity to attend seminars/workshops, possible full-time employment, willing to act as a professional reference, willing to complete paperwork for educational credit, willing to provide letters of recommendation.

Contact Write, call, or fax Dr. Patrick J. Russolillo, Director, Psychological Services. Phone: 860-638-2562. Fax: 860-638-2564. In-person interview required. Applicants must submit a formal organization application, letter of interest, resume, personal reference. Applications are accepted continuously.

CORNERSTONE FOUNDATION
90 Burns Avenue
San Ignacio, Cayo Belize

General Information Nonprofit humanitarian organization working to strengthen community, educate all age levels, provide basic needs, and empower citizens to improve their livelihood through grassroots mobilization. Established in 1999. Number of employees: 7. Number of internship applications received each year: 200.

Internships Available ▶ *1–4 HIV/AIDS education interns:* responsibilities include educating all community members about HIV and AIDS, concentrating more heavily on advocacy to change social conditions that lead to poor HIV health; recruiting and training community members and adolescent volunteers to do HIV/AIDS outreach on an informal basis, specifically targeting at-risk populations. Candidates should have ability to work independently, analytical skills, computer skills, editing skills, oral communication skills, organizational skills, research skills, self-motivation, strong interpersonal skills, strong leadership ability, writing skills, flexibility and a strong interest in working with grassroots activities. Duration is 3–12 months. Unpaid. Open to recent high school graduates, college sophomores, college juniors, college seniors, recent college graduates, career changers, individuals reentering the workforce. ▶ *1–10 Jump Start Program interns:* responsibilities include organizing projects and activities for pre-school age children and mothers with a focus on learning English in order to prepare them for school, where English is the taught language. Candidates should have ability to work independently, analytical skills, oral communication skills, organizational skills, self-motivation, strong interpersonal skills, strong leadership ability, written communication skills, flexibility and a strong interest in working with grassroots activities. Duration is 3-months in summer only. Unpaid. Open to recent high school graduates, college sophomores, college juniors, college seniors, recent college graduates, career changers, individuals reentering the workforce. ▶ *1–4 adult literacy coordinators:* responsibilities include coordinating existing basic literacy courses and English as a Second Language Program with the National Communication Skills Program, networking, recruiting and training instructors, and working to initiate new classes in surrounding villages. Candidates should have ability to work independently, analytical skills, office skills, oral communication skills, organizational skills, self-motivation, strong interpersonal skills, strong leadership ability, writing skills, flexibility and strong interest in working with grassroots activities. Duration is 3–12 months. Unpaid. Open to recent high school graduates, college freshmen, college sophomores, college juniors, college seniors, recent college graduates, career changers, individuals reentering the workforce. ▶ *1–4 community development coordinators:* responsibilities include assessing programs and providing ways and means to weave community and program initiatives together, to encourage community ownership of Cornerstone programs, and to inspire and support program initiatives. Candidates should have ability to work independently, analytical skills, computer skills, knowledge of field, office skills, oral communication skills, organizational skills, self-motivation, strong interpersonal skills, strong leadership ability, flexibility and a strong interest working with grassroots activities. Duration is 3–12 months. Unpaid. Open to recent high school graduates, college sophomores, college juniors, college seniors, recent college graduates, career changers, individuals reentering the workforce. ▶ *1–4 computer program coordinators:* responsibilities include assessing and working one-on-one with children and adults with a wide range of mental and physical disabilities; providing life skills training, establishing learning environments, and stimulating physical activity. Candidates should have ability to work independently, analytical skills, computer skills, oral communication skills, organizational skills, self-motivation, strong interpersonal skills, strong leadership ability, written communication skills, flexibility and a strong interest working with grassroots activities. Duration is 3–12 months. Unpaid. Open to recent high school graduates, college sophomores, college juniors, college seniors, recent college graduates, career changers, individuals reentering the workforce. ▶ *1–4 disaster, food, medical, relief/aid coordinators:* responsibilities include working with the ministry of Human Development and the Red Cross as well as the government hospital and traditional healers to complete assessments, find and receive proper treatment for clients, network with facilities and organizations abroad, and fund-raise. Candidates should have ability to work independently, analytical skills, computer skills, experience in the field, office skills, oral communication skills, organizational skills, research skills, self-motivation, strong interpersonal skills, strong leadership ability, written communication skills, flexibility and strong interest in working with grassroots activities. Duration is 3–12 months. Unpaid. Open to recent high school graduates, college freshmen, college sophomores, college juniors, college seniors, recent college graduates, career changers, individuals reentering the workforce. ▶ *1–4 environmental project coordinators:* responsibilities include teaching children environmental awareness and conservation, assisting in river and village clean-up campaigns, helping develop interpretive trails, and networking and cooperating with other environmental agencies including assisting with their projects and organic gardens. Candidates should have ability to work independently, analytical skills, oral communication skills, organizational skills, self-motivation, strong interpersonal skills, strong leadership ability, flexibility and a strong interest working with grassroots activities. Duration is 3–12 months. Unpaid. Open to recent high school graduates, college sophomores, college juniors, college seniors, recent college graduates, career changers, individuals reentering the workforce. ▶ *Up to 10 generations of culture interns:* responsibilities include being matched with a Belizian youth and elderly companion in order to learn about cultural distinctions and generational differences and facilitate the sharing and documenting of ideas between the generations. Candidates should have ability to work independently, analytical skills, oral communication skills, organizational skills, self-motivation, strong interpersonal skills, strong leadership ability, writing skills, flexibility and a strong interest in working with people of another culture. Duration is 3 weeks. Unpaid. Open to recent high school graduates, college sophomores, college juniors, college seniors, recent college graduates, career changers, individuals reentering the workforce. ▶ *1–4 media program interns:* responsibilities include interviewing, writing, and marketing for publications and an Internet Web site; includes one tourism-based magazine, a youth educational newsletter, and a women's empowerment newsletter; contributing as a desktop publisher or Web site designer. Candidates should have ability to work independently, analytical skills, computer skills, editing skills, office skills, oral communication skills, organizational skills, research skills, self-motivation, strong interpersonal skills, strong leadership ability, writing skills, flexibility and a strong interest working with grassroots activities. Duration is 3–12 months. Unpaid. Open to recent high school graduates, college sophomores, college juniors, college seniors, recent college graduates, career changers, individuals reentering the workforce. ▶ *Up to 10 natural healing interns:* responsibilities include exploring the environment of the Belizean rainforest and receiving an introduction to its healing resources; determining the role natural healing plays within Belizean culture. Candidates should have ability to work independently, analytical skills, oral communication skills, organizational skills, self-motivation, strong interpersonal skills, strong leadership ability, writing skills, flexibility and a strong interest in working with grassroots activities. Duration is 3 weeks. Unpaid. Open to recent high school graduates, college sophomores, college juniors, college seniors, recent college graduates, career changers. ▶ *1–4 women's program coordinators:* responsibilities include working with the ministry of Human Development and other women's organizations to develop women's programs including domestic violence outreach, community activism; helping publish a women's newsletter and educational activities. Candidates should have ability to work independently, analytical skills, office skills, oral communication skills, organizational skills, self-motivation, strong interpersonal skills, strong leadership ability, writing skills, flexibility and a strong interest in working with grassroots activities. Duration is 3–12 months. Unpaid. Open to recent high school graduates, college freshmen, college sophomores, college juniors, college seniors, recent college graduates, career changers, individuals reentering the workforce. ▶ *1–4 youth development coordinators:* responsibilities include designing and implementing youth programs for students who attend feeding program; coordinating other activities, including but not limited to the mural project, summer fun activities, arts and crafts, sports, music, monthly newsletter, life skills courses. Candidates should have ability to work independently, analytical skills, oral communication skills, organizational skills, self-motivation, strong interpersonal skills, strong leadership ability, written communication skills, flexibility and a strong interest in working with grassroots activities. Duration is 3–12 months. Unpaid. Open to recent high school graduates, college sophomores, college juniors, college seniors, recent college graduates, career changers, individuals reentering the workforce. International applications accepted.

Benefits Housing at a cost, meals at a cost, on-the-job training, willing to act as a professional reference, willing to complete paperwork for educational credit, willing to provide letters of recommendation.

International Internships Available.

Contact Write, call, fax, e-mail, or through World Wide Web site Rocio Zaiden, Development Director, San Ignacio Town, Cayo District Belize. Phone: 501-824-2373. Fax: 501-824-2373. E-mail: csvolunteers@hotmail.com. Applicants must submit a formal organization application, letter of interest. Application deadline: March 1 for summer, November 1 for spring. World Wide Web: http://www.peacecorner.org/cornerstone.htm.

COUNTERPOINT SHELTERS AND CRISIS CENTER
715 Inkster Road
Inkster, Michigan 48141

General Information Social service agency that provides a wide range of services including drug abuse prevention and a runaway shelter. Established in 1975. Number of employees: 30. Unit of Starfish Family Services, Inkster, Michigan. Number of internship applications received each year: 40.

Internships Available ▶ *4–6 counseling or group work interns:* responsibilities include working with non-adjudicated teens toward family reunification, helping teens with independent living skills, and performing group work; crisis line and crisis drop-in counseling. Candidates should have ability to work with others, college courses in field, knowledge of field, oral communication skills, plan to pursue career in field, self-motivation, written communication skills. Duration is 1–2 semesters. Unpaid. Open to college freshmen, college sophomores, college juniors, college seniors, graduate students, career changers. ▶ *1 youth assistance group worker.* Candidates should have ability to work independently, oral communication skills, self-motivation, written communication skills, group work skills. Duration is flexible. Unpaid. Open to college freshmen, college sophomores, college juniors, college seniors, recent college graduates, graduate students, law students, career changers. ▶ *4–6 youth care workers/counselors:* responsibilities include managing floor in residential program for 1-6 adolescents, conducting intakes, performing crisis management and individual, family, and group counseling. Candidates should have ability to work independently, ability to work with others, knowledge of field, oral communication skills, plan to pursue career in field, written communication skills, background in social work/psychology. Duration is flexible. Unpaid. Open to college freshmen, college sophomores, college juniors, college seniors. International applications accepted.

Benefits Names of contacts, on-the-job training, opportunity to attend seminars/workshops, possible full-time employment, willing to act as a professional reference, willing to complete paperwork for educational credit, willing to provide letters of recommendation.

Contact Write, call, fax, or e-mail Sheree Askew, Clinical/Marketing Specialist. Phone: 313-563-5005. Fax: 313-563-4765. E-mail: saskew@sfish.org. In-person interview required. Applicants must submit a formal organization application, resume, personal reference, letter of recommendation, TB tests, criminal records check, drug screening; academic transcripts desirable. Applications are accepted continuously. World Wide Web: http://www.sfishonline.org.

CREATIVE RESPONSE TO CONFLICT
PO Box 271
Nyack, New York 10960

General Information Program established by the New York Quaker Project on Community Conflict to provide specially designed activities in which participants experience ways to examine conflicts and develop solutions. Established in 1972. Number of employees: 6. Number of internship applications received each year: 25.

Internships Available ▶ *2 interns:* responsibilities include facilitating small groups within workshops, helping to gather materials for use with activities, and sharing administrative duties. Candidates should have knowledge of field, oral communication skills, plan to pursue career in field, strong interpersonal skills, ability to work well with children, commitment to nonviolence. Duration is 3–12 months. Unpaid. Open to college seniors, recent college gradu-

Creative Response to Conflict (continued)

ates, graduate students, law students, career changers, individuals reentering the workforce, retired teachers. International applications accepted.
Benefits Formal training, on-the-job training, opportunity to attend seminars/workshops, tuition assistance, willing to complete paperwork for educational credit, willing to provide letters of recommendation.
Contact Write, call, fax, or e-mail Priscilla Prutzman, Executive Director. Phone: 845-353-1796. Fax: 845-358-4924. E-mail: ccrcnyack@aol.com. In-person interview recommended (telephone interview accepted). Applicants must submit a letter of interest, resume, personal reference, three letters of recommendation. Applications are accepted continuously. World Wide Web: http://www.ccrcglobal.org.

CRISIS SUPPORT SERVICES
PO Box 9102
Berkeley, California 94709

General Information Nonprofit, volunteer-based agency that operates a 24-hour telephone crisis line, community education and training, grief counseling, in-home senior outreach, and therapy group for those who have attempted suicide. Established in 1966. Number of employees: 16. Number of internship applications received each year: 60.
Internships Available ▶ *Counselors:* responsibilities include answering 24-hour crisis line; mental health interns also co-facilitate groups and provide individual and family counseling. Candidates should have ability to work independently, oral communication skills, self-motivation, strong interpersonal skills, written communication skills. Duration is one year (minimum 4 hours per week). Unpaid. Open to adults 19 and over. International applications accepted.
Benefits Formal training, on-the-job training, opportunity to attend seminars/workshops, willing to act as a professional reference, willing to complete paperwork for educational credit, willing to provide letters of recommendation.
Contact Write, call, fax, or through World Wide Web site Chrissy Brewer, Clinical Director. Phone: 510-848-1515. Fax: 510-486-0443. In-person interview required. Applicants must submit a formal organization application, three letters of recommendation. Applications are accepted continuously. World Wide Web: http://www.crisissupport.org.

THE CUBA AMERICA JEWISH MISSION
1442A Walnut Street, #224
Berkeley, California 94709

General Information Nonprofit organization that assists in the revitalization of Jewish life in Cuba by working to improve physical and spiritual well-being and to assist new Cuban settlers in Israel. Established in 1997. Number of employees: 3. Number of internship applications received each year: 5.
Internships Available ▶ *1 executive assistant:* responsibilities include answering requests for information, developing programming, working on newsletter, coordinating and developing volunteer programs, clerical duties, bookkeeping, and fund-raising. Candidates should have ability to work independently, analytical skills, editing skills, office skills, oral communication skills, organizational skills, personal interest in the field, self-motivation, strong interpersonal skills, strong leadership ability, writing skills, Spanish skills (helpful), knowledge of Word, Excel, and Quicken. Duration is flexible. Position available as unpaid or paid. Open to recent high school graduates, college freshmen, college sophomores, college juniors, college seniors, recent college graduates, graduate students, law students, career changers, individuals reentering the workforce. ▶ *1 grant writer:* responsibilities include grant writing to obtain funding for both administration and programming. Candidates should have analytical skills, computer skills, editing skills, knowledge of field, personal interest in the field, research skills, self-motivation, writing skills, previous experience with grant writing in or out of school. Duration is flexible . Position available as unpaid or paid. Open to college sophomores, college

juniors, college seniors, recent college graduates, graduate students, law students, career changers, individuals reentering the workforce. International applications accepted.
Benefits On-the-job training, willing to act as a professional reference, willing to complete paperwork for educational credit, willing to provide letters of recommendation.
Contact Write, fax, e-mail, or through World Wide Web site June Safran, Executive Director. Fax: 510-527-2514. E-mail: june@thecajm.org. No phone calls. In-person interview recommended (telephone interview accepted). Applicants must submit a letter of interest, resume, two writing samples. Applications are accepted continuously. World Wide Web: http://www.thecajm.org.

DANIEL WEBSTER COUNCIL, BOY SCOUTS: OUTDOOR EDUCATION & OUTREACH DIVISION
571 Holt Avenue
Manchester, New Hampshire 03109

General Information Outdoor adventure education/counseling program for troubled youths; national outreach program for at-risk and developmentally disabled youth. Established in 1984. Number of employees: 5. Number of internship applications received each year: 12.
Internships Available ▶ *Adventure program assistants:* responsibilities include designing and implementing outdoor adventure-based counseling programs. Candidates should have ability to work with others, experience in the field, oral communication skills, personal interest in the field, self-motivation, strong leadership ability. Duration is 9.5 months (beginning in fall). $800 per month. Open to recent college graduates, graduate students.
Benefits Formal training, free housing, names of contacts, opportunity to attend seminars/workshops, possible full-time employment, travel reimbursement, willing to act as a professional reference, willing to complete paperwork for educational credit, willing to provide letters of recommendation, stipend and grocery allowance.
Contact Write, call, or e-mail John Rainville, Director of Outdoor Education and Outreach Program. Phone: 603-625-6431. E-mail: jrainvil@bsamail.org. In-person interview recommended (telephone interview accepted). Applicants must submit a letter of interest, resume, two personal references. Application deadline: August 15.

D.C. RAPE CRISIS CENTER
PO Box 34125
Washington, District of Columbia 20043

General Information Private nonprofit agency offering 24-hour crisis counseling, companion services, and community education programs on related issues. Established in 1972. Number of employees: 17. Number of internship applications received each year: 50.
Internships Available ▶ *1–2 administration interns:* responsibilities include coordinating the workshop program, database management, and assisting in planning the Center's annual gala. Candidates should have ability to work with others, office skills, oral communication skills, organizational skills, self-motivation, written communication skills. Duration is flexible. Unpaid. Open to high school seniors, recent high school graduates, college freshmen, college sophomores, college juniors, college seniors, recent college graduates, individuals reentering the workforce. ▶ *2 community education interns:* responsibilities include assisting with coordinating Sexual Assault Awareness Month, self-defense classes, and other community education projects; some interns, depending on experience, have the option of being trained to conduct presentations. Candidates should have ability to work with others, knowledge of field, oral communication skills, organizational skills, self-motivation, written communication skills. Duration is flexible (3 months minimum). Unpaid. Open to high school seniors, recent high school graduates, college freshmen, college sophomores, college juniors, college seniors, recent college graduates, graduate students, career changers, individuals reentering the workforce. ▶ *3–5 counseling and advocacy interns:* responsibilities include assisting with volunteer schedule and other volunteer-related projects, attending training sessions for professionals on sexual abuse, and assisting the counseling and advocacy depart-

ment by working on ongoing projects including updating the referral guide to the library; summer interns can be trained to work on 24-hour crisis hot line. Candidates should have office skills, oral communication skills, organizational skills, personal interest in the field, self-motivation, strong interpersonal skills. Duration is flexible (3 months minimum). Unpaid. Open to high school seniors, recent high school graduates, college freshmen, college sophomores, college juniors, college seniors, recent college graduates, career changers, individuals reentering the workforce. ▶ *2 development interns:* responsibilities include assisting with fund-raising projects, including direct mail, phone-a-thons, and special projects and events. Candidates should have ability to work independently, computer skills, office skills, organizational skills, self-motivation, strong interpersonal skills. Duration is flexible (3 months minimum). Unpaid. Open to high school seniors, recent high school graduates, college freshmen, college sophomores, college juniors, college seniors, recent college graduates, career changers, individuals reentering the workforce. International applications accepted.

Benefits Formal training, names of contacts, opportunity to attend seminars/workshops, travel reimbursement, willing to act as a professional reference, willing to complete paperwork for educational credit, willing to provide letters of recommendation.

Contact Write, call, fax, or e-mail Karen Bailey, Executive Assistant. Phone: 202-232-0789 Ext. 221. Fax: 202-387-3812. E-mail: dcrccintern@hotmail.com. In-person interview recommended (telephone interview accepted). Applicants must submit a formal organization application, letter of interest, resume. Applications are accepted continuously. World Wide Web: http://www.dcrcc.org.

ECUMENICAL SOCIAL MINISTRIES
201 North Weber Street
Colorado Springs, Colorado 80903

General Information Nonprofit human services agency that provides basic emergency services, food, rental assistance, job assistance, medicine, and clothing. Established in 1982. Number of employees: 12. Number of internship applications received each year: 20.

Internships Available ▶ *1–10 social work interns:* responsibilities include assisting low-income families in rent or utilities, and working in direct services to provide assistance in counseling, goal setting, and financial planning. Candidates should have ability to work independently, computer skills, personal interest in the field, plan to pursue career in field, self-motivation, strong interpersonal skills. Duration is flexible. Unpaid. Open to high school seniors, college freshmen, college sophomores, college juniors, college seniors, recent college graduates, graduate students, career changers, individuals reentering the workforce. International applications accepted.

Benefits On-the-job training, willing to act as a professional reference, willing to complete paperwork for educational credit, willing to provide letters of recommendation.

Contact Write, call, fax, or e-mail Marcia Hanscom, Volunteer Director. Phone: 719-228-6785. Fax: 719-636-3452. E-mail: esmmarcia@juno.com. In-person interview required. Applicants must submit a formal organization application, letter of interest, resume, two personal references. Applications are accepted continuously.

ELIZABETH STONE HOUSE
PO Box 59
Jamaica Plain, Massachusetts 02130

General Information Emergency shelter for battered women and their children; provides residential mental health alternative for women in emotional distress and their children and transitional housing and economic development programs. Established in 1974. Number of employees: 20. Number of internship applications received each year: 150.

Internships Available ▶ *1–5 administrative/direct service interns:* responsibilities include providing support to outreach coordinator, fund-raiser, administrative coordinator, and direct service staff. Candidates should have ability to work independently, ability to work with others, computer skills, office skills, oral communication skills, organizational skills, personal interest in the field, self-

motivation, written communication skills. Duration is flexible. Unpaid. Open to recent high school graduates, college freshmen, college sophomores, college juniors, college seniors, recent college graduates, graduate students, law students, career changers, individuals reentering the workforce. ▶ *Child-care interns:* responsibilities include coordinating children's activities with child-care worker and supervisor. Candidates should have ability to work with others, experience in the field, oral communication skills, plan to pursue career in field, self-motivation. Duration is flexible. Unpaid. Open to college freshmen, college sophomores, college juniors, college seniors, recent college graduates, graduate students, law students, career changers, individuals reentering the workforce. ▶ *5–10 direct service co-advocates:* responsibilities include providing emotional support to women in the program and attending at least one weekly house meeting. Candidates should have ability to work independently, personal interest in the field, self-motivation, strong interpersonal skills, strong leadership ability. Duration is minimum of 6 months. Unpaid. Open to college freshmen, college sophomores, college juniors, college seniors, recent college graduates, graduate students, law students, career changers, individuals reentering the workforce. ▶ *Donation interns:* responsibilities include creating holding spaces for donations, coordinating all receiving and distribution of donations to residents, and sending appropriate thank you notes. Candidates should have ability to work independently, oral communication skills, personal interest in the field, self-motivation, written communication skills. Duration is flexible. Unpaid. Open to college freshmen, college sophomores, college juniors, college seniors, recent college graduates, graduate students, law students, career changers, individuals reentering the workforce. International applications accepted.

Benefits On-the-job training, opportunity to attend seminars/workshops, willing to act as a professional reference, willing to complete paperwork for educational credit, willing to provide letters of recommendation.

Contact Write, call, fax, or e-mail Lila Bucklin, Direct Service Advocate/Volunteer/Intern Coordinator. Phone: 617-427-9801 Ext. 401. Fax: 617-427-6252. E-mail: info@elizabethstone.org. In-person interview recommended (telephone interview accepted). Applicants must submit a formal organization application. Application deadline: May 30 for fall.

THE EMPOWER PROGRAM
1312 8th Street, NW
Washington, District of Columbia 20001

General Information Nonprofit educational organization that works with youth, ages 10-21, to prevent gender-based violence, such as sexual harassment, sexual assault, dating violence, and bullying. Established in 1992. Number of employees: 8. Number of internship applications received each year: 25.

Internships Available ▶ *1–2 program assistants/development assistants:* responsibilities include participation in various aspects of organization's program development, fund-raising and research, events planning, and editing publication. Candidates should have ability to work independently, computer skills, editing skills, office skills, oral communication skills, organizational skills, personal interest in the field, research skills, self-motivation, strong interpersonal skills, writing skills. Duration is flexible. Unpaid. Open to high school students, recent high school graduates, college freshmen, college sophomores, college juniors, college seniors, recent college graduates, graduate students, law students, career changers, individuals reentering the workforce. International applications accepted.

Benefits Names of contacts, on-the-job training, opportunity to attend seminars/workshops, possible full-time employment, willing to act as a professional reference, willing to complete paperwork for educational credit, willing to provide letters of recommendation.

Contact Write, call, fax, e-mail, or through World Wide Web site Sydney Campbell, Office Manager, 1312 8th Street, NW, Washington, District of Columbia 20001. Phone: 202-232-8200. Fax: 202-234-1901. E-mail: empower@empowered.org. In-person interview recommended (telephone interview accepted). Applicants must submit a letter of interest, resume, writing sample. Application

The Empower Program (continued)
deadline: March 31 for summer, August 1 for fall, November 30 for spring. World Wide Web: http://www.empowered.org.

FAIR ACRES FAMILY YMCA
2600 Grand Avenue
Carthage, Missouri 64836

General Information Nonprofit organization that promotes family harmony and health. Established in 1990. Number of employees: 55. Number of internship applications received each year: 3.
Internships Available ▶ *1–7 camp counselors:* responsibilities include organizing and supervising activities for a group of 15 school-age children. Candidates should have ability to work with others, knowledge of field, organizational skills, personal interest in the field. Duration is 13 weeks. $5.25–$5.50 per hour. Open to recent high school graduates, college freshmen, college sophomores, college juniors, college seniors. ▶ *1–5 fitness center attendants:* responsibilities include assisting fitness center users in the proper usage of fitness center machines and free weights. Candidates should have ability to work independently, ability to work with others, oral communication skills, personal interest in the field, knowledge of fitness. Duration is 3–12 months. Position available as unpaid or at $5.30–$6.30 per hour. Open to recent high school graduates, college freshmen, college sophomores, college juniors, college seniors, individuals reentering the workforce. ▶ *1–5 youth coordinators:* responsibilities include creating and coordinating activities for pre-school through school-age youth. Candidates should have ability to work independently, ability to work with others, knowledge of field, oral communication skills, written communication skills. Duration is 3 months. Position available as unpaid or paid. Open to recent high school graduates, college freshmen, college sophomores, college juniors, college seniors, recent college graduates, career changers. International applications accepted.
Benefits Names of contacts, on-the-job training, opportunity to attend seminars/workshops, possible full-time employment, willing to act as a professional reference, willing to complete paperwork for educational credit, willing to provide letters of recommendation.
Contact Write, call, or fax Debby Orr, Business Services Director. Phone: 417-358-1070. Fax: 417-358-1102. In-person interview recommended (telephone interview accepted). Applicants must submit a formal organization application, three personal references, three letters of recommendation. Application deadline: May 15 for summer, August 1 for fall, December 1 for spring.

FAMILY YMCA
465 West Sixth Avenue
Lancaster, Ohio 43130

General Information Nonprofit organization providing fitness, health, social, and recreational opportunities for children, adults, and families. Established in 1920. Number of employees: 75. Number of internship applications received each year: 4.
Internships Available ▶ *1–2 program interns:* responsibilities include assisting with programs in youth sports, recreation, and childcare. Candidates should have ability to work independently, ability to work with others, oral communication skills, personal interest in the field, self-motivation, strong leadership ability, written communication skills. Duration is flexible. Position available as unpaid or paid. Open to college freshmen, college sophomores, college juniors, college seniors, recent college graduates, graduate students, law students, career changers. International applications accepted.
Benefits Job counseling, names of contacts, on-the-job training, opportunity to attend seminars/workshops, willing to act as a professional reference, willing to complete paperwork for educational credit, willing to provide letters of recommendation, YMCA membership.
Contact Write, call, or fax Randall Au, Director of Operations. Phone: 740-654-0616. Fax: 740-654-4206. In-person interview required. Applicants must submit a formal organization applica-

tion, letter of interest, resume, high school diploma, academic transcripts, 1-3 personal references. Applications are accepted continuously.

FEDERATION EMPLOYMENT AND GUIDANCE SERVICE (FEGS)
315 Hudson Street
New York, New York 10013

General Information One of the largest not-for-profit human services organizations in the country, providing vocational, educational, and rehabilitation services for clients with physical, psychiatric, and developmental disabilities; provides employment services, vocational rehabilitation, services for high school drop-out prevention, and services for new immigrants. Established in 1934. Number of employees: 2,700. Number of internship applications received each year: 350.
Internships Available ▶ *200 interns:* responsibilities include working on special projects as developed and arranged between the intern and the agency. Candidates should have knowledge of field, oral communication skills, organizational skills, personal interest in the field, plan to pursue career in field, strong interpersonal skills, written communication skills. Duration is flexible (preferably 2 semesters). Unpaid. Open to college freshmen, college sophomores, college juniors, college seniors, recent college graduates, graduate students, law students, career changers, individuals reentering the workforce. International applications accepted.
Benefits Formal training, job counseling, on-the-job training, opportunity to attend seminars/workshops, possible full-time employment, willing to act as a professional reference, willing to complete paperwork for educational credit, willing to provide letters of recommendation, extensive training program.
Contact Write, call, or e-mail Ms. Karen Zuckerman, Assistant Vice President, 315 Hudson Street, 9th Floor, New York, New York 10013. Phone: 212-366-8228. E-mail: kzuckerman@fegs.org. In-person interview required. Applicants must submit a formal organization application, letter of interest, resume, two letters of recommendation. Applications are accepted continuously. World Wide Web: http://www.fegs.org.

FLORENCE CRITTENTON CENTER
234 East Avenue 33
Los Angeles, California 90031-1937

General Information Residential treatment center for abused and neglected teenage girls and teen mothers and group home for severely emotionally disturbed adolescents; provides residents with educational, vocational, parenting, and life skills. Established in 1892. Number of employees: 105. Number of internship applications received each year: 30.
Internships Available ▶ *5–10 cuddlers:* responsibilities include changing, feeding, playing, supervising, and other duties associated with caring for infants and toddlers in Child Development Center. Candidates should have personal interest in the field, strong interpersonal skills, some knowledge/experience with children preferred. Duration is 2 hours per week for about 3 months. Unpaid. Open to college freshmen, college sophomores, college juniors, college seniors, recent college graduates, graduate students, law students, career changers, individuals reentering the workforce, adults over 18 years of age. ▶ *20–25 mentors:* responsibilities include developing a long term one-on-one relationship with teenage girl who has suffered severe abuse or neglect; acting as a role model and mentor. Candidates should have self-motivation, strong interpersonal skills, strong leadership ability, ability to handle disturbed behavior. Duration is 8 hours per month for six months to one year. Unpaid. Open to college freshmen, college sophomores, college juniors, college seniors, recent college graduates, graduate students, law students, career changers, individuals reentering the workforce, females over 18 years of age. ▶ *2–3 readers/storytellers:* responsibilities include reading to residents as well as their infants and toddlers one night a week. Candidates should have oral communication skills, personal interest in the field, self-motivation, strong interpersonal skills, ability to handle disturbed behavior. Duration is 1 hour per week for approximately 3 months. Unpaid. Open to college freshmen, col-

lege sophomores, college juniors, college seniors, recent college graduates, graduate students, law students, career changers, individuals reentering the workforce, adults over 18 years of age. ▶ *20–25 tutors:* responsibilities include working one-on-one with a resident, tutoring on various high school subjects which include math, literacy, English, and history. Candidates should have ability to work with others, oral communication skills, personal interest in the field, self-motivation, ability to handle disturbed behavior. Duration is 1 hour per week for approximately 3 months. Unpaid. Open to recent high school graduates, college freshmen, college sophomores, college juniors, college seniors, recent college graduates, graduate students, law students, career changers, individuals reentering the workforce, adults over 18 years of age. ▶ *4–5 workshop coordinators:* responsibilities include conducting workshops/ activities with residents on cultural, artistic, athletic, vocational, or clinical topics (according to the interests of the volunteer). Candidates should have oral communication skills, strong interpersonal skills, strong leadership ability, knowledge of topic/ activity. Duration is flexible. Unpaid. Open to college freshmen, college sophomores, college juniors, college seniors, recent college graduates, graduate students, law students, career changers, individuals reentering the workforce, adults over 18 years of age. International applications accepted.

Benefits Formal training, on-the-job training, possible full-time employment, willing to act as a professional reference, willing to complete paperwork for educational credit, willing to provide letters of recommendation, experience working with at-risk youth.

Contact Write, call, fax, or e-mail Kristin Collins, Volunteer Services and Special Projects Coordinator, PO Box 31219, Los Angeles, California 90031-1937. Phone: 323-225-4211 Ext. 209. Fax: 323-225-1602. E-mail: kristin@florencecrittenton.com. In-person interview required. Applicants must submit a formal organization application, three personal references, TB test, criminal clearance check required. Applications are accepted continuously. World Wide Web: http://www.florencecrittenton.com.

4C'S OF ALAMEDA COUNTY
22351 City Center Drive, Suite 200
Hayward, California 94541

General Information Private nonprofit organization offering child-care services. Established in 1972. Number of employees: 93.

Internships Available ▶ *Human resources interns:* responsibilities include maintaining HRIS, maintaining personnel files, assisting with preparation of payroll, conducting new hire orientation, and processing all employment verification requests. Candidates should have ability to work with others, computer skills, office skills, oral communication skills, organizational skills, written communication skills, ability to maintain confidentiality. Duration is 1 semester. Unpaid. Open to college freshmen, college sophomores, college juniors, college seniors, recent college graduates, graduate students.

Benefits Formal training, job counseling, on-the-job training, opportunity to attend seminars/workshops, possible full-time employment, willing to act as a professional reference, willing to complete paperwork for educational credit, willing to provide letters of recommendation.

Contact Write, fax, or e-mail Jennifer Tanroco, Human Resources Assistant. Fax: 514-538-1736. E-mail: hrdept@4c-alameda.org. No phone calls. In-person interview required. Applicants must submit a resume. Applications are accepted continuously. World Wide Web: http://www.4c-alameda.org.

FOURTH WORLD MOVEMENT
7600 Willow Hill Drive
Landover, Maryland 20785

General Information International organization that develops partnerships between very poor families and other citizens through civic, educational, and cultural projects; projects maintained by culturally diverse corps of full-time, long-term volunteers. Established in 1957. Number of employees: 10. Unit of International Movement ATD Fourth World, Pierrelaye, France. Number of internship applications received each year: 100.

Internships Available ▶ *2–6 FWM volunteers:* responsibilities include working on projects emphasizing education, creative expression, and civic involvement undertaken in partnership with families in persistent poverty. Candidates should have ability to work independently, self-motivation, strong interpersonal skills, sense of commitment and community. Duration is 2–20 years. $3200–$6500 per year. Open to those who have completed 3-month FWM internship. ▶ *4–12 Fourth World interns:* responsibilities include living and working with the full-time volunteers at Washington-area center, with shorter stays at the New York center; participating in office and manual work and in programs with poor children and their families; learning the Movement's history and approach through videos, readings, and discussions; planning and evaluating meetings; writing regular reports about experiences. Candidates should have ability to work independently, ability to work with others, self-motivation, one year employment or college experience, patience, willingness to question one's knowledge, sense of humor. Duration is 2-3 months (possible 2 year commitment). Unpaid. Open to U.S. citizens 19 years or older, high school graduates. International applications accepted.

Benefits Formal training, free housing, names of contacts, on-the-job training, opportunity to attend seminars/workshops, willing to act as a professional reference, willing to complete paperwork for educational credit, willing to provide letters of recommendation, possibility of long-term international commitment.

Contact Write, e-mail, or through World Wide Web site Denis Jay, Internship Coordinator. E-mail: fourthworld@erols.com. No phone calls. In-person interview recommended (telephone interview accepted). Applicants must submit a formal organization application, letter of interest, resume, three letters of recommendation, self-addressed stamped envelope (55 cents). Application deadline: May 15 for summer, August 15 for fall, December 15 for spring. Fees: $25. World Wide Web: http://www.atd-fourthworld.org.

GIRL SCOUTS OF PALM GLADES COUNCIL, INC.
1224 West Indiantown Road
Jupiter, Florida 33458

General Information Organization that strives to instill leadership qualities in young women, to develop their self-esteem, to help them to reach their fullest potential, and to prepare them to be caring, confident, and resourceful citizens. Established in 1912. Number of employees: 25. Unit of Girl Scouts of the USA, New York, New York. Number of internship applications received each year: 5.

Internships Available ▶ *1 accounting assistant:* responsibilities include journal entries, accounts payable, cash receipts, and assistance with bank records. Candidates should have ability to work independently, analytical skills, office skills, research skills, strong interpersonal skills, knowledge of Word and Excel. Duration is flexible (20 hours per week). $8–$10 per hour. Open to college freshmen, college sophomores, college juniors, college seniors, recent college graduates, career changers, individuals reentering the workforce. ▶ *1 marketing/communications intern:* responsibilities include assisting director of communications with all aspects of public relations, publicity, and promotion media. Candidates should have ability to work independently, college courses in field, computer skills, editing skills, oral communication skills, organizational skills, strong interpersonal skills, writing skills. Duration is one semester minimum. Unpaid. Open to college sophomores, college juniors, college seniors. International applications accepted.

Benefits Job counseling, names of contacts, possible full-time employment, willing to complete paperwork for educational credit, willing to provide letters of recommendation.

Contact Write, fax, e-mail, or through World Wide Web site Lisa Johnson, Director, Marketing and Communications. Fax: 561-427-0187. E-mail: ljohnson@gspgc.org. In-person interview recommended (telephone interview accepted). Applicants must submit a letter of interest, resume, writing sample. Applications are accepted continuously. World Wide Web: http://gspgc.org.

GIRL SCOUTS OF RIVERLAND COUNCIL
2710 Quarry Road
LaCrosse, Wisconsin 54601

General Information Youth organization. Established in 1943. Number of employees: 15. Unit of Girl Scouts of the USA, New York, New York. Number of internship applications received each year: 3.

Internships Available ▶ *2–4 Girl Scout facilitators:* responsibilities include recruitment of Girl Scouts from target populations and providing programming for troops. Candidates should have ability to work independently, ability to work with others, oral communication skills, self-motivation, strong leadership ability, written communication skills. Duration is 12–26 weeks. Position available as unpaid or at $1500–$3000 per duration of internship. Open to recent high school graduates, college freshmen, college sophomores, college juniors, college seniors, recent college graduates, graduate students, career changers, individuals reentering the workforce. ▶ *1 MIS intern:* responsibilities include assisting in all MIS operations. Candidates should have ability to work independently, computer skills, oral communication skills, organizational skills, personal interest in the field, strong interpersonal skills. Duration is 2 semesters. $5–$6 per hour. ▶ *1–2 program directors:* responsibilities include organization of on-site camp and tripping program for resident campers. Candidates should have ability to work independently, ability to work with others, oral communication skills, strong leadership ability, written communication skills. Duration is 10–13 weeks. $1500–$2000 per duration of internship. Open to college freshmen, college sophomores, college juniors, college seniors, recent college graduates. ▶ *1–3 program specialists:* responsibilities include planning and implementation of Girl Scouting program activities such as badge workshops, Gold and Silver Award Banquet, resident and day camping opportunities. Candidates should have ability to work independently, organizational skills, personal interest in the field, self-motivation, written communication skills. Duration is 12–16 weeks. Position available as unpaid or at $1500–$3000 per semester. Open to college freshmen, college sophomores, college juniors, college seniors, recent college graduates, graduate students, career changers, individuals reentering the workforce. ▶ *1 training assistant:* responsibilities include conducting adult education trainings in the volunteer management system. Candidates should have ability to work independently, computer skills, oral communication skills, organizational skills, self-motivation, strong interpersonal skills, strong leadership ability, written communication skills. Duration is 1–2 semesters. Position available as unpaid or paid. Open to college juniors, recent college graduates. International applications accepted.

Benefits Job counseling, names of contacts, on-the-job training, opportunity to attend seminars/workshops, possible full-time employment, willing to act as a professional reference, willing to complete paperwork for educational credit, willing to provide letters of recommendation.

Contact Write, call, or e-mail Sarah Resch, Chief Program Officer. Phone: 608-784-3693. Fax: 608-784-3613. E-mail: campehawee@yahoo.com. In-person interview recommended (telephone interview accepted). Applicants must submit a letter of interest, resume, personal reference. Applications are accepted continuously. World Wide Web: http://www.gsriverland.com.

GIRL SCOUTS OF SOUTHWESTERN NEW YORK
2661 Horton Road
Jamestown, New York 14701

General Information Organization that provides girls with contemporary developmental experiences to inspire the highest ideals of character and conduct and fosters development into happy, resourceful, and contributing adult women. Established in 1930. Number of employees: 13. Unit of Girl Scouts of the USA, New York, New York. Number of internship applications received each year: 1.

Internships Available ▶ *1–3 outreach managers:* responsibilities include assisting with the delivery of community outreach programs for girls in underserved areas. Candidates should have oral communication skills, organizational skills, personal interest in the field, self-motivation, strong interpersonal skills, strong leader-

ship ability, writing skills. Unpaid. Open to college freshmen, college sophomores, college juniors, college seniors, recent college graduates, graduate students, law students, career changers, individuals reentering the workforce. ▶ *1–2 program assistants:* responsibilities include assisting with the design and delivery of programs for girls ages 5-17. Candidates should have ability to work with others, oral communication skills, organizational skills, strong leadership ability. Duration is flexible. Unpaid. Open to high school students. ▶ *Summer resident camp interns:* responsibilities include administrative duties, camp direction, unit leading, and a variety of other duties. Candidates should have oral communication skills, organizational skills, personal interest in the field, self-motivation, strong interpersonal skills, strong leadership ability. $6–$9 per hour. Open to high school seniors, recent high school graduates, college freshmen, college sophomores, college juniors, college seniors, recent college graduates, graduate students, law students, career changers. ▶ *1–3 training assistants:* responsibilities include designing and delivering volunteer training to groups of 10-45 adults. Candidates should have oral communication skills, organizational skills, research skills, self-motivation, strong interpersonal skills, strong leadership ability. Unpaid. Open to recent high school graduates, college freshmen, college sophomores, college juniors, college seniors, recent college graduates, graduate students, law students, career changers, individuals reentering the workforce. International applications accepted.

Benefits Names of contacts, opportunity to attend seminars/workshops, possible full-time employment, travel reimbursement, willing to complete paperwork for educational credit, willing to provide letters of recommendation.

Contact Write, call, fax, or e-mail Lisa Lane-Gniewecki, Executive Director. Phone: 716-665-2225. Fax: 716-661-9704. E-mail: gsswny@yahoo.com. In-person interview recommended (telephone interview accepted). Applicants must submit a resume. Applications are accepted continuously.

GIRLS INCORPORATED OF GREATER LOWELL
220 Worthen Street
Lowell, Massachusetts 01852

General Information Nonprofit organization that provides after-school programs for girls ages 6–18 in the greater Lowell area. Established in 1945. Number of employees: 11. Affiliate of Girls Incorporated, New York, New York. Number of internship applications received each year: 2.

Internships Available ▶ *1–2 program counselors:* responsibilities include developing and implementing educational, cultural, and recreational programs for girls at least 6 years old. Candidates should have ability to work independently, ability to work with others, personal interest in the field, self-motivation. Duration is 3–12 months. Position available as unpaid or at $9 per hour. Open to high school seniors, recent high school graduates, college freshmen, college sophomores, college juniors, college seniors, recent college graduates, graduate students, career changers, individuals reentering the workforce, individuals at least 18 years old. International applications accepted.

Benefits Formal training, names of contacts, on-the-job training, opportunity to attend seminars/workshops, willing to act as a professional reference, willing to complete paperwork for educational credit, willing to provide letters of recommendation.

Contact Write, call, fax, or e-mail Carol S. Duncan, Executive Director. Phone: 978-458-6529. Fax: 978-458-4837. E-mail: ggrlowell@aol.com. In-person interview required. Applicants must submit a letter of interest, resume. Applications are accepted continuously.

GIRLS INCORPORATED OF HUNTSVILLE
PO Box 3066
Huntsville, Alabama 35804

General Information Youth agency providing informal education programs, services, and activities to girls ages 5–19. Established in 1972. Number of employees: 20. Unit of Girls Incorporated, New York, New York.

Internships Available ▶ *1–3 Operation Smart volunteers:* responsibilities include facilitating hands-on science and math activities relevant to technology with girls. Candidates should have analytical skills, knowledge of field, personal interest in the field, self-motivation, strong interpersonal skills, experience desirable. Duration is 8 weeks. Unpaid. Open to recent high school graduates, college freshmen, college sophomores, college juniors, college seniors, recent college graduates, graduate students, career changers, high school juniors and seniors. International applications accepted.

Benefits Formal training, names of contacts, on-the-job training, opportunity to attend seminars/workshops, possible full-time employment, willing to complete paperwork for educational credit, willing to provide letters of recommendation.

Contact Write, call, or e-mail Mildred Henderson, Executive Director. Phone: 256-851-9911. Fax: 256-851-9930. E-mail: smalone@hiwaay.net. In-person interview required. Applicants must submit a letter of interest, resume, three personal references, letter of recommendation, background check required. Application deadline: May 1 for summer; continuous for other positions.

GIRLS INCORPORATED OF METROPOLITAN DALLAS
2040 Empire Central Drive
Dallas, Texas 75235

General Information Nonprofit agency that strives to assist economically disadvantaged girls ages 6-18. Established in 1968. Number of employees: 60. Affiliate of Girls Incorporated, New York, New York. Number of internship applications received each year: 4.

Internships Available ▶ *1 public relations assistant:* responsibilities include contacting media, writing press releases, maintaining media list, and assisting with special events. Candidates should have computer skills, oral communication skills, organizational skills, strong interpersonal skills, written communication skills. Duration is flexible. Unpaid. ▶ *1 special events assistant:* responsibilities include working on major fund-raising event and working with volunteers, corporate sponsors, and graphic artists/printers. Candidates should have computer skills, oral communication skills, organizational skills, strong interpersonal skills, writing skills. Duration is flexible. Unpaid. Open to college freshmen, college sophomores, college juniors, college seniors, recent college graduates, graduate students, career changers, individuals reentering the workforce.

Benefits Names of contacts, opportunity to attend seminars/workshops, possible full-time employment, travel reimbursement, willing to act as a professional reference, willing to provide letters of recommendation.

Contact Write, call, or e-mail Lynette Smith, Director of Special Events. Phone: 214-654-4530. E-mail: lsmith@girlsincdallas.org. In-person interview required. Applicants must submit a formal organization application, letter of interest, resume, three personal references, letter of recommendation (optional). Application deadline: May 1 for summer, July 1 for fall, December 1 for spring. World Wide Web: http://www.girlsincdallas.org.

GIRLS INCORPORATED OF ST. LOUIS
4746 Carter Avenue
St. Louis, Missouri 63115

General Information Established in 1865. Number of employees: 50. Affiliate of Girls Incorporated, New York, New York. Number of internship applications received each year: 2.

Internships Available ▶ *1–10 Center instructors:* responsibilities include providing workshops for after school and summer participants in the areas of dance, science, art, music, sports, sewing, culinary arts, health, drama, computers, fitness and entrepreneurship; must be proficient in at least two areas. Candidates should have ability to work independently, analytical skills, computer skills, oral communication skills, organizational skills, personal interest in the field, self-motivation, strong interpersonal skills, strong leadership ability, written communication skills. Duration is 10-week summer program (40 hours per week) or one year (September to September). Position available as unpaid or at $7–$10 per hour. Open to college freshmen, college sophomores, college juniors, college seniors, recent college graduates, graduate students, law students, career changers, individuals reentering the workforce.

▶ *1–3 outreach instructors:* responsibilities include providing workshops for children on various topics relating to drug abuse, pregnancy prevention, and safety session preventing physical abuse. Candidates should have ability to work independently, analytical skills, computer skills, knowledge of field, oral communication skills, organizational skills, personal interest in the field, research skills, self-motivation, strong interpersonal skills, strong leadership ability, written communication skills. Duration is one year (September to September). Position available as unpaid or at $8–$10 per hour. Open to college sophomores, college juniors, college seniors, recent college graduates, graduate students, law students, career changers, individuals reentering the workforce.

Benefits On-the-job training, possible full-time employment, willing to act as a professional reference, willing to provide letters of recommendation.

Contact Write, call, or fax Andriette J. Fields, Program Director. Phone: 314-385-8088. Fax: 314-385-6540. In-person interview recommended (telephone interview accepted). Applicants must submit a letter of interest, resume, personal reference.

GLADNEY CENTER FOR ADOPTION
6300 John Ryan Drive
Fort Worth, Texas 76132-4122

General Information Adoption agency and maternity home. Established in 1887. Number of employees: 65. Number of internship applications received each year: 20.

Internships Available ▶ *1–2 admissions interns:* responsibilities include answering inquiry calls and making professional assessment of client's needs; direct contact with young women, mostly over the phone, interested in pursuing an adoption plan for their unborn child; admitting birth mothers to the program that is most appropriate for their needs. Candidates should have office skills, oral communication skills, organizational skills, personal interest in the field, self-motivation, strong interpersonal skills. Duration is 1–2 semesters. Unpaid. Open to college juniors, college seniors, graduate students. ▶ *1–2 birth parent services interns:* responsibilities include answering inquiry calls and making professional assessment of client's needs; direct contact with young women and their families planning adoption for their unborn child; attending weekly case management meetings. Candidates should have office skills, oral communication skills, organizational skills, personal interest in the field, self-motivation, strong interpersonal skills. Duration is 1–2 semesters. Unpaid. Open to graduate students. ▶ *1–2 domestic adoption interns:* responsibilities include phone contact and counseling with adoptive families; assisting caseworker with maintaining files to adhere to licensing standards; making home visits to clients in the Metroplex; attending weekly case management meetings. Candidates should have office skills, oral communication skills, organizational skills, personal interest in the field, self-motivation, strong interpersonal skills. Duration is 1–2 semesters. Unpaid. Open to graduate students. ▶ *1 international program intern:* responsibilities include observing and assisting with international adoption casework including conducting orientations and post-placement supervision; assisting with maintenance of international child registry database, adoptive family pre-adoption education program, international post-placement process, and adoptive parent survey process. Candidates should have ability to work with others, office skills, oral communication skills, organizational skills, personal interest in the field. Duration is 1–2 semesters. Unpaid. Open to college freshmen, college sophomores, college juniors, college seniors. ▶ *1 post-adoption intern:* responsibilities include answering post-adoption line and being available to answer post-adoption related questions of birth mothers, adult adoptees, and adoptive parents; co-facilitating a monthly birth parent support group, answering letters from birth parents; coordinating ongoing non-identifying communication between adoptive parents and birth parents. Candidates should have oral communication skills, organizational skills, personal interest in the field, self-motivation, strong interpersonal skills, written communication skills. Duration is 1–2 semesters. Unpaid. Open to college juniors, college seniors, graduate students. ▶ *1–2 residential birth parent services interns:* responsibilities include direct contact with young women living in maternity home and planning adoption for their children,

Gladney Center for Adoption (continued)

assisting houseparents with planning of weekly activities, attending weekly dorm meetings, and observing weekly group counseling meeting. Candidates should have office skills, oral communication skills, personal interest in the field, self-motivation, strong interpersonal skills. Duration is 1–2 semesters. Unpaid. Open to college freshmen, college sophomores, college juniors, college seniors. ▶ *1–2 transitional care program interns:* responsibilities include assisting transitional care coordinator with recruiting new transitional care families; assuring all current families meet licensing standards; placing children with families; obtaining medical records for children; obtaining necessary supplies for families; arranging placement of children with adoptive families. Candidates should have ability to work with others, office skills, oral communication skills, organizational skills, personal interest in the field, self-motivation. Duration is 1–2 semesters. Unpaid. Open to college freshmen, college sophomores, college juniors, college seniors.

Benefits Formal training, on-the-job training, willing to complete paperwork for educational credit, first aid and CPR training provided for some internships.

Contact Write, call, fax, e-mail, or through World Wide Web site Hannah Powell, Human Resources Assistant. Phone: 817-922-6000. Fax: 817-922-5955. E-mail: jobline@gladney.org. In-person interview required. Applicants must submit a formal organization application, resume, three personal references, negative TB-PPD test, rubella screen, drug screen, background check, first aid and CPR training required for some internships (paid for by organization). Applications are accepted continuously. World Wide Web: http://www.gladney.org.

GOLDEN CRADLE ADOPTION SERVICES
1050 Kings Highway North, Suite 201
Cherry Hill, New Jersey 08034

General Information Private, nonprofit, New Jersey licensed agency that provides adoption and maternity services to men and women faced with an unplanned pregnancy and to people seeking to build families through adoption. Established in 1980. Number of employees: 10. Number of internship applications received each year: 5.

Internships Available ▶ *1 public relations/marketing intern:* responsibilities include reviewing and revising all marketing materials and developing short-term and long-range marketing plans for the organization. Candidates should have ability to work with others, college courses in field, computer skills, plan to pursue career in field, self-motivation, writing skills. Duration is flexible. Unpaid. ▶ *1–2 research analysts:* responsibilities include gathering and analyzing data to review services and provide improvements for clients. Candidates should have college courses in field, computer skills, research skills, self-motivation, written communication skills. Duration is flexible. Unpaid. ▶ *1–3 social work interns:* responsibilities include handling client caseload by following a birth parent or adoptive parent through the adoption process, following New Jersey regulations regarding adoption. Candidates should have computer skills, declared college major in field, plan to pursue career in field, strong interpersonal skills, writing skills. Duration is flexible. Unpaid. Open to college juniors, college seniors, recent college graduates, graduate students, career changers. International applications accepted.

Benefits Formal training, names of contacts, on-the-job training, possible full-time employment, travel reimbursement, willing to complete paperwork for educational credit, willing to provide letters of recommendation.

Contact Write, call, fax, e-mail, or through World Wide Web site Jared N. Rolsky, Executive Director. Phone: 856-667-2229. Fax: 856-667-5437. E-mail: info@goldencradle.org. In-person interview required. Applicants must submit a letter of interest, resume. Applications are accepted continuously. World Wide Web: http://www.goldencradle.org.

GOOD SHEPHERD/MCMAHON SERVICES
7 West Burnside Avenue
Bronx, New York 10453

General Information Foster care program that provides out-of-home placement services for abused and neglected children and adolescents. Established in 1937. Number of employees: 70. Division of Good Shepherd Services, New York, New York. Number of internship applications received each year: 12.

Internships Available ▶ *3–5 social work assistants:* responsibilities include assisting staff in providing services to children and families and developing arts and crafts projects. Candidates should have ability to work independently, oral communication skills, personal interest in the field, self-motivation, strong interpersonal skills, written communication skills, valid driver's license, Spanish ability, willingness to do field work, use public transportation, and make inner city home visits. Duration is flexible. Unpaid. Open to college juniors, college seniors, recent college graduates, graduate students.

Benefits Job counseling, opportunity to attend seminars/workshops, travel reimbursement, willing to complete paperwork for educational credit, willing to provide letters of recommendation.

Contact Write, call, or fax Sheila Kelly, Family Activity Supervisor. Phone: 718-561-4340 Ext. 203. Fax: 718-561-3839. In-person interview recommended (telephone interview accepted). Applicants must submit a formal organization application, letter of interest, resume, two personal references, two letters of recommendation, Central State Registry clearance; fingerprinting (depending on position). Application deadline: April 1 for summer.

GRASSROOTS INTERNATIONAL
179 Boylston Street, 4th Floor
Boston, Massachusetts 02130

General Information Organization that provides cash grants and material aid to community organizations for social change in Haiti, Mexico, Eritrea, Brazil, the West Bank, and Gaza strip. Established in 1983. Number of employees: 9. Number of internship applications received each year: 150.

Internships Available ▶ *1 Brazil program intern:* responsibilities include performing research related to Latin America and the Caribbean. Candidates should have ability to work independently, computer skills, oral communication skills, organizational skills, research skills, writing skills, fluency in Portuguese. Duration is 1 semester. Unpaid. ▶ *1 Latin America and Caribbean Program intern:* responsibilities include program support and research related to Latin America and the Caribbean, specifically Mexico and Haiti. Candidates should have ability to work independently, oral communication skills, research skills, written communication skills, fluency in Spanish, French, and/or Haitian Creole. Duration is 1 semester. Unpaid. ▶ *1 The Middle East and Horn of Africa intern:* responsibilities include program support and research related to the Middle East and the Horn of Africa, specifically Eritrea and Palestine. Candidates should have ability to work independently, computer skills, oral communication skills, organizational skills, research skills, writing skills. Duration is 1 semester. Unpaid. ▶ *1 advocacy intern:* responsibilities include implementing policy advocacy strategies, preparing and distributing campaign materials, drafting position papers, and organizing grassroots international constituents. Candidates should have ability to work independently, computer skills, experience in the field, oral communication skills, organizational skills, written communication skills. Duration is 1 semester. Unpaid. ▶ *1 communications/media program assistant:* responsibilities include monitoring the international electronic and print media. Candidates should have ability to work independently, analytical skills, computer skills, oral communication skills, organizational skills, research skills, writing skills. Duration is 1 semester. Unpaid. ▶ *1 leadership intern.* Candidates should have ability to work independently, computer skills, oral communication skills, organizational skills, strong leadership ability, writing skills. Duration is 1 semester. Unpaid. Open to college freshmen, college sophomores, college juniors, college seniors, recent college graduates, graduate students, career changers. International applications accepted.

Benefits Formal training, names of contacts, opportunity to attend seminars/workshops, willing to complete paperwork for educational credit, willing to provide letters of recommendation.

Contact Write, fax, e-mail, or through World Wide Web site Internship Coordinator. Phone: 617-524-1400. Fax: 617-524-5525. E-mail: jobs@grassrootsonline.org. In-person interview recommended (telephone interview accepted). Applicants must submit a letter of interest, resume. Applications are accepted continuously. World Wide Web: http://www.grassrootsonline.org.

GREEN CHIMNEYS CHILDREN'S SERVICES, INC.
Caller Box 719, 400 Doansburg Road
Brewster, New York 10509

General Information Voluntary, nonsectarian multiservice agency and residential treatment center dedicated to basic education for children and daily living skills programs for adults. Established in 1947. Number of employees: 350. Number of internship applications received each year: 30.

Internships Available ▶ *1–6 education interns:* responsibilities include teaching assistant duties in special education classroom setting. Candidates should have ability to work independently, knowledge of field, oral communication skills, personal interest in the field, strong interpersonal skills, written communication skills. Duration is 3–5 months. Position available as unpaid or paid. ▶ *1–6 farm interns:* responsibilities include assisting with farm science, riding, and greenhouse programs; assisting the professional staff with teaching the students while participating in daily chores, daily living skills programs, public programming events, academic studies, horticultural projects, athletics and recreational activities, and other outdoor activities. Candidates should have ability to work independently, experience in the field, oral communication skills, personal interest in the field, strong interpersonal skills, written communication skills. Duration is 3 months minimum; June 1-August 31 for summer, September 1-December 30 for fall, January 3-May 31 for winter/spring. Position available as unpaid or paid. Open to college juniors, college seniors, recent college graduates, graduate students. International applications accepted.

Benefits Free housing, free meals, opportunity to attend seminars/workshops, possible full-time employment, willing to complete paperwork for educational credit, willing to provide letters of recommendation.

Contact Write, call, fax, or e-mail Ms. Jackie Ryan, Intern Coordinator, Caller Box 719, Doansburg Road. Phone: 845-279-2995 Ext. 158. Fax: 845-279-2714. E-mail: jryan@greenchimneys.org. In-person interview recommended (telephone interview accepted). Applicants must submit a formal organization application, resume, three personal references. Applications are accepted continuously. World Wide Web: http://www.greenchimneys.org.

HABITAT FOR HUMANITY INTERNATIONAL
322 West Lamar Street
Americus, Georgia 31709

General Information Nonprofit, Christian housing ministry dedicated to the elimination of poverty housing worldwide. Established in 1976. Number of employees: 600. Number of internship applications received each year: 150.

Internships Available ▶ *3 HFHI volunteers/interns:* responsibilities include general administrative duties in field of interest; some project work; may also include data entry, filing, research, customer service, and training. Candidates should have computer skills, office skills, oral communication skills, strong interpersonal skills, written communication skills. Duration is year-round. Paid. Open to recent high school graduates, college freshmen, college sophomores, college juniors, college seniors, recent college graduates, graduate students, law students, career changers, individuals reentering the workforce. ▶ *3 construction volunteers/interns:* responsibilities include working with volunteers in restoring HFHI housing to an accepted standard; repairing corporate buildings; and working with various tools. Candidates should have ability to work independently, ability to work with others, self-motivation, some construction experience (preferred). Duration is year-round. Food stipend of $56 per week. Open to recent high school graduates, college freshmen, college sophomores, college juniors, college seniors, recent college graduates, law

students, career changers, individuals reentering the workforce. ▶ *1 international training intern:* responsibilities include supporting and promoting quality international training and education and designing and presenting training materials. Candidates should have oral communication skills, strong interpersonal skills, writing skills, experience in adult education. Duration is 3–12 months. $450 per month. ▶ *2 summer youth blitz interns:* responsibilities include logistics coordination, media communication, preparing morning reflections, communication with participants, program advisers, and community-team building, discussion facilitation and liaison between all parties; involves travel. Candidates should have oral communication skills, strong interpersonal skills, strong leadership ability, written communication skills, experience working with youth ages 16-18, must have valid driver's license. Duration is May to August. Food stipend of $56 per week. Open to college juniors, college seniors, recent college graduates, graduate students. International applications accepted.

Benefits Free housing, willing to complete paperwork for educational credit.

Contact Write, call, fax, or e-mail Volunteer Staffing. Phone: 229-924-6935 Ext. 2952. Fax: 229-924-0641. E-mail: hrstaffing@hfhi.org. Telephone interview required. Applicants must submit a formal organization application, resume, two personal references. Applications are accepted continuously. World Wide Web: http://habitat.org.

HABITAT FOR HUMANITY LAKE COUNTY, IL
315 North Martin Luther King Jr. Avenue
Waukegan, Illinois 60085

General Information Nonprofit homebuilder and social service provider. Established in 1989. Number of employees: 7. Affiliate of Habitat for Humanity International, Americus, Georgia.

Internships Available ▶ *1–2 construction manager interns:* responsibilities include assisting construction manager with building homes from permitting through final punch list while working with volunteers; both on-site and office responsibilities. Candidates should have ability to work independently, computer skills, experience in the field, oral communication skills, strong interpersonal skills, strong leadership ability. Duration is 6 months–1 year. Unpaid. Open to recent college graduates, graduate students, career changers, individuals reentering the workforce. ▶ *1 family services intern:* responsibilities include coordinating activities to assist in Family Services Department; includes presenting information at meetings; interpreting documents; coordinating information; writing letters; and meeting with clients. Candidates should have ability to work independently, computer skills, declared college major in field, organizational skills, strong interpersonal skills, written communication skills. Duration is 6 months-1 year. Unpaid. Open to college seniors, recent college graduates, graduate students, career changers. ▶ *1 legal assistant intern:* responsibilities include assisting in real estate closings, corporate law issues, risk management issues, and family law. Candidates should have ability to work independently, college courses in field, computer skills, experience in the field, self-motivation, written communication skills. Duration is 6 months-1 year. Unpaid. Open to recent college graduates, graduate students, law students, career changers, individuals reentering the workforce. ▶ *1 public relations intern:* responsibilities include assisting resource development director in promoting organization through media, events, and written publications; many "hands-on" and creative opportunities. Candidates should have ability to work independently, computer skills, editing skills, experience in the field, oral communication skills, written communication skills. Duration is 6 months–1 year. Unpaid. Open to college seniors, recent college graduates, graduate students, career changers, individuals reentering the workforce. ▶ *Resource development interns:* responsibilities include researching and writing grants; coordinating and overseeing data entry, mailings; writing manuals for groups working on house with Habitat. Candidates should have computer skills, oral communication skills, organizational skills, research skills, strong interpersonal skills, writing skills. Duration is 6 months–1 year. Unpaid. Open to recent college graduates, graduate students, career changers, individuals reentering the workforce. International applications accepted.

Habitat for Humanity Lake County, IL (continued)
Benefits Formal training, names of contacts, on-the-job training, opportunity to attend seminars/workshops, possible full-time employment, willing to act as a professional reference, willing to complete paperwork for educational credit, willing to provide letters of recommendation, free meals (limited), networking opportunities.
Contact Write, call, fax, e-mail, or through World Wide Web site Julie Donovan, Executive Director, 315 Martin Luther King Jr. Avenue, Waukegan 60085. Phone: 847-623-1020. Fax: 847-623-1038. E-mail: julie@habitatlc.org. Telephone interview required. Applicants must submit a letter of interest, resume, academic transcripts, writing sample, personal reference. Application deadline: April 1 for summer, November 1 for winter. World Wide Web: http://www.habitatlc.org.

HAP ENTERPRISES, INC.
310 Wayne Street
Beaver, Pennsylvania 15009

General Information Nonprofit organization providing services to individuals with developmental disabilities. Established in 1970. Number of employees: 165. Number of internship applications received each year: 10.
Internships Available ▶ *2 marketing interns:* responsibilities include working on newsletter, special events, news and festive articles, press releases, marketing materials, and media relations. Candidates should have ability to work independently, college courses in field, computer skills, experience in the field, oral communication skills, personal interest in the field, plan to pursue career in field, written communication skills. Duration is flexible. Unpaid. Open to college sophomores, college juniors, college seniors, recent college graduates, graduate students.
Benefits On-the-job training, opportunity to attend seminars/workshops, travel reimbursement, willing to act as a professional reference, willing to complete paperwork for educational credit, willing to provide letters of recommendation.
Contact Call or e-mail Robert L. Bickerton, Director of Marketing. Phone: 724-728-0440. Fax: 724-728-8312. E-mail: rbickerton@hapenterprises.org. In-person interview recommended (telephone interview accepted). Applicants must submit a letter of interest, resume. Applications are accepted continuously. World Wide Web: http://www.hapenterprises.org.

HARBEL PREVENTION AND RECOVERY CENTER
5807 Harford Road
Baltimore, Maryland 21214

General Information State-certified substance abuse prevention and treatment program that provides early intervention/prevention/treatment services through individual, family, and group counseling, school outreach, and tutoring. Established in 1970. Number of employees: 40. Unit of HARBEL Community Organization, Baltimore, Maryland. Number of internship applications received each year: 15.
Internships Available ▶ *1–2 GED/vocational interns.* Candidates should have ability to work with others, computer skills, oral communication skills, personal interest in the field, self-motivation, written communication skills. Duration is 1–2 semesters. Unpaid. Open to college freshmen, college sophomores, college juniors, college seniors. ▶ *2–3 addiction counselor interns:* responsibilities include providing individual and group counseling in outpatient substance abuse program that serves adults and adolescents. Candidates should have college courses in field, knowledge of field, plan to pursue career in field, strong interpersonal skills, written communication skills. Duration is 2 semester (required). Unpaid. Open to graduate students. ▶ *Tutors:* responsibilities include providing one-on-one tutoring services to high risk middle/senior high students. Candidates should have ability to work independently, ability to work with others, oral communication skills, personal interest in the field, self-motivation, ability to act as a positive drug-free role model. Duration is flexible; normally minimum of 1 semester. Unpaid. Open to high school students, recent high school graduates, college sophomores, college juniors,

college seniors, recent college graduates, graduate students, law students, career changers, individuals reentering the workforce. International applications accepted.
Benefits Names of contacts, opportunity to attend seminars/workshops, willing to act as a professional reference, willing to complete paperwork for educational credit, willing to provide letters of recommendation.
Contact Call Patricia Stabile, Director. Phone: 410-444-2100. Fax: 410-426-1140. E-mail: harbelprc@yahoo.com. In-person interview required. Applicants must submit a formal organization application, letter of interest, resume, tutoring program requires 3 references and in-person interview only. Application deadline: July 1 for addiction counselors; continuous for tutors. World Wide Web: http://phoenix.goucher.edu/~harbel/hprc.htm.

HARBOR, INC.
PO Box 1903
Smithfield, North Carolina 27577

General Information Domestic violence/sexual assault/displaced homemaker agency. Established in 1984. Number of employees: 11. Number of internship applications received each year: 5.
Internships Available ▶ *1 crisis counselor.* Candidates should have ability to work independently, analytical skills, college courses in field, computer skills, knowledge of field, organizational skills, research skills, self-motivation, strong interpersonal skills, writing skills, must have car for use at agency. Duration is flexible. Unpaid. Open to college seniors, recent college graduates, graduate students. International applications accepted.
Benefits Names of contacts, on-the-job training, possible full-time employment, travel reimbursement, willing to act as a professional reference, willing to complete paperwork for educational credit, willing to provide letters of recommendation.
Contact Write or e-mail Keri Christensen, Executive Director. Fax: 919-938-4515. E-mail: harborinc2002@aol.com. No phone calls. In-person interview recommended (telephone interview accepted). Applicants must submit a formal organization application, letter of interest, resume, three personal references, must have car for use at the agency.

HARDEE COUNTY FAMILY YMCA
610 West Orange Street
Wauchula, Florida 33873

General Information Organization that offers programs to help strengthen local families. Number of employees: 25. Unit of Sarasota Family YMCA, Inc., Sarasota, Florida. Number of internship applications received each year: 2.
Internships Available ▶ *8 child-care workers:* responsibilities include supervising children ages 5-12. Candidates should have ability to work with others, knowledge of field, personal interest in the field, plan to pursue career in field, strong leadership ability. Duration is 3 months in summer or one semester. Unpaid. Open to high school seniors, recent high school graduates, college freshmen, college sophomores, college juniors, college seniors, recent college graduates, graduate students, law students, career changers, individuals reentering the workforce. ▶ *1 office/administration intern:* responsibilities include working on computer, organization/filing, and front desk. Candidates should have ability to work independently, computer skills, office skills, oral communication skills, organizational skills, strong interpersonal skills. Duration is one summer or semester. Unpaid. Open to high school seniors, recent high school graduates, college freshmen, college sophomores, college juniors, college seniors, recent college graduates, graduate students, career changers, individuals reentering the workforce. ▶ *2 sports/fitness interns:* responsibilities include assisting in youth sports and fitness programs including coordinating programs, maintaining equipment, overseeing fitness floor, and possibly teaching classes. Candidates should have knowledge of field, personal interest in the field, self-motivation, strong interpersonal skills, strong leadership ability, basic computer skills. Duration is one summer or semester. Unpaid. Open to high school seniors, recent high school graduates, college freshmen, college sophomores, college juniors, college seniors, recent college graduates, graduate students, career changers, individuals reentering the workforce. International applications accepted.

Benefits Names of contacts, possible full-time employment, willing to act as a professional reference, willing to complete paperwork for educational credit, willing to provide letters of recommendation, free membership in YMCA.
Contact Write or call Bonny Perry, Executive Director. Phone: 863-773-6445. In-person interview required. Applicants must submit a formal organization application, resume, two personal references, 2 professional references; criminal background check required. Applications are accepted continuously.

HARTFORD FOOD SYSTEM
509 Wethersfield Avenue
Hartford, Connecticut 06114

General Information Community food-advocacy organization that develops and operates food programs designed to assist lower-income families; includes policy, farming, and nutrition. Established in 1978. Number of employees: 7. Number of internship applications received each year: 40.
Internships Available ▶ *1–2 food policy research assistants:* responsibilities include investigating policies and issues related to food, agriculture, or nutrition. Candidates should have computer skills, oral communication skills, personal interest in the field, research skills, self-motivation, writing skills. Duration is 6–12 months. $200–$250 per week. Open to college seniors, recent college graduates, graduate students, law students, career changers. ▶ *4–8 organic farm interns:* responsibilities include general farm duties on a 16-acre community-supported agriculture farm that grows organic produce for and with lower-income urban families. Candidates should have ability to work independently, ability to work with others, oral communication skills, personal interest in the field, self-motivation, ability to perform hard physical labor. Duration is 2–8 months. $150–$200 per week. Open to college freshmen, college sophomores, college juniors, college seniors, recent college graduates, graduate students, career changers. International applications accepted.
Benefits Health insurance, names of contacts, opportunity to attend seminars/workshops, possible full-time employment, travel reimbursement, willing to act as a professional reference, willing to complete paperwork for educational credit, willing to provide letters of recommendation, stipend, possibility of housing.
Contact Write, call, or e-mail Mr. Mark Winne, Executive Director. Phone: 860-296-9325. E-mail: info@hartfordfood.org. In-person interview recommended (telephone interview accepted). Applicants must submit a letter of interest, resume, writing sample, 2-3 personal references. Application deadline: March 1 for organic farm interns; continuous for all other positions. World Wide Web: http://www.hartfordfood.org.

HELP LINE TELEPHONE SERVICES/JEWISH BOARD OF FAMILY AND CHILDREN'S SERVICES
3 West 29th Street, 10th Floor
New York, New York 10001

General Information Telephone crisis hot line. Established in 1970. Number of employees: 3. Number of internship applications received each year: 5.
Internships Available ▶ *1–2 database assistants:* responsibilities include assisting in setting up and maintaining databases. Candidates should have ability to work with others, analytical skills, computer skills, experience in the field, office skills, oral communication skills, organizational skills, research skills. Duration is flexible. Unpaid. Open to college juniors, college seniors, recent college graduates, graduate students, career changers, individuals reentering the workforce. ▶ *1–2 research assistants for fund-raising:* responsibilities include assisting the executive director with research necessary to seek funding and writing grants. Candidates should have analytical skills, computer skills, oral communication skills, personal interest in the field, self-motivation, written communication skills. Duration is flexible. Position available as unpaid or at $12 per hour. Open to college juniors, college seniors, graduate students, law students. International applications accepted.
Benefits Names of contacts, on-the-job training, opportunity to attend seminars/workshops, willing to act as a professional refer-

ence, willing to complete paperwork for educational credit, willing to provide letters of recommendation, opportunity to work independently with excellent supervision.
Contact Write, call, fax, or e-mail Heather Stokes, CSW, Director, 3 West 29th Street, 10th Floor. Phone: 212-684-4480 Ext. 206. Fax: 212-684-4483. E-mail: hstokes@jbfcs.org. In-person interview required. Applicants must submit a resume, two writing samples, two letters of recommendation. Applications are accepted continuously. World Wide Web: http://www.helpline.org.

HEMLOCK GIRL SCOUT COUNCIL
350 Hale Avenue
Harrisburg, Pennsylvania 17105

General Information Youth services organization that focuses on the growth and development of girls ages 5-17 and the training and support of adults who work with them. Established in 1963. Number of employees: 45. Unit of Girl Scouts of the USA, New York, New York. Number of internship applications received each year: 4.
Internships Available ▶ *1–3 field aides:* responsibilities include supporting adults, promoting the delivery of programs, and providing special activities for girls. Duration is flexible. Position available as unpaid or paid. ▶ *1–10 resident camp counselors:* responsibilities include developing and implementing weekly outdoor thematic programs for girls ages 6-17. Candidates should have ability to work with others, oral communication skills, self-motivation, strong leadership ability. Duration is June 17 through August 12. $165–$220 per week. Open to college sophomores, college juniors, college seniors. International applications accepted.
Benefits Names of contacts, opportunity to attend seminars/workshops, possible full-time employment, travel reimbursement, willing to complete paperwork for educational credit, willing to provide letters of recommendation.
Contact Write, fax, or e-mail Mr. Randall K. Cline, Executive Director. Fax: 717-234-5097. E-mail: rcline@hgsc.org. No phone calls. In-person interview recommended (telephone interview accepted). Applications are accepted continuously. World Wide Web: http://www.hgsc.org.

HERBERT HOOVER BOYS AND GIRLS CLUB
2901 North Grand Avenue
St. Louis, Missouri 63107

General Information Organization providing educational, sports, personal development, and cultural programs for youths aged 6-18. Established in 1967. Number of employees: 29. Unit of Boys & Girls Clubs of America, Atlanta, Georgia. Number of internship applications received each year: 40.
Internships Available ▶ *1–2 computer instructors:* responsibilities include giving computer instruction to youth and assisting in computer club and resource center. Candidates should have ability to work independently, computer skills, knowledge of field, oral communication skills, strong interpersonal skills. Duration is 12 months. $15–$25 per hour. Open to college seniors, recent college graduates, graduate students, career changers. ▶ *1–3 tutors:* responsibilities include providing tutoring and homework assistance in resource center. Candidates should have computer skills, knowledge of field, oral communication skills, strong interpersonal skills, strong leadership ability. Duration is 9 months. Position available as unpaid or at $6–$11 per hour. Open to college juniors, college seniors, recent college graduates, graduate students. ▶ *8–20 youth group counselors:* responsibilities include supervising and planning activities of group summer day camp; providing counseling and guidance as needed to include appropriate age-specific programs and support. Candidates should have ability to work independently, college courses in field, oral communication skills, organizational skills, plan to pursue career in field, self-motivation, strong leadership ability, written communication skills. Duration is 3 months. $5.50–$8 per hour. Open to recent high school graduates, college freshmen, college sophomores, college juniors, college seniors, recent college graduates, graduate students, career changers, individuals reentering the workforce. International applications accepted.

Herbert Hoover Boys and Girls Club (continued)

Benefits Formal training, names of contacts, on-the-job training, possible full-time employment, willing to complete paperwork for educational credit, willing to provide letters of recommendation. **Contact** Write, call, fax, or e-mail Debra M. B. Harris, Director of Operations. Phone: 314-652-8300. Fax: 314-652-8007. E-mail: debra@hhbgc.org. In-person interview required. Applicants must submit a resume. Application deadline: May 1 for summer, August 1 for fall. World Wide Web: http://www.hhbgc.org.

HILLEL: THE FOUNDATION FOR JEWISH CAMPUS LIFE
1640 Rhode Island Avenue, NW
Washington, District of Columbia 20036

General Information Jewish foundation that promotes religious, social, educational, and recreational student activities, focusing on leadership development. Established in 1923. Number of employees: 68. Number of internship applications received each year: 500.
Internships Available ▶ *1 Arline and David L. Bittker Fellowship:* responsibilities include Jewish identity and awareness programming, networking with Jewish student leaders from around the world, developing leadership programs through conferences, national initiatives, and grants programs; working with students on the Hillel Board of Directors. Candidates should have ability to work independently, oral communication skills, organizational skills, personal interest in the field, plan to pursue career in field, self-motivation, strong interpersonal skills, strong leadership ability, writing skills, creativity. Duration is 1 year. $22,500 per year. ▶ *1 Bronfman Fellow:* responsibilities include serving as personal assistant to the president and international director of Hillel, helping coordinate site visits, working on major fund-raising initiatives, and interaction with major leaders of the Jewish community. Candidates should have ability to work with others, oral communication skills, personal interest in the field, writing skills, multitasking ability. Duration is 1 year. $22,500 per year. ▶ *1 Hillel Tzedek Fellow:* responsibilities include overseeing campuses involved in community service initiatives, training and developing new programs for those students and supervisors, planning major Jewish public policy conference as well as social justice programming pieces for other student conferences, and administering grants for student programs. Candidates should have ability to work independently, analytical skills, computer skills, oral communication skills, organizational skills, personal interest in the field, self-motivation, strong interpersonal skills, strong leadership ability, writing skills. Duration is 1 year. $22,500 per year. ▶ *65–100 Hillel's Steinhardt Jewish Campus Service Corps:* responsibilities include promoting Jewish involvement to previously unaffiliated Jewish students on campus; creating involving programs to encourage Jewish students to interact with other Jews in social, educational, or community service settings; working with Jewish leaders on campus to connect them to their Judaism. Candidates should have ability to work independently, computer skills, oral communication skills, self-motivation, strong interpersonal skills, strong leadership ability, written communication skills, creativity. Duration is 11 months. $21,000–$23,000 per duration of internship. ▶ *1 Israel Fellow:* responsibilities include promoting Israel advocacy on campus; assisting students and campus professionals in creating Israel programs and addressing Israel issues on campus. Candidates should have ability to work independently, ability to work with others, computer skills, oral communication skills, personal interest in the field, written communication skills, must have spent time in Israel. Duration is 1 year. $22,500 per year. ▶ *1 Iyyun Fellowship:* responsibilities include serving as educational and programming resource to Jewish college students; assisting in development of the Jewish learning component of all Hillel conferences. Candidates should have ability to work independently, ability to work with others, college courses in field, editing skills, knowledge of field, organizational skills, writing skills. Duration is 1 year. $22,500 per year. ▶ *1 Samuel and Helene Soref Fellowship:* responsibilities include Jewish identity and awareness programming; working with Jewish student leaders from small Jewish campus communities; helping create pieces of student conferences; administering grants for student programs. Candidates

should have ability to work independently, ability to work with others, oral communication skills, personal interest in the field, written communication skills. Duration is 1 year. $22,500 per year. Open to college seniors, recent college graduates. International applications accepted.
Benefits Formal training, health insurance, names of contacts, on-the-job training, opportunity to attend seminars/workshops, possible full-time employment, willing to act as a professional reference, willing to provide letters of recommendation.
International Internships Available in Montreal, Canada; Toronto, Canada; Vancouver, Canada; Jerusalem, Israel; Tel Aviv, Israel; Montevideo, Uruguay.
Contact Write, call, fax, e-mail, or through World Wide Web site Rachel Gurshman, Assistant Director of Human Resources. Phone: 202-449-6500 Ext. 6559. Fax: 202-449-6459. E-mail: rgurshman@hillel.org. Telephone interview required. Applicants must submit a formal organization application, resume, academic transcripts, writing sample, two letters of recommendation, Internet application (for Jewish Campus Service Corps), photograph. Application deadline: March 1. Fees: $25. World Wide Web: http://www.hillel.org.

HILLSIDE CHILDREN'S CENTER
1337 East Main Street
Rochester, New York 14609

General Information Local leader in caring for young people with a wide range of emotional, behavioral, or life circumstance problems through a variety of comprehensive, family-centered services. Established in 1837. Number of employees: 5,000. Affiliate of Crestwood Children's Center, Scottsville, New York. Number of internship applications received each year: 50.
Internships Available ▶ *4–8 YFDS interns:* responsibilities include working directly with youth and staff; counseling; being responsible for supervising youth in everyday living situations; observation of staff working with youth. Candidates should have ability to work with others, knowledge of field, oral communication skills, organizational skills, personal interest in the field, plan to pursue career in field, self-motivation, writing skills. Duration is flexible. Unpaid. Open to college sophomores, college juniors, college seniors. ▶ *3–6 education interns:* responsibilities include working with youth in classroom settings; helping with problem subjects; assisting teacher in teaching; tutoring; observation of classroom. Candidates should have ability to work with others, college courses in field, computer skills, knowledge of field, oral communication skills, organizational skills, personal interest in the field, plan to pursue career in field, self-motivation, writing skills. Duration is flexible. Unpaid. Open to college freshmen, college sophomores, college juniors, college seniors. ▶ *1–3 recreation department interns:* responsibilities include helping recreation department; supervising youth and running activities that keep the youth busy and active. Candidates should have ability to work with others, college courses in field, knowledge of field, oral communication skills, organizational skills, personal interest in the field, plan to pursue career in field, self-motivation, written communication skills. Duration is 1 or 2 semesters or summer. Unpaid. Open to college freshmen, college sophomores, college juniors, college seniors, graduate students, career changers. ▶ *Social work interns:* responsibilities include following a BSW, MSW employee, learning the role of a social worker or family service primary; working directly with youth; counseling, working on files, advocating, and observing. Candidates should have ability to work independently, ability to work with others, college courses in field, computer skills, knowledge of field, oral communication skills, organizational skills, personal interest in the field, plan to pursue career in field, research skills, self-motivation, strong leadership ability, writing skills. Duration is flexible. Unpaid. Open to college juniors, college seniors.
Benefits Formal training, names of contacts, on-the-job training, opportunity to attend seminars/workshops, possible full-time employment, willing to complete paperwork for educational credit, willing to provide letters of recommendation.
Contact Call or e-mail Terry Bourgeois, Intern Specialist. Phone: 716-654-4529. Fax: 716-654-4460. E-mail: tbourgeo@hillside.com. In-person interview required. Applicants must submit a formal

organization application, letter of interest, resume, orientation and 2-hour crisis awareness training. Application deadline: April 1 for summer, July 1 for fall, November 1 for spring. World Wide Web: http://www.hillside.com.

THE HOME FOR LITTLE WANDERERS
271 Huntington Avenue
Boston, Massachusetts 02115

General Information Nonprofit child and family welfare organization providing multidisciplinary services ranging from prevention to residential programs, schools, and home-based support. Established in 1799. Number of employees: 904. Number of internship applications received each year: 50.
Internships Available ▶ *8–15 direct-care interns:* responsibilities include mentoring kids with emotional and behavioral issues, running activity groups, tutoring or planning activities for kids (depending on site of position). Candidates should have ability to work with others, experience in the field, oral communication skills, organizational skills, personal interest in the field, self-motivation. Duration is September 1-May 1. Unpaid. Open to college sophomores, college juniors, college seniors, recent college graduates, graduate students, career changers. ▶ *1–3 human resources interns:* responsibilities include helping with recruitment, job fairs, sorting resumes, recruiting database, Web sites, corporate and community relations, orientations, and paper work compliance. Candidates should have ability to work with others, computer skills, organizational skills, personal interest in the field, self-motivation, writing skills. Duration is 10 weeks. Unpaid. Open to college sophomores, college juniors, college seniors, recent college graduates, career changers. ▶ *10–20 school helpers:* responsibilities include helping with elementary-age children in classrooms and with after school programs, tutoring, activities, co-leading after school groups, in-school mentoring, and classroom support. Candidates should have ability to work with others, experience in the field, oral communication skills, organizational skills, personal interest in the field, self-motivation. Duration is 8 months (September-May) on a weekly basis; hours 9-5. Unpaid. Open to college freshmen, college sophomores, college juniors, college seniors, recent college graduates, graduate students, career changers, individuals reentering the workforce. International applications accepted.
Benefits On-the-job training, opportunity to attend seminars/workshops, possible full-time employment, willing to act as a professional reference, willing to complete paperwork for educational credit, willing to provide letters of recommendation.
Contact E-mail or through World Wide Web site Sarah Attie, Volunteers and Intern Manager. Phone: 617-585-7521. Fax: 617-437-8500. E-mail: sattie@thehome.org. In-person interview required. Applicants must submit a formal organization application, resume, three letters of recommendation. Application deadline: April 1 for graduate level (fall to spring) may be direct care or school helper position, August 1 for fall (1 semester), September 1 for undergraduate level (fall to spring) may be direct care or school helper, December 1 for spring (1 semester). World Wide Web: http://www.thehome.org.

HOME FREE
3409 Kilmer Lane
Plymouth, Minnesota 55441

General Information Organization that provides services for battered women and their children including safe temporary housing, advocacy, information, support, and referrals. Established in 1980. Number of employees: 30. Division of Missions, Inc., Plymouth, Minnesota. Number of internship applications received each year: 10.
Internships Available ▶ *1 children's advocate interns:* responsibilities include providing direct services and recreational activities for children; helping them to express their feelings and needs; assessing children's needs in cooperation with staff and mothers; and modeling non-violent disciplinary options. Candidates should have ability to work independently, plan to pursue career in field, self-motivation, strong interpersonal skills. Duration is flexible. Unpaid. Open to high school seniors, recent high school graduates, college freshmen, college sophomores, college juniors, college seniors, recent college graduates, graduate students, career

changers, individuals reentering the workforce. ▶ *1–3 legal advocate interns:* responsibilities include providing crisis support to women who have been assaulted by their partners; accompanying women to Order for Protection filings and hearings in family/criminal court; providing other individual and systems advocacy. Candidates should have ability to work independently, computer skills, oral communication skills, self-motivation, strong interpersonal skills, written communication skills. Duration is flexible. Unpaid. Open to recent high school graduates, college freshmen, college sophomores, college juniors, college seniors, recent college graduates, graduate students, law students, career changers, individuals reentering the workforce. ▶ *1–2 women's advocate interns:* responsibilities include providing advocacy in a battered women's shelter, individual and systems advocacy including the criminal justice system; facilitating cooperative living in the shelter, providing support to shelter residents, and answering the crisis line. Candidates should have ability to work independently, office skills, oral communication skills, self-motivation, strong interpersonal skills, strong leadership ability, written communication skills. Duration is flexible. Unpaid. Open to recent high school graduates, college freshmen, college sophomores, college juniors, college seniors, recent college graduates, graduate students, law students, career changers, individuals reentering the workforce. International applications accepted.
Benefits Formal training, on-the-job training, opportunity to attend seminars/workshops, willing to act as a professional reference, willing to complete paperwork for educational credit, willing to provide letters of recommendation, work-related travel reimbursement.
Contact Write, call, or e-mail Kari Hitchcock, Volunteer Coordinator. Phone: 763-545-7080 Ext. 11. Fax: 763-545-7071. E-mail: hfoffice@slate.homefreeprograms.org. In-person interview required. Applicants must submit a formal organization application, letter of interest, two letters of recommendation. Applications are accepted continuously.

H.O.M.E. INC.
PO Box 10
Orland, Maine 04472-0010

General Information Corporation dedicated to "helping people to help themselves" by providing education, an outlet for the sale of crafts, and health care to low-income individuals in addition to job training and housing. Established in 1970. Number of employees: 50. Number of internship applications received each year: 15.
Internships Available ▶ *1 adult volunteer program intern:* responsibilities include clearing land, gathering hay, painting houses, putting up fences, and working on repairs with low-income families. Candidates should have ability to work independently, oral communication skills, self-motivation, strong interpersonal skills, writing skills. Duration is 6–12 months. Unpaid. Open to high school seniors, recent high school graduates, individuals reentering the workforce. ▶ *2 farm assistants:* responsibilities include working with Cashmere goats, sheep, work horses, and all phases of farm life; training horses to work as team; gardening; cutting hay; general barn duties. Candidates should have ability to work independently, ability to work with others, knowledge of field, oral communication skills, personal interest in the field, self-motivation, written communication skills, flexibility. Duration is 6–12 months. Unpaid. Open to recent high school graduates, recent college graduates, career changers, individuals reentering the workforce. ▶ *2 house construction interns:* responsibilities include learning construction and carpentry and building homes. Candidates should have ability to work independently, oral communication skills, self-motivation, strong interpersonal skills, willingness to learn and follow instructions. Duration is 3–24 months. Unpaid. Open to recent high school graduates, recent college graduates, career changers, individuals reentering the workforce. ▶ *2 wood harvesting/processing interns:* responsibilities include operating saw and shingle mill and harvesting wood with horses. Candidates should have ability to work independently, oral communication skills, self-motivation, strong interpersonal skills, written communication skills. Duration is 6–24 months. Unpaid. Open to recent high school graduates, individuals reentering the workforce. ▶ *2*

H.O.M.E. Inc. (continued)

woodworking/cabinet makers: responsibilities include learning cabinetry and woodworking from start to finish. Candidates should have ability to work independently, oral communication skills, self-motivation, strong interpersonal skills, written communication skills. Duration is 6–24 months. Unpaid. Open to recent high school graduates, recent college graduates, career changers, individuals reentering the workforce. International applications accepted.

Benefits Free housing, free meals, opportunity to attend seminars/workshops, possible full-time employment, willing to complete paperwork for educational credit, willing to provide letters of recommendation, possible small stipend after training.

Contact Write, call, or e-mail Fr. Randy Eldridge, OHR, Volunteer Coordinator. Phone: 207-469-7961 Ext. 24. Fax: 207-469-1023. E-mail: padre@acadia.net. Applicants must submit a letter of interest, resume, two personal references, two letters of recommendation. Application deadline: February 1 for summer, July 1 for fall, November 1 for spring. World Wide Web: http://www.homecoop.net.

HOPE FAMILY RESOURCES, INC.
81 Pondfield Road, PMB 353
Bronxville, New York 10708

General Information Comprehensive counseling care and education agency strengthening the well-being of laypersons and clergy/religious with faith and reason through family centers, counselor formation programs, and media. Established in 1985. Number of employees: 8. Number of internship applications received each year: 12.

Internships Available ▶ *2–4 Counseling Enrichment and Practice interns:* responsibilities include field instruction assignments of study and direct counseling service in the New York metropolitan area. Candidates should have ability to work independently, ability to work with others, oral communication skills, organizational skills, plan to pursue career in field, written communication skills. Duration is one year (September to August). Unpaid. Open to college seniors, recent college graduates, graduate students, career changers, students and alumni of faith-based/universities or seminaries preferred. ▶ *2–4 mental health management interns:* responsibilities include coordination, communications, data-entry, paraprofessional counseling, research, fund-raising, and translation (if possible). Candidates should have computer skills, personal interest in the field, plan to pursue career in field, self-motivation, strong interpersonal skills, writing skills, bilingual or multi-lingual ability (a plus). Duration is one year (April to March). Unpaid. Open to recent high school graduates, college freshmen, college sophomores, college juniors, college seniors, recent college graduates, graduate students, career changers, students or alumni of faith-based high schools, universities, or seminaries preferred. International applications accepted.

Benefits Formal training, free meals, housing at a cost, job counseling, on-the-job training, opportunity to attend seminars/workshops, possible full-time employment, travel reimbursement, willing to act as a professional reference, willing to complete paperwork for educational credit, vacation time, liability insurance (for counseling positions).

Contact Write, call, or e-mail Dr. Denise Mari, Counseling Director, PO Box 128, Eastchester, New York 10709. Phone: 914-793-9508. E-mail: team@hopeforme.org. In-person interview required. Applicants must submit a letter of interest, resume, academic transcripts, two writing samples, three personal references, statement of adequate physical and psychological health; police/background clearance required. Application deadline: April 1 for mental health management interns, September 1 for counseling interns. Fees: $20. World Wide Web: http://www.hopeforme.org.

HOPE FOR KIDS, INC.
1001 University Drive
State College, Pennsylvania 16804

General Information Therapeutic foster care program. Established in 1997. Number of employees: 9. Number of internship applications received each year: 40.

Internships Available ▶ *1–5 case manager assistants:* responsibilities include assisting with case management, school placements, family visits and interventions, intake meeting, counseling arrangements, and aftercare/transition plans. Candidates should have ability to work independently, college courses in field, computer skills, knowledge of field, office skills, oral communication skills, organizational skills, self-motivation, strong interpersonal skills, written communication skills. Duration is flexible. Unpaid. Open to college seniors. ▶ *1 fund-raiser/event coordinator assistant:* responsibilities include assisting with fund-raising and event coordination. Candidates should have ability to work independently, computer skills, knowledge of field, office skills, oral communication skills, organizational skills, research skills, self-motivation, strong interpersonal skills, writing skills. Duration is flexible. Unpaid. Open to college seniors. ▶ *1–2 missions interns:* responsibilities include assisting with coordination of trips to El Salvador to partake in mission trip to feed the street children. Candidates should have ability to work independently, office skills, oral communication skills, personal interest in the field, strong interpersonal skills, writing skills. Duration is flexible. Unpaid. International applications accepted.

Benefits On-the-job training, travel reimbursement, willing to act as a professional reference, willing to complete paperwork for educational credit, willing to provide letters of recommendation.

International Internships Available in San Salvador, El Salvador.

Contact Write, call, fax, or e-mail Celeste Glass, Clinical Supervisor, PO Box 1331, State College, Pennsylvania 16804. Phone: 814-861-4673. Fax: 814-861-5077. E-mail: bgold1703@aol.com. In-person interview recommended (telephone interview accepted). Applicants must submit a letter of interest, resume, three personal references. Applications are accepted continuously. World Wide Web: http://hopeforkidsinc.net.

HOUSING ASSISTANCE COUNCIL
1025 Vermont Avenue, NW, Suite 606
Washington, District of Columbia 20005

General Information National nonprofit organization concerned with rural low-income housing. Established in 1971. Number of employees: 39. Number of internship applications received each year: 20.

Internships Available ▶ *Up to 2 interns:* responsibilities include data entry and/or analysis depending on organization's needs. Candidates should have ability to work independently, ability to work with others, analytical skills, personal interest in the field, research skills, writing skills. Duration is 1-5 months (usually summer). Position available as unpaid or at minimum wage or above. Open to high school students, recent high school graduates, college freshmen, college sophomores, college juniors, college seniors, recent college graduates, graduate students, law students, career changers, individuals reentering the workforce. International applications accepted.

Benefits On-the-job training, opportunity to attend seminars/workshops, possible full-time employment, willing to act as a professional reference, willing to complete paperwork for educational credit, willing to provide letters of recommendation.

Contact E-mail or through World Wide Web site Mary Stover, Research and Information Director. E-mail: mary@ruralhome.org. No phone calls. In-person interview recommended (telephone interview accepted). Applicants must submit a letter of interest, resume, writing sample, three personal references. Applications are accepted continuously. World Wide Web: http://www.ruralhome.org.

IMMIGRATION AND REFUGEE SERVICES OF AMERICA
1717 Massachusetts Avenue, NW, Suite 200
Washington, District of Columbia 20036

General Information Nonsectarian network of nonprofit agencies providing direct services and advocacy for migrant individuals and families of all nationalities. Established in 1922. Number of employees: 55. Number of internship applications received each year: 300.

Internships Available ▶ *2 IRSA-USCR communications/media interns:* responsibilities include assisting communications director in forging and maintaining links with print, radio, and television media; helping prepare and distribute press releases and media information packets; assisting in setting up of press conferences, briefings, and other events; researching current news developments concerning refugees and immigrants; tracking organization in the news; producing and distributing reprints of articles; answering inquiries about the organization's work; assisting in media database management. Candidates should have ability to work independently, computer skills, oral communication skills, personal interest in the field, writing skills, enthusiasm, positive attitude. Duration is 10 week minimum (at least 20 hours per week). Unpaid. ▶ *1 ISRA fund-raising/development intern:* responsibilities include researching potential funding sources for many different projects; assisting in direct mail campaigns; researching and developing a strategy for soliciting sponsorship for the 2003 survey; identifying opportunities for public visibility; tracking the organization in the news; answering inquiries about working with refugees; attending meetings; working with donor management database. Candidates should have ability to work independently, computer skills, personal interest in the field, writing skills, enthusiasm, positive attitude. Duration is 10 week minimum (at least 20 hours per week). Unpaid. ▶ *1 Project Himilo intern:* responsibilities include researching, tracking, and monitoring national, state, and local program opportunities and policy matters in employment, health care, justice, housing, and other relevant issues relating to the lives of the Somali refugees and immigrants in the U.S.; conducting organizational development assessment surveys of local Somali community-based organizations; analyzing and evaluating data gleaned from assessment surveys; assisting with prospect research, proposal development, program development, and program evaluation; organizing, attending, and reporting on refugee resettlement meetings, conferences, and related activities; providing general administrative support. Candidates should have ability to work independently, computer skills, experience in the field, personal interest in the field, research skills, strong interpersonal skills, writing skills, flexibility, sense of humor. Duration is 10 week minimum (at least 20 hours per week). Unpaid. ▶ *U.S. refugee resettlement interns:* responsibilities include researching, tracking, and monitoring international, national, state, and local program opportunities and policy matters in employment, health care, justice, housing, and other relevant issues; conducting long-term refugee satisfaction survey; assisting with needs assessments, proposal development, program development, casework, administration, and program evaluation; organizing, attending, and reporting on refugee resettlement meetings, conferences, and related activities; providing general administrative support. Candidates should have ability to work independently, ability to work with others, computer skills, knowledge of field, personal interest in the field, research skills, self-motivation, writing skills. Duration is 10 week minimum (at least 20 hours per week). Unpaid. ▶ *3–6 USCR research interns:* responsibilities include working in Africa, eastern Asia, southern Asia, North America, Europe, former Soviet Union, or the Middle East on relevant refugee situational projects with policy analysts. Candidates should have ability to work independently, computer skills, knowledge of field, personal interest in the field, research skills, writing skills, experience with Nexis-Lexis and Web based research (preferred), knowledge of a foreign language (a plus). Duration is 10 week minimum (at least 20 hours per week). Unpaid. ▶ *1 congressional liaison intern:* responsibilities include researching current legislation affecting refugees and asylum seekers, attending Congressional and governmental meetings of relevance to asylum in the U.S. or assistance abroad, maintaining a database of congressional and governmental contacts, helping organize meetings and briefings, and providing clerical support. Candidates should have ability to work independently, computer skills, personal interest in the field, research skills, writing skills, experience with Nexis-Lexis, Thomas, and Web-based research (preferred). Duration is 10 week minimum (at least 20 hours per week). Unpaid. ▶ *1 journalism intern:* responsibilities include writing, covering policy related events, editing, assisting with developing and soliciting material, and administrative support. Candidates should have ability to work independently, ability to work with others, computer skills, editing skills, knowledge

of field, personal interest in the field, research skills, writing skills. Duration is 10 week minimum (at least 20 hours per week). Unpaid. Open to college sophomores, college juniors, college seniors, recent college graduates, graduate students, career changers. International applications accepted.
Benefits On-the-job training, willing to act as a professional reference, willing to complete paperwork for educational credit, willing to provide letters of recommendation, local travel reimbursement, occasional travel opportunities.
Contact Write, fax, or e-mail Meheret Mellese, Program Assistant. Fax: 202-797-2363. E-mail: mmellese@irsa-uscr.org. In-person interview recommended (telephone interview accepted). Applicants must submit a resume, two personal references, one 3- to 5-page writing sample, cover letter indicating internship preferred, names and contact information of 2 references. Application deadline: January 15 for winter/spring, April 15 for summer, August 15 for fall. World Wide Web: http://www.refugeesusa.org.

INCARCERATED MOTHER'S PROGRAM
1968 Second Avenue, 2nd Floor
New York, New York 10029

General Information Program designed to strengthen the family unit to prevent children from being placed in foster care. Established in 1986. Number of employees: 43. Division of Edwin Gould Services For Children and Families, New York, New York. Number of internship applications received each year: 15.
Internships Available ▶ *1–6 intern/volunteers:* responsibilities include establishing consistent relationships with assigned families, facilitating program activities and group dynamics, and facilitating individual sessions with assigned youth. Candidates should have knowledge of field, oral communication skills, personal interest in the field, self-motivation, strong interpersonal skills, strong leadership ability, must be available for Saturday activities and meetings. Duration is 6–12 months. Unpaid. Open to college juniors, college seniors, recent college graduates, graduate students, law students, career changers, individuals reentering the workforce. International applications accepted.
Benefits Willing to act as a professional reference, willing to complete paperwork for educational credit, willing to provide letters of recommendation.
Contact Write, call, or fax Alexandra Badia, Teen Program Coordinator. Phone: 212-410-4200 Ext. 134. Fax: 212-410-4345. In-person interview required. Applicants must submit a formal organization application, letter of interest, resume, 3 professional references. Applications are accepted continuously.

INTERNATIONAL RESCUE COMMITTEE–ATLANTA RESETTLEMENT OFFICE
4151 Memorial Drive, Suite 201-C
Decatur, Georgia 30032

General Information Nonsecular refugee settlement organization that helps refugees find jobs and accommodation and adjust during their first 90 days in the U.S. Established in 1933. Number of employees: 52. Branch of International Rescue Committee, New York, New York. Number of internship applications received each year: 40.
Internships Available ▶ *5–10 IRC-Atlanta interns:* responsibilities include various tasks working with refugees primarily from Africa, the Middle East, Asia, and Eastern Europe. Candidates should have ability to work independently, ability to work with others, oral communication skills, organizational skills, self-motivation. Duration is flexible. Unpaid. Open to high school students and up. International applications accepted.
Benefits Possible full-time employment, willing to act as a professional reference, willing to complete paperwork for educational credit, willing to provide letters of recommendation.
Contact Write, call, fax, or e-mail Ann Taylor, Volunteer Coordinator, 4151 Memorial Drive, Suite 201-C, Decatur, Georgia 30032. Phone: 404-292-7731 Ext. 26. Fax: 404-292-5325. E-mail: ann@atl.intrescom.org. In-person interview required. Applicants must submit a letter of interest, resume. Applications are accepted continuously. World Wide Web: http://www.theIRC.org.

INTERNATIONAL SERVICE EXTENSION OF THE YMCA
6300 Westpark, Suite 600
Houston, Texas 77057

General Information Community service organization with local associations worldwide. Established in 1974. Unit of YMCA of the USA, Chicago, Illinois. Number of internship applications received each year: 100.
Internships Available ▶ *25–30 English teachers:* responsibilities include teaching English in a community-based YMCA in Taiwan. Candidates should have knowledge of field, oral communication skills, personal interest in the field, strong interpersonal skills, written communication skills, willingness to live in another culture for 1 year. Duration is 1 year. NT$26,000–NT$31,000 per month (approximately $795–$950 U.S. dollars). Open to recent college graduates, graduate students, law students, career changers. International applications accepted.
Benefits Health insurance, names of contacts, possible full-time employment, willing to provide letters of recommendation, orientations in U.S. and Taiwan, paid vacation, airfare reimbursed, subsidized housing.
International Internships Available in Taiwan.
Contact Write, call, or e-mail Patty Schnabel, Program Director. Phone: 713-339-9015 Ext. 338. Fax: 281-842-9077. E-mail: kpsmile@flash.net. In-person interview required. Applicants must submit a formal organization application, letter of interest, academic transcripts, three letters of recommendation. Application deadline: June 1 for fall placement. Fees: $50. World Wide Web: http://www.ymca.net.

JEWISH FAMILY AND CHILDREN'S SERVICES
2150 Post Street
San Francisco, California 94115

General Information Multifunction social service and mental health organization that provides multiple programs including counseling, homecare, adoptions, and emigrant resettlement; the oldest ongoing charity west of the Mississippi. Established in 1850.
Internships Available ▶ *Academic year interns:* responsibilities include working in counseling, case management, homecare, adoptions, or emigrant resettlement. Candidates should have enrollment in a clinical training program. Duration is 1 academic year. Unpaid. Open to 2nd-year graduate students or postgraduate students. ▶ *Summer interns:* responsibilities include Jewish communal work. Duration is 10 weeks. $200 per week. Open to Jewish undergraduate students.
Contact Write, call, fax, or e-mail Yael Moses, Supervisor, Adult Services, 2150 Post Street, San Francisco, California 94115. Phone: 415-449-1234. Fax: 415-449-1253. E-mail: yaelm@jfcs.org. Applicants must submit a letter of interest, resume. Application deadline: May 15 for summer, June 30 for academic year. World Wide Web: http://www.jfcs.org.

JEWISH FAMILY SERVICE OF SOUTHERN MIDDLESEX COUNTY
52 Condordia Shopping Center
Monroe Township, New Jersey 08831

General Information Family social service agency offering individual, family, and couples therapy; socialization groups; provides meals on wheels for the elderly. Number of employees: 8. Branch of Jewish Family Service of Southern Middlesex County, East Brunswick, New Jersey. Number of internship applications received each year: 10.
Internships Available ▶ *1–2 geriatric interns:* responsibilities include working with older adults in socialization groups, assisting with social services, helping with publicity for groups. Candidates should have oral communication skills, personal interest in the field, plan to pursue career in field, strong interpersonal skills, written communication skills, college courses in field (helpful). Duration is May to September. Unpaid. Open to college juniors, college seniors, recent college graduates, graduate students.

Benefits Opportunity to attend seminars/workshops, willing to act as a professional reference, willing to complete paperwork for educational credit, willing to provide letters of recommendation.
Contact E-mail Tony Ehrlich,, Director. Phone: 609-395-7979. Fax: 609-395-7129. E-mail: jfsmonroe@aol.com. In-person interview required. Applicants must submit a resume, three personal references. Applications are accepted continuously.

JOBS FOR YOUTH
50 East Washington, 4th Floor
Chicago, Illinois 60602

General Information Job readiness agency that helps young men and women from low-income families become a part of the economic mainstream and provides the business community with motivated entry-level workers. Established in 1979. Number of employees: 40. Number of internship applications received each year: 40.
Internships Available ▶ *5–10 assessment interns:* responsibilities include overseeing assessment portion of program; providing orientation to all incoming clients; monitoring test taking; and interviewing all prospective clients and enrolling them in a workshop or GED classes. Candidates should have oral communication skills, organizational skills, personal interest in the field, strong interpersonal skills. Duration is flexible. Unpaid. Open to college juniors, college seniors.
Benefits On-the-job training, possible full-time employment, willing to act as a professional reference, willing to complete paperwork for educational credit, willing to provide letters of recommendation.
Contact Call or e-mail Kristin Anderson, Director of Volunteer Services. Phone: 312-499-2929. E-mail: kristin@jfychicago.org. In-person interview required. Applicants must submit a letter of interest, resume. Applications are accepted continuously. World Wide Web: http://www.jfychicago.org.

JOINT ACTION IN COMMUNITY SERVICE, INC., SAN FRANCISCO REGIONAL OFFICE
703 Market Street, Suite 406
San Francisco, California 94103

General Information National nonprofit organization serving at-risk youth ages 16-24. Established in 1967. Number of employees: 8. Unit of Joint Action in Community Service, Washington, District of Columbia. Number of internship applications received each year: 80.
Internships Available ▶ *1–2 resource development interns:* responsibilities include researching resources for at-risk youth ages 16-24; creating user friendly resource book and locating contacts at social services agencies. Candidates should have ability to work independently, computer skills, oral communication skills, research skills, strong interpersonal skills, writing skills. Duration is minimum 1 semester/quarter or summer, 4 hours per week. Unpaid. Open to college sophomores, college juniors, college seniors, recent college graduates, graduate students, career changers, individuals reentering the workforce. ▶ *1–3 youth services interns:* responsibilities include making outreach calls to at-risk youth ages 16-24 and providing support, resources and referrals based on needs, such as job search assistance or locating housing. Candidates should have office skills, oral communication skills, personal interest in the field, plan to pursue career in field, self-motivation, strong interpersonal skills. Duration is minimum 1 semester/quarter or summer, 4–8 hours per week. Unpaid. Open to college juniors, college seniors, recent college graduates, graduate students, career changers, individuals reentering the workforce.
Benefits Formal training, willing to act as a professional reference, willing to complete paperwork for educational credit, willing to provide letters of recommendation, opportunity to gain experience in social services.
Contact Write, call, fax, or e-mail Amy Casella, Deputy Regional Director. Phone: 415-222-6905. Fax: 415-543-3108. E-mail: amy@jacsinc.org. In-person interview recommended (telephone interview accepted). Applicants must submit a letter of interest, resume. Applications are accepted continuously. World Wide Web: http://www.jacsinc.org.

JOINT ACTION IN COMMUNITY SERVICE (JACS)
Suite 810E, The Curtis Center, 170 South Independence Mall West
Philadelphia, Pennsylvania 19106-3315

General Information Youth service organization that provides support services to students from the Job Corps program. Established in 1967. Number of employees: 4. Branch of Joint Action in Community Service, Washington, District of Columbia. Number of internship applications received each year: 10.

Internships Available ▶ *1–2 client outreach/office assistants:* responsibilities include contacting former Job Corps students and conducting needs assessments, locating resources for use by staff, and various administrative tasks. Candidates should have ability to work independently, office skills, oral communication skills, self-motivation, strong interpersonal skills, written communication skills. Duration is 2–12 months. Unpaid. Open to college freshmen, college sophomores, college juniors, college seniors, recent college graduates, graduate students, law students, career changers, individuals reentering the workforce, retirees, must be 18 or over. International applications accepted.

Benefits Formal training, job counseling, names of contacts, on-the-job training, opportunity to attend seminars/workshops, willing to act as a professional reference, willing to complete paperwork for educational credit, willing to provide letters of recommendation, stipend for travel and meal expenses.

Contact Write, call, fax, or e-mail Stefanie Eshleman, Deputy Regional Director, Suite 810E, The Curtis Center, 170 South Independence Mall West, Philadelphia, Pennsylvania 19106-3315. Phone: 215-861-5530. Fax: 215-861-5535. E-mail: seshleman@doleta. gov. In-person interview recommended (telephone interview accepted). Applicants must submit a formal organization application, letter of interest, resume, two personal references. Applications are accepted continuously. World Wide Web: http://www. jacsinc.org.

KOSCIUSKO COMMUNITY YMCA
1401 East Smith Street
Warsaw, Indiana 46580

General Information Organization that provides health, fitness, aquatics, and social services to the community. Established in 1961. Number of employees: 140. Unit of YMCA of the USA, Chicago, Illinois.

Internships Available ▶ *1–5 day camp counselors:* responsibilities include working hands-on with children in daily camp. Candidates should have ability to work independently, personal interest in the field, self-motivation, strong interpersonal skills, strong leadership ability. Duration is 5–12 weeks. Position available as unpaid or at $6–$7 per hour. Open to college freshmen, college sophomores, college juniors, college seniors. ▶ *1–5 physical department interns:* responsibilities include organizing classes and programs; marketing, hiring, training, and supervising staff; creating new programs and evaluating current programs; performing other duties in the physical department. Candidates should have ability to work independently, oral communication skills, organizational skills, self-motivation, strong interpersonal skills, written communication skills. Duration is as needed. Position available as unpaid or at $6–$7 per hour. Open to college freshmen, college sophomores, college juniors, college seniors, recent college graduates. International applications accepted.

Benefits Formal training, job counseling, names of contacts, opportunity to attend seminars/workshops, possible full-time employment, willing to complete paperwork for educational credit, willing to provide letters of recommendation.

Contact Write, call, fax, or e-mail Tom Garland, Executive Director. Phone: 574-269-9622. Fax: 574-269-1396. E-mail: tgarland@kcymca. org. In-person interview required. Applicants must submit a resume, three personal references. Application deadline: May 1 for summer. World Wide Web: http://www.kcymca.org.

LACASA/ ZACHARIAS CENTER (LAKE COUNTY COUNCIL AGAINST SEXUAL ASSAULT)
4275 Old Grand Avenue
Gurnee, Illinois 60031

General Information Comprehensive sexual abuse/sexual assault center. Established in 1981. Number of employees: 18. Unit of Illinois Coalition Against Sexual Assault (ICASA), Springfield, Illinois. Number of internship applications received each year: 10.

Internships Available ▶ *1–2 advocacy interns:* responsibilities include medical and court advocacy for survivors of sexual assault in Lake County; includes hotline work and medical advocacy at hospitals. Candidates should have ability to work independently, ability to work with others, computer skills, oral communication skills, organizational skills, personal interest in the field, self-motivation. Duration is 6 months minimum. Unpaid. Open to recent high school graduates, college freshmen, college sophomores, college juniors, college seniors, recent college graduates, graduate students, law students. ▶ *1–3 clinical interns:* responsibilities include providing client-centered, trauma-based individual and group counseling to non-offending survivors of sexual assault and sexual abuse, ages 3 through adult. Candidates should have ability to work independently, ability to work with others, knowledge of field, oral communication skills, personal interest in the field, self-motivation, writing skills, feminist philosophy, trauma-based model. Duration is 6 months minimum. Unpaid. Open to graduate students. International applications accepted.

Benefits Formal training, names of contacts, on-the-job training, opportunity to attend seminars/workshops, willing to act as a professional reference, willing to complete paperwork for educational credit, willing to provide letters of recommendation.

Contact Call Caroline F. "Cecy" Wren, Director of Client Services, 4275 Old Grand Avenue, Gurnee, Illinois 60031. Phone: 847-244-1187 Ext. 32. Fax: 847-244-6380. In-person interview required. Applicants must submit a letter of interest, resume, three personal references, successful completion of state-required volunteer training course (40 hours). Applications are accepted continuously. World Wide Web: http://www.info@lacasagurnee.org.

L'ARCHE MOBILE INC.
151 South Ann Street
Mobile, Alabama 36604

General Information Christian community that provides permanent family-like homes for people with a mental handicap. Established in 1974. Number of employees: 25. Affiliate of International Federation of L'Arche, Montreal, Quebec, Canada. Number of internship applications received each year: 2.

Internships Available ▶ *1–3 house assistants:* responsibilities include working as a team to try to meet the needs of the men and women with a handicap who reside in the home; includes personal care of daily activities and providing companionship. Candidates should have ability to work independently, oral communication skills, self-motivation, strong interpersonal skills, written communication skills, must have a high school degree. Duration is flexible. Position available as unpaid or paid. Open to recent high school graduates, college freshmen, college sophomores, college juniors, college seniors, recent college graduates, graduate students, law students, career changers, individuals reentering the workforce. International applications accepted.

Benefits Formal training, free housing, free meals, health insurance, job counseling, on-the-job training, possible full-time employment, willing to complete paperwork for educational credit, willing to provide letters of recommendation.

Contact Write, call, fax, e-mail, or through World Wide Web site Dennis O'Keefe, Executive Director. Phone: 251-438-2094. Fax: 251-438-2094. E-mail: larchmob@hotmail.com. Telephone interview required. Applicants must submit a formal organization application, letter of interest, resume, 2-3 letters of recommendation. Applications are accepted continuously. World Wide Web: http://www2.acan.net/~larchmob/.

LATIN AMERICAN ART RESOURCE PROJECT
7044 Woodville Road
Mt. Airy, Maryland 21771

General Information Development program that teaches artists, artisans, and art educators in disadvantaged Central American communities how to make art and artisanry with low-cost local resources. Established in 1994. Number of employees: 3. Number of internship applications received each year: 20.

Internships Available ▶ *1–3 development interns:* responsibilities include preparation of indigenous materials for demonstration purposes; organizing workshops and program presentations; project documentation; fund-raising for specific projects; conducted at U.S. site with possible follow-through in Honduras. Candidates should have office skills, oral communication skills, personal interest in the field, research skills, strong interpersonal skills, written communication skills, emotional maturity. Duration is 1–3 months. Unpaid. Open to recent high school graduates, college freshmen, college sophomores, college juniors, college seniors, recent college graduates, graduate students, law students, career changers, individuals reentering the workforce, social and community workers. ▶ *1–3 studio interns:* responsibilities include preparation of art materials, assistance with art projects, photographic documentation; some office duties, studio maintenance; U.S. site with possible follow-through in Honduras. Candidates should have ability to work with others, office skills, personal interest in the field, self-motivation, honesty and responsibility, aptitude for manual skills. Duration is 1–3 months. Unpaid. Open to recent high school graduates, college freshmen, college sophomores, college juniors, college seniors, recent college graduates, graduate students, law students, career changers, individuals reentering the workforce, young artists, art students. International applications accepted.

Benefits Housing at a cost, job counseling, meals at a cost, names of contacts, on-the-job training, opportunity to attend seminars/workshops, possible full-time employment, willing to act as a professional reference, willing to complete paperwork for educational credit, willing to provide letters of recommendation, tutorials and classes included in program cost; possibility of reduction of program cost.

International Internships Available in Honduras.

Contact Write, call, e-mail, or through World Wide Web site Mr. William Swetcharnik, Program Director. Phone: 301-831-7286. E-mail: swetcharnik@hood.edu. In-person interview recommended (telephone interview accepted). Applicants must submit a formal organization application, letter of interest, resume, academic transcripts, two personal references, two letters of recommendation, fee ranging from $2200-$4800, depending on number of months of participation (may be partially waived in some circumstances). Applications are accepted continuously. Fees: $100. World Wide Web: http://www.hood.edu/academic/art/laarp.

LITTLE BROTHERS–FRIENDS OF THE ELDERLY
355 North Ashland
Chicago, Illinois 60607

General Information National nonprofit voluntary organization committed to relieving isolation and loneliness among the elderly. Established in 1959. Number of employees: 40. Affiliate of International Federation of Little Brothers of the Poor, Paris, France. Number of internship applications received each year: 45.

Internships Available ▶ *1 Spanish-speaking program assistant:* responsibilities include developing and nurturing friendships with diverse Hispanic elderly and planning and executing various social activities. Candidates should have ability to work independently, knowledge of field, oral communication skills, personal interest in the field, self-motivation, strong interpersonal skills, valid driver's license, fluency in Spanish. Duration is 12 months. $600 monthly stipend. Open to college seniors, recent college graduates, career changers, individuals reentering the workforce. ▶ *1–3 art therapy interns:* responsibilities include facilitating the development of integrated art projects into the Rochelle vacation schedule; developing calendar of art projects for homebound celebrations; maintaining a visiting relationship with a core of elderly who have a desire for artistic expression in their lives; participating in program and evaluation meetings. Candidates should have ability to work independently, knowledge of field, oral communication skills, personal interest in the field, self-motivation, strong interpersonal skills. Duration is 3–12 months. Unpaid. Open to college seniors, recent college graduates, graduate students, career changers, individuals reentering the workforce. ▶ *1–20 intergenerational visiting program interns:* responsibilities include organizing activities for the elderly, giving daily living assistance, driving, and conducting special summer projects. Candidates should have ability to work independently, college courses in field, knowledge of field, oral communication skills, organizational skills, personal interest in the field, self-motivation, strong interpersonal skills. Duration is 9–12 months. Unpaid. Open to college freshmen, college sophomores, college juniors, college seniors, recent college graduates, graduate students, career changers, individuals reentering the workforce. ▶ *1–2 marketing interns:* responsibilities include research, the development of a marketing plan (including a budget) and supporting materials, and implementation of the plan. Candidates should have ability to work independently, oral communication skills, personal interest in the field, research skills, self-motivation, writing skills. Duration is 3–12 months. Unpaid. Open to college freshmen, college sophomores, college juniors, college seniors, recent college graduates, graduate students, career changers. ▶ *1–3 photography interns:* responsibilities include visiting the elderly in their homes during holiday parties and at special gatherings; photographing the elderly who are visited and/or those who attend the celebrations; taking responsibility for the development of the photographs, identifying and cataloging each shot according to date and whether it was an individual shot or taken at a Little Brothers event. Candidates should have ability to work independently, oral communication skills, personal interest in the field, self-motivation, strong interpersonal skills. Duration is 3–12 months. Unpaid. Open to college freshmen, college sophomores, college juniors, college seniors, recent college graduates, graduate students, career changers, individuals reentering the workforce. ▶ *1–4 program assistants:* responsibilities include developing and nurturing friendship with diverse elderly individuals and planning and executing various social activities. Candidates should have ability to work independently, knowledge of field, oral communication skills, personal interest in the field, self-motivation, strong interpersonal skills, valid driver's license, coursework in premed, nursing, gerontology, psychology, sociology (preferred). Duration is 12 months. $600 monthly stipend. Open to college juniors, college seniors, recent college graduates, graduate students, career changers, individuals reentering the workforce. ▶ *1–3 public relations interns:* responsibilities include working in the areas of marketing/public relations and fund-raising. Candidates should have ability to work independently, ability to work with others, editing skills, knowledge of field, oral communication skills, personal interest in the field, research skills, self-motivation, writing skills. Duration is 3–12 months. Unpaid. Open to college freshmen, college sophomores, college juniors, college seniors, recent college graduates, graduate students, career changers, individuals reentering the workforce. ▶ *1–8 summer vacation interns:* responsibilities include creating a family atmosphere for the elderly, organizing activities, giving daily living assistance, and driving in a country setting. Candidates should have oral communication skills, organizational skills, personal interest in the field, self-motivation, strong interpersonal skills. Duration is 7 weeks. $200 stipend. Open to college freshmen, college sophomores, college juniors, college seniors, recent college graduates, graduate students, career changers, individuals reentering the workforce. ▶ *1–3 summers in the city: homebound activities interns:* responsibilities include interacting with the elderly and preparing and/or assisting with various group activities. Candidates should have ability to work independently, oral communication skills, organizational skills, strong interpersonal skills. Duration is 6–12 weeks. Room and $1200 stipend for every six-week commitment. Open to college freshmen, college sophomores, college juniors, college seniors, recent college graduates, graduate students, career changers. International applications accepted.

Benefits Health insurance, names of contacts, on-the-job training, opportunity to attend seminars/workshops, possible full-time employment, willing to act as a professional reference, will-

ing to complete paperwork for educational credit, willing to provide letters of recommendation, room and board for summer vacation interns, room and health insurance for program assistants.
International Internships Available in France; Berlin, Germany; Dublin, Ireland; Acapulco, Mexico; Barcelona, Spain.
Contact Write, call, fax, e-mail, or through World Wide Web site Ms. Christine Bertrand, Intergenerational Coordinator. Phone: 312-455-1000. Fax: 312-455-9674. E-mail: cbertrand.chi@littlebrothers. org. In-person interview recommended (telephone interview accepted). Applicants must submit a letter of interest, resume, two personal references, two letters of recommendation, 2-3 writing samples for public relations interns. Applications are accepted continuously. World Wide Web: http://www.littlebrothers.org/chicago.

LITTLE BROTHERS–FRIENDS OF THE ELDERLY
3305 Washington Street
Boston, Massachusetts 02130

General Information National, non-profit voluntary organization committed to relieving isolation and loneliness among the elderly. Established in 1979. Number of employees: 4. Affiliate of International Federation of Little Brothers of the Poor, Paris, France. Number of internship applications received each year: 20.
Internships Available ▶ *1–2 photography interns:* responsibilities include visiting and photographing the elderly at home, during holiday parties, and at special gatherings; developing photographs, including identifying and cataloging according to date and event type. Candidates should have ability to work independently, knowledge of field, oral communication skills, personal interest in the field, self-motivation, strong interpersonal skills. Duration is 3–12 months. Unpaid. Open to college freshmen, college sophomores, college juniors, college seniors, recent college graduates, graduate students, career changers, individuals reentering the workforce. ▶ *1–2 public relations/marketing interns:* responsibilities include developing projects in the areas of marketing, public relations, and fund-raising. Candidates should have ability to work independently, ability to work with others, college courses in field, editing skills, knowledge of field, oral communication skills, organizational skills, personal interest in the field, research skills, self-motivation, writing skills. Duration is 3–12 months. Unpaid. Open to college sophomores, college juniors, college seniors, recent college graduates, career changers, individuals reentering the workforce. ▶ *1–2 summer in the city interns:* responsibilities include working on a team; planning and organizing activities for individuals or small groups. Candidates should have ability to work independently, oral communication skills, organizational skills, personal interest in the field, self-motivation, strong interpersonal skills. Duration is 1–3 months. Unpaid. Open to college freshmen, college sophomores, college juniors, college seniors, recent college graduates, graduate students, career changers, individuals reentering the workforce. ▶ *1–2 visiting interns:* responsibilities include developing and nurturing friendship with diverse elderly individuals, planning and executing various activities, and being responsible for a special project. Candidates should have ability to work independently, knowledge of field, oral communication skills, organizational skills, personal interest in the field, self-motivation, strong interpersonal skills, valid driver's license. Duration is 1 year, (can be renewed for a second year). $600 monthly stipend. Open to college juniors, college seniors, recent college graduates, graduate students, career changers, individuals reentering the workforce. International applications accepted.
Benefits Health insurance, names of contacts, on-the-job training, opportunity to attend seminars/workshops, willing to act as a professional reference, willing to complete paperwork for educational credit, willing to provide letters of recommendation.
International Internships Available in France; Berlin, Germany; Dublin, Ireland; Acapulco, Mexico; Barcelona, Spain.
Contact Write, call, fax, e-mail, or through World Wide Web site Rene Morrissette, Assistant Director. Phone: 617-524-8882. Fax: 617-524-8905. E-mail: rmorrissette.bos@littlebrothers.org. In-person interview recommended (telephone interview accepted). Applicants must submit a letter of interest, resume, two personal references,

two letters of recommendation, 2-3 writing samples (for public relations marketing interns). Applications are accepted continuously. World Wide Web: http://www.littlebrothers.org/boston.

LIVING IN SAFE ALTERNATIVES, INC.–PLAINVILLE GROUP HOME
50 Bank Street
Plainville, Connecticut 06062-2703

General Information Group home setting in a residential community serving the social, emotional, educational, and therapeutic needs of abused, abandoned, neglected, and adjudicated adolescent females; strong focus on teaching independent living skills. Established in 1972. Number of employees: 17. Division of Living in Safe Alternatives, Inc., Plainville, Connecticut. Number of internship applications received each year: 8.
Internships Available ▶ *1–2 occupational therapy interns:* responsibilities include teaching life skills to clients, assessing and testing client's life skills ability, providing groups and individual life skill counseling, writing, and implementing life skill work plan for clients. Candidates should have college courses in field, knowledge of field, oral communication skills, personal interest in the field, plan to pursue career in field, self-motivation, strong interpersonal skills, written communication skills. Duration is 1–2 semesters. Unpaid. Open to college juniors, college seniors, graduate students. ▶ *1–2 social work/counseling interns:* responsibilities include helping provide individual and group counseling to clients, implementing psychological testing to clients, writing and implementing client treatment plans, performing family therapy, and monitoring psychotropic medication of clients. Candidates should have knowledge of field, oral communication skills, plan to pursue career in field, self-motivation, strong interpersonal skills, written communication skills. Duration is 1–2 semesters. Unpaid. Open to recent college graduates, graduate students, only those working toward MSW or MA in counseling. ▶ *1–2 youth worker interns:* responsibilities include interaction with and observation of clients, communication with on-duty staff weekly, participation in supervision, and one self-directed workshop or group with clients. Candidates should have knowledge of field, oral communication skills, personal interest in the field, self-motivation, strong interpersonal skills, written communication skills. Duration is 1–2 semesters. Unpaid. Open to college juniors, college seniors, recent college graduates, graduate students. International applications accepted.
Benefits Formal training, names of contacts, on-the-job training, opportunity to attend seminars/workshops, possible full-time employment, willing to act as a professional reference, willing to complete paperwork for educational credit, willing to provide letters of recommendation.
Contact Write, call, or fax Sonia Cruz, Program Coordinator, 50 Bank Street, Plainville, Connecticut 08062-2703. Phone: 860-747-9930. Fax: 860-793-2231. In-person interview required. Applicants must submit a formal organization application, letter of interest, resume, three personal references, letter of recommendation, current physical exam (including PPD), police and DCF background check required. Application deadline: November 1 for spring.

LUTHERAN VOLUNTEER CORPS
1226 Vermont Avenue, NW
Washington, District of Columbia 20005

General Information Nonprofit organization that places individuals in full-time volunteer assignments; placements include: advocacy, health, legal, environmental, social services, education, and youth child services. Established in 1979. Number of employees: 90. Unit of Luther Place Memorial Church, Washington, District of Columbia. Number of internship applications received each year: 145.
Internships Available ▶ *100 volunteers:* responsibilities include various duties according to position; positions available in ten U.S. cities. Candidates should have ability to work with others, organizational skills, personal interest in the field, self-motivation, flexibility and maturity. Duration is 1–2 years. Monthly stipend. Open to college seniors, recent college graduates, career changers, individuals reentering the workforce.

Lutheran Volunteer Corps (continued)

Benefits Free housing, free meals, health insurance, names of contacts, on-the-job training, opportunity to attend seminars/workshops, travel reimbursement, willing to act as a professional reference, willing to provide letters of recommendation, possibility of eligibility for AmeriCorps.

Contact Write, call, fax, e-mail, or through World Wide Web site Jen Neeper, Recruitment Coordinator, 1226 Vermont Avenue, Washington, District of Columbia 20005. Phone: 202-387-3222. Fax: 202-667-0037. E-mail: staff@lvchome.org. Telephone interview required. Applicants must submit a formal organization application, academic transcripts, three personal references, one essay. Application deadline: applications accepted February 1 to May 15. World Wide Web: http://www.lvchome.org.

MAINE CENTERS FOR WOMEN, WORK, AND COMMUNITY
Stoddard House, University of Maine at Augusta, 46 University Drive
Augusta, Maine 04330-9410

General Information Program providing a range of comprehensive support, pre-employment, education, training, self-employment, and employment services and resources designed to assist displaced homemakers and single parents in developing marketable skills and in making the transition to economically viable paid employment. Established in 1978. Number of employees: 32. Unit of The University of Maine at Augusta, Augusta, Maine. Number of internship applications received each year: 3.

Internships Available ▶ *1–10 interns:* responsibilities include working in program planning and direct service, management information systems assistance, self-employment, workforce literacy, economic and leadership development training, and advocacy; may also focus on research and public policy issues relating to women's economic development. Candidates should have ability to work independently, computer skills, knowledge of field, organizational skills, strong interpersonal skills, written communication skills. Duration is 3–12 months. Unpaid. Open to college juniors, college seniors, recent college graduates, graduate students, law students, career changers, individuals reentering the workforce. International applications accepted.

Benefits Job counseling, names of contacts, on-the-job training, opportunity to attend seminars/workshops, willing to act as a professional reference, willing to complete paperwork for educational credit, willing to provide letters of recommendation, reimbursement for job-related travel expenses.

Contact Write, call, fax, or e-mail Ms. Eloise Vitelli, Associate Director. Phone: 207-621-3432. Fax: 207-621-3429. E-mail: evitelli@maine.edu. In-person interview required. Applicants must submit a formal organization application, letter of interest, resume, 2 personal references or letters of recommendation. Applications are accepted continuously. World Wide Web: http://www.womenworkandcommunity.org.

MAKE-A-WISH FOUNDATION OF CENTRAL AND SOUTHERN ARIZONA
711 East Northern Avenue
Phoenix, Arizona 85020

General Information Nonprofit organization that grants wishes to children age 2½–18 who suffer from life-threatening illnesses. Established in 1980. Number of employees: 6. Unit of Make-A-Wish Foundation of America, Phoenix, Arizona. Number of internship applications received each year: 5.

Internships Available ▶ *1 intern:* responsibilities include assisting staff in all aspects of program administration. Candidates should have ability to work with others, computer skills, oral communication skills, self-motivation, written communication skills, ability to work well with children and to interact with volunteers. Duration is flexible. Unpaid. Open to college freshmen, college sophomores, college juniors, college seniors, recent college graduates, graduate students. International applications accepted.

Benefits Names of contacts, on-the-job training, opportunity to attend seminars/workshops, possible full-time employment, will-ing to act as a professional reference, willing to complete paperwork for educational credit, willing to provide letters of recommendation, good nonprofit experience.

Contact Write, call, fax, e-mail, or through World Wide Web site Volunteer Manager, 711 East Northern Avenue, Phoenix, Arizona 85020. Phone: 602-395-9474 Ext. 132. Fax: 602-395-0722. E-mail: csaz@makeawishcsaz.org. In-person interview recommended (telephone interview accepted). Applicants must submit a letter of interest, resume, personal reference, two letters of recommendation. Application deadline: June 1 for fall, October 1 for spring. World Wide Web: http://www.wish.org/centralaz.

MANHATTAN EMERGENCY SHELTER, INC.
831 Leavenworth
Manhattan, Kansas 66502

General Information Temporary emergency shelter and transitional living facility for those in need (homeless). Established in 1985. Number of employees: 11. Number of internship applications received each year: 5.

Internships Available ▶ *1–3 assistant case workers:* responsibilities include assisting client services director in helping guests regain their independence and self-sufficiency. Candidates should have ability to work independently, analytical skills, computer skills, knowledge of field, office skills, oral communication skills, organizational skills, personal interest in the field, plan to pursue career in field, self-motivation, strong interpersonal skills, strong leadership ability, writing skills. Duration is flexible. Unpaid. Open to high school seniors, recent high school graduates, college freshmen, college sophomores, college juniors, college seniors, individuals reentering the workforce. International applications accepted.

Benefits Free meals, names of contacts, on-the-job training, opportunity to attend seminars/workshops, possible full-time employment, willing to act as a professional reference, willing to complete paperwork for educational credit, willing to provide letters of recommendation.

Contact Write, call, fax, or e-mail Junell Norris, Executive Director, PO Box 896, Manhattan, Kansas 66505-0896. Phone: 785-537-3113. Fax: 785-537-1380. E-mail: junellnorris@hotmail.com. In-person interview recommended (telephone interview accepted). Applicants must submit a formal organization application, letter of interest, resume, academic transcripts, portfolio, two personal references, two letters of recommendation. Application deadline: April 1 for summer, December 1 for spring. World Wide Web: http://www.mesi.interkan.net/mes.

MARYHAVEN CENTER OF HOPE
1010 Route 112
Port Jefferson Station, New York 11776

General Information Not-for-profit, non-sectarian agency committed to serving both children and adults who are mentally and physically challenged by establishing, maintaining, and operating progressive programs and services which are residential, therapeutic, and vocational in nature; goal is the attainment of normalization in all aspects of life for each individual in its care. Established in 1931. Number of employees: 1,065. Affiliate of Catholic Health Services of Long Island, Melville, New York. Number of internship applications received each year: 40.

Internships Available ▶ *Applied behavior specialist assistants:* responsibilities include following up on behavior plan at sites, reporting to ABS, collecting data, and reporting results. Duration is flexible. Unpaid. ▶ *Applied behavior specialist interns:* responsibilities include data collection, analysis, and functional assessments. Duration is flexible. Position available as unpaid or at $7 per hour. ▶ *Home touch coordinators:* responsibilities include tracking goals, billing sheets for monthly services to consumers, petty cash, mileage for staff; liaison between staff, families, and consumers; reviewing documentation for completion and accuracy. Duration is flexible. Unpaid. ▶ *Human resource specialist interns:* responsibilities include recruiting, clerical tasks, benefit administration, and special projects. Duration is flexible. Position available as unpaid or at $7 per hour. ▶ *Recreational therapist interns:* responsibilities include assisting in running groups, special projects, and outings; needs assessments for individual consumers. Duration is flexible. Unpaid. ▶ *Service coordinators:* responsibilities include consumer contact; overseeing training in work setting, case notes, and observing consumers during free time activities. Duration is flexible. Unpaid. ▶ *Social worker interns:* responsibilities include individual sessions, crisis intervention techniques. Duration is flexible. Unpaid. ▶ *Special education teacher interns:* responsibilities include classroom management; IEP development, leading to special education certification. Duration is flexible. Unpaid. ▶ *Vocational instructor interns:* responsibilities include assisting in running groups, assisting with thrift shop, performing evaluations on consumers, individual assessments for work readiness and skills. Duration is flexible. Unpaid. ▶ *Vocational rehabilitation counselor interns:* responsibilities include consumer contact, overseeing training in work setting, case notes, and observing consumers during free time activities. Duration is Flexible. Unpaid. Open to recent high school graduates, college freshmen, college sophomores, college juniors, college seniors, recent college graduates, graduate students, law students, career changers, individuals reentering the workforce. International applications accepted.

Benefits Formal training, names of contacts, on-the-job training, opportunity to attend seminars/workshops, possible full-time employment, willing to act as a professional reference, willing to complete paperwork for educational credit, willing to provide letters of recommendation.

Contact Write, call, fax, or e-mail Elizabeth Schultz, Human Resource Manager. Phone: 631-474-4120 Ext. 277. Fax: 631-474-0826. E-mail: eschultz@maryhaven.org. In-person interview recommended (telephone interview accepted). Applicants must submit a formal organization application, resume, academic transcripts, personal reference, course curriculum, TB testing required (upon acceptance). Applications are accepted continuously.

MCGAW YMCA CHILD CARE CENTER
1420 Maple Avenue
Evanston, Illinois 60201

General Information Organization that provides developmental programs for children ages 6 weeks to 6th grade. Number of employees: 80. Unit of McGaw YMCA, Evanston, Illinois. Number of internship applications received each year: 50.

Internships Available ▶ *1–15 child-care workers:* responsibilities include monitoring safety of preschool and/or school age children, planning programs, helping program run smoothly, and maintaining care of equipment and supplies. Candidates should have personal interest in the field, minimum age 16 years, experience in child care desirable. Duration is flexible. $5.15–$10 per hour. Open to high school students, recent high school graduates, college freshmen, college sophomores, college juniors, college seniors, recent college graduates, graduate students, law students, career changers, individuals reentering the workforce. International applications accepted.

Benefits Possible full-time employment, willing to complete paperwork for educational credit, YMCA membership.

Contact Write, call, or fax Director, School's Out Program. Phone: 847-475-8580. Fax: 847-733-2562. In-person interview required. Applicants must submit a formal organization application, academic transcripts, three letters of recommendation. Applications are accepted continuously.

MEALS ON WHEELS OF SAN FRANCISCO, INC.
1375 Fairfax Avenue
San Francisco, California 94124

General Information Human/social services organization serving nutritious food to homebound elderly of San Francisco. Established in 1970. Number of employees: 50. Affiliate of Meals on Wheels Association of America, Washington, District of Columbia. Number of internship applications received each year: 5.

Internships Available ▶ *1 Web site developer:* responsibilities include developing, designing, and maintaining organization's Web site. Candidates should have computer skills, editing skills, knowledge of field, writing skills. Duration is 1 year. Unpaid. Open to high school seniors, recent high school graduates, college freshmen, college sophomores, college juniors, college seniors, recent college graduates, graduate students, career changers, individuals reentering the workforce. ▶ *1–2 database management interns:* responsibilities include database management/entry for fundraising system. Candidates should have ability to work independently, analytical skills, computer skills, office skills, research skills, self-motivation. Duration is 1 year. Unpaid. Open to recent high school graduates, college freshmen, college sophomores, college juniors, college seniors, career changers. ▶ *1–2 development assistants:* responsibilities include assisting in development/fundraising office with grant applications, direct mail pieces, special events, public relations, marketing and communications. Candidates should have ability to work independently, ability to work with others, analytical skills, computer skills, oral communication skills, organizational skills, personal interest in the field, self-motivation, written communication skills. Duration is 20-40 hours per week. Unpaid. Open to college juniors, college seniors, recent college graduates, graduate students.

Benefits Free meals, names of contacts, on-the-job training, opportunity to attend seminars/workshops, possible full-time employment, travel reimbursement, willing to act as a professional reference, willing to complete paperwork for educational credit, willing to provide letters of recommendation.

Contact Write, call, fax, or e-mail Jessica Sweedler, Director of Marketing and Communications, 1375 Fairfax Avenue, San Francisco, California 94124. Phone: 415-920-1111 Ext. 233. Fax: 415-920-1110. E-mail: jsweedler@mowsf.org. Applicants must submit a letter of interest, resume, two personal references. Applications are accepted continuously. World Wide Web: http://www.mowsf.org.

METRO ATLANTA YMCA
100 Edgewood Avenue, NE, Suite 1100
Atlanta, Georgia 30303

General Information Nonprofit agency dedicated to providing programs and services that develop spirit, mind, and body. Established in 1858. Number of employees: 2,500.

Internships Available ▶ *Courtesy Center representatives:* responsibilities include front desk, front-line public relations to members. Candidates should have ability to work with others, oral communication skills, organizational skills, strong leadership ability. Duration is 1 semester. Position available as unpaid or paid. Open to recent high school graduates, college freshmen, college sophomores, college juniors, college seniors, recent college graduates, graduate students, law students, career changers, individuals reentering the workforce. ▶ *Aquatics interns:* responsibilities include lifeguarding, swim instruction, program planning, and class organization. Candidates should have ability to work with others, knowledge of field, organizational skills, self-motivation, strong leadership ability, written communication skills. Duration is seasonal. Position available as unpaid or paid. Open to high school seniors, recent high school graduates, college freshmen, college sophomores, college juniors, college seniors, recent college graduates, graduate students, law students, career changers, individuals reentering the workforce. ▶ *Camp interns:* responsibilities include working in arts and crafts, equestrian, environmental studies, and leadership training with 3-16 year olds; working as counselors or bus drivers. Candidates should have ability to work independently, ability to work with others, personal interest in the field, self-motivation, strong leadership ability. Duration is seasonal. Position available as unpaid or paid. Open to high school seniors, recent high school graduates, college freshmen, college sophomores, college juniors, college seniors, recent college graduates, graduate students, law students, career changers, individuals reentering the workforce. ▶ *Clerical interns:* responsibilities include human resources, data entry, filing, organizing, communications, public relations. Candidates should have ability to work with others, editing skills, oral communication skills, writing skills. Position available as unpaid or paid. Open to recent high school graduates, college freshmen, college sophomores, college juniors, college seniors, recent college graduates, graduate students, law students, career changers, individuals reentering the workforce. ▶ *Education interns:* responsibilities include acting as pre-school teacher's assistants, child-care site monitors, after-school enrichment, and tutoring. Candidates should have ability to work with others, college courses in field, knowledge of field,

Metro Atlanta YMCA (continued)

plan to pursue career in field, strong leadership ability, completion at least two years of college or be in process of completing second year of college. Duration is 1 semester. Unpaid. Open to college sophomores, college juniors, college seniors, recent college graduates. ▶ *Membership representatives:* responsibilities include signing-up new members, telling the YMCA story, developing relationships with members and organizations. Candidates should have ability to work with others, oral communication skills, self-motivation, strong leadership ability. Duration is 1 semester. Position available as unpaid or paid. Open to recent high school graduates, college freshmen, college sophomores, college juniors, college seniors, recent college graduates, graduate students, law students, career changers, individuals reentering the workforce. ▶ *Sports/recreation interns (coaches, monitors, referees):* responsibilities include climbing wall, ropes course, dance, gymnastics, volleyball, basketball, soccer, tennis, and sports clinic instructors. Candidates should have ability to work independently, ability to work with others, experience in the field, knowledge of field, strong leadership ability. Duration is sports season (includes volleyball, basketball, soccer, gymnastics, tennis). Unpaid. Open to high school seniors, recent high school graduates, college freshmen, college sophomores, college juniors, college seniors, recent college graduates, graduate students, law students, career changers, individuals reentering the workforce. ▶ *Wellness interns:* responsibilities include working as an aerobics instructor, wellness coach, or personal trainer. Candidates should have college courses in field, knowledge of field, personal interest in the field. Duration is 1 semester. Position available as unpaid or paid. Open to recent high school graduates, college freshmen, college sophomores, college juniors, college seniors, recent college graduates, career changers.

Benefits Formal training, on-the-job training, opportunity to attend seminars/workshops, possible full-time employment, willing to act as a professional reference, willing to complete paperwork for educational credit, willing to provide letters of recommendation, possible minimum wage/stipend.

Contact Fax or e-mail Nicky Rosenbluth, Staff Development Director. Fax: 404-527-7693. E-mail: careers@ymcaatlanta.org. No phone calls. In-person interview recommended (telephone interview accepted). Applicants must submit a formal organization application, letter of interest, resume, personal reference, letter of recommendation, criminal background check required. Applications are accepted continuously. World Wide Web: http://www.ymcaatlanta.org.

METRO FAMILY YMCA
2831 Southwest Barbur Boulevard
Portland, Oregon 97201

General Information Organization that promotes Christian principles through programs that build healthy bodies, minds, and spirits for all. Established in 1977. Number of employees: 140. Branch of YMCA of Columbia-Willamette, Portland, Oregon. Number of internship applications received each year: 12.

Internships Available ▶ *4 adult health/fitness/cardiac rehabilitation interns:* responsibilities include teaching land and water classes and overseeing weight room, cardiovascular and health education, social events, and program operations. Candidates should have college courses in field, oral communication skills, personal interest in the field, plan to pursue career in field, self-motivation, strong interpersonal skills. Duration is 10 weeks or 1 semester (20-40 hours per week). Unpaid. Open to college freshmen, college sophomores, college juniors, college seniors, recent college graduates, graduate students, career changers. ▶ *4 child-care program interns:* responsibilities include assisting teachers, teaching students, and performing administrative duties. Candidates should have declared college major in field, experience in the field, oral communication skills, personal interest in the field, strong interpersonal skills, strong leadership ability. Duration is 10 weeks or 1 semester. Unpaid. Open to college sophomores, college juniors, college seniors. ▶ *1 corporate site intern:* responsibilities include assisting program directors at corporate health and fitness sites; teaching fitness; and conducting weight orientations, health education, and incentive programs. Candidates should have college courses in

field, experience in the field, oral communication skills, self-motivation, strong interpersonal skills, strong leadership ability. Duration is 1 semester. Unpaid. Open to college juniors, college seniors. ▶ *4 youth sports and aquatics interns:* responsibilities include assisting program director in youth sports program and with special events; coordinating programs; performing administrative duties; and teaching. Candidates should have college courses in field, experience in the field, oral communication skills, personal interest in the field, strong interpersonal skills, strong leadership ability. Duration is 10 weeks or 1 semester. Unpaid. Open to college freshmen, college sophomores, college juniors, college seniors, recent college graduates, graduate students. International applications accepted.

Benefits Formal training, job counseling, names of contacts, on-the-job training, opportunity to attend seminars/workshops, possible full-time employment, willing to complete paperwork for educational credit, willing to provide letters of recommendation.

Contact Write or e-mail Erika Johnson, Program Director. Fax: 503-294-3381. E-mail: ejohnson@ymca-portland.org. No phone calls. In-person interview recommended (telephone interview accepted). Applicants must submit a letter of interest, resume. Application deadline: March 1 for spring, May 1 for summer, August 1 for fall, November 1 for winter. World Wide Web: http://www.ymca-portland.org.

METROPOLITAN YMCA OF THE ORANGES
2 Babcock Place
Livingston, New Jersey 07052

General Information Association that seeks to improve the quality of community life by fostering healthful living, developing responsible leaders and citizens, strengthening the family unit, promoting the quality of all persons, protecting the environment, and uniting community members and community organizations to solve contemporary problems. Established in 1886. Number of employees: 10. Number of internship applications received each year: 10.

Internships Available ▶ *2–3 athletics interns:* responsibilities include developing, teaching, and implementing sports programs. Candidates should have experience in the field, organizational skills, personal interest in the field, strong interpersonal skills, strong leadership ability. Duration is flexible. Position available as unpaid or paid. ▶ *2–3 child-care interns:* responsibilities include teaching children ages 6 weeks–5 years. Candidates should have college courses in field, knowledge of field, organizational skills, personal interest in the field, strong interpersonal skills. Duration is flexible. Position available as unpaid or paid. ▶ *2–3 environmental education interns:* responsibilities include developing, teaching, and implementing programs in environmental education. Candidates should have college courses in field, organizational skills, personal interest in the field, strong interpersonal skills, strong leadership ability. Duration is flexible. Position available as unpaid or paid. ▶ *Up to 5 marketing/public relations interns:* responsibilities include working directly with the marketing director to help implement marketing strategies at YMCA branches. Candidates should have ability to work with others, college courses in field, computer skills, editing skills, oral communication skills, writing skills. Duration is 6 months-1 year. Position available as unpaid or paid. Open to college freshmen, college sophomores, college juniors, college seniors, recent college graduates, graduate students, law students, career changers, individuals reentering the workforce. International applications accepted.

Benefits Names of contacts, opportunity to attend seminars/workshops, possible full-time employment, travel reimbursement, willing to complete paperwork for educational credit, willing to provide letters of recommendation.

Contact Write, call, fax, or e-mail Rick Gorab, Senior Vice President and COO, 2 Babcock Place, West Orange, New Jersey 07052. Phone: 973-535-1478. Fax: 973-758-9622. E-mail: rgorab@metroymcas.org. In-person interview required. Applicants must submit a resume. Application deadline: March 1 for summer, October 1 for winter. World Wide Web: http://www.metroymcas.org.

METUCHEN–EDISON YMCA
65 High Street
Metuchen, New Jersey 08840

General Information Community-based YMCA that offers membership privileges and programming services to build body, mind, and spirit for all persons in the community. Established in 1921. Number of employees: 200. Number of internship applications received each year: 2.
Internships Available ► *2–4 child-care classroom teachers:* responsibilities include assisting in day-care center, kindergarten class, or pre-school program. Candidates should have oral communication skills, personal interest in the field, strong interpersonal skills, strong leadership ability, written communication skills. Duration is 4 weeks (minimum). Paid. Open to high school seniors, recent high school graduates, college freshmen, college sophomores, college juniors, college seniors, recent college graduates, career changers, individuals reentering the workforce. ► *1–3 fitness directors:* responsibilities include conducting fitness testing and demonstrating Nautilus, free weight, and cardiorespiratory equipment. Candidates should have knowledge of field, oral communication skills, self-motivation, strong interpersonal skills, strong leadership ability. Duration is flexible. Paid. Open to college freshmen, college sophomores, college juniors, college seniors, recent college graduates, graduate students, career changers, individuals reentering the workforce. International applications accepted.
Benefits Formal training, names of contacts, on-the-job training, opportunity to attend seminars/workshops, possible full-time employment, travel reimbursement, willing to act as a professional reference, willing to complete paperwork for educational credit, willing to provide letters of recommendation, national YMCA job listings provided.
Contact Write, call, fax, or e-mail Megan Powers, Branch Executive Director. Phone: 732-548-2044. Fax: 732-549-0910. E-mail: mpmetedisonymca1@aol.com. In-person interview required. Applicants must submit a formal organization application, resume, two personal references, criminal background check required. Applications are accepted continuously.

MIDDLE EARTH
98 Grove Street
Somerville, New Jersey 08876

General Information Nonprofit community-based organization with a mission to provide adolescents with prevention, intervention, and crisis services to enable them to develop into responsible and productive members of the community. Established in 1972. Number of employees: 15. Number of internship applications received each year: 5.
Internships Available ► *Alternative to Incarceration Case Managers:* responsibilities include coordination of all aspects of the participant's case such as liaison work with the Probation Division, the schools, involved agencies, and the family; providing informal one-to-one counseling, crisis intervention, and development of individual program plans; monitoring progress on the level system and initiating consequences for non-compliance. Candidates should have ability to work with others, college courses in field, oral communication skills, organizational skills, personal interest in the field, self-motivation, strong leadership ability. Duration is 1 semester. Position available as unpaid or paid. Open to college juniors, college seniors, graduate students. ► *Agency-wide interns:* responsibilities include supervising mentoring at drop-in-centers, supervising community services projects, and serving the agency where needed. Candidates should have ability to work with others, college courses in field, knowledge of field, oral communication skills, personal interest in the field, research skills, self-motivation, strong leadership ability, writing skills. Duration is 1 semester. Position available as unpaid or paid. Open to college freshmen, college sophomores, college juniors, college seniors, recent college graduates, graduate students, law students. ► *Mentors:* responsibilities include spending 2-5 hours per week with each client; services include: outreach to adolescent and or family, mentoring, life skills, 24-hour crisis support and counseling. Candidates should have ability to work with others, college courses in field, knowledge of field, oral communication skills, organizational skills, personal interest in the field, self-motivation, strong leader-

ship ability, writing skills. Duration is 1 semester. Position available as unpaid or paid. Open to college freshmen, college sophomores, college juniors, college seniors, recent college graduates, graduate students.
Benefits On-the-job training, opportunity to attend seminars/ workshops, possible full-time employment, travel reimbursement, willing to act as a professional reference, willing to complete paperwork for educational credit, willing to provide letters of recommendation.
Contact Write, call, or fax Gary Hrynoweski, Senior Case Manager. Phone: 908-725-7223. Fax: 908-722-5411. In-person interview required. Applicants must submit a letter of interest, resume, personal reference. Applications are accepted continuously.

MIDDLE EARTH, INC.
299 Jacksonville Road
Warminister, Pennsylvania 18974

General Information Day treatment center and alternative high school. Established in 1973. Number of employees: 14. Number of internship applications received each year: 12.
Internships Available ► *3 criminal justice interns:* responsibilities include conducting informal counseling and working with probation officers. Duration is dependent on university requirements. Unpaid. Open to college sophomores, college juniors, college seniors, recent college graduates, graduate students. ► *3 educational interns:* responsibilities include teaching in classroom setting. Duration is flexible. Unpaid. Open to college sophomores, college juniors, college seniors, recent college graduates, graduate students. ► *3 psychology interns.* Duration is flexible. Unpaid. Open to college juniors, college seniors, recent college graduates, graduate students. ► *3–5 social services interns:* responsibilities include working one-on-one with adolescents. Duration is dependent on university requirements. Unpaid. Open to college sophomores, college juniors, college seniors, recent college graduates, graduate students. Candidates for all positions should have ability to work independently, oral communication skills, organizational skills, personal interest in the field, self-motivation, strong interpersonal skills. International applications accepted.
Benefits Formal training, names of contacts, on-the-job training, opportunity to attend seminars/workshops, possible full-time employment, willing to act as a professional reference, willing to complete paperwork for educational credit, willing to provide letters of recommendation, lunch provided at no cost.
Contact Write, call, or fax Ms. Elizabeth A. Quigley, Director of Educational Programming. Phone: 215-443-0280. Fax: 215-443-0245. In-person interview recommended (telephone interview accepted). Applications are accepted continuously.

MOHAWK VALLEY COMMUNITY ACTION AGENCY, INC.
207 North James Street
Rome, New York 13440

General Information Community action agency that offers a range of human services programs to benefit low/moderate income families and individuals. Established in 1966. Number of employees: 290. Number of internship applications received each year: 10.
Internships Available ► *1–2 public information interns:* responsibilities include working with area news organizations to promote the agency and to educate the public about the various programs and services offered. Candidates should have editing skills, knowledge of field, oral communication skills, research skills, writing skills. Duration is 6–12 months. Unpaid. Open to recent high school graduates, college freshmen, college sophomores, college juniors, college seniors, recent college graduates. International applications accepted.
Benefits Names of contacts, possible full-time employment, travel reimbursement, willing to complete paperwork for educational credit, willing to provide letters of recommendation.
Contact Write, call, or fax Richard E. Weltz, Deputy Director. Phone: 315-339-5640. Fax: 315-339-2981. E-mail: rweltz@mvcaa. com. In-person interview required. Applicants must submit a

formal organization application, resume. Applications are accepted continuously. World Wide Web: http://mvcaa.com.

MONTGOMERY COUNTY COMMUNITY CORRECTIONS
11651 Nebel Street
Rockville, Maryland 20852

General Information Agency that provides effective community correctional alternatives between probation/parole supervision and security confinement for male and female adult offenders. Established in 1972. Number of employees: 70. Division of Montgomery County Department of Corrections and Rehabilitation, Rockville, Maryland. Number of internship applications received each year: 50.
Internships Available ▶ *2 CART interns:* responsibilities include working in the Community Accountability and Treatment Services Program, verifying participant's whereabouts, collecting and testing urine, assisting in group treatment facilitation of life skills and substance-abuse education, performing crisis intervention, and assisting in home visits in the community. Candidates should have ability to work independently, declared college major in field, oral communication skills, personal interest in the field, self-motivation, strong interpersonal skills. Duration is minimum 4 months, maximum 1 year. $5.15 per hour (24 hours per week).
▶ *6 Prerelease Center interns:* responsibilities include supervising adult offenders residing in a community correctional facility preparing for release and recreational trips, collecting and testing urine, coordinating employment, performing resident verifications, and participating as a treatment team member. Candidates should have declared college major in field, oral communication skills, personal interest in the field, self-motivation, strong interpersonal skills, written communication skills. Duration is 4–12 months. $5.15 per hour. Open to college juniors, college seniors, recent college graduates, graduate students, law students, career changers, individuals reentering the workforce. International applications accepted.
Benefits Formal training, job counseling, on-the-job training, opportunity to attend seminars/workshops, possible full-time employment, willing to act as a professional reference, willing to complete paperwork for educational credit, willing to provide letters of recommendation, room and board option.
Contact Write, call, fax, or e-mail Carl D. Hamstead, Organizational Development Manager. Phone: 301-468-4200. Fax: 301-468-4420. E-mail: carl.hamstead@co.mo.md.us. In-person interview recommended (telephone interview accepted). Applicants must submit a formal organization application. Application deadline: November 1 for spring; continuous for other positions. World Wide Web: http://www.montgomerycountyjobs.com.

MORRIS AREA GIRL SCOUT COUNCIL
1579 Sussex Turnpike
Randolph, New Jersey 07869

General Information Agency that recruits and retains girls and adults into the Girl Scouting organization and provides fun and interesting programs so that girls can become happy, resourceful citizens. Established in 1912. Number of employees: 50. Unit of Girl Scouts of the USA, New York, New York. Number of internship applications received each year: 1.
Internships Available ▶ *1 fund development intern:* responsibilities include researching funding sources and writing proposals. Candidates should have ability to work independently, computer skills, personal interest in the field, plan to pursue career in field, research skills, written communication skills. Duration is 3–10 weeks. Unpaid. Open to high school seniors, recent high school graduates, college freshmen, college sophomores, college juniors, college seniors, recent college graduates, career changers, individuals reentering the workforce. International applications accepted.
Benefits On-the-job training, possible full-time employment, willing to complete paperwork for educational credit, willing to provide letters of recommendation.
Contact Write, fax, or e-mail Martha Krall, Membership Services Director. Fax: 973-927-7683. E-mail: gsboard@magsc.org. No phone calls. In-person interview recommended (telephone interview accepted). Applicants must submit a letter of interest, two letters of recommendation. Applications are accepted continuously. World Wide Web: http://magsc.org.

MY SISTER'S HOUSE (ATLANTA UNION MISSION)
921 Howell Mill Road
Atlanta, Georgia 30318

General Information Christian rehabilitation program for homeless women and their children, providing each family with their own 2-room efficiency apartment during their 6-month stay, a 4-phase therapeutic program to help mothers move towards self-sufficiency and independent living, and a therapeutic child development center. Established in 1938. Number of employees: 30. Unit of Atlanta Union Mission, Atlanta, Georgia. Number of internship applications received each year: 15.
Internships Available ▶ *4–6 child-care providers:* responsibilities include supervising and caring for children in child development center (nursery, preschool, or after school), preparing developmentally appropriate lessons and teaching art and educational activities, and acting as a role model by demonstrating positive interactions and social behavior. Candidates should have ability to work with others, experience in the field, oral communication skills, organizational skills, personal interest in the field, strong leadership ability. Duration is 6–12 months. Unpaid. Open to high school seniors, recent high school graduates, college freshmen, college sophomores, college juniors, college seniors, recent college graduates, graduate students, career changers, individuals reentering the workforce. ▶ *4–6 counseling/social work interns:* responsibilities include providing therapeutic activities that promote the welfare of the clients and/or their children such as recordkeeping, case management, intake, group, individual therapy, and educational classes. Candidates should have college courses in field, knowledge of field, oral communication skills, strong interpersonal skills, strong leadership ability, written communication skills. Duration is 6–12 months. Unpaid. Open to college seniors, recent college graduates, graduate students, career changers, individuals reentering the workforce. ▶ *2 food service assistants:* responsibilities include assisting food service coordinator in the overall operation of kitchen in facility, serving homeless women and children in emergency shelter and long-term program, menu-planning, instruction in food handling/safety, supervision of program clients working in kitchen, and cooking. Candidates should have experience in the field, oral communication skills, plan to pursue career in field, strong interpersonal skills, strong leadership ability, college or vocational courses in field. Duration is 6–12 months. Unpaid. Open to recent high school graduates, college freshmen, college sophomores, college juniors, college seniors, recent college graduates, graduate students, career changers, individuals reentering the workforce. International applications accepted.
Benefits Free meals, names of contacts, on-the-job training, opportunity to attend seminars/workshops, possible full-time employment, willing to act as a professional reference, willing to complete paperwork for educational credit, willing to provide letters of recommendation.
Contact Write, call, fax, e-mail, or through World Wide Web site Terry Freeman, Program Director. Phone: 404-669-0138. Fax: 404-762-0240. E-mail: terry.freeman@myaum.org. In-person interview recommended (telephone interview accepted). Applicants must submit a resume. Applications are accepted continuously. World Wide Web: http://www.aumcares.org.

MY SISTER'S PLACE
PO Box 29596
Washington, District of Columbia 20017

General Information Temporary shelter for battered women and their children; services include children's programs, a 24-hour hot line, support groups, transitional housing, financial assistance, community education, public relations, and administration. Established in 1979. Number of employees: 25. Number of internship applications received each year: 25.
Internships Available ▶ *1 SOS center assistant:* responsibilities include supervising children, screening potential clients over the

phone, assisting with case management, accompanying clients to court, assisting with support groups, and performing administrative work. Candidates should have college courses in field, knowledge of field, office skills, oral communication skills, personal interest in the field, plan to pursue career in field, self-motivation, strong interpersonal skills, written communication skills, ability to work in fast-paced environment. Duration is at least one semester. Unpaid. Open to college juniors, college seniors, recent college graduates, graduate students, law students, career changers, individuals reentering the workforce. ▶ *1–2 administration interns:* responsibilities include providing general administrative help. Candidates should have ability to work independently, ability to work with others, office skills, self-motivation. Duration is at least one semester. Unpaid. Open to recent high school graduates, college freshmen, college sophomores, college juniors, college seniors, recent college graduates, graduate students, law students, career changers, individuals reentering the workforce. ▶ *1–2 hot line interns:* responsibilities include answering hot line, assisting residents, and crisis counseling. Candidates should have ability to work independently, ability to work with others, oral communication skills, personal interest in the field, self-motivation. Duration is at least one semester. Unpaid. Open to college juniors, college seniors, recent college graduates, graduate students, law students, career changers, individuals reentering the workforce. ▶ *1–2 public relations interns:* responsibilities include assisting with community education, Latino outreach, events, public speaking, newsletter, governmental research, and public relations. Candidates should have ability to work independently, computer skills, editing skills, office skills, oral communication skills, organizational skills, personal interest in the field, research skills, self-motivation, strong interpersonal skills, writing skills, women's issues background, bilingual ability (a plus). Duration is at least one semester. Unpaid. Open to college sophomores, college juniors, college seniors, recent college graduates, graduate students, law students, career changers, individuals reentering the workforce.

Benefits Formal training, job counseling, names of contacts, opportunity to attend seminars/workshops, possible full-time employment, willing to complete paperwork for educational credit, willing to provide letters of recommendation, training in crisis counseling.

Contact Write, call, fax, or e-mail Arnita Green-Williams, Volunteer Program Director. Phone: 202-529-5261. Fax: 202-529-5984. E-mail: agreen@mysistersplacedc.org. In-person interview required. Applicants must submit a letter of interest, resume, writing sample (public relations interns). Application deadline: April 1 for summer, July 1 for fall, November 1 for winter.

NATIONAL CENTER FOR MISSING AND EXPLOITED CHILDREN
699 Prince Street
Alexandria, Virginia 22314

General Information Nonprofit organization whose mission is to find missing children and prevent child victimization. Established in 1984. Number of employees: 180. Number of internship applications received each year: 75.

Internships Available ▶ *1 ICMEC intern:* responsibilities include promoting and distributing information; participating in design and development of small projects and one central project; researching and analyzing articles and information; assisting with general inquiries; and communicating with the public and officials. Candidates should have ability to work independently, analytical skills, computer skills, editing skills, office skills, oral communication skills, research skills, strong interpersonal skills, written communication skills, minimum 2.5 GPA. Duration is 2 to 3 months (minimum 22.5 hours per week). Unpaid. Open to college juniors, college seniors, recent college graduates. ▶ *1 NetSmartz marketing intern:* responsibilities include assisting with the logistics of one national and six regional press events and conferences, assisting with identifying organizations to partner with, following-up with potential partners, tracking organizations, preparing background materials to be sent to potential partners, and assisting with testing programs. Candidates should have ability to work independently, computer skills, editing skills, office skills, oral communication skills, research skills, strong interpersonal skills, writing skills,

minimum 2.5 GPA, courses in public relations, marketing, or communications. Duration is 2 to 3 months (8 hours minimum per week). Unpaid. Open to college juniors, college seniors, recent college graduates. ▶ *7–10 case assistant interns:* responsibilities include providing technical assistance to law enforcement, families, social service, and courts in issues related to missing and exploited children; searching databases; networking with law enforcement and state agencies to assist in bringing cases to resolution. Candidates should have ability to work independently, analytical skills, computer skills, editing skills, office skills, oral communication skills, plan to pursue career in field, strong interpersonal skills, written communication skills, minimum 2.5 GPA. Duration is 3 to 4 months (15 hours per week). Unpaid. Open to college juniors, college seniors, recent college graduates, graduate students, law students. ▶ *2–4 international case assistant interns:* responsibilities include providing technical assistance to law enforcement, families, social services, and attorneys in missing and exploited children issues; assisting in routine case management and follow-up to bring cases to resolution. Candidates should have ability to work independently, computer skills, editing skills, office skills, oral communication skills, plan to pursue career in field, research skills, writing skills, minimum 2.5 GPA. Duration is 2 to 3 months (15 hours per week). Unpaid. Open to college juniors, college seniors, recent college graduates, graduate students, law students. ▶ *2–4 legal interns:* responsibilities include researching; handling issues on child welfare, juvenile justice, children in court, child sexual exploitation, and missing children; cataloging legal and other material; monitoring hearings and professional meetings. Candidates should have ability to work independently, computer skills, oral communication skills, research skills, writing skills, minimum 2.5 GPA. Duration is 2 to 3 months (minimum 15 hours per week). Unpaid. Open to law students. ▶ *2–3 legal/public policy assistants:* responsibilities include researching on lexis-nexis or at law library; handling issues related to child welfare, juvenile justice, children in court, child sexual exploitation, and missing children; researching new statutes, cases, and journal/press articles; cataloging material; monitoring hearings and meetings. Candidates should have ability to work independently, analytical skills, computer skills, editing skills, oral communication skills, research skills, writing skills, experience with American government and child-related courses (preferred). Duration is 2 to 3 months (25 hours per week). Unpaid. Open to law students who have completed one year (2.5 GPA minimum). ▶ *1–2 public affairs assistant interns:* responsibilities include placing missing child photos with photo partners, preparation of case files for publication, advising parents of photo replacements, notifying partners of children recovered, reviewing videos and updating library, supplying Spanish network with cases, and assisting in searching for cases for major print and television media. Candidates should have ability to work independently, computer skills, knowledge of field, office skills, oral communication skills, personal interest in the field, plan to pursue career in field, research skills, writing skills, minimum 2.5 GPA, Spanish fluency (desired). Duration is 2 to 3 months (15 hours per week). Unpaid. Open to college juniors, college seniors, recent college graduates. International applications accepted.

Benefits On-the-job training, opportunity to attend seminars/workshops, willing to complete paperwork for educational credit, reimbursement for parking/public transportation costs.

Contact Write, fax, e-mail, or through World Wide Web site Internship Coordinator. Fax: 703-274-2095. E-mail: interns@ncmec.org. No phone calls. Telephone interview required. Applicants must submit a formal organization application, resume, academic transcripts, writing sample. Application deadline: March 15 for summer, August 15 for fall, December 10 for spring. World Wide Web: http://www.missingkids.com.

NCO YOUTH AND FAMILY SERVICES
1305 West Oswego Road
Naperville, Illinois 60540

General Information Licensed child welfare agency providing individual, family, and group counseling, prevention services,

NCO Youth and Family Services (continued)

crisis programs for runaways, and boys group home. Established in 1971. Number of employees: 17. Number of internship applications received each year: 25.

Internships Available ▶ *1 counselor intern:* responsibilities include providing individual, family, and group counseling. Candidates should have ability to work independently, analytical skills, college degree in related field, oral communication skills, strong interpersonal skills, written communication skills. Duration is 9 months (fall to spring). Unpaid. Open to second year students in master's program. ▶ *2 youth worker interns:* responsibilities include working on activities with shelter residents. Candidates should have ability to work independently, declared college major in field, oral communication skills, strong interpersonal skills, strong leadership ability. Duration is flexible. Unpaid. Open to college seniors. International applications accepted.

Benefits Names of contacts, on-the-job training, opportunity to attend seminars/workshops, possible full-time employment, willing to act as a professional reference, willing to complete paperwork for educational credit, willing to provide letters of recommendation.

Contact Write, call, or fax Ms. Beverly Garrett, Executive Director, 1305 West Oswego Road, Naperville, Illinois 60540. Phone: 630-961-2992. Fax: 630-961-7251. In-person interview required. Applicants must submit a letter of interest, resume, academic transcripts, three personal references. Application deadline: March 1 for fall counselor intern. World Wide Web: http://www.NCOYOUTH.org.

NEIGHBORS HELPING NEIGHBORS, INC.
443 39th Street, Suite 202
Brooklyn, New York 11232

General Information Neighborhood preservation and housing advocacy organization that provides home ownership education/counseling, landlord/tenant education/counseling, and community economic development assistance. Established in 1982. Number of employees: 8. Number of internship applications received each year: 10.

Internships Available ▶ *1–4 research assistant/special projects interns:* responsibilities include researching one or more aspects of a particular project or program in development related to neighborhood preservation, economic development, and/or homeownership education and services. Candidates should have ability to work independently, analytical skills, computer skills, editing skills, office skills, oral communication skills, organizational skills, personal interest in the field, research skills, self-motivation, writing skills. Duration is flexible. Unpaid. Open to college juniors, college seniors, recent college graduates, graduate students, law students, career changers, individuals reentering the workforce, retired adults. International applications accepted.

Benefits Names of contacts, on-the-job training, opportunity to attend seminars/workshops, possible full-time employment, willing to act as a professional reference, willing to complete paperwork for educational credit, willing to provide letters of recommendation, possibility of honorarium or stipend for research assistant/special projects positions.

Contact Write, fax, or e-mail Lisa-Nicolle Grist, Executive Director. Fax: 718-686-7948. E-mail: nhnhelp@erols.com. No phone calls. In-person interview recommended (telephone interview accepted). Applicants must submit a letter of interest, resume, writing sample. Applications are accepted continuously. World Wide Web: http://www.nhnhome.org.

OLD FIRST REFORMED CHURCH
4th and Race Streets
Philadelphia, Pennsylvania 19106

General Information Church with strong community outreach component, including homeless shelter, summer day camp, job program for teenagers, and urban workcamp program. Established in 1727. Number of employees: 4. Unit of United Church of Christ, Cleveland, Ohio. Number of internship applications received each year: 15.

Internships Available ▶ *4 summer staff interns:* responsibilities include staffing summer day camp or teen jobs program. Candidates should have oral communication skills, self-motivation, strong interpersonal skills, strong leadership ability, strong ability to work with children. Duration is 2 months. $150 per week. ▶ *1 volunteer:* responsibilities include working with homeless shelter, youth groups, urban workcamp program; generally serving as welcoming presence for inclusive church community. Candidates should have computer skills, oral communication skills, organizational skills, personal interest in the field, self-motivation, strong interpersonal skills, writing skills. Duration is 1 year. $150 per week. Open to recent high school graduates, college freshmen, college sophomores, college juniors, college seniors, recent college graduates, graduate students, career changers, individuals reentering the workforce. International applications accepted.

Benefits Free housing, health insurance, job counseling, on-the-job training, opportunity to attend seminars/workshops, willing to act as a professional reference, willing to complete paperwork for educational credit, willing to provide letters of recommendation, catastrophic insurance, free meals for summer interns, AmeriCorps educational credit.

Contact Write, call, fax, or e-mail Rev. Geneva M. Butz, Pastor. Phone: 215-922-4566. Fax: 215-922-6366. E-mail: oldfirst@oldfirstucc.org. In-person interview recommended (telephone interview accepted). Applicants must submit a formal organization application, letter of interest, resume, three personal references, additional application to the United Church of Christ Office of Voluntary Service. Application deadline: May 1 for summer.

OLIVET BOYS AND GIRLS CLUB OF READING AND BERKS COUNTIES
1161 Pershing Boulevard
Reading, Pennsylvania 19611

General Information Youth development agency. Established in 1898. Number of employees: 75. Unit of Boys & Girls Clubs of America, Atlanta, Georgia. Number of internship applications received each year: 10.

Internships Available ▶ *1–3 drug and alcohol education assistants:* responsibilities include assisting with drug and alcohol education programs at the club and in outreach programs, assisting in HIV/AIDS education programs and individual guidance programs at seasonal retreats and at week-long residential camps. Duration is flexible (usually 10 weeks). Position available as unpaid or paid. Open to college freshmen, college sophomores, college juniors, college seniors. ▶ *1–4 education assistants:* responsibilities include assisting with the planning and operation of homework centers, tutoring and publicizing the center, working with literacy programs, and expanding current computer programs. Candidates should have ability to work with others, computer skills, written communication skills. Duration is flexible (usually 10 weeks). Position available as unpaid or paid. Open to college freshmen, college sophomores, college juniors, college seniors, recent college graduates, graduate students. ▶ *1–3 physical education assistants:* responsibilities include assisting with the planning and implementation of physical education activities for the facilities including gym and fitness rooms, and supervising and maintaining safety levels of all program equipment. Duration is flexible (usually 10 weeks). Position available as unpaid or paid. Open to college freshmen, college sophomores, college juniors, college seniors. ▶ *Program assistants:* responsibilities include assisting in providing recreation, education, and guidance programs for children ages 6-18. Candidates should have knowledge of field, personal interest in the field, plan to pursue career in field, self-motivation. Duration is 1 semester. Unpaid. Open to college juniors, college seniors, recent college graduates.

Benefits On-the-job training, opportunity to attend seminars/workshops, possible full-time employment, willing to provide letters of recommendation.

Contact Write Richard G. DeGroote, Vice President. Fax: 610-373-8815. No phone calls. In-person interview required. Applicants must submit a letter of interest, resume. Applications are accepted continuously.

OPERATION CROSSROADS AFRICA
34 Mount Morris Park
New York, New York 10027

General Information International nonprofit, nongovernmental volunteer organization. Established in 1957. Number of employees: 2. Number of internship applications received each year: 250.
Internships Available ▶ *150–200 Crossroads volunteers (Africa or Brazil):* responsibilities include living and working with group of 8-10 volunteers in rural African village or in Salvador, Bahia (Brazil) performing agriculture, education, community health, construction, or women's development projects. Candidates should have knowledge of field, oral communication skills, personal interest in the field, strong interpersonal skills, willingness to experience another culture. Duration is mid-June to mid-August. Unpaid. Open to high school seniors, recent high school graduates, college freshmen, college sophomores, college juniors, college seniors, recent college graduates, graduate students, individuals reentering the workforce, must be at least 17 years of age. International applications accepted.
Benefits Free housing, free meals, health insurance, on-the-job training, travel reimbursement, willing to act as a professional reference, willing to complete paperwork for educational credit, willing to provide letters of recommendation, limited number of scholarships available.
International Internships Available in Brazil; Gambia; Ghana; Kenya; Malawi; Senegal; South Africa; Uganda; United Republic of Tanzania.
Contact Write, call, e-mail, or through World Wide Web site Willis Logan, Chairman. Phone: 212-289-1949. Fax: 212-289-2526. E-mail: oca@igc.org. Applicants must submit a formal organization application, three letters of recommendation, participation fee of $3500 (upon acceptance). Application deadline: February 1. Fees: $25. World Wide Web: http://www.igc.org/oca.

OXFAM AMERICA
26 West Street
Boston, Massachusetts 02111

General Information Nonprofit international agency that funds self-help development and disaster relief projects in Africa, Asia, and the Americas and produces and distributes educational materials for people in the U.S. on issues of hunger and sustainable development. Established in 1970. Number of employees: 100. Number of internship applications received each year: 1,000.
Internships Available ▶ *30 interns/volunteers:* responsibilities include providing clerical support, computer-based tasks, writing project summaries, translations, and helping with educational campaigns and events depending on the availability of special projects; no overseas assignments; working in what is essentially an office environment. Candidates should have analytical skills, computer skills, editing skills, office skills, organizational skills, research skills, writing skills, evidence of interest in issues of poverty and hunger, experience or involvement in community or campus events that educate around these issues (preferred), foreign languages (Spanish, French, or Portuguese preferred). Duration is flexible. Unpaid. Open to high school students, recent high school graduates, college freshmen, college sophomores, college juniors, college seniors, recent college graduates, graduate students, law students, career changers, individuals reentering the workforce. International applications accepted.
Benefits Opportunity to attend seminars/workshops, willing to complete paperwork for educational credit, willing to provide letters of recommendation, career exploration potential, pre-professional skill development.
Contact Write, call, e-mail, or through World Wide Web site Ms. Diana Hughes, Coordinator of Volunteer and Intern Program. Phone: 617-728-2468. E-mail: dhughes@oxfamamerica.org. In-person interview recommended (telephone interview accepted). Applicants must submit one-side resume, half-page letter of interest indicating availability. Applications are accepted continuously. World Wide Web: http://www.oxfamamerica.org.

PARENTAL STRESS CENTER
5877 Commerce Street
Pittsburgh, Pennsylvania 15206

General Information Family services organization. Established in 1975. Number of employees: 110. Number of internship applications received each year: 20.
Internships Available ▶ *1–3 MIS interns:* responsibilities include database management, network support, multi-media production, (depends on intern's expertise). Candidates should have ability to work with others, analytical skills, computer skills, experience in the field, written communication skills. Duration is flexible. Position available as unpaid or paid. Open to college juniors, college seniors, recent college graduates, graduate students, law students, career changers. ▶ *1–2 development/marketing assistants:* responsibilities include development of marketing material, contacts with various media, preparation of fund-raising materials, and personal contact. Candidates should have computer skills, oral communication skills, organizational skills, self-motivation, writing skills. Duration is flexible. Position available as unpaid or paid. Open to college juniors, college seniors, recent college graduates, graduate students, law students, career changers. ▶ *2–6 facilitator of parenting education interns:* responsibilities include supervising, planning, and facilitating various parenting education classes and marketing classes and working with individual families. Candidates should have ability to work with others, computer skills, experience in the field, self-motivation, written communication skills. Duration is flexible. Position available as unpaid or paid. Open to college juniors, college seniors, recent college graduates, graduate students, law students, career changers, individuals reentering the workforce. ▶ *1–4 family support counselors:* responsibilities include providing family support services, parenting education, and counseling. Candidates should have ability to work independently, organizational skills, plan to pursue career in field, self-motivation, strong interpersonal skills, written communication skills. Duration is flexible. Position available as unpaid or paid. Open to college juniors, college seniors, recent college graduates, graduate students, law students, career changers. International applications accepted.
Benefits Formal training, job counseling, names of contacts, on-the-job training, opportunity to attend seminars/workshops, possible full-time employment, willing to act as a professional reference, willing to complete paperwork for educational credit, willing to provide letters of recommendation.
Contact Write, call, fax, e-mail, or through World Wide Web site Timothy P. Snyder, Executive Director. Phone: 412-361-4800. Fax: 412-361-4801. E-mail: tps@pscfamily.net. In-person interview recommended (telephone interview accepted). Applicants must submit a letter of interest, resume, academic transcripts, writing sample, three personal references. Applications are accepted continuously. World Wide Web: http://www.pscfamily.net.

PATHFINDERS
1614 East Kane Place
Milwaukee, Wisconsin 53202

General Information Social service agency that provides short-term crisis intervention, counseling, and shelter programs for adolescents aged 11-17. Established in 1970. Number of employees: 20. Unit of The Counseling Center of Milwaukee, Inc., Milwaukee, Wisconsin. Number of internship applications received each year: 30.
Internships Available ▶ *1–20 assistant advocates:* responsibilities include providing direct one-on-one contact with teenage clients, telephone crisis counseling, facilitating groups, performing intake assessments, and general management tasks. Candidates should have ability to work independently, ability to work with others, oral communication skills, personal interest in the field, self-motivation, written communication skills. Duration is 4 months. Unpaid. Open to recent high school graduates, college freshmen, college sophomores, college juniors, college seniors, career changers, individuals reentering the workforce. ▶ *1–4 graduate student therapist interns:* responsibilities include providing direct one-on-one therapy with teenage clients and their families. Candidates should have ability to work independently, college degree in related field, oral communication skills, personal inter-

Pathfinders (continued)

est in the field, strong interpersonal skills, written communication skills. Duration is 1–2 semesters. Unpaid. Open to graduate students. ▶ *1–6 peer advocates:* responsibilities include providing direct one-on-one contact with teenage clients, positive peer role modeling, facilitating groups, and telephone crisis counseling. Candidates should have ability to work independently, oral communication skills, self-motivation, strong interpersonal skills, written communication skills. Duration is 3 months. Unpaid. Open to high school students. International applications accepted.

Benefits Formal training, free meals, names of contacts, on-the-job training, opportunity to attend seminars/workshops, possible full-time employment, willing to act as a professional reference, willing to complete paperwork for educational credit, willing to provide letters of recommendation.

Contact Write, call, fax, or e-mail Lisa Gumm, Assistant Director. Phone: 414-271-1560. Fax: 414-271-1831. E-mail: pflisa@execpc.com. In-person interview required. Applicants must submit a formal organization application, two personal references. Application deadline: January 9 for spring, May 15 for summer, August 21 for fall.

PENNSYLVANIA COUNSELING SERVICES
6079 Main Street
East Petersburg, Pennsylvania 17520

General Information Counseling clinics featuring outpatient and inpatient drug and alcohol, family based, and intensive services; also offers alternative school and community resources. Established in 1983. Number of employees: 350. Branch of Pennsylvania Counseling, Lebanon, Pennsylvania. Number of internship applications received each year: 10.

Internships Available ▶ *2–4 pre-doctoral interns in clinical/counseling psychology:* responsibilities include performing the duties of a psychologist including psychotherapy, consultation, and individual, group, and family psychological assessment all while supervised by psychologists. Candidates should have college degree in related field, knowledge of field, oral communication skills, strong interpersonal skills, written communication skills, completed classwork by start of internship. Duration is 1 year (August to August). $18,400 per year. Open to graduate students in clinical psychology. International applications accepted.

Benefits Formal training, health insurance, meals at a cost, on-the-job training, opportunity to attend seminars/workshops, possible full-time employment, willing to act as a professional reference, willing to complete paperwork for educational credit, willing to provide letters of recommendation, bonus possible per 12 months.

Contact Write, call, fax, e-mail, or through World Wide Web site Dr. John C. Grisbacher, Director of Internships. Phone: 717-560-1908. Fax: 717-560-4941. E-mail: jcgrisbacher@pacounseling.com. In-person interview recommended (telephone interview accepted). Applicants must submit a formal organization application, resume, personal reference, three letters of recommendation. Application deadline: April 15. World Wide Web: http://pacounseling.com.

PEOPLE MAKING A DIFFERENCE THROUGH COMMUNITY SERVICE, INC.
PO Box 120189
Boston, Massachusetts 02112-0189

General Information Organization that involves and engages people through meaningful, hands-on work that meets the needs of charities in Greater Boston. Established in 1992. Number of employees: 1. Number of internship applications received each year: 3.

Internships Available ▶ *1–2 development assistants:* responsibilities include assisting board development committee with biannual appeals and special events for grassroots support. Candidates should have ability to work independently, ability to work with others, computer skills, knowledge of field, office skills, organizational skills, research skills, self-motivation. Duration is flexible. Unpaid. Open to college seniors, recent college graduates, graduate students, career changers. ▶ *1–3 program project coordinators:* responsibilities include assisting with all aspects of service program:

volunteer recruitment, project development, planning, evaluation, participation, and fund-raising. Candidates should have ability to work with others, computer skills, experience in the field, organizational skills, personal interest in the field, self-motivation. Duration is flexible. Unpaid. Open to college juniors, college seniors, recent college graduates, graduate students.

Benefits Names of contacts, on-the-job training, opportunity to attend seminars/workshops, willing to act as a professional reference, willing to complete paperwork for educational credit, willing to provide letters of recommendation.

Contact Write, e-mail, or through World Wide Web site Lori Tsuruda, Founder and Executive Director. E-mail: lori@pmd.org. No phone calls. In-person interview required. Applicants must submit a letter of interest, resume, academic transcripts, three personal references, two letters of recommendation, participation in at least one PMD community service project prior to application (offered on a weekly basis). Applications are accepted continuously. World Wide Web: http://www.pmd.org.

PHOENIXVILLE AREA YMCA
400 East Pothouse Road
Phoenixville, Pennsylvania 19460

General Information Organization that provides the community with services that promote healthy spirits, minds, and bodies. Established in 1952. Number of employees: 200. Number of internship applications received each year: 3.

Internships Available ▶ *1–3 aquatic interns:* responsibilities include teaching preschool, youth, and adult swim programs; conducting aquatic fitness and/or therapeutic program; assisting with staff scheduling; assisting with management of outdoor pool complex during summer internship. Candidates should have experience in the field, oral communication skills, personal interest in the field, self-motivation, strong interpersonal skills, strong leadership ability. Duration is summer or 1-3 semesters. Position available as unpaid or paid. Open to college freshmen, college sophomores, college juniors, college seniors, recent college graduates, graduate students, PHEAA work-study eligibles. ▶ *2–5 child-care interns:* responsibilities include assisting with staffing schedules, designing lesson plans for various age groups, assisting in provider care, learning state licensing requirements, developing a promotional piece for services offered. Candidates should have knowledge of field, plan to pursue career in field, self-motivation, strong interpersonal skills, strong leadership ability, written communication skills. Duration is one summer or 1-3 semesters. Position available as unpaid or paid. Open to high school seniors, college freshmen, college sophomores, college juniors, college seniors, recent college graduates, individuals pursuing child-care certificates. ▶ *1–3 community and family recreation interns:* responsibilities include designing lesson plan for outdoor education, designing youth and/or family special events, creating promotional strategy for youth and/or family programs, assisting in day camp program during summer internship. Candidates should have ability to work independently, oral communication skills, personal interest in the field, self-motivation, strong interpersonal skills, strong leadership ability. Duration is one summer or 1-3 semesters. Position available as unpaid or paid. Open to college freshmen, college sophomores, college juniors, college seniors, recent college graduates, PHEAA work-study eligibles. ▶ *1 corporate office intern:* responsibilities include basic accounting, data entry, answering phones, filing, word processing, spreadsheets. Candidates should have computer skills, office skills, organizational skills, plan to pursue career in field, self-motivation, strong interpersonal skills. Duration is 1 summer or 1 semester. Unpaid. Open to college sophomores, college juniors, college seniors, graduate students, PHEAA work-study eligibles. ▶ *1 financial development intern:* responsibilities include entering data into donor database, assisting with fund-raising events, assisting with organizing annual appeal, researching and writing grant proposals. Candidates should have ability to work independently, computer skills, personal interest in the field, research skills, strong interpersonal skills, writing skills. Duration is 1–3 semesters. Position available as unpaid or paid. Open to college juniors, college seniors, graduate students, PHEAA work-study eligibles. ▶ *1–3 health and fitness interns:* responsibilities include designing individualized fitness programs, orienting clients on equipment use, developing fitness-related bulletin boards, developing and implementing fitness incentive program, fitness testing. Candidates should have knowledge of field, organizational skills, plan to pursue career in field, self-motivation, strong interpersonal skills, strong leadership ability. Duration is one summer or 1-3 semesters. Unpaid. Open to high school seniors, college juniors, college seniors, recent college graduates, graduate students, PHEAA work-study eligibles. ▶ *1–2 member services representatives:* responsibilities include greeting members, parents, guests; taking payments; taking class registrations; dispensing information; assisting with security issues; answering phones. Candidates should have ability to work independently, computer skills, oral communication skills, self-motivation, strong interpersonal skills, strong leadership ability. Duration is 1 summer or 1-3 semesters. Position available as unpaid or paid. Open to recent high school graduates, college freshmen, college sophomores, college juniors, college seniors, recent college graduates, individuals reentering the workforce, PHEAA work-study eligibles. ▶ *1 public relations intern:* responsibilities include writing press releases, duplication of public relations materials, design of fliers, sign painting, and special event decorations. Candidates should have computer skills, editing skills, knowledge of field, self-motivation, strong interpersonal skills, written communication skills. Duration is summer or 1-3 semesters. Unpaid. Open to college sophomores, college juniors, college seniors, recent college graduates, graduate students, PHEAA work-study eligibles. ▶ *1 youth sports assistant:* responsibilities include assisting in organizing youth sports leagues; entering registration into league database; coordinating use of fields/facilities; working in sports camps during summer; monitoring league activities and standings. Candidates should have knowledge of field, oral communication skills, personal interest in the field, self-motivation, strong interpersonal skills, strong leadership ability. Duration is 1-3 semesters or 1 summer. Position available as unpaid or paid. Open to PHEAA work-study eligibles.

Benefits Job counseling, names of contacts, on-the-job training, opportunity to attend seminars/workshops, possible full-time employment, willing to complete paperwork for educational credit, willing to provide letters of recommendation.

Contact Write, call, fax, or e-mail Nanette Paolella, Human Resources Director, 2460 Boulevard of the Generals, Norristown, Pennsylvania 19403. Phone: 610-539-9190. Fax: 610-539-8650. E-mail: npaolella@phoenixvilleareaymca.org. In-person interview recommended (telephone interview accepted). Applicants must submit a letter of interest, resume, two personal references, two letters of recommendation. Applications are accepted continuously. World Wide Web: http://www.phoenixvilleareaymca.org.

PRESBYTERIAN CHILD WELFARE AGENCY
116 Buckhorn Lane
Buckhorn, Kentucky 41721

General Information Agency that provides residential care for abused children. Established in 1902. Number of employees: 385.

Internships Available ▶ *2–4 case workers:* responsibilities include working with abused and neglected children. Candidates should have ability to work independently, computer skills, oral communication skills, self-motivation, strong interpersonal skills, strong leadership ability, written communication skills. Duration is 6 months to 2 years. Paid. Open to college juniors, college seniors, recent college graduates, graduate students, career changers. ▶ *3–5 child-care specialists or social workers:* responsibilities include performing diverse child-care duties. Candidates should have ability to work independently, analytical skills, college courses in field, computer skills, experience in the field, office skills, oral communication skills, plan to pursue career in field, self-motivation, strong interpersonal skills, strong leadership ability, written communication skills. Duration is 6 months to 2 years. Paid. Open to college juniors, college seniors, recent college graduates, graduate students, career changers. ▶ *1–3 therapists:* responsibilities include supervising case workers and house parents. Candidates should have ability to work independently, college courses in field, computer skills, knowledge of field, oral communication skills, organizational skills, self-motivation, strong interpersonal skills,

strong leadership ability, written communication skills. Duration is 1–2 years. Paid. Open to college seniors, recent college graduates, graduate students. International applications accepted.

Benefits Free housing, job counseling, names of contacts, opportunity to attend seminars/workshops, possible full-time employment, willing to complete paperwork for educational credit, willing to provide letters of recommendation, reimbursement for some expenses.

Contact Write, call, fax, or e-mail Patty Wilder, Human Resources Coordinator. Phone: 606-398-7000. Fax: 606-398-7912. E-mail: patty. wilder@buckhorn.org. In-person interview required. Applicants must submit a resume, personal reference. Applications are accepted continuously. World Wide Web: http://www. buckhornchildren.org.

PRISONERS AID ASSOCIATION OF MARYLAND, INC.
204 East 25th Street
Baltimore, Maryland 21218

General Information Social service agency primarily working with inmates and ex-offenders who are usually destitute and homeless . Established in 1869. Number of employees: 12. Number of internship applications received each year: 10.

Internships Available ▶ *1–5 client advocates:* responsibilities include working closely with clients to contact social service programs, keep appointments, stay on their schedules, and become stable and self sufficient. Candidates should have ability to work independently, computer skills, oral communication skills, strong interpersonal skills, written communication skills. Duration is year-round (minimum 6-week commitment). Unpaid. Open to college freshmen, college sophomores, college juniors, college seniors, recent college graduates, graduate students, law students, career changers, individuals reentering the workforce. ▶ *Counselors:* responsibilities include counseling for behavior and life style changes. Candidates should have computer skills, oral communication skills, personal interest in the field, self-motivation, strong interpersonal skills, written communication skills. Duration is year-round (minimum 6-week commitment). Unpaid. Open to college juniors, college seniors, recent college graduates, graduate students, law students, career changers, individuals reentering the workforce. ▶ *Junior case managers:* responsibilities include helping clients establish goals, get into treatment programs, and follow through on goal achievement. Candidates should have ability to work independently, oral communication skills, self-motivation, strong interpersonal skills, written communication skills. Duration is year-round (minimum 6-week commitment). Unpaid. Open to college sophomores, college juniors, college seniors, recent college graduates, graduate students, law students, career changers, individuals reentering the workforce. International applications accepted.

Benefits Names of contacts, possible full-time employment, willing to act as a professional reference, willing to complete paperwork for educational credit, willing to provide letters of recommendation.

Contact Write, call, fax, or e-mail Malinda Miles, Executive Director. Phone: 410-662-0359. Fax: 410-662-0358. E-mail: prisonersaid@ hotmail.com. In-person interview recommended (telephone interview accepted). Applicants must submit a resume. Applications are accepted continuously.

PROGRAM FOR AID TO VICTIMS OF SEXUAL ASSAULT, INC. (PAVSA)
Building for Women, 32 East First Street, Suite 200
Duluth, Minnesota 55802

General Information Program offering crisis intervention and support advocacy to victims/survivors of sexual assault and their friends and family and sexual assault education to the community, professionals, and schools. Established in 1975. Number of employees: 5. Number of internship applications received each year: 15.

Internships Available ▶ *1–3 advocate interns:* responsibilities include assisting in crisis intervention, assisting in coordinating volunteers, one-to-one advocacy, and systems advocacy; will design a project

Program for Aid to Victims of Sexual Assault, Inc. (PAVSA) (continued)

for term of the internship in conjunction with agency needs. Candidates should have ability to work independently, oral communication skills, organizational skills, personal interest in the field, self-motivation, strong interpersonal skills. Duration is 3–12 months. Unpaid. Open to college sophomores, college juniors, college seniors, recent college graduates, graduate students, law students, career changers. ▶ *1–2 researchers:* responsibilities include initiating and completing research project under supervision of staff members and presenting results to staff and community. Candidates should have ability to work independently, analytical skills, computer skills, research skills, self-motivation, strong interpersonal skills, written communication skills. Duration is 3–12 months. Unpaid. Open to college juniors, college seniors, recent college graduates, graduate students, law students, career changers. International applications accepted.

Benefits Formal training, job counseling, names of contacts, opportunity to attend seminars/workshops, willing to act as a professional reference, willing to complete paperwork for educational credit, willing to provide letters of recommendation, mileage reimbursement for work-related activities.

Contact Write, call, fax, or e-mail Beth Olson, Program Coordinator. Phone: 218-726-1442. Fax: 218-720-4890. E-mail: pavsa@pavsa. org. In-person interview recommended (telephone interview accepted). Applicants must submit a formal organization application, resume, three personal references, criminal history background check required; participation in 40 hours of training in either March or October. Applications are accepted continuously. World Wide Web: http://www.pavsa.org.

PROJECT BREAD–THE WALK FOR HUNGER
160 North Washington Street
Boston, Massachusetts 02114

General Information Leading hunger-relief organization in Massachusetts. Number of employees: 40.

Internships Available ▶ *1–3 communications interns:* responsibilities include working with editors and reporters, scheduling guests, assisting with publicity and public relations, maintaining a database, and conducting evaluation of public relations activities and making recommendations for improvement. Candidates should have oral communication skills, organizational skills, self-motivation, writing skills, excellent follow through skills, and an interest in helping others. Duration is 1 semester (spring or summer). Small stipend. Open to college freshmen, college sophomores, college juniors, college seniors, recent college graduates.

Benefits Willing to complete paperwork for educational credit.

Contact Fax or e-mail Sarah Wheeler, Intern Coordinator. Fax: 617-248-8877. E-mail: info@projectbread.org. In-person interview required. Applicants must submit a letter of interest, resume. Applications are accepted continuously. World Wide Web: http://www.projectbread.org.

THE RAPE CRISIS CENTER OF CENTRAL MASSACHUSETTS, INC.
799 West Boylston Street
Worcester, Massachusetts 01606

General Information Program providing comprehensive services to survivors of sexual assault and their concerned others as well as education geared toward ending violence against women. Established in 1973. Number of employees: 18. Number of internship applications received each year: 10.

Internships Available ▶ *Counselors:* responsibilities include providing legal and medical advocacy, on-call hot line coverage, face-to-face counseling, and opportunity for facilitating support groups. Duration is 6–12 months. Unpaid. Open to individuals 18 or older. International applications accepted.

Benefits Formal training, names of contacts, opportunity to attend seminars/workshops, possible full-time employment, travel reimbursement, willing to complete paperwork for educational credit, willing to provide letters of recommendation.

Contact Write, call, or fax Heidi LeBoeuf-Mahoney, Director of Counseling Services. Phone: 508-852-7600. Fax: 508-852-7870.

In-person interview required. Applicants must submit volunteer questionnaire. Application deadline: February 10 for spring, August 31 for fall.

THE RAPE CRISIS CENTER OF CENTRAL MASSACHUSETTS, INC.
275 Nichols Road
Fitchburg, Massachusetts 01420

General Information Program providing comprehensive services to survivors of sexual assault and their concerned others as well as education geared toward ending violence against women. Established in 1973. Number of employees: 14. Number of internship applications received each year: 10.

Internships Available ▶ *10 counselors:* responsibilities include providing legal and medical advocacy, on-call hotline coverage, and face-to-face counseling; opportunity for facilitating support groups. Duration is 6 months minimum. Unpaid. Open to individuals at least 18 years of age. International applications accepted.

Benefits Formal training, names of contacts, opportunity to attend seminars/workshops, possible full-time employment, travel reimbursement, willing to complete paperwork for educational credit, willing to provide letters of recommendation.

Contact Write, call, or fax Heidi LeBoeuf-Mahoney, Director of Counseling Services. Phone: 978-343-5683. Fax: 978-343-5478. In-person interview required. Applicants must submit volunteer questionnaire. Application deadline: March 31 for spring, August 31 for fall.

REFUGEE AND IMMIGRATION SERVICES
1615 Kecoughtan Road
Hampton, Virginia 23661

General Information Nonprofit organization providing accommodation for refugee housing, employment, and ESL tutoring; refugees are assisted in acquiring a variety of services. Established in 1975. Number of employees: 14. Unit of Catholic Diocese of Richmond, Richmond, Virginia. Number of internship applications received each year: 10.

Internships Available ▶ *1–6 ESL interns:* responsibilities include ESL tutoring, teaching ESL work site classes, office work, assistance in preparing ESL training workshops, or publishing a newsletter. Candidates should have ability to work with others, college courses in field, office skills, organizational skills, personal interest in the field, plan to pursue career in field, self-motivation. Duration is 1–12 months. Unpaid. Open to college sophomores, college juniors, college seniors, recent college graduates, graduate students, career changers, individuals reentering the workforce. ▶ *1–4 law interns:* responsibilities include assisting immigration lawyer. Candidates should have college courses in field, computer skills, office skills, oral communication skills, plan to pursue career in field, written communication skills. Duration is 1–12 months. Unpaid. Open to 2nd year law students only. ▶ *1–6 social science interns:* responsibilities include assisting caseworkers in providing social services for refugees, including counseling, transportation, and possibly interpreting. Candidates should have ability to work independently, college courses in field, office skills, organizational skills, plan to pursue career in field, strong interpersonal skills. Duration is 1–12 months. Unpaid. Open to college freshmen, college sophomores, college juniors, college seniors, recent college graduates, graduate students, career changers, individuals reentering the workforce. International applications accepted.

Benefits Job counseling, on-the-job training, opportunity to attend seminars/workshops, possible full-time employment, willing to act as a professional reference, willing to complete paperwork for educational credit, willing to provide letters of recommendation.

Contact Write, call, fax, or e-mail Karen Kurilko, Regional Director. Phone: 757-247-3600. Fax: 757-247-1070. E-mail: kkurilko@hrris.org. In-person interview recommended (telephone interview accepted). Applicants must submit a formal organization application, resume, two personal references, two letters of recommendation. Applications are accepted continuously. World Wide Web: http://www.richmonddiocese.org/ris/.

REGINA RESCUE MISSION, INC.
2076 Scarth Street
Regina, Saskatchewan S4P 3H1 Canada

General Information Nonprofit organization that exists to rescue people from poverty, addiction, and sin, by offering emergency help, life changing recovery programs, and the Gospel message. Established in 2000. Number of employees: 4. Unit of Association of Gospel Rescue Missions, North Kansas City, Missouri. Number of internship applications received each year: 1.

Internships Available ▶ *2–4 interns:* responsibilities include learning all aspects of rescue mission work from vision to implementation, administration, development (fund-raising), chaplaincy work, budgeting, short range and long range planning, and building operations/kitchen, maintenance, janitorial, vehicle, security, volunteerism, human resources. Candidates should have ability to work independently, organizational skills, personal interest in the field, self-motivation, strong interpersonal skills. Duration is flexible. $200 Canadian dollars per month. Open to college freshmen, college sophomores, college juniors, college seniors, recent college graduates, graduate students, law students, career changers, individuals reentering the workforce, must be a born-again Christian. International applications accepted.

Benefits Formal training, free housing, free meals, on-the-job training, willing to act as a professional reference, willing to complete paperwork for educational credit, willing to provide letters of recommendation, participation in "Rescue College" (see www.agrm.org).

International Internships Available.

Contact Write, fax, or e-mail Michelle Porter, Associate Director, PO Box 3356 Stn Main, Regina, Saskatchewan S4P 3H1 Canada. Fax: 425-740-7738. E-mail: porter@sprint.ca. No phone calls. In-person interview recommended (telephone interview accepted). Applicants must submit a letter of interest, resume, two personal references, must be able to sign doctrinal statement, 2 letters of recommendation (1 from pastor, 1 from college). Applications are accepted continuously. World Wide Web: http://www.agrm.org/.

RESOURCE CENTER FOR WOMEN
1301 Seminole Boulevard, Suite 150
Largo, Florida 33770

General Information Displaced homemaker, and single parent organization, providing Pinellas and Pasco County clients with: personal and career counseling, pre-employment training, personal growth and assertiveness training, decision-making and problem-solving techniques, parenting classes, professional career placement services, and referrals for other services. Established in 1977. Number of employees: 12. Number of internship applications received each year: 10.

Internships Available ▶ *1–3 assistant intake counselors:* responsibilities include screening clients, scheduling intake counseling appointments, referring clients to available community services, and assisting with case management and clerical tasks. Candidates should have ability to work independently, ability to work with others, oral communication skills, organizational skills, personal interest in the field, written communication skills, ability to work with multiple demands from clients undergoing stress while keeping calm and a sense of humor. Duration is flexible. Unpaid. Open to college seniors, recent college graduates, graduate students, retired professionals. ▶ *1 community development/media representative:* responsibilities include assisting with public relations, preparing news releases and public service announcements, and maintaining speaker's bureau. Candidates should have ability to work independently, ability to work with others, computer skills, editing skills, knowledge of field, oral communication skills, personal interest in the field, plan to pursue career in field, research skills, written communication skills. Duration is flexible. Unpaid. Open to college seniors, recent college graduates, graduate students. ▶ *1–3 community/agency outreach interns:* responsibilities include visiting community sites and interviewing potential clients, distributing material, and providing information and referrals for various needs of clients. Candidates should have ability to work independently, ability to work with others, computer skills, edit-

ing skills, oral communication skills, self-motivation, written communication skills. Duration is flexible. Unpaid. Open to college seniors, recent college graduates, graduate students, volunteers with professional skills. ▶ *1–3 job developer interns:* responsibilities include developing and maintaining a network of job/employment contacts and monitoring placement services files. Candidates should have editing skills, oral communication skills, organizational skills, personal interest in the field, research skills, self-motivation, strong interpersonal skills, written communication skills, human resources knowledge, knowledge of business/employment field. Duration is flexible. Unpaid. Open to college seniors, recent college graduates, graduate students, volunteers with professional skills. ▶ *1–3 personal growth counselor interns:* responsibilities include intake interviews; serving as teaching assistant in career and personal growth classes; referrals to other agencies; short-term individual counseling assistance; and short-term group experience. Candidates should have ability to work independently, ability to work with others, college courses in field, knowledge of field, oral communication skills, personal interest in the field, plan to pursue career in field, self-motivation, written communication skills. Duration is flexible. Unpaid. Open to recent college graduates, graduate students. ▶ *1 research assistant:* responsibilities include conducting statistical/demographic research (national/state/local), grant and subject research, and setting up libraries. Candidates should have ability to work independently, analytical skills, computer skills, editing skills, office skills, organizational skills, research skills, self-motivation, writing skills. Duration is flexible. Unpaid. Open to college seniors, recent college graduates, graduate students, retired professionals/volunteers. International applications accepted.

Benefits Formal training, job counseling, names of contacts, on-the-job training, opportunity to attend seminars/workshops, possible full-time employment, travel reimbursement, willing to act as a professional reference, willing to complete paperwork for educational credit, willing to provide letters of recommendation.

Contact Write or fax Ms. Susan Olsen, Executive Director. Phone: 727-586-1110. Fax: 727-585-4089. In-person interview recommended (telephone interview accepted). Applicants must submit a letter of interest, resume, three personal references, three letters of recommendation, background check required. Application deadline: May 1 for summer interns; continuous for all others.

ROCKY MOUNTAIN VILLAGE
2644 Alvarado Road
Empire, Colorado 80438

General Information Nonprofit organization that provides services for children and adults with physical and/or mental disabilities. Established in 1951. Number of employees: 10. Program of Easter Seals Colorado, Lakewood, Colorado. Number of internship applications received each year: 3.

Internships Available ▶ *1–10 camp counselors:* responsibilities include caring for the health, safety, and happiness of 1-3 people with developmental disabilities. Candidates should have ability to work with others, knowledge of field, oral communication skills, personal interest in the field. Duration is 1 summer. $200 per week plus bonus if entire season completed. Open to high school seniors, recent high school graduates, college freshmen, college sophomores, college juniors, college seniors, recent college graduates, graduate students, law students, career changers, individuals reentering the workforce. ▶ *1 office assistant:* responsibilities include assisting with answering phones, camp paperwork, and other office work. Candidates should have ability to work independently, ability to work with others, computer skills, office skills, oral communication skills, written communication skills. Duration is 1 summer. $200 per week plus bonus if entire season completed. Open to high school seniors, recent high school graduates, college freshmen, college sophomores, college juniors, college seniors, recent college graduates, graduate students, law students, career changers, individuals reentering the workforce. ▶ *1 program intern:* responsibilities include working with the assistant director to coordinate, develop, and implement programs for summer residential coed camp for people with disabilities. Candidates should have experience in the field, organizational skills, personal interest in the field, strong interpersonal skills,

Rocky Mountain Village (continued)

strong leadership ability. Duration is 1 summer. $200 per week with $300 bonus if entire season completed. Open to college freshmen, college sophomores, college juniors, college seniors, recent college graduates, graduate students. ▶ *1 public relations intern:* responsibilities include working with computer specialist to develop weekly camp newsletter and developing press releases. Candidates should have ability to work independently, ability to work with others, computer skills, experience in the field, writing skills, newsletter/layout skills. Duration is 1 summer. Position available as unpaid or at $200 per week with $200 bonus if entire season completed. Open to recent high school graduates, college freshmen, college sophomores, college juniors, college seniors, recent college graduates, graduate students. International applications accepted.

Benefits Formal training, free housing, free meals, on-the-job training, willing to act as a professional reference, willing to complete paperwork for educational credit, willing to provide letters of recommendation.

Contact Write, call, fax, e-mail, or through World Wide Web site Ms. Melissa Huber, Assistant Director, 2644 Alvarado Road, PO Box 115, Empire, Colorado 80438. Phone: 303-569-2333 Ext. 316. Fax: 303-569-3857. E-mail: huberm@cess.org. In-person interview recommended (telephone interview accepted). Applicants must submit a formal organization application, letter of interest, resume, total of 3 personal references/letters of recommendation. Applications are accepted continuously. World Wide Web: http://www.eastersealsco.org.

SAFEHOUSE DENVER, INC.
1649 Downing Street
Denver, Colorado 80218

General Information Domestic violence outreach and shelter facility, serving women and children who are victims of domestic violence. Established in 1977. Number of employees: 26. Number of internship applications received each year: 100.

Internships Available ▶ *Development/administrative assistants:* responsibilities include letter writing, data entry, and event organizing. Candidates should have ability to work independently, ability to work with others, computer skills, office skills, organizational skills, research skills, self-motivation, writing skills. Duration is 16–52 weeks. Unpaid. Open to college seniors, recent college graduates, graduate students, career changers, individuals reentering the workforce. ▶ *1–3 outreach advocates:* responsibilities include answering the crisis line, co-facilitating groups, working on indirect projects, attending staff meetings, attending court sessions, participating in supervisions, and advocacy services to women or children. Candidates should have ability to work independently, computer skills, oral communication skills, organizational skills, self-motivation, strong interpersonal skills, written communication skills. Duration is 24–52 weeks. Unpaid. Open to college seniors, recent college graduates, graduate students, career changers. ▶ *2–3 shelter advocates:* responsibilities include answering the 24-hour crisis line, maintaining a safe and secure residential facility, and individual case management and advocacy. Candidates should have ability to work independently, college courses in field, knowledge of field, personal interest in the field, self-motivation, strong interpersonal skills. Duration is 24–52 weeks. Unpaid. Open to college seniors, recent college graduates, graduate students, career changers. International applications accepted.

Benefits Formal training, on-the-job training, opportunity to attend seminars/workshops, willing to act as a professional reference, willing to provide letters of recommendation.

Contact Write, call, or fax Mollie Hill, Director of Outreach Services, PO Box 19888, Denver, Colorado 80218. Phone: 303-318-9959. Fax: 303-318-9979. E-mail: safhsedenver@earthlink.net. In-person interview required. Applicants must submit a letter of interest, resume, personal reference. Applications are accepted continuously. Fees: $15. World Wide Web: http://www.safehouse-denver.com.

ST. ELIZABETH SHELTER
804 Alarid Street
Sante Fe, New Mexico 87505

General Information Shelter serving homeless men, women, and families; also has transitional programs. Established in 1986. Number of employees: 26. Number of internship applications received each year: 10.

Internships Available ▶ *6 direct-service interns:* responsibilities include taking in homeless guests, organizing meals, processing donations, providing case management, and other duties integral to running the shelter. Candidates should have ability to work independently, personal interest in the field, self-motivation, strong interpersonal skills, Spanish speaking ability and valid driver's license (a plus). Duration is 6–12 months. $70 per week. Open to recent college graduates, graduate students, law students, career changers, individuals reentering the workforce, individuals with 2 years of college or work experience. International applications accepted.

Benefits Free housing, free meals, health insurance, names of contacts, on-the-job training, opportunity to attend seminars/workshops, possible full-time employment, willing to act as a professional reference, willing to complete paperwork for educational credit, willing to provide letters of recommendation, $1200 exit stipend upon successful completion of 12 months.

Contact Write, call, fax, e-mail, or through World Wide Web site Maria Lopez, Program Manager. Phone: 505-982-6611. Fax: 505-982-5347. E-mail: mlopez@steshelter.org. Telephone interview required. Applicants must submit a formal organization application, letter of interest, resume, three personal references. Application deadline: 2-6 months in advance of desired starting date. World Wide Web: http://www.steshelter.org.

SAN DIEGO YOUTH AND COMMUNITY SERVICES
3255 Wing Street
San Diego, California 92110

General Information Local social service agency that provides innovative responses to emerging social problems including support services for at-risk children and their families. Established in 1970. Number of employees: 180. Number of internship applications received each year: 70.

Internships Available ▶ *5–8 AOD interns specialists:* responsibilities include planning, implementing, and supervising peer education, mediation, and after-school recreational activities for at-risk youth. Candidates should have ability to work independently, ability to work with others, oral communication skills, personal interest in the field, self-motivation. Duration is 3–6 months. Unpaid. Open to college freshmen, college sophomores, college juniors, college seniors, recent college graduates, graduate students, law students, career changers, individuals reentering the workforce. ▶ *3–6 HIV prevention and education interns:* responsibilities include co-facilitating group discussion of HIV/AIDS and related prevention issues; assisting in coordinating and implementing HIV/AIDS related group activities; providing input toward maintaining a dynamic curriculum. Candidates should have ability to work with others, knowledge of field, oral communication skills, personal interest in the field, written communication skills. Duration is 3–6 months. Unpaid. Open to college juniors, college seniors, recent college graduates, graduate students. ▶ *2–3 case manager interns:* responsibilities include providing assistance to agency social workers and case managers for youth in probation group home or teen recovery center. Candidates should have ability to work independently, knowledge of field, oral communication skills, self-motivation, strong interpersonal skills, writing skills. Duration is 3–6 months. Unpaid. Open to college juniors, college seniors, recent college graduates, graduate students. ▶ *10–11 community development specialist interns:* responsibilities include assisting in neighborhood locations frequented by youth; creating opportunities for youth to receive education on drug and alcohol abuse and treatment, HIV/AIDS and other STI's, and information and referrals. Candidates should have ability to work independently, experience in the field, oral communication skills, strong interpersonal skills, written communication skills. Duration is 3–6 months. Unpaid. Open to recent high school graduates, college freshmen, college sophomores, college juniors, college seniors, recent college graduates, graduate students, law students, career changers, individuals reentering the workforce. ► *1–4 counselor interns:* responsibilities include providing general counseling and advocacy services to those in need and maintaining client records; facilitating off-site counseling groups as assigned. Candidates should have ability to work independently, knowledge of field, oral communication skills, personal interest in the field, self-motivation, strong interpersonal skills, written communication skills. Duration is 9–12 months. Unpaid. Open to those working toward MFT license. ► *5–6 emergency teen shelter interns:* responsibilities include supervising shelter residents in milieu and recreational trips, group therapy, and assessing case files. Candidates should have ability to work independently, knowledge of field, oral communication skills, personal interest in the field, self-motivation, strong interpersonal skills, written communication skills. Duration is 3–6 months. Unpaid. Open to college freshmen, college sophomores, college juniors, college seniors, recent college graduates, graduate students, law students, career changers, individuals reentering the workforce. ► *10–12 foster and adoptions interns:* responsibilities include mentoring and tutoring foster and adopted students in reading and math and working with youth during after school program; co-facilitating groups and assisting in developing life plan goals. Candidates should have ability to work independently, oral communication skills, personal interest in the field, self-motivation, strong interpersonal skills, written communication skills. Duration is 3–6 months. Unpaid. Open to recent high school graduates, college freshmen, college sophomores, college juniors, college seniors, recent college graduates, graduate students, law students, career changers, individuals reentering the workforce. ► *1–4 mobile health clinic volunteers:* responsibilities include counseling HIV-positive youth, collecting data, and developing and distributing promotional and educational materials. Candidates should have ability to work independently, ability to work with others, experience in the field, oral communication skills, self-motivation, written communication skills. Duration is 3–6 months. Unpaid. Open to recent high school graduates, college freshmen, college sophomores, college juniors, college seniors, recent college graduates, graduate students, law students, career changers, individuals reentering the workforce. International applications accepted.

Benefits Formal training, job counseling, names of contacts, on-the-job training, opportunity to attend seminars/workshops, possible full-time employment, willing to act as a professional reference, willing to complete paperwork for educational credit, willing to provide letters of recommendation, free meals (depending on center where intern works).

Contact Write, call, fax, or e-mail Jean Stein, Volunteer Services Administrator, 3255 Wing Street, San Diego, California 92110. Phone: 619-221-8600 Ext. 271. Fax: 619-221-8611. E-mail: volunteer@ sdycs.org. In-person interview recommended (telephone interview accepted). Applicants must submit a formal organization application, letter of interest, resume, three personal references, TB test and background check required. Applications are accepted continuously. World Wide Web: http://www.sdycs.org.

SARAH HEINZ HOUSE
One Heinz Street
Pittsburgh, Pennsylvania 15212

General Information Youth recreation center for children ages 7-18. Established in 1901. Number of employees: 55. Unit of Boys & Girls Clubs of America, Atlanta, Georgia. Number of internship applications received each year: 15.

Internships Available ► *1–7 day camp counselors:* responsibilities include supervising children, planning and implementing programs or activities, and counseling children. Duration is June to August. $1000 per duration of internship. ► *1–10 resident camp counselors:* responsibilities include supervising children, planning and implementing programs or activities, and counseling children. Duration is June to July (boys), July to August (girls). $900–$1000 per duration of internship. Candidates for all positions should have ability to work independently, personal interest in the field, self-motivation, strong interpersonal skills, strong leadership ability. Open to high school seniors, recent high school gradu-

ates, college freshmen, college sophomores, college juniors, college seniors, recent college graduates, graduate students, career changers, individuals reentering the workforce.

Benefits Formal training, on-the-job training, willing to act as a professional reference, willing to complete paperwork for educational credit, willing to provide letters of recommendation, free housing, meals, and health insurance (at resident camp only).

Contact Write, call, fax, or e-mail Jennifer L. Roberts, Program Director. Phone: 412-231-2377. Fax: 412-231-2428. E-mail: roberts@ sarahheinzhouse.com. In-person interview required. Applicants must submit a formal organization application, resume, three personal references. Application deadline: May 31. World Wide Web: http://www.sarahheinzhouse.org.

SARASOTA FAMILY YMCA, INC.
1 South School Avenue, Suite 301
Sarasota, Florida 34237

General Information Organization that offers programs to help strengthen local families including sports, wellness, fitness, and human services. Established in 1947. Number of employees: 800.

Internships Available ► *Child care workers/summer camp staff:* responsibilities include supervising children ages 5-12 and working with director to enhance the programs offered. Candidates should have ability to work with others, declared college major in field, knowledge of field, personal interest in the field, plan to pursue career in field. Duration is 3 months in summer or 1 semester. Unpaid. ► *Office/administrative interns:* responsibilities include working with members at front desk, computer work, filing, organization, and general administrative work. Candidates should have ability to work independently, computer skills, office skills, organizational skills, strong interpersonal skills. Duration is 1 semester. Unpaid. ► *Social services assistants:* responsibilities include working in one of many social services programs including youth residential, foster case program, counseling programs, alternative education programs for teens, and various other areas. Candidates should have ability to work with others, computer skills, declared college major in field, personal interest in the field, plan to pursue career in field, self-motivation. Duration is 1 semester. Unpaid. ► *Sports/fitness interns:* responsibilities include assisting with youth sports and fitness programs for all ages, assisting in coordinating programs, teaching classes, maintaining equipment, and overseeing fitness floor. Candidates should have ability to work with others, declared college major in field, knowledge of field, plan to pursue career in field, strong leadership ability. Duration is 3 months in summer or 1 semester. Unpaid. Open to college juniors, college seniors. International applications accepted.

Benefits Names of contacts, on-the-job training, possible full-time employment, willing to act as a professional reference, willing to complete paperwork for educational credit, willing to provide letters of recommendation, free YMCA membership.

Contact Call, fax, or e-mail Marti McKenna, Vice President, Human Resources, One South School Avenue, Suite 301, Sarasota, Florida 34237. Phone: 941-951-2916 Ext. 1064. Fax: 941-365-2311. E-mail: mmckenna@sarasota-ymca.org. In-person interview required. Applicants must submit a formal organization application, resume, two personal references. Applications are accepted continuously. World Wide Web: http://www.sarasota-ymca.org.

SELF RELIANCE FOUNDATION
529 14th Street, NW, Suite 740
Washington, District of Columbia

General Information Nonprofit Hispanic community outreach organization. Established in 1979. Number of employees: 20. Number of internship applications received each year: 30.

Internships Available ► *1 development assistant:* responsibilities include assisting in developing Spanish-language community outreach campaigns. Candidates should have ability to work independently, computer skills, editing skills, office skills, oral communication skills, organizational skills, research skills, self-motivation, strong interpersonal skills, strong leadership ability, writing skills. Duration is 3–6 months. Unpaid. Open to college freshmen, college sophomores, college juniors, college seniors. ► *1 information and referral specialist:* responsibilities include taking calls from Spanish speakers needing information or com-

Self Reliance Foundation *(continued)*

munity services. Candidates should have ability to work independently, computer skills, office skills, oral communication skills, organizational skills, research skills, strong interpersonal skills. Duration is 3–6 months. Unpaid. Open to college freshmen, college sophomores, college juniors, college seniors. ► *1 production studio intern:* responsibilities include assisting in Spanish-language educational video productions. Candidates should have analytical skills, computer skills, editing skills, office skills, oral communication skills, organizational skills, personal interest in the field, research skills, self-motivation, strong interpersonal skills, strong leadership ability, writing skills. Duration is 3–6 months. Unpaid. Open to college sophomores, college juniors, college seniors, recent college graduates. International applications accepted.
Benefits Formal training, on-the-job training, opportunity to attend seminars/workshops, possible full-time employment, willing to act as a professional reference, willing to complete paperwork for educational credit, willing to provide letters of recommendation, travel reimbursement in DC area.
Contact Write, call, e-mail, or through World Wide Web site Maite Arce, Deputy Director. Phone: 202-661-8087. Fax: 202-661-8017. E-mail: maite@selfreliancefoundation.org. In-person interview required. Applicants must submit a formal organization application, resume. Applications are accepted continuously. World Wide Web: http://www.selfreliancefoundation.org.

SERVICE LEAGUE OF SAN MATEO COUNTY
727 Middlefield Road
Redwood City, California 94063

General Information Organization that provides services to San Mateo jail inmates, their families, and those released from jail. Established in 1961. Number of employees: 25. Number of internship applications received each year: 6.
Internships Available ► *1 assistant release counselor:* responsibilities include interviewing and assisting former inmates and their families with counseling and emergency needs and maintaining computer client records and statistics. Candidates should have computer skills, oral communication skills, organizational skills, plan to pursue career in field, self-motivation, strong interpersonal skills. Duration is 6 months minimum; flexible hours (minimum 8 hours per week). Unpaid. Open to college juniors, college seniors, recent college graduates. ► *1 assistant to jail coordinator:* responsibilities include assisting jail coordinators, responding to inmate requests in county jail as appropriate, acting as liaison between inmate and family. Candidates should have ability to work independently, declared college major in field, oral communication skills, organizational skills, self-motivation, strong interpersonal skills, personal interest or knowledge of field, strong sense of self. Duration is 9 months (school year); flexible hours (minimum 8 hours per week). Unpaid. Open to college sophomores, college juniors, college seniors, recent college graduates, individuals age 21 or older.
Benefits On-the-job training, willing to act as a professional reference, willing to complete paperwork for educational credit, willing to provide letters of recommendation.
Contact Write or call Ernestine Gemmet, Office Manager. Phone: 650-364-4664. Fax: 650-365-6817. E-mail: egemmet@serviceleague. org. Applicants must submit a formal organization application, letter of interest, three letters of recommendation. Applications are accepted continuously.

SOUTHEAST PREVENTION SERVICES
7D Zetterower Avenue
Statesboro, Georgia 30458

General Information Center that acts as a lending library, produces newsletters, holds workshops and conferences related to substance abuse prevention as it relates to risk and protective factors, and provides research-based prevention programs for youth. Established in 1991. Number of employees: 2. Subsidiary of Pineland MH/MR/SA Community Service Board, Statesboro, Georgia. Number of internship applications received each year: 8.

Internships Available ► *2 health educator/evaluator specialists:* responsibilities include developing and presenting educational offerings, assisting with survey implementation and tabulation of results, serving on planning committee for educational workshops or conferences, assisting with gathering data for programs. Candidates should have oral communication skills, personal interest in the field, research skills, self-motivation, written communication skills. Duration is August to December, January to May, and May to August. Unpaid. Open to college seniors, graduate students. International applications accepted.
Benefits Names of contacts, on-the-job training, opportunity to attend seminars/workshops, travel reimbursement, willing to provide letters of recommendation.
Contact Write or e-mail Charlotte Mallard, Program Manager, PO Box 1038, Statesboro, Georgia 30459. Phone: 912-764-2475. Fax: 912-489-8552. E-mail: seprevention@hotmail.com. In-person interview required. Applicants must submit a letter of interest, resume. Application deadline: May 1 for summer, August 1 for fall, December 1 for spring.

SPRING LAKE RANCH, INC.
Spring Lake Road
Cuttingsville, Vermont 05738

General Information Therapeutic community for emotionally disturbed adults. Established in 1933. Number of employees: 35. Number of internship applications received each year: 20.
Internships Available ► *1–6 work leaders/house advisers:* responsibilities include leading work crews in a safe manner so that residents will have a challenging, meaningful, enjoyable experience; overseeing practical aspects of house residents' lives and giving them support and guidance in reaching their goals; and participating in and contributing to the ranch community. Candidates should have oral communication skills, organizational skills, personal interest in the field, self-motivation, strong interpersonal skills. Duration is 6 months or longer. $193 per week. Open to recent college graduates, graduate students, career changers, individuals reentering the workforce, individuals 21 or older (college degree not necessary).
Benefits Free housing, free meals, health insurance, on-the-job training, opportunity to attend seminars/workshops, possible full-time employment, willing to provide letters of recommendation, vacation and sick time.
Contact Write, call, fax, or e-mail Ms. Lynn McDermott, Personnel Director, PO Box 310, Cuttingsville, Vermont 05738. Phone: 802-492-3322. Fax: 802-492-3331. E-mail: lynnslr@mindspring. com. In-person interview recommended (telephone interview accepted). Applicants must submit a resume. Applications are accepted continuously. World Wide Web: http://www.spring-lake-ranch.org.

STARLIGHT CHILDREN'S FOUNDATION OF NY*NJ*CT
1560 Broadway, Suite 600
New York, New York 10036

General Information Organization that brightens the lives of seriously ill children between the ages of 4 and 18 through a variety of programs, including wish granting and various activities in and out of hospital pediatric wards. Established in 1985. Number of employees: 8. Unit of Starlight Children's Foundation International, Los Angeles, California. Number of internship applications received each year: 100.
Internships Available ► *1–3 children's services interns:* responsibilities include maintaining hospital party and outpatient activities programs, scheduling parties and entertainment for parties, distributing outpatient tickets, maintaining donor correspondence, and assisting with granting of wishes. Duration is 3 months minimum. Unpaid. ► *1–2 marketing and event interns:* responsibilities include working closely with fund-raising associate by assisting with the planning and implementation of special events, maintaining donor correspondence, and soliciting various items and donations; also assists with promotions, newsletters, and marketing. Duration is 3 months minimum. Unpaid. Candidates for all positions should have office skills, oral communication skills,

organizational skills, self-motivation, strong interpersonal skills, written communication skills. Open to college sophomores, college juniors, college seniors, recent college graduates. International applications accepted.
Benefits Formal training, on-the-job training, willing to complete paperwork for educational credit, willing to provide letters of recommendation.
Contact Write, call, fax, or e-mail Michele Hall, Program Manager. Phone: 212-354-2878. Fax: 212-354-2977. E-mail: michele@starlightnyc. org. In-person interview recommended (telephone interview accepted). Applicants must submit a formal organization application, letter of interest, resume, three personal references. Application deadline: March 31 for summer; continuous for fall and winter. World Wide Web: http://www.starlight.org.

STRIDES THERAPEUTIC RIDING
PO Box 572455
Tarzana, California 91357-2455

General Information Organization providing therapeutic horsemanship for the disabled. Established in 1987. Number of employees: 2. Unit of North American Riding for the Handicapped Association (NARHA), Denver, Colorado. Number of internship applications received each year: 15.
Internships Available ▶ *2–3 program assistants:* responsibilities include assisting with lessons for disabled riders, horse and track care, and horse training (if qualified). Candidates should have ability to work independently, ability to work with others, oral communication skills, self-motivation, strong leadership ability, riding experience (preferred). Duration is 2–4 months. Unpaid. Open to high school seniors, recent high school graduates, college freshmen, college sophomores, college juniors, college seniors, recent college graduates, graduate students, law students, career changers, individuals reentering the workforce, elderly persons in good physical condition. International applications accepted.
Benefits Formal training, housing at a cost, job counseling, names of contacts, on-the-job training, opportunity to attend seminars/workshops, possible full-time employment, willing to act as a professional reference, willing to complete paperwork for educational credit, willing to provide letters of recommendation, insurance for accident or injury on the job.
Contact Write, call, fax, e-mail, or through World Wide Web site Nora Fischbach, Program Director. Phone: 818-341-4737. Fax: 818-705-2201. E-mail: strides@onebox.com. In-person interview recommended (telephone interview accepted). Applicants must submit a formal organization application, letter of interest, resume, two personal references. Applications are accepted continuously. World Wide Web: http://www.strides.org.

TAHIRIH JUSTICE CENTER
PO Box 7638
Falls Church, Virginia 22040

General Information Nonprofit human rights organization aiding women who are fleeing gender persecution and are seeking asylum in the United States. Established in 1997. Number of employees: 6. Number of internship applications received each year: 60.
Internships Available ▶ *2–4 VAWA legal and outreach interns:* responsibilities include legal research; legal writing including memos, affidavits, and client-related correspondence; outreach to immigrants and domestic violence communities. Candidates should have ability to work independently, computer skills, office skills, organizational skills, personal interest in the field, plan to pursue career in field, research skills, self-motivation, writing skills. Unpaid. Open to graduate students, law students. ▶ *1–2 human rights legal interns:* responsibilities include interviewing clients, gathering evidence, drafting affidavits and legal memoranda, researching legal and country conditions. Candidates should have analytical skills, editing skills, knowledge of field, personal interest in the field, strong interpersonal skills, writing skills. Duration is 3–4 months. Unpaid. Open to law students, career changers. ▶ *2–4 office administration interns:* responsibilities include general office administration duties, research, representation of organization at conferences, and speaking engagements. Candidates should have ability to work with others, office skills, oral communication

skills, personal interest in the field, research skills, writing skills. Unpaid. Open to recent high school graduates, college freshmen, college sophomores, college juniors, college seniors, recent college graduates. International applications accepted.
Benefits Names of contacts, on-the-job training, opportunity to attend seminars/workshops, possible full-time employment, willing to act as a professional reference, willing to complete paperwork for educational credit, willing to provide letters of recommendation.
Contact Write, call, fax, e-mail, or through World Wide Web site Barfonce Baldwin, Office Manager. Phone: 703-237-4554. Fax: 703-237-4574. E-mail: justice@tahirih.org. In-person interview recommended (telephone interview accepted). Applicants must submit a letter of interest, resume, writing sample. Application deadline: March 30 for summer, September 1 for fall, November 30 for spring. World Wide Web: http://www.tahirih.org.

TEEN LINE
PO Box 48750
Los Angeles, California 90048

General Information Organization that provides teen-to-teen hot line and associated community outreach services. Established in 1981. Number of employees: 6. Unit of Cedars-Sinai Medical Center, Los Angeles, California. Number of internship applications received each year: 20.
Internships Available ▶ *2–4 administrative interns:* responsibilities include assisting program manager with all administrative tasks; some research involved. Candidates should have ability to work independently, computer skills, organizational skills, self-motivation, strong interpersonal skills, written communication skills. Duration is flexible (minimum of 12 weeks in summer and minimum of 6 months during the year). Unpaid. Open to high school students, recent high school graduates, college freshmen, college sophomores, college juniors, college seniors, recent college graduates. ▶ *6 resource associates:* responsibilities include facilitating meetings of adolescents and supervising their work on teen hot line. Candidates should have analytical skills, knowledge of field, oral communication skills, organizational skills, personal interest in the field, strong interpersonal skills. Duration is 6 months. Unpaid. Open to graduate students. International applications accepted.
Benefits Formal training, on-the-job training, opportunity to attend seminars/workshops, possible full-time employment, willing to complete paperwork for educational credit, willing to provide letters of recommendation.
Contact Write, call, fax, or e-mail Jenni Kim-Harris, Program Manager. Phone: 310-423-3401 Ext. 2. Fax: 310-423-0456. E-mail: teenlineca@aol.com. In-person interview recommended (telephone interview accepted). Applicants must submit a resume. Applications are accepted continuously. World Wide Web: http://www. teenlineonline.org.

TEEN RESPONSE, INC.
6758 Bramble Avenue
Cincinnati, Ohio 45227

General Information Nonprofit youth-serving community organization engaged in building leadership skills and positive self-esteem in youth 10-16 years of age. Established in 1993. Number of employees: 5. Number of internship applications received each year: 100.
Internships Available ▶ *1–2 youth social workers:* responsibilities include working directly with youth and engaging them in productive activities to foster personal growth and build positive self-esteem and developing activities for this process; working as a role-model/mentor for youth in group and one-on-one settings. Candidates should have ability to work independently, oral communication skills, personal interest in the field, self-motivation, strong interpersonal skills, written communication skills. Duration is 3–12 months. Unpaid. Open to college freshmen, college sophomores, college juniors, college seniors, recent college graduates. International applications accepted.
Benefits Free housing, names of contacts, on-the-job training, opportunity to attend seminars/workshops, willing to act as a

Teen Response, Inc. (continued)

professional reference, willing to complete paperwork for educational credit, willing to provide letters of recommendation.
Contact Write, call, or e-mail Mark Wooten, Administrative Assistant, PO Box 9555, Cincinnati, Ohio 45209-0555. Phone: 513-272-8222. Fax: 513-272-8222. E-mail: teenresponseinc@netzero. net. In-person interview recommended (telephone interview accepted). Applicants must submit a formal organization application, letter of interest, resume, writing sample, three personal references. Applications are accepted continuously. World Wide Web: http://www.teenresponseinc.com.

THISTLEDEW CAMP
62741 County Road 551
Togo, Minnesota 55723

General Information Residential correctional camp for juvenile males that offers short-term program for nonserious offenders including a special education program, work experience, recreation, and a comprehensive high-adventure portion. Established in 1955. Number of employees: 57. Unit of Minnesota Department of Corrections, St. Paul, Minnesota. Number of internship applications received each year: 15.
Internships Available ▶ *2–6 challenge interns:* responsibilities include assisting director of high adventure challenge program including training of students on high ropes course, rock climbing, helping in supervision of a 3-day solo experience, and participating in 2- or 3-week long wilderness treks; possible modes of travel are canoeing, backpacking, or cross-country skiing. Candidates should have ability to work with others, personal interest in the field. Duration is 12 weeks. $412 per duration of internship. Open to college juniors, college seniors. ▶ *2–6 residential interns:* responsibilities include assisting professional staff with counseling and report writing, working some afternoons and evenings helping to supervise students in work and recreational activities; also includes involvement in a week-long wilderness expedition with a graduating group. Candidates should have ability to work with others, personal interest in the field. Duration is 12 weeks. $412 per duration of internship. Open to college juniors, college seniors. ▶ *2–3 school interns:* responsibilities include assisting professional staff in providing treatment and education for juvenile boys ages 13 to 17 years; can also fulfill student teaching requirements at Thistledew. Candidates should have ability to work independently, ability to work with others, oral communication skills, personal interest in the field, written communication skills. Duration is 12 weeks. $412 per duration of internship. Open to college juniors, college seniors. ▶ *1–6 therapeutic adventure interns:* responsibilities include assisting professional staff in the facilitation of rock climbing, solo, wilderness travel skills and expedition. Candidates should have ability to work independently, oral communication skills, personal interest in the field, self-motivation, strong interpersonal skills, written communication skills, ability to handle extensive wilderness travel and rigorous physical activity. Duration is minimum of 3 months. $412 per duration of internship. Open to college juniors, college seniors, graduate students. International applications accepted.
Benefits Formal training, free housing, free meals, names of contacts, on-the-job training, opportunity to attend seminars/ workshops, possible full-time employment, willing to complete paperwork for educational credit, willing to provide letters of recommendation.
Contact Write, call, fax, or e-mail Christine Phillips, Personnel Officer. Phone: 218-376-4411. Fax: 218-376-4679. E-mail: cphillips@thistledewcamp.com. In-person interview recommended (telephone interview accepted). Applicants must submit a formal organization application, letter of interest, resume, two personal references, Mantoux Test (TB) plus a physical exam and background check required. Applications are accepted continuously. World Wide Web: http://www.thistledewcamp.com.

TRAVELERS AID
60 Walton Street, #200
Atlanta, Georgia 30303

General Information Nonprofit social service agency working with people in crisis, preventing homelessness. Established in

1900. Number of employees: 16. Unit of Travelers Aid International, Washington, District of Columbia. Number of internship applications received each year: 10.
Internships Available ▶ *1–3 development associates:* responsibilities include assisting with fund-raising and working on annual campaign. Candidates should have ability to work independently, oral communication skills, personal interest in the field, research skills, self-motivation, written communication skills. Duration is 6–12 months. Position available as unpaid or paid. Open to college freshmen, college sophomores, college juniors, college seniors, graduate students. ▶ *1–4 social work interns:* responsibilities include intake assessment, case management, crisis intervention, resource development with a variety of client populations. Candidates should have ability to work independently, oral communication skills, strong interpersonal skills, written communication skills, must be enrolled in BSW or MSW program. Duration is flexible. Unpaid. Open to college juniors, college seniors, graduate students. ▶ *1–3 volunteer coordinator associates:* responsibilities include helping to coordinate the volunteer program. Candidates should have experience in the field, oral communication skills, self-motivation, strong interpersonal skills, written communication skills. Duration is 6–12 months. Unpaid. Open to college freshmen, college sophomores, college juniors, college seniors, recent college graduates, graduate students. International applications accepted.
Benefits Names of contacts, on-the-job training, opportunity to attend seminars/workshops, possible full-time employment, travel reimbursement, willing to act as a professional reference, willing to complete paperwork for educational credit, willing to provide letters of recommendation.
Contact Call, fax, or e-mail Kay Bernier, Associate Director, 60 Walton Street, #200, Atlanta, Georgia 30303. Phone: 404-817-7070 Ext. 14. Fax: 404-817-9922. E-mail: kaybernier@hotmail. com. Applicants must submit a resume, two writing samples, 3 personal references or letters of recommendation, in-person or telephone interview. Application deadline: May 1 for summer, November 1 for January.

UNITED WAY OF WACO
PO Box 2027
Waco, Texas 76703

General Information Clearinghouse for pledges that are allocated to member agencies. Established in 1923. Number of employees: 1. Number of internship applications received each year: 4.
Internships Available ▶ *1 intern:* responsibilities include record-keeping, sending out press notices, and assisting in the placing of volunteers in member agencies. Candidates should have office skills, written communication skills, computer skills (helpful). Duration is flexible. Unpaid. Open to high school students, recent high school graduates, college freshmen, college sophomores, college juniors, college seniors, recent college graduates, graduate students, law students, career changers, individuals reentering the workforce. International applications accepted.
Benefits Names of contacts, possible full-time employment, willing to complete paperwork for educational credit, willing to provide letters of recommendation.
Contact Write, call, or fax Dorothy Wienecke, Communication Coordinator/Volunteer Center Director. Phone: 254-752-2753. Fax: 254-752-2769. In-person interview recommended (telephone interview accepted). Applicants must submit a resume. Applications are accepted continuously.

UNIVERSITY FOR THE STUDY OF HUMAN GOODNESS/HUMAN SERVICE ALLIANCE
3983 Old Greensboro Road
Winston-Salem, North Carolina 27101

General Information Organization whose mission is to expand others' capacity to serve. Established in 1987. Number of internship applications received each year: 100.
Internships Available ▶ *10–30 service learning interns/servant leadership interns:* responsibilities include working in various areas including nonprofit management; restaurant management/marketing; video production; volunteer management; and public speaking.

Candidates should have ability to work independently, ability to work with others, oral communication skills, self-motivation, strong leadership ability, written communication skills. Duration is January-December or July-June; co-ops and summer internships also available. Unpaid. Open to recent high school graduates, college freshmen, college sophomores, college juniors, college seniors, recent college graduates, graduate students, law students, career changers, individuals reentering the workforce, retirees. International applications accepted.

Benefits Free housing, free meals, job counseling, on-the-job training, opportunity to attend seminars/workshops, willing to act as a professional reference, willing to provide letters of recommendation, free tuition for program.

Contact Write, call, fax, e-mail, or through World Wide Web site Joanna White, Dean of Admissions. Phone: 336-761-8745. Fax: 336-722-7882. E-mail: jwhite@ufhg.org. In-person interview recommended (telephone interview accepted). Applicants must submit a formal organization application, three personal references, questionnaire, full-length photo. Application deadline: June 1 for mid-July entry, December 1 for January entry. World Wide Web: http://www.ufhg.org.

UPPER BUCKS YMCA
151 South 14th Street
Quakertown, Pennsylvania 18951

General Information Social service organization that provides programs in health, fitness, aquatics, and child care. Established in 1969. Number of employees: 100. Number of internship applications received each year: 2.

Internships Available ▶ *1 camp counselor:* responsibilities include planning activities and ensuring safety and welfare of campers ages 5-12. Candidates should have oral communication skills, strong interpersonal skills, written communication skills, declared major in education or human services. Duration is 3½ months. $6–$7 per hour. ▶ *2 child-care interns:* responsibilities include working in a team-teaching situation and caring for the safety of the children. Candidates should have college courses in field, oral communication skills, plan to pursue career in field, strong interpersonal skills, strong leadership ability, background in early childhood, human services, or education. Duration is 3 months. $6 per hour. ▶ *1 physical instructor:* responsibilities include setting up weight training and fitness programs, supervising workout programs, and coaching children in sports. Candidates should have ability to work independently, ability to work with others, knowledge of field, oral communication skills, personal interest in the field. Duration is flexible. Unpaid. Open to college freshmen, college sophomores, college juniors, college seniors, recent college graduates, graduate students, law students, career changers, individuals reentering the workforce. International applications accepted.

Benefits Names of contacts, opportunity to attend seminars/workshops, possible full-time employment, travel reimbursement, willing to complete paperwork for educational credit, willing to provide letters of recommendation, CPR and first aid training, YMCA membership.

Contact Write, call, or fax Pat Hess, Child Care Director. Phone: 215-536-8409. Fax: 215-538-2943. In-person interview required. Application deadline: May 1 for summer, August 1 for fall, December 1 for winter. Fees: $20.

U.S. COMMITTEE FOR REFUGEES
1717 Massachusetts Avenue, NW, Suite 200
Washington, District of Columbia 20036

General Information Sister agency of Immigration and Refugee Services of America, working primarily to insure that the protection and assistance needs of refugees and internally displaced persons overseas are met.

Internships Available ▶ *1 communication intern:* responsibilities include assisting communications officer in forging links with print, radio, and television media; assisting media database management; tracking organization in the news; answering inquiries about organization. Candidates should have editing skills, knowledge of field, oral communication skills, personal interest in the field, writing skills. Duration is 12 weeks minimum. $75–$100 monthly

stipend . Open to college juniors, college seniors, recent college graduates, graduate students, career changers. ▶ *1 fund-raising/development intern:* responsibilities include researching potential funding sources, assisting direct mailing campaigns, tracking IRSA organization in the news, answering inquiries about IRSA work, attending meetings on behalf of development staff, working with donor management database. Candidates should have ability to work independently, computer skills, personal interest in the field, writing skills, enthusiasm, positive attitude. Duration is 12 week minimum. $75–$100 monthly stipend. Open to college freshmen, college sophomores, college juniors, college seniors, recent college graduates, graduate students, career changers. ▶ *1 government liaison intern:* responsibilities include drafting correspondence and making calls related to advocacy efforts; providing written summaries of bills and regulations; drafting informational memos and action alerts to partner agencies; attending congressional hearings, mark-ups, and briefings; researching legal issues on migration; arranging meetings with congressional staff; providing clerical support. Candidates should have knowledge of field, personal interest in the field, research skills, writing skills, ability to work well under pressure, graduate-level course work in law (preferred). Duration is 12 weeks minimum. $75–$100 monthly stipend. Open to college seniors, recent college graduates, graduate students, law students. ▶ *6 research interns:* responsibilities include researching current refugee situations for newsletter articles, reports, and annual survey; areas of research are: Africa, Latin America, Asia, North America, Europe, the former Soviet Union, and the Middle East; other responsibilities include attending meetings of relevance to region, responding to public inquiries, and some clerical support. Candidates should have ability to work independently, computer skills, editing skills, research skills, writing skills. Duration is 12 weeks minimum. $75–$100 monthly stipend. Open to college juniors, college seniors, recent college graduates, graduate students, career changers.

Benefits On-the-job training, willing to act as a professional reference, willing to complete paperwork for educational credit, willing to provide letters of recommendation.

Contact Write, fax, or e-mail Meheret Mellese, Program Assistant. Fax: 202-347-3418. E-mail: mmellese@irsa-uscr.org. Applicants must submit a letter of interest, resume, writing sample of 3-5 pages, 2 references (names and contact information only). Application deadline: April 15 for summer, August 1 for fall, December 10 for spring. World Wide Web: http://www.refugees.org.

VALLEY YOUTH HOUSE
524 Walnut Street
Allentown, Pennsylvania 18101

General Information Youth services organization that provides preventative and responsive services for troubled young people and families; offers emergency shelter, long-term care, counseling, guidance, information, preparation for adulthood, and referral. Established in 1973. Number of employees: 186. Number of internship applications received each year: 40.

Internships Available ▶ *3–4 administration interns:* responsibilities include performing program audits, assisting in the planning and execution of the Project Child Conference (community conference on child abuse), coordinating community resources, completing agency research, and assisting in agency grant writing. Candidates should have declared college major in field, oral communication skills, organizational skills, self-motivation, strong interpersonal skills, written communication skills. Duration is 1–3 semesters. Unpaid. Open to college seniors, graduate students. ▶ *8–10 bachelor's-level clinical counseling interns:* responsibilities include becoming familiar with the policies, practices, and protocols of the agency; conducting entry and intake interviews with clients; providing individual counseling; participating in family counseling as an observer; providing ongoing behavior management and client supervision; accompanying clients to appointments and activities; providing direct in-person client services; providing all appropriate and required timely documentation; performing case management; and participating in weekly undergraduate intern group supervision. Candidates should have declared college major in field, oral communication skills, self-motivation, strong interpersonal skills, written communication

Valley Youth House (continued)

skills. Duration is 1–3 semesters. Unpaid. Open to college juniors, college seniors. ▶ *10–15 master's-level clinical counseling interns:* responsibilities include performing direct, in-person client service; successfully engaging and maintaining clients through the treatment process; completing adolescent and parent intake interviews and their subsequent dictation; providing individual, parent, family, and group counseling services within the context of office-based or outreach services according to treatment plans; providing ongoing case coordination; assessing and collecting client fees; completing necessary documentation; participating in weekly supervision and biweekly group supervision. Candidates should have ability to work independently, declared college major in field, oral communication skills, self-motivation, strong interpersonal skills, written communication skills. Duration is 2–3 semesters. Unpaid. Open to graduate students. International applications accepted.

Benefits Names of contacts, on-the-job training, opportunity to attend seminars/workshops, possible full-time employment, travel reimbursement, willing to act as a professional reference, willing to complete paperwork for educational credit, willing to provide letters of recommendation.

Contact Write, call, fax, or e-mail Marcella Kraybill-Greggo, Internship Coordinator. Phone: 610-432-6481. Fax: 610-432-6648. E-mail: marcellak@valleyyouthhouse.org. In-person interview required. Applicants must submit a formal organization application, resume. Application deadline: April 30 for summer, July 30 for fall (until slots are filled), December 20 for spring.

VINCENTIAN SERVICE CORPS–CENTRAL
4330 Olive Street
St. Louis, Missouri 63108

General Information Faith-based volunteer program for lay women and men who want to work with those at an economic disadvantage while living in a community with other members and experiencing a simple lifestyle. Established in 1984. Number of employees: 2. Affiliate of Vincentian Service Corps, New York, New York. Number of internship applications received each year: 12.

Internships Available ▶ *4 child-care workers (infant to kindergarten):* responsibilities include developing relationships with the children and their parents; assisting in planning and executing the daily activities designed for emotional, social, educational, and physical development of assigned children. Candidates should have ability to work with others, knowledge of field, oral communication skills, personal interest in the field, self-motivation. Duration is 1 year (full- time). $100 monthly stipend. Open to college seniors, recent college graduates, career changers, individuals reentering the workforce, individuals interested in young children. ▶ *1–2 high school instructors:* responsibilities include teaching 5 periods a day, preparing for assemblies, group sessions, guiding students, and completing paper work for class. Candidates should have ability to work independently, analytical skills, experience in the field, oral communication skills, organizational skills, self-motivation, strong interpersonal skills, strong leadership ability, writing skills. Duration is 1 year. $100 monthly stipend. Open to recent college graduates, graduate students. ▶ *1–2 outreach ministry for inner city children interns:* responsibilities include tutoring, coaching sports/recreational activities, summer camp, and teaching. Candidates should have oral communication skills, organizational skills, self-motivation, strong interpersonal skills, strong leadership ability. Duration is 1 year. $100 monthly stipend. Open to recent college graduates. ▶ *1 shelter assistant:* responsibilities include assisting women in moving from an abusive situation and attaining job and parenting skills; helping them learn how to handle conflict and live in positive relationships. Candidates should have knowledge of field, oral communication skills, personal interest in the field, strong interpersonal skills, strong leadership ability. Duration is August to July. $100 monthly stipend. Open to recent college graduates, graduate students, law students, career changers. ▶ *6–12 skills trainers:* responsibilities include training and direct care for clients regarding everyday activities, plus helping to maintain the daily household operations; helping clients build social skills. Candidates should have ability to work with others,

oral communication skills, personal interest in the field, self-motivation. Duration is 1 year (full-time). $100 monthly stipend. Open to college seniors, recent college graduates, graduate students, law students, career changers, individuals reentering the workforce, anyone able to work with handicapped people. ▶ *10–20 volunteers:* responsibilities include working with parishes, schools, clinics, and social service agencies in urban areas. Candidates should have ability to work with others, oral communication skills, self-motivation, written communication skills, desire to experience community. Duration is 1 year. $100 monthly stipend. Open to college seniors, recent college graduates, graduate students, career changers.

Benefits Free housing, health insurance, opportunity to attend seminars/workshops, possible full-time employment, travel reimbursement, tuition assistance, willing to complete paperwork for educational credit.

Contact Write, call, fax, e-mail, or through World Wide Web site Sr. Mary Catherine Dunn, D.C., Director. Phone: 314-533-4770 Ext. 103. Fax: 314-533-3226. E-mail: vsccentral@dcwcp.org. Telephone interview required. Applicants must submit a formal organization application, academic transcripts, 5 personal references. Application deadline: May 31 for fall. World Wide Web: http://www.vscorps.org.

VISITING NEIGHBORS, INC.
611 Broadway, 5th Floor, Suite 510
New York, New York 10012

General Information Organization that fosters independence for senior citizens living in their homes through neighbor assistance and an escort and shopping program. Established in 1972. Number of employees: 14. Number of internship applications received each year: 6.

Internships Available ▶ *1–6 psychology interns:* responsibilities include working with professional staff on small caseload while providing mental stimulation, encouragement, and physical independence to people over 60. Candidates should have ability to work independently, analytical skills, oral communication skills, personal interest in the field, self-motivation, strong interpersonal skills, written communication skills. Duration is 6–12 months. Unpaid. ▶ *1–6 public relations and communications interns:* responsibilities include working on newsletter and putting together press kit. Candidates should have ability to work independently, oral communication skills, self-motivation, strong interpersonal skills, writing skills. Duration is flexible. Unpaid. ▶ *1–6 social work interns:* responsibilities include working in office, in field with clients, and managing a caseload in size corresponding to intern's level of experience and maturity. Candidates should have ability to work independently, oral communication skills, personal interest in the field, self-motivation, strong interpersonal skills, writing skills. Duration is flexible. Unpaid. Open to high school students, recent high school graduates, college freshmen, college sophomores, college juniors, college seniors, recent college graduates, graduate students, law students, career changers, individuals reentering the workforce. International applications accepted.

Benefits On-the-job training, willing to act as a professional reference, willing to complete paperwork for educational credit, willing to provide letters of recommendation.

Contact Write, call, fax, e-mail, or through World Wide Web site Ms. Cynthia Maurer, Executive Director, 611 Broadway, 5th Floor, Suite 510. Phone: 212-260-6200. Fax: 212-260-2962. E-mail: hsquarevn@aol.com. In-person interview required. Applicants must submit a formal organization application, letter of interest, 2 personal references and/or letters of recommendation. Applications are accepted continuously. World Wide Web: http://www.visitingneighbors.org.

VOLUNTEERS FOR PEACE
1034 Tiffany Road
Belmont, Vermont 05730

General Information Placement service that places North Americans in 1500 work camps worldwide. Established in 1981. Number of employees: 3. Number of internship applications received each year: 600.

Internships Available ▶ *1,200–1,400 international work campers:* responsibilities include living with an international group of 12-20 persons and becoming involved in a community service project. Candidates should have organizational skills, self-motivation, strong interpersonal skills, intercultural experience. Duration is 2 to 3 weeks each program; interns normally register for multiple camps. Unpaid. Open to individuals age 15 or over. International applications accepted.

Benefits Free housing, meals at a cost, opportunity to attend seminars/workshops, willing to complete paperwork for educational credit, inexpensive international experience.

International Internships Available.

Contact Write, call, fax, e-mail, or through World Wide Web site Amy Bannon, Outgoing Placement Director, 1034 Tiffany Road. Phone: 802-259-2759. Fax: 802-259-2922. E-mail: vfp@vfp.org. Applicants must submit a formal organization application, $200 for room and board upon acceptance. Applications are accepted continuously. World Wide Web: http://www.vfp.org.

VOLUNTEERS OF AMERICA
1660 Duke Street
Alexandria, Virginia 22314

General Information National, nonprofit, spiritually-based organization providing comprehensive human services and affordable housing for families, the elderly, and people with disabilities. Established in 1896. Number of employees: 76. Number of internship applications received each year: 35.

Internships Available ▶ *1–3 international services interns:* responsibilities include program development, research, grant writing, representation at international agency briefings. Candidates should have ability to work independently, analytical skills, knowledge of field, research skills, written communication skills. Duration is flexible. Unpaid. Open to college seniors, recent college graduates, graduate students, individuals reentering the workforce, exchange students. ▶ *1–3 public policy interns:* responsibilities include representation at coalition meetings, attending hearings on Capitol Hill, contributing articles to monthly newsletter, and a variety of other possibilities. Candidates should have ability to work with others, analytical skills, knowledge of field, research skills, self-motivation, written communication skills. Duration is flexible. Unpaid. Open to college juniors, college seniors, recent college graduates, graduate students, law students. International applications accepted.

Benefits Travel reimbursement, willing to act as a professional reference, willing to complete paperwork for educational credit, willing to provide letters of recommendation.

Contact Write, call, or e-mail Christine Fall, Public Policy Assistant. Phone: 703-341-5000. Fax: 703-341-7000. E-mail: cfall@voa.org. Telephone interview required. Applicants must submit a resume, writing sample. Applications are accepted continuously. World Wide Web: http://www.volunteersofamerica.org.

WASHINGTON COMMUNITY YMCA/YWCA
121 East Main Street
Washington, Iowa 52353

General Information Organization that provides health, recreation, and social programs including full-service child care. Established in 1925. Number of employees: 50.

Internships Available ▶ *1 child caregiver:* responsibilities include providing child care. Duration is flexible. Position available as unpaid or paid. ▶ *1 health/fitness intern:* responsibilities include working with individuals and groups on health and wellness. Duration is 6–12 weeks. Position available as unpaid or paid. ▶ *2–3 summer camp/school age child-care interns.* Duration is one summer. Position available as unpaid or paid. ▶ *1–2 youth physical programs interns:* responsibilities include setting up, administering, and implementing youth sports for kindergarten through sixth grades. Duration is 1–3 months. Position available as unpaid or paid. Candidates for all positions should have oral communication skills, creativity. Open to college freshmen, college sophomores, college juniors, college seniors. International applications accepted.

Benefits Possible full-time employment, willing to complete paperwork for educational credit, willing to provide letters of recommendation.

Contact Write, call, or fax Jennifer Chalupa, Executive Director. Phone: 319-653-2141. Fax: 319-653-2142. In-person interview required. Applicants must submit a formal organization application, letter of interest, resume, three letters of recommendation. Application deadline: April 13 for summer; continuous for other positions.

WASHINGTON COUNTY YOUTH SERVICES BUREAU/BOYS & GIRLS CLUB
38 Elm Street, PO Box 627
Montpelier, Vermont 05601

General Information Alcohol/drug abuse outpatient treatment program for youth; provides individual/family counseling programs, Teen Center, after-school program, and statewide coalitions. Established in 1974. Number of employees: 35. Number of internship applications received each year: 4.

Internships Available ▶ *1–3 after-school programs counselors:* responsibilities include helping to facilitate group activities for adolescents. Candidates should have knowledge of field, oral communication skills, self-motivation, strong interpersonal skills, an interest in working with youth. Duration is 10–12 months. Unpaid. Open to college juniors, college seniors, recent college graduates, graduate students, individuals reentering the workforce. ▶ *1 drug counselor:* responsibilities include counseling individuals and families where drug use/abuse is an issue. Candidates should have ability to work independently, ability to work with others, college courses in field, knowledge of field, oral communication skills, organizational skills, self-motivation, an interest in working with youth. Duration is 10 to 12 months (20 hours a week). Unpaid. Open to college seniors, recent college graduates, graduate students, career changers. ▶ *1–2 individual/family counselors:* responsibilities include working with the family counselor and youth on a variety of issues. Candidates should have college courses in field, knowledge of field, oral communication skills, self-motivation, strong interpersonal skills, an interest in working with youth. Duration is 10 to 12 months (20 hours a week). Unpaid. Open to recent college graduates, graduate students, individuals reentering the workforce. International applications accepted.

Benefits Formal training, on-the-job training, opportunity to attend seminars/workshops, possible full-time employment, travel reimbursement, willing to act as a professional reference, willing to complete paperwork for educational credit, willing to provide letters of recommendation.

Contact Write, call, fax, or e-mail Tom Howard, Executive Director. Phone: 802-229-9151. Fax: 802-229-2508. E-mail: wcysb@adelphia. net. In-person interview required. Applicants must submit a letter of interest, resume, three letters of recommendation. Applications are accepted continuously.

WAYNESBORO YMCA
810 East Main Street
Waynesboro, Pennsylvania 17268

General Information Worldwide fellowship united by a common loyalty to Jesus Christ for the purpose of building Christian personality and a Christian society. Established in 1915. Number of employees: 60. Unit of YMCA of the USA, Chicago, Illinois. Number of internship applications received each year: 2.

Internships Available ▶ *1–3 assistant aquatic supervisors:* responsibilities include teaching programs for 6-36 month olds, 3-5 year olds, 6-12 year olds; teaching water exercise for adults and seniors, conducting arthritis water program, performing administrative duties, supervising housekeeping of pool area, maintaining records of swimming lesson participants, and keeping monthly statistical summaries. Candidates should have ability to work independently, knowledge of field, personal interest in the field, self-motivation, strong interpersonal skills, certification in CPR, first aid, and lifeguard. Duration is 3–12 months. Position available as unpaid or at $5.75–$6.50 per hour. Open to college freshmen, college sophomores, college juniors, college seniors, recent college graduates, graduate students, career changers, individuals reentering the workforce. ▶ *1–3 day camp counselors:* responsibilities include directing small group of youth ages 6-12; organizing and implementing daily activities and special events. Candidates should have abil-

Waynesboro YMCA (continued)

ity to work with others, organizational skills, personal interest in the field, strong leadership ability, CPR and first aid training (provided). Duration is June to August. Position available as unpaid or at $5.65–$6 per hour. Open to high school seniors, recent high school graduates, college freshmen, college sophomores, college juniors, college seniors, recent college graduates, graduate students. ▶ *1–2 fitness consultants:* responsibilities include assessing members' fitness status and needs and designing an exercise program to meet those needs; cleaning equipment; and overseeing fitness center. Candidates should have ability to work independently, analytical skills, oral communication skills, personal interest in the field, self-motivation, strong interpersonal skills. Duration is flexible. Unpaid. Open to college freshmen, college sophomores, college juniors, college seniors, recent college graduates, graduate students, individuals reentering the workforce. ▶ *1–2 group supervisors:* responsibilities include overseeing and assisting in the operation of an after-school program for school-age children. Candidates should have ability to work independently, experience in the field, oral communication skills, plan to pursue career in field, strong interpersonal skills, interest in aiding children socially and emotionally. Duration is 9 months. Position available as unpaid or at $5.65–$5.85 per hour. Open to high school seniors, recent high school graduates, college freshmen, college sophomores, college juniors, college seniors, recent college graduates, graduate students, individuals reentering the workforce. ▶ *1 sport coordinator:* responsibilities include organizing, planning, and implementing sport leagues and camps in the summer; responsible for adult and youth sport programs. Candidates should have knowledge of field, oral communication skills, organizational skills, self-motivation, strong leadership ability. Duration is May to August. Unpaid. Open to college juniors, college seniors, recent college graduates, graduate students. ▶ *1–2 summer playground supervisors:* responsibilities include organizing, planning, and implementing daily activities for youth 5 years to 6th grade (held off-site at several community sites); responsible for children during their scheduled time. Candidates should have oral communication skills, organizational skills, personal interest in the field, self-motivation, strong interpersonal skills. Duration is early June to early August (8 weeks). Position available as unpaid or at $5.65–$7.50 per hour. Open to high school seniors, recent high school graduates, college freshmen, college sophomores, college juniors, college seniors, recent college graduates. International applications accepted.

Benefits Names of contacts, on-the-job training, opportunity to attend seminars/workshops, possible full-time employment, willing to act as a professional reference, willing to complete paperwork for educational credit, willing to provide letters of recommendation.

Contact Write, call, fax, or e-mail H. Alan Smith, Associate Executive Director. Phone: 717-762-6012. Fax: 717-762-4368. E-mail: alansmith@wboy.org. In-person interview required. Applicants must submit a letter of interest, resume, three personal references. Application deadline: April 1 for summer, July 1 for fall, October 1 for winter. World Wide Web: http://www.wboy.org.

WEDIKO CHILDREN'S SERVICES
72-74 East Dedham Street
Boston, Massachusetts 02118

General Information Organization that operates a 45-day summer Residential Treatment Program for emotionally disturbed children in southern New Hampshire; located on a 450-acre camp-like setting. Established in 1934. Number of employees: 7. Number of internship applications received each year: 300.

Internships Available ▶ *70–100 activity assistants:* responsibilities include working in a residential psycho-educational treatment program serving children and adolescents (ages 7-18) with serious emotional and behavioral disabilities. Candidates should have organizational skills, self-motivation, strong interpersonal skills, strong leadership ability, strong desire to work with special needs children. Duration is late June to late August. $1400–$1700 per duration of internship. ▶ *70–100 direct-care staff:* responsibilities include working as part of a team of 6-8 adults; each team is responsible for a group of 8-10 children/adolescents. Candidates

should have oral communication skills, self-motivation, strong interpersonal skills, strong leadership ability, strong desire to work with special needs children. Duration is late June to late August. $1400–$1700 per duration of internship. ▶ *70–100 direct-care/teaching assistants:* responsibilities include planning and implementing active, learner-centered language arts, math and science curricula. Candidates should have oral communication skills, self-motivation, strong interpersonal skills, strong leadership ability, written communication skills. Duration is late June to late August. $1400–$1700 per duration of internship. Open to college sophomores, college juniors, college seniors, recent college graduates, graduate students, law students, career changers. International applications accepted.

Benefits Formal training, free housing, free meals, job counseling, on-the-job training, opportunity to attend seminars/workshops, possible full-time employment, willing to act as a professional reference, willing to provide letters of recommendation, AmeriCorps education award ($1250).

Contact Write, call, or e-mail Bonnie Thompson, Summer Program Coordinator. Phone: 617-292-9200. Fax: 617-292-9275. E-mail: bthompson@wediko.org. In-person interview recommended (telephone interview accepted). Applicants must submit a formal organization application, letter of recommendation. Applications are accepted continuously. World Wide Web: http://www.wediko.org.

WITTENBRAKER YMCA
1201 Church Street
New Castle, Indiana 47362

General Information Community service center offering all types of activities, educational services, and community events. Established in 1924. Number of employees: 100. Branch of YMCA of the USA, Chicago, Illinois. Number of internship applications received each year: 10.

Internships Available ▶ *1–5 aquatics staff interns:* responsibilities include pool maintenance, swim lesson instruction, lifeguarding, water aerobics instruction, special event planning, and working with youth. Candidates should have ability to work independently, ability to work with others, knowledge of field, oral communication skills, self-motivation, appropriate certificates. Position available as unpaid or paid. Open to college sophomores, college juniors, college seniors, recent college graduates, graduate students. ▶ *1–5 fitness staff interns:* responsibilities include fitness assessments, personal training, developing workout programs, helping with special events, and working with youth. Candidates should have ability to work independently, college courses in field, computer skills, knowledge of field, oral communication skills, personal interest in the field, self-motivation, strong interpersonal skills, writing skills. Position available as unpaid or paid. Open to college freshmen, college sophomores, college juniors, college seniors, recent college graduates, graduate students. ▶ *1–5 sports programs interns:* responsibilities include working with adults and youth; developing sports programs; supervising and organizing programs for YMCA sports director; and all duties associated with wellness/fitness aquatics. Candidates should have ability to work independently, college courses in field, computer skills, knowledge of field, oral communication skills, organizational skills, personal interest in the field, self-motivation, strong interpersonal skills, writing skills. Duration is flexible. Position available as unpaid or paid. Open to college freshmen, college sophomores, college juniors, college seniors, recent college graduates, graduate students. International applications accepted.

Benefits Formal training, job counseling, names of contacts, on-the-job training, opportunity to attend seminars/workshops, possible full-time employment, willing to act as a professional reference, willing to complete paperwork for educational credit, willing to provide letters of recommendation.

Contact Write, call, fax, or e-mail Stephanie Kampmeier, Wellness Director. Phone: 765-529-3804. Fax: 765-529-4575. E-mail: steph570@hotmail.com. In-person interview recommended (telephone interview accepted). Applicants must submit a letter of interest, resume, three personal references. Applications are accepted continuously.

WOMEN IN COMMUNITY SERVICE
1111 3rd Avenue, Room 800
Seattle, Washington 98101

General Information Organization that strives to reduce poverty by promoting self-reliance. Established in 1964. Number of employees: 4. Unit of Women in Community Service, Alexandria, Virginia. Number of internship applications received each year: 20.

Internships Available ▶ *2–4 youth program interns:* responsibilities include guiding former Job Corps students (ages 16-24) in making life transitions. Candidates should have computer skills, oral communication skills, organizational skills, self-motivation, strong interpersonal skills, written communication skills. Duration is 2–6 months. Unpaid. Open to recent high school graduates, college freshmen, college sophomores, college juniors, college seniors, recent college graduates, graduate students, career changers, individuals reentering the workforce. International applications accepted.

Benefits On-the-job training, opportunity to attend seminars/workshops, willing to act as a professional reference, willing to complete paperwork for educational credit, willing to provide letters of recommendation.

Contact Write, call, fax, or e-mail Kathryn Pursch, Community Resource Specialist. Phone: 206-553-2082. Fax: 206-553-6151. E-mail: newvolunteers@aol.com. In-person interview recommended (telephone interview accepted). Applicants must submit a formal organization application, two personal references. Applications are accepted continuously. World Wide Web: http://www.wics.org.

THE WOMEN'S CENTER
133 Park Street, NE
Vienna, Virginia 22180

General Information Private nonprofit group of professionals offering individual counseling and psychotherapy, career counseling, separation and divorce services, support and therapy groups, legal and financial education, workshops, and educational programs. Established in 1974. Number of employees: 95. Number of internship applications received each year: 20.

Internships Available ▶ *1–2 career services interns:* responsibilities include helping to implement career programs, researching, and assisting with the annual conference and the mentoring program. Candidates should have ability to work independently, ability to work with others, office skills, oral communication skills, organizational skills, written communication skills. Duration is 3–6 months. Unpaid. Open to college freshmen, college sophomores, college juniors, college seniors, recent college graduates, graduate students, career changers, individuals reentering the workforce. ▶ *2 development interns:* responsibilities include assisting with fundraising and proposal writing, foundation research, and corporate solicitation. Candidates should have ability to work with others, oral communication skills, personal interest in the field, written communication skills. Duration is 3–6 months. Unpaid. Open to college freshmen, college sophomores, college juniors, college seniors, recent college graduates, graduate students, career changers, individuals reentering the workforce. ▶ *3–6 information/intake interns:* responsibilities include assisting callers by providing information and referrals to meet needs, making counseling appointments, and researching community resources. Candidates should have ability to work independently, oral communication skills, strong interpersonal skills, interest in psychology, social work, and/or women's studies. Duration is 3–12 months. Unpaid. Open to college juniors, college seniors, recent college graduates, graduate students, career changers. ▶ *3 public relations interns:* responsibilities include assisting with developing and implementing marketing strategies, publicity, and media contacts for special events; performing research; making press calls; promoting programs; and participating in program planning. Candidates should have ability to work with others, oral communication skills, personal interest in the field, written communication skills. Duration is flexible. Unpaid. Open to college freshmen, college sophomores, college juniors, college seniors, recent college graduates, graduate students, career changers, individuals reentering the workforce. ▶ *14 therapy/clinical interns:* responsibilities include individual and group psychotherapy and assisting with workshop presentation; some interns also providing career counseling. Duration is 8 months. Unpaid. Open to individuals completing master's degree in social work or professional counseling or a doctorate degree in psychology. International applications accepted.

Benefits On-the-job training, opportunity to attend seminars/workshops, willing to act as a professional reference, willing to complete paperwork for educational credit, willing to provide letters of recommendation.

Contact Write, call, fax, or e-mail Ms. Gale Gearhart, Director of Administration. Phone: 703-281-4928 Ext. 244. Fax: 703-242-1454. E-mail: ggearhart@thewomenscenter.org. In-person interview recommended (telephone interview accepted). Applicants must submit a letter of interest, resume. Applications are accepted continuously. World Wide Web: http://www.thewomenscenter.org.

YAI/NATIONAL INSTITUTE FOR PEOPLE WITH DISABILITIES
460 West 34th Street
New York, New York 10001

General Information Social services agency working with people with mental retardation and/or developmental disabilities in a variety of settings to promote independence and inclusion. Established in 1957. Number of employees: 4,500. Number of internship applications received each year: 150.

Internships Available ▶ *20–30 counselors:* responsibilities include working with adults with developmental disabilities in a residential group home; teaching daily living skills and providing informal counseling. Candidates should have ability to work independently, ability to work with others, personal interest in the field, plan to pursue career in field, related experience a plus but not required. Duration is flexible. Position available as unpaid or paid. Open to recent high school graduates, college freshmen, college sophomores, college juniors, college seniors, recent college graduates, graduate students, career changers, individuals reentering the workforce. ▶ *2–4 human resources interns:* responsibilities include working in fast-paced office with recruitment or benefits team to assist in human resources functions for large not-for-profit agency. Candidates should have ability to work independently, ability to work with others, computer skills, office skills, personal interest in the field. Duration is flexible. Unpaid. Open to college freshmen, college sophomores, college juniors, college seniors, recent college graduates, individuals reentering the workforce. ▶ *10–20 job coaches:* responsibilities include working with adults with mental retardation; providing job training skills and follow-up counseling. Candidates should have ability to work independently, ability to work with others, computer skills, knowledge of field, personal interest in the field, plan to pursue career in field. Duration is flexible. Unpaid. Open to college freshmen, college sophomores, college juniors, college seniors, recent college graduates, graduate students, career changers, individuals reentering the workforce. ▶ *20–30 teacher/teacher assistants:* responsibilities include working with adults with mental retardation in a classroom-setting; providing hands-on teaching of daily living skills and community integration. Candidates should have ability to work independently, ability to work with others, personal interest in the field, plan to pursue career in field, experience a plus but not required. Duration is flexible. Position available as unpaid or paid. Open to recent high school graduates, college freshmen, college sophomores, college juniors, college seniors, recent college graduates, graduate students, career changers, individuals reentering the workforce. International applications accepted.

Benefits Formal training, job counseling, names of contacts, on-the-job training, opportunity to attend seminars/workshops, possible full-time employment, willing to act as a professional reference, willing to complete paperwork for educational credit, willing to provide letters of recommendation.

Contact Write, call, fax, e-mail, or through World Wide Web site Human Resources. Phone: 212-273-6165. Fax: 212-563-4836. E-mail: careers@yai.org. In-person interview recommended (telephone interview accepted). Applicants must submit a formal organization application, letter of interest, resume, four letters of recommendation. Applications are accepted continuously. World Wide Web: http://www.yai.org.

YMCA/MENTOR DULUTH
302 West First Street
Duluth, Minnesota 55802

General Information   Program that works with youth and families (usually low income, single parent households) to provide adult mentors for children. Established in 1882. Number of employees: 200. Number of internship applications received each year: 5.
Internships Available   ▶ *100 AmeriCorps interns:* responsibilities include direct and indirect service; working with underprivileged youth, human needs, and volunteerism. Candidates should have ability to work independently, computer skills, personal interest in the field, strong interpersonal skills, experience working with youth. Duration is 1 year. Educational stipend and living allowance. Open to recent high school graduates, college freshmen, college sophomores, college juniors, college seniors, recent college graduates, graduate students, law students, career changers, individuals reentering the workforce, individuals 18 years of age, retired persons. ▶ *6–8 human services interns:* responsibilities include working with families using interviewing skills; performing casework; maintaining contact with adult volunteers and families; planning, implementing, and evaluating special programs/activities. Candidates should have ability to work independently, college degree in related field, oral communication skills, self-motivation, strong interpersonal skills. Duration is 6–12 months. Unpaid. Open to graduate students. International applications accepted.
Benefits   Names of contacts, possible full-time employment, travel reimbursement, willing to complete paperwork for educational credit, willing to provide letters of recommendation, free YMCA membership.
Contact   Write, call, or e-mail Mr. Blair Gagne, Program Director. Phone: 218-722-4745 Ext. 125. E-mail: bgagne@duluthymca.org. In-person interview required. Applicants must submit a resume, three personal references. Applications are accepted continuously.

YMCA OF GREATER TOLEDO, WEST BRANCH
2020 Tremainsville
Toledo, Ohio 43613

General Information   Organization that institutes Christian principles through programs that build a healthy spirit, mind, and body for all. Established in 1865. Number of employees: 120. Unit of YMCA of Greater Toledo, Toledo, Ohio. Number of internship applications received each year: 5.
Internships Available   ▶ *1–3 outdoor pool manager interns/assistant manager interns:* responsibilities include marketing; budgeting; hiring, supervising, and evaluating a staff of 30–45; and maintaining daily operations and upkeep of pool. Candidates should have ability to work with others, experience in the field, oral communication skills, self-motivation, strong leadership ability. Duration is 5–9 months. $6–$7.50 per hour. Open to college sophomores, college juniors, college seniors. ▶ *1–2 program director interns:* responsibilities include helping to plan, budget, and manage the program department for youth sports, teens, aquatics, family programming, and fitness; helping prepare flyers, newsletters, and brochures; performing public relations duties. Candidates should have ability to work with others, experience in the field, oral communication skills, organizational skills, plan to pursue career in field, self-motivation. Duration is 6–9 months. Position available as unpaid or paid. Open to college juniors, college seniors.
Benefits   Formal training, names of contacts, opportunity to attend seminars/workshops, possible full-time employment, willing to act as a professional reference, willing to complete paperwork for educational credit, willing to provide letters of recommendation, national YMCA job listings provided.
Contact   Write, call, or fax David Thompson, Executive Director. Phone: 419-475-3496. Fax: 419-475-8837. In-person interview recom-

mended (telephone interview accepted). Applicants must submit a formal organization application. Application deadline: March 1 for summer.

YMCA OF METROPOLITAN MOBILE, INC.
PO Box 2272
Mobile, Alabama 36652

General Information   Organization that provides instruction and assistance in the areas of health/wellness, community service, youth and adult sports, aquatics programming, and child care. Established in 1856. Number of employees: 400. Number of internship applications received each year: 15.
Internships Available   ▶ *2–4 administrative interns:* responsibilities include assisting executive director in developing membership appreciation special events, dealing with member service issues, leading customer service training for staff. Candidates should have oral communication skills, organizational skills, self-motivation, strong interpersonal skills, written communication skills. Duration is as required by intern's school. Unpaid. Open to college freshmen, college sophomores, college juniors, college seniors, recent college graduates, graduate students. ▶ *1–14 child-care/summer day camp interns:* responsibilities include assisting with administration and planning of summer day camp and child-care programs. Candidates should have ability to work with others, oral communication skills, organizational skills. Unpaid. Open to high school students, recent high school graduates, college freshmen, college sophomores, college juniors, college seniors, recent college graduates, graduate students, law students, career changers, individuals reentering the workforce. ▶ *2–4 fitness interns:* responsibilities include assisting fitness director in fitness testing, program implementation, and senior and women's programs. Candidates should have knowledge of field, oral communication skills, self-motivation, strong interpersonal skills, written communication skills. Duration is as required by intern's school. Unpaid. Open to college freshmen, college sophomores, college juniors, college seniors, recent college graduates, graduate students. ▶ *2–14 youth sports interns:* responsibilities include assisting in planning and administration of YMCA youth sports programs. Candidates should have ability to work independently, ability to work with others, analytical skills, knowledge of field, oral communication skills, organizational skills, personal interest in the field, plan to pursue career in field, self-motivation, strong leadership ability, writing skills. Duration is fall, spring, or summer semesters. Unpaid. Open to high school students, recent high school graduates, college freshmen, college sophomores, college juniors, college seniors, recent college graduates, graduate students, law students, career changers, individuals reentering the workforce. International applications accepted.
Benefits   On-the-job training, possible full-time employment, willing to act as a professional reference, willing to complete paperwork for educational credit, willing to provide letters of recommendation.
Contact   Write, fax, or e-mail Patrick Davenport, Vice President of Operations/COO, PO Box 2272, Mobile, Alabama 36652. Fax: 251-438-1174. E-mail: pdavenport@ymcasalabama.org. No phone calls. In-person interview recommended (telephone interview accepted). Applicants must submit a formal organization application, letter of interest, resume, personal reference, drug test; criminal background check required. Applications are accepted continuously.

YMCA SAFE PLACE SERVICES
2400 Crittenden Drive
Louisville, Kentucky 40217

General Information   Agency that provides emergency shelter counseling and case management care to teens with serious family problems. Established in 1974. Number of employees: 40. Unit of YMCA of Greater Louisville, Louisville, Kentucky. Number of internship applications received each year: 25.
Internships Available   ▶ *2 administrative interns:* responsibilities include assisting in the development of grant and foundation proposals and performing quality assurance studies. Candidates should have computer skills, editing skills, office skills, organizational skills, research skills, writing skills. Duration is 1–2 semesters.

Unpaid. Open to college freshmen, college sophomores, college juniors, college seniors, recent college graduates. ▶ *1–2 clerical interns:* responsibilities include filing, typing, and performing computer work. Candidates should have analytical skills, computer skills, office skills, research skills, self-motivation, writing skills. Duration is 1–2 semesters. Unpaid. Open to recent high school graduates, college freshmen, college sophomores, college juniors, college seniors, recent college graduates, graduate students, career changers. ▶ *1–2 education teachers:* responsibilities include teaching and tutoring of homeless youth during after-school hours. Candidates should have oral communication skills, personal interest in the field, self-motivation, strong interpersonal skills, written communication skills. Duration is 1–2 semesters. Unpaid. Open to college juniors, college seniors, recent college graduates, graduate students. ▶ *2–4 social workers/counselors:* responsibilities include counseling individuals, groups, and families; presenting life skills; and conducting informal discussions with youth. Candidates should have ability to work independently, office skills, oral communication skills, plan to pursue career in field, self-motivation, strong interpersonal skills, written communication skills. Duration is 1–2 semesters. Unpaid. Open to graduate students working toward master's degree in social work-related field. ▶ *4–6 youth workers:* responsibilities include supervising 8-10 youths in meal preparation, chores, and recreation. Candidates should have oral communication skills, self-motivation, strong interpersonal skills, strong leadership ability, written communication skills. Duration is 1–2 semesters. Position available as unpaid or at $8–$9 per hour. Open to high school graduates (at least associate degree desirable), must be 21 or over. International applications accepted.

Benefits Formal training, free meals, names of contacts, opportunity to attend seminars/workshops, possible full-time employment, willing to act as a professional reference, willing to complete paperwork for educational credit, willing to provide letters of recommendation.

Contact Write, fax, or e-mail Sonny M. Hatfield, Director of Counseling Services. Fax: 502-635-1443. E-mail: shatfield@ymcalouisville.org. No phone calls. In-person interview required. Applicants must submit a resume. Applications are accepted continuously. World Wide Web: http://www.ymcalouisville.org.

YOUTH AND SHELTER SERVICES, INC.
420 Kellogg, PO Box 1628
Ames, Iowa 50010

General Information Organization that exists to help children, youth, and families solve problems, grow, and become self-sufficient, responsible, contributing members of society. Established in 1976. Number of employees: 180. Number of internship applications received each year: 20.

Internships Available ▶ *Administrative interns:* responsibilities include duties in various departments including public relations, conference planning, or general administration. Candidates should have ability to work with others, college courses in field, computer skills, editing skills, office skills, organizational skills. Duration is 1 semester or 1 summer. Unpaid. Open to college freshmen, college sophomores, college juniors, college seniors. ▶ *Human services interns:* responsibilities include assisting with various programs including foster care, residential center, drug treatment, and day care. Candidates should have college courses in field, personal interest in the field, plan to pursue career in field, strong interpersonal skills. Duration is 1 semester or 1 summer. Unpaid. Open to college juniors, college seniors. International applications accepted.

Benefits Formal training, names of contacts, opportunity to attend seminars/workshops, possible full-time employment, willing to complete paperwork for educational credit, willing to provide letters of recommendation.

Contact Write, call, fax, e-mail, or through World Wide Web site Phyllis Craig, Volunteer Coordinator. Phone: 515-233-3141. Fax: 515-233-2440. E-mail: pcraig@yss.ames.ia.us. In-person interview recommended (telephone interview accepted). Applicants must submit a formal organization application, letter of interest, resume,

2-3 personal references. Application deadline: May 1 for summer, August 1 for fall, December 30 for spring. World Wide Web: http://www.yss.ames.ia.us.

YOUTH ENRICHMENT SERVICES (YES)
PO Box 105
West Islip, New York 11795

General Information Youth services organization. Established in 1987. Number of employees: 60. Number of internship applications received each year: 10.

Internships Available ▶ *2–5 bookkeeper/administrative assistant interns:* responsibilities include working under the direction of executive director and administrative assistant; grant development, bookkeeping, fiscal responsibilities, vouchering. Candidates should have ability to work independently, analytical skills, computer skills, organizational skills, self-motivation, written communication skills. Duration is flexible. Unpaid. Open to high school seniors, recent high school graduates, college freshmen, college sophomores, college juniors, college seniors, recent college graduates, individuals reentering the workforce. ▶ *1–2 executive director interns:* responsibilities include working with the executive director on budgeting, planning, fiscal implementation, grant writing, program development, monitoring, evaluation, community liaison, meetings, and special initiatives. Candidates should have ability to work independently, college courses in field, computer skills, plan to pursue career in field, strong interpersonal skills, strong leadership ability. Duration is flexible. Unpaid. Open to college juniors, college seniors, recent college graduates, graduate students, law students, career changers, individuals reentering the workforce. ▶ *2–5 program coordinator interns:* responsibilities include assisting and training with the staff program coordinators and the executive director; outreach, delivery of direct services, community liaison. Candidates should have ability to work with others, computer skills, oral communication skills, organizational skills, self-motivation, strong leadership ability. Duration is flexible. Unpaid. Open to high school students, recent high school graduates, college freshmen, college sophomores, college juniors, college seniors, recent college graduates, graduate students, law students, career changers, individuals reentering the workforce. ▶ *1–2 senior program coordinator interns:* responsibilities include overseeing programs; some budgeting, staff training, and supervision; community liaison, outreach, meetings, and program scheduling; all under senior program coordinator's direction. Candidates should have ability to work with others, computer skills, oral communication skills, organizational skills, self-motivation, strong leadership ability. Duration is flexible. Unpaid. Open to college sophomores, college juniors, college seniors, recent college graduates, graduate students, law students, career changers, individuals reentering the workforce. International applications accepted.

Benefits Formal training, names of contacts, on-the-job training, opportunity to attend seminars/workshops, possible full-time employment, willing to act as a professional reference, willing to complete paperwork for educational credit, willing to provide letters of recommendation.

Contact Write, call, fax, e-mail, or through World Wide Web site Mary Ann Pfeiffer, Executive Director. Phone: 631-587-5172. Fax: 631-661-2973. E-mail: yesletters@aol.com. In-person interview recommended (telephone interview accepted). Applicants must submit a formal organization application, letter of interest, resume, academic transcripts, three personal references. Applications are accepted continuously. World Wide Web: http://www.yesnews.org.

YOUTH OPPORTUNITIES UPHELD
172 Lincoln Street
Worcester, Massachusetts 01605

General Information Nonprofit organization that provides troubled adolescents and families with opportunities to deal with problems in ways that promote development as individuals and as contributing members of society. Established in 1970. Number of employees: 20. Number of internship applications received each year: 150.

Internships Available ▶ *10–35 court mentor program interns:* responsibilities include working as an outreach counselor for

Youth Opportunities Upheld (continued)

"court-involved" or at-risk adolescents who are struggling with individual or family problems, filing weekly/monthly reports, attending weekly staff meeting, and organizing activities. Candidates should have ability to work independently, self-motivation, strong interpersonal skills, strong leadership ability. Duration is 6–12 months. Unpaid. Open to college freshmen, college sophomores, college juniors, college seniors, graduate students. ▶ *Educational counselors:* responsibilities include working in an alternative school for troubled adolescents, tutoring, participating in sports or activities, and monitoring behaviors on a daily point sheet. Candidates should have ability to work with others, oral communication skills, organizational skills, personal interest in the field, writing skills. Duration is one academic year. Unpaid. Open to college freshmen, college sophomores, college juniors, college seniors, graduate students. ▶ *8 graduate clinical interns:* responsibilities include performing individual/family counseling, assessments, observations, and therapy sessions. Candidates should have analytical skills, college degree in related field, plan to pursue career in field, strong interpersonal skills. Duration is one academic year. Unpaid. Open to graduate students. ▶ *Residential counselors:* responsibilities include working in a residential home for troubled adolescents, attending group meetings, working as an advocate to youth, and participating in activities that are set up for youth. Candidates should have oral communication skills, personal interest in the field, self-motivation, strong interpersonal skills. Duration is one academic year. Unpaid. Open to college freshmen, college sophomores, college juniors, college seniors, graduate students. ▶ *2 teen parent counselors:* responsibilities include assisting staff in planning group activities, spending time with teenage mothers, assisting in weekly menu planning, and participating as a positive role model. Candidates should have oral communication skills, personal interest in the field, strong interpersonal skills, written communication skills. Duration is one academic year. Unpaid. Open to college freshmen, college sophomores, college juniors, college seniors, graduate students. International applications accepted.

Benefits Formal training, names of contacts, opportunity to attend seminars/workshops, possible full-time employment, travel reimbursement, willing to act as a professional reference, willing to complete paperwork for educational credit, willing to provide letters of recommendation.

Contact Write, call, or fax Lenore Johnson, Coordinator of Mentoring and Prevention Services. Phone: 508-770-0511 Ext. 114. Fax: 508-770-0875. E-mail: johnsonl@youinc.org. In-person interview required. Applicants must submit a formal organization application, letter of interest, resume, three letters of recommendation, criminal records check required. Applications are accepted continuously. World Wide Web: http://www.youinc.org.

YWCA/DOMESTIC VIOLENCE PREVENTION CENTER
626 Church Street
Lynchburg, Virginia 24504

General Information Organization that serves battered women and their children and seeks to eliminate abuse. Established in 1978. Number of employees: 20. Unit of YWCA of the USA, New York, New York. Number of internship applications received each year: 5.

Internships Available ▶ *3–6 interns:* responsibilities include providing casework assistance with both children and adults. Candidates should have ability to work independently, ability to work with others, computer skills, office skills, oral communication skills, personal interest in the field, self-motivation, written communication skills. Duration is 1 semester. Unpaid. Open to college seniors, graduate students, individuals reentering the workforce. International applications accepted.

Benefits Formal training, on-the-job training, opportunity to attend seminars/workshops, possible full-time employment, travel reimbursement, willing to act as a professional reference, willing to complete paperwork for educational credit, willing to provide letters of recommendation.

Contact Write, call, or fax Sheila Andrews, DVPC Director. Phone: 434-528-1041. Fax: 434-847-2529. In-person interview required. Applicants must submit a resume. Applications are accepted continuously.

YWCA OF DAYTON OHIO
141 West Third Street
Dayton, Ohio 45402

General Information Organization whose mission is to provide the tools for women to achieve self-sufficiency and create a safer environment; programs include shelter services for domestic violence, homeless, pregnant/parent teens and childcare and teen services. Established in 1870. Number of employees: 80. Affiliate of YWCA of the USA, New York, New York.

Internships Available ▶ *1–2 Girls Inc. summer interns:* responsibilities include assisting with teaching Girls Inc. curriculum, "day camp" activities, and field trips; for more information on Girls Inc., refer to National Web site, www.girlsinc.org. Candidates should have ability to work independently, ability to work with others, oral communication skills, plan to pursue career in field, major in education, human service, or social service related field. Duration is 8–12 weeks. Position available as unpaid or at $8–$8.50 per hour. Open to college juniors, college seniors. International applications accepted.

Benefits On-the-job training, possible full-time employment, willing to act as a professional reference, willing to complete paperwork for educational credit, willing to provide letters of recommendation.

Contact Call, fax, or e-mail Susan Gartner, Teen Manager. Phone: 937-461-5550 Ext. 124. Fax: 937-222-0610. E-mail: sgartner@ywcadayton.org. In-person interview required. Applicants must submit a formal organization application, letter of interest, resume, three personal references. Application deadline: May 15. World Wide Web: http://www.ywcadayton.org.

YWCA OF GREATER HARRISBURG
1101 Market Street
Harrisburg, Pennsylvania 17103

General Information Organization that actively serves as an advocate and resource to the community on issues that impact women and children and provides services to empower women, including violence intervention and prevention, child care, and housing. Established in 1894. Number of employees: 100. Number of internship applications received each year: 10.

Internships Available ▶ *8 advocate interns:* responsibilities include working the hot line, attending emergency hospital and preliminary hearing in sexual assault and domestic violence cases, research, case management, and documentation. Candidates should have analytical skills, oral communication skills, self-motivation, strong interpersonal skills, written communication skills. Duration is flexible (spring, summer, and fall programs). Unpaid. Open to high school seniors, recent high school graduates, college freshmen, college sophomores, college juniors, college seniors, recent college graduates, graduate students, law students, career changers, individuals reentering the workforce, must be 18 years or older. ▶ *1–4 assistant group supervisors:* responsibilities include assisting in classroom management; providing interesting, challenging educational opportunities for children ages 2 months to 12 years; writing lesson plans; producing displays; interacting with children; and meeting with teachers. Candidates should have ability to work with others, knowledge of field, self-motivation, written communication skills. Duration is flexible (spring, summer, and fall programs). Unpaid. Open to recent high school graduates, college freshmen, college sophomores, college juniors, college seniors, recent college graduates, graduate students, law students, career changers, individuals reentering the workforce. ▶ *1 education specialist:* responsibilities include grant writing and responding to community organizations' requests for information and training in the areas of sexual assault, domestic violence, and anti-violence. Duration is flexible (spring, summer, and fall programs). Unpaid. Open to high school students, recent high school graduates, college freshmen, college sophomores, college juniors, college seniors, recent college graduates, graduate students, law students, career changers, individuals reentering the workforce. International applications accepted.

Benefits Formal training, names of contacts, possible full-time employment, willing to complete paperwork for educational credit, willing to provide letters of recommendation.

Contact Write, call, fax, or e-mail Jennifer Cooper, Assistant Director of Violence and Prevention Services. Phone: 717-238-7273. Fax: 717-238-4533. E-mail: jcooper@ywcahbg.org. In-person interview required. Applicants must submit a formal organization application, resume. Applications are accepted continuously.

YWCA OF ST. PAUL
375 Selby Avenue
St. Paul, Minnesota 55102-1822

General Information Nonprofit membership-based organization dedicated to the advancement of women and families. Established in 1907. Number of employees: 117. Affiliate of YWCA of the USA, New York, New York. Number of internship applications received each year: 20.

Internships Available ▶ *1–3 case manager interns:* responsibilities include assisting case managers in providing direction to homeless women by helping them develop plans to eliminate barriers to self-sufficiency through education/employment and stabilized housing. Candidates should have ability to work independently, college courses in field, oral communication skills, personal interest in the field, strong interpersonal skills. Duration is 3 months (minimum). Unpaid. Open to college juniors, college seniors, recent college graduates, graduate students. ▶ *1–3 child enrichment center interns:* responsibilities include participating in the children's program by developing and implementing activities appropriate to the curriculum and providing support to the child development specialists. Candidates should have ability to work independently, analytical skills, experience in the field, personal interest in the field, self-motivation, strong interpersonal skills. Duration is 3 months (minimum). Unpaid. Open to college freshmen, college sophomores, college juniors, college seniors, recent college graduates, graduate students, career changers, individuals reentering the workforce. ▶ *1 child-care intern:* responsibilities include assisting in the preparation, implementation, and evaluation of a school-age child-care program. Candidates should have experience in the field, oral communication skills, personal interest in the field, strong interpersonal skills, strong leadership ability. Duration is 3 months (minimum). Unpaid. Open to college freshmen, college sophomores, college juniors, college seniors, recent college graduates, graduate students, career changers. ▶ *1–2 girls' programming interns:* responsibilities include researching, developing, and delivering programs for girls ages 7-14; becoming a positive role model and mentor for girls in the program. Candidates should have oral communication skills, organizational skills, personal interest in the field, strong interpersonal skills, strong leadership ability. Duration is 3 months (minimum). Unpaid. Open to college freshmen, college sophomores, college juniors, college seniors, recent college graduates, graduate students, career changers, individuals reentering the workforce. ▶ *1 housing intake intern:* responsibilities include assisting with day-to-day operations of a transitional housing program, including staffing the intake phone line and providing program support. Candidates should have ability to work independently, office skills, oral communication skills, personal interest in the field, strong interpersonal skills, written communication skills. Duration is 3 months (minimum). Unpaid. Open to college freshmen, college sophomores, college juniors, college seniors, recent college graduates, graduate students, career changers, individuals reentering the workforce. ▶ *1 mentoring project intern:* responsibilities include assisting in coordinating and leading group mentoring for girls. Candidates should have ability to work independently, ability to work with others, computer skills, experience in the field, oral communication skills, organizational skills, strong leadership ability. Duration is 3 months (minimum). Unpaid. Open to college sophomores, college juniors, college seniors, recent college graduates, graduate students, career changers, individuals reentering the workforce. ▶ *1 support services intern:* responsibilities include assisting in monitoring the school attendance of elementary-age students who are part of a family

intervention project and maintaining accurate information pertaining to their progress. Candidates should have ability to work independently, college courses in field, oral communication skills, personal interest in the field, strong interpersonal skills. Duration is 3 months (minimum). Unpaid. Open to college juniors, college seniors, recent college graduates, graduate students, career changers, individuals reentering the workforce. ▶ *1 volunteer coordinator intern:* responsibilities include recruiting, screening, and training potential volunteers, and assisting with volunteer program management. Candidates should have ability to work independently, computer skills, office skills, oral communication skills, organizational skills, personal interest in the field, strong interpersonal skills, written communication skills. Duration is 3 months (minimum). Unpaid. Open to college freshmen, college sophomores, college juniors, college seniors, recent college graduates, career changers, individuals reentering the workforce. ▶ *1 youth achievers intern:* responsibilities include helping facilitate an after-school program, developing and implementing behavior management techniques, and implementing individual service plans for youth and families. Candidates should have experience in the field, oral communication skills, personal interest in the field, strong interpersonal skills, strong leadership ability. Duration is 3 months (minimum). Unpaid. Open to college sophomores, college juniors, college seniors, recent college graduates, graduate students, career changers. International applications accepted.

Benefits Names of contacts, on-the-job training, opportunity to attend seminars/workshops, possible full-time employment, travel reimbursement, willing to act as a professional reference, willing to complete paperwork for educational credit, willing to provide letters of recommendation.

Contact Write, call, fax, or e-mail JoAnne Peters, Volunteer Services Coordinator. Phone: 651-265-0722. Fax: 651-222-6307. E-mail: volunteer@ywcaofstpaul.org. In-person interview recommended (telephone interview accepted). Applicants must submit a formal organization application, letter of interest, resume, three personal references, criminal background check required (paid for by YWCA). Applications are accepted continuously. World Wide Web: http://www.ywcaofstpaul.org.

YWCA OF WESTERN NEW YORK
190 Franklin Street
Buffalo, New York 14202

General Information Membership movement of women of diverse beliefs, faiths, and values committed to the empowerment of women. Established in 1870. Number of employees: 100.

Internships Available ▶ *2 assistant case managers:* responsibilities include conducting intake interviews, documenting files, scheduling presentations, and facilitating workshops. Candidates should have experience in social service setting. Duration is flexible. Unpaid. Open to individuals with at least associate degree. ▶ *1–5 child-care assistants:* responsibilities include assisting in planning activities for children ages 6 weeks-5 years and working cooperatively with teachers and parents. Duration is flexible. Position available as unpaid or paid. Open to individuals with at least associate degree. ▶ *2 child-care curriculum developers:* responsibilities include developing a curriculum for children ages 6 weeks-12 years in science, math, health, safety, and social studies. Candidates should have minimum one year of experience working with children. Duration is flexible. Unpaid. Open to individuals with associate degree in early childhood education. ▶ *15 extended-day program aides:* responsibilities include developing weekly program plans for children ages 5-12; researching reference articles and organizations; establishing a library system of articles, games, and crafts; and working with children. Candidates should have minimum one year of experience with school-age children. Duration is 9 months. Position available as unpaid or paid. Open to individuals with high school diploma. ▶ *1–2 grant research assistants:* responsibilities include researching funding opportunities and compiling required data. Candidates should have written communication skills. Duration is flexible. Unpaid. Open to individuals with high school diploma. ▶ *1 health and wellness assistant:* responsibilities include teaching fitness classes; marketing programs, outreach events, and demonstrations; and assisting with mailings

YWCA of Western New York (continued)

and filing. Duration is 8–10 weeks. Unpaid. Open to individuals with high school diploma. ▶ *1 residence program aide:* responsibilities include performing crisis management, coordinating resident services, recording behavioral data, directing facility supervision services, monitoring medications, and alternating as group team leader. Candidates should have experience in residence community setting. Duration is flexible. Unpaid. Open to individuals with at least associate degree. ▶ *1–2 special events/public relations interns:* responsibilities include assisting in the arrangement and promotion of special events and helping with publicity. Candidates should have ability to work independently, computer skills, oral communication skills, organizational skills, research skills, self-motivation, strong interpersonal skills, written communication skills. Duration is flexible. Unpaid. Open to individuals with high school diploma. ▶ *2 teen center program aide interns:* responsibili-

ties include performing outreach, facilitating group discussion and workshops, and communicating with teens about available services. Duration is flexible. Unpaid. Open to individuals with at least 2 years of post-secondary education. International applications accepted.

Benefits Formal training, opportunity to attend seminars/workshops, possible full-time employment, willing to complete paperwork for educational credit, willing to provide letters of recommendation.

Contact Write, call, or fax Donna Mostiller, Human Resources Manager. Phone: 716-852-6120. Fax: 716-852-1629. In-person interview required. Applicants must submit a letter of interest, resume, three letters of recommendation, writing sample (for grant research position). Applications are accepted continuously. World Wide Web: http://www.ywca-wny.org.

INFORMATION

GENERAL

ACCURACY IN MEDIA
4455 Connecticut Avenue, NW, Suite 330
Washington, District of Columbia 20008

General Information Nonprofit educational organization whose purpose is to monitor bias and inaccuracies in the news media through a newsletter and news column. Established in 1969. Number of employees: 10. Number of internship applications received each year: 50.

Internships Available ▶ *1 assistant MIS manager:* responsibilities include assisting MIS chief with maintenance of office computer systems. Candidates should have ability to work independently, computer skills, office skills, organizational skills, personal interest in the field, self-motivation, strong interpersonal skills. Duration is 3–6 months. Position available as unpaid or at $125 per week. Open to high school students, recent high school graduates, college freshmen, college sophomores, college juniors, college seniors, recent college graduates, graduate students, law students, career changers, individuals reentering the workforce.
▶ *1 assistant Web master:* responsibilities include assisting Web master with maintaining and designing Web sites. Candidates should have ability to work independently, analytical skills, computer skills, editing skills, organizational skills, personal interest in the field, research skills, self-motivation, strong interpersonal skills, strong leadership ability, writing skills. Duration is 3–12 months. Position available as unpaid or at $125 per week. Open to high school students, recent high school graduates, college freshmen, college sophomores, college juniors, college seniors, recent college graduates, graduate students, law students, career changers, individuals reentering the workforce. ▶ *1 graphic artist:* responsibilities include creating and designing advertising and marketing materials. Candidates should have ability to work independently, computer skills, editing skills, personal interest in the field, plan to pursue career in field, self-motivation, writing skills. Duration is 3–12 months. $125 per week. Open to recent high school graduates, college freshmen, college sophomores, college juniors, college seniors, recent college graduates, graduate students. ▶ *1–2 marketing assistants:* responsibilities include assisting with marketing, public relations, and advertising for the organization, with a focus on the Internet. Candidates should have ability to work independently, analytical skills, computer skills, editing skills, oral communication skills, organizational skills, personal interest in the field, plan to pursue career in field, self-motivation, strong interpersonal skills, writing skills. Duration is 3–6 months. Position available as unpaid or at $125 per week. Open to high school students, recent high school graduates, college freshmen, college sophomores, college juniors, college seniors, recent college graduates, graduate students, law students, career changers, individuals reentering the workforce. ▶ *1–2 writers:* responsibilities include researching and writing articles for the organization's Web site. Candidates should have ability to work independently, analytical skills, computer skills, editing skills, organizational skills, personal interest in the field, research skills, self-motivation, strong interpersonal skills, writing skills. Duration is 3–6 months. Position available as unpaid or at $125 per week. Open to high school students, recent high school graduates, college freshmen, college sophomores, college juniors, college seniors, recent college graduates, graduate students, law students, career changers, individuals reentering the workforce.

Benefits On-the-job training, opportunity to attend seminars/workshops, possible full-time employment, willing to act as a professional reference, willing to complete paperwork for educational credit, willing to provide letters of recommendation.
Contact Write, fax, e-mail, or through World Wide Web site Mr. Don Irvine, Executive Director. Fax: 202-364-4098. E-mail: aimintern@yahoo.com. No phone calls. In-person interview recommended (telephone interview accepted). Applicants must submit a formal organization application, letter of interest, resume, academic transcripts, two writing samples. Application deadline: March 31 for summer, August 15 for fall, October 31 for spring. World Wide Web: http://www.aim.org/.

BLACK SPEAKERS ONLINE
235 East Queen Street
Inglewood, California 90301

General Information Organization that offers a directory of black speakers from a wide range of budgets, geographical areas, topics, talents, and entertainments. Established in 1996. Number of employees: 10. Division of Speakers Etcetera, Inglewood, California. Number of internship applications received each year: 150.

Internships Available ▶ *15–20 university services interns:* responsibilities include marketing speakers and services to universities. Candidates should have ability to work independently, analytical skills, oral communication skills, self-motivation, strong interpersonal skills. Duration is September 1 to March 1. Commission. Open to college sophomores, college juniors, graduate students, career changers.

Benefits Names of contacts, opportunity to attend seminars/workshops, possible full-time employment, travel reimbursement, willing to act as a professional reference, willing to complete paperwork for educational credit, willing to provide letters of recommendation.
Contact E-mail Raoul Davis, Director University Services, 812 Brook Hill Road, Richmond 23227. Fax: 310-671-0123. E-mail: speakersblack@hotmail.com. No phone calls. Telephone interview required. Applicants must submit a formal organization application, resume. Application deadline: June 1. World Wide Web: http://www.blackspeakers.net.

CENTER FOR INVESTIGATIVE REPORTING, INC.
131 Steuart Street, Suite 600
San Francisco, California 94105

General Information Nonprofit organization producing television and print media reports on national and international issues including the environment, science, public health, constitutional government-freedom of information, social justice, international affairs, economic and financial issues, and the public trust. Established in 1977. Number of employees: 10. Number of internship applications received each year: 100.

Internships Available ▶ *4–6 interns:* responsibilities include working closely with staff reporters on tasks including research, information organization, story development, and production. Candidates should have analytical skills, oral communication skills, personal interest in the field, plan to pursue career in field, self-motivation, written communication skills. Duration is 5 months. Monthly stipend of $500. Open to college freshmen, college sophomores, college juniors, college seniors, recent college graduates, graduate students, law students, career changers, individuals reentering the workforce. International applications accepted.

Center for Investigative Reporting, Inc. (continued)

Benefits Names of contacts, opportunity to attend seminars/ workshops, possible full-time employment, willing to complete paperwork for educational credit, willing to provide letters of recommendation.
Contact Write, call, fax, e-mail, or through World Wide Web site Intern Coordinator. Phone: 415-543-1200. Fax: 415-543-8311. E-mail: center@cironline.org. Applicants must submit a letter of interest, resume, 2-3 writing samples. Application deadline: May 1 for summer/fall (July to November), December 1 for winter/ spring (February to June). World Wide Web: http://www. muckraker.org.

THE CHRISTOPHERS
12 East 48th Street
New York, New York 10017

General Information Nonprofit media organization. Established in 1945. Number of employees: 35. Number of internship applications received each year: 100.
Internships Available ▶ *1–2 editorial interns:* responsibilities include copyediting, fact checking, research, some writing, and general office duties including but not limited to filing, photocopying, and data entry. Candidates should have ability to work independently, editing skills, personal interest in the field, research skills, strong interpersonal skills, writing skills. Duration is one semester, winter (5 weeks), or summer (10-12 weeks). Unpaid. Open to college sophomores, college juniors, college seniors. International applications accepted.
Benefits Willing to act as a professional reference, willing to provide letters of recommendation.
Contact Write or e-mail Regina Pappalardo, Youth Coordinator. Phone: 212-759-4050. Fax: 212-759-6946. E-mail: youth@christophers. org. In-person interview required. Applicants must submit a letter of interest, resume, 2 or more writing samples. Applications are accepted continuously. World Wide Web: http://www. christophers.org.

NAPLES FREE-NET
2655 Northbrooke Drive
Naples, Florida 34119

General Information Community-oriented free Internet service provider, homeport for local nonprofit organizations and provider of introductory education on how to use the Internet. Established in 1995. Number of internship applications received each year: 30.
Internships Available ▶ *Interns:* responsibilities include developing Web sites, programming, surveys, and office assistance to an ISP community network. Candidates should have ability to work with others, computer skills, oral communication skills, self-motivation, written communication skills, Web skills. Duration is flexible. Unpaid. Open to high school students, recent high school graduates, college freshmen, college sophomores, college juniors, college seniors, recent college graduates, graduate students, law students, career changers, individuals reentering the workforce. International applications accepted.
Benefits Housing at a cost, names of contacts, on-the-job training, opportunity to attend seminars/workshops, willing to act as a professional reference, willing to complete paperwork for educational credit, willing to provide letters of recommendation.
Contact E-mail or through World Wide Web site Dr. Melody Hainsworth, Internship Committee Chair. Fax: 941-513-9696. E-mail: intern@naples.net. No phone calls. Telephone interview required. Applicants must submit a letter of interest, resume, e-mail correspondence. Applications are accepted continuously. World Wide Web: http://www.naples.net.

NATIONAL SECURITY AND NATURAL RESOURCES NEWS SERVICE
1100 Connecticut Avenue, NW, Suite 1310
Washington, District of Columbia 20036

General Information Nonprofit news service that works to increase and improve the major news media coverage of military, arms control, and international security stories as well as environmental and natural resources stories. Established in 1990. Number of employees: 6. Unit of Public Education Center, Inc., Washington, District of Columbia. Number of internship applications received each year: 30.
Internships Available ▶ *2–6 National Security News Service journalism and research interns:* responsibilities include assisting reporters with investigative stories on the military and defense industries and environmental issues. Duration is 1 semester. Unpaid. ▶ *2–6 natural resources news service journalism and research interns:* responsibilities include assisting reporters with investigative stories on the environment (both foreign and domestic) for eventual publication in the major news media. Duration is 2 months. Unpaid. ▶ *2–6 science news service interns:* responsibilities include assisting reporters with investigative stories about science issues (both foreign and domestic) for eventual publication in the major media. Duration is 2 months. Unpaid. Candidates for all positions should have ability to work independently, oral communication skills, personal interest in the field, research skills, self-motivation, writing skills. Open to college juniors, college seniors, recent college graduates, graduate students. International applications accepted.
Benefits Job counseling, names of contacts, on-the-job training, travel reimbursement, willing to complete paperwork for educational credit, willing to provide letters of recommendation.
Contact Write, call, fax, or e-mail Sarah Banner, Intern Coordinator. Phone: 202-466-4310. Fax: 202-466-4344. E-mail: banner@ publicedcenter.org. Telephone interview required. Applicants must submit a letter of interest, resume, writing sample. Application deadline: April 30 for summer, November 30 for spring. World Wide Web: http://www.publicedcenter.org.

UNIVERSITY DIRECTORIES
PO Box 8830
Chapel Hill, North Carolina 27515

General Information Publisher of campus telephone directories. Established in 1974. Number of employees: 30. Unit of The Village Companies, Chapel Hill, North Carolina. Number of internship applications received each year: 1,100.
Internships Available ▶ *350 sales interns.* Candidates should have ability to work independently, oral communication skills, self-motivation, strong interpersonal skills, strong leadership ability. Duration is 10 weeks. Commission. Open to college freshmen, college sophomores, college juniors, college seniors, recent college graduates, graduate students.
Benefits Formal training, job counseling, names of contacts, opportunity to attend seminars/workshops, possible full-time employment, willing to complete paperwork for educational credit, willing to provide letters of recommendation.
Contact Write, call, fax, e-mail, or through World Wide Web site Yvonne Knutson, National Recruiting Manager. Phone: 800-743-5556 Ext. 143. Fax: 919-968-8513. E-mail: yknutson@vilcom.com. In-person interview recommended (telephone interview accepted). Applicants must submit a letter of interest, resume. Application deadline: April 15 for summer. World Wide Web: http://www. universitydirectories.com.

WORLD COMPLIANCE, INC.
123 Southeast 3rd Avenue, #143
Miami, Florida 33131

General Information Information technology company that distributes state of the art Know-Your-Customer database to financial institutions; identifies suspected terrorists, money laundering, and fraud. Established in 2001. Number of employees: 7. Number of internship applications received each year: 150.
Internships Available ▶ *1–2 marketing interns:* responsibilities include assisting director of marketing, campaign research (design execution and analysis), customer retention programs, customer relationship management, and e-mail marketing campaign. Candidates should have computer skills, declared college major in field, experience in the field, office skills, self-motivation, strong interpersonal skills. Duration is 3–9 months. Position available as unpaid or at $500–$1500 per month. Open to college seniors, recent college graduates, graduate students. ▶ *4 research specialists:* responsibilities include maintaining online database; research-

ing information sources online; identification, evaluation, and integration of information about individuals or companies involved in money laundering, fraud, and other financial crimes. Candidates should have ability to work independently, analytical skills, computer skills, office skills, self-motivation. Duration is 6–12 months. Position available as unpaid or at $500–$1500 per month. Open to college juniors, college seniors, individuals reentering the workforce. International applications accepted.

Benefits Housing at a cost, on-the-job training, opportunity to attend seminars/workshops, possible full-time employment, willing to act as a professional reference, willing to provide letters of recommendation.

Contact E-mail Dirk Mohrmann, President. Fax: 305-513-5676. E-mail: dirkm@worldcompliance.com. No phone calls. Telephone interview required. Applicants must submit a formal organization application. Applications are accepted continuously. World Wide Web: http://www.worldcompliance.com.

MOTION PICTURE AND SOUND RECORDING INDUSTRIES

ASSISTANT DIRECTORS TRAINING PROGRAM
14724 Ventura Boulevard, Suite 775
Sherman Oaks, California 91403

General Information Training program that provides 400 days of paid, on-the-job training, supplemented by classroom seminars, in the work of second assistant directors. Established in 1965. Number of employees: 3. Unit of Directors Guild–Producer Training Plan, Sherman Oaks, California. Number of internship applications received each year: 800.

Internships Available ▶ *15–25 assistant director trainees:* responsibilities include assisting with administrative procedures in motion picture and television production, attending regular seminars that cover subjects pertinent to second assistant director work, and working with various studio and production companies. Candidates should have ability to work independently, oral communication skills, organizational skills, self-motivation, strong interpersonal skills, stamina. Duration is 400 days. $550–$680 per week. Open to college sophomores, college juniors, college seniors, recent college graduates, graduate students, law students, career changers, individuals reentering the workforce, high school graduates with at least 2 years work experience and least 21 years old. International applications accepted.

Benefits Formal training, health insurance, job counseling, names of contacts, on-the-job training, opportunity to attend seminars/workshops, possible full-time employment.

Contact Write, call, e-mail, or through World Wide Web site R. John Slosser, Administrator. Phone: 818-386-2545. E-mail: mail@trainingplan.org. In-person interview required. Applicants must submit a formal organization application, resume, academic transcripts, writing sample. Application deadline: November 15 for internship beginning following June. Fees: $75. World Wide Web: http://www.dgptp.org.

ASSOCIATION OF INDEPENDENT VIDEO AND FILMMAKERS–FOUNDATION FOR INDEPENDENT VIDEO AND FILM
304 Hudson Street, 6th Floor
New York, New York 10013

General Information Trade association of 5000 independent media professionals that provides advocacy and information services; also an educational nonprofit organization offering informational and networking events for filmmakers, and the publisher of a national magazine, *The Independent.* Established in 1975. Number of employees: 10. Number of internship applications received each year: 100.

Internships Available ▶ *1 editorial intern:* responsibilities include assisting the Independent Film and Video Monthly editorial staff; researching and writing. Candidates should have ability to work independently, ability to work with others, computer skills, editing skills, knowledge of field, office skills, research skills, self-motivation, written communication skills. Duration is year-round. $100 per month. Open to college juniors, college seniors, recent college graduates, graduate students, career changers. ▶ *2–4 information services interns:* responsibilities include assisting with research, filing, and data entry in Filmmaker Resource Library; assisting with seminar and event coordination. Candidates should have ability to work independently, computer skills, knowledge of field, office skills, oral communication skills, organizational skills, personal interest in the field, research skills, self-motivation, strong interpersonal skills, written communication skills. Duration is year-round (up to 16 hours per week). $100 per month. Open to high school seniors, recent high school graduates, college freshmen, college sophomores, college juniors, college seniors, recent college graduates, graduate students, career changers, individuals reentering the workforce. ▶ *1–2 membership interns:* responsibilities include assisting with research and mailings, including database maintenance. Candidates should have ability to work independently, computer skills, knowledge of field, office skills, research skills, writing skills. Duration is year-round (up to 16 hours per week). Unpaid. Open to college freshmen, college sophomores, college juniors, college seniors, recent college graduates, graduate students, individuals reentering the workforce. International applications accepted.

Benefits Job counseling, names of contacts, opportunity to attend seminars/workshops, willing to act as a professional reference, willing to complete paperwork for educational credit, willing to provide letters of recommendation, membership in AIVF, selection of free publications in library, stipend of $100 a month with a 10-hour Web commitment.

Contact Write, fax, e-mail, or through World Wide Web site Bo Mehrad, Information Services Associate. Fax: 212-463-8519. E-mail: bo@aivf.org. No phone calls. In-person interview required. Applicants must submit a formal organization application, letter of interest, resume. Applications are accepted continuously. World Wide Web: http://www.aivf.org.

BEACH ASSOCIATES
200 North Glebe Road, Suite 720
Arlington, Virginia 22203

General Information Video production company that specializes in organizational communications. Established in 1979. Number of employees: 13. Number of internship applications received each year: 20.

Internships Available ▶ *1 new media intern:* responsibilities include digitizing and editing video, designing and developing WWW pages and CD-ROMS, working on live Webcast events and designing and maintaining promotional materials. Candidates should have ability to work independently, analytical skills, computer skills, organizational skills, self-motivation. Duration is 1 semester. Unpaid. Open to college juniors, college seniors, only those receiving college credit for internships. ▶ *1 production assistant intern:* responsibilities include entering scripts, answering the phone, logging and labeling tapes, gripping on ENG and EFP shoots, operating teleprompter, editing, running errands, dubbing, typing, making travel arrangements, faxing, copying, bulking tapes, shipping packages, and filing. Candidates should have ability to work with others, college courses in field, computer skills, knowledge of field, office skills, oral communication skills, organizational skills, personal interest in the field, self-motivation, written communication skills. Duration is 1 semester. Unpaid. Open to college sophomores, college juniors, college seniors, recent college graduates.

Benefits Formal training, names of contacts, on-the-job training, opportunity to attend seminars/workshops, willing to act as a professional reference, willing to complete paperwork for educational credit, willing to provide letters of recommendation, free parking.

Contact Write, call, fax, e-mail, or through World Wide Web site Ms. Kay Leonard, Executive Vice President/General Manager. Phone: 703-812-8813. Fax: 703-812-9710. E-mail: kleonard@

Beach Associates (continued)
beachassociates.com. Telephone interview required. Applicants must submit a letter of interest, resume. Applications are accepted continuously. World Wide Web: http://www.beachassociates.com.

BUZZCO ASSOCIATES, INC.
33 Bleecker Street
New York, New York 10012

General Information   Traditional animation company specializing in all forms of 2-D animation with projects ranging from corporate sales films, cable network IDs, network public service announcements, and national and regional commercials. Established in 1985. Number of employees: 5. Number of internship applications received each year: 25.

Internships Available ▶ *1–3 interns:* responsibilities include performing production research and assisting film editorial staff. Candidates should have ability to work with others, plan to pursue career in field, self-motivation. Duration is 1–6 months. Unpaid. Open to high school seniors, recent high school graduates, college freshmen, college sophomores, college juniors, college seniors, recent college graduates, individuals reentering the workforce.

Benefits Job counseling, names of contacts, possible full-time employment, willing to complete paperwork for educational credit, willing to provide letters of recommendation, access to facilities.

Contact Write, call, fax, e-mail, or through World Wide Web site Ms. Candy Kugel, Director, Producer. Phone: 212-473-8800. Fax: 212-473-8891. E-mail: info@buzzzco.com. In-person interview required. Applicants must submit a letter of interest. Application deadline: 6 weeks prior to start of internship. World Wide Web: http://www.buzzzco.com.

ENCORE VIDEO PRODUCTIONS, INC.
811 Main Street
Myrtle Beach, South Carolina 29577

General Information   Film/motion picture company and nonlinear post production company that has done a variety of motion picture, television, corporate, and government projects; complete script-to-screen service. Established in 1980. Number of employees: 4. Number of internship applications received each year: 50.

Internships Available ▶ *1 camera assistant/video/editor intern:* responsibilities include assisting in all aspects of motion picture production and studio/field work. Candidates should have college courses in field, editing skills, knowledge of field, personal interest in the field, plan to pursue career in field, writing skills. Duration is flexible. Unpaid. Open to college freshmen, college sophomores, college juniors, college seniors, recent college graduates, graduate students. International applications accepted.

Benefits On-the-job training, willing to act as a professional reference, willing to complete paperwork for educational credit, willing to provide letters of recommendation, travel with company.

Contact Write, call, fax, or e-mail Kimberly Kay Bagnal, Office Manager. Phone: 843-448-9900. Fax: 843-448-9235. E-mail: kimberly@encorevideo.biz. Applicants must submit a letter of interest, resume. Applications are accepted continuously. World Wide Web: http://www.encorevideo.biz.

FILM/VIDEO ARTS
462 Broadway, Suite 520
New York, New York 10013

General Information   Nonprofit organization that offers subsidized rates to independent film and video makers, holds classes in multimedia and Web construction, and provides production and post-production equipment and services in film and video. Established in 1968. Number of employees: 9. Number of internship applications received each year: 500.

Internships Available ▶ *10–12 interns:* responsibilities include answering phones; scheduling and admitting clients to post-production rooms; performing administrative responsibilities related to signing up students for classes; assisting public relations director, controller, executive director, and membership coordinator as needed. Duration is 6 months. Unpaid. Open to

college freshmen, college sophomores, college juniors, college seniors, recent college graduates, graduate students, law students, career changers, individuals reentering the workforce. International applications accepted.

Benefits Formal training, opportunity to attend seminars/workshops, possible full-time employment, willing to complete paperwork for educational credit, willing to provide letters of recommendation, opportunity to use equipment and facility for personal non-commercial projects on a standby basis.

Contact Write, call, fax, e-mail, or through World Wide Web site Jennifer Gauthier, Internship Coordinator. Phone: 212-941-8787. Fax: 212-219-8924. E-mail: internships@fva.com. In-person interview required. Applicants must submit a formal organization application, letter of interest, resume, sample work (recommended). Applications are accepted continuously. World Wide Web: http://www.fva.com.

FILMWORKS LABORATORY, INC.
523 Colorado Avenue
Santa Monica, California 90401

General Information   Post production boutique offering lab, telecine, editing, sound, and duplication. Established in 1996. Number of employees: 10. Number of internship applications received each year: 100.

Internships Available ▶ *2–4 post production interns:* responsibilities include breaking down film lab rolls and prepping film for telecine, dubs, addressing mailers, answering phones, ordering lunches, and client services. Candidates should have ability to work independently, college courses in field, organizational skills, personal interest in the field, plan to pursue career in field, strong interpersonal skills. Duration is 1–2 semesters. $6.75 per hour. Open to college freshmen, college sophomores, college juniors, college seniors, recent college graduates.

Benefits Job counseling, possible full-time employment, willing to act as a professional reference, willing to complete paperwork for educational credit, willing to provide letters of recommendation.

Contact Write or fax Victoria English, Vice President. Fax: 310-451-2660. E-mail: post@filmworkslaboratory.com. No phone calls. In-person interview required. Applicants must submit a resume. Applications are accepted continuously. World Wide Web: http://www.filmworkslaboratory.com.

HISTORIC FILMS
211 Third Street
Greenport, New York 11944

General Information   Historic stock footage library specializing in archival film and musical performances. Established in 1991. Number of employees: 9. Number of internship applications received each year: 50.

Internships Available ▶ *1–2 research assistants:* responsibilities include video research, logging of images, tape to tape transfer, and various other duties. Candidates should have ability to work independently, analytical skills, office skills, organizational skills, personal interest in the field, research skills. Duration is 6–12 weeks. Unpaid. Open to recent high school graduates, college freshmen, college sophomores, college juniors, college seniors, recent college graduates, graduate students.

Benefits Names of contacts, on-the-job training, possible full-time employment, willing to act as a professional reference, willing to complete paperwork for educational credit, willing to provide letters of recommendation.

Contact Write, call, fax, e-mail, or through World Wide Web site Kevin Rice, Research Director/Internship Coordinator. Phone: 631-477-9700. Fax: 631-477-9800. E-mail: kevin@historicfilms.com. In-person interview recommended (telephone interview accepted). Applicants must submit a letter of interest, resume. Applications are accepted continuously. World Wide Web: http://www.historicfilms.com.

HYBRID FILMS
116 University Place, Suite 2
New York, New York 10003

General Information Independent documentary film and television production company; films have been broadcast internationally on networks including A&E, Court TV, and the BBC. Established in 1995. Number of employees: 3. Number of internship applications received each year: 100.
Internships Available ▶ *1–5 production/edit interns:* responsibilities include logging, transcribing, and digitizing video material; production assistance; general office duties; research for future projects. Candidates should have ability to work independently, computer skills, office skills, personal interest in the field, research skills, self-motivation. Duration is at least 3 months. Unpaid. Open to college freshmen, college sophomores, college juniors, college seniors, recent college graduates, graduate students, career changers. International applications accepted.
Benefits Job counseling, names of contacts, on-the-job training, possible full-time employment, travel reimbursement, willing to act as a professional reference, willing to complete paperwork for educational credit, willing to provide letters of recommendation.
Contact Write, call, fax, or e-mail Courtney Reilly, Production Manager. Phone: 212-463-9908. Fax: 212-675-6344. E-mail: internships@hybridfilms.tv. In-person interview recommended (telephone interview accepted). Applicants must submit a letter of interest, resume. Applications are accepted continuously. World Wide Web: http://hybridfilms.tv.

LEFRAK PRODUCTIONS, INC.
40 West 57th Street, Suite 409
New York, New York 10019

General Information Film and television development company headed by an independent producer. Established in 1980. Number of employees: 5. Number of internship applications received each year: 50.
Internships Available ▶ *5–7 interns:* responsibilities include performing general office work, attending the theater, and looking for new project ideas. Candidates should have ability to work independently, computer skills, knowledge of field, office skills, oral communication skills, organizational skills, plan to pursue career in field, research skills, self-motivation, strong interpersonal skills, written communication skills. Duration is 3 months (full-time or part-time). Unpaid. Open to college freshmen, college sophomores, college juniors, college seniors, recent college graduates, graduate students, law students, career changers. International applications accepted.
Benefits Formal training, job counseling, on-the-job training, possible full-time employment, willing to act as a professional reference, willing to complete paperwork for educational credit, willing to provide letters of recommendation.
Contact Call or fax Melissa Sarrocco, Internship Coordinator. Phone: 212-541-9444. Fax: 212-974-8205. In-person interview recommended (telephone interview accepted). Applicants must submit a resume. Applications are accepted continuously.

LIGHTHOUSE PRODUCTIONS
120 El Camino Drive, Suite 212
Beverly Hills, California 90212

General Information Feature film and television production company. Established in 1974. Number of employees: 2. Number of internship applications received each year: 150.
Internships Available ▶ *2–4 story development interns:* responsibilities include script coverage and general assistant responsibilities (phone, fax, copy machine). Candidates should have analytical skills, office skills, oral communication skills, plan to pursue career in field, writing skills. Duration is 10–15 weeks. Unpaid. Open to college juniors, college seniors, recent college graduates, graduate students. International applications accepted.
Benefits Formal training, job counseling, willing to complete paperwork for educational credit, willing to provide letters of recommendation.
Contact Write or fax Michael Phillips, Producer. Fax: 310-859-7511. E-mail: lighthouse38@hotmail.com. No phone calls. In-person interview recommended (telephone interview accepted). Applicants must submit a formal organization application, resume, writing sample. Application deadline: February 1 for spring, May 1 for summer and fall, December 1 for winter.

LIGHTSTORM ENTERTAINMENT, INC.
919 Santa Monica Boulevard
Santa Monica, California 90401

General Information Company that develops and produces0 feature films and television shows. Established in 1990. Number of employees: 20. Unit of Twentieth Century Fox Film Corp., Los Angeles, California. Number of internship applications received each year: 100.
Internships Available ▶ *4–5 development interns:* responsibilities include script analysis, data entry, research assistance, and general office support. Candidates should have ability to work independently, analytical skills, college courses in field, computer skills, office skills, oral communication skills, organizational skills, personal interest in the field, research skills, self-motivation, strong interpersonal skills, writing skills. Duration is 3–4 months. Unpaid.
▶ *2–3 production interns:* responsibilities include inventory and archiving of production-related materials; research assistance. Candidates should have ability to work independently, college courses in field, computer skills, office skills, oral communication skills, organizational skills, plan to pursue career in field, research skills, self-motivation, strong interpersonal skills, written communication skills. Duration is 3–4 months. Unpaid. Open to college juniors, college seniors, graduate students. International applications accepted.
Benefits Job counseling, on-the-job training, willing to act as a professional reference, willing to complete paperwork for educational credit, willing to provide letters of recommendation.
Contact Write, fax, or e-mail Tom Cohen, Creative Executive. Fax: 310-656-6102. E-mail: tomc@lightstormla.com. No phone calls. In-person interview recommended (telephone interview accepted). Applicants must submit a letter of interest, resume, two writing samples, two personal references, analytical writing sample (for development applicants). Application deadline: April 1 for summer, July 1 for fall, December 1 for spring.

LOVETT PRODUCTIONS, INC.
155 Sixth Avenue, 10th Floor
New York, New York 10013

General Information Independent production company that produces documentary and reality programming, video news releases, industrials, and independent films. Established in 1989. Number of employees: 5. Number of internship applications received each year: 100.
Internships Available ▶ *4–6 production office assistants:* responsibilities include assisting in all aspects of pre- and post-production, research, writing, logging, labeling, videotaping, dubbing, and phones. Candidates should have ability to work independently, ability to work with others, oral communication skills, personal interest in the field, plan to pursue career in field, self-motivation, written communication skills. Duration is 3–4 months. Unpaid. Open to college freshmen, college sophomores, college juniors, college seniors, recent college graduates, graduate students, law students, career changers, individuals reentering the workforce. International applications accepted.
Benefits Willing to act as a professional reference, willing to complete paperwork for educational credit, stipend for food and transportation ($13 per day), willing to provide references and recommendations based on performance.
Contact Write, call, fax, or e-mail Brian Glazer, Internship Coordinator/Production Manager. Phone: 212-242-8999. Fax: 212-242-7347. E-mail: brianglazer@lovettproductions.com. In-person interview recommended (telephone interview accepted). Applicants must submit a letter of interest, resume. Applications are accepted continuously. World Wide Web: http://www.lovettproductions.com.

MAYSLES FILMS, INC.
250 West 54th Street, PH
New York, New York 10019

General Information   Leading force in non-fiction film, making over a dozen documentaries as well as producing reality commercials and infomercials. Established in 1962. Number of employees: 9. Number of internship applications received each year: 50.

Internships Available ▶ *3–5 office production interns:* responsibilities include assisting in all aspects of production research, dubbing, spot checking, working in the library, assisting with distribution (preparing orders), and assisting with press files. Candidates should have organizational skills, personal interest in the field, self-motivation, written communication skills. Duration is 1 semester. Unpaid. Open to high school students, college freshmen, college sophomores, college juniors, college seniors, recent college graduates. International applications accepted.

Benefits Travel reimbursement, willing to complete paperwork for educational credit, willing to provide letters of recommendation.

Contact Write, call, or fax Internship Coordinator. Phone: 212-582-6050. Fax: 212-586-2057. In-person interview required. Applicants must submit a resume, cover letter. Applications are accepted continuously. World Wide Web: http://www.mayslesfilms.com.

MCT MANAGEMENT/BOLD! MARKETING AND PROMOTION
333 West 52nd Street, Suite 1003
New York, New York 10019

General Information   Music management and promotion company. Established in 1987. Number of employees: 7. Number of internship applications received each year: 25.

Internships Available ▶ *Artist management assistants:* responsibilities include general office responsibilities and music duplication. Candidates should have computer skills, experience in the field, office skills, oral communication skills, self-motivation, some technical competence. Duration is flexible. Unpaid. Open to college seniors, recent college graduates, career changers. ▶ *Promotion assistants:* responsibilities include promotion details, including calls to radio stations, generation of reports, and general office responsibilities. Candidates should have computer skills, oral communication skills, personal interest in the field, self-motivation, strong interpersonal skills. Duration is flexible. Unpaid. Open to college freshmen, college sophomores, college juniors, college seniors, recent college graduates, career changers. International applications accepted.

Benefits On-the-job training, possible full-time employment, willing to act as a professional reference, willing to complete paperwork for educational credit, willing to provide letters of recommendation, unique experience in music industry.

Contact Write, fax, or e-mail Gregg DeMammos, Human Resource Manager. Fax: 212-315-4601. E-mail: mailbox@mctbold.com. No phone calls. In-person interview required. Applicants must submit a resume. Applications are accepted continuously.

METRO-GOLDWYN-MAYER/UNITED ARTISTS
1350 Sixth Avenue, 24th Floor
New York, New York 10019

General Information   Movie company that releases first-run films into the domestic market. Established in 1924. Number of employees: 60. Branch of Metro Goldwyn Mayer, Santa Monica, California. Number of internship applications received each year: 500.

Internships Available ▶ *3–5 interns:* responsibilities include working in publicity and promotions departments. Candidates should have college courses in field, computer skills, office skills, oral communication skills, organizational skills, personal interest in the field, research skills, strong interpersonal skills, ability to handle heavy phones in hectic office environment. Duration is 1 semester. Unpaid. Open to college freshmen, college sophomores, college juniors, college seniors.

Benefits Names of contacts, willing to complete paperwork for educational credit, willing to provide letters of recommendation.

Contact Write, call, or fax Intern Coordinator. Phone: 212-708-0300. Fax: 212-582-2846. In-person interview required. Applicants must submit a letter of interest, resume. Applications are accepted continuously. World Wide Web: http://www.mgm.com.

NASSAU COUNTY OFFICE OF CINEMA AND TELEVISION PROMOTION
400 County Seat Drive
Mineola, New York 11501

General Information   Film commission that scouts locations and facilitates film production, commercials, videos, and still photography; also runs the Long Island International Film Expo. Established in 1989. Number of employees: 6. Unit of Nassau County Department of Sports, Entertainment and Tourism, Mineola, New York. Number of internship applications received each year: 40.

Internships Available ▶ *1 data entry intern:* responsibilities include updating and entering data into film database. Candidates should have ability to work with Office Suite program. Duration is flexible. Unpaid. Open to high school seniors, recent high school graduates, college freshmen, college sophomores, college juniors, college seniors, recent college graduates, graduate students, law students, career changers, individuals reentering the workforce. ▶ *1–4 film coordinators:* responsibilities include contacting clients by phone, scouting locations, researching, updating files, following up on film shoots, assisting with permit procedures, and helping with Long Island International Film Expo. Candidates should have ability to work independently, oral communication skills, personal interest in the field, self-motivation, strong interpersonal skills. Duration is flexible. Unpaid. Open to high school seniors, recent high school graduates, college freshmen, college sophomores, college juniors, college seniors, recent college graduates, graduate students, law students, career changers, individuals reentering the workforce. ▶ *3 location photographers:* responsibilities include photographing locations, mansions, and parks. Candidates should have personal interest in the field. Duration is flexible. Unpaid. Open to recent high school graduates, college freshmen, college sophomores, college juniors, college seniors, recent college graduates, graduate students, law students, career changers, individuals reentering the workforce.

Benefits Formal training, names of contacts, willing to complete paperwork for educational credit, willing to provide letters of recommendation.

Contact Write, call, fax, or e-mail Ms. Debra Markowitz, Director. Phone: 516-571-3168. Fax: 516-571-5801. E-mail: debfilm@aol.com. In-person interview recommended (telephone interview accepted). Applicants must submit a resume. Applications are accepted continuously. World Wide Web: http://www.nassaucountynydevelopment.org.

NORTHWEST FILM CENTER
1219 Southwest Park Avenue
Portland, Oregon 97205

General Information   Regional media arts center serving the Northwest with film and video exhibitions, continuing education, artist-in-the-schools programs, and fellowships programs. Established in 1972. Number of employees: 15. Unit of Portland Art Museum, Portland, Oregon. Number of internship applications received each year: 100.

Internships Available ▶ *3–4 education interns:* responsibilities include working at the equipment room desk and assisting with preparations for film classes. Candidates should have ability to work independently, knowledge of field, oral communication skills, organizational skills, strong interpersonal skills, written communication skills. Duration is 1 semester. Unpaid. Open to recent high school graduates, college freshmen, college sophomores, college juniors, college seniors, recent college graduates, graduate students, law students, career changers. ▶ *1–4 education/equipment interns:* responsibilities include assisting with equipment rental program and helping students with film and video equipment. Candidates should have ability to work independently, knowledge of field, organizational skills, personal interest in the field, self-motivation, strong interpersonal skills. Duration is 1 semester.

Unpaid. Open to recent high school graduates, college freshmen, college sophomores, college juniors, college seniors, recent college graduates, graduate students, law students, career changers.
▶ *1–4 exhibition program and festival assistants:* responsibilities include performing a wide variety of tasks related to promoting a major media arts organization. Candidates should have office skills, organizational skills, personal interest in the field, research skills, self-motivation, strong interpersonal skills. Duration is 1 semester. Unpaid. Open to college freshmen, college sophomores, college juniors, college seniors, recent college graduates, graduate students, law students, career changers, individuals reentering the workforce. International applications accepted.

Benefits Names of contacts, opportunity to attend seminars/ workshops, willing to act as a professional reference, willing to complete paperwork for educational credit, willing to provide letters of recommendation, opportunity to attend screenings and events and to take classes on a standby basis.

Contact Write or e-mail Internship Coordinator. Fax: 503-294-0874. E-mail: info@nwfilm.org. In-person interview recommended (telephone interview accepted). Applicants must submit a letter of interest, resume. Application deadline: May 10 for summer, August 10 for fall, December 10 for winter. World Wide Web: http://www.nwfilm.org.

OPEN CITY FILMS/ BLOW UP PICTURES
44 Hudson Street, 2nd Floor
New York, New York 10013

General Information Independent film production company. Established in 1993. Number of employees: 8. Number of internship applications received each year: 200.

Internships Available ▶ *4–6 interns:* responsibilities include assisting in all areas of office operations including phones, script reading, research, development, and production. Candidates should have ability to work independently, computer skills, office skills, personal interest in the field, research skills, written communication skills. Duration is 3–4 months. Unpaid. Open to college freshmen, college sophomores, college juniors, college seniors. International applications accepted.

Benefits Willing to act as a professional reference, willing to complete paperwork for educational credit, willing to provide letters of recommendation.

Contact Write, fax, or e-mail Lauryn Siegel, Office Manager. Fax: 212-587-1950. E-mail: oc@opencityfilms.com. No phone calls. Applicants must submit a letter of interest, resume. Applications are accepted continuously. World Wide Web: http://www.blowuppictures.com.

ORANGE RECORDINGS
2248 Panorama Terrace
Los Angeles, California 90039

General Information Record label company; wholesale and retail of recorded music, indie, rock, garage genres. Established in 1997. Number of employees: 5. Number of internship applications received each year: 25.

Internships Available ▶ *2–3 public relations/marketing interns:* responsibilities include press (music) follow up, phone calls to schedule reviews, interviews, sales tracking, public relations, marketing new releases, and everything to do with the music business. Candidates should have ability to work with others, knowledge of field, oral communication skills, personal interest in the field, plan to pursue career in field, written communication skills. Duration is flexible. Position available as unpaid or at $8–$10 per hour. Open to high school students, recent high school graduates, college freshmen, college sophomores, college juniors, college seniors, recent college graduates, graduate students, law students, career changers, individuals reentering the workforce. International applications accepted.

Benefits Job counseling, names of contacts, on-the-job training, opportunity to attend seminars/workshops, possible full-time employment, willing to act as a professional reference, willing to complete paperwork for educational credit, willing to provide letters of recommendation.

Contact Write, fax, e-mail, or through World Wide Web site Ron Sievers, President. Fax: 443-659-1483. E-mail: ron@orangerecordings.

com. No phone calls. In-person interview recommended (telephone interview accepted). Applicants must submit a letter of interest, resume. Applications are accepted continuously. World Wide Web: http://www.orangerecordings.com.

SEASIDE PRODUCTIONS
1411 5th Street, Suite 405
Santa Monica, California 90401

General Information Feature film production company. Established in 1995. Number of employees: 1. Subsidiary of Europa Corporation, Paris, France.

Internships Available ▶ *3–5 development interns.* Candidates should have analytical skills, computer skills, office skills, oral communication skills, writing skills. Duration is flexible. Unpaid. Open to college freshmen, college sophomores, college juniors, college seniors. International applications accepted.

Benefits Free meals, names of contacts, on-the-job training, willing to act as a professional reference, willing to complete paperwork for educational credit, willing to provide letters of recommendation.

Contact Fax India Osborne, Vice President of Production. Fax: 310-395-2890. E-mail: indiao@europacorp-us.com. No phone calls. In-person interview recommended (telephone interview accepted). Applicants must submit a letter of interest, resume. Applications are accepted continuously.

SIMON & GOODMAN PICTURE COMPANY
2095 Broadway, Suite 402
New York, New York 10023

General Information Documentary film company. Established in 1987. Number of employees: 4. Number of internship applications received each year: 250.

Internships Available ▶ *3–6 interns:* responsibilities include assisting producers and editors on film shoots, logging tapes, research, and miscellaneous office duties. Candidates should have ability to work with others, college courses in field, knowledge of field, office skills, self-motivation, strong interest in documentary films. Duration is 1 semester. Unpaid. Open to undergraduate or graduate film students, recent graduates. International applications accepted.

Benefits Names of contacts, on-the-job training, opportunity to attend seminars/workshops, possible full-time employment, willing to act as a professional reference, willing to complete paperwork for educational credit, willing to provide letters of recommendation, possible attendance at film shoots.

Contact Write, fax, or e-mail Internship Coordinator. Fax: 212-721-0922. E-mail: sgpic@aol.com. No phone calls. In-person interview recommended (telephone interview accepted). Applicants must submit a letter of interest, resume, international applicants must have proof of housing in New York City. Applications are accepted continuously. World Wide Web: http://www.sgpic.com.

S.O.S. PRODUCTIONS, INC.
753 Harmon Avenue
Columbus, Ohio 43223

General Information Film, audio, video, and postproduction facility that makes television commercials and corporate videos. Established in 1981. Number of employees: 26. Number of internship applications received each year: 50.

Internships Available ▶ *1 audio post-production intern:* responsibilities include recording, editing, and working in sound design. Candidates should have college courses in field, oral communication skills, personal interest in the field, self-motivation, strong interpersonal skills, students must be receiving college credit, must have own vehicle and valid driver's license. Duration is 1 semester. $50 per week. ▶ *1–2 production interns:* responsibilities include setting-up and wrapping video film equipment; understanding the purpose of each production service and the planning and execution phases of the production process; and assisting in building, lighting, and striking sets. Candidates should have college courses in field, oral communication skills, plan to pursue career in field, self-motivation, strong interpersonal skills, students must be receiving college credit, must have own vehicle and valid driver's license.

S.O.S. Productions, Inc. (continued)
Duration is 10 weeks. $50 per week. Open to college freshmen, college sophomores, college juniors, college seniors.
Benefits Names of contacts, on-the-job training, possible full-time employment, willing to act as a professional reference, willing to complete paperwork for educational credit, willing to provide letters of recommendation.
Contact Write, fax, or e-mail Virginia Hayes, Production Manager. Fax: 614-221-3836. E-mail: vhayes@sostv.com. No phone calls. In-person interview required. Applicants must submit a letter of interest, resume. Applications are accepted continuously.

SPIRITUAL LIFE MUSIC
56 Walker Street, 3rd Floor
New York, New York 10013

General Information Independent record label. Established in 1999. Number of employees: 5. Number of internship applications received each year: 40.
Internships Available ▶ *2–3 interns:* responsibilities include working in many facets of the industry. Candidates should have ability to work independently, analytical skills, knowledge of field, oral communication skills, organizational skills, personal interest in the field, self-motivation, strong interpersonal skills. Duration is 1–2 semesters. Unpaid. Open to high school seniors, recent high school graduates, college freshmen, college sophomores, college juniors, college seniors, recent college graduates, career changers. International applications accepted.
Benefits On-the-job training, possible full-time employment, willing to act as a professional reference, willing to complete paperwork for educational credit, willing to provide letters of recommendation.
Contact Call, fax, or e-mail Christina Freund, Business Affairs. Phone: 212-226-1628. Fax: 212-226-2017. E-mail: christina@spirituallifemusic.com. In-person interview recommended (telephone interview accepted). Applicants must submit a resume. Applications are accepted continuously.

WOMEN MAKE MOVIES, INC.
462 Broadway, 5th Floor
New York, New York 10013

General Information National women's media organization that facilitates the production, promotion, and distribution of films and videotapes by and about women. Established in 1972. Number of employees: 14. Number of internship applications received each year: 200.
Internships Available ▶ *1–5 distribution assistants:* responsibilities include working in distribution department; maintaining database and mailing lists; keeping up in-house video library; working in shipping room; and maintaining promotional files. Candidates should have ability to work with others, computer skills, office skills, oral communication skills, organizational skills, personal interest in the field, plan to pursue career in field, written communication skills. Duration is 1 semester. Unpaid. ▶ *1 general office assistant:* responsibilities include working with assistant office manager updating and maintaining lists on computer database, general office duties, and responding to general information requests. Candidates should have computer skills, office skills, oral communication skills, plan to pursue career in field, strong interpersonal skills, written communication skills. Duration is 1 semester. Unpaid. ▶ *1–2 graphic production assistants:* responsibilities include producing one-sheets and other promotional pieces from templates. Candidates should have ability to work with others, knowledge of field, office skills, oral communication skills, personal interest in the field, research skills, written communication skills, knowledge of Macintosh-based Quark Xpress and PhotoShop, and PC-based Front Page. Duration is 1 semester. Unpaid. ▶ *1–2 production assistants:* responsibilities include researching and updating grant files and other filmmaker resources; assisting with management of project files and program databases; and assisting with media workshops. Candidates should have ability to work independently, ability to work with others, computer skills, knowledge of field, office skills, oral communication skills, plan to pursue career in field, written communication skills. Duration

is 1 semester. Unpaid. ▶ *1–3 promotions assistants:* responsibilities include assisting sales and marketing staff with outreach to community-based and academic organizations; assisting with production and mailing of promotional materials; designing fliers; and doing online research. Candidates should have ability to work with others, computer skills, editing skills, office skills, oral communication skills, research skills, writing skills, knowledge of Internet and/or desktop publishing. Duration is 1 semester. Unpaid. Open to college freshmen, college sophomores, college juniors, college seniors, recent college graduates, graduate students. International applications accepted.
Benefits Names of contacts, opportunity to attend seminars/workshops, travel reimbursement, willing to complete paperwork for educational credit, willing to provide letters of recommendation, access to film collection, resource files, and independent filmmaking network, invitations to screenings and receptions.
Contact Write, fax, e-mail, or through World Wide Web site Talar Attarian. Fax: 212-925-2052. E-mail: info@wmm.com. No phone calls. In-person interview recommended (telephone interview accepted). Applicants must submit a formal organization application, letter of interest, resume, writing sample. Applications are accepted continuously. World Wide Web: http://www.wmm.com.

NEWSPAPER PUBLISHERS

THE ADVOCATE
PO Box 588
Baton Rouge, Louisiana 70821

General Information Publisher of daily newspaper. Established in 1907. Number of employees: 571. Number of internship applications received each year: 20.
Internships Available ▶ *2 reporter interns:* responsibilities include reporting the news. Candidates should have ability to work with others, computer skills, experience in the field, personal interest in the field, self-motivation, writing skills. Duration is 2 years. $11.10–$13.53 per hour. Open to college seniors, recent college graduates. International applications accepted.
Benefits Health insurance, possible full-time employment, travel reimbursement, willing to act as a professional reference, willing to provide letters of recommendation.
Contact Write, call, fax, or e-mail Jason Jacobs. Phone: 225-388-0171. Fax: 225-388-0397. E-mail: jjacobs@theadvocate.com. In-person interview required. Applicants must submit a formal organization application, resume, portfolio, writing sample, three personal references. Applications are accepted continuously. World Wide Web: http://www.2theadvocate.com.

AMERICAN PRESS
PO Box 2893
Lake Charles, Louisiana 70602

General Information Daily independent and family-owned newspaper. Established in 1895. Number of employees: 200. Number of internship applications received each year: 50.
Internships Available ▶ *1 editorial intern:* responsibilities include newswriting, reporting, feature writing, and working with top editors. Candidates should have declared college major in field, personal interest in the field, plan to pursue career in field, self-motivation, written communication skills. Duration is 2-3 months in summer. $7.50 per hour. Open to college freshmen, college sophomores, college juniors, college seniors. International applications accepted.
Benefits Formal training, on-the-job training, possible full-time employment, willing to act as a professional reference, willing to complete paperwork for educational credit, willing to provide letters of recommendation, opportunity to work with top editors.
Contact Write, fax, e-mail, or through World Wide Web site Mr. Brett Downer, Editor. Fax: 337-494-4070. E-mail: bdowner@americanpress.com. No phone calls. Applicants must submit a let-

ter of interest, resume, 5 writing samples. Application deadline: March 30. World Wide Web: http://www.americanpress.com.

AMERICAN YOUTH WORK CENTER/YOUTH TODAY
1200 17th Street, NW, 4th Floor
Washington, District of Columbia 20036

General Information National monthly newspaper for professionals concerned with youth, especially at-risk, out-of-school youth; topics may include child welfare, juvenile justice, child labor, and substance abuse. Established in 1983. Number of employees: 11. Number of internship applications received each year: 100.

Internships Available ▶ *1–2 reporter interns:* responsibilities include gathering and analyzing information, writing short articles, preparing regular features and proofreading copy, covering meetings on Capitol Hill and meetings sponsored by public policy organizations, and performing some administrative duties. Candidates should have ability to work independently, college courses in field, computer skills, editing skills, knowledge of field, office skills, oral communication skills, organizational skills, plan to pursue career in field, research skills, self-motivation, strong interpersonal skills, writing skills. Duration is full-time summer or part-time or full-time year-round. $6.50 per hour. Open to high school students, recent high school graduates, college freshmen, college sophomores, college juniors, college seniors, recent college graduates. International applications accepted.

Benefits Names of contacts, on-the-job training, opportunity to attend seminars/workshops, possible full-time employment, willing to act as a professional reference, willing to complete paperwork for educational credit, willing to provide letters of recommendation.

International Internships Available.

Contact Write, call, fax, or e-mail John Kelly, Intern Coordinator. Phone: 202-785-0764 Ext. 110. Fax: 202-728-0657. E-mail: jkelly@youthtoday.org. In-person interview recommended (telephone interview accepted). Applicants must submit a letter of interest, resume, two writing samples. Applications are accepted continuously.

ANCHORAGE DAILY NEWS
PO Box 149001
Anchorage, Alaska 99514

General Information General circulation daily newspaper. Established in 1946. Number of employees: 530. Unit of The McClatchy Company, Sacramento, California. Number of internship applications received each year: 400.

Internships Available ▶ *1 copy editor intern:* responsibilities include layout, headlines, editing. Candidates should have computer skills, editing skills, experience in the field, organizational skills, writing skills, ability to meet deadlines. Duration is 12 weeks, June 1-August 31. $9.50 per hour. Open to college juniors, college seniors, recent college graduates, graduate students, career changers, individuals reentering the workforce. ▶ *1 photographer intern:* responsibilities include acting as general assignment photographer; reporting to photo editor; 40 hours/week, overtime as needed on occasion. Candidates should have ability to work independently, experience in the field, oral communication skills, strong interpersonal skills, written communication skills. Duration is 12 weeks, June 1-August 31 (slightly flexible start/stop dates). $9.50 per hour. Open to college sophomores, college juniors, college seniors, recent college graduates, graduate students, career changers, individuals reentering the workforce. ▶ *2 reporting interns:* responsibilities include acting as general assignment reporter, 40 hours/week plus overtime as occasionally needed; reporting, writing, meeting deadlines; reports to metro or feature editor. Candidates should have college courses in field, experience in the field, oral communication skills, research skills, strong interpersonal skills, writing skills. Duration is 12 weeks. $9.50 per hour. Open to college juniors, college seniors, recent college graduates, graduate students, career changers, individuals reentering the workforce.

Benefits Job counseling, names of contacts, on-the-job training, opportunity to attend seminars/workshops, possible full-time employment, travel reimbursement, willing to complete paperwork

for educational credit, small grant toward getting to and returning from Anchorage, assistance in finding lodging.

Contact Write or e-mail Ms. Kathleen Macknicki, Internship Coordinator. Fax: 907-258-2157. E-mail: kmacknicki@adn.com. No phone calls. Applicants must submit a letter of interest, resume, portfolio, at least 6 writing samples. Application deadline: January 1 for summer. World Wide Web: http://www.adn.com.

ANN ARBOR NEWS
340 East Huron
Ann Arbor, Michigan 48106-1147

General Information Daily newspaper publisher. Established in 1838. Number of employees: 400. Unit of Newhouse Newspapers. Number of internship applications received each year: 60.

Internships Available ▶ *1–2 reporters/copy editors:* responsibilities include performing copy desk work, covering breaking news, and interviewing for features. Candidates should have ability to work with others, college courses in field, editing skills, experience in the field, plan to pursue career in field, writing skills. Duration is 3 months. $500–$525 per week. Open to college sophomores, college juniors, college seniors, recent college graduates, graduate students. ▶ *1–2 sales representatives:* responsibilities include selling classified or display advertising space to contract advertisers and acting as salespersons during summer. Candidates should have ability to work independently, oral communication skills, personal interest in the field, self-motivation, strong interpersonal skills, written communication skills. Duration is 3 months. $12–$15 per hour. Open to college sophomores, college juniors, college seniors.

Benefits Formal training, on-the-job training, possible full-time employment, willing to act as a professional reference, willing to complete paperwork for educational credit.

Contact Write, call, or e-mail Richard W. Fitzgerald, Managing Editor/Ypsilanti, 301 West Michigan Avenue, Suite 201, Ypsilanti, Michigan 48197. Phone: 734-482-4863. Fax: 734-482-2096. E-mail: rfitzgerald@annarbornews.com. Applicants must submit a letter of interest, resume, four writing samples, two personal references, 2 writing references. Application deadline: January 15 for summer. World Wide Web: http://aa.mlive.com.

THE ANNISTON STAR
PO Box 189
Anniston, Alabama 36202

General Information Newspaper. Established in 1883. Number of employees: 100. Number of internship applications received each year: 200.

Internships Available ▶ *3 editorial interns:* responsibilities include working as reporters or copy editors. Candidates should have ability to work with others, computer skills, editing skills, oral communication skills, personal interest in the field, writing skills. Duration is 12 weeks. $350 per week. Open to college juniors, college seniors, recent college graduates, graduate students. International applications accepted.

Benefits Job counseling, on-the-job training, possible full-time employment, willing to complete paperwork for educational credit, willing to provide letters of recommendation.

Contact Write, fax, or e-mail Troy Turner, Managing Editor. Fax: 256-235-3535. E-mail: tturner@annistonstar.com. No phone calls. Applicants must submit a letter of interest, resume, 3-5 writing samples. Application deadline: January 30. World Wide Web: http://www.annistonstar.com.

ARKANSAS DEMOCRAT-GAZETTE
121 East Capitol Avenue
Little Rock, Arkansas 72201

General Information Daily statewide newspaper. Number of employees: 500. Subsidiary of Wehco Media, Little Rock, Arkansas. Number of internship applications received each year: 400.

Internships Available ▶ *2–4 photography, graphics, design, copyediting interns.* Candidates should have editing skills, knowledge of field, plan to pursue career in field, writing skills. Duration is May/June to August/September. Paid. Open to college sophomores, college juniors, college seniors. ▶ *4–6 reporting interns:* responsibilities include reporting in the news, features, business, or sports

Arkansas Democrat-Gazette (continued)

department. Candidates should have college courses in field, experience in the field, oral communication skills, plan to pursue career in field, research skills, writing skills. Duration is May/June to August/September. Paid. Open to college sophomores, college juniors, college seniors, graduate students. International applications accepted.

Benefits Names of contacts, on-the-job training, possible full-time employment, willing to act as a professional reference, willing to provide letters of recommendation, opportunity to gain experience.

Contact Write or e-mail Mr. Todd Stone, City Editor, 121 East Capitol Avenue, Little Rock, Arkansas 72201. E-mail: todd_stone@adg.ardemgaz.com. Applicants must submit a letter of interest, resume, three personal references, 8-10 work samples (articles, graphics, photos). Application deadline: November 1. World Wide Web: http://www.ardemgaz.com.

THE ATLANTA JOURNAL–CONSTITUTION
72 Marietta Street, NW
Atlanta, Georgia 30303

General Information Major daily metropolitan newspaper. Established in 1898. Number of employees: 500. Unit of Cox Enterprises, Inc., Atlanta, Georgia. Number of internship applications received each year: 500.

Internships Available ▶ *News interns:* responsibilities include working in department that matches an intern's area of skill or experience, such as reporting, copy editing, photography, or graphic arts. Candidates should have previous professional daily experience with deadlines, preferably on a newspaper, must have worked on campus newspaper or other publications. Duration is 10 weeks in summer, winter positions possible. $550 per week. Open to college juniors, college seniors, recent college graduates, graduate students. International applications accepted.

Benefits Job counseling, on-the-job training, opportunity to attend seminars/workshops, possible full-time employment, willing to complete paperwork for educational credit, willing to provide letters of recommendation, mentor system that aids professional growth.

Contact Write, e-mail, or through World Wide Web site Angela Tuck, Director of News Personnel and Staff Development. E-mail: atuck@ajc.com. No phone calls. Applicants must submit a resume, personal reference, 500-word essay (see Web site or write for details), copies of 5-10 news clips or samples of photos/graphics/headlines. Application deadline: December 15 for summer. World Wide Web: http://www.ajc.com/services/internships.

BEE PUBLICATIONS
5564 Main Street
Williamsville, New York 14221

General Information Publications agency, including 9 newspapers, that reports on local government, schools, sports, and other community activities in a professional manner. Established in 1879. Number of employees: 60. Number of internship applications received each year: 8.

Internships Available ▶ *1–5 reporters:* responsibilities include rewriting press releases, editing copy, and writing features, news, and sports stories. Duration is 1 semester or summer. Unpaid. Open to college freshmen, college sophomores, college juniors, college seniors.

Benefits Formal training, possible full-time employment, willing to complete paperwork for educational credit.

Contact Write, call, fax, or e-mail Mr. David Sherman, Managing Editor, PO Box 150, Buffalo, New York 14231-0150. Phone: 716-632-4700. Fax: 716-633-8601. E-mail: dsherman@beenews.com. In-person interview required. Applicants must submit a letter of interest, resume. Applications are accepted continuously. World Wide Web: http://www.beenews.com.

THE BIRMINGHAM NEWS
2200 Fourth Avenue North
Birmingham, Alabama 35203

General Information Newspaper recognized regionally and nationally for its reporting and commentary. Established in 1888. Number of employees: 643. Unit of Advance Publications, Staten Island, New York. Number of internship applications received each year: 100.

Internships Available ▶ *2 fall sports interns:* responsibilities include working as a beginning sports reporter. Candidates should have ability to work independently, ability to work with others, college courses in field, computer skills, knowledge of field, plan to pursue career in field, research skills, self-motivation, writing skills, minimum B average in course work. Duration is 16 weeks. $400 per week. Open to college sophomores, college juniors, college seniors. ▶ *3 summer advertising interns:* responsibilities include working as a beginning/regular salesperson. Candidates should have ability to work independently, computer skills, office skills, oral communication skills, self-motivation, writing skills. Duration is 10–12 weeks. $6 per hour. Open to college sophomores, college juniors. ▶ *4 summer news interns:* responsibilities include working as a beginning reporter. Candidates should have ability to work independently, ability to work with others, college courses in field, computer skills, knowledge of field, plan to pursue career in field, research skills, writing skills, minimum B average in course work. Duration is 10–12 weeks. $400 per week. Open to college sophomores, college juniors.

Benefits Formal training, job counseling, on-the-job training, possible full-time employment, travel reimbursement, willing to complete paperwork for educational credit, willing to provide letters of recommendation.

Contact Write, call, or fax Mr. Randy Henderson, Assistant Managing Editor (for news internships). Phone: 205-325-2210. Fax: 205-325-2283. Applicants must submit a letter of interest, resume, 8-10 writing samples. Application deadline: January 15 for summer, April 1 for fall. World Wide Web: http://www.al.com.

BIRMINGHAM POST-HERALD
2200 Fourth Avenue, North
Birmingham, Alabama 35203-3802

General Information Daily afternoon newspaper in Birmingham, Alabama. Established in 1921. Number of employees: 58. Subsidiary of Scripps Howard Company, Cincinnati, Ohio. Number of internship applications received each year: 80.

Internships Available ▶ *1 photographic intern:* responsibilities include working as a beginning photographer. Candidates should have ability to work independently, ability to work with others, college courses in field, knowledge of field, plan to pursue career in field. Duration is 12 weeks. $300 per week. Open to college freshmen, college sophomores, college juniors. ▶ *2 reporting interns:* responsibilities include working as a beginning reporter. Candidates should have ability to work independently, college courses in field, computer skills, oral communication skills, plan to pursue career in field, strong interpersonal skills, writing skills. Duration is 12 weeks. $300 per week. Open to college sophomores, college juniors.

Benefits On-the-job training, possible full-time employment, willing to act as a professional reference, willing to complete paperwork for educational credit, willing to provide letters of recommendation.

Contact Write, fax, or e-mail Becky Gallagher, Public Service Director. Fax: 205-325-2410. E-mail: mailbox@postherald.com. No phone calls. Applicants must submit a letter of interest, resume, three personal references, five writing samples. Application deadline: January 31 for summer, June 1 for fall. World Wide Web: http://www.postherald.com.

THE BOSTON GLOBE
135 Morrissey Boulevard
Boston, Massachusetts 02107

General Information Newspaper. Established in 1872. Number of employees: 2,200. Subsidary of The New York Times, New York, New York. Number of internship applications received each year: 200.

Internships Available ▶ *2 business summer interns:* responsibilities include accounts payable and payroll (accounting intern); advertising sales (advertising intern). Candidates should have ability to work independently, analytical skills, computer skills, knowledge of field, office skills, oral communication skills, organizational skills, personal interest in the field, self-motivation, written communication skills. Duration is 13 weeks. $570 per week. Open to college sophomores, college juniors. ▶ *2 one-year interns:* responsibilities include advertising sales or advertising design. Candidates should have ability to work independently, analytical skills, college degree in related field, computer skills, knowledge of field, office skills, oral communication skills, organizational skills, plan to pursue career in field, self-motivation, strong interpersonal skills, written communication skills. Duration is 1 year. $24,000–$41,000 per year. Open to recent college graduates. ▶ *15 summer editorial interns:* responsibilities include general assignment reporting for 13 interns; editorial design position and photography position also available. Candidates should have editing skills, writing skills, experience with school newspaper, previous internship at a daily or weekly newspaper. $601 per week. Open to college sophomores, college juniors.

Benefits On-the-job training, opportunity to attend seminars/workshops, health insurance for one-year internship.

Contact Write, fax, e-mail, or through World Wide Web site Tia Purnell, Assistant Manager, Human Resources, PO Box 2378, Boston, Massachusetts 02107. Phone: 617-929-2021. Fax: 617-929-3376. E-mail: collegerecruiting@globe.com. Applicants must submit a formal organization application, letter of interest, resume, in-person interview (if selected). Application deadline: February 15 for business summer and one-year interns, November 5 for summer editorial interns. World Wide Web: http://www.boston.com/extranet.

BUCKS COUNTY COURIER TIMES
8400 Route 13
Levittown, Pennsylvania 19057

General Information Suburban Philadelphia newspaper with a circulation of over 70,000. Established in 1910. Number of employees: 300. Unit of Calkins Media, Inc., Levittown, Pennsylvania. Number of internship applications received each year: 100.

Internships Available ▶ *1 copy editor:* responsibilities include copyediting daily newspaper copy. Candidates should have ability to work with others, analytical skills, computer skills, editing skills, knowledge of field, written communication skills. Duration is 12 weeks (June to August). $365 per week. ▶ *1 feature writer:* responsibilities include writing and editing features. Candidates should have analytical skills, computer skills, editing skills, research skills, strong interpersonal skills, writing skills. Duration is 12 weeks (June to August). $365 per week. ▶ *1 photographer/graphics person:* responsibilities include photo or graphic (computer) work. Candidates should have analytical skills, organizational skills, personal interest in the field, self-motivation, strong interpersonal skills. Duration is 12 weeks (June to August). $365 per week. ▶ *Reporters:* responsibilities include reporting for daily newspaper. Candidates should have analytical skills, personal interest in the field, research skills, self-motivation, strong interpersonal skills, writing skills. Duration is 12 weeks (June to August). $365 per week. ▶ *1 sports writer:* responsibilities include writing features covering sports events and editing. Candidates should have analytical skills, computer skills, editing skills, personal interest in the field, research skills, strong interpersonal skills, writing skills. Duration is 12 weeks (June to August). $365 per week. Open to college juniors, college seniors, recent college graduates, graduate students.

Benefits Names of contacts, willing to complete paperwork for educational credit, willing to provide letters of recommendation, car expenses.

Contact Write, call, fax, or e-mail Jackie Massott, Internship Coordinator. Phone: 215-949-4189. Fax: 215-949-4177. E-mail: jmassott@phillyburbs.com. In-person interview recommended (telephone interview accepted). Applicants must submit a formal organization application, letter of interest, resume, published writing samples. Application deadline: February 1 for summer. World Wide Web: http://www.bcct-gpn.com.

BUFFALO NEWS
1 News Plaza, PO Box 100
Buffalo, New York 14240

General Information Publisher of daily newspaper. Established in 1880. Number of employees: 1,000. Unit of Berkshire Hathaway, Inc., Omaha, Nebraska. Number of internship applications received each year: 100.

Internships Available ▶ *3 copy editors:* responsibilities include editing news stories and verifying facts and grammar. Candidates should have college courses in field, editing skills, knowledge of field, writing skills, experience on school newspaper. Duration is one summer (usually 3 months). $342 per week. Open to college sophomores, college juniors, college seniors, graduate students. ▶ *Photographer:* responsibilities include replacing vacationing staffer. Candidates should have knowledge of field, oral communication skills, written communication skills, experience on school newspaper. Duration is one summer (usually 3 months). $342 per week. Open to college sophomores, college juniors, college seniors, graduate students. ▶ *11 reporters:* responsibilities include replacing vacationing staffers. Candidates should have computer skills, oral communication skills, writing skills, experience on school newspaper. Duration is 3 months. $342 per week. Open to college sophomores, college juniors, college seniors, graduate students. ▶ *3–4 salespeople:* responsibilities include selling retail advertising. Candidates should have ability to work independently, analytical skills, college courses in field, knowledge of field, office skills, oral communication skills, organizational skills, personal interest in the field, self-motivation, strong interpersonal skills, written communication skills. Duration is June–August. $342 per week. Open to college freshmen, college sophomores, college juniors, college seniors.

Benefits Willing to complete paperwork for educational credit, willing to provide letters of recommendation.

Contact Write Stephen W. Bell, Managing Editor. E-mail: sbell@buffnews.com. No phone calls. In-person interview required. Applicants must submit a formal organization application, letter of interest, resume, 4-6 writing samples. Application deadline: December 1 for summer. World Wide Web: http://www.buffalo.com.

CALLER-TIMES
820 Lower North Broadway
Corpus Christi, Texas 78401

General Information Daily newspaper providing coverage in a 10-county area in southern Texas. Established in 1883. Number of employees: 400. Unit of EW Scripps, Cincinnati, Ohio. Number of internship applications received each year: 40.

Internships Available ▶ *3 newsroom interns.* Candidates should have editing skills, research skills, self-motivation, strong interpersonal skills, written communication skills. Duration is 10 weeks. $280–$300 per week. Open to college sophomores, college juniors, college seniors.

Benefits Names of contacts, possible full-time employment, willing to provide letters of recommendation.

Contact Write, call, fax, e-mail, or through World Wide Web site Mr. Nick Jimenez, PO Box 9136, Corpus Christi, Texas 78469. Phone: 361-886-3787. Fax: 361-886-3732. E-mail: jimenezn@caller.com. In-person interview recommended (telephone interview accepted). Applicants must submit a letter of interest, resume, writing sample. Application deadline: January 30 for summer. World Wide Web: http://www.caller.com.

COLUMBUS LEDGER–ENQUIRER
17 West 12th Street
Columbus, Georgia 31901

General Information Newspaper. Established in 1828. Number of employees: 250. Unit of Knight Ridder, San Jose, California. Number of internship applications received each year: 75.

Internships Available ▶ *1–4 1-4 newsroom reporters:* responsibilities include working as a professional journalist writing on deadline. Candidates should have ability to work independently, editing skills, oral communication skills, plan to pursue career in field, writing skills. Duration is 10–12 weeks. Paid. Open to recent high school graduates, college freshmen, college sophomores, college juniors, college seniors, graduate students.

Benefits Housing at a cost, job counseling, names of contacts, on-the-job training, opportunity to attend seminars/workshops, possible full-time employment, willing to act as a professional reference, willing to complete paperwork for educational credit, willing to provide letters of recommendation.

Contact Write or e-mail Susan Catron, Managing Editor. Phone: 706-571-8557. Fax: 706-576-6290. E-mail: scatron@ledger-enquirer.com. In-person interview recommended (telephone interview accepted). Applicants must submit a formal organization application, letter of interest, resume, portfolio, personal reference, 10 writing samples. Application deadline: January 15 for summer. World Wide Web: http://www.ledger-enquirer.com.

CONNECTICUT POST
410 State Street
Bridgeport, Connecticut 06604

General Information Daily newspaper. Established in 1883. Number of employees: 525. Subsidiary of Media News Group, Inc., Denver, Colorado. Number of internship applications received each year: 60.

Internships Available ▶ *Interns:* responsibilities include performing the duties of an entry-level reporter; also copy desk and photography work. Candidates should have computer skills, editing skills, oral communication skills, plan to pursue career in field, research skills, writing skills. Duration is based on school guidelines. Unpaid. Open to college freshmen, college sophomores, college juniors, college seniors, high school students over age 16.

Benefits On-the-job training, willing to act as a professional reference, willing to complete paperwork for educational credit, willing to provide letters of recommendation.

Contact Write, call, fax, or e-mail Cindy Simoneau, Assistant Managing Editor, 410 State Street, Bridgeport, Connecticut 06604. Phone: 203-330-6391. Fax: 203-367-8158. E-mail: csimoneau@ctpost.com. In-person interview recommended (telephone interview accepted). Applicants must submit a resume, three writing samples, letter of recommendation, 1 personal reference from an academic advisor. Applications are accepted continuously.

THE DAILY MINING GAZETTE
PO Box 368
Houghton, Michigan 49931

General Information Daily newspaper. Number of employees: 75. Unit of Ogden Newspapers, Wheeling, West Virginia. Number of internship applications received each year: 20.

Internships Available ▶ *1 staff writer/intern:* responsibilities include general assignment reporting. Candidates should have ability to work independently, college courses in field, computer skills, oral communication skills, organizational skills, personal interest in the field, plan to pursue career in field, self-motivation, strong interpersonal skills, written communication skills. Duration is mid-May to mid-August. $5.50 per hour. Open to college freshmen, college sophomores, college juniors, college seniors, recent college graduates.

Benefits On-the-job training, possible full-time employment, travel reimbursement, willing to complete paperwork for educational credit.

Contact E-mail Bruce Heisel, Managing Editor. Phone: 906-483-2210. Fax: 906-482-2726. E-mail: bheisel@mininggazette.com. Telephone interview required. Applicants must submit a letter of interest, resume, writing sample. Applications are accepted continuously. World Wide Web: http://www.mininggazette.com.

THE DALLAS MORNING NEWS
508 Young Street
Dallas, Texas 75202

General Information Newspaper with daily circulation of 520,000 and Sunday circulation of 785,000. Established in 1885. Number of employees: 2,000. Unit of Belo Corporation, Dallas, Texas. Number of internship applications received each year: 400.

Internships Available ▶ *4 copy editors.* Candidates should have ability to work with others, analytical skills, college courses in field, editing skills, experience in the field, plan to pursue career in field, writing skills. Duration is 12 weeks. $535 per week. ▶ *1–2 graphic artists.* Candidates should have ability to work with others, college courses in field, computer skills, knowledge of field, research skills, self-motivation. Duration is 12 weeks. $535 per week. ▶ *2 photographers.* Candidates should have ability to work with others, college courses in field, knowledge of field, plan to pursue career in field, self-motivation, knowledge of digital cameras. Duration is 12 weeks. $535 per week. ▶ *7–10 reporters.* Candidates should have ability to work with others, analytical skills, college courses in field, editing skills, experience in the field, plan to pursue career in field, writing skills. Duration is 12 weeks. $535 per week. Open to college freshmen, college sophomores, college juniors, college seniors, recent college graduates, graduate students.

Benefits Housing at a cost, job counseling, on-the-job training, opportunity to attend seminars/workshops, possible full-time employment, willing to act as a professional reference, willing to complete paperwork for educational credit, willing to provide letters of recommendation.

Contact Write or through World Wide Web site Sue F. Smith, Deputy Managing Editor, Communications Center, PO Box 655237, Dallas, Texas 75265. No phone calls. Applicants must submit a letter of interest, resume, portfolio, three personal references, 7-10 writing samples, cover letter. Application deadline: November 15 for summer. World Wide Web: http://www.dallasnews.com.

DELAWARE COUNTY DAILY TIMES
500 Mildred Avenue
Primos, Pennsylvania 19018

General Information Seven-day-per-week newspaper serving Delaware County. Established in 1876. Number of employees: 140. Unit of The Journal Register Company, Trenton, New Jersey. Number of internship applications received each year: 50.

Internships Available ▶ *1–3 reporters:* responsibilities include covering fires, school board meetings, corporate events, and features. Candidates should have ability to work independently, ability to work with others, computer skills, personal interest in the field, self-motivation, writing skills. Duration is 3 months. Paid. Open to college freshmen, college sophomores, college juniors, college seniors, recent college graduates.

Benefits Possible full-time employment, travel reimbursement, willing to act as a professional reference, willing to complete paperwork for educational credit, willing to provide letters of recommendation.

Contact Write, call, fax, or e-mail Linda DeMeglio, Managing Editor. Phone: 610-622-8817. Fax: 610-622-8887. E-mail: ldemeglio@delcotimes.com. In-person interview recommended (telephone interview accepted). Applicants must submit a letter of interest, resume, 3 to 6 writing samples. Application deadline: March 1 for summer. World Wide Web: http://www.delcotimes.com.

DEMOCRAT AND CHRONICLE
55 Exchange Boulevard
Rochester, New York 14614

General Information Newspaper that serves the Rochester, New York area. Number of employees: 900. Unit of Gannett Co., Inc., McLean, Virginia.

Internships Available ▶ *1 business reporting intern.* Candidates should have analytical skills, organizational skills, research skills, self-motivation, written communication skills, valid driver's license.

Duration is 10 weeks during summer. $500 per week. ▶ *1 copyediting intern*. Candidates should have analytical skills, editing skills, organizational skills, research skills, self-motivation, written communication skills, valid driver's license. Duration is 10 weeks during summer. $500 per week.
Benefits On-the-job training, willing to complete paperwork for educational credit.
Contact Write Dow Jones Newspaper Fund (through college placement office). No phone calls. Applicants must submit drug test; apply through college placement office. Application deadline: deadlines, set by the DOW Jones Newspaper Fund, may be obtained through college placement director. World Wide Web: http://www.democratandchronicle.com.

DENVER POST CORPORATION
1560 Broadway
Denver, Colorado 80202

General Information Publisher of general circulation newspaper. Established in 1892. Number of employees: 268. Unit of Media News Group, Inc., Denver, Colorado. Number of internship applications received each year: 300.
Internships Available ▶ *3–7 interns:* responsibilities include reporting news, editing copy, graphics, or photography in a department commensurate with intern's skills and interests. Candidates should have computer skills, experience in the field, oral communication skills, organizational skills, plan to pursue career in field, research skills, self-motivation, strong interpersonal skills, writing skills. Duration is 10 weeks. $460 per week. Open to students who have completed their junior year of college (minimum). International applications accepted.
Benefits On-the-job training, possible full-time employment, willing to act as a professional reference, willing to complete paperwork for educational credit, willing to provide letters of recommendation, reimbursement for travel while on assignment, health insurance after 30 days.
Contact Write, e-mail, or through World Wide Web site Internship Recruiter. E-mail: living@denverpost.com. No phone calls. Telephone interview required. Applicants must submit a letter of interest, resume, list of three personal references; reporting applicants should include a portfolio of no more than 5 clips; photography applicants should provide a portfolio with primarily color slides and a self-addressed stamped envelope for return of slides. Application deadline: October 31 for summer. World Wide Web: http://www.denverpost.com.

DES MOINES REGISTER
715 Locust Street
Des Moines, Iowa 50309

General Information Daily and Sunday statewide newspaper. Established in 1826. Unit of Gannett Co., Inc., McLean, Virginia. Number of internship applications received each year: 200.
Internships Available ▶ *1 art intern:* responsibilities include producing informational graphics for the daily and Sunday newspaper. Candidates should have ability to work with others, college courses in field, plan to pursue career in field, self-motivation, written communication skills, Macintosh skills. Duration is 12 weeks in summer. $10.62 per hour. ▶ *3 copy editor interns:* responsibilities include editing copy and stories, writing headlines and doing layouts (2 nightside news copy desk positions; 1 sports copy desk position). Candidates should have ability to work with others, college courses in field, computer skills, editing skills, plan to pursue career in field, self-motivation, layout/design skills. Duration is 12 weeks in summer. $10.75 per hour. ▶ *1 photo intern:* responsibilities include shooting photos on deadline and for enterprise stories. Candidates should have ability to work with others, college courses in field, computer skills, plan to pursue career in field, self-motivation, strong visual skills. Duration is 12 weeks in summer. $10.75 per hour. ▶ *5 reporting interns:* responsibilities include reporting stories, both breaking news and enterprise, for the daily and Sunday Register. Candidates should have ability to work with others, college courses in field, plan to pursue career in field, research skills, writing skills. Duration is 12 weeks in summer. $10.75 per hour. ▶ *1 sports reporter:* responsibilities include providing coverage of high school and collegiate sports. Candidates

should have ability to work with others, college courses in field, plan to pursue career in field, research skills, writing skills. Duration is 12 weeks in summer. $10.75 per hour. Open to college juniors, college seniors.
Benefits Formal training, names of contacts, on-the-job training, opportunity to attend seminars/workshops, possible full-time employment, willing to complete paperwork for educational credit, willing to provide letters of recommendation, reimbursement of work-related travel expenses.
Contact Write or e-mail Diane E. Graham, Managing Editor/ Staff Development, PO Box 957, Des Moines, Iowa 50311. E-mail: dgraham@dmreg.com. No phone calls. Applicants must submit a letter of interest, resume, 8-10 work samples, 2-3 personal references. Application deadline: April 1 for fall, December 1 for summer. World Wide Web: http://www.desmoinesregister.com.

DETROIT FREE PRESS
600 West Fort Street
Detroit, Michigan 48226

General Information One of the nation's 20 largest newspapers; winner of 8 Pulitzer Prizes. Established in 1831. Number of employees: 300. Unit of Knight Ridder, San Jose, California. Number of internship applications received each year: 450.
Internships Available ▶ *Interns:* responsibilities include working in the areas Web producing, feature writing in health and entertainment, news writing, editorial page writing, copy editing, business, and sports writing. Duration is 12 weeks. $541 per week. Open to college sophomores, college juniors, college seniors, recent college graduates, graduate students, career changers.
Benefits Formal training, job counseling, names of contacts, on-the-job training, opportunity to attend seminars/workshops, possible full-time employment, willing to complete paperwork for educational credit, willing to provide letters of recommendation.
Contact Write, call, fax, e-mail, or through World Wide Web site Mr. Joe Grimm, Recruiting and Development Editor. Phone: 313-222-6490. Fax: 313-222-5981. E-mail: grimm@freepress.com. In-person interview recommended (telephone interview accepted). Applicants must submit a letter of interest, resume, portfolio, three personal references, 6 work samples. Application deadline: December 1 for summer. World Wide Web: http://www.freep.com/jobspage.

DULUTH NEWS TRIBUNE
424 West First Street
Duluth, Minnesota 55802

General Information Daily morning newspaper. Number of employees: 300. Division of Knight Ridder, San Jose, California. Number of internship applications received each year: 400.
Internships Available ▶ *10 Ridder Fellows:* responsibilities include positions available in news, sports, and features reporting; photography, graphic arts, copy editing, and page design. Candidates should have ability to work independently, ability to work with others, oral communication skills, plan to pursue career in field, self-motivation, written communication skills, ability to work under deadline pressure. Duration is one summer (8 weeks). $440 per week. Open to college sophomores, college juniors, college seniors. International applications accepted.
Benefits Free housing, names of contacts, on-the-job training, opportunity to attend seminars/workshops, possible full-time employment, willing to act as a professional reference, willing to complete paperwork for educational credit, willing to provide letters of recommendation.
Contact Write, call, or e-mail Holly Gruber, Intern Coordinator. Phone: 218-720-4106. Fax: 218-720-4120. E-mail: hgruber@ duluthnews.com. Telephone interview required. Applicants must submit a resume, portfolio, four personal references, essay (1 page) on motivation for internship, 10-15 writing samples. Application deadline: December 1.

ELYRIA CHRONICLE–TELEGRAM
225 East Avenue
Elyria, Ohio 44035

General Information Daily and Sunday newspaper. Established in 1829. Number of employees: 50. Unit of Lorain County Printing and Publishing Company, Elyria, Ohio. Number of internship applications received each year: 125.

Internships Available ▶ *1 copy desk intern:* responsibilities include design, pagination, copyediting, and writing headlines. Candidates should have college courses in field, computer skills, editing skills, knowledge of field, self-motivation, writing skills. Duration is 3 months. $325 per week. Open to college freshmen, college sophomores, college juniors, college seniors. ▶ *2–3 newsroom interns:* responsibilities include reporting and writing. Candidates should have ability to work independently, ability to work with others, plan to pursue career in field, research skills, self-motivation, writing skills. Duration is 3–4 months. $325 per week. Open to college freshmen, college sophomores, college juniors, college seniors. ▶ *1 photo department intern:* responsibilities include taking photos for paper. Candidates should have ability to work independently, ability to work with others, college courses in field, knowledge of field, plan to pursue career in field, self-motivation. Duration is 3 months. $325 per week. Open to college freshmen, college sophomores, college juniors, college seniors, recent college graduates. International applications accepted.

Benefits Job counseling, names of contacts, possible full-time employment, travel reimbursement, willing to act as a professional reference, willing to provide letters of recommendation.

Contact Write, fax, or e-mail Mr. Rudy Dicks, Managing Editor. Phone: 440-329-7126. Fax: 440-329-7282. E-mail: rdicks@ohio. net. In-person interview required. Applicants must submit a letter of interest, resume, three personal references, 8-10 writing samples. Application deadline: February 1 for summer. World Wide Web: http://www.chronicletelegram.com.

EMPIRE STATE WEEKLIES
2010 Empire Boulevard
Webster, New York 14580

General Information Group of weekly community newspapers serving eastern Monroe and western Wayne counties. Established in 1863. Number of employees: 25. Number of internship applications received each year: 8.

Internships Available ▶ *2 editorial interns:* responsibilities include assisting with general editorial duties. Candidates should have ability to work independently, computer skills, editing skills, oral communication skills, personal interest in the field, self-motivation, strong interpersonal skills, writing skills. Duration is 3–6 months. Unpaid. Open to high school seniors, recent high school graduates, college freshmen, college sophomores, college juniors, college seniors, recent college graduates. International applications accepted.

Benefits Job counseling, on-the-job training, possible full-time employment, willing to complete paperwork for educational credit, willing to provide letters of recommendation.

Contact Write, call, or e-mail Michael B. Sorenson, Managing Editor. Phone: 585-671-1533. Fax: 585-671-7067. E-mail: websterherald@empirestateweeklies.com. In-person interview recommended (telephone interview accepted). Applicants must submit a letter of interest, resume, three writing samples, three personal references. Application deadline: February 15 for spring, April 15 for summer, July 15 for fall.

THE FRESNO BEE
1626 E Street
Fresno, California 93786

General Information Newspaper. Established in 1922. Number of employees: 156. Branch of The McClatchy Company, Sacramento, California. Number of internship applications received each year: 115.

Internships Available ▶ *2–3 general assignment reporters:* responsibilities include general assignment reporting, probably including police, city government, and feature stories. Candidates should have ability to work independently, ability to work with others, computer skills, plan to pursue career in field, self-motivation, writing skills. Duration is 12 weeks (June to August). $413 per week. Open to college sophomores, college juniors, college seniors, recent college graduates, not open to those who have had previous internships at Fresno Bee. ▶ *1 photography intern:* responsibilities include general assignments including sports. Candidates should have ability to work with others, college courses in field, computer skills, plan to pursue career in field, self-motivation, photographic skills. Duration is 12 weeks (June to August). $400 per week. Open to college sophomores, college juniors, college seniors, recent college graduates.

Benefits On-the-job training, possible full-time employment, willing to act as a professional reference, willing to complete paperwork for educational credit, willing to provide letters of recommendation.

Contact Write, call, e-mail, or through World Wide Web site Rich Marshall, Senior Editor. Phone: 559-441-6443. Fax: 559-441-6640. E-mail: rmarshal@fresnobee.com. Telephone interview required. Applicants must submit a letter of interest, resume, 3-5 writing samples. Application deadline: January 10. World Wide Web: http://www.fresnobee.com.

THE GAZETTE
30 South Prospect Street
Colorado Springs, Colorado 80903

General Information Daily newspaper. Established in 1872. Number of employees: 500. Unit of Freedom Communications, Irvine, California. Number of internship applications received each year: 200.

Internships Available ▶ *1 photo intern:* responsibilities include all tasks of a staff photographer. Candidates should have ability to work independently, ability to work with others, computer skills, knowledge of field, oral communication skills, personal interest in the field, self-motivation, writing skills. Duration is 3 months. $10 per hour. Open to college freshmen, college sophomores, college juniors, college seniors, recent college graduates, graduate students. ▶ *4–6 reporting interns:* responsibilities include various duties from year to year; refer to Web site for information on number of openings, pay, and types of internships available. Candidates should have ability to work independently, computer skills, experience in the field, oral communication skills, plan to pursue career in field, self-motivation, writing skills. Duration is 10 weeks. $10 per hour. Open to college juniors, college seniors, recent college graduates, graduate students.

Benefits Formal training, job counseling, on-the-job training, opportunity to attend seminars/workshops, possible full-time employment, willing to complete paperwork for educational credit.

Contact Write, e-mail, or through World Wide Web site Connie Steele, Newsroom Administrator, 30 South Prospect Street, Colorado Springs, Colorado 80903. Fax: 719-636-0202. E-mail: csteele@gazette.com. No phone calls. Applicants must submit a letter of interest, resume, 6 writing samples. Application deadline: November 30 for summer; continuous for photo interns. World Wide Web: http://www.gazette.com/other/interns.php.

GAZETTE COMMUNICATIONS
PO Box 511
Cedar Rapids, Iowa 52406

General Information Multimedia company publishing regional newspaper. Established in 1883. Number of employees: 750. Unit of Gazette Communications, Cedar Rapids, Iowa. Number of internship applications received each year: 300.

Internships Available ▶ *2–3 KCRG-TV News interns:* responsibilities include shadowing reporters, assignment editors, photographers, and producers through the television new gathering process; will learn all aspects of news gathering process, but will also focus on intern's interest. Candidates should have ability to work independently, ability to work with others, college courses in field, oral communication skills, organizational skills, self-motivation. Duration is 1 semester. Unpaid. Open to college juniors, college seniors. ▶ *2 advertising interns:* responsibilities include working with display and classified advertising; planning and conducting sales presentations; coordinating ad design and layouts. Candidates should have ability to work independently, ability to work with others, college courses in field, computer skills, oral communication skills, organizational skills, personal interest in the field, plan to pursue career in field, self-motivation, written communication skills. Duration is May to August. $7.50 per hour. Open to college sophomores, college juniors. ▶ *3–4 news reporting interns:* responsibilities include general reporting responsibilities. Candidates should have ability to work independently, college courses in field, computer skills, knowledge of field, oral communication skills, plan to pursue career in field, self-motivation, writing skills. Duration is 3 months in fall, spring, or summer. $8 per hour. Open to college sophomores, college juniors, college seniors. ▶ *3–4 photo interns:* responsibilities include taking photos for stories in newspaper. Candidates should have ability to work independently, ability to work with others, declared college major in field, knowledge of field, oral communication skills, plan to pursue career in field, self-motivation. Duration is 3 months in fall, spring, or summer. $8 per hour. Open to college sophomores, college juniors, college seniors, recent college graduates. ▶ *1 public relations intern:* responsibilities include assisting with "Newspaper in Education" projects and events, attending editor's coffees, assisting with "In your Neighborhood" projects, in-house promotions, and other related efforts. Candidates should have ability to work independently, computer skills, knowledge of field, oral communication skills, personal interest in the field, self-motivation, strong interpersonal skills, written communication skills. Duration is 1 summer. $7–$7.50 per hour. Open to college sophomores, college juniors.

Benefits Possible full-time employment, willing to complete paperwork for educational credit, willing to provide letters of recommendation.

Contact Write, fax, or e-mail Patricia Thoms, Employment Manager. Fax: 319-368-8834. E-mail: gazcohr@gazettecommunications.com. No phone calls. In-person interview recommended (telephone interview accepted). Applicants must submit a letter of interest, resume, 6 news clips, photo portfolio. Application deadline: January 1 for summer (reporters and photographers), March 15 for advertising and public relations (summer term only), May 1 for fall (reporters and photographers), September 1 for winter (reporters and photographers). World Wide Web: http://www.gazettecommunications.com.

HIGH COUNTRY NEWS
Box 1090
Paonia, Colorado 81428

General Information Paper that covers the communities and environment of the Rocky Mountain West, the Southwest, the Great Basin, California, and the Pacific Northwest; circulation is 23,000. Established in 1970. Number of employees: 25. Number of internship applications received each year: 75.

Internships Available ▶ *6 editorial interns:* responsibilities include writing news briefs and stories for Western Roundup section, looking for story leads in news releases and newspapers, sorting mail, and answering telephone calls. Candidates should have research skills, self-motivation, strong interpersonal skills, writing skills, knowledge of High Country News and the West. Duration is 4 months. Stipend of $500 per month. Open to college seniors, recent college graduates, graduate students, law students, career changers, individuals reentering the workforce.

Benefits Free housing, names of contacts, on-the-job training, opportunity to attend seminars/workshops, travel reimbursement, willing to complete paperwork for educational credit, willing to provide letters of recommendation.

Contact Write, call, e-mail, or through World Wide Web site Matt Jenkins, Assistant Editor, PO Box 1090, Paonia, Colorado 81428. Phone: 970-527-4898. E-mail: matt@hcn.org. Telephone interview required. Applicants must submit a letter of interest, resume, three writing samples. Application deadline: March 1 for summer (May 3-August 27), June 30 for fall (August 30-December 17), October 27 for spring (January 5-April 30). World Wide Web: http://www.hcn.org.

HONOLULU ADVERTISER
Box 3110
Honolulu, Hawaii 96802

General Information Morning/afternoon newspaper with circulation of 150,000. Established in 1856. Number of employees: 150. Affiliate of Gannett Co., Inc., McLean, Virginia. Number of internship applications received each year: 50.

Internships Available ▶ *2–3 interns:* responsibilities include working in the newsroom learning various reporting and editing techniques. Candidates should have ability to work with others, experience in the field, plan to pursue career in field, self-motivation, writing skills. Duration is 10–13 weeks. $10 per hour. Open to college freshmen, college sophomores, college juniors, college seniors, recent college graduates, graduate students, only those with ties to Hawaii.

Benefits On-the-job training, possible full-time employment, willing to act as a professional reference.

Contact Write, call, or e-mail Shauna Goya, Intern Coordinator. Phone: 808-535-2425. Fax: 808-525-8037. E-mail: sgoya@honoluluadvertiser.com. Applicants must submit a letter of interest, resume, three personal references, letter of recommendation, 6 writing samples; test will be arranged for finalists. Application deadline: November 1. World Wide Web: http://www.honoluluadvertiser.com.

LANCASTER NEWSPAPERS
8 West King Street, PO Box 1328
Lancaster, Pennsylvania 17608-1328

General Information Community newspaper with a circulation of 90,000 daily and 110,000 Sunday. Established in 1794. Number of employees: 550. Number of internship applications received each year: 30.

Internships Available ▶ *1–2 advertising/marketing interns:* responsibilities include selling advertising and working on marketing projects. Candidates should have ability to work with others, computer skills, knowledge of field, oral communication skills, plan to pursue career in field, written communication skills. Duration is 13 weeks from May to August. Salary commensurate with experience. ▶ *1 information services intern:* responsibilities include PC and Macintosh system support, installation, and troubleshooting. Candidates should have ability to work independently, ability to work with others, analytical skills, computer skills, knowledge of field, plan to pursue career in field. Duration is 13 weeks. $7.50 per hour. ▶ *6–9 reporters:* responsibilities include general assignment reporting. Candidates should have computer skills, editing skills, knowledge of field, writing skills. Duration is 13 weeks. $7.50–$9 per hour. Open to college freshmen, college sophomores, college juniors, college seniors.

Benefits Formal training, possible full-time employment, travel reimbursement, willing to provide letters of recommendation.

Contact Write, fax, or e-mail Tonya Nevling, Human Resources Manager. Phone: 717-291-8681. Fax: 717-293-4311. E-mail: humanresources@lnpnews.com. Applicants must submit a letter of interest, resume, 3 writing samples (for reporters). Application deadline: December 31 for summer. World Wide Web: http://www.lancasteronline.com.

LAS VEGAS REVIEW-JOURNAL
PO Box 70
Las Vegas, Nevada 89125

General Information Daily newspaper with circulation of 188,000. Established in 1905. Number of employees: 764. Unit of Donrey Media Group Newspaper Division, Las Vegas, Nevada. Number of internship applications received each year: 50.

Internships Available ▶ *1–3 reporters:* responsibilities include general assignment reporting. Candidates should have college courses in field, computer skills, editing skills, research skills, strong interpersonal skills, writing skills. Duration is 3 months in summer. $10 per hour. Open to college juniors, college seniors, recent college graduates, graduate students, journalism majors.

Benefits Names of contacts, possible full-time employment, willing to complete paperwork for educational credit.

Las Vegas Review-Journal (continued)

Contact Write, fax, or e-mail Charles Zobell, Managing Editor, PO Box 70, Las Vegas, Nevada 89125-0070. Fax: 702-383-4676. E-mail: charles_zobell@lvrj.com. No phone calls. In-person interview recommended (telephone interview accepted). Applicants must submit a letter of interest, resume, two writing samples. Application deadline: March 15 for summer. World Wide Web: http://www.lvrj.com.

LEXINGTON HERALD-LEADER
100 Midland Avenue
Lexington, Kentucky 40508

General Information Pulitzer prize-winning newspaper covering central and eastern Kentucky with daily circulation of about 120,000 and Sunday circulation of about 165,000. Number of employees: 520. Unit of Knight Ridder, San Jose, California. Number of internship applications received each year: 300.
Internships Available ▶ *1 copy editing intern:* responsibilities include editing copy and writing headlines. Candidates should have college courses in field, computer skills, editing skills, knowledge of field, writing skills, must have own transportation. Duration is 10 weeks in summer (40 hours per week). $450 per week. Open to college freshmen, college sophomores, college juniors, college seniors. ▶ *1 design desk intern:* responsibilities include layout and design. Candidates should have ability to work independently, college courses in field, computer skills, knowledge of field, personal interest in the field, must have own transportation. Duration is 10 weeks in summer (40 hours per week). $450 per week. Open to college freshmen, college sophomores, college juniors, college seniors, recent college graduates. ▶ *1 photo intern.* Candidates should have ability to work with others, knowledge of field, personal interest in the field, self-motivation, must have own transportation. Duration is 10 weeks in summer (40 hours per week). $450 per week. Open to college freshmen, college sophomores, college juniors, college seniors, recent college graduates, graduate students. ▶ *4 reporting interns:* responsibilities include reporting and writing stories. Candidates should have college courses in field, experience in the field, oral communication skills, personal interest in the field, writing skills, must have own transportation. Duration is 10 weeks in summer. $450 per week. Open to college freshmen, college sophomores, college juniors, college seniors, recent college graduates. International applications accepted.
Benefits On-the-job training, opportunity to attend seminars/workshops, possible full-time employment, willing to act as a professional reference, willing to complete paperwork for educational credit, willing to provide letters of recommendation, reimbursement for mileage and other job-related expenses while on assignment.
Contact Write Liz Petros. Phone: 859-231-3305. Fax: 859-231-1363. E-mail: lpetros@herald-leader.com. Applicants must submit a letter of interest, resume, 5-10 writing samples, telephone interview (for finalists). Application deadline: November 15. World Wide Web: http://www.kentucky.com.

LIMA NEWS
3515 Elida Road, PO Box 690
Lima, Ohio 45802-0690

General Information Newspaper. Number of employees: 36. Unit of Freedom Communications, Irvine, California. Number of internship applications received each year: 50.
Internships Available ▶ *2 photographers.* Candidates should have ability to work independently, knowledge of field, plan to pursue career in field, self-motivation, strong interpersonal skills. Duration is 3 months (year-round). $300 per week. Open to college freshmen, college sophomores, college juniors, college seniors.
Benefits On-the-job training, possible full-time employment, willing to act as a professional reference, willing to complete paperwork for educational credit.
Contact Write or e-mail Craig Orosz, Photo Editor. E-mail: corosz@limanews.com. No phone calls. In-person interview required. Applicants must submit a letter of interest, resume, three personal references, three letters of recommendation, 6-10 writing clips. Applications are accepted continuously. World Wide Web: http://www.limanews.com.

MIDWEST SUBURBAN PUBLISHING
6901 West 159th Street
Tenley Park, Illinois 60477

General Information Publisher of Daily Southtown and Star Publications. Established in 1901. Unit of Hollinger International, Toronto, Canada. Number of internship applications received each year: 100.
Internships Available ▶ *Interns.* Duration is 12 weeks in summer. Paid. Open to college freshmen, college sophomores, college juniors, college seniors, graduate students. International applications accepted.
Benefits Possible full-time employment, willing to complete paperwork for educational credit, willing to provide letters of recommendation, possible travel reimbursement.
Contact Write, fax, or e-mail John Hector, Metro Editor. Fax: 708-633-5999. E-mail: jhector@dailysouthtown.com. No phone calls. In-person interview recommended (telephone interview accepted). Applicants must submit a letter of interest, resume, writing clips. Applications are accepted continuously. World Wide Web: http://www.dailysouthtown.com.

MILWAUKEE JOURNAL SENTINEL
333 West State Street
Milwaukee, Wisconsin 53203

General Information Publisher of largest newspaper in Wisconsin with daily circulation of 278,300 and Sunday circulation of 461,000. Established in 1837. Number of employees: 1,500. Subsidiary of Journal Communications, Milwaukee, Wisconsin. Number of internship applications received each year: 500.
Internships Available ▶ *Newsroom interns:* responsibilities include working in areas of copy editing, reporting, graphics, design, or photography. Candidates should have major in journalism (preferred), previous internship or newsroom experience (preferred). Duration is 12 weeks. $450 per week. Open to college juniors, college seniors, recent college graduates, graduate students. International applications accepted.
Benefits Job counseling, on-the-job training, opportunity to attend seminars/workshops, possible full-time employment, willing to act as a professional reference, willing to complete paperwork for educational credit, willing to provide letters of recommendation, reimbursement for mileage and other job-related expenses while on assignment.
Contact Write or e-mail Marilyn Krause, Senior Editor/Administration. E-mail: mkrause@journalsentinel.com. No phone calls. Applicants must submit a resume, portfolio, cover letter, 5-6 writing clips, in-person or telephone interview. Application deadline: November 1 for summer. World Wide Web: http://www.jsonline.com.

THE NEWS & OBSERVER
215 South McDowell Street, PO Box 191
Raleigh, North Carolina 27601

General Information Newspaper. Established in 1894. Number of employees: 1,000. Unit of The McClatchy Company, Sacramento, California. Number of internship applications received each year: 300.
Internships Available ▶ *1 fall visual internship:* responsibilities include page design and creation of graphic elements for daily newspaper. Candidates should have ability to work independently, ability to work with others, experience in the field, personal interest in the field, plan to pursue career in field, self-motivation. Duration is 12 weeks. $450 per week. Open to college sophomores, college juniors, college seniors, recent college graduates, graduate students. ▶ *8 newsroom reporters, copy editors, and graphic artists:* responsibilities include reporting, editing, or designing for the daily newspaper. Candidates should have knowledge of field, personal interest in the field, self-motivation, strong interpersonal

skills. Duration is 10 weeks. $450 per week. Open to college sophomores, college juniors, college seniors, recent college graduates, graduate students, career changers.
Benefits Formal training, job counseling, on-the-job training, opportunity to attend seminars/workshops, willing to act as a professional reference, willing to complete paperwork for educational credit, willing to provide letters of recommendation.
Contact Through World Wide Web site Susan Spring, Director of Operations. Fax: 919-836-5911. No phone calls. Applicants must submit a formal organization application, letter of interest, resume, personal reference, 500-word autobiography, 6 writing samples; interview may be required. Application deadline: July 1 for fall, November 1 for summer. World Wide Web: http://www.newsobserver.com.

THE NEWS-COURIER
PO Box 670
Athens, Alabama 35612

General Information Newspaper. Number of employees: 30. Unit of Community Newspaper Holdings, Inc., Birmingham, Alabama. Number of internship applications received each year: 8.
Internships Available ▶ *1 reporter:* responsibilities include interviews, meeting coverage, writing stories, and some photography. Candidates should have editing skills, organizational skills, plan to pursue career in field, self-motivation, written communication skills. Duration is 3 months. $5.30–$5.75 per hour. International applications accepted.
Benefits On-the-job training, possible full-time employment.
Contact Write or fax Sonny Turner, Editor, PO Box 670, Athens, Alabama 35612. Fax: 256-233-7753. No phone calls. In-person interview recommended (telephone interview accepted). Applicants must submit a letter of interest, resume, three personal references, 5 writing samples. Applications are accepted continuously.

NEWSDAY
235 Pinelawn Road
Melville, New York 11747-4250

General Information Nation's sixth largest daily newspaper with a circulation of over 577,000 and 675,000 on Sunday. Established in 1945. Number of employees: 1,000. Subsidiary of The Tribune Company, Chicago, Illinois. Number of internship applications received each year: 200.
Internships Available ▶ *20–30 reporters, librarians, photographers, graphic interns, and copy editors:* responsibilities include covering spot news, writing features, reporting, taking photographs, library work, on-line Internet research, and artwork. Candidates should have ability to work independently, ability to work with others, editing skills, knowledge of field, writing skills. Duration is 10 weeks in summer (full-time); spring and fall positions part-time (2 days per week). Position available as unpaid or at $525 per week for summer positions; spring and fall positions unpaid. Open to college juniors, college seniors, graduate students.
Benefits Opportunity to attend seminars/workshops, willing to complete paperwork for educational credit, willing to provide letters of recommendation, travel reimbursement while on assignment.
Contact Write, call, e-mail, or through World Wide Web site Walter Middlebrook, Jr., Associate Editor for Recruitment. Phone: 631-843-2637. E-mail: jobs@newsday.com. Applicants must submit a formal organization application, letter of interest, resume, academic transcripts, three letters of recommendation, writing test (included on application), portfolio (graphics and photography interns), writing samples (reporters, librarians, or editors), Dow Jones test for copyeditors (recommended). Application deadline: May 31 for fall, November 15 for summer, November 8 for spring. World Wide Web: http://www.newsday.com/about/jobs/jobinter/htm.

THE NEWS-SENTINEL
600 West Main Street
Fort Wayne, Indiana 46802

General Information Newspaper published in the afternoon Monday through Saturday. Unit of Knight Ridder, San Jose, California. Number of internship applications received each year: 200.
Internships Available ▶ *1–2 general assignment reporter interns.* Candidates should have computer skills, organizational skills, plan to pursue career in field, self-motivation, writing skills. Duration is 10–12 weeks. Position available as unpaid or at $400 per week. Open to college sophomores, college juniors, college seniors, recent college graduates, graduate students, career changers. ▶ *1–2 photographer interns.* Candidates should have computer skills, organizational skills, plan to pursue career in field, self-motivation, writing skills, some photography experience (preferred). Duration is 10–12 weeks. Position available as unpaid or at $400 per week. Open to college sophomores, college juniors, college seniors, graduate students, career changers.
Benefits Formal training, job counseling, on-the-job training, opportunity to attend seminars/workshops, possible full-time employment, travel reimbursement, willing to act as a professional reference, willing to complete paperwork for educational credit, willing to provide letters of recommendation.
Contact Write Richard Griffis, Managing Editor. Fax: 260-461-8817. E-mail: rgriffis@news-sentinel.com. No phone calls. In-person interview recommended (telephone interview accepted). Applicants must submit a letter of interest, resume, portfolio, 6-8 writing samples. Application deadline: December 1 for summer. World Wide Web: http://www.news-sentinel.com.

THE NEW YORK TIMES
229 West 43rd Street
New York, New York 10036

General Information Newspaper. Established in 1851. Number of employees: 4,000. Number of internship applications received each year: 300.
Internships Available ▶ *3 copy editors:* responsibilities include editing stories and writing headlines for publication. Candidates should have ability to work independently, analytical skills, computer skills, editing skills, knowledge of field, oral communication skills, plan to pursue career in field, research skills, self-motivation, strong interpersonal skills, writing skills. Duration is end of May to beginning of August. $700 per week. Open to college juniors, college seniors, graduate students. ▶ *1 design intern:* responsibilities include producing page layouts for publication. Candidates should have ability to work independently, computer skills, knowledge of field, oral communication skills, organizational skills, plan to pursue career in field, self-motivation, writing skills. Duration is end of May to beginning of August. $700 per week. Open to college juniors, college seniors, graduate students. ▶ *1 graphics intern:* responsibilities include producing graphics for publication. Candidates should have ability to work independently, analytical skills, computer skills, knowledge of field, oral communication skills, organizational skills, plan to pursue career in field, research skills, self-motivation, strong interpersonal skills, writing skills. Duration is end of May to beginning of August . $700 per week. Open to college juniors, college seniors, graduate students. ▶ *1 photographer.* Candidates should have ability to work independently, knowledge of field, oral communication skills, plan to pursue career in field, strong interpersonal skills, written communication skills. Duration is end of May to beginning of August. $700 per week. Open to college juniors, college seniors, graduate students. ▶ *4 reporters:* responsibilities include reporting and writing stories for publication. Candidates should have ability to work independently, analytical skills, computer skills, knowledge of field, oral communication skills, plan to pursue career in field, research skills, self-motivation, strong interpersonal skills, writing skills. Duration is end of May to beginning of August. $700 per week. Open to college seniors, graduate students. International applications accepted.
Benefits Job counseling, names of contacts, on-the-job training, opportunity to attend seminars/workshops, possible full-time employment, travel reimbursement, willing to act as a profes-

sional reference, willing to complete paperwork for educational credit, willing to provide letters of recommendation, $300 monthly housing subsidy.
Contact Write, call, or e-mail Sheila Rule, Senior Manager, Recruiting. Phone: 212-556-4143. E-mail: rulesh@nytimes.com. Applicants must submit a letter of interest, resume, portfolio, 8-10 writing samples; previous internship required. Application deadline: November 15. World Wide Web: http://www.nytimes.com.

OMAHA WORLD-HERALD COMPANY
1334 Dodge Street
Omaha, Nebraska 68102

General Information Mass circulation newspaper. Established in 1865. Number of employees: 800. Number of internship applications received each year: 100.
Internships Available ▶ *4 advertising interns:* responsibilities include sales, production, and special projects. Candidates should have computer skills, declared college major in field, knowledge of field, personal interest in the field, self-motivation, writing skills. Duration is 12 weeks. $400 per week. ▶ *4–6 news interns:* responsibilities include writing news and feature stories and editing copy. Candidates should have analytical skills, editing skills, personal interest in the field, self-motivation, writing skills. Duration is 12 weeks. $400 per week. Open to college juniors, college seniors. International applications accepted.
Benefits Formal training, job counseling, on-the-job training, opportunity to attend seminars/workshops, possible full-time employment, willing to act as a professional reference, willing to complete paperwork for educational credit, willing to provide letters of recommendation, some mentoring, $1000 scholarship.
Contact Write, call, fax, or e-mail Jeff Gauger, Assistant Manager Editor. Phone: 800-284-6397. Fax: 402-345-0183. E-mail: jgauger@owh.com. In-person interview recommended (telephone interview accepted). Applicants must submit a letter of interest, resume, 4-6 examples of work. Application deadline: November 1 for summer.

ORLANDO SENTINEL
633 North Orange Avenue
Orlando, Florida 32801

General Information Newspaper. Established in 1876. Number of employees: 1,500. Subsidiary of Tribune Company, Chicago, Illinois. Number of internship applications received each year: 250.
Internships Available ▶ *6–8 interns:* responsibilities include working in various areas including reporting, editing, photography, or graphic arts. Candidates should have ability to work with others, analytical skills, experience in the field, plan to pursue career in field, research skills, writing skills. Duration is 10–12 weeks. $500 per week. Open to college juniors, college seniors, graduate students, individuals with previous internships in journalism.
Benefits On-the-job training, opportunity to attend seminars/workshops, possible full-time employment, willing to act as a professional reference, willing to complete paperwork for educational credit.
Contact Write, e-mail, or through World Wide Web site Mr. Dana S. Eagles, Recruitment and Staff Development Editor. E-mail: deagles@orlandosentinel.com. No phone calls. Applicants must submit a letter of interest, resume, three personal references, five work samples. Application deadline: November 15 for summer, November 1 for winter (sports only). World Wide Web: http://www.orlandosentinel.com.

THE OTTAWA HERALD
104 South Cedar Street
Ottawa, Kansas 66067

General Information Daily newspaper. Established in 1896. Number of employees: 36.
Internships Available ▶ *2 reporter/photographer interns:* responsibilities include working on general assignments with opportunities for copyediting. Candidates should have experience with a school publication. Duration is up to 12 weeks in the summer. $8 per hour. Open to college freshmen, college sophomores, college juniors, college seniors, recent college graduates, graduate students.
Benefits On-the-job training, travel reimbursement, willing to act as a professional reference, willing to complete paperwork for educational credit, willing to provide letters of recommendation.
Contact Write, fax, e-mail, or through World Wide Web site Jeanny Sharp, Editor and Publisher. Phone: 785-242-4700. Fax: 785-242-9420. E-mail: jsharp@ottawaherald.com. In-person interview recommended (telephone interview accepted). Applicants must submit a letter of interest, resume, clips (for reporters), samples (for photographers). Applications are accepted continuously. World Wide Web: http://www.ottawaherald.com.

THE PALM BEACH POST
2751 South Dixie Highway
West Palm Beach, Florida 33405

General Information Daily newspaper. Number of employees: 1,200. Unit of Cox Newspapers, Inc., Atlanta, Georgia. Number of internship applications received each year: 400.
Internships Available ▶ *2 photography interns:* responsibilities include working as full-time photographer. Candidates should have ability to work independently, ability to work with others, knowledge of field, oral communication skills, plan to pursue career in field, self-motivation, former photo internship. Duration is 16 weeks. Paid. ▶ *3 summer reporting interns (metro or sports):* responsibilities include working in the same capacity as a full-time reporter. Candidates should have ability to work independently, ability to work with others, experience in the field, oral communication skills, personal interest in the field, plan to pursue career in field, self-motivation, writing skills. Duration is 10–12 weeks. Paid. Open to college freshmen, college sophomores, college juniors, college seniors, graduate students. International applications accepted.
Benefits Job counseling, names of contacts, on-the-job training, opportunity to attend seminars/workshops, willing to act as a professional reference, willing to complete paperwork for educational credit, willing to provide letters of recommendation.
Contact Write Lynn Kalber, Director of Administration/Newsroom, 2751 South Dixie Highway, West Palm Beach, Florida 33405. E-mail: lkalber@pbpost.com. No phone calls. Applicants must submit a letter of interest, resume, portfolio, writing sample. Application deadline: April 1 for fall, December 1 for summer. World Wide Web: http://www.palmbeachpost.com.

PEORIA JOURNAL STAR
1 News Plaza
Peoria, Illinois 61643

General Information Newspaper with a circulation of 87,900 Monday–Friday, 106,000 Saturday, and 112,600 Sunday. Established in 1855. Number of employees: 400. Unit of Copley Newspapers, Inc., La Jolla, California. Number of internship applications received each year: 300.
Internships Available ▶ *2 news interns:* responsibilities include reporting assigned stories. Candidates should have ability to work with others, college courses in field, experience in the field, oral communication skills, self-motivation, written communication skills, reporting skills. Duration is 2–4 months. $275 per week. Open to college juniors, college seniors, recent college graduates, graduate students.
Benefits On-the-job training, possible full-time employment, willing to complete paperwork for educational credit, willing to provide letters of recommendation.
Contact Write, fax, e-mail, or through World Wide Web site Jerry D. McDowell, City Editor. Fax: 309-686-3296. E-mail: jmcdowell@pjstar.com. In-person interview recommended (telephone interview accepted). Applicants must submit a letter of interest, resume, 5-10 writing samples, 3-5 personal references. Application deadline: February 15 for summer, July 30 for fall, November 30 for spring. World Wide Web: http://www.pjstar.com.

PHILADELPHIA INQUIRER
400 North Broad Street
Philadelphia, Pennsylvania 19130

General Information Major metropolitan newspaper that offers a strong investigative approach to issues and a solid national and foreign report. Established in 1829. Number of employees: 525. Unit of Knight Ridder, San Jose, California. Number of internship applications received each year: 500.
Internships Available ▶ *5 Art Peters Programs interns:* responsibilities include training on copy desk, reporting. Candidates should have ability to work independently, editing skills, plan to pursue career in field, self-motivation, strong interpersonal skills, written communication skills. Duration is 1 summer. $662 per week. Open to college freshmen, college sophomores, college juniors, college seniors, graduate students (between semesters). ▶ *1 Knight Ridder Minority Specialty Development Program intern:* responsibilities include working with editors and reporters. Candidates should have ability to work independently, computer skills, oral communication skills, research skills, self-motivation, strong interpersonal skills, strong leadership ability, written communication skills. Duration is 1 year. $819 per week. Open to recent college graduates, graduate students. ▶ *1 minority graphics intern:* responsibilities include graphics and page design. Candidates should have computer skills, oral communication skills, self-motivation, strong interpersonal skills, written communication skills. Duration is 10 weeks. $662 per week. Open to college freshmen, college sophomores, college juniors, college seniors, recent college graduates, graduate students. ▶ *1 minority photojournalism intern:* responsibilities include shooting assignments in news, features, and sports. Candidates should have ability to work independently, analytical skills, experience in the field, oral communication skills, plan to pursue career in field, self-motivation, strong interpersonal skills, strong leadership ability, written communication skills. Duration is 1 summer. $662 per week. Open to college freshmen, college sophomores, college juniors, college seniors, graduate students. International applications accepted.
Benefits Formal training, job counseling, names of contacts, opportunity to attend seminars/workshops, possible full-time employment, willing to act as a professional reference, willing to complete paperwork for educational credit, willing to provide letters of recommendation, ongoing evaluations.
Contact Write Oscar Miller, Director of Recruiting. Phone: 215-854-5102. Fax: 215-854-2578. E-mail: omiller@phillynews.com. In-person interview recommended (telephone interview accepted). Applicants must submit a resume, portfolio, three personal references, 8-10 writing samples. Application deadline: November 15 for summer interns, December 1 for Knight Ridder intern. World Wide Web: http://www.phillynews.com.

REGIONAL NEWS
12243 South Harlem Avenue
Palos Heights, Illinois 60463

General Information Weekly suburban newspaper with paid circulation. Established in 1941. Number of employees: 30. Number of internship applications received each year: 20.
Internships Available ▶ *1 display advertising/outside sales intern:* responsibilities include performing primarily outside and some telephone sales. Candidates should have ability to work independently, college courses in field, experience in the field, oral communication skills, personal interest in the field, self-motivation, strong interpersonal skills. Duration is 11–13 weeks. $8.50 per hour plus commission. Open to college juniors, college seniors, recent college graduates, graduate students, career changers with sales experience.
Benefits Formal training, job counseling, names of contacts, on-the-job training, possible full-time employment, travel reimbursement, willing to act as a professional reference, willing to complete paperwork for educational credit, willing to provide letters of recommendation, phone and car allowances.
Contact Write Mr. Charles Richards, Publisher and Owner. Fax: 708-448-4012. No phone calls. In-person interview required. Applicants must submit a formal organization application, letter of interest, resume. Application deadline: April 15.

RICHMOND TIMES-DISPATCH
300 East Franklin Street
Richmond, Virginia 23219

General Information Newspaper with daily circulation of approximately 195,000 and Sunday circulation of 240,000. Established in 1850. Number of employees: 900. Unit of Media General, Richmond, Virginia. Number of internship applications received each year: 180.
Internships Available ▶ *1 graphics intern:* responsibilities include using PC graphics illustration and free-hand illustration in news department. Candidates should have ability to work independently, computer skills, personal interest in the field, self-motivation, strong interpersonal skills, writing skills. Duration is 10 weeks (May to August). $445 per week. ▶ *6 news department editorial interns:* responsibilities include writing, reporting, editing, and processing information. Candidates should have analytical skills, editing skills, plan to pursue career in field, self-motivation, strong interpersonal skills, writing skills. Duration is 10 weeks (May to August). $445 per week. ▶ *1 photo intern:* responsibilities include taking news and feature photographs and conducting photo lab work. Candidates should have ability to work independently, computer skills, knowledge of field, plan to pursue career in field, strong interpersonal skills, writing skills. Duration is 10 weeks (September to November). $445 per week. Open to college juniors, college seniors, recent college graduates, graduate students.
Benefits Job counseling, names of contacts, on-the-job training, possible full-time employment, willing to provide letters of recommendation, opportunity to attend periodic intern meetings that include speakers from the newsroom and other departments.
Contact Write or e-mail Mr. John A. Dillon, Deputy Managing Editor, PO Box 85333, Richmond, Virginia 23293. E-mail: jdillon@timesdispatch.com. In-person interview recommended (telephone interview accepted). Applicants must submit a letter of interest, resume, 5-8 writing samples, 2-3 personal references. Application deadline: January 10 for summer, June 12 for photo intern, December 10 for spring. World Wide Web: http://www.timesdispatch.com.

ROLL CALL
50 F Street, NW, Suite 700
Washington, District of Columbia 20001

General Information Thrice-weekly newspaper covering Capitol Hill. Established in 1955. Number of employees: 40. Unit of The Economist, London, United Kingdom. Number of internship applications received each year: 50.
Internships Available ▶ *4 editorial interns:* responsibilities include assisting editors and reporters with research and reporting; some independent reporting and writing; some general office duties. Candidates should have computer skills, plan to pursue career in field, research skills, self-motivation, writing skills. Duration is one summer or semester. Unpaid. Open to college freshmen, college sophomores, college juniors, college seniors, recent college graduates, graduate students. International applications accepted.
Benefits On-the-job training, possible full-time employment, willing to act as a professional reference, willing to complete paperwork for educational credit, willing to provide letters of recommendation.
Contact Write, call, fax, or e-mail Doug Fruehling, Managing Editor. Phone: 202-349-4150. Fax: 202-824-0902. E-mail: dwf@rollcall.com. Telephone interview required. Applicants must submit a letter of interest, resume, two writing samples. Application deadline: March 1 for summer, July 31 for fall, November 15 for spring. World Wide Web: http://www.rollcall.com.

THE SAGINAW NEWS
203 South Washington Avenue
Saginaw, Michigan 48607

General Information Newspaper with a circulation of 50,000 daily and 60,000 Sunday papers in eastern and mid-Michigan. Established in 1859. Number of internship applications received each year: 100.
Internships Available ▶ *1–2 news interns.* Candidates should have ability to work independently, oral communication skills, self-

motivation, strong interpersonal skills, writing skills. Duration is 3–4 months. $10.40 per hour. Open to college freshmen, college sophomores, college juniors, college seniors, recent college graduates. ► *1 photography intern:* responsibilities include daily duties of a newspaper staff photographer. Candidates should have ability to work independently, computer skills, plan to pursue career in field, self-motivation. Duration is 3-6 months (spring, summer, fall). $10.40 per hour. Open to college freshmen, college sophomores, college juniors, college seniors, recent college graduates, graduate students.

Benefits Names of contacts, on-the-job training, possible full-time employment, willing to act as a professional reference.

Contact Write or e-mail Jodi McFarland, Assistant Metro Editor. Phone: 989-776-9675. Fax: 989-752-3115. E-mail: jmcfarland@ thesaginawnews.com. In-person interview required. Applicants must submit a letter of interest, resume, three personal references, 6 writing samples. Applications are accepted continuously.

THE ST. AUGUSTINE RECORD
1 News Place
St. Augustine, Florida 32086

General Information Daily newspaper in northeast Florida. Established in 1894. Number of employees: 100. Unit of Morris Communications Corporation, Augusta, Georgia.

Internships Available ► *5 interns.* Candidates should have ability to work with others, experience in the field. Duration is 1 semester. Paid. Open to college juniors, college seniors, recent college graduates, graduate students.

Benefits Willing to act as a professional reference, willing to complete paperwork for educational credit, willing to provide letters of recommendation.

Contact Fax, e-mail, or through World Wide Web site Jim Baltzelle, Editor. Fax: 904-819-3558. E-mail: jbaltzelle@staugustinerecord. com. No phone calls. Applications are accepted continuously. World Wide Web: http://www.staugustine.com.

ST. PAUL PIONEER PRESS
345 Cedar Street
St. Paul, Minnesota 55101

General Information Award-winning daily newspaper covering the Twin Cities area. Established in 1849. Number of employees: 1,000. Unit of Knight Ridder, San Jose, California. Number of internship applications received each year: 300.

Internships Available ► *1 Native American newsroom intern.* Duration is 12 weeks. $580 per week. ► *3–5 newsroom interns:* responsibilities include positions available in reporting, copy editing, graphic design, new media, photography, page design/layout. Duration is 10 weeks. $580 per week. Candidates for all positions should have ability to work independently, ability to work with others, knowledge of field, self-motivation, writing skills. Open to college sophomores, college juniors, college seniors, recent college graduates, graduate students.

Benefits Job counseling, on-the-job training, opportunity to attend seminars/workshops, possible full-time employment, willing to act as a professional reference, willing to provide letters of recommendation.

Contact Write, call, or e-mail Rubèn Rosario, Columnist/Internship Coordinator. Phone: 651-228-5454. Fax: 651-228-2159. E-mail: rrosario@pioneerpress.com. In-person interview recommended (telephone interview accepted). Applicants must submit a letter of interest, resume, portfolio, three personal references, 2–page personal essay, 6–8 writing samples. Application deadline: December 30. World Wide Web: http://www.pioneerplanet.com.

ST. PETERSBURG TIMES
490 First Avenue South
St. Petersburg, Florida 33701-4204

General Information Independent metropolitan daily newspaper covering west-central Florida. Established in 1884. Number of employees: 1,500. Number of internship applications received each year: 500.

Internships Available ► *12–18 summer interns:* responsibilities include working either in the newsroom, design and graphics, or business departments performing hands-on newspaper tasks. Candidates should have ability to work with others, analytical skills, experience in the field, oral communication skills, organizational skills, written communication skills. Duration is 10–12 weeks. $450 per week. Open to college sophomores, college juniors, college seniors, recent college graduates.

Benefits On-the-job training, possible full-time employment, willing to act as a professional reference, willing to provide letters of recommendation, scholarships available for returning students.

Contact Write, call, or e-mail Nancy Waclawek, Director of Corporate Giving, PO Box 1121, St. Petersburg, Florida 33731. Phone: 727-893-8780. Fax: 727-892-2257. E-mail: waclawek@sptimes. com. Applicants must submit a letter of interest, resume, three personal references, 5-6 clips (reporting interns), portfolio samples (art/design/photography interns). Application deadline: December 1 for news and marketing interns; February 15 for all other departments. World Wide Web: http://www.sptimes.com/ internship.

SAN FRANCISCO BAY GUARDIAN
135 Mississippi Street
San Francisco, California 94107

General Information San Francisco-based liberal alternative news and arts/entertainment weekly paper. Established in 1966. Number of employees: 100. Number of internship applications received each year: 175.

Internships Available ► *3 arts and entertainment journalism interns:* responsibilities include sorting mail and faxes, compiling and writing "superlists," becoming a staff writer for the calendar section, and writing preview blurbs and short reviews by pitch or on assignment. Candidates should have ability to work independently, computer skills, oral communication skills, plan to pursue career in field, research skills, self-motivation, strong interpersonal skills, written communication skills, demonstrable or background interest in either music, theater, or film, knowledge of San Francisco area (helpful). Duration is 4 months (2 days per week). Unpaid. Open to recent high school graduates, college freshmen, college sophomores, college juniors, college seniors, recent college graduates, graduate students. ► *1 culture intern:* responsibilities include writing, editing, research, fact-checking, and light office work. Candidates should have ability to work with others, editing skills, oral communication skills, plan to pursue career in field, research skills, self-motivation, writing skills, sense of humor, knowledge of San Francisco area. Duration is 4 months (2 days per week). Unpaid. Open to recent high school graduates, college freshmen, college sophomores, college juniors, college seniors, recent college graduates, graduate students, law students, career changers, individuals reentering the workforce. ► *4–6 news interns:* responsibilities include writing, researching, checking facts, and assisting in the newsroom. Candidates should have ability to work independently, ability to work with others, analytical skills, computer skills, oral communication skills, personal interest in the field, research skills, self-motivation, written communication skills, knowledge of San Francisco area. Duration is 4 months (2 days per week). Unpaid. Open to recent high school graduates, college freshmen, college sophomores, college juniors, college seniors, recent college graduates, graduate students, law students, career changers, individuals reentering the workforce. ► *1 online department intern:* responsibilities include writing and researching stories and working on Web site. Candidates should have ability to work independently, analytical skills, computer skills, editing skills, knowledge of field, oral communication skills, personal interest in the field, research skills, self-motivation, strong interpersonal skills, strong leadership ability, writing skills, design and/or html skills. Duration is 4 months (2 days per week). Unpaid. Open to high school seniors, recent high school graduates, college freshmen, college sophomores, college juniors, college seniors, recent college graduates, graduate students, law students, career changers, individuals reentering the workforce. International applications accepted.

Benefits Job counseling, names of contacts, on-the-job training, opportunity to attend seminars/workshops, willing to act as a

professional reference, willing to complete paperwork for educational credit, willing to provide letters of recommendation.
Contact Through World Wide Web site Corbett Miller, Editorial Coordinator. Phone: 415-255-3100. Fax: 415-255-8762. E-mail: corbett@sfbg.com. In-person interview recommended (telephone interview accepted). Applicants must submit a resume, three writing samples, cover letter. Application deadline: April 15 for summer, August 15 for fall, December 15 for spring. World Wide Web: http://www.sfbg.com.

THE SEATTLE TIMES
1120 John Street, PO Box 70
Seattle, Washington 98111

General Information Newspaper. Established in 1896. Number of employees: 2,000. Number of internship applications received each year: 600.
Internships Available ▶ *1–3 Blethen Family Internships for Minority Journalists:* responsibilities include reporting, photography, copy desk, arts/graphic assignments. Candidates should have computer skills, editing skills, experience in the field, plan to pursue career in field, writing skills. Duration is flexible. Paid. Open to college sophomores, college juniors, college seniors, recent college graduates. ▶ *Residency interns:* responsibilities include reporting, photography, copy desk, and arts/graphics. Candidates should have computer skills, editing skills, experience in the field, plan to pursue career in field, writing skills. Duration is 3 years. $525 per week. Open to recent college graduates, journalists with limited daily newspaper experience. ▶ *12 summer interns:* responsibilities include reporting, photography, arts/graphics, and copy desk duties. Candidates should have computer skills, editing skills, knowledge of field, plan to pursue career in field, research skills, writing skills. Duration is 12 weeks. $525 per week. Open to college freshmen, college sophomores, college juniors, college seniors, recent college graduates, graduate students.
Benefits Job counseling, on-the-job training, possible full-time employment, willing to act as a professional reference, willing to provide letters of recommendation, possibility of health insurance.
Contact Write, call, fax, e-mail, or through World Wide Web site Danyelle Lesch, Internship Coordinator. Phone: 206-464-2414. Fax: 206-464-2261. E-mail: newsinternships@seattletimes.com. Applicants must submit a letter of interest, resume, 5-7 samples of published work, formal application (upon hire). Application deadline: November 1 for summer interns; continuous for other positions. World Wide Web: http://seattletimes.com/internships.

THE STATE NEWSPAPER
PO Box 1333
Columbia, South Carolina 29202

General Information Newspaper that serves South Carolina with a daily circulation of 120,000. Established in 1891. Number of employees: 500. Unit of Knight Ridder, San Jose, California. Number of internship applications received each year: 150.
Internships Available ▶ *1 copy editor:* responsibilities include editing copy and writing headlines. Candidates should have ability to work independently, college courses in field, editing skills, oral communication skills, plan to pursue career in field, written communication skills. Duration is 10–12 weeks. $375 per week. Open to college sophomores, college juniors. ▶ *1–2 reporting interns:* responsibilities include covering events and writing stories. Candidates should have ability to work independently, oral communication skills, organizational skills, plan to pursue career in field, writing skills. Duration is 10-12 weeks in summer. $375 per week. Open to college freshmen, college sophomores, college juniors. International applications accepted.
Benefits Job counseling, names of contacts, on-the-job training, opportunity to attend seminars/workshops, possible full-time employment, willing to complete paperwork for educational credit, willing to provide letters of recommendation.
Contact Write, fax, or e-mail Paul Osmundson, Assistant Managing Editor. Fax: 803-771-8430. E-mail: posmundson@thestate.com. No phone calls. Applicants must submit a letter of interest, resume, three personal references, five writing samples. Application deadline: January 1 for summer. World Wide Web: http://www.thestate.com.

THE TAMPA TRIBUNE
200 South Parker Street
Tampa, Florida 33606

General Information Newspaper that publishes a morning edition, Monday to Sunday, with a circulation of about 265,000. Number of employees: 500. Unit of Media General, Richmond, Virginia. Number of internship applications received each year: 200.
Internships Available ▶ *1 copyeditor intern.* Candidates should have editing skills, knowledge of field, plan to pursue career in field, strong interpersonal skills, writing skills, experience in copyediting (AP style grammar and English). Duration is 10 weeks in summer. $480 per week. Open to college freshmen, college sophomores, college juniors, college seniors, graduate students. ▶ *1 design intern.* Candidates should have computer skills, experience in the field, oral communication skills, research skills, strong interpersonal skills, written communication skills. Duration is 10 weeks. $400 per week. Open to college freshmen, college sophomores, college juniors, college seniors, recent college graduates, graduate students. ▶ *1 photography intern.* Candidates should have computer skills, experience in the field, oral communication skills, plan to pursue career in field, strong interpersonal skills, photo skills. Duration is 10 weeks. $480 per week. Open to college freshmen, college sophomores, college juniors, college seniors, recent college graduates, graduate students. ▶ *2 reporter interns:* responsibilities include reporting and handling all aspects of news gathering and writing. Candidates should have ability to work with others, experience in the field, oral communication skills, organizational skills, plan to pursue career in field, written communication skills. Duration is 10 weeks. $480 per week. Open to college freshmen, college sophomores, college juniors, college seniors, graduate students.
Benefits On-the-job training, willing to act as a professional reference, willing to provide letters of recommendation, professional experience.
Contact Write, call, or e-mail Beverly Dominick, News Recruiting and Training Manager, PO Box 191, Tampa, Florida 33601. Phone: 813-259-7633. E-mail: bdominick@tamptrib.com. Applicants must submit a formal organization application, letter of interest, resume, three personal references, 6 writing samples, at least 1 letter of recommendation. Application deadline: December 1. World Wide Web: http://www.tampatrib.com.

TIMES LEADER
15 North Main Street
Wilkes-Barre, Pennsylvania 18711

General Information Newspaper. Number of employees: 200. Unit of Knight Ridder, San Jose, California. Number of internship applications received each year: 24.
Internships Available ▶ *2–6 interns:* responsibilities include reporting, copy editing, photography, or page design. Candidates should have computer skills, knowledge of field, plan to pursue career in field, research skills, self-motivation, strong interpersonal skills, written communication skills. Duration is 6–12 weeks. Position available as unpaid or at $300 per week. Open to college freshmen, college sophomores, college juniors, college seniors, recent college graduates, graduate students.
Benefits On-the-job training, willing to complete paperwork for educational credit.
Contact Write, fax, or e-mail Pamela C. Turfa, Intern Coordinator, 15 North Main Street, Wilkes-Barre, Pennsylvania 18711. Phone: 570-829-7177. Fax: 570-970-7446. E-mail: pamt@leader.net. Applicants must submit a letter of interest, resume, three personal references, 3 to 5 writing samples, portfolio (photography applicants). Application deadline: March 1. World Wide Web: http://www.timesleader.com.

TOLEDO BLADE
541 North Superior Street
Toledo, Ohio 43660

General Information Publisher of newspaper with daily circulation of 145,000 and Sunday circulation of 200,000. Established

Toledo Blade (continued)

in 1836. Number of employees: 750. Division of Block Communications, Inc., Toledo, Ohio. Number of internship applications received each year: 300.

Internships Available ▶ *4 city desk reporters:* responsibilities include general assignment reporting. Candidates should have ability to work independently, ability to work with others, college courses in field, computer skills, editing skills, knowledge of field, oral communication skills, plan to pursue career in field, research skills, written communication skills. Duration is 13 weeks in summer only. $512 per week. ▶ *4 photographers:* responsibilities include taking, processing, and printing pictures. Candidates should have ability to work independently, ability to work with others, college courses in field, computer skills, oral communication skills, personal interest in the field, plan to pursue career in field, written communication skills, advanced photography skills, accuracy a must. Duration is 1 semester. $512 per week. Open to college juniors, college seniors, recent college graduates, graduate students.

Benefits On-the-job training, possible full-time employment, willing to act as a professional reference, willing to complete paperwork for educational credit, willing to provide letters of recommendation.

Contact Write or e-mail Luann Sharp, Assistant Managing Editor. E-mail: luannsharp@theblade.com. No phone calls. Telephone interview required. Applicants must submit a formal organization application, letter of interest, resume, three personal references, writing samples. Application deadline: January 15 for city desk positions; continuous for photographer positions. World Wide Web: http://www.toledoblade.com.

THE VINDICATOR
PO Box 780
Youngstown, Ohio 44501-0780

General Information Daily newspaper with circulation of about 78,000. Established in 1869. Number of employees: 400. Number of internship applications received each year: 35.

Internships Available ▶ *6 copy editors:* responsibilities include editing stories for content, spelling, grammar, accuracy, and style; writing headlines; learning basics of design and pagination. Candidates should have ability to work independently, computer skills, editing skills, self-motivation, strong interpersonal skills, writing skills. Duration is 12–15 weeks. $300 per week. Open to college sophomores, college juniors, college seniors. ▶ *5 general assignment reporters:* responsibilities include substantive contributions to the daily work of a newspaper in reporting, copy desk, photography, and design/graphics. Candidates should have ability to work independently, ability to work with others, computer skills, editing skills, knowledge of field, writing skills. Duration is 12 weeks. $300 per week. Open to college sophomores, college juniors, college seniors. ▶ *1 page designer:* responsibilities include design and pagination. Candidates should have ability to work independently, computer skills, knowledge of field, organizational skills, self-motivation, strong interpersonal skills. Duration is 12 weeks. $300 per week. Open to college sophomores, college juniors, college seniors, recent college graduates.

Benefits On-the-job training, possible full-time employment, willing to complete paperwork for educational credit.

Contact Write, call, or e-mail Ernest A. Brown, Jr., Assistant Regional Editor/Intern Coordinator, Youngstown, Ohio. Phone: 330-747-1471 Ext. 1304. Fax: 330-747-6712. E-mail: ebrown@vindy.com. In-person interview required. Applicants must submit a letter of interest, resume, three writing samples, two personal references. Application deadline: March 31 for summer; contact for deadlines for other positions.

THE WASHINGTON POST
1150 15th Street, NW
Washington, District of Columbia 20071

General Information Newspaper publisher. Established in 1877. Number of employees: 3,500. Unit of The Washington Post Co., Washington, District of Columbia. Number of internship applications received each year: 600.

Internships Available ▶ *3–4 copy editors:* responsibilities include working on foreign, national, metro, sports, and business copy desks. Candidates should have ability to work with others, computer skills, editing skills, knowledge of field, personal interest in the field, writing skills. Duration is 12 weeks (June to August). $894.75 per week. ▶ *1 editorial page writer/copy editor.* Candidates should have ability to work with others, editing skills, personal interest in the field, research skills, written communication skills. Duration is 12 weeks (June to August). $813.40 per week. ▶ *1 news artist:* responsibilities include designing pages and producing graphics and maps. Candidates should have ability to work with others, computer skills, editing skills, knowledge of field, research skills, writing skills. Duration is 12 weeks (June to August). $813.40 per week. ▶ *1 page designer:* responsibilities include designing pages for news and features sections. Candidates should have ability to work with others, computer skills, editing skills, knowledge of field, oral communication skills, writing skills. Duration is 12 weeks (June to August). $894.75 per week. ▶ *1 photographer:* responsibilities include shooting photos and working inside the photo department. Candidates should have ability to work independently, ability to work with others, experience in the field, oral communication skills, personal interest in the field. Duration is 12 weeks (June to August). $813.40 per week. ▶ *12–14 reporters:* responsibilities include reporting and writing stories for metro, business, sports, and style sections. Candidates should have ability to work independently, knowledge of field, research skills, strong interpersonal skills, writing skills. Duration is 12 weeks (June to August). $813.40 per week. Open to college juniors, college seniors, graduate students. International applications accepted.

Benefits Formal training, job counseling, names of contacts, opportunity to attend seminars/workshops, possible full-time employment, willing to act as a professional reference, willing to provide letters of recommendation, reimbursement of work-related travel expenses.

Contact Write, e-mail, or through World Wide Web site Cheryl G. Butler, Summer News Program. E-mail: butlerc@washpost.com. No phone calls. In-person interview recommended (telephone interview accepted). Applicants must submit a formal organization application, resume, academic transcripts, portfolio, two letters of recommendation, 6-8 writing samples or photo/graphics portfolio. Application deadline: November 1. World Wide Web: http://www.washingtonpost.com/intern.

THE WASHINGTON TIMES
3600 New York Avenue, NE
Washington, District of Columbia 20002

General Information Publisher of daily newspaper. Established in 1982. Number of employees: 850. Number of internship applications received each year: 320.

Internships Available ▶ *1 copy editor:* responsibilities include editing copy, writing headlines and captions, formatting stories. Candidates should have ability to work independently, ability to work with others, editing skills, knowledge of field, oral communication skills, plan to pursue career in field, self-motivation, writing skills. Duration is 8 weeks. $300 per week. Open to college sophomores, college juniors, college seniors, recent college graduates. ▶ *7 editorial writers:* responsibilities include reporting and writing news and feature stories. Candidates should have ability to work with others, knowledge of field, plan to pursue career in field, research skills, self-motivation, writing skills. Duration is 8 weeks. $300 per week. Open to college sophomores, college juniors, college seniors. ▶ *1 graphic artist:* responsibilities include page design and production (QuarkXpress) of news and features, production of information graphics, and story illustration. Candidates should have ability to work independently, ability to work with others, college courses in field, computer skills, personal interest in the field, self-motivation. Duration is 8 weeks. $300 per week. Open to college sophomores, college juniors, college seniors. ▶ *1 photographer:* responsibilities include photographing daily news assignments according to newspaper deadlines. Candidates should have ability to work with others, computer skills, declared college major in field, experience in the field, plan to pursue career in field, self-motivation. Duration is 8 weeks. $300 per week. Open to college sophomores, college juniors, college seniors. ▶ *7* *reporters:* responsibilities include reporting and writing news and feature stories. Candidates should have ability to work with others, knowledge of field, oral communication skills, plan to pursue career in field, self-motivation, writing skills. Duration is 8 weeks. $300 per week. Open to college sophomores, college juniors, college seniors.

Benefits On-the-job training, possible full-time employment, willing to complete paperwork for educational credit.

Contact Write or e-mail Kenneth M. McIntyre, Assistant Managing Editor. E-mail: jlea@washingtontimes.com. No phone calls. Applicants must submit a letter of interest, resume, 5-10 writing samples, 5-10 samples of photos or graphics (if relevant). Application deadline: December 31 for summer. World Wide Web: http://www.washingtontimes.com.

WATERBURY REPUBLICAN-AMERICAN
389 Meadow Street
Waterbury, Connecticut 06702

General Information Newspaper publishing daily and Sunday editions. Established in 1844. Number of employees: 320. Number of internship applications received each year: 50.

Internships Available ▶ *1–2 advertising sales interns:* responsibilities include selling advertising to clients. Candidates should have ability to work independently, office skills, oral communication skills, organizational skills, plan to pursue career in field, self-motivation, strong interpersonal skills, written communication skills, must have own transportation, valid driver's license. Duration is 2–3 months. Paid. ▶ *1–2 graphics designers:* responsibilities include creating advertisements for clients. Candidates should have ability to work independently, ability to work with others, college courses in field, computer skills, plan to pursue career in field, self-motivation, prior graphics course work/experience preferred (Adobe Illustrator or other graphics software), multi-ad creator. Duration is 2–3 months. Paid. ▶ *1–2 photographers:* responsibilities include photographing news-related events and people. Candidates should have ability to work independently, ability to work with others, analytical skills, declared college major in field, experience in the field, oral communication skills, organizational skills, plan to pursue career in field, self-motivation, written communication skills. Duration is 2–4 months. Paid. ▶ *1–3 reporters:* responsibilities include collecting and reporting news. Candidates should have ability to work independently, ability to work with others, analytical skills, computer skills, declared college major in field, oral communication skills, organizational skills, plan to pursue career in field, research skills, self-motivation, writing skills. Duration is 2–4 months. Paid. Open to college sophomores, college juniors, college seniors, graduate students.

Benefits On-the-job training, opportunity to attend seminars/workshops, possible full-time employment, willing to act as a professional reference, willing to complete paperwork for educational credit, willing to provide letters of recommendation.

Contact Write, fax, or e-mail Patricia D. Nagle, Personnel Manager. Fax: 203-573-9432. E-mail: pnagle@rep-am.com. No phone calls. In-person interview required. Applicants must submit a formal organization application, letter of interest, resume, portfolio (if applicable). Applications are accepted continuously.

WINSTON-SALEM JOURNAL
PO Box 3159
Winston-Salem, North Carolina 27102

General Information Daily newspaper serving 9 counties in northwestern North Carolina. Established in 1897. Number of employees: 463. Unit of Media General, Richmond, Virginia. Number of internship applications received each year: 75.

Internships Available ▶ *1 advertising salesperson:* responsibilities include selling and laying out ads and customer relations. Candidates should have college courses in field, experience in the field, organizational skills, plan to pursue career in field, strong interpersonal skills. Duration is flexible. $275 per week. ▶ *1 marketing and creative services intern:* responsibilities include assisting marketing department with creative services special projects. Duration is flexible. $300 per week. ▶ *3–4 newspaper reporters:* responsibilities include general assignment reporting. Candidates should have college courses in field, experience in the field, plan to pursue

career in field, self-motivation, writing skills. Duration is 10–12 weeks. $375 per week. ▶ *1 photographer:* responsibilities include taking photos, performing general assignments, and developing and printing film. Candidates should have ability to work independently, college courses in field, experience in the field, plan to pursue career in field. Duration is flexible. $375 per week. Open to college juniors, college seniors returning to school in the fall. International applications accepted.

Benefits Formal training, possible full-time employment, travel reimbursement.

Contact Write, call, fax, or e-mail Randy Noftle, Director of Human Resources. Phone: 336-727-7330. Fax: 336-727-4096. E-mail: rnoftle@wsjournal.com. In-person interview recommended (telephone interview accepted). Applicants must submit a formal organization application, letter of interest, resume, academic transcripts, two letters of recommendation. Application deadline: December 31 for summer. World Wide Web: http://www.wsjournal.com.

NEWSPAPER, PERIODICAL, BOOK, AND DATABASE PUBLISHERS

AGORA, INC.
14 West Mt. Vernon Place
Baltimore, Maryland 21201

General Information International publisher of investment, travel, and health-related consumer publications with affiliated offices in Florida, New Mexico, London, Paris, and Ireland. Established in 1979. Number of employees: 180. Number of internship applications received each year: 400.

Internships Available ▶ *Copy writers:* responsibilities include working with promotional advertising material, brochures, newsletter articles, special reports, and bulletins. Candidates should have ability to work independently, computer skills, editing skills, research skills, writing skills. Duration is flexible. $10 to $15 per day, or $6 to $8 per hour. ▶ *Editorial associates:* responsibilities include research, fact checking, correcting copy, and administrative duties. Candidates should have ability to work independently, ability to work with others, computer skills, editing skills, oral communication skills, personal interest in the field, written communication skills. Duration is flexible. $10 to $15 per day, or $6 to $8 per hour. ▶ *Graphic design interns.* Candidates should have ability to work independently, college courses in field, knowledge of field, office skills, personal interest in the field, self-motivation, knowledge of Quark, Illustrator, PhotoShop, PageMaker, and Word. Duration is flexible. $10 to $15 per day, or $6 to $8 per hour. ▶ *Marketing interns:* responsibilities include print buying, customer correspondence, and general administrative duties. Candidates should have ability to work independently, ability to work with others, computer skills, oral communication skills, personal interest in the field, written communication skills. Duration is flexible. $10 to $15 per day, or $6 to $8 per hour. Open to college freshmen, college sophomores, college juniors, college seniors, graduate students. International applications accepted.

Benefits Opportunity to attend seminars/workshops, possible full-time employment, willing to complete paperwork for educational credit, willing to provide letters of recommendation, free housing for out-of-state and international interns.

International Internships Available in France; Waterford, Ireland.

Contact Write, fax, or e-mail Elizabeth Zepp, Personnel Specialist. Fax: 410-783-8455. E-mail: ezepp@agora-inc.com. No phone calls. Applicants must submit a letter of interest, resume, cover letter indicating placement preference. Applications are accepted continuously. World Wide Web: http://www.agora-inc.com.

ARCHAE EDITIONS
Box 444, Prince Street Station
New York, New York 10012-0008

General Information Nonprofit organization that produces alternative materials and literature (books, prints, audios, videos, and film). Established in 1977. Number of employees: 1. Number of internship applications received each year: 50.
Internships Available ▶ *5–10 collaborative assistants.* Duration is flexible. Unpaid. Open to college juniors, college seniors, recent college graduates, graduate students. ▶ *8–10 interns:* responsibilities include collaborating with a productive full-time artist/writer (usually Richard Kostelanetz) in the project-centered production of books, videotapes, films, holograms, and audiotapes for exhibition and production. Candidates should have ability to work independently, computer skills, editing skills, plan to pursue career in field, self-motivation, desire to complete a project that should prominently display the intern's name. Duration is flexible. Unpaid. Open to college sophomores, college juniors, college seniors, recent college graduates, career changers. International applications accepted.
Benefits Job counseling, names of contacts, on-the-job training, possible full-time employment, willing to complete paperwork for educational credit, willing to provide letters of recommendation, projects on which interns can put their names.
Contact Write, e-mail, or through World Wide Web site Mr. Richard Kostelanetz, Director of Literature and Media. E-mail: rkostelanetz@bigfoot.com. No phone calls. In-person interview recommended (telephone interview accepted). Applicants must submit a letter of interest, resume. Applications are accepted continuously. World Wide Web: http://www.richardkostelanetz.com.

ART PAPERS MAGAZINE
PO Box 5748
Atlanta, Georgia 31107

General Information Nonprofit organization and publisher of ART PAPERS Magazine brings readers diverse, independent, and award-winning coverage of contemporary art and culture. Established in 1977. Number of employees: 6. Number of internship applications received each year: 50.
Internships Available ▶ *1 advertising intern:* responsibilities include organizing and researching information for potential current advertisers and contacting potential advertisers. Candidates should have ability to work independently, analytical skills, computer skills, editing skills, office skills, oral communication skills, organizational skills, research skills, self-motivation, writing skills, strong interest in sales and marketing (experience preferred). Duration is 1 semester (minimum). Unpaid. ▶ *2 editorial interns:* responsibilities include assisting editors with correspondence and communication with contributing writers; copy editing; assisting in management of articles through production; updating and maintaining records and archives. Candidates should have ability to work independently, computer skills, editing skills, knowledge of field, research skills, writing skills. Duration is 1 semester (minimum); 6-12 month residency available. Unpaid. ▶ *1 finance and operations intern:* responsibilities include researching contacts for potential sponsors and donors; assisting with basic accounting functions; and working to create beneficial partnerships with other organizations. Candidates should have ability to work independently, college courses in field, computer skills, experience in the field, organizational skills, research skills, writing skills, Quickbooks and Excel. Duration is 1 semester (minimum). Unpaid. ▶ *1 marketing and development intern:* responsibilities include developing marketing campaigns to reach new vendors and subscribers; researching, identifying, and contacting potential subscribers; developing, marketing, and implementing circulation expansion projects; researching and identifying potential advertisers. Candidates should have ability to work independently, computer skills, organizational skills, research skills, writing skills, background or experience in marketing, database experience a plus. Duration is 1 semester (minimum). Unpaid. Open to college juniors, college seniors, recent college graduates, graduate students.

Benefits Willing to act as a professional reference, willing to complete paperwork for educational credit, willing to provide letters of recommendation.
Contact Write, call, fax, or e-mail Development Manager. Phone: 404-588-1837 Ext. 11. Fax: 404-588-1836. E-mail: circulation@artpapers.org. In-person interview recommended (telephone interview accepted). Applicants must submit a letter of interest, resume, academic transcripts, three personal references, two letters of recommendation, 1 writing sample (editorial intern); portfolio (graphic intern). Applications are accepted continuously. World Wide Web: http://www.artpapers.org.

BARRICADE BOOKS
185 Bridge Plaza North, Suite 308A
Fort Lee, New Jersey 07024

General Information Publishing company. Established in 1991. Number of employees: 10. Number of internship applications received each year: 100.
Internships Available ▶ *1–2 publisher's assistants:* responsibilities include general office support and entry-level editorial and publicity tasks. Candidates should have office skills, oral communication skills, personal interest in the field, self-motivation, writing skills. Duration is 3 months. $25 per day. Open to college sophomores, college juniors, college seniors, recent college graduates, graduate students. International applications accepted.
Benefits On-the-job training, willing to act as a professional reference, willing to complete paperwork for educational credit, willing to provide letters of recommendation.
Contact Write, call, fax, e-mail, or through World Wide Web site Jeff Nordstedt, Internship Coordinator. Phone: 201-944-7600. Fax: 201-944-6363. E-mail: jeff@barricadebooks.com. Applicants must submit a letter of interest, resume. Application deadline: May 1 for summer, December 1 for spring. World Wide Web: http://www.barricadebooks.com.

BEACON PRESS
25 Beacon Street
Boston, Massachusetts 02108

General Information Publisher of trade and scholarly nonfiction. Established in 1854. Number of employees: 30. Unit of Unitarian Universalist Association, Boston, Massachusetts. Number of internship applications received each year: 300.
Internships Available ▶ *Interns:* responsibilities include working in various departments including marketing, publicity, editing, and business. Candidates should have ability to work independently, analytical skills, computer skills, office skills, oral communication skills, organizational skills, self-motivation, written communication skills, editing and research skills (helpful). Duration is flexible. Unpaid. Open to college freshmen, college sophomores, college juniors, college seniors, recent college graduates, graduate students, career changers, individuals reentering the workforce. International applications accepted.
Benefits Job counseling, names of contacts, on-the-job training, possible full-time employment, willing to complete paperwork for educational credit, willing to provide letters of recommendation.
Contact Write, fax, or e-mail Christopher Vyce, Assistant to the Director. Fax: 617-723-3097. E-mail: cvyce@beacon.org. No phone calls. Applicants must submit a letter of interest, resume, cover letter. Application deadline: March 1 for summer, June 1 for fall, October 1 for winter, December 1 for spring.

BEAVER COUNTY TIMES
400 Fair Avenue
Beaver, Pennsylvania 15009

General Information County-wide newspaper with a weekday circulation of 43,000 and a Sunday circulation of 52,000. Number of employees: 300.
Internships Available ▶ *Copy editor interns:* responsibilities include duties essentially the same as staff members. Candidates should have knowledge of pagination. Duration is 13 weeks in summer. Paid. ▶ *Editorial interns.* Duration is one summer between junior

and senior year. Paid. ▶ *Photography interns:* responsibilities include duties essentially the same as those performed by regular staff members. Duration is 13 weeks. Paid.
Contact Write or e-mail Internship Coordinator. Phone: 724-775-3200. Fax: 724-775-4180. E-mail: ldelauter@timesonline.com. Applicants must submit samples of work. World Wide Web: http://www.timesonline.com.

BENT LIGHT MEDIA
637 South Broadway, Suite 334B
Boulder, Colorado 80305

General Information Publishing house. Established in 1998. Number of employees: 6. Number of internship applications received each year: 20.
Internships Available ▶ *3–6 marketing interns:* responsibilities include pitch development, marketing to individual sectors, researching markets, ad and press kit design, book development through marketing, and interacting with fair participants. Candidates should have ability to work independently, ability to work with others, editing skills, oral communication skills, research skills, self-motivation. Duration is 2–4 months. Unpaid. Open to college freshmen, college sophomores, college juniors, college seniors, recent college graduates, graduate students, individuals reentering the workforce. ▶ *3–6 publishing interns:* responsibilities include contacting and working with authors during manuscript process; day-to-day office duties including editing, writing, filing, and working with others in publishing. Candidates should have ability to work with others, editing skills, office skills, self-motivation, writing skills. Duration is 2–4 months. Unpaid. Open to high school seniors, recent high school graduates, college freshmen, college sophomores, college juniors, college seniors, recent college graduates, graduate students, career changers, individuals reentering the workforce. International applications accepted.
Benefits Formal training, on-the-job training, opportunity to attend seminars/workshops, possible full-time employment, willing to act as a professional reference, willing to complete paperwork for educational credit, willing to provide letters of recommendation.
Contact Write, call, fax, or e-mail Dee Anderson, General Manager. Phone: 303-543-8532. Fax: 303-543-1023. E-mail: dee@toursforfree.com. In-person interview recommended (telephone interview accepted). Applicants must submit a letter of interest, resume. Application deadline: January 15 for spring, April 15 for summer, July 15 for fall, October 15 for winter. World Wide Web: http://www.toursforfree.com.

BIBLICAL ARCHAEOLOGY SOCIETY
4710 41st Street, NW
Washington, District of Columbia 20016

General Information Nonprofit nondenominational, educational organization publishing 3 magazines and producing other media and tours on archaeology and the Bible. Established in 1975. Number of employees: 25. Number of internship applications received each year: 50.
Internships Available ▶ *1–2 editorial assistants:* responsibilities include clerical duties, letter writing, photo searches, proofreading, corrections to publications, and correspondence. Candidates should have ability to work with others, computer skills, office skills, oral communication skills, research skills, written communication skills. Duration is minimum of one summer or one semester. Position available as unpaid or at $7–$8 per hour. Open to college freshmen, college sophomores, college juniors, college seniors, recent college graduates, graduate students, career changers, individuals reentering the workforce. International applications accepted.
Benefits Names of contacts, on-the-job training, possible full-time employment, travel reimbursement, willing to act as a professional reference, willing to complete paperwork for educational credit, willing to provide letters of recommendation.
Contact Write, fax, or e-mail James Onley, Personnel Manager, 4710 41st Street, NW, Washington, District of Columbia 20016. Fax: 202-364-2636. E-mail: operations@bib-arch.org. In-person interview recommended (telephone interview accepted). Applicants

must submit a letter of interest, resume, writing sample. Applications are accepted continuously. World Wide Web: http://www.biblicalarchaeology.org.

BOSTON MAGAZINE
300 Massachusetts Avenue
Boston, Massachusetts 02115

General Information Publisher of city/regional magazine. Established in 1962. Number of employees: 50. Unit of Metrocorp, Inc., Philadelphia, Pennsylvania. Number of internship applications received each year: 300.
Internships Available ▶ *3 advertising sales interns:* responsibilities include assisting account executives and sales assistant with client contact and management of materials, including soliciting and preparing media packets. Candidates should have ability to work independently, computer skills, office skills, oral communication skills, personal interest in the field, strong interpersonal skills. Duration is 1 semester. Unpaid. ▶ *1–2 art interns:* responsibilities include assisting art director and associate with monthly productions, extensive photo research, and trafficking artwork. Candidates should have computer skills, oral communication skills, personal interest in the field, self-motivation, strong interpersonal skills, writing skills. Duration is 1 semester. Unpaid. ▶ *5–10 editorial interns:* responsibilities include working in direct positions with writers and editors, performing basic research, tracking and calling sources for information, and working on story development. Candidates should have ability to work with others, computer skills, research skills, self-motivation, writing skills. Duration is 1 semester. Unpaid. ▶ *2 marketing interns:* responsibilities include assisting in event coordination, sales materials preparation, working with advertising clients, proofreading and writing marketing sections of the magazine. Candidates should have ability to work with others, computer skills, office skills, personal interest in the field, writing skills. Duration is 1 semester. Unpaid. ▶ *2 promotions/special projects interns:* responsibilities include helping in organizing functions sponsored by the magazine, working with the production manager, helping service the various advertising and promotion needs of the manager, and compiling and writing monthly press reports. Candidates should have ability to work independently, computer skills, office skills, organizational skills, personal interest in the field, strong interpersonal skills. Duration is 1–4 months. Unpaid. Open to college freshmen, college sophomores, college juniors, college seniors, recent college graduates.
Benefits Names of contacts, opportunity to attend seminars/workshops, possible full-time employment, willing to complete paperwork for educational credit, willing to provide letters of recommendation.
Contact Write, fax, or e-mail Michelle Watts, Executive Coordinator. Fax: 617-262-4925. E-mail: mwatts@bostonmagazine.com. No phone calls. Applicants must submit a letter of interest, resume, 2-3 writing samples for editorial positions. Application deadline: March 15 for summer, August 1 for fall, November 21 for spring. World Wide Web: http://www.bostonmagazine.com.

THE BUREAU OF NATIONAL AFFAIRS, INC.
1231 25th Street, NW, 4th Floor, S-100
Washington, District of Columbia 20037-1164

General Information Private publisher of print and electronic news and specialized news and information services covering developments in business, economics, law, taxation, employee relations, environmental protection, and other public policy issues. Established in 1947. Number of employees: 1,600. Number of internship applications received each year: 100.
Internships Available ▶ *2 editorial interns:* responsibilities include clipping the wire service, copyediting, proofreading, and reporting. Candidates should have ability to work with others, analytical skills, editing skills, research skills, self-motivation, writing skills. Duration is 15 to 18 hours per week in spring and fall. $11.50–$12 per hour. Open to college juniors, college seniors. International applications accepted.
Benefits Formal training, possible full-time employment, willing to complete paperwork for educational credit.

The Bureau of National Affairs, Inc. (continued)

Contact Write, call, fax, or e-mail Anthony A. Harris, Employment Director, 1250 23rd Street, NW, 4th Floor, Washington, District of Columbia 20037-1164. Phone: 202-261-1566. Fax: 202-261-1583. E-mail: tharris@bna.com. In-person interview recommended (telephone interview accepted). Applicants must submit a letter of interest, resume, 4 newsclips (preferably published). Application deadline: May 1 for fall, November 1 for spring. World Wide Web: http://www.bna.com.

CAPE COD LIFE
PO Box 1385
Pocasset, Massachusetts 02559-1385

General Information Publisher of Cape Cod Life, a bimonthly regional lifestyle magazine designed to capture the unique spirit of Cape Cod, Martha's Vineyard, and Nantucket; also publishes annual Cape Cod Home, Living and Gardening on the Cape and Islands. Established in 1979. Number of employees: 19. Number of internship applications received each year: 20.
Internships Available ▶ *1–2 editorial interns:* responsibilities include performing editorial tasks including research, fact checking, proofreading, editing, and writing. Candidates should have ability to work independently, organizational skills, personal interest in the field, research skills, writing skills, knowledge of or interest in the region (Cape Cod, Martha's Vineyard, and Nantucket). Duration is flexible. Unpaid. Open to college freshmen, college sophomores, college juniors, college seniors.
Benefits Possible full-time employment, willing to complete paperwork for educational credit, willing to provide letters of recommendation.
Contact Write, fax, e-mail, or through World Wide Web site Jennifer Sperry, Associate Editor, Pocasset, Massachusetts 02559-1385. Fax: 508-564-4470. E-mail: editorial@capecodlife.com. No phone calls. In-person interview recommended (telephone interview accepted). Applicants must submit a letter of interest, resume, three writing samples, three personal references, letter of recommendation. Application deadline: March 27 for summer. World Wide Web: http://www.capecodlife.com.

CHARLESBRIDGE PUBLISHING
85 Main Street
Watertown, Massachusetts 02472

General Information Publisher of school books that help children use reason and creative thinking to learn and solve problems, as well as trade fiction and nonfiction picture books. Established in 1979. Number of employees: 30. Number of internship applications received each year: 100.
Internships Available ▶ *4 editorial assistants:* responsibilities include researching, editing, proofreading, writing, and revising manuscripts. Candidates should have analytical skills, editing skills, oral communication skills, organizational skills, research skills, writing skills. Duration is 1 semester. Unpaid. Open to college juniors, college seniors, recent college graduates, graduate students, career changers, individuals reentering the workforce. ▶ *1 graphic arts assistant:* responsibilities include creating illustrations, designing layouts, communicating with editors, evaluating the graphic potential of stories, and researching accuracy of illustrations. Candidates should have ability to work independently, ability to work with others, oral communication skills, research skills, self-motivation, experience in graphic arts, sensitivity to text/art interface in children's picture books. Duration is 1 semester. Unpaid. Open to college sophomores, college juniors, college seniors, recent college graduates, graduate students, individuals reentering the workforce. ▶ *1 marketing intern:* responsibilities include researching, writing, compiling data, planning, surveying, e-mail campaign analysis, communicating with sales, editorial and administration. Candidates should have computer skills, oral communication skills, self-motivation, strong interpersonal skills, written communication skills. Duration is 1 semester. Unpaid. Open to college sophomores, college juniors, college seniors, recent college graduates, graduate students, law students, career changers.

Benefits On-the-job training, opportunity to attend seminars/workshops, willing to act as a professional reference, willing to complete paperwork for educational credit, willing to provide letters of recommendation.
Contact Write or e-mail Ms. Elena Dworkin Wright, Managing Editor. E-mail: schooleditorial@charlesbridge.com. No phone calls. In-person interview recommended (telephone interview accepted). Applicants must submit a letter of interest, resume, 2-3 art samples (graphic art interns), 1 writing sample (editorial interns). Applications are accepted continuously. World Wide Web: http://www.charlesbridge.com.

CHILDREN'S PRESSLINE
227 West 29th Street, 14th Floor
New York, New York 10001

General Information Nonprofit youth journalism program. Established in 2001. Number of employees: 3. Number of internship applications received each year: 10.
Internships Available ▶ *2–3 editorial assistants:* responsibilities include editing, research, transcribing, oral and written communications, and some office support. Candidates should have ability to work independently, computer skills, editing skills, oral communication skills, organizational skills, personal interest in the field, plan to pursue career in field, research skills, self-motivation, strong interpersonal skills, strong leadership ability, writing skills. Duration is flexible. Unpaid. Open to recent high school graduates, college freshmen, college sophomores, college juniors, college seniors, recent college graduates, graduate students, law students, career changers, individuals reentering the workforce. International applications accepted.
Benefits Job counseling, names of contacts, on-the-job training, opportunity to attend seminars/workshops, possible full-time employment, travel reimbursement, willing to act as a professional reference, willing to complete paperwork for educational credit, willing to provide letters of recommendation, possibility of part-time employment.
Contact Write, call, fax, or e-mail Katina Paron, Program Director. Phone: 212-760-2772. Fax: 212-760-1142. E-mail: kparon@cplmedia.org. In-person interview required. Applicants must submit a letter of interest, resume, writing sample, two personal references, letter of recommendation. Applications are accepted continuously. World Wide Web: http://www.cplmedia.org.

THE CHRONICLE OF THE HORSE
108 The Plains Road, PO Box 46
Middleburg, Virginia 20118

General Information Weekly sport horse magazine with primary focus on news and additional articles on horse care, rider profiles, and how-to information on all English horse sports and breeding. Established in 1937. Number of employees: 20. Number of internship applications received each year: 25.
Internships Available ▶ *3 editorial interns:* responsibilities include proofreading, editing, writing, and working on special projects/assignments. Candidates should have ability to work with others, editing skills, oral communication skills, personal interest in the field, research skills, self-motivation, writing skills, knowledge of horse sports. Duration is 3–5 months. $6.50 per hour. Open to college freshmen, college sophomores, college juniors, college seniors, recent college graduates. International applications accepted.
Benefits Names of contacts, on-the-job training, possible full-time employment, travel reimbursement, willing to act as a professional reference, willing to complete paperwork for educational credit, willing to provide letters of recommendation.
Contact Write, call, e-mail, or through World Wide Web site Beth Rasin, Assistant Editor. Phone: 540-687-6341. Fax: 540-687-3937. E-mail: bethr@chronofhorse.com. In-person interview required. Applicants must submit a resume, writing sample, letter of interest including equestrian background. Applications are accepted continuously. World Wide Web: http://www.chronofhorse.com.

CITY LIMITS
120 Wall Street, 20th Floor
New York, New York 10005

General Information New York's urban affairs news magazine. Established in 1976. Number of employees: 12. Unit of City Limits Community Information Service, New York, New York. Number of internship applications received each year: 30.
Internships Available ▶ *1–3 editorial interns:* responsibilities include research, reporting, and writing for City Limits magazine and the City Limits weekly bulletin. Candidates should have ability to work independently, analytical skills, experience in the field, oral communication skills, research skills, self-motivation, writing skills, reporting experience (preferred). Duration is 3–5 months. Unpaid. Open to college freshmen, college sophomores, college juniors, college seniors, recent college graduates, graduate students, career changers. International applications accepted.
Benefits Job counseling, names of contacts, on-the-job training, opportunity to attend seminars/workshops, possible full-time employment, willing to act as a professional reference, willing to complete paperwork for educational credit, willing to provide letters of recommendation.
Contact Write, call, fax, or e-mail Matt Pacenza, Associate Editor. Phone: 212-479-3351. Fax: 212-344-6457. E-mail: matt@citylimits.org. In-person interview recommended (telephone interview accepted). Applicants must submit a letter of interest, resume, published writing samples (if possible). Applications are accepted continuously. World Wide Web: http://www.citylimits.org.

COLUMBIA JOURNALISM REVIEW
Journalism Building, Columbia University
New York, New York 10027

General Information National monitor of the news media. Established in 1961. Number of employees: 11. Number of internship applications received each year: 100.
Internships Available ▶ *6 interns:* responsibilities include research and other duties as needed. Candidates should have ability to work independently, ability to work with others, computer skills, oral communication skills, plan to pursue career in field, research skills, written communication skills. Duration is 3–5 months. $8 per hour. Open to college freshmen, college sophomores, college juniors, college seniors, recent college graduates, graduate students, career changers, individuals reentering the workforce. International applications accepted.
Benefits Opportunity to attend seminars/workshops, willing to act as a professional reference, willing to complete paperwork for educational credit, willing to provide letters of recommendation.
Contact Write, call, fax, or e-mail Brent Cunningham, Managing Editor, Journalism Building, Columbia University. Phone: 212-854-1882. Fax: 212-854-8580. E-mail: cjr@columbia.edu. Applicants must submit a letter of interest, resume, three writing samples, two letters of recommendation or two reference contacts. Applications are accepted continuously. World Wide Web: http://www.cjr.org.

CONGRESSIONAL QUARTERLY, INC.
1414 22nd Street, NW
Washington, District of Columbia 20037

General Information Company that publishes accurate, timely, and objective information on Congress and national politics; services include a weekly magazine and research reports, daily, weekly, and annual publications, and an online product "CQ.com" as well as books and directories. Established in 1945. Number of employees: 275. Subsidiary of Times Publishing Company, St. Petersburg, Florida. Number of internship applications received each year: 200.
Internships Available ▶ *Interns:* responsibilities include working on the news media service and performing duties in the editorial, marketing, and advertising departments. Candidates should have computer skills, knowledge of field, office skills, oral communication skills, strong interpersonal skills, writing skills. Duration is 3 months. Position available as unpaid or paid. Open to college juniors, college seniors, recent college graduates, graduate students, law students. International applications accepted.

Benefits Names of contacts, opportunity to attend seminars/workshops, willing to complete paperwork for educational credit, willing to provide letters of recommendation.
Contact Write, call, fax, or e-mail Annette M. Billings, Director of Human Resources. Phone: 202-822-1452. Fax: 202-293-1487. E-mail: abillings@cq.com. Applicants must submit a letter of interest, resume, three writing samples. Applications are accepted continuously.

CONNECTICUT MAGAZINE
35 Nutmeg Drive
Trumbull, Connecticut 06611

General Information General interest regional magazine with a circulation of 90,000. Established in 1971. Number of employees: 26. Unit of Journal Register Company, Trenton, New Jersey. Number of internship applications received each year: 75.
Internships Available ▶ *2–4 editorial interns:* responsibilities include working on monthly calendar and dining guide sections, checking facts, researching, typing correspondence, answering phones, and taking responsibility for various special projects. Candidates should have editing skills, oral communication skills, organizational skills, personal interest in the field, self-motivation, writing skills. Duration is 1 semester. Unpaid. Open to college freshmen, college sophomores, college juniors, college seniors, recent college graduates, graduate students, career changers, individuals reentering the workforce. International applications accepted.
Benefits Job counseling, names of contacts, willing to act as a professional reference, willing to complete paperwork for educational credit, willing to provide letters of recommendation.
Contact Write, call, fax, e-mail, or through World Wide Web site Cathy P. Ross, Calendar Editor. Phone: 203-380-6600 Ext. 326. Fax: 203-380-6612. E-mail: cross@connecticutmag.com. In-person interview recommended (telephone interview accepted). Applicants must submit a letter of interest, resume, 2-3 writing samples. Applications are accepted continuously. World Wide Web: http://www.connecticutmag.com.

DAVID R. GODINE, PUBLISHER, INC.
9 Hamilton Place
Boston, Massachusetts 02108

General Information Book publisher specializing in high-quality books on art, typography, and photography, as well as poetry, fiction, reprints of classics, and children's literature; publishes 25 titles per year. Established in 1970. Number of employees: 6. Number of internship applications received each year: 150.
Internships Available ▶ *3 interns:* responsibilities include general office work to assist with publicity, editing, and sales duties. Candidates should have editing skills, oral communication skills, organizational skills, plan to pursue career in field, written communication skills, Quark Xpress, PhotoShop, and HTML skills. Duration is 4 months minimum (20-25 hours per week minimum). Unpaid. Open to college juniors, college seniors, recent college graduates, graduate students. International applications accepted.
Benefits Formal training, job counseling, names of contacts, on-the-job training, opportunity to attend seminars/workshops, willing to act as a professional reference, willing to complete paperwork for educational credit, willing to provide letters of recommendation, accessible by subway.
Contact Write Carl W. Scarbrough, Director of Publicity. No phone calls. In-person interview recommended (telephone interview accepted). Applicants must submit a letter of interest, resume. Application deadline: March 1 for summer, June 1 for fall, October 1 for spring. World Wide Web: http://www.godine.com.

DR. ANDREW WEIL'S SELF HEALING
42 Pleasant Street
Watertown, Massachusetts 02472

General Information Consumer health newsletter. Established in 1995. Number of employees: 6. Number of internship applications received each year: 30.
Internships Available ▶ *1–2 editorial interns:* responsibilities include assisting with fact-checking articles for accuracy, assisting editors with research, maintaining research files, assisting with other edito-

Dr. Andrew Weil's Self Healing (continued)

rial projects, writing short articles, and other clerical duties. Candidates should have college courses in field, personal interest in the field, research skills, self-motivation, written communication skills. Duration is 1 semester. Unpaid. Open to college sophomores, college juniors, college seniors, graduate students. **Benefits** Travel reimbursement, willing to act as a professional reference, willing to complete paperwork for educational credit, willing to provide letters of recommendation.
Contact Write, fax, or e-mail Jessica Cerretani, Research Editor. Phone: 617-926-0200 Ext. 368. Fax: 617-923-4009. E-mail: jcerretani@ bodyandsoulmag.com. In-person interview required. Applicants must submit a letter of interest, resume. Application deadline: April 1 for summer, August 1 for fall, December 1 for spring. World Wide Web: http://www.drweilselfhealing.com.

EARL G. GRAVES, LTD./BLACK ENTERPRISE MAGAZINE
130 Fifth Avenue
New York, New York 10011

General Information Publishing and ancillary products company. Established in 1970. Number of employees: 100. Number of internship applications received each year: 400.
Internships Available ▶ *4–6 editorial interns:* responsibilities include receiving assignments from the section editor and working as staff writer. Candidates should have analytical skills, editing skills, experience in the field, oral communication skills, personal interest in the field, plan to pursue career in field, research skills, writing skills. Duration is 10 weeks. Paid. Open to college sophomores, college juniors, college seniors, graduate students. International applications accepted.
Benefits Job counseling, names of contacts, on-the-job training, opportunity to attend seminars/workshops, possible full-time employment, willing to act as a professional reference, willing to complete paperwork for educational credit, willing to provide letters of recommendation.
Contact Write or e-mail Natalie M. Hibbert, Employment and Benefits Programs Manager. E-mail: careers@blackenterprise.com. No phone calls. In-person interview recommended (telephone interview accepted). Applicants must submit a formal organization application, letter of interest, resume, as many writing samples as possible. Application deadline: January 30. World Wide Web: http://www.blackenterprise.com.

ELSEVIER HEALTH SCIENCE
11830 Westline Industrial Drive
St. Louis, Missouri 63146

General Information Publisher of medical/health science textbooks, reference books, and journals and producer of videos, multimedia products, and seminars/conferences. Established in 1906. Number of employees: 850. Subsidiary of Harcourt Health Sciences, Chestnut Hill, Massachusetts. Number of internship applications received each year: 50.
Internships Available ▶ *Editorial interns:* responsibilities include reviewing manuscripts, phone surveying reviewers and synopsizing comments, obtaining copyright permissions, arranging for freelance photographers, and working for an editor responsible for developing a manuscript for a text or reference book in the health science field. Candidates should have editing skills, oral communication skills, plan to pursue career in field, research skills, writing skills. Duration is flexible. $7.50 per hour. ▶ *Marketing interns:* responsibilities include copywriting and/or editing. Candidates should have editing skills, oral communication skills, plan to pursue career in field, research skills, writing skills. Duration is flexible. $7.50 per hour. ▶ *Production interns:* responsibilities include dealing with print vendors, cost containment, quality control, and electronic product development. Candidates should have computer skills, editing skills, oral communication skills, plan to pursue career in field, writing skills. Duration is flexible. $7.50 per hour. Open to college freshmen, college sophomores, college juniors, college seniors. International applications accepted.
Benefits Possible full-time employment, willing to complete paperwork for educational credit.

Contact Write, fax, or through World Wide Web site Human Resources. Fax: 314-432-0779. No phone calls. In-person interview required. Applicants must submit a formal organization application, letter of interest, resume. Applications are accepted continuously. World Wide Web: http://www.elsevier.com.

ENERGIZE, INC.
5450 Wissahickon Avenue
Philadelphia, Pennsylvania 19144

General Information Training, consulting, and publishing firm that specializes in volunteerism and assists international, national, state, and local organizations in developing citizen participation programs; publishes and distributes more than 65 books via a direct mailing catalog and a major Web site. Established in 1977. Number of employees: 5. Number of internship applications received each year: 10.
Internships Available ▶ *1–2 marketing assistants:* responsibilities include print and cyberspace marketing and research, editorial, and reporting duties. Candidates should have computer skills, personal interest in the field, research skills, written communication skills. Duration is flexible. Unpaid. Open to college freshmen, college sophomores, college juniors, college seniors, recent college graduates, graduate students, career changers, individuals reentering the workforce. International applications accepted.
Benefits Job counseling, names of contacts, on-the-job training, opportunity to attend seminars/workshops, willing to act as a professional reference, willing to complete paperwork for educational credit, willing to provide letters of recommendation.
Contact Write or e-mail Ms. Susan J. Ellis, President. Phone: 215-438-8342. Fax: 215-438-0434. E-mail: susan@energizeinc.com. In-person interview required. Applicants must submit a letter of interest, resume. Applications are accepted continuously. World Wide Web: http://www.energizeinc.com.

ENTERTAINMENT DESIGN AND LIGHTING DIMENSIONS MAGAZINES
249 West 17th Street, 3rd Floor
New York, New York 10011

General Information Publisher of leading trade magazines for the entertainment technology industry, covering all aspects of sound, lighting, set design, costume, architectural and themed entertainment applications. Established in 1967. Number of employees: 75. Division of Intertec Publishing Corporation, Overland Park, Kansas. Number of internship applications received each year: 35.
Internships Available ▶ *1 publishing/editorial intern:* responsibilities include supporting promotions and marketing projects, assisting with production, circulation, and advertising activities, and providing support for editorial projects and activities. Candidates should have computer skills, office skills, oral communication skills, personal interest in the field, strong interpersonal skills, writing skills. Duration is 8–10 weeks. Minimum wage to $10 per hour. ▶ *6–12 technical theater interns at BLMC:* responsibilities include technical assistance with production of Broadway Lighting Master Classes Seminar, hanging and focusing lights, running A/V equipment, and related preparatory administrative and office work. Candidates should have ability to work with others, office skills, personal interest in the field, theater lighting experience (a strong preference). Position available as unpaid or paid. Open to recent high school graduates, college freshmen, college sophomores, college juniors, college seniors, recent college graduates, graduate students, individuals reentering the workforce.
Benefits Names of contacts, on-the-job training, willing to complete paperwork for educational credit.
Contact Write, fax, or e-mail Florence Dobransky, Internship Coordinator, 32 West 18th Street, 11th Floor, New York, New York 10011-4612. Fax: 212-206-3798. E-mail: fdobransky@primediabusiness. com. No phone calls. In-person interview recommended (telephone interview accepted). Applicants must submit a letter of interest, letter of recommendation, resume (if applicable). Application deadline: May 15 for summer. World Wide Web: http://www. etecnyc.net.

ENTERTAINMENT WEEKLY
1675 Broadway
New York, New York 10019

General Information Weekly magazine covering popular entertainment. Established in 1990. Number of employees: 200. Subsidiary of Time, Inc., New York, New York. Number of internship applications received each year: 750.
Internships Available ▶ *1 art intern:* responsibilities include assisting design editors in various tasks and maintaining art archives. Candidates should have ability to work independently, ability to work with others, college courses in field, computer skills, knowledge of field, office skills, oral communication skills, organizational skills, personal interest in the field, plan to pursue career in field, self-motivation. Duration is 3–5 months. $10 per hour. Open to college juniors, college seniors, recent college graduates, graduate students. ▶ *3 editorial interns:* responsibilities include assisting editors in various tasks, such as inputting stories, transcribing interviews, running copy, and handling reader mail. Candidates should have ability to work independently, ability to work with others, college courses in field, computer skills, editing skills, knowledge of field, office skills, oral communication skills, organizational skills, personal interest in the field, plan to pursue career in field, research skills, self-motivation, writing skills, love of entertainment. Duration is 3–5 months. $10 per hour. Open to college seniors, recent college graduates, graduate students. ▶ *2 ew.com interns:* responsibilities include updating editorial databases, performing research, and inputting database changes. Candidates should have ability to work independently, computer skills, office skills, oral communication skills, research skills, written communication skills. Duration is 5–6 months. $10 per hour. Open to college seniors, recent college graduates, graduate students. ▶ *1 photo intern:* responsibilities include assisting photo editors in various tasks including obtaining photos, contacting photographers, and maintaining archives. Candidates should have ability to work independently, ability to work with others, college courses in field, computer skills, knowledge of field, office skills, oral communication skills, organizational skills, personal interest in the field, plan to pursue career in field, self-motivation. Duration is 3 months (approximate). $10 per hour. Open to college juniors, college seniors, recent college graduates, graduate students.
Benefits On-the-job training, possible full-time employment, willing to act as a professional reference, willing to complete paperwork for educational credit.
Contact Write, call, or fax Ms. Annabel Bentley, Director of Research Services. Phone: 212-522-5558. Fax: 212-522-6104. In-person interview required. Applicants must submit a letter of interest, resume, 4-5 previously published clips, 5 writing samples. Application deadline: February 15 for summer, June 15 for fall, October 15 for spring. World Wide Web: http://ew.com.

E/THE ENVIRONMENTAL MAGAZINE
28 Knight Street
Norwalk, Connecticut 06851

General Information Magazine serving as a clearinghouse of information, news, and commentary on environmental issues, geared toward both the general public and dedicated environmentalists for the purpose of promoting environmental awareness and activism. Established in 1990. Number of employees: 8. Number of internship applications received each year: 100.
Internships Available ▶ *4 advertising interns:* responsibilities include assisting in advertisement sales, handling mailings, proofing ads, and computer work. Duration is flexible. Unpaid. Open to college freshmen, college sophomores, college juniors, college seniors, recent college graduates, graduate students, career changers. ▶ *4 editorial interns:* responsibilities include keying articles, proofreading, responding to editorial phone calls, correspondence, and performing library and phone research; will have opportunity to write and publish articles, possible travel for stories, Internet research, and conducting product reviews. Duration is 2 months minimum. Unpaid. Open to recent high school graduates, college freshmen, college sophomores, college juniors, college seniors, recent college graduates, graduate students, career changers, individuals reentering the workforce. Candidates for all positions

should have ability to work independently, oral communication skills, self-motivation, strong interpersonal skills, written communication skills. International applications accepted.
Benefits Job counseling, names of contacts, opportunity to attend seminars/workshops, possible full-time employment, willing to act as a professional reference, willing to complete paperwork for educational credit, willing to provide letters of recommendation, some free meals.
Contact Write, call, fax, e-mail, or through World Wide Web site Brian Howard, Managing Editor. Phone: 203-854-5559 Ext. 109. Fax: 203-866-0602. E-mail: info@emagazine.com. In-person interview recommended (telephone interview accepted). Applicants must submit a letter of interest, resume, two writing samples. Applications are accepted continuously. World Wide Web: http://www.emagazine.com.

F & W PUBLICATIONS, INC.
4700 East Galbraith Road
Cincinnati, Ohio 45236

General Information Book and magazine publisher of self-help materials in the art, writing, crafts, design, and woodworking fields. Established in 1910. Number of employees: 300. Number of internship applications received each year: 150.
Internships Available ▶ *4–5 editorial assistants:* responsibilities include copyediting, proofreading, researching, writing and editorial planning. Candidates should have ability to work with others, college courses in field, computer skills, editing skills, organizational skills, plan to pursue career in field, research skills, self-motivation, writing skills. Duration is 10–12 weeks. $350 per week. Open to college juniors, graduate students, students returning to school after internship ends (required). ▶ *1 graphic design assistant:* responsibilities include working on basic design assignments on MAC software, contributing to book and magazine layouts. Candidates should have ability to work independently, ability to work with others, declared college major in field, oral communication skills, organizational skills, plan to pursue career in field, experience with Quark Xpress, Illustrator, and PhotoShop packages (required). Duration is 10-12 weeks (May to August or June to September). $350 per week. Open to college juniors, graduate students, students returning to school after internship ends (required). ▶ *1 marketing/conference assistant:* responsibilities include analysis, financial, or copywriting, research , and planning mailings. Candidates should have ability to work with others, analytical skills, computer skills, oral communication skills, organizational skills, plan to pursue career in field, research skills, self-motivation, writing skills. Duration is 10-12 weeks (May to August or June to September). $350 per week. Open to college juniors, graduate students, students returning to school after internship ends (required). ▶ *1 production intern:* responsibilities include assembling advertising materials, ordering corporate stationary/business cards, data entry, correspondence, and organization of book production materials. Candidates should have ability to work with others, computer skills, editing skills, knowledge of field, office skills, oral communication skills, organizational skills. Duration is 10–12 weeks. $350 per week. Open to college juniors, graduate students.
Benefits Job counseling, on-the-job training, possible full-time employment, willing to act as a professional reference, willing to complete paperwork for educational credit.
Contact Write, e-mail, or through World Wide Web site Debbie Carroll, Human Resources Recruiter. Fax: 513-891-7195. E-mail: debbie.carroll@fwpubs.com. No phone calls. In-person interview recommended (telephone interview accepted). Applicants must submit a letter of interest, resume, 1-3 samples of work (design interns), 2-3 writing samples. Application deadline: January 15 for summer. World Wide Web: http://www.fwpublications.com.

FANTAGRAPHICS BOOKS, INC.
7563 Lake City Way, NE
Seattle, Washington 98115

General Information Publisher of original comic books and book collections, book collections of classic comic strips and underground comic books, and a trade magazine about the comics industry. Established in 1976. Number of employees: 30. Number of internship applications received each year: 25.

Fantagraphics Books, Inc. (continued)

Internships Available ▶ *3–4 editorial interns:* responsibilities include typesetting, proofreading, copyediting, writing copy, and assisting in promotional work. Candidates should have computer skills, editing skills, knowledge of field, office skills, organizational skills, personal interest in the field, written communication skills. Duration is variable. Unpaid. Open to recent high school graduates, college freshmen, college sophomores, college juniors, college seniors, recent college graduates, graduate students, law students, career changers, individuals reentering the workforce, must be 18 or older. International applications accepted.
Benefits Names of contacts, possible full-time employment, willing to complete paperwork for educational credit, willing to provide letters of recommendation.
Contact Write or fax Milo George, Managing Editor. Fax: 206-524-2104. No phone calls. Applicants must submit a letter of interest, resume. Application deadline: April 1 for summer/fall, October 1 for winter/spring. World Wide Web: http://www.fantagraphics.com.

FARRAR, STRAUS, AND GIROUX
19 Union Square West
New York, New York 10003

General Information General trade book publisher. Established in 1946. Number of employees: 100. Number of internship applications received each year: 250.
Internships Available ▶ *Interns:* responsibilities include working in different departments. Candidates should have ability to work with others, computer skills, office skills, oral communication skills, personal interest in the field, written communication skills. Duration is flexible. Unpaid. Open to college freshmen, college sophomores, college juniors, college seniors, recent college graduates, graduate students. International applications accepted.
Benefits Possible full-time employment, willing to complete paperwork for educational credit, willing to provide letters of recommendation.
Contact Call Ms. Peggy Miller, Coordinator of Interns. Phone: 212-741-6900. In-person interview required. Applicants must submit a resume. Applications are accepted continuously.

FOREIGN AFFAIRS MAGAZINE
58 East 68th Street
New York, New York 10021

General Information Bimonthly journal devoted to international affairs and U.S. foreign policy. Established in 1922. Number of employees: 15. Division of Council on Foreign Relations, New York, New York. Number of internship applications received each year: 400.
Internships Available ▶ *1 academic-year intern:* responsibilities include editing, proofreading, and layout for articles to be published in magazine; research and fact checking; writing press releases; assisting with art acquisition; archiving; screening unsolicited manuscripts. Candidates should have analytical skills, editing skills, personal interest in the field, self-motivation, strong interpersonal skills, writing skills. Duration is 10 months. $27,000 per year. Open to college seniors, recent college graduates, graduate students, law students. ▶ *2 semester interns:* responsibilities include copyediting and proofreading, fact-checking, screening unsolicited manuscripts, and assisting editors. Candidates should have ability to work independently, editing skills, personal interest in the field, research skills, strong interpersonal skills, writing skills. Duration is 3 months. Unpaid. Open to college juniors, college seniors, recent college graduates, graduate students, law students. International applications accepted.
Benefits Formal training, health insurance, names of contacts, on-the-job training, opportunity to attend seminars/workshops, possible full-time employment, willing to act as a professional reference, willing to provide letters of recommendation, attendance at Council on Foreign Relations events.
Contact Write or call Editorial Assistant. Phone: 212-434-9507. Applicants must submit a letter of interest, resume, three writing samples, three letters of recommendation. Application deadline:

early December for spring semester interns, March 28 for academic-year interns, May 16 for fall semester interns. World Wide Web: http://www.foreignaffairs.org.

FOREIGN POLICY MAGAZINE
1779 Massachusetts Avenue, NW
Washington, District of Columbia 20036

General Information Bimonthly magazine on global politics, economics, and ideas. Established in 1970. Number of employees: 25. Unit of Carnegie Endowment for International Peace, Washington, District of Columbia. Number of internship applications received each year: 120.
Internships Available ▶ *1–3 editorial assistants:* responsibilities include research, reviewing manuscripts, fact checking and proofreading articles for publication, and assisting in all aspects of magazine publication. Candidates should have computer skills, research skills, writing skills, strong research skills in a foreign language desirable. Duration is 3–4 months. Unpaid. Open to college juniors, college seniors, recent college graduates, graduate students, law students. International applications accepted.
Benefits Opportunity to attend seminars/workshops, willing to complete paperwork for educational credit, willing to provide letters of recommendation, reimbursement of local travel expenses.
Contact Through World Wide Web site Verena Ringler, Internship Coordinator. Phone: 202-939-2246. Fax: 202-483-4430. E-mail: editor@ceip.org. In-person interview recommended (telephone interview accepted). Applicants must submit a letter of interest, resume, one writing sample, or various clips, totaling 5-10 pages. Application deadline: April 1 for summer, August 1 for fall, November 1 for spring. World Wide Web: http://www.foreignpolicy.com.

FOREIGN SERVICE JOURNAL
2101 E Street, NW
Washington, District of Columbia 20037

General Information Monthly journal that informs readers about foreign affairs from an insider's perspective; circulation 13,000. Established in 1918. Number of employees: 36. Unit of American Foreign Service Association, Washington, District of Columbia. Number of internship applications received each year: 150.
Internships Available ▶ *Editorial interns (spring and fall):* responsibilities include editing, writing, research, fact-checking, proof-reading, and administrative work; opportunity to write article for Journal. Duration is one semester (at least 2 full days per week). $300 stipend. Open to individuals 18 years or older, (college juniors, seniors, with native-level English fluency preferred). ▶ *Editorial interns (summer):* responsibilities include editing, writing, research, fact-checking, proof-reading, and administrative work; opportunity to write article for Journal. Duration is one summer (full-time). $500 stipend. Open to individuals 18 years or older, (college juniors, seniors with native-level English fluency preferred). Candidates for all positions should have computer skills, editing skills, office skills, organizational skills, research skills, writing skills, publications experience (a plus), HTML (a plus), strong interest in international affairs. International applications accepted.
Benefits On-the-job training, opportunity to attend seminars/workshops, willing to act as a professional reference, willing to complete paperwork for educational credit, willing to provide letters of recommendation.
Contact Write, call, fax, e-mail, or through World Wide Web site Internship Coordinator. Phone: 202-338-4045 Ext. 511. Fax: 202-338-8244. E-mail: journal@afsa.org. Applicants must submit a letter of interest, resume, writing sample. Application deadline: April 15 for summer, July 15 for fall, November 15 for spring. World Wide Web: http://www.nafsa.org/intern/journalism.cfm.

FRIENDS JOURNAL
1216 Arch Street 2A
Philadelphia, Pennsylvania 19107

General Information Monthly religious periodical with emphasis on social action, spiritual nurturing, news/features, poetry, and book reviews. Established in 1955. Number of employees: 12. Number of internship applications received each year: 25.

Internships Available ▶ *1–3 editorial assistants:* responsibilities include editing, proofreading, writing, working on the computer, possible Web site work, and office tasks. Candidates should have ability to work independently, computer skills, editing skills, organizational skills, self-motivation, written communication skills. Duration is flexible. Unpaid. ▶ *1–3 office assistants:* responsibilities include assisting with development and circulation tasks and assisting editors. Candidates should have ability to work independently, ability to work with others, computer skills, office skills, organizational skills, self-motivation. Duration is flexible. Unpaid. Open to college freshmen, college sophomores, college juniors, college seniors, recent college graduates, graduate students, career changers, individuals reentering the workforce. International applications accepted.

Benefits Names of contacts, on-the-job training, possible full-time employment, willing to act as a professional reference, willing to complete paperwork for educational credit, willing to provide letters of recommendation.

Contact Write, call, fax, e-mail, or through World Wide Web site Susan Corson-Finnerty, Publisher and Executive Editor, 1216 Arch Street, 2A, Philadelphia, Pennsylvania 19107. Phone: 215-563-8629. Fax: 215-568-1377. E-mail: publisher_exec_ed@friendsjournal.org. In-person interview recommended (telephone interview accepted). Applicants must submit a letter of interest, resume, three personal references, 2-3 writing samples. Applications are accepted continuously. World Wide Web: http://www.friendsjournal.org.

HARPERCOLLINS PUBLISHERS
10 East 53rd Street, 20th Floor
New York, New York 10022

General Information Broad based publisher of academic, business, and professional, children's, general interest, religious, and spiritual books with significant publishing interests in North America, Canada, Europe, Australia, and Asia. Established in 1817. Number of employees: 800. Subsidiary of News Corporation, New York, New York. Number of internship applications received each year: 500.

Internships Available ▶ *8 rotational interns:* responsibilities include providing administrative support in various departments and creating an original book idea that is presented at the end of the internship. Candidates should have ability to work with others, office skills, oral communication skills, personal interest in the field, plan to pursue career in field, written communication skills. Duration is 10 weeks in summer. Paid. Open to college juniors, college seniors.

Contact E-mail Human Resources Manager, New York. E-mail: collrec@harpercollins.com. No phone calls. In-person interview required. Applicants must submit a letter of interest, resume, writing sample, two personal references. Application deadline: April 25. World Wide Web: http://www.harpercollins.com.

HARPER'S MAGAZINE FOUNDATION
666 Broadway, 11th Floor
New York, New York 10012

General Information Magazine publisher. Established in 1850. Number of employees: 35. Number of internship applications received each year: 100.

Internships Available ▶ *4 editorial interns:* responsibilities include assisting a section editor (Readings, Forum, or Articles and Annotations), participating in the general tasks required to run a magazine, and working on the Harper's Index. Candidates should have computer skills, oral communication skills, organizational skills, personal interest in the field, research skills, writing skills. Duration is summer (3 months), fall (4 months), or winter (5 months). Unpaid. Open to college freshmen, college sophomores, college juniors, college seniors, recent college graduates, graduate students, law students, career changers, individuals reentering the workforce. International applications accepted.

Benefits Formal training, names of contacts, on-the-job training, possible full-time employment, willing to complete paperwork for

educational credit, willing to provide letters of recommendation, transportation within New York City (unlimited Metro Card).

Contact Write, call, fax, e-mail, or through World Wide Web site Rachel Monahan, Assistant Editor. Phone: 212-420-5720. Fax: 212-228-5889. E-mail: rachel@harpers.org. In-person interview recommended (telephone interview accepted). Applicants must submit a formal organization application, resume. Application deadline: February 15 for summer, June 15 for fall, October 15 for winter. World Wide Web: http://www.harpers.org.

HILL STREET PRESS
191 East Broad Street, Suite 209
Athens, Georgia 30601-2848

General Information Independent publisher of literary and trade fiction and nonfiction related to the diverse American South. Established in 1998. Number of employees: 4. Number of internship applications received each year: 40.

Internships Available ▶ *4–5 editorial interns:* responsibilities include evaluating unsolicited manuscripts, proofreading, editorial research, technical preparation of manuscripts, drafting rejection letters, general office duties, and product development. Candidates should have ability to work independently, computer skills, editing skills, office skills, research skills, self-motivation, interest in the literature of the American South. Duration is 1 semester. Unpaid. ▶ *2 marketing assistants:* responsibilities include maintaining databases and Web sites, developing review lists, production of advertising copy, mass mailings, special events publicity. Candidates should have computer skills, office skills, organizational skills, research skills, strong interpersonal skills, writing skills. Duration is 1 semester. Unpaid. Open to college sophomores, college juniors, college seniors, recent college graduates, graduate students, career changers.

Benefits Names of contacts, on-the-job training, willing to act as a professional reference, willing to complete paperwork for educational credit, willing to provide letters of recommendation.

Contact Write Judy J. Long, Vice President/Editor-in-Chief, 191 East Broad Street, Suite 209, Athens, Georgia 30601-2848. Fax: 706-613-7204. No phone calls. In-person interview recommended (telephone interview accepted). Applicants must submit a letter of interest, resume, two writing samples. Applications are accepted continuously. World Wide Web: http://www.hillstreetpress.com.

HISPANIC LINK JOURNALISM FOUNDATION
1420 N Street, NW
Washington, District of Columbia 20005

General Information News service based in Washington, D.C., that publishes the national newsweekly *Hispanic Link Weekly Report* (in English), and syndicates 3 columns weekly (in English and Spanish) through the Los Angeles Times syndicate to approximately 70 newspapers and magazines in the U.S. and Latin America. Established in 1980. Number of employees: 5. Number of internship applications received each year: 40.

Internships Available ▶ *1–2 fellowships:* responsibilities include writing for *Hispanic Link Weekly Report* and other media outlets. Candidates should have analytical skills, oral communication skills, plan to pursue career in field, research skills, written communication skills. Duration is 1 year. $25,000 stipend for duration of internship. ▶ *2–3 reporting interns:* responsibilities include a variety of tasks ranging from office and basic media training to full reporting, editing, and marketing training. Candidates should have personal interest in the field, plan to pursue career in field. Duration is flexible. Unpaid. Open to anyone interested regardless of education. International applications accepted.

Benefits Formal training, job counseling, names of contacts, on-the-job training, travel reimbursement, willing to act as a professional reference, willing to complete paperwork for educational credit, willing to provide letters of recommendation, direct contact with potential employers provided (for paid interns only), health insurance (fellowships only).

Contact Write, call, fax, or e-mail Hector Ericksen-Mendoza, Executive Director. Phone: 202-238-0705. Fax: 202-238-0706. E-mail: hector@hispaniclink.org. Telephone interview required. Applicants must submit a formal organization application, letter of interest, resume, three personal references, 3-10 writing clips. Application deadline: January 1 for winter/spring, May 1 for summer/fall. World Wide Web: http://www.hispaniclink.org.

HOUGHTON MIFFLIN COMPANY
222 Berkeley Street
Boston, Massachusetts 02116-3764

General Information Publisher of college textbooks and educational software. Established in 1834. Number of employees: 1,196. Unit of Vivendi Universal, Paris, France.

Internships Available ▶ *12 interns:* responsibilities include working in editorial, marketing, and advertising, production art and design, production, rights and permissions, custom publishing, or software development. Candidates should have computer skills, oral communication skills, written communication skills. Duration is 3 months (June-August), 35 hours per week. $9 per hour. Open to college sophomores, college juniors. International applications accepted.

Benefits Opportunity to attend seminars/workshops, possible full-time employment, willing to complete paperwork for educational credit.

Contact Through World Wide Web site Beth Gottfried, Administrator, Boston, Massachusetts 02116-3764. No phone calls. Telephone interview required. Applicants must submit a letter of interest, resume. Application deadline: March 31. World Wide Web: http://www.hmco.com.

HUNTER HOUSE, INC., PUBLISHERS
PO Box 2914
Alameda, California 94501

General Information Independent book publishing company that specializes in health, social issues, self-help/psychology, and women's issues. Established in 1978. Number of employees: 8. Number of internship applications received each year: 20.

Internships Available ▶ *1-4 editorial interns:* responsibilities include copyediting manuscripts, proofreading page proofs, confirming resource information for particular books, compiling contacts, drafting letters, soliciting endorsements for upcoming books, logging and helping to evaluate manuscript submissions, and conducting library and bookstore research. Candidates should have computer skills, editing skills, plan to pursue career in field, research skills, written communication skills. Duration is 3 months minimum (20 hours per week). Unpaid. Open to college freshmen, college sophomores, college juniors, college seniors, recent college graduates, career changers. ▶ *1 editorial/marketing intern:* responsibilities include following one project through editorial finalization and then working on the same book in marketing and publicity. Candidates should have ability to work independently, ability to work with others, computer skills, editing skills, experience in the field, personal interest in the field, research skills, written communication skills. Duration is 3 months minimum (20 hours per week). Unpaid. Open to college freshmen, college sophomores, college juniors, college seniors, individuals reentering the workforce. ▶ *1 marketing intern:* responsibilities include compiling lists of contacts who will review the book, researching direct mail lists, writing promotional copy, updating marketing database, organizing direct mailings. Candidates should have analytical skills, computer skills, oral communication skills, self-motivation, strong interpersonal skills, written communication skills. Duration is 3 months minimum (20 hours per week). Unpaid. Open to college juniors, college seniors, recent college graduates, individuals reentering the workforce. ▶ *1 publicity intern:* responsibilities include writing, designing, and mailing promotional new book announcement fliers; choosing relevant media for newly released books and mailing review copies to this list; assisting with book, radio, television, and print interviews for authors; helping to write and mail press kits; contacting book stores to schedule and organize author events and signings. Candidates should have computer skills, experience in the field, oral communication skills, self-motivation, written communication skills. Duration is 3 months minimum (20 hours per week). Unpaid. Open to college sophomores, college juniors, college seniors, recent college gradu-

ates, individuals reentering the workforce. ▶ *1 publisher's assistant intern:* responsibilities include assisting the publisher with business analysis and modeling, long-term plans and project schedules, and with daily activities related to operations and book acquisitions. Candidates should have ability to work with others, analytical skills, office skills, organizational skills, research skills, literacy with either spreadsheets, databases, and scheduling software, or Internet and HTML. Duration is 3 months minimum (20 hours per week). Unpaid. Open to college seniors, recent college graduates, graduate students, career changers, individuals reentering the workforce. International applications accepted.

Benefits Names of contacts, on-the-job training, willing to complete paperwork for educational credit, willing to provide letters of recommendation.

Contact Write, fax, e-mail, or through World Wide Web site Internship Coordinator, PO Box 2914, Alameda, California 94501-0914. Fax: 510-865-4295. E-mail: hhi@hunterhouse.com. No phone calls. In-person interview recommended (telephone interview accepted). Applicants must submit a formal organization application, letter of interest, resume, two personal references. Applications are accepted continuously. World Wide Web: http://www.hunterhouse.com/.

ISLAND PRESS
1718 Connecticut Avenue, NW, Suite 300
Washington, District of Columbia 20009

General Information Nonprofit publisher of books about the environment for professionals, students, and general readers. Established in 1978. Number of employees: 26. Number of internship applications received each year: 300.

Internships Available ▶ *1-2 marketing interns:* responsibilities include assisting marketing staff with exhibit preparation, mailings, and contacting vendors. Candidates should have ability to work independently, computer skills, office skills, oral communication skills, plan to pursue career in field, written communication skills. Duration is 3-4 months. $60 per week. Open to college juniors, college seniors, recent college graduates, graduate students. ▶ *1-2 production/design interns:* responsibilities include assisting in design work for environmental books and supporting production team. Candidates should have college courses in field, computer skills, office skills, personal interest in the field, plan to pursue career in field. Duration is 3-4 months. $60 per week. Open to college juniors, college seniors, recent college graduates, graduate students. ▶ *1-3 publicity intern:* responsibilities include assisting in all steps of publicity campaign execution; responsible for all book review receipts and distribution in-house and to authors; general department support. Candidates should have ability to work independently, computer skills, oral communication skills, organizational skills, self-motivation, written communication skills, ability to juggle multiple tasks. Duration is 3-4 months minimum (longer preferred); 20 hours per week (flexible). $60 per week. Open to recent high school graduates, college freshmen, college sophomores, college juniors, college seniors, recent college graduates, individuals reentering the workforce. International applications accepted.

Benefits On-the-job training, possible full-time employment, willing to act as a professional reference, willing to complete paperwork for educational credit, willing to provide letters of recommendation, stipend.

Contact Write, e-mail, or through World Wide Web site Jen Mase, Human Resources Manager, 1718 Connecticut Avenue, NW, Suite 300, Washington, District of Columbia 20009. E-mail: resumes@islandpress.org. No phone calls. In-person interview recommended (telephone interview accepted). Applicants must submit a letter of interest, resume, two writing samples. Application deadline: January 15 for spring, April 30 for summer, August 31 for fall. World Wide Web: http://www.islandpress.org.

IVAN R. DEE, PUBLISHER
1332 North Halsted Street
Chicago, Illinois 60622-2694

General Information Book publisher. Established in 1988. Number of employees: 10. Unit of Rowman & Littlefield Publishing Group, Lanham, Maryland. Number of internship applications received each year: 800.

Internships Available ▶ *1 computer intern:* responsibilities include assisting with databases, updating information, hardware troubleshooting, and editing and assisting with Web site. Candidates should have ability to work independently, ability to work with others, knowledge of field, self-motivation, experience with Microsoft Access and Excel, basic programming skills. Duration is 5–6 months. $6–$10 per hour. ▶ *2–4 general internships in publishing:* responsibilities include proofreading, marketing, operational duties, marketing, production, editorial, and special projects. Candidates should have ability to work independently, analytical skills, oral communication skills, personal interest in the field, self-motivation, written communication skills. Duration is 5–6 months. Unpaid. ▶ *1 marketing intern:* responsibilities include assisting publicist and sales director with special projects including correspondence, phone calls, research, and assisting with events. Candidates should have ability to work independently, oral communication skills, personal interest in the field, research skills, strong interpersonal skills, written communication skills. Duration is 5–6 months. Unpaid. ▶ *1–2 publicity interns:* responsibilities include assisting publicist with special projects including research, correspondence, and assisting with events. Candidates should have ability to work independently, oral communication skills, personal interest in the field, research skills, strong interpersonal skills, written communication skills. Duration is 5–6 months. Unpaid. Open to college juniors, college seniors, recent college graduates, graduate students. International applications accepted.

Benefits On-the-job training, opportunity to attend seminars/workshops, possible full-time employment, willing to act as a professional reference, willing to complete paperwork for educational credit, willing to provide letters of recommendation, $10 per day to cover lunch and transportation costs.

Contact Write, fax, e-mail, or through World Wide Web site Vicki Hsu, Production Editor/Internship Coordinator. Fax: 312-787-6269. E-mail: intern@ivanrdee.com. No phone calls. In-person interview recommended (telephone interview accepted). Applicants must submit a letter of interest, resume. Applications are accepted continuously. World Wide Web: http://www.ivanrdee.com.

JOHN F. BLAIR PUBLISHER
1406 Plaza Drive
Winston-Salem, North Carolina 27103

General Information General trade publisher. Established in 1954. Number of employees: 10. Number of internship applications received each year: 12.

Internships Available ▶ *1–2 sales and marketing interns:* responsibilities include database maintenance, mailing of samples and other information, and Internet research. Candidates should have ability to work independently, computer skills, oral communication skills, personal interest in the field, self-motivation, written communication skills. Duration is flexible. Unpaid. Open to college freshmen, college sophomores, college juniors, college seniors, recent college graduates, graduate students. International applications accepted.

Benefits Job counseling, names of contacts, on-the-job training, willing to act as a professional reference, willing to complete paperwork for educational credit, willing to provide letters of recommendation.

Contact Write or e-mail Ed Southern, Sales Director. Fax: 336-768-9194. E-mail: southern@blairpub.com. No phone calls. In-person interview recommended (telephone interview accepted). Applicants must submit a letter of interest, resume. Applications are accepted continuously. World Wide Web: http://www.blairpub.com.

JOHN WILEY & SONS, INC.
111 River Street
Hoboken, New Jersey 07030

General Information Largest and oldest independent publishing company in North America. Established in 1807. Number of employees: 950. Number of internship applications received each year: 300.

Internships Available ▶ *2–3 editorial assistants:* responsibilities include assisting product development, conducting market research and comparative analysis on competing books, and contacting professors as potential reviewers for manuscripts. Candidates should have ability to work independently, analytical skills, computer skills, knowledge of field, office skills, oral communication skills, organizational skills, personal interest in the field, research skills, self-motivation, strong interpersonal skills, written communication skills. Duration is 9 weeks in summer. $300 per week. ▶ *1–2 finance assistants:* responsibilities include assisting in corporate finance department and working in several areas including accounts payable, royalties, and payroll. Candidates should have analytical skills, computer skills, experience in the field, office skills, organizational skills, personal interest in the field, ability to work with numbers. Duration is 9 weeks in summer. $300 per week. ▶ *2–4 information technology interns:* responsibilities include software/hardware trouble shooting, basic network wiring, light applications development, and basic support call responding. Candidates should have ability to work independently, declared college major in field, experience in the field, office skills, oral communication skills, plan to pursue career in field, self-motivation, strong interpersonal skills, writing skills, knowledge of Word, Lotus, NT/Novell Server, Sun Solaris, Unix, and databases. Duration is 9 weeks in summer. $350 per week. ▶ *2–3 marketing assistants:* responsibilities include building a database of target sales opportunities, conducting telephone research, assisting in preparation of material for national sales meeting, and Internet marketing. Candidates should have ability to work independently, analytical skills, computer skills, office skills, oral communication skills, organizational skills, plan to pursue career in field, research skills, self-motivation, strong interpersonal skills, writing skills. Duration is 9 weeks in summer. $300 per week. ▶ *1–3 new media assistants:* responsibilities include assisting with research, development, and/or pilot implementation including new publishing technologies; Internet research, Web development, project tracking, and Web site quality assurance. Candidates should have ability to work independently, analytical skills, college courses in field, computer skills, knowledge of field, office skills, oral communication skills, organizational skills, plan to pursue career in field, research skills, self-motivation, strong interpersonal skills, writing skills. Duration is 9 weeks in summer. $300 per week. ▶ *1–2 production assistants:* responsibilities include trafficking manuscripts through production process, interacting with vendors, authors, and creative department. Candidates should have computer skills, office skills, oral communication skills, organizational skills, personal interest in the field, strong interpersonal skills, written communication skills. Duration is 9 weeks in summer. $300 per week. Open to college juniors.

Benefits Names of contacts, on-the-job training, opportunity to attend seminars/workshops, possible full-time employment, willing to act as a professional reference, willing to provide letters of recommendation, stipend.

Contact Write, e-mail, or through World Wide Web site Internship Coordinator. E-mail: opportunities@wiley.com. No phone calls. In-person interview required. Applicants must submit a letter of interest, resume. Application deadline: March 1. World Wide Web: http://www.wiley.com.

JONES AND BARTLETT PUBLISHERS
40 Tall Pine Drive
Sudbury, Massachusetts 01776

General Information Educational publishing company. Established in 1983. Number of employees: 100. Number of internship applications received each year: 20.

Internships Available ▶ *1 Paul Prindle Publishing Internship:* responsibilities include various activities in editorial, production, and especially in marketing and sales; mostly administrative.

Jones and Bartlett Publishers (continued)

Candidates should have computer skills, office skills, plan to pursue career in field, research skills, strong interpersonal skills, written communication skills. Duration is 2–3 months. $8 per hour. Open to recent high school graduates, college freshmen, college sophomores, college juniors, college seniors.

Benefits On-the-job training.

Contact E-mail Kathy Precourt, Human Resources Director. Fax: 978-443-8000. E-mail: kprecourt@jbpub.com. In-person interview recommended (telephone interview accepted). Applicants must submit a formal organization application, writing sample, letter of recommendation. Application deadline: April 30. World Wide Web: http://www.jbpub.com.

LOS ANGELES MAGAZINE
5900 Wilshire Boulevard, 10th Floor
Los Angeles, California 90036

General Information City magazine that focuses on local issues, problems, people, trends, events, and lifestyles, and highlights options and opportunities available in the southern California area. Established in 1960. Number of employees: 50. Unit of Emmis Communications, Indianapolis, Indiana. Number of internship applications received each year: 50.

Internships Available ▶ *4–6 editorial interns:* responsibilities include fact checking, researching, and performing basic clerical duties. Candidates should have ability to work independently, oral communication skills, plan to pursue career in field, research skills, writing skills. Duration is 2–3 months. Unpaid. Open to college juniors, college seniors.

Benefits Willing to complete paperwork for educational credit, willing to provide letters of recommendation.

Contact Write, fax, or e-mail Mr. Eric Mercado, Research Editor. Fax: 323-801-0105. E-mail: emercado@lamag.com. No phone calls. In-person interview recommended (telephone interview accepted). Applicants must submit a letter of interest, resume, writing sample. Application deadline: April 1 for summer, July 31 for fall, October 31 for winter, December 1 for spring. World Wide Web: http://www.lamag.com.

METRO NEW MEDIA, INC.
55 Perry Street, #1M
New York, New York 10014

General Information Company that publishes New York Theatre Wire (www.nytheatre-wire.com) and Curator's Choice (www.nymuseums.com). Established in 1996. Number of employees: 2. Number of internship applications received each year: 70.

Internships Available ▶ *1 Web design intern:* responsibilities include general Web design and systems development; Greenwich Village location. Duration is 1–2 semesters. Unpaid. ▶ *1 journalism intern:* responsibilities include working directly with publisher and leading New York theater journalists and editors. Unpaid.

Benefits On-the-job training, opportunity to attend seminars/workshops, willing to act as a professional reference, willing to complete paperwork for educational credit, willing to provide letters of recommendation.

Contact E-mail Internship Coordinator. E-mail: metro@nytheatre-wire.com. No phone calls. Applicants must submit a letter of interest, resume. Applications are accepted continuously. World Wide Web: http://www.nytheatre-wire.com.

MIDDLE EAST RESEARCH AND INFORMATION PROJECT, INC. (MERIP)
1500 Massachusetts Avenue, NW, Suite 119
Washington, District of Columbia 20005

General Information Nonprofit organization seeking to educate the public about the contemporary Middle East in such areas as peace, human rights, politics, and social justice; major program is the Middle East Report, a quarterly magazine that provides an independent look at the region and U.S. policy. Established in 1971. Number of employees: 4. Number of internship applications received each year: 80.

Internships Available ▶ *1 intern:* responsibilities include assisting the editorial staff in producing the Middle East Report.

Candidates should have background in journalism or publications. Duration is flexible. Unpaid. Open to college juniors, college seniors, recent college graduates, career changers, individuals reentering the workforce. International applications accepted.

Benefits Job counseling, names of contacts, opportunity to attend seminars/workshops, willing to act as a professional reference, willing to complete paperwork for educational credit, willing to provide letters of recommendation, opportunity to hear summer lunch speakers.

Contact Write, fax, e-mail, or through World Wide Web site Intern Coordinator. Fax: 202-223-3604. E-mail: ctoensing@merip.org. In-person interview recommended (telephone interview accepted). Applicants must submit a letter of interest, resume. Applications are accepted continuously. World Wide Web: http://www.merip.org.

MILKWEED EDITIONS
1011 Washington Avenue South, Suite 300
Minneapolis, Minnesota 55415-1246

General Information Nonprofit literary press. Established in 1984. Number of employees: 10. Number of internship applications received each year: 50.

Internships Available ▶ *2–5 publishing interns:* responsibilities include reading and critiquing unsolicited manuscripts; using proofreader's marks; researching markets, new books, funding opportunities, and authors; proofing books scheduled for reprint; reading galleys critically; administrative duties; library fact-checking. Candidates should have computer skills, knowledge of field, oral communication skills, personal interest in the field, self-motivation, writing skills. Duration is 12 weeks (3 days per week). Unpaid. Open to college seniors, recent college graduates, graduate students, law students, career changers, individuals reentering the workforce. International applications accepted.

Benefits Names of contacts, willing to act as a professional reference, willing to complete paperwork for educational credit, willing to provide letters of recommendation.

Contact Write, call, fax, or e-mail Internship Coordinator. Phone: 612-332-3192. Fax: 612-215-2550. E-mail: develop@milkweed.org. In-person interview recommended (telephone interview accepted). Applicants must submit a letter of interest, resume, two letters of recommendation. Applications are accepted continuously. World Wide Web: http://www.milkweed.org.

MILWAUKEE MAGAZINE
417 East Chicago Street
Milwaukee, Wisconsin 53202

General Information Magazine that entertains readers, keeps them informed on important regional issues, and helps them get the most from their city. Established in 1979. Number of employees: 35. Subsidiary of Quad/Graphics Inc., Sussex, Wisconsin. Number of internship applications received each year: 25.

Internships Available ▶ *1–3 editorial interns:* responsibilities include researching special projects, reporting, and some writing. Candidates should have analytical skills, experience in the field, self-motivation, strong interpersonal skills, written communication skills, demonstrated interest in magazine journalism (highly recommended). Duration is 1 semester or summer. Unpaid. Open to college sophomores, college juniors, college seniors, recent college graduates, graduate students, career changers.

Benefits Names of contacts, on-the-job training, willing to act as a professional reference, willing to complete paperwork for educational credit, willing to provide letters of recommendation, possibility of part-time or freelance employment.

Contact Write or e-mail Natalie Dorman, Associate Editor. E-mail: natalie.dorman@qg.com. No phone calls. In-person interview recommended (telephone interview accepted). Applicants must submit a letter of interest, resume, three personal references, 5 writing samples. Application deadline: March 1 for summer, November 1 for spring. World Wide Web: http://www.milwaukeemagazine.com.

MOMENT MAGAZINE
4710 41st Street, NW
Washington, District of Columbia 20016

General Information   Independent Jewish bimonthly magazine that covers political, artistic, social, religious, and cultural issues affecting the Jewish world. Established in 1975. Number of employees: 20. Unit of Jewish Educational Ventures. Number of internship applications received each year: 40.
Internships Available   ► *1–2 editorial assistants:* responsibilities include proofreading, writing, performing administrative tasks, research, and fact checking. Candidates should have ability to work independently, ability to work with others, computer skills, office skills, oral communication skills, personal interest in the field, research skills, written communication skills. Duration is 3 months minimum (15-20 hours per week). Position available as unpaid or paid. Open to college sophomores, college juniors, college seniors, recent college graduates. International applications accepted.
Benefits   Names of contacts, willing to complete paperwork for educational credit, willing to provide letters of recommendation.
Contact   Write, call, fax, or e-mail James Onley, Personnel Manager. Phone: 800-221-4644. Fax: 202-364-2636. E-mail: operations@bib-arch.org. In-person interview recommended (telephone interview accepted). Applicants must submit a letter of interest, resume, writing samples (helpful). Applications are accepted continuously. World Wide Web: http://www.momentmag.com.

MOTHER JONES MAGAZINE
731 Market Street, Suite 600
San Francisco, California 94103

General Information   Magazine that specializes in investigative reporting and political analysis. Established in 1976. Number of employees: 50. Number of internship applications received each year: 500.
Internships Available   ► *6–10 editorial interns:* responsibilities include fact checking and reporting support, research, and reporting assistance on investigative research projects for both magazine and Web site. Candidates should have editing skills, research skills, writing skills. Duration is 4 months (minimum). $100 per month stipend; after 4 months, interns are reviewed for the Mother Jones fellowship which requires an additional 4–8-month commitment and pays a larger stipend. Open to recent college graduates, graduate students. International applications accepted.
Benefits   Names of contacts, opportunity to attend seminars/workshops, willing to complete paperwork for educational credit, willing to provide letters of recommendation.
Contact   Write, fax, e-mail, or through World Wide Web site Internship Coordinator. Fax: 415-665-6696. E-mail: intern@motherjones.com. No phone calls. In-person interview recommended (telephone interview accepted). Applicants must submit a letter of interest, resume, three writing samples, names and phone numbers of 3 personal references. Applications are accepted continuously. World Wide Web: http://www.motherjones.com.

MS. MAGAZINE
433 South Beverly Drive
Beverly Hills, California 90212

General Information   Feminist magazine with focus on international news, health, arts, work, and books. Established in 1972. Number of employees: 25. Subsidiary of Feminist Majority Foundation, Beverly Hills, California. Number of internship applications received each year: 200.
Internships Available   ► *3–4 editorial interns:* responsibilities include answering phones, responding to e-mails, doing research for editors, attending weekly editorial meetings, some writing. Candidates should have ability to work with others, knowledge of field, oral communication skills, research skills, self-motivation, written communication skills. Duration is one fall, spring, or summer. Unpaid. Open to college sophomores, college juniors, college seniors, career changers, individuals reentering the workforce. ► *3–4 marketing interns:* responsibilities include supporting the Marketing Circulation Department in marketing and promotion activities. Candidates should have ability to work independently, ability to

work with others, analytical skills, computer skills, office skills, oral communication skills, organizational skills, personal interest in the field, research skills, self-motivation, written communication skills. Duration is one fall, spring, or summer. Unpaid. Open to recent high school graduates, college sophomores, college juniors, college seniors, graduate students, career changers, individuals reentering the workforce. International applications accepted.
Benefits   On-the-job training, willing to act as a professional reference, willing to complete paperwork for educational credit, willing to provide letters of recommendation, academic credit.
Contact   Write, e-mail, or through World Wide Web site Jaclyn Leader, Internship Coordinator. Fax: 310-556-2514. E-mail: jleader@feminist.org. No phone calls. Telephone interview required. Applicants must submit a letter of interest, resume, writing sample, two letters of recommendation. Applications are accepted continuously. World Wide Web: http://www.msmagazine.com.

NATIONAL JOURNAL.COM
1501 M Street, NW, Suite 300
Washington, District of Columbia 20005

General Information   Publishing company that covers politics, government, and technology. Established in 1998. Number of employees: 10. Division of National Journal Group, Inc., Washinton, District of Columbia. Number of internship applications received each year: 100.
Internships Available   ► *1 intern:* responsibilities include editing columns and features, assisting in managing public opinion polling database, assisting with syndication projects, monitoring news wires, and creating and implementing site features. Candidates should have editing skills, writing skills, knowledge of Web, Internet, and HTML, experience in politics and media, familiarity with AP style. Duration is 1 semester. $7 per hour. Open to college freshmen, college sophomores, college juniors, college seniors.
Benefits   Opportunity to attend seminars/workshops, willing to act as a professional reference, willing to complete paperwork for educational credit, willing to provide letters of recommendation.
Contact   Write, fax, e-mail, or through World Wide Web site Drew Sullivan, Managing Editor. Fax: 202-454-8940. E-mail: dsullivan@nationaljournal.com. No phone calls. In-person interview recommended (telephone interview accepted). Applicants must submit a letter of interest, resume, three writing samples, three personal references. Applications are accepted continuously. World Wide Web: http://www.nationaljournal.com.

NATIONAL NEWS BUREAU
PO Box 43039
Philadelphia, Pennsylvania 19129

General Information   Organization that handles the syndication of feature materials for newspapers, periodicals, and magazines. Established in 1979. Number of employees: 14. Number of internship applications received each year: 200.
Internships Available   ► *4–8 interns:* responsibilities include interviewing and reviewing and writing travel stories. Candidates should have ability to work independently, self-motivation, strong interpersonal skills. Duration is 1 semester. Paid. Open to recent high school graduates, college freshmen, college sophomores, college juniors, college seniors, recent college graduates, graduate students, career changers. International applications accepted.
Benefits   Formal training, free housing, health insurance, names of contacts, on-the-job training, opportunity to attend seminars/workshops, possible full-time employment, travel reimbursement, willing to complete paperwork for educational credit, willing to provide letters of recommendation.
International Internships   Available.
Contact   Write or e-mail Mr. Harry Jay Katz, Publisher. Fax: 215-893-5394. E-mail: hjaykatz@aol.com. No phone calls. In-person interview required. Applicants must submit a letter of interest, resume, copy of valid passport and/or driver's license. Applications are accepted continuously. World Wide Web: http://www.nationalnewsbureau.com.

THE NATION INSTITUTE
33 Irving Place, 8th Floor
New York, New York 10003

General Information Nonprofit foundation, affiliated with The Nation magazine, that supports research, conferences, seminars, educational programs, and independent media with an emphasis on social justice, civil liberties, cultural politics, and peace. Established in 1966. Number of employees: 5. Affiliate of The Nation Magazine, New York, New York. Number of internship applications received each year: 400.

Internships Available ▶ *24 interns:* responsibilities include checking facts; research; reading and evaluating manuscripts; assisting the advertising, circulation, and the promotional staff; filing; photocopying; and running errands. Candidates should have ability to work with others, computer skills, knowledge of field, personal interest in the field, plan to pursue career in field, research skills, writing skills. Duration is 1 semester. $150 per week. Open to recent high school graduates, college freshmen, college sophomores, college juniors, college seniors, recent college graduates, graduate students, law students, career changers, individuals reentering the workforce. International applications accepted.

Benefits Job counseling, names of contacts, on-the-job training, opportunity to attend seminars/workshops, willing to act as a professional reference, willing to complete paperwork for educational credit, willing to provide letters of recommendation, small stipend provided.

Contact Write, call, or e-mail Richard Kim, Internship Director. Phone: 212-209-5400. E-mail: rkim@nationinstitute.com. Applicants must submit a letter of interest, resume, two writing samples, two letters of recommendation. Application deadline: March 28 for summer, July 18 for fall, November 7 for winter/spring. World Wide Web: http://www.thenation.com.

NEW MOON PUBLISHING
34 East Superior Street, #200
Duluth, Minnesota 55802

General Information Magazine publisher. Established in 1992. Number of employees: 15. Number of internship applications received each year: 12.

Internships Available ▶ *1–2 business administration interns:* responsibilities include database entry, telephone, assisting with day-to day-management at small publishing company. Candidates should have ability to work independently, computer skills, oral communication skills, personal interest in the field, self-motivation, strong interpersonal skills, writing skills. Duration is spring, fall, or summer semester. Unpaid. Open to high school seniors, college freshmen, college sophomores, college juniors, college seniors. ▶ *1–3 editorial interns:* responsibilities include some writing, researching, editing, and acquiring material; maintaining files; inputting submissions; researching and securing artwork; working with Girls Editorial Board; working with adult and girl contributors; contributing to planning and organizing of upcoming issues. Candidates should have ability to work independently, analytical skills, computer skills, editing skills, oral communication skills, organizational skills, personal interest in the field, research skills, self-motivation, strong interpersonal skills, strong leadership ability, writing skills, commitment to girls' and women's issues. Duration is fall, spring, or summer semester. Unpaid. Open to high school students, recent high school graduates, college freshmen, college sophomores, college juniors, college seniors, recent college graduates, graduate students, career changers, individuals reentering the workforce. ▶ *1 general communications intern:* responsibilities include developing communications and administrative systems via sources research; development, and organization. Candidates should have ability to work independently, computer skills, knowledge of field, office skills, organizational skills, research skills, writing skills. Duration is one spring, fall, summer. Unpaid. Open to college sophomores, college juniors, college seniors, recent college graduates, graduate students. ▶ *1–2 marketing/e-commerce interns:* responsibilities include researching and implementing traffic-building strategies; continual development of site based on customer feedback; assisting in all administrative functions of online catalog. Candidates should have ability to work independently, computer skills, office skills, organizational skills,

strong interpersonal skills, knowledge of Web design, HTML, and on-line marketing. Duration is flexible. Unpaid. Open to college juniors, college seniors, recent college graduates, graduate students. ▶ *1–2 public relations interns:* responsibilities include updating press list, researching media outlets, writing and distributing press releases, developing fact sheet and brochures. Candidates should have ability to work independently, ability to work with others, analytical skills, college courses in field, computer skills, editing skills, knowledge of field, oral communication skills, organizational skills, personal interest in the field, research skills, self-motivation, written communication skills, commitment to girls' and women's issues. Duration is fall, spring, or summer semester. Unpaid. Open to college juniors, college seniors, recent college graduates, graduate students, career changers. ▶ *1–2 social science/research/advocacy interns:* responsibilities include engaging in action projects that have critical strategic contacts and raise awareness of equality issues. Candidates should have ability to work independently, analytical skills, computer skills, personal interest in the field, research skills, writing skills. Duration is one fall, summer, spring. Unpaid. Open to college juniors, college seniors, recent college graduates, graduate students. ▶ *1–3 turn beauty inside out interns:* responsibilities include fund-raising, outreach, planning, community project organizing, and researching funders. Candidates should have ability to work independently, office skills, oral communication skills, organizational skills, research skills, writing skills. Duration is one spring, fall, summer. Unpaid. Open to college sophomores, college juniors, college seniors, recent college graduates, graduate students, career changers. International applications accepted.

Benefits Names of contacts, on-the-job training, willing to act as a professional reference, willing to complete paperwork for educational credit, willing to provide letters of recommendation.

Contact Write, call, fax, or e-mail Deb Mylin, Managing Editor. Phone: 218-728-5507 Ext. 21. Fax: 218-728-0314. E-mail: girl@newmoon.org. In-person interview recommended (telephone interview accepted). Applicants must submit a letter of interest, resume, three writing samples. Application deadline: March 1 for summer, May 1 for fall, October 1 for spring. World Wide Web: http://www.newmoon.org.

THE NEW REPUBLIC
1331 H Street, NW, Suite 700
Washington, District of Columbia 20005

General Information Weekly journal of opinion. Established in 1914. Number of employees: 30. Number of internship applications received each year: 100.

Internships Available ▶ *3 reporters/researchers:* responsibilities include reading unsolicited manuscripts, proofreading, checking facts, handling editor's correspondence, periodic phone coverage, running errands, and writing short articles and editorials. Candidates should have ability to work independently, analytical skills, editing skills, office skills, oral communication skills, personal interest in the field, research skills, self-motivation, strong interpersonal skills, writing skills, journalism background (preferred). Duration is one summer or one academic year. $300 per week. Open to college seniors, recent college graduates, graduate students, law students. International applications accepted.

Benefits Health insurance, job counseling, names of contacts, possible full-time employment, willing to act as a professional reference, willing to provide letters of recommendation, opportunity to attend lunches with prominent political figures.

Contact Write or e-mail Internship Coordinator. E-mail: tnr@aol.com. No phone calls. Applicants must submit a letter of interest, resume, two letters of recommendation, in-person or telephone interview (for finalists), 2 writing samples (one opinion piece, one reported piece). Application deadline: April 15. World Wide Web: http://www.thenewrepublic.com.

NEWSWEEK
251 West 57th Street
New York, New York 10019

General Information Major weekly news magazine. Established in 1933. Number of employees: 400. Unit of Washington Post

Company, Washington, District of Columbia. Number of internship applications received each year: 500.

Internships Available ▶ *2 photo interns:* responsibilities include conducting Internet searches for published photos. Candidates should have knowledge of field, organizational skills, personal interest in the field, self-motivation, strong interpersonal skills. Duration is 13 weeks. $600 per week. ▶ *8–12 summer interns:* responsibilities include researching, copy flow, reporting, and occasional writing. Candidates should have ability to work with others, personal interest in the field, research skills, writing skills, one previous internship at a significant paper or magazine. Duration is June to August (13 weeks). $594 per week. Open to college juniors, college seniors, recent college graduates, graduate students. International applications accepted.

Benefits On-the-job training, possible full-time employment, opportunity to attend editorial meetings and luncheons with editors.

Contact Write or through World Wide Web site Marcus Mabry, Chief of Correspondents. No phone calls. Applicants must submit a resume, cover letter, names and phone numbers of 2 references, 5 published writing samples (editorial positions), 2 writing samples (public relations positions). Application deadline: December 15 for summer. World Wide Web: http://www.newsweek.com.

PENGUIN PUTNAM INC.
375 Hudson Street
New York, New York 10014

General Information Adult and children's trade book publisher. Established in 1838. Number of employees: 800. Division of Pearson plc, London, United Kingdom. Number of internship applications received each year: 300.

Internships Available ▶ *5–8 art department interns:* responsibilities include paste and mechanical work, light design work, corrections, and packaging of originals; also some light clerical work involved in the day-to-day operations of the office. Candidates should have office skills, oral communication skills, personal interest in the field, self-motivation, strong interpersonal skills, Quark, PhotoShop, and Illustrator skills. Duration is 1 summer or semester. Minimum wage. ▶ *8–10 editorial interns:* responsibilities include reading and evaluating unsolicited manuscripts, drafting and sending rejection letters, research, and general office support. Candidates should have editing skills, oral communication skills, personal interest in the field, self-motivation, strong interpersonal skills, writing skills. Duration is 1 summer or semester. Minimum wage. ▶ *4–6 marketing interns:* responsibilities include special projects within the department including creating marketing databases, working on seasonal catalogs, updating reading group guides, and general office support. Candidates should have office skills, oral communication skills, personal interest in the field, self-motivation, strong interpersonal skills, writing skills. Duration is 1 summer or semester. Minimum wage. ▶ *4–6 publicity interns:* responsibilities include special projects within the department including working directly with media contacts, updating press materials, and general office support. Candidates should have office skills, oral communication skills, personal interest in the field, self-motivation, strong interpersonal skills, written communication skills. Duration is 1 summer or semester. Minimum wage. ▶ *15–20 publishing interns:* responsibilities include working in a department such as editorial, art, marketing, online, production, sales, subsidiary rights, contracts, and publicity. Candidates should have office skills, oral communication skills, personal interest in the field, self-motivation, strong interpersonal skills, written communication skills. Duration is 1 summer or semester. Minimum wage. Open to college freshmen, college sophomores, college juniors, college seniors, graduate students, law students. International applications accepted.

Benefits On-the-job training, willing to complete paperwork for educational credit.

Contact Write, fax, or e-mail Latoya Sims, Human Resources Assistant. Fax: 212-366-2930. E-mail: jobs@penguinputnam.com. In-person interview required. Applicants must submit a letter of interest, resume. Application deadline: January 15 for spring, February 28 for summer, August 31 for fall. World Wide Web: http://www.penguinputnam.com.

PHILADELPHIA MAGAZINE
1818 Market Street, 36th Floor
Philadelphia, Pennsylvania 19103

General Information City magazine covering local politics, news, and entertainment. Established in 1908. Number of employees: 150. Unit of Metro Corporation, New York, New York. Number of internship applications received each year: 500.

Internships Available ▶ *2–3 art interns:* responsibilities include assisting designers, photographers, and stylists. Candidates should have ability to work independently, computer skills, knowledge of field, organizational skills, strong interpersonal skills. Duration is 1 semester or summer. Unpaid. Open to high school seniors, college freshmen, college sophomores, college juniors, college seniors, recent college graduates. ▶ *6–7 editorial interns:* responsibilities include assisting writers with research, functioning as a general editorial assistant, fact checking, reporting, and writing brief articles. Candidates should have ability to work independently, analytical skills, oral communication skills, organizational skills, research skills, strong interpersonal skills. Duration is 1 semester or summer. Unpaid. Open to high school seniors, college freshmen, college sophomores, college juniors, college seniors, recent college graduates, graduate students, career changers. International applications accepted.

Benefits Job counseling, names of contacts, possible full-time employment, willing to act as a professional reference, willing to complete paperwork for educational credit, willing to provide letters of recommendation.

Contact Write or e-mail Victor Fiorillo, Research Editor. Fax: 215-656-3502. E-mail: victor@phillymag.com. No phone calls. In-person interview recommended (telephone interview accepted). Applicants must submit a letter of interest, resume, 3-5 writing samples. Applications are accepted continuously. World Wide Web: http://www.phillymag.com.

POHLY & PARTNERS
27 Melcher Street, Floor 2
Boston, Massachusetts 02210

General Information Custom publisher of magazines and online content. Established in 1987. Number of employees: 35. Number of internship applications received each year: 100.

Internships Available ▶ *1–2 ad sales/marketing interns:* responsibilities include supporting ad sales department, client contacts, and maintaining database. Candidates should have ability to work independently, ability to work with others, computer skills, oral communication skills, research skills, written communication skills, must be receiving academic credit. Duration is 1 semester. Unpaid. ▶ *2–3 editorial interns:* responsibilities include fact-checking and writing as assigned. Candidates should have ability to work independently, oral communication skills, plan to pursue career in field, self-motivation, writing skills, must be receiving academic credit. Duration is 1 semester. Unpaid. ▶ *1 marketing intern:* responsibilities include supporting marketing communications program, maintaining database, and doing analysis. Candidates should have ability to work independently, oral communication skills, research skills, strong interpersonal skills, writing skills, must be receiving academic credit. Duration is 1 semester. Unpaid. Open to college juniors, college seniors, graduate students. International applications accepted.

Benefits On-the-job training, possible full-time employment, willing to act as a professional reference, willing to complete paperwork for educational credit, willing to provide letters of recommendation.

Contact Write, e-mail, or through World Wide Web site Karen English, Senior Editor. E-mail: karene@pohlypartners.com. No phone calls. In-person interview recommended (telephone interview accepted). Applicants must submit a letter of interest, resume, writing samples (for editorial internship). Applications are accepted continuously. World Wide Web: http://www.pohlypartners.com.

PRINTED MATTER, INC.
535 West 22nd Street
New York, New York 10011

General Information Nonprofit arts organization whose mission is to foster the appreciation, dissemination, and understanding of artists' books and related publications by artists. Established in 1976. Number of employees: 5. Number of internship applications received each year: 10.

Internships Available ▶ *1–4 interns:* responsibilities include assisting with daily and ongoing operations including exhibits and special events. Candidates should have ability to work independently, ability to work with others, oral communication skills, organizational skills, personal interest in the field, self-motivation. Duration is minimum of 3 months. Unpaid. Open to college freshmen, college sophomores, college juniors, college seniors, recent college graduates, graduate students, law students, career changers. International applications accepted.

Benefits On-the-job training, willing to act as a professional reference, willing to complete paperwork for educational credit, willing to provide letters of recommendation.

Contact Write, call, fax, or e-mail Max Schumann, Manager. Phone: 212-925-0325. Fax: 212-925-0464. E-mail: mschumann@ printedmatter.org. In-person interview recommended (telephone interview accepted). Applicants must submit a letter of interest, resume. Applications are accepted continuously. World Wide Web: http://www.printedmatter.org.

RANDOM HOUSE, INC.
1745 Broadway
New York, New York 10019

General Information General trade book publisher. Established in 1925. Number of employees: 1,800. Division of Bertelsmann, Gutersloh, Germany. Number of internship applications received each year: 1,000.

Internships Available ▶ *20–25 summer interns:* responsibilities include working in one of the major publishing groups or functional areas. Candidates should have knowledge of field, office skills, oral communication skills, personal interest in the field, self-motivation, written communication skills. Duration is 10 weeks. $300 per week. Open to college juniors. International applications accepted.

Benefits Job counseling, opportunity to attend seminars/ workshops, possible full-time employment.

Contact Through World Wide Web site Internship Coordinator. No phone calls. In-person interview required. Applicants must submit a letter of interest, resume. Application deadline: March 31. World Wide Web: http://www.randomhouse.com/careers.

RESOURCE PUBLICATIONS, INC.
160 East Virginia Street, Suite 290
San Jose, California 95112-5876

General Information Communications firm dealing in resources for ministry, education, and personal growth. Established in 1973. Number of employees: 29. Number of internship applications received each year: 100.

Internships Available ▶ *1 advertising intern:* responsibilities include developing all aspects of special projects in display advertising sales and marketing. Candidates should have ability to work independently, oral communication skills, organizational skills, strong interpersonal skills, written communication skills. Duration is 10 weeks. Paid. ▶ *1 design intern:* responsibilities include designing book covers and layouts for brochures and advertisements. Candidates should have ability to work independently, ability to work with others, college courses in field, computer skills, knowledge of field, written communication skills. Duration is 10–12 weeks. $500 per duration of internship. Open to college juniors, college seniors. ▶ *1 editorial intern:* responsibilities include performing copyediting and product packaging/production projects. Candidates should have computer skills, editing skills, organizational skills, research skills, written communication skills. Duration is 10–12 weeks. Position available as unpaid or paid. Open to high school students. ▶ *1 marketing intern:* responsibilities include conducting market research, developing literature,

and planning and executing promotional efforts. Candidates should have oral communication skills, organizational skills, plan to pursue career in field, written communication skills. Duration is 10–12 weeks. Position available as unpaid or paid. Open to high school students, college juniors, college seniors, recent college graduates, graduate students, individuals reentering the workforce. ▶ *1 sales intern:* responsibilities include planning and executing sales campaigns via telephone, exhibits, formal sales conferences, and related activities. Candidates should have knowledge of field, oral communication skills, organizational skills, strong interpersonal skills, written communication skills. Duration is 10–12 weeks. Position available as unpaid or at $8–$10 per hour. Open to college juniors, college seniors, recent college graduates, graduate students, career changers, individuals reentering the workforce.

Benefits On-the-job training, possible full-time employment, willing to act as a professional reference, willing to complete paperwork for educational credit, willing to provide letters of recommendation, commissions on sales for some positions.

Contact Write, fax, e-mail, or through World Wide Web site Mr. William Burns, President. Fax: 408-287-8748. E-mail: wjb@rpinet. com. No phone calls. In-person interview required. Applicants must submit a letter of interest, resume. Applications are accepted continuously. World Wide Web: http://www.rpinet.com/.

RODALE INC.
33 East Minor Street
Emmaus, Pennsylvania 18098

General Information International publisher of healthy active living content; magazine titles include *Prevention, Men's Health,* and *Runner's World;* book titles include *Dr. Shapiro's Picture Perfect Weight Loss.* Established in 1930. Number of employees: 750. Number of internship applications received each year: 2,000.

Internships Available ▶ *Summer interns:* responsibilities include writing, editing, editorial research, marketing, public relations, graphic design, and Web development. Candidates should have computer skills, experience in the field, oral communication skills, organizational skills, self-motivation, strong interpersonal skills, written communication skills. Duration is 11 weeks (typically early June through mid-August). Position available as unpaid or at $425 per week (undergraduate level); $600 per week (graduate level). Open to college juniors, college seniors, recent college graduates, graduate students. International applications accepted.

Benefits Formal training, job counseling, meals at a cost, names of contacts, on-the-job training, opportunity to attend seminars/ workshops, possible full-time employment, willing to act as a professional reference, willing to complete paperwork for educational credit, willing to provide letters of recommendation, free health club access, discounted publications.

Contact Write, fax, e-mail, or through World Wide Web site Internship Program Manager, 33 East Minor Street, Emmaus, Pennsylvania 18098. Fax: 610-967-9209. E-mail: hr3@rodale.com. No phone calls. In-person interview recommended (telephone interview accepted). Applicants must submit a letter of interest, resume, three writing samples, portfolio (if applicable). Application deadline: February 1. World Wide Web: http://www.rodale. com.

RUGGED LAND
276 Canal Street, 5th Floor
New York, New York 10013

General Information Book publishing and film development company. Established in 2001. Number of employees: 4.

Internships Available ▶ *1–3 interns:* responsibilities include research, writing, office work; exposure to all aspects of book publishing and film production including editorial, marketing, publicity, and subsidiary rights. Candidates should have ability to work independently, oral communication skills, research skills, strong interpersonal skills, writing skills, journalism experience preferred, but not essential. Duration is fall (September to December), spring (January to April), or summer (May to August) minimum 3 days per week. Unpaid. Open to college freshmen, college sophomores, college juniors, college seniors, recent college graduates. International applications accepted.

Benefits Names of contacts, willing to act as a professional reference, willing to complete paperwork for educational credit, willing to provide letters of recommendation.

Contact Write, fax, e-mail, or through World Wide Web site Webster Stone, Managing Partner. Fax: 212-334-5749. E-mail: wstone@ruggedland.com. No phone calls. In-person interview recommended (telephone interview accepted). Applicants must submit a letter of interest, resume, writing sample. Applications are accepted continuously. World Wide Web: http://www.ruggedland.com.

RUNNING PRESS
125 South 22nd Street
Philadelphia, Pennsylvania 19103

General Information General book publisher mainly of nonfiction, children's titles, art, and gift books. Established in 1972. Number of employees: 80. Unit of Perseus Books Group, New York, New York. Number of internship applications received each year: 30.

Internships Available ▶ *1–2 assistants to associate publisher:* responsibilities include working with the associate publisher as well as with the editorial, sales, production, legal, and publicity departments. Candidates should have computer skills, personal interest in the field, research skills, strong interpersonal skills, writing skills. Duration is flexible. Unpaid. Open to college freshmen, college sophomores, college juniors, college seniors, recent college graduates. ▶ *2 design interns:* responsibilities include developing design concepts, scanning artwork, layout and design for book pages, and researching illustrator/photographer candidates. Candidates should have college courses in field, computer skills, oral communication skills, personal interest in the field, self-motivation, knowledge of Quark Xpress and PhotoShop. Duration is flexible. Unpaid. Open to college sophomores, college juniors, college seniors. ▶ *3–4 editorial interns:* responsibilities include assisting with general editorial work. Candidates should have computer skills, editing skills, oral communication skills, personal interest in the field, research skills, writing skills. Duration is flexible. Unpaid. Open to college sophomores, college juniors, college seniors, recent college graduates, graduate students. ▶ *1 production intern:* responsibilities include assisting in daily administrative duties in the production department including some communication with vendors; distribution and/or trafficking materials; coordinating bound galleys; some data entry on computer. Candidates should have ability to work with others, computer skills, office skills, organizational skills, personal interest in the field, writing skills. Duration is 3–4 months. Unpaid. Open to college sophomores, college juniors, college seniors, recent college graduates, graduate students, law students. ▶ *2–3 publicity interns:* responsibilities include providing support to publicity director, publicist and publicity assistant; handling publicity campaign for assigned title(s); drafting pitch letters, press releases; organizing mailing; making follow-up calls to media to pitch title(s); and clipping and filing reviews. Candidates should have computer skills, oral communication skills, personal interest in the field, self-motivation, strong interpersonal skills, written communication skills. Duration is 12 weeks. Unpaid. Open to college sophomores, college juniors, college seniors, recent college graduates, graduate students. ▶ *1–2 special sales interns:* responsibilities include assisting with day-to-day operations of the special sales department including order taking, customer service, and computer work. Candidates should have computer skills, oral communication skills, personal interest in the field, self-motivation, writing skills. Duration is 12 weeks. Unpaid. Open to college sophomores, college juniors, college seniors, recent college graduates, graduate students. International applications accepted.

Benefits Names of contacts, on-the-job training, possible full-time employment, willing to act as a professional reference, willing to complete paperwork for educational credit, willing to provide letters of recommendation, hands-on experience.

Contact Write, call, fax, or e-mail Joelle Herr, Managing Editor. Phone: 215-567-5080 Ext. 223. Fax: 215-568-2919. E-mail: jherr@runningpress.com. In-person interview recommended (telephone interview accepted). Applicants must submit a letter of interest,

resume, writing sample. Applications are accepted continuously. World Wide Web: http://www.runningpress.com.

SAN DIEGO COMMUNITY NEWSPAPER GROUP
4645 Cass Street
San Diego, California 92169

General Information Publisher of six community newspapers and assorted specialty publications. Established in 1988. Number of employees: 30. Division of Mannis Communications, Inc., San Diego, California. Number of internship applications received each year: 100.

Internships Available ▶ *12 editorial interns:* responsibilities include researching and compiling information for editorials and articles, putting together calendars and obituaries, occasionally gathering editorial information for the senior editor, and writing news and feature articles. Candidates should have ability to work independently, ability to work with others, computer skills, office skills, oral communication skills, written communication skills, knowledge of Associated Press style guidelines. Duration is 9–12 weeks. Unpaid. Open to college freshmen, college sophomores, college juniors, college seniors, recent college graduates, career changers, individuals reentering the workforce. International applications accepted.

Benefits Names of contacts, on-the-job training, possible full-time employment, willing to act as a professional reference, willing to complete paperwork for educational credit, willing to provide letters of recommendation.

Contact Write, call, fax, or e-mail John Gregory, Editor-in-Chief, PO Box 9550, San Diego, California 92169. Phone: 858-270-3103 Ext. 142. Fax: 858-270-9325. E-mail: mail@sdnews.com. In-person interview recommended (telephone interview accepted). Applicants must submit a formal organization application, letter of interest, resume, 1-3 writing samples, 1-3 personal references, letter of recommendation (optional). Application deadline: May 15 for summer, August 20 for fall, December 15 for winter. World Wide Web: http://www.sdnews.com.

SAN DIEGO DAILY TRANSCRIPT
2131 Third Avenue
San Diego, California 92101

General Information Newspaper and Web-based publisher of business information and content. Established in 1886. Number of employees: 80. Unit of Transcript Publishing Co., San Diego, California. Number of internship applications received each year: 50.

Internships Available ▶ *1–3 editorial interns:* responsibilities include writing, reporting, and researching. Candidates should have plan to pursue career in field, research skills, self-motivation, writing skills, major in journalism. Duration is 3 months. $560 per week. Open to college seniors, recent college graduates, graduate students, law students, career changers. ▶ *1–3 summer interns:* responsibilities include writing, reporting, and researching. Candidates should have ability to work with others, editing skills, oral communication skills, personal interest in the field, research skills, self-motivation, writing skills. Duration is 2–3 months. Unpaid. Open to college juniors, college seniors, graduate students, law students. International applications accepted.

Benefits On-the-job training, opportunity to attend seminars/workshops, possible full-time employment, willing to act as a professional reference, willing to provide letters of recommendation.

Contact Write, call, or e-mail Adriana Gutierrez, Human Resources Manager. Phone: 619-232-4381. Fax: 619-236-8126. E-mail: gutierrez@sddt.com. In-person interview recommended (telephone interview accepted). Applicants must submit a formal organization application, letter of interest, resume, three writing samples, three personal references. Application deadline: one month prior to start of semester. World Wide Web: http://www.sddt.com.

THE SAN DIEGO UNION-TRIBUNE
350 Camino de la Reina
San Diego, California 92108

General Information   Publishing and information services. Number of employees: 1,500. Unit of Copley Newspapers, Inc., La Jolla, California. Number of internship applications received each year: 250.

Internships Available   ▶ *1–4 interns:* responsibilities include working as professional reporter, photographer, page designer, and copyeditor. Candidates should have experience in the field, plan to pursue career in field, research skills, self-motivation, writing skills, fluency in a second language that is spoken in San Diego (a plus). Duration is 10–12 weeks. Position available as unpaid or at $460 per week for summer interns; academic-year interns unpaid . Open to college juniors, college seniors, recent college graduates, graduate students.

Benefits   On-the-job training, opportunity to attend seminars/workshops, willing to complete paperwork for educational credit.

Contact   Write, call, e-mail, or through World Wide Web site Carol Goodhue, Training and Development Coordinator, PO Box 120191, San Diego, California 92112-0191. Phone: 619-293-1261. E-mail: carol.goodhue@uniontrib.com. Telephone interview required. Applicants must submit a letter of interest, resume, 6 samples of published newspaper stories. Application deadline: November 15 for paid summer interns; continuous for unpaid interns. World Wide Web: http://www.uniontrib.com.

SCHNEIDER PUBLISHING
11835 West Olympic Boulevard, Suite 1265
Los Angeles, California 90064

General Information   Magazine publisher. Established in 1988. Number of employees: 9. Number of internship applications received each year: 50.

Internships Available   ▶ *1–3 office assistants:* responsibilities include flexible duties depending on the intern's interest and experience; general assistance with office tasks. Candidates should have ability to work independently, analytical skills, editing skills, office skills, oral communication skills, organizational skills, personal interest in the field, research skills, self-motivation, strong interpersonal skills, writing skills, experience with computers (desirable). Duration is flexible. Position available as unpaid or at $6 per hour. Open to high school seniors, recent high school graduates, college freshmen, college sophomores, college juniors, college seniors, recent college graduates, graduate students. International applications accepted.

Benefits   On-the-job training, possible full-time employment, willing to act as a professional reference, willing to complete paperwork for educational credit, willing to provide letters of recommendation, small stipend.

Contact   Write, fax, or e-mail Ann Shepphird, Managing Editor, 11835 West Olympic Boulevard, Suite 1265, Los Angeles, California 90064. Fax: 310-577-3715. E-mail: ann@schneiderpublishing.com. No phone calls. In-person interview recommended (telephone interview accepted). Applicants must submit a letter of interest, resume. Applications are accepted continuously.

SCIENCE MAGAZINE
1200 New York Avenue, NW
Washington, District of Columbia 20005

General Information   Nonprofit educational magazine. Established in 1880. Number of employees: 120. Subsidiary of American Association for the Advancement of Science, Washington, District of Columbia. Number of internship applications received each year: 40.

Internships Available   ▶ *1 intern:* responsibilities include news writing and editing. Candidates should have ability to work with others, analytical skills, editing skills, oral communication skills, research skills, self-motivation, writing skills, knowledge of science. Duration is January 1 to June 30 or July 1 to December 31. $400 per week. Open to college seniors, recent college graduates, graduate students, career changers. International applications accepted.

Benefits   Opportunity to attend seminars/workshops, travel reimbursement, willing to act as a professional reference, willing to provide letters of recommendation.

International Internships   Available in Cambridge, United Kingdom.

Contact   Write, call, fax, or e-mail Eliot Marshall, Senior Writer. Phone: 202-326-6589. Fax: 202-371-9227. E-mail: emarshal@aaas.org. Applicants must submit a letter of interest, resume, two personal references, 3-5 writing samples. Application deadline: March 1 for summer, October 1 for winter. World Wide Web: http://www.sciencemag.org.

SCIENCE NEWS MAGAZINE
1719 N Street, NW
Washington, District of Columbia 20036

General Information   Weekly newsmagazine covering science. Established in 1922. Number of employees: 20. Unit of Science Service, Inc., Washington, District of Columbia. Number of internship applications received each year: 80.

Internships Available   ▶ *3 science writer interns:* responsibilities include researching and writing short news stories and longer features for weekly magazine. Candidates should have ability to work independently, college courses in field, plan to pursue career in field, research skills, self-motivation, writing skills. Duration is 3–4 months. $1800 per month. Open to college seniors, recent college graduates, graduate students, career changers. International applications accepted.

Benefits   Job counseling, names of contacts, on-the-job training, willing to act as a professional reference, willing to complete paperwork for educational credit, willing to provide letters of recommendation, opportunity to write/publish stories.

Contact   Write Keith Haglund, Internship Coordinator. Fax: 202-659-0365. No phone calls. Applicants must submit a letter of interest, resume, at least 3 examples of journalistic writing. Application deadline: February 1 for summer, June 15 for fall, October 15 for spring. World Wide Web: http://www.sciencenews.org.

SMITHSONIAN INSTITUTION PRESS
750 Ninth Street, NW, #4300
Washington, District of Columbia 20560-0950

General Information   Publishing arm of the Smithsonian Institution that annually produces 80–100 publications relating to Smithsonian collections and research interests. Established in 1846. Number of employees: 38. Unit of Smithsonian Institution, Washington, District of Columbia. Number of internship applications received each year: 20.

Internships Available   ▶ *1–2 Smithsonian Contributions and Studies series interns:* responsibilities include proofing, editing, and coding files for upload to Web site, as well as proofing and editing of manuscripts in progress. Candidates should have college courses in field, computer skills, editing skills, knowledge of field, self-motivation, written communication skills. Duration is 8–12 weeks. Unpaid. Open to college sophomores, college juniors, college seniors, recent college graduates, graduate students. ▶ *1–2 acquisitions interns:* responsibilities include working on development of books on scholarly subjects for adults, researching the locations of outstanding photographs and illustrations for manuscripts, assisting with the correlation and preparation for publication of book projects. Candidates should have computer skills, office skills, personal interest in the field, research skills, strong interpersonal skills, written communication skills. Duration is 8–12 weeks. Unpaid. Open to college sophomores, college juniors, college seniors, recent college graduates. ▶ *1–2 marketing interns:* responsibilities include assisting marketing staff with preparing print advertisements, flyers, and brochures for direct mail, publicity kits, sales kits, and jacket copy; sending books out for review by media and course adoption. Candidates should have ability to work with others, computer skills, office skills, oral communication skills, writing skills. Duration is 8–12 weeks. Unpaid. Open to college sophomores, college juniors, college seniors, recent college graduates.

Benefits   Job counseling, names of contacts, opportunity to attend seminars/workshops, possible full-time employment, willing to complete paperwork for educational credit, willing to provide letters of recommendation, one-on-one professional mentor/student involvement.

Contact Write or e-mail Mr. Prospero M. Hernandez, Internship Coordinator, 750 Ninth Street, NW #4300, Washington, District of Columbia 20560-0950. E-mail: phernandez@sipress.si.edu. In-person interview recommended (telephone interview accepted). Applicants must submit a formal organization application, resume, academic transcripts, two letters of recommendation, personal essay. Application deadline: April 1 for summer, July 1 for fall, October 1 for spring. World Wide Web: http://www.sipress.si. edu.

SOUTH CAROLINA PRESS ASSOCIATION FOUNDATION
PO Box 11429
Columbia, South Carolina 29211

General Information One of the nation's oldest state press associations; members include all daily newspapers and nearly every weekly newspaper in South Carolina. Established in 1875. Number of internship applications received each year: 15.
Internships Available ▶ *1–3 summer interns:* responsibilities include working in either editorial, advertising, or photography positions. Candidates should have ability to work independently, computer skills, personal interest in the field, plan to pursue career in field, research skills, self-motivation, writing skills, previous newspaper experience and working knowledge of newspaper software and/or camera equipment, darkroom, computer photo experience (beneficial), preference given to journalism, advertising, or communications majors. Duration is 10 weeks. $3000 per duration of internship. Open to any South Carolina college or university student who has completed the sophomore year by the start of internship.
Benefits On-the-job training, approved travel expenses involved in work assignments and additional work will be funded by intern's host newspaper.
Contact Write, call, e-mail, or through World Wide Web site William C. Rogers, Secretary. Phone: 888-SCPRESS. Fax: 803-551-0903. E-mail: jroberts@scpress.org. Applicants must submit a formal organization application, resume, academic transcripts, letter of recommendation from college advisor (director of communication/journalism major); maximum of 6 newspaper work samples; list of college activities; list of college scholarships or awards received; statement of interest (maximum 250 words). Application deadline: January 30. World Wide Web: http://www. scpress.org.

SOUTHERN PROGRESS CORPORATION
PO Box 2581
Birmingham, Alabama 35202

General Information Magazine and book publisher specializing in lifestyle publications. Established in 1886. Number of employees: 1,400. Subsidiary of AOL Time Warner, Inc., New York, New York. Number of internship applications received each year: 600.
Internships Available ▶ *1–2 accounting interns:* responsibilities include general accounting functions. Candidates should have analytical skills, computer skills, declared college major in field, knowledge of field, organizational skills. Duration is 3–5 months. $10 per hour. ▶ *4–6 advertising interns:* responsibilities include writing ad copy, selecting promotional items, and assisting sales team with sales calls. Candidates should have ability to work independently, ability to work with others, college courses in field, organizational skills, personal interest in the field, written communication skills. Duration is 3–5 months. $10 per hour. ▶ *12–15 editorial interns:* responsibilities include writing, proofreading, editing, and research. Candidates should have ability to work with others, editing skills, experience in the field, personal interest in the field, research skills, writing skills. Duration is 3–5 months. $10 per hour. ▶ *2–3 graphic design interns:* responsibilities include designing promotional material for advertising department. Candidates should have ability to work independently, computer skills, declared college major in field, knowledge of field, organizational skills. Duration is 3–5

months. $10 per hour. ▶ *2–4 marketing interns:* responsibilities include maintaining vendor performance records, report-tracking, and special research projects. Candidates should have analytical skills, computer skills, knowledge of field, organizational skills, personal interest in the field, research skills. Duration is 3–5 months. $10 per hour. ▶ *2 new media interns:* responsibilities include designing and updating magazine Internet sites. Candidates should have ability to work with others, computer skills, knowledge of field, plan to pursue career in field, self-motivation, written communication skills, familiarity with HTML, major in graphic design or new media (a plus). Duration is 3–5 months. $10 per hour. ▶ *1–2 test kitchens interns:* responsibilities include preparing recipes for taste testing and photography. Candidates should have ability to work independently, ability to work with others, knowledge of field, culinary arts degree preferred. Duration is 8–10 weeks. $10 per hour. Open to college juniors, college seniors, recent college graduates, graduate students.
Benefits Job counseling, names of contacts, on-the-job training, opportunity to attend seminars/workshops, possible full-time employment, willing to complete paperwork for educational credit, willing to provide letters of recommendation, reimbursement of work-related travel expenses.
Contact Write, fax, or through World Wide Web site Ms. Holly Hughey, Student Intern Coordinator. Fax: 205-455-6750. No phone calls. In-person interview required. Applicants must submit a letter of interest, resume, letter of recommendation, design samples, at least 5 writing samples (for creative position). Application deadline: February 15 for summer, June 15 for fall, September 15 for winter/spring. World Wide Web: http://www.southernprogress. com.

SURFACE MAGAZINE
70 Washington Street, #807
Brooklyn, New York 11201

General Information National lifestyle magazine exploring emerging trends in fashion, interiors, architecture, art, graphics, film, and music. Established in 1994. Number of employees: 15. Unit of Surface Magazine, San Francisco, California. Number of internship applications received each year: 500.
Internships Available ▶ *1–4 advertising/promotions interns:* responsibilities include updating and managing databases; conducting media research; planning and execution of promotional events. Candidates should have ability to work independently, computer skills, oral communication skills, organizational skills, self-motivation, writing skills. Duration is 3–6 months. Unpaid. Open to college freshmen, college sophomores, college juniors, college seniors, recent college graduates, graduate students. ▶ *1–2 editorial interns:* responsibilities include researching, developing, writing, and editing editorial content. Candidates should have ability to work independently, computer skills, editing skills, plan to pursue career in field, research skills, writing skills. Duration is 3–6 months. Unpaid. Open to college juniors, college seniors, recent college graduates, graduate students.
Benefits Formal training, on-the-job training, willing to act as a professional reference, willing to complete paperwork for educational credit, willing to provide letters of recommendation.
Contact Fax or e-mail Jennifer Keller, Internship Director. Fax: 718-488-0651. E-mail: jkeller@surfarcmag.com. No phone calls. In-person interview required. Applicants must submit a letter of interest, resume, three personal references, portfolio (graphic designers), writing samples (editorial positions). Applications are accepted continuously. World Wide Web: http://www.surfacemag. com.

TEACHER MAGAZINE
6935 Arlington Road, Suite 100
Bethesda, Maryland 20814-5281

General Information National magazine that covers K-12 education and reports on the teaching profession, school policy and culture, and the people who influence education. Established in 1989. Number of employees: 10. Unit of Editorial Projects in Education, Inc., Bethesda, Maryland. Number of internship applications received each year: 50.

Teacher Magazine (continued)

Internships Available ▶ *1 editorial intern:* responsibilities include researching and writing "Calendar" section; writing short articles and sidebars; proofreading and fact-checking articles; and assisting staff with special projects. Candidates should have ability to work independently, editing skills, oral communication skills, research skills, writing skills, attention to detail. Duration is 12-15 weeks (15 hours per week). $6 per hour. Open to college sophomores, college juniors, college seniors, recent college graduates, graduate students. International applications accepted.

Benefits On-the-job training, willing to act as a professional reference, willing to complete paperwork for educational credit, opportunity to write and publish short articles.

Contact Write or e-mail Samantha Stainburn, Managing Editor. E-mail: sstain@epe.org. No phone calls. Telephone interview required. Applicants must submit a resume, three writing samples, cover letter. Application deadline: April 1 for summer, August 1 for fall, November 18 for spring. World Wide Web: http://www.teachermagazine.org.

TIKKUN MAGAZINE
2342 Shattuck Avenue, #1200
Berkeley, California 94704

General Information Bimonthly Jewish critique of politics, culture, and society; influence is not limited to the Jewish population. Established in 1986. Number of employees: 8. Unit of Institute for Labor and Mental Health, Oakland, California. Number of internship applications received each year: 30.

Internships Available ▶ *3–6 editorial, production, and publishing interns:* responsibilities include reading unsolicited manuscripts, writing evaluations and rejection letters, handling author correspondence, proofreading galleys, performing independent research project; assisting with production of magazine, soliciting advertising, organizing outside conferences, lectures, seminars, and teach-ins; assisting in office administration. Candidates should have ability to work independently, editing skills, office skills, oral communication skills, personal interest in the field, self-motivation, strong interpersonal skills, written communication skills. Duration is flexible; prefer a commitment of at least three months. Unpaid. Open to college freshmen, college sophomores, college juniors, college seniors, recent college graduates, graduate students, law students, career changers, individuals reentering the workforce. International applications accepted.

Benefits Job counseling, names of contacts, on-the-job training, possible full-time employment, willing to act as a professional reference, willing to complete paperwork for educational credit, willing to provide letters of recommendation, free books.

Contact Write, call, or e-mail Judy Tergis, Office Manager, 2107 Van Ness Avenue, Suite 302, San Francisco, California 94109. Phone: 510-644-1200. Fax: 510-644-1255. E-mail: magazine@tikkun.org. In-person interview recommended (telephone interview accepted). Applicants must submit a letter of interest, resume. Applications are accepted continuously. World Wide Web: http://www.tikkun.org.

TIMBER PRESS, INC.
133 SW 2nd Avenue, Suite 450
Portland, Oregon 97204

General Information Book publisher. Established in 1978. Number of employees: 30. Number of internship applications received each year: 30.

Internships Available ▶ *1–2 interns:* responsibilities include researching, writing, and designing promotional materials; maintenance of daily content on Web site; press kit assembly; shipping and miscellaneous tasks for publicity, sales, and other departments. Candidates should have computer skills, oral communication skills, personal interest in the field, research skills, self-motivation, written communication skills. Duration is 3 months. Unpaid. Open to college sophomores, college juniors, college seniors, recent college graduates, graduate students, career changers, individuals reentering the workforce.

Benefits Formal training, names of contacts, on-the-job training, opportunity to attend seminars/workshops, willing to act as a

professional reference, willing to complete paperwork for educational credit, willing to provide letters of recommendation.

Contact Write, call, fax, e-mail, or through World Wide Web site Maureen Tingley, Publicist. Phone: 503-227-2878 Ext. 109. Fax: 503-227-3070. E-mail: maureen@timberpress.com. In-person interview recommended (telephone interview accepted). Applicants must submit a letter of interest, resume, three personal references. Application deadline: February 1 for spring, March 1 for summer, August 1 for fall, November 1 for winter. World Wide Web: http://www.timberpress.com.

WASHINGTONIAN MAGAZINE
1828 L Street, NW, Suite 200
Washington, District of Columbia 20036

General Information General interest magazine that focuses on the people and issues of Washington, DC. Established in 1965. Number of employees: 60. Number of internship applications received each year: 200.

Internships Available ▶ *1–3 advertising/account executive interns:* responsibilities include phone sales and updating and researching ad files. Candidates should have ability to work independently, computer skills, office skills, oral communication skills, personal interest in the field, self-motivation, strong interpersonal skills, written communication skills. Duration is 3–5 months. Approximately $5 per hour (tax free). Open to undergraduates. ▶ *1–2 art interns:* responsibilities include assisting with production and in-house design assignments using PhotoShop and QuarkXpress. Candidates should have college courses in field, computer skills, oral communication skills, personal interest in the field, strong interpersonal skills. Duration is 2–3 months. Unpaid. Open to college freshmen, college sophomores, college juniors, college seniors, graduate students. ▶ *4–5 editorial/interns:* responsibilities include fact checking, research, and writing. Candidates should have ability to work independently, experience in the field, organizational skills, personal interest in the field, research skills, self-motivation, writing skills. Duration is 3–5 months. $6.15 per hour. Open to college freshmen, college sophomores, college juniors, college seniors, recent college graduates, graduate students, career changers. International applications accepted.

Benefits Names of contacts, opportunity to attend seminars/workshops, willing to act as a professional reference, willing to complete paperwork for educational credit, willing to provide letters of recommendation.

Contact Write, call, fax, or through World Wide Web site Cindy Rich, Assistant Editor. Phone: 202-296-3600. Fax: 202-862-3526. In-person interview recommended (telephone interview accepted). Applicants must submit a letter of interest, resume, three writing samples, three personal references. Application deadline: March 1 for summer positions, November 1 for January positions. World Wide Web: http://www.washingtonian.com.

WEIDER PUBLICATIONS–MEN'S FITNESS MAGAZINE
21100 Erwin Street
Woodland Hills, California 91367

General Information National fitness magazine. Established in 1975. Number of employees: 500. Division of America Media, Inc., Woodland Hills, California. Number of internship applications received each year: 75.

Internships Available ▶ *1–2 art interns:* responsibilities include working in the Art Department with art and photo assistants, helping to organize the art library, working with contributors, and assisting in the general monthly production cycle of the magazine. Candidates should have ability to work with others, college courses in field, computer skills, organizational skills, personal interest in the field, plan to pursue career in field, experience with Macs, PhotoShop, and Quark (a plus). Duration is 3–4 months. Unpaid. Open to college freshmen, college sophomores, college juniors, college seniors, student must be receiving school credit for internship (preference given to students from Los Angeles area).

Benefits Possible full-time employment, willing to act as a professional reference, willing to complete paperwork for educational credit, willing to provide letters of recommendation.

Contact Fax or e-mail Charlie Knudtson, Art Assistant, 21100 Erwin Street, Woodland Hills, California 91367. Phone: 818-226-0105. Fax: 818-883-9286. E-mail: charles.knudtson@weiderpub.com. In-person interview recommended (telephone interview accepted). Applicants must submit a letter of interest, resume. Applications are accepted continuously. World Wide Web: http://www.mensfitness.com.

WILSON QUARTERLY
1 Woodrow Wilson Plaza, 1300 Pennsylvania Avenue, NW
Washington, District of Columbia 20004-3027

General Information General interest quarterly magazine focusing on humanities-related topics and providing a comprehensive survey of the latest scholarly research in a broad range of subject areas. Established in 1976. Number of employees: 6. Subsidiary of Woodrow Wilson International Center for Scholars, Washington, District of Columbia. Number of internship applications received each year: 200.
Internships Available ▶ *1–3 editorial interns:* responsibilities include fact checking, background and art research, phone work, and some basic office duties, including delivering packages and photocopying. Candidates should have ability to work independently, office skills, oral communication skills, organizational skills, research skills, written communication skills. Duration is 4–12 months. $400–$800 per month. Open to college sophomores, college juniors, college seniors, recent college graduates, graduate students.
Benefits Job counseling, names of contacts, willing to act as a professional reference, willing to complete paperwork for educational credit, willing to provide letters of recommendation, reimbursement of expenses related to editorial research.
Contact Write Mr. James Carman, Managing Editor. Applicants must submit a letter of interest, resume, three writing samples, list of personal references. Application deadline: March 15 for summer, July 15 for fall, October 15 for spring. World Wide Web: http://www.wilsonquarterly.com.

WIRED MAGAZINE
520 Third Street, Third Floor
San Francisco, California 94107

General Information Magazine. Established in 1993. Number of employees: 80. Division of Conde Nast Publications, New York, New York. Number of internship applications received each year: 300.
Internships Available ▶ *1 editorial intern:* responsibilities include reporting articles for publication, administrative duties, and research. Candidates should have ability to work independently, analytical skills, computer skills, editing skills, knowledge of field, office skills, oral communication skills, organizational skills, personal interest in the field, research skills, self-motivation, strong interpersonal skills, writing skills. Duration is 4 months. $10 per hour. ▶ *1 reporting intern.* Duration is 4 months. $10 per hour. ▶ *1 research intern:* responsibilities include researching and fact checking articles in the magazine, story idea generation, and writing and reporting stories for publications. Candidates should have ability to work independently, ability to work with others, analytical skills, computer skills, editing skills, knowledge of field, office skills, organizational skills, personal interest in the field, research skills, self-motivation, writing skills. Duration is 4 months. $10 per hour. Open to recent college graduates, graduate students, individuals reentering the workforce. International applications accepted.
Benefits Meals at a cost, on-the-job training, possible full-time employment.
Contact Write or fax Jennifer Hillner, Editor. Fax: 415-276-5100. In-person interview required. Applicants must submit a letter of interest, resume, two personal references, professional references, 2-3 writing samples. Application deadline: February 1 for spring, June 1 for summer, October 1 for winter. World Wide Web: http://www.wired.com/wired.

WOMEN EXPRESS, INC.
PO Box 120-027
Boston, Massachusetts 02112-0027

General Information Publisher of *Teen Voices* and Teen Voices Online, a teen feminist magazine. Established in 1988. Number of employees: 11. Number of internship applications received each year: 300.

Internships Available ▶ *2–3 business management/human resources interns:* responsibilities include assisting in daily operation of organization, setting up and improving administrative systems, helping recruiting volunteers and interns, managing hours compliance, and coordinating staff and related events. Candidates should have ability to work independently, computer skills, office skills, organizational skills, self-motivation, written communication skills. Duration is 4-6 months (12-16 hours per week). Unpaid. Open to college freshmen, college sophomores, college juniors, college seniors, recent college graduates, graduate students, career changers, individuals reentering the workforce. ▶ *1–2 business/accounting interns:* responsibilities include assisting in financial oversight of Women Express; working with associate director and audit committee of Board of Directors to prepare expense reports; helping manage accounts payable and receivable; collections; deposits. Candidates should have ability to work independently, ability to work with others, college degree in related field, computer skills, declared college major in field, knowledge of field, office skills, oral communication skills, organizational skills, written communication skills, knowledge of Peachtree preferred but will train if necessary. Duration is 4-6 months (12-16 hours per week). Unpaid. Open to college juniors, college seniors, recent college graduates, graduate students, law students, career changers, individuals reentering the workforce. ▶ *2–3 circulation/marketing interns:* responsibilities include coordinating customer service, fulfillment of subscriptions and direct mail, and helping conceptualize a renewal service and other ways to retain subscribers and attract new ones. Candidates should have ability to work independently, ability to work with others, computer skills, office skills, oral communication skills, organizational skills, research skills, self-motivation, written communication skills, knowledge of databases and postal system (helpful). Duration is 4-6 months (12-16 hours per week). Unpaid. Open to college freshmen, college sophomores, college juniors, college seniors, recent college graduates, graduate students, law students, career changers, individuals reentering the workforce. ▶ *2–3 editorial assistants:* responsibilities include working with managing editor to manage editorial process, arranging editorial meetings, ensuring deadlines are met, managing submissions, writing editorials, and acting as a liaison to teen writers. Candidates should have ability to work independently, ability to work with others, computer skills, editing skills, knowledge of field, organizational skills, personal interest in the field, research skills, writing skills. Duration is 4-6 months (12-16 hours per week). Unpaid. Open to college sophomores, college juniors, college seniors, recent college graduates, graduate students, law students, career changers, individuals reentering the workforce. ▶ *10–15 editorial mentors:* responsibilities include working directly with low-skilled teens on the teen editorial board as a mentor and resource; helping teens to research and write sections of the magazines; compiling resources; fact checking, content and development; communicating with writers. Candidates should have ability to work independently, editing skills, knowledge of field, oral communication skills, organizational skills, personal interest in the field, research skills, self-motivation, strong interpersonal skills, strong leadership ability, written communication skills, experience working with at-risk teens (helpful). Duration is 4-6 months (6-10 hours per week). Unpaid. Open to college sophomores, college juniors, college seniors, recent college graduates, graduate students, law students, career changers, individuals reentering the workforce. ▶ *1–2 executive director assistants:* responsibilities include assisting the executive director in a variety of aspects of the organization, filing, phone work, xeroxing, and coordinating larger projects. Candidates should have analytical skills, personal interest in the field, self-motivation, strong interpersonal skills, strong leadership ability, writing skills. Duration is 4 to 6 months (12 to 16 hours per week). Unpaid. Open to college juniors, college seniors, recent college gradu-

Women Express, Inc. (continued)

ates, graduate students, law students, career changers, individuals reentering the workforce. ▶ *1–2 graphic design interns:* responsibilities include designing materials including flyers, invitations, brochures, posters for Teen Voices, fund-raising and teen programs; special supplements in the magazine, program books. Candidates should have ability to work independently, college degree in related field, computer skills, declared college major in field, knowledge of field, organizational skills, personal interest in the field, plan to pursue career in field, Quark Express skills (essential). Duration is 4-6 months (12-16 hours per week). Unpaid. Open to college freshmen, college sophomores, college juniors, college seniors, recent college graduates, graduate students, law students, career changers, individuals reentering the workforce. ▶ *1–2 public relations interns:* responsibilities include promoting WE/Teen Voices magazine on a local and national level; coordinating public relations for national and local media; writing press releases, attending press conferences; managing media contacts and database. Candidates should have ability to work independently, ability to work with others, experience in the field, oral communication skills, organizational skills, self-motivation, strong leadership ability, written communication skills. Duration is 4–6 months. Unpaid. Open to college juniors, college seniors, recent college graduates, graduate students, law students, career changers, individuals reentering the workforce. ▶ *1–2 publishing interns:* responsibilities include assisting in marketing Teen Voices to bookstores and consumers; researching advertising leads; assessing costs and benefits; writing copy for advertisements; manage a distribution and newsstand sales; working closely with distribution. Candidates should have ability to work independently, ability to work with others, analytical skills, knowledge of field, oral communication skills, organizational skills, research skills, self-motivation, written communication skills, marketing, sales or publishing experience (preferred). Duration is 4-6 months (12-16 hours per week). Unpaid. Open to college freshmen, college sophomores, college juniors, college seniors, recent college graduates, graduate students, career changers, individuals reentering the workforce. ▶ *4–5 special events/fund-raising interns:* responsibilities include assisting with all fund-raising activities including foundation research, grant writing, donor management and special campaigns and events; working with fund-raising committee of the Board of Directors. Candidates should have analytical skills, computer skills, office skills, oral communication skills, written communication skills. Duration is 4-6 months (12-16 hours per week). Unpaid. Open to college freshmen, college sophomores, college juniors, college seniors, recent college graduates, graduate students, law students, career changers, individuals reentering the workforce. ▶ *1–2 teen programs interns:* responsibilities include working with and supervising high-risk adolescent girls in three programs; teaching life and job skills; working with families, logistics, transportation; scheduling training sessions; supporting mentors; providing crisis intervention. Candidates should have ability to work independently, knowledge of field, oral communication skills, self-motivation, strong leadership ability, written communication skills, Masters level social work (preferred), experience in working with teens strongly recommended. Duration is 4-6 months (12-16 hours per week). Unpaid. Open to college freshmen, college sophomores, college juniors, college seniors, recent college graduates, graduate students, individuals reentering the workforce. International applications accepted.

Benefits Names of contacts, on-the-job training, opportunity to attend seminars/workshops, possible full-time employment, willing to act as a professional reference, willing to complete paperwork for educational credit, willing to provide letters of recommendation.

Contact Write, call, fax, e-mail, or through World Wide Web site Carole Allen, Associate Director, 515 Washington Street, 6th Floor, Boston, Massachusetts 02111. Phone: 617-426-5505. Fax: 617-426-5577. E-mail: hr@teenvioces.com. In-person interview recommended (telephone interview accepted). Applicants must submit a letter of interest, resume, writing sample, portfolio (for graphic design position). Applications are accepted continuously. World Wide Web: http://www.teenvoices.com.

RADIO BROADCASTING

CLEAR CHANNEL RADIO–ATLANTA
1819 Peachtree Street, Suite 700
Atlanta, Georgia 30309

General Information Radio stations. Established in 1974. Number of employees: 180. Unit of Clear Channel Communications, San Antonio, Texas. Number of internship applications received each year: 300.
Internships Available ▶ *15 interns:* responsibilities include assisting radio stations personnel with listener activities including promotions, marketing, contests, sales, and research. Candidates should have ability to work independently, college courses in field, personal interest in the field, plan to pursue career in field, strong interpersonal skills. Duration is 1 semester. Unpaid. Open to college sophomores, college juniors, college seniors, graduate students, must be 18 years old.
Benefits Names of contacts, on-the-job training, possible full-time employment, willing to act as a professional reference, willing to complete paperwork for educational credit, willing to provide letters of recommendation.
Contact Write or e-mail Dr. Susan DeBonis, Director of Research. Fax: 404-367-1100. E-mail: susandebonis@clearchannel.com. No phone calls. In-person interview required. Applicants must submit a letter of interest, resume, approval for internship from institution. Applications are accepted continuously.

INFINITY BROADCASTING OF MN
625 2nd Avenue South, Suite 550
Minneapolis, Minnesota 55402

General Information Commercial radio consisting of WCCO-AM, 102.9 Lite FM, Mix 104.1, and KCCO-AM. Number of employees: 150. Number of internship applications received each year: 150.
Internships Available ▶ *12–20 promotions and marketing interns:* responsibilities include assisting in all aspects of the promotions department, including reviewing qualitative research, assisting in copywriting, assisting with the coordination and execution of events, and creating promotional signage. Candidates should have ability to work with others, computer skills, office skills, oral communication skills, organizational skills, personal interest in the field, plan to pursue career in field, research skills, self-motivation, written communication skills. Duration is every 4 months (3 periods per year). Unpaid. Open to college freshmen, college sophomores, college juniors, college seniors, must be pursuing internship for credit. International applications accepted.
Benefits Names of contacts, on-the-job training, willing to complete paperwork for educational credit.
Contact Write, call, fax, or e-mail Chris Kalis, Promotion Director. Phone: 612-337-1029. Fax: 612-339-5653. E-mail: kalis@infinitybroadcasting.com. In-person interview recommended (telephone interview accepted). Applicants must submit a letter of interest, resume. Applications are accepted continuously.

KEUN/KJJB RADIO
330 West Laurel Avenue
Eunice, Louisiana 70535

General Information Radio and cable television programming. Established in 1952. Number of employees: 10. Number of internship applications received each year: 5.
Internships Available ▶ *1–2 interns:* responsibilities include radio work and public relations. Candidates should have ability to work independently, computer skills, plan to pursue career in field, self-motivation, writing skills. Duration is 3–12 months. Unpaid. Open to recent high school graduates, college freshmen, college sophomores, college juniors, college seniors, recent college graduates, graduate students, individuals reentering the workforce. International applications accepted.

Benefits Job counseling, names of contacts, opportunity to attend seminars/workshops, possible full-time employment, willing to complete paperwork for educational credit, willing to provide letters of recommendation.

Contact Write, fax, or e-mail Mr. Karl Rene De Rouen, President and General Manager. E-mail: karl@keunworldwide.com. No phone calls. Telephone interview required. Applicants must submit a formal organization application, resume, personal reference. Application deadline: 6 months prior to start of internship. World Wide Web: http://www.keunworldwide.com.

KFAN RADIO
7900 Xerxes Avenue South, Suite 102
Minneapolis, Minnesota 55431

General Information All sports-talk station in the Twin Cities and surrounding areas. Established in 1991. Number of employees: 300. Subsidiary of Clear Channel Communications, San Antonio, Texas. Number of internship applications received each year: 50.

Internships Available ▶ *10 promotions assistants:* responsibilities include working with programming and on-air talent, live remotes, broadcasts, contesting/merchandising, public relations, client relations, event planning and implementation, and writing opportunities. Candidates should have ability to work independently, ability to work with others, computer skills, office skills, oral communication skills, organizational skills, personal interest in the field, self-motivation, strong leadership ability. Duration is January to May; May to August; August to December. Unpaid. Open to high school students, college freshmen, college sophomores, college juniors, college seniors, recent college graduates, must be working for academic credit. International applications accepted.

Benefits Names of contacts, on-the-job training, opportunity to attend seminars/workshops, possible full-time employment, travel reimbursement, willing to act as a professional reference, willing to complete paperwork for educational credit, willing to provide letters of recommendation.

Contact Write, call, fax, e-mail, or through World Wide Web site Jessie Barghultz, Promotions Coordinator, 7900 Xerxes Avenue South, Suite 102. Phone: 952-820-4343. Fax: 952-820-4241. E-mail: jessiebarghultz@clearchannel.com. Applicants must submit a letter of interest, resume. Applications are accepted continuously. World Wide Web: http://www.kfan.com.

KJNP AM-FM RADIO-TV
2501 Mission Road, PO Box 56359
North Pole, Alaska 99705-1359

General Information Christian radio and television station spreading the gospel of Jesus Christ throughout Alaska and the Northern Hemisphere. Established in 1967. Unit of Evangelistic Missionary Fellowship, Lakewood, Colorado. Number of internship applications received each year: 4.

Internships Available ▶ *1 TV technician:* responsibilities include taking meter readings on transmitter; airing prerecorded programs (entails cueing and rewinding tapes before airing) directly off the satellite, commercials, public service announcements, and interlude tapes between programs; maintaining TV log; and monitoring all equipment in control room during air time. Candidates should have ability to work independently, ability to work with others, self-motivation. Duration is minimum of 3 months. Unpaid. Open to recent high school graduates, college freshmen, college sophomores, college juniors, college seniors, recent college graduates, graduate students, law students, career changers, individuals reentering the workforce. ▶ *1 camera operator:* responsibilities include operating cameras for live public service format program, preparing set to go on the air, escorting guests to the set, and helping out in other areas of the station. Candidates should have ability to work with others. Duration is flexible. Unpaid. Open to high school students, recent high school graduates, college freshmen, college sophomores, college juniors, college seniors, recent college graduates, graduate students, law students, career changers, individuals reentering the workforce. ▶ *Engineering interns:* responsibilities include maintaining electronic equipment and calibrating transmitters. Candidates should have ability to work independently, ability to work with others, self-

motivation. Duration is flexible. Unpaid. Open to recent high school graduates, college freshmen, college sophomores, college juniors, college seniors, recent college graduates, graduate students, law students, career changers, individuals reentering the workforce. ▶ *Maintenance interns:* responsibilities include maintaining grounds and buildings, cutting wood, removing snow in winter, and some carpentry work. Candidates should have ability to work independently, ability to work with others, self-motivation. Duration is flexible. Unpaid. Open to high school students, recent high school graduates, college freshmen, college sophomores, college juniors, college seniors, recent college graduates, graduate students, law students, career changers, individuals reentering the workforce. ▶ *1 radio technician:* responsibilities include making sure stations are on the air, following and keeping logs for both the AM and FM stations, answering the lobby telephone, and helping in other areas of the station. Candidates should have ability to work with others, oral communication skills. Duration is 1 year. Unpaid. Open to high school seniors, recent high school graduates, college freshmen, college sophomores, college juniors, college seniors, recent college graduates, graduate students, law students, career changers, individuals reentering the workforce. ▶ *1 receptionist intern:* responsibilities include answering 5 incoming telephone lines and intercom calls and directing to proper departments, greeting guests and tourists, monitoring AM/FM/TV, answering 2-way system, keeping coffee and hot water supplied, keeping lobby area clean, typing Trapline Chatter messages that are aired over radio, and performing office work. Candidates should have ability to work with others, oral communication skills, self-motivation, written communication skills. Duration is flexible. Unpaid. Open to recent high school graduates, college freshmen, college sophomores, college juniors, college seniors, recent college graduates, graduate students, law students, career changers, individuals reentering the workforce. International applications accepted.

Benefits Free housing, on-the-job training, willing to complete paperwork for educational credit, willing to provide letters of recommendation.

Contact Write, call, fax, or e-mail Ms. Julie K. Beaver, Executive Secretary. Phone: 907-488-2216. Fax: 907-488-5246. E-mail: kjnp@mosquitonet.com. Applicants must submit a formal organization application, letter of interest, three professional or personal references. Applications are accepted continuously. World Wide Web: http://www.mosquitonet.com/~kjnp.

KSRC-FM STAR 102
508 Westport Road, Suite 202
Kansas City, Missouri 64111

General Information Radio station. Number of employees: 80. Unit of Infinity/CBS/Viacom. Number of internship applications received each year: 20.

Internships Available ▶ *1–5 promotions interns:* responsibilities include customer service, interaction with the public at events, organizing items, filing, computer database work, phoning listeners, and various other duties. Candidates should have ability to work with others, college courses in field, computer skills, office skills, oral communication skills, organizational skills, plan to pursue career in field, self-motivation, writing skills. Duration is 1 semester. Unpaid. Open to college freshmen, college sophomores, college juniors, college seniors.

Benefits Willing to act as a professional reference, willing to complete paperwork for educational credit, willing to provide letters of recommendation.

Contact Write Jamie Harris, Promotions Coordinator. No phone calls. In-person interview recommended (telephone interview accepted). Applicants must submit a letter of interest, resume. Applications are accepted continuously. World Wide Web: http://www.Star102.com.

SHADOW BROADCAST SERVICES
201 Route 17 North, 9th Floor
Rutherford, New Jersey 07070

General Information Traffic, news, sports, weather, and programming services. Established in 1977. Number of employees: 100.

Division of Westwood One, New York, New York. Number of internship applications received each year: 30.

Internships Available ► *7 sports interns:* responsibilities include keeping up on sports scores and stats, faxing stations, and informing announcers of sports information. Candidates should have ability to work independently, ability to work with others, oral communication skills, personal interest in the field, writing skills. Duration is 6-week program throughout the year. $50 per duration of internship. ► *7–14 traffic interns:* responsibilities include phone calls, faxing, writing, collecting information, and listening for information. Candidates should have ability to work independently, oral communication skills, personal interest in the field, strong interpersonal skills. Duration is 1 semester. $50 per duration of internship. Open to college freshmen, college sophomores, college juniors, college seniors, graduate students. **Benefits** Possible full-time employment, willing to act as a professional reference, willing to complete paperwork for educational credit, willing to provide letters of recommendation.

Contact Write, call, fax, or e-mail Sal Cowan, Intern Coordinator, 201 Route 17 North, 9th Floor, Rutherford, New Jersey 07070. Phone: 201-939-1888. Fax: 201-939-1043. E-mail: sal_cowan@ metronetworks.com. In-person interview required. Applicants must submit a resume. Application deadline: May 1 for summer, December 1 for winter/spring.

WALK FM/AM
66 Colonial Drive
Patchogue, New York 11772

General Information Commercial FM/AM radio station offering programming to Long Island's adult audiences. Established in 1951. Number of employees: 40. Unit of Clear Channel Communications, Dallas, Texas. Number of internship applications received each year: 30.

Internships Available ► *1–2 engineering department interns:* responsibilities include assisting the chief engineer and ITM manager with studio, station, and computer operations. Candidates should have ability to work independently, ability to work with others, analytical skills, college courses in field, computer skills, office skills, oral communication skills, organizational skills, personal interest in the field, plan to pursue career in field, self-motivation. Duration is 1 semester. Unpaid. Open to college freshmen, college sophomores, college juniors, college seniors, individuals receiving academic credit for internship. ► *2–5 news department interns:* responsibilities include assisting with information gathering, news writing, and traffic coordination. Candidates should have ability to work independently, ability to work with others, analytical skills, computer skills, editing skills, knowledge of field, oral communication skills, organizational skills, personal interest in the field, research skills, self-motivation, writing skills. Duration is 8–12 weeks. Unpaid. Open to college freshmen, college sophomores, college juniors, college seniors, graduate students, law students, individuals receiving academic credit for internship. ► *2–4 programming interns:* responsibilities include assisting the program director on a daily basis with music, scheduling, airshift scheduling, contesting, and cross-promotions. Candidates should have ability to work independently, ability to work with others, computer skills, editing skills, office skills, oral communication skills, organizational skills, plan to pursue career in field, self-motivation, writing skills. Duration is 1 semester. Unpaid. Open to high school students, recent high school graduates, college freshmen, college sophomores, college juniors, college seniors, individuals receiving academic credit for internship. ► *2–12 promotion department interns:* responsibilities include assisting at station and with public appearances, meeting and greeting, and helping set up and breakdown sound equipment. Candidates should have oral communication skills, personal interest in the field, self-motivation, strong interpersonal skills, clean personal appearance, ability to work weekends. Duration is 6–8 weeks. Unpaid. Open to college freshmen, college sophomores, college juniors, college seniors, graduate students, law students, individuals receiving academic credit for internship. International applications accepted.

Benefits Formal training, job counseling, names of contacts, on-the-job training, possible full-time employment, willing to act

as a professional reference, willing to complete paperwork for educational credit, willing to provide letters of recommendation. **Contact** Write, call, fax, e-mail, or through World Wide Web site Bill Terry, Intern Coordinator, PO Box 230, Patchogue, New York 11772. Phone: 631-475-5200. Fax: 631-475-9016. E-mail: bterry@ walkradio.com. In-person interview recommended (telephone interview accepted). Applicants must submit a resume. Application deadline: April 30 for summer; continuous for positions during academic year. World Wide Web: http://www.WALKRADIO. com.

WCTC-AM/WMGQ-FM
78 Veronica Avenue
Somerset, New Jersey 08873

General Information WCTC-AM is a news/talk station serving the central New Jersey area. WMGQ-FM is a stereo music station featuring adult contemporary programming. Established in 1946. Number of employees: 50. Unit of Greater Media, Inc., New Brunswick, New Jersey. Number of internship applications received each year: 40.

Internships Available ► *10–15 marketing and promotions interns:* responsibilities include writing marketing proposals and attending events. Candidates should have ability to work independently, office skills, oral communication skills, organizational skills, self-motivation, strong interpersonal skills, written communication skills. Duration is flexible (need summer interns). Unpaid. Open to recent high school graduates, college freshmen, college sophomores, college juniors, college seniors, recent college graduates. ► *1 news reporter:* responsibilities include gathering and writing news stories. Duration is one semester (24 hours per week). Unpaid. Open to college juniors, college seniors, recent college graduates, graduate students.

Benefits Formal training, job counseling, names of contacts, possible full-time employment, willing to act as a professional reference, willing to complete paperwork for educational credit, willing to provide letters of recommendation.

Contact Write, call, fax, or e-mail David Kirby, Director of Communications. Phone: 732-249-2600 Ext. 230. Fax: 732-249-7515. E-mail: dkirby@greaterrvb.com. In-person interview required. Applicants must submit a letter of interest, resume. Applications are accepted continuously.

THE WESTWOOD ONE RADIO NETWORKS
524 West 57th Street, 1st Floor
New York, New York 10019

General Information America's largest radio network providing over 150 news, sports, music, talk, and entertainment programs; features; live events; 24-hour formats; and Shadow Broadcast services. Number of employees: 100.

Internships Available ► *2 artist relations/programming interns:* responsibilities include working in the programming and production departments; contacting artist representatives, including publicists and record company personnel; researching the artists being interviewed, including assembling and reviewing artist biographies and other source material. Candidates should have office skills, oral communication skills, organizational skills, self-motivation, strong interpersonal skills, written communication skills, major in broadcasting (helpful). Duration is 1 semester. Unpaid. Open to college freshmen, college sophomores, college juniors, college seniors, only those earning academic credit.

Benefits Job counseling, names of contacts, possible full-time employment, willing to act as a professional reference, willing to complete paperwork for educational credit, willing to provide letters of recommendation, $50 stipend.

Contact E-mail Pam Green, Senior Director of Artist Relations. Phone: 212-975-2106. Fax: 212-262-3960. E-mail: ww1pgreen@aol. com. In-person interview required. Applicants must submit a letter of interest, resume. Applications are accepted continuously.

WGN-RADIO 720
435 North Michigan Avenue
Chicago, Illinois 60611

General Information Radio station featuring a progressive and flexible full-service news/talk and sports format. Established in 1924. Number of employees: 120. Unit of Tribune Company, Chicago, Illinois. Number of internship applications received each year: 2,000.

Internships Available ▶ *2 news interns:* responsibilities include answering phones, researching and writing stories, taking feeds, and assisting with major event coverage. Candidates should have analytical skills, computer skills, editing skills, plan to pursue career in field, self-motivation, written communication skills. Duration is 14 weeks. $75 per week. Open to college sophomores, college juniors, college seniors, recent college graduates, graduate students, law students, career changers, individuals reentering the workforce. ▶ *2 programming interns:* responsibilities include booking guests, generating ideas, screening phones, producing audio, editing, completing promotional and programming paperwork, maintaining computerized music library, and completing special projects. Candidates should have editing skills, experience in the field, plan to pursue career in field, research skills, strong interpersonal skills, written communication skills. Duration is 14 weeks. $75 per week. Open to college sophomores, college juniors, college seniors, recent college graduates, graduate students, law students, career changers, individuals reentering the workforce. ▶ *1 promotion intern:* responsibilities include preparing weekly press releases, writing and scheduling promotional announcements, working promotional events, writing for monthly listener newsletter, and compiling and editing community calendar newspaper column. Candidates should have ability to work independently, computer skills, knowledge of field, plan to pursue career in field, strong interpersonal skills, writing skills. Duration is 14 weeks. $75 per week. Open to college sophomores, college juniors, college seniors, recent college graduates, graduate students, career changers, individuals reentering the workforce. ▶ *1 sales intern:* responsibilities include preparation of sales presentations, training in strategies, prospecting, follow-up, promotional/marketing activities, and research. Candidates should have computer skills, oral communication skills, plan to pursue career in field, research skills, self-motivation, strong interpersonal skills. Duration is 14 weeks. Unpaid. Open to college seniors, recent college graduates, graduate students, law students, career changers, individuals reentering the workforce. ▶ *1 sports intern:* responsibilities include covering sports events; answering phones; and researching, writing, and producing stories. Candidates should have editing skills, experience in the field, plan to pursue career in field, research skills, self-motivation, strong interpersonal skills. Duration is 14 weeks. $75 per week. Open to college sophomores, college juniors, college seniors, recent college graduates, graduate students, law students, career changers, individuals reentering the workforce. International applications accepted.

Benefits Formal training, job counseling, names of contacts, opportunity to attend seminars/workshops, possible full-time employment, willing to act as a professional reference, willing to complete paperwork for educational credit, willing to provide letters of recommendation.

Contact Write, fax, e-mail, or through World Wide Web site Kurt Vanderah, Producer, 435 North Michigan, Chicago, Illinois 60611. Fax: 312-222-3072. E-mail: kurtvanderah@wgnradio.com. No phone calls. In-person interview required. Applicants must submit a letter of interest, resume. Application deadline: January 1 for spring, April 1 for summer, July 1 for fall, October 1 for winter. World Wide Web: http://wgnradio.com.

WJXA 92.9 FM/WMAK 96.3 FM
504 Rosedale Avenue
Nashville, Tennessee 37211

General Information Commercial radio station featuring soft rock and oldies music. Established in 1948. Number of employees: 50. Division of South Central Communications, Evansville, Indiana. Number of internship applications received each year: 50.

Internships Available ▶ *2 accounting/general business interns:* responsibilities include working on spreadsheets, filing, accounts payable, accounts receivable, and word processing. Duration is flexible. Unpaid. Open to recent high school graduates, college freshmen, career changers. ▶ *2 promotions interns:* responsibilities include assisting promotions director with internal and external sales promotions and station-involved events. Candidates should have ability to work with others, oral communication skills, personal interest in the field, self-motivation, written communication skills. Duration is flexible. Unpaid. ▶ *2 retail marketing interns:* responsibilities include assisting retail marketing director. Candidates should have ability to work independently, ability to work with others, computer skills, editing skills, oral communication skills, personal interest in the field, research skills, written communication skills. Unpaid. International applications accepted.

Benefits Names of contacts, on-the-job training, possible full-time employment, willing to complete paperwork for educational credit, willing to provide letters of recommendation.

Contact Write Sarah Robison, Business Manager, PO Box 40596, Nashville, Tennessee 37204. Fax: 615-259-4594. No phone calls. In-person interview recommended (telephone interview accepted). Applicants must submit a formal organization application, resume, writing sample, two personal references, two letters of recommendation, evidence of enrollment in credit-bearing program. Applications are accepted continuously.

WMMR-FM
1 Bala Plaza
Bala-Cynwyd, Pennsylvania 19004

General Information Album-oriented rock station providing entertainment, music, news, and public affairs programming to eastern Pennsylvania, New Jersey, and Delaware. Established in 1968. Unit of Greater Media, Inc., New Brunswick, New Jersey. Number of internship applications received each year: 40.

Internships Available ▶ *5–7 programming/promotions interns:* responsibilities include pulling and filing music, assisting the traffic and continuity department, answering correspondence, handling phone requests and giveaways, and preparing broadcast packs for remote broadcasts. Candidates should have ability to work independently, computer skills, office skills, oral communication skills, self-motivation, strong interpersonal skills. Duration is flexible. Unpaid. Open to college freshmen, college sophomores, college juniors, college seniors, individuals receiving college credit.

Benefits Names of contacts, possible full-time employment, willing to complete paperwork for educational credit, willing to provide letters of recommendation.

Contact Write, call, fax, or e-mail Eric Simon, Intern Coordinator. Phone: 610-771-9752. Fax: 610-771-9710. E-mail: esimon@greaterphila.com. In-person interview required. Applicants must submit a letter of interest, resume. Applications are accepted continuously. World Wide Web: http://www.wmmr.com.

WOPP-AM
1101 Cameron Road
Opp, Alabama 36467

General Information Commercial radio station broadcasting music, news, weather, and sports. Established in 1980. Number of employees: 9. Number of internship applications received each year: 20.

Internships Available ▶ *2 news interns:* responsibilities include gathering news. Candidates should have computer skills, oral communication skills, plan to pursue career in field, research skills, strong interpersonal skills, written communication skills. Duration is 3 months. Unpaid. ▶ *1 production intern:* responsibilities include producing promos and some commercials. Candidates should have ability to work independently, computer skills, editing skills, oral communication skills, personal interest in the field, writing skills. Unpaid. ▶ *1 sales intern:* responsibilities include selling and writing ads. Candidates should have knowledge of field, office skills, plan to pursue career in field, self-motivation, writing skills. Commission of 25%. Open to college freshmen, college sophomores, college juniors, college seniors. International applications accepted.

WOPP-AM (continued)

Benefits On-the-job training, opportunity to attend seminars/workshops, willing to act as a professional reference, willing to complete paperwork for educational credit, willing to provide letters of recommendation, sales interns earn commission and are reimbursed gas money.

Contact Write, fax, or e-mail Mr. Robert H. Boothe, General Manager. Fax: 334-493-4546. E-mail: wopp@wopp.com. No phone calls. Applicants must submit a resume, four personal references. Applications are accepted continuously. World Wide Web: http://www.wopp.com.

WOR RADIO
1440 Broadway
New York, New York 10018

General Information Radio station. Established in 1989. Number of employees: 100. Division of Buckley Broadcasting, Greenwich, Connecticut. Number of internship applications received each year: 75.

Internships Available ► *8 radio station interns:* responsibilities include assisting station personnel with hands-on jobs in any of the following departments: programming, engineering, or marketing. Candidates should have college courses in field, knowledge of field, self-motivation, strong interpersonal skills, writing skills. Duration is 1 semester (requires 2 full days per week in fall and spring semesters and 3 full days per week in summer). $10 per day. Open to college juniors, college seniors.

Benefits Opportunity to attend seminars/workshops, possible full-time employment, willing to act as a professional reference, willing to complete paperwork for educational credit, willing to provide letters of recommendation.

Contact Write, call, fax, or e-mail Ms. Weleskie Dias, Internship Coordinator. Phone: 212-642-4538. Fax: 212-642-4486. E-mail: wdias@wor710.com. In-person interview required. Applicants must submit a letter of interest, resume. Applications are accepted continuously. World Wide Web: http://www.wor710.com.

WOTX 102.3 FM AND WTIL 107.7 FM
37 Redington Road, PO Box 875
Concord, New Hampshire 03302-0875

General Information Commercial radio stations with full-service format serving the over-30 audience in the capital city region of south central New Hampshire with a heavy emphasis on news, talk, sports, and community affairs. Established in 1946. Number of employees: 10. Unit of Vox Radio Group, Claremont, New Hampshire.

Internships Available ► *1 news department intern:* responsibilities include assisting in covering, writing, editing, and rewriting local and state news. Candidates should have ability to work with others, college courses in field, oral communication skills, personal interest in the field, writing skills. Duration is 3 months minimum. Unpaid. Open to college sophomores, college juniors, college seniors, recent college graduates, graduate students. ► *1 promotion intern/radio station:* responsibilities include coordinating station promotion events. Candidates should have ability to work independently, oral communication skills, strong interpersonal skills. Duration is flexible. Unpaid. Open to high school students, recent high school graduates, college freshmen, college sophomores, college juniors, college seniors, recent college graduates. ► *1 sales department intern:* responsibilities include assisting sales manager with sales, research, sales service, and promotions. Candidates should have oral communication skills, plan to pursue career in field, self-motivation, strong interpersonal skills, written communication skills, major in communications, marketing or business. Duration is 3 months minimum. Unpaid. Open to college sophomores, college juniors, college seniors, recent college graduates, graduate students. International applications accepted.

Benefits Job counseling, names of contacts, on-the-job training, willing to complete paperwork for educational credit, willing to provide letters of recommendation.

Contact Write, fax, e-mail, or through World Wide Web site Bob Lipman, Operations Manager, PO Box 875, Concord, New Hampshire 03302-0875. Fax: 603-224-6404. E-mail: rlipman@

1077thepulse.com. No phone calls. In-person interview required. Applicants must submit a letter of interest, resume, two letters of recommendation. Applications are accepted continuously. World Wide Web: http://outlaw1023.net.

WRDX–CLEAR CHANNEL COMMUNICATIONS
3001 Philadelphia Pike
Claymont, Delaware 19703

General Information Radio broadcasting company. Established in 1997. Number of employees: 25. Division of Clear Channel Communications, San Antonio, Texas. Number of internship applications received each year: 30.

Internships Available ► *10–15 promotions assistants:* responsibilities include database, live broadcasts, learning in-studio broadcasts set up, and executing promotions. Candidates should have ability to work independently, ability to work with others, office skills, oral communication skills, personal interest in the field, self-motivation. Duration is flexible. Position available as unpaid or paid. Open to high school seniors, recent high school graduates, college freshmen, college sophomores, college juniors, college seniors, individuals reentering the workforce. International applications accepted.

Benefits Formal training, job counseling, names of contacts, on-the-job training, possible full-time employment, willing to act as a professional reference, willing to complete paperwork for educational credit, willing to provide letters of recommendation.

Contact Call or e-mail Rich Gallo, Assistant Promotions Director. Phone: 302-793-4200 Ext. 302. Fax: 302-793-4204. E-mail: richatwrdx@aol.com. In-person interview required. Applicants must submit a resume. Applications are accepted continuously. World Wide Web: http://www.wrdx.com.

WRQX FM MIX 107.3
4400 Jenifer Street, NW
Washington, District of Columbia 20015

General Information Organization that includes three radio stations. WRQX-FM is an adult contemporary station; WJZW-FM is a jazz station; WMAL-AM is a major market news station featuring news, talk, weather, and traffic reporting. Established in 1990. Number of employees: 150. Division of Disney–ABC, Inc., New York, New York. Number of internship applications received each year: 20.

Internships Available ► *2–3 advertising sales interns:* responsibilities include assisting with proposals, researching clients, organizing and producing proposals, and accompanying sales staff on presentations. Candidates should have ability to work independently, computer skills, office skills, oral communication skills, strong interpersonal skills, written communication skills. Duration is 1 semester. Unpaid. Open to college juniors, college seniors. ► *1–3 marketing/promotion interns:* responsibilities include coordinating contests, assisting with the execution of promotions, researching promotional opportunities, and attending promotions. Candidates should have ability to work independently, computer skills, office skills, oral communication skills, organizational skills, personal interest in the field, plan to pursue career in field, self-motivation, strong interpersonal skills. Duration is 1 semester. Unpaid. Open to college juniors, college seniors. ► *2–3 morning show interns:* responsibilities include helping the morning show producer with day-to-day operations; must be available from 5:30 a.m. to at least 10:00 a.m. Candidates should have ability to work with others, college courses in field, office skills, oral communication skills, organizational skills, plan to pursue career in field. Duration is 1 semester. Unpaid. Open to college juniors, college seniors, graduate students. ► *2–3 news interns:* responsibilities include operating newsroom computer system, conducting research and story checks, performing telephone interviews, and typing. Candidates should have ability to work independently, computer skills, editing skills, research skills, strong interpersonal skills, written communication skills. Duration is 1 semester. Unpaid. Open to college juniors, college seniors. International applications accepted.

Benefits Names of contacts, possible full-time employment, willing to act as a professional reference, willing to complete paperwork for educational credit.

Contact Write, call, fax, e-mail, or through World Wide Web site Renee Sharrow, Promotion and Marketing Assistant. Phone: 202-895-2405. Fax: 202-686-3070. E-mail: renee.l.sharrow@abc.com. In-person interview required. Applicants must submit a formal organization application, letter of interest, resume, two letters of recommendation, example of work (for WMAL position). Applications are accepted continuously. World Wide Web: http://www.mix1073FM.com.

SOFTWARE PUBLISHERS

CAPTIVA SOFTWARE
10145 Pacific Heights Boulevard, 6th Floor
San Diego, California 92121

General Information Company whose products cover a continuum of needs in the information capture marketplace from toolkits to complete solutions. Established in 1989. Number of employees: 70. Number of internship applications received each year: 100.
Internships Available ▶ *1–2 human resources interns:* responsibilities include providing clerical and administrative assistance with projects within the HR department; includes data entry, filing, copying and organizing various pieces of data. Candidates should have ability to work independently, computer skills, office skills, personal interest in the field, self-motivation, written communication skills. Duration is 30–90 days. Unpaid. Open to college freshmen, college sophomores, college juniors, college seniors, recent college graduates. ▶ *1 public relations and marketing intern:* responsibilities include writing press releases and case studies; media relations and story pitching for article placements; research on Enterprise Content Management (ECM) market; marketing research for company presentations; and other projects as needed. Candidates should have declared college major in field, plan to pursue career in field, research skills, self-motivation, excellent writing skills a must. Duration is 3–6 months. Unpaid. Open to college juniors, college seniors, recent college graduates, graduate students. International applications accepted.
Benefits On-the-job training, possible full-time employment, willing to act as a professional reference, willing to complete paperwork for educational credit, willing to provide letters of recommendation.
Contact E-mail or through World Wide Web site Human Resources. E-mail: careers@captivasoftware.com. No phone calls. In-person interview recommended (telephone interview accepted). Applicants must submit a formal organization application, resume. Applications are accepted continuously. World Wide Web: http://www.captivasoftware.com.

ELECTRONIC ARTS
209 Redwood Shores Parkway
Redwood City, California 94065-1175

General Information Independent developer and publisher of interactive entertainment software for personal computers and advanced entertainment systems including PlayStation2 Computer Entertainment System and Nintendo GameCube. Established in 1982. Number of internship applications received each year: 1,000.
Internships Available ▶ *Computer graphic artists:* responsibilities include producing bit map graphics, 3D shapes, and computer animation by creating new art and/or retouching existing art. Candidates should have ability to work with others, college courses in field, computer skills, knowledge of field, self-motivation, knowledge of 3D graphics programs. Duration is 3 months for summer interns; 6 months for co-ops. $2050–$2306.25 per month. Open to college sophomores, college juniors, college seniors, graduate students. ▶ *Online developers.* Candidates should have knowledge of field, plan to pursue career in field, self-motivation, strong interpersonal skills, knowledge of JAVA, HTML, JAVA Script, PERL, and CGI. Duration is 3 months for summer interns; 6 months for co-ops. $2562.50–$2989.58 per month. Open to college freshmen, college sophomores, college juniors, college seniors. ▶ *Software engineers:* responsibilities include programming specific features into the game; testing, debugging, and documenting code contributions. Candidates should have ability to work with others, analytical skills, college courses in field, computer skills, plan to pursue career in field, knowledge of C and C++, gaming industry experience. Duration is 3 months for summer interns, 6 months for co-ops. $2562.50–$2989.58 per month. Open to college sophomores, college juniors, college seniors, graduate students, those with one year remaining in school.
Benefits On-the-job training, opportunity to attend seminars/workshops, willing to act as a professional reference, willing to complete paperwork for educational credit, willing to provide letters of recommendation, mandated disability plan, health club membership, housing stipend, reimbursement for bike and helmet.
Contact E-mail or through World Wide Web site Internship Coordinator, 209 Redwood Shores Parkway, Redwood City, California 94065-1175. E-mail: interns@ea.com. In-person interview recommended (telephone interview accepted). Applicants must submit a resume, portfolio, additional requirements located on Web site. Application deadline: February 28 for summer. World Wide Web: http://www.jobs.ea.com.

PPP INFOTECH LIMITED
No. 9/1, Manjolai First Street, Kalaimagal Nagar,
Ekkaduthangal
Chennai (Madras), Tamil Nadu 600 097 India

General Information Software company developing software technologies for computer networking, Internet, and Intranet for more than 10,000 customers in 80 countries with substantial sales in America and Europe. Established in 1995. Number of employees: 25. Number of internship applications received each year: 5.
Internships Available ▶ *2–4 consultant-marketing interns:* responsibilities include promoting and marketing software products; talking to several organizations over Internet chat, phone, and e-mail; meeting decision makers of companies; may also take part in media campaigns for the locality. Candidates should have ability to work independently, computer skills, office skills, oral communication skills, personal interest in the field, strong leadership ability, written communication skills. Duration is 3–6 months. Position available as unpaid or at payment on commission basis. Open to college freshmen, college sophomores, recent college graduates, graduate students, career changers, individuals reentering the workforce. International applications accepted.
Benefits Housing at a cost, job counseling, meals at a cost, names of contacts, on-the-job training, tuition assistance, willing to act as a professional reference, willing to complete paperwork for educational credit, willing to provide letters of recommendation.
International Internships Available.
Contact Call or e-mail B. Parameshwar Babu, Director. E-mail: pbabu@pppindia.com. Telephone interview required. Applicants must submit a letter of interest, resume, interview over e-mail and Internet chat is preferred. Applications are accepted continuously. Fees: $25. World Wide Web: http://www.pppinfotech.com.

TELECOMMUNICATIONS

AT&T
200 Laurel Avenue, Room D32B03
Middletown, New Jersey 07748

General Information Telecommunication company. Established in 1885. Number of internship applications received each year: 1,000.
Internships Available ▶ *50–100 interns.* Candidates should have coursework in computer science, computer engineering, or electrical engineering, GPA of 3.0 or above. Duration is 12 weeks in summer. Salary depends on intern's level of education . Open to college sophomores, college juniors, college seniors, graduate students. International applications accepted.

AT&T (*continued*)

Benefits On-the-job training, opportunity to attend seminars/workshops, travel reimbursement, willing to act as a professional reference, willing to provide letters of recommendation, opportunity to work with renowned scientist.

Contact Through World Wide Web site Internship Coordinator. Telephone interview required. Applicants must submit a formal organization application, letter of interest, resume, academic transcripts, personal reference, letter of recommendation. Application deadline: April 15. World Wide Web: http://www.att.com/hr.

BLACK ENTERTAINMENT TELEVISION
1235 W Street, NE
Washington, District of Columbia 20018

General Information Telecommunications company consisting of cable network channel, 2 magazines, pay per view channel, and other venues of mass communication. Established in 1980. Number of employees: 530. Number of internship applications received each year: 600.

Internships Available ▶ *40–60 interns:* responsibilities include various duties according to departmental needs. Candidates should have computer skills, oral communication skills, organizational skills, plan to pursue career in field, strong interpersonal skills. Duration is 1 semester. Unpaid. Open to high school seniors, college freshmen, college sophomores, college juniors, college seniors, graduate students, law students. International applications accepted.

Benefits On-the-job training, possible full-time employment, willing to complete paperwork for educational credit.

Contact Write or fax Nikki Gainey, Internship Coordinator. Fax: 202-608-2589. E-mail: nikki.gainey@bet.net. In-person interview recommended (telephone interview accepted). Applicants must submit a formal organization application, letter of interest, resume, academic transcripts, three letters of recommendation, verification from school that internship is for academic credit. Application deadline: March 27 for summer, July 3 for fall, November 13 for spring. World Wide Web: http://www.bet.com.

GEOSPATIAL INFORMATION AND TECHNOLOGY ASSOCIATION (GITA)
14456 East Evans Avenue
Aurora, Colorado 80014-1409

General Information Educational association serving professionals using geospatial information and technology in infrastructure-based industries (utilities, telecommunications, oil and gas pipeline, local government). Established in 1979. Number of employees: 11. Number of internship applications received each year: 20.

Internships Available ▶ *Up to 9 interns:* responsibilities include working with GITA corporate members, using their geospatial information and technology skills in the workplace at their facilities; interns may also find their own opportunities. Candidates should have college courses in field, computer skills, knowledge of field, personal interest in the field, plan to pursue career in field, self-motivation. Duration is dependent on internship arranged. Paid at up to $2000 per year. Open to college juniors, college seniors, graduate students. International applications accepted.

Benefits Names of contacts, on-the-job training, possible full-time employment.

International Internships Available.

Contact Write, call, fax, e-mail, or through World Wide Web site Gina Holler, Membership Coordinator, 14456 East Evans Avenue, Aurora, Colorado 80014. Phone: 303-337-0513. Fax: 303-337-1001. E-mail: gholler@gita.org. Applicants must submit a formal organization application, letter of interest, academic transcripts, three personal references, three letters of recommendation. Application deadline: December 15 for summer. World Wide Web: http://www.gita.org.

G4 MEDIA, LLC
11444 West Olympic Boulevard, 11th Floor
Los Angeles, California 90064

General Information Cable network station dedicated to the video game industry. Established in 2000. Number of employees: 250. Subsidiary of Comcast Corporation, Philadelphia, Pennsylvania. Number of internship applications received each year: 75.

Internships Available ▶ *15–20 media interns.* Candidates should have college courses in field, computer skills, oral communication skills, personal interest in the field, plan to pursue career in field, strong interpersonal skills. Duration is 1–2 semesters. Unpaid. Open to college juniors, college seniors, graduate students, law students. International applications accepted.

Benefits Job counseling, on-the-job training, opportunity to attend seminars/workshops, possible full-time employment, willing to act as a professional reference, willing to complete paperwork for educational credit, G4 media products.

International Internships Available in Japan.

Contact Write, fax, or e-mail Monica Hayes, Human Resources Generalist. Fax: 310-481-3498. E-mail: jobs@g4media.com. No phone calls. In-person interview recommended (telephone interview accepted). Applicants must submit a formal organization application, resume, proof from university/college of eligibility for course credit. Applications are accepted continuously. World Wide Web: http://www.g4tv.com.

SBC/AMERITECH
222 North Meridian Street, Room 120
Indianapolis, Indiana 46226

General Information Organization responsible for the planning, designing, construction, and maintenance of the telecommunication network and installing and maintaining communication services to customers. Number of internship applications received each year: 200.

Internships Available ▶ *Management trainees:* responsibilities include telecommunications engineering, installation, switch technologies, and operator services (both technical and supervisory). Candidates should have analytical skills, oral communication skills, personal interest in the field, self-motivation, strong interpersonal skills, strong leadership ability. Duration is 3 months. $1650 per month (minimum). Open to college juniors, college seniors, graduate students.

Benefits Job counseling, names of contacts, on-the-job training, opportunity to attend seminars/workshops, possible full-time employment, travel reimbursement.

Contact Write, fax, or through World Wide Web site J. A. Mayhen, Staffing Consultant, 220 N. Meridan Street, Room 120, Indianapolis, Indiana 46226. Fax: 317-265-1460. No phone calls. In-person interview recommended (telephone interview accepted). Applicants must submit a formal organization application, resume, academic transcripts. Applications are accepted continuously. World Wide Web: http://www.sbc.com.

TELEVISION BROADCASTING

ABC NEWS NIGHTLINE
1717 DeSales Street, NW
Washington, District of Columbia 20036

General Information Television news, broadcast journalism company. Established in 1980. Number of employees: 35. Number of internship applications received each year: 400.

Internships Available ▶ *4–6 interns:* responsibilities include helping to manage the enormous flow of information that comes into the office every day; participating in all editorial conferences with access to all areas of the broadcast. Candidates should have oral communication skills, self-motivation, strong interpersonal skills, written communication skills, desire to learn more about broadcast

journalism. Duration is 8–12 weeks. Unpaid. Open to college juniors, college seniors, graduate students, law students, must be receiving academic credit. International applications accepted.
Benefits Names of contacts, on-the-job training, opportunity to attend seminars/workshops, willing to act as a professional reference, willing to complete paperwork for educational credit, willing to provide letters of recommendation, occasional free meals, some travel reimbursement.
Contact Write, call, e-mail, or through World Wide Web site Intern Coordinator, 1717 DeSales Street, NW, Washington, District of Columbia 20036. Phone: 202-222-7000. Fax: 202-222-7976. E-mail: niteline@abcnews.com. Telephone interview required. Applicants must submit a formal organization application, letter of interest, resume, academic transcripts, two letters of recommendation, letter from university confirming eligibility to receive credit. Application deadline: March 15 for summer, July 1 for fall, October 1 for winter, November 15 for spring semester I; February 1 for spring semester II. World Wide Web: http://www.abcnews.com.

ACADEMY OF TELEVISION ARTS AND SCIENCES
5220 Lankershim Boulevard
North Hollywood, California 91601-3109

General Information Service and awards organization that presents the annual primetime Emmy awards; provides activities for television industry members; and fosters competition for college students in the form of a paid summer internship program which places students with Los Angeles-based television stations, production companies, studios, and other television-related venues. Established in 1946. Number of employees: 52. Number of internship applications received each year: 1,050.
Internships Available ▶ *27–29 interns:* responsibilities include working as an intern in one of 27 categories: Agency, Traditional Animation, Computer Generated Animation, Art Direction, Broadcast Advertising and Promotion, Business Affairs, Casting, Children's Programming and Development, Cinematography, Commercials, Costume Design, Development, Documentary/Reality Production, Editing, Entertainment News, Episodic Series, Movies for Television, Music, Network Programming Management, Production Management, Public Relations and Publicity, Sound, Syndication/Distribution, Television Directing-Single Camera, Television Directing–Multi-Camera, Television Scriptwriting, and Videotape Post Production. Candidates should have college courses in field, knowledge of field, oral communication skills, plan to pursue career in field, self-motivation, written communication skills, employment authorization and a social security card to receive stipend (if international student). Duration is 8 weeks. $2500 per duration of internship. Open to college freshmen, college sophomores, college juniors, college seniors, recent college graduates, graduate students, law students. International applications accepted.
Benefits Job counseling, opportunity to attend seminars/workshops, willing to act as a professional reference, willing to provide letters of recommendation, $500 housing/travel supplement for non-L.A. County residents.
Contact Write, call, fax, e-mail, or through World Wide Web site Internships. Phone: 818-754-2830. Fax: 818-761-8524. E-mail: internships@emmys.org. Applicants must submit a formal organization application, letter of interest, resume, academic transcripts, writing sample, three letters of recommendation, videotaped interview if selected as a finalist, portfolio may be required (depending on category). Application deadline: March 15 for summer. World Wide Web: http://www.emmys.tv.

AMERICA'S MOST WANTED/STF PRODUCTIONS, INC.
5151 Wisconsin Avenue, NW
Washington, District of Columbia 20016

General Information Major television production company. Subsidiary of Fox Television Stations, Inc., Los Angeles, California.
Internships Available ▶ *Hot line interns:* responsibilities include attending weekly show meeting; assisting in hot line department; opportunities to interact with personnel in all major aspects of production, cross-train between departments, and "pitch" a story.

Candidates should have ability to work independently, ability to work with others, oral communication skills, personal interest in the field, research skills, self-motivation, writing skills. Duration is one semester (15-20 hours per week). Unpaid. ▶ *Missing children interns:* responsibilities include attending weekly show meeting; assisting in Missing Children Department; opportunities to interact with personnel in all major aspects of production, cross-train between departments, and "pitch" a story. Duration is one semester (15-20 hours per week). Unpaid. ▶ *News interns:* responsibilities include attending weekly show meeting; assisting in News Department; opportunities to identify, research and "pitch" a story and assist in its development and final production, if selected; interacting with personnel in all major aspects of television production; cross-training opportunities. Candidates should have ability to work independently, ability to work with others, personal interest in the field, research skills, self-motivation, writing skills. Duration is one semester (15-20 hours per week). Unpaid. ▶ *Production interns:* responsibilities include attending weekly show meeting, assisting in production; opportunities to pitch stories for production, interact with personnel in all major aspects of television production, and cross-training between production and News, Publicity, Hot line and Missing Children. Candidates should have ability to work independently, ability to work with others, personal interest in the field, research skills, self-motivation, writing skills. Duration is one semester (15-20 hours per week). Unpaid. ▶ *Publicity interns:* responsibilities include attending weekly show meeting; assisting in Publicity Department; opportunities to assist in development and final production, interact with personnel in all major aspects of television production, cross-train between departments, and "pitch" a story. Candidates should have ability to work independently, ability to work with others, personal interest in the field, research skills, self-motivation, writing skills. Duration is one semester (15-20 hours per week). Unpaid. Open to college sophomores, college juniors, college seniors.
Benefits On-the-job training, willing to complete paperwork for educational credit.
Contact Write or call Intern Coordinator. Phone: 202-204-2600. E-mail: intern@amw.com. Applicants must submit a formal organization application, resume, writing sample, signed letter from college or university indicating that academic credit will be received for the internship. Applications are accepted continuously.

ARKANSAS EDUCATIONAL TELECOMMUNICATIONS NETWORK
PO Box 1250
Conway, Arkansas 72033

General Information Public television station providing PBS programs, educational shows and materials; also produces local programming. Established in 1961. Number of employees: 100. Number of internship applications received each year: 80.
Internships Available ▶ *4 K-12 services interns:* responsibilities include video library review and update and researching, designing, and writing summaries for teacher's guides. Candidates should have ability to work independently, ability to work with others, analytical skills, computer skills, research skills, writing skills. Duration is 1 semester. Unpaid. Open to college freshmen, college sophomores, college juniors, college seniors, recent college graduates, graduate students, career changers, individuals reentering the workforce. ▶ *1–2 accounting office assistant interns:* responsibilities include assisting with researching invoices, keying and processing payable vouchers, and reconciling fund records; helping reconcile monthly bank statements and preparing monthly trade account statements. Candidates should have college courses in field, computer skills, knowledge of field, office skills, good typing skills, good math skills. Duration is 1 semester. Unpaid. Open to college sophomores, college juniors, college seniors, recent college graduates, graduate students, career changers, individuals reentering the workforce. ▶ *1 broadcast management intern:* responsibilities include general administration duties and research assistance (labor law questions, political concerns, grant applications, donor prospects). Candidates should have analytical skills, computer skills, organizational skills, research skills, strong leadership ability, writing skills. Duration is 1 semester. Unpaid. Open to college sophomores, college juniors, college seniors, recent

Arkansas Educational Telecommunications Network (continued)
college graduates, graduate students, law students, career changers, individuals reentering the workforce. ▶ *1–2 development interns:* responsibilities include assisting with events, with mailings to members and volunteers, updating computer files, research assistance on special projects, and providing administrative and clerical support. Candidates should have ability to work independently, ability to work with others, computer skills, editing skills, office skills, oral communication skills, organizational skills, research skills, self-motivation, writing skills. Duration is 1 semester. Unpaid. Open to high school students, recent high school graduates, college freshmen, college sophomores, college juniors, college seniors, recent college graduates, graduate students, law students, career changers, individuals reentering the workforce. ▶ *1–2 general business interns:* responsibilities include performing general finance/administration office duties; assisting in accounting processes, personnel/payroll duties, and purchasing activities. Candidates should have college courses in field, computer skills, knowledge of field, office skills, oral communication skills, written communication skills. Duration is 1 semester. Unpaid. Open to college freshmen, college sophomores, college juniors, college seniors, recent college graduates, graduate students, career changers, individuals reentering the workforce. ▶ *2 graphics interns:* responsibilities include programming research for monthly Program Guide; layout and design for brochures, flyers, and newsletters; photography; assisting with assembly of scenery for AETN productions; and assisting Web designer. Candidates should have college courses in field, knowledge of field, personal interest in the field, research skills, familiarity with computer graphic programs. Duration is 1 semester. Unpaid. Open to college freshmen, college sophomores, college juniors, college seniors, recent college graduates, graduate students, career changers, individuals reentering the workforce. ▶ *1 human resource intern:* responsibilities include assisting with annual employee performance evaluations, scheduling employee training, composing job advertisements, collecting/reporting applicant statistics, and contracts for professional services. Candidates should have computer skills, office skills, oral communication skills, organizational skills, writing skills. Duration is 1 semester. Unpaid. Open to college sophomores, college juniors, college seniors, recent college graduates, graduate students, law students, career changers, individuals reentering the workforce. ▶ *2 membership interns:* responsibilities include data entry, telephone customer service, handling member correspondence, running weekly mailings and reports, packaging and mailing premiums, and sorting and labeling bulk mailings. Candidates should have ability to work independently, ability to work with others, computer skills, editing skills, office skills, oral communication skills, organizational skills, self-motivation, ability to follow directions, good ability with numbers. Duration is 1 semester. Unpaid. Open to high school students, recent high school graduates, college freshmen, college sophomores, college juniors, college seniors, recent college graduates, graduate students, law students, career changers, individuals reentering the workforce. ▶ *2 outreach/publicist interns:* responsibilities include research, writing program features and news/press releases, preparing and mailing outreach information packets, and assisting in preparation of outreach events. Candidates should have computer skills, editing skills, personal interest in the field, research skills, writing skills. Duration is 1 semester. Unpaid. Open to recent high school graduates, college freshmen, college sophomores, college juniors, college seniors, recent college graduates, graduate students, career changers, individuals reentering the workforce. ▶ *3 postsecondary services interns:* responsibilities include designing multimedia presentations; evaluating technology training; and analyzing basic skills needs. Candidates should have ability to work independently, ability to work with others, analytical skills, organizational skills, self-motivation. Duration is 1 semester. Unpaid. Open to college freshmen, college sophomores, college juniors, college seniors, recent college graduates, graduate students, career changers, individuals reentering the workforce. ▶ *6 production assistant interns:* responsibilities include operating studio cameras under supervision, arranging studio sets, lighting sets, floor directing, assistant directing, and assisting videographics in the field. Candidates should have ability to work with others, knowledge of field, oral communication skills, plan to pursue career in field. Duration is

1 semester. Unpaid. Open to college sophomores, college juniors, college seniors, recent college graduates, graduate students. ▶ *5 production interns:* responsibilities include assisting in business aspects of production, preparing programs for broadcast, and with phone supervision during live broadcasts; screening and transcribing video tapes. Candidates should have analytical skills, computer skills, office skills, personal interest in the field, research skills, strong interpersonal skills. Duration is 1 semester. Unpaid. Open to college freshmen, college sophomores, college juniors, college seniors, recent college graduates, graduate students. ▶ *2 program assistant interns:* responsibilities include performing general office duties; working in video library, preparing film and videotape programs for shipping, and maintaining program records in database. Candidates should have ability to work independently, analytical skills, computer skills, office skills, organizational skills, must be good with numbers. Duration is 1 semester. Unpaid. Open to college freshmen, college sophomores, college juniors, college seniors, recent college graduates, graduate students, career changers, individuals reentering the workforce. ▶ *1 purchasing intern:* responsibilities include assisting in keying updates to vendor database, writing specifications for sealed bids, research and proposals, lease and land management, and risk management/insurance. Candidates should have ability to work independently, organizational skills, writing skills, good math and customer service skills. Duration is 1 semester. Unpaid. Open to college freshmen, college sophomores, college juniors, college seniors, recent college graduates, graduate students, career changers, individuals reentering the workforce. ▶ *2 viewer services assistant interns:* responsibilities include performing general office duties, working on department files, and preparing responses to viewer inquiries. Candidates should have computer skills, office skills, oral communication skills, research skills, strong interpersonal skills, written communication skills. Duration is 1 semester. Unpaid. Open to recent high school graduates, college freshmen, college sophomores, college juniors, college seniors, recent college graduates, graduate students, career changers, individuals reentering the workforce. International applications accepted.
Benefits On-the-job training, willing to act as a professional reference, willing to complete paperwork for educational credit, willing to provide letters of recommendation.
Contact Write, call, or fax Mechelle Williams, Intern Coordinator. Phone: 800-662-2386 Ext. 43. Fax: 501-852-2280. In-person interview recommended (telephone interview accepted). Applicants must submit a formal organization application, resume, letter of recommendation, writing samples (for communications and programming positions). Application deadline: April 1 for summer, June 15 for fall, October 30 for spring. World Wide Web: http://www.aetn.org.

AT&T BROADBAND
14 Burr Street
Framingham, Massachusetts 01701

General Information Original programming department of AT&T Broadband of New England providing video training and local programming to communities in Massachusetts, New Hampshire, and Connecticut. Established in 1980. Number of employees: 225. Unit of AT&T Broadband, Andover, Massachusetts. Number of internship applications received each year: 50.
Internships Available ▶ *3–5 marketing interns:* responsibilities include event marketing, public relations liaison, and production assistance. Candidates should have ability to work independently, ability to work with others, oral communication skills, organizational skills, research skills, self-motivation, writing skills. Duration is 2–5 months. Unpaid. Open to college seniors, graduate students. ▶ *30 television production interns:* responsibilities include working on video production crews. Candidates should have ability to work independently, ability to work with others, computer skills, editing skills, oral communication skills, self-motivation, written communication skills. Duration is 3–5 months. Unpaid. Open to college freshmen, college sophomores, college juniors, college seniors, recent college graduates, graduate students, career changers, individuals reentering the workforce. International applications accepted.

Benefits Names of contacts, on-the-job training, opportunity to attend seminars/workshops, possible full-time employment, willing to act as a professional reference, willing to complete paperwork for educational credit, willing to provide letters of recommendation.
Contact Write, fax, or e-mail Peter Strzetelski, Manager of Learning and Development. Fax: 508-879-5468. E-mail: peter_strzetelski@cable.comcast.com. No phone calls. In-person interview recommended (telephone interview accepted). Applicants must submit a letter of interest, resume. Application deadline: May 1 for summer, July 1 for fall, November 1 for spring. World Wide Web: http://www.att3.com.

BAY NEWS 9 CABLE STATION
7901 66th Street North
Pinellas Park, Florida 33781

General Information Television news station serving the Bay area of Florida. Number of employees: 105. Division of Bright House Networks, Syracuse, New York.
Internships Available ▶ *Interns:* responsibilities include working at assignment desk, associate production, and clerical duties as needed. Unpaid. Open to students of journalism, television production, or graphic arts, in junior year (minimum) or 4 year program or having completed one year of technical training.
Contact Write, fax, or e-mail Human Resource Manager. Fax: 727-437-2031. E-mail: lucar@baynews9.com. No phone calls. Applicants must submit a letter of interest, resume, evidence of college credit for internship. World Wide Web: http://www.baynews9.com.

BNNTV/CAMERAPLANET
253 Fifth Avenue, Seventh Floor
New York, New York 10016

General Information Television, film, Web, and news production company. Established in 1983. Number of employees: 30. Number of internship applications received each year: 50.
Internships Available ▶ *15–20 Camera Planet interns:* responsibilities include working with CameraPlanet.com staff to develop and upload user video to Web site. Candidates should have ability to work independently, ability to work with others, analytical skills, office skills, oral communication skills, organizational skills, self-motivation, written communication skills. Duration is 3 months. Unpaid. Open to college sophomores, college juniors, college seniors, recent college graduates, graduate students, career changers, individuals reentering the workforce. ▶ *3 computer technology interns.* Candidates should have personal interest in the field. Duration is 3 months. Unpaid. Open to recent high school graduates, college freshmen, college sophomores, college juniors, college seniors, graduate students. ▶ *5 development interns:* responsibilities include working with TV and film development division to research and develop story ideas. Candidates should have ability to work independently, ability to work with others, analytical skills, oral communication skills, research skills, self-motivation, writing skills. Duration is 3 months. Unpaid. Open to college freshmen, college sophomores, college juniors, college seniors, recent college graduates, career changers, individuals reentering the workforce. ▶ *5 film development interns.* Candidates should have personal interest in the field. Duration is 3 months. Unpaid. Open to college freshmen, college sophomores, college juniors, college seniors, recent college graduates, graduate students. ▶ *1 graphics intern.* Candidates should have personal interest in the field. Duration is 3 months. Unpaid. Open to college freshmen, college sophomores, college juniors, college seniors, recent college graduates, graduate students. ▶ *1 public relations intern.* Candidates should have personal interest in the field. Duration is 3 months. Unpaid. Open to college freshmen, college sophomores, college juniors, college seniors, recent college graduates, graduate students. ▶ *5–10 television/production development interns.* Candidates should have personal interest in the field. Duration is 3 months. Unpaid. Open to college freshmen, college sophomores, college juniors, college seniors, recent college graduates, graduate students. International applications accepted.
Benefits On-the-job training, opportunity to attend seminars/workshops, possible full-time employment, willing to act as a

professional reference, willing to complete paperwork for educational credit, willing to provide letters of recommendation.
Contact Call, fax, or e-mail Melanie Blair, Intern Coordinator. Phone: 212-779-0500. Fax: 212-532-5554. E-mail: melanie@cameraplanet.com. In-person interview recommended (telephone interview accepted). Applicants must submit a formal organization application, resume. Application deadline: January for spring, May for summer, September for fall. World Wide Web: http://www.bnntv.com.

CENTRAL FLORIDA NEWS 13
64 East Concord Street
Orlando, Florida 32801

General Information Twenty-four hour local news television station. Established in 1997. Number of employees: 100. Number of internship applications received each year: 50.
Internships Available ▶ *3–8 news interns:* responsibilities include assisting reporters on stories, helping answer newsroom phones, helping research information, helping write copy, and learning the writing, editing, and producing process. Candidates should have knowledge of field, oral communication skills, plan to pursue career in field, self-motivation, writing skills. Duration is 1 semester. Unpaid. ▶ *1–3 promotions interns:* responsibilities include helping, write, edit, and produce promotional materials for broadcast; assisting in community relations projects; helping create story ideas for promotional materials. Candidates should have ability to work with others, editing skills, knowledge of field, self-motivation, writing skills. Duration is 1 semester. Unpaid. Open to college juniors, college seniors. International applications accepted.
Benefits Names of contacts, on-the-job training, willing to act as a professional reference, willing to complete paperwork for educational credit.
Contact Write, fax, or e-mail Jennifer Cook, Executive Producer. Fax: 407-513-1399. E-mail: jcook@cfnew13.com. No phone calls. In-person interview recommended (telephone interview accepted). Applicants must submit a letter of interest, resume. Applications are accepted continuously.

CHARLIE ROSE SHOW
499 Park Avenue, 11th Floor
New York, New York 10022

General Information Nightly television program featuring one-on-one interviews and roundtable discussions. Established in 1991. Number of employees: 15. Unit of Bloomberg, New York, New York. Number of internship applications received each year: 150.
Internships Available ▶ *9–11 production interns:* responsibilities include helping with research for upcoming guests, meeting and greeting guests, maintaining the green room and studio, and basic office duties. Candidates should have computer skills, knowledge of field, office skills, organizational skills, research skills, self-motivation. Duration is 1 semester. Unpaid. Open to college juniors, college seniors, recent college graduates, graduate students. International applications accepted.
Benefits Possible full-time employment, willing to act as a professional reference, willing to complete paperwork for educational credit, willing to provide letters of recommendation, onsite shoots, free snacks/food, contact with celebrities.
Contact Write or fax David G. Huppert, Research/Internship Coordinator. Phone: 212-940-1600. Fax: 212-940-1909. E-mail: dhuppert@bloomberg.com. In-person interview required. Applicants must submit a letter of interest, resume. Applications are accepted continuously. World Wide Web: http://www.charlierose.com.

CHARTER COMMUNICATIONS–WCTR CHANNEL 3
95 Higgins Street
Worcester, Massachusetts 01606

General Information Cable company servicing 22 central Massachusetts communities. Established in 1975. Number of employees: 400. Unit of Charter Communications, St. Louis, Missouri. Number of internship applications received each year: 30.
Internships Available ▶ *2–4 production assistants for news:* responsibilities include running camera and audio, writing scripts, editing,

Charter Communications–WCTR Channel 3 (continued)

co-producing, directing, and floor directing. Candidates should have ability to work with others, college courses in field, computer skills, experience in the field, oral communication skills, personal interest in the field, self-motivation. Duration is 1 semester. Unpaid. Open to college juniors, college seniors, recent college graduates. ▶ *2–4 production assistants for programming production:* responsibilities include hands-on experience in all phases of television production (studio and remotes). Candidates should have declared college major in field, oral communication skills, plan to pursue career in field, self-motivation, strong interpersonal skills, ability to work days, nights, or weekends. Duration is one semester (minimum 18 hours per week). Unpaid. Open to college juniors, college seniors, recent college graduates, graduate students. International applications accepted.

Benefits On-the-job training, possible full-time employment, willing to complete paperwork for educational credit.

Contact Write, call, fax, or e-mail Bill Jackson, Production Manager. Phone: 508-853-1515. Fax: 508-854-5065. E-mail: bjackson@ greatermediaworc.com. In-person interview recommended (telephone interview accepted). Applicants must submit a formal organization application, letter of interest, resume. Application deadline: May 1 for summer, August 1 for fall, December 1 for spring; first come, first serve for all deadlines. World Wide Web: http://www.chartercom.com.

CNN AMERICA, INC.
820 1st Street, NE
Washington, District of Columbia 20002

General Information Cable news network offering 24 hours of news and information programming daily. Established in 1980. Number of employees: 300. Unit of AOL Time Warner, Inc., New York, New York. Number of internship applications received each year: 500.

Internships Available ▶ *15–20 departmental interns:* responsibilities include assisting with production needs, conducting research, and learning about booking guests and show research. Duration is 12–15 weeks. Unpaid. ▶ *5–10 rotation interns:* responsibilities include assisting writers, producers, video librarians, and field crews. Duration is 12–15 weeks. Unpaid. Candidates for all positions should have ability to work independently, college courses in field, oral communication skills, plan to pursue career in field, self-motivation, strong interpersonal skills. Open to college juniors, college seniors, graduate students. International applications accepted.

Benefits Formal training, names of contacts, opportunity to attend seminars/workshops, willing to complete paperwork for educational credit.

International Internships Available in London, United Kingdom.

Contact Write, call, e-mail, or through World Wide Web site Jennifer Gibson, Human Resources Coordinator. Phone: 202-515-2916. E-mail: jennifer.gibson@turner.com. Applicants must submit a formal organization application, letter of interest, resume, academic transcripts, two letters of recommendation, 1–2 page essay. Application deadline: March 1 for summer, July 1 for fall, November 1 for spring. World Wide Web: http://www.turnerjobs.com.

COMCAST
27800 Franklin Road
Southfield, Michigan 48034

General Information Cable television local programming department producing local origination programming. Established in 1981. Number of employees: 15. Division of Comcast, Philadelphia, Pennsylvania. Number of internship applications received each year: 15.

Internships Available ▶ *1–3 newsmaker interns:* responsibilities include learning video production, editing, and camera work. Candidates should have ability to work independently, ability to work with others, analytical skills, computer skills, knowledge of field, office skills, oral communication skills, organizational skills, personal interest in the field, plan to pursue career in field, research skills, self-motivation, strong leadership ability, writing

skills. Duration is minimum of 3 to 4 months. Unpaid. Open to recent high school graduates, college freshmen, college sophomores, college juniors, college seniors, recent college graduates, graduate students, individuals reentering the workforce. International applications accepted.

Benefits Formal training, on-the-job training, opportunity to attend seminars/workshops, possible full-time employment, willing to act as a professional reference, willing to complete paperwork for educational credit, willing to provide letters of recommendation.

Contact Write, fax, or e-mail Trista Sutton, Producer. Fax: 248-359-6750. E-mail: trista_sutton@cable.comcast.com. No phone calls. In-person interview required. Applicants must submit a letter of interest, resume. Application deadline: January 5 for spring, March 1 for summer, October 1 for winter.

COMCAST
12345G Sunrise Valley Drive
Reston, Virginia 20191

General Information Television studio and mobile unit providing locally produced television programming for a cable television community channel. Established in 1970. Number of employees: 28. Unit of Comcast Corporation, Philadelphia, Pennsylvania. Number of internship applications received each year: 20.

Internships Available ▶ *3 TV production interns:* responsibilities include learning camera editing and possibly directing. Candidates should have ability to work independently, ability to work with others, personal interest in the field, self-motivation. Duration is 1 semester. Unpaid. Open to high school students, recent high school graduates, college freshmen, college sophomores, college juniors, college seniors, recent college graduates, graduate students, career changers, individuals reentering the workforce.

Benefits On-the-job training, willing to act as a professional reference, willing to complete paperwork for educational credit, willing to provide letters of recommendation.

Contact Write or call Dan Nicholson, Manager of Production Services. Phone: 703-758-8099. In-person interview recommended (telephone interview accepted). Applicants must submit a letter of interest, resume. Applications are accepted continuously.

COMCAST CABLE–CHANNEL 26
1111 Anderson Drive
San Rafael, California 94901

General Information Public access and local origination facility where professional and nonprofessional community programming is produced. Established in 1976. Number of employees: 5. Department of Comcast Cable, San Rafael, California. Number of internship applications received each year: 20.

Internships Available ▶ *4 access interns:* responsibilities include assisting access coordinator and programming. Candidates should have ability to work independently, ability to work with others, knowledge of field, office skills, organizational skills, personal interest in the field. Duration is flexible; minimum of 130 hours per semester required. Unpaid. ▶ *4 productions interns:* responsibilities include working for staff productions, overseeing automated playback system, office maintenance, and working as part of crew on public access productions. Candidates should have ability to work independently, ability to work with others, office skills, organizational skills, personal interest in the field. Duration is flexible; minimum of 140 hours per semester. Unpaid. Open to recent high school graduates, college freshmen, college sophomores, college juniors, college seniors, recent college graduates, graduate students, career changers, individuals reentering the workforce.

Benefits Job counseling, opportunity to attend seminars/workshops, willing to complete paperwork for educational credit, willing to provide letters of recommendation, informal training in television production.

Contact Write or call Ms. Jennifer Kloepping, Producer/Director. Phone: 415-258-0136. In-person interview recommended (telephone interview accepted). Applicants must submit a formal organization application, two personal references. Application deadline: May 15 for summer, August 15 for fall, December 15 for spring. World Wide Web: http://communityprogramming.marin.org.

COMEDY CENTRAL
1775 Broadway, 10th Floor
New York, New York 10019

General Information Advertiser-supported basic cable comedy service. Established in 1991. Number of employees: 300. Unit of Time Warner and Viacom, New York, New York. Number of internship applications received each year: 800.

Internships Available ▶ *1–2 advertising/marketing interns:* responsibilities include occasionally attending radio record sessions, assisting off-air producer on various tape projects, maintaining advertising portfolio and radio tape library, processing bills, and organizing budget book. Candidates should have computer skills, office skills. Duration is one summer. Unpaid. Open to college freshmen, college sophomores, college juniors, college seniors. ▶ *1 affiliate relations intern:* responsibilities include supporting affiliate sales group. Candidates should have computer skills, oral communication skills, self-motivation, strong interpersonal skills, written communication skills. Duration is one summer. Unpaid. Open to college freshmen, college sophomores, college juniors, college seniors. ▶ *1 affiliate relations intern (Chicago and Los Angeles):* responsibilities include gaining distribution and maintaining customer base via creative marketing and promotional campaigns. Candidates should have personal interest in comedy. Duration is 1 semester. Unpaid. Open to college freshmen, college sophomores, college juniors, college seniors. ▶ *2 corporate communication/public relations interns:* responsibilities include assisting in day-to-day public relations effort/events, maintaining network press digest, updating press releases and executive and talent bio photo files, maintaining press tape library, general office support, and coordinating press kits. Candidates should have office skills, writing skills. Duration is 1 semester. Unpaid. Open to college freshmen, college sophomores, college juniors, college seniors. ▶ *1 corporate communications intern (Los Angeles and New York).* Candidates should have personal interest in comedy. Duration is 1 semester. Unpaid. Open to college freshmen, college sophomores, college juniors, college seniors. ▶ *1 development intern (New York and Los Angeles):* responsibilities include assisting in evaluating current series scripts, unsolicited submissions, and writing samples. Candidates should have sense of humor and personal interest in stand-up comedy. Duration is 1 semester. Unpaid. Open to college freshmen, college sophomores, college juniors, college seniors. ▶ *1 enterprises intern:* responsibilities include signing, recording, releasing, and marketing comedian's CDs. Candidates should have personal interest in comedy. Duration is 1 semester. Unpaid. Open to college freshmen, college sophomores, college juniors, college seniors. ▶ *1 finance intern.* Duration is 1 semester. Unpaid. ▶ *1–2 human resources interns:* responsibilities include assisting in development of human resources administrative filing system, assisting in various human resources projects, providing general office support, and assisting in development of recruitment database. Candidates should have computer skills, office skills. Duration is 1 semester. Unpaid. Open to college freshmen, college sophomores, college juniors, college seniors. ▶ *1 off-air creative intern.* Duration is 1 semester. Unpaid. ▶ *1–2 on-air creative interns:* responsibilities include providing general office support, assisting at external shoots and screenings, helping production assistants, and assisting on occasional off-lining. Candidates should have strong interpersonal skills, flexible schedule. Duration is 1 semester. Unpaid. Open to college freshmen, college sophomores, college juniors, college seniors. ▶ *Online/enterprise interns:* responsibilities include assisting in updating games horoscopes and videoclips, basic HTML site maintenance, media acquisition of video images, and providing ideas/feedback in site maintenance and development. Candidates should have written communication skills, knowledge of Word, Excel, Explorer, Netscape, HTML, and PhotoShop, some experience in JAVA script and Premiere (preferred). Duration is 1 semester. Unpaid. Open to college freshmen, college sophomores, college juniors, college seniors. ▶ *2–3 production interns:* responsibilities include providing basic office support, copying and labeling various programs for other departments, helping organize program cart sheets, and maintaining prop closet and reel library. Candidates should have ability to work independently, computer skills, oral communication skills, self-motivation, strong interpersonal skills, written communication skills. Duration is 1 semester. Unpaid.

Open to college freshmen, college sophomores, college juniors, college seniors. ▶ *1 programming and acquisitions intern.* Candidates should have personal interest in comedy. Duration is 1 semester. Unpaid. Open to college freshmen, college sophomores, college juniors, college seniors. ▶ *1 talent intern:* responsibilities include working on laugh riots submissions. Candidates should have sense of humor and personal interest in stand-up comedy. Duration is spring semester. Unpaid. Open to college freshmen, college sophomores, college juniors, college seniors.

Benefits On-the-job training, possible full-time employment, willing to act as a professional reference, willing to complete paperwork for educational credit, willing to provide letters of recommendation, small travel stipend, opportunity to attend show tapings and planned intern trips.

Contact Fax or through World Wide Web site Human Resources Coordinator. Fax: 212-767-4257. No phone calls. In-person interview required. Applicants must submit a letter of interest, resume, verification of school credit for internship, statement indicating hours available and department of interest. Applications are accepted continuously. World Wide Web: http://www.comedycentral. com.

C-SPAN
400 North Capitol Street, NW, Suite 650
Washington, District of Columbia 20001

General Information Organization that provides audience access to live gavel-to-gavel proceedings of the U.S. House of Representatives, the U.S. Senate, and to other forums where public policy is discussed, debated, and decided, without editing, commentary, or analysis and with a balanced presentation of points-of-view. Established in 1979. Number of employees: 260.

Internships Available ▶ *1 "Washington Journal" intern:* responsibilities include developing specific live and taped programs for morning program, *The Washington Journal*; greeting guests, setting up studio/green room, follow-up with guests, and research. Candidates should have ability to work independently, computer skills, oral communication skills, personal interest in the field, self-motivation, strong interpersonal skills. Duration is 10–12 weeks. Unpaid. ▶ *1–2 affiliate relations interns:* responsibilities include maintaining and improving carriage of C-SPAN networks among cable affiliates through affiliate promotions and relationships with cable contacts at the corporate level. Candidates should have ability to work independently, computer skills, oral communication skills, personal interest in the field, strong interpersonal skills, written communication skills. Duration is 10–12 weeks. Unpaid. ▶ *1–2 book TV interns:* responsibilities include working with book TV on C-SPAN2 which explores the world of nonfiction books including recently published biographies and historical works, politics or culture, older history books, books about current events and public issues. Candidates should have analytical skills, computer skills, organizational skills, personal interest in the field, research skills, self-motivation. Duration is 10–12 weeks. Unpaid. ▶ *1 community relations intern:* responsibilities include supporting targeted community marketing efforts to cable companies across the country; developing educational materials and outreach programs. Candidates should have ability to work independently, computer skills, oral communication skills, personal interest in the field, strong interpersonal skills, written communication skills. Duration is 10–12 weeks. Unpaid. ▶ *1–2 engineering interns:* responsibilities include being responsible for overall technical quality of C-SPAN's products; working with other departments to purchase and repair technical equipment; tracking new technologies and recommending ways C-SPAN can use these technologies. Candidates should have ability to work independently, ability to work with others, computer skills, editing skills, oral communication skills, organizational skills, personal interest in the field, research skills, self-motivation, writing skills. Duration is 10–12 weeks. Unpaid. ▶ *1–2 field producers:* responsibilities include developing programming ideas by researching specific areas of government, its history and the process, as well as coordinating logistical aspects required in production. Candidates should have analytical skills, computer skills, organizational skills, personal interest in the field, research skills, self-motivation. Duration is 10–12 weeks. Unpaid. ▶ *1–2 human resources interns:* responsibilities include working in

C-SPAN (continued)

benefits, employee records, payroll, and employee relations. Candidates should have ability to work independently, computer skills, editing skills, experience in the field, oral communication skills, organizational skills, research skills, self-motivation, strong interpersonal skills, writing skills. Duration is 10–12 weeks. Unpaid. ▶ *1–2 marketing interns:* responsibilities include providing creative direction and developing support materials that promote the network to cable operators, educators, and viewers; generating ads and publications. Candidates should have computer skills, editing skills, organizational skills, personal interest in the field, self-motivation, writing skills. Duration is 10–12 weeks. Unpaid. ▶ *1–2 media relations interns:* responsibilities include communicating C-SPAN's mission, programming, style, and content to national media outlets. Candidates should have computer skills, office skills, organizational skills, personal interest in the field, research skills, self-motivation. Duration is 10–12 weeks. Unpaid. ▶ *1–2 new media interns:* responsibilities include developing and managing contracts and initiating business relationships relating to C-SPAN products, videotapes, transcripts, and online services. Candidates should have computer skills, editing skills, experience in the field, organizational skills, research skills, writing skills. Duration is 10–12 weeks. Unpaid. ▶ *1–2 programming operations editorial interns:* responsibilities include working with producers in developing daily schedule, tracking House and Senate floor debate, script-writing, voice-overs, scheduling breaks, coordinating final programming that airs on C-SPAN. Candidates should have computer skills, oral communication skills, personal interest in the field, self-motivation, strong interpersonal skills. Duration is 10–12 weeks. Unpaid. ▶ *1–2 programming operations technical interns:* responsibilities include technical aspects of setting the networks on-air, including program direction, master control, camera, lighting, audio and on-air promotions. Candidates should have ability to work with others, knowledge of field, oral communication skills, personal interest in the field, self-motivation, strong leadership ability. Duration is 10–12 weeks. Unpaid. ▶ *1–2 radio interns:* responsibilities include broadcasting a mix of daily programs similar in style to those found on the C-SPAN television networks, including congressional hearings, speeches, debates, and forum discussions. Candidates should have ability to work independently, computer skills, editing skills, oral communication skills, organizational skills, personal interest in the field, research skills, self-motivation, strong interpersonal skills, writing skills. Duration is 10–12 weeks. Unpaid. Open to college juniors, college seniors. International applications accepted.

Benefits Job counseling, names of contacts, possible full-time employment, willing to complete paperwork for educational credit.

Contact Write, call, fax, e-mail, or through World Wide Web site Angela P. Seldon, Human Resources Senior Specialist. Phone: 202-626-4868. Fax: 202-737-3323. E-mail: aseldon@c-span.org. In-person interview recommended (telephone interview accepted). Applicants must submit a letter of interest, resume, interactive application available. Applications are accepted continuously. World Wide Web: http://www.c-span.org.

GW MEDIA GROUP
303 Camarillo
Placentia, California 92870

General Information Television, film, and news production company; portfolio includes: Today's Lifestyles TV Travel Show and Lake Night King's TV Comedy. Established in 1987. Number of employees: 32. Number of internship applications received each year: 70.

Internships Available ▶ *2–4 Web interns:* responsibilities include assisting in maintaining, developing, and updating of the ONTV2 Web site with TV show archives and special guests sites. Candidates should have ability to work independently, editing skills, research skills, self-motivation, writing skills. Duration is 6–8 weeks. Unpaid. Open to recent high school graduates, college freshmen, college sophomores, college juniors, college seniors, recent college graduates, graduate students, career changers, individuals reentering the workforce. ▶ *2–4 field producers:* responsibilities include assisting in developing production segment ideas, researching specific

areas of America's dining and leisure habits, and coordinating logistics needed for productions. Candidates should have ability to work with others, computer skills, personal interest in the field, research skills, writing skills. Duration is 6–8 weeks. Unpaid. Open to recent high school graduates, college freshmen, college sophomores, college juniors, college seniors, graduate students, career changers, individuals reentering the workforce. ▶ *2–4 production interns:* responsibilities include assisting on productions including setup, strike, gaining experience on cameras, audio, and lighting equipment. Candidates should have ability to work with others, personal interest in the field, plan to pursue career in field, research skills. Duration is 6–8 weeks. Unpaid. Open to recent high school graduates, college freshmen, college sophomores, college juniors, college seniors, recent college graduates, graduate students, career changers, individuals reentering the workforce. International applications accepted.

Benefits Formal training, free housing, free meals, job counseling, on-the-job training, opportunity to attend seminars/workshops, possible full-time employment, willing to act as a professional reference, willing to complete paperwork for educational credit, willing to provide letters of recommendation.

Contact Write, e-mail, or through World Wide Web site Gregory Juaren, Operations Supervisor, PO Box 122, Placentia 92870. Phone: 714-381-5464. E-mail: gwmediatv@lycos.com. In-person interview recommended (telephone interview accepted). Applicants must submit a letter of interest, resume, two personal references. Applications are accepted continuously. World Wide Web: http://www.ontv2.com.

HOME BOX OFFICE
1100 Avenue of the Americas, H3
New York, New York 10036

General Information Subscriber-based cable television channel. Established in 1972. Number of employees: 2,000. Unit of AOL Time Warner, Inc., New York, New York. Number of internship applications received each year: 1,500.

Internships Available ▶ *50–75 communications interns:* responsibilities include duties relating to all areas of communications including production, original programming, advertising, marketing, finance, computers, human resources, public relations, accounting, and photography. Candidates should have computer skills, office skills, oral communication skills, personal interest in the field, strong interpersonal skills, writing skills. Duration is 10–12 weeks. Stipend of $500 upon successful completion of internship. ▶ *2–4 human resources interns:* responsibilities include recruiting, reviewing resumes, and conducting phone interviews. Candidates should have ability to work independently, computer skills, office skills, oral communication skills, organizational skills, strong interpersonal skills. Duration is 10–12 weeks. $500 per duration of internship. Open to college sophomores, college juniors, college seniors.

Benefits Possible full-time employment, willing to complete paperwork for educational credit, willing to provide letters of recommendation.

Contact Write, fax, or through World Wide Web site Internship Coordinator, 1100 Avenue of the Americas, New York, New York 10036. Fax: 212-512-1520. No phone calls. In-person interview required. Applicants must submit a letter of interest, resume, formal letter from college or university stating that intern will receive academic credit. Applications are accepted continuously. World Wide Web: http://www.HBO.com.

JAZBO PRODUCTIONS
185 Pier Avenue, Suite 106
Santa Monica, California 90405

General Information Golden Globe-winning feature film and television production company involved in the development of feature films and made-for-television productions for the networks and major studios. Established in 1985. Number of employees: 1. Number of internship applications received each year: 150.

Internships Available ▶ *1–2 assistants to the president:* responsibilities include assisting with general office duties and management of scripts, videotapes, and concept treatments; story analysis of scripts; screening potential projects; Web research and produc-

tion back-up. Candidates should have ability to work independently, computer skills, oral communication skills, organizational skills, self-motivation, written communication skills. Duration is 4–6 months. Unpaid. Open to college sophomores, college juniors, college seniors, recent college graduates, graduate students, law students, career changers, individuals reentering the workforce. **Benefits** Job counseling, names of contacts, on-the-job training, opportunity to attend seminars/workshops, possible full-time employment, willing to act as a professional reference, willing to complete paperwork for educational credit, willing to provide letters of recommendation.
Contact Write, call, fax, or e-mail Ms. Jill Marti, President. Phone: 310-664-6004. Fax: 310-664-3656. E-mail: jazbo.inc@verizon.net. In-person interview recommended. Applicants must submit a formal organization application, letter of interest, resume, personal reference, 2-3 professional references. Applications are accepted continuously.

THE JERRY SPRINGER SHOW
454 North Columbus Drive
Chicago, Illinois 60611

General Information One-hour daily syndicated talk show working its 10th season as one of America's most popular talk shows. Established in 1991. Number of employees: 60. Number of internship applications received each year: 800.
Internships Available ▶ *6–12 production interns:* responsibilities include researching and interviewing prospective guests for the show, researching possible show topics on the Internet and over the phone, being involved in all show day procedures, and working with guests who will be appearing on the program. Candidates should have ability to work with others, oral communication skills, organizational skills, plan to pursue career in field, research skills. Duration is minimum of 3 months (30 hours per week). Unpaid. Open to recent high school graduates, college freshmen, college sophomores, college juniors, college seniors, recent college graduates, graduate students, career changers. ▶ *1 technical intern:* responsibilities include assisting in the control room during taping, working closely with the assistant director on various production elements, production paperwork, assisting the director/ assistant director, stage managers, delivering shows for satellite transmission when necessary. Candidates should have college courses in field, oral communication skills, organizational skills, plan to pursue career in field. Duration is minimum of 3 months (24 hours per week). Unpaid. Open to college freshmen, college sophomores, college juniors, college seniors, recent college graduates. ▶ *10–15 universal interns:* responsibilities include working in various areas including research, audience, production, business office, editing, and viewer mail. Candidates should have ability to work with others, office skills, oral communication skills, plan to pursue career in field. Duration is minimum of 3 months (24 hours per week). Unpaid. Open to recent high school graduates, college freshmen, college sophomores, college juniors, college seniors, recent college graduates. International applications accepted.
Benefits On-the-job training, possible full-time employment, willing to act as a professional reference, willing to complete paperwork for educational credit, willing to provide letters of recommendation.
Contact Write, call, fax, or e-mail Nathan Kotterman, Internship Coordinator. Phone: 312-321-5390. Fax: 312-321-5353. E-mail: springerpa@hotmail.com. In-person interview recommended (telephone interview accepted). Applicants must submit a formal organization application, letter of interest, resume. Applications are accepted continuously. World Wide Web: http://www.jerryspringer.com.

KCRA-TV
3 Television Circle
Sacramento, California 95814

General Information Commercial broadcast television station. Established in 1945. Number of employees: 230. Unit of Hearst-Argyle Television, Inc., New York, New York. Number of internship applications received each year: 100.

Internships Available ▶ *2 commercial production assistants:* responsibilities include production of commercial spots, promotions, public service announcements, and some special programming. Candidates should have college courses in field, computer skills, editing skills, personal interest in the field, research skills, self-motivation. Duration is 1 semester. Unpaid. Open to college sophomores, college juniors, college seniors, recent college graduates, graduate students. ▶ *1 community relations assistant:* responsibilities include providing clerical support for public relations functions and KCRA-TV scholarship program, preparing community calendar, and assisting in production of public affairs programming. Candidates should have ability to work independently, computer skills, office skills, organizational skills, personal interest in the field, strong interpersonal skills, writing skills. Duration is one fall semester. Unpaid. Open to college sophomores, college juniors, college seniors, recent college graduates, graduate students. ▶ *1 consumer reporter assistant:* responsibilities include researching stories, setting up locations, accompanying reporters on assignment, and researching case files and records. Candidates should have college courses in field, computer skills, personal interest in the field, research skills, self-motivation, written communication skills. Duration is 1 semester. Unpaid. Open to college juniors, college seniors, recent college graduates, graduate students. ▶ *2 editing assistants:* responsibilities include working with the engineering supervisor and staff in transferring video and audio reports to master library tapes. Candidates should have ability to work with others, computer skills, oral communication skills, organizational skills, personal interest in the field, self-motivation. Duration is 1 semester. Unpaid. Open to college sophomores, college juniors, college seniors, recent college graduates, graduate students. ▶ *5 general news assistants:* responsibilities include working at the assignment desk answering reporters' phones, researching stories, accompanying reporters and/or photographers on assignments, and assisting news producers with production chores. Candidates should have college courses in field, computer skills, editing skills, personal interest in the field, research skills, written communication skills. Duration is 1 semester. Unpaid. Open to college sophomores, college juniors, college seniors, recent college graduates, graduate students. ▶ *1 graphics assistant:* responsibilities include working with art department in non-broadcast artwork including sales prices, printwork, set building and design, and computer graphics. Candidates should have college courses in field, computer skills, editing skills, plan to pursue career in field, self-motivation. Duration is 1 semester. Unpaid. Open to college sophomores, college juniors, college seniors, recent college graduates, graduate students. ▶ *1–3 news producer assistants:* responsibilities include performing news production functions including tearing scripts, recording and logging news feeds, answering telephones, researching news stories, and writing. Candidates should have ability to work with others, computer skills, personal interest in the field, research skills, self-motivation, written communication skills. Duration is 1 semester. Unpaid. Open to college sophomores, college juniors, college seniors, recent college graduates, graduate students. ▶ *2 news special projects interns:* responsibilities include researching story ideas and assisting reporters and photographers in researching information for series and special projects. Candidates should have computer skills, organizational skills, personal interest in the field, research skills, self-motivation, written communication skills. Duration is 1 semester. Unpaid. Open to college sophomores, college juniors, college seniors, recent college graduates, graduate students. ▶ *1 promotions assistant:* responsibilities include assisting with production of on-air promotional spots including field, studio, and post production work; creating outside media work (newspaper ads and radio spots); and producing public service announcements. Candidates should have ability to work with others, college courses in field, computer skills, plan to pursue career in field, self-motivation. Duration is 1 semester. Unpaid. Open to college sophomores, college juniors, college seniors, recent college graduates, graduate students. ▶ *1 sales assistant:* responsibilities include working on sales research, typing rough formats for sales promotion information; opportunities to accompany account executives on sales calls. Candidates should have computer skills, office skills, organizational skills, personal interest in the field, self-motivation, strong interpersonal skills, writing skills. Duration is 1 semester. Unpaid. Open to col-

KCRA-TV (continued)

lege sophomores, college juniors, college seniors, recent college graduates, graduate students. ▶ *1–3 sports assistants:* responsibilities include compiling scores, researching stories and game information, monitoring televised games, and accompanying reporter and photographer in the field. Duration is 1 semester. Unpaid. Open to college sophomores, college juniors, college seniors, recent college graduates, graduate students.
Benefits On-the-job training, possible full-time employment, willing to complete paperwork for educational credit.
Contact Write, call, fax, or e-mail Julia Seabourn, Newsroom/Internship Program Administrative Assistant. Phone: 916-325-3287. Fax: 916-441-4050. E-mail: jseabourn@hearst.com. In-person interview recommended (telephone interview accepted). Applicants must submit a formal organization application, letter of interest, resume. Application deadline: April 6 for summer, July 13 for fall, November 23 for spring. World Wide Web: http://www.thekcrachannel.com.

KGO TELEVISION ABC, INC.
900 Front Street
San Francisco, California 94111

General Information Television station. Number of employees: 230. Affiliate of Disney–ABC, Inc., New York, New York. Number of internship applications received each year: 100.
Internships Available ▶ *News Research/"Seven On Your Side" interns:* responsibilities include assisting staff with research, collecting information from online services, maintaining news database, following up viewer letters, and other duties as assigned. Candidates should have ability to work independently, oral communication skills, plan to pursue career in field, research skills, written communication skills. Duration is 1 semester. $6.75 per hour. ▶ *Accounting/finance interns:* responsibilities include spreadsheet work; general office support; opportunities to assist with preparation of operation plan, capital budget, and/or annual and quarterly forecasts. Candidates should have ability to work independently, computer skills, knowledge of field, oral communication skills, organizational skills, written communication skills, familiarity with MS Office (helpful). Duration is 1 semester. $6.75 per hour. ▶ *Graphics interns:* responsibilities include visual research; general office support. Candidates should have ability to work independently, computer skills, knowledge of field, oral communication skills, written communication skills, creative talent, sense of humor. Duration is 1 semester. $6.75 per hour. ▶ *Human resources interns:* responsibilities include assisting in daily operations; may include projects in benefits, compensation, and/or recruitment. Candidates should have ability to work independently, oral communication skills, organizational skills, personal interest in the field, strong interpersonal skills, written communication skills, knowledge of MS Word and Excel (helpful). Duration is 1 semester. $6.75 per hour. ▶ *Information systems interns:* responsibilities include providing internal support for desktop applications, operating systems, and network troubleshooting. Candidates should have ability to work independently, analytical skills, computer skills, personal interest in the field, strong interpersonal skills, knowledge of operating systems and Novell NetWare. Duration is 1 semester. $6.75 per hour. ▶ *Marketing research interns:* responsibilities include working with Nielsen overnight reports, keeping track of ratings, creating new graphs, updating programming schedules, and general office duties. Candidates should have ability to work independently, computer skills, oral communication skills, personal interest in the field, written communication skills, attention to detail, knowledge of MS Office (helpful), marketing/research major (preferred). Duration is 1 semester. $6.75 per hour. ▶ *News/assignment desk interns:* responsibilities include monitoring news sources; screening, answering, and following up phone calls; updating source lists, and other duties as assigned. Candidates should have ability to work independently, ability to work with others, oral communication skills, plan to pursue career in field, written communication skills. Duration is 1 semester. $6.75 per hour. ▶ *News/weather interns:* responsibilities include assisting staff with preparation of on-air graphics and information. Candidates should have ability to work independently, computer skills, declared college major in field, oral communication skills, plan to pursue

career in field, written communication skills, familiarity with DIFAX products, domestic data bulletins, and Netscape a plus. Duration is 1 semester. $6.75 per hour. ▶ *On-air promotions interns:* responsibilities include assisting with pre-production duties such as logging tapes, searching for footage, and setting up promo shots; performing supervised edit sessions; assisting as assigned on location; other duties. Candidates should have ability to work independently, knowledge of field, personal interest in the field, strong interpersonal skills, energy and enthusiasm, ability to work well under pressure. Duration is 1 semester. $6.75 per hour. ▶ *Public affairs interns:* responsibilities include assisting community relations manager and director of public affairs; general office correspondence; selecting and writing 10 Second Community Calendar announcements; other duties as assigned. Candidates should have ability to work independently, oral communication skills, personal interest in the field, strong interpersonal skills, writing skills. Duration is 1 semester. $6.75 per hour. ▶ *Sales interns:* responsibilities include assisting in daily operations of broadcast sales office; general office support. Candidates should have ability to work independently, computer skills, oral communication skills, personal interest in the field, written communication skills, attention to detail, knowledge of Windows (helpful), marketing/communications major (preferred). Duration is 1 semester. $6.75 per hour. ▶ *Sports interns:* responsibilities include assisting the staff in daily operations, which may include watching and logging televised games, reviewing sports footage, and general office support. Candidates should have knowledge of field, oral communication skills, organizational skills, personal interest in the field, strong interpersonal skills, written communication skills. Duration is 1 semester. $6.75 per hour. Open to college juniors, college seniors, graduate students. International applications accepted.
Benefits On-the-job training, willing to complete paperwork for educational credit.
Contact Call Carrie L. Hess, Human Resources Administrator. Phone: 415-954-7774. Fax: 415-954-7514. E-mail: carrie.hess@abc.com. In-person interview required. Applicants must submit a formal organization application, letter of interest, resume, academic transcripts, two letters of recommendation. Applications are accepted continuously. World Wide Web: http://www.abc7news.com.

KGTV/SAN DIEGO'S 10
4600 Air Way
San Diego, California 92102

General Information Broadcasting television station whose main goal is to provide a sense of leadership to the citizens of the San Diego community. Established in 1953. Number of employees: 75. Affiliate of McGraw-Hill Companies, New York, New York. Number of internship applications received each year: 180.
Internships Available ▶ *1–3 sales/research interns:* responsibilities include working in research and sales departments and being involved with the Neilson overnights, program schedule, creating sales presentations, and learning about the advertising aspects of television. Candidates should have ability to work independently, computer skills, organizational skills, personal interest in the field, plan to pursue career in field, strong interpersonal skills. Duration is 12–15 weeks. Unpaid. Open to college freshmen, college sophomores, college juniors, college seniors, graduate students, must be earning school credit. International applications accepted.
Benefits Meals at a cost, names of contacts, on-the-job training, possible full-time employment, willing to act as a professional reference, willing to complete paperwork for educational credit, willing to provide letters of recommendation.
Contact Write, fax, e-mail, or through World Wide Web site Alex Welch, Local Sales Assistant. Fax: 619-266-2296. E-mail: alex_welch@kgtv.com. No phone calls. In-person interview recommended (telephone interview accepted). Applicants must submit a letter of interest, resume. Applications are accepted continuously. World Wide Web: http://www.thesandiegochannel.com.

KQED INC.
2601 Mariposa Street
San Francisco, California 94110

General Information Public broadcasting company that includes KQED-TV and KQED-FM. Established in 1954. Number of employees: 230. Number of internship applications received each year: 100.

Internships Available ▶ *1 KQED Media Education Project intern:* responsibilities include working at the Center for Education and Lifelong Learning on such tasks as writing/editing publications, researching media, dubbing videotapes, and developing educational workshops. Candidates should have ability to work independently, computer skills, oral communication skills, research skills, written communication skills, minimum GPA of 2.5, experience with PC or Macintosh word processing and desktop publishing applications, Spanish skills a plus. Duration is flexible, minimum of 15 hours per week. Unpaid. ▶ *1 KQED TV Web intern:* responsibilities include participating in maintenance and development of the CELL Web site, researching and updating content, assisting program development staff and Web manager. Candidates should have ability to work independently, oral communication skills, organizational skills, written communication skills, minimum GPA of 2.5, strong computer skills including HTML programming, desktop publishing, and telecommunications. Duration is flexible, typically 4 months in spring, fall, or summer. Unpaid. ▶ *1 KQED TV program publicity intern:* responsibilities include assisting the publicist, filing program information and press clips, proofreading, research, writing, and organizing and preparing mailings. Candidates should have oral communication skills, organizational skills, self-motivation, strong interpersonal skills, writing skills, minimum GPA of 2.5, attention to detail, flexibility, Macintosh and/or PC proficiency, humor and enthusiasm. Duration is 1 semester (15-20 hours per week). Unpaid. ▶ *2 KQED educational services interns:* responsibilities include working in KQED's Center for Education and Lifelong Learning, writing and editing publications, doing audience research, developing educational content, and facilitating outreach activities. Candidates should have ability to work independently, computer skills, oral communication skills, research skills, self-motivation, written communication skills, major in education or related experience (preferred), Spanish skills a plus, knowledge of word processing and desktop publishing desirable, minimum GPA of 2.5. Duration is flexible, minimum of 15 hours. Unpaid. ▶ *1 KQED human resources intern:* responsibilities include developing effective communication techniques, HTML Web maintenance, events planning, employee relations, diversity training, benefits administration, recruiting, and customer services. Candidates should have computer skills, oral communication skills, organizational skills, self-motivation, writing skills, minimum GPA of 2.5, major in liberal arts, strong English and grammatical skills. Duration is flexible (16-24 hours per week); typically 4 months in spring, fall, or summer. Unpaid. ▶ *2 KQED-FM news interns:* responsibilities include researching, reporting, sound gathering, producing news and feature stories, and attending seminars and workshops on a variety of topics. Candidates should have oral communication skills, strong interpersonal skills, written communication skills, minimum GPA of 2.5, major in journalism, communications, or broadcasting, or strong writing experience. Duration is 4 months, minimum of 16-24 hours per week. Unpaid. Open to college juniors, college seniors, graduate students. International applications accepted.

Benefits Formal training, job counseling, names of contacts, opportunity to attend seminars/workshops, willing to complete paperwork for educational credit.

Contact Write, fax, e-mail, or through World Wide Web site Katherine Yamamoto, Labor Relations Manager. Fax: 415-553-2183. E-mail: hr@kqed.org. No phone calls. In-person interview recommended (telephone interview accepted). Applicants must submit a letter of interest, resume, proof of eligibility to receive college credit; women and minorities strongly encouraged to apply. Applications are accepted continuously. World Wide Web: http://www.kqed.org/HR.

KSDK NEWS CHANNEL 5
1000 Market Street
St. Louis, Missouri 63101

General Information NBC-affiliated news source for St. Louis. Established in 1947. Number of employees: 155. Unit of Gannett, Arlington, Virginia. Number of internship applications received each year: 400.

Internships Available ▶ *1 assignment desk intern:* responsibilities include answering phones and making calls, primary story research. Candidates should have ability to work independently, college courses in field, computer skills, knowledge of field, oral communication skills, organizational skills, personal interest in the field, plan to pursue career in field, research skills, self-motivation, strong interpersonal skills, written communication skills. Duration is flexible by semester. Unpaid. Open to college freshmen, college sophomores, college juniors, college seniors, graduate students. ▶ *1 community relations/news intern:* responsibilities include working on projects for community relations department as well as news. Candidates should have ability to work independently, analytical skills, college courses in field, computer skills, knowledge of field, oral communication skills, organizational skills, personal interest in the field, plan to pursue career in field, research skills, self-motivation, strong interpersonal skills, strong leadership ability, written communication skills. Duration is flexible. Unpaid. Open to college freshmen, college sophomores, college juniors, college seniors. ▶ *1 program/magazine show intern:* responsibilities include assisting with production of *Show Me St. Louis.* Candidates should have ability to work independently, ability to work with others, college courses in field, computer skills, knowledge of field, oral communication skills, organizational skills, personal interest in the field, plan to pursue career in field, research skills, self-motivation, strong leadership ability, written communication skills. Duration is flexible. Unpaid. Open to college freshmen, college sophomores, college juniors, college seniors, graduate students. ▶ *1 research/special projects intern:* responsibilities include working on various stories, working as reporters' assistants, and working with producers. Candidates should have ability to work independently, ability to work with others, college courses in field, computer skills, knowledge of field, oral communication skills, organizational skills, personal interest in the field, plan to pursue career in field, research skills, self-motivation, written communication skills. Duration is flexible by semester. Unpaid. Open to college freshmen, college sophomores, college juniors, college seniors, graduate students. ▶ *1 sports intern:* responsibilities include researching sports stories and tracking games. Candidates should have ability to work independently, ability to work with others, college courses in field, computer skills, knowledge of field, oral communication skills, organizational skills, personal interest in the field, research skills, self-motivation, written communication skills. Duration is flexible by semester. Unpaid. Open to college freshmen, college sophomores, college juniors, college seniors, graduate students. International applications accepted.

Benefits Formal training, job counseling, names of contacts, on-the-job training, opportunity to attend seminars/workshops, possible full-time employment, willing to act as a professional reference, willing to complete paperwork for educational credit, willing to provide letters of recommendation, mileage reimbursement while on assignment.

Contact Write, call, fax, e-mail, or through World Wide Web site Ava Ehrlich, Executive Producer. Phone: 314-444-5120. Fax: 314-444-5164. E-mail: aehrlich@ksdk.gannett.com. In-person interview recommended (telephone interview accepted). Applicants must submit a letter of interest, resume, academic transcripts, letter of recommendation, 3 writing samples (broadcast). Application deadline: March 10 for summer/fall, December 1 for winter/spring. World Wide Web: http://ksdk.com.

KTLA-TV
5800 Sunset Boulevard
Los Angeles, California 90028

General Information Broadcast company. Number of employees: 358. Unit of Tribune Company, Chicago, Illinois. Number of internship applications received each year: 500.

KTLA-TV (continued)

Internships Available ► *2 human resources interns:* responsibilities include recruiting next term's interns (recruiting, screening, interviews), job fairs, and various office work. Candidates should have computer skills, office skills, personal interest in the field, self-motivation. Duration is 2 to 3 months (10 to 20 hours per week). Unpaid. Open to college sophomores, college juniors, college seniors. ► *10–25 news interns:* responsibilities include getting daily live broadcast on air, assisting with material and tapes (coordinating, locating, organizing); involves areas of sports, news, and entertainment. Candidates should have college courses in field, knowledge of field, personal interest in the field, self-motivation, strong interpersonal skills. Duration is 2.5 to 3.5 months (10 to 20 hours per week). Unpaid. Open to college sophomores, college juniors, college seniors, recent college graduates, career changers. ► *2–6 sales interns:* responsibilities include scheduling and airing of commercials; overlaps with marketing. Candidates should have personal interest in the field, self-motivation, strong interpersonal skills. Duration is 2 to 3 months (10 to 20 hours per week). Unpaid. Open to college freshmen, college sophomores, college juniors, college seniors. International applications accepted.

Benefits Names of contacts, opportunity to attend seminars/workshops, willing to act as a professional reference, willing to complete paperwork for educational credit, willing to provide letters of recommendation.

Contact Call, fax, or e-mail Human Resources. Phone: 323-460-5540. Fax: 323-460-5527. E-mail: ktla-hr@tribune.com. In-person interview recommended (telephone interview accepted). Applicants must submit a letter of interest, resume, letter of recommendation, documentation of eligibility to receive class credit. Application deadline: April 15 for summer, July 15 for fall, December 15 for spring. World Wide Web: http://www.ktla.com.

KUED-TV
101 Wasatch Drive, University of Utah
Salt Lake City, Utah 84112

General Information Television station whose goal is to be a vital community resource in the areas of public discourse, education, community service, and the arts by providing alternative, noncommercial television programs that educate, enlighten, and entertain. Established in 1958. Number of employees: 107. Unit of University of Utah, Salt Lake City, Utah. Number of internship applications received each year: 10.

Internships Available ► *1 intern:* responsibilities include performing studio and field production lighting, audio work, off- and on-line editing; and rotating among administrative, development, and creative services departments. Candidates should have college courses in field, knowledge of field, oral communication skills, organizational skills, personal interest in the field, strong interpersonal skills, written communication skills. Duration is 1 summer. $1500 per duration of internship. Open to college juniors, college seniors. International applications accepted.

Benefits Formal training.

Contact Write or e-mail Christy Dunn, Human Resources Officer. E-mail: cdunn@media.utah.edu. No phone calls. In-person interview required. Applicants must submit a letter of interest, resume. Application deadline: April 24. World Wide Web: http://www.media.utah.edu.

KVIE-TV
PO Box 6, 2595 Capitol Oaks Drive
Sacramento, California 95833

General Information Public television station serving the nation's 21st-largest media market; covers Sacramento, CA and 28 surrounding counties; strives to educate, enlighten, and entertain its viewers and members. Established in 1959. Number of employees: 91. Number of internship applications received each year: 50.

Internships Available ► *1–3 local production interns:* responsibilities include research on the Internet and phone interviews. Candidates should have ability to work independently, ability to work with others, computer skills, oral communication skills,

research skills, written communication skills. Duration is flexible (at least 2 months). Unpaid. Open to college freshmen, college sophomores, college juniors, college seniors, recent college graduates, graduate students, career changers, individuals reentering the workforce. ► *1 marketing and public relations assistant:* responsibilities include distributing media material, demographic and statistical research, Web page maintenance, filing, and data input. Candidates should have ability to work independently, computer skills, oral communication skills, organizational skills, personal interest in the field, research skills, self-motivation, strong interpersonal skills, written communication skills. Duration is flexible. Unpaid. Open to college freshmen, college sophomores, college juniors, college seniors. ► *1–2 outreach assistants:* responsibilities include assisting the coordinator in planning RTL workshops and outreach events, community contact, drafting letters, data entry, assisting with newsletter, drafting forms, and project evaluations. Candidates should have ability to work independently, computer skills, office skills, oral communication skills, organizational skills, personal interest in the field, research skills, self-motivation, strong interpersonal skills, written communication skills. Duration is flexible. Unpaid. Open to high school seniors, recent high school graduates, college freshmen, college sophomores, college juniors, college seniors, recent college graduates, career changers, individuals reentering the workforce. ► *3–5 production interns:* responsibilities include assisting with productions and membership drives. Candidates should have ability to work independently, college courses in field, computer skills, office skills, oral communication skills, personal interest in the field, plan to pursue career in field, research skills, self-motivation, strong interpersonal skills, writing skills. Duration is flexible. Unpaid. Open to college freshmen, college sophomores, college juniors, college seniors. ► *3–5 research/production interns:* responsibilities include office work and researching for productions and membership drives. Candidates should have ability to work independently, computer skills, office skills, oral communication skills, organizational skills, research skills, self-motivation, writing skills. Duration is flexible. Unpaid. Open to college freshmen, college sophomores, college juniors, college seniors. ► *1–2 special events interns:* responsibilities include assisting with organizing and implementing special events and on-air auctions including follow-up with donors, speakers, and vendors; solicitation of items for auction(s); preparing written correspondence; helping with set-up and tear-down of events; and graphic and Web design. Candidates should have ability to work independently, computer skills, office skills, oral communication skills, organizational skills, personal interest in the field, research skills, self-motivation, strong interpersonal skills, written communication skills. Duration is flexible. Unpaid. Open to college freshmen, college sophomores, college juniors, college seniors.

Benefits Formal training, job counseling, names of contacts, on-the-job training, opportunity to attend seminars/workshops, possible full-time employment, willing to act as a professional reference, willing to complete paperwork for educational credit, willing to provide letters of recommendation, reimbursement of work-related travel expenses.

Contact Write, call, fax, e-mail, or through World Wide Web site Ms. Lillian Nelson, Volunteer Intern Coordinator. Phone: 916-641-3593. Fax: 916-929-7215. E-mail: lnelson@kvie.org. In-person interview recommended (telephone interview accepted). Applicants must submit a letter of interest, resume, personal reference. Applications are accepted continuously. World Wide Web: http://www.kvie.org.

LATE SHOW WITH DAVID LETTERMAN
1697 Broadway
New York, New York 10019

General Information Nightly talk/comedy/variety program. Established in 1993. Number of employees: 90. Unit of Worldwide Pants Incorporated, New York, New York. Number of internship applications received each year: 750.

Internships Available ► *14–15 interns:* responsibilities include working with specific departments including writing, production, talent, research, music, finance, and audience development, mailroom/audio department and as a floater. Candidates should have office skills, oral communication skills, organizational skills, plan to pursue career in field, strong interpersonal skills. Duration is approximately 3-4 months (depending on semester). Unpaid. Open to college sophomores, college juniors, college seniors. International applications accepted.

Benefits Names of contacts, on-the-job training, possible full-time employment, willing to act as a professional reference, willing to complete paperwork for educational credit, willing to provide letters of recommendation, exposure to a nationally-aired TV production.

Contact Write, call, or fax Janice Penino, Director, Human Resources. Phone: 212-975-5806. Fax: 212-975-4734. In-person interview required. Applicants must submit a resume, must be receiving college credit. Application deadline: March 1 for summer, June 1 for fall, October 1 for spring. World Wide Web: http://www.cbs.com.

MIDLAND COMMUNITY TELEVISION NETWORK
1710 West St. Andrews
Midland, Michigan 48640

General Information Public access, government access, television station. Number of employees: 6. Unit of City of Midland, Midland, Michigan. Number of internship applications received each year: 6.

Internships Available ▶ *1–2 video production assistants:* responsibilities include working in shooting (camera), editing, multi-camera directing. Candidates should have ability to work independently, ability to work with others, computer skills, knowledge of field, plan to pursue career in field, degree in broadcasting. Duration is one year (July to July). $7–$8 per hour. Open to recent college graduates.

Benefits On-the-job training, opportunity to attend seminars/workshops, willing to act as a professional reference, willing to complete paperwork for educational credit, willing to provide letters of recommendation.

Contact Write, call, or e-mail Ron Beacom, Director. Phone: 989-837-3474. Fax: 989-837-3478. E-mail: rbeacom@midland-mi.org. In-person interview recommended (telephone interview accepted). Applicants must submit a resume, videotape. Applications are accepted continuously.

THE NEWSHOUR WITH JIM LEHRER/PBS
3620 South 27th Street
Arlington, Virginia 22202

General Information Public television's nightly newscast. Established in 1975. Number of employees: 150. Unit of MacNeil/Lehrer Productions, Arlington, Virginia. Number of internship applications received each year: 250.

Internships Available ▶ *7 broadcast desk assistants:* responsibilities include producing a nightly television news program in the areas of research, newsdesk, wires, and setup unit. Candidates should have office skills, oral communication skills, organizational skills, plan to pursue career in field, research skills, strong interpersonal skills. Duration is 6 months (January-July or July-January). $8 per hour plus overtime. ▶ *1 online desk assistant:* responsibilities include organizing and distributing show transcripts and viewer mail, encoding transcripts into HTML, digitizing audio, updating Web site indexes, and assisting editorial and production staff with several projects. Candidates should have computer skills, organizational skills, plan to pursue career in field, strong interpersonal skills, writing skills. Duration is 6 months. $8.50 per hour. Open to recent college graduates, career changers. International applications accepted.

Benefits Possible full-time employment, willing to act as a professional reference, willing to provide letters of recommendation, breakfast meetings with senior producers, on-air correspondents, and reporters twice a month.

Contact Write, call, or through World Wide Web site Desk Assistant Coordinator. Phone: 703-998-2150. Fax: 703-998-4154. In-person interview recommended (telephone interview accepted). Applicants must submit a formal organization application, letter of interest, resume, writing sample, 3 personal references or letters of recommendation. Application deadline: May 1 for July-January, November 1 for January-July. World Wide Web: http://www.pbs.org/newshour.

NJN, THE NEW JERSEY NETWORK
25 South Stockton Street, PO Box 777
Trenton, New Jersey 08625-0777

General Information Public television company. Established in 1970. Number of employees: 160. Number of internship applications received each year: 250.

Internships Available ▶ *30–35 interns:* responsibilities include researching and setting up field reports, working the news desk and crew logistics, compiling and archiving news video, interviewing newsmakers in the field (for advanced interns), and acting as production assistants. Candidates should have ability to work independently, college courses in field, computer skills, editing skills, office skills, oral communication skills, personal interest in the field, plan to pursue career in field, research skills, self-motivation, strong interpersonal skills, written communication skills, experience in field (preferred). Duration is flexible, usually 15 hours per week (year-round). Unpaid. Open to college freshmen, college sophomores, college juniors, college seniors, career changers. International applications accepted.

Benefits On-the-job training, opportunity to attend seminars/workshops, possible full-time employment, willing to act as a professional reference, willing to complete paperwork for educational credit, willing to provide letters of recommendation.

Contact Write, call, fax, e-mail, or through World Wide Web site Steve McPhillips, Director, Human Resources. Phone: 609-777-5014. Fax: 609-633-0254. E-mail: smcphil@njn.org. Applicants must submit a letter of interest, resume, writing sample, in-person interview recommended. Applications are accepted continuously. World Wide Web: http://www.njn.net.

PUBLIC INTEREST VIDEO NETWORK
6308 Tone Drive
Bethesda, Maryland 20817

General Information Media center producing public television documentaries and assisting issue-oriented nonprofit organizations and government agencies in using the media. Established in 1979. Number of employees: 3. Number of internship applications received each year: 10.

Internships Available ▶ *2 production assistants:* responsibilities include assisting producer/director in field production, research, editing, graphics, distribution, and office-related matters. Candidates should have ability to work independently, ability to work with others, editing skills, office skills, research skills, self-motivation, written communication skills, Media-100 video editing, PhotoShop, After Affects, and Mac computer experience a plus. Duration is 3 or more months. Unpaid. Open to college sophomores, college juniors, college seniors, recent college graduates, graduate students, career changers. International applications accepted.

Benefits Job counseling, names of contacts, on-the-job training, possible full-time employment, travel reimbursement, willing to act as a professional reference, willing to complete paperwork for educational credit, willing to provide letters of recommendation, filming on location across the U.S.

Contact Write, call, fax, e-mail, or through World Wide Web site Mr. Arlen Slobodow, Director. Phone: 301-263-1110. Fax: 301-320-4929. E-mail: info@publicinterestvideo.com. In-person interview recommended (telephone interview accepted). Applicants must submit a letter of interest, resume, three personal references. Application deadline: March 1 for summer (recommended deadline); continuous for academic year positions. World Wide Web: http://www.publicinterestvideo.com.

RADIO & TELEVISION NEWS DIRECTORS FOUNDATION
1600 K Street, NW, #700
Washington, District of Columbia 20006

General Information Nonprofit foundation. Number of employees: 12. Unit of Radio & Television News Directors Foundation, Washington, District of Columbia. Number of internship applications received each year: 50.

Internships Available ▶ *2 Capitol Hill interns:* responsibilities include following newsworthy congressional activities and helping to coordinate broadcast coverage of these activities. Candidates

Radio & Television News Directors Foundation (continued)
should have college courses in field, knowledge of field, personal interest in the field, plan to pursue career in field, self-motivation, written communication skills. Duration is March to May or June to August. $1000 per month. Open to recent college graduates, graduate students. International applications accepted.

Benefits Names of contacts, on-the-job training, opportunity to attend seminars/workshops, possible full-time employment.

Contact Write, call, e-mail, or through World Wide Web site Karen Jackson Bullitt, Program Coordinator, 1600 K Street, NW, #700, Washington, District of Columbia 20006. Phone: 202-467-5218. Fax: 202-223-4007. E-mail: karenb@rtndf.org. Applicants must submit a formal organization application, resume, three letters of recommendation. Application deadline: January 12 for spring, April 4 for summer. World Wide Web: http://www.rtndf.org.

SCI FI CHANNEL
100 Universal City Plaza, Building 1440, 32nd Floor
Universal City, California 91608

General Information Company that develops and distributes television programming. Established in 1992. Number of employees: 20. Division of Vivendi Universal, Universal City, California. Number of internship applications received each year: 100.

Internships Available ▶ *5–10 television development/programming interns:* responsibilities include sitting in on development meetings with writers and producers, watching tapes, reading scripts, research, phones, filing, copying, faxing, and other various duties. Candidates should have desire for career as a TV development executive or TV producer. Duration is Flexible (year-round openings). Unpaid. Open to college freshmen, college sophomores, college juniors, college seniors, graduate students. International applications accepted.

Benefits On-the-job training, opportunity to attend seminars/workshops, willing to act as a professional reference, willing to complete paperwork for educational credit, willing to provide letters of recommendation, opportunity to attend meetings with writers and producers.

Contact Write, call, fax, or e-mail Zig Gauthier, Vice President, Alternative Programming. Phone: 818-777-6957. Fax: 818-866-1420. E-mail: zig.gauthier@unistudios.com. In-person interview recommended (telephone interview accepted). Applicants must submit a resume. Applications are accepted continuously. World Wide Web: http://www.scifi.com.

SESAME WORKSHOP
One Lincoln Plaza
New York, New York 10023

General Information Not-for-profit company using media to educate children and families worldwide; sponsors programs for traditional and new media; engages in publishing, product licensing, and community outreach; producer of Sesame Street. Established in 1969. Number of employees: 350. Number of internship applications received each year: 500.

Internships Available ▶ *10–20 interns:* responsibilities include working in book publishing, graphic design, administrative, and various production departments. Candidates should have ability to work independently, analytical skills, college courses in field, editing skills, knowledge of field, office skills, oral communication skills, organizational skills, personal interest in the field, plan to pursue career in field, research skills, self-motivation, strong interpersonal skills, strong leadership ability, writing skills, knowledge of Microsoft Office, PhotoShop, Quark, Mac, PC. Duration is 3 months. Daily stipend. Open to college freshmen, college sophomores, college juniors, college seniors, graduate students, law students, must be currently enrolled in college or university. International applications accepted.

Benefits Opportunity to attend seminars/workshops, possible full-time employment, willing to act as a professional reference, willing to complete paperwork for educational credit, willing to provide letters of recommendation.

Contact Write, fax, or e-mail Internship Coordinator, One Lincoln Plaza, Fourth Floor, New York, New York 10023. Fax: 212-875-6113. E-mail: human.resources@sesameworkshop.org. No phone calls. In-person interview recommended (telephone interview accepted). Applicants must submit a letter of interest, resume, letter from advisor confirming school enrollment. Application deadline: April 1 for summer, August 1 for fall, December 1 for spring/winter. World Wide Web: http://www.sesameworkshop.org.

STUDIO ONE
4300 Dartmouth Drive, PO Box 7307
Grand Forks, North Dakota 58202

General Information One-hour broadcast in which students produce news, weather, sports, and entertainment segments and interview guests ranging from local people to international celebrities. Established in 1987. Number of employees: 35. Division of University of North Dakota Television Center, Grand Forks, North Dakota. Number of internship applications received each year: 120.

Internships Available ▶ *Assistant news directors:* responsibilities include serving on the Studio One Executive Council, the Board of Directors, and providing leadership to the news team; working with the news director to make decisions about stories and newscast content. Candidates should have ability to work with others, knowledge of field, oral communication skills, organizational skills, strong leadership ability, ability to project a professional presence on television. Duration is 1 semester. Unpaid. Open to college freshmen, college sophomores, college juniors, college seniors, recent college graduates, graduate students, law students. ▶ *6–8 marketing staff interns:* responsibilities include building an audience, promoting the show, working with guests during the live show production, and assisting with recruiting. Candidates should have knowledge of field, oral communication skills, organizational skills, strong interpersonal skills, written communication skills. Duration is 1 semester. Unpaid. Open to college freshmen, college sophomores, college juniors, college seniors, recent college graduates, graduate students, law students, career changers. ▶ *News anchors:* responsibilities include working as a field reporter and presenting the news during the live telecast. Candidates should have knowledge of field, oral communication skills, research skills, strong interpersonal skills, strong leadership ability, written communication skills. Duration is 1 semester. Unpaid. Open to college sophomores, college juniors, college seniors, recent college graduates. ▶ *8–10 photographers:* responsibilities include shooting and editing tape segments for members of the news and programming teams; working with the news director and executive director. Candidates should have oral communication skills, organizational skills, strong interpersonal skills, written communication skills, ability to remain positive during challenging situations. Duration is 1 semester. Unpaid. Open to college freshmen, college sophomores, college juniors, college seniors, recent college graduates, graduate students, law students, career changers. International applications accepted.

Benefits Formal training, on-the-job training, opportunity to attend seminars/workshops, willing to act as a professional reference, willing to complete paperwork for educational credit, willing to provide letters of recommendation.

Contact Write, call, fax, e-mail, or through World Wide Web site Lori Shafer, Internship Coordinator. Phone: 701-777-2489. Fax: 701-777-4342. E-mail: lori_shafer@und.edu. In-person interview required. Application deadline: March 14 for fall, November 1 for spring. World Wide Web: http://www.und.edu/dept/studio1.

THINKTVNETWORK/GREATER DAYTON PUBLIC TELEVISION
110 South Jefferson Street
Dayton, Ohio 45402-2415

General Information Television station comprising 2 public broadcasting stations: WPTD and WPTO. Established in 1959. Number of employees: 50. Number of internship applications received each year: 15.

Internships Available ▶ *3–4 interns:* responsibilities include working in areas of production, engineering, or marketing/administration. Candidates should have ability to work independently, computer skills, editing skills, office skills, oral communication skills, organizational skills, personal interest in the field, plan to pursue career in field, research skills, self-motivation, strong interpersonal skills, writing skills, experience or college courses in field. Duration is flexible. $6–$7 per hour. Open to college juniors, college seniors.

Benefits Formal training, names of contacts, possible full-time employment, willing to complete paperwork for educational credit, willing to provide letters of recommendation.

Contact Write, fax, or e-mail Ms. Jennifer Casson, Office and Personnel Manager. Fax: 937-220-1642. E-mail: jennifer_casson@wptd.pbs.org. No phone calls. In-person interview required. Applicants must submit a formal organization application, letter of interest, resume. Applications are accepted continuously. World Wide Web: http://www.thinktv.org.

TURNER BROADCASTING SYSTEM, INC.
1 CNN Center, 9 North
Atlanta, Georgia 30303

General Information News, entertainment, and sports company. Established in 1970. Number of employees: 15,000. Subsidiary of AOL Time Warner, Inc., New York, New York. Number of internship applications received each year: 500.

Internships Available ▶ *News, entertainment, sports interns:* responsibilities include opportunities as described on Web site. Candidates should have oral communication skills, personal interest in the field, strong interpersonal skills, written communication skills. Duration is 3–4 months. Unpaid. Open to college juniors, college seniors, graduate students. International applications accepted.

Benefits Names of contacts, opportunity to attend seminars/workshops, willing to complete paperwork for educational credit.

International Internships Available in Brussels, Belgium; Rio de Janeiro, Brazil; Santiago, Chile; Bejing, China; Cairo, Egypt; Paris, France; Berlin, Germany; Hong Kong; New Delhi, India; Jerusalem, Israel; Rome, Italy; Tokyo, Japan; Nairobi, Kenya; Mexico City, Mexico; Manila, Philippines; Seoul, Republic of Korea; Moscow, Russian Federation; London, United Kingdom.

Contact Through World Wide Web site Internship Coordinator. No phone calls. Telephone interview required. Applicants must submit a formal organization application, letter of interest, resume, three personal references. Application deadline: March 1 for summer, August 15 for fall, November 15 for spring. World Wide Web: http://www.turnerjobs.com.

VIACOM CORP.
1170 Soldiers Field Road
Boston, Massachusetts 02134

General Information Broadcast television and AM–FM radio stations serving the Boston area. Established in 1921. Number of employees: 300. Affiliate of Viacom Corp., New York, New York. Number of internship applications received each year: 200.

Internships Available ▶ *1–2 BZ Productions interns:* responsibilities include learning how commercials and promotional spots are made, field and studio production skills, post- production techniques, and an overview of writing, directing, producing and editing; learning the terminology and uses of production equipment, logging and labeling tapes, and organizing production office, working closely with the TV Sales Department. Candidates should have knowledge of field, oral communication skills, organizational skills, personal interest in the field, self-motivation, strong interpersonal skills. Duration is 1 semester (Monday through Friday). Unpaid. Open to college sophomores, college juniors, college seniors, graduate students. ▶ *1–2 Centro interns:* responsibilities include researching future show topics working with community groups, and translating segments from English to Spanish. Candidates should have editing skills, oral communication skills, research skills, written communication skills, knowledge of Spanish language. Duration is 1 semester. Unpaid. Open to college sophomores, college juniors, college seniors, graduate students. ▶ *1–3 WBZ Newsradio: news interns:* responsibilities include assisting WBZ Newsradio news department in news gathering, writing, audio production, and administration. Days needed: Monday-Friday 8am-11pm, plus possible weekend work (flexible). Candidates should have oral communication skills, personal interest in the field, research skills, self-motivation, strong interpersonal skills,

written communication skills. Duration is 1 semester (flexible from Monday through Friday, 8am to 11pm , plus possible weekend work). Unpaid. Open to college sophomores, college juniors, college seniors, graduate students. ▶ *1–4 WBZ-TV News: Assignment Desk interns:* responsibilities include assisting assignment editors, reporters, and producers in gathering news stories, pre-interviewing, researching, viewing/logging tapes, and extensive phone work to help cultivate news stories. Candidates should have oral communication skills, personal interest in the field, research skills, self-motivation, strong interpersonal skills, ability to work in a hectic environment. Duration is 1 semester (variable weekdays, nights, weekends). Unpaid. Open to college sophomores, college juniors, college seniors, graduate students. ▶ *1–3 WBZ-TV News: I-Team interns:* responsibilities include documenting research, pre-interviewing subjects, taking telephone tips, researching and developing tips, and logging tapes. Candidates should have ability to work independently, computer skills, office skills, oral communication skills, personal interest in the field, research skills, strong interpersonal skills, written communication skills. Duration is 1 semester (Monday through Friday). Unpaid. Open to college sophomores, college juniors, college seniors, graduate students. ▶ *1–3 WBZ-TV: promotions/creative services interns:* responsibilities include learning how a TV station uses their own air to achieve strategic marketing goals and objectives; learning the logistics and language of promotion; gaining a working knowledge of television production, from the creative writing process, to field producing, to post production in the edit room; learning how to develop and execute news topicals, news serials, and public service announcement. Days needed: Monday-Friday. Candidates should have computer skills, office skills, oral communication skills, personal interest in the field, strong interpersonal skills, writing skills. Duration is 1 semester (Monday through Friday). Unpaid. Open to college sophomores, college juniors, college seniors, graduate students. ▶ *1 arts and entertainment intern:* responsibilities include researching stories, organizing A&E incoming correspondence, responding to phone calls and press releases, and coordinating Web site information. Candidates should have ability to work independently, office skills, oral communication skills, organizational skills, research skills, writing skills. Duration is 1 semester. Unpaid. Open to college sophomores, college juniors, college seniors, graduate students. ▶ *1–2 consumer unit/health interns:* responsibilities include assisting in story development and research, handling viewer phone calls and mail, logging tapes, and assisting on field shoots. Candidates should have computer skills, oral communication skills, organizational skills, personal interest in the field, research skills, written communication skills. Duration is 1 semester. Unpaid. Open to college sophomores, college juniors, college seniors, recent college graduates. ▶ *1 news media (Web) intern:* responsibilities include assisting Webmaster in site development, design, and upkeep; learning how Web site content is maintained and updated; using HTML; helping design graphics for the site; learning how ad space is used by the sales departments; answering or forwarding numerous daily e-mail requests; developing skills in current Web design/publishing software, including Adobe PhotoShop, Allair HomeSite, Netscape Navigator/Communicator, Microsoft Internet Explorer, and Microsoft Office. Candidates should have computer skills, knowledge of field, personal interest in the field, self-motivation, strong interpersonal skills, HTML experience. Duration is 1 semester (Monday through Friday). Unpaid. Open to college sophomores, college juniors, college seniors, graduate students. ▶ *1–2 public relations/affairs interns:* responsibilities include writing and maintaining updated biographies, photos, and press materials; tracking station press coverage for monthly reports; scheduling speaking engagements for talent; coordinating publicity elements of special events and broadcasts including telethons, network, and syndication talent visits; assisting in planning and execution of photo shoots; distributing press releases to media and maintaining the media database; updating and coordinating materials for the station's Web site with the Webmaster. Candidates should have ability to work independently, computer skills, oral communication skills, personal interest in the field, strong interpersonal skills, written communication skills. Duration is 1 semester (Monday through Friday). Unpaid. Open to college sophomores, college juniors, college seniors, graduate students. ▶ *1–3 sales promotions*

Viacom Corp. (continued)

interns: responsibilities include assisting sales and promotion departments with creation, development, and execution of promotion campaigns for radio advertisers, and assisting with daily prize distribution. Candidates should have ability to work independently, ability to work with others, office skills, oral communication skills, organizational skills, written communication skills. Unpaid. Open to college sophomores, college juniors, college seniors, graduate students. ▶ *1–7 sports interns:* responsibilities include logging games as they are recorded off TV and satellite, logging highlight feeds, answering phones, and occasionally assisting talent in the field. Candidates should have analytical skills, editing skills, knowledge of field, oral communication skills, organizational skills, personal interest in the field, research skills, self-motivation. Duration is 1 semester. Unpaid. Open to college sophomores, college juniors, college seniors, graduate students. ▶ *1–2 television programming interns:* responsibilities include working with programming coordinator to facilitate flow of program information; answering viewer inquiries; working with research director to compile data to be used to help sell advertising. Candidates should have ability to work with others, office skills, oral communication skills, organizational skills, research skills, written communication skills, Microsoft Excel experience (preferred). Unpaid. Open to college sophomores, college juniors, college seniors, graduate students. ▶ *1–3 videotape library interns:* responsibilities include computer archiving; providing file footage for news producers, writers, and editors; maintaining beta log book; and producing "special archives" pitch reels. Candidates should have computer skills, oral communication skills, organizational skills, research skills, strong interpersonal skills. Duration is 1 semester. Unpaid. Open to college sophomores, college juniors, college seniors, graduate students. ▶ *1–3 weather/special projects interns:* responsibilities include participation in data collection and interpretation for development of weather and science reports; working with producers; making phone calls and setting up interviews to be used in stories. Candidates should have analytical skills, knowledge of field, oral communication skills, personal interest in the field, research skills, self-motivation, strong leadership ability, written communication skills, computer skills a plus. Duration is 1 semester. Unpaid. Open to college sophomores, college juniors, college seniors, graduate students. International applications accepted.
Benefits Opportunity to attend seminars/workshops, willing to complete paperwork for educational credit, willing to provide letters of recommendation.
Contact Write, call, fax, e-mail, or through World Wide Web site Andrea Naper, Internship Program Manager. Phone: 617-787-7113. Fax: 617-787-7275. E-mail: abnaper@boston.cbs.com. In-person interview recommended (telephone interview accepted). Applicants must submit a resume, academic transcripts, formal application (portion of which must be completed by intern/faculty advisor). Application deadline: March 15 for summer, July 15 for fall, November 15 for spring. World Wide Web: http://www.wbz.com.

WCAU-TV, CHANNEL 10 TELEVISION, INVESTIGATIVE UNIT
10 Monument Road
Bala Cynwyd, Pennsylvania 19004

General Information Investigative unit that prepares reports for television and helps people with complaints about products, services, and institutions. Number of employees: 3. Unit of NBC 10, Bala Cynwyd, Pennsylvania. Number of internship applications received each year: 50.
Internships Available ▶ *1–5 researcher interns:* responsibilities include researching and setting up news stories; coming up with story ideas, handling viewer communication, logging tapes, and assisting in investigations. Candidates should have ability to work independently, ability to work with others, oral communication skills, organizational skills, research skills, self-motivation. Duration is 1 semester. Unpaid. Open to college juniors, college seniors, must be receiving college credit.
Benefits Formal training, possible full-time employment, willing to complete paperwork for educational credit, willing to provide letters of recommendation.

Contact Write, call, fax, or through World Wide Web site Joanne Wilder, Director of Press and Community Relations. Phone: 610-668-5645. Fax: 610-668-7092. Applicants must submit a letter of interest, resume, application (available on Web site). World Wide Web: http://www.nbc10.com.

WCHS-TV
1301 Piedmont Road
Charleston, West Virginia 25301

General Information Commercial television station broadcasting in a competitive top-50 market. Established in 1958. Number of employees: 100. Unit of Sinclair Broadcast Group, Baltimore, Maryland. Number of internship applications received each year: 40.
Internships Available ▶ *6–15 news interns:* responsibilities include performing off-air reporting duties such as gathering and writing news stories and running the teleprompter. Candidates should have college courses in field, computer skills, editing skills, plan to pursue career in field, strong interpersonal skills, writing skills. Duration is 200 hours. Unpaid. Open to college freshmen, college sophomores, college juniors, college seniors, recent college graduates, graduate students, law students, career changers, individuals reentering the workforce. International applications accepted.
Benefits Possible full-time employment, willing to act as a professional reference, willing to complete paperwork for educational credit, willing to provide letters of recommendation.
Contact Write, call, fax, or e-mail Ms. Jessica Worstell, News Administrative Assistant. Phone: 304-345-4115. Fax: 304-345-1849. E-mail: jworstel@sbgnet.com. In-person interview recommended (telephone interview accepted). Applicants must submit a resume. Applications are accepted continuously. World Wide Web: http://www.wchstv.com.

WCIU-TV CHANNEL 26
26 North Halsted
Chicago, Illinois 60661

General Information Independent television broadcasting station that features some local production. Established in 1964. Number of employees: 100. Unit of Weigel Broadcasting, Chicago, Illinois. Number of internship applications received each year: 100.
Internships Available ▶ *1 newsroom intern.* Candidates should have ability to work independently, ability to work with others, editing skills, experience in the field, self-motivation, writing skills. Duration is 10-15 weeks (20-40 hours per week). Unpaid. ▶ *1–3 programming/production assistants:* responsibilities include working on on-air productions and taping. Candidates should have ability to work with others, editing skills, oral communication skills, self-motivation, writing skills. Duration is 10-15 weeks (20-40 hours per week). Unpaid. ▶ *1 public relations intern:* responsibilities include developing promotion campaigns. Candidates should have ability to work with others, editing skills, oral communication skills, self-motivation, writing skills. Duration is 10-15 weeks (20-40 hours per week). Unpaid. Open to college freshmen, college sophomores, college juniors.
Benefits On-the-job training, possible full-time employment, willing to act as a professional reference, willing to complete paperwork for educational credit, willing to provide letters of recommendation.
Contact Write, fax, or e-mail Ms. Lilli Scheye, Internship Coordinator, 28 North Halsted, Chicago, Illinois 60661. Fax: 312-705-2656. E-mail: lscheye@wciu.com. No phone calls. In-person interview required. Applicants must submit a formal organization application, letter of interest, resume, writing sample, two personal references. Applications are accepted continuously.

WCNC-TV/NBC6
1001 Wood Ridge Center Drive
Charlotte, North Carolina 28217

General Information Television station. Number of employees: 200. Subsidiary of BECO Coporation, Dallas, Texas. Number of internship applications received each year: 200.

Internships Available ► *Interns:* responsibilities include weekly evaluation; participation in intern newscasts; workshops; completion of beat calls and projects; specific positions available in reporting, producing, new media, assignment desk, editing, photography, sports, weather, art, promotions and community affairs. Candidates should have ability to work independently, oral communication skills, plan to pursue career in field, research skills, self-motivation, written communication skills. Duration is 1–2 semesters. Paid. Open to college juniors, college seniors, graduate students. International applications accepted.

Benefits Names of contacts, willing to act as a professional reference, willing to complete paperwork for educational credit, willing to provide letters of recommendation.

Contact E-mail Greg Shepperd, Planning Editor. Fax: 704-357-4975. E-mail: gshepperd@nbc6.com. No phone calls. In-person interview recommended (telephone interview accepted). Applicants must submit a formal organization application, letter of interest, resume, letter of recommendation. Applications are accepted continuously. World Wide Web: http://www.nbc6.com.

WDAF-TV
3030 Summit
Kansas City, Missouri 64108

General Information FOX affiliate that provides diverse programming, including sports and entertainment, with emphasis on local news. Established in 1949. Number of employees: 215. Unit of News Corporation, Los Angeles, California. Number of internship applications received each year: 40.

Internships Available ► *1–2 art/graphics interns:* responsibilities include working on AVA Paintbox or Macintosh. Candidates should have ability to work independently, college courses in field, computer skills, oral communication skills, self-motivation. Duration is one summer or one semester. Unpaid. Open to college juniors, college seniors. ► *1–2 community relations/public relations interns:* responsibilities include writing and producing public service announcements, helping with events, writing press releases, assisting in field and studio shoots, and performing clerical responsibilities. Candidates should have ability to work independently, college courses in field, computer skills, organizational skills, strong interpersonal skills, writing skills. Duration is one summer or one semester. Unpaid. Open to college juniors, college seniors. ► *1–3 creative services interns:* responsibilities include writing on-air voice-over copy, assisting in field and studio shoots, editing, producing audio carts, and performing various other duties. Candidates should have ability to work independently, college courses in field, computer skills, oral communication skills, self-motivation, writing skills. Duration is 1 semester. Unpaid. Open to college juniors, college seniors. ► *3–5 news interns.* Candidates should have computer skills, oral communication skills, plan to pursue career in field, self-motivation, strong interpersonal skills, writing skills. Duration is one summer or one semester. Unpaid. Open to college juniors, college seniors. ► *1–2 sports interns.* Candidates should have computer skills, oral communication skills, plan to pursue career in field, self-motivation, strong interpersonal skills, writing skills. Duration is one summer or one semester. Unpaid. International applications accepted.

Benefits Job counseling, names of contacts, on-the-job training, possible full-time employment, willing to complete paperwork for educational credit, willing to provide letters of recommendation.

Contact Write or fax Gail Lang, Human Resources Director. Fax: 816-932-9193. In-person interview required. Applicants must submit a letter of interest, resume, three personal references, three letters of recommendation. Applications are accepted continuously. World Wide Web: http://www.wdaftv4.com.

WDBJ TELEVISION, INC.
2807 Hershberger Road
Roanoke, Virginia 24017

General Information CBS affiliate with a potential viewing audience of over 1 million each week in portions of Virginia, West Virginia, and North Carolina. Established in 1955. Number of employees: 120. Unit of Schurz Communications, Inc., South Bend, Indiana. Number of internship applications received each year: 25.

Internships Available ► *1 engineering intern:* responsibilities include assisting with master control and maintenance observation. Candidates should have ability to work independently, ability to work with others, declared college major in field, self-motivation. Duration is flexible. Unpaid. Open to college juniors, college seniors. ► *1–2 news interns:* responsibilities include assisting with reporting and producing. Candidates should have ability to work independently, ability to work with others, computer skills, declared college major in field, self-motivation, writing skills. Duration is flexible. Unpaid. Open to college juniors, college seniors. ► *1–2 production interns:* responsibilities include learning camera techniques, lighting, audio, tape editing, studio set-up, electronic field production, and character generator. Candidates should have ability to work independently, ability to work with others, computer skills, declared college major in field. Duration is flexible. Unpaid. Open to college juniors, college seniors. ► *1 sales intern:* responsibilities include working with business community to sell broadcast air time. Candidates should have computer skills, declared college major in field, oral communication skills, strong interpersonal skills, written communication skills. Duration is flexible. Unpaid. International applications accepted.

Benefits Possible full-time employment, willing to complete paperwork for educational credit.

Contact Write, fax, e-mail, or through World Wide Web site Ms. Monica L. Taylor, Personnel Manager, 2001 Colonial Avenue, Roanoke, Virginia 24015. Fax: 540-344-5097. E-mail: mtaylor@wdbj7.com. No phone calls. In-person interview required. Applicants must submit a formal organization application, letter of interest, resume, letter of recommendation. Applications are accepted continuously. World Wide Web: http://www.wdbj7.com.

WDCQ-TV
1961 Delta Road
University Center, Michigan 48710

General Information Professional TV and radio stations (PBS and NPR) providing academic preparation for work in telecommunications industry. Established in 1964. Number of employees: 30. Unit of Delta College, University Center, Michigan.

Internships Available ► *1–2 TV field/studio production interns:* responsibilities include assisting in producing and editing on-air productions. Duration is 4–6 months. Position available as unpaid or paid. ► *1 radio intern:* responsibilities include on-air programming, fund-raising on-air, and assisting with production of audio tapes. Duration is 4–6 months. Position available as unpaid or paid. Candidates for all positions should have ability to work independently, computer skills, knowledge of field, oral communication skills, written communication skills. Open to college freshmen, college sophomores, college juniors, college seniors.

Benefits Formal training, job counseling, names of contacts, willing to complete paperwork for educational credit, willing to provide letters of recommendation.

Contact Write, call, or e-mail Mr. Kent Wieland, Production Manager, Delta Broadcasting. Phone: 989-686-9350. E-mail: kwwielan@alpha.delta.edu. Applicants must submit a letter of interest, resume. Applications are accepted continuously. World Wide Web: http://www.delta.edu/broadcasting.

WDIV-TV
550 West Lafayette Boulevard
Detroit, Michigan 48226

General Information Commercial television station. Number of employees: 200. Unit of Post-Newsweek Stations, Detroit, Michigan. Number of internship applications received each year: 250.

Internships Available ► *5–8 news department interns:* responsibilities include assisting in various areas including assignment desk, sports, and special projects. Candidates should have ability to work with others, college courses in field, oral communication skills, plan to pursue career in field, self-motivation, written communication skills. Duration is 1 semester. Unpaid. ► *2–3 programming department interns:* responsibilities include assisting producers with field and studio shoots, research, writing scripts, screening and logging tapes, audience booking, organizing edit sessions, and researching and gathering materials for editorials and documentaries.

WDIV-TV (continued)

Candidates should have college courses in field, oral communication skills, plan to pursue career in field, self-motivation, writing skills. Duration is 1 semester. Unpaid. ▶ *1 research department intern:* responsibilities include creating sales onesheets; maintaining research wall, weekly sweeps tracking report, and news promotable ratings/calendars; recording and viewing of competitors' newscast promotables; assisting in assembly or presentations; typing various reports and assisting in analysis; miscellaneous projects. Candidates should have ability to work with others, college courses in field, computer skills, oral communication skills, plan to pursue career in field, self-motivation, written communication skills. Duration is 1 semester. Unpaid. ▶ *1 sales department intern:* responsibilities include maintenance of matrix sales software; monitoring daily newspapers and radio to establish new leading sourcing; monitoring local TV competitors to establish new promotional ideas; maintenance of client contracts and weekly updates of sales sports for account executives; assisting in writing sales orders, on client calls, with development of client news packages, and with sales rating seminar. Candidates should have ability to work with others, college courses in field, computer skills, oral communication skills, plan to pursue career in field, self-motivation, written communication skills. Duration is 1 semester. Unpaid. Open to college juniors, college seniors, graduate students.

Benefits On-the-job training, willing to complete paperwork for educational credit.

Contact Write, call, or fax Barbara Zielinski, Human Resources Administrator. Phone: 313-222-0468. Fax: 313-222-0471. In-person interview required. Applicants must submit a formal organization application, resume. Application deadline: April 1 for summer, October 1 for winter.

WEWB-TV
14 Corporate Woods Boulevard
Albany, New York 12211

General Information WEWB-TV (WB45) is the capital region's affiliate for Warner Brothers Television (The 'WB') and Tribune Broadcasting. Established in 1999. Number of employees: 13. Unit of Tribune Broadcasting Company, Chicago, Illinois. Number of internship applications received each year: 50.

Internships Available ▶ *2–3 marketing/sales interns:* responsibilities include working in the fast-paced environment of a growing TV station; participating in station events, assisting station staff and learning how WB affiliate operates. Candidates should have computer skills, office skills, oral communication skills, research skills, strong interpersonal skills, writing skills. Duration is 1 semester. Unpaid. Open to college freshmen, college sophomores, college juniors, college seniors.

Benefits On-the-job training, willing to act as a professional reference, willing to complete paperwork for educational credit, willing to provide letters of recommendation.

Contact Fax or e-mail Dan Sher, Marketing/Public Relations Director. Fax: 518-431-3155. E-mail: dsher@tribune.com. No phone calls. In-person interview recommended (telephone interview accepted). Applicants must submit a letter of interest, resume. Applications are accepted continuously. World Wide Web: http://www.wb45.com.

WEWS-TV 5
3001 Euclid Avenue
Cleveland, Ohio 44115

General Information Television station. Established in 1947. Number of employees: 187. Unit of Scripps Howard Company, Cincinnati, Ohio. Number of internship applications received each year: 175.

Internships Available ▶ *1 Akron News Bureau intern:* responsibilities include working as the assignment desk editor in Akron. Candidates should have ability to work independently, oral communication skills, self-motivation, strong interpersonal skills, written communication skills. Duration is 1 quarter or semester. Unpaid. Open to college sophomores, college juniors, graduate students, law students. ▶ *1–3 Good Morning Cleveland interns:* responsibilities include hands-on experience in the production of a live daily morning news/talk show; duties range from researching topics, helping viewers, and assisting at assignment desk to keeping show records. Candidates should have ability to work independently, ability to work with others, computer skills, oral communication skills, organizational skills, research skills, self-motivation, strong leadership ability. Duration is 1 quarter or semester. Unpaid. Open to college juniors, college seniors, graduate students. ▶ *1 editing intern:* responsibilities include working with editors, receiving and cataloging video materials from all over the world, and learning to edit stories that are to appear on the air. Candidates should have ability to work independently, oral communication skills, organizational skills, self-motivation, strong interpersonal skills. Duration is 1 quarter or semester. Unpaid. Open to college juniors, college seniors, graduate students, law students. ▶ *3–6 investigators/troubleshooters:* responsibilities include conducting phone work, giving referrals to viewers who call helpline, accompanying field reporters, and assisting the investigative team with research. Candidates should have ability to work independently, oral communication skills, organizational skills, research skills, self-motivation, strong interpersonal skills, strong leadership ability, written communication skills, interest in investigative and consumer reporting and producing. Duration is 1 quarter or semester. Unpaid. Open to college juniors, college seniors, graduate students, law students. ▶ *6–8 news assignment desk interns:* responsibilities include answering phone calls, placing calls to local law enforcement or story contacts, and communicating with field news crews. Candidates should have ability to work independently, computer skills, oral communication skills, organizational skills, research skills, self-motivation, strong interpersonal skills, strong leadership ability, writing skills. Duration is 1 quarter or semester. Unpaid. Open to college juniors, college seniors, graduate students, law students. ▶ *1 production intern.* Candidates should have oral communication skills, self-motivation, strong interpersonal skills. Duration is 1 quarter or semester. Unpaid. Open to college juniors, college seniors, graduate students. ▶ *2 promotion interns:* responsibilities include assisting with the coordination of station events and special projects, answering viewer calls and letters, sending out promotional materials, writing movie promos, scheduling and maintaining public service announcements, and performing general office duties. Candidates should have ability to work independently, computer skills, oral communication skills, organizational skills, plan to pursue career in field, self-motivation, strong interpersonal skills, strong leadership ability, written communication skills. Duration is 1 quarter or semester. Unpaid. Open to college juniors, college seniors, graduate students. ▶ *1–3 sales interns:* responsibilities include typing, filing, checking sales orders, assisting the sales managers on special projects, assisting the account executives, and occasionally accompanying account executives on sales calls. Candidates should have computer skills, office skills, oral communication skills, organizational skills, self-motivation, strong interpersonal skills, written communication skills. Duration is 1 quarter or semester. Unpaid. Open to college juniors, college seniors, graduate students. ▶ *3 sports interns:* responsibilities include clearing the sports wires, shot-sheeting and timing interviews, monitoring afternoon sports feeds, helping keep the sports director informed on breaking events, and periodically accompanying the sports producer on stories. Candidates should have ability to work independently, oral communication skills, self-motivation, strong interpersonal skills, written communication skills, knowledge of sports helpful. Duration is 1 quarter or semester. Unpaid. Open to college juniors, college seniors, graduate students, law students. International applications accepted.

Benefits Possible full-time employment, willing to complete paperwork for educational credit, hands-on experience.

Contact Write, fax, or e-mail Ms. Moreen Bailey Frater, Community Affairs Director. Phone: 216-431-5555. Fax: 216-361-1762. E-mail: bailey@wews.com. In-person interview required. Applicants must submit a letter of interest, resume. Applications are accepted continuously. World Wide Web: http://www.newsnet5.com.

WGAL 8 (TV)
1300 Columbia Avenue
Lancaster, Pennsylvania 17604-7127

General Information Television station, affiliated with NBC, emphasizing news, public affairs, and programming. Established in 1949. Number of employees: 150. Unit of Hearst-Argyle Television, Inc., New York, New York. Number of internship applications received each year: 100.

Internships Available ▶ *1–2 creative services interns:* responsibilities include working as production assistant on commercial, promotional, and public service announcement shoots and updating Web site data. Candidates should have computer skills, declared college major in field, oral communication skills, organizational skills, personal interest in the field, self-motivation, strong interpersonal skills, writing skills, audio and video editing skills, knowledge of field cameras. Duration is 1 semester. Unpaid. Open to college juniors, college seniors, graduate students, applicants must attend school or have home residence in viewing area. ▶ *4–6 news interns:* responsibilities include accompanying reporters and assisting the assignment editor and newscast producers. Candidates should have ability to work independently, oral communication skills, organizational skills, strong leadership ability, writing skills. Duration is 1 semester. Unpaid. Open to college juniors, college seniors, graduate students, applicants must be attending school or have home residence in viewing area. ▶ *1–2 sports interns:* responsibilities include assisting department staff. Candidates should have ability to work independently, declared college major in field, knowledge of field, oral communication skills, personal interest in the field, self-motivation, strong interpersonal skills, writing skills, video editing skills. Duration is 1 semester. Unpaid. Open to college juniors, college seniors, graduate students, applicants must attend school or have home residence in viewing area. ▶ *1–2 weather interns:* responsibilities include preparing weather data and learning about broadcasting. Candidates should have ability to work independently, ability to work with others, analytical skills, computer skills, declared college major in field, oral communication skills, organizational skills, self-motivation, written communication skills. Duration is 1 semester. Unpaid. Open to college juniors, college seniors, graduate students, applicants must attend school or have home residence in viewing area.

Benefits On-the-job training, possible full-time employment, willing to complete paperwork for educational credit.

Contact Write, call, fax, e-mail, or through World Wide Web site Juliet Finkey, Internship Coordinator. Phone: 717-393-5851 Ext. 255. Fax: 717-393-9484. E-mail: news8@wgal.com. In-person interview required. Applicants must submit a letter of interest, resume. Application deadline: up to one year in advance, particularly for summer positions. World Wide Web: http://www.thewgalchannel.com.

WHYY, INC.
Independence Mall West, 150 North Sixth Street
Philadelphia, Pennsylvania 19106

General Information Public television and radio station. Established in 1954. Number of employees: 221. Number of internship applications received each year: 200.

Internships Available ▶ *1–2 Radio Times interns:* responsibilities include assisting staff with radio production duties and with library research relating to upcoming interview guests on the local public affairs program produced by WHYY-FM. Candidates should have ability to work independently, ability to work with others, college courses in field, computer skills, editing skills, research skills. Duration is 1 semester. Unpaid. Open to college sophomores, college juniors, college seniors. ▶ *1–3 TV news interns for "Twelve Tonight":* responsibilities include assisting the news and editorial staff with monitoring scanners and 2-way radio calls, performing clerical duties, and preparing stories to air in the Wilmington, DE office. Candidates should have ability to work with others, college courses in field, computer skills, research skills, writing skills. Duration is 1 semester. Unpaid. Open to college sophomores, college juniors, college seniors. ▶ *2–5 TV production interns:* responsibilities include assisting staff with library research and related duties, assisting with operating character generator/teleprompter, logging tapes, typing and filing scripts, and performing general office duties. Candidates should have ability to work with others, college courses in field, computer skills, editing skills, research skills, self-motivation, writing skills. Duration is 1 semester. Unpaid. Open to college sophomores, college juniors, college seniors. ▶ *1–2 Voices in the Family interns.* Candidates should have college courses in field, computer skills, editing skills, research skills, strong interpersonal skills. Duration is 1 semester. Unpaid. Open to college sophomores, college juniors, college seniors. ▶ *2–3 WHYY-FM news interns:* responsibilities include assisting reporters with writing broadcast copy, handling phone calls, setting up interviews, and gathering research material and sound bites for broadcast. Candidates should have ability to work independently, college courses in field, computer skills, editing skills, research skills, writing skills. Duration is 1 semester. Unpaid. Open to college juniors, college seniors. ▶ *1–3 development/fund-raising interns:* responsibilities include assisting staff with choosing premiums for pledge drives, calling to obtain samples, writing and designing premium brochures, assisting with market research, and updating reports using Lotus 123. Candidates should have ability to work independently, ability to work with others, computer skills, office skills, oral communication skills, writing skills. Duration is 1 semester. Unpaid. Open to college sophomores, college juniors, college seniors. ▶ *1 foundation/grants research intern:* responsibilities include assisting grants writer in establishing a coordinated and unified approach to soliciting support for WHYY, researching the many funding services to which WHYY could apply, and composing brief profiles of potential donors. Candidates should have ability to work independently, computer skills, research skills, self-motivation, writing skills. Duration is 1 semester. Unpaid. Open to college sophomores, college juniors, college seniors. ▶ *1 human resources assistant:* responsibilities include assisting staff with administrative, recruitment, benefits, and training needs. Candidates should have college courses in field, computer skills, oral communication skills, personal interest in the field, plan to pursue career in field, strong interpersonal skills. Duration is 1 semester. Unpaid. Open to college sophomores, college juniors, college seniors. ▶ *1 marketing intern:* responsibilities include assisting marketing/sales representatives with database research for client presentations, performing market research and audience research projects, and assisting with administrative duties as needed. Candidates should have ability to work independently, ability to work with others, computer skills, office skills, oral communication skills, research skills. Duration is 1 semester. Unpaid. ▶ *1–2 member services interns:* responsibilities include responding to member service calls and requests, assisting with premium shipments and inventory maintenance, assisting with fund-raisers, and performing general office duties. Candidates should have ability to work independently, ability to work with others, computer skills, oral communication skills, self-motivation, writing skills. Duration is 1 semester. Unpaid. Open to college sophomores, college juniors, college seniors. ▶ *1–2 public information/public relations interns:* responsibilities include assisting publicists with writing press releases and pieces for company newsletter, updating mailing lists and press clips, and assisting with special events and promotional activities. Candidates should have ability to work with others, college courses in field, computer skills, editing skills, writing skills. Duration is 1 semester. Unpaid. Open to college sophomores, college juniors, college seniors.

Benefits Possible full-time employment, willing to complete paperwork for educational credit.

Contact Write, call, fax, e-mail, or through World Wide Web site Ms. Sandra W. Chatfield, Community Relations Manager. Phone: 215-351-1261. Fax: 215-574-1477. E-mail: schatfield@whyy.org. In-person interview required. Applicants must submit a formal organization application, letter of interest, resume, writing sample. Applications are accepted continuously. World Wide Web: http://www.whyy.org.

WJBK-TV
Box 2000
Southfield, Michigan 48037

General Information Television station. Number of employees: 220. Division of Fox Television Stations, Inc., Los Angeles, California. Number of internship applications received each year: 100.

Internships Available ▶ *1 community service intern:* responsibilities include helping in the actual production of public service announcements for community groups, contacting and preinterviewing guests, and producing videotapes and other visuals. Candidates should have college courses in field, oral communication skills, strong interpersonal skills, writing skills. Duration is minimum of 12 weeks at 15 hours per week. Unpaid. ▶ *2 creative services interns:* responsibilities include working in marketing, advertising, or public relations; writing ad copy; and aiding with scheduling promotional materials. Candidates should have ability to work with others, college courses in field, office skills, oral communication skills, self-motivation, written communication skills. Duration is minimum of 12 weeks at 15 hours per week. Unpaid. ▶ *1 graphics intern:* responsibilities include working with state-of-the-art equipment and learning typesetting, keylining, photographic reproduction methods, set design, and on-air graphics. Candidates should have ability to work independently, computer skills, experience in the field, oral communication skills, plan to pursue career in field, major in arts. Duration is minimum of 12 weeks at 15 hours per week. Unpaid. ▶ *10–12 news interns:* responsibilities include working on assignment, specialty reporting, making recommendations for coverage, conducting extensive research for potential stories, and working closely with medical and consumer reporters. Candidates should have computer skills, oral communication skills, self-motivation, strong interpersonal skills. Duration is minimum of 12 weeks at 15 hours per week. Unpaid. ▶ *2 program interns:* responsibilities include assisting in all levels of production, learning control room procedures, and special events programming. Candidates should have ability to work with others, college courses in field, oral communication skills, self-motivation. Duration is minimum of 12 weeks at 15 hours per week. Unpaid. ▶ *1 public relations intern:* responsibilities include assisting in coordinating speaking engagements and personal appearances for on-air talent and coordinating special events. Candidates should have office skills, strong interpersonal skills, writing skills. Duration is minimum of 12 weeks at 15 hours per week. Unpaid. ▶ *4 sports interns:* responsibilities include assisting sports director and staff and working at sports events to provide help as needed. Candidates should have oral communication skills, organizational skills, personal interest in the field, strong interpersonal skills. Duration is minimum of 12 weeks at 15 hours per week. Unpaid. Open to college juniors, college seniors, graduate students.

Benefits Willing to complete paperwork for educational credit.
Contact Write Ms. Valerie Poma, Intern Coordinator. E-mail: vpoma037@fox.com. In-person interview required. Applicants must submit portfolio (for graphics interns). Application deadline: March 31 for summer, July 31 for fall, November 30 for winter.

WMAR-TV
6400 York Road
Baltimore, Maryland 21212

General Information Television station affiliate of ABC network. Established in 1947. Number of employees: 200. Unit of Scripps Howard Company, Cincinnati, Ohio. Number of internship applications received each year: 150.

Internships Available ▶ *1 creative services intern:* responsibilities include assisting promotion producers for news and entertainment promotion. Duration is 1 semester. Unpaid. Open to college juniors, college seniors, graduate students, applicants must be eligible for course credit for internship. ▶ *3 news interns:* responsibilities include assisting in all aspects of news, reporting, producing, writing, and assignment functions. Duration is 1 semester. Unpaid. Open to college juniors, college seniors, graduate students, applicants must be eligible for course credit for internship. ▶ *1 production intern:* responsibilities include directing show preparation including pre-production of video pack-

ages, writing, editing, and post production. Duration is 1 semester. Unpaid. Open to college juniors, college seniors, graduate students. ▶ *1 public affairs intern:* responsibilities include assisting with public service announcements and production of local public affairs programs. Duration is 1 semester. Unpaid. Open to college juniors, college seniors, graduate students, applicants must be eligible for course credit for internship. ▶ *1 sales intern:* responsibilities include working on development of sales promotions and presentations and possibly in research. Duration is 1 semester. Unpaid. Open to college juniors, college seniors, graduate students, applicants must be eligible for course credit for internship. ▶ *1 sports production intern:* responsibilities include covering area sports events. Duration is 1 semester. Unpaid. Open to college juniors, college seniors, graduate students, applicants must be eligible for course credit for internship. Candidates for all positions should have ability to work independently, college courses in field, computer skills, oral communication skills, strong interpersonal skills, writing skills.

Benefits Willing to complete paperwork for educational credit.
Contact Write Terry Jackson, Programming Coordinator/Administrative Assistant. No phone calls. In-person interview required. Applicants must submit a formal organization application, writing sample. Application deadline: January 1 for spring, May 1 for summer, September 1 for fall.

WNYW-FOX TELEVISION
205 East 67th Street
New York, New York 10021

General Information Television station with a hands-on training program for individuals interested in obtaining experience in various fields of TV broadcasting. Established in 1986. Number of employees: 250. Unit of Fox, Inc., Los Angeles, California. Number of internship applications received each year: 600.

Internships Available ▶ *35–40 interns:* responsibilities include working in one of the following departments depending on intern's interest: human resources, sales, traffic, 10 o'clock/evening news, "Good Day New York", programming, or newsroom. Candidates should have ability to work with others, knowledge of field, oral communication skills, personal interest in the field, plan to pursue career in field, written communication skills. Duration is flexible. Unpaid. Open to college juniors, college seniors. International applications accepted.

Benefits Opportunity to attend seminars/workshops, willing to complete paperwork for educational credit, $5 per day travel stipend.
Contact Write or call Ms. Roselyn Barranda, Human Resources Recruiter. Phone: 212-452-5700. In-person interview required. Applicants must submit a letter of interest, resume, letter from academic institution stating eligibility for internship. Applications are accepted continuously.

WPRI-TV/WNAC-TV
25 Catamore Boulevard
East Providence, Rhode Island 02914

General Information Broadcast television station that handles news, commercial production, and promotion. Established in 1954. Number of employees: 123. Affiliate of LIN Television, Providence, Rhode Island. Number of internship applications received each year: 50.

Internships Available ▶ *1 business intern:* responsibilities include billing, filing, copying payables and collections, organizing files, handling incoming and outgoing mail, and distributing traffic logs and faxes. Candidates should have ability to work independently, computer skills, knowledge of field, office skills, organizational skills, research skills, self-motivation, strong interpersonal skills, writing skills. Duration is 1 semester. Unpaid. ▶ *1–2 engineering interns:* responsibilities include operation of videotape machines and audio equipment; dubbing commercials, television shows, and public service announcements. Candidates should have ability to work independently, ability to work with others, computer skills, declared college major in field, editing skills, knowledge of field, organizational skills, self-motivation. Duration is 1 semester. Unpaid. ▶ *4–8 news interns:* responsibilities include assisting producer in newsroom work. Candidates should have computer skills, editing skills, knowledge of field, oral communication skills, plan to pursue career in field, research skills, self-motivation, strong interpersonal skills, writing skills. Duration is 3–4 months. Unpaid. ▶ *4–8 production interns:* responsibilities include working in studio and assisting with lighting, sets, and camera work. Candidates should have college courses in field, computer skills, plan to pursue career in field, research skills, self-motivation, strong interpersonal skills, writing skills. Duration is 1 semester. Unpaid. ▶ *1–2 production producer interns:* responsibilities include rough scriptwriting for commercials. Candidates should have ability to work independently, computer skills, editing skills, knowledge of field, organizational skills, research skills, self-motivation, strong interpersonal skills, writing skills. Duration is 1 semester. Unpaid. ▶ *Programming interns:* responsibilities include organizing tapes for daily air on both stations, maintaining the film library, organizing incoming information from both networks, and distributing and answering viewer mail. Candidates should have ability to work independently, analytical skills, computer skills, editing skills, knowledge of field, organizational skills, plan to pursue career in field, research skills, self-motivation, strong interpersonal skills, writing skills. Duration is 1 semester. Unpaid. ▶ *2–4 promotion interns:* responsibilities include assisting producer and writing. Candidates should have ability to work independently, computer skills, knowledge of field, research skills, self-motivation, strong interpersonal skills, writing skills. Duration is 1 semester. Unpaid. ▶ *1–2 public affairs interns:* responsibilities include researching and writing public service announcements; updating the Web site; and reviewing incoming public service announcements and doing post-production on them. Candidates should have ability to work independently, computer skills, editing skills, knowledge of field, office skills, research skills, self-motivation, strong interpersonal skills, writing skills. Duration is 1 semester. Unpaid. ▶ *1–2 research and marketing interns:* responsibilities include preparing charts and graphs using Neilsen information for sales and station use, preparing presentations for account executives. Candidates should have ability to work independently, computer skills, editing skills, office skills, organizational skills, research skills, strong interpersonal skills, writing skills. Duration is 1 semester. Unpaid. ▶ *3–5 sports interns:* responsibilities include learning to write for sports broadcasting, editing and archiving sports highlights, and charting games and incoming video feeds. Candidates should have ability to work independently, computer skills, editing skills, knowledge of field, office skills, organizational skills, plan to pursue career in field, strong interpersonal skills, writing skills. Duration is 1 semester. Unpaid. Open to college freshmen, college sophomores, college juniors, college seniors. International applications accepted.

Benefits Formal training, on-the-job training, possible full-time employment, willing to complete paperwork for educational credit, willing to provide letters of recommendation.

Contact Write, fax, e-mail, or through World Wide Web site Mr. Richard Lynch, Internship Coordinator. Fax: 401-434-3761. E-mail: rlynch@wpri.com. No phone calls. In-person interview required. Applicants must submit a letter of interest, resume, 2-3 writing samples. Application deadline: January 1 for spring, May 1 for summer, September 1 for fall. World Wide Web: http://www.wpri.com.

WPTA-TV
PO Box 2121, 3401 Butler Road
Ft. Wayne, Indiana 46808

General Information Television broadcast facility. Established in 1957. Number of employees: 90. Division of Granite Broadcasting, New York, New York. Number of internship applications received each year: 20.

Internships Available ▶ *1–2 accounting/billing/payables interns:* responsibilities include working in the business office, generating and inputting financial information into system, and generating and balancing financial reports. Candidates should have ability to work independently, ability to work with others, computer skills, office skills, organizational skills, plan to pursue career in field, self-motivation. Duration is flexible. Unpaid. ▶ *1 community affairs intern:* responsibilities include learning and applying skills related to production of public service announcements,

organizational skills related to community projects. Candidates should have ability to work independently, ability to work with others, computer skills, knowledge of field, self-motivation. Duration is flexible. Unpaid. ▶ *2–3 news production assistants:* responsibilities include working with news producers and reporters in learning skills for producing news stories. Candidates should have ability to work independently, computer skills, editing skills, plan to pursue career in field, self-motivation, writing skills. Duration is flexible. Unpaid. ▶ *2–3 production assistants:* responsibilities include working with producers, directors, and photographers in production of news and programming. Candidates should have ability to work independently, ability to work with others, computer skills, plan to pursue career in field, self-motivation. Duration is flexible. Unpaid. ▶ *1–2 sales assistants:* responsibilities include learning to sell advertising and place orders into computerized system. Candidates should have ability to work independently, computer skills, oral communication skills, plan to pursue career in field, self-motivation, strong interpersonal skills. Duration is flexible. Unpaid. Open to college sophomores, college juniors, college seniors. International applications accepted.

Benefits On-the-job training, possible full-time employment, willing to act as a professional reference, willing to complete paperwork for educational credit.

Contact Write Deborah J. Sand, Human Resources Manager. No phone calls. In-person interview recommended (telephone interview accepted). Applicants must submit a letter of interest, letter from college providing criteria and approval for college credit. Applications are accepted continuously.

WPVI-TV
4100 City Line Avenue
Philadelphia, Pennsylvania 19131

General Information Television station that broadcasts local news 4 hours per day and an additional 4 to 6 hours weekly of other local shows. Established in 1948. Number of employees: 220. Unit of American Broadcasting Company, Inc., New York, New York. Number of internship applications received each year: 100.

Internships Available ▶ *1–2 "Sunday Live" interns:* responsibilities include booking guests and generating theme for weekly show. Duration is 1 semester. Unpaid. Open to college juniors, college seniors. ▶ *1–2 creative services interns:* responsibilities include assisting with press releases, program schedules, and on-air promotions. Duration is 1 semester. Unpaid. Open to college juniors, college seniors. ▶ *6–8 news department interns:* responsibilities include serving as production assistants to newscast, segment producers, and assignment editor. Duration is 1 semester. Unpaid. Open to college juniors, college seniors. ▶ *3–5 public affairs department interns:* responsibilities include working as production assistants to producers, photographers, and editors working on the magazine shows "Prime Time", "Visions", "Fast Forward", and a variety of other studio programs. Duration is 1 semester. Unpaid. Open to college juniors, college seniors, graduate students. Candidates for all positions should have personal interest in the field, self-motivation, strong interpersonal skills, eligibility to receive academic credit.

Benefits Job counseling, names of contacts, willing to complete paperwork for educational credit, willing to provide letters of recommendation.

Contact Write, call, or fax Ms. Linda Munich, Director of Public Affairs. Phone: 215-878-9700. Fax: 215-581-4515. In-person interview required. Applicants must submit a formal organization application, letter of interest, resume, signature of academic advisor or school representative. Applications are accepted continuously. World Wide Web: http://www.wpvi.com.

WRDW-TV
1301 Georgia Avenue
North Augusta, South Carolina 29841

General Information Broadcast commercial CBS-network affiliate television station. Established in 1954. Number of employees: 85. Unit of Gray Communications, Inc., Albany, Georgia. Number of internship applications received each year: 10.

WRDW-TV (continued)

Internships Available ▶ *News-production interns:* responsibilities include news writing, story setup, field interviews, telephone interviews, videotape editing. Candidates should have declared college major in field, oral communication skills, plan to pursue career in field, self-motivation, strong interpersonal skills, written communication skills. Duration is 6–9 weeks. Unpaid. Open to college juniors, college seniors.

Benefits Job counseling, willing to act as a professional reference, willing to complete paperwork for educational credit, willing to provide letters of recommendation.

Contact Write or e-mail Estelle Parsley, Director of News and Operations, PO Box 1212, Augusta, Georgia 30903. Fax: 803-279-8316. E-mail: estelle.parsley@wrdw.com. No phone calls. In-person interview recommended (telephone interview accepted). Applicants must submit a letter of interest, resume, drug screening required. Applications are accepted continuously. World Wide Web: http://www.wrdw.com.

WTIU-TV
Radio-TV Building, Indiana University
Bloomington, Indiana 47405

General Information Public television station serving south central Indiana with a full schedule of national and local programming. Established in 1969. Number of employees: 60. Unit of Indiana University Bloomington, Bloomington, Indiana. Number of internship applications received each year: 25.

Internships Available ▶ *1–4 local production assistants:* responsibilities include assisting with production of local programs in public affairs, business, and sports. Candidates should have ability to work with others, computer skills, oral communication skills, organizational skills, written communication skills. Duration is flexible. Unpaid. ▶ *1–2 promotions assistants:* responsibilities include assisting with on-air promotion production. Candidates should have ability to work independently, computer skills, editing skills, organizational skills, strong interpersonal skills, written communication skills. Duration is flexible. Unpaid. ▶ *1 public information assistant:* responsibilities include assisting with publications and non-broadcast promotion. Candidates should have computer skills, editing skills, oral communication skills, organizational skills, research skills, written communication skills. Duration is flexible. Unpaid. ▶ *1–2 videographers:* responsibilities include assisting with field shoots and studio productions. Candidates should have ability to work independently, computer skills, editing skills, self-motivation. Duration is flexible. Open to college sophomores, college juniors, college seniors.

Benefits Job counseling, names of contacts, on-the-job training, possible full-time employment, willing to complete paperwork for educational credit, willing to provide letters of recommendation.

Contact Write, fax, or through World Wide Web site Phil Meyer, Station Manager. Fax: 812-855-0729. No phone calls. In-person interview required. Applicants must submit a letter of interest, resume, writing sample, two letters of recommendation. Applications are accepted continuously. World Wide Web: http://www.wtiu.indiana.edu.

WTVF NEWS
474 James Robertson Parkway
Nashville, Tennessee 37219

General Information CBS television affiliate that produces and airs local newscasts, current events, entertainment, and public service shows. Number of employees: 200. Unit of Landmark Community, Norfolk, Virginia. Number of internship applications received each year: 60.

Internships Available ▶ *1–4 Newschannel 5+ interns:* responsibilities include scheduling guests, camera operation, some editing, answering phones, greeting guests, limited writing, switcher operation, graphics and audio tasks. Candidates should have ability to work independently, editing skills, oral communication skills, plan to pursue career in field, self-motivation, strong interpersonal skills. Duration is 1 semester. Unpaid. Open to college sophomores, college juniors, college seniors, must be receiving college credit. ▶ *4–5 Talk of the Town interns:* responsibilities include answering viewer calls and letters, assisting with studio floor direction, typing daily show lists, assisting guests on outside remotes, and filling recipe requests. Candidates should have oral communication skills, organizational skills, plan to pursue career in field, self-motivation, strong interpersonal skills. Duration is 1 semester. Unpaid. Open to college freshmen, college sophomores, college juniors, college seniors, must be receiving college credit. ▶ *Consumer interns:* responsibilities include researching consumer advocacy field and working closely with government agencies and viewers. Candidates should have personal interest in the field, self-motivation. Duration is 1 semester. Unpaid. Open to college sophomores, college juniors, college seniors, must be receiving college credit. ▶ *7–10 news department interns:* responsibilities include answering phones, making beat calls, calling to verify facts, writing stories, and logging video feeds, going out with reporters and photographers on stories, editing videotape, and ripping scripts. Candidates should have oral communication skills, plan to pursue career in field, self-motivation, strong interpersonal skills, written communication skills. Duration is length of school term. Unpaid. Open to college freshmen, college sophomores, college juniors, college seniors, must be receiving college credit. ▶ *Sports interns:* responsibilities include dealing with sports industry. Candidates should have personal interest in the field, self-motivation, must be able to work weekends. Duration is 1 semester. Unpaid. Open to college sophomores, college juniors, college seniors, must be receiving college credit. International applications accepted.

Benefits Names of contacts, possible full-time employment, willing to act as a professional reference, willing to complete paperwork for educational credit, willing to provide letters of recommendation.

Contact Write, call, or fax Ms. Neysa Ellery Taylor, Assignment Editor. Phone: 615-248-5281. Fax: 615-244-9883. In-person interview recommended (telephone interview accepted). Applicants must submit a letter of interest, resume. Applications are accepted continuously. World Wide Web: http://www.newchannel5.com.

WUSA TV9 (CBS AFFILIATE)
4100 Wisconsin Avenue, NW
Washington, District of Columbia 20016

General Information Television news station. Established in 1949. Number of employees: 200. Subsidiary of Gannett Co., Inc., McLean, Virginia. Number of internship applications received each year: 200.

Internships Available ▶ *1 Medical Unit intern:* responsibilities include assisting medical producer and or medical reporter in story research, logging tapes, and general production responsibilities such as: filing medical archive tapes, updating medical unit portion of station's Web page, and returning viewer calls/emails/letters. Candidates should have ability to work independently, computer skills, editing skills, oral communication skills, organizational skills, research skills, self-motivation, strong interpersonal skills, written communication skills. Duration is 4 months in spring, summer, or fall. Unpaid. Open to college juniors, college seniors, recent college graduates. ▶ *1 news assignment desk intern:* responsibilities include assisting assignment editors and reporters in story research, gaining experience in broadcast news gathering, assignment desk operation, and field production. Candidates should have college courses in field, computer skills, organizational skills, plan to pursue career in field, strong interpersonal skills, written communication skills. Duration is 4 months in summer, fall, or spring. Unpaid. Open to college juniors, college seniors, graduate students. ▶ *2 sports unit interns:* responsibilities include helping to coordinate video footage of sports highlights; gaining knowledge and experience in interviewing, field, live studio, and post-production techniques; participating in field shoots at sports locations such as Redskins Park, the MCI Center, and Camden Yards. Candidates should have computer skills, knowledge of field, organizational skills, personal interest in the field, research skills. Duration is 4 months in summer, fall, or spring. Unpaid. Open to college juniors, college seniors, graduate students. ▶ *1 weather unit intern:* responsibilities include learning weather graphics (WSI Weather Pro), Doppler Radar, and SLM (street level mapping); using newsroom computers to read and analyze raw computer guidance and write forecasts from this data; learning how to pursue a shot for on air use and to sort and post Difax maps and Alphanumeric data. Candidates should have analytical skills, college courses in field, computer skills, knowledge of field, oral communication skills, organizational skills, plan to pursue career in field, research skills, self-motivation, strong interpersonal skills, written communication skills. Duration is 4 months in spring, summer, or fall. Unpaid. Open to college juniors, college seniors, recent college graduates.

Benefits Willing to act as a professional reference, willing to provide letters of recommendation, free parking.

Contact Write, call, e-mail, or through World Wide Web site Sarah Laslo, Human Resources Administrator. Phone: 202-895-5884. Fax: 202-895-5666. E-mail: slaslo@wusatv9.com. Telephone interview required. Applicants must submit a letter of interest, resume, letter from college/university verifying academic credit for internship. Application deadline: March 15 for summer, June 15 for fall, October 15 for spring semester. World Wide Web: http://www.wusatv9.com.

WWSB
1477 Tenth Street
Sarasota, Florida 34236

General Information ABC affiliate, television news and programming. Established in 1971. Number of employees: 100. Division of Southern Broadcasting Corporation, Sarasota, Florida. Number of internship applications received each year: 30.

Internships Available ▶ *News interns.* Candidates should have ability to work independently, college courses in field, oral communication skills, plan to pursue career in field, self-motivation, strong interpersonal skills. Duration is 1 semester. Unpaid. Open to college students with at least 6 credit hours of communication or journalism. International applications accepted.

Benefits On-the-job training, possible full-time employment, willing to act as a professional reference, willing to provide letters of recommendation.

Contact Write, fax, or e-mail Kay Miller, News Director. Phone: 941-923-8840. Fax: 941-923-8709. E-mail: kmiller@wwsb.com. In-person interview required. Applicants must submit a letter of interest, resume, must be receiving college credit. Applications are accepted continuously.

WXIX-TV 19
19 Broadcast Plaza, 635 West 7th Street
Cincinnati, Ohio 45203

General Information Broadcasting station offering the Cincinnati TV market a variety of entertainment programming, including the Fox network and local programming and news. Established in 1968. Number of employees: 120. Unit of Raycom Media, Inc., Montgomery, Alabama.

Internships Available ▶ *3–4 news interns:* responsibilities include shadowing reporters and photographers on news stories, updating assignment desk files, making beat calls to police and fire departments, following up on news stories, and tape dubbing on VHS machines. Candidates should have coursework in journalism, broadcasting, communications, or public relations. Duration is minimum of 10 hours per week. Unpaid. Open to college juniors, college seniors, only those earning college credit. ▶ *Sales promotion interns:* responsibilities include assisting in sales promotion and event execution, assisting with various client-related projects and reports, assisting in coordination of commercial production, updating and maintaining sales promotion event calendar, and attending weekly sales and promotion meetings. Candidates should have coursework in related areas of study. Duration is minimum of 10 hours per week. Unpaid. Open to college juniors, college seniors, only those earning college credit. ▶ *Sports interns:* responsibilities include logging videotape of games and sporting events, accompanying photographers to gather sound for stories, gathering score and sporting event information, tape dubbing on VHS and Beta machines, and assisting in preparation for Ten O'clock News and Sports Wrap . Candidates should have coursework in related areas of study. Duration is minimum of 4 weeks. Unpaid. Open to college juniors, college seniors, only those earning college credit. ▶ *Weather interns:* responsibilities include helping prepare daily weather show; making forecasts, drawing graphics, performing weather analysis by plotting maps, research through Internet and National Weather Service, and searching for weather scenes on BASYS computer system. Candidates should have course work in meteorology or related areas. Duration is minimum of 10 hours per week. Unpaid. Open to college juniors, college seniors.

Benefits Names of contacts, possible full-time employment, willing to complete paperwork for educational credit, willing to provide letters of recommendation.

Contact Write, fax, e-mail, or through World Wide Web site Lisa Slattery, Payroll Benefits Administrator. Fax: 513-421-0341. E-mail: hr@fox19.com. No phone calls. Applicants must submit a letter of interest, resume. Applications are accepted continuously. World Wide Web: http://www.fox19.com.

MANUFACTURING

GENERAL

AGOGO THREADS
17888 West 53rd Drive
Golden, Colorado 80403

General Information Women's clothing manufacturer. Established in 2001. Number of employees: 6. Number of internship applications received each year: 6.
Internships Available ▶ *1–2 administrative assistants:* responsibilities include administrative work, answering phones, and general office work. Candidates should have ability to work with others, analytical skills, computer skills, office skills, oral communication skills, organizational skills, written communication skills. Duration is 3–6 semesters. Position available as unpaid or at minimum wage to $7.50 per hour. Open to high school seniors, recent high school graduates, college freshmen, college sophomores, college juniors, college seniors, recent college graduates, individuals reentering the workforce.
Benefits Formal training, job counseling, on-the-job training, possible full-time employment, travel reimbursement, willing to act as a professional reference, willing to complete paperwork for educational credit, willing to provide letters of recommendation.
Contact Fax or e-mail Messiah Jacobs, President. Fax: 413-778-3949. E-mail: mj@agogothreads.com. No phone calls. In-person interview required. Applicants must submit a resume, three personal references, 3 work or job references. Applications are accepted continuously. World Wide Web: http://www.agogothreads.com.

APPLE COMPUTER, INC.
1 Infinite Loop, MS 84-3CE
Cupertino, California 95014

General Information Computer company whose mission is to bring the best personal computing products and support to students, educators, designers, scientists, engineers, business persons, and consumers in 140 countries around the world. Established in 1977. Number of employees: 9,000. Number of internship applications received each year: 6,000.
Internships Available ▶ *Finance interns.* Candidates should have ability to work independently, ability to work with others, analytical skills, college courses in field, experience in the field, oral communication skills, written communication skills. Duration is 3 months. Paid. Open to college juniors, college seniors, graduate students, MBA students. ▶ *Hardware engineering interns.* Candidates should have ability to work independently, ability to work with others, college courses in field, computer skills, experience in the field, organizational skills, self-motivation. Duration is 3 months. Paid. Open to college sophomores, college juniors, graduate students, college seniors enrolled in graduate programs. ▶ *Information systems and technology interns.* Candidates should have ability to work independently, ability to work with others, college courses in field, computer skills, experience in the field, oral communication skills. Duration is 3 months. Paid. Open to college sophomores, college juniors, graduate students, college seniors enrolled in graduate programs. ▶ *Marketing interns.* Candidates should have ability to work independently, ability to work with others, computer skills, experience in the field, oral communication skills, written communication skills. Duration is 3 months. Paid. Open to college seniors, graduate students, MBA students. ▶ *Systems software engineering interns.* Candidates should have ability to work independently, ability to work with others, college courses in field, computer skills, experience in the field, oral communication skills, self-motivation. Duration is 3 months. Paid. Open to college sophomores, college juniors, graduate students, college seniors enrolled in graduate programs. International applications accepted.
Benefits Health insurance, housing at a cost, opportunity to attend seminars/workshops, possible full-time employment, travel reimbursement, willing to act as a professional reference, willing to provide letters of recommendation, training, competitive salary.
Contact Write, fax, e-mail, or through World Wide Web site University Relations. Fax: 408-974-5957. E-mail: applejobs@apple.com. No phone calls. Telephone interview required. Applicants must submit a resume. Applications are accepted continuously. World Wide Web: http://www.apple.com.

BIC CORPORATION
500 Bic Drive
Milford, Connecticut 06460

General Information Manufacturer of writing instruments, lighters, and shavers. Established in 1958. Number of employees: 950. Subsidiary of Societe Bic, Clichy, France. Number of internship applications received each year: 100.
Internships Available ▶ *3–4 interns:* responsibilities include assisting in various departments (marketing, manufacturing, engineering, information technology, or accounting/finance) according to intern's abilities and departmental needs. Candidates should have analytical skills, computer skills, knowledge of field, oral communication skills, organizational skills, self-motivation, strong interpersonal skills, strong leadership ability, written communication skills. Duration is flexible. Paid. ▶ *2–3 sales/marketing interns:* responsibilities include assisting in marketing department according to intern's abilities and departmental needs. Candidates should have analytical skills, computer skills, knowledge of field, oral communication skills, organizational skills, research skills, self-motivation, strong interpersonal skills, strong leadership ability, written communication skills. Duration is flexible. Paid. Open to college juniors, college seniors, recent college graduates, graduate students.
Benefits Health insurance, job counseling, on-the-job training, possible full-time employment, travel reimbursement, access to company store and company activities, breakfast and lunch at cost.
Contact Write, fax, e-mail, or through World Wide Web site Paul Moyher, Corporate Human Resources Manager. Fax: 203-783-2200. E-mail: jobs@bicworld.com. No phone calls. In-person interview required. Applicants must submit a letter of interest, resume, three personal references. Applications are accepted continuously. World Wide Web: http://www.bicworld.com.

THE BOEING COMPANY–ST. LOUIS
PO Box 516, Mailcode S2761740
St. Louis, Missouri 63166-0516

General Information Defense contractor and producer of military aircraft and missiles. Number of employees: 20,000. Division of The Boeing Company, Seattle, Washington. Number of internship applications received each year: 3,000.
Internships Available ▶ *5–25 business administration interns:* responsibilities include working on a variety of assignments including accounting contracts and pricing, logistics, estimating, and business operations. Candidates should have analytical skills, computer skills, oral communication skills, personal interest in the field, self-motivation, written communication skills. Duration

is 10–13 weeks. Paid. ▶ *Electrical engineering/computer science/computer engineering interns:* responsibilities include working on a variety of assignments such as mission systems software designing programs, testing operational flight programs for avionic systems, and supporting flight test and hardware integration. Candidates should have ability to work with others, analytical skills, college courses in field, computer skills, oral communication skills, self-motivation. Duration is 10–13 weeks. Paid. ▶ *5–10 industrial engineering interns:* responsibilities include working on a variety of assignments including production methods engineering, liaison engineering, human factors, and strategic modernization. Candidates should have analytical skills, oral communication skills, organizational skills, personal interest in the field, self-motivation, strong interpersonal skills. Duration is 10–13 weeks. Paid. ▶ *10–30 mechanical/aerospace engineering interns:* responsibilities include working on a variety of assignments including flight test engineering, structural definition, liaison engineering, and design development. Candidates should have ability to work with others, analytical skills, computer skills, declared college major in field, oral communication skills, organizational skills, personal interest in the field, plan to pursue career in field, self-motivation. Duration is 10–13 weeks. Paid. Open to college juniors, college seniors.
Benefits Formal training, health insurance, housing at a cost, job counseling, on-the-job training, opportunity to attend seminars/workshops, possible full-time employment, travel reimbursement, tuition assistance, willing to complete paperwork for educational credit, relocation assistance.
Contact Through World Wide Web site Internship Coordinator. Applicants must submit electronic application: www.boeing.com/employment/college/. Application deadline: February 1 for summer, April 1 for fall, September 1 for spring. World Wide Web: http://www.boeing.com.

CAROLYN RAY
578 Nepperhan Avenue
Yonkers, New York 10701

General Information Manufacturer of fabrics and wallcoverings for interior designers and architects. Established in 1979. Number of employees: 4. Number of internship applications received each year: 20.
Internships Available ▶ *1–2 general assistants:* responsibilities include sample-making, clerical duties, customer service, studio production, maintenance, and organization. Candidates should have ability to work independently, ability to work with others, oral communication skills, organizational skills, personal interest in the field, self-motivation. Duration is flexible. Unpaid. Open to high school students, recent high school graduates, college freshmen, college sophomores, college juniors, college seniors, recent college graduates, graduate students, career changers, individuals reentering the workforce. ▶ *1–5 studio interns:* responsibilities include assisting with production of handpainted fabrics and sample making for both fabrics and wallcovering. Candidates should have ability to work independently, ability to work with others, analytical skills, editing skills, organizational skills, personal interest in the field, research skills, self-motivation, artistic interest. Duration is flexible. Position available as unpaid or paid. Open to high school students, recent high school graduates, college freshmen, college sophomores, college juniors, college seniors, recent college graduates, graduate students, law students, career changers, individuals reentering the workforce. International applications accepted.
Benefits Job counseling, names of contacts, on-the-job training, opportunity to attend seminars/workshops, possible full-time employment, willing to act as a professional reference, willing to complete paperwork for educational credit, willing to provide letters of recommendation, reimbursement of local travel expenses.
Contact Write, fax, or e-mail Rachael Zumbo, Internship Coordinator. Fax: 914-476-0677. E-mail: carolyn-ray@msn.com. In-person interview recommended (telephone interview accepted). Applicants must submit a letter of interest, resume, portfolio, two letters of recommendation. Applications are accepted continuously.

CNH GLOBAL N.V.
700 State Street
Racine, Wisconsin 53404

General Information Manufacturer of agricultural and industrial equipment. Established in 1999. Unit of Fiat, Turin, Italy.
Internships Available ▶ *40 interns:* responsibilities include working in field of interest: accounting, engineering, finance, human resources, logistics, product evaluation, programming, purchasing, sales, service, or service parts. Candidates should have computer skills, oral communication skills, strong interpersonal skills, written communication skills, personal transportation, agricultural background (a plus). Duration is 3 months (average). Paid. Open to college sophomores, college juniors, college seniors, graduate students. International applications accepted.
Benefits Housing at a cost, on-the-job training, opportunity to attend seminars/workshops, possible full-time employment, travel reimbursement, willing to act as a professional reference, willing to complete paperwork for educational credit, willing to provide letters of recommendation.
Contact Through World Wide Web site Manager, Employment and Staffing. No phone calls. In-person interview recommended (telephone interview accepted). Applicants must submit a formal organization application, resume, academic transcripts, cover letter. Applications are accepted continuously. World Wide Web: http://www.cnh.com.

DESIGNTECH INTERNATIONAL
7955 Cameron Brown Court
Springfield, Virginia 22153

General Information Company that develops and markets innovative consumer electronic products designed to enhance, protect, and simplify the lives of consumers. Established in 1986. Number of employees: 100. Number of internship applications received each year: 50.
Internships Available ▶ *2–3 engineering (electric and mechanical) interns:* responsibilities include involvement with design of new products, primarily in the smart home electronic and auto security areas. Candidates should have ability to work independently, analytical skills, college courses in field, computer skills, knowledge of field, personal interest in the field, plan to pursue career in field, self-motivation. Duration is 6–12 months. $500–$1000 per month. Open to college seniors, recent college graduates, graduate students. ▶ *2–3 marketing interns:* responsibilities include developing and packaging material for new products, public relations campaigns, sales analyses, and marketing programs. Candidates should have ability to work independently, analytical skills, computer skills, knowledge of field, writing skills. Duration is 6–12 months. $500–$1000 per month. Open to college juniors, college seniors, recent college graduates, graduate students. ▶ *2–3 operations and finance interns:* responsibilities include working on projects involving manufacturing processes, inventory controls, and financial analysis. Candidates should have ability to work independently, analytical skills, college courses in field, experience in the field, self-motivation, written communication skills. Duration is 6–12 months. $500–$1000 per month. Open to college seniors, recent college graduates, graduate students. ▶ *1–2 product designers:* responsibilities include product designing of consumer electronics, concepts, CAD work, model making. Candidates should have ability to work with others, computer skills, declared college major in field, knowledge of field, personal interest in the field, plan to pursue career in field, self-motivation. Duration is 6–12 months. $500–$1000 per month. Open to college seniors, recent college graduates, graduate students. International applications accepted.
Benefits Formal training, free housing, names of contacts, on-the-job training, possible full-time employment, willing to complete paperwork for educational credit, willing to provide letters of recommendation.
Contact Write, fax, e-mail, or through World Wide Web site Mark Gottlieb, Chairman. Fax: 703-866-2001. E-mail: info@designtech-intl.com. No phone calls. Applicants must submit a formal organization application, letter of interest, resume. Applications are accepted continuously. World Wide Web: http://www.designtech-intl.com.

ELIZABETH DOW
155 6th Avenue, 4th Floor
New York, New York 10013

General Information Manufacturer of handpainted wallcoverings and interior decorative painting. Established in 1992. Number of employees: 10. Number of internship applications received each year: 750.

Internships Available ▶ *10–12 interns:* responsibilities include sampling, painting, and studio work (art and design interns); database entry and followup (marketing/managerial interns). Candidates should have ability to work independently, ability to work with others, oral communication skills, organizational skills, personal interest in the field, self-motivation, Macintosh skills. Duration is flexible. Position available as unpaid or at minimum wage. Open to high school students, recent high school graduates, college freshmen, college sophomores, college juniors, college seniors, recent college graduates, graduate students, career changers, individuals reentering the workforce. International applications accepted.

Benefits Possible full-time employment, willing to act as a professional reference, willing to complete paperwork for educational credit, willing to provide letters of recommendation.

Contact Write, call, fax, or e-mail Xavier Santana, Internship Coordinator. Phone: 212-463-0144. Fax: 212-463-0824. E-mail: edowltd@aol.com. In-person interview recommended (telephone interview accepted). Applicants must submit a letter of interest, resume, personal reference, two letters of recommendation, portfolio (optional). Application deadline: continuous, but as early as possible for summer. World Wide Web: http://www.elizabethdow.com.

FASTENAL COMPANY
307 North Clinton
Trenton, New Jersey 08638

General Information Full-line industrial and construction supplier. Established in 1967. Number of employees: 45. Branch of Fastenal Company, Winona, Minnesota.

Internships Available ▶ *1–2 operations interns:* responsibilities include order fulfillment to customers and on-time deliveries, maintaining inventory through cycle counts, and organizing inventory accuracy. Candidates should have knowledge of field, organizational skills, self-motivation, strong interpersonal skills, strong leadership ability. Position available as unpaid or paid. Open to college juniors, college seniors. ▶ *1–2 sales interns:* responsibilities include inside sales, outside sales, customer service requests; learning all aspects of running a business. Candidates should have oral communication skills, organizational skills, personal interest in the field, self-motivation, strong interpersonal skills, strong leadership ability. Position available as unpaid or paid. Open to college juniors, college seniors, recent college graduates. International applications accepted.

Benefits On-the-job training, opportunity to attend seminars/workshops, possible full-time employment.

Contact E-mail or through World Wide Web site Ruth Procopio, Northeast Marketing Development Manager, 1225 Mid Valley Drive, Jessup, Pennsylvania 18434. Phone: 570-307-0992 Ext. 157. Fax: 570-307-0449. E-mail: rprocopi@fastenal.com. Applicants must submit a formal organization application, resume. Applications are accepted continuously. World Wide Web: http://www.fastenal.com.

HALLMARK CARDS, INC.
PO Box 419580
Kansas City, Missouri 64141

General Information Personal expression company that designs, manufactures, and distributes greeting cards as well as albums, ornaments, collectibles, gift wrap, partyware, and related products. Established in 1910. Number of employees: 5,500. Number of internship applications received each year: 1,500.

Internships Available ▶ *1–5 financial analysts:* responsibilities include assisting with cash management, financial plans, forecasts, internal auditing, and other projects that may be individual or team-based. Candidates should have analytical skills, college courses in field, computer skills, plan to pursue career in field, self-motivation, strong interpersonal skills. Duration is 10-12 weeks in summer. Paid. Open to college juniors, graduate students. ▶ *3 information technology analysts:* responsibilities include applying technical training (including programming) to solve problems in specific business area: trouble-shooting, implementation, needs analysis, design/program minor systems; some Web development opportunities. Candidates should have college courses in field, computer skills, oral communication skills, plan to pursue career in field, strong interpersonal skills, strong leadership ability. Duration is 10-12 weeks in summer. Paid. Open to college juniors. ▶ *Up to 10 manufacturing interns:* responsibilities include working with industrial, mechanical, and electrical engineering staff; assisting in productivity improvement efforts in a variety of plant operations. Candidates should have analytical skills, college courses in field, oral communication skills, plan to pursue career in field, strong interpersonal skills, strong leadership ability. Duration is 10–12 weeks. Paid. Open to college sophomores, college juniors. ▶ *1–8 marketing associates:* responsibilities include assisting with strategic product development and product management by gathering, analyzing, and evaluating information. Candidates should have analytical skills, college courses in field, oral communication skills, plan to pursue career in field, strong interpersonal skills, strong leadership ability. Duration is 10-12 weeks in summer. Paid. Open to college juniors, graduate students.

Benefits Job counseling, meals at a cost, on-the-job training, possible full-time employment, travel reimbursement, 50% discount on Hallmark products in company store (20% discount at Halls Plaza, Halls Crown Center, and associated stores), business travel accident insurance, paid holidays.

Contact Write, fax, or e-mail College Relations. Fax: 816-274-4299. E-mail: hcolle1@hallmark.com. No phone calls. In-person interview required. Applicants must submit a formal organization application, letter of interest, resume, academic transcripts, two personal references. Application deadline: January 15 for summer. World Wide Web: http://www.hallmark.com.

HONEST TEA
5019 Wilson Lane
Bethesda, Maryland 20814

General Information Manufacturer and marketer of bottled iced tea and tea bags. Established in 1998. Number of employees: 6. Number of internship applications received each year: 100.

Internships Available ▶ *3–12 sales/marketing interns:* responsibilities include sales and marketing through events and sampling. Candidates should have ability to work independently, organizational skills, self-motivation, strong interpersonal skills. Duration is 10–13 weeks. $300 per week. Open to college sophomores, college juniors, college seniors, recent college graduates.

Benefits On-the-job training, possible full-time employment, willing to act as a professional reference, willing to provide letters of recommendation.

Contact Fax or e-mail Kara Farwell, Marketing. Fax: 301-652-3557. E-mail: kara@honesttea.com. No phone calls. Applicants must submit a letter of interest, resume. Application deadline: May 1. World Wide Web: http://www.honesttea.com.

INTERNATIONAL FLAVORS & FRAGRANCES
521 West 57th Street
New York, New York 10019

General Information Manufacturer of flavors, fragrances and aroma chemicals. Number of employees: 203. Number of internship applications received each year: 15.

Internships Available ▶ *1 fragrance evaluation intern:* responsibilities include helping with brochure preparation, samples distribution, classification, and bottles preparation. Candidates should have ability to work independently, ability to work with others, office skills, organizational skills, self-motivation. Duration is 1 year. $15 per day. Open to college freshmen, college sophomores, college juniors, college seniors, graduate students. ▶ *1–3 marketing interns:* responsibilities include market analysis, working on MS Word. Candidates should have ability to work with others, computer skills, office skills, oral communication skills, personal interest in the field, written communication skills. Duration is 2–6 months.

$15 per day. Open to college freshmen, college sophomores, college juniors, college seniors, graduate students, career changers. ▶ *1–2 public relations/advertising interns:* responsibilities include assisting director of advertising and public relations with all department functions including both administrative and corporate responsibilities. Candidates should have ability to work independently, computer skills, editing skills, office skills, oral communication skills, organizational skills, plan to pursue career in field, research skills, self-motivation, strong interpersonal skills, strong leadership ability, writing skills, major in advertising, marketing, or communications. Duration is flexible. $15 per day. Open to college freshmen, college sophomores, college juniors, college seniors, recent college graduates, graduate students. International applications accepted.

Benefits On-the-job training, travel reimbursement, willing to act as a professional reference, willing to complete paperwork for educational credit, willing to provide letters of recommendation, meal allowance.

International Internships Available.

Contact Write, call, or fax Ms. Kashmira Palkhivala, Director, Human Resources. Phone: 212-708-7217. Fax: 212-708-7119. In-person interview recommended (telephone interview accepted). Applicants must submit a formal organization application, letter of interest, resume. Applications are accepted continuously.

KIMBERLY-CLARK CORPORATION
2100 Winchester Road
Neenah, Wisconsin 54956-0999

General Information Manufacturer of personal care, tissue, and health-care products. Established in 1872. Number of employees: 5,100. Number of internship applications received each year: 800.

Internships Available ▶ *10–15 MIS interns (business systems):* responsibilities include assisting a new system development team or a production support team in the design, modification, and testing of automated systems. Candidates should have ability to work independently, college courses in field, oral communication skills, plan to pursue career in field, self-motivation, strong interpersonal skills, strong leadership ability, written communication skills, minimum overall GPA of 3.0 (preferred), knowledge of at least 1 programming language. Duration is 3 months in summer. $18–$20 per hour. Open to college juniors. ▶ *5–10 MIS interns (computer services):* responsibilities include assisting technology-related teams in the support, trouble shooting, and testing of computing and telecommunications infrastructure. Candidates should have ability to work independently, college courses in field, oral communication skills, plan to pursue career in field, research skills, self-motivation, strong interpersonal skills, strong leadership ability, written communication skills, minimum overall GPA of 3.0 (preferred). Duration is 3 months in summer. $18–$20 per hour. Open to college juniors. ▶ *35–45 electrical engineering co-ops:* responsibilities include application of electrical engineering skills to a manufacturing environment working with automated manufacturing equipment including programmable controllers, analog and digital motor controllers, and discrete control hardware. Candidates should have declared college major in field, oral communication skills, self-motivation, strong interpersonal skills, written communication skills, minimum GPA of 3.0, completed basic circuits course. Duration is 3–6 months. $15.75–$22.25 per hour. Open to college sophomores, college juniors, college seniors. ▶ *12–14 finance interns:* responsibilities include working on various projects including cost, competitive and financial analysis, budgeting and forecasting, and financial controls. Candidates should have analytical skills, oral communication skills, plan to pursue career in field, self-motivation, strong interpersonal skills, strong leadership ability, written communication skills, minimum overall GPA of 3.2 (preferred), major in finance or accounting. Duration is 3 months in summer. $17–$19 per hour. Open to college juniors, college seniors. ▶ *15–25 logistics interns:* responsibilities include supporting logistics and the supply chain by controlling materials from the vendor to and through the production facility, warehouse, and customer. Candidates should have analytical skills, oral communication skills, organizational skills, self-motivation, strong interpersonal skills, written communication

skills, minimum overall GPA of 3.0 (preferred). Duration is 3–6 months. $17–$19 per hour. Open to college sophomores, college juniors, college seniors. ▶ *35–45 mechanical engineering co-ops:* responsibilities include applying mechanical engineering skills to a manufacturing environment through CAD design, familiarization with plant safety, documentation, and participation on a project team. Candidates should have college courses in field, oral communication skills, self-motivation, strong interpersonal skills, written communication skills, minimum GPA of 3.0, completed basic drafting course. Duration is 3–6 months. $15.75–$22.25 per hour. Open to college sophomores, college juniors, college seniors. ▶ *25–35 research and development co-ops:* responsibilities include product, process, or materials development. Candidates should have college courses in field, oral communication skills, self-motivation, strong interpersonal skills, written communication skills, minimum GPA of 3.0. Duration is 3–6 months. $15.75–$22.25 per hour. Open to college sophomores, college juniors, college seniors. ▶ *5–10 research and development interns:* responsibilities include product, process, or materials development. Candidates should have college courses in field, oral communication skills, self-motivation, strong interpersonal skills, written communication skills, minimum GPA of 3.0 (preferred); major in chemical engineering, biomedical engineering, chemistry, biochemistry, or material science. Duration is 3–6 months. $15.75–$22.25 per hour. Open to college sophomores, college juniors.

Benefits Formal training, on-the-job training, opportunity to attend seminars/workshops, possible full-time employment, travel reimbursement.

Contact Through World Wide Web site Kay Keberlein, Recruiting Assistant. Phone: 920-721-2602. Fax: 920-721-4219. E-mail: kkeber@kcc.com. In-person interview recommended (telephone interview accepted). Applicants must submit a letter of interest, resume, academic transcripts. Application deadline: February 1 for summer; continuous for co-op positions. World Wide Web: http://www.kimberly-clark.com.

KRAFT FOODS, INC.
Three Lakes Drive
Northfield, Illinois 60093

General Information Consumer packaged goods company. Established in 1903. Number of employees: 1,500. Subsidiary of Altria Group, Inc., New York, New York. Number of internship applications received each year: 400.

Internships Available ▶ *12–15 assistant brand manager summer interns:* responsibilities include marketing project encompassing marketing analysis, design, and execution; summary presentation to supervisors at conclusion. Candidates should have ability to work independently, oral communication skills, self-motivation, strong interpersonal skills, strong leadership ability, written communication skills. Duration is 12 weeks. Paid. Open to graduate students. ▶ *20–25 assistant research scientist summer interns.* Candidates should have ability to work independently, analytical skills, declared college major in field, oral communication skills, plan to pursue career in field, research skills, self-motivation, strong interpersonal skills, written communication skills. Duration is 3 months. Paid. Open to college juniors, college seniors, graduate students. ▶ *5–10 financial associates.* Candidates should have ability to work independently, analytical skills, computer skills, declared college major in field, oral communication skills, plan to pursue career in field, self-motivation, strong interpersonal skills, written communication skills. Duration is 3 months. Paid. Open to college juniors, graduate students. ▶ *6–9 human resources summer interns:* responsibilities include assignments vary depending on location, department, or plant. Candidates should have ability to work independently, analytical skills, college courses in field, computer skills, knowledge of field, oral communication skills, organizational skills, personal interest in the field, plan to pursue career in field, self-motivation, strong interpersonal skills, writing skills. Duration is 3 months. Paid. Open to college juniors, graduate students. ▶ *5–10 information systems interns.* Candidates should have analytical skills, computer skills, oral communication skills, plan to pursue career in field, self-motivation, strong interpersonal skills. Duration is 3 months. Paid. Open to college juniors, graduate students.

Kraft Foods, Inc. (continued)

Benefits Formal training, housing at a cost, on-the-job training, opportunity to attend seminars/workshops, possible full-time employment, travel reimbursement, willing to act as a professional reference, willing to complete paperwork for educational credit, willing to provide letters of recommendation.
Contact Fax or through World Wide Web site Nina Swanson, Senior Manager, Staffing and University Relations, Three Lakes Drive, Northfield, Illinois 60093. Fax: 847-646-8960. No phone calls. In-person interview required. Applicants must submit a formal organization application, resume, three personal references, drug test and background screening required. Application deadline: February 1 for summer. World Wide Web: http://www.kraftfoods.com/careers.

MATTEL, INC.
333 Continental Boulevard, MS-M1-0210
El Segundo, California 90245

General Information Worldwide leader in the design, manufacture, and marketing of family products. Established in 1945. Number of employees: 2,200. Number of internship applications received each year: 250.
Internships Available ▶ *8–12 marketing interns:* responsibilities include assisting with the management of the product development process from concept to retail distribution; recommending marketing actions for assigned brand based on evaluation of product analysis, testing, and sales performance. Candidates should have college degree in related field, oral communication skills, plan to pursue career in field, self-motivation, strong leadership ability, written communication skills. Duration is 10-12 weeks in summer. $900–$1100 per week. ▶ *2–4 senior financial analyst interns:* responsibilities include financial planning and analysis at corporate level, comprehensive financial forecasting, analysis of actual results, analysis of new business ventures and divestitures, capital expenditure analysis, preparation of presentations to senior management, and special reports. Candidates should have analytical skills, oral communication skills, plan to pursue career in field, self-motivation, strong interpersonal skills, written communication skills. Duration is 10-12 weeks in summer. $900–$1100 per week. Open to graduate students. International applications accepted.
Benefits Names of contacts, on-the-job training, opportunity to attend seminars/workshops, possible full-time employment, travel reimbursement, willing to act as a professional reference, willing to complete paperwork for educational credit, willing to provide letters of recommendation, on-site fitness center, half-day Fridays, "picnics in the park", toy discounts.
Contact Write or e-mail Corporate Staffing, Attn: Internships. E-mail: interns@mattel.com. No phone calls. In-person interview required. Applicants must submit a formal organization application, letter of interest, resume, personal references (once selected). Application deadline: March 1. World Wide Web: http://www.mattel.com.

NATIONAL STARCH AND CHEMICAL COMPANY
10 Finderne Avenue
Bridgewater, New Jersey 08807

General Information Leading manufacturer of adhesives, specialty chemicals, resins, electronic materials, specialty food, and industrial starches. Established in 1895. Number of employees: 1,200. Unit of Imperial Chemical Industries, Bridgewater, New Jersey. Number of internship applications received each year: 1,000.
Internships Available ▶ *15–20 summer interns:* responsibilities include working at World Headquarters in Bridgewater, NJ, or at one of major manufacturing plants in Indiana, Illinois, North Carolina, South Carolina, or Missouri. Candidates should have analytical skills, computer skills, oral communication skills, organizational skills, personal interest in the field, research skills, self-motivation, strong interpersonal skills, strong leadership ability, written communication skills, major in chemistry, chemical engineering, food science, MIS/CIS, polymer science, or mate-

rial science. Duration is 3 months. Competitive salary. Open to college sophomores, college juniors, college seniors, graduate students.
Benefits On-the-job training, opportunity to attend seminars/workshops, possible full-time employment, travel reimbursement.
Contact Write, fax, or e-mail Colleen Twill, Graduate Development Manager, 10 Finderne Avenue, Bridgewater, New Jersey 08807. Fax: 908-685-6956. E-mail: colleen.twill@nstarch.com. No phone calls. In-person interview required. Applicants must submit a letter of interest, resume, academic transcripts. Application deadline: February 28. World Wide Web: http://www.nationalstarch.com.

OSHKOSH B'GOSH, INC.
112 Otter Avenue, PO Box 300
Oshkosh, Wisconsin 54902

General Information Manufacturer, marketer, and retailer of children's wear and menswear. Established in 1895. Number of employees: 335. Number of internship applications received each year: 200.
Internships Available ▶ *1–3 associate merchandisers:* responsibilities include coordinating and developing new and existing sales aids; assisting merchandise manager in development of seasonal lot numbers forecasts, analysis of seasonal product costing, and working with designers and artists in all aspects of line development. Candidates should have ability to work independently, ability to work with others, analytical skills, college courses in field, computer skills, oral communication skills, plan to pursue career in field, self-motivation, written communication skills. Duration is 10–12 weeks. Paid. Open to college juniors, college seniors, recent college graduates, graduate students. ▶ *1–2 designers:* responsibilities include assisting the design team in all related functions of seasonal line development; assuming a supporting role in communication and maintaining information in Web PDM and other related documents to the design and success of the finished procedure. Candidates should have ability to work independently, ability to work with others, analytical skills, college courses in field, computer skills, editing skills, knowledge of field, oral communication skills, organizational skills, personal interest in the field, plan to pursue career in field, research skills, written communication skills. Duration is 3 months. Paid. Open to college sophomores, college juniors, college seniors, recent college graduates, graduate students. ▶ *1 import associate:* responsibilities include working with factory, agent, and mill to replicate desired fabric; implementing and maintaining tracking system; ensuring on-time delivery of salesman samples. Candidates should have ability to work independently, ability to work with others, analytical skills, college courses in field, computer skills, office skills, oral communication skills, organizational skills, plan to pursue career in field, self-motivation, written communication skills. Duration is 10–12 weeks. Paid. Open to college juniors, college seniors, recent college graduates, graduate students. ▶ *1 product development associate:* responsibilities include gathering information needed from suppliers; completing purchasing and shipping tasks; organizing and maintaining all fabric, color, and documentation systems. Candidates should have ability to work independently, ability to work with others, analytical skills, college courses in field, computer skills, office skills, oral communication skills, organizational skills, plan to pursue career in field, research skills, self-motivation, writing skills. Duration is 10–12 weeks. Paid. Open to college juniors, college seniors, recent college graduates.
Benefits On-the-job training, possible full-time employment, willing to act as a professional reference, willing to complete paperwork for educational credit, willing to provide letters of recommendation.
Contact Write, fax, e-mail, or through World Wide Web site Andrea Kessler, Recruiter, 112 Otter Avenue, PO Box 300, Oshkosh 54903. Fax: 920-231-8621. E-mail: jobs@bgosh.com. In-person interview recommended (telephone interview accepted). Applicants must submit a letter of interest, resume, portfolio, personal reference. Applications are accepted continuously. World Wide Web: http://www.oshkoshbgosh.com.

OWENS CORNING WORLD HEADQUARTERS
One Owens Corning Parkway
Toledo, Ohio 43659

General Information Manufacturing company providing complete building material systems and advanced glass fiber used in more than 40,000 composite end-use applications. Established in 1938. Number of employees: 1,000. Number of internship applications received each year: 1,500.

Internships Available ▶ *1–6 finance interns:* responsibilities include working in the area of audit, business analysis, tax, external reporting, and corporate accounting. Candidates should have ability to work independently, ability to work with others, analytical skills, computer skills, knowledge of field, oral communication skills, organizational skills, plan to pursue career in field, self-motivation, writing skills, major in accounting or finance. Duration is one summer. $13–$16 per hour. ▶ *1–3 human resources interns:* responsibilities include assisting with training and development programs; supporting compensation and benefits projects. Candidates should have ability to work independently, computer skills, knowledge of field, oral communication skills, organizational skills, self-motivation, strong interpersonal skills, major in human resources. Duration is one summer. $12.19–$15 per hour. ▶ *1–5 information systems interns:* responsibilities include working on analysis, design, technology application, and release testing/deployment activities. Candidates should have ability to work independently, ability to work with others, analytical skills, computer skills, declared college major in field, oral communication skills, organizational skills, personal interest in the field, self-motivation. Duration is one summer. $14–$17 per hour. ▶ *1–5 manufacturing engineer interns:* responsibilities include working in chemical, mechanical, ceramic, and manufacturing technology. Candidates should have ability to work independently, analytical skills, college courses in field, computer skills, oral communication skills, organizational skills, plan to pursue career in field, self-motivation, strong interpersonal skills, written communication skills, technical expertise. Duration is one summer. $15.60–$19.20 per hour. ▶ *1–3 sales/marketing interns:* responsibilities include working in specific geographic area within 200-300 mile radius of Toledo, analyzing the market, identifying major general contractors, determining products they are purchasing and why they are purchasing them. Candidates should have ability to work independently, analytical skills, college courses in field, computer skills, knowledge of field, oral communication skills, organizational skills, self-motivation, strong interpersonal skills, written communication skills, ability to establish relationships. Duration is one summer. $12–$15 per hour. Open to college juniors, college seniors.

Benefits On-the-job training, opportunity to attend seminars/workshops, possible full-time employment, travel reimbursement, possibility of relocation or housing assistance.

Contact Through World Wide Web site Elizabeth Polak, University Relations Leader, One Owens Corning Parkway, Toledo, Ohio 43659. E-mail: resume@owenscorning.com. No phone calls. In-person interview required. Applicants must submit a formal organization application, resume. Application deadline: March 1. World Wide Web: http://www.owenscorning.com.

PELLA CORPORATION
102 Main Street
Pella, Iowa 50219

General Information One of the largest manufacturer of Pella windows and doors. Established in 1925. Number of employees: 7,500. Number of internship applications received each year: 1,000.

Internships Available ▶ *3–6 accounting interns:* responsibilities include estimating costs, pricing products, analyzing profits, annual financial statements, budgeting processes, financial analysis, and financial statement preparation. Candidates should have analytical skills, computer skills, declared college major in field, oral communication skills, organizational skills, written communication skills, technical skills, MS Excel. Duration is flexible. $2300–$2600 per duration of internship. Open to college juniors, college seniors. ▶ *30–40 engineering coops.* Candidates should have computer skills, declared college major in field, organizational skills, strong interpersonal skills, strong leadership ability, experi-

ence in fixture-machine design, auto-CAD. Duration is flexible. $2400–$3000 per duration of internship. Open to college sophomores, college juniors, college seniors. ▶ *2 human resource co-ops:* responsibilities include recruitment, selection, benefits compensation, and training and development. Candidates should have knowledge of field, oral communication skills, organizational skills, strong interpersonal skills, strong leadership ability. Duration is flexible. $2300–$2600 per duration of internship. Open to college juniors, college seniors. ▶ *5–8 information technology interns:* responsibilities include supporting user-requested changes to database; reports. Candidates should have ability to work with others, analytical skills, computer skills, programming and design experience a plus. Duration is flexible. $2500–$2800 per duration of internship. Open to college juniors, college seniors. ▶ *3 marketing coops:* responsibilities include marketing communications, merchandising, market research, customer satisfaction programs, market support services, technical publications, and/or product line management. Candidates should have analytical skills, declared college major in field, oral communication skills, organizational skills, strong interpersonal skills, written communication skills, Excel and Word proficiency, understanding of spreadsheets and regression analysis, presentation skills. Duration is flexible. $2200–$2600 per duration of internship. Open to college juniors, college seniors.

Benefits Health insurance, housing at a cost, on-the-job training, opportunity to attend seminars/workshops, possible full-time employment, travel reimbursement, tuition assistance, willing to act as a professional reference, willing to complete paperwork for educational credit, willing to provide letters of recommendation, dental insurance, holiday pay, vacation pay.

Contact Through World Wide Web site Alison Van Vark, College Relations Coordinator, 102 Main Street, Pella, Iowa 50219. No phone calls. In-person interview required. Applicants must submit a resume, academic transcripts. Applications are accepted continuously. World Wide Web: http://www.pella.com.

SGI (SILICON GRAPHICS, INC.)
1600 Amphitheatre Parkway
Mountain View, California 94043-1351

General Information Leading supplier of high-performance interactive computing systems; offers a broad range of products from desktop workstations to servers and high-end supercomputers. Established in 1982. Number of employees: 4,500. Number of internship applications received each year: 1,500.

Internships Available ▶ *Business development interns:* responsibilities include identifying strategic alliances; negotiation and management of partner contracts; conducting research and competitive analysis. Paid. ▶ *Financial analyst interns:* responsibilities include budgeting, expense control and accounting, cost accounting, and revenue planning. Paid. ▶ *Hardware engineering interns:* responsibilities include microprocessor design, logic design, mask layout, CAD, computer systems design, or mechanical engineering. Paid. ▶ *Human resources interns:* responsibilities include planning and implementing wage reviews, meetings, focus groups, management reports, recruiting, and training. Paid. ▶ *Information systems interns:* responsibilities include opportunities to work as a business analyst, programming analyst, network analyst, database administrator, desktop support, or systems administrator. Paid. ▶ *Manufacturing interns:* responsibilities include forecasting and analyzing product transitions, developing material plan, strategizing and implementing processes throughout the manufacturing cycle. Paid. ▶ *Marketing interns:* responsibilities include opportunities in areas of product, strategic, service, and/or technical marketing. Paid. ▶ *Software engineering interns:* responsibilities include working on operating systems, applications, supercomputing applications, compiler design, or graphics system software. Paid. ▶ *Support/service interns:* responsibilities include UNIX and/or NT technical product support. Paid. Candidates for all positions should have computer skills, declared college major in field, experience in the field, self-motivation, strong interpersonal skills. Open to college sophomores, college juniors, college seniors, graduate students.

Benefits Names of contacts, on-the-job training, opportunity to attend seminars/workshops, possible full-time employment, travel reimbursement, willing to act as a professional reference, willing

SGI (Silicon Graphics, Inc.) (continued)

to complete paperwork for educational credit, willing to provide letters of recommendation, internal marketing of strong performers to hiring managers, housing subsidy, paid holidays, access to fitness facilities.
Contact Write, fax, e-mail, or through World Wide Web site Intern Program Manager. Fax: 650-932-0820. E-mail: krohna@sgi.com. No phone calls. In-person interview recommended (telephone interview accepted). Applicants must submit a letter of interest, resume. Applications are accepted continuously. World Wide Web: http://www.sgi.com.

SUSQUEHANNA PFALTZGRAFF COMPANY
140 East Market Street
York, Pennsylvania 17401

General Information Privately-held, diversified media and dinnerware manufacturing company. Established in 1811. Number of employees: 1,800.
Internships Available ▶ *2 accounting interns:* responsibilities include assisting in preparing financial statements, business forecasting, product costing, and the monthly closing. Candidates should have analytical skills, computer skills, declared college major in field, oral communication skills, strong interpersonal skills, written communication skills. Duration is 10–12 weeks. $8.50 per hour. ▶ *1 human resources intern:* responsibilities include exposure to all facets of a human resources department (recruiting, benefits, payroll, HRIS, compensation, training). Candidates should have college courses in field, computer skills, office skills, oral communication skills, plan to pursue career in field, strong interpersonal skills. Duration is 10–12 weeks. $8.50 per hour. ▶ *1 marketing intern:* responsibilities include assisting marketing manager with special projects. Candidates should have computer skills, declared college major in field, oral communication skills, strong interpersonal skills, written communication skills. Duration is 12 weeks. $8.50 per hour. Open to college juniors, college seniors, recent college graduates. International applications accepted.
Benefits On-the-job training, possible full-time employment, willing to act as a professional reference, willing to complete paperwork for educational credit.
Contact Write, fax, or e-mail Corporate Human Resources, 140 East Market Street, York, Pennsylvania 17401. Fax: 717-852-2594. E-mail: corp.hr@suspfz.com. No phone calls. In-person interview required. Applicants must submit a letter of interest, resume. Application deadline: April 15 for summer.

TRACY WATTS , INC.
305 West 20th Street
New York, New York 10011

General Information Millinery studio that produces hat collections for high-end retailers and custom costumes work. Established in 1993. Number of employees: 2. Number of internship applications received each year: 30.
Internships Available ▶ *2 intern/assistants:* responsibilities include assisting in all aspects of the business such as dealing with buyers and stylists, hand-finishing production, running errands to garment district, and answering telephone. Candidates should have ability to work independently, computer skills, personal interest in the field, self-motivation, strong interpersonal skills, design or art background. Duration is 12 weeks (summer, fall, or spring). Unpaid. Open to college freshmen, college sophomores, college juniors, college seniors, recent college graduates, graduate students, career changers. International applications accepted.
Benefits Job counseling, names of contacts, on-the-job training, opportunity to attend seminars/workshops, possible full-time employment, willing to act as a professional reference, willing to complete paperwork for educational credit, willing to provide letters of recommendation, exposure to retail buyers, designers, and fashion magazine editors; learning custom techniques of millinery production; free lunch daily; free hats.
Contact Write, fax, or e-mail Ms. Tracy Watts, President. Phone: 212-727-7349. Fax: 212-229-0471. E-mail: tracywatts@nyc.rr.com. In-person interview required. Applicants must submit a letter of interest, resume, portfolio, letter of recommendation, cover letter, work samples. Applications are accepted continuously. World Wide Web: http://www.tracywatts.com.

TRANS-LUX CORPORATION
110 Richards Avenue
Norwalk, Connecticut 06854

General Information Leading manufacturer, distributor, and servicer of real-time electronic information displays for use in the indoor and outdoor markets; owner of movie theater chain in southwest United States. Established in 1930. Number of employees: 225. Number of internship applications received each year: 400.
Internships Available ▶ *1–3 PC support interns:* responsibilities include performing a variety of PC support duties; supporting the user community through troubleshooting, upgrades, and installations. Candidates should have ability to work independently, experience in the field, self-motivation, strong interpersonal skills. Duration is flexible. Position available as unpaid or at $10–$15 per hour. Open to college juniors, college seniors. ▶ *3–6 accounting interns:* responsibilities include assisting with general accounting duties which may include account analysis, consolidation of bank requisitions, and preparing property tax returns. Candidates should have analytical skills, college courses in field, computer skills, knowledge of field, personal interest in the field, retail-oriented background. Duration is flexible. Unpaid. Open to college sophomores, college juniors, college seniors, graduate students. ▶ *1–3 business development internship:* responsibilities include assisting the sales and marketing departments with business development work, including identifying contacts and sources for key markets; duties may also include development of database. Candidates should have computer skills, knowledge of field, oral communication skills, personal interest in the field, research skills, strong interpersonal skills. Duration is flexible. Position available as unpaid or at $10–$12 per hour. Open to college sophomores, college juniors, college seniors, graduate students. ▶ *6–9 electrical engineering interns:* responsibilities include assisting the engineering department with hardware and software design projects, design completion, prototyping, and other functions or special projects. Candidates should have ability to work independently, ability to work with others, analytical skills, college courses in field, computer skills, knowledge of field, oral communication skills, organizational skills, self-motivation, specific programming experience for software positions. Duration is flexible. Unpaid. Open to college juniors, college seniors, graduate students. ▶ *6–9 engineering department interns:* responsibilities include assisting the engineering department with hardware and software design projects, design completion, prototyping, and other functions or special projects. Candidates should have ability to work independently, ability to work with others, analytical skills, college courses in field, computer skills, knowledge of field, oral communication skills, organizational skills, personal interest in the field, self-motivation, specific programming experience for software positions. Duration is flexible. Position available as unpaid or at $12–$15 per hour. Open to college juniors, college seniors, recent college graduates, graduate students. ▶ *1–3 human resources interns:* responsibilities include assisting a busy human resources department by performing a variety of entry-level professional duties. Candidates should have ability to work independently, analytical skills, computer skills, office skills, oral communication skills, organizational skills, personal interest in the field, research skills, self-motivation, strong interpersonal skills, writing skills. Duration is flexible. Position available as unpaid or paid. Open to college juniors, college seniors, recent college graduates, graduate students. ▶ *1–3 manufacturing timestudy interns:* responsibilities include determining standards for the subassemblies and final assemblies of manufacturing process; other duties may include serving as back-up bidder for FC's. Candidates should have ability to work with others, analytical skills, knowledge of field, personal interest in the field, research skills. Duration is flexible. Position available as unpaid or at $12–$15 per hour. Open to college juniors, college seniors, recent college graduates, graduate students. ▶ *1–3 programming interns:* responsibilities include assisting the MIS Department's application development staff in modifying programs written in RPG400. Candidates should have

college courses in field, computer skills, knowledge of field. Duration is flexible. Position available as unpaid or at $10–$15 per hour. Open to college sophomores, college juniors, college seniors, graduate students. ▶ *1–3 sales and marketing intern:* responsibilities include working with sales and marketing professionals, as well as other departments, on a variety of projects including development of sales training programs and redesign of systems. Candidates should have analytical skills, oral communication skills, organizational skills, personal interest in the field, strong interpersonal skills, written communication skills. Duration is flexible. Unpaid. Open to college juniors, college seniors, graduate students. International applications accepted.

Benefits Job counseling, names of contacts, on-the-job training, opportunity to attend seminars/workshops, possible full-time employment, willing to act as a professional reference, willing to complete paperwork for educational credit, willing to provide letters of recommendation.

Contact Write, fax, or e-mail Lisa Charest, Human Resources Generalist. Fax: 203-857-0299. E-mail: internships@trans-lux.com. In-person interview recommended (telephone interview accepted). Applicants must submit a formal organization application, letter of interest, resume. Application deadline: January 30 for spring, May 30 for summer, September 30 for fall. World Wide Web: http://www.trans-lux.com.

PHARMACEUTICAL AND MEDICINE MANUFACTURING

ABBOTT LABORATORIES
College Relations, Department 39K, Building AP51, 200 Abbott Park Road
Abbott Park, Illinois 60064-6208

General Information Global, diversified company dedicated to the discovery, development, manufacture, and marketing of health-care products and services. Established in 1888. Number of employees: 75,000. Number of internship applications received each year: 10,000.

Internships Available ▶ *Computing and information science interns:* responsibilities include supporting day-to-day responsibilities related to application development, technical support, data processing operations, and business systems. Duration is May to August. $12.75–$17 per hour. Open to college freshmen, college sophomores, college juniors, college seniors, graduate students. ▶ *Engineering interns:* responsibilities include supporting day-to-day operations in areas of engineering including chemical, software, manufacturing, hazardous waste, telecommunications, hardware, mechanical, electrical, materials or environmental development, and support of production processes and systems. Duration is May to August. $12.75–$17 per hour. Open to college freshmen, college sophomores, college juniors, college seniors, graduate students. ▶ *Finance and accounting interns:* responsibilities include supporting day-to-day responsibilities in corporate, division, or plant-level financial planning and analysis; manufacturing; general accounting or financial reporting. Duration is May to August. $11–$14.50 per hour. Open to college freshmen, college sophomores, college juniors, college seniors, graduate students. ▶ *Human resources interns:* responsibilities include supporting day-to-day responsibilities in areas including compensation and benefits, employee relations, training and development, staffing, and work/family life and diversity. Duration is May to August. $11–$14.50 per hour. Open to college freshmen, college sophomores, college juniors, college seniors, graduate students. ▶ *Production/operations management interns:* responsibilities include supporting day-to-day operations in areas including scale-up, process development, quality control, production planning, or packaging of products and instrument systems. Duration is May to August. $11.25–$15 per hour. Open to college freshmen, college sophomores, college juniors, college seniors, graduate students. ▶ *Sales and marketing interns:* responsibilities include supporting day-to-day responsibilities in marketing. Duration is May to August. $11–$14.50 per hour. Open to college freshmen, college sophomores, college juniors, college seniors, graduate students, MBA students. ▶ *70–90 science and research development interns:* responsibilities include supporting day-to-day operations in synthetic organic chemistry, analytical chemistry, molecular biology, virology, immunology, pharmacology, pharmacy, physiology, biochemistry, toxicology, pathology, research data management, or analytical services. Duration is May to August. $12.25–$16.25 per hour. Open to college freshmen, college sophomores, college juniors, college seniors, graduate students. International applications accepted.

Benefits Formal training, free housing, free meals, names of contacts, on-the-job training, opportunity to attend seminars/workshops, possible full-time employment, travel reimbursement for interns outside 40-mile radius of site.

Contact Through World Wide Web site Amy Alderson, Recruiter, College Relations, College Relations Department 39K, Building AP51, 200 Abbott Park Road, Abbott Park, Illinois 60064-6208. Phone: 847-935-3707. Fax: 847-937-9646. E-mail: amy.alderson@abbott.com. In-person interview recommended (telephone interview accepted). Applicants must submit a resume, apply on line at www.abbott.com. Application deadline: April 1. World Wide Web: http://www.abbott.com.

OTHER SERVICES

BUSINESS, PROFESSIONAL, LABOR, POLITICAL, AND OTHER ORGANIZATIONS

A. E. SCHWARTZ & ASSOCIATES
PO Box 79228
Waverley, Massachusetts 02479-0228

General Information Comprehensive training and consulting organization offering over 40 management and professional training programs to managers and support staff nationally and internationally. Established in 1982. Number of employees: 12. Number of internship applications received each year: 1,200.
Internships Available ▶ *3–5 business technology interns:* responsibilities include developing new version of commercial Web site; maintaining and posting new data; researching and installing new software/hardware; creating solutions and generating information for end-users, partners, and registrants; developing systems for tracking and project management; managing corporate e-mail and autoresponders. Candidates should have ability to work independently, computer skills, oral communication skills, organizational skills, written communication skills, Internet knowledge and experience. Duration is flexible (minimum 16-24 hours weekly). Position available as unpaid or paid. Open to college sophomores, college juniors, college seniors, recent college graduates, graduate students, career changers. ▶ *3–5 graphic designers:* responsibilities include creating new design concepts; designing flyers, book covers, sales materials, catalog, and exhibit materials including specialty and promotional items; writing, editing, and copyediting; providing camera-ready output and overseeing printing; Internet Web design. Candidates should have ability to work independently, analytical skills, computer skills, declared college major in field, oral communication skills, organizational skills, written communication skills, Internet knowledge and experience. Duration is flexible (minimum 16-24 hours weekly). Position available as unpaid or paid. Open to college sophomores, college juniors, college seniors, recent college graduates, graduate students, career changers, individuals reentering the workforce. ▶ *3–5 publishing interns:* responsibilities include coordinating marketing and placement of new releases online; researching supplemental information; editing, developing, writing, and evaluating new and existing materials. Candidates should have ability to work independently, ability to work with others, analytical skills, computer skills, editing skills, oral communication skills, organizational skills, written communication skills, Internet knowledge and experience. Duration is flexible (minimum 16-24 hours weekly). Position available as unpaid or paid. Open to college sophomores, college juniors, college seniors, recent college graduates, graduate students, career changers, individuals reentering the workforce. ▶ *3–5 sales/ marketing interns:* responsibilities include developing strategies and new distribution outlets, networking with sponsoring organizations to arrange programs, developing contacts, researching new distribution avenues (Internet emphasis), developing and maintaining computer systems for mail projects, placing advertisements, and handling correspondence. Candidates should have ability to work independently, ability to work with others, oral communica-

tion skills, organizational skills, personal interest in the field, self-motivation, Internet knowledge and experience. Duration is flexible (minimum 16-24 hours weekly). Position available as unpaid or paid. Open to college sophomores, college juniors, college seniors, recent college graduates, graduate students, career changers, individuals reentering the workforce. ▶ *3–5 writers/editors:* responsibilities include assisting in the writing, editing, and copyediting of new and existing materials (online and offline); researching supplemental information; writing articles for training and management journals; and compiling, writing, and editing manuscripts and training manuals. Candidates should have ability to work independently, ability to work with others, analytical skills, computer skills, editing skills, oral communication skills, organizational skills, written communication skills, Internet knowledge and experience. Duration is flexible (minimum 16-24 hours weekly). Position available as unpaid or paid. Open to college sophomores, college juniors, college seniors, recent college graduates, graduate students, career changers, individuals reentering the workforce. International applications accepted.
Benefits Formal training, on-the-job training, possible full-time employment, willing to act as a professional reference, willing to complete paperwork for educational credit, willing to provide letters of recommendation, opportunity to attend seminars/workshops/meetings, travel stipend for some positions.
Contact Write, fax, e-mail, or through World Wide Web site Mr. Andrew E. Schwartz, CEO. Fax: 617-926-0660. E-mail: interns@ aeschwartz.com. In-person interview recommended (telephone interview accepted). Applicants must submit a letter of interest, resume, writing sample, 3 personal and professional references (names and phone numbers). Applications are accepted continuously. World Wide Web: http://www.aeschwartz.com.

AFRICA ACTION
1634 Eye Street, NW, Suite 5810
Washington, District of Columbia 20006

General Information National organization that works for political, economic, and social justice in Africa through the provision of accessible information and analysis; works with the mobilization of public pressure to change the policies and policy-making processes of U.S. and multinational institutions toward Africa. Established in 1978. Number of employees: 5. Number of internship applications received each year: 20.
Internships Available ▶ *1–2 research assistants:* responsibilities include drafting position papers, researching information for Web site, attending and reporting on constituent meetings. Candidates should have college courses in field, computer skills, knowledge of field, oral communication skills, research skills, self-motivation, written communication skills. Duration is 2–12 months. Unpaid. Open to graduate students. International applications accepted.
Benefits Names of contacts, opportunity to attend seminars/workshops, willing to act as a professional reference, willing to complete paperwork for educational credit, willing to provide letters of recommendation.
Contact Write, fax, or e-mail Brenda Payne, Administrator. Fax: 202-546-1545. No phone calls. Telephone interview required. Applicants must submit a formal organization application, resume, two writing samples, two letters of recommendation, 1-to 2-page essay describing goals and objectives in seeking an internship with Africa Action. Application deadline: June 1 for fall (September), October 1 for winter (January). World Wide Web: http://www.africaaction.org.

AMERICAN ASSOCIATION OF ADVERTISING AGENCIES
405 Lexington Avenue, 18th Floor
New York, New York 10174-1801

General Information National trade association of the advertising industry with more than 575 members nationwide. Established in 1917. Number of employees: 100. Number of internship applications received each year: 450.
Internships Available ▶ *70–90 multicultural advertising interns:* responsibilities include performing duties in account management, art direction, interactive technologies, copywriting, research, broadcast production, graphic design, traffic, print product, and media in New York, Chicago, Boston, Detroit, Dallas, Seattle, Philadelphia, Portland, Los Angeles, or San Francisco. Candidates should have ability to work independently, ability to work with others, analytical skills, computer skills, knowledge of field, oral communication skills, organizational skills, personal interest in the field, plan to pursue career in field, research skills, self-motivation, writing skills. Duration is 70 weeks. $350–$400 per week. Open to college juniors, college seniors, graduate students.
Benefits Names of contacts, opportunity to attend seminars/ workshops, possible full-time employment, willing to act as a professional reference, willing to complete paperwork for educational credit, willing to provide letters of recommendation, 70% payment of housing and transportation costs.
Contact Write, call, fax, e-mail, or through World Wide Web site Tiffany R. Warren, Manager of Diversity Programs. Phone: 800-676-9333. Fax: 212-573-8968. E-mail: maip@aaaa.org. In-person interview required. Applicants must submit a formal organization application, resume, academic transcripts, two letters of recommendation, 2-3 writing or creative samples (for art/ copywriting positions). Application deadline: January. World Wide Web: http://www.aaaa.org.

AMERICAN ASSOCIATION OF UNIVERSITY WOMEN EDUCATIONAL FOUNDATION
1111 16th Street, NW
Washington, District of Columbia 20036-4873

General Information Foundation that provides funding for educational programs that directly benefit women and girls; groundbreaking research on gender bias in schools; fellowships and grants for outstanding women from around the globe; and vital community action projects. Established in 1881. Number of employees: 90. Unit of AAUW, Washington, District of Columbia. Number of internship applications received each year: 30.
Internships Available ▶ *1 Eleanor Roosevelt teacher fellowships and community action grants intern:* responsibilities include assisting with the management and assessment of funding programs. Duration is flexible. Unpaid. ▶ *1 communications intern:* responsibilities include assisting the coordinator with monitoring and managing the flow of materials between the two staffs; editing and writing articles, press releases, and creative briefs for meetings; and other programmatic, technical, and administrative projects. Duration is flexible. Unpaid. ▶ *2 development interns:* responsibilities include working with the staff to analyze contribution systems, determine donor trends, and research potential funders; writing text for proposals, donor profiles, and publications. Duration is flexible. Unpaid. ▶ *1 gender equity research intern:* responsibilities include assisting in the coordination of commissioned research reports currently in production. Duration is flexible. Unpaid. ▶ *1 higher education fellowships intern:* responsibilities include working with the senior program officer on program assessment projects and the development of a major Colleges of Teacher Education initiative. Duration is flexible. Unpaid. ▶ *1 international fellowships intern:* responsibilities include assisting the senior program officer with assessment and evaluation efforts. Duration is flexible. Unpaid. ▶ *1 multicultural initiatives and higher education intern:* responsibilities include assisting the associate director and coordinator of multicultural initiatives and the program officer for career development grants and selected professions fellowships to assess grant programs; researching and writing articles on minority women in higher education; and coordinating conferences and meetings. Duration is flexible. Unpaid. Open to college freshmen, college sophomores, college juniors, college seniors, recent college graduates, graduate students.
Benefits Formal training, job counseling, names of contacts, opportunity to attend seminars/workshops, possible full-time employment, willing to complete paperwork for educational credit, willing to provide letters of recommendation, small stipend, computer courses on all levels, career development lunches, networking opportunities.
Contact Write, call, fax, or e-mail Jai Fawn Burrello, Internship Coordinator. Phone: 202-785-7700. Fax: 202-872-1413. E-mail: aauwjobs@aauw.org. In-person interview recommended (telephone interview accepted). Applicants must submit a letter of interest, resume, writing sample. Applications are accepted continuously. World Wide Web: http://www.aauw.org.

AMERICAN COUNCIL FOR THE UNITED NATIONS UNIVERSITY
4421 Garrison Street, NW
Washington, District of Columbia 20016

General Information Nonprofit corporation that provides support for the United Nations University, an autonomous organization of the United Nations that focuses intellectual resources on world problems; global, decentralized, non-degree granting, postgraduate research institution; manages the Millennium Project on futures research and global change. Established in 1976. Number of employees: 3. Affiliate of United Nations University, Tokyo, Japan. Number of internship applications received each year: 100.
Internships Available ▶ *5–8 Millennium Project interns:* responsibilities include assisting with research and editing in social and technological fields, entering data, attending meetings and conferences, reviewing and reading documents, helping develop studies, and Web site improvements. Candidates should have analytical skills, computer skills, editing skills, organizational skills, research skills, writing skills. Duration is 2½ months to 1 year (preferably full-time). Unpaid. Open to college juniors, college seniors, recent college graduates, graduate students, law students, career changers, individuals reentering the workforce, preference given to graduate students. ▶ *1–2 Webmaster's assistants:* responsibilities include maintaining and improving Web site, assisting global research on future of global change, attending conferences, and finding the best ideas and experts. Candidates should have analytical skills, computer skills, editing skills, organizational skills, research skills, writing skills. Duration is 2½ months to 1 year (preferably full-time for 1 semester). Unpaid. Open to college juniors, college seniors, recent college graduates, graduate students, career changers, individuals reentering the workforce. ▶ *1–2 general interns:* responsibilities include providing liaison services between U.S. research institutions and the United Nations University programs. Candidates should have computer skills, editing skills, office skills, oral communication skills, organizational skills, self-motivation. Duration is flexible (preferably full-time for one semester). Unpaid. Open to college juniors, college seniors, recent college graduates, graduate students, law students, career changers, individuals reentering the workforce, preference given to graduate students. ▶ *2–3 video interns:* responsibilities include scanning Internet and other sources for images and video footage; assisting in editing and production for documentaries on global change. Candidates should have analytical skills, computer skills, editing skills, organizational skills, video skills. Duration is 2½ months to 1 year (preferably full-time for 1 semester). Unpaid. Open to college juniors, college seniors, recent college graduates, graduate students, career changers, individuals reentering the workforce. International applications accepted.
Benefits Formal training, job counseling, names of contacts, on-the-job training, opportunity to attend seminars/workshops, possible full-time employment, willing to act as a professional reference, willing to complete paperwork for educational credit, willing to provide letters of recommendation, work-related travel reimbursement.
International Internships Available in Buenos Aires, Argentina; Beijing, China; Cairo, Egypt; Maduri, India; Rome, Italy; Tokyo, Japan; Moscow, Russian Federation; London, United Kingdom.

American Council for the United Nations University (continued)

Contact Write, call, fax, e-mail, or through World Wide Web site Jerome C. Glenn, Executive Director. Phone: 202-686-5179. Fax: 202-686-5179. E-mail: jglenn@igc.org. In-person interview recommended (telephone interview accepted). Applicants must submit a letter of interest, resume. Applications are accepted continuously. World Wide Web: http://www.millennium-project.org.

THE AMERICAN ENTERPRISE INSTITUTE (AEI)
1150 17th Street, NW
Washington, District of Columbia 20036

General Information Public policy making organization. Established in 1943. Number of employees: 180. Number of internship applications received each year: 1,000.

Internships Available ▶ *40 interns:* responsibilities include working in one of the following areas: economic policy, foreign and defense studies, political and social studies, public relations, The American Enterprise magazine, communications, seminars and conferences, publications, publications marketing, information systems, marketing, and accounting. Candidates should have computer skills, personal interest in the field, research skills, self-motivation, written communication skills. Duration is flexible (usually one semester). Unpaid. Open to college juniors, college seniors, graduate students, law students. International applications accepted.

Benefits Free meals, names of contacts, opportunity to attend seminars/workshops, possible full-time employment, willing to act as a professional reference, willing to provide letters of recommendation.

Contact Write, fax, e-mail, or through World Wide Web site Robert Lutz, Intern Coordinator. Phone: 202-862-5800. Fax: 202-862-7171. E-mail: intern@aei.org. Applicants must submit a letter of interest, resume, academic transcripts, 500-word writing sample. Application deadline: April 1 for summer, September 15 for fall, December 1 for spring. World Wide Web: http://www.aei.org.

AMERICAN FEDERATION OF TEACHERS
555 New Jersey Avenue, NW
Washington, District of Columbia 20001

General Information Public employee labor union. Established in 1916. Number of employees: 350. Number of internship applications received each year: 150.

Internships Available ▶ *Interns:* responsibilities include research, writing, support for policy development and resources for affiliates. Candidates should have ability to work independently, knowledge of field, organizational skills, strong interpersonal skills, writing skills. $280 per week. Open to college sophomores, college juniors, college seniors, recent college graduates, graduate students, law students. International applications accepted.

Benefits On-the-job training, opportunity to attend seminars/workshops, willing to complete paperwork for educational credit, willing to provide letters of recommendation, health insurance (if necessary).

Contact Write, fax, or e-mail Patricia Olshefski, Director, PSRP Department. Fax: 202-879-4597. E-mail: intern@aft.org. No phone calls. Applicants must submit a resume, academic transcripts, writing sample, letter of recommendation, letter of interest indicating type of experience desired and reason for applying. Application deadline: March 1 for summer, July 1 for fall, November 1 for winter. World Wide Web: http://www.aft.org.

AMERICAN FOREIGN SERVICE ASSOCIATION
2101 E Street, NW
Washington, District of Columbia 20037

General Information Professional association and labor union representing members of the U.S. Foreign Service in labor-management relations, in promoting and advancing the diplomatic profession, and securing popular support for an active and effective U.S. foreign policy. Established in 1924. Number of employees: 25.

Internships Available ▶ *1 advocacy and legislative affairs intern:* responsibilities include drafting letters to Congress and opinion leaders, calling congressional staff members, and working with community leaders. Candidates should have ability to work independently, ability to work with others, computer skills, self-motivation, writing skills. Duration is 1 semester (16 hours per week, minimum). $300 stipend (fall and spring interns); $500 (summer interns). Open to college freshmen, college sophomores, college juniors, college seniors. ▶ *1 editorial/research assistant (Foreign Service Journal):* responsibilities include editing, writing, fact-checking and proofreading for the Foreign Service Journal; opportunity to write an article for the Journal in addition to some administrative work. Candidates should have computer skills, editing skills, research skills, writing skills, knowledge of HTML (a plus), native-level fluency in English (required), interest in international affairs with coursework in the field (preferable), publications experience (a plus). Duration is 1 semester. $300 stipend (fall and spring interns); $500 stipend (summer interns). Open to college freshmen, college sophomores, college juniors, college seniors, recent college graduates, graduate students. ▶ *1 legislative affairs intern:* responsibilities include helping maintain database, analyzing and summarizing legislation, attending hearings, working with grassroots and coalition organizations, and helping develop and implement legislative strategy. Candidates should have analytical skills, computer skills, editing skills, organizational skills, research skills, self-motivation, writing skills, general understanding of the legislative process and politics in general. Duration is 1 semester. $300 stipend (fall and spring interns); $500 stipend (summer interns). Open to college freshmen, college sophomores, college juniors, college seniors. ▶ *1 public affairs intern:* responsibilities include interviewing Foreign Service personnel, drafting articles and other materials, and placing articles in newspapers and magazines. Candidates should have ability to work independently, editing skills, oral communication skills, self-motivation, strong interpersonal skills, writing skills, some exposure to international affairs is desirable. Duration is 1 semester. $300 stipend (fall and spring interns); $500 stipend (summer interns). Open to college freshmen, college sophomores, college juniors, college seniors. ▶ *1 publications marketing/advertising intern (Foreign Service Journal):* responsibilities include helping design and operate a marketing campaign; gaining experience in promoting a supplement, print advertising, direct mailing, phone skills, as well as overall production, circulation, and distribution of magazine. Candidates should have computer skills, ability to work hard, dependability, detail-orientation, general understanding of marketing and advertising. Duration is 1 semester (16-24 hours per week). $300 stipend (fall and spring interns); $500 stipend (summer interns). Open to college freshmen, college sophomores, college juniors, college seniors. International applications accepted.

Benefits Willing to act as a professional reference, willing to complete paperwork for educational credit, willing to provide letters of recommendation, stipends available.

Contact Write, call, fax, e-mail, or through World Wide Web site Intern Coordinator. Phone: 202-338-4045. Fax: 202-338-6820. E-mail: afsa@afsa.org. In-person interview recommended (telephone interview accepted). Applicants must submit a letter of interest, resume, writing sample. Applications are accepted continuously. World Wide Web: http://www.afsa.org.

AMERICAN ISRAEL PUBLIC AFFAIRS COMMITTEE (AIPAC)
440 First Street, NW, Suite 600
Washington, District of Columbia 20001

General Information Bipartisan organization that lobbies Congress and the Administration on legislation that affects the U.S.-Israel relationship. Established in 1954. Number of employees: 100. Number of internship applications received each year: 300.

Internships Available ▶ *10–25 interns:* responsibilities include a variety of tasks and positions, including research, writing, public relations, legislative work, and event planning. Candidates should have computer skills, office skills, oral communication skills, research skills, writing skills, knowledge of/interest in the Middle East. Duration is one semester (minimum of 16 hours per week) or summer (full-time). Unpaid. Open to college freshmen, college sophomores, college juniors, college seniors, recent college graduates, graduate students.

Benefits Job counseling, opportunity to attend seminars/workshops, willing to act as a professional reference, willing to complete paperwork for educational credit, willing to provide letters of recommendation, stipend for summer positions (full-time).
International Internships Available in Jerusalem, Israel.
Contact Write, call, fax, e-mail, or through World Wide Web site Rachel Murov, Internship Coordinator. Phone: 202-639-5327. Fax: 202-347-4918. E-mail: rachel_murov@aipac.org. Applicants must submit a letter of interest, resume, writing sample, two letters of recommendation, passport-size photo. Application deadline: January 15 for spring, April 1 for summer, September 15 for fall, December 1 for winter. World Wide Web: http://www.aipac.org.

AMERICAN JUDICATURE SOCIETY
180 North Michigan Avenue, Suite 600
Chicago, Illinois 60601

General Information Society that strives to maintain and enhance the independence and effectiveness of the judicial system. Established in 1913. Number of employees: 15. Number of internship applications received each year: 50.
Internships Available ▶ *1–2 law clerks:* responsibilities include legal research and writing and assisting in the publication of various journals/newsletters. Candidates should have ability to work independently, analytical skills, computer skills, editing skills, research skills, writing skills. Duration is 2–3 months. Unpaid. Open to law students. ▶ *1–2 research assistants:* responsibilities include library research, writing reports, and collating and cataloging information. Candidates should have analytical skills, college courses in field, computer skills, office skills, research skills, writing skills. Duration is 2–3 months. Unpaid. Open to college juniors, college seniors. International applications accepted.
Benefits On-the-job training, possible full-time employment, willing to act as a professional reference, willing to complete paperwork for educational credit, willing to provide letters of recommendation, opportunity to develop legal and social science research skills.
Contact Write, e-mail, or through World Wide Web site Malia Reddick, Director of Research. Fax: 312-558-9175. E-mail: mreddick@ajs.org. No phone calls. In-person interview required. Applicants must submit a letter of interest, resume, writing sample, two personal references, two letters of recommendation. Application deadline: April 1 for summer, August 1 for fall, December 1 for spring. World Wide Web: http://www.ajs.org.

AMERICAN OUTLOOK MAGAZINE
5395 Emerson Way
Indianapolis, Indiana 46226

General Information Nonprofit futurist public policy think tank. Established in 1961. Number of employees: 50. Division of Hudson Institute, Indianapolis, Indiana. Number of internship applications received each year: 30.
Internships Available ▶ *2–3 editorial assistants:* responsibilities include assisting with production of *American Outlook&OR magazine and other Hudson Institute publications. Candidates should have analytical skills, computer skills, editing skills, research skills, writing skills. Duration is 3–4 months. Unpaid. Open to college seniors, recent college graduates, graduate students. International applications accepted.*
Benefits On-the-job training, willing to act as a professional reference, willing to complete paperwork for educational credit, willing to provide letters of recommendation.
Contact Write, fax, or e-mail Sam Karnick, Editor-in-Chief. Fax: 317-545-9639. E-mail: sam@hudson.org. No phone calls. In-person interview required. Applicants must submit a letter of interest, resume, three writing samples. Application deadline: January 1 for spring, May 1 for summer, August 1 for fall, November 1 for winter. World Wide Web: http://www.americanoutlook.org.

AMERICAN SOCIETY OF COMPOSERS, AUTHORS, AND PUBLISHERS
1 Lincoln Plaza, Floor 6
New York, New York 10023-7129

General Information Membership organization of over 70,000 composers, songwriters, lyricists, and music publishers; ASCAP's function is to protect the rights of its members by licensing and paying royalties for the public performances of their copyrighted works. Established in 1914. Number of employees: 700. Number of internship applications received each year: 30.
Internships Available ▶ *10–20 interns:* responsibilities include diverse tasks structured to reflect the intern's interests, talents, and skills level. Candidates should have analytical skills, computer skills, oral communication skills, strong interpersonal skills, written communication skills. Duration is flexible. Unpaid. Open to high school students, recent high school graduates, college freshmen, college sophomores, college juniors, college seniors, recent college graduates, graduate students, law students, career changers, individuals reentering the workforce. International applications accepted.
Benefits Possible full-time employment, willing to complete paperwork for educational credit, willing to provide letters of recommendation.
Contact Write, e-mail, or through World Wide Web site Manny Valderas, Human Resources Administrator. Fax: 212-874-8480. E-mail: jobline@ascap.com. No phone calls. In-person interview required. Applicants must submit a letter of interest, resume. Applications are accepted continuously. World Wide Web: http://www.ascap.com.

AMERICAN SOCIETY OF MAGAZINE EDITORS
919 Third Avenue, 22nd Floor
New York, New York 10022

General Information Professional society for magazine editors that provides a forum for the discussion of matters of mutual concern. Established in 1963. Number of employees: 3. Unit of Magazine Publishers of America, New York, New York. Number of internship applications received each year: 175.
Internships Available ▶ *40 editorial interns:* responsibilities include performing entry-level editorial tasks. Candidates should have college courses in field, editing skills, knowledge of field, plan to pursue career in field, writing skills, previous magazine experience. Duration is 10 weeks in summer. Stipend of $325 per week. Open to college juniors. International applications accepted.
Benefits Housing at a cost, opportunity to attend seminars/workshops, willing to act as a professional reference, willing to provide letters of recommendation, distribution of resumes to ASME members.
Contact Write, fax, e-mail, or through World Wide Web site Marlene Kahan, Executive Director. Fax: 212-906-0128. E-mail: asme@magazine.org. No phone calls. Applicants must submit a formal organization application, letter of interest, resume, three writing samples, letter of recommendation. Application deadline: November 15. Fees: $25. World Wide Web: http://www.asme.magazine.org.

AMIDEAST
1730 M Street, NW, Suite 1100
Washington, District of Columbia 20036

General Information Private, nonprofit organization promoting cooperation and understanding between Americans and the people of the Middle East and North Africa through education and development programs. Established in 1951. Number of employees: 53. Number of internship applications received each year: 100.
Internships Available ▶ *1 editorial research intern:* responsibilities include assisting in writing, researching, and marketing of quarterly professional periodical and other resources for overseas educational advisers and organizing and maintaining advising resource collections. Duration is flexible. Paid. ▶ *1 intern for special projects-short-term training:* responsibilities include researching short-term training programs, responding to trainees' requests, maintaining accurate records, corresponding with trainers and the field offices,

and providing general program support. Candidates should have ability to work independently, ability to work with others, computer skills, office skills, oral communication skills, written communication skills. Duration is 1 month. Paid. ▶ *1 public relations/fund-raising intern:* responsibilities include researching international companies and compiling information to support fund-raising, public relations, and marketing products and services; researching, writing, and proofreading newsletters, annual report, flyers, and press releases; updating computerized mailing/donor lists. Candidates should have ability to work independently, ability to work with others, computer skills, office skills, oral communication skills, written communication skills. Duration is flexible. Paid. ▶ *2 publications interns:* responsibilities include researching, writing, editing, and producing educational materials; processing publications orders; and developing and implementing marketing activities. Candidates should have ability to work independently, ability to work with others, computer skills, office skills, oral communication skills, written communication skills. Duration is flexible (3 months minimum). Paid. ▶ *1 study abroad intern:* responsibilities include researching markets, developing advertisements and promotional materials, preparing mass mailings, and responding to requests for information. Candidates should have ability to work independently, ability to work with others, computer skills, office skills, oral communication skills, written communication skills. Duration is 1 semester. Paid. Open to college freshmen, college sophomores, college juniors, college seniors. International applications accepted.

Benefits Willing to complete paperwork for educational credit, willing to provide letters of recommendation.

Contact Write, call, e-mail, or through World Wide Web site Shawnte Jefferies, Personnel Assistant. Phone: 202-776-9600. E-mail: personnel@amideast.org. In-person interview recommended (telephone interview accepted). Applicants must submit a letter of interest, resume. Applications are accepted continuously. World Wide Web: http://www.amideast.org.

ASHOKA: INNOVATORS FOR THE PUBLIC
1700 North Moore Street, Suite 2000
Arlington, Virginia 22209-1903

General Information International, nonprofit organization presenting fellowships to individuals with creative ideas for social change in Asia, Latin America, Central Europe, Africa, and North America. Established in 1980. Number of employees: 52. Number of internship applications received each year: 100.

Internships Available ▶ *Interns:* responsibilities include working in areas of development, recruitment and selection of fellows, fellowship support services, environmental education, citizen-based initiative, social marketing, finance, research, computers, and administration; working in offices dealing with Latin America, Asia, Central Europe, Africa, and North America. Candidates should have ability to work independently, ability to work with others, computer skills, oral communication skills, research skills, self-motivation, writing skills, language ability (French, Spanish, Portuguese, Thai or other Asian language a plus), entrepreneurial spirit. Duration is flexible (minimum of 12 hours per week preferred). Unpaid. Open to college freshmen, college sophomores, college juniors, college seniors, recent college graduates, graduate students, law students, career changers, individuals reentering the workforce. International applications accepted.

Benefits Names of contacts, opportunity to attend seminars/workshops, possible full-time employment, willing to complete paperwork for educational credit, willing to provide letters of recommendation.

Contact Write, fax, e-mail, or through World Wide Web site Jim Scrivani, Internship Coordinator. Phone: 703-527-8300 Ext. 276. Fax: 703-527-8383. E-mail: interns@ashoka.org. In-person interview recommended (telephone interview accepted). Applicants must submit a letter of interest, resume, cover letter. Applications are accepted continuously. World Wide Web: http://www.ashoka.org.

ASIAN AMERICAN ECONOMIC DEVELOPMENT ENTERPRISES, INC. (AAEDE)
216 West Garvey Avenue, Unit E
Monterey Park, California 91754

General Information Nonprofit organization aiding small business owners in the community via workshops and individual consultation and providing the community with job fairs and volunteer opportunities. Established in 1977. Number of employees: 3. Number of internship applications received each year: 40.

Internships Available ▶ *1–2 community liaisons:* responsibilities include contacting various media and community organizations by sending out press releases, compiling press kits, arranging radio and television interviews, and making new media and association contacts for AAEDE. Candidates should have oral communication skills, organizational skills, self-motivation, writing skills. Duration is 8-12 hours per week. Position available as unpaid or paid. ▶ *2–3 conference coordinator assistants:* responsibilities include participating in all aspects of conference planning, including design and selection of invitations, sponsorship, speaker arrangements, lecture materials, lecture hall preparation, volunteer recruitment, and room set-up planning. Candidates should have ability to work with others, oral communication skills, organizational skills, self-motivation, creative and detail-oriented nature. Duration is 8-12 hours per week. Position available as unpaid or paid. ▶ *2–3 newsletter publication assistants:* responsibilities include gathering and evaluating information for newsletter, writing articles, editing submissions, reporting on community events, supporting design and layout, compiling graphic boards, interacting with the printer, and assisting with bulk mail. Candidates should have ability to work independently, ability to work with others, computer skills, editing skills, research skills, writing skills. Duration is 8-12 hours per week. Unpaid. ▶ *2–3 research/special project assistants:* responsibilities include gathering and evaluating business and/or demographic information for programs and grant applications, attending community meetings, evaluating proposals, and interacting with small business clients. Candidates should have analytical skills, computer skills, oral communication skills, research skills, writing skills, foreign language skills and business experience helpful. Duration is 8-12 hours per week. Unpaid. Open to college freshmen, college sophomores, college juniors, college seniors, recent college graduates, graduate students.

Benefits Opportunity to attend seminars/workshops, willing to act as a professional reference, willing to complete paperwork for educational credit, willing to provide letters of recommendation.

Contact Write, call, fax, e-mail, or through World Wide Web site Van Truong, Program Manager, 216 West Garvey Avenue, Unit E, Monterey Park, California 91754. Phone: 626-572-7021. Fax: 626-572-6533. E-mail: vt@aaede.org. In-person interview recommended (telephone interview accepted). Applicants must submit a letter of interest, resume. Applications are accepted continuously. World Wide Web: http://www.aaede.org.

ASIAN AMERICAN JOURNALISTS ASSOCIATION
1182 Market Street, Suite 320
San Francisco, California 94102

General Information National nonprofit organization that encourages Asian-American students to pursue journalism careers, seeks to increase employment of and provide support for Asian-American journalists, and promotes fair and accurate coverage of Asian-American issues. Established in 1981. Number of employees: 7. Number of internship applications received each year: 200.

Internships Available ▶ *1 Siani Lee broadcast internship:* responsibilities include operating in a news department in a variety of areas such as breaking news, sports, entertainment, or the tape library. Candidates should have ability to work with others, college courses in field, oral communication skills, plan to pursue career in field, self-motivation, written communication skills. Duration is summer. $2500 per duration of internship. Open to college freshmen, college sophomores, college juniors, college seniors. ▶ *3 Stanford Chen interns:* responsibilities include working in small to medium-sized newspapers or broadcast stations throughout the US; one position awarded to resident of Pacific Northwest. Candidates should have oral communication skills, personal interest in the field, plan to pursue career in field, self-motivation, writing skills. Duration is flexible. $1500 per duration of internship. Open to college juniors, college seniors. ▶ *30–40 student media projects interns:* responsibilities include creating a newspaper, television broadcasting, radio programming, and working on a Web site. Candidates should have ability to work with others, oral communication skills, research skills, self-motivation, written communication skills. Duration is week-long internship at AAJA National Convention. Unpaid. Open to college freshmen, college sophomores, college juniors, college seniors, recent college graduates.

Benefits Job counseling, names of contacts, willing to complete paperwork for educational credit, willing to provide letters of recommendation, opportunity to attend annual convention.

Contact Write or e-mail Ms. Lila Chwee, Student Programs Coordinator. Phone: 415-346-2051. Fax: 415-346-6343. E-mail: lilac@aaja.org. In-person interview recommended (telephone interview accepted). Applicants must submit a formal organization application, resume, academic transcripts, two personal references, letter of recommendation. Application deadline: March 10 for fall, April 7 for summer. World Wide Web: http://www.aaja.org.

ASIAN PACIFIC AMERICAN DISPUTE RESOLUTION CENTER
1145 Wilshire Boulevard, Suite 100
Los Angeles, California 90017

General Information Center that provides mediation and conciliation services to individuals, organizations, and businesses that are interested in resolving disputes outside the court system. Established in 1989. Number of employees: 7. Number of internship applications received each year: 100.

Internships Available ▶ *5 AmeriCorps VISTA Interns:* responsibilities include serving in one of five API social service agencies; creating an outreach strategy in their own agency and for the entire collaborative, as well as having choice to write grants, develop volunteer programs, or develop curriculum. Candidates should have oral communication skills, organizational skills, personal interest in the field, self-motivation, strong interpersonal skills, strong leadership ability. Duration is one year (40 hours per week). $700 per month. Open to college sophomores, college juniors, college seniors, recent college graduates, graduate students, law students, career changers, individuals reentering the workforce. ▶ *1–5 conflict resolution specialists:* responsibilities include conducting intake interviews, interacting with clients, and performing casework; observing and participating in mediation (with complete training provided by Center); assisting with community education, public presentation, and outreach programs. Candidates should have oral communication skills, organizational skills, personal interest in the field, self-motivation, strong interpersonal skills, written communication skills. Duration is 16 weeks (12-15 hours per week). Unpaid. Open to college juniors, college seniors, recent college graduates, graduate students, law students, career changers. ▶ *1 development specialist:* responsibilities include assisting in the creation of a database with contact information on community organizations as well as corporations in the local area; assisting with grant writing for the Center; supporting the day-to-day activities and special projects. Candidates should have ability to work independently, organizational skills, research skills, self-motivation, strong interpersonal skills, writing skills. Duration is 10–12 weeks. Unpaid. Open to college juniors, college seniors, recent college graduates, graduate students, law students, career changers, individuals reentering the workforce. ▶ *Language specialists:* responsibilities include translating casework (applications, evaluations), outreach materials (flyers, presentations, brochures) and recruitment materials (flyers, paperwork) into language of expertise. Candidates should have editing skills, written communication skills, competence in a foreign language (especially in an Asian language). Duration is 8–10 weeks. Unpaid. Open to college juniors, college seniors, recent college graduates, graduate students, law students, career changers. ▶ *1 peer mediation intern:* responsibilities include assisting in compiling and packaging of peer mediation curriculum, researching and networking

with other programs, and other projects assigned by the peer mediation coordinator; after training, intern will assist at local high school. Candidates should have oral communication skills, organizational skills, personal interest in the field, self-motivation, strong interpersonal skills. Duration is 4 months (10-12 hours per week). Unpaid. Open to college juniors, college seniors, recent college graduates, graduate students, law students, career changers, individuals reentering the workforce. International applications accepted.

Benefits Formal training, on-the-job training, opportunity to attend seminars/workshops, willing to complete paperwork for educational credit, willing to provide letters of recommendation, parking validation.

Contact Write, call, fax, or e-mail Monica Zi, Volunteer Coordinator. Phone: 213-250-8190. Fax: 213-250-8195. E-mail: apadrc@sbcglobal.net. In-person interview recommended (telephone interview accepted). Applicants must submit a letter of interest, resume, application form. Applications are accepted continuously. World Wide Web: http://www.apadrc.org.

ASSOCIATION FOR CHILDHOOD EDUCATION INTERNATIONAL
17904 Georgia Avenue, Suite 215
Olney, Maryland 20832

General Information Not-for-profit professional membership association of educators concerned with children from infancy through early adolescence. Established in 1892. Number of employees: 14. Number of internship applications received each year: 5.

Internships Available ▶ *2 office interns.* Candidates should have computer skills, oral communication skills, self-motivation, strong interpersonal skills, written communication skills, interest in learning about nonprofit operations. Duration is 3–6 weeks. Position available as unpaid or paid. Open to college juniors, college seniors, recent college graduates, graduate students, career changers, individuals reentering the workforce. International applications accepted.

Benefits Names of contacts, on-the-job training, willing to act as a professional reference, willing to complete paperwork for educational credit, willing to provide letters of recommendation.

Contact Fax, e-mail, or through World Wide Web site Marilyn Gardner, Director of Marketing and Membership. Fax: 301-570-2212. E-mail: aceimemb@aol.com. No phone calls. In-person interview recommended (telephone interview accepted). Applicants must submit a formal organization application, letter of interest. Applications are accepted continuously. World Wide Web: http://www.acei.org.

ATLANTIC COUNCIL OF THE UNITED STATES
910 17th Street, NW, Suite 1000
Washington, District of Columbia 20006

General Information National, nonprofit, nonpartisan center for the formation of foreign policy. Established in 1961. Number of employees: 40. Number of internship applications received each year: 250.

Internships Available ▶ *15–20 John A. Baker interns:* responsibilities include scholarly research, administrative and/or office tasks, computer entry and application, weekly Intern Discussion Series roundtables, and a research project. Candidates should have computer skills, knowledge of field, office skills, personal interest in the field, research skills, written communication skills. Duration is 10–15 weeks. Unpaid. Open to college freshmen, college sophomores, college juniors, college seniors, recent college graduates, graduate students. International applications accepted.

Benefits Job counseling, names of contacts, opportunity to attend seminars/workshops, possible full-time employment, willing to complete paperwork for educational credit, willing to provide letters of recommendation, weekly Intern Discussion Series roundtables.

Contact Write, fax, e-mail, or through World Wide Web site Internship Coordinator. Fax: 202-463-7241. E-mail: internships@acus.org. Telephone interview required. Applicants must submit a letter of interest, resume, academic transcripts, writing sample, two letters of recommendation. Application deadline: March 30 for summer (priority); however, applications are received on a continuous basis, June 30 for fall, November 15 for spring (priority). World Wide Web: http://www.acus.org.

AUSTRALIAN EMBASSY
1601 Massachusetts Avenue, NW
Washington, District of Columbia 20036

General Information   Diplomatic mission representing Australia in the United States. Established in 1946. Number of employees: 350. Unit of Department of Foreign Affairs and Trade, Canberra, Australia. Number of internship applications received each year: 50.

Internships Available   ▶ *1 congressional liaison intern:* responsibilities include assistance with research on U.S. and domestic and foreign trade policy and congressional activities of relevance to Australia; reporting on hearings and legislative developments; and general administrative cuties. Candidates should have ability to work independently, organizational skills, research skills, strong interpersonal skills, writing skills, knowledge of Access database (desirable). Duration is one summer or semester. Unpaid. Open to college freshmen, college sophomores, college juniors, college seniors, international applicants who have A1 or A2 visa, Greencard, or INS authorization. ▶ *1 cultural relations intern:* responsibilities include assisting with basic event management, database tasks, administrative assistance, and research; requires commitment to work outside normal working hours. Candidates should have ability to work independently, ability to work with others, oral communication skills, personal interest in the field, written communication skills, knowledge of Microsoft Access and ability to create Web pages is advantage. Duration is one summer or semester. Unpaid. Open to college freshmen, college sophomores, college juniors, college seniors, international students who have A1 or A2 visa, Greencard, or INS authorization. ▶ *1 public affairs intern:* responsibilities include assisting with writing embassy news briefs and posting on Web site, assisting with writing quarterly newsletter, compiling embassy fact sheets, and research in library and Internet. Candidates should have ability to work independently, research skills, strong interpersonal skills, writing skills, interest in field of public relations, journalism, and/or international relations. Duration is one summer or semester. Unpaid. Open to college juniors, college seniors, international applicants who have A1 or A2 visa, Greencard, or INS authorization. International applications accepted.

Benefits   Willing to complete paperwork for educational credit, willing to provide letters of recommendation.

Contact   Write, fax, or e-mail Intern Coordinator. Fax: 202-797-3414. E-mail: public.affairs@austemb.org. In-person interview required. Applicants must submit a letter of interest, resume, three writing samples. Application deadline: March 30 for summer, August 15 for fall, December 1 for spring. World Wide Web: http://www.austemb.org/.

BRAZILIAN-AMERICAN CHAMBER OF COMMERCE, INC.
509 Madison Avenue, 3rd Floor
New York, New York 10022

General Information   Bilateral trade association aiming to foster better business relations between Brazil and the U.S. Established in 1969. Number of employees: 5. Number of internship applications received each year: 20.

Internships Available   ▶ *2–3 membership marketing interns:* responsibilities include contacting potential members over the phone, researching for annual publication, and handling business information requests. Candidates should have oral communication skills, organizational skills, self-motivation, strong interpersonal skills, written communication skills. Duration is one summer, spring, or fall semester (minimum 25 hours per week). $600 stipend per month. Open to college seniors and graduate students at U.S. universities.

Benefits   Job counseling, names of contacts, on-the-job training, opportunity to attend seminars/workshops, willing to act as a professional reference, willing to complete paperwork for educational credit, willing to provide letters of recommendation.

Contact   Write, fax, or e-mail Sueli Bonaparte, Executive Director, 509 Madison Avenue, 3rd Floor, New York, New York 10022. Fax: 212-751-7692. E-mail: membership@brazilcham.com. No phone calls. In-person interview recommended (telephone interview accepted). Applicants must submit a letter of interest, resume, academic transcripts, writing sample, letter of recommendation. Applications are accepted continuously. World Wide Web: http://www.brazilcham.com.

BUSINESS INFORMATION SERVICE FOR NEWLY INDEPENDENT STATES (BISNIS)
1401 Constitution Avenue, NW, Ronald Reagan Building
Washington, District of Columbia 20230

General Information   U.S. government-funded organization that assists U.S. companies seeking to export U.S. products or services or to establish business cooperation in the former Soviet Union. Established in 1992. Number of employees: 15. Unit of United States Department of Commerce, Washington, District of Columbia. Number of internship applications received each year: 15.

Internships Available   ▶ *1–3 interns:* responsibilities include answering public inquiries on NIS commercial issues; researching and writing reports and/or articles; assisting with trade events and visiting delegations; and administrative support. Candidates should have ability to work independently, computer skills, editing skills, oral communication skills, personal interest in the field, research skills, writing skills. Duration is one semester (20 hours per week). Unpaid. Open to college freshmen, college sophomores, college juniors, college seniors, graduate students, law students, must be U.S. citizen.

Benefits   Names of contacts, opportunity to attend seminars/workshops, willing to act as a professional reference, willing to complete paperwork for educational credit, willing to provide letters of recommendation, language class participation.

Contact   Write, call, fax, or e-mail Joan Morgan, Intern Coordinator. Phone: 202-482-2709. Fax: 202-482-2293. E-mail: bisnis@ita.doc.gov. In-person interview recommended (telephone interview accepted). Applicants must submit a letter of interest, resume, academic transcripts, 1-2 writing samples. Applications are accepted continuously. World Wide Web: http://www.bisnis.doc.gov.

CAMPAIGN FOR U.N. REFORM
420 7th Street, Suite C
Washington, District of Columbia 20003

General Information   Political lobbying organization. Established in 1975. Number of employees: 3. Number of internship applications received each year: 100.

Internships Available   ▶ *3–8 research associates/interns:* responsibilities include attending coalition meetings; writing press releases; analyzing voting patterns of Congress in regards to UN related votes; document duplication and distribution on Capitol Hill; researching UN related issues. Candidates should have ability to work with others, computer skills, oral communication skills, self-motivation, writing skills. Duration is 1–4 months. $5 per day. Open to college freshmen, college sophomores, college juniors, college seniors, recent college graduates, graduate students. International applications accepted.

Benefits   Formal training, names of contacts, on-the-job training, opportunity to attend seminars/workshops, travel reimbursement, willing to act as a professional reference, willing to complete paperwork for educational credit, willing to provide letters of recommendation.

Contact   Write, fax, or e-mail Don Kraus, Executive Director, 420 7th Street, Suite C, Washington, District of Columbia 20003. Fax: 202-546-8703. E-mail: dkraus@cunr.org. In-person interview recommended (telephone interview accepted). Applicants must submit a letter of interest, resume, writing sample. Applications are accepted continuously. World Wide Web: http://www.cunr.org.

CANADIAN EMBASSY
501 Pennsylvania Avenue, NW
Washington, District of Columbia 20001

General Information Embassy that provides students the opportunity for involvement in governmental affairs in order to gain a general understanding of the Canada/U.S. bilateral relationship. Established in 1936. Number of employees: 250. Number of internship applications received each year: 400.
Internships Available ▶ *2–5 economics interns:* responsibilities include working in various areas such as energy, trade, science, defense, and OLIFI. Candidates should have computer skills, oral communication skills, organizational skills, research skills, strong interpersonal skills, writing skills, U.S. or Canadian citizenship. Duration is January to December. Unpaid. Open to college sophomores, college juniors, college seniors, recent college graduates, graduate students, law students. ▶ *2–5 politics interns:* responsibilities include working in congressional relations and the environment. Candidates should have ability to work with others, computer skills, oral communication skills, organizational skills, research skills, writing skills, U.S. or Canadian citizenship. Duration is January to December. Unpaid. Open to college juniors, college seniors, recent college graduates, graduate students, law students. ▶ *5 public affairs interns:* responsibilities include working in various areas such as relations, special events, cultural relations, press, and publications. Candidates should have ability to work with others, computer skills, oral communication skills, organizational skills, research skills, writing skills, U.S. or Canadian citizenship. Duration is 1 semester. Unpaid. Open to college sophomores, college juniors, college seniors, recent college graduates, graduate students. International applications accepted.
Benefits Job counseling, names of contacts, opportunity to attend seminars/workshops, willing to complete paperwork for educational credit, willing to provide letters of recommendation, networking opportunities, access to gym.
Contact Write, call, fax, e-mail, or through World Wide Web site Ingrid S. Summa, Internship Coordinator. Phone: 202-682-1740 Ext. 7530. Fax: 202-682-7791. E-mail: ingrid.summa@dfait-maeci.gc.ca. Telephone interview required. Applicants must submit a letter of interest, resume, academic transcripts, writing sample, three letters of recommendation. Application deadline: March 15 for summer, July 15 for fall, November 15 for winter/spring. World Wide Web: http://www.canadianembassy.org.

CARIBBEAN LATIN AMERICAN ACTION
1818 N Street, NW, Suite 310
Washington, District of Columbia 20036

General Information Organization that promotes economic development in the Caribbean basin countries. Established in 1978. Number of employees: 12. Number of internship applications received each year: 35.
Internships Available ▶ *1–4 interns:* responsibilities include researching, writing, editing, conference planning, acting as a congressional liaison, and making regional contacts. Candidates should have ability to work independently, knowledge of field, oral communication skills, research skills, self-motivation, written communication skills, Spanish fluency a plus. Duration is 1 semester. Unpaid. Open to college freshmen, college sophomores, college juniors, college seniors, graduate students. International applications accepted.
Benefits Names of contacts, opportunity to attend seminars/workshops, possible full-time employment, willing to complete paperwork for educational credit, willing to provide letters of recommendation.
Contact Write or e-mail Internship Coordinator. Fax: 202-822-0075. E-mail: info@claa.org. In-person interview recommended (telephone interview accepted). Applicants must submit a formal organization application, letter of interest, resume, academic transcripts, writing sample. Applications are accepted continuously. World Wide Web: http://www.claa.org.

CAUX SCHOLARS PROGRAM
1156 15th Street, NW, Suite 910
Washington, District of Columbia 20005

General Information Program that trains young adults in the theory and practice of conflict transformation in the international context. Established in 1991. Number of employees: 8. Unit of MRA/Initiatives of Change, Washington, District of Columbia. Number of internship applications received each year: 30.
Internships Available ▶ *1–10 Caux Scholars:* responsibilities include attending course held in Switzerland in conflict transformation at a cost of $2300; working 10 hours per week in practical conference support. Candidates should have oral communication skills, personal interest in the field, self-motivation, strong interpersonal skills. Duration is 1 month (July to August). Unpaid. Open to college juniors, college seniors, recent college graduates, graduate students, law students, career changers. ▶ *1 Caux Scholars Program intern:* responsibilities include mailing information, working on production of reports and brochures, helping with mailings, maintaining database, handling phone and written inquiries, and attending Executive Committee and Advisory Board meetings. Candidates should have ability to work independently, computer skills, research skills, self-motivation, strong interpersonal skills, written communication skills. Duration is flexible (generally fall to summer). Unpaid. Open to college juniors, college seniors, recent college graduates, graduate students. International applications accepted.
Benefits Job counseling, names of contacts, opportunity to attend seminars/workshops, travel reimbursement, willing to complete paperwork for educational credit, willing to provide letters of recommendation, housing may be provided at no cost.
International Internships Available in Australia; United Kingdom.
Contact Write, call, fax, e-mail, or through World Wide Web site Ms. N. Sherman, Program Director. Phone: 202-872-9077. Fax: 202-872-9137. E-mail: cauxsp@aol.com. In-person interview recommended (telephone interview accepted). Applicants must submit a formal organization application, letter of interest, resume, essay, either 2 personal references or 2 letters of recommendation. Application deadline: April 1 for summer. Fees: $25. World Wide Web: http://www.cauxscholars.org.

CDS INTERNATIONAL, INC.
871 United Nations Plaza, 15th Floor
New York, New York 10017-1814

General Information Organization that prepares young professionals for the challenges of international business through a variety of internships and professional development programs. Established in 1968. Number of employees: 20. Number of internship applications received each year: 500.
Internships Available ▶ *60–80 Congress-Bundestag Youth Exchange for Young Professionals participants:* responsibilities include 2 months of German language training, 4 months at an institution of higher education, and a 5-month internship; interns live with host families in Germany; for more information see www.cdsintl.org/sipintro.html. Candidates should have ability to work independently, knowledge of field, plan to pursue career in field, self-motivation, strong interpersonal skills, strong leadership ability, sincere intercultural interest paired with interest, goals, and experience in a business, technical, agricultural, or vocational field, individuals in other fields invited to apply. Duration is 1 year (July-July). Stipend available. Open to recent high school graduates, college freshmen, college sophomores, college juniors, college seniors, recent college graduates, U.S. citizens between 18 and 24 years old (no former CBYX high school scholarship recipients). ▶ *Gear Up!-the Automotive Industry Internships (Germany):* responsibilities include placement in Saxony region in Germany; for more information see www.cdsintl.org/gearup.html. Candidates should have ability to work independently, college courses in field, knowledge of field, personal interest in the field, plan to pursue career in field, self-motivation, strong interpersonal skills, strong leadership ability, German language skills. Duration is 5 months (July to December). Compensation covers basic living expenses. Open to college juniors, college seniors, recent college graduates, graduate students, young professionals (engineering students).

CDS International, Inc. (continued)

▶ *20 Robert Bosch Foundation Fellowships:* responsibilities include 4-month internship placement in public sector; 5-month internship placement in private sector in Germany; various seminars throughout Europe; intended for U.S. citizens with graduate training (or equivalent experience) in business administration, economics, journalism/mass communication, law, political science, and public affairs/public policy; for more information, visit www.cdsintl.org/rbfpintro.html. Candidates should have ability to work independently, college degree in related field, experience in the field, oral communication skills, plan to pursue career in field, self-motivation, strong interpersonal skills, strong leadership ability, written communication skills, German language skills not required. Duration is 9 months (September-May). Stipend available. Open to recent college graduates, graduate students, law students, young American professionals aged 23-34. ▶ *10 Schott summer interns (Germany):* responsibilities include placements in a variety of business/marketing, engineering, IT and physical sciences fields at Schott Glas in Mainz, Germany; for more information see please visit www.schottintro.html. Candidates should have ability to work independently, ability to work with others, college courses in field, experience in the field, office skills, oral communication skills, personal interest in the field, plan to pursue career in field, self-motivation, German language proficiency, relevant work experience. Duration is 3 months. Compensation covers basic living expenses abroad; limited stipends available for 1-month language course. Open to college juniors, college seniors, recent college graduates, graduate students, young professionals aged 30 or younger. ▶ *10 Work Immersion Study Program (WISP) participants:* responsibilities include placement in a variety of business and technical fields; program starts with a one-month language course and is followed by a 2-month internship with a German host company. Candidates should have college courses in field, knowledge of field, plan to pursue career in field, self-motivation, at least one semester of German language. Duration is 3 months. scholarship program; paid internship. Open to community college students only. ▶ *Culinary arts and hospitality interns (Switzerland):* responsibilities include placements in culinary arts, hospitality management and related fields; for more information see www.cdsintl.org/capsintro.html. Candidates should have ability to work independently, college degree in related field, knowledge of field, personal interest in the field, plan to pursue career in field, self-motivation, strong interpersonal skills, strong leadership ability. Duration is 18 months. Compensation covers basic living expenses abroad. Open to recent college graduates, degree-holding American professionals, must be U.S. citizen and aged 21-30. ▶ *Independent work-abroad programs (Germany and Switzerland).* Candidates should have declared college major in field, experience in the field, oral communication skills, plan to pursue career in field, self-motivation, strong interpersonal skills, intercultural interest, language proficiency, college degree (for Switzerland). Duration is 2–18 months. Position available as unpaid or paid. Open to college freshmen, college sophomores, college juniors, college seniors, recent college graduates, graduate students, young professionals. ▶ *Interns (Argentina):* responsibilities include placements in Cordoba or Buenos Aires; for more information visit www.cdsintl.org/sipaintro.html. Candidates should have ability to work independently, college courses in field, experience in the field, oral communication skills, personal interest in the field, plan to pursue career in field, self-motivation, strong interpersonal skills, Spanish language skills, major in business, marketing, engineering, computer science, or hotel management/tourism. Duration is 3 months. Unpaid. Open to college juniors, college seniors, recent college graduates, graduate students, young professionals. ▶ *Interns (Germany):* responsibilities include placements in business, finance, technical, and engineering fields; for more information see www.cdsintl.org/intintro.html. Candidates should have ability to work independently, college courses in field, knowledge of field, oral communication skills, plan to pursue career in field, self-motivation, strong interpersonal skills, strong leadership ability, written communication skills, German language skills, intercultural interest. Duration is 3–18 months. Compensation covers basic living expenses abroad; limited number of stipends for language course. Open to college juniors, college seniors, recent college graduates, graduate students, young

professionals. ▶ *Summer interns (Ecuador):* responsibilities include placements in business/finance, hotel management/tourism, computer science, engineering, social work/humanitarian, and environmental fields; see www.cdsinti.org/sipeintro.html for more details. Candidates should have declared college major in field, personal interest in the field, plan to pursue career in field, self-motivation, Spanish language skills, intercultural interest. Duration is 3 months. Unpaid. Open to college juniors, college seniors, recent college graduates, graduate students, young professionals, must be U.S. citizen. ▶ *Summer interns (Germany):* responsibilities include placements in a variety of business, technical and engineering fields; for more information visit www.cdsintl.org/sipintro.html. Candidates should have college courses in field, knowledge of field, office skills, oral communication skills, plan to pursue career in field, self-motivation, strong interpersonal skills, intercultural interest, German language skills. Duration is 2–3 months. Compensation covers basic living expenses; limited stipends available for 1-month language course. Open to college juniors, college seniors, recent college graduates, graduate students, young professionals, must be 30 years or under. International applications accepted.

Benefits Housing at a cost, on-the-job training, opportunity to attend seminars/workshops, willing to provide letters of recommendation, opportunity to live and work in another country, assistance in securing necessary work authorizations, scholarships for some programs, health insurance for some programs.

International Internships Available in Argentina; Ecuador; Germany; Switzerland; Turkey.

Contact Write, call, fax, e-mail, or through World Wide Web site Mary Jones, Program Assistant, Internships Abroad. Phone: 212-497-3500. Fax: 212-497-3535. E-mail: usabroad@cdsintl.org. In-person interview recommended (telephone interview accepted). Applicants must submit a formal organization application, letter of interest, resume, academic transcripts, two letters of recommendation, essay, writing samples may be required; please see individual application guidelines for required materials. Application deadline: February 1 for Schott summer interns and Gear Up! program, October 15 for Robert Bosch Fellows program, December 1 for Congress-Bundestag Youth Exchange for Young Professionals, December 15 for summer interns in Germany and work immersion study program; March 1 for summer interns in Equador. World Wide Web: http://www.cdsintl.org.

CENTER FOR CALIFORNIA STUDIES
6000 J Street
Sacramento, California 95819-6081

General Information Applied research institute at California State University, Sacramento. Established in 1984. Number of employees: 75. Division of California State University, Sacramento, California. Number of internship applications received each year: 1,000.

Internships Available ▶ *64 Capital Fellows:* responsibilities include working as full-time paid staff assistant to senior executive branch staff, judicial administration officials, and members of the California Assembly and Senate. Candidates should have analytical skills, personal interest in the field, research skills, strong interpersonal skills, strong leadership ability, writing skills. Duration is one year (September/October to August/September). $1882 per month. Open to college seniors, recent college graduates, graduate students, law students, career changers. International applications accepted.

Benefits Formal training, on-the-job training, opportunity to attend seminars/workshops, possible full-time employment, tuition assistance, willing to act as a professional reference, willing to complete paperwork for educational credit, willing to provide letters of recommendation, health and dental benefits, enrollment fees provided, 12 graduate credits from the Government and Public Policy Departments at CSUS.

Contact Write, call, fax, e-mail, or through World Wide Web site Robert Gregg, Outreach Coordinator. Phone: 916-278-6906. Fax: 916-278-5199. E-mail: calstudies@csus.edu. In-person interview required. Applicants must submit a formal organization application, academic transcripts, two writing samples, two letters of recommendation. Application deadline: February 25. World Wide Web: http://www.csus.edu/calst.

CENTER FOR COMMUNICATION, INC.
271 Madison Avenue, Suite 700
New York, New York 10016

General Information Nonprofit organization that encourages university students to meet professionals in communications industries by sponsoring seminars featuring professionals in print and broadcast journalism, book and magazine publishing, advertising, public relations, and new technologies. Established in 1980. Number of employees: 6. Number of internship applications received each year: 100.

Internships Available ▶ *2–4 interns:* responsibilities include researching senior topics; collecting newsclips; compiling suggested reading lists; helping to promote, support, and publicize activities; and participating in all aspects of seminar production. Candidates should have ability to work independently, computer skills, research skills, self-motivation, strong interpersonal skills, strong career interest in the media. Duration is up to 10 weeks. $250 per spring or fall internship (2 days per week); $500 per summer internship (4 days per week). Open to college sophomores, college juniors, college seniors, recent college graduates, graduate students. International applications accepted.

Benefits Names of contacts, opportunity to attend seminars/ workshops, willing to act as a professional reference, willing to complete paperwork for educational credit, willing to provide letters of recommendation.

Contact Write or through World Wide Web site Frank Argellier, Director of Student Affairs. Fax: 212-686-6393. E-mail: frank@ cencom.org. No phone calls. In-person interview required. Applicants must submit a letter of interest, resume, two personal references, 1 or 2 letters of recommendation. Applications are accepted continuously. World Wide Web: http://www.cencom. org.

CENTER FOR FOLKLIFE & CULTURAL HERITAGE
750 9th Street, NW, Suite 4100
Washington, District of Columbia 20560

General Information Center that engages in cultural conservation and representation activities that promote continuity, integrity, and equity for traditional ethnic, tribal, regional, minority, and working-class cultures in the U.S. and abroad through scholarly research, professional advocacy, and public programs. Established in 1967. Number of employees: 45. Unit of Smithsonian Institution, Washington, District of Columbia. Number of internship applications received each year: 200.

Internships Available ▶ *1–25 interns:* responsibilities include organizing and handling written, audio, and visual documentation and logistics for public programs, educational resources, publications, and recordings; performing computer input for archivist; following up field work by organizing and compiling reports and documentation; following up with potential participants by securing necessary information related to festival presentation; and acquiring and disseminating information from and to festival staff. Candidates should have ability to work with others, office skills, organizational skills, personal interest in the field, self-motivation. Duration is 1–12 months. Unpaid. Open to high school students, recent high school graduates, college freshmen, college sophomores, college juniors, college seniors, recent college graduates, graduate students, law students, career changers, individuals reentering the workforce. International applications accepted.

Benefits Names of contacts, on-the-job training, opportunity to attend seminars/workshops, willing to act as a professional reference, willing to complete paperwork for educational credit, willing to provide letters of recommendation.

Contact Write, call, fax, or e-mail Ms. Arlene Reiniger, Program Specialist, Intern Coordinator. Phone: 202-275-1180. Fax: 202-275-1119. E-mail: arlene@folklife.si.edu. Applicants must submit a formal organization application, academic transcripts, writing sample, two letters of recommendation. Application deadline: March 15 for summer; continuous for other seasons. World Wide Web: http://sss.si.edu/folklife.

CENTER FOR NATIONAL POLICY
1 Massachusetts Avenue, NW, Suite 333
Washington, District of Columbia 20001-1401

General Information Public policy organization dedicated to advancing America's common goals. Established in 1981. Number of employees: 15. Number of internship applications received each year: 200.

Internships Available ▶ *1–2 communications interns:* responsibilities include assisting with event planning and management of databases; assisting with press research and publicity. Candidates should have computer skills, editing skills, oral communication skills, organizational skills, self-motivation, written communication skills. Duration is 3 months. Unpaid. Open to college freshmen, college sophomores, college juniors, college seniors. ▶ *1–2 foreign policy interns:* responsibilities include assisting in policy research, event planning, publicity, general office support work, and database management. Candidates should have ability to work with others, analytical skills, oral communication skills, organizational skills, research skills, self-motivation, written communication skills. Duration is 3 months. Unpaid. Open to college freshmen, college sophomores, college juniors, college seniors, recent college graduates. International applications accepted.

Benefits Job counseling, names of contacts, opportunity to attend seminars/workshops, willing to act as a professional reference, willing to complete paperwork for educational credit, willing to provide letters of recommendation, possibility of stipend.

Contact Write, fax, or e-mail Alex Sunshine, Events Coordinator. Fax: 202-682-1818. E-mail: alex.sunshine@cnponline.org. No phone calls. Telephone interview required. Applicants must submit a letter of interest, resume, academic transcripts, writing sample. Applications are accepted continuously. World Wide Web: http:// www.cnponline.org.

CENTER FOR STRATEGIC AND BUDGETARY ASSESSMENTS
1730 Rhode Island Avenue, NW, Suite 912
Washington, District of Columbia 20036

General Information Organization that analyzes the defense budget, military strategy and policies, and other issues and educates the media, government, and public on these issues. Established in 1983. Number of employees: 12. Number of internship applications received each year: 200.

Internships Available ▶ *1–3 research assistants:* responsibilities include supporting staff research, performing office and administrative tasks. Candidates should have ability to work independently, computer skills, knowledge of field, office skills, oral communication skills, written communication skills. Duration is 10–12 weeks. $300–$400 per week. Open to college juniors, college seniors.

Benefits Names of contacts, opportunity to attend seminars/ workshops, willing to complete paperwork for educational credit, willing to provide letters of recommendation.

Contact Write, call, fax, or through World Wide Web site Intern Coordinator. Phone: 202-331-7990. Fax: 202-331-8019. E-mail: info@csbaonline.org. Applicants must submit a letter of interest, resume, writing sample (3-4 pages). Application deadline: April 15 for summer, August 1 for fall, November 15 for spring. World Wide Web: http://www.csbaonline.org.

CENTER FOR STRATEGIC & INTERNATIONAL STUDIES
1800 K Street, NW
Washington, District of Columbia 20006

General Information Public policy research organization dedicated to analysis and policy impact. Established in 1962. Number of employees: 180. Number of internship applications received each year: 600.

Internships Available ▶ *1 Anne Armstrong Leadership Award:* responsibilities include research, data collection, and administrative duties; available through Abshire-Inamori Leadership Academy; contact Terucha Achterburg . Candidates should have declared college major in field, oral communication skills, research skills, strong leadership ability, writing skills, minimum GPA of 3.5 in area of concentration. Duration is 3 months. $3000 per duration

Center for Strategic & International Studies (continued)
of internship. Open to college sophomores, college juniors, college seniors, recent college graduates. ▶ *60–70 interns:* responsibilities include research, data collection, and administrative duties. Candidates should have ability to work independently, college courses in field, computer skills, editing skills, knowledge of field, organizational skills, personal interest in the field, research skills, writing skills. Duration is 10–15 weeks. Position available as unpaid or paid. Open to college juniors, college seniors, recent college graduates, graduate students, law students. International applications accepted.

Benefits Job counseling, opportunity to attend seminars/workshops, possible full-time employment, travel reimbursement, willing to complete paperwork for educational credit, willing to provide letters of recommendation.

Contact Write, call, fax, or e-mail Denise Payne, Intern Coordinator, 1800 K Street, NW, Suite 400, Washington, District of Columbia 20006. Phone: 202-887-0200 Ext. 3290. Fax: 202-775-3199. E-mail: internships@csis.org. Applicants must submit a letter of interest, resume, 1 writing sample (1150 words maximum). Application deadline: March 1 for summer, July 1 for fall, November 1 for spring. World Wide Web: http://www.csis.org.

CENTER FOR STUDENT MISSIONS
PO Box 900
Dana Point, California 92629

General Information Organization that facilitates Christian mission and service trips in several urban locations throughout the U.S. and Canada. Established in 1988. Number of employees: 3. Number of internship applications received each year: 150.

Internships Available ▶ *50–60 city hosts:* responsibilities include hosting and leading suburban and rural church youth and adult groups during short-term mission and service trips (two to six days) in the inner-cities of Chicago, Washington, DC, Houston, Los Angeles, Toronto, San Francisco, Nashville, Philadelphia, and Seattle. Candidates should have ability to work independently, oral communication skills, self-motivation, strong interpersonal skills, strong leadership ability, youth ministry experience or desire for experience, strong Christian faith. Duration is 3–11 months. $425 per month. Open to college freshmen, college sophomores, college juniors, college seniors, recent college graduates, graduate students, career changers.

Benefits Formal training, free housing, free meals, on-the-job training, possible full-time employment, willing to act as a professional reference, willing to complete paperwork for educational credit, willing to provide letters of recommendation.

International Internships Available in Toronto, Canada.

Contact Write, call, fax, e-mail, or through World Wide Web site Kyle Becchetti, Vice President of Operations. Phone: 949-248-8200. Fax: 949-248-7753. E-mail: info@csm.org. In-person interview required. Applicants must submit a formal organization application, four personal references. Applications are accepted continuously. World Wide Web: http://www.csm.org.

CENTER OF CONCERN
1225 Otis Street, NE
Washington, District of Columbia 20017

General Information Social justice research organization. Established in 1971. Number of employees: 15. Number of internship applications received each year: 100.

Internships Available ▶ *2–3 Global Women's Project interns:* responsibilities include research and communication on gender and international trade issues. Candidates should have ability to work independently, college courses in field, knowledge of field, office skills, research skills, written communication skills. Duration is flexible. Unpaid. Open to college juniors, college seniors, recent college graduates, graduate students. ▶ *1 development intern:* responsibilities include analyzing and tracking donors, researching grant prospects and opportunities, and assisting in strategic planning for appeals. Candidates should have ability to work independently, ability to work with others, computer skills, personal interest in the field, self-motivation, written communication skills. Duration is flexible. Unpaid. Open to college seniors, recent col-

lege graduates, graduate students. ▶ *2–3 foreign aid and international financial institutions project interns:* responsibilities include monitoring relevant institutional activities, drafting memos summarizing developments, attending meetings, and assisting with library research and general support work. Candidates should have ability to work independently, college courses in field, knowledge of field, research skills, self-motivation, written communication skills. Duration is flexible. Unpaid. Open to college juniors, college seniors, recent college graduates, graduate students, law students. ▶ *1 global justice education intern:* responsibilities include assisting with outreach to schools and dissemination of educational materials for secondary schools and universities. Candidates should have ability to work independently, computer skills, oral communication skills, organizational skills, writing skills. Duration is flexible. Unpaid. Open to college juniors, college seniors, recent college graduates, graduate students, career changers. ▶ *2–3 international economics research interns:* responsibilities include surveying literature, assisting with research, networking, and general support on economic issues. Candidates should have ability to work independently, college courses in field, knowledge of field, research skills, self-motivation, written communication skills. Duration is flexible. Unpaid. Open to college seniors, recent college graduates, graduate students.

Benefits Free meals, names of contacts, opportunity to attend seminars/workshops, willing to act as a professional reference, willing to complete paperwork for educational credit, willing to provide letters of recommendation, exposure to international networks and Washington, D.C. international development community, possibility of travel reimbursement.

Contact Write, fax, e-mail, or through World Wide Web site Candy Warner, Director of Administration. Fax: 202-832-9494. E-mail: cwarner@coc.org. No phone calls. Telephone interview required. Applicants must submit a letter of interest, resume, writing sample. Applications are accepted continuously. World Wide Web: http://www.coc.org.

CENTER ON POLICY ATTITUDES
1779 Massachusetts Avenue, NW, Suite 510
Washington, District of Columbia 20036

General Information Research organization, think tank, and public opinion polling organization devoted to the study of public and elite attitudes on foreign and domestic public policy. Established in 1992. Number of employees: 8. Affiliate of University of Maryland, College Park, College Park, Maryland. Number of internship applications received each year: 125.

Internships Available ▶ *1–2 Web site interns:* responsibilities include assisting the Webmaster in maintaining and updating COPA's Web site, and assisting in small research tasks as needed. Candidates should have ability to work independently, ability to work with others, college courses in field, computer skills, editing skills, research skills, writing skills. Duration is 1 semester. $10 per hour. Open to college juniors, college seniors, recent college graduates. ▶ *1–2 office interns:* responsibilities include assisting in office support by filing; maintaining database mailing lists and press lists; and assisting on small research projects as needed. Candidates should have ability to work with others, computer skills, office skills, organizational skills, personal interest in the field, research skills. Duration is 1–2 semesters. $7 per hour. Open to college sophomores, college juniors, college seniors, recent college graduates, graduate students. International applications accepted.

Benefits Travel reimbursement, willing to act as a professional reference, willing to provide letters of recommendation.

Contact Write or fax Research Associate, 1779 Massachusetts Avenue, NW, Suite 510, Washington, District of Columbia 20036. Fax: 202-232-1159. In-person interview recommended (telephone interview accepted). Applicants must submit a letter of interest, resume. Applications are accepted continuously. World Wide Web: http://www.policyattitudes.org.

CITIZENS FOR PARTICIPATION IN POLITICAL ACTION (CPPAX)
43 Winter Street, 7th Floor
Boston, Massachusetts 02108

General Information Multi-issue, progressive, grassroots political organization with a current focus on economic democracy, including fair taxes, adequate human services, cuts in military budget, economic and labor rights issues, campaign finance reform, reform of managed health-care system, and public education funding. Established in 1962. Number of employees: 5. Number of internship applications received each year: 60.

Internships Available ▶ *1–2 economic democracy interns:* responsibilities include researching, writing, and organizing for a fair economy and assisting with campaign for single-payer national health-care plan. Duration is flexible. Unpaid. ▶ *1–2 electoral action interns:* responsibilities include researching and organizing candidates and ballot questions, concentrating on campaign finance reform. Duration is flexible. Unpaid. ▶ *1–2 events planning interns:* responsibilities include planning annual membership convention and other events throughout the year. Duration is flexible. Unpaid. ▶ *1–2 fund-raising interns:* responsibilities include aiding development staff in all areas of grassroots fund-raising and researching and writing grant proposals. Duration is flexible. Unpaid. ▶ *Nonprofit management interns:* responsibilities include assisting with database management, learning rudimentary bookkeeping, recruiting and training volunteers, and helping with strategic planning. Duration is flexible. Unpaid. ▶ *1–2 peace and new priorities interns:* responsibilities include performing congressional research, member organizing for peace, and organizing campaign for the rights of oppressed people in Burma. Duration is flexible. Unpaid. ▶ *1–2 publications interns:* responsibilities include researching, writing, and producing publications. Duration is flexible. Unpaid. Open to high school students, recent high school graduates, college freshmen, college sophomores, college juniors, college seniors, recent college graduates, graduate students, law students, career changers, individuals reentering the workforce. International applications accepted.

Benefits On-the-job training, travel reimbursement, willing to act as a professional reference, willing to complete paperwork for educational credit, willing to provide letters of recommendation.

Contact Write, call, fax, or e-mail Dennis Burke, Executive Director. Phone: 617-426-3040. Fax: 617-426-8389. E-mail: cppax@cppax.org. In-person interview recommended (telephone interview accepted). Applicants must submit a letter of interest, resume. Applications are accepted continuously. World Wide Web: http://www.cppax.org.

CLIENTLOGIC
3102 West End Avenue, Suite 1000
Nashville, Tennessee 37203

General Information International provider of customer management solutions, including customer care, fulfillment, and marketing services with operations in ten countries. Established in 1998. Number of employees: 80. Subsidiary of Onex Corporation, Toronto, Ontario, Canada. Number of internship applications received each year: 500.

Internships Available ▶ *1–3 Flash/HTML designers:* responsibilities include creation of Flash demos and animations, Web programming and design (HTML), graphics creation. Candidates should have ability to work independently, computer skills, editing skills, organizational skills, personal interest in the field, self-motivation, skilled Flash and HTML programmer with an eye for design, inquisitive learner, Web experience, proficient in Net research. Duration is 3–9 months. Unpaid. Open to recent high school graduates, college freshmen, college sophomores, college juniors, college seniors, recent college graduates, graduate students, law students, career changers, individuals reentering the workforce. ▶ *1–3 Web programming and design analysts:* responsibilities include Web programming and design (HTML), graphics creation, online research, competitor Web site analysis/tracking. Candidates should have computer skills, knowledge of field, organizational skills, personal interest in the field, skilled HTML programmer with an eye for design, Web experience, inquisitive learner, proficient in Net research. Duration is 3–9 months. Unpaid. Open to college freshmen, college sophomores, college juniors, college seniors, recent college graduates, graduate students, law students, career changers, individuals reentering the workforce. ▶ *1–3 events and trade show planners:* responsibilities include event planning, conference evaluation, trade show coordination (giveaways, collateral, booth), business report composition. Candidates should have ability to work with others, computer skills, office skills, oral communication skills, organizational skills, personal interest in the field, detail-orientation, planning skills, ability to be an inquisitive learner, Net research proficiency, event experience (preferred, but not required). Duration is 3–9 months. Unpaid. Open to recent high school graduates, college freshmen, college sophomores, college juniors, college seniors, recent college graduates, graduate students, law students, career changers, individuals reentering the workforce. ▶ *1–2 marketing support (high school helpers):* responsibilities include support for marketing and PR team including organization, research, promotions, events, and trade show preparation. Candidates should have computer skills, office skills, organizational skills, self-motivation, strong interpersonal skills. Duration is 3–9 months. Unpaid. Open to high school students, recent high school graduates. ▶ *1–2 media relations analysts:* responsibilities include media outreach, press release composition, online research, market monitoring, media planning, business report composition. Candidates should have experience in the field, oral communication skills, organizational skills, personal interest in the field, strong interpersonal skills, written communication skills, PR/MarCom/media experience, avid reader, inquisitive learner, proficient in Net research. Duration is 3–9 months. Unpaid. Open to college freshmen, college sophomores, college juniors, college seniors, recent college graduates, graduate students, law students, career changers, individuals reentering the workforce. ▶ *1–4 public relations/marketing analysts:* responsibilities include press releases, award applications, sales presentations, online research, PR outreach, copywriting, market monitoring, media planning, business report composition. Candidates should have office skills, oral communication skills, organizational skills, personal interest in the field, strong interpersonal skills, written communication skills, PR experience, avid reader, inquisitive learner, proficient in Net research. Duration is 3–9 months. Unpaid. Open to high school seniors, recent high school graduates, college freshmen, college sophomores, college juniors, college seniors, recent college graduates, graduate students, law students, career changers, individuals reentering the workforce. ▶ *1–2 sales information analysts:* responsibilities include sales presentations, proposal log, online prospecting database, sales support. Candidates should have ability to work with others, computer skills, office skills, organizational skills, self-motivation. Duration is 3–9 months. Unpaid. Open to high school seniors, recent high school graduates, college freshmen, college sophomores, college juniors, college seniors, recent college graduates, graduate students, law students, career changers, individuals reentering the workforce. ▶ *1–3 strategic research analysts (business intelligence):* responsibilities include online research, business outreach, market and trend analysis, product planning, and business report composition. Candidates should have analytical skills, organizational skills, personal interest in the field, research skills, writing skills, must be avid reader, inquisitive learner, proficient in Net research. Duration is 3–9 months. Unpaid. Open to college freshmen, college sophomores, college juniors, college seniors, recent college graduates, graduate students, law students, career changers, individuals reentering the workforce. International applications accepted.

Benefits Job counseling, names of contacts, on-the-job training, opportunity to attend seminars/workshops, possible full-time employment, willing to act as a professional reference, willing to complete paperwork for educational credit, willing to provide letters of recommendation, substantive work, fun/relaxed environment, business travel reimbursement, team outings, networking, flexible schedules.

International Internships Available in The Hague, Netherlands.

Contact Write, fax, or e-mail Ms. Channing Rollo, Manager of Business Intelligence, 3102 West End Avenue, Suite 1000, Nashville, Tennessee 37203. Phone: 615-301-7100. Fax: 615-301-7150. E-mail: internship@clientlogic.com. In-person interview recommended

ClientLogic (continued)

(telephone interview accepted). Applicants must submit a letter of interest, resume, writing sample. Applications are accepted continuously. World Wide Web: http://www.clientlogic.com.

COALITION FOR AMERICAN LEADERSHIP ABROAD
AFSA Building, 2101 E Street, NW
Washington, District of Columbia 20037

General Information   Association whose goal is to promote American engagement in world affairs and act as resource for foreign affairs. Established in 1996. Number of employees: 4.
Internships Available   ▶ *2–3 advocacy and legislative affairs interns:* responsibilities include drafting letters to Congress, working with local community leaders, and grassroots campaign work. Candidates should have ability to work with others, computer skills, editing skills, self-motivation, writing skills. Duration is (minimum of 16 hours per week) one summer or semester. Position available as unpaid or at $200–$300 per duration of internship. Open to college sophomores, college juniors, college seniors, recent college graduates, graduate students, law students. International applications accepted.
Benefits Job counseling, opportunity to attend seminars/ workshops, willing to act as a professional reference, willing to complete paperwork for educational credit, willing to provide letters of recommendation.
Contact Write, call, fax, e-mail, or through World Wide Web site Harry Blaney, President. Phone: 202-944-5519. Fax: 202-338-6820. E-mail: colead@afsa.org. In-person interview recommended (telephone interview accepted). Applicants must submit a letter of interest, resume, academic transcripts, 2-page writing sample. Application deadline: March 15 for summer, July 15 for fall, October 15 for spring. World Wide Web: http://www.colead.org.

COMMITTEE FOR ECONOMIC DEVELOPMENT
2000 L Street, NW, Suite 700
Washington, District of Columbia 20036

General Information Nonprofit, nonpartisan, business-sponsored policy organization involving 250 of the nation's business and education leaders; develops in-depth studies that are distributed to Congress, the Administration, and state, local, and public- and private-sector leaders. Established in 1942. Number of employees: 20. Number of internship applications received each year: 75.
Internships Available ▶ *2–4 research interns:* responsibilities include researching prospective legislation, attending and summarizing meetings and hearings, and compiling statistics and other data in connection with CED publications and studies in progress. Candidates should have analytical skills, computer skills, research skills, writing skills, college courses in economics. Duration is flexible. $1000 per duration of internship. Open to college sophomores, college juniors, college seniors, recent college graduates. International applications accepted.
Benefits Opportunity to attend seminars/workshops, travel reimbursement, willing to complete paperwork for educational credit, willing to provide letters of recommendation, opportunity to attend congressional hearings and other events.
Contact Write, call, fax, e-mail, or through World Wide Web site Jeff Loesel, Intern Coordinator. Phone: 202-296-5860. Fax: 202-223-0776. E-mail: jeff.loesel@ced.org. Applicants must submit a letter of interest, resume, academic transcripts, writing sample. Application deadline: March 20 for summer; continuous for all other positions. World Wide Web: http://www.ced.org.

COMPETITIVE ENTERPRISE INSTITUTE
1001 Connecticut Avenue, NW, Suite 1250
Washington, District of Columbia 20036

General Information Pro-market public interest group dedicated to free enterprise and limited government. Established in 1984. Number of employees: 25. Number of internship applications received each year: 250.
Internships Available ▶ *4–10 interns:* responsibilities include research and writing, issue tracking, and assisting policy managers; some administrative functions. Candidates should have analyti-

cal skills, editing skills, personal interest in the field, research skills, self-motivation, written communication skills, understanding of free market principles and policy approaches. Duration is flexible, especially during fall and winter. Unpaid. Open to college juniors, college seniors, recent college graduates, graduate students, law students. International applications accepted.
Benefits Job counseling, on-the-job training, opportunity to attend seminars/workshops, possible full-time employment, willing to act as a professional reference, willing to complete paperwork for educational credit, willing to provide letters of recommendation.
Contact Fax or e-mail Intern Coordinator. Fax: 202-331-0640. E-mail: internmgr@cei.org. No phone calls. Telephone interview required. Applicants must submit a letter of interest, resume, brief writing sample. Application deadline: April 1 for summer, June 30 for fall, November 1 for winter. World Wide Web: http://www. cei.org.

THE CONGRESSIONAL INSTITUTE, INC.
401 Wythe Street
Alexandria, Virginia 22314

General Information Public policy educational and research organization. Established in 1987. Number of employees: 6. Number of internship applications received each year: 24.
Internships Available ▶ *2–3 general interns:* responsibilities include research, meeting planning, database entry, and general office tasks; working on Web site research, layout, and design. Candidates should have computer skills, office skills, oral communication skills, organizational skills, strong interpersonal skills, writing skills. Duration is 1 semester. Position available as unpaid or at $6.50–$8 per hour. Open to recent high school graduates, college freshmen, college sophomores, college juniors, college seniors, recent college graduates.
Benefits Names of contacts, on-the-job training, opportunity to attend seminars/workshops, possible full-time employment, willing to act as a professional reference, willing to complete paperwork for educational credit, willing to provide letters of recommendation, some free meals.
Contact Write, call, fax, or e-mail Karen Bronson, Executive Director. Phone: 703-837-8812. Fax: 703-837-8817. E-mail: change_leader@conginst.org. In-person interview recommended (telephone interview accepted). Applicants must submit a letter of interest, resume, writing sample, three personal references, two letters of recommendation. Application deadline: April 15 for summer, August 1 for fall, December 1 for spring. World Wide Web: http://www.conginst.org.

CONGRESSIONAL MANAGEMENT FOUNDATION
513 Capitol Court, NE, Suite 300
Washington, District of Columbia 20002

General Information Nonprofit, nonpartisan organization dedicated to helping Congress become a better-managed, more effective institution by tailoring private sector management tools to the congressional environment. Established in 1977. Number of employees: 7. Number of internship applications received each year: 100.
Internships Available ▶ *2–4 interns:* responsibilities include assisting professional staff in all aspects of current projects including research, writing, survey tabulation and analysis, and general office support. Candidates should have analytical skills, computer skills, oral communication skills, personal interest in the field, self-motivation, strong interpersonal skills, writing skills. Duration is minimum of 3 months (20 to 40 hours per week). Unpaid. Open to college sophomores, college juniors, college seniors, recent college graduates, graduate students. International applications accepted.
Benefits Job counseling, names of contacts, on-the-job training, opportunity to attend seminars/workshops, willing to act as a professional reference, willing to complete paperwork for educational credit, willing to provide letters of recommendation.
Contact Write, call, fax, or e-mail Sarah Hopson, Intern Coordinator. Phone: 202-546-0100. Fax: 202-547-0936. E-mail: cfm@cfmweb. org. Telephone interview required. Applicants must submit a let-

ter of interest, resume, 2-5 page writing sample. Application deadline: March 15 for summer; continuous for fall and spring. World Wide Web: http://www.cmfweb.org.

CONGRESSIONAL RESEARCH SERVICE
Library of Congress, 101 Independence Avenue, SE
Washington, District of Columbia 20540-7000

General Information Organization that works exclusively for Congress conducting research, analyzing legislation, and providing information at the request of committees, members, and their staffs. Established in 1946. Number of employees: 700. Unit of Library of Congress, Washington, District of Columbia. Number of internship applications received each year: 500.
Internships Available ▶ *Interns:* responsibilities include performing reference duties in response to inquiries related to public policy; assisting in the development, planning, and coordinating of seminars; briefing programs for members of Congress and their staffs. Candidates should have analytical skills, research skills, writing skills, some background in policy issues involving defense, foreign policy, environmental topics, taxes, and the economy. Duration is flexible. Unpaid. Open to college juniors, college seniors, recent college graduates, graduate students.
Benefits Formal training, job counseling, on-the-job training, opportunity to attend seminars/workshops, willing to act as a professional reference, willing to complete paperwork for educational credit, willing to provide letters of recommendation.
Contact Write, e-mail, or through World Wide Web site Bernevia McCalip, Internship Coordinator. E-mail: bmccalip@crs.loc.gov. No phone calls. Applicants must submit a letter of interest, resume. Applications are accepted continuously. World Wide Web: http://www.loc.gov/crsinfo.

CONGRESSMAN JOHN T. DOOLITTLE
U.S. House of Representatives, 2410 Rayburn House Office Building
Washington, District of Columbia 20515

General Information Congressional office.
Internships Available ▶ *Interns:* responsibilities include assisting members of Congressman Doolittle's staff with daily responsibilities in either the Washington, DC office or the Roseville, CA office. Unpaid.
Contact Write, call, fax, or through World Wide Web site Intern Coordinator. Phone: 202-225-2511. Fax: 202-225-5444. World Wide Web: http://www.house.gov/doolittle/.

CO-OP AMERICA
1612 K Street, NW, Suite 600
Washington, District of Columbia 20006

General Information Nonprofit consumer education organization teaching consumers, businesses, and investors how to use their economic power to create a more socially just and environmentally sustainable world. Established in 1982. Number of employees: 35. Number of internship applications received each year: 250.
Internships Available ▶ *1 CABN Listings editor/coordinator:* responsibilities include setting milestones and final goals for each publication with managing director; handling special case processing; tracking and correspondence with members; verifying listing information when needed; working with membership coordinator, managing director, and screening coordinator to review progress; helping members edit their listings; serving on screening team. Candidates should have oral communication skills, organizational skills, self-motivation, strong leadership ability, written communication skills, familiarity with PC office applications, must be able to type fast. Duration is 3–4 months. $150-$300 per month; Everett positions are $230 per week for 10 weeks; $150 monthly stipend for additional weeks . Open to college sophomores, college juniors, college seniors, recent college graduates, graduate students, career changers, individuals reentering the workforce. ▶ *1 Green business intern:* responsibilities include Web design. Candidates should have computer skills, office skills, organizational skills, personal interest in the field, self-motivation, writing skills. Duration is 2–4 months. $150-$300 per month; Everett positions

are $230 per week for 10 weeks. Open to college juniors, college seniors, recent college graduates, graduate students, career changers, individuals reentering the workforce. ▶ *1 Shareholder Action Network Research and Advocacy intern:* responsibilities include researching corporate activities and positions on social, economic, and environmental concerns; writing articles and action alerts; scanning Web for related press; updating Web site; interviewing shareholder activists and helping SAN team strategies. Candidates should have ability to work independently, oral communication skills, personal interest in the field, research skills, written communication skills. Duration is 3–6 months. $150-$300 per month; Everett positions are $230 per week for 10 weeks. Open to college sophomores, college juniors, college seniors, recent college graduates, graduate students, law students, individuals reentering the workforce, PhD students. ▶ *1–5 Woodwise assistants:* responsibilities include coordinating student campus projects at participating schools nationally; researching and working with publishers and advertisers of magazines. Candidates should have computer skills, oral communication skills, organizational skills, personal interest in the field, self-motivation, written communication skills. Duration is one semester or summer. $150-$300 per month; Everett summer positions are $230 per week for 10 weeks. Open to college sophomores, college juniors, college seniors, recent college graduates, graduate students. ▶ *1 public education and media interns:* responsibilities include writing press releases, editorials, and fact sheets; tracking clips; pitch calling; research; and developing media lists. Candidates should have ability to work independently, ability to work with others, editing skills, personal interest in the field, research skills, self-motivation, written communication skills. Duration is one semester or summer (10 weeks). $150-$920 per month; Everett positions are $230 per week for 10 weeks. Open to college sophomores, college juniors, college seniors, recent college graduates, graduate students, career changers, individuals reentering the workforce. ▶ *1 publications intern:* responsibilities include assisting in writing, researching, editing, and proofing for the "America Quarterly" magazine, "Real Money" newsletter, and "2004 National Green Pages," as well as assisting with content for the publications Web sites. Candidates should have ability to work independently, experience in the field, research skills, self-motivation, written communication skills. Duration is mid-June to July/August. $150-$300 per month; Everett summer positions are $230 per week for 10 weeks. Open to college sophomores, college juniors, college seniors, graduate students. International applications accepted.
Benefits On-the-job training, opportunity to attend seminars/workshops, possible full-time employment, willing to act as a professional reference, willing to complete paperwork for educational credit, willing to provide letters of recommendation, flexible work environment.
Contact Write or e-mail Internship Coordinator, 1612 K Street, Suite 600, Washington, District of Columbia 20006. Phone: 202-872-5307. Fax: 202-331-8166. E-mail: internships@coopamerica.org. In-person interview recommended (telephone interview accepted). Applicants must submit a letter of interest, resume, two writing samples, 2-3 personal references. Application deadline: April 1 for summer; continuous for other positions. World Wide Web: http://www.coopamerica.org.

COUNCIL ON HEMISPHERIC AFFAIRS
1730 M Street, NW, Suite 1010
Washington, District of Columbia 20036

General Information Research and information organization that analyzes and monitors diplomatic, economic, social, human rights, political, trade, development, environmental, social justice, drug, and military trends in U.S.-Latin American and U.S.-Canadian relations. Established in 1975. Number of employees: 19. Number of internship applications received each year: 500.
Internships Available ▶ *2–4 Canadian-U.S. relations research associates:* responsibilities include researching U.S.-Canadian political and economic relations, as well as Canadian-Latin American relations; drafting and publishing articles that spotlight bilateral issues. Candidates should have ability to work independently, editing skills, knowledge of field, oral communication skills, organizational skills, strong leadership ability, writing skills. Duration is 18 weeks

Council on Hemispheric Affairs (continued)

or 14 weeks in summer. Unpaid. Open to high school seniors, recent high school graduates, college freshmen, college sophomores, college juniors, college seniors, recent college graduates, graduate students, law students, career changers, individuals reentering the workforce. ▶ *2–4 Caribbean Affairs research associates:* responsibilities include monitoring, researching, and preparing draft articles for publication on U.S.-Caribbean economic and political issues; researching Caribbean basic developmental and democracy-building projects. Candidates should have ability to work independently, analytical skills, computer skills, editing skills, oral communication skills, research skills, strong leadership ability, written communication skills. Duration is 18 weeks or 14 weeks in summer. Paid. Open to high school seniors, recent high school graduates, college freshmen, college sophomores, college juniors, college seniors, recent college graduates, graduate students, law students, career changers, individuals reentering the workforce. ▶ *15–20 U.S.-Latin American relations research associates:* responsibilities include research, writing, and by-line publishing of articles on pressing regional topics, as well as some light administrative duties. Candidates should have ability to work independently, ability to work with others, analytical skills, computer skills, editing skills, knowledge of field, oral communication skills, personal interest in the field, research skills, self-motivation, strong leadership ability, writing skills. Duration is 18 weeks or 14 weeks in summer. Unpaid. Open to high school seniors, recent high school graduates, college freshmen, college sophomores, college juniors, college seniors, recent college graduates, graduate students, law students, career changers, individuals reentering the workforce, academics on sabbatical, retirees. ▶ *1–2 computer-based research associates:* responsibilities include taking a leadership position in both creating literature on hemispheric substantive issues and distributing them via the Internet, supervising e-mail flow, and editing the organization's Web site. Candidates should have ability to work independently, analytical skills, computer skills, editing skills, oral communication skills, organizational skills, written communication skills. Duration is 18 weeks or 14 weeks in summer. Unpaid. Open to high school seniors, recent high school graduates, college freshmen, college sophomores, college juniors, college seniors, recent college graduates, graduate students, law students, career changers, individuals reentering the workforce. ▶ *3–5 economic affairs research associates:* responsibilities include monitoring economic indicators, interviewing international and regional lending agency officers, and drafting and publishing professional economic analyses and op-ed articles for the media. Candidates should have ability to work independently, ability to work with others, analytical skills, computer skills, editing skills, oral communication skills, writing skills. Duration is 18 weeks or 14 weeks in summer. Unpaid. Open to high school seniors, recent high school graduates, college freshmen, college sophomores, college juniors, college seniors, recent college graduates, graduate students, law students, career changers, individuals reentering the workforce. ▶ *1–2 freedom of press research associates:* responsibilities include monitoring issues of freedom of the press and media responsibility throughout the hemisphere. Candidates should have ability to work independently, ability to work with others, experience in the field, oral communication skills, writing skills. Duration is 18 weeks or 14 weeks in summer. Unpaid. Open to high school seniors, recent high school graduates, college freshmen, college sophomores, college juniors, college seniors, recent college graduates, graduate students, law students, career changers, individuals reentering the workforce. ▶ *2–4 hemispheric security affairs research associates:* responsibilities include monitoring U.S. and Canadian military sales policies to Latin America; evaluating patterns of the Pentagon's cooperation with Latin American military institutions and the relationship of hemispheric armed forces with their civilian governments. Candidates should have ability to work independently, ability to work with others, analytical skills, editing skills, oral communication skills, research skills. Duration is 18 weeks or 14 weeks in summer. Unpaid. Open to high school seniors, recent high school graduates, college freshmen, college sophomores, college juniors, college seniors, recent college graduates, graduate students, law students, career changers, individuals reentering the workforce. ▶ *Hemispheric trade research associates:* responsibilities include research, preparing reports, publishing by-line articles. Candidates should have ability to work independently, computer skills, editing skills, oral communication skills, organizational skills, self-motivation, strong interpersonal skills, writing skills. Duration is 18 weeks or 14 weeks in summer. Unpaid. Open to high school seniors, recent high school graduates, college freshmen, college sophomores, college juniors, college seniors, recent college graduates, graduate students, law students, career changers, individuals reentering the workforce. ▶ *2–4 institutional affairs research associates:* responsibilities include representing the organization's interests and positions to other organizations and the media. Candidates should have ability to work independently, analytical skills, computer skills, editing skills, oral communication skills, writing skills. Duration is 18 weeks or 14 weeks in summer. Unpaid. Open to high school seniors, recent high school graduates, college freshmen, college sophomores, college juniors, college seniors, recent college graduates, graduate students, law students, career changers, individuals reentering the workforce. ▶ *2–4 public analysis and information research associates:* responsibilities include public writing; political and economic themes for publication in print and electronic media. Candidates should have ability to work independently, analytical skills, computer skills, editing skills, knowledge of field, oral communication skills, organizational skills, strong interpersonal skills, writing skills, journalism background (helpful). Duration is 18 weeks or 14 weeks in summer. Unpaid. Open to high school seniors, recent high school graduates, college freshmen, college sophomores, college juniors, college seniors, recent college graduates, graduate students, law students, career changers, individuals reentering the workforce. International applications accepted.

Benefits Formal training, job counseling, names of contacts, on-the-job training, opportunity to attend seminars/workshops, possible full-time employment, willing to act as a professional reference, willing to complete paperwork for educational credit, willing to provide letters of recommendation, occasional meals and recreational trips.

Contact Write, call, fax, e-mail, or through World Wide Web site Secretary for Internships. Phone: 202-216-9261. Fax: 202-216-6035. E-mail: coha@coha.org. In-person interview recommended (telephone interview accepted). Applicants must submit a formal organization application, letter of interest, resume, academic transcripts, writing sample, two personal references, two letters of recommendation. Applications are accepted continuously. World Wide Web: http://www.coha.org.

CROHN'S AND COLITIS FOUNDATION OF AMERICA
386 Park Avenue South
New York, New York 10016

General Information Foundation whose mission is to stimulate and encourage innovative basic biomedical and clinical research of inflammatory bowel disease. Established in 1967. Number of employees: 39. Number of internship applications received each year: 12.

Internships Available ▶ *1–16 student research fellowship awards:* responsibilities include conducting full-time research with mentor investigating a subject relevant to inflammatory bowel disease. Candidates should have major in a medical field. Duration is 10 weeks in the spring. $2500 per duration of internship. Open to college juniors, college seniors, recent college graduates, graduate students.

Benefits Opportunity to attend seminars/workshops, willing to act as a professional reference, willing to complete paperwork for educational credit, willing to provide letters of recommendation.

Contact Write, call, fax, e-mail, or through World Wide Web site Carol Cox, Manager of Research Programs. Phone: 800-932-2423. Fax: 212-779-4098. E-mail: info@ccfa.org. Applicants must submit a formal organization application. Application deadline: March 15. World Wide Web: http://www.ccfa.org.

CSEA
143 Washington Avenue
Albany, New York 12210

General Information Political lobbying organization working on behalf of 265,000 public, private, and active retired labor union members. Established in 1912. Number of employees: 250. Affiliate of AFSCME Local 1000, AFL-CIO. Number of internship applications received each year: 30.

Internships Available   ▶ *2–3 legislative and political action interns.* Candidates should have ability to work independently, ability to work with others, analytical skills, self-motivation, writing skills. Duration is January to June. Paid. Open to college freshmen, college sophomores, college juniors, college seniors, recent college graduates. International applications accepted.

Benefits Formal training, on-the-job training, opportunity to attend seminars/workshops, possible full-time employment, willing to act as a professional reference, willing to complete paperwork for educational credit, willing to provide letters of recommendation.

Contact Write, call, fax, or e-mail Michael J. Neidl, III, Legislative Coordinator. Phone: 518-436-8622. Fax: 518-427-1677. E-mail: neidl@cseainc.org. Applicants must submit a letter of interest, resume, writing sample, in-person interview (in special circumstances telephone interview considered). Application deadline: November 15. World Wide Web: http://www.csea.net.

DAVIS & COMPANY, INC.
11 Harristown Road
Glen Rock, New Jersey 07452

General Information Firm that helps companies improve performance by reaching, engaging, and motivating employees; services include communication consulting, implementation, training/learning, evaluation, and measurement; has extensive experience building awareness about key business issues, including organizational change, business strategy, vision, mission, process improvement, and reward and recognition. Established in 1984. Number of employees: 17. Number of internship applications received each year: 100.

Internships Available   ▶ *2 interns:* responsibilities include writing short articles for newsletters, research, organizing media lists, and attending client meetings; could also entail designing graphics and Web site support. Candidates should have declared college major in field, oral communication skills, plan to pursue career in field, strong interpersonal skills, written communication skills, enthusiasm, good attitude. Duration is 2–3 months. Position available as unpaid or at $7–$10 per hour. Open to college juniors, college seniors, recent college graduates, graduate students.

Benefits Job counseling, on-the-job training, opportunity to attend seminars/workshops, possible full-time employment, travel reimbursement, willing to complete paperwork for educational credit, willing to provide letters of recommendation.

Contact Write, fax, or e-mail Ms. Ellen Van Den Heuvel, Director of Human Resources and Administration. Fax: 201-445-5122. E-mail: ellen.vandenheuvel@davisandco.com. No phone calls. In-person interview required. Applicants must submit a letter of interest, resume. Applications are accepted continuously. World Wide Web: http://www.davisandco.com.

DEMOCRATIC NATIONAL COMMITTEE
430 South Capital Street, SE
Washington, District of Columbia 20003

General Information Administrative body of the Democratic Party whose primary job is to organize the national convention and assist state and local organizations with the election of candidates. Established in 1848. Number of employees: 175. Number of internship applications received each year: 300.

Internships Available   ▶ *Up to 50 interns:* responsibilities include various assignments depending on department. Candidates should have ability to work independently, oral communication skills, strong interpersonal skills, strong leadership ability, written communication skills, must be a democrat. Duration is 2–3 months. Unpaid. Open to college freshmen, college sophomores, college juniors, college seniors, recent college graduates, graduate students. International applications accepted.

Benefits Formal training, job counseling, opportunity to attend seminars/workshops, possible full-time employment, willing to complete paperwork for educational credit, willing to provide letters of recommendation.

Contact Write, call, fax, e-mail, or through World Wide Web site Belen Mendoza, Intern Coordinator. Phone: 202-479-5152. Fax: 202-479-5125. E-mail: mendozab@dnc.org. Applicants must submit a formal organization application, resume, two personal references, letter of recommendation. Application deadline: April 15 for summer; continuous for fall and spring. World Wide Web: http://www.democrats.org.

DEMOCRATIC SENATORIAL CAMPAIGN COMMITTEE
120 Maryland Avenue, NE
Washington, District of Columbia 20002

General Information Organization that supports and assists Democratic candidates running for the U.S. Senate. Established in 1959. Number of employees: 40. Branch of Democratic National Committee, Washington, District of Columbia. Number of internship applications received each year: 100.

Internships Available   ▶ *3–6 interns:* responsibilities include providing administrative support to the political, finance, research, or press departments. Candidates should have ability to work independently, computer skills, oral communication skills, research skills, strong interpersonal skills, written communication skills. Duration is 1 semester or summer. Unpaid. Open to college freshmen, college sophomores, college juniors, college seniors, recent college graduates. International applications accepted.

Benefits Names of contacts, opportunity to attend seminars/workshops, possible full-time employment, willing to act as a professional reference, willing to complete paperwork for educational credit, willing to provide letters of recommendation.

Contact Write, fax, e-mail, or through World Wide Web site Bradley Katz, Research Assistant. Fax: 202-969-0394. E-mail: katz@dscc.org. No phone calls. Applicants must submit a letter of interest, resume, writing sample, letter of recommendation. Applications are accepted continuously. World Wide Web: http://www.dscc.org.

DOW JONES NEWSPAPER FUND
PO Box 300
Princeton, New Jersey 08543-0300

General Information Private foundation that promotes journalism careers. Established in 1959. Number of employees: 4. Number of internship applications received each year: 600.

Internships Available   ▶ *12 business reporting interns:* responsibilities include attending a training program; working at a daily newspaper as a business reporter. Candidates should have ability to work independently, analytical skills, college courses in field, oral communication skills, personal interest in the field, plan to pursue career in field, self-motivation, strong interpersonal skills, writing skills. Duration is 11 weeks in summer (includes one week of training). $325–$605 per week. Open to college sophomores, college juniors. ▶ *100 editing interns:* responsibilities include attending a 2-week training program and working as a copy editor at a daily newspaper. Candidates should have analytical skills, college courses in field, computer skills, editing skills, oral communication skills, personal interest in the field, plan to pursue career in field, research skills, writing skills. Duration is 10 weeks in summer (includes 1-2 weeks of training). $325 per week minimum. Open to college juniors, college seniors, graduate students.

Benefits Formal training, possible full-time employment, $1000 scholarship for those returning to college following the internship, some travel reimbursement.

Contact Write, call, fax, e-mail, or through World Wide Web site Richard Holden, Editing Intern Program. Phone: 609-452-2820. Fax: 609-520-5804. E-mail: newsfund@wsj.dowjones.com. Telephone interview required. Applicants must submit a formal organization application, resume, academic transcripts, two personal references, essay and a test. Application deadline: November 1. World Wide Web: http://www.DJNewspaperFund.dowjones.com.

ECONOMIC STRATEGY INSTITUTE
1401 H Street, NW, Suite 560
Washington, District of Columbia 20005

General Information Nonprofit public policy research organization specializing in international trade issues. Established in 1989. Number of employees: 15. Number of internship applications received each year: 150.
Internships Available ▶ *1–4 research assistants:* responsibilities include assisting research associates and senior staff with trade policy research, performing general office duties, and assisting with publications. Candidates should have ability to work independently, ability to work with others, analytical skills, oral communication skills, research skills, writing skills. Duration is 3-4 months in summer or anytime during the academic year. Unpaid. Open to college juniors, college seniors, recent college graduates, graduate students, law students, career changers, individuals reentering the workforce. International applications accepted.
Benefits Opportunity to attend seminars/workshops, willing to act as a professional reference, willing to complete paperwork for educational credit, willing to provide letters of recommendation, work-related travel reimbursement.
Contact Write, call, fax, e-mail, or through World Wide Web site Ulrika Swanson, Senior Research Associate. Phone: 202-326-8547. Fax: 202-289-1319. E-mail: rswanson@econstrat.org. In-person interview recommended (telephone interview accepted). Applicants must submit a letter of interest, resume, writing sample. Applications are accepted continuously. World Wide Web: http://www.econstrat.org.

ELIZABETH GLASER PEDIATRIC AIDS FOUNDATION
2950 31st Street, Suite 125
Santa Monica, California 90405

General Information Foundation providing funds for research programs related to pediatric HIV/AIDS and motivating participants to consider future careers in this field. Established in 1989. Number of employees: 25. Branch of Elizabeth Glaser Pediatric AIDS Foundation, New York, New York. Number of internship applications received each year: 100.
Internships Available ▶ *Interns:* responsibilities include performing independent research in basic medical, clinical, epidemiological, or psychosocial areas relating to pediatric AIDS. Stipend upon completion of internship. International applications accepted.
Benefits Job counseling, names of contacts.
International Internships Available.
Contact Write, call, fax, e-mail, or through World Wide Web site Mr. Chris Hudnall, Program Coordinator. Phone: 310-314-1459. Fax: 310-314-1469. E-mail: chris@pedaids.org. Applicants must submit a formal organization application, resume, academic transcripts, letter of sponsorship from MD, PhD, or LCSW who has expertise in pediatric HIV/AIDS; statement of purpose from applicant, documentation from school registrar of full-time educational status, abbreviated curriculum vitae of sponsor. World Wide Web: http://www.pedaids.org.

EMBASSY OF FRANCE, ASSISTANT PROGRAM, CULTURAL SERVICES DEPARTMENT
4101 Reservoir Road, NW
Washington, District of Columbia 20007

General Information Diplomatic mission representing France in the United States. Number of internship applications received each year: 1,500.
Internships Available ▶ *20–23 Chateaubriand Fellows:* responsibilities include writing a dissertation in humanities or social sciences. Duration is 9 months. 1600 euros per month. Open to graduate students, only PhD candidates enrolled in an American university. ▶ *Interns (France):* Candidates should have ability to work independently, ability to work with others, oral communication skills, self-motivation, written communication skills, basic fluency in French. Duration is 3 months minimum. Position available as unpaid or paid. Open to college freshmen, college sophomores, college juniors, college seniors, recent college graduates, gradu-

ate students, law students, individuals only between 18 and 30 years of age and enrolled in an American university. ▶ *1,500 teaching assistantships:* responsibilities include teaching in French primary and secondary schools. Candidates should have ability to work independently, oral communication skills, organizational skills, self-motivation, strong leadership ability, basic fluency in French. Duration is October 1 to March 30 (at least). 740 euros per month. Open to college freshmen, college sophomores, college juniors, college seniors, graduate students, only U.S. citizens under 35 years of age. International applications accepted.
Benefits On-the-job training, free introductory courses provided to facilitate assistants' integration and introduction to their jobs, health insurance and a round-trip ticket to France (Chateaubriand Fellowships).
International Internships Available in France.
Contact Write, call, fax, e-mail, or through World Wide Web site Ambassade de France aux Etats-Unis, Assistant Program, Service Culturel/SCULE, Washington 20007. Phone: 202-944-6448. Fax: 202-944-6268. E-mail: assistant@frenchculture.org. Applicants must submit a formal organization application, resume, academic transcripts, 2 academic recommendations, 1 copy of medical certificate, 2 passport or ID photos. Application deadline: continuous for interns (France), January 15 for teaching assistantships and Chateaubriand Fellows. World Wide Web: http://www.info-france-usa.org/visitingfrance/teach.asp.

EMIGRE MEMORIAL GERMAN INTERNSHIP PROGRAMS (EMGIP)
PO Box 345
Durham, New Hampshire 03824

General Information Program that sends students from non-German speaking countries to work, live, and study in German Parliaments. Established in 1965. Number of employees: 1. Number of internship applications received each year: 25.
Internships Available ▶ *Up to 6 Deutscher Bundestag interns (Berlin):* responsibilities include work-study in the administrative, legislative research, and political areas of the Parliament. Candidates should have ability to work independently, analytical skills, college courses in field, computer skills, editing skills, knowledge of field, oral communication skills, organizational skills, personal interest in the field, plan to pursue career in field, research skills, self-motivation, strong interpersonal skills, writing skills, high fluency in German. Duration is 3 months. $1000–$2000 per duration of internship. Open to college sophomores, college juniors, college seniors, recent college graduates, graduate students, law students, young professionals. ▶ *5 Landtag interns:* responsibilities include work-study in German state legislatures. Candidates should have ability to work independently, analytical skills, college courses in field, computer skills, editing skills, knowledge of field, office skills, oral communication skills, organizational skills, personal interest in the field, plan to pursue career in field, research skills, self-motivation, strong interpersonal skills, writing skills, at least a 90% written and spoken German fluency. Duration is 1–2 months. Position available as unpaid or at stipend of $200 to $1000 per internship. Open to college freshmen, college sophomores, college juniors, college seniors, recent college graduates, graduate students, law students. International applications accepted.
Benefits Names of contacts, on-the-job training, opportunity to attend seminars/workshops, willing to act as a professional reference, willing to provide letters of recommendation, possibility of subsidized housing.
International Internships Available in Berlin, Germany; Dresden, Germany; Erfurt, Germany; Mainz, Germany; Schwerin, Germany; Wiesbaden, Germany.
Contact Write Prof. George K. Romoser, Director. No phone calls. In-person interview recommended (telephone interview accepted). Applicants must submit a formal organization application, letter of interest, resume, academic transcripts, three letters of recommendation, in-person interview required for finalists. Application deadline: February 11. Fees: $150.

ETHICS AND PUBLIC POLICY CENTER
1015 15th Street, NW, Suite 900
Washington, District of Columbia 20005

General Information Public policy center established to clarify and reinforce the bond between the Judeo-Christian moral tradition and the public debate over domestic and foreign policy issues. Established in 1976. Number of employees: 25. Number of internship applications received each year: 50.

Internships Available ▶ *1–2 Evangelical Christians in the third world interns:* responsibilities include supporting the projec tresearch advisor in his role of identifying and locating essential research resources, and distributing resources to researchers in the field; active participation in pioneering research. Candidates should have ability to work independently, computer skills, organizational skills, research skills, strong interpersonal skills, written communication skills. Duration is 3–6 months. Unpaid. Open to college freshmen, college sophomores, college juniors, college seniors, recent college graduates, graduate students. ▶ *1–2 Islam and democracy interns:* responsibilities include supporting the project in research, writing, and some administrative tasks. Candidates should have ability to work independently, analytical skills, editing skills, office skills, personal interest in the field, research skills, self-motivation, writing skills. Duration is 3–6 months. Unpaid. Open to college freshmen, college sophomores, college juniors, college seniors, recent college graduates. ▶ *1–2 biotechnology and democracy interns:* responsibilities include supporting the project in research, writing, and some administrative tasks. Candidates should have ability to work independently, analytical skills, computer skills, oral communication skills, personal interest in the field, research skills, self-motivation, writing skills. Duration is 3–6 months. Unpaid. Open to college freshmen, college sophomores, college juniors, college seniors, recent college graduates, law school graduates. ▶ *1–5 center project interns:* responsibilities include library research, reading and summarizing results, attending seminars related to projects, and typing and organizing research. Candidates should have ability to work independently, computer skills, editing skills, research skills, strong interpersonal skills, written communication skills. Duration is 3–6 months. Unpaid. Open to college freshmen, college sophomores, college juniors, college seniors, recent college graduates, graduate students, law students, individuals reentering the workforce. International applications accepted.

Benefits Names of contacts, opportunity to attend seminars/workshops, possible full-time employment, willing to complete paperwork for educational credit, willing to provide letters of recommendation, reimbursement of daily travel expenses.

Contact Write, call, fax, or e-mail Intern Coordinator. Phone: 202-682-1200. Fax: 202-408-0632. E-mail: ethics@eppc.org. Telephone interview required. Applicants must submit a letter of interest, resume. Applications are accepted continuously. World Wide Web: http://www.eppc.org.

THE EURASIA FOUNDATION
1350 Connecticut Avenue, NW, Suite 1000
Washington, District of Columbia 20036

General Information Nonprofit grantmaking foundation. Established in 1993. Number of employees: 25. Number of internship applications received each year: 40.

Internships Available ▶ *1 communications intern:* responsibilities include helping maintain database; helping maintain/update Web site; providing writing and editing support for publications. Candidates should have ability to work independently, computer skills, editing skills, personal interest in the field, writing skills. Duration is 1–4 semesters. $8 per hour. ▶ *1 government relations intern:* responsibilities include background research on political figures and offices; helping to maintain database; scheduling and some correspondence for director of government relations; helping with logistics in hosting events. Candidates should have ability to work independently, ability to work with others, computer skills, editing skills, personal interest in the field, research skills. Duration is 1–2 years. $8 per hour. ▶ *1 program development intern:* responsibilities include researching support for grant programs, developing proposals and grant-related evaluations, and working with grant database and other administrative functions. Candidates should have ability to work independently, computer skills, knowledge of field, personal interest in the field, research skills, writing skills. Duration is 1–4 semesters. $8 per hour. Open to college juniors, college seniors, graduate students.

Benefits Job counseling, names of contacts, on-the-job training, opportunity to attend seminars/workshops, willing to act as a professional reference, willing to complete paperwork for educational credit, willing to provide letters of recommendation.

Contact Write, fax, or e-mail Martin Varghese, Human Resources Assistant. Fax: 202-234-7377. E-mail: resumes@eurasia.org. No phone calls. In-person interview required. Applicants must submit a letter of interest, resume, writing sample. Applications are accepted continuously. World Wide Web: http://www.eurasia.org.

FARM SANCTUARY
3100 Aikens Road
Watkins Glen, New York 14891

General Information National, nonprofit organization dedicated to ending animal agriculture abuses through public education programs, legislation, farm animal cruelty investigations, and campaigns, in addition to running shelters that provide 24-hour emergency rescue, rehabilitation, and permanent care for hundreds of animals. Established in 1986. Number of employees: 25. Number of internship applications received each year: 200.

Internships Available ▶ *6 interns:* responsibilities include farm chores/barn cleaning, office work, and conducting educational tours. Candidates should have ability to work independently, ability to work with others, personal interest in the field, self-motivation, commitment to vegetarianism. Duration is 1–3 months. Unpaid. Open to high school students, recent high school graduates, college freshmen, college sophomores, college juniors, college seniors, recent college graduates, graduate students, law students, career changers, individuals reentering the workforce. International applications accepted.

Benefits Free housing, job counseling, names of contacts, possible full-time employment, willing to complete paperwork for educational credit, willing to provide letters of recommendation.

Contact Write, call, fax, e-mail, or through World Wide Web site Michelle Waffner, Education Program Manager, PO Box 150, Watkins Glen, New York 14891. Phone: 607-583-4512. Fax: 607-583-4349. E-mail: education@farmsanctuary.org. Telephone interview required. Applicants must submit a formal organization application, two letters of recommendation. Applications are accepted continuously. World Wide Web: http://www.farmsanctuary.org.

FEDERAL BUREAU OF INVESTIGATION, FBI ACADEMY
Quantico, Virginia 22135

General Information Academy that trains FBI personnel and other members of the law enforcement community and is viewed as one of the world's premier law enforcement institutions of higher learning.

Internships Available ▶ *FBI Academy interns:* responsibilities include assignments by individual training unit; tasks will vary with background and education of student, needs of unit, and work assigned; duties involve research development and updating work projects, usually related to student's educational endeavors. Candidates should have analytical skills, computer skills, writing skills, ability to qualify under FBI employee standards, minimum GPA 3.0, ability to pass a polygraph and drug test as part of background investigation. Duration is one semester (minimum of 12 weeks) full-time 8:00 am to 4:30 pm Monday to Friday unless otherwise specified. Unpaid. Open to U.S. citizens at least 18 years old, college juniors, college seniors, or graduate students (preferred).

Contact Through World Wide Web site Internship Coordinator. Applicants must submit materials as specified on Web site: www.fbi.gov/employment/intern.htm. Application deadline: March 1 of the previous year for spring; July 20 of the previous year for summer, November 11 of the previous year for fall. World Wide Web: http://www.fbi.gov/employment/academy.htm.

FEDERAL BUREAU OF INVESTIGATION (FBI) HEADQUARTERS
J. Edgar Hoover Building, 935 Pennsylvania Avenue, NW
Washington, District of Columbia 20535-0001

General Information Principal investigative arm of the U.S. Department of Justice with the authority and responsibility to investigate specific crimes assigned to it and to provide other law enforcement agencies with cooperative services. Established in 1908.
Internships Available ▶ *Honors Internship Program:* responsibilities include working with Special Agents and Professional Support personnel on important cases and procedures; initial orientation followed by assignment to a division based on intern's academic discipline, potential contribution, and the needs of the Bureau. Candidates should have minimum GPA of 3.0; students must be returning to their campus following the program. Duration is early June to mid-August. Unpaid. Open to undergraduates enrolled in junior year at time of application, graduate-level students (must be enrolled in school and attending full time), only U.S. citizens. ▶ *Presidential Management (PMI) Interns.* Candidates should have clear interest and commitment to a career in analysis and management of public policies and programs. Duration is initital two-year full -time service appointment after which individual is eligible for permanent federal government position. Paid. Open to graduate students from variety of disciplines who are completing or expecting to complete a master's or doctoral-level degree during the current academic year.
Benefits Travel expenses to and from Washington, DC, information and assistance on housing (Honors Program).
Contact Through World Wide Web site Internship Coordinator. Applicants must submit materials as specified on Web site: www.fbi.gov/employment/intern.htm. World Wide Web: http://www.fbi.gov.

FINNEGAN FOUNDATION
3600 Raymond Street
Reading, Pennsylvania 19605

General Information Foundation that provides practical training in government and politics by offering internships in Harrisburg, Pennsylvania. Established in 1961. Number of employees: 1. Number of internship applications received each year: 50.
Internships Available ▶ *5–10 interns:* responsibilities include various positions in the many departments of state government. Candidates should have ability to work independently, ability to work with others, analytical skills, research skills, self-motivation, writing skills. Duration is 8-10 weeks in summer. Paid. Open to college freshmen, college sophomores, college juniors, college seniors.
Benefits Opportunity to attend seminars/workshops, willing to act as a professional reference, willing to complete paperwork for educational credit, willing to provide letters of recommendation.
Contact Write, call, fax, e-mail, or through World Wide Web site William C. Baer, Administrator. Phone: 610-929-4582. Fax: 610-921-3075. E-mail: bbam200@aol.com. Applicants must submit a formal organization application, letter of interest, academic transcripts, personal reference, letter of recommendation, essay on varied topics. Application deadline: February 1. World Wide Web: http://members.aol.com/JAFINNEGAN.

FOOD AND ALLIED SERVICE TRADES DEPARTMENT, AFL-CIO
1925 K Street, NW, Suite 400
Washington, District of Columbia 20006-1132

General Information Labor organization providing research support services for affiliated unions. Established in 1975. Number of employees: 15. Unit of AFL-CIO, Washington, District of Columbia. Number of internship applications received each year: 100.
Internships Available ▶ *3 interns:* responsibilities include gathering and analyzing information on public and private organizations; researching to assist affiliated unions in organizing and bargaining programs (research is based on a wide range of sources including the Internet, CD data, information sources, publica-

tions, and publicly available information from government sources). Candidates should have ability to work independently, personal interest in the field, research skills, writing skills, commitment to social justice. Duration is 1–14 weeks. $150 per week. Open to college freshmen, college sophomores, college juniors, college seniors, graduate students, law students. International applications accepted.
Benefits Job counseling, names of contacts, on-the-job training, opportunity to attend seminars/workshops, possible full-time employment, willing to act as a professional reference, willing to complete paperwork for educational credit, willing to provide letters of recommendation.
Contact Write, fax, or e-mail Mr. Gene Bruskin, Secretary/Treasurer. Fax: 202-737-7208. E-mail: gbruskin@fastaflcio.org. Applicants must submit a letter of interest, resume, writing sample. Applications are accepted continuously. World Wide Web: http://www.fastaflcio.org.

FOOD FIRST/ INSTITUTE FOR FOOD AND DEVELOPMENT POLICY
398 60th Street
Oakland, California 94618-1212

General Information Nonprofit people's think tank. Established in 1975. Number of employees: 9. Number of internship applications received each year: 35.
Internships Available ▶ *1–2 membership and development assistants:* responsibilities include assisting with keeping track of members, member relations, and correspondence. Candidates should have computer skills, office skills, oral communication skills, personal interest in the field, plan to pursue career in field, written communication skills. Duration is 3–12 months. Unpaid. Open to college juniors, college seniors, recent college graduates, career changers, individuals reentering the workforce. ▶ *1 publishing intern:* responsibilities include all aspects of publishing. Candidates should have computer skills, editing skills, office skills, plan to pursue career in field, self-motivation, written communication skills. Duration is 3–12 months. Unpaid. Open to college juniors, college seniors, recent college graduates, graduate students, career changers, individuals reentering the workforce. ▶ *5–10 research interns:* responsibilities include library and Internet research on issues of hunger and poverty. Candidates should have ability to work independently, analytical skills, research skills, self-motivation, writing skills. Duration is 3-12 months (10 hours per week minimum). Unpaid. Open to college sophomores, college juniors, college seniors, recent college graduates, graduate students, law students, career changers, individuals reentering the workforce. International applications accepted.
Benefits Free meals, names of contacts, on-the-job training, willing to act as a professional reference, willing to complete paperwork for educational credit, willing to provide letters of recommendation.
Contact Write, call, fax, e-mail, or through World Wide Web site Marilyn Borchardt, Development Director. Phone: 510-654-4400. Fax: 510-654-4551. E-mail: marbor@foodfirst.org. Telephone interview required. Applicants must submit a formal organization application, letter of interest, resume, writing sample, two personal references. Applications are accepted continuously. World Wide Web: http://www.foodfirst.org.

FOREIGN POLICY ASSOCIATION
470 Park Avenue South, 2nd Floor, North
New York, New York 10016-6819

General Information National, nonprofit organization that educates Americans about significant world issues by providing impartial, nonpartisan publications, programs, and forums to increase public awareness of international matters. Established in 1918. Number of employees: 24. Number of internship applications received each year: 450.
Internships Available ▶ *1–2 editorial interns:* responsibilities include assisting with fact checking, resource lists, and updates for publications and performing minimal clerical tasks. Candidates should have ability to work independently, computer skills, personal interest in the field, self-motivation, written communication skills. Dura-

tion is 8–10 weeks. Unpaid. Open to college juniors, college seniors, recent college graduates. ▶ *1–2 sales and fulfillment interns:* responsibilities include data entry with Microsoft Access, assistance with promotional mailings, and minimal clerical tasks. Candidates should have ability to work independently, analytical skills, computer skills, organizational skills, research skills, self-motivation. Duration is 8–12 weeks. Position available as unpaid or paid. Open to college freshmen, college sophomores, career changers, individuals reentering the workforce. International applications accepted.
Benefits Job counseling, names of contacts, on-the-job training, possible full-time employment, travel reimbursement, willing to act as a professional reference, willing to complete paperwork for educational credit, willing to provide letters of recommendation, free admission to events and free publications.
Contact Write, fax, or through World Wide Web site Director of appropriate department. Fax: 212-481-9275. No phone calls. In-person interview required. Applicants must submit a letter of interest, resume. Applications are accepted continuously. World Wide Web: http://www.fpa.org.

FOREIGN POLICY RESEARCH INSTITUTE
1528 Walnut Street, Suite 610
Philadelphia, Pennsylvania 19102

General Information Independent, nonprofit organization devoted to scholarly research and public education on international affairs; publishes an academic quarterly journal. Established in 1955. Number of employees: 10. Number of internship applications received each year: 300.
Internships Available ▶ *1–2 administrative assistants:* responsibilities include general office assistance, conference preparation, public relations, development. Candidates should have computer skills, knowledge of field, office skills, organizational skills, personal interest in the field. Duration is 1 semester. Position available as unpaid or paid. Open to recent high school graduates, college freshmen, college sophomores, college juniors, college seniors, recent college graduates, graduate students. ▶ *1 editorial assistant:* responsibilities include proofreading, fact-checking, assisting in publication of Orbis, FPRI's journal of world affairs. Candidates should have computer skills, editing skills, knowledge of field, organizational skills, personal interest in the field, research skills. Duration is 1 semester. Position available as unpaid or paid. Open to college freshmen, college sophomores, college juniors, college seniors, recent college graduates, graduate students. ▶ *4–6 research assistants:* responsibilities include maintaining data files, conducting literature searches, compiling indices, general office/research help. Candidates should have computer skills, knowledge of field, organizational skills, personal interest in the field, research skills, writing skills. Duration is 1 semester. Position available as unpaid or paid. Open to college freshmen, college sophomores, college juniors, college seniors, recent college graduates, graduate students. International applications accepted.
Benefits Opportunity to attend seminars/workshops, willing to complete paperwork for educational credit, willing to provide letters of recommendation, use of library resources, salary for those eligible for Pennsylvania state work-study only.
Contact Write, fax, or e-mail Internship Coordinator. Fax: 215-732-4401. E-mail: intern@fpri.org. No phone calls. Applicants must submit a letter of interest, resume, writing sample, two letters of recommendation. Application deadline: April 1 for summer, December 1 for spring. World Wide Web: http://www.fpri.org.

GERMAN-AMERICAN BUSINESS COUNCIL
1524 18th Street, Suite 2
Washington, District of Columbia 20036

General Information Nonprofit organization offering seminars and workshops on German-American business relations. Established in 1990. Number of employees: 2. Number of internship applications received each year: 50.
Internships Available ▶ *1–2 administrative interns:* responsibilities include organizing seminars/workshops, membership correspondence, and a variety of administrative tasks. Candidates should have ability to work independently, computer skills, office skills, organizational skills, research skills, written communication skills, must be able to speak German. Duration is 3–12

months. Unpaid. Open to college freshmen, college sophomores, college juniors, college seniors, recent college graduates, graduate students. International applications accepted.
Benefits On-the-job training, opportunity to attend seminars/workshops, willing to complete paperwork for educational credit, willing to provide letters of recommendation.
Contact Call or e-mail Sabine Creamer, Director of Administration and Programs. Phone: 202-332-7700. Fax: 202-408-9369. E-mail: gabc.creamer@worldnet.att.net. In-person interview recommended (telephone interview accepted). Applicants must submit a resume. Application deadline: 3 months in advance (recommended). World Wide Web: http://www.washgabc.com.

HERBERT SCOVILLE, JR. PEACE FELLOWSHIP
110 Maryland Avenue, NE, Suite 409
Washington, District of Columbia 20002

General Information Fellowship named for the late Dr. Herbert Scoville Jr., a longtime nuclear arms control activist in both government and private life, who devoted special attention to encouraging young people interested in arms control and disarmament issues; brings 2-4 fellows per semester to Washington, D.C., to serve as project assistants at one of 23 arms control/disarmament groups. Established in 1987. Number of employees: 1. Number of internship applications received each year: 60.
Internships Available ▶ *2–4 Scoville Peace fellows:* responsibilities include serving as special project assistant and working on research and/or advocacy in the field of peace and security. Candidates should have ability to work with others, oral communication skills, personal interest in the field, plan to pursue career in field, research skills, written communication skills. Duration is 6–9 months. Stipend of $1800 per month. Open to recent college graduates, graduate students, career changers.
Benefits Health insurance, travel reimbursement.
Contact Call, e-mail, or through World Wide Web site Mr. Paul Revsine, Program Director. Phone: 202-543-4100 Ext. 124. E-mail: scoville@clw.org. In-person interview required. Applicants must submit a letter of interest, resume, two personal references, two letters of recommendation, 2 essays with requirements that can be obtained by accessing Web site or calling for information. Application deadline: February 1 for fall, October 15 for spring. World Wide Web: http://www.scoville.org.

HERITAGE FOUNDATION
214 Massachusetts Avenue, NE
Washington, District of Columbia 20002

General Information Conservative think tank whose mission is to formulate and promote public policies based on the principles of free enterprise, limited government, individual freedom, traditional American values, and a strong national defense. Established in 1973. Number of employees: 180. Number of internship applications received each year: 700.
Internships Available ▶ *40–50 academic year interns:* responsibilities include performing a variety of research and administrative assignments, attending public lectures and conferences, and assisting with computer and other projects. Duration is 2–12 weeks. $10 per day expense stipend (spring and fall). Open to college sophomores, college juniors, college seniors, recent college graduates, graduate students. ▶ *40–50 summer interns:* responsibilities include performing a variety of research and administrative assignments, attending public lectures and conferences, and assisting with computer and other projects. Duration is 10 weeks. Position available as unpaid or at $250 per week. Open to college juniors, college seniors, recent college graduates. Candidates for all positions should have ability to work independently, ability to work with others, computer skills, research skills, self-motivation, writing skills. International applications accepted.
Benefits Formal training, job counseling, names of contacts, opportunity to attend seminars/workshops, possible full-time employment, willing to complete paperwork for educational credit, willing to provide letters of recommendation.
Contact Write, call, e-mail, or through World Wide Web site Intern Coordinator. Phone: 202-608-6032. E-mail: internships@heritage.org. Applicants must submit a formal organization application, letter of interest, resume, writing sample, two letters of

Heritage Foundation (continued)

recommendation. Application deadline: March 1 for summer; continuous for fall and spring. World Wide Web: http://www.heritage.org/internships.

HOSTELLING INTERNATIONAL–AMERICAN YOUTH HOSTELS
733 15th Street, NW, Suite 840
Washington, District of Columbia 20005

General Information Nonprofit organization dedicated to helping all people gain a greater understanding of the world and its people through the development and operation of hostels and coordination of educational and recreational programs. Established in 1934. Number of employees: 37. Unit of International Youth Hostel Federation, United Kingdom. Number of internship applications received each year: 150.
Internships Available ▶ *1–4 HI-AYH hostel interns:* responsibilities include educational program development, designing materials and displays, and working with local volunteers. Candidates should have ability to work with others, college courses in field, oral communication skills, research skills, writing skills, knowledge of languages, travel experience. Duration is 1 semester. Position available as unpaid or at $100–$150 per week. Open to college freshmen, college sophomores, college juniors, college seniors, recent college graduates, graduate students. ▶ *2–4 HI-AYH national office interns:* responsibilities include developing program models, researching nonprofit models, working with regional and hostel volunteers and staff, and updating publications and Web site. Candidates should have office skills, oral communication skills, organizational skills, personal interest in the field, strong interpersonal skills, writing skills, experience in research and proposal development. Duration is minimum of 12 weeks. $150 per week stipend and housing offered. Open to college seniors, recent college graduates, graduate students. ▶ *2–30 regional HI-AYH council offices interns:* responsibilities include assisting with program development, marketing, and special events. Candidates should have ability to work independently, declared college major in field, oral communication skills, written communication skills, major in education, marketing, nonprofit administration, or recreation desired, travel experience a plus. Duration is 1 semester. $100–$150 per week. Open to college sophomores, college juniors, college seniors, recent college graduates, graduate students. International applications accepted.
Benefits Opportunity to attend seminars/workshops, willing to act as a professional reference, willing to complete paperwork for educational credit, willing to provide letters of recommendation, stipends and housing provided for some positions.
Contact Write, fax, e-mail, or through World Wide Web site Internship Coordinator. Fax: 202-783-6171. No phone calls. Applicants must submit a letter of interest, resume, two letters of recommendation. Application deadline: February 1 for spring, May 22 for summer, September 1 for winter. World Wide Web: http://www.hiusa.org.

HOUSTON INTERNATIONAL PROTOCOL ALLIANCE
901 Bagby, Suite 100
Houston, Texas 77002

General Information Nonprofit organization that serves as the protocol office for the city of Houston, working closely with the mayor's office to serve the local consular corps, visiting dignitaries, and the Sister City program. Established in 1983. Number of employees: 6. Department of Greater Houston Convention & Visitors Bureau, Houston, Texas. Number of internship applications received each year: 40.
Internships Available ▶ *7–10 protocol interns:* responsibilities include research, event coordination, day-to-day administrative tasks, special projects, and drafting correspondence. Candidates should have organizational skills, personal interest in the field, research skills, self-motivation, strong interpersonal skills, written communication skills. Duration is 3-6 months with option of extending past six months. Unpaid. Open to college freshmen,

college sophomores, college juniors, college seniors, recent college graduates, graduate students. International applications accepted.
Benefits Job counseling, names of contacts, willing to act as a professional reference, willing to complete paperwork for educational credit, willing to provide letters of recommendation, free parking.
Contact Write, call, fax, or e-mail Diana Santana, Protocol Manager. Phone: 713-227-3395. Fax: 713-227-3399. E-mail: dsantana@ghcvb.org. In-person interview recommended (telephone interview accepted). Applicants must submit a letter of interest, resume, writing sample. Application deadline: April 15 for summer, July 15 for fall, November 15 for spring. World Wide Web: http://www.houston-guide.com/protocol/.

INDEPENDENT PROGRESSIVE POLITICS NETWORK
PO Box 1041
Bloomfield, New Jersey 07003

General Information Organization that brings together individuals and groups in support of a progressive third-party movement.
Internships Available ▶ *Web development interns.* Candidates should have computer skills, written communication skills. Duration is flexible. Unpaid. ▶ *Editorial interns:* responsibilities include editing and/or writing articles for the *Independent Politics News.* Duration is flexible. Unpaid. ▶ *Special projects interns:* responsibilities include handling special projects, administrative support, and coordinating activities of the speakers bureau. Duration is flexible. Unpaid. ▶ *Youth outreach interns:* responsibilities include organizing and overseeing the Youth Involvement Task Force. Duration is flexible. Unpaid.
Contact Write, call, fax, or e-mail Ted Glick. Phone: 973-338-5398. Fax: 973-338-2210. E-mail: indpol@igc.org. Applicants must submit a letter of interest, resume, description of experience with activism/organizing. Applications are accepted continuously.

INDIGENOUS TOURISM RIGHTS INTERNATIONAL
366 North Prior Avenue, Suite 205
St. Paul, Minnesota 55104

General Information Nonprofit indigenous organization working on tourism issues. Established in 1995. Number of employees: 3. Unit of The Tides Center, San Francisco, California. Number of internship applications received each year: 20.
Internships Available ▶ *1 Spanish translator intern:* responsibilities include translating newsletters, articles, and documents from Spanish to English and English to Spanish. Candidates should have ability to work independently, oral communication skills, self-motivation, strong interpersonal skills, written communication skills, Spanish/English fluency. Duration is 3 months (8-15 hours per week). Unpaid. Open to college freshmen, college sophomores, college juniors, college seniors, recent college graduates, graduate students, law students, career changers. ▶ *1 biodiversity and technical assistance intern:* responsibilities include helping the technical assistance director with research and communications in new community-based program providing resources to organization in Los Angeles. Candidates should have computer skills, self-motivation, Spanish skills (helpful). Duration is 3 months (8-15 hours per week). Unpaid. Open to college sophomores, college juniors, college seniors, recent college graduates, graduate students, law students. ▶ *1 communications and networking intern:* responsibilities include assisting with the Global Information Network, including sending out action alerts, recruiting new members, updating database, assisting with Web development, and facilitating Web discussions. Candidates should have ability to work independently, office skills, oral communication skills, self-motivation, written communication skills, interest in environmental or international issues. Duration is 3 months (8-15 hours per week). Unpaid. Open to college sophomores, college juniors, college seniors, recent college graduates, graduate students, law students, career changers. ▶ *1 fund-raising intern:* responsibilities include assisting with researching foundations, grantwriting, and updating the fund-raising database. Candidates should have ability to work independently, ability to work with others, office skills, self-motivation, writing skills, experience/interest in environmental

or international issues. Duration is 3 months (8-15 hours per week). Unpaid. Open to college sophomores, college juniors, college seniors, recent college graduates, graduate students, law students, career changers. ▶ *1 graphic design/publications intern:* responsibilities include assisting in developing PR packet to be used during outreach, recruitment, and grantwriting. Candidates should have computer skills, self-motivation, Spanish skills (helpful). Duration is 3 months (8-15 hours per week). Unpaid. Open to college sophomores, college juniors, college seniors, recent college graduates, graduate students, law students. International applications accepted.

Benefits On-the-job training, opportunity to attend seminars/workshops, willing to act as a professional reference, willing to complete paperwork for educational credit, willing to provide letters of recommendation.

Contact Write, call, fax, or e-mail Cyndy Harrison, Office Administrator. Phone: 651-644-9984. Fax: 651-644-2720. E-mail: cyndy@tourismrights.org. In-person interview required. Applicants must submit a letter of interest, resume, personal reference. Application deadline: January 15 for spring, May 15 for summer, September 15 for fall. World Wide Web: http://www.tourismrights.org.

INITIATIVE FOR SOCIAL ACTION AND RENEWAL EURASIA (ISAR)
1601 Connecticut Avenue, NW, Suite 301
Washington, District of Columbia 20009

General Information Nonprofit, nongovernmental organization that supports environmental groups and projects in the former Soviet Union. Established in 1983. Number of employees: 11. Number of internship applications received each year: 75.

Internships Available ▶ *Interns:* responsibilities include focusing on individual projects, answering telephones, filing, entering data, and processing requests for information. Candidates should have editing skills, knowledge of field, office skills, personal interest in the field, writing skills. Duration is 3–6 months. Position available as unpaid or paid. Open to college freshmen, college sophomores, college juniors, college seniors, recent college graduates, graduate students. International applications accepted.

Benefits Job counseling, names of contacts, opportunity to attend seminars/workshops, possible full-time employment, willing to complete paperwork for educational credit, willing to provide letters of recommendation, office training, reimbursement of local travel expenses to and from ISAR.

Contact Write or through World Wide Web site Olga Segars, Office Manager. Fax: 202-667-3291. E-mail: olga@isar.org. No phone calls. In-person interview recommended (telephone interview accepted). Applicants must submit a letter of interest, resume. Applications are accepted continuously. World Wide Web: http://www.isar.org.

INSTITUTE FOR POLICY STUDIES
733 15th Street, NW, Suite 1020
Washington, District of Columbia 20005

General Information Progressive, nonprofit, public policy research institute that conducts research and public outreach on a range of domestic and foreign policy issues. Established in 1963. Number of employees: 24. Number of internship applications received each year: 200.

Internships Available ▶ *1 Drug Policy Project intern:* responsibilities include helping to foster a paradigm shift replacing the punitive and coercive "social control model" of drug policy with a public health and community economic development model. Candidates should have ability to work independently, computer skills, editing skills, organizational skills, research skills, self-motivation, written communication skills. Duration is flexible. Unpaid. Open to college freshmen, college sophomores, college juniors, college seniors, graduate students. ▶ *1 Global Economy Project intern:* responsibilities include producing policy papers related to the international division of labor, global job crisis, and the enforcement of international labor rights; monitoring the social and economic impact of the North American Free Trade Agreement. Candidates should have ability to work independently,

ability to work with others, editing skills, oral communication skills, personal interest in the field, research skills, self-motivation, writing skills. Unpaid. Open to college freshmen, college sophomores, college juniors, college seniors, graduate students, law students. ▶ *1 Human Rights Award Event intern:* responsibilities include marketing and planning the annual fall event marking the presentation of the international and domestic human rights award to a distinguished group or individual, engaging in extensive networking with the human rights community in Washington, D.C. Candidates should have ability to work independently, computer skills, editing skills, oral communication skills, organizational skills, personal interest in the field, self-motivation, strong interpersonal skills, strong leadership ability, writing skills. Duration is flexible. Unpaid. Open to college freshmen, college sophomores, college juniors, college seniors, graduate students, law students. ▶ *1 Miriam Pemberton Economic Conversion Project intern:* responsibilities include research, writing, organizing, and dealing with administrative hassles related to the conversion of military resources to civilian use. Candidates should have ability to work independently, ability to work with others, computer skills, editing skills, office skills, oral communication skills, research skills, writing skills. Duration is flexible. Unpaid. Open to college freshmen, college sophomores, college juniors, college seniors, recent college graduates, graduate students, law students, career changers. ▶ *1 Pathways to the 21st Century intern:* responsibilities include outlining analysis of this century and laying the foundation for the next. Candidates should have ability to work independently, ability to work with others, computer skills, editing skills, office skills, oral communication skills, organizational skills, research skills, self-motivation, strong leadership ability, writing skills. Duration is flexible. Unpaid. Open to college freshmen, college sophomores, college juniors, college seniors, recent college graduates, graduate students, law students. ▶ *1 Progressive Challenge intern:* responsibilities include participating in progressive politics and debates. Candidates should have ability to work independently, ability to work with others, computer skills, editing skills, organizational skills, personal interest in the field, research skills, self-motivation, writing skills, knowledge of Internet (a plus). Duration is flexible. Unpaid. Open to college freshmen, college sophomores, college juniors, college seniors, graduate students, law students. ▶ *1 Social Action Leadership School for Activists intern:* responsibilities include coordinating training sessions and engaging in extensive outreach to the activist community. Candidates should have ability to work with others, computer skills, office skills, oral communication skills, organizational skills, personal interest in the field, strong leadership ability, writing skills. Duration is flexible. Unpaid. Open to college freshmen, college sophomores, college juniors, college seniors, graduate students, law students. ▶ *1 Sustainable Energy and Economy Network intern:* responsibilities include researching and writing independent projects. Candidates should have ability to work independently, ability to work with others, computer skills, editing skills, organizational skills, personal interest in the field, research skills, self-motivation, writing skills, background in gender studies, environmental issues, micro credit, or activities of the Bretton Woods Institutions. Duration is flexible. Unpaid. Open to college freshmen, college sophomores, college juniors, college seniors, graduate students, law students. ▶ *1 United Nations Project intern:* responsibilities include research and assisting in crafting memos and op-eds to reverse anti-UN policies. Candidates should have analytical skills, computer skills, editing skills, office skills, oral communication skills, organizational skills, research skills, self-motivation, strong leadership ability, writing skills. Duration is flexible. Unpaid. Open to college freshmen, college sophomores, college juniors, college seniors, recent college graduates, graduate students, law students. ▶ *1 campaign for migrant and domestic workers intern:* responsibilities include publicizing the plight of domestic and migrant workers and producing literature on workers' legal rights. Candidates should have analytical skills, computer skills, editing skills, oral communication skills, organizational skills, personal interest in the field, research skills, strong interpersonal skills, writing skills. Duration is flexible. Unpaid. Open to college sophomores, college juniors, college seniors, recent college graduates, graduate students, law students. ▶ *1 corporate accountability/national tax policy/feminist agenda project intern:* responsibilities include assisting in writing briefing papers

Institute for Policy Studies (continued)

and articles intended to apply a liberal analysis to tax policy and to promote more responsible corporate behavior with respect to pay equity and prevention of sexual harassment and working jointly with Center for Advancement of Public Policy on these issues. Candidates should have ability to work independently, ability to work with others, computer skills, editing skills, oral communication skills, organizational skills, personal interest in the field, research skills, writing skills. Duration is flexible. Unpaid. Open to college freshmen, college sophomores, college juniors, college seniors, graduate students, law students. ▶ *1 press/public relations intern:* responsibilities include assisting the media office in developing databases and media outreach strategies; helping respond to inquiries from the press; outreach to Congress, the media, grassroots groups, and other policy-making organizations. Candidates should have ability to work independently, computer skills, editing skills, office skills, oral communication skills, organizational skills, research skills, writing skills. Duration is flexible. Unpaid. Open to college freshmen, college sophomores, college juniors, college seniors, graduate students, law students. International applications accepted.
Benefits Job counseling, names of contacts, opportunity to attend seminars/workshops, possible full-time employment, willing to complete paperwork for educational credit, willing to provide letters of recommendation, travel stipend for Social Action Leadership School for Activists position.
Contact Write, fax, e-mail, or through World Wide Web site Ms. Dorian Lipscombe, Director of Administration. Fax: 202-387-7915. E-mail: dorian@igc.org. No phone calls. In-person interview recommended (telephone interview accepted). Applicants must submit a formal organization application, letter of interest, resume, academic transcripts, writing sample, two letters of recommendation. Application deadline: April 15 for summer. World Wide Web: http://www.ips-dc.org.

INTERHEMISPHERIC RESOURCE CENTER
PO Box 2178
Silver City, New Mexico 88062

General Information   Private, nonprofit research and analysis policy institute producing books, policy reports, and periodicals on U.S. foreign policy, U.S.–Latin America relations. Established in 1979. Number of employees: 9. Number of internship applications received each year: 50.
Internships Available ▶ *1–4 research interns:* responsibilities include working with staff writers compiling information on U.S. foreign policy and U.S.-Latin America relations. Candidates should have ability to work independently, ability to work with others, computer skills, knowledge of field, organizational skills, personal interest in the field, research skills, written communication skills. Duration is 3 months. Unpaid. Open to recent high school graduates, college freshmen, college sophomores, college juniors, college seniors, recent college graduates, graduate students. International applications accepted.
Benefits Free housing, names of contacts, on-the-job training, opportunity to attend seminars/workshops, possible full-time employment, willing to complete paperwork for educational credit, willing to provide letters of recommendation.
Contact Write, fax, e-mail, or through World Wide Web site Siri Khalsa, Administrative Assistant. Fax: 505-388-0619. E-mail: siri@irc-online.org. No phone calls. Telephone interview required. Applicants must submit a letter of interest, resume, three writing samples, 3 letters of recommendation, including 2 from professors. Applications are accepted continuously. World Wide Web: http://www.irc-online.org.

INTERNATIONAL ASSOCIATION TO UNITE THE DEMOCRACIES
Hall of States, Suite 601 C, 444 North Capitol Street, NW
Washington, District of Columbia 20001

General Information   Educational association with a history of commitment and support for world order and democracy. Established in 1940. Number of employees: 1. Number of internship applications received each year: 50.

Internships Available ▶ *1–3 interns:* responsibilities include research on specific international issues related to AUD's mission, goals, and projects; duties include: program development, event planning, newsletter writing and editing, specific research; possibility of tailoring project to student's needs and interests. Candidates should have college courses in field, computer skills, editing skills, personal interest in the field, research skills, writing skills. Duration is 1–6 months. Position available as unpaid or paid. Open to college seniors, recent college graduates, graduate students. International applications accepted.
Benefits Free housing, opportunity to attend seminars/workshops, willing to act as a professional reference, willing to complete paperwork for educational credit, willing to provide letters of recommendation, small stipend.
Contact Write, fax, or e-mail Marielle Reiss, Office Manager, PO Box 77164, Washington, District of Columbia 20013-7164. Phone: 202-347-9465. Fax: 202-347-9464. E-mail: atunite@aol.com. Applicants must submit a formal organization application, letter of interest, resume. Application deadline: April 15 for summer, August 15 for fall, December 15 for spring. World Wide Web: http://www.unionnow.org.

INTERNATIONAL BUSINESS–GOVERNMENT COUNSELLORS, INC. (IBC)
818 Connecticut Avenue, NW, 12th Floor
Washington, District of Columbia 20006

General Information   International government relations firm that provides research and analysis to clients from major international corporations; also manages several trade associations. Established in 1972. Number of employees: 20. Number of internship applications received each year: 30.
Internships Available ▶ *1 association management intern:* responsibilities include assisting with membership development, meeting planning, publications, correspondence, Web page and database management, and research. Candidates should have ability to work independently, computer skills, office skills, oral communication skills, self-motivation, strong interpersonal skills. Duration is 3 months (flexible). Unpaid. ▶ *3 interns:* responsibilities include attending congressional hearings and other trade-related meetings, performing basic research on a variety of issues, and providing written summaries. Candidates should have ability to work independently, computer skills, knowledge of field, research skills, self-motivation, written communication skills. Duration is 3 months (flexible). Unpaid. Open to college sophomores, college juniors, college seniors. International applications accepted.
Benefits Job counseling, on-the-job training, opportunity to attend seminars/workshops, willing to act as a professional reference, willing to complete paperwork for educational credit, willing to provide letters of recommendation.
Contact Write or e-mail Ms. Mary Fromyer, Intern Supervisor. Phone: 202-872-8181. Fax: 202-872-8696. E-mail: mfromyer@ibgc.com. Telephone interview required. Applicants must submit a letter of interest, resume, academic transcripts, writing sample. Applications are accepted continuously. World Wide Web: http://www.ibgc.com.

INTERNATIONAL CENTER
731 8th Street, SE
Washington, District of Columbia 20003

General Information   Nonprofit organization dedicated to promoting good governance and development through direct contacts with all levels of governments, institutions, and individuals; has established major initiatives in settling regional conflicts, fostering bilateral relations, supporting democratic movements, and has provided seeds for reforestation projects in over 130 countries; has recently started water purification projects in Central America. Established in 1977. Number of employees: 12. Number of internship applications received each year: 200.
Internships Available ▶ *2–4 Korea Project: KISON interns:* responsibilities include providing journalists, academics, NGO staff, and government officials of South Korea with information on several issues, including regional security of the Korea peninsula and northeast Asia. Candidates should have ability to work independently,

analytical skills, editing skills, research skills, written communication skills. Duration is 4–12 months. Unpaid. Open to college juniors, college seniors, recent college graduates, graduate students. ▶ *4–8 New Forests Project interns:* responsibilities include conducting research, writing project proposals, translating documents into Spanish/French, packaging tree seeds for worldwide distribution, assisting with fund-raising projects, editing electronic newsletters, managing databases, and project coordination. Candidates should have ability to work independently, ability to work with others, computer skills, editing skills, oral communication skills, organizational skills, personal interest in the field, research skills, self-motivation, writing skills. Duration is 4–12 months. Unpaid. Open to college freshmen, college sophomores, college juniors, college seniors, recent college graduates, graduate students, law students. ▶ *4–10 Russia Commission interns:* responsibilities include assisting with all programs of the Commission on U.S.-Russian relations, hosting foreign visitors, conducting translations, assisting with international business and marketing projects, editing electronic newsletters, conducting research, and managing databases. Candidates should have ability to work independently, ability to work with others, analytical skills, computer skills, editing skills, written communication skills. Duration is 3–4 months. Unpaid. Open to college juniors, college seniors, recent college graduates, graduate students, law students. ▶ *2–3 Vietnam Trade Council interns:* responsibilities include assisting with all aspects of the U.S.-Vietnam Trade Council, hosting foreign officials in Washington D.C., organizing meetings and conferences, conducting research, and compiling statistics for briefing books. Candidates should have ability to work independently, ability to work with others, analytical skills, computer skills, knowledge of field, oral communication skills, organizational skills, personal interest in the field, research skills, strong leadership ability, writing skills. Duration is 4–12 months. Unpaid. Open to college juniors, college seniors, recent college graduates, graduate students. International applications accepted.
Benefits Names of contacts, opportunity to attend seminars/workshops, possible full-time employment, travel reimbursement, willing to act as a professional reference, willing to complete paperwork for educational credit, willing to provide letters of recommendation.
Contact Write, call, fax, e-mail, or through World Wide Web site Erick Toledo. Phone: 202-547-3800 Ext. 110. Fax: 202-546-4784. E-mail: icnfp@erols.com. In-person interview recommended (telephone interview accepted). Applicants must submit a letter of interest, resume, writing sample. Application deadline: March 31 for summer, June 15 for fall, November 15 for spring. World Wide Web: http://www.internationalcenter.com.

INTERNATIONAL FOUNDATION OF EMPLOYEE BENEFIT PLANS
18700 West Bluemound Road, PO Box 69
Brookfield, Wisconsin 53008-0069

General Information Nonprofit educational association serving the employee benefits industry as an information clearinghouse. Established in 1954. Number of employees: 148. Number of internship applications received each year: 1,000.
Internships Available ▶ *200 interns:* responsibilities include assisting with diverse duties in employee benefits and benefit administration. Candidates should have ability to work independently, computer skills, oral communication skills, personal interest in the field, strong interpersonal skills, written communication skills. Duration is usually 1 summer (between sophomore/junior year and junior/senior year); open to discussing availability. $7–$12 per hour. Open to college sophomores. International applications accepted.
Benefits Formal training, job counseling, opportunity to attend seminars/workshops, possible full-time employment, willing to complete paperwork for educational credit, willing to provide letters of recommendation, use of all services of the Foundation, including the library.
International Internships Available in Toronto, Canada.
Contact Write, call, fax, e-mail, or through World Wide Web site Dorothy D. Ellis, Administrative Assistant, 18700 West Bluemound Road, PO Box 69, Brookfield, Wisconsin 53008-0069. Phone: 262-786-6710 Ext. 8218. Fax: 262-786-8670. E-mail: dorothye@ifebp.org. In-person interview required. Application deadline: March 30. World Wide Web: http://www.ifebp.org.

INTERNATIONAL RADIO AND TELEVISION SOCIETY FOUNDATION, INC.
420 Lexington Avenue, Suite 1601
New York, New York 10170

General Information Organization providing a forum for all segments of the communication industry, as a business that entertains, informs, educates, and serves the American public in a meaningful way. Number of employees: 6. Number of internship applications received each year: 600.
Internships Available ▶ *35 summer fellows:* responsibilities include extensive one-week orientation to broadcasting, cable, advertising, and new media; taking a number of related field trips and learning networking skills by attending industry social events; eight weeks of full-time "real world" experience through placements with NY-based corporations in a variety of areas. Candidates should have major in communications or demonstrated strong interest in field through extracurricular activities or other practical experience. Duration is nine weeks (June to August). Stipend of $320 per week. Open to college juniors, college seniors, graduate students, full-time, currently enrolled students only.
Benefits Free housing, reimbursement for travel to NYC.
Contact Write, call, fax, or through World Wide Web site Michele Marsala, Manager of Academic Programs. Phone: 212-867-6650. Fax: 212-867-6653. Applicants must submit a formal organization application. World Wide Web: http://www.irts.org.

INTERNATIONAL TRADE ADMINISTRATION
14th Street and Constitution Avenue, NW, Room 7417
Washington, District of Columbia 20230

General Information International trade organization that assists small and medium-sized businesses in exporting overseas and formulates and implements U.S. foreign trade policy. Established in 1980. Number of employees: 1,745. Unit of United States Department of Commerce, Washington, District of Columbia. Number of internship applications received each year: 300.
Internships Available ▶ *1 student temporary employment program intern:* responsibilities include assisting with advising on international economic policy, administering international trade treaties, monitoring imports and exports, promoting exports, and many other trade-related functions. Candidates should have ability to work with others, computer skills, oral communication skills, written communication skills, U.S. citizenship. Duration is 3–12 months. Paid. ▶ *30–40 volunteer interns:* responsibilities include assisting with advising on international economic policy, administering international trade treaties, monitoring imports and exports, promoting exports, and many other trade-related functions. Candidates should have U.S. citizenship. Duration is flexible. Unpaid. Open to high school students, college freshmen, college sophomores, college juniors, college seniors, graduate students, law students.
Benefits Formal training, possible full-time employment, willing to complete paperwork for educational credit, willing to provide letters of recommendation, health benefits for qualifying students.
Contact Fax or e-mail Tina James, Human Resources Specialist. Fax: 202-482-1903. E-mail: tina_james@ita.doc.gov. No phone calls. Applicants must submit a resume, academic transcripts. Applications are accepted continuously.

INTERNATIONAL TRADE ADMINISTRATION, U.S. AND FOREIGN COMMERCIAL SERVICE
2012 HCHB, 14th and Constitution Avenue, NW
Washington, District of Columbia 20230

General Information International network of commercial specialists in 70 countries that promotes the export of U.S. goods and services. Established in 1980. Number of employees: 100. Unit of United States Department of Commerce, Washington, District of Columbia. Number of internship applications received each year: 50.

International Trade Administration, U.S. and Foreign Commercial Service (continued)

Internships Available ▶ *4 commercial service trade mission interns:* responsibilities include assisting project managers plan, organize, and recruit small to medium size U.S. companies for participation in overseas trade missions. Candidates should have ability to work independently, computer skills, oral communication skills, research skills, strong interpersonal skills, written communication skills. Duration is year-round (flexible). Unpaid. ▶ *2 international buyer program interns:* responsibilities include assisting project officer coordinate worldwide promotion of selected U.S. trade shows. Candidates should have ability to work with others, computer skills, oral communication skills, personal interest in the field, written communication skills. Duration is year-round (flexible). Unpaid. ▶ *2–3 multi-state/catalog exhibition program interns:* responsibilities include assisting project managers plan, organize, and recruit small to medium size U.S. companies to participate in catalog show exhibitions designed to penetrate foreign markets. Candidates should have ability to work independently, computer skills, oral communication skills, research skills, strong interpersonal skills, written communication skills. Duration is year-round (flexible). Unpaid. ▶ *2 trade fair certification interns:* responsibilities include helping program staff review and select international trade shows for support by U.S. Department of Commerce overseas staff and coordinating domestic promotion of shows to potential exhibitors. Candidates should have analytical skills, computer skills, oral communication skills, research skills, strong interpersonal skills, written communication skills. Duration is year-round (flexible). Unpaid. Open to college freshmen, college sophomores, college juniors, college seniors, graduate students, must be U.S. citizen.

Benefits On-the-job training, willing to act as a professional reference, willing to complete paperwork for educational credit, willing to provide letters of recommendation, international marketing experience.

Contact Write, call, fax, or e-mail Bobby Jones, Confidential Assistant, Export Promotion Services, 2810 HCHB, 14th and Constitution Avenue, NW, Washington, District of Columbia 20230. Phone: 202-482-3741. Fax: 202-482-2526. E-mail: bobby.jones@mail. doc.gov. Telephone interview required. Applicants must submit a formal organization application, letter of interest. Applications are accepted continuously. World Wide Web: http://www.ita.doc. gov/doctm/doctm.html.

INVESTOR RESPONSIBILITY RESEARCH CENTER
1350 Connecticut Avenue, NW, Suite 700
Washington, District of Columbia 20036-1701

General Information Research organization that reports to nearly 400 institutional investors on a wide range of questions relating to the role of business in society. Established in 1972. Number of employees: 80. Number of internship applications received each year: 100.

Internships Available ▶ *6–8 CGS interns:* responsibilities include extracting data from proxy materials filed by U.S. corporations and writing related analysis. Candidates should have computer skills, research skills, self-motivation, writing skills. Duration is 2–3 months. Unpaid. Open to college freshmen, college sophomores, college juniors, college seniors. ▶ *3–5 GSS interns (GRS-international).* Candidates should have analytical skills, plan to pursue career in field, research skills, writing skills, attention to detail, experience with databases and MS Word (preferred), major in business, finance, economics, international relations, or languages. Duration is year-round (minimum of 30 hours per week and a 6-month commitment). Unpaid. Open to college freshmen, college sophomores, college juniors, college seniors, recent college graduates, graduate students, law students, career changers. ▶ *1–2 corporate benching service interns.* Candidates should have research skills, self-motivation, writing skills, attention to detail, familiarity with Lexis/Nexis and experience working with databases (a plus), interest in role of business in society. Duration is flexible (at least 20 hours per week part-time, 35 hours per week full-time). $10 per hour. Open to college freshmen, college sophomores, college juniors, college seniors, recent college graduates, graduate students, law students, career changers. ▶ *Research*

analyst interns (GRS-domestic): responsibilities include writing reports or articles; compiling databases on selected topics; and working on surveys concerning stockholders, questions relating to social responsibility, and corporate governance issues. Candidates should have analytical skills, personal interest in the field, research skills, self-motivation, writing skills, attention to detail, experience with databases and MS Word (preferred), major in business, finance, economics, or general liberal arts. Duration is year-round (minimum of 20-30 hours per week and at least 2-6 month commitment). Position available as unpaid or at $10 per hour (students receiving academic credit are not paid). Open to college freshmen, college sophomores, college juniors, college seniors, recent college graduates, graduate students, law students, career changers. International applications accepted.

Benefits On-the-job training, possible full-time employment, willing to act as a professional reference, willing to complete paperwork for educational credit, willing to provide letters of recommendation, transportation stipend to/from work locally.

Contact Write, fax, e-mail, or through World Wide Web site Charine Adams, Director, Human Resources, 1350 Connecticut Avenue, NW Suite 700, Washington, District of Columbia 20036-1701. Fax: 202-833-3555. E-mail: hr@irrc.com. No phone calls. In-person interview recommended (telephone interview accepted). Applicants must submit a letter of interest, resume, writing sample. Application deadline: January 15 for spring, corporate benching service interns. World Wide Web: http://irrc.com.

IOWA GOVERNOR'S OFFICE
State Capitol
Des Moines, Iowa 50319

General Information Executive branch of Iowa state government. Number of employees: 35. Number of internship applications received each year: 30.

Internships Available ▶ *First Lady's Office interns:* responsibilities include working with First Lady's personal assistant in areas of scheduling, constituent response, telephone duties, and communications with media. Candidates should have oral communication skills, strong interpersonal skills, written communication skills, computer literacy and email communication skills (strongly recommended). Duration is summer, fall, or winter (minimum 16 hours per week). Unpaid. Open to high school seniors, college freshmen, college sophomores, college juniors, college seniors. ▶ *Casework interns:* responsibilities include handling casework calls, researching referrals for calls, filing casework, and drafting responses. Candidates should have office skills, oral communication skills, research skills, written communication skills, strong people skills. Duration is summer, fall, or spring (minimum 16 hours per week). Unpaid. Open to high school seniors, college freshmen, college sophomores, college juniors, college seniors. ▶ *Communications interns:* responsibilities include assisting in writing press releases and advisories, setting up press conferences, calling to media, and reporting on weekly press clippings. Candidates should have oral communication skills, research skills, written communication skills, background in communications or journalism. Duration is summer, fall, or spring (minimum 16 hours per week). Unpaid. Open to high school seniors, college freshmen, college sophomores, college juniors, college seniors, graduate students, law students. ▶ *Law clerk interns:* responsibilities include legal research, responding to prisoner letters, extradition filing, and clemency work. Candidates should have analytical skills, research skills, self-motivation, written communication skills. Duration is summer, fall, or spring (minimum 16 hours per week). Unpaid. Open to law students, undergraduates interested in attending law school. ▶ *Policy interns:* responsibilities include policy research, establishing policy files, outreach work with interest groups, and policy development. Candidates should have oral communication skills, personal interest in the field, research skills, written communication skills, background in political science, humanities, or liberal arts. Duration is summer, fall, or spring (minimum 16 hours per week). Unpaid. Open to high school seniors, college sophomores, college juniors, college seniors, recent college graduates, graduate students, law students. ▶ *Secretarial interns:* responsibilities include copying, filing, data entry, dictation, answering phone and mail. Candidates should have computer skills, office skills, oral communication skills, written communication skills. Duration is summer, fall, or winter (minimum of 16 hours per week). Unpaid. Open to high school seniors, college freshmen, college sophomores, college juniors, college seniors.

Benefits Willing to complete paperwork for educational credit.

Contact Write, call, fax, or e-mail Elisabeth Buck, Deputy Chief of Staff. Phone: 515-281-0201. Fax: 515-281-6611. E-mail: elis.buck@igov.state.ia.us. Applicants must submit a formal organization application, resume. Application deadline: May 1 for summer, July 1 for fall, December 1 for spring. World Wide Web: http://www.state.governor.state.ia.us.

JAMESTOWN FOUNDATION
4516 43rd Street, NW
Washington, District of Columbia 20016

General Information Nonprofit organization specializing in increasing Western understanding of the former Soviet Union and China through the monitoring of political, economic, and social trends. Established in 1983. Number of employees: 10. Number of internship applications received each year: 30.

Internships Available ▶ *1–4 research assistants:* responsibilities include providing administrative and research support for Foundation staff. Candidates should have ability to work independently, computer skills, office skills, research skills, writing skills, Arabic, Chinese, Russian, or central Asian language skills (helpful). Duration is 1 semester. Unpaid. Open to college freshmen, college sophomores, college juniors, college seniors, graduate students. International applications accepted.

Benefits Job counseling, on-the-job training, opportunity to attend seminars/workshops, willing to complete paperwork for educational credit, willing to provide letters of recommendation.

Contact Write, call, fax, or e-mail Mindy Lairmore, Intern Coordinator. Phone: 202-483-8888. Fax: 202-483-8337. E-mail: pubs@jamestown.org. In-person interview recommended (telephone interview accepted). Applicants must submit a letter of interest, resume. Applications are accepted continuously. World Wide Web: http://www.jamestown.org.

JAPAN-AMERICA SOCIETY OF WASHINGTON, DC
1020 19th Street, NW, LL #40
Washington, District of Columbia 20036

General Information Organization dedicated to promoting a better understanding between Japan and the United States through programs and services. Established in 1957. Number of employees: 5. Affiliate of National Association of Japan America Societies, Washington, District of Columbia. Number of internship applications received each year: 20.

Internships Available ▶ *2–3 interns:* responsibilities include various office duties in membership programs and services. Candidates should have ability to work independently, office skills, oral communication skills, organizational skills, self-motivation, written communication skills. Duration is minimum of 8 weeks. Unpaid. Open to college freshmen, college sophomores, college juniors, college seniors, graduate students. International applications accepted.

Benefits Job counseling, names of contacts, opportunity to attend seminars/workshops, possible full-time employment, willing to complete paperwork for educational credit, willing to provide letters of recommendation, travel reimbursement related to internship assignments.

Contact Write, fax, or e-mail Internship Coordinator, 1020 19th Street, LL #40, Washington, District of Columbia 20036. Fax: 202-833-2456. E-mail: jaswdc@us-japan.org. No phone calls. In-person interview recommended (telephone interview accepted). Applicants must submit a letter of interest, resume. Application deadline: March 31 for summer, July 31 for fall, November 30 for spring. World Wide Web: http://www.us-japan.org.

JEFFERSON GOVERNMENT RELATIONS
1615 L Street, NW, Suite 650
Washington, District of Columbia 20036

General Information Professional services firm bringing talent and depth to many areas, including congressional relations, regulatory affairs, health care, federal marketing, crisis communications, infrastructure, cities, state, and local public affairs. Established in 1987. Number of employees: 25. Number of internship applications received each year: 500.

Internships Available ▶ *1–4 interns:* responsibilities include reporting to group supervisors, conducting professional and administrative duties, and conducting research for current clients or new business activity; depending upon internship selected, opportunities exist for entry-level accounting duties, human resource management, government relations, and health care. Candidates should have analytical skills, oral communication skills, plan to pursue career in field, research skills, written communication skills, an interest in public policy, government, politics, regulatory and environmental issues, or personnel and human resources. Duration is usually 2 to 4 months; renewable. Unpaid. Open to college freshmen, college sophomores, college juniors, college seniors, recent college graduates, graduate students, law students. International applications accepted.

Benefits Names of contacts, willing to act as a professional reference, willing to complete paperwork for educational credit, willing to provide letters of recommendation, $150 per month transportation reimbursement.

Contact Write, call, fax, or e-mail Ms. Andrea Whetzel, Executive Assistant. Phone: 202-626-8227. Fax: 202-626-8593. E-mail: awhetzel@jeffersongr.com. In-person interview recommended (telephone interview accepted). Applicants must submit a letter of interest, resume, academic transcripts, writing sample. Applications are accepted continuously. World Wide Web: http://www.jeffersongr.com.

JOHN KERRY FOR PRESIDENT
197 Portland Street
Boston, Massachusetts 02114

General Information Presidential campaign. Established in 2003. Number of employees: 50. Number of internship applications received each year: 50.

Internships Available ▶ *25–30 interns:* responsibilities include data entry, mailings, office management, and student outreach. Candidates should have ability to work independently, ability to work with others, self-motivation, strong leadership ability. Duration is flexible. Unpaid. Open to high school students, recent high school graduates, college freshmen, college sophomores, college juniors, college seniors, recent college graduates.

Benefits On-the-job training, willing to act as a professional reference, willing to complete paperwork for educational credit, willing to provide letters of recommendation.

Contact Call or e-mail Ayanna Pressley, Volunteer/Intern Coordinator. Phone: 617-367-1551. Fax: 617-523-2033. E-mail: students@johnkerry.com. In-person interview recommended (telephone interview accepted). Applicants must submit a resume. Applications are accepted continuously. World Wide Web: http://www.johnkerry.com.

JUNIOR ACHIEVEMENT OF ORANGE COUNTY/ INLAND EMPIRE
301 East 17th Street, Suite 202
Costa Mesa, California 92627

General Information Nonprofit organization dedicated to educating and inspiring young people to value free enterprise, business, and economics to improve the quality of their lives. Established in 1919. Number of employees: 4. Division of Junior Achievement of Southern California, Inc., Los Angeles, California.

Internships Available ▶ *1–2 marketing/development interns:* responsibilities include assisting executive director in marketing and fundraising, community outreach, newsletter, and special events. Candidates should have computer skills, oral communication skills, personal interest in the field, research skills, self-motivation, strong interpersonal skills, presentation skills. Duration is flexible. Unpaid.
▶ *1–2 program interns:* responsibilities include assisting program managers with recruiting, training, monitoring volunteers; administration and data entry. Candidates should have computer skills, oral communication skills, organizational skills, personal interest in

Junior Achievement of Orange County/ Inland Empire (continued)

the field, strong interpersonal skills, presentation skills. Duration is flexible. Unpaid. Open to college juniors, college seniors, recent college graduates, graduate students.

Benefits On-the-job training, possible full-time employment, willing to act as a professional reference, willing to complete paperwork for educational credit, willing to provide letters of recommendation.

Contact Write, fax, or e-mail Dennis Young, President. Fax: 949-515-2508. E-mail: dyoung@jasocal.org. No phone calls. In-person interview required. Applicants must submit a letter of interest, resume, two personal references. Applications are accepted continuously. World Wide Web: http://www.ja.org.

KENNAN INSTITUTE FOR ADVANCED RUSSIAN STUDIES
1300 Pennsylvania Avenue, NW
Washington, District of Columbia 20004-3027

General Information Institute that sponsors domestic and foreign scholars to conduct research in residence on topics related to the former Soviet Union. Established in 1974. Number of employees: 10. Unit of Woodrow Wilson International Center for Scholars, Washington, District of Columbia. Number of internship applications received each year: 80.

Internships Available ▶ *10–15 research interns:* responsibilities include providing research assistance for a scholar in residence, conducting research, translating, editing, some photocopying, summarizing research articles, compiling bibliographies, and writing reports. Candidates should have ability to work independently, editing skills, knowledge of field, organizational skills, research skills, Russian language ability. Duration is 3–9 months. $3.50–$6 per hour. Open to college juniors, college seniors, recent college graduates, graduate students. ▶ *1 staff intern:* responsibilities include providing assistance to various staff members, and researching assignments. Candidates should have ability to work independently, college courses in field, office skills, organizational skills, research skills, Russian or Ukrainian language skills. Duration is 3 months minimum. $3.50–$6 per hour. Open to recent college graduates, graduate students. International applications accepted.

Benefits Opportunity to attend seminars/workshops, willing to complete paperwork for educational credit, willing to provide letters of recommendation, subsidy for using Washington, DC metro.

Contact Write, call, fax, or e-mail Ms. Jennifer Giglio, Program Associate, 1300 Pennsylvania Avenue, NW, Washington, District of Columbia 20004-3027. Phone: 202-691-4246. Fax: 202-691-4247. E-mail: giglioje@wwic.si.edu. In-person interview recommended (telephone interview accepted). Applicants must submit a letter of interest, resume. Applications are accepted continuously. World Wide Web: http://wwics.si.edu.

KOREA ECONOMIC INSTITUTE
1201 F Street, Suite 910
Washington, District of Columbia 20004

General Information Institute that promotes an understanding with respect to economic relations between the United States and the Republic of Korea. Established in 1982. Number of employees: 9. Affiliate of Korea Institute for International Economics Policy, Seoul, Republic of Korea.

Internships Available ▶ *2 operations and research interns:* responsibilities include attending conferences, programs, and hearings; preparing short reports; assisting with planning and conduct of conferences and programs; providing research and administrative support to staff; and maintaining organization of KEI library. Candidates should have computer skills, office skills, organizational skills, writing skills, background in political science and/or economics, interest in the Asia-Pacific (especially Korea), attention to detail, professional demeanor. Duration is year-round (minimum of 30 hours per week). Unpaid. Open to college sophomores, college juniors, college seniors, graduate students. International applications accepted.

Benefits Opportunity to attend seminars/workshops, willing to act as a professional reference, willing to complete paperwork for educational credit, willing to provide letters of recommendation.

Contact Write, fax, or e-mail Ms. Caroline G. Cooper, Director of Congressional Affairs and Trade Policy. Fax: 202-464-1987. E-mail: cgc@keia.org. No phone calls. Applicants must submit application and recommendation form which may be downloaded from organization Web site, brief writing sample. Application deadline: March 25 for summer, June 15 for fall, November 1 for spring. World Wide Web: http://www.keia.org.

LAFAYETTE URBAN ENTERPRISE ASSOCIATION
337 Columbia Street, PO Box 277
Lafayette, Indiana 47902

General Information Independent, nonpartisan, nonprofit organization established to direct zone activities and reinvestment. Established in 1993. Number of employees: 4. Number of internship applications received each year: 20.

Internships Available ▶ *1 community development intern:* responsibilities include assisting the executive director with design, implementation, and administration of community projects and organizational programs; interacting with zone businesses and residents to gather information for LUEA projects and programs; creating spreadsheets and generating reports for zone programs; writing, editing, and revising press releases and articles for publications such as the quarterly newsletter, IN THE ZONE; creating presentational media; Web site maintenance; and general administrative support duties. Candidates should have ability to work independently, ability to work with others, computer skills, office skills, oral communication skills, writing skills. Duration is 1 semester or longer. $6–$7 per hour. Open to college freshmen, college sophomores, college juniors, college seniors, recent college graduates, graduate students. International applications accepted.

Benefits Job counseling, names of contacts, on-the-job training, willing to act as a professional reference, willing to complete paperwork for educational credit, willing to provide letters of recommendation.

Contact Write, fax, or e-mail Dennis Carson, Executive Director, PO Box 277, Lafayette, Indiana 47902. Fax: 765-742-6276. E-mail: info@luea.org. No phone calls. In-person interview recommended (telephone interview accepted). Applicants must submit a letter of interest, resume. Application deadline: March 1 for summer, July 1 for fall, November 1 for spring. World Wide Web: http://www.luea.org.

LARCHMONT LITERARY AGENCY
444 North Larchmont Boulevard, #200
Los Angeles, California 90004

General Information Literary agency that represents screenwriters and directors for film work. Established in 1998. Number of employees: 3. Number of internship applications received each year: 20.

Internships Available ▶ *2 interns:* responsibilities include answering phones, reading screenplays, xeroxing, filing, and writing synopses of screenplays. Candidates should have ability to work with others, computer skills, oral communication skills, plan to pursue career in field, written communication skills. Duration is 3 months minimum. Unpaid. Open to college seniors, recent college graduates, graduate students.

Benefits Names of contacts, on-the-job training, opportunity to attend seminars/workshops, willing to act as a professional reference, willing to provide letters of recommendation.

Contact Write, call, or fax Alexandra Booke, Story Editor. Phone: 323-856-3070. Fax: 323-856-3071. E-mail: jm@larchmontlit.com. In-person interview required. Applicants must submit a letter of interest, resume, writing sample, personal reference, letter of recommendation. Applications are accepted continuously.

LEGACY INTERNATIONAL'S GLOBAL YOUTH VILLAGE
1020 Legacy Drive
Bedford, Virginia 24523

General Information International youth training program in a camp setting that focuses on cross-cultural understanding and leadership training and offers workshops in conflict resolution, the arts, ESOL, international relations, and other programs. Established in 1979. Number of employees: 9. Unit of Legacy International, Bedford, Virginia. Number of internship applications received each year: 40.

Internships Available ▶ *7–10 counselors/program specialists:* responsibilities include live-in cabin counseling plus other duties depending on the intern's skills. Candidates should have ability to work with others, experience in the field, oral communication skills, organizational skills, personal interest in the field, strong leadership ability. Duration is 4 weeks (June to July). Position available as unpaid or at $900–$1200 per duration of internship. Open to college juniors, college seniors, recent college graduates, graduate students, career changers, individuals reentering the workforce, must be 21 years or older. ▶ *6 food service interns:* responsibilities include learning how a food service operation works while serving as a prep cook in Legacy's vegetarian kitchen; meals prepared using whole foods, served family style, with an international flare. Candidates should have ability to work independently, ability to work with others, oral communication skills, personal interest in the field, self-motivation. Duration is 4 weeks (June—July). $900–$1200 per duration of internship. Open to college sophomores, college juniors, college seniors, recent college graduates, graduate students, career changers, individuals reentering the workforce, must be 20 years or older. International applications accepted.

Benefits Formal training, free housing, free meals, health insurance, names of contacts, on-the-job training, possible full-time employment, willing to act as a professional reference, willing to complete paperwork for educational credit, willing to provide letters of recommendation, laundry service, stipend based on qualifications.

Contact Write, fax, e-mail, or through World Wide Web site Leila Baz, Staff Director. Fax: 540-297-1860. E-mail: staff@legacyintl. org. No phone calls. Telephone interview required. Applicants must submit a formal organization application, resume, 2-3 professional references with phone/fax numbers. Applications are accepted continuously. World Wide Web: http://www. globalyouthvillage.org.

LIBERTARIAN PARTY OF NORTH CAROLINA
1821 Hillanddale Road, 1B-253
Durham, North Carolina 27705

General Information Political party. Established in 1971. Number of employees: 1. Affiliate of Libertarian Party, Washington, District of Columbia. Number of internship applications received each year: 3.

Internships Available ▶ *1–8 interns:* responsibilities include grassroots political activity. Candidates should have ability to work independently, ability to work with others, personal interest in the field. Duration is flexible. Unpaid. Open to high school students, college freshmen, college sophomores, college juniors, college seniors, recent college graduates, graduate students, law students.

Benefits Names of contacts, on-the-job training, willing to act as a professional reference, willing to complete paperwork for educational credit, willing to provide letters of recommendation.

Contact Write, call, or e-mail Sean Haugh, Executive Director, Durham. Phone: 919-286-0152. E-mail: director@lpnc.org. In-person interview recommended (telephone interview accepted). Applicants must submit a letter of interest. Applications are accepted continuously. World Wide Web: http://www.lpnc.org.

LM SERVICES, LLC
131 West 33rd Street
New York, New York 10001

General Information Global company that designs, sources, and distributes infants' and children's clothing under the brands Little Me and Ralph Lauren. Established in 1914. Number of employees: 620. Subsidiary of S. Schwab Company, Inc. Number of internship applications received each year: 150.

Internships Available ▶ *2–6 Little Me design interns:* responsibilities include setting up merchandise approval and design package system; working with the merchandising staff on all licensed products; maintaining color system; and participating in showroom preps for line reviews. Candidates should have ability to work independently, ability to work with others, college courses in field, oral communication skills, organizational skills, personal interest in the field, self-motivation, strong leadership ability, must be earning academic credit. Duration is spring, summer, or fall semesters. Unpaid. Open to college freshmen, college sophomores, college juniors, college seniors. ▶ *Little Me merchandising interns:* responsibilities include assisting designers in making presentation boards; tabbing colors for prints and stripes; copying materials used for recordkeeping, file submits; attending design meetings as well as tracking samples needed from showrooms. Candidates should have ability to work independently, ability to work with others, college courses in field, oral communication skills, organizational skills, personal interest in the field, self-motivation, strong leadership ability. Duration is spring, summer, or fall semesters. Unpaid. ▶ *1–2 Ralph Lauren Childrenswear merchandising interns:* responsibilities include assisting the merchandising staff with daily maintenance of the line list, communications with design on fabric approvals/trimsheet updates; sample tracking; and price comparisons. Candidates should have ability to work independently, ability to work with others, computer skills, oral communication skills, organizational skills, personal interest in the field, self-motivation, strong leadership ability, must be earning academic credit. Duration is spring, summer, or fall semester. Unpaid. Open to college sophomores, college juniors, college seniors. ▶ *2–3 Ralph Lauren Childrenswear retail analysis interns:* responsibilities include assisting the department with management meeting packets, database administration, analyzing end of month reports, developing various reports/spreadsheets, and general day-to-day analytical activities. Candidates should have ability to work independently, ability to work with others, analytical skills, computer skills, knowledge of field, office skills, oral communication skills, organizational skills, personal interest in the field, self-motivation, strong leadership ability, written communication skills, finance and economic majors; must be earning academic credit. Duration is spring, summer, or fall semester. Unpaid. ▶ *30–40 Ralph Lauren Childrenswear retail merchandising interns:* responsibilities include managing, marketing, and merchandising the Ralph Lauren Childrenswear in-store shop presentations with the guidance and supervision of a merchandise coordinator. Candidates should have ability to work independently, ability to work with others, oral communication skills, organizational skills, personal interest in the field, self-motivation, strong leadership ability, must be earning academic credit. Duration is spring, summer, or fall semester. Unpaid. Open to college sophomores, college juniors, college seniors. ▶ *3–4 Ralph Lauren Childrenswear showroom sales interns:* responsibilities include assisting key account managers with market preparation; coordinating pamphlets and setting up showrooms for appointments; tracking weekly orders; data entry; and other projects relating to the retail business. Candidates should have ability to work independently, ability to work with others, computer skills, office skills, oral communication skills, organizational skills, personal interest in the field, self-motivation, strong leadership ability, must be earning academic credit. Duration is spring, summer, or fall semester. Unpaid. Open to college sophomores, college juniors, college seniors. ▶ *2–3 marketing interns (Ralph Lauren Childrenswear and Little Me):* responsibilities include maintaining periodical library; updating competitive binder; conducting product research; signing samples in and out for editorial purposes; assisting in the coordination of the sample room (when needed); and developing various spreadsheets requiring data entry. Candidates should have ability to work independently, ability to work with others,

LM Services, LLC (continued)

college courses in field, computer skills, knowledge of field, office skills, oral communication skills, organizational skills, self-motivation, strong leadership ability, writing skills, must be earning academic credit. Duration is spring, summer or fall semester. Unpaid. Open to college sophomores, college juniors, college seniors.

Benefits Names of contacts, on-the-job training, possible full-time employment, willing to act as a professional reference, willing to complete paperwork for educational credit, willing to provide letters of recommendation.

Contact Write, fax, or e-mail Ruby Hovsepian, Internship Manager. Fax: 212-643-2790. E-mail: rhovsepian@sschwab.com. No phone calls. In-person interview recommended (telephone interview accepted). Applicants must submit a letter of interest, resume, verification letter from school. Applications are accepted continuously.

MELPOMENE INSTITUTE FOR WOMEN'S HEALTH RESEARCH
1010 University Avenue
St. Paul, Minnesota 55104

General Information Organization helping girls and women of all ages to link physical activity and health through research, education, and publication. Established in 1982. Number of employees: 15. Number of internship applications received each year: 50.

Internships Available ▶ *3–6 interns:* responsibilities include a variety of assignments in health research, marketing/public relations, or computer projects depending on intern's background and interests. Candidates should have ability to work independently, ability to work with others, oral communication skills, personal interest in the field, writing skills, experience with PC's (helpful). Duration is 13-15 weeks (10-12 hours per week). Unpaid. Open to college freshmen, college sophomores, college juniors, college seniors, recent college graduates, graduate students, career changers, individuals reentering the workforce. International applications accepted.

Benefits Names of contacts, on-the-job training, opportunity to attend seminars/workshops, willing to act as a professional reference, willing to complete paperwork for educational credit, willing to provide letters of recommendation, opportunity to contribute to research on women's health, small stipend.

Contact Write, call, fax, e-mail, or through World Wide Web site Maureen Moo-Dodge, Director of Internships, 1010 University Avenue, St. Paul, Minnesota 55104. Phone: 651-642-1951. Fax: 651-642-1871. E-mail: health@melpomene.org. In-person interview recommended (telephone interview accepted). Applicants must submit a formal organization application, letter of interest, resume, two writing samples, three personal references, outline of expectations for internship. Application deadline: April 1 for summer, June 1 for fall, October 1 for winter. World Wide Web: http://www.melpomene.org.

MERIDIAN INTERNATIONAL CENTER–EDUCATIONAL AND VISITOR SERVICES
1630 Crescent Place, NW
Washington, District of Columbia 20009

General Information Service promoting international understanding through exchange of people, ideas, and the arts. Established in 1960. Number of employees: 100. Number of internship applications received each year: 50.

Internships Available ▶ *1–2 Resources Center interns:* responsibilities include maintaining and developing information for programming of international visitors, conducting research on several different subjects, distributing program information for resource forums, and escorting international visitors to DC appointments. Candidates should have computer skills, office skills, oral communication skills, organizational skills, research skills, self-motivation, written communication skills. Duration is 6–12 months. Unpaid. Open to college juniors, college seniors, recent college graduates, graduate students. ▶ *1 The Hospitality Information Service (THIS) intern:* responsibilities include assisting in maintaining database with assistants and volunteers, administrative duties, and

assisting in program coordination for diplomats. Candidates should have ability to work with others, computer skills, office skills, oral communication skills, self-motivation, foreign language skills (helpful). Duration is 1–3 months. Unpaid. Open to college freshmen, college sophomores, college juniors, college seniors, graduate students. ▶ *2–3 arts and communications interns:* responsibilities include helping with press and public relations, planning cultural programs and receptions, assisting staff with exhibitions, and monitoring galleries. Candidates should have ability to work independently, ability to work with others, computer skills, experience in the field, oral communication skills, plan to pursue career in field, written communication skills. Duration is 2–3 months. Unpaid. Open to college juniors, college seniors, recent college graduates, graduate students. ▶ *2–3 development interns:* responsibilities include assisting in planning large fund-raising galas and other special events, assisting with public relations and media relations, and providing support for all development staff. Candidates should have computer skills, office skills, oral communication skills, self-motivation, strong interpersonal skills, written communication skills, must have excellent English language skills. Duration is 3–12 months. Unpaid. Open to college sophomores, college juniors, college seniors, recent college graduates, graduate students. ▶ *1–2 international classroom interns:* responsibilities include assisting with creating, improving, and expanding Meridian's collection of curriculum aids for use by D.C. public school educators instructing students about international issues and events. Candidates should have ability to work independently, computer skills, office skills, oral communication skills, personal interest in the field, research skills, strong interpersonal skills, written communication skills. Duration is 3–6 months. Unpaid. Open to college sophomores, college juniors, college seniors. ▶ *1–2 visitor services assistants:* responsibilities include working with volunteer corps, acting as a liaison between international visitors and volunteers, scheduling cultural events, assisting in conferences and workshops, and maintaining records. Candidates should have ability to work independently, ability to work with others, computer skills, office skills, oral communication skills, written communication skills. Duration is flexible. Unpaid. Open to high school students, recent high school graduates, college freshmen, college sophomores, college juniors, college seniors, recent college graduates, graduate students. ▶ *1 world affairs intern:* responsibilities include assisting in conference registration; coordinating variety of lectures, briefings, discussions, and seminars with an international theme. Candidates should have office skills, oral communication skills, organizational skills, personal interest in the field, plan to pursue career in field, written communication skills, data entry skills. Duration is 1–3 months. Unpaid. Open to high school students, college freshmen, college sophomores, college juniors, college seniors, recent college graduates, graduate students. International applications accepted.

Benefits Formal training, job counseling, names of contacts, on-the-job training, opportunity to attend seminars/workshops, possible full-time employment, willing to act as a professional reference, willing to complete paperwork for educational credit, willing to provide letters of recommendation.

Contact Write, fax, or through World Wide Web site Intern Coordinator. Fax: 202-667-1475. No phone calls. Telephone interview required. Applicants must submit a letter of interest, resume. Applications are accepted continuously. World Wide Web: http://www.meridian.org.

THE MIDDLE EAST INSTITUTE
1761 N Street, NW
Washington, District of Columbia 20036

General Information Nonprofit organization dedicated to improving public knowledge and understanding of the politics, economics, cultures, languages, and religions of the Middle East, North Africa, Caucasus, and Central Asia; publishing the Middle East Journal; teaching Arabic, Hebrew, Persian, and Turkish languages; presenting cultural and political programs; and operating the Keiser Library. Established in 1946. Number of employees: 15. Number of internship applications received each year: 100.

Internships Available ▶ *1 development intern:* responsibilities include helping maintain records, increasing fund-raising activities, and

writing articles about MEI lectures. Candidates should have ability to work independently, computer skills, editing skills, office skills, organizational skills, research skills, strong interpersonal skills, writing skills. Duration is 1 semester. Unpaid. Open to college freshmen, college sophomores, college juniors, college seniors, recent college graduates. ▶ *1–2 library interns:* responsibilities include compiling bibliographies, researching topics for patrons, answering telephone inquiries on the Middle East, and writing for the Institute's Web site. Candidates should have ability to work independently, computer skills, office skills, oral communication skills, organizational skills, research skills, strong interpersonal skills, writing skills. Duration is 1 semester. Unpaid. Open to college freshmen, college sophomores, college juniors, college seniors, recent college graduates. ▶ *2–3 programs interns:* responsibilities include research for conferences and seminars, helping to administer public events, correspondence, and writing articles about MEI. Candidates should have ability to work independently, oral communication skills, research skills, strong interpersonal skills, writing skills. Duration is 1 semester. Unpaid. Open to college freshmen, college sophomores, college juniors, college seniors, recent college graduates, graduate students. ▶ *3–4 publication interns:* responsibilities include proofreading book reviews, helping compile the journal's "Bibliography of Periodical Literature," drafting book annotations for publication in the Middle East Journal, maintaining two databases, and writing articles about MEI lectures. Candidates should have ability to work independently, computer skills, editing skills, organizational skills, plan to pursue career in field, research skills, writing skills. Duration is 1 semester. Unpaid. Open to college freshmen, college sophomores, college juniors, college seniors, recent college graduates, graduate students. International applications accepted.
Benefits Names of contacts, opportunity to attend seminars/workshops, willing to complete paperwork for educational credit, willing to provide letters of recommendation, 1 language course tuition-free, 1 year free membership in organization, reimbursement of local travel expenses.
Contact Write, call, fax, e-mail, or through World Wide Web site Talal Belrhiti, Internship Coordinator. Phone: 202-785-0191. Fax: 202-452-8876. E-mail: ast-ed@mideasti.org. In-person interview recommended (telephone interview accepted). Applicants must submit a letter of interest, resume, academic transcripts, writing sample, letter of recommendation. Applications are accepted continuously. World Wide Web: http://www.mideasti.org.

NATIONAL ASSOCIATION FOR COMMUNITY MEDIATION
1527 New Hampshire Avenue, NW
Washington, District of Columbia 20036

General Information An organization of community mediation programs and volunteer mediations whose goals are to provide a compelling voice in policy making, legislative arenas, and network support. Established in 1994. Number of employees: 4. Number of internship applications received each year: 20.
Internships Available ▶ *2–3 interns:* responsibilities include research, information gathering, networking, maintaining communication with related national organizations, creating a profile of state mediation associations and activities in their states, and additional administrative and clerical tasks as needed. Candidates should have ability to work independently, computer skills, oral communication skills, research skills, strong interpersonal skills, written communication skills, background or experience in mediation or conflict resolution. Duration is 3–6 months. Position available as unpaid or paid. Open to college juniors, college seniors, recent college graduates, graduate students, law students, law school graduates, career changers. International applications accepted.
Benefits Names of contacts, on-the-job training, opportunity to attend seminars/workshops, travel reimbursement, willing to act as a professional reference, willing to complete paperwork for educational credit, willing to provide letters of recommendation, possibility of stipend.
Contact Write, fax, or e-mail Craig Coletta, Coordinator, 1527 New Hampshire Avenue, NW, Washington, District of Columbia 20036. Fax: 202-667-8629. E-mail: nafcm@nafcm.org. No phone calls.

Telephone interview required. Applicants must submit a letter of interest, resume, three personal references. Applications are accepted continuously. World Wide Web: http://www.nafcm.org.

NATIONAL ASSOCIATION OF COLLEGIATE DIRECTORS OF ATHLETICS (NACDA)
24651 Detroit Road
Westlake, Ohio 44145

General Information Largest association of collegiate athletics administrators with a membership of more than 6,100 individuals and more than 1,600 institutions throughout the United States, Canada, and Mexico. Established in 1965. Number of employees: 10. Number of internship applications received each year: 50.
Internships Available ▶ *3–4 administrative interns:* responsibilities include assisting with a wide range of activities and duties, including one of NACDA's main undertakings, its annual convention, which requires months of preparation to make the event successful. Candidates should have computer skills, oral communication skills, plan to pursue career in field, self-motivation, strong interpersonal skills, written communication skills. Duration is one summer (May to August) or 10 months (September-July 1). $100 per week. Open to college freshmen, college sophomores, college juniors, college seniors, recent college graduates, graduate students, career changers, individuals reentering the workforce. International applications accepted.
Benefits Willing to act as a professional reference, willing to complete paperwork for educational credit, willing to provide letters of recommendation.
Contact Write, call, fax, or e-mail Becky Parke, Assistant Administrator/Association Liaison, PO Box 16428, Cleveland, Ohio 44116. Phone: 440-892-4000. Fax: 440-892-4007. E-mail: bparke@nacda.com. In-person interview recommended (telephone interview accepted). Applicants must submit a letter of interest, resume. Applications are accepted continuously. World Wide Web: http://www.nacda.com.

NATIONAL ASSOCIATION OF ELECTED AND APPOINTED OFFICIALS (NALEO) EDUCATIONAL FUND
1122 Washington Boulevard, 3rd Floor
Los Angeles, California 90015

General Information Nonprofit organization that promotes participation in the American political process. Established in 1981. Number of employees: 26. Number of internship applications received each year: 300.
Internships Available ▶ *Up to 10 Ford Motor Company Fellows:* responsibilities include working with a member of the House of Representatives in Washington, D.C. Duration is June 23 to August 3. Stipend of $1200. Open to recent college graduates, graduate students, law students, college seniors graduating in May. ▶ *10–14 Shell Legislative Internships:* responsibilities include participating in the legislative process with an elected or appointed official from intern's home state. Duration is June 23 to August 2. Stipend of $1500. Open to college juniors, college seniors, recent college graduates. Candidates for all positions should have ability to work independently, analytical skills, computer skills, editing skills, office skills, oral communication skills, organizational skills, research skills, self-motivation, strong interpersonal skills, strong leadership ability, writing skills.
Benefits Free housing, free meals, names of contacts, opportunity to attend seminars/workshops, possible full-time employment, travel reimbursement, willing to act as a professional reference, willing to provide letters of recommendation.
Contact Write, call, fax, e-mail, or through World Wide Web site Lourdes Ferrer, Deputy Director of Constituency Services. Phone: 213-747-7607 Ext. 127. Fax: 213-747-7664. E-mail: lferrer@naleo.org. Telephone interview required. Applicants must submit a formal organization application, resume, academic transcripts, two writing samples, two letters of recommendation. Application deadline: March 7 for Shell Legislative Internship Program, March 14 for Ford Motor Company Fellows Program. World Wide Web: http://www.naleo.org.

THE NATIONAL CENTER FOR PUBLIC POLICY RESEARCH
777 North Capitol Street, NE, Suite 803
Washington, District of Columbia 20002

General Information   Resource center for conservative activists, journalists, and policymakers that seeks to promote enlightened and reasoned debate on diverse public policy issues; dedicated to the principles of a strong defense, free competitive enterprise, and individual liberty. Established in 1982. Number of employees: 7. Number of internship applications received each year: 100.
Internships Available   ▶ *3–5 research assistants:* responsibilities include researching a topic of interest concerning U.S. domestic policy and/or international relations and general office support. Candidates should have ability to work independently, office skills, organizational skills, research skills, self-motivation, writing skills. Duration is flexible (37.5 hours per week). $6–$7 per hour. Open to college freshmen, college sophomores, college juniors, college seniors, recent college graduates, graduate students.
Benefits   Job counseling, names of contacts, on-the-job training, opportunity to attend seminars/workshops, possible full-time employment, willing to act as a professional reference, willing to complete paperwork for educational credit, willing to provide letters of recommendation.
Contact   Write, fax, or e-mail David Almasi, Executive Director. Fax: 202-408-7773. E-mail: dalmasi@nationalcenter.org. No phone calls. Telephone interview required. Applicants must submit a formal organization application, letter of interest, resume, writing sample, personal reference. Applications are accepted continuously. World Wide Web: http://www.nationalcenter.org.

NATIONAL FOUNDATION FOR WOMEN LEGISLATORS
910 16th Street, NW, Suite 100
Washington, District of Columbia 20005

General Information   501(c)(3) nonprofit, nonpartisan foundation providing leadership training and issue education to women who hold and/or run for elected office at all state and federal levels. Established in 1938. Number of employees: 9. Number of internship applications received each year: 30.
Internships Available   ▶ *15 general interns.* Candidates should have ability to work independently, analytical skills, computer skills, editing skills, office skills, oral communication skills, organizational skills, research skills, self-motivation, strong interpersonal skills, strong leadership ability, writing skills, ability to be a team player. Duration is year-round. Position available as unpaid or paid. Open to college juniors, college seniors, recent college graduates, graduate students, law students, career changers, individuals reentering the workforce. International applications accepted.
Benefits   Names of contacts, on-the-job training, opportunity to attend seminars/workshops, possible full-time employment, willing to act as a professional reference, willing to complete paperwork for educational credit, willing to provide letters of recommendation.
Contact   Write, call, fax, e-mail, or through World Wide Web site Julie Swayney, Intern Coordinator, 910 16th Street, NW Suite 100, Washington 20005. Phone: 202-337-3565 Ext. 1010. Fax: 202-293-5430. E-mail: nfwl@erols.com. In-person interview recommended (telephone interview accepted). Applicants must submit a letter of interest, resume. Applications are accepted continuously. World Wide Web: http://www.womenlegislators.org.

NATIONAL INSTITUTE FOR PUBLIC POLICY
3031 Javier Road, Suite 300
Fairfax, Virginia 22031

General Information   Organization providing historically-based strategic analysis, policy research, and education in the international security field. Established in 1981. Number of employees: 20. Number of internship applications received each year: 50.
Internships Available   ▶ *1–2 research support interns:* responsibilities include researching and writing educational materials, assisting with editing of the journal *Comparative Strategy,* and assisting with organizing conferences. Candidates should have college courses in field, knowledge of field, personal interest in the field,

research skills. Duration is flexible. Position available as unpaid or paid. Open to recent college graduates, graduate students.
Benefits   Job counseling, names of contacts, opportunity to attend seminars/workshops, possible full-time employment, willing to complete paperwork for educational credit, willing to provide letters of recommendation.
Contact   Write, call, fax, or e-mail Mr. John J. Kohout, III, Vice President. Phone: 703-698-0563. Fax: 703-698-0566. E-mail: john.kohout@nipp.org. In-person interview required. Applicants must submit a letter of interest, resume, writing sample. Applications are accepted continuously. World Wide Web: http://www.nipp.org.

NATIONAL INSTITUTE OF STANDARDS AND TECHNOLOGY
100 Bureau Drive
Gaithersburg, Maryland 20899

General Information   Non-regulatory, federal agency that conducts research that advances the nation's technology infrastructure and is needed by U.S. industry to improve products and services. Established in 1901. Number of employees: 3,000. Unit of United States Department of Commerce, Washington, District of Columbia. Number of internship applications received each year: 200.
Internships Available   ▶ *100–120 summer undergraduate research fellows (SURF):* responsibilities include working on an ongoing research project under the guidance of a NIST scientist or engineer from one of seven NIST laboratories. Candidates should have college courses in field, personal interest in the field, plan to pursue career in field, research skills, self-motivation. Duration is 9–12 weeks. $3000–$4000 per duration of internship. Open to college freshmen, college sophomores, college juniors, college seniors, recent college graduates.
Benefits   Free housing, names of contacts, on-the-job training, opportunity to attend seminars/workshops, possible full-time employment, travel reimbursement, willing to act as a professional reference, willing to provide letters of recommendation.
Contact   E-mail or through World Wide Web site Anita Sweigert, Administrative Assistant. Phone: 301-975-4200. E-mail: anita.sweigert@nist.gov. Applicants must submit a formal organization application, letter of interest, resume, academic transcripts, two letters of recommendation. Application deadline: February 15. World Wide Web: http://www.nist.gov.

NATIONAL JOURNALISM CENTER
800 Maryland Avenue, NE
Washington, District of Columbia 20002

General Information   Organization that provides training to reporters in order to improve the field of investigative reporting. Established in 1977. Number of employees: 9. Unit of Education and Research Institute, Washinton, District of Columbia. Number of internship applications received each year: 300.
Internships Available   ▶ *10–30 interns:* responsibilities include researching and writing articles for the Center and acting as reporters on staff at Washington Metropolitan-area media outlets. Candidates should have analytical skills, oral communication skills, plan to pursue career in field, research skills, strong interpersonal skills, written communication skills. Duration is 1–3 months. $100 per week. Open to college juniors, college seniors, recent college graduates. ▶ *75–80 journalism interns:* responsibilities include researching, reporting, writing, and some administrative tasks. Candidates should have ability to work independently, analytical skills, editing skills, organizational skills, plan to pursue career in field, research skills, self-motivation, strong interpersonal skills, writing skills. Duration is 12 weeks. $100 per week. Open to college juniors, college seniors, recent college graduates, career changers.
Benefits   Housing at a cost, job counseling, names of contacts, opportunity to attend seminars/workshops, willing to act as a professional reference, willing to complete paperwork for educational credit, willing to provide letters of recommendation, access to in-house job bank, resume referral provided.

Contact Write, call, fax, or e-mail Mr. Malcolm A. Kline, Editor. Phone: 202-544-1333. Fax: 202-544-5368. E-mail: mal@nationaljournalismcenter.org. In-person interview recommended (telephone interview accepted). Applicants must submit a formal organization application, letter of interest, resume, 2-3 writing samples. Application deadline: February 1 for spring, May 1 for summer, September 1 for fall, November 26 for winter. World Wide Web: http://www.nationaljournalismcenter.org.

NATIONAL OPINION RESEARCH CENTER
55 East Monroe Street, Suite 1800
Chicago, Illinois 60603

General Information Social science research center that studies health, education, labor, alcohol and drug abuse, and other areas of public policy interest; located at University of Chicago. Established in 1941. Number of employees: 500. Number of internship applications received each year: 175.
Internships Available ▶ *5 summer interns:* responsibilities include assisting project staff in coding, editing, and data entry of questionnaires; preparing interviewer training materials; questionnaire design; and instrument testing. Candidates should have ability to work independently, ability to work with others, analytical skills, personal interest in the field, plan to pursue career in field, written communication skills. Duration is 10 weeks. $9.50–$11.50 per hour. Open to college juniors, college seniors, recent college graduates, graduate students. International applications accepted.
Benefits Formal training, names of contacts, on-the-job training, opportunity to attend seminars/workshops, possible full-time employment, willing to act as a professional reference, willing to complete paperwork for educational credit, willing to provide letters of recommendation.
Contact Write, fax, e-mail, or through World Wide Web site Dennis Dew, Survey Director, 55 East Monroe Street, Suite 1800 NORC, Chicago, Illinois 60603. Fax: 312-759-4004. E-mail: norc-intern@norcmail.uchicago.edu. No phone calls. Telephone interview required. Applicants must submit a letter of interest, resume, 5-page writing sample. Application deadline: April 15 for summer. World Wide Web: http://www.norc.uchicago.edu.

NATIONAL SECURITY ARCHIVE, THE GEORGE WASHINGTON UNIVERSITY
Gelman Library, Suite 701, 2130 H Street, NW
Washington, District of Columbia 20037

General Information Nonprofit research institute, library, and publisher providing scholars, journalists, librarians, students, and other researchers with unclassified and declassified government documents for research and informed debate. Established in 1985. Number of employees: 25. Number of internship applications received each year: 150.
Internships Available ▶ *5–10 interns:* responsibilities include performing library and archival research; building chronology of events; obtaining, ordering, and cataloging government documents; and entering computer data. Candidates should have ability to work independently, college courses in field, computer skills, knowledge of field, research skills, writing skills. Duration is 2 months. Unpaid. Open to college freshmen, college sophomores, college juniors, college seniors, recent college graduates, graduate students. International applications accepted.
Benefits Possible full-time employment, willing to complete paperwork for educational credit, willing to provide letters of recommendation.
Contact Write, fax, or e-mail Ms. Sue Bechtel, Administrator. Fax: 202-994-7005. E-mail: sbechtel@gwu.edu. No phone calls. Applicants must submit a letter of interest, resume, writing sample. Application deadline: March 15 for summer (suggested), July 15 for fall (suggested), December 1 for spring (suggested). World Wide Web: http://www.nsarchive.org.

NATIONAL TREASURY EMPLOYEES UNION
1750 H Street, NW
Washington, District of Columbia 20006

General Information Union of federal government employees representing employee interests on Capitol Hill, in court, in negotiations, and in the news media. Established in 1938. Number of employees: 65. Number of internship applications received each year: 20.
Internships Available ▶ *1 public relations intern:* responsibilities include using computer software, desktop publishing and graphic designs. Duration is flexible. Paid. ▶ *1 staff writer intern:* responsibilities include developing written materials. Duration is flexible. Paid. Open to college juniors, college seniors, recent college graduates, graduate students. International applications accepted.
Benefits Names of contacts, willing to complete paperwork for educational credit, willing to provide letters of recommendation.
Contact Write, call, or fax Sheila McCormick, Internship Coordinator. Phone: 202-572-5500 Ext. 7034. Fax: 202-572-5643. In-person interview recommended (telephone interview accepted). Applicants must submit a letter of interest, resume. Applications are accepted continuously. World Wide Web: http://www.nteu.org.

NETWORK IN SOLIDARITY WITH THE PEOPLE OF GUATEMALA
1830 Connecticut Avenue, NW
Washington, District of Columbia 20009

General Information Organization that educates North Americans to work for justice in Guatemala, to support Guatemala's grassroots movement, and to reorient U.S. policy towards Guatemala. Established in 1981. Number of employees: 4. Number of internship applications received each year: 30.
Internships Available ▶ *10–15 human rights monitors:* responsibilities include monitoring human rights in Guatemalan villages and acting as a link to U.S. sister communities. Candidates should have ability to work independently, analytical skills, self-motivation, strong interpersonal skills, strong leadership ability, Spanish speaking ability. Duration is 6–12 months. $250 per month. Open to college freshmen, college sophomores, college juniors, college seniors, recent college graduates, graduate students, law students, career changers, individuals reentering the workforce. ▶ *1–2 interns:* responsibilities include researching and writing of grassroots education material and supporting grassroots campaigns encouraging respect of human rights in Guatemala. Candidates should have ability to work independently, ability to work with others, computer skills, personal interest in the field, written communication skills, knowledge of Spanish (preferred). Unpaid. Open to college sophomores, college juniors, college seniors, recent college graduates, graduate students.
Benefits Names of contacts, on-the-job training, opportunity to attend seminars/workshops, travel reimbursement, willing to act as a professional reference, willing to complete paperwork for educational credit, willing to provide letters of recommendation, additional benefits for human rights monitors (in Guatemala): health insurance, free housing, free meals, formal training.
International Internships Available in Guatemala.
Contact Write, call, fax, e-mail, or through World Wide Web site Jennifer Morley, U.S. Program Coordinator, Guatemala Accompaniment Project. Phone: 202-265-8713. Fax: 202-223-8221. E-mail: nisguagap@igc.org. Telephone interview required. Applicants must submit a formal organization application, resume, writing sample, three personal references. Application deadline: January 2 for February training, May 1 for June training, September 1 for October training. World Wide Web: http://www.nisgua.org.

NEW YORK COMMITTEE FOR OCCUPATIONAL SAFETY AND HEALTH
275 Seventh Avenue
New York, New York 10001

General Information Organization of labor unions and safety and health activists that provides training programs, educational materials, and technical assistance. Established in 1979. Number of employees: 11.
Internships Available ▶ *3 interns:* responsibilities include performing duties in the areas of research, legislative work, training, and technical assistance. Candidates should have ability to work independently, computer skills, organizational skills, research skills, self-motivation, written communication skills. Duration is 3-6

New York Committee for Occupational Safety and Health (continued)

months (year-round). Unpaid. Open to college juniors, college seniors, recent college graduates, graduate students.
Benefits Job counseling, names of contacts, opportunity to attend seminars/workshops, possible full-time employment, travel reimbursement, willing to provide letters of recommendation.
Contact Write, call, fax, or e-mail Joel Shufro, Director. Phone: 212-627-3900 Ext. 15. Fax: 212-627-9812. E-mail: jshufro@nycosh.org. In-person interview recommended (telephone interview accepted). Applicants must submit a letter of interest, resume, writing sample, two personal references. Applications are accepted continuously. World Wide Web: http://www.nycosh.org.

NEW YORK UNION SEMESTER, QUEENS COLLEGE
25 West 43rd Street, 19th Floor
New York, New York 10036

General Information Program that provides students with the opportunity to intern with a union for a semester while studying at Queens College. Established in 1999. Number of employees: 1. Unit of Queens College Labor Resource Center, New York, New York. Number of internship applications received each year: 50.
Internships Available ▶ *20–25 activist interns:* responsibilities include various duties dependent on specific positions. Candidates should have ability to work independently, ability to work with others, oral communication skills, personal interest in the field, self-motivation, strong leadership ability. Duration is February to May or September to December. $210 per week. Open to college juniors, college seniors, recent college graduates, graduate students, law students, career changers. ▶ *20–50 interns:* responsibilities include working with unions, typically writing articles for a union newsletter, advocating on behalf of the legal rights of immigrant workers, assisting in anti-sweatshop campaigns, investigating occupational health and safety violations, or working in a community outreach center. Candidates should have ability to work independently, oral communication skills, personal interest in the field, strong interpersonal skills, written communication skills. Duration is August to December. Stipend of $210 per week. Open to college sophomores, college juniors, college seniors, recent college graduates. International applications accepted.
Benefits Formal training, job counseling, names of contacts, on-the-job training, opportunity to attend seminars/workshops, possible full-time employment, tuition assistance, willing to act as a professional reference, willing to complete paperwork for educational credit, willing to provide letters of recommendation.
Contact Write, call, fax, e-mail, or through World Wide Web site Johanna Jones, Program Coordinator. Phone: 212-827-0200. Fax: 212-827-5955. E-mail: unionsemester@qc.edu. Telephone interview required. Applicants must submit a formal organization application, academic transcripts, three personal references, essay (assigned), 1 writing sample (optional). Application deadline: June 15 for fall, November 15 for spring. World Wide Web: http://www.qc.edu/unionsemester.

NON-PROFIT HOUSING ASSOCIATION OF NORTHERN CALIFORNIA
369 Pine Street, Suite 350
San Francisco, California 94104

General Information Association of nonprofit housing developers in northern California. Established in 1979. Number of employees: 5. Number of internship applications received each year: 10.
Internships Available ▶ *1 writer/researcher:* responsibilities include researching relevant housing issues such as child development, education, and need for affordable housing, and producing written work on the subject. Candidates should have ability to work independently, analytical skills, college courses in field, computer skills, editing skills, experience in the field, office skills, oral communication skills, organizational skills, plan to pursue career in field, research skills, self-motivation, strong interpersonal skills, writing skills. Duration is dependent upon availability. Position

available as unpaid or at a variable stipend. Open to recent college graduates, graduate students. International applications accepted.
Benefits On-the-job training, opportunity to attend seminars/workshops, possible full-time employment, travel reimbursement, willing to act as a professional reference, willing to complete paperwork for educational credit, willing to provide letters of recommendation, commuter benefit.
Contact Write, call, or e-mail Dianne J. Spaulding, Executive Director. Phone: 415-989-8160. Fax: 415-989-8166. E-mail: dianne@nonprofithousing.org. In-person interview required. Applicants must submit a letter of interest, resume. Applications are accepted continuously. World Wide Web: http://www.nonprofithousing.org.

NORTHEAST–MIDWEST INSTITUTE
218 D Street, SE
Washington, District of Columbia 20003

General Information Nonprofit research and public education organization that develops public policy, provides technical assistance, sponsors regional conferences, and distributes publications. Established in 1977. Number of employees: 20. Number of internship applications received each year: 25.
Internships Available ▶ *2 interns:* responsibilities include working in various departments including Brownfields, Energy, Great Lakes/Ecosystems, Smart Growth, and Upper Mississippi. Candidates should have oral communication skills, organizational skills, writing skills. Duration is one summer. Unpaid. International applications accepted.
Benefits Names of contacts, opportunity to attend seminars/workshops, willing to provide letters of recommendation.
Contact Write or fax Heather Lockridge, Administrative Assistant. Fax: 202-544-0043. No phone calls. In-person interview recommended (telephone interview accepted). Applicants must submit a letter of interest, resume, academic transcripts, writing sample. Application deadline: May 1. World Wide Web: http://www.nemw.org.

OHIO LEGISLATIVE SERVICE COMMISSION, RIFFE CENTER FOR GOVERNMENT AND THE ARTS
77 South High Street, 9th Floor
Columbus, Ohio 43215-6136

General Information Non-partisan organization providing the members of the Ohio General Assembly with legal, bill-drafting, research, and other support services. Established in 1953. Number of employees: 135. Unit of Ohio General Assembly, Columbus, Ohio. Number of internship applications received each year: 200.
Internships Available ▶ *27 legislative interns:* responsibilities include providing general staff assistance to elected officials including assisting with constituent work; performing legislative research; writing press releases, newspaper columns, and speeches; attending committee meetings. Candidates should have ability to work independently, analytical skills, oral communication skills, self-motivation, strong interpersonal skills, written communication skills. Duration is 13 months (December 1 to December 31 of the following year). $24,500–$25,500 per year. ▶ *2 telecommunications interns:* responsibilities include working in Ohio State House telecommunications studio; working as production assistants for production of televised legislative sessions and with video production, editing, audio, floor directing, and lighting; and conducting studio tours for the public. Candidates should have college degree in related field, oral communication skills, self-motivation, strong interpersonal skills, written communication skills, video production experience. Duration is 13 months (December 1 to December 31 of the following year). $24,500–$25,500 per year. Open to individuals with at least a bachelor's degree by start of internship. International applications accepted.
Benefits Formal training, health insurance, names of contacts, on-the-job training, opportunity to attend seminars/workshops, possible full-time employment, willing to act as a professional reference, willing to provide letters of recommendation, leave time.

Contact Write, call, e-mail, or through World Wide Web site Rachel Faherty, Internship Coordinator. Phone: 614-466-3615. E-mail: rfaherty@lsc.state.oh.us. In-person interview required. Applicants must submit a formal organization application, resume, academic transcripts, three letters of recommendation, 2-4-page typewritten autobiographical statement. Application deadline: April 1 for legislative interns, May 31 for telecommunications interns. World Wide Web: http://www.lsc.state.oh.us.

PARLIAMENTARY MONITORING GROUP (PMG)
Church Square House, 5 Spin Street, 10th Floor
Cape Town 8001 South Africa

General Information Independent, not-for-profit organization that monitors parliamentary committees and provides summary reports of committee meetings on the Internet. Established in 1995. Number of employees: 9. Affiliate of Institute for Democracy in South Africa (IDASA), Cape Town, South Africa. Number of internship applications received each year: 50.
Internships Available ▶ *1 parliamentary monitor:* responsibilities include attendance at daily parliamentary committee meeting and writing detailed reports of the proceedings which are published on Web site. Candidates should have ability to work with others, analytical skills, computer skills, personal interest in the field, self-motivation, writing skills. Duration is February to June or August to November. Unpaid. Open to recent college graduates, graduate students, law students. International applications accepted.
Benefits On-the-job training, willing to act as a professional reference, willing to complete paperwork for educational credit, willing to provide letters of recommendation.
International Internships Available.
Contact E-mail Ms. Gaile Moosmann, Managing Editor, 307 Westminster House, 122 Long Market Street, Cape Town 8001 South Africa. Phone: 27-21-4658885. Fax: 27-21-4658887. E-mail: info@pmg.org.za. Applicants must submit a letter of interest, resume, two letters of recommendation. Applications are accepted continuously. World Wide Web: http://www.pmg.org.za.

PERENNIAL STRATEGY GROUP
1455 Pennsylvania Avenue, NW, Suite 225
Washington, District of Columbia 20004

General Information Government relations firm. Established in 2002. Number of employees: 7. Number of internship applications received each year: 100.
Internships Available ▶ *1-2 legal research assistants:* responsibilities include research, writing, mail outs, assisting in office projects, occasional answering of phones, at times assisting at political events, administrative duties. Candidates should have ability to work independently, ability to work with others, office skills, research skills, self-motivation, writing skills. Duration is 12-40 hours per week. Position available as unpaid or at $7–$9 per hour. Open to college freshmen, college sophomores, college juniors, college seniors, recent college graduates, law students. International applications accepted.
Benefits Names of contacts, on-the-job training, possible full-time employment, willing to act as a professional reference, willing to complete paperwork for educational credit, willing to provide letters of recommendation.
Contact Call, fax, or e-mail Andrea DeArment, Office Manager. Phone: 202-638-5090. Fax: 202-638-5564. E-mail: andrea@perennialsg.com. In-person interview recommended (telephone interview accepted). Applicants must submit a resume, writing sample (desirable). Applications are accepted continuously. World Wide Web: http://perennialsg.com.

PRESBYTERIAN CHURCH (USA), PRESBYTERIAN HISTORICAL SOCIETY
425 Lombard Street
Philadelphia, Pennsylvania 19147-1516

General Information Archives that collect and preserve official records and personal papers of the Presbyterian Church, serve the administrative needs of the Presbyterian Church, and provide access to academic and other researchers. Established in 1852.

Number of employees: 25. Unit of Presbyterian Church (USA), Louisville, Kentucky. Number of internship applications received each year: 5.
Internships Available ▶ *1 archives intern:* responsibilities include processing archival collections and assisting with reference questions. Candidates should have ability to work independently, college courses in field, organizational skills, personal interest in the field, research skills, written communication skills. Duration is flexible. Position available as unpaid or at $7.50–$9 per hour. Open to college freshmen, college sophomores, college juniors, college seniors, graduate students, career changers. International applications accepted.
Benefits On-the-job training, willing to act as a professional reference, willing to complete paperwork for educational credit, willing to provide letters of recommendation.
Contact Write, fax, or e-mail Margery N. Sly, Deputy Director. Fax: 215-627-0509. E-mail: msly@history.pcusa.org. No phone calls. In-person interview recommended (telephone interview accepted). Applicants must submit a letter of interest, resume, writing sample, three personal references. Applications are accepted continuously. World Wide Web: http://www.history.pcusa.org.

PROCTER & GAMBLE COMPANY
Miami Valley Laboratories, Box 538707
Cincinnati, Ohio 45253-8707

General Information International, technically-based company engaged in the research, development, manufacture, and sale of consumer products in five Global Business Units: health care, baby and family care, beauty care, fabric and home care, and snacks and beverages. Established in 1837. Number of internship applications received each year: 100.
Internships Available ▶ *20–30 doctoral summer interns:* responsibilities include performing duties as full-time researcher at one corporate technical center in Cincinnati. Candidates should have ability to work with others, analytical skills, knowledge of field, oral communication skills, plan to pursue career in field, strong leadership ability, written communication skills. Duration is 10–12 weeks. $875 per week for graduating seniors; salary for graduate students commensurate with schooling. Open to graduate students, graduating seniors going on to graduate school.
Benefits Formal training, on-the-job training, opportunity to attend seminars/workshops, local transportation from housing to work site, affordable university housing available.
Contact E-mail or through World Wide Web site Brenda Cromer, Recruiting Coordinator. Fax: 513-627-2266. E-mail: doctoral.im@pg.com. No phone calls. Telephone interview required. Applicants must submit a letter of interest, resume, two letters of recommendation, application as posted on Web site. Application deadline: March 1 for summer. World Wide Web: http://www.pg.com/jobs/jobs_us/sectionmain.jhtml.

PROJECT VOTE SMART
One Common Ground
Philipsburg, Montana 59858

General Information National library of political information on over 13,000 candidates and elected officials per election cycle. Established in 1988. Number of employees: 25. Number of internship applications received each year: 100.
Internships Available ▶ *5–10 National Political Awareness Test assistants:* responsibilities include conducting ongoing research of political issues to be included in the presidential, congressional, gubernatorial, and state legislative National Political Awareness Tests; administering NPATs to campaigns and candidates. Candidates should have ability to work independently, ability to work with others, oral communication skills, organizational skills, research skills, written communication skills. Duration is 10 weeks. Unpaid. Open to recent high school graduates, college freshmen, college sophomores, college juniors, college seniors, recent college graduates, graduate students, law students. ▶ *2–5 Web researchers:* responsibilities include researching new and changed links, reviewing link suggestions from the Web site, and entering new links and descriptions into the database. Candidates should have ability to work independently, computer skills, editing skills, knowledge of field, office skills, organizational skills. Duration is 10 weeks.

Project Vote Smart (continued)

Unpaid. Open to high school seniors, college freshmen, college sophomores, college juniors, college seniors, recent college graduates, graduate students, law students. ▶ *2–5 facilities assistants:* responsibilities include assisting in all areas including lodge and kitchen management and general maintenance. Candidates should have ability to work independently, knowledge of field, oral communication skills, organizational skills, self-motivation, strong interpersonal skills, strong leadership ability. Duration is 10 weeks. Unpaid. Open to recent high school graduates, college freshmen, college sophomores, college juniors, college seniors, recent college graduates, graduate students. ▶ *1 management assistant:* responsibilities include assisting in all areas of managing a nonprofit organization. Candidates should have ability to work independently, computer skills, office skills, oral communication skills, organizational skills, strong interpersonal skills. Duration is 10 weeks. Unpaid. Open to recent high school graduates, college freshmen, college sophomores, college juniors, college seniors, recent college graduates, graduate students, law students. ▶ *2 membership assistants:* responsibilities include working in all aspects of the membership department; includes data entry, bulk mailing, research, and statistical analysis; contacting members and vendors; and processing special requests. Candidates should have ability to work independently, analytical skills, computer skills, editing skills, office skills, oral communication skills, organizational skills, research skills, strong interpersonal skills. Duration is 10 weeks. Unpaid. Open to recent high school graduates, college freshmen, college sophomores, college juniors, college seniors, recent college graduates, graduate students, law students. ▶ *2–4 performance evaluation assistants:* responsibilities include maintaining and updating evaluations by special interest groups; researching new interest groups and adding new ratings. Candidates should have ability to work independently, computer skills, editing skills, office skills, oral communication skills, organizational skills, personal interest in the field, research skills. Duration is 10 weeks. Unpaid. Open to recent high school graduates, college freshmen, college sophomores, college juniors, college seniors, recent college graduates, graduate students, law students. ▶ *2 public information/media assistants:* responsibilities include maintaining contacts with national media; publicizing PVS through news releases and presentations; and PSAS print development. Candidates should have ability to work independently, computer skills, editing skills, knowledge of field, office skills, oral communication skills, organizational skills, strong interpersonal skills, written communication skills. Duration is 10 weeks. Unpaid. Open to recent high school graduates, college freshmen, college sophomores, college juniors, college seniors, recent college graduates, graduate students, law students. ▶ *10–15 research and hot line assistants:* responsibilities include answering Voter's Research Hotline; researching special requests made by callers; researching potential presidential candidates and other elected officials; and updating candidate database. Candidates should have ability to work independently, computer skills, oral communication skills, organizational skills, research skills, strong interpersonal skills, written communication skills. Duration is 10 weeks. Unpaid. Open to recent high school graduates, college freshmen, college sophomores, college juniors, college seniors, recent college graduates, graduate students, law students. International applications accepted.

Benefits Formal training, free housing, free meals, on-the-job training, possible full-time employment, willing to act as a professional reference, willing to complete paperwork for educational credit, willing to provide letters of recommendation, scholarships available.

Contact Write, call, fax, e-mail, or through World Wide Web site Lisa Coligan, Internship Coordinator. Phone: 406-859-VOTE. Fax: 406-859-8680. E-mail: intern@vote-smart.org. Telephone interview required. Applicants must submit a formal organization application, letter of interest, resume, three personal references. Application deadline: May 1 for summer; continuous for all other positions. World Wide Web: http://www.vote-smart.org.

PUBLIC FORUM INSTITUTE
2300 M Street, NW, Suite 900
Washington, District of Columbia 20037

General Information Nonpartisan, independent public policy group specializing in the development of public forums to debate major issues on the national agenda and maintaining a strong emphasis on social security and budget issues, trade, energy, and economic policy. Established in 1978. Number of employees: 8. Number of internship applications received each year: 200.

Internships Available ▶ *2–4 congressional policy forum interns:* responsibilities include researching speakers issued for policy forums, attending congressional hearings, and working on survey reports. Candidates should have ability to work independently, computer skills, organizational skills, personal interest in the field, self-motivation, strong interpersonal skills. Duration is flexible. Unpaid. Open to college freshmen, college sophomores, college juniors, college seniors, individuals reentering the workforce. ▶ *1–2 media associates:* responsibilities include reporting to communication director, press conferences, pitching position development, public policy editorial development, and writing press/reporter research. Candidates should have computer skills, plan to pursue career in field, self-motivation, strong interpersonal skills, written communication skills. Duration is 2–3 months. Unpaid. Open to college freshmen, college sophomores, college juniors, college seniors, recent college graduates, graduate students, law students, career changers, individuals reentering the workforce. ▶ *1–2 public affairs associates:* responsibilities include working with senior vice president for business development; proposal writing, team presentations, corporate research, and new ideas creation. Candidates should have oral communication skills, plan to pursue career in field, self-motivation, strong interpersonal skills, written communication skills. Duration is 1–3 months. Unpaid. Open to college freshmen, college sophomores, college juniors, college seniors, recent college graduates, graduate students, career changers, business school students. ▶ *4–6 summer associates:* responsibilities include joining a team of 3 professional staff and being fully integrated into the activities of that team; working primarily on national public policy summits. Candidates should have ability to work independently, computer skills, organizational skills, personal interest in the field, self-motivation, strong interpersonal skills. Duration is flexible. Unpaid. Open to college freshmen, college sophomores, college juniors, college seniors, recent college graduates, individuals reentering the workforce. ▶ *2–3 summer project associates:* responsibilities include public policy event planning for congressional summits on topical issues; grassroots public relations and outreach work (no phone answering/mail handling). Candidates should have computer skills, oral communication skills, organizational skills, self-motivation, strong interpersonal skills. Duration is 2–3 months. Unpaid. Open to college freshmen, college sophomores, college juniors.

Benefits Names of contacts, on-the-job training, opportunity to attend seminars/workshops, possible full-time employment, willing to act as a professional reference, willing to complete paperwork for educational credit, willing to provide letters of recommendation.

Contact Write, call, fax, e-mail, or through World Wide Web site Anne C. Neel, Vice President of Personnel. Phone: 202-467-2774. Fax: 202-293-5717. E-mail: anne@pfidc.org. In-person interview recommended (telephone interview accepted). Applicants must submit a formal organization application, letter of interest, two personal references. Application deadline: March 31 for summer, August 31 for fall, November 30 for January term, December 31 for spring. World Wide Web: http://www.publicforuminstitute.org.

QUAKER UNITED NATIONS OFFICE
777 United Nations Plaza, 5th Floor
New York, New York 10017

General Information Organization that represents the world body of the Religious Society of Friends (Quakers) at the United Nations. Established in 1948. Number of employees: 6. Number of internship applications received each year: 50.

Internships Available ▶ *2 interns:* responsibilities include providing program and administrative office support for staff by following the schedule of meetings and stream of documents around the activities of the General Assembly; monitoring, researching, and interpreting one or more substantial issues of interest to intern and QUNO; and assisting with office tasks, including mailings, filing, phones, and assisting visitors. Candidates should have college courses in field, office skills, oral communication skills, organizational skills, personal interest in the field, writing skills. Duration is 1 year. $16,000 per year. Open to recent college graduates or the equivalent. International applications accepted.

Benefits Health insurance, opportunity to attend seminars/workshops, travel reimbursement, willing to act as a professional reference, willing to provide letters of recommendation, 20 days vacation.

Contact Write, call, fax, e-mail, or through World Wide Web site Internship Coordinator. Phone: 212-682-2745. Fax: 212-983-0034. E-mail: qunony@afsc.org. Applicants must submit writing sample, application (available by e-mail), 4 personal references and/or letters of recommendation. Application deadline: February 6. World Wide Web: http://www.quno.org.

RAND
1700 Main Street, PO Box 2138
Santa Monica, California 90407-2138

General Information Private, nonprofit institution for research and analysis on issues affecting national security and the public welfare. Established in 1948. Number of employees: 1,100. Number of internship applications received each year: 400.

Internships Available ▶ *20–25 summer associates:* responsibilities include conducting research related to dissertation and discussing problems of mutual interest with RAND researchers; positions available in Santa Monica, CA, Arlington, VA, and Pittsburgh, PA. Candidates should have ability to work independently, ability to work with others, analytical skills, oral communication skills, research skills, written communication skills. Duration is 12 weeks. Stipend. Open to graduate students enrolled full time who have completed at least 2 years of graduate work leading to a doctorate or professional degree. International applications accepted.

Benefits Names of contacts, on-the-job training, opportunity to attend seminars/workshops, possible full-time employment, travel reimbursement, willing to complete paperwork for educational credit, willing to provide letters of recommendation, opportunity to conduct independent research.

Contact Write, fax, e-mail, or through World Wide Web site Sally Sleeper, Director, Graduate Student Summer Associate Program. Phone: 412-683-2300 Ext. 4914. Fax: 412-683-2800. E-mail: summerdirector@rand.org. Applicants must submit a letter of interest, resume, names and e-mail addresses of 3 academic references. Application deadline: February 1. World Wide Web: http://www.rand.org/edu_fellowships/gsap.

REPORTERS COMMITTEE FOR FREEDOM OF THE PRESS
1815 North Fort Myer Drive, Suite 900
Arlington, Virginia 22209

General Information Organization that helps reporters around the country gather and cover the news and advises them about First Amendment and freedom of information rights. Established in 1970. Number of employees: 10. Number of internship applications received each year: 75.

Internships Available ▶ *1 journalism intern (broadcast):* responsibilities include covering media law issues that affect broadcasters such as cameras in courtrooms. Duration is 1 one semester (possibility of part-time). Small stipend available. ▶ *1 journalism intern (news gathering):* responsibilities include assisting in editing publications, covering legal issues that involve journalists but do not fall within traditional media law categories, and covering legal problems encountered by American journalists abroad. Duration is flexible. Small stipend available. Open to college juniors, college seniors, recent college graduates, graduate students, law students, career changers. Candidates for all positions should have editing skills,

personal interest in the field, self-motivation, strong interpersonal skills, writing skills. International applications accepted.

Benefits Formal training, on-the-job training, opportunity to attend seminars/workshops, willing to act as a professional reference, willing to complete paperwork for educational credit, willing to provide letters of recommendation.

Contact Write, call, or e-mail Ms. Rebecca Daugherty, Internship Coordinator. Phone: 703-807-2100. E-mail: rdaugherty@reporterscommittee.org. Applicants must submit a letter of interest, resume, writing sample. Application deadline: January 31 for summer, March 31 for fall, October 31 for winter/spring. World Wide Web: http://www.rcfp.org.

ROBERT BOSCH FOUNDATION FELLOWSHIP PROGRAM, CDS INTERNATIONAL, INC.
871 United Nations Plaza, 15th Floor
New York, New York 10017

General Information Fellowship program in Germany for American citizens in the fields of business, economics, journalism, law, mass communications, political science, and public affairs/public policy. Established in 1968. Number of employees: 23. Number of internship applications received each year: 250.

Internships Available ▶ *20 executive level interns:* responsibilities include performing various duties dependent upon field of specialization. Candidates should have ability to work independently, analytical skills, experience in the field, oral communication skills, personal interest in the field, strong leadership ability. Duration is 9 months (September to June). Stipend of 1800 euros per month. Open to recent college graduates, graduate students, law students.

Benefits Health insurance, opportunity to attend seminars/workshops, travel reimbursement, tuition assistance, German language training, stipend of 1800 euros per month.

International Internships Available in Germany.

Contact Through World Wide Web site Ms. Jeanne Fahey, Program Officer. Phone: 212-497-3518. Fax: 212-497-3535. E-mail: jfahey@cdsintl.org. In-person interview required. Applicants must submit a formal organization application, letter of interest, resume, academic transcripts, two letters of recommendation, statement of purpose. Application deadline: October 15 for September of the following year. World Wide Web: http://www.cdsintl.org.

ROYAL PALM TOURS, INC.
PO Box 60079
Fort Myers, Florida 33906-6079

General Information Tour company primarily creating and operating special interest programs in the fields of nature-based, cultural, and heritage tourism; also offers consulting and tourism industry workshops. Established in 1980. Number of employees: 6. Number of internship applications received each year: 100.

Internships Available ▶ *1 student intern:* responsibilities include hands-on participation in tour research, product development, pricing, sales and marketing, and operations; visitations to related agencies. Candidates should have ability to work independently, computer skills, knowledge of field, office skills, oral communication skills, organizational skills, personal interest in the field, plan to pursue career in field, research skills, strong interpersonal skills, written communication skills, major in tourism, leisure studies, or commercial recreation. Duration is 3–4 months. Unpaid. Open to college juniors, college seniors, recent college graduates. International applications accepted.

Benefits Formal training, housing at a cost, job counseling, meals at a cost, names of contacts, on-the-job training, opportunity to attend seminars/workshops, willing to act as a professional reference, willing to provide letters of recommendation, supplementary part-time paid employment.

Contact Write or e-mail Ron Drake, President. Phone: 239-368-0760. Fax: 239-368-7141. E-mail: rptours@aol.com. Telephone interview required. Applicants must submit a formal organization application, letter of interest, resume, four writing samples,

Royal Palm Tours, Inc. (continued)

three personal references, strengths and weaknesses evaluation. Applications are accepted continuously. World Wide Web: http://www.royalpalmtours.com.

SEARCH FOR COMMON GROUND
1601 Connecticut Avenue, NW, Suite 200
Washington, District of Columbia 20009

General Information Nonprofit organization that specializes in domestic and international conflict resolution. Established in 1982. Number of employees: 60. Number of internship applications received each year: 500.

Internships Available ▶ *5–10 interns:* responsibilities include planning conferences; making travel arrangements; administrative support; and researching, writing, editing, and proofreading on any of the following programs: Search for Common Ground in Macedonia, Burundi, Angola, Democratic Republic of Congo, the Middle East, Ukraine, West Africa, or U.S.; Common Ground Productions, arts and culture, communications, Web editing. Candidates should have ability to work with others, editing skills, office skills, oral communication skills, organizational skills, personal interest in the field, research skills, self-motivation, writing skills, experience living in a mentioned international area or speaking its language is helpful. Duration is 3–4 months. Unpaid. Open to college freshmen, college sophomores, college juniors, college seniors, recent college graduates, graduate students, career changers. International applications accepted.

Benefits Names of contacts, on-the-job training, opportunity to attend seminars/workshops, possible full-time employment, travel reimbursement, willing to complete paperwork for educational credit, willing to provide letters of recommendation.

International Internships Available in Brussels, Belgium.

Contact Write, fax, e-mail, or through World Wide Web site Nancy Toubia, Human Resources Generalist. Fax: 202-232-6718. E-mail: search@sfcg.org. No phone calls. In-person interview recommended (telephone interview accepted). Applicants must submit a letter of interest, resume, two writing samples. Application deadline: February 1 for summer, April 1 for fall, September 1 for spring. World Wide Web: http://www.sfcg.org.

SERENDIPITY LITERARY AGENCY, LLC
732 Fulton Street
Brooklyn, New York 11238

General Information Literary agency representing authors of adult fiction and non-fiction. Established in 2000. Number of employees: 3. Number of internship applications received each year: 150.

Internships Available ▶ *2–3 interns:* responsibilities include reading manuscripts, logging mail, preparing publisher submission letters, and tracking submissions to publisher. Candidates should have computer skills, editing skills, office skills, self-motivation, writing skills, ability to work some evening and weekend events. Duration is up to a year. Unpaid. Open to college juniors, college seniors, recent college graduates, graduate students, career changers. International applications accepted.

Benefits On-the-job training, opportunity to attend seminars/workshops, willing to act as a professional reference, willing to complete paperwork for educational credit, willing to provide letters of recommendation.

Contact Write, fax, or e-mail Regina Brooks, President. Phone: 718-230-7689. Fax: 718-230-7829. E-mail: rbrooks@serendipitylit.com. In-person interview recommended (telephone interview accepted). Applicants must submit a formal organization application, resume, writing sample, two personal references. Applications are accepted continuously. World Wide Web: http://www.serendipitylit.com.

SHORE FACTS MARKETING RESEARCH
PO Box 1759
Ocean City, Maryland 21843

General Information Firm that provides market research for clients in resort retail industries by using psychographic and demographic data, focus group interviews, videotape analysis,

and extensive mail and personal interviews. Established in 1987. Number of employees: 5. Number of internship applications received each year: 65.

Internships Available ▶ *2 Internet researchers:* responsibilities include using the Web to conduct research. Candidates should have ability to work independently, ability to work with others, computer skills, personal interest in the field, research skills, self-motivation. Duration is flexible. Unpaid. Open to high school seniors, recent high school graduates, college freshmen, college sophomores, college juniors, college seniors, recent college graduates, graduate students, law students, career changers, individuals reentering the workforce. ▶ *2 administrative assistants:* responsibilities include working with small business owner to facilitate running of market research firm. Candidates should have ability to work independently, organizational skills, personal interest in the field, self-motivation, strong interpersonal skills. Duration is flexible. Unpaid. Open to high school seniors, recent high school graduates, college freshmen, college sophomores, college juniors, college seniors, recent college graduates, graduate students, law students, career changers, individuals reentering the workforce. ▶ *3 computer analysis interns:* responsibilities include collecting, processing, and interpreting market research data on IBM and Macintosh computers. Candidates should have ability to work independently, ability to work with others, computer skills, oral communication skills, personal interest in the field, self-motivation. Duration is flexible. Unpaid. Open to high school seniors, recent high school graduates, college freshmen, college sophomores, college juniors, college seniors, recent college graduates, graduate students, law students, career changers, individuals reentering the workforce. ▶ *4 interviewers:* responsibilities include interviewing subjects on a variety of research topics and writing summations of the findings. Candidates should have ability to work independently, oral communication skills, research skills, self-motivation, strong interpersonal skills. Duration is flexible. Unpaid. Open to college freshmen, college sophomores, college juniors, college seniors, recent college graduates, graduate students, law students, career changers. ▶ *1–2 management major interns:* responsibilities include organizing and structuring work flow at busy market research firm. Candidates should have office skills, oral communication skills, organizational skills, personal interest in the field, strong interpersonal skills. Duration is flexible. Unpaid. Open to college freshmen, college sophomores, college juniors, college seniors, recent college graduates, graduate students, law students, career changers, individuals reentering the workforce. ▶ *2–3 videographers:* responsibilities include videotaping market research sessions and editing film. Candidates should have ability to work independently, ability to work with others, knowledge of field, personal interest in the field, self-motivation, video skills. Duration is flexible. Unpaid. Open to high school seniors, recent high school graduates, college freshmen, college sophomores, college juniors, college seniors, recent college graduates, graduate students, law students, career changers, individuals reentering the workforce. International applications accepted.

Benefits Formal training, job counseling, names of contacts, opportunity to attend seminars/workshops, willing to act as a professional reference, willing to complete paperwork for educational credit, willing to provide letters of recommendation, health club membership.

Contact Write, call, or fax Mr. Paul D. Jankovic, Owner/Publisher. Phone: 410-524-5351. Fax: 302-539-1232. E-mail: ecprg@aol.com. Applicants must submit a letter of interest, resume. Applications are accepted continuously. World Wide Web: http://www.ecusa.com.

SOCIALIST PARTY USA
339 Lafayette Street, Room 303
New York, New York 11001

General Information Political party. Established in 1901. Number of employees: 3. Number of internship applications received each year: 15.

Internships Available ▶ *1–2 campaign clearinghouse interns:* responsibilities include press relations, fund-raising, light paperwork; will provide on-the-spot training. Candidates should have office skills, oral communication skills, personal interest in the field, self-motivation, strong leadership ability, written communication skills. Duration is one summer or semester. Unpaid. Open to high school students, college freshmen, college sophomores, college juniors, college seniors, graduate students.

Benefits Free meals, opportunity to attend seminars/workshops, travel reimbursement, willing to complete paperwork for educational credit, willing to provide letters of recommendation.

Contact Write, call, fax, e-mail, or through World Wide Web site Greg Pason, National Secretary, 339 Lafayette Street, Room 303. Phone: 212-982-4586. Fax: 212-982-4586. E-mail: natsec@sp-usa. org. In-person interview recommended (telephone interview accepted). Applicants must submit a letter of interest. Applications are accepted continuously. World Wide Web: http://www.votesocialist.org.

SOCIETY FOR INTERNATIONAL DEVELOPMENT–WASHINGTON CHAPTER
1875 Connecticut Avenue, NW, Suite 720
Washington, District of Columbia 20009-5728

General Information Nonpolitical, nonprofit membership organization with over 65 chapters around the world providing ways in which those interested in development can exchange ideas, information, and experiences with others. Established in 1957. Number of employees: 5. Unit of Society for International Development International, Rome, Italy. Number of internship applications received each year: 100.

Internships Available ▶ *2–4 interns:* responsibilities include writing for newsletter, serving as liaison with SID work groups, organizing program and events, attending informational and educational programs, promoting SID among prospective members, and assisting with general office duties. Candidates should have oral communication skills, strong interpersonal skills, writing skills. Duration is 1 semester. Unpaid. Open to college sophomores, college juniors, college seniors, recent college graduates, graduate students. International applications accepted.

Benefits Opportunity to attend seminars/workshops, willing to complete paperwork for educational credit, willing to provide letters of recommendation, excellent networking contacts.

Contact Write, call, fax, or e-mail Alina Zyszkowski, Executive Director. Phone: 202-884-8590. Fax: 202-884-8499. E-mail: sid@aed. org. In-person interview recommended (telephone interview accepted). Applicants must submit a resume, writing sample, three personal references. Applications are accepted continuously. World Wide Web: http://www.sidw.org.

SOCIETY OF PROFESSIONAL JOURNALISTS
3909 North Meridian Street
Indianapolis, Indiana 46208

General Information Organization that serves the professional needs of journalists and students pursuing careers in journalism. Established in 1909. Number of employees: 15.

Internships Available ▶ *2 Pulliam/Kilgore interns:* responsibilities include researching and writing about freedom of information issues. Candidates should have ability to work independently, computer skills, editing skills, research skills, writing skills. Duration is 10 weeks in summer. $400 per week. Open to college juniors, college seniors, recent college graduates, graduate students, law students. International applications accepted.

Benefits Names of contacts, opportunity to attend seminars/workshops, possible full-time employment, willing to complete paperwork for educational credit.

Contact Write, call, fax, or e-mail Jeff Mohl, Magazine Editor. Phone: 317-927-8000. Fax: 317-920-4789. E-mail: jmohl@spj.org. Applicants must submit a formal organization application, resume, 5 writing samples, essay on assigned topic. Application deadline: March 1. World Wide Web: http://www.spj.org.

SPORTING GOODS MANUFACTURERS ASSOCIATION
1150 17th Street, NW, Suite 407
Washington, District of Columbia 20036

General Information Trade association that promotes sports participation for all people and fosters sports products industry

growth. Established in 1906. Number of employees: 5. Number of internship applications received each year: 15.

Internships Available ▶ *1 intern:* responsibilities include performing legislative research, attending congressional hearings, handling oral and written public inquiries, and event planning. Candidates should have ability to work independently, ability to work with others, computer skills, knowledge of field, office skills, oral communication skills, writing skills. Duration is 2–5 months. Paid. Open to college sophomores, college juniors, college seniors.

Benefits Opportunity to attend seminars/workshops, willing to complete paperwork for educational credit, willing to provide letters of recommendation.

Contact Write, call, or fax John Loving, Manager of Government Relations. Phone: 202-775-1762. Fax: 202-296-7462. In-person interview recommended (telephone interview accepted). Applicants must submit a resume, cover letter. Applications are accepted continuously. World Wide Web: http://www.sgma.com.

SUCCESS QUEST COMMUNICATIONS-SQC
22720 Hawk Hill Loop
Land O Lakes, Florida 34639

General Information Company that provides Web site design and consulting and technical job placement. Established in 1999. Number of employees: 11. Number of internship applications received each year: 50.

Internships Available ▶ *Interns.* Candidates should have ability to work independently, analytical skills, computer skills, editing skills, knowledge of field, personal interest in the field, plan to pursue career in field, research skills, self-motivation. Position available as unpaid or paid. Open to recent high school graduates, college freshmen, college sophomores, college juniors, college seniors, recent college graduates, graduate students, career changers, individuals reentering the workforce. International applications accepted.

Benefits Possible full-time employment, willing to provide letters of recommendation.

Contact E-mail Mr. Dana Hansen, President. Phone: 813-727-3881. E-mail: kissedoff2002@hotmail.com. Telephone interview required. Applicants must submit a letter of interest, resume, e-mail questionnaire. Applications are accepted continuously. World Wide Web: http://www.kissedoff.com.

TIBET JUSTICE CENTER
2288 Fulton #312
Berkeley, California 94704

General Information Nonprofit membership group promoting self-determination for the Tibetan people and advocating human rights, environmental protection, and peaceful resolution through legal research, analysis, and education. Established in 1989. Number of employees: 2. Number of internship applications received each year: 30.

Internships Available ▶ *Interns:* responsibilities include general organizational assistance, research, writing, and editing. Candidates should have ability to work independently, organizational skills, personal interest in the field, research skills, writing skills. Duration is flexible; full time in summer, part time during school semester. Unpaid. Open to college freshmen, college sophomores, college juniors, college seniors, recent college graduates, graduate students, law students. International applications accepted.

Benefits Job counseling, names of contacts, willing to act as a professional reference, willing to complete paperwork for educational credit, willing to provide letters of recommendation.

Contact Write, call, fax, or e-mail Minnie Cancellaro, Executive Director. Phone: 510-486-0588. Fax: 510-548-3785. E-mail: minnie@tibetjustice.org. In-person interview recommended (telephone interview accepted). Applicants must submit a resume, 1 writing sample (optional). Applications are accepted continuously. World Wide Web: http://www.tibetjustice.org.

TRADE INFORMATION CENTER (TIC)
14th Street and Constitution Avenue, NW, Mail Stop RRB-TIC
Washington, District of Columbia 20230

General Information Organization that is the first stop for a company seeking export assistance from the federal government. Established in 1992. Number of employees: 25. Unit of International Trade Administration, Washington, District of Columbia.
Internships Available ▶ *6–8 interns:* responsibilities include assisting with counseling U.S. companies, responding to public inquiries for export information, synthesizing information from overseas embassies for public dissemination, maintaining and updating databases, and assisting in special projects. Candidates should have computer skills, personal interest in the field, writing skills, knowledge of Web tools such as Dreamweaver, Lotus Notes, HTML, JAVA, Flash, Adobe Photo Shop, and Adobe Illustrator (helpful). Duration is flexible by quarter or semester. Unpaid. Open to college sophomores, college juniors, college seniors, graduate students, law students, currently enrolled students only.
Benefits Opportunity to attend seminars/workshops, willing to act as a professional reference, willing to complete paperwork for educational credit, willing to provide letters of recommendation.
Contact Fax, e-mail, or through World Wide Web site Susan Lusi, Intern Coordinator, Washington 20230. Phone: 800-USA-TRADE. Fax: 202-482-4473. E-mail: susan_lusi@ita.doc.gov. Applicants must submit a letter of interest, resume, academic transcripts, 1-2 page writing sample. Applications are accepted continuously. World Wide Web: http://www.export.gov/tic.

TUITION PAINTERS
114 King Street, Suite 200
Alexandria, Virginia 22314

General Information Entrepreneurial development company. Established in 1996. Number of employees: 200. Number of internship applications received each year: 1,500.
Internships Available ▶ *125–150 management/marketing interns:* responsibilities include running own small business, receiving training and support from the company, but bearing responsibility for all marketing and sales, employee management and supervision, and public relations. Candidates should have ability to work independently, oral communication skills, organizational skills, self-motivation, strong interpersonal skills, strong leadership ability. Duration is March to August. Commission-based salary. Open to college freshmen, college sophomores, college juniors. ▶ *125–150 marketing and production representatives:* responsibilities include running the day-to-day operations of a business including marketing, sales, hiring, and managing employees. Candidates should have ability to work independently, ability to work with others, oral communication skills, self-motivation, strong leadership ability, written communication skills. Duration is May to August. $8000–$10,000 per duration of internship. Open to college freshmen, college sophomores, college juniors, college seniors. International applications accepted.
Benefits Formal training, job counseling, names of contacts, on-the-job training, opportunity to attend seminars/workshops, possible full-time employment, willing to act as a professional reference, willing to complete paperwork for educational credit, willing to provide letters of recommendation.
International Internships Available in Ontario, Canada.
Contact Through World Wide Web site Barry Lake, President. Phone: 866-Pay-4-College. Fax: 703-838-2629. E-mail: blake@tuitionpainters.com. In-person interview required. Application deadline: February 1. World Wide Web: http://www.tuitionpainters.com.

UNITED NATIONS ASSOCIATION OF THE USA
801 2nd Avenue
New York, New York 10017

General Information Nonprofit, nonpartisan, national organization dedicated to strengthening the United Nations system and to enhancing U.S. participation in the UN and other international institutions. Established in 1964. Number of employees:

40. Affiliate of United Nations, New York, New York. Number of internship applications received each year: 200.

Internships Available ▶ *2–3 Adopt-A-Minefield interns:* responsibilities include extensive research and writing related to landmines. Candidates should have ability to work independently, computer skills, research skills, written communication skills. Duration is minimum of 6 weeks. Unpaid. Open to college freshmen, college sophomores, college juniors, college seniors, recent college graduates. ▶ *2–4 American NGO Coalition for the International Criminal Court interns:* responsibilities include researching ICC issues in the U.S.; writing reports, briefs, and letters. Candidates should have ability to work independently, personal interest in the field, plan to pursue career in field, research skills, writing skills. Duration is minimum of 6 weeks. Unpaid. Open to college freshmen, college sophomores, college juniors, college seniors, recent college graduates, graduate students, law students. ▶ *2–4 Business Council for the UN interns:* responsibilities include establishing a partnership between the business community and the UN. Candidates should have ability to work independently, computer skills, office skills, oral communication skills, research skills, strong interpersonal skills, writing skills. Duration is minimum of 4 weeks. Unpaid. Open to college freshmen, college sophomores, college juniors, college seniors, recent college graduates, graduate students, individuals reentering the workforce. ▶ *1 Council of Organizations intern:* responsibilities include assisting the liaison of the UNAUSA and performing research. Candidates should have computer skills, office skills, organizational skills, clerical skills. Duration is flexible. Unpaid. Open to college freshmen, college sophomores, college juniors, college seniors. ▶ *1–2 Global Health Initiative interns:* responsibilities include research, writing, preparing outreach, and maintaining Web site. Candidates should have ability to work independently, personal interest in the field, research skills, written communication skills. Duration is minimum of 6 weeks. Unpaid. Open to college juniors, college seniors, recent college graduates, graduate students, career changers, individuals reentering the workforce. ▶ *6 Model UN and education interns:* responsibilities include researching the global issues and the work of the United Nations and adapting this information for use by the public; collecting materials for distribution to chapters, preparing responses to public inquiries, or assisting with outreach programs; researching and writing background papers about international issues; and assisting with the development of international affairs-related programs for youth. Candidates should have ability to work independently, editing skills, oral communication skills, research skills, strong leadership ability, writing skills. Duration is flexible. Unpaid. Open to high school students, recent high school graduates, college freshmen, college sophomores, college juniors, college seniors, recent college graduates, graduate students. ▶ *4 communication department interns:* responsibilities include writing, fact-checking, proofreading, and monitoring new developments in the UN. Candidates should have computer skills, editing skills, oral communication skills, research skills, strong interpersonal skills, writing skills. Duration is flexible. Unpaid. Open to college freshmen, college sophomores, college juniors, college seniors, recent college graduates, graduate students. ▶ *2–4 development interns:* responsibilities include assisting in identifying potential speakers and guests for chairman's council members and researching and writing profiles of individuals, foundations, and other funding sources. Candidates should have computer skills, oral communication skills, organizational skills, research skills, strong interpersonal skills, written communication skills. Duration is minimum of 6 weeks. Unpaid. Open to college freshmen, college sophomores, college juniors, college seniors, recent college graduates, graduate students. ▶ *2–4 executive office interns:* responsibilities include providing research and analysis on issues of global significance and preparing materials for meetings and conferences. Candidates should have ability to work independently, ability to work with others, computer skills, office skills, oral communication skills, organizational skills, research skills, writing skills. Duration is minimum of 6 weeks. Unpaid. Open to college seniors, recent college graduates, graduate students. ▶ *2–3 media relations and public affairs interns:* responsibilities include research on UN issues; distributing documents and press releases; writing on both internal and external publications. Candidates should have ability to work independently, editing skills, oral communication skills,

organizational skills, personal interest in the field, written communication skills. Duration is minimum of 6 weeks. Unpaid. Open to high school seniors, recent high school graduates, college freshmen, college sophomores, college juniors, college seniors, recent college graduates, graduate students. ▶ *2–4 national membership interns:* responsibilities include assisting with training and support to network of community-based chapters and statewide divisions, especially in areas of board developmen, fund-raising, and recruitment. Candidates should have ability to work independently, computer skills, office skills, oral communication skills, organizational skills, written communication skills. Duration is flexible. Unpaid. Open to high school seniors, recent high school graduates, college freshmen, college sophomores, college juniors, college seniors, recent college graduates, graduate students. ▶ *4 policy studies department interns:* responsibilities include performing independent research, maintaining correspondence with other organizations, and public outreach. Candidates should have ability to work independently, computer skills, editing skills, oral communication skills, research skills, writing skills. Duration is flexible (20-35 hours per week). Unpaid. Open to college seniors, recent college graduates, graduate students, law students. International applications accepted.
Benefits Opportunity to attend seminars/workshops, willing to act as a professional reference, willing to complete paperwork for educational credit, willing to provide letters of recommendation, U.N. Headquarters passes.
Contact Write, fax, e-mail, or through World Wide Web site Gary Su, Intern Coordinator. Fax: 212-682-9185. E-mail: gsu@unausa. org. No phone calls. Telephone interview required. Applicants must submit a formal organization application, letter of interest, resume, writing sample, two letters of recommendation. Application deadline: March 15 for summer; continuous for other positions. World Wide Web: http://www.unausa.org.

UNITED NATIONS HEADQUARTERS INTERNSHIP PROGRAM, OFFICE OF HUMAN RESOURCES MANAGEMENT
United Nations Secretariat, Room S-2570
New York, New York 10017

General Information Organization that promotes understanding of major problems confronting the world and how the United Nations attempts to find solutions. Established in 1945. Number of employees: 14,000. Number of internship applications received each year: 2,000.
Internships Available ▶ *120 interns:* responsibilities include carrying out an assignment in the department or office of the Secretariat that has selected the intern. Candidates should have analytical skills, computer skills, personal interest in the field, research skills, self-motivation. Duration is 2 months in spring, summer, or fall. Unpaid. Open to law students, graduate students under the age of 30. International applications accepted.
Benefits Meals at a cost, opportunity to attend seminars/ workshops, willing to provide letters of recommendation, opportunity to attend meetings.
Contact Write, e-mail, or through World Wide Web site Internship Coordinator, United Nations Secretariat, Room S-2590D, New York, New York 10017. Phone: 212-963-7522. Fax: 212-963-3683. E-mail: ohrm_interns@un.org. Applicants must submit a resume, academic transcripts, 2 copies of formal application in English or French, short essay in English or French stating reason for seeking the internship. Application deadline: four to twelve months prior to start of internship. World Wide Web: http://www. un.org.

UNITED NATIONS POPULATION FUND
220 East 42nd Street, 16th Floor
New York, New York 10017

General Information Nonprofit organization that is part of the UN common system. Established in 1969. Number of employees: 300. Number of internship applications received each year: 60.
Internships Available ▶ *Interns:* responsibilities include working under supervision of senior staff member in multilateral population activities. Candidates should have personal interest in the

field, proficiency in English, fluency in French, Spanish, or Arabic (a plus). Duration is year-round. Unpaid. Open to individuals with first year master's level degree in social science field with concentration in population studies. International applications accepted.
Benefits On-the-job training, opportunity to attend seminars/ workshops, willing to act as a professional reference, willing to provide letters of recommendation.
Contact Write, call, fax, e-mail, or through World Wide Web site Bertha del Carpio, Personnel Assistant, 220 East 42nd Street 16th Floor, New York, New York 10017. Phone: 212-297-5356. Fax: 212-297-4908. E-mail: carpio@unfpa.org. Applicants must submit a formal organization application, letter of interest, resume, proof of medical insurance. Applications are accepted continuously. World Wide Web: http://www.unfpa.org.

UNIVERSITY OF MARYLAND/CENTER FOR INTERNATIONAL DEVELOPMENT AND CONFLICT MANAGEMENT
Room 0145, Tydings Hall
College Park, Maryland 20742-7231

General Information Research center and think tank focusing on issues of ethnopolitical conflict, conflict management, development, and information technology. Established in 1981. Number of employees: 30. Unit of University of Maryland, College Park, College Park, Maryland. Number of internship applications received each year: 10.
Internships Available ▶ *1–3 research assistants/conflict interns:* responsibilities include providing support for research on minority groups, international organizations, and events of cooperation and conflict using online and library resources; statistical and qualitative analysis of human rights, social movements and events data in the U.S. and world-wide; Web site updates; logistic support for seminars and conferences organized under the auspices of CIDCM projects. Candidates should have ability to work independently, ability to work with others, computer skills, research skills, self-motivation, written communication skills. Duration is 3–12 months. Position available as unpaid or at $7–$12 per hour. Open to college seniors, recent college graduates, graduate students, career changers. International applications accepted.
Benefits Job counseling, names of contacts, on-the-job training, opportunity to attend seminars/workshops, willing to act as a professional reference, willing to provide letters of recommendation, possible stipends.
Contact Write, fax, or e-mail Ms. Joanne Manrique, Program Coordinator. Fax: 301-314-9256. E-mail: cidcm@cidcm.umd.edu. No phone calls. In-person interview recommended (telephone interview accepted). Applicants must submit a letter of interest, resume, academic transcripts, three personal references, letter of recommendation. Applications are accepted continuously. World Wide Web: http://www.cidcm.umd.edu/.

THE URBAN INSTITUTE
2100 M Street, NW
Washington, District of Columbia 20037

General Information Private, nonprofit, nonpartisan public policy research organization. Established in 1968. Number of employees: 400. Number of internship applications received each year: 500.
Internships Available ▶ *5–15 temporary research assistants:* responsibilities include assisting senior researchers in public policy research, data gathering, literature reviews, telephone survey work, and statistical analyses using a software package such as SAS or SPSS. Candidates should have analytical skills, college courses in field, computer skills, plan to pursue career in field, research skills, writing skills. Duration is flexible. $10–$16 per hour. Open to college freshmen, college sophomores, college juniors, college seniors, graduate students. International applications accepted.
Benefits On-the-job training, opportunity to attend seminars/ workshops, possible full-time employment, willing to act as a professional reference, willing to complete paperwork for educational credit, willing to provide letters of recommendation.

The Urban Institute (continued)
Contact Write, fax, e-mail, or through World Wide Web site Tammy Pritt, Human Resources Associate. Fax: 202-887-5189. E-mail: resumes@ui.urban.org. No phone calls. In-person interview recommended (telephone interview accepted). Applicants must submit a formal organization application, letter of interest, resume, academic transcripts, writing sample, three personal references. Applications are accepted continuously. World Wide Web: http://www.urban.org.

U.S. OLYMPIC COMMITTEE
1 Olympic Plaza
Colorado Springs, Colorado 80909-5760

General Information Nonprofit sports organization promoting sports in the U.S. and sending teams to the Olympics. Established in 1978. Number of employees: 500. Number of internship applications received each year: 750.
Internships Available ▶ *25 Colorado Springs interns:* responsibilities include working in broadcasting, sports administration, sport science, accounting, journalism and public relations, computer science, or marketing department. Duration is 1 semester. Housing, meals, and pay combined equal $8.50 per hour. ▶ *3 Lake Placid interns:* responsibilities include working in sports administration or sport science department. Duration is 1 semester. Housing, meals and pay combined equal $8.50 per hour. ▶ *3 San Diego interns:* responsibilities include working in sports administration or sport science department. Duration is 1 semester. Housing, meals, and pay combined equal $8.50 per hour. Candidates for all positions should have ability to work independently, college courses in field, computer skills, knowledge of field, office skills, oral communication skills, personal interest in the field, plan to pursue career in field, self-motivation, strong interpersonal skills, writing skills. Open to college juniors, college seniors, graduate students.
Benefits On-the-job training, opportunity to attend seminars/workshops, possible full-time employment, willing to complete paperwork for educational credit, exposure to Olympic movement.
Contact Write, call, fax, or e-mail Manager of Intern Program, 1 Olympic Plaza, Colorado Springs, Colorado 80909. Phone: 719-866-2597 Ext. 2597. Fax: 719-578-4817. E-mail: internprog@usoc.org. Telephone interview required. Applicants must submit a formal organization application, letter of interest, resume, three letters of recommendation, 6 writing samples (for journalism positions), official academic transcripts (unofficial printouts are not acceptable). Application deadline: February 15 for summer, June 1 for fall, October 1 for winter/spring. World Wide Web: http://www.usolympicteam.com.

U.S. TERM LIMITS
10 G Street, NE, Suite 410
Washington, District of Columbia 20002

General Information Non-partisan issue advocacy organization. Established in 1992. Number of employees: 15. Number of internship applications received each year: 50.
Internships Available ▶ *4–5 interns:* responsibilities include research for USTL's political staff, assistance to media relations director, and some clerical chores including preparing mass mailings. Candidates should have computer skills, oral communication skills, personal interest in the field, research skills, written communication skills. Duration is flexible. $800 per month (full-time), $400 per month (part-time). Open to college freshmen, college sophomores, college juniors, college seniors, recent college graduates.
Benefits On-the-job training, opportunity to attend seminars/workshops, willing to act as a professional reference, willing to complete paperwork for educational credit, willing to provide letters of recommendation.
Contact Write, call, fax, e-mail, or through World Wide Web site Kurt A. Gardinier, Intern Coordinator/Media Relations Director, 10 G Street, NE, Suite 410, Washington, District of Columbia 20002. Phone: 202-379-3000 Ext. 109. Fax: 202-379-3010. E-mail: kagardinier@ustermlimits.org. Applicants must submit a letter of interest, resume, writing sample, personal reference. Applications are accepted continuously. World Wide Web: http://www.ustermlimits.org.

U.S.-UKRAINE FOUNDATION
733 15th Street, NW, Suite 1026
Washington, District of Columbia 20005

General Information Nonprofit, non-governmental organization established to facilitate democratic development, free market reform, and to enhance human rights in the Ukraine. Established in 1991. Number of employees: 13. Number of internship applications received each year: 40.
Internships Available ▶ *1–4 interns:* responsibilities include reporting on congressional hearings and other events, Web site maintenance, office management, and program support; other responsibilities depend upon interests and skills of intern. Candidates should have ability to work with others, computer skills, office skills, personal interest in the field, self-motivation, written communication skills. Duration is flexible (usually one summer or one semester). Unpaid. Open to college freshmen, college sophomores, college juniors, college seniors, recent college graduates, graduate students, law students, career changers. International applications accepted.
Benefits On-the-job training, opportunity to attend seminars/workshops, willing to act as a professional reference, willing to complete paperwork for educational credit, willing to provide letters of recommendation.
Contact Write, fax, e-mail, or through World Wide Web site Motrya Mac, Intern Coordinator, 733 15th Street, NW, Suite 1026, Washington, District of Columbia 20005. Fax: 202-347-4267. E-mail: usuf@usukraine.org. No phone calls. In-person interview recommended (telephone interview accepted). Applicants must submit a letter of interest, resume. Applications are accepted continuously. World Wide Web: http://www.usukraine.org.

VARSITY MANAGEMENT
1896 Tice Valley Boulevard
Walnut Creek, California 94595

General Information Summer management program/house painting business. Established in 1993. Number of employees: 1,000. Number of internship applications received each year: 1,800.
Internships Available ▶ *150–200 summer managers:* responsibilities include attending training program; working in marketing, sales, management, client relations, or recruiting. Candidates should have ability to work independently, oral communication skills, self-motivation, strong interpersonal skills, strong leadership ability. Duration is 3-6 months (part-time in spring, full-time in summer). $5000–$40,000 per duration of internship. Open to recent high school graduates, college freshmen, college sophomores, college juniors, college seniors, recent college graduates. International applications accepted.
Benefits Formal training, names of contacts, on-the-job training, opportunity to attend seminars/workshops, possible full-time employment, tuition assistance, willing to act as a professional reference, willing to complete paperwork for educational credit, willing to provide letters of recommendation.
Contact Call, fax, e-mail, or through World Wide Web site Roland Thoms, President. Phone: 925-937-0434. Fax: 925-937-0499. E-mail: jobs@varsitystudent.com. In-person interview recommended (telephone interview accepted). Applicants must submit a formal organization application. Application deadline: March 20. World Wide Web: http://www.varsitystudent.com.

VAULT
150 West 22nd Street
New York, New York 10011

General Information Career services firm. Established in 1996. Number of employees: 40. Number of internship applications received each year: 600.
Internships Available ▶ *5–7 content summer associates:* responsibilities include working on various business-oriented writing projects; some research is also required. Candidates should have ability to

work with others, computer skills, organizational skills, research skills, writing skills. Position available as unpaid or paid. Open to college freshmen, college sophomores, college juniors, college seniors, recent college graduates, graduate students, law students, career changers. ▶ *1 junior network administrator:* responsibilities include supporting over 40 user desktops, administering NT domain, and performing backups. Candidates should have knowledge of field, oral communication skills, written communication skills, strong PC troubleshooting skills for a variety of software and hardware, basic UNIX skills. Duration is flexible. $10 per hour. Open to college freshmen, college sophomores, college juniors, college seniors, recent college graduates, graduate students, law students. ▶ *1–3 marketing/sales interns:* responsibilities include creating marketing materials, product management, customer service, campaign implementation, prospecting leads, planning client events. Candidates should have ability to work independently, oral communication skills, research skills, strong interpersonal skills, written communication skills. Duration is 3 months or longer (40 hours per week). $500 per month. Open to college freshmen, college sophomores, college juniors, college seniors. International applications accepted.

Benefits Names of contacts, on-the-job training, possible full-time employment, travel reimbursement, willing to act as a professional reference, willing to complete paperwork for educational credit, willing to provide letters of recommendation.

Contact Write or e-mail Marcy Lerner, Vice President of Content. E-mail: mlerner@staff.vault.com. No phone calls. In-person interview required. Applicants must submit a letter of interest, resume. Applications are accepted continuously. World Wide Web: http://www.vault.com.

VIA
PO Box 20266
Stanford, California 94309

General Information Private, nonprofit, nonsectarian organization dedicated to increasing understanding between the United States and Asia. Established in 1963. Number of employees: 12. Number of internship applications received each year: 40.

Internships Available ▶ *2–4 volunteer English resources in Indonesia:* responsibilities include assisting non-government organization, editing brochures and periodicals in English, providing English language support to the organization. Candidates should have ability to work independently, ability to work with others, experience in the field, personal interest in the field, self-motivation. Duration is 1–2 years. Living stipend varies by post. Open to recent college graduates, graduate students, career changers, must have bachelor's degree. ▶ *10–16 volunteer English teachers (summer):* responsibilities include teaching English in Vietnam, western China, or academic volunteer program in Bali, Indonesia. Candidates should have ability to work independently, ability to work with others, oral communication skills, personal interest in the field, self-motivation. Duration is 2 months. Unpaid. Open to college freshmen, college sophomores, college juniors, college seniors. ▶ *20–30 volunteer English teachers in Asia:* responsibilities include teaching English language instruction at university level to government officials, social science researchers, students in schools for the handicapped, and at orphanages. Candidates should have ability to work independently, ability to work with others, personal interest in the field, self-motivation, at least one course in language of host country, ESL training. Duration is 1–2 years. Living stipend varies by post. Open to recent college graduates, career changers, must have bachelor's degree.

Benefits Formal training, health insurance, possible full-time employment, willing to provide letters of recommendation, scholarships to cover participation fee, transportation to host country, stipend to cover cost of living including room and board.

International Internships Available in China; Indonesia; Viet Nam.
Contact Write, call, fax, e-mail, or through World Wide Web site Ann Le, Program Director. Phone: 650-723-3228. Fax: 650-725-1805. E-mail: info@viaprograms.org. In-person interview required. Applicants must submit a formal organization application, participation fee upon acceptance of $1975 for one year and summer,

$975 for two years, participation in training program. Application deadline: February 13 for June/July departure. World Wide Web: http://www.viaprograms.org.

VISIONS IN ACTION
2710 Ontario Road, NW
Washington, District of Columbia 20009

General Information Nonprofit organization that places volunteers with other nonprofit organizations, development organizations, research institutes, health centers, and the progressive press in the countries of Uganda, Tanzania, South Africa, Burkina Faso, and Mexico. Established in 1988. Number of employees: 8. Number of internship applications received each year: 250.

Internships Available ▶ *10–20 Mexico summer program volunteers:* responsibilities include participation in group project supporting local community development efforts in the state of Oaxaca; participation in various learning and cultural activities in Oaxaca and Chiapas. Candidates should have ability to work with others, personal interest in the field. Duration is 6 weeks (June-July). Unpaid. Open to high school seniors, recent high school graduates, college freshmen, college sophomores, college juniors, college seniors, recent college graduates, graduate students, law students, career changers, individuals reentering the workforce, must be 18 years of age or older. ▶ *10–20 Tanzania summer program volunteers:* responsibilities include participation in a group project involving appropriate technology, learning how to build solar cookers, biogas systems, and participation in a five-day safari to the Serengeti and Ngorongoro Crater. Candidates should have ability to work with others, personal interest in the field. Duration is 7 weeks (June-July). Unpaid. Open to high school seniors, recent high school graduates, college freshmen, college sophomores, college juniors, college seniors, recent college graduates, graduate students, law students, career changers, individuals reentering the workforce, must be 18 years of age or older. ▶ *20–30 U.S. office interns:* responsibilities include working in areas of recruitment, international administration, public relations, finance, fund-raising, research, Internet, newsletter, or conference organizing. Candidates should have computer skills, office skills, oral communication skills, organizational skills, research skills, written communication skills. Duration is 3 months. Unpaid. Open to college freshmen, college sophomores, college juniors, college seniors, recent college graduates, graduate students, law students, career changers, individuals reentering the workforce. ▶ *50–100 community development workers:* responsibilities include working with communities in low-income areas. Candidates should have oral communication skills, organizational skills, personal interest in the field, strong interpersonal skills, written communication skills. Duration is 6–12 months. Unpaid. Open to college juniors, college seniors, recent college graduates, graduate students, law students, career changers. ▶ *10–20 democratization trainers/election monitors:* responsibilities include training voters on their rights and voting procedures, monitoring elections, leading voting workshops, and observing ballot counting. Candidates should have analytical skills, oral communication skills, organizational skills, personal interest in the field, strong interpersonal skills, written communication skills. Duration is 6–12 months. Unpaid. Open to college juniors, college seniors, recent college graduates, graduate students, law students, career changers. ▶ *30–60 health professionals:* responsibilities include working in a clinic, lab, or hospital. Candidates should have analytical skills, knowledge of field, personal interest in the field, strong interpersonal skills. Duration is 6–12 months. Unpaid. Open to college juniors, college seniors, recent college graduates, graduate students, law students, career changers. ▶ *30–60 journalists:* responsibilities include working for a newspaper, magazine, or radio/television station. Candidates should have ability to work independently, knowledge of field, oral communication skills, research skills, written communication skills. Duration is 6–12 months. Unpaid. Open to college juniors, college seniors, recent college graduates, graduate students, law students, career changers. ▶ *10–20 microfinance specialists:* responsibilities include working with local microfinance institutions providing small loans for income-generating projects. Candidates should have computer skills, experience in the field, office skills, strong leadership ability. Duration is 1–2 years.

Visions In Action (continued)

Unpaid. Open to recent college graduates, graduate students, law students. ▶ *50–100 program assistants:* responsibilities include writing, research, administration, and organizing office-based assistance in areas of human rights, environment, children, women, housing, social work, or democratization. Candidates should have ability to work with others, computer skills, office skills, oral communication skills, personal interest in the field, written communication skills. Duration is 6–12 months. Unpaid. Open to college juniors, college seniors, recent college graduates, graduate students, law students, career changers. ▶ *40–80 project managers:* responsibilities include managing rural and urban development projects. Candidates should have knowledge of field, oral communication skills, organizational skills, strong leadership ability, written communication skills. Duration is 6–12 months. Unpaid. Open to college juniors, college seniors, recent college graduates, graduate students, law students, career changers. ▶ *40–80 public health educators:* responsibilities include performing research, educating, and designing communication material. Candidates should have office skills, oral communication skills, personal interest in the field, strong interpersonal skills, written communication skills. Duration is 6–12 months. Unpaid. Open to college juniors, college seniors, recent college graduates, graduate students, law students, career changers. ▶ *40–80 researchers:* responsibilities include assisting with research in either a natural or social science discipline. Candidates should have analytical skills, computer skills, office skills, research skills, writing skills. Duration is 6–12 months. Unpaid. Open to college juniors, college seniors, recent college graduates, graduate students, law students, career changers. ▶ *30–60 youth group coordinators:* responsibilities include leading community service projects, sports, and vocational training. Candidates should have ability to work with others, oral communication skills, organizational skills, personal interest in the field, self-motivation, strong leadership ability. Duration is 6–12 months. Unpaid. Open to college juniors, college seniors, recent college graduates, graduate students, law students, career changers. International applications accepted.

Benefits Formal training, job counseling, names of contacts, on-the-job training, opportunity to attend seminars/workshops, possible full-time employment, willing to act as a professional reference, willing to complete paperwork for educational credit, willing to provide letters of recommendation, monthly stipend of $50–$100 for international placements.

International Internships Available in Burkina Faso; Mexico; South Africa; Uganda; United Republic of Tanzania.

Contact Write, call, fax, e-mail, or through World Wide Web site Program Coordinator. Phone: 202-625-7402. Fax: 202-588-9344. E-mail: visions@igc.org. Telephone interview required. Applicants must submit a formal organization application, resume, two letters of recommendation. Application deadline: March 15 for Tanzania and Mexico 6-7 week summer programs, April 1 for July departure (South Africa, Mexico, Tanzania), June 1 for September 1st departure (Uganda), October 1 for January departure (South Africa, Mexico). Fees: $45. World Wide Web: http://www.visionsinaction.org.

WASHINGTON INSTITUTE FOR NEAR EAST POLICY
1828 L Street, NW, Suite 1050
Washington, District of Columbia 20036

General Information Research institute that analyzes U.S. policy in the Middle East. Established in 1985. Number of employees: 35. Number of internship applications received each year: 250.

Internships Available ▶ *5–6 research assistants:* responsibilities include preparing reports and assisting with seminars and conferences. Candidates should have ability to work with others, analytical skills, college courses in field, research skills, written communication skills. Duration is 1 year. $23000–$27000 per year plus extensive benefits. Open to recent college graduates. ▶ *1–8 research interns:* responsibilities include carrying out directed research and administrative duties (including seminars). Duration is flexible (at least 4 days per week preferred). Position available as unpaid or paid. Open to college freshmen, college

sophomores, college juniors, college seniors, recent college graduates, graduate students. International applications accepted.

Benefits On-the-job training, opportunity to attend seminars/workshops, possible full-time employment, willing to act as a professional reference, willing to complete paperwork for educational credit, willing to provide letters of recommendation, health insurance and job counseling for research assistants, opportunity to attend Institute events.

Contact Write, fax, e-mail, or through World Wide Web site Patrick Clawson, Deputy Director. Phone: 202-452-0650. Fax: 202-223-5364. E-mail: patrickc@washingtoninstitute.org. In-person interview recommended (telephone interview accepted). Applicants must submit a letter of interest, resume, writing sample, explanation of knowledge of Middle East (suggested). Application deadline: February 1 for research assistants, March 1 for interns (summer). World Wide Web: http://www.washingtoninstitute.org.

THE WINANT AND CLAYTON VOLUNTEERS, INC.
109 East 50th Street
New York, New York 10022

General Information International reciprocal exchange program between the U.S. and the U.K. Established in 1948. Number of employees: 1. Affiliate of St. Bartholomew's Church, New York, New York. Number of internship applications received each year: 75.

Internships Available ▶ *20 volunteers:* responsibilities include working in youth clubs, centers for the homeless, rehabilitation and drug-crisis centers, programs for the elderly, and early childhood day care. Candidates should have ability to work independently, oral communication skills, self-motivation, strong interpersonal skills, strong leadership ability, maturity and flexibility. Duration is 9 weeks (7 weeks volunteering; 2 weeks independent travel). Unpaid. Open to U.S. citizens 18 or older.

Benefits Free housing, 2 weeks independent travel, opportunity to see United Kingdom and live and work in another culture, small stipend available (paid in British pounds); applicant is responsible for airfare.

International Internships Available in United Kingdom.

Contact Write, call, or fax Ms. Nanette Rousseau. Phone: 212-378-0271. Fax: 212-378-0281. In-person interview recommended (telephone interview accepted). Applicants must submit a formal organization application, letter of interest, resume, two writing samples, five personal references. Application deadline: January 31 for summer. Fees: $35. World Wide Web: http://www.winantclaytonvolunteer.org.

WOMEN IN GOVERNMENT
2600 Virginia Avenue, NW, Suite 709
Washington, District of Columbia 20037

General Information Nonprofit educational association for elected women in state government. Established in 1989. Number of employees: 10. Number of internship applications received each year: 150.

Internships Available ▶ *1–3 project intern(s):* responsibilities include working in all departments of the organization including policy, development, program, and administrative. Candidates should have ability to work independently, oral communication skills, self-motivation, strong interpersonal skills, written communication skills. Duration is 3–5 months. Position available as unpaid or paid. Open to recent high school graduates, college freshmen, college sophomores, college juniors, college seniors. International applications accepted.

Benefits On-the-job training, opportunity to attend seminars/workshops, willing to act as a professional reference, willing to complete paperwork for educational credit, willing to provide letters of recommendation.

Contact Write, fax, e-mail, or through World Wide Web site Sarah Bollinger, Manager, Legislative Services. Fax: 202-333-0875. E-mail: sbollinger@womeningovernment.org. No phone calls. In-person interview recommended (telephone interview accepted). Applicants must submit a letter of interest, resume. Applications are accepted continuously. World Wide Web: http://www.womeningovernment.org.

WOMEN'S CAMPAIGN FUND
734 15th Street, NW, Suite 500
Washington, District of Columbia 20005

General Information Political action committee. Established in 1974. Number of employees: 4. Number of internship applications received each year: 75.

Internships Available ▶ *2 communications interns:* responsibilities include political research and writing, developing and updating the Web page, writing press releases, and providing follow-up to media contacts. Candidates should have computer skills, editing skills, office skills, oral communication skills, plan to pursue career in field, research skills, self-motivation, written communication skills. Duration is 3 months. Unpaid. ▶ *2–3 development interns:* responsibilities include assisting development department with all aspects of fund-raising, including event planning and high donor solicitation, maintaining and updating contributor lists and databases, and processing of contributions. Candidates should have computer skills, office skills, organizational skills, personal interest in the field, strong interpersonal skills, written communication skills. Duration is 3 months. Unpaid. ▶ *3–4 political interns:* responsibilities include political research and tracking, event planning, list development for candidate fund-raising activities, and providing administrative support. Candidates should have ability to work independently, ability to work with others, office skills, oral communication skills, personal interest in the field, writing skills. Duration is 3 months. Unpaid. Open to college freshmen, college sophomores, college juniors, college seniors. International applications accepted.

Benefits On-the-job training, possible full-time employment, willing to act as a professional reference, willing to complete paperwork for educational credit, willing to provide letters of recommendation, metro checks.

Contact Write, call, fax, or e-mail Monica Cash, Office Manager, 734 15th Street NW, Suite 500, Washington, District of Columbia 20005. Phone: 202-393-8164. Fax: 202-393-0649. E-mail: monica@wcfonline.org. In-person interview recommended (telephone interview accepted). Applicants must submit a letter of interest, resume, personal reference. Applications are accepted continuously. World Wide Web: http://www.wcfonline.org.

WOMEN'S INSTITUTE FOR FREEDOM OF THE PRESS
1940 Calvert Street, NW
Washington, District of Columbia 20009-1502

General Information Institute dedicated to researching and publishing new ideas and perspectives on expanding the communications system to make it more democratic, especially to increase the communication of women with each other and with the general public. Established in 1972. Number of employees: 1. Number of internship applications received each year: 12.

Internships Available ▶ *2 archives interns:* responsibilities include categorizing historic women's papers for research. Candidates should have ability to work independently, analytical skills, organizational skills, personal interest in the field, written communication skills. Duration is flexible. Unpaid. Open to high school students, recent high school graduates, college freshmen, college sophomores, college juniors, college seniors, recent college graduates, graduate students, law students, career changers, individuals reentering the workforce. ▶ *2–4 computer/online specialists:* responsibilities include surveying current uses of electronic communications for women's issues and equality, including management of Web site and new uses of computer video and audio. Candidates should have ability to work independently, analytical skills, computer skills, knowledge of field, organizational skills, personal interest in the field. Duration is flexible. Unpaid. Open to high school students, recent high school graduates, college freshmen, college sophomores, college juniors, college seniors, recent college graduates, graduate students, law students, career changers, individuals reentering the workforce, computer technologists. ▶ *1–2 editors:* responsibilities include editing an issue of associates newsletter. Candidates should have ability to work independently, computer skills, editing skills, personal interest in the field, self-motivation, writing skills. Duration is flexible. Unpaid.

Open to high school students, recent high school graduates, college freshmen, college sophomores, college juniors, recent college graduates, graduate students, law students, career changers, individuals reentering the workforce. ▶ *2–4 organizational liaisons:* responsibilities include acting as WIFP liaison with other women's groups and media change/democracy organizations; attending meetings, conferences, and press conferences. Candidates should have ability to work independently, computer skills, editing skills, personal interest in the field, self-motivation, writing skills. Duration is flexible. Unpaid. Open to high school students, recent high school graduates, college freshmen, college sophomores, college juniors, college seniors, recent college graduates, graduate students, law students, career changers, individuals reentering the workforce. ▶ *1–5 writers:* responsibilities include writing articles on WIFP work and ongoing projects. Candidates should have analytical skills, organizational skills, personal interest in the field, self-motivation, written communication skills. Duration is flexible. Unpaid. Open to high school students, recent high school graduates, college freshmen, college sophomores, college juniors, college seniors, recent college graduates, graduate students, law students, career changers, individuals reentering the workforce. International applications accepted.

Benefits Opportunity to attend seminars/workshops, willing to act as a professional reference, willing to complete paperwork for educational credit, willing to provide letters of recommendation.

Contact Write, e-mail, or through World Wide Web site Dr. Martha Leslie Allen, Director. Fax: 202-986-6355. E-mail: director@wifp.org. No phone calls. Applicants must submit a letter of interest, resume. Applications are accepted continuously. World Wide Web: http://www.wifp.org.

WOMEN'S POLICY, INC.
409 12th Street, SW, Suite 310
Washington, District of Columbia 20024

General Information Public policy research and publications organization that monitors congressional action affecting women and children. Established in 1995. Number of employees: 5. Affiliate of The George Washington University, Washington, District of Columbia. Number of internship applications received each year: 30.

Internships Available ▶ *1 intern:* responsibilities include attending congressional hearings, writing articles and fact sheets, other duties associated with newsletter publications, and miscellaneous clerical duties. Candidates should have ability to work independently, ability to work with others, analytical skills, computer skills, office skills, oral communication skills, organizational skills, research skills, written communication skills. Duration is flexible. Unpaid. Open to college sophomores, college juniors, college seniors, recent college graduates.

Benefits Names of contacts, on-the-job training, opportunity to attend seminars/workshops, willing to act as a professional reference, willing to complete paperwork for educational credit, willing to provide letters of recommendation, opportunity to attend projects and events with congressional caucus for women's issues.

Contact Write, call, fax, e-mail, or through World Wide Web site Jennifer Lockwood-Shabat, Internship Coordinator, 409 12th Street, SW, Suite 310, Washington, District of Columbia 20024. Phone: 202-554-2323. Fax: 202-554-2346. E-mail: webmaster@womenspolicy.org. In-person interview recommended (telephone interview accepted). Applicants must submit a letter of interest, resume, writing sample, three personal references, telephone interview recommended. Application deadline: April 1 for summer, August 1 for fall, November 15 for winter/spring. World Wide Web: http://www.womenspolicy.org.

WOODROW WILSON INTERNATIONAL CENTER FOR SCHOLARS
One Woodrow Wilson Plaza, 1300 Pennsylvania Avenue, NW
Washington, District of Columbia 20004-3027

General Information Public policy research institute. Established in 1968. Number of employees: 90. Unit of Smithsonian Institution, Washington, District of Columbia. Number of internship applications received each year: 700.

Internships Available ▶ *50–60 research assistants:* responsibilities include searching for source materials at area institutions; analysis and summarization of research materials; compilation of bibliographies; proofreading and editing of written work; clarification of quotations in response to references. Candidates should have college courses in field, computer skills, editing skills, office skills, organizational skills, personal interest in the field, research skills, writing skills. Duration is 3–9 months. Position available as unpaid or at $5 per hour stipend. Open to college juniors, college seniors, recent college graduates, graduate students, law students. International applications accepted.

Benefits Opportunity to attend seminars/workshops, willing to act as a professional reference, willing to complete paperwork for educational credit, willing to provide letters of recommendation, discounted meals.

Contact Write, call, fax, e-mail, or through World Wide Web site Internship Coordinator. Phone: 202-691-4053. Fax: 202-691-4001. E-mail: internships@wwic.si.edu. In-person interview recommended (telephone interview accepted). Applicants must submit a letter of interest, resume, academic transcripts, two letters of recommendation. Applications are accepted continuously. World Wide Web: http://wwics.si.edu/.

WORLD AFFAIRS COUNCILS OF AMERICA
1800 K Street, Suite 1014
Washington, District of Columbia 20006

General Information Nongovernmental, nonprofit, nonpartisan organization composed of over 80 independent world affairs councils and affiliated educational institutions located throughout the U.S. whose purpose is to improve the quality of citizen education in international affairs. Established in 1960. Number of employees: 3. Number of internship applications received each year: 25.

Internships Available ▶ *1 general intern:* responsibilities include locating speakers on a wide range of topics connected with world affairs (foreign policy, environmental issues, and defense), maintaining records on World Affairs Councils and updating information on an ongoing basis, handling telephone inquiries regarding the work of the WACs, and updating the database of information, embassies, and think tanks. Candidates should have ability to work with others, computer skills, editing skills, organizational skills, personal interest in the field, writing skills. Duration is one semester or summer. Unpaid. Open to college sophomores, college juniors, college seniors.

Benefits Job counseling, names of contacts, willing to complete paperwork for educational credit, willing to provide letters of recommendation.

Contact Write, call, or e-mail Francesca Martonffy, Internship Coordinator, Washington, District of Columbia 20006. Phone: 202-833-4557. Fax: 202-833-4555. E-mail: ncwao@aol.com. Applicants must submit a letter of interest, resume, writing sample. Applications are accepted continuously. World Wide Web: http://www.worldaffairscouncils.org.

WORLD FEDERALIST ASSOCIATION
418 7th Street, SE
Washington, District of Columbia 20003

General Information Organization working to transform the United Nations into a democratic world federation capable of protecting the environment, abolishing war, and protecting human rights. Established in 1947. Number of employees: 13. Number of internship applications received each year: 100.

Internships Available ▶ *5 International Criminal Court interns:* responsibilities include research, writing briefs and fact sheets, updating Web pages, calling congressional offices, participating in lobby visits, and attending and summarizing meetings. Candidates should have knowledge of field, oral communication skills, personal interest in the field, research skills, strong interpersonal skills, written communication skills. Duration is minimum of 2-3 months (3 months for summer). $10 per day. ▶ *5 Partners Program/National Activism interns:* responsibilities include media and legislative work, contacting grassroots leaders, assisting with meeting and project

coordination, helping craft lobbying strategy, and seeking new activists. Candidates should have knowledge of field, oral communication skills, personal interest in the field, research skills, written communication skills, background in international issues (preferred). Duration is minimum of 2-3 months (3 months for summer). $10 per day. ▶ *5 United Nations Peace Operations interns:* responsibilities include research, writing briefs and fact sheets, updating Web pages, calling congressional offices, participating in lobby visits, and attending and summarizing meetings. Candidates should have knowledge of field, oral communication skills, personal interest in the field, research skills, written communication skills. Duration is minimum of 2-3 months (3 months for summer). $10 per day. ▶ *5 environmental advocacy interns:* responsibilities include research, attending and reporting on NGO and other meetings, writing briefs and fact sheets, participating in lobby visits, organizing conferences, and some communications work. Candidates should have knowledge of field, oral communication skills, personal interest in the field, research skills, written communication skills. Duration is minimum of 2-3 months (3 months for summer). $10 per day. ▶ *5 issues media interns:* responsibilities include drafting press releases, maintaining media databases, and contributing to campaign strategies. Candidates should have knowledge of field, oral communication skills, personal interest in the field, research skills, written communication skills, background in media (useful). Duration is 2-3 days per week. $10 per day. Open to college freshmen, college sophomores, college juniors, college seniors, recent college graduates, graduate students, law students, career changers. International applications accepted.

Benefits On-the-job training, opportunity to attend seminars/workshops, possible full-time employment, willing to act as a professional reference, willing to complete paperwork for educational credit, willing to provide letters of recommendation, networking with other peace/justice organizations both nationally and internationally.

Contact E-mail or through World Wide Web site Christian W. Hansson, Internship Coordinator, 418 Seventh Street, SE, Washington, District of Columbia 20003. E-mail: internships@wfa.org. In-person interview recommended (telephone interview accepted). Applicants must submit a letter of interest, resume, writing sample. Application deadline: January 20 for spring, March 1 for summer, August 15 for fall. World Wide Web: http://www.wfa.org.

WORLD FEDERALIST MOVEMENT
United Nations Office, 777 United Nations Plaza, 12th Floor
New York, New York 10017

General Information Non-governmental organization that works for world order through international law, a strengthened UN, and a more democratic and participatory system of global governance. Established in 1947. Number of employees: 18.

Internships Available ▶ *General interns:* responsibilities include research, writing memos, assisting with reports, administrative tasks, attending meeting and workshops with UN delegates and representatives of NGOs. Duration is 4-6 months (part-time). Position available as unpaid or paid. Open to college juniors, college seniors, recent college graduates, graduate students. International applications accepted.

Benefits Names of contacts, on-the-job training, opportunity to attend seminars/workshops, willing to complete paperwork for educational credit, willing to provide letters of recommendation.

Contact Write, call, fax, e-mail, or through World Wide Web site Victoria Clarke, Program Associate. Phone: 212-599-2542. Fax: 212-599-1332. E-mail: wfm1@igc.org. Applicants must submit a resume, 500-word essay discussing how global governance should be modified or strengthened in order to address global problems. Application deadline: April 30. World Wide Web: http://www.wfm.org.

ENVIRONMENT, CONSERVATION, AND WILDLIFE ORGANIZATIONS

ALLIANCE FOR THE WILD ROCKIES
PO Box 8731
Missoula, Montana 59807

General Information Organization whose aim is to preserve and protect the remaining wilderness and biodiversity of the Northern Rockies bio-region by empowering regional conservationists and informing the public about the loss of wildlands. Established in 1988. Number of employees: 1. Number of internship applications received each year: 20.
Internships Available ▶ *1–2 ecosystem defense interns:* responsibilities include administering the Forest Watch program that includes reviewing timber sales, mining, and other development proposals; filing written appeals when necessary. Candidates should have ability to work with others, computer skills, knowledge of field, office skills, oral communication skills, personal interest in the field, research skills, self-motivation, strong leadership ability, written communication skills. Duration is 1–2 semesters. Unpaid.
▶ *1–3 outreach/education interns:* responsibilities include staffing AWR office, supervising volunteers, and public outreach. Candidates should have ability to work independently, computer skills, editing skills, knowledge of field, office skills, oral communication skills, personal interest in the field, research skills, self-motivation, strong interpersonal skills, written communication skills. Duration is 1-2 semesters (15-20 hours per week). Unpaid. Open to high school students, recent high school graduates, college freshmen, college sophomores, college juniors, college seniors, recent college graduates, graduate students, law students, career changers, individuals reentering the workforce. International applications accepted.
Benefits Formal training, job counseling, names of contacts, on-the-job training, opportunity to attend seminars/workshops, willing to act as a professional reference, willing to complete paperwork for educational credit, willing to provide letters of recommendation.
Contact Write, call, fax, or e-mail Michael Garrity, Executive Director. Phone: 406-721-5420. Fax: 406-721-9917. E-mail: awr@wildrockiesalliance.org. In-person interview recommended (telephone interview accepted). Applicants must submit a letter of interest, resume, writing sample, three personal references. Applications are accepted continuously. World Wide Web: http://www.wildrockiesalliance.org.

AMERICAN FARMLAND TRUST
1200 18th Street, NW, Suite 800
Washington, District of Columbia 20036

General Information Nonprofit land conservation organization focused on working lands (agricultural). Established in 1980. Number of employees: 54. Number of internship applications received each year: 200.
Internships Available ▶ *3 development interns:* responsibilities include identifying and researching potential funders, analyzing data, writing profiles on event attendees, creating a donor survey, and collecting information on potential project partners. Candidates should have ability to work independently, computer skills, personal interest in the field, research skills, self-motivation, written communication skills. Duration is 1 one semester (part-time). $500 per semester. ▶ *1 events intern:* responsibilities include assisting manager of major gifts events with all aspects of event planning and preparation. Candidates should have computer skills, office skills, organizational skills, personal interest in the field, plan to pursue career in field, strong interpersonal skills, written communication skills. Duration is 1 semester. $500 per semester. Open

to college sophomores, college juniors, college seniors, recent college graduates. International applications accepted.
Benefits Names of contacts, on-the-job training, opportunity to attend seminars/workshops, possible full-time employment, willing to act as a professional reference, willing to complete paperwork for educational credit, willing to provide letters of recommendation.
Contact E-mail Andrea Caserta, Prospect Research Specialist. E-mail: acaserta@farmland.org. No phone calls. Telephone interview required. Applicants must submit a letter of interest, resume, writing sample, three personal references. Applications are accepted continuously. World Wide Web: http://www.farmland.org.

THE AMERICAN FLORAL ENDOWMENT
11 Glen-Ed Professional Park
Glen Carbon, Illinois 62034

General Information National research foundation established to secure contributions for funding research and education relevant to floriculture, the results of which benefit the industry and general public. Established in 1961. Number of employees: 10. Number of internship applications received each year: 50.
Internships Available ▶ *1–50 Mosmiller interns.* Candidates should have ability to work independently, knowledge of field, oral communication skills, self-motivation, strong interpersonal skills, strong leadership ability, written communication skills, must have an interest in a career as a retail florist or wholesaler and demonstrate an understanding of the basic skills required for a career in either or both career paths. Duration is 10–16 weeks. $2000 scholarship upon completion of internship. Open to college freshmen, college sophomores, college juniors, college seniors, recent college graduates, graduate students. ▶ *5–50 Vic and Margaret Ball interns.* Candidates should have ability to work independently, knowledge of field, oral communication skills, self-motivation, strong interpersonal skills, strong leadership ability, written communication skills, must be interested in a career as a commercial grower and demonstrate a basic understanding of the fundamental skills. Duration is 3–6 months. $4000 scholarship upon completion of 4-month internship; $6000 scholarship upon completion of 6-month internship; 3-month summer experience ($1500). Open to college freshmen, college sophomores, college juniors, college seniors, graduate students.
Benefits Paid internship in addition to scholarships up to $6000.
International Internships Available.
Contact Write, call, e-mail, or through World Wide Web site Steven F. Martinez, Executive Vice President, #11, Glen Ed Professional Park, Glen Carbon, Illinois 62034. Phone: 618-692-0045. Fax: 618-692-4045. E-mail: afe@endowment.org. Applicants must submit a formal organization application, letter of interest, academic transcripts, letter of recommendation from advisor. Application deadline: March 1 for fall/winter, November 1 for summer/spring. World Wide Web: http://www.endowment.org.

AMERICAN FORESTS
910 17th Street, NW, Suite 600
Washington, District of Columbia 20006

General Information Organization dedicated to ensuring the benefits of trees and forests for future generations. Established in 1875. Number of employees: 30. Number of internship applications received each year: 300.
Internships Available ▶ *1 communications/publications intern:* responsibilities include research and writing articles and press releases. Duration is flexible. $50 per week. ▶ *1 marketing intern (DC):* responsibilities include developing partnerships for tree planting. Duration is flexible. $50 per week. ▶ *1–2 policy interns:* responsibilities include writing and research. Duration is flexible. $50 per week. ▶ *1 policy research intern:* responsibilities include assisting with planning of policy and workshops. Duration is 8–10 weeks. $50 per week. ▶ *2 program services interns:* responsibilities include developing partnerships for tree planting. Duration is flexible. $50 per week. ▶ *1 urban forestry intern:* responsibilities include research and acting as community liaison. Duration is flexible. $50 per week. Open to college sophomores, college juniors, college seniors, recent college graduates, graduate students. International applications accepted.

Benefits Opportunity to attend seminars/workshops, possible full-time employment, willing to complete paperwork for educational credit, willing to provide letters of recommendation, opportunity to write for publications and present own seminar.

Contact Write, fax, or e-mail Lu Rose, Vice President of Administration. Fax: 202-955-4588. E-mail: lrose@amfor.org. No phone calls. In-person interview recommended (telephone interview accepted). Applicants must submit a letter of interest, resume, writing sample. Applications are accepted continuously. World Wide Web: http://www.amfor.org.

AMERICAN HIKING SOCIETY
1422 Fenwick Lane
Silver Spring, Maryland 20910

General Information National voice for America's hikers that promotes and protects foot trails and the hiking experience. Established in 1976. Number of employees: 7. Number of internship applications received each year: 100.

Internships Available ► *1–2 conservation and policy interns:* responsibilities include tracking and analyzing legislation, attending and reporting on congressional hearings, surveying member organizations, developing outreach events, recreation research, mailings, and working with conservation coalitions and other organization support tools. Candidates should have ability to work independently, college courses in field, knowledge of field, organizational skills, research skills, written communication skills. Duration is 2–3 months. Position available as unpaid or at $500 per duration of internship. ► *1–2 trail programs interns:* responsibilities include research, writing, and outreach related to programs including National Trails Day, Winter Trails, and Volunteer Vacations; corporate and foundation grant research; communications; drafting promotional materials; and assisting in planning special events. Candidates should have ability to work independently, oral communication skills, organizational skills, personal interest in the field, written communication skills. Duration is 2–3 months. Position available as unpaid or at $500 per duration of internship. Open to college freshmen, college sophomores, college juniors, college seniors, recent college graduates, graduate students, law students, career changers. International applications accepted.

Benefits On-the-job training, opportunity to attend seminars/workshops, possible full-time employment, willing to act as a professional reference, willing to complete paperwork for educational credit, willing to provide letters of recommendation.

Contact Write, call, or e-mail Office Manager. Phone: 301-565-6704. Fax: 301-565-6714. E-mail: info@americanhiking.org. Telephone interview required. Applicants must submit a letter of interest, resume, writing sample. Application deadline: April 15 for summer, August 15 for fall, December 15 for spring. World Wide Web: http://www.americanhiking.org.

AMERICAN HORTICULTURAL SOCIETY
7931 East Boulevard Drive
Alexandria, Virginia 22308-1300

General Information Society that promotes excellence in horticulture through information, education, training, publications, and leadership. Established in 1922. Number of employees: 20. Number of internship applications received each year: 25.

Internships Available ► *1 editorial interns:* responsibilities include researching and writing short articles; proofreading and fact checking; coordinating author and photographer submissions. Candidates should have ability to work independently, college courses in field, computer skills, editing skills, research skills, writing skills. Duration is 3–12 months. $8 per hour. ► *1 horticultural database intern:* responsibilities include horticultural research and data entry, proof reading, and preparing reports. Candidates should have ability to work independently, college courses in field, computer skills, organizational skills, research skills, written communication skills. Duration is 6–12 months. $8 per hour. ► *5 horticultural interns:* responsibilities include garden maintenance, visitor and member services, creation of seasonal exhibits and displays. Candidates should have ability to work independently, college courses in field, oral communication skills, self-motivation, strong interpersonal

skills, written communication skills. Duration is 3–6 months. $8 per hour. Open to college freshmen, college sophomores, college juniors, college seniors, recent college graduates, graduate students, career changers.

Benefits Job counseling, names of contacts, on-the-job training, opportunity to attend seminars/workshops, willing to act as a professional reference, willing to complete paperwork for educational credit, willing to provide letters of recommendation, job lists provided when available.

Contact Write, call, fax, e-mail, or through World Wide Web site Tom Underwood, Director of Gardens and Buildings. Phone: 703-768-5700 Ext. 112. Fax: 703-768-8700. E-mail: tunderwood@ahs.org. In-person interview recommended (telephone interview accepted). Applicants must submit a formal organization application, resume, academic transcripts, three personal references. Applications are accepted continuously. World Wide Web: http://www.ahs.org.

AMERICAN RIVERS
1025 Vermont Avenue, NW #720
Washington, District of Columbia 20005

General Information Nonprofit membership organization that represents 22,000 members nationwide and is dedicated to protecting and restoring America's river systems and fostering a river stewardship ethic by seeking federal and state protection for rivers through legal and legislation advocacy; covers nationally significant rivers, hydropower policy reform, western water issues, urban rivers, and clean water issues. Established in 1973. Number of employees: 48. Number of internship applications received each year: 75.

Internships Available ► *4 communications interns:* responsibilities include working as a media intern with the Media Affairs Campaign involving production of promotional materials, press releases, and media correspondence; monitoring the news; maintaining slides, photos, videotapes, and the media database, or working as a Web assistant with American Rivers Online Campaign; assisting with daily Web site maintenance, coding graphics design, content development, and brainstorming new ways to use the Internet to communicate organizational message. Candidates should have computer skills, editing skills, oral communication skills, plan to pursue career in field, writing skills. Duration is 3 months (approximately 30 hours per week). $1500 stipend. ► *6–12 conservation interns:* responsibilities include legislative research, grassroots organizing through contact with national environmental and river groups, working on various conservation programs, responding to requests from river activists, researching American Rivers issues in preparation of written materials, and various long term projects; may work with Corps Reform Campaign, Hydropower Campaign, Legislative/Public Policy Campaign, Rivers Unplugged Campaign, or Wild and Scenic Rivers Campaign. Candidates should have analytical skills, computer skills, knowledge of field, personal interest in the field, research skills, writing skills. Duration is 3 months (approximately 30 hours per week). $1500 stipend. Open to college sophomores, college juniors, college seniors, recent college graduates, graduate students, law students. International applications accepted.

Benefits Names of contacts, opportunity to attend seminars/workshops, willing to act as a professional reference, willing to complete paperwork for educational credit, willing to provide letters of recommendation, opportunity to work with senior-level staff and have significant impact on important projects.

Contact Write, fax, e-mail, or through World Wide Web site Anne Hoffert, Internship Coordinator. Fax: 202-347-9240. E-mail: ahoffert@amrivers.org. No phone calls. Applicants must submit a letter of interest, resume, writing sample, three personal references. Applications are accepted continuously. World Wide Web: http://www.amrivers.org.

ANACOSTIA WATERSHED SOCIETY
4302 Baltimore Avenue
Bladensburg, Maryland 20710

General Information Small environmental group whose purpose is to restore the Anacostia River, an urban river in Washington, D.C., by organizing volunteers to perform stream cleanups, tree planting, and water quality monitoring. Established in 1989. Number of employees: 7. Number of internship applications received each year: 15.

Internships Available ▶ *1–2 assistant project managers:* responsibilities include organizing volunteers to perform stream cleanups, water quality monitoring, newsletter writing, and tree planting. Candidates should have ability to work independently, ability to work with others, computer skills, office skills, personal interest in the field, writing skills. Duration is 1–3 semesters. Unpaid. Open to college sophomores, college juniors, college seniors, recent college graduates, graduate students. International applications accepted.

Benefits On-the-job training, opportunity to attend seminars/workshops, willing to act as a professional reference, willing to complete paperwork for educational credit, willing to provide letters of recommendation.

Contact Write, call, fax, e-mail, or through World Wide Web site Mr. James Connolly, Executive Director. Phone: 301-699-6204. Fax: 301-699-3317. E-mail: jim@anacostiaws.org. In-person interview recommended (telephone interview accepted). Applicants must submit a letter of interest, resume. Applications are accepted continuously. World Wide Web: http://www.anacostiaws.org.

THE ANTARCTICA PROJECT
1630 Connecticut Avenue, NW, 3rd Floor
Washington, District of Columbia 20009

General Information Organization working to preserve Antarctica and its flora and fauna by educating the public and governments on Antarctic conservation. Established in 1982. Number of employees: 3. Unit of Antarctic and Southern Ocean Coalition (ASOC), Washington, District of Columbia. Number of internship applications received each year: 30.

Internships Available ▶ *1–2 interns:* responsibilities include conducting research and writing on a variety of conservation issues, attending relevant meetings, helping communicate with members, and some administrative duties. Candidates should have ability to work independently, ability to work with others, declared college major in field, knowledge of field, oral communication skills, research skills, self-motivation, written communication skills. Duration is 1–4 months. Unpaid. Open to college sophomores, college juniors, college seniors, recent college graduates, graduate students, law students. International applications accepted.

Benefits On-the-job training, opportunity to attend seminars/workshops, willing to act as a professional reference, willing to complete paperwork for educational credit, willing to provide letters of recommendation.

Contact Write, fax, or e-mail Josh Stevens, Associate. Phone: 202-518-2046. Fax: 202-387-4823. E-mail: josh.antarctica@igc.org. In-person interview recommended (telephone interview accepted). Applicants must submit a letter of interest, resume, writing sample. Applications are accepted continuously. World Wide Web: http://www.asoc.org.

APPALACHIAN MOUNTAIN CLUB, VOLUNTEER TRAILS PROGRAM
PO Box 298
Gorham, New Hampshire 03581

General Information Recreation/conservation organization that sponsors weekly volunteer-based camps, providing backcountry service projects in New York, New England, and other locations. Established in 1876. Number of employees: 100. Unit of Appalachian Mountain Club, Boston, Massachusetts. Number of internship applications received each year: 250.

Internships Available ▶ *Trail crew leaders:* responsibilities include leading trail crews of people 50 years of age or older, teen programs, and women's programs (inquire for other special groups). Candidates should have oral communication skills, organizational skills, self-motivation, strong interpersonal skills, strong leadership ability. Duration is mid-May to late August. Paid.
▶ *200 week-long and weekend volunteers:* responsibilities include maintaining and brushing trails; strenuous physical work to stabilize the treadway through the use of water bars, step stones, and drainage cleaning; positions located at worksites in the northeastern U.S. Candidates should have self-motivation, strong interpersonal skills. Duration is 1 to 2 weeks (mid-June through September). Unpaid. Open to individuals ages 16 and up. International applications accepted.

Benefits Willing to complete paperwork for educational credit.

Contact Write, call, fax, e-mail, or through World Wide Web site Kim Marion, North Country Volunteer Coordinator. Phone: 603-466-2721 Ext. 192. Fax: 603-466-2822. E-mail: kmarion@amcinfo.org. Applicants must submit a formal organization application. Application deadline: April 1 for trail crew leaders; continuous for all other positions. World Wide Web: http://www.outdoors.org.

ARLINGTONIANS FOR A CLEAN ENVIRONMENT (ACE)
3308 South Stafford Street
Arlington, Virginia 22206

General Information Organization working to improve the environment of Arlington County, Virginia together with local government and community organizations to achieve and maintain a clean and sustainable community. Established in 1978. Number of employees: 2. Number of internship applications received each year: 12.

Internships Available ▶ *ACE Project Watershed Watch program assistants:* responsibilities include recruiting volunteers, organizing and implementing volunteer projects including stream cleanups, invasive plant removal, storm drain marking, organizing and delivering classroom and community presentations about watersheds, documenting outcome of events, and office work. Candidates should have ability to work with others, organizational skills, computer skills including experience with Microsoft Work and Access, multi-tasking, public speaking experience, interest and/or experience with environmental or outdoor education, and Spanish speaking ability (desirable). Duration is 12 weeks in spring, summer, or fall. Stipend. Open to recent high school graduates, college freshmen, college sophomores, college juniors, college seniors, recent college graduates, career changers, individuals reentering the workforce.

Benefits On-the-job training, opportunity to attend seminars/workshops, travel reimbursement, willing to act as a professional reference, willing to complete paperwork for educational credit, willing to provide letters of recommendation.

Contact Fax, e-mail, or through World Wide Web site Elenor Hodges, Executive Director. Phone: 703-228-6427. Fax: 703-228-6407. E-mail: office@arlingtonenvironment.org. Applicants must submit a letter of interest, resume, two writing samples, three personal references. Application deadline: April 1 for summer, July 1 for fall, November 1 for spring. World Wide Web: http://www.arlingtonenvironment.org.

ASPEN CENTER FOR ENVIRONMENTAL STUDIES
100 Puppy Smith Street
Aspen, Colorado 81611

General Information Private, nonprofit environmental education center located within the Hallam Lake Nature Preserve whose mission is to inspire a life-long commitment to the preservation of the natural world by educating for environmental stewardship, conserving and restoring the balance of natural communities, and advancing the ethic that the earth must be respected and nurtured. Established in 1968. Number of employees: 12. Number of internship applications received each year: 150.

Internships Available ▶ *12 summer naturalist interns:* responsibilities include leading off-site interpretive hikes at the Maroon Bells, Snowmass, and on top of Aspen Mountain, teaching environmental education programs for children and adults, maintaining trails, assisting with cutthroat trout project, and caring for resident birds of prey. Candidates should have ability to work with others, college courses in field, experience in the field, oral communication skills, personal interest in the field, self-motivation. Duration is June through September. $125 per week. Open to college juniors, college seniors, recent college graduates, graduate students. International applications accepted.

Benefits Formal training, free housing, on-the-job training, opportunity to attend seminars/workshops, possible full-time employment, willing to act as a professional reference, willing to complete paperwork for educational credit, willing to provide letters of recommendation, tuition-free participation in Natural Field School courses.
Contact Write, call, fax, e-mail, or through World Wide Web site Internship Coordinator. Phone: 970-925-5756. Fax: 970-925-4819. E-mail: aces@aspennature.org. Applicants must submit a formal organization application, resume, in-person or telephone interview for qualified applicants. Application deadline: March 1. World Wide Web: http://www.aspennature.org.

ASSATEAGUE ISLAND NATIONAL SEASHORE
7206 National Seashore Lane
Berlin, Maryland 21811

General Information National seashore committed to preservation and interpretation of the natural environment. Established in 1965. Number of employees: 50. Unit of United States National Park Service, Washington, District of Columbia. Number of internship applications received each year: 70.
Internships Available ▶ *1–2 environmental education interns:* responsibilities include providing information to visitors, creating and presenting environmental education programs on- and off-site to grade levels kindergarten through middle-school. Candidates should have oral communication skills, self-motivation, strong interpersonal skills, biology or education major. Duration is end of August through October. Unpaid. ▶ *1–4 interpretive naturalists:* responsibilities include providing information to visitors through guided walks, recreational demonstrations, campfires, illustrated evening programs, aquarium duty, children's activities, and visitor center duty. Candidates should have oral communication skills, self-motivation, strong interpersonal skills, biology or education major. Duration is early June to late August. Unpaid. ▶ *1–2 resource management interns:* responsibilities include providing service to researchers, scientists, or park biologists in a variety of activities. Candidates should have ability to work with others, declared college major in field, self-motivation, ability to work under physically demanding circumstances. Duration is early June to late August. Unpaid. Open to college sophomores, college juniors, college seniors, recent college graduates, graduate students, career changers.
Benefits Formal training, free housing, job counseling, on-the-job training, opportunity to attend seminars/workshops, willing to complete paperwork for educational credit, willing to provide letters of recommendation, information on the application process for seasonal employment, worker's compensation, uniform provided, $12 per day provided for food.
Contact Write, fax, or e-mail Ms. Liz Davis, Park Ranger. Fax: 410-641-1099. E-mail: liz_davis@nps.gov. No phone calls. Telephone interview required. Applicants must submit a letter of interest, resume, academic transcripts, two letters of recommendation. Applications are accepted continuously. World Wide Web: http://www.nps.gov/asis/.

AUDUBON CENTER OF THE NORTH WOODS
PO Box 530
Sandstone, Minnesota 55072

General Information Environmental education center that stresses the positive relationship between people and nature; programs combine natural history, outdoor skills, and ethics and serve youth, college, and adult audiences. Established in 1968. Number of employees: 31. Number of internship applications received each year: 40.
Internships Available ▶ *4–6 environmental education interns:* responsibilities include leading residential programs for children and adults and assisting with eco-tours, outdoor recreation trips, gear care, curriculum development, and maintenance; teaching in an outdoor setting is a strong component of position. Candidates should have ability to work independently, ability to work with others, college courses in field, knowledge of field, oral communication skills, self-motivation. Duration is 5–12 months. $300–

$550 per month. Open to college seniors, recent college graduates, graduate students. ▶ *4–6 summer environmental education interns:* responsibilities include residential environmental instruction for summer youth camps, dorm supervision, camping/canoeing trips, assistance with teacher workshops and adult/family programs, gear care, and maintenance. Candidates should have ability to work with others, knowledge of field, oral communication skills, personal interest in the field, self-motivation, strong leadership ability. Duration is 3–4 months. $500–$550 per month. Open to college sophomores, college juniors, college seniors, recent college graduates, graduate students. ▶ *1 summer wildlife rehabilitation intern:* responsibilities include care, feeding, and maintenance of education and rehabilitation animals, initial first aid and stabilization of rehabilitation animals, contact with general public. Candidates should have ability to work independently, knowledge of field, organizational skills, self-motivation, strong interpersonal skills. Duration is 3–4 months. $300–$400 per month. Open to college juniors, college seniors, recent college graduates, graduate students. ▶ *1–2 wildlife interns:* responsibilities include care/feeding/training of educational raptors and reptiles, educational programming with captive animals, care/feeding of animals in rehabilitation, development of educational materials, maintenance, and adventure programming. Candidates should have ability to work independently, ability to work with others, experience in the field, oral communication skills, organizational skills, self-motivation. Duration is 6–12 months. $300–$550 per month. Open to college juniors, college seniors, recent college graduates, graduate students. International applications accepted.
Benefits Formal training, free housing, free meals, names of contacts, on-the-job training, opportunity to attend seminars/workshops, possible full-time employment, willing to act as a professional reference, willing to complete paperwork for educational credit, willing to provide letters of recommendation, graduate credits in environmental education.
Contact Write, call, fax, or e-mail Intern Coordinator. Phone: 320-245-2648. Fax: 320-245-5272. E-mail: audubonl@audubon-center.org. In-person interview recommended (telephone interview accepted). Applicants must submit a letter of interest, resume, three personal references. Applications are accepted continuously. World Wide Web: http://www.audubon-center.org.

AUDUBON NATURALIST SOCIETY
8940 Jones Mill Road
Chevy Chase, Maryland 20815

General Information Independent, nonprofit, environmental education and conservation organization serving the metropolitan Washington, D.C. region. Established in 1897. Number of employees: 30. Number of internship applications received each year: 100.
Internships Available ▶ *5–10 environmental education interns:* responsibilities include co-teaching children's classes in environmental education, maintaining a classroom, assisting with the upkeep of a 40-acre wildlife sanctuary, and undertaking an independent project. Candidates should have ability to work independently, ability to work with others, personal interest in the field, self-motivation, strong leadership ability, experience working with children. Duration is 3 months in summer. $1200–$2400 per duration of internship. Open to college freshmen, college sophomores, college juniors, college seniors, recent college graduates, graduate students, career changers. International applications accepted.
Benefits Formal training, free housing, names of contacts, on-the-job training, opportunity to attend seminars/workshops, willing to act as a professional reference, willing to complete paperwork for educational credit, willing to provide letters of recommendation.
Contact Write, call, fax, or e-mail Children's and Family Program Coordinator. Phone: 301-652-9188 Ext. 15. Fax: 301-951-7179. E-mail: avernor@audubonnaturalist.org. In-person interview recommended (telephone interview accepted). Applicants must submit a letter of interest, resume, three personal references, two letters of recommendation. Application deadline: March 15.

AULLWOOD AUDUBON CENTER AND FARM
1000 Aullwood Road
Dayton, Ohio 45414

General Information Nature center and organic farm dedicated to educating the public about environmental issues through the presentation of formal and informal tours. Established in 1957. Number of employees: 16. Division of National Audubon Society, New York, New York. Number of internship applications received each year: 70.

Internships Available ▶ *Administrative assistant interns:* responsibilities include fiscal planning; networking with other Audubon groups; tracking projects; teaching; and participating in meetings, activities, and special events. Candidates should have ability to work independently, computer skills, office skills, oral communication skills, organizational skills, written communication skills. Duration is flexible. $120 per week. Open to college sophomores, college juniors, college seniors, recent college graduates, graduate students. ▶ *Environmental education interns:* responsibilities include teaching youth and school groups, assisting with educational program development and teaching materials preparation, and involvement with all aspects of operations. Candidates should have college courses in field, experience in the field, oral communication skills, organizational skills, strong interpersonal skills, written communication skills. Duration is flexible. $120 per week. Open to college sophomores, college juniors, college seniors, recent college graduates, graduate students. ▶ *Maintenance interns:* responsibilities include working in close contact with the maintenance staff in dealing with special problems of the sanctuary. Candidates should have ability to work independently, knowledge of field, self-motivation, experience with power equipment and vehicle maintenance. Duration is flexible. $120 per week. Open to college sophomores, college juniors, college seniors, recent college graduates. ▶ *Museum store interns:* responsibilities include contacts with suppliers and assisting with daily store operations. Candidates should have ability to work independently, computer skills, office skills, oral communication skills, organizational skills, strong interpersonal skills. Duration is flexible. $120 per week. Open to college sophomores, college juniors, college seniors, recent college graduates, graduate students. ▶ *Organic agriculture interns:* responsibilities include involvement in all aspects of farm work, including farm chores, organic vegetable garden, marketing, and record keeping. Candidates should have ability to work independently, oral communication skills, organizational skills, personal interest in the field, self-motivation, ability to lift 40–60 pounds repeatedly. Duration is flexible. $120 per week. Open to college sophomores, college juniors, college seniors, recent college graduates, graduate students. International applications accepted.

Benefits Formal training, free housing, job counseling, names of contacts, opportunity to attend seminars/workshops, possible full-time employment, willing to complete paperwork for educational credit, willing to provide letters of recommendation.

Contact Write, call, e-mail, or through World Wide Web site Ms. Alison J. Verey, Intern Coordinator. Phone: 937-890-7360. Fax: 937-890-2382. E-mail: averey@audubon.org. In-person interview recommended (telephone interview accepted). Applicants must submit a formal organization application, resume, three personal references. Applications are accepted continuously. World Wide Web: http://www.aullwood.center.audubon.org.

BARRIER ISLAND ENVIRONMENTAL EDUCATION CENTER
2810 Seabrook Island Road
John's Island, South Carolina 29455-6219

General Information Resident environmental education center serving elementary and middle school students in 3- or 5-day sessions; subjects include marine biology, forest ecology, sensory awareness, and Indian life. Established in 1981. Number of employees: 16. Division of Saint Christopher Camp and Conference Center, John's Island, South Carolina. Number of internship applications received each year: 50.

Internships Available ▶ *14 naturalist interns:* responsibilities include performing tasks similar to those of regular teaching staff in the morning and afternoon, leading afternoon recreation activities, running evening programs, and program development. Candidates should have ability to work independently, computer skills, experience in the field, oral communication skills, organizational skills, plan to pursue career in field, self-motivation, strong interpersonal skills, strong leadership ability, writing skills, BA/BS in education or biology/science-related field. Duration is August to May. Paid. Open to recent college graduates, graduate students, career changers. International applications accepted.

Benefits Free housing, free meals, names of contacts, on-the-job training, possible full-time employment, willing to complete paperwork for educational credit, willing to provide letters of recommendation, temporary health insurance/medical allowance program.

Contact Write, call, fax, e-mail, or through World Wide Web site Jim Koenig, Director. Phone: 843-768-1337. Fax: 843-768-0918. E-mail: bieec@aol.com. Applicants must submit a formal organization application, resume (including educational and employment histories) and a recent photo. Application deadline: August 15. World Wide Web: http://www.stchristopher.org.

BAYSHORE DISCOVERY PROJECT (SCHOONER A.J. MEERWALD)
2800 High Street
Port Norris, New Jersey 08349

General Information Organization whose mission is to motivate people to care for the history, culture, and environment of the Bayshore region through education, preservation, and example. Established in 1988. Number of employees: 22. Number of internship applications received each year: 100.

Internships Available ▶ *2–3 onboard education interns:* responsibilities include presenting Delaware Estuary-specific learning stations to kids grades 4-12 as well as participating in shipboard maintenance and vessel operations. Candidates should have college courses in field, experience in the field, oral communication skills, personal interest in the field, strong interpersonal skills, some boat experience, strong environmental ethic. Duration is one summer, fall, or spring. $500 per month. Open to college freshmen, college sophomores, college juniors, college seniors, recent college graduates, graduate students, career changers.

Benefits Formal training, free housing, free meals, on-the-job training, possible full-time employment, willing to act as a professional reference, willing to complete paperwork for educational credit, willing to provide letters of recommendation.

Contact Write, call, fax, or e-mail Kristoffer Whitney, Education Programs Coordinator. Phone: 856-785-2060. Fax: 856-785-2893. E-mail: ajmeerwald@snip.net. Telephone interview required. Applicants must submit a letter of interest, resume, 3 professional references. Application deadline: March 16 for spring (March-June), June 16 for summer (June-August), August 16 for fall (August-October/November). World Wide Web: http://www.ajmeerwald.org.

BLACKWATER NATIONAL WILDLIFE REFUGE
2145 Key Wallace Drive
Cambridge, Maryland 21613

General Information Refuge providing a resting and feeding area for migratory waterfowl, habitat for threatened and endangered species (bald eagle, Delmarva fox squirrel), and wildlife-oriented recreation for the public. Established in 1933. Number of employees: 25. Unit of Fish & Wildlife Service Region V, Hadley, Massachusetts. Number of internship applications received each year: 20.

Internships Available ▶ *1 fall or spring intern:* responsibilities include greeting the public, answering questions, showing films in the auditorium, acting as cashier, giving orientation talks to youth groups, assisting with wetland environmental education programs, preparing and presenting refuge slide program, guiding bus and trail tours, and answering letters and information requests. Duration is 3–6 months. Unpaid. ▶ *1 summer or winter intern:* responsibilities include greeting the public, answering questions, showing films in the auditorium, acting as cashier, giving orientation talks to youth groups, assisting with wetland environmental education programs, preparing and presenting refuge slide program, guiding bus and trail tours, and answering letters and information requests. Duration is 12–16 weeks. Unpaid. Candidates for all positions should have ability to work independently, ability to work with others, computer skills, oral communication skills, self-motivation, written communication skills. Open to college freshmen, college sophomores, college juniors, college seniors, recent college graduates, graduate students, career changers, individuals reentering the workforce. International applications accepted.

Benefits Free housing, names of contacts, on-the-job training, opportunity to attend seminars/workshops, willing to act as a professional reference, willing to complete paperwork for educational credit, willing to provide letters of recommendation.

Contact Write, call, fax, or e-mail Maggie Briggs, Outdoor Recreation Planner. Phone: 410-228-2677. Fax: 410-221-7738. E-mail: maggie_briggs@fws.gov. In-person interview recommended (telephone interview accepted). Applicants must submit a formal organization application, resume, three personal references. Application deadline: March 31 for summer, June 30 for fall, December 30 for spring. World Wide Web: http://www.blackwater. fws.gov/.

BLUE OCEAN SOCIETY FOR MARINE CONSERVATION
118 Pleasant Street
Portsmouth, New Hampshire 03801

General Information Nonprofit organization dedicated to promoting marine conservation through public education, information resources, and marine research in New England focusing on the Gulf of Maine. Established in 2000. Number of employees: 4. Number of internship applications received each year: 30.

Internships Available ▶ *3–6 marine education interns:* responsibilities include working with naturalists aboard whale watch boats, collecting data, and educating passengers; assisting in data analysis, event planning and fund-raising, writing articles and helping plan special events, completing a special project involving research, conservation, or education. Candidates should have ability to work with others, computer skills, knowledge of field, oral communication skills, self-motivation, written communication skills. Duration is May to August, September or October; fall, winter, spring positions also available; suggested commitment for all is 10-12 weeks. Unpaid. Open to college freshmen, college sophomores, college juniors, college seniors, recent college graduates, graduate students, individuals reentering the workforce, high school seniors and recent high school graduates who live locally. International applications accepted.

Benefits Formal training, job counseling, names of contacts, on-the-job training, opportunity to attend seminars/workshops, willing to act as a professional reference, willing to complete paperwork for educational credit, willing to provide letters of recommendation.

Contact Call, e-mail, or through World Wide Web site Jen Hafner, Vice President, Portsmouth, New Hampshire. Phone: 603-431-0260. Fax: 603-431-0260. E-mail: info@blueoceansociety.org. In-person interview recommended (telephone interview accepted). Applicants must submit a formal organization application, letter of interest, resume, 2 provided recommendation forms. Application deadline: March 1 for summer; continuous for fall, winter, and spring. World Wide Web: http://www.blueoceansociety.org.

THE BOSPAS FOREST FARM
Oficina de Correo
Ibarra Ecuador

General Information Farm dedicated to growing a variety of crops and trees organically and sustainably, focusing on diversity rather than on mono culture, using agroforestry and permaculture techniques. Established in 1999. Number of employees: 4. Unit of The International Vetiver Network, Leesburg, Virginia. Number of internship applications received each year: 5.

Internships Available ▶ *1–2 Bospas Arboretum establishment assistants:* responsibilities include researching the tree species in the area, setting up an inventory of tree species, making descriptions of trees, preparing and painting signs. Candidates should have ability to work independently, ability to work with others, knowledge of field, personal interest in the field, basic Spanish skills. Duration is 1 month. Unpaid. ▶ *1–2 general farm activities assistants:* responsibilities include planting trees, compost making, general maintenance, construction work, irrigation system, machete work. Candidates should have ability to work with others, knowledge of field, basic Spanish skills. Duration is 1 month. Unpaid. Open to college seniors, recent college graduates, graduate students. International applications accepted.

Benefits Housing at a cost, meals at a cost, names of contacts, on-the-job training, willing to provide letters of recommendation.

International Internships Available.

Contact Write or e-mail Piet P. Sabbe. E-mail: bospasforest@ gardener.com. No phone calls. Applicants must submit a letter of interest, two writing samples, two letters of recommendation. Applications are accepted continuously. World Wide Web: http:// www.ecuativer.com/bospas.

BOWMAN'S HILL WILDFLOWER PRESERVE
PO Box 685, 1635 River Road
New Hope, Pennsylvania 18938-0685

General Information Natural preserve that grows, cares for, and exhibits a living collection of Pennsylvania's native plants and provides educational programs, exhibits, and literature centered on regional flora. Established in 1934. Number of employees: 9. Number of internship applications received each year: 60.

Internships Available ▶ *1–3 preserve interns:* responsibilities include leading tours and field trips, growing wildflowers, assisting with nursery operations, collecting and storing seeds, maintaining plant collection and trail system, completing an assigned project, maintaining a daily journal, weeding, planting, pruning, and performing trail work. Candidates should have ability to work independently, knowledge of field, oral communication skills, plan to pursue career in field, self-motivation, strong interpersonal skills. Duration is 10–15 weeks. $7–$8 per hour. Open to college sophomores, college juniors, college seniors, recent college graduates, graduate students, career changers, individuals reentering the workforce. International applications accepted.

Benefits Formal training, names of contacts, on-the-job training, opportunity to attend seminars/workshops, possible full-time employment, willing to act as a professional reference, willing to complete paperwork for educational credit, willing to provide letters of recommendation.

Contact Write, call, fax, e-mail, or through World Wide Web site Gabrielle Sivitz, Intern Coordinator, PO Box 685, New Hope, Pennsylvania 18938-0685. Phone: 215-862-2924. Fax: 215-862-1846. E-mail: bhwp@bhwp.org. In-person interview recommended (telephone interview accepted). Applicants must submit a formal organization application. Application deadline: February 13 for summer. World Wide Web: http://www.bhwp.org.

BUREAU OF LAND MANAGEMENT, COOS BAY DISTRICT, UMPQUA RESOURCE AREA
1300 Airport Lane
North Bend, Oregon 97459

General Information Federal agency that manages natural resources on over 270 million acres of public lands for the people of the United States; employs people in many fields including natural resources, administration, and computer resources. Established in 1946. Number of employees: 200. Unit of Bureau of Land Management, Washington, District of Columbia. Number of internship applications received each year: 10.

Internships Available ▶ *1–2 interpretive education interns:* responsibilities include developing and implementing interpretive and environmental education programs; developing interpretive exhibit, brochures, and panels; and assisting staff. Candidates should have ability to work independently, ability to work with others, oral communication skills, organizational skills, personal interest in the field, writing skills. Duration is May to September (40 hours per week). Unpaid. ▶ *2–4 seasonal recreation technical interns:* responsibilities include operating the park entrance station, performing day-to-day maintenance, giving group tours and formal presentations to the public. Candidates should have ability to work independently, ability to work with others, oral communication skills, organizational skills, personal interest in the field, written communication skills. Duration is May to September (40 hours per week). Unpaid. ▶ *1–6 summer natural resource interns:* responsibilities include giving small group tours and presentations, working in the gift shop, developing educational programs, creating displays, and maintaining site. Candidates should have ability to work with others, oral communication skills, personal interest in the field, self-motivation, written communication skills. Duration is May to September (40 hours per week). Unpaid. Open to recent high school graduates, college freshmen, college sophomores, college juniors, college seniors, recent college graduates, graduate students, law students, career changers, individuals reentering the workforce, must be 18 years or older. International applications accepted.

Benefits Formal training, free housing, job counseling, names of contacts, on-the-job training, opportunity to attend seminars/workshops, willing to act as a professional reference, willing to complete paperwork for educational credit, willing to provide letters of recommendation, reimbursement of on-site travel expenses, $75 stipend per week; preference to volunteers for regular positions.

Contact Write, call, fax, or e-mail Robert Golden, Park Ranger. Phone: 541-756-0100. Fax: 541-751-4303. E-mail: robert_golden@or.blm.gov. Applicants must submit a letter of interest, resume, three personal references. Application deadline: May 1.

BUREAU OF LAND MANAGEMENT, PRICE FIELD OFFICE
125 South, 600 West
Price, Utah 84501

General Information Federal agency responsible for managing and administering the use of public lands located primarily in the western United States and Alaska. Established in 1946. Number of employees: 40. Unit of Bureau of Land Management, Salt Lake City, Utah.

Internships Available ▶ *2–4 recreation/archaeology interns:* responsibilities include taking inventory of use and users of Nine Mile Canyon, developing and providing interpretive information to visitors, participating in inventory and recording of cultural sites, monitoring impact of visitation on cultural sites, light maintenance of recreation facilities, and identifying need for facilities development. Candidates should have ability to work independently, oral communication skills, personal interest in the field, research skills, self-motivation. Duration is up to 6 months (minimum of 8 weeks). Unpaid. Open to college freshmen, college sophomores, college juniors, college seniors, recent college graduates, graduate students, career changers, individuals reentering the workforce. ▶ *2 recreation/paleontology interns:* responsibilities include taking inventory of recreation use and users, developing and providing educational information to visitors, participating in discovery and recording of fossil sites, monitoring impacts of visitation on paleontological sites, performing light maintenance of recreation facilities, identifying future development needs, and working with CEU Prehistoric Museum in laboratory and field preparation of specimens. Candidates should have ability to work independently, ability to work with others, oral communication skills, personal interest in the field, self-motivation, written communication skills. Duration is Easter through Labor Day (or 8-week time frames). Unpaid. Open to college freshmen, college sophomores, college juniors, college seniors, recent college graduates, graduate students, career changers, individuals reentering the workforce, retirees. ▶ *2–6 river ranger/recreation interns:* responsibilities include conducting compliance checks of private and commercial river runners and monitoring resource conditions. Candidates should have ability to work independently, analytical skills, oral communication skills, self-motivation, strong interpersonal skills, writing skills. Duration is up to 6 months (minimum of 8 weeks). Unpaid. Open

to college freshmen, college sophomores, college juniors, college seniors, recent college graduates, graduate students, career changers, individuals reentering the workforce, retirees. International applications accepted.

Benefits Free housing, job counseling, names of contacts, on-the-job training, opportunity to attend seminars/workshops, possible full-time employment, willing to act as a professional reference, willing to complete paperwork for educational credit, willing to provide letters of recommendation, worker's compensation, possibility of subsistence pay for food.

Contact Write, call, fax, or e-mail Mr. Dennis J. Willis, Outdoor Recreation Planner, 125 South 600 West, Price, Utah 84501. Phone: 435-636-3600. Fax: 435-636-3657. E-mail: dennis_willis@blm.gov. Telephone interview required. Applicants must submit a formal organization application, letter of interest. Applications are accepted continuously. World Wide Web: http://www.blm.gov/utah/price.

BUREAU OF LAND MANAGEMENT, UPPER MISSOURI RIVER BREAKS NATIONAL MONUMENT
Airport Road
Lewistown, Montana 59457

General Information Area maintaining 150-mile scenic, historic, and natural resource along the Missouri River which includes a major part of the Lewis and Clark National Historic Trail as well as the Nez Perce National Historic Trail. Established in 1946. Number of employees: 30. Unit of Bureau of Land Management, Lewiston, Montana. Number of internship applications received each year: 20.

Internships Available ▶ *1–2 campground hosts:* responsibilities include imparting rules and knowledge to visitors, performing light maintenance, and providing emergency assistance. Duration is May to September. Unpaid. Open to college freshmen, college sophomores, college juniors, college seniors, recent college graduates, graduate students, law students, career changers, individuals reentering the workforce, retired personnel. ▶ *6 river rangers:* responsibilities include staffing visitor center and remote river launch points, registering river boaters, providing visitor services including resource interpretation, conducting river patrols, and maintaining recreation sites. Duration is 14 weeks. Unpaid. Open to college freshmen, college sophomores, college juniors, college seniors, recent college graduates, graduate students, law students, career changers, retired personnel. ▶ *1–2 visitor center hosts:* responsibilities include protecting resources, running slide programs, and operating visitor services including resource interpretation. Duration is April to September. Unpaid. Open to college freshmen, college sophomores, college juniors, college seniors, recent college graduates, graduate students, law students, career changers, individuals reentering the workforce, retired personnel. Candidates for all positions should have ability to work independently, oral communication skills, personal interest in the field, self-motivation, strong interpersonal skills.

Benefits Free housing, on-the-job training, willing to complete paperwork for educational credit, willing to provide letters of recommendation, reimbursement for living expenses.

Contact Write or call Sandra M. Padilla, Lead Park Ranger. Phone: 406-538-7461. Fax: 406-538-1904. E-mail: spadilla@mt.blm.gov. Telephone interview required. Applicants must submit a formal organization application, letter of interest, academic transcripts. Application deadline: April 1 for summer. World Wide Web: http://www.mt.blm.gov/ldo.

CARIBBEAN CONSERVATION CORPORATION
4424 Northwest 13th Street, Suite A1
Gainesville, Florida 32609

General Information Organization that is dedicated to the conservation of sea turtles and related marine and coastal wildlife through research, training, advocacy, education, and protection of natural areas. Established in 1959. Number of employees: 8. Number of internship applications received each year: 200.

Internships Available ▶ *8 green turtle research assistants:* responsibilities include assisting scientists with research on the green turtle, monitoring turtle nesting beach, tagging turtles and recording

Caribbean Conservation Corporation (continued)
data, working with volunteer groups on turtle projects, and educating tourists about turtles. Candidates should have oral communication skills, plan to pursue career in field, research skills, strong interpersonal skills, background/experience with turtles preferred. Duration is minimum of 2 months, beginning in June, ending in late October. Unpaid. ▶ *4–6 leatherback turtle research assistants:* responsibilities include assisting scientists with research on the leatherback turtle, monitoring turtle nesting beach, tagging turtles and recording data, working with volunteer groups on turtle projects, and educating tourists about turtles. Candidates should have oral communication skills, plan to pursue career in field, research skills, strong interpersonal skills, background/experience with turtles preferred, ability to speak English and Spanish at conversational levels. Duration is 2 months or more, beginning in March, ending in late May. Unpaid. Open to college freshmen, college sophomores, college juniors, college seniors, recent college graduates, graduate students, career changers. International applications accepted.

Benefits Formal training, free housing, free meals, willing to complete paperwork for educational credit, willing to provide letters of recommendation.

International Internships Available in Costa Rica.

Contact Write, fax, e-mail, or through World Wide Web site Dan Evans, Field Program Coordinator. Fax: 352-375-2449. E-mail: resprog@ccturtle.org. No phone calls. Telephone interview required. Applicants must submit a formal organization application, letter of interest, resume, three personal references. Application deadline: April 1 for green turtle research assistants, December 31 for leatherback turtle research assistants. World Wide Web: http://www.ccturtle.org.

CAROLINA RAPTOR CENTER, INC.
PO Box 16443
Charlotte, North Carolina 28297

General Information Nonprofit organization that exists to provide public education and contribute research on the importance of raptors and to care for sick, injured, and orphaned raptors. Established in 1981. Number of employees: 15. Number of internship applications received each year: 30.

Internships Available ▶ *3–5 environmental educators:* responsibilities include assisting with the care of trained birds of prey, presenting programs at site and elsewhere, and helping with displays and exhibits. Candidates should have ability to work independently, computer skills, oral communication skills, organizational skills, personal interest in the field, self-motivation, strong interpersonal skills, writing skills. Duration is minimum of 120 hours. Unpaid. ▶ *3–5 nonprofit administration interns:* responsibilities include assisting with volunteer administration, membership processing including database updating, ongoing fund-raiser funds processing, and other administrative duties. Candidates should have ability to work independently, computer skills, office skills, oral communication skills, organizational skills, personal interest in the field, self-motivation, strong interpersonal skills, written communication skills. Duration is minimum of 120 hours. Unpaid. ▶ *3–5 raptor care interns:* responsibilities include caring for, feeding, and training nonreleasable raptors. Candidates should have ability to work independently, ability to work with others, organizational skills, personal interest in the field, self-motivation. Duration is minimum of 120 hours. Unpaid. ▶ *5–7 raptor rehabilitators:* responsibilities include assisting with care, feeding, and releasing to the wild injured and orphaned raptors. Candidates should have ability to work independently, ability to work with others, organizational skills, personal interest in the field, self-motivation, written communication skills. Duration is minimum of 120 hours. Unpaid. Open to high school students, recent high school graduates, college freshmen, college sophomores, college juniors, college seniors, recent college graduates, graduate students, career changers, individuals reentering the workforce. International applications accepted.

Benefits Names of contacts, on-the-job training, opportunity to attend seminars/workshops, willing to complete paperwork for educational credit, willing to provide letters of recommendation.

Contact Write, fax, e-mail, or through World Wide Web site Lori Sparkman, Director of Volunteer Programs. Fax: 704-875-8814. E-mail: lorisparkman@birdsofprey.org. No phone calls. In-person interview recommended (telephone interview accepted). Applicants must submit a formal organization application, letter of interest, resume, three personal references. Applications are accepted continuously. World Wide Web: http://www.birdsofprey.org.

CARRYING CAPACITY NETWORK
2000 P Street, NW, Suite 310
Washington, District of Columbia 20036

General Information Informational network striving to make the public aware of such issues as environmental degradation, resource conservation, and population stabilization. Established in 1989. Number of employees: 4. Number of internship applications received each year: 50.

Internships Available ▶ *1–2 staff/program assistants:* responsibilities include providing general office support, giving telephone assistance, maintaining the database, offering membership and research support, working on independent projects, and assisting with staff projects. Candidates should have ability to work independently, computer skills, oral communication skills, personal interest in the field, research skills, self-motivation, writing skills. Duration is minimum of 3 months. $7–$8.50 per hour. Open to college freshmen, college sophomores, college juniors, college seniors.

Benefits Opportunity to attend seminars/workshops, possible full-time employment, willing to complete paperwork for educational credit, willing to provide letters of recommendation.

Contact Fax Robin Lazaro, Network Coordinator. Fax: 202-296-4609. No phone calls. In-person interview recommended (telephone interview accepted). Applicants must submit a letter of interest, resume. Applications are accepted continuously. World Wide Web: http://www.carryingcapacity.org.

CENTER FOR ENVIRONMENTAL HEALTH
528 61st Street, Suite A
Oakland, California 94609

General Information Nonprofit environmental and public health organization. Established in 1996. Number of employees: 6. Number of internship applications received each year: 35.

Internships Available ▶ *1–2 interns:* responsibilities include assistance in various programmatic, administrative, and fundraising projects. Candidates should have oral communication skills, organizational skills, research skills, strong interpersonal skills, written communication skills. Duration is 2–12 months. $300 per month. Open to college freshmen, college sophomores, college juniors, college seniors, recent college graduates, graduate students, law students, individuals reentering the workforce. ▶ *1 project coordinator assistant:* responsibilities include assisting Health Care Without Harm (HCWH) project coordinator in local and national coalition work with research, networking, and general assistance. Candidates should have ability to work with others, computer skills, office skills, oral communication skills, organizational skills, self-motivation. Duration is 3–12 months. $300 per month. Open to college sophomores, college juniors, college seniors, recent college graduates, graduate students. ▶ *1 staff scientist assistant:* responsibilities include assisting staff scientist with programmatic research and reporting; assisting in day-to-day office activities. Candidates should have ability to work with others, computer skills, oral communication skills, organizational skills, research skills, written communication skills. Duration is 3–12 months. $300 per month. Open to college freshmen, college sophomores, college juniors, college seniors, recent college graduates, graduate students, law students, career changers, individuals reentering the workforce. International applications accepted.

Benefits Names of contacts, on-the-job training, opportunity to attend seminars/workshops, possible full-time employment, travel reimbursement, willing to act as a professional reference, willing to complete paperwork for educational credit, willing to provide letters of recommendation.

Contact Write, call, fax, e-mail, or through World Wide Web site Michael Green, Executive Director. Phone: 510-594-9864. Fax: 510-594-9863. E-mail: ceh@cehca.org. In-person interview required.

Applicants must submit a letter of interest, resume, writing sample, three personal references. Application deadline: January 20 for spring, May 20 for summer. World Wide Web: http://www.cehca.org.

CENTER FOR HEALTH, ENVIRONMENT, AND JUSTICE
PO Box 6806
Falls Church, Virginia 22040-6806

General Information Organization that assists grassroots citizens' groups in the fight against pollution. Established in 1981. Number of employees: 15. Number of internship applications received each year: 100.
Internships Available ▶ *1–2 development interns:* responsibilities include assisting with all aspects of development including grant writing, prospect research, and major donor activities. Candidates should have ability to work independently, editing skills, knowledge of field, oral communication skills, organizational skills, personal interest in the field, plan to pursue career in field, self-motivation, strong interpersonal skills, strong leadership ability, writing skills. Duration is flexible. Unpaid. Open to college seniors, recent college graduates, graduate students, career changers, individuals reentering the workforce. ▶ *1–5 grassroots organizing interns:* responsibilities include assisting with a variety of tasks including communication with local communities and answering phone inquiries. Candidates should have ability to work independently, analytical skills, oral communication skills, organizational skills, plan to pursue career in field, self-motivation, strong interpersonal skills, strong leadership ability. Duration is flexible. Position available as unpaid or paid. Open to college freshmen, college sophomores, college juniors, college seniors, recent college graduates, graduate students, career changers, individuals reentering the workforce. ▶ *1–2 journalism interns:* responsibilities include researching and updating a guidebook, working with editor of quarterly magazine. Candidates should have ability to work independently, computer skills, editing skills, organizational skills, personal interest in the field, plan to pursue career in field, self-motivation, strong interpersonal skills, strong leadership ability, writing skills. Duration is flexible. Unpaid. Open to college juniors, college seniors, graduate students, career changers, individuals reentering the workforce. ▶ *4–6 national campaign organizing interns:* responsibilities include working on and helping with organizing two national campaigns: Stop Dioxin Exposure Campaign and Health Care Without Harm Campaign. Candidates should have ability to work independently, analytical skills, computer skills, editing skills, office skills, oral communication skills, organizational skills, plan to pursue career in field, research skills, self-motivation, strong interpersonal skills, strong leadership ability, writing skills. Duration is flexible. Paid. Open to college juniors, college seniors, recent college graduates, graduate students, law students, career changers, individuals reentering the workforce. ▶ *1–3 nonprofit management interns:* responsibilities include assisting with a variety of tasks including marketing, public relations, schedule coordinating, and other activities. Candidates should have ability to work independently, computer skills, office skills, oral communication skills, organizational skills, plan to pursue career in field, self-motivation, strong interpersonal skills, strong leadership ability. Duration is flexible. Unpaid. Open to college seniors, recent college graduates, graduate students, career changers, individuals reentering the workforce. ▶ *1–4 research interns:* responsibilities include researching, compiling, and distributing information to activists in response to written and telephone inquiries. Candidates should have ability to work independently, analytical skills, computer skills, organizational skills, plan to pursue career in field, research skills, self-motivation, strong interpersonal skills, strong leadership ability, writing skills. Duration is flexible. Unpaid. Open to college sophomores, college juniors, college seniors, recent college graduates, graduate students, career changers, individuals reentering the workforce. ▶ *1–5 science interns:* responsibilities include compiling toxicity profiles on common chemicals found at contaminated sites. Candidates should have ability to work independently, ability to work with others, analytical skills, computer skills, plan to pursue career in field, research skills, self-motivation, written communication skills. Duration is flexible. Paid. Open to

college juniors, college seniors, recent college graduates, graduate students, career changers, individuals reentering the workforce. International applications accepted.
Benefits Formal training, job counseling, names of contacts, opportunity to attend seminars/workshops, possible full-time employment, willing to complete paperwork for educational credit, willing to provide letters of recommendation, small transportation stipend.
Contact Write, e-mail, or through World Wide Web site Ms. Sharon Franklin, Administrator. Fax: 703-237-8389. E-mail: sfranklin@chej.org. No phone calls. Telephone interview required. Applicants must submit a letter of interest, resume. Application deadline: March 15 for summer, October 31 for winter, December 15 for spring. World Wide Web: http://www.chej.org.

CENTER FOR URBAN HORTICULTURE/ WASHINGTON PARK ARBORETUM
University of Washington, Box 354115
Seattle, Washington 98195-4115

General Information Division within college whose mission is research, teaching, and public service in urban horticulture with programs that center on urban plant selection, placement, restoration, and management. Established in 1980. Number of employees: 40. Unit of College of Forest Resources, University of Washington, Seattle, Washington. Number of internship applications received each year: 20.
Internships Available ▶ *1 curatorial intern:* responsibilities include field inventory and mapping, label making and placement, plant records data entry, and herbarium documentation. Candidates should have oral communication skills, written communication skills, computer literacy, attention to detail, working knowledge of botanical nomenclature and systematic botany, interest in woody ornamental plants. Duration is 3–6 months. $7–$8 per hour. Open to college freshmen, college sophomores, college juniors, college seniors, graduate students. ▶ *1–2 public education for adults interns:* responsibilities include planning, coordinating, and implementing public symposium and outreach curriculum; writing and editing newsletters, developing interpretive displays, leading tours, and co-instructing public courses. Candidates should have computer skills, editing skills, plan to pursue career in field, strong interpersonal skills, writing skills, background in horticulture, knowledge of Web software (helpful). Duration is 3–4 months. $8 per hour. Open to college juniors, college seniors, graduate students. ▶ *1 youth education assistant:* responsibilities include assisting with development, promotion, instruction, and evaluation of educational programs for youth, families, adults, and the general public which includes group tours, workshops, and summer camps. Candidates should have plan to pursue career in field, self-motivation, strong interpersonal skills, major in education, horticulture, or ecological studies. Duration is 3–5 months. $7–$9 per hour. Open to college freshmen, college sophomores, college juniors, college seniors, graduate students. International applications accepted.
Benefits Formal training, opportunity to attend seminars/workshops, possible full-time employment, willing to act as a professional reference, willing to complete paperwork for educational credit, willing to provide letters of recommendation.
Contact Write, call, fax, e-mail, or through World Wide Web site Sue Nicol, Outreach Coordinator. Phone: 206-685-8033. Fax: 206-685-2692. E-mail: snicol@u.washington.edu. Telephone interview required. Applicants must submit a resume, two personal references, letter of interest indicating which position desired. Application deadline: March 31. World Wide Web: http://www.urbanhort.org.

CENTRAL WISCONSIN ENVIRONMENTAL STATION/UNIVERSITY OF WISCONSIN–STEVENS POINT
10186 County Road MM
Amherst Junction, Wisconsin 54407

General Information Environmental station that provides a foundation for appreciation and understanding of the environment, and develops the skills and attitudes needed to deal with

Central Wisconsin Environmental Station/University of Wisconsin–Stevens Point (continued)

present and future environmental problems. Established in 1975. Number of employees: 15. Unit of University of Wisconsin–Stevens Point, Stevens Point, Wisconsin. Number of internship applications received each year: 20.

Internships Available ▶ *3–4 environmental education interns:* responsibilities include providing instruction in environmental studies for groups of K-12 students, directing K-12 programs one day per week, being involved in a variety of administrative responsibilities, working with weekend groups, and performing other duties as necessary. Candidates should have oral communication skills, personal interest in the field, self-motivation, strong interpersonal skills, written communication skills, understanding of ecological concepts. Duration is 1 semester. Position available as unpaid or paid. Open to college juniors, college seniors, recent college graduates, graduate students, career changers, must be Wisconsin resident or attending Wisconsin state university.

Benefits Formal training, on-the-job training, opportunity to attend seminars/workshops, willing to act as a professional reference, willing to complete paperwork for educational credit, willing to provide letters of recommendation, some meals provided, possible housing allowance.

Contact E-mail Patty Dreier, Director. Phone: 715-824-2428. Fax: 715-824-3201. E-mail: cwes@uwsp.edu. In-person interview recommended (telephone interview accepted). Applicants must submit a formal organization application, letter of interest, resume, academic transcripts, three personal references. Application deadline: July 1 for fall, December 1 for spring. World Wide Web: http://www.uwsp.edu/cnr/cwes.

CHATTAHOOCHEE/OCONEE NATIONAL FOREST
1755 Cleveland Highway
Gainesville, Georgia 30501

General Information Forest service whose purpose is caring for the land and serving the people. Number of employees: 160. Unit of United States Forest Service, Washington, District of Columbia. Number of internship applications received each year: 5.

Internships Available ▶ *2 interpreters:* responsibilities include providing visitors with information. Candidates should have ability to work independently, declared college major in field, oral communication skills, plan to pursue career in field, research skills, strong interpersonal skills. Duration is 10 weeks. Unpaid. ▶ *2 recreation assistants:* responsibilities include developing recreational programs. Candidates should have ability to work independently, ability to work with others, college courses in field, oral communication skills, plan to pursue career in field, self-motivation, major in outdoor education. Duration is 10 weeks. Unpaid. Open to college freshmen, college sophomores, college juniors, college seniors.

Benefits Formal training, names of contacts, opportunity to attend seminars/workshops, possible full-time employment, willing to complete paperwork for educational credit, willing to provide letters of recommendation, small fee for travel and meals.

Contact Write, call, or fax Ms. Luana W. Kitchens, Human Resources Program Manager. Phone: 770-297-3016. Fax: 770-297-3011. In-person interview recommended (telephone interview accepted). Applicants must submit a letter of interest, resume. Application deadline: April 1 for summer. World Wide Web: http://www.fs.fed.us.

CHEQUAMEGON NATIONAL FOREST, THE GREAT DIVIDE DISTRICT
PO Box 896
Hayward, Wisconsin 54843

General Information National forest focusing on natural resource management and emphasizing multiple use and conservation of resources including wildlife, recreation, timber, wilderness, water, and soil. Established in 1905. Number of employees: 35. Unit of United States Forest Service, Washington, District of Columbia. Number of internship applications received each year: 30.

Internships Available ▶ *1–2 biological assistants:* responsibilities include working outdoors in all types of weather with biological technician; gathering field information; doing maintenance work; working with chainsaws, brush saws, and driving a tractor. Candidates should have ability to work independently, ability to work with others, experience in the field, personal interest in the field, plan to pursue career in field, self-motivation. Duration is June to August. $9 per hour. Open to college sophomores, college juniors, college seniors, recent college graduates, graduate students. ▶ *1–2 recreation interns:* responsibilities include assisting recreation technician with campground maintenance, trail maintenance, working with the public, giving accurate information. Candidates should have ability to work independently, ability to work with others, personal interest in the field, self-motivation. Duration is June to September. Position available as unpaid or at $10 per hour. Open to college sophomores, college juniors, college seniors, recent college graduates, graduate students. ▶ *1 wilderness ranger intern:* responsibilities include working in the Rainbow Lake and Porcupine Wilderness areas, meeting with the public, constructing new trails, maintaining campsites, and engaging in other resource management projects. Candidates should have ability to work independently, ability to work with others, knowledge of field, oral communication skills, personal interest in the field, self-motivation, strong leadership ability, map reading skills, outdoor experience. Duration is June to September. Position available as unpaid or at $10 per hour. Open to college juniors, college seniors, recent college graduates, graduate students. International applications accepted.

Benefits Formal training, names of contacts, on-the-job training, opportunity to attend seminars/workshops, willing to act as a professional reference, willing to complete paperwork for educational credit, willing to provide letters of recommendation, stipend $20–$25 per day for meals.

Contact Write, call, fax, or e-mail Ms. Kathy M. Moe, Biological Technician. Phone: 715-634-4821. Fax: 715-634-3769. E-mail: kmoe@fs.fed.us. Telephone interview required. Applicants must submit a letter of interest, resume, two personal references, two letters of recommendation. Application deadline: February 28 for summer.

CHEWONKI FOUNDATION, INC.
485 Chewonki Neck Road
Wiscasset, Maine 04578

General Information Year-round environmental education center offering summer camp, wilderness expeditions, trips and workshops for families, individuals, and school programs; located on the coast of Maine. Established in 1915. Number of employees: 60. Number of internship applications received each year: 25.

Internships Available ▶ *2–4 camp counselors:* responsibilities include serving as resident counselor in cabin with 8–10 boys, activity instructor, and assistant wilderness trip leader. Candidates should have knowledge of field, personal interest in the field, self-motivation, strong interpersonal skills, strong leadership ability. Duration is 8-10 weeks in summer. $1000–$2600 per duration of internship. Open to high school students, recent high school graduates, college freshmen, college sophomores, college juniors, college seniors, recent college graduates, graduate students. ▶ *2–4 environmental education interns:* responsibilities include working in wilderness encampments with school groups; teaching camping and related wilderness skills and natural history. Candidates should have college courses in field, oral communication skills, personal interest in the field, self-motivation, strong interpersonal skills, strong leadership ability. Duration is 12–15 weeks. $100–$250 per week. Open to college seniors, graduate students, career changers, individuals reentering the workforce. International applications accepted.

Benefits Free housing, free meals, names of contacts, on-the-job training, possible full-time employment, willing to act as a professional reference, willing to complete paperwork for educational credit, willing to provide letters of recommendation.

Contact Write, call, fax, e-mail, or through World Wide Web site Dick Thomas, Camp Director. Phone: 207-882-7323. Fax: 207-882-4074. E-mail: info@chewonki.org. In-person interview recommended (telephone interview accepted). Applicants must submit a formal organization application, resume, 3 personal references or letters of recommendation. Applications are accepted continuously. World Wide Web: http://www.chewonki.org.

CHINCOTEAGUE NATIONAL WILDLIFE REFUGE
PO Box 62, 8231 Beach Road
Chincoteague, Virginia 23336

General Information Wildlife refuge located on a barrier island off the Eastern Shore of Virginia that has 14,000 acres of beach, saltmarsh, freshwater marsh, and maritime forest; migrating and wintering area for waterfowl; home or stopover for 1 endangered and 2 threatened species. Established in 1943. Number of employees: 25. Division of U.S. Fish and Wildlife Service, Department of the Interior, Washington, District of Columbia. Number of internship applications received each year: 50.
Internships Available ▶ *1 fall biology intern:* responsibilities include assisting with wildlife population censuses and surveys; vegetation sampling; operating deer hunter check station; and assisting in other routine duties. Candidates should have ability to work independently, college courses in field, knowledge of field, personal interest in the field, self-motivation, written communication skills. Duration is 8–12 weeks. Stipend of $120 per week (variable). ▶ *1–2 spring and fall environmental education interns:* responsibilities include developing and conducting environmental education programs for various school groups; assisting with development of environmental education materials for teachers; and assisting with teacher workshops. Candidates should have ability to work independently, college courses in field, oral communication skills, organizational skills, personal interest in the field, writing skills. Duration is 10–13 weeks. Stipend of $120 per week (variable). ▶ *2–6 spring and summer biology interns:* responsibilities include assisting with wildlife population censuses and surveys; collecting and recording information in support of the refuge's piping plover program; studying adult arrival and nest survey data; assisting in routing piping plover management including construction of predator exclosures; and other routine duties. Candidates should have ability to work independently, college courses in field, knowledge of field, personal interest in the field, strong interpersonal skills, written communication skills. Duration is 8–12 weeks. Stipend of $120 per week (variable). ▶ *2 spring, summe, and fall interpretive interns:* responsibilities include staffing the visitor center; developing and conducting interpretive programs and other informational materials. Candidates should have ability to work independently, knowledge of field, oral communication skills, organizational skills, personal interest in the field, written communication skills. Duration is 10–13 weeks. Stipend of $120 per week (variable). Open to college juniors, college seniors, recent college graduates, graduate students, career changers, individuals reentering the workforce. International applications accepted.
Benefits Free housing, names of contacts, willing to complete paperwork for educational credit, willing to provide letters of recommendation.
Contact Write, call, fax, or e-mail Mr. John D. Schroer, Refuge Manager, PO Box 62, 8231 Beach Road. Phone: 757-336-6122. Fax: 757-336-5273. E-mail: r5rw_chnwr@mail.fws.gov. Applicants must submit a letter of interest, resume, telephone interview for finalists. Application deadline: January 15 for spring, March 15 for summer, July 15 for fall. World Wide Web: http://chinco.fws.gov.

CINCINNATI NATURE CENTER
4949 Tealtown Road
Milford, Ohio 45150

General Information Private, nonprofit environmental education center with three sites, including farms and large natural area totaling 1,425 acres. Established in 1966. Number of employees: 40. Number of internship applications received each year: 20.
Internships Available ▶ *6 environmental education interns:* responsibilities include teaching youth from pre-school through high school about environmental concepts in a natural or farm setting using a hands-on, experiential approach; assisting with special events; developing and conducting programs for the general public; helping with grounds work, chores, and other tasks related to operating a nature center and/or educational farm. Candidates should have college courses in field, knowledge of field, oral communication skills, personal interest in the field, self-motivation, strong interpersonal skills, written communication skills, must have transportation and valid driver's license and insurance. Duration is one semester (40 hours per week with the possibility of an extension). $175 per week. Open to college freshmen, college sophomores, college juniors, college seniors, recent college graduates, graduate students, career changers, individuals reentering the workforce. ▶ *1–2 farm interns:* responsibilities include assisting with chores on an educational farm including care and maintenance of crops, livestock, and gardens. Candidates should have ability to work independently, ability to work with others, personal interest in the field, self-motivation. Duration is flexible. $105 per week. Open to college freshmen, college sophomores, college juniors, college seniors, graduate students, individuals reentering the workforce.
Benefits Free housing, on-the-job training, opportunity to attend seminars/workshops, willing to act as a professional reference, willing to complete paperwork for educational credit, willing to provide letters of recommendation, $15 per week gas reimbursement if the internship takes place at a site other than where housing is offered.
Contact Write, call, fax, or e-mail Connie Brockman, Education Director. Phone: 513-831-1711 Ext. 27. Fax: 513-831-8052. E-mail: cbrockman@cincynature.org. In-person interview recommended (telephone interview accepted). Applicants must submit a letter of interest, resume, writing sample, three personal references. Application deadline: August 15 for fall semester, December 1 for spring semester; continuous for farm interns. World Wide Web: http://www.cincynature.org.

CISPUS LEARNING CENTER
2142 Cispus Road
Randle, Washington 98377-9305

General Information Outdoor education learning facility used by school groups for environmental education; offers teacher training and a challenge course. Established in 1981. Number of employees: 20. Unit of Association of Washington School Principals, Olympia, Washington. Number of internship applications received each year: 24.
Internships Available ▶ *1–2 challenge course facilitators:* responsibilities include facilitating groups on the challenge ropes course. Candidates should have ability to work independently, oral communication skills, organizational skills, personal interest in the field, strong interpersonal skills, strong leadership ability, experience with youth. Duration is 12–16 weeks. $500 per month. Open to college juniors, college seniors, recent college graduates, graduate students, career changers, individuals reentering the workforce. International applications accepted.
Benefits Formal training, free housing, free meals, names of contacts, on-the-job training, opportunity to attend seminars/workshops, willing to act as a professional reference, willing to complete paperwork for educational credit, willing to provide letters of recommendation, orientation.
Contact Write, call, e-mail, or through World Wide Web site Jesse Garner, Challenge Course Business Manager. Phone: 360-497-7131. E-mail: cispusropes@cispus.org. Telephone interview required. Applicants must submit a formal organization application, letter of interest, resume, three personal references. Applications are accepted continuously. World Wide Web: http://www.cispus.org.

CLIMATE INSTITUTE
333½ Pennsylvania Avenue, SE
Washington, District of Columbia 20003

General Information Organization serving as a link between scientists and policymakers on the issues of climate change and stratospheric ozone depletion. Established in 1986. Number of employees: 8. Number of internship applications received each year: 30.
Internships Available ▶ *2–5 research assistants:* responsibilities include assisting with projects, Web site operations, and working with international partners. Candidates should have ability to work independently, ability to work with others, office skills, research

skills, writing skills. Duration is flexible. Unpaid. Open to high school students, recent high school graduates, college freshmen, college sophomores, college juniors, college seniors, recent college graduates, graduate students, law students, career changers, individuals reentering the workforce. International applications accepted.

Benefits Job counseling, names of contacts, opportunity to attend seminars/workshops, possible full-time employment, willing to act as a professional reference, willing to complete paperwork for educational credit, willing to provide letters of recommendation, interns serving in Washington participate in Gordon MacDonald Environmental Leadership dinner/seminars.

Contact Write, fax, or e-mail John Topping, President, 333½ Pennsylvania Avenue, SE, Washington, District of Columbia 20003-1148. Fax: 202-547-0111. E-mail: jtopping@climate.org. In-person interview recommended (telephone interview accepted). Applicants must submit a letter of interest, resume, writing sample. Applications are accepted continuously. World Wide Web: http://www.climate.org.

CLINIC FOR THE REHABILITATION OF WILDLIFE (C.R.O.W.)
PO Box 150
Sanibel Island, Florida 33957

General Information Nonprofit wildlife rehabilitation center and veterinary hospital dedicated to the care of injured, ill, and orphaned native and migratory wildlife of Lee County. Established in 1968. Number of employees: 5. Number of internship applications received each year: 100.

Internships Available ▶ *2–4 externs:* responsibilities include participating on rehabilitative team. Candidates should have ability to work with others, personal interest in the field, self-motivation, background in natural science and/or veterinary field (recommended), willingness to participate with staff in manual labor (a must). Duration is 6–8 weeks. Unpaid. Open to college sophomores, college juniors, college seniors, recent college graduates, graduate students, career changers. ▶ *1–2 fellows:* responsibilities include organizing and supporting volunteers and externs with daily cleaning, feeding, and rehabilitation of wildlife patients in outside compounds; assisting veterinarian as needed with clinic duties. Candidates should have oral communication skills, organizational skills, personal interest in the field, self-motivation, strong interpersonal skills, prior externship with C.R.O.W. (preferred), background in natural science or experience with animals, willingness to perform manual labor. Duration is 6 months. Stipend of $500 per month. Open to college freshmen, college sophomores, college juniors, college seniors, recent college graduates, graduate students, career changers. International applications accepted.

Benefits Free housing, on-the-job training, willing to act as a professional reference, willing to complete paperwork for educational credit, willing to provide letters of recommendation.

Contact Write, call, or e-mail Dr. PJ Deitschel, Externships. Phone: 941-472-3644. E-mail: crowclinic@aol.com. Telephone interview required. Applicants must submit a formal organization application, letter of interest, resume, academic transcripts, 2 recommendations (1 must be from a veterinarian if vet student). Applications are accepted continuously. World Wide Web: http://www.crowclinic.org.

CLYDE E. BUCKLEY WILDLIFE SANCTUARY
1305 Germany Road
Frankfort, Kentucky 40601

General Information Wildlife sanctuary and Audubon center working to teach the public about the environment through hands-on experience and to encourage the potential of native flora and fauna through sound wildlife management. Established in 1967. Number of employees: 2. Unit of National Audubon Society, New York, New York. Number of internship applications received each year: 30.

Internships Available ▶ *6 sanctuary operations interns:* responsibilities include assisting with nature interpretation, environmental

education, wildlife management, caretaking, maintenance, administration, exhibits, photography, gift shop operations, fund-raising, and creative writing. Candidates should have ability to work independently, ability to work with others, computer skills, knowledge of field, oral communication skills, self-motivation. Duration is 10 weeks. $3.85–$5.15 per hour. Open to college freshmen, college sophomores, college juniors, college seniors, recent college graduates, graduate students, career changers, individuals reentering the workforce.

Benefits Formal training, free housing, opportunity to attend seminars/workshops, willing to complete paperwork for educational credit, utilities, uniforms.

Contact Write, call, fax, or e-mail Mr. Timothy Williams, Sanctuary Manager. Phone: 859-873-5711. Fax: 859-873-5711. E-mail: twilliams@audubon.org. In-person interview recommended (telephone interview accepted). Applicants must submit a resume, two personal references, two letters of recommendation, letter describing reason for internship and potential contribution to programs (include interests and hobbies). Application deadline: February 15 for spring, May 15 for summer, August 15 for fall.

COLORADO WILDLIFE FEDERATION
445 Union Boulevard, Suite 302
Lakewood, Colorado 80228-1243

General Information Conservation education organization that focuses on issues affecting Colorado's wildlife and conservation programs for children. Established in 1953. Number of employees: 3. Affiliate of National Wildlife Federation, Vienna, Virginia. Number of internship applications received each year: 30.

Internships Available ▶ *1 conservation advocacy intern:* responsibilities include assisting staff and Board of Directors by working on various conservation advocacy campaigns, including off-road vehicles and mule deer herd health. Candidates should have ability to work independently, analytical skills, college courses in field, computer skills, editing skills, knowledge of field, office skills, oral communication skills, organizational skills, personal interest in the field, research skills, self-motivation, strong interpersonal skills, writing skills. Duration is year-round. Position available as unpaid or at $7–$10 per hour. Open to college freshmen, college sophomores, college juniors, college seniors, recent college graduates, graduate students, law students, career changers. ▶ *1–4 education interns:* responsibilities include visiting 2nd through 8th grade classrooms in the Denver metropolitan area to bring conservation education programming to students, and leading outdoor education programs for the students at Two Ponds National Wildlife Refuge in Arvada, Colorado. Candidates should have ability to work independently, knowledge of field, oral communication skills, personal interest in the field, research skills, self-motivation, strong interpersonal skills, ability to work with children. Duration is one semester. Position available as unpaid or at $8 per hour. Open to recent high school graduates, college freshmen, college sophomores, college juniors, college seniors, recent college graduates, graduate students, law students, career changers, individuals reentering the workforce. International applications accepted.

Benefits Job counseling, names of contacts, on-the-job training, opportunity to attend seminars/workshops, willing to complete paperwork for educational credit, willing to provide letters of recommendation, mileage reimbursement for delivering programs.

Contact Write, call, fax, e-mail, or through World Wide Web site Michael Brogan, Director of Education. Phone: 303-987-0400. Fax: 303-987-0200. E-mail: education@coloradowildlife.org. In-person interview recommended (telephone interview accepted). Applicants must submit a letter of interest, resume. Applications are accepted continuously. World Wide Web: http://www.coloradowildlife.org.

COMMUNITY ENVIRONMENTAL CENTER
43-10 11th Street
Long Island City, New York 11101

General Information Not-for-profit energy conservation and environmental education center. Established in 1994. Number of employees: 40. Number of internship applications received each year: 40.

Internships Available ▶ *1–2 construction management interns (technical services):* responsibilities include developing construction management documentation, quality management, and performing field inspections. Candidates should have ability to work independently, computer skills, experience in the field, oral communication skills, self-motivation, writing skills, major or degree in construction management or related field, ability to travel. Duration is 3–6 months. Position available as unpaid or at $12 per hour. Open to college seniors, recent college graduates, graduate students. ▶ *1–2 energy interns (technical services):* responsibilities include developing heating distribution and system specifications, performing building performance analyses, assisting in construction management and designing, and conducting energy audits. Candidates should have ability to work independently, oral communication skills, organizational skills, personal interest in the field, writing skills, degree or major in energy, mechanical engineering or related field, experience in doing energy audits on buildings, ability to travel. Duration is 3–6 months. Position available as unpaid or at $12 per hour. Open to college seniors, recent college graduates, graduate students. ▶ *1–2 fund-raising support/office support interns:* responsibilities include research of urban environmental issues; preparation of informational materials, including writing, editing, and layout; miscellaneous projects (e.g., educational programs, technical analyses, policy). Candidates should have ability to work independently, ability to work with others, editing skills, personal interest in the field, research skills, writing skills. Duration is one semester or one summer. Position available as unpaid or at $8 per hour. Open to high school students, recent high school graduates, college freshmen, college sophomores, college juniors, college seniors, individuals reentering the workforce. International applications accepted.

Benefits On-the-job training, opportunity to attend seminars/workshops, possible full-time employment, willing to act as a professional reference, willing to complete paperwork for educational credit, willing to provide letters of recommendation.

Contact Write, call, fax, or e-mail Lynn Grace, Director of the Learning Center/Outreach, 43-10 11th Street, Long Island City, New York 11101. Phone: 718-784-1444 Ext. 107. Fax: 718-784-8347. E-mail: lgrace@cecenter.org. In-person interview required. Applicants must submit a letter of interest, resume. Applications are accepted continuously.

THE CONSERVANCY OF SOUTHWEST FLORIDA
1450 Merrihue Drive
Naples, Florida 34102

General Information Locally based, nonprofit conservation organization whose efforts are primarily focused on ecological research, environmental protection, and environmental education; operates two nature centers, a wildlife rehabilitation clinic, and offers many environment programs and activities for the public. Established in 1964. Number of employees: 57. Number of internship applications received each year: 200.

Internships Available ▶ *1–2 Museum of Natural History/Naples Nature Center Conservation Associates:* responsibilities include working in museum research and exhibit interpretation and design, outdoors on nature trails, and delivering programs. Candidates should have ability to work independently, computer skills, knowledge of field, oral communication skills, personal interest in the field, self-motivation, strong interpersonal skills. Duration is 6–9 months. $125 per week. Open to college juniors, college seniors, recent college graduates, graduate students. ▶ *1 environmental policy conservation associate (Fort Myers office):* responsibilities include assisting in all aspects of research and investigations of environmental issues. Candidates should have ability to work independently, ability to work with others, oral communication skills, personal interest in the field, self-motivation, written communication skills, must provide own housing. Duration is 3–6 months. $125 per week. Open to recent college graduates, graduate students, law school graduates. ▶ *1 environmental policy conservation associate (Naples office):* responsibilities include assisting in all aspects of research and investigations of environmental issues. Candidates should have ability to work independently, ability to work with others, oral communication skills, personal interest in the field, self-motivation, written communication skills. Duration is 3–9 months. $125 per

week. Open to recent college graduates, graduate students, law students. ▶ *1 environmental science conservation associate:* responsibilities include working on current field and/or office projects. Candidates should have analytical skills, college degree in related field, oral communication skills, plan to pursue career in field, research skills, written communication skills. Duration is 3–9 months. $125 per week. Open to recent college graduates, graduate students, law students. ▶ *1–3 naturalist conservation associates (Briggs):* responsibilities include teaching marine and estuarine ecology programs as well as environmental education programs for summer programs and adult visitors; assisting in development of and implementation of summer programs and community outreach programs; supervising nature center; leading outdoor excursions, guided local-tour and canoe trips within Rookery Bay National Estuarine Reserve and other south Florida ecosystems. Candidates should have ability to work independently, college courses in field, knowledge of field, oral communication skills, organizational skills, personal interest in the field, self-motivation, strong interpersonal skills, physical ability to hike and canoe. Duration is 3–9 months. $125 per week. Open to college juniors, college seniors, recent college graduates, graduate students. ▶ *1–2 school programs conservation associates:* responsibilities include teaching the natural science of Florida ecology to preschool and elementary school children; providing field trips for children focusing on south Florida ecology and environmental science; planning day-long and occasional week-long children's events; assisting staff in developing new programs including ecotourism and community education for all ages. Candidates should have ability to work independently, ability to work with others, college courses in field, computer skills, oral communication skills, organizational skills, personal interest in the field, self-motivation, experience with children. Duration is 6–9 months. $125 per week. Open to college juniors, college seniors, recent college graduates, graduate students. ▶ *4 sea turtle research conservation associates:* responsibilities include monitoring and recording loggerhead sea turtle nesting information, measuring and tagging nesting turtles, securing the nest, and relocating when necessary. Candidates should have ability to work independently, declared college major in field, oral communication skills, personal interest in the field, self-motivation, strong interpersonal skills, ability to work in hot, buggy conditions. Duration is May to August or May to October. $125 per week. Open to college seniors, recent college graduates, graduate students. ▶ *4–9 summer camp conservation associates:* responsibilities include teaching the natural science of Florida ecology to preschool, elementary, and middle school students; some outdoor work in hot and buggy conditions; assisting staff with developing camp curricula. Candidates should have ability to work independently, college courses in field, oral communication skills, personal interest in the field, self-motivation, strong interpersonal skills, favorable attitude towards children. Duration is May to August only. $125 per week. Open to college juniors, college seniors, recent college graduates, graduate students. ▶ *4–5 wildlife rehabilitation conservation associates:* responsibilities include assisting in care and treatment of injured, sick, and orphaned Florida wildlife and cleaning and maintaining facilities. Candidates should have ability to work independently, college courses in field, experience in the field, personal interest in the field, self-motivation, strong interpersonal skills. Duration is 6–9 months. $125 per week. Open to college juniors, college seniors, recent college graduates, graduate students. International applications accepted.

Benefits Formal training, free housing, job counseling, names of contacts, on-the-job training, opportunity to attend seminars/workshops, possible full-time employment, willing to act as a professional reference, willing to complete paperwork for educational credit, willing to provide letters of recommendation, uniform shirts furnished, accident insurance at no cost.

Contact Write, call, fax, e-mail, or through World Wide Web site Sharon L. Truluck, Human Resources Director. Phone: 941-262-0304 Ext. 213. Fax: 941-262-0672. E-mail: internships@conservancy.org. Telephone interview required. Applicants must submit a formal organization application, letter of interest, resume, academic transcripts, three personal references, three letters of recommendation. Applications are accepted continuously. World Wide Web: http://www.conservancy.org.

CORAL CAY CONSERVATION, LTD.
The Tower, 13th Floor, 125 High Street, Colliers Wood
London SW19 2JG United Kingdom

General Information   Coral reef and tropical forest conservation organization. Established in 1986. Number of employees: 20. Number of internship applications received each year: 80.

Internships Available ▶ *1–12 head office/science/foundation interns:* responsibilities include data management, report production, administration, teaching (presentations), and statistical analysis. Candidates should have ability to work independently, analytical skills, computer skills, editing skills, office skills, oral communication skills, organizational skills, research skills, self-motivation, strong interpersonal skills, written communication skills. Duration is flexible. Unpaid. Open to college seniors, recent college graduates, graduate students, law students, career changers, individuals reentering the workforce. ▶ *16–20 marine expedition leaders (Honduras, Fiji, Philippines, and Malaysia):* responsibilities include managing, administering, and leading a major conservation project site with up to 40 volunteers and local staff. Candidates should have computer skills, knowledge of field, oral communication skills, organizational skills, personal interest in the field, self-motivation, strong interpersonal skills, strong leadership ability, written communication skills, diving experience required. Duration is 6 months. Unpaid. Open to graduate students, law students, career changers, individuals reentering the workforce, management professionals. ▶ *3 medical officers (Honduras, Philippines, Fiji, Malaysia):* responsibilities include serving on a remote conservation project site; responsible for care of up to 35 volunteers and local staff. Candidates should have ability to work independently, college degree in related field, computer skills, knowledge of field, oral communication skills, organizational skills, strong interpersonal skills, strong leadership ability, written communication skills. Duration is 4 months. Unpaid. Open to recent college graduates, graduate students, career changers, must be nurse, doctor, or paramedic. ▶ *4–8 project scientists/science officers (Honduras, Fiji, Philippines, Malaysia):* responsibilities include coordinating day-to-day scientific program for Caribbean Indo Pacific coral reef conservation project; science officers train volunteer divers in marine ecology and organize survey work; project scientists oversee all of above and organize community work and represent Coral Cay Conservation at conferences. Candidates should have college degree in related field, computer skills, knowledge of field, oral communication skills, organizational skills, personal interest in the field, research skills, self-motivation, strong interpersonal skills, strong leadership ability, written communication skills. Duration is 3–6 months. Unpaid. Open to recent college graduates, graduate students. ▶ *2 rainforest conservation expedition leaders (Philippines):* responsibilities include managing, administering, and leading a major conservation project site with up to 20 volunteers and local staff. Candidates should have computer skills, knowledge of field, oral communication skills, organizational skills, personal interest in the field, self-motivation, strong interpersonal skills, strong leadership ability, written communication skills, trekking experience required. Duration is 6 months. Unpaid. Open to graduate students, law students, career changers, individuals reentering the workforce, management professionals. ▶ *3 scuba instructors (Philippines, Fiji, Honduras, Malaysia):* responsibilities include diving instruction and coordination of safe diving activity in remote marine conservation site. Candidates should have knowledge of field, oral communication skills, organizational skills, strong interpersonal skills, strong leadership ability, must have relevant PADI scuba certification. Duration is 3 or more months. Unpaid. Open to recent high school graduates, college freshmen, college sophomores, college juniors, college seniors, recent college graduates, graduate students, law students, career changers, individuals reentering the workforce. International applications accepted.

Benefits   Free housing, free meals, names of contacts, on-the-job training, opportunity to attend seminars/workshops, possible full-time employment, willing to act as a professional reference, willing to complete paperwork for educational credit, willing to provide letters of recommendation, free housing and meals for field staff, travel reimbursement (only) for London office interns.

International Internships   Available in Fiji; Honduras; Malaysia; Philippines; London, United Kingdom.
Contact   Write, call, fax, e-mail, or through World Wide Web site Tanya Blackburn, Public Relations and Information Officer. Phone: 44-870-750-0668 Ext. 210. Fax: 44-870-750-0667. E-mail: tb@coralcay. org. In-person interview required. Applicants must submit a formal organization application, letter of interest, resume, academic transcripts, portfolio, personal reference, letter of recommendation, professional reference. Applications are accepted continuously. World Wide Web: http://www.coralcay.org.

CORKSCREW SWAMP SANCTUARY
375 Sanctuary Road
Naples, Florida 34120

General Information   11,000-acre wilderness area in southwest Florida providing preservation, protection, and public education; home to old-growth bald cypress forest and Florida's largest nesting colony of endangered wood storks. Established in 1954. Number of employees: 23. Unit of National Audubon Society, New York, New York. Number of internship applications received each year: 200.

Internships Available ▶ *2–4 naturalist educators:* responsibilities include environmental education and interpretation tasks, program development and staffing, and maintenance of visitor center. Candidates should have ability to work independently, ability to work with others, oral communication skills, personal interest in the field, some experience in environmental area, education background recommended. Duration is 6-8 months (start late August/early September). $150 per week. Open to college juniors, college seniors, recent college graduates, graduate students, career changers. ▶ *2–4 resource management team members:* responsibilities include resource management fieldwork, exotic plant removal, trail maintenance, staffing and maintenance of visitor center and grounds. Candidates should have ability to work independently, ability to work with others, personal interest in the field. Duration is 6 months. $150 per week. Open to college freshmen, college sophomores, college juniors, college seniors, recent college graduates, graduate students, career changers.

Benefits   Formal training, free housing, job counseling, names of contacts, on-the-job training, willing to complete paperwork for educational credit, willing to provide letters of recommendation, job lists provided when available, $50 allowance for necessary clothing/uniform.

Contact   Write, fax, or e-mail Laurel Chaplin, Education Director. Fax: 239-348-9155. E-mail: lchaplin@audubon.org. No phone calls. Telephone interview required. Applicants must submit a letter of interest, resume, three personal references. Applications are accepted continuously. World Wide Web: http://www.audubon. org/local/sanctuary/corkscrew.

DEEP PORTAGE CONSERVATION RESERVE
2197 Nature Center Drive, NW
Hackensack, Minnesota 56452

General Information   6000-acre forest and conservation education center that conducts programs in environmental education. Established in 1973. Number of employees: 22. Number of internship applications received each year: 40.

Internships Available ▶ *6–8 field instructors:* responsibilities include counseling 350 campers per summer on woods and wildlife outdoor skills. Candidates should have ability to work independently, analytical skills, oral communication skills, organizational skills, personal interest in the field, plan to pursue career in field, research skills, self-motivation, strong interpersonal skills, strong leadership ability. Duration is June 8 to August 15. $150–$225 per week. Open to college freshmen, college sophomores, college juniors, college seniors, recent college graduates, graduate students, career changers. International applications accepted.

Benefits   Formal training, free housing, free meals, job counseling, names of contacts, opportunity to attend seminars/workshops, possible full-time employment, willing to complete paperwork for educational credit, willing to provide letters of recommendation.

Contact   Write, call, fax, e-mail, or through World Wide Web site Dale Yerger, Director. Phone: 218-682-2325. Fax: 218-682-3121. E-mail: portage@uslink.net. In-person interview recommended (telephone interview accepted). Applicants must submit a resume, three personal references. Application deadline: May 1. World Wide Web: http://www.deep-portage.org.

DELAWARE NATURE SOCIETY (ASHLAND NATURE CENTER)
PO Box 700, Brackenville and Barley Mill Road
Hockessin, Delaware 19707

General Information Environmental education and advocacy organization. Established in 1964. Number of employees: 70. Number of internship applications received each year: 5.
Internships Available ▶ *1–3 environmental education interns:* responsibilities include teaching and co-teaching children's classes and leading or assisting with field trips. Candidates should have ability to work with others, computer skills, knowledge of field, oral communication skills, personal interest in the field, ability to work with children, outdoor skills. Duration is 1–12 months. Position available as unpaid or paid. Open to college juniors, college seniors, recent college graduates, graduate students, career changers. ▶ *1–2 stream watch interns:* responsibilities include assisting with stream watch workshops, participating in research, and preparing educational displays or articles. Candidates should have college courses in field, computer skills, oral communication skills, personal interest in the field, plan to pursue career in field, research skills, written communication skills, strong science background. Duration is 1–12 months. Paid. Open to college juniors, college seniors, recent college graduates, graduate students, career changers, individuals reentering the workforce. International applications accepted.
Benefits Formal training, on-the-job training, opportunity to attend seminars/workshops, possible full-time employment, willing to act as a professional reference, willing to complete paperwork for educational credit, willing to provide letters of recommendation.
Contact Write, call, fax, e-mail, or through World Wide Web site Linda Young, Communications Coordinator, PO Box 700, Hockessin, Delaware 19707. Phone: 302-239-2334 Ext. 10. Fax: 302-239-2473. E-mail: lindaY@dnsashland.org. In-person interview required. Applicants must submit a formal organization application, letter of interest, resume, two personal references, two letters of recommendation. Applications are accepted continuously. World Wide Web: http://www.delawarenaturesociety.org.

DELAWARE WATER GAP NATIONAL RECREATION AREA
294 Old Milford Road
Milford, Pennsylvania 18337

General Information Organization devoted to conserving scenery, natural and historic objects, and wildlife for the enjoyment of future generations. Established in 1965. Number of employees: 128. Unit of United States National Park Service, Washington, District of Columbia. Number of internship applications received each year: 15.
Internships Available ▶ *1 geographic information systems laboratory assistant:* responsibilities include developing and implementing various software tools to facilitate spatial data creation, managing and analyzing within a GIS, assisting in development of GIS analytical procedure, and assisting in development of network communications. Candidates should have ability to work independently, ability to work with others, college courses in field, computer skills, organizational skills, self-motivation. Duration is 12–14 weeks. Unpaid. Open to college sophomores, college juniors, college seniors, recent college graduates, graduate students, career changers, individuals reentering the workforce. ▶ *1 resource assistant:* responsibilities include assisting with divisional activities that may include wildlife, fisheries, vegetation monitoring/management, trails development, water resources planning, wetland studies, and cultural landscape. Candidates should have ability to work independently, ability to work with others, college courses in field, computer skills, knowledge of field, oral communication skills, self-motivation, written communication skills. Duration is 3 months minimum. Unpaid. Open to college juniors, college seniors, recent college graduates, graduate students. ▶ *2*

water quality assistants: responsibilities include measuring water quality in streams and rivers, maintaining and calibrating equipment, performing data entry, and analyzing data. Candidates should have ability to work independently, ability to work with others, analytical skills, computer skills, knowledge of field, organizational skills. Duration is 12 weeks. Unpaid. Open to college juniors, college seniors, recent college graduates, graduate students. International applications accepted.
Benefits Free housing, job counseling, names of contacts, willing to complete paperwork for educational credit, willing to provide letters of recommendation, worker's compensation, potential stipend.
Contact Write or fax Patrick J. Lynch, Chief, Division of Research and Resource Planning. Fax: 570-296-4706. E-mail: patrick_lynch@nps.gov. No phone calls. In-person interview recommended (telephone interview accepted). Applicants must submit a letter of interest, resume. Application deadline: February 15 for spring/summer, November 1 for winter. World Wide Web: http://www.nps.gov/dewa.

DOLPHIN RESEARCH CENTER
58901 Overseas Highway
Grassy Key, Florida 33050-6019

General Information Organization dedicated to teaching, learning, and caring for marine mammals and the environment. Established in 1984. Number of employees: 80. Number of internship applications received each year: 100.
Internships Available ▶ *1 animal care and training intern:* responsibilities include assisting trainers during dolphin and sea lion training sessions; conducting segments of public sessions or workshops; assisting with data collection for research, repair, and maintenance of training equipment; food preparation; assisting with husbandry procedures. Candidates should have ability to work with others, knowledge of field, oral communication skills, organizational skills, personal interest in the field, self-motivation. Duration is 3–4 months. Unpaid. Open to college freshmen, college sophomores, college juniors, college seniors, recent college graduates, career changers. ▶ *1 animal husbandry/medical intern:* responsibilities include food and vitamin prep; stocking and inventorying food and husbandry supplies; fish delivery assistance; training and supervising other volunteers/interns; maintaining husbandry and medical files; assisting with medical procedures and observations; assisting with data collection for ongoing research. Candidates should have ability to work independently, experience in the field, oral communication skills, organizational skills, plan to pursue career in field, strong interpersonal skills. Duration is 3–4 months. Unpaid. Open to college sophomores, college juniors, college seniors, recent college graduates, career changers. ▶ *1 development and membership intern:* responsibilities include assisting with development and membership with annual giving campaigns; assisting with developing and implementing lapses and special appeals; and assisting with letter writing and correspondence to members. Candidates should have ability to work independently, computer skills, editing skills, knowledge of field, office skills, oral communication skills, organizational skills, strong interpersonal skills, writing skills. Duration is 3–4 months. Unpaid. Open to college freshmen, college sophomores, college juniors, college seniors, recent college graduates, graduate students, career changers. ▶ *1 dolphin/child therapy intern:* responsibilities include supporting dolphin-assisted therapy staff; preparation and maintenance of session equipment; assisting program participants and families; recording session notes and maintaining records; preparing program folders; assisting with data collection for ongoing research. Candidates should have ability to work with others, college courses in field, knowledge of field, oral communication skills, plan to pursue career in field. Duration is 3–4 months. Unpaid. Open to college freshmen, college sophomores, college juniors, college seniors, recent college graduates, career changers. ▶ *1–2 education interns:* responsibilities include supporting education staff; assisting with coordination of students in week-long DolphinLab classes; handling information requests and correspondence; preparing DolphinLab participant notebooks; assisting and/or teaching seminars and community outreach presentations; recording minutes for department meetings. Candidates

Dolphin Research Center (continued)

should have college courses in field, oral communication skills, personal interest in the field, plan to pursue career in field, strong interpersonal skills. Duration is 3–4 months. Unpaid. Open to college sophomores, college juniors, college seniors, recent college graduates, career changers. ▶ *1 guest programs intern:* responsibilities include assisting with educating and entertaining guests; narrating training sessions; teaching workshops; photographing program participants; food preparation; and other responsibilities. Candidates should have ability to work with others, oral communication skills, organizational skills, personal interest in the field, self-motivation. Duration is 3–4 months. Unpaid. Open to college freshmen, college sophomores, college juniors, college seniors, recent college graduates, graduate students, career changers. ▶ *1–2 research interns:* responsibilities include preparation and maintenance of research equipment; coordinating and assisting with data collection for ongoing research; summarizing and analyzing research data; maintaining records; training and supervising other volunteers/interns in data collection. Candidates should have ability to work independently, ability to work with others, computer skills, knowledge of field, oral communication skills, plan to pursue career in field. Duration is 3–4 months. Unpaid. Open to college sophomores, college juniors, college seniors, recent college graduates, graduate students. ▶ *1 visual communications intern:* responsibilities include videoing and photographing dolphin and sea lion sessions, public interactive programs, and seminars; creating and maintaining archives and databases; and creating visual products for use in general, educational, and/or outreach program. Candidates should have computer skills, plan to pursue career in field, self-motivation, strong interpersonal skills, visual creativity. Duration is 3–4 months. Unpaid. Open to recent high school graduates, college freshmen, college sophomores, college juniors, college seniors, recent college graduates, career changers, individuals reentering the workforce. International applications accepted.
Benefits Formal training, on-the-job training, opportunity to attend seminars/workshops, possible full-time employment, willing to act as a professional reference, willing to complete paperwork for educational credit, willing to provide letters of recommendation.
Contact Write, call, fax, e-mail, or through World Wide Web site Mary Ackroyd, Volunteer Resources. Phone: 305-289-1121 Ext. 230. Fax: 305-743-7627. E-mail: drc-vr@dolphins.org. Telephone interview required. Applicants must submit a formal organization application, resume, academic transcripts, two letters of recommendation, volunteer application with the intern application. Application deadline: February 1 for summer, June 1 for fall, October 1 for winter. World Wide Web: http://www.dolphins.org.

ECOLOGICAL CENTER LOS CUARTOS
Torre Basques 10-16
Aguascolientes 20139 Mexico

General Information Center for environmental education and community-based environmental programs. Established in 1992. Number of employees: 15. Affiliate of Centro Mexicano para la Filantropia CEMEFI, Mexico. Number of internship applications received each year: 22.
Internships Available ▶ *1–2 environmental educators:* responsibilities include collaborating in environmental education of children, participation in camps, education, and organization. Candidates should have ability to work independently, knowledge of field, oral communication skills, organizational skills, personal interest in the field, self-motivation, strong interpersonal skills, strong leadership ability, written communication skills, fluency in Spanish. Duration is 8–14 weeks. Unpaid. Open to recent high school graduates, college freshmen, college sophomores, college juniors, college seniors, recent college graduates, graduate students, law students, career changers, individuals reentering the workforce. International applications accepted.
Benefits Formal training, free housing, free meals, on-the-job training, opportunity to attend seminars/workshops, possible full-time employment, willing to provide letters of recommendation.
International Internships Available.

Contact Write, call, fax, e-mail, or through World Wide Web site Martin Barbarena Cruz, Chairman. Phone: 52-4-9650138. Fax: 52-4-9650087. E-mail: info@cuartos.org.mx. Applicants must submit a letter of interest, resume. Applications are accepted continuously. World Wide Web: http://www.cuartos.org.mx.

EDUCATIONAL COMMUNICATIONS, INC.
PO Box 351419
Los Angeles, California 90035-9119

General Information Environmental media programs and conservation organization specializing in ecological activism and television and radio production and distribution; also promotes ecotourism. Established in 1958. Number of employees: 1. Unit of Educational Communications, Idyllwild, California. Number of internship applications received each year: 25.
Internships Available ▶ *Interns:* responsibilities include working in a variety of areas including ecological and environmental activism, administration, networking, organizing research, fund-raising, public speaking, membership development, writing, producing, editing, directing television and radio productions, distribution, publishing, journalism, and broadcasting. Candidates should have ability to work independently, ability to work with others, personal interest in the field, English speaking/understanding ability. Duration is flexible (prefer 3 days per week for tv editing, one day per week for ecological activism). Unpaid. Open to high school students, recent high school graduates, college freshmen, college sophomores, college juniors, college seniors, recent college graduates, graduate students, law students, career changers, individuals reentering the workforce. International applications accepted.
Benefits Housing at a cost, names of contacts, on-the-job training, opportunity to attend seminars/workshops, willing to act as a professional reference, willing to complete paperwork for educational credit, willing to provide letters of recommendation, referrals provided, opportunity to produce and host own television and radio shows, overseas travel in exchange for shooting and editing television shows.
International Internships Available.
Contact Write, call, or e-mail Leslie Lewis, Administrative Assistant. Phone: 310-559-9160. Fax: 310-559-9160. E-mail: ecnp@aol.com. Telephone interview required. Applicants must submit a letter of interest. Applications are accepted continuously. World Wide Web: http://www.ecoprojects.org.

EL MALPAIS NATIONAL CONSERVATION AREA AND NATIONAL MONUMENT
2001 East Santa Fe Avenue
Grants, New Mexico 87020

General Information Area designated by Congress to preserve the natural geology and cultural resources surrounding Grant's Lava Flows; land includes 2 wilderness areas. Number of employees: 5. Unit of Bureau of Land Management, Albuquerque Field Office, Albuquerque, New Mexico. Number of internship applications received each year: 12.
Internships Available ▶ *1–2 backcountry rangers:* responsibilities include patrolling NCA backcountry/wilderness by vehicle or on foot, keeping a written patrol log, writing reports, providing visitors with accurate information, giving guided tours, assisting with maintenance, and staffing visitor center. Duration is 3 months (flexible). Unpaid. ▶ *1–2 visitor information specialists:* responsibilities include staffing the visitor center desk, responding to visitor questions, selling Cooperating Association books and materials, patrolling NCA by vehicle or on foot, keeping a written patrol log, writing reports as necessary, giving guided tours, and assisting with maintenance. Duration is 3 months (flexible). Unpaid. Candidates for all positions should have computer skills, oral communication skills, personal interest in the field, strong interpersonal skills, written communication skills.
Benefits Free housing, willing to complete paperwork for educational credit, willing to provide letters of recommendation.
Contact Write or call Ms. Karen Davis, Volunteer Coordinator/ Park Ranger. Phone: 505-287-7911. Fax: 505-285-5041. E-mail:

karen_davis@blm.gov. Applicants must submit a formal organization application, resume, two personal references. Applications are accepted continuously.

ENDANGERED SPECIES COALITION
1101 14th Street, NW, Suite 1400
Washington, District of Columbia 20005

General Information Environmental organization working to protect endangered species and the Endangered Species Act. Established in 1982. Number of employees: 6. Number of internship applications received each year: 60.

Internships Available ▶ *1–3 organizing interns:* responsibilities include contacting activists and environmental groups via phone, e-mail, or fax on endangered species issues; keeping up with legislation on endangered species issues; assisting with daily office activities and database maintenance; helping answer requests for information. Candidates should have ability to work independently, ability to work with others, knowledge of field, oral communication skills, organizational skills, personal interest in the field, self-motivation, strong leadership ability, writing skills. Duration is 1 semester. Position available as unpaid or paid. Open to college freshmen, college sophomores, college juniors, college seniors, recent college graduates. International applications accepted.

Benefits On-the-job training, willing to act as a professional reference, willing to complete paperwork for educational credit, willing to provide letters of recommendation.

Contact Write, fax, or e-mail Beth Lowell, Northeast Organizer, 1101 14th Street, NW, Suite 1001. Phone: 202-772-3234. Fax: 202-756-2804. E-mail: blowell@stopextinction.org. In-person interview recommended (telephone interview accepted). Applicants must submit a letter of interest, resume, one-page writing sample. Applications are accepted continuously. World Wide Web: http://www.stopextinction.org.

ENVIRONMENTAL AND ENERGY STUDY INSTITUTE
122 C Street, NW, Suite 600
Washington, District of Columbia 20001-2109

General Information Nonpartisan public policy research and analysis organization that strives to produce better informed congressional debates and to generate credible and innovative policies for environmentally sustainable development. Established in 1984. Number of employees: 11. Number of internship applications received each year: 120.

Internships Available ▶ *3 legislative interns:* responsibilities include researching for institute reports, publications, and projects; attending congressional hearings and other meetings; reporting on proceedings to EESI staff and assisting in administrative work; setting up and attending meetings with other organizations and congressional offices; and assisting with congressional briefings on climate change, energy efficiency, and transportation. Candidates should have oral communication skills, personal interest in the field, self-motivation, strong interpersonal skills, written communication skills. Duration is flexible. Unpaid. Open to college freshmen, college sophomores, college juniors, college seniors, graduate students. International applications accepted.

Benefits Names of contacts, possible full-time employment, willing to complete paperwork for educational credit, willing to provide letters of recommendation, leadership skills.

Contact Write, call, fax, or e-mail Claire Suen, Intern Coordinator. Phone: 202-628-1400. Fax: 202-628-1825. E-mail: csuen@eesi.org. In-person interview recommended (telephone interview accepted). Applicants must submit a letter of interest, resume. Applications are accepted continuously. World Wide Web: http://www.eesi.org.

ENVIRONMENTAL DEFENSE
257 Park Avenue South
New York, New York 10010

General Information Nonprofit national advocacy organization with over 300,000 members working to develop economical and viable solutions to tough environmental problems.

Established in 1967. Number of employees: 85. Number of internship applications received each year: 200.

Internships Available ▶ *4–6 legal interns:* responsibilities include working on issues involving fisheries management, land use issues integrated with issues of air pollution and traffic congestion, legislative issues, policy/legal research, and policy analysis. Candidates should have ability to work independently, analytical skills, computer skills, declared college major in field, editing skills, knowledge of field, office skills, oral communication skills, organizational skills, personal interest in the field, plan to pursue career in field, research skills, self-motivation, strong interpersonal skills, strong leadership ability, written communication skills. Duration is May 31 to August 31. Position available as unpaid or at $450–$500 per week. Open to recent college graduates, graduate students, law students, career changers. International applications accepted.

Benefits Names of contacts, opportunity to attend seminars/workshops, travel reimbursement, willing to act as a professional reference, willing to complete paperwork for educational credit, willing to provide letters of recommendation.

Contact Write, call, fax, or e-mail Maxine Adams, Intern Recruiter. Phone: 212-505-2100. Fax: 212-533-6748. E-mail: maxineadams@environmentaldefense.org. In-person interview recommended (telephone interview accepted). Applicants must submit a formal organization application, letter of interest, resume, academic transcripts, writing sample, two personal references, two letters of recommendation. Applications are accepted continuously.

EXOTIC FELINE BREEDING COMPOUND, INC.
HCR 1, Box 84
Rosamond, California 93560

General Information Nonprofit organization dedicated to the preservation and propagation of rare and endangered felines through breeding, research, and education. Established in 1977. Number of employees: 5. Number of internship applications received each year: 3.

Internships Available ▶ *1–3 keepers:* responsibilities include cleaning cages, behavioral observation, completion of health charts, dietary preparation, assisting in medical procedures, educational talks with public, and office procedures. Candidates should have ability to work independently, ability to work with others, analytical skills, declared college major in field, personal interest in the field, plan to pursue career in field. Duration is flexible. Unpaid. Open to college freshmen, college sophomores, college juniors, college seniors, recent college graduates, graduate students. International applications accepted.

Benefits Housing at a cost, on-the-job training, willing to act as a professional reference, willing to complete paperwork for educational credit, willing to provide letters of recommendation.

Contact Write, call, fax, or e-mail Sandra Masek, Director/General Manager, HCR 1, Box 84, Rosamond, California 93560. Phone: 661-256-3793. Fax: 661-256-6867. E-mail: info@cathouse-fcc.org. Applicants must submit a letter of interest, resume, letter of recommendation. Applications are accepted continuously. World Wide Web: http://www.cathouse-fcc.org.

FAIRVIEW LAKE ENVIRONMENTAL EDUCATION CENTER–YMCA
1035 Fairview Lake Road
Newton, New Jersey 07860

General Information Residential facility that offers a hands-on approach to education and presents all-age courses dealing with life sciences, ecology, technical wilderness skills, and recreation. Established in 1915. Number of employees: 40. Branch of Metropolitan YMCA of the Oranges, Livingston, New Jersey. Number of internship applications received each year: 10.

Internships Available ▶ *1–3 naturalist interns:* responsibilities include participating in training, observing courses, teaching, aiding in maintenance, designing displays, and submitting paperwork. Duration is 3 months (fall); 3-5 months (spring). $200 per week. Open to college seniors, recent college graduates, graduate students. ▶ *2 recreational interns:* responsibilities include teaching, participating in training including team building, challenge, boat-

Fairview Lake Environmental Education Center–YMCA (continued)
ing, archery, and hiking. Duration is 3 months. $150 per week. Open to college freshmen, college sophomores, college juniors, college seniors, recent college graduates, graduate students. Candidates for all positions should have ability to work with others, college courses in field, oral communication skills, personal interest in the field. International applications accepted.

Benefits Formal training, free housing, free meals, opportunity to attend seminars/workshops, possible full-time employment, willing to complete paperwork for educational credit, willing to provide letters of recommendation, opportunity to receive certifications in first aid, CPR, and lifeguarding.

Contact Write, call, fax, or e-mail Ms. Christina Henriksen, Environmental Education Director. Phone: 973-383-9282. Fax: 973-383-6386. E-mail: fairviewlake@metroymcas.org. In-person interview recommended (telephone interview accepted). Applicants must submit a letter of interest, resume. Application deadline: February 1 for spring; continuous for fall. World Wide Web: http://www.fairviewlake.org.

FENTON RANCH
26473 Highway 126
Jemez Springs, New Mexico 87025

General Information Residential facility that houses the environmental education program for a Manzano Day School, a private elementary school. Established in 1974. Number of employees: 5. Unit of Manzano Day School, Albuquerque, New Mexico. Number of internship applications received each year: 80.

Internships Available ▶ *1–2 environmental education interns:* responsibilities include teaching environmental education programs to elementary-aged children, designing curriculums, facilitating free time, keeping journals, supervising meals, and playing with children outdoors. Candidates should have ability to work independently, ability to work with others, oral communication skills, organizational skills, personal interest in the field, self-motivation, strong leadership ability. Duration is 7 weeks (early April to mid- May) or 11 weeks (mid-August to late October). $200 per week. Open to college sophomores, college juniors, college seniors, recent college graduates, graduate students, career changers.

Benefits Free housing, free meals, on-the-job training, travel reimbursement, willing to act as a professional reference, willing to complete paperwork for educational credit, willing to provide letters of recommendation.

Contact Write, call, or e-mail Kestrel Mandras, Fenton Director, 1801 Central Avenue NW, Albuquerque 87104. Phone: 505-243-6659. Fax: 505-243-4711. E-mail: km@mds.k12.nm.us. Telephone interview required. Applicants must submit a formal organization application, letter of interest, resume, three personal references. Application deadline: March 1 for spring, July 15 for fall. World Wide Web: http://www.mds.k12.nm.us/home/programs/fenton/fenton.html.

FERNWOOD NATURE CENTER
13988 Range Line Road
Niles, Michigan 49120

General Information Nature Center and botanical garden working to educate people about the natural environment and to create environmental awareness and appreciation. Established in 1963. Number of employees: 15. Number of internship applications received each year: 15.

Internships Available ▶ *1 seasonal naturalist:* responsibilities include leading nature walks for children, teaching classes, and maintaining trails and displays. Candidates should have college courses in field, experience in the field, oral communication skills, personal interest in the field, strong interpersonal skills, experience or interest in working with children. Duration is 8 months (March to November). $220–$250 per week. Open to college juniors, college seniors, recent college graduates, graduate students, career changers, individuals reentering the workforce.

Benefits Formal training, free housing, job counseling, names of contacts, on-the-job training, opportunity to attend seminars/workshops, travel reimbursement, willing to act as a professional reference, willing to complete paperwork for educational credit, willing to provide letters of recommendation.

Contact Write, call, or e-mail Ms. Wendy E. Jones, Head Naturalist. Phone: 616-695-6491. E-mail: nature@remc11.k12.mi.us. In-person interview recommended (telephone interview accepted). Applicants must submit a letter of interest, resume, three personal references. Application deadline: February 1. World Wide Web: http://www.fernwoodbotanical.org.

FIVE RIVERS ENVIRONMENTAL EDUCATION CENTER
5 Rivers Center, Game Farm Road
Delmar, New York 12054

General Information Environmental center providing education programs to the public and schools. Established in 1973. Number of employees: 5. Unit of New York State Department of Environmental Conservation, Albany, New York. Number of internship applications received each year: 75.

Internships Available ▶ *8 naturalist interns:* responsibilities include teaching environmental programs and conducting other projects. Candidates should have oral communication skills, personal interest in the field, self-motivation, strong interpersonal skills, written communication skills. Duration is 10–12 weeks. $200 per week. Open to college freshmen, college sophomores, college juniors, college seniors, recent college graduates, graduate students, career changers, individuals reentering the workforce.

Benefits Formal training, free housing, job counseling, names of contacts, on-the-job training, opportunity to attend seminars/workshops, travel reimbursement, willing to act as a professional reference, willing to complete paperwork for educational credit, willing to provide letters of recommendation, worker's compensation.

Contact Write, call, or e-mail Ms. Anita Sanchez, Senior Environmental Educator. Phone: 518-475-0291. E-mail: amsanche@gw.dec.state.ny.us. In-person interview recommended (telephone interview accepted). Applicants must submit a formal organization application, resume, three personal references. Applications are accepted continuously.

FRANCIS BEIDLER FORREST
336 Sanctuary Road
Harleyville, South Carolina 29448

General Information Nonprofit environmental organization. Established in 1977. Number of employees: 10. Unit of National Audubon Society, New York, New York. Number of internship applications received each year: 30.

Internships Available ▶ *1–2 naturalist interns:* responsibilities include leading interpretive walks for all ages on 1-1/2 mile boardwalk through virgin swamp forest; leading half-day canoe trips; running visitor center desk; wildlife and sanctuary management as needed; independent project; assisting with ongoing special events and research; maintenance. Candidates should have ability to work independently, declared college major in field, oral communication skills, plan to pursue career in field, self-motivation, strong interpersonal skills. Duration is 3 months. $200 per week. Open to college juniors, college seniors, recent college graduates, graduate students, career changers, individuals reentering the workforce.

Benefits Free housing, on-the-job training, willing to act as a professional reference, willing to complete paperwork for educational credit, willing to provide letters of recommendation.

Contact Write, call, fax, e-mail, or in person Michael Dawson, Center Director. Phone: 843-462-2150. Fax: 843-462-2713. E-mail: mdawson@audubon.org. Telephone interview required. Applicants must submit a letter of interest, resume, three personal references. Application deadline: January 1 for spring, April 15 for summer, July 15 for fall. World Wide Web: http://www.beidlerForest.com.

FRIENDS OF THE EARTH
1025 Vermont Avenue, NW, Suite 300
Washington, District of Columbia 20005

General Information Independent global advocacy organization working to protect the Earth from environmental disaster,

preserve biological, cultural, and ethnic diversity, and empower citizens and help them develop an effective voice in decisions affecting their environment and lives. Established in 1969. Number of employees: 27. Number of internship applications received each year: 250.
Internships Available ▶ *6 fellowships:* responsibilities include working with project directors from Eco-Team, Global Team, Journalism, Communications and Marketing, and Community Health and Environment Team in researching, writing, lobbying, and assisting with administrative support on a variety of topics, including taxation and consumption, corporate accountability, water resource protection, ozone layer protection, Northwest rivers and wetlands, and trade and international banking/monetary policy. Duration is 6 months. $1200 per month. Open to recent college graduates, graduate students, law students. ▶ *5 interns:* responsibilities include working with project directors from Eco-Team, Global Team, Journalism, Communications and Marketing, and Community Health and Environment Team in researching, writing, lobbying, and assisting with administrative support on a variety of topics, including consumption and taxation, corporate accountability, water resource protection, ozone layer protection, Northwest rivers and wetlands, and trade and international banking/monetary policy. Duration is 3–6 months. Unpaid. Open to college seniors, recent college graduates, graduate students, law students. Candidates for all positions should have ability to work independently, computer skills, knowledge of field, oral communication skills, research skills, written communication skills. International applications accepted.
Benefits Names of contacts, on-the-job training, opportunity to attend seminars/workshops, willing to complete paperwork for educational credit, willing to provide letters of recommendation, possible travel reimbursement.
Contact Write, fax, or e-mail Intern Coordinator. Fax: 202-783-0444. E-mail: jobs@foe.org. No phone calls. Applicants must submit a letter of interest, resume, one 3-page writing sample. Applications are accepted continuously. World Wide Web: http://www.foe.org/FOE.

FUND FOR ANIMALS, INC.
8121 Georgia Avenue, Suite 301
Silver Spring, Maryland 20910

General Information Nonprofit animal protection organization that focuses on companion animal and wildlife issues. Established in 1967. Number of employees: 13. Unit of The Fund for Animals, New York, New York. Number of internship applications received each year: 30.
Internships Available ▶ *1–5 interns:* responsibilities include performing a variety of tasks in the legal, legislative, outreach, campaign, and administrative departments. Candidates should have strong interest in animal advocacy. Duration is minimum of 3 months. Position available as unpaid or at $500 per internship or academic credit. Open to high school students, recent high school graduates, college freshmen, college sophomores, college juniors, college seniors, recent college graduates, graduate students, law students, career changers, individuals reentering the workforce. International applications accepted.
Benefits Formal training, opportunity to attend seminars/workshops, willing to complete paperwork for educational credit, willing to provide letters of recommendation, reimbursement for work-related travel expenses.
Contact Write, call, fax, or e-mail Jennifer Allen, Program Coordinator. Phone: 301-585-2591 Ext. 206. Fax: 301-585-2595. E-mail: jallen@fund.org. In-person interview recommended (telephone interview accepted). Applicants must submit a letter of interest, resume, writing sample, two letters of recommendation, completed questionnaire. Applications are accepted continuously. World Wide Web: http://www.fund.org.

GENESEE VALLEY OUTDOOR LEARNING CENTER
1717 Rayville Road
Parkton, Maryland 21120

General Information Experiential learning center that offers ropes course and environmental programs for school children,

those with special needs, at-risk youth, and corporations. Number of employees: 20. Number of internship applications received each year: 10.
Internships Available ▶ *10–15 challenge course interns:* responsibilities include educating groups, maintenance, and other educational requirements as needed; 5–6 day work week; occasional evenings. Candidates should have ability to work independently, personal interest in the field, self-motivation, strong interpersonal skills, strong leadership ability, current first aid and CPR certifications. Duration is minimum of 3 months. Position available as unpaid or paid. Open to high school students, recent high school graduates, college freshmen, college sophomores, college juniors, college seniors, recent college graduates, graduate students, law students, career changers, individuals reentering the workforce. ▶ *8–10 instructors:* responsibilities include educating groups, maintenance and other educational requirements as needed; 5-6 day work week, some evenings. Candidates should have ability to work independently, oral communication skills, personal interest in the field, self-motivation, strong interpersonal skills, strong leadership ability, current first aid and CPR certifications. Duration is minimum of 3 months. $180–$250 per week. Open to recent high school graduates, college freshmen, college sophomores, college juniors, college seniors, recent college graduates, graduate students, law students, career changers, individuals reentering the workforce. ▶ *1 youth camp director:* responsibilities include directing 7 and 8 year-old camp (day), overseeing instructors and CITs and program; 5-day work week; educational requirements as needed. Candidates should have experience in the field, oral communication skills, personal interest in the field, self-motivation, strong interpersonal skills, strong leadership ability. Duration is June 17 to August 30. $180 to $250 per week, depending on experience level . Open to college freshmen, college sophomores, college juniors, college seniors, recent college graduates, graduate students, law students, career changers, individuals reentering the workforce. International applications accepted.
Benefits Formal training, free housing, free meals, on-the-job training, possible full-time employment, willing to act as a professional reference, willing to complete paperwork for educational credit, willing to provide letters of recommendation, health insurance assistance.
Contact Write, call, fax, e-mail, or through World Wide Web site Marcia Denmark, Supervisor of Program and Personnel, Parkton, Maryland 21120. Phone: 410-343-0101. Fax: 410-343-1451. E-mail: info@geneseevalley.org. In-person interview recommended (telephone interview accepted). Applicants must submit a formal organization application, letter of interest, resume, three personal references. Application deadline: March 15 for spring, May 31 for summer, August 23 for fall. World Wide Web: http://www.geneseevalley.org.

GEORGE WASHINGTON & JEFFERSON NATIONAL FORESTS
5162 Valleypointe Parkway
Roanoke, Virginia 24019-3050

General Information Organization responsible for the management of the George Washington and Jefferson National Forests, including recreation, wildlife, timber, wilderness, watershed, range, and cultural resources. Established in 1940. Number of employees: 364. Number of internship applications received each year: 15.
Internships Available ▶ *Interns:* responsibilities include working in cultural resources, range, recreation, timber, or wildlife. Candidates should have ability to work independently, knowledge of field, oral communication skills, plan to pursue career in field, self-motivation, strong interpersonal skills, written communication skills. Duration is 1–3 months. Unpaid. Open to college freshmen, college sophomores, college juniors, college seniors, recent college graduates, graduate students.
Benefits On-the-job training, willing to complete paperwork for educational credit, willing to provide letters of recommendation.
Contact Write, call, or fax Dave Collins, Program Coordinator. Phone: 540-265-5166. Fax: 540-265-5145. In-person interview recommended (telephone interview accepted). Applications are accepted continuously.

GEORGIA 4-H ENVIRONMENTAL EDUCATION PROGRAM
350 Rock Eagle Road
Eatonton, Georgia 31024

General Information   Environmental education center that services school-age children from the Southeast during the school year, instructing students and teachers in science and outdoor education. Established in 1979. Number of employees: 50. Unit of University of Georgia, College of Agricultural and Environmental Science, Athens, Georgia. Athens, Georgia. Number of internship applications received each year: 10.

Internships Available   ▶ *1–4 environmental education instructors:* responsibilities include teaching environmental/outdoor education classes to primarily 4th-8th grade students, including ecology, living history, outdoor skills; night classes, and team-building; other duties (lab work, trail maintenance) as assigned. Candidates should have ability to work independently, oral communication skills, organizational skills, personal interest in the field, self-motivation, strong interpersonal skills, strong leadership ability, written communication skills. Duration is fall or spring seasons (usually 12-15 weeks). $180 per week. Open to college juniors, college seniors, recent college graduates.

Benefits   Formal training, free housing, free meals, health insurance, names of contacts, on-the-job training, possible full-time employment, willing to complete paperwork for educational credit, willing to provide letters of recommendation.

Contact   Write, call, fax, or e-mail Donna Stewart, Environmental Education Coordinator. Phone: 706-484-2862. Fax: 706-484-2888. E-mail: donnast@uga.edu. Applicants must submit a letter of interest, resume, three personal references. Application deadline: December 15 for spring.

GLACIER INSTITUTE
PO Box 7457
Kalispell, Montana 59904

General Information   Outdoor education organization dedicated to raising awareness for and appreciation of Glacier National Park and its surroundings. Established in 1983. Number of employees: 50. Number of internship applications received each year: 50.

Internships Available   ▶ *1 assistant program director:* responsibilities include assisting in management of the environmental education facility including overseeing food preparation and purchase and some teaching. Candidates should have ability to work independently, oral communication skills, organizational skills, self-motivation, strong interpersonal skills, strong leadership ability. Duration is 7–8 months. $600–$700 per month. Open to recent college graduates, graduate students, career changers. ▶ *2–3 interns:* responsibilities include providing administrative and field backup to instructors teaching college-level courses in and around Glacier National Park and teaching a basic outdoor education curriculum in a day camp setting. Candidates should have oral communication skills, organizational skills, personal interest in the field, self-motivation, strong interpersonal skills, strong leadership ability. Duration is 3–7 months. $200–$500 per month. Open to college juniors, college seniors, recent college graduates, graduate students, career changers. ▶ *5–6 interns/teachers:* responsibilities include teaching an environmental education curriculum to fifth and sixth graders in a residential setting, or working with adults on day-long or multiple day courses. Candidates should have ability to work with others, oral communication skills, personal interest in the field, self-motivation, strong leadership ability, written communication skills. Duration is 2-3 months in spring, fall, or summer. $200–$600 per month. Open to college juniors, college seniors, recent college graduates, graduate students, career changers. ▶ *2–3 teachers/naturalists:* responsibilities include teaching an environmental education curriculum to fifth and sixth graders in a residential setting; assisting in instruction and administrative duties for summer camps, elderhostels, writing workshops, and teacher training workshops. Candidates should have ability to work independently, ability to work with others, oral communication skills, personal interest in the field, self-motivation. Duration is 7–8 months. $500–$600 per month. Open

to college juniors, college seniors, recent college graduates, graduate students, career changers. International applications accepted.

Benefits   Formal training, free housing, free meals, names of contacts, on-the-job training, opportunity to attend seminars/workshops, possible full-time employment, willing to act as a professional reference, willing to complete paperwork for educational credit, willing to provide letters of recommendation.

Contact   Write, call, fax, e-mail, or through World Wide Web site R. J. Devitt, Program Director. Phone: 406-755-1211. Fax: 406-755-7154. E-mail: glacinst@digisys.net. In-person interview recommended (telephone interview accepted). Applicants must submit a formal organization application, letter of interest, resume, writing sample, three personal references. Application deadline: January 20 for spring and summer, March 1 for fall. World Wide Web: http://www.glacierinstitute.org.

GLEN HELEN OUTDOOR EDUCATION CENTER
1075 State Route 343
Yellow Springs, Ohio 45387

General Information   Residential environmental education center for elementary school-age children. Established in 1956. Number of employees: 10. Unit of Antioch University, Yellow Springs, Ohio. Number of internship applications received each year: 100.

Internships Available   ▶ *10 naturalist interns:* responsibilities include planning and leading small groups of elementary school-age students in residential environmental education programs; opportunity to care for a bird of prey at raptor center. Candidates should have ability to work independently, personal interest in the field, self-motivation, strong interpersonal skills, strong leadership ability. Duration is mid-August to mid-December or early January to early June. $250 per month. Open to college juniors, college seniors, recent college graduates, graduate students, career changers. International applications accepted.

Benefits   Formal training, free housing, free meals, names of contacts, on-the-job training, opportunity to attend seminars/workshops, tuition assistance, willing to complete paperwork for educational credit, willing to provide letters of recommendation, opportunity to purchase health insurance, 12 undergraduate credits or 10 graduate credits through Antioch University.

Contact   Write, call, fax, or e-mail Sue Feller, Assistant Director. Phone: 937-767-7648. Fax: 937-767-6655. E-mail: bwhaley@antioch-college.edu. In-person interview recommended (telephone interview accepted). Applicants must submit a formal organization application, academic transcripts, three personal references. Applications are accepted continuously. World Wide Web: http://www.glenhelen.org.

GORE RANGE NATURAL SCIENCE SCHOOL
PO Box 250
Red Cliff, Colorado 81649

General Information   Non-advocacy, nonprofit organization that raises environmental awareness and inspires stewardship through natural science learning experiences in the Rocky Mountain ecosystem. Established in 1998. Number of employees: 15. Number of internship applications received each year: 40.

Internships Available   ▶ *3–7 summer naturalists:* responsibilities include leading nature hikes and teaching natural history and ecology classes for groups of all ages. Candidates should have college courses in field, oral communication skills, personal interest in the field, self-motivation, strong leadership ability, written communication skills. Duration is June to September 1. $150 per week. Open to college seniors, recent college graduates. ▶ *2–4 winter naturalists:* responsibilities include leading interpretive snowshoe hikes and teaching natural history and winter ecology programs for groups of all ages. Candidates should have experience in the field, oral communication skills, research skills, self-motivation, strong interpersonal skills, strong leadership ability. Duration is December 1 to April 1. $150 per week. Open to recent college graduates. International applications accepted.

Benefits   Formal training, free housing, names of contacts, on-the-job training, opportunity to attend seminars/workshops, possible full-time employment, willing to act as a professional reference, willing to provide letters of recommendation.

Contact Call, e-mail, or through World Wide Web site Steven Wiseman, Interpretive Programs Coordinator. Phone: 970-827-9725. Fax: 970-827-9730. E-mail: wiseman@gorerange.org. In-person interview recommended (telephone interview accepted). Applicants must submit a formal organization application, letter of interest, resume, three personal references. Application deadline: March 1 for summer, September 1 for winter. World Wide Web: http://www.gorerange.org.

GREAT VALLEY NATURE CENTER
PO Box 82
Devault, Pennsylvania 19432

General Information Center that provides environmental education and recreational experience for school children, organized groups, and the general public. Established in 1974. Number of employees: 7. Number of internship applications received each year: 50.

Internships Available ▶ *1 animal caretaker/educator:* responsibilities include taking care of large animal collection used for educational programs. Candidates should have ability to work independently, ability to work with others, knowledge of field, self-motivation. Duration is flexible. $150–$200 per week. Open to high school seniors, recent high school graduates, college freshmen, college sophomores, college juniors, college seniors, recent college graduates, graduate students, career changers, individuals reentering the workforce. ▶ *1 marketing/public relations intern:* responsibilities include marketing all facets of Nature Center, including making contacts, brochures, television, newspapers, and radio promotion. Candidates should have ability to work independently, ability to work with others, editing skills, oral communication skills, self-motivation, writing skills. Duration is flexible. $150–$200 per week. Open to college juniors, college seniors, graduate students. ▶ *5–10 teachers:* responsibilities include teaching educational programs to school groups and the general public, proposing exhibits, and caring for the animals; possibility of leading adventure programs (canoeing, rock climbing). Candidates should have ability to work independently, ability to work with others, knowledge of field, oral communication skills, personal interest in the field. Duration is flexible. $150–$200 per week. Open to recent high school graduates, college freshmen, college sophomores, college juniors, college seniors, recent college graduates, graduate students, career changers, individuals reentering the workforce. International applications accepted.

Benefits On-the-job training, opportunity to attend seminars/workshops, possible full-time employment, willing to act as a professional reference, willing to complete paperwork for educational credit, willing to provide letters of recommendation.

Contact Write, call, fax, or e-mail Janet Zeis, Intern Coordinator. Phone: 610-935-9777. Fax: 610-935-0130. E-mail: gvncee@nni.com. In-person interview recommended (telephone interview accepted). Applicants must submit a formal organization application, letter of interest, resume. Applications are accepted continuously. World Wide Web: http://www.gvnc.org.

GREEN MOUNTAIN CLUB
4711 Waterbury-Stowe Road
Waterbury Center, Vermont 05677

General Information Organization that promotes hiking in the Green Mountains, maintains trails, and protects the Long Trail Corridor. Established in 1910. Number of employees: 12. Number of internship applications received each year: 100.

Internships Available ▶ *12–18 Long Trail patrol interns:* responsibilities include building hiking trails with simple hand tools, learning techniques for constructing with stone and logs, and working closely with a small crew. Candidates should have ability to work independently, personal interest in the field, self-motivation, strong interpersonal skills, willingness to live outdoors for a week at a time. Duration is flexible (opportunities available June through September). $200–$240 per week. Open to recent high school graduates, college freshmen, college sophomores, college juniors, college seniors, recent college graduates, career changers, individuals reentering the workforce, individuals 18 years and older. ▶ *15–20 backcountry caretakers:* responsibilities include educating public on mountain ecology and safety; maintaining wilderness campsites and hiking trails. Candidates should have ability to work independently, oral communication skills, personal interest in the field, self-motivation, strong interpersonal skills. Duration is flexible (opportunities available May through October). $200–$240 per week. Open to recent high school graduates, college freshmen, college sophomores, college juniors, college seniors, recent college graduates, graduate students, career changers, individuals reentering the workforce, individuals 18 years and older. ▶ *3 education programs interns:* responsibilities include developing displays, brochures, presentations, and slide shows on the social, ecological, and physical aspects of the Long Trail System and its management. Candidates should have computer skills, editing skills, experience in the field, office skills, organizational skills, self-motivation, writing skills. Duration is 1–6 months. Unpaid. Open to recent high school graduates, college freshmen, college sophomores, college juniors, college seniors, recent college graduates, graduate students, career changers, individuals reentering the workforce. ▶ *2 outdoor leadership interns:* responsibilities include helping run groups of volunteers who camp in the Vermont mountains; building primitive hiking trails. Candidates should have ability to work with others, personal interest in the field, self-motivation. Duration is July to September (full-time). Unpaid. Open to individuals 18 years and older. ▶ *5–10 recreation/resource management interns.* Candidates should have ability to work independently, personal interest in the field, self-motivation, strong interpersonal skills. Duration is flexible (year-round). Position available as unpaid or paid. Open to recent high school graduates, college freshmen, college sophomores, college juniors, college seniors, recent college graduates, graduate students, career changers, individuals reentering the workforce. International applications accepted.

Benefits Free housing, job counseling, names of contacts, on-the-job training, opportunity to attend seminars/workshops, possible full-time employment, travel reimbursement, tuition assistance, willing to act as a professional reference, willing to complete paperwork for educational credit, willing to provide letters of recommendation, office space, computer use, free board for outdoor leadership interns.

Contact Write, call, or e-mail Mr. Dave Hardy, Director of Field Programs. Phone: 802-244-7037. E-mail: dave@greenmountainclub.org. In-person interview recommended (telephone interview accepted). Applicants must submit a letter of interest, resume, two personal references. Applications are accepted continuously. World Wide Web: http://www.greenmountainclub.org.

HAWK MOUNTAIN SANCTUARY
1700 Hawk Mountain Road
Kempton, Pennsylvania 19529

General Information Privately supported wildlife preserve maintaining a 2500-acre Appalachian mountain reserve visited by 80,000 people per year, including 8,000 children in organized groups. Established in 1934. Number of employees: 14. Number of internship applications received each year: 60.

Internships Available ▶ *Conservation science interns:* responsibilities include assisting with census of flora and fauna populations, maintaining databases, analyzing and preparing technical and nontechnical reports, participating in some interpretative activities for visitors, conducting an independent research project including final report. Candidates should have ability to work with others, personal interest in the field. Duration is 4 months. $600 per month. Open to college juniors, college seniors, recent college graduates, graduate students. International applications accepted.

Benefits Formal training, free housing, job counseling, names of contacts, opportunity to attend seminars/workshops, willing to complete paperwork for educational credit, willing to provide letters of recommendation.

Contact Write, call, or e-mail Kyle McCarty, Intern Coordinator. Phone: 570-943-3411. Fax: 570-943-2284. E-mail: mccarty@hawkmtn.org. In-person interview recommended (telephone interview accepted). Applicants must submit a formal organization application, letter of interest, resume, self-addressed envelope. Application deadline: 2 months prior to start of internship. World Wide Web: http://www.hawkmountain.org.

HAWTHORNE VALLEY FARM VISITING STUDENTS PROGRAM
327CR 21C
Ghent, New York 12075

General Information Residential farm/environmental education program that follows the Waldorf educational philosophy; biodynamic dairy farm with commercial processing dairy, bakery, full health food store, gardens and CSA and K-12 Waldorf School. Established in 1972. Number of employees: 11. Branch of Hawthorne Valley Association, Inc., Ghent, New York. Number of internship applications received each year: 20.

Internships Available ▶ *3–4 interns:* responsibilities include planning and implementing outdoor programs for elementary school children including baking bread, pressing cider, gardening, and feeding animals. Candidates should have oral communication skills, organizational skills, personal interest in the field, self-motivation, strong interpersonal skills, strong leadership ability, maturity, experience working with children (helpful). Duration is 3–18 months. $200 per month stipend. Open to college freshmen, college sophomores, college juniors, college seniors, recent college graduates, graduate students, career changers, individuals reentering the workforce.

Benefits Formal training, free housing, free meals, opportunity to attend seminars/workshops, possible full-time employment, willing to act as a professional reference, willing to complete paperwork for educational credit, willing to provide letters of recommendation, opportunity to observe Waldorf school classes K-12 and participate in biodynamic agriculture and community cultural events.

Contact Write, call, fax, e-mail, or through World Wide Web site Nick Franceschelli, Director, 327 Route 21C, Ghent, New York 12075. Phone: 518-672-4790. Fax: 518-672-7608. E-mail: vsp@taconic.net. In-person interview recommended (telephone interview accepted). Applicants must submit a formal organization application, letter of interest, resume, 3 personal references showing work with children. Applications are accepted continuously.

HEAL THE BAY
3220 Nebraska Avenue
Santa Monica, California 90404

General Information Nonprofit environmental organization dedicated to making Santa Monica Bay and southern California coastal waters safe and healthy for people and marine life. Established in 1985. Number of employees: 22. Number of internship applications received each year: 70.

Internships Available ▶ *15–20 interns:* responsibilities include doing research and fieldwork in science, law and policy, community programs, development, education, and communications. Candidates should have oral communication skills, organizational skills, strong interpersonal skills, strong leadership ability, written communication skills, strong sense of responsibility. Duration is minimum of 8-10 hours per week. Unpaid. Open to college freshmen, college sophomores, college juniors, college seniors, recent college graduates, graduate students, law students, career changers, individuals reentering the workforce. International applications accepted.

Benefits Formal training, names of contacts, on-the-job training, opportunity to attend seminars/workshops, possible full-time employment, willing to act as a professional reference, willing to complete paperwork for educational credit, willing to provide letters of recommendation.

Contact Write, call, fax, or e-mail Tom Galassi, Volunteer Coordinator. Phone: 310-453-0395 Ext. 145. Fax: 310-453-7927. E-mail: programs@healthebay.org. In-person interview recommended (telephone interview accepted). Applicants must submit a letter of interest, resume, letter of recommendation. Applications are accepted continuously. World Wide Web: http://www.healthebay.org.

HRS CLEARWATER
112 Little Market Street
Poughkeepsie, New York 12471

General Information Organization that provides environment education and celebration of Hudson River estuary. Established in 1966. Number of employees: 23. Number of internship applications received each year: 100.

Internships Available ▶ *3–8 education interns:* responsibilities include helping teach students of many ages about Hudson River ecology and helping to sail and maintain the boat. Candidates should have oral communication skills, personal interest in the field, self-motivation, strong interpersonal skills, ability to live on a boat. Duration is 1–2 months. $50–$100 per week. Open to recent high school graduates, college sophomores, college juniors, college seniors, recent college graduates, graduate students, career changers, individuals reentering the workforce.

Benefits Free housing, free meals.

Contact Write, call, fax, or e-mail Sarah Slack, Educator. Phone: 845-454-7673. Fax: 845-454-7953. E-mail: slack@clearwater.org. In-person interview recommended (telephone interview accepted). Applicants must submit a letter of interest, resume, two personal references. Application deadline: February 28 for spring, April 15 for summer, July 30 for fall. World Wide Web: http://www.clearwater.org.

IDAHO RIVERS UNITED
PO Box 633
Boise, Idaho 83701

General Information Citizens' nonprofit river conservation organization working on wild and scenic rivers, water policy, and salmon restoration. Established in 1987. Number of employees: 5. Number of internship applications received each year: 10.

Internships Available ▶ *1–4 conservation assistants:* responsibilities include duties related to intern's interests and abilities, primarily helping staff with research, advocacy, and outreach on hydropower, wild and scenic rivers, salmon restoration, and public land watershed conservation. Candidates should have analytical skills, oral communication skills, personal interest in the field, research skills, strong interpersonal skills, written communication skills. Duration is 1 summer, spring or fall. Position available as unpaid or paid. Open to college sophomores, college juniors, college seniors, recent college graduates, graduate students, law students, career changers, individuals reentering the workforce.

Benefits Names of contacts, on-the-job training, opportunity to attend seminars/workshops, possible full-time employment, travel reimbursement, willing to act as a professional reference, willing to complete paperwork for educational credit, willing to provide letters of recommendation.

Contact Write, call, fax, or e-mail Jenna Borovansky, Conservation Director. Phone: 208-343-7481. Fax: 208-343-9376. E-mail: jenna@idahorivers.org. In-person interview recommended (telephone interview accepted). Applicants must submit a letter of interest, resume. Applications are accepted continuously. World Wide Web: http://www.idahorivers.org.

INSTITUTE FOR AGRICULTURE AND TRADE POLICY (IATP)
Environment and Agriculture Program, 2105 First Avenue South
Minneapolis, Minnesota 55404-2505

General Information Institute promoting resilient family farms, rural communities, and ecosystems around the world through research and education, science and technology, and advocacy.

Internships Available ▶ *Interns:* responsibilities include conducting research on environmental, agricultural, and trade policy issues; developing "how-to" literature on organizing forestry cooperatives; design and maintenance of Web pages; intern may work on any of a variety of ongoing projects. Duration is minimum of 3 months (full- or part-time). Unpaid.

Benefits Names of contacts, willing to act as a professional reference, willing to complete paperwork for educational credit, some positions may offer small stipends.

Contact Write, call, fax, e-mail, or through World Wide Web site Char Greenwald, Internship Coordinator. Phone: 612-870-3411. Fax: 612-870-4846. E-mail: cgreenwald@iatp.org. World Wide Web: http://www.iatp.org.

INTERNATIONAL CRANE FOUNDATION
PO Box 447
Baraboo, Wisconsin 53913

General Information Nonprofit foundation dedicated to the preservation of cranes and the wetlands on which they depend. Established in 1973. Number of employees: 30. Number of internship applications received each year: 200.

Internships Available ▶ *2 aviculture associates:* responsibilities include caring for and breeding cranes, completing one independent project under the supervision of a full-time employee, and supervising the volunteer chick parent program with emphasis on chick rearing. Candidates should have ability to work independently, ability to work with others, computer skills, knowledge of field, oral communication skills, personal interest in the field, research skills, self-motivation, writing skills. Duration is 6 months. $650 per month. ▶ *3 aviculture interns:* responsibilities include caring for and breeding cranes and completing an independent project under the supervision of a full-time employee. Candidates should have ability to work independently, ability to work with others, computer skills, knowledge of field, oral communication skills, personal interest in the field, self-motivation. Duration is 6 months. $350 per month. Open to college juniors, college seniors, recent college graduates. International applications accepted.

Benefits Free housing, names of contacts, on-the-job training, possible full-time employment, willing to act as a professional reference, willing to complete paperwork for educational credit, willing to provide letters of recommendation.

Contact Write or e-mail Kelly Maguire, Aviculturist. E-mail: kelly@savingcranes.org. No phone calls. Applicants must submit a letter of interest, resume, three letters of recommendation, telephone interview (if selected as a finalist). Applications are accepted continuously. World Wide Web: http://www.savingcranes.org.

JACKSON HOLE CONSERVATION ALLIANCE
PO Box 2728
Jackson, Wyoming 83001

General Information Local, nonprofit membership organization dedicated to protecting Jackson Hole's wildlife, scenery, and open spaces through land-use planning, citizen involvement, and natural resource conservation. Established in 1979. Number of employees: 11. Number of internship applications received each year: 75.

Internships Available ▶ *1–2 education and outreach intern:* responsibilities include working on an independent project of mutual interest to both the intern and the Alliance; helping with the day-to-day office administration of a nonprofit grassroots organization; assisting at meetings and special events; coordinating volunteers; maintaining community contacts; working on land-use planning and resource conservation issues; organizing fund-raising events, educational forums, and field trips. Candidates should have ability to work independently, computer skills, oral communication skills, organizational skills, strong interpersonal skills, written communication skills. Duration is 3–4 months. $650 per month. Open to college juniors, college seniors, recent college graduates, graduate students, law students, career changers, individuals reentering the workforce. International applications accepted.

Benefits Formal training, job counseling, names of contacts, on-the-job training, opportunity to attend seminars/workshops, possible full-time employment, travel reimbursement, willing to act as a professional reference, willing to complete paperwork for educational credit, willing to provide letters of recommendation.

Contact Write, call, fax, e-mail, or through World Wide Web site Kathy Berry, Outreach Director. Phone: 307-733-9417. Fax: 307-733-9008. E-mail: kathy@jhalliance.org. In-person interview recommended (telephone interview accepted). Applicants must submit a letter of interest, resume, two personal references. Application deadline: April 1 for summer, October 15 for winter. World Wide Web: http://www.jhalliance.com.

JACKSON HOLE LAND TRUST
PO Box 2897
Jackson, Wyoming 83001

General Information Trust organized to protect open space on private land in Jackson Hole through voluntary nongovernmental means. Established in 1981. Number of employees: 11. Number of internship applications received each year: 60.

Internships Available ▶ *4 interns:* responsibilities include office work, research, errands, field work, GIS, public relations. Candidates should have ability to work with others, oral communication skills, research skills, self-motivation, writing skills. Duration is June 1 through August 31; September 1 through November 30; December 1 through February 28; March 1 through May 31. $5.15 per hour. Open to college freshmen, college sophomores, college juniors, college seniors, recent college graduates, graduate students, law students, career changers, individuals reentering the workforce.

Benefits Names of contacts, on-the-job training, opportunity to attend seminars/workshops, possible full-time employment, travel reimbursement, willing to act as a professional reference, willing to complete paperwork for educational credit, willing to provide letters of recommendation.

Contact Write, call, fax, e-mail, or through World Wide Web site Susan J. Hall, Intern Coordinator. Phone: 307-733-4707. Fax: 307-733-4144. E-mail: susan@jhlandtrust.org. In-person interview recommended (telephone interview accepted). Applicants must submit a letter of interest, resume, writing sample. Application deadline: February 1 for spring, May 1 for summer, August 1 for fall, November 1 for winter. World Wide Web: http://www.jhlandtrust.org.

KAUA'I NATIONAL WILDLIFE REFUGE COMPLEX
PO Box 1128
Kilauea, Hawaii 96754

General Information Cmplex of refuges that promotes conservation of wildlife, wildlife habitat, and cultural resources through environmental education and interpretation. Established in 1985. Number of employees: 9. Unit of Hawaiian and Pacific Islands National Wildlife Refuge Complex, Honolulu, Hawaii. Number of internship applications received each year: 30.

Internships Available ▶ *1–2 biological interns:* responsibilities include assisting with waterbird and/or seabird population surveys, nest monitoring, banding, and habital management activities. Candidates should have ability to work independently, ability to work with others, computer skills, declared college major in field, experience in the field, research skills, ability to perform physically demanding chores, often in inclement weather. Duration is 3–5 months. $175 per week. ▶ *1–2 visitor services interns:* responsibilities include greeting, orienting, and educating visiting public and school groups; performing daily maintenance tasks, including opening and closing the refuge; and counting fee monies. Candidates should have ability to work independently, oral communication skills, plan to pursue career in field, research skills, strong interpersonal skills, writing skills. Duration is 3–5 months. $175 per week. Open to college juniors, college seniors, recent college graduates, graduate students, individuals reentering the workforce.

Benefits Formal training, free housing, job counseling, names of contacts, on-the-job training, travel reimbursement, willing to act as a professional reference, willing to complete paperwork for educational credit, willing to provide letters of recommendation.

Contact Write, call, fax, or e-mail Kathy Batha, Park Ranger. Phone: 808-828-1413. Fax: 808-828-6634. E-mail: kathy_batha@fws.gov. In-person interview recommended (telephone interview accepted). Applicants must submit a letter of interest, resume, two personal references. Application deadline: March 31 for summer, June 30 for fall, November 15 for winter.

LAND TRUST ALLIANCE
1331 H Street, NW, Suite 400
Washington, District of Columbia 20005-4734

General Information National organization of local and regional land conservation groups providing information, education,

Land Trust Alliance (continued)

technical assistance, public policy advocacy, and public education. Established in 1982. Number of employees: 45. Number of internship applications received each year: 50.

Internships Available ▶ *1–3 Land Trust Research interns:* responsibilities include providing a wide range of information services to LTA staff and other land conservation professionals. Candidates should have ability to work with others, oral communication skills, personal interest in the field, research skills, self-motivation, written communication skills. Duration is one semester or year. Unpaid. Open to college seniors, recent college graduates, graduate students, law students, career changers, individuals reentering the workforce. ▶ *1–2 public policy interns:* responsibilities include working with the public policy director on policy issues of concern to land conservationists. Candidates should have oral communication skills, written communication skills. Position available as unpaid or paid.

Benefits Job counseling, names of contacts, on-the-job training, opportunity to attend seminars/workshops, possible full-time employment, willing to act as a professional reference, willing to complete paperwork for educational credit, willing to provide letters of recommendation.

Contact Write, fax, e-mail, or through World Wide Web site Rob Aldrich, Director of Information Services. Fax: 202-638-4730. E-mail: raldrich@lta.org. No phone calls. In-person interview recommended (telephone interview accepted). Applicants must submit a letter of interest, resume, 3-4 personal references, writing sample (for advanced candidates). Applications are accepted continuously. World Wide Web: http://www.lta.org.

LEAGUE OF CONSERVATION VOTERS
1920 L Street, NW, Suite 800
Washington, District of Columbia 20036

General Information Bipartisan political arm of the environmental community. Established in 1970. Number of employees: 38. Number of internship applications received each year: 500.

Internships Available ▶ *1–5 Education Fund interns:* responsibilities include researching, assisting with training, coordinating trips, grassroots programming. Candidates should have ability to work independently, ability to work with others, computer skills, editing skills, oral communication skills, organizational skills, research skills, self-motivation, writing skills. Duration is 3–6 months. $1100 monthly stipend. Open to college freshmen, college sophomores, college juniors, college seniors, recent college graduates. ▶ *1–2 campaigns interns:* responsibilities include researching voting records and legislation and assisting with campaign-related activities. Candidates should have ability to work independently, ability to work with others, analytical skills, computer skills, organizational skills, personal interest in the field, research skills, self-motivation. Duration is 6 months. $1100 monthly stipend. ▶ *1–2 communications interns:* responsibilities include researching stories for news reporters, drafting press releases, and assisting with media relations and media plans. Candidates should have ability to work independently, ability to work with others, college courses in field, computer skills, editing skills, oral communication skills, personal interest in the field, plan to pursue career in field, research skills, self-motivation, writing skills. Duration is 3–6 months. $1100 monthly stipend. Open to college juniors, college seniors, recent college graduates. ▶ *1–2 development interns:* responsibilities include research, Web site assistance, event coordination assistance, administrative work. Candidates should have ability to work with others, computer skills, editing skills, office skills, oral communication skills, research skills, self-motivation. Duration is 3–6 months. $1100 monthly stipend. Open to college juniors, college seniors, recent college graduates. ▶ *1–5 policy and lobbying interns:* responsibilities include researching congressional voting records and environmental legislation and studying and reporting on congressional candidates. Candidates should have ability to work independently, ability to work with others, college courses in field, personal interest in the field, plan to pursue career in field, research skills, written communication skills. Duration is 6 months. $1100 monthly stipend. Open to recent college graduates. International applications accepted.

Benefits Opportunity to attend seminars/workshops, possible full-time employment, willing to act as a professional reference, willing to provide letters of recommendation.

Contact Write, call, or fax Intern Coordinator. Phone: 202-785-8683. Fax: 202-835-0491. Applicants must submit a letter of interest, resume, writing sample, three personal references, telephone or in-person interview. Application deadline: February 1 for spring, April 1 for summer, December 1 for winter. World Wide Web: http://www.lcv.org.

LINSLY OUTDOOR CENTER
2425 Route 168
Georgetown, Pennsylvania 15043

General Information Outdoor center that builds teamwork, self-esteem, and trust through a variety of programs that provide adventure, environmental education, and a unique outdoor experience for groups of all ages. Established in 1987. Number of employees: 8. Unit of Linsly School, Wheeling, West Virginia. Number of internship applications received each year: 50.

Internships Available ▶ *6 instructors/interns:* responsibilities include teaching and developing adventure, challenge, and environmental education programs for all age groups, supervising day and evening programs, and assisting in daily operations. Candidates should have ability to work independently, ability to work with others, organizational skills, self-motivation, strong leadership ability. Duration is 3-4 months in spring, summer, or fall. $180–$210 per week. Open to college freshmen, college sophomores, college juniors, college seniors, recent college graduates, graduate students, career changers.

Benefits Formal training, free housing, names of contacts, possible full-time employment, willing to act as a professional reference, willing to complete paperwork for educational credit, willing to provide letters of recommendation, some free meals.

Contact Write, call, e-mail, or through World Wide Web site Jeff Hasis, Director. Phone: 724-899-2100. E-mail: loc1@timesnet.net. In-person interview recommended (telephone interview accepted). Applicants must submit a formal organization application, letter of interest, resume, three personal references. Applications are accepted continuously. World Wide Web: http://www.linsly.org.

LONG LAKE CONSERVATION CENTER
28952 438th Lane
Palisade, Minnesota 56469

General Information Residential conservation/environmental education facility providing activities and learning units designed to heighten and enhance students' appreciation of and sensitivity toward the environment. Established in 1963. Number of employees: 18. Unit of Aitkin County Parks Commission, Aitkin, Minnesota. Number of internship applications received each year: 50.

Internships Available ▶ *4–8 naturalist interns:* responsibilities include teaching, leading adolescents in environmental education programs and activities, and supervising groups of students. Candidates should have ability to work independently, oral communication skills, organizational skills, personal interest in the field, strong interpersonal skills, written communication skills. Duration is 3–12 months. $100 per week. Open to recent high school graduates, college freshmen, college sophomores, college juniors, college seniors, recent college graduates, graduate students, career changers, individuals reentering the workforce. International applications accepted.

Benefits Free housing, free meals, job counseling, names of contacts, on-the-job training, willing to act as a professional reference, willing to complete paperwork for educational credit, willing to provide letters of recommendation.

Contact Write, call, fax, or e-mail Pam Carlson, Administration Coordinator, 28952 438th Lane. Phone: 800-450-5522. Fax: 218-768-2309. E-mail: llcc@mlecmn.net. Applicants must submit a formal organization application, resume, academic transcripts, letter of recommendation, essay describing philosophy on environmental education. Applications are accepted continuously. World Wide Web: http://www.llcc.org.

MANTI–LA SAL NATIONAL FOREST, MONTICELLO RANGER DISTRICT
PO Box 820
Monticello, Utah 84535

General Information Ranger district located on the Colorado Plateau near Moab, Utah, that manages numerous Anasazi ruins and the Dark Canyon Wilderness. Established in 1906. Number of employees: 15. Unit of Manti–La Sal National Forest, Price, Utah. Number of internship applications received each year: 15.

Internships Available ▶ *2–3 archaeological assistants:* responsibilities include assisting with office and fieldwork including surveying, identifying, and recording archaeological sites and ruins; projects and tasks undertaken can be negotiated depending on interests and skills. Candidates should have ability to work with others, college courses in field, computer skills, office skills, self-motivation, writing skills, driver's license. Duration is 2–4 months. Unpaid. Open to recent high school graduates, college freshmen, college sophomores, college juniors, college seniors, recent college graduates, graduate students, career changers, individuals reentering the workforce, seniors/retirees. ▶ *2–3 recreation site maintenance interns:* responsibilities include making public contacts, collecting and evaluating visitor use data, and assisting with recreation/trails/campground maintenance programs. Candidates should have ability to work independently, ability to work with others, oral communication skills, driver's license, physical fitness (lifting, hiking). Duration is 2–4 months. Position available as unpaid or paid. Open to individuals 18 years or older. ▶ *2 wilderness rangers:* responsibilities include making public contacts, providing information, and collecting and evaluating visitor use data. Candidates should have ability to work independently, ability to work with others, self-motivation, good physical condition (hiking), outdoor skills (map reading, backpacking, 4x4 driving). Unpaid. Open to college freshmen, college sophomores, college juniors, college seniors, recent college graduates, graduate students, career changers, individuals reentering the workforce, seniors/retirees. International applications accepted.

Benefits Free housing, job counseling, on-the-job training, travel reimbursement, willing to complete paperwork for educational credit, willing to provide letters of recommendation, possible subsistence reimbursement.

Contact Write, call, or e-mail Donald Irwin, District Archaeologist. Phone: 435-587-2041. E-mail: dcirwin@fs.fed.us. Applicants must submit informal application. Application deadline: April 30 for summer.

MERCK FAMILY FUND
303 Adams Street
Milton, Massachusetts 02186-4253

General Information Private grantmaking foundation committed to the preservation of the environment through protection of eastern ecosystems, sustainable economics, and a concern for socially and economically disadvantaged people; supports youth and organizes urban greening projects in Boston, Providence, and New York. Established in 1954. Number of employees: 3. Number of internship applications received each year: 70.

Internships Available ▶ *1 foundation intern:* responsibilities include conducting extensive written and phone outreach with nonprofit groups; assisting with office administration; and participating in research projects related to sustainable economics, eastern forest ecosystems, urban greening, and youth organizing. Candidates should have ability to work independently, office skills, organizational skills, personal interest in the field, research skills, self-motivation, strong interpersonal skills, written communication skills, familiarity with the Foundation's program areas, familiarity with Macintosh computers and Internet research. Duration is 3–8 months. $1400 per month for 4-day work week or $11.50 per hour for fewer hours. Open to college juniors, college seniors, recent college graduates, graduate students, law students, career changers.

Benefits Job counseling, names of contacts, on-the-job training, opportunity to attend seminars/workshops, willing to act as a professional reference, willing to complete paperwork for educational credit, willing to provide letters of recommendation.

Contact Write, fax, e-mail, or through World Wide Web site Betsy Caruso, Fund Administrator. Fax: 617-696-7262. E-mail: merck@merckff.org. No phone calls. In-person interview required. Applicants must submit a letter of interest, resume, writing sample, list of 3 references. Application deadline: March 1 for summer, June 1 for fall, October 1 for spring. World Wide Web: http://www.merckff.org.

MERCK FOREST AND FARMLAND CENTER
Box 86, Route 315
Rupert, Vermont 05768

General Information Center that teaches about land stewardship and sustainability by providing programs, access, and demonstrations on over 3130 acres of working farm and forest land. Established in 1950. Number of employees: 12. Number of internship applications received each year: 50.

Internships Available ▶ *1–5 resource assistants:* responsibilities include environmental education, farm chores, forest and trail management, Visitor Center duties, and seasonal work including maple sugaring, lambing, and organic gardening. Candidates should have ability to work independently, ability to work with others, personal interest in the field, self-motivation. Duration is 4–6 months. $75 per week. Open to recent high school graduates, college freshmen, college sophomores, college juniors, college seniors, recent college graduates, graduate students, law students, career changers, individuals reentering the workforce, must be 18 or older. International applications accepted.

Benefits Free housing, on-the-job training, opportunity to attend seminars/workshops, willing to complete paperwork for educational credit, willing to provide letters of recommendation, free organic farm products.

Contact Write, call, fax, or e-mail Ken Smith, Executive Director. Phone: 802-394-7836. Fax: 802-394-2519. E-mail: merck@vermontel.net. In-person interview recommended (telephone interview accepted). Applicants must submit a letter of interest, resume. Applications are accepted continuously. World Wide Web: http://www.merckforest.org.

MONTANA WILDLIFE FEDERATION
PO Box 1175
Helena, Montana 59624

General Information Statewide grassroots conservation organization working to protect and enhance wildlife, habitat, and wildlife values; lobbies state and federal agencies, the state legislature, and the congressional delegation to affect policy and management decisions. Established in 1935. Number of employees: 11. Affiliate of National Wildlife Federation, Missoula, Montana. Number of internship applications received each year: 10.

Internships Available ▶ *1–2 legislative interns:* responsibilities include assisting the MWF lobbyist during state legislative years; researching bills pertinent to MWF work; organizing grassroots support, in some cases testifying; organizing press coverage and developing voting record. Candidates should have ability to work with others, computer skills, oral communication skills, organizational skills, research skills, written communication skills. Duration is 5–6 months. $500–$1000 per month. ▶ *1–2 program coordinators:* responsibilities include maintaining grassroots activist database, managing phonetree operation, writing editorials and letters to the editor, managing the phone fund-raising program including personnel management, working with the Education Committee on special projects, and event planning. Candidates should have computer skills, office skills, oral communication skills, organizational skills, research skills, written communication skills. Duration is 5–6 months. $500–$1000 per month. Open to college freshmen, college sophomores, college juniors, college seniors, recent college graduates, graduate students, law students, career changers, individuals reentering the workforce. International applications accepted.

Benefits Formal training, job counseling, names of contacts, on-the-job training, opportunity to attend seminars/workshops, possible full-time employment, travel reimbursement, willing to act as a professional reference, willing to complete paperwork for educational credit, willing to provide letters of recommendation, assistance in locating housing.

Montana Wildlife Federation (continued)

Contact Write or e-mail Deb Lane, Comptroller. E-mail: dlane@ mtwf.org. In-person interview recommended (telephone interview accepted). Applicants must submit a letter of interest, resume, three personal references. Application deadline: April 15 for summer, June 15 for fall. World Wide Web: http://www.montanawildlife. com.

MOUNTAIN TRAIL OUTDOOR SCHOOL
PO Box 250
Hendersonville, North Carolina 28793-0250

General Information Outdoor school that educates and inspires students of all ages to protect the natural and human environment. Established in 1991. Number of employees: 15. Unit of Kanuga Conference Center, Hendersonville, North Carolina. Number of internship applications received each year: 50.
Internships Available ▶ *2–4 outdoor environmental education interns:* responsibilities include teaching natural history classes, environmental awareness, and adventure activities, and assisting with training and program development. Candidates should have knowledge of field, oral communication skills, organizational skills, personal interest in the field, strong interpersonal skills, strong leadership ability, experience and/or desire to work with youth. Duration is 4–5 months. $200 per week. Open to college freshmen, college sophomores, college juniors, college seniors, recent college graduates, graduate students. International applications accepted.
Benefits Formal training, free housing, free meals, job counseling, names of contacts, on-the-job training, opportunity to attend seminars/workshops, possible full-time employment, willing to act as a professional reference, willing to complete paperwork for educational credit, willing to provide letters of recommendation, limited health insurance.
Contact Write, call, e-mail, or through World Wide Web site Paul Bockoven, Director, Outdoor Education. Phone: 828-692-9136. Fax: 828-696-3589. E-mail: mtos@kanuga.org. Telephone interview required. Applicants must submit a formal organization application, letter of interest, resume, three letters of recommendation. Application deadline: January 1 for spring, June 1 for fall. World Wide Web: http://www.kanuga.org/mtos.htm.

NACUL CENTER FOR ECOLOGICAL ARCHITECTURE
592 Main Street
Amherst, Massachusetts 01002

General Information Center that researches and develops ecological architecture designs including sustainable communities, solar buildings, and other socially responsible projects. Established in 1970. Number of employees: 4. Number of internship applications received each year: 25.
Internships Available ▶ *3–6 architectural interns:* responsibilities include drafting, researching, model building, office work, photography, and design. Candidates should have ability to work with others, college courses in field, computer skills, office skills, personal interest in the field, research skills, self-motivation. Duration is 3–12 months. Unpaid. Open to college freshmen, college sophomores, college juniors, college seniors, recent college graduates, graduate students. International applications accepted.
Benefits Formal training, on-the-job training, opportunity to attend seminars/workshops, possible full-time employment, willing to act as a professional reference, willing to complete paperwork for educational credit, willing to provide letters of recommendation.
Contact Write, call, fax, e-mail, or through World Wide Web site Tullio Inglese, Director. Phone: 413-256-8025. Fax: 413-253-2451. E-mail: info@nacul.com. In-person interview recommended (telephone interview accepted). Applicants must submit a formal organization application, resume, portfolio. Applications are accepted continuously. World Wide Web: http://nacul.com.

NATIONAL AQUARIUM IN BALTIMORE
Pier 3, 501 East Pratt Street
Baltimore, Maryland 21202

General Information State-of-the-art aquatic institution dedicated to the conservation and preservation of the environment. Established in 1981. Number of employees: 350. Number of internship applications received each year: 240.
Internships Available ▶ *20–40 interns:* responsibilities include working in aquarist, community and government affairs, conservation, conservation education, development/membership, herpetology, horticulture, information systems, library, marine animal rescue program, marine mammal training, media relations, publications, retail sales, or water quality; working with staff on daily duties and special events. Candidates should have ability to work with others, college courses in field, knowledge of field, oral communication skills, personal interest in the field, plan to pursue career in field. Duration is 120 hours. Unpaid. Open to college freshmen, college sophomores, college juniors, college seniors, graduate students. International applications accepted.
Benefits Names of contacts, on-the-job training, opportunity to attend seminars/workshops, willing to act as a professional reference, willing to complete paperwork for educational credit, willing to provide letters of recommendation, uniform, 30% discount at gift shop and on food service.
Contact Write, call, fax, e-mail, or through World Wide Web site Kathy Siegfried, Internship Coordinator. Phone: 410-576-3888. Fax: 410-659-0116. E-mail: intern@aqua.org. Telephone interview required. Applicants must submit a formal organization application, letter of interest, academic transcripts, e-mail interview if necessary (international students). Application deadline: April 1 for summer and fall, November 1 for winter and spring. World Wide Web: http://www.aqua.org.

NATIONAL CAPITAL REGION–ROCK CREEK PARK
3545 Williamsburg Lane, NW
Washington, District of Columbia 20008

General Information Service devoted to the preservation of land, historic landscapes, and wildlife for enjoyment and education of the public. Established in 1890. Number of employees: 100. Unit of United States Department of Interior, Washington, District of Columbia. Number of internship applications received each year: 25.
Internships Available ▶ *1–2 assistant curators:* responsibilities include care and cataloging of park archives including flora and fauna, photos, and other materials relating to park history. Candidates should have ability to work independently, computer skills, editing skills, knowledge of field, office skills, oral communication skills, organizational skills, plan to pursue career in field, research skills, self-motivation, strong interpersonal skills, writing skills. Duration is flexible. Unpaid. ▶ *1 historian:* responsibilities include researching and cataloging information. Candidates should have ability to work independently, ability to work with others, computer skills, editing skills, oral communication skills, personal interest in the field, plan to pursue career in field, research skills, self-motivation, writing skills. Duration is flexible. Unpaid. ▶ *1–3 interpreters/educators:* responsibilities include interpreting historic sites and/or natural environment, preparing programs, researching, assisting with planetarium operation and animal care. Candidates should have ability to work independently, ability to work with others, computer skills, oral communication skills, personal interest in the field, research skills, self-motivation, strong leadership ability, writing skills. Duration is flexible. Unpaid. ▶ *1 librarian:* responsibilities include installation of library cataloging system, replacing books, and deleting out-of-date volumes. Candidates should have ability to work independently, ability to work with others, computer skills, editing skills, office skills, personal interest in the field, self-motivation, writing skills. Duration is flexible. Unpaid. ▶ *2–4 maintenance workers:* responsibilities include maintaining grounds and facilities. Candidates should have ability to work independently. Duration is flexible. Unpaid. ▶ *1 resource management specialist:* responsibilities include maintaining and monitoring natural resources for public use. Candidates should have ability to work independently, ability to work with others, computer skills, personal interest in the field, plan to pursue career in field,

research skills, self-motivation. Duration is flexible. Unpaid. ▶ *1–3 visitor information specialists:* responsibilities include answering telephones, typing, filing, taking reservations, bookstore sales, updating bulletin board, and preparing monthly activity guide. Candidates should have ability to work with others, computer skills, oral communication skills, personal interest in the field, plan to pursue career in field, research skills, self-motivation, writing skills. Duration is flexible. Unpaid. Open to high school students, recent high school graduates, college freshmen, college sophomores, college juniors, college seniors, recent college graduates, graduate students, law students, career changers, individuals reentering the workforce.

Benefits Formal training, job counseling, names of contacts, on-the-job training, opportunity to attend seminars/workshops, possible full-time employment, willing to act as a professional reference, willing to complete paperwork for educational credit, willing to provide letters of recommendation, small stipend occasionally available, limited housing available.

Contact Write, call, fax, e-mail, or through World Wide Web site Mr. Dwight Madison, Supervisory Park Ranger. Phone: 202-895-6222. Fax: 202-895-6230. E-mail: dwight_madison@nps.gov. In-person interview recommended (telephone interview accepted). Applicants must submit a letter of interest, resume, three personal references, three letters of recommendation. Applications are accepted continuously. World Wide Web: http://www.nps.gov/rocr.

NATIONAL PARKS CONSERVATION ASSOCIATION
1300 19th Street, NW, Suite 300
Washington, District of Columbia 20036

General Information National environmental organization dedicated to protecting and enhancing the national park system. Established in 1919. Number of employees: 100. Number of internship applications received each year: 75.

Internships Available ▶ *1–3 interns:* responsibilities include researching issues pertaining to natural and cultural resource policies and providing research support for staff; attending and collecting information from congressional hearings. Candidates should have knowledge of field, oral communication skills, personal interest in the field, research skills, self-motivation, strong interpersonal skills, written communication skills. Duration is 10-14 weeks (35 hours per week). $8.25–$11.43 per hour. Open to college seniors, recent college graduates, graduate students, law students, career changers. International applications accepted.

Benefits Names of contacts, opportunity to attend seminars/workshops, possible full-time employment, willing to act as a professional reference, willing to complete paperwork for educational credit, willing to provide letters of recommendation.

Contact Write, call, fax, or e-mail Jessica Butts, Intern Coordinator, 1300 19th Street, NW Suite 300, Washington, District of Columbia 20036. Phone: 202-454-3382. Fax: 202-659-8183. E-mail: interns@npca.org. In-person interview recommended (telephone interview accepted). Applicants must submit a formal organization application, resume, academic transcripts, writing sample, three personal references, cover letter. Application deadline: May 1 for summer, August 1 for fall, December 1 for winter/spring. World Wide Web: http://www.npca.org.

NATIONAL WILDLIFE FEDERATION
11100 Wildlife Center Drive
Reston, Virginia 20190

General Information Nation's largest nonprofit, member-supported conservation education organization. Established in 1936. Number of employees: 200. Number of internship applications received each year: 500.

Internships Available ▶ *8–15 interns:* responsibilities include researching environmental policy issues; attending congressional hearings, briefings, and seminars; lobbying on environmental legislation; and routine office work; areas covered include endangered habitat, water quality, wetlands, land stewardship, international development, and sustainable communities; positions in the department of education may have additional responsibilities plus working with programs such as school yard habitat, backyard habitat, and campus ecology. Candidates should have ability to work with others, college degree in related field,

experience in the field, oral communication skills, writing skills, interest in environmental issues, volunteer experience valued. Duration is 20–48 weeks. $320–$410 per week. Open to college juniors, college seniors, recent college graduates, graduate students, law students, career changers. International applications accepted.

Benefits Formal training, health insurance, names of contacts, on-the-job training, opportunity to attend seminars/workshops, possible full-time employment, travel reimbursement, willing to act as a professional reference, willing to complete paperwork for educational credit, willing to provide letters of recommendation.

Contact Write, fax, e-mail, or through World Wide Web site Aline Mota Brito, Internship Coordinator. Fax: 703-438-6468. E-mail: brito@nwf.org. No phone calls. In-person interview recommended (telephone interview accepted). Applicants must submit a letter of interest, resume, writing sample, 3-5 academic or professional references. Application deadline: March 15. World Wide Web: http://www.nwf.org/nwf.

NATIONAL WILDLIFE FEDERATION CAMPUS ECOLOGY PROGRAM
11100 Wildlife Center Drive
Reston, Virginia 20190-5362

General Information Program that supports practical conservation projects on college and university campuses by assisting with project implementation, providing training, and documenting lessons learned nationally and beyond. Established in 1936. Number of employees: 250. Number of internship applications received each year: 60.

Internships Available ▶ *10–20 campus ecology fellowships:* responsibilities include identifying environmentally sustainable projects/programs on fellow's campus; determining the best action to achieve identified goals; and taking steps to implement this action plan. Candidates should have ability to work independently, computer skills, oral communication skills, organizational skills, personal interest in the field, self-motivation, strong interpersonal skills, strong leadership ability, written communication skills. Duration is one academic year. Stipends up to $1200 per semester. Open to college freshmen, college sophomores, college juniors, college seniors, recent college graduates, graduate students, law students. ▶ *5–10 program interns:* responsibilities include working in backyard wildlife habitat, NatureLink, schoolyard habitats, and as habitat stewards; assisting staff; offering presentations; sending information to, and responding to e-mail/phone/mail requests from general public. Candidates should have ability to work independently, oral communication skills, organizational skills, personal interest in the field, strong interpersonal skills, written communication skills. Duration is 6 months (full-time). $275 per week. Open to recent college graduates, graduate students. ▶ *2–4 special projects interns:* responsibilities include assistance with various projects, possibly including resource development, research, database development, and Web maintenance. Candidates should have ability to work independently, office skills, personal interest in the field, research skills, writing skills. Duration is flexible. Unpaid. Open to high school students, recent high school graduates, college freshmen, college sophomores, college juniors, college seniors, recent college graduates, graduate students, law students, career changers, individuals reentering the workforce. International applications accepted.

Benefits Job counseling, on-the-job training, opportunity to attend seminars/workshops, possible full-time employment, willing to act as a professional reference, willing to complete paperwork for educational credit, willing to provide letters of recommendation.

Contact Write, call, e-mail, or through World Wide Web site Kathy Cacciola, Coordinator. Phone: 703-438-6318. Fax: 703-438-6468. E-mail: cacciola@nwf.org. Telephone interview required. Applicants must submit a formal organization application, resume, two personal references, three letters of recommendation, grant proposal. Application deadline: see Web site for deadline. World Wide Web: http://www.nwf.org/campus ecology.

NEW ENGLAND SMALL FARM INSTITUTE/ NORTHEAST WORKERS ON ORGANIC FARMS
PO Box 608, 275 Jackson Street
Belchertown, Massachusetts 01007

General Information   Small farm demonstration and training center that manages public farmland and advocates for sustainable agriculture in New England. Established in 1978. Number of employees: 10. Number of internship applications received each year: 200.

Internships Available   ▶ *80–100 farm apprentices/Northeast Workers on Organic Farms (NEWOOF):* responsibilities include farm work; specific responsibilities vary at each farm. Candidates should have ability to work independently, ability to work with others, personal interest in the field, self-motivation, ability to do hard physical work and work with flexible schedule. Duration is 1 growing season, or other as negotiated. Position available as unpaid or paid. Open to recent high school graduates, college freshmen, college sophomores, college juniors, college seniors, recent college graduates, graduate students, career changers, individuals reentering the workforce.

Benefits   Names of contacts, on-the-job training, other benefits negotiated with individual farms including housing, meals, and stipends.

Contact   Write, call, fax, e-mail, or through World Wide Web site Roz Cook, Program Coordinator. Phone: 413-323-4531. Fax: 413-323-9594. E-mail: newoof@smallfarm.org. Applicants must submit a formal organization application, additional application materials may be required depending on position. Applications are accepted continuously. Fees: $10. World Wide Web: http://www.smallfarm.org.

NEW ENGLAND WILD FLOWER SOCIETY
180 Hemenway Road
Framingham, Massachusetts 01701-2699

General Information   Private, nonprofit plant conservation organization dedicated to the conservation of temperate North American plants; offers programs in education, horticulture, research, habitat preservation, and conservation advocacy. Established in 1900. Number of employees: 30. Number of internship applications received each year: 30.

Internships Available   ▶ *2 education interns:* responsibilities include assisting with children's and family programs, leading tours, curriculum development, exhibit preparation, special projects, and community outreach. Candidates should have ability to work independently, ability to work with others, experience in the field, oral communication skills, personal interest in the field, U.S. citizenship. Duration is mid-May to August 31. Position available as unpaid or at $8–$10 per hour. Open to college juniors, college seniors, recent college graduates. ▶ *1 native plant horticulture intern:* responsibilities include general maintenance duties in a garden setting, rigorous physical labor, native plant identification, and standard horticultural practices. Candidates should have ability to work independently, ability to work with others, experience in the field, personal interest in the field, self-motivation, U.S. citizenship. Duration is 6 months (March 19-August 31). $230 per week. Open to college juniors, college seniors, recent college graduates, graduate students, career changers, individuals reentering the workforce. ▶ *2 plant conservation fellows:* responsibilities include gaining experience in plant conservation program activities on- and off-site, including both administrative and field work activities such as natural areas management, assisting with regional rare plant monitoring program, and record-keeping. Candidates should have ability to work independently, ability to work with others, experience in the field, personal interest in the field, self-motivation, U.S. citizenship. Duration is 6 months (March to August). $230 per week. Open to college juniors, college seniors, recent college graduates, graduate students, career changers, individuals reentering the workforce. ▶ *1 propagation and nursery management intern:* responsibilities include native plant identification, native plant propagation, seed collection, record-keeping, production and sales, and public information duties. Candidates should have ability to work independently, ability to work with others, knowledge of field, personal interest in the field,

self-motivation, U.S. citizenship. Duration is 6 months (March-August). $230 per week. Open to college juniors, college seniors, recent college graduates, graduate students, career changers, individuals reentering the workforce.

Benefits   Formal training, free housing, names of contacts, opportunity to attend seminars/workshops, willing to complete paperwork for educational credit, willing to provide letters of recommendation, worker's compensation.

Contact   Write, call, fax, e-mail, or through World Wide Web site Tom Smarr, Horticulturist. Phone: 508-877-7630 Ext. 3404. Fax: 508-877-3658. E-mail: tsmarr@newfs.org. In-person interview recommended (telephone interview accepted). Applicants must submit a formal organization application, resume, two letters of recommendation, application can be downloaded from Web site. Application deadline: February 10 for spring/summer interns. World Wide Web: http://www.newfs.org/~newfs/.

NORTH CAROLINA BOTANICAL GARDEN
Campus Box 3375, Totten Center, UNC-CH
Chapel Hill, North Carolina 27599-3375

General Information   Regional center for research, conservation, and interpretation of plants, particularly those native to the southeastern U.S., as well as horticultural plants with traditional uses or those of special botanical interest. Established in 1960. Number of employees: 25. Unit of The University of North Carolina at Chapel Hill, Chapel Hill, North Carolina. Number of internship applications received each year: 35.

Internships Available   ▶ *1 garden collections and native plant propagation intern:* responsibilities include horticultural maintenance, development, and interpretation of display collections focusing on native plants in Garden Commons, Plant Families Garden, wildflower borders and nature trail system; seed collecting, cleaning, and processing; native plant propagation; and working with volunteers. Candidates should have ability to work independently, computer skills, personal interest in the field, self-motivation, strong interpersonal skills. Duration is 3–12 months. $8.21 per hour. ▶ *1 herb garden and education outreach intern:* responsibilities include horticultural maintenance, development and interpretation of the Mercer Reeves Hubbard Herb Garden; planning and implementing horticultural therapy programs for persons with special needs; assisting in environmental education outreach programs in public schools; and working with volunteers. Candidates should have ability to work independently, computer skills, personal interest in the field, self-motivation, strong interpersonal skills. Duration is 3–12 months. $8.21 per hour. ▶ *1 native habitat gardens and plant records intern:* responsibilities include horticultural maintenance; development and interpretation of Native Habitat Gardens that highlight native southeast U.S. flora; implementing weekly "What's In Bloom?" interpretive display; assisting with plant label and records database; assisting with overall Garden interpretation strategy; working with volunteers. Candidates should have ability to work independently, computer skills, knowledge of field, personal interest in the field, self-motivation, strong interpersonal skills. Duration is 3–12 months. $8.21 per hour. ▶ *1 public education and tour guide intern:* responsibilities include assessment of existing programs and development of additional on-site education programs for pre- and school-age children; planning and preparing pre- and post-visit materials; and working with volunteer tour guide training, scheduling, and program presentations. Candidates should have ability to work independently, computer skills, personal interest in the field, self-motivation, strong interpersonal skills. Duration is 3–12 months. $8.21 per hour. Open to recent high school graduates, college freshmen, college sophomores, college juniors, college seniors, recent college graduates, graduate students, career changers, individuals reentering the workforce. International applications accepted.

Benefits   Job counseling, names of contacts, on-the-job training, opportunity to attend seminars/workshops, possible full-time employment, willing to act as a professional reference, willing to complete paperwork for educational credit, willing to provide letters of recommendation, flexible start and end dates.

Contact   Write, call, fax, or e-mail Mr. James L. Ward. Phone: 919-962-0522. Fax: 919-962-3531. E-mail: wardjl@email.unc.edu. In-person interview recommended (telephone interview accepted). Applicants must submit a formal organization application, letter of interest, resume, three personal references. Applications are accepted continuously. World Wide Web: http://www.unc.edu/depts/ncbg.

NORTH CASCADES INSTITUTE
810 State Route 20
Sedro Woolley, Washington 98284-9394

General Information Environmental education organization dedicated to increasing understanding and appreciation of the natural, historical, and cultural landscapes of the Pacific Northwest through field seminars, school programs, watershed education, summer camps, and other programs. Established in 1986. Number of employees: 13. Number of internship applications received each year: 40.
Internships Available ▶ *6–8 environmental education interns:* responsibilities include teaching in environmental education programs for youth. Candidates should have ability to work independently, oral communication skills, personal interest in the field, self-motivation, strong interpersonal skills, written communication skills, current first aid and CPR certification. Duration is 7–10 weeks. Unpaid. Open to college juniors, college seniors, recent college graduates, graduate students. International applications accepted.
Benefits Formal training, free housing, free meals, job counseling, names of contacts, on-the-job training, opportunity to attend seminars/workshops, willing to act as a professional reference, willing to complete paperwork for educational credit, willing to provide letters of recommendation, materials and college credit.
Contact Write, call, fax, e-mail, or through World Wide Web site Christina Dyson, Office Assistant. Phone: 360-856-5700 Ext. 209. Fax: 360-856-1934. E-mail: nci@ncascades.org. In-person interview recommended (telephone interview accepted). Applicants must submit a formal organization application, letter of interest, resume, three personal references. Applications are accepted continuously. World Wide Web: http://www.ncascades.org.

NORTHWEST COALITION FOR ALTERNATIVES TO PESTICIDES
PO Box 1393
Eugene, Oregon 97440

General Information Nonprofit 5-state grassroots membership organization that works to protect people and the environment by advancing healthy solutions to pest problems. Established in 1977. Number of employees: 9. Number of internship applications received each year: 15.
Internships Available ▶ *1–2 program assistants:* responsibilities include assisting with NCAP's program work including researching and writing articles for NCAP's quarterly "Journal of Pesticide Reform" and other research to benefit specific program; each intern has a special project, depending on skills and interests. Candidates should have ability to work independently, computer skills, office skills, oral communication skills, organizational skills, personal interest in the field, research skills, self-motivation, strong interpersonal skills, writing skills. Duration is flexible. Unpaid. Open to high school students, recent high school graduates, college freshmen, college sophomores, college juniors, college seniors, recent college graduates, graduate students, law students, career changers, individuals reentering the workforce. International applications accepted.
Benefits Names of contacts, on-the-job training, willing to act as a professional reference, willing to complete paperwork for educational credit, willing to provide letters of recommendation.
Contact Write, call, or e-mail Megan Kemple, Public Education Coordinator. Phone: 541-344-5044 Ext. 20. Fax: 541-344-6923. E-mail: info@pesticide.org. In-person interview recommended (telephone interview accepted). Applicants must submit a letter of interest. Applications are accepted continuously. World Wide Web: http://www.pesticide.org.

NUCLEAR INFORMATION AND RESOURCE SERVICE
1424 16th Street, NW, Suite 404
Washington, District of Columbia 20036

General Information Organization that assists citizens and communities concerned with the dangers of nuclear power and radioactive waste by promoting safe energy and energy alternatives. Established in 1978. Number of employees: 7. Number of internship applications received each year: 75.
Internships Available ▶ *1 communications intern:* responsibilities include helping run and improve Web site, improving and operating e-mail and Internet capabilities, designing and building databases, updating press contacts, and writing information sheets. Candidates should have computer skills, personal interest in the field, strong interpersonal skills. Duration is flexible. Unpaid. ▶ *1 radiation and health hazard intern.* Candidates should have ability to work with others, oral communication skills, research skills, writing skills. Duration is flexible. Unpaid. ▶ *Radioactive waste interns.* Candidates should have ability to work independently, experience in the field, oral communication skills, personal interest in the field, strong interpersonal skills, written communication skills. Duration is flexible. Unpaid. ▶ *1 reactor watchdog intern.* Candidates should have ability to work independently, ability to work with others, oral communication skills, personal interest in the field. Duration is flexible. Unpaid. Open to high school students, recent high school graduates, college freshmen, college sophomores, college juniors, college seniors, recent college graduates, graduate students, law students, career changers, individuals reentering the workforce.
Benefits Names of contacts, opportunity to attend seminars/workshops, possible full-time employment, willing to complete paperwork for educational credit, willing to provide letters of recommendation.
Contact Write, fax, or e-mail Don Keesing, Administrative Coordinator. Fax: 202-462-2183. E-mail: nirsnet@nirs.org. No phone calls. Applicants must submit a resume, writing sample. Applications are accepted continuously. World Wide Web: http://www.nirs.org.

THE OJAI FOUNDATION
9739 Ojai-Santa Paula Road
Ojai, California 93023

General Information Nonprofit organization whose purpose is to offer a center for education, renewal, and the honoring of life's many passages. Established in 1974. Number of employees: 8. Number of internship applications received each year: 10.
Internships Available ▶ *1–2 center management interns:* responsibilities include acting as administrative assistant to the leadership council, attending meetings and events both on and off the land, and special project upon completion of program. Candidates should have experience in the field, oral communication skills, organizational skills, self-motivation, strong leadership ability, written communication skills. Duration is 6–7 months. Unpaid. Open to recent high school graduates, college freshmen, college sophomores, college juniors, college seniors, recent college graduates, graduate students, career changers, individuals reentering the workforce, those interested in business management or starting their own center. ▶ *1–2 land stewardship interns:* responsibilities include participation in meetings and staff councils, hands-on activities and projects on the land, research assignments, and special project upon completion of program. Candidates should have ability to work independently, ability to work with others, experience in the field, oral communication skills, personal interest in the field, self-motivation. Duration is 6–7 months. Unpaid. Open to recent high school graduates, college freshmen, college sophomores, college juniors, college seniors, recent college graduates, graduate students, career changers, individuals reentering the workforce, those interested in alternative gardening, landscaping, land management, and community practices. International applications accepted.

The Ojai Foundation (continued)

Benefits Free housing, on-the-job training, opportunity to attend seminars/workshops, willing to act as a professional reference, willing to provide letters of recommendation, living in community close to the earth.

Contact Write, fax, or e-mail Marlow Hotchkiss, Director. Phone: 805-646-8343 Ext. 104. Fax: 805-646-2456. E-mail: ojaifdn@jetlink. net. Applicants must submit a letter of interest, resume, two personal references, in-person interview (for finalists). Applications are accepted continuously. World Wide Web: http:// ojaifoundation.org.

OREGON ENVIRONMENTAL COUNCIL
520 SW 6th Avenue, Suite 940
Portland, Oregon 97204-1535

General Information Nonprofit environmental organization. Established in 1968. Number of employees: 11. Number of internship applications received each year: 50.

Internships Available ► *1–2 environmental policy research assistants:* responsibilities include researching environmental policy issues, writing reports and summaries, and assisting OEC program staff. Candidates should have ability to work independently, computer skills, personal interest in the field, research skills, writing skills. Duration is 2–3 months. Unpaid. Open to college freshmen, college sophomores, college juniors, college seniors, recent college graduates, graduate students, law students. International applications accepted.

Benefits Willing to act as a professional reference, willing to complete paperwork for educational credit, willing to provide letters of recommendation.

Contact Write, fax, e-mail, or through World Wide Web site Clare Naber, Volunteer/Internship Coordinator. Fax: 503-222-1405. E-mail: clare@orcouncil.org. No phone calls. Telephone interview required. Applicants must submit a letter of interest, resume, personal reference. Applications are accepted continuously. World Wide Web: http://www.orcouncil.org.

OREGON MUSEUM OF SCIENCE AND INDUSTRY SCIENCE CAMPS
508 Southwest 13th Street
Redmond, Oregon 97756

General Information Organization that teaches natural history, outdoor skills, and environmental science to students of all ages in a residential camp setting in the desert, the Cascade Mountains, and on the Pacific coast. Established in 1951. Number of employees: 50. Division of Oregon Museum of Science and Industry, Portland, Oregon. Number of internship applications received each year: 30.

Internships Available ► *2 administration interns:* responsibilities include assisting with office administration, data presentation, and other duties as necessary to help facilitate the smooth operation of an educational facility. Candidates should have ability to work independently, computer skills, knowledge of field, office skills, research skills, writing skills. Duration is 3 months. $15–$20 per day. ► *8 naturalist interns:* responsibilities include reviewing available curriculum and becoming proficient in teaching those subjects, developing and organizing program materials and displays, aiding in logistics for field programs, and being a positive role model for students. Candidates should have knowledge of field, organizational skills, personal interest in the field, self-motivation, strong interpersonal skills, strong leadership ability. Duration is 3 months. $15–$20 per day. Open to college juniors, college seniors, recent college graduates, graduate students. International applications accepted.

Benefits Free housing, free meals, on-the-job training, opportunity to attend seminars/workshops, possible full-time employment, willing to act as a professional reference, willing to complete paperwork for educational credit, willing to provide letters of recommendation.

Contact Write, call, fax, or e-mail Kayla Chitwood, Programming Coordinator. Phone: 541-504-2538. Fax: 541-504-2538. E-mail: sciencecamps@omsi.edu. In-person interview recommended (telephone interview accepted). Applicants must submit a formal organization application, letter of interest, resume, three personal references, letter of recommendation. Applications are accepted continuously. World Wide Web: http://www.omsi.com.

PACIFIC ENVIRONMENT AND RESOURCES CENTER
1440 Broadway, Suite 306
Oakland, California 94612

General Information Nonprofit organization that employs grassroots activism and environmental advocacy and is committed to global environmental improvement projects around the Pacific Rim. Established in 1987. Number of employees: 11. Number of internship applications received each year: 20.

Internships Available ► *1 administrative intern:* responsibilities include letter writing, typing, organizing files and information, answering phones, filling requests for information, assisting with mailings and databases, and helping with other miscellaneous tasks. Candidates should have ability to work independently, ability to work with others, computer skills, office skills, oral communication skills, organizational skills, research skills, writing skills. Duration is 3 months. Unpaid. Open to college freshmen, college sophomores, college juniors, college seniors, recent college graduates, graduate students, career changers, individuals reentering the workforce. ► *1 communications intern:* responsibilities include writing/assisting with press releases, publications, Web site design, updating and monitoring on-line news sources, and assisting with publication of on-line newsletter. Candidates should have computer skills, editing skills, office skills, oral communication skills, research skills, written communication skills. Duration is 1–9 months. Unpaid. Open to college freshmen, college sophomores, college juniors, college seniors, recent college graduates, graduate students, career changers. ► *1 development/fund-raising intern:* responsibilities include duties based on organization's requirements and intern's interest. Candidates should have ability to work independently, analytical skills, computer skills, editing skills, oral communication skills, research skills, self-motivation, written communication skills. Duration is 1–9 months. Unpaid. Open to college freshmen, college sophomores, college juniors, college seniors, recent college graduates, graduate students, career changers. ► *1–5 independent project interns:* responsibilities include working with a project director on an issue that relates to a PERC project. Candidates should have ability to work independently, analytical skills, oral communication skills, research skills, self-motivation, writing skills. Duration is 4 months. Unpaid. Open to college freshmen, college sophomores, college juniors, college seniors, recent college graduates, graduate students, career changers, individuals reentering the workforce. ► *1–5 project assistants:* responsibilities include researching and summarizing information on a particular subject of interest to the intern and relevant to a Pacific environment project. Candidates should have ability to work independently, oral communication skills, organizational skills, research skills, self-motivation, written communication skills. Duration is 3–9 months. Unpaid. Open to college freshmen, college sophomores, college juniors, college seniors, recent college graduates, graduate students, career changers, individuals reentering the workforce. International applications accepted.

Benefits Job counseling, names of contacts, possible full-time employment, willing to act as a professional reference, willing to complete paperwork for educational credit, willing to provide letters of recommendation, opportunity to work with experts, structured supervision, opportunity to learn about global environmental issues.

Contact Write, fax, e-mail, or through World Wide Web site John Carroll, Administrative Assistant. Fax: 510-251-8838. E-mail: info@ pacificenvironment.org. No phone calls. In-person interview recommended (telephone interview accepted). Applicants must submit a formal organization application, letter of interest, resume. Applications are accepted continuously. World Wide Web: http:// www.pacificenvironment.org.

PEACE VALLEY NATURE CENTER
170 Chapman Road
Doylestown, Pennsylvania 18901

General Information Center that promotes environmental awareness through a variety of educational experiences; serves as a wildlife sanctuary where citizens of southeast Pennsylvania can enjoy natural beauty. Established in 1975. Number of employees: 4. Unit of Bucks County Department of Parks and Recreation, Langhorne, Pennsylvania. Number of internship applications received each year: 25.

Internships Available ▶ *2 naturalist interns:* responsibilities include observing and teaching environmental education programs to children of all ages, completing and presenting an approved project, writing a newsletter article on a natural history topic, filling out weekly diary, assisting in all aspects of nature center operations. Candidates should have ability to work independently, knowledge of field, oral communication skills, personal interest in the field, plan to pursue career in field, self-motivation, strong interpersonal skills, strong leadership ability, writing skills. Duration is 10–12 weeks. $5.15 per hour. Open to college freshmen, college sophomores, college juniors, college seniors, recent college graduates, graduate students, career changers.

Benefits Formal training, free housing, names of contacts, on-the-job training, opportunity to attend seminars/workshops, willing to act as a professional reference, willing to complete paperwork for educational credit, willing to provide letters of recommendation.

Contact Write, call, fax, or e-mail Gail Hill, Environmental Education Director. Phone: 215-345-7860. Fax: 215-345-4529. E-mail: ghill@co.bucks.pa.us. In-person interview recommended (telephone interview accepted). Applicants must submit a formal organization application, letter of interest, resume, two personal references. Application deadline: February 2 for spring, April 21 for summer, July 28 for fall.

PEOPLE FOR THE ETHICAL TREATMENT OF ANIMALS (PETA)
501 Front Street
Norfolk, Virginia 23510

General Information International animal rights organization whose mission is to oppose and expose all forms of animal abuse and exploitation. Established in 1980. Number of employees: 99. Number of internship applications received each year: 50.

Internships Available ▶ *13 interns:* responsibilities include helping with grassroots outreach activities including demonstrations and tabling events, office work, preparing mailings, creating props, working on special projects, and on-line research. Candidates should have ability to work with others, oral communication skills, personal interest in the field. Duration is flexible. $50 per week. Open to individuals at least 18 years of age. International applications accepted.

Benefits Free housing, free meals, on-the-job training, opportunity to attend seminars/workshops, possible full-time employment, travel reimbursement, willing to act as a professional reference, willing to complete paperwork for educational credit.

Contact Write, call, fax, e-mail, or through World Wide Web site Vicki Carey, Human Resources Director, 501 Front Street, Norfolk, Virginia 23510. Phone: 757-622-7382 Ext. 1416. Fax: 757-628-0789. E-mail: vickic@fsap.org. Applicants must submit a formal organization application, letter of interest, resume, three letters of recommendation, 2-page essay discussing interest in animal rights and expectations of internship, driving record (if available). Applications are accepted continuously. World Wide Web: http://www.peta.org.

PILOT MOUNTAIN STATE PARK
1792 Pilot Knob Park Road
Pinnacle, North Carolina 27043-9201

General Information State park that preserves North Carolina's natural heritage and provides recreation opportunities for park visitors. Established in 1968. Number of employees: 7. Unit of North Carolina Department of ENR, Division of Parks and Recreation, Raleigh, North Carolina. Number of internship applications received each year: 4.

Internships Available ▶ *2–5 park interns:* responsibilities include participating in park operation, environmental education programs, resource management, trail work, visitor contact, and outdoor projects. Candidates should have ability to work independently, ability to work with others, oral communication skills, personal interest in the field, self-motivation, written communication skills. Duration is arranged with academic institution. Position available as unpaid or paid. Open to recent high school graduates, college freshmen, college sophomores, college juniors, college seniors, recent college graduates, graduate students, law students, career changers, individuals reentering the workforce, must be age 18 or older. International applications accepted.

Benefits Names of contacts, on-the-job training, willing to act as a professional reference, willing to complete paperwork for educational credit, willing to provide letters of recommendation, recreational opportunities (hiking, canoeing, family camp ground, and rock climbing).

Contact Write, call, fax, or e-mail Janet Pearson, Volunteer Manager. Phone: 336-325-2355. Fax: 336-325-2751. E-mail: pilotmtn@surry.net. In-person interview recommended (telephone interview accepted). Applicants must submit a letter of interest, three personal references. Application deadline: March 1 for summer (paid position); continous for other positions. World Wide Web: http://ils.unc.edu/parkproject/pimo.html.

PLANET DRUM FOUNDATION
PO Box 31251
San Francisco, California 94131

General Information Nonprofit ecological education organization promoting the ideas of bioregionalism and urban sustainability through publications, workshops, lectures, performances, and hands-on environmental work. Established in 1973. Number of employees: 5.

Internships Available ▶ *Ecuador Restoration Project assistants:* responsibilities include assisting in various areas of urban sustainability in Ecuador's coastal cities with projects including re-vegetation of hillsides, water supply and purity, ecology education, alternative energy and more. Duration is year-round. Unpaid. ▶ *Administrative assistants:* responsibilities include running Planet Drum's office, acting as assistant to the director, arranging appointments, conducting research, sorting archival materials, organizing the library, responding to telephone requests, and leading bulk mail parties. Duration is 3 months minimum (20 hours per week). Unpaid. ▶ *Art and design assistants:* responsibilities include helping with the design and layout for flyers, notices to members, project photo albums, displays for tabling, and Web page; taking photos. Candidates should have sense of humor. Duration is 3 months minimum (20 hours per week). Unpaid. ▶ *Editorial assistants:* responsibilities include helping with the Planet Drum Pulse newsletter and other publications. Candidates should have ability to work independently, ability to work with others, editing skills, writing skills. Duration is 3 months minimum (20 hours per week). Unpaid. ▶ *Event coordinator assistants:* responsibilities include helping to plan benefit events or the Shasta Bioregional Gathering (a long-weekend event); includes obtaining donations, promotion to media and attendees, and scheduling workshops, speakers, and entertainment. Duration is 3 months minimum (20 hours per week). Unpaid. International applications accepted.

Benefits Names of contacts, on-the-job training, opportunity to attend seminars/workshops, willing to complete paperwork for educational credit, willing to provide letters of recommedation, access to library, small stipend for local travel, opportunity to complete a project.

International Internships Available in Bahia de Caraquez, Ecuador.

Contact Write, call, fax, or e-mail Judy Goldhaft, Managing Director. Phone: 415-285-6556. Fax: 415-285-6563. E-mail: planetdrum@igc.org. In-person interview recommended (telephone interview accepted). Applicants must submit a formal organization application, resume. Applications are accepted continuously. World Wide Web: http://www.planetdrum.org.

POCONO ENVIRONMENTAL EDUCATION CENTER
RR 2, Box 1010
Dingmans Ferry, Pennsylvania 18328

General Information Center that advances environmental awareness, knowledge, and skills through education. Established in 1968. Number of employees: 35. Number of internship applications received each year: 300.

Internships Available ▶ *1 development intern:* responsibilities include assisting director of development with management of membership and volunteer services, coordinating special events, and researching funding sources. Candidates should have ability to work independently, ability to work with others, analytical skills, computer skills, knowledge of field, office skills, organizational skills, personal interest in the field, research skills, self-motivation, written communication skills. Duration is 6–10 months. Position available as unpaid or at $500–$800 per month. Open to college juniors, college seniors, recent college graduates, graduate students, career changers, individuals reentering the workforce. ▶ *6–10 environmental education instructors:* responsibilities include teaching environment/outdoor education to people of all ages, developing programs and activities, performing daily operations and procedures, and assisting with support services. Candidates should have ability to work independently, ability to work with others, college courses in field, computer skills, knowledge of field, office skills, oral communication skills, organizational skills, personal interest in the field, self-motivation. Duration is 6–10 months. Position available as unpaid or at $700–$800 per month. Open to college seniors, recent college graduates, graduate students, career changers. ▶ *2–4 environmental education interns:* responsibilities include teaching environment/outdoor education/recreation opportunities to all visitors and guests, assisting in all daily operations and support services. Candidates should have ability to work with others, knowledge of field, office skills, oral communication skills, personal interest in the field, self-motivation. Duration is 3–6 months. $500–$700 per month. Open to college sophomores, college juniors, college seniors, recent college graduates, graduate students, career changers, individuals reentering the workforce. ▶ *1–2 program planning interns:* responsibilities include scheduling group's program/activities, coordinating cabins, facilities, staff, and food-service arrangements; designing weekly schedules, and teaching environment/outdoor education to people of all ages. Candidates should have ability to work independently, ability to work with others, analytical skills, computer skills, knowledge of field, office skills, oral communication skills, organizational skills, personal interest in the field, self-motivation, written communication skills. Duration is 6–10 months. Position available as unpaid or at $500–$800 per month. Open to college juniors, college seniors, recent college graduates, graduate students, career changers. ▶ *1 public relations intern:* responsibilities include writing press releases, designing layout for promotional materials, maintaining a darkroom, and assisting with programs and activities. Candidates should have ability to work independently, computer skills, editing skills, knowledge of field, office skills, oral communication skills, organizational skills, personal interest in the field, self-motivation, strong interpersonal skills, writing skills. Duration is 6–10 months. Position available as unpaid or at $500–$800 per month. Open to college juniors, college seniors, recent college graduates, graduate students, career changers. International applications accepted.

Benefits Formal training, free housing, free meals, job counseling, names of contacts, on-the-job training, opportunity to attend seminars/workshops, tuition assistance, willing to act as a professional reference, willing to complete paperwork for educational credit, willing to provide letters of recommendation.

Contact Write, call, fax, e-mail, or through World Wide Web site Ms. Florence Mauro, Director of Education. Phone: 570-828-2319. Fax: 570-828-9695. E-mail: fmauro@peec.org. In-person interview recommended (telephone interview accepted). Applicants must submit a letter of interest, resume, two personal references, 2 writing samples (for public relations interns). Application deadline: March 1 for summer, June 1 for fall, October 1 for winter/spring. World Wide Web: http://www.peec.org.

POK-O-MACCREADY OUTDOOR EDUCATION CENTER
112 Reber Road North
Willsboro, New York 12996

General Information Outdoor education center in the Adirondacks that allows children in grades 5–12 to participate in activities including pond study, pioneer living, rock climbing, cross-country skiing, winter camping, environmental study, and overnight hikes. Established in 1973. Number of employees: 9. Division of Pok-O-MacCready Camps, Inc., Willsboro, New York. Number of internship applications received each year: 12.

Internships Available ▶ *2–4 outdoor educator interns:* responsibilities include teaching and facilitating groups of middle-school children in different aspects of outdoor education, work projects as necessary. Candidates should have ability to work independently, oral communication skills, personal interest in the field, self-motivation, strong interpersonal skills, experience in outdoor activities; working with children a plus. Duration is 2–4 months. $100–$150 per month. Open to recent high school graduates, college freshmen, college sophomores, college juniors, college seniors, recent college graduates. International applications accepted.

Benefits Formal training, free housing, free meals, possible full-time employment, willing to act as a professional reference, willing to complete paperwork for educational credit, willing to provide letters of recommendation, worker's compensation.

Contact Write, call, fax, or e-mail Ben Moss, Director of Outdoor Education. Phone: 518-963-7967. Fax: 518-963-4165. E-mail: pmoec02@aol.com. Telephone interview required. Applicants must submit a letter of interest, resume. Applications are accepted continuously. World Wide Web: http://www.pokomac.com.

POPULATION CONNECTION
1400 16th Street, NW, Suite 320
Washington, District of Columbia 20036

General Information National nonprofit membership organization that works to mobilize broad public support for a sustainable balance of the earth's people, environment, and resources. Established in 1968. Number of employees: 30. Number of internship applications received each year: 70.

Internships Available ▶ *1 field and outreach fellow:* responsibilities include grassroots organizing, coordinating exhibits, and public speaking. Candidates should have ability to work independently, computer skills, editing skills, oral communication skills, organizational skills, personal interest in the field, self-motivation, strong interpersonal skills. Duration is January 1 to June 15 or July 1 to December 15. $750 bi-weekly. Open to recent college graduates, graduate students. ▶ *1–2 government relations fellows:* responsibilities include monitoring legislation and influencing public policy. Candidates should have ability to work independently, ability to work with others, analytical skills, computer skills, oral communication skills, personal interest in the field, self-motivation, written communication skills. Duration is January to June and July to December. $750 bi-weekly. Open to recent college graduates, graduate students. ▶ *1–2 media/communications fellows:* responsibilities include researching, writing, and marketing publications and general media work. Candidates should have computer skills, editing skills, office skills, personal interest in the field, research skills, writing skills. Duration is January to June and July to December. $750 bi-weekly. Open to recent college graduates, graduate students. ▶ *1–2 population education fellows:* responsibilities include developing and marketing teaching materials and teacher training. Candidates should have ability to work independently, computer skills, editing skills, organizational skills, personal interest in the field, research skills, written communication skills. Duration is January to June and July to December. $750 bi-weekly. Open to recent college graduates, graduate students. ▶ *1–2 research interns:* responsibilities include researching and writing reports. Candidates should have ability to work independently, analytical skills, computer skills, editing skills, research skills, writing skills. Duration is flexible. Unpaid. Open to recent college graduates. International applications accepted.

Benefits Job counseling, on-the-job training, possible full-time employment, willing to act as a professional reference, willing to complete paperwork for educational credit, willing to provide letters of recommendation, health insurance for paid fellowships.
Contact Write, call, fax, e-mail, or through World Wide Web site Jay Keller, Internship/Fellowship Coordinator, 1400 15th Street, NW, Suite 320, Washington, District of Columbia 20036. Phone: 202-323-2200. Fax: 202-332-2302. E-mail: jay@populationconnection. org. Applicants must submit a letter of interest, resume, three reference names, titles, and phone numbers, two writing samples (totaling 3-5 pages). Application deadline: April 15 for July-December paid fellowships, October 1 for January-June paid fellowships; continuous for all unpaid positions. World Wide Web: http://www.populationconnection.org.

POWDER RIVER BASIN RESOURCE COUNCIL
23 North Scott, Suite 19
Sheridan, Wyoming 82801

General Information Nonprofit membership conservation/agriculture organization promoting stewardship of Wyoming's natural resources and quality of life through organizing, public education, and lobbying. Established in 1973. Number of employees: 6. Affiliate of Western Organization Resource Council, Billings, Montana. Number of internship applications received each year: 50.
Internships Available ▶ *1–2 project assistants:* responsibilities include assisting with research; compiling information; drafting materials connected with resource issues such as water development, energy development, waste management, and sustainable agriculture; evaluating conservation policies; and increasing citizen involvement in decision making. Candidates should have ability to work independently, ability to work with others, research skills, self-motivation, writing skills. Duration is 3 months. $200–$250 per month. Open to college freshmen, college sophomores, college juniors, college seniors, recent college graduates, graduate students, law students, career changers, individuals reentering the workforce. International applications accepted.
Benefits Formal training, housing at a cost, meals at a cost, names of contacts, willing to complete paperwork for educational credit, willing to provide letters of recommendation, staff car for travel.
Contact Write, call, fax, e-mail, or through World Wide Web site Kevin Lind, Director. Phone: 307-672-5809. Fax: 307-672-5800. E-mail: klind@powderriverbasin.org. In-person interview recommended (telephone interview accepted). Applicants must submit a letter of interest, resume, three personal references, one-page writing sample. Applications are accepted continuously. World Wide Web: http://www.powderriverbasin.org.

RANDALL DAVEY AUDUBON CENTER
PO Box 9314
Santa Fe, New Mexico 87504

General Information Environmental education center advocating environmental issues that affect the southwest United States. Established in 1983. Number of employees: 7. Unit of National Audubon Society, New York, New York. Number of internship applications received each year: 60.
Internships Available ▶ *1–3 environmental education interns:* responsibilities include assisting in planning and teaching environmental education classes for students, staffing the visitor center, leading interpretive walks, assisting with the maintenance of building and grounds, and assisting with newsletter writing and production. Candidates should have ability to work independently, oral communication skills, personal interest in the field, strong interpersonal skills. Duration is 3 months. $125 per week. Open to college freshmen, college sophomores, college juniors, college seniors, recent college graduates, graduate students.
Benefits Formal training, free housing, job counseling, names of contacts, on-the-job training, opportunity to attend seminars/workshops, willing to act as a professional reference, willing to complete paperwork for educational credit, willing to provide letters of recommendation, use of staff car.
Contact Write, call, fax, or e-mail Jessica Lagalo, Education Manager. Phone: 505-983-4609. Fax: 505-983-2355. E-mail: jlagalo@audubon.org. Telephone interview required. Applicants must

submit a letter of interest, resume, 2-3 personal references or letters of recommendation. Application deadline: February 15 for summer, June 24 for fall, November 15 for spring. World Wide Web: http://www.audubon.org.

THE RAPTOR CENTER AT THE VERMONT INSTITUTE OF NATURAL SCIENCE
27023 Church Hill Road
Woodstock, Vermont 05091-9720

General Information Living museum of birds of prey and rehabilitation facility for all birds. Established in 1987. Number of employees: 4. Number of internship applications received each year: 100.
Internships Available ▶ *1–2 wildlife care interns:* responsibilities include assisting with medical care of rehabilitation birds and providing captive management and husbandry for over 70 birds and reptiles used for education. Candidates should have ability to work independently, knowledge of field, oral communication skills, organizational skills, personal interest in the field, self-motivation, strong interpersonal skills, must be 18 years or older, have valid driver's license, able to climb stairs and lift up to 40 pounds, work in all weather conditions. Duration is 3-8 months (40 hours per week). Unpaid. Open to college freshmen, college sophomores, college juniors, college seniors, recent college graduates, graduate students, law students, career changers, individuals reentering the workforce. International applications accepted.
Benefits Formal training, free housing, names of contacts, on-the-job training, opportunity to attend seminars/workshops, willing to act as a professional reference, willing to complete paperwork for educational credit, willing to provide letters of recommendation, food allowance ($400 per month).
Contact Write, call, fax, or e-mail Mike Pratt, Director, Wildlife Services. Phone: 802-457-2779 Ext. 125. Fax: 802-457-1053. E-mail: mpratt@vinsweb.org. Telephone interview required. Applicants must submit a letter of interest, resume, two letters of recommendation. Application deadline: March 15 for summer (May-August), July 1 for fall (September-December), December 15 for winter and spring. World Wide Web: http://www.vinsweb.org.

RHODODENDRON SPECIES BOTANICAL GARDEN
PO Box 3798
Federal Way, Washington 98063

General Information Botanical garden dedicated to the conservation, research, acquisition, evaluation, cultivation, public display, and distribution of rhododendron species; provides education relating to the genus; and serves as a unique resource to scientific, horticultural, and educational communities worldwide. Established in 1964. Number of employees: 8. Number of internship applications received each year: 40.
Internships Available ▶ *1 garden maintenance propagation intern:* responsibilities include assisting with caring for a 22-acre garden, including proper pruning and planting techniques, landscape design, weed control, garden renovation, irrigation, and plant identification; assisting with propagation including grafting, cuttings, seed sowing, and hand pollination; assisting with greenhouse operation, transplanting, and inventory control. Candidates should have ability to work independently, computer skills, oral communication skills, organizational skills, personal interest in the field, plan to pursue career in field, self-motivation, strong interpersonal skills, written communication skills. Duration is 6 months. $8 per hour. Open to college freshmen, college sophomores, college juniors, college seniors, recent college graduates, graduate students, career changers. ▶ *1 retail management intern:* responsibilities include managing and operating plant sales pavilion including purchasing, pricing and displaying plant material, maintaining and stocking facility, creating labels and signage, supervising volunteer assistants, and record-keeping; assisting with mail order plant sales and data entry. Candidates should have ability to work independently, college courses in field, computer skills, knowledge of field, oral communication skills, organizational skills, personal interest in the field, self-motivation, strong interpersonal skills, written communication skills. Duration is 2

Rhododendron Species Botanical Garden (continued)
months (March to May). $8 per hour. Open to college sophomores, college juniors, college seniors, recent college graduates, graduate students.
Benefits Formal training, job counseling, on-the-job training, willing to act as a professional reference, willing to complete paperwork for educational credit, willing to provide letters of recommendation.
Contact Write, call, fax, e-mail, or through World Wide Web site Tracy Osborn, Internship Coordinator. Phone: 253-838-4646. Fax: 253-838-4686. E-mail: rsf@rhodygarden.org. In-person interview recommended (telephone interview accepted). Applicants must submit a letter of interest, resume, three letters of recommendation. Application deadline: March 1 for spring, June 1 for summer, September 2 for fall. World Wide Web: http://www.rhodygarden.org.

RIVERBEND ENVIRONMENTAL EDUCATION CENTER
1950 Spring Mill Road
Gladwyne, Pennsylvania 19035

General Information Environmental education center emphasizing awareness, appreciation, and understanding of the environment. Established in 1974. Number of employees: 6. Number of internship applications received each year: 150.
Internships Available ▶ *3 Riverbend Exploration Camp environmental education interns:* responsibilities include attending one-week training session, assisting staff with summer day camp, greeting and speaking with public visitors, leading nature walks, assisting with upkeep and cleaning of facilities. Candidates should have ability to work independently, personal interest in the field, self-motivation, strong interpersonal skills, knowledge of basic environmental concepts, experience with children. Duration is 13 weeks (June to August). Salary commensurate with qualifications. Open to college sophomores, college juniors, college seniors, recent college graduates, graduate students, career changers. ▶ *3 development interns:* responsibilities include assisting staff with all administrative facets of fund-raising including membership, special events, foundation and corporate research, grantwriting, and reporting. Candidates should have ability to work with others, computer skills, office skills, organizational skills, research skills, writing skills. Unpaid. Open to college sophomores, college juniors, college seniors, recent college graduates, graduate students, career changers. ▶ *7–10 environmental educators:* responsibilities include planning and leading week-long day camp programs for children ages 4-14. Candidates should have ability to work with others, oral communication skills, personal interest in the field, self-motivation, knowledge of environmental concepts, experience educating children. Duration is June to August. Salary commensurate with qualifications. Open to college seniors, recent college graduates, graduate students, career changers, individuals reentering the workforce, individuals with experience equivalent to college degree (acceptable). ▶ *3–50 habitat interns:* responsibilities include assisting habitat manager with the upkeep, planning, and planting of 30-acre wildlife habitat, including being outside and working with equipment of various sizes. Candidates should have ability to work independently, ability to work with others, oral communication skills, personal interest in the field, self-motivation. Duration is variable. Unpaid. Open to high school students, recent high school graduates, college freshmen, college sophomores, college juniors, college seniors, recent college graduates, graduate students, career changers, individuals reentering the workforce. ▶ *3 seasonal environmental education interns:* responsibilities include teaching classes in schools, organized groups, and public; maintaining teaching areas; planning and preparing classes and public programs from assigned environmental concepts; assisting in developing and revising classes and programs; maintaining small animal cages; assisting with promotion of programs via press releases, newsletter, and articles; assisting with development and implementation of large public events; and assisting with office duties. Candidates should have ability to work independently, personal interest in the field, plan to pursue career in field, self-motivation, strong interpersonal skills, knowledge of basic environmental concepts. Duration is January-June, June-

September, or September-December (40 hours per week). Salary commensurate with qualifications. Open to college sophomores, college juniors, college seniors, recent college graduates, career changers, individuals reentering the workforce. ▶ *3–10 summer junior interns:* responsibilities include assisting with day-to-day operations of summer day camp with environmental themes, including working with groups of children. Candidates should have ability to work with others, oral communication skills, personal interest in the field, self-motivation. Duration is June to August (dates flexible). Unpaid. Open to high school seniors, recent high school graduates, college freshmen, college sophomores, college juniors, college seniors, recent college graduates, graduate students, law students, career changers, individuals reentering the workforce. International applications accepted.
Benefits Formal training, job counseling, names of contacts, on-the-job training, opportunity to attend seminars/workshops, possible full-time employment, willing to act as a professional reference, willing to complete paperwork for educational credit, willing to provide letters of recommendation, introduction to administration of other environmental centers, opportunity to visit other environmental centers in the region, possibility of free housing.
Contact Write, call, fax, e-mail, or through World Wide Web site Stacy Carr, Director of Children's Programs. Phone: 610-527-5234. Fax: 610-527-1161. E-mail: scarr@riverbendeec.org. In-person interview recommended (telephone interview accepted). Applicants must submit a letter of interest, resume, three personal references. Applications are accepted continuously. World Wide Web: http://www.gladwyne.com/riverbend/.

SAN FRANCISCO BAY NATIONAL WILDLIFE REFUGE COMPLEX
PO Box 524
Newark, California 94560

General Information Refuge whose mission is to protect, enhance, and maximize natural resources and educate the public on the value of those resources. Established in 1972. Number of employees: 25. Number of internship applications received each year: 30.
Internships Available ▶ *8 environmental education assistants:* responsibilities include conducting workshops for teachers and helping environmental education specialists conduct field trips for elementary school classes. Candidates should have ability to work independently, knowledge of field, oral communication skills, organizational skills, self-motivation, strong interpersonal skills. Duration is 3–4 months. $100 per week. Open to college juniors, college seniors, recent college graduates, graduate students, career changers, individuals reentering the workforce. ▶ *4 public use assistants:* responsibilities include helping the public use staff with daily operations such as managing the visitor center, office work, some interpretation for visitors, volunteer recruitment, and training. Candidates should have ability to work independently, analytical skills, computer skills, office skills, oral communication skills, organizational skills, personal interest in the field, research skills, self-motivation, strong interpersonal skills, writing skills. Duration is 3–5 months. $100 per week. Open to college juniors, college seniors, recent college graduates, graduate students, career changers. ▶ *6–8 resource management/biology interns:* responsibilities include monitoring and surveying endangered species, habitat restoration work, data entry, and report writing. Candidates should have ability to work independently, ability to work with others, computer skills, declared college major in field, experience in the field, personal interest in the field, research skills. Duration is 3–5 months. $100 per week. Open to college juniors, college seniors, recent college graduates, graduate students, career changers. International applications accepted.
Benefits Free housing, on-the-job training, travel reimbursement, willing to complete paperwork for educational credit, willing to provide letters of recommendation, accident insurance.
Contact Write, call, fax, e-mail, or through World Wide Web site John McClure, Volunteer Coordinator. Phone: 510-792-0222. Fax: 510-792-5828. E-mail: john_mcclure@fws.gov. Applicants must submit formal application through the Student Conservation

Association, 603-543-1700. Applications are accepted continuously. World Wide Web: http://www.r1.fws.gov/sfbnwr/sfbnwr.html.

SARETT NATURE CENTER
2300 Benton Center Road
Benton Harbor, Michigan 49022

General Information Nature center designed to provide environmental education for the surrounding school districts, as well as an outlet for natural history education of the general public. Established in 1970. Number of employees: 8. Unit of Michigan Audubon Society, Lansing, Michigan. Number of internship applications received each year: 20.

Internships Available ▶ *2 naturalist interns:* responsibilities include teaching diverse natural history programs to school groups, primarily preschool through sixth grade; leading interpretive nature walks; and teaching cross-country skiing. Candidates should have ability to work independently, ability to work with others, college courses in field, knowledge of field, oral communication skills. Duration is 3–5 months. $6 per hour. Open to college sophomores, college juniors, college seniors, recent college graduates.

Benefits Free housing, job counseling, names of contacts, on-the-job training, opportunity to attend seminars/workshops, willing to complete paperwork for educational credit, willing to provide letters of recommendation.

Contact Write, call, fax, or e-mail Dianne Braybrook, Chief Naturalist. Phone: 269-927-4832. Fax: 269-927-2742. E-mail: sarett@sarett.com. Applicants must submit a letter of interest, resume, three personal references. Applications are accepted continuously. World Wide Web: http://www.sarett.com.

SAVE AMERICA'S FORESTS
4 Library Court, SE
Washington, District of Columbia 20003

General Information Environmental and forest protection education and lobbying organization. Established in 1989. Number of employees: 6.

Internships Available ▶ *2–4 interns:* responsibilities include research, writing, office tasks, lobbying, organizing for legislation. Candidates should have analytical skills, knowledge of field, office skills, oral communication skills, strong interpersonal skills, writing skills. Duration is 1 semester. Position available as unpaid or paid. Open to college sophomores, college juniors, college seniors, recent college graduates, graduate students, law students, career changers.

Benefits On-the-job training, possible full-time employment, willing to act as a professional reference, willing to complete paperwork for educational credit, willing to provide letters of recommendation, possibility of stipend.

Contact Write, call, e-mail, or through World Wide Web site Internship Coordinator, 4 Library Court, SE, Washington, District of Columbia 20003. Phone: 202-544-9219. E-mail: intern@saveamericasforests.org. Telephone interview required. Applicants must submit a letter of interest, resume, two writing samples, 2 personal references or letters of recommendation. Applications are accepted continuously. World Wide Web: http://www.saveamericasforests.org.

SAVE THE SOUND, INC.
20 Marshall Street
Norwalk, Connecticut 06854

General Information Environmental, nonprofit organization dedicated to the protection, restoration, and appreciation of Long Island Sound and its watershed through programs in education, research, and advocacy. Established in 1972. Number of employees: 8. Number of internship applications received each year: 60.

Internships Available ▶ *1 habitat restoration field intern:* responsibilities include conducting field surveys (from land and water) at selected sites around the Long Island Sound to identify stormwater and sewer outfalls and other sources of pollution and habitat degradation, and collecting data to assess the impact of those sources on nearby coastal habitats. Candidates should have computer skills, BS degree in marine science, biology, ecology, environmental science or a related field (preferred, but upper-level undergraduates with appropriate coursework/work experience will be considered), must have valid driver's license, transportation, and valid Connecticut or New York Safe Boating Certificate. Duration is 10 weeks from May to September (20 to 30 hours per week). Unpaid. ▶ *1 marketing assistants:* responsibilities include assisting in the development of a three-year public relations plan. Candidates should have ability to work with others, computer skills, office skills, oral communication skills, writing skills. Duration is flexible. Unpaid. Open to college freshmen, college sophomores, college juniors, college seniors, recent college graduates, graduate students, career changers. ▶ *1 membership database assistant:* responsibilities include inputting membership data into the database and maintaining current membership information. Candidates should have ability to work independently, computer skills, office skills, organizational skills, self-motivation. Duration is flexible. Unpaid. Open to high school seniors, recent high school graduates, college freshmen, college sophomores, college juniors, college seniors, career changers. ▶ *1–2 water quality research interns:* responsibilities include identifying algae from water samples in lab and analyzing pigment content and nutrients of samples to track algae blooms. Candidates should have ability to work independently, analytical skills, knowledge of field, personal interest in the field, basic understanding of lab skills and science-related topics. Duration is flexible. Unpaid. Open to college freshmen, college sophomores, college juniors, college seniors, recent college graduates, graduate students, career changers.

Benefits Opportunity to attend seminars/workshops, willing to act as a professional reference, willing to complete paperwork for educational credit, willing to provide letters of recommendation.

Contact Write, fax, or e-mail Leah Lopez, Staff Attorney. Phone: 203-354-0036. Fax: 203-354-0041. E-mail: llopez@savethesound.org. In-person interview recommended (telephone interview accepted). Applicants must submit a formal organization application, letter of interest, resume, writing sample, 3 references, list of applicable coursework (for habitat restoration and water quality positions). Application deadline: May 1 for habitat restoration and water quality field interns; continuous for all other positions. World Wide Web: http://www.savethesound.org.

SCENIC AMERICA
801 Pennsylvania Avenue, SE, #300
Washington, District of Columbia 20003

General Information Organization that educates the public about the need to protect and improve the visual environment through research and technical assistance to local and state activists and concerned citizens. Established in 1978. Number of employees: 7. Number of internship applications received each year: 60.

Internships Available ▶ *1 policy intern:* responsibilities include research on billboard control and other issues; preparing and follow-up on scenic news e-newsletter; meetings with other nonprofits and government officials; improving resource center and databases. Candidates should have ability to work independently, ability to work with others, oral communication skills, research skills, writing skills, professionalism and a genuine interest in policy issues. Duration is 10–18 weeks. $100 per week. ▶ *1 program intern:* responsibilities include working on scenic conservation projects; research and writing correspondence; attending meetings. Candidates should have ability to work independently, ability to work with others, computer skills, oral communication skills, research skills, written communication skills, genuine interest in organization's issues. Duration is 10–18 weeks. $100 per week. Open to college freshmen, college sophomores, college juniors, college seniors, graduate students, law students. International applications accepted.

Benefits Names of contacts, on-the-job training, opportunity to attend seminars/workshops, willing to act as a professional reference, willing to complete paperwork for educational credit, willing to provide letters of recommendation.

Contact Write, call, fax, or e-mail Meg Maguire, President. Phone: 202-543-6200. Fax: 202-543-9130. E-mail: scenic@scenic.org. In-person interview recommended (telephone interview accepted). Applicants

Scenic America (continued)

must submit a letter of interest, resume, writing sample, three personal references. Applications are accepted continuously. World Wide Web: http://www.scenic.org.

SEATTLE AUDUBON SOCIETY
8050 35th Avenue, NE
Seattle, Washington 98115

General Information Society protecting birds and the natural environment by involving volunteers and the community in education, advocacy, preservation, science, and enjoyment. Established in 1916. Number of employees: 12. Unit of National Audubon Society, New York, New York. Number of internship applications received each year: 10.

Internships Available ▶ *1 Northwest Shade-Grown Coffee Campaign intern:* responsibilities include researching various facets of coffee industry, consumer habits, and market trends to determine best cities in which to spread the word about shade-grown coffee; doing public outreach and marketing for the campaign; communicating with campaign members, media, and the public; coordinating special projects. Candidates should have ability to work independently, oral communication skills, research skills, self-motivation, strong interpersonal skills, writing skills. Duration is 10 weeks (20 hours per week) or 200 hours within a similar time period. Unpaid. Open to college juniors, college seniors, recent college graduates, graduate students, law students, career changers, individuals reentering the workforce. ▶ *2–3 Web site interns:* responsibilities include assisting the Web site committee chair, maintaining and adding to Web site. Candidates should have ability to work independently, analytical skills, computer skills, knowledge of field, self-motivation, homesite HTML editor and Dreamweaver design tool experience desired. Duration is 10 weeks (20 hours per week). Unpaid. Open to college juniors, college seniors, recent college graduates, graduate students, career changers. ▶ *2–3 communications interns:* responsibilities include assisting with efforts to publicize events, initiatives and programs; assisting with the maintenance of media database and news clip file; general writing and research to support programs, events, and initiatives; coordinating with 30 committees about their publicity needs. Candidates should have ability to work independently, ability to work with others, college courses in field, organizational skills, plan to pursue career in field, writing skills. Duration is 10 weeks (20 hours per week). Unpaid. Open to college juniors, college seniors, recent college graduates, graduate students, career changers, individuals reentering the workforce. ▶ *2–3 conservation interns:* responsibilities include projects in at least two of the following areas: urban habitat, aquatics, forests, shade-grown coffee, and wildlife and salmon recovery. Candidates should have analytical skills, computer skills, oral communication skills, personal interest in the field, self-motivation, written communication skills. Duration is 10 weeks (20 hours per week). Unpaid. Open to college seniors, recent college graduates, graduate students, law students, career changers. ▶ *2–3 education interns:* responsibilities include assisting with at least one of the following programs: Summer Nature Camp or Spring Curriculum Planning for Nature Camp; school-based program for 3rd-5th graders; clubs for high schoolers; and educational kit programs. Candidates should have knowledge of field, oral communication skills, organizational skills, strong interpersonal skills, strong leadership ability. Duration is 10 weeks (20 hours per week). Unpaid. Open to college seniors, recent college graduates, graduate students, law students, career changers. ▶ *1 technology intern:* responsibilities include assisting the technology committee chair in overseeing the operations of computer software and hardware and maintaining Web site. Candidates should have ability to work independently, analytical skills, computer skills, experience in the field, self-motivation. Duration is 10 weeks (20 hours per week). Unpaid. Open to recent college graduates, graduate students, career changers. ▶ *2–3 volunteer, membership, or development programs interns:* responsibilities include assisting the volunteer coordinator and Volunteer Committee with multiple elements of program: recruiting, screening, orientation, training, recognizing, communicating, publicizing, managing the database, and budgeting; assisting the executive director with development projects; assisting membership committee to develop loyalty in current members and attract new members to the chapter. Candidates should have ability to work independently, computer skills, oral communication skills, plan to pursue career in field, strong interpersonal skills, writing skills. Duration is 10 weeks (20 hours per week). Unpaid. Open to college seniors, recent college graduates, graduate students, law students, career changers. International applications accepted.
Benefits Job counseling, names of contacts, on-the-job training, opportunity to attend seminars/workshops, possible full-time employment, willing to act as a professional reference, willing to complete paperwork for educational credit, willing to provide letters of recommendation.
Contact Write, call, fax, e-mail, or through World Wide Web site Lorraine Hartmann, Volunteer Coordinator. Phone: 206-523-8243 Ext. 12. Fax: 206-528-7779. E-mail: lorraineh@seattleaudubon.org. In-person interview recommended (telephone interview accepted). Applicants must submit a formal organization application, letter of interest, resume, two personal references, letters of recommendation preferred. Applications are accepted continuously. World Wide Web: http://www.seattleaudubon.org.

SHARON AUDUBON CENTER
325 Cornwall Bridge Road
Sharon, Connecticut 06069

General Information 1200-acre sanctuary providing environmental education, wildlife rehabilitation, and nature enjoyment. Established in 1961. Number of employees: 6. Unit of National Audubon Society, New York, New York. Number of internship applications received each year: 100.

Internships Available ▶ *1–2 bird banding interns (MAPS) project):* responsibilities include operating mist-netting and banding (Monitoring Avian Productivity and Survivorship) stations in Connecticut and New York, following two weeks of intensive training. Candidates should have ability to work independently, knowledge of field, organizational skills, personal interest in the field, research skills, strong interpersonal skills, birding skills. Duration is 12 weeks. $200 per week. Open to college juniors, college seniors, recent college graduates. ▶ *2 environmental education interns:* responsibilities include teaching a wide variety of environmental and natural history topics to on-site and outreach audiences, assisting with curriculum development and exhibits, rehabilitating injured and orphaned birds, and participating in many other facets of a nature center's day-to-day operations. Candidates should have oral communication skills, personal interest in the field, self-motivation, strong interpersonal skills, strong leadership ability. Duration is 3 months. $150 per week. Open to college juniors, college seniors, recent college graduates, graduate students. ▶ *1–3 research apprentices:* responsibilities include assisting in ongoing projects, including breeding bird census, biological monitoring, data entering, habitat management, and researching/writing management plans for tracts of land. Candidates should have personal interest in the field, plan to pursue career in field, research skills, self-motivation, strong interpersonal skills. Duration is 8–12 weeks. $150–$200 per week. Open to college juniors, college seniors, recent college graduates, graduate students. ▶ *1–2 summer naturalists:* responsibilities include teaching and designing curriculum for week-long summer nature programs for children ages 4–14. Candidates should have experience in the field, oral communication skills, personal interest in the field, self-motivation, strong interpersonal skills, strong leadership ability. Duration is 11–12 weeks. $200 per week. Open to college juniors, college seniors, recent college graduates, graduate students. International applications accepted.
Benefits Free housing, names of contacts, opportunity to attend seminars/workshops, willing to act as a professional reference, willing to complete paperwork for educational credit, willing to provide letters of recommendation, worker's compensation, Audubon Summer Camp scholarship eligibility.
Contact Write, call, fax, or e-mail Mr. Joseph Markow, Environmental Education Specialist. Phone: 860-364-0520. Fax: 860-364-5792. E-mail: jmarkow@audubon.org. Telephone interview required. Applicants must submit a letter of interest, resume, three personal references. Applications are accepted continuously. World Wide Web: http://www.audubon.org/local/sanctuary/sharon.

SHAVER'S CREEK ENVIRONMENTAL CENTER, PENNSYLVANIA STATE UNIVERSITY
RR 1, Box 325, Discovery Road
Petersburg, Pennsylvania 16669

General Information Center providing exemplary day and residential environmental education and outdoor adventure programming. Established in 1976. Number of employees: 20. Unit of Division of Continuing and Distance Education, Pennsylvania State University, University Park, Pennsylvania. Number of internship applications received each year: 75.

Internships Available ▶ *4–6 environmental education interns:* responsibilities include participating in all aspects of the Center's operation which may include summer camps, school programs, visitor center operations, live animal care and handling, public natural and cultural history walks, volunteer training and supervision, adventure and recreational programs, weekend festivals and events, teacher and pre-teacher workshops, team building programs, curriculum and program development, and writing articles for newsletter. Candidates should have organizational skills, personal interest in the field, plan to pursue career in field, strong interpersonal skills, strong leadership ability, background in education or natural sciences helpful. Duration is January to May, June to August, or September to December. $150–$175 per week. Open to college freshmen, college sophomores, college juniors, college seniors, recent college graduates, graduate students, career changers. International applications accepted.

Benefits Formal training, free housing, on-the-job training, opportunity to attend seminars/workshops, possible full-time employment, willing to act as a professional reference, willing to complete paperwork for educational credit, willing to provide letters of recommendation, assistance with resume preparation, access to the Internet, meals during residential programs.

Contact Write, call, fax, e-mail, or through World Wide Web site Doug Wentzel, Internship Coordinator. Phone: 814-863-2000. Fax: 814-865-2706. E-mail: shaverscreek@outreach.psu.edu. Telephone interview required. Applicants must submit a formal organization application, letter of interest, resume, three personal references, 3 letters of recommendation (international applicants only). Application deadline: March 1 for summer, July 1 for fall, November 1 for spring. World Wide Web: http://www.shaverscreek.org.

SIERRA CLUB
408 C Street, NE
Washington, District of Columbia 20002

General Information Organization dedicated to the preservation and enjoyment of the environment. Established in 1892. Number of employees: 40. Unit of Sierra Club, San Francisco, California. Number of internship applications received each year: 200.

Internships Available ▶ *6–10 issue-oriented interns:* responsibilities include performing research on a specific environmental issue (public lands and wilderness, toxics and environmental quality, energy and global warming, population, human rights, trade) to be used in the education of the public and Congress; attending congressional hearings, meetings with other environmental groups, and other strategy sessions; and other administrative duties. Candidates should have ability to work independently, computer skills, oral communication skills, personal interest in the field, research skills, writing skills, ability to work in a busy office. Duration is 1 semester. Unpaid. Open to college freshmen, college sophomores, college juniors, college seniors, recent college graduates, graduate students, law students, career changers. ▶ *1–3 media interns:* responsibilities include helping set up press conferences, issuing press releases, and ensuring that journalists receive timely information; writing op-ed articles for newspapers on environmental issues. Candidates should have ability to work independently, computer skills, editing skills, oral communication skills, personal interest in the field, writing skills, ability to work in a busy office. Duration is 1 semester. Unpaid. Open to college freshmen, college sophomores, college juniors, college seniors, recent college graduates, graduate students. ▶ *1–3 political interns:* responsibilities include helping with the endorsement process of individuals running for Congress and checking voting records. Candidates should have ability to work independently, computer skills, oral communication skills, personal interest in the field, research skills, strong interpersonal skills, writing skills. Duration is 1 semester. Unpaid. Open to college freshmen, college sophomores, college juniors, college seniors, recent college graduates, graduate students, law students. International applications accepted.

Benefits Names of contacts, opportunity to attend seminars/workshops, possible full-time employment, willing to act as a professional reference, willing to complete paperwork for educational credit, willing to provide letters of recommendation, 4 summer college stipends.

Contact Write, fax, or e-mail Joanne Tait, Executive Coordinator. Fax: 202-547-6009. E-mail: dc-internships@sierraclub.org. No phone calls. Applicants must submit a letter of interest, resume, writing sample. Application deadline: March 15 for summer. World Wide Web: http://www.sierraclub.org.

SIERRA CLUB, SAN FRANCISCO BAY CHAPTER
2530 San Pablo Avenue, Suite I
Berkeley, California 94702

General Information Nonprofit environmental organization. Established in 1892. Number of employees: 15. Division of Sierra Club, San Francisco, California. Number of internship applications received each year: 6.

Internships Available ▶ *1–2 conservation interns:* responsibilities include acting as advisor to Science Student Coalition (high school students), staff to Environmental Justice Committee, and liaison to local urban creeks advocacy organizations; some office administration; other special projects according to intern's interests. Candidates should have ability to work independently, oral communication skills, personal interest in the field, strong interpersonal skills, written communication skills. Duration is one or more semesters. Unpaid. Open to recent high school graduates, college freshmen, college sophomores, college juniors, college seniors. International applications accepted.

Benefits Willing to act as a professional reference, willing to complete paperwork for educational credit, willing to provide letters of recommendation, possible federal work-study.

Contact Write, call, fax, or e-mail Jonna Papaefthimiou, Volunteer Coordinator. Phone: 510-848-0800. Fax: 510-848-3303. E-mail: jonna@sfbaysc.org. In-person interview recommended (telephone interview accepted). Applicants must submit a letter of interest, resume, writing sample. Applications are accepted continuously. World Wide Web: http://sfbay.sierraclub.org.

SLIDE RANCH
2025 Shoreline Highway
Muir Beach, California 94965

General Information Environmental farm and wilderness-based teaching center; serves wide variety of schools, organizations, and families from both the local affluent area and also from low-income, urban, under-served populations. Established in 1970. Number of employees: 14. Number of internship applications received each year: 100.

Internships Available ▶ *6 teachers-in-residence:* responsibilities include planning lessons and teaching groups and families, gardening, caring for various farm animals, and various community responsibilities. Candidates should have ability to work with others, oral communication skills, personal interest in the field, self-motivation, experience and interest in community living situation, educational skills. Duration is February 1 to December 20. $300 per month. Open to anyone with interest in outdoor education (do not need college degree). International applications accepted.

Benefits Formal training, free housing, free meals, names of contacts, on-the-job training, opportunity to attend seminars/workshops, possible full-time employment, willing to act as a professional reference, willing to complete paperwork for educational credit, willing to provide letters of recommendation.

Contact Write, call, fax, e-mail, or through World Wide Web site Program Coordinator. Phone: 415-381-6155. Fax: 415-381-5762. E-mail: admin@slideranch.org. In-person interview recommended (telephone interview accepted). Applicants must submit a letter

Slide Ranch (continued)

of interest, resume, three personal references, personal statement. Application deadline: September 30. World Wide Web: http://www.slideranch.org.

SOCIETY OF AMERICAN FORESTERS
5400 Grosvenor Lane
Bethesda, Maryland 20814

General Information   Professional organization founded to advance the science, education, technology, and practice of forestry. Established in 1900. Number of employees: 29. Number of internship applications received each year: 8.
Internships Available ▶ *1 Henry Clepper Forest Policy intern:* responsibilities include preparing background reports on current resource issues; assisting, preparing, and developing recommendations to Congress; monitoring federal environmental and natural resources legislation; providing liaison support with environmental and natural resource organizations. Candidates should have ability to work independently, knowledge of field, oral communication skills, research skills, self-motivation, written communication skills. Duration is 6 months starting July or January. $1000 per month. Open to college seniors, recent college graduates, graduate students. International applications accepted.
Benefits   Names of contacts, opportunity to attend seminars/workshops, willing to provide letters of recommendation, association with established professionals in SAF and other organizations.
Contact   Write, call, fax, or e-mail Rita Neznek, Government Affairs Manager. Phone: 301-897-8720 Ext. 115. Fax: 301-897-3690. E-mail: neznekr@safnet.org. Applicants must submit a letter of interest, resume, academic transcripts, writing sample, 1-3 personal references. Applications are accepted continuously. World Wide Web: http://www.safnet.org.

SOMERSET COUNTY PARK COMMISSION ENVIRONMENTAL EDUCATION CENTER
190 Lord Stirling Road
Basking Ridge, New Jersey 07920

General Information   Environmental education center/park providing leisure learning opportunities for the public, schools, and scouting groups. Established in 1971. Number of employees: 15. Division of Somerset County Park Commission, North Branch, New Jersey. Number of internship applications received each year: 30.
Internships Available ▶ *3–4 maintenance crew interns:* responsibilities include assisting the maintenance department with trail maintenance and repair, landscaping, and various outdoor assignments within an outdoor park setting. Candidates should have ability to work with others, personal interest in the field, self-motivation, trailwork experience and experience with hand tools preferred. Duration is 8 weeks. $7.95 per hour. Open to high school seniors, recent high school graduates, college freshmen, college sophomores, college juniors, college seniors, recent college graduates, graduate students, career changers, individuals reentering the workforce. ▶ *7–8 seasonal naturalist assistants:* responsibilities include assisting in presentation of environmental projects and teaching various kinds of environmental education programs to all age ranges of public. Candidates should have ability to work independently, ability to work with others, experience in the field, oral communication skills, environmental education background preferred. Duration is 10–11 weeks. $8.95 per hour. Open to college freshmen, college sophomores, college juniors, college seniors, recent college graduates, graduate students, career changers, individuals reentering the workforce.
Benefits   Job counseling, names of contacts, on-the-job training, possible full-time employment, willing to act as a professional reference, willing to complete paperwork for educational credit, willing to provide letters of recommendation.
Contact   Write, call, fax, e-mail, or through World Wide Web site Kurt Bender, Environmental Science Supervisor. Phone: 908-766-2489 Ext. 332. Fax: 908-766-2687. E-mail: kbbender@parks.co.somerset.nj.us. In-person interview recommended (telephone interview accepted). Applicants must submit a formal organiza-

tion application, letter of interest, resume. Application deadline: May 30 for summer. World Wide Web: http://www.park.co.somerset.nj.us.

SOUTHFACE ENERGY INSTITUTE
241 Pine Street
Atlanta, Georgia 30308

General Information   Private, nonprofit energy and environmental education and research organization concentrating on energy efficient and sustainable building practices, community design, alternative energy technologies, sustainable landscaping, urban wildlife habitat development, and water conservation. Established in 1978. Number of employees: 15. Number of internship applications received each year: 300.
Internships Available ▶ *12–16 interns:* responsibilities include assisting staff with ongoing activities; working on special projects, such as hands-on workshops or government-sponsored projects; and working on independent projects. Candidates should have oral communication skills, research skills, self-motivation, strong interpersonal skills, written communication skills, enthusiasm about environmental issues and willingness to be involved in a wide variety of projects, computer skills (useful). Duration is 3–6 months. $335–$435 per month. Open to recent high school graduates, college freshmen, college sophomores, college juniors, college seniors, recent college graduates, graduate students, career changers, individuals reentering the workforce. International applications accepted.
Benefits   Formal training, free housing, job counseling, names of contacts, on-the-job training, opportunity to attend seminars/workshops, possible full-time employment, willing to act as a professional reference, willing to complete paperwork for educational credit, willing to provide letters of recommendation.
Contact   Write, call, fax, e-mail, or through World Wide Web site Ms. Aziza Cooper, Internship Coordinator. Phone: 404-872-3549 Ext. 114. Fax: 404-872-5009. E-mail: aziza@southface.org. In-person interview recommended (telephone interview accepted). Applicants must submit a formal organization application, resume, two personal references, statement of intent. Applications are accepted continuously. World Wide Web: http://www.southface.org.

SQUAM LAKES NATURAL SCIENCE CENTER
PO Box 173
Holderness, New Hampshire 03245

General Information   Center whose mission is to advance understanding of ecology by exploring New Hampshire's natural world. Established in 1966. Number of employees: 35. Number of internship applications received each year: 40.
Internships Available ▶ *1 island caretaker and education intern:* responsibilities include caretaking, working with visitors, natural history interpretation. Candidates should have ability to work independently, oral communication skills, personal interest in the field, self-motivation, strong interpersonal skills, ability to deal with unusual living arrangement (on island for most of summer). Duration is mid-June to Labor Day (minimum of 5 nights per week on island). $100 per week. ▶ *4–5 summer education/animal care interns:* responsibilities include 15-minute animal presentations ("mini-talks") to general public; some work on special events and projects; helping care for live animal collection; working with docents; rotation in Science Center Day Camp. Candidates should have ability to work independently, ability to work with others, oral communication skills, personal interest in the field, self-motivation, courses in environmental education, education, or natural sciences. Duration is June 1 to August 30 (some flexibility). $100 per week. Open to college juniors, college seniors, recent college graduates, graduate students, career changers, individuals reentering the workforce.
Benefits   Free housing, names of contacts, on-the-job training, opportunity to attend seminars/workshops, willing to act as a professional reference, willing to complete paperwork for educational credit, willing to provide letters of recommendation, opportunity to work with live animals.
Contact   Write, fax, e-mail, or through World Wide Web site Amy Yeakel, Director of Education. Fax: 603-968-2229. E-mail: amy.yeakel@nhnature.org. No phone calls. In-person interview recom-

mended (telephone interview accepted). Applicants must submit a formal organization application, letter of interest, resume, personal reference, two letters of recommendation. Application deadline: February 15 for summer. World Wide Web: http://www. nhnature.org.

STUDENT CONSERVATION ASSOCIATION (SCA)
PO Box 550, 689 River Road
Charlestown, New Hampshire 03603

General Information Nonprofit organization that places interns year-round in expense-paid conservation projects in national parks, national historic sites, forests, and wildlife refuges nationwide. Established in 1957. Number of employees: 80. Number of internship applications received each year: 5,000.
Internships Available ▶ *60–70 Hudson Valley conservation corps participants.* Candidates should have college courses in field, research skills, strong interpersonal skills, strong leadership ability, qualifications as specified on Web site. Duration is 3–10 months. $250-$300 per week plus paid child care. Open to college juniors, college seniors, recent college graduates, graduate students, law students, career changers. ▶ *80–120 Northeast residential conservation corps participants:* responsibilities include outdoor conservation project including trail construction and maintenance (spring/summer months); conducting environmental education programs in local schools and community groups (winter months). Candidates should have oral communication skills, personal interest in the field, self-motivation, strong interpersonal skills, qualifications as specified on Web site. Duration is 5–10 months. $60 per week stipend; education award of up to $4725. Open to recent high school graduates, college freshmen, college sophomores, college juniors, college seniors, recent college graduates, those 18 and 25 years old only. ▶ *150–200 conservation crew leaders:* responsibilities include managing all aspects of 3-5 week high school trail crew, training and leading 6-8 high school youth in national park or forest. Candidates should have experience in the field, oral communication skills, strong interpersonal skills, strong leadership ability, qualifications as specified on Web site. Duration is 2-3 months in summer. $300–$500 per week. Open to college seniors, recent college graduates, graduate students, law students, career changers, individuals reentering the workforce, must be 21 or older. ▶ *1,500 environmental and cultural resource management interns:* responsibilities include resource management duties ranging from backcountry patrol, wildlife ecology, forestry, and environmental education to archaeology and historical interpretation. Candidates should have ability to work independently, organizational skills, self-motivation, strong interpersonal skills, qualifications as specified on Web site (varies by position). Duration is 12–52 weeks. $50–$250 per week. Open to recent high school graduates, college freshmen, college sophomores, college juniors, college seniors, recent college graduates, graduate students, law students, career changers, individuals reentering the workforce, individuals at least 18 years of age. ▶ *28–40 fire education corps (team leaders):* responsibilities include leading seasonal intern team in a three phase project, attending public events and community meetings, canvassing, risk evaluations, youth education, GIS, media interviews, fuels-mitigation, and analyzing the project. Candidates should have oral communication skills, organizational skills, self-motivation, strong interpersonal skills, strong leadership ability, U.S. citizenship, valid driver's license, minimum current CPR and standard first aid certification. Duration is 8–12 months. $160 weekly stipend. Open to college juniors, college seniors, recent college graduates, graduate students, law students, career changers, must be 21years. ▶ *125–175 fire education corps (team members):* responsibilities include participating in Field-Season phase of a community wildland fire education project; attending events and community meetings, youth-education days, fuels-reduction projects, media spots, canvassing, and conducting local home-risk evaluations; special projects. Candidates should have computer skills, oral communication skills, organizational skills, self-motivation, strong interpersonal skills, U.S. citizenship, valid driver's license, minimum current CPR and standard first aid certification. Duration is 11–13 weeks. $50 weekly stipend for food. Open to recent high school graduates, college freshmen, college sophomores, college juniors, college seniors,

recent college graduates, graduate students, law students, career changers, individuals reentering the workforce. International applications accepted.
Benefits Formal training, free housing, health insurance, names of contacts, on-the-job training, opportunity to attend seminars/workshops, possible full-time employment, travel reimbursement, tuition assistance, willing to complete paperwork for educational credit, uniform stipend, weekly living allowance, eligibility for AmeriCorps educational awards, loan deferment.
International Internships Available in Canada; Mexico.
Contact Write, call, fax, e-mail, or through World Wide Web site Recruitment Office. Phone: 603-543-1700. Fax: 603-543-1828. E-mail: internships@thesca.org. Telephone interview required. Applicants must submit a formal organization application, resume, academic transcripts, three letters of recommendation, application and additional requirements available on Web site; $20 application fee (U.S., Canada, and Mexico); $40 application fee (other international). Applications are accepted continuously. World Wide Web: http://www.theSCA.org.

SULLYS HILL NATIONAL GAME PRESERVE
PO Box 286
Fort Totten, North Dakota 58335

General Information National wildlife refuge system, part of the larger national system of lands totaling 93 million acres; manages wildlife, habitat and people for a variety of opportunities. Established in 1904. Number of employees: 4. Unit of Devils Lake Wetland Management District Complex, Devils Lake, North Dakota. Number of internship applications received each year: 20.
Internships Available ▶ *1–5 environmental education interns:* responsibilities include environmental education, public recreation, wildlife management. Candidates should have ability to work independently, ability to work with others, oral communication skills, personal interest in the field, self-motivation, written communication skills. Duration is flexible. Unpaid. Open to recent high school graduates, college freshmen, college sophomores, college juniors, college seniors, recent college graduates, graduate students, career changers, individuals reentering the workforce. ▶ *1 park or refuge ranger intern:* responsibilities include visitor relations, wildlife refuge management and maintenance, assisting in events and workshops. Candidates should have ability to work independently, ability to work with others, knowledge of field, oral communication skills, organizational skills, personal interest in the field. Duration is May 1 to October 1. Unpaid. Open to college sophomores, college juniors, college seniors, recent college graduates, graduate students, individuals reentering the workforce. ▶ *2–3 wildlife biologist interns:* responsibilities include wildlife surveys, habitat inventories, wildlife studies, species management. Candidates should have ability to work independently, computer skills, oral communication skills, personal interest in the field, plan to pursue career in field, strong interpersonal skills. Duration is flexible (April 15 to October 15). Unpaid. Open to college freshmen, college sophomores, college juniors, college seniors, recent college graduates, graduate students. International applications accepted.
Benefits Formal training, free housing, job counseling, names of contacts, on-the-job training, travel reimbursement, willing to act as a professional reference, willing to complete paperwork for educational credit, willing to provide letters of recommendation, food stipend.
Contact Write, call, fax, or e-mail Joe Maxwell, Refuge Manager, PO Box 286, Fort Totten, North Dakota 58335. Phone: 701-766-4272. Fax: 701-662-8612. E-mail: joe_maxwell@fws.gov. Telephone interview required. Applicants must submit a letter of interest, resume, three personal references. Application deadline: April 30 for summer, August 15 for fall, December 1 for spring.

SURFRIDER FOUNDATION
120½ South El Camino Real, #207
San Clemente, California 92672

General Information Nonprofit environmental organization dedicated to the protection, preservation, and restoration of the world's oceans, waves, and beaches through conservation, activ-

Surfrider Foundation (continued)

ism, research, and education. Established in 1984. Number of employees: 18. Number of internship applications received each year: 50.

Internships Available ▶ *Chapter interns/volunteers:* responsibilities include working in local communities with chapter leaders on local issues; areas available include administrative, public relations/media, legal counsel, membership services, events/fund-raisers, literature distribution, newsletter publication, research. Candidates should have oral communication skills, organizational skills, personal interest in the field, strong interpersonal skills, strong leadership ability. Duration is flexible. Unpaid. Open to high school seniors, recent high school graduates, college freshmen, college sophomores, college juniors, college seniors, recent college graduates, law students. ▶ *4–5 national interns/volunteers:* responsibilities include working in Southern California area in administrative chapter development, events/fund-raisers, legislative analysis, program research, cataloging and archiving, public speaking, report writing, newsletter, or membership development. Candidates should have computer skills, office skills, oral communication skills, organizational skills, research skills, strong interpersonal skills, written communication skills. Duration is flexible. Unpaid. Open to high school seniors, recent high school graduates, college freshmen, college sophomores, college juniors, college seniors, recent college graduates, graduate students, law students.

Benefits Possible full-time employment, willing to act as a professional reference, willing to complete paperwork for educational credit, willing to provide letters of recommendation.

Contact Write or e-mail Michelle Kremer, Deputy Executive Director, PO Box 6010, San Clemente, California 92674-6010. Fax: 949-492-8142. E-mail: mkremer@surfrider.org. No phone calls. Telephone interview required. Applicants must submit a letter of interest, resume, three writing samples. Applications are accepted continuously. World Wide Web: http://www.surfrider.org.

THREE LAKES NATURE CENTER AND AQUARIUM
400 Sausiluta Drive
Richmond, Virginia 23227

General Information Facility providing environmental education in many areas through visitation, public and school programs, and group tours. Established in 1992. Number of employees: 4. Subsidiary of Henrico County Division of Recreation and Parks, Richmond, Virginia. Number of internship applications received each year: 10.

Internships Available ▶ *2 nature center interns:* responsibilities include participating in all aspects of nature center operation including program planning and implementation, exhibit design and fabrication, and animal care and maintenance. Candidates should have ability to work independently, oral communication skills, organizational skills, personal interest in the field, self-motivation, strong leadership ability. Duration is flexible. Unpaid. Open to college freshmen, college sophomores, college juniors, college seniors, graduate students. International applications accepted.

Benefits Formal training, names of contacts, willing to provide letters of recommendation.

Contact Write, call, fax, or e-mail Mr. Tom Thorp, Nature Program Coordinator. Phone: 804-261-8230. Fax: 804-266-6938. E-mail: tt-threelakes@juno.com. In-person interview recommended (telephone interview accepted). Applicants must submit a letter of interest, resume. Applications are accepted continuously. World Wide Web: http://www.co.henrico.va.us/rec/31nature.htm.

TREES FOR TOMORROW NATURAL RESOURCES EDUCATION CENTER
519 Sheridan Street East
Eagle River, Wisconsin 54521

General Information Natural resource education center teaching fourth graders through adults about the wise use and management of forests, wildlife, water, and soil resources. Established in 1944. Number of employees: 23. Number of internship applications received each year: 30.

Internships Available ▶ *4 naturalist interns:* responsibilities include teaching student groups ranging from fourth graders to adults about the importance of conserving natural resources (forests, wildlife, water, soil, and energy) through hands-on activities and guided tours of managed forest areas and industries. Candidates should have ability to work with others, oral communication skills, self-motivation, strong leadership ability, written communication skills. Duration is 9 months (August 24-June 1). $700 per month. Open to college juniors, college seniors, recent college graduates, graduate students, law students, career changers, individuals reentering the workforce. ▶ *1 outreach naturalist:* responsibilities include presenting natural resource programs to resorts and campgrounds on behalf of Trees For Tomorrow and the U.S. Forest Service. Candidates should have ability to work independently, college courses in field, knowledge of field, oral communication skills, self-motivation. Duration is May to August. $650 per month. Open to college seniors, recent college graduates, graduate students. International applications accepted.

Benefits Formal training, free housing, free meals, health insurance, job counseling, names of contacts, on-the-job training, opportunity to attend seminars/workshops, possible full-time employment, willing to act as a professional reference, willing to complete paperwork for educational credit, willing to provide letters of recommendation.

Contact Write, call, fax, e-mail, or through World Wide Web site Ms. Sandy Lotto, Intern Coordinator. Phone: 800-838-9472. Fax: 715-479-2318. E-mail: trees@nnex.net. Telephone interview required. Applicants must submit a letter of interest, resume, list of 3 contacts. Application deadline: April 11 for summer, May 15 for nine-month position. World Wide Web: http://www.treesfortomorrow.com.

TREES NEW YORK
51 Chambers Street, Suite 1412 A
New York, New York 10007

General Information Nonprofit organization dedicated to the preservation, improvement, and increase of New York's urban forest through advocacy education, publishing, and direct community service. Established in 1979. Number of employees: 7. Number of internship applications received each year: 50.

Internships Available ▶ *1–2 interns:* responsibilities include projects relating to organization's programs, general office duties, some desktop publishing and computer work. Candidates should have ability to work independently, computer skills, organizational skills, self-motivation, written communication skills, interest in urban forestry, forestry, nonprofit management, and environmental studies (these applicants will be given priority), teaching and marketing experience. Duration is flexible. Position available as unpaid or paid. Open to college freshmen, college sophomores, college juniors, college seniors, recent college graduates, graduate students, career changers, individuals reentering the workforce. International applications accepted.

Benefits Names of contacts, willing to act as a professional reference, willing to complete paperwork for educational credit, willing to provide letters of recommendation.

Contact Write, call, fax, e-mail, or through World Wide Web site Leslie Fitzpatrick. Phone: 212-227-1887. Fax: 212-732-5325. E-mail: treesny@treesny.com. In-person interview required. Applicants must submit a resume, cover letter indicating preference in time frame. Applications are accepted continuously. World Wide Web: http://www.treesny.com.

TRUSTEES OF RESERVATIONS, WESTERN REGION
PO Box 792
Stockbridge, Massachusetts 01262

General Information Organization that preserves properties of scenic, historical, and ecological value throughout Massachusetts for public use and enjoyment. Established in 1891. Number of employees: 11. Unit of Trustees of Reservations, Beverly, Massachusetts. Number of internship applications received each year: 30.

Internships Available ▶ *1–3 historic site interns:* responsibilities include working with the historic resources manager to gain professional experience in the daily administration of historic

properties and collections management. Candidates should have ability to work independently, oral communication skills, self-motivation, strong interpersonal skills, written communication skills, availability to work weekends. Duration is 10–15 weeks. Position available as unpaid or at $300 per week. Open to college juniors, college seniors, recent college graduates, graduate students. **Benefits** Free housing, willing to act as a professional reference, willing to complete paperwork for educational credit, willing to provide letters of recommendation.
Contact Write Will Garrison, Historic Resources Manager. E-mail: wgarrison@ttor.org. No phone calls. In-person interview recommended (telephone interview accepted). Applicants must submit a letter of interest, resume. Application deadline: March 15 for summer. World Wide Web: http://www.thetrustees.org.

TURNBULL NATIONAL WILDLIFE REFUGE
26010 South Smith Road
Cheney, Washington 99004-9326

General Information Refuge and breeding ground for migratory birds and other wildlife. Established in 1937. Number of employees: 16. Unit of United States Fish and Wildlife Service, Portland, Oregon, Portland, Oregon. Number of internship applications received each year: 10.
Internships Available ▶ *1 biological aide:* responsibilities include assisting with wildlife and habitat monitoring and bird banding. Candidates should have ability to work independently, ability to work with others, college courses in field, computer skills, research skills, self-motivation. Duration is 4 months (beginning May 1). Position available as unpaid or paid. Open to college juniors, college seniors, recent college graduates, individuals reentering the workforce. ▶ *1 clerical/administration intern:* responsibilities include clerical duties including answering phones, filing, typing, personnel actions (helping with vacancy announcements, payroll), public information, and permit preparation. Candidates should have ability to work independently, computer skills, office skills, oral communication skills, organizational skills, strong interpersonal skills, written communication skills. Duration is 3–6 months. Unpaid. Open to college freshmen, college sophomores, college juniors, college seniors, recent college graduates, graduate students, individuals reentering the workforce. ▶ *1–2 environmental education assistants:* responsibilities include conducting environmental education activities for refuge visitors, assisting groups in conducting field study activities, and preparing and presenting programs on wildlife, wildflowers, and ecology. Candidates should have college courses in field, oral communication skills, personal interest in the field, self-motivation, strong interpersonal skills, written communication skills. Duration is 3 months. Unpaid. Open to college freshmen, college sophomores, college juniors, college seniors, recent college graduates, graduate students, individuals reentering the workforce.
Benefits Job counseling, names of contacts, on-the-job training, willing to act as a professional reference, willing to complete paperwork for educational credit, willing to provide letters of recommendation, free housing if available.
Contact Write, call, fax, or e-mail Ms. Nancy J. Curry, Refuge Manager. Phone: 509-235-4723. Fax: 509-235-4703. E-mail: nancy_curry@fws.gov. Telephone interview required. Applicants must submit a formal organization application, letter of interest, resume, three personal references, letter of recommendation. Application deadline: March 1 for spring, May 1 for summer, August 1 for fall. World Wide Web: http://www.r1.fws.gov/turnbull/turnbull.html.

TURTLE MOUNTAIN ENVIRONMENTAL LEARNING CENTER
#2 Lake Metigoshe State Park
Bottineau, North Dakota 58318

General Information Environmental education program for diverse age groups that emphasizes learning in an outdoor environment. Established in 1985. Number of employees: 1. Unit of Lake Metigoshe State Park, Bottineau, North Dakota. Number of internship applications received each year: 20.

Internships Available ▶ *2 naturalist interns:* responsibilities include facilitating group activities and discussions in teaching environmental awareness. Candidates should have ability to work independently, ability to work with others, oral communication skills, personal interest in the field, self-motivation, desire to share nature with all age groups. Duration is April 1 to June 5, May 25 to September 5, August 25 to November 1. $160 per week. Open to college freshmen, college sophomores, college juniors, college seniors, recent college graduates, career changers, individuals reentering the workforce. International applications accepted.
Benefits Free housing, names of contacts, on-the-job training, opportunity to attend seminars/workshops, willing to act as a professional reference, willing to complete paperwork for educational credit, willing to provide letters of recommendation, reimbursement of work-related travel expenses, uniforms provided.
Contact Write, call, fax, e-mail, or through World Wide Web site Greg Hansen, TMELC Coordinator. Phone: 701-263-4514. Fax: 701-263-4648. E-mail: tmelc@state.nd.us. Applicants must submit a letter of interest, resume, academic transcripts, three personal references, telephone interview if selected. Application deadline: February 28 for spring, April 1 for summer, August 1 for fall. World Wide Web: http://www.state.nd.us/ndparks/Parks/Metigoshe/TMELC.htm.

UNIVERSITY OF RHODE ISLAND, ENVIRONMENTAL EDUCATION CENTER
W. Alton Jones Campus, 401 Victory Highway
West Greenwich, Rhode Island 02817

General Information Organization dedicated to educating school-age children about the environment, ecology, cultural history, farming, and group building. Established in 1964. Number of employees: 5. Department of University of Rhode Island, Kingston, Rhode Island.
Internships Available ▶ *1 animal and garden manager:* responsibilities include overseeing the day-to-day functions of an historic, working farm including facilities maintenance, animal care, chores, and gardening; carrying out all duties in a manner that makes the farm, animals, and gardens as safe and accessible as possible to children. Candidates should have ability to work independently, knowledge of field, personal interest in the field, self-motivation, strong interpersonal skills, previous experience caring for farm animals and gardens. Duration is mid-March to mid-September. $250–$300 per week. Open to college freshmen, college sophomores, college juniors, college seniors, recent college graduates, graduate students. ▶ *3–5 field teachers/naturalists:* responsibilities include planning and teaching outdoor lessons in forest and wetland ecology, team building, outdoor skills, environmental issues, farming, and Native American and pioneer history on 2300-acre wilderness campus; teaching outdoor lessons in farming, animal care, gardening, and pioneer history on 300-acre historic farm. Candidates should have knowledge of field, oral communication skills, personal interest in the field, strong interpersonal skills, strong leadership ability. Duration is 4–9 months. Minimum stipend of $250 per week . Open to recent college graduates, graduate students. ▶ *1 nurse's assistant/EMT:* responsibilities include assisting RN in injury and illness assessment, dispensing medication, and operating camp infirmary. Candidates should have declared college major in field, knowledge of field, oral communication skills, self-motivation, strong interpersonal skills. Duration is mid-June to mid-August. $300–$400 per week. Open to college sophomores, college juniors, college seniors, graduate students, nursing students or EMT's. ▶ *16 summer camp naturalists/counselors:* responsibilities include leading campers ages 8-13 during seven six-day residential camping programs; counselors may teach up to seven themes or lead natural and cultural history and sensory awareness, canoeing, no-trace camping and survival skills, conservation activities, and new games. Candidates should have ability to work with others, knowledge of field, oral communication skills, strong leadership ability, CPR and first aid. Duration is 9 weeks (mid-June to mid-August). Stipend of $195-$319 per week. Open to college freshmen, college sophomores, college juniors, college seniors, recent college graduates, graduate students. ▶ *10 teen expedition leaders:* responsibilities include leading week-long sessions of the Teen

University of Rhode Island, Environmental Education Center (continued)

Expeditions program; planning and implementing canoeing, kayaking, backpacking, and rock climbing trips for participants ages 12-17. Candidates should have ability to work with others, experience in the field, oral communication skills, organizational skills, self-motivation, strong leadership ability, strong skills in at least one of the following: canoeing, kayaking, backpacking, or rock climbing. Duration is mid-June to late August. Stipend of $200-$305 per week. Open to college sophomores, college juniors, college seniors, recent college graduates, graduate students. International applications accepted.

Benefits Formal training, free housing, free meals, on-the-job training, willing to act as a professional reference, willing to complete paperwork for educational credit, willing to provide letters of recommendation.

Contact Write, call, fax, e-mail, or through World Wide Web site Mr. John Jacques, Manager. Phone: 401-397-3304 Ext. 6043. Fax: 401-397-3293. E-mail: urieec@etal.uri.edu. In-person interview recommended (telephone interview accepted). Applicants must submit a formal organization application, letter of interest, resume, 3 professional references. Application deadline: January 15 for spring, May 15 for summer, July 30 for fall, November 15 for winter. World Wide Web: http://www.uri.edu/ajc/eec.

UPHAM WOODS 4-H ENVIRONMENTAL CENTER
N194 County Road North
Wisconsin Dells, Wisconsin 53965

General Information Youth camp and environmental education facility where youth and adults gain first-hand experience in natural sciences, citizenship, and group living. Established in 1941. Number of employees: 7. Subsidiary of University of Wisconsin Extension/Youth Development, Madison, Wisconsin. Number of internship applications received each year: 20.

Internships Available ▶ *3–5 teaching naturalists:* responsibilities include teaching all ages of youth environmental education and youth development skills. Candidates should have computer skills, oral communication skills, organizational skills, personal interest in the field, strong interpersonal skills, strong leadership ability. Duration is 4–12 months. $250–$300 per week depending on certifications such as for lifeguarding or completion of degree(s). Open to college juniors, college seniors, recent college graduates, graduate students, career changers. International applications accepted.

Benefits Free housing, job counseling, names of contacts, willing to complete paperwork for educational credit, willing to provide letters of recommendation, most meals provided.

Contact Write, call, fax, or e-mail Director. Phone: 608-254-6461. Fax: 608-253-7140. E-mail: upham@chorus.net. In-person interview recommended (telephone interview accepted). Applicants must submit a letter of interest, resume. Application deadline: February 1 for spring, March 1 for summer, November 1 for winter.

U.S. FISH AND WILDLIFE SERVICE
103 East Plumtree Road
Sunderland, Massachusetts 01375

General Information Federal agency conserving the nation's natural resources. Established in 1871. Number of employees: 2. Unit of U.S. Fish and Wildlife Service Northeast Regional Office, Hadley, Massachusetts. Number of internship applications received each year: 6.

Internships Available ▶ *1 environmental database manager:* responsibilities include managing and updating databases on the management activities of the Connecticut River Migratory Fish Restoration Program. Candidates should have ability to work independently, computer skills, organizational skills, personal interest in the field, self-motivation, experience with data. Duration is flexible (year-round). Unpaid. Open to high school students, recent high school graduates, college freshmen, college sophomores, college juniors, college seniors, recent college graduates, graduate students, law students, career changers, individuals reentering the workforce, retirees. ▶ *1–5 migratory fish count coordinators:* responsibilities include assembling and reporting daily migratory fish counts by calling seven dams and recording their data on migratory fish.

Candidates should have ability to work independently, ability to work with others, computer skills, office skills, oral communication skills, organizational skills. Duration is May 1 to August 1. Unpaid. Open to high school students, recent high school graduates, college freshmen, college sophomores, college juniors, college seniors, recent college graduates, graduate students, law students, career changers, individuals reentering the workforce, retirees. ▶ *1 technical assistant:* responsibilities include assisting field technician with a wide variety of duties related to fisheries management; some field work available. Candidates should have ability to work independently, ability to work with others, oral communication skills, organizational skills, personal interest in the field, self-motivation. Duration is flexible (year-round). Unpaid. Open to college freshmen, college sophomores, college juniors, college seniors, recent college graduates, graduate students, law students, career changers, individuals reentering the workforce, retirees. International applications accepted.

Benefits Job counseling, names of contacts, on-the-job training, willing to act as a professional reference, willing to complete paperwork for educational credit, willing to provide letters of recommendation.

Contact Write, call, e-mail, or through World Wide Web site Janice N. Rowan, Coordinator. Phone: 413-548-9138. Fax: 413-548-9622. E-mail: jan_rowan@fws.gov. In-person interview recommended (telephone interview accepted). Applicants must submit a letter of interest, resume. Applications are accepted continuously. World Wide Web: http://www.fws.gov/r5crc.

U.S. FOREST SERVICE, PIKE AND SAN ISABEL FORESTS, SOUTH PARK DISTRICT
PO Box 219
Fairplay, Colorado 80440

General Information National forest district with 4 broad missions: research, international forestry, state and private forestry, and managing forest resources in a way that will best meet the needs of its visitors without impairing the productivity of the land. Established in 1905. Number of employees: 40. Unit of Pike & San Isabel National Forests, Pueblo, Colorado. Number of internship applications received each year: 40.

Internships Available ▶ *1–2 hosts (Wilkerson Pass Visitor Center).* Candidates should have ability to work independently, ability to work with others, knowledge of field, oral communication skills, self-motivation, strong leadership ability. Duration is May through September or longer depending on weather (40 hours per week). Position available as unpaid or at $70 per week. Open to recent high school graduates, college freshmen, college sophomores, college juniors, college seniors, recent college graduates, graduate students, career changers, individuals reentering the workforce, retirees. ▶ *2–4 naturalists/interpreters:* responsibilities include developing and conducting interpretive programs at Wilkerson Pass and 21 campgrounds; writing news releases; assisting with the maintenance of interpretive center; operating book sales outlet; providing visitor information; and conducting various independent projects including creating publications, fliers, children's programs, photography exhibits, and district projects. Candidates should have ability to work independently, computer skills, oral communication skills, organizational skills, plan to pursue career in field, self-motivation, strong interpersonal skills, writing skills. Duration is end of May–end of September (2 months minimum). Position available as unpaid or at $70 per week (40 hours per week). Open to recent high school graduates, college freshmen, college sophomores, college juniors, college seniors, recent college graduates, graduate students, law students, career changers, individuals reentering the workforce, individuals 18 years or older. International applications accepted.

Benefits Formal training, free housing, job counseling, names of contacts, opportunity to attend seminars/workshops, tuition assistance, willing to complete paperwork for educational credit, willing to provide letters of recommendation, specific information on USFS hiring methods and applications.

Contact Write, call, or e-mail Rebecca J. Anderson, Interpretive Specialist. Phone: 719-836-3852. E-mail: banderson05@fs.fed.us. Applicants must submit a letter of interest, resume, writing sample, volunteer application. Application deadline: March (applications preferred). World Wide Web: http://www.fs.fed.us/r2/psicc/sopa.

U.S. FOREST SERVICE, STANISLAUS NATIONAL FOREST
#1 Pinecrest Lake Road
Pinecrest, California 95364

General Information Land management agency. Established in 1906. Number of employees: 60. Unit of United States Department of Agriculture, National Forest Service, Washington, District of Columbia. Number of internship applications received each year: 50.

Internships Available ▶ *1–10 natural resource interpretive assistants:* responsibilities include researching, preparing, presenting, and evaluating programs including guided walks, talks, or campfire programs; assisting other interpreters of natural resources with set-up and children's activities; working with a wide variety of audiences. Candidates should have ability to work independently, knowledge of field, oral communication skills, self-motivation, strong interpersonal skills, written communication skills. Duration is usually June-September (other times throughout the year may be available). $17 per day. Open to high school students, recent high school graduates, college freshmen, college sophomores, college juniors, college seniors, recent college graduates, graduate students, law students, career changers, individuals reentering the workforce, retirees. ▶ *1 recreation technician:* responsibilities include assisting in developing a recreation program; cleaning restrooms, picking up trash and litter, installing stoves, picnic tables and sign posts; describing rules, regulations, and recreational opportunities to the public. Candidates should have ability to work independently, ability to work with others, oral communication skills, ability to work on feet for extended periods, ability to lift and carry 40 pounds. Duration is 10–14 weeks. $17 per day. Open to high school students, recent high school graduates, college freshmen, college sophomores, college juniors, college seniors, recent college graduates, graduate students, law students, career changers, individuals reentering the workforce. ▶ *4–8 wilderness interns:* responsibilities include wilderness monitoring work requiring multiple day trips into the wilderness backcountry to gather the data needed to restore and protect special lands. Candidates should have ability to work independently, ability to work with others, analytical skills, personal interest in the field, writing skills, must have own backpacking equipment, be physically fit, and skilled at map and compass use and reconnaissance. Duration is mid-June to mid-August. $17 per day. Open to college freshmen, college sophomores, college juniors, college seniors. ▶ *1 writer/ editor/graphics designer:* responsibilities include completing annual newsletter, Junior Ranger newsletter, information displays, brochures, and handouts. Candidates should have ability to work independently, computer skills, editing skills, knowledge of field, writing skills, experience with IBM computer graphics programs. Duration is flexible. $17 per day. Open to high school students, recent high school graduates, college freshmen, college sophomores, college juniors, college seniors, recent college graduates, graduate students, law students, career changers, individuals reentering the workforce, retirees. International applications accepted.

Benefits Formal training, free housing, job counseling, names of contacts, on-the-job training, opportunity to attend seminars/ workshops, willing to act as a professional reference, willing to complete paperwork for educational credit, willing to provide letters of recommendation.

Contact Write, call, fax, or e-mail Joy Barney, Interpretive Specialist/Environmental Education Coordinator, #1 Pinecrest Lake Road, Pinecrest, California 95364. Phone: 209-965-3434. Fax: 209-965-3372. E-mail: jbarney@fs.fed.us. In-person interview recommended (telephone interview accepted). Applicants must submit a formal organization application, two personal references. Applications are accepted continuously.

U.S. NAVY MARINE MAMMAL PROGRAM
53560 Hull Street, Code 2351
San Diego, California 92152

General Information Program that trains dolphins and sea lions for the U.S. Navy. Established in 1959. Number of employees: 250. Number of internship applications received each year: 100.

Internships Available ▶ *12 animal care and training interns:* responsibilities include diet preparation, sanitation, equipment and facility maintenance; possibly assisting marine animal training staff in husbandry and open ocean training. Candidates should have ability to work independently, ability to work with others, declared college major in field, knowledge of field, plan to pursue career in field, self-motivation. Duration is 16 weeks (40 hours per week). Unpaid. Open to college sophomores, college juniors, college seniors, recent college graduates.

Benefits Formal training, job counseling, on-the-job training, opportunity to attend seminars/workshops, possible full-time employment, willing to act as a professional reference, willing to complete paperwork for educational credit, willing to provide letters of recommendation.

Contact Write, fax, or e-mail Erika Putman, Coordinator of Volunteer Opportunities, Space and Naval Warfare Systems Center, Code 2351, 53560 Hull Street, San Diego, California 92152. Phone: 619-767-4100. Fax: 619-553-2678. E-mail: putman@spawar.navy.mil. Telephone interview required. Applicants must submit a letter of interest, resume, academic transcripts, three letters of recommendation, proof of U.S. citizenship and medical insurance. Application deadline: March 1 for summer, June 15 for fall, October 15 for spring. World Wide Web: http://www.spawar.navy.mil/sandiego/technology/mammals/.

VOLUNTEERS FOR OUTDOOR COLORADO
600 South Marion Parkway
Denver, Colorado 80209

General Information Organization that seeks to instill a personal sense of responsibility for the stewardship of Colorado's public lands, working in partnership with federal, state, and local land management agencies and other nonprofits to organize volunteers on projects statewide, year-round. Established in 1984. Number of employees: 7. Number of internship applications received each year: 35.

Internships Available ▶ *100–150 VOC Network interns:* responsibilities include working for federal, state, and local management agencies or other nonprofit agencies in Colorado backcountry, environmental education, recreation, botany, and research/field work. Candidates should have personal interest in the field. Duration is flexible. Position available as unpaid or paid. Open to high school students, recent high school graduates, college freshmen, college sophomores, college juniors, college seniors, recent college graduates, graduate students, law students, career changers, individuals reentering the workforce. International applications accepted.

Benefits On-the-job training and housing or a stipend for most positions.

Contact Write, call, fax, e-mail, or through World Wide Web site Wendy Hodges, VOC Network Coordinator. Phone: 303-715-1010. Fax: 303-715-1212. E-mail: voc@voc.org. Applicants must submit materials requested directly from the agency hiring. Applications are accepted continuously. World Wide Web: http://www.voc.org.

WETLANDS INSTITUTE
1075 Stone Harbor Boulevard
Stone Harbor, New Jersey 08247-1424

General Information Private, nonprofit organization dedicated to public education and scientific research concerning intertidal salt marshes and other coastal ecosystems. Established in 1969. Number of employees: 15. Number of internship applications received each year: 60.

Internships Available ▶ *2 aquarist interns:* responsibilities include maintaining aquariums in exhibit building, collecting specimens, and interpreting exhibits for visitors. Candidates should have ability to work independently, college courses in field, knowledge of

field, personal interest in the field, self-motivation. Duration is one summer. Unpaid. Open to college freshmen, college sophomores, college juniors, college seniors, recent college graduates, graduate students, individuals reentering the workforce. ▶ *2–6 environmental education interns:* responsibilities include teaching summer nature classes and assisting with public programs. Candidates should have knowledge of field, oral communication skills, personal interest in the field, self-motivation, strong interpersonal skills, written communication skills. Duration is 3 months. Position available as unpaid or paid. Open to college freshmen, college sophomores, college juniors, college seniors, recent college graduates, graduate students, career changers, individuals reentering the workforce. ▶ *2 horticulture interns:* responsibilities include maintaining, improving, and cataloging gardens on the grounds; identifying indigenous salt marsh plants; educating visitors. Candidates should have ability to work independently, ability to work with others, college courses in field, oral communication skills, personal interest in the field, self-motivation, strong leadership ability. Duration is 3 months. Unpaid. Open to college freshmen, college sophomores, college juniors, college seniors, recent college graduates, graduate students. ▶ *10–20 research interns:* responsibilities include assisting visiting researchers with projects. Candidates should have ability to work with others, college courses in field, computer skills, knowledge of field, personal interest in the field, self-motivation. Duration is May to August/September. Position available as unpaid or at $3600 for 12 weeks. Open to college freshmen, college sophomores, college juniors, college seniors, recent college graduates, graduate students. International applications accepted.
Benefits Formal training, on-the-job training, opportunity to attend seminars/workshops, willing to act as a professional reference, willing to complete paperwork for educational credit, willing to provide letters of recommendation, limited housing; qualifying students may receive housing for 12 weeks and a $3600 stipend.
Contact Write, fax, or through World Wide Web site Intern Coordinator. Fax: 609-368-3871. In-person interview recommended (telephone interview accepted). Applicants must submit a formal organization application, resume, academic transcripts, letter stating personal goals, one academic reference. Application deadline: March 15 for summer, September 1 for fall, December 1 for spring. World Wide Web: http://www.wetlandsinstitute.org.

WILDERNESS EDUCATION INSTITUTE
2260 Baseline Road, Suite 205
Boulder, Colorado 80302

General Information Nonprofit environmental educational summer camps for youth. Established in 1996. Number of employees: 1. Number of internship applications received each year: 10.
Internships Available ▶ *2 environmental education/adventure interns:* responsibilities include developing and teaching environmental lesson plans, planning backpacking trips, facilitating team building, and mentoring youth aged 8-17 in residential summer camp settings. Candidates should have passion for kids, environmental science, summer camp experience a plus. Duration is June 15 to August 15. Unpaid. Open to individuals 17-18.
Benefits On-the-job training, opportunity to attend seminars/workshops, willing to act as a professional reference, willing to complete paperwork for educational credit, willing to provide letters of recommendation.
Contact Through World Wide Web site Rob Alexander, Executive Director. Telephone interview required. Applicants must submit a letter of interest, resume, academic transcripts, fee to cover room and board. Application deadline: February 28. World Wide Web: http://www.weiprograms.org.

WILDLIFE CONSERVATION SOCIETY/BRONX ZOO
Education Department, 2300 Southern Boulevard
Bronx, New York 10460-1099

General Information Society devoted to the conservation of wildlife and habitats through conservation, education, and science; also sponsors girls for planet earth summit that brings

together 40 girls ages 14-17 from across the country. Established in 1895. Number of employees: 600. Number of internship applications received each year: 200.
Internships Available ▶ *2 Girls for Planet Earth Summit interns:* responsibilities include preparing educational materials; daily and overnight supervision during the entire summit is required. Candidates should have oral communication skills, organizational skills, strong interpersonal skills, strong leadership ability, experience in teaching/working with children, interest in wildlife and ecology, and ability to relate to high school students. Duration is June 30 to August 8 (30 to 35 hours per week). $2500 per duration of internship. Open to college juniors, college seniors, recent college graduates, graduate students, teachers. ▶ *1–2 distance learning interns:* responsibilities include helping set up, coordinate, and breakdown videoconferencing equipment; helping administer and deliver distance learning programs for K-12 classrooms. Candidates should have oral communication skills, organizational skills, personal interest in the field, strong interpersonal skills, written communication skills. Duration is 1 semester. Position available as unpaid or at $8–$10 per hour. Open to college juniors, college seniors, recent college graduates, graduate students. ▶ *2 fall/spring teaching interns:* responsibilities include assisting staff in teaching school groups who come to the zoo by teaching principles of zoology, ecology, and conservation science. Candidates should have knowledge of field, oral communication skills, strong interpersonal skills, experience working with children. Duration is 18–20 weeks. $8–$10 per hour. Open to college juniors, college seniors, recent college graduates, graduate students. ▶ *10 summer teaching interns:* responsibilities include helping to run conservation-based summer camp at the zoo, leading children in crafts, games, songs, and demonstrating live animals. Candidates should have knowledge of field, oral communication skills, strong interpersonal skills, experience working with children. Duration is 11 weeks. $8–$10 per hour. Open to college juniors, college seniors, recent college graduates, graduate students.
Benefits Formal training, on-the-job training.
Contact Write, fax, e-mail, or through World Wide Web site Ms. Ilyssa Gillman, Intern Coordinator. Fax: 718-365-3300. E-mail: igillman@wcs.org. No phone calls. In-person interview required. Applicants must submit a letter of interest, resume, letter of recommendation, application from Web site. Applications are accepted continuously. World Wide Web: http://www.wcs.org.

WILDLIFE SOCIETY
5410 Grosvenor Lane
Bethesda, Maryland 20814-2197

General Information Society whose mission is to enhance the scientific, technical, managerial, and educational capabilities and achievements of wildlife professionals. Established in 1937. Number of employees: 12. Number of internship applications received each year: 15.
Internships Available ▶ *2 policy interns:* responsibilities include researching conservation issues, preparing background information for use in testimony or comments, attending briefings and hearings, writing for and assisting with the preparation of publications, and assisting with the routine activities of the Society. Candidates should have knowledge of field, research skills, self-motivation, writing skills, course work in wildlife, natural resources, biology, or management (preferred). Duration is 6 months. $1000 per month. Open to college seniors, recent college graduates, graduate students. International applications accepted.
Benefits Willing to provide letters of recommendation.
Contact Write, call, fax, e-mail, or through World Wide Web site Thomas M. Franklin, Wildlife Policy Director. Phone: 301-897-9770. Fax: 301-530-2471. E-mail: tws@wildlife.org. In-person interview recommended (telephone interview accepted). Applicants must submit a letter of interest, resume, academic transcripts, two writing samples, three personal references. Applications are accepted continuously. World Wide Web: http://www.wildlife.org.

WOLF RIDGE ENVIRONMENTAL LEARNING CENTER
6282 Cranberry Road
Finland, Minnesota 55603

General Information Residential environmental school for students of all ages whose mission is to teach stewardship, promote a quality environment through educational programs, and awaken the natural curiosity of the human mind. Established in 1971. Number of employees: 55. Number of internship applications received each year: 50.
Internships Available ▶ *16 student naturalists:* responsibilities include teaching ecology, cultural history, and recreation classes; participating in diplomatic liaison relationships; participating in seminars; conducting formal evening slide presentations; enrolling in a post-baccalaureate program in environmental education offered through the University of Minnesota, Duluth. Candidates should have ability to work independently, analytical skills, college degree in related field, knowledge of field, oral communication skills, organizational skills, personal interest in the field, plan to pursue career in field, research skills, self-motivation, strong interpersonal skills, strong leadership ability, written communication skills, desire to learn, willingness and ability to work alone and engage in physical activity. Duration is 9 months. Stipend of $3500. Open to recent college graduates, graduate students, career changers. International applications accepted.
Benefits Formal training, free housing, free meals, job counseling, names of contacts, on-the-job training, opportunity to attend seminars/workshops, tuition assistance, willing to act as a professional reference, willing to complete paperwork for educational credit, willing to provide letters of recommendation, post-baccalaureate certificate in environmental education through University of Minnesota, Duluth.
Contact Write, call, fax, e-mail, or through World Wide Web site Joe Walewski, Director of Naturalist Training. Phone: 218-353-7414. Fax: 218-353-7762. E-mail: mail@wolf-ridge.org. Telephone interview required. Applicants must submit a formal organization application, letter of interest, resume, academic transcripts, three personal references. Application deadline: March 31. World Wide Web: http://www.wolf-ridge.org.

WOODCOCK NATURE CENTER
56 Deer Run Road
Wilton, Connecticut 06897

General Information Organization that provides year-round youth programs focused on native species of flora and fauna found on site. Established in 1973. Number of employees: 4. Number of internship applications received each year: 30.
Internships Available ▶ *6 environmental education interns:* responsibilities include planning and teaching environmental/natural education and outdoor recreation programs to children ages 4-11 during day camp; participating in daily operation and maintenance of WNC and preserve. Candidates should have experience in the field, personal interest in the field, self-motivation, courses in environmental science, biology, elementary education, or related field (preferred), CPR, Standard First Aid (desired). Duration is June 2 to August 22 (off July 4 week). $200–$275 per week. Open to college sophomores, college juniors, college seniors, recent college graduates, graduate students, career changers, individuals reentering the workforce.
Benefits Possibility of free housing.
Contact Write, call, or e-mail John McLeran, Co-Director. Phone: 203-762-7280. E-mail: woodcock.natrue.ctr@snet.net. In-person interview recommended (telephone interview accepted). Applicants must submit a resume, three personal references, cover letter. Applications are accepted continuously. World Wide Web: http://www.woodcocknaturecenter.org.

WOOD LAKE NATURE CENTER
6710 Lake Shore Drive
Richfield, Minnesota 55423

General Information Natural area with 150 acres of fields, woods, marsh, and restored prairie preserved by the city of Richfield to give children and adults a place to explore, observe, and learn about the natural world. Established in 1970. Number of employees: 7. Division of City of Richfield, Recreation Services, Richfield, Minnesota. Number of internship applications received each year: 50.
Internships Available ▶ *1–2 naturalist interns:* responsibilities include leading environmental education activities for individuals of all ages. Candidates should have college courses in field, knowledge of field, oral communication skills, plan to pursue career in field, self-motivation, strong interpersonal skills. Duration is flexible (10 weeks or more). Position available as unpaid or paid. Open to college juniors, college seniors, recent college graduates, graduate students, law students, career changers, individuals reentering the workforce. ▶ *1–2 summer interns:* responsibilities include teaching classes, supervising volunteers, exhibit design, and animal care. Candidates should have ability to work independently, knowledge of field, oral communication skills, plan to pursue career in field, self-motivation, strong interpersonal skills. Duration is June through August. Position available as unpaid or at stipend of $150 per week. Open to college juniors, college seniors, recent college graduates, graduate students, career changers, individuals reentering the workforce.
Benefits Formal training, job counseling, names of contacts, on-the-job training, opportunity to attend seminars/workshops, willing to act as a professional reference, willing to complete paperwork for educational credit, willing to provide letters of recommendation.
Contact Write, call, fax, e-mail, or through World Wide Web site Mr. Tom Moffatt, Naturalist/Intern Coordinator. Phone: 612-861-9365. Fax: 612-861-9367. E-mail: tmoffatt@ci.richfield.mn.us. In-person interview recommended (telephone interview accepted). Applicants must submit a formal organization application, letter of interest, resume, academic transcripts, three personal references, criminal background check required. Application deadline: February 1 for spring, May 1 for summer, August 1 for fall, December 1 for winter. World Wide Web: http://www.ci.richfield.mn.us/RecreationServices/WoodLake/.

YMCA BECKET–CHIMNEY CORNERS OUTDOOR CENTER
748 Hamilton Road
Becket, Massachusetts 01223

General Information 1200-acre outdoor center in Berkshire Mountains serving over 10,000 guests annually in retreat, environmental education, adventure, and family camp programs. Established in 1903. Number of employees: 350. Number of internship applications received each year: 30.
Internships Available ▶ *Program instructors:* responsibilities include leading recreation and education programs; providing general support and administrative procedures specific to the outdoor center programs. Candidates should have ability to work with others, personal interest in the field, strong leadership ability. Duration is 2–12 months. $270 per week. Open to recent high school graduates, college freshmen, college sophomores, college juniors, college seniors, recent college graduates, career changers, individuals reentering the workforce. International applications accepted.
Benefits Formal training, free housing, free meals, job counseling, names of contacts, on-the-job training, opportunity to attend seminars/workshops, possible full-time employment, willing to act as a professional reference, willing to complete paperwork for educational credit, willing to provide letters of recommendation, free use of the facility when not working.
Contact Write, call, fax, or e-mail Eric Grimes, Director of Outdoor Environmental Education. Phone: 413-623-8991. Fax: 413-623-5890. E-mail: egrimes@bccymca.org. Telephone interview required. Applicants must submit a formal organization application, letter of interest, resume, three personal references. Applications are accepted continuously. World Wide Web: http://www.bccymca.org.

YMCA CAMP KERN
5291 State Route 350
Oregonia, Ohio 45054

General Information Camp operating as a residential outdoor education center. Established in 1910. Number of employees:

YMCA Camp Kern (continued)

30. Branch of Dayton YMCA, Dayton, Ohio. Number of internship applications received each year: 8.

Internships Available ▶ *3 naturalist interns:* responsibilities include teaching and leading activities dealing with natural history, pioneer, and Native American topics. Candidates should have oral communication skills, personal interest in the field, self-motivation, strong interpersonal skills, desire to work with children. Duration is one fall or spring. $110 per week. Open to college freshmen, college sophomores, college juniors, college seniors, recent college graduates, graduate students, law students, career changers, individuals reentering the workforce. International applications accepted.

Benefits Free housing, free meals, names of contacts, opportunity to attend seminars/workshops, possible full-time employment, willing to complete paperwork for educational credit, willing to provide letters of recommendation.

Contact Write, call, fax, or e-mail Dave Moran, Director of Outdoor Education. Phone: 513-932-3756. Fax: 513-932-8607. E-mail: dmoran@daytonymca.org. In-person interview recommended (telephone interview accepted). Applicants must submit a letter of interest, resume. Applications are accepted continuously. World Wide Web: http://www.campkern.org.

YMCA CAMP WIDJIWAGAN'S ENVIRONMENTAL EDUCATION PROGRAM
3788 North Arm Road
Ely, Minnesota 55731-9604

General Information Educational facility that uses a wilderness-based program to teach about the environment. Established in 1973. Number of employees: 18. Unit of YMCA of Greater St. Paul, St. Paul, Minnesota. Number of internship applications received each year: 15.

Internships Available ▶ *2–4 naturalist interns:* responsibilities include leading students in grades 4-9, helping co-lead small group activities for 10 students, serving in program support roles, and assisting with curriculum as part of independent intern project development. Candidates should have oral communication skills, organizational skills, personal interest in the field, self-motivation, strong interpersonal skills. Duration is 1 semester. $120–$160 per month. Open to college sophomores, college juniors, college seniors, recent college graduates. International applications accepted.

Benefits Free meals, willing to complete paperwork for educational credit, willing to provide letters of recommendation, extensive training and staff development, possibility of seasonal, full-time employment.

Contact Write, call, or e-mail Ms. Karen Pick, Senior Program Director–Camp Widjiwagan. Phone: 218-365-2117. Fax: 218-365-2018. E-mail: widji@spacestar.org. Applicants must submit a formal organization application, resume, personal reference, letter of recommendation. Application deadline: June 10 for fall, August 15 for winter. World Wide Web: http://www.mtn.org/widji.

SOCIAL ADVOCACY ORGANIZATIONS

ACADEMY FOR EDUCATIONAL DEVELOPMENT
1825 Connecticut Avenue, NW
Washington, District of Columbia 20009

General Information Nonprofit organization committed to solving critical social issues within the U.S. and around the world through education, social marketing, research, training, policy analysis, and innovative program design and management. Established in 1961. Number of employees: 740. Number of internship applications received each year: 350.

Internships Available ▶ *Interns:* responsibilities include working in various areas of the organization. Candidates should have computer skills, editing skills, oral communication skills, organizational skills, written communication skills. Duration is flexible. Position available as unpaid or at wage based on academic status, work experience, and project budget; non-paid internships provide academic credit and/or work experience. Open to college freshmen, college sophomores, college juniors, college seniors, graduate students, international students who have U.S. work permit. International applications accepted.

Benefits On-the-job training, possible full-time employment, willing to act as a professional reference, willing to complete paperwork for educational credit.

Contact Fax or e-mail Tanya Unwalla, Human Resources Coordinator. Phone: 202-884-8502. Fax: 202-884-8413. E-mail: employ@aed.org. In-person interview recommended (telephone interview accepted). Applicants must submit a letter of interest, resume, references and writing samples (if selected). Applications are accepted continuously. World Wide Web: http://www.aed.org.

ACCURACY IN ACADEMIA
4455 Connecticut Avenue
Washington, District of Columbia 20008

General Information Nonprofit organization dedicated to fighting political correctness and defending free speech on college campuses nationwide. Established in 1985. Number of employees: 8. Number of internship applications received each year: 75.

Internships Available ▶ *2 writer/research interns:* responsibilities include writing and research for newspaper the "Campus Report" and for Web page; assisting with conference planning on an as needed basis. Candidates should have ability to work independently, analytical skills, computer skills, editing skills, knowledge of field, office skills, oral communication skills, organizational skills, personal interest in the field, plan to pursue career in field, research skills, self-motivation, strong interpersonal skills, writing skills. Duration is 8–16 weeks. $25 per day. Open to high school students, recent high school graduates, college freshmen, college sophomores, college juniors, college seniors, recent college graduates, graduate students, law students, career changers, individuals reentering the workforce.

Benefits On-the-job training, opportunity to attend seminars/workshops, possible full-time employment, willing to act as a professional reference, willing to complete paperwork for educational credit, willing to provide letters of recommendation.

Contact Write, fax, or e-mail Executive Director. Phone: 202-364-3085. Fax: 202-364-4098. E-mail: aimintern@yahoo.com. In-person interview recommended (telephone interview accepted). Applicants must submit a formal organization application, letter of interest, resume, two letters of recommendation, 2 writing samples (for writing positions). Application deadline: March 31 for summer, August 15 for fall, November 15 for winter/spring. World Wide Web: http://www.academia.org.

THE ACTIVISM CENTER AT WETLANDS PRESERVE
PO Box 344
New York, New York 10108

General Information Multi-issue activism organization that uses public education and creative protest to challenge the abuse of animals, the environment, and human beings by corporations and governments worldwide. Established in 1989. Number of internship applications received each year: 200.

Internships Available ▶ *Animal rights legislative internship:* responsibilities include lobbying legislators and consulates on local, state, federal, and international animal rights issues; conducting research; organizing voters in critical legislative districts; acting as group liaison to organizations working on local, state, federal, and international animal rights issues. Candidates should have ability to work independently, editing skills, organizational skills, research skills, self-motivation, writing skills. Duration is flexible. Unpaid. ▶ *Animal rights resource and outreach interns:* responsibilities include serving as resource librarian to resource center of hundreds of books, videos, and informational files on animal rights issues; writing articles on organization's animal rights activities for "Wetlands Works" newsletter; contacting student groups to arrange presentations at schools. Candidates should have organizational skills, personal interest in the field, writing skills. Duration is flexible. Unpaid. ▶ *Anti-fur interns:* responsibilities include working with staff and volunteers to organize anti-fur protests and other events, and developing educational materials for activists and the public, including a boycott/protest target list of stores that sell fur in NYC; conducting extensive research and developing detailed files on the NYC fur industry, working on legislative campaigns and ballot initiatives to ban the sale of fur and to ban fur farming and trapping. Candidates should have ability to work independently, ability to work with others, computer skills, organizational skills, personal interest in the field, research skills. Duration is flexible. Unpaid. ▶ *Anti-sweatshop interns:* responsibilities include working with the Global Sweatshop Coalition on direct solidarity campaign with workers on the bottom rung of the global economic ladder to defend fair wages and decent working conditions and uphold the rights of workers, both within the U.S. and abroad to organize and unionize. Candidates should have oral communication skills, organizational skills, personal interest in the field, self-motivation, strong leadership ability, writing skills. Duration is flexible. Unpaid. ▶ *1–4 computer maintenance interns:* responsibilities include maintain and administer small network of Macintosh, Windows, and Linux machines; troubleshoot all machines; install new hardware and software, secure donations of new equipment. Candidates should have ability to work independently, computer skills, knowledge of field, self-motivation. Duration is flexible. Unpaid. ▶ *1–10 data managers:* responsibilities include preparing written instructions for use with all databases; instructing high school interns in data entry; supervising and assessing work of assistants; and completing several hours of data entry weekly. Candidates should have ability to work with others, computer skills, editing skills, knowledge of field, office skills, organizational skills, knowledge of Microsoft Excel, Filemaker Pro, Access (strongly preferred), knowledge of MYSQL also helpful. Duration is flexible. Unpaid. ▶ *Earth and animal liberation political prisoner support interns:* responsibilities include generating media attention, public support, and legal assistance for people unjustly jailed for involvement in environmental and animal rights activism. Candidates should have ability to work with others, oral communication skills, research skills, self-motivation, written communication skills. Duration is flexible. Unpaid. ▶ *Fund-raising/development interns:* responsibilities include researching and implementing fund-raising and organizational development strategies to support human rights, animal rights, and environmental projects. Candidates should have knowledge of field, office skills, organizational skills, research skills, strong interpersonal skills, strong leadership ability. Unpaid. ▶ *Graphic designer and/or Web designer:* responsibilities include laying out brochures, reports, posters, and pamphlets; creating logos; designing and/or coding Web sites on human, animal, and environmental justice issues. Candidates should have ability to work independently, computer skills, experience in the field, self-motivation, artistic/graphic design skills. Duration is flexible. Unpaid. ▶ *Indigenous rights interns:* responsibilities include working with interns, volunteers, and staff on organizing demonstrations, rallies, and marches against corporations involved in the destruction of indigenous homelands in Colombia, Ecuador, and Burma; organizing educational forums on a broad range of indigenous rights issues; networking with local, national, and international human rights and environmental groups. Candidates should have ability to work with others, oral communication skills, personal interest in the field, self-motivation, strong leadership ability, writing skills. Duration is flexible. Unpaid. ▶ *1–6 internship outreach/recruitment assistants:* responsibilities include processing internship applications; responding to intern inquiries; posting information on internship program to internship Web sites and activism listservers; arranging, coordinating, and staffing information booths at concerts, street fairs, and other events to publicize Wetlands internships; coordinating mailings to high school and college internship programs and student organizations. Candidates should have office skills, oral communication skills, organizational skills, research skills, strong interpersonal skills. Duration is flexible. Unpaid. ▶ *Media relations interns:* responsibilities include maintaining database of contact information for over 600 news organizations; drafting media advisories and news releases; conducting interviews with media; and pitching stories to media through oral communication. Candidates should have ability to work independently, computer skills, editing skills, oral communication skills, personal interest

in the field, writing skills. Duration is flexible. Unpaid. ▶ *Novice activist interns for the environment and human and animal rights:* responsibilities include working on a variety of projects as the need arises in order to gain exposure to a wide range of issues and tasks, issues will include fighting sweatshop labor, working for legislation against animal cruelty, defending rainforests, and campaigning against the first trade. Candidates should have ability to work independently, ability to work with others, personal interest in the field, self-motivation. Duration is flexible. Unpaid. ▶ *Protest photographers/videographers:* responsibilities include attending conferences, rallies, marches, demonstrations and other events, taking photos and/or short video to be used by mainstream and independent media to document protest activities; videographers may also develop produced programs for video and public access TV. Candidates should have ability to work independently, knowledge of field, personal interest in the field, self-motivation. Unpaid. ▶ *1–6 protest/direct action/civil disobedience interns:* responsibilities include working with an affinity group in organizing direct actions, protests, and street theater events; taking on responsibilities including researching issues and targets; scouting locations; researching, building and/or acquiring special equipment, creating banners, signs, literature, press releases, and press packets; recruiting participants for the action and supporting roles; alerting media to the upcoming event. Candidates should have ability to work with others, personal interest in the field, self-motivation, strong leadership ability. Duration is flexible. Unpaid. Open to any interested person. International applications accepted.

Benefits Names of contacts, on-the-job training, opportunity to attend seminars/workshops, willing to act as a professional reference, willing to complete paperwork for educational credit, willing to provide letters of recommendation.

International Internships Available.

Contact Write, call, fax, e-mail, or through World Wide Web site Adam Weissman, Internship Program Coordinator. Phone: 212-947-7744. Fax: 212-947-7773. E-mail: adam@wetlands-preserve.org. In-person interview recommended (telephone interview accepted). Applicants must submit a formal organization application. Applications are accepted continuously. World Wide Web: http://www.wetlands-preserve.org/activismcenter.html.

ADC RESEARCH INSTITUTE
4201 Connecticut Avenue, NW, Suite 300
Washington, District of Columbia 20008

General Information Grassroots civil rights organization that defends the rights of Arab-Americans, promotes Arab heritage, and addresses Middle East issues. Established in 1980. Number of employees: 13.

Internships Available ▶ *1–2 American Committee on Jerusalem interns:* responsibilities include assisting on projects and campaigns which defend the rights of Palestinians, Muslims, and Christians; educating the public and policymakers for a balanced viewpoint in Jerusalem; monitoring media coverage of Palistinian issues; administrative duties. Candidates should have computer skills, oral communication skills, research skills, writing skills, knowledge of the history of Jerusalem and current Middle East politics. Duration is 1 summer or semester (June 1 to July 31 or longer). $1000 for graduate students; $750 for undergraduates for summer; prorated for semesters. Open to college sophomores, college juniors, college seniors, recent college graduates, graduate students, law students. ▶ *2 education and outreach interns:* responsibilities include working closely with director of educational programs in mobilizing grassroots network of ADC activists; campaigning for Arab-American issues; responding to requests from educators and activists; developing lesson plans; working with peace and human rights organizations on Middle East issues, Palestinian rights, and the humanitarian crisis in Iraq; writing articles for ADC newsletter. Candidates should have writing skills, knowledge of Arab world or Arab-American community. Duration is 1-2 semesters or 10-week summer term. Position available as unpaid or at $800 stipend for graduate students; $500 for undergraduates during summer term; prorated during semester. Open to college sophomores, college juniors, college seniors, recent college graduates, graduate students. ▶ *Government affairs interns:* responsibilities include assisting government affairs director in monitoring Congress and administration

ADC Research Institute (continued)

on Arab-American issues (Middle East and civil rights), researching legislation, attending hearings, and writing for ADC newsletter. Candidates should have knowledge of field, research skills, writing skills. Duration is 1-2 semesters or one summer (10 weeks). Position available as unpaid or at $800 for graduate students; $500 for undergraduates for summer; prorated for semesters. Open to college juniors, college seniors, recent college graduates, graduate students, law students, career changers. ▶ *1–2 information systems interns:* responsibilities include organizing Internet workshop and assisting in all aspects of registration process for national convention. Candidates should have ability to work independently, oral communication skills, research skills, extensive knowledge/willingness to learn, and good computer instincts. Duration is flexible (full-time during summer). $800 stipend for graduate students; $500 for undergraduates during summer; prorated during semester. Open to college sophomores, college juniors, college seniors, recent college graduates, graduate students. ▶ *4 legal interns:* responsibilities include working closely with attorney on immigration law, civil and human rights law, international law, and treaties; screening new cases as they come into the office; legal research; drafting client letters and press releases. Candidates should have ability to work independently, analytical skills, research skills, writing skills, 1-2 years of law school, strong commitment to civil rights and diversity. Duration is 1-2 semesters or 10-week summer term. Position available as unpaid or at $800 for 10-week summer term; prorated during semester. Open to graduate students, law students. ▶ *4 media and publications interns:* responsibilities include writing articles for ADC Times; conducting research; producing and/or updating publications; helping write, edit, and design Annual Activity Report; maintaining video book library and filing system; monitoring media; responding to public and media information requests. Candidates should have knowledge of field, research skills, writing skills. Duration is 1-2 semesters or 10-week summer term. Position available as unpaid or at $800 for graduate students; $500 for undergraduates during summer term; prorated for semesters. Open to college sophomores, college juniors, college seniors, recent college graduates, graduate students. ▶ *2 organizing and special events interns:* responsibilities include assisting the director with work involving the national network of local chapters, organizing regional conferences, and monitoring and mobilizing activists to work on projects. Candidates should have computer skills, knowledge of field, oral communication skills, organizational skills, written communication skills. Duration is 1-2 semesters or 10-week summer term. Position available as unpaid or at $800 for graduate students; $500 for undergraduates during summer; prorated for semesters. Open to college sophomores, college juniors, college seniors, recent college graduates, graduate students. ▶ *15 summer interns:* responsibilities include attending meetings and conferences of government officials; emphasis on educational programs located around Washington, D.C.; working with legal, media, education, and organizing departments in relation to projects and campaigns; working with ADC programs and campaigns in legal, education, media, and political action. Candidates should have knowledge of field, writing skills. Duration is 10 weeks (June 1 to July 31 or longer). Position available as unpaid or at $750 stipend for undergraduates; $1000 stipend for graduate and law students. Open to college sophomores, college juniors, college seniors, recent college graduates, graduate students, law students. International applications accepted.

Benefits Names of contacts, on-the-job training, opportunity to attend seminars/workshops, willing to complete paperwork for educational credit, willing to provide letters of recommendation, one day per week of leadership development skills for summer interns, introduction to Washington, assistance with locating roommates and/or housing, opportunity to attend meetings with Congress, administration officials, Arab embassies, and American organizations.

Contact Write, call, fax, or e-mail Mr. Marvin Wingfield, Director of Education and Outreach. Phone: 202-244-2990. Fax: 202-244-3196. E-mail: marvinw@adc.org. Applicants must submit a letter of interest, resume, academic transcripts, two letters of recommendation, 2-page essay. Application deadline: January 15

for legal department interns; continuous for fall and spring, March 1 for summer. World Wide Web: http://www.adc.org.

ADVOCATES FOR YOUTH
1025 Vermont Avenue, NW, Suite 200
Washington, District of Columbia 20005

General Information National organization dedicated exclusively to the advancement of adolescent sexual and reproductive health.

Internships Available ▶ *Interns.* Duration is 3 month (minimum of 35 hours per week) part-time positions may be available. Position available as unpaid or paid.

Contact Write Director of Internships. Applicants must submit a letter of interest, resume. Applications are accepted continuously. World Wide Web: http://www.advocatesforyouth.org.

AIDS ACTION
1906 Sunderland Place, NW
Washington, District of Columbia 20036

General Information National organization devoted solely to lobbying the federal government for AIDS policy, legislation, and funding. Established in 1984. Number of employees: 17. Number of internship applications received each year: 25.

Internships Available ▶ *1–3 Pedro Zamora fellows:* responsibilities include updating/writing policy briefs on various issues; researching variety of health and civil rights issues related to HIV; attending congressional hearings and coalition meetings; monitoring voting records. Candidates should have ability to work with others, analytical skills, knowledge of field, oral communication skills, research skills, self-motivation, written communication skills. Duration is 10–24 weeks. Position available as unpaid or at $300 per week. Open to recent high school graduates, college freshmen, college sophomores, college juniors, college seniors, recent college graduates, graduate students. International applications accepted.

Benefits Names of contacts, opportunity to attend seminars/workshops, possible full-time employment, willing to act as a professional reference, willing to complete paperwork for educational credit.

Contact Write, call, fax, e-mail, or through World Wide Web site Scott Brawley, Fellowship Coordinator. Phone: 202-530-8030 Ext. 3047. Fax: 202-530-8031. E-mail: sbrawley@aidsaction.org. In-person interview required. Applicants must submit a formal organization application, letter of interest, resume, two personal references, letter of recommendation. Application deadline: April 15 for summer, July 15 for fall, December 1 for spring. World Wide Web: http://www.aidsaction.org.

ALASKA CIVIL LIBERTIES UNION
PO Box 201844
Anchorage, Alaska 99520-1844

General Information Nonprofit, non-partisan organization dedicated to protecting the guarantees of civil liberties in the Bill of Rights and Alaska Constitution through public education, litigation, and political lobbying. Established in 1983. Number of employees: 3. Affiliate of American Civil Liberties Union, New York, New York. Number of internship applications received each year: 4.

Internships Available ▶ *1 law clerk:* responsibilities include researching and drafting legal memoranda, assisting volunteer attorneys with filing pleadings, monitoring legislative committee hearings, and researching/drafting testimony and position papers on legislation affecting civil liberties. Candidates should have ability to work independently, analytical skills, oral communication skills, personal interest in the field, research skills, writing skills. Duration is one quarter, semester, or summer (flexible). Unpaid. Open to graduate students, law students. International applications accepted.

Benefits Names of contacts, willing to act as a professional reference, willing to complete paperwork for educational credit, willing to provide letters of recommendation, free housing (when available).

Contact Write, fax, or e-mail Jennifer Rudinger, Executive Director, PO Box 201844, Anchorage, Alaska 99520-1844. Fax: 907-258-0288. E-mail: akclu@alaska.net. No phone calls. Telephone interview required. Applicants must submit a letter of interest, resume, academic transcripts. Applications are accepted continuously. World Wide Web: http://www.aclu.org.

ALLIANCE FOR HEALTH REFORM
1444 Eye Street, NW, Suite 910
Washington, District of Columbia 20005

General Information Nonpartisan, not-for-profit organization that strives to educate news media, congressional staff, and others about issues in health reform. Established in 1991. Number of employees: 7. Number of internship applications received each year: 50.
Internships Available ▶ *2–3 interns:* responsibilities include helping with seminar logistics; performing research on all aspects of health reform; carrying out general administrative duties; working closely with experienced policy professionals, congressional staffers, administrators, journalists, and other members of the policy community. Candidates should have ability to work with others, college courses in field, oral communication skills, organizational skills, personal interest in the field, research skills, written communication skills. Duration is 2 months minimum. Position available as unpaid or paid. Open to college freshmen, college sophomores, college juniors, college seniors, recent college graduates, graduate students, law students, career changers, individuals reentering the workforce. International applications accepted.
Benefits Opportunity to attend seminars/workshops, willing to complete paperwork for educational credit, willing to provide letters of recommendation.
Contact Write, fax, e-mail, or through World Wide Web site Ms. Nancy Peavy, Director of Operations. Fax: 202-789-2233. E-mail: npeavy@allhealth.org. In-person interview recommended (telephone interview accepted). Applicants must submit a letter of interest, resume, academic transcripts, writing sample, two personal references. Application deadline: March 1 for summer, November 1 for winter. World Wide Web: http://www.allhealth.org.

ALLIANCE FOR JUSTICE
11 Dupont Circle, NW, 2nd Floor
Washington, District of Columbia 20036

General Information Association of national, regional, and local organizations working for the public interest to provide equal access to government forums for all groups and individuals. Established in 1979. Number of employees: 30. Number of internship applications received each year: 200.
Internships Available ▶ *1–2 Everett interns:* responsibilities include general office duties, working mostly with First Monday Coordinator on First Monday event (held the first Monday in October of each year). Candidates should have ability to work with others, computer skills, oral communication skills, organizational skills, research skills, written communication skills. Duration is June to August. Paid. Open to college freshmen, college sophomores, college juniors, college seniors, graduate students, law students. ▶ *1–2 fellowship interns:* responsibilities include researching records of judicial nominees, providing technical assistance on laws governing lobbying and electoral activities by nonprofits, organizing national "First Monday" conferences promoting public interest work, and analyzing legal issues that affect the public interest community. Candidates should have computer skills, oral communication skills, organizational skills, research skills, writing skills. Duration is 1 August to September—one year. $32,000 per year. Open to law school graduates. ▶ *Winter interns:* responsibilities include general office duties. Candidates should have computer skills, oral communication skills, organizational skills, research skills, writing skills. Duration is school year—flexible. Unpaid. Open to college freshmen, college sophomores, college juniors, college seniors, graduate students, law students. International applications accepted.

Benefits Names of contacts, on-the-job training, opportunity to attend seminars/workshops, willing to act as a professional reference, willing to complete paperwork for educational credit, willing to provide letters of recommendation.
Contact Write, fax, or e-mail Alicia Holmes, Director of Administration. Fax: 202-822-6068. E-mail: alliance@afj.org. No phone calls. In-person interview recommended (telephone interview accepted). Applicants must submit a letter of interest, resume, writing sample. Application deadline: February 1 for summer, October 1 for winter. World Wide Web: http://www.afj.org.

ALTERNATIVES TO MARRIAGE PROJECT
PO Box 991010
Boston, Massachusetts 02199

General Information National, nonprofit organization working for fairness and equality for unmarried people including those who choose not to marry, cannot marry, or live together before marriage. Established in 1998. Number of employees: 1. Number of internship applications received each year: 50.
Internships Available ▶ *1 project intern:* responsibilities include helping with general office and clerical work and helping with other projects. Candidates should have computer skills, oral communication skills, personal interest in the field, self-motivation. Duration is 1 semester. Unpaid. Open to recent high school graduates, college freshmen, college sophomores, college juniors, college seniors, recent college graduates, graduate students, law students, career changers, individuals reentering the workforce. International applications accepted.
Benefits Job counseling, on-the-job training, willing to act as a professional reference, willing to complete paperwork for educational credit, willing to provide letters of recommendation, informal friendly environment.
Contact E-mail or through World Wide Web site Dorian Solot, Executive Director. Phone: 781-793-0296. Fax: 781-394-6625. E-mail: dsolot@unmarried.org. Telephone interview required. Applicants must submit three personal references, application or resume and cover letter. Application deadline: March 30 for summer; continuous for other positions. World Wide Web: http://www.unmarried.org.

AMERICAN CIVIL LIBERTIES UNION
125 Broad Street, 18th Floor
New York, New York 10004

General Information Public interest, nonprofit organization. Established in 1920. Number of employees: 200. Number of internship applications received each year: 250.
Internships Available ▶ *1–2 college interns:* responsibilities include various research projects for attorneys in legal department, as well as other projects assigned by paralegal including intake correspondence. Candidates should have computer skills, personal interest in the field, research skills, self-motivation, strong interpersonal skills, written communication skills. Duration is 10–12 weeks. Unpaid. Open to recent high school graduates, college freshmen, college sophomores, college juniors, college seniors, recent college graduates. International applications accepted.
Benefits Opportunity to attend seminars/workshops, willing to act as a professional reference, willing to complete paperwork for educational credit.
Contact Write or call Undergraduate Internship Coordinator. Phone: 212-549-2610. Fax: 212-549-2651. Applicants must submit a letter of interest, resume, 5-page non-fiction writing sample. Application deadline: March 1 for summer, August 1 for fall, November 1 for spring. World Wide Web: http://www.aclu.org.

AMERICAN FORUM IN WASHINGTON
National Press Building, 529 14th Street, NW, Suite 1071
Washington, District of Columbia 20045

General Information Progressive, nonprofit media organization that publishes articles on quality of life issues and provides a resource for progressives to disseminate social commentary to the media. Established in 1981. Number of employees: 6. Number of internship applications received each year: 60.

American Forum in Washington (continued)

Internships Available ▶ *2–3 editorial assistants:* responsibilities include editing and proofing of articles and related research; contacting authors and tracking in-office article status; developing press releases, PSAs, and audio and video scripts. Candidates should have ability to work independently, ability to work with others, editing skills, office skills, written communication skills. Duration is 1 semester (minimum 14 hours per week). Unpaid. ▶ *2–4 media interns:* responsibilities include surveying media; researching and writing reports; analyzing usage data; preparing media packets for print, broadcast, and online media outlets. Candidates should have ability to work independently, oral communication skills, personal interest in the field, research skills, strong interpersonal skills. Duration is 1 semester minimum (14 hours per week). Unpaid. ▶ *1–3 state organizers:* responsibilities include developing reports, board volunteer events, organizational affiliations, policy updates and related information, assisting with state meeting and member building. Candidates should have oral communication skills, organizational skills, strong interpersonal skills, strong leadership ability, written communication skills. Duration is minimum 14 hours per week. Unpaid. Open to recent high school graduates, college freshmen, college sophomores, college juniors, college seniors, recent college graduates, graduate students, career changers. International applications accepted.

Benefits Names of contacts, opportunity to attend seminars/workshops, possible full-time employment, willing to act as a professional reference, willing to complete paperwork for educational credit, willing to provide letters of recommendation.

Contact Write, call, fax, or e-mail Lutrecia N. Borders, Intern Coordinator. Phone: 202-638-1431. Fax: 202-638-1434. E-mail: forum@mediaforum.org. In-person interview recommended (telephone interview accepted). Applicants must submit a letter of interest, resume, academic transcripts. Applications are accepted continuously. World Wide Web: http://www.mediaforum.org.

AMERICAN FRIENDS SERVICE COMMITTEE
1501 Cherry Street
Philadelphia, Pennsylvania 19102-1479

General Information Nonprofit organization. Established in 1917. Number of employees: 350. Number of internship applications received each year: 40.

Internships Available ▶ *20 Mexico project volunteers:* responsibilities include volunteer work in rural Mexico. Candidates should have ability to work with others, oral communication skills, self-motivation, Spanish skills. Duration is June 29 to August 18. Unpaid. Open to recent high school graduates, college freshmen, college sophomores, college juniors, college seniors, recent college graduates, graduate students, law students, law school graduates, individuals reentering the workforce.

Benefits Opportunity to attend seminars/workshops, willing to provide letters of recommendation.

International Internships Available in Xilitla, Mexico.

Contact Call or e-mail Kate Houston, Recruitment Coordinator. Phone: 215-241-7295. Fax: 215-241-7026. E-mail: mexsummer@afsc.org. Applicants must submit a formal organization application, resume, 4 references, $1250 to cover housing and meals. Application deadline: March 1. World Wide Web: http://www.afsc.org/upcoming/mexsumr.htm.

AMERICAN FRIENDS SERVICE COMMITTEE– ARIZONA AREA PROGRAM
931 North Fifth Avenue
Tucson, Arizona 85705

General Information Nonprofit social justice and peace organization. Established in 1917. Number of employees: 2. Branch of American Friends Service Committee, Philadelphia, Pennsylvania. Number of internship applications received each year: 10.

Internships Available ▶ *1 community intern:* responsibilities include contributing to current projects; planning, publicizing, and facilitating conferences and workshops; supporting coalitions and other groups; helping maintain area program office in Tucson; creating a personal project in consultation with program coordinator; promoting peace and justice. Candidates should have ability to work independently, analytical skills, computer skills, oral communication skills, organizational skills, personal interest in the field, self-motivation, strong interpersonal skills, writing skills. Duration is 9 to 12 months. $650–$800 per month. Open to recent high school graduates, recent college graduates. International applications accepted.

Benefits Health insurance, names of contacts, on-the-job training, opportunity to attend seminars/workshops, travel reimbursement, willing to act as a professional reference, willing to complete paperwork for educational credit, willing to provide letters of recommendation.

Contact Write, call, fax, or e-mail Caroline Isaacs, Program Coordinator, 931 North Fifth Avenue, Tucson, Arizona 85705. Phone: 520-623-9141. Fax: 520-623-5901. E-mail: afscazcj@azstarnet.com. In-person interview recommended (telephone interview accepted). Applicants must submit a resume, writing sample, three personal references. Application deadline: April 1. World Wide Web: http://www.afsc.org/az.htm.

AMERICAN HUMANE
63 Inverness Drive East
Englewood, Colorado 80112

General Information National organization dedicated to identifying and preventing animal and child abuse and neglect; provides advocacy, research, training, technical assistance, and other services in the areas of animal and child protection. Established in 1877. Number of employees: 65. Number of internship applications received each year: 10.

Internships Available ▶ *1 marketing intern:* responsibilities include project management of a range of existing cause marketing programs with corporate sponsors, evaluating market opportunities, and creating proposals. Candidates should have ability to work independently, computer skills, oral communication skills, research skills, written communication skills. Duration is flexible. Position available as unpaid or paid. ▶ *1 public relations intern:* responsibilities include preparing press releases and articles, contacting media, using online services to create mailing lists, and participating in campaign/event planning. Candidates should have ability to work independently, analytical skills, oral communication skills, research skills, strong interpersonal skills, written communication skills. Duration is flexible. Position available as unpaid or paid. Open to college juniors, college seniors, recent college graduates.

Benefits Possible full-time employment, willing to act as a professional reference, willing to complete paperwork for educational credit, willing to provide letters of recommendation, stipend may be available.

Contact Write, fax, e-mail, or through World Wide Web site Ginger Moore, Human Resources Manager. Fax: 303-792-5333. E-mail: gingerm@americanhumane.org. No phone calls. In-person interview recommended (telephone interview accepted). Applicants must submit a letter of interest, resume, 2 personal references/letters of recommendation. Applications are accepted continuously. World Wide Web: http://www.americanhumane.org.

AMERICAN JEWISH CONGRESS, GOVERNMENTAL AND PUBLIC AFFAIRS OFFICE
1001 Connecticut Avenue, NW, Suite 407
Washington, District of Columbia 20036

General Information National community relations organization dedicated to protecting the religious, civil, political, and economic rights of all Americans. Established in 1918. Number of employees: 3. Unit of American Jewish Congress, New York, New York. Number of internship applications received each year: 50.

Internships Available ▶ *3–4 legislative interns:* responsibilities include attending and reporting on congressional committee hearings and interest group coalition meetings and performing administrative duties. Candidates should have ability to work with others, office skills, oral communication skills, personal interest in the field, self-motivation, written communication skills. Duration is 3 months minimum. Unpaid. ▶ *1 public policy institute intern:*

responsibilities include helping with development activities of regional office, writing policy papers generated from regional public policy institute, and administrative activities. Candidates should have oral communication skills, personal interest in the field, self-motivation, strong interpersonal skills, written communication skills. Duration is year-round. Unpaid. Open to college freshmen, college sophomores, college juniors, college seniors, recent college graduates. International applications accepted.

Benefits Names of contacts, opportunity to attend seminars/workshops, possible full-time employment, travel reimbursement, willing to act as a professional reference, willing to complete paperwork for educational credit, willing to provide letters of recommendation.

International Internships Available in Jerusalem, Israel.

Contact Write, call, or fax Charles D. Brooks, Director. Phone: 202-466-9661. Fax: 202-466-9665. E-mail: washrep@ajcongress. org. Telephone interview required. Applicants must submit a formal organization application, letter of interest, resume, writing sample. Applications are accepted continuously. World Wide Web: http://www.ajcongress.org.

AMERICANS FOR DEMOCRATIC ACTION
1625 K Street, NW, Suite 210
Washington, District of Columbia 20006

General Information Nation's oldest liberal lobbying group that combines grassroots organizing with lobbying on various issues at local, state, and national levels. Established in 1947. Number of employees: 10. Number of internship applications received each year: 100.

Internships Available ▶ *4–10 legislative interns:* responsibilities include researching, writing, helping with mailings, and following one or two issues on Capitol Hill. Candidates should have ability to work independently, analytical skills, computer skills, editing skills, knowledge of field, office skills, organizational skills, personal interest in the field, research skills, self-motivation, strong interpersonal skills, writing skills. Duration is flexible. Unpaid. Open to high school students, recent high school graduates, college freshmen, college sophomores, college juniors, college seniors, recent college graduates, graduate students, law students, career changers, individuals reentering the workforce. International applications accepted.

Benefits Names of contacts, opportunity to attend seminars/workshops, possible full-time employment, willing to act as a professional reference, willing to complete paperwork for educational credit, willing to provide letters of recommendation.

Contact Write, call, fax, e-mail, or through World Wide Web site Valerie Dulk-Jacobs, Special Assistant to the Director. Phone: 202-785-5980. Fax: 202-785-5969. E-mail: valerie@adaction.com. In-person interview recommended (telephone interview accepted). Applicants must submit a resume, one-page letter of interest indicating legislative issues important and career plans. Application deadline: May 1 for summer, August 1 for fall, December 1 for spring. World Wide Web: http://www.adaction.org.

AMERICAN WOMAN'S ECONOMIC DEVELOPMENT CORPORATION
216 East 45th Street
New York, New York 10017

General Information Not-for-profit organization that provides training, counseling, and technical assistance to women who own or would like start their own businesses. Established in 1976. Number of employees: 15. Number of internship applications received each year: 100.

Internships Available ▶ *1 administration intern:* responsibilities include supporting assistant to executive secretary of president and CEO. Candidates should have ability to work independently, computer skills, oral communication skills, organizational skills, research skills, self-motivation, strong interpersonal skills, writing skills. Unpaid. ▶ *1–2 development assistants:* responsibilities include researching and identifying potential funders and grant writing. Candidates should have ability to work independently, computer skills, editing skills, oral communication skills, research skills, strong interpersonal skills, writing skills. Duration is flexible.

Unpaid. ▶ *1–2 program coordinators:* responsibilities include working with training or counseling director on program logistics, including assisting with registration, mailings, and publicity; and interfacing with clients and instructors. Candidates should have ability to work independently, computer skills, oral communication skills, self-motivation, strong interpersonal skills, written communication skills. Duration is flexible. Unpaid. Open to college freshmen, college sophomores, college juniors, college seniors.

Benefits Opportunity to attend seminars/workshops, willing to act as a professional reference, willing to complete paperwork for educational credit, willing to provide letters of recommendation.

Contact Write, fax, or e-mail Ms. Roseanne Antonucci, Executive Director. Fax: 212-986-7114. E-mail: rlantonucci@awed.org. No phone calls. In-person interview required. Applicants must submit a letter of interest, resume, three personal references, telephone interview acceptable for out-of-town candidates. Application deadline: March 30 for summer; continuous for fall, winter, and spring. World Wide Web: http://www.awed.org.

AMNESTY INTERNATIONAL, MIDWEST REGION
53 West Jackson, Suite 731
Chicago, Illinois 60604-3607

General Information Grassroots international human rights organization that trains and organizes membership, functions as a liaison with the media, and organizes fund-raising and special events. Established in 1961. Number of employees: 10. Unit of Amnesty International USA, New York, New York. Number of internship applications received each year: 50.

Internships Available ▶ *1–2 OUTFRONT human rights interns:* responsibilities include coordination of various outreach projects promoting international LGBT human rights and the work of the OUTFRONT Program. Candidates should have ability to work independently, ability to work with others, computer skills, editing skills, office skills, oral communication skills, organizational skills, personal interest in the field, research skills, self-motivation, written communication skills. Duration is 1–12 months. Unpaid. Open to high school students, recent high school graduates, college freshmen, college sophomores, college juniors, college seniors, recent college graduates. ▶ *1–2 death penalty abolition interns:* responsibilities include working with death penalty coordinator on death penalty-related projects in region. Candidates should have ability to work independently, computer skills, editing skills, knowledge of field, office skills, oral communication skills, organizational skills, personal interest in the field, research skills, self-motivation, strong interpersonal skills, strong leadership ability, writing skills. Duration is flexible. Unpaid. Open to high school students, recent high school graduates, college freshmen, college sophomores, college juniors, college seniors, recent college graduates, graduate students, law students. ▶ *1–2 membership development interns:* responsibilities include maintaining and recruiting members by managing lists, phone, and e-mail; developing and sending membership information; contacting group coordinators; data entry; and assisting in event planning. Candidates should have ability to work independently, computer skills, editing skills, office skills, oral communication skills, organizational skills, personal interest in the field, research skills, self-motivation, strong interpersonal skills, writing skills. Duration is 1–6 months. Unpaid. Open to high school students, recent high school graduates, college freshmen, college sophomores, college juniors, college seniors, recent college graduates, graduate students, law students. ▶ *1–2 office/ general administrative interns:* responsibilities include working in a not-for-profit office environment, organizing various information including international reports, country specific materials (written and audio-visual), and other office duties. Candidates should have ability to work independently, ability to work with others, analytical skills, computer skills, editing skills, office skills, oral communication skills, organizational skills, personal interest in the field, self-motivation, writing skills. Duration is 3 to 6 months (2-3 days a week). Unpaid. Open to high school students, recent high school graduates, college freshmen, college sophomores, college juniors, college seniors. ▶ *1 women's human rights intern:* responsibilities include attending Women's Convention Coalition meetings, assisting in passing resolution through City Council, arranging Alderman visits, outreach to ally

Amnesty International, Midwest Region (continued)

organizations, answering general requests, mailings help, and general office work. Candidates should have ability to work independently, computer skills, knowledge of field, office skills, oral communication skills, organizational skills, personal interest in the field, research skills, self-motivation, strong interpersonal skills, written communication skills. Duration is 1–6 months. Unpaid. Open to college freshmen, college sophomores, college juniors, college seniors, recent college graduates, graduate students, law students, career changers. International applications accepted. **Benefits** Opportunity to attend seminars/workshops, willing to complete paperwork for educational credit, willing to provide letters of recommendation.

International Internships Available in London, United Kingdom. **Contact** Write, call, fax, or e-mail Audrey Randall, Office Administrator. Phone: 312-427-2060. Fax: 312-427-2589. E-mail: arandall@aiusa.org. In-person interview recommended (telephone interview accepted). Applicants must submit a formal organization application, letter of interest, resume, two personal references, 1-2 letters of recommendation for interns 3 months or longer. Applications are accepted continuously. World Wide Web: http://www.amnesty-usa.org.

AMNESTY INTERNATIONAL USA, WASHINGTON OFFICE
600 Pennsylvania Avenue, SE, 5th Floor
Washington, District of Columbia 20003

General Information Organization conducting a worldwide movement working impartially for the release of prisoners of conscience, fair and prompt trials for political prisoners, and an end to torture and executions. Established in 1961. Number of employees: 55. Unit of Amnesty International USA, New York, New York. Number of internship applications received each year: 500.

Internships Available ▶ *2 African affairs interns:* responsibilities include monitoring and providing information on developments in the region, participating in projects that promote human rights policy in the region. Candidates should have ability to work independently, computer skills, office skills, oral communication skills, organizational skills, personal interest in the field, research skills, strong interpersonal skills, writing skills. Duration is minimum of 3 months. Unpaid. Open to college freshmen, college sophomores, college juniors, college seniors, recent college graduates, graduate students, law students, career changers. ▶ *2 Asian affairs interns:* responsibilities include monitoring and providing information on developments in the region, participating in projects that promote human rights policy in the region. Candidates should have ability to work independently, computer skills, office skills, oral communication skills, organizational skills, personal interest in the field, research skills, strong interpersonal skills, writing skills. Duration is minimum of 3 months. Unpaid. Open to college freshmen, college sophomores, college juniors, college seniors, recent college graduates, graduate students, law students, career changers. ▶ *4 European/Middle Eastern affairs interns:* responsibilities include monitoring and providing information on developments in the region and participating in projects that promote human rights policy in the region. Candidates should have ability to work independently, computer skills, office skills, oral communication skills, organizational skills, personal interest in the field, research skills, strong interpersonal skills, writing skills. Duration is minimum of 3 months. Paid. Open to college freshmen, college sophomores, college juniors, college seniors, recent college graduates, graduate students, law students, career changers. ▶ *2 Latin American affairs interns:* responsibilities include monitoring and providing information on developments in the region and participating in projects that promote human rights policy in the region. Candidates should have ability to work independently, computer skills, office skills, oral communication skills, organizational skills, personal interest in the field, research skills, strong interpersonal skills, writing skills. Duration is minimum of 3 months. Unpaid. Open to college freshmen, college sophomores, college juniors, college seniors, recent college graduates, graduate students. ▶ *1–2 Program to Abolish the Death Penalty interns:* responsibilities include assisting in creating training materials for organizing against the

death penalty and providing research on the death penalty and related issues in the U.S. and internationally. Candidates should have ability to work independently, computer skills, office skills, oral communication skills, organizational skills, personal interest in the field, research skills, strong interpersonal skills, writing skills. Duration is minimum of 3 months. Unpaid. Open to college freshmen, college sophomores, college juniors, college seniors, recent college graduates, graduate students. ▶ *3 campaign interns:* responsibilities include assisting with all aspects of campaigns and crisis response including planning, materials preparation, event coordination, and evaluation. Candidates should have ability to work independently, computer skills, office skills, oral communication skills, organizational skills, personal interest in the field, research skills, strong interpersonal skills, writing skills. Duration is minimum of 3 months. Unpaid. Open to college freshmen, college sophomores, college juniors, college seniors, recent college graduates, graduate students. ▶ *2–3 country specialists:* responsibilities include assisting in the recruitment, training, and servicing of volunteer country specialists. Candidates should have ability to work independently, computer skills, office skills, oral communication skills, organizational skills, personal interest in the field, strong interpersonal skills, writing skills. Duration is minimum of 3 months. Unpaid. Open to college freshmen, college sophomores, college juniors, college seniors, recent college graduates, graduate students. ▶ *1 grassroots advocacy intern:* responsibilities include assisting in promoting the legislative priorities of AIUSA, providing information to AISUA members and groups that are lobbying the congressional representatives, and assisting in developing online human rights actions. Candidates should have ability to work independently, computer skills, office skills, oral communication skills, organizational skills, personal interest in the field, research skills, strong interpersonal skills, writing skills. Duration is minimum of 3 months. Unpaid. Open to college freshmen, college sophomores, college juniors, college seniors, recent college graduates, graduate students, law students, career changers. ▶ *2 human rights and the environment interns:* responsibilities include providing research on cases involving environmental and human rights violations and assisting in grassroots organizing strategies. Candidates should have ability to work independently, computer skills, office skills, oral communication skills, organizational skills, personal interest in the field, research skills, strong interpersonal skills, writing skills. Duration is minimum of 3 months. Unpaid. Open to college freshmen, college sophomores, college juniors, college seniors, recent college graduates, graduate students. ▶ *1 media relations intern:* responsibilities include assisting the press officer with all aspects of work to ensure media coverage of human rights issues. Candidates should have ability to work independently, computer skills, office skills, oral communication skills, organizational skills, personal interest in the field, strong interpersonal skills, writing skills. Duration is minimum of 3 months. Unpaid. Open to college freshmen, college sophomores, college juniors, college seniors, recent college graduates, graduate students. ▶ *3–4 mid-Atlantic regional office interns:* responsibilities include working to mobilize, motivate, and support AIUSA members in their efforts to publicize and eliminate worldwide human rights abuses. Candidates should have ability to work independently, computer skills, office skills, oral communication skills, organizational skills, personal interest in the field, research skills, strong interpersonal skills, writing skills. Duration is minimum of 3 months. Unpaid. Open to college freshmen, college sophomores, college juniors, college seniors, recent college graduates, graduate students. ▶ *3–4 national field program interns:* responsibilities include assisting in the coordination of national training programs and the development of activists tools and assisting in grassroots organizing strategies. Candidates should have ability to work independently, office skills, oral communication skills, organizational skills, personal interest in the field, research skills, strong interpersonal skills, writing skills. Duration is minimum of 3 months. Unpaid. Open to college freshmen, college sophomores, college juniors, college seniors, recent college graduates, graduate students. ▶ *1 new media Web site intern:* responsibilities include updating Web pages, creating new pages including graphic work, helping produce online events, site maintenance, and running log file reports. Candidates should have ability to work independently, ability to work with others, computer skills, oral communication skills, organizational skills, personal interest in the field, writing skills, Web development skills (preferred). Duration is minimum of 3 months . Unpaid. Open to high school seniors, college freshmen, college sophomores, college juniors, college seniors, recent college graduates, graduate students. ▶ *1–2 refugee interns:* responsibilities include providing research and documentation to be used to support asylum claims, maintaining resource materials and database files, and responding to information requests. Candidates should have ability to work independently, ability to work with others, office skills, oral communication skills, organizational skills, personal interest in the field, research skills, writing skills. Duration is minimum of 3 months. Unpaid. Open to college freshmen, college sophomores, college juniors, college seniors, recent college graduates, graduate students. ▶ *1 women's program intern:* responsibilities include representing Women's Program at events, meetings, and networking opportunities; conducting outreach to women's organizations; maintaining events calendar; research; and compilation of materials. Candidates should have ability to work independently, ability to work with others, office skills, oral communication skills, organizational skills, personal interest in the field, research skills, writing skills. Duration is minimum of 3 months. Unpaid. Open to college freshmen, college sophomores, college juniors, college seniors, recent college graduates, graduate students. International applications accepted.

Benefits Job counseling, names of contacts, opportunity to attend seminars/workshops, travel reimbursement, willing to act as a professional reference, willing to complete paperwork for educational credit, willing to provide letters of recommendation.

Contact Write, call, fax, or e-mail Toni Coverton, Acting Office Manager. Phone: 202-544-0200. Fax: 202-546-7142. E-mail: tcoverto@ aiusa.org. Telephone interview required. Applicants must submit a letter of interest, resume, writing sample, two letters of recommendation. Application deadline: February 15 for spring, April 15 for summer, August 15 for fall, November 30 for winter. World Wide Web: http://amnesty-usa.org.

ANIMAL PROTECTION INSTITUTE
1122 S Street
Sacramento, California 95814

General Information Animal advocacy organization. Established in 1968. Number of employees: 19. Number of internship applications received each year: 40.

Internships Available ▶ *1–2 animal advocacy interns:* responsibilities include assisting program and legal staff with advocacy campaigns by conducting research, writing publications, drafting member action alerts, and lobbying public officials. Candidates should have ability to work independently, analytical skills, plan to pursue career in field, research skills, strong interpersonal skills, written communication skills. Duration is 40 hours per week during summer; variable during school year. Position available as unpaid or at $7-$12 per hour (for summer positions only). Open to college juniors, college seniors, recent college graduates, graduate students, law students. ▶ *2–6 animal care (primates) interns:* responsibilities include animal care at the Texas Snow Monkey Sanctuary in Dilley, Texas; physical labor for rescued primates (vervets, baboons, and snow monkeys). Candidates should have ability to work with others, college courses in field, experience in the field, personal interest in the field, plan to pursue career in field, self-motivation. Duration is 2–6 months. Unpaid. Open to college juniors, college seniors, graduate students. ▶ *1–2 legal interns:* responsibilities include assisting legal staff with research; writing agency comments; drafting model legislation; and lobbying public officials. Candidates should have ability to work independently, analytical skills, plan to pursue career in field, research skills, strong interpersonal skills, writing skills. Duration is 2–6 months. Position available as unpaid or at $9–$12 per hour. Open to law students.

Benefits On-the-job training, opportunity to attend seminars/workshops, possible full-time employment, willing to act as a professional reference, willing to complete paperwork for educational credit, willing to provide letters of recommendation, housing provided for animal care positions.

Contact Write, fax, or e-mail Nicole Paquette, Director of Legal and Government Affairs, PO Box 22505, Sacramento, California

95822. Fax: 916-447-3070. E-mail: npaquette@api4animals.org. No phone calls. In-person interview recommended (telephone interview accepted). Applicants must submit a letter of interest, resume, writing sample, three personal references. Application deadline: January 31 for spring; continuous for school-year positions, March 15 for summer. World Wide Web: http://www.api4animals.org.

ARAB AMERICAN INSTITUTE
1600 K Street, NW, Suite 601
Washington, District of Columbia 20006

General Information Organization that nurtures and encourages direct participation of Arab Americans in political and civic life in the U.S. Established in 1985. Number of employees: 15. Number of internship applications received each year: 75.

Internships Available ▶ *3–4 interns:* responsibilities include assisting in Government Relations, Communications, or Community Relations Departments; setting up meetings, assisting with logistics of special events, helping the Institute build its action network; some clerical work, research, and writing. Candidates should have ability to work independently, college courses in field, computer skills, knowledge of field, research skills, writing skills. Duration is minimum 6 weeks in winter, spring, summer, or fall. Position available as unpaid or at $500–$1000 per month. Open to college freshmen, college sophomores, college juniors, college seniors, recent college graduates, graduate students. International applications accepted.

Benefits Opportunity to attend seminars/workshops, possible full-time employment, willing to complete paperwork for educational credit, willing to provide letters of recommendation.

Contact Write, call, fax, or e-mail Dianne L. Davidson, Office Manager. Phone: 202-429-9210. Fax: 202-429-9214. E-mail: ddavidson@ aaiusa.org. In-person interview recommended (telephone interview accepted). Applicants must submit a resume, writing sample, cover letter listing dates of availability and requesting either paid or for-school-credit position. Application deadline: April 15 for summer, August 9 for fall, December 13 for spring. World Wide Web: http://www.aaiusa.org.

THE ARMS CONTROL ASSOCIATION
1726 M Street, NW, Suite 201
Washington, District of Columbia 20036

General Information Independent research organization dedicated to raising public knowledge of arms control and related national security issues. Established in 1971. Number of employees: 9. Number of internship applications received each year: 200.

Internships Available ▶ *1–3 foreign affairs/national security interns:* responsibilities include research support and clerical duties. Candidates should have ability to work with others, analytical skills, computer skills, office skills, personal interest in the field, research skills, self-motivation. Duration is 1 semester. Unpaid. Open to college freshmen, college sophomores, college juniors, college seniors, recent college graduates, graduate students. International applications accepted.

Benefits Job counseling, meals at a cost, names of contacts, on-the-job training, opportunity to attend seminars/workshops, possible full-time employment, travel reimbursement, willing to act as a professional reference, willing to complete paperwork for educational credit, willing to provide letters of recommendation, $10 per day lunch/transit stipend.

Contact Write, call, fax, e-mail, or through World Wide Web site Andrew Howells, Assistant to the Executive Director. Phone: 202-463-8270. Fax: 202-463-8273. E-mail: aca@armscontrol.org. In-person interview recommended (telephone interview accepted). Applicants must submit a letter of interest, resume, 1 writing sample (3-5 pages). Application deadline: April 15 for summer, August 15 for fall, December 15 for winter/spring. World Wide Web: http://www.armscontrol.org.

ASIAN PACIFIC AMERICAN INSTITUTE FOR CONGRESSIONAL STUDIES (APAICS)
1001 Connecticut Avenue, Suite 835
Washington, District of Columbia 20036

General Information Non-partisan, nonprofit, educational organization whose mission is to promote the participation of Asian American and Pacific Islanders in the political process. Established in 1995. Number of employees: 2. Number of internship applications received each year: 100.
Internships Available ▶ *1–3 interns:* responsibilities include obtaining updates on legislation, regulations, and court decisions affecting the Asian American and Pacific Islander communities; research, writing political briefings, program administration, and general office work. Candidates should have ability to work independently, organizational skills, personal interest in the field, strong interpersonal skills, written communication skills. Duration is flexibe (year-round). Unpaid. Open to college freshmen, college sophomores, college juniors, college seniors, recent college graduates, graduate students, law students. ▶ *10–15 summer interns (Washington DC):* responsibilities include placements in Congress, federal agencies, and institutions that further the mission of APAICS. Candidates should have oral communication skills, personal interest in the field, self-motivation, strong interpersonal skills, strong leadership ability, written communication skills, minimum GPA of 3.3. Duration is June 13-August 7. $2500 stipend. Open to college freshmen, college sophomores, college juniors, college seniors, recent college graduates, graduate students, law students, minimum 18 years of age. International applications accepted.
Benefits Opportunity to attend seminars/workshops, willing to act as a professional reference, willing to complete paperwork for educational credit, willing to provide letters of recommendation.
Contact Write, call, fax, or e-mail Internship Coordinator. Phone: 202-296-9200. Fax: 202-296-9236. E-mail: apaics@apaics.org. Telephone interview required. Applicants must submit a formal organization application, resume, academic transcripts, writing sample, two letters of recommendation, materials as specified on Web site. Application deadline: January 31 for summer program; continuous for all other time frames. World Wide Web: http://www.apaics.org.

ASSOCIATION FOR WOMEN IN SCIENCE (AWIS)
1200 New York Avenue, NW, Suite 650
Washington, District of Columbia 20005

General Information Nonprofit organization whose mission is to expand education and employment opportunities in science for girls and women. Established in 1971. Number of employees: 7. Number of internship applications received each year: 150.
Internships Available ▶ *Interns:* responsibilities include helping to develop chapter activities and plan AWIS events; assisting with grant proposal writing; legislative analysis; assisting with magazine production, membership services, and research; obtaining resources/statistics on issues of women in science; Web site maintenance. Candidates should have ability to work independently, office skills, research skills, strong interpersonal skills, written communication skills. Duration is flexible. Paid. Open to college freshmen, college sophomores, college juniors, college seniors, recent college graduates, graduate students. International applications accepted.
Benefits Opportunity to attend seminars/workshops, willing to complete paperwork for educational credit, willing to provide letters of recommendation.
Contact Write or e-mail Intern Coordinator. E-mail: awis@awis.org. Applicants must submit a letter of interest, resume. Applications are accepted continuously. World Wide Web: http://www.awis.org.

BASTROP CHILDREN'S ADVOCACY CENTER
1002 Chestnut Street
Bastrop, Texas 78602

General Information Private, nonprofit, community site providing forensic interviewing, individual, group, and family counseling for abuse survivors and their families; also coordinates agencies involved in civic and criminal investigation of child abuse.

Established in 1992. Number of employees: 5. Affiliate of Children's Advocacy Centers of Texas, Austin, Texas. Number of internship applications received each year: 5.
Internships Available ▶ *2–3 clinical interns:* responsibilities include individual, group, and family counseling; outreach activities including community and in-school presentations; home visits; advocacy; basic office work; computer work. Candidates should have ability to work independently, analytical skills, declared college major in field, knowledge of field, oral communication skills, plan to pursue career in field, self-motivation, strong interpersonal skills, writing skills, must provide own transportation. Duration is as educational contract requires. Unpaid. Open to college seniors, recent college graduates, graduate students, post graduates seeking contact hours for licensure.
Benefits On-the-job training, opportunity to attend seminars/workshops, willing to act as a professional reference, willing to complete paperwork for educational credit, willing to provide letters of recommendation, possibility of mileage reimbursement to/from home in neighboring counties.
Contact Write, call, or e-mail Shelley Mathews, Executive Director, PO Box 1098, Bastrop 78602. Phone: 512-321-6161. Fax: 512-303-3985. E-mail: cacbastrop@austin.rr.com. In-person interview required. Applicants must submit a letter of interest, resume, academic transcripts, 1-2 recommendations (may be from professors). Applications are accepted continuously. World Wide Web: http://www.childrensadvocacycenter.org.

BETTER GOVERNMENT ASSOCIATION
28 East Jackson Boulevard, Suite 1900
Chicago, Illinois 60604

General Information Nationally recognized public interest organization that collaborates with local and national print and broadcast news organizations to investigate waste, corruption, and inefficiency in government. Established in 1923. Number of employees: 4. Number of internship applications received each year: 150.
Internships Available ▶ *3–5 interns:* responsibilities include conducting background research, interviews, litigation searches, surveillance, and administrative duties. Candidates should have ability to work independently, analytical skills, research skills, self-motivation, strong interpersonal skills, desire to work in the public interest. Duration is flexible. Unpaid. Open to college juniors, college seniors, recent college graduates, graduate students, law students. ▶ *1–3 legal interns:* responsibilities include researching, analyzing, and developing legal theory; investigating waste, fraud, and corruption in government; and performing general office duties. Candidates should have ability to work independently, analytical skills, organizational skills, personal interest in the field, research skills, self-motivation, written communication skills. Duration is flexible. Unpaid. Open to law students. International applications accepted.
Benefits Job counseling, names of contacts, opportunity to attend seminars/workshops, possible full-time employment, willing to act as a professional reference, willing to complete paperwork for educational credit, willing to provide letters of recommendation, leadership skills.
Contact Write, call, fax, e-mail, or through World Wide Web site Terrance A. Norton, Executive Director. Phone: 312-427-8330. Fax: 312-427-8340. E-mail: terrance_norton@hotmail.com. Applicants must submit a letter of interest, resume. Application deadline: January 15 for spring, May 30 for summer, September 1 for fall. World Wide Web: http://www.bettergov.org.

BIRTHING THE FUTURE
PO Box 1040
Bayfield, Colorado 81122

General Information Organization dedicated to inspiring, fostering, and advocating vision and practical models for the healing and well being of life on the planet through birth activism.
Internships Available ▶ *2 interns:* responsibilities include office work including phone, writing, e-mail, and Web work; supervised, independent work on a project of intern's choosing that supports organization's mission. Candidates should have skills in marketing and sales, research, Web design, graphics, or creative

writing, video production, design, and photography skills (beneficial but not required). Duration is minimum of 8 weeks (approximately 30 hours per week). Unpaid.

Benefits Free housing, hands-on experience in organizational, financial, and day-to-day aspects of child birth, mid-wifery, and birth activism.

Contact Write, call, fax, or e-mail Suzanne Arms, President. Phone: 970-884-4090. Fax: 970-884-9141. E-mail: suzanne@ birthingthefuture.com. Applicants must submit resume focusing on relevant skills and experience, personal letter about oneself, including interest, availability, and length of internship desired, photo of applicant. Applications are accepted continuously. World Wide Web: http://www.birthingthefuture.com.

BREAD FOR THE WORLD AND BREAD FOR THE WORLD INSTITUTE
50 F Street NW, Suite 500
Washington, District of Columbia 20001

General Information Nonprofit anti-hunger advocacy organization that addresses U.S. public policy affecting the hungry. Established in 1974. Number of employees: 60. Number of internship applications received each year: 100.

Internships Available ▶ *1–2 annual hunger report interns:* responsibilities include assisting with publishing a major reference guide on global hunger. Candidates should have ability to work independently, analytical skills, computer skills, editing skills, knowledge of field, oral communication skills, organizational skills, personal interest in the field, research skills, self-motivation, strong interpersonal skills, strong leadership ability, writing skills. Duration is 3 months or 1-2 years. Unpaid. Open to college sophomores, college juniors, college seniors, recent college graduates, graduate students. ▶ *1 church relations intern:* responsibilities include carrying out promotional efforts to churches and denominational representatives in support of BFW legislation. Candidates should have ability to work independently, computer skills, knowledge of field, office skills, oral communication skills, organizational skills, personal interest in the field, self-motivation, strong interpersonal skills, writing skills. Duration is 8–10 weeks. Unpaid. Open to college freshmen, college sophomores, college juniors, college seniors, recent college graduates. ▶ *1–3 development interns:* responsibilities include assisting with fund-raising for both the general budget and special projects. Candidates should have ability to work independently, computer skills, office skills, oral communication skills, personal interest in the field, self-motivation, strong interpersonal skills, writing skills. Duration is 3 months or 1-2 years. Unpaid. Open to college freshmen, college sophomores, college juniors, college seniors, recent college graduates. ▶ *1 domestic hunger issues intern:* responsibilities include assisting with developing and communicating policy and legislative strategy on domestic hunger issues. Candidates should have ability to work independently, analytical skills, college courses in field, computer skills, editing skills, knowledge of field, oral communication skills, personal interest in the field, research skills, self-motivation, strong interpersonal skills, writing skills. Duration is 3 months or 1-2 years. Unpaid. Open to college freshmen, college sophomores, college juniors, college seniors, recent college graduates. ▶ *1 human resources intern.* Candidates should have ability to work independently, college courses in field, computer skills, oral communication skills, organizational skills, plan to pursue career in field, research skills, self-motivation, strong interpersonal skills, writing skills. Duration is 3 months or 1 year. Unpaid. Open to college freshmen, college sophomores, college juniors, college seniors, recent college graduates, graduate students, career changers. ▶ *1 international hunger issues intern:* responsibilities include assisting with research and lobbying support. Candidates should have ability to work independently, computer skills, editing skills, knowledge of field, oral communication skills, organizational skills, personal interest in the field, plan to pursue career in field, research skills, self-motivation, strong interpersonal skills, strong leadership ability, writing skills. Duration is 3 months or 1-2 years. Unpaid. Open to college sophomores, college juniors, college seniors, recent college graduates, graduate students. ▶ *1 media intern:* responsibilities include using a variety of media to fulfill objectives. Candidates should have ability to work independently, computer skills,

knowledge of field, oral communication skills, personal interest in the field, self-motivation, strong interpersonal skills, writing skills. Duration is 3 months or 1-2 years. Unpaid. Open to college freshmen, college sophomores, college juniors, college seniors, recent college graduates. ▶ *1–3 organizing interns:* responsibilities include assisting with building a strong grassroots lobbying network by working on specific projects or in a specific region of the country. Candidates should have ability to work independently, computer skills, knowledge of field, oral communication skills, organizational skills, personal interest in the field, self-motivation, strong interpersonal skills, writing skills. Duration is 3 months or 1-2 years. Unpaid. Open to college freshmen, college sophomores, college juniors, college seniors, recent college graduates. ▶ *1–5 stipend interns:* responsibilities include serving in any capacity where needed in any of the above positions. Candidates should have ability to work independently, computer skills, office skills, oral communication skills, personal interest in the field, self-motivation, strong interpersonal skills, written communication skills. Duration is 1 year. $17,595 per year plus medical and dental benefits. Open to recent college graduates, graduate students, career changers. International applications accepted.

Benefits Job counseling, names of contacts, opportunity to attend seminars/workshops, possible full-time employment, willing to complete paperwork for educational credit, willing to provide letters of recommendation, reimbursement of work-related travel expenses.

Contact Write, call, fax, e-mail, or through World Wide Web site Ms. Katherine Simmons, Human Resources Manager. Phone: 202-639-9400. Fax: 202-639-9401. E-mail: human.resources@bread. org. Applicants must submit a formal organization application, letter of interest, resume, academic transcripts, writing sample, three letters of recommendation. Application deadline: April 1 for summer, July 1 for fall, November 1 for winter and spring. World Wide Web: http://www.bread.org.

CALIFORNIA NATIONAL ORGANIZATION FOR WOMEN
926 J Street, Suite 424
Sacramento, California 95814

General Information Women's rights organization working primarily on legislation in the state of California. Established in 1972. Number of employees: 6. Branch of National Organization for Women (National Action Center), Washington, District of Columbia. Number of internship applications received each year: 35.

Internships Available ▶ *1–3 California NOW interns:* responsibilities include communication with local chapters, specific short- or long-term projects as assigned, depending on intern's interests. Candidates should have ability to work independently, computer skills, oral communication skills, research skills, writing skills. Duration is flexible. Unpaid. Open to high school students, recent high school graduates, college freshmen, college sophomores, college juniors, college seniors, recent college graduates, graduate students, law students, career changers, individuals reentering the workforce. International applications accepted.

Benefits On-the-job training, opportunity to attend seminars/ workshops, travel reimbursement, willing to act as a professional reference, willing to complete paperwork for educational credit, willing to provide letters of recommendation.

Contact Write, call, fax, or e-mail Mandy Benson, Field Director. Phone: 916-442-3414. Fax: 916-442-6942. E-mail: fielddir@canow. org. In-person interview recommended (telephone interview accepted). Applicants must submit a letter of interest. Applications are accepted continuously. World Wide Web: http://www. canow.org.

CAMPAIGN FOR TOBACCO-FREE KIDS
1400 Eye Street, NW, Suite 1200
Washington, District of Columbia 20005

General Information Organization dedicated to protecting children from tobacco addiction and exposure to secondhand smoke.

Campaign for Tobacco-Free Kids (continued)
Internships Available ▶ *Interns:* responsibilities include assisting on substantive projects in a variety of areas, including constituency relations, communications, and research. Candidates should have writing skills, attention to detail, responsibility, strong writing skills, ability to multi-task. Duration is minimum 12 weeks, 15 hours per week. Paid. Open to high school students, college freshmen, college sophomores, college juniors, college seniors, recent college graduates.
Benefits Willing to complete paperwork for educational credit.
Contact Fax or e-mail Internship Coordinator. Fax: 202-296-5427. E-mail: jobs@tobaccofreekids.org. No phone calls. Applicants must submit a letter of interest, resume, two writing samples, two personal references, 2 references. Applications are accepted continuously. World Wide Web: http://tobaccofreekids.org.

CARAL–CALIFORNIA ABORTION & REPRODUCTIVE RIGHTS ACTION LEAGUE
32 Monterey Boulevard
San Francisco, California 94131

General Information Political lobbying, educational organization dedicated to creating and sustaining a constituency that uses the political process to guarantee the full range of reproductive rights to all women. Established in 1978. Number of employees: 9. Affiliate of National Abortion and Reproductive Rights Action League, Washington, District of Columbia. Number of internship applications received each year: 25.
Internships Available ▶ *1–3 grassroots organizing interns:* responsibilities include coordinating volunteers, supervising and directing campaign strategy implementation, legislative alert organizing, event work, and writing. Candidates should have ability to work with others, oral communication skills, personal interest in the field, self-motivation, written communication skills, Mac computer skills (preferred), ability to work in busy environment, ability to be a team player. Duration is 15-20 hours per week. Unpaid. Open to high school students, recent high school graduates, college freshmen, college sophomores, college juniors, college seniors, recent college graduates, graduate students, law students, individuals reentering the workforce. ▶ *Legislative interns:* responsibilities include tracking local, state, and national legislation on abortion and other reproductive health issues; designing fact sheets, writing newsletter articles, and developing other educational material on existing and pending legislation. Candidates should have Mac computer skills (preferred). Duration is 10 hours per week. Unpaid. ▶ *Political interns:* responsibilities include helping with electoral strategy, public education, and candidate endorsements for elections; participation in grassroots efforts surrounding targeted races of CARAL- endorsed candidates. Candidates should have Mac computer skills (preferred). Duration is 20 hours per week. Unpaid.
Benefits Formal training, names of contacts, on-the-job training, opportunity to attend seminars/workshops, possible full-time employment, willing to act as a professional reference, willing to complete paperwork for educational credit, willing to provide letters of recommendation, work and travel stipends.
Contact Write, call, fax, e-mail, or through World Wide Web site Nora Dye, Administrative Coordinator, 32 Monterey Boulevard, San Francisco, California 94131. Phone: 415-334-1502 Ext. 301. Fax: 415-334-6510. E-mail: caral@aol.com. Applicants must submit a letter of interest, resume. Applications are accepted continuously. World Wide Web: http://www.caral.org or www.choice.org.

THE CARTER CENTER
One Copenhill, 453 Freedom Parkway
Atlanta, Georgia 30307

General Information Nonprofit organization, founded by Jimmy and Rosalynn Carter, dedicated to resolving conflicts, promoting democracy, and fighting disease, hunger, poverty, and oppression throughout the world. Established in 1982. Number of employees: 150. Unit of Emory University, Atlanta, Georgia. Number of internship applications received each year: 300.
Internships Available ▶ *Graduate assistants:* responsibilities include duties focusing on issues concerning democratization and develop-

ment, global health, and urban revitalization. Candidates should have ability to work independently, college courses in field, knowledge of field, research skills, writing skills. Duration is 10 weeks (40 hours per week). Stipend of $3000. Open to graduate and professional students who have completed at least one year of graduate study. ▶ *Interns:* responsibilities include duties focusing on issues concerning democratization and development, global health, and urban revitalization, including some office administration. Candidates should have college courses in field, computer skills, research skills, writing skills, interest in contemporary international and domestic issues. Duration is at least 15 weeks (minimum of 20 hours per week). Unpaid. Open to college juniors, college seniors, recent college graduates, graduate students. International applications accepted.
Benefits Formal training, job counseling, names of contacts, opportunity to attend seminars/workshops, willing to complete paperwork for educational credit, willing to provide letters of recommendation, possibility of financial aid.
Contact Write, call, fax, or through World Wide Web site Director, Educational Program. Phone: 404-420-5151. Fax: 404-420-5196. Applicants must submit a formal organization application, resume, academic transcripts, writing sample, two letters of recommendation, short essay describing interest in field. Application deadline: March 15 for summer, June 15 for fall, October 15 for spring. World Wide Web: http://www.cartercenter.org.

CENTER FOR ALASKAN COASTAL STUDIES
PO Box 2225
Homer, Alaska 99603

General Information Nonprofit, grassroots organization that fosters responsible interactions with natural surroundings through environmental education, stewardship, and research. Established in 1982. Number of employees: 10.
Internships Available ▶ *2 summer naturalist interns:* responsibilities include leading natural history tours and participating in research or environmental education projects. Candidates should have college courses in field, oral communication skills, personal interest in the field, strong interpersonal skills, written communication skills, group leadership/teaching experience. Duration is June 1 to August 15 or 31. $1000–$1200 per month. Open to college juniors, college seniors, recent college graduates, graduate students.
Benefits Free housing, names of contacts, on-the-job training, opportunity to attend seminars/workshops, willing to act as a professional reference, willing to complete paperwork for educational credit, willing to provide letters of recommendation.
Contact Write, call, fax, e-mail, or through World Wide Web site Marilyn Sigman, Executive Director. Phone: 907-235-6667. Fax: 907-235-6668. E-mail: cacs@xyz.net. Telephone interview required. Applicants must submit a letter of interest, resume, three letters of recommendation. Application deadline: February 20. World Wide Web: http://www.akcoastalstudies.org.

CENTER FOR ARMS CONTROL AND NON-PROLIFERATION
322 4th Street, NE
Washington, District of Columbia 20002

General Information Organization founded by Leo Szilard and other pioneers of nuclear weapons to stop the nuclear arms race; has prepared an agenda for action advocating the reduction of danger posed by weapons of mass destruction, the strengthening and reform of multilateral conflict resolution and peacekeeping, and the revision of the military budget to meet current circumstances. Established in 1980. Number of employees: 18. Number of internship applications received each year: 90.
Internships Available ▶ *2 interns:* responsibilities include assisting with research, writing factsheets, networking at meetings, attending debates, and sharing daily administrative duties. Candidates should have ability to work independently, analytical skills, computer skills, editing skills, knowledge of field, office skills, personal interest in the field, self-motivation, written communication skills. Duration is 3–6 months. Position available as unpaid or paid. Open to college sophomores, college juniors, college

seniors, recent college graduates, graduate students, law students, career changers, individuals reentering the workforce. International applications accepted.

Benefits Job counseling, opportunity to attend seminars/workshops, travel reimbursement, willing to complete paperwork for educational credit, willing to provide letters of recommendation.

Contact Write, call, fax, e-mail, or through World Wide Web site Erik Floden, Intern Coordinator/Policy Analyst, 110 Maryland Avenue, NE, Suite 409. Phone: 202-546-0795. Fax: 202-566-5142. E-mail: efloden@clw.org. In-person interview recommended (telephone interview accepted). Applicants must submit a letter of interest, resume, writing sample, two letters of recommendation. Application deadline: March 15 for summer positions; continuous for other positions. World Wide Web: http://www.armscontrolcenter.org/terrorism/about/employment.html.

THE CENTER FOR DEFENSE INFORMATION
1779 Massachusetts Avenue, NW
Washington, District of Columbia 20036

General Information Nonprofit think tank NGO focusing on defense and international affairs. Established in 1972. Number of employees: 30. Number of internship applications received each year: 400.

Internships Available ▶ *5 research/television/computer interns:* responsibilities include writing, research, working in communications and television production, and assisting with computer systems administration. Candidates should have ability to work with others, computer skills, editing skills, organizational skills, personal interest in the field, research skills, self-motivation, writing skills, driver's license. Duration is 3–5 months. Position available as unpaid or paid. Open to college freshmen, college sophomores, college juniors, college seniors, recent college graduates, graduate students, individuals reentering the workforce. International applications accepted.

Benefits Names of contacts, on-the-job training, opportunity to attend seminars/workshops, willing to act as a professional reference, willing to complete paperwork for educational credit, willing to provide letters of recommendation.

Contact Write, fax, e-mail, or through World Wide Web site Steve Welsh, Internship Coordinator, 1779 Massachusetts Avenue, NW #615, Washington, District of Columbia 20036. Phone: 202-332-0600 Ext. 119. Fax: 202-462-4559. E-mail: internships@cdi.org. Applicants must submit a letter of interest, resume, academic transcripts, writing sample, two letters of recommendation. Application deadline: March 1 for summer (check Web site), July 1 for fall (check Web site), October 1 for spring (check Web site). World Wide Web: http://www.cdi.org.

CENTER FOR EQUAL OPPORTUNITY
14 Pidgeon Hill Drive, Suite 500
Sterling, Virginia 20165

General Information Nonprofit research organization specializing in race, ethnicity, language issues, and assimilation. Established in 1995. Number of employees: 5. Number of internship applications received each year: 12.

Internships Available ▶ *3–6 research assistants:* responsibilities include conducting research for senior staff, contributing to reports, and other writing assignments. Candidates should have ability to work with others, personal interest in the field, research skills, self-motivation, writing skills. Duration is 3 months. Unpaid. Open to college freshmen, college sophomores, college juniors, college seniors, recent college graduates, graduate students, law students.

Benefits Names of contacts, opportunity to attend seminars/workshops, willing to act as a professional reference, willing to complete paperwork for educational credit, willing to provide letters of recommendation.

Contact Write, call, fax, e-mail, or through World Wide Web site David Gersten, Executive Director. Phone: 703-421-5443. Fax: 703-421-6401. E-mail: dgersten@ceousa.org. Telephone interview required. Applicants must submit a letter of interest, resume, writing sample. Applications are accepted continuously. World Wide Web: http://www.ceousa.org.

CENTER FOR NONPROLIFERATION STUDIES
Monterey Institute of International Studies, 425 Van Buren
Monterey, California 93940

General Information Largest nongovernmental organization in U.S. devoted exclusively to research and training in nonproliferation issues; striving to combat the spread of weapons of mass destruction through training and information dissemination. Established in 1989. Number of employees: 65. Unit of Monterey Institute of International Studies, Monterey, California. Number of internship applications received each year: 40.

Internships Available ▶ *Nonproliferation internships (DC office):* responsibilities include researching chemical and biological weapons nonproliferation issues; monitoring events in Congress, administration, and media; collecting documents and testimony; assisting with outreach activities. Candidates should have computer skills, office skills, research skills. Duration is 5 months. $7–$9 per hour. Open to college seniors, recent college graduates, graduate students. ▶ *5–10 summer undergraduate internships in nonproliferation studies:* responsibilities include research assistance for one of the following projects: East Asia Nonproliferation; Proliferation Research and Assessment Program; Newly Independent States Nonproliferation; Chemical and Biological Nonproliferation; Education. Candidates should have ability to work independently, personal interest in the field, research skills, writing skills. Duration is 2–4 months. $7 per hour. Open to college juniors, college seniors. International applications accepted.

Benefits On-the-job training, opportunity to attend seminars/workshops, willing to provide letters of recommendation.

Contact E-mail or through World Wide Web site Fred Wehling, Education Coordinator. Fax: 831-647-6522. E-mail: fwehling@miis.edu. Applicants must submit a letter of interest, resume, academic transcripts, two letters of recommendation. Application deadline: March 1 for summer (Monterey), June 29 for fall (DC), November 8 for winter/spring (DC). World Wide Web: http://cns.miis.edu.

CENTER FOR POLICY ALTERNATIVES
1875 Connecticut Avenue, NW, Suite 710
Washington, District of Columbia 20009

General Information Organization that provides state policymakers with effective alternative models on cutting-edge issues, promotes informed leadership among public officials and advocates, and provides assistance and public education. Established in 1974. Number of employees: 20. Number of internship applications received each year: 300.

Internships Available ▶ *7–10 interns:* responsibilities include research, writing, and administrative work. Candidates should have personal interest in the field, research skills, self-motivation, strong interpersonal skills, writing skills. Duration is flexible. Unpaid. Open to college freshmen, college sophomores, college juniors, college seniors, recent college graduates, graduate students. International applications accepted.

Benefits Opportunity to attend seminars/workshops, possible full-time employment, willing to complete paperwork for educational credit, willing to provide letters of recommendation.

Contact Write, call, fax, or e-mail Maxine Somerville, Internship Coordinator. Phone: 202-387-6030. Fax: 202-387-8529. E-mail: hr@cfpa.org. In-person interview recommended (telephone interview accepted). Applicants must submit a letter of interest, resume, academic transcripts, writing sample (4-5 pages maximum), at least one personal reference, at least one letter of recommendation. Application deadline: March 1 for summer, November 1 for spring. World Wide Web: http://www.stateaction.org.

CENTER FOR THE STUDY OF CONFLICT, INC.
5846 Bellona Avenue
Baltimore, Maryland 21212

General Information Center that performs research on abstract conflict resolution, applies the findings to discover ways to stop violence at all levels, and distributes the results. Established in 1982. Number of employees: 1. Number of internship applications received each year: 20.

Center for the Study of Conflict, Inc. (continued)
Internships Available ▶ *1 fund-raiser:* responsibilities include writing and editing grant proposals and fund-raising letters and researching prospects. Candidates should have ability to work independently, computer skills, oral communication skills, personal interest in the field, research skills, writing skills. Duration is flexible. Unpaid. Open to college freshmen, college sophomores, college juniors, college seniors, recent college graduates, graduate students, career changers, individuals reentering the workforce. ▶ *Indexers of files:* responsibilities include indexing letters and forms in files; reading, phoning, and library research. Candidates should have ability to work independently, analytical skills, college courses in field, computer skills, knowledge of field, research skills. Duration is flexible. Unpaid. Open to college freshmen, college sophomores, college juniors, college seniors, recent college graduates, graduate students, career changers, individuals reentering the workforce. ▶ *2–4 research assistants:* responsibilities include library research, copyediting, writing, fund-raising, and office work (including typing). Candidates should have ability to work independently, computer skills, editing skills, research skills, self-motivation, writing skills. Duration is flexible. Unpaid. Open to college freshmen, college sophomores, college juniors, college seniors, recent college graduates, graduate students, law students, career changers, individuals reentering the workforce. International applications accepted.
Benefits Names of contacts, on-the-job training, willing to act as a professional reference, willing to complete paperwork for educational credit, willing to provide letters of recommendation.
Contact Write or call Dr. Richard Wendell Fogg, Director. Phone: 410-323-7656. Applicants must submit application materials obtained by calling or writing. Application deadline: April 15.

CENTER FOR THE STUDY OF SOCIAL STRUCTURES
2502 Orella Street
Santa Barbara, California 93105-3899

General Information Nonprofit organization working to change the social structure of the American government to form kinder and freer government; believes that all early childhood and college education should be free; drugs should be decriminalized and heavily taxed; and less money should be spent on the military. Established in 1981. Number of internship applications received each year: 20.
Internships Available ▶ *"Idea Marketing" interns/volunteers:* responsibilities include duties as listed on the Web site. Candidates should have oral communication skills, personal interest in the field, honesty, integrity, and warm cheerful personality. Duration is flexible. Position available as unpaid or paid. Open to anyone interested in improving social structures. International applications accepted.
Benefits Job counseling, names of contacts, possible full-time employment, willing to act as a professional reference, willing to complete paperwork for educational credit, willing to provide letters of recommendation.
International Internships Available.
Contact Write, fax, e-mail, or through World Wide Web site William B. Hackett, Director/Founder, 2502 Orella Street, Santa Barbara, California 93105-3899. Phone: 805-898-0502. Fax: 805-687-0082. E-mail: center@rain.org. Applicants must submit letter explaining how the applicant could contribute to the organization. Applications are accepted continuously. World Wide Web: http://www.rain.org/~center.

CENTER FOR WOMEN POLICY STUDIES (CWPS)
1211 Connecticut Avenue, NW, Suite 312
Washington, District of Columbia 20036

General Information Public policy research and advocacy organization that advances the rights of women. Established in 1972. Number of employees: 12. Number of internship applications received each year: 150.
Internships Available ▶ *1–3 policy research/program assistants:* responsibilities include assisting with library research, fact checking, data entry, and supporting various programs; working on

policy analysis and advocacy programs. Candidates should have ability to work with others, computer skills, knowledge of field, research skills, writing skills. Duration is 2–3 months. Unpaid. Open to college seniors, recent college graduates, graduate students, law students, career changers, individuals reentering the workforce. International applications accepted.
Benefits Opportunity to attend seminars/workshops, willing to complete paperwork for educational credit, willing to provide letters of recommendation.
Contact Write, fax, e-mail, or through World Wide Web site Leslie R. Wolfe, President. Fax: 202-296-8962. E-mail: cwps@centerwomenpolicy.org. No phone calls. In-person interview recommended (telephone interview accepted). Applicants must submit a letter of interest, resume. Applications are accepted continuously. World Wide Web: http://www.centerwomenpolicy.org.

CHICAGO FOUNDATION FOR WOMEN
230 West Superior, Suite 400
Chicago, Illinois 60610-3536

General Information Foundation dedicated to increasing resources and opportunities for women and girls; the Foundation has awarded over $9 million to hundreds of programs serving women and girls in the greater Chicago area. Established in 1985. Number of employees: 14. Affiliate of Women's Funding Network, San Francisco, California. Number of internship applications received each year: 50.
Internships Available ▶ *1 Jessica Eve Patt intern:* responsibilities include assisting with special projects and administrative support in development department, interacting with leaders in women's philanthropic and social service advocacy community. Candidates should have computer skills, office skills, oral communication skills, organizational skills, personal interest in the field, strong interpersonal skills. Duration is 12–24 months. $10–$12 per hour. Open to recent high school graduates, college freshmen, college sophomores, college juniors, college seniors, recent college graduates, graduate students, law students, career changers, individuals reentering the workforce. ▶ *1 communications intern:* responsibilities include assisting communications department with development of materials for large annual fund-raising event; conducting outreach and marketing around event. Candidates should have computer skills, oral communication skills, personal interest in the field, research skills, strong interpersonal skills, written communication skills. Duration is 4–5 months. $10–$12 per hour. Open to college freshmen, college sophomores, college juniors, college seniors, recent college graduates, graduate students, career changers, individuals reentering the workforce. ▶ *1 program/public policy intern:* responsibilities include providing administrative support to grant-making and technical assistance programs; research projects coordinated with grantee organizations and peers in philanthropic field. Candidates should have analytical skills, college courses in field, organizational skills, research skills, self-motivation, strong interpersonal skills. Duration is 3–5 months. $1000–$2000 per duration of internship. Open to recent college graduates, graduate students. International applications accepted.
Benefits Names of contacts, opportunity to attend seminars/workshops, possible full-time employment, travel reimbursement, willing to complete paperwork for educational credit, willing to provide letters of recommendation.
Contact Write, fax, or e-mail Erin Hustings, Internship Coordinator/Executive Assistant to the Directors, 230 West Superior, Suite 400, Chicago, Illinois 60610-3636. Fax: 312-266-0990. E-mail: ehustings@cfw.org. No phone calls. In-person interview required. Applicants must submit a letter of interest, resume. Applications are accepted continuously. World Wide Web: http://www.cfw.org.

CHILDREN NOW
1212 Broadway, 5th Floor
Oakland, California 94612

General Information Independent, nonpartisan research and action organization dedicated to improving children's lives.
Internships Available ▶ *1 Internet intern:* responsibilities include working with Internet coordinator to develop and implement a strategic marketing plan for organization's Web sites, developing outreach materials, helping to develop and promote collateral

media opportunities at Web portals and related commercial Web sites, and re-purpose and repairage content using Macromedia Dream Weaver and Adobe PhotoShop tools. Candidates should have ability to work independently, computer skills, organizational skills, writing skills, willingness to comply with established file-naming schemes, commitment to children's advocacy issues, experience with basic HTML. Duration is 10 weeks in summer (40 hours per week). $300 weekly stipend. ▶ *1 children and the media intern:* responsibilities include assisting in organization and coordination of events, briefings, and convenings; updating database; researching content for staff; assisting Internet coordinator in content development; writing letters to industry leaders, academics, and advocates; assisting department with mailings, proofreading, and reports. Candidates should have ability to work independently, computer skills, organizational skills, research skills, writing skills. Duration is 10 weeks in summer (40 hours per week). $300 weekly stipend. ▶ *1 nonprofit fund-raising intern:* responsibilities include researching and reporting on prospective sources of funding; participating in general department planning and fund-raising efforts. Candidates should have ability to work independently, computer skills, organizational skills, research skills, writing skills, interest in children's issues, desire to learn about non-profit fund-raising. Duration is 10 weeks in summer (40 hours per week). $300 weekly stipend. ▶ *1 policy intern I:* responsibilities include two main components: Child Indicators Project and Easy Care and Education Project; conducting on-line and library research and data collection about factors influencing child well-being; writing fact sheets and/or papers; developing advocacy tools for Children Now's family of Web sites. Candidates should have ability to work independently, computer skills, organizational skills, research skills, writing skills, strong background in college-level statistics or public health research, Microsoft Excel, attention to detail. Duration is 10 weeks in summer (40 hours per week). $300 weekly stipend.
Contact Write, fax, or e-mail Internship Coordinator. Fax: 510-763-1974. E-mail: jjones@childrennow.org. No phone calls. World Wide Web: http://www.childrennow.org.

CHILDREN'S DEFENSE FUND
25 E Street, NW
Washington, District of Columbia 20001

General Information Advocacy organization that exists to provide a strong voice for children; goals are achieved by educating the public about children's needs and encouraging preventive investment in children before they get sick, get into trouble, drop out of school, or suffer from family breakdown. Established in 1969. Number of employees: 110. Number of internship applications received each year: 450.
Internships Available ▶ *60–100 interns:* responsibilities include duties from general office tasks to extensive researching and writing. Candidates should have ability to work with others, computer skills, office skills, research skills, writing skills, flexibility. Duration is flexible. Unpaid. Open to high school students, recent high school graduates, college freshmen, college sophomores, college juniors, college seniors, recent college graduates, graduate students, law students, career changers, individuals reentering the workforce. International applications accepted.
Benefits On-the-job training, opportunity to attend seminars/workshops, possible full-time employment, willing to act as a professional reference, willing to complete paperwork for educational credit, willing to provide letters of recommendation.
Contact Write, call, fax, or e-mail Kristin Peterson, Internship Coordinator. Phone: 202-628-8787. Fax: 202-662-3570. E-mail: kpeterson@childrensdefense.org. Telephone interview required. Applicants must submit a formal organization application, letter of interest, resume, three personal references. Applications are accepted continuously. World Wide Web: http://www.childrensdefense.org.

CITIZEN ADVOCACY CENTER
238 North York Road
Elmhurst, Illinois 60126

General Information Organization that educates citizens about civil tools to initiate actions to stimulate citizen awareness and involvement, monitor local government, help citizens on issues of public significance, and litigate on behalf of citizens to sustain access to justice. Established in 1994. Number of employees: 3. Number of internship applications received each year: 150.
Internships Available ▶ *4–10 interns:* responsibilities include writing articles and brochures, researching local government issues, attending meetings, facilitating community programs and grass-roots activism. Candidates should have ability to work independently, ability to work with others, personal interest in the field, research skills, self-motivation, writing skills. Duration is 8–10 weeks. Unpaid. Open to high school students, recent high school graduates, college freshmen, college sophomores, college juniors, college seniors, recent college graduates, graduate students, law students, career changers, individuals reentering the workforce. International applications accepted.
Benefits On-the-job training, willing to act as a professional reference, willing to complete paperwork for educational credit, willing to provide letters of recommendation.
Contact Write, call, fax, or e-mail Ms. Terry Pastika, Community Lawyer. Phone: 630-833-4080. Fax: 630-833-4083. E-mail: tpastika@citizenadvocacycenter.org. In-person interview recommended (telephone interview accepted). Applicants must submit a letter of interest, resume. Application deadline: March 1 for summer; continuous for other positions. World Wide Web: http://www.citizenadvocacycenter.org.

CITIZENS AGAINST GOVERNMENT WASTE
1301 Connecticut Avenue, NW, Suite 400
Washington, District of Columbia 20036

General Information One million member private, nonpartisan, nonprofit organization dedicated to educating Americans about waste, fraud, and abuse in the federal government. Established in 1984. Number of employees: 16. Number of internship applications received each year: 60.
Internships Available ▶ *2 corporate development/membership interns:* responsibilities include providing support for fund-raising activities including helping research potential corporate and individual donors. Candidates should have ability to work independently, computer skills, oral communication skills, research skills, strong interpersonal skills, written communication skills. Duration is flexible. Unpaid. ▶ *1 finance/accounting intern:* responsibilities include aiding finance/human resources department in payroll and accounting issues. Candidates should have ability to work with others, computer skills, office skills, oral communication skills, organizational skills. Duration is flexible. Unpaid. ▶ *2 government affairs interns:* responsibilities include monitoring hearings, summarizing essential testimony and votes taken during committee meetings, tracking legislation, and writing news articles. Candidates should have ability to work independently, computer skills, oral communication skills, strong interpersonal skills, written communication skills. Duration is flexible. Unpaid. ▶ *2 grassroots interns:* responsibilities include visiting Capitol Hill, attending coalition meetings, writing articles for bi-weekly grassroots newsletter, and keeping abreast of the current political agenda. Candidates should have ability to work independently, computer skills, oral communication skills, strong interpersonal skills, written communication skills. Duration is flexible. Unpaid. ▶ *1 health and science policy intern:* responsibilities include assisting director of health and science with research, trading legislation, writing regarding Medicare, health savings accounts, prescription drugs, and price controls. Candidates should have ability to work independently, computer skills, research skills, writing skills. Duration is flexible. Unpaid. ▶ *2 media interns:* responsibilities include assisting in answering press and public information requests, producing and distributing press releases, and maintaining media database. Candidates should have ability to work independently, computer skills, oral communication skills, research skills, writing skills. Duration is flexible. Unpaid. ▶ *2 research interns:* responsibilities include formulating policy papers and collecting data for original investigative studies, researching and writing for annual "Pig Book", "Prime Cuts", and special projects. Candidates should have ability to work independently, computer skills, oral communication skills, research skills, strong interpersonal skills, written communication skills. Duration is flexible. Unpaid. Open to college

Citizens Against Government Waste (continued)

freshmen, college sophomores, college juniors, college seniors, recent college graduates. International applications accepted.
Benefits Names of contacts, opportunity to attend seminars/workshops, willing to act as a professional reference, willing to complete paperwork for educational credit, willing to provide letters of recommendation.
Contact Write, call, fax, e-mail, or through World Wide Web site Mark Carpenter, Intern Coordinator. Phone: 202-467-5300. Fax: 202-467-4253. E-mail: interns@cagw.org. Telephone interview required. Applicants must submit a letter of interest, resume, writing sample. Applications are accepted continuously. World Wide Web: http://www.cagw.org.

CITIZENS FOR A SOUND ECONOMY AND CSE FOUNDATION
1900 M Street, NW, Suite 500
Washington, District of Columbia 20036

General Information Organization working to educate and mobilize citizens to promote market-based solutions for public policy issues such as tax and budget policy, trade policy, and regulatory policy. Established in 1984. Number of employees: 25. Number of internship applications received each year: 200.
Internships Available ▶ *1 public affairs intern:* responsibilities include assisting with press conferences, special events, op-ed and article placement, and event follow-up. Candidates should have oral communication skills, personal interest in the field, self-motivation, strong interpersonal skills, writing skills. Duration is flexible. Unpaid. Open to college freshmen, college sophomores, college juniors, college seniors. ▶ *1–2 research interns:* responsibilities include assisting with the researching, writing, and editing of organizational reports and publications. Candidates should have ability to work independently, editing skills, research skills, self-motivation, written communication skills. Duration is flexible. Unpaid. Open to college sophomores, college juniors, college seniors. International applications accepted.
Benefits Opportunity to attend seminars/workshops, willing to complete paperwork for educational credit, willing to provide letters of recommendation.
Contact Write, call, fax, or e-mail Nicole M. Thompson, Intern Coordinator. Phone: 202-783-3870. Fax: 202-783-4687. E-mail: nthompson@cse.org. Telephone interview required. Applicants must submit a formal organization application, letter of interest, resume, academic transcripts, writing sample. Applications are accepted continuously. World Wide Web: http://www.cse.org.

CITIZENS FOR TAX JUSTICE
1311 L Street, NW
Washington, District of Columbia 20005

General Information Research and advocacy organization. Established in 1979. Number of employees: 9. Number of internship applications received each year: 100.
Internships Available ▶ *2 research interns:* responsibilities include research, writing, representing organization at coalition meetings. Candidates should have ability to work independently, analytical skills, computer skills, editing skills, office skills, oral communication skills, organizational skills, personal interest in the field, research skills, self-motivation, strong interpersonal skills, strong leadership ability, writing skills. Duration is 10 weeks during summer. Stipend of $230 per week. Open to college freshmen, college sophomores, college juniors, college seniors, recent college graduates, (college sophomores and juniors preferred).
Benefits Opportunity to attend seminars/workshops, possible full-time employment, willing to act as a professional reference, willing to complete paperwork for educational credit, willing to provide letters of recommendation.
Contact Write, fax, or through World Wide Web site Will Gomaa, Intern Coordinator, 1311 L Street, NW, Washington, District of Columbia 20005. Fax: 202-638-3486. No phone calls. Telephone interview required. Applicants must submit a letter of interest, resume, writing sample, three personal references. Application deadline: March 15. World Wide Web: http://www.ctj.org.

CITIZENS' NETWORK FOR FOREIGN AFFAIRS (CNFA)
1111 19th Street, NW, Suite 900
Washington, District of Columbia 20036

General Information Nonprofit, nonpartisan organization dedicated to stimulating international economic growth in developing and emerging world markets. Established in 1986. Number of employees: 17. Number of internship applications received each year: 500.
Internships Available ▶ *4–5 interns:* responsibilities include staff support, researching, and attending and reporting on meetings. Candidates should have ability to work independently, computer skills, knowledge of field, research skills, self-motivation, written communication skills. Duration is 5 months in spring, 4 months in fall, 3 months in summer. $1000 per month. Open to college juniors, college seniors, recent college graduates. International applications accepted.
Benefits Formal training, job counseling, names of contacts, on-the-job training, opportunity to attend seminars/workshops, possible full-time employment, willing to complete paperwork for educational credit, willing to provide letters of recommendation.
Contact Write, call, fax, e-mail, or through World Wide Web site Dollie Eleam, Internship Coordinator. Phone: 202-296-3920. Fax: 202-296-3948. E-mail: intern@cnfa.org. Applicants must submit a letter of interest, resume, writing sample, three letters of recommendation. Application deadline: April 1 for summer, July 1 for fall, November 1 for spring. World Wide Web: http://www.cnfa.org.

COALITION FOR THE INTERNATIONAL CRIMINAL COURT
777 United Nations Plaza, 12th Floor
New York, New York 10017

General Information Program promoting a fair, effective, and independent International Criminal Court; ratification and implementation of the Rome Statute for the ICC; NGO network building. Established in 1995. Number of employees: 16. Unit of World Federalist Movement, New York, New York. Number of internship applications received each year: 300.
Internships Available ▶ *2–6 legal interns:* responsibilities include legal research and background research related to the ratification and implementation of the Rome Statute for the International Criminal Court. Candidates should have ability to work independently, analytical skills, editing skills, research skills, strong interpersonal skills, writing skills. Duration is flexible. Unpaid. Open to graduate students, law students. ▶ *10–12 outreach, media, research, and design interns:* responsibilities include miscellaneous duties relating to the International Criminal Court campaign, promoting international human rights through international law, and NGO networking. Candidates should have computer skills, editing skills, personal interest in the field, research skills, strong interpersonal skills, writing skills. Duration is flexible. Unpaid. Open to high school students, recent high school graduates, college freshmen, college sophomores, college juniors, college seniors, recent college graduates, graduate students. International applications accepted.
Benefits Names of contacts, opportunity to attend seminars/workshops, possible full-time employment, willing to act as a professional reference, willing to complete paperwork for educational credit, willing to provide letters of recommendation, reimbursement of assignment-related expenses.
International Internships Available in Brussels, Belgium; Mexico City, Mexico; Lima, Peru.
Contact Fax or e-mail Joydeep Sengupta, Outreach/Communications Associate. Fax: 212-599-1332. E-mail: cicc6@icgnow.org. No phone calls. In-person interview recommended (telephone interview accepted). Applicants must submit a formal organization application, letter of interest, resume, writing sample. Applications are accepted continuously. World Wide Web: http://www.iccnow.org.

COMMON CAUSE
1250 Connecticut Avenue, NW
Washington, District of Columbia 20036

General Information Nonprofit, nonpartisan citizens' lobbying group working to promote honesty, accountability, and ethics in government. Established in 1970. Number of employees: 40. Number of internship applications received each year: 150.

Internships Available ► *1 Web/Internet Communications intern:* responsibilities include working on the design and maintenance of the Common Cause Web site; working on writing and sending CauseNet alerts. Candidates should have computer skills, editing skills, knowledge of field, research skills, writing skills. Unpaid. Open to high school seniors, recent high school graduates, college freshmen, college sophomores, college juniors, college seniors, recent college graduates. ► *3 campaign finance research interns:* responsibilities include helping staff collect and analyze reports of political contributions to candidates and political parties, and gathering research material about PACs and other large political donors. Candidates should have ability to work independently, computer skills, knowledge of field, organizational skills, research skills, self-motivation. Unpaid. Open to high school seniors, college freshmen, college sophomores, college juniors, college seniors, recent college graduates, graduate students. ► *20–25 grassroots interns:* responsibilities include organizing grassroots effort, research, public relations, and legislation. Candidates should have ability to work independently, oral communication skills, self-motivation, strong interpersonal skills, written communication skills. Unpaid. Open to high school students, recent high school graduates, college freshmen, college sophomores, college juniors, college seniors, recent college graduates, graduate students, law students. ► *1 issue mail intern:* responsibilities include issuing mail correspondence and assisting the governing board representative. Candidates should have ability to work independently, computer skills, editing skills, oral communication skills, writing skills. Unpaid. Open to college freshmen, college sophomores, college juniors, college seniors, recent college graduates, graduate students. ► *2–3 legislative policy interns:* responsibilities include assisting lobbying staff and researching issues development. Candidates should have analytical skills, computer skills, oral communication skills, organizational skills, strong interpersonal skills, written communication skills. Unpaid. Open to college freshmen, college sophomores, college juniors, college seniors, recent college graduates, graduate students, law students. ► *3 media communication interns:* responsibilities include assisting in producing, proofing, and editing press releases; booking radio talk shows; answering requests for information. Candidates should have editing skills, oral communication skills, personal interest in the field, strong interpersonal skills. Unpaid. Open to college freshmen, college sophomores, college juniors, college seniors, recent college graduates, graduate students. ► *1 membership and fund-raising intern:* responsibilities include assisting membership/fund-raising staff. Candidates should have ability to work with others, office skills, oral communication skills, personal interest in the field. Unpaid. Open to college freshmen, college sophomores, college juniors, college seniors, recent college graduates, graduate students. ► *2 state issues interns:* responsibilities include assisting 43 state organizations and activists across the country in grassroots campaigns and legislative battles. Candidates should have ability to work independently, oral communication skills, research skills, strong interpersonal skills, written communication skills. Unpaid. Open to recent high school graduates, college freshmen, college sophomores, college juniors, college seniors. International applications accepted.

Benefits Job counseling, opportunity to attend seminars/workshops, willing to act as a professional reference, willing to complete paperwork for educational credit, willing to provide letters of recommendation, daily travel expenses paid.

Contact Write, call, fax, e-mail, or through World Wide Web site Kathleen Grant, Director of Outreach and Youth Initiatives. Phone: 202-833-1200. Fax: 202-659-3716. E-mail: kgrant@commoncause.org. Applicants must submit a formal organization application, resume, writing sample. Applications are accepted continuously. World Wide Web: http://www.commoncause.org.

THE CONGRESSIONAL HUNGER CENTER
229½ Pennsylvania Avenue, SE
Washington, District of Columbia 20003

General Information National, nonprofit organization that develops leaders in the fight against hunger. Established in 1993. Number of employees: 9. Number of internship applications received each year: 150.

Internships Available ► *20–24 Bill Emerson National Hunger Fellows:* responsibilities include working at field site (6 months) and policy site (6 months) addressing hunger and poverty from a grass-roots local and national policy level. Candidates should have ability to work with others, organizational skills, personal interest in the field, research skills, strong leadership ability, writing skills. Duration is 1 year beginning in August. $10,000 per year. Open to recent college graduates, graduate students, law students, career changers, individuals reentering the workforce. ► *Interns:* responsibilities include working on one of several projects, depending on the intern's interests. Candidates should have ability to work independently, oral communication skills, strong interpersonal skills, written communication skills. Duration is flexible. Position available as unpaid or paid. Open to individuals 18 years of age or older.

Benefits Formal training, free housing, health insurance, names of contacts, on-the-job training, opportunity to attend seminars/workshops, travel reimbursement, willing to act as a professional reference, willing to provide letters of recommendation.

International Internships Available.

Contact Call, e-mail, or through World Wide Web site John Kelly, Co-Director, 229½ Pennsylvania Avenue, SE, Washington, District of Columbia 20003. Phone: 202-547-7022. E-mail: fellows@hungercenter.org. In-person interview required. Applicants must submit a formal organization application, resume, two letters of recommendation, personal statement and essay on leadership. Application deadline: January 15 for national fellows program; continuous for internship program. World Wide Web: http://www.hungercenter.org.

CONSERVATION LAW FOUNDATION
62 Summer Street
Boston, Massachusetts 02110-1016

General Information Nonprofit regional environmental advocacy organization. Number of employees: 50. Number of internship applications received each year: 50.

Internships Available ► *1–3 general interns:* responsibilities include maintaining news clippings, helping staff with record keeping and occasional mailings, assisting advocates with library or Internet research in CLF project areas, and writing projects. Candidates should have ability to work independently, computer skills, research skills, self-motivation, strong interpersonal skills, writing skills. Duration is minimum of 3 months (at least 12 hours per week). Unpaid. Open to college freshmen, college sophomores, college juniors, college seniors, recent college graduates. ► *1–4 legal interns/legal associates:* responsibilities include working closely with CLF's staff of 20 attorneys, as well as with experts in technical fields including science and resource economics and legal research and writing; see Web site for more information. Candidates should have ability to work independently, knowledge of field, research skills, self-motivation, written communication skills. Duration is one semester or summer. Position available as unpaid or at $1500 for 12 weeks full-time work (applicable to summer); work study also available. Open to law students. ► *1 membership intern:* responsibilities include data entry, mailings and other administrative work, Internet research, copy editing, publicity, promotion material design, event-planning, and community organizing. Candidates should have ability to work independently, organizational skills, personal interest in the field, self-motivation, written communication skills. Duration is minimum of 3 months. Unpaid. Open to college sophomores, college juniors, college seniors, recent college graduates.

Benefits Willing to act as a professional reference, willing to complete paperwork for educational credit, willing to provide letters of recommendation.

Contact Write, call, fax, or e-mail Lily Orr, Volunteer Liaison. Phone: 617-350-0990 Ext. 711. Fax: 617-350-4030. E-mail: lorr@clf.

Conservation Law Foundation (continued)
org. In-person interview required. Applicants must submit a letter of interest, resume, writing sample, academic transcripts may be required. Applications are accepted continuously. World Wide Web: http://www.clf.org.

CONSUMER ENERGY COUNCIL OF AMERICA
2000 L Street, NW, Suite 802
Washington, District of Columbia 20036

General Information Research and policy organization that promotes consumer interests in policy issues, conducts research, and builds coalitions between public and private sectors; issues include utility industry restructuring, energy distribution in the developing world, telecommunications policy, and pricing policies. Established in 1973. Number of employees: 7. Number of internship applications received each year: 200.
Internships Available ▶ *2–4 research assistants:* responsibilities include researching policies, drafting letters, tracking legislation, reviewing literature, compiling and analyzing data, preparing tables and charts, editing, proofreading, assisting in drafting proposals, assisting in project development, and some general office work. Candidates should have ability to work independently, analytical skills, computer skills, editing skills, office skills, oral communication skills, organizational skills, research skills, self-motivation, strong interpersonal skills, strong leadership ability, writing skills. Duration is flexible (usually 3 months). Position available as unpaid or paid. Open to college sophomores, college juniors, college seniors, recent college graduates, graduate students. International applications accepted.
Benefits Job counseling, names of contacts, on-the-job training, opportunity to attend seminars/workshops, possible full-time employment, travel reimbursement, willing to act as a professional reference, willing to complete paperwork for educational credit, willing to provide letters of recommendation, stipends may be available based on project funding.
Contact Write, fax, e-mail, or through World Wide Web site Internship Coordinator. Phone: 202-659-0404. Fax: 202-659-0407. E-mail: outreach@cecarf.org. In-person interview recommended. Applicants must submit a letter of interest, resume, GPA, 2 in-depth writing samples, 3 references. Applications are accepted continuously. World Wide Web: http://www.cecarf.org.

CONSUMER FEDERATION OF AMERICA
1424 16th Street, NW, Suite 604
Washington, District of Columbia 20036

General Information Nonprofit public interest organization seeking to advocate consumer interest for product safety, telecommunications, protection against consumer scams, advertising, insurance, real estate, banking, health care, and utility deregulation before Congress, federal regulatory agencies, and the courts. Established in 1967. Number of employees: 15. Number of internship applications received each year: 50.
Internships Available ▶ *2 general interns:* responsibilities include research, working on legislation, attending occasional coalition meetings and briefings on Capitol Hill, as well as working with regulatory agencies. Candidates should have ability to work independently, office skills, organizational skills, personal interest in the field, research skills, written communication skills. Duration is 1 semester. $25 weekly stipend for undergraduates working full-time, $50 weekly stipend for graduates and law students working full-time; salary negotiable. Open to college freshmen, college sophomores, college juniors, college seniors, recent college graduates, graduate students, law students. International applications accepted.
Benefits Names of contacts, opportunity to attend seminars/workshops, travel reimbursement, willing to act as a professional reference, willing to complete paperwork for educational credit, willing to provide letters of recommendation.
Contact Write, call, or through World Wide Web site Susan Peschin, Project Director. Phone: 202-387-6121. Fax: 202-265-7987. E-mail: speschin@consumerfed.org. Applicants must submit

a letter of interest, resume, writing sample. Applications are accepted continuously. World Wide Web: http://www.consumerfed. org.

DC COALITION AGAINST DOMESTIC VIOLENCE–VICTIM ADVOCACY PROGRAM
500 Indiana Avenue, NW, #4235
Washington, District of Columbia 20001

General Information Court-based advocacy program for victims of domestic violence. Number of employees: 3. Number of internship applications received each year: 100.
Internships Available ▶ *8–10 domestic violence victim advocates:* responsibilities include crisis intervention and emotional support; referrals to other community services; information about the legal process; also advocates within the justice system on behalf of victims of domestic violence. Candidates should have ability to work independently, oral communication skills, personal interest in the field, self-motivation, strong interpersonal skills. Duration is 1 semester. Unpaid. Open to college freshmen, college sophomores, college juniors, college seniors, recent college graduates, graduate students, law students, survivors of domestic violence. International applications accepted.
Benefits Formal training, on-the-job training, willing to act as a professional reference, willing to complete paperwork for educational credit, willing to provide letters of recommendation.
Contact Call or e-mail Christina Principe, Program Director. Phone: 202-879-7851. Fax: 202-879-1191. E-mail: dvadv09@desc. gov. In-person interview recommended (telephone interview accepted). Applicants must submit a formal organization application, resume, three personal references. Application deadline: May 1 for summer, August 1 for fall, December 1 for spring. World Wide Web: http://www.dccadv.org.

THE DEVELOPMENT GAP
927 15th Street, NW, Fourth Floor
Washington, District of Columbia 20005

General Information Organization that works for grassroots input into economic policymaking, and organizes opposition to imposition of economic policy from Washington. Established in 1977. Number of employees: 5. Number of internship applications received each year: 60.
Internships Available ▶ *4–8 interns:* responsibilities include conducting research and writing reports on the impact of World Bank/IMF programs; assisting with organizing events. Candidates should have experience in the field, oral communication skills, personal interest in the field, research skills, self-motivation, written communication skills. Duration is flexible. Unpaid. Open to recent college graduates, graduate students, career changers. International applications accepted.
Benefits Names of contacts, on-the-job training, opportunity to attend seminars/workshops, willing to act as a professional reference, willing to complete paperwork for educational credit, willing to provide letters of recommendation, reimbursement of local transportation expenses.
Contact Write or e-mail Stephanie Weinberg, Internship Coordinator. Phone: 202-898-1566. Fax: 202-898-1612. E-mail: sweinberg@ developmentgap.org. Applicants must submit a letter of interest, resume, writing sample. Application deadline: May 1 for summer, December 1 for winter/spring. World Wide Web: http:// www.developmentgap.org.

THE EDUCATION TRUST, INC.
1725 K Street, NW, Suite 200
Washington, District of Columbia 20006

General Information Education advocacy group dedicated to closing the achievement gap . Established in 1990. Number of employees: 45. Number of internship applications received each year: 200.
Internships Available ▶ *2–5 interns:* responsibilities include duties as described on Web site. Candidates should have ability to work independently, knowledge of field, oral communication skills, research skills, strong interpersonal skills, writing skills. Duration

is one semester on summer. Modest stipend. Open to college juniors, college seniors, recent college graduates, graduate students, career changers.
Benefits Opportunity to attend seminars/workshops, willing to act as a professional reference, willing to complete paperwork for educational credit, willing to provide letters of recommendation.
Contact Write, fax, or e-mail Charles Williams, Internship Coordinator. Fax: 202-293-2605. E-mail: cwilliams@edtrust.org. No phone calls. Telephone interview required. Applicants must submit a letter of interest, resume, writing sample, two personal references. Application deadline: April 1 for summer, July 1 for fall, November 1 for spring. World Wide Web: http://www.edtrust.org.

EQUALITY FLORIDA
1222 South Dale Mabry, #652
Tampa, Florida 33629

General Information State-wide education and advocacy organization that works to achieve social, political, and economic justice and is dedicated to ending discrimination based on sexual orientation, race, class, and gender. Established in 1997. Number of employees: 7. Number of internship applications received each year: 30.
Internships Available ▶ *1–2 communications interns:* responsibilities include drafting press releases, writing for newsletter, being included in Media Watch project which monitors and responds to bias and bigotry in press coverage. Candidates should have ability to work with others, computer skills, editing skills, research skills, writing skills, strong personal commitment to diversity and to advancing lesbian, gay, bisexual, and transgender rights. Duration is one semester and summer. Unpaid. Open to college freshmen, college sophomores, college juniors, college seniors, recent college graduates, graduate students, law students, career changers.
▶ *1–2 development interns:* responsibilities include working closely with the director of development on creating membership appeals and soliciting support from major donors. Candidates should have computer skills, organizational skills, strong leadership ability, written communication skills, strong personal commitment to diversity and advancing lesbian, gay, bisexual and transgender rights. Duration is one semester or summer. Unpaid. Open to college freshmen, college sophomores, college juniors, college seniors, recent college graduates, graduate students, law students, career changers.
▶ *5–6 field interns:* responsibilities include working on ongoing voter registration and identification efforts within Florida's LGBT community and will be especially involved in all electoral mobilization efforts. Candidates should have ability to work with others, oral communication skills, organizational skills, written communication skills, strong personal commitment to diversity and to advancing lesbian, gay, bisexual, and transgender rights. Duration is one semester and summer. Unpaid. Open to college freshmen, college sophomores, college juniors, college seniors, recent college graduates, graduate students, law students, career changers. ▶ *1–2 information technology management interns:* responsibilities include working with director of operations to organize and coordinate all project management, accounting, legal, computer systems, physical site (office), and human resources needs. Candidates should have computer skills, office skills, organizational skills, self-motivation, strong interpersonal skills, writing skills. Duration is one semester or summer. Unpaid. Open to college freshmen, college sophomores, college juniors, college seniors, recent college graduates, graduate students, career changers. ▶ *1–2 leadership development interns:* responsibilities include working with director of operations to plan, implement, and conduct leadership conferences at the local community level and at the statewide level. Candidates should have computer skills, office skills, organizational skills, self-motivation, strong interpersonal skills, strong leadership ability. Duration is one semester or summer. Unpaid. Open to college freshmen, college sophomores, college juniors, college seniors, recent college graduates, graduate students, career changers. ▶ *1–2 legislative interns:* responsibilities include assignment in Tallahassee and working in lobbying and legislative research. Candidates should have analytical skills, oral communication skills, research skills, written communication skills, strong personal commitment to diversity and to advancing lesbian, gay, transgender, and bisexual rights. Duration is one semester or

summer. Unpaid. Open to college freshmen, college sophomores, college juniors, college seniors, recent college graduates, graduate students, law students, career changers. International applications accepted.
Benefits Names of contacts, on-the-job training, opportunity to attend seminars/workshops, willing to act as a professional reference, willing to complete paperwork for educational credit, willing to provide letters of recommendation.
Contact Write, call, fax, e-mail, or through World Wide Web site Vonn New, Director of Operations. Phone: 813-870-3735 Ext. 214. Fax: 813-870-1499. E-mail: vonn@eqfl.org. In-person interview recommended (telephone interview accepted). Applicants must submit a formal organization application, letter of interest, resume, three personal references, two letters of recommendation. Applications are accepted continuously. World Wide Web: http://www.eqfl.org.

EQUAL JUSTICE USA/QUIXOTE CENTER
3502 Varnum Street
Brentwood, Maryland 20722

General Information Multi-issue social justice organization working for structural change in the Catholic church and civil society. Established in 1976. Number of employees: 22. Number of internship applications received each year: 15.
Internships Available ▶ *Interns:* responsibilities include grassroots organizing, fund-raising, office tasks, phone banking, research, advocacy, and other duties. Candidates should have ability to work independently, computer skills, office skills, oral communication skills, self-motivation. Duration is flexible. Position available as unpaid or paid. Open to high school students, recent high school graduates, college freshmen, college sophomores, college juniors, college seniors, recent college graduates, graduate students, law students, career changers, individuals reentering the workforce. International applications accepted.
Benefits Names of contacts, on-the-job training, opportunity to attend seminars/workshops, willing to act as a professional reference, willing to complete paperwork for educational credit, willing to provide letters of recommendation.
Contact Call, fax, or e-mail Trisha Kendall, Coordinator, PO Box 5206, Hyattsville, Maryland 20782. Phone: 301-699-0042. Fax: 301-864-2182. E-mail: trishak@quixote.org. In-person interview recommended (telephone interview accepted). Applicants must submit a letter of interest, resume, writing sample. Applications are accepted continuously. World Wide Web: http://www.quixote.org/ej.

FAMILIES U.S.A. FOUNDATION
1334 G Street, NW, 3rd Floor
Washington, District of Columbia 20005

General Information National health-care consumer advocacy organization engaged in the fight for affordable health and long-term care for all American families, in areas including policy research, field organizing, lobbying, and media operations. Established in 1982. Number of employees: 30. Number of internship applications received each year: 300.
Internships Available ▶ *1 field organizing intern:* responsibilities include working with more than 200 state and local organizations that are involved in consumer health issues, helping provide a wide array of technical assistance on issues such as Medicaid and managed care, using innovative on-line and teleconferencing techniques to communicate with these groups. Candidates should have ability to work independently, oral communication skills, organizational skills, personal interest in the field, self-motivation, written communication skills. Duration is one semester (possibly longer if internship successful). $6.15 per hour. Open to college juniors, college seniors, recent college graduates, graduate students, law students, individuals reentering the workforce.
▶ *2 health policy interns:* responsibilities include engaging in health policy research on issues such as consumer protections in managed care, the devolution of federal health programs such as Medicare and Medicaid, access and affordability issues, and analysis of federal and state health-care legislation. Candidates should have ability to work independently, editing skills, personal interest in the field, research skills, self-motivation, written communication

Families U.S.A. Foundation (continued)

skills. Duration is one semester (possibly longer if internship successful). $6.15 per hour. Open to college seniors, recent college graduates, graduate students. ▶ *2 media interns:* responsibilities include contacting media, interviewing individuals with health-care stories, helping with media events, and monitoring media. Candidates should have ability to work independently, oral communication skills, organizational skills, personal interest in the field, strong interpersonal skills, written communication skills. Duration is one semester (possibly longer if internship successful). $6.15 per hour. Open to college sophomores, college juniors, college seniors, recent college graduates, career changers, individuals reentering the workforce. International applications accepted.
Benefits On-the-job training, opportunity to attend seminars/workshops, willing to act as a professional reference, willing to complete paperwork for educational credit, willing to provide letters of recommendation.
Contact Write, fax, e-mail, or through World Wide Web site Internship Program Coordinator, 1334 G Street, NW, 3rd Floor. Fax: 202-347-2417. E-mail: mrosenblatt@familiesusa.org. No phone calls. Telephone interview required. Applicants must submit a letter of interest, resume, writing sample (2-3 pages). Application deadline: March 15 for summer, July 15 for fall, December 1 for winter/spring. World Wide Web: http://www.familiesusa.org.

FARM SANCTUARY–WEST
19080 Newville Road
Orland, California 95963

General Information National, nonprofit organization dedicated to ending animal agricultural abuses through public education programs, legislation, farm animal cruelty investigations and campaigns, in addition to providing shelters for rescuing, rehabilitating, and providing permanent care for hundreds of animals. Established in 1993. Number of employees: 6. Branch of Farm Sanctuary, Watkins Glen, New York. Number of internship applications received each year: 200.
Internships Available ▶ *4 interns:* responsibilities include farm chores/barn cleaning and conducting educational tours. Candidates should have ability to work with others, personal interest in the field, self-motivation, commitment to vegetarianism. Duration is 1–3 months. Unpaid. Open to high school students, recent high school graduates, college freshmen, college sophomores, college juniors, college seniors, recent college graduates, graduate students, law students, career changers, individuals reentering the workforce. International applications accepted.
Benefits Free housing, job counseling, names of contacts, possible full-time employment, willing to complete paperwork for educational credit, willing to provide letters of recommendation.
Contact Write, call, fax, e-mail, or through World Wide Web site Michelle Waffner, Education Program Manager, PO Box 150, Watkins Glen, New York 14891. Phone: 607-583-4512. Fax: 607-583-4349. E-mail: education@farmsanctuary.org. Telephone interview required. Applicants must submit a formal organization application, two letters of recommendation. Applications are accepted continuously. World Wide Web: http://www.farmsanctuary.org.

FEDERATION FOR AMERICAN IMMIGRATION REFORM (FAIR)
1666 Connecticut Avenue, NW, Suite 400
Washington, District of Columbia 20009

General Information Nonprofit public education organization. Established in 1979. Number of employees: 25. Number of internship applications received each year: 100.
Internships Available ▶ *Web site development intern:* responsibilities include reporting to director of special projects and working with Webmaster; helping to develop e-mail database into an automated information system designed to inform an interested public on immigration issues and to identify activists; may also work on Web site redesign and updating. Candidates should have self-motivation, word processing and database program experience, experience with Internet searches and e-mail communications (desirable), HTML knowledge (a plus). Duration is 3-months (at least 32 hours per week). $8 per hour. ▶ *1 government relations*

intern: responsibilities include tracking and analyzing legislation; conducting research; distributing information to Hill staff; assisting with Hill mailings; attending, taking notes, and reporting on Hill committee hearings; filing, faxing, and some general office duties. Candidates should have ability to work independently, knowledge of field, oral communication skills, personal interest in the field, self-motivation, written communication skills, MS Word experience, familiarity and comfort with goals of organization. Duration is 12-16 weeks (flexible full-time hours); position generally available year-round. $8 per hour. Open to college sophomores, college juniors, college seniors, recent college graduates, graduate students, law students. ▶ *1 law intern:* responsibilities include heavy research, primarily in the areas of immigration law, constitutional law, and administrative law; writing briefs, editing, and cite checking law review articles. Candidates should have ability to work independently, analytical skills, college courses in field, organizational skills, research skills, written communication skills, student status in a JD program, demonstrated or strong interest in helping citizens fight illegal immigration and control mass immigration. Duration is 12-16 weeks during summer. Minimum $10 per hour depending on experience. Open to law students. ▶ *1 media relations intern:* responsibilities include updating the media database, scheduling radio shows, faxing background material to television, radio, and print press; maintaining the video library, attending and helping plan press conferences, filing and writing articles for the newsletter. Candidates should have ability to work independently, computer skills, organizational skills, personal interest in the field, self-motivation, written communication skills, familiarity and comfort with goals of organization. Duration is usually a 6-month position but can be flexible. $8 per hour. Open to college freshmen, college sophomores, college juniors, college seniors, recent college graduates, graduate students, law students. ▶ *1 membership development/fund-raising intern:* responsibilities include coordination and production of 6-month appreciation gift mailings, assisting with round table meeting planning, drafting articles for the monthly newsletter, assisting with major donor mailings, and foundation research. Candidates should have ability to work independently, office skills, organizational skills, plan to pursue career in field, self-motivation, written communication skills, Internet experience, MS Word. Duration is 12-16 weeks (flexible full-time hours). $8 per hour. Open to recent high school graduates, college freshmen, college sophomores, college juniors, college seniors, recent college graduates. International applications accepted.
Benefits Job counseling, on-the-job training, opportunity to attend seminars/workshops, possible full-time employment, travel reimbursement, willing to act as a professional reference, willing to complete paperwork for educational credit, willing to provide letters of recommendation.
Contact Write, fax, e-mail, or through World Wide Web site Intern Coordinator. Fax: 202-387-3447. E-mail: jobs@fairus.org. In-person interview recommended (telephone interview accepted). Applicants must submit a letter of interest, resume, writing sample, 2–3 personal references, academic transcripts (helpful). Application deadline: April 30 for summer, July 1 for fall; continuous for winter/spring positions. World Wide Web: http://www.fairus.org.

FEDERATION OF AMERICAN SCIENTISTS
1717 K Street NW, Suite 209
Washington, District of Columbia 20036

General Information Nonprofit, privately funded organization engaged in analysis and advocacy on the consequences of science and technology on public policy. Established in 1945. Number of employees: 16. Number of internship applications received each year: 150.
Internships Available ▶ *Interns:* responsibilities include assisting project director with various projects of intern's choice and some administrative work; consult Web site for more information. Candidates should have ability to work independently, computer skills, knowledge of field, self-motivation, strong interpersonal skills, written communication skills. Duration is flexible. Position available as unpaid or paid. Open to high school seniors, recent high school graduates, college freshmen, college sophomores, col-

lege juniors, college seniors, recent college graduates, graduate students, law students, career changers. International applications accepted.

Benefits On-the-job training, opportunity to attend seminars/workshops, willing to act as a professional reference, willing to complete paperwork for educational credit, willing to provide letters of recommendation, stipend depending on hours per week worked and funding availability.

Contact Write, fax, or e-mail Sarah Mason, Organization Manager. Fax: 202-675-1010. E-mail: fas@fas.org. No phone calls. In-person interview required. Applicants must submit a letter of interest, resume, writing sample, personal reference, three personal references. Applications are accepted continuously. World Wide Web: http://www.fas.org.

FELLOWSHIP OF RECONCILIATION
PO Box 271
Nyack, New York 10960

General Information National interfaith peace and justice organization committed to active nonviolence as a means of personal, and social change. Established in 1915. Number of employees: 27. Number of internship applications received each year: 50.

Internships Available ▶ *1 Interfaith Peacebuilder Program intern:* responsibilities include assisting in all aspects of program management and development; focusing on delegations assigned throughout the year. Candidates should have ability to work with others, office skills, oral communication skills, writing skills, strong commitment to mission of FOR, interest and previous experience with Israel/Palestine (preferred), ability to handle single living situation, working knowledge of Arabic and/or Hebrew (useful). Duration is September to August. $650 per month. ▶ *1 Peacemaker Training Institute intern:* responsibilities include assisting in developing network of young activists and implementing youth nonviolence program. Candidates should have ability to work independently, oral communication skills, organizational skills, written communication skills, strong commitment to mission of FOR, ability to travel throughout the year. Duration is September to August. $650 per month. ▶ *1 nonviolence training intern:* responsibilities include assisting training coordinator in providing training and support for trainers, working with an FOR task force, updating and publishing FOR Trainers Directory, organizing training events and facilitating workshops, and revising curriculum. Candidates should have computer skills, office skills, oral communication skills, organizational skills, self-motivation, strong interpersonal skills. Duration is September to August. $650 per month. ▶ *1 task force on Latin America and the Caribbean intern:* responsibilities include assisting staff organize participation in demonstrations and other events; developing and organizing media activist training; staffing outreach efforts; assisting in organizing speaking tours; maintaining e-mail and other contact information on activists; assisting with production of newsletter; developing and carrying out a project to scan and post studies and documents. Candidates should have ability to work independently, oral communication skills, organizational skills, strong interpersonal skills, written communication skills, strong commitment to the mission of FOR, fluency in Spanish (desirable). Duration is September to August. $650 per month. Open to individuals 21 and over.

Benefits Free housing, health insurance, on-the-job training, opportunity to attend seminars/workshops, willing to act as a professional reference, willing to complete paperwork for educational credit, willing to provide letters of recommendation, 4 weeks vacation and paid holidays.

Contact Write, call, fax, e-mail, or through World Wide Web site Yvonne Royster, Administrative Assistant. Phone: 845-358-4601. Fax: 845-358-4924. E-mail: for@forusa.org. Telephone interview required. Applicants must submit a formal organization application, resume, personal reference, three personal references. Application deadline: March 31. World Wide Web: http://www.forusa.org.

FEMINIST MAJORITY AND FEMINIST MAJORITY FOUNDATION (CALIFORNIA OFFICE)
433 South Beverly Drive
Beverly Hills, California 90212

General Information Nonprofit research and advocacy organizations dedicated to promoting equality for women. Established in 1987. Number of employees: 20. Number of internship applications received each year: 300.

Internships Available ▶ *5–10 interns:* responsibilities include researching, writing, analyzing policy, organizing demonstrations and pro-choice rock-and-roll concerts, and clinic defense. Candidates should have ability to work independently, ability to work with others, knowledge of field, self-motivation, strong leadership ability, written communication skills. Duration is 2 months minimum. Unpaid. Open to college freshmen, college sophomores, college juniors, college seniors, recent college graduates, graduate students, law students.

Benefits Job counseling, names of contacts, on-the-job training, possible full-time employment, willing to act as a professional reference, willing to complete paperwork for educational credit, willing to provide letters of recommendation.

Contact Write, call, fax, e-mail, or through World Wide Web site Jaclyn Leader, Internship Coordinator. Phone: 310-556-2500. Fax: 310-556-2509. E-mail: jleader@feminist.org. Applicants must submit a letter of interest, resume, writing sample, two personal references, two letters of recommendation, telephone or in-person interview (for finalists). Applications are accepted continuously. World Wide Web: http://www.feminist.org.

FEMINIST MAJORITY AND FEMINIST MAJORITY FOUNDATION (VIRGINIA OFFICE)
1600 Wilson Boulevard, Suite 801
Arlington, Virginia 22209

General Information Nonprofit research and advocacy organization dedicated to promoting equality for women. Established in 1987. Number of employees: 30. Number of internship applications received each year: 150.

Internships Available ▶ *4–10 interns:* responsibilities include monitoring press conferences and congressional hearings; researching, writing, and analyzing policy; organizing demonstrations; constructing and updating Web site; advocacy on women's rights violations outside of the U.S. Candidates should have ability to work independently, ability to work with others, oral communication skills, self-motivation, written communication skills. Duration is minimum of 2 months. Stipend of $8 per hour for administrative work (maximum 10 hours per week). Open to college freshmen, college sophomores, college juniors, college seniors. International applications accepted.

Benefits Names of contacts, on-the-job training, willing to act as a professional reference, willing to complete paperwork for educational credit, willing to provide letters of recommendation, computer training provided.

Contact Write, call, e-mail, or through World Wide Web site Diane Greenhalgh, Grassroots Organizer, Web Team. Phone: 703-522-2214. Fax: 703-522-2219. E-mail: internship@feminist.org. Telephone interview required. Applicants must submit a letter of interest, resume, writing sample, two letters of recommendation. Applications are accepted continuously. World Wide Web: http://www.feminist.org/intern.

FIGHT CRIME: INVEST IN KIDS
2000 P Street, NW, Suite 240
Washington, District of Columbia 20036

General Information Nonprofit, bipartisan anti-crime and child advocacy organization led by police chiefs, sheriffs, prosecutors and victims of violence. Established in 1996. Number of employees: 20. Number of internship applications received each year: 50.

Internships Available ▶ *1–3 interns:* responsibilities include possible positions in media, federal policy, state policy, outreach, and research; please see Web site for openings. Candidates should have ability to work with others, knowledge of field, oral communication skills, personal interest in the field, written com-

Fight Crime: Invest in Kids (continued)

munication skills. Duration is flexible (usually semester). $125 per week. Open to college freshmen, college sophomores, college juniors, college seniors. International applications accepted.
Benefits Willing to act as a professional reference, willing to complete paperwork for educational credit, willing to provide letters of recommendation, opportunity to attend events on Capitol Hill.
Contact Write, fax, or e-mail Intern Coordinator, 2000 P Street, NW Suite 240, Washington 20036. Fax: 202-776-0110. E-mail: info@ fightcrime.org. No phone calls. Telephone interview required. Applicants must submit a letter of interest, resume, writing sample. Application deadline: March 15 for summer, August 1 for fall, November 15 for winter/spring. World Wide Web: http://www. fightcrime.org.

FRIENDS COMMITTEE ON NATIONAL LEGISLATION
245 Second Street, NE
Washington, District of Columbia 20002

General Information Lobbying organization guided by Quaker religious beliefs that attempts to bring spiritual values to public policy decisions. Established in 1943. Number of employees: 22. Number of internship applications received each year: 30.
Internships Available ▶ *3 legislative interns:* responsibilities include attending coalition meetings, answering constituent phone calls and letters, contributing to FCNL's newsletter, writing issue papers, drafting documents and letters for legislative advocacy, preparing FCNL's weekly legislative action message, and performing general administrative work. Candidates should have ability to work independently, analytical skills, computer skills, editing skills, office skills, oral communication skills, organizational skills, personal interest in the field, research skills, self-motivation, strong interpersonal skills, writing skills. Duration is 11 months. Paid. Open to recent college graduates, graduate students, law students. International applications accepted.
Benefits Health insurance, on-the-job training, opportunity to attend seminars/workshops, possible full-time employment, willing to act as a professional reference, willing to complete paperwork for educational credit, willing to provide letters of recommendation.
Contact Write, fax, e-mail, or through World Wide Web site Internship Coordinator. Fax: 202-547-6019. E-mail: fcnl@fcnl.org. No phone calls. Telephone interview required. Applicants must submit a formal organization application, academic transcripts, four personal references. Application deadline: applicants for September through July position must apply between January 1 and March 1. World Wide Web: http://www.fcnl.org.

FRIENDS FOR A NON-VIOLENT WORLD
1050 Selby Avenue
St. Paul, Minnesota 55104

General Information Organization that provides education about non-violence and peacemaking. Established in 1981. Number of employees: 2. Number of internship applications received each year: 15.
Internships Available ▶ *2 summer peace interns:* responsibilities include coordinating one major project such as organizing our week-long summer camp; office work; participation in study group. Candidates should have knowledge of field, office skills, organizational skills, self-motivation, strong interpersonal skills, passion for non-violence. Duration is June 15-August 30. $1575 per duration of internship. Open to college freshmen, college sophomores, college juniors, college seniors, recent college graduates, graduate students, law students, career changers, individuals reentering the workforce.
Benefits Formal training, on-the-job training, opportunity to attend seminars/workshops, willing to act as a professional reference, willing to complete paperwork for educational credit, willing to provide letters of recommendation, support from mentors.
Contact Write, call, fax, e-mail, or through World Wide Web site Executive Director, 1050 Selby Avenue, St. Paul, Minnesota 55104. Phone: 651-917-0383. Fax: 651-917-0379. E-mail: info@fnvw.org.

In-person interview recommended (telephone interview accepted). Applicants must submit a letter of interest, resume, three personal references. Application deadline: April 1 for summer; continuous for fall/spring. World Wide Web: http://www.fnvw.org.

FRIENDS OF THE THIRD WORLD
611 West Wayne Street
Fort Wayne, Indiana 46802-2167

General Information Organization that advocates nonviolent voluntary action against the root causes of poverty. Established in 1972. Number of employees: 1.
Internships Available ▶ *1–2 coffee project interns:* responsibilities include coordinating the purchase, grinding, roasting, packing, and shipping of fair trade coffee and other products. Duration is 12 months. Unpaid. Open to individuals at least 18 year of age. ▶ *1–2 event organizers:* responsibilities include editing and writing; media work and supervision of other local volunteers; contacting for recruitment and contributions; events including student workday, World Food Day event, and international festival. Candidates should have ability to work independently, oral communication skills, self-motivation, strong interpersonal skills, written communication skills. Duration is 6–12 months. Unpaid. Open to high school seniors, recent high school graduates, college freshmen, college sophomores, college juniors, college seniors, recent college graduates, graduate students, law students, career changers, individuals reentering the workforce. ▶ *1–2 graphic artist editor/ printers:* responsibilities include working with unskilled trainees and community volunteers to produce newsletters, catalogs, and event materials. Candidates should have computer skills, self-motivation, strong interpersonal skills, writing skills, artistic ability. Duration is 6 months to 2 years. Unpaid. Open to college sophomores, college juniors, college seniors, recent college graduates, graduate students, law students, career changers, individuals reentering the workforce. ▶ *1–2 handicraft marketing interns:* responsibilities include communicating with low-income producers of handmade crafts, writing and presenting information, developing and implementing marketing displays. Candidates should have ability to work independently, oral communication skills, personal interest in the field, written communication skills. Duration is 2 months to 2 years. Unpaid. Open to high school students, recent high school graduates, college freshmen, college sophomores, college juniors, college seniors, recent college graduates, graduate students, law students, career changers, individuals reentering the workforce. International applications accepted.
Benefits On-the-job training, opportunity to attend seminars/ workshops, willing to act as a professional reference, willing to complete paperwork for educational credit, willing to provide letters of recommendation, free housing and meals and small stipend with commitment of at least 3 months, possibility of student loan deferment.
Contact Marian Waltz, Volunteer Coordinator. Phone: 260-422-6821. Fax: 260-422-1650. E-mail: fotw@igc.org. Telephone interview required. Applicants must submit a formal organization application, personal reference. Applications are accepted continuously. World Wide Web: http://www.friendsofthethirdworld.org.

GAY AND LESBIAN VICTORY FUND
1705 DeSales Street, NW, Suite 500
Washington, District of Columbia 20036

General Information National donor network committed to electing qualified, openly gay and lesbian candidates to public office. Established in 1991. Number of employees: 15. Number of internship applications received each year: 40.
Internships Available ▶ *3 interns:* responsibilities include duties coincident with interest and experience of intern; positions available in the areas of media relations, fund-raising, campaign management, and research. Candidates should have ability to work independently, ability to work with others, computer skills, oral communication skills, organizational skills, personal interest in the field, self-motivation, written communication skills. Duration is flexible. Position available as unpaid or at $400–$800 per month.

Open to college sophomores, college juniors, college seniors, recent college graduates, graduate students, law students, career changers, individuals reentering the workforce.
Benefits Job counseling, names of contacts, possible full-time employment, willing to act as a professional reference, willing to complete paperwork for educational credit, willing to provide letters of recommendation, networking opportunities, stipend.
Contact Write, call, fax, e-mail, or through World Wide Web site Meghan Duffy, Intern Coordinator. Phone: 202-842-8679. Fax: 202-289-3863. E-mail: mduffy@victoryfund.org. In-person interview recommended (telephone interview accepted). Applicants must submit a formal organization application, letter of interest, resume, two personal references, application can be downloaded through Web site. Applications are accepted continuously. World Wide Web: http://www.victoryfund.org.

GLOBAL EXCHANGE
2017 Mission Street, Room 303
San Francisco, California 94110

General Information Nonprofit research, education, action center devoted to international human rights. Established in 1988. Number of employees: 45. Number of internship applications received each year: 400.
Internships Available ▶ *2 alternative trade interns:* responsibilities include overseeing craft booth at Bay Area fairs and festivals and researching and writing materials about country conditions and alternative trade. Candidates should have ability to work independently, oral communication skills, personal interest in the field, self-motivation, strong interpersonal skills. Duration is 4–12 weeks. Unpaid. Open to college freshmen, college sophomores, college juniors, college seniors, recent college graduates, career changers. ▶ *4 campaign program interns:* responsibilities include organizing and promoting campaign to end Cold War against Cuba and campaign to promote peace in Mexico. Candidates should have ability to work independently, analytical skills, editing skills, organizational skills, research skills, self-motivation, strong leadership ability, writing skills. Duration is 4–12 weeks. Unpaid. Open to college seniors, recent college graduates, graduate students. ▶ *1–2 fund-raising interns:* responsibilities include researching private and corporate foundations, developing ways to reach new members, and cultivating existing members. Candidates should have computer skills, office skills, oral communication skills, organizational skills, personal interest in the field, research skills, self-motivation, writing skills. Duration is 8–12 weeks. Unpaid. Open to college freshmen, college sophomores, college juniors, college seniors, recent college graduates, graduate students. ▶ *4 human rights interns:* responsibilities include organizing around the issues of human rights, corporate accountability, and the global economy. Candidates should have ability to work independently, analytical skills, organizational skills, personal interest in the field, plan to pursue career in field, research skills, self-motivation, strong interpersonal skills, strong leadership ability, written communication skills. Duration is 8–12 weeks. Unpaid. Open to recent college graduates, graduate students, law students. ▶ *2 media interns:* responsibilities include writing and distributing promotional articles on the work of Global Exchange, developing media contacts, developing and distributing promotional materials for Global Exchange Speakers Bureau. Candidates should have computer skills, editing skills, oral communication skills, research skills, strong interpersonal skills, writing skills. Duration is 8–10 weeks. Unpaid. Open to college juniors, college seniors, recent college graduates, graduate students, career changers. ▶ *2–10 reality tours interns:* responsibilities include developing information packets about areas to be visited (Cuba, Mexico, Central America), inputting data, producing flyers, answering phones, typing, and mailing. Candidates should have computer skills, office skills, oral communication skills, organizational skills, research skills, writing skills. Duration is 1–6 months. Unpaid. Open to college sophomores, college juniors, recent college graduates. ▶ *2 research interns:* responsibilities include researching role of global corporations and economic institutions such as WTO, World Bank, and IMF in the global economy; researching and writing about GMO's, high tech industries, and China in the global economy. Candidates should have analytical skills, computer

skills, office skills, research skills, self-motivation, writing skills. Duration is 4–12 weeks. Unpaid. Open to college seniors, recent college graduates, graduate students. International applications accepted.
Benefits Names of contacts, on-the-job training, opportunity to attend seminars/workshops, willing to act as a professional reference, willing to complete paperwork for educational credit, willing to provide letters of recommendation.
International Internships Available in San Cristobal de las Casas, Mexico.
Contact Write, call, e-mail, or through World Wide Web site Intern Coordinator. Phone: 415-255-7296 Ext. 227. E-mail: interns@globalexchange.org. Telephone interview required. Applicants must submit a formal organization application, letter of interest, resume, academic transcripts, two letters of recommendation. Application deadline: April 1 for summer positions; continuous for other positions. World Wide Web: http://www.globalexchange.org.

HADASSAH, THE WOMEN'S ZIONIST ORGANIZATION
5100 Wisconsin Avenue, NW, Suite 250
Washington, District of Columbia 20016

General Information Political lobbying organization that promotes women's rights and the security of Israel. Established in 1912. Number of employees: 2. Branch of Hadassah Zionist Women's Organization of America, New York, New York. Number of internship applications received each year: 15.
Internships Available ▶ *1–4 interns:* responsibilities include representing Hadassah at coalition meetings, congressional hearings, and events; reporting in writing to Hadassah staff about events attended. Candidates should have ability to work independently, ability to work with others, knowledge of field, oral communication skills, personal interest in the field, writing skills. Duration is one summer or semester. Unpaid. Open to recent high school graduates, college freshmen, college sophomores, college juniors, college seniors.
Benefits Job counseling, names of contacts, opportunity to attend seminars/workshops, possible full-time employment, travel reimbursement, willing to act as a professional reference, willing to complete paperwork for educational credit, willing to provide letters of recommendation.
International Internships Available in Jerusalem, Israel.
Contact Write, fax, or e-mail Marla Gilson, Director. Phone: 202-363-4600. Fax: 202-363-4651. E-mail: mgilson@hadassah.org. In-person interview recommended (telephone interview accepted). Applicants must submit a letter of interest, resume, writing sample. Applications are accepted continuously. World Wide Web: http://www.hadassah.org.

HEARTS AND MINDS NETWORK, INC.
3074 Broadway
New York, New York 10027

General Information Nonprofit organization addressing poverty, the environment, human rights, addictions, and other major issues and providing a clearinghouse of information for the public, locally, nationally, and internationally. Established in 1996. Number of employees: 20. Number of internship applications received each year: 100.
Internships Available ▶ *5 Web site design and development volunteers/interns:* responsibilities include Web site editing, design, management, promotion, Web site hosting, software. Candidates should have ability to work independently, ability to work with others, computer skills, knowledge of field, personal interest in the field, self-motivation. Duration is 4–50 weeks. Unpaid. Open to high school students, recent high school graduates, college freshmen, college sophomores, college juniors, college seniors, recent college graduates, graduate students, law students, career changers, individuals reentering the workforce, retirees. ▶ *3 accounting and financial management volunteers/interns:* responsibilities include bookkeeping, accounting, analysis and reporting, or socially-responsible investing. Candidates should have ability to work independently, ability to work with others, analytical skills, computer skills,

Hearts and Minds Network, Inc. (continued)

knowledge of field, self-motivation. Duration is 4–50 weeks. Unpaid. Open to high school students, recent high school graduates, college freshmen, college sophomores, college juniors, college seniors, recent college graduates, graduate students, law students, career changers, individuals reentering the workforce, retirees. ► *4 computers/technical support volunteers/interns:* responsibilities include providing technical support for computers, printers, software, and Web site. Candidates should have ability to work independently, computer skills, personal interest in the field, self-motivation, strong interpersonal skills. Duration is 4–50 weeks. Unpaid. Open to high school students, recent high school graduates, college freshmen, college sophomores, college juniors, college seniors, recent college graduates, graduate students, law students, career changers, individuals reentering the workforce, retirees. ► *19 creative and graphic design volunteers/interns:* responsibilities include arts management, creative writing, fine art, illustration, or photography for Web site, campaigns, or print publications (5 positions); art direction and graphic design for Web site, ad campaigns, or print publications (5 positions); doing promotional writing for Web site, ad campaigns, or print publications (4 positions); copywriting (4 positions). Candidates should have ability to work independently, knowledge of field, self-motivation. Duration is 4–50 weeks. Unpaid. Open to high school students, recent high school graduates, college freshmen, college sophomores, college juniors, college seniors, recent college graduates, graduate students, law students, career changers, individuals reentering the workforce, retirees. ► *5 education volunteers/interns:* responsibilities include teaching economically disadvantaged high school students writing, art, and Web site design. Candidates should have ability to work independently, personal interest in the field, self-motivation, strong interpersonal skills. Duration is 4–50 weeks. Unpaid. Open to high school students, recent high school graduates, college freshmen, college sophomores, college juniors, college seniors, recent college graduates, graduate students, law students, law school graduates, career changers, individuals reentering the workforce, retirees. ► *5 fund-raising/events planning/ad sales volunteers/interns:* responsibilities include fund-raising through direct mailing, corporate, foundation, or personal solicitation; planning cultural and fund-raising events; may also include selling ads for Web site and/or print publications. Candidates should have ability to work independently, computer skills, oral communication skills, personal interest in the field, self-motivation, strong interpersonal skills. Duration is 4–50 weeks. Unpaid. Open to high school students, recent high school graduates, college freshmen, college sophomores, college juniors, college seniors, recent college graduates, graduate students, law students, career changers, individuals reentering the workforce, retirees. ► *8–10 general volunteers/interns:* responsibilities include working in any combination of other position offerings. Candidates should have ability to work independently, ability to work with others, organizational skills, personal interest in the field, self-motivation. Duration is 4–50 weeks. Unpaid. Open to high school students, recent high school graduates, college freshmen, college sophomores, college juniors, college seniors, recent college graduates, graduate students, law students, career changers, individuals reentering the workforce, retirees. ► *3 interior design or carpentry volunteers/interns:* responsibilities include designing and drafting improvements for Hearts & Minds office space or building in changes. Duration is 4–50 weeks. Unpaid. ► *15 journalism volunteers/interns:* responsibilities include research, writing, and editing articles. Candidates should have ability to work independently, ability to work with others, computer skills, personal interest in the field, self-motivation, writing skills. Duration is 4–50 weeks. Unpaid. Open to high school students, recent high school graduates, college freshmen, college sophomores, college juniors, college seniors, recent college graduates, graduate students, law students, career changers, individuals reentering the workforce, retirees. ► *5 law and regulatory compliance volunteers/interns:* responsibilities include employee, volunteer, member, and government relations; advice on copyrights; avoiding libel, liability, and other legal exposure; regulatory compliance. Candidates should have ability to work independently, knowledge of field, personal interest in the field, self-motivation. Duration is 4–50 weeks. Unpaid. Open to high school students, recent high school graduates, college freshmen,

college sophomores, college juniors, college seniors, recent college graduates, graduate students, law students, career changers, individuals reentering the workforce, retirees. ► *7 marketing and publishing volunteers/interns:* responsibilities include strategy planning, circulation promotion, production, direct mailing, and/or other marketing activities. Candidates should have ability to work independently, computer skills, personal interest in the field, self-motivation, strong interpersonal skills. Duration is 4–50 weeks. Unpaid. Open to high school students, recent high school graduates, college freshmen, college sophomores, college juniors, college seniors, recent college graduates, graduate students, law students, career changers, individuals reentering the workforce, retirees. ► *4 marketing/research volunteers/interns:* responsibilities include strategic planning, surveys, and focus groups to evaluate effectiveness of organization; research and reporting on social issues. Candidates should have ability to work independently, analytical skills, computer skills, personal interest in the field, strong interpersonal skills. Duration is 4–50 weeks. Unpaid. Open to high school students, recent high school graduates, college freshmen, college sophomores, college juniors, college seniors, recent college graduates, graduate students, law students, career changers, individuals reentering the workforce, retirees. ► *7 office volunteers/interns:* responsibilities include office management, phone calls, photocopying, running errands, faxing, word processing, and desk top publishing. Candidates should have ability to work independently, ability to work with others, computer skills, office skills, self-motivation. Duration is 4–50 weeks. Unpaid. Open to high school students, recent high school graduates, college freshmen, college sophomores, college juniors, college seniors, recent college graduates, graduate students, law students, career changers, individuals reentering the workforce, retirees. ► *3 personnel/volunteer recruitment and relations volunteers/interns:* responsibilities include recruiting, communicating with, and supervising volunteers and interns at the office and all over the world (via phone and e-mail). Candidates should have ability to work independently, computer skills, personal interest in the field, self-motivation, strong interpersonal skills. Duration is 4–50 weeks. Unpaid. Open to high school students, recent high school graduates, college freshmen, college sophomores, college juniors, college seniors, recent college graduates, graduate students, law students, career changers, individuals reentering the workforce, retirees. ► *5 public relations/advertising volunteers/interns:* responsibilities include working on public service ad campaigns regarding the environment, homelessness, addictions, child abuse, and other important issues; working on campaigns to promote Hearts & Minds publications; or contacting major media and writing press releases and other marketing materials. Candidates should have oral communication skills, personal interest in the field, self-motivation, strong interpersonal skills, written communication skills. Duration is 4–50 weeks. Unpaid. Open to high school students, recent high school graduates, college freshmen, college sophomores, college juniors, college seniors, recent college graduates, graduate students, law students, career changers, individuals reentering the workforce, retirees. International applications accepted.

Benefits Job counseling, on-the-job training, opportunity to attend seminars/workshops, willing to act as a professional reference, willing to complete paperwork for educational credit, willing to provide letters of recommendation, advice on resume and cover letter, cooperation for independent study, local (commuting) travel reimbursed.

Contact Write, call, fax, e-mail, or through World Wide Web site Volunteer/Internship Manager. Phone: 212-280-0333. Fax: 212-280-0336. E-mail: help@change.net. In-person interview recommended (telephone interview accepted). Applicants must submit a letter of interest, resume, three personal references, samples helpful for graphic design, writing, art, and photography applicants. Applications are accepted continuously. World Wide Web: http://www.change.net.

INSTITUTE FOR WOMEN'S POLICY RESEARCH
1707 L Street, NW, Suite 750
Washington, District of Columbia 20036

General Information Nonprofit research organization that works primarily on issues related to equal opportunity and economic and social justice for women. Established in 1987. Number of employees: 24. Number of internship applications received each year: 200.

Internships Available ▶ *1–2 communications interns:* responsibilities include working with the communications department to assist with conference planning, publicizing WPR to media and public, and assisting with production of publications. Candidates should have ability to work independently, computer skills, oral communication skills, personal interest in the field, self-motivation, written communication skills. Duration is 10–13 weeks. Position available as unpaid or paid. Open to college freshmen, college sophomores, college juniors, college seniors, recent college graduates, graduate students, law students, individuals reentering the workforce. ▶ *1 development intern:* responsibilities include assisting director of development and membership coordinator with grant research, preparing reports and proposals, direct mail, special events, and outreach efforts. Candidates should have ability to work independently, ability to work with others, computer skills, oral communication skills, personal interest in the field, written communication skills. Duration is 10–12 weeks. Position available as unpaid or paid. Open to college freshmen, college sophomores, college juniors, college seniors, recent college graduates, graduate students, individuals reentering the workforce. ▶ *2–4 research interns:* responsibilities include performing literature reviews, collecting data and resources, preparing reports and summaries, attending relevant meetings and congressional hearings, and providing general office support. Candidates should have ability to work independently, ability to work with others, computer skills, office skills, oral communication skills, organizational skills, personal interest in the field, research skills, self-motivation, writing skills. Duration is 10–12 weeks. Position available as unpaid or paid. Open to college freshmen, college sophomores, college juniors, college seniors, recent college graduates, graduate students, law students, individuals reentering the workforce. International applications accepted.

Benefits Opportunity to attend seminars/workshops, travel reimbursement, willing to act as a professional reference, willing to complete paperwork for educational credit, willing to provide letters of recommendation.

Contact Write, e-mail, or through World Wide Web site Vanessa Melamede, Research Program Coordinator. Fax: 202-833-4362. E-mail: vanessa@iwpr.org. No phone calls. Telephone interview required. Applicants must submit a letter of interest, resume, writing sample, three personal references. Application deadline: March 1 for summer, August 15 for fall, December 5 for spring. World Wide Web: http://www.iwpr.org.

INTERNATIONAL CAMPAIGN FOR TIBET
1825 K Street, NW, Suite 520
Washington, District of Columbia 20006

General Information Human rights and Tibetan advocacy organization. Established in 1988. Number of employees: 15. Number of internship applications received each year: 50.

Internships Available ▶ *1–2 interns:* responsibilities include answering phones, assisting campaigns coordinator and other staff with light research, responding to general inquiries from members, and coordinating distribution of campaign materials. Candidates should have ability to work independently, office skills, personal interest in the field, research skills, strong interpersonal skills, written communication skills. Duration is 3–6 months. $500–$800 per month. Open to college sophomores, college juniors, college seniors, recent college graduates, graduate students. International applications accepted.

Benefits Opportunity to attend seminars/workshops, willing to complete paperwork for educational credit, willing to provide letters of recommendation, small stipend per month.

Contact Write, fax, or e-mail Van Ly, Program Associate. Fax: 202-785-4343. E-mail: vanl@savetibet.org. No phone calls. Applicants must submit a letter of interest, resume, writing sample. Application deadline: March 15 for summer, July 15 for fall, November 15 for spring. World Wide Web: http://www.savetibet.org.

INTERNATIONAL ECONOMIC DEVELOPMENT COUNCIL
734 15th Street, NW, Suite 800
Washington, District of Columbia 20005

General Information Nonprofit membership association that serves public and private sector practitioners in economic development and provides information to its members to help improve local economies. Established in 1967. Number of employees: 30. Number of internship applications received each year: 35.

Internships Available ▶ *5–8 interns:* responsibilities include assisting with research projects on economic development trends and topics, tracking legislation, writing newsletter articles, and completing survey analyses. Candidates should have ability to work independently, organizational skills, plan to pursue career in field, research skills, strong interpersonal skills, writing skills. Duration is flexible (minimum commitment of 2 months). Position available as unpaid or at $8.50–$10.50 per hour. Open to college juniors, college seniors, recent college graduates, graduate students, PhD candidates. International applications accepted.

Benefits Names of contacts, on-the-job training, opportunity to attend seminars/workshops, possible full-time employment, willing to act as a professional reference, willing to complete paperwork for educational credit, willing to provide letters of recommendation, practical work experience, opportunity to have work published.

Contact Write, fax, e-mail, or through World Wide Web site Louise Anderson. Fax: 202-223-4745. E-mail: landerson@iedconline.org. No phone calls. Telephone interview required. Applicants must submit a letter of interest, resume, writing sample. Application deadline: first Friday in March for summer; continuous for other seasons. World Wide Web: http://www.iedonline.org.

INTERNATIONAL HUMAN RIGHTS LAW GROUP
1200 18th Street, NW, Suite 602
Washington, District of Columbia 20036

General Information Nonprofit organization of human rights and legal professionals engaged in human rights advocacy, litigation, and training around the world. Established in 1978. Number of employees: 28. Number of internship applications received each year: 200.

Internships Available ▶ *6–8 legal/graduate interns:* responsibilities include assisting attorneys in program work; legal research projects; writing, summarizing, and analyzing reports. Candidates should have ability to work independently, analytical skills, experience in the field, research skills, self-motivation, writing skills. Duration is 10–12 weeks. Unpaid. Open to graduate students, law students, career changers. ▶ *2–3 undergraduate interns:* responsibilities include researching, writing, and administrative duties. Candidates should have oral communication skills, personal interest in the field, research skills, self-motivation, strong interpersonal skills, writing skills. Duration is 10–12 weeks. Unpaid. Open to college sophomores, college juniors, college seniors, recent college graduates. International applications accepted.

Benefits Names of contacts, opportunity to attend seminars/workshops, willing to act as a professional reference, willing to complete paperwork for educational credit, willing to provide letters of recommendation, opportunity to learn how human rights organization works.

International Internships Available in Bosnia and Herzegovina; Burundi; Cambodia; D.R.C., Congo; Morocco; Nigeria.

Contact Write, fax, e-mail, or through World Wide Web site Internship Coordinator, 1200 18th Street, NW, Suite 602, Washington, District of Columbia 20036. Fax: 202-822-4606. E-mail: humanrights@hrlawgroup.org. No phone calls. Telephone interview required. Applicants must submit a letter of interest, resume, three letters of recommendation, 5-page writing sample. Application deadline: March 1 for summer, August 31 for fall, December 31 for spring. World Wide Web: http://www.hrlawgroup.org.

JOBS WITH JUSTICE
501 Third Street, NW
Washington, District of Columbia 20001-2797

General Information National coalition of labor unions and religious, civil rights, women's, student, farm, and community organizations working together at the local level to defend and expand the rights of working people. Established in 1987. Number of employees: 9.

Internships Available ▶ *2–3 interns:* responsibilities include organizing student-labor outreach, assisting national staff in providing support services to local coalitions, helping in preparation for trainings, and general administrative support. Candidates should have ability to work with others, computer skills, office skills, self-motivation, interest in the labor movement and/or issues affecting working people, desktop publishing, database, and Web experience (a plus). Duration is summer, spring, winter, or fall semester (full- or part-time). Position available as unpaid or paid. Open to high school students, recent high school graduates, college freshmen, college sophomores, college juniors, college seniors, recent college graduates, graduate students, career changers, individuals reentering the workforce. International applications accepted.

Benefits Job counseling, willing to act as a professional reference, willing to complete paperwork for educational credit, willing to provide letters of recommendation, small stipend (depending on need).

Contact Write, call, fax, e-mail, or through World Wide Web site Sian Lewis, Office Coordinator, 501 Third Street, NW, Washington, District of Columbia 20001. Phone: 202-434-1106. Fax: 202-434-1477. E-mail: sian@jwj.org. Applicants must submit a letter of interest, resume. Applications are accepted continuously. World Wide Web: http://www.jwj.org.

JUSTICEWORKS COMMUNITY, INC.
1012 Eighth Avenue
Brooklyn, New York 11215

General Information Nonprofit agency whose mission is to effect more humane criminal justice policy through public education, advocacy, and community organizing. Established in 1992. Number of employees: 6. Number of internship applications received each year: 8.

Internships Available ▶ *1 community organizing intern:* responsibilities include making educational presentations recruiting community members to public actions and the larger social justice movement. Candidates should have computer skills, oral communication skills, personal interest in the field, strong interpersonal skills, writing skills. Duration is September to June (2 semesters). Unpaid. Open to recent college graduates, graduate students, law students, career changers. ▶ *2 development assistants:* responsibilities include researching foundations both at Foundation Center and on line; assisting with annual special event preparations. Candidates should have ability to work independently, computer skills, oral communication skills, research skills, writing skills. Duration is one semester to one year. Unpaid. Open to college juniors, college seniors, recent college graduates, graduate students, career changers. ▶ *2 media assistants:* responsibilities include maintaining media database; scanning print media for articles related to mission of JWC. Candidates should have ability to work independently, computer skills, editing skills, oral communication skills, personal interest in the field, research skills, strong interpersonal skills, writing skills, ability to craft press releases and media advisories. Duration is one semester to one year. Unpaid. Open to college juniors, college seniors, recent college graduates, graduate students. ▶ *1 research intern:* responsibilities include research, primarily on the Internet, on the current status of mandatory minimum sentencing laws (state-by-state) as well as the existence of alternatives to incarceration (state-by-state). Candidates should have ability to work independently, analytical skills, computer skills, research skills, written communication skills, ability to access and maximize information on the Internet. Duration is one semester to one year. Unpaid. Open to college seniors, graduate students, law students. International applications accepted.

Benefits Names of contacts, opportunity to attend seminars/workshops, willing to act as a professional reference, willing to complete paperwork for educational credit, willing to provide letters of recommendation.

Contact Write, call, fax, or e-mail Mary-Elizabeth Fitzgerald, Executive Director. Phone: 718-499-6704. Fax: 718-832-2832. E-mail: mefitzgerald@justiceworks.org. In-person interview required. Applicants must submit a letter of interest, resume, academic transcripts, writing sample, three letters of recommendation. Application deadline: May 1 for summer, December 1 for spring. World Wide Web: http://www.justiceworks.org.

KOREAN AMERICAN COALITION
3727 West 6th Street, Suite 515
Los Angeles, California 90020

General Information Nonprofit community advocacy organization. Established in 1983. Number of employees: 15. Number of internship applications received each year: 80.

Internships Available ▶ *4–6 corporate interns:* responsibilities include working with KAC and a designated multinational corporation. Candidates should have college courses in field, knowledge of field, oral communication skills, self-motivation, strong interpersonal skills, written communication skills. Duration is 2 months. $1000 per duration of internship. Open to college sophomores, college juniors, non-graduating college seniors. ▶ *1–4 legal interns:* responsibilities include working in law office 4 days per week and KAC office 1 day per week. Candidates should have computer skills, knowledge of field, office skills, oral communication skills, personal interest in the field, self-motivation, strong interpersonal skills, written communication skills. Duration is 2 months. $1000 per duration of internship. Open to college freshmen, college sophomores, college juniors. ▶ *2–5 media interns:* responsibilities include working with KAC and local news service. Candidates should have knowledge of field, office skills, oral communication skills, strong interpersonal skills, writing skills. Duration is 2 months. $1000 per duration of internship. Open to college freshmen, college sophomores, college juniors, non-graduating college seniors. ▶ *2–4 political interns:* responsibilities include working with KAC and a local political office in various functions. Candidates should have knowledge of field, office skills, oral communication skills, self-motivation, strong interpersonal skills, writing skills. Duration is 2 months. $1000 per duration of internship. Open to college freshmen, college sophomores, college juniors, non-graduating college seniors. International applications accepted.

Benefits Names of contacts, opportunity to attend seminars/workshops, possible full-time employment, willing to act as a professional reference, willing to complete paperwork for educational credit, willing to provide letters of recommendation.

Contact Write, call, fax, or e-mail Debbie Sheen, Program Coordinator. Phone: 213-365-5999 Ext. 108. Fax: 213-380-7990. E-mail: kac_debbie@hotmail.com. Telephone interview required. Applicants must submit a formal organization application, resume, academic transcripts, two letters of recommendation, two essays. Application deadline: late February for summer. Fees: $10.

LAWYERS' COMMITTEE FOR CIVIL RIGHTS UNDER LAW
1401 New York Avenue, NW, Suite 400
Washington, District of Columbia 20005

General Information Civil rights litigation and advocacy organization. Established in 1963. Number of employees: 40. Number of internship applications received each year: 300.

Internships Available ▶ *Graduate interns:* responsibilities include assisting in public policy research, locating experts, and other project-related activities. Candidates should have analytical skills, college courses in field, organizational skills, research skills, writing skills. Duration is flexible. Unpaid. Open to graduate students. ▶ *10–15 law student interns:* responsibilities include legal research and writing, assisting attorneys with case investigation and trial preparation, working with civil rights and/or community based organizations, interviewing clients and witnesses. Candidates should have ability to work independently, ability to work with others, personal interest in the field, research skills, writing skills, evidence of community service or civil rights interest. Duration is flexible. Unpaid. Open to law students. ▶ *Undergraduate interns:* responsibilities include assisting administrative and attorney employees with administrative tasks, desktop publishing, non-legal writing and research, filing, and some clerical work. Candidates should have ability to work independently, ability to work with others, office skills, personal interest in the field, self-motivation, evidence of community service or civil rights interest. Duration is flexible. Unpaid. Open to college freshmen, college sophomores, college juniors, college seniors, recent college graduates, graduate students, career changers, individuals reentering the workforce. International applications accepted.

Benefits Names of contacts, on-the-job training, opportunity to attend seminars/workshops, possible full-time employment, travel reimbursement, willing to act as a professional reference, willing to complete paperwork for educational credit, willing to provide letters of recommendation.

Contact Write, call, fax, e-mail, or through World Wide Web site Nancy Anderson, Intern Coordinator. Phone: 202-662-8600. Fax: 202-783-0857. E-mail: nanderson@lawyerscomm.org. In-person interview recommended (telephone interview accepted). Applicants must submit a letter of interest, resume, writing sample, three personal references. Applications are accepted continuously. World Wide Web: http://www.lawyerscomm.org.

MARCH OF DIMES BIRTH DEFECTS FOUNDATION, OFFICE OF GOVERNMENT AFFAIRS
1146 19th Street, NW, 6th Floor
Washington, District of Columbia 20036

General Information Nonprofit organization that is dedicated to the prevention of birth defects through research, public health education, advocacy, and community service. Established in 1938. Number of employees: 11. Unit of National Office March of Dimes, White Plains, New York. Number of internship applications received each year: 25.

Internships Available ▶ *School-year interns:* responsibilities include assisting with monitoring, tracking, and reporting on public policy issues; researching and drafting letters, position papers, testimony, and legislative updates; attending and monitoring congressional hearings, markups, and meetings; and providing general office support. Candidates should have knowledge of field, personal interest in the field, research skills, self-motivation, strong interpersonal skills, writing skills. Duration is one semester or summer. Position available as unpaid or paid. Open to college sophomores, college juniors, college seniors, recent college graduates, graduate students.

Benefits Willing to complete paperwork for educational credit.

Contact Write, call, fax, or e-mail Susan Langley, Office Manager, 1146 19th Street, NW 6th Floor, Washington, District of Columbia 20036. Phone: 202-659-1800. Fax: 202-296-2964. E-mail: slangley@marchofdimes.com. In-person interview recommended (telephone interview accepted). Applicants must submit a letter of interest, resume, writing sample, three letters of recommendation. Applications are accepted continuously. World Wide Web: http://www.modimes.org.

MARIJUANA POLICY PROJECT
PO Box 77492, Capitol Hill
Washington, District of Columbia 20013

General Information Political lobbying organization for marijuana policy reform at the state and national levels. Established in 1995. Number of employees: 13. Number of internship applications received each year: 75.

Internships Available ▶ *1 communications intern:* responsibilities include research, writing, and administration. Candidates should have computer skills, editing skills, oral communication skills, research skills, writing skills. Duration is 4 months. $8–$10 per hour. Open to college freshmen, college sophomores, college juniors, college seniors, recent college graduates, graduate students, law students. ▶ *Federal policies intern:* responsibilities include research, writing, and administration. Candidates should have computer skills, oral communication skills, personal interest in the field, research skills, self-motivation, written communication skills. Duration is 4 months (spring, summer, or fall). $8–$10 per hour. Open to college freshmen, college sophomores, college juniors, college seniors, recent college graduates, graduate students, law students. ▶ *1 state policies intern:* responsibilities include research, writing, and administration. Candidates should have computer skills, oral communication skills, personal interest in the field, research skills, self-motivation, written communication skills. Duration is 4 months. $8–$10 per hour. Open to college sophomores, college juniors, college seniors, recent college graduates, graduate students, law students. International applications accepted.

Benefits Possible full-time employment, willing to act as a professional reference, willing to complete paperwork for educational credit, willing to provide letters of recommendation.

Contact E-mail Chad Thevenot, Grants Manager. E-mail: chad@mpp.org. No phone calls. Applicants must submit a letter of interest, resume. Applications are accepted continuously. World Wide Web: http://www.mpp.org.

MASSACHUSETTS PUBLIC INTEREST RESEARCH GROUPS
29 Temple Place
Boston, Massachusetts 02111-1305

General Information Nonprofit, nonpartisan organization involved in research, organizing, and advocacy for statewide environmental and consumer protection reforms. Established in 1972. Number of employees: 40. Number of internship applications received each year: 70.

Internships Available ▶ *2–5 program interns:* responsibilities include conducting research; preparing investigative reports; drafting public education materials; working with media and coalition groups to build support for issues through public education programs; representing MASSPIRG on issues specific to coalition and other local organizations; preparing testimony for government hearings on pending legislation. Candidates should have ability to work independently, ability to work with others, computer skills, oral communication skills, organizational skills, personal interest in the field, self-motivation, writing skills. Duration is flexible. Position available as unpaid or paid. Open to college freshmen, college sophomores, college juniors, college seniors, recent college graduates, graduate students, law students, career changers. International applications accepted.

Benefits Names of contacts, on-the-job training, opportunity to attend seminars/workshops, possible full-time employment, willing to act as a professional reference, willing to complete paperwork for educational credit, willing to provide letters of recommendation, small stipend.

Contact Write, call, fax, e-mail, or through World Wide Web site Stephanie Gros, Executive Assistant. Phone: 617-292-4800. Fax: 617-292-8057. E-mail: steph.gros@masspirg.org. In-person interview recommended (telephone interview accepted). Applicants must submit a letter of interest, resume. Applications are accepted continuously. World Wide Web: http://www.masspirg.org.

METRO JUSTICE OF ROCHESTER
36 St. Paul Street, Room 112
Rochester, New York 14604

General Information Multi-issue community organization focusing on economic justice, antiracism, Latin American solidarity, health care, labor, women's issues, and environmental issues. Established in 1965. Number of employees: 2. Number of internship applications received each year: 10.

Internships Available ▶ *2–3 interns:* responsibilities include assisting with a substantial research project that aids the community in some way; includes media relations, recruitment technologies, campaign strategies, and database maintenance. Candidates should have ability to work with others, oral communication skills, research skills, self-motivation, written communication skills. Duration is 1–2 semesters. Unpaid. Open to high school seniors, recent high school graduates, college sophomores, college juniors, college seniors, recent college graduates, graduate students, law students, career changers, individuals reentering the workforce.

Metro Justice of Rochester (continued)
Benefits Willing to complete paperwork for educational credit, willing to provide letters of recommendation.
Contact Write, call, fax, or e-mail Jon Greenbaum, Organizer. Phone: 585-325-2560. Fax: 585-325-2561. E-mail: metroj@frontiernet. net. In-person interview recommended (telephone interview accepted). Applicants must submit a letter of interest. Applications are accepted continuously. World Wide Web: http://www. metrojustice.org.

NATIONAL ABORTION AND REPRODUCTIVE RIGHTS ACTION LEAGUE OF OHIO
614 West Superior Avenue, Suite 608
Cleveland, Ohio 44113

General Information Political lobbying group, grassroots organization, and education foundation. Established in 1979. Number of employees: 2. Affiliate of National Abortion and Reproductive Rights Action League, Washington, District of Columbia. Number of internship applications received each year: 5.
Internships Available ▶ *1–3 interns:* responsibilities include assisting with educational, grassroots organizing, and lobbying projects; providing staff support as needed. Candidates should have ability to work independently, organizational skills, research skills, strong interpersonal skills, writing skills, must be pro-choice. Duration is flexible. Unpaid. Open to high school students, recent high school graduates, college freshmen, college sophomores, college juniors, college seniors, recent college graduates, graduate students, law students, career changers, individuals reentering the workforce, medical students.
Benefits On-the-job training, opportunity to attend seminars/ workshops, willing to act as a professional reference, willing to complete paperwork for educational credit, willing to provide letters of recommendation.
Contact Write, call, fax, or e-mail Kellie Copeland. Phone: 216-522-0169. Fax: 216-522-0044. E-mail: choice@naralohio.org. In-person interview required. Applicants must submit a letter of interest, resume. Applications are accepted continuously. World Wide Web: http://www.naralohio.org.

NATIONAL ASIAN PACIFIC AMERICAN LEGAL CONSORTIUM
1140 Connecticut Avenue, NW, Suite 1200
Washington, District of Columbia 20036

General Information Civil rights organization that advances the legal and civil rights of Asian-Pacific Americans through litigation, advocacy, public education, and public policy development. Established in 1991. Number of employees: 12. Number of internship applications received each year: 100.
Internships Available ▶ *1–2 communications interns:* responsibilities include assisting the communications staff and program staff with implementing media strategies; writing press releases and media alerts; assisting with writing and editing of newsletter and other publications; arranging and implementing press conferences; performing some administrative work. Candidates should have ability to work with others, computer skills, editing skills, research skills, writing skills. Duration is 1 semester. Unpaid. Open to high school seniors, recent high school graduates, college freshmen, college sophomores, college juniors, college seniors, recent college graduates, graduate students, career changers, individuals reentering the workforce. ▶ *1–2 development interns:* responsibilities include researching grant opportunities, assisting with proposal writing, and assisting with individual donors program as needed. Candidates should have ability to work independently, oral communication skills, organizational skills, self-motivation, strong interpersonal skills, written communication skills. Duration is January to June or June to November/December. Unpaid. Open to college seniors, graduate students, career changers. ▶ *1–10 law student interns:* responsibilities include assisting the executive director and legal staff on special research projects; writing policy statements, legislative alerts, and news articles; reviewing and assisting in preparation of amicus briefs; attending congressional hearings and representing NAPALC at coalition meetings; some

administrative work. Candidates should have analytical skills, computer skills, editing skills, organizational skills, research skills, writing skills. Duration is 1 semester. Unpaid. Open to law students. ▶ *1–10 undergraduate and graduate interns:* responsibilities include assisting consortium's executive director, associate director, and legal staff on special research projects; writing legislative alerts, press releases, and news articles; attending congressional hearings and representing NAPALC at coalition meetings; some administrative work. Candidates should have ability to work with others, computer skills, editing skills, research skills, writing skills. Duration is 10 weeks or 1 semester. Unpaid. Open to college juniors, college seniors, graduate students.
Benefits Job counseling, names of contacts, on-the-job training, opportunity to attend seminars/workshops, possible full-time employment, travel reimbursement, willing to act as a professional reference, willing to complete paperwork for educational credit, willing to provide letters of recommendation.
Contact Write, call, fax, e-mail, or through World Wide Web site Mr. Vincent Eng, Legal Director. Phone: 202-296-2300. Fax: 202-296-2318. E-mail: veng@napalc.org. Telephone interview required. Applicants must submit a letter of interest, resume, one 2–5 page writing sample. Applications are accepted continuously. World Wide Web: http://www.napalc.org.

NATIONAL ASSOCIATION FOR EQUAL OPPORTUNITY IN HIGHER EDUCATION
8701 Georgia Avenue, Suite 200
Silver Spring, Maryland 20910

General Information Organization whose objective is to implement programs and policies which affect minority student enrollment, using diverse strategies to ensure an increase of Black students into HBCU establishments. Established in 1969. Number of employees: 36. Number of internship applications received each year: 300.
Internships Available ▶ *100–200 interns:* responsibilities include policy writing, research, computer services. Candidates should have ability to work independently, ability to work with others, analytical skills, college courses in field, computer skills, office skills, oral communication skills, personal interest in the field, research skills, self-motivation, written communication skills. Duration is 10 weeks in summer (various hours during the fall and spring). $500–$550 per week. Open to college freshmen, college sophomores, college juniors, college seniors, graduate students, law students, medical students. International applications accepted.
Benefits Housing at a cost, job counseling, names of contacts, on-the-job training, opportunity to attend seminars/workshops, possible full-time employment, travel reimbursement, willing to act as a professional reference, willing to complete paperwork for educational credit, willing to provide letters of recommendation.
International Internships Available in Dominican Republic.
Contact Write, call, fax, e-mail, or through World Wide Web site Dr. Jacquelyn Madry-Taylor, Senior Advisor for Federal Grants and Programs, 8701 Georgia Avenue, Suite 200, Silver Spring, Maryland 20910. Phone: 301-650-2440. Fax: 301-495-3306. E-mail: jtaylor@ nafeo.org. Telephone interview required. Applicants must submit a formal organization application, resume, academic transcripts, writing sample, two letters of recommendation. Application deadline: March 31 for summer. World Wide Web: http://www. nafeo.org.

NATIONAL CENTER FOR FAIR AND OPEN TESTING (FAIRTEST)
342 Broadway
Cambridge, Massachusetts 02139

General Information Public education and advocacy organization fighting race, gender, and class bias in standardized exams and promoting assessment methods that are fair, accurate, and educationally sound. Established in 1985. Number of employees: 6. Number of internship applications received each year: 25.
Internships Available ▶ *2–3 interns:* responsibilities include researching and writing for a current project or campaign related to civil rights and educational testing, preparing a report on test coaching, researching challenges to tests and test misuses, and

organizing and assisting families in coping with high stakes testing. Candidates should have personal interest in the field, strong interpersonal skills, computer skills (helpful). Duration is flexible. Position available as unpaid or at small stipend. Open to high school students, college freshmen, college sophomores, college juniors, college seniors, graduate students, career changers, individuals reentering the workforce.

Benefits Names of contacts, willing to complete paperwork for educational credit, willing to provide letters of recommendation.

Contact Write Internship Coordinator. Applicants must submit a letter of interest, resume, writing sample. Applications are accepted continuously.

NATIONAL CENTER FOR LESBIAN RIGHTS
870 Market Street, Suite 570
San Francisco, California 94102

General Information Legal and advocacy organization for LGBT communities, including immigration, full civil and human rights; provides litigation, legal resources, and community education to more than 1,500 LGBT members nationwide. Established in 1977. Number of employees: 11. Number of internship applications received each year: 50.

Internships Available ▶ *1–3 law clerks:* responsibilities include contact with inquiring calls and e-mails made by nationwide members of gay, lesbian, and transgender communities; issues vary from adoption by same sex couples, second parent adoptions, LGBT rights in the workplace, and human rights; proofreading existing manuals with law resources/cases/information on the above-mentioned. Candidates should have college courses in field, editing skills, knowledge of field, oral communication skills, research skills, writing skills. Duration is 1 semester. Work-study available. Open to law students. International applications accepted.

Benefits On-the-job training, opportunity to attend seminars/workshops, willing to act as a professional reference, willing to complete paperwork for educational credit, willing to provide letters of recommendation.

Contact Write or e-mail Courtney Joslin, Staff Attorney. Fax: 415-239-8442. E-mail: joslin@nclrights.org. No phone calls. Applicants must submit a letter of interest, resume, academic transcripts. Applications are accepted continuously. World Wide Web: http://www.nclrights.org.

NATIONAL COMMITTEE FOR RESPONSIVE PHILANTHROPY
2001 S Street, NW, Suite 620
Washington, District of Columbia 20009

General Information Organization committed to making philanthropy more responsive to the economically, socially, and politically disenfranchised. Established in 1976. Number of employees: 10. Number of internship applications received each year: 150.

Internships Available ▶ *2–4 research interns:* responsibilities include public interest research, organizing, and policy advocacy; assisting with information gathering, data analysis, and report writing; helping with administrative tasks; accountability for self-directed duties are 85% program and 15% administrative. Candidates should have ability to work independently, analytical skills, computer skills, personal interest in the field, research skills, self-motivation, writing skills. Duration is 3-12 months. $10 per hour. Open to college freshmen, college sophomores, college juniors, college seniors, recent college graduates, graduate students. International applications accepted.

Benefits On-the-job training, opportunity to attend seminars/workshops, possible full-time employment, willing to act as a professional reference, willing to complete paperwork for educational credit, willing to provide letters of recommendation.

Contact Write, call, fax, e-mail, or through World Wide Web site Jeff Krehely, Research Coordinator. Phone: 202-387-9177. Fax: 202-332-5084. E-mail: jeff@ncrp.org. In-person interview recommended (telephone interview accepted). Applicants must submit a letter of interest, resume, writing sample, three personal references. Applications are accepted continuously. World Wide Web: http://www.ncrp.org.

NATIONAL CONSUMERS LEAGUE
1701 K Street, NW, Suite 1200
Washington, District of Columbia 20006

General Information Private, nonprofit membership consumer advocacy organization. Established in 1899. Number of employees: 20. Number of internship applications received each year: 50.

Internships Available ▶ *1 communications intern:* responsibilities include writing consumer-friendly articles, drafting press releases, developing press outreach materials and lists, marketing publications, assisting in Web design and publication layout. Candidates should have ability to work independently, ability to work with others, editing skills, oral communication skills, self-motivation, writing skills. Duration is minimum of 8 weeks (minimum 20 hours per week). Unpaid. Open to college juniors, college seniors, recent college graduates, graduate students, career changers, individuals reentering the workforce. ▶ *1 events coordinator intern:* responsibilities include planning and expediting events, communicating with speakers and attendees, developing and implementing event budgets, negotiating event contracts, working on site with hotel and catering staff, maintaining accurate records and files. Candidates should have ability to work independently, ability to work with others, oral communication skills, organizational skills, self-motivation, written communication skills. Duration is minimum 8 weeks (minimum 20 hours per week). Unpaid. Open to college juniors, college seniors, recent college graduates, graduate students, career changers, individuals reentering the workforce. ▶ *2–3 public policy interns:* responsibilities include working on issues in food and drug safety, health care, child labor, consumer fraud, financial services, telecommunications, or e-commerce. Candidates should have ability to work independently, ability to work with others, computer skills, oral communication skills, self-motivation, written communication skills. Duration is minimum of 8 weeks (minimum 20 hours per week). Unpaid. Open to college juniors, college seniors, recent college graduates, graduate students, law students, career changers, individuals reentering the workforce. International applications accepted.

Benefits Job counseling, names of contacts, on-the-job training, opportunity to attend seminars/workshops, willing to act as a professional reference, willing to complete paperwork for educational credit, willing to provide letters of recommendation, opportunity to contribute to League publications.

Contact Write, call, fax, or e-mail Ms. Sara Cooper, Executive Vice President. Phone: 202-835-3323 Ext. 111. Fax: 202-835-0747. E-mail: intern@nclnet.org. Telephone interview required. Applicants must submit a formal organization application, letter of interest, resume, writing sample, letter of recommendation. Applications are accepted continuously. World Wide Web: http://www.nclnet.org.

NATIONAL COUNCIL FOR RESEARCH ON WOMEN
11 Hanover Square
New York, New York 10005

General Information Working alliance of centers and individuals actively involved in feminist research, policy analysis, advocacy, and innovative programs for women and girls. Established in 1981. Number of employees: 9. Number of internship applications received each year: 50.

Internships Available ▶ *3–5 interns:* responsibilities include administrative duties, including: database maintenance, fulfilling orders, mail merges, and organization; networking with others in the field, getting an introduction to nonprofits, and gaining access to women-centered goings-on around the world; depending on skills and experience, intern will take on substantive projects. Candidates should have ability to work independently, oral communication skills, personal interest in the field, strong interpersonal skills, written communication skills. Duration is 3 months (at least 2-3 days per week). $10 per day for public transit and lunch. Open to recent high school graduates, college freshmen, college sophomores, college juniors, college seniors, recent college graduates, graduate students, law students, career changers. International applications accepted.

Benefits On-the-job training, opportunity to attend seminars/workshops, willing to act as a professional reference, willing to complete paperwork for educational credit, willing to provide letters of recommendation.

National Council for Research on Women (continued)

Contact Write, call, fax, or e-mail Elizabeth Horton. Phone: 212-785-7335. Fax: 212-785-7350. E-mail: lhorton@ncrw.org. In-person interview recommended (telephone interview accepted). Applicants must submit a resume, writing sample, two personal references. Applications are accepted continuously. World Wide Web: http://www.ncrw.org.

NATIONAL COUNCIL OF JEWISH WOMEN– LEGISLATIVE OFFICE
1707 L Street, NW, Suite 950
Washington, District of Columbia 20036

General Information Legislative branch office of a large membership organization with a service and advocacy mission. Established in 1893. Number of employees: 5. Branch of National Council of Jewish Women, New York, New York. Number of internship applications received each year: 20.
Internships Available ▶ *1–2 legislative interns:* responsibilities include assisting staff with substantive hands-on lobbying and tracking legislative issues. Candidates should have analytical skills, oral communication skills, personal interest in the field, research skills, self-motivation, strong interpersonal skills, written communication skills, progressive stance on social issues. Duration is flexible. Position available as unpaid or paid. Open to college sophomores, college juniors, college seniors, recent college graduates, graduate students, law students. International applications accepted.
Benefits Job counseling, on-the-job training, opportunity to attend seminars/workshops, travel reimbursement, willing to act as a professional reference, willing to complete paperwork for educational credit, willing to provide letters of recommendation.
International Internships Available in Israel.
Contact Write, call, fax, or e-mail Carolyn Ratner, Senior Legislative Associate, 1707 L Street, NW, Suite 950, Washington, District of Columbia 20036. Phone: 202-296-2588. Fax: 202-331-7792. E-mail: action@ncjwdc.org. In-person interview recommended (telephone interview accepted). Applicants must submit a letter of interest, resume, writing sample. Application deadline: February 1 for summer, November 1 for spring. World Wide Web: http://www.ncjw.org.

NATIONAL CRIME PREVENTION COUNCIL
1000 Connecticut Avenue, NW, 13th Floor
Washington, District of Columbia 20036

General Information Organization that helps focus the power of the individual and the community in the fight against crime. Established in 1980. Number of employees: 70. Number of internship applications received each year: 200.
Internships Available ▶ *6 interns:* responsibilities include working in any of the following programs: communities, research, press relations, public service, policing, prevention, education, state services, human resources, finance, and production. Candidates should have ability to work independently, ability to work with others, computer skills, knowledge of field, office skills, oral communication skills, personal interest in the field, research skills, self-motivation, writing skills. Duration is one summer. $8 per hour. Open to high school students, college freshmen, college sophomores, college juniors, college seniors, recent college graduates, graduate students, law students.
Benefits Opportunity to attend seminars/workshops, possible full-time employment, travel reimbursement, willing to act as a professional reference, willing to complete paperwork for educational credit, willing to provide letters of recommendation.
Contact Write, call, fax, or e-mail Vernon Banks, Human Resources Assistant. Phone: 202-466-6272. Fax: 202-296-1356. E-mail: hr-intern@ncpc.org. Telephone interview required. Applicants must submit a letter of interest, resume, writing sample. Application deadline: March 31. World Wide Web: http://www.ncpc.org.

NATIONAL CRIMINAL JUSTICE ASSOCIATION
720 7th Street, NW, Third Floor
Washington, District of Columbia 20001-3716

General Information Nonprofit, membership-based criminal justice association representing state and local government interests in public safety and crime control to Congress, federal executive, and private and public agencies. Established in 1971. Number of employees: 8. Number of internship applications received each year: 100.
Internships Available ▶ *1 graduate intern:* responsibilities include researching, writing, and developing a quarterly policy report; and assisting staff with other projects. Candidates should have analytical skills, editing skills, knowledge of field, oral communication skills, research skills, self-motivation, writing skills. Duration is fall, spring, or summer. Unpaid. Open to graduate students. ▶ *1–2 undergraduate interns:* responsibilities include researching and writing articles for the monthly association newsletter; attending hearings, press conferences, and Supreme Court sessions; possibly assisting staff with grant projects. Candidates should have ability to work independently, analytical skills, editing skills, personal interest in the field, research skills, self-motivation, writing skills. Duration is fall, spring, or summer. Unpaid. Open to college sophomores, college juniors, college seniors. International applications accepted.
Benefits On-the-job training, opportunity to attend seminars/workshops, willing to act as a professional reference, willing to complete paperwork for educational credit, willing to provide letters of recommendation, opportunity to attend congressional hearings, Supreme Court briefings and Justice Department meetings.
Contact Write, call, fax, e-mail, or through World Wide Web site Linda Lee, Staff Associate/Editor, 720 7th Street, NW, 3rd Floor, Washington, District of Columbia 20001-3716. Phone: 202-628-8550. Fax: 202-628-0080. E-mail: llee@ncja.org. Telephone interview required. Applicants must submit a letter of interest, resume, academic transcripts, writing sample, 2 personal references or 2 letters of recommendation. Applications are accepted continuously. World Wide Web: http://www.ncja.org.

NATIONAL ORGANIZATION FOR VICTIM ASSISTANCE (NOVA)
1730 Park Road, NW
Washington, District of Columbia 20010

General Information Private, nonprofit, 501(c)(3) organization of victim and witness assistance programs and practitioners, criminal justice agencies and professionals, mental health professionals, researchers, former victims and survivors, and others committed to the recognition and implementation of victim rights and services. Established in 1975. Number of employees: 8. Number of internship applications received each year: 30.
Internships Available ▶ *1–5 conference assistants:* responsibilities include assisting the conference coordinator with logistics of preparing a national victims conference of approximately 2000 participants. Candidates should have computer skills, office skills, oral communication skills, strong interpersonal skills, written communication skills. Duration is flexible. Unpaid. Open to high school students, recent high school graduates, college freshmen, college sophomores, college juniors, college seniors, recent college graduates, graduate students, law students, career changers, individuals reentering the workforce. ▶ *1 legislative assistants/lobbyist:* responsibilities include assisting in monitoring proposed federal and state legislation and promoting passage of designated bills to assist victims of crime. Candidates should have ability to work with others, oral communication skills, personal interest in the field, research skills, self-motivation, written communication skills. Duration is flexible. Unpaid. Open to college freshmen, college sophomores, college juniors, college seniors, recent college graduates, graduate students, law students, career changers, individuals reentering the workforce. ▶ *Office assistants:* responsibilities include assisting in general office duties including answering phones and victim letters; mailings; special projects. Candidates should have office skills, personal interest in the field, strong interpersonal skills, writing skills. Duration is flexible. Unpaid. Open to high school students, recent high school graduates, college freshmen, college sophomores, college juniors, college seniors, recent college graduates, graduate students, law students, career changers, individuals reentering the workforce. ▶ *Victim advocates/crisis intervenors:* responsibilities include working directly with victims of crime by phone, mail, or in person; possibility of participating in a 40-hour training to learn crisis intervention.

Candidates should have ability to work independently, oral communication skills, personal interest in the field, strong interpersonal skills, writing skills. Duration is flexible. Unpaid. Open to high school students, recent high school graduates, college freshmen, college sophomores, college juniors, college seniors, recent college graduates, graduate students, law students, career changers, individuals reentering the workforce. International applications accepted.

Benefits Formal training, names of contacts, on-the-job training, opportunity to attend seminars/workshops, willing to act as a professional reference, willing to complete paperwork for educational credit, willing to provide letters of recommendation, flexible hours, input in designing the internship, development of long-lasting skills, free housing (when available).

Contact Write, call, fax, e-mail, or through World Wide Web site Cheryl Guidry Tyiska, Director of Victim Services, 1730 Park Road, NW, Washington, District of Columbia 20010. Phone: 202-232-6682. Fax: 202-462-2255. E-mail: cheryl@trynova.org. In-person interview recommended (telephone interview accepted). Applicants must submit a letter of interest, resume, personal reference. Applications are accepted continuously. World Wide Web: http://www.trynova.org.

NATIONAL ORGANIZATION FOR WOMEN (NATIONAL ACTION CENTER)
733 15th Street, NW, 2nd Floor
Washington, District of Columbia 20005

General Information Feminist organization working to ensure full equality for women and to end discrimination. Established in 1966. Number of employees: 35. Number of internship applications received each year: 200.

Internships Available ▶ *1–2 Internet/LAN interns:* responsibilities include assisting in programming and maintaining NOW's Web page and working with membership services. Candidates should have ability to work with others, computer skills, experience in the field, organizational skills, research skills, self-motivation. Duration is 1 semester. Unpaid. Open to college freshmen, college sophomores, college juniors, college seniors, recent college graduates, graduate students. ▶ *1 comptroller assistant:* responsibilities include maintaining a nonprofit organization's cash flow by assisting comptroller in daily book maintenance and organizing for yearly audit. Candidates should have ability to work independently, analytical skills, college courses in field, computer skills, office skills, organizational skills. Duration is 1 semester. Unpaid. Open to college sophomores, college juniors, college seniors, recent college graduates. ▶ *1–2 direct mail/fund-raising/development interns:* responsibilities include researching, writing, creating ads, working on product catalog, grant writing and research. Candidates should have ability to work independently, computer skills, research skills, strong interpersonal skills, written communication skills. Duration is 1 semester. Unpaid. Open to college sophomores, college juniors, college seniors, recent college graduates, graduate students, individuals reentering the workforce. ▶ *1–4 field organizing interns:* responsibilities include working on special projects in areas including welfare rights, lesbian rights, racial diversity, violence against women, and state and chapter development. Candidates should have ability to work with others, oral communication skills, organizational skills, personal interest in the field, written communication skills. Duration is 1 semester. Unpaid. Open to high school seniors, recent high school graduates, college freshmen, college sophomores, college juniors, college seniors, recent college graduates, graduate students. ▶ *1–3 government relations interns:* responsibilities include lobbying, attending meetings, and performing legislative research and writing. Candidates should have ability to work independently, analytical skills, organizational skills, self-motivation, strong interpersonal skills, written communication skills. Duration is 14 weeks. Unpaid. Open to college sophomores, college juniors, college seniors, recent college graduates, graduate students. ▶ *1–3 legal interns:* responsibilities include researching, writing, analysis, and policy drafts. Candidates should have analytical skills, knowledge of field, oral communication skills, organizational skills, research skills, self-motivation. Duration is 8–10 weeks. Unpaid. Open to law students. ▶ *1–2 membership/database interns:* responsibilities include database

development and membership processing. Candidates should have ability to work independently, analytical skills, computer skills, self-motivation, strong interpersonal skills, database design skills (preferred). Duration is 1 semester. Unpaid. Open to recent high school graduates, college freshmen, college sophomores, college juniors, college seniors, recent college graduates, graduate students, career changers, individuals reentering the workforce. ▶ *1–2 political action interns:* responsibilities include assisting NOW in PAC organizing, meeting with candidates, candidate research, processing endorsement requests, and managing Federal Election Commission materials. Candidates should have analytical skills, computer skills, organizational skills, self-motivation, strong interpersonal skills, written communication skills. Duration is 1 semester. Unpaid. Open to college freshmen, college sophomores, college juniors, college seniors, recent college graduates. ▶ *2–4 press/communications interns:* responsibilities include researching and writing articles for the *National NOW Times,* assisting in maintaining press clippings, drafting press releases. Candidates should have editing skills, research skills, self-motivation, strong interpersonal skills, writing skills. Duration is 1 semester. Unpaid. Open to college freshmen, college sophomores, college juniors, college seniors, recent college graduates, graduate students, individuals reentering the workforce. International applications accepted.

Benefits Names of contacts, on-the-job training, opportunity to attend seminars/workshops, possible full-time employment, willing to act as a professional reference, willing to complete paperwork for educational credit, willing to provide letters of recommendation, formal training in grassroots organizing.

Contact Write, call, fax, e-mail, or through World Wide Web site Intern Coordinator. Phone: 202-628-8669. Fax: 202-785-8576. E-mail: nowinterns@aol.com. Telephone interview required. Applicants must submit a formal organization application, letter of interest, resume, 1-2 letters of recommendation, one-page writing sample. Application deadline: March 15 for summer, July 30 for fall, November 20 for spring. World Wide Web: http://www.now.org.

NATIONAL PARTNERSHIP FOR WOMEN AND FAMILIES
1875 Connecticut Avenue, NW, Suite 650
Washington, District of Columbia 20009

General Information Nonprofit, nonpartisan organization that uses public education and advocacy to promote fairness in the workplace, quality health care, and policies that help women and men meet the dual demands of work and family. Founded as the Women's Legal Defense Fund, the National Partnership has grown from a small group of volunteers into one of the nation's most powerful and effective advocates for women and families; works with business, government, unions, nonprofit organizations, and the media, and is a voice of fairness, a source for solutions, and a force for change. Established in 1971. Number of employees: 28. Number of internship applications received each year: 250.

Internships Available ▶ *1–2 Action Council and Membership interns:* responsibilities include membership recruitment and fund-raising; expanding the National Partnership's membership in the Action Council through implementation of small fund-raising events, creation of fund-raising solicitations, follow-up of pledges, and administrative duties associated with the daily operations of the development department; conducting research regarding current and potential major donors. Candidates should have ability to work independently, computer skills, oral communication skills, organizational skills, research skills, written communication skills. Duration is 8-10 weeks (10-20 hours per week during academic year; full-time during summer). Unpaid. Open to college juniors, college seniors, recent college graduates, graduate students. ▶ *1–2 annual luncheon interns:* responsibilities include assisting in the production of the annual luncheon, including coordinating invitation and follow-up mailings to guests, tracking responses, assisting with logistics, and other luncheon related duties. Candidates should have ability to work independently, computer skills, oral communication skills, organizational skills, research skills, written communication skills. Duration is 8-10 weeks (10-20 hours per week during academic year; full-time during summer). Unpaid.

National Partnership for Women and Families (continued)

Open to college juniors, college seniors, recent college graduates, graduate students. ▶ *Up to 2 communications interns:* responsibilities include researching, writing, and assisting with quarterly newsletter production; attending inside and outside meetings and press events; responding to requests for information from the media and public; producing and distributing daily clip packets; and maintaining filing systems. Candidates should have ability to work independently, computer skills, oral communication skills, organizational skills, research skills, written communication skills. Duration is 8-10 weeks (10-20 hours per week during academic year; full-time during summer). Unpaid. Open to college juniors, college seniors, recent college graduates, graduate students. ▶ *2–3 law clerks for Health Program:* responsibilities include assisting with the National Partnership's advocacy efforts to improve women's access to affordable, quality health care; researching and analyzing women's health issues, monitoring federal and state legislation, and attending and reporting back to staff about relevant congressional hearings, briefings, and other meetings. Candidates should have ability to work independently, editing skills, personal interest in the field, research skills, self-motivation, writing skills. Duration is 8-10 weeks (10-20 hours per week during academic year; full time during summer). Unpaid. Open to graduate students, law students. ▶ *2–3 law clerks for Work and Family Program:* responsibilities include assisting the National Partnership's advocacy efforts in the areas of equal employment opportunities, family-friendly workplace policy, expansion of the Family and Medical Leave Act, and employment barriers affecting low-income women; working on ensuring effective enforcement of federal agencies responsible for enforcing anti-discrimination laws, and attending and reporting back to staff about relevant congressional hearings, briefings, and other meetings. Candidates should have ability to work independently, editing skills, personal interest in the field, research skills, self-motivation, writing skills. Duration is 8-10 weeks (10-20 hours per week during academic year; full-time during summer). Unpaid. Open to law students. ▶ *2–4 law clerks for workplace fairness:* responsibilities include assisting the National Partnership's advocacy efforts in the areas of equal employment opportunities, employment barriers affecting low-income women, and the civil rights impact of welfare reform; legal research and writing in support of monitoring of EEO enforcement; advocacy of broader laws and legal interpretations; amicus litigation; coalition advocacy; and public education about laws and proposals in this area. Candidates should have ability to work independently, editing skills, personal interest in the field, research skills, self-motivation, writing skills. Duration is 8-10 weeks (10-20 hours per week during academic year; full-time during summer). Unpaid. Open to law students. ▶ *2–4 work and family interns:* responsibilities include assisting with the National Partnership's advocacy efforts in the areas of equal employment opportunities, family-friendly workplace policy, expansion of the Family and Medical Leave Act, and barriers affecting low-income women; ensuring effective enforcement of federal agencies responsible for enforcing anti-discrimination laws, monitoring and developing legislative initiatives on employment issues, and public education. Candidates should have ability to work independently, computer skills, oral communication skills, organizational skills, research skills, written communication skills. Duration is 8-10 weeks (10-20 hours per week during academic year; full-time during summer). Unpaid. Open to college juniors, college seniors, recent college graduates, graduate students, law students. ▶ *2–4 workplace fairness interns:* responsibilities include assisting with the National Partnership's advocacy efforts in the areas of equal employment opportunities, such as affirmative action, employment barriers affecting low-income women, particularly welfare recipients, and the civil rights impact of welfare policy changes at the national and state levels; also assisting in monitoring enforcement of federal anti-discrimination laws, advocating for legislation on employment issues, representation of the National Partnership in coalitions, research and writing, and educating the public about laws and proposals in the area, including developing fact sheets and other informational materials. Candidates should have ability to work independently, computer skills, oral communication skills, personal interest in the field, research skills, written communication skills. Duration is 8-10 weeks (10-20 hours per week during

academic year; full time during summer). Unpaid. Open to college freshmen, college sophomores, college juniors, college seniors, recent college graduates, graduate students. International applications accepted.
Benefits Job counseling, names of contacts, on-the-job training, opportunity to attend seminars/workshops, willing to act as a professional reference, willing to complete paperwork for educational credit, willing to provide letters of recommendation.
Contact Write, call, fax, or e-mail Ms. Helen Seery McBride, Director of Administration. Phone: 202-986-2600. Fax: 202-986-2539. E-mail: hmcbride@nationalpartnership.org. Applicants must submit a letter of interest, resume, academic transcripts, writing sample, 3-4 references. Application deadline: March 15 for summer, July 15 for fall, November 15 for spring. World Wide Web: http://www.nationalpartnership.org.

NATIONAL PEACE FOUNDATION
666 11th Street, NW, Suite 202
Washington, District of Columbia 20001

General Information Grassroots network of women who are dedicated to a peaceful future, locally and globally. Established in 1982. Number of employees: 6. Number of internship applications received each year: 40.
Internships Available ▶ *1–2 interns:* responsibilities include nonprofit management including reception work, membership retention, membership database entry, and letters to members. Candidates should have ability to work with others, office skills, oral communication skills, self-motivation, written communication skills. Duration is one summer or semester. Small stipend. Open to graduate students. International applications accepted.
Benefits Opportunity to attend seminars/workshops, travel reimbursement, willing to act as a professional reference, willing to provide letters of recommendation.
Contact Write or fax Kathleen Lansing, Deputy Director. Fax: 202-783-7040. No phone calls. In-person interview recommended (telephone interview accepted). Applicants must submit a resume, writing sample, cover letter. Application deadline: early August for fall, April 15 for summer, December 1 for spring. World Wide Web: http://www.nationalpeace.org.

NATIONAL STUDENT CAMPAIGN AGAINST HUNGER AND HOMELESSNESS
233 North Pleasant Street, Suite 32
Amherst, Massachusetts 01002

General Information Coalition of student and community members who are working to end hunger and homelessness through education, service, and organizing; trains students to create or improve service programs, promotes campus and community collaborations, and initiates programs to fight poverty. Established in 1985. Number of employees: 4. Unit of Center for Public Interest Research, Boston, Massachusetts. Number of internship applications received each year: 50.
Internships Available ▶ *2–4 Annual Hunger Cleanup interns:* responsibilities include publicizing community service work-a-thon to campuses across the country and coordinating fundraising efforts for the cleanup. Candidates should have oral communication skills, personal interest in the field, self-motivation, strong interpersonal skills. Duration is flexible (at least one semester). Unpaid. Open to high school seniors, recent high school graduates, college freshmen, college sophomores, college juniors, college seniors, recent college graduates, graduate students, law students, career changers, individuals reentering the workforce. ▶ *1–2 Internet interns:* responsibilities include updating and expanding existing Web site; building list serve, utilizing Internet to build network student participants. Candidates should have ability to work independently, computer skills, personal interest in the field, self-motivation, written communication skills, creativity. Duration is 1 semester. Unpaid. Open to high school seniors, recent high school graduates, college freshmen, college sophomores, college juniors, college seniors, recent college graduates, graduate students, career changers, individuals reentering the workforce. ▶ *2 National Conference interns:* responsibilities include helping to organize the annual national student conference held each October. Candidates

should have ability to work independently, oral communication skills, personal interest in the field, self-motivation, strong interpersonal skills. Duration is flexible; at least fall semester; summer internships also available. Unpaid. Open to high school seniors, recent high school graduates, college freshmen, college sophomores, college juniors, college seniors, recent college graduates, graduate students, law students, career changers, individuals reentering the workforce. ▶ *2 food salvage interns:* responsibilities include developing food salvage programs that ensure unused high school and college campus cafeteria food will go to those members of the local community who are in need of it. Candidates should have oral communication skills, personal interest in the field, self-motivation, strong interpersonal skills, written communication skills. Duration is flexible; at least one semester. Unpaid. Open to high school seniors, recent high school graduates, college freshmen, college sophomores, college juniors, college seniors, recent college graduates, graduate students, career changers, individuals reentering the workforce. ▶ *1–3 public policy interns:* responsibilities include developing network around local and national legislation that addresses the problems of hunger and homelessness, researching current legislation, and writing monthly action alert. Candidates should have ability to work independently, editing skills, personal interest in the field, research skills, writing skills. Duration is at least 1 semester/quarter. Unpaid. Open to high school seniors, recent high school graduates, college freshmen, college sophomores, college juniors, college seniors, recent college graduates, graduate students, law students, career changers, individuals reentering the workforce. ▶ *2 publication interns:* responsibilities include updating project manuals and developing a series of fact sheets on hunger and homelessness. Candidates should have ability to work independently, ability to work with others, editing skills, research skills, writing skills. Duration is flexible; at least one semester. Unpaid. Open to high school seniors, recent high school graduates, college freshmen, college sophomores, college juniors, college seniors, recent college graduates, graduate students, career changers, individuals reentering the workforce. International applications accepted.

Benefits Job counseling, names of contacts, on-the-job training, opportunity to attend seminars/workshops, possible full-time employment, willing to act as a professional reference, willing to complete paperwork for educational credit, willing to provide letters of recommendation, opportunity for meaningful project experience, chance to make a difference in lives of others, possibility of free housing for National Conference interns.

Contact Write, call, fax, e-mail, or through World Wide Web site Jennifer Hecker, Organizing Director. Phone: 800-664-8647. Fax: 413-256-6435. E-mail: info@studentsagainsthunger.org. In-person interview recommended (telephone interview accepted). Applicants must submit a letter of interest, resume. Applications are accepted continuously. World Wide Web: http://www.studentsagainsthunger.org.

NATIONAL TAXPAYERS UNION
108 North Alfred Street
Alexandria, Virginia 22314

General Information Public interest group that works for tax relief, constitutional limits on taxes and spending, taxpayers' rights, and reduction of government waste. Established in 1969. Number of employees: 15. Number of internship applications received each year: 100.

Internships Available ▶ *2–4 associate policy analysts:* responsibilities include conducting long-term research on fiscal policy issues. Candidates should have ability to work independently, analytical skills, computer skills, personal interest in the field, research skills, writing skills. Duration is minimum of 10 weeks. Position available as unpaid or at $225 per week. ▶ *2 legislative aides:* responsibilities include assisting lobbying staff with mailings, visits to legislators, and calls to congressional aides. Candidates should have knowledge of field, office skills, oral communication skills, personal interest in the field, strong interpersonal skills, written communication skills. Duration is minimum of 10 weeks. Position available as unpaid or at $200 per week. ▶ *2 researchers:* responsibilities include researching cost impact of fiscal policies. Candidates should have computer skills, office skills, oral communication

skills, research skills, strong interpersonal skills. Duration is minimum of 10 weeks. Position available as unpaid or at $180 per week. Open to college sophomores, college juniors, college seniors, graduate students, law students. International applications accepted.

Benefits Names of contacts, opportunity to attend seminars/workshops, willing to act as a professional reference, willing to complete paperwork for educational credit, willing to provide letters of recommendation.

Contact Write, fax, e-mail, or through World Wide Web site Jeff Dircksen, Director of Congressional Analysis. Fax: 703-683-5722. E-mail: dircksen@ntu.org. Telephone interview required. Applicants must submit a letter of interest, resume, two writing samples, personal reference. Applications are accepted continuously. World Wide Web: http://www.ntu.org.

NATIONAL WHISTLEBLOWER CENTER
3238 P Street, NW
Washington, District of Columbia 20007

General Information Nonprofit educational and advocacy organization committed to environmental protection, nuclear safety, government accountability, and protecting the rights of employee whistle blowers. Established in 1988. Number of employees: 6. Number of internship applications received each year: 100.

Internships Available ▶ *1–10 law clerks:* responsibilities include significant legal research and writing projects, assisting at trials, and performing all the work of an associate attorney. Candidates should have ability to work independently, ability to work with others. Duration is 10 weeks (minimum). Unpaid. Open to college freshmen, college sophomores, college juniors, college seniors, law students. International applications accepted.

Benefits Opportunity to attend seminars/workshops, willing to act as a professional reference, willing to complete paperwork for educational credit, willing to provide letters of recommendation, one-on-one supervision from an attorney.

Contact Write, call, fax, e-mail, or through World Wide Web site Karima Brooker, Internship Coordinator, 3238 P Street, NW, Washington, District of Columbia 20007. Phone: 202-342-6980. Fax: 202-342-6984. E-mail: whistle@whistleblowers.org. Telephone interview required. Applicants must submit a letter of interest, resume. Application deadline: March 1 for summer, September 1 for January positions, December 1 for spring. World Wide Web: http://www.whistleblowers.org.

NATIONAL WOMEN'S HEALTH NETWORK
514 10th Street, NW, Suite 400
Washington, District of Columbia 20004

General Information Organization that provides information on women's health issues and advocates for women's health by functioning as a watchdog over federal agencies. Established in 1975. Number of employees: 5. Number of internship applications received each year: 100.

Internships Available ▶ *5 women's health advocacy interns:* responsibilities include working in the clearinghouse and on special projects and attending meetings and conferences. Candidates should have oral communication skills, organizational skills, personal interest in the field, research skills, self-motivation, strong interpersonal skills, writing skills. Duration is 10 weeks (minimum). Position available as unpaid or at $160 per week for spring/fall only; no summer stipend. Open to college freshmen, college sophomores, college juniors, college seniors, recent college graduates, graduate students, law students, career changers, individuals reentering the workforce. International applications accepted.

Benefits Names of contacts, opportunity to attend seminars/workshops, willing to act as a professional reference, willing to complete paperwork for educational credit, willing to provide letters of recommendation.

Contact Write, call, or fax Stephanie Donne, Clearinghouse Coordinator. Phone: 202-347-1140. Fax: 202-347-1168. Telephone interview required. Applicants must submit a letter of interest, resume, writing sample. Application deadline: continuous for spring and fall, March 15 for summer. World Wide Web: http://www.womenshealthnetwork.org.

NATIONAL WOMEN'S JUSTICE COALITION, INC.
GPO Box 3148
Canberra ACT 2601 Australia

General Information Organization that provides networking, capacity building, and lobbying to promote women's legal equality in Australia. Established in 1995. Number of employees: 4. Number of internship applications received each year: 50.

Internships Available ▶ *1–4 interns:* responsibilities include general administrative duties, research, and public relations tasks (updating records, Web research, and dealing with public inquiries). Candidates should have ability to work independently, analytical skills, computer skills, editing skills, experience in the field, office skills, oral communication skills, organizational skills, personal interest in the field, research skills, self-motivation, strong interpersonal skills, strong leadership ability, writing skills. Duration is 1–2 semesters. Unpaid. Open to recent college graduates, graduate students, law students, individuals reentering the workforce, people interested in the role/aims of the organization. International applications accepted.

Benefits Names of contacts, on-the-job training, willing to act as a professional reference, willing to complete paperwork for educational credit, willing to provide letters of recommendation.

International Internships Available.

Contact Call or e-mail Shawanah Tasneem, Intern Coordinator, GPO Box 3148, Canberra 2601 Australia. Phone: 61-2-6247-2075. Fax: 61-2-6257-3070. E-mail: nwjc@nwjc.org.au. In-person interview recommended (telephone interview accepted). Applicants must submit a formal organization application, resume, two personal references. Applications are accepted continuously. World Wide Web: http://www.nwjc.org.au.

NATIONAL WOMEN'S POLITICAL CAUCUS
1634 Eye Street, NW, Suite 310
Washington, District of Columbia 20006

General Information National bipartisan grassroots organization dedicated to the advancement of women through appointed and elected public office; operates a nonprofit, leadership development, education, and research arm and conducts extensive training seminars designed to train women for potential candidacy. Established in 1971. Number of employees: 3. Number of internship applications received each year: 100.

Internships Available ▶ *1–2 interns:* responsibilities include working in media and communications, political and electoral politics, membership, grassroots organizing, or development and fundraising. Candidates should have ability to work independently, computer skills, office skills, oral communication skills, personal interest in the field, research skills, strong interpersonal skills, writing skills. Duration is 1 semester. Unpaid. Open to college freshmen, college sophomores, college juniors, college seniors, recent college graduates, graduate students. International applications accepted.

Benefits Names of contacts, on-the-job training, opportunity to attend seminars/workshops, willing to act as a professional reference, willing to complete paperwork for educational credit, willing to provide letters of recommendation, opportunity to gain leadership skills.

Contact Write, call, fax, or e-mail Jenny Johnson, Intern Coordinator. Phone: 202-785-1100. Fax: 202-785-3605. E-mail: info@nwpc.org. Telephone interview required. Applicants must submit a letter of interest, resume, writing sample. Applications are accepted continuously. World Wide Web: http://www.nwpc.org.

NETWORK
801 Pennsylvania Avenue, SE, Suite 460
Washington, District of Columbia 20003

General Information National Catholic social justice lobby whose members seek to influence national legislation for healthcare reform, affordable housing, economic conversion, deficit reduction, and global collaboration for equitable and sustainable development. Established in 1971. Number of employees: 14. Number of internship applications received each year: 20.

Internships Available ▶ *1 associate field organizer:* responsibilities include representing staff at coalition meetings, activating grassroots organizing, communicating with membership, and assisting with administrative tasks. Duration is 11 months. $8162 per duration of internship. ▶ *2 associate lobbyists:* responsibilities include representing staff at coalition meetings, conveying legislative information to staff, lobbying, and assisting with administrative work. Duration is 11 months. $8162 per duration of internship. Candidates for all positions should have ability to work with others, computer skills, oral communication skills, personal interest in the field, self-motivation, written communication skills. Open to recent college graduates, career changers, individuals reentering the workforce.

Benefits Names of contacts, on-the-job training, opportunity to attend seminars/workshops, possible full-time employment, willing to complete paperwork for educational credit, willing to provide letters of recommendation, full health benefits.

Contact Write, call, fax, e-mail, or through World Wide Web site Mark Torma, Associate Coordinator. Phone: 202-547-5556. Fax: 202-547-5510. E-mail: mtorma@networklobby.org. Telephone interview required. Applicants must submit a formal organization application, resume, two personal references. Application deadline: February 1. World Wide Web: http://www.networklobby.org.

NEW HAVEN/LEÓN SISTER CITY PROJECT
608 Whitney Avenue
New Haven, Connecticut 06511

General Information Progressive binational grassroots organization that fosters a partnership between the communities of Greater New Haven, Connecticut and León, Nicaragua. Established in 1984. Number of employees: 3. Number of internship applications received each year: 8.

Internships Available ▶ *Peace and justice volunteers:* responsibilities include working shoulder-to-shoulder with residents of Léon, sharing expertise and knowledge in fields including agriculture, social work, medicine, weaving, marketing, and computers. Candidates should have knowledge of field, oral communication skills, personal interest in the field, self-motivation, moderate proficiency in Spanish. Duration is 1–12 months. Unpaid. Open to recent high school graduates, college freshmen, college sophomores, college juniors, college seniors, recent college graduates, graduate students, law students, career changers, professionals from all areas of work. International applications accepted.

Benefits Housing at a cost, meals at a cost, names of contacts, possible full-time employment, willing to act as a professional reference, willing to complete paperwork for educational credit, willing to provide letters of recommendation.

International Internships Available in Léon, Nicaragua.

Contact Write, call, fax, e-mail, or through World Wide Web site Program Director. Phone: 203-562-1607. Fax: 203-624-1683. E-mail: nh@newhavenleon.org. In-person interview recommended (telephone interview accepted). Applicants must submit a formal organization application, letter of interest, resume. Applications are accepted continuously. World Wide Web: http://www.newhavenleon.org.

NEW YORK PUBLIC INTEREST RESEARCH GROUP
107 Washington Avenue
Albany, New York 12210

General Information Nonpartisan, not-for-profit research and advocacy organization established and directed by New York state college and university students that works for consumer protection, environmental preservation, and reform in health care, education, and government. Established in 1973. Number of employees: 60. Number of internship applications received each year: 60.

Internships Available ▶ *6–10 legislative associates:* responsibilities include researching issues, tracking legislation, organizing public support, and advocating positions in the New York legislature. Candidates should have ability to work independently, ability to work with others, oral communication skills, self-motivation, strong leadership ability, writing skills. Duration is 1 semester. $400 per month. Open to college juniors, college seniors, graduate students. International applications accepted.

Benefits Formal training, names of contacts, opportunity to attend seminars/workshops, possible full-time employment, travel reimbursement, willing to complete paperwork for educational credit, willing to provide letters of recommendation.
Contact Write, call, or fax Mr. Blair Horner, Legislative Director. Phone: 518-436-0876. Fax: 518-432-6178. E-mail: bhorner@nypirg.org. In-person interview recommended (telephone interview accepted). Applicants must submit a formal organization application, writing sample. Application deadline: November 1.

NORTH CAROLINA CENTER FOR PUBLIC POLICY RESEARCH
PO Box 430
Raleigh, North Carolina 27602

General Information Public policy research center that studies state government policies and procedures and attempts to educate the public. Established in 1977. Number of employees: 6.
Internships Available ▶ *2 research interns:* responsibilities include keeping up with legislation, writing and researching articles, and performing data entry. Candidates should have personal interest in the field, plan to pursue career in field, research skills, writing skills. Duration is 10 weeks. Unpaid. Open to college juniors, college seniors, recent college graduates, graduate students. International applications accepted.
Benefits Willing to act as a professional reference, willing to complete paperwork for educational credit, willing to provide letters of recommendation.
Contact Write, call, fax, or e-mail Policy Analyst. Phone: 919-832-2839. Fax: 919-832-2847. E-mail: rosebud@nccppr.org. In-person interview recommended (telephone interview accepted). Applicants must submit a resume, academic transcripts, writing sample. Application deadline: March 31 for summer; continuous for all other positions. World Wide Web: http://www.nccppr.com.

OCTOBER 22 COALITION TO STOP POLICE BRUTALITY
PO Box 2627
New York, New York 10009

General Information Community-based nonprofit group fighting police brutality. Established in 1996. Number of employees: 4. Number of internship applications received each year: 6.
Internships Available ▶ *2 office assistants:* responsibilities include communication with local grassroots organizations, families of people killed by police, lawyers, and researchers on police. Candidates should have ability to work with others, oral communication skills, personal interest in the field. Duration is 1 semester. Unpaid. Open to college freshmen, college sophomores, college juniors, college seniors. International applications accepted.
Benefits On-the-job training, willing to act as a professional reference, willing to complete paperwork for educational credit, willing to provide letters of recommendation.
Contact Write, call, or e-mail Kathryn Lee, Managing Director, 263 East 10th Street, Apartment 1, New York 10009. Phone: 212-477-8062. E-mail: no1022@aol.com. In-person interview recommended (telephone interview accepted). Applicants must submit a letter of interest. Applications are accepted continuously. World Wide Web: http://www.october22.org.

OHIO CITIZEN ACTION
614 West Superior, Suite 1200
Cleveland, Ohio 44113

General Information State's largest environmental, consumer advocacy and nonprofit grassroots group. Established in 1975. Number of employees: 85. Number of internship applications received each year: 30.
Internships Available ▶ *10–30 community organizers/grassroots organizers:* responsibilities include educating and involving the public on environmental and political issues through petitioning, fundraising, and letter writing campaigns. Candidates should have ability to work independently, oral communication skills, organizational skills, personal interest in the field, self-motivation, strong interpersonal skills, strong leadership ability. Duration is flexible.

$350–$425 per week. Open to high school seniors, recent high school graduates, college freshmen, college sophomores, college juniors, college seniors, recent college graduates, graduate students, law students, career changers, individuals reentering the workforce. International applications accepted.
Benefits Formal training, health insurance, job counseling, names of contacts, on-the-job training, opportunity to attend seminars/workshops, possible full-time employment, travel reimbursement, willing to act as a professional reference, willing to complete paperwork for educational credit, willing to provide letters of recommendation.
Contact Write, call, fax, e-mail, or through World Wide Web site Brandon Milne, Staff Director. Phone: 216-861-5200. Fax: 216-694-6904. E-mail: bmilne@ohiocitizen.org. In-person interview recommended (telephone interview accepted). Applicants must submit a formal organization application, resume, call 216-623-3952 for interview. Applications are accepted continuously. World Wide Web: http://ohiocitizen.org.

ORGANIZATION OF CHINESE AMERICANS
1001 Connecticut Avenue, NW, Suite 601
Washington, District of Columbia 20036

General Information National, nonprofit advocacy organization of concerned Chinese Americans dedicated to securing social justice, equal opportunity, and equal treatment of Chinese Americans. Established in 1973. Number of employees: 10. Number of internship applications received each year: 120.
Internships Available ▶ *1–4 congressional interns:* responsibilities include attending subcommittee hearings, tracking legislation, research, writing articles and press releases, and office duties. Candidates should have ability to work independently, ability to work with others, analytical skills, computer skills, editing skills, office skills, oral communication skills, research skills, self-motivation, strong leadership ability, writing skills. Duration is 10 weeks. Paid. ▶ *1–4 government interns:* responsibilities include attending subcommittee hearings, tracking legislation, research, writing articles and press releases, and office duties. Candidates should have ability to work independently, ability to work with others, analytical skills, computer skills, editing skills, office skills, oral communication skills, research skills, self-motivation, strong leadership ability, writing skills. Duration is 10 weeks. Paid. ▶ *1–4 national office interns:* responsibilities include writing press releases and articles; attending meetings. Candidates should have ability to work independently, analytical skills, computer skills, editing skills, office skills, oral communication skills, organizational skills, research skills, self-motivation, strong interpersonal skills, writing skills. Duration is 10 weeks. Paid. Open to college freshmen, college sophomores, college juniors, college seniors.
Benefits Opportunity to attend seminars/workshops, willing to act as a professional reference, willing to complete paperwork for educational credit, willing to provide letters of recommendation, stipend of $2000.
Contact Write, call, fax, or e-mail Keith McAllister, Director of Technology. Phone: 202-223-5500. Fax: 202-296-0540. E-mail: oca@ocanatl.org. Telephone interview required. Applicants must submit a formal organization application, resume, academic transcripts, writing sample, two personal references, cover letters, essay (typed and double-spaced) explaining interest in internship. Application deadline: March 24 for summer, July 15 for fall, November 15 for spring. World Wide Web: http://www.ocanatl.org.

OVARIAN CANCER NATIONAL ALLIANCE
910 17th Street, NW, Suite 413
Washington, District of Columbia 20006

General Information Nonprofit organization working at the national level to increase public and professional understanding of ovarian cancer and to advocate for increased research for more effective diagnostics and treatment. Established in 1997. Number of employees: 9. Number of internship applications received each year: 10.
Internships Available ▶ *1–2 staff assistants:* responsibilities include working closely with the public education director and communications coordinator; handling consumer correspondence, data entry, statistics, and information gathering; outreach; writ-

Ovarian Cancer National Alliance (continued)

ing and working with constituent groups. Candidates should have ability to work independently, computer skills, writing skills, interest in women's and health issues. Duration is one summer or semester. Stipend. Open to college freshmen, college sophomores, college juniors, college seniors, recent college graduates, career changers.

Benefits On-the-job training, opportunity to attend seminars/workshops, willing to act as a professional reference, willing to complete paperwork for educational credit, willing to provide letters of recommendation.

Contact Write, call, fax, e-mail, or through World Wide Web site Jennifer Schenfeld, Program Assistant. Phone: 202-331-1332. Fax: 202-331-2292. E-mail: ocna@ovariancancer.org. In-person interview recommended (telephone interview accepted). Applicants must submit a resume, writing sample, two personal references. Applications are accepted continuously. World Wide Web: http://www.ovariancancer.org.

OWL: THE VOICE OF MIDLIFE AND OLDER WOMEN
666 11th Street, NW, Suite 700
Washington, District of Columbia 20001

General Information National membership organization that strives to improve the status and quality of life for women, midlife and older. Established in 1980. Number of employees: 8. Number of internship applications received each year: 15.

Internships Available ▶ *1 communications/public relations intern.* Candidates should have analytical skills, editing skills, oral communication skills, research skills, strong interest in women's issues, positive attitude, computer skills (helpful). Duration is flexible (3 month minimum, 16 hours per week). Unpaid. ▶ *1 development/fund-raising intern.* Candidates should have oral communication skills, organizational skills, research skills, strong interpersonal skills, written communication skills, strong interest in women's issues, positive attitude, computer skills (helpful). Duration is flexible (3 month minimum, 16 hours per week). Unpaid. ▶ *1 organizing and advocacy intern.* Candidates should have analytical skills, oral communication skills, organizational skills, self-motivation, writing skills, strong interest in women's issues, positive attitude, computer skills (helpful). Duration is flexible (3 month minimum, 16 hours per week). Unpaid. ▶ *1 public policy and research intern.* Candidates should have ability to work independently, analytical skills, oral communication skills, research skills, writing skills, strong interest in women's issues, positive attitude, computer skills (helpful). Duration is flexible (3 month minimum, 16 hours per week). Unpaid. Open to college sophomores, college juniors, college seniors, recent college graduates, graduate students, law students, career changers, individuals reentering the workforce, non-traditional students. International applications accepted.

Benefits Opportunity to attend seminars/workshops, possible full-time employment, travel reimbursement, willing to act as a professional reference, willing to complete paperwork for educational credit, willing to provide letters of recommendation, willing to design special projects to match intern's academic targets.

Contact Write, call, fax, or e-mail Laurie M. Young, Executive Director, 666 11th Street, NW, Suite 700, Washington, District of Columbia 20001. Phone: 800-825-3695. Fax: 202-638-2356. E-mail: lyoung@owl-national.org. In-person interview recommended (telephone interview accepted). Applicants must submit a letter of interest, resume, two writing samples, personal reference, letter of recommendation. Applications are accepted continuously. World Wide Web: http://www.owl-national.org.

PARTNERS FOR LIVABLE COMMUNITIES
1429 21st Street, NW
Washington, District of Columbia 20036

General Information Nonprofit organization working to improve the livability of communities by promoting quality of life, economic development, and social equity. Established in 1978. Number of employees: 8. Number of internship applications received each year: 50.

Internships Available ▶ *1–2 Creative City Public Policy Writers:* responsibilities include public policy research and documentation for Partners' publication on the Creative City; documenting best practices in participating cities; analyzing and documenting success of Creative City initiatives. Candidates should have ability to work independently, computer skills, editing skills, research skills, writing skills. Duration is flexible. Position available as unpaid or paid. Open to recent college graduates, graduate students, career changers, individuals reentering the workforce. ▶ *2–4 interns:* responsibilities include assisting in research, writing, event coordinating, and information management. Candidates should have ability to work independently, ability to work with others, computer skills, editing skills, oral communication skills, organizational skills, personal interest in the field, research skills, self-motivation, writing skills. Duration is flexible (typically 3-4 months). Position available as unpaid or paid. Open to college freshmen, college sophomores, college juniors, college seniors, recent college graduates, graduate students, law students, career changers, individuals reentering the workforce.

Benefits Names of contacts, opportunity to attend seminars/workshops, willing to act as a professional reference, willing to complete paperwork for educational credit, willing to provide letters of recommendation, possibility of stipend.

Contact Write, call, fax, or e-mail Laura Durham, Senior Program Officer. Phone: 202-887-5990. Fax: 202-466-4845. E-mail: partners@livable.com. In-person interview recommended (telephone interview accepted). Applicants must submit a letter of interest, resume, writing sample, statement indicating ates available and goals for internship experience. Applications are accepted continuously. World Wide Web: http://www.livable.com.

PARTNERSHIP FOR PUBLIC SERVICE
1725 Eye Street, NW, Suite 900
Washington, District of Columbia 20006

General Information Nonprofit, nonpartisan organization dedicated to revitalizing the federal civil service. Established in 2001. Number of employees: 25. Number of internship applications received each year: 250.

Internships Available ▶ *3–4 Partnership for Public Service Fellows:* responsibilities include contributing to all divisions of organization; providing administrative support to programming, legislative, and communication divisions. Candidates should have ability to work independently, analytical skills, computer skills, editing skills, office skills, oral communication skills, organizational skills, personal interest in the field, research skills, self-motivation, strong interpersonal skills, strong leadership ability, written communication skills. Duration is 3–4 months. Position available as unpaid or at stipend of $750-$1000 per month. Open to college freshmen, college sophomores, college juniors, college seniors, recent college graduates, graduate students, law students. International applications accepted.

Benefits Formal training, on-the-job training, opportunity to attend seminars/workshops, willing to act as a professional reference, willing to complete paperwork for educational credit, willing to provide letters of recommendation.

Contact Write, call, fax, e-mail, or through World Wide Web site Shari Katz, Internship Coordinator. Phone: 202-775-9111. Fax: 202-775-8885. E-mail: skatz@ourpublicservice.org. Telephone interview required. Applicants must submit a resume, academic transcripts, two writing samples, three personal references. Application deadline: March 1 for summer, July 20 for fall, November 15 for winter. World Wide Web: http://www.ourpublicservice.org.

PEACE ACTION AND PEACE ACTION EDUCATION FUND
1819 H Street, NW, Room 425
Washington, District of Columbia 20006

General Information Grassroots peace and justice organization that seeks to promote global security by converting to a peace economy and stopping the nuclear arms race and conventional arms trade. Established in 1957. Number of employees: 16. Number of internship applications received each year: 100.

Internships Available ▶ *1–2 communication interns:* responsibilities include research, writing, desktop and Web publishing, coalition meetings, some event organizing, and administrative work. Duration is 3 months. Small stipend. ▶ *1–2 organizing department interns:* responsibilities include assisting with event organizing, research, writing, desk top publishing, Web publishing, some administrative work. Duration is 3 months. Small stipend. Candidates for all positions should have ability to work independently, ability to work with others, computer skills, organizational skills, personal interest in the field, written communication skills. Open to high school seniors, recent high school graduates, college freshmen, college sophomores, college juniors, college seniors, recent college graduates, graduate students, law students, career changers, individuals reentering the workforce. International applications accepted.

Benefits Names of contacts, on-the-job training, opportunity to attend seminars/workshops, possible full-time employment, travel reimbursement, willing to act as a professional reference, willing to complete paperwork for educational credit, willing to provide letters of recommendation.

Contact Write, call, fax, e-mail, or through World Wide Web site Carrie Benzschawel, Program Associate. Phone: 202-862-9740 Ext. 3041. Fax: 202-862-9762. E-mail: cbenzschawel@peace-action.org. Telephone interview required. Applicants must submit a letter of interest, resume, writing sample, 2-3 personal references. Applications are accepted continuously. World Wide Web: http://www.peace-action.org.

PEOPLE FOR THE AMERICAN WAY FOUNDATION
2000 M Street, NW, #400
Washington, District of Columbia 20036

General Information Nonprofit, 300,000-member, progressive, nonpartisan, constitutional liberties organization. Established in 1980. Number of employees: 90. Number of internship applications received each year: 300.

Internships Available ▶ *5–6 Everett Public Service Internships:* responsibilities include writing, research, grassroots organizing, congressional monitoring. Candidates should have ability to work independently, ability to work with others, computer skills, oral communication skills, research skills, writing skills. Duration is 10 weeks. $220–$250 per week. Open to college freshmen, college sophomores, college juniors, college seniors, recent college graduates, graduate students, law students. ▶ *5–10 interns:* responsibilities include writing, grassroots organizing, researching, monitoring legislation, performing media relations, marketing, and development work. Candidates should have ability to work with others, computer skills, oral communication skills, research skills, written communication skills. Duration is 2–12 months. Position available as unpaid or at $7.50–$10 per hour. Open to recent high school graduates, college freshmen, college sophomores, college juniors, college seniors, recent college graduates, graduate students, law students, career changers, individuals reentering the workforce. International applications accepted.

Benefits Job counseling, opportunity to attend seminars/workshops, possible full-time employment, willing to act as a professional reference, willing to complete paperwork for educational credit, willing to provide letters of recommendation.

Contact Write, call, fax, e-mail, or through World Wide Web site Ms. Judy Green, Senior Vice President for Personnel. Phone: 202-467-2306. Fax: 202-293-2672. E-mail: jgreen@pfaw.org. Telephone interview required. Applicants must submit a letter of interest, resume. Application deadline: April 30 for summer. World Wide Web: http://www.pfaw.org.

PHYSICIANS FOR HUMAN RIGHTS
100 Boylston Street, Suite 702
Boston, Massachusetts 02116

General Information Organization that promotes health by protecting human rights; has sent over 100 medical and forensic teams to dozens of countries to investigate war crimes, reports of torture, disappearances, and extrajudicial executions; prison conditions; landmines; use of chemical weapons, and other areas. Established in 1986. Number of employees: 30. Number of internship applications received each year: 30.

Internships Available ▶ *5–15 interns (in Boston and DC offices):* responsibilities include possibility of researching cases of health professionals and others whose international human rights are violated, assisting in organization of advocacy actions and educational events on health and human rights, drafting letters and background materials, and researching topics of special interest to the organization in the field of health and human rights. Candidates should have ability to work independently, ability to work with others, computer skills, personal interest in the field, writing skills. Duration is minimum of 2 months. Unpaid. Open to recent high school graduates, college freshmen, college sophomores, college juniors, college seniors, recent college graduates. International applications accepted.

Benefits Names of contacts, opportunity to attend seminars/workshops, willing to complete paperwork for educational credit.

Contact Write, fax, or e-mail Kathleen Carspecken, Internship Coordinator. Phone: 617-695-0041 Ext. 201. Fax: 617-695-0307. E-mail: kcarspecken@phrusa.org. In-person interview recommended (telephone interview accepted). Applicants must submit a letter of interest, resume, 3-5 page writing sample. Applications are accepted continuously. World Wide Web: http://www.phrusa.org/.

PHYSICIANS FOR SOCIAL RESPONSIBILITY–LOS ANGELES
3250 Wilshire Boulevard, Suite 1400
Los Angeles, California 90010

General Information Organization that works toward creating a world free of nuclear weapons, global environmental pollution, and gun violence. Established in 1970. Number of employees: 5. Unit of Physicians for Social Responsibility, Washington, District of Columbia. Number of internship applications received each year: 8.

Internships Available ▶ *3 assistant environmental/health care policy organizers:* responsibilities include media outreach, creating publications and databases, organizing public events, research, promoting computer networks, and building grassroots support. Candidates should have computer skills, office skills, organizational skills, personal interest in the field, research skills, written communication skills. Duration is flexible. Unpaid. International applications accepted.

Benefits On-the-job training, opportunity to attend seminars/workshops, travel reimbursement, willing to act as a professional reference, willing to complete paperwork for educational credit, willing to provide letters of recommendation, paid parking, possible employment.

Contact E-mail Kim Zanti, Membership Coordinator. Phone: 213-386-4901 Ext. 113. Fax: 213-386-4184. E-mail: kzanti@psr.org. In-person interview recommended (telephone interview accepted). Applicants must submit a letter of interest, resume. Applications are accepted continuously. World Wide Web: http://www.psrla.org.

POLARIS PROJECT
Washington, District of Columbia

General Information Community-based research and advocacy organization working to combat the trafficking of women and children. Established in 2002. Number of employees: 3. Number of internship applications received each year: 40.

Internships Available ▶ *Development interns:* responsibilities include helping in grant research and proposal writing and in coordinating fund-raising events. Candidates should have ability to work independently, computer skills, editing skills, oral communication skills, organizational skills, research skills, self-motivation, strong interpersonal skills, strong leadership ability, written communication skills. Duration is 1–12 months. Unpaid. Open to college freshmen, college sophomores, college juniors, college seniors, recent college graduates, graduate students, law students, career changers. ▶ *Research interns:* responsibilities include conducting research and writing report drafts for www.HumanTrafficking.com. Candidates should have ability to work independently, ability to work with others, analytical skills, computer skills, editing skills, organizational skills, personal interest in the field, research skills, self-motivation, writing skills. Duration is 1–12 months.

Polaris Project (continued)

Unpaid. Open to college freshmen, college sophomores, college juniors, college seniors, recent college graduates, graduate students, law students, career changers. ▶ *Technology interns:* responsibilities include helping maintain and build organizational and program Web sites. Candidates should have ability to work independently, ability to work with others, computer skills, organizational skills, self-motivation. Duration is 1–12 months. Unpaid. Open to college sophomores, college juniors, college seniors, recent college graduates, graduate students, law students, career changers. International applications accepted.

Benefits On-the-job training, opportunity to attend seminars/workshops, willing to act as a professional reference, willing to complete paperwork for educational credit, willing to provide letters of recommendation.

Contact Call, e-mail, or through World Wide Web site Katherine Chon, Co-Executive Director. Phone: 202-547-7909. Fax: 202-547-6654. E-mail: intern@polarisproject.org. In-person interview recommended (telephone interview accepted). Applicants must submit a letter of interest, resume, writing sample, three personal references, sign-up for Grassroots Network at www.polarisproject.org. Applications are accepted continuously. World Wide Web: http://www.PolarisProject.org.

THE POPULATION INSTITUTE
107 2nd Street, NE
Washington, District of Columbia 20002

General Information Nonprofit grassroots organization specializing in the link between international population and environmental issues. Established in 1969. Number of employees: 18. Number of internship applications received each year: 50.

Internships Available ▶ *1 World Population Awareness Week coordinator:* responsibilities include organizing events and establishing network of contacts for this officially sponsored week. Candidates should have ability to work independently, computer skills, editing skills, oral communication skills, organizational skills, self-motivation, strong interpersonal skills, strong leadership ability, writing skills. Duration is 1 year. $2000 per month. ▶ *1–2 field coordinators:* responsibilities include planning and implementing trips around the nation for the president of the Institute and maintaining contact with educators and community organizations. Candidates should have ability to work independently, computer skills, office skills, oral communication skills, organizational skills, self-motivation, strong interpersonal skills, strong leadership ability, writing skills. Duration is 1 year. $2000 per month. ▶ *1 media fellow:* responsibilities include maintaining a press list, acting as liaison with media, writing, reporting, proofreading, and editing. Candidates should have ability to work independently, computer skills, editing skills, oral communication skills, research skills, self-motivation, strong interpersonal skills, writing skills. Duration is 1 year. $2000 per month. ▶ *1–2 public policy fellows:* responsibilities include assisting with legislative alerts and informing legislators and key staff about population issues. Candidates should have ability to work independently, analytical skills, college courses in field, computer skills, oral communication skills, organizational skills, self-motivation, strong interpersonal skills, strong leadership ability. Duration is 1 year. $2000 per month. Open to college freshmen, college sophomores, college juniors, college seniors, recent college graduates, graduate students, those 21 to 25 years old only.

Benefits Formal training, names of contacts, on-the-job training, opportunity to attend seminars/workshops, willing to act as a professional reference, willing to complete paperwork for educational credit, willing to provide letters of recommendation, health and dental coverage, paid vacation, sick leave.

Contact Write, call, fax, e-mail, or through World Wide Web site Education Coordinator. Phone: 202-544-3300. Fax: 202-544-0068. E-mail: web@populationinstitute.org. In-person interview required. Applicants must submit a letter of interest, resume, academic transcripts, three letters of recommendation. Application deadline: April 15. World Wide Web: http://www.populationinstitute.org.

PROGRESSIVE ACTION NETWORK (EAST COAST AND MIDWEST INTERNS)
1341 G Street, NW, Suite 600
Washington, District of Columbia 20005

General Information Network providing stable funding for progressive political organizations, mobilizing mass numbers of people to participate in the political process, and developing activism and membership development careers. Established in 1978. Number of employees: 2. Number of internship applications received each year: 50.

Internships Available ▶ *25–50 field and phone outreach staff interns:* responsibilities include educating and fund-raising by phone or by doing neighborhood outreach; positions available in New Jersey, Minnesota, Washington, Iowa, Wisconsin, and Indiana. Candidates should have analytical skills, oral communication skills, personal interest in the field, self-motivation, strong interpersonal skills, ability to learn quickly, desire to work with people. Duration is minimum of 2 months. $9–$11 per hour, plus bonus (either full-time or part-time). Open to high school seniors, recent high school graduates, college freshmen, college sophomores, college juniors, college seniors, recent college graduates, graduate students, law students, career changers, individuals reentering the workforce.

Benefits Formal training, health insurance, opportunity to attend seminars/workshops, possible full-time employment, willing to act as a professional reference, willing to complete paperwork for educational credit, willing to provide letters of recommendation, relocation opportunity, career placement, reimbursement for job-related travel expenses.

Contact Write, fax, or e-mail Barbara Helmick, Executive Director. Phone: 202-624-1720. Fax: 202-737-9197. In-person interview recommended (telephone interview accepted). Applicants must submit other materials as listed in Web site. Applications are accepted continuously. World Wide Web: http://www.progressiveaction.org.

PUBLIC CITIZEN'S CONGRESS WATCH
215 Pennsylvania Avenue, SE
Washington, District of Columbia 20003

General Information Consumer organization concerned with lobbying, organizing, and researching consumer rights and government and corporate accountability. Established in 1971. Number of employees: 16. Unit of Public Citizen, Washington, District of Columbia. Number of internship applications received each year: 50.

Internships Available ▶ *2 field/grassroots interns.* Duration is 3–4 months. Unpaid. ▶ *1–2 research interns:* responsibilities include researching legislation, making phone calls to Congress, organizing conferences and rallies, and assisting with office duties. Candidates should have organizational skills, research skills. Duration is 3–4 months. Unpaid. Open to college freshmen, college sophomores, college juniors, college seniors, recent college graduates, graduate students, law students. International applications accepted.

Benefits Formal training, possible full-time employment, willing to complete paperwork for educational credit.

Contact Write, call, or fax Tamar Scialo, Executive Assistant. Phone: 202-454-5186. Fax: 202-547-7392. In-person interview recommended (telephone interview accepted). Applicants must submit a letter of interest, resume, writing sample. Applications are accepted continuously. World Wide Web: http://www.citizen.org.

PUBLIC CITIZEN'S CRITICAL MASS ENERGY PROJECT
215 Pennsylvania Avenue, SE
Washington, District of Columbia 20003

General Information Project that opposes nuclear power and promotes cleaner, safer energy alternatives, and sustainable agriculture; researches and writes studies on energy issues, food irradiation, and nuclear waste; lobbies Congress; monitors relevant federal and state agencies; initiates litigation; and works with press and citizen groups; also works against public water privatization. Established in 1974. Number of employees: 15. Unit of Public Citizen, Washington, District of Columbia. Number of internship applications received each year: 40.

Internships Available ▶ *2–4 interns:* responsibilities include researching and writing reports on energy-related food and water policy or legal matters, helping in a lobbying campaign, working with the media and/or providing assistance to local safe energy organizations, performing some administrative tasks, and helping with organizing. Candidates should have ability to work independently, computer skills, oral communication skills, organizational skills, personal interest in the field, research skills, self-motivation, strong interpersonal skills, strong leadership ability, writing skills, commitment to progressive causes. Duration is flexible. Position available as unpaid or paid. Open to college sophomores, college juniors, college seniors, recent college graduates, graduate students, law students, career changers, individuals reentering the workforce. International applications accepted.

Benefits Names of contacts, on-the-job training, opportunity to attend seminars/workshops, willing to complete paperwork for educational credit, willing to provide letters of recommendation.

Contact Write, fax, e-mail, or through World Wide Web site Dennis Roy, Internship Coordinator. Fax: 202-547-7392. E-mail: cmep@citizen.org. No phone calls. In-person interview recommended (telephone interview accepted). Applicants must submit a letter of interest, resume, writing sample. Applications are accepted continuously. World Wide Web: http://www.citizen.org/cmep.

PUBLIC POLICY DEPARTMENT OF THE GENERAL FEDERATION OF WOMEN'S CLUBS
1734 N Street, NW
Washington, District of Columbia 20036-0246

General Information Advocacy branch of GFWC. Number of employees: 1. Number of internship applications received each year: 45.

Internships Available ▶ *1–2 research assistants:* responsibilities include researching policy positions and gathering relevant materials; findings will be used by GFWC national committee to determine if resolutions need to be amended and updated; attending meetings with the department director. Candidates should have ability to work independently, analytical skills, computer skills, organizational skills, research skills, self-motivation, writing skills, strong background in political science. Duration is 1 semester. Unpaid. Open to college freshmen, college sophomores, college juniors, college seniors, recent college graduates, graduate students, law students, individuals reentering the workforce. International applications accepted.

Benefits Job counseling, names of contacts, on-the-job training, possible full-time employment, travel reimbursement, willing to act as a professional reference, willing to complete paperwork for educational credit, willing to provide letters of recommendation, small stipend commensurate with experience and availability.

Contact Call, fax, or e-mail Sarah Albert, Public Policy Director. Phone: 202-347-3168. Fax: 202-835-0246. E-mail: legislation@gfwc.org. Applicants must submit a letter of interest, resume, two personal references. Applications are accepted continuously. World Wide Web: http://www.gfwc.org.

QUAKER PEACE CENTRE
3 Rye Road
Cape Town 7700 South Africa

General Information Peace center. Established in 1988. Number of employees: 26. Number of internship applications received each year: 20.

Internships Available ▶ *Administrative/fieldwork interns.* Candidates should have computer skills, knowledge of field, office skills, organizational skills, personal interest in the field, strong interpersonal skills. Duration is 6–12 months. Unpaid. Open to recent college graduates, graduate students, career changers. International applications accepted.

Benefits Opportunity to attend seminars/workshops, willing to act as a professional reference, willing to provide letters of recommendation.

International Internships Available.

Contact Write or e-mail Miss Bonita Louis, Administrator. Fax: 27-021-686-8167. E-mail: bonita@qpc.org.za. No phone calls. Applicants must submit a formal organization application, letter of interest, resume. Applications are accepted continuously. World Wide Web: http://www.quaker.org/capetown/.

RAINFOREST RELIEF
338 Prospect Place
Brooklyn, New York 11238

General Information Rainforest preservation/conservation organization working to reduce the demand for rainforest-destructive materials through education and direct action. Established in 1989. Number of internship applications received each year: 20.

Internships Available ▶ *1–10 Banana Co-Op interns:* responsibilities include working with Banana Project coordinator to assist four Wöes in Talamanca, Costa Rica, with stabilizing their production and processing of organic, shade-grown bananas and banana products and finding markets. Candidates should have ability to work with others, oral communication skills, organizational skills, knowledge of Spanish (helpful). Duration is 1–12 months. Unpaid. Open to high school seniors, recent high school graduates, college freshmen, college sophomores, college juniors, college seniors, recent college graduates, graduate students, law students, career changers, individuals reentering the workforce. ▶ *National Waterfronts interns:* responsibilities include research planned and started waterfront construction projects around the country to prevent use of uncertified rainforest woods; contacting architects, planners, and municipal officials to help generate long-term policies. Candidates should have ability to work independently, computer skills, oral communication skills, research skills, self-motivation, written communication skills. Duration is 12 months. Unpaid. Open to college freshmen, college sophomores, college juniors, college seniors, recent college graduates, graduate students, law students, career changers, individuals reentering the workforce. ▶ *1 New Jersey waterfronts campaign assistant:* responsibilities include contacting all waterfront towns in NJ and working to convince them to pass policies to ban the use of unsustainable rainforest woods for boardwalking, piers, pilings, and bulkheads; organizing with other groups. Candidates should have ability to work independently, oral communication skills, organizational skills, self-motivation, strong interpersonal skills, written communication skills. Duration is 3–6 months. Unpaid. Open to recent high school graduates, college freshmen, college sophomores, college juniors, college seniors, recent college graduates, graduate students, career changers, individuals reentering the workforce. ▶ *1–3 New York City: Campaign Assistants:* responsibilities include assisting director with campaign to end the use of unsustainable rainforest woods by NYC; organizing in schools; projects; letter campaigns; outreach; meetings. Candidates should have ability to work independently, oral communication skills, organizational skills, strong interpersonal skills, strong leadership ability. Duration is 6–12 months. Unpaid. Open to recent high school graduates, college freshmen, college sophomores, college juniors, college seniors, recent college graduates, graduate students, career changers, individuals reentering the workforce. ▶ *1–2 graphics interns:* responsibilities include working with director to design, produce, and print brochures, pamphlets, buttons, stickers, and other graphic pieces. Candidates should have ability to work independently, ability to work with others, computer skills, self-motivation, graphic and design experience. Duration is 3–12 months. Unpaid. Open to high school students, recent high school graduates, college freshmen, college sophomores, college juniors, college seniors, recent college graduates, graduate students, career changers, individuals reentering the workforce. ▶ *1 import-export data intern:* responsibilities include compiling and organizing data obtained through imports database on rainforest wood imports by company name, location, species, and products; generating reports. Candidates should have ability to work independently, computer skills, organizational skills, research skills, self-motivation, writing skills. Duration is 3–6 months. Unpaid. Open to high school seniors, recent high school graduates, college freshmen, college sophomores, college juniors, college seniors, recent college graduates, gradu-

Rainforest Relief (continued)

ate students, career changers, individuals reentering the workforce. ▶ *1 media intern:* responsibilities include assisting director in "marketing" positions on rainforest destruction to newspapers, magazines, home improvement programs, and other media; keeping track of articles/videotapes. Candidates should have ability to work independently, oral communication skills, research skills, self-motivation, strong interpersonal skills, written communication skills. Duration is 3–6 months. Unpaid. Open to recent high school graduates, college freshmen, college sophomores, college juniors, college seniors, recent college graduates, graduate students, career changers, individuals reentering the workforce. ▶ *1–2 office manager's assistants:* responsibilities include clerical work, organizing the office, light bookkeeping, responding to information requests, organizing meetings, scheduling and booking presentations. Candidates should have computer skills, office skills, oral communication skills, strong interpersonal skills, written communication skills. Duration is 6–12 months. Unpaid. Open to high school seniors, recent high school graduates, college freshmen, college sophomores, college juniors, college seniors, recent college graduates, graduate students, career changers, individuals reentering the workforce. ▶ *1–2 presentations coordinators:* responsibilities include assisting director (and later other presenters) in outreach for presentations in schools, colleges, and community groups; keeping track of scheduled presentations and donations. Candidates should have oral communication skills, organizational skills, self-motivation, strong interpersonal skills, written communication skills. Duration is 3–12 months. Unpaid. Open to high school students, recent high school graduates, college freshmen, college sophomores, college juniors, college seniors, recent college graduates, graduate students, career changers, individuals reentering the workforce. ▶ *4 set construction interns:* responsibilities include researching and identifying rainforest plywood used for set construction in NYC and school theaters nationwide; working with construction unions, producers, and directors to end the practice. Candidates should have ability to work independently, computer skills, oral communication skills, self-motivation, strong interpersonal skills, written communication skills. Duration is 6–12 months. Unpaid. Open to high school students, recent high school graduates, college freshmen, college sophomores, college juniors, college seniors, recent college graduates, graduate students, career changers, individuals reentering the workforce. ▶ *2–3 special events assistants:* responsibilities include working with director and development staff to help coordinate special events; marketing events via the media and outreach to businesses, the community, and donors; organizing volunteers for the event. Candidates should have ability to work with others, computer skills, oral communication skills, self-motivation, strong leadership ability. Duration is 6–12 months. Unpaid. Open to high school seniors, recent high school graduates, college freshmen, college sophomores, college juniors, college seniors, recent college graduates, career changers, individuals reentering the workforce. ▶ *1–5 telephone outreach interns:* responsibilities include calling people who have expressed an interest in organization and converting them to "Member" status. Candidates should have ability to work independently, ability to work with others, oral communication skills, self-motivation, good phone skills. Duration is 1–12 months. Position available as unpaid or paid. Open to high school students, recent high school graduates, college freshmen, college sophomores, college juniors, college seniors, recent college graduates, career changers, individuals reentering the workforce. International applications accepted.

Benefits Names of contacts, on-the-job training, opportunity to attend seminars/workshops, possible full-time employment, travel reimbursement, willing to act as a professional reference, willing to complete paperwork for educational credit, willing to provide letters of recommendation, possibility of part-time employment, free meals at office.

International Internships Available in Costa Rica; Quito, Ecuador; Kalimantan, Indonesia; Milan, Italy.

Contact Write, call, fax, or e-mail Tim Keating, Executive Director, PO Box 150566, Brooklyn, New York 11215. Phone: 718-398-3760. Fax: 718-398-3760. E-mail: relief@igc.org. In-person interview recommended (telephone interview accepted). Applicants must

submit a letter of interest, resume. Applications are accepted continuously. World Wide Web: http://www.rainforestrelief.org.

RELIGIOUS ACTION CENTER OF REFORM JUDAISM
2027 Massachusetts Avenue, NW
Washington, District of Columbia 20036

General Information Organization that advocates social justice and religious liberty, serves as a Reform Jewish movement advocate in the nation's capital, and monitors legislation of concern to American Jewish communities. Established in 1961. Number of employees: 20. Unit of Union of American Hebrew Congregations, New York, New York. Number of internship applications received each year: 30.

Internships Available ▶ *5 legislative assistants:* responsibilities include representing the Center in various coalitions, monitoring legislation, participating in visits to offices of senators and representatives, preparing educational and programmatic materials for congregations, and performing administrative work. Candidates should have ability to work with others, personal interest in the field, plan to pursue career in field, self-motivation, strong leadership ability, written communication skills. Duration is 1 year. $1700 per month. Open to recent college graduates. International applications accepted.

Benefits Health insurance, names of contacts, opportunity to attend seminars/workshops, travel reimbursement, willing to act as a professional reference, willing to provide letters of recommendation.

Contact Write, call, fax, e-mail, or through World Wide Web site Barbara Weinstein, Legislative Director. Phone: 202-387-2800. Fax: 202-667-9070. E-mail: bweinstein@uahc.org. Applicants must submit a formal organization application, resume, academic transcripts, writing sample, two letters of recommendation. Application deadline: March 15. World Wide Web: http://www.rac.org.

RESOURCE CENTER FOR NONVIOLENCE
515 Broadway
Santa Cruz, California 95060

General Information Organization that offers a wide-ranging educational program in the history, theory, methodology, and current practice of nonviolence as a source for personal and social change. Established in 1976. Number of employees: 7. Unit of Eschaton Foundation, Santa Cruz, California. Number of internship applications received each year: 20.

Internships Available ▶ *2–6 interns:* responsibilities include engaging in personal study, planning and directing the program, participating in events, and working on community education in the theory and practice of nonviolence. Candidates should have ability to work independently, analytical skills, computer skills, knowledge of field, oral communication skills, organizational skills, personal interest in the field, self-motivation, strong interpersonal skills, strong leadership ability, written communication skills. Duration is flexible. Unpaid. Open to college sophomores, college juniors, college seniors, recent college graduates, graduate students, career changers. International applications accepted.

Benefits Job counseling, names of contacts, on-the-job training, opportunity to attend seminars/workshops, willing to act as a professional reference, willing to complete paperwork for educational credit, willing to provide letters of recommendation.

Contact Write, call, fax, e-mail, or through World Wide Web site Intern Coordinator. Phone: 831-423-1626. Fax: 831-423-8716. E-mail: intern@rcnv.org. In-person interview recommended (telephone interview accepted). Applicants must submit a formal organization application, two letters of recommendation, essay question. Applications are accepted continuously. World Wide Web: http://www.rcnv.org.

RESULTS
440 First Street, NW, Suite 450
Washington, District of Columbia 20001

General Information Grassroots citizens lobbying group working to create the political will to end hunger and poverty. Established in 1980. Number of employees: 20. Number of internship applications received each year: 50.

Internships Available ▶ *1 administrative intern:* responsibilities include office support, communications, lobbying, and research. Candidates should have ability to work with others, analytical skills, computer skills, editing skills, office skills, organizational skills, research skills, self-motivation, writing skills. Duration is flexible. Unpaid. ▶ *1 conference intern:* responsibilities include supporting the annual Washington conference for volunteers. Candidates should have computer skills, office skills, organizational skills, self-motivation, strong interpersonal skills, writing skills. Duration is 1 summer or spring. Unpaid. ▶ *1 development intern:* responsibilities include research into fund-raising and compiling material for donors. Candidates should have computer skills, office skills, oral communication skills, organizational skills, writing skills. Duration is flexible. Unpaid. ▶ *1 domestic legislative intern:* responsibilities include researching and grass roots support. Candidates should have ability to work with others, computer skills, editing skills, oral communication skills, organizational skills, research skills, writing skills. Duration is flexible. Unpaid. ▶ *1 global legislative intern:* responsibilities include research and grassroots support. Candidates should have ability to work with others, computer skills, editing skills, oral communication skills, organizational skills, research skills, writing skills. Duration is flexible. Unpaid. Open to college freshmen, college sophomores, college juniors, college seniors, graduate students. International applications accepted.

Benefits Formal training, on-the-job training, travel reimbursement, willing to act as a professional reference, willing to complete paperwork for educational credit, willing to provide letters of recommendation, possible health insurance, possibility of small stipend.

Contact Write, call, fax, e-mail, or through World Wide Web site Internship Coordinator, 440 First Street, NW, Suite 450, Washington, District of Columbia 20001. Phone: 202-783-7100. Fax: 202-783-2818. E-mail: results@results.org. Applicants must submit a letter of interest, resume, writing sample. Applications are accepted continuously. World Wide Web: http://www.resultsusa.org.

THE RUTHERFORD INSTITUTE
PO Box 7482
Charlottesville, Virginia 22906-7482

General Information Nonprofit, legal, and educational civil liberties organization specializing in the defense of constitutional and human rights. Established in 1982. Number of employees: 25. Number of internship applications received each year: 40.

Internships Available ▶ *5 summer interns:* responsibilities include participation in an intensive course in constitutional law and providing research and writing for litigation in state and federal courts and for educational resources. Candidates should have ability to work independently, analytical skills, computer skills, editing skills, organizational skills, personal interest in the field, plan to pursue career in field, research skills, self-motivation, written communication skills. Duration is 8–10 weeks. Position available as unpaid or at $200–$400 per week. Open to law students.

Benefits On-the-job training, travel reimbursement, willing to act as a professional reference, willing to complete paperwork for educational credit, willing to provide letters of recommendation, housing stipend of $300 per month.

Contact Write, call, fax, or e-mail Candice Mills Jones, Internship Program Coordinator, PO Box 7482, Charlottesville, Virginia 22906-7482. Phone: 434-978-3888. Fax: 434-978-1789. E-mail: candicej@rutherford.org. Applicants must submit a letter of interest, resume, writing sample, two personal references. Application deadline: February 14 for 1st-year law students, November 15 for 2nd- and 3rd-year law students. World Wide Web: http://www.rutherford.org.

SEATTLE YOUTH INVOLVEMENT NETWORK
2017 East Spruce Street
Seattle, Washington 98122

General Information Organization that advocates for youth in order to create positive changes in the community through civic involvement, leadership development, and volunteer service. Established in 1992. Number of employees: 4. Number of internship applications received each year: 8.

Internships Available ▶ *1–2 fund-raising interns:* responsibilities include assisting with grant writing, special events, and other fund-raising activities. Candidates should have ability to work independently, computer skills, office skills, organizational skills, strong interpersonal skills, writing skills, some interest or experience in fund-raising. Duration is flexible. $7 per hour. Open to high school students. ▶ *1 program intern:* responsibilities include working with youth to design and implement forums, service projects, publications, and activities in the community. Candidates should have ability to work independently, computer skills, organizational skills, strong interpersonal skills, strong leadership ability, written communication skills. Duration is flexible. $7.01 per hour. Open to high school students only.

Benefits Names of contacts, on-the-job training, possible full-time employment, willing to act as a professional reference, willing to complete paperwork for educational credit, willing to provide letters of recommendation.

Contact Write, fax, e-mail, or through World Wide Web site Liz Vivian, Executive Director, 2017 East Spruce Street, Seattle, Washington 98122. Fax: 206-323-8731. E-mail: liz@seattleyouth.org. No phone calls. In-person interview recommended (telephone interview accepted). Applicants must submit a letter of interest, resume, criminal records check required. Applications are accepted continuously. World Wide Web: http://www.seattleyouth.org.

SELF-HELP CREDIT UNION
301 West Main Street
Durham, North Carolina 27701

General Information Organization that creates ownership and wealth-building opportunities among North Carolina's disadvantaged populations through loans to home and business owners. Established in 1980. Number of employees: 100. Number of internship applications received each year: 75.

Internships Available ▶ *Charter school interns:* responsibilities include assisting with evaluation of financial data and maintenance of databases; research projects targeted to "business side" of charter schools; projects related to federal and state funding sources, energy efficiency projects, and educational management organizations. Candidates should have ability to work independently, ability to work with others, analytical skills, computer skills, knowledge of field, oral communication skills, written communication skills, understanding of lending and the public education sector/charter school industry. Duration is 8 to 10 weeks in the summer. Position available as unpaid or at $12 per hour. Open to graduate students. ▶ *Commercial generalist interns:* responsibilities include assisting loan officers on small business loan transactions related to Self-Help's community development mission, providing support for the development of an internal resource guide on lending policies and procedures, compiling and tracking historical and future data regarding loan inquiries, and project to determine how much time spent in pre-post-approval processing by loan officer. Candidates should have ability to work independently, computer skills, knowledge of field, organizational skills, some Spanish skills. Duration is 8 to 10 weeks in the summer. Position available as unpaid or at $10 per hour for undergraduates; $12 per hour for graduate students. Open to college seniors, recent college graduates, graduate students. ▶ *Community facilities fund interns:* responsibilities include extensive research, analysis, data compilation, and reporting; researching and developing markets for Community Facility Fund in area of child-care lending. Candidates should have ability to work independently, ability to work with others, analytical skills, computer skills, knowledge of field, oral communication skills, research skills, written communication skills. Duration is 8 to 10 weeks in the summer. Position available as unpaid or at $10–$12 per hour. Open to college sophomores, college juniors, college seniors, graduate students.

Self-Help Credit Union (continued)

▶ *Credit union operations interns:* responsibilities include reviewing and upgrading "disaster recovery" plan, assisting in providing quality service to customers, and some clerical and administrative duties as needed; developing, distributing, collecting, and summarizing deposit and loan customer service survey; assisting information and technology team. Candidates should have ability to work independently, ability to work with others, computer skills, office skills, oral communication skills, writing skills, strong attention to detail. Duration is 8 to 10 weeks in the summer. Position available as unpaid or at $10 per hour. Open to college juniors, college seniors. ▶ *Information services interns:* responsibilities include serving in support role to IT, troubleshooting network and printing problems, Web design, and Internet research. Candidates should have ability to work independently, ability to work with others, college courses in field, knowledge of field, experience in Win NT, MS Access, UNIX, and programming. Duration is 8 to 10 weeks in the summer. Position available as unpaid or at $10–$12 per hour. Open to college juniors, college seniors, graduate students. ▶ *New market interns:* responsibilities include providing research for the New Market Tax Credit program (currently under development at Self-Help), investigating and implementing procedures for updating mailing lists, and updating filing procedures; researching, developing, and refining business plans for target markets. Candidates should have ability to work independently, ability to work with others, analytical skills, computer skills, knowledge of field, oral communication skills, organizational skills, research skills, written communication skills, ability to perform interviews with customers. Duration is 8 to 10 weeks in the summer. Position available as unpaid or at $12 per hour. Open to graduate students, graduates in business, law, public policy, or planning. ▶ *Predatory legal research and policy interns:* responsibilities include research and writing position papers, researching abusive lending practices through literature searches, and researching and writing in support of regulatory and legislative agendas. Candidates should have ability to work independently, ability to work with others, analytical skills, knowledge of field, oral communication skills, organizational skills, research skills, self-motivation, written communication skills. Duration is 8-10 weeks in the summer. Position available as unpaid or at $12 per hour. Open to law students, 1-L's (welcome to apply). ▶ *Predatory lending policy interns:* responsibilities include assisting with predatory lending campaign in NC, communicating with media, assisting with press events, outreach to ally groups, some database work, and developing Web materials. Candidates should have ability to work independently, analytical skills, computer skills, oral communication skills, organizational skills, research skills, strong interpersonal skills, written communication skills. Duration is 8 to 10 weeks in the summer. Position available as unpaid or at $10 per hour. Open to college freshmen, college sophomores, college juniors, college seniors, graduate students. ▶ *Predatory lending research interns:* responsibilities include conducting research in home mortgage market, performing statistical analysis, and developing reports with predatory lending policy implications. Candidates should have ability to work independently, ability to work with others, analytical skills, computer skills, knowledge of field, oral communication skills, organizational skills, research skills, self-motivation, written communication skills. Duration is 8 to 10 weeks in the summer. Position available as unpaid or at $12 per hour. Open to graduate students, graduates in public policy, business, economics, or planning. ▶ *Real estate development interns:* responsibilities include assisting the project coordinator and marketing director in everyday duties, researching elderly housing development options, preparing an application for a national housing grant program, enhancement of Web site, developing home buyer satisfaction survey, and performing various commercial real estate tasks as needed. Candidates should have ability to work independently, ability to work with others, computer skills, knowledge of field, oral communication skills, organizational skills, research skills, self-motivation, written communication skills, active interest in community development and real estate. Duration is 8 to 10 weeks in the summer. Position available as unpaid or at $10–$12 per hour. Open to college seniors, graduate students, graduates in business, public policy, law, or regional/city planning. ▶ *Resource/policy research interns:*

responsibilities include conducting impact survey, researching borrowers, analyzing data and writing borrower case histories, updating media contacts database, and developing system for chronicling self-help presentation and honors awards. Candidates should have ability to work independently, ability to work with others, computer skills, knowledge of field, organizational skills, research skills. Duration is 8 to 10 weeks in the summer. Position available as unpaid or at $12 per hour. Open to graduate students. ▶ *Sustainable development interns:* responsibilities include assisting with urban or rural sustainable development efforts through research, marketing, and networking; assisting commercial team to more effectively reach sustainable businesses as loan customers. Candidates should have ability to work independently, knowledge of field, research skills, writing skills, active interest in the relationship between the environment and economic development. Duration is 8 to 10 weeks in the summer. Position available as unpaid or at $12 per hour. Open to graduates in city/regional planning, MBA, law, or public policy (preferred).
Benefits On-the-job training, possible full-time employment, willing to complete paperwork for educational credit, willing to provide letters of recommendation.
Contact Write, e-mail, or through World Wide Web site Internship Program, PO Box 3619, Durham, North Carolina 27701. E-mail: internships@self-help.org. No phone calls. In-person interview required. Applicants must submit a letter of interest, resume, writing sample. Applications are accepted continuously. World Wide Web: http://www.self-help.org.

SOUTHEAST ASIA RESOURCE ACTION CENTER (SEARAC)
1628 16th Street, NW, 3rd Floor
Washington, District of Columbia 20009-3099

General Information National capacity-building and advocacy organization for Americans of Cambodian, Laotian, and Vietnamese descent. Established in 1979. Number of employees: 6. Number of internship applications received each year: 20.
Internships Available ▶ *1 intern:* responsibilities include conducting research, assisting public education and advocacy efforts, responding to requests for information, attending public meetings, contributing articles for publication, and administrative duties. Candidates should have computer skills, research skills, self-motivation, strong interpersonal skills, written communication skills, multicultural sensitivity, interest in community and public service, knowledge of Southeast Asia, knowledge of immigrant issues. Duration is 1–2 semesters. Unpaid. Open to college sophomores, college juniors, college seniors, recent college graduates, graduate students, law students, career changers, individuals reentering the workforce. International applications accepted.
Benefits Job counseling, names of contacts, on-the-job training, opportunity to attend seminars/workshops, willing to act as a professional reference, willing to complete paperwork for educational credit, willing to provide letters of recommendation.
Contact Write, call, fax, e-mail, or through World Wide Web site Ms. Eloise Needleman, Administrative Manager. Phone: 202-667-4690. Fax: 202-667-6449. E-mail: searac@searac.org. In-person interview recommended (telephone interview accepted). Applicants must submit a formal organization application, letter of interest, resume, writing sample. Applications are accepted continuously. World Wide Web: http://www.searac.org.

SPEAK OUT
PO Box 99096
Emeryville, California 94662

General Information Nonprofit national speakers and artists agency providing 200 speakers and artists who address issues of social, economic, and political justice, working primarily through campuses and community groups. Established in 1990. Number of employees: 5. Affiliate of Institute for Democratic Education and Culture, Oakland, California. Number of internship applications received each year: 10.
Internships Available ▶ *2 interns:* responsibilities include working alongside staff members on specific projects, setting up speak-

ing engagements, coordinating tour schedules, working on publicity campaigns and grant writing, and performing some basic office work. Candidates should have ability to work independently, computer skills, office skills, oral communication skills, writing skills. Duration is minimum of one month commitment. Unpaid. Open to high school students, recent high school graduates, college freshmen, college sophomores, college juniors, college seniors. **Benefits** Names of contacts, on-the-job training, willing to act as a professional reference, willing to complete paperwork for educational credit, willing to provide letters of recommendation. **Contact** Write, call, fax, e-mail, or through World Wide Web site Lolan Sevilla, Program Coordinator. Phone: 510-601-0182. Fax: 510-601-0183. E-mail: speakout@igc.org. Applicants must submit a formal organization application, letter of interest, resume, writing sample, letter of recommendation. Applications are accepted continuously. World Wide Web: http://www.speakersandartists.org.

STUDENT ACTION WITH FARMWORKERS
1317 West Pettigrew Street
Durham, North Carolina 27705

General Information Social justice, nonprofit organization linking students and farmworkers to learn about each others lives, share resources and skills, and improve conditions for farmworkers. Established in 1992. Number of employees: 6. Number of internship applications received each year: 90.
Internships Available ▶ *30 Into the Fields Program interns:* responsibilities include teaching English as a second language, health education, mentoring and tutoring, legal assistance, immigration assistance (depends on placement preferences). Candidates should have analytical skills, oral communication skills, organizational skills, personal interest in the field, strong interpersonal skills, bilingual ability (Spanish and English). Duration is June 1 to August 10. $1200 per duration of internship. Open to college freshmen, college sophomores, college juniors, college seniors, recent college graduates, graduate students, law students. International applications accepted.
Benefits Formal training, free housing, job counseling, names of contacts, on-the-job training, opportunity to attend seminars/ workshops, travel reimbursement, tuition assistance, willing to act as a professional reference, willing to complete paperwork for educational credit, willing to provide letters of recommendation, $1500 scholarship.
Contact Call, e-mail, or through World Wide Web site Libby Manley, Program Director. Phone: 919-660-3652. Fax: 919-681-7600. E-mail: levante@duke.edu. In-person interview recommended (telephone interview accepted). Applicants must submit a formal organization application, resume, two personal references, personal statement. Application deadline: February 10 for summer. Fees: $15. World Wide Web: http://www.saf-unite.org.

STUDENT PUGWASH USA
2029 P Street, Suite 301
Washington, District of Columbia 20036

General Information National, nonprofit educational organization that provides a wide range of activities for university and select high school students to promote the socially responsible application of science and technology. Established in 1979. Number of employees: 2. Number of internship applications received each year: 15.
Internships Available ▶ *1–2 editorial/research interns:* responsibilities include researching science, technology, and society issues; producing and publishing one to two issue brief(s); compiling resource materials; and assisting staff with Web site maintenance. Candidates should have computer skills, research skills, self-motivation, strong interpersonal skills, writing skills. Duration is 3–4 months. Unpaid. ▶ *1–2 marketing/communications interns:* responsibilities include assisting with research for and design of outreach and program materials; designing program and event posters and flyers; and managing database of media contacts, members, and organizations. Candidates should have college courses in field, computer skills, organizational skills, research skills, self-motivation, written communication skills. Duration is 3–4 months. Unpaid. ▶ *1–2 student organizer interns:* responsibili-

ties include helping plan and organize national conference; researching science, technology, and society issues; providing general support for nationwide chapter program; possibility of publishing issue brief. Candidates should have computer skills, personal interest in the field, research skills, self-motivation, strong interpersonal skills, written communication skills. Duration is 3-4 months (year-round). Unpaid. Open to college freshmen, college sophomores, college juniors, college seniors, recent college graduates, graduate students, law students. International applications accepted.
Benefits Formal training, job counseling, names of contacts, opportunity to attend seminars/workshops, possible full-time employment, willing to complete paperwork for educational credit, willing to provide letters of recommendation.
Contact Write, call, fax, e-mail, or through World Wide Web site Susan Veres, Executive Director. Phone: 202-429-8900. Fax: 202-429-8905. E-mail: spusa@spusa.org. In-person interview recommended (telephone interview accepted). Applicants must submit a letter of interest, resume, writing sample. Application deadline: May 15 for summer, August 16 for fall, December 13 for spring. World Wide Web: http://www.spusa.org/pugwash/.

THIRD MILLENNIUM: ADVOCATES FOR THE FUTURE, INC.
330 West 38th Street, Suite 1705
New York, New York 10018

General Information National, nonprofit advocacy and educational organization started by young Americans concerned about the long-term future of the U.S.; purpose is to redirect America's political focus from the next election cycle to the next generation cycle, addressing the issues of the national debt, crime, the environment, race relations, and health care from a generational perspective. Established in 1993. Number of employees: 3. Number of internship applications received each year: 15.
Internships Available ▶ *2 general interns:* responsibilities include researching grants, writing press releases, researching congressional testimony, and administrative work. Candidates should have ability to work independently, oral communication skills, personal interest in the field, research skills, self-motivation, written communication skills. Duration is flexible. Unpaid. Open to college freshmen, college sophomores, college juniors, college seniors, recent college graduates.
Benefits Names of contacts, opportunity to attend seminars/workshops, possible full-time employment, travel reimbursement, willing to act as a professional reference, willing to complete paperwork for educational credit, willing to provide letters of recommendation, opportunity to write op-ed pieces and meet future leaders.
Contact Write, call, fax, or e-mail Cindy Ng, Director of Operations, Third Millennium, 330 West 38th Street, Suite 1705, New York, New York 10018. Phone: 212-760-4240. Fax: 212-760-8102. E-mail: cindyng@thirdmil.org. Applicants must submit a letter of interest, resume. Applications are accepted continuously. World Wide Web: http://www.thirdmil.org.

TOXICS ACTION CENTER
29 Temple Place
Boston, Massachusetts 02111

General Information Organization that provides organizing assistance to neighborhood groups battling toxics and pollution in their communities. Number of employees: 5. Number of internship applications received each year: 35.
Internships Available ▶ *1–3 Nuke-Free New England interns:* responsibilities include working to pressure utility and government officials to close down nuclear power plants; (internships also available in Portland, ME and West Hartford, CT). Candidates should have oral communication skills, organizational skills, personal interest in the field, self-motivation, strong interpersonal skills, written communication skills. Duration is flexible. Position available as unpaid or paid. Open to college freshmen, college sophomores, college juniors, college seniors, recent college graduates, graduate students, law students. ▶ *1 Web page intern:* responsibilities include helping set up and manage organization's

Toxics Action Center (continued)

Web page, establishing links to other sites and publicizing resources to grassroots groups. Candidates should have computer skills, oral communication skills, organizational skills, personal interest in the field, self-motivation, written communication skills. Duration is flexible. Position available as unpaid or paid. Open to college freshmen, college sophomores, college juniors, college seniors, recent college graduates, graduate students, law students. ▶ *3 conference interns:* responsibilities include working with staff to set up training conferences for local activists in MA, CT, and ME; (internships also available in Portland, ME and West Hartford, CT). Candidates should have ability to work with others, oral communication skills, personal interest in the field, self-motivation, written communication skills. Duration is flexible. Position available as unpaid or paid. Open to college freshmen, college sophomores, college juniors, college seniors, recent college graduates, graduate students, law students. ▶ *1 legal manual intern:* responsibilities include researching and preparing a manual to guide over 400 neighborhood groups that are battling toxic pollution in their communities in legal and organizational matters. Candidates should have ability to work independently, organizational skills, personal interest in the field, self-motivation, writing skills. Duration is flexible. Position available as unpaid or paid. Open to graduate students, law students. ▶ *1–3 pesticides interns:* responsibilities include working with community activists to help stop pesticide exposure from agricultural sources, right-of-way spraying, and use by municipalities; (internships also available in Portland, ME and West Hartford (CT). Candidates should have oral communication skills, organizational skills, personal interest in the field, self-motivation, strong interpersonal skills, written communication skills. Duration is flexible. Position available as unpaid or paid. Open to college freshmen, college sophomores, college juniors, college seniors, recent college graduates, graduate students, law students. ▶ *1–2 recycling interns:* responsibilities include working with residents to develop and implement effective municipal recycling campaigns. Candidates should have oral communication skills, organizational skills, personal interest in the field, self-motivation, strong interpersonal skills, written communication skills. Duration is flexible. Position available as unpaid or paid. Open to college freshmen, college sophomores, college juniors, college seniors, recent college graduates, graduate students, law students. International applications accepted.

Benefits Names of contacts, on-the-job training, opportunity to attend seminars/workshops, possible full-time employment, willing to act as a professional reference, willing to complete paperwork for educational credit, willing to provide letters of recommendation, possibility of small stipend.

Contact Write, call, fax, or through World Wide Web site Heidi Blankenship, Administrator. Phone: 617-292-4821. Fax: 617-292-8057. Applicants must submit a letter of interest, resume. Applications are accepted continuously. World Wide Web: http://www.toxicsaction.org.

TRAPROCK PEACE CENTER
103A Keets Road
Deerfield, Massachusetts 01342

General Information Local and regional peace education center. Established in 1979. Number of employees: 2. Number of internship applications received each year: 5.

Internships Available ▶ *1–2 community organizer interns:* responsibilities include phone calls, flyering, planning and organizing events, general office work, maintenance, visiting schools and festivals. Candidates should have ability to work independently, computer skills, oral communication skills, personal interest in the field, strong interpersonal skills, written communication skills. Duration is 3 months. Unpaid. Open to college freshmen, college sophomores, college juniors, college seniors, recent college graduates, graduate students, career changers, individuals reentering the workforce. International applications accepted.

Benefits Free housing, names of contacts, on-the-job training, opportunity to attend seminars/workshops, willing to act as a professional reference, willing to provide letters of recommendation.

Contact Write or through World Wide Web site Sunny Miller, Director. Phone: 413-773-7427. In-person interview recommended

(telephone interview accepted). Applicants must submit a letter of interest, resume, two personal references, two letters of recommendation. Applications are accepted continuously. World Wide Web: http://www.traprockpeace.org.

20/20 VISION
1828 Jefferson Place, NW
Washington, District of Columbia 20036

General Information Nonprofit lobbying and citizen education organization whose goal is to revitalize democracy by creating persistent, strategic citizen action, persuading decision-makers to protect the earth by preserving the environment and promoting disarmament. Established in 1986. Number of employees: 8. Number of internship applications received each year: 200.

Internships Available ▶ *1–3 outreach interns:* responsibilities include assisting with general office responsibilities and working on specific projects within the legislation, media, field, development, promotion, and membership departments as priorities dictate. Candidates should have ability to work independently, editing skills, oral communication skills, personal interest in the field, research skills, self-motivation, strong interpersonal skills, writing skills. Duration is 2-3 months minimum. Position available as unpaid or paid. Open to college freshmen, college sophomores, college juniors, college seniors, recent college graduates, graduate students. International applications accepted.

Benefits Job counseling, names of contacts, opportunity to attend seminars/workshops, travel reimbursement, willing to complete paperwork for educational credit, willing to provide letters of recommendation.

Contact Write, call, fax, e-mail, or through World Wide Web site Rebecca Zimmerman, Peace and Environment Fellow. Phone: 202-833-2020. Fax: 202-833-5307. E-mail: vision@2020vision.org. In-person interview recommended (telephone interview accepted). Applicants must submit a letter of interest, resume, writing sample. Applications are accepted continuously. World Wide Web: http://www.2020vision.org.

U.S.–ASIA INSTITUTE
232 East Capitol Street, NE
Washington, District of Columbia 20003

General Information Private, non-governmental organization that promotes dialogue on international issues of common interest to the United States and participating Asian nations. Established in 1979. Number of employees: 5. Number of internship applications received each year: 80.

Internships Available ▶ *1–2 staff assistants:* responsibilities include assisting staff in organizing various programs; performing research and office work; attending and reporting on congressional hearings, seminars, and workshops. Candidates should have editing skills, knowledge of field, office skills, personal interest in the field, research skills, self-motivation. Duration is 3 months minimum (preferred). Unpaid. Open to college juniors, college seniors, recent college graduates, graduate students. International applications accepted.

Benefits Opportunity to attend seminars/workshops, willing to complete paperwork for educational credit, willing to provide letters of recommendation.

Contact Write, call, fax, or e-mail Joji Konoshima, President. Phone: 202-544-3181. Fax: 202-543-1748. E-mail: usasiai@aol.com. In-person interview recommended (telephone interview accepted). Applicants must submit a letter of interest, resume, academic transcripts, cover letter, 1 writing sample (3-5 pages). Applications are accepted continuously.

U.S. PUBLIC INTEREST RESEARCH GROUP (PIRG)
218 D Street, SE
Washington, District of Columbia 20003

General Information National lobbying office for network of statewide consumer, environmental, and campaign finance reform public interest watchdog organizations. Established in 1983. Number of employees: 35. Number of internship applications received each year: 100.

Internships Available ▶ *1–2 administrative interns:* responsibilities include working with administrative director on day-to-day management of the organization including computer systems, filing systems, publications, and other administrative tasks. Candidates should have ability to work independently, ability to work with others, computer skills, office skills, oral communication skills, written communication skills. Duration is 1 semester. Unpaid. Open to college freshmen, college sophomores, college juniors, college seniors, recent college graduates. ▶ *1–3 campaign interns:* responsibilities include coordinating media events, coordinating grassroots campaign activities, and working with campaign offices across the United States. Candidates should have ability to work independently, oral communication skills, organizational skills, strong interpersonal skills, written communication skills. Duration is 1 semester. Unpaid. Open to college freshmen, college sophomores, college juniors, college seniors, recent college graduates. ▶ *4–8 legislative interns:* responsibilities include conducting research, preparing investigative reports, coordinating media events, coordinating grassroots campaigns, monitoring legislation, and coordinating coalitions. Candidates should have ability to work independently, ability to work with others, oral communication skills, organizational skills, self-motivation, written communication skills. Duration is 1 semester. Unpaid. Open to college freshmen, college sophomores, college juniors, college seniors, recent college graduates, graduate students, law students. International applications accepted.
Benefits Opportunity to attend seminars/workshops, possible full-time employment, willing to act as a professional reference, willing to complete paperwork for educational credit, willing to provide letters of recommendation, various training sessions, brown bag lunch discussions; will be part of campus work-study programs.
Contact Write, call, fax, or e-mail Rick Trilsch, Intern Coordinator. Phone: 202-546-9707 Ext. 312. Fax: 202-546-2461. E-mail: uspirg@pirg.org. In-person interview recommended (telephone interview accepted). Applicants must submit a letter of interest, resume, 1–3 page writing sample. Applications are accepted continuously. World Wide Web: http://www.uspirg.org.

VANGUARD COMMUNICATIONS
2121 K Street, NW, Suite 300
Washington, District of Columbia 20037

General Information Company that develops and implements advocacy communications campaigns to help resolve the world's most pressing problems. Established in 1987. Number of employees: 31. Number of internship applications received each year: 50.
Internships Available ▶ *Interns:* responsibilities include drafting and distributing press releases, monitoring client news coverage, media database maintenance, assisting in news release production, contacting reporters, editing correspondence, and assisting office personnel. Candidates should have office skills, oral communication skills, strong interpersonal skills, written communication skills, previous work/internships experience and knowledge of Microsoft Word (preferred), major in mass communications, public relations, journalism, or related subject required. Duration is 6–8 weeks. Unpaid. Open to college freshmen, college sophomores, college juniors, college seniors, graduate students. International applications accepted.
Benefits On-the-job training, willing to complete paperwork for educational credit, reimbursement for Metro expenses.
Contact Write, fax, or e-mail Tracy Ferrell, Internship Coordinator. Fax: 202-331-9420. E-mail: tferrell@vancomm.com. No phone calls. In-person interview recommended (telephone interview accepted). Applicants must submit a resume, two writing samples, cover letter. Applications are accepted continuously. World Wide Web: http://www.vancomm.com.

THE VEGETARIAN RESOURCE GROUP
PO Box 1463
Baltimore, Maryland 21203

General Information Public interest group that educates the public about the various aspects of vegetarianism, including health, environment, and ethics. Established in 1982. Number of employees: 8. Number of internship applications received each year: 20.
Internships Available ▶ *1–4 interns:* responsibilities include writing for *The Vegetarian Journal* and performing research, Web-related activities, outreach work, and clerical duties. Candidates should have ability to work independently, ability to work with others, computer skills, organizational skills, personal interest in the field, self-motivation, writing skills. Duration is 1–16 weeks. Unpaid. Open to high school students, recent high school graduates, college freshmen, college sophomores, college juniors, college seniors, recent college graduates, graduate students, law students, career changers, individuals reentering the workforce. International applications accepted.
Benefits Free housing, names of contacts, on-the-job training, opportunity to attend seminars/workshops, possible full-time employment, travel reimbursement, willing to act as a professional reference, willing to complete paperwork for educational credit, willing to provide letters of recommendation.
Contact Write or e-mail Mr. Charles Stahler. Phone: 410-366-8343. E-mail: vrg@vrg.org. In-person interview recommended (telephone interview accepted). Applicants must submit a letter of interest, resume, writing sample. Applications are accepted continuously. World Wide Web: http://www.vrg.org.

VOICES FOR CHILDREN
2851 Meadow Lark Drive
San Diego, California 92123

General Information Nonprofit children's advocacy for those in foster care. Established in 1980. Number of employees: 23. Affiliate of National Court Appointed Special Advocate Association, Seattle, Washington. Number of internship applications received each year: 200.
Internships Available ▶ *20 IEP educational surrogates:* responsibilities include reviewing and evaluating progress of foster children within the school site; interviewing child, teachers, and staff; attending individual education program meetings. Candidates should have ability to work independently, ability to work with others, oral communication skills, research skills, written communication skills, ability to maintain objectivity. Duration is one year (after training). Unpaid. Open to college juniors, college seniors, recent college graduates, graduate students, law students, career changers, individuals reentering the workforce, must be 21 years or older. ▶ *20–30 case assessment program interns:* responsibilities include reading, reviewing, and summarizing court case files of foster children and making recommendations as to type of advocate needed. Candidates should have ability to work independently, analytical skills, research skills, written communication skills, ability to make objective recommendations. Duration is as needed. Unpaid. Open to recent college graduates, graduate students, law students, career changers, individuals reentering the workforce, must be 21 years or older. ▶ *150–200 court-appointed special advocates:* responsibilities include advocacy for abused and neglected children in foster care through juvenile court system, providing continuity and support; interviewing all parties; preparing written reports for the court. Candidates should have ability to work independently, oral communication skills, personal interest in the field, research skills, strong interpersonal skills, written communication skills. Duration is 1 year to 18 months (after training). Unpaid. Open to college juniors, college seniors, recent college graduates, graduate students, law students, career changers, individuals reentering the workforce, must be 21 years or older. ▶ *50 court-appointed special monitors:* responsibilities include monitoring and evaluating the progress of dependent children of juvenile court (in foster care); interviewing parties; preparing written reports for court. Candidates should have ability to work independently, oral communication skills, personal interest in the field, research skills, strong interpersonal skills, written communication skills. Duration is 2 years (after training). Unpaid. Open to college juniors, college seniors, recent college graduates, graduate students, law students, career changers, individuals reentering the workforce, must be 21 years or older.

Voices for Children (continued)

Benefits Formal training, on-the-job training, opportunity to attend seminars/workshops, travel reimbursement, willing to act as a professional reference, willing to complete paperwork for educational credit, 44-hour training in social services and juvenile court law and court procedures.

Contact Write, call, e-mail, or through World Wide Web site Gary B. Cagle, Volunteer Recruitment Coordinator. Phone: 858-569-2019. Fax: 858-569-7151. E-mail: garyc@voices4children.com. In-person interview required. Applicants must submit a formal organization application, three personal references, criminal background check required. Applications are accepted continuously. World Wide Web: http://www.voices4children.com.

WASHINGTON OFFICE ON AFRICA
212 East Capitol Street
Washington, District of Columbia 20003

General Information Progressive advocacy organization for a just U.S. policy toward Africa. Established in 1972. Number of employees: 2. Number of internship applications received each year: 40.

Internships Available ▶ *1–2 research and advocacy interns:* responsibilities include engaging with other Africa-related advocacy organizations on advocacy strategy; drafting briefing documents for grassroots constituency; Capitol Hill lobbying; and related office work. Candidates should have ability to work independently, ability to work with others, analytical skills, oral communication skills, personal interest in the field, written communication skills. Duration is 2–6 months. Unpaid. Open to college sophomores, college juniors, college seniors, graduate students. International applications accepted.

Benefits Opportunity to attend seminars/workshops, willing to act as a professional reference, willing to complete paperwork for educational credit, willing to provide letters of recommendation, reimbursement of work-related travel expenses.

Contact Write, fax, e-mail, or through World Wide Web site Leon P. Spencer, Executive Director. Fax: 202-547-7505. E-mail: woa@igc.org. No phone calls. In-person interview recommended (telephone interview accepted). Applicants must submit a formal organization application, letter of interest, resume, writing sample, two letters of recommendation. Applications are accepted continuously. World Wide Web: http://www.woaafrica.org.

WASHINGTON OFFICE ON LATIN AMERICA
1630 Connecticut Avenue, NW, #200
Washington, District of Columbia 20009

General Information Nongovernmental organization aiming to help shape foreign policy that advances human rights and political and economic development in Latin America. Established in 1974. Number of employees: 17. Number of internship applications received each year: 300.

Internships Available ▶ *7 interns:* responsibilities include monitoring U.S. foreign policy and events in the region, assisting administrative staff with clerical duties, and actively participating in day-to-day operations of human rights organization. Candidates should have college courses in field, computer skills, office skills, personal interest in the field, research skills, writing skills, must be Spanish-speaking. Duration is 1 semester or summer. Unpaid. Open to college freshmen, college sophomores, college juniors, college seniors, recent college graduates. International applications accepted.

Benefits Job counseling, names of contacts, possible full-time employment, willing to complete paperwork for educational credit, willing to provide letters of recommendation.

Contact Write, call, fax, or through World Wide Web site Jana Kurtz, Internship Coordinator, 1630 Connecticut Avenue, NW #200, Washington, District of Columbia 20009. Phone: 202-797-2171. Fax: 202-797-2172. E-mail: wola@wola.org. Applicants must submit a letter of interest, resume, writing sample, two personal references, telephone interview for finalists only. Application deadline: March 15 for summer, August 1 for fall, December 1 for spring. World Wide Web: http://www.wola.org.

WASHINGTON PEACE CENTER
1426 9th Street, NW, Suite 306
Washington, District of Columbia 20001

General Information Multi-issue, grassroots, anti-racist organization working for nonviolent social change through education and action. Established in 1963. Number of employees: 2. Number of internship applications received each year: 100.

Internships Available ▶ *1–3 interns:* responsibilities include developing programs and materials in support of educational events and direct actions; community outreach and development to further social justice initiatives such as economic literacy, anti-racism education, and anti-military campaigns. Candidates should have ability to work independently, ability to work with others, computer skills, strong leadership ability, writing skills, commitment to social justice. Duration is 1 semester. Unpaid. Open to high school seniors, recent high school graduates, college freshmen, college sophomores, college juniors, college seniors, recent college graduates, graduate students. International applications accepted.

Benefits Opportunity to attend seminars/workshops, willing to act as a professional reference, willing to complete paperwork for educational credit, willing to provide letters of recommendation.

Contact Write, call, fax, or e-mail Coordinator. Phone: 202-234-2000. Fax: 202-234-7064. E-mail: wpc@igc.org. In-person interview recommended (telephone interview accepted). Applicants must submit a letter of interest, resume, personal history in social justice activism and/or social service projects. Application deadline: April 1 for summer, November 1 for spring; continuous for remainder of year. World Wide Web: http://www.washingtonpeacecenter.org.

WEST VIRGINIA KIDS COUNT FUND
1031 Quarrier Street, Suite 313
Charleston, West Virginia 25301

General Information Advocacy group that seeks to improve the lives of West Virginia's at-risk children by mobilizing the private and public sectors to create prevention and early intervention programs, policies, and strategies; creates and maintains a statewide network of child advocates; and collects, analyzes, and disseminates information about at-risk children to the public through the media. Established in 1989. Number of employees: 3. Unit of Kids Count–Annie E. Casey Foundation, Baltimore, Maryland. Number of internship applications received each year: 2.

Internships Available ▶ *1 communications intern:* responsibilities include writing fact sheets, media releases, compiling information, organizing media contacts, compiling media results, working on desktop publishing and Web site maintenance. Candidates should have ability to work with others, analytical skills, computer skills, oral communication skills, plan to pursue career in field, research skills, written communication skills. Duration is flexible. Unpaid. Open to college juniors, college seniors, graduate students. International applications accepted.

Benefits Names of contacts, opportunity to attend seminars/workshops, travel reimbursement, willing to complete paperwork for educational credit, willing to provide letters of recommendation, networking opportunities with professionals in the field.

Contact E-mail Missy Menefee, Communications Coordinator. E-mail: missymenefee@wvkidscountfund.org. No phone calls. In-person interview recommended (telephone interview accepted). Applications are accepted continuously. World Wide Web: http://www.wvkidscountfund.org.

WIDER OPPORTUNITIES FOR WOMEN, INC.
1001 Connecticut Avenue, NW, Suite 930
Washington, District of Columbia 20036

General Information Organization that works nationally and in Washington, D.C., to achieve economic self-sufficiency for women through public policy advocacy and program service delivery. Established in 1964. Number of employees: 6. Number of internship applications received each year: 100.

Internships Available ▶ *2–4 Nontraditional Occupations for Women Project interns:* responsibilities include case management, evaluation, administration, and organizing. Candidates should have ability to work with others, computer skills, oral communication skills, organizational skills, personal interest in the field, self-motivation. Duration is one summer. Unpaid. ▶ *1–3 public policy interns:* responsibilities include researching and analyzing public policies for their impact on women's employment and training; representing WOW at briefings, hearings, and other meetings relating to legislative agenda; State Organizing for Family Economic Self-Sufficiency Projects; updating grassroots network of women's employment training organizations on legislation and soliciting their support when necessary. Candidates should have analytical skills, computer skills, personal interest in the field, research skills, self-motivation, written communication skills. Duration is one summer. Unpaid. Open to college freshmen, college sophomores, college juniors, college seniors, graduate students. International applications accepted.

Benefits Job counseling, names of contacts, willing to complete paperwork for educational credit, willing to provide letters of recommendation, assistance with resume preparation, stipend of $10 per day to cover transportation and lunch.

Contact Write, fax, e-mail, or through World Wide Web site Vivian Staples, Office Manager, 815 15th Street, NW, Suite 916, Washington, District of Columbia 20005-3104. Fax: 202-464-1660. E-mail: info@ wowonline.org. In-person interview recommended (telephone interview accepted). Applicants must submit a resume, writing sample, cover letter. Applications are accepted continuously. World Wide Web: http://www.wowonline.org.

WOMEN'S INTERNATIONAL LEAGUE FOR PEACE AND FREEDOM
1213 Race Street
Philadelphia, Pennsylvania 19107-1691

General Information Organization devoted to ending sexism, racism, classism, oppression, militarism, and all forms of violence. Established in 1915. Number of employees: 8. Division of Women's International League for Peace and Freedom, Geneva, Switzerland. Number of internship applications received each year: 100.

Internships Available ▶ *1–3 communications interns:* responsibilities include maintaining the content and design of the organization's Web site; researching and linking to other online political and peace activist resources. Candidates should have ability to work independently, computer skills, organizational skills, research skills, writing skills. Duration is 12 weeks (minimum 20 hours per week). Position available as unpaid or at $117 per week. Open to high school seniors, recent high school graduates, college freshmen, college sophomores, college juniors, college seniors, recent college graduates, law students, career changers, individuals reentering the workforce. ▶ *1–2 development interns:* responsibilities include working with development director and staff on funding WILPF national political campaign; includes coordinating, fund-raising, appeal letters, and grant research. Candidates should have ability to work independently, ability to work with others, oral communication skills, organizational skills, research skills, writing skills. Duration is 12 weeks (minimum 20 hours per week). Position available as unpaid or at $117 per week. Open to high school seniors, recent high school graduates, college freshmen, college sophomores, college juniors, college seniors, recent college graduates, graduate students, law students, career changers, individuals reentering the workforce. ▶ *1–3 membership assistants:* responsibilities include helping members organize new branches and strengthen existing branches and participating in all phases of campaigning from keeping records to bringing in new members. Candidates should have ability to work independently, oral communication skills, self-motivation, strong interpersonal skills, strong leadership ability, written communication skills. Duration is 12 weeks (minimum 20 hours per week). Position available as unpaid or at $117 per week. Open to high school seniors, recent high school graduates, college freshmen, college sophomores, college juniors, college seniors, recent college graduates, graduate students, law students, career changers, individuals reentering the workforce. ▶ *1–3 national program assistants:* responsibilities include working

with branches around the country; tracking legislation; working with program coordinator to develop and implement national programs. Candidates should have ability to work independently, ability to work with others, oral communication skills, research skills, self-motivation, writing skills. Duration is 12 weeks (minimum 20 hours per week). Position available as unpaid or at $117 per week. Open to high school seniors, recent high school graduates, college freshmen, college sophomores, college juniors, college seniors, recent college graduates, graduate students, law students, career changers, individuals reentering the workforce. ▶ *1 publications assistant:* responsibilities include assisting the editor in locating and soliciting copy, editing news, researching and writing stories, checking facts, and using desktop publishing programs. Candidates should have ability to work independently, computer skills, editing skills, oral communication skills, research skills, writing skills. Duration is 12 weeks (minimum 20 hours per week). Position available as unpaid or at $117 per week. Open to college freshmen, college sophomores, college juniors, college seniors, recent college graduates, graduate students, career changers, individuals reentering the workforce. International applications accepted.

Benefits Formal training, on-the-job training, opportunity to attend seminars/workshops, possible full-time employment, willing to act as a professional reference, willing to complete paperwork for educational credit, willing to provide letters of recommendation.

International Internships Available in Geneva, Switzerland.

Contact Write, call, fax, e-mail, or through World Wide Web site Jody Dodd, Leadership/Outreach Coordinator. Phone: 215-563-7110. Fax: 215-563-5527. E-mail: jdodd@wilpf.org. In-person interview recommended (telephone interview accepted). Applicants must submit a letter of interest, resume, writing sample. Application deadline: May 1 for summer, August 1 for fall, December 1 for spring. World Wide Web: http://www.wilpf.org.

WORKING FAMILIES PARTY
88 Third Avenue, 4th Floor
Brooklyn, New York 11217

General Information Grassroots political party focusing on issues of economic justice, democratic political reform, and investment in education and children. Established in 1998. Number of employees: 25. Number of internship applications received each year: 200.

Internships Available ▶ *Interns:* responsibilities include working at state office in Brooklyn, or for upstate offices in Syracuse, Rochester, Buffalo, and Albany; assisting with electoral campaigns, planning, fund-raising, canvassing, direct mailing, and administrative duties. Candidates should have ability to work independently, oral communication skills, self-motivation, strong interpersonal skills, strong leadership ability, written communication skills, commitment to social and economic justice. Duration is flexible. $250 per week. Open to recent high school graduates, college freshmen, college sophomores, college juniors, college seniors, recent college graduates, graduate students, law students, career changers, individuals reentering the workforce.

Benefits Possible full-time employment, willing to act as a professional reference, willing to complete paperwork for educational credit, willing to provide letters of recommendation.

Contact Write, call, fax, e-mail, or through World Wide Web site Rachel Berkson, Intern Director. Phone: 718-222-3796. Fax: 718-246-3718. E-mail: rsber@hotmail.com. Applicants must submit a letter of interest, resume. Applications are accepted continuously. World Wide Web: http://www.workingfamiliesparty.org.

WORLD HUNGER ECUMENICAL ARIZONA TASK FORCE (WHEAT)
1714 East Roma Avenue
Phoenix, Arizona 85016

General Information Nonprofit organization that educates, advocates, and empowers individuals to action in the fight against hunger. Established in 1979. Number of employees: 5. Number of internship applications received each year: 25.

World Hunger Ecumenical Arizona Task Force (WHEAT) (continued)

Internships Available ▶ *1–2 communication interns:* responsibilities include assisting in all stages of disseminating WHEAT reports and analyses to news media; establishing and maintaining relationship with print, broadcast, and electronic media. Candidates should have ability to work independently, oral communication skills, strong interpersonal skills, written communication skills, attention to detail. Duration is flexible. Unpaid. Open to high school seniors, recent high school graduates, college freshmen, college sophomores, college juniors, college seniors, recent college graduates, graduate students, law students, career changers, individuals reentering the workforce. ▶ *1–2 local and global food security issues interns:* responsibilities include assisting in researching, preparing, and distributing information on how legislative proposals would affect families, the federal budget, states, and third world countries. Candidates should have computer skills, oral communication skills, organizational skills, personal interest in the field, research skills, self-motivation, strong leadership ability, writing skills, strong Internet skills, familiarity with tax and budget concepts, fluency in a foreign language (helpful), quantitative analytic skills (required). Duration is flexible. Unpaid. Open to recent high school graduates, college freshmen, college sophomores, college juniors, college seniors, recent college graduates, graduate students, law students, career changers. ▶ *1–3 nonprofit event planning interns:* responsibilities include scheduling, set up, and content of various events; gathering appropriate materials for use as hand outs; helping maintain contacts with state civic, religious, and community action organizations; helping plan annual conference workshops and seminars. Candidates should have ability to work independently, analytical skills, oral communication skills, organizational skills, self-motivation, strong leadership ability. Duration is flexible. Unpaid. Open to high school seniors, recent high school graduates, college freshmen, college sophomores, college juniors, college seniors, recent college graduates, graduate students, law students, career changers, individuals reentering the workforce. ▶ *1–2 nonprofit fund-raising interns:* responsibilities include identifying potential contributors, preparing reports and proposals to funders, and maintaining information on grants to WHEAT; conducting research on foundations and new funding sources. Candidates should have ability to work independently, computer skills, office skills, oral communication skills, organizational skills, personal interest in the field, research skills, self-motivation, strong leadership ability, writing skills. Duration is flexible. Unpaid. Open to high school seniors, recent high school graduates, college freshmen, college sophomores, college juniors, college seniors, recent college graduates, graduate students, law students, career changers, individuals reentering the workforce. ▶ *1–2 nonprofit management interns:* responsibilities include assisting with staff recruitment process; preparing reconciliations of bi-weekly time sheets; ordering supplies and coding invoices; assisting staff with computer and/or software-related problems and doing preventive maintenance; working in all aspects of executive-level leadership; program and board oversight opportunities. Candidates should have ability to work independently, computer skills, oral communication skills, organizational skills, personal interest in the field, self-motivation, strong interpersonal skills, strong leadership ability. Duration is flexible. Unpaid. Open to high school seniors, recent high school graduates, college freshmen, college sophomores, college juniors, college seniors, recent college graduates, graduate students, law students, career changers, individuals reentering the workforce. ▶ *1–2 nonprofit marketing and promotion interns:* responsibilities include developing materials for use in press kits and corporate information packets; researching specific subjects; assisting in preparation of materials for presentations; collecting and analyzing data from range of sources to track state economics and finances. Candidates should have ability to work independently, computer skills, oral communication skills, organizational skills, self-motivation, strong leadership ability. Duration is flexible. Unpaid. Open to high school seniors, recent high school graduates, college freshmen, college sophomores, college juniors, college seniors, recent college graduates, graduate students, law students, career changers, individuals reentering the workforce. ▶ *1–2 outreach campaigns interns:* responsibilities include helping maintain communication with partner groups and others; tracking use of creative outreach

strategies; helping develop new materials; helping research state and local policies affecting ability of individuals to obtain economic security. Candidates should have ability to work independently, computer skills, oral communication skills, organizational skills, self-motivation, strong leadership ability. Duration is flexible. Unpaid. Open to high school seniors, recent high school graduates, college freshmen, college sophomores, college juniors, college seniors, recent college graduates, graduate students, law students, career changers, individuals reentering the workforce. ▶ *1–2 state/federal policy watch interns:* responsibilities include following process of legislative proposals; responding to requests for information on WHEAT projects; assisting in monitoring federal budget process and implications of budget proposals on programs involving low-income families and individuals. Candidates should have ability to work independently, computer skills, oral communication skills, organizational skills, self-motivation, strong leadership ability. Duration is flexible. Unpaid. Open to high school seniors, recent high school graduates, college freshmen, college sophomores, college juniors, college seniors, recent college graduates, graduate students, law students, career changers, individuals reentering the workforce. International applications accepted.

Benefits Formal training, names of contacts, on-the-job training, opportunity to attend seminars/workshops, possible full-time employment, travel reimbursement, willing to act as a professional reference, willing to complete paperwork for educational credit, willing to provide letters of recommendation.

Contact Write, call, fax, e-mail, or through World Wide Web site Dr. Tamera Zivic, Executive Director. Phone: 602-955-5076. Fax: 602-955-5290. E-mail: wheat@hungerhurts.org. In-person interview recommended (telephone interview accepted). Applicants must submit a formal organization application, letter of interest, resume, academic transcripts, two personal references, two letters of recommendation. Applications are accepted continuously. World Wide Web: http://www.hungerhurts.org.

YES! MAGAZINE AND POSITIVE FUTURES NETWORK
284 Madrona Way, NE, Suite 116
Bainbridge Island, Washington 98110

General Information Independent, nonprofit organization dedicated to supporting people's active engagement in creating a just, sustainable, and compassionate world. Established in 1996. Number of employees: 14. Number of internship applications received each year: 30.

Internships Available ▶ *1–2 editorial interns:* responsibilities include researching and writing (short) pieces for publication in Yes!; fact checking and copyediting articles received for publication; researching story leads and facts on the Internet; carrying out other special projects when determined. Candidates should have editing skills, organizational skills, research skills, self-motivation, written communication skills. Duration is 3 months or longer. Unpaid. ▶ *1 network/conference intern:* responsibilities include assisting in all areas pertaining to hosting a retreat for social activists, including involvement in the invitation and network process, promotion, logistics, scheduling, and carrying out other projects when determined. Candidates should have oral communication skills, research skills, self-motivation, strong interpersonal skills, written communication skills. Duration is 3 months or longer. Unpaid. ▶ *1 outreach/marketing intern:* responsibilities include assisting in planning and executing promotional and educational efforts; working with magazine retail outlets; assisting in public relations efforts; assisting both Major Donor and Yes! for youth education program outreach efforts. Candidates should have computer skills, office skills, oral communication skills, organizational skills, research skills, self-motivation. Duration is 3 months or longer. Unpaid. Open to recent high school graduates, college freshmen, college sophomores, college juniors, college seniors, recent college graduates, graduate students, law students, career changers, individuals reentering the workforce.

Benefits Free housing, health insurance, names of contacts, on-the-job training, willing to act as a professional reference, willing to complete paperwork for educational credit, willing to provide letters of recommendation.

Contact Write, call, or e-mail Kathleen Peel, Office Manager, PO Box 10818, Bainbridge Island, Washington 98110. Phone: 800-937-4451. E-mail: internships@futurenet.org. In-person interview recommended (telephone interview accepted). Applicants must submit a letter of interest, resume, three personal references, 2-3 writing samples. Applications are accepted continuously. World Wide Web: http://www.yesmagazine.org.

YOUTHNOISE
2000 M Street, NW, Suite 500
Washington, District of Columbia 20036

General Information Place where teens learn, share, and connect with each other to help change the world; creating local and global positive change by volunteering, fund-raising, and speaking out. Established in 2001. Number of employees: 12. Unit of Save the Children Federation, Westport, Connecticut.
Internships Available ▶ *1 Web site developer intern:* responsibilities include Web site development using PHP and light system; administration tasks. Candidates should have ability to work independently, ability to work with others, personal interest in the field, self-motivation, knowledge of MS SQL server, PostgreSQL, and Linus (desired). Duration is flexible (3 to 6 months). Unpaid. Open to college freshmen, college sophomores, college juniors, college seniors, recent college graduates, graduate students. ▶ *1–2 Web site production interns:* responsibilities include designing and building Web pages and graphics; working with site team to conceptualize, implement, and test new site features and functionalities; performing site maintenance. Candidates should have ability to work independently, ability to work with others, knowledge of field, self-motivation, hand coding HTML, Flash and ActionScript skills (desired). Duration is flexible (3 to 6 months). Unpaid. Open to recent high school graduates, college freshmen, college sophomores, college juniors, college seniors, recent college graduates. ▶ *1 development intern:* responsibilities include working closely with development director to help broaden base of financial support, foundation research, major donor prospecting, and earned income market research. Candidates should have analytical skills, oral communication skills, organizational skills, research skills, strong leadership ability, written communication skills. Duration is flexible (3-6 months). Unpaid. Open to high school seniors, recent high school graduates, college freshmen, college sophomores, college juniors, college seniors, recent college graduates, graduate students. ▶ *1–2 editorial interns:* responsibilities include researching issues to be featured on Web site, writing and fact checking articles for teen audience, helping identify active young people to profile, interviewing subjects, and interacting with users of the site to help ensure a safe environment. Candidates should have editing skills, personal interest in the field, research skills, writing skills, major in journalism/communications (preferred). Duration is flexible (3 to 6 months). Unpaid. Open to high school students, recent high school graduates, college freshmen, college sophomores, college juniors, college seniors. ▶ *1 graphic design intern (marketing):* responsibilities include creating teen-friendly Web pages for marketing promotion; creating online banner ads, print ads, flyers, and brochures; administrative duties as needed. Candidates should have ability to work independently, computer skills, oral communication skills, strong interpersonal skills, experience in HTML, Flash, PhotoShop, Illustrator, InDesign/Pagemaker/Quark Express (preferred), URLs and/or work samples. Duration is flexible (3 to 6 months). Unpaid. Open to high school students, recent high school graduates, college freshmen, college sophomores, college juniors, college seniors, recent college graduates, graduate students, career changers, individuals reentering the workforce. ▶ *1–2 graphic design interns (Web):* responsibilities include designing fun, professional quality Web graphics, pages, and special features for teen audience; creating Flash movies; assisting with basic site maintenance.

Candidates should have ability to work independently, ability to work with others, knowledge of field, self-motivation, hand coding HTML and other scripting skills (desired). Duration is flexible (3 to 6 months). Unpaid. Open to high school seniors, recent high school graduates, college freshmen, college sophomores, college juniors, college seniors, recent college graduates, graduate students. ▶ *1 marketing intern:* responsibilities include brainstorming and developing new marketing/promotional concepts; writing and editing marketing content for teen audience; identifying new potential marketing partners; administrative duties as needed. Candidates should have computer skills, personal interest in the field, research skills, self-motivation, strong interpersonal skills, written communication skills. Duration is flexible (3 to 6 months). Unpaid. Open to high school students, recent high school graduates, college freshmen, college sophomores, college juniors, college seniors, recent college graduates, graduate students, career changers, individuals reentering the workforce. ▶ *1 policy intern:* responsibilities include researching and reporting on youth-related policy issues and trends; writing "action alerts" designed to compel teens to speakout and create positive local, national, and global change. Candidates should have analytical skills, knowledge of field, research skills, strong interpersonal skills, writing skills. Duration is flexible (3-6 months). Unpaid. Open to college sophomores, college juniors, college seniors, recent college graduates, graduate students, law students. International applications accepted.
Benefits On-the-job training, willing to act as a professional reference, willing to complete paperwork for educational credit, willing to provide letters of recommendation.
Contact Write, fax, or e-mail Intern Coordinator. Fax: 202-293-1778. E-mail: jobs@youthnoisemail.com. No phone calls. Applicants must submit a letter of interest, resume, two personal references, URLs and/or work samples (for graphic design position). Applications are accepted continuously. World Wide Web: http://www.youthNOISE.com.

YOUTH VENTURE
1700 North Moore Street, Suite 2000
Arlington, Virginia 22209

General Information National, not-for-profit organization that enables young people (ages 12-20) to create, lead, and launch their own organizations, clubs, or businesses that make a difference in their community. Established in 1995. Number of employees: 7. Number of internship applications received each year: 50.
Internships Available ▶ *Interns:* responsibilities include working with national and regional staff in communications, Web site development and maintenance, and research or outreach. Candidates should have ability to work independently, computer skills, editing skills, office skills, oral communication skills, research skills, self-motivation, strong interpersonal skills, written communication skills. Duration is flexible. Unpaid. Open to high school students, recent high school graduates, college freshmen, college sophomores, college juniors, college seniors, recent college graduates, graduate students, law students, career changers, individuals reentering the workforce.
Benefits Names of contacts, on-the-job training, opportunity to attend seminars/workshops, willing to act as a professional reference, willing to complete paperwork for educational credit, willing to provide letters of recommendation.
Contact Write, call, fax, e-mail, or through World Wide Web site Lorenley Baez, Program Assistant. Phone: 703-527-4126 Ext. 315. Fax: 703-527-8383. E-mail: info@youthventure.org. In-person interview recommended (telephone interview accepted). Applicants must submit a letter of interest, resume, personal reference. Applications are accepted continuously. World Wide Web: http://www.youthventure.org.

PROFESSIONAL, SCIENTIFIC, AND TECHNICAL SERVICES

GENERAL

ACOLYTE SYSTEMS, INC.
176 Madison Avenue, 3rd Floor
New York, New York 10016

General Information Developer, designer, and marketer of wireless lighting systems and devices that can be customized for a wide variety of applications.
Internships Available ▶ *Accounting interns:* responsibilities include assisting financial officer; assisting with general accounting tasks; keeping notes on meetings and interviews; working with supervisor to create project based on student's educational objective; clerical and office tasks as needed. Candidates should have college level accounting knowledge, skills, and abilities, knowledge of general accounting software, typing skills, punctuality, professionalism. Duration is 3 to 6 months (flexible to school schedule). Unpaid. ▶ *Business administration interns:* responsibilities include assisting chief executive officer; scheduling meetings; handling corporate correspondence; keeping notes on meetings and interviews; working with supervisor to create project based on student's educational objective; clerical and office tasks as needed. Candidates should have organizational skills, knowledge of general office software and typing skills, punctuality, professionalism. Duration is 3-6 months (flexible to school schedule) 30 to 40 hours per week. Unpaid. ▶ *Publicity interns (public relations department):* responsibilities include assisting publicity staff; creating and maintaining information databases; helping write and distribute press releases; keeping notes on meetings and interviews; writing with supervisor to create project based on student's educational objective; clerical and office tasks as needed. Candidates should have organizational skills, knowledge of general office software, typing skills, punctuality, professionalism. Duration is 3 to 6 months (flexible to school schedule) 30-40 hours per week. Unpaid.
Benefits Possible full-time employment, travel stipend.
Contact Fax or e-mail Internship Coordinator. Phone: 888-ACOLYTE. Fax: 212-629-6931. E-mail: info@888acolyte.com. Applicants must submit resume (faxed) to the attention of staff member listed on Web site as contact for position of interest or e-mail resume. Applications are accepted continuously. World Wide Web: http://www.smartlyte.com.

ADNET SYSTEMS, INC.
11260 Roger Bacon Drive, Suite 403
Reston, Virginia 20190

General Information Company providing a wide range of technical and administrative support services primarily to government agencies including NASA, Department of Transportation, Department of Labor, U.S. Army, and others. Established in 1991. Number of employees: 6. Branch of ADNET Systems, Inc., Potomac, Maryland. Number of internship applications received each year: 500.
Internships Available ▶ *25–40 Department of Transportation student interns:* responsibilities include supporting various projects within a wide range of DOT offices. Candidates should have computer skills, office skills, oral communication skills, strong interpersonal skills, written communication skills. Duration is June to August (10 weeks). $400–$450 per week. Open to college freshmen, college sophomores, college juniors, college seniors, graduate students, law students. ▶ *NASA visiting student interns:* responsibilities include working within the Goddard Space Flight Center on projects related to computer science. Candidates should have computer skills, experience in the field, office skills, personal interest in the field, plan to pursue career in field, written communication skills. Duration is June to Aguust (10 weeks). $6–$6.50 per hour. Open to high school students, recent high school graduates, college sophomores, college juniors, college seniors, graduate students. International applications accepted.
Benefits Free housing, opportunity to attend seminars/workshops, possible full-time employment, travel reimbursement, willing to act as a professional reference, willing to complete paperwork for educational credit, willing to provide letters of recommendation.
Contact E-mail or through World Wide Web site Heather Robertson, Director, Education Programs. Phone: 703-787-9361. Fax: 703-709-7219. E-mail: education.programs@adnet-sys.com. Applicants must submit a formal organization application, resume, academic transcripts, personal reference. Application deadline: January 28 for NASA Visiting Student interns, March 8 for Department of Transportation interns. World Wide Web: http://www.adnet-sys.com.

AMERICAN PSYCHOLOGICAL ASSOCIATION
750 First Street, NE
Washington, District of Columbia 20002-4242

General Information Scientific and professional organization representing psychology in the U.S.; the largest association of psychologists worldwide, with a membership greater than 150,000.
Internships Available ▶ *5 Congressional Fellows:* responsibilities include working as legislative assistant on the staff of a member of Congress or congressional committee; conducting legislative or oversight work, assisting in hearings and debates, preparing briefs, and writing speeches. Candidates should have ability to work with others, oral communication skills, self-motivation, written communication skills, demonstrated competence in scientific and/or professional psychology. Duration is 1 year. Stipend from $48,500 to $64,400 depending upon years of post-doctoral experience. Open to APA members (or applicants for membership) with a doctorate in psychology at the time of application, minimum of 2 years post-doctoral experience (preferred). ▶ *1 Science Policy Fellow:* responsibilities include working as special assistant in an executive branch research funding/coordinating office. Candidates should have ability to work independently, ability to work with others, oral communication skills, written communication skills, demonstrated competence in scientific psychology, sensitivity toward policy issues, and a strong interest in applying psychological knowledge to national science policy issues. Duration is 1 year. $53,900. Open to APA members (or applicants for membership) with a doctorate in psychology with one year post-doctoral experience. ▶ *Public interest policy interns:* responsibilities include working on public interest issues pertaining to children, women, ethnic minorities, HIV/AIDS, disabilities, aging, lesbian/bisexual concerns, media, and/or violence. Duration is 15-20

hours per week (minimum). $14.50 per hour. Open to doctoral students in psychology or related field, in at least second year of training.
Benefits Up to $3000 per fellow for relocation to Washington DC and travel expenses during year.
Contact Through World Wide Web site Internship Coordinator. Phone: 800-374-2721 Ext. 6062. Applicants must submit materials as detailed on Web site. Application deadline: mid-January for Science Fellowship Program, January 1 for Congressional Fellowship Program, May 7 for public interest policy interns. World Wide Web: http://www.apa.org.

AMERICAN STANDARDS TESTING BUREAU, INC.
40 Water Street
New York, New York 10004

General Information Technical and management consulting firm. Established in 1916. Number of employees: 900. Number of internship applications received each year: 1,000.
Internships Available ▶ *3–6 interns:* responsibilities include performing duties consistent with intern's interests and skills. Candidates should have computer skills, organizational skills, self-motivation, strong interpersonal skills, writing skills, declared college major in project accounting, international business, or engineering (particularly welcome). Duration is 1 semester. Position available as unpaid or paid. Open to college juniors, college seniors, recent college graduates, graduate students, law students, career changers, individuals reentering the workforce. ▶ *6–10 management or marketing trainees.* Candidates should have oral communication skills, organizational skills, plan to pursue career in field, research skills, strong interpersonal skills, written communication skills. Duration is 6–12 months. Position available as unpaid or paid. Open to college seniors, recent college graduates, graduate students, law students, career changers, individuals reentering the workforce. International applications accepted.
Benefits Possible full-time employment, willing to complete paperwork for educational credit, willing to provide letters of recommendation.
International Internships Available in Brazil; Greece; Republic of Korea; Russian Federation; Spain.
Contact Write, fax, or e-mail Dr. John Zimmerman, Director of Professional Staffing, PO Box 583, New York, New York 10274. Fax: 212-825-2250. E-mail: worldteck@aol.com. No phone calls. In-person interview required. Applicants must submit a formal organization application, resume, three personal references, letter of recommendation. Applications are accepted continuously.

ANIMAL BEHAVIOR CENTER OF NEW YORK
89-10 Eliot Avenue
Rego Park, New York 11374

General Information Not-for-profit applied animal behavior treatment and teaching center. Established in 1992. Number of employees: 15. Subsidiary of American Foundation for Animal Rescue, Inc., Rego Park, New York. Number of internship applications received each year: 100.
Internships Available ▶ *12 canine behavior counselors (CBC):* responsibilities include lectures, case studies, videotape, training dogs, instruction (private and group), rounds, off-site trips to veterinarian hospitals and shelters. Candidates should have ability to work independently, analytical skills, oral communication skills, personal interest in the field, plan to pursue career in field, strong interpersonal skills. Duration is 1–3 months. Unpaid. Open to recent high school graduates, college freshmen, college sophomores, college juniors, college seniors, recent college graduates, graduate students, career changers, individuals reentering the workforce. International applications accepted.
Benefits Formal training, housing at a cost, job counseling, on-the-job training, opportunity to attend seminars/workshops, possible full-time employment, willing to act as a professional reference, willing to complete paperwork for educational credit, willing to provide letters of recommendation.
Contact Write, call, fax, e-mail, or through World Wide Web site Robert DeFranco, Executive Director, 89-10 Elitot Avenue, Rego Park, New York 11374. Phone: 718-205-0200. Fax: 718-205-3962. E-mail: abcny@canines.com. In-person interview recommended (telephone interview accepted). Applicants must submit a formal organization application, $3000 program fee (upon acceptance). Applications are accepted continuously. Fees: $50. World Wide Web: http://www.canines.com.

ARNOLD ARBORETUM OF HARVARD UNIVERSITY
125 Arborway
Jamaica Plain, Massachusetts 02130

General Information Facility whose mission is to increase knowledge of woody plants through research and disseminate this knowledge through educational programs. Established in 1872. Number of employees: 60. Unit of Harvard University, Cambridge, Massachusetts. Number of internship applications received each year: 100.
Internships Available ▶ *10 grounds maintenance interns:* responsibilities include assisting with the care and maintenance of the Living Collections which includes pruning, weeding, mulching, mowing, and various renovation projects. Candidates should have ability to work independently, college courses in field, knowledge of field, organizational skills, personal interest in the field, self-motivation, strong interpersonal skills, strong leadership ability. Duration is April/May to mid-August. $8 per hour. Open to college freshmen, college sophomores, college juniors, college seniors, recent college graduates, graduate students, career changers, individuals reentering the workforce. ▶ *2 nursery and greenhouse interns:* responsibilities include assisting with all duties related to the propagation and production of woody ornamental plants. Candidates should have ability to work independently, college courses in field, knowledge of field, personal interest in the field, self-motivation, strong interpersonal skills. Duration is end of May to mid-August. $8 per hour. Open to college freshmen, college sophomores, college juniors, college seniors, recent college graduates, graduate students, career changers, individuals reentering the workforce. ▶ *2 plant records interns:* responsibilities include assisting with the mapping, labeling, and curation of all woody plants of the Living Collections. Candidates should have ability to work independently, computer skills, organizational skills, personal interest in the field, self-motivation, strong interpersonal skills, plant identification skills. Duration is end of May to mid-August. $8 per hour. Open to college sophomores, college juniors, college seniors, recent college graduates, graduate students, career changers. International applications accepted.
Benefits Formal training, job counseling, on-the-job training, opportunity to attend seminars/workshops, possible full-time employment, willing to act as a professional reference, willing to complete paperwork for educational credit, willing to provide letters of recommendation.
Contact Write, call, fax, e-mail, or through World Wide Web site Tom Akin, Internship Coordinator. Phone: 617-524-1718 Ext. 112. Fax: 617-524-1418. E-mail: takin@arnarb.harvard.edu. Telephone interview required. Applicants must submit a formal organization application. Application deadline: February 1. World Wide Web: http://www.arboretum.harvard.edu.

AUTOMOTIVE RESTORATION, INC.
1785 Barnum Avenue
Stratford, Connecticut 06614

General Information Antique and classic automobile restoration shop that performs panel fabrication, woodwork, upholstery, body, paint, and mechanical work; includes management, appraisal, and evaluation. Established in 1977. Number of employees: 38. Number of internship applications received each year: 50.
Internships Available ▶ *1–2 general office interns:* responsibilities include bookkeeping, invoicing, research, documentation, and business management. Candidates should have ability to work with others, computer skills, office skills, oral communication skills, research skills, written communication skills. Duration is flexible. $6 to $15 per hour commensurate with experience and ability. Open to recent high school graduates, college freshmen, college sophomores, college juniors, college seniors, recent college graduates, graduate students, law students, career changers, individuals reentering the workforce, must be 18 or older. ▶ *4 restoration apprentices:* responsibilities include assisting tradespeople in areas

Automotive Restoration, Inc. (continued)

including panel fabrication, photography, research, documentation, upholstery, older vehicle mechanics, vintage race mechanics, paint/body, assembly/detail, and woodwork. Candidates should have ability to work with others, analytical skills, oral communication skills, self-motivation, written communication skills, technical interests and educational background. Duration is flexible. $6 to $15 per hour commensurate with experience and ability. Open to high school seniors, recent high school graduates, college freshmen, college sophomores, college juniors, college seniors, recent college graduates, graduate students, career changers, individuals reentering the workforce, must be 18 or older. International applications accepted.

Benefits Names of contacts, on-the-job training, opportunity to attend seminars/workshops, possible full-time employment, travel reimbursement, willing to act as a professional reference, willing to complete paperwork for educational credit, willing to provide letters of recommendation.

Contact Write, call, fax, e-mail, or through World Wide Web site Mrs. Denise Cutrone, Human Resources, 1785 Barnum Avenue, Stratford, Connecticut 06497. Phone: 203-377-6745. Fax: 203-386-0486. E-mail: kent@auto-restore.com. In-person interview recommended (telephone interview accepted). Applicants must submit a letter of interest, resume. Applications are accepted continuously. World Wide Web: http://www.automotiverestorations.com.

BATTELLE MEMORIAL INSTITUTE
505 King Avenue
Columbus, Ohio 43201

General Information Provider of innovative science and technology solutions for government and commercial customers worldwide and management of three national laboratories for the U.S. Department of Energy. Established in 1923. Number of employees: 1,800. Number of internship applications received each year: 200.

Internships Available ▶ *Co-ops:* responsibilities include working on an assignment directly related to intern's field of study. Duration is one academic term (full-time). Paid. ▶ *Internships:* responsibilities include assignments that may or may not be directly related to intern's college major. Duration is 3 months to 3 years; part- or full-time. Paid. Open to college freshmen, college sophomores, college juniors, college seniors.

Benefits Possible full-time employment.

Contact Through World Wide Web site Internship Coordinator. Applicants must submit materials as specified on Web site. Applications are accepted continuously. World Wide Web: http://www.battelle.org.

BENETECH
480 California Avenue, Suite 201
Palo Alto, California 94306-1609

General Information Nonprofit developer of technology to address social needs. Established in 1989. Number of employees: 13. Number of internship applications received each year: 100.

Internships Available ▶ *1–3 marketing interns:* responsibilities include researching and pursuing marketing opportunities for social benefit projects. Candidates should have ability to work independently, analytical skills, computer skills, oral communication skills, personal interest in the field, research skills, self-motivation, strong interpersonal skills, written communication skills. Duration is 1 summer or 1 semester. Position available as unpaid or at $10–$15 per hour. Open to college juniors, college seniors, graduate students. ▶ *1–3 software interns:* responsibilities include programming and testing reading systems and other adaptive tools for people with disabilities. Candidates should have analytical skills, computer skills, personal interest in the field, research skills, self-motivation, programming experience. Duration is 1 summer or 1 semester. Position available as unpaid or at $8–$15 per hour. Open to college sophomores, college juniors, college seniors, recent college graduates, graduate students, individuals with disabilities are encouraged to apply. ▶ *1–3 technology for social needs interns:* responsibilities include researching social applications of technology, analyzing needs, and developing funding applications. Candidates should have ability to work independently, oral communication skills, research skills, self-motivation, strong interpersonal skills, written communication skills. Duration is 1 summer or 1 semester. Position available as unpaid or at $8–$12 per hour. Open to recent high school graduates, college sophomores, college juniors, college seniors, graduate students, law students. International applications accepted.

Benefits On-the-job training, possible full-time employment, willing to act as a professional reference, willing to provide letters of recommendation.

Contact Write, fax, or e-mail Jane Simchuk, Manager of Administration, 480 California Avenue, Suite 201, Palo Alto, California 94306-1609. Fax: 650-603-8887. E-mail: jane@benetech.org. No phone calls. Telephone interview required. Applicants must submit a letter of interest, resume, writing sample, letter of recommendation. Application deadline: May 15 for summer. World Wide Web: http://www.benetech.org.

CENTER FOR COASTAL STUDIES, INC.
59 Commercial Street, PO Box 1036
Provincetown, Massachusetts 02657

General Information Marine mammal/habitat/coastal ecology research organization. Established in 1976. Number of employees: 15. Number of internship applications received each year: 50.

Internships Available ▶ *2–4 research interns:* responsibilities include data collection, entry, and some analysis; an independent project. Candidates should have ability to work independently, ability to work with others, computer skills, personal interest in the field, research skills, self-motivation, written communication skills. Duration is 3–5 months. $500 per month. Open to college juniors, college seniors, recent college graduates, graduate students, must be pursuing career in marine animal research. International applications accepted.

Benefits On-the-job training, willing to act as a professional reference, willing to complete paperwork for educational credit, willing to provide letters of recommendation.

Contact Write, e-mail, or through World Wide Web site Internship Coordinator. Phone: 508-487-3622. Fax: 508-487-4695. E-mail: ccs@coastalstudies.org. Telephone interview required. Applicants must submit a letter of interest, resume, academic transcripts, two letters of recommendation. Application deadline: October 31 for winter (January-May). Fees: $10. World Wide Web: http://www.coastalstudies.org.

CLEANEVENT USA, INC.
8350 Parkline Boulevard, Suite 100
Orlando, Florida 32809

General Information Provider of cleaning and waste management services to venues and events. Established in 1997. Number of employees: 25. Number of internship applications received each year: 200.

Internships Available ▶ *2 event coordinators:* responsibilities include assisting in event planning, administration, payroll, dispatching, recruiting, and job costing. Candidates should have ability to work independently, ability to work with others, computer skills, oral communication skills, high energy level. Duration is 5–12 months. $1000 per month. Open to college seniors, recent college graduates. International applications accepted.

Benefits Names of contacts, on-the-job training, possible full-time employment, willing to act as a professional reference, willing to complete paperwork for educational credit, willing to provide letters of recommendation, travel, meals, and lodging provided (during events).

Contact Write, fax, or e-mail Human Resource Manager. Fax: 407-856-0131. E-mail: hr@cleaneventusa.com. No phone calls. Telephone interview required. Applicants must submit a letter of interest, resume. Applications are accepted continuously. World Wide Web: http://www.cleaneventusa.com.

CONSUMER ELECTRONICS ASSOCIATION
2500 Wilson Boulevard
Arlington, Virginia 22201

General Information Association representing 1000 companies making products that give consumers access to entertainment, education, and information; producer, sponsor, and manager of the International Consumer Electronics show. Established in 1924. Number of employees: 120. Number of internship applications received each year: 2,500.

Internships Available ► *1–2 Web services interns:* responsibilities include managing and maintaining new and existing content on various CEA Web sites; facilitating the creation of new Web-based content management tools using SQL, ASP, and HTML; and assisting with day-to-day management and maintenance of CEA's Web sites. Candidates should have ability to work with others, computer skills, oral communication skills, knowledge of HTML and JavaScript. Duration is 6 months. $12–$14 per hour. Open to college sophomores, college juniors, college seniors, recent college graduates, graduate students, career changers. ► *1 communications intern:* responsibilities include writing press releases and other promotional materials, assisting with scheduling press conferences for CEA, assisting maintenance of the PR contact database, researching new media contacts, and providing general support for the communications staff. Candidates should have experience in the field, oral communication skills, organizational skills, plan to pursue career in field, writing skills. Duration is summer (May to August). $10 per hour. Open to college sophomores, college juniors, college seniors. ► *1 conferences intern:* responsibilities include assisting with the fall conference and board retreat; managing service request forms and fulfillment of services for VIP buyers and government guests; performing database management, and making travel arrangements for government guests. Candidates should have computer skills, office skills, oral communication skills, organizational skills, strong interpersonal skills, written communication skills. Duration is fall semester. $10 per hour. Open to college sophomores, college juniors, college seniors. ► *1 editorial intern:* responsibilities include writing short articles for Vision Magazine, helping edit copy, and helping collect artwork for Vision; researching information on potential Hall of Fame candidates; and writing biographies for Hall of Fame nominees. Candidates should have editing skills, experience in the field, oral communication skills, research skills, writing skills. Duration is summer (May to August). $9 per hour. Open to college sophomores, college juniors, college seniors. ► *1 graphics intern:* responsibilities include assisting staff with day-to-day graphics requests including small design projects, camera-ready materials, and scanning of needed graphics. Candidates should have ability to work independently, computer skills, experience in the field, oral communication skills, plan to pursue career in field, knowledge of Quark Xpress, Adobe PhotoShop, and Adobe Illustrator. Duration is summer (May to August) and/or fall semester. $10 per hour. Open to college sophomores, college juniors, college seniors. ► *1–2 information technology interns:* responsibilities include providing hands-on end-user PC/technical support, trouble-shooting network, and assisting with e-mail and PC problems; working with staff to assess needs and to identify and implement solutions. Candidates should have ability to work with others, computer skills, experience in the field, oral communication skills, plan to pursue career in field, customer service skills. Duration is 6 months. $10–$12 per hour. Open to college sophomores, college juniors, college seniors, recent college graduates. ► *1 library intern:* responsibilities include answering in-depth reference questions; contributing to daily current awareness listing, database management, indexing and abstracting, cataloging, and online searching of information services; day-to-day library functions including shelving, checking-in magazines, and answering ready-reference questions. Candidates should have computer skills, experience in the field, plan to pursue career in field, research skills, customer service skills and Web knowledge. Duration is summer (May to August), fall or spring semester. $10 per hour. Open to recent college graduates, graduate students. ► *1 marketing intern:* responsibilities include working closely with the marketing department staff on marketing strategy, promotion campaigns for CEA/CES events, and writing promotional copy; coordinating design work with graphics staff; coordinating mail house and printing processes; and assisting in staffing local CEA events. Candidates should have ability to work with others, knowledge of field, office skills, oral communication skills, organizational skills, written communication skills. Duration is summer (May to August) and/or fall semester. $10–$12 per hour. Open to college juniors, college seniors, recent college graduates, graduate students. ► *1 sales intern:* responsibilities include assisting with correspondence, faxing, mailing, data entry, telemarketing, and prospecting using knowledge gained from the exhibitor profile, needs, and requirements. Candidates should have oral communication skills, plan to pursue career in field, research skills, self-motivation, strong interpersonal skills, written communication skills. Duration is summer and fall semesters. $10–$12 per hour. Open to college sophomores, college juniors, college seniors, recent college graduates. ► *1 technology policy intern:* responsibilities include supporting and working on federal technology issues; monitoring events and hearings; tracking state and federal legislation; researching and writing; Web site support; drafting position papers; issues include broadband, privacy, digital download, and recording rights. Candidates should have knowledge of field, oral communication skills, personal interest in the field, research skills, written communication skills. Duration is summer (May to August). $10 per hour. Open to college juniors, college seniors, graduate students, law students. International applications accepted.
Benefits Formal training, names of contacts, on-the-job training, opportunity to attend seminars/workshops, possible full-time employment, willing to act as a professional reference, willing to complete paperwork for educational credit, willing to provide letters of recommendation.
Contact E-mail or through World Wide Web site Amy Hegeman, Human Resources Specialist. Fax: 703-907-7056. E-mail: ceajobs@ce.org. No phone calls. In-person interview required. Applicants must submit a resume, three personal references, 2 writing samples for communications and editorial positions. Applications are accepted continuously. World Wide Web: http://www.ce.org.

CREATIVE PRODUCERS GROUP
4818 Washington Boulevard
St. Louis, Missouri 63108

General Information Marketing communications company specializing in meetings, video, events, and Web for Fortune 500 firms. Established in 1985. Number of employees: 35. Number of internship applications received each year: 30.
Internships Available ► *1–2 graphic design interns:* responsibilities include logo design, print work, Web design. Candidates should have computer skills, declared college major in field, knowledge of field, oral communication skills, self-motivation, written communication skills. Duration is 1 semester. Unpaid. ► *1 production intern:* responsibilities include assisting producers and project managers with the production of major meetings, tours, and events. Candidates should have knowledge of field, oral communication skills, organizational skills, plan to pursue career in field, self-motivation, written communication skills. Duration is 1 semester. Unpaid. ► *1–2 sales and marketing interns:* responsibilities include research, writing press releases, assisting sales people with proposals and presentations. Candidates should have analytical skills, declared college major in field, knowledge of field, oral communication skills, self-motivation, written communication skills. Duration is 1 semester. Unpaid. ► *1–3 video interns:* responsibilities include dubs, video library assistance, production assistance, Media 100 editing, stock footage location. Candidates should have declared college major in field, knowledge of field, oral communication skills, organizational skills, self-motivation, written communication skills. Duration is 1 semester. Unpaid. Open to college sophomores, college juniors, college seniors.
Benefits On-the-job training, willing to act as a professional reference, willing to complete paperwork for educational credit, willing to provide letters of recommendation.
Contact Write, e-mail, or through World Wide Web site Amy M. J. Elz, Manager, Marketing and Special Projects. Fax: 314-367-5510. E-mail: internships@getcreative.com. No phone calls. In-person interview required. Applicants must submit a formal

Creative Producers Group (continued)

organization application, letter of interest, resume. Applications are accepted continuously. World Wide Web: http://www.getcreative.com.

EQUINE SPECIALTY HOSPITAL, INC./AURORA EQUINE VETERINARY SERVICE
17434 Rapids Road
Mantua, Ohio 44255

General Information Equine veterinary medical and surgical hospital and field service. Established in 1976. Number of employees: 25. Number of internship applications received each year: 12.
Internships Available ▶ *2–3 equine veterinary interns:* responsibilities include duties as described at http://www.aaep.org/avenues.php. Candidates should have ability to work independently, oral communication skills, self-motivation, strong interpersonal skills, written communication skills. Duration is 1 year. $20,000–$25,000 per year. Open to graduates of veterinary college eligible for licensure in Ohio. International applications accepted.
Benefits Formal training, free housing, health insurance, on-the-job training, opportunity to attend seminars/workshops, possible full-time employment, willing to complete paperwork for educational credit, willing to provide letters of recommendation.
International Internships Available.
Contact Write or e-mail Arthur E. Segedy, DVM. Phone: 440-834-0811. E-mail: equinehospital@netscape.net. In-person interview recommended (telephone interview accepted). Applicants must submit a formal organization application, letter of interest, resume, three personal references. Applications are accepted continuously. World Wide Web: http://www.aaep.org.

GROBIT MEDIA
1025 North Fillmore Street, Suite 280
Arlington, Virginia 22201

General Information Digital media contact design and development firm specializing in consumer products. Established in 2001. Number of employees: 2. Number of internship applications received each year: 12.
Internships Available ▶ *1–4 digital artists and illustrators:* responsibilities include creating graphical assets that will be used for digital media design and content purposes. Candidates should have ability to work independently, computer skills, knowledge of field, oral communication skills, organizational skills, personal interest in the field, self-motivation, strong interpersonal skills, written communication skills, proficiency in PhotoShop and Freehand required, experience with Adobe Illustrator, Adobe After Effects, DVD studio pro a plus. Unpaid. Open to high school students, recent high school graduates, college freshmen, college sophomores, college juniors, college seniors, recent college graduates, graduate students, individuals reentering the workforce. ▶ *1–4 market research and business development interns:* responsibilities include creating and executing marketing and business development plans. Candidates should have ability to work independently, analytical skills, college courses in field, computer skills, editing skills, knowledge of field, office skills, oral communication skills, organizational skills, personal interest in the field, research skills, self-motivation, strong interpersonal skills, written communication skills. Unpaid. Open to college juniors, college seniors, recent college graduates, graduate students, MBA students. International applications accepted.
Benefits Names of contacts, on-the-job training, possible full-time employment, willing to act as a professional reference, willing to complete paperwork for educational credit, willing to provide letters of recommendation.
Contact E-mail Greg Schraff, Managing Partner. Fax: 703-248-8814. E-mail: gregschraff@grobit.com. No phone calls. In-person interview recommended (telephone interview accepted). Applicants must submit a letter of interest, resume, portfolio. Applications are accepted continuously. World Wide Web: http://www.grobit.com.

HAGYARD DAVIDSON MCGEE
4250 Iron Works Pike
Lexington, Kentucky 40511

General Information Equine hospital. Established in 1876. Number of employees: 250. Number of internship applications received each year: 20.
Internships Available ▶ *2–5 veterinarians.* Candidates should have ability to work independently, oral communication skills, self-motivation, strong interpersonal skills. Duration is July 1 to June 30. Paid. Open to college seniors, veterinary college graduates. International applications accepted.
Benefits Formal training, free housing, health insurance, on-the-job training, opportunity to attend seminars/workshops, possible full-time employment, travel reimbursement, willing to act as a professional reference, willing to provide letters of recommendation.
Contact Write or e-mail Nicole L. Tomlinson, Internship Coordinator. Phone: 859-255-8741. Fax: 859-253-0196. E-mail: n.nltfarrier@verizon.net. In-person interview recommended (telephone interview accepted). Applicants must submit a letter of interest, resume, academic transcripts, portfolio, three letters of recommendation. Application deadline: December 1. World Wide Web: http://www.hagyard.com.

HEWITT ASSOCIATES LLC
100 Half Day Road
Lincolnshire, Illinois 60069

General Information Consulting firm specializing in human resource solutions that help clients get the most from design, financing, communication, administration, delivery of human resources, compensation, and benefit plans. Established in 1940. Number of employees: 13,000. Number of internship applications received each year: 1,000.
Internships Available ▶ *12–20 actuarial consultants:* responsibilities include using analytical and communication skills to help clients address various employee benefit issues, pension valuations, merger and acquisition strategy, union negotiation support, design of executive retirement plans, and financial analysis of health-care benefits. Candidates should have ability to work independently, analytical skills, plan to pursue career in field, self-motivation, strong interpersonal skills. Duration is 10–12 weeks. Competitive salary. ▶ *10–25 business analysts:* responsibilities include working on teams delivering pension, 401(k), or health and welfare benefits to clients' employees; testing the computer systems that support the benefit plans; researching client problems; benefit calculations; and analyzing data. Candidates should have ability to work independently, ability to work with others, analytical skills, self-motivation, detail orientation and flexibility. Duration is 10–12 weeks. Competitive salary. ▶ *8–10 information systems interns:* responsibilities include formulating and recommending strategies for the use of computer and communications technology to support all of the practices within Hewitt Associates, including PeopleSoft, Lotus Notes, and internal systems. Candidates should have ability to work independently, ability to work with others, analytical skills, knowledge of field, SQL, C++, Visual Basic, Windows NT, Access, networking, and database administration experience. Duration is 10–12 weeks. Competitive salary. ▶ *8–10 programmer analysts:* responsibilities include working on teams to deliver the technology that administers clients' benefit plans, tailoring Hewitt's customized systems and software to clients' requirements, developing system specifications, customizing programs, converting data, and designing and implementing interactive systems including voice-response and Internet. Candidates should have ability to work independently, ability to work with others, analytical skills, self-motivation, COBOL, JCL knowledge. Duration is 10–12 weeks. Competitive salary. Open to individuals entering senior year of college. International applications accepted.
Benefits Free housing, free meals, on-the-job training, opportunity to attend seminars/workshops, possible full-time employment, willing to act as a professional reference, willing to complete paperwork for educational credit, willing to provide letters of recommendation.
Contact Write, fax, or through World Wide Web site Kathy Loverude, Recruiting Consultant, 100 Half Day Road, Lincolnshire, Illinois 60069. Fax: 847-575-1178. E-mail: careers@hewitt.com. No

phone calls. In-person interview required. Applicants must submit a letter of interest, resume, academic transcripts, formal application (for in-person interviews, first round); telephone interview (for second round of interviews). Application deadline: January 15 for summer. World Wide Web: http://www.hewitt.com.

LITTLETON LARGE ANIMAL CLINIC
8025 South Santa Fe Drive
Littleton, Colorado 80120

General Information Equine hospital/with 24-hour emergency service. Established in 1950. Number of employees: 50. Number of internship applications received each year: 40.

Internships Available ▶ *4 veterinary post-graduate interns:* responsibilities include treatment of all assigned cases. Candidates should have college degree in related field, knowledge of field, oral communication skills, personal interest in the field, plan to pursue career in field, must be fully licensed by state of Colorado. Duration is one year (June to June). $900-$1300 per month plus quarterly increase of $200 per month. Open to recent college graduates. ▶ *1 veterinary technician intern:* responsibilities include monitoring ICU patients, taking radiographs, administering and monitoring anesthesia, and aiding veterinarian with receiving emergencies. Candidates should have knowledge of field, plan to pursue career in field, self-motivation, strong interpersonal skills. Duration is January-June or July-December. $950 per month. Open to certified veterinary technicians. International applications accepted.

Benefits Free housing, health insurance, opportunity to attend seminars/workshops, possible full-time employment, travel reimbursement, willing to act as a professional reference, willing to complete paperwork for educational credit, willing to provide letters of recommendation.

Contact Write, call, fax, e-mail, or through World Wide Web site Dawn Ermish, Intern/Extern Coordinator. Phone: 303-794-6359 Ext. 20. Fax: 303-794-9466. E-mail: llacequine@qwest.net. Applicants must submit a formal organization application, letter of interest, resume, academic transcripts, portfolio, three letters of recommendation. Application deadline: December 1. World Wide Web: http://www.littletonequine.com.

MERRITT & ASSOCIATES EQUINE HOSPITAL
26996 North Darrell Road
Wauconda, Illinois 60084

General Information Equine veterinary hospital. Established in 1996. Number of employees: 20. Number of internship applications received each year: 12.

Internships Available ▶ *2 interns.* Candidates should have ability to work with others, college degree in related field, oral communication skills, organizational skills, plan to pursue career in field, self-motivation. Duration is one year (July 1-June 30). $22,000-$24,000 per year. Open to veterinary school graduate. International applications accepted.

Benefits Formal training, health insurance, on-the-job training, opportunity to attend seminars/workshops, willing to act as a professional reference, willing to complete paperwork for educational credit, willing to provide letters of recommendation, continuing education allowance, vacation, and sick days.

Contact E-mail Amy Raia, Practice Manager. Phone: 847-526-9550. Fax: 847-526-9552. E-mail: merrittequine@ameritech.net. Applicants must submit a formal organization application, letter of interest, resume, academic transcripts, three letters of recommendation, telephone interview initially followed by in-person interview if appropriate. Application deadline: April 1. World Wide Web: http://www.merrittequine.com.

THE NATIONAL ACADEMIES
500 5th Street, NW
Washington, District of Columbia 20001

General Information Non-governmental science, engineering, and medical policy organization. Established in 1863. Number of employees: 1,300. Number of internship applications received each year: 600.

Internships Available ▶ *15–20 Christine Mirzayan Science and Technology Policy interns:* responsibilities include involvement with analysis and creation of science and technology policy and familiarization with interaction of science, technology, and government by working on a science and technology policy study. Candidates should have ability to work independently, oral communication skills, personal interest in the field, self-motivation, strong interpersonal skills, written communication skills. Duration is 12 weeks (January); 10 weeks (June); 12 weeks (September). Stipend of $4800-$5700. Open to graduate students, law students, those currently or about to enroll or recent graduates from graduate degree program (MS, MBA, JD, MD, PhD, DVM). International applications accepted.

Benefits Job counseling, on-the-job training, opportunity to attend seminars/workshops, travel reimbursement, willing to complete paperwork for educational credit.

Contact E-mail or through World Wide Web site Deborah D. Stine, Program Director. Phone: 202-334-2455. Fax: 202-334-1667. E-mail: internship@nas.edu. Applicants must submit application and reference form on-line. Application deadline: March 1 for June session, June 1 for September session, November 1 for January session. World Wide Web: http://www.nationalacademies.org/internship.

ORGANIZERS' COLLABORATIVE
PO Box 400897
Cambridge, Massachusetts 02140

General Information Organization that develops free software, Web sites and publishes information to help social change organizations become more effective in their use of electronic mail, databases, and the Internet. Established in 1999. Number of employees: 1. Number of internship applications received each year: 25.

Internships Available ▶ *1–2 Web application and software developers:* responsibilities include developing Web-based national directory of social change-related e-mail lists and software development. Candidates should have ability to work independently, oral communication skills, self-motivation, strong interpersonal skills, Web/software experience using HTML, PHP, PERL, JAVA script, Visual Basic, Filemaker, or GTK. Duration is 2–9 months (start September, January, or June). Position available as unpaid or paid. Open to high school students, recent high school graduates, college freshmen, college sophomores, college juniors, college seniors, graduate students, law students, career changers, individuals reentering the workforce. ▶ *1 Web site promotion, e-fund-raising intern:* responsibilities include increasing visibility and traffic of group's Web sites and enhancing online fund-raising capacity. Candidates should have ability to work independently, computer skills, oral communication skills, self-motivation, written communication skills. Duration is 2-9 months (start September, January, or June). Unpaid. Open to high school students, recent high school graduates, college freshmen, college sophomores, college juniors, college seniors, recent college graduates, graduate students, law students, career changers, individuals reentering the workforce. ▶ *1 development associate/event organizer:* responsibilities include prospect research on potential donors, media work, and organizing annual fund-raising event. Candidates should have ability to work independently, oral communication skills, self-motivation, written communication skills. Duration is 2-9 months (start September, January or June). Unpaid. Open to high school students, recent high school graduates, college freshmen, college sophomores, college juniors, college seniors, recent college graduates, graduate students, law students, career changers, individuals reentering the workforce. ▶ *1–2 graphic designers (Web):* responsibilities include helping produce art work and graphics for Web site, brochures, and publications. Candidates should have ability to work independently, oral communication skills, self-motivation, strong interpersonal skills, experience with PhotoShop, Fireworks, Quark Xpress, or Illustrator helpful. Duration is 2–9 months (start September, January, or June). Unpaid. Open to high school students, recent high school graduates, college freshmen, college sophomores, college juniors, college seniors, recent college graduates, graduate students, law students, career changers, individuals reentering the workforce. ▶ *1 nonprofit office man-*

Organizers' Collaborative (continued)

agement intern: responsibilities include nonprofit bookkeeping, office organization, and government and foundation reporting. Candidates should have ability to work independently, office skills, oral communication skills, organizational skills, self-motivation, written communication skills. Duration is 2-9 months (start September, January, or June). Unpaid. Open to high school students, recent high school graduates, college freshmen, college sophomores, college juniors, college seniors, recent college graduates, graduate students, law students, career changers, individuals reentering the workforce. ▶ *1–2 social movement specialists (Internet):* responsibilities include acting as issue specialists (housing, rights, peace) using e-mail to recruit editors for national online directory of social change resources. Candidates should have ability to work independently, computer skills, oral communication skills, self-motivation, strong interpersonal skills. Duration is 2 to 9 months (start September, January, or June). Unpaid. Open to high school students, recent high school graduates, college freshmen, college sophomores, college juniors, college seniors, recent college graduates, graduate students, law students, career changers, individuals reentering the workforce. ▶ *1–2 technical writing/user supporters:* responsibilities include revising manuals for software and creating technical tips sheets to make computers/Internet accessible to grassroots groups. Candidates should have ability to work independently, computer skills, self-motivation, writing skills. Duration is 2-9 months (start September, January, or June). Unpaid. Open to high school students, recent high school graduates, college freshmen, college sophomores, college juniors, college seniors, recent college graduates, graduate students, law students, career changers, individuals reentering the workforce. International applications accepted.
Benefits Travel reimbursement, willing to act as a professional reference, willing to complete paperwork for educational credit, willing to provide letters of recommendation, some stipends available.
Contact Write or e-mail Rich Cowan, Director. Phone: 617-426-1228 Ext. 108. Fax: 617-695-1295. E-mail: oc@organizenow.net. Applicants must submit a resume, brief cover letter indicating how many hours available to work and relevant experience with computers, politics, or social change activism. Application deadline: April 10 for summer, August 1 for fall, December 1 for winter/spring. World Wide Web: http://organizenow.net.

PERFORMANCE EQUINE ASSOCIATES
15257 Highway 377
Whitesboro, Texas 76273

General Information Equine veterinary hospital. Established in 2000. Number of employees: 17. Number of internship applications received each year: 12.
Internships Available ▶ *1–3 veterinary interns:* responsibilities include treatment of horses under the supervision of the doctors on staff. Candidates should have college degree in related field. Duration is one year (July to June). $24,000 per year. Open to recent college graduates. International applications accepted.
Benefits Free housing, health insurance, on-the-job training, possible full-time employment, willing to act as a professional reference, willing to complete paperwork for educational credit, willing to provide letters of recommendation.
Contact Write Dr. Lane Easter. No phone calls. Applicants must submit a letter of interest, resume, academic transcripts, two letters of recommendation. Application deadline: January 31. World Wide Web: http://performanceequineassoc.com.

PERFORMANCE RESEARCH
25 Mill Street, Queen Anne Square
Newport, Rhode Island 02840

General Information Market research firm specializing in quantitatively and qualitatively evaluating the effectiveness of sports and special event sponsorships. Established in 1985. Number of employees: 30. Number of internship applications received each year: 400.
Internships Available ▶ *1–2 market research interns:* responsibilities include travel and data collecting at sporting events, conducting personal interviews, performing data entry, designing surveys, and generating reports. Candidates should have ability to work independently, oral communication skills, research skills, self-motivation, strong interpersonal skills, writing skills, some experience with word processing and graphics applications on the computer (preferred). Duration is 12–15 weeks. $2000 stipend. Open to college juniors, college seniors, recent college graduates, graduate students. International applications accepted.
Benefits Job counseling, names of contacts, possible full-time employment, willing to act as a professional reference, willing to complete paperwork for educational credit, willing to provide letters of recommendation, stipend paid upon completion of internship, work-related travel reimbursement.
Contact Write, fax, e-mail, or through World Wide Web site Mr. Marc Porter, Internship Coordinator. Fax: 401-848-0110. E-mail: mporter@performanceresearch.com. No phone calls. In-person interview required. Applicants must submit a letter of interest, resume, writing sample. Application deadline: February 15 for spring, April 15 for summer, July 15 for fall, November 15 for winter. World Wide Web: http://www.performanceresearch.com.

PIONEER HI-BRED INTERNATIONAL
400 Locust Street, Suite 700, PO Box 14454
Des Moines, Iowa 50306-3454

General Information World leader in the discovery, development, and delivery of elite crop genetics. Established in 1926. Number of employees: 2,000. Subsidiary of DuPont, Wilmington, Delaware. Number of internship applications received each year: 1,000.
Internships Available ▶ *35–40 product advancement trial interns.* Candidates should have ability to work independently, college courses in field, knowledge of field, oral communication skills, personal interest in the field, plan to pursue career in field, self-motivation, strong interpersonal skills, strong leadership ability, written communication skills. Duration is 6 months. $9–$12 per hour plus a $1000 stipend upon successful completion of internship. Open to college sophomores, college juniors, college seniors, recent college graduates. ▶ *50 professional interns:* responsibilities include participating in development activities organized by Pioneer and completing and presenting a project at the end of the internship. Candidates should have analytical skills, college courses in field, computer skills, experience in the field, oral communication skills, strong interpersonal skills, strong leadership ability, written communication skills. Duration is 3 months. $9–$12 per hour plus a $1000 stipend if returning to school. Open to college sophomores, college juniors, college seniors. International applications accepted.
Benefits Formal training, job counseling, on-the-job training, opportunity to attend seminars/workshops, possible full-time employment, travel reimbursement, tuition assistance, willing to act as a professional reference, willing to complete paperwork for educational credit, willing to provide letters of recommendation.
International Internships Available.
Contact Write, e-mail, or through World Wide Web site Carla Cain, Employment Services Manager, 400 Locust Street, Suite 700, PO Box 14454. Fax: 515-334-6555. E-mail: carla.cain@pioneer.com. No phone calls. In-person interview recommended (telephone interview accepted). Applicants must submit a formal organization application, letter of interest, academic transcripts, writing sample, personal reference, letter of recommendation, resume that can be scanned. Applications are accepted continuously. World Wide Web: http://www.pioneer.com.

PRESENTATION TESTING, INC.
330 West 38th Street, Suite 1705
New York, New York 10018

General Information Company that gathers and analyzes audience response to help perfect the message. Established in 2002. Number of employees: 3. Number of internship applications received each year: 15.
Internships Available ▶ *1–2 general interns:* responsibilities include participating in all areas of a small start-up company including researching potential clients; preparing for sales meetings, assist-

ing in delivery of consulting services and dial groups. Duration is flexible. Unpaid. Open to college sophomores, college juniors, college seniors, recent college graduates.

Benefits Names of contacts, opportunity to attend seminars/workshops, willing to act as a professional reference, willing to complete paperwork for educational credit, willing to provide letters of recommendation.

Contact Write, call, fax, or e-mail Cindy Ng, Director of Operations. Phone: 212-760-4358. Fax: 212-760-8102. E-mail: cindyng@presentationtesting.com. Applicants must submit a letter of interest, resume. Applications are accepted continuously. World Wide Web: http://www.PresentationTesting.com.

PRO-FOUND SOFTWARE, INC.
500 Frank W. Burr Boulevard, Glenpointe Centre West
Teaneck, New Jersey 07666

General Information Technology consulting firm specializing in software development and system connectivity. Established in 1989. Number of employees: 8. Number of internship applications received each year: 1,000.

Internships Available ▶ *2 software consultants:* responsibilities include working with senior professionals and industry-leading clients in all aspects of software development from requirements definition through design and implementation. Candidates should have ability to work independently, ability to work with others, college courses in field, computer skills, experience in the field, personal interest in the field. Duration is 3–12 months. $500–$650 per week. Open to college sophomores, college juniors, college seniors, recent college graduates, graduate students. International applications accepted.

Benefits Opportunity to attend seminars/workshops, possible full-time employment, willing to complete paperwork for educational credit, willing to provide letters of recommendation, opportunity to co-publish articles and utilize and extend cutting-edge tools and components in software laboratory.

Contact Write, call, fax, e-mail, or through World Wide Web site Traci Dare, Internship Coordinator. Phone: 201-928-0400. Fax: 201-928-1122. E-mail: tdare@pro-found.com. In-person interview recommended (telephone interview accepted). Applicants must submit a letter of interest, resume. Applications are accepted continuously. World Wide Web: http://www.pro-found.com.

RIC INTERNATIONAL
432 Columbia Street, Suite B10
Cambridge, Massachusetts 02141-1041

General Information Language services company. Established in 1991. Number of employees: 9. Number of internship applications received each year: 300.

Internships Available ▶ *2–4 market research interns:* responsibilities include quantifying and qualifying the needs of specific market segments (government or private) for technical translation services; developing sales and marketing recommendations based on these findings. Candidates should have ability to work independently, analytical skills, oral communication skills, self-motivation, strong interpersonal skills, telephone skills. Duration is 10–12 weeks. Position available as unpaid or at $300–$500 per duration of internship. Open to college juniors, college seniors, recent college graduates, graduate students, career changers. International applications accepted.

Benefits On-the-job training, possible full-time employment, willing to act as a professional reference, willing to complete paperwork for educational credit, willing to provide letters of recommendation.

Contact Write, fax, e-mail, or through World Wide Web site Internship Coordinator. Fax: 617-344-5639. E-mail: internship@ricintl.com. No phone calls. In-person interview required. Applicants must submit a letter of interest, resume, 2-3 page proposal on ideas for the position. Application deadline: April 7 for summer, July 1 for fall. World Wide Web: http://www.ricintl.com.

RISK ANALYSIS GROUP
4641 Burnet Avenue
Sherman Oaks, California 91403

General Information Risk and security consulting firm. Established in 2001. Number of internship applications received each year: 3,000.

Internships Available ▶ *1 administrative assistant:* responsibilities include answering phones, composing and typing routine correspondence, organizing and maintaining files, sending out faxes, assistance with various projects, research, dictation, memos, and other duties as assigned. Candidates should have computer skills, editing skills, office skills, research skills, strong interpersonal skills, writing skills. Duration is 3–12 months. Unpaid. Open to college freshmen, college sophomores, college juniors, college seniors, recent college graduates, graduate students, law students, career changers. ▶ *1 corporate sponsorship sales intern:* responsibilities include creating annual, quarterly, monthly and weekly sales reports; pursuing new business and sales leads through cold calling, internal and external networking, and participation in trade shows; filing all contact data, correspondence, estimates, and proposals for new businesses and maintenance on existing business accounts; and customer service. Candidates should have ability to work independently, oral communication skills, research skills, self-motivation, strong interpersonal skills. Duration is 3–12 months. Unpaid. Open to college freshmen, college sophomores, college juniors, college seniors, recent college graduates, graduate students, law students, career changers. ▶ *1 editorial assistant:* responsibilities include proofreading newsletter and magazine articles; assisting editorial process for newsletter and special reports; editing/writing short news items for publication; editing marketing material; editorial projects; recordkeeping; confirming research data; and ensuring that deadlines are met. Candidates should have analytical skills, editing skills, knowledge of field, research skills, self-motivation, writing skills. Duration is 3–12 months. Unpaid. Open to college freshmen, college sophomores, college juniors, college seniors, recent college graduates, graduate students, law students, career changers. ▶ *2 human resources assistants:* responsibilities include informational probing, pre-screening of potential candidates, interviewing potential candidates, employment/reference checks, background checks, organizing and maintaining files, working with human resources management, typing, assisting with various projects and other duties as assigned. Candidates should have computer skills, oral communication skills, organizational skills, research skills, strong interpersonal skills. Duration is 3–12 months. Unpaid. Open to college freshmen, college sophomores, college juniors, college seniors, graduate students, law students, career changers. ▶ *2 human resources recruiter assistants:* responsibilities include helping review resumes, screening qualified candidates, e-mailing questionnaires to qualified candidates, scanning resumes from resume databases, preliminary phone screens, scheduling interviews, posting internships on the Internet, handling miscellaneous administrative work, and organizing and maintaining files. Candidates should have computer skills, oral communication skills, organizational skills, research skills, strong interpersonal skills, written communication skills. Duration is 3–12 months. Unpaid. Open to college freshmen, college sophomores, college juniors, college seniors, recent college graduates, graduate students, law students, career changers. ▶ *5 junior consultants:* responsibilities include development and implementation of programs and projects, brainstorming and creative meetings, internal site development, surveys and assessments, researching and evaluating resources, analyzing policy issues and contexts, demographic analysis, fact sheet preparation, database and information management, assisting with various projects and other assigned duties. Candidates should have analytical skills, organizational skills, plan to pursue career in field, research skills, strong leadership ability, written communication skills. Duration is 3–24 months. Unpaid. Open to college freshmen, college sophomores, college juniors, college seniors, recent college graduates, graduate students, law students, career changers. ▶ *1 marketing/public relations assistant:* responsibilities include working on internal/external communications, newsletters, investor relations, and Web site development; composing sales letters and various types of correspondence; planning, promoting, and

Risk Analysis Group (continued)

implementing events and services; creating promotional materials; qualitative/quantitative research; department mailings. Candidates should have oral communication skills, organizational skills, research skills, self-motivation, strong interpersonal skills, written communication skills. Duration is 3–12 months. Unpaid. Open to college freshmen, college sophomores, college juniors, college seniors, recent college graduates, graduate students, law students, career changers. ▶ *1 programming assistant:* responsibilities include assisting senior programmer; assisting with content and layout of Web site; helping manage, maintain, and edit Web site; database maintenance; and work with IT department. Candidates should have ability to work with others, analytical skills, college courses in field, computer skills, knowledge of field, research skills. Duration is 3–12 months. Unpaid. Open to college freshmen, college sophomores, college juniors, college seniors, recent college graduates, graduate students, law students, career changers. ▶ *3 research assistants:* responsibilities include information probing, organizing and maintaining files and databases, working with management, typing, project assistance, and other duties as assigned. Candidates should have ability to work independently, analytical skills, computer skills, organizational skills, research skills, writing skills. Duration is 3–12 months. Unpaid. Open to college freshmen, college sophomores, college juniors, college seniors, recent college graduates, graduate students, law students, career changers. ▶ *5 research assistants IV (telecommuting):* responsibilities include conducting demographic analysis to provide critical input, informational probing, organizing and maintaining files and database, working with management, assisting with various projects, typing, and other duties as assigned. Candidates should have analytical skills, computer skills, office skills, organizational skills, research skills, self-motivation. Duration is 3–12 months. Unpaid. Open to college freshmen, college sophomores, college juniors, college seniors, recent college graduates, graduate students, law students, career changers. ▶ *1 sales assistant:* responsibilities include contacting executives and directors of companies, cold calling, maintaining business contacts, generating leads and follow-ups, informational probing, organizing and maintaining files, working with management, and assisting with projects. Candidates should have oral communication skills, organizational skills, research skills, self-motivation, strong interpersonal skills. Duration is 3–12 months. Unpaid. Open to college freshmen, college sophomores, college juniors, college seniors, recent college graduates, graduate students, law students, career changers. ▶ *2 training assistants:* responsibilities include assisting trainers in coordinating, mentoring, and managing trainees; assessment of individual skills, abilities, and experience in order to develop training plans, online courses, and live e-classes; scheduling, conducting, and coordinating training sessions; updating and improving curriculum; record and report evaluations of activities and report statistics. Candidates should have oral communication skills, organizational skills, strong interpersonal skills, strong leadership ability, writing skills. Duration is 3–12 months. Unpaid. Open to college freshmen, college sophomores, college juniors, college seniors, recent college graduates, graduate students, law students, career changers.
Benefits Formal training, job counseling, on-the-job training, opportunity to attend seminars/workshops, possible full-time employment, willing to act as a professional reference, willing to complete paperwork for educational credit, willing to provide letters of recommendation.
Contact Write or e-mail Catherine Rhee, Director. E-mail: catherine@riskanalysisgroup.com. No phone calls. In-person interview required. Applicants must submit a formal organization application, letter of interest, resume, academic transcripts, three writing samples, 3 to 5 personal references. Applications are accepted continuously. World Wide Web: http://www.riskanalysisgroup.com.

SMITHSONIAN INSTITUTION, OFFICE OF SPONSORED PROJECTS
750 Ninth Street, NW, Suite 9200
Washington, District of Columbia 20001

General Information Unit that provides assistance to Smithsonian staff who are seeking, or have obtained, grants or other external funding for sponsored projects. Established in 1846. Number of employees: 16. Unit of Smithsonian Institution, Washington, District of Columbia. Number of internship applications received each year: 20.
Internships Available ▶ *Grants and contract administration interns:* responsibilities include helping research, curatorial, and educational staff find funding, prepare proposals, and administer grants and contracts. Candidates should have ability to work independently, office skills, self-motivation, strong interpersonal skills, positive attitude. Duration is variable (minimum 2 months, 10-15 hours per week). Unpaid. Open to high school students, recent high school graduates, college freshmen, college sophomores, college juniors, college seniors, recent college graduates, graduate students, law students, career changers, individuals reentering the workforce. International applications accepted.
Benefits Opportunity to attend seminars/workshops, possible full-time employment, willing to act as a professional reference, willing to complete paperwork for educational credit, willing to provide letters of recommendation, travel reimbursement to and from work.
Contact Write, call, fax, or e-mail Karen Otiji, Internship Coordinator. Phone: 202-275-0677. Fax: 202-275-0497. E-mail: kareno@osp.si.edu. Telephone interview required. Applicants must submit a formal organization application, resume, academic transcripts, personal reference, essay, cover letter indicating proposed internship dates and internship objectives. Applications are accepted continuously. World Wide Web: http://www.si.edu.

SMITHSONIAN INSTITUTION, OFFICE OF THE CHIEF TECHNOLOGY OFFICER
Arts and Industries Building, 900 Jefferson Drive, SW, Room 2224
Washington, District of Columbia 20560-0433

General Information Unit that provides Smithsonian's central computing and telecommunications services and training as well as leadership in information technology. Established in 1846. Number of employees: 150. Unit of Smithsonian Institution, Washington, District of Columbia. Number of internship applications received each year: 50.
Internships Available ▶ *Interns:* responsibilities include providing technical support to several mainframe systems and network servers doing computer training, helping to maintain e-mail and Web services, assisting with image scanning and the development of multimedia documents. Candidates should have computer skills, knowledge of field, interest in computer help desk operations, e-mail, programming languages, or network design. Duration is flexible. Position available as unpaid or paid. Open to high school students, recent high school graduates, college freshmen, college sophomores, college juniors, college seniors, recent college graduates, graduate students, law students, career changers, individuals reentering the workforce, must be 16 years or older. International applications accepted.
Benefits On-the-job training, opportunity to attend seminars/workshops, willing to complete paperwork for educational credit, willing to provide letters of recommendation, practical experience with an information technology services unit.
Contact Write, fax, e-mail, or through World Wide Web site Sherri Manning, Internship Coordinator, Arts and Industries Building 900 Jefferson Drive, SW, Room 2225, Washington, District of Columbia 20560-0433. Fax: 202-633-9466. E-mail: mannings@oit.si.edu. No phone calls. Applicants must submit a formal organization application, letter of interest, resume, academic transcripts, personal reference, essay. Applications are accepted continuously. World Wide Web: http://www.si.edu/organiza/offices/oit/start.htm.

TOXIKON
15 Wiggins Avenue
Bedford, Massachusetts 01730

General Information Environmental chemistry and toxicology (mammalion and in vitro) contract testing labs. Established in 1977. Number of employees: 90. Number of internship applications received each year: 35.

Internships Available ▶ *2–3 assistant environmental chemistry lab technicians:* responsibilities include extracting and analyzing inorganic, environmental samples, including oil and grease and total petroleum hydrocarbons, according to method and within the framework of Toxikon SOP's and QAP and in a timely manner; analyses include nitrates, nitrites, sulfates, acidity, alkalinity, turbidity, conductivity, pH, DO, Suspended Solids, Total Solids, BOD; maintaining complete and thorough records of all extractions, sample preparations and analysis; entering analyses data into SAM as soon as they are complete; maintaining a current work order due table; ensuring proper method validation and performance within all required QA/QC, EPA and GLP guidelines. Duration is 40 hours per week in summer (May—August). $10 per hour plus overtime potential. Open to college juniors, college seniors, recent college graduates. ▶ *1 assistant in vitro lab technician:* responsibilities include setting up and conducting various tests for in vitro studies conducted under FDA, ISO/EN, GLP and other guidelines for the department; Ames Assays, water testing, microbial penetration; this position supports the microbiology and cell culture labs; responsible for all equipment utilized and assigned, including calibration and maintenance logs. Duration is 40 hours per week in summer (May—August). $10 per hour plus overtime potential. Open to college juniors, college seniors, recent college graduates. ▶ *1 assistant in vivo lab technician:* responsibilities include animal testing (small rodents such as mice, guinea pigs, hamsters) conducted under appropriate guidelines (FDA, EPA, GLP, ISO) for medical product registration; includes preparation of reagents and testing solutions as well as maintaining complete documentation testing data; working with mice, rats, hamsters, rabbits, guinea pigs and dogs under the direction of a senior lab technician. Duration is 40 hours per week in summer (May—August). $10 per hour plus overtime potential. Open to college juniors, college seniors, recent college graduates, individuals experienced with animal handling. ▶ *1 log-in assistant:* responsibilities include receiving and logging samples on the computer; assisting with sample return and disposal; reviewing contracts and filing; preparing bottle orders for environmental chemistry division and assisting with the toxicology log-in, including microbiology and cell culture departments. Duration is 40 hours per week in summer (May—August). $10 per hour plus overtime potential. Open to college juniors, college seniors, recent college graduates. Candidates for all positions should have ability to work independently, ability to work with others, college courses in field, knowledge of field, organizational skills, plan to pursue career in field, self-motivation, ability to work in a fast-paced production lab environment while meeting or exceeding project due dates.
Benefits Formal training, job counseling, names of contacts, on-the-job training, possible full-time employment, willing to act as a professional reference, willing to complete paperwork for educational credit, willing to provide letters of recommendation.
Contact Write, fax, e-mail, or through World Wide Web site Human Resources Generalist. Fax: 781-271-1137. E-mail: hr@toxikon. com. No phone calls. In-person interview recommended (telephone interview accepted). Applicants must submit a formal organization application, letter of interest, resume, academic transcripts, portfolio, three personal references. Applications are accepted continuously. World Wide Web: http://www.toxikon.com.

VINTAGE RACING SERVICES, INC.
1785 Barnum Avenue
Stratford, Connecticut 06614

General Information Company that performs vintage race car restoration, sales, maintenance, and track support. Established in 1985. Number of employees: 8. Number of internship applications received each year: 5.
Internships Available ▶ *1–2 general office interns:* responsibilities include bookkeeping, invoicing, research, documentation, and business management. Candidates should have ability to work with others, computer skills, office skills, oral communication skills, research skills, written communication skills. Duration is flexible. $6 to $15 per hour commensurate with experience and ability. Open to recent high school graduates, college freshmen, college sophomores, college juniors, college seniors, recent college gradu-

ates, graduate students, law students, career changers, individuals reentering the workforce, must be 18 years or older. ▶ *3 race car technicians:* responsibilities include vintage race car preparation, trackside maintenance, system design, component repair/ design and fabrication, repair and maintenance. Candidates should have ability to work with others, analytical skills, personal interest in the field, self-motivation, written communication skills, willingness to travel within U.S. Duration is flexible. $7 to $25 per hour commensurate with experience and ability. Open to high school seniors, recent high school graduates, college freshmen, college sophomores, college juniors, college seniors, recent college graduates, graduate students, law students, career changers, individuals reentering the workforce, must be 18 years or older. International applications accepted.
Benefits Names of contacts, on-the-job training, opportunity to attend seminars/workshops, possible full-time employment, travel reimbursement, willing to act as a professional reference, willing to complete paperwork for educational credit, willing to provide letters of recommendation.
Contact Write, call, fax, e-mail, or through World Wide Web site Mrs. Denise Cutrone, Human Resources. Phone: 203-377-6745 Ext. 10. Fax: 203-386-0486. E-mail: kent@auto-restore.com. In-person interview recommended (telephone interview accepted). Applicants must submit a letter of interest, resume. Applications are accepted continuously. World Wide Web: http://www.vintageracingservices. com.

VIRGINIA EQUINE IMAGING
PO Box 835
Middleburg, Virginia 20118

General Information Veterinary diagnostic imaging and sports medicine practice. Established in 1997. Number of employees: 8. Number of internship applications received each year: 8.
Internships Available ▶ *1 diagnostic imaging intern (veterinarian):* responsibilities include all aspects of diagnostic imaging, lameness examination work-ups, referral letters, client communication, and emergency work. Candidates should have ability to work independently, college degree in related field, experience in the field, oral communication skills, self-motivation, strong interpersonal skills, strong leadership ability, writing skills. Duration is 1 year (starting in June). $18,000 per duration of internship. Open to veterinarians. International applications accepted.
Benefits Formal training, health insurance, job counseling, names of contacts, on-the-job training, opportunity to attend seminars/ workshops, travel reimbursement, willing to act as a professional reference, willing to provide letters of recommendation.
Contact E-mail Dr. Kent Allen, Veterinarian. Phone: 540-687-4663. Fax: 540-687-4665. E-mail: vaequine@aol.com. In-person interview required. Applicants must submit a formal organization application, letter of interest, resume, academic transcripts, portfolio, two personal references, three letters of recommendation. Application deadline: January 1.

ADVERTISING AND PUBLIC RELATIONS

THE ADVERTISING CLUB
235 Park Avenue South, Sixth Floor
New York, New York 10003

General Information Premier organization for all communications professionals in New York; offers its members a forum to exchange ideas, learn, make connections, recognize excellence, and give back to build a stronger advertising and marketing community. Established in 1896. Number of employees: 9. Unit of American Advertising Federation, Washington, District of Columbia. Number of internship applications received each year: 500.
Internships Available ▶ *Account management interns:* responsibilities include assisting account executives in serving clients;

The Advertising Club (continued)

coordinating all aspects of campaigns; acting as liaison between agency and clients; planning ads for publication. Candidates should have computer skills, oral communication skills, strong interpersonal skills, writing skills. Duration is 10 weeks. Position available as unpaid or paid. Open to undergraduate students entering junior/senior year. ► *Account planners:* responsibilities include researching and understanding ways in which consumers make decisions, how they operate in a category, relate to a brand, and perceive its competition. Candidates should have analytical skills, oral communication skills, research skills, written communication skills. Duration is 10 weeks in summer. Position available as unpaid or paid. Open to students entering junior or senior year. ► *Creative interns:* responsibilities include assisting art directors <u>and</u> designers; copywriting (for some positions). Candidates should have computer skills, proficiency in QuarkXpress and Adobe PhotoShop, comprehension of stats, mock-ups, film production, and mechanical production (helpful). Duration is 10 weeks in summer. Position available as unpaid or paid. Open to students entering junior or senior year. ► *Media interns:* responsibilities include assisting media planners with preparation of general advertising plans; exploring alternative media options including interactive media. Candidates should have analytical skills, computer skills, mathematical skills, good presentation skills. Duration is 10 weeks in summer. Position available as unpaid or paid. Open to students entering junior/senior year. ► *Publishing interns:* responsibilities include assisting promotion/marketing staff with trade shows/events, creation of collateral materials, presentation, and in-house marketing duties. Candidates should have oral communication skills, organizational skills, written communication skills, knowledge of Word, Excel, PowerPoint, Quark. Duration is 10 weeks in summer. Position available as unpaid or paid. Open to students entering junior or senior year.

Benefits Names of contacts, opportunity to attend seminars/workshops.

Contact Through World Wide Web site Internship Coordinator. Telephone interview required. Applicants must submit a resume, academic transcripts, writing sample, two letters of recommendation, portfolio (for creative internship positions); formal application available on Web site. Application deadline: March 6 for summer. World Wide Web: http://www.theadvertisingclub.org.

AIGNER ASSOCIATES PR INC./SPECIAL EVENTS, INC.
250 Everett Street
Boston, Massachusetts 02134

General Information Public relations and strategic marketing company. Established in 1984. Number of employees: 8. Number of internship applications received each year: 80.

Internships Available ► *2 account coordinators:* responsibilities include assisting with media contacts, office support, writing, and helping with special event production. Candidates should have computer skills, oral communication skills, self-motivation, strong interpersonal skills, written communication skills. Duration is 1 semester. Unpaid. Open to college freshmen, college sophomores, college juniors, college seniors.

Benefits Names of contacts, possible full-time employment, willing to complete paperwork for educational credit, willing to provide letters of recommendation.

Contact Write, call, or fax Melissa Prusinski, Intern Coordinator. Phone: 617-254-9500. Fax: 617-254-3700. E-mail: mprusinski@aignerassoc.com. In-person interview required. Applicants must submit a letter of interest, resume, two writing samples. Application deadline: January 1 for spring, May 1 for summer, August 1 for fall. World Wide Web: http://www.aignerassoc.com.

ALTICOR, INC. FAMILY OF COMPANIES
7575 Fulton Street East
Ada, Michigan 49355-0001

General Information One of the world's largest network marketing companies, marketing products and services through independent distributors in the U.S. and more than 60 other countries and territories. Established in 1959. Number of employees: 6,000. Number of internship applications received each year: 600.

Internships Available ► *15–30 summer interns:* responsibilities include working in any of the following departments: accounting, marketing, chemistry, biology, chemical and electrical engineering, and/or purchasing. Candidates should have declared college major in field, minimum GPA of 3.0. Duration is 12-13 weeks. $15 per hour (average). Open to college juniors, graduate students, college seniors with term or semester remaining.

Benefits Travel reimbursement, willing to complete paperwork for educational credit, discounts on Amway products, housing assistance program.

Contact Write, fax, or e-mail Cindy Molnar, Recruiter. Fax: 616-787-0368. E-mail: cindy.molnar@altcor.com. No phone calls. In-person interview required. Applicants must submit a letter of interest, resume, academic transcripts. Application deadline: January 31 (recommended). World Wide Web: http://www.alticor.com.

COMCAST
1030 Higgins Road, Suite 100
Park Ridge, Illinois 60068

General Information Cable advertising company that sells local air time on cable networks such as CNN, ESPN, and BET, and produces commercials. Number of employees: 50. Unit of AT&T Broadband, Denver, Colorado.

Internships Available ► *5 TV production interns:* responsibilities include assisting in location and studio production of commercials, set-up and breakdown of all equipment, and audio monitoring. Candidates should have ability to work with others, college courses in field, computer skills, knowledge of field, plan to pursue career in field. Duration is flexible (16 weeks minimum, 3 days per week). Unpaid. ► *6 copywriting interns:* responsibilities include assisting producers and writing ad copy. Candidates should have college courses in field, computer skills, knowledge of field, personal interest in the field, plan to pursue career in field, writing skills. Duration is 3–6 months. Unpaid. ► *Marketing and sales research interns:* responsibilities include implementing and producing advertising proposals, developing sales presentations, marketing related products, and promotional events. Candidates should have college courses in field, computer skills, organizational skills, plan to pursue career in field, research skills, writing skills. Duration is flexible. Unpaid. Open to college juniors, college seniors, recent college graduates, graduate students.

Benefits Willing to complete paperwork for educational credit, willing to provide letters of recommendation.

Contact Write, fax, or e-mail Greg Scott, Production Supervisor. Fax: 847-292-0164. E-mail: scott.greg@broadband.att.com. No phone calls. In-person interview required. Applicants must submit a resume. Applications are accepted continuously.

BERNSTEIN-REIN ADVERTISING
4600 Madison, Suite 1500
Kansas City, Missouri 64112

General Information Full-service advertising agency. Established in 1964. Number of employees: 340. Number of internship applications received each year: 200.

Internships Available ► *1–2 account management interns:* responsibilities include attending internal strategy meetings, coordinating daily operations of accounts, and writing conference reports. Candidates should have college courses in field, knowledge of field, office skills, oral communication skills, organizational skills, personal interest in the field, plan to pursue career in field, written communication skills. Duration is June to August. $8 per hour. ► *1–2 creative interns:* responsibilities include working as a copywriter or art director; conceiving and executing print, outdoor, and broadcast advertising; creating logos and taglines; selecting talent; and attending commercial shoots and edits; see Web site for additional assignments. Candidates should have ability to work with others, college courses in field, computer skills, knowledge of field, personal interest in the field, writing skills, graphic design/art experience. Duration is June to August. $8 per hour. ► *1 database/direct mail marketing intern.* Candidates should have analytical skills, computer skills, knowledge of field, oral communication skills, research skills, writing skills. Duration is June to August. $8 per hour. ▶ *1–2 media interns:* responsibilities include researching media, targeting markets, developing budgets, projecting ratings, assisting in post-buy analyses, attending meetings with national media representatives, and researching new media trends. Candidates should have analytical skills, computer skills, knowledge of field, office skills, organizational skills, research skills. Duration is June to August. $8 per hour. Open to college students entering their senior year.

Benefits On-the-job training, possible full-time employment, willing to complete paperwork for educational credit.

Contact Write, fax, or e-mail Shannan McKee, Manager of Human Resources. Fax: 816-531-5708. E-mail: shannan_mckee@bradv. com. No phone calls. In-person interview required. Applicants must submit a formal organization application, letter of interest, resume, writing sample, three personal references. Application deadline: March 1. World Wide Web: http://www.bernstein-rein. com.

BOZELL & JACOBS, LLC
13801 FNB Parkway
Omaha, Nebraska 68154

General Information Full-service advertising and public relations firm. Established in 1921. Number of employees: 50. Number of internship applications received each year: 100.

Internships Available ▶ *5–8 advertising and public relations interns:* responsibilities include working closely with advertising and public relations professionals, assisting with client projects, and working on a team to develop a complete campaign for client. Candidates should have ability to work with others, knowledge of field, oral communication skills, personal interest in the field, self-motivation, written communication skills, relevant course work or professional experience. Duration is 12 weeks in summer. $7 per hour. Open to college sophomores, college juniors, college seniors, recent college graduates, graduate students. International applications accepted.

Benefits Possible full-time employment, willing to complete paperwork for educational credit, willing to provide letters of recommendation.

Contact Write, fax, or e-mail Katy Briggs, Internship Coordinator. Fax: 402-965-4308. E-mail: kbriggs@bozelljacobs.com. No phone calls. In-person interview recommended (telephone interview accepted). Applicants must submit a formal organization application, letter of interest, resume, academic transcripts, writing sample, letter of recommendation, portfolio (for creative positions). Application deadline: March 1. World Wide Web: http://www. bozelljacobs.com/summerintern.

BRETT SINGER & ASSOCIATES, LLC/DAVID GERSTEN & ASSOCIATES, INC.
240 West 44th Street
New York, New York 10036

General Information Entertainment publicity office focusing mostly on theater (Broadway, off-Broadway, tours). Established in 1995. Number of employees: 5. Number of internship applications received each year: 25.

Internships Available ▶ *1–3 publicity interns:* responsibilities include clerical work (copying, filing, typing), Internet research, and heavy phone work. Candidates should have ability to work with others, office skills, oral communication skills, organizational skills, personal interest in the field. Duration is flexible. Position available as unpaid or at $50 per week. Open to high school students, recent high school graduates, college freshmen, college sophomores, college juniors, college seniors, recent college graduates, graduate students, (college students/recent graduates preferred). International applications accepted.

Benefits Job counseling, names of contacts, on-the-job training, opportunity to attend seminars/workshops, possible full-time employment, travel reimbursement, willing to act as a professional reference, willing to complete paperwork for educational credit, willing to provide letters of recommendation.

Contact Write, fax, or e-mail Brett Singer, President, 240 West 44th Street. Phone: 212-575-0263. Fax: 212-575-2240. E-mail: interns@brettsinger.com. In-person interview recommended (telephone interview accepted). Applicants must submit a letter of interest, resume. Applications are accepted continuously. World Wide Web: http://www.brettsinger.com.

BROWN-MILLER COMMUNICATIONS
1114 Jones Street
Martinez, California 94553

General Information Full-service public relations agency serving the health food and agriculture industries; emphasizes creativity, strong writing skills, thorough research, and persistent work. Established in 1987. Number of employees: 8. Number of internship applications received each year: 50.

Internships Available ▶ *1 account coordinator:* responsibilities include writing press releases and magazine articles, answering phones and making media calls, coordinating special events, preparing monthly activity reports, supervising account timelines, tracking press clippings, coordinating product mailing, performing database updates, running errands, researching, and filing. Candidates should have computer skills, oral communication skills, personal interest in the field, self-motivation, writing skills. Duration is 1 semester. Unpaid. Open to individuals with two years of college-related course experience in public relations, journalism, English, or communications. International applications accepted.

Benefits Job counseling, travel reimbursement, willing to complete paperwork for educational credit, willing to provide letters of recommendation, writing and editing skills enhancement, exposure to media relations.

Contact Write, fax, or e-mail Internship Coordinator. Fax: 925-370-9811. E-mail: bmc@brownmillerpr.com. No phone calls. In-person interview recommended (telephone interview accepted). Applicants must submit a letter of interest, resume, two writing samples. Applications are accepted continuously. World Wide Web: http://www.brownmillerpr.com.

BRYAN FARRISH RADIO PROMOTION
14230 Ventura Boulevard, 2nd Floor
Sherman Oaks, California 91423

General Information Music airplay promotion with radio interview publicity and syndication. Established in 1998. Number of employees: 8. Number of internship applications received each year: 50.

Internships Available ▶ *1–7 music airplay promotion interns:* responsibilities include contacting artists by phone/e-mail; data entry; and calling radio stations. Duration is flexible. Unpaid. ▶ *1–2 radio publicity interns:* responsibilities include contacting potential guests for radio publicity campaigns by phone/e-mail. Duration is flexible. Unpaid. Candidates for all positions should have oral communication skills, typing skills. Open to individuals over age 21.

Benefits Job counseling, names of contacts, on-the-job training, opportunity to attend seminars/workshops, possible full-time employment, willing to act as a professional reference, willing to complete paperwork for educational credit, willing to provide letters of recommendation, CDs and passes to artist performances.

Contact Call Intern Assistant. Phone: 818-905-8038 Ext. 14. Fax: 818-905-9149. E-mail: jobs@radio-media.com. In-person interview required. Applications are accepted continuously. World Wide Web: http://www.radio-media.com.

BURSON-MARSTELLER
230 Park Avenue South
New York, New York 10003

General Information Global perception management firm focused on delivering measurable business results to its clients through a full range of consulting and communications disciplines. Established in 1953. Number of employees: 400. Unit of WPP, New York, New York. Number of internship applications received each year: 80.

Internships Available ▶ *10–15 public relations interns:* responsibilities include working as part of a team, creating media lists, writ-

Burson-Marsteller (continued)

ing press materials, pitching stories to media, helping with logistics and staffing of press conferences and/or special events, conducting research, and monitoring media; positions also available in Chicago, DC, and California. Candidates should have oral communication skills, personal interest in the field, written communication skills, minimum GPA of 3.0 or equivalent, participation in extracurricular activities. Duration is 10 weeks. Paid. Open to college juniors, college seniors. International applications accepted.
Benefits Opportunity to attend seminars/workshops, possible full-time employment.
Contact Fax, e-mail, or through World Wide Web site Nikita Green, Recruitment Manager. Phone: 212-614-4000. Fax: 212-598-6964. E-mail: nikita_green@nyc.bm.com. Applicants must submit a letter of interest, resume, academic transcripts, writing sample, 2 essays on assigned topics; application materials can be e-mailed. Application deadline: February 3. World Wide Web: http://www.bm.com.

CAIRNS & ASSOCIATES
641 Lexington Avenue, 32nd Floor
New York, New York 10021

General Information Full-service public relations and integrated marketing agency. Established in 1983. Number of employees: 18. Number of internship applications received each year: 100.
Internships Available ▶ *2–6 interns:* responsibilities include preparing media lists and coordinating press mailings, contacting editors and television producers, maintaining press clippings, preparing client reports, writing press materials, and conducting research projects. Candidates should have knowledge of field, oral communication skills, personal interest in the field, research skills, self-motivation, written communication skills. Duration is 1 semester. Unpaid. Open to college sophomores, college juniors, college seniors, recent college graduates, graduate students.
Benefits Job counseling, names of contacts, on-the-job training, opportunity to attend seminars/workshops, possible full-time employment, willing to complete paperwork for educational credit, willing to provide letters of recommendation, participation in mentor program.
Contact Write, fax, or e-mail Karen Bertiger, Human Resource Manager, 641 Lexington Avenue, 32nd Floor, New York, New York 10022. Fax: 212-319-3956. E-mail: kbertiger@cairnsny.com. No phone calls. In-person interview required. Applicants must submit a letter of interest, resume. Applications are accepted continuously.

CANAAN PUBLIC RELATIONS
75 South Broadway, Suite 470
White Plains, New York 10601

General Information Full-service public relations firm with two major divisions: travel, hospitality, and entertainment; beauty, health, and fitness. Established in 1977. Number of employees: 1. Number of internship applications received each year: 50.
Internships Available ▶ *1–3 interns:* responsibilities include assisting account executive, preparing press kits, editing, writing, and helping plan events. Candidates should have office skills, oral communication skills, organizational skills, self-motivation, strong interpersonal skills, written communication skills. Duration is flexible. $15 per day. Open to college seniors, recent college graduates, graduate students. International applications accepted.
Benefits Formal training, names of contacts, opportunity to attend seminars/workshops, possible full-time employment, travel reimbursement, willing to complete paperwork for educational credit, willing to provide letters of recommendation.
International Internships Available.
Contact Write, fax, or e-mail Jed Canaan, President, 75 South Broadway, Suite 470, White Plains, New York 10601. Phone: 914-304-4080. Fax: 914-304-4083. E-mail: jedc@canaanpr.com. In-person interview required. Applicants must submit a letter of interest, resume. Applications are accepted continuously. World Wide Web: http://www.canaanpr.com.

CLARKE & COMPANY
535 Boylston Street, 4th Floor
Boston, Massachusetts 02116

General Information Public relations firm. Established in 1977. Number of employees: 30. Number of internship applications received each year: 100.
Internships Available ▶ *Business to business/consumer interns:* responsibilities include fully supporting the activities of two busy practice groups including drafting releases, mailing-list development, and other activities. Candidates should have college courses in field, computer skills, office skills, organizational skills, written communication skills. Duration is 1 semester. Position available as unpaid or paid. ▶ *Public affairs/crisis interns:* responsibilities include fully supporting the activities of the public affairs and crisis divisions; drafting releases, research, event attendance, and list development. Candidates should have college courses in field, computer skills, organizational skills, research skills, written communication skills. Duration is 1 semester. Position available as unpaid or paid. Open to college juniors, college seniors, recent college graduates.
Benefits On-the-job training, willing to act as a professional reference, willing to complete paperwork for educational credit, willing to provide letters of recommendation, possibility of stipend.
Contact Write or e-mail Carolyn Alberto, Internship Manager. Fax: 617-536-8524. E-mail: calberto@clarkeco.com. No phone calls. In-person interview required. Applicants must submit a letter of interest, resume. Applications are accepted continuously. World Wide Web: http://www.clarkeco.com.

COLE HENDERSON DRAKE
426 Marietta Street
Atlanta, Georgia 30313

General Information Advertising agency. Established in 1969. Number of employees: 30. Number of internship applications received each year: 30.
Internships Available ▶ *1 Wendy's High School Heisman intern:* responsibilities include managing client program including client contact, ad materials, public relations, and event planning. Candidates should have ability to work independently, ability to work with others, college courses in field, plan to pursue career in field, self-motivation, strong leadership ability. Duration is one semester (fall only). $1500 per duration of internship. ▶ *1 account planning intern:* responsibilities include overall view of account planning; developing and presenting a project; assisting planner. Candidates should have ability to work independently, analytical skills, college courses in field, plan to pursue career in field, self-motivation, strong leadership ability. Duration is 1 semester. $500 per duration of internship. ▶ *1 client services intern:* responsibilities include overview of account management; developing and presenting a project; assisting account manager in analysis, recommendations, and client programs. Candidates should have college courses in field, plan to pursue career in field, self-motivation, strong interpersonal skills, strong leadership ability. Duration is 1 semester. $500 per duration of internship. ▶ *1 creative intern:* responsibilities include assisting creative department. Candidates should have ability to work independently, computer skills, declared college major in field, experience in the field, plan to pursue career in field, solid knowledge of PhotoShop, QuarkXpress and Illustrator. Duration is 1 semester. $500 per duration of internship. ▶ *1 media planning intern:* responsibilities include overview of media planning; developing and presenting a project; assisting planners. Candidates should have ability to work independently, college courses in field, plan to pursue career in field, self-motivation, strong leadership ability, writing skills. Duration is 1 semester. $500 per duration of internship. ▶ *1 public relations intern:* responsibilities include agency and client press releases, assisting with new business, and other related public relation duties. Candidates should have ability to work independently, ability to work with others, college courses in field, plan to pursue career in field, self-motivation, written communication skills. $500 per duration of internship. Open to college juniors, college seniors, recent college graduates, graduate students. International applications accepted.

Benefits Willing to act as a professional reference, willing to complete paperwork for educational credit, willing to provide letters of recommendation.

Contact Write, call, fax, or e-mail April Voris, Client Services Manager. Phone: 404-892-4500. Fax: 404-892-4522. E-mail: avoris@chdatlanta.com. In-person interview recommended (telephone interview accepted). Applicants must submit a letter of interest, resume, portfolio, two writing samples. Application deadline: March 28 for summer, July 31 for fall, October 31 for spring. World Wide Web: http://www.chdatlanta.com.

COMMONWEALTH CONSULTANTS
8321 Old Courthouse Road, #250
Vienna, Virginia 22182

General Information Company that specializes in local political and corporate public relations, fund-raising, and lobbying. Established in 1996. Number of employees: 5. Number of internship applications received each year: 40.

Internships Available ▶ *1–2 student interns:* responsibilities include answering phones, database management, helping with fund-raising events, and general office duties. Candidates should have ability to work with others, computer skills, knowledge of field, oral communication skills, organizational skills, personal interest in the field, must have reliable transportation. Duration is one semester (15 hours per week). Unpaid. Open to college sophomores, college juniors, college seniors, recent college graduates. International applications accepted.

Benefits Names of contacts, on-the-job training, travel reimbursement, willing to act as a professional reference, willing to complete paperwork for educational credit, willing to provide letters of recommendation.

Contact Write, fax, or e-mail Ajay Jain, Account Representative. Fax: 703-827-0571. E-mail: ajain@cwconsult.com. No phone calls. In-person interview required. Applicants must submit a letter of interest, resume. Applications are accepted continuously. World Wide Web: http://www.cwconsult.com.

CONE
90 Canal Street
Boston, Massachusetts 02114

General Information Public relations/communications firm that seeks to find true alignments between companies and their customers and to create programs and communications to build image, understanding, and sales. Established in 1980. Number of employees: 50. Division of Omnicom Group. Inc., New York, New York. Number of internship applications received each year: 100.

Internships Available ▶ *12–16 account service interns:* responsibilities include engaging in all aspects of strategic marketing communications while linked to a team through which the intern will be exposed to all areas of account service. Candidates should have college courses in field, computer skills, experience in the field, oral communication skills, organizational skills, personal interest in the field, plan to pursue career in field, research skills, self-motivation, strong interpersonal skills, writing skills. Duration is 3 months. Unpaid. Open to college juniors, college seniors, graduate students. International applications accepted.

Benefits Job counseling, names of contacts, opportunity to attend seminars/workshops, willing to act as a professional reference, willing to complete paperwork for educational credit, willing to provide letters of recommendation, assistance with resume preparation and interviews, networking opportunities.

Contact Write, fax, or e-mail Wendy Krampf, Human Resources Associate. Fax: 617-523-3955. E-mail: internships@coneinc.com. In-person interview required. Applicants must submit a letter of interest, resume. Application deadline: May 1 for summer, August 1 for fall, December 1 for spring. World Wide Web: http://www.coneinc.com.

COOPER COMMUNICATIONS, INC.
5350 Topanga Canyon Boulevard
Woodland Hills, California 91364-1718

General Information Marketing/public relations firm specializing in corporate public relations, strategic planning, marketing, and media relations. Established in 1982. Number of employees: 8. Number of internship applications received each year: 50.

Internships Available ▶ *Public relations interns:* responsibilities include composing correspondence, creating media lists, placing media follow-up calls, assembling press kits, database management, research, and general office support. Candidates should have editing skills, oral communication skills, writing skills, knowledge of Word and Excel (preferred), ability to multitask. Duration is 1-2 semesters (approximately 15 hours per week). Unpaid. Open to college freshmen, college sophomores, college juniors, college seniors. International applications accepted.

Benefits On-the-job training, possible full-time employment, willing to act as a professional reference, willing to complete paperwork for educational credit, willing to provide letters of recommendation.

Contact Write, fax, or e-mail Abby Sturgeon, Account Executive. Fax: 818-348-8230. E-mail: abby@coopercommunications.net. No phone calls. In-person interview recommended (telephone interview accepted). Applicants must submit a letter of interest, resume. Applications are accepted continuously. World Wide Web: http://coopercommunications.net.

C. PAUL LUONGO COMPANY, PUBLIC RELATIONS AND MARKETING
441 Stuart Street
Boston, Massachusetts 02116

General Information Public relations firm and marketing agency that offers corporate, product, and financial publicity consulting and marketing communications services throughout the U.S. and Canada. Established in 1964. Number of employees: 6. Number of internship applications received each year: 100.

Internships Available ▶ *1–2 assistant to president interns:* responsibilities include new business and media research, telephone contacts. Candidates should have ability to work independently, analytical skills, computer skills, editing skills, office skills, oral communication skills, organizational skills, research skills, self-motivation, strong interpersonal skills, strong leadership ability, writing skills. Duration is 3–6 months. Unpaid. Open to recent high school graduates, college freshmen, college sophomores, college juniors, college seniors, recent college graduates, graduate students, law students, career changers, individuals reentering the workforce.
▶ *1–2 assistants to president:* responsibilities include administrative duties, telephones, research for new business, new business telephone contacts, some editing of articles and papers, and filing. Candidates should have computer skills, editing skills, office skills, oral communication skills, research skills, self-motivation, writing skills. Duration is minimum 3 months and up to one year. Unpaid. Open to high school students, recent high school graduates, college freshmen, college sophomores, college juniors, college seniors, recent college graduates, graduate students, law students, career changers, individuals reentering the workforce. ▶ *1 intern:* responsibilities include performing a variety of public relations activities. Candidates should have ability to work independently, analytical skills, computer skills, editing skills, office skills, oral communication skills, organizational skills, research skills, self-motivation, strong interpersonal skills, strong leadership ability, writing skills. Duration is 3 months minimum. Unpaid. Open to high school seniors, recent high school graduates, college freshmen, college sophomores, college juniors, college seniors, recent college graduates, graduate students, law students, career changers, individuals reentering the workforce. International applications accepted.

Benefits Formal training, job counseling, names of contacts, on-the-job training, possible full-time employment, willing to act as a professional reference, willing to complete paperwork for educational credit, willing to provide letters of recommendation.

C. Paul Luongo Company, Public Relations and Marketing (continued)
Contact Write, call, fax, e-mail, or through World Wide Web site Mr. C. Paul Luongo, President. Phone: 617-266-4210. Fax: 617-266-2211. E-mail: cpaul@cpaulluongo.com. In-person interview recommended (telephone interview accepted). Applicants must submit a letter of interest, resume. Applications are accepted continuously. World Wide Web: http://www.cpaulluongo.com.

CREATIVE EVENT PLANNING
1040 First Avenue, Suite 105
New York, New York 10022

General Information Corporate event planning, public relations, and marketing company. Established in 1989. Number of employees: 2.
Internships Available ▶ *1–2 administrative assistants:* responsibilities include greeting clients, typing proposals, Internet research, comparing analysis between locations, and talking to vendors. Candidates should have computer skills, English skills. Duration is flexible. Position available as unpaid or paid. Open to college freshmen, college sophomores, college juniors, college seniors, recent college graduates, graduate students, career changers, individuals reentering the workforce. ▶ *1–2 assistant planners:* responsibilities include general computer work, answering phones, writing proposals, Internet research, and event preparation. Candidates should have ability to work independently, ability to work with others, computer skills, organizational skills, self-motivation, written communication skills. Duration is April to October or beyond. Position available as unpaid or paid. Open to college freshmen, college sophomores, college juniors, college seniors, recent college graduates, graduate students, career changers, individuals reentering the workforce. ▶ *1–2 marketing assistants:* responsibilities include e-mailing newsletters and correspondence and enhancing print presentations for marketing material. Candidates should have computer skills, English skills. Duration is flexible. Position available as unpaid or paid. Open to college freshmen, college sophomores, college juniors, college seniors, recent college graduates, graduate students, career changers, individuals reentering the workforce. ▶ *1–2 sales assistants:* responsibilities include calling past clients, finding new clients through warm and cold leads by phone, follow up data, sending marketing materials/press kits, and entering information into database. Candidates should have ability to work independently, knowledge of field, oral communication skills, self-motivation, strong interpersonal skills, strong leadership ability. Duration is minimum of 6 months. Position available as unpaid or paid. Open to college juniors, college seniors, recent college graduates, graduate students, career changers, individuals reentering the workforce. International applications accepted.
Contact Write, call, or fax Lynn Silverman, Owner. Phone: 212-421-9080. Fax: 212-421-7838. Applicants must submit a letter of interest, resume.

CREATIVE MANAGEMENT SERVICES
906 D Street, NE
Washington, District of Columbia 20002

General Information Communications company producing advertising, marketing, public relations, video productions, and event planning for large and small companies and the government. Established in 1980. Number of employees: 2. Number of internship applications received each year: 100.
Internships Available ▶ *1 special assistant to the president:* responsibilities include interviewing talent; handling client bookings; making arrangements for travel and wardrobe; accompanying owner to photo shoots, TV bookings, fashion shows, and parties; and assisting with events planning and writing/advertising services. Candidates should have ability to work independently, ability to work with others, analytical skills, computer skills, office skills, oral communication skills, organizational skills, self-motivation, strong leadership ability, writing skills. Duration is 3 months or 1 semester. Unpaid. Open to high school students, recent high school graduates, college freshmen, college sophomores, college juniors, college seniors, recent college graduates, graduate students, law students, career changers, individuals reentering the workforce.

Benefits Job counseling, names of contacts, on-the-job training, willing to act as a professional reference, willing to complete paperwork for educational credit, willing to provide letters of recommendation, lunch provided.
Contact Write, call, or e-mail Ms. Anne Schwab, President. Phone: 202-333-3560. Fax: 202-544-2856. E-mail: crmgtser@aol.com. In-person interview recommended (telephone interview accepted). Applicants must submit a letter of interest, resume. Applications are accepted continuously.

CROMARTY AND COMPANY
246 West End Avenue, Suite 12A
New York, New York 10023

General Information Theatrical press agency serving a wide range of Broadway, off-Broadway, music, and dance clients by handling publicity needs. Established in 1987. Number of employees: 5. Number of internship applications received each year: 200.
Internships Available ▶ *1–2 interns:* responsibilities include assisting press agents in all aspects of publicity, including writing and mailing press releases and other materials, attending opening nights and interviews, and assisting in the office. Candidates should have ability to work independently, college courses in field, computer skills, editing skills, knowledge of field, office skills, oral communication skills, organizational skills, personal interest in the field, plan to pursue career in field, self-motivation, strong interpersonal skills, strong leadership ability, writing skills. Duration is 4 months. $50–$100 per week. Open to college freshmen, college sophomores, college juniors, college seniors, recent college graduates, graduate students, career changers, individuals reentering the workforce. International applications accepted.
Benefits Names of contacts, possible full-time employment, travel reimbursement, willing to complete paperwork for educational credit, willing to provide letters of recommendation, reimbursement for lunch on work days, small stipend.
Contact Write, e-mail, or through World Wide Web site Peter Cromarty, Internship Coordinator, PO Box 237154, New York, New York 10023. E-mail: peterc@cromarty.com. No phone calls. In-person interview recommended (telephone interview accepted). Applicants must submit a letter of interest, resume, writing sample. Application deadline: April 1 for summer, September 1 for fall, November 1 for winter. World Wide Web: http://www.cromarty.com.

DYE, VAN MOL, AND LAWRENCE
209 Seventh Avenue North
Nashville, Tennessee 37219

General Information Full-service marketing and communications firm that specializes in national, regional, and local public relations and community activities. Established in 1980. Number of employees: 50. Number of internship applications received each year: 85.
Internships Available ▶ *1–2 interns:* responsibilities include research and writing, arranging special events and meetings, and calling the media. Candidates should have ability to work with others, oral communication skills, organizational skills, research skills, self-motivation, writing skills. Duration is 3-5 months in fall, spring, or summer. $7–$8 per hour. Open to college juniors, college seniors, recent college graduates, graduate students.
Benefits Formal training, names of contacts, willing to complete paperwork for educational credit, willing to provide letters of recommendation.
Contact Write or e-mail Kristen Smithson, Internship Coordinator. Phone: 615-244-1818. E-mail: kristen.smithson@dvl.com. In-person interview required. Applicants must submit a letter of interest, resume, formal application (sent to applicant by DVL). Application deadline: March 15 for summer, July 15 for fall, November 1 for spring. World Wide Web: http://www.dvl.com.

DYKEMAN ASSOCIATES, INC.
4115 Rawlins
Dallas, Texas 75219

General Information Full-service marketing, public relations, and video production firm. Established in 1974. Number of employees: 5. Number of internship applications received each year: 75.

Internships Available ▶ *3–4 interns:* responsibilities include assisting with production of collateral materials, video production, and ad preparation; compiling media lists; contacting media; setting up programs for speakers; creating proposals for business prospects; and monitoring presentations to clients. Candidates should have analytical skills, college courses in field, computer skills, organizational skills, plan to pursue career in field, self-motivation, writing skills, dependability. Duration is 1 semester to 1 year. $12 per hour in barter dollars. Open to college juniors, college seniors, recent college graduates, graduate students. International applications accepted.

Benefits Formal training, job counseling, names of contacts, on-the-job training, opportunity to attend seminars/workshops, possible full-time employment, willing to complete paperwork for educational credit, willing to provide letters of recommendation, job listings, barter dollars (in lieu of cash) for salary.

Contact Write, fax, or e-mail Ms. Alice Dykeman, President/CEO. Fax: 214-528-0241. E-mail: adykeman@airmail.net. No phone calls. In-person interview recommended (telephone interview accepted). Applicants must submit a letter of interest, resume, four writing samples, two personal references, two letters of recommendation. Application deadline: March 15 for summer, June 15 for fall, November 15 for spring. World Wide Web: http://www.dykemanassoc.com.

EAST COAST PROMOTION AND RESEARCH GROUP
PO Box 1759
Ocean City, Maryland 21843

General Information Broad-based marketing and research business. Established in 1976. Number of employees: 10.

Internships Available ▶ *2 accounting interns:* responsibilities include tracking billing and financial records of busy advertising agency. Unpaid. ▶ *2 administrative assistants:* responsibilities include helping coordinate agency activities. Unpaid. ▶ *2 advertising interns:* responsibilities include helping develop advertising campaigns for new and existing advertising clients. Duration is 1–3 semesters. Unpaid. ▶ *2 computer science interns:* responsibilities include laying out and designing advertising campaigns on IBM and Macintosh computers. Duration is 8–10 weeks. Unpaid. ▶ *2 copy writers:* responsibilities include developing a theme and writing copy for advertising campaign. Unpaid. ▶ *3 graphic design interns:* responsibilities include developing a concept for an advertising campaign and laying out and designing ads on Macintosh and IBM computers. Unpaid. ▶ *1 human resource intern:* responsibilities include scheduling and updating personnel-related information. Unpaid. ▶ *2 management interns.* Unpaid. ▶ *4 marketing research interns:* responsibilities include conducting market research projects. Unpaid. ▶ *2 photography interns:* responsibilities include shooting black-and-white and color photographs for advertising and public relations campaigns. Unpaid. ▶ *3 public relations interns:* responsibilities include creating, writing, and servicing public relations campaigns for agency clients. Unpaid. ▶ *2 public relations writers:* responsibilities include developing marketing and sales promotion projects for advertising agency clients. Unpaid. International applications accepted.

Benefits Job counseling, names of contacts, opportunity to attend seminars/workshops, possible full-time employment, willing to complete paperwork for educational credit, willing to provide letters of recommendation, health club membership available, orientation program.

Contact Write, call, fax, or e-mail Mr. Paul Jankovic, President. Phone: 410-524-5351. Fax: 302-539-1232. E-mail: ecprg@aol.com. Applicants must submit a letter of interest, resume. Applications are accepted continuously. World Wide Web: http://www.ecusa.com.

THE EDELMAN GROUP
50 Broad Street, Suite 2001
New York, New York 10004

General Information Firm that specializes in design, advertising, and marketing for corporate clients. Established in 1982. Number of employees: 6. Number of internship applications received each year: 200.

Internships Available ▶ *1 accounting assistant:* responsibilities include invoicing, billing, and reconciling accounts. Candidates should have ability to work independently, computer skills, oral communication skills, organizational skills, personal interest in the field, plan to pursue career in field. Duration is 1 semester. Unpaid. Open to college freshmen, college sophomores, college juniors, college seniors, recent college graduates. ▶ *1–2 graphic design interns:* responsibilities include photo research, preparing artwork for presentation, and some design work. Candidates should have ability to work independently, ability to work with others, personal interest in the field, plan to pursue career in field, self-motivation, previous study of design and/or fine art. Duration is flexible. Unpaid. Open to college freshmen, college sophomores, college juniors, college seniors, recent college graduates. ▶ *1 receptionist/office intern:* responsibilities include answering telephone calls from clients and using fax and copying machines. Candidates should have ability to work with others, computer skills, office skills, oral communication skills, personal interest in the field, written communication skills. Duration is 1 semester. Unpaid. Open to high school seniors, college freshmen, college sophomores. ▶ *1 sales assistant:* responsibilities include assisting salesperson with research, lead qualification, and telemarketing. Candidates should have computer skills, oral communication skills, personal interest in the field, research skills, self-motivation, strong interpersonal skills. Duration is flexible. Unpaid. Open to college freshmen, college sophomores, college juniors, college seniors. International applications accepted.

Benefits Formal training, possible full-time employment, willing to complete paperwork for educational credit, willing to provide letters of recommendation.

Contact Write or e-mail Sandra Gibbs, Office Administrator. Fax: 212-825-1900. E-mail: sandy@edelmangroup.com. No phone calls. In-person interview recommended (telephone interview accepted). Applicants must submit a resume, two personal references, portfolio (graphic design positions). Applications are accepted continuously. World Wide Web: http://www.edelmangroup.com.

EISNER, PETROU, AND ASSOCIATES
509 South Exeter Street
Baltimore, Maryland 21202

General Information Full-service marketing communications agency specializing in technology, travel/tourism/hospitality, health care, business-to-business public relations, and special events. Established in 1986. Number of employees: 22. Affiliate of Eisner Communications, Baltimore, Maryland. Number of internship applications received each year: 100.

Internships Available ▶ *1–3 public relations interns (Baltimore office):* responsibilities include research; special events planning and implementation; and assisting with media relations and client contact. Candidates should have knowledge of field, oral communication skills, organizational skills, personal interest in the field, strong interpersonal skills, written communication skills, major in public relations/communications, previous public relations class work or internship experience. Duration is 1 semester. Position available as unpaid or paid. ▶ *1–3 public relations interns (Washington office):* responsibilities include research; special events planning and implementation; assisting in media relations and client contact. Candidates should have ability to work independently, knowledge of field, oral communication skills, organizational skills, personal interest in the field, strong interpersonal skills, writing skills, major in public relations/journalism, previous public relations class work or internship experience. Duration is 1 semester. Position available as unpaid or paid. Open to college juniors, college seniors, recent college graduates. International applications accepted.

Benefits Names of contacts, opportunity to attend seminars/workshops, possible full-time employment, travel reimbursement,

Eisner, Petrou, and Associates (continued)

willing to complete paperwork for educational credit, willing to provide letters of recommendation, possible college credit and/or stipend, Metro Card.
Contact Write, fax, or e-mail Erin Clark, Account Supervisor. Fax: 410-752-3550. E-mail: info@eisnerpetrou.com. No phone calls. In-person interview recommended (telephone interview accepted). Applicants must submit a letter of interest, resume, writing sample, two personal references. Application deadline: April 15 for summer, July 15 for fall, November 15 for spring. World Wide Web: http://www.eisnerpetrou.com.

FENTON COMMUNICATIONS
1320 18th Street, NW
Washington, District of Columbia 20036

General Information Issue-oriented public relations firm committed to representing socially responsible clients. Established in 1981. Number of employees: 30. Number of internship applications received each year: 200.
Internships Available ▶ *2–4 public relations interns:* responsibilities include program work (campaign strategy brainstorming, writing, conducting research, organizing press conferences); administrative work; developing media lists; monitoring media coverage. Candidates should have experience in the field, office skills, oral communication skills, personal interest in the field, writing skills. Duration is one semester (full-time). Position available as unpaid or at $1200 per month. Open to college freshmen, college sophomores, college juniors, college seniors, recent college graduates, graduate students. International applications accepted.
Benefits Formal training, job counseling, opportunity to attend seminars/workshops, possible full-time employment, willing to complete paperwork for educational credit, willing to provide letters of recommendation, opportunity to attend press conferences, YMCA membership, Metro passes.
Contact Write, fax, e-mail, or through World Wide Web site Erin Visser, Human Resource Manager, 1320 18th Street, NW, Washington, District of Columbia 20030. Fax: 202-822-4787. E-mail: fenton@fenton.com. No phone calls. Telephone interview required. Applicants must submit a letter of interest, resume, 2-3 writing samples. Applications are accepted continuously. World Wide Web: http://www.fenton.com.

FORTUNE PUBLIC RELATIONS
2319 California Street
Berkeley, California 94703

General Information Restaurant and food products public relations firm. Established in 1986. Number of employees: 2. Number of internship applications received each year: 20.
Internships Available ▶ *1 publicist trainee:* responsibilities include copywriting, client contact, press kit design and production, media list development, media follow-up calls, and general office duties. Candidates should have ability to work independently, knowledge of field, oral communication skills, writing skills, IBM or PC computer skills. Duration is flexible. Unpaid. Open to college seniors, recent college graduates, graduate students, career changers, individuals reentering the workforce. International applications accepted.
Benefits Job counseling, names of contacts, on-the-job training, opportunity to attend seminars/workshops, willing to act as a professional reference, willing to complete paperwork for educational credit, willing to provide letters of recommendation, possibility of part-time employment.
Contact Write, call, fax, or e-mail Tom Walton, Co-owner. Phone: 510-548-1097. Fax: 510-841-7006. E-mail: fortunepr@aol.com. In-person interview recommended (telephone interview accepted). Applicants must submit a resume. Applications are accepted continuously. World Wide Web: http://www.fortunepublicrelations. com.

THE GOLF DIGEST COMPANIES
4 Times Square, 7th Floor
New York, New York 10036

General Information Department responsible for all public relations and publicity for *Golf Digest, Golf for Women, Golf World, and Golf World Business.* Established in 1950. Number of employees: 100. Unit of Advance Magazine Publishers, Inc., New York, New York. Number of internship applications received each year: 100.
Internships Available ▶ *1–2 communications interns:* responsibilities include assisting the communications staff in all areas of publicity, including media relations and special events. Candidates should have ability to work independently, ability to work with others, computer skills, oral communication skills, organizational skills, self-motivation, written communication skills. Duration is 3–4 months. $150 per week. Open to college freshmen, college sophomores, college juniors, college seniors, recent college graduates.
Benefits Names of contacts, opportunity to attend seminars/ workshops, willing to act as a professional reference, willing to complete paperwork for educational credit, willing to provide letters of recommendation.
Contact Write, fax, or e-mail Karen Affinito, Public Relations Manager. Fax: 212-286-5344. E-mail: karen.affinito@golfdigest. com. No phone calls. In-person interview recommended (telephone interview accepted). Applicants must submit a letter of interest, resume. Application deadline: April 15 for summer, July 15 for fall, November 15 for spring. World Wide Web: http://www. golfdigest.com.

HALSTEAD COMMUNICATIONS
329 East 82nd Street
New York, New York 10028

General Information Company providing public relations for education and nonprofit organizations. Established in 1980. Number of employees: 6. Number of internship applications received each year: 250.
Internships Available ▶ *1 public relations intern:* responsibilities include writing pitch letters and press releases, pitching stories to print and broadcast media, word processing, compiling and updating databases, generating mailing lists, and conducting mailings. Candidates should have computer skills, office skills, oral communication skills, organizational skills, personal interest in the field, self-motivation, writing skills, creativity and flexibility, knowledge of MS-Office (preferred). Duration is flexible; (about 40 hours per week). Position available as unpaid or at $10–$12 per hour. Open to college juniors, college seniors, recent college graduates.
Benefits Job counseling, names of contacts, on-the-job training, opportunity to attend seminars/workshops, possible full-time employment, travel reimbursement, willing to act as a professional reference, willing to complete paperwork for educational credit, willing to provide letters of recommendation.
Contact Write, call, fax, or e-mail Heidi Reinholdt, Internship Coordinator. Phone: 212-734-2190. Fax: 212-517-7284. E-mail: reinholdt@halsteadpr.com. In-person interview recommended (telephone interview accepted). Applicants must submit a resume, writing sample, cover letter stating interest and availability. Application deadline: call for deadlines. World Wide Web: http://www. halsteadpr.com.

HILL AND KNOWLTON, INC.
466 Lexington Avenue, 3rd Floor
New York, New York 10017

General Information Headquarters of global public relations firm. Established in 1927. Number of employees: 150. Number of internship applications received each year: 700.
Internships Available ▶ *Fall/winter interns:* responsibilities include working on assignments and attending regular employee seminars and office events; internships available in New York City, Washington (DC), Chicago, Houston, Los Angeles, San Francisco, Sacramento, Tampa, and Ft. Lauderdale. Candidates should have oral communication skills, organizational skills, personal interest in the field, written communication skills, previous academic or work

experience in public relations or communications field helpful. Duration is flexible. $10 per hour. ▶ *6–12 summer interns:* responsibilities include working with one or two supervisors as part of account teams; exposure to practice specialties within the public relations profession including media relations, financial relations, marketing and crisis communications, and health care; research; preparing and presenting proposals; internships available in New York City, Washington (DC), Chicago, Houston, Los Angeles, San Francisco, Sacramento, Tampa, and Ft. Lauderdale. Candidates should have oral communication skills, organizational skills, personal interest in the field, written communication skills, previous academic or work experience in public relations or communication field helpful. Duration is mid-June to mid-August (8-10 week minimum). $10 per hour. Open to college juniors, college seniors, recent college graduates, graduate students. International applications accepted.
Benefits Formal training, opportunity to attend seminars/workshops, possible full-time employment, willing to complete paperwork for educational credit, willing to provide letters of recommendation.
Contact E-mail or through World Wide Web site Donna Renella, Senior Managing Director, Recruitment. E-mail: careers@hillandknowlton.com. Telephone interview required. Applicants must submit a letter of interest, resume, 1 specified essay. Application deadline: March 1 for summer, July 30 for fall, October 15 for winter. World Wide Web: http://www.hillandknowlton.com.

HWH PUBLIC RELATIONS/NEW MEDIA
1414 Avenue of the Americas
New York, New York 10019

General Information Public relations agency. Established in 1980. Number of employees: 25. Number of internship applications received each year: 200.
Internships Available ▶ *1–2 graphic design interns:* responsibilities include working with New Media team on Web design, graphic design, Internet, and Flash projects. Candidates should have ability to work independently, ability to work with others, computer skills, knowledge of field, personal interest in the field. Duration is 1 semester. Unpaid. Open to college sophomores, college juniors, college seniors. ▶ *5–7 public relations interns:* responsibilities include writing press releases, researching and compiling media lists, phone pitching, arranging media appointments, administrative tasks. Candidates should have ability to work independently, ability to work with others, computer skills, knowledge of field, office skills, oral communication skills, writing skills. Duration is 1 semester; (minimum of 15 hours per week required). Unpaid. Open to college juniors, college seniors.
Benefits Travel reimbursement, willing to act as a professional reference, willing to complete paperwork for educational credit, willing to provide letters of recommendation.
Contact Write, call, fax, e-mail, or through World Wide Web site Carrie Gray, Intern Coordinator. Phone: 212-355-5049. Fax: 212-593-0065. E-mail: carrieg@hwhpr.com. In-person interview required. Applicants must submit a letter of interest, resume, writing sample. Application deadline: March 1 for summer, June 30 for fall, October 31 for spring. World Wide Web: http://www.hwhpr.com.

JACKSINA COMPANY
1501 Broadway, Suite 1508
New York, New York 10036

General Information Publicity, public relations, and marketing company whose expertise is concentrated in the entertainment field with specific attention to the promoting, publicizing, and marketing of Broadway shows and films; also works in the music industry. Established in 1978. Number of employees: 4.
Internships Available ▶ *Account associates.* Candidates should have ability to work independently, office skills, oral communication skills, personal interest in the field, self-motivation, strong interpersonal skills, written communication skills. Duration is one summer. Unpaid. Open to college freshmen, college sophomores, college juniors, college seniors. International applications accepted.

Benefits Free meals, job counseling, on-the-job training, opportunity to attend seminars/workshops, possible full-time employment, travel reimbursement, willing to act as a professional reference, willing to complete paperwork for educational credit, willing to provide letters of recommendation.
Contact Write, call, fax, or e-mail Judy Jacksina. Phone: 212-221-8361. Fax: 212-221-8369. E-mail: thejacksinaco@mindspring.com. In-person interview recommended (telephone interview accepted). Applicants must submit a resume. Applications are accepted continuously.

J & L MARKETING, INC.
1860 Campus Place
Louisville, Kentucky 40299

General Information Marketing and advertising arm for the automobile industry. Established in 1991. Number of employees: 150.
Internships Available ▶ *Promotion coordinators:* responsibilities include leading and organizing marketing promotions at automotive dealerships, conducting sales meetings, greeting and qualifying customers based on buying needs and habits, and maintaining an upbeat sales atmosphere. Candidates should have ability to work independently, oral communication skills, organizational skills, personal interest in the field, self-motivation, strong interpersonal skills. Duration is up to one year. $12–$14 per hour. Open to college freshmen, college sophomores, college juniors.
Benefits Formal training, on-the-job training, travel reimbursement, willing to act as a professional reference, willing to complete paperwork for educational credit.
Contact Call or e-mail Jessica Lukawski, National Recruiter. Phone: 800-346-9117 Ext. 126. Fax: 502-261-9155. E-mail: jlukawski@jandlmarketing.com. In-person interview recommended (telephone interview accepted). Applicants must submit a formal organization application, resume. Applications are accepted continuously. World Wide Web: http://www.jandlmarketing.com.

KCSA PUBLIC RELATIONS WORLDWIDE
800 Second Avenue
New York, New York 10017

General Information Public relations agency specializing in public and investor relations, corporate communications, and marketing communications. Established in 1969. Number of employees: 50. Number of internship applications received each year: 400.
Internships Available ▶ *3–5 public relations interns:* responsibilities include working with various groups. Candidates should have ability to work with others, computer skills, oral communication skills, personal interest in the field, self-motivation, written communication skills. Duration is flexible. Unpaid. Open to college sophomores, college juniors, college seniors.
Benefits Formal training, job counseling, on-the-job training, possible full-time employment, travel reimbursement, willing to complete paperwork for educational credit, willing to provide letters of recommendation.
Contact Write, fax, or e-mail Managing Partner. Phone: 212-896-1238. Fax: 212-986-3380. E-mail: vchung@kcsa.com. In-person interview required. Applicants must submit a letter of interest, resume. Application deadline: early January for spring, August 15 for summer, September 15 for fall. World Wide Web: http://www.kcsa.com.

LEVINE COMMUNICATIONS OFFICE
10333 Ashton Avenue
Los Angeles, California 90024

General Information Entertainment public relations firm. Established in 1983. Number of employees: 4. Number of internship applications received each year: 500.
Internships Available ▶ *1–25 interns:* responsibilities include writing press releases, assembling media lists, writing pitch letters, pitching stories to media, working events, administrative duties, research. Candidates should have oral communication skills, organizational skills, self-motivation, strong interpersonal skills, writing skills. Duration is 295 total hours. Unpaid. Open to high

Levine Communications Office (continued)

school students, recent high school graduates, college freshmen, college sophomores, college juniors, college seniors, recent college graduates, graduate students, law students, career changers, individuals reentering the workforce. International applications accepted.

Benefits Job counseling, names of contacts, on-the-job training, opportunity to attend seminars/workshops, willing to act as a professional reference, willing to complete paperwork for educational credit, willing to provide letters of recommendation.

Contact Write, call, fax, e-mail, or through World Wide Web site Ottilia Makgatho, Internship Coordinator. Phone: 310-248-6222 Ext. 14. Fax: 310-248-6227. E-mail: ottilia@levinepr.com. In-person interview recommended (telephone interview accepted). Applicants must submit a formal organization application, letter of interest, resume. Applications are accepted continuously. World Wide Web: http://www.levinepr.com.

LIGGETT-STASHOWER PUBLIC RELATIONS
1228 Euclid Avenue
Cleveland, Ohio 44115

General Information Public relations division of one of the largest communications firms in the Midwest serving clients nationwide. Established in 1980. Number of employees: 95. Unit of Liggett-Stashower Inc., Cleveland, Ohio. Number of internship applications received each year: 100.

Internships Available ▶ *1–2 public relations interns:* responsibilities include assisting with media relations, contacting print editors and broadcast journalists on telephone, and assisting on general assignments as needed. Candidates should have computer skills, knowledge of field, oral communication skills, plan to pursue career in field, writing skills, formal education in public relations, membership in PRSSA (a plus). Duration is 1 summer or fall semester. Minimum wage stipend. Open to college juniors, college seniors. International applications accepted.

Benefits Formal training, names of contacts, on-the-job training, opportunity to attend seminars/workshops, willing to act as a professional reference, willing to complete paperwork for educational credit, willing to provide letters of recommendation.

Contact Write, fax, or e-mail Brenda Stolarski, Business Manager. Fax: 216-736-8118. E-mail: bstolarski@liggett.com. No phone calls. In-person interview required. Applicants must submit a letter of interest, resume, portfolio, three writing samples. Application deadline: March 1 for summer, July 1 for fall. World Wide Web: http://www.liggett.com.

LINDY PROMOTIONS, INC.
4343 Montgomery Avenue, Suite 5
Bethesda, Maryland 20814

General Information Promotions and event planning company. Number of employees: 3. Number of internship applications received each year: 400.

Internships Available ▶ *1–4 marketing interns:* responsibilities include various administrative duties, grassroots marketing in the D.C. metropolitan area, writing press releases, helping with planning and execution of events, assisting with mailings, advertising sales for monthly newsletter. Candidates should have ability to work independently, computer skills, office skills, organizational skills, personal interest in the field, research skills, self-motivation, strong interpersonal skills, strong leadership ability, writing skills. Duration is 3–4 months. Unpaid. Open to college sophomores, college juniors, college seniors.

Benefits Names of contacts, on-the-job training, possible full-time employment, willing to act as a professional reference, willing to complete paperwork for educational credit, willing to provide letters of recommendation.

Contact Write, fax, or e-mail Becky Dilling, Event Coordinator, 4343 Montgomery Avenue, Suite 5, Bethesda, Maryland 20814. Fax: 301-652-7714. E-mail: becky@lindypromo.com. In-person interview recommended (telephone interview accepted). Applicants must submit a letter of interest, resume. World Wide Web: http://www.lindypromo.com.

LORD, SULLIVAN & YODER PUBLIC RELATIONS
250 Old Wilson Bridge Road
Columbus, Ohio 43085

General Information Full-service marketing communications and public relations firm. Established in 1965. Number of employees: 75.

Internships Available ▶ *1 intern:* responsibilities include writing news releases, Web site copy, assisting management in new business and client research, developing media lists and editorial calendars, media relations, attending internal and client meetings, and others tasks as appropriate. Candidates should have computer skills, organizational skills, research skills, self-motivation, writing skills, (preference is given to communications majors). Duration is one summer (flexible). $10 per hour. Open to college sophomores, college juniors. International applications accepted.

Benefits Job counseling, on-the-job training, opportunity to attend seminars/workshops, possible full-time employment, travel reimbursement, willing to act as a professional reference, willing to complete paperwork for educational credit, willing to provide letters of recommendation, $1500 scholarship.

Contact Call, e-mail, or through World Wide Web site Marty Hatfield, Senior Account Executive. Phone: 614-825-8500. Fax: 614-846-2780. E-mail: mhatfield@lsy.com. Applicants must submit a formal organization application, letter of interest, resume, three writing samples, two letters of recommendation, completed case study. Application deadline: March 15 for summer. World Wide Web: http://www.lsy.com.

MAGNET COMMUNICATIONS
110 Fifth Avenue
New York, New York 10011

General Information Public relations agency providing full-service communications services including media relations, special events, strategic planning and research, creative services, corporate management, and crisis management. Established in 2000. Number of employees: 150. Division of Havas Advertising, Paris, France. Number of internship applications received each year: 500.

Internships Available ▶ *5–10 interns:* responsibilities include writing press materials, pitching stories, researching and fact-checking, and coordinating special events. Candidates should have ability to work with others, computer skills, oral communication skills, plan to pursue career in field, self-motivation, written communication skills. Duration is 3 months in fall, summer, or spring. Position available as unpaid or at $7–$10 per hour. Open to college juniors, college seniors, recent college graduates. International applications accepted.

Benefits Formal training, names of contacts, on-the-job training, opportunity to attend seminars/workshops, possible full-time employment, willing to complete paperwork for educational credit, willing to provide letters of recommendation.

Contact Write, e-mail, or through World Wide Web site Intern Coordinator. E-mail: hrjobs@magnet.com. No phone calls. In-person interview required. Applicants must submit a formal organization application, letter of interest, resume, three writing samples. Application deadline: February 28 for summer; continuous for other positions. World Wide Web: http://www.magnet.com.

MANNING, SELVAGE & LEE
1170 Peachtree Street, 4th Floor
Atlanta, Georgia 30309

General Information International global public relations firm. Established in 1965. Number of employees: 40. Division of Publicis Groupe, SA, New York, New York. Number of internship applications received each year: 200.

Internships Available ▶ *1–2 summer interns (Georgia):* responsibilities include media monitoring, clip reports, media list compilation, pitching, and research. Candidates should have experience in the field, organizational skills, strong interpersonal skills, written communication skills, overall GPA of 3.0 or higher. Duration is 1 summer. $10 per hour. ▶ *Summer interns (New York):* responsibilities include assignment to work in a specific practice group and also to work with other interns to complete a public relations program for a client; completion of a basic training program. Candidates should have declared college major in field, overall GPA of 3.0 or higher. Duration is 8 weeks (full-time). $10 per hour. Open to individuals who have completed junior or senior year of college. International applications accepted.

Benefits Formal training, names of contacts, on-the-job training, opportunity to attend seminars/workshops, possible full-time employment, willing to act as a professional reference, willing to complete paperwork for educational credit, willing to provide letters of recommendation.

Contact E-mail or through World Wide Web site Jenni Sasser, Director of Human Resources. Phone: 404-870-6802. Fax: 404-870-6869. E-mail: hr.atl@mslpr.com. In-person interview required. Applicants must submit a formal organization application, letter of interest, resume, 2-3 writing samples, 2-3 letters or recommendation, electronic application and other materials as specified on Web site. Application deadline: February 15. World Wide Web: http://www.mslpr.com.

MAXIMUM EXPOSURE PR
50 Tice Boulevard
Woodcliff Lake, New Jersey 07677

General Information Public relations firm servicing a wide variety of interests including consumer products, professionals, business-to-business services, and nonprofit organizations. Established in 1986. Number of employees: 5.

Internships Available ▶ *Public relations interns:* responsibilities include assisting account executives in all aspects of public relations and performing clerical work. Candidates should have ability to work independently, ability to work with others, computer skills, office skills, oral communication skills, organizational skills, plan to pursue career in field, self-motivation, written communication skills. Duration is year-round. Unpaid. Open to college freshmen, college sophomores, college juniors, college seniors. International applications accepted.

Benefits On-the-job training, willing to act as a professional reference, willing to complete paperwork for educational credit, willing to provide letters of recommendation.

Contact Write or e-mail Andrea Pass, Vice President. E-mail: andrea@maximumexposurepr.com. No phone calls. In-person interview required. Applicants must submit a resume, three writing samples. Applications are accepted continuously. World Wide Web: http://www.maximumexposurepr.com.

M80 SERVICES
2400 Hyperion Avenue
Los Angeles, California 90027

General Information Marketing company specializing in online grassroots marketing, promotions and publicity, lifestyle marketing, imaging and design for record labels, studios, and corporate brands. Established in 1998. Number of employees: 14. Number of internship applications received each year: 100.

Internships Available ▶ *5–10 assistant directors:* responsibilities include marketing, research, networking, outreach, reporting, collateral distribution, promotions, database management, design, and client relations. Candidates should have computer skills, organizational skills, plan to pursue career in field, research skills, self-motivation, written communication skills. Duration is 1 semester. Unpaid. Open to recent high school graduates, college freshmen, college sophomores, college juniors, college seniors, graduate students. International applications accepted.

Benefits Names of contacts, on-the-job training, willing to act as a professional reference, willing to complete paperwork for educational credit, willing to provide letters of recommendation.

Contact E-mail Joe Muran, Vice President Marketing, Research and Development. E-mail: joey@m801m.com. No phone calls. In-person interview recommended (telephone interview accepted). Applicants must submit a resume, writing sample. Applications are accepted continuously. World Wide Web: http://www.m80im.com.

MITCH SCHNEIDER ORGANIZATION
14724 Ventura Boulevard, Suite 410
Sherman Oaks, California 91403

General Information Music public relations company. Established in 1995. Number of employees: 15. Number of internship applications received each year: 150.

Internships Available ▶ *5–10 interns:* responsibilities include assisting in writing news items, organizing mailings, making follow-up phone calls, updating computer database information, and researching media and various business contacts. Candidates should have ability to work with others, computer skills, office skills, oral communication skills, organizational skills, personal interest in the field, plan to pursue career in field, research skills, self-motivation, written communication skills. Duration is 3 months (15 hours minimum per week). Unpaid. Open to college freshmen, college sophomores, college juniors, college seniors, graduate students.

Benefits Job counseling, names of contacts, opportunity to attend seminars/workshops, possible full-time employment, willing to act as a professional reference, willing to complete paperwork for educational credit, willing to provide letters of recommendation, opportunity to attend music-related events and receive company products.

Contact Write, fax, e-mail, or through World Wide Web site Kerry McGovern, Internship Coordinator. Fax: 818-380-0430. E-mail: msoorg@aol.com. No phone calls. In-person interview recommended (telephone interview accepted). Applicants must submit a letter of interest, resume, completed internship application. Applications are accepted continuously. World Wide Web: http://www.msopr.com.

MIXED MEDIA
20 Lockmere Road
Cranston, Rhode Island 02910

General Information Publicity and promotion company specializing in the music industry. Established in 1989. Number of employees: 1. Number of internship applications received each year: 10.

Internships Available ▶ *1–2 publicity assistants:* responsibilities include press kit assembly; telephone/fax/e-mail solicitations to the media about new recordings/cds; promotion of musicians to industry-related contacts (distributors, other record companies, booking agents, managers). Candidates should have ability to work independently, computer skills, office skills, oral communication skills, personal interest in the field, self-motivation, strong interpersonal skills, written communication skills. Duration is 1–2 semesters. Unpaid. Open to college freshmen, college sophomores, college juniors, college seniors.

Benefits Names of contacts, on-the-job training, willing to act as a professional reference, willing to complete paperwork for educational credit, willing to provide letters of recommendation, possibility of part-time employment, opportunity to attend concerts and record release performances.

Contact Call, fax, or e-mail Ginny Shea, President. Phone: 401-942-8025. Fax: 401-942-5487. E-mail: ginny@mixed-media.org. In-person interview recommended (telephone interview accepted). Applicants must submit a resume. Applications are accepted continuously.

M. SILVER ASSOCIATES, INC.
747 Third Avenue, 23rd Floor
New York, New York 10017-2803

General Information Public relations/marketing communications consultants to travel, consumer, and tourism industries worldwide. Established in 1960. Number of employees: 24. Number of internship applications received each year: 100.

Internships Available ▶ *2–4 fall/winter/spring interns:* responsibilities include assisting account group with daily workload necessary to serving clients, attending staff/creative meetings, conducting on-line research, writing press releases, preparing and disseminating press releases, press kits, and photographs; using ACT database to initiate, track, and report on media contact; assisting with press trip invitations, itineraries, and trips. Duration is 1

M. Silver Associates, Inc. (continued)

semester. $6-8 per hour depending on experience plus a stipend to reimburse for expenses. Open to college sophomores, college juniors, college seniors, only those studying toward a public relations/communications degree or having completed other PR internship. ► *2–3 summer interns:* responsibilities include assisting account group with daily work load necessary to serving clients; attending staff/creative meetings; conducting on-line research; writing press releases; preparing and disseminating press releases, press kits, and photographs; using ACT database to initiate, track, and report on media contact; assisting with press trip invitations, itineraries, and trips. Duration is end of May semester through mid-August. $200 stipend per week. Open to college sophomores, college juniors, only those studying toward public relations/communications degree or having completed other PR internship. Candidates for all positions should have college courses in field, computer skills, experience in the field, oral communication skills, organizational skills, written communication skills.

Benefits Job counseling, names of contacts, on-the-job training, opportunity to attend seminars/workshops, possible full-time employment, willing to act as a professional reference, willing to complete paperwork for educational credit, willing to provide letters of recommendation, opportunity to attend staff meetings/creative sessions and to be a fully participating accounts group member; stipend for travel and lunch.

Contact Write, call, fax, e-mail, or through World Wide Web site Vivian DiMare, Operations Administrator/Internship Coordinator. Phone: 212-754-6500 Ext. 204. Fax: 212-754-6698. E-mail: vivian@msilver-pr.com. In-person interview recommended (telephone interview accepted). Applicants must submit a letter of interest, resume, 1 or 2 letters of recommendation. Applications are accepted continuously. World Wide Web: http://www.msilver-pr.com.

NATIONAL CANCER INSTITUTE, OFFICE OF COMMUNICATIONS
Building 31, Room 10A28, 31 Center Drive, MSC 2580
Bethesda, Maryland 20892-2580

General Information Organization responsible for developing and managing communications activities of the National Cancer Institute and disseminating information to the public, the press, and health professionals. Established in 1937. Number of employees: 5,000. Unit of National Institute of Health, Bethesda, Maryland. Number of internship applications received each year: 50.

Internships Available ► *1–10 health communication interns:* responsibilities include planning, developing, evaluating, and promoting education and information programs to target audiences; preparing and carrying out national education campaigns; and pretesting and evaluating health education materials. Candidates should have computer skills, knowledge of field, oral communication skills, organizational skills, self-motivation, written communication skills. Duration is 6 months-1 year. $1500–$2100 per month. ► *1–3 science writing interns:* responsibilities include handling inquiries from reporters, writing news and feature articles and fact sheets for the press and public, and attending scientific meetings. Candidates should have analytical skills, computer skills, oral communication skills, organizational skills, writing skills, knowledge of science. Duration is 6 months-1 year. $1500–$2100 per month. Open to graduate students.

Benefits Formal training, health insurance, on-the-job training, opportunity to attend seminars/workshops, willing to act as a professional reference, willing to complete paperwork for educational credit, willing to provide letters of recommendation, reimbursement of on-the-job travel expenses, free parking, paid government holidays.

Contact Write, e-mail, or through World Wide Web site Internship Director. Fax: 301-496-7096. E-mail: nciinterndirector@mail.nih.gov. No phone calls. Telephone interview required. Applicants must submit a formal organization application, letter of interest, resume, academic transcripts, two writing samples, letter of recommendation, 1 personal reference from advisor/Dean stating student status and expected date of graduation. Application deadline:

March 15 for July—December term, September 15 for January—June term. World Wide Web: http://internship.cancer.gov.

NORTH CAROLINA AMATEUR SPORTS
PO Box 12727
Research Triangle Park, North Carolina 27709

General Information Organization that promotes the Olympic movement through amateur sports, produces the State Games of North Carolina and Cycle North Carolina, sponsors state conferences on the Olympic movement and amateur sports, and attracts national and international events and conferences to North Carolina. Established in 1983. Number of employees: 5. Number of internship applications received each year: 30.

Internships Available ► *1 Cycle North Carolina Assistant Ride Director:* responsibilities include assisting with event management, equipment procurement and distribution, recruitment, scheduling and supervising of volunteers, coordinating logistics, assisting with event promotion, processing entries, and distributing entry confirmations. Candidates should have ability to work with others, oral communication skills, organizational skills, self-motivation, strong leadership ability, written communication skills. Duration is August through October. Paid. Open to college juniors, college seniors, recent college graduates, graduate students, career changers. ► *1 competition intern:* responsibilities include State Games of North Carolina equipment procurement, venue set-up, temporary warehouse organization, communications planning and implementation. Candidates should have ability to work independently, ability to work with others, oral communication skills, organizational skills, self-motivation. Duration is mid-May through mid-July. $200 per week. Open to college freshmen, college sophomores, college juniors, college seniors, recent college graduates, graduate students. ► *Data services intern:* responsibilities include State Games of North Carolina entry processing, validation and roster verification, weekly entry summary reports, and registration reports. Candidates should have ability to work independently, ability to work with others, computer skills, oral communication skills, organizational skills, written communication skills. Duration is mid-May through mid-July. $200 per week. Open to college freshmen, college sophomores, college juniors, college seniors, recent college graduates, graduate students. ► *1 marketing intern:* responsibilities include marketing and media/promotions for the State Games of North Carolina including sponsor fulfillment, signage, merchandise and ticket distribution, sports information, and event results. Candidates should have ability to work independently, computer skills, oral communication skills, organizational skills, writing skills. Duration is mid-May through mid-July. $200 per week. Open to college freshmen, college sophomores, college juniors, college seniors, recent college graduates, graduate students. ► *1 special events intern:* responsibilities include planning, organizing, and implementing special programs and projects associated with the State Games of North Carolina, including Celebration of Athletes, VIP Reception, Sportsmanship Program, and Host Hotel Program. Candidates should have ability to work independently, ability to work with others, oral communication skills, organizational skills, personal interest in the field, strong leadership ability, written communication skills. Duration is mid-May through mid-July. $200 per week. Open to college freshmen, college sophomores, college juniors, college seniors, recent college graduates, graduate students. ► *1 volunteer coordinator:* responsibilities include recruiting, training, supervising, and assigning 1000-2000 volunteers who work with the State Games. Candidates should have computer skills, oral communication skills, organizational skills, self-motivation, strong interpersonal skills, written communication skills. Duration is 8–10 weeks. $150–$200 per week. Open to college freshmen, college sophomores, college juniors, college seniors, recent college graduates, graduate students. ► *Volunteer services intern:* responsibilities include recruiting, training, supervising, and assigning volunteers for the State Games of North Carolina. Candidates should have ability to work independently, computer skills, oral communication skills, organizational skills, self-motivation, written communication skills. Duration is mid-May through mid-July. $200 per week. Open to college freshmen, college sophomores, college juniors, college seniors, recent college graduates, graduate students.

Benefits Job counseling, names of contacts, on-the-job training, opportunity to attend seminars/workshops, possible full-time employment, travel reimbursement, willing to act as a professional reference, willing to complete paperwork for educational credit, willing to provide letters of recommendation.

Contact Write, call, fax, e-mail, or through World Wide Web site Ty Martin, Assistant Director of Operations. Phone: 919-361-1133 Ext. 2. Fax: 919-361-2559. E-mail: ty.martin@ncsports.org. In-person interview recommended (telephone interview accepted). Applicants must submit a formal organization application, letter of interest, resume, three personal references. Application deadline: July 1 for Cycle North Carolina position; February 15 for other positions. World Wide Web: http://www.ncsports.org.

OCEAN CITY ADVERTISING AGENCY
PO Box 1759
Ocean City, Maryland 21843

General Information Full-service advertising agency that serves the resort area by providing advertising, public relations, sales promotion, photography, and market research services. Established in 1976. Number of employees: 10. Number of internship applications received each year: 100.

Internships Available ▶ *2 accounting interns:* responsibilities include tracking billing and financial records of busy advertising agency. Candidates should have computer skills, knowledge of field, personal interest in the field, self-motivation, strong interpersonal skills. Duration is 1–2 semesters. Unpaid. ▶ *2 advertising interns:* responsibilities include helping develop advertising campaigns for new and existing advertising clients. Candidates should have computer skills, oral communication skills, personal interest in the field, self-motivation, strong interpersonal skills, strong leadership ability. Duration is flexible. Unpaid. ▶ *2 computer science interns:* responsibilities include laying out and designing advertising campaigns on IBM and Macintosh computers. Candidates should have ability to work independently, computer skills, knowledge of field, personal interest in the field, self-motivation, strong interpersonal skills. Duration is 1–2 semesters. Unpaid. ▶ *2 copy writers:* responsibilities include developing a theme and writing copy for advertising campaign. Candidates should have computer skills, personal interest in the field, self-motivation, writing skills. Duration is 1–2 semesters. Unpaid. ▶ *3 graphic design interns:* responsibilities include developing a concept for an advertising campaign and laying out and designing ads on Macintosh and IBM computers. Candidates should have ability to work independently, college courses in field, computer skills, knowledge of field, personal interest in the field, self-motivation. Duration is 1–2 semesters. Unpaid. ▶ *2 human resources interns:* responsibilities include scheduling personnel records. Candidates should have ability to work with others, office skills, organizational skills, personal interest in the field, self-motivation, strong leadership ability. Duration is flexible. Unpaid. ▶ *2 management interns:* responsibilities include helping control functional aspects of a growing business. Candidates should have ability to work independently, organizational skills, personal interest in the field, self-motivation, strong interpersonal skills, strong leadership ability. Duration is 1–2 semesters. Unpaid. ▶ *4 marketing research interns:* responsibilities include conducting market research projects. Candidates should have ability to work independently, computer skills, oral communication skills, organizational skills, personal interest in the field, strong interpersonal skills. Duration is 1–2 semesters. Unpaid. ▶ *2 photography interns:* responsibilities include shooting black-and-white and color photographs for advertising and public relations campaigns. Candidates should have ability to work independently, knowledge of field, organizational skills, personal interest in the field, self-motivation, strong interpersonal skills. Duration is 1–2 semesters. Unpaid. ▶ *3 public relations interns:* responsibilities include creating, writing, and servicing public relations campaigns for agency clients. Candidates should have ability to work independently, computer skills, self-motivation, strong interpersonal skills, writing skills. Duration is 1–2 semesters. Unpaid. ▶ *2 public relations writers:* responsibilities include writing press releases for advertising agency clients. Candidates should have ability to work with others, computer skills, editing skills, personal interest in the field, writing skills. Duration is flexible.

Unpaid. ▶ *2 videographers:* responsibilities include helping to shoot video. Candidates should have ability to work independently, ability to work with others, experience in the field, personal interest in the field, self-motivation, photo skills. Duration is 1–2 semesters. Unpaid. Open to college freshmen, college sophomores, college juniors, college seniors, recent college graduates, graduate students, law students, career changers. International applications accepted.

Benefits Formal training, job counseling, names of contacts, opportunity to attend seminars/workshops, possible full-time employment, willing to act as a professional reference, willing to complete paperwork for educational credit, willing to provide letters of recommendation, health club membership available.

Contact Write or fax Mr. Paul Jankovic, President. Phone: 410-524-5351. Fax: 302-539-1232. E-mail: ecprg@aol.com. Applicants must submit a letter of interest, resume. Applications are accepted continuously. World Wide Web: http://www.ecusa.com.

PERFORMANCE MARKETING
3122 Fire Road, Suite 200
Egg Harbor Township, New Jersey 08234

General Information Advertising and marketing consulting company. Established in 2001. Number of employees: 4. Number of internship applications received each year: 30.

Internships Available ▶ *1–4 marketing interns:* responsibilities include assisting in the planning and execution of advertising campaigns; press release distribution and writing; scheduling and organization of special events; and other duties as assigned. Candidates should have computer skills, oral communication skills, personal interest in the field, self-motivation, written communication skills. Duration is flexible. Paid. Open to college freshmen, college sophomores, college juniors, college seniors, recent college graduates, graduate students.

Benefits On-the-job training, possible full-time employment, willing to act as a professional reference, willing to complete paperwork for educational credit, willing to provide letters of recommendation, stipend for travel and lunch.

Contact Write, call, fax, or e-mail Scott A. Middlekauff, Account Executive. Phone: 609-646-0414. Fax: 609-646-1350. E-mail: smiddlekauff@callpm.com. In-person interview required. Applicants must submit a letter of interest, resume. Applications are accepted continuously.

THE PETE SANDERS GROUP
230 West 41st Street, Suite 1802
New York, New York 10036

General Information Public relations firm specializing in entertainment with clients including Broadway musical "Chicago," "Def Poetry Jam", "The Miracle Worker", and others. Established in 1990. Number of employees: 7. Number of internship applications received each year: 40.

Internships Available ▶ *2 press interns:* responsibilities include direct contact with the media, setting up and supervising press interviews, editing press releases, assisting in special events planning, and general office duties. Candidates should have ability to work independently, computer skills, editing skills, office skills, oral communication skills, personal interest in the field, self-motivation, strong interpersonal skills, writing skills, major in communications, journalism, theater, or English. Duration is 8 weeks minimum (generally 1 semester or winter break). Unpaid. Open to college sophomores, college juniors, college seniors, recent college graduates. International applications accepted.

Benefits Free meals, on-the-job training, opportunity to attend seminars/workshops, possible full-time employment, travel reimbursement, willing to act as a professional reference, willing to complete paperwork for educational credit, willing to provide letters of recommendation, some complimentary theater tickets.

Contact Write, call, fax, or e-mail Glenna Freedman, Internship Supervisor, 230 West 41st Street, Suite 1802, New York, New York 10036. Phone: 212-730-0067. Fax: 212-730-0394. E-mail: gbfpress@aol.com. Applicants must submit a letter of interest, resume, in-person interview preferred; telephone interview occasionally acceptable. Applications are accepted continuously.

QUALLY AND COMPANY, INC.
2238 Central Street
Evanston, Illinois 60201-5724

General Information   Integrated advertising agency specializing in new product development, new product introductions, and repositioning of existing products and services. Established in 1979. Number of employees: 4. Number of internship applications received each year: 175.

Internships Available   ▶ *2–3 art directors:* responsibilities include performing art, design, production, and general tasks. Candidates should have ability to work independently, analytical skills, computer skills, editing skills, experience in the field, organizational skills, plan to pursue career in field, self-motivation. Duration is 3–9 months. Unpaid. ▶ *2 copy writers:* responsibilities include performing various writing assignments and general tasks. Candidates should have ability to work independently, ability to work with others, analytical skills, college courses in field, computer skills, editing skills, knowledge of field, organizational skills, plan to pursue career in field, research skills, self-motivation, writing skills. Duration is 3–6 months. Unpaid. Open to college juniors, college seniors, recent college graduates, graduate students, law students, career changers. ▶ *2–3 graphic designers:* responsibilities include assisting with art direction and computer production and performing general tasks. Candidates should have ability to work independently, ability to work with others, analytical skills, college courses in field, computer skills, knowledge of field, organizational skills, plan to pursue career in field, self-motivation. Duration is 3–6 months. Unpaid. Open to college juniors, college seniors, recent college graduates, graduate students, career changers. ▶ *2 new business development interns:* responsibilities include assisting with new business development, direct mail, account service, and public relations. Candidates should have ability to work independently, analytical skills, computer skills, knowledge of field, office skills, oral communication skills, personal interest in the field, research skills, self-motivation, strong interpersonal skills, written communication skills. Duration is 3–6 months. Unpaid. Open to college juniors, college seniors, recent college graduates, graduate students, law students, career changers. ▶ *1 research intern:* responsibilities include researching for new and existing businesses and performing general tasks. Candidates should have analytical skills, computer skills, declared college major in field, editing skills, knowledge of field, organizational skills, personal interest in the field, research skills, self-motivation, writing skills. Duration is 3–6 months. Unpaid. Open to college juniors, college seniors, recent college graduates, graduate students, law students, career changers. International applications accepted.

Benefits   Formal training, job counseling, names of contacts, on-the-job training, opportunity to attend seminars/workshops, possible full-time employment, willing to act as a professional reference, willing to complete paperwork for educational credit, willing to provide letters of recommendation, networking opportunities.

Contact   Write, call, or e-mail Mr. Robert Qually, President/Creative Director, 1187 Wilmette Avenue, Suite 201, Wilmette, Illinois 60091-2719. Phone: 847-864-4154. E-mail: quallycompany@hotmail.com. In-person interview recommended (telephone interview accepted). Applicants must submit a letter of interest, resume, portfolio, three personal references, three letters of recommendation, 10 writing samples (copywriter position). Application deadline: nine months in advance of desired internship.

QUIET RESORTS PUBLIC RELATIONS
PO Box 505
Bethany Beach, Delaware 19930

General Information   Public relations firm operating weekly and seasonal newspapers in local resort towns and providing publicity services. Established in 1989. Number of employees: 6. Number of internship applications received each year: 45.

Internships Available   ▶ *2 Internet graduate student interns:* responsibilities include designing Web page layout. Candidates should have ability to work independently, ability to work with others, analytical skills, computer skills, personal interest in the field, self-motivation. Duration is flexible. Unpaid. Open to graduate students. ▶ *2–3 Web page designers.* Candidates should have ability to work independently, ability to work with others, computer skills, organizational skills, personal interest in the field. Duration is flexible. Unpaid. Open to high school seniors, recent high school graduates, college freshmen, college sophomores, college juniors, college seniors, recent college graduates, graduate students, law students, career changers, individuals reentering the workforce. ▶ *2 administrative assistants:* responsibilities include working with owner, publisher, and editor. Candidates should have ability to work independently, office skills, oral communication skills, self-motivation, strong interpersonal skills. Duration is 1–2 semesters. Unpaid. Open to high school seniors, recent high school graduates, college freshmen, college sophomores, college juniors, college seniors, recent college graduates, graduate students, law students, career changers, individuals reentering the workforce. ▶ *3 advertising layout interns:* responsibilities include creating comprehensive campaigns and performing typesetting duties. Candidates should have ability to work independently, computer skills, personal interest in the field, self-motivation, strong interpersonal skills, strong leadership ability. Duration is 1–2 semesters. Unpaid. Open to college freshmen, college sophomores, college juniors, college seniors, recent college graduates, graduate students, law students, career changers, individuals reentering the workforce. ▶ *4 advertising/sales interns:* responsibilities include developing sales leads in a local territory; contact with local businesses by mail, phone, and personal interviews; and creating advertising ideas for the clients. Candidates should have ability to work independently, oral communication skills, self-motivation, strong interpersonal skills, written communication skills. Duration is 1–2 semesters. Unpaid. Open to college freshmen, college sophomores, college juniors, college seniors, recent college graduates, graduate students, law students, career changers. ▶ *2 circulation interns:* responsibilities include overseeing the organization and distribution of newsletters, pamphlets, and magazines to the local market and by direct mail. Candidates should have ability to work independently, analytical skills, computer skills, organizational skills, self-motivation, strong interpersonal skills. Duration is flexible. Unpaid. Open to high school seniors, recent high school graduates, college freshmen, college sophomores, college juniors, college seniors, graduate students, law students, career changers, individuals reentering the workforce. ▶ *2 editorial interns:* responsibilities include developing newsworthy topics, interviewing subjects, writing stories, and helping with production and organization. Candidates should have personal interest in the field, self-motivation, strong interpersonal skills, writing skills. Duration is flexible. Unpaid. Open to recent high school graduates, college freshmen, college sophomores, college juniors, college seniors, recent college graduates, graduate students, law students, career changers, individuals reentering the workforce. ▶ *2 photography interns:* responsibilities include developing photographic opportunities. Candidates should have ability to work independently, ability to work with others, knowledge of field, personal interest in the field, self-motivation, photo skills. Duration is 1–2 semesters. Unpaid. Open to high school seniors, recent high school graduates, college freshmen, college sophomores, college juniors, college seniors, recent college graduates, graduate students, law students, career changers, individuals reentering the workforce. ▶ *3 production interns:* responsibilities include designing, typesetting, and pasting-up ads and articles for newsletters, newspapers, and brochures. Candidates should have ability to work independently, computer skills, office skills, personal interest in the field, strong interpersonal skills. Duration is 1–2 semesters. Unpaid. Open to college freshmen, college sophomores, college juniors, college seniors, recent college graduates, graduate students, law students, career changers. ▶ *4 reporters:* responsibilities include developing and following up on news and feature topics of local interest. Candidates should have ability to work with others, computer skills, editing skills, oral communication skills, writing skills. Duration is 1–2 semesters. Unpaid. Open to recent high school graduates, college freshmen, college sophomores, college juniors, college seniors, recent college graduates, graduate students, law students, career changers. ▶ *2 typesetters:* responsibilities include designing, laying out, and composing advertisements on Macintosh or IBM-compatible computers. Candidates should have ability to work independently, computer skills, office skills, organizational skills, personal interest in the field, self-motivation, strong interpersonal skills. Duration is flexible. Unpaid. Open to

recent high school graduates, college freshmen, college sophomores, college juniors, college seniors, recent college graduates, graduate students, law students, career changers, individuals reentering the workforce. International applications accepted.
Benefits Formal training, names of contacts, opportunity to attend seminars/workshops, possible full-time employment, willing to act as a professional reference, willing to complete paperwork for educational credit, willing to provide letters of recommendation, health club membership available.
Contact Write, call, fax, or e-mail Mr. Paul D. Jankovic. Phone: 410-524-5351. Fax: 302-539-1232. E-mail: ecprg@aol.com. Applicants must submit a letter of interest, resume. Applications are accepted continuously. World Wide Web: http://www.ecusa.com.

ROGERS & COWAN- NY
640 5th Avenue, 5th Floor
New York, New York 10019

General Information Publicity agency. Established in 1950. Number of employees: 30. Unit of Weber Shandwick North America, Inc., New York, New York. Number of internship applications received each year: 150.
Internships Available ▶ *3–8 interns:* responsibilities include assisting publicists with research, writing copy for news releases and feature stories, helping coordinate photo shoots, and aiding in the organization and preparation of special client events. Candidates should have computer skills, office skills, oral communication skills, strong interpersonal skills, written communication skills. Duration is one quarter or semeseter. Unpaid. Open to college freshmen, college sophomores, college juniors, college seniors, graduate students. International applications accepted.
Benefits Possible full-time employment, willing to complete paperwork for educational credit, willing to provide letters of recommendation.
Contact Write, fax, or e-mail Shannon Nelson, Human Resources Benefits Coordinator, 1888 Century Park East, 5th Floor, Los Angeles, California 90067. Fax: 310-284-2070. E-mail: internship@ webershandwick.com. No phone calls. Applicants must submit a letter of interest, resume, telephone interview followed by in-person interview (if appropriate). Applications are accepted continuously. World Wide Web: http://www.rogersandcowan.com.

ROSEN GROUP
30 West 26th Street
New York, New York 10010

General Information Public relations firm specializing in media, publishing, and liquor promotions. Established in 1984. Number of employees: 14. Number of internship applications received each year: 50.
Internships Available ▶ *2 office interns:* responsibilities include writing, copying, and performing phone work and research. Candidates should have ability to work with others, oral communication skills, personal interest in the field, plan to pursue career in field, written communication skills. Duration is 1 semester. $7–$8 per hour. Open to college juniors, college seniors, recent college graduates. International applications accepted.
Benefits On-the-job training, possible full-time employment, willing to act as a professional reference, willing to complete paperwork for educational credit, willing to provide letters of recommendation.
Contact Write, call, or e-mail Ms. Lori Rosen, President. Phone: 212-255-8455. E-mail: lori@rosengrouppr.com. In-person interview required. Applicants must submit a letter of interest, resume. Applications are accepted continuously. World Wide Web: http://www.rosengrouppr.com.

RUDER FINN, INC.
301 East 57th Street
New York, New York 10022

General Information Full-service independently owned public relations agency. Established in 1948. Number of employees: 325. Number of internship applications received each year: 300.
Internships Available ▶ *8–15 executive trainees:* responsibilities include assisting public relations account team on variety of tasks including media monitoring, preparing clip reports, research, media follow-up, and other assignments. Duration is 4 months. $21,000 per year salary; pro-rated for 4 months spent in program. Open to college seniors, recent college graduates, graduate students, law students, career changers. ▶ *3–5 summer interns:* responsibilities include assisting public relations account team on variety of tasks including media monitoring, research, preparing clip reports, and other assignments. Duration is 2–3 months. $10 per hour. Open to college juniors. Candidates for all positions should have ability to work with others, analytical skills, oral communication skills, organizational skills, research skills, written communication skills.
Benefits Formal training, job counseling, on-the-job training, opportunity to attend seminars/workshops, possible full-time employment, willing to provide letters of recommendation.
Contact Write, call, fax, e-mail, or through World Wide Web site Ms. Sheridan Falvo, Senior Associate, Human Resources. Phone: 212-715-1696. Fax: 212-583-2779. E-mail: falvos@ruderfinn.com. In-person interview recommended (telephone interview accepted). Applicants must submit a formal organization application, resume, academic transcripts, three writing samples, two letters of recommendation. Application deadline: March 3 for summer (June-August or June-October), August 1 for fall (October-February), December 1 for winter (February-June). World Wide Web: http://www.ruderfinn.com.

SALLY FISCHER PUBLIC RELATIONS
330 West 58th Street, Suite 509
New York, New York 10019

General Information Small public relations firm specializing in the areas of design, fashion, food, publishing, and entertainment. Established in 1989. Number of employees: 10. Number of internship applications received each year: 75.
Internships Available ▶ *3–4 junior publicist trainees:* responsibilities include direct involvement in all aspects of public relations, including special events, media and client relations, and writing. Candidates should have ability to work independently, computer skills, office skills, oral communication skills, personal interest in the field, self-motivation, strong interpersonal skills, written communication skills, ability to work in fast-paced environment. Duration is flexible. Unpaid. Open to college freshmen, college sophomores, college juniors, college seniors, recent college graduates, graduate students, law students. International applications accepted.
Benefits Names of contacts, on-the-job training, possible full-time employment, travel reimbursement, willing to act as a professional reference, willing to complete paperwork for educational credit, willing to provide letters of recommendation.
Contact Write, fax, or e-mail Gina Nisi, Assistant to President/ Intern Coordinator. Phone: 212-246-2977. Fax: 212-246-8116. E-mail: gina@sallyfischerpr.com. In-person interview recommended (telephone interview accepted). Applicants must submit a letter of interest, resume. Application deadline: January 1 for spring, May 1 for summer. World Wide Web: http://www.sallyfpr.com.

SHIRLEY HERZ ASSOCIATES
165 West 46th Street, Suite 910
New York, New York 10036

General Information Public relations firm for Broadway and off-Broadway shows, projects, and institutions. Established in 1972. Number of employees: 4. Number of internship applications received each year: 200.
Internships Available ▶ *2–4 interns:* responsibilities include aiding five press agents, answering phones, and writing press releases. Candidates should have ability to work independently, ability to work with others, computer skills, editing skills, office skills, oral communication skills, organizational skills, research skills, self-motivation, writing skills. Duration is 1 semester. Unpaid. Open to college freshmen, college sophomores, college juniors, college seniors. International applications accepted.
Benefits Formal training, possible full-time employment, willing to complete paperwork for educational credit, willing to provide letters of recommendation.

Shirley Herz Associates (continued)

Contact Write, call, or fax Bob Lasko, Intern Coordinator. Phone: 212-221-8466. Fax: 212-921-8023. In-person interview required. Applicants must submit a letter of interest, resume. Applications are accepted continuously.

SILVERMAN MEDIA & MARKETING GROUP, INC.
100 Crossways Park West, Suite 111
Woodbury, New York 11797

General Information Media and marketing company specializing in public relations, integrated marketing, special event creation and management, celebrity representation, and charitable foundations; focuses on sports, entertainment, nonprofit, travel, special events, TV shows, home video, automotive, and new product publicity and promotion. Established in 1984. Number of employees: 6. Number of internship applications received each year: 200.

Internships Available ▶ *1–3 public relations/special events assistants:* responsibilities include assisting with media research and contact, phone work, event and account coordination, writing of press releases, and general office duties. Candidates should have office skills, oral communication skills, plan to pursue career in field, self-motivation, strong interpersonal skills, written communication skills. Duration is 3–4 months. Unpaid. Open to college freshmen, college sophomores, college juniors, college seniors, recent college graduates, graduate students, law students, career changers, individuals reentering the workforce.

Benefits Job counseling, names of contacts, on-the-job training, possible full-time employment, willing to act as a professional reference, willing to complete paperwork for educational credit, willing to provide letters of recommendation, $15 per day travel reimbursement.

Contact Write, call, fax, or e-mail Morgan Futch, Accountant Executive. Phone: 516-495-5280. Fax: 516-495-5281. E-mail: smmgmorgan@aol.com. In-person interview required. Applicants must submit a letter of interest, resume, photo at time of interview to attach to resume, proof of lodging in the Long Island/NYC area prior to interview. Applications are accepted continuously. World Wide Web: http://www.silverman-media.com.

SMITHSONIAN OFFICE OF PUBLIC AFFAIRS
1000 Jefferson Drive, SW, Room 354
Washington, District of Columbia 20560-0033

General Information Office of the Smithsonian that informs the public and staff through publications and media relations about exhibitions, programs, and research activities. Number of employees: 16. Unit of Smithsonian Institution, Washington, District of Columbia.

Internships Available ▶ *Media relations interns:* responsibilities include updating mailing lists of journalists, newspapers, and magazines; organizing materials and filling information kits for journalists; and writing news releases and other informational materials. Duration is flexible. Unpaid. ▶ *Publications interns:* responsibilities include writing features, news stories, and column items. Candidates should have research skills, writing skills, interviewing skills. Duration is flexible. Unpaid. Open to high school students, college freshmen, college sophomores, college juniors, college seniors, recent college graduates, graduate students. International applications accepted.

Benefits Willing to act as a professional reference, willing to complete paperwork for educational credit.

Contact Write, call, or fax Bill Holmes, Administrative Officer, 1000 Jefferson Drive, SW Room 354, Washington, District of Columbia 20560-0033. Phone: 202-357-2627. Fax: 202-357-3346. Applicants must submit a formal organization application, academic transcripts, personal reference, essay, by-lined writing samples (for publications positions). Applications are accepted continuously. World Wide Web: http://www.si.edu.

SPIDER SPLAT CONSULTING, INC.
20 Park Plaza, Suite 515
Boston, Massachusetts 02116

General Information Strategic Internet consultancy focused on clients outsourced online advertising and marketing program management. Established in 1997. Number of employees: 14. Number of internship applications received each year: 1,000.

Internships Available ▶ *5–10 advertising interns:* responsibilities include online advertising, ad copy creation, account management, analysis of conversions, and marketing document creation. Candidates should have analytical skills, organizational skills, research skills, writing skills, Excel, Word, and Outlook (intermediate level skills). Duration is flexible (minimum 20 hour per week commitment for 6 months). Position available as unpaid or paid. Open to college juniors, college seniors, recent college graduates, graduate students. ▶ *5–10 webmaster interns.* Duration is flexible (minimum 20 hours per week for 6 months). Position available as unpaid or paid. Open to college seniors, recent college graduates, graduate students.

Benefits Job counseling, on-the-job training, opportunity to attend seminars/workshops, possible full-time employment, willing to act as a professional reference, willing to complete paperwork for educational credit, willing to provide letters of recommendation.

Contact Write, fax, e-mail, or through World Wide Web site Human Resources Director. Fax: 617-507-5934. E-mail: internjobs@spidersplat.com. No phone calls. In-person interview required. Applicants must submit a resume, online application. Applications are accepted continuously. World Wide Web: http://www.spidersplat.com.

SPORTS ILLUSTRATED, COMMUNICATIONS DEPARTMENT
135 West 50th Street, 3rd Floor
New York, New York 10020-1393

General Information Department responsible for all public relations and publicity for Sports Illustrated, Sports Illustrated for Kids, and SI.com. Established in 1954. Number of employees: 400. Unit of Time, Inc., New York, New York. Number of internship applications received each year: 300.

Internships Available ▶ *1–4 communications interns:* responsibilities include assisting the communications staff in all areas of publicity, including media relations and special events. Duration is one semester or summer. Unpaid. Open to college sophomores, college juniors, college seniors, those only able to receive college credit or equivalent for internship. ▶ *1 sports marketing intern:* responsibilities include assisting the sports marketing department in all areas of outreach including research and planning. Duration is one semester or summer. Unpaid. Open to college sophomores, college seniors, graduate students, those only able to receive college credit or equivalent for internship. Candidates for all positions should have ability to work independently, ability to work with others, computer skills, knowledge of field, oral communication skills, self-motivation, written communication skills.

Benefits Job counseling, names of contacts, opportunity to attend seminars/workshops, possible full-time employment, travel reimbursement, willing to act as a professional reference, willing to complete paperwork for educational credit, willing to provide letters of recommendation, meal stipend ($6 per day).

Contact Write or fax Sheryl L. Spain, Associate Director of Communications. Fax: 212-522-4832. No phone calls. In-person interview recommended (telephone interview accepted). Applicants must submit a letter of interest, resume, 1-3 writing samples (published material when possible), 2 professional references from previous employers. Application deadline: March 1 for summer, August 15 for fall, November 15 for spring. World Wide Web: http://www.si.com.

THINKCREATIVE
304 West College Avenue
Tallahassee, Florida 32301

General Information Marketing consulting firm providing services associated with a full-service marketing, public relations, and interactive agency. Established in 1995. Number of employees: 12. Number of internship applications received each year: 45.

Internships Available ▶ *6 interns.* Candidates should have organizational skills, personal interest in the field, self-motivation. Duration is 2 semesters. Unpaid. Open to college freshmen, college sophomores, college juniors, college seniors, recent college graduates, graduate students. International applications accepted.

Benefits Formal training, job counseling, willing to act as a professional reference, willing to complete paperwork for educational credit, willing to provide letters of recommendation, free lunches (2 days per week).

Contact Call, e-mail, or through World Wide Web site Brian Ramos, Vice President of Client Services. Phone: 850-656-7050 Ext. 14. E-mail: bramos@thinkcreative.com. In-person interview recommended (telephone interview accepted). Applicants must submit a resume, work samples (for creative positions). Application deadline: March 1 for summer, June 30 for fall, November 30 for spring. World Wide Web: http://www.thinkcreative.com.

WEBER SHANDWICK
640 5th Avenue
New York, New York 10019

General Information Full-service communications agency. Established in 1974. Number of employees: 250. Division of InterPublic Group, New York, New York. Number of internship applications received each year: 750.

Internships Available ▶ *6–10 public relations interns:* responsibilities include writing, researching, and performing media relations activities. Candidates should have ability to work independently, ability to work with others, plan to pursue career in field, research skills, self-motivation, written communication skills. Duration is 10 weeks. $10 and up per hour. Open to college juniors, college seniors, recent college graduates, graduate students. International applications accepted.

Benefits Formal training, job counseling, names of contacts, on-the-job training, opportunity to attend seminars/workshops, possible full-time employment, willing to act as a professional reference, willing to complete paperwork for educational credit.

Contact Write, fax, or e-mail Human Resources. Fax: 212-445-8095. E-mail: jobsnewyork@webershandwick.com. No phone calls. In-person interview recommended (telephone interview accepted). Applicants must submit a formal organization application, letter of interest, resume. Application deadline: March 31 for summer. World Wide Web: http://www.webershandwick.com.

WEBER SHANDWICK
676 North St. Clair, Suite 1000
Chicago, Illinois 60611-3110

General Information Consumer public relations firm. Number of employees: 150. Subsidiary of Weber Shandwick Worldwide, Minneapolis, Minnesota. Number of internship applications received each year: 1,000.

Internships Available ▶ *14–18 interns:* responsibilities include working on 2-3 accounts, compiling media lists, pitching, market research, vendor coordination, writing, editing, and daily clip reports. Candidates should have oral communication skills, plan to pursue career in field, strong interpersonal skills, written communication skills, major in journalism, communications, public relations, or related fields. Duration is 3 months. Paid. Open to college juniors, college seniors, recent college graduates, graduate students, career changers. International applications accepted.

Benefits Names of contacts, on-the-job training, possible full-time employment, willing to act as a professional reference, willing to complete paperwork for educational credit, willing to provide letters of recommendation.

Contact E-mail Intern Coordinator, 676 North St. Clair, Suite 1000, Chicago, Illinois 60611-3110. E-mail: internships@webershandwick.com. No phone calls. In-person interview required. Applicants must submit a letter of interest, resume, test for writing and proofreading skills. Applications are accepted continuously. World Wide Web: http://www.webershandwick.com.

WIDMEYER COMMUNICATIONS
1825 Connecticut Avenue, NW, Fifth Floor
Washington, District of Columbia 20009

General Information Public relations firm. Established in 1987. Number of employees: 70. Number of internship applications received each year: 150.

Internships Available ▶ *1–3 fellows:* responsibilities include writing for media (press releases); writing for client; event planning; participating in strategy and planning sessions; assisting with general business operations; and research. Candidates should have computer skills, knowledge of field, oral communication skills, research skills, self-motivation, strong interpersonal skills, writing skills. Duration is 3 months. $10 per hour. Open to recent college graduates, graduate students. International applications accepted.

Benefits Health insurance, on-the-job training, opportunity to attend seminars/workshops, possible full-time employment, willing to act as a professional reference, willing to provide letters of recommendation.

Contact Write, e-mail, or through World Wide Web site Laura Hamra, Human Resources. Phone: 202-667-0901. Fax: 202-667-0902. E-mail: fellowships@widmeyer.com. In-person interview required. Applicants must submit a letter of interest, resume, two writing samples. Applications are accepted continuously. World Wide Web: http://www.widmeyer.com.

ARCHITECTURAL, ENGINEERING, AND DESIGN SERVICES

AMERICAN & INTERNATIONAL DESIGNS, INC.
1100 South Avenue, Suite 2
Staten Island, New York 10314

General Information Interior design firm that specializes in restaurant, health-care, medical, corporate facilities and the luxury home market. Established in 1980. Number of employees: 5. Number of internship applications received each year: 400.

Internships Available ▶ *3–4 CAD operator/3/0 modeling operators:* responsibilities include developing space plans; drawing floor plans, furniture plans, tile plans, window elevations, and general drafting and plotting. Candidates should have college courses in field, computer skills, experience in the field, organizational skills, plan to pursue career in field. Duration is 8–10 weeks. Unpaid. Open to college juniors, college seniors, recent college graduates, graduate students. ▶ *2–4 administrative interns:* responsibilities include working directly with the administrator, assisting in minutes of meetings, project management, and expediting and tracking interior design projects. Candidates should have ability to work independently, computer skills, office skills, oral communication skills, organizational skills, written communication skills. Unpaid. Open to recent high school graduates. ▶ *1 advertising assistant:* responsibilities include preparing and coordinating media kits for distribution on TV Magazine Books; editorials of current interior design projects. Candidates should have computer skills, declared college major in field, experience in the field, knowledge of field, personal interest in the field, writing skills. Duration is 3–8 weeks. Unpaid. Open to college juniors, college seniors, recent college graduates, graduate students. ▶ *2 bookkeeper/accounting assistants:* responsibilities include assisting in maintaining financial books for 3 divisions, preparing budgets, and keeping intern time sheets. Candidates should have ability to work independently, college courses in field, experience in the field, office skills, organizational skills, plan to pursue career in field. Duration is 6–10 weeks. Unpaid. Open to college sophomores, college juniors, college seniors, recent college graduates, graduate students. ▶ *2 computer and technical information interns:* responsibilities include researching new products, assisting in training on new software, installing updates, reviewing all equipment and new

American & International Designs, Inc. (continued)

contracts, maintaining supplies, and Web site development. Candidates should have ability to work with others, experience in the field, office skills, plan to pursue career in field, research skills. Duration is 8–10 weeks. Unpaid. Open to college juniors, college seniors, recent college graduates, graduate students. ▶ *3 graphic design interns:* responsibilities include designing graphics for collateral materials, brochures, inserts, press kits, tear sheets, Web site, mailings, and presentations. Candidates should have ability to work independently, computer skills, experience in the field, organizational skills, plan to pursue career in field, research skills, writing skills. Duration is 8–12 weeks. Unpaid. Open to college juniors, college seniors, recent college graduates, graduate students, individuals reentering the workforce. ▶ *5–10 junior interior designer interns:* responsibilities include working with design team to develop and administrate interior design projects. Candidates should have college courses in field, computer skills, office skills, organizational skills, plan to pursue career in field, 3D skills, auto CAD, rendering drafting skills. Duration is 6–8 weeks. Unpaid. Open to college juniors, college seniors, recent college graduates, graduate students. ▶ *2 librarian interns:* responsibilities include maintaining product libraries, updating all literature, coordinating samples, distributing information to all in-house staff, updating presentation boards, and maintaining photo library. Candidates should have ability to work independently, computer skills, office skills, organizational skills, self-motivation, strong interpersonal skills. Duration is 6 weeks. Unpaid. Open to high school seniors, recent high school graduates, college freshmen, college sophomores, college juniors, college seniors, recent college graduates. ▶ *2–4 marketing information interns:* responsibilities include launching new design trends and services for the hospitality industries, organizing and developing press kits, attending trade shows and local seminars, coordinating and purchasing mailing lists, assisting in the development of collateral material for information requests. Candidates should have ability to work independently, college courses in field, computer skills, oral communication skills, plan to pursue career in field, strong interpersonal skills. Duration is 8–10 weeks. Unpaid. Open to college juniors, college seniors, recent college graduates, graduate students. ▶ *2 personnel assistants:* responsibilities include maintaining and updating procedures manual, reviewing general procedures with staff, reviewing time sheets, developing daily schedules, preparing letters of recommendation, assisting in job placements, and working with principles. Candidates should have computer skills, office skills, oral communication skills, research skills, strong interpersonal skills, strong leadership ability. Duration is 8–10 weeks. Unpaid. Open to recent high school graduates, college freshmen, college juniors, college seniors. ▶ *4 photographer interns:* responsibilities include photographing projects in progress in several mediums; digital black and white for marketing media; press shots; Web site publication. Candidates should have ability to work independently, analytical skills, college courses in field, computer skills, editing skills, experience in the field, plan to pursue career in field. Duration is 3–12 weeks. Unpaid. Open to college sophomores, college seniors, recent college graduates, graduate students. ▶ *4 public relations interns:* responsibilities include organizing and developing case studies of recent completed jobs, writing public relations news about company and products, vendor public relations, and attending and promoting grand openings. Candidates should have ability to work independently, computer skills, oral communication skills, plan to pursue career in field, research skills, written communication skills. Duration is 6–8 weeks. Unpaid. Open to college juniors, college seniors, recent college graduates, graduate students.

Benefits Formal training, free meals, job counseling, on-the-job training, opportunity to attend seminars/workshops, possible full-time employment, travel reimbursement, willing to act as a professional reference, willing to complete paperwork for educational credit, willing to provide letters of recommendation.

Contact Write, fax, or through World Wide Web site Alex Reyes, Internship Coordinator, 900 South Avenue, Staten Island, New York 10314. Fax: 718-317-9627. E-mail: susanharann@aol.com. No phone calls. In-person interview recommended (telephone interview accepted). Applicants must submit a formal organization application, resume, personal reference, portfolio (occasionally). Applica-

tion deadline: January 30 for spring, May 1 for summer, July 15 for fall, September 15 for winter. World Wide Web: http://www.designamericanyc.com.

BAE SYSTEMS/INFORMATION AND ELECTRONIC WARFARE SECTOR
95 Canal Street, PO Box 2029
Nashua, New Hampshire 03061-2029

General Information Designer and developer of advanced defense electronics. Established in 1951. Number of employees: 4,500. Number of internship applications received each year: 1,000.

Internships Available ▶ *Co-ops:* responsibilities include performing various tasks to meet the needs of the organization; positions available in missile/weapon systems development, software engineering, programming, Web development, database/applications development, communications engineering, and circuit analysis. Duration is 4-6 months; generally 1 semester (full-time); may include summer or winter break and return on an alternating semester basis. Position available as unpaid or paid. ▶ *Interns:* responsibilities include performing various tasks to meet the needs of the organization; positions available in missile/weapon systems development, software engineering, programming, Web development, database/applications development, communications engineering, and circuit analysis. Duration is summer or winter break (full-time). Position available as unpaid or paid. Candidates for all positions should have ability to work with others, computer skills, oral communication skills, written communication skills, major in computer science, electrical engineering, computer engineering, electronics, information systems, and finance. Open to college juniors, college seniors.

Benefits Partial benefits for co-ops.

Contact Through World Wide Web site Internship Coordinator. Applicants must submit a resume. Applications are accepted continuously. World Wide Web: http://www.na.baesystems.com.

BURNS AND MCDONNELL
9400 Ward Parkway
Kansas City, Missouri 64114

General Information Consulting firm for engineering, architectural, and environmental projects. Established in 1898. Number of employees: 1,700. Number of internship applications received each year: 50.

Internships Available ▶ *1–3 architectural interns:* responsibilities include assisting architects on different projects. Duration is 1 summer. Paid. ▶ *3–5 civil engineering interns:* responsibilities include assisting senior engineers with projects. Duration is 1 summer. Paid. ▶ *3–5 electrical engineering interns:* responsibilities include assisting senior electrical engineers with lighting, electrical instruments and control, and a variety of other duties. Duration is 1 summer. Paid. ▶ *1–3 environmental engineer interns:* responsibilities include assisting senior engineer with waste management and water and air pollution control projects. Duration is 1 summer. Paid. ▶ *5–8 mechanical engineering interns:* responsibilities include assisting senior mechanical engineers with projects. Duration is 1 summer. Paid. Candidates for all positions should have computer skills, oral communication skills, organizational skills, plan to pursue career in field, strong interpersonal skills, written communication skills. Open to college freshmen, college sophomores, college juniors, college seniors. International applications accepted.

Benefits Job counseling, names of contacts, on-the-job training, opportunity to attend seminars/workshops, possible full-time employment, travel reimbursement, willing to complete paperwork for educational credit, willing to provide letters of recommendation.

Contact Write, call, fax, e-mail, or through World Wide Web site Melissa L. Lavin, College Recruiter. Phone: 816-822-3441. Fax: 816-822-3516. E-mail: mlavin@burnsmcd.com. Applicants must submit a resume, academic transcripts. Application deadline: April 1. World Wide Web: http://www.burnsmcd.com.

ENGINEERING MINISTRIES INTERNATIONAL
110 South Weber, Suite 104
Colorado Springs, Colorado 80903

General Information Provider of free engineering and architecture services to missionaries in developing countries; nonprofit Christian ministry whose mission is to involve design professionals in missions. Established in 1981. Number of employees: 24. Number of internship applications received each year: 75.

Internships Available ▶ *4–8 architectural missionary interns:* responsibilities include a 2-week missions trip for conceptual design of a ministry facility; office duties such as programming master plans and construction documents; raising support to cover intern's expenses. Candidates should have ability to work with others, declared college major in field. Duration is 3–8 months. Unpaid. ▶ *6–10 architectural overseas missionary interns:* responsibilities include designing and drawing missionary facilities in India, Uganda, or Guatemala; design, AutoCad, and travel; raising support to cover intern's expenses. Candidates should have ability to work with others, computer skills, declared college major in field. Duration is 3–6 months. Unpaid. ▶ *5–8 civil engineering missionary interns:* responsibilities include a 2-week missions trip/site visit to a developing country; helping a missionary by designing a water, wastewater, drainage system, or road; raising support to cover intern's expenses. Candidates should have ability to work with others, declared college major in field. Duration is 3–8 months. Unpaid. ▶ *4–12 construction management missionary interns:* responsibilities include overseeing construction of a needed ministry facility in India, Uganda, or Guatemala for a missionary; budgeting, scheduling, conflict resolution, managing both work teams and nationals; intern must raise own support. Candidates should have ability to work with others, declared college major in field. Duration is 3–12 months. Unpaid. ▶ *8–10 engineering overseas missionary interns:* responsibilities include designing needed facilities for missionaries in India or Guatemala; structural or water resources engineering design; raising support to cover intern's expenses. Candidates should have ability to work independently, ability to work with others, declared college major in field. Duration is 3–6 months. Unpaid. ▶ *1 network administrator/Webmaster intern:* responsibilities include network administration for a 25-computer network running Windows NT small business server; Web page design and updating; raising support to cover intern's expenses. Candidates should have ability to work independently, college courses in field, computer skills, knowledge of field, self-motivation. Duration is 3–8 months. Unpaid. ▶ *4–8 structural engineering missionary interns:* responsibilities include a 2-week missions trip/site visit to conceptually design a ministry facility; office duties such as structural design of small buildings and drawing construction documents; raising support to cover intern's expenses. Candidates should have ability to work with others, declared college major in field. Duration is 3–8 months. Unpaid. ▶ *2–4 surveying missionary interns (overseas):* responsibilities include surveying property for missionary facilities in India or Guatemala; AutoCad, and raising support to cover intern's expenses. Candidates should have ability to work with others, declared college major in field. Duration is 3–8 months. Unpaid. Open to college juniors, college seniors, recent college graduates, graduate students, career changers, individuals reentering the workforce. International applications accepted.

Benefits Housing at a cost, job counseling, names of contacts, on-the-job training, opportunity to attend seminars/workshops, willing to act as a professional reference, willing to complete paperwork for educational credit, willing to provide letters of recommendation, international travel, mentoring.

International Internships Available in Calgary, Canada; Guatemala City, Guatemala; Mussoorie, India; Kampala, Uganda.

Contact Write, call, e-mail, or through World Wide Web site Christy Taylor, Intern Director. Phone: 719-633-2078. Fax: 719-633-2970. E-mail: intern@emiusa.org. Telephone interview required. Applicants must submit a formal organization application, letter of interest, resume, written Christian testimony. Application deadline: January 20 for summer, April 20 for fall, September 15 for spring. World Wide Web: http://www.emiusa.org.

GENSLER
One Rockefeller Plaza, Suite 500
New York, New York 10020

General Information Architecture and design firm offering a full range of services including strategic consulting, master planning, and program management.

Internships Available ▶ *Summer or school-year interns:* responsibilities include working in various positions available in 24 global offices; see Web site for details. Paid.

Contact Through World Wide Web site Internship Coordinator. Applicants must submit a resume, cover letter (do not include portfolio or work samples). Application deadline: between March 1 and April 30 for summer; continuous for school year positions. World Wide Web: http://www.gensler.com.

GME CONSULTANTS
14000 21st Avenue North
Minneapolis, Minnesota 55447

General Information Geotechnical materials and environmental engineering consulting firm. Established in 1981. Number of employees: 85. Number of internship applications received each year: 10.

Internships Available ▶ *4–6 field services technicians:* responsibilities include providing quality control testing and inspections for various construction projects. Candidates should have ability to work independently, knowledge of field, personal interest in the field, self-motivation, strong interpersonal skills, writing skills. Duration is 4–6 months. $11–$12 per hour. Open to college freshmen, college sophomores, college juniors, college seniors, recent college graduates, graduate students, individuals reentering the workforce. International applications accepted.

Benefits Formal training, on-the-job training, opportunity to attend seminars/workshops, possible full-time employment, willing to act as a professional reference, willing to complete paperwork for educational credit, willing to provide letters of recommendation.

Contact Write, fax, or e-mail Tammy Hakanson, Field Services Manager, 14000 21st Avenue North, Minneapolis, Minnesota 55447. Fax: 763-559-0720. E-mail: thakanson@gmeconsultants.com. No phone calls. In-person interview recommended (telephone interview accepted). Applicants must submit a resume. Applications are accepted continuously. World Wide Web: http://www.gmeconsultants.com.

HARLEYELLIS
26913 Northwestern Highway, Suite 200
Southfield, Michigan 48034-3476

General Information Full-service, planning, architecture, engineering, management, and interiors firm that serves corporate, university, health care, science and research, automotive, and industrial clients throughout the Midwest. Established in 1909. Number of employees: 300. Number of internship applications received each year: 150.

Internships Available ▶ *1–2 architecture co-ops:* responsibilities include opportunity to gain exposure and familiarity with basic construction materials and methods through CADD, training, and field observation and opportunities. Candidates should have ability to work with others, analytical skills, computer skills, declared college major in field, oral communication skills, plan to pursue career in field. Duration is 3 months (minimum). $11–$14 per hour. ▶ *1–2 civil engineer co-ops:* responsibilities include assisting in designing site layouts, grading, and utilities including storm and sanitary sewers and watermains, CADD drafting and field measuring. Candidates should have ability to work with others, analytical skills, computer skills, declared college major in field, oral communication skills, personal interest in the field. Duration is 3 months (minimum). $11–$15 per hour. ▶ *1–2 electrical engineer co-ops:* responsibilities include assisting engineers in field data collection, calculations, code research, and other design engineering tasks; preparing CAD generated documents. Candidates should have ability to work with others, analytical skills, computer skills, declared college major in field, oral communication skills, personal interest in the field. Duration is 3 months (minimum).

HARLEYELLIS *(continued)*

$11–$15 per hour. ▶ *2 facilities management co-ops:* responsibilities include performing basic CAD/CAFM design applications (AutoCAD), assisting in preparing limited calculations (e.g. building areas, space/department allocations), and gathering dimensionally accurate on-site data for CAD applications. Candidates should have ability to work with others, computer skills, oral communication skills, self-motivation, declared college major in architecture, interior architecture, facilities management, or interior design. Duration is 3 months (minimum). $11–$15 per hour. ▶ *2 mechanical engineer co-ops:* responsibilities include developing basic understanding of building design as it relates to mechanical engineering, performing limited mechanical engineering design calculations, developing familiarity with engineering drawings and specifications, CADD, and field measurement. Candidates should have ability to work with others, analytical skills, computer skills, declared college major in field, oral communication skills, personal interest in the field. Duration is 3 months (minimum). $11–$15 per hour. ▶ *1–2 structural engineer co-ops:* responsibilities include assisting in preparation of project structural analysis and design, construction documents (CAD generated), and project written documentation; assisting in gathering on-site data and developing an understanding of the design process. Candidates should have ability to work with others, analytical skills, computer skills, declared college major in field, oral communication skills, personal interest in the field. Duration is 3 months (minimum). $11–$15 per hour. Open to college juniors, college seniors.

Benefits On-the-job training, opportunity to attend seminars/workshops, possible full-time employment, willing to act as a professional reference, willing to complete paperwork for educational credit, willing to provide letters of recommendation, flextime work schedule.

Contact Write, fax, e-mail, or through World Wide Web site Carolyn C. Palmer, Principal. Fax: 248-262-1552. E-mail: ccpalmer@harleyellis.com. In-person interview recommended (telephone interview accepted). Applicants must submit a letter of interest, resume, academic transcripts. Applications are accepted continuously. World Wide Web: http://www.harleyellis.com.

PROGRAM FOR WOMEN IN SCIENCE AND ENGINEERING
Iowa State University, 210 Lab of Mechanics
Ames, Iowa 50011-2131

General Information Program working to increase the number of women in science and engineering. Established in 1986. Number of employees: 5. Unit of Iowa State University of Science and Technology, Ames, Iowa. Number of internship applications received each year: 140.

Internships Available ▶ *10–40 high school interns:* responsibilities include working on an independent research project under the supervision of science or engineering faculty or staff. Candidates should have ability to work with others, analytical skills, oral communication skills, personal interest in the field, plan to pursue career in field, self-motivation, written communication skills. Duration is 6 weeks. $1800 per duration of internship. Open to individuals between junior and senior year in high school. ▶ *20–30 undergraduate interns:* responsibilities include working on an independent research project under the supervision of science or engineering faculty or staff. Candidates should have ability to work with others, analytical skills, college courses in field, knowledge of field, oral communication skills, organizational skills, personal interest in the field, plan to pursue career in field, self-motivation, written communication skills. Duration is 8 weeks. $3000 per duration of internship. Open to college freshmen, college sophomores, college juniors, college seniors. International applications accepted.

Benefits Housing at a cost, meals at a cost, opportunity to attend seminars/workshops, willing to provide letters of recommendation, opportunity to be part of state-of-the-art scientific research.

Contact Write, call, fax, e-mail, or through World Wide Web site Karen Zunkel, Director. Phone: 515-294-0966. Fax: 515-294-8627. E-mail: pwse@iastate.edu. Applicants must submit a formal organization application, academic transcripts, writing sample, two personal references, two letters of recommendation. Application deadline: February 1 for summer. World Wide Web: http://www.iastate.edu/~pwse_info/.

SHIVE-HATTERY, INC.
115 3rd Street, SE, 9th Floor
Cedar Rapids, Iowa 52401

General Information Engineering and architectural consulting firm. Established in 1962. Unit of Shive-Hattery, Inc., Cedar Rapids, Iowa. Number of internship applications received each year: 20.

Internships Available ▶ *5–10 architect interns:* responsibilities include working under the guidance of a registered professional architect to learn the intricacies of architecture from concept through construction. Candidates should have ability to work independently, analytical skills, college courses in field, computer skills, knowledge of field, oral communication skills, organizational skills, personal interest in the field, plan to pursue career in field, research skills, self-motivation, strong interpersonal skills, strong leadership ability, written communication skills. Duration is flexible. Salary dependent on level of education and experience. Open to college sophomores, college juniors, college seniors, recent college graduates. ▶ *5–10 engineering interns:* responsibilities include working under the guidance of a registered professional engineer. Candidates should have ability to work independently, analytical skills, college courses in field, computer skills, knowledge of field, oral communication skills, organizational skills, personal interest in the field, plan to pursue career in field, research skills, self-motivation, strong interpersonal skills, strong leadership ability, written communication skills. Duration is flexible. Salary dependent on level of education and experience. Open to college sophomores, college juniors, college seniors, recent college graduates, individuals reentering the workforce. ▶ *5–10 landscape architect interns:* responsibilities include working in any of the following engineering areas: civil, mechanical, electrical, or architectural; duties may include land survey, CAD design, or going to actual job sites. Candidates should have ability to work independently, analytical skills, college courses in field, computer skills, editing skills, knowledge of field, oral communication skills, organizational skills, personal interest in the field, plan to pursue career in field, research skills, self-motivation, strong interpersonal skills, strong leadership ability, written communication skills. Duration is flexible. Salary dependent on level of education and experience. Open to college sophomores, college juniors, college seniors, recent college graduates.

Benefits On-the-job training, opportunity to attend seminars/workshops, possible full-time employment, travel reimbursement, willing to complete paperwork for educational credit, worker's compensation.

Contact Write, fax, e-mail, or through World Wide Web site Gloria J. Frost, Vice President/Director of Human Resources, 115 3rd Street, SE, 9th Floor, Box 1599, Cedar Rapids, Iowa 52401. Fax: 800-854-8270. E-mail: gfrost@shive-hattery.com. No phone calls. In-person interview recommended (telephone interview accepted). Applicants must submit a formal organization application, resume. Applications are accepted continuously. World Wide Web: http://www.shive-hattery.com.

WALDEN ASSOCIATES
16 Spring Street
Oyster Bay, New York 11771

General Information Environmental/civil engineering consulting firm. Established in 1995. Number of employees: 10.

Internships Available ▶ *1–2 environmental engineers or geologists:* responsibilities include field work, investigations, writing reports, CADD, GIS, project work. Candidates should have ability to work independently, computer skills, oral communication skills, personal interest in the field, self-motivation, written communication skills. Duration is flexible. $10–$18 per hour. Open to college freshmen, college sophomores, college juniors, college seniors, recent college graduates, graduate students, preference given to Long Island residents.

Benefits On-the-job training, opportunity to attend seminars/workshops, possible full-time employment, willing to act as a

professional reference, willing to complete paperwork for educational credit, willing to provide letters of recommendation.

Contact Write, call, fax, or e-mail Bob Keane, Project Manager. Phone: 516-624-7200. Fax: 516-624-3219. E-mail: jobs@walden-assoc.com. Telephone interview required. Applicants must submit a resume. Applications are accepted continuously. World Wide Web: http://www.walden-assoc.com.

WASHINGTON INTERNSHIPS FOR STUDENTS OF ENGINEERING (WISE)
1828 L Street, NW, Suite 906
Washington, District of Columbia 20036

General Information Program set-up to match engineering students with suitable internships; sponsored by WISE, ANS, ASCE, ASME, IEEE, NSPE and SAE and AIChE (which acts as the program administrator). Established in 1980. Number of internship applications received each year: 75.

Internships Available ▶ *13–15 WISE interns:* responsibilities include researching and completing a paper on a current and topical engineering-related public policy issue; meeting with congressional committees, executive office departments, and corporate government affairs offices daily. Candidates should have ability to work independently, research skills, self-motivation, strong leadership ability, writing skills, membership in an engineering society (required by most of the sponsoring societies). Duration is June to August (10 weeks). $2100 stipend. Open to college juniors, college seniors, recent graduates beginning study in an engineering policy-related master's program.

Benefits Free housing, interaction with leaders in Congress and administration, industry, and prominent non-governmental organizations.

Contact Write, call, fax, e-mail, or through World Wide Web site Allian Pratt, Program Manager, Washington, District of Columbia 20005-3314. Phone: 202-785-3756. Fax: 202-429-9417. E-mail: pratta@asme.org. Applicants must submit a formal organization application, academic transcripts, two writing samples, two personal references, two letters of recommendation. Application deadline: December 12. World Wide Web: http://www.wise-intern.org.

LEGAL SERVICES

AMERICAN ASSOCIATION OF TRIAL LAWYERS (ATLA)
1050 31st Street, NW
Washington, District of Columbia 20007

General Information Organization that safeguards victims' rights and strengthens civil justice through education and dissemination of information critical to the health and safety of the American public. Established in 1946. Number of internship applications received each year: 300.

Internships Available ▶ *1–10 interns:* responsibilities include working in public affairs, state affairs, legal affairs, media relations, meetings/conventions, continuing legal education, publications, production, and foundations. Candidates should have analytical skills, computer skills, editing skills, office skills, organizational skills, personal interest in the field, plan to pursue career in field, research skills, writing skills. Duration is one summer. Paid. Open to college freshmen, college sophomores, college juniors, college seniors, recent college graduates, graduate students. International applications accepted.

Benefits Names of contacts, on-the-job training, opportunity to attend seminars/workshops, willing to act as a professional reference, willing to complete paperwork for educational credit.

Contact Write or fax Irene Cardon, Associate Director, Human Resources. Fax: 202-333-2861. Applicants must submit a letter of interest, resume. Application deadline: March 1. World Wide Web: http://www.atla.org.

AMERICAN BAR ASSOCIATION
740 15th Street, NW
Washington, District of Columbia 20005

General Information National voluntary association of attorneys with primary goals of professional and public service, as well as improvement of the judicial system. Established in 1878. Number of employees: 180. Unit of American Bar Association, Chicago, Illinois.

Internships Available ▶ *2–4 Center for Immigration Law and Representation interns:* responsibilities include doing various tasks in immigration benefits and procedures including interviewing, legal research, and case preparation, in either Washington, D.C. or Harlingen, Texas. Duration is 1 semester or 1 summer (for Washington, DC interns) 2-3 months (Harlingen, TX interns). Position available as unpaid or paid. Open to law students. ▶ *Central and East European Law Initiative interns:* responsibilities include researching, writing, and legal assesments (lawyers). Candidates should have ability to work independently, self-motivation, strong interpersonal skills, writing skills, training/experience in international affairs (preferred). Duration is 15 hours per week minimum during school year; full-time in summer. Unpaid. Open to college freshmen, college sophomores, college juniors, college seniors, law students, attorneys. ▶ *6 Commission on Mental and Physical Disability Law interns.* Duration is fall, spring, or summer semester. Position available as unpaid or paid. Open to college freshmen, college sophomores, college juniors, college seniors, law students. ▶ *1 Division for Media Relations and Public Affairs intern:* responsibilities include participating in press briefings, news conferences, strategic planning, event publicity, interview placements, and other duties. Candidates should have demonstrated interest in public relations. Duration is one academic term (part-time). Unpaid. Open to college sophomores, college juniors, college seniors. ▶ *6 Government Public Sector Lawyers Division interns:* responsibilities include helping with the division's publications, assisting in award program, and a wide variety of clerical and administrative tasks. Candidates should have self-motivation, strong leadership ability. Duration is 1 semester or 1 summer. Unpaid. Open to college juniors, college seniors, law students. ▶ *1–3 Governmental Affairs Office interns:* responsibilities include working with the staff, conducting research, and writing memoranda on legislative and policy issues. Candidates should have research skills, writing skills. Duration is part-time during school year; full-time during summer. Unpaid. Open to college freshmen, college sophomores, college juniors, college seniors. ▶ *1 Immigration and Pro Bono Development intern.* Candidates should have immigration law experience/coursework. Duration is 10-20 hours per week for length of school year. Unpaid. Open to law students in second or third year. ▶ *1–5 Public Services Division interns:* responsibilities include compiling information for directories and other databases; coordinating survey development, distribution, and results; assisting with mailings, copying, and faxing. Duration is 8–10 weeks. Position available as unpaid or paid. Open to college freshmen, college sophomores, college juniors, college seniors, undergraduates and first-year law students (project internships only), second and third-year law students (eligible for 1 Public Service Summer Internship). ▶ *6 Section of Dispute Resolution interns:* responsibilities include various tasks in mediation, arbitration, and other non-litigious forms of dispute resolution. Unpaid. Open to college freshmen, college sophomores, college juniors, college seniors. ▶ *1–4 Section of Individual Rights and Responsibilities interns:* responsibilities include conducting legal research; assisting in monitoring state and federal legislative developments on various civil rights, civil liberties, and human rights issues; and writing newsletter articles for the Section newsletter. Candidates should have personal interest in the field, research skills, writing skills. Duration is 1 semester. Unpaid. Open to college juniors, college seniors, law students. ▶ *1–4 Section of International Law and Practice interns:* responsibilities include conducting legal research; assisting in monitoring state and federal legislative developments on various civil rights, civil liberties, and human rights issues; and writing newsletter articles for the Section. Candidates should have personal interest in the field. Duration is 1 academic term or summer. Unpaid. Open to college freshmen, college sophomores, college juniors, college seniors. ▶ *1 Standing Committee on Law*

and National Security intern: responsibilities include assisting with daily operation of standing committee business, responding to requests, organizing monthly breakfast meeting, and other tasks as necessary. Duration is 2-3 days per week. Unpaid. Open to college freshmen, college sophomores, college juniors, college seniors, graduate students. International applications accepted.
Benefits Opportunity to attend seminars/workshops, possible full-time employment, willing to act as a professional reference, willing to complete paperwork for educational credit, willing to provide letters of recommendation.
Contact Write, call, fax, or through World Wide Web site Internship Coordinator. Phone: 202-662-1010. Fax: 202-662-1032. Applicants must submit a letter of interest, resume. Applications are accepted continuously. World Wide Web: http://www.abanet.org.

AMERICAN BAR ASSOCIATION–CENTRAL EUROPEAN AND EURASIAN LAW INITIATIVE (CEELI)
740 15th Street, NW
Washington, District of Columbia 20005-1022

General Information Program that provides legal reform in Central and Eastern Europe and the former Soviet states. Established in 1990. Number of employees: 35. Unit of American Bar Association, Chicago, Illinois. Number of internship applications received each year: 400.
Internships Available ▶ *2–16 interns:* responsibilities include providing administrative and research support for one of CEELI's departments. Candidates should have ability to work independently, computer skills, research skills, self-motivation, strong interpersonal skills, training and/or experience in international affairs (preferred). Duration is minimum of one semester (12-20 hours per week) or one summer (full-time). Unpaid. Open to recent college graduates, graduate students, law students, attorneys. International applications accepted.
Benefits Opportunity to attend seminars/workshops, willing to act as a professional reference, willing to complete paperwork for educational credit, willing to provide letters of recommendation, access to internal ABA job postings for full-time employment.
Contact Write, fax, or e-mail Susan Henderson, Recruitment Assistant. Fax: 202-662-1597. E-mail: internships@abaceeli.org. No phone calls. In-person interview recommended (telephone interview accepted). Applicants must submit a letter of interest, resume, brief writing sample (5 page maximum). Applications are accepted continuously. World Wide Web: http://www.abanet.org/ceeli.

AMERICAN SOCIETY OF INTERNATIONAL LAW
2223 Massachusetts Avenue, NW
Washington, District of Columbia 20008

General Information Professional organization that engages in the exploration of international legal issues, including economic and private transactions, the environment, armed conflicts, human rights, dispute resolution, space, and the United Nations system. Established in 1906. Number of employees: 18. Number of internship applications received each year: 150.
Internships Available ▶ *1–3 financial office assistants:* responsibilities include assisting the controllers office with accounting functions. Candidates should have computer skills, knowledge of field, office skills, organizational skills, self-motivation. Duration is 8–10 weeks. Unpaid. Open to college freshmen, college sophomores, college juniors. ▶ *1 library/research assistant:* responsibilities include helping to maintain the ASIL Web site, assisting staff and the Washington legal community with their information needs, and general library activities. Candidates should have ability to work with others, computer skills, office skills, oral communication skills, research skills, self-motivation, writing skills. Duration is one semester or summer. Unpaid. Open to college sophomores, college juniors, college seniors, graduate students, law students. ▶ *1 meetings assistant:* responsibilities include database development, correspondence with panelists and exhibitors, Internet research on panelists and exhibitors, assisting with CLE administration for the Annual Meeting, and other administrative functions associated with the meeting planning. Candidates should have ability to work independently, computer skills, office skills, oral communication skills, organizational skills, research skills, self-motivation, strong interpersonal skills, writing skills. Duration is one semester or summer. Unpaid. Open to college juniors, college seniors, graduate students, law students. ▶ *1 publications intern:* responsibilities include bluebooking citations, desktop publishing, and formatting text for ASIL publications including ITProceedings of the Annual Meeting and IT Studies in Transnational Legal Policy series. Candidates should have ability to work independently, computer skills, editing skills, organizational skills, research skills, strong bluebooking and citation checking skills. Duration is one semester or summer. Unpaid. Open to law students. ▶ *1 research assistant—American Journal of International Law.* Duration is one semester or one summer (minimum). Position available as unpaid or paid. Open to second- and third-year law students. ▶ *1–3 sales and marketing assistants:* responsibilities include assisting in the promotion of the Society's programs and publications, conducting market research, and assisting in the development and implementation of marketing strategies. Candidates should have computer skills, oral communication skills, organizational skills, research skills, strong interpersonal skills, written communication skills. Duration is 1 semester or summer. Unpaid. Open to college juniors, college seniors, graduate students, law students. International applications accepted.
Benefits Opportunity to attend seminars/workshops, possible full-time employment, willing to act as a professional reference, willing to complete paperwork for educational credit, willing to provide letters of recommendation, assistance with development of legal analysis skills available for some positions.
Contact Write or fax Internship Coordinator. Fax: 202-797-7133. No phone calls. In-person interview recommended (telephone interview accepted). Applicants must submit a letter of interest, resume, list of three references (one work, one academic, one personal reference) with telephone numbers. Application deadline: April 1 for summer, August 1 for fall, December 1 for spring. World Wide Web: http://www.asil.org.

ANIMAL LEGAL DEFENSE FUND
127 Fourth Street
Petaluma, California 94952-3005

General Information National nonprofit public interest law organization dedicated to protecting animals and establishing their legal rights through litigation. Established in 1979. Number of employees: 20. Number of internship applications received each year: 100.
Internships Available ▶ *2 Eleanor Seiling Legal Clerkship interns:* responsibilities include legal research and preparation of pleadings in cases currently being handled by ALDF; placement is in ALDF's Rockville, Maryland office. Candidates should have analytical skills, computer skills, oral communication skills, research skills, writing skills, administrative law coursework, previous law clerking experience. Duration is 10 weeks in summer. $3500 per duration of internship. Open to second-year law students only.
Benefits On-the-job training, possible full-time employment, willing to act as a professional reference, willing to provide letters of recommendation.
Contact Write, call, fax, e-mail, or through World Wide Web site Pamela Miller, Office Administrator, 6930 Carroll Avenue, Suite 800, Takoma Park, Maryland 20912. Phone: 301-891-6790. Fax: 301-891-6707. E-mail: pmiller@aldf.org. In-person interview required. Applicants must submit a letter of interest, resume, writing sample, three personal references. Application deadline: April 15 for summer, November 30 for spring. World Wide Web: http://www.aldf.org.

ASSOCIATION OF LEGAL AID ATTORNEYS/UAW 2325
568 Broadway, Room 702A
New York, New York 10012-3225

General Information Oldest and largest major union of lawyers in the U.S., who each year represent some 300,000 indigent New Yorkers in criminal, civil, and juvenile cases. Established in 1969. Number of employees: 750.

Internships Available ▶ *Interns:* responsibilities include exposure to wide variety of activities including HQ administration, criminal law, criminal justice policy (e.g. police abuse, drug law reform), political action, union meetings, and collective bargaining. Duration is one fall, spring and/or summer. Unpaid.
Benefits Willing to complete paperwork for educational credit.
Contact E-mail George Albro, Secretary Treasurer. Phone: 212-343-0708. E-mail: galbro@legal-aid.org. Applicants must submit resume and cover letter indicating time of year desired (via e-mail only). Applications are accepted continuously. World Wide Web: http://www.alaa.org.

AYUDA, INC.
1736 Columbia Road, NW
Washington, District of Columbia 20009

General Information Nonprofit community-based agency that provides legal assistance on immigration and domestic violence matters to the low-income, foreign-born population of Washington, DC metropolitan area. Established in 1971. Number of employees: 15. Number of internship applications received each year: 350.
Internships Available ▶ *4–6 domestic violence legal assistants:* responsibilities include conducting initial interviews with battered women, drafting legal documents, preparing clients for trial, conducting case investigations, assisting at counsel table during trial, attending community outreach activities. Candidates should have ability to work independently, computer skills, experience in the field, office skills, oral communication skills, organizational skills, plan to pursue career in field, research skills, strong interpersonal skills, writing skills, proficiency in Spanish required. Duration is 10–12 weeks. Unpaid. Open to college sophomores, college juniors, college seniors, recent college graduates, graduate students, law students, individuals reentering the workforce.
▶ *5–8 immigration legal assistants:* responsibilities include working in areas of political asylum, naturalization, relative petition, adjustment of status, advance parole, and suspension of deportation. Candidates should have ability to work independently, organizational skills, plan to pursue career in field, self-motivation, strong interpersonal skills, writing skills, proficiency in Spanish (required), proficiency in French (desired). Duration is 10–12 weeks. Unpaid. Open to college freshmen, college sophomores, college juniors, college seniors, recent college graduates, graduate students, law students, career changers, individuals reentering the workforce.
▶ *1–2 public relations interns:* responsibilities include drafting grant proposals, creating annual report, developing media contacts, and working on fund-raising projects. Candidates should have ability to work independently, computer skills, editing skills, office skills, organizational skills, research skills, self-motivation, strong interpersonal skills, writing skills. Duration is 10–12 weeks. Unpaid. Open to college freshmen, college sophomores, college juniors, college seniors, recent college graduates, graduate students, law students. International applications accepted.
Benefits Opportunity to attend seminars/workshops, willing to act as a professional reference, willing to complete paperwork for educational credit, willing to provide letters of recommendation, help in obtaining fellowships.
Contact Write, call, fax, or e-mail Vilma Cabrera, Volunteer Coordinator. Phone: 202-387-2870 Ext. 10. Fax: 202-387-0324. E-mail: vcabrera@ayudainc.org. In-person interview recommended (telephone interview accepted). Applicants must submit a formal organization application, letter of interest, resume, 2–3 personal references. Application deadline: January 15 for spring, March 15 for summer, September 10 for fall.

BET TZEDEK LEGAL SERVICES
145 South Fairfax Avenue, Suite 200
Los Angeles, California 90036

General Information Legal services organization providing free legal services to poor and low-income residents of Los Angeles County, focusing primarily on senior citizens. Established in 1973. Number of employees: 54. Number of internship applications received each year: 100.
Internships Available ▶ *1–2 marketing/development interns:* responsibilities include assisting in special event production, direct mail solicitation, and telephone follow-up. Candidates should have abil-

ity to work independently, computer skills, office skills, organizational skills, strong interpersonal skills, writing skills, good phone skills, high-energy, and people-oriented disposition. Duration is 10-12 weeks (20 hours per week during summer; 8 hours per week during academic year). Unpaid. Open to college sophomores, college juniors, college seniors, recent college graduates, graduate students, career changers. ▶ *1–2 nonprofit fund accounting interns:* responsibilities include working hands-on with computerized accounts payable and receivable documentation, assisting in the input and accounting functions specific to nonprofit organizations with multiple funding sources, receiving training in the use and function of spreadsheet applications, and organizing data for review and taking part in the data analysis process. Candidates should have ability to work with others, office skills, oral communication skills, organizational skills, general accounting and/or bookkeeping background (helpful), 10-key experience, moderate typing skills, familiarity with computers. Duration is 10-12 weeks (8 hours per week). Unpaid. Open to college freshmen, college sophomores, college juniors, college seniors, recent college graduates, graduate students, career changers, individuals reentering the workforce. ▶ *7–9 prescreeners/legal assistants:* responsibilities include prescreening clients by phone for financial and case type eligibility, making appropriate referrals, conducting in-person interviews, writing letters on behalf of clients, and other client advocacy under the direction of supervising attorneys. Candidates should have ability to work independently, analytical skills, oral communication skills, plan to pursue career in field, strong interpersonal skills, written communication skills, demonstrable commitment to community service, understanding of the problems of the poor. Duration is 11-12 weeks (20 hours per week during summer, 8 hours per week during academic year). Unpaid. Open to college freshmen, college sophomores, college juniors, recent college graduates, college seniors (during academic year only).
Benefits Formal training, on-the-job training, willing to act as a professional reference, willing to complete paperwork for educational credit, willing to provide letters of recommendation.
Contact Write, call, fax, or e-mail Ms. Robin Sommerstein, Human Resource Director/Volunteer Coordinator. Phone: 323-549-5814. Fax: 323-939-1040. E-mail: rsommerstein@bettzedek.org. In-person interview recommended (telephone interview accepted). Applicants must submit a letter of interest, resume. Application deadline: April 15 for summer, September 10 for fall. World Wide Web: http://www.bettzedek.org.

CALIFORNIA RURAL LEGAL ASSISTANCE
21 Carr Street
Watsonville, California 95076

General Information Law office funded by federal, state, county, and city government, providing free legal advice to qualifying low-income people in the areas of unemployment, housing, welfare law, and education. Established in 1968. Number of employees: 13. Number of internship applications received each year: 50.
Internships Available ▶ *2–3 legal interns:* responsibilities include handling case work, conducting client intake, advising and referral, preparing legal materials, and working closely with staff attorneys; special research projects are also possible. Candidates should have ability to work with others, analytical skills, computer skills, oral communication skills, research skills, self-motivation, writing skills. Duration is 2 quarters (minimum of 10 hours per week). Unpaid. Open to college freshmen, college sophomores, college juniors, college seniors, recent college graduates, graduate students, law students. International applications accepted.
Benefits Willing to complete paperwork for educational credit, willing to provide letters of recommendation, one-on-one supervision by an attorney.
Contact Write, fax, or e-mail Shirley Conner, Intern Coordinator. Fax: 831-724-7530. E-mail: watsonville@crla.org. No phone calls. In-person interview recommended (telephone interview accepted). Applicants must submit a letter of interest, resume. Applications are accepted continuously.

CENTER FOR INTERNATIONAL LEGAL STUDIES
Schweigmuhlweg 6B
Salzburg Austria

General Information Legal publication, research, and training institute whose essential purpose is the promotion of information dissemination and the administration of post-graduate programs. Established in 1976. Number of employees: 15. Number of internship applications received each year: 50.
Internships Available ▶ *10–20 international law interns:* responsibilities include a variety of legal work. Candidates should have analytical skills, personal interest in the field, plan to pursue career in field, research skills, self-motivation, strong interpersonal skills. Duration is 2–3 months. Position available as unpaid or at $800–$1000 per month. Open to graduate students. ▶ *10–20 summer externs:* responsibilities include a variety of legal work. Candidates should have analytical skills, office skills, personal interest in the field, research skills, self-motivation, strong interpersonal skills. Duration is 1 month. Unpaid. Open to law students. International applications accepted.
Benefits Free housing, free meals, on-the-job training, willing to complete paperwork for educational credit.
International Internships Available.
Contact Write or e-mail Christian Campbell, Schweigmuhlueg 6B, Salzburg 5020 Austria. E-mail: christian.campbell@cils.or.at. Applicants must submit a formal organization application, resume, academic transcripts, two letters of recommendation, statement of interest. Application deadline: December 1 for spring. Fees: $200. World Wide Web: http://www.cils.org.

CONNECTICUT JUDICIAL BRANCH
2275 Silas Deane Highway
Rocky Hill, Connecticut 06067

General Information Branch of government consisting of 22 courts dealing with criminal and civil matters statewide. Established in 1976. Number of employees: 2,400. Branch of State of Connecticut Court Support Services, Bridgeport, Connecticut. Number of internship applications received each year: 900.
Internships Available ▶ *200 interns:* responsibilities include court coverage including contacts with clients; working with court personnel; assisting probation officers and court investigators; interns are assigned to adult probation, judicial matters, family division, and States Attorney and Public Defenders offices statewide. Candidates should have ability to work with others, oral communication skills, personal interest in the field, written communication skills, ability to maintain a high level of confidentiality, must be student in good standing. Duration is 1 or 2 semesters contingent on major and departmental requirements. Unpaid. Open to college sophomores, college juniors, college seniors, graduate students, law students, must disclose any pending matter before the court to intern coordinator. International applications accepted.
Benefits Formal training, health insurance, job counseling, on-the-job training, possible full-time employment, travel reimbursement, willing to act as a professional reference, willing to complete paperwork for educational credit, willing to provide letters of recommendation.
Contact Write, call, or e-mail Mrs. Robyn N. Oliver, Program Coordinator. Phone: 860-757-2270. E-mail: robyn.oliver@jud.state. ct.us. Applicants must submit materials obtained by calling or writing. Applications are accepted continuously. World Wide Web: http://www.jud.state.ct.us.

COUNCIL FOR COURT EXCELLENCE
1717 K Street, NW, Suite 510
Washington, District of Columbia 20036

General Information Nonprofit, nonpartisan civic organization working to improve the administration of justice in local and federal courts through studies of judicial branch performance and advocacy of related reforms, and through public education about courts. Established in 1982. Number of employees: 6. Number of internship applications received each year: 60.
Internships Available ▶ *3 interns:* responsibilities include working on priority projects related to court performance in areas such as criminal justice, child abuse and neglect, civil justice, and community education about the courts. Candidates should have computer skills, office skills, research skills, self-motivation, strong interpersonal skills, writing skills. Duration is one summer. Unpaid. Open to college freshmen, college sophomores, college juniors, college seniors, recent college graduates, graduate students, law students, individuals reentering the workforce. International applications accepted.
Benefits Job counseling, names of contacts, on-the-job training, opportunity to attend seminars/workshops, possible full-time employment, willing to act as a professional reference, willing to complete paperwork for educational credit, willing to provide letters of recommendation, commuting costs paid.
Contact Write, call, fax, e-mail, or through World Wide Web site Ms. Priscilla Skillman, Assistant Director. Phone: 202-785-5917. Fax: 202-785-5922. E-mail: skillman@courtexcellence.org. In-person interview recommended (telephone interview accepted). Applicants must submit a letter of interest, resume, writing sample. Applications are accepted continuously. World Wide Web: http://www. courtexcellence.org.

DISABILITY RIGHTS ADVOCATES
449 15th Street, Suite 303
Oakland, California 94612

General Information Legal advocacy organization that supports the rights of persons with disabilities in litigation relating to the Americans with Disabilities Act. Number of employees: 21. Number of internship applications received each year: 50.
Internships Available ▶ *Fall law clerks.* Candidates should have ability to work independently, ability to work with others, analytical skills, computer skills, oral communication skills, personal interest in the field, writing skills. Duration is 1 semester. Position available as unpaid or paid. Open to law students. ▶ *1–8 law clerks.* Candidates should have ability to work independently, ability to work with others, analytical skills, computer skills, personal interest in the field, writing skills. Duration is June 1 to August 31. Position available as unpaid or at $8–$12 per hour. Open to recent college graduates, graduate students, law students. International applications accepted.
Benefits On-the-job training, possible full-time employment, willing to complete paperwork for educational credit, willing to provide letters of recommendation, travel to and from work reimbursed.
Contact Write, fax, or e-mail Caroline Amimo, Office Administrator. Fax: 510-451-8511. E-mail: carolinea@dralegal.org. No phone calls. Applicants must submit a resume, writing sample, 5-page writing sample. Application deadline: April 1. World Wide Web: http:// www.dralegal.org.

GEORGETOWN UNIVERSITY LAW CENTER–CRIMINAL JUSTICE CLINIC
111 F Street, NW
Washington, District of Columbia 20001-2095

General Information Clinic providing representation to indigent criminal defendants in District of Columbia. Established in 1989. Number of employees: 18. Number of internship applications received each year: 400.
Internships Available ▶ *10 investigative interns:* responsibilities include meeting investigative needs of 2 clinic attorneys in all aspects of investigations, including assessing government's cases, interviewing potential witnesses, gathering relevant paperwork, serving subpoenas, collecting evidence, and other field work. Candidates should have oral communication skills, organizational skills, self-motivation, strong interpersonal skills, strong leadership ability, written communication skills. Duration is 1 semester or summer. Unpaid. Open to college freshmen, college sophomores, college juniors, college seniors, recent college graduates, graduate students, law students. International applications accepted.
Benefits Formal training, job counseling, names of contacts, on-the-job training, opportunity to attend seminars/workshops, travel reimbursement, willing to act as a professional reference, willing to complete paperwork for educational credit, willing to provide letters of recommendation, membership in fitness center.

Contact Write, call, fax, e-mail, or through World Wide Web site Rebecca O'Brien, Investigations Supervisor. Phone: 202-662-9589. Fax: 202-662-9681. E-mail: obrienra@law.georgetown.edu. Telephone interview required. Applicants must submit a formal organization application, two personal references. Application deadline: March 15 for 1st round fall, April 1 for summer, July 1 for 2nd round fall, December 1 for spring. World Wide Web: http://www.law.georgetown.edu/clinics/cjc/iip.html.

HALT–AN ORGANIZATION OF AMERICANS FOR LEGAL REFORM
1612 K Street, NW, Suite 510
Washington, District of Columbia 20006

General Information National nonprofit membership organization dedicated to making the civil legal system more accessible, less costly, and more equitable. Established in 1978. Number of employees: 7. Number of internship applications received each year: 200.

Internships Available ▶ *2–4 interns:* responsibilities include working in all aspects of organization on projects with extensive research and writing. Candidates should have computer skills, editing skills, office skills, personal interest in the field, research skills, writing skills. Duration is 1 semester. Position available as unpaid or at $210–$300 per week. Open to recent high school graduates, college freshmen, college sophomores, college juniors, college seniors, recent college graduates, graduate students, law students. International applications accepted.

Benefits Willing to act as a professional reference, willing to complete paperwork for educational credit, willing to provide letters of recommendation.

Contact Write, fax, e-mail, or through World Wide Web site Internship Coordinator. Fax: 202-887-9699. E-mail: internships@halt.org. Applicants must submit a letter of interest, resume, writing sample of 3 to 10 pages. Applications are accepted continuously. World Wide Web: http://www.halt.org.

HIV & AIDS LEGAL SERVICES ALLIANCE, INC.
3550 Wilshire Boulevard, Suite 750
Los Angeles, California 90010

General Information Nonprofit legal service program for people with HIV or AIDS. Established in 1997. Number of employees: 13. Number of internship applications received each year: 75.

Internships Available ▶ *2–4 interns/law clerks:* responsibilities include assisting staff attorneys in providing direct legal services on a wide range of issues including discrimination, benefits, housing, immigration, debtor relief, and testamentary. Candidates should have ability to work independently, computer skills, knowledge of field, self-motivation, strong interpersonal skills, demonstrated commitment to public service. Duration is May to June (full-time) or up to 10 hours per week during school year. Unpaid. Open to law students.

Benefits Formal training, job counseling, on-the-job training, opportunity to attend seminars/workshops, willing to act as a professional reference, willing to complete paperwork for educational credit, willing to provide letters of recommendation.

Contact Write, call, fax, or e-mail Laurie Aronoff, Director of Volunteer Programs. Phone: 213-201-1492. Fax: 213-201-1594. E-mail: laronoff@apla.org. In-person interview recommended (telephone interview accepted). Applicants must submit a letter of interest, resume, letters of recommendation (preferred). Application deadline: February 15 for summer; continuous for other positions.

JUDICIAL INTERNSHIP PROGRAM, SUPREME COURT OF THE UNITED STATES
Office of the Administrative Assistant to the Chief Justice, Room 5
Washington, District of Columbia 20543

General Information Office that assists the Chief Justice in fulfilling non-adjudicatory responsibilities. Established in 1972. Number of employees: 350. Number of internship applications received each year: 150.

Internships Available ▶ *1–3 judicial interns:* responsibilities include routine office tasks; monitoring research on the federal judicial system; helping prepare memoranda, correspondence, background research for articles and speeches; monitoring and summarizing benefits with international judicial visitors. Candidates should have ability to work with others, analytical skills, oral communication skills, research skills, self-motivation, written communication skills, some course work in constitutional law or the Supreme Court (preferred). Duration is 1 semester. Unpaid. Open to college juniors, college seniors. International applications accepted.

Benefits Opportunity to attend seminars/workshops, willing to act as a professional reference, willing to complete paperwork for educational credit, willing to provide letters of recommendation, $1000 stipend may be available for interns who are returning to academic studies.

Contact Write, call, or fax Judicial Fellow. Phone: 202-479-3415. Fax: 202-479-3484. Telephone interview required. Applicants must submit a formal organization application, resume, academic transcripts, writing sample, three letters of recommendation, candidate statement describing experience, skills, and reason for application, and essay of 2 pages or more. Application deadline: March 10 for summer, June 10 for fall, October 20 for winter. World Wide Web: http://www.supremecourtus.gov.

KOHN, KOHN AND COLAPINTO, P.C.
3233 P Street, NW
Washington, District of Columbia 20007-2756

General Information Public interest law firm specializing in representation of whistle-blowers; represents employees who were fired or retaliated against for making disclosures regarding nuclear safety, corporate or government misconduct, environmental protection, or health and safety violations. Established in 1988. Number of employees: 7. Number of internship applications received each year: 100.

Internships Available ▶ *6–8 legal interns:* responsibilities include significant legal research and writing projects, assisting at trials, and performing all the work of an associate attorney. Candidates should have ability to work independently, ability to work with others, analytical skills, oral communication skills, research skills, written communication skills. Duration is 10 weeks in summer; flexible at other times of year. Unpaid. Open to college juniors, college seniors, recent college graduates, graduate students, law students. International applications accepted.

Benefits Willing to act as a professional reference, willing to complete paperwork for educational credit, willing to provide letters of recommendation, one-on-one supervision from an attorney.

Contact Write, call, fax, e-mail, or through World Wide Web site Karima Brooker, Internship Coordinator. Phone: 202-342-6980. Fax: 202-342-6984. E-mail: kb@kkc.com. Telephone interview required. Applicants must submit a resume, cover letter. Application deadline: March 1 for summer, June 1 for fall, September 1 for January positions, December 1 for spring. World Wide Web: http://www.whistleblowers.org.

LAMBDA LEGAL DEFENSE AND EDUCATION FUND, INC.
3325 Wilshire Boulevard, #1300
Los Angeles, California 90010

General Information National organization committed to achieving full recognition of the civil rights of lesbians, gay men, bisexuals, transgenders, and people with HIV/AIDS through impact litigation, education, and public policy work. Established in 1973. Number of employees: 10. Branch of Lambda Legal Defense and Education Fund, Inc., New York, New York. Number of internship applications received each year: 75.

Internships Available ▶ *1–3 interns:* responsibilities include handling intake of callers, researching legal matters and classifying them into subject-matter files, utilizing programs such as Lexis or Westlaw, and legal research and writing. Candidates should have ability to work with others, computer skills, personal interest in the field, research skills, self-motivation, writing skills. Duration is summer, fall, or winter/spring semester. Unpaid. Open to law students. International applications accepted.

Lambda Legal Defense and Education Fund, Inc. (continued)

Benefits Opportunity to attend seminars/workshops, travel reimbursement, willing to act as a professional reference, willing to complete paperwork for educational credit, willing to provide letters of recommendation.

Contact Write or e-mail Stefan Johnson, Intake Coordinator. Phone: 213-382-7600. Fax: 213-351-6050. E-mail: sjohnson@ lambdalegal.org. Applicants must submit a letter of interest, resume, writing sample. Application deadline: February 15 for summer, August 15 for fall, November 15 for winter/spring. World Wide Web: http://www.lambdalegal.org.

LAMBDA LEGAL DEFENSE AND EDUCATION FUND, INC.
Southern Regional Office, 1447 Peachtree Street, Suite 1004
Atlanta, Georgia 30309

General Information National organization committed to achieving full recognition of the civil righs of lesbians, gay men, bisexuals, the transgender, and people with HIV/AIDS through impact litigation, education, and public policy work. Established in 1973. Number of employees: 5. Unit of Lambda Legal–Headquarters, New York, New York. Number of internship applications received each year: 50.

Internships Available ▶ *1–3 academic year interns:* responsibilities include research, writing, client intake, and special projects. Duration is 3–6 months. Paid at up to $10 per hour. ▶ *1–3 summer interns:* responsibilities include research, writing, client intake, and special projects. Duration is June to August. Unpaid. Candidates for all positions should have analytical skills, college courses in field, personal interest in the field, research skills, writing skills. Open to law students. International applications accepted.

Benefits Formal training, job counseling, names of contacts, on-the-job training, opportunity to attend seminars/workshops, willing to act as a professional reference, willing to complete paperwork for educational credit, willing to provide letters of recommendation.

Contact Write Greg Nevins, Staff Attorney. Phone: 404-897-1880. Fax: 404-897-1884. In-person interview recommended (telephone interview accepted). Applicants must submit a letter of interest, resume, academic transcripts, writing sample. Application deadline: April 30 for summer; continuous for academic-year positions. World Wide Web: http://www.lambdalegal.org.

LAMBDA LEGAL DEFENSE AND EDUCATION FUND, INC. (MIDWEST REGION)
11 East Adams, Suite 1008
Chicago, Illinois 60603-6303

General Information Established in 1973. Number of employees: 12. Branch of Lambda Legal Defense and Education Fund, Inc., New York, New York.

Internships Available ▶ *Legal help desk interns:* responsibilities include handling and documenting intake calls under direction of help desk coordinator; speaking with callers regarding potential cases, identifying key facts, recording vital information for attorney review, and connecting callers to legal and social services. Candidates should have ability to work independently, computer skills, oral communication skills, personal interest in the field, strong interpersonal skills, written communication skills, ability to maintain confidentiality a must. Duration is fall, spring, and summer semesters. Unpaid. Open to recent high school graduates, college freshmen, college sophomores, college juniors, college seniors, recent college graduates, graduate students, law students, career changers. ▶ *1–3 legal interns:* responsibilities include assisting attorneys with ongoing cases; researching, drafting, and/or completing amicus curiae briefs on all areas of sexual orientation, gender identity, and HIV discrimination; researching case materials in library; summarizing briefs, testimony, and depositions. Candidates should have ability to work independently, knowledge of field, personal interest in the field, research skills, writing skills. Duration is one summer (10-12 weeks). $4500 per duration of internship. Open to law students. International applications accepted.

Benefits Names of contacts, on-the-job training, willing to act as a professional reference, willing to provide letters of recommendation, completion of paperwork for educational credit (for legal internship only).

Contact Write, call, fax, e-mail, or through World Wide Web site RoiAnn Phillips, Outreach Associate. Phone: 312-663-4413. Fax: 312-663-4307. E-mail: lldefmro@lambdalegal.org. In-person interview required. Applicants must submit a letter of interest, resume, 1 writing sample required (for legal internship only). 2–3 personal references. Application deadline: January 1 for summer legal interns; continuous for help desk interns, July 1 for fall legal interns. World Wide Web: http://www.lambdalegal.org.

LANSNER AND KUBITSCHEK
325 Broadway, Suite 201
New York, New York 10007

General Information Public interest law firm in the areas of family law, civil rights, and social security. Established in 1991. Number of employees: 15.

Internships Available ▶ *3–4 fall/spring interns:* responsibilities include interviewing clients, drafting briefs, researching legal issues, tracking down witnesses, and attending court hearings. Candidates should have analytical skills, personal interest in the field, research skills, strong interpersonal skills, writing skills. Duration is one semester (minimum of 10 hours per week). Unpaid. Open to college seniors, recent college graduates, graduate students, law students. ▶ *6–8 summer associates:* responsibilities include interviewing clients, drafting briefs, researching legal issues, tracking down witnesses, attending court hearings, tracking client files, and conducting social security hearings. Candidates should have analytical skills, research skills, strong interpersonal skills, written communication skills. Duration is June to August. Unpaid. Open to law students. ▶ *8–10 winter interns:* responsibilities include drafting briefs, researching legal issues, attending court hearings, and preparing client files. Candidates should have analytical skills, personal interest in the field, research skills, strong interpersonal skills, writing skills. Duration is 3 weeks in January (full-time). Unpaid. Open to college sophomores, college juniors, college seniors. International applications accepted.

Benefits Names of contacts, on-the-job training, opportunity to attend seminars/workshops, willing to act as a professional reference, willing to complete paperwork for educational credit, willing to provide letters of recommendation, possibility of academic credit for summer associates.

Contact Write, call, fax, e-mail, or through World Wide Web site Katie Roberson-Young, Paralegal. Phone: 212-349-0900. Fax: 212-349-0694. E-mail: katie@lanskub.com. In-person interview recommended (telephone interview accepted). Applicants must submit a letter of interest, resume, writing sample. Applications are accepted continuously. World Wide Web: http://www. lansnerkubitschek.com.

LAW OFFICES OF PAUL STRAUSS AND ASSOCIATES
601 Pennsylvania Avenue, NW, Suite 900
Washington, District of Columbia 20004

General Information Law office. Established in 1993. Number of employees: 6. Number of internship applications received each year: 100.

Internships Available ▶ *3–5 interns/paralegals/law clerks:* responsibilities include assisting attorneys in all aspects of cases, includung preparation for litigation, preparing witnesses, and investigating facts. Candidates should have ability to work independently, analytical skills, computer skills, editing skills, office skills, oral communication skills, organizational skills, self-motivation, strong interpersonal skills, strong leadership ability, written communication skills. Unpaid. Open to college freshmen, college sophomores, college juniors, college seniors, recent college graduates, graduate students, law students, career changers. International applications accepted.

Benefits Formal training, on-the-job training, possible full-time employment, willing to complete paperwork for educational credit, willing to provide letters of recommendation, subsidized housing available.

Contact Call or e-mail Richard Bianco, Supervising Attorney. Phone: 202-220-3100. E-mail: strausslaw@aol.com. Applicants must submit a letter of interest, resume. Applications are accepted continuously.

THE LEGAL AID SOCIETY, CRIMINAL DEFENSE DIVISION
49 Thomas Street, 2nd Floor
New York, New York 10013

General Information Organization that provides free legal assistance to indigent clients in all areas of the law including criminal defense, juvenile, appeals, and civil. Established in 1876. Number of employees: 250. Division of Legal Aid Society, New York, New York. Number of internship applications received each year: 300.
Internships Available ▶ *30–40 investigator interns:* responsibilities include locating, interviewing, and taking written statements from witnesses in the field; background checks and research; serving subpoenas; and assisting attorneys in preparing for court. Candidates should have ability to work independently, oral communication skills, personal interest in the field, strong interpersonal skills, written communication skills, commitment to community service and advocacy for the indigent. Duration is 1–2 semesters. Unpaid. Open to college sophomores, college juniors, college seniors, recent college graduates, graduate students, law students. International applications accepted.
Benefits Formal training, job counseling, opportunity to attend seminars/workshops, possible full-time employment, willing to act as a professional reference, willing to complete paperwork for educational credit, willing to provide letters of recommendation.
Contact Write, call, fax, or e-mail Peter Lane, Intern Coordinator. Phone: 212-732-5000. Fax: 212-693-1149. E-mail: plane@legal-aid.org. In-person interview recommended (telephone interview accepted). Applicants must submit a formal organization application, resume, two personal references, two letters of recommendation. Application deadline: February 15 for spring, March 15 for summer, September 15 for fall. World Wide Web: http://www.legal-aid.org.

LEGAL AID SOCIETY, JUVENILE RIGHTS DIVISION
304 Park Avenue South, 6th Floor
New York, New York 10010

General Information Division representing children in neglect, abuse, and juvenile delinquency proceedings in city's five borough Family Courts. Established in 1962. Number of employees: 8. Division of Legal Aid Society, New York, New York.
Internships Available ▶ *Child advocacy interns:* responsibilities include assisting with monitoring compliance with court orders; gathering records from social workers, foster parents, schools, and health professionals; writing letters, drafting motions and orders; serving subpoenas. Duration is flexible. Unpaid. Open to high school seniors, college freshmen, college sophomores, college juniors, college seniors, recent college graduates. ▶ *Clerical interns:* responsibilities include clerical duties as needed. Duration is flexible. Unpaid. Open to high school students, college freshmen, college sophomores, college juniors, college seniors, recent college graduates. ▶ *Legal interns:* responsibilities include being paired with attorneys to help prepare cases for court, drafting motions and orders, conducting legal research and writing briefs, and assisting with client interviews. Duration is flexible. Unpaid. Open to law students. ▶ *Paralegal interns:* responsibilities include assisting with monitoring compliance with court orders, writing letters, drafting motions and orders, and serving subpoenas. Duration is flexible. Unpaid. Open to college freshmen, college sophomores, college juniors, college seniors, individuals in paralegal program at school. Candidates for all positions should have ability to work independently, ability to work with others, oral communication skills, organizational skills, written communication skills. International applications accepted.
Benefits Names of contacts, on-the-job training, opportunity to attend seminars/workshops, possible full-time employment, will-

ing to act as a professional reference, willing to complete paperwork for educational credit, willing to provide letters of recommendation.
Contact Fax, e-mail, or through World Wide Web site Veronique Questel, Intern Coordinator. Fax: 646-654-7080. E-mail: vvquestel@legal-aid.org. In-person interview recommended (telephone interview accepted). Applicants must submit a formal organization application, letter of interest, resume, confidentiality agreement. Applications are accepted continuously. World Wide Web: http://www.legal-aid.org.

LEGAL SERVICES FOR PRISONERS WITH CHILDREN
1540 Market Street, Suite 490
San Francisco, California 94102

General Information Organization that provides training, technical assistance, advocacy, and litigation support to legal service offices and to prisoners and their families, and advocates throughout California. Established in 1978. Number of employees: 9. Number of internship applications received each year: 75.
Internships Available ▶ *Interns:* responsibilities include handling client intake, responding to requests for assistance from prisoners and their families, conducting legal research, and writing. Candidates should have ability to work independently, ability to work with others, oral communication skills, personal interest in the field, research skills, written communication skills. Duration is flexible. Unpaid. Open to college juniors, college seniors, recent college graduates, graduate students, law students. International applications accepted.
Benefits Job counseling, names of contacts, travel reimbursement, willing to act as a professional reference, willing to complete paperwork for educational credit, willing to provide letters of recommendation.
Contact Write or e-mail Yvonne Cooks, Intern Coordinator. Fax: 415-552-3150. E-mail: info@prisonerswithchildren.org. No phone calls. Applicants must submit a letter of interest, resume, writing sample. Applications are accepted continuously. World Wide Web: http://www.prisonerswithchildren.org.

MIGRANT LEGAL ACTION PROGRAM
1001 Connecticut Avenue, NW, Suite 915
Washington, District of Columbia 20036

General Information National support and advocacy center providing legal representation to migrant and seasonal farm workers nationwide concerning employment conditions, health, housing, education, wages, public benefits, and general welfare. Established in 1970. Number of employees: 5. Number of internship applications received each year: 120.
Internships Available ▶ *2–4 law student interns:* responsibilities include legal research and writing under the supervision of a staff attorney. Duration is 1-2 semesters or 1 summer. Unpaid. Open to law students. ▶ *1 undergraduate intern:* responsibilities include assisting staff in a variety of research, writing, and some clerical duties. Duration is 1-2 semesters or 1 summer. Unpaid. Open to college sophomores, college juniors, college seniors, recent college graduates. Candidates for all positions should have ability to work independently, ability to work with others, oral communication skills, research skills, self-motivation, written communication skills.
Benefits Names of contacts, opportunity to attend seminars/workshops, willing to complete paperwork for educational credit, willing to provide letters of recommendation.
Contact Write or call Mr. Roger C. Rosenthal, Executive Director. Phone: 202-775-7780. In-person interview recommended (telephone interview accepted). Applicants must submit a letter of interest, resume, writing sample, two personal references. Application deadline: March 1 for summer, August 15 for fall, November 15 for spring. World Wide Web: http://www.mlap.org.

NATIVE AMERICAN RIGHTS FUND
1506 Broadway
Boulder, Colorado 80302

General Information Nonprofit law firm that represents tribes and individuals on tribal issues including land, water, and recognition. Established in 1970. Number of employees: 40. Number of internship applications received each year: 30.
Internships Available ▶ *5 summer law clerks:* responsibilities include conducting legal research and writing projects on issues of Indian law, procedure, and policy (work setting is either Boulder, CO; Anchorage, AK; or Washington, DC). Candidates should have ability to work with others, college courses in field, plan to pursue career in field, research skills, written communication skills, background in Native American issues (preferred). Duration is 10–12 weeks. $15 per hour. Open to second-year law students. International applications accepted.
Benefits Formal training, names of contacts, on-the-job training, travel reimbursement, willing to act as a professional reference, willing to complete paperwork for educational credit, willing to provide letters of recommendation.
Contact Write, call, fax, or e-mail Ms. Lorna Babby, Staff Attorney, 1506 Broadway, Boulder, Colorado 80301. Phone: 303-447-8760. Fax: 303-443-7776. E-mail: babby@narf.org. Applicants must submit a letter of interest, resume, academic transcripts, writing sample, three letters of recommendation. Application deadline: October 15. World Wide Web: http://www.narf.org.

NEW YORK STATE BAR ASSOCIATION
One Elk Street
Albany, New York 12207

General Information Official organization of lawyers in New York that strives to aid the administration of justice, promote legal reforms, and apply legal knowledge and experience for public benefit. Established in 1876. Number of employees: 115. Number of internship applications received each year: 20.
Internships Available ▶ *1 public relations intern:* responsibilities include writing news releases, preparing backgrounders, scripting broadcast public service announcements, assisting with special events, learning how to conduct research through databases, handling requests for materials produced by the department and available to the public, writing news and feature stories for the monthly newspaper and the staff publication, and assisting with photography. Candidates should have ability to work independently, computer skills, knowledge of field, office skills, personal interest in the field, research skills, writing skills, major in journalism or public relations. Duration is 10 weeks. $8 per hour for summer interns. Open to college juniors and seniors who are residents of the northeastern United States.
Benefits Formal training, job counseling, opportunity to attend seminars/workshops, travel reimbursement, willing to complete paperwork for educational credit, willing to provide letters of recommendation.
Contact Write or e-mail Mr. Brad Carr, Director of Media Services and Public Affairs. Fax: 518-463-4276. E-mail: bcarr@nysba.org. No phone calls. In-person interview required. Applicants must submit a letter of interest, resume, three writing samples. Application deadline: April 1. World Wide Web: http://www.nysba.org.

NOW LEGAL DEFENSE AND EDUCATION FUND
395 Hudson Street, 5th Floor
New York, New York 10014

General Information Public interest law and policy office working to expand women's rights. Established in 1970. Number of employees: 50. Number of internship applications received each year: 400.
Internships Available ▶ *5–10 fall and spring legal interns:* responsibilities include performing legal research and writing and assisting with litigation and legislative projects. Candidates should have ability to work independently, ability to work with others, computer skills, research skills, self-motivation, writing skills. Duration is 1 semester. $12 per hour. Open to law students. ▶ *6–8 legal interns (New York City):* responsibilities include performing legal research and writing and assisting with litigation and legislative projects.

Candidates should have editing skills, oral communication skills, research skills, self-motivation, writing skills. Duration is 10 weeks in summer. $420 per week. Open to law students. ▶ *1–2 legal interns (Washington, D.C.):* responsibilities include performing legal research and writing and assisting with legislative and policy analysis. Duration is June to August. $350 per week. Open to law students. ▶ *2–5 undergraduate summer and semester interns:* responsibilities include working in the areas of fund-raising/development/media/communications/World Wide Web, intake, and judicial education at both the New York and D.C. offices. Candidates should have computer skills, editing skills, oral communication skills, research skills, writing skills. Duration is dependent on internship. Position available as unpaid or at $230 per week during summer. Open to college freshmen, college sophomores, college juniors, college seniors. International applications accepted.
Benefits Names of contacts, on-the-job training, opportunity to attend seminars/workshops, possible full-time employment, willing to act as a professional reference, willing to complete paperwork for educational credit, willing to provide letters of recommendation.
Contact Write, fax, e-mail, or through World Wide Web site Lauryn Fraas, Program Assistant. Fax: 212-226-1066. E-mail: njep@nowldef.org. No phone calls. In-person interview recommended (telephone interview accepted). Applicants must submit a letter of interest, resume, writing sample, three personal references. Application deadline: February 1 for summer (undergraduates and first-year law students); January 2 (summer second- and third-year law students); continuous for all other positions. World Wide Web: http://www.nowldef.org.

OFFICE OF GENERAL COUNSEL
1600 Defense, Pentagon
Washington, District of Columbia 20301-1600

General Information Office that advises high-level policymakers in the Office of the Secretary of Defense and works closely with the military, the Departments of Justice, State, Treasury, and other government agencies. Number of employees: 80. Unit of Office of the Secretary of Defense, Washington, District of Columbia. Number of internship applications received each year: 200.
Internships Available ▶ *10–13 honors legal interns:* responsibilities include assisting with drafting and commenting on legislation, regulations, congressional testimony, litigation materials, and legal opinions, and assisting with the formulation of Department of Defense legal policy on topics of current interest. Candidates should have ability to work independently, ability to work with others, oral communication skills, plan to pursue career in field, research skills, written communication skills. Duration is 10–13 weeks in summer. $470–$575 per week. Open to first and second-year law students.
Benefits Job counseling, names of contacts, willing to complete paperwork for educational credit, willing to provide letters of recommendation.
Contact Write, call, or e-mail Kimberly M. Lenzer, Internship Coordinator. Phone: 703-614-6852. E-mail: grants@dodge.osd.mil. Applicants must submit a letter of interest, resume, writing sample, form (OF)6-12, statement of class rank and law school transcripts for 2nd-year law students, undergraduate transcripts for both 1st and 2nd-year law students. Application deadline: January 7 for first-year law students, November 20 for second-year law students.

PUBLIC DEFENDER SERVICE FOR THE DISTRICT OF COLUMBIA
633 Indiana Avenue, NW
Washington, District of Columbia 20004

General Information Independent government agency that provides criminal defense for indigent clients of the District of Columbia. Established in 1970. Number of employees: 200. Number of internship applications received each year: 600.
Internships Available ▶ *25–30 case assistants:* responsibilities include working with a staff trial attorney, interviewing witnesses, taking statements, photographing crime scenes, and assisting

attorney with trial preparations. Candidates should have ability to work independently, analytical skills, oral communication skills, organizational skills, personal interest in the field, self-motivation, strong interpersonal skills, written communication skills. Duration is 12 weeks. Unpaid. Open to college freshmen, college sophomores, college juniors, college seniors, recent college graduates, graduate students, law students, career changers, individuals reentering the workforce. ▶ *5 fellowship investigators:* responsibilities include working with a staff trial attorney, interviewing witnesses, taking statements, photographing crime scenes, and assisting attorney with trial preparations. Candidates should have ability to work independently, experience in the field, oral communication skills, self-motivation, strong interpersonal skills, written communication skills, Spanish speaking ability and writing fluency. Duration is 16 weeks. $1000–$2500 per duration of internship. Open to college sophomores, college juniors, college seniors, recent college graduates, graduate students, law students, career changers, individuals reentering the workforce. ▶ *40 investigators:* responsibilities include working with a staff trial attorney, interviewing witnesses, taking statements, and assisting the attorney with trial preparations. Candidates should have ability to work independently, analytical skills, oral communication skills, organizational skills, personal interest in the field, self-motivation, strong interpersonal skills, written communication skills. Duration is 12 weeks. Unpaid. Open to college freshmen, college sophomores, college juniors, college seniors, recent college graduates, graduate students, law students, career changers, individuals reentering the workforce. International applications accepted.

Benefits Formal training, job counseling, names of contacts, on-the-job training, opportunity to attend seminars/workshops, possible full-time employment, travel reimbursement, willing to act as a professional reference, willing to complete paperwork for educational credit, willing to provide letters of recommendation.

Contact Write, call, fax, e-mail, or through World Wide Web site Christian Pipe, Internship Coordinator. Phone: 800-341-2582. Fax: 202-626-8437. E-mail: internship@pdsdc.org. In-person interview recommended (telephone interview accepted). Applicants must submit a formal organization application, letter of interest, resume, essay, 2 personal references or 2 letters of recommendation. Application deadline: February 1 for spring quarter (priority), April 1 for summer (priority), July 1 for fall (priority), December 1 for spring semester(priority). World Wide Web: http://pdsdc.org.

PUBLIC DEFENDER SERVICE FOR THE DISTRICT OF COLUMBIA, MENTAL HEALTH DIVISION
St. Elizabeths Hospital, Cottage 2
Washington, District of Columbia 20032

General Information Independent government public interest law office that specializes in representing indigent clients facing civil and criminal commitment to D.C. area mental institutions. Established in 1970. Number of employees: 12. Division of Public Defender Service for the District of Columbia, Washington, District of Columbia. Number of internship applications received each year: 100.

Internships Available ▶ *14 investigators:* responsibilities include interviewing clients and witnesses; helping attorneys prepare cases for court; documenting all investigations; gathering and organizing medical and legal records; executing subpoenas; testifying in court. Candidates should have ability to work independently, analytical skills, oral communication skills, organizational skills, personal interest in the field, self-motivation, strong interpersonal skills, writing skills. Duration is 10-12 weeks minimum (at least 2 days per week during academic year; at least 3 days per week in summer). Unpaid. ▶ *2 social work interns:* responsibilities include assisting social worker in securing necessary social services for clients; meeting with clients; contacting providers; assisting clients with appointments; various other duties. Candidates should have ability to work independently, oral communication skills, organizational skills, personal interest in the field, self-motivation, strong interpersonal skills, writing skills. Duration is 10-12 weeks minimum (2 days per week to full-time). Unpaid. Open to col-

lege freshmen, college sophomores, college juniors, college seniors, recent college graduates, graduate students, law students, career changers. International applications accepted.

Benefits Formal training, on-the-job training, opportunity to attend seminars/workshops, willing to act as a professional reference, willing to complete paperwork for educational credit, willing to provide letters of recommendation, reimbursement of work-related travel expenses.

Contact Write, call, fax, or e-mail Carolyn Slenska, Chief Investigator. Phone: 202-645-4999. Fax: 202-645-7761. E-mail: cslenska@pdsdc.org. In-person interview recommended (telephone interview accepted). Applicants must submit a letter of interest, resume, two letters of recommendation, one 3-4 page writing sample. Application deadline: March 30 for summer; continuous for all other positions.

PUBLIC INTEREST CLEARINGHOUSE
47 Kearny Street, Suite 705
San Francisco, California 94108

General Information Support organization for legal services throughout California and Nevada. Established in 1979. Number of employees: 8.

Internships Available ▶ *1–2 interns:* responsibilities include working with attorneys and staff to provide general support for the organization. Candidates should have ability to work independently, computer skills, office skills, organizational skills, self-motivation. Duration is one semester or summer. Unpaid. Open to college sophomores, college juniors, college seniors, recent college graduates. ▶ *1–2 legal interns:* responsibilities include working with attorneys on the Coordination Project, the Public Interest Law Program, and the Technology Project; interns will research and write on issues with state wide implications for legal service programs and provide general support to their supervising attorney; responsibilities will vary depending on project. Candidates should have ability to work independently, oral communication skills, personal interest in the field, strong interpersonal skills, written communication skills. Duration is one semester (varies according to school schedule). Unpaid. Open to law students. International applications accepted.

Benefits Job counseling, on-the-job training, opportunity to attend seminars/workshops, willing to act as a professional reference, willing to complete paperwork for educational credit, willing to provide letters of recommendation, possibility of work-study funding.

Contact Write, fax, or e-mail Amy Hamill, Public Interest Law Program Director. Fax: 415-834-0202. E-mail: ahamill@pic.org. No phone calls. In-person interview required. Applicants must submit a letter of interest, resume, three personal references. Applications are accepted continuously. World Wide Web: http://www.pic.org.

RICHARD P. DIEGUEZ, ATTORNEY AND COUNSELLOR AT LAW
192 Garden Street, Suite 2
Roslyn Heights, New York 11577-1012

General Information Entertainment law practice and entertainment industry educational organization. Established in 1987. Number of employees: 3. Number of internship applications received each year: 100.

Internships Available ▶ *1 law clerk:* responsibilities include assisting with client intake, file maintenance, legal research, investigation, negotiation, and contract review. Candidates should have analytical skills, office skills, oral communication skills, organizational skills, research skills, writing skills. Duration is flexible. Unpaid. Open to college juniors, college seniors, recent college graduates, graduate students, law students, career changers. ▶ *2–4 management assistants:* responsibilities include developing and implementing marketing and promotional campaigns for entertainment industry educational organizations; industry research; phone contact with producers, publishers, recording artists, managers, agents, and media. Candidates should have ability to work independently, oral communication skills, organizational skills, self-motivation, strong interpersonal skills, strong leadership ability.

Richard P. Dieguez, Attorney and Counsellor at Law (continued)

Duration is flexible. Unpaid. Open to high school students, recent high school graduates, college freshmen, college sophomores, college juniors, college seniors, recent college graduates, graduate students, career changers, individuals reentering the workforce. International applications accepted.

Benefits Job counseling, names of contacts, on-the-job training, opportunity to attend seminars/workshops, willing to act as a professional reference, willing to complete paperwork for educational credit, willing to provide letters of recommendation, hands-on experience.

Contact Richard P. Dieguez, Esq., 192 Garden Street, Suite 2, Roslyn Heights, New York 11877-1012. Phone: 516-621-6424. E-mail: rpdieguez@rpdieguez.com. In-person interview recommended (telephone interview accepted). Applicants must submit a letter of interest, resume, academic transcripts, writing sample, three personal references, additional requirements found on Web site at http://www.rpdieguez.com/rpd_internships.html. Application deadline: early August for fall, early January for spring, April for summer. World Wide Web: http://www.rpdieguez.com.

SONOMA COUNTY LEGAL SERVICES FOUNDATION
1212 4th Street, Suite I
Santa Rosa, California 95404

General Information Foundation that provides legal education, referrals, and services to youth and families, especially on the lower end of the economic scale. Established in 1973. Number of employees: 2. Number of internship applications received each year: 4.

Internships Available ► *1–3 legal education assistants:* responsibilities include contacting schools and community groups to arrange speakers on legal topics, contacting attorneys to schedule their participation, providing appropriate resource materials, and follow-up. Duration is flexible (minimum of 3 months desirable). Unpaid. ► *1–3 legal program assistants:* responsibilities include working with clients who have legal issues to help them resolve these with local resources, on their own, or by referral to attorneys; contacting attorneys regarding these cases, recruiting attorneys, and following-up with clients. Duration is flexible (minimum of 3 months desirable). Unpaid. Candidates for all positions should have ability to work independently, ability to work with others, office skills, oral communication skills, personal interest in the field, self-motivation. Open to high school students, recent high school graduates, college freshmen, college sophomores, college juniors, college seniors, recent college graduates, graduate students, law students, career changers, individuals reentering the workforce, seniors. International applications accepted.

Benefits Names of contacts, on-the-job training, opportunity to attend seminars/workshops, travel reimbursement, willing to act as a professional reference, willing to complete paperwork for educational credit, willing to provide letters of recommendation.

Contact Write, call, fax, or e-mail Toni Novak, Executive Director. Phone: 707-546-2924. Fax: 707-546-0263. E-mail: sclsf@sonic.net. In-person interview recommended (telephone interview accepted). Applicants must submit a letter of interest, resume. Applications are accepted continuously.

SOUTHERN CENTER FOR HUMAN RIGHTS
83 Poplar Street, NW
Atlanta, Georgia 30303

General Information Nonprofit law office. Established in 1979. Number of employees: 23. Number of internship applications received each year: 100.

Internships Available ► *5–10 human rights interns:* responsibilities include legal research and writing for death penalty and prisoner's rights cases; case investigation. Candidates should have personal interest in the field, research skills, self-motivation, strong interpersonal skills, writing skills. Duration is 2–6 months. Unpaid. Open to college seniors, recent college graduates, law students. International applications accepted.

Benefits Job counseling, on-the-job training, opportunity to attend seminars/workshops, travel reimbursement, willing to act as a

professional reference, willing to complete paperwork for educational credit, willing to provide letters of recommendation.

Contact Write, e-mail, or through World Wide Web site Ty Alper, Staff Attorney. Phone: 404-688-1202. Fax: 404-688-9440. E-mail: rights@schr.org. Telephone interview required. Applicants must submit a letter of interest, resume, writing sample, three personal references. Applications are accepted continuously. World Wide Web: http://www.schr.org.

STUDENT PRESS LAW CENTER
1815 North Fort Myer Drive, Suite 900
Arlington, Virginia 22209

General Information Nonprofit corporation that provides free legal assistance to student journalists and advisers and publishes materials explaining students' First Amendment rights. Established in 1974. Number of employees: 5. Number of internship applications received each year: 200.

Internships Available ► *2–3 legal newswriting interns:* responsibilities include writing, editing, and laying out magazine. Candidates should have ability to work with others, editing skills, organizational skills, personal interest in the field, writing skills, student media experience (preferred). Duration is 1 semester or summer. $2500 stipend for full-semester interns; $1800 stipend for summer interns plus possible $600 scholarship. Open to college sophomores, college juniors, college seniors, recent college graduates, graduate students. ► *1–2 media law interns:* responsibilities include researching and writing opinions and articles and making client contact. Candidates should have ability to work independently, analytical skills, personal interest in the field, research skills, strong interpersonal skills, written communication skills. Duration is 1 semester or summer. $500 per week for full-time interns; $10 per hour for part-time interns. Open to law students. International applications accepted.

Benefits Job counseling, opportunity to attend seminars/workshops, willing to act as a professional reference, willing to complete paperwork for educational credit, willing to provide letters of recommendation.

Contact Write, e-mail, or through World Wide Web site Mr. Mark Goodman, Executive Director. E-mail: splc@splc.org. Applicants must submit a letter of interest, resume, two personal references, newswriting clips (for journalism applicants); legal writing sample (law applicants). Application deadline: February 1 for summer (suggested date), June 1 for fall (suggested date), November 1 for spring (suggested date). World Wide Web: http://www.splc.org.

VICTIM-WITNESS ASSISTANCE PROGRAM–OFFICE OF THE DISTRICT ATTORNEY, COUNTY OF LOS ANGELES
Volunteer Services, 3204 Rosemead Boulevard, Suite 200
El Monte, California 91731

General Information Office that provides a broad range of services to victims and witnesses of crime. Established in 1977. Number of employees: 94. Number of internship applications received each year: 125.

Internships Available ► *30–40 student interns/volunteers:* responsibilities include contacting victims; providing resource referrals; explaining court procedures; providing court escort; providing case status and disposition; notifying families; assisting victims with information about obtaining crime reports, witness fees, property return; arranging for restitution or translation; assisting children, elderly, and handicapped. Candidates should have analytical skills, oral communication skills, personal interest in the field, self-motivation, strong interpersonal skills, written communication skills. Duration is 1 summer, 6 months, or 1 year. Unpaid. Open to college freshmen, college sophomores, college juniors, college seniors, recent college graduates, graduate students, law students, career changers, individuals over 18 years of age. International applications accepted.

Benefits Formal training, job counseling, names of contacts, opportunity to attend seminars/workshops, possible full-time

employment, willing to complete paperwork for educational credit, willing to provide letters of recommendation.
Contact Write, call, fax, or e-mail Victoria Carter, Volunteer Coordinator. Phone: 626-927-2500. Fax: 626-569-9541. E-mail: vcarter@da.co.la.ca.us. In-person interview required. Applicants must submit a formal organization application, two personal references. Applications are accepted continuously.

VOLUNTEER LEGAL SERVICES PROGRAM
465 California Street, Suite 1100
San Francisco, California 94104

General Information Legal services program. Established in 1977. Number of employees: 25. Affiliate of Bar Association of San Francisco, San Francisco, California. Number of internship applications received each year: 20.
Internships Available ▶ *1–2 legal interns:* responsibilities include conducting project evaluations, staffing the Homeless Advocacy Project, updating training manuals, and researching legal issues. Candidates should have ability to work independently, computer skills, oral communication skills, personal interest in the field, written communication skills. Duration is flexible. Unpaid. Open to recent college graduates, law students, career changers. ▶ *1–2 media interns:* responsibilities include identifying and developing news stories; interviewing clients, staff, and volunteers; writing and distributing press releases; organizing and maintaining media archive; writing and editing articles for various internal publications. Candidates should have ability to work independently, oral communication skills, personal interest in the field, self-motivation, writing skills. Duration is flexible. Unpaid. Open to college seniors, recent college graduates, graduate students, law students, career changers. International applications accepted.
Benefits Opportunity to attend seminars/workshops, willing to act as a professional reference, willing to complete paperwork for educational credit, willing to provide letters of recommendation.
Contact Fax or e-mail Amanda Chavez, Director of Volunteer and Holistic Services. Fax: 415-477-2390. E-mail: achavez@sfbar.org. No phone calls. In-person interview required. Applicants must submit a letter of interest, resume, writing sample. Applications are accepted continuously. World Wide Web: http://www.sfbar.org/vlsp.

WASHINGTON AREA LAWYERS FOR THE ARTS
1120 Connecticut Avenue, NW, #260
Washington, District of Columbia 20036

General Information Organization that provides legal assistance to artists and training to attorneys and artists. Established in 1983. Number of employees: 4. Number of internship applications received each year: 100.
Internships Available ▶ *2–3 art law interns:* responsibilities include counseling artists/clients by telephone and helping them discern their legal needs; preparing summaries of facts, issues, and applicable laws for the director of legal services; possibly sitting in on client consultations; organizing workshops and symposia on legal issues and the arts. Candidates should have ability to work independently, college courses in field, computer skills, knowledge of field, oral communication skills, research skills, copyright background (helpful). Duration is 1–4 months. Unpaid. Open to law students. ▶ *1–2 marketing interns.* Candidates should have interest in media relations and arts management, event production skills. Duration is flexible. Unpaid. Open to college freshmen, college sophomores, college juniors, college seniors.
Benefits Formal training, job counseling, on-the-job training, opportunity to attend seminars/workshops, willing to act as a professional reference, willing to complete paperwork for educational credit, willing to provide letters of recommendation.
Contact Write, call, fax, or e-mail John D. Malloy, Director of Legal Services. Phone: 202-429-0960. Fax: 202-429-0965. E-mail: legalservices@thewala.org. In-person interview required. Applicants must submit a letter of interest, resume, academic transcripts, one 1- to 5- page writing sample. Application deadline: January 8 for spring, March 1 for summer, September 1 for fall. World Wide Web: http://www.thewala.org.

WASHINGTON LEGAL FOUNDATION
2009 Massachusetts Avenue, NW
Washington, District of Columbia 20036

General Information Public interest law firm advocating free enterprise and working to restore balance to the judiciary through original litigation and distribution of multiple publications. Established in 1977. Number of employees: 20. Number of internship applications received each year: 100.
Internships Available ▶ *1–3 law clerks:* responsibilities include legal research, assisting in preparation of briefs, and writing comments and petitions to regulatory agencies. Candidates should have ability to work independently, editing skills, plan to pursue career in field, written communication skills, excellent legal research and analytical skills a must. Duration is full-time in summer; 15 hours per week during school semesters. Paid at hourly rate depending on experience. Open to second- and third-year law students only. ▶ *1–3 legal policy interns:* responsibilities include production of nationally distributed legal policy publications; monitoring and analysis of developments in federal and state courts, legislatures, and regulatory agencies; assisting in setting up and promoting bi-weekly press briefing events; assisting with outreach to and expansion of Foundation's national pro bono network. Candidates should have editing skills, oral communication skills, research skills, written communication skills, interest in intersection between law and public policy. Duration is flexible (minimum 15 hours per week during spring and fall semesters); full-time in summer. Position available as unpaid or at competitive salary. Open to recent college graduates, graduate students, law students. ▶ *1–5 public affairs interns:* responsibilities include researching, marketing, database maintenance, filing, and donor correspondence. Candidates should have ability to work with others, computer skills, organizational skills, self-motivation, written communication skills. Duration is flexible (3 months minimum preferred). Position available as unpaid or at hourly rate depending on experience. Open to college juniors, college seniors, graduate students. International applications accepted.
Benefits Names of contacts, possible full-time employment, willing to act as a professional reference, willing to complete paperwork for educational credit, willing to provide letters of recommendation.
Contact Write, e-mail, or through World Wide Web site Ms. Constance Claffey Larcher, President. Fax: 202-588-0371. E-mail: administration@wlf.org. No phone calls. In-person interview required. Applicants must submit a letter of interest, resume, writing sample (legal policy position). Applications are accepted continuously. World Wide Web: http://www.wlf.org.

WOMEN'S LAW PROJECT
125 South 9th Street, Suite 300
Philadelphia, Pennsylvania 19107

General Information Nonprofit feminist public interest law firm. Established in 1974. Number of employees: 9. Number of internship applications received each year: 40.
Internships Available ▶ *10–15 telephone counselors:* responsibilities include performing telephone counseling including interviewing callers to identify legal problems; counseling callers on strategies for solving legal problems; providing information; recording information in database. Candidates should have ability to work with others, analytical skills, computer skills, oral communication skills, self-motivation. Duration is minimum of one semester (fall, spring, summer). Unpaid. Open to recent high school graduates, college freshmen, college sophomores, college juniors, college seniors, recent college graduates, graduate students, career changers, individuals reentering the workforce. International applications accepted.
Benefits On-the-job training, willing to act as a professional reference, willing to complete paperwork for educational credit, willing to provide letters of recommendation.
Contact E-mail Kathy Kaib, Program Associate. Fax: 215-928-9848. E-mail: kkaib@womenslawproject.org. No phone calls. In-person interview recommended (telephone interview accepted). Applicants must submit a formal organization application, letter of interest, resume. Applications are accepted continuously.

SCIENTIFIC RESEARCH AND DEVELOPMENT SERVICES

AMERICAN ASSOCIATION FOR THE ADVANCEMENT OF SCIENCE
1200 New York Avenue, NW, Suite 100
Washington, District of Columbia 20005

General Information Nonprofit scientific association, publisher of SCIENCE Magazine. Established in 1848. Number of employees: 400. Number of internship applications received each year: 200.
Internships Available ▶ *Interns:* responsibilities include various positions depending on specific needs of the department. Candidates should have computer skills, knowledge of field, oral communication skills, personal interest in the field, strong interpersonal skills, written communication skills. Duration is 3–5 months. Position available as unpaid or paid. Open to college seniors, recent college graduates, graduate students, individuals reentering the workforce.
Benefits Opportunity to attend seminars/workshops, possible full-time employment, willing to act as a professional reference, willing to complete paperwork for educational credit, willing to provide letters of recommendation, paid holidays when they fall on regularly scheduled work day.
Contact Write, e-mail, or through World Wide Web site Yvette Robinson, Personnel Assistant, 1200 New York Avenue, NW, #102, Washington, District of Columbia 20005. Fax: 202-682-1630. E-mail: hrtemp@aaas.org. No phone calls. In-person interview required. Applicants must submit a letter of interest, resume, 2-3 writing samples, 2-3 letters of recommendation. Application deadline: April 1 for summer, November 1 for fall. World Wide Web: http://www.aaas.org.

AMERICAN GEOGRAPHICAL SOCIETY
120 Wall Street, Suite 100
New York, New York 10005

General Information Organization that encourages geographical research and field work and makes it available to policy makers, the media, and the public to reduce geographical illiteracy in the United States; publishes a scholarly journal, a magazine, and a newsletter; maintains programs of educational travel, volunteer teaching, economic geography, and geographic information service and speakers. Established in 1851. Number of employees: 4. Number of internship applications received each year: 35.
Internships Available ▶ *3–6 editorial, research, and/or administrative interns.* Candidates should have ability to work independently, computer skills, oral communication skills, self-motivation, strong interpersonal skills, writing skills. Duration is 10 weeks minimum. Unpaid. Open to college freshmen, college sophomores, college juniors, college seniors, recent college graduates, graduate students, exceptional high school seniors. International applications accepted.
Benefits Formal training, job counseling, names of contacts, on-the-job training, opportunity to attend seminars/workshops, willing to act as a professional reference, willing to complete paperwork for educational credit, willing to provide letters of recommendation.
Contact Write, call, fax, e-mail, or through World Wide Web site Ms. Mary Lynne Bird, Executive Director. Phone: 212-422-5456. Fax: 212-422-5480. E-mail: mlbird@amergeog.org. In-person interview recommended (telephone interview accepted). Applicants must submit a letter of interest, resume, writing sample, two letters of recommendation. Applications are accepted continuously. World Wide Web: http://amergeog.org.

ARGONNE NATIONAL LABORATORY, DIVISION OF EDUCATIONAL PROGRAMS
9700 South Cass Avenue
Argonne, Illinois 60439

General Information Laboratory conducting research in a wide variety of disciplines including biological, environmental, medical, and materials sciences and ceramics, chemistry, physics, engineering, computer science, mathematics, and reactor and energy technologies. Number of employees: 3,500. Number of internship applications received each year: 600.
Internships Available ▶ *20–250 interns:* responsibilities include working on a research project with a staff scientist. Candidates should have oral communication skills, research skills, self-motivation, strong interpersonal skills, written communication skills. Duration is one semester (can be extended). $400 per week. Open to college sophomores, college juniors, college seniors, recent college graduates.
Benefits Free housing, opportunity to attend seminars/workshops, possible full-time employment, travel reimbursement, willing to complete paperwork for educational credit, willing to provide letters of recommendation.
Contact Write, fax, e-mail, or through World Wide Web site Ms. Lisa Reed, Program Coordinator. Fax: 630-252-3193. E-mail: lreed@dep.anl.gov. No phone calls. Applicants must submit a formal organization application, academic transcripts, three letters of recommendation. Application deadline: February 1 for summer, March 15 for fall, October 15 for spring. World Wide Web: http://www.dep.anl.gov.

ASPRS: THE IMAGING AND GEOSPATIAL INFORMATION SOCIETY
5410 Grosvenor Lane, Suite 210
Bethesda, Maryland 20814-2160

General Information Scientific association serving over 7,000 professional members around the world, with a mission to advance knowledge and improve understanding of mapping sciences and to promote responsible applications of photogrammetry, remote sensing, GIS, and supporting technologies. Established in 1934.
Internships Available ▶ *Leica geosystems interns:* responsibilities include carrying out a small research project of intern's choice or working on existing LH systems project as a team member; submission of final report upon completion of internship. Candidates should have ability to work with others, research skills, self-motivation, enrollment in an accredited college or university and membership of ASPRS. Duration is 3 months. $2500 stipend. Open to graduate students of photogrammetry and remote sensing.
Benefits Allowance for travel and living expenses for the period of the internship.
International Internships Available in Heerbrugg, Switzerland.
Contact Write, e-mail, or through World Wide Web site ASPRS Scholarship Administrator. Phone: 301-493-0290. Fax: 301-493-0208. E-mail: scholarships@asprs.org. Applicants must submit a formal organization application, academic transcripts, a research proposal (maximum 1000 words) stating significance of the research, proposed methodology, expected results and schedule. Application deadline: first Monday in December. World Wide Web: http://www.asprs.org.

BERMUDA BIOLOGICAL STATION FOR RESEARCH, INC.
17 Biological Lane
Ferry Reach, St. George's Bermuda

General Information Research and education center for oceanography, marine biology, and global climate change. Established in 1903. Number of employees: 100. Number of internship applications received each year: 150.
Internships Available ▶ *10 graduate interns:* responsibilities include conducting research with technical staff or independently. Candidates should have acceptance into graduate program by recognized university, thesis proposal must have been approved by advisor at

that university, must have faculty supervisor at BBSR and approved funding. Duration is 3 months to 3 years. Unpaid. Open to graduate students. ▶ *8 undergraduate research interns:* responsibilities include conducting independent research project. Candidates should have ability to work independently, college courses in field, knowledge of field, research skills, strong interpersonal skills. Duration is August to November only. Room and board is deducted from salary of approximately $265 per week. Open to college juniors, college seniors. ▶ *3–6 volunteer interns:* responsibilities include working 40 hours per week in lab of scientist who pays intern's room and board. Candidates should have computer skills, knowledge of field, organizational skills, personal interest in the field, self-motivation, strong interpersonal skills. Duration is 3–4 months. Unpaid. Open to college juniors, college seniors, recent college graduates, graduate students. International applications accepted.

Benefits Opportunity to attend seminars/workshops, possible full-time employment, willing to act as a professional reference, willing to complete paperwork for educational credit, willing to provide letters of recommendation, free room and board for volunteer interns.

International Internships Available.

Contact E-mail or through World Wide Web site Helle Patterson, Education Officer, 17 Biological Lane, Ferry Reach, St. George's GEO1 Bermuda. E-mail: hpatt@bbsr.edu. No phone calls. Applicants must submit a formal organization application, letter of interest, resume, academic transcripts, letter of recommendation. Application deadline: March 15 for research experience (undergraduate); no application deadline for graduate or volunteer interns. World Wide Web: http://www.bbsr.edu/.

CARNEGIE INSTITUTION OF WASHINGTON
5251 Broad Branch Road, NW
Washington, District of Columbia 20015

General Information Science research organization. Established in 1902. Number of employees: 100. Number of internship applications received each year: 80.

Internships Available ▶ *10–15 interns in geoscience:* responsibilities include research. Candidates should have ability to work independently, analytical skills, college courses in field, oral communication skills, research skills, self-motivation. Duration is June to August (10 weeks). $3500 per duration of internship. Open to college freshmen, college sophomores, college juniors.

Benefits Free housing, on-the-job training, opportunity to attend seminars/workshops, travel reimbursement, willing to act as a professional reference, willing to provide letters of recommendation.

Contact E-mail or through World Wide Web site Dr. Bill Minarik, Summer Education Coordinator. Fax: 202-478-8901. E-mail: summer-internships@gl.ciw.edu. No phone calls. Applicants must submit a formal organization application, resume, academic transcripts, three letters of recommendation. Application deadline: March 14. World Wide Web: http://www.gl.ciw.edu/interns.

CIIT CENTERS FOR HEALTH RESEARCH
6 Davis Drive, PO Box 12137
Research Triangle Park, North Carolina 27709-2137

General Information Not-for-profit scientific research institute dedicated to providing an improved scientific basis for understanding and assessing the potential adverse effects of chemicals, pharmaceuticals, and consumer products on human health. Established in 1976. Number of employees: 150. Number of internship applications received each year: 100.

Internships Available ▶ *5–10 summer interns:* responsibilities include working in research laboratories on projects under the direction of a CIIT scientist; conducting an independent research project and presenting findings in a seminar. Candidates should have ability to work independently, ability to work with others, college courses in field, oral communication skills, research skills, self-motivation. Duration is 12–15 weeks. $480 per week. Open to college sophomores, college juniors, college seniors. International applications accepted.

Benefits Formal training, on-the-job training, opportunity to attend seminars/workshops, travel reimbursement, willing to act

as a professional reference, willing to complete paperwork for educational credit, willing to provide letters of recommendation.

Contact Write, e-mail, or through World Wide Web site Rusty Bramlage, Director, Human Resources. Phone: 919-558-1331. Fax: 919-558-1430. E-mail: bramlage@ciit.org. Telephone interview required. Applicants must submit a formal organization application, two letters of recommendation. Application deadline: March 1. World Wide Web: http://www.ciit.org.

CROW CANYON ARCHAEOLOGICAL CENTER
23390 Road K
Cortez, Colorado 81321

General Information Archaeological center that initiates and conducts significant archaeological research in the Southwest and shares the results through innovative public and professional education, open communication with Native Americans, and partnerships with institutions having common interests. Established in 1983. Number of employees: 49. Number of internship applications received each year: 100.

Internships Available ▶ *3–6 education interns:* responsibilities include assisting in teaching lay participants ranging in age from 4th graders to senior citizens about anthropological/archaeological concepts and methods, serving as docent at excavation sites, assisting in planning and implementing field trips, and developing lesson plan or research project. Candidates should have knowledge of field, oral communication skills, plan to pursue career in field, research skills, self-motivation, strong interpersonal skills. Duration is 8–11 weeks. Stipend. ▶ *4–6 field interns:* responsibilities include excavating and recording architectural and non-architectural contexts, mapping with a total station, site photography, instructing and supervising lay participants in basic excavation techniques and archaeological concepts. Candidates should have ability to work independently, ability to work with others, experience in the field, oral communication skills, organizational skills, research skills. Duration is 8–11 weeks. Stipend. ▶ *4 lab interns:* responsibilities include processing, cataloging, and analyzing a variety of archaeological samples, artifacts, maps and other records; collections and database management; maintenance of a small research library; instructing and supervising lay participants ranging in age from 4th graders to senior citizens in laboratory research. Candidates should have analytical skills, computer skills, experience in the field, organizational skills, research skills, strong interpersonal skills. Duration is 8–11 weeks. Stipend. Open to college juniors, college seniors, recent college graduates, graduate students.

Benefits Free housing, free meals, names of contacts, on-the-job training, travel reimbursement, willing to act as a professional reference, willing to complete paperwork for educational credit, willing to provide letters of recommendation, modest weekly stipend, training in archaeological field and laboratory techniques, experiential teaching program.

Contact Write, fax, e-mail, or through World Wide Web site Human Resources. Fax: 970-565-4859. E-mail: interns@crowcanyon. org. No phone calls. Telephone interview required. Applicants must submit a formal organization application, three personal references, three letters of recommendation. Applications are accepted continuously. World Wide Web: http://www.crowcanyon. org.

HARVARD SCHOOL OF PUBLIC HEALTH, DIVISION OF BIOLOGICAL SCIENCES
665 Huntington Avenue, Building 1-1204-A
Boston, Massachusetts 02115-6021

General Information Molecular biology research training center. Established in 1923. Number of employees: 2. Division of Harvard University, Cambridge, Massachusetts. Number of internship applications received each year: 130.

Internships Available ▶ *10–16 summer interns:* responsibilities include laboratory-based molecular biology research. Candidates should have analytical skills, college courses in field, knowledge of field, plan to pursue career in field, self-motivation, strong interpersonal skills. Duration is June 9 to August 15. $3782 per

Harvard School of Public Health, Division of Biological Sciences (continued)
duration of internship. Open to minority students at college junior or senior level, must be U.S. citizen or permanent resident.
Benefits Free housing, travel reimbursement, graduate-level training for research careers.
Contact Write, call, fax, e-mail, or through World Wide Web site William Alley, Internship Coordinator, 665 Huntington Avenue, Building 1, Room 1312, Boston 02115-6018. Phone: 617-432-4822. Fax: 617-432-0433. E-mail: balley@hsph.harvard.edu. Applicants must submit a formal organization application, letter of interest, academic transcripts, two letters of recommendation. Application deadline: February 14. World Wide Web: http://www.hsph.harvard.edu/sip.

INSTITUTE OF ECOSYSTEM STUDIES (IES)
Box R
Millbrook, New York 12545-0178

General Information Ecological research and education institute. Established in 1983. Number of employees: 120. Number of internship applications received each year: 200.
Internships Available ▶ *8–10 research experiences for undergraduates interns:* responsibilities include working closely with a mentor scientist, developing and conducting an independent ecological research project and writing a paper for an Institute publication, and presenting results at a formal symposium. Duration is 12 weeks. $3600 per duration of internship. Open to college freshmen, college sophomores, college juniors, first semester seniors.
Benefits Free housing, names of contacts, opportunity to attend seminars/workshops, possible full-time employment, willing to complete paperwork for educational credit, willing to provide letters of recommendation.
Contact Write, call, fax, e-mail, or through World Wide Web site Heather Dahl, Undergraduate Research Program Coordinator. Phone: 845-677-7600 Ext. 326. Fax: 845-677-6455. E-mail: dahlh@ecostudies.org. Applicants must submit a formal organization application, resume, online application at www.ecostudies.org/education/reu/reu1.html. Application deadline: February 15 for summer. World Wide Web: http://www.ecostudies.org.

LAMONT-DOHERTY EARTH OBSERVATORY
Room 103A Oceanography
Palisades, New York 10964

General Information Organization involved in geological, oceanographic, environmental, and climatic research. Established in 1948. Number of employees: 550. Unit of Columbia University, New York, New York. Number of internship applications received each year: 170.
Internships Available ▶ *16–20 summer interns:* responsibilities include undertaking research projects in oceanography, marine geophysics, geochemistry, geology, and environmental science. Candidates should have analytical skills, computer skills, knowledge of field, personal interest in the field, written communication skills, 2 semesters of calculus. Duration is 10 weeks. $2530 per duration of internship. Open to college sophomores, college juniors.
Benefits Free housing, names of contacts, opportunity to attend seminars/workshops, willing to complete paperwork for educational credit, willing to provide letters of recommendation, travel reimbursement (for travel over 200 miles).
Contact Write or e-mail Dr. Dallas Abbott, Summer Internship Program Director. E-mail: dallas@ldeo.columbia.edu. No phone calls. Applicants must submit a formal organization application, letter of interest, academic transcripts, writing sample, three letters of recommendation. Application deadline: March 10 for summer. World Wide Web: http://www.ldeo.columbia.edu/~dallas/abbott_sum.html.

LAWRENCE LIVERMORE NATIONAL LABORATORY, UNDERGRADUATE SUMMER INSTITUTE
PO Box 808, L-231
Livermore, California 94551-0808

General Information Research facility providing scientific and technological expertise; dedicated to global security, the environment, and the future scientific needs of the nation. Established in 1985. Number of employees: 9,000. Number of internship applications received each year: 100.
Internships Available ▶ *25 interns:* responsibilities include attending lectures on fusion, lasers, computational modeling, physics, chemistry, engineering, and national security; working on research project in field. Candidates should have personal interest in the field, plan to pursue career in field, major in applied science field, experience in a lab science setting in previous summers (preferred). Duration is 10 weeks. $19–$21 per hour. Open to college sophomores, college juniors, college seniors, must be returning to college in the fall following the internship.
Benefits Health insurance, opportunity to attend seminars/workshops, possible full-time employment, travel reimbursement, willing to act as a professional reference, opportunity to work on research projects.
Contact Write, call, fax, e-mail, or through World Wide Web site Lynda Allen, Secretary. Phone: 925-422-1748. Fax: 925-422-3160. E-mail: allen48@llnl.gov. Applicants must submit a formal organization application, letter of interest, resume, academic transcripts, two personal references. Application deadline: January 1. World Wide Web: http://www.llnl.gov/usi/.

LINCOLN LABORATORY, MASSACHUSETTS INSTITUTE OF TECHNOLOGY
244 Wood Street
Lexington, Massachusetts 02420-9108

General Information Research and development center whose primary focus is in the field of advanced electronics; research includes space surveillance, tactical systems, satellite communications, and radar and air traffic control systems. Established in 1951. Number of employees: 2,300. Branch of Massachusetts Institute of Technology, Cambridge, Massachusetts.
Internships Available ▶ *35–45 summer research assistants:* responsibilities include designing hardware, conducting scientific programming, developing software, analyzing data, and offering technical support. Candidates should have analytical skills, computer skills, plan to pursue career in field, research skills, minimum 3.5 GPA, major in physics, mathematics, electrical engineering, or computer science. Duration is 10 weeks. Competitive salary. Open to college seniors, recent college graduates, graduate students, rising college seniors.
Benefits Formal training, housing at a cost, job counseling, on-the-job training, opportunity to attend seminars/workshops, possible full-time employment, travel reimbursement, willing to provide letters of recommendation.
Contact Write, fax, or through World Wide Web site Mr. Paul F. Hezel, Human Resources Representative. Fax: 781-981-7086. In-person interview recommended (telephone interview accepted). Applicants must submit a letter of interest, resume, academic transcripts, U.S. citizenship, 2 letters of recommendation (following interview). Application deadline: March 15 for summer. World Wide Web: http://www.ll.mit.edu.

LUNAR AND PLANETARY INSTITUTE
3600 Bay Area Boulevard
Houston, Texas 77058-1113

General Information Institute whose goal is to facilitate methods for the distribution of results of current planetary science research to the worldwide scientific community. Established in 1968. Number of employees: 60. Unit of Universities Space Research Association, Columbia, Maryland. Number of internship applications received each year: 166.
Internships Available ▶ *10–12 interns:* responsibilities include participating actively in lunar/planetary research with scientists at the Institute and the NASA Johnson Space Center in such areas as cosmic dust characterization, meteorite fall statistics, planetary rigolith studies, Mars soil analog chemistry, trace element partitioning studies, volcano morphology characterization, planetary volcanism and thermal histories, thermal and mechanical modeling of planetary interiors, database management systems, and search for micro-organisms in geologic samples, and astrobiology. Candidates should have ability to work independently, college

courses in field, computer skills, experience in the field, plan to pursue career in field, 50 semester hours of credit. Duration is 10 weeks. $500 per week. Open to college sophomores, college juniors, college seniors. International applications accepted.
Benefits Housing at a cost, opportunity to attend seminars/ workshops, up to $1000 travel allowance.
Contact Write, fax, or e-mail Ms. Jodi J. Jordan, Executive Administrator. Fax: 281-486-2173. E-mail: jordan@lpi.usra.edu. No phone calls. Applicants must submit a letter of interest, academic transcripts, three letters of recommendation, biographical sketch including goals, career plans, scientific interests, reason for application, major field of study; application available on line. Application deadline: February 3 for summer. World Wide Web: http://www.lpi.usra.edu/lpiintern.html.

MARIA MITCHELL OBSERVATORY
3 Vestal Street
Nantucket, Massachusetts 02554

General Information Observatory that runs an active, diverse program in astronomical research and an educational outreach program. Established in 1908. Number of employees: 7. Unit of Maria Mitchell Association, Nantucket, Massachusetts. Number of internship applications received each year: 100.
Internships Available ▶ *6 summer research assistants:* responsibilities include performing scientific research and participating in public and educational programs. Candidates should have ability to work independently, ability to work with others, computer skills, oral communication skills, personal interest in the field, plan to pursue career in field, research skills, self-motivation, written communication skills. Duration is 10–15 weeks. $1300 per month. Open to college freshmen, college sophomores, college juniors, college seniors, must be U.S. citizen or have permanent residency.
Benefits Free housing, job counseling, names of contacts, on-the-job training, opportunity to attend seminars/workshops, travel reimbursement, tuition assistance, willing to complete paperwork for educational credit, willing to provide letters of recommendation.
Contact Write, call, fax, or e-mail Dr. Vladimir Strelnitski, Director. Phone: 508-228-9273. Fax: 508-228-1031. E-mail: vladimir@mmo.org. Telephone interview required. Applicants must submit a formal organization application, letter of interest, resume, academic transcripts, three letters of recommendation. Application deadline: February 1 for summer. World Wide Web: http://www.mmo.org.

MARINE ENVIRONMENTAL RESEARCH INSTITUTE
PO Box 1652
Blue Hill, Maine 04614

General Information Non-profit marine science research facility. Established in 1991. Number of employees: 12. Number of internship applications received each year: 50.
Internships Available ▶ *3–4 education interns:* responsibilities include leading educational boat and field trips, conducting in-house programs, and writing educational materials. Candidates should have knowledge of field, oral communication skills, strong interpersonal skills, strong leadership ability, written communication skills. Duration is 10 weeks. $1200 per duration of internship. Open to college juniors, college seniors, recent college graduates, graduate students. ▶ *1–2 research interns:* responsibilities include assisting in field research (collection of samples); seal stranding response; lab research (seal necropsy, tissue banking); data management. Candidates should have ability to work with others, computer skills, knowledge of field, oral communication skills, research skills, written communication skills. Duration is 10–12 weeks. $1200 per duration of internship. Open to college seniors, recent college graduates, graduate students. International applications accepted.
Benefits Free housing, job counseling, willing to act as a professional reference, willing to provide letters of recommendation.
Contact Write, call, fax, or e-mail Internship Coordinator. Phone: 207-374-2135. Fax: 207-374-2931. E-mail: meriedu@downeast.net. Telephone interview required. Applicants must submit a letter of interest, resume, three personal references. Application deadline: March 1 for research interns, March 21 for education interns. World Wide Web: http://meriresearch.org.

METHODIST RESEARCH INSTITUTE AT CLARIAN HEALTH PARTNERS
PO Box 1367
Indianapolis, Indiana 46206

General Information Research program designed to pair students in the sciences with biomedical researchers.
Internships Available ▶ *Summer student research program interns:* responsibilities include designing and implementing a biomedical research study including analyzing data, preparing research report, and giving an oral presentation; learning to prepare a manuscript for submission to a peer reviewed journal. Candidates should have oral communication skills, research skills, written communication skills, minimum 3.0 GPA (or equivalent). Duration is 12 weeks (40 hours per week). $8.50 per hour. Open to college juniors, college seniors, graduate students in science, medical students.
Contact Call or e-mail Dr. Karen Spear, Program Coordinator. Phone: 317-962-8765. E-mail: kspear@clarian.org. Applicants must submit a formal organization application, interview, physical evaluation. Application deadline: February.

MOTE MARINE LABORATORY
1600 Ken Thompson Parkway
Sarasota, Florida 34236

General Information Independent nonprofit organization dedicated to research in marine and environmental sciences. Established in 1955. Number of employees: 200. Number of internship applications received each year: 300.
Internships Available ▶ *2–5 business interns:* responsibilities include business and financial duties, including bookkeeping, accounts payable, and accounts receivable. Candidates should have ability to work independently, ability to work with others, computer skills, office skills, organizational skills, plan to pursue career in field, self-motivation. Duration is 8–16 weeks. Unpaid. Open to college juniors, college seniors. ▶ *2–3 communications interns:* responsibilities include press release writing, preparation of articles for newsletters and magazines, and office assistance. Candidates should have ability to work with others, college courses in field, computer skills, editing skills, written communication skills. Duration is 8–16 weeks. Unpaid. Open to college sophomores, college juniors, college seniors, recent college graduates. ▶ *2–5 development office interns:* responsibilities include administrative duties in marketing/ development office. Candidates should have ability to work independently, college courses in field, computer skills, office skills, oral communication skills, plan to pursue career in field, self-motivation, strong interpersonal skills, written communication skills. Duration is 8–16 weeks. Unpaid. Open to college juniors, college seniors. ▶ *2–5 education interns:* responsibilities include assisting as instructors and designing education program. Candidates should have ability to work independently, ability to work with others, college courses in field, oral communication skills, plan to pursue career in field, strong leadership ability. Duration is 8–16 weeks. Unpaid. Open to college sophomores, college juniors, college seniors, recent college graduates. ▶ *20–50 research interns:* responsibilities include various duties depending on assigned research area including tissue processing, sediment and water analysis, animal monitoring, data entry, and report writing. Candidates should have ability to work independently, plan to pursue career in field, research skills, self-motivation. Duration is 8–16 weeks. Unpaid. Open to recent high school graduates, college sophomores, college juniors, college seniors. International applications accepted.
Benefits Housing at a cost, on-the-job training, opportunity to attend seminars/workshops, willing to act as a professional reference, willing to complete paperwork for educational credit, willing to provide letters of recommendation, free aquarium admission, gift shop discount, a few scholarships available at $150 per week.
Contact Write, call, fax, or e-mail Andrea Davis, Coordinator of Volunteer/Intern Services. Phone: 941-388-4441. Fax: 941-388-4312. E-mail: adavis@mote.org. Applicants must submit a formal

Mote Marine Laboratory (continued)

organization application, academic transcripts, writing sample. Applications are accepted continuously. World Wide Web: http://www.mote.org.

NATIONAL ASTRONOMY AND IONOSPHERE CENTER (NAIC)/ARECIBO OBSERVATORY
Cornell University, 504 Space Sciences Building
Ithaca, New York 14853-6801

General Information   Center for atmospheric sciences, radar, and radio astronomy that operates the world's largest single dish radio telescope (located in Puerto Rico). Established in 1963. Number of employees: 10. Unit of Cornell University. Number of internship applications received each year: 150.
Internships Available   ▶ *8 summer research assistants:* responsibilities include participation in research projects including searches for pulsars; studies of galaxies, giant stars, or interstellar medium; investigation of ionized portions of the earth's atmosphere; mapping planets or other members of the solar system; and developing projects for instrumentation or software. Candidates should have ability to work independently, ability to work with others, college courses in field, computer skills, knowledge of field, research skills, self-motivation. Duration is 10 weeks. $1600–$2267 per month. Open to college freshmen, college sophomores, college juniors, college seniors, first- or second -year graduate students. International applications accepted.
Benefits   Formal training, housing at a cost, meals at a cost, opportunity to attend seminars/workshops, travel reimbursement, willing to complete paperwork for educational credit, willing to provide letters of recommendation.
Contact   Write, fax, e-mail, or through World Wide Web site Ms. Jill Morrison, Assistant to the Director. Phone: 607-255-3735. Fax: 607-255-8803. E-mail: jtm14@cornell.edu. Applicants must submit a formal organization application, letter of interest, academic transcripts, three letters of recommendation. Application deadline: February 5. World Wide Web: http://www.naic.edu.

NATIONAL CENTER FOR TOXICOLOGICAL RESEARCH (NCTR)
3900 NCTR Road
Jefferson, Arkansas 72079

General Information   Center that conducts peer-reviewed biological research relevant to the current and future needs of the Food and Drug Administration. Established in 1971. Number of employees: 600. Unit of Food and Drug Administration, Rockville, Maryland. Number of internship applications received each year: 55.
Internships Available   ▶ *8–10 student interns:* responsibilities include participating part-time on-site at NCTR in biological research experiments under the mentorship of an NCTR scientist (while full-time student at an accredited college or university). Candidates should have ability to work independently, ability to work with others, analytical skills, college courses in field, editing skills, oral communication skills, plan to pursue career in field, research skills, self-motivation, writing skills. Duration is 1 year. $12,800–$20,735 stipend per year (part-time). Open to college sophomores, college juniors, college seniors, graduate students, only those from local area. ▶ *15–19 summer student research program interns:* responsibilities include conducting biological research studies (may involve laboratory animals, probably rodents), preparing written reports, and making an oral presentation of research results under mentorship of an NCTR scientist. Candidates should have ability to work independently, ability to work with others, analytical skills, college courses in field, oral communication skills, personal interest in the field, research skills, self-motivation, writing skills. Duration is 10 weeks. $1455–$2770 per month. Open to college freshmen, college sophomores, college juniors, college seniors, recent college graduates, graduate students, pre-postdoctoral students.
Benefits   On-the-job training, opportunity to attend seminars/workshops.
Contact   Write, call, fax, e-mail, or through World Wide Web site Linda McCamant, Program Manager, Oak Ridge Institute for Science and Education (ORISE), Oak Ridge 37831-0117. Phone: 860-

576-1089. Fax: 860-241-5219. E-mail: mccamanl@orau.org. In-person interview required. Applicants must submit a formal organization application, letter of interest, academic transcripts, writing sample, three personal references, three letters of recommendation. Application deadline: February 15 for summer student research program; continuous for student interns. World Wide Web: http://www.nctr.fda.gov.

NATIONAL SPACE SOCIETY
600 Pennsylvania Avenue, SE, Suite 201
Washington, District of Columbia 20003

General Information   Independent international educational nonprofit organization dedicated to the creation of a spacefaring civilization with 50 chapters and members in more than 35 countries. Established in 1974. Number of employees: 5. Number of internship applications received each year: 10.
Internships Available   ▶ *1 journalism intern:* responsibilities include assisting editor of AD ASTRA with publication tasks, selection of images, and maintenance of AD ASTRA index; updating the media contacts database. Candidates should have ability to work independently, computer skills, editing skills, personal interest in the field, research skills, writing skills, minimum GPA of 3.0. Duration is June 1 to August 1 . Unpaid. ▶ *1 public outreach intern:* responsibilities include assisting with responding to inquiries from members and the public and contributing to the planning and coordination of NSS outreach events and programs. Candidates should have ability to work independently, computer skills, oral communication skills, organizational skills, research skills, written communication skills, minimum GPA of 3.0. Duration is June 1 to August 1. Unpaid. ▶ *1 public policy intern:* responsibilities include attending congressional briefings and assisting NSS staff with organization and distribution of testimony, tracking legislation, and political action events. Candidates should have ability to work independently, computer skills, oral communication skills, organizational skills, research skills, written communication skills, minimum GPA of 3.0. Duration is June 1 to August 1. Unpaid. Open to college sophomores, college juniors. International applications accepted.
Benefits   Names of contacts, on-the-job training, opportunity to attend seminars/workshops, willing to act as a professional reference, willing to complete paperwork for educational credit, willing to provide letters of recommendation.
Contact   Write, fax, e-mail, or through World Wide Web site Internship Coordinator, 600 Pennsylvania Avenue, SE Suite 201, Washington, District of Columbia 20003. Phone: 202-543-1900. Fax: 202-546-4189. E-mail: nsshq@nss.org. Applicants must submit a formal organization application, letter of interest, resume, academic transcripts, letter of recommendation. Application deadline: March 15 for summer; continuous for academic-year positions. World Wide Web: http://www.nss.org.

OFFICE OF SCIENCE, U.S. DEPARTMENT OF ENERGY
SC-1, 1000 Independence Avenue, SW
Washington, District of Columbia 20585-0118

General Information   Multidisciplinary-science federal government agency. Established in 1977. Number of employees: 3,000. Division of United States Department of Energy, Washington, District of Columbia. Number of internship applications received each year: 1,600.
Internships Available   ▶ *90–150 Community College Institute of Science and Technology interns:* responsibilities include various scientific/engineering research projects with a mentor scientist. Candidates should have minimum GPA of 3.25. Duration is ten-week summer term. $400 per week. Open to college freshmen, college sophomores, full-time community college students (at least 18 years old). ▶ *40–100 pre-service interns:* responsibilities include variety of scientific/engineering research projects with a mentor scientist and master teacher. Candidates should have minimum GPA of 3.0, must plan to teach K12 science/maths. Duration is 10-week summer term. $400 per week. Open to college juniors, college seniors, graduate students working toward K-12 teaching certification, at least 18 years old. ▶ *40–70 science undergraduate*

laboratory interns: responsibilities include science/engineering research with a mentor scientist. Candidates should have minimum GPA of 2.5. Duration is one summer (10 weeks) or one semester (16 weeks). $400 per week. Open to college freshmen, college sophomores, college juniors, college seniors, must be U.S. citizen or permanent resident and at least 18 years old.

Benefits Opportunity to attend seminars/workshops, travel reimbursement, willing to complete paperwork for educational credit, housing assistance.

Contact Call or e-mail Todd Clark. Phone: 202-586-7174. Fax: 202-586-8054. E-mail: todd.clark@science.doe.gov. Applicants must submit online application: https://applicationlink.labworks.org/applicationlink/default.htm. Application deadline: February 1 for summer, August 1 for fall, November 1 for spring. World Wide Web: http://www.scied.science.doe.gov.

PRINCETON PLASMA PHYSICS LABORATORY
PO Box 451, MS-40
Princeton, New Jersey 08543-0451

General Information Research (experimental and theoretical) collaborative national center for science and innovation leading to an attractive energy source. Established in 1950. Number of employees: 600. Unit of Princeton University, Princeton, New Jersey. Number of internship applications received each year: 300.

Internships Available ▶ *25 National Undergraduate Fellowship Program interns:* responsibilities include scientific research (experimental or theoretical) depending on intern's interest. Candidates should have analytical skills, college courses in field, computer skills, plan to pursue career in field, research skills. Duration is 10 weeks in summer. $4800 per duration of internship. Open to college juniors.

Benefits Housing at a cost, meals at a cost, names of contacts, opportunity to attend seminars/workshops, travel reimbursement, willing to act as a professional reference, willing to provide letters of recommendation, one-week introductory course in plasma physics.

Contact Write, e-mail, or through World Wide Web site James Morgan, Program Administrator. Fax: 609-243-2112. E-mail: jmorgan@pppl.gov. Applicants must submit a formal organization application, academic transcripts, two letters of recommendation, personal statement indicating research interests. Application deadline: February 1. World Wide Web: http://www.pppl.gov.

RUTGERS COOPERATIVE EXTENSION OF
HUNTERDON COUNTY
PO Box 2900, 4 Gauntt Place
Flemington, New Jersey 08822

General Information Program that provides information to commercial farmers to allow them to make good pest control decisions. Unit of Rutgers, The State University of New Jersey, New Brunswick, New Brunswick, New Jersey.

Internships Available ▶ *4–6 integrated pest management field technicians:* responsibilities include collecting data to monitor pest levels on fruit crops in commercial orchards; interns trained in methods of detecting and quantifying insects and disease using various field scouting techniques. Candidates should have ability to work independently, computer skills, oral communication skills, personal interest in the field, self-motivation, strong interpersonal skills. Duration is May to August. $7–$9 per hour. Open to high school seniors, recent high school graduates, college freshmen, college sophomores, college juniors, college seniors, recent college graduates, graduate students, career changers, individuals reentering the workforce. International applications accepted.

Benefits Names of contacts, on-the-job training, opportunity to attend seminars/workshops, travel reimbursement, willing to act as a professional reference, willing to complete paperwork for educational credit, willing to provide letters of recommendation.

Contact Write, call, fax, or e-mail Meredith Compton, IPM Program Associate. Phone: 908-788-1338. Fax: 908-806-4735. E-mail: macompton@aesop.rutgers.edu. In-person interview recommended (telephone interview accepted). Applicants must submit a formal

organization application, letter of interest, resume, 2-3 personal references. Application deadline: May 1. World Wide Web: http://www.rce.rutgers.edu.

SMITHSONIAN ENVIRONMENTAL RESEARCH
CENTER
647 Contees Wharf Road, PO Box 28
Edgewater, Maryland 21037

General Information Research facility that advances stewardship of the biosphere through interdisciplinary research and educational outreach; SERC's scientists study a variety of interconnected ecosystems at the Center's primary research site in Maryland and at affiliated sites around the world. Established in 1965. Number of employees: 100. Branch of Smithsonian Institution, Washington, District of Columbia. Number of internship applications received each year: 200.

Internships Available ▶ *1–4 environmental and ecology education interns:* responsibilities include conducting nature tours on Center's trails, leading groups on canoe trips in tidal wetlands, assisting education staff with teacher workshops and environmental education programs. Candidates should have ability to work with others, college courses in field, computer skills, oral communication skills, plan to pursue career in field, self-motivation. Duration is 10–16 weeks. $350 per week. Open to college sophomores, college juniors, college seniors, recent college graduates, graduate students. ▶ *1–4 environmental engineering interns:* responsibilities include assisting SERC engineers in the fields of computers, micrometeorology, nutrient and water flows, and light in ecosystems. Candidates should have ability to work independently, ability to work with others, analytical skills, college courses in field, computer skills, research skills. Duration is 10–16 weeks. $350 per week. Open to college freshmen, college sophomores, college juniors, college seniors, recent college graduates, graduate students. ▶ *1–30 environmental research interns:* responsibilities include working on a specific project under the supervision of the Center's professional staff; projects include terrestrial and estuarine environmental research and are tailored to provide the maximum educational benefit to each participant. Candidates should have ability to work independently, ability to work with others, analytical skills, college courses in field, computer skills, research skills. Duration is 10–16 weeks. $350 per week. Open to college freshmen, college sophomores, college juniors, college seniors, recent college graduates, graduate students. International applications accepted.

Benefits Housing at a cost, names of contacts, on-the-job training, opportunity to attend seminars/workshops, possible full-time employment, willing to complete paperwork for educational credit, willing to provide letters of recommendation, access to the Smithsonian Institution.

Contact Write, call, e-mail, or through World Wide Web site Ms. Kim Sproat. Phone: 443-482-2217. Fax: 443-482-2380. E-mail: SERCintern@ssi.edu. Applicants must submit a formal organization application, academic transcripts, two letters of recommendation, personal essay. Application deadline: February 1 for summer (priority consideration), June 1 for fall, November 15 for spring (priority consideration). World Wide Web: http://www.serc.si.edu/internship/index.htm.

SMITHSONIAN TROPICAL RESEARCH INSTITUTE
1100 Jefferson Drive, Suite 3123
Washington, District of Columbia 20560-0705

General Information Center for basic research on tropical ecosystems that includes modern labs and a network of field stations located in the Republic of Panama. Unit of Smithsonian Institution, Washington, District of Columbia. Number of internship applications received each year: 300.

Internships Available ▶ *Interns:* responsibilities include working at marine or terrestrial research stations on projects that match intern's interests and future career goals. Candidates should have college courses in field, knowledge of field, personal interest in the field, plan to pursue career in field. Duration is flexible. Position available as unpaid or at stipend (on limited basis). Open to

Smithsonian Tropical Research Institute (continued)
individuals completing undergraduate studies or beginning graduate studies in areas related to the interests of STRI staff. International applications accepted.
Benefits Opportunity to attend seminars/workshops, willing to complete paperwork for educational credit.
International Internships Available in Panama.
Contact Write Internship Coordinator, Office of Education, PO Box 37012, Quad, Suite 3123, 705, Washington, District of Columbia 20013-7012. Applicants must submit a formal organization application, resume, academic transcripts, personal reference, letter outlining interests, qualifications, and how travel to Panama and room and board expenses while working there will be paid. Applications are accepted continuously. World Wide Web: http://www.si.edu/stri.

SOUTHWEST RESEARCH INSTITUTE (SWRI)
6220 Culebra Road
San Antonio, Texas 78238-5166

General Information Institute that researches and develops technology in science and engineering fields. Established in 1947. Number of employees: 2,800. Number of internship applications received each year: 1,000.
Internships Available ▶ *20–40 student analysts:* responsibilities include assisting senior-level analysts on current projects. Candidates should have ability to work independently, college courses in field, computer skills, oral communication skills, plan to pursue career in field, self-motivation, strong interpersonal skills, strong leadership ability. Duration is flexible. $10–$20 per hour. ▶ *20–40 student engineers:* responsibilities include assisting senior-level engineers on current projects. Candidates should have ability to work independently, college courses in field, computer skills, oral communication skills, strong interpersonal skills, written communication skills. Duration is flexible. $11–$20 per hour. ▶ *10–15 student scientists:* responsibilities include assisting senior-level scientists on current projects. Candidates should have ability to work independently, computer skills, oral communication skills, strong interpersonal skills, written communication skills, major in physical science. Duration is flexible. $11–$17 per hour. Open to college sophomores, college juniors, college seniors, graduate students.
Benefits Formal training, job counseling, names of contacts, possible full-time employment, travel reimbursement, willing to complete paperwork for educational credit, willing to provide letters of recommendation, competitive salaries based on semester hours completed; free housing for summer positions for students outside the San Antonio area.
Contact Write, call, fax, e-mail, or through World Wide Web site Ernest C. Gomez, Student Employment Coordinator. Phone: 210-522-3503. Fax: 210-522-3990. E-mail: egomez@swri.org. Applicants must submit a formal organization application, academic transcripts, resume recommended. Applications are accepted continuously. World Wide Web: http://www.swri.org.

UNIVERSITY OF CALIFORNIA, LAWRENCE LIVERMORE NATIONAL LABORATORY
PO Box 808
Livermore, California 94551

General Information Government research and development agency. Established in 1952. Number of employees: 7,000. Number of internship applications received each year: 1,500.
Internships Available ▶ *6–12 ASCI Pipeline interns:* responsibilities include individual project designed according to the student's abilities and skills within the discipline of high-performance computing, programming, network administration, graphics, and database management. Candidates should have ability to work independently, ability to work with others, plan to pursue career in field, self-motivation, major in computer science. Duration is May to September. $18–$24 per hour. Open to college sophomores, college juniors, college seniors, graduate students, U.S. citizens (required). ▶ *20–25 High-Energy-Density Physics Program (HEDP) interns:* responsibilities include preparatory work for experimental, theoretical, and computational research in hydrodynamics, atomic,

plasma, and inertial confinement physics; and radiation/particle transport as applied to the evolution of complex systems. Candidates should have ability to work independently, ability to work with others, analytical skills, declared college major in field, plan to pursue career in field, self-motivation. Duration is May to September. $18–$24 per hour. Open to college juniors, college seniors, graduate students, U.S. citizens (required). ▶ *3–6 Interns for Defense Technologies (IDT):* responsibilities include work in nuclear, mechanical, electrical, and materials engineering. Candidates should have ability to work independently, ability to work with others, analytical skills, declared college major in field, plan to pursue career in field, self-motivation. Duration is May to September. $18–$24 per hour. Open to college sophomores, college juniors, college seniors, graduate students, U.S. citizens (required). ▶ *20–30 Internships in Terascale Simulation Technology (ITST):* responsibilities include preparation for employment as computational scientists. Candidates should have ability to work independently, ability to work with others, college degree in related field, computer skills, plan to pursue career in field, self-motivation. Duration is May to September. $4480–$5860 per month. Open to advanced undergraduate and preferably graduate students; computer science (visualization, modeling, graphics) and mathematics majors; must be U.S. citizen. ▶ *6–8 LLNL College Cyber Defenders (CCD) Program participants:* responsibilities include learning the concepts and gaining skills in information technologies and protection in a distributed environment (such as the Internet). Candidates should have ability to work independently, ability to work with others, college courses in field, computer skills, self-motivation. Duration is May to September. $15–$24 per hour. Open to college sophomores, college juniors, college seniors, graduate students, individuals with U.S. citizenship (required), computer related 2-4 year degrees. ▶ *2–4 Laser Science and Technology Student Program (LSTSP) participants:* responsibilities include hands-on experience in laser and optics projects. Candidates should have ability to work independently, ability to work with others, analytical skills, plan to pursue career in field, self-motivation, major in laser science, optics, or optical engineering. Duration is May to September. $20–$30 per hour. Open to college juniors, college seniors, graduate students, U.S. citizens (required). ▶ *20–25 Nuclear Science Internship Program participants:* responsibilities include training and access to unique nuclear science expertise, equipment, and facilities, by establishing collaborations with key academic institutions. Candidates should have ability to work independently, ability to work with others, computer skills, declared college major in field, plan to pursue career in field, self-motivation. Duration is May to September. $20–$30 per hour. Open to college juniors, college seniors, graduate students, individuals with U.S. citizenship (required), actinide, material, and/or nuclear science majors. ▶ *5–10 Physics and Advanced Technologies Interns (PAII):* responsibilities include experimental, theoretical, and computational research in a wide range of physics technology programs. Candidates should have ability to work independently, ability to work with others, analytical skills, declared college major in field, plan to pursue career in field, self-motivation. Duration is May to September. $20–$30 per hour. Open to college juniors, college seniors, graduate students. ▶ *300–400 Scholars Employment Program interns:* responsibilities include working in state of the art facilities at a National Security laboratory in a variety of science and engineering programs. Candidates should have ability to work independently, college courses in field, computer skills, plan to pursue career in field, self-motivation. Duration is May to September. $15–$24 per hour. Open to college freshmen, college sophomores, college juniors, college seniors, recent college graduates, graduate students, U.S. citizens (required).

Benefits Health insurance, opportunity to attend seminars/workshops, possible full-time employment, travel reimbursement.

Contact Through World Wide Web site Summer Employment Manager, PO Box 808 L-275, Livermore, California 94551. Fax: 925-423-0984. No phone calls. Applicants must submit a formal organization application, resume, academic transcripts, company-designed interest form. Application deadline: February 28 for summer. World Wide Web: http://internships.llnl.gov.

U.S. NATIONAL ARBORETUM
3501 New York Avenue, NE
Washington, District of Columbia 20002

General Information Agency that conducts research, provides education, and conserves and displays trees, shrubs, flowers, and other plants to enhance the environment. Established in 1927. Number of employees: 100. Branch of U.S. Department of Agriculture, Beltsville, Maryland. Number of internship applications received each year: 30.

Internships Available ▶ *1 Asian collection intern:* responsibilities include gardening and maintenance experience throughout the collection and maintaining plant records. Candidates should have ability to work independently, ability to work with others, computer skills, knowledge of field, self-motivation. Duration is 1 year. $9.14 per hour. Open to high school seniors, recent high school graduates, college freshmen, college sophomores, college juniors, college seniors, recent college graduates, graduate students, career changers, individuals reentering the workforce. ▶ *1 Fern Valley native plant collection intern:* responsibilities include assisting in maintenance of the collection, including planting, weeding, watering, pruning, and propagation. Candidates should have ability to work independently, ability to work with others, knowledge of field, self-motivation. Duration is 3 months. $9.14 per hour. Open to recent high school graduates, college freshmen, college sophomores, college juniors, college seniors, recent college graduates, graduate students, career changers, individuals reentering the workforce. ▶ *1 Friendship Garden intern:* responsibilities include maintenance of residential garden setting. Candidates should have ability to work independently, knowledge of field, self-motivation, strong interpersonal skills, strong leadership ability. Duration is 8 months (2 days per week). $9.14 per hour. Open to recent high school graduates, college freshmen, college sophomores, college juniors, college seniors, recent college graduates, graduate students, career changers, individuals reentering the workforce. ▶ *1 conifer collection intern:* responsibilities include gardening and maintenance experience throughout the collection and maintaining plant records. Candidates should have ability to work independently, ability to work with others, computer skills, knowledge of field, self-motivation. Duration is 3 months. $9.14 per hour. Open to recent high school graduates, college freshmen, college sophomores, college juniors, college seniors, recent college graduates, graduate students, career changers, individuals reentering the workforce. ▶ *1 engineering intern:* responsibilities include surveying and mapping utility systems, specifically drainage systems and fields. Candidates should have ability to work independently, computer skills, knowledge of field, self-motivation. Duration is 3 months. $9.14 per hour. Open to recent high school graduates, college freshmen, college sophomores, college juniors, college seniors, recent college graduates, graduate students, career changers, individuals reentering the workforce. ▶ *1 floral and nursery plants research (germplasm) intern:* responsibilities include care of germplasm, watering, seed and cutting propagation, and weeding/mowing greenhouse and field areas. Candidates should have ability to work independently, knowledge of field, research skills, self-motivation. Duration is 5 months. $9.14 per hour. Open to recent high school graduates, college freshmen, college sophomores, college juniors, college seniors, recent college graduates, graduate students, career changers, individuals reentering the workforce. ▶ *1 floral and nursery plants research (molecular biology) intern:* responsibilities include assisting with tissue culture, acclimation of plants to greenhouse conditions, and DNA and serological analysis. Candidates should have ability to work independently, ability to work with others, knowledge of field, research skills, self-motivation. Duration is 5 months. $9.14 per hour. Open to recent high school graduates, college freshmen, college sophomores, college juniors, college seniors, recent college graduates, graduate students, career changers, individuals reentering the workforce. ▶ *1 floral and nursery plants research (shrub breeding) intern:* responsibilities include examination of genetic diversity in selected genera, assisting with plant breeding work, plant maintenance, and plant tissue culture. Candidates should have ability to work independently, ability to work with others, knowledge of field, research skills, self-motivation. Duration is 3 months. $9.14 per hour. Open to recent high school graduates, college freshmen, college sophomores, college juniors, college seniors, recent college graduates, graduate students, career changers, individuals reentering the workforce. ▶ *1-2 high visibility areas interns:* responsibilities include assisting with all aspects of garden maintenance including watering, planting, weeding, and fertilizing. Candidates should have ability to work independently, knowledge of field, oral communication skills, self-motivation. Duration is 3-6 months. $9.14 per hour. Open to recent high school graduates, college freshmen, college sophomores, college juniors, college seniors, recent college graduates, graduate students, career changers, individuals reentering the workforce. ▶ *1 holly/magnolia collection intern:* responsibilities include assisting in all aspects of collection management including record-keeping, mapping, weeding, pruning, watering, and general care. Duration is 3 months. $9.14 per hour. Open to recent high school graduates, college freshmen, college sophomores, college juniors, college seniors, recent college graduates, graduate students, career changers, individuals reentering the workforce. ▶ *1 integrated pest management intern:* responsibilities include working with a wide variety of plants and the insects and diseases that attack them; inspection of plants, application of non-chemical controls, and assistance in teaching IPM theories to professionals and home gardeners. Candidates should have ability to work independently, ability to work with others, knowledge of field, oral communication skills, self-motivation, written communication skills. Duration is 9 months to 1 year. $9.14 per hour. Open to recent high school graduates, college freshmen, college sophomores, college juniors, college seniors, recent college graduates, graduate students, career changers, individuals reentering the workforce. ▶ *1 marketing intern:* responsibilities include reviewing and analyzing the Arboretum's fee-based activities and developing a marketing plan to maximize their impact and income. Candidates should have ability to work independently, computer skills, office skills, self-motivation, written communication skills. Duration is 3 months. $9.14 per hour. Open to recent high school graduates, college freshmen, college sophomores, college juniors, college seniors, recent college graduates, graduate students, career changers, individuals reentering the workforce. ▶ *1 national herb garden intern:* responsibilities include assisting with garden maintenance, propagation, planting, and watering. Candidates should have computer skills, knowledge of field, self-motivation, strong interpersonal skills, interest in herbs and antique roses. Duration is 10 months. $9.14 per hour. Open to recent high school graduates, college freshmen, college sophomores, college juniors, college seniors, recent college graduates, graduate students, career changers, individuals reentering the workforce. ▶ *1 plant records intern:* responsibilities include entering accession, location, source, descriptive data, and references in database (BG-BASE); record-keeping and field work. Candidates should have ability to work independently, computer skills, knowledge of field, self-motivation, written communication skills. Duration is 1 year. $9.14 per hour. Open to recent high school graduates, college freshmen, college sophomores, college juniors, college seniors, recent college graduates, graduate students, career changers, individuals reentering the workforce. International applications accepted.

Benefits On-the-job training, opportunity to attend seminars/workshops, willing to act as a professional reference, willing to complete paperwork for educational credit, willing to provide letters of recommendation.

Contact Write, call, fax, e-mail, or through World Wide Web site Kari Iddings, Internship Coordinator. Phone: 202-245-4521. Fax: 202-245-4575. E-mail: iddingsk@ars.usda.gov. In-person interview recommended (telephone interview accepted). Applicants must submit a formal organization application, resume, academic transcripts, 3 professional references. Application deadline: January for IPM and herb garden interns, February for all other positions. World Wide Web: http://www.usna.usda.gov.

WHITNEY LABORATORY
9505 Ocean Shore Boulevard
St. Augustine, Florida 32086

General Information Marine biomedical research laboratory. Established in 1975. Number of employees: 50. Unit of University of Florida, Gainesville, Florida. Number of internship applications received each year: 150.

Whitney Laboratory (continued)

Internships Available ▶ *10–12 Whitney Summer Undergraduate Research Program interns:* responsibilities include participating in research training in cell, molecular, and neuro biology using marine organisms; planning and executing research program. Candidates should have ability to work independently, ability to work with others, analytical skills, personal interest in the field, plan to pursue career in field, self-motivation. Duration is 10 weeks. $250–$300 per week. Open to college freshmen, college sophomores, college juniors, college seniors. International applications accepted.

Benefits Formal training, free housing, job counseling, names of contacts, opportunity to attend seminars/workshops, travel reimbursement, willing to act as a professional reference, willing to provide letters of recommendation.

Contact Write, call, fax, e-mail, or through World Wide Web site William R. Buzzi, Education Coordinator. Phone: 904-461-4011. Fax: 904-461-4008. E-mail: wrb@whitney.ufl.edu. Applicants must submit a formal organization application, letter of interest, resume, academic transcripts, two letters of recommendation, prioritized list of research interests. Application deadline: February 28 for summer, July 1 for fall, November 1 for winter/spring. World Wide Web: http://http://www.whitney.ufl.edu.

PUBLIC ADMINISTRATION

GENERAL

ALASKA STATE PARKS
550 West 7th Avenue, Suite 1380
Anchorage, Alaska 99501-3561

General Information State agency that maintains parks and provides outdoor recreation facilities. Established in 1970. Number of employees: 194. Division of State of Alaska Department of Natural Resources, Anchorage, Alaska. Number of internship applications received each year: 100.
Internships Available ▶ *1–14 ranger assistants:* responsibilities include assisting staff in daily operations involving facility maintenance, visitor contacts, and construction projects. Duration is May to September. Unpaid. Open to individuals reentering the workforce, must be at least 18 years old. ▶ *1–2 trail crew members:* responsibilities include maintaining park trails and public facilities and assisting with construction or repair of any new or old facilities (training provided). Duration is May to September. Unpaid. Open to college freshmen, college sophomores, college juniors, college seniors, recent college graduates, individuals reentering the workforce, must be at least 18 years old. ▶ *15–20 volunteer interns:* responsibilities include various duties at park facilities depending on current needs and intern's abilities. Duration is 1 summer (May to September). Unpaid. Open to college freshmen, college sophomores, college juniors, college seniors, recent college graduates, graduate students, career changers, individuals reentering the workforce, individuals age 18 or older. Candidates for all positions should have ability to work independently, ability to work with others, college courses in field, knowledge of field, personal interest in the field, self-motivation, good physical condition.
Benefits Free housing, on-the-job training, willing to complete paperwork for educational credit, expense allowance to cover food costs.
Contact Write, call, fax, e-mail, or through World Wide Web site Lynn Wibbenmeyer, Volunteer Coordinator. Phone: 907-269-8708. Fax: 907-269-8907. E-mail: volunteer@dnr.state.ak.us. Telephone interview required. Applicants must submit a formal organization application, letter of interest, resume, academic transcripts, personal reference, three letters of recommendation. Application deadline: April 1 for summer, August 1 for winter. World Wide Web: http://www.alaskastateparks.org.

CALIFORNIA EXECUTIVE FELLOWS, JUDICIAL ADMINISTRATION FELLOWS, CALIFORNIA SENATE FELLOWS, CALIFORNIA ASSEMBLY FELLOWS
Center for California Studies, CSU Sacramento, 6000 J Street
Sacramento, California 95819-6081

General Information Public policy, public service, and curricular support unit devoted to promoting the understanding of California's history, cultures, and public policies. Established in 1984. Number of employees: 75. Unit of California State University, Sacramento, Sacramento, California. Number of internship applications received each year: 1,000.
Internships Available ▶ *18 Assembly Fellows:* responsibilities include assuming the role of a professional staff team member in Assembly branch of California's state government. Candidates should have ability to work independently, analytical skills, computer skills, knowledge of field, office skills, oral communication skills, personal interest in the field, strong interpersonal skills, written communication skills. Duration is 11 months. $1882 per month. ▶ *18 Executive Fellows:* responsibilities include assuming the role of a professional staff team member in the Executive branch of California's state government. Candidates should have ability to work independently, analytical skills, computer skills, knowledge of field, office skills, oral communication skills, personal interest in the field, strong interpersonal skills, written communication skills. Duration is 11 months. $1882 per month. ▶ *10 Judicial Administration Fellows:* responsibilities include assuming the role of a professional staff team member in Judicial branch of California's state government. Candidates should have ability to work with others, knowledge of field, oral communication skills, personal interest in the field, written communication skills. Duration is 11 months. $1882 per month. ▶ *18 Senate Fellows:* responsibilities include assuming the role of a professional staff team member in Senate branch of California's state government. Candidates should have ability to work with others, knowledge of field, oral communication skills, personal interest in the field, written communication skills. Duration is 11 months. $1882 per month. Open to college seniors, recent college graduates, graduate students, law students, career changers, must have completed 4-year degree by August. International applications accepted.
Benefits Formal training, health insurance, on-the-job training, opportunity to attend seminars/workshops, possible full-time employment, tuition assistance, willing to act as a professional reference, willing to complete paperwork for educational credit, willing to provide letters of recommendation, dental and vision care, 12 units of graduate credit for fellows who fulfill academic requirements.
Contact Write, call, fax, e-mail, or through World Wide Web site Robert Gregg, Outreach Coordinator, Center for California Studies CSU Sacramento, 6000 J Street, Sacramento, California 95819-6081. Phone: 916-278-6906. Fax: 916-278-5199. E-mail: calstudies@csus.edu. In-person interview required. Applicants must submit a formal organization application, academic transcripts, writing sample, three letters of recommendation. Application deadline: February 25. World Wide Web: http://www.csus.edu/calst.

CENTRAL INTELLIGENCE AGENCY
Recruitment Center, Student Programs, L 100, LF7
Washington, District of Columbia 20505

General Information Agency involved in information collection, processing, analysis, and reporting. Established in 1947.
Internships Available ▶ *Graduate studies interns:* responsibilities include becoming acquainted with professional intelligence analysts and participating in substantive agency work. Candidates should have analytical skills, declared college major in field, oral communication skills, self-motivation, strong leadership ability, written communication skills. Duration is flexible. $17.55–$23.64 per hour. Open to college seniors, graduate students. ▶ *Student trainees:* responsibilities include participating in substantive agency assignments commensurate with intern's academic training and ability. Candidates should have analytical skills, declared college major in field, oral communication skills, self-motivation, strong leadership ability, written communication skills. Duration is 3 semesters. $14.16–$17.55 per hour. Open to college sophomores. ▶ *Summer internships:* responsibilities include working with professionals and viewing the role of the agency while gaining work experience. Candidates should have analytical skills, declared college major in field, oral communication skills, self-motivation, strong

Central Intelligence Agency (continued)

interpersonal skills, written communication skills. Duration is 2 summers (minimum of 90 days), or 1 summer and 1 semester. $14.16–$17.55 per hour. Open to college sophomores, college juniors.
Benefits Formal training, health insurance, names of contacts, on-the-job training, opportunity to attend seminars/workshops, possible full-time employment, travel reimbursement, willing to complete paperwork for educational credit, willing to provide letters of recommendation, vacation and sick days accrual.
Contact Through World Wide Web site Personnel Representative, L100 LF7, Washington, District of Columbia 20505. No phone calls. Applicants must submit a letter of interest, resume, formal application provided following review of cover letter/resume. Application deadline: April 1 for fall, August 1 for spring, November 1 for summer. World Wide Web: http://www.cia.gov.

CITY OF NEW YORK/PARKS & RECREATION
830 Fifth Avenue, Room 309
New York, New York 10021

General Information Local government agency responsible for 28,000 acres of green space; oversees cultural, athletic, and social events. Established in 1934. Number of employees: 2,200. Number of internship applications received each year: 1,000.
Internships Available ▶ *100–200 interns:* responsibilities include working in the areas of public administration, recreation, environmental science, computer operations, photography, architecture, landscape architecture, engineering, urban planning, revenue, accounting, commissioner's staff, recruiting, historical signs program, press/marketing, and forestry; locations in all five boroughs. Candidates should have oral communication skills, organizational skills, self-motivation, strong interpersonal skills, written communication skills. Duration is flexible. Position available as unpaid or paid. Open to high school students, recent high school graduates, college freshmen, college sophomores, college juniors, college seniors, recent college graduates, graduate students, law students, individuals reentering the workforce. International applications accepted.
Benefits On-the-job training, opportunity to attend seminars/workshops, possible full-time employment, travel reimbursement, willing to act as a professional reference, willing to complete paperwork for educational credit, willing to provide letters of recommendation, participation in monthly speaker series; some stipends may be available for federal work-study participants.
Contact Write, call, fax, e-mail, or through World Wide Web site Leslie Nusblatt, Intern Coordinator. Phone: 212-360-8257. Fax: 212-360-8200. E-mail: leslie.nusblatt@parks.nyc.gov. In-person interview required. Applicants must submit a letter of interest, resume, 1-3 writing samples (on specific occasions). Applications are accepted continuously. World Wide Web: http://www.nyc.gov/parks.

CITY OF PHOENIX, BUDGET AND RESEARCH DEPARTMENT
200 West Washington Street, 14th Floor
Phoenix, Arizona 85003-1611

General Information Department that assists in allocation of city resources to provide efficient, effective, and economical municipal services; develops the city's annual budget and capital improvement program by monitoring expenditures and revenues; and conducts management research analysis. Established in 1913. Number of employees: 30. Department of City of Phoenix, Phoenix, Arizona. Number of internship applications received each year: 90.
Internships Available ▶ *1–4 management interns:* responsibilities include conducting municipal research and analysis of administrative and organizational problems, policies, and practices; providing staff assistance for city council and subcommittees. Candidates should have analytical skills, oral communication skills, plan to pursue career in field, research skills, written communication skills, satisfactory completion of all courses for a master's degree in public or business administration or a closely related field prior to first day of program year. Duration is 1 year. $30,992–$45,053

per year. Open to graduate students, law students, career changers, individuals reentering the workforce. International applications accepted.
Benefits Formal training, health insurance, job counseling, opportunity to attend seminars/workshops, possible full-time employment, tuition assistance, dental insurance.
Contact Write, call, e-mail, or through World Wide Web site Cecile Pettle, Budget and Research Director. Phone: 602-262-4800. E-mail: julie.flaskenid@phoenix.gove. In-person interview required. Applicants must submit a formal organization application, letter of interest, resume, writing sample. World Wide Web: http://phoenix.gov.

CONGRESSMAN BILL THOMAS
2208 Rayburn House Office Building
Washington, District of Columbia 20515

General Information Republican U.S. Congressman serving the 22nd Congressional District of California; Chairman of Committee on Ways and Means. Number of employees: 8. Number of internship applications received each year: 150.
Internships Available ▶ *10 interns:* responsibilities include legislative research and basic office duties. Candidates should have office skills. Duration is minimum of 6 weeks. Position available as unpaid or paid. Open to college freshmen, college sophomores, college juniors, college seniors. International applications accepted.
Benefits Opportunity to attend seminars/workshops, possible full-time employment, willing to complete paperwork for educational credit.
Contact Write, call, or fax Mary Sue Englund, Intern Coordinator. Phone: 202-225-2915. Fax: 202-225-2908. Applicants must submit a letter of interest, resume, writing sample. Applications are accepted continuously. World Wide Web: http://www.house.gov/billthomas.

CONGRESSMAN MICHAEL BILIRAKIS
2269 Rayburn House Office Building
Washington, District of Columbia 20515

General Information Congressional office. Established in 1982. Number of employees: 9. Number of internship applications received each year: 20.
Internships Available ▶ *1–3 legislative interns:* responsibilities include assisting legislative staff with daily operations from running errands to attending legislative hearings. Candidates should have ability to work with others, computer skills, research skills, self-motivation, writing skills. Duration is 6 weeks minimum. Unpaid. Open to college freshmen, college sophomores, college juniors, college seniors, recent college graduates, graduate students, law students. International applications accepted.
Benefits Names of contacts, opportunity to attend seminars/workshops, willing to complete paperwork for educational credit, willing to provide letters of recommendation.
Contact Write, call, or fax Carrie Melvin, Legislative Correspondent. Phone: 202-225-5755. Fax: 202-225-4085. Applicants must submit a letter of interest, resume, writing sample, 3 letters of recommendation or personal references; telephone interview accepted. Application deadline: January 15 for spring, April 15 for summer, August 15 for fall. World Wide Web: http://www.house.gov/bilirakis.

CONGRESSWOMAN DIANA DEGETTE
U.S. House of Representatives, Room 1530 Longworth
Washington, District of Columbia 20515

General Information Democratic U.S. Congresswoman serving the 1st Congressional District of Colorado. Established in 1997. Number of employees: 9. Number of internship applications received each year: 50.
Internships Available ▶ *1–5 interns:* responsibilities include assisting staff, answering phones, opening mail, conducting research, answering letters, and attending meetings and hearings. Candidates should have ability to work independently, office skills, oral communication skills, personal interest in the field, research skills, self-motivation, writing skills. Duration is minimum of 8 weeks. Unpaid. Open to recent high school graduates, college fresh-

men, college sophomores, college juniors, college seniors, recent college graduates, graduate students, law students, career changers, individuals reentering the workforce. International applications accepted.

Benefits Job counseling, names of contacts, on-the-job training, opportunity to attend seminars/workshops, willing to act as a professional reference, willing to complete paperwork for educational credit, willing to provide letters of recommendation, opportunity to observe how Congress works and take part in legislative initiatives.

Contact Write, call, fax, or e-mail Steve Plevniak, Intern Coordinator. Phone: 202-225-4431. Fax: 202-225-5657. E-mail: degette@mail.house.gov. In-person interview recommended (telephone interview accepted). Applicants must submit a letter of interest, resume, writing sample. Applications are accepted continuously. World Wide Web: http://www.house.gov/degette.

CONGRESSWOMAN SLAUGHTER
469 Rayburn House Office Building, (NY-28)
Washington, District of Columbia 20515

General Information Democratic member of the United States House of Representatives. Established in 1986. Number of employees: 10. Unit of United States House of Representatives, Washington, District of Columbia. Number of internship applications received each year: 20.

Internships Available ▶ *1–2 interns:* responsibilities include drafting constituent letters, attending committee hearings, administrative duties, research projects. Candidates should have oral communication skills, organizational skills, research skills, strong interpersonal skills, writing skills, interest in government/legislative process. Duration is flexible. Unpaid. Open to college freshmen, college sophomores, college juniors, college seniors. International applications accepted.

Benefits Opportunity to attend seminars/workshops, willing to complete paperwork for educational credit, willing to provide letters of recommendation.

Contact Write, call, fax, or through World Wide Web site Mary Beth Walker, Office Manager, Washington, District of Columbia 20515. Phone: 202-225-3615. Fax: 202-225-7822. Telephone interview required. Applicants must submit a formal organization application, letter of interest, resume, academic transcripts, writing sample, two letters of recommendation. Application deadline: January 5 for spring, March 30 for summer, July 31 for fall, November 3 for winter. World Wide Web: http://www.house.gov/slaughter/.

DEMOCRATIC CAUCUS OF THE HOUSE OF REPRESENTATIVES
200 West Washington Street, Room 149
Indianapolis, Indiana 46204-2786

General Information Group consisting of the collective membership of state representatives affiliated with the Democratic Party of the House of Representatives. Number of employees: 75. Unit of State of Indiana, Indiana. Number of internship applications received each year: 70.

Internships Available ▶ *15–20 constituent/caucus services interns:* responsibilities include working with a full-time legislative assistant in support of 3 or 4 state representatives, drafting constituent letters, conducting legislative and constituent problem research, attending committee meetings, summarizing legislation, and preparing material for newsletters. Candidates should have ability to work with others, oral communication skills, personal interest in the field, strong leadership ability, written communication skills. Duration is 3–4 months. $275 per week. ▶ *3 media services interns:* responsibilities include working with the caucus media director in assisting all Democratic state representatives with media relations, research, writing news releases, setting up press conferences, taping and sending radio feeds, and coordinating photograph sessions with visiting constituents. Candidates should have oral communication skills, personal interest in the field, strong interpersonal skills, writing skills. Duration is 3–4 months. $275 per week. ▶ *1–2 ways and means interns:* responsibilities include assisting the Democratic fiscal analyst in working for the chief

Democratic member of the Ways and Means Committee and following meetings of the Committee. Candidates should have analytical skills, oral communication skills, personal interest in the field, research skills, written communication skills. Duration is 3–4 months. $275 per week. Open to college juniors, college seniors, recent college graduates, graduate students.

Benefits Possible full-time employment, willing to complete paperwork for educational credit.

Contact Write, call, fax, e-mail, or through World Wide Web site Stacey Wybiral, Internship Director. Phone: 317-232-0243. Fax: 317-233-8184. E-mail: swybiral@iga.state.in.us. In-person interview required. Applicants must submit a formal organization application, letter of interest, resume, academic transcripts, two letters of recommendation. Application deadline: October 16. World Wide Web: http://www.state.in.us/legislative/house_democrats.

ECONOMIC RESEARCH SERVICE, US DEPARTMENT OF AGRICULTURE
1800 M Street, NW
Washington, District of Columbia 20036-5831

General Information Federal agency that provides economic and social science research and analysis for use by decision makers in areas relating to agriculture, food, natural resources, and rural America. Established in 1961. Number of employees: 425. Unit of United States Department of Agriculture, Washington, District of Columbia. Number of internship applications received each year: 150.

Internships Available ▶ *1–3 computer specialists:* responsibilities include assisting in development of agency Internet or Intranet services; assisting in development of Windows database application programs; assisting in the development and validation of relational databases; and assisting in the development of standard system operating procedures. Candidates should have analytical skills, declared college major in field, organizational skills, personal interest in the field, plan to pursue career in field, knowledge of Internet technologies, client-server databases, Visual C++, database and spreadsheet software. Duration is flexible within period of May to August. $9-$10 per hour, depending on education level. Open to college sophomores, college juniors, college seniors, continuing students only (enrolled in school in fall). ▶ *15–20 economics assistants/economists:* responsibilities include assisting economists in developing and presenting economic research and analysis, conducting literature searches, collecting and analyzing information using a variety of software packages to develop spreadsheets, creating graphics and text for documents. Candidates should have analytical skills, college courses in field, computer skills, knowledge of field, plan to pursue career in field, research skills. Duration is flexible within period of May to August. $10–$20 per hour, depending on education level. Open to college sophomores, college juniors, college seniors, graduate students, continuing students only (enrolled in school in fall). International applications accepted.

Benefits On-the-job training, opportunity to attend seminars/workshops, willing to act as a professional reference, willing to complete paperwork for educational credit, computer training, public transit subsidy.

Contact Write, call, fax, or e-mail Kate Muir, Human Resources Coordinator, 1800 M Street, NW, Room 4151, Washington, District of Columbia 20036-5831. Phone: 202-694-5014. Fax: 202-694-5757. E-mail: erssummerinterns@ers.usda.gov. Applicants must submit a formal organization application, resume, academic transcripts, application form available on Web site. Application deadline: March 1. World Wide Web: http://www.ers.usda.gov.

FEDERAL RESERVE BANK OF NEW YORK
33 Liberty Street
New York, New York 10045

General Information One of the 12 regional banks which along with the Federal Reserve Board in Washington, D.C. comprise the Federal Reserve System, and are responsible for implementing the nation's monetary policy through a variety of techniques including buying and selling U.S. Government securities in the

Federal Reserve Bank of New York (continued)

open market. Established in 1913. Number of employees: 3,500. Number of internship applications received each year: 2,500.

Internships Available ▶ *12 graduate summer analysts:* responsibilities include assignment to one particular department for the summer, but will have frequent opportunities to complete projects by collaboration with other analysts and employers around the banks; examples of past assignments include participation in risk examinations, developing reports and databases, and conducting economic research with senior level economists. Candidates should have analytical skills, computer skills, oral communication skills, plan to pursue career in field, written communication skills, strong academic record. Duration is 12–14 weeks. $1300 per week. Open to students pursuing master's degree in business, economics, finance, public policy, or related disciplines. ▶ *12 undergraduate summer interns:* responsibilities include assignment to one particular department for the summer, but have frequent opportunities to complete projects by collaborating with other analysts and employees from around the banks; examples of past assignments include participating in risk examinations, developing reports and databases, and conducting economic research with senior level economists. Candidates should have analytical skills, computer skills, oral communication skills, plan to pursue career in field, research skills, self-motivation, background in business, finance, or related field, strong academic record. Duration is 12–14 weeks. $400–$600 per week. Open to students who have completed junior year of college by beginning of internship.

Benefits Formal training, meals at a cost, on-the-job training, opportunity to attend seminars/workshops, possible full-time employment, willing to act as a professional reference, willing to complete paperwork for educational credit.

Contact Write, e-mail, or through World Wide Web site Internship Coordinator. E-mail: campus@ny.frb.org. No phone calls. In-person interview recommended (telephone interview accepted). Applicants must submit a formal organization application, letter of interest, resume, academic transcripts, writing sample. Application deadline: January 31 for summer. World Wide Web: http://www.newyorkfed.org.

FEDERAL RESERVE BOARD OF GOVERNORS
20th and Constitution Avenue, NW, MS 129
Washington, District of Columbia 20551

General Information Central banking system of the U.S. whose primary function is the formulation of monetary policy to foster stable economic conditions and long-term economic growth. Established in 1913. Number of employees: 1,650. Number of internship applications received each year: 500.

Internships Available ▶ *Division of Information Technology interns:* responsibilities include writing and testing software, assisting with hardware and software installation, designing Web pages and PowerPoint presentations, writing documentation for applications being developed or modified, performing routine office functions. Candidates should have major in computer science, economics, finance, business administration, or a related discipline. Duration is approximately June 1 to September 1. Position available as unpaid or paid. Open to college students who have completed their sophomore, junior, or senior year. ▶ *Division of Research and Statistics/Division of Monetary Affairs interns:* responsibilities include research projects according to individual interests, aptitude, and experience (graduate students); assisting in research projects conducted by economists at the Board (undergraduates). Candidates should have analytical skills, computer skills, knowledge of field, oral communication skills, research skills, written communication skills. Duration is approximately June 1 to September 1 (paid interns) or 10-12 weeks in summer (unpaid interns). Position available as unpaid or paid. Open to graduate students working toward doctoral degrees in economics and undergraduates majoring in economics, finance, mathematics, statistics, or computer science.

Benefits Willing to complete paperwork for educational credit.
Contact Write or through World Wide Web site Recruitment Section. No phone calls. Applicants must submit application on line. Application deadline: March 1. World Wide Web: http://www.federalreserve.gov.

GEOSCIENTISTS-IN-THE-PARKS PROGRAM, GEOLOGIC RESOURCES DIVISION, NATIONAL PARK SERVICE
12795 West Almeda Parkway
Lakewood, Colorado 80228

General Information The Geologic Resources Division provides geologic expertise to National Parks and coordinates the Geologist-in-the-Parks Program. Established in 1995. Division of United States National Park Service, Washington, District of Columbia. Number of internship applications received each year: 300.

Internships Available ▶ *1–4 earth scientists/geologists:* responsibilities include interpreting area geology, producing educational materials, or assisting in resource management. Candidates should have ability to work independently, knowledge of field, oral communication skills, self-motivation, strong interpersonal skills. Duration is flexible. Unpaid. Open to college juniors, college seniors, recent college graduates, graduate students. ▶ *1 geologist or geology intern:* responsibilities include assisting in evaluating and coordinating growing geoscience program. Candidates should have college courses in field, oral communication skills, self-motivation, strong interpersonal skills, written communication skills. Duration is negotiable for summer. Unpaid. Open to college juniors, college seniors, recent college graduates, graduate students. ▶ *1 geologist/guide (park interpreter):* responsibilities include presenting volcano talks, staffing visitor center, interpretive roving, collecting park entrance fees, special projects on geologic interpretation and resource management. Candidates should have ability to work independently, college courses in field, knowledge of field, oral communication skills, self-motivation, interest and/or experience in interpretation and/or education. Duration is May-August. Position available as unpaid or at stipend of $7 per day up to $2500 for 12 weeks. Open to college juniors, college seniors, recent college graduates, graduate students. ▶ *20–100 geologist/hydrologists/air quality specialists:* responsibilities include basic interpretation of the area's physical and integrated natural resources to park visitors; conducting inventories and monitoring geologic features and sites; identifying, cataloging, and caring for geologic specimens; incorporating geology (e.g., information, protection of special features, resource management, hazards) into park actions and planning documents; summarizing scientific literature; developing informative museum or visitor displays; writing teacher guides; mapping geologic resources; and conducting research (e.g., in stratigraphy, slope stability, sedimentology, volcanology, paleontology, caves, soil). Candidates should have ability to work independently, college courses in field, oral communication skills, self-motivation, strong interpersonal skills, written communication skills. Duration is 1–9 months. Position available as unpaid or paid. Open to college freshmen, college sophomores, college juniors, college seniors, recent college graduates, graduate students. ▶ *1 interpreter (park guide):* responsibilities include providing technical paleontological assistance on paleo projects, excavations, inventories, monitoring, curation, measuring stratigraphic sections, and paleo databases. Candidates should have ability to work independently, ability to work with others, declared college major in field, organizational skills, self-motivation. Duration is one summer. Unpaid. Open to college juniors, college seniors, recent college graduates, graduate students. ▶ *1 physical science/geology intern:* responsibilities include providing assistance with one or more physical science projects which vary from year to year; may include geologic mapping, paleontological sampling, glacier data collection, water quality monitoring, and evaluating impacts from air pollution. Candidates should have ability to work independently, ability to work with others, analytical skills, declared college major in field, organizational skills, self-motivation. Duration is early May to late September. Position available as unpaid or paid. Open to college juniors, college seniors, recent college graduates, graduate students. ▶ *1–50 researcher/resource managers:* responsibilities include conducting research projects in stratigraphy, slope stability, sedimentology, groundwater hydrology, geomorphology, or volcanology. Candidates should have ability to work independently, ability to work with others, declared college major in field, knowledge of field, research skills, self-

motivation. Duration is flexible. Stipend of $7 per day up to $2500 for 12 weeks of work. Open to graduate students. International applications accepted.
Benefits Free housing, willing to complete paperwork for educational credit.
Contact Through World Wide Web site Judy Geniac, GIP Program Manager. Phone: 303-969-2015. Fax: 303-987-6792. E-mail: judy_geniac@nps.gov. Applicants must submit materials as detailed on Web site. Applications are accepted continuously. World Wide Web: http://www2.nature.nps.gov/grd/geojob.

HOUSE EDUCATIONAL PROGRAMS
45A State Office Building
St. Paul, Minnesota 55155

General Information Office that provides educational experiences in the legislative process. Established in 1975. Number of employees: 1. Division of Minnesota House of Representatives, St. Paul, Minnesota. Number of internship applications received each year: 75.
Internships Available ▶ *25–50 legislative interns:* responsibilities include research, corresponding, writing news releases, designing or compiling surveys, telephoning, providing constituent services, monitoring committee meetings, or following the status of a bill. Candidates should have ability to work with others, office skills, oral communication skills, organizational skills, personal interest in the field, research skills, written communication skills. Duration is 3–5 months. Unpaid. Open to recent high school graduates, college freshmen, college sophomores, college juniors, college seniors, recent college graduates, graduate students, law students, career changers, individuals reentering the workforce. International applications accepted.
Benefits On-the-job training, opportunity to attend seminars/ workshops, willing to act as a professional reference, willing to complete paperwork for educational credit, willing to provide letters of recommendation.
Contact Write, call, fax, or e-mail Josh D. Gackle, Educational Programs Coordinator. Phone: 651-296-7452. Fax: 651-215-3903. E-mail: josh.gackle@house.mn. In-person interview recommended (telephone interview accepted). Applicants must submit a formal organization application, resume. Applications are accepted continuously. World Wide Web: http://www.house.leg.state.mn.us.

ILLINOIS LEGISLATIVE STAFF INTERNSHIP PROGRAM
University of Illinois, 1 University Plaza, MS 478
Springfield, Illinois 62703-5407

General Information Program providing experience in a legislative environment. Established in 1963. Number of employees: 254. Number of internship applications received each year: 100.
Internships Available ▶ *45–55 graduate public service interns.* Candidates should have ability to work independently, ability to work with others, computer skills, oral communication skills, writing skills. Duration is 21 months. $850 per month during the academic months; $1700 per month during the summer. Open to recent college graduates, graduate students, law students. ▶ *20 partisan staff interns:* responsibilities include researching issues, drafting bills, analyzing bills and agency budget requests to prepare for committee and floor action; providing general staff work for the party they serve. Candidates should have oral communication skills, writing skills. Duration is August to June (10½ months). $2026 per month. Open to college seniors, recent college graduates, graduate students, law students. ▶ *3 research interns:* responsibilities include researching a variety of questions on public issues for legislators. Candidates should have oral communication skills, research skills, writing skills. Duration is August to June (10½ months). $2026 per month. Open to college seniors, recent college graduates, graduate students, law students. ▶ *1 science writing intern:* responsibilities include answering a variety of inquiries from legislators and publishing articles on scientific topics in legislative newsletter. Candidates should have college courses in field, oral communication skills, research skills, writing skills. Dura-

tion is August to June (10½ months). $2026 per month. Open to college seniors, recent college graduates, graduate students, law students.
Benefits Health insurance, opportunity to attend seminars/ workshops, possible full-time employment, tuition assistance, willing to complete paperwork for educational credit, 8 hours of graduate credit.
Contact Write, call, fax, e-mail, or through World Wide Web site Ms. Kim Hayden, Acting Director of Graduate Intern Programs, University of Illinois, One University Plaza, MS 478, Springfield, Illinois 62703-5407. Phone: 217-206-6158. Fax: 217-206-7508. E-mail: aldrich.ann@uis.edu. In-person interview required. Applicants must submit a formal organization application, resume, academic transcripts, writing sample, three letters of recommendation. Application deadline: February 1. World Wide Web: http://ilsip.uis.edu.

INTERNATIONAL CITY/COUNTY MANAGEMENT ASSOCIATION
777 North Capitol Street, NE, Suite 500
Washington, District of Columbia 20002-4201

General Information Association that promotes and supports professional management of local governments, advocates the council-manager form of government, and collects and publishes data and information on local government, primarily in the U.S. Established in 1914. Number of employees: 115. Number of internship applications received each year: 200.
Internships Available ▶ *Environmental program interns:* responsibilities include working on grant- and contract-funded environmental projects; assisting with meetings, workshops, and conference planning; and preparing articles and case studies on local government environmental issues. Candidates should have college courses in field, computer skills, office skills, oral communication skills, self-motivation, writing skills. Duration is flexible. $10–$11 per hour. ▶ *Inquiry service interns:* responsibilities include receiving and responding to requests for information, reading and abstracting new documents to be added to database, and working on special research, writing, and general projects involving other departments. Candidates should have computer skills, oral communication skills, personal interest in the field, research skills, self-motivation, writing skills. Duration is flexible. $10–$11 per hour. ▶ *International interns:* responsibilities include assisting with recruiting for overseas assignments; researching and writing for quarterly newsletter, arranging seminars, study tours, and on-the-job training for overseas officials. Duration is flexible. $9–$11 per hour. ▶ *Management information publications/urban management interns:* responsibilities include researching and writing brief descriptions of local government programs, making phone calls to collect information for the Software Reference Guide, and helping assemble mailings. Candidates should have computer skills, oral communication skills, research skills, self-motivation, written communication skills. Duration is flexible. $9–$11 per hour. Open to college freshmen, college sophomores, college juniors, college seniors, graduate students. International applications accepted.
Benefits Opportunity to attend seminars/workshops, willing to act as a professional reference, willing to complete paperwork for educational credit, willing to provide letters of recommendation.
Contact Write, fax, or e-mail Steven Taylor, Intern Coordinator, 777 North Capitol Street, NE Suite 500, Washington, District of Columbia 20002-4201. Fax: 202-962-3500. E-mail: staylor@icma.org. No phone calls. In-person interview recommended (telephone interview accepted). Applicants must submit a letter of interest, resume, two writing samples. Application deadline: March 1 for summer, July 31 for fall, November 1 for spring. World Wide Web: http://icma.org.

MASSACHUSETTS OFFICE OF CONSUMER AFFAIRS AND BUSINESS REGULATION
10 Park Plaza, Suite 5170
Boston, Massachusetts 02116

General Information State's watchdog charged with educating and informing consumers; oversees nine state agencies including the divisions of banks, insurance, telecommunications, and

Massachusetts Office of Consumer Affairs and Business Regulation (continued)
energy. Established in 1969. Number of employees: 44. Number of internship applications received each year: 100.
Internships Available ▶ *1–5 consumer information specialists:* responsibilities include receiving training in consumer protection laws, assisting in research, staffing consumer hot line, answering consumer e-mails and written correspndence. Candidates should have ability to work independently, analytical skills, computer skills, office skills, oral communication skills, organizational skills, research skills, self-motivation, strong interpersonal skills, strong leadership ability, writing skills. Duration is 6 months. Position available as unpaid or at $10 per hour. Open to college freshmen, college sophomores, college juniors, college seniors, graduate students, law students. International applications accepted.
Benefits On-the-job training, opportunity to attend seminars/workshops, willing to act as a professional reference, willing to complete paperwork for educational credit, willing to provide letters of recommendation.
Contact Write, call, fax, or e-mail Andrea Saia, Director of Consumer Education. Phone: 617-973-8700. Fax: 617-973-8799. E-mail: andrea.saia@state.ma.us. In-person interview recommended (telephone interview accepted). Applicants must submit a letter of interest, resume. Application deadline: March 15 for summer (recommended), July 1 for fall (recommended), November 15 for winter (recommended). World Wide Web: http://www.state.ma.us/consumer/.

MICHIGAN HOUSE OF REPRESENTATIVES–REPUBLICAN CAUCUS SERVICES
South House Office Building, 7th Floor
Lansing, Michigan 48909-7514

General Information State legislative office that provides services in media relations, research, legislative analysis, and planning events. Established in 1833. Number of employees: 250. Unit of Michigan Legislature, Lansing, Michigan, Lansing, Michigan. Number of internship applications received each year: 100.
Internships Available ▶ *5 central staff interns:* responsibilities include answering constituent concerns, assisting with district events and media relations, and performing detailed analysis of legislation. Candidates should have ability to work independently, ability to work with others, computer skills, office skills, oral communication skills, personal interest in the field, written communication skills. Duration is 1 semester. Unpaid. ▶ *1–30 representative staff interns:* responsibilities include scheduling, tracking legislation, and performing general office duties. Candidates should have office skills, oral communication skills, personal interest in the field, self-motivation, strong interpersonal skills, written communication skills. Duration is 1 semester. Unpaid. Open to high school students, recent high school graduates, college freshmen, college sophomores, college juniors, college seniors, graduate students. International applications accepted.
Benefits Names of contacts, possible full-time employment, willing to complete paperwork for educational credit, willing to provide letters of recommendation.
Contact Write, call, or fax Sean Ruban, Communications Analyst. Phone: 517-373-4698. Fax: 517-373-8402. In-person interview recommended (telephone interview accepted). Applicants must submit a formal organization application, letter of interest, resume. Applications are accepted continuously.

MICHIGAN STATE DEPARTMENT OF CIVIL SERVICE
400 South Pine Street
Lansing, Michigan 48909

General Information State government merit system administering all government operations. Established in 1946. Number of internship applications received each year: 1,200.
Internships Available ▶ *1,000 student interns:* responsibilities include working with engineers, doctors, attorneys, social workers, chemists, conservation officers, animal health inspectors, and other state job categories, including information technology, accounting, and marketing. Duration is flexible. Position available as unpaid or paid. Open to college freshmen, college

sophomores, college juniors, college seniors, graduate students, law students. International applications accepted.
Benefits Possible full-time employment, travel reimbursement, referrals provided, possibility of stipend.
Contact Write, call, fax, or through World Wide Web site Personnel Management Specialist/Student Programs. Phone: 517-335-0300. Fax: 517-241-8815. Applicants must submit a formal organization application, letter of interest, resume. Applications are accepted continuously. World Wide Web: http://www.state.mi.us/mdcs.

MISSOURI LEGISLATIVE INTERN PROGRAM
State Capitol
Jefferson City, Missouri 65101

General Information Program that selects the best students in related fields at Missouri institutions of higher education and provides interns an opportunity to gain valuable practical experience in the government process. Established in 1972. Unit of Missouri State Government, Jefferson City, Missouri. Number of internship applications received each year: 125.
Internships Available ▶ *100–125 legislative interns:* responsibilities include working with legislators and their staff. Candidates should have ability to work with others, computer skills, oral communication skills, research skills, written communication skills. Duration is 1 semester (part-time and full-time); January to mid-May. Unpaid. Open to college juniors, college seniors, recent college graduates, graduate students, law students. International applications accepted.
Benefits Opportunity to attend seminars/workshops, willing to act as a professional reference, willing to complete paperwork for educational credit, willing to provide letters of recommendation.
Contact Write, call, fax, or e-mail Representative Jeneé Lowe. Phone: 573-851-2437. Fax: 573-526-5759. E-mail: jlowe@services.state.mo.us. In-person interview recommended (telephone interview accepted). Applicants must submit a formal organization application, letter of interest, resume, academic transcripts, three letters of recommendation. Application deadline: December 1 for spring.

MONTANA LEGISLATIVE COUNCIL
PO Box 201706
Helena, Montana 59620-1706

General Information Council that provides legislating services. Established in 1957. Number of employees: 55. Unit of Montana Legislature, Helena, Montana. Number of internship applications received each year: 11.
Internships Available ▶ *11 interns:* responsibilities include assisting legislators. Candidates should have college course in general government. Duration is January to April (in odd-numbered years). Unpaid. Open to college juniors, college seniors, only those enrolled in a Montana school.
Benefits On-the-job training, willing to complete paperwork for educational credit.
Contact Write, call, fax, or e-mail David D. Bohyer, Director, Research and Policy Analysis. Phone: 406-444-3064. Fax: 406-444-3036. E-mail: dbohyer@state.mt.us. Applicants must submit application materials to intern coordinator at the college or university. Application deadline: November 1 of even-numbered year (preferred). World Wide Web: http://www.leg.state.mt.us.

MONTGOMERY COUNTY COMMISSION FOR WOMEN
401 North Washington Street, Suite 100
Rockville, Maryland 20850

General Information Government unit that conducts research and advocacy activities for women's issues, and operates a counseling and career center primarily for women. Established in 1972. Number of employees: 18. Department of Montgomery County Government, Rockville, Maryland. Number of internship applications received each year: 25.
Internships Available ▶ *7–8 counseling interns:* responsibilities include providing individual psychosocial or career counseling to adults; co-leading groups; special projects. Candidates should have college degree in related field, knowledge of field, plan to

pursue career in field, self-motivation, strong interpersonal skills. Duration is 2 semesters (20 hours per week). Unpaid. Open to individuals enrolled in a graduate-level program for counseling or social work who are using this experience as part of a formal practicum or internship approved by their university for credit. ▶ *4–6 information and referral specialists:* responsibilities include providing intake for counseling center; making referrals to local resources; assisting individuals in person and by phone find information and resources to meet their needs. Candidates should have computer skills, oral communication skills, personal interest in the field, research skills, strong interpersonal skills. Duration is 1–2 semesters. Unpaid. Open to college seniors, recent college graduates, career changers, individuals reentering the workforce.

Benefits Formal training, on-the-job training, opportunity to attend seminars/workshops, willing to act as a professional reference, willing to complete paperwork for educational credit, willing to provide letters of recommendation, supervision for university-based practica and internships.

Contact Write, call, fax, or e-mail Janice Herold, Clinical Supervisor. Phone: 240-777-8317. Fax: 301-279-1318. E-mail: janice.herold@co.mo.md.us. In-person interview required. Applicants must submit a resume, two personal references, letter of interest that indicates time of availability. Applications are accepted continuously. World Wide Web: http://www.montgomerycountymd.gov/cfw.

NATIONAL SECURITY AGENCY
9800 Savage Road
Fort George G. Meade, Maryland 20755-6779

General Information Federal government agency that provides foreign signals intelligence to decision-makers and protects U.S. national security information systems. Established in 1952. Number of internship applications received each year: 1,800.

Internships Available ▶ *Computer science interns:* responsibilities include performing a variety of programming and analysis functions, including systems design, computer security research, systems programming, computer security systems design, applications analysis, application, and evaluation. Candidates should have ability to work independently, ability to work with others, college courses in field, knowledge of field, personal interest in the field, minimum GPA of 3.0 preferred. Duration is June through August 31. $29,130 per year. Open to college juniors, graduate students. ▶ *Electrical or computer engineering interns:* responsibilities include working as part of a small team to develop advanced communication security and foreign signals intelligence collection and processing systems, including fundamental research through advanced development, small to large system design and prototype development, developmental test and evaluation, field installation, and operational support. Candidates should have ability to work independently, ability to work with others, college courses in field, minimum GPA of 3.0 preferred. Duration is June through August 31. $29,130 per year. Open to college juniors, graduate students. ▶ *4 foreign language summer program interns.* Candidates should have language skills as determined. Duration is 12 weeks. $14 per hour. Open to college juniors, college seniors, graduate students. ▶ *16 intelligence analyst interns.* Candidates should have college major in political science, history, or international relations. Duration is 12 weeks. $14 per hour. Open to college juniors, college seniors, graduate students. ▶ *25–35 mathematics interns:* responsibilities include using advanced concepts to solve cryptologic problems and helping develop and evaluate code and cipher systems. Candidates should have ability to work independently, ability to work with others, college courses in field, personal interest in the field, minimum 3.5 GPA. Duration is June through August 31. $14–$24 per hour. Open to college juniors, graduate students, exceptional mathematics students in their freshman or sophomore year of college.

Benefits Opportunity to attend seminars/workshops, possible full-time employment, travel reimbursement, willing to complete paperwork for educational credit, annual and sick leave.

Contact Write, fax, e-mail, or through World Wide Web site Julie Darling, Summer Program Manager, 9800 Savage Road, Attention: MB3, Suite 6779, PO Box 1661, Fort George G. Meade, Maryland 20755-6779. Phone: 800-669-0703. Fax: 410-854-4593.

E-mail: jdarl2@nsa.gov. In-person interview required. Applicants must submit a resume, academic transcripts, 2 letters of recommendation (for mathematics interns); security processing required. Application deadline: October 15 for summer mathematics interns, November 15 for all other positions. World Wide Web: http://www.nsa.gov.

NEW YORK DEPARTMENT OF CITYWIDE ADMINISTRATIVE SERVICES
1 Center Street, 24th Floor, Rooms 24-25
New York, New York 10007

General Information Program addressing issues in New York City government. Established in 1969. Number of employees: 6. Division of New York City Government, New York, New York. Number of internship applications received each year: 250.

Internships Available ▶ *25 government scholars program interns:* responsibilities include assisting with administrative problem solving, research and policy consultation; planning direct service delivery; and attending weekly seminars that examine crucial issues facing city government. Duration is 10 weeks. $3535 per duration of internship. Open to college sophomores, college juniors. ▶ *25 urban fellows program interns:* responsibilities include assisting with policy analysis and review, direct service delivery, fieldwork, and computer applications; and working in areas such as human services, criminal justice, health, housing, transportation, and economic development. Duration is 9 months. $25,000 per duration of internship. Open to recent college graduates, graduate students, individuals within 2 years of college graduation. Candidates for all positions should have ability to work independently, computer skills, oral communication skills, personal interest in the field, self-motivation, strong interpersonal skills, strong leadership ability, writing skills.

Benefits Job counseling, names of contacts, opportunity to attend seminars/workshops, possible full-time employment, willing to provide letters of recommendation.

Contact Write, call, fax, or through World Wide Web site Ms. Barbara Simmons, Director of Fellowship Programs. Phone: 212-669-3695. Fax: 212-669-3688. Applicants must submit a formal organization application, letter of interest, resume, academic transcripts, two writing samples, two letters of recommendation, application available via Web site. Application deadline: January 3 for government scholars, January 10 for urban fellows. World Wide Web: http://www.ci.nyc.ny.us/html/dcas/html/intern/html.

NEW YORK STATE ASSEMBLY INTERNS COMMITTEE
104-A Legislative Office Building
Albany, New York 12248

General Information Program that seeks to provide experiential learning for students and services to elected members and staff of the New York State Assembly. Established in 1971. Number of employees: 6. Unit of New York State Assembly, Albany, New York. Number of internship applications received each year: 190.

Internships Available ▶ *10 graduate interns:* responsibilities include performing research necessary to the development of legislative issues for standing committees and commission offices. Candidates should have research skills, self-motivation, strong interpersonal skills, C+ average, strong interest in state government. Duration is January to June. $11,500 per duration of internship. Open to students within one year of graduating from graduate school and recent graduates from graduate school. ▶ *150 session interns:* responsibilities include participating in the daily operation of a state legislator's office; attending Assembly sessions, committee meetings, and public hearings; and researching proposed legislation and constituent problems. Candidates should have ability to work independently, self-motivation, strong interpersonal skills, writing skills, C+ average, interest in state government. Duration is January to mid-May. $3500 per duration of internship. Open to college juniors, college seniors, college sophomores of exceptional academic standing. International applications accepted.

Benefits Formal training, health insurance, job counseling, names of contacts, on-the-job training, opportunity to attend seminars/workshops, possible full-time employment, willing to act as a

New York State Assembly Interns Committee (continued)
professional reference, willing to complete paperwork for educational credit, willing to provide letters of recommendation.
Contact Write, call, fax, e-mail, or through World Wide Web site James A. Murphy, Director. Phone: 518-455-4704. Fax: 518-455-4705. E-mail: intern@assembly.state.ny.us. Applicants must submit a formal organization application, letter of interest, resume, academic transcripts, writing sample, two letters of recommendation, letter from college/university authorizing internship. Application deadline: November 1. World Wide Web: http://assembly.state.ny.us:/internship/.

NEW YORK STATE COUNCIL ON THE ARTS
175 Varick Street, 3rd Floor
New York, New York 10014

General Information State agency engaged in the funding of nonprofit cultural organizations. Established in 1960. Number of employees: 40. Unit of State of New York, Albany, New York. Number of internship applications received each year: 15.
Internships Available ▶ *Staff support services interns:* responsibilities include a variety of clerical work, including writing, drafting, and data entry; directing staff support services; recruiting and working with placement institutions; and serving as staff representative to agency and outside entities. Duration is flexible. Unpaid. Open to college freshmen, college sophomores, college juniors, college seniors, graduate students, individuals reentering the workforce.
Benefits Willing to complete paperwork for educational credit.
Contact Write, call, or fax Ms. Marnee Geller, Personnel Associate, 175 Varick Street, 3rd floor, New York, New York 10014. Phone: 212-627-2989. Fax: 212-620-5911. In-person interview required. Applicants must submit a letter of interest, resume. Applications are accepted continuously. World Wide Web: http://www.nysca.org.

NEW YORK STATE SENATE STUDENT PROGRAMS OFFICE
State Capitol, Room 416, 90 South Swan Street
Albany, New York 12247

General Information Program promoting public service career options with the legislature. Established in 1965. Number of employees: 2. Unit of New York State Senate-The State Legislature, Albany, New York.
Internships Available ▶ *1 James L. Biggane Finance Fellow:* responsibilities include placement with senate finance/fiscal studies, working among a strong group of fiscal analysts, acquiring skills, and employing the previous life skills of the fellow. Candidates should have self-motivation, interest in finance. Duration is approximately 10 months (September through late July). $29,500 stipend for duration of fellowship. Open to persons at mid-career, at least 35 years of age at time of application. ▶ *1 Richard J. Roth Journalism Fellow:* responsibilities include researching and writing in Senate press office. Candidates should have analytical skills, editing skills, oral communication skills, research skills, writing skills, New York residency or enrollment at a New York state college or university. Duration is approximately 10 months (September through late July). $29,500 stipend for duration of fellowship. Open to recent college graduates, graduate students, graduating seniors with degree in journalism or communications. ▶ *1 Richard Wiebe Public Service Fellow:* responsibilities include expert-level participation in the routines and specialty areas of a legislative office, including research, analysis, synthesis, and legislative and/or constituent casework. Candidates should have analytical skills, editing skills, oral communication skills, research skills, written communication skills, New York residency or enrollment in a New York university. Duration is approximately 10 months (September through late July). $29,500 stipend for duration of fellowship. Open to graduate students, law students. ▶ *9 legislative fellows:* responsibilities include expert-level participation in the routines and specialty areas of a legislative office, including research, analysis, synthesis, and legislative and/or constituent casework. Candidates should have analytical skills, editing skills, oral communication skills, research skills, written communication skills,

New York residency or enrollment in a New York university. Duration is approximately 10 months (September through late July). $29,500 stipend for duration of fellowship. Open to individuals who have completed one year of graduate school. ▶ *61 session assistants:* responsibilities include assisting with legislative routines, analyses, and representation. Candidates should have analytical skills, editing skills, oral communication skills, research skills, written communication skills, New York residency or enrollment in a New York college or university. Duration is approximately 4 months (January through late April/early May). $3500 stipend for duration of internship. Open to college sophomores, college juniors, college seniors.
Benefits Some benefits provided.
Contact Write, call, fax, or e-mail James A. Utermark, Director. Phone: 518-455-2611. Fax: 518-426-6827. E-mail: students@senate.state.ny.us. In-person interview required. Applicants must submit a formal organization application, resume, academic transcripts, four writing samples, indication of preferred areas of placement, 3 academic references. Application deadline: last Friday in October for graduate fellows, first Friday in May for undergraduates. World Wide Web: http://www.senate.state.ny.us.

OFFICE OF LEGISLATIVE RESEARCH AND GENERAL COUNSEL
436 State Capitol Building
Salt Lake City, Utah 84114

General Information Office providing professional staff resources to the state legislature. Established in 1948. Number of employees: 65. Unit of Utah State Legislature, Salt Lake City, Utah. Number of internship applications received each year: 75.
Internships Available ▶ *45–65 legislative interns:* responsibilities include providing staff and research services to individual legislators. Candidates should have ability to work independently, analytical skills, college courses in field, computer skills, oral communication skills, organizational skills, personal interest in the field, research skills, self-motivation, strong interpersonal skills, written communication skills. Duration is 45 days. $1800 per duration of internship. Open to college juniors, college seniors, recent college graduates, preference given to students from Utah colleges.
Benefits Willing to act as a professional reference, willing to provide letters of recommendation, class credit.
Contact Write, fax, or e-mail Jerry D. Howe, Intern Coordinator, 436 State Capitol Building, Salt Lake City, Utah 89114. Fax: 801-538-1712. E-mail: jhowe@le.state.ut.us. No phone calls. Applicants must submit a resume, academic transcripts, writing sample, three personal references. Application deadline: October 31.

OFFICE OF THE ATTORNEY GENERAL OF MARYLAND, CONSUMER PROTECTION DIVISION
200 St. Paul Place
Baltimore, Maryland 21202

General Information State government agency. Number of employees: 46. Number of internship applications received each year: 300.
Internships Available ▶ *Mediation interns:* responsibilities include mediation of disputes filed by consumers against business entities such as retailers, repair shops, service providers, landlords, and home builders. Candidates should have ability to work with others, analytical skills, computer skills, oral communication skills, personal interest in the field, written communication skills. Duration is at least 1 semester. Paid. Open to college freshmen, college sophomores, college juniors, college seniors, graduate students, law students, career changers.
Benefits Willing to act as a professional reference, willing to complete paperwork for educational credit, willing to provide letters of recommendation, educational credit or $9 per day stipend.
Contact Write, call, or e-mail Ronnie Sanderson, Mediation Supervisor. Phone: 410-576-6355. Fax: 410-576-7040. E-mail: rsanderson@oag.state.md.us. In-person interview required. Applicants must submit a formal organization application, letter of interest, 2-3 personal references. Applications are accepted continuously. World Wide Web: http://www.oag.state.md.us.

OFFICE OF THE SPEAKER OF THE HOUSE
H-232 The Capitol
Washington, District of Columbia 20515

General Information Congressional Leadership Office including press, public affairs, administration, strategic planning, information technology, and executive scheduling departments. Number of employees: 35. Number of internship applications received each year: 100.

Internships Available ▶ *3–7 congressional interns:* responsibilities include critical research; preparing memos and press releases; attending hearings, briefings, and lectures; performing administrative duties; shadowing staffers to meetings; designing and improving computer systems. Candidates should have ability to work with others, computer skills, office skills, oral communication skills, research skills, self-motivation. Duration is 6 weeks to 3 months (180 working days maximum). Unpaid. Open to college freshmen, college sophomores, college juniors, college seniors, recent college graduates, graduate students, law students, juniors and seniors (preferred). International applications accepted.

Benefits Job counseling, names of contacts, on-the-job training, opportunity to attend seminars/workshops, willing to act as a professional reference, willing to complete paperwork for educational credit, willing to provide letters of recommendation, lecture series, photo opportunities, attendance at hearings and joint sessions of Congress.

Contact Call or e-mail Kristina Moore, Staff Assistant, Office of Administration. Phone: 202-225-0600. Fax: 202-226-1996. E-mail: kristina.moore@mail.house.gov. In-person interview recommended (telephone interview accepted). Applicants must submit a formal organization application, letter of interest, resume, two personal references, two letters of recommendation. Application deadline: April 15 for summer (recommended), July 15 for fall (recommended), November 15 for spring (recommended).

OFFICE OF U.S. SENATOR JEFF BINGAMAN
United States Senate
Washington, District of Columbia 20510

General Information U.S. Senate office. Number of employees: 50. Number of internship applications received each year: 30.

Internships Available ▶ *3–6 fall and spring interns:* responsibilities include writing letters, conducting research, and greeting constituents. Duration is 4 months. Unpaid. ▶ *10–16 summer interns:* responsibilities include writing letters, conducting research, and greeting constituents. Duration is 5–6 weeks. Position available as unpaid or at $600 per duration of internship. Candidates for all positions should have computer skills, office skills, oral communication skills, self-motivation, strong interpersonal skills, writing skills. Open to undergraduates who are residents of or attending college in New Mexico.

Benefits On-the-job training, opportunity to attend seminars/workshops, willing to act as a professional reference, willing to complete paperwork for educational credit, willing to provide letters of recommendation, possibility of paid housing (summer interns).

Contact Write, call, fax, e-mail, or through World Wide Web site David Pike, Intern Coordinator. Phone: 202-224-5521. Fax: 202-224-2852. E-mail: david_pike@bingaman.senate.gov. Applicants must submit a formal organization application, resume, writing sample, three letters of recommendation. Application deadline: March 31 for summer; continuous for fall and spring. World Wide Web: http://bingaman.senate.gov.

OHIO STATE PARKS
1952 Belcher, Building C-3
Columbus, Ohio 43224

General Information State agency overseeing the operation of 73 state parks. Established in 1949. Number of employees: 3,000. Division of Ohio Department of Natural Resources, Columbus, Ohio.

Internships Available ▶ *100–200 adopt-a-trail volunteers:* responsibilities include adopting a trail to maintain on a regular basis. Candidates should have ability to work independently, ability to work with others, knowledge of field, oral communication skills, personal interest in the field, self-motivation. Duration is flexible, up to 1 year. Unpaid. Open to high school students, recent high school graduates, college freshmen, college sophomores, college juniors, college seniors, recent college graduates, graduate students, law students, career changers. ▶ *100–300 campground hosts:* responsibilities include welcoming people, performing public relations work, helping maintain campgrounds, and leading group activities. Candidates should have ability to work independently, analytical skills, oral communication skills, organizational skills, personal interest in the field, self-motivation, strong interpersonal skills, strong leadership ability. Duration is up to 6 months (April 1 to October 31). Unpaid. Open to college juniors, college seniors, recent college graduates, career changers, retired people, avid campers. ▶ *Green teens:* responsibilities include working in state parks, assisting staff with interpretive programs, trail maintenance, leading youth groups on hiking trips, and light maintenance. Candidates should have ability to work independently, oral communication skills, personal interest in the field, self-motivation, strong interpersonal skills. Duration is flexible; can be year-round depending on projects. Unpaid. Open to high school students, individuals 12 to 18 years of age with parental permission. ▶ *200–400 groups volunteers:* responsibilities include working with various groups including the camera club, garden club, horseman's groups, and scouts in trail maintenance and park beautification. Candidates should have ability to work independently, knowledge of field, oral communication skills, personal interest in the field, self-motivation, strong interpersonal skills, strong leadership ability. Duration is flexible, up to 1 year. Unpaid. Open to high school students, recent high school graduates, college freshmen, college sophomores, college juniors, college seniors, recent college graduates, graduate students, law students, career changers. ▶ *Individual volunteers-in-parks:* responsibilities include a wide variety of work opportunities in state parks and nature centers designed to meet the needs of the individual and the park/nature center. Candidates should have ability to work independently, knowledge of field, oral communication skills, personal interest in the field, self-motivation, strong interpersonal skills. Duration is flexible; can be year-round. Unpaid. Open to recent high school graduates, college freshmen, college sophomores, college juniors, college seniors, recent college graduates, graduate students, career changers, individuals reentering the workforce. International applications accepted.

Benefits Formal training, housing at a cost, job counseling, on-the-job training, opportunity to attend seminars/workshops, willing to act as a professional reference, willing to complete paperwork for educational credit, willing to provide letters of recommendation, worker's compensation, opportunity to learn first-hand about careers in natural resources and parks.

Contact Write, call, fax, or e-mail Mr. Jim Henahan, Community Partnerships Manager. Phone: 614-265-6561. Fax: 614-261-8407. E-mail: jim.henahan@dnr.state.oh.us. In-person interview recommended (telephone interview accepted). Applicants must submit a formal organization application, letter of interest, resume, three letters of recommendation. Applications are accepted continuously. World Wide Web: http://www.ohiostateparks.org.

SAN MATEO COUNTY PLANNING AND BUILDING DIVISION
455 County Center
Redwood City, California 94063

General Information Government division that regulates land use and development in unincorporated San Mateo county. Established in 1856. Number of employees: 50. Division of County of San Mateo, Redwood City, California. Number of internship applications received each year: 5.

Internships Available ▶ *1–2 planning interns:* responsibilities include assisting and coordinating various current planning research projects. Candidates should have ability to work independently, analytical skills, declared college major in field, oral communication skills, research skills, writing skills. Duration is flexible. Unpaid. Open to college freshmen, college sophomores, college juniors, college seniors, recent college graduates. ▶ *3–5 research interns:* responsibilities include assisting with literature and telephone surveys, organizing and interpreting data, writing let-

San Mateo County Planning and Building Division (continued)

ters and reports, and some clerical work on a variety of projects in Long Range Planning and Current Planning departments. Candidates should have ability to work with others, analytical skills, oral communication skills, personal interest in the field, research skills, written communication skills. Duration is 10 weeks to 1 year. Unpaid. Open to college juniors, college seniors, recent college graduates, graduate students, career changers. International applications accepted.

Benefits Names of contacts, on-the-job training, opportunity to attend seminars/workshops, willing to complete paperwork for educational credit, willing to provide letters of recommendation.

Contact Write, call, or fax Dave Holbrook, Senior Planner/ Internship Coordinator. Phone: 650-363-4161. Fax: 650-363-4849. In-person interview recommended (telephone interview accepted). Applicants must submit a letter of interest, resume. Applications are accepted continuously. World Wide Web: http://www.co. sanmateo.ca.us/planning.

SECURITIES AND EXCHANGE COMMISSION
450 5th Street, NW, M/S 0103
Washington, District of Columbia 20549

General Information Commission that regulates national securities markets, stockbrokers, investment companies, and investment advisors, and prescribes certain disclosure requirements for companies that issue stocks and securities to the public. Established in 1934. Number of employees: 3,000. Number of internship applications received each year: 1,000.

Internships Available ▶ *Advanced commitment program interns:* responsibilities include providing legal research and other assistance to staff attorneys. Candidates should have ability to work independently, analytical skills, knowledge of field, oral communication skills, personal interest in the field, plan to pursue career in field, writing skills. Duration is maximum of 14 months. Paid. Open to third-year law students, recent law student graduates without Bar membership. ▶ *5–25 research assistants:* responsibilities include providing research and other assistance to professional staff members. Candidates should have oral communication skills, personal interest in the field, research skills, self-motivation, writing skills. Duration is 8-12 weeks in summer. Position available as unpaid or at $550–$650 per week. Open to college freshmen, college sophomores, college juniors, college seniors. ▶ *Student observer program interns:* responsibilities include assisting attorneys in research and memoranda of legal cases. Candidates should have ability to work independently, analytical skills, oral communication skills, plan to pursue career in field, research skills, written communication skills. Duration is 10 weeks. Unpaid. Open to third-year law students. ▶ *40–100 summer honors program interns:* responsibilities include participating in topical seminars on various aspects of federal securities laws, taking part in a series of educational lectures and meetings, and working with an assigned attorney on a variety of projects. Candidates should have ability to work independently, analytical skills, personal interest in the field, research skills, self-motivation, writing skills. Duration is 10 weeks. $650–$750 per week. Open to first- and second-year law students. International applications accepted.

Benefits Formal training, job counseling, names of contacts, on-the-job training, opportunity to attend seminars/workshops, possible full-time employment, travel reimbursement, willing to complete paperwork for educational credit, willing to provide letters of recommendation.

Contact Write, call, fax, e-mail, or through World Wide Web site Jodi Wells, Recruiting Assistant. Phone: 202-942-7320. Fax: 202-942-9619. E-mail: recruit@sec.gov. In-person interview recommended (telephone interview accepted). Applicants must submit a letter of interest, resume, academic transcripts, three personal references, one 5-10 page writing sample (for legal interns). Application deadline: November 15 for 2nd year legal interns; March 1 for all other positions. World Wide Web: http://www.sec. gov/jobs.shtml.

SENATE REPUBLICAN POLICY COMMITTEE
347 Russell Senate Office Building
Washington, District of Columbia 20510

General Information Committee that assists U.S. Senators and their staffs in aspects of the legislative process, distributes legislative background papers, and provides closed-circuit broadcasting of Senate floor activities. Established in 1946. Number of employees: 17. Unit of United States Senate, Washington, District of Columbia. Number of internship applications received each year: 50.

Internships Available ▶ *3–4 legislative interns:* responsibilities include assisting the RPC staff with a full range of office tasks; answering phones and providing general clerical assistance, as well as conducting legislative research to assist in the compilation of policy papers and other timely projects. Candidates should have computer skills, editing skills, knowledge of field, office skills, organizational skills, personal interest in the field, research skills, self-motivation, strong interpersonal skills, writing skills, verbal communication skills. Duration is 1–2 semesters. $500 per month. Open to recent high school graduates, college freshmen, college sophomores, college juniors, college seniors, recent college graduates, graduate students, law students. International applications accepted.

Benefits Names of contacts, opportunity to attend seminars/ workshops, possible full-time employment, willing to act as a professional reference, willing to complete paperwork for educational credit, willing to provide letters of recommendation.

Contact Write, call, e-mail, or through World Wide Web site Craig Cheney, Administrative Director. Phone: 202-224-2946. E-mail: mailbox@rpc.senate.gov. Telephone interview required. Applicants must submit a formal organization application, letter of interest, resume, three letters of recommendation, one 3-to 5-page writing sample. Application deadline: March 15 for summer, July 1 for fall, November 30 for spring. World Wide Web: http://rpc. senate.gov.

SENATOR JAMES M. INHOFE
453 Russell Senate Office Building
Washington, District of Columbia 20510

General Information Congressional office representing the State of Oklahoma. Established in 1994. Number of employees: 24. Number of internship applications received each year: 30.

Internships Available ▶ *2–4 spring/fall interns:* responsibilities include administrative duties, correspondence, attending hearings, preparing reports, and running errands. Duration is 10 weeks. Unpaid. Open to college sophomores, college juniors, college seniors, recent college graduates, graduate students, law students, career changers. ▶ *10–12 summer interns:* responsibilities include meeting constituent requests, correspondence, attending hearings and briefings, research, and assisting Senator and staff as needed. Duration is 6 weeks. Position available as unpaid or at $1200 per duration of internship. Open to college sophomores, college juniors, college seniors, recent college graduates. Candidates for all positions should have oral communication skills, personal interest in the field, research skills, strong interpersonal skills, strong leadership ability, writing skills. International applications accepted.

Benefits Opportunity to attend seminars/workshops, willing to act as a professional reference, willing to complete paperwork for educational credit, willing to provide letters of recommendation.

Contact Write, call, e-mail, or through World Wide Web site Suzanne Meledeo, Intern Coordinator. Phone: 202-224-4721. E-mail: suzanne_meledeo@inhofe.senate.gov. Applicants must submit a formal organization application, letter of interest, resume, academic transcripts, writing sample, three personal references, three letters of recommendation. Application deadline: March 15 for summer, August 15 for fall, December 15 for spring. World Wide Web: http://www.senate.gov/~inhofe/.

SENATOR LARRY E. CRAIG
United States Senate
Washington, District of Columbia 20510-1203

General Information Personal office of Republican Senator from Idaho. Number of employees: 22. Number of internship applications received each year: 100.

Internships Available ▶ *5–6 legislative interns:* responsibilities include working with legislative correspondent to research issues; composing correspondence; attending committee hearings; sitting in and taking notes on meetings; and completing small projects; may also include opening, sorting, and delivering mail; answering phone; greeting constituents; running errands; and other clerical duties. Candidates should have ability to work independently, computer skills, oral communication skills, organizational skills, personal interest in the field, research skills, self-motivation, strong interpersonal skills, written communication skills. Duration is 1 semester. $1000 per month. Open to college freshmen, college sophomores, college juniors, college seniors, recent college graduates, graduate students, law students, Idahoans or students attending Idaho institutions (preferred).

Benefits On-the-job training, willing to act as a professional reference, willing to complete paperwork for educational credit, willing to provide letters of recommendation, DC political experience for Idaho students.

Contact Write, call, e-mail, or through World Wide Web site Christopher Hartwell, Intern Coordinator, Hart Building, Room 520, Washington 20510. Phone: 202-224-2752. Fax: 202-228-1067. E-mail: chris_hartwell@craig.senate.gov. In-person interview recommended (telephone interview accepted). Applicants must submit a formal organization application, letter of interest, resume, academic transcripts, 1-2 writing samples, 2-3 personal references. Application deadline: March 15 for summer (May-August), July 1 for fall (September-December), November 15 for spring (January-May). World Wide Web: http://craig.senate.gov.

SONOMA COUNTY ECONOMIC DEVELOPMENT BOARD
401 College Avenue, Suite D
Santa Rosa, California 95401-5119

General Information Public agency charged with developing policies and programs to enhance the local economy and quality of life. Established in 1957. Number of employees: 10. Department of County of Sonoma, Santa Rosa, California. Number of internship applications received each year: 600.

Internships Available ▶ *2 public policy interns:* responsibilities include researching the following areas: technology/connectivity policy, sustainable business practices, and high tech industry support policies and programs. Candidates should have ability to work independently, oral communication skills, self-motivation, strong interpersonal skills, writing skills. Duration is one year (beginning in summer). $36,600 per year. Open to college seniors, recent college graduates, graduate students, law students. International applications accepted.

Benefits Formal training, job counseling, names of contacts, on-the-job training, opportunity to attend seminars/workshops, willing to act as a professional reference, willing to complete paperwork for educational credit, willing to provide letters of recommendation, opportunity to work with leaders in business, government, and education.

Contact Write Ben G. Stone, Coordinator, 401 College Avenue, Suite D, Santa Rosa, California 95401-5148. E-mail: edb@sonoma-county.org. No phone calls. In-person interview required. Applicants must submit a letter of interest, resume. Application deadline: January 31. World Wide Web: http://www.sonoma-co.org.

SOUTH DAKOTA LEGISLATURE–LEGISLATIVE RESEARCH COUNCIL
500 East Capitol
Pierre, South Dakota 57501-5070

General Information Legislative service agency that provides nonpartisan research and legal services to the 105 members of the South Dakota legislature. Established in 1951. Number of employees: 25. Number of internship applications received each year: 40.

Internships Available ▶ *22 legislative interns:* responsibilities include serving as partisan staff to legislators, conducting research on issues facing the legislature, tracking and responding to legislators' constituent requests, monitoring and summarizing legislative meetings and legislation, and performing general office administration. Candidates should have office skills, organizational skills, research skills, self-motivation, strong interpersonal skills, writing skills. Duration is 7–8 weeks during January-March legislative session. $4000 per duration of internship. Open to college freshmen, college sophomores, college juniors, college seniors, graduate students, law students. International applications accepted.

Benefits Names of contacts, willing to act as a professional reference, willing to complete paperwork for educational credit, willing to provide letters of recommendation.

Contact Write or call Mr. David Ortbahn, Principal Research Analyst. Phone: 605-773-3251. In-person interview recommended (telephone interview accepted). Applicants must submit a formal organization application, academic transcripts, three letters of recommendation. Application deadline: October 15 for winter (January to March). World Wide Web: http://www.legis.state.sd.us.

STATE OF ILLINOIS, OFFICE OF THE GOVERNOR
½ State House
Springfield, Illinois 62706

General Information Governing agency of Illinois.

Internships Available ▶ *8–16 James H. Dunn, Jr. Memorial Fellowships:* responsibilities include gaining experience in various areas including policy analysis and program administration as part of a public sector management training program. Candidates should have ability to work with others, computer skills, office skills, oral communication skills, personal interest in the field, self-motivation. Duration is August 1 to July 31. $26,700 per year. Open to individuals possessing a bachelor's degree. ▶ *100 Michael Curry summer interns:* responsibilities include working in the Governor's Office and in various agencies under the Governor's jurisdiction learning, firsthand, the operations of Illinois State Government; placements in Springfield and Chicago. Candidates should have ability to work with others, computer skills, office skills, oral communication skills, writing skills. Duration is 10 weeks. $1200 per month. Open to college juniors, college seniors, recent college graduates, graduate students, law students, Illinois residents only. ▶ *2 Vito Marzullo Internships:* responsibilities include gaining experience in various areas including policy analysis and program administration as part of public sector management training program. Candidates should have ability to work with others, computer skills, office skills, oral communication skills, personal interest in the field, self-motivation. Duration is August 1 to July 31. $26,700 per year. Open to Illinois residents possessing a bachelor's degree.

Benefits Health insurance, on-the-job training, possible full-time employment, travel reimbursement, willing to act as a professional reference, willing to complete paperwork for educational credit, willing to provide letters of recommendation, life insurance, paid holidays, sick and vacation days (for full-year positions).

Contact Write, call, or through World Wide Web site Kathy Herrington, Internship Coordinator. Phone: 217-782-5213. In-person interview recommended (telephone interview accepted). Applicants must submit a formal organization application, academic transcripts, two writing samples, three letters of recommendation. Application deadline: January 31. World Wide Web: http://www.state.il.us/gov/officeinternship.htm.

STATE OF NEW MEXICO, OFFICE OF THE GOVERNOR
State Capitol Building, Suite 400
Santa Fe, New Mexico 87501

General Information Executive branch of state government. Number of employees: 40. Number of internship applications received each year: 50.

State of New Mexico, Office of the Governor (continued)

Internships Available ▶ *1–2 communications interns:* responsibilities include tracking current events, creating press releases, and holding press conferences. Candidates should have ability to work with others, declared college major in field, oral communication skills, plan to pursue career in field, research skills, written communication skills. Duration is 1 semester. Position available as unpaid or paid. Open to college juniors, college seniors, recent college graduates, graduate students. ▶ *1–2 constituent services interns:* responsibilities include constituent casework, including advocacy and liaison between state and federal agencies. Candidates should have oral communication skills, strong interpersonal skills, strong desire to help people. Duration is flexible. Position available as unpaid or paid. Open to college juniors, college seniors, recent college graduates, graduate students, career changers, individuals reentering the workforce. ▶ *1 executive administration intern:* responsibilities include general administration for the governor. Candidates should have computer skills, office skills, oral communication skills, organizational skills, strong interpersonal skills. Duration is 1 semester. Position available as unpaid or paid. Open to college juniors, college seniors, recent college graduates, graduate students, career changers, individuals reentering the workforce. ▶ *1–2 legal interns:* responsibilities include assisting Legal Counsel of Office of the Governor. Candidates should have analytical skills, college courses in field, knowledge of field, personal interest in the field, research skills, written communication skills. Duration is 1 semester. Position available as unpaid or paid. Open to college seniors, recent college graduates, graduate students, law students, individuals reentering the workforce. ▶ *1 legislative affairs intern:* responsibilities include research and administration. Candidates should have ability to work with others, oral communication skills, organizational skills, research skills, written communication skills. Duration is 1 semester. Position available as unpaid or paid. Open to college juniors, college seniors, recent college graduates, graduate students, law students. ▶ *1–3 public policy interns:* responsibilities include research and administration. Candidates should have ability to work independently, computer skills, office skills, organizational skills, research skills. Duration is 1 semester. Position available as unpaid or paid. Open to college juniors, college seniors, recent college graduates, graduate students.

Benefits On-the-job training, willing to act as a professional reference, willing to complete paperwork for educational credit, willing to provide letters of recommendation.

Contact E-mail or through World Wide Web site J.R. Morgan, Intern Coordinator. Phone: 505-467-2238. Fax: 505-467-2226. E-mail: jr.morgan@state.nm.us. In-person interview recommended (telephone interview accepted). Applicants must submit a formal organization application, resume, writing sample, personal reference, letter of recommendation. Application deadline: March 15 for summer, June 15 for fall, September 15 for spring. World Wide Web: http://www.governor.state.nm.us.

STATE OF SOUTH DAKOTA BUREAU OF PERSONNEL
500 East Capitol Avenue
Pierre, South Dakota 57501

General Information Bureau that administers the human resources management system for the State of South Dakota and its employees including recruitment and selection, job analysis, training, payroll compensation, and employee benefits. Number of employees: 65. Number of internship applications received each year: 2,000.

Internships Available ▶ *Interns:* responsibilities include positions in various divisions including wildlife and games, fish, and parks; see Web site for details. Position available as unpaid or paid. Open to college sophomores, college juniors, college seniors, graduate students.

Contact Write, call, fax, e-mail, or through World Wide Web site Bureau of Personnel. Phone: 605-773-3148. Fax: 605-773-4344. E-mail: bopinfo@state.ed.us. Applicants must submit a formal organization application, resume. Application deadline: February 3 for summer, July 19 for fall, November 1 for spring. World Wide Web: http://www.sttate.sd.us/bop.

UNITED STATES SECRET SERVICE
950 H Street, NW, Suite 7400
Washington, District of Columbia 20223

General Information Government office of investigative and protective operations. Established in 1865. Number of employees: 5,600. Unit of United States Department of Treasury, Washington, District of Columbia. Number of internship applications received each year: 130.

Internships Available ▶ *10–15 student volunteer interns:* responsibilities include assisting agents with various tasks and administrative duties. Candidates should have ability to work with others, college courses in field, office skills, oral communication skills, plan to pursue career in field, self-motivation. Duration is 1 semester. Unpaid. Open to college freshmen, college sophomores, college juniors, college seniors.

Benefits Job counseling, names of contacts, on-the-job training, possible full-time employment, willing to complete paperwork for educational credit, willing to provide letters of recommendation.

Contact Write or fax Trumaine Mathis, Human Resources Specialist. Fax: 202-406-5613. No phone calls. In-person interview recommended (telephone interview accepted). Applicants must submit a letter of interest, resume, background check required. Application deadline: January 15 for summer, April 15 for fall, August 15 for spring. World Wide Web: http://www.jobweb.org/employer/ussecret.htm.

U.S. SENATOR DIANNE FEINSTEIN
11111 Santa Monica Boulevard, Suite 915
Los Angeles, California 90025

General Information One of the four district offices representing Senator Feinstein in the state of California. Established in 1992. Number of employees: 8. Number of internship applications received each year: 20.

Internships Available ▶ *6–8 interns:* responsibilities include working with staff members, answering constituent inquiries, assisting with correspondence, and special projects. Candidates should have ability to work independently, ability to work with others, knowledge of field, office skills, oral communication skills, organizational skills, research skills, self-motivation, writing skills. Duration is May through August/September. Unpaid. Open to college freshmen, college sophomores, college juniors, college seniors. International applications accepted.

Benefits Names of contacts, on-the-job training, opportunity to attend seminars/workshops, possible full-time employment, willing to act as a professional reference, willing to complete paperwork for educational credit, willing to provide letters of recommendation.

Contact Write or call Olyvia Rodriguez, Intern Coordinator, 11111 Santa Monica Boulevard, Suite 915, Los Angeles, California 90025. Phone: 310-914-7300. In-person interview recommended (telephone interview accepted). Applicants must submit a formal organization application, letter of interest, resume, writing sample, three personal references. Application deadline: April 20. World Wide Web: http://www.feinstein.senate.gov.

U.S. SENATOR MAX BAUCUS
511 Hart Building
Washington, District of Columbia 20510

General Information Represents state of Montana in U.S. Senate. Established in 1978. Number of employees: 30.

Internships Available ▶ *6 legislative interns:* responsibilities include writing statements, attending hearings and briefings, and researching legislation. Candidates should have ability to work with others, organizational skills, personal interest in the field, research skills, self-motivation, writing skills. Duration is 1 semester or 1 summer. Unpaid. Open to college freshmen, college sophomores, college juniors, college seniors, recent college graduates, graduate students, law students.

Benefits Job counseling, on-the-job training, opportunity to attend seminars/workshops, possible full-time employment, willing to act as a professional reference, willing to complete paperwork for educational credit, willing to provide letters of recommendation.

Contact Write or call Nancy Hadley, Intern Coordinator. Phone: 202-224-2651. Applicants must submit a formal organization application, writing sample, two personal references. Applications are accepted continuously.

WASHINGTON STATE GOVERNOR'S INTERNSHIP PROGRAM
521 Capitol Way, South
Olympia, Washington 98504-7500

General Information State government. Established in 1985. Number of employees: 2. Unit of Washington State Department of Personnel, Olympia, Washington. Number of internship applications received each year: 25.

Internships Available ▶ *5–10 executive fellows:* responsibilities include reporting to or assisting mid-management at a professional or managerial level. Candidates should have college degree in related field, oral communication skills, organizational skills, strong interpersonal skills, strong leadership ability, writing skills. Duration is 1–2 years. $2249-$2831 (executive fellows I); $2468-$3134 (executive fellows II). Open to graduate students, law students, permanent state employees. ▶ *10–15 undergraduate interns:* responsibilities include working in information technology, social work, research and analysis, transportation, vocational rehabilitation, or special projects. Candidates should have computer skills, oral communication skills, self-motivation, strong interpersonal skills, writing skills. Duration is 3–6 months. $1873–$2148 per month. Open to college freshmen, college sophomores, college juniors, college seniors, permanent state employees. International applications accepted.

Benefits Formal training, health insurance, on-the-job training, opportunity to attend seminars/workshops, possible full-time employment, travel reimbursement, willing to act as a professional reference, willing to complete paperwork for educational credit, willing to provide letters of recommendation, vacation, sick leave, and other employee benefits.

Contact Write, call, fax, e-mail, or through World Wide Web site Heather Rehaume, Program Assistant. Phone: 360-664-6291. Fax: 360-586-4694. E-mail: heatherr@dop.wa.gov. In-person interview required. Applicants must submit a letter of interest, resume, academic transcripts, two letters of recommendation, 300-word essay (executive fellows only); supplemental questionnaire. Applications are accepted continuously. World Wide Web: http://hr.dop.wa.gov/gip.

YOUTH ADVOCACY AND INVOLVEMENT OFFICE, NORTH CAROLINA DEPARTMENT OF ADMINISTRATION
1319 Mail Service Center
Raleigh, North Carolina 27699-1319

General Information State government agency that serves as an advocate for children and youth; seeks to enhance the quality of life for North Carolina's children and youth through policy reviews, legislative recommendations, and positive intervention through leadership educational opportunities. Established in 1969. Number of employees: 9. Division of North Carolina Department of Administration, Raleigh, North Carolina. Number of internship applications received each year: 350.

Internships Available ▶ *75 interns.* Candidates should have knowledge of field, oral communication skills, personal interest in the field, strong interpersonal skills, written communication skills. Duration is 10 weeks. $6.75 per hour. Open to college freshmen, college sophomores, college juniors, college seniors, graduate students, law students, North Carolina residents only.

Benefits Formal training, job counseling, names of contacts, opportunity to attend seminars/workshops, willing to complete paperwork for educational credit, willing to provide letters of recommendation.

Contact Write, call, e-mail, or through World Wide Web site Karen Bass, Internship Coordinator. Phone: 919-733-9296. E-mail: karen.bass@ncmail.net. Telephone interview required. Applicants must submit a formal organization application, letter of interest, resume, academic transcripts. Application deadline: February 2 for summer. World Wide Web: http://www.doa.state.nc.us/doa/yaio/intern.htm.

REAL ESTATE AND RENTAL AND LEASING

GENERAL

CROWN CAPITAL FINANCIAL CORPORATION
540 Pacific Avenue
San Francisco, California 94133

General Information Commercial real estate/real estate merchant and mortgage banking organization. Established in 1977. Number of internship applications received each year: 200.
Internships Available ▶ *1–2 interns:* responsibilities include working directly for owner principals, assisting in commercial real estate investment and mortgage banking business. Candidates should have analytical skills, computer skills, personal interest in the field, self-motivation, strong interpersonal skills, writing skills. Duration is 3–6 months. $500–$1000 per month. Open to college sophomores, college juniors, college seniors, recent college graduates.
Benefits On-the-job training, willing to act as a professional reference, willing to complete paperwork for educational credit, willing to provide letters of recommendation, working directly with senior principals of the company.
Contact Write, fax, or e-mail David W. Yancey, President. Phone: 415-398-6330 Ext. 349. Fax: 415-398-6057. E-mail: dyancey@crowncapital.com. Telephone interview required. Applicants must submit a letter of interest, resume, academic transcripts, SAT scores. Application deadline: February 1 for spring, April 1 for summer, July 1 for fall, November 1 for winter. World Wide Web: http://crowncapital.com.

HARVEY PROPERTY MANAGEMENT COMPANY, INC.
6931 Arlington Road, Suite 500
Bethesda, Maryland 20814

General Information Commercial property management and development company. Established in 1987. Number of employees: 10. Number of internship applications received each year: 10.

Internships Available ▶ *1 commercial property management intern:* responsibilities include interaction with tenants, government officials, contractors, and owners; researching and establishing databases; learning all aspects of the property management business including legal and financial. Candidates should have ability to work independently, office skills, oral communication skills, personal interest in the field, plan to pursue career in field, research skills, written communication skills. Duration is 12–52 weeks. Unpaid. Open to high school students, college freshmen, college sophomores, college juniors, graduate students.

Benefits On-the-job training, opportunity to attend seminars/workshops, possible full-time employment, willing to act as a professional reference, willing to complete paperwork for educational credit, willing to provide letters of recommendation.

Contact Write, fax, or e-mail Avi Halpert, Vice President, Property Management. Fax: 301-907-0394. E-mail: avih@harveycompanies.com. No phone calls. In-person interview recommended (telephone interview accepted). Applicants must submit a resume, 2 business letters. Applications are accepted continuously.

RETAIL TRADE

GENERAL

ABC CARPET & HOME
888 Broadway
New York, New York 10003

General Information Home furnishings company. Established in 1889. Number of employees: 500. Number of internship applications received each year: 100.
Internships Available ▶ *2–3 furniture buying office interns:* responsibilities include writing purchase orders, following up on shipments, ticketing merchandise on floor, data entry, communication with manufacturers and staff. Candidates should have ability to work independently, oral communication skills, self-motivation, strong interpersonal skills, written communication skills. Duration is flexible. Stipend of $15 per day. Open to college freshmen, college sophomores, college juniors, college seniors. ▶ *2–3 human resources interns:* responsibilities include file maintenance and updating, wage surveys, job description projects, orientation video, newsletter articles, benefits surveys, and compensation projects. Candidates should have ability to work independently, computer skills, oral communication skills, organizational skills, self-motivation, strong interpersonal skills, written communication skills. Duration is flexible. Stipend of $15 per day. Open to college freshmen, college sophomores, college juniors, college seniors. ▶ *2–3 linens buying office interns:* responsibilities include writing purchase orders, following up on shipments, ticketing merchandise on floor, data entry, communication with manufacturers and store staff. Candidates should have ability to work independently, oral communication skills, self-motivation, strong interpersonal skills, written communication skills. Duration is flexible. Stipend of $15 per day. Open to college freshmen, college sophomores, college juniors, college seniors. ▶ *2–4 visual interns:* responsibilities include assisting visual merchandising team in floor displays. Candidates should have ability to work independently, oral communication skills, organizational skills, self-motivation, strong interpersonal skills. Duration is flexible. Stipend of $15 per day. Open to college freshmen, college sophomores, college juniors, college seniors, recent college graduates.
Benefits Possible full-time employment, willing to act as a professional reference, willing to complete paperwork for educational credit, willing to provide letters of recommendation.
Contact E-mail Carrie Gorman, Assistant Director. E-mail: hr@abchome.com. No phone calls. In-person interview recommended (telephone interview accepted). Applicants must submit a formal organization application, resume, must be able to work legally in the U.S. Applications are accepted continuously. World Wide Web: http://www.abchome.com.

BMW OF NORTH AMERICA, INC.
300 Chestnut Ridge Road
Woodcliff Lake, New Jersey 07677-7731

General Information Sales and marketing of automobiles, motorcycles, and parts. Established in 1976. Number of employees: 1,100. Subsidiary of BMW, AG, Munich, Germany. Number of internship applications received each year: 500.
Internships Available ▶ *10–12 interns:* responsibilities include positions in sales, engineering, finance, distribution, marketing, administration, service, MIS, and legal. Candidates should have analytical skills, college courses in field, computer skills, organizational skills, self-motivation, strong interpersonal skills, written com-munication skills. Duration is 3 months (minimum), usually summer, but possible opportunities throughout the year. $1076 bi-weekly. Open to college juniors, college seniors, law students. International applications accepted.
Benefits Formal training, job counseling, names of contacts, on-the-job training, travel reimbursement, willing to complete paperwork for educational credit, willing to provide letters of recommendation.
Contact Write, fax, or e-mail Intern Coordinator. Fax: 201-307-0992. E-mail: internships@bmwna.com. No phone calls. Applicants must submit a letter of interest, resume, in-person interview for U.S. applicants; telephone interview for international applicants. Application deadline: at least 4 months before desired start date. World Wide Web: http://www.bmwusa.com.

BRIDGESTONE/FIRESTONE, INC.
180 Sheree Boulevard, Suite 2000
Exton, Pennsylvania 19341

General Information Retail tire and automotive service provider. Established in 1900. Number of employees: 15. Division of Bridgestone Americas Holding, Inc., Nashville, Tennessee. Number of internship applications received each year: 100.
Internships Available ▶ *8–20 retail sales and management interns:* responsibilities include sales, customer satisfaction, following the development plan, and team building. Candidates should have declared college major in field, oral communication skills, plan to pursue career in field, self-motivation, strong interpersonal skills. Duration is June to August. $10–$12 per hour. Open to college juniors, college seniors. International applications accepted.
Benefits Formal training, health insurance, names of contacts, on-the-job training, possible full-time employment, willing to act as a professional reference, willing to complete paperwork for educational credit, willing to provide letters of recommendation.
Contact Write, call, fax, or e-mail Bob Smith, Manager of Recruiting and Retention. Phone: 610-594-5415. Fax: 610-594-6251. E-mail: rsmith@bfusa.com. In-person interview required. Applicants must submit a formal organization application, resume, academic transcripts, 2-3 personal references; pre-employment drug testing and physical required. Application deadline: May 15. World Wide Web: http://www.bfmastercare.com.

GRANDY FARM MARKET
PO Box 673
Grandy, North Carolina 27939

General Information Retail outlet for fruits and vegetables, frozen yogurt, and baked goods. Established in 1987. Number of employees: 25.
Internships Available ▶ *2–4 retail produce interns:* responsibilities include creating product displays, stocking, acting as rotation cashier, and providing customer service. Candidates should have ability to work independently, ability to work with others, oral communication skills, personal interest in the field, self-motivation. Duration is 4–6 months. $5.50–$6.50 per hour. Open to high school seniors, recent high school graduates, college freshmen, college sophomores, college juniors, college seniors, recent college graduates, graduate students. ▶ *2 retail produce trainees:* responsibilities include carrying out various tasks and responsibilities involved in the retail of fresh produce and baked goods; duties are similar to those in a supermarket, but in a farm market atmosphere. Candidates should have personal interest in the field, self-motivation, strong interpersonal skills. Duration is flexible

(prefer 6 months). $5.50–$6.50 per hour. Open to recent high school graduates, college freshmen, college sophomores, college juniors, college seniors, recent college graduates. International applications accepted.

Benefits Free housing, meals at a cost, on-the-job training, willing to act as a professional reference, willing to complete paperwork for educational credit, willing to provide letters of recommendation.

Contact Write, call, or e-mail Colon Grandy, Jr., Owner. Phone: 252-453-2658. E-mail: grandyfarmmkt@hotmail.com. Telephone interview required. Applicants must submit a formal organization application, resume, academic transcripts, three personal references, letter of recommendation. Application deadline: May 15.

THE HOME DEPOT, CORPORATE OFFICE
2455 Paces Ferry Road
Atlanta, Georgia 30339

General Information Retailer of hardware, home improvement, and garden/patio supplies. Established in 1979. Number of employees: 5,000. Number of internship applications received each year: 40.

Internships Available ▶ *8–12 Building Better Health Interns:* responsibilities include assisting in coordination of wellness events, facility supervision, instruction of fitness and nutrition classes, writing articles for newsletters, promoting wellness program through incentive and motivational programs, and coordinating community resources in the field. Candidates should have ability to work independently, knowledge of field, oral communication skills, self-motivation, strong interpersonal skills, written communication skills. Duration is 15 weeks, (40 hours per week). Position available as unpaid or at up to $1000 stipend at end of 15-week internship. Open to college juniors, college seniors, recent college graduates, graduate students, career changers. International applications accepted.

Benefits Free meals, job counseling, on-the-job training, willing to act as a professional reference, willing to complete paperwork for educational credit, willing to provide letters of recommendation.

Contact Write, call, fax, or e-mail Steven McLelland, Wellness Coordinator, 2455 Paces Ferry Road, Atlanta, Georgia 30339. Phone: 770-433-8211 Ext. 17133. Fax: 770-384-4123. E-mail: steven_mclelland@homedepot.com. In-person interview recommended (telephone interview accepted). Applicants must submit a formal organization application, resume, letter of recommendation. Application deadline: March 15 for summer, October 1 for spring.

INTERIOR DESIGN COLLECTIONS
39 East 12th Street, Suite 205
New York, New York 10003

General Information Multi-line sales company representing high-end interior product lines selling to interior designers and architects. Established in 1990. Number of employees: 3. Number of internship applications received each year: 60.

Internships Available ▶ *1–4 IDC associates:* responsibilities include client interaction on phone and at field/sales meetings; administration duties; computer work for customer contact; new client lists and rating; sample coordinating. Candidates should have ability to work independently, computer skills, office skills, oral communication skills, organizational skills, self-motivation, strong interpersonal skills. Duration is 6-12 weeks (2-4 days per week). Unpaid. Open to college sophomores, college juniors, college seniors, recent college graduates, graduate students, career changers. International applications accepted.

Benefits Formal training, job counseling, names of contacts, on-the-job training, opportunity to attend seminars/workshops, possible full-time employment, willing to act as a professional reference, willing to complete paperwork for educational credit, willing to provide letters of recommendation, in-town travel reimbursement; most lunch and job expenses paid.

Contact Write, call, or fax Xenia Psihas. Phone: 212-995-9154. Fax: 212-995-8288. Telephone interview required. Applicants must

submit a letter of interest, resume. Application deadline: February 28 for spring, March 30 for summer, July 30 for fall, November 30 for winter.

JC PENNEY COMPANY, INC.
6501 Legacy Drive
Plano, Texas 75024-3698

General Information Multibillion dollar organization with retail department stores, a catalog business, Eckerd Drug stores, and JC Penney Direct Marketing Services. Established in 1902. Number of employees: 3,600. Number of internship applications received each year: 5,000.

Internships Available ▶ *4 summer brand design interns:* responsibilities include developing and designing artwork, including prints, patterns, and graphic designs, to be utilized in a private brand strategy. Candidates should have college courses in field, oral communication skills, plan to pursue career in field, strong interpersonal skills, minimum 3.0 GPA (preferred), familiarity with U4ia textile design software (a plus). Duration is 10 weeks. $11.50 per hour. ▶ *12–18 summer information systems interns:* responsibilities include Internet technology, client/server technology, relational databases, and object-oriented technology. Candidates should have college courses in field, declared college major in field, plan to pursue career in field, minimum 3.0 GPA (preferred), experience with Visual Basic, C++, JAVA, HTML, and COBOL. Duration is 10 weeks. $16.50 per hour. ▶ *100 summer merchandise management interns:* responsibilities include participating in decision-making involving customer service, inventory flow, marketing, presentation, and merchandise. Candidates should have personal interest in the field, plan to pursue career in field, strong interpersonal skills, strong leadership ability, 3.0 minimum GPA (preferred), retail experience (a plus). Duration is 10 weeks. $11.50 per hour. Open to college juniors, college seniors. International applications accepted.

Benefits Formal training, opportunity to attend seminars/workshops, possible full-time employment, travel reimbursement and free housing for some positions.

Contact Write, call, fax, or through World Wide Web site Michael Silipo, College Relations Manager, PO Box 10001, Dallas 75301-8115. Phone: 972-431-2316. Fax: 972-431-2320. In-person interview required. Applicants must submit a formal organization application, letter of interest, resume, portfolio required for some positions. Application deadline: April 1. World Wide Web: http://www.jcpenney.com.

LANDS' END
5 Lands' End Lane
Dodgeville, Wisconsin 53595

General Information Direct merchant/e-commerce merchant of traditionally-styled classic casualwear for the family and products for bed and bath; accessories are offered to customers through regular mailing of catalogs and through the Internet. Established in 1963. Number of employees: 8,000. Number of internship applications received each year: 1,500.

Internships Available ▶ *1–2 Web design interns:* responsibilities include working with the Internet team in creating daily and weekly feature content for the business divisions or special projects, including banners, product page images, or content for affiliate programs; designing Internet-ready graphics, including GIFs, JPEGs, and animated GIFs. Candidates should have ability to work independently, college courses in field, computer skills, self-motivation, strong interpersonal skills, strong leadership ability. Duration is 3–6 months. $12–$15 per hour. ▶ *1–2 apparel design interns:* responsibilities include working with seasoned designers to learn how to design and develop product by interpreting concepts into themes, developing color, fabrication, silhouettes, and mood for upcoming seasons; conducting market research; and drawing flat sketches and illustrations. Candidates should have ability to work independently, college courses in field, strong interpersonal skills, understanding of textile construction, ability to do flat drawings and sketches. Duration is 3 months. $12 per hour. ▶ *2–3 art direction interns:* responsibilities include learning the process behind designing, developing and producing, and selling concepts and layouts; editing film and working with layout revisions; gaining exposure to the process behind a photo shoot. Candidates should have ability to work independently, college courses in field, experience in the field, self-motivation, strong interpersonal skills, strong leadership ability. Duration is 3–6 months. $12 per hour. ▶ *3 corporate fitness interns:* responsibilities include assisting with adult recreation leagues, tournaments, and wellness programs; teaching aerobics classes (land and water), doing fitness evaluations; supervising floor and pool area of the Activity Center; and educating employees on a variety of health-related topics. Candidates should have college courses in field, knowledge of field, self-motivation, strong interpersonal skills, strong leadership ability. Duration is 3 months. Paid. ▶ *1–2 employee services interns:* responsibilities include developing and implementing campus recruitment plans, attending job fairs, townhall events and open houses, and planning special events to attract segments of the population that would be interested in seasonal employment opportunities. Candidates should have ability to work independently, college courses in field, knowledge of field, strong interpersonal skills, strong leadership ability. Duration is June to December. $12 per hour. ▶ *4–6 information services interns:* responsibilities include developing programs and documentation, coding, testing, and debugging programs, and developing specifications and test plans. Candidates should have college courses in field, computer skills, self-motivation, strong interpersonal skills, strong leadership ability. Duration is 3–6 months. $15 per hour. ▶ *2–4 inventory interns:* responsibilities include pre-season planning and forecasting, extensive sales trend analysis, learning inventory concepts and strategies for direct marketing, and tracking the manufacturing process. Candidates should have ability to work independently, analytical skills, self-motivation, strong interpersonal skills, strong leadership ability. Duration is 3 months. $12 per hour. ▶ *3–6 marketing and MBA interns:* responsibilities include forecasting circulation, response, demand, advertising costs, and profits across multiple channels; and collecting, reporting, and analyzing data related to understanding customer behavior. Candidates should have analytical skills, college courses in field, computer skills, research skills, self-motivation, strong interpersonal skills. Duration is 3 months. $12–$25 per hour. ▶ *1–2 media relations interns:* responsibilities include working with either the product team or corporate team on public relations campaigns; developing and maintaining relationships with major national and business media; researching and writing public relation materials including fact sheets, captions, press releases, memos, and cover letters; and developing a media list and learning how to "pitch" a story to the media. Candidates should have ability to work with others, college courses in field, self-motivation, writing skills. Duration is 3 months. $12 per hour. ▶ *2–4 merchandising interns:* responsibilities include assisting merchants in driving specific categories through product development, developing competitive analysis for team reviews, and understanding the levers that affect the business. Candidates should have analytical skills, college courses in field, computer skills, knowledge of field, plan to pursue career in field, self-motivation, strong interpersonal skills. Duration is 3 months. $12 per hour. ▶ *3–5 operations management interns:* responsibilities include providing managerial support in distribution centers, taking on a leadership role within call centers operations, and coaching and developing an internal work force. Candidates should have ability to work independently, college courses in field, self-motivation, strong interpersonal skills, strong leadership ability. Duration is June to December. $12 per hour. ▶ *2–3 quality interns:* responsibilities include assisting with product and specification development, fit evaluation, and testing of fabrics. Candidates should have ability to work independently, college courses in field, self-motivation, strong interpersonal skills, strong leadership ability, background in clothing and textiles. Duration is 3 months. $12 per hour. ▶ *2–4 retail store management interns:* responsibilities include assisting with store operations including merchandising, monitoring inventory levels, accountability for overall operations, and setting up and executing store and advertising plans. Candidates should have ability to work independently, experience in the field, self-motivation, strong interpersonal skills, strong leadership ability. Duration is 3 months. $12 per hour. Open to college juniors, college seniors.

Benefits Formal training, job counseling, names of contacts, on-the-job training, opportunity to attend seminars/workshops,

possible full-time employment, travel reimbursement, willing to act as a professional reference, willing to complete paperwork for educational credit, willing to provide letters of recommendation, clothing/merchandise discounts, access to on-site fitness facility, payment of housing security deposit.
Contact Write, call, fax, or through World Wide Web site Regina Lord, Intern Coordinator, 5 Lands' End Lane, Dodgeville, Wisconsin 53595. Phone: 608-935-4928. Fax: 608-935-4831. In-person interview recommended (telephone interview accepted). Applicants must submit a resume, portfolio, video conference (where applicable), online application, 2-3 writing samples (for certain positions). Application deadline: March 1 for summer, August 1 for fall, December 1 for spring. World Wide Web: http://www.landsend.com.

RICH'S/LAZARUS/GOLDSMITH'S DEPARTMENT STORES
223 Perimeter Center Parkway
Atlanta, Georgia 30346

General Information Traditional retail department store that emphasizes dynamic store environments, diverse merchandise selection, and superior customer service. Established in 1867. Number of employees: 20,000. Unit of Federated Department Stores, Inc., Cincinnati, Ohio. Number of internship applications received each year: 600.
Internships Available ▶ *35 sales management interns:* responsibilities include management, visual merchandising, human resources, business analysis, and store-line support exposure. Candidates should have ability to work independently, ability to work with others, analytical skills, computer skills, knowledge of field, oral communication skills, organizational skills, personal interest in the field, plan to pursue career in field, self-motivation, strong leadership ability. Duration is 10 weeks. $13 per hour. Open to college sophomores, college juniors, college seniors. International applications accepted.
Benefits Formal training, on-the-job training, possible full-time employment, willing to act as a professional reference, willing to complete paperwork for educational credit, willing to provide letters of recommendation.
Contact Write, fax, e-mail, or through World Wide Web site Kate Coon-Linard, Manager, New Talent. Fax: 770-913-5114. E-mail: kcoon@fds.com. No phone calls. In-person interview required. Applicants must submit a resume. Application deadline: April 1 for summer. World Wide Web: http://www.retailology.com/college.

SAKS FIFTH AVENUE
611 Fifth Avenue
New York, New York 10022

General Information Retail company. Established in 1924. Number of employees: 1,400. Division of Saks, Inc., Birmingham, Alabama. Number of internship applications received each year: 3,500.
Internships Available ▶ *7–27 New York store interns:* responsibilities include all aspects of store-line retail, including customer service, operations, merchandising, management, and selling; 70% selling floor experience and 30% classes. Candidates should have analytical skills, knowledge of field, oral communication skills, organizational skills, strong interpersonal skills, strong leadership ability, problem-solving and decision-making skills, minimum GPA of 3.0, work experience (preferred). Duration is one fall (September to January); one summer (June to August). $10 per hour. Open to college juniors, college seniors, recent college graduates.
Benefits Formal training, housing at a cost, job counseling, meals at a cost, names of contacts, on-the-job training, opportunity to attend seminars/workshops, possible full-time employment, willing to act as a professional reference, willing to complete paperwork for educational credit, willing to provide letters of recommendation, discount shopping privilege.
Contact Write, call, fax, or e-mail Peter Goldschmidt, Internship Coordinator. Phone: 212-940-4910. Fax: 212-940-2992. E-mail: peter_goldschmidt@s5a.com. In-person interview required. Applicants

Saks Fifth Avenue (continued)

must submit a resume, academic transcripts, two personal references, cover letter. Application deadline: March 1 for fall, December 1 for summer.

SHERWIN-WILLIAMS
10740 C Broadway Avenue
Cleveland, Ohio 44125

General Information Company specializing in the sale of paint coatings and related products to wholesale and commercial markets. Established in 1866. Number of employees: 1,500. Unit of Sherwin-Williams Company, Cleveland, Ohio. Number of internship applications received each year: 300.
Internships Available ▶ *30–50 summer interns:* responsibilities include servicing customers; performing basic administrative tasks including processing audit applications, receiving payments on accounts, and processing paperwork; performing tasks assigned by manager, and preparing and providing written projects. Candidates should have college courses in field, oral communication skills, personal interest in the field, self-motivation, strong interpersonal skills, interest in sales/marketing as a career. Duration is 10–12 weeks. $8.50–$9 per hour. Open to college juniors, college seniors.
Benefits Formal training, names of contacts, on-the-job training, possible full-time employment, willing to act as a professional reference, willing to complete paperwork for educational credit, willing to provide letters of recommendation, management training program.
Contact Write, fax, e-mail, or through World Wide Web site Josh Dunn. Fax: 216-341-1032. E-mail: josh.dunn@sherwin.com. No phone calls. In-person interview required. Applicants must submit a formal organization application, letter of interest, resume. Applications are accepted continuously. World Wide Web: http://www.sherwin.com.

SHERWIN-WILLIAMS
10440 East Northwest Highway
Dallas, Texas 75238

General Information Division that distributes Sherwin-Williams branded architectural coatings, industrial maintenance products, industrial finishes, and related items. Established in 1866. Number of employees: 100. Division of The Sherwin-Williams Company, Cleveland, Ohio.
Internships Available ▶ *1–100 summer co-op interns:* responsibilities include working with customer service, merchandising, credit, and sales areas; assisting store manager in maintaining good customer relations, market development, and inventory management. Candidates should have oral communication skills, organizational skills, personal interest in the field, self-motivation, strong interpersonal skills, strong leadership ability. Duration is one summer (9-12 weeks). $8–$8.50 per hour. Open to college sophomores, college juniors, college seniors. International applications accepted.
Benefits Formal training, names of contacts, on-the-job training, opportunity to attend seminars/workshops, possible full-time employment, willing to complete paperwork for educational credit, willing to provide letters of recommendation.
Contact Write, call, fax, e-mail, or through World Wide Web site Ron Novak, Area Human Resources Manager. Phone: 214-553-

3938. Fax: 214-553-3937. E-mail: rdnovak@sherwin.com. In-person interview required. Applicants must submit a formal organization application, letter of interest, resume. Applications are accepted continuously. World Wide Web: http://www.sherwin-williams.com.

THE SOUTHWESTERN COMPANY
2457 Atrium Way
Nashville, Tennessee 37214

General Information Summer work program for college students. Established in 1855. Number of employees: 75. Division of Southwestern/Great American, Inc., Nashville, Tennessee.
Internships Available ▶ *Student sales interns.* Candidates should have ability to work independently, ability to work with others, oral communication skills, self-motivation, willingness to work hard. Duration is 12–14 weeks. Commission. Open to college freshmen, college sophomores, college juniors, college seniors, graduate students. International applications accepted.
Benefits Formal training, job counseling, on-the-job training, possible full-time employment, willing to complete paperwork for educational credit, willing to provide letters of recommendation, access to full-service placement office.
International Internships Available in Bristol, United Kingdom.
Contact Write, call, or through World Wide Web site Trey Campbell, Public Relations/Sales Promotions Manager. Phone: 615-391-2801. E-mail: trey.campbell@southwestern.com. In-person interview recommended (telephone interview accepted). Applicants must submit a formal organization application, letter of interest, resume, follow-up interviews. Application deadline: June 1. World Wide Web: http://www.southwestern.com.

THE WET SEAL, INC.
26972 Burbank
Foothill Ranch, California 92610

General Information Fashion retail company. Established in 1962. Number of employees: 525. Number of internship applications received each year: 60.
Internships Available ▶ *Interns.* Candidates should have ability to work independently, analytical skills, college courses in field, college degree in related field, computer skills, declared college major in field, editing skills, knowledge of field, office skills, oral communication skills, organizational skills, personal interest in the field, plan to pursue career in field, research skills, self-motivation, strong interpersonal skills, strong leadership ability, written communication skills. Unpaid. Open to college freshmen, college sophomores, college juniors, college seniors.
Benefits On-the-job training, possible full-time employment, willing to act as a professional reference, willing to complete paperwork for educational credit, willing to provide letters of recommendation.
Contact Write, call, fax, or e-mail Diana Dowell, Recruitment Coordinator. Phone: 949-699-4867. Fax: 949-699-4722. E-mail: diana.dowell@wetseal.com. In-person interview required. Applicants must submit a formal organization application, letter of interest, resume, proof of eligibility for internships from current school. Applications are accepted continuously. World Wide Web: http://www.wetsealinc.com.

TRANSPORTATION

GENERAL

AMERICA WEST AIRLINES
4000 East Sky Harbor Boulevard
Phoenix, Arizona 85034

General Information Major U.S. carrier. Established in 1983. Number of employees: 11,000. Number of internship applications received each year: 100.
Internships Available ▶ *Interns:* responsibilities include working in public relations, communications, marketing, sales, or finance.

Candidates should have analytical skills, college courses in field, computer skills, written communication skills. Duration is flexible. Position available as unpaid or paid. Open to college freshmen, college sophomores, college juniors, college seniors, graduate students.
Benefits Willing to complete paperwork for educational credit, travel stipend.
Contact Write, fax, or e-mail Connie Razza, Internship Coordinator. Fax: 480-693-8813. E-mail: employment@americawest.com. No phone calls. In-person interview required. Applicants must submit a letter of interest, resume. Applications are accepted continuously. World Wide Web: http://www.americawest.com.

UTILITIES

GENERAL

LORD INTERNATIONAL
PO Box 164
New Port Richey, Florida 35656

General Information Independent power producer of renewable electricity. Established in 1975. Number of employees: 20. Number of internship applications received each year: 20.
Internships Available ▶ *1–10 electrical engineering manager/trainees:* responsibilities include electrical engineering management training during the development process of utility grade renewable electric power plants in U.S. and Europe; planning, costing, plant development and operation management. Candidates should have college courses in field, oral communication skills, plan to pursue career in field, written communication skills. Duration is 1 year. Unpaid. Open to college seniors, recent college graduates, graduate students. ▶ *1–5 general manager (trainees/assistants):* responsibilities include learning electric utility industry operations, government and investor relations, and accounting and financial statement protection for new plants. Candidates should have ability to work independently, analytical skills, computer skills, editing skills, office skills, oral communication skills, organizational skills, personal interest in the field, plan to pursue career in field, self-motivation, strong leadership ability, written communication skills. Duration is 1 year. Unpaid. Open to college seniors, recent college graduates, graduate students. ▶ *1–10 investment officers:* responsibilities include assisting in creating all financial statements for initial power plant start-ups worldwide; entry level relations with investors during private placements. Candidates should have ability to work independently, college courses in field, organizational skills, written communication skills, major in finance. Duration is 1–2 years. Unpaid. Open to college seniors, graduate students, career changers. International applications accepted.
Benefits Names of contacts, opportunity to attend seminars/workshops, possible full-time employment, tuition assistance, willing to act as a professional reference, willing to complete paperwork for educational credit, willing to provide letters of recommendation.
International Internships Available.
Contact Write R. B. O'Donnell, President. No phone calls. Telephone interview required. Applicants must submit a resume. Applications are accepted continuously.

MINNESOTA POWER
30 West Superior Street
Duluth, Minnesota 55802

General Information Diversified electric utility company that uses fossil fuel and hydro power to generate electricity; has interests in power marketing, telecommunications, coal mining, and natural gas. Established in 1923. Number of employees: 1,500. Number of internship applications received each year: 100.
Internships Available ▶ *5–10 interns:* responsibilities include working in information technology, engineering, accounting, drafting, financial, power trading, or telecommunications. Candidates should have ability to work with others, college courses in field, computer skills, writing skills, minimum GPA of 3.0. Duration is 6–12 months. $10.60 per hour. Open to college freshmen, college sophomores, college juniors, college seniors, vocational students.
Benefits Willing to complete paperwork for educational credit.

Contact Through World Wide Web site Kim Lucarelli, Human Resource Specialist. Fax: 218-723-3944. E-mail: klucarelli@mnpower. com. No phone calls. Applicants must submit application materials as specified on Web site during available periods only. Application deadline: consult Web site for deadlines. World Wide Web: http://www.mnpower.com.

NATIONAL FUEL GAS COMPANY
10 Lafayette Square
Buffalo, New York 14203

General Information Diversified energy company whose $35 billion in assets is distributed among six segments: exploration and production, utility, pipeline and storage, energy marketing, international, and timber. Established in 1902. Number of employees: 2,000. Number of internship applications received each year: 500.
Internships Available ▶ *1 engineering co-op (Buffalo, NY):* responsibilities include assisting experienced engineers in a wide variety of work projects that include replacement project planning and design, pipeline network computer simulation, unit cost analysis, and cost estimating. Duration is summer (May to August). $12 per hour. ▶ *1–2 engineering co-ops (Erie, PA):* responsibilities include assisting experienced engineers in a wide variety of work projects that include replacement project planning and design, pipeline network computer simulation, unit cost analysis, and cost estimating. Duration is summer (May to August). $12 per hour. Candidates for all positions should have ability to work independently, computer skills, oral communication skills, self-motivation, strong interpersonal skills, major in mechanical or civil engineering. Open to college juniors, college seniors, graduate students. International applications accepted.
Benefits Possible full-time employment.
Contact Write, fax, or e-mail Catherine Martorana, Human Resources Coordinator. Phone: 716-857-7385. Fax: 716-857-7195. E-mail: jobs@natfuel.com. In-person interview required. Applicants must submit a resume, academic transcripts. Application deadline: March 1. World Wide Web: http://www.natfuel.com.

WOLF CREEK NUCLEAR OPERATING CORPORATION
1550 Oxen Lane, NE, PO Box 411
Burlington, Kansas 66839-0411

General Information Commercial nuclear electric power generating station. Established in 1987. Number of employees: 1,000. Number of internship applications received each year: 20.
Internships Available ▶ *1–4 engineering trainees:* responsibilities include assisting engineers in daily operations of nuclear power plant; assigned projects as needed to complete mission of work group. Candidates should have ability to work with others, analytical skills, college courses in field, computer skills, oral communication skills, personal interest in the field, self-motivation, written communication skills. Duration is 7 months. $13.50 per hour. Open to college juniors, college seniors.
Benefits On-the-job training, opportunity to attend seminars/workshops, possible full-time employment, travel reimbursement.
Contact Write, fax, or e-mail David O. Reynolds, Human Resources Staff Specialist, 1550 Oxen Lane, NE, PO Box 411, Burlington, Kansas 66839-0411. Fax: 620-364-4186. E-mail: dareyno@wcnoc. com. No phone calls. Applicants must submit a letter of interest, resume, academic transcripts. Application deadline: February 28 for summer/fall, September 30 for spring/summer.

FIELD OF INTEREST INDEX

Business and Financial Operations

Community and Social Services

Office and Administration

Personal Care and Service

Transportation, Tourism, and Lodging Attendants

Production

Sales

Transportation and Material Moving Occupations

GEOGRAPHIC INDEX

INTERNATIONAL INTERNSHIPS INDEX

ACADEMIC LEVEL REQUIRED INDEX

COLLEGE SENIORS

INTERNATIONAL APPLICANTS ACCEPTED INDEX

PAID INTERNSHIPS INDEX

POSSIBILITY OF PERMANENT EMPLOYMENT INDEX

EMPLOYER INDEX

Notes

Notes

Notes

Notes

Notes

Notes

Notes

Notes

Notes

Notes

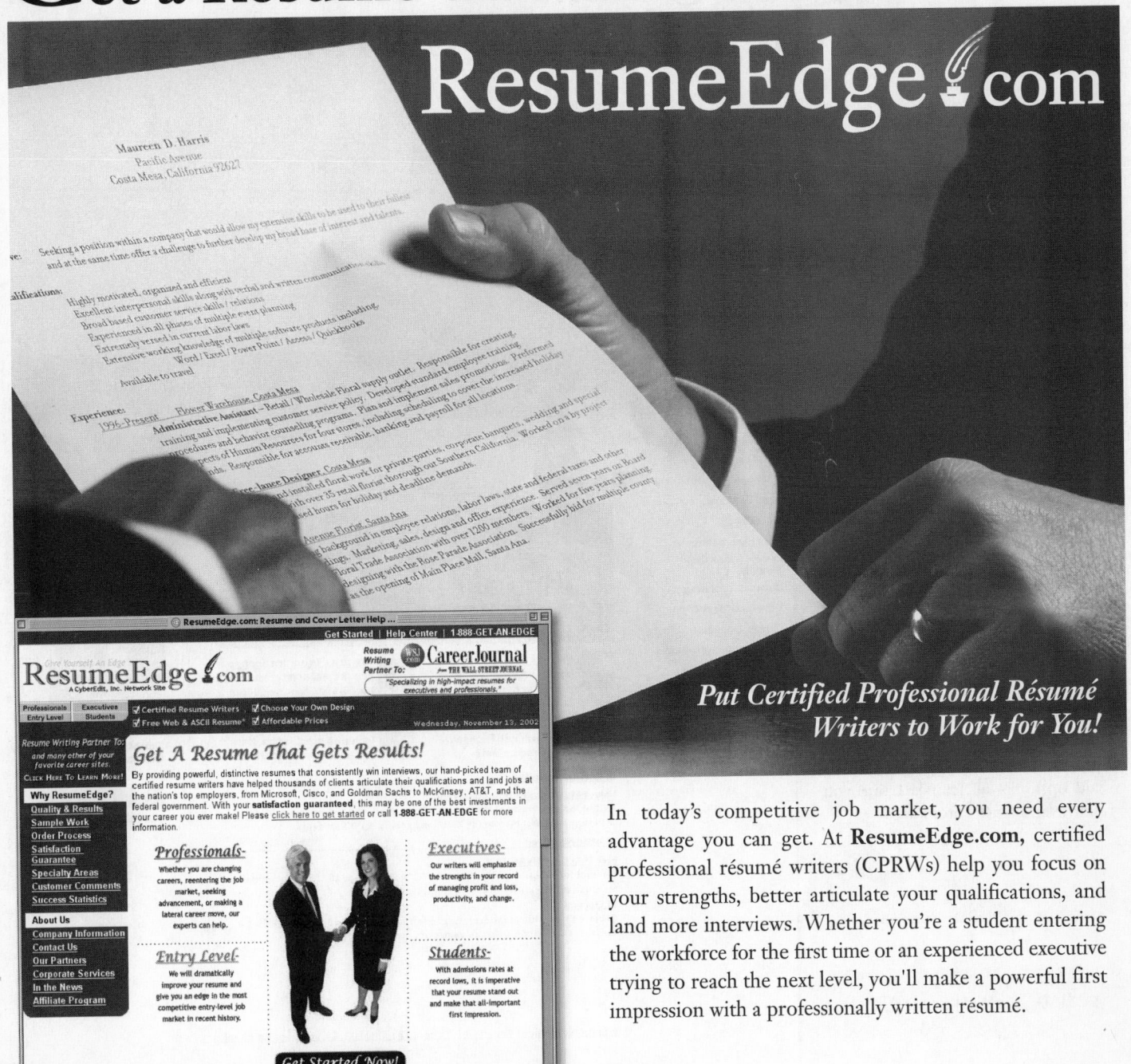

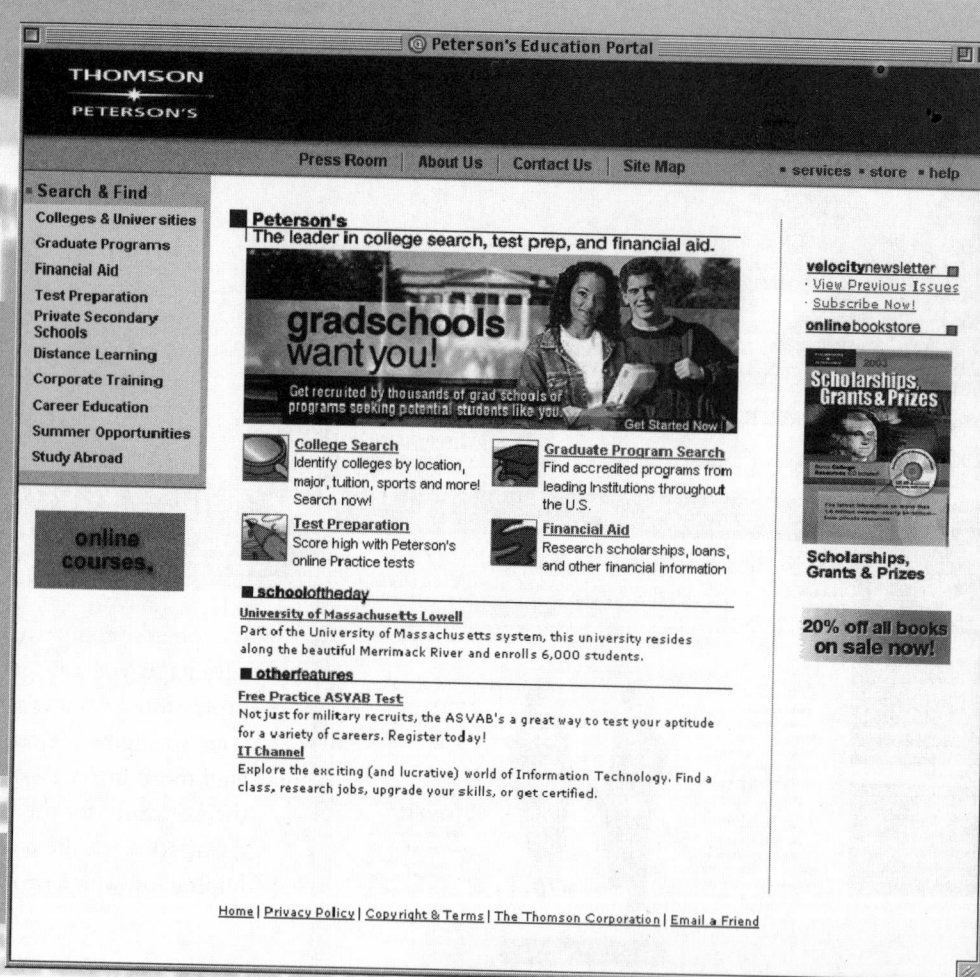